CONSTITUTIONAL LAW IN CONTEMPORARY AMERICA

Volume 2: Civil Rights and Liberties

DAVID SCHULTZ
PROFESSOR OF POLITICAL SCIENCE
HAMLINE UNIVERSITY

JOHN R. VILE
DEAN and PROFESSOR OF POLITICAL SCIENCE
MIDDLE TENNESSEE STATE UNIVERSITY

MICHELLE D. DEARDORFF
DEPARTMENT HEAD AND ADOLPH S. OCHS PROFESSOR OF GOVERNMENT
UNIVERSITY OF TENNESSEE AT CHATTANOOGA

WEST ACADEMIC PUBLISHING

444 Cedar Street, Suite 700
St. Paul, MN 55101
1-877-888-1330

Printed in the United States of America

ISBN: 978-1-68328-556-4

Preface

Volume II of *Constitutional Law in Contemporary America* introduces students to the key conflicts and debates surrounding the civil rights and liberties issues that are addressed in the Bill of Rights (as subsequently applied to the states) and in the Reconstruction Amendments. Collectively, the three of us have more than 85 years of teaching constitutional law to undergraduate, graduate, and law students at a variety of institutions. With this experience as a backdrop, we have designed this book to meet the needs of current political science students and professors. We realized that while every constitutional law class is organized differently, and that every professor emphasizes points or legal issues in a unique fashion, there are some key cases that all professors teach, that issues that were important to constitutional law twenty years ago have been replaced with new issues more relevant to contemporary America, and that textbooks need to be affordable so that they can be supplemented with other resources. With the help of West Academic Publishing, we have designed these two volumes to address these classroom needs.

In both volumes of *Constitutional Law in Contemporary America*, we have chosen Supreme Court cases that are most generally accepted as part of the constitutional canon and that illuminate the central concepts usually covered in constitutional law classes. In defining this canon, we have relied heavily upon a survey conducted by the Law and Politics section of the American Political Science Association. We have edited these cases carefully in order to highlight the primary political conflicts reflected within the Constitution and to include significant concurring and dissenting opinions. To help students gain a clearer understanding of the Constitution and to demonstrate how state and federal courts sometimes address issues differently in a federal system, we have included some cases that state courts have decided on the basis of state constitutional grounds. We have also included several lower federal court cases to demonstrate how Supreme Court decisions are implemented and challenged. Our focus here, as it is for most political scientists, is to use constitutional law as a means of explaining and describing American government. Although we think that students who use these volumes will learn legal thinking, we have not emphasized this as prominently as most law school texts, but have sought primarily to discuss both the law and the politics of the Constitution as a way of clarifying and imparting an understanding of American government and the political process.

While grounded firmly in the existing traditional canon of cases, this volume expands this canon to incorporate such topics by: exploring the freedom of speech beyond mere doctrinal development to types of speech regulation, with a special emphasis on the rights of students; providing an historical overview of the incorporation of the Bill of Rights; carefully examining the development of search and seizure law in the context of the War on Drugs and the War on Terror; including the barriers against the use excessive force by the state; broadly covering the Equal Protection Clause, including race, gender, affirmative action, alienage, disabilities, sexual orientation and identity, and indigency; examining state constitutional responses to state funding of public education; introducing the development of privacy rights in a wide context, including reproductive rights and the right to die; and, examining the state action requirement. This volume also features a chapter on constitutional personhood that encompasses issues as diverse as slavery, abortion, animals, robots, and space aliens, and a chapter on the Second Amendment that examines gun rights. As students read these cases and primary documents, they will be examining the expansion of citizenship rights to larger groups of citizens, the tensions between liberty and stability in society and the constant conflicts between societal equality and personal liberty.

To help students understand the context in which cases are decided, we have begun each chapter with a timeline that notes relevant political developments, court decisions, and national events connected to the topic. The book also provides a topical introduction to each chapter and to each major area of law discussed within the chapter. We have provided contextual introductions to the cases, connected them to longer lines of precedent in the "Related Cases" feature, and provided questions that tie the case back to the larger issues of law and political science. We have also written a glossary containing terms with which students typically struggle and included a bibliography to enable students to continue their own learning through additional research. To meet our own interests, the flexible organization of the text ensures that professors can teach the cases and chapters in any order to achieve their own pedagogical objectives.

Many individuals and many institutions have come together to enable us to complete this book. David Schultz would like to thank Claude Teweles at Roxbury Publishing Company, the original publisher who signed this book and subsequently sold the book to Oxford University Press, which has in turn passed it on to West. In addition, Paul C. Barthlomew, whose original two volumes on constitutional law, which were published in 1978 and form the basis of part of our project, also deserves acknowledgment. David would also like to thank his many undergraduate constitutional law students over the years as well as his law students. Both groups have helped him focus his thoughts. Nate Hackman, his first constitutional law teacher at the State University of New York at Binghamton, remains a big influence on his thinking. Finally, he thanks his wife for her patience in talking about the law more than he should.

Michelle D. Deardorff is indebted to the colleagues with whom she has argued these constitutional issues over the years, most particularly Paul Folger of Heartland Community College, the late Isaiah Madison of Jackson State University, Jilda Aliotta of the University of Hartford, and Angela Kupenda of Mississippi College School of Law. She is appreciative of the late Augustus Jones, Jr., of Miami University who first introduced her to constitutional law and transitioned from being her professor to a valued co-author in her life. Stephen Hoffmann and Phil Loy of Taylor University must be thanked for feeding her enjoyment of political science and for encouraging her to pursue graduate school. Her parents, Earl and Fonda Donaldson, encouraged her curiosity and analytical skills by never rejecting her questions and letting her take risks—both intellectual and physical; she is very grateful for their continuing support. The wonderful political scientists who compose the American Political Science Association's Political Science Education organized section have transformed her pedagogy. Most significantly, she thanks the students at Millikin University, Jackson State University, and the University of Tennessee at Chattanooga whom it has been her honor and privilege to teach over the last twenty-five years. Their enduring excitement and engagement in these topics have made the classroom a "sacred place" to which it is always a pleasure to return. Finally, her husband, David Deardorff, has made her a better writer and a more thoughtful teacher; this has been the best collaboration of her life.

John R. Vile thanks his family members, especially his parents Ralph and Joanna, his wife Linda, and his daughters Virginia and Rebekah, for their continuing affection and support. He thanks his teachers at the College of William and Mary and the University of Virginia and NEH seminar directors at Princeton University and the University of Iowa who contributed to his own understanding of the Constitution; he will forever be indebted to Henry J. Abraham at Virginia, and Alpheus T. Mason and Walter Murphy of Princeton. He further appreciates his supervisors and colleagues, especially those at Middle Tennessee State University, who have facilitated his ongoing research, his students at McNeese State University, Middle Tennessee State University, and Vanderbilt University whose questions have sharpened his understanding of the Constitution, and his colleagues at the American Mock Trial Association for their continuing devotion to developing undergraduate thinking and advocacy skills. While adding his thanks to Claude Teweles, he further acknowledges the role of Kenneth Holland, now at Ball State University, and Mary Volcansek, at Texas Christian University, who first conceived of this project, and the many editors and publishers who, in helping him with other works, also contributed to constitutional knowledge.

All of us owe a great debt of gratitude to those colleagues and professionals at West Academic who have helped us improve this case law book in wonderful ways. Our executive editor, James Cahoy, has been a faithful supporter of this project, asking us the difficult questions regarding our purpose and intent and ensuring that we have a common voice when the three of us often had different visions that needed to be accommodated. Heather Sieve and Laura Holle, the publication specialists, helped us keep to the necessary deadlines and bring this edition to print.

This book is very different from the one that was initially proposed many years ago. A large weight of these changes are born by the many helpful reviewers that read this text in its many iterations and communicated to us the ways in which this book could be enhanced and approved. To that end, we are very grateful to all the anonymous reviewers who offered their time and outstanding suggestions.

Last but not least, we offer our collective thanks to those who labored to create, ratify, amend, and interpret the U.S. Constitution. Because of their efforts, we continue to enjoy the "blessings of liberty," the appreciation and understanding of which we hope these volumes will further perpetuate.

David Schultz,
Professor,
Hamline University,
University of Minnesota School of Law

John R. Vile,
Professor of Political Science and Dean,
University Honors College,
Middle Tennessee State University

Michelle D. Deardorff,
Adolph S. Ochs Professor of Government and
Department Head,
University of Tennessee at Chattanooga

July 4, 2017

Summary of Contents

Table of Contents

Table of Cases

The Constitution of the United States of America

Preamble

We the people of the United States, in order to form a more perfect union, establish justice, insure domestic tranquility, provide for the common defense, promote the general welfare, and secure the blessings of liberty to ourselves and our posterity, do ordain and establish this Constitution for the United States of America.

Article I

Section 1. All legislative powers herein granted shall be vested in a Congress of the United States, which shall consist of a Senate and House of Representatives.

Section 2. The House of Representatives shall be composed of members chosen every second year by the people of the several states, and the electors in each state shall have the qualifications requisite for electors of the most numerous branch of the state legislature.

No person shall be a Representative who shall not have attained to the age of twenty five years, and been seven years a citizen of the United States, and who shall not, when elected, be an inhabitant of that state in which he shall be chosen.

Representatives and direct taxes shall be apportioned among the several states which may be included within this union, according to their respective numbers, which shall be determined by adding to the whole number of free persons, including those bound to service for a term of years, and excluding Indians not taxed, three fifths of all other Persons. The actual Enumeration shall be made within three years after the first meeting of the Congress of the United States, and within every subsequent term of ten years, in such manner as they shall by law direct. The number of Representatives shall not exceed one for every thirty thousand, but each state shall have at least one Representative; and until such enumeration shall be made, the state of New Hampshire shall be entitled to chuse three, Massachusetts eight, Rhode Island and Providence Plantations one, Connecticut five, New York six, New Jersey four, Pennsylvania eight, Delaware one, Maryland six, Virginia ten, North Carolina five, South Carolina five, and Georgia three.

When vacancies happen in the Representation from any state, the executive authority thereof shall issue writs of election to fill such vacancies.

The House of Representatives shall choose their speaker and other officers; and shall have the sole power of impeachment.

Section 3. The Senate of the United States shall be composed of two Senators from each state, chosen by the legislature thereof, for six years; and each Senator shall have one vote.

Immediately after they shall be assembled in consequence of the first election, they shall be divided as equally as may be into three classes. The seats of the Senators of the first class shall be vacated at the expiration of the second year, of the second class at the expiration of the fourth year, and the third class at the expiration of the sixth year, so that one third may be chosen every second year; and if vacancies happen by resignation, or otherwise, during the recess of the legislature of any state, the executive thereof may make temporary appointments until the next meeting of the legislature, which shall then fill such vacancies.

No person shall be a Senator who shall not have attained to the age of thirty years, and been nine years a citizen of the United States and who shall not, when elected, be an inhabitant of that state for which he shall be chosen.

The Vice President of the United States shall be President of the Senate, but shall have no vote, unless they be equally divided.

The Senate shall choose their other officers, and also a President pro tempore, in the absence of the Vice President, or when he shall exercise the office of President of the United States.

The Senate shall have the sole power to try all impeachments. When sitting for that purpose, they shall be on oath or affirmation. When the President of the United States is tried, the Chief Justice shall preside: And no person shall be convicted without the concurrence of two thirds of the members present.

Judgment in cases of impeachment shall not extend further than to removal from office, and disqualification to hold and enjoy any office of honor, trust or profit under the United States: but the party convicted shall nevertheless be liable and subject to indictment, trial, judgment and punishment, according to law.

Section 4. The times, places and manner of holding elections for Senators and Representatives, shall be prescribed in each state by the legislature thereof; but the Congress may at any time by law make or alter such regulations, except as to the places of choosing Senators.

The Congress shall assemble at least once in every year, and such meeting shall be on the first Monday in December, unless they shall by law appoint a different day.

Section 5. Each House shall be the judge of the elections, returns and qualifications of its own members, and a majority of each shall constitute a quorum to do business; but a smaller number may adjourn from day to day, and may be authorized to compel the attendance of absent members, in such manner, and under such penalties as each House may provide.

Each House may determine the rules of its proceedings, punish its members for disorderly behavior, and, with the concurrence of two thirds, expel a member.

Each House shall keep a journal of its proceedings, and from time to time publish the same, excepting such parts as may in their judgment require secrecy; and the yeas and nays of the members of either House on any question shall, at the desire of one fifth of those present, be entered on the journal.

Neither House, during the session of Congress, shall, without the consent of the other, adjourn for more than three days, nor to any other place than that in which the two Houses shall be sitting.

Section 6. The Senators and Representatives shall receive a compensation for their services, to be ascertained by law, and paid out of the treasury of the United States. They shall in all cases, except treason, felony and breach of the peace, be privileged from arrest during their attendance at the session of their respective Houses, and in going to and returning from the same; and for any speech or debate in either House, they shall not be questioned in any other place.

No Senator or Representative shall, during the time for which he was elected, be appointed to any civil office under the authority of the United States, which shall have been created, or the emoluments whereof shall have been increased during such time: and no person holding any office under the United States, shall be a member of either House during his continuance in office.

Section 7. All bills for raising revenue shall originate in the House of Representatives; but the Senate may propose or concur with amendments as on other Bills.

Every bill which shall have passed the House of Representatives and the Senate, shall, before it become a law, be presented to the President of the United States; if he approve he shall sign it, but if not he shall return it, with his objections to that House in which it shall have originated, who shall enter the objections at large on their journal, and proceed to reconsider it. If after such reconsideration two thirds of that House shall agree to pass the bill, it shall be sent, together with the objections, to the other House, by which it shall likewise be reconsidered, and if approved by two thirds of that House, it shall become a law. But in all such cases the votes of both Houses shall be determined by yeas and nays, and the names of the persons voting for and against the bill shall be entered on the journal of each House respectively. If any bill shall not be returned by the President within ten days (Sundays excepted) after it shall have been presented to him, the same shall be a law, in like manner as if he had signed it, unless the Congress by their adjournment prevent its return, in which case it shall not be a law.

Every order, resolution, or vote to which the concurrence of the Senate and House of Representatives may be necessary (except on a question of adjournment) shall be presented to the President of the United States; and before the same shall take effect, shall be approved by him, or being disapproved by him, shall be repassed by two thirds of the Senate and House of Representatives, according to the rules and limitations prescribed in the case of a bill.

Section 8. The Congress shall have power to lay and collect taxes, duties, imposts and excises, to pay the debts and provide for the common defense and general welfare of the United States; but all duties, imposts and excises shall be uniform throughout the United States;

To borrow money on the credit of the United States;

To regulate commerce with foreign nations, and among the several states, and with the Indian tribes;

To establish a uniform rule of naturalization, and uniform laws on the subject of bankruptcies throughout the United States;

To coin money, regulate the value thereof, and of foreign coin, and fix the standard of weights and measures;

To provide for the punishment of counterfeiting the securities and current coin of the United States;

To establish post offices and post roads;

To promote the progress of science and useful arts, by securing for limited times to authors and inventors the exclusive right to their respective writings and discoveries;

To constitute tribunals inferior to the Supreme Court;

To define and punish piracies and felonies committed on the high seas, and offenses against the law of nations;

To declare war, grant letters of marque and reprisal, and make rules concerning captures on land and water;

To raise and support armies, but no appropriation of money to that use shall be for a longer term than two years;

To provide and maintain a navy;

To make rules for the government and regulation of the land and naval forces;

To provide for calling forth the militia to execute the laws of the union, suppress insurrections and repel invasions;

To provide for organizing, arming, and disciplining, the militia, and for governing such part of them as may be employed in the service of the United States, reserving to the states respectively, the appointment of the officers, and the authority of training the militia according to the discipline prescribed by Congress;

To exercise exclusive legislation in all cases whatsoever, over such District (not exceeding ten miles square) as may, by cession of particular states, and the acceptance of Congress, become the seat of the government of the United States, and to exercise like authority over all places purchased by the consent of the legislature of the state in which the same shall be, for the erection of forts, magazines, arsenals, dockyards, and other needful buildings;—And

To make all laws which shall be necessary and proper for carrying into execution the foregoing powers, and all other powers vested by this Constitution in the government of the United States, or in any department or officer thereof.

Section 9. The migration or importation of such persons as any of the states now existing shall think proper to admit, shall not be prohibited by the Congress prior to the year one thousand eight hundred and eight, but a tax or duty may be imposed on such importation, not exceeding ten dollars for each person.

The privilege of the writ of habeas corpus shall not be suspended, unless when in cases of rebellion or invasion the public safety may require it.

No bill of attainder or ex post facto Law shall be passed.

No capitation, or other direct, tax shall be laid, unless in proportion to the census or enumeration herein before directed to be taken.

No tax or duty shall be laid on articles exported from any state.

No preference shall be given by any regulation of commerce or revenue to the ports of one state over those of another: nor shall vessels bound to, or from, one state, be obliged to enter, clear or pay duties in another.

No money shall be drawn from the treasury, but in consequence of appropriations made by law; and a regular statement and account of receipts and expenditures of all public money shall be published from time to time.

No title of nobility shall be granted by the United States: and no person holding any office of profit or trust under them, shall, without the consent of the Congress, accept of any present, emolument, office, or title, of any kind whatever, from any king, prince, or foreign state.

Section 10. No state shall enter into any treaty, alliance, or confederation; grant letters of marque and reprisal; coin money; emit bills of credit; make anything but gold and silver coin a tender in payment of debts; pass any bill of attainder, ex post facto law, or law impairing the obligation of contracts, or grant any title of nobility.

No state shall, without the consent of the Congress, lay any imposts or duties on imports or exports, except what may be absolutely necessary for executing it's inspection laws: and the net produce of all duties and imposts, laid by any state on imports or exports, shall be for the use of the treasury of the United States; and all such laws shall be subject to the revision and control of the Congress.

No state shall, without the consent of Congress, lay any duty of tonnage, keep troops, or ships of war in time of peace, enter into any agreement or compact with another state, or with a foreign power, or engage in war, unless actually invaded, or in such imminent danger as will not admit of delay.

Article II

Section 1. The executive power shall be vested in a President of the United States of America. He shall hold his office during the term of four years, and, together with the Vice President, chosen for the same term, be elected, as follows:

Each state shall appoint, in such manner as the Legislature thereof may direct, a number of electors, equal to the whole number of Senators and Representatives to which the State may be entitled in the Congress: but no Senator or Representative, or person holding an office of trust or profit under the United States, shall be appointed an elector.

The electors shall meet in their respective states, and vote by ballot for two persons, of whom one at least shall not be an inhabitant of the same state with themselves. And they shall make a list of all the persons voted for, and of the number of votes for each; which list they shall sign and certify, and transmit sealed to the seat of the government of the United States, directed to the President of the Senate. The President of the Senate shall, in the presence of the Senate and House of Representatives, open all the certificates, and the votes shall then be counted. The person having the greatest number of votes shall be the President, if such number be a majority of the whole number of electors appointed; and if there be more than one who have such majority, and have an equal number of votes, then the House of Representatives shall immediately choose by ballot one of them for President; and if no person have a majority, then from the five highest on the list the said House shall in like manner choose the President. But in choosing the President, the votes shall be taken by States, the representation from each state having one vote; A quorum for this purpose shall consist of a member or members from two thirds of the states, and a majority of all the states shall be necessary to a choice. In every case, after the choice of the President, the person having the greatest number of votes of the electors shall be the Vice President. But if there should remain two or more who have equal votes, the Senate shall choose from them by ballot the Vice President.

The Congress may determine the time of choosing the electors, and the day on which they shall give their votes; which day shall be the same throughout the United States.

No person except a natural born citizen, or a citizen of the United States, at the time of the adoption of this Constitution, shall be eligible to the office of President; neither shall any person be eligible to that office who shall not have attained to the age of thirty five years, and been fourteen Years a resident within the United States.

In case of the removal of the President from office, or of his death, resignation, or inability to discharge the powers and duties of the said office, the same shall devolve on the Vice President, and the Congress may by law provide for the case of removal, death, resignation or inability, both of the President and Vice President, declaring what officer shall then act as President, and such officer shall act accordingly, until the disability be removed, or a President shall be elected.

The President shall, at stated times, receive for his services, a compensation, which shall neither be increased nor diminished during the period for which he shall have been elected, and he shall not receive within that period any other emolument from the United States, or any of them.

Before he enter on the execution of his office, he shall take the following oath or affirmation:—"I do solemnly swear (or affirm) that I will faithfully execute the office of President of the United States, and will to the best of my ability, preserve, protect and defend the Constitution of the United States."

Section 2. The President shall be commander in chief of the Army and Navy of the United States, and of the militia of the several states, when called into the actual service of the United States; he may require the opinion, in writing, of the principal officer in each of the executive departments, upon any subject relating to the duties of their respective offices, and he shall have power to grant reprieves and pardons for offenses against the United States, except in cases of impeachment.

He shall have power, by and with the advice and consent of the Senate, to make treaties, provided two thirds of the Senators present concur; and he shall nominate, and by and with the advice and consent of the Senate, shall appoint ambassadors, other public ministers and consuls, judges of the Supreme Court, and all other officers of the United States, whose appointments are not herein otherwise provided for, and which shall be established by law: but the Congress may by law vest the appointment of such inferior officers, as they think proper, in the President alone, in the courts of law, or in the heads of departments.

The President shall have power to fill up all vacancies that may happen during the recess of the Senate, by granting commissions which shall expire at the end of their next session.

Section 3. He shall from time to time give to the Congress information of the state of the union, and recommend to their consideration such measures as he shall judge necessary and expedient; he may, on extraordinary occasions, convene both Houses, or either of them, and in case of disagreement between them, with respect to the time of adjournment, he may adjourn them to such time as he shall think proper; he shall receive ambassadors and other public ministers; he shall take care that the laws be faithfully executed, and shall commission all the officers of the United States.

Section 4. The President, Vice President and all civil officers of the United States, shall be removed from office on impeachment for, and conviction of, treason, bribery, or other high crimes and misdemeanors.

Article III

Section 1. The judicial power of the United States, shall be vested in one Supreme Court, and in such inferior courts as the Congress may from time to time ordain and establish. The judges, both of the supreme and inferior courts, shall hold their offices during good behaviour, and shall, at stated times, receive for their services, a compensation, which shall not be diminished during their continuance in office.

Section 2. The judicial power shall extend to all cases, in law and equity, arising under this Constitution, the laws of the United States, and treaties made, or which shall be made, under their authority;—to all cases affecting ambassadors, other public ministers and consuls;—to all cases of admiralty and maritime jurisdiction;—to controversies to which the United States shall be a party;—to controversies between two or more states;—between a state and citizens of another state;—between citizens of different states;—between citizens of the same state claiming lands under grants of different states, and between a state, or the citizens thereof, and foreign states, citizens or subjects.

In all cases affecting ambassadors, other public ministers and consuls, and those in which a state shall be party, the Supreme Court shall have original jurisdiction. In all the other cases before mentioned, the Supreme Court shall have appellate jurisdiction, both as to law and fact, with such exceptions, and under such regulations as the Congress shall make.

The trial of all crimes, except in cases of impeachment, shall be by jury; and such trial shall be held in the state where the said crimes shall have been committed; but when not committed within any state, the trial shall be at such place or places as the Congress may by law have directed.

Section 3. Treason against the United States, shall consist only in levying war against them, or in adhering to their enemies, giving them aid and comfort. No person shall be convicted of treason unless on the testimony of two witnesses to the same overt act, or on confession in open court.

The Congress shall have power to declare the punishment of treason, but no attainder of treason shall work corruption of blood, or forfeiture except during the life of the person attainted.

Article IV

Section 1. Full faith and credit shall be given in each state to the public acts, records, and judicial proceedings of every other state. And the Congress may by general laws prescribe the manner in which such acts, records, and proceedings shall be proved, and the effect thereof.

Section 2. The citizens of each state shall be entitled to all privileges and immunities of citizens in the several states.

A person charged in any state with treason, felony, or other crime, who shall flee from justice, and be found in another state, shall on demand of the executive authority of the state from which he fled, be delivered up, to be removed to the state having jurisdiction of the crime.

No person held to service or labor in one state, under the laws thereof, escaping into another, shall, in consequence of any law or regulation therein, be discharged from such service or labor, but shall be delivered up on claim of the party to whom such service or labor may be due.

Section 3. New states may be admitted by the Congress into this union; but no new states shall be formed or erected within the jurisdiction of any other state; nor any state be formed by the junction of two or more states, or parts of states, without the consent of the legislatures of the states concerned as well as of the Congress.

The Congress shall have power to dispose of and make all needful rules and regulations respecting the territory or other property belonging to the United States; and nothing in this Constitution shall be so construed as to prejudice any claims of the United States, or of any particular state.

Section 4. The United States shall guarantee to every state in this union a republican form of government, and shall protect each of them against invasion; and on application of the legislature, or of the executive (when the legislature cannot be convened) against domestic violence.

Article V

The Congress, whenever two thirds of both houses shall deem it necessary, shall propose amendments to this Constitution, or, on the application of the legislatures of two thirds of the several states, shall call a convention for proposing amendments, which, in either case, shall be valid to all intents and purposes, as part of this Constitution, when ratified by the legislatures of three fourths of the several states, or by conventions in three fourths thereof, as the one or the other mode of ratification may be proposed by the Congress; provided that no amendment which may be made prior to the year one thousand eight hundred and eight shall in any manner affect the first and fourth clauses in the ninth section of the first article; and that no state, without its consent, shall be deprived of its equal suffrage in the Senate.

Article VI

All debts contracted and engagements entered into, before the adoption of this Constitution, shall be as valid against the United States under this Constitution, as under the Confederation.

This Constitution, and the laws of the United States which shall be made in pursuance thereof; and all treaties made, or which shall be made, under the authority of the United States, shall be the supreme law of the land; and the judges in every state shall be bound thereby, anything in the Constitution or laws of any State to the contrary notwithstanding.

The Senators and Representatives before mentioned, and the members of the several state legislatures, and all executive and judicial officers, both of the United States and of the several states, shall be bound by oath or affirmation, to support this Constitution; but no religious test shall ever be required as a qualification to any office or public trust under the United States.

Article VII

The ratification of the conventions of nine states, shall be sufficient for the establishment of this Constitution between the states so ratifying the same.

Done in convention by the unanimous consent of the states present the seventeenth day of September in the year of our Lord one thousand seven hundred and eighty seven and of the independence of the United States of America the twelfth. In witness whereof We have hereunto subscribed our Names,

G. Washington—Presidt. and deputy from Virginia

New Hampshire: John Langdon, Nicholas Gilman

Massachusetts: Nathaniel Gorham, Rufus King

Connecticut: Wm: Saml. Johnson, Roger Sherman

New York: Alexander Hamilton

New Jersey: Wil: Livingston, David Brearly, Wm. Paterson, Jona: Dayton

Pennsylvania: B. Franklin, Thomas Mifflin, Robt. Morris, Geo. Clymer, Thos. FitzSimons, Jared Ingersoll, James Wilson, Gouv Morris

Delaware: Geo: Read, Gunning Bedford jun, John Dickinson, Richard Bassett, Jaco: Broom

Maryland: James McHenry, Dan of St Thos. Jenifer, Danl Carroll

Virginia: John Blair--, James Madison Jr.

North Carolina: Wm. Blount, Richd. Dobbs Spaight, Hu Williamson

South Carolina: J. Rutledge, Charles Cotesworth Pinckney, Charles Pinckney, Pierce Butler

Georgia: William Few, Abr Baldwin

BILL OF RIGHTS

Amendment I

Congress shall make no law respecting an establishment of religion, or prohibiting the free exercise thereof; or abridging the freedom of speech, or of the press; or the right of the people peaceably to assemble, and to petition the Government for a redress of grievances.

Amendment II

A well regulated Militia, being necessary to the security of a free State, the right of the people to keep and bear Arms, shall not be infringed.

Amendment III

No Soldier shall, in time of peace be quartered in any house, without the consent of the Owner, nor in time of war, but in a manner to be prescribed by law.

Amendment IV

The right of the People to be secure in their persons, houses, papers, and effects, against unreasonable searches and seizures, shall not be violated, and no Warrants shall issue, but upon probable cause, supported by Oath or affirmation, and particularity describing the place to be searched, and the persons or things to be seized.

Amendment V

No person shall be held to answer for a capital, or otherwise infamous crime, unless on a presentment or indictment of a Grand Jury, except in cases arising in the land or naval forces, or in the Militia, when in actual service in time of War or public danger; nor shall any person be subject for the same offence to be twice put in jeopardy of life or limb; nor shall be compelled in any criminal case to be a witness against himself, nor be deprived of life, liberty, or property, without due process of law; nor shall private property be taken for public use, without just compensation.

Amendment VI

In all criminal prosecutions, the accused shall enjoy the right to a speedy and public trial, by an impartial jury of the State and district wherein the crime shall have been committed, which district shall have been previously ascertained by law, and to be informed of the nature and cause of the accusation; to be confronted with the witnesses against him; to have compulsory process for obtaining witnesses in his favor, and to have Assistance of Counsel for his defence.

Amendment VII

In Suits at common law, where the value in controversy shall exceed twenty dollars, the right of trial by jury shall be preserved, and no fact tried by a jury, shall be otherwise re-examined in any Court of the United States, than according to the rules of the common law.

Amendment VIII

Excessive bail shall not be required, nor excessive fines imposed, nor cruel and unusual punishments inflicted.

Amendment IX

The enumeration in the Constitution, of certain rights, shall not be construed to deny or disparage others retained by the people.

Amendment X

The powers not delegated to the United States by the Constitution, nor prohibited by it to the States, are reserved to the States respectively, or to the people.

OTHER AMENDMENTS TO THE CONSTITUTION

Amendment XI (Ratified in 1795)

The Judicial power of the United States shall not be construed to extend to any suit in law or equity, commenced or prosecuted against one of the United States by Citizens of another State, or by Citizens or Subjects of any Foreign State.

Amendment XII (Ratified in 1804)

The Electors shall meet in their respective states and vote by ballot for President and Vice-President, one of whom, at least, shall not be an inhabitant of the same state with themselves; they shall name in their ballots the person voted for as President, and in distinct ballots the person voted for as Vice-President, and they shall make distinct lists of all persons voted for as President, and of all persons voted for as Vice-President, and of the number of votes for each, which lists they shall sign and certify, and transmit sealed to the seat of the government of the United States, directed to the President of the Senate;—The President of the Senate shall, in the presence of the Senate and House of Representatives, open all the certificates and the votes shall then be counted;—The person having the greatest number of votes for President, shall be the President, if such number be a majority of the whole number of Electors appointed; and if no person have such majority, then from the persons having the highest numbers not exceeding three on the list of those voted for as President, the House of Representatives shall choose immediately, by ballot, the President. But in choosing the President, the votes shall be taken by states, the representation from each state having one vote; a quorum for this purpose shall consist of a member or members from two-thirds of the states, and a majority of all the states shall be necessary to a choice. And if the House of Representatives shall not choose a President whenever the right of choice shall devolve upon then, before the fourth day of March next following, then the Vice-President shall act as President, as in the case of the death or other constitutional disability of the President.—The person having the greatest number of votes as Vice-President, shall be the Vice-President, if such number be a majority of the whole number of Electors appointed, and if no person have a majority, then from the two highest numbers on the list, the Senate shall choose the Vice-President; a quorum for the purpose shall consist of two-thirds of the whole number of Senators, and a majority of the whole number shall be necessary to a choice. But no person constitutionally ineligible to the office of President shall be eligible to that of Vice-President of the United States.

Amendment XIII (Ratified in 1865)

Section 1. Neither slavery nor involuntary servitude, except as a punishment for crime whereof the party shall have been duly convicted, shall exist within the United States, or any place subject to their jurisdiction.

Section 2. Congress shall have power to enforce this article by appropriate legislation.

Amendment XIV (Ratified in 1868)

Section 1. All persons born or naturalized in the United States, and subject to the jurisdiction thereof, are citizens of the United States and of the State wherein they reside. No State shall make or enforce any law which shall abridge the privileges or immunities of citizens of the United States; nor shall any State deprive any person of life, liberty, or property, without due process of law; nor deny to any person within its jurisdiction the equal protection of the laws.

Section 2. Representatives shall be apportioned among the several States according to their respective numbers, counting the whole number of persons in each State, excluding Indians not taxed. But when the right to vote at any election for the choice of electors for President and Vice President of the United States, Representatives in Congress, the Executive and Judicial officers of a State, or the members of the Legislature thereof, is denied to any of the male inhabitants of such State, being twenty-one years of age, and citizens of the United States, or in any way abridged, except for participation in rebellion, or other crime, the basis of representation therein shall be reduced in the proportion which the number of such male citizens shall bear to the whole number of male citizens twenty-one years of age in such State.

Section 3. No person shall be a Senator or Representative in Congress, or elector of President and Vice President, or hold any office, civil or military, under the United States, or under any State, who, having previously taken an oath, as a member of Congress, or as an officer of the United States, or as a member of any State legislature, or as an executive or judicial officer of any State, to support the Constitution of the United States, shall have engaged in insurrection or rebellion against the same, or given aid or comfort to the enemies thereof. But Congress may by a vote of two-thirds of each House, remove such disability.

Section 4. The validity of the public debt of the United States, authorized by law, including debts incurred for payment of pensions and bounties for services in suppressing insurrection or rebellion, shall not be questioned. But neither the United States nor any State shall assume or pay any debt or obligation incurred in aid of insurrection or rebellion against the United States, or any claim for the loss or emancipation of any slave; but all such debts, obligations and claims shall be held illegal and void.

Section 5. The Congress shall have power to enforce, by appropriate legislation, the provisions of this article.

Amendment XV (Ratified in 1870)

Section 1. The right of citizens of the United States to vote shall not be denied or abridged by the United States or by any State on account of race, color, or previous condition of servitude.

Section 2. The Congress shall have power to enforce this article by appropriate legislation.

Amendment XVI (Ratified in 1913)

The Congress shall have power to lay and collect taxes on incomes, from whatever source derived, without apportionment among the several States, and without regard to any census or enumeration.

Amendment XVII (Ratified in 1913)

The Senate of the United States shall be composed of two Senators from each State, elected by the people thereof for six years; and each Senator shall have one vote. The electors in each State shall have the qualifications requisite for electors of the most numerous branch of the State legislatures.

When vacancies happen in the representation of any State in the Senate, the executive authority of such State shall issue writs of election to fill such vacancies: Provided, That the legislature of any State may empower the executive thereof to make temporary appointments until the people fill the vacancies by election as the legislature may direct.

This amendment shall not be so construed as to affect the election or term of any Senator chosen before it becomes valid as part of the Constitution.

Amendment XVIII (Ratified in 1919) (Repealed in 1933 by Amendment XXI)

Section 1. After one year from the ratification of this article the manufacture, sale, or transportation of intoxicating liquors within, the importation thereof into, or the exportation thereof from the United States and all territory subject to the jurisdiction thereof for beverage purposes is hereby prohibited.

Section 2. The Congress and the several States shall have concurrent power to enforce this article by appropriate legislation.

Section 3. This article shall be inoperative unless it shall have been ratified as an amendment to the Constitution by the legislatures of the several States as provided in the Constitution, within seven years from the date of the submission hereof to the States by the Congress.

Amendment XIX (Ratified in 1920)

The right of citizens of the United States to vote shall not be denied or abridged by the United States or by any State on account of sex.

Congress shall have power to enforce this article by appropriate legislation.

Amendment XX (Ratified in 1933)

Section 1. The terms of the President and Vice President shall end at noon on the 20th day of January, and the terms of Senators and Representatives at noon on the 3d day of January, of the years in which such terms would have ended if this article had not been ratified; and the terms of their successors shall then begin.

Section 2. The Congress shall assemble at least once in every year, and such meeting shall begin at noon on the 3d day of January, unless they shall by law appoint a different day.

Section 3. If, at the time fixed for the beginning of the term of the President, the President elect shall have died, the Vice President elect shall become President. If a President shall not have been chosen before the time fixed for the beginning of his term, or if the President elect shall have failed to qualify, then the Vice President elect shall act as President until a President shall have qualified; and the Congress may by law provide for the case wherein neither a President elect nor a Vice President elect shall have qualified, declaring who shall then act as President, or the manner in which one who is to act shall be selected, and such person shall act accordingly until a President or Vice President shall have qualified.

Section 4. The Congress may by law provide for the case of the death of any of the persons from whom the House of Representatives may choose a President whenever the right of choice shall have devolved upon them, and for the case of the death of any of the persons from whom the Senate may choose a Vice President whenever the right of choice shall have devolved upon them.

Section 5. Sections 1 and 2 shall take effect on the 15th day of October following the ratification of this article.

Section 6. This article shall be inoperative unless it shall have been ratified as an amendment to the Constitution by the legislatures of three-fourths of the several States within seven years from the date of its submission.

Amendment XXI (Ratified in 1933)

Section 1. The eighteenth article of amendment to the Constitution of the United States is hereby repealed.

Section 2. The transportation or importation into any State, Territory, or possession of the United States for delivery or use therein of intoxicating liquors, in violation of the laws thereof, is hereby prohibited.

Section 3. This article shall be inoperative unless it shall have been ratified as an amendment to the Constitution by conventions in the several States, as provided in the Constitution, within seven years from the date of the submission hereof to the States by the Congress.

Amendment XXII (Ratified in 1951)

Section 1. No person shall be elected to the office of the President more than twice, and no person who has held the office of President, or acted as President, for more than two years of a term to which some other person was elected President shall be elected to the office of the President more than once. But this Article shall not apply to any person holding the office of President when this Article was proposed by the Congress, and shall not prevent any person who may be holding the office of President, or acting as President, during the term within which this Article becomes operative from holding the office of President or acting as President during the remainder of such term.

Section 2. This Article shall be inoperative unless it shall have been ratified as an amendment to the Constitution by the legislatures of three-fourths of the several States within seven years from the date of its submission to the States by the Congress.

Amendment XXIII (Ratified in 1961)

Section 1. The District constituting the seat of Government of the United States shall appoint in such manner as the Congress may direct:

A number of electors of President and Vice President equal to the whole number of Senators and Representatives in Congress to which the District would be entitled if it were a State, but in no event more than the least populous State; they shall be in addition to those appointed by the States, but they shall be considered, for the purposes of the election of President and Vice President, to be electors appointed by a State; and they shall meet in the District and perform such duties as provided by the twelfth article of amendment.

Section 2. The Congress shall have power to enforce this article by appropriate legislation.

Amendment XXIV (Ratified in 1964)

Section 1. The right of citizens of the United States to vote in any primary or other election for President or Vice President, for electors for President or Vice President, or for Senator or Representative in Congress, shall not be denied or abridged by the United States or any State by reason of failure to pay any poll tax or other tax.

Section 2. The Congress shall have power to enforce this article by appropriate legislation.

Amendment XXV (Ratified in 1967)

Section 1. In case of the removal of the President from office or of his death or resignation, the Vice President shall become President.

Section 2. Whenever there is a vacancy in the office of the Vice President, the President shall nominate a Vice President who shall take office upon confirmation by a majority vote of both Houses of Congress.

Section 3. Whenever the President transmits to the President pro tempore of the Senate and the Speaker of the House of Representatives his written declaration that he is unable to discharge the powers and duties of his office, and until he transmits to them a written declaration to the contrary, such powers and duties shall be discharged by the Vice President as Acting President.

Section 4. Whenever the Vice president and a majority of either the principal officers of the executive departments or of such other body as Congress may by law provide, transmit to the President pro tempore of the Senate and the Speaker of the House of Representatives their written declaration that the President is unable to discharge the powers and duties of his office, the Vice President shall immediately assume the powers and duties of the office as Acting President.

Thereafter, when the President transmits to the President pro tempore of the Senate and the Speaker of the House of Representatives his written declaration that no inability exists, he shall resume the powers and duties of his office unless the Vice President and a majority of either the principal officers of the executive department or of such other body as Congress may by law provide, transmit within four days to the President pro tempore of the Senate and the Speaker of the House of Representatives their written declaration that the President is unable to discharge the powers and duties of his office. Thereupon Congress shall decide the issue, assembling within forty-eight hours for that purpose if not in session. If the Congress, within twenty-one days after receipt of the latter written declaration, or, if Congress is not in session, within twenty-one days after Congress is required to assemble, determines by two-thirds vote of both Houses that the President is unable to discharge the powers and duties of his office, the Vice President shall continue to discharge the same as Acting President; otherwise, the President shall resume the powers and duties of his office.

Amendment XXVI (Ratified in 1971)

Section 1. The right of citizens of the United States, who are eighteen years of age or older, to vote shall not be denied or abridged by the United States or by any State on account of age.

Section 2. The Congress shall have power to enforce this article by appropriate legislation.

Amendment XXVII (Ratified in 1992)

No law varying the compensation for the services of the Senators and Representatives shall take effect until an election of Representatives shall have intervened.

CONSTITUTIONAL LAW IN CONTEMPORARY AMERICA

Volume 2: Civil Rights and Liberties

CHAPTER I

Creating the Modern Federal Judiciary: Incorporation and Interpretation of the Bill of Rights

---

Timeline: Incorporation and Interpretation of the Bill of Rights

1776 The Declaration of Independence includes lack of judicial independence for the colonies as one of its grievances against King George III.

1786 The Annapolis Convention issues a call for a constitutional convention.

1787 The Constitutional Convention meets in Philadelphia.

1788 *The Federalist Papers* are published, arguing that the judiciary will be "the least dangerous branch" of the new government.

1789 George Washington nominates John Jay as the first chief justice of the United States.

1789 Congress adopts the Judiciary Act, which outlines the federal court system with three tiers and six Supreme Court justices. Connecticut's Oliver Ellsworth, who had attended the Constitutional Convention, is a key author.

Congress proposes the Bill of Rights.

1790 The Supreme Court holds its first session in the Royal Exchange Building in New York City.

1791 The Bill of Rights is ratified by the states.

1828 Andrew Jackson is elected president.

1833 In *Barron v. Baltimore* the Supreme Court rules that neither the Fifth Amendment nor any part of the Bill of Rights applies to the states.

1860 Abraham Lincoln is elected president.

1865 The Civil War ends and Reconstruction begins.

1866 Congress enacts the Civil Rights Act of 1866.

1868 The Fourteenth Amendment is ratified.

1870 The Fifteenth Amendment is ratified.

1873 In the *Slaughterhouse Cases* the Supreme Court rules that the Privileges or Immunities Clause of the Fourteenth Amendment does not protect the rights of individuals against a state.

1876 Reconstruction ends with the withdrawal of the federal troops from the South.

1884 In *Hurtado v. People of State of California* the Supreme Court rules that the grand jury requirement of the Fifth Amendment does not apply to state criminal trials.

1897 The Supreme Court rules in *Chicago, B. & Q. R. Co. v. City of Chicago* that the Fifth Amendment's Just Compensation Clause applies to the states.

1917 United States enters World War I.

1917 Congress enacts the Espionage Act of 1917.

1925 In *Gitlow v. New York* the Supreme Court rules that the First Amendment Free Speech Clause was incorporated through the Fourteenth Amendment to apply to the states.

1932 The Supreme Court rules in *Powell v. Alabama* that the Sixth Amendment right to counsel applies to the states.

1932 Franklin Roosevelt is elected president.

1933 Tennessee Valley Authority is created by Congress.

1936 In *Ashwander v. Tennessee Valley Authority* the Supreme Court declares several principles that apply to the Court's interpretation of constitutional issues.

1937 In *Palko v. Connecticut* the Supreme Court rules that the Fifth Amendment's protection against double jeopardy does not apply to the states.

1938 The Supreme Court declares in *United States v. Carolene Products Co.* that it will give greater scrutiny to laws that affect or impinge on rights protected by the Bill of Rights.

1940 Congress enacts the Smith Act.

1940 In *Cantwell v. Connecticut* the Supreme Court rules that the First Amendment's Free Exercise Clause was incorporated by the Fourteenth Amendment to apply to the states.

1941 Japanese attack U.S. naval base at Pearl Harbor.

1942 President Roosevelt issues Executive Order interning Japanese Americans into camps.

1942 In *Skinner v. Oklahoma* the Supreme Court rules that the right to reproduce is a fundamental right.

1944 In *Korematsu v. U.S.*, the Supreme Court rules that the use of the race by the government is a suspect classification that will be examined with heightened or strict scrutiny.

1947 The Supreme Court rules in *Adamson v. California* that the right against self-incrimination in the Fifth Amendment does not apply to the states.

1949 In *Wolf v. Colorado* the Supreme Court rules that the Fourth Amendment's exclusionary rule does not apply to states.

1953 Earl Warren becomes chief justice.

1956 William Brennan becomes an associate justice.

1961 The Supreme Court rules in *Mapp v. Ohio* that the Fourth Amendment's exclusionary rule applies to the states.

1963 In *Gideon v. Wainwright* the Court determines that the Fourth Amendment requires that state provide an attorney for an indigent person accused of a criminal offense.

1965 The Supreme Court rules in *Griswold v. Connecticut* that the Ninth Amendment includes a right to privacy granting married couples the right to purchase contraceptives.

1969 In *Benton v. Maryland* the Supreme Court rules that the Fifth Amendment's double jeopardy provision applies to the states.

2008 The Supreme Court rules in *District of Columbia v. Heller* that the Second Amendment protects an individual right to own guns.

2010 In *McDonald v. City of Chicago Illinois*, the Supreme Courts rules that the Second Amendment is incorporated by the Due Process Clause of the Fourteenth Amendment to apply to states.

NOTE TO STUDENTS

The first part of this chapter duplicates materials in volume I. Students who have read that volume may still want to use this section for review.

INTRODUCTION

In 1976 the United States celebrated the bicentennial of the Declaration of Independence, and eleven years later it celebrated the bicentennial of the U.S. Constitution. These two documents were themselves grounded in hundreds of years of prior history, much of which originated in Great Britain. Although American constitutional law largely focuses on U.S. Supreme Court decisions, these decisions are best understood against this background and history.

THE ENGLISH BACKGROUND OF THE U.S. LEGAL SYSTEM

Fifty-five delegates met at the **Constitutional Convention** in Philadelphia in the summer of 1787 to draft the Constitution of the United States. The delegates from twelve of the existing thirteen states who assembled at this convention were chosen by state legislatures, each operating under its own constitution. These constitutions, in turn, replaced earlier charters from England and compacts, or agreements, that states had made to govern themselves.

Because it operated according to the principle that its legislative branch, the Parliament, was sovereign, the British mother country had no written constitution that was unchangeable by ordinary legislative means. It did, however, have a long history of attempting to restrain arbitrary power. This history was reflected in documents like the **Magna Carta** of 1215 and the English Bill of Rights of 1689. Individuals of English descent particularly associated the first of these documents with the principle of "no taxation without representation." In time, American colonists interpreted this principle to mean that the English Parliament could not tax them unless and until it had seated colonial representatives. As the British imposed taxes and trade restrictions on the colonies to pay for the expenses they had incurred in defending the colony in the French and Indian War (1754–1763), the colonists remonstrated and petitioned the English King before ultimately calling two Continental Congresses.

Declaration of Independence:

We hold these truths to be self-evident, that all men are created equal, that they are endowed by their Creator with certain unalienable Rights, that among these are Life, Liberty and the pursuit of Happiness. That to secure these rights, Governments are instituted among Men, deriving their just powers from the consent of the governed.

THE DECLARATION OF INDEPENDENCE

In 1776 the Second Continental Congress decided to declare the colonists' independence from Britain. When this body had commissioned Thomas Jefferson to write the **Declaration of Independence** to explain why the colonists were cutting their ties to the mother country, the Virginian drew upon the British legal heritage and upon the **natural rights** philosophy of British **social contract** theorists, most notably John Locke. Jefferson declared that people were "created equal," that governments were designed to secure their rights of "life, liberty and the pursuit of happiness," and that legitimate government rested "on the consent of the governed" rather than on the divine right of kings or hereditary succession. The Declaration further affirmed the right of the people to alter or replace the government, by peaceful means when they were available and by revolutionary means when they were not.

THE ARTICLES OF CONFEDERATION

Recognizing that the colonies would need a superintending government if they wanted to avoid a **state of nature** where they might be at constant war with one another, the Second Continental Congress drafted a document known as the Articles of Confederation. It created a unicameral Congress, in which each state was represented equally. Because the states were still jealous of their individual identities, the Articles continued to vest primary sovereignty, or power, in the states. Nine or more of the thirteen states needed to agree on most key legislative matters, and the Articles required them to act unanimously in amending the document.

Despite some signal accomplishments—most notably the victory in the Revolutionary War and the adoption of the Northwest Resolution of 1787 providing for the admission of further states—the Articles proved to be largely inadequate. Congress lacked key domestic powers, and America's prestige was quickly deteriorating abroad. The requirement for unanimity blocked needed amendments.

Preamble, U.S. Constitution:

We the People of the United States, in Order to form a more perfect Union, establish Justice, insure domestic Tranquility, provide for the common defence, promote the general Welfare, and secure the Blessings of Liberty to ourselves and our Posterity, do ordain and establish this Constitution for the United States.

A NEW CONSTITUTION

In these circumstances, delegates from a meeting of five states who had discussed interstate navigation and commerce at Annapolis, Maryland, issued a call for a constitutional convention. Support for this convention was strengthened in the winter of 1786–1787, when the government under the Articles of Confederation responded lethargically to a taxpayer revolt in Massachusetts known as Shays' Rebellion. Although Congress had called the Convention to strengthen the **Articles of Confederation**, which the state legislatures had formally adopted in 1781, the Constitutional Convention of 1787 instead created an entirely new Constitution, which it hoped would establish "a more perfect Union."

The document outlined its purposes in its opening paragraph, known as the Preamble. A key purpose of the new constitution, often particularly associated with the judiciary, was to "establish justice." Grievances against perceived judicial abuses had played a prominent part in events leading up to the Declaration of Independence from England.

The new constitution replaced the **unicameral** congress under the Articles of Confederation, in which each state had a single vote, with a **bicameral c**ongress in which states were represented according to population in one house and equally in the other. While establishing a **federal system** that maintained existing states, the new constitution further enlarged the powers of Congress at the expense of states, which had been largely sovereign under the Articles of Confederation. It then balanced congressional powers with powerful executive and judicial branches. The Framers entrusted Congress with the powers to make the laws, the president with the power to enforce them, and the judiciary with the power to interpret them.

Article III, Sec. 1:

The judicial Power of the United States, shall be vested in one supreme Court, and in such inferior Courts as the Congress may from time to time ordain and establish.

The Organization and Operation of the Federal Judicial System

The Constitution outlines the powers of the three branches of government in its first three of seven main divisions, known as articles. Article I thus describes the legislative branch, Article II the executive branch, and Article III the judicial branch. Although this order arguably gives primacy to the legislative branch, casebooks commonly begin with the judicial branch because its written decisions are critical to understanding the roles of the other two branches.

Article III's description of the judicial branch is far leaner than Article I's description of the legislative branch or Article II's description of the executive branch. Section 1 of Article III vests "[t]he judicial Power of the United States" in one Supreme Court and in such other courts as Congress shall create. This terse language left a good deal to the discretion of the other two branches, especially with regard to the establishment and organization of lower federal courts.

The first Congress that met under the new constitution consisted of a number of delegates who had attended the Constitutional Convention of 1787. It adopted a Judiciary Act that continues to serve as the basic outline for this system. The first reading in the first volume of this casebook includes selections from this act, which mirrored the hierarchical system that most states had already established and that continues today.

The Judiciary Act of 1789 and subsequent laws provide for federal cases to begin in **U.S. District Courts**, of which there are currently ninety-four. These courts are trial courts, or courts of **original** jurisdiction, where lawyers argue their cases and judges hear them for the first time. Each state has from one to four U.S. District Courts. On some occasions, laws provide for three-judge district courts, but more typically a single federal judge presides over each of these courts. Consistent with guarantees in the Sixth and Seventh Amendments to the U.S. Constitution, defendants before such courts have the right to jury trials.

U.S. District Courts, like the courts above them, have jurisdiction over (i.e., the authority to hear) both civil and criminal cases. **Civil cases** involve suits by individual citizens, who have grievances against one another. **Plaintiffs** bring the suits, and **defendants** respond to them (losing parties who appeal cases become **appellants,** while winning parties against whom they filed such appeals are **appellees**). Individuals might bring matters involving breaches of contracts, torts (wrongful actions that have caused damages), libel, and so on, for which they generally seek monetary damages. Criminal cases involve charges that the government, as the **prosecution,** brings against persons alleged to have violated the law: defendants. Criminal conviction may result in fines, jail sentences, or, in extreme cases, the death penalty.

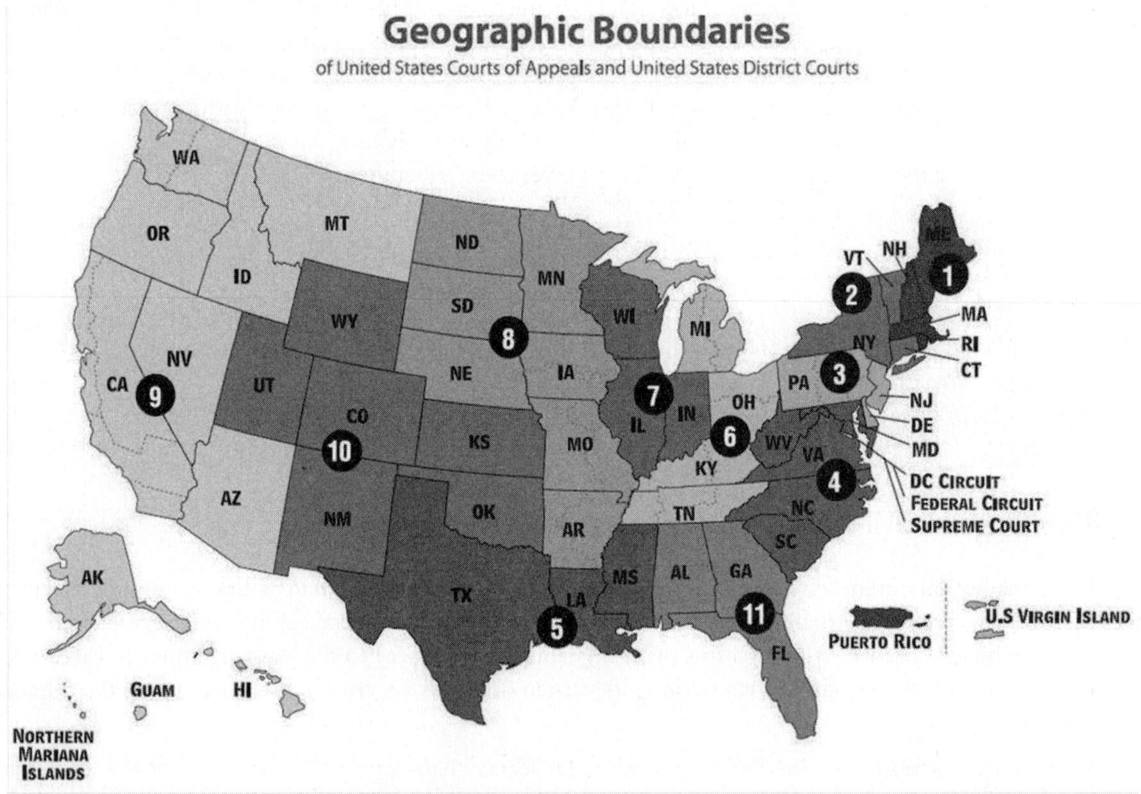

A system of **U.S. Circuit Courts** (there are eleven numbered circuits, a D.C. circuit, and a specialized circuit) constitutes the next level. These are chiefly courts of **appellate jurisdiction.** They are so designated because they review judgments on appeal from the district courts. Either side in a civil case may file such appeals, but since the Fifth Amendment prohibits double jeopardy, only individuals who are convicted can file appeals in criminal cases. Judges of the courts of appeal usually meet in panels of three, although sometimes they meet ***en banc,*** or as a whole. Under the Judiciary Act of 1789, Supreme Court justices had to "ride circuit" and serve as judges on these courts in addition to their duties in the capital. Although justices nominally remain in charge of such circuits and sometimes oversee special appeals from them, the law no longer requires this onerous duty of circuit-riding that not only tested the endurance but also threatened the physical health of the early justices.

Individuals or entities who lose their cases in the circuit courts, in one of three specialized federal courts (the Court of Military Appeals, the Court of Claims, or the Court of International Trade), or in a state's highest court (usually, but not always, designated as a state supreme court) on matters involving the U.S. Constitution may in turn appeal to the **U.S. Supreme Court.** Like the Capitol Building and the White House, the Supreme Court is located in Washington, D.C. Although the Constitution does not specify the number of justices on this Court, Congress has set the number at nine since the Civil War.

STRUCTURE OF THE FEDERAL COURTS

U.S. SUPREME COURT
U.S. Appellate Courts (13 Circuits)
Highest State Appellate Court
Court of International Trade
U.S. District Court (94 Courts)
Court of Military Appeals
State Appellate Courts
Court of Claims
State and Local Trial Courts

The **chief justice** presides over the Supreme Court. Whereas the House of Representatives chooses its own speaker, the president appoints a new chief justice when the current chief leaves office. The **chief justice** is regarded as ***primus inter pares***, or first among equals. The chief oversees the administration of the federal courts and directs its secret discussion of cases in chambers. By tradition, if the chief votes with the majority on the case, he may either write the decision personally or choose the justice who will write the Court's opinion; when the chief is in the minority, the ranking member of the majority exercises the same privilege.

In addition to a limited number of cases of original jurisdiction (cases it hears for the first time), which the U.S. Constitution assigns to it, the Supreme Court accepts cases from the U.S. circuit courts, from specialized federal courts, or, in cases involving federal jurisdiction, from the states' highest courts, through writs, or petitions, the most common of which is a **writ of certiorari**. In the past, the Court relied more heavily on **writs of appeal**, which the Court was technically required to hear, and on **writs of certification**, through which lower courts requested the Supreme Court to clarify an ambiguous provision of the law.

Congress has granted the Court discretion to decide which cases it will hear. It currently operates according to the **rule of four.** Under this rule, the Court will not listen to a case unless four or more members vote to do so. Of the thousands of petitions that the Court receives each year, it generally schedules oral arguments in fewer than seventy-five. When the Supreme Court accepts a case, it invites the parties to present oral arguments, the justices meet together in conference and vote in secret, opinions are written and reviewed, and the Court subsequently issues its decision.

Because the Supreme Court is not an elected branch, it is inappropriate for individuals to "lobby" the Court by arranging private meetings with justices and attempting to extract promises from them. Moreover, because the Court's members are not elected, individuals and organizations have no cause to give them campaign contributions. With the Court's permission, groups that are interested in cases may file ***amicus curiae***, or friend of the court, **briefs** in which they present arguments for the side they support. These briefs may provide background information about the effect of the general point of law—as on matters involving abortion or affirmative action—that the facts of an individual case or cases might not otherwise reveal.

Because it stands at the top of the federal judicial hierarchy, the U.S. Supreme Court is the most influential court in the land. Accordingly, almost all the decisions in this and most other constitutional law casebooks are taken from its decisions. Most opinions will feature a **majority**, or plurality, opinion on behalf of the Court. Many will also feature **concurring** and **dissenting opinions**. Justices who write concurring opinions agree with the ruling in the case but not necessarily with the reasoning. Dissenters believe that the Court has ruled incorrectly and make their appeal to the larger audience who will read such decisions.

Article II, Sec. 2:

"He [the President] . . . shall nominate, and by and with the Advice and Consent of the Senate, shall appoint . . . Judges of the supreme Court. . . ."

Article III, Sec. 1:

The Judges, both of the supreme and inferior Courts, shall hold their Offices during good Behavior, and shall, at stated Times, receive for their Services a Compensation which shall not be diminished during their Continuance in Office.

The Appointment, Confirmation, and Tenure of Judges and Justices

The judiciary is the only one of the three branches of the national government whose members (excluding civil servants, staffs, and political appointees) are appointed rather than elected. Supporters of the **Virginia** (large-state) **Plan** at the Constitutional Convention of 1787 had advocated legislative appointment of judges and justices, whereas advocates of the **New Jersey** (small-state) **Plan** had favored executive appointment. Ultimately, the Convention compromised by providing that the president would make such appointments, and the Senate would be asked to provide its "advice and consent"; by contrast, many states outline minimal qualifications but allow for the election of judges. In a well-known variant of this, often called the **Missouri Plan**, after its state of origination, governors appoint judges who are subsequently subject to electoral approval or disapproval.

Probably because federal judges are appointed rather than elected, the Constitution does not outline age, residency, and citizenship requirements for members of the judiciary as it does for Congress and the presidency. For example, there is no requirement that a Justice be an attorney. In modern times, it is practically inconceivable that these bodies would not at a minimum seek an individual with a law degree. Despite the absence of a constitutionally specified requirement to do so, presidents have increasingly nominated to the Supreme Court individuals who have served in lower courts, where they are likely to have established a record, which the president can evaluate in attempting to predict the kind of justices they would be.

Congress exercises far more scrutiny when deciding whether to confirm members of the judiciary than it does when confirming cabinet officers, and it typically extends greater scrutiny to nominees for the Supreme

Court than to nominees for lower courts. Senators know that the Constitution specifies that judges and justices will serve "**during good behavior.**" This means that they will be in office until they die, retire, or, as specified in Article II, Section 4, of the Constitution, are impeached and convicted of "Treason, Bribery, or other high Crimes and Misdemeanors." Although a score of federal judges have been impeached and convicted, Congress has yet to remove a U.S. Supreme Court justice through the mechanism of **impeachment** and conviction.

The Constitution intended for judges and justices to be independent. In addition to specifying a requirement for "good behavior," the Constitution prevented members of Congress from cutting judicial salaries in retaliation once they were in office. Article III does allow Congress to increase judicial salaries to enable judges who serve during long time periods to keep pace with inflation.

Because judges and justices will interpret and apply the Constitution and laws that are made under it, presidential candidates often describe the kinds of judicial appointments they will make. President Richard Nixon indicated that he would favor judges who favored law and order. In the election of 2008, Republican candidate John McCain stressed that he favored judges who would interpret the Constitution strictly, whereas Democrat Barack Obama stressed the need for judges to be compassionate. In 2016, presidential candidate Hillary Clinton promised to keep the Court on a progressive path, while Donald Trump released a potential list of possible Supreme Court nominees who he believed would, like the recently departed Justice Antonin Scalia, interpreted the Constitution conservatively and roll back the Court's abortion decision in *Roe v. Wade* (1973).

The Senate Judiciary Committee now televises its confirmation hearings, and special interest lobby groups increasingly weigh in to influence such votes. The hearings in the Reagan administration involving Robert Bork, a strong advocate of original intent, took partisan controversy to a new level of bitterness; commentators still refer to the possibility that a judicial nominee will be "Borked," or rejected by the Senate on partisan grounds. The bitter acrimony recurred when George H. W. Bush nominated Clarence Thomas. Only the second African American to be nominated for such a post, Thomas was much more conservative than the African American justice who was retiring, Thurgood Marshall. Critics not only challenged Thomas's ideology but aired allegations that he had engaged in sexual harassment. After classic "he said, she said" testimony from a former government employee, Anita Hill, the Senate confirmed Thomas, and he serves on the Court today.

When they contemplate federal judicial appointments, presidents clearly have to consider the Senate's response. Presidents might purposely seek out individuals without a long paper trail that can be used against them, but presidents are just as likely to seek someone with a known judicial philosophy with which they agree. Sometimes presidents sacrifice some perceived ideological compatibility in order to select individuals they think will have a greater chance of being confirmed. Even after outgoing President Barack Obama nominated Merrick Garland, a judge on the U.S. Court of Appeals for the D.C. Circuit, who was generally regarded as a moderate, to replace Antonin Scalia who died on February 13, 2016, Republicans who held sway in the Senate, blocked the nomination and refused even to hold hearings in hopes that a Republican President would be able to make the appointment.

The Federalist Explains the Judicial Branch

In understanding the judicial branch, it is helpful to appreciate what the American Founders intended for it to accomplish. The second reading in the first chapter of the first volume of this casebook is an essay from *The Federalist*, an outstanding series of essays that Alexander Hamilton, James Madison, and John Jay authored under the pseudonym Publius. Publius defended the proposed Constitution of 1787 against **Anti-Federalist** critics, who had focused in part on fears that the new government had overly empowered the judiciary. In *Federalist* No. 78, Alexander Hamilton, who had served as a delegate to the Constitutional Convention from New York and was among the passionate advocates of a stronger national government, defended the exercise of judicial review and attempted to minimize its negative effects. He associated judicial power with constitutional supremacy rather than with judicial supremacy. He also attempted to defend both the process of appointing judges and justices and the lifetime tenure that most of them will have.

Article III, Sec. 2, para. 1:

The judicial Power shall extend to all Cases, in Law and Equity, arising under this Constitution, the Laws of the United States, and Treaties made, or which shall be made, under their authority; to all Cases affecting Ambassadors, other public Ministers and Consuls; to all Cases of admiralty and maritime Jurisdiction; to Controversies to which the United States shall be a Party; to Controversies between two or more states; between a State and Citizens of another State; between Citizens of different States between Citizens of the same State claiming Lands under Grants of different States, and between a State, or the Citizens thereof, and foreign States, Citizens or Subjects.

The Jurisdiction and Power of Federal Courts

Members of the legislative and executive branches typically campaign by committing themselves in advance to certain policies and programs. They may advocate stronger defense, better health care, or better schools and highways; they may identify themselves as pro-life or pro-choice on abortion, or stick with more general themes like maintaining a healthy economy or advocating change. Politicians effectively act as policy entrepreneurs, hoping to identify and champion the issues or themes that will strike a responsive chord with their constituencies.

Although they ultimately wield tremendous powers, federal judges and justices do not run for office, and while they might be willing to share their general philosophies of decision making and constitutional interpretation with congressional committees, judicial nominees commonly refuse to answer questions about issues that they think are likely to come before their courts. Such nominees recognize that members of the public expect them to uphold the law without fear or favor, and they understand that they will immediately lose credibility if they precommit themselves to one side or another.

In outlining "judicial power" in Article III, the U.S. Constitution continually refers to "cases" and "controversies." This language helps explain why judges must necessarily be more passive than members of the other branches of government. They must wait for controversies to reveal themselves in conflicts between individual litigants before they can either hear them or attempt to resolve them.

Drawing from English legal history, Article III extends the judicial power to a variety of cases in both "**law and equity**." The former cases are the more familiar controversies involving levying fines and punishments. By contrast, equity jurisdiction is wider, allowing courts to intervene to prevent impending harms. An individual bringing damages because a neighbor's tree fell on his or her house would be bringing a case under "law," whereas an individual seeking an **injunction**, or judicial order, forbidding a neighbor from chopping down a tree without first securing protection for the residence would be bringing a case in "equity."

Between Judicial Activism and Judicial Restraint: Methods of Constitutional Interpretation

The Supreme Court exercises the power to interpret the laws and the Constitution. Differing approaches to interpreting the Constitution, like differing approaches to purely literary works or to holy books—the Bible, for example—can lead to different interpretations of these documents' meaning. Opponents of path-breaking judicial decisions often describe them as products of an "activist" court and call for judicial "restraint." The judges against whom the charges are made may see themselves as simply carrying out the job that they believe the Constitution has entrusted to them. Some jurists will distinguish between judicial "**interpretivism**," which largely focuses on the words and original meaning of the Constitution, while "**noninterpretivists**" will consider their mandate to be wider. In recent years, judges have raised the question of whether it is appropriate to look to foreign jurisdictions for ascertaining trends, as, for example, in matters related to capital punishment.

After more than two hundred years, the words of the Constitution are sometimes not only difficult to interpret in their own right but even more difficult to apply to contemporary situations. Different provisions might call for different approaches. No list of interpretive methods is likely to be exhaustive, or to serve equally for all provisions, but the following approaches are among the most common:

1. **Focus on the meaning of words:** Although every judge and justice pays considerable attention to the specific words of the Constitution, some consider this approach to be primary. Justice Hugo Lafayette Black was thus famous for observing that the words in the First Amendment providing that "Congress shall make no law" relative to speech meant precisely that.

2. **Original intent**: Often in combination with the focus on words, interpreters of the Constitution often seek to ascertain what words, phrases, and constitutional arrangements meant when they were originally proposed, ratified, and/or subsequently amended. Contemporary dictionaries and public statements of leading Framers might prove useful, although they are often contradictory.

3. **Precedent**: Citing the legal doctrine of ***stare decisis***, judges are especially likely to adhere to established precedents. Such adherence promotes stability in the law. Continuing adherence to a bad precedent, or series of precedents, can likewise perpetuate constitutional misunderstandings.

4. **Constitutional principles**: Judges often refer to principles that they believe are either stated, or implicit, within the Constitution. Examples include separation of church and state (a principle that observers often use to explain the Establishment Clause of the First Amendment), one person-one vote (used in legislative apportionment cases to require districts of approximately equal populations), and separation of powers. Of course, cases often involve conflicting principles among which judges and justices must choose. Judges sometimes liken their work to "balancing" various principles and considerations.

5. **Considerations of public policy**: Although legislators and executives are presumably the most likely to consider public policy implications of proposed legislation, judges often recognize that their decisions will have public policy consequences. They also recognize that they are ultimately dependent on the political branches for enforcement of their decisions.

6. **Living Constitution**: Often contrasted with original intent, advocates of a living constitution are likely to point to the difficulty of amending the Constitution and of the need for judicial interpretations that help keep the Constitution in touch with the times. In overturning more than fifty years of racial segregation in education, the Court observed in *Brown v. Board of Education* (1954) that education had a much larger role to play in society than it did at the time that the Court had approved the doctrine of "separate but equal."

This list is far from exhaustive, but students generally understand court decisions best when they know the methods the judges applied to get to them. Students will want to pay particular attention to the method of interpretation when they do the "reasoning" section of their case briefs.

Theories of Constitutional Interpretation

Interpretive Technique	Interpretivism	Noninterpretivism
Focus on the meaning of words	Use the plain meaning of the words to interpret the Constitution	
Original intent	Use the intent of the Framers, who drafted and ratified the document, such as the Constitution or a specific Amendment, to interpret the Constitution	
Precedent		Interpret the Constitution consistent with previous case law and decisions; avoid overturning past decisions unless clearly wrong.
Constitutional principles		Use neutral principles of law or basic values such as "separation of powers" to interpret the Constitution.
Considerations of public policy		Matters of social policy or public welfare should be used to clarify the meaning of specific constitutional texts.
Living Constitution		Read the Constitution in light of what it means today or in light of evolving values.

The Development of Judicial Review of National Legislation

Americans had brought a system of **common law** with them from England. Under this system, judges filled in gaps or interpreted ambiguous provisions of law while deciding cases. Cases in turn served as precedents that built upon one another. Under the British system of **parliamentary sovereignty**, the judicial role was fairly circumscribed by deference to the legislature.

The judiciary had arguably played a larger role in America, where it had once examined colonial laws to see that they were aligned with those of the motherland. Moreover, the new Constitution created a system embodying **separation of powers** and **checks and balances.** Separation of powers distributes powers among the three branches of government, each of which should adhere to the Constitution, but none of which can claim fully to embody the will of "We the People."

The framers of the Constitution fully expected that courts would interpret the laws. This is called **statutory interpretation**. When courts so interpret the laws, the law-making authority is free to adopt laws that state their intentions more clearly. In a 5–4 ruling in *Ledbetter v. Goodyear Tire and Rubber Co., Inc.* (550 U.S. 618, 2007), the Supreme Court rejected Lilly Ledbetter's sex discrimination claim under Title VII of the Civil Rights Act of

1964. She had filed a suit within 180 days of learning that the Goodyear Tire & Rubber Company was paying comparable male workers more than it paid her, but long after she was initially hired. The Court interpreted the law to require individuals to file suit within 180 days of the initial violation; Congress responded in early 2009 by passing the Lilly Ledbetter Fair Pay Restoration Act allowing employees to file claims within 180 days of their most recent paycheck.

Many Founders hoped, and some feared, that in addition to interpreting laws, courts would also exercise the power, now known as **judicial review**, to review the constitutionality of laws that arose in cases before them and strike down laws that they considered to be unconstitutional. Unless courts reverse themselves in such cases, lawmakers cannot override exercises of judicial review simply by adopting new laws. Instead, they must utilize the difficult power of constitutional amendment, as they did, for example, when adopting the Fourteenth Amendment to overturn the Supreme Court decision in *Dred Scott v. Sandford* (60 U.S. (19 How.) 393, 1857) declaring that blacks were not, and could not become, citizens of the United States. Consistent with common law antecedents, courts have established both the extent and the limitations of the power of judicial review through a process of case precedents, which are the subject of this chapter.

Also consistent with Hamilton's arguments in *Federalist* No. 78, Section 25 of the Judiciary Acts empowered the Supreme Court, when deciding on cases or controversies, to decide whether laws or actions that brought cases before them are constitutional or unconstitutional. Although the Court's power to review state laws for their conformity with the national Constitution is almost certainly essential to the perpetuation of a federal government, which attends to the interests of the entire nation, the power to review and invalidate national laws is more problematic because it pits the judgment of one unelected branch of government against that of one or both other branches that are more directly accountable to the people. Alexander Bickel, a prominent twentieth-century scholar, termed this the "countermajoritarian difficulty." *Marbury v. Madison* (5 U.S. (1 Cranch) 137, 1803), which is the first case in the first volume of this casebook, represents Chief Justice John Marshall's attempt to establish and justify the exercise of such power, which it has exercised ever since.

It is important to recognize that judicial review did not originate with *Marbury v. Madison.* Rather, this case represented the culmination of a series of precedents, some of which had originated a century before in Great Britain. State courts had repeatedly exercised the power of invalidating state statutes. North Carolina, Rhode Island, and New Jersey (*Holmes v. Walton,* 1780) are prime examples of this. Moreover, in *Hylton v. United States* (3 Dallas 171, 1796), the carriage tax case, the Supreme Court had assumed, but had not exercised, the power to declare an act of Congress unconstitutional.

Incorporation and the Bill of Rights

One of the clearest and best ways to understand judicial review, methods of constitutional interpretation, and how the Supreme Court has used this power to facilitate its power and influence is to look at how it has employed it to **incorporate** the various provisions of the Bill of Rights to the states.

During the battle over ratification of the Constitution, the omission of a bill of rights attracted criticism from the Anti-Federalists, who feared that the new national government would threaten individual liberty. Despite Alexander Hamilton's assurances in *Federalist* No. 84 that no bill of rights was necessary because the national government would not have the power to restrict individual rights, James Madison promised to introduce such language in Congress as amendments to the Constitution. In 1789 James Madison honored his promise, offering seventeen amendments in the House of Representatives, ten of which, once ratified in December 1791, became the Bill of Rights. Insofar as the Constitution's purpose was to establish the national government, these amendments were designed to restrict the national government's actions that would deprive citizens of civil liberties.

However, among the original seventeen amendments Madison offered, which passed in House on August 24, 1789, was one amendment that was meant to place limits on state power. It read: "No State shall infringe the right of trial by jury in criminal cases, nor the rights of conscience, nor the freedom of speech, or of the press." The Senate did not concur, rejecting this amendment as unnecessary. Did this mean that states were free to disregard the Bill of Rights? Even though Virginia and other states had their own bills of rights, this question was open until the Marshall Court addressed the matter in *Barron v. Baltimore* (32 U.S. 243, 1833), where Justice Marshall ruled that neither the Fifth Amendment's Just Compensation Clause nor any provision of the Bill of Rights applied to the states.

This chapter and the cases in it examine two important issues. The first looks to the incorporation of the Bill of Rights to apply to the individual states. This discussion allows the development of an understanding of how the Bill of Rights gradually came to exert limits on state power. For defenders of states' rights, like the Anti-Federalists, subjecting the states to the same constitutional limitations that were imposed on the national government was an encroachment on their sovereignty. Next, the chapter examines the modern interpretation of the Bill of Rights as a tool to limit both state (including local government) and federal authority. This discussion explores how the Supreme Court has come to give meaning to what the Bill of Rights says, especially in terms of the level of analysis or judicial scrutiny brought to bear to protect certain types of rights. At least since the New Deal, the assumption has been that the Court is a guardian not primarily of economic rights (as it was prior to the New Deal) but of individual rights such as freedom of speech or religion. This chapter looks at how the Court has adopted its modern framework and tools of scrutiny to protect rights. The chapter investigates two important concepts, suspect classifications and fundamental rights, that the Court has utilized as it has accepted its modern role as a defender of individual rights.

One lesson that should come from the cases in this chapter is that the nature of American democracy and the role of the Supreme Court in it have dramatically changed over time. Thus, the assumption that American courts have always focused on the protection of individual rights, at least the types of rights thought of today, such as freedom of speech, press, or criminal due process, is mistaken. The Court did little in its first 150 years to protect many of the rights now taken for granted. Instead, the Constitution designated the political processes to protect individual rights through a series of constitutional mechanisms such as checks and balances and separation of powers that were supposed to prevent the tyranny of the majority, or majority faction (Madison's phrase in *Federalist* No. 10), from having its way.

The original 1787 Constitution was based on the assumption that the federal government would be strictly limited by the Constitution. Some rights, such as habeas corpus, would be protected in Article I, 9 against encroachment by Congress or in Article I, 10 against the states, and Article IV would also protect some individual rights from state encroachment. However, the Founders largely addressed possible federal rather than state encroachments on individual rights. Perhaps the biggest constitutional revolution really came between 1787 when the original Constitution was adopted, and in 1791, when the Bill of Rights was ratified by the states. When James Madison, Alexander Hamilton, and John Jay penned the *Federalist Papers* in 1787, they wrote them for publication in a newspaper to encourage New York State legislators to adopt the new proposed Constitution. Far from simple political propaganda, the eighty-five *Federalist Papers* became an important gloss regarding what the Framers thought about and intended when they wrote the Constitution. In fact, over the years many scholars and Supreme Court justices have turned to these writings as an interpretive aid. Among the most important papers, *Federalist* No. 10 (along with No. 51, also written by Madison) is seen as particularly insightful into the design of the Constitution.

According to Madison in *Federalist* No. 10, there are three competing goals that political society needs to address. First, there is the need to preserve a republican form of government. This is a government premised at least in part upon majority rule. A second goal is the protection of individual liberty. The third is to limit the threat of factions to both republican government and individual liberty. Madison defined a faction as a "number of citizens, whether amounting to a majority or minority of the whole, who are united and actuated by some common impulse of passion, or of interest, adverse to the rights of other citizens, or to the permanent and aggregate interests of the community."

Factions, if they are composed simply of a numeric minority of the population can be handled by majority rule and elections. That is, the majority can outvote them. The real problem though is what to do with majority factions. Madison contends that one cannot eliminate the causes of faction because their causes are rooted in human nature. The issue is how to control their effects. In a critical passage in *Federalist* No. 10, Madison summarizes the political or sociological dilemma the proposed constitution was meant to address.

> If a faction consists of less than a majority, relief is supplied by the republican principle, which enables the majority to defeat its sinister views by regular vote. It may clog the administration, it may convulse the society; but it will be unable to execute and mask its violence under the forms of the Constitution. When a majority is included in a faction, the form of popular government, on the other hand, enables it to sacrifice to its ruling passion or interest both the public good and the rights of other citizens. To secure the public good and private rights against the danger of such a faction, and at the same time to preserve the spirit and the form of popular government, is then the great object to which our inquiries are directed.

The issue then is how to preserve individual liberty and republican government from the threats of majority faction.

In both *Federalist* Nos. 10 and 51 Madison describes the solution to this problem. It involved using numerous institutional remedies, including checks and balances, separation of powers, federalism, and bicameralism to control the effects of factions and to make it difficult for any one group to amass too much political power. The original constitutional solution was thus to use the political process to police the machinery of government against majority factions.

However, the construction of a bill of rights represented not only a triumph for the Anti-Federalists, but also recognition that the political process itself cannot police itself to protect rights. Instead, the creation of the Bill of Rights was supposed to take certain rights out of the political process and grant special powers to the courts to protect them. As Justice Jackson stated in *West Virginia v. Barnette* (319 U.S. 624, 1943): "The very purpose of a Bill of Rights was to withdraw certain subjects from the vicissitudes of political controversy, to place them beyond the reach of majorities and officials and to establish them as legal principles to be applied by the courts. One's right to . . . freedom of worship . . . and other fundamental rights may not be submitted to vote; they depend on the outcome of no elections." The adoption of the Bill of Rights, thus, was a major change in how American democracy and the courts were supposed to operate.

However, did the adoption of the Bill of Rights take politics out of rights? As one reads the cases in this chapter, one should ask this question. To what extent are rights really entrenched against majorities, and how successful or vigilant has the Supreme Court been as a defender of the Bill of Rights?

States and the Bill of Rights

Two often contradictory trends emerged early on in the American republic. On the one hand, property rights were deemed very important and often were afforded special protection in the law, or at least in many of the constitutional decisions issued by the Supreme Court under Chief Justice John Marshall. A discussion of how the early Supreme Court protected property rights is found in volume one. On the other hand, states regularly used eminent domain to take private property for a variety of public uses, often without paying compensation to the owner. During the American Revolutionary War, states regularly confiscated private property to facilitate the war effort, while during the early nineteenth century, states encouraged economic development by permitting uncompensated takings. In Massachusetts, the Mill Acts permitted the flooding of adjacent property, and state judges upheld laws that denied owners compensation for losses due to the floods. In an effort to defend their rights against uncompensated takings, landowners turned to the federal courts for relief, hoping that eventually Marshall and the Supreme Court would extend constitutional protections to their properties. These two trends collided in *Barron v. Baltimore* (32 U.S. 243, 1833), a case in which the Court did not come to the defense of property rights but ruled that the Bill of Rights did not apply to the states. This meant that a state government, or in this case, a city, could take the property of an owner without paying for it.

In many ways, *Barron* is not an easy case. While the First Amendment is clear in stating that "Congress [a branch of the national government] shall make no law. . .," the Fifth Amendment contains no similar restrictive language. Thus, it is conceivable that one reading of this amendment would suggest that the takings clause should also limit state action. However, Marshall offers a persuasive argument that the first eight amendments clearly apply only to the national government, as evidenced by the language and text of the Ninth and Tenth Amendments. Are you persuaded by his logic? Should the rejection of Madison's amendment to restrict state encroachments on individual rights bear on interpretations regarding application of the Bill of Rights to the states?

As a result of *Barron*, were states free to disregard individual rights if they did not have their own bills of rights to protect them? While the answer is yes in one sense, Article IV, Section 2, of the Constitution also contains a potentially significant clause that seems to guard individual rights. The Privileges or Immunities Clause states: "The citizens of each state shall be entitled to all privileges and immunities of citizens in the several states." What exactly were these privileges and immunities? Supreme Court Justice Bushrod Washington (a nephew of George Washington), while writing as a circuit court judge in *Corfield v. Coryell* (6 F.Cas. 546, 1823), attempted to answer this question.

> The inquiry is, what are the privileges and immunities of citizens in the several states? We feel no hesitation in confining these expressions to those privileges and immunities which are, in their nature, fundamental; which belong, of right, to the citizens of all free governments; and which have, at all times, been enjoyed by the citizens of the several states which compose this Union, from the time of their becoming free, independent, and sovereign. What these fundamental principles are, it would perhaps be more tedious than difficult to enumerate. They may, however, be all comprehended under the following general heads: Protection by the government; the enjoyment of life and liberty, with the right to acquire and possess property of every kind, and to pursue and obtain happiness and safety; subject nevertheless to such restraints as the government may justly prescribe for the general good of the whole. The right of a citizen of one state to pass through, or to reside in any other state, for purposes of trade, agriculture, professional pursuits, or otherwise; to claim the benefit of the writ of habeas corpus; to institute and maintain actions of any kind in the courts of the state; to take, hold and dispose of property, either real or personal; and an exemption from higher taxes or impositions than are paid by the other citizens of the state; may be mentioned as some of the particular privileges and immunities of citizens, which are clearly embraced by the general description of privileges deemed to be fundamental: to which may be added, the elective franchise, as regulated and established by the laws or constitution of the state in which it is to be exercised.

Arguably, such privileges and immunities might encompass many of the protections found in the Bill of Rights, but the Supreme Court in *Barron* ignored this decision and seemed uninterested in cataloging a list of **fundamental rights** that were protected against state intrusion.

BARRON V. BALTIMORE

32 U.S. 243, 7 Peters 243, 8 L.Ed. 672 (1833)

The city of Baltimore in the process of paving certain streets around the waterfront had diverted the course of some streams. The net result had been the depositing of so much silt and sediment around a wharf owned by Barron that the water was too shallow to afford dockage. Barron, who had sued for $4500 damages, using the provision of the Fifth Amendment of the Constitution. that forbids deprivation of property without just compensation as a basis for his claim, lost in the lower courts.

Vote: No dissent

CHIEF JUSTICE MARSHALL delivered the opinion of the Court.

. . . The Constitution was ordained and established by the people of the United States for themselves, for their own government, and not for the government of the individual States. Each State established a Constitution for itself, and, in that Constitution, provided such limitations and restrictions on the powers of its particular government as its judgment dictated. The people of the United States framed such a government for the United States as they supposed best adapted to their situation, and best calculated to their interests. The powers they conferred on this government were to be exercised by itself; and the limitations on power, if expressed in general terms, are naturally, and, we think, necessarily applicable to the government created by the instrument. They are limitations of power granted in the instrument itself; not of distinct governments, framed by different persons and for different purposes.

If these propositions be correct, the Fifth Amendment must be understood as restraining the power of the general government, not as applicable to the States. In their several constitutions they have imposed such restrictions on their respective governments as their own wisdom suggested; such as they deemed most proper for themselves. It is a subject on which they judge exclusively, and with which others interfere no further than they are supposed to have a common interest.

The counsel for the plaintiff in error insists that the Constitution was intended to secure the people of the several States against the undue exercise of power by their respective State governments; as well as against that which might be attempted by their general government. In support of this argument he relies on the inhibitions contained in the tenth section of the first article.

We think that section affords a strong if not a conclusive argument in support of the opinion already indicated by the court.

The preceding section contains restrictions which are obviously intended for the exclusive purpose of restraining the exercise of power by the departments of the general government. Some of them use language applicable only to Congress; others are expressed in general terms. The third clause, for example, declares that "no bill of attainder or *ex post facto* law shall be passed." No language can be more general; yet the demonstration is complete that it applies solely to the government of the United States. In addition to the general arguments furnished by the instrument itself, some of which have been already suggested, the succeeding section, the avowed purpose of which is to restrain State legislation, contains in terms the very prohibition. It declares that "no State shall pass any bill of attainder or *ex post facto* law." This provision, then, of the ninth section, however comprehensive its language, contains no restriction on state legislation. . . .

If the original Constitution, in the ninth and tenth sections of the first article, draws this plain and marked line of discrimination between the limitations it imposes on the powers of the general government, and on those of the States; if in every inhibition intended to act on State power, words are employed which directly express that intent,—some strong reason must be assigned for departing from this safe and judicious course in framing the amendments, before that departure can be assumed.

We search in vain for that reason.

. . . In almost every convention by which the Constitution was adopted, amendments to guard against the abuse of power were recommended. These amendments demanded security against the apprehended encroachments of the general government, not against those of the local governments. . .

FOR DISCUSSION

After *Barron,* what mechanisms existed at the state level to protect individual rights? Do you think Anti-Federalists were correct in their assertions that states were not dangers to individual freedom or that adequate controls were in place to protect individual rights at this level of government?

The Bill of Rights and Fourteenth Amendment

The Fourteenth Amendment was originally proposed in Congress by Representative John Bingham of Ohio on June 13, 1866, and ratified on July 28, 1868. The amendment offered constitutional protection to the rights of the recently freed slaves, and it overturned the Supreme Court decision in *Dred Scott v. Sandford* (60 U.S. 393, 1857), which had declared that African Americans could never be citizens. The amendment represented an additional effort to protect the rights of the freed slaves. In addition to clarifying U.S. citizenship, Section 1 of the Fourteenth Amendment had three critical provisions: a privileges or immunities clause, a due process clause, and an equal protection clause.

Some argued that the Privileges or Immunities Clause served either to protect the rights Justice Washington described in *Corfield v. Coryell* (4 Wash. C.C. 380, 1823) against state encroachment, or to serve as a broader platform for reversing *Barron* to apply the Bill of Rights to the states. Support for the former claim could be found in the language of the Civil Rights Act of 1866, which referred to many of the rights found in *Corfield* and which the act sought to protect for the newly freed slaves. Concern among some that the civil rights act was unconstitutional had prompted certain members of Congress to push for the Fourteenth Amendment. However, in the *Slaughterhouse Cases*, the Court rejected a broad interpretation of the intent of the Fourteenth Amendment.

The Slaughterhouse Cases (83 U.S. 36, 1873), decided only five years after the adoption of the Fourteenth Amendment, were the first interpretation of that amendment. At this time, "due process" still basically meant procedure. Substantive due process, by which the "what" of governmental activity as well as the "how" can be questioned, came later, although in *Dred Scott v. Sandford* (60 U.S. 393, 1856) the Court had alluded to substantive due process.

In the *Slaughterhouse Cases* the Court ruled that the Privileges or Immunities Clause did not serve to protect individuals from state encroachment of the Bill of Rights. It also effectively ruled against the idea that the Bill of Rights applied to the states. Reaching this conclusion was consistent with *Barron.* In the rest of the opinion, the Court distinguished sharply between the privileges and immunities of state citizenship and of federal citizenship, noting that only the latter were protected from transgression by the states in the Fourteenth Amendment. With respect to the former, the Court noted that these would be determined as cases arose. In fact, with the occasional exception of a case such as *Saenz v. Roe* (526 U.S. 489, 1999), which voided durational residency laws to collect welfare or public assistance in order to protect the right to interstate travel, the Court rarely has found a state statute to conflict with the Privileges or Immunities Clause of the Fourteenth

Amendment. In general, the test of such a privilege is that it be derived from federal law (including, of course, the Constitution) and that it be a concomitant of citizenship. In this latter respect this provision differs from most of the guarantees of the Constitution, which are enjoyed by "persons," citizens and noncitizens alike.

Yet if the Privileges or Immunities Clause did not extend the Bill of Rights to the states, perhaps another part of the Fourteenth Amendment did? Did the Due Process Clause offer any protection? In *Hurtado v. People of State of California* (110 U.S. 516, 1884) the Court confronted this question. *Hurtado*, like *Barron*, rejected claims that the protections of the Fifth Amendment imposed restrictions on states. In this case, the Court ruled that the grand jury provisions for indictment did not should apply to the states. Yet the dissents in the *Slaughterhouse Cases* and the emerging substantive due process decisions in cases such as *Munn v. Illinois* (94 U.S. 113, 1877) and *Muglar v. Kansas* (123 U.S. 623, 1887) revealed a concern for the protection of property and economic rights. Concern for property rights and efforts to protect some fundamental rights finally paid off in *Chicago, B. & Q. R. Co. v. City of Chicago* (166 U.S. 226, 1897), where a more economically minded Court under Chief Justice Melvin Fuller issued the first decision incorporating the Bill of Rights to apply to the states via the Fourteenth Amendment's Due Process Clause thus beginning a long slow erosion of the effects of *Barron.*

Chicago, B. & Q. R. Co. v. City of Chicago began an intense and prolonged debate on two fronts. First, it was one of several decisions (discussed in volume one) that extended significant legal protections to property rights under the Fourteenth Amendment during a time when the amendment, while originally written to protect the rights of newly freed slaves, was largely ignored as a tool to fight racial discrimination and Jim Crow laws. Second *Chicago, B. & Q. R. Co. v. City of Chicago* is first in a litany of Supreme Court cases regarding whether the adoption of the Fourteenth Amendment's Due Process Clause was meant to apply the Bill of Rights to the states. In regard to this second point, three answers were possible.

First, some argue that the Due Process Clause does not incorporate any of the Bill of Rights amendments to the states. This position was rejected in *Chicago, B. & Q. R. Co. v. City of Chicago.* A second answer is the **incorporation thesis**. This is the claim that the Due Process Clause incorporated all of the Bill of Rights provisions to apply to the states. Justice Hugo Black, especially in *Adamson v. California* (332 U.S. 46, 1947), argued this. However, with the exception of Black and perhaps John Marshall Harlan, no other justices have adopted this position. Finally, the third answer is **selective incorporation**. This is the claim that the Due Process Clause incorporates only the most essential provisions of the Bill of Rights, like some of the more important criminal due process guarantees. The Court first adopted this approach in *Chicago, B. & Q. R. Co. v. City of Chicago* and then in *Gitlow v. New York* (268 U.S. 652, 1925).

Gitlow's significance lies not so much in the Court's failure to overturn Gitlow's conviction for seditious speech under New York State's Criminal Anarchy Law but in its statement that:

> For present purposes we may and do assume that freedom of speech and of the press—which are protected by the First Amendment from abridgment by Congress—are among the fundamental personal rights and "liberties" protected by the due process clause of the Fourteenth Amendment from impairment by the states. . .

Most scholars consider this ruling, not *Chicago, B. & Q. R. Co. v. City of Chicago,* to be the first clear case of incorporation, or at least the case that began the modern debate about incorporation. The question that emerged out of *Gitlow* was whether only the Free Speech and Free Press Clauses applied to the states or whether other protections in the First Amendment similarly applied. The debate on the Court after *Gitlow,* which was framed with respect to that question, often sought to determine whether some rights were more fundamental than others and thereby deserving to be extended to protection against state encroachment.

In deciding which rights should be applied to the states, the Court had to decide whether all rights have equal value and weight, or whether some deserve more protection or carry greater weight than others? In arguing cases, some lawyers say that the rights to free speech, freedom of religion, and so on are in the First Amendment because they are of transcendent importance. This is not, however, the reason for their placement there (states simply did not ratify the first two proposals), and the Bill of Rights provides no explicit hierarchy for rights that it articulates.

In *Palko v. State of Connecticut* (302 U.S. 319, 1937), Justice Cardozo rejects claims that the Self-incrimination Clause of the Fifth Amendment applies to the states. The holding in *Palko* is that the only provisions of the Bill of Rights that are applicable to the states through the Due Process Clause of the Fourteenth Amendment are those that are of the very essence of a **scheme of ordered liberty**. This claim tries to demarcate some provisions as enjoying greater constitutional status than others.

The next case, *Cantwell v. Connecticut* (310 U.S. 296, 1940), one of many involving Jehovah's Witnesses, ruled that the concept of liberty expressed in the First Amendment also included freedom of religion. In balancing the state's interest in preserving the peace against freedom of religion, the Court tipped the balance toward in the latter in the light of the unwarranted administrative censorship of religion provided by the statute in question.

Standing in contrast to assertions that the Fourteenth Amendment only selectively incorporated some Bill of Rights provisions that were deemed more fundamental or important were claims that the Due Process Clause fully incorporated all of the provisions. Justice Black is best known for arguing the **incorporation** thesis, with his dissent in *Adamson v. People of State of California* (332 U.S. 46, 1947) best articulating this position. To defend his claim, Black's dissent offers an analysis of the debates on the passage of the Fourteenth Amendment, to which he attached a long-detailed appendix discussing the debates and adoption of that Amendment. Black attempted to show that the authors of the Fourteenth Amendment intended to protect all the provisions of the Bill of Rights against state action. Even if Black is historically correct, and many historians dispute his assertion, his position on total incorporation has never gained a majority on the Court.

Are you persuaded that the First Amendment does or should incorporate all the Bill of Rights protections to the states? Or perhaps Justice Washington was correct that other rights besides those found in the Bill of Rights should be protected against state encroachment? Or do you think Justice Cardozo was correct in asserting that only certain rights that are more important than others should receive such protection? Do you think that some rights are more fundamental than others? If so, on what basis?

Criminal due process decisions have been central to the incorporation of the Bill of Rights. The next four cases in this chapter, beginning with *Powell v. Alabama* (287 U.S. 45, 1932), show how the Court applied the selective incorporation theory in the area of criminal due process; *Powell v. Alabama, the first "Scottsboro Boys" case to reach the Supreme Court*—the second was *Norris v. Alabama* (294 U.S. 587, 1987)—involved allegations of rape of two white women against a number of African-American minors. The Court ruled that the right to counsel articulated in the Sixth Amendment applied to the states given the presence of certain circumstances, which included a racially-charged hostile environment, a rush to judgment, and relatively uneducated defendants. In *Betts v. Brady* (316 U.S. 455, 1942), however, the Court refused, however, to extend protection for the right of counsel against the states in all circumstances. Related cases ruled that the Fourteenth Amendment's Due Process Clause invalidated activities by a state that elicited self-incrimination insofar as the incriminatory statements were found to be part of a coerced confession and thus a denial of "essential fairness," which also included the guarantee of a fair jury trial. As the Court has noted, a denial by a state of rights or privileges specifically embodied in several of the first eight amendments may, in certain circumstances, or in connection with other elements, operate, in a given case, to deprive a person of due process of law in violation of the Fourteenth Amendment.

In *Gideon v. Wainwright* (372 U.S. 335, 1963), the case that follows *Powell v. Alabama* in this casebook, the Court applied the guarantee of counsel in the Sixth Amendment to all cases in the state courts, capital and noncapital alike, thus extending the "Gitlow doctrine." This includes cases in which a defendant could not afford a lawyer. In *Wolf v. Colorado* (338 U.S. 25, 1949), the next case in this text, the Court refused to extend the exclusionary rule, which it had fashioned in *Weeks v. United States* (232 U.S. 383, 1914) as a way of enforcing the Fourth Amendment protections against unreasonable searches and seizures, to the states. The net result of *Wolf* was that unreasonable searches and seizures were forbidden but the evidence thus secured could be admitted in state courts. *Wolf* is an unusual case in that the Court set forth a very specific point—that the security of one's privacy against arbitrary intrusion by the police is basic to a free society, in other words, is "fundamental"—but, having set down this doctrine, refused to implement or enforce it by excluding evidence that had been illegally secured.

Finally, *Mapp v. Ohio* (367 U.S. 643, 1961) overturned *Wolf.* Do the arguments in *Gideon* and *Mapp* for incorporation rest on the same grounds? While *Gideon* may assert more constitutional grounds or find that application of the Sixth Amendment rests upon arguments that are grounded in the law or in the needs of protecting the accused, some of the reasoning in *Mapp* seems more premised upon policy or pragmatic grounds. Specifically, one cannot have dual standards, with one rule applying to the federal government and another to states. Do you agree with this logic? Is Justice Clark correct in his claims about the problems that would occur with a dual standard? Or is Clark making his claims for incorporation by appealing to the logic of *Palko,* namely, that the exclusionary rule really does represent a "concept of ordered liberty"? The previous criminal due process cases should have demonstrated convincingly the many differing positions that the Court has taken when it comes to the incorporation debate.

Much of the incorporation debate revolved around textually explicit provisions of the Bill of Rights and their application to the states. But as will be recalled from *Corfield* and *Chicago, B. & Q. R. Co. v. City of Chicago,* there were also some who believed that states should be prevented from impinging upon a host of fundamental rights. In *Griswold v. Connecticut* (381 U.S. 479, 1965), the Court draws upon the Ninth Amendment to decide if a right to privacy exists and whether it limits states.

Griswold is one of a very small number of cases that use the Ninth Amendment to support a holding. In addition to a right to privacy, are there any other rights that you think should be protected from state encroachment (or incorporated via the Fourteenth Amendment) that are not textually explicit in the Bill of Rights? How would one justify which additional rights to include? Would they have to be rights that are deemed to be part of a concept of ordered liberty, or is there some other rationale for their inclusion? Could one cite the intent of the Framers as textual support for the rights to be included? Recall that the Anti-Federalists wanted a Bill of Rights to limit federal action, not state action. The congressional debates on the Ninth Amendment are thin in terms of what additional rights should be protected. Maybe the additional rights are the economic ones that were discussed in *Corfield*? Many constitutions in other countries protect economic rights, such as those to work or own property or obtain health care. Does the Bill of Rights, specifically the Ninth Amendment, also protect them?

What Has Been Incorporated?

So far the Court has not ruled that either the Third Amendment provision limiting the quartering of troops in private homes, the Fifth Amendment requirement for grand jury indictments, or the Seventh Amendment right to jury trials is incorporated to apply to the states through the Fourteenth Amendment. Otherwise, the rest of the Bill of Rights now applies to the states. The most recent incorporation took place with in *McDonald v. City of Chicago, Illinois,* 561 U.S. 742 (2010), ruling that the Second Amendment right to bear arms also applied to the states.

First Amendment

- religion, establishment: *Everson v. Board of Education of the Township of Ewing* (330 U.S. 1, 1947); free exercise, *Cantwell v. Connecticut* (310 U.S. 296, 1940)
- freedom of speech and the press: *Gitlow v. New York* (268 U.S. 652, 1925); press, specifically: *Near v. Minnesota* (283 U.S. 697, 1931)
- assembly: *DeJonge v. Oregon* (299 U.S. 353, 1937)

Second Amendment

- right to bear arms: *McDonald v. City of Chicago, Illinois,* 561 U.S. 742 (2010)

Fourth Amendment

- search and seizure: *Wolf v. Colorado* (338 U.S. 25, 1949), exclusionary rule applied in *Mapp v. Ohio* (367 U.S. 643, 1961)
- issuance of warrant, *Ker v. California* (374 U.S. 23, 1963)

Fifth Amendment

- double jeopardy: *Benton v. Maryland* (395 U.S. 784, 1969)
- self-incrimination: *Malloy v. Hogan* (378 U.S. 1, 1964)
- private property (decided without use of the incorporation doctrine): *Chicago, Burlington & Quincy Railroad Co. v. Chicago* (166 U.S. 226, 1897)

Sixth Amendment

- speedy trial: *Klopfer v. North Carolina* (386 U.S. 213, 1967)
- public trial (decided using the Due Process Clause of the Fourteenth Amendment without use of the incorporation doctrine): *In re Oliver* (333 U.S. 257, 1948)
- trial by jury: *Duncan v. Louisiana* (391 U.S. 145, 1968)
- impartial jury: *Parker v. Gladden* (385 U.S. 363, 1966)
- confront witnesses: *Pointer v. Texas* (380 U.S. 400, 1965)
- compulsory process for witness testimony (subpoena): *Washington v. Texas* (388 U.S. 14, 1967)
- counsel, in capital cases: *Powell v. Alabama* (287 U.S. 45, 1932); in felony cases: *Gideon v. Wainwright* (372 U.S. 335, 1963); in any case in which imprisonment may be a penalty, *Argersinger v. Hamlin* (407 U.S. 25, 1972)

Eighth Amendment

- excessive fines: *Cooper Industries, Inc., v. Leatherman Tool Group, Inc.* (532 U.S. 424, 2001)
- cruel and unusual punishment: *Robinson v. California* (370 U.S. 660, 1962)

Ninth Amendment

- "other [rights] retained by the people": *Griswold v. Connecticut* (381 U.S. 479, 1965), in which the court found the right to privacy to be one such "other" right.

SLAUGHTERHOUSE CASES

83 U.S. 36, 16 Wall. 36, 21 L.Ed. 394 (1873)

The Slaughterhouse Cases, the first cases brought to the Supreme Court under the Fourteenth Amendment, arose under a Louisiana statute of 1869 regulating the business of slaughtering livestock in New Orleans. The highly corrupt state legislature of the Reconstruction period had granted a monopoly to the facilities of one corporation. Other butchers were to have access to these facilities on payment of a reasonable fee, but the net result was that more than a thousand persons and companies were prevented from continuing in the business.

Vote: 5–4

JUSTICE MILLER delivered the opinion of the Court.

. . . The plaintiffs in error accepting this issue, allege that the statute is a violation of the Constitution of the United States in these several particulars:—

That it creates an involuntary servitude forbidden by the thirteenth article of amendment;

That it abridges the privileges and immunities of citizens of the United States;

That it denies to the plaintiffs the equal protection of the laws; and,

That it deprives them of their property without due process of law; contrary to the provisions of the first section of the fourteenth article of amendment. . . . The next observation is more important in view of the arguments of counsel in the present case. It is, that the distinction between citizenship of the United States and citizenship of a State is clearly recognized and established. Not only may a man be a citizen of the United States without being a citizen of a State, but an important element is necessary to convert the former into the latter. He must reside within the State to make him a citizen of it, but it is only necessary that he should be born or naturalized in the United States to be a citizen of the Union.

It is quite clear, then, that there is a citizenship of the United States, and a citizenship of a State, which are distinct from each other, and which depend upon different characteristics or circumstances in the individual.

We think this distinction and its explicit recognition in this amendment of great weight in this argument, because the next paragraph of this same section, which is the one mainly relied on by the plaintiffs in error, speaks only of privileges and immunities of citizens of the United States, and does not speak of those of citizens of the several States. The argument, however, in favor of the plaintiffs rests wholly on the assumption that the citizenship is the same, and the privileges and immunities guaranteed by the clause are the same.

The language is, "No State shall make or enforce any law which shall abridge the privileges or immunities of citizens of the United States." It is a little remarkable, if this clause was intended as a protection to the citizen of a State against the legislative power of his own State, that the word citizen of the State should be left out when it is so carefully used, and used in contradistinction to citizens of the United States, in the very sentence which preceded it. It is too clear for argument that the change in phraseology was adopted understandingly and with a purpose.

Of the privileges and immunities of the citizen of the United States, and of the privileges and immunities of the citizen of the State, and what they respectively are, we will presently consider; but we wish to state here that it is only the former which are placed by this clause under the protection of the Federal Constitution, and that the latter, whatever they may be, are not intended to have any additional protection by this paragraph of the amendment.

If, then, there is a difference between the privileges and immunities belonging to a citizen of the United States as such, and those belonging to the citizen of the State as such, the latter must rest for their security and protection where they have heretofore rested; for they are not embraced by this paragraph of the amendment. . . .

Having shown that the privileges and immunities relied on in the argument are those which belong to citizens of the States as such, and that they are left to the State governments for security and protection, and not by this article placed under the special care of the Federal government, we may hold ourselves excused from defining the privileges and immunities of citizens of the United States which no State can abridge, until some case involving those privileges may make it necessary to do so.

But lest it should be said that no such privileges and immunities are to be found if those we have been considering are excluded, we venture to suggest some which owe their existence to the Federal Government, its national character, its Constitution, or its laws.

One of these is well described in the case of *Crandall v. Nevada*, 73 U.S. 35 (1867). It is said to be the right of the citizen of this great country, protected by implied guarantees of its Constitution, "to come to the seat of government to assert any claim he may have upon that government, to transact any business he may have with it, to seek its protection, to share its offices, to engage in administering its functions. He has the right of free access to its seaports, through which all operations of foreign commerce are conducted, to the sub-treasuries, land offices, and courts of justice in the several states."

Another privilege of a citizen of the United States is to demand the care and protection of the Federal government over his life, liberty, and property when on the high seas or within the jurisdiction of a foreign government. Of this there can be no doubt, nor that the right depends upon his character as a citizen of the United States. The right to peaceably assemble and petition for redress of grievances, the privilege of the writ of habeas corpus, are rights of the citizen guaranteed by the Federal Constitution. The right to use the navigable waters of the United States, however they may penetrate the territory of the several States, all rights secured to our citizens by treaties with foreign nations, are dependent upon citizenship of the United States, and not citizenship of a State. One of these privileges is conferred by the very article under consideration. It is that a citizen of the United States, can of his own volition, become a citizen of any State of the Union by a bona fide residence therein, with the same rights as other citizens of that State. To these may be added the rights secured by the thirteenth and fifteenth articles of amendment, and by the other clause of the fourteenth, next to be considered. . . .

The argument has not been much pressed in these cases that the defendant's charter deprives the plaintiffs of their property without due process of law, or that it denies to them the equal protection of the law. The first of these paragraphs has been in the Constitution since the adoption of the Fifth Amendment, as a restraint upon the federal power. It is also to be found in some form of expression in the Constitutions of nearly all of the States, as a restraint upon the power of the States. This law, then, has practically been the same as it now is during the existence of the government, except so far as the present amendment may place the restraining power over the States in this matter in the hands of the Federal government.

We are not without judicial interpretation, therefore, both State and national, of the meaning of this clause. And it is sufficient to say that under no construction of that provision that we have ever seen, or any that we deem admissible, can the restraint imposed by the State of Louisiana upon the exercise of their trade by the butchers of New Orleans be held to be a deprivation of property within the meaning of that provision.

"Nor shall any State deny to any person within its jurisdiction the equal protection of the laws."

In the light of the history of these amendments, and the pervading purpose of them, which we have already discussed, it is not difficult to give a meaning to this clause. The existence of laws in the States where the newly emancipated Negroes resided, which discriminated with gross injustice and hardship against them as a class, was the evil to be remedied by this clause, and by it such laws are forbidden.

If, however, the States did not conform their laws to its requirements, then by the fifth section of the article of amendment Congress was authorized to enforce it by suitable legislation. We doubt very much whether any action of a State not directed by way of discrimination against the Negroes as a class, or on account of their race, will ever be held to come within the purview of this provision. It is so clearly a provision for that race and that emergency, that a strong case would be necessary for its application to any other. But as it is a State that is to be dealt with, and not alone the validity of its laws, we may safely leave that matter until Congress shall have exercised its power, or some case of State oppression, by denial of equal justice in its courts, shall have claimed a decision at our hands. We find no such case in the one before us, and do not deem it necessary to go over the argument again, as it may have relation to this particular clause of the amendment. . . .

Judgment affirmed.

JUSTICE FIELD dissented, with the concurrence of CHIEF JUSTICE CHASE, and JUSTICES SWAYNE and BRADLEY.

What then, are the privileges and immunities which are secured against abridgement by State legislation?

The terms, privileges and immunities, are not new in the amendment; they were in the Constitution before the amendment was adopted. They are found in the second section of the fourth article, which declares that "the citizens of each State shall be entitled to all privileges and immunities of citizens in the several States," and they have been the subject of frequent consideration in judicial decisions. In *Corfield v. Coryell,* 4 Wash. C.C. 380 (1823), Mr. Justice Washington said he had "no hesitation in confining these expressions to those privileges and immunities which were, in their nature, fundamental; which belong of right to citizens of all free governments, and which have at all times been enjoyed by the citizens of the several States which compose the Union, from the time of their becoming free, independent, and sovereign;" and, in considering what those fundamental privileges were, he said that perhaps it would be more tedious than difficult to enumerate them, but that they might be "all comprehended under the following general heads; protection by the government; the enjoyment of life and liberty, with the right to acquire and possess property of every kind, and to pursue and obtain happiness and safety, subject, nevertheless to such restraints as the government may justly prescribe for the general good of the whole." This appears to me to be a sound construction of the clause in question. The privileges and immunities designated are those *which of right belong to the citizens of all free governments.* Clearly among these must be placed the right to pursue a lawful employment in a lawful manner, without other restraint than such as equally affects all persons. In the discussions in Congress upon the passage of the Civil Rights Act repeated reference was made to this language of Mr. Justice Washington. It was cited by Senator Trumbull with the observation that it enumerated the very rights belonging to a citizen of the United States set forth in the first section of the act, and with the statement that all persons born in the United States being declared by the act citizens of the United States, would thenceforth be entitled to the rights of citizens, and that these were the great fundamental rights set forth in the act; and that they were set forth "as appertaining to every freeman." . . .

This equality of right, with exemption from all disparaging and partial enactments, in the lawful pursuits of life, throughout the whole country, is the distinguishing privilege of citizens of the United States. To them, everywhere, all pursuits, all professions, all avocations are open without other restrictions than such as are imposed equally upon all others of the same age, sex, and condition. The State may prescribe such regulations for every pursuit and calling of life as will promote the public health, secure the good order and advance the general prosperity of society, but when once prescribed, the pursuit or calling must be free to be followed by every citizen who is within the conditions designated, and will conform to the regulations. This is the fundamental idea upon which our institutions rest, and unless adhered to in the legislation of the country our government will be a republic only in name. The Fourteenth Amendment, in my judgment, makes it essential to the validity of the legislation of every State that this equality of right should be respected. How widely this equality has been departed from, how entirely rejected and trampled upon by the act of Louisiana, I have already shown. And it is to be a matter of profound regret that its validity is recognized by a majority of this court, for by it the right of free labor, one of the most sacred and imprescriptible rights of man, is violated. . . . That only is a free government, in the American sense of the term, under which the inalienable right of every citizen to pursue his happiness is unrestrained, except by just, equal, and impartial laws.

JUSTICES SWAYNE and BRADLEY also filed separate dissenting opinions.

FOR DISCUSSION

Did the Court effectively read the Privileges or Immunities Clause out of the Constitution? What rights are protected by this clause of the Fourteenth Amendment as a result of this decision?

RELATED CASE

***Crandall* v. *Nevada:* 6 Wall. 35 (1868).**

A state cannot impose a tax on persons leaving the state by any common carrier to be collected by the carrier because this would transgress the rights of U.S. citizens to move freely about the country.

HURTADO V. PEOPLE OF STATE OF CALIFORNIA

110 U.S. 516, 4 S.Ct. 111, 28 L.Ed. 232 (1884)

Hurtado was indicted for murder based on a clause in the California constitution that allowed for such indictments without a grand jury, relying instead on the filing of a writ of information by a prosecutor. Upon his conviction Hurtado appealed, contending that this form of indictment violated his Fourteenth Amendment due process rights. The Supreme Court upheld his conviction.

Vote: 9–0

JUSTICE MATTHEWS delivered the opinion of the Court.

The constitution of the United States was ordained, it is true, by descendants of Englishmen, who inherited the traditions of the English law and history; but it was made for an undefined and expanding future, and for a people gathered, and to be gathered, from many nations and of many tongues; and while we take just pride in the principles and institutions of the common law, we are not to forget that in lands where other systems of jurisprudence prevail, the ideas and processes of civil justice are also not unknown. Due process of law, in spite of the absolutism of continental governments, is not alien to that Code which survived the Roman empire as the foundation of modern civilization in Europe, and which has given us that fundamental maxim of distributive justice, *suum cuique tribuere* [to harm no one, to give each his own]. There is nothing in *Magna Charta*, rightly construed as a broad charter of public right and law, which ought to exclude the best ideas of all systems and of every age; and as it was the characteristic principle of the common law to draw its inspiration from every fountain of justice, we are not to assume that the sources of its supply have been exhausted. On the contrary, we should expect that the new and various experiences of our own situation and system will mould and shape it into new and not useful forms.

The concessions of *Magna Charta* were wrung from the king as guaranties against the oppressions and usurpations of his prerogative. It did not enter into the minds of the barons to provide security against their own body or in favor of the commons by limiting the power of parliament; so that bills of attainder, *ex post facto* laws, laws declaring forfeitures of estates, and other arbitrary acts of legislation which occur so frequently in English history, were never regarded as inconsistent with the law of the land; for notwithstanding what was attributed to Lord Coke in *Bonham's Case*, 8 Reporter, 115, 118a (1610), the omnipotence of parliament over the common law was absolute, even against common right and reason. The actual and practical security for English liberty against legislative tyranny was the power of a free public opinion represented by the commons. In this country written constitutions were deemed essential to protect the rights and liberties of the people against the encroachments of power delegated to their governments, and the provisions of *Magna Charta* were incorporated into bills of rights, They were limitations upon all the powers of government, legislative as well as executive and judicial. It necessarily happened, therefore, that as these broad and general maxims of liberty and justice held in our system a different place and performed a different function from their position and office in English constitutional history and law, they would receive and justify a corresponding and more comprehensive interpretation. Applied in England only as guards against executive usurpation and tyranny, here they have become bulwarks also against arbitrary legislation; but in that application, as it would be incongruous to measure and restrict them by the ancient customary English law, they must be held to guaranty, not particular forms of procedure, but the very substance of individual rights to life, liberty, and property. Restraints that could be fastened upon executive authority with precision and detail, might prove obstructive and injurious when imposed on the just and necessary discretion of legislative power; and while, in every instance, laws that violated express and specific injunctions and prohibitions might without embarrassment be judicially declared to be void, yet any general principle or maxim founded on the essential nature of law, as a just and reasonable expression of the public will, and of government as instituted by popular consent and for the general good, can only be applied to cases coming clearly within the scope of its spirit and purpose, and not to legislative provisions merely establishing forms and modes of attainment. Such regulations, to adopt a sentence of Burke's "may alter the mode and application, but have no power over the substance of original justice."

Such is the often repeated doctrine of this court. In *Munn* v. *Illinois*, 94 U.S. 113 (1877), the chief justice, delivering the opinion of the court, said: "A person has no property, no vested interest, in any rule of the common law. That is only one of the forms of municipal law, and is no more sacred than any other. Rights of property which have been created by the common law cannot be taken away without due process; but the law itself, as a rule of conduct, may be changed at the will or even at the whim of the legislature, unless prevented by constitutional limitations. Indeed, the great office of statutes is to remedy defects in the common law as they are developed, and to adapt it to the changes of time and circumstances." And in *Walker* v. *Sauvinet*, 92 U.S. 90 (1875), the court said: "A trial by jury in suits at common law pending in state courts is not, therefore, a privilege or immunity of national citizenship which the states are forbidden by the fourteenth amendment to abridge. A state cannot deprive a person of his property without due process of law; but this does not necessarily imply that all trials in the state courts affecting the property of persons must be by jury. This requirement of the constitution is met if the trial is had according to the settled course of judicial proceedings. Due process of law is process according to the law of the land. This process in the states is regulated by the law of the state." In *Kennard* v. *Louisiana ex rel. Morgan*, 92 U.S. 480 (1875), the question was whether a mode of trying the title to an office, in which was no provision for a jury, was due process of law. Its validity was affirmed. The chief justice, after reciting the various steps in the proceeding, said: "From this it appears that ample provision has been made for the trial of the contestation before a court of competent jurisdiction; for bringing the party against whom the proceeding is had before the court and notifying him of the case he is required to meet; for giving him an opportunity to be heard in his defense; for the deliberation and judgment of the court; for an appeal from this judgment to the highest court of the state, and for hearing and judgment there. A mere statement of the facts carries with it a complete answer to all the constitutional objections urged against the validity of the act." And Mr. Justice Miller, in *Davidson v. New Orleans*, 96 U.S. 97 (1878), after showing the difficulty, if not the impossibility, of framing a definition of this constitutional phrase which should be "at once perspicuous, comprehensive, and satisfactory," and thence deducing the wisdom "in the ascertaining of the intent and application of such an important phrase in the federal constitution, by the gradual process of judicial inclusion and exclusion, as the cases presented for decision shall require," says, however, that "it is not possible to hold that a party has, without due process of law, been deprived of his property, when, as regards the issues affecting it, he has by the laws of the state fair trial in a court of justice, according to the modes of proceeding applicable to such a case."

We are to construe this phrase in the fourteenth amendment by the *usus loquendi* [usage in speaking] of the constitution itself. The same words are contained in the fifth amendment. That article makes specific and express provision for perpetuating the institution of the grand jury, so far as relates to prosecutions for the more aggravated crimes under the laws of the United States. It declares that "no person shall be held to answer for a capital or otherwise infamous crime, unless on a presentment or indictment of a grand jury, except in cases arising in the land or naval forces, or in the militia when in actual service in time of war or public danger; nor shall any person be subject for the same offense to be twice put in jeopardy of life or limb; nor shall he be compelled in any criminal case to be a witness against himself." It then immediately adds: "nor be deprived of life, liberty, or property without due process of law." According to a recognized canon of interpretation, especially applicable to formal and solemn instruments of constitutional law, we are forbidden to assume, without clear reason to the contrary, that any part of this most important amendment is superfluous. The natural and obvious inference is that, in the sense of the constitution, "due process of law" was not meant or intended to include, *ex vi termini* [by the force of the term], the institution and procedure of a grand jury in any case. The conclusion is equally irresistible, that when the same phrase was employed in the fourteenth amendment to restrain the action of the states, it was used in the same sense and with no greater extent; and that if in the adoption of that amendment it had been part of its purpose to perpetuate the institution of the grand jury in all the states, it would have embodied, as did the fifth amendment, express declarations to that effect. Due process of law in the latter refers to that law of the land which derives its authority from the legislative powers conferred upon congress by the constitution of the United States, exercised within the limits therein prescribed, and interpreted according to the principles of the common law. In the fourteenth amendment, by parity of reason, it refers to that law of the land in each state which derives its authority from the inherent and reserved powers of the state, exerted within the limits of those fundamental principles of liberty and justice which lie at the base of all our civil and political institutions, and the greatest security for which resides in the right of the people to make their own laws, and alter them at their pleasure. "The fourteenth amendment," as was said by Mr. Justice Bradley in *Missouri* v. *Lewis*, 101 U.S. 22 (1879), "does not profess to secure to all persons in the United States the benefit of the same laws and the same remedies. Great diversities in these respects may exist in two states separated only by an imaginary line. On one side of this line there may be a right of trial by jury, and on the other side no such right. Each state prescribes its own modes of judicial proceeding."

FOR DISCUSSION

Why does the Court refer to English history to explain what due process means? Did the Court in this case effectively freeze the meaning of due process to the meaning accepted in British law? What does the Court say due process guarantees in this case?

CHICAGO, B. & Q. R. CO. v. CITY OF CHICAGO

166 U.S. 226, 17 S.Ct. 581, 41 L.Ed. 979 (1897)

The City of Chicago used its power of eminent domain to condemn a right of way owned by the Chicago, Burlington & Quincy Railroad Company, a corporation of Illinois. In a jury trial to determine the compensation owned to the railroad company, a jury awarded the plaintiff one dollar. The railroad company objected and appealed, and the award was sustained. The case was appealed to the U.S. Supreme Court claiming a violation of the Fourteenth Amendment's Due Process Clause.

Vote: No dissent

JUSTICE HARLAN delivered the opinion of the Court.

The questions presented on this writ of error relate to the jurisdiction of this court to re-examine the final judgment of the supreme court of Illinois, and to certain rulings of the state court, which, it is alleged, were in disregard of that part of the fourteenth amendment declaring that no state shall deprive any person of his property without due process of law, or deny the equal protection of the laws to any person within its jurisdiction.

By an ordinance of the city council of Chicago approved October 9, 1880, it was ordained that Rockwell street, in that city, be opened and widened from West Eighteenth street to West Nineteenth street by condemning therefore, in accordance with the above act of April 10, 1872, certain parcels of land owned by individuals, and also certain parts of the right of way in that city of the Chicago, Burlington & Quincy Railroad Company, a corporation of Illinois.

In execution of that ordinance a petition was filed by the city, November 12, 1890, in the circuit court of Cook county, Ill., for the condemnation of the lots, pieces, or parcels of land and property proposed to be taken or damaged for the proposed improvement, and praying that the just compensation required for private property taken or damaged be ascertained by a jury.

The parties interested in the property described in the petition, including the Chicago, Burlington & Quincy Railroad Company, were admitted as defendants in the proceeding. In their verdict the jury fixed the just compensation to be paid to the respective individual owners of the lots, pieces, and parcels of land and property sought to be taken or damaged by the proposed improvements, and fixed one dollar as just compensation to the railroad company in respect of those parts of its right of way described in the city's petition as necessary to be used for the purposes of the proposed street.

Thereupon the railroad company moved for a new trial. The motion was overruled, and a final judgment was rendered in execution of the award by the jury. That judgment was affirmed by the supreme court of the state.

It is proper now to inquire whether the due process of law enjoined by the fourteenth amendment requires compensation to be made or adequately secured to the owner of private property taken for public use under the authority of a state.

But if, as this court has adjudged, a legislative enactment, assuming arbitrarily to take the property of one individual and give it to another individual, would not be due process of law, as enjoined by the fourteenth amendment, it must be that the requirement of due process of law in that amendment is applicable to the direct appropriation by the state to public use, and without compensation, of the private property of the citizen. The legislature may prescribe a form of procedure to be observed in the taking of private property for public use, but it is not due process of law if provision be not made for compensation. Notice to the owner to appear in some judicial tribunal and show cause why his property shall not be taken for public use without compensation would be a mockery of justice. Due process of law, as applied to judicial proceedings instituted for the taking of private property for public use means. therefore, such process as recognizes the right of the owner to be compensated if his property be wrested from him and transferred to the public. The mere form of the proceeding instituted against the owner, even if he be admitted to defend, cannot convert the process used into due process of law, if the necessary result be to deprive him of his property without compensation.

In *Fletcher v. Peck*, 10 U.S. 87 (1810), this court, speaking by Chief Justice Marshall, said: "It may well be doubted whether the nature of society and of government does not prescribe some limits to the legislative power; and, if any be prescribed, where are they to be found, if the property of an individual, fairly and honestly acquired, may be seized without compensation? To the legislature all legislative power is granted, but the question whether the act of transferring the property of an individual to the public be in the nature of legislative power is well worthy of serious reflection."

In *Loan Ass'n v. Topeka,* 87 U.S. 655 (1874), Mr. Justice Miller, delivering the judgment of this court, after observing that there were private rights in every free government beyond the control of the state, and that a government, by whatever name it was called, under which the property of citizens was at the absolute disposition and unlimited control of any depository of power, was, after all, but a despotism, said: "The theory of our governments, state and national, is opposed to the deposit of unlimited power anywhere. The executive, the legislative, and the judicial branches of these governments are all of limited and defined powers. There are limitations on such power, which grow out of the essential nature of all free governments, implied reservations of individual rights, without which the social compact could not exist, and which are respected by all governments entitled to the name." No court, he said, would hesitate to adjudge void any statute declaring that "the homestead now owned by A. should no longer be his, but should henceforth be the property of B." In accordance with these principles it was held in that case that the property of the citizen could not be taken under the power of taxation to promote private objects, and, therefore, that a statute authorizing a town to issue its bonds in aid of a manufacturing enterprise of individuals was void because the object was a private, not a public, one.

In our opinion, a judgment of a state court, even if it be authorized by statute, whereby private property is taken for the state or under its direction for public use, without compensation made or secured to the owner, is, upon principle and authority, wanting in the due process of law required by the fourteenth amendment of the constitution of the United States, and the affirmance of such judgment by the highest court of the state is a denial by that state of a right secured to the owner by that instrument.

FOR DISCUSSION

Why does the Fourteenth Amendment guarantee to owners just compensation for property taken by the government? Is the decision in this case really based on the Fourteenth Amendment or on some other reasoning?

GITLOW V. NEW YORK

268 U.S. 652, 45 S.Ct. 625, 69 L.Ed. 1138 (1925)

Benjamin Gitlow had been indicted for the statutory crime of criminal anarchy under a 1902 New York State law that proscribed advocating the overthrow of organized government by forceful means. Gitlow was a member of a left-wing political group, and in 1920 he was arrested for the publication of a document, The Left-Wing Manifesto, that urged the use of class strikes and other measures to institute socialism in the United States. Gitlow challenged the validity of the state criminal anarchy law under the Fourteenth Amendment.

Vote: 7–2

JUSTICE SANFORD delivered the opinion of the Court.

. . . The precise question presented, and the only question which we can consider under this writ of error, then, is whether the statute, as construed and applied in this case by the state courts, deprived the defendant of his liberty of expression, in violation of the due process clause of the Fourteenth Amendment. The statute does not penalize the utterance or publication of abstract "doctrine" or academic discussion having no quality of incitement to any concrete action. It is not aimed against mere historical or philosophical essays. It does not restrain the advocacy of changes in the form of government by constitutional and lawful means. What it prohibits is language advocating, advising, or teaching the overthrow of organized government by unlawful means. These words imply urging to action. Advocacy is defined in the *Century Dictionary* as: "1. The act of pleading for, supporting, or recommending; active espousal." It is not the abstract "doctrine" of overthrowing organized government by unlawful means which is denounced by the statute, but the advocacy of action for the accomplishment of that purpose.

The Manifesto, plainly, is neither the statement of abstract doctrine nor, as suggested by counsel, mere prediction that industrial disturbances and revolutionary mass strikes will result spontaneously in an inevitable process of evolution in the economic system. It advocates and urges in fervent language mass action which shall progressively foment industrial disturbances, and, through political mass strikes and revolutionary mass action, overthrow and destroy organized parliamentary government. It concludes with a call to action in these words: "The proletariat revolution and the Communist reconstruction of society—the struggle for these—is now indispensable. . . . The Communist International calls the proletariat of the world to the final struggle!" This is not the expression of philosophical abstraction, the mere prediction of future events; it is the language of direct incitement.

The means advocated for bringing about the destruction of organized parliamentary government, namely, mass industrial revolts usurping the functions of municipal government, political mass strikes directed against the parliamentary state, and revolutionary mass action for its final destruction, necessarily imply the use of force and violence, and in their essential nature are inherently unlawful in a constitutional government of law and order. That the jury were warranted in finding that the Manifesto advocated not merely the abstract doctrine of overwhelming organized government by force, violence, and unlawful means, but action to that end, is clear.

For present purposes we may and do assume that freedom of speech and of the press—which are protected by the First Amendment from abridgement by Congress—are among the fundamental personal rights and "liberties" protected by the due process clause of the Fourteenth Amendment from impairment by the states. . . .

It is a fundamental principle, long established, that freedom of speech and of the press which is secured by the Constitution does not confer an absolute right to speak or publish, without responsibility, whatever one may choose, or an unrestricted and unbridled license that gives immunity for every possible use of language, and prevents the punishment of those who abuse this freedom. . . . Reasonably limited, it was said by Story . . .

this freedom is an inestimable privilege in a free government; without such limitation, it might become the scourge of the republic.

That a state, in the exercise of its police power, may punish those who abuse this freedom by utterances inimical to the public welfare, tending to corrupt public morals, incite to crime, or disturb the public peace, is not open to question. . . . Thus it was held by this court in the *Fox v. Washington,* 236 U.S. 273 (1915), case, that a state may punish publications advocating and encouraging a breach of its criminal laws; and, in the *Gilbert v. Minnesota,* 254 U.S. 325 (1920), case, that a state may punish utterances teaching or advocating that its citizens should not assist the United States in prosecuting or carrying on war with its public enemies.

And, for yet more imperative reasons, a state may punish utterances endangering the foundations of organized government and threatening its overthrow by unlawful means. These imperil its own existence as a constitutional state. Freedom of speech and press, said Story . . ., does not protect disturbances of the public peace or the attempt to subvert the government. It does not protect publications or teachings which tend to subvert or imperil the government, or to impede or hinder it in the performance of its governmental duties. . . . It does not protect publications prompting the overthrow of government by force; the punishment of those who publish articles which tend to destroy organized society being essential to the security of freedom and the stability of the state. . . . And a state may penalize utterances which openly advocate the overthrow of the representative and constitutional form of government of the United States and the several states, by violence or other unlawful means. . . . In short, this freedom does not deprive a state of the primary and essential right of self-preservation, which so long as human governments endure, they cannot be denied. . . .

By enacting the present statute the state has determined, through its legislative body, that utterances advocating the overthrow of organized government by force, violence, and unlawful means, are so inimical to the general welfare, and involve such danger of substantive evil, that they may be penalized in the exercise of its police power. That determination must be given great weight. Every presumption is to be indulged in favor of the validity of the statute. . . . That utterances inciting to the overthrow of organized government by unlawful means present a sufficient danger of substantive evil to bring their punishment within the range of legislative discretion is clear. Such utterances, by their very nature, involve danger to the public peace and to the security of the state. They threaten breaches of the peace and ultimate revolution. And the immediate danger is none the less real and substantial because the effect of a given utterance cannot be accurately foreseen. The state cannot reasonably be required to measure the danger from every such utterance in the nice balance of a jeweler's scale. A single revolutionary spark may kindle a fire that, smoldering for a time, may burst into a sweeping and destructive conflagration. It cannot be said that the state is acting arbitrarily or unreasonably when, in the exercise of its judgment as to the measures necessary to protect the public peace and safety, it seeks to extinguish the spark without waiting until it has enkindled the flame or blazed into the conflagration. It cannot reasonably be required to defer the adoption of measures for its own peace and safety until the revolutionary utterances lead to actual disturbances of the public peace or imminent and immediate danger of its own destruction; but it may, in the exercise of its judgment, suppress the threatened danger of its incipiency. . . .

We cannot hold that the present statute is an arbitrary or unreasonable exercise of the police power of the state, unwarrantably infringing the freedom of speech or press; and we must and do sustain its constitutionality. . . .

JUSTICE HOLMES dissented, joined by JUSTICE BRANDEIS.

Mr. Justice Brandeis and I are of opinion that this judgment should be reversed. The general principle of free speech, it seems to me, must be taken to be included in the Fourteenth Amendment, in view of the scope that has been given to the word "liberty" as there used, although perhaps it may be accepted with a somewhat larger latitude of interpretation than is allowed to Congress by the sweeping language that governs, or ought to govern, the laws of the United States. If I am right, then I think that the criterion sanctioned by the full court in

Schenck v. United States, 249 U.S. 47 (1919), applies: "The question in every case is whether the words used are used in such circumstances and are of such a nature as to create a clear and present danger that they will bring about the substantive evils that [the state] has a right to prevent." It is true that in my opinion this criterion was departed from in *Abrams v. United States,* 250 U.S. 616 (1919), but the convictions that I express in that case are too deep for it to be possible for me as yet to believe that it and *Schaefer v. United States,* 251 U.S. 466 (1960), have settled the law. If what I think the correct test is applied, it is manifest that there was no present danger of an attempt to overthrow the government by force on the part of the admittedly small minority who shared the defendant's views. It is said that this Manifesto was more than a theory, that it was an incitement. Every idea is an incitement. It offers itself for belief, and if believed, it is acted on unless some other belief outweighs it, or some failure of energy stifles the movement at its birth. The only difference between the expression of an opinion and an incitement in the narrower sense is the speaker's enthusiasm for the result. Eloquence may set fire to reason. But whatever may be thought of the redundant discourse before us, it had no chance of starting a present conflagration. If, in the long run, the beliefs expressed in proletarian dictatorship are destined to be accepted by the dominant forces of the community, the only meaning of free speech is that they should be given their chance and have their way.

If the publication of this document has been laid as an attempt to induce an uprising against government at once, and not at some indefinite time in the future, it would have presented a different question. The object would have been one with which the law might deal, subject to the doubt whether there was any danger that the publication could produce any result; or, in other words, whether it was not futile and too remote from possible consequences. But the indictment alleges the publication and nothing more.

FOR DISCUSSION

What reason does the Court give for ruling that freedom of speech is protected against state encroachment by the Due Process Clause? Do both the majority and dissents agree on this point? Where is the disagreement between the two?

RELATED CASES

***Meyer v. Nebraska:* 262 U.S. 390 (1923).**

In upholding the right to teach foreign languages, the majority held that "Liberty" includes the right of a person to engage in occupations of his choosing, to marry, to acquire useful knowledge, to worship God and to enjoy those privileges long recognized as essential to the orderly pursuit of happiness by free men.

***Pierce v. Society of Sisters:* 268 U.S. 510 (1925).**

The Court ruled that a state compulsory education act that requires, in general, that children between eight and sixteen years of age be sent to the public school in the area where they reside is an unreasonable interference with the liberty of the parents and guardians to direct the upbringing of the children and in that respect violates the Fourteenth Amendment.

Palko v. State of Connecticut

302 U.S. 319, 58 S.Ct. 149, 82 L.Ed. 288 (1937)

Frank Palka (misspelled as Palko in Court records) was convicted of murder in the second degree in a California state court. The state appealed the conviction, it was reversed, and a new trial was ordered at which Palka was convicted of first-degree murder. Palka appealed, claiming a violation of the Eighth Amendment Double Jeopardy Clause. The Supreme Court upheld his conviction.

Vote: 8–1

Justice Cardozo delivered the opinion of the Court.

The execution of the sentence will not deprive appellant of his life without the process of law assured to him by the Fourteenth Amendment of the Federal Constitution.

The argument for appellant is that whatever is forbidden by the Fifth Amendment is forbidden by the Fourteenth also. The Fifth Amendment, which is not directed to the States, but solely to the federal government, creates immunity from double jeopardy. No person shall be "subject for the same offense to be twice put in jeopardy of life or limb." The Fourteenth Amendment ordains, "nor shall any State deprive any person of life, liberty, or property, without due process of law." To retry a defendant, though under one indictment and only one, subjects him, it is said, to double jeopardy in violation of the Fifth Amendment, if the prosecution is one on behalf of the United States. From this the consequence is said to follow that there is a denial of life or liberty without due process of law, if the prosecution is one on behalf of the people of a state. Thirty-five years ago a like argument was made to this court in *Dreyer v. Illinois*, 187 U.S. 71 (1902), and was passed without consideration of its merits as unnecessary to a decision. The question is now here.

We do not find it profitable to mark the precise limits of the prohibition of double jeopardy in federal prosecutions. The subject was much considered in *Kepner v. United States*, 195 U.S. 100, decided in 1904 by a closely divided court. The view was there expressed for a majority of the court that the prohibition was not confined to jeopardy in a new and independent case. It forbade jeopardy in the same case if the new trial was at the instance of the government and not upon defendant's motion. All this may be assumed for the purpose of the case at hand, though the dissenting opinions show how much was to be said in favor of a different ruling. Right-minded men, as we learn from those opinions, could reasonably, even if mistakenly, believe that a second trial was lawful in prosecutions subject to the Fifth Amendment, if it was all in the same case. Even more plainly, right-minded men could reasonably believe that in espousing that conclusion they were not favoring a practice repugnant to the conscience of mankind. Is double jeopardy in such circumstances, if double jeopardy it must be called, a denial of due process forbidden to the States? The tyranny of labels must not lead us to leap to a conclusion that a word which in one set of facts may stand for oppression or enormity is of like effect in every other.

We have said that in appellant's view the Fourteenth Amendment is to be taken as embodying the prohibitions of the Fifth. His thesis is even broader. Whatever would be a violation of the original bill of rights (Amendments 1 to 8) if done by the federal government is now equally unlawful by force of the Fourteenth Amendment if done by a state. There is no such general rule.

The Fifth Amendment provides, among other things, that no person shall be held to answer for a capital or otherwise infamous crime unless on presentment or indictment of a grand jury. This court has held that, in prosecutions by a state, presentment or indictment by a grand jury may give way to informations at the instance of a public officer. *Hurtado v. California*, 110 U.S. 516 (1884). The Fifth Amendment provides also that no person shall be compelled in any criminal case to be a witness against himself. This court has said that, in prosecutions by a state, the exemption will fail if the state elects to end it. The Sixth Amendment calls for a jury trial in criminal cases and the Seventh for a jury trial in civil cases at common law where the value in controversy shall exceed $20. This court has ruled that consistently with those amendments trial by jury may be modified by a state or abolished altogether As to the Fourth Amendment, one should refer, and as to other provisions of the Sixth, to *West v. Louisiana*, 194 U.S. 258 (1904).

On the other hand, the due process clause of the Fourteenth Amendment may make it unlawful for a state to abridge by its statutes the freedom of speech which the First Amendment safeguards against encroachment by the Congress (*De Jonge v. Oregon*, 299 U.S. 353 (1937), or the like freedom of the press (*Grosjean v. American Press Co.*, 297 U.S. 233 (1936); *Near v. Minnesota*, 283 U.S. 697 (1931), or the free exercise of religion or the right of peaceable assembly, without which speech would be unduly trammeled (De *Jonge v. Oregon*; *Herndon v. Lowry*, 301 U.S. 242 (1937)), or the right of one accused of crime to the benefit of counsel (*Powell v. Alabama*, 287 U.S. 45 (1932)). In these and other situations immunities that are valid as against the federal government by force of the specific pledges of particular amendments have been found to be implicit in the concept of ordered liberty, and thus, through the Fourteenth Amendment, become valid as against the states.

We reach a different plane of social and moral values when we pass to the privileges and immunities that have been taken over from the earlier articles of the Federal Bill of Rights and brought within the Fourteenth Amendment by a process of absorption. These in their origin were effective against the federal government alone. If the Fourteenth Amendment has absorbed them, the process of absorption has had its source in the belief that neither liberty nor justice would exist if they were sacrificed. This is true, for illustration, of freedom of thought and speech. Of that freedom one may say that it is the matrix, the indispensable condition, of nearly every other form of freedom. With rare aberrations a pervasive recognition of that truth can be traced in our history, political and legal. So it has come about that the domain of liberty, withdrawn by the Fourteenth Amendment from encroachment by the states, has been enlarged by latter-day judgments to include liberty of the mind as well as liberty of action. The extension became, indeed, a logical imperative when once it was recognized, as long ago it was, that liberty is something more than exemption from physical restraint, and that even in the field of substantive rights and duties the legislative judgment, if oppressive and arbitrary, may be overridden by the courts. Fundamental too in the concept of due process, and so in that of liberty, is the thought that condemnation shall be rendered only after trial. The hearing, moreover, must be a real one, not a sham or a pretense. For that reason, ignorant defendants in a capital case were held to have been condemned unlawfully when in truth, though not in form, they were refused the aid of counsel. The decision did not turn upon the fact that the benefit of counsel would have been guaranteed to the defendants by the provisions of the Sixth Amendment if they had been prosecuted in a federal court. The decision turned upon the fact that in the particular situation laid before us in the evidence the benefit of counsel was essential to the substance of a hearing.

Our survey of the cases serves, we think, to justify the statement that the dividing line between them, if not unfaltering throughout its course, has been true for the most part to a unifying principle. On which side of the line the case made out by the appellant has appropriate location must be the next inquiry and the final one. Is that kind of double jeopardy to which the statute has subjected him a hardship so acute and shocking that our policy will not endure it? Does it violate those "fundamental principles of liberty and justice which lie at the base of all our civil and political institutions"? The answer surely must be "no." What the answer would have to be if the state were permitted after a trial free from error to try the accused over again or to bring another case against him, we have no occasion to consider. We deal with the statute before us and no other. The state is not attempting to wear the accused out by a multitude of cases with accumulated trials. It asks no more than this, that the case against him shall go on until there shall be a trial free from the corrosion of substantial legal error. This is not cruelty at all, nor even vexation in any immoderate degree. If the trial had been infected with error adverse to the accused, there might have been review at his instance, and as often as necessary to purge the vicious taint. A reciprocal privilege, subject at all times to the discretion of the presiding judge has now been granted to the state. There is here no seismic innovation. The edifice of justice stands, its symmetry, to many, greater than before.

The conviction of appellant is not in derogation of any privileges or immunities that belong to him as a citizen of the United States.

There is argument in his behalf that the privileges and immunities clause of the Fourteenth Amendment as well as the due process clause has been flouted by the judgment.

FOR DISCUSSION

What rights does the Due Process Clause protect against state encroachment? Does Justice Cardozo's discussion make that clear?

CANTWELL V. CONNECTICUT

310 U.S. 296, 60 S.Ct. 900, 84 L.Ed. 1213 (1940)

Jesse Cantwell and his two sons, who were Jehovah's Witnesses, went from house to house in Cassius Street in New Haven, Connecticut, selling books. Part of their procedure was to play a record that described the books. They were convicted of violating a statute that required a permit from the secretary of the Public Welfare Council before making solicitations for money for alleged religious purposes.

Vote: 9–0

JUSTICE ROBERTS delivered the opinion of the Court.

. . . We hold that the statute, as construed and applied to the appellants, deprives them of their liberty without due process of law in contravention of the Fourteenth Amendment. The fundamental concept of liberty embodied in that Amendment embraces the liberties guaranteed by the First Amendment. The First Amendment declares that Congress shall make no law respecting an establishment of religion or prohibiting the free exercise thereof. The Fourteenth Amendment has rendered the legislatures of the states as incompetent as Congress to enact such laws. The constitutional inhibition of legislation on the subject of religion has a double aspect. On the one hand, it forestalls compulsion by law of the acceptance of any creed or the practice of any form of worship. Freedom of conscience and freedom to adhere to such religious organization or form of worship as the individual may choose cannot be restricted by law. On the other hand, it safeguards the free exercise of the chosen form of religion. Thus the Amendment embraces two concepts—freedom to believe and freedom to act.

The first is absolute but, in the nature of things, the second cannot be. Conduct remains subject to regulation for the protection of society. The freedom to act must have appropriate definition to preserve the enforcement of that protection. In every case the power to regulate must be so exercised as not, in attaining a permissible end, unduly to infringe the protected freedom. No one would contest the proposition that a State may not, by statute, wholly deny the right to preach or to disseminate religious views. Plainly such a previous and absolute restraint would violate the terms of the guarantee. It is equally clear that a State may by general and non-discriminatory legislation regulate the times, the places, and the manner of soliciting upon its streets, and of holding meetings thereon; and may in other respects safeguard the peace, good order and comfort of the community, without unconstitutionally invading the liberties protected by the Fourteenth Amendment. The appellants are right in their insistence that the Act in question is not such a regulation. If a certificate is procured, solicitation is permitted without restraint, but, in the absence of a certificate, solicitation is altogether prohibited. . . . Nothing we have said is intended even remotely to imply that, under the cloak of religion, persons may, with impunity, commit frauds upon the public. Certainly penal laws are available to punish such conduct. Even the exercise of religion may be at some slight inconvenience in order that the state may protect its citizens from fraudulent solicitation by requiring a stranger in the community, before permitting him publicly to solicit funds for any purpose, to establish his identity and his authority to act for the cause which he purports to represent. The State is likewise free to regulate the time and manner of solicitation generally, in the interest of public safety, peace, comfort or convenience. But to condition the solicitation of aid for the perpetuation of religious views or systems upon a license, the grant of which rests in the exercise of a determination by state authority as to what is a religious cause, is to lay a forbidden burden upon the exercise of liberty protected by the Constitution. . . .

The offense known as breach of the peace embraces a great variety of conduct destroying or menacing public order and tranquility. It includes not only violent acts but acts and words likely to produce violence in others. No one would have the hardihood to suggest that the principle of freedom of speech sanctions incitement to riot or that religious liberty connotes the privilege to exhort others to physical attack upon those belonging to another sect. When clear and present danger of riot, disorder, interference with traffic upon the public streets, or other immediate threat to public safety, peace, or order, appears, the power of the State to prevent or punish is obvious. Equally obvious is it that a State may not unduly suppress free communication of views, religious or other, under the guise of conserving desirable conditions. Here we have a situation analogous to a conviction under a statute sweeping in a great variety of conduct under a general and indefinite characterization, and leaving to the executive and judicial branches too wide a discretion in its application. . . .

The essential characteristic of these liberties is that under their shield many types of life, character, opinion and belief can develop unmolested and unobstructed. Nowhere is this shield more necessary than in our own country for a people composed of many races and many creeds. There are limits to the exercise of these liberties. The danger in these times from the coercive activities of those who in the delusion of racial or religious conceit would incite violence and breaches of the peace in order to deprive others of their equal right to the exercise of their liberties, is emphasized by events familiar to all. These and other transgressions of those limits the States appropriately may punish. . . .

FOR DISCUSSION

Does the incorporation of freedom of religion to apply to states mean that they are prohibited from imposing any restrictions on religious practice? Does incorporation imply an absolute protection for rights against state interference?

RELATED CASES

Hamilton v. Regents of the University of California: **293 U.S. 245 (1934).**

Requiring students at a state university to take a course in military science and tactics is not a deprivation of liberty without due process.

Jamison v. Texas: **318 U.S. 413 (1943).**

The right to distribute handbills on religious subjects on the public streets cannot be prohibited at all times, at all places, and under all circumstances. Here an ordinance of Dallas was held void.

***Largent v. Texas:* 318 U.S. 418 (1943).**

Requiring a permit for the distribution of religious handbills is prior restraint and void. These handbills "seek in a lawful fashion to promote the raising of funds for religious purposes." Such handbills are to be distinguished from commercial handbills. Distribution of the latter can be regulated or prohibited.

ADAMSON V. PEOPLE OF STATE OF CALIFORNIA

332 U.S. 46, 67 S.Ct. 1672, 91 L.Ed. 1903 (1947)

In *Adamson* a majority of the Court rejected claims that the Fifth Amendment's guarantee against self-incrimination applies to states and therefore precludes the prosecution in a murder trial from asking the accused about prior offenses if he or she takes the witness stand. In dissent, Justice Black makes the case for the total incorporation of the Bill of Rights to apply to the states.

Vote: 5–4

JUSTICE BLACK dissenting.

The first 10 amendments were proposed and adopted largely because of fear that Government might unduly interfere with prized individual liberties. The people wanted and demanded a Bill of Rights written into their Constitution. The amendments embodying the Bill of Rights were intended to curb all branches of the Federal Government in the fields touched by the amendments—Legislative, Executive, and Judicial. The Fifth, Sixth, and Eighth Amendments were pointedly aimed at confining exercise of power by courts and judges within precise boundaries, particularly in the procedure used for the trial of criminal cases. Past history provided strong reasons for the apprehensions which brought these procedural amendments into being and attest the wisdom of their adoption. For the fears of arbitrary court action sprang largely from the past use of courts in the imposition of criminal punishments to suppress speech, press, and religion. Hence the constitutional limitations of courts' powers were, in the view of the Founders, essential supplements to the First Amendment, which was itself designed to protect the widest scope for all people to believe and to express the most divergent political, religious, and other views.

But these limitations were not expressly imposed upon state court action. In 1833, *Barron v. Baltimore*, 32 U.S. 423, was decided by this Court. It specifically held inapplicable to the states that provision of the Fifth Amendment which declares: "nor shall private property be taken for public use, without just compensation." In deciding the particular point raised, the Court there said that it could not hold that the first eight amendments applied to the states. This was the controlling constitutional rule when the Fourteenth Amendment was proposed in 1866.

My study of the historical events that culminated in the Fourteenth Amendment, and the expressions of those who sponsored and favored, as well as those who opposed its submission and passage, persuades me that one of the chief objects that the provisions of the Amendment's first section, separately, and as a whole, were intended to accomplish was to make the Bill of Rights, applicable to the states. With full knowledge of the import of the *Barron* decision, the framers and backers of the Fourteenth Amendment proclaimed its purpose to be to overturn the constitutional rule that case had announced. This historical purpose has never received full consideration or exposition in any opinion of this Court interpreting the Amendment.

Investigation of the cases relied upon in *Twining v. New Jersey*, 211 U.S. 78 (1908), to support the conclusion there reached that neither the Fifth Amendment's prohibition of compelled testimony, nor any of the Bill of Rights, applies to the States, reveals an unexplained departure from this salutary practice. Neither the briefs nor opinions in any of these cases, except *Maxwell v. Dow*, 176 U.S. 581 (1900), make reference to the legislative and contemporary history for the purpose of demonstrating that those who conceived, shaped, and brought about the adoption of the Fourteenth Amendment intended it to nullify this Court's decision in *Barron v. Baltimore*, 32 U.S. 243 (1833), and thereby to make the Bill of Rights applicable to the States. In *Maxwell v. Dow*, the issue turned on whether the Bill of Rights guarantee of a jury trial was, by the Fourteenth Amendment, extended to trials in state courts. In that case counsel for appellant did cite from the speech of Senator Howard, which so emphatically stated the understanding of the framers of the Amendment—the Committee on Reconstruction for which he spoke—that the Bill of Rights was to be made applicable to the states by the Amendment's first section. The Court's opinion in *Maxwell v. Dow*, acknowledged that counsel had "cited from the speech of one of the Senators," but indicated that it was not advised what other speeches were made in the Senate or in the House. The Court considered, moreover, that "What individual Senators or Representatives may have urged in debate, in regard to the meaning to be given to a proposed constitutional amendment, or bill, or resolution, does not furnish a firm ground for its proper construction, nor is it important as explanatory of the grounds upon which the members voted in adopting it."

In the *Twining* case itself, the Court was cited to a then recent book, Guthrie, *Fourteenth Amendment to the Constitution* (1898). A few pages of that work recited some of the legislative background of the Amendment, emphasizing the speech of Senator Howard. But Guthrie did not emphasize the speeches of Congressman Bingham, nor the part he played in the framing and adoption of the first section of the Fourteenth Amendment. Yet Congressman Bingham may, without extravagance, be called the Madison of the first section of the Fourteenth Amendment. In the *Twining* opinion the Court explicitly declined to give weight to the historical demonstration that the first section of the Amendment was intended to apply to the states the several protections of the Bill of Rights. It held that that question was "no longer open" because of previous decisions of this Court which, however, had not appraised the historical evidence on that subject. The Court admitted that its action had resulted in giving "much less effect to the 14th Amendment than some of the public men active in framing it" had intended it to have. With particular reference to the guarantee against compelled testimony, the Court stated that "Much might be said in favor of the view that the privilege was guaranteed against state impairment as a privilege and immunity of national citizenship, but, as has been shown, the decisions of this court have foreclosed that view." Thus the Court declined and again today declines, to appraise the relevant historical evidence of the intended scope of the first section of the Amendment. Instead it relied upon previous cases, none of which had analyzed the evidence showing that one purpose of those who framed, advocated, and adopted the Amendment had been to make the Bill of Rights applicable to the States. None of the cases relied upon by the Court today made such an analysis.

For this reason, I am attaching to this dissent, an appendix which contains a resume, by no means complete, of the Amendment's history. In my judgment that history conclusively demonstrates that the language of the first section of the Fourteenth Amendment, taken as a whole, was thought by those responsible for its submission to the people, and by those who opposed its submission, sufficiently explicit to guarantee that thereafter no state could deprive its citizens of the privileges and protections of the Bill of Rights. Whether this Court ever will, or whether it now should, in the light of past decisions, give full effect to what the Amendment was intended to accomplish is not necessarily essential to a decision here. However that may be, our prior decisions, including *Twining*, do not prevent our carrying out that purpose, at least to the extent of making applicable to the states, not a mere part, as the Court has, but the full protection of the Fifth Amendment's provision against compelling evidence from an accused to convict him of crime. And I further contend that the "natural law" formula which the Court uses to reach its conclusion in this case should be abandoned as an incongruous excrescence on our Constitution. I believe that formula to be itself a violation of our Constitution, in that it subtly conveys to courts, at the expense of legislatures, ultimate power over public policies in fields where no specific provision of the Constitution limits legislative power. And my belief seems to be in accord with the views expressed by this Court, at least for the first two decades after the Fourteenth Amendment was adopted.

FOR DISCUSSION

Does Justice Black provide a good argument for total incorporation of the entire Bill of Rights? Should all of them apply or, as Justice Cardozo argued, are some more important or fundamental?

POWELL V. ALABAMA

287 U.S. 45, 53 S.Ct. 55, 77 L.Ed. 158 (1932)

This was the first of the famous Scottsboro cases. Powell was one of nine African American youths who were indicted for the rape of two white girls. Six days after the date of the crime, they were tried in a community where the attitude was one of great hostility. The accused were not represented by counsel; the judge simply appointed "all members of the bar" to defend them. The proceedings were challenged as denying due process to the defendants.

Vote: 7–2

JUSTICE SUTHERLAND delivered the opinion of the Court.

. . . *First.* The record shows that immediately upon the return of the indictment defendants were arraigned and pleaded not guilty. Apparently they were not asked whether they had, or were able to employ, counsel, or wished to have counsel appointed; or whether they had friends or relatives who might assist in that regard if communicated with. That it would not have been an idle ceremony to have given the defendants reasonable opportunity to communicate with their families and endeavor to obtain counsel is demonstrated by the fact that very soon after conviction, able counsel appeared in their behalf.

It is hardly necessary to say that, the right to counsel being conceded, a defendant should be afforded a fair opportunity to secure counsel of his own choice. Not only was that not done here, but such designation of counsel as was attempted was either so indefinite or so close upon the trial as to amount to a denial of effective and substantial aid in that regard. This will be amply demonstrated by a brief review of the record. . . .

Nor do we think the situation was helped by what occurred on the morning of the trial. At that time, as appears from the colloquy printed above, Mr. Roddy stated to the court that he did not appear as counsel, but that he would like to appear along with counsel that the court might appoint; that he had not been given an opportunity to prepare the case; that he was not familiar with the procedure in Alabama, but merely came down as a friend of the people who were interested; that he thought the boys would be better off if he should step entirely out of the case. Mr. Moody, a member of the local bar, expressed a willingness to help Mr. Roddy in anything he could do under the circumstances. To this the court responded:

"All right, all the lawyers that will; of course I would not require a lawyer to appear if—." And Mr. Moody continued, "I am willing to do that for him as a member of the bar; I will go ahead and help do anything I can do." With this dubious understanding, the trials immediately proceeded. The defendants, young, ignorant, illiterate, surrounded by hostile sentiment, haled back and forth under guard of soldiers, charged with an atrocious crime regarded with especial horror in the community where they were to be tried, were thus put in peril of their lives within a few moments after counsel for the first time charged with any degree of responsibility began to represent them.

"It is not enough to assume that counsel thus precipitated into the case thought there was no defense, and exercised their best judgment in proceeding to trial without preparation. Neither they nor the court could say what a prompt and thoroughgoing investigation might disclose as to the facts. No attempt was made to investigate. No opportunity to do so was given. Defendants were immediately hurried to trial. . . . Under the circumstances disclosed, we hold that defendants were not accorded the right of counsel in any substantial sense. To decide otherwise, would simply be to ignore actualities.

Second. The Constitution of Alabama provides that in all criminal prosecutions the accused shall enjoy the right to have the assistance of counsel; and a state statute requires the court in a capital case, where the defendant is unable to employ counsel, to appoint counsel for him. The state supreme court held that these provisions had not been infringed, and with that holding we are powerless to interfere. The question, however, which is our duty, and within our power, to decide, is whether the denial of the assistance of counsel contravenes the due process clause of the Fourteenth Amendment to the federal Constitution.

While the question has never been categorically determined by this court, a consideration of the nature of the right and a review of the expressions of this and other courts, makes it clear that the right to the aid of counsel is of this fundamental character.

It has never been doubted by this court, or any other so far as we know, that notice and hearing are preliminary steps essential to the passing of an enforceable judgment, and that they, together with a legally competent tribunal having jurisdiction of the case, constitute basic elements of the constitutional requirement of due process of law. . . .

What, then, does a hearing include? Historically and in practice, in our own country at least, it has always included the right to the aid of counsel when desired and provided by the party asserting the right. The right to be heard would be, in many cases, of little avail if it did not comprehend the right to be heard by counsel. Even the intelligent and educated layman has small and sometimes no skill in the science of law. If charged with crime, he is incapable, generally, of determining for himself whether the indictment is good or bad. He is unfamiliar with the rules of evidence. Left without the aid of counsel, he may be put on trial without a proper charge, and convicted upon incompetent evidence, or evidence irrelevant to the issue or otherwise inadmissible. He lacks both the skill and knowledge adequately to prepare his defense, even though he have a perfect one. He requires the guiding hand of counsel at every step in the proceedings against him. Without it, though he be not guilty, he faces the danger of conviction because he does not know how to establish his innocence. If that be true of men of intelligence, how much more true is it of the ignorant and illiterate, or those of feeble intellect. If in any case, in civil or criminal, a state or federal court were arbitrarily to refuse to hear a party by counsel, employed by and appearing for him, it reasonably may not be doubted that such a refusal would be a denial of a hearing, and, therefore, of due process in the constitutional sense.

In the light of the facts outlined in the forepart of this opinion—the ignorance and illiteracy of the defendants, their youth, the circumstances of public hostility, the imprisonment and the close surveillance of the defendants by the military forces, the fact that their friends and families were all in other states and communication with them necessarily difficult, and above all that they stood in deadly peril of their lives—we think the failure of the trial court to give them reasonable time and opportunity to secure counsel was a clear denial of due process.

But passing that, and assuming their inability, even if opportunity had been given, to employ counsel, as the trial court evidently did assume, we are of opinion that, under the circumstances just stated, the necessity of counsel was so vital and imperative that the failure of the trial court to make an effective appointment of counsel was likewise a denial of due process within the meaning of the Fourteenth Amendment. Whether this would be so in other criminal prosecutions, or under other circumstances, we need not determine. All that is necessary now to decide, as we do decide, is that in a capital case, where the defendant is unable to employ counsel, and is incapable adequately of making his own defense because of ignorance, feeblemindedness, illiteracy, or the like, it is the duty of the court, whether requested or not, to assign counsel for him as a necessary requisite of due process of law; and that duty is not discharged by an assignment at such a time or under such circumstances as to preclude the giving of effective aid in the preparation and trial of the case. To hold otherwise would be to ignore the fundamental postulate, already adverted to, "that there are certain immutable principles of justice which inhere in the very idea of free government which no member of the Union may disregard." . . . In a case such as this, whatever may be the rule in other cases, the right to have counsel appointed, when necessary, is a logical corollary from the constitutional right to be heard by counsel. . . .

The judgments must be reversed, and the causes remanded for further proceedings not inconsistent with this opinion.

Judgments reversed.

JUSTICE BUTLER dissented, with the concurrence of JUSTICE MCREYNOLDS.

If correct, the ruling that the failure of the trial court to give petitioners time and opportunity to secure counsel was denial of due process is enough, and with this the opinion should end. But the Court goes on to declare that "the failure of the trial court to make an effective appointment of counsel was likewise a denial of due process within the meaning of the Fourteenth Amendment." This is an extension of federal authority into a field hitherto occupied exclusively by the several states. Nothing before the Court calls for a consideration of the point. It was not suggested below and petitioners do not ask for its decision here. The Court, without being called upon to consider it, adjudges without a hearing an important constitutional question concerning criminal procedure in state courts. . . .

FOR DISCUSSION

Is the impetus for incorporation in this case driven by the law and the Fourteenth Amendment or by the facts of this case? Would there have been less need for incorporation if states actually did protect the rights of their citizens? Can we trust states to treat their citizens fairly and to respect their rights?

RELATED CASE

***Chandler v. Fretag:* 348 U.S. 3 (1954).**

An accused must be given the opportunity to secure counsel, or there is a denial of due process under the Fourteenth Amendment. "Regardless of whether petitioner would have been entitled to the appointment of counsel, his right to be heard through his own counsel was unqualified."

***Chessman v. Teets, Warden:* 354 U.S. 156 (1957).**

Refusal of an accused to be represented by counsel at the trial does not constitute a waiver of his right to counsel at the settlement proceedings.

***Moore v. Michigan:* 355 U.S. 155 (1957).**

Where a person convicted of murder in a state court has not intelligently and understandingly waived the benefit of counsel and where the circumstances show that his rights could not have been fairly protected without counsel, there is denial of due process under the Fourteenth Amendment.

GIDEON V. WAINWRIGHT

372 U.S. 335, 83 S.Ct. 792, 9 L.Ed. 2d 799 (1963)

Clarence Earl Gideon was charged in a Florida state court with having broken and entered a poolroom with intent to commit a misdemeanor. This is a noncapital felony under Florida law. The defendant had appeared in court without funds and without counsel and had asked the court to appoint counsel for him. This was denied because the law of Florida permitted appointment of counsel for indigent defendants only in capital cases. Gideon conducted his own defense, was convicted, and was sentenced to prison. Subsequently he applied for a writ of habeas corpus on the ground that the trial court's refusal to appoint counsel denied him rights under the Constitution. The state supreme court denied all relief.

Vote: 9–0

JUSTICE BLACK delivered the opinion of the Court.

Treating due process as "a concept less rigid and more fluid than those envisaged in other specific and particular provisions of the Bill of Rights," the Court held that refusal to appoint counsel under the particular facts and circumstances in the *Betts v. Brady,* 316 U.S. 455 (1942), case was not so "offensive to the common and fundamental ideas of fairness" as to amount to a denial of due process. Since the facts and circumstances of the two cases are so nearly indistinguishable, we think the *Betts v. Brady* holding if left standing would require us to reject Gideon's claim that the Constitution guarantees him the assistance of counsel. Upon full reconsideration we conclude that *Betts v. Brady* should be overruled.

Not only these precedents but also reason and reflection require us to recognize that in our adversary system of criminal justice, any person haled into court, who is too poor to hire a lawyer, cannot be assured a fair trial unless counsel is provided for him. This seems to us to be an obvious truth. Governments, both state and federal, quite properly spend vast sums of money to establish machinery to try defendants accused of crime. Lawyers to prosecute are everywhere deemed essential to protect the public's interest in an orderly society. Similarly, there are few defendants charged with crime, few indeed, who fail to hire the best lawyers they can get to prepare and present their defenses. That government hires lawyers to prosecute and defendants who have the money hire lawyers to defend are the strongest indications of the widespread belief that lawyers in criminal courts are necessities, not luxuries. The right of one charged with crime to counsel may not be deemed fundamental and essential to fair trials in some countries, but it is in ours. From the very beginning, our state and national constitutions and laws have laid great emphasis on procedural and substantive safeguards designed to assure fair trials before impartial tribunals in which every defendant stands equal before the law. This noble ideal cannot be realized if the poor man charged with crime has to face his accusers without a lawyer to assist him. . . .

Reversed.

JUSTICE HARLAN concurred.

In agreeing with the Court that the right to counsel in a case such as this should now be expressly recognized as a fundamental right embraced in the Fourteenth Amendment, I wish to make a further observation. When we hold a right or immunity, valid against the Federal Government, to be "implicit in the concept of ordered liberty" and thus valid against the States, I do not read our past decisions to suggest that by so holding, we automatically carry over an entire body of federal law and apply it in full sweep to the States. Any such concept would disregard the frequently wide disparity between the legitimate interests of the States and of the Federal Government, the divergent problems that they face, and the significantly different consequences of their actions. In what is done today I do not understand the Court to depart from the principles laid down in

Palko v. Connecticut, 302 U.S. 319 (1937), or to embrace the concept that the Fourteenth Amendment "incorporates" the Sixth Amendment as such.

On these premises I join in the judgment of the Court.

FOR DISCUSSION

Why is a right to counsel important? When and under what circumstances is that right protected in this case? Is it in all cases? All criminal? Only some criminal?

WOLF V. COLORADO

338 U.S. 25, 69 S.Ct. 1359, 93 L.Ed. 1782 (1949)

Police officers went to the office of a physician and, without a warrant, took his appointment book. From this source they obtained the names of patients who later testified against the physician, and he was found guilty of illegal practice. The Court on certiorari had to determine whether a conviction in a state court for a state offense denies due process under the Fourteenth Amendment when the evidence used for conviction was obtained under circumstances that would have rendered it inadmissible in a prosecution for violation of a federal law in a federal court because it violated the guarantee against search and seizure under the Fourth Amendment as applied in Weeks v. United States, 232 U.S. 383 (1914).

Vote: 6–3

JUSTICE FRANKFURTER delivered the opinion of the Court.

To rely on a tidy formula for the easy determination of what is a fundamental right for purposes of legal enforcement may satisfy a longing for certainty but ignores the movements of a free society. It belittles the scale of the conception of due process. The real clue to the problem confronting the judiciary in the application of the Due Process Clause is not to ask where the line is once and for all to be drawn but to recognize that it is for the Court to draw it by the gradual and empiric process of "inclusion and exclusion." *Davidson v. New Orleans,* 96 U.S. 97, 104 (1878). This was the Court's insight when first called upon to consider the problem; to this insight the Court has on the whole been faithful as case after case has come before it since *Davidson v. New Orleans* was decided.

The security of one's privacy against arbitrary intrusion by the police—which is at the core of the Fourth Amendment—is basic to a free society. It is therefore implicit in "the concept of ordered liberty" and as such enforceable against the States through the Due Process Clause. The knock at the door, whether by day or by night, as a prelude to a search, without authority of law but solely on the authority of the police, did not need the commentary of recent history to be condemned as inconsistent with the conception of human rights enshrined in the history and the basic constitutional documents of English-speaking peoples. Accordingly, we have no hesitation in saying that were a State affirmatively to sanction such police incursion into privacy it would run counter to the guaranty of the Fourteenth Amendment. But the ways of enforcing such a basic right raise questions of a different order. How such arbitrary conduct should be checked, what remedies against it should be afforded, the means by which the right should be made effective, are all questions that are not to be so dogmatically answered as to preclude the varying solutions which spring from an allowable range of judgment on issues not susceptible of quantitative solution.

In *Weeks v. United States*, 232 U.S. 383 (1914), this Court held that in a federal prosecution the Fourth Amendment barred the use of evidence secured through an illegal search and seizure. This ruling was made for the first time in 1914. It was not derived from the explicit requirements of the Fourth Amendment; it was not based on legislation expressing Congressional policy in the enforcement of the Constitution. The decision was a matter of judicial implication. Since then it has been frequently applied and we stoutly adhere to it. But the immediate question is whether the basic right to protection against arbitrary intrusion by the police demands the exclusion of logically relevant evidence obtained by an unreasonable search and seizure because, in a federal prosecution for a federal crime, it would be excluded. As a matter of inherent reason, one would suppose this to be an issue as to which men with complete devotion to the protection of the right of privacy might give different answers. When we find that in fact most of the English-speaking world does not regard as vital to such protection the exclusion of evidence thus obtained, we must hesitate to treat this remedy as an essential ingredient of the right. The contrariety of views of the States is particularly impressive in view of the careful reconsideration which they have given the problem in the light of the *Weeks* decision.

We hold, therefore, that in a prosecution in a State court for a State crime the Fourteenth Amendment does not forbid the admission of evidence obtained by an unreasonable search and seizure. And though we have interpreted the Fourth Amendment to forbid the admission of such evidence, a different question would be presented if Congress under its legislative powers were to pass a statute purporting to negate the *Weeks* doctrine. We would then be faced with the problem of the respect to be accorded the legislative judgment on an issue as to which, in default of that judgment, we have been forced to depend upon our own. Problems of a converse character, also not before us, would be presented should Congress under Section 5 of the Fourteenth Amendment undertake to enforce the rights there guaranteed by attempting to make the *Weeks* doctrine binding upon the States.

Affirmed.

[The appendix of the opinion includes a listing of the states of the Union and their attitudes on the *Weeks* doctrine. Australia, Canada, England, India, and Scotland are also included.]

JUSTICE BLACK concurred

I agree with the conclusion of the Court that the Fourth Amendment's prohibition of "unreasonable searches and seizures" is enforceable against the states. Consequently, I should be for reversal of this case if I thought the Fourth Amendment not only prohibited "unreasonable searches and seizures," but also, of itself, barred the use of evidence so unlawfully obtained. But I agree with what appears to be a plain implication of the Court's opinion that the federal exclusionary rule is not a command of the Fourth Amendment but is a judicially created rule of evidence which Congress might negate. . . . This leads me to concur in the Court's judgment of affirmance.

It is not amiss to repeat my belief that the Fourteenth Amendment was intended to make the Fourth Amendment in its entirety applicable to the states. The Fourth Amendment was designed to protect people against unrestrained searches and seizures by sheriffs, policemen and other law enforcement officers. Such protection is an essential in a free society.

JUSTICE RUTLEDGE dissented, joined by JUSTICE MURPHY.

As Congress and this Court are, in my judgment, powerless to permit the admission in federal courts of evidence seized in defiance of the Fourth Amendment, so I think state legislators and judges—if subject to the Amendment, as I believe them to be—may not lend their offices to the admission in state courts of evidence thus seized. Compliance with the Bill of Rights betokens more than lip service. The Court makes the illegality of this search and seizure its inarticulate premise of decision. I acquiesce in that premise and think the conviction should be reversed.

JUSTICE MURPHY dissented, joined by JUSTICE RUTLEDGE.

The conclusion is inescapable that but one remedy exists to deter violations of the search and seizure clause. That is the rule which excludes illegally obtained evidence. Only by exclusion can we impress upon the zealous prosecutor that violation of the Constitution will do him no good. And only when that point is driven home can the prosecutor be expected to emphasize the importance of observing constitutional demands in his instructions to the police.

I cannot believe that we should decide due process questions by simply taking a poll of the rules in various jurisdictions, even if we follow the *Palko* "test." Today's decision will do inestimable harm to the cause of fair police methods in our cities and states. Even more important, perhaps, it must have tragic effect upon public respect for our judiciary. For the Court now allows what is indeed shabby business: lawlessness by officers of the law.

Since the evidence admitted was secured in violation of the Fourth Amendment, the judgment should be reversed.

JUSTICE DOUGLAS also dissented.

FOR DISCUSSION

Does it make practical sense for the federal government to be restricted by the exclusionary rule but not the states? Does such a dual system of protection effectively mean that the rule lacks force?

MAPP V. OHIO

367 U.S. 643, 81 S.Ct. 1684, 6 L.Ed. 1081 (1961)

Police officers in Cleveland requested admittance to the Mapp residence to search for a fugitive who was reportedly hiding in the home. Further, the police had word that a large amount of illegal paraphernalia was hidden there. The officers entered the house forcefully without a warrant and searched the entire house from the basement to the second floor and ultimately found materials that resulted in Mapp's conviction for possessing obscenity. Mapp challenged the use of this evidence by the state.

Vote: 6–3

JUSTICE CLARK delivered the opinion of the Court.

. . . Seventy-five years ago, in *Boyd v. United States,* 116 U.S. 616, 630 (1886), considering the Fourth and Fifth Amendments as running "almost into each other" on the facts before it, this Court held that the doctrines of those Amendments "apply to all invasions on the part of the government and its employees of the sanctity of a man's home and the privacies of life. . . ."

Less than 30 years after *Boyd,* this Court, in *Weeks v. United States,* 232 U.S. 383 (1914), stated that "the 4th Amendment . . . put the courts of the United States and Federal officials, in the exercise of their power and authority, under limitations and restraints [and] forever secure[d] the people, their persons, houses, papers, and effects, against all unreasonable searches and seizures under the guise of law . . . and the duty of giving to it force and effect is obligatory upon all entrusted under our Federal system with the enforcement of the laws." . . . In 1949, 35 years after *Weeks* was announced, this Court, in *Wolf v. People of State of Colorado,* 338 U.S. 25 (1949), again for the first time, discussed the effect of the Fourth Amendment upon the States through the operation of the Due Process Clause of the Fourteenth Amendment. It said: "[W]e have no hesitation in saying that were a State affirmatively to sanction such police incursion into privacy it would run counter to the guaranty of the Fourteenth Amendment." Nevertheless, after declaring that the "security of one's privacy against arbitrary intrusion by the police" is "implicit in the 'concept of ordered liberty' and as such enforceable against the States through the Due Process Clause," cf. *Palko v. State of Connecticut,* 302 U.S. 319 (1937), and announcing that it "stoutly adhere[d]" to the *Weeks* decision, the Court decided that the *Weeks* exclusionary rule would not then be imposed upon the States as "an essential ingredient of the right." The Court's reasons for not considering essential to the right to privacy, as a curb imposed upon the States by the Due Process Clause, that which decades before had been posited as part and parcel of the Fourth Amendment's limitation upon federal encroachment of individual privacy, were bottomed on factual considerations.

. . . Today we once again examine *Wolf's* constitutional documentation of the right to privacy free from unreasonable state intrusion, and, after its dozen years on our books, are led by it to close the only courtroom door remaining open to evidence secured by official lawlessness in flagrant abuse of that basic right, reserved to all persons as a specific guarantee against that very same unlawful conduct. We hold that all evidence obtained by searches and seizures in violation of the Constitution is, by that same authority, inadmissible in a state court.

Since the Fourth Amendment's right of privacy has been declared enforceable against the States through the Due Process Clause of the Fourteenth, it is enforceable against them by the same sanction of exclusion as is used against the Federal Government. . . .

Moreover, our holding that the exclusionary rule is an essential part of both the Fourth and Fourteenth Amendments is not only the logical dictate of prior cases, but it also makes very good sense. There is no war between the Constitution and common sense. . . .

The ignoble shortcut to conviction left open to the State tends to destroy the entire system of constitutional restraints on which the liberties of the people rest. Having once recognized that the right to privacy embodied in the Fourth Amendment is enforceable against the States, and that the right to be secure against rude invasions of privacy by state officers is, therefore, constitutional in origin, we can no longer permit that right to remain an empty promise. Because it is enforceable in the same manner and to like effect as other basic rights secured by the Due Process Clause, we can no longer permit it to be revocable at the whim of any police officer who, in the name of law enforcement itself, chooses to suspend its enjoyment. Our decision, founded on reason and truth, gives to the individual no more than that which the Constitution guarantees him, to the police officer no less than that to which honest law enforcement is entitled, and, to the courts, that judicial integrity so necessary in the true administration of justice.

The judgment of the Supreme Court of Ohio is reversed and the cause remanded for further proceedings not inconsistent with this opinion.

Reversed and remanded.

JUSTICE BLACK concurred.

. . . I am still not persuaded that the Fourth Amendment, standing alone, would be enough to bar the introduction into evidence against an accused of papers and effects seized from him in violation of its commands. For the Fourth Amendment does not itself contain any provision expressly precluding the use of such evidence, and I am extremely doubtful that such a provision could properly be inferred from nothing more than the basic command against unreasonable searches and seizures. Reflection on the problem, however, in the light of cases coming before the Court since *Wolf,* has led me to conclude that when the Fourth Amendment's ban against unreasonable searches and seizures is considered together with the Fifth Amendment's ban against compelled self-incrimination, a constitutional basis emerges which not only justifies but actually requires the exclusionary rule. . . .

JUSTICE DOUGLAS concurred.

. . . The only remaining remedy, if exclusion of the evidence is not required, is an action of trespass by the homeowner against the offending officer. Mr. Justice Murphy showed how onerous and difficult it would be for the citizen to maintain that action and how meagre the relief even if the citizen prevails. The truth is that trespass actions against officers who make unlawful searches and seizures are mainly illusory remedies.

. . . Once evidence, inadmissible in a federal court, is admissible in a state court a "double standard" exists which, as the Court points out, leads to "working arrangements" that undercut federal policy and reduce some aspects of law enforcement to shabby business. The rule that supports that practice does not have the force of reason behind it.

JUSTICE HARLAN, whom JUSTICE FRANKFURTER and JUSTICE WHITTAKER joined, dissented.

In overruling the *Wolf* case the Court, in my opinion, has forgotten the sense of judicial restraint which, with due regard for *stare decisis,* is one element that should enter into deciding whether a past decision of this Court should be overruled. Apart from that I also believe that the *Wolf* rule represents sounder Constitutional doctrine than the new rule which now replaces it.

From the Court's statement of the case one would gather that the central, if not controlling, issue on this appeal is whether illegally state-seized evidence is Constitutionally admissible in a state prosecution, an issue which would of course face us with the need for re-examining *Wolf.* However, such is not the situation. For, although that question was indeed raised here and below among appellant's subordinate points, the new and pivotal issue brought to the Court by this appeal is whether § 2905.34 of the Ohio Revised Code making criminal the *mere* knowing possession or control of obscene material, and under which appellant has been convicted, is consistent with the rights of free thought and expression assured against state action by the Fourteenth Amendment. That was the principal issue which was decided by the Ohio Supreme Court, which was tendered by appellant's Jurisdictional Statement, and which was briefed and argued in this Court.

In this posture of things, I think it fair to say that five members of this Court have simply "reached out" to overrule *Wolf.* With all respect for the views of the majority, and recognizing that *stare decisis* carries different weight in Constitutional adjudication than it does in nonconstitutional decision, I can perceive no justification for regarding this case as an appropriate occasion for re-examining *Wolf.* . . .

FOR DISCUSSION

What reasons does the court give in *Mapp* for reversing *Wolf?* Are these grounds based on legal or practical concerns?

GRISWOLD V. CONNECTICUT

381 U.S. 479, 85 S.Ct. 1678, 14 L.Ed. 2d 510 (1965)

Estelle Griswold, the executive director of Planned Parenthood, had instructed married couples about birth control contrary to a Connecticut that made it illegal to use, sell, or counsel others on the use of birth control. Griswold was convicted for violation of the law; she appealed the conviction.

Vote: 7–2

JUSTICE DOUGLAS delivered the opinion of the Court.

Coming to the merits, we are met with a wide range of questions that implicate the Due Process Clause of the Fourteenth Amendment. Overtones of some arguments suggest that *Lochner v. State of New York,* 198 U.S. 45 (1905), should be our guide. But we decline that invitation as we did in *West Coast Hotel Co. v. Parrish,* 300 U.S. 379 (1937). We do not sit as a super-legislature to determine the wisdom, need, and propriety of laws that touch economic problems, business affairs, or social conditions. This law, however, operates directly on an intimate relation of husband and wife and their physician's role in one aspect of that relation.

The association of people is not mentioned in the Constitution nor in the Bill of Rights. The right to educate a child in a school of the parents' choice—whether public or private or parochial—is also not mentioned. Nor is the right to study any particular subject or any foreign language. Yet the First Amendment has been construed to include certain of those rights.

By *Pierce v. Society of Sisters,* 268 U.S. 510 (1925), the right to educate one's children as one chooses is made applicable to the States by the force of the First and Fourteenth Amendments. By *Meyer v. State of Nebraska,* 262 U.S. 390 (1923), the same dignity is given the right to study the German language in a private school. In other words, the State may not, consistently with the spirit of the First Amendment, contract the spectrum of available knowledge. The right of freedom of speech and press includes not only the right to utter or to print, but the right to distribute, the right to receive, the right to read and freedom of inquiry, freedom of thought, and freedom to teach—indeed the freedom of the entire university community. Without those peripheral rights the specific rights would be less secure. And so we reaffirm the principle of the *Pierce* and the *Meyer* cases.

In *NAACP v. State of Alabama,* 357 U.S. 449 (1958), we protected the "freedom to associate and privacy in one's associations," noting that freedom of association was a peripheral First Amendment right. Disclosure of membership lists of a constitutionally valid association, we held, was invalid "as entailing the likelihood of a substantial restraint upon the exercise by petitioner's members of their right to freedom of association." In other words, the First Amendment has a penumbra where privacy is protected from governmental intrusion. In like context, we have protected forms of "association" that are not political in the customary sense but pertain to the social, legal, and economic benefit of the members. We held it not permissible to bar a lawyer from practice, because he had once been a member of the Communist Party. The man's "association with that Party" was not shown to be "anything more than a political faith in a political party" and was not action of a kind proving bad moral character.

Those cases involved more than the "right of assembly"—a right that extends to all irrespective of their race or ideology. The right of "association," like the right of belief (*West Virginia State Board of Education v. Barnette,* 319 U.S. 624 (1943)) is more than the right to attend a meeting; it includes the right to express one's attitudes or philosophies by membership in a group or by affiliation with it or by other lawful means. Association in that context is a form of expression of opinion; and while it is not expressly included in the First Amendment its existence is necessary in making the express guarantees fully meaningful.

The foregoing cases suggest that specific guarantees in the Bill of Rights have penumbras, formed by emanations from those guarantees that help give them life and substance. Various guarantees create zones of privacy. The right of association contained in the penumbra of the First Amendment is one, as we have seen. The Third Amendment in its prohibition against the quartering of soldiers "in any house" in time of peace without the consent of the owner is another facet of that privacy. The Fourth Amendment explicitly affirms the "right of the people to be secure in their persons, houses, papers, and effects, against unreasonable searches and seizures." The Fifth Amendment in its Self-Incrimination Clause enables the citizen to create a zone of privacy which government may not force him to surrender to his detriment. The Ninth Amendment provides: "The enumeration in the Constitution, of certain rights, shall not be construed to deny or disparage others retained by the people."

The Fourth and Fifth Amendments were described in *Boyd v. United States,* 116 U.S. 616 (1886), as protection against all governmental invasions "of the sanctity of a man's home and the privacies of life." We recently referred in *Mapp v. Ohio,* 367 U.S. 643 (1961), to the Fourth Amendment as creating a "right to privacy, no less important than any other right carefully and particularly reserved to the people."

"The principles laid down in this opinion (by Lord Camden in *Entick v. Carrington*, 19 How.St.Tr. 1029 (1765)) affect the very essence of constitutional liberty and security. They reach further than the concrete form of the case then before the court, with its adventitious circumstances; they apply to all invasions on the part of the government and its employees of the sanctity of a man's home and the privacies of life. It is not the breaking of his doors, and the rummaging of his drawers, that constitutes the essence of the offense; but it is the invasion of his indefeasible right of personal security, personal liberty and private property, where that right has never been forfeited by his conviction of some public offense—it is the invasion of this sacred right which underlies and constitutes the essence of Lord Camden's judgment. Breaking into a house and opening boxes and drawers are circumstances of aggravation; but any forcible and compulsory extortion of a man's own testimony, or of his private papers to be used as evidence to convict him of crime, or to forfeit his goods, is within the condemnation of that judgment. In this regard the fourth and fifth amendments run almost into each other."

We have had many controversies over these penumbral rights of "privacy and repose."

The present case, then, concerns a relationship lying within the zone of privacy created by several fundamental constitutional guarantees. And it concerns a law which, in forbidding the use of contraceptives rather than regulating their manufacture or sale, seeks to achieve its goals by means having a maximum destructive impact upon that relationship. Such a law cannot stand in light of the familiar principle, so often applied by this Court, that a "governmental purpose to control or prevent activities constitutionally subject to state regulation may not be achieved by means which sweep unnecessarily broadly and thereby invade the area of protected freedoms." Would we allow the police to search the sacred precincts of marital bedrooms for telltale signs of the use of contraceptives? The very idea is repulsive to the notions of privacy surrounding the marriage relationship.

We deal with a right of privacy older than the Bill of Rights—older than our political parties, older than our school system. Marriage is a coming together for better or for worse, hopefully enduring, and intimate to the degree of being sacred. It is an association that promotes a way of life, not causes; a harmony in living, not political faiths; a bilateral loyalty, not commercial or social projects. Yet it is an association for as noble a purpose as any involved in our prior decisions.

Reversed.

JUSTICE GOLDBERG, whom CHIEF JUSTICE WARREN and JUSTICE BRENNAN join, concurring.

I agree with the Court that Connecticut's birth—control law unconstitutionally intrudes upon the right of marital privacy, and I join in its opinion and judgment. Although I have not accepted the view that 'due process' as used in the Fourteenth Amendment includes all of the first eight Amendments (see my concurring opinion in *Pointer v. Texas,* 380 U.S. 400 (1965), and the dissenting opinion of Mr. Justice Brennan in *Cohen v. Hurley,* 366 U.S. 117 (1961). I do agree that the concept of liberty protects those personal rights that are fundamental, and is not confined to the specific terms of the Bill of Rights. My conclusion that the concept of liberty is not so restricted and that it embraces the right of marital privacy though that right is not mentioned explicitly in the Constitution is supported both by numerous decisions of this Court, referred to in the Court's opinion, and by the language and history of the Ninth Amendment. In reaching the conclusion that the right of marital privacy is protected, as being within the protected penumbra of specific guarantees of the Bill of Rights, the Court refers to the Ninth Amendment. I add these words to emphasize the relevance of that Amendment to the Court's holding.

FOR DISCUSSION

What does the Ninth Amendment protect? Can you generate a list of rights not otherwise listed in the first eight amendments that should also be protected by the Eighth? What does a right to privacy include?

OTIS MCDONALD V. CITY OF CHICAGO, ILLINOIS

561 U.S. 742, 130 S.Ct. 3020, 177 L.Ed. 2d 894 (2010)

Located in Chapter III, page 441.

FOR DISCUSSION

Is there a difference in how the various Justices in the majority would incorporate the Second or any Amendment to apply to the states? Is this approach advocated by Justice Thomas more faithful to original intent? What was the original intent of the Fourteenth Amendment's Framers when it came to guns or any of the other Bill of Rights protections?

Interpretation of the Bill of Rights

In addition to the issue of incorporating the Bill of Rights provisions to apply to the states, a related question concerns how the Supreme Court should interpret these provisions as well as the meaning of the Constitution. While the opening of this chapter discusses the debates over the meaning of the Constitution, matters of interpretation also are important when it comes to the Bill of Rights. What does freedom of speech, for example, include? Does it include the right falsely to cry fire in a crowded theater? Answering this question requires ascertaining what speech is and what freedom means. Answering these questions, as well as seeking to understand what the rest of the Bill of Rights means, is the subject of the remainder of this book.

But there is a second issue: the judiciary's attitude toward the government and individual rights. When a law, rule, or policy is challenged as violating a provision of the Bill of Rights, such as the First Amendment Free Exercise Clause, how much scrutiny of it should the judiciary offer, and how much deference should judges give to Congress or a state legislature in presuming that it is or is not constitutional? The Supreme Court has addressed this issue in a series of cases that describe its approach to constitutional questions. In *Ashwander v. Tennessee Valley Authority* (297 U.S. 288, 1936), the Court seems to suggest that a presumption should be given to constitutionality of an act by the government and that declaring acts invalid on constitutional grounds should be avoided. Instead, the preference is to resolve disputes on statutory or other grounds. In part the reasons for this are grounded in separation of powers and judicial deference to Congress and the president. Moreover, while statutory decisions can be overridden by Congress, constitutional decisions cannot, short of constitutional amendments.

However, do the presumptions in the ***Ashwander* rules** apply across the board? Should the Court give the same presumptions of constitutionality to all legislation? From the 1870s or 1880s until the New Deal, the

Court, employing doctrines such as economic or substantive due process or liberty of contract, seemed to give more exacting scrutiny to economic legislation or regulation than to other types of government action (This topic is discussed in volume one). But after the invalidation of many parts of Roosevelt's first New Deal legislation enacted in 1933, the president in 1937 proposed what has been called a court-packing plan, an attempt to seat on the Court justices more sympathetic to his policies. While the part of the Judiciary Reorganization Bill of 1937 that embodied the plan was stripped from act before it was passed by Congress, the Court seemed to get the message. A combination of new justices and changed attitudes on the bench (a backing down or retreat?) led to what appeared to be a new judicial philosophy that gave less scrutiny to economic legislation and more to other individual rights. *United States v. Carolene Products* (304 U.S. 144, 1938), especially the famous footnote number 4 [quoted later in the presentation of the case], highlights this switch in judicial or constitutional philosophy.

Carolene Products is one of the most important Supreme Court cases of the twentieth century, but not because of either its facts or its holding. Instead, it is because of the dicta in footnote number 4. Hinted at in note 4 are different levels of judicial scrutiny or examination of legislation depending on the subject matter. In general, legislation affecting Bill of Rights protections such as freedom of speech or religion are examined more carefully than laws seeking to regulate the economy.

The origins of the concept or idea that the federal courts will examine legislation with varying levels of analysis originated with *McCulloch v. Maryland* (17 U.S. 316, 1819). Chief Justice Marshall, in upholding the power of the federal government to charter a national bank, turned to the Necessary and Proper Clause to find a constitutional basis for this legislation. In interpreting what "necessary" meant in Article I, Section 8, Clause 18, Marshall wrote:

> Congress is authorized to pass all laws 'necessary and proper' to carry into execution the powers conferred on it. These words, 'necessary and proper,' in such an instrument, are probably to be considered as synonymous. Necessarily, powers must here intend such powers as are suitable and fitted to the object; such as are best and most useful in relation to the end proposed. If this be not so, and if congress could use no means but such as were absolutely indispensable to the existence of a granted power, the government would hardly exist; at least, it would be wholly inadequate to the purposes of its formation.

This reading of the Constitution implies that the Court would give wide deference to congressional construction of its own power. The presumption would be that unless an act was clearly against the plain text of the Constitution, it would be upheld. *McCulloch* is thus the origin of what has come to be described as **rational basis review**. Under a rational basis test, plaintiffs wishing to challenge the constitutionality of a law bear the burden of showing that it is unconstitutional. The presumption will be that the law is constitutional unless one can show that there is no rational basis for the law. It is not hard to show a rational basis for almost any law. Thus, this level of analysis or scrutiny is exceedingly deferential to legislation.

However, while the Court examines most laws from a rational basis perspective, it subjects others to more intense analysis. After the Civil War, beginning with the federal courts (and before this with some state courts, such as in *Wynehamer v. People* (13 N.Y. 485, 1856), judges began to examine some laws with even more closely than usual, that is, with heightened or **strict scrutiny**. The origins of this type of analysis can be found in efforts by the federal courts in examining economic legislation or that which affected the regulation of the economy, including that of workplaces.

In cases such as *Mugler v. Kansas* (123 U.S. 623, 1887) and *Lochner v. New York* (198 U.S. 45, 1905), the Supreme Court enunciated the doctrine of substantive due process, liberty of contract, or economic due process and demanded that the government demonstrate special reasons for the legislation. As the Court stated in *Mugler* when striking down a state law banning alcohol sales:

> It does not at all follow that every statute enacted ostensibly for the promotion of these ends is to be accepted as a legitimate exertion of the police powers of the state. There are, of necessity, limits beyond which legislation cannot rightfully go. While every possible presumption is to be indulged in favor of the validity of a statute, the courts must obey the constitution rather than the law-making department of government, and must, upon their own responsibility, determine whether, in any particular case, these limits have been passed.

Mugler suggested that a stricter or heightened form of analysis would be used by the federal courts when they examined some types of legislation. As would become characteristic of the period on the Court known as the *Lochner* era, legislation engaging in economic regulation, including that of interstate commerce, received more searching scrutiny than a rational basis analysis.

With the New Deal and *Carolene Products,* things would change. *Carolene Products* was the most explicit of a host of decisions by the Supreme Court revealing that it would no longer give more heightened scrutiny to economic legislation, such as that which regulated the interstate shipment of filled milk (i.e., skimmed milk modified to resemble milk or cream). Instead, it would receive the rational basis examination similar to that described in *McCulloch.* Yet footnote number 4 of *Carolene Products* hinted at using a more heightened or strict scrutiny not for economic legislation but for classes of laws implicating Bill of Rights protections, race, and rules governing the political process. This new test would be described as *strict scrutiny.*

Under a **strict scrutiny** test, the burdens of proof are reversed. If one can show that a law implicates a provision in the Bill of Rights, such as a right to freedom of speech, instead of the federal courts presuming the constitutionality of a law, the Court presumes it to be unconstitutional unless the government can make three showings.

First, the government must demonstrate that it has a **compelling interest** in adopting a specific law. Although there is no set definition of what constitutes a compelling interest, the courts have accepted the prevention of corruption, or the appearance of corruption, in cases involving political campaign donations.

Second, the government must show that the law or rule adopted is "narrowly tailored" to achieve that goal or interest. If the government action regulates or prohibits too much or fails to address essential aspects of the compelling interest, then the rule is not considered to be narrowly tailored. For example, if the government, in an effort to prevent violence, also prohibits peaceful political demonstrations, the law would be deemed too overbroad, that is, not tailored narrowly enough to secure the compelling governmental interest it was asserting.

Finally, the law or policy must be the **least restrictive means** to securing the governmental interest it addresses. Put another way, there cannot be a less restrictive way to effectively achieve the compelling government interest than that which is proposed by the law. For example, if the government wished to prevent the sale of obscene materials and did that by banning all works of literature containing four-letter words, this would not be the least restrictive means to achieving that objective. Unless the government can meet all three prongs of the strict scrutiny test, the law, policy, or rule will be presumed to be unconstitutional.

While *Carolene Products* launched the modern dual standard of strict and rational basis scrutiny, it left unanswered several questions. For one, what specifically should strict scrutiny apply to? The dicta in footnote 4 said such scrutiny should apply to the Bill of Rights, but a wider application of strict scrutiny to other matters was suggested as well. Such as what? Second, are these two standards of analysis (strict and rational basis) the only two levels of scrutiny? *Korematsu v. United States* (323 U.S. 214, 1944) and *Skinner v. Oklahoma* (316 U.S. 535, 1942), partially answered the first question.

Korematsu is an important case on several scores. It is famous for upholding the internment program that resulted in the forced removal of over 100,000 Japanese-Americans to camps in the Southwest and elsewhere, which contemporary scholars widely regard as the product of racial animus and fear during World War II.

Second, near the beginning of *Korematsu* the Court declares the use of race as a basis for governmental mandates to be suspect. Specifically the Court stated: "[A]ll legal restrictions which curtail the civil rights of a single racial group are immediately suspect. That is not to say that all such restrictions are unconstitutional. It is to say that courts must subject them to the most rigid scrutiny."

Korematsu is famous for the origins of the concept of **suspect classifications**. Under this doctrine, the use of certain suspect classifications would be examined under strict scrutiny. In the Equal Protection jurisprudence of the Fourteen Amendment, the concept of suspect classification would be used to invalidate racially discriminatory legislation. Beyond race, the Supreme Court would also find other classifications, such as religion, to be suspect, hence subject to strict scrutiny. Eventually, the Court would find gender to be **semi-suspect**, inviting it to create a third or intermediate level of analysis. The use of strict and intermediate level scrutiny to examine racial and other forms of classification is discussed in more detail in Chapter VII, which covers the concept of equal protection.

The irony of *Korematsu* is that despite declaring race to be suspect, it upheld the Japanese relocation program. Eventually, in the 1990s, Congress recognized that errors of the policy and compensated living victims for their losses.

Unlike *Korematsu,* which contended that certain ways of classifying individuals are suspect, *Skinner v. Oklahoma* follows on the earlier discussion of the Ninth Amendment, *Carolene Products*, and *Palko* in seeking to determine whether some rights (both those textually explicit and not in the Constitution or Bill of Rights) deserve to be given special protection by the courts. In this case, the Court finds that while a right to reproduction is nowhere mentioned in the Constitution, it nonetheless is a fundamental right deserving of constitutional protection.

Skinner should be read in the context of another case, *Buck v. Bell* (274 U.S. 200, 1927), where Justice Holmes, speaking for the majority, upheld a Virginia law calling for the sterilization of those deemed to be "feebleminded." Although historians have questioned the validity of these claims, Carrie Buck, a woman tested to have the IQ of a nine-year-old, became pregnant as a result of a rape. The Court asserted her mother had also had a very low IQ. In upholding the Virginia law, Holmes declared "[t]hree generations of imbeciles are enough" and ruled that it was in the best interests of society and the victim that she be sterilized. Criticism of the *Buck* decision, or at least its dicta, and reaction to the Nazi eugenics program in Germany during World War II contributed to a reevaluation of reproduction as a fundamental right.

Skinner described procreation as a fundamental right subject to strict scrutiny analysis. With *Skinner* and *Korematsu*, the Supreme Court articulated two major categories of legislation that would be subject to strict scrutiny: the use of suspect classifications and legislation affecting fundamental rights. Following World War II and through the Warren and Burger years, the Court undertook a process of creating or listing suspect or semi-suspect classes and fundamental rights that would be given the level of analysis suggested by *Carolene Products* footnote number 4. The framework set out in *Ashwander*, *Carolene Products, Korematsu,* and *Skinner* continues to define the basic approach the Court uses today to examine and interpret constitutional questions.

Constitutional Analysis Framework

Level of Analysis	Application	Test
Rational Basis	Ordinary legislation, economic regulation	Plaintiffs challenging a law must show that (1) the government lacked a legitimate interest and (2) the means was not rationally related to serving that interest.
Intermediate scrutiny	Classifications based on gender, alienage, or illegitimacy	Government must show that (1) it has an important interest in enacting the legislation and (2) that the classification was substantially related to securing that interest.
Strict scrutiny	Classifications based on race or religion, fundamental rights including marriage, procreation, interstate travel, voting, and access to justice	Government must show that (1) it has a compelling interest in enacting the legislation; (2) the law is narrowly tailored; and (3) the law as written is the least restrictive means of securing that interest.

ASHWANDER V. TENNESSEE VALLEY AUTHORITY

297 U.S. 288, 56 S.Ct. 466, 80 L.Ed. 688 (1936)

Shareholders of a power company sued the latter, contending that its sale of power lines to the federal government was illegal in that the Tennessee Valley Authority lacked the constitutional authority to purchase and dispose of hydroelectric power. While the Court in a majority opinion by Chief Justice Hughes upheld the sale of the power lines, it refused to rule on the broader constitutional questions raised by the shareholders. Justice Brandeis' concurrence offered clarification on the Court's constitutional adjudication.

Vote: 8–1

JUSTICE BRANDEIS (concurring).

Considerations of propriety, as well as long-established practice, demand that we refrain from passing upon the constitutionality of an act of Congress unless obliged to do so in the proper performance of our judicial function, when the question is raised by a party whose interests entitle him to raise it.

The Court has frequently called attention to the great gravity and delicacy of its function in passing upon the validity of an act of Congress; and has restricted exercise of this function by rigid insistence that the jurisdiction of federal courts is limited to actual cases and controversies; and that they have no power to give advisory opinions. On this ground it has in recent years ordered the dismissal of several suits challenging the constitutionality of important acts of Congress.

The Court developed, for its own governance in the cases confessedly within its jurisdiction, a series of rules under which it has avoided passing upon a large part of all the constitutional questions pressed upon it for decision. They are:

1. The Court will not pass upon the constitutionality of legislation in a friendly, nonadversary, proceeding, declining because to decide such questions is legitimate only in the last resort, and as a necessity in the determination of real, earnest, and vital controversy between individuals. It never was the thought that, by means of a friendly suit, a party beaten in the legislature could transfer to the courts an inquiry as to the constitutionality of the legislative act.

2. The Court will not anticipate a question of constitutional law in advance of the necessity of deciding it. It is not the habit of the court to decide questions of a constitutional nature unless absolutely necessary to a decision of the case.

3. The Court will not formulate a rule of constitutional law broader than is required by the precise facts to which it is to be applied.

4. The Court will not pass upon a constitutional question although properly presented by the record, if there is also present some other ground upon which the case may be disposed of. This rule has found most varied application. Thus, if a case can be decided on either of two grounds, one involving a constitutional question, the other a question of statutory construction or general law, the Court will decide only the latter. Appeals from the highest court of a state challenging its decision of a question under the Federal Constitution are frequently dismissed because the judgment can be sustained on an independent state ground.

5. The Court will not pass upon the validity of a statute upon complaint of one who fails to show that he is injured by its operation. Among the many applications of this rule, none is more striking than the denial of the right of challenge to one who lacks a personal or property right. Thus, the challenge by a public official interested only in the performance of his official duty will not be entertained.

6. The Court will not pass upon the constitutionality of a statute at the instance of one who has availed himself of its benefits.

7. When the validity of an act of the Congress is drawn in question, and even if a serious doubt of constitutionality is raised, it is a cardinal principle that this Court will first ascertain whether a construction of the statute is fairly possible by which the question may be avoided.

FOR DISCUSSION

Do you agree with Justice Brandeis that the Court should avoid basing its decisions on constitutional grounds when possible? Why? Is there a constitutional basis for this assertion? How might checks and balance, separation of powers, or the difficultly in amending the Constitution play into this reasoning?

UNITED STATES V. CAROLENE PRODUCTS CO.

304 U.S. 144, 58 S.Ct. 778, 82 L.Ed. 1234 (1938)

Carolene Products Company was fined for a violation of a federal law that prohibited the shipment of filled milk across state borders. The company, which had in fact shipped a compound of condensed milk made with coconut oil, appealed the fine. The case challenged the authority of the federal government to regulate the practice in question; the company contended that such regulation lay outside the government's power to control interstate commerce. The Supreme Court upheld the law and the fine.

Vote: 8–1

JUSTICE STONE delivered the opinion of the Court:

The question for decision is whether the "Filled Milk Act" of Congress of March 4, 1923, which prohibits the shipment in interstate commerce of skimmed milk compounded with any fat or oil other than milk fat, so as to resemble milk or cream, transcends the power of Congress to regulate interstate commerce or infringes the Fifth Amendment.

But such we think is not the purpose or construction of the statutory characterization of filled milk as injurious to health and as a fraud upon the public. There is no need to consider it here as more than a declaration of the legislative findings deemed to support and justify the action taken as a constitutional exertion of the legislative power, aiding informed judicial review, as do the reports of legislative committees, by revealing the rationale of the legislation. Even in the absence of such aids, the existence of facts supporting the legislative judgment is to be presumed, for regulatory legislation affecting ordinary commercial transactions is not to be pronounced unconstitutional unless in the light of the facts made known or generally assumed it is of such a character as to preclude the assumption that it rests upon some rational basis within the knowledge and experience of the legislators.[4]

Nor need we enquire whether similar considerations enter into the review of statutes directed at particular religious, or national, or racial minorities; whether prejudice against discrete and insular minorities may be a special condition, which tends seriously to curtail the operation of those political processes ordinarily to be relied upon to protect minorities, and which may call for a correspondingly more searching judicial inquiry.

FOR DISCUSSION

Does footnote number 4 change the presumptions of constitutionality described in *Ashwander*? Does the footnote create several classes or instances in which the Court will not apply normal deference as outlined by *Ashwander*? Is that change in deference warranted?

KOREMATSU V. UNITED STATES

323 U.S. 214, 65 S.Ct. 193, 89 L.Ed. 194 (1944)

Korematsu, an American citizen by birth of Japanese descent, was convicted of violation of a presidential order that directed all persons of Japanese ancestry to evacuate an area in California. The evacuees were then transferred to War Relocation Centers. Of approximately 112,000 persons affected, about 70,000 were reported as having been born in the United States. This order was issued in pursuance of an executive order based on an act of Congress. Korematus challenged this specified exercise of the war power

[4] There may be narrower scope for operation of the presumption of constitutionality when legislation appears on its face to be within a specific prohibition of the Constitution, such as those of the first ten Amendments, which are deemed equally specific when held to be embraced within the Fourteenth.

It is unnecessary to consider now whether legislation which restricts those political processes which can ordinarily be expected to bring about repeal of undesirable legislation, is to be subjected to more exacting judicial scrutiny under the general prohibitions of the Fourteenth Amendment than are most other types of legislation. [Stone proceeded to cite cases relative to the right to vote, on restraints upon the dissemination of information; on interferences with political organizations and prohibitions of peaceable assembly.]

Vote: 6–3

JUSTICE BLACK delivered the opinion of the Court.

The petitioner, an American citizen of Japanese descent, was convicted in a federal district court for remaining in San Leandro, California, a Military Area, contrary to Civilian Exclusion Order No. 34 of the Commanding General of the Western Command, U.S. Army, which directed that after May 9, 1942, all persons of Japanese ancestry should be excluded from that area. No question was raised as to petitioner's loyalty to the United States. The Circuit Court of Appeals affirmed, and the importance of the constitutional question involved caused us to grant certiorari.

It should be noted, to begin with, that all legal restrictions which curtail the civil rights of a single racial group are immediately suspect. That is not to say that all such restrictions are unconstitutional. It is to say that courts must subject them to the most rigid scrutiny. Pressing public necessity may sometimes justify the existence of such restrictions; racial antagonism never can.

In the instant case prosecution of the petitioner was begun by information charging violation of an Act of Congress, of March 21, 1942, 56 Stat. 173, which provides that ". . . whoever shall enter, remain in, leave, or commit any act in any military area or military zone prescribed, under the authority of an Executive order of the President, by the Secretary of War, or by any military commander designated by the Secretary of War, contrary to the restrictions applicable to any such area or zone or contrary to the order of the Secretary of War or any such military commander, shall, if it appears that he knew or should have known of the existence and extent of the restrictions or order and that his act was in violation thereof, be guilty of a misdemeanor and upon conviction shall be liable to a fine of not to exceed $5,000 or to imprisonment for not more than one year, or both, for each offense."

Exclusion Order No.34, which the petitioner knowingly and admittedly violated, was one of a number of military orders and proclamations, all of which were substantially based upon Executive Order No.9066, 7 Fed. Reg. 1407. That order, issued after we were at war with Japan, declared that "the successful prosecution of the war requires every possible protection against espionage and against sabotage to national-defense material, national-defense premises, and national-defense utilities. . . ."

One of the series of orders and proclamations, a curfew order, which like the exclusion order here was promulgated pursuant to Executive Order 9066, subjected all persons of Japanese ancestry in prescribed West Coast military areas to remain in their residences from 8 p.m. to 6 a.m. As is the case with the exclusion order here, that prior curfew order was designed as a "protection against espionage and against sabotage." In *Kiyoshi Hirabayashi v. United States,* 320 U.S. 81 (1943), we sustained a conviction obtained for violation of the curfew order. The Hirabayashi conviction and this one thus rest on the same 1942 Congressional Act and the same basic executive and military orders, all of which orders were aimed at the twin dangers of espionage and sabotage.

The 1942 Act was attacked in the *Hirabayashi* case as an unconstitutional delegation of power; it was contended that the curfew order and other orders on which it rested were beyond the war powers of the Congress, the military authorities and of the President, as Commander-in-Chief of the Army; and finally that to apply the curfew order against none but citizens of Japanese ancestry amounted to a constitutionally prohibited discrimination solely on account of race. To these questions, we gave the serious consideration which their importance justified. We upheld the curfew order as an exercise of the power of the government to take steps necessary to prevent espionage and sabotage in an area threatened by Japanese attack.

In the light of the principles we announced in the *Hirabayashi* case, we are unable to conclude that it was beyond the war power of Congress and the Executive to exclude those of Japanese ancestry from the West Coast war area at the time they did. True, exclusion from the area in which one's home is located is a far greater deprivation than constant confinement to the home from 8 p.m. to 6 a.m. Nothing short of apprehension by the proper military authorities of the gravest imminent danger to the public safety can constitutionally justify either. But exclusion from a threatened area, no less than curfew, has a definite and close relationship to the prevention of espionage and sabotage. The military authorities, charged with the primary responsibility of defending our shores, concluded that curfew provided inadequate protection and ordered exclusion. They did so, as pointed out in our *Hirabayashi* opinion, in accordance with Congressional authority to the military to say who should, and who should not, remain in the threatened areas. . . .

It is said that we are dealing here with the case of imprisonment of a citizen in a concentration camp solely because of his ancestry, without evidence or inquiry concerning his loyalty and good disposition towards the United States. Our task would be simple, our duty clear, were this a case involving the imprisonment of a loyal citizen in a concentration camp because of racial prejudice. Regardless of the true nature of the assembly and relocation centers—and we deem it unjustifiable to call them concentration camps with all the ugly connotations that term implies—we are dealing specifically with nothing but an exclusion order. To cast this case into outlines of racial prejudice, without reference to the real military dangers which were presented, merely confuses the issue. Korematsu was not excluded from the Military Area because of hostility to him or his race. He was excluded because we are at war with the Japanese Empire, because the properly constituted military authorities feared an invasion of our West Coast and felt constrained to take proper security measures, because they decided that the military urgency of the situation demanded that all citizens of Japanese ancestry be segregated from the West Coast temporarily, and finally, because Congress, reposing its confidence in this time of war in our military leaders—as inevitably it must—determined that they should have the power to do just this. There was evidence of disloyalty on the part of some, the military authorities considered that the need for action was great, and time was short. We cannot—by availing ourselves of the calm perspective of hindsight—now say that at that time these actions were unjustified.

Affirmed.

FOR DISCUSSION

What does it mean for the Court to view legal restrictions based on race as suspect? Does that mean that race can never be the basis of any legislation or government policy? Does *Korematsu* suggest that the Constitution is "color blind" in that it declares all use of race to be unconstitutional? Some would argue yes, while others contend that some benign or remedial uses of race, such as in the case of affirmative action, are permissible. This topic and question is more fully discussed in Chapter VII, on equal protection.

RELATED CASES

***Santiago v. Nogueras:* 214 U.S. 260 (1909).**

The president may establish a system of civil government for conquered territory. Such authority "is found in the laws applicable to conquest and cession. That authority is the military power, under the control of the President as Commander-in-Chief." Statutes passed by Congress may supersede presidential orders. The specific question here involved a land title, and the location was Puerto Rico.

***Hirabayashi v. United States:* 320 U.S. 81 (1943).**

The Court held valid curfew regulations for persons of Japanese ancestry as a proper military measure to prevent espionage and sabotage. The Court noted that "in time of war residents having ethnic affiliation with an invading enemy may be a greater source of danger than those of a different ancestry."

***Ex parte Mitsuye Endo:* 323 U.S. 283 (1944).**

An American citizen of Japanese ancestry who had been in custody in a War Relocation Center could not be longer detained and must be unconditionally released after her loyalty had been conceded. The purpose was to protect the war effort against possible sabotage; when that purpose had been achieved, those involved had to be released. This case, decided the same day as *Korematsu,* arose out of the Relocation Center at Tule Lake, California.

***Montgomery Ward and Co. v. United States,* 326 U.S. 690 (1945).**

After a federal court of appeals had found that Montgomery Ward was engaged in production and thus subject to seizure under presidential order as authorized by the Smith-Connally Act of 1943, the Supreme Court dismissed the case as **moot** because the company's properties had been returned to it. The statute in question was also known as the War Labor Disputes Act. The president had put the secretary of war in charge of Montgomery Ward.

SKINNER V. OKLAHOMA

316 U.S. 535, 62 S.Ct. 1110, 86 L.Ed. 1655 (1942)

The state of Oklahoma passed a law providing for the mandatory sterilization of any individual convicted of a crime and deemed a habitual criminal. Skinner was convicted first of stealing chickens and then a few years later of robbery. When the Oklahoma attorney general directed that a vasectomy be performed on Skinner, the plaintiff challenged the order, which was then affirmed by the Supreme Court of Oklahoma in a 5–4 decision.

Vote: 9-0

JUSTICE DOUGLAS delivered the opinion of the Court.

This case touches a sensitive and important area of human rights. Oklahoma deprives certain individuals of a right which is basic to the perpetuation of a race—the right to have offspring. Oklahoma has decreed the enforcement of its law against petitioner, overruling his claim that it violated the Fourteenth Amendment. Because that decision raised grave and substantial constitutional questions, we granted the petition for certiorari.

Several objections to the constitutionality of the Act have been pressed upon us. It is urged that the Act cannot be sustained as an exercise of the police power in view of the state of scientific authorities respecting inheritability of criminal traits. It is argued that the Act is penal in character and that the sterilization provided for is cruel and unusual punishment and violative of the Fourteenth Amendment. We pass those points without intimating an opinion on them, for there is a feature of the Act which clearly condemns it. That is its failure to meet the requirements of the equal protection clause of the Fourteenth Amendment.

But the instant legislation runs afoul of the equal protection clause, though we give Oklahoma that large deference which the rule of the foregoing cases requires. We are dealing here with legislation which involves one of the basic civil rights of man. Marriage and procreation are fundamental to the very existence and survival of the race. The power to sterilize, if exercised, may have subtle, farreaching and devastating effects. In evil or reckless hands it can cause races or types which are inimical to the dominant group to wither and disappear. There is no redemption for the individual whom the law touches. Any experiment which the State conducts is to his irreparable injury. He is forever deprived of a basic liberty. We mention these matters not to reexamine the scope of the police power of the States. We advert to them merely in emphasis of our view that strict scrutiny of the classification which a State makes in a sterilization law is essential, lest unwittingly or otherwise invidious discriminations are made against groups or types of individuals in violation of the constitutional guaranty of just and equal laws. The guaranty of equal protection of the laws is a pledge of the protection of equal laws. When the law lays an unequal hand on those who have committed intrinsically the same quality of offense and sterilizes one and not the other, it has made as an invidious a discrimination as if it had selected a particular race or nationality for oppressive treatment. Sterilization of those who have thrice committed grand larceny with immunity for those who are embezzlers is a clear, pointed, unmistakable discrimination. Oklahoma makes no attempt to say that he who commits larceny by trespass or trick or fraud has biologically inheritable traits which he who commits embezzlement lacks. Oklahoma's line between larceny by fraud and embezzlement is determined, as we have noted, with reference to the time when the fraudulent intent to convert the property to the taker's own use arises. We have not the slightest basis for inferring that that line has any significance in eugenics nor that the inheritability of criminal traits follows the neat legal distinctions which the law has marked between those two offenses. In terms of fines and imprisonment the crimes of larceny and embezzlement rate the same under the Oklahoma code. Only when it comes to sterilization are the pains and penalties of the law different. The equal protection clause would indeed be a formula of empty words if such conspicuously artificial lines could be drawn.

Reversed.

CHIEF JUSTICE STONE, concurring.

I concur in the result, but I am not persuaded that we are aided in reaching it by recourse to the equal protection clause.

If Oklahoma may resort generally to the sterilization of criminals on the assumption that their propensities are transmissible to future generations by inheritance, I seriously doubt that the equal protection clause requires it to apply the measure to all criminals in the first instance, or to none.

Moreover, if we must presume that the legislature knows—what science has been unable to ascertain—that the criminal tendencies of any class of habitual offenders are transmissible regardless of the varying mental characteristics of its individuals, I should suppose that we must likewise presume that the legislature, in its wisdom, knows that the criminal tendencies of some classes of offenders are more likely to be transmitted than those of others. And so I think the real question we have to consider is not one of equal protection, but whether the wholesale condemnation of a class to such an invasion of personal liberty, without opportunity to any individual to show that his is not the type of case which would justify resort to it, satisfies the demands of due process.

There are limits to the extent to which the presumption of constitutionality can be pressed, especially where the liberty of the person is concerned (see *United States v. Carolene Products Co.*, 304 U.S. 144, 152, n. 4, 1938) and where the presumption is resorted to only to dispense with a procedure which the ordinary dictates of prudence would seem to demand for the protection of the individual from arbitrary action. Although petitioner here was given a hearing to ascertain whether sterilization would be detrimental to his health, he was given none to discover whether his criminal tendencies are of an inheritable type. Undoubtedly a state may, after appropriate inquiry, constitutionally interfere with the personal liberty of the individual to prevent the transmission by inheritance of his socially injurious tendencies. But until now we have not been called upon to say that it may do so without giving him a hearing and opportunity to challenge the existence as to him of the only facts which could justify so drastic a measure.

There are limits to the extent to which a legislatively represented majority may conduct biological experiments at the expense of the dignity and personality and natural powers of a minority—even those who have been guilty of what the majority define as crimes. But this Act falls down before reaching this problem, which I mention only to avoid the implication that such a question may not exist because not discussed. On it I would also reserve judgment

FOR DISCUSSION

What other fundamental rights exist? If the right to procreate is a fundamental right, is a right not to reproduce (abortion) equally protected as a fundamental right? Is marriage a fundamental right? If so, does it also apply to individuals of the same sex?

GLOSSARY

Advisory Opinions: Opinions that advise what a court would do in hypothetical situations; U.S. courts do not issue advisory opinions.

Advice and Consent: Constitutional term for the Senate's role in deciding whether to accept or reject treaties and presidential nominations to the judiciary and other posts.

***Amicus Curiae* Briefs**: "friend of the court" briefs filed by nonparties to a suit who want to have a court consider their views on the matter.

Appellants: Losing parties in legal actions who file appeals.

Appellate Jurisdiction: The jurisdiction of higher courts to review judgments of lower trial courts. Courts generally limit appellate review to questions of law rather than determinations of facts.

Appellees: Winning parties in legal actions against whom appeals are filed.

Articles of Confederation: The government for the thirteen states that preceded the U.S. Constitution. Ratified in 1781, the Articles remained in effect until 1789.

***Ashwander* Rules.** A series of rules guiding the Supreme Court's interpretation that seek to avoid, when possible, decisions based on constitutional grounds. The basis for this rule resides in judicial restraint and presumptions of legislative deference found in the concepts of separation of powers.

***Carolene Products* Footnote Number** 4. This refers to Justice Stone's footnote number 4 in *United States v. Carolene Products,* where the Court articulates a constitutional approach to legislation that gives less presumption to a law's validity when it affects the Bill of Rights, the rights of discrete and insular minorities, and the operation of the political process.

Cases and Controversies: Language used in Article III that courts have interpreted to avoid giving advisory opinions when no litigants in a case have concrete interests at stake.

Checks and Balances: A system of government in which various branches and levels of government are designed to prevent abuse of powers by the others.

Chief Justice of the United States: Designated by the Constitution to preside over the U.S. Supreme Court, the chief is generally considered to be *primus inter pares*, or first among equals. By tradition the chief either writes or assigns opinions when the chief is in the majority. The chief also presides over trials of presidential impeachments.

Civil Cases: Cases that involve disputes between private individuals.

Common Law: The system of judge-made, or judge-discovered, law prominent in Great Britain, that has been adapted to the system of most U.S. states. Louisiana uses a civil law system, based on French and Spanish codes.

Concurring Opinion: An opinion in which a judge or justice indicates agreement with a court's decision but adds further explanation, sometimes justifying a decision on alternate grounds.

Constitutional Convention of 1787: A convention of fifty-five delegates from twelve of the thirteen states (all but Rhode Island) that wrote the Constitution. Copies of the document were sent to state conventions for ratification, and it became effective in 1789.

Declaration of Independence: Drafted largely by Thomas Jefferson for the Second Continental Congress, the statement of the American colonists' reasons for declaring their independence from Britain. The document is probably most famous for articulating the natural rights doctrine that "all men are created equal" and that they are endowed with the rights of "life, liberty, and the pursuit of happiness."

Declaratory Judgment: A judgment of law (not to be confused with advisory opinions) that stems from an actual case and is binding on the parties.

Defendants: Individuals responding either to civil cases filed against them or to government charges of criminal wrongdoing.

Delegated Powers: To justify exercises of powers, departments of government must be able trace them directly to enumerations of power within the Constitution. Most congressional powers are listed in Article I, Section 8. Delegated powers may form the basis of implied powers.

Dissenting Opinion: An opinion in which a judge or justice disagrees with the majority opinion and explains the jurist's reasoning in hopes of persuading others that the opinion is wrong.

During Good Behavior: The constitutional provision according to which judges and justices will serve until they die, retire, or are impeached, convicted, and removed from office.

En Banc: A meeting of all members of a court, typically a U.S. circuit court, whose members more typically serve on three-judge panels.

Federal System: Divides government between a national government and states. A federal government requires a national constitution to delineate the boundaries and respective responsibilities of the two governing entities. In federal systems, both the national and state governments can act directly on the states.

Federalists: Individuals who supported ratification of the U.S. Constitution. They designated their opponents as Anti-Federalists. One of the first two political parties in the United States subsequently took this name.

Fundamental Rights. Rights of individuals explicitly described in the Constitution or the Bill of Rights, as well outside of plain text of both, which the Supreme Court has declared to be so important that legislation affecting them must be subject to strict scrutiny. These latter rights include marriage, procreation, voting, interstate travel, and access to justice.

Impeachment: A constitutional mechanism through which the president, judges, and other civil offices may be charged by the House of Representatives for "Treason, Bribery, or other High Crimes and Misdemeanors." Impeachment leads to a trial in the U.S. Senate, where a two-thirds vote is required to convict and remove from office an impeached person.

Incorporation. The theory that with the adoption of the Due Process Clause of the Fourteenth Amendment, some or all of the provisions of the Bill of Rights also limit the actions of state and local governments.

Intermediate Level Scrutiny. The test the Court uses to examine legislation that classifies individuals on the basis of gender or alienage, or with respect to illegitimacy. The government must show that it had an important interest in enacting the legislation and that the classification substantially furthers that interest.

Interpretivism: A name sometimes given to the position that jurists who believe their task to be limited to ascertaining and applying the original understanding of constitutional words. Noninterpretivists are more likely to supplement this understanding from extraconstitutional sources.

Judicial Activism and Judicial Restraint: Contrasting styles of judicial interpretation, the first stressing a broad judicial responsibility and the latter typically more deferential to judgments made by the two elected branches of government.

Judicial Review: A power not directly stated in the U.S. Constitution, but based both on constitutional principles and on long-standing precedents by which courts determine whether laws brought before them in cases are consistent with the Constitution. Courts may exercise such review over both state and federal legislation.

Jurisdiction: The scope of a court's authority. Article III of the Constitution grants both original and appellate jurisdiction to the Supreme Court, with the latter being subject to "such Exceptions . . . as the Congress shall make."

Justiciability: Before a Court will deliver an opinion, the parties must show that the controversy that brings them before the Court and/or the remedy they seek is one that is appropriate for judges to address.

Law and Equity: Two divisions of English law, both of which are entrusted in the United States to review by the Supreme Court.

Magna C[h]arta: A document signed by King John in England with his noblemen in England in 1215 and generally regarded as the origin of the British Parliament, and subsequent representative institutions, and of the idea of written constitutionalism.

Majority Opinion: An opinion that reflects a Supreme Court majority and has the effect of operative law.

Missouri Plan: An arrangement adopted in some states whereby the governor appoints judges, who are later subject to a popular vote as to whether they should be retained or removed from office.

Moot: Describing cases that have been effectively settled before they can be adjudicated; courts refuse to hear moot cases because they no longer present a live "case or controversy."

Natural Rights: Rights like "life, liberty, and the pursuit of happiness," which are mentioned in the Declaration of Independence and are thought to belong to individuals by reason of their personhood. Just governments incorporate natural rights into civil rights.

New Jersey Plan: A plan offered by small states at the Constitutional Convention of 1787 advocating equal state representation in a unicameral congress. This plan favored presidential appointment of federal judges.

Original Intent: A method of constitutional interpretation that emphasizes the intent of those who wrote, ratified, and/or amended the Constitution.

Original Jurisdiction: The location, in the legal system, of cases that arrive before a court for their first hearing. The U.S. Supreme Court exercises relatively little original jurisdiction because most cases come to it on appeal.

Parliamentary Sovereignty: Under British law, the legislative body, or Parliament, is thought to be supreme. Americans rejected this notion as incompatible with natural rights and with a system of checks and balances.

Political Questions: Issues on which courts will refuse to rule on the grounds that they are matters for the two political, or elected, branches to handle.

***Primus Inter Pares*:** First among equals. Often used to describe the role of the chief justice of the United States.

Prosecution: Representative of the government in criminal cases.

Rational Basis Test. The basic test the Court uses to examine most legislation or economic legislation adopted by the government. Under this test, plaintiffs must show that the government lacked a rational basis in adopting the legislation.

Recusal: The stepping aside of a judge who has a personal stake or interest in a case. Judges are expected to recuse themselves when such conditions exist.

Rule of Four: The Supreme Court will not accept review of a case unless four of the nine justices agree that they want to hear it. The rule points to the wide discretion that the Court has in setting its own docket.

Scheme of Ordered Liberty. A theory of selective incorporation developed in *Palko v. State of Connecticut* (1937) stating that the Fourteenth Amendment's Due Process Clause protects only certain rights against state encroachment.

Selective Incorporation. The theory that the Due Process Clause of the Fourteenth Amendment applies only certain parts or sections of the Bill of Rights to state and local governments. Using this theory, the Supreme Court has incorporated all but the Second, Third, and parts of the Seventh Amendment.

SemiSuspect Classification. Any classification based on gender, alienage, or illegitimacy, which is automatically subject to an intermediate level of scrutiny.

Separation of Powers: Characteristic of a system that divides powers among various branches of government in order to prevent abuses by any of them. The U.S. Constitution divides the national government into legislative, executive, and judicial branches.

Social Contract: The idea that just governments are based on the consent of the governed. Social contract theorists, most notably Thomas Hobbes, John Locke, and Jean-Jacques Rousseau, argued that if individuals found themselves in a lawless state of nature, they would form a social contract to escape the unpleasantness of a society without laws.

Standing: Before courts will accept a case, parties must establish that they have a proper interest in the case. This showing is called standing.

Stare Decisis: Let [the precedent] stand. Many court decisions are based on the belief that judges should as much as possible adhere to existing precedents.

State of Nature: A hypothetical prepolitical state in which laws would not be established, settled, known, or impartially enforced.

Statutory Interpretation: The power that courts exercise to determine the meaning of legislation.

Strict Scrutiny. The test the Court uses to examine legislation that relies on suspect classifications or limits fundamental rights. The government must show that it has a compelling interest, and also that the law addressing that interest is both narrowly tailored and the least restrictive means of securing that interest.

Supremacy Clause: The provision in Article VI that affirms the supremacy of the Constitution over conflicting state laws.

Suspect Classification. Classifications based on race or religion and thus are subject to strict scrutiny are described as suspect.

Unicameral Legislature: A lawmaking body that has a single house, or chamber.

U.S. Circuit Courts: Courts that sit midway between the ninety-four U.S. District Courts and the U.S. Supreme Court. There are currently eleven numbered circuits, a D.C. circuit, and a specialized circuit.

U.S. District Courts: Federal trial courts, of which there are currently ninety-four.

U.S. Supreme Court: The highest court in the federal system, with power over both lower state courts and federal courts. Housed in Washington, D.C., the Court has eight associate justices and a chief justice.

Virginia Plan: The first plan introduced at the Constitutional Convention of 1787. It favored a bicameral Congress in which states would be represented according to population. It introduced the idea of separation of powers among the legislative, executive, and judicial branches. It called for legislative appointment of judges.

Writ of Appeal: A petition, which the Supreme Court used to be obligated to accept, under which litigants could request review of their cases by the Court.

Writ of Certification: A writ in which a lower court asks a higher court to clarify a matter of law.

Writ of Certiorari: The most common writ, or petition, by which cases come before the U.S. Supreme Court for appellate review.

Writ of Mandamus: A judicial order directed to an executive official ordering the official to produce or deliver a document.

SELECTED BIBLIOGRAPHY

Abraham, Henry J. and Barbara A. Perry. 2003. *Freedom and the Court: Civil Rights & Liberties in the United States*, 8th ed. Lawrence: University Press of Kansas.

Barnett, Randy E. 1989. *The Rights Retained by the People: The History and Meaning of the Ninth Amendment.* Fairfax, VA: George Mason University Press.

Bobbitt, Philip. 1991. *Constitutional Interpretation.* Cambridge, MA: Blackwell.

Bodenhamer, David J., and James W. Ely, Jr. 2008. *The Bill of Rights in Modern American after 200 Years.* Revised and Expanded edition. Bloomington: Indiana University Press.

Ely, John Hart. 1980. *Democracy and Distrust: A Theory of Judicial Review.* Cambridge, MA: Harvard University Press.

Farrand, Max, ed. 1966. *The Records of the Federal Convention of 1787*, vol. 2. New Haven, CT: Yale University Press.

Green, Christopher. 2015. *Equal Citizenship, Civil Rights, and the Constitution: The Original Sense of the Privileges or Immunities Clause.* London: Routledge.

Kahn, Ronald. 1994. *The Supreme Court and Constitutional Theory.* Lawrence: University Press of Kansas.

Kelly, Alfred, Winfred A. Harbison, and Herman Belz. 1991. *The American Constitution: Its Origins and Development.* New York: W. W. Norton.

Levy, Leonard W. 1989. *Original Intent and the Framers' Constitution.* New York: Macmillan.

Perry, Michael J. 1999. *We the People: The Fourteenth Amendment and the Supreme Court.* New York: Oxford University Press.

Schwartz, Bernard. 1993. *A History of the Supreme Court.* New York: Oxford University Press.

Stone, Geoffrey R., and Richard A. Epstein. 1992. *The Bill of Rights in the Modern States.* Chicago: University of Chicago Press.

Tribe, Laurence H., and Michael C. Dorf. 1991. *On Reading the Constitution.* Cambridge, MA: Harvard University Press.

CHAPTER II

The First Amendment and Religion

Timeline: The First Amendment and Religion

1620 Pilgrims seeking religious freedom arrive in Massachusetts.

1633 The charter of Rhode Island provides for "liberty of conscience."

1688 The Toleration Act limits persecution of Protestant dissenters in England.

1692 The Salem witch trials demonstrate the dangers of an improper mixture of church and state.

1774 British adoption of the Quebec Act, which recognizes Catholicism in Canada, leads to fears of an established church in the thirteen colonies.

1776 The Virginia Declaration of Rights extends religious freedom beyond mere "toleration."

1786 Virginia adopts the Statute for Religious Freedom, largely written by Thomas Jefferson

1789 The New Constitution prohibits religious tests for federal offices.

1791 The states ratify the First Amendment.

1802 Thomas Jefferson writes a letter in which he calls for "a wall of separation between church and state."

1833 *Barron v. Baltimore* decides that the provisions of the Bill of Rights limit only the national government. Massachusetts becomes the last state to disestablish an official church.

1838 The Massachusetts Supreme Court upholds the last known American blasphemy conviction (under state law) in *Commonwealth v. Kneeland.*

1864 The United States adds the words "In God we Trust" to its currency.

1868 The Fourteenth Amendment alters the relationship between the national government and the states.

1875 President Ulysses S. Grant proposes a constitutional amendment (called the Blaine Amendment) to limit aid to parochial schools.

1879 *Reynolds v. United States* distinguishes between religious belief and religious actions in upholding the conviction of a bigamist.

1899 In *Bradfield v. Roberts* the Court upholds the constitutionality of a federal expenditure on a religious hospital.

1925 *Pierce v. Society of Sisters* establishes the right of parents to send their children to parochial schools.

1930 *Cochrane v. Board of Education* allows states to provide secular textbooks for children in parochial schools.

1940 *Minersville School District v. Gobitis* allows public schools to require the pledge of allegiance.

1943 *West Virginia Board of Education v. Barnette* reverses course and rules against compulsory flag salutes in public schools.

1947 The Supreme Court applies the Establishment Clause to the states in *Everson v. Board of Education of Ewing Township* but allows states to provide reimbursement for bus transportation to parochial schools.

1953 Intent on heightening differences between the United States and communist nations, Congress adds the words "under God" to the pledge of allegiance.

1960 John F. Kennedy, a Roman Catholic, assures the Greater Houston Ministerial Association that, as president, his responsibility would be to uphold the Constitution, including the First Amendment. A few months later, in 1961, he becomes the first Roman Catholic ever to hold that office.

1962 *Engel v. Vitale* strikes down public prayer in public schools.

1963 *Abington v. Schempp* extends the ban in *Engel* to Bible reading, recitations of the Lord's Prayer, and other devotional exercises in public schools. *Sherbert v. Verner* decides that a state must extend unemployment benefits to an individual who loses a job because of religious objections to working on Saturdays.

1968 *Flast v. Cohen* opens the door for a limited number of taxpayer suits in cases involving alleged violations of the Establishment Clause.

1970 *Walz v. Tax Commission of the City of New York* upholds a property tax exemption as a way of lessening entanglement between church and state.

1971 *Lemon v. Kurtzman* formulates the three-pronged *Lemon* test, which is used in this case to strike down aid to parochial schools. *Tilton v. Richardson* allows for federal monies for construction on religious college campuses but requires that the buildings be devoted to secular purposes.

1972 *Wisconsin v. Yoder* allows Amish parents to exempt their children from public education beyond the eighth grade.

1980 *Stone v. Graham* voids a Kentucky law that requires the Ten Commandments to be posted in public school classrooms.

1983 In *Marsh v. Chambers* the Supreme Court allows Nebraska to continue hiring a chaplain to begin its legislative sessions with prayer.

1984 *Lynch v. Donnelly* allows the display of a religious crèche on public property as part of a display that includes a variety of secular Christmas symbols.

1985 *Wallace v. Jaffree* strikes down an Alabama law that encourages public school students to use a moment of silence for prayer.

1990 In *Employment Division, Department of Human Resources v. Smith* the Court rejects the application of the compelling state interest test in cases where a religious practice violates a general criminal law.

1992 *Lee v. Weisman* extends the ban on public prayer to public school graduations.

1995 In a case that combines concerns about the establishment clause and freedom of speech, the Court rules in *Rosenberger v. Rector and Visitors of the University of Virginia* that a state college cannot ban use of student activity funds to religious organizations.

1993 Congress adopts the Religious Freedom Restoration Act.

1997 *City of Boerne v. Flores* decides that in the Religious Freedom Restoration Act, Congress has improperly attempted to revise the Fourteenth Amendment.

2000 *Santa Fe Independent School District v. Doe* strikes down public prayers at public school football games.

2002 *Good News Club v. Milford Central School* prohibits a public school from barring access to religious groups that wanted to use the limited public forum it had created for other groups that wanted to meet on campus after school.

2004 In *Elk Grove Unified School District v. Newdow* the Supreme Court overturns a lower court decision that public schools cannot use the words "under God" in the pledge of allegiance on the ground that the noncustodial parent who brought the claim lacked proper standing.

2005 *Cutter v. Wilkinson* upholds a provision of the Religious Land Use and Institutionalized Persons Act of 2000.

2009 In his inaugural address, President Barack Obama specifically mentions the rights of nonbelievers.

2011 *Arizona Christian School v. Winn* denies standing to Arizona taxpayers challenging state tax credits for individuals who provide scholarships for children to attend religious schools.

2014 *Burwell v. Hobby Lobby Stores,* rules that the mandate to provide contraceptive coverage under the Affordable Care Act violates the rights of closely-held corporations under the Religious Freedom Restoration Act.

2015 *Equal Employment Opportunity Commission v. Abercrombie & Fitch Stores* says that employer may be liable for damages if it denies employment to an otherwise eligible employee out of concern that she will wear a hijab.

INTRODUCTION

Issues involving religion and politics are frequently so controversial that it is common to hear warnings about speaking about either at social gatherings. Mixed with issues of law, these matters can be even more explosive, but no less critical. Early political documents such as the Declaration of Independence and the Northwest Ordinance refer to the Deity, but the text of the Constitution of 1787 makes no explicit mention of God, although Article VII was accompanied by the statement that the states present adopted the document "in the year of our Lord one thousand seven hundred and eighty-seven."

Article VI of the document includes a specific prohibition against "**test oaths**" (affirming certain religious beliefs), which certain states then required, as a condition for public office. Another difference from some early state constitutions is that the U.S. Constitution does not exclude members of the clergy from running for political office. The Constitution arguably extends some recognition to Sunday, the traditional Christian day of rest, by not counting it toward the number of days that the president has to sign or veto a bill, but it includes no requirements for worship, then or on any other day. Perhaps more surprisingly, the original constitution contains no explicit protections for religious liberty; and at the time of its adoption, although the trend within the states had been toward religious disestablishment, some states continued to support established churches through tax monies and laws.

Anti-Federalists, who opposed ratification of the U.S. Constitution, argued that a bill of rights was necessary to rein in the powers of the new government over matters like religion and speech, over which the Anti-Federalists thought the national government should have no control. James Madison, a leading supporter of constitutional ratification and the author of a "free exercise" clause in the earlier Virginia Declaration of Rights, eventually shepherded the proposed bill of rights through the first Congress, in part because he thought it could do no harm (and might do some good) and in part because he believed that such a concession was necessary to forestall the possibility of a second constitutional convention that might undo the work of the first. The states ratified ten of twelve amendments that Congress sent to them. In addition to protecting freedoms of speech, press, peaceable assembly, and petition, the First Amendment contains two clauses designed to protect religious liberty.

First Amendment:

Congress shall make no law respecting an establishment of religion, or prohibiting the free exercise thereof . . . .

The Religion Clauses of the First Amendment

The first of the two clauses related to religion prohibits any law "respecting an establishment of religion," and the second prohibits any restriction on the free exercise of religion. Because the Bill of Rights initially was construed to apply to the national government, in the early days of the republic there was no attempt to apply either clause directly to state and local governments. Thus, the first clause did not eliminate state religious establishments; indeed, by specifically prohibiting congressional action, it initially assured that states could continue to keep official churches in place. Similarly, the test oath provision in Article VI initially did not void state religious qualifications for voting or holding office.

The Framers of the U.S. Constitution were clearly committed to religious liberty. They believed the best way to preserve such freedom was to allow people to worship free of state dictates. The most perplexing questions of church-state relations lie at the intersection of the two religion clauses. Courts must often decide whether deference to the religious beliefs of one group is an "establishment" of religion or whether a generally applicable law that disproportionately affects members of one denomination interferes with the free exercise of that set of believers. Sometimes a decision hinges on whether the Court regards a case as chiefly focusing on one clause or the other.

Consistent with the order of the First Amendment, this chapter treats the Establishment Clause first and then the Free Exercise clause. It is important to recognize, however, that the clauses are side by side in the First Amendment and that many cases will require the clauses to be balanced. Moreover, it is common to find cases in which issues of free exercise are inextricably tied to issues related to freedom of speech and press or other values articulated in the Bill of Rights.

The Establishment Clause

Beginnings

Although individuals who were seeking their own religious freedom founded a number of the American colonies, some of the same individuals were intent on developing Christian commonwealths, where only the orthodox could practice their religion without restraint. Such restrictions were soon challenged in the name of "soul liberty" by Roger Williams, a Baptist who founded Rhode Island, and other dissenters. By the time of the American Revolution, there was special pressure in states where the new Episcopal Church (part of the Anglican Communion, of which the only other member at the time was the Church of England) had been established to avoid charges of treason. Nevertheless, some colonists favored continuing the support of ministers, especially those who contributed to educating the youth—a function that was then more frequently private than governmental.

In Virginia, faced with support for such an establishmentarian measure backed by popular governor Patrick Henry, James Madison, who went on to become the primary author and sponsor of the Bill of Rights, circulated a petition (his Memorial and Remonstrance Against Religious Assessments) that ultimately rallied popular support against the proposal. Madison subsequently helped secure support for the Virginia Statute for Religious Freedom, which his friend Thomas Jefferson had authored. The new law disestablished the Anglican Church in Virginia and laid the groundwork for the federal policy of **separation of church and state**. Madison later became the chief author of the Bill of Rights.

In 1802, during his presidency, Jefferson wrote a letter to the Danbury Baptist Association in Connecticut in which he opined that the First Amendment created a "wall of separation" between church and state, thus resurrecting a phrase that Roger Williams had used earlier. It was arguably easier to coin a phrase than to explain its meaning, and when in office Jefferson himself did not always practice strict separation of church and state. Moreover, although the American founders had disestablished religion at the national level, the society was largely Christian and Protestant. George Washington and John Adams were among those who believed that religious influence was necessary to the development of the civic virtues that were essential to republican government. Joseph Story, one of the most important early justices on the U.S. Supreme Court, not only favored mild state religious establishments, like those of his native Massachusetts, but also thought that the influence of religion should be felt through the application of common law principles, which in turn came largely from Christian Great Britain. By contrast, Jefferson did not believe that the common law, which continued to have a strong influence on American law, embodied distinctly Christian principles.

Protestantism had an important influence in nineteenth- and early twentieth- century America. A Protestant ethos, which often included prayers and readings from the King James Version of the Bible, was so pervasive in the developing system of public schools that Roman Catholics often felt the need to establish separate parochial schools. In general, American Catholics found that the principle of separation of church and state was used to deny state aid to their denominational schools even though Congress never proposed, and the states never ratified, a clarifying amendment (the Blaine Amendment) that more specifically articulated this principle.

The Establishment Clause and Religious Exercises in the Public Schools

Through most of the nineteenth century, issues of religion in the schools were dealt with under state constitutions, but in the twentieth century justices began using the Due Process Clause of the Fourteenth Amendment to apply provisions of the First Amendment to such controversies. In the first major establishment case, *Everson v. Board of Education of Ewing Township* (1947), the Supreme Court had to assess the constitutionality of state provision of bus transportation for students attending parochial schools. Justice Hugo L. Black articulated a **strict separationist** view: that the Establishment Clause was intended to deny governmental expenditures on behalf of religion. Black also cited the "wall of separation" analogy. In the case at hand, however, he upheld the aid by deciding that it was not directed to schools per se but to the students and their parents and was similar to providing police or fire protection to such institutions.

What about the pervasively Protestant religious practices in public schools? These received their first major test before the Supreme Court in *Engel v. Vitale* (1962), where the Court examined the constitutionality of a prayer that the New York State Board of Regents composed for schoolchildren to say at the beginning of each day. This time Justice Black's decision more closely matched his separationistic rhetoric. The Court ruled that the public prayer was a religious exercise that according to the First and Fourteenth Amendments, should not be allowed in public schools. Within a year, the Court would extend this ban to other devotional exercises.

In time, the Court's attempt to insulate public schools from religious exercises probably accelerated student flight from such schools, as an increasing number of Protestants questioned whether a completely secular environment was adequate for their children's education. In the meantime, the Court continued to confront issues, most generated by traditional Catholic schools, relative to the constitutionality of state aid to those institutions. Practical and constitutional issues were often tied together; many states recognized that it was easier to help keep the schools afloat than to absorb the added costs that would accompany the enrollment of parochial school students in public schools.

The Development and Application of the *Lemon* Test and Other Approaches

Few cases ultimately proved to be more important in this First Amendment field than *Lemon v. Kurtzman* (403 U.S. 602, 1971), in which the Court had to rule on the constitutionality of a number of state provisions intended to funnel aid to nonpublic schools run by religious denominations. In ruling on devotional exercises in public schools, the Court had already decided that such exercises were unconstitutional if they did not have a clear secular (nonreligious) purpose or if they had the primary (chief) effect of either advancing or inhibiting religion. In *Walz v. Tax Commission* (397 U.S. 664, 1970), the Court had further upheld a state property tax exemption for churches on the basis that such an exemption was less likely to lead to "excessive entanglement" than the monitoring that tax payments would require. In *Lemon*, the Court added this test to form the three-pronged "*Lemon* test," which has become at once one of the Court's most pervasive and most controversial tests in the establishment area.

Overlying controversy over the *Lemon* test is the degree to which decisions relative to students should apply to other contexts involving adults. In *Marsh v. Chambers* (463 U.S. 783, 1983), the Court largely ignored the *Lemon* test in allowing Nebraska to continue to pay a chaplain to open each session with prayer. The Court cited a long history of such practices dating back to the first Congress but leaving uncertainty about how the Court would decide when such historical practice were to be discontinued.

Two years later, however, the Court relied in *Wallace v. Jaffree* (472 U.S. 38, 1985) on the secular purpose prong of the *Lemon* test to strike down an Alabama law that specifically sanctioned the use of prayer in a previously legislated moment of silence for school students. Moreover, Justice Sandra Day O'Connor used the occasion to articulate a rival **endorsement test** in her concurring opinion. She argued that a law was inappropriate when the government either intentionally or unintentionally endorsed a religion so that nonmembers would feel like outsiders. For his part, Justice William Rehnquist, who later became chief justice, took direct aim at the wall of separation analogy, which he called "Jefferson's misleading metaphor." In a far more **accommodationist** stance, which he attempted to bolster through his reading of debates over the Bill of Rights, Rehnquist concluded that the Establishment Clause was intended to prohibit a national church or the preference of one religious denomination over another. He did not think the clause required strict neutrality between religion and irreligion.

Nonetheless, the Court often seeks to use the principle of **neutrality** in matters related to church and state. Such a principle is largely implicit in the prong of the *Lemon* test that requires that the primary effect of a law neither advance nor inhibit religion. In *Zelman v. Simmons Harris* (536 U.S. 639, 2002), Chief Justice Rehnquist used this principle, and earlier precedents relative to tax deductions for educational expenses, to justify a voucher system that parents could use to send their children to parochial schools. The amounts in question were certainly much larger than those in *Everson v. Board of Education* (330 U.S. 1, 1947), but one might argue that the effect in enhancing parental choice was the same. As dissenters pointed out, however, the decision seemed to violate prior judicial statements relative to the Establishment Clause stating that no amount of money, large or small, should be directed to religious institutions.

Symbolic Displays on Public Properties

Religious adherents often convey their beliefs through the use of symbols. Such symbols are, in turn, often associated with holidays or events that blend spiritual and sacred elements. Increasingly, such symbols are also becoming flashpoints for controversy. As in the area of prayer, the Court has been especially wary of religious displays in public school settings, where students may be unable to distinguish between respectful recognition of religious beliefs and governmental endorsement, but it has been less consistent when schoolchildren were not directly involved.

A lead case is *Lynch v. Donnelly* (465 U.S. 668, 1984), in which the Court ruled that a city could display a manger scene as part of a wider Christmas display. Some observers hailed the decision as a reasonable accommodation of religion, while others scoffed at the so-called reindeer rule, which appeared to sanction religious displays only when they were surrounded by secular symbols. Just five years later, in *County of Allegheny v. American Civil Liberties Union* (492 U.S. 573, 1989), the Court outlawed the display of a solitary crèche inside a county courthouse while allowing a display of a Christmas tree, a menorah, and other such symbols outside a city hall.

The companion decisions in *Van Orden v. Perry* (545 U.S. 677, 2005) and *McCreary v. American Civil Liberties Union* (545 U.S. 844, 2005) point to subtle distinctions that the Court must sometimes draw in this area. Thus, in the first case, the Court upheld a monument to the Ten Commandments on the grounds of the Texas State Capitol, while in the second it disallowed a posting of the Ten Commandments in county courthouses. The decisions pit familiar arguments over the *Lemon* test, the endorsement test, and accommodationism in another context. The Court continues to weigh the circumstances of individual cases in a manner that might not be conducive to establishing clear rules.

One Candidate's View

The section on the Establishment Clause ends with a selection that takes readers beyond the Court and back to the distinction between a culture and a nation. Although the Constitution guarantees that there will be no officially established religion, it cannot necessarily change public attitudes. Until 1960, only one Roman Catholic (Al Smith in 1924) had run for president, and he did not win. John F. Kennedy's Catholicism was thus perceived to be a significant liability, and some members of the Protestant clergy warned that, if elected, Kennedy would be subject to a foreign sovereign (the pope is the head of the Vatican State as well as head of the Roman Catholic Church). In a speech to the Greater Houston Ministerial Association in September 1960, Kennedy addressed these fears, endorsing separation of church and state and indicating that if elected, he would be president of people of all denominations. His speech is widely credited with allaying fears among many voters and helping him win the election.

THOMAS JEFFERSON, THE VIRGINIA ACT FOR ESTABLISHING RELIGIOUS FREEDOM

1786

One of the three accomplishments that Thomas Jefferson wanted recorded on his tombstone (the others were writing the Declaration of Independence and founding the University of Virginia) was the Virginia Statute for Religious Liberty, a strong affirmation of the value of religious liberty. James Madison, who would father the U.S. Bill of Rights, was the political figure who did the most to get this legislation adopted by the Virginia legislature. The statute continues to provide a strong rationale for the need for church-state separation.

Well aware that Almighty God hath created the mind free; that all attempts to influence it by temporal punishments or burdens, or by civil incapacitations, tend only to beget habits of hypocrisy and meanness, and are a departure from the plan of the Holy Author of our religion, who being Lord both of body and mind, yet chose not to propagate it by coercions on either, as was in his Almighty power to do; that the impious presumption of legislators and rulers, civil as well as ecclesiastical, who, being themselves but fallible and uninspired men, have assumed dominion over the faith of others, setting up their own opinions and modes of thinking as the only true and infallible, and as such endeavoring to impose them on others, hath established and maintained false religions over the greatest part of the world, and through all time; that to compel a man to furnish contributions of money for the propagation of opinions which he disbelieves, is sinful and tyrannical; that even the forcing him to support this or that teacher of his own religious persuasion, is depriving him of the comfortable liberty of giving his contributions to the particular pastor whose morals he would make his pattern, and whose powers he feels most persuasive to righteousness, and is withdrawing from the ministry those temporal rewards, which proceeding from an approbation of their personal conduct, are an additional incitement to earnest and unremitting labors for the instruction of mankind; that our civil rights have no dependence on our religious opinions, more than our opinions in physics or geometry; that, therefore, the proscribing any citizen as unworthy [of] the public confidence by laying upon him an incapacity of being called to the offices of trust and emolument, unless he profess or renounce this or that religious opinion, is depriving him injuriously of those privileges and advantages to which in common with his fellow citizens he has a natural right; that it tends also to corrupt the principles of that very religion it is meant to encourage, by bribing, with a monopoly of worldly honors and emoluments, those who will externally profess and conform to it; that though indeed these are criminal who do not withstand such temptation, yet neither are those innocent who lay the bait in their way; that to suffer the civil magistrate to intrude his powers into the field of opinion and to restrain the profession or propagation of principles, on the supposition of their ill tendency, is a dangerous fallacy, which at once destroys all religious liberty, because he being of course judge of that tendency, will make his opinions the rule of judgment, and approve or condemn the sentiments of others only as they shall square with or differ from his own; that it is time enough for the rightful purposes of civil government, for its officers to interfere when principles break out into overt acts against peace and good order; and finally, that truth is great and will prevail if left to herself, that she is the proper and sufficient antagonist to error, and has nothing to fear from the conflict, unless by human interposition disarmed of her natural weapons, free argument and debate, errors ceasing to be dangerous when it is permitted freely to contradict them.

Be it therefore enacted by the General Assembly, That no man shall be compelled to frequent or support any religious worship, place, or ministry whatsoever, nor shall be enforced, restrained, molested, or burdened in his body or goods, nor shall otherwise suffer on account of his religious opinions or belief; but that all men shall be free to profess, and by argument to maintain, their opinions in matters of religion, and that the same shall in nowise diminish, enlarge, or affect their civil capacities.

And though we well know this Assembly, elected by the people for the ordinary purposes of legislation only, have no powers equal to our own and that therefore to declare this act irrevocable would be of no effect in law, yet we are free to declare, and do declare, that the rights hereby asserted are of the natural rights of mankind, and that if any act shall be hereafter passed to repeal the present or to narrow its operation, such act will be an infringement of natural right.

FOR DISCUSSION

To what degree is the Virginia statute based on theological propositions? Are there some conceptions of God that are incompatible with religious liberty?

JOSEPH STORY, COMMENTARIES ON THE CONSTITUTION

§§ 1865–1873, 1833

Joseph Story served as an early Supreme Court justice (1811–1845). His *Commentaries on the Constitution* remain among the most useful interpretations of that document. Whereas Jefferson and Madison stressed complete separation of church and state, Story was much more sympathetic to mild religious establishments, at least at the state level. Thus Jefferson argued for a secular state, but Story believed that Christian principles were incorporated into the common law, which the United States had adapted from England.

§ 1866. The real difficulty lies in ascertaining the limits, to which government may rightfully go in fostering and encouraging religion. Three cases may easily be supposed. One, where a government affords aid to a particular religion, leaving all persons free to adopt any other; another, where it creates an ecclesiastical establishment for the propagation of the doctrines of a particular sect of that religion, leaving a like freedom to all others; and a third, where it creates such an establishment, and excludes all persons, not belonging to it, either wholly, or in part, from any participation in the public honours, trusts, emoluments, privileges, and immunities of the state. For instance, a government may simply declare, that the Christian religion shall be the religion of the state, and shall be aided, and encouraged in all the varieties of sects belonging to it; or it may declare, that the Catholic or Protestant religion shall be the religion of the state, leaving every man to the free enjoyment of his own religious opinions; or it may establish the doctrines of a particular sect, as of Episcopalians, as the religion of the state, with a like freedom; or it may establish the doctrines of a particular sect, as exclusively the religion of the state, tolerating others to a limited extent, or excluding all, not belonging to it, from all public honours, trusts, emoluments, privileges, and immunities.

§ 1867. Now, there will probably be found few persons in this, or any other Christian country, who would deliberately contend, that it was unreasonable, or unjust to foster and encourage the Christian religion generally, as a matter of sound policy, as well as of revealed truth. In fact, every American colony, from its foundation down to the revolution, with the exception of Rhode Island (if, indeed, that state be an exception), did openly, by the whole course of its laws and institutions, support and sustain, in some form, the Christian religion; and almost invariably gave a peculiar sanction to some of its fundamental doctrines. And this has continued to be the case in some of the states down to the present period, without the slightest suspicion, that it was against the principles of public law, or republican liberty. Indeed, in a republic, there would seem to be a peculiar propriety in viewing the Christian religion, as the great basis, on which it must rest for its support and permanence, if it be, what it has ever been deemed by its truest friends to be, the religion of liberty. Montesquieu has remarked, that the Christian religion is a stranger to mere despotic power. The mildness so frequently recommended in the gospel is incompatible with the despotic rage, with which a prince punishes his subjects, and exercises himself in cruelty. . . . . it is certainly true, that the parent country has acted upon it [religious liberty] with a severe and vigilant zeal; and in most of the colonies the same rigid jealousy has been maintained almost down to our own times. Massachusetts, while she has promulgated in her BILL OF RIGHTS the importance and necessity of the public support of religion, and the worship of God, has authorized the legislature to require it only for Protestantism. The language of that bill of rights is remarkable for its pointed affirmation of the duty of government to support Christianity, and the reasons for it. "As," says the third article, "the happiness of a people, and the good order and preservation of civil government, essentially depend upon piety, religion, and morality; and as these cannot be generally diffused through the community, but by the institution of the public worship of God, and of public instructions in piety, religion, and morality; therefore, to promote their happiness and to secure the good order and preservation of their government, the people of this Commonwealth have a right to invest their legislature with power to authorize, and require, and the legislature shall from time to time authorize and require, the several towns, parishes, &c. &c. to make suitable provision at their own expense for the institution of the public worship of God, and for the support and maintenance of public *protestant* teachers of piety, religion, and morality, in all cases where such provision shall not be made voluntarily." Afterwards there follow provisions, prohibiting any superiority of one sect over another, and securing to all citizens the free exercise of religion.

§ 1868. Probably at the time of the adoption of the constitution, and of the amendment to it, now under consideration, the general, if not the universal, sentiment in America was, that Christianity ought to receive encouragement from the state, so far as was not incompatible with the private rights of conscience, and the freedom of religious worship. An attempt to level all religions, and to make it a matter of state policy to hold all in utter indifference, would have created universal disapprobation, if not universal indignation.

§ 1869. It yet remains a problem to be solved in human affairs, whether any free government can be permanent, where the public worship of God, and the support of religion, constitute no part of the policy or duty of the state in any assignable shape. . . .

§ 1870. But the duty of supporting religion, and especially the Christian religion, is very different from the right to force the consciences of other men, or to punish them for worshipping God in the manner, which, they believe, their accountability to him requires. It has been truly said, that "religion, or the duty we owe to our Creator, and the manner of discharging it, can be dictated only by reason and conviction, not by force or violence." Mr. Locke himself, who did not doubt the right of government to interfere in matters of religion, and especially to encourage Christianity, at the same time has expressed his opinion of the right of private judgment, and liberty of conscience, in a manner becoming his character, as a sincere friend of civil and religious liberty. "No man, or society of men," says he, "have any authority to impose their opinions or interpretations on any other, the meanest Christian; since, in matters of religion, every man must know, and believe, and give an account for himself." The rights of conscience are, indeed, beyond the just reach of any human power. They are given by God, and cannot be encroached upon by human authority, without a criminal disobedience of the precepts of natural, as well as of revealed religion.

§ 1871. The real object of the amendment was, not to countenance, much less to advance Mahometanism, or Judaism, or infidelity, by prostrating Christianity; but to exclude all rivalry among Christian sects, and to prevent any national ecclesiastical establishment, which should give to an hierarchy the exclusive patronage of the national government. It thus cut off the means of religious persecution, (the vice and pest of former ages,) and of the subversion of the rights of conscience in matters of religion, which had been trampled upon almost from the days of the Apostles to the present age. . . . .

§ 1872. [Omitted.]

§ 1873. It was under a solemn consciousness of the dangers from ecclesiastical ambition, the bigotry of spiritual pride, and the intolerance of sects, thus exemplified in our domestic, as well as in foreign annals, that it was deemed advisable to exclude from the national government all power to act upon the subject. The situation, too, of the different states equally proclaimed the policy, as well as the necessity of such an exclusion. In some of the states, episcopalians constituted the predominant sect; in others, presbyterians; in others, congregationalists; in others, quakers; and in others again, there was a close numerical rivalry among contending sects. It was impossible, that there should not arise perpetual strife and perpetual jealousy on the subject of ecclesiastical ascendancy, if the national government were left free to create a religious establishment. The only security was in extirpating the power. But this alone would have been an imperfect security, if it had not been followed up by a declaration of the right of the free exercise of religion, and a prohibition (as we have seen) of all religious tests. Thus, the whole power over the subject of religion is left exclusively to the state governments, to be acted upon according to their own sense of justice, and the state constitutions; and the Catholic and the

Protestant, the Calvinist and the Arminian, the Jew and the Infidel, may sit down at the common table of the national councils, without any inquisition into their faith, or mode of worship.

Story, Joseph. *Commentaries on the Constitution of the United States.* 3 vols. Boston, 1833. Taken from The Founder's Constitution, http://press-pubs.uchicago.edu/founders/documents/amendI_religions69,html. The University of Chicago Press.

FOR DISCUSSION

While modern Americans typically associate religious freedom with religious disestablishment, some nations, like England and France, continue to provide for both freedom and a mild form of religious establishment. How can one account for such distinctions? Is one system more likely than another to foster, or inhibit, the development of robust religious institutions within society?

EVERSON V. BOARD OF EDUCATION OF EWING TOWNSHIP

330 U.S. 1, 67 S.Ct. 504, 91 L.Ed. 711 (1947)

A statute of the state of New Jersey authorized local school districts to make rules and contracts for the transportation of children to and from schools. Here the township board of education had authorized reimbursement to parents of money they had expended for the transportation of their children on regular buses operated by the public transportation system. Some of these children attended Catholic parochial schools. The appellant, a district taxpayer, challenged the right of the board to reimburse the parents of parochial school children under the First and Fourteenth Amendments.

Vote: 5–4

JUSTICE BLACK delivered the opinion of the Court.

. . . The "establishment of religion" clause of the First Amendment means at least this: Neither a state nor the Federal Government can set up a church. Neither can pass laws which aid one religion, aid all religions, or prefer one religion over another. Neither can force nor influence a person to go to or to remain away from church against his will or force him to profess a belief or disbelief in any religion. No person can be punished for entertaining or professing religious beliefs or disbeliefs, for church attendance or non-attendance. No tax in any amount, large or small, can be levied to support any religious activities or institutions, whatever they may be called, or whatever form they may adopt to teach or practice religion. Neither a state nor the Federal Government can, openly or secretly, participate in the affairs of any religious organization or groups and vice versa. In the words of Jefferson, the clause against establishment of religion by law was intended to erect "a wall of separation between Church and State." . . .

Measured by these standards, we cannot say that the First Amendment prohibits New Jersey from spending tax-raised funds to pay the bus fares of parochial school pupils as a part of a general program under which it pays the fares of pupils attending public and other schools. It is undoubtedly true that children are helped to get to church schools. There is even a possibility that some of the children might not be sent to the church schools if the parents were compelled to pay their childrens' bus fares out of their own pockets when transportation to a public school would have been paid for by the State. The same possibility exists where the state requires a local transit company to provide reduced fares to school children including those attending parochial schools, or where a municipally owned transportation system undertakes to carry all school children free of charge.

Moreover, state-paid policemen, detailed to protect children going to and from church schools from the very real hazards of traffic, would serve much the same purpose and accomplish much the same result as state provisions intended to guarantee free transportation of a kind which the state deems to be best for the school children's welfare. And parents might refuse to risk their children to the serious danger of traffic accidents going to and from parochial schools, the approaches to which were not protected by policemen. Similarly, parents might be reluctant to permit their children to attend schools which the state had cut off from such general government services as ordinary police and fire protection, connections for sewage disposal, public highways and sidewalks. Of course, cutting off church schools from these services, so separate and so indisputably marked off from the religious function, would make it far more difficult for the schools to operate. But such is obviously not the purpose of the First Amendment. That Amendment requires the state to be a neutral in its relations with groups of religious believers and nonbelievers; it does not require the state to be their adversary. State power is no more to be used so as to handicap religions than it is to favor them.

This court has said that parents may, in the discharge of their duty under state compulsory education laws, send their children to a religious rather than a public school if the school meets the secular educational requirements which the state has power to impose. It appears that these parochial schools meet New Jersey's requirements. The state contributes no money to the schools. It does not support them. Its legislation, as applied, does no more than provide a general program to help parents get their children, regardless of their religion, safely and expeditiously to and from accredited schools.

The First Amendment has erected a wall between church and state. That wall must be kept high and impregnable. We could not approve the slightest breach. New Jersey has not breached it here.

Affirmed.

JUSTICE JACKSON, dissenting.

It is of no importance in this situation whether the beneficiary of this expenditure of tax-raised funds is primarily the parochial school and incidentally the pupil, or whether the aid is directly bestowed on the pupil with indirect benefits to the school. The state cannot maintain a Church and it can no more tax its citizens to furnish free carriage to those who attend a Church. The prohibition against establishment of religion cannot be circumvented by a subsidy, bonus or reimbursement of expense to individuals for receiving religious instruction and indoctrination.

This freedom was first in the Bill of Rights because it was first in the forefathers' minds; it was set forth in absolute terms, and its strength is its rigidity. It was intended not only to keep the states' hands out of religion, but to keep religion's hands off the state, and above all, to keep bitter religious controversy out of public life by denying to every denomination any advantage from getting control of public policy or the public purse. Those great ends I cannot but think are immeasurably compromised by today's decision.

But we cannot have it both ways. Religious teaching cannot be a private affair when the state seeks to impose regulations which infringe on it indirectly, and a public affair when it comes to taxing citizens of one faith to aid another, or those of no faith to aid all. If these principles seem harsh in prohibiting aid to Catholic education, it must not be forgotten that it is the same Constitution that alone assures Catholics the right to maintain these schools at all when predominant local sentiment would forbid them, *Pierce v. Society of Sisters,* 268 U.S. 510 (1925). Nor should I think that those who have done so well without this aid would want to see this separation between Church and State broken down. If the state may aid these religious schools, it may therefore regulate them. Many groups have sought aid from tax funds only to find that it carried political controls with it. Indeed this Court has declared that "It is hardly lack of due process for the Government to regulate that which it subsidizes."

JUSTICE RUTLEDGE dissenting, joined by JUSTICES FRANKFURTER, JACKSON and BURTON.

. . . Does New Jersey's action furnish support for religion by use of the taxing power? Certainly it does, if the test remains undiluted as Jefferson and Madison made it, that money taken by taxation from one is not to be used or given to support another's religious training or belief, or indeed one's own. Today as then the furnishing of "contributions of money for the propagation of opinions which he disbelieves" is the forbidden exaction; and the prohibition is absolute for whatever measure brings that consequence and whatever amount may be sought or given to that end.

The funds used here were raised by taxation. The Court does not dispute, nor could it, that their use does in fact give aid and encouragement—to religious instruction. It only concludes that this aid is not "support" in law. But Madison and Jefferson were concerned with aid and support in fact, not as a legal conclusion "entangled in precedents". . . . Here parents pay money to send their children to parochial schools and funds raised by taxation are used to reimburse them. This not only helps the children to get to school and the parents to send them. It aids them in a particular school to secure, namely, religious training and teaching.

New Jersey's action therefore exactly fits the type of exaction and the kind of evil at which Madison and Jefferson struck. Under the test they framed it cannot be said that the cost of transportation is no part of the cost of education or of the religious instruction given. That it is a substantial and a necessary element is shown most plainly by the continuing and increasing demand for the state to assume it. Nor is there pretense that it relates only to the secular instruction given in religious schools or that any attempt is or could be made toward allocating proportional shares as between the secular and the religious instruction. It is precisely because the instruction is religious and relates to a particular faith, whether one or another, that parents send their children to religious schools under the *Pierce* doctrine. And the very purpose of the state's contribution is to defray the cost of conveying the pupil to the place where he will receive not simply secular, but also and primarily religious, teaching and guidance.

Finally, transportation, where it is needed, is as essential to education as any other element. Its cost is as much a part of the total expense, except at times in amount, as the cost of textbooks, of school lunches, of athletic equipment, of writing and other materials; indeed of all other items composing the total burden. Now as always the core of the educational process is the teacher-pupil relationship. Without this the richest equipment and facilities would go for naught.

But we are told that the New Jersey statute is valid in its present application because the appropriation is for a public, not a private purpose, namely, the promotion of education, and the majority accept this idea in the conclusion that all we have here is "public welfare legislation." If that is true and the Amendment's force can be thus destroyed, what has been said becomes all the more pertinent. For then there could be no possible objection to more extensive support of religious education by New Jersey.

If the fact alone be determinative that religious schools are engaged in education, thus promoting the general and individual welfare, together with the legislature's decision that the payment of public moneys for their aid makes their work a public function, then I can see no possible basis, except one of dubious legislative policy, for the state's refusal to make full appropriation for support of private, religious schools, just as is done for public instruction. There could not be, on that basis, valid constitutional objection.

We have here then one substantial issue, not two. To say that New Jersey's appropriation and her use of the power of taxation for raising the funds appropriated are not for public purposes but are for private ends, is to say that they are for the support of religion and religious teaching. Conversely, to say that they are for public purposes is to say that they are not for religious ones.

This is precisely for the reason that education which includes religious training and teaching, and its support, have been made matters of private right and function, not public, by the very terms of the First

Amendment. That is the effect not only in its guaranty of religion's free exercise, but also in the prohibition of establishments. It was on this basis of the private character of the function of religious education that this Court held parents entitled to send their children to private, religious schools. *Pierce v. Society of Sisters*. Now it declares in effect that the appropriation of public funds to defray part of the cost of attending those schools is for a public purpose. If so, I do not understand why the state cannot go farther or why this case approaches the verge of its power.

Our constitutional policy is exactly the opposite. It does not deny the value or the necessity for religious training, teaching or observance. Rather it secures their free exercise. But to that end it does deny that the state can undertake or sustain them in any form or degree. For this reason the sphere of religious activity, as distinguished from the secular intellectual liberties, has been given the twofold protection and, as the state cannot forbid, neither can it perform or aid in performing the religious function. The dual prohibition makes that function altogether private. It cannot be made a public one by legislative act. This was the very heart of Madison's Remonstrance, as it is of the Amendment itself.

No one conscious of religious values can be unsympathetic toward the burden which our constitutional separation puts on parents who desire religious instruction mixed with secular for their children. They pay taxes for others' children's education, at the same time the added cost of instruction for their own. Nor can one happily see benefits denied to children which others receive, because in conscience they or their parents for them desire a different kind of training others do not demand.

Hardship in fact there is which none can blink. But, for assuring to those who undergo it the greater, the most comprehensive freedom, it is one written by design and firm intent into our basic law. . . .

. . . Like St. Paul's freedom, religious liberty with a great price must be bought. And for those who exercise it most fully, by insisting upon religious education for their children mixed with secular, by the terms of our Constitution the price is greater than for others. . . .

FOR DISCUSSION

Is there a disconnect, as the dissenters charge, in this case between Black's rhetoric and his decision? Is it appropriate to distinguish between monies that go directly to students and/or parents and monies that go directly to parochial schools? To what degree was it appropriate for Justice Black to interpret the First Amendment with reference to the church-state controversy in Virginia?

RELATED CASES

***Illinois ex rel. McCollum v. Board of Education of Champaign County:* 333 U.S. 203 (1948).**

The Court struck down a program whereby public schools allowed religious teachers to instruct students in grades four through nine on school property and during school hours.

***Zorach v. Clauson:* 343 U.S. 306 (1952).**

The Court upheld a New York City program that released students who, with their parents' consent, went off campus during the school day to receive religious instruction.

ENGEL V. VITALE

370 U.S. 421, 82 S.Ct. 1261, 8 L.Ed.2d 601 (1962)

Following a recommendation of the New York State Board of Regents, the New Hyde Park Board of Education directed that the following prayer be said aloud by each class in the presence of a teacher at the beginning of each school day: "Almighty God, we acknowledge our dependence upon Thee, and we beg Thy blessings upon us, our parents, our teachers and our country." This action was challenged by the parents of ten pupils as violating the Establishment Clause of the First Amendment as applied to the states through the Due Process Clause of the Fourteenth Amendment.

Vote: 6–1

JUSTICE BLACK delivered the opinion of the Court.

We think that by using its public school system to encourage recitation of the Regents' prayer, the State of New York has adopted a practice wholly inconsistent with the Establishment Clause.

There can, of course, be no doubt that New York's program of daily classroom invocation of God's blessings as prescribed in the Regents' prayer is a religious activity. It is a solemn avowal of divine faith and supplication for the blessings of the Almighty. The nature of such a prayer has always been religious; none of the respondents has denied this and the trial court expressly so found:

The religious nature of prayer was recognized by Jefferson and has been concurred in by theological writers, the United States Supreme Court and state courts and administrative officials, including New York's Commissioner of Education. A committee of the New York Legislature has agreed.

The Board of Regents as *amicus curiae,* the respondents and intervenors all concede the religious nature of prayer, but seek to distinguish this prayer because it is based on our spiritual heritage.

The petitioners contend among other things that the state laws requiring or permitting use of the Regents' prayer must be struck down as a violation of the Establishment Clause because that prayer was composed by governmental officials as a part of a governmental program to further religious beliefs. For this reason, petitioners argue, the State's use of the Regents' prayer in its public school system breaches the constitutional wall of separation between Church and State. We agree with that contention since we think that the constitutional prohibition against laws respecting an establishment of religion must at least mean that in this country it is no part of the business of government to compose official prayers for any group of the American people to recite as a part of a religious program carried on by government.

The First Amendment was added to the Constitution to stand as a guarantee that neither the power nor the prestige of the Federal Government would be used to control, support or influence the kinds of prayer the American people can say that the people's religions must not be subjected to the pressures of government for change each time a new political administration is elected to office. Under that Amendment's prohibition against governmental establishment of religion, as reinforced by the provisions of the Fourteenth Amendment, government in this country, be it state or federal, is without power to prescribe by law any particular form of prayer which is to be used as an official prayer in carrying on any program of governmentally sponsored religious activity.

There can be no doubt that New York's state prayer program officially establishes the religious beliefs embodied in the Regents' prayer. The respondents' argument to the contrary, which is largely based upon the contention that the Regents' prayer is "non-denominational" and the fact that the program, as modified and approved by state courts, does not require all pupils to recite the prayer but permits those who wish to do so to remain silent or be excused from the room, ignores the essential nature of the program's constitutional defects. Neither the fact that the prayer may be denominationally neutral, nor the fact that its observance on the part of the students is voluntary can serve to free it from the limitations of the Establishment Clause, as it might from the Free Exercise Clause, of the First Amendment, both of which are operative against the States by virtue of the Fourteenth Amendment. Although these two clauses may in certain instances overlap, they forbid two quite different kinds of governmental encroachment upon religious freedom. The Establishment Clause, unlike the Free Exercise Clause, does not depend upon any showing of direct governmental compulsion and is violated by the enactment of laws which establish an official religion whether those laws operate directly to coerce nonobserving individuals or not. . . .

JUSTICE DOUGLAS, concurring.

Prayers of course may be so long and of such a character as to amount to an attempt at the religious instruction that was denied the public schools by the *McCollum* case. But New York's prayer is of a character that does not involve any element of proselytizing as in the *McCollum v. Board of Education*, 333 U.S. 203 (1948), case.

The question presented by this case is therefore an extremely narrow one. It is whether New York oversteps the bounds when it finances a religious exercise.

What New York does on the opening of its public schools is what we do when we open court. Our Marshal has from the beginning announced the convening of the Court and then added "God save the United States and this honorable court." That utterance is a supplication, a prayer in which we, the judges, are free to join, but which we need not recite any more than the students need recite the New York prayer.

What New York does on the opening of its public schools is what each House of Congress does at the opening of each day's business. Reverend Frederick B. Harris is Chaplain of the Senate; Reverend Bernard Braskamp is Chaplain of the House. Guest chaplains of various denominations also officiate.

In New York the teacher who leads in prayer is on the public payroll; and the time she takes seems minuscule as compared with the salaries appropriated by state legislatures and Congress for chaplains to conduct prayers in the legislative halls. Only a bare fraction of the teacher's time is given to reciting this short 22-word prayer, about the same amount of time that our Marshal spends announcing the opening of our sessions and offering a prayer for this Court. Yet for me the principle is the same, no matter how briefly the prayer is said, for in each of the instances given the person praying is a public official on the public payroll, performing a religious exercise in a governmental institution. It is said that the element of coercion is inherent in the giving of this prayer. If that is true here, it is also true of the prayer with which this Court is convened, and with those that open the Congress. Few adults, let alone children, would leave our courtroom or the Senate or the House while those prayers are being given. Every such audience is in a sense a "captive" audience.

At the same time I cannot say that to authorize this prayer is to establish a religion in the strictly historic meaning of those words. A religion is not established in the usual sense merely by letting those who chose to do so say the prayer that the public school teacher leads. Yet once government finances a religious exercise it inserts a divisive influence into our communities. The New York court said that the prayer given does not conform to all of the tenets of the Jewish, Unitarian, and Ethical Culture groups. One of petitioners is an agnostic.

"We are a religious people whose institutions presuppose a Supreme Being." *Zorach v. Clauson,* 343 U.S. 306 (1952). . . . Under our Bill of Rights free play is given for making religion an active force in our lives. But "if a religious leaven is to be worked into the affairs of our people, it is to be one by individuals and groups, not by the Government." *McGowan v. Maryland,* 366 U.S. 420 (1961). By reason of the First Amendment government is commanded "to have no interest in theology or ritual" for on those matters "government must be neutral." The First Amendment leaves the Government in a position not of hostility to religion but of neutrality. The philosophy is that the atheist or agnostic—the non-believer—is entitled to go his own way. The philosophy is that if government interferes in matters spiritual, it will be a divisive force. The First Amendment teaches that a government neutral in the field of religion better serves all religious interests.

My problem today would be uncomplicated but for *Everson v. Board of Education,* 330 U.S. 1 (1947), which allowed taxpayers' money to be used to pay "the bus fares of parochial school pupils as a part of a general program under which" the fares of pupils attending public and other schools were also paid. The Everson case seems in retrospect to be out of line with the First Amendment. . . .

JUSTICE STEWART, dissenting.

With all respect, I think the Court has misapplied a great constitutional principle. I cannot see how an "official religion" is established by letting those who want to say a prayer say it. On the contrary, I think that to deny the wish of these school children to join in reciting this prayer is to deny them the opportunity of sharing in the spiritual heritage of our Nation.

The Court's historical review of the quarrels over the Book of Common Prayer in England throws no light for me on the issue before us in this case. England had then and has now an established church. Equally unenlightening, I think, is the history of the early establishment and later rejection of an official church in our own States. For we deal here not with the establishment of a state church, which would, of course, be constitutionally impermissible, but with whether school children who want to begin their day by joining in prayer must be prohibited from doing so. Moreover, I think that the Court's task, in this as in all areas of constitutional adjudication, is not responsibly aided by the uncritical invocation of metaphors like the "wall of separation," a phrase nowhere to be found in the Constitution. What is relevant to the issue here is not the history of an established church in sixteenth century England or in eighteenth century America, but the history of the religious traditions of our people, reflected in countless practices of the institutions and officials of our government.

[Stewart describes a number of such practices.]

Countless similar examples could be listed, but there is no need to belabor the obvious. It was all summed up by this Court just ten years ago in a single sentence: "We are a religious people whose institutions presuppose a Supreme Being." *Zorach v. Clauson*. . . .

I do not believe that this Court, or the Congress, or the President has by the actions and practices I have mentioned established an "official religion" in violation of the Constitution. And I do not believe the State of New York has done so in this case. What each has done has been to recognize and to follow the deeply entrenched and highly cherished spiritual traditions of our Nation—traditions which come down to us from those who almost two hundred years ago avowed their "firm reliance on the Protection of Divine Providence" when they proclaimed the freedom and independence of this brave new world.

FOR DISCUSSION

This case generated very shrill criticism, which some observers have continued to repeat, from individuals who feared that the Court was "kicking God out of schools." Should the Court have waited for further evidence of the effect that "voluntary" prayer had on nonparticipants before declaring that such prayers were automatically a violation of the Establishment Clause? How would you respond to those who believe that this decision led to moral decline?

RELATED CASES

***School District of Abington Township, Pennsylvania v. Schempp:* 374 U.S. 203 (1963).**

Further extended the Engel ban on prayer to include devotional readings of the Lord's Prayer and daily readings from the Bible in public schools.

***Lee v. Weisman:* 505 U.S. 577 (1992).**

The Court struck down the practice of inviting members of the clergy to deliver prayers at public high school graduations.

***Santa Fe Independent School District v. Doe:* 530 U.S. 290 (2000).**

Struck down the practice of student-led prayer at public school sporting events.

LEMON V. KURTZMAN

403 U.S. 602, 91 S.Ct. 2105, 29 L.Ed.2d 745 (1971)

As school expenses rose and some parents of children in parochial school sought relief, states, aware of the money such institutions saved the states, sometimes tried to help the schools. This case deals with attempts by Rhode Island and Pennsylvania to offer such assistance. In *Abington v. Schempp*, 374 U.S. 203 (1963), the Court indicated that it would examine challenges brought under the Establishment Clause to see whether such measures had a clear secular (as opposed to a religious) purpose and whether their primary effect was either to advance or inhibit religion. This case is most significant for adding a third prong, that of excessive entanglement, to formulate what is now known as the *Lemon* test.

Vote: 7–1

CHIEF JUSTICE BURGER delivered the opinion of the Court.

These two appeals raise questions as to Pennsylvania and Rhode Island statutes providing state aid to church-related elementary and secondary schools. Both statutes are challenged as violative of the Establishment and Free Exercise Clauses of the First Amendment and the Due Process Clause of the Fourteenth Amendment.

Pennsylvania has adopted a statutory program that provides financial support to nonpublic elementary and secondary schools by way of reimbursement for the cost of teachers' salaries, textbooks, and instructional materials in specified secular subjects. Rhode Island has adopted a statute under which the State pays directly to teachers in nonpublic elementary schools a supplement of 15% of their annual salary. Under each statute state aid has been given to church-related educational institutions. We hold that both statutes are unconstitutional.

I

[Burger reviews the details of both state programs.]

II

In *Everson v. Board of Education,* 330 U.S. 1 (1947), this Court upheld a state statute that reimbursed the parents of parochial school children for bus transportation expenses. There Mr. Justice Black, writing for the majority, suggested that the decision carried to "the verge" of forbidden territory under the Religion Clauses. Candor compels acknowledgment, moreover, that we can only dimly perceive the lines of demarcation in this extraordinarily sensitive area of constitutional law.

The language of the Religion Clauses of the First Amendment is at best opaque, particularly when compared with other portions of the Amendment. Its authors did not simply prohibit the establishment of a state church or a state religion, an area history shows they regarded as very important and fraught with great dangers. Instead they commanded that there should be "no law *respecting* an establishment of religion." A law may be one "respecting" the forbidden objective while falling short of its total realization. A law "respecting" the proscribed result, that is, the establishment of religion, is not always easily identifiable as one violative of the Clause. A given law might not *establish* a state religion but nevertheless be one "respecting" that end in the sense of being a step that could lead to such establishment and hence offend the First Amendment.

In the absence of precisely stated constitutional prohibitions, we must draw lines with reference to the three main evils against which the Establishment Clause was intended to afford protection: "sponsorship, financial support, and active involvement of the sovereign in religious activity." *Walz* v. *Tax Commission,* 397 U.S. 664 (1970).

Every analysis in this area must begin with consideration of the cumulative criteria developed by the Court over many years. Three such tests may be gleaned from our cases. First, the statute must have a secular legislative purpose; second, its principal or primary effect must be one that neither advances nor inhibits religion, *Board of Education v. Allen,* 392 U.S. 236 (1968); finally, the statute must not foster "an excessive government entanglement with religion." *Walz.*

Inquiry into the legislative purposes of the Pennsylvania and Rhode Island statutes affords no basis for a conclusion that the legislative intent was to advance religion. On the contrary, the statutes themselves clearly state that they are intended to enhance the quality of the secular education in all schools covered by the compulsory attendance laws. There is no reason to believe the legislatures meant anything else. A State always has a legitimate concern for maintaining minimum standards in all schools it allows to operate. As in *Allen,* we find nothing here that undermines the stated legislative intent; it must therefore be accorded appropriate deference.

In *Allen* the Court acknowledged that secular and religious teachings were not necessarily so intertwined that secular textbooks furnished to students by the State were in fact instrumental in the teaching of religion. The legislatures of Rhode Island and Pennsylvania have concluded that secular and religious education are identifiable and separable. In the abstract we have no quarrel with this conclusion.

The two legislatures, however, have also recognized that church-related elementary and secondary schools have a significant religious mission and that a substantial portion of their activities is religiously oriented. They have therefore sought to create statutory restrictions designed to guarantee the separation between secular and religious educational functions and to ensure that State financial aid supports only the former. All these provisions are precautions taken in candid recognition that these programs approached, even if they did not intrude upon, the forbidden areas under the Religion Clauses. We need not decide whether these legislative precautions restrict the principal or primary effect of the programs to the point where they do not offend the Religion Clauses, for we conclude that the cumulative impact of the entire relationship arising under the statutes in each State involves excessive entanglement between government and religion.

III

In *Walz* v. *Tax Commission,* the Court upheld state tax exemptions for real property owned by religious organizations and used for religious worship. That holding, however, tended to confine rather than enlarge the area of permissible state involvement with religious institutions by calling for close scrutiny of the degree of entanglement involved in the relationship. The objective is to prevent, as far as possible, the intrusion of either into the precincts of the other.

Our prior holdings do not call for total separation between church and state; total separation is not possible in an absolute sense. Some relationship between government and religious organizations is inevitable. *Zorach* v. *Clauson,* 343 U.S. 306 (1952); *Sherbert* v. *Verner,* 374 U.S. 398 (1963). Fire inspections, building and zoning regulations, and state requirements under compulsory school-attendance laws are examples of necessary and permissible contacts. Indeed, under the statutory exemption before us in *Walz,* the State had a continuing burden to ascertain that the exempt property was in fact being used for religious worship. Judicial caveats against entanglement must recognize that the line of separation, far from being a "wall," is a blurred, indistinct, and variable barrier depending on all the circumstances of a particular relationship.

This is not to suggest, however, that we are to engage in a legalistic minuet in which precise rules and forms must govern. A true minuet is a matter of pure form and style, the observance of which is itself the substantive end. Here we examine the form of the relationship for the light that it casts on the substance.

In order to determine whether the government entanglement with religion is excessive, we must examine the character and purposes of the institutions that are benefited, the nature of the aid that the State provides, and the resulting relationship between the government and the religious authority. Mr. Justice Harlan, in a separate opinion in *Walz,* echoed the classic warning as to "programs, whose very nature is apt to entangle the state in details of administration . . . ." Here we find that both statutes foster an impermissible degree of entanglement.

(a) *Rhode Island program*

The District Court made extensive findings on the grave potential for excessive entanglement that inheres in the religious character and purpose of the Roman Catholic elementary schools of Rhode Island, to date the sole beneficiaries of the Rhode Island Salary Supplement Act.

The church schools involved in the program are located close to parish churches. This understandably permits convenient access for religious exercises since instruction in faith and morals is part of the total educational process. The school buildings contain identifying religious symbols such as crosses on the exterior and crucifixes, and religious paintings and statues either in the classrooms or hallways. Although only approximately 30 minutes a day are devoted to direct religious instruction, there are religiously oriented extracurricular activities. Approximately two-thirds of the teachers in these schools are nuns of various religious orders. Their dedicated efforts provide an atmosphere in which religious instruction and religious vocations are natural and proper parts of life in such schools. Indeed, as the District Court found, the role of teaching nuns in enhancing the religious atmosphere has led the parochial school authorities to attempt to maintain a one-to-one ratio between nuns and lay teachers in all schools rather than to permit some to be staffed almost entirely by lay teachers.

On the basis of these findings the District Court concluded that the parochial schools constituted "an integral part of the religious mission of the Catholic Church." The various characteristics of the schools make them "a powerful vehicle for transmitting the Catholic faith to the next generation." This process of inculcating religious doctrine is, of course, enhanced by the impressionable age of the pupils, in primary schools particularly. In short, parochial schools involve substantial religious activity and purpose.

The substantial religious character of these church-related schools gives rise to entangling church-state relationships of the kind the Religion Clauses sought to avoid. Although the District Court found that concern for religious values did not inevitably or necessarily intrude into the content of secular subjects, the considerable religious activities of these schools led the legislature to provide for careful governmental controls and surveillance by state authorities in order to ensure that state aid supports only secular education.

The dangers and corresponding entanglements are enhanced by the particular form of aid that the Rhode Island Act provides. Our decisions from *Everson* to *Allen* have permitted the States to provide church-related schools with secular, neutral, or nonideological services, facilities, or materials. Bus transportation, school lunches, public health services, and secular textbooks supplied in common to all students were not thought to offend the Establishment Clause. We note that the dissenters in *Allen* seemed chiefly concerned with the pragmatic difficulties involved in ensuring the truly secular content of the textbooks provided at state expense.

In *Allen* the Court refused to make assumptions, on a meager record, about the religious content of the textbooks that the State would be asked to provide. We cannot, however, refuse here to recognize that teachers have a substantially different ideological character from books. In terms of potential for involving some aspect of faith or morals in secular subjects, a textbook's content is ascertainable, but a teacher's handling of a subject is not. We cannot ignore the danger that a teacher under religious control and discipline poses to the separation of the religious from the purely secular aspects of pre-college education. The conflict of functions inheres in the situation.

We need not and do not assume that teachers in parochial schools will be guilty of bad faith or any conscious design to evade the limitations imposed by the statute and the First Amendment. We simply recognize that a dedicated religious person, teaching in a school affiliated with his or her faith and operated to inculcate its tenets, will inevitably experience great difficulty in remaining religiously neutral. Doctrines and faith are not inculcated or advanced by neutrals. With the best of intentions such a teacher would find it hard to make a total separation between secular teaching and religious doctrine. What would appear to some to be essential to good citizenship might well for others border on or constitute instruction in religion. Further difficulties are inherent in the combination of religious discipline and the possibility of disagreement between teacher and religious authorities over the meaning of the statutory restrictions.

A comprehensive, discriminating, and continuing state surveillance will inevitably be required to ensure that these restrictions are obeyed and the First Amendment otherwise respected. Unlike a book, a teacher cannot be inspected once so as to determine the extent and intent of his or her personal beliefs and subjective acceptance of the limitations imposed by the First Amendment. These prophylactic contacts will involve excessive and enduring entanglement between state and church.

(b) *Pennsylvania program*

[The Court examines this program and arrives at similar conclusions.]

IV

A broader base of entanglement of yet a different character is presented by the divisive political potential of these state programs. In a community where such a large number of pupils are served by church-related schools, it can be assumed that state assistance will entail considerable political activity. Partisans of parochial schools, understandably concerned with rising costs and sincerely dedicated to both the religious and secular educational missions of their schools, will inevitably champion this cause and promote political action to achieve their goals. Those who oppose state aid, whether for constitutional, religious, or fiscal reasons, will inevitably respond and employ all of the usual political campaign techniques to prevail. Candidates will be forced to declare and voters to choose. It would be unrealistic to ignore the fact that many people confronted with issues of this kind will find their votes aligned with their faith.

Ordinarily political debate and division, however vigorous or even partisan, are normal and healthy manifestations of our democratic system of government, but political division along religious lines was one of the principal evils against which the First Amendment was intended to protect. The potential divisiveness of such conflict is a threat to the normal political process. . . .

V

In *Walz* it was argued that a tax exemption for places of religious worship would prove to be the first step in an inevitable progression leading to the establishment of state churches and state religion. That claim could not stand up against more than 200 years of virtually universal practice imbedded in our colonial experience and continuing into the present.

The progression argument, however, is more persuasive here. We have no long history of state aid to church-related educational institutions comparable to 200 years of tax exemption for churches. Indeed, the state programs before us today represent something of an innovation. We have already noted that modern governmental programs have self-perpetuating and self-expanding propensities. These internal pressures are only enhanced when the schemes involve institutions whose legitimate needs are growing and whose interests have substantial political support. Nor can we fail to see that in constitutional adjudication some steps, which when taken were thought to approach "the verge," have become the platform for yet further steps. A certain momentum develops in constitutional theory and it can be a "downhill thrust" easily set in motion but difficult to retard or stop. Development by momentum is not invariably bad; indeed, it is the way the common law has grown, but it is a force to be recognized and reckoned with. The dangers are increased by the difficulty of perceiving in advance exactly where the "verge" of the precipice lies. As well as constituting an independent evil against which the Religion Clauses were intended to protect, involvement or entanglement between government and religion serves as a warning signal.

JUSTICE WHITE, concurring in the judgments in No. 153 and No. 89 and dissenting in Nos. 569 and 570.

No one in these cases questions the constitutional right of parents to satisfy their state-imposed obligation to educate their children by sending them to private schools, sectarian or otherwise, as long as those schools meet minimum standards established for secular instruction. The States are not only permitted, but required by the Constitution, to free students attending private schools from any public school attendance obligation. *Pierce v. Society of Sisters,* 268 U.S. 510 (1925). The States may also furnish transportation for students, *Everson v. Board of Education,* 330 U.S. 1 (1947), and books for teaching secular subjects to students attending parochial and other private as well as public schools, *Board of Education v. Allen,* 392 U.S. 23 (1968); we have also upheld arrangements whereby students are released from public school classes so that they may attend religious instruction. *Zorach v. Clauson,* 343 U.S. 306 (1952). Outside the field of education, we have upheld Sunday closing laws, *McGowan v. Maryland,* 366 U.S. 420 (1961), state and federal laws exempting church property and church activity from taxation, *Walz v. Tax Commission,* 397 U.S. 664 (1970), and governmental grants to religious organizations for the purpose of financing improvements in the facilities of hospitals managed and controlled by religious orders. *Bradfield v. Roberts,* 175 U.S. 291 (1899).

Our prior cases have recognized the dual role of parochial schools in American society: they perform both religious and secular functions. Our cases also recognize that legislation having a secular purpose and extending governmental assistance to sectarian schools in the performance of their secular functions does not constitute "law[s] respecting an establishment of religion" forbidden by the First Amendment merely because a secular program may incidentally benefit a church in fulfilling its religious mission. That religion may indirectly benefit from governmental aid to the secular activities of churches does not convert that aid into an impermissible establishment of religion.

This much the Court squarely holds in the *Tilton v. Richardson,* 403 U.S. 672 (1971), case, where it also expressly rejects the notion that payments made directly to a religious institution are, without more, forbidden by the First Amendment. In *Tilton,* the Court decides that the Federal Government may finance the separate function of secular education carried on in a parochial setting. It reaches this result although sectarian institutions undeniably will obtain substantial benefit from federal aid; without federal funding to provide adequate facilities for secular education, the student bodies of those institutions might remain stationary or even decrease in size and the institutions might ultimately have to close their doors.

It is enough for me that the States and the Federal Government are financing a separable secular function of overriding importance in order to sustain the legislation here challenged. That religion and private interests other than education may substantially benefit does not convert these laws into impermissible establishments of religion.

FOR DISCUSSION

To what degree does the legislative purpose prong of the *Lemon* test require the Court to examine legislative "motives" (something it does not generally do)? To what extent do you think this and the other two prongs of the test are grounded in historical precedent and experience? Do you think it would be desirable to incorporate the actual words of the *Lemon* test into the First Amendment?

RELATED CASES

***Tilton v. Richardson*: 403 U.S. 672 (1971).**

The Court upheld provisions of the Higher Education Facilities Act of 1963, which permitted federal aid for construction of secular buildings at church-related colleges and universities.

***Mueller v. Allen*: 463 U.S. 388 (1983).**

The Court upheld a voucher program that permitted parents to deduct up to $700 a year for educational expenses.

***Witters v. Washington Department of Services for the Blind*: 474 U.S. 481 (1986).**

A unanimous Court allowed for state vocational monies to be spent on to permit a disabled student to attend a Bible school.

***Locke v. Davey*: 540 U.S. 712 (2004).**

The Court held that a state could, under a state constitutional provision, withhold scholarship money from a student who planned to pursue a theology degree.

***Zobrest v. Catalina Foothills School District*: 509 U.S. 1 (1993).**

The Court ruled that allowing a sign language interpreter to accompany a student to a parochial school was permissible.

***Zelman v. Simmon-Harris*: 536 U.S. 639 (2002).**

The Court upheld a Cleveland school voucher system that parents could use to send children to parochial schools.

MARSH V. CHAMBERS

463 U.S. 782, 103 S.Ct. 3330, 77 L.Ed.3d 1019 (1983)

Although the Supreme Court commonly applies the Lemon test to most Establishment Clause cases, *Marsh* demonstrates that this does not always happen. The case is fascinating because it involves prayer in the state legislature rather than in the classroom.

Vote: 6–3

CHIEF JUSTICE BURGER delivered the opinion of the Court.

The question presented is whether the Nebraska Legislature's practice of opening each legislative day with a prayer by a chaplain paid by the State violates the Establishment Clause of the First Amendment.

I

The Nebraska Legislature begins each of its sessions with a prayer offered by a chaplain who is chosen biennially by the Executive Board of the Legislative Council and paid out of public funds. Robert E. Palmer, a Presbyterian minister, has served as chaplain since 1965 at a salary of $319.75 per month for each month the legislature is in session.

Ernest Chambers is a member of the Nebraska Legislature and a taxpayer of Nebraska. Claiming that the Nebraska Legislature's chaplaincy practice violates the Establishment Clause of the First Amendment, he brought this action under 42 U.S.C. § 1983, seeking to enjoin enforcement of the practice. After denying a motion to dismiss on the ground of legislative immunity, the District Court held that the Establishment Clause was not breached by the prayers, but was violated by paying the chaplain from public funds. It therefore enjoined the legislature from using public funds to pay the chaplain; it declined to enjoin the policy of beginning sessions with prayers. Cross-appeals were taken.

The Court of Appeals for the Eighth Circuit rejected arguments that the case should be dismissed on Tenth Amendment, legislative immunity, standing, or federalism grounds. On the merits of the chaplaincy issue, the court refused to treat respondent's challenges as separable issues as the District Court had done. Instead, the Court of Appeals assessed the practice as a whole because "[parsing] out [the] elements" would lead to "an incongruous result."

Applying the three-part test of *Lemon* v. *Kurtzman,* 403 U.S. 602 (1971), as set out in *Committee for Public Education & Religious Liberty* v. *Nyquist,* 413 U.S. 756 (1973), the court held that the chaplaincy practice violated all three elements of the test: the purpose and primary effect of selecting the same minister for 16 years and publishing his prayers was to promote a particular religious expression; use of state money for compensation and publication led to entanglement. Accordingly, the Court of Appeals modified the District Court's injunction and prohibited the State from engaging in any aspect of its established chaplaincy practice.

We granted certiorari limited to the challenge to the practice of opening sessions with prayers by a state-employed clergyman, and we reverse.

II

The opening of sessions of legislative and other deliberative public bodies with prayer is deeply embedded in the history and tradition of this country. From colonial times through the founding of the Republic and ever since, the practice of legislative prayer has coexisted with the principles of disestablishment and religious freedom. In the very courtrooms in which the United States District Judge and later three Circuit Judges heard and decided this case, the proceedings opened with an announcement that concluded, "God save the United States and this Honorable Court." The same invocation occurs at all sessions of this Court.

The tradition in many of the Colonies was, of course, linked to an established church, but the Continental Congress, beginning in 1774, adopted the traditional procedure of opening its sessions with a prayer offered by a paid chaplain. Although prayers were not offered during the Constitutional Convention, the First Congress, as one of its early items of business, adopted the policy of selecting a chaplain to open each session with prayer. Thus, on April 7, 1789, the Senate appointed a committee "to take under consideration the manner of electing Chaplains." On April 9, 1789, a similar committee was appointed by the House of Representatives. On April

25, 1789, the Senate elected its first chaplain; the House followed suit on May 1, 1789. A statute providing for the payment of these chaplains was enacted into law on September 22, 1789.

On September 25, 1789, three days after Congress authorized the appointment of paid chaplains, final agreement was reached on the language of the Bill of Rights. Clearly the men who wrote the First Amendment Religion Clauses did not view paid legislative chaplains and opening prayers as a violation of that Amendment, for the practice of opening sessions with prayer has continued without interruption ever since that early session of Congress. It has also been followed consistently in most of the states, including Nebraska, where the institution of opening legislative sessions with prayer was adopted even before the State attained statehood.

Standing alone, historical patterns cannot justify contemporary violations of constitutional guarantees, but there is far more here than simply historical patterns. In this context, historical evidence sheds light not only on what the draftsmen intended the Establishment Clause to mean, but also on how they thought that Clause applied to the practice authorized by the First Congress—their actions reveal their intent. An Act "passed by the first Congress assembled under the Constitution, many of whose members had taken part in framing that instrument, . . . is contemporaneous and weighty evidence of its true meaning." *Wisconsin v. Pelican Ins. Co.*, 127 U.S. 265 (1888).

In *Walz v. Tax Comm'n,* 397 U.S. 664 (1970), we considered the weight to be accorded to history: "It is obviously correct that no one acquires a vested or protected right in violation of the Constitution by long use, even when that span of time covers our entire national existence and indeed predates it. Yet an unbroken practice . . . is not something to be lightly cast aside."

No more is Nebraska's practice of over a century, consistent with two centuries of national practice, to be cast aside. It can hardly be thought that in the same week Members of the First Congress voted to appoint and to pay a chaplain for each House and also voted to approve the draft of the First Amendment for submission to the states, they intended the Establishment Clause of the Amendment to forbid what they had just declared acceptable. In applying the First Amendment to the states through the Fourteenth Amendment, *Cantwell v. Connecticut,* 310 U.S. 296 (1940), it would be incongruous to interpret that Clause as imposing more stringent First Amendment limits on the states than the draftsmen imposed on the Federal Government.

This unique history leads us to accept the interpretation of the First Amendment draftsmen who saw no real threat to the Establishment Clause arising from a practice of prayer similar to that now challenged. We conclude that legislative prayer presents no more potential for establishment than the provision of school transportation, *Everson* v. *Board of Education,* 330 U.S. 1 (1947), beneficial grants for higher education, *Tilton* v. *Richardson,* 403 U.S. 672 (1971), or tax exemptions for religious organizations, *Walz.*

Respondent cites Justice Brennan's concurring opinion in *Abington School Dist.* v. *Schempp,* 374 U.S. 203 (1963), and argues that we should not rely too heavily on "the advice of the Founding Fathers" because the messages of history often tend to be ambiguous and not relevant to a society far more heterogeneous than that of the Framers. Respondent also points out that John Jay and John Rutledge opposed the motion to begin the first session of the Continental Congress with prayer.

We do not agree that evidence of opposition to a measure weakens the force of the historical argument; indeed it infuses it with power by demonstrating that the subject was considered carefully and the action not taken thoughtlessly, by force of long tradition and without regard to the problems posed by a pluralistic society. Jay and Rutledge specifically grounded their objection on the fact that the delegates to the Congress "were so divided in religious sentiments . . . that [they] could not join in the same act of worship." Their objection was met by Samuel Adams, who stated that "he was no bigot, and could hear a prayer from a gentleman of piety and virtue, who was at the same time a friend to his country."

This interchange emphasizes that the delegates did not consider opening prayers as a proselytizing activity or as symbolically placing the government's "official seal of approval on one religious view." Rather, the Founding Fathers looked at invocations as "conduct whose . . . effect . . . [harmonized] with the tenets of some or all religions." *McGowan v. Maryland* (1961). The Establishment Clause does not always bar a state from regulating conduct simply because it "harmonizes with religious canons." Here, the individual claiming injury by the practice is an adult, presumably not readily susceptible to "religious indoctrination," or peer pressure.

In light of the unambiguous and unbroken history of more than 200 years, there can be no doubt that the practice of opening legislative sessions with prayer has become part of the fabric of our society. To invoke Divine guidance on a public body entrusted with making the laws is not, in these circumstances, an "establishment" of religion or a step toward establishment; it is simply a tolerable acknowledgment of beliefs widely held among the people of this country. As Justice Douglas observed, "[we] are a religious people whose institutions presuppose a Supreme Being." *Zorach v. Clauson,* 343 U.S. 306 (1952).

III

We turn then to the question of whether any features of the Nebraska practice violate the Establishment Clause. Beyond the bare fact that a prayer is offered, three points have been made: first, that a clergyman of only one denomination—Presbyterian—has been selected for 16 years; second, that the chaplain is paid at public expense; and third, that the prayers are in the Judeo-Christian tradition. Weighed against the historical background, these factors do not serve to invalidate Nebraska's practice.

The Court of Appeals was concerned that Palmer's long tenure has the effect of giving preference to his religious views. We cannot, any more than Members of the Congresses of this century, perceive any suggestion that choosing a clergyman of one denomination advances the beliefs of a particular church. To the contrary, the evidence indicates that Palmer was reappointed because his performance and personal qualities were acceptable to the body appointing him. Palmer was not the only clergyman heard by the legislature; guest chaplains have officiated at the request of various legislators and as substitutes during Palmer's absences. Absent proof that the chaplain's reappointment stemmed from an impermissible motive, we conclude that his long tenure does not in itself conflict with the Establishment Clause.

Nor is the compensation of the chaplain from public funds a reason to invalidate the Nebraska Legislature's chaplaincy; remuneration is grounded in historic practice initiated, as we noted earlier, by the same Congress that drafted the Establishment Clause of the First Amendment.

The content of the prayer is not of concern to judges where, as here, there is no indication that the prayer opportunity has been exploited to proselytize or advance any one, or to disparage any other, faith or belief. That being so, it is not for us to embark on a sensitive evaluation or to parse the content of a particular prayer.

The unbroken practice for two centuries in the National Congress and for more than a century in Nebraska and in many other states gives abundant assurance that there is no real threat "while this Court sits," *Panhandle Oil Co.* v. *Mississippi ex rel. Knox,* 277 U.S. 218 (1928).

JUSTICE BRENNAN, with whom JUSTICE MARSHALL joins, dissenting.

The Court today has written a narrow and, on the whole, careful opinion. In effect, the Court holds that officially sponsored legislative prayer, primarily on account of its "unique history," is generally exempted from the First Amendment's prohibition against "an establishment of religion." The Court's opinion is consistent with dictum in at least one of our prior decisions, and its limited rationale should pose little threat to the overall fate of the Establishment Clause. Moreover, disagreement with the Court requires that I confront the fact that some 20 years ago, in a concurring opinion in one of the cases striking down official prayer and ceremonial Bible reading in the public schools, I came very close to endorsing essentially the result reached by the Court today.

Nevertheless, after much reflection, I have come to the conclusion that I was wrong then and that the Court is wrong today. I now believe that the practice of official invocational prayer, as it exists in Nebraska and most other state legislatures, is unconstitutional. It is contrary to the doctrine as well the underlying purposes of the Establishment Clause, and it is not saved either by its history or by any of the other considerations suggested in the Court's opinion.

FOR DISCUSSION

To what degree do you think the Court should be influenced by historical precedent? Does the Court use such precedent appropriately in this case? Should it make a difference whether the state paid a chaplain or whether such an individual prayed without such remuneration? Would the practice have been more or less acceptable if the position been had rotated among different denominations?

WALLACE V. JAFFREE

472 U.S. 38, 105 S.Ct. 2479, 86 L.Ed.2d 29 (1985)

This review of an Alabama law, apparently designed to signal that classroom moments of silence could be used for school prayer, is perhaps more important for the stances that the justices outlined on the Establishment Clause than for the decision itself. Justice John Paul Stevens largely relied on the *Lemon* test; Justice Sandra Day O'Connor outlined an endorsement test; and Justice Rehnquist cited history both to refute the idea that the Establishment Clause created a wall of separation between church and state and to show that the goals of the clause were more modest than the Court had recognized.

Vote: 6–3

JUSTICE STEVENS wrote the majority opinion.

I

Appellee Ishmael Jaffree is a resident of Mobile County, Alabama. On May 28, 1982, he filed a complaint on behalf of three of his minor children; two of them were second-grade students and the third was then in kindergarten. The complaint named members of the Mobile County School Board, various school officials, and the minor plaintiffs' three teachers as defendants. The complaint alleged that the appellees brought the action "seeking principally a declaratory judgment and an injunction restraining the Defendants and each of them from maintaining or allowing the maintenance of regular religious prayer services or other forms of religious observances in the Mobile County Public Schools in violation of the First Amendment as made applicable to states by the Fourteenth Amendment to the United States Constitution." The complaint further alleged that two of the children had been subjected to various acts of religious indoctrination "from the beginning of the school year in September, 1981"; that the defendant teachers had "on a daily basis" led their classes in saying certain prayers in unison; that the minor children were exposed to ostracism from their peer group class members if they did not participate; and that Ishmael Jaffree had repeatedly but unsuccessfully requested that the devotional services be stopped. The original complaint made no reference to any Alabama statute.

II

Our unanimous affirmance of the Court of Appeals' judgment concerning § 16–1–20.2 makes it unnecessary to comment at length on the District Court's remarkable conclusion that the Federal Constitution imposes no obstacle to Alabama's establishment of a state religion. Before analyzing the precise issue that is presented to us, it is nevertheless appropriate to recall how firmly embedded in our constitutional jurisprudence is the proposition that the several States have no greater power to restrain the individual freedoms protected by the First Amendment than does the Congress of the United States.

The State of Alabama, no less than the Congress of the United States, must respect that basic truth.

III

When the Court has been called upon to construe the breadth of the Establishment Clause, it has examined the criteria developed over a period of many years. Thus, in *Lemon v. Kurtzman,* 403 U.S. 602 (1971), we wrote: "Every analysis in this area must begin with consideration of the cumulative criteria developed by the Court over many years. Three such tests may be gleaned from our cases. First, the statute must have a secular legislative purpose; second, its principal or primary effect must be one that neither advances nor inhibits religion, *Board of Education v. Allen,* 392 U.S. 236 (1968); finally, the statute must not foster " 'an excessive government entanglement with religion.' "

It is the first of these three criteria that is most plainly implicated by this case. As the District Court correctly recognized, no consideration of the second or third criteria is necessary if a statute does not have a clearly secular purpose. For even though a statute that is motivated in part by a religious purpose may satisfy the first criterion, the First Amendment requires that a statute must be invalidated if it is entirely motivated by a purpose to advance religion.

In applying the purpose test, it is appropriate to ask "whether government's actual purpose is to endorse or disapprove of religion." In this case, the answer to that question is dispositive. For the record not only provides us with an unambiguous affirmative answer, but it also reveals that the enactment of § 16–1–20.1 was not motivated by any clearly secular purpose—indeed, the statute had *no* secular purpose.

IV

The sponsor of the bill that became § 16–1–20.1, Senator Donald Holmes, inserted into the legislative record—apparently without dissent—a statement indicating that the legislation was an "effort to return voluntary prayer" to the public schools. Later Senator Holmes confirmed this purpose before the District Court. In response to the question whether he had any purpose for the legislation other than returning voluntary prayer to public schools, he stated: "No, I did not have no other purpose in mind." The State did not present evidence of *any* secular purpose.

The unrebutted evidence of legislative intent contained in the legislative record and in the testimony of the sponsor of § 16–1–20.1 is confirmed by a consideration of the relationship between this statute and the two other measures that were considered in this case. The District Court found that the 1981 statute and its 1982 sequel had a common, nonsecular purpose. The wholly religious character of the later enactment is plainly evident from its text. When the differences between § 16–1–20.1 and its 1978 predecessor, § 16–1–20, are examined, it is equally clear that the 1981 statute has the same wholly religious character.

The legislative intent to return prayer to the public schools is, of course, quite different from merely protecting every student's right to engage in voluntary prayer during an appropriate moment of silence during the schoolday. The 1978 statute already protected that right, containing nothing that prevented any student from engaging in voluntary prayer during a silent minute of meditation. Appellants have not identified any secular purpose that was not fully served by § 16–1–20 before the enactment of § 16–1–20.1. Thus, only two conclusions are consistent with the text of § 16–1–20.1: (1) the statute was enacted to convey a message of state endorsement and promotion of prayer; or (2) the statute was enacted for no purpose. No one suggests that the statute was nothing but a meaningless or irrational act.

We must, therefore, conclude that the Alabama Legislature intended to change existing law and that it was motivated by the same purpose that the Governor's answer to the second amended complaint expressly admitted; that the statement inserted in the legislative history revealed; and that Senator Holmes' testimony frankly described. The legislature enacted § 16–1–20.1, despite the existence of § 16–1–20 for the sole purpose of expressing the State's endorsement of prayer activities for one minute at the beginning of each schoolday. The addition of "or voluntary prayer" indicates that the State intended to characterize prayer as a favored practice. Such an endorsement is not consistent with the established principle that the government must pursue a course of complete neutrality toward religion.

The importance of that principle does not permit us to treat this as an inconsequential case involving nothing more than a few words of symbolic speech on behalf of the political majority. For whenever the State itself speaks on a religious subject, one of the questions that we must ask is "whether the government intends to convey a message of endorsement or disapproval of religion." The well-supported concurrent findings of the District Court and the Court of Appeals—that § 16–1–20.1 was intended to convey a message of state approval of prayer activities in the public schools—make it unnecessary, and indeed inappropriate, to evaluate the practical significance of the addition of the words "or voluntary prayer" to the statute. Keeping in mind, as we must, "both the fundamental place held by the Establishment Clause in our constitutional scheme and the myriad, subtle ways in which Establishment Clause values can be eroded," we conclude that § 16–1–20.1 violates the First Amendment.

The judgment of the Court of Appeals is affirmed.

JUSTICE POWELL, concurring.

I concur in the Court's opinion and judgment that Ala. Code § 16–1–20.1 (Supp. 1984) violates the Establishment Clause of the First Amendment. My concurrence is prompted by Alabama's persistence in attempting to institute state-sponsored prayer in the public schools by enacting three successive statutes. I agree fully with Justice O'Connor's assertion that some moment-of-silence statutes may be constitutional, a suggestion set forth in the Court's opinion as well.

I write separately to express additional views and to respond to criticism of the three-pronged *Lemon* test. *Lemon v. Kurtzman,* 403 U.S. 602 (1971) identifies standards that have proved useful in analyzing case after case both in our decisions and in those of other courts. It is the only coherent test a majority of the Court has ever adopted. Only once since our decision in *Lemon,* have we addressed an Establishment Clause issue without resort to its three-pronged test. See *Marsh v. Chambers,* 463 U.S. 783 (1983). *Lemon* has not been overruled or its test modified. Yet, continued criticism of it could encourage other courts to feel free to decide Establishment Clause cases on an ad hoc basis.

JUSTICE O'CONNOR, concurring in the judgment.

Nothing in the United States Constitution as interpreted by this Court or in the laws of the State of Alabama prohibits public school students from voluntarily praying at any time before, during, or after the schoolday. Alabama has facilitated voluntary silent prayers of students who are so inclined by enacting Ala. Code § 16–1–20 (Supp. 1984), which provides a moment of silence in appellees' schools each day. The parties to these proceedings concede the validity of this enactment. At issue in these appeals is the constitutional validity of an additional and subsequent Alabama statute, which both the District Court and the Court of Appeals concluded was enacted solely to officially encourage prayer during the moment of silence. I agree with the judgment of the Court that, in light of the findings of the courts below and the history of its enactment, § 16–1–20.1 of the Alabama Code violates the Establishment Clause of the First Amendment. In my view, there can be little doubt that the purpose and likely effect of this subsequent enactment is to endorse and sponsor voluntary prayer in the public schools. I write separately to identify the peculiar features of the Alabama law that render it invalid, and to explain why moment of silence laws in other States do not necessarily manifest the same infirmity. I also write to explain why neither history nor the Free Exercise Clause of the First Amendment validates the Alabama law struck down by the Court today.

I

The Religion Clauses of the First Amendment, coupled with the Fourteenth Amendment's guarantee of ordered liberty, preclude both the Nation and the States from making any law respecting an establishment of religion or prohibiting the free exercise thereof. *Cantwell v. Connecticut,* 310 U.S. 296 (1940). Although a distinct jurisprudence has enveloped each of these Clauses, their common purpose is to secure religious liberty. See *Engel v. Vitale,* 370 U.S. 421 (1962). On these principles, the Court has been and remains unanimous.

As these cases once again demonstrate, however, "it is far easier to agree on the purpose that underlies the First Amendment's Establishment and Free Exercise Clauses than to obtain agreement on the standards that should govern their application." *Walz v. Tax Comm'n,* 397 U.S. 664 (1970). It once appeared that the Court had developed a workable standard by which to identify impermissible government establishments of religion. See *Lemon v. Kurtzman,* 403 U.S. 602 (1971). Under the now familiar *Lemon* test, statutes must have both a secular legislative purpose and a principal or primary effect that neither advances nor inhibits religion, and in addition they must not foster excessive government entanglement with religion. Despite its initial promise, the *Lemon* test has proved problematic. The required inquiry into "entanglement" has been modified and questioned, see *Mueller v. Allen,* 463 U.S. 388 (1983), and in one case we have upheld state action against an Establishment Clause challenge without applying the *Lemon* test at all. *Marsh v. Chambers,* 463 U.S. 783 (1983). The author of *Lemon* himself apparently questions the test's general applicability. See *Lynch v. Donnelly,* 465 U.S. 668 (1984). Justice Rehnquist today suggests that we abandon *Lemon* entirely, and in the process limit the reach of the Establishment Clause to state discrimination between sects and government designation of a particular church as a "state" or "national" one.

Perhaps because I am new to the struggle, I am not ready to abandon all aspects of the *Lemon* test. I do believe, however, that the standards announced in *Lemon* should be reexamined and refined in order to make them more useful in achieving the underlying purpose of the First Amendment.

The *Lynch* concurrence suggested that the religious liberty protected by the Establishment Clause is infringed when the government makes adherence to religion relevant to a person's standing in the political community. Direct government action endorsing religion or a particular religious practice is invalid under this approach because it "sends a message to nonadherents that they are outsiders, not full members of the political community, and an accompanying message to adherents that they are insiders, favored members of the political community." Under this view, *Lemon*'s inquiry as to the purpose and effect of a statute requires courts to examine whether government's purpose is to endorse religion and whether the statute actually conveys a message of endorsement.

The endorsement test is useful because of the analytic content it gives to the *Lemon*-mandated inquiry into legislative purpose and effect. In this country, church and state must necessarily operate within the same community. Because of this coexistence, it is inevitable that the secular interests of government and the religious interests of various sects and their adherents will frequently intersect, conflict, and combine. A statute that ostensibly promotes a secular interest often has an incidental or even a primary effect of helping or hindering a sectarian belief. Chaos would ensue if every such statute were invalid under the Establishment Clause. For example, the State could not criminalize murder for fear that it would thereby promote the Biblical command against killing. The task for the Court is to sort out those statutes and government practices whose purpose and effect go against the grain of religious liberty protected by the First Amendment.

The endorsement test does not preclude government from acknowledging religion or from taking religion into account in making law and policy. It does preclude government from conveying or attempting to convey a message that religion or a particular religious belief is favored or preferred. Such an endorsement infringes the religious liberty of the nonadherent, for "[when] the power, prestige and financial support of government is placed behind a particular religious belief, the indirect coercive pressure upon religious minorities to conform to the prevailing officially approved religion is plain." *Engel v. Vitale.* At issue today is whether state moment of silence statutes in general, and Alabama's moment of silence statute in particular, embody an impermissible endorsement of prayer in public schools.

A

Twenty-five states permit or require public school teachers to have students observe a moment of silence in their classrooms.

A state-sponsored moment of silence in the public schools is different from state-sponsored vocal prayer or Bible reading. First, a moment of silence is not inherently religious. Silence, unlike prayer or Bible reading, need not be associated with a religious exercise. Second, a pupil who participates in a moment of silence need not compromise his or her beliefs. During a moment of silence, a student who objects to prayer is left to his or her own thoughts, and is not compelled to listen to the prayers or thoughts of others. For these simple reasons, a moment of silence statute does not stand or fall under the Establishment Clause according to how the Court regards vocal prayer or Bible reading

By mandating a moment of silence, a State does not necessarily endorse any activity that might occur during the period. "[Whether] a government activity communicates endorsement of religion is not a question of simple historical fact. Although evidentiary submissions may help answer it, the question is, like the question whether racial or sex-based classifications communicate an invidious message, in large part a legal question to be answered on the basis of judicial interpretation of social facts." The relevant issue is whether an objective observer, acquainted with the text, legislative history, and implementation of the statute, would perceive it as a state endorsement of prayer in public schools. A moment of silence law that is clearly drafted and implemented so as to permit prayer, meditation, and reflection within the prescribed period, without endorsing one alternative over the others, should pass this test.

B

The analysis above suggests that moment of silence laws in many States should pass Establishment Clause scrutiny because they do not favor the child who chooses to pray during a moment of silence over the child who chooses to meditate or reflect. Alabama Code § 16–1–20.1 (Supp. 1984) does not stand on the same footing. However deferentially one examines its text and legislative history, however objectively one views the message attempted to be conveyed to the public, the conclusion is unavoidable that the purpose of the statute is to endorse prayer in public schools. I accordingly agree with the Court of Appeals, that the Alabama statute has a purpose which is in violation of the Establishment Clause, and cannot be upheld.

CHIEF JUSTICE BURGER, dissenting.

Some who trouble to read the opinions in these cases will find it ironic—perhaps even bizarre—that on the very day we heard arguments in the cases, the Court's session opened with an invocation for Divine protection. Across the park a few hundred yards away, the House of Representatives and the Senate regularly open each session with a prayer. These legislative prayers are not just one minute in duration, but are extended, thoughtful invocations and prayers for Divine guidance. They are given, as they have been since 1789, by clergy appointed as official chaplains and paid from the Treasury of the United States. Congress has also provided chapels in the Capitol, at public expense, where Members and others may pause for prayer, meditation—or a moment of silence.

Inevitably some wag is bound to say that the Court's holding today reflects a belief that the historic practice of the Congress and this Court is justified because members of the Judiciary and Congress are more in need of Divine guidance than are schoolchildren. Still others will say that all this controversy is "much ado about nothing," since no power on earth—including this Court and Congress—can stop any teacher from opening the schoolday with a moment of silence for pupils to meditate, to plan their day—or to pray if they voluntarily elect to do so.

JUSTICE REHNQUIST, dissenting.

Thirty-eight years ago this Court, in *Everson v. Board of Education,* 330 U.S. 1 (1947), summarized its exegesis of Establishment Clause doctrine thus: "In the words of Jefferson, the clause against establishment of religion by law was intended to erect 'a wall of separation between church and State.' *Reynolds v. United States,* 98 U.S. 145 (1879)."

This language from *Reynolds*, a case involving the Free Exercise Clause of the First Amendment rather than the Establishment Clause, quoted from Thomas Jefferson's letter to the Danbury Baptist Association the phrase "I contemplate with sovereign reverence that act of the whole American people which declared that their legislature should 'make no law respecting an establishment of religion, or prohibiting the free exercise thereof,' thus building a wall of separation between church and State."

It is impossible to build sound constitutional doctrine upon a mistaken understanding of constitutional history, but unfortunately the Establishment Clause has been expressly freighted with Jefferson's misleading metaphor for nearly 40 years. Thomas Jefferson was of course in France at the time the constitutional Amendments known as the Bill of Rights were passed by Congress and ratified by the States. His letter to the Danbury Baptist Association was a short note of courtesy, written 14 years after the Amendments were passed by Congress. He would seem to any detached observer as a less than ideal source of contemporary history as to the meaning of the Religion Clauses of the First Amendment.

Jefferson's fellow Virginian, James Madison, with whom he was joined in the battle for the enactment of the Virginia Statute of Religious Liberty of 1786, did play as large a part as anyone in the drafting of the Bill of Rights. He had two advantages over Jefferson in this regard: he was present in the United States, and he was a leading Member of the First Congress. But when we turn to the record of the proceedings in the First Congress leading up to the adoption of the Establishment Clause of the Constitution, including Madison's significant contributions thereto, we see a far different picture of its purpose than the highly simplified "wall of separation between church and State."

[Rehnquist summarizes how Madison responded to Anti-Federalist criticisms by proposing the Bill of Rights.]

The language Madison proposed for what ultimately became the Religion Clauses of the First Amendment was this: "The civil rights of none shall be abridged on account of religious belief or worship, nor shall any national religion be established, nor shall the full and equal rights of conscience be in any manner, or on any pretext, infringed."

[Rehnquist followed with an extensive review of the foundations of the First Amendment.]

It seems indisputable from these glimpses of Madison's thinking, as reflected by actions on the floor of the House in 1789, that he saw the Amendment as designed to prohibit the establishment of a national religion, and perhaps to prevent discrimination among sects. He did not see it as requiring neutrality on the part of government between religion and irreligion. Thus the Court's opinion in *Everson*—while correct in bracketing Madison and Jefferson together in their exertions in their home State leading to the enactment of the Virginia Statute of Religious Liberty—is totally incorrect in suggesting that Madison carried these views onto the floor of the United States House of Representatives when he proposed the language which would ultimately become the Bill of Rights.

The repetition of this error in the Court's opinion in *Illinois ex rel. McCollum v. Board of Education,* 333 U.S. 203 (1948), and *Engel v. Vitale,* 370 U.S. 421 (1962), does not make it any sounder historically. Finally, in *Abington School District v. Schempp,* 374 U.S. 203 (1963), the Court made the truly remarkable statement that "the views of Madison and Jefferson, preceded by Roger Williams, came to be incorporated not only in the Federal Constitution but likewise in those of most of our States." On the basis of what evidence we have, this statement is demonstrably incorrect as a matter of history. And its repetition in varying forms in succeeding opinions of the Court can give it no more authority than it possesses as a matter of fact; *stare decisis* may bind courts as to matters of law, but it cannot bind them as to matters of history.

[Rehnquist engages in an extensive review of governmental acknowledgments of religion in U.S. history.]

It would seem from this evidence that the Establishment Clause of the First Amendment had acquired a well-accepted meaning: it forbade establishment of a national religion, and forbade preference among religious sects or denominations. Indeed, the first American dictionary defined the word "establishment" as "the act of establishing, founding, ratifying or ordaining," such as in "[the] episcopal form of religion, so called, in England." 1 N. Webster, *American Dictionary of the English Language* (1st ed. 1828). The Establishment Clause did not require government neutrality between religion and irreligion nor did it prohibit the Federal Government from providing nondiscriminatory aid to religion. There is simply no historical foundation for the proposition that the Framers intended to build the "wall of separation" that was constitutionalized in *Everson.*

Notwithstanding the absence of a historical basis for this theory of rigid separation, the wall idea might well have served as a useful albeit misguided analytical concept, had it led this Court to unified and principled results in Establishment Clause cases. The opposite, unfortunately, has been true; in the 38 years since *Everson* our Establishment Clause cases have been neither principled nor unified. Our recent opinions, many of them hopelessly divided pluralities, have with embarrassing candor conceded that the "wall of separation" is merely a "blurred, indistinct, and variable barrier," which "is not wholly accurate" and can only be "dimly perceived." *Lemon* v. *Kurtzman,* 403 U.S. 602 (1971); *Tilton v. Richardson,* 403 U.S. 672 (1971); *Wolman v. Walter,* 433 U.S. 229 (1977); *Lynch v. Donnelly,* 465 U.S. 668 (1984).

[Rehnquist further reviews what he considered to be inconsistencies in interpreting the Establishment Clause.]

The Framers intended the Establishment Clause to prohibit the designation of any church as a "national" one. The Clause was also designed to stop the Federal Government from asserting a preference for one religious denomination or sect over others. Given the "incorporation" of the Establishment Clause as against the States via the Fourteenth Amendment in *Everson,* States are prohibited as well from establishing a religion or discriminating between sects. As its history abundantly shows, however, nothing in the Establishment Clause requires government to be strictly neutral between religion and irreligion, nor does that Clause prohibit Congress or the States from pursuing legitimate secular ends through nondiscriminatory sectarian means.

The Court strikes down the Alabama statute because the State wished to "characterize prayer as a favored practice." It would come as much of a shock to those who drafted the Bill of Rights as it will to a large number of thoughtful Americans today to learn that the Constitution, as construed by the majority, prohibits the Alabama Legislature from "endorsing" prayer. George Washington himself, at the request of the very Congress which passed the Bill of Rights, proclaimed a day of "public thanksgiving and prayer, to be observed by acknowledging with grateful hearts the many and signal favors of Almighty God." History must judge whether it was the Father of his Country in 1789, or a majority of the Court today, which has strayed from the meaning of the Establishment Clause.

FOR DISCUSSION

This case is perhaps best known for the justices' articulation of rival approaches to interpreting the Establishment Clause. What are the approaches of the majority? Of Justice O'Connor? Of the dissenters? What are the central strengths and weaknesses of each approach? How, if at all, are these approaches linked to different methods of constitutional interpretation? Is there a way of deciding which method works best within a given area of the law? If so, what is it?

SANTA FE INDEPENDENT SCHOOL DISTRICT V. DOE

530 U.S. 290, 120 S.Ct. 2266, 147 L.Ed.2d 295 (2000)

In *Lee v. Weisman* (505 U.S. 577, 1992), the Court decided that a school district had violated the Establishment Clause by selecting a member of the clergy to deliver invocations and benedictions at high school graduations. The opinion, written by Justice Anthony Kennedy, is probably most notable for Kennedy's concern that the practice had a coercive effect on students in attendance, who would have to decide whether to stand and/or bow their heads during such prayers. In dissent, Justice Antonin Scalia argued that the Court had no way of assessing psychological coercion and that it should limit its concerns to actual coercion through threat of law or penalty or to actual financial support of such activities. In *Santa Fe*, the school attempted to avoid the implications of Lee by allowing students to decide whether to pray at football games and to choose the individuals who would deliver such prayers.

Vote: 6–3

JUSTICE STEVENS delivered the opinion of the Court.

Prior to 1995, the Santa Fe High School student who occupied the school's elective office of student council chaplain delivered a prayer over the public address system before each varsity football game for the entire season. This practice, along with others, was challenged in District Court as a violation of the Establishment Clause of the First Amendment. While these proceedings were pending in the District Court, the school district adopted a different policy that permits, but does not require, prayer initiated and led by a student at all home games. The District Court entered an order modifying that policy to permit only nonsectarian, nonproselytizing prayer. The Court of Appeals held that, even as modified by the District Court, the football prayer policy was invalid. We granted the school district's petition for certiorari to review that holding.

I

The Santa Fe Independent School District (District) is a political subdivision of the State of Texas, responsible for the education of more than 4,000 students in a small community in the southern part of the State. The District includes the Santa Fe High School, two primary schools, an intermediate school and the junior high school. Respondents are two sets of current or former students and their respective mothers. One family is Mormon and the other is Catholic. The District Court permitted respondents (Does) to litigate anonymously to protect them from intimidation or harassment.

Respondents commenced this action in April 1995 and moved for a temporary restraining order to prevent the District from violating the Establishment Clause at the imminent graduation exercises. In their complaint the Does alleged that the District had engaged in several proselytizing practices, such as promoting attendance at a Baptist revival meeting, encouraging membership in religious clubs, chastising children who held minority religious beliefs, and distributing Gideon Bibles on school premises. They also alleged that the District allowed students to read Christian invocations and benedictions from the stage at graduation ceremonies, and to deliver overtly Christian prayers over the public address system at home football games.

On May 10, 1995, the District Court entered an interim order addressing a number of different issues. With respect to the impending graduation, the order provided that "non-denominational prayer" consisting of "an invocation and/or benediction" could be presented by a senior student or students selected by members of the graduating class. The text of the prayer was to be determined by the students, without scrutiny or preapproval by school officials. References to particular religious figures "such as Mohammed, Jesus, Buddha, or the like" would be permitted "as long as the general thrust of the prayer is non-proselytizing."

In response to that portion of the order, the District adopted a series of policies over several months dealing with prayer at school functions. The policies enacted in May and July for graduation ceremonies provided the format for the August and October policies for football games. The May policy provided: "The board has chosen to permit the graduating senior class, with the advice and counsel of the senior class principal or designee, to elect by secret ballot to choose whether an invocation and benediction shall be part of the graduation exercise. If so chosen the class shall elect by secret ballot, from a list of student volunteers, students to deliver nonsectarian, nonproselytizing invocations and benedictions for the purpose of solemnizing their graduation ceremonies."

The parties stipulated that after this policy was adopted, "the senior class held an election to determine whether to have an invocation and benediction at the commencement [and that the] class voted, by secret ballot, to include prayer at the high school graduation." In a second vote the class elected two seniors to deliver the invocation and benediction.

In July, the District enacted another policy eliminating the requirement that invocations and benedictions be "nonsectarian and nonproselytising," but also providing that if the District were to be enjoined from enforcing that policy, the May policy would automatically become effective.

The August policy, which was titled "Prayer at Football Games," was similar to the July policy for graduations. It also authorized two student elections, the first to determine whether "invocations" should be delivered, and the second to select the spokesperson to deliver them. Like the July policy, it contained two parts, an initial statement that omitted any requirement that the content of the invocation be "nonsectarian and nonproselytising," and a fallback provision that automatically added that limitation if the preferred policy should be enjoined. On August 31, 1995, according to the parties' stipulation, "the district's high school students voted to determine whether a student would deliver prayer at varsity football games. . . . The students chose to allow a student to say a prayer at football games." A week later, in a separate election, they selected a student "to deliver the prayer at varsity football games."

The final policy (October policy) is essentially the same as the August policy, though it omits the word "prayer" from its title, and refers to "messages" and "statements" as well as "invocations." It is the validity of that policy that is before us.

We granted the District's petition for certiorari, limited to the following question: "Whether petitioner's policy permitting student-led, student-initiated prayer at football games violates the Establishment Clause." We conclude, as did the Court of Appeals, that it does.

II

The first Clause in the First Amendment to the Federal Constitution provides that "Congress shall make no law respecting an establishment of religion, or prohibiting the free exercise thereof." The Fourteenth Amendment imposes those substantive limitations on the legislative power of the States and their political subdivisions. In *Lee v. Weisman,* 505 U.S. 577 (1992), we held that a prayer delivered by a rabbi at a middle school graduation ceremony violated that Clause. Although this case involves student prayer at a different type of school function, our analysis is properly guided by the principles that we endorsed in *Lee.*

In this case the District first argues that this principle is inapplicable to its October policy because the messages are private student speech, not public speech. It reminds us that "there is a crucial difference between *government* speech endorsing religion, which the Establishment Clause forbids, and *private* speech endorsing religion, which the Free Speech and Free Exercise Clauses protect." We certainly agree with that distinction, but we are not persuaded that the pregame invocations should be regarded as "private speech."

These invocations are authorized by a government policy and take place on government property at government-sponsored school-related events. Of course, not every message delivered under such circumstances is the government's own. We have held, for example, that an individual's contribution to a government-created forum was not government speech. Although the District relies heavily on *Rosenberger v. Rector and Visitors of the University of Virginia,* 515 U.S. 819 (1995), and similar cases involving such forums, it is clear that the pregame ceremony is not the type of forum discussed in those cases. The Santa Fe school officials simply do not "evince either 'by policy or by practice,' any intent to open the [pregame ceremony] to 'indiscriminate use,' . . . by the student body generally." *Hazelwood School Dist. v. Kuhlmeier,* 484 U.S. 260 (1988). Rather, the school allows only one student, the same student for the entire season, to give the invocation. The statement or invocation, moreover, is subject to particular regulations that confine the content and topic of the student's message.

Granting only one student access to the stage at a time does not, of course, necessarily preclude a finding that a school has created a limited public forum. Here, however, Santa Fe's student election system ensures that only those messages deemed "appropriate" under the District's policy may be delivered. That is, the majoritarian process implemented by the District guarantees, by definition, that minority candidates will never prevail and that their views will be effectively silenced.

Like the student referendum for funding [of student activities] in *Board of Regents of Univ. of Wis. System v. Southworth,* 529 U.S. 217 (2000), this student election does nothing to protect minority views but rather places the students who hold such views at the mercy of the majority. Because "fundamental rights may not be submitted to vote; they depend on the outcome of no elections," *West Virginia Bd. of Ed. v. Barnette,* 319 U.S. 624 (1943), the District's elections are insufficient safeguards of diverse student speech.

In *Lee,* the school district made the related argument that its policy of endorsing only "civic or nonsectarian" prayer was acceptable because it minimized the intrusion on the audience as a whole. We rejected that claim by explaining that such a majoritarian policy "does not lessen the offense or isolation to the objectors. At best it narrows their number, at worst increases their sense of isolation and affront." Similarly, while Santa Fe's majoritarian election might ensure that *most* of the students are represented, it does nothing to protect the minority; indeed, it likely serves to intensify their offense.

Moreover, the District has failed to divorce itself from the religious content in the invocations. It has not succeeded in doing so, either by claiming that its policy is " 'one of neutrality rather than endorsement' " or by characterizing the individual student as the "circuit-breaker" in the process. Contrary to the District's repeated assertions that it has adopted a "hands-off" approach to the pregame invocation, the realities of the situation plainly reveal that its policy involves both perceived and actual endorsement of religion. In this case, as we found in *Lee,* the "degree of school involvement" makes it clear that the pregame prayers bear "the imprint of the State and thus put school-age children who objected in an untenable position."

The District has attempted to disentangle itself from the religious messages by developing the two-step student election process. The text of the October policy, however, exposes the extent of the school's entanglement. The elections take place at all only because the school "board *has chosen to permit* students to deliver a brief invocation and/or message." The elections thus "shall" be conducted "by the high school student council" and "upon advice and direction of the high school principal." The decision whether to deliver a message is first made by majority vote of the entire student body, followed by a choice of the speaker in a separate, similar majority election. Even though the particular words used by the speaker are not determined by those votes, the policy mandates that the "statement or invocation" be "consistent with the goals and purposes of this policy," which are "to solemnize the event, to promote good sportsmanship and student safety, and to establish the appropriate environment for the competition."

In addition to involving the school in the selection of the speaker, the policy, by its terms, invites and encourages religious messages. The policy itself states that the purpose of the message is "to solemnize the event." A religious message is the most obvious method of solemnizing an event. Moreover, the requirements that the message "promote good citizenship" and "establish the appropriate environment for competition" further narrow the types of message deemed appropriate, suggesting that a solemn, yet nonreligious, message, such as commentary on United States foreign policy, would be prohibited. Indeed, the only type of message that is expressly endorsed in the text is an "invocation"—a term that primarily describes an appeal for divine assistance. In fact, as used in the past at Santa Fe High School, an "invocation" has always entailed a focused religious message. Thus, the expressed purposes of the policy encourage the selection of a religious message, and that is precisely how the students understand the policy.

The actual or perceived endorsement of the message, moreover, is established by factors beyond just the text of the policy. Once the student speaker is selected and the message composed, the invocation is then delivered to a large audience assembled as part of a regularly scheduled, school-sponsored function conducted on school property. The message is broadcast over the school's public address system, which remains subject to the control of school officials. It is fair to assume that the pregame ceremony is clothed in the traditional indicia of school sporting events, which generally include not just the team, but also cheerleaders and band members dressed in uniforms sporting the school name and mascot. The school's name is likely written in large print across the field and on banners and flags. The crowd will certainly include many who display the school colors and insignia on their school T-shirts, jackets, or hats and who may also be waving signs displaying the school name. It is in a setting such as this that "the board has chosen to permit" the elected student to rise and give the "statement or invocation."

In this context the members of the listening audience must perceive the pregame message as a public expression of the views of the majority of the student body delivered with the approval of the school administration. In cases involving state participation in a religious activity, one of the relevant questions is "whether an objective observer, acquainted with the text, legislative history, and implementation of the statute, would perceive it as a state endorsement of prayer in public schools."

According to the District, the secular purposes of the policy are to "foster free expression of private persons . . . as well [as to] solemnize sporting events, promote good sportsmanship and student safety, and establish an appropriate environment for competition." We note, however, that the District's approval of only one specific kind of message, an "invocation," is not necessary to further any of these purposes. Additionally, the fact that only one student is permitted to give a content-limited message suggests that this policy does little to "foster free expression." Furthermore, regardless of whether one considers a sporting event an appropriate occasion for solemnity, the use of an invocation to foster such solemnity is impermissible when, in actuality, it constitutes prayer sponsored by the school. And it is unclear what type of message would be both appropriately "solemnizing" under the District's policy and yet non-religious.

Most striking to us is the evolution of the current policy from the long-sanctioned office of "Student Chaplain" to the candidly titled "Prayer at Football Games" regulation. This history indicates that the District intended to preserve the practice of prayer before football games.

School sponsorship of a religious message is impermissible because it sends the ancillary message to members of the audience who are nonadherents "that they are outsiders, not full members of the political community, and an accompanying message to adherents that they are insiders, favored members of the political community." *Lynch* v. *Donnelly,* 465 U.S. 668 (1984). The delivery of such a message—over the school's public address system, by a speaker representing the student body, under the supervision of school faculty, and pursuant to a school policy that explicitly and implicitly encourages public prayer—is not properly characterized as "private" speech.

III

The District next argues that its football policy is distinguishable from the graduation prayer in *Lee* because it does not coerce students to participate in religious observances. Its argument has two parts: first, that there is no impermissible government coercion because the pregame messages are the product of student choices; and second, that there is really no coercion at all because attendance at an extracurricular event, unlike a graduation ceremony, is voluntary.

The reasons just discussed explaining why the alleged "circuit-breaker" mechanism of the dual elections and student speaker do not turn public speech into private speech also demonstrate why these mechanisms do not insulate the school from the coercive element of the final message. In fact, this aspect of the District's argument exposes anew the concerns that are created by the majoritarian election system. The parties' stipulation clearly states that the issue resolved in the first election was "whether a student would deliver prayer at varsity football games," and the controversy in this case demonstrates that the views of the students are not unanimous on that issue.

One of the purposes served by the Establishment Clause is to remove debate over this kind of issue from governmental supervision or control. We explained in *Lee* that the "preservation and transmission of religious beliefs and worship is a responsibility and a choice committed to the private sphere." The two student elections authorized by the policy, coupled with the debates that presumably must precede each, impermissibly invade that private sphere.

The District further argues that attendance at the commencement ceremonies at issue in *Lee* "differs dramatically" from attendance at high school football games, which it contends "are of no more than passing interest to many students" and are "decidedly extracurricular," thus dissipating any coercion. Attendance at a high school football game, unlike showing up for class, is certainly not required in order to receive a diploma. Moreover, we may assume that the District is correct in arguing that the informal pressure to attend an athletic event is not as strong as a senior's desire to attend her own graduation ceremony.

There are some students, however, such as cheerleaders, members of the band, and, of course, the team members themselves, for whom seasonal commitments mandate their attendance, sometimes for class credit. The District also minimizes the importance to many students of attending and participating in extracurricular activities as part of a complete educational experience. As we noted in *Lee*, "law reaches past formalism." To assert that high school students do not feel immense social pressure, or have a truly genuine desire, to be involved in the extracurricular event that is American high school football is "formalistic in the extreme."

Even if we regard every high school student's decision to attend a home football game as purely voluntary, we are nevertheless persuaded that the delivery of a pregame prayer has the improper effect of coercing those present to participate in an act of religious worship. For "the government may no more use social pressure to enforce orthodoxy than it may use more direct means." As in *Lee*, "what to most believers may seem nothing more than a reasonable request that the nonbeliever respect their religious practices, in a school context may appear to the nonbeliever or dissenter to be an attempt to employ the machinery of the State to enforce a religious orthodoxy." The constitutional command will not permit the District "to exact religious conformity from a student as the price" of joining her classmates at a varsity football game.

CHIEF JUSTICE REHNQUIST, with whom JUSTICES SCALIA and THOMAS join, dissenting.

The Court distorts existing precedent to conclude that the school district's student-message program is invalid on its face under the Establishment Clause. But even more disturbing than its holding is the tone of the Court's opinion; it bristles with hostility to all things religious in public life. Neither the holding nor the tone of the opinion is faithful to the meaning of the Establishment Clause, when it is recalled that George Washington himself, at the request of the very Congress which passed the Bill of Rights, proclaimed a day of "public thanksgiving and prayer, to be observed by acknowledging with grateful hearts the many and signal favors of Almighty God."

We do not learn until late in the Court's opinion that respondents in this case challenged the district's student-message program at football games before it had been put into practice.

The Court, venturing into the realm of prophecy, decides that it "need not wait for the inevitable" and invalidates the district's policy on its face.

Even if it were appropriate to apply the *Lemon* test here, the district's student-message policy should not be invalidated on its face. The policy at issue here may be applied in an unconstitutional manner, but it will be time enough to invalidate it if that is found to be the case. I would reverse the judgment of the Court of Appeals.

FOR DISCUSSION

To what degree is it appropriate for the Court to consider students at a football game and/or a graduation ceremony to be members of a "captive audience"? What, if anything, could or should a court do if confronted with a case that arose because a crowd of students or parents began reciting the Lord's Prayer in unison at such an event?

ZELMAN V. SIMMONS HARRIS

536 U.S. 639, 122 S.Ct. 2460, 153 L.Ed. 2d 604 (2002)

This case deals with a pilot project scholarship program that directed state money for poor parents in Cleveland, Ohio, to use toward tuition and tutoring at public and private schools of the parents' choosing. Most participating families had chosen parochial schools. The U.S. Circuit Court had ruled that the program violated the Establishment Clause.

Vote: 5–4

CHIEF JUSTICE REHNQUIST delivered the opinion of the Court.

The program has been in operation within the Cleveland City School District since the 1996–1997 school year. In the 1999–2000 school year, 56 private schools participated in the program, 46 (or 82%) of which had a religious affiliation. None of the public schools in districts adjacent to Cleveland have elected to participate. More than 3,700 students participated in the scholarship program, most of whom (96%) enrolled in religiously affiliated schools. Sixty percent of these students were from families at or below the poverty line. . . .

The Establishment Clause of the First Amendment, applied to the States through the Fourteenth Amendment, prevents a State from enacting laws that have the "purpose" or "effect" of advancing or inhibiting religion. There is no dispute that the program challenged here was enacted for the valid secular purpose of providing educational assistance to poor children in a demonstrably failing public school system. Thus, the question presented is whether the Ohio program nonetheless has the forbidden "effect" of advancing or inhibiting religion.

To answer that question, our decisions have drawn a consistent distinction between government programs that provide aid directly to religious schools, and programs of true private choice, in which government aid reaches religious schools only as a result of the genuine and independent choices of private individuals. While our jurisprudence with respect to the constitutionality of direct aid programs has "changed significantly" over the past two decades, our jurisprudence with respect to true private choice programs has remained consistent and unbroken. Three times we have confronted Establishment Clause challenges to neutral government programs that provide aid directly to a broad class of individuals, who, in turn, direct the aid to religious schools or institutions of their own choosing. Three times we have rejected such challenges.

In *Mueller v. Allen*, 463 U.S. 388 (1983), we rejected an Establishment Clause challenge to a Minnesota program authorizing tax deductions for various educational expenses, including private school tuition costs, even though the great majority of the program's beneficiaries (96%) were parents of children in religious schools. We began by focusing on the class of beneficiaries, finding that because the class included "*all* parents," including parents with "children [who] attend nonsectarian private schools or sectarian private schools," the program was "not readily subject to challenge under the Establishment Clause." Then, viewing the program as a whole, we emphasized the principle of private choice, noting that public funds were made available to religious schools "only as a result of numerous, private choices of individual parents of school-age children." This, we said, ensured that " 'no imprimatur of state approval' can be deemed to have been conferred on any particular religion, or on religion generally." . . .

That the program was one of true private choice, with no evidence that the State deliberately skewed incentives toward religious schools, was sufficient for the program to survive scrutiny under the Establishment Clause.

In *Witters v. Washington Department of Services for the Blind*, 474 U.S. 481 (1986), we used identical reasoning to reject an Establishment Clause challenge to a vocational scholarship program that provided tuition aid to a student studying at a religious institution to become a pastor. . . .

Finally, in *Zobrest v. Catalina Foothills School District*, 509 U.S. 1 (1993), we applied *Mueller* and *Witters* to reject an Establishment Clause challenge to a federal program that permitted sign-language interpreters to assist deaf children enrolled in religious schools. Reviewing our earlier decisions, we stated that "government programs that neutrally provide benefits to a broad class of citizens defined without reference to religion are not readily subject to an Establishment Clause challenge." . . .

Mueller, *Witters*, and *Zobrest* thus make clear that where a government aid program is neutral with respect to religion, and provides assistance directly to a broad class of citizens who, in turn, direct government aid to religious schools wholly as a result of their own genuine and independent private choice, the program is not readily subject to challenge under the Establishment Clause. A program that shares these features permits government aid to reach religious institutions only by way of the deliberate choices of numerous individual recipients. The incidental advancement of a religious mission, or the perceived endorsement of a religious message, is reasonably attributable to the individual recipient, not to the government, whose role ends with the disbursement of benefits. . . .

We believe that the program challenged here is a program of true private choice, consistent with *Mueller*, *Witters*, and *Zobrest*, and thus constitutional. As was true in those cases, the Ohio program is neutral in all respects toward religion. It is part of a general and multifaceted undertaking by the State of Ohio to provide educational opportunities to the children of a failed school district. It confers educational assistance directly to a broad class of individuals defined without reference to religion, *i.e.*, any parent of a school-age child who resides in the Cleveland City School District. The program permits the participation of *all* schools within the district, religious or nonreligious. Adjacent public schools also may participate and have a financial incentive to do so. Program benefits are available to participating families on neutral terms, with no reference to religion. The only preference stated anywhere in the program is a preference for low-income families, who receive greater assistance and are given priority for admission at participating schools.

There are no "financial incentives" that "skew" the program toward religious schools. . . .

Respondents suggest that even without a financial incentive for parents to choose a religious school, the program creates a "public perception that the State is endorsing religious practices and beliefs." But we have repeatedly recognized that no reasonable observer would think a neutral program of private choice, where state aid reaches religious schools solely as a result of the numerous independent decisions of private individuals, carries with it the *imprimatur* of government endorsement.

There also is no evidence that the program fails to provide genuine opportunities for Cleveland parents to select secular educational options for their school-age children. Cleveland schoolchildren enjoy a range of educational choices: They may remain in public school as before, remain in public school with publicly funded tutoring aid, obtain a scholarship and choose a religious school, obtain a scholarship and choose a nonreligious private school, enroll in a community school, or enroll in a magnet school. That 46 of the 56 private schools now participating in the program are religious schools does not condemn it as a violation of the Establishment Clause. . . .

Justice Souter speculates that because more private religious schools currently participate in the program, the program itself must somehow discourage the participation of private nonreligious schools. But Cleveland's preponderance of religiously affiliated private schools certainly did not arise as a result of the program; it is a phenomenon common to many American cities. . . . Indeed, by all accounts the program has captured a remarkable cross-section of private schools, religious and nonreligious. It is true that 82% of Cleveland's participating private schools are religious schools, but it is also true that 81% of private schools in Ohio are religious schools. . . .

Respondents and Justice Souter claim that even if we do not focus on the number of participating schools that are religious schools, we should attach constitutional significance to the fact that 96% of scholarship recipients have enrolled in religious schools. They claim that this alone proves parents lack genuine choice, even if no parent has ever said so. We need not consider this argument in detail, since it was flatly rejected in *Mueller*, where we found it irrelevant that 96% of parents taking deductions for tuition expenses paid tuition at religious schools. Indeed, we have recently found it irrelevant even to the constitutionality of a direct aid program that a vast majority of program benefits went to religious schools. The constitutionality of a neutral educational aid program simply does not turn on whether and why, in a particular area, at a particular time, most private schools are run by religious organizations, or most recipients choose to use the aid at a religious school. . . .

Respondents finally claim that we should look to *Committee for Public Ed. & Religious Liberty v. Nyquist,* 413 U.S. 756 (1973), to decide these cases. We disagree for two reasons. First, the program in *Nyquist* was quite different from the program challenged here. *Nyquist* involved a New York program that gave a package of benefits exclusively to private schools and the parents of private school enrollees. . . .

Second, were there any doubt that the program challenged in *Nyquist* is far removed from the program challenged here, we expressly reserved judgment with respect to "a case involving some form of public assistance (*e.g.*, scholarships) made available generally without regard to the sectarian-nonsectarian, or public-nonpublic nature of the institution benefited." That, of course, is the very question now before us, and it has since been answered, first in *Mueller*, then in *Witters*, and again in *Zobrest*. To the extent the scope of *Nyquist* has remained an open question in light of these later decisions, we now hold that *Nyquist* does not govern neutral educational assistance programs that, like the program here, offer aid directly to a broad class of individual recipients defined without regard to religion.

In sum, the Ohio program is entirely neutral with respect to religion. It provides benefits directly to a wide spectrum of individuals, defined only by financial need and residence in a particular school district. It permits such individuals to exercise genuine choice among options public and private, secular and religious. The program is therefore a program of true private choice. In keeping with an unbroken line of decisions rejecting challenges to similar programs, we hold that the program does not offend the Establishment Clause.

The judgment of the Court of Appeals is reversed.

It is so ordered.

JUSTICE O'CONNOR, concurring.

While I join the Court's opinion, I write separately for two reasons. First, although the Court takes an important step, I do not believe that today's decision, when considered in light of other longstanding government programs that impact religious organizations and our prior Establishment Clause jurisprudence, marks a dramatic break from the past. Second, given the emphasis the Court places on verifying that parents of voucher students in religious schools have exercised "true private choice," I think it is worth elaborating on the Court's conclusion that this inquiry should consider all reasonable educational alternatives to religious schools that are available to parents. To do otherwise is to ignore how the educational system in Cleveland actually functions.

I

These cases are different from prior indirect aid cases in part because a significant portion of the funds appropriated for the voucher program reach religious schools without restrictions on the use of these funds. The share of public resources that reach religious schools is not, however, as significant as respondents suggest. Data from the 1999–2000 school year indicate that 82 percent of schools participating in the voucher program were religious and that 96 percent of participating students enrolled in religious schools, but these data are incomplete. These statistics do not take into account all of the reasonable educational choices that may be available to students in Cleveland public schools. When one considers the option to attend community schools, the percentage of students enrolled in religious schools falls to 62.1 percent. If magnet schools are included in the mix, this percentage falls to 16.5 percent.

Even these numbers do not paint a complete picture. . . . Even if one assumes that all voucher students come from low-income families and that each voucher student used up the entire $2,250 voucher, at most $8.2 million of public funds flowed to religious schools under the voucher program in 1999–2000. . . .

Although $ 8.2 million is no small sum, it pales in comparison to the amount of funds that federal, state, and local governments already provide religious institutions. . . .

These tax exemptions . . . are just part of the picture. Federal dollars also reach religiously affiliated organizations through public health programs such as Medicare and Medicaid, through educational programs such as the Pell Grant program, and the G.I. Bill of Rights; and through child care programs such as the Child Care and Development Block Grant Program (CCDBG). Medicare and Medicaid provide federal funds to pay for the healthcare of the elderly and the poor, respectively and the G.I. Bills subsidize higher education of low-income individuals and veterans; and the CCDBG program finances child care for low-income parents. These programs are well-established parts of our social welfare system, and can be quite substantial.

A significant portion of the funds appropriated for these programs reach religiously affiliated institutions, typically without restrictions on its subsequent use. . . .

Against this background, the support that the Cleveland voucher program provides religious institutions is neither substantial nor atypical of existing government programs. While this observation is not intended to justify the Cleveland voucher program under the Establishment Clause, it places in broader perspective alarmist claims about implications of the Cleveland program and the Court's decision in these cases.

II

Nor does today's decision signal a major departure from this Court's prior Establishment Clause jurisprudence. A central tool in our analysis of cases in this area has been the *Lemon* test. As originally formulated, a statute passed this test only if it had "a secular legislative purpose," if its "principal or primary effect" was one that "neither advanced nor inhibited religion," and if it did "not foster an excessive government entanglement with religion." In *Agostini v. Felton,* 521 U.S. 203 (1997), we folded the entanglement inquiry into the primary effect inquiry. This made sense because both inquiries rely on the same evidence, and the degree of entanglement has implications for whether a statute advances or inhibits religion. . . .

. . . Such a refinement of the *Lemon* test surely does not betray *Everson v. Board of Education*, 330 U.S. 1 (1947).

III

There is little question in my mind that the Cleveland voucher program is neutral as between religious schools and nonreligious schools. Justice Souter rejects the Court's notion of neutrality, proposing that the neutrality of a program should be gauged not by the opportunities it presents but rather by its effects. In particular, a "neutrality test . . . [should] focus on a category of aid that may be directed to religious as well as secular schools, and ask whether the scheme favors a religious direction." Justice Souter doubts that the Cleveland program is neutral under this view. He surmises that the cap on tuition that voucher schools may charge low-income students encourages these students to attend religious rather than nonreligious private voucher schools. But Justice Souter's notion of neutrality is inconsistent with that in our case law. As we put it in *Agostini*, government aid must be "made available to both religious and secular beneficiaries on a nondiscriminatory basis."

I do not agree that the nonreligious schools have failed to provide Cleveland parents reasonable alternatives to religious schools in the voucher program. For nonreligious schools to qualify as genuine options for parents, they need not be superior to religious schools in every respect. They need only be adequate substitutes for religious schools in the eyes of parents. The District Court record demonstrates that nonreligious schools were able to compete effectively with Catholic and other religious schools in the Cleveland voucher program. The best evidence of this is that many parents with vouchers selected nonreligious private schools over religious alternatives and an even larger number of parents send their children to community and magnet schools rather than seeking vouchers at all. Moreover, there is no record evidence that any voucher-eligible student was turned away from a nonreligious private school in the voucher program, let alone a community or magnet school.

. . . Even if national statistics were relevant for evaluating the Cleveland program, Justice Souter ignores evidence which suggests that, at a national level, nonreligious private schools may target a market for different, if not higher, quality of education. For example, nonreligious private schools are smaller; have smaller class sizes, have more highly educated teachers, and have principals with longer job tenure than Catholic schools.

Additionally, Justice Souter's theory that the Cleveland voucher program's cap on the tuition encourages low-income student to attend religious schools ignores that these students receive nearly double the amount of tuition assistance under the community schools program than under the voucher program and that none of the community schools is religious.

In my view the more significant finding in these cases is that Cleveland parents who use vouchers to send their children to religious private schools do so as a result of true private choice. . . .

I find the Court's answer to the question whether parents of students eligible for vouchers have a genuine choice between religious and nonreligious schools persuasive. In looking at the voucher program, all the choices available to potential beneficiaries of the government program should be considered. In these cases, parents who were eligible to apply for a voucher also had the option, at a minimum, to send their children to community schools. Yet the Court of Appeals chose not to look at community schools, let alone magnet schools, when evaluating the Cleveland voucher program. That decision was incorrect. . . . .

Considering all the educational options available to parents whose children are eligible for vouchers, including community and magnet schools, the Court finds that parents in the Cleveland schools have an array of nonreligious options. Not surprisingly, respondents present no evidence that any students who were candidates for a voucher were denied slots in a community school or a magnet school. Indeed, the record suggests the opposite with respect to community schools.

JUSTICE THOMAS, concurring.

Frederick Douglass once said that "education . . . means emancipation. It means light and liberty. It means the uplifting of the soul of man into the glorious light of truth, the light by which men can only be made free." Today many of our inner-city public schools deny emancipation to urban minority students. Despite this Court's observation nearly 50 years ago in *Brown v. Board of Education*, 347 U.S. 483 (1954), that "it is doubtful that any child may reasonably be expected to succeed in life if he is denied the opportunity of an education," urban children have been forced into a system that continually fails them. These cases present an example of such failures. Besieged by escalating financial problems and declining academic achievement, the Cleveland City School District was in the midst of an academic emergency when Ohio enacted its scholarship program.

I

[Citing the *Lemon* Test] I agree with the Court that Ohio's program easily passes muster under our stringent test, but, as a matter of first principles, I question whether this test should be applied to the States.

. . . On its face, this provision [the Establishment Clause] places no limit on the States with regard to religion. The Establishment Clause originally protected States, and by extension their citizens, from the imposition of an established religion by the Federal Government. Whether and how this Clause should constrain state action under the Fourteenth Amendment is a more difficult question.

The Fourteenth Amendment fundamentally restructured the relationship between individuals and the States and ensured that States would not deprive citizens of liberty without due process of law. . . . As Justice Harlan noted, the Fourteenth Amendment "added greatly to the dignity and glory of American citizenship, and to the security of personal liberty." When rights are incorporated against the States through the Fourteenth Amendment they should advance, not constrain, individual liberty.

Consequently, in the context of the Establishment Clause, it may well be that state action should be evaluated on different terms than similar action by the Federal Government. . . . Thus, while the Federal Government may "make no law respecting an establishment of religion," the States may pass laws that include or touch on religious matters so long as these laws do not impede free exercise rights or any other individual religious liberty interest. By considering the particular religious liberty right alleged to be invaded by a State, federal courts can strike a proper balance between the demands of the Fourteenth Amendment on the one hand and the federalism prerogatives of States on the other.

Whatever the textual and historical merits of incorporating the Establishment Clause, I can accept that the Fourteenth Amendment protects religious liberty rights. But I cannot accept its use to oppose neutral programs of school choice through the incorporation of the Establishment Clause. There would be a tragic irony in converting the Fourteenth Amendment's guarantee of individual liberty into a prohibition on the exercise of educational choice.

II

The wisdom of allowing States greater latitude in dealing with matters of religion and education can be easily appreciated in this context. Respondents advocate using the Fourteenth Amendment to handcuff the State's ability to experiment with education. But without education one can hardly exercise the civic, political, and personal freedoms conferred by the Fourteenth Amendment. . . .

In addition to expanding the reach of the scholarship program, the inclusion of religious schools makes sense given Ohio's purpose of increasing educational performance and opportunities. Religious schools, like other private schools, achieve far better educational results than their public counterparts. . . .

Although one of the purposes of public schools was to promote democracy and a more egalitarian culture, failing urban public schools disproportionately affect minority children most in need of educational opportunity. . . .

While the romanticized ideal of universal public education resonates with the cognoscenti who oppose vouchers, poor urban families just want the best education for their children, who will certainly need it to function in our high-tech and advanced society. . . .

Converting the Fourteenth Amendment from a guarantee of opportunity to an obstacle against education reform distorts our constitutional values and disserves those in the greatest need.

As Frederick Douglass poignantly noted "no greater benefit can be bestowed upon a long benighted people, than giving to them, as we are here earnestly this day endeavoring to do, the means of an education."

JUSTICE STEVENS, dissenting.

Is a law that authorizes the use of public funds to pay for the indoctrination of thousands of grammar school children in particular religious faiths a "law respecting an establishment of religion" within the meaning of the First Amendment? In answering that question, I think we should ignore three factual matters that are discussed at length by my colleagues.

First, the severe educational crisis that confronted the Cleveland City School District when Ohio enacted its voucher program is not a matter that should affect our appraisal of its constitutionality. . . .

Second, the wide range of choices that have been made available to students *within the public school system* has no bearing on the question whether the State may pay the tuition for students who wish to reject public education entirely and attend private schools that will provide them with a sectarian education. . . .

Third, the voluntary character of the private choice to prefer a parochial education over an education in the public school system seems to me quite irrelevant to the question whether the government's choice to pay for religious indoctrination is constitutionally permissible. . . .

JUSTICE SOUTER, with whom JUSTICES STEVENS, GINSBURG, and BREYER join, dissenting.

The applicability of the Establishment Clause to public funding of benefits to religious schools was settled in *Everson v. Board of Ed. of Ewing* (1947), which inaugurated the modern era of establishment doctrine. The Court stated the principle in words from which there was no dissent: "No tax in any amount, large or small, can be levied to support any religious activities or institutions, whatever they may be called, or whatever form they may adopt to teach or practice religion."

I

[Souter reviews previous Supreme Court decisions on the subject.]

II

Although it has taken half a century since *Everson* to reach the majority's twin standards of neutrality and free choice, the facts show that, in the majority's hands, even these criteria cannot convincingly legitimize the Ohio scheme.

A

Consider first the criterion of neutrality. As recently as two Terms ago, a majority of the Court recognized that neutrality conceived of as evenhandedness toward aid recipients had never been treated as alone sufficient to satisfy the Establishment Clause, *Mitchell v. Helms,* 530 U.S. 793 (2000). But at least in its limited significance, formal neutrality seemed to serve some purpose. Today, however, the majority employs the neutrality criterion in a way that renders it impossible to understand.

Neutrality in this sense refers, of course, to evenhandedness in setting eligibility as between potential religious and secular recipients of public money. Thus, for example, the aid scheme in *Witters* provided an eligible recipient with a scholarship to be used at any institution within a practically unlimited universe of schools; it did not tend to provide more or less aid depending on which one the scholarship recipient chose, and there was no indication that the maximum scholarship amount would be insufficient at secular schools. Neither did any condition of Zobrest's interpreter's subsidy favor religious education.

In order to apply the neutrality test, then, it makes sense to focus on a category of aid that may be directed to religious as well as secular schools, and ask whether the scheme favors a religious direction. Here, one would ask whether the voucher provisions, allowing for as much as $2,250 toward private school tuition (or a grant to a public school in an adjacent district), were written in a way that skewed the scheme toward benefiting religious schools.

This, however, is not what the majority asks. The majority looks not to the provisions for tuition vouchers, but to every provision for educational opportunity: "The program permits the participation of *all* schools within the district, [as well as public schools in adjacent districts], religious or nonreligious." The majority then finds confirmation that "participation of *all* schools" satisfies neutrality by noting that the better part of total state educational expenditure goes to public schools, thus showing there is no favor of religion.

The illogic is patent. If regular, public schools (which can get no voucher payments) "participate" in a voucher scheme with schools that can, and public expenditure is still predominantly on public schools, then the majority's reasoning would find neutrality in a scheme of vouchers available for private tuition in districts with no secular private schools at all. "Neutrality" as the majority employs the term is, literally, verbal and nothing more. . . .

Why the majority does not simply accept the fact that the challenge here is to the more generous voucher scheme and judge its neutrality in relation to religious use of voucher money seems very odd. It seems odd, that is, until one recognizes that comparable schools for applying the criterion of neutrality are also the comparable schools for applying the other majority criterion, whether the immediate recipients of voucher aid have a genuinely free choice of religious and secular schools to receive the voucher money. And in applying this second criterion, the consideration of "*all* schools" is ostensibly helpful to the majority position.

B

The majority addresses the issue of choice the same way it addresses neutrality, by asking whether recipients or potential recipients of voucher aid have a choice of public schools among secular alternatives to religious schools. Again, however, the majority asks the wrong question and misapplies the criterion. The majority has confused choice in spending scholarships with choice from the entire menu of possible educational placements, most of them open to anyone willing to attend a public school. . . .

If, contrary to the majority, we ask the right question about genuine choice to use the vouchers, the answer shows that something is influencing choices in a way that aims the money in a religious direction: of 56 private schools in the district participating in the voucher program (only 53 of which accepted voucher students in 1999–2000), 46 of them are religious; 96.6% of all voucher recipients go to religious schools, only 3.4% to nonreligious ones. . . .

There is, in any case, no way to interpret the 96.6% of current voucher money going to religious schools as reflecting a free and genuine choice by the families that apply for vouchers. The 96.6% reflects, instead, the fact that too few nonreligious school desks are available and few but religious schools can afford to accept more than a handful of voucher students. And contrary to the majority's assertion, public schools in adjacent districts hardly have a financial incentive to participate in the Ohio voucher program, and none has. For the overwhelming number of children in the voucher scheme, the only alternative to the public schools is religious. And it is entirely irrelevant that the State did not deliberately design the network of private schools for the sake of channeling money into religious institutions. The criterion is one of genuinely free choice on the part of the private individuals who choose, and a Hobson's choice is not a choice, whatever the reason for being Hobsonian.

III

I do not dissent merely because the majority has misapplied its own law, for even if I assumed *arguendo* that the majority's formal criteria were satisfied on the facts, today's conclusion would be profoundly at odds with the Constitution. Proof of this is clear on two levels. The first is circumstantial, in the now discarded symptom of violation, the substantial dimension of the aid. The second is direct, in the defiance of every objective supposed to be served by the bar against establishment.

A

The scale of the aid to religious schools approved today is unprecedented, both in the number of dollars and in the proportion of systemic school expenditure supported. Each measure has received attention in previous cases. On one hand, the sheer quantity of aid, when delivered to a class of religious primary and secondary schools, was suspect on the theory that the greater the aid, the greater its proportion to a religious school's existing expenditures, and the greater the likelihood that public money was supporting religious as well as secular instruction. . . .

B

It is virtually superfluous to point out that every objective underlying the prohibition of religious establishment is betrayed by this scheme, but something has to be said about the enormity of the violation. I anticipated these objectives earlier, in discussing *Everson*, which cataloged them, the first being respect for freedom of conscience. Jefferson described it as the idea that no one "shall be compelled to . . . support any religious worship, place, or ministry whatsoever," even a "teacher of his own religious persuasion," and Madison thought it violated by any " 'authority which can force a citizen to contribute three pence . . . of his property for the support of any . . . establishment.' " Madison's objection to three pence has simply been lost in the majority's formalism.

As for the second objective, to save religion from its own corruption, Madison wrote of the " 'experience . . . that ecclesiastical establishments, instead of maintaining the purity and efficacy of Religion, have had a contrary operation.' "

The risk is already being realized. In Ohio, for example, a condition of receiving government money under the program is that participating religious schools may not "discriminate on the basis of . . . religion," which means the school may not give admission preferences to children who are members of the patron faith; children of a parish are generally consigned to the same admission lotteries as non-believers. . . .

For perspective on this foot-in-the-door of religious regulation, it is well to remember that the money has barely begun to flow. . . .

When government aid goes up, so does reliance on it; the only thing likely to go down is independence. . . .

JUSTICE BREYER, with whom JUSTICES STEVENS and SOUTER join, dissenting.

I join Justice Souter's opinion, and I agree substantially with Justice Stevens. I write separately, however, to emphasize the risk that publicly financed voucher programs pose in terms of religiously based social conflict. I do so because I believe that the Establishment Clause concern for protecting the Nation's social fabric from religious conflict poses an overriding obstacle to the implementation of this well-intentioned school voucher program. . . .

I

The First Amendment begins with a prohibition, that "Congress shall make no law respecting an establishment of religion," and a guarantee, that the government shall not prohibit "the free exercise thereof." These Clauses embody an understanding, reached in the 17th century after decades of religious war, that liberty and social stability demand a religious tolerance that respects the religious views of all citizens, permits those citizens to "worship God in their own way," and allows all families to "teach their children and to form their characters" as they wish. The Clauses reflect the Framers' vision of an American Nation free of the religious strife that had long plagued the nations of Europe. Whatever the Framers might have thought about particular 18th century school funding practices, they undeniably intended an interpretation of the Religion Clauses that would implement this basic First Amendment objective.

[Breyer proceeds to examine case precedents.]

When it decided these 20th century Establishment Clause cases, the Court did not deny that an earlier American society might have found a less clear-cut church/state separation compatible with social tranquility. Indeed, historians point out that during the early years of the Republic, American schools—including the first public schools—were Protestant in character. Their students recited Protestant prayers, read the King James version of the Bible, and learned Protestant religious ideals. Those practices may have wrongly discriminated against members of minority religions, but given the small number of such individuals, the teaching of Protestant religions in schools did not threaten serious social conflict.

The 20th century Court was fully aware, however, that immigration and growth had changed American society dramatically since its early years. . . .

The 20th century Court was also aware that political efforts to right the wrong of discrimination against religious minorities in primary education had failed; in fact they had exacerbated religious conflict. . . .

These historical circumstances suggest that the Court, applying the Establishment Clause through the Fourteenth Amendment to 20th century American society, faced an interpretive dilemma that was in part practical. The Court appreciated the religious diversity of contemporary American society. It realized that the status quo favored some religions at the expense of others. And it understood the Establishment Clause to prohibit (among other things) any such favoritism. Yet *how* did the Clause achieve that objective? Did it simply require the government to give each religion an equal chance to introduce religion into the primary schools—a kind of "equal opportunity" approach to the interpretation of the Establishment Clause? Or, did that Clause avoid government favoritism of some religions by insisting upon "separation"—that the government achieve equal treatment by removing itself from the business of providing religious education for children? This interpretive choice arose in respect both to religious activities in public schools and government aid to private education.

In both areas the Court concluded that the Establishment Clause required "separation," in part because an "equal opportunity" approach was not workable. . . . .

With respect to government aid to private education, did not history show that efforts to obtain equivalent funding for the private education of children whose parents did not hold popular religious beliefs only exacerbated religious strife?. . .

The upshot is the development of constitutional doctrine that reads the Establishment Clause as avoiding religious strife, *not* by providing every religion with an *equal opportunity* (say, to secure state funding or to pray in the public schools), but by drawing fairly clear lines of *separation* between church and state—at least where the heartland of religious belief, such as primary religious education, is at issue.

II

The principle underlying these cases—avoiding religiously based social conflict—remains of great concern. As religiously diverse as America had become when the Court decided its major 20th century Establishment Clause cases, we are exponentially more diverse today. America boasts more than 55 different religious groups and subgroups with a significant number of members. . . .

III

I concede that the Establishment Clause currently permits States to channel various forms of assistance to religious schools, for example, transportation costs for students, computers, and secular texts. States now certify the nonsectarian educational content of religious school education. Yet the consequence has not been great turmoil. . . .

School voucher programs differ, however, in both *kind* and *degree* from aid programs upheld in the past. They differ in kind because they direct financing to a core function of the church: the teaching of religious truths to young children. For that reason the constitutional demand for "separation" is of particular constitutional concern.

Vouchers also differ in *degree*. The aid programs recently upheld by the Court involved limited amounts of aid to religion. But the majority's analysis here appears to permit a considerable shift of taxpayer dollars from public secular schools to private religious schools. That fact, combined with the use to which these dollars will be put, exacerbates the conflict problem. State aid that takes the form of peripheral secular items, with prohibitions against diversion of funds to religious teaching, holds significantly less potential for social division. In this respect as well, the secular aid upheld in *Mitchell* differs dramatically from the present case. Although it was conceivable that minor amounts of money could have, contrary to the statute, found their way to the religious activities of the recipients, that case is at worst the camel's nose, while the litigation before us is the camel itself.

IV

I do not believe that the "parental choice" aspect of the voucher program sufficiently offsets the concerns I have mentioned. . . .

V

The Court, in effect, turns the clock back. It adopts, under the name of "neutrality," an interpretation of the Establishment Clause that this Court rejected more than half a century ago. In its view, the parental choice that offers each religious group a kind of equal opportunity to secure government funding overcomes the

Establishment Clause concern for social concord. An earlier Court found that "equal opportunity" principle insufficient; it read the Clause as insisting upon greater separation of church and state, at least in respect to primary education. In a society composed of many different religious creeds, I fear that this present departure from the Court's earlier understanding risks creating a form of religiously based conflict potentially harmful to the Nation's social fabric. Because I believe the Establishment Clause was written in part to avoid this kind of conflict, and for reasons set forth by Justice Souter and Justice Stevens, I respectfully dissent.

FOR DISCUSSION

How would you compare the ruling in this case with the Court's decision in *Everson v. Board of Education*? Are all parents and students equally entitled to the benefits of a parochial school education, or should such an education be limited to those who can afford directly to pay for it?

VAN ORDEN V. PERRY

543 U.S.1135, 125 S.Ct. 1240, 160 L.Ed.2d 1092 (2005)

In *Stone v. Graham* (449 U.S. 39, 1980), the Supreme Court ruled that Kentucky could not display the Ten Commandments in school classrooms. *Van Orden* is knottier because it involves the display of a monument with these commandments on the grounds of the Texas State Capitol.

Vote: 5–4

CHIEF JUSTICE REHNQUIST announced the judgment of the Court and delivered an opinion, in which JUSTICES SCALIA, KENNEDY, and THOMAS join.

The question here is whether the Establishment Clause of the First Amendment allows the display of a monument inscribed with the Ten Commandments on the Texas State Capitol grounds. We hold that it does.

The 22 acres surrounding the Texas State Capitol contain 17 monuments and 21 historical markers commemorating the "people, ideals, and events that compose Texan identity." Tex. H. Con. Res. 38, 77th Leg. (2001). The monolith challenged here stands 6-feet high and 3-feet wide. It is located to the north of the Capitol building, between the Capitol and the Supreme Court building. Its primary content is the text of the Ten Commandments. An eagle grasping the American flag, an eye inside of a pyramid, and two small tablets with what appears to be an ancient script are carved above the text of the Ten Commandments. Below the text are two Stars of David and the superimposed Greek letters Chi and Rho, which represent Christ. The bottom of the monument bears the inscription "PRESENTED TO THE PEOPLE AND YOUTH OF TEXAS BY THE FRATERNAL ORDER OF EAGLES OF TEXAS 1961."

The legislative record surrounding the State's acceptance of the monument from the Eagles—a national social, civic, and patriotic organization—is limited to legislative journal entries. After the monument was accepted, the State selected a site for the monument based on the recommendation of the state organization responsible for maintaining the Capitol grounds. The Eagles paid the cost of erecting the monument, the dedication of which was presided over by two state legislators.

Petitioner Thomas Van Orden is a native Texan and a resident of Austin. At one time he was a licensed lawyer, having graduated from Southern Methodist Law School. Van Orden testified that, since 1995, he has encountered the Ten Commandments monument during his frequent visits to the Capitol grounds. His visits are typically for the purpose of using the law library in the Supreme Court building, which is located just northwest of the Capitol building.

Forty years after the monument's erection and six years after Van Orden began to encounter the monument frequently, he sued numerous state officials in their official capacities under Rev. Stat. § 1979, 42 U.S.C. § 1983, seeking both a declaration that the monument's placement violates the Establishment Clause and an injunction requiring its removal. After a bench trial, the District Court held that the monument did not contravene the Establishment Clause. It found that the State had a valid secular purpose in recognizing and commending the Eagles for their efforts to reduce juvenile delinquency. The District Court also determined that a reasonable observer, mindful of the history, purpose, and context, would not conclude that this passive monument conveyed the message that the State was seeking to endorse religion. The Court of Appeals affirmed the District Court's holdings with respect to the monument's purpose and effect. We granted certiorari and now affirm.

Our cases, Januslike, point in two directions in applying the Establishment Clause. One face looks toward the strong role played by religion and religious traditions throughout our Nation's history.

The other face looks toward the principle that governmental intervention in religious matters can itself endanger religious freedom.

This case, like all Establishment Clause challenges, presents us with the difficulty of respecting both faces. Our institutions presuppose a Supreme Being, yet these institutions must not press religious observances upon their citizens. One face looks to the past in acknowledgment of our Nation's heritage, while the other looks to the present in demanding a separation between church and state. Reconciling these two faces requires that we neither abdicate our responsibility to maintain a division between church and state nor evince a hostility to religion by disabling the government from in some ways recognizing our religious heritage.

These two faces are evident in representative cases both upholding and invalidating laws under the Establishment Clause.

Whatever may be the fate of the *Lemon* test in the larger scheme of Establishment Clause jurisprudence, we think it not useful in dealing with the sort of passive monument that Texas has erected on its Capitol grounds. Instead, our analysis is driven both by the nature of the monument and by our Nation's history.

[Rehnquist proceeds to cite examples from this history.]

In this case we are faced with a display of the Ten Commandments on government property outside the Texas State Capitol. Such acknowledgments of the role played by the Ten Commandments in our Nation's heritage are common throughout America. We need only look within our own Courtroom. Since 1935, Moses has stood, holding two tablets that reveal portions of the Ten Commandments written in Hebrew, among other lawgivers in the south frieze. Representations of the Ten Commandments adorn the metal gates lining the north and south sides of the Courtroom as well as the doors leading into the Courtroom. Moses also sits on the exterior east facade of the building holding the Ten Commandments tablets.

Similar acknowledgments can be seen throughout a visitor's tour of our Nation's Capital. [Rehnquist cites several examples.]

Our opinions, like our building, have recognized the role the Decalogue plays in America's heritage. The Executive and Legislative Branches have also acknowledged the historical role of the Ten Commandments. These displays and recognitions of the Ten Commandments bespeak the rich American tradition of religious acknowledgments.

Of course, the Ten Commandments are religious—they were so viewed at their inception and so remain. The monument, therefore, has religious significance. According to Judeo-Christian belief, the Ten

Commandments were given to Moses by God on Mt. Sinai. But Moses was a lawgiver as well as a religious leader. And the Ten Commandments have an undeniable historical meaning, as the foregoing examples demonstrate. Simply having religious content or promoting a message consistent with a religious doctrine does not run afoul of the Establishment Clause.

There are, of course, limits to the display of religious messages or symbols. For example, we held unconstitutional a Kentucky statute requiring the posting of the Ten Commandments in every public schoolroom. *Stone v. Graham,* 449 U.S. 39 (1980). In the classroom context, we found that the Kentucky statute had an improper and plainly religious purpose. As evidenced by *Stone*'s almost exclusive reliance upon two of our school prayer cases, *School Dist. of Abington Township v. Schempp,* 364 U.S. 298 (1963), and *Engel v. Vitale,* 370 U.S. 421 (1962), it stands as an example of the fact that we have "been particularly vigilant in monitoring compliance with the Establishment Clause in elementary and secondary schools," *Edwards v. Aguillard,* 482 U.S. 578 (1987). Neither *Stone* itself nor subsequent opinions have indicated that *Stone*'s holding would extend to a legislative chamber, see *Marsh v. Chambers,* 463 U.S. 783 (1983), or to capitol grounds. The placement of the Ten Commandments monument on the Texas State Capitol grounds is a far more passive use of those texts than was the case in *Stone,* where the text confronted elementary school students every day. Indeed, Van Orden, the petitioner here, apparently walked by the monument for a number of years before bringing this lawsuit. The monument is therefore also quite different from the prayers involved in *Schempp* and *Lee v. Weisman,* 505 U.S. 577 (1992). Texas has treated her Capitol grounds monuments as representing the several strands in the State's political and legal history. The inclusion of the Ten Commandments monument in this group has a dual significance, partaking of both religion and government. We cannot say that Texas' display of this monument violates the Establishment Clause of the First Amendment.

JUSTICE SCALIA, concurring.

I join the opinion of the Chief Justice because I think it accurately reflects our current Establishment Clause jurisprudence—or at least the Establishment Clause jurisprudence we currently apply some of the time. I would prefer to reach the same result by adopting an Establishment Clause jurisprudence that is in accord with our Nation's past and present practices, and that can be consistently applied—the central relevant feature of which is that there is nothing unconstitutional in a State's favoring religion generally, honoring God through public prayer and acknowledgment, or, in a nonproselytizing manner, venerating the Ten Commandments.

JUSTICE THOMAS, concurring.

The Court holds that the Ten Commandments monument found on the Texas State Capitol grounds does not violate the Establishment Clause. Rather than trying to suggest meaninglessness where there is meaning, the Chief Justice rightly recognizes that the monument has "religious significance." He properly recognizes the role of religion in this Nation's history and the permissibility of government displays acknowledging that history. For those reasons, I join the Chief Justice's opinion in full.

This case would be easy if the Court were willing to abandon the inconsistent guideposts it has adopted for addressing Establishment Clause challenges, and return to the original meaning of the Clause. I have previously suggested that the Clause's text and history "resist incorporation" against the States. If the Establishment Clause does not restrain the States, then it has no application here, where only state action is at issue.

Even if the Clause is incorporated, or if the Free Exercise Clause limits the power of States to establish religions, our task would be far simpler if we returned to the original meaning of the word "establishment" than it is under the various approaches this Court now uses. The Framers understood an establishment "necessarily [to] involve actual legal coercion."

There is no question that, based on the original meaning of the Establishment Clause, the Ten Commandments display at issue here is constitutional. In no sense does Texas compel petitioner Van Orden to do anything. The only injury to him is that he takes offense at seeing the monument as he passes it on his way to the Texas Supreme Court Library. He need not stop to read it or even to look at it, let alone to express support for it or adopt the Commandments as guides for his life. The mere presence of the monument along his path involves no coercion and thus does not violate the Establishment Clause.

Returning to the original meaning would do more than simplify our task. It also would avoid the pitfalls present in the Court's current approach to such challenges. This Court's precedent elevates the trivial to the proverbial "federal case," by making benign signs and postings subject to challenge. Yet even as it does so, the Court's precedent attempts to avoid declaring all religious symbols and words of longstanding tradition unconstitutional, by counterfactually declaring them of little religious significance. Even when the Court's cases recognize that such symbols have religious meaning, they adopt an unhappy compromise that fails fully to account for either the adherent's or the nonadherent's beliefs, and provides no principled way to choose between them. Even worse, the incoherence of the Court's decisions in this area renders the Establishment Clause impenetrable and incapable of consistent application. All told, this Court's jurisprudence leaves courts, governments, and believers and nonbelievers alike confused—an observation that is hardly new.

JUSTICE STEVENS, with whom JUSTICE GINSBURG joins, dissenting.

The sole function of the monument on the grounds of Texas' State Capitol is to display the full text of one version of the Ten Commandments. The monument is not a work of art and does not refer to any event in the history of the State. It is significant because, and only because, it communicates the following message:

[Stevens follows with the text of the Ten Commandments]

Viewed on its face, Texas' display has no purported connection to God's role in the formation of Texas or the founding of our Nation; nor does it provide the reasonable observer with any basis to guess that it was erected to honor any individual or organization. The message transmitted by Texas' chosen display is quite plain: This State endorses the divine code of the "Judeo-Christian" God.

I

In my judgment, at the very least, the Establishment Clause has created a strong presumption against the display of religious symbols on public property.

Government's obligation to avoid divisiveness and exclusion in the religious sphere is compelled by the Establishment and Free Exercise Clauses, which together erect a wall of separation between church and state. This metaphorical wall protects principles long recognized and often recited in this Court's cases. The first and most fundamental of these principles, one that a majority of this Court today affirms, is that the Establishment Clause demands religious neutrality—government may not exercise a preference for one religious faith over another. This essential command, however, is not merely a prohibition against the government's differentiation among religious sects. We have repeatedly reaffirmed that neither a State nor the Federal Government "can constitutionally pass laws or impose requirements which aid all religions as against non-believers, and neither can aid those religions based on a belief in the existence of God as against those religions founded on different beliefs." *Torcaso v. Watkins*, 367 U.S. 488, 495 (1961). This principle is based on the straightforward notion that governmental promotion of orthodoxy is not saved by the aggregation of several orthodoxies under the State's banner.

Acknowledgments of this broad understanding of the neutrality principle are legion in our cases. Strong arguments to the contrary have been raised from time to time, perhaps the strongest in then-Justice Rehnquist's scholarly dissent in *Wallace v. Jaffree,* 472 U.S. 38 (1985). Powerful as his argument was, we squarely rejected it and thereby reaffirmed the principle that the Establishment Clause requires the same respect for the atheist as it does for the adherent of a Christian faith. As we wrote, "the Court has unambiguously concluded that the individual freedom of conscience protected by the First Amendment embodies the right to select any religious faith or none at all."

In restating this principle, I do not discount the importance of avoiding an overly strict interpretation of the metaphor so often used to define the reach of the Establishment Clause. The plurality is correct to note that "religion and religious traditions" have played a "strong role . . . throughout our nation's history." This Court has often recognized "an unbroken history of official acknowledgment . . . of the role of religion in American life." Given this history, it is unsurprising that a religious symbol may at times become an important feature of a familiar landscape or a reminder of an important event in the history of a community. The wall that separates the church from the State does not prohibit the government from acknowledging the religious beliefs and practices of the American people, nor does it require governments to hide works of art or historic memorabilia from public view just because they also have religious significance.

This case, however, is not about historic preservation or the mere recognition of religion. The issue is obfuscated rather than clarified by simplistic commentary on the various ways in which religion has played a role in American life, and by the recitation of the many extant governmental "acknowledgments" of the role the Ten Commandments played in our Nation's heritage. Surely, the mere compilation of religious symbols, none of which includes the full text of the Commandments and all of which are exhibited in different settings, has only marginal relevance to the question presented in this case.

The monolith displayed on Texas Capitol grounds cannot be discounted as a passive acknowledgment of religion, nor can the State's refusal to remove it upon objection be explained as a simple desire to preserve a historic relic. This Nation's resolute commitment to neutrality with respect to religion is flatly inconsistent with the plurality's wholehearted validation of an official state endorsement of the message that there is one, and only one, God.

JUSTICE SOUTER, with whom JUSTICES STEVENS and GINSBURG join, dissenting.

Although the First Amendment's Religion Clauses have not been read to mandate absolute governmental neutrality toward religion *Sherbert v. Verner,* 374 U.S. 398 (1963), the Establishment Clause requires neutrality as a general rule, *e.g., Everson v. Board of Ed. of Ewing,* 330 U.S. 1 (1947), and thus expresses Madison's condemnation of "employing Religion as an engine of Civil policy." A governmental display of an obviously religious text cannot be squared with neutrality, except in a setting that plausibly indicates that the statement is not placed in view with a predominant purpose on the part of government either to adopt the religious message or to urge its acceptance by others.

[Souter cites *Stone v. Graham* (449 U.S. 39, 1980) and other precedents.]

What these observations underscore are the simple realities that the Ten Commandments constitute a religious statement, that their message is inherently religious, and that the purpose of singling them out in a display is clearly the same.

FOR DISCUSSION

Do you think the Court would have decided this decision the same way if the issue had involved accepting a new monument that was to be donated rather than one that was already on the premises? Should a religious display on public property have to have the patina of history surrounding it before it is appropriate? Do you think a state could decide to accept a religious monument from one religious group and reject a comparable gift from another? What if a state said its decision was based on aesthetic reasons, but the Court did not accept this explanation?

McCreary v. American Civil Liberties Union

545 U.S. 844, 125 S.Ct. 2722, 162 L.Ed.2d 729 (2005)

As in the preceding case, *Van Orden v. Perry*, to which this case was a companion, the issue involved the posting of the Ten Commandments on public property, only here the text was displayed as part of a larger exhibit in a county courthouse.

Vote: 5–4

Justice Souter delivered the opinion of the Court.

Executives of two counties posted a version of the Ten Commandments on the walls of their courthouses. After suits were filed charging violations of the Establishment Clause, the legislative body of each county adopted a resolution calling for a more extensive exhibit meant to show that the Commandments are Kentucky's "precedent legal code." The result in each instance was a modified display of the Commandments surrounded by texts containing religious references as their sole common element. After changing counsel, the counties revised the exhibits again by eliminating some documents, expanding the text set out in another, and adding some new ones.

The issues are whether a determination of the counties' purpose is a sound basis for ruling on the Establishment Clause complaints, and whether evaluation of the counties' claim of secular purpose for the ultimate displays may take their evolution into account. We hold that the counties' manifest objective may be dispositive of the constitutional enquiry, and that the development of the presentation should be considered when determining its purpose.

I

[Souter reviews the history of the displays in McCreary and Pulaski counties.]

II

A

Ever since *Lemon v. Kurtzman*, 403 U.S. 602 (1971), summarized the three familiar considerations for evaluating Establishment Clause claims, looking to whether government action has "a secular legislative purpose" has been a common, albeit seldom dispositive, element of our cases. Though we have found government action motivated by an illegitimate purpose only four times since *Lemon*, and "the secular purpose requirement alone may rarely be determinative . . ., it nevertheless serves an important function."

The touchstone for our analysis is the principle that the "First Amendment mandates governmental neutrality between religion and religion, and between religion and nonreligion." When the government acts with the ostensible and predominant purpose of advancing religion, it violates that central Establishment Clause value of official religious neutrality, there being no neutrality when the government's ostensible object is to take sides.

B

Despite the intuitive importance of official purpose to the realization of Establishment Clause values, the Counties ask us to abandon *Lemon*'s purpose test, or at least to truncate any enquiry into purpose here. Their first argument is that the very consideration of purpose is deceptive: according to them, true "purpose" is unknowable, and its search merely an excuse for courts to act selectively and unpredictably in picking out evidence of subjective intent. The assertions are as seismic as they are unconvincing.

C

After declining the invitation to abandon concern with purpose wholesale, we also have to avoid the Counties' alternative tack of trivializing the enquiry into it. The Counties would read the cases as if the purpose enquiry were so naive that any transparent claim to secularity would satisfy it, and they would cut context out of the enquiry, to the point of ignoring history, no matter what bearing it actually had on the significance of current circumstances. There is no precedent for the Counties' arguments, or reason supporting them.

1

Lemon said that government action must have "a secular . . . purpose," and after a host of cases it is fair to add that although a legislature's stated reasons will generally get deference, the secular purpose required has to be genuine, not a sham, and not merely secondary to a religious objective.

2

The Counties' second proffered limitation can be dispatched quickly. They argue that purpose in a case like this one should be inferred, if at all, only from the latest news about the last in a series of governmental actions, however close they may all be in time and subject. But the world is not made brand new every morning, and the Counties are simply asking us to ignore perfectly probative evidence; they want an absentminded objective observer, not one presumed to be familiar with the history of the government's actions and competent to learn what history has to show.

III

This case comes to us on appeal from a preliminary injunction. We accordingly review the District Court's legal rulings *de novo*, and its ultimate conclusion for abuse of discretion.

We take *Stone v. Graham*, 449 U.S. 39 (1980), as the initial legal benchmark, our only case dealing with the constitutionality of displaying the Commandments. *Stone* recognized that the Commandments are an "instrument of religion" and that, at least on the facts before it, the display of their text could presumptively be understood as meant to advance religion: although state law specifically required their posting in public school classrooms, their isolated exhibition did not leave room even for an argument that secular education explained their being there. But *Stone* did not purport to decide the constitutionality of every possible way the Commandments might be set out by the government, and under the Establishment Clause detail is key. Hence, we look to the record of evidence showing the progression leading up to the third display of the Commandments.

A

The display rejected in *Stone* had two obvious similarities to the first one in the sequence here: both set out a text of the Commandments as distinct from any traditionally symbolic representation, and each stood alone, not part of an arguably secular display. *Stone* stressed the significance of integrating the Commandments into a secular scheme to forestall the broadcast of an otherwise clearly religious message, and for good reason, the Commandments being a central point of reference in the religious and moral history of Jews and Christians. They proclaim the existence of a monotheistic god (no other gods). They regulate details of religious obligation (no graven images, no sabbath breaking, no vain oath swearing). And they unmistakably rest even the universally accepted prohibitions (as against murder, theft, and the like) on the sanction of the divinity proclaimed at the beginning of the text. Displaying that text is thus different from a symbolic depiction, like tablets with 10 roman numerals, which could be seen as alluding to a general notion of law, not a sectarian conception of faith. Where the text is set out, the insistence of the religious message is hard to avoid in the absence of a context plausibly suggesting a message going beyond an excuse to promote the religious point of view. The display in *Stone* had no context that might have indicated an object beyond the religious character of the text, and the Counties' solo exhibit here did nothing more to counter the sectarian implication than the postings at issue in *Stone*. Actually, the posting by the Counties lacked even the *Stone* display's implausible disclaimer that the Commandments were set out to show their effect on the civil law. What is more, at the ceremony for posting the framed Commandments in Pulaski County, the county executive was accompanied by his pastor, who testified to the certainty of the existence of God. The reasonable observer could only think that the Counties meant to emphasize and celebrate the Commandments' religious message.

This is not to deny that the Commandments have had influence on civil or secular law; a major text of a majority religion is bound to be felt. The point is simply that the original text viewed in its entirety is an unmistakably religious statement dealing with religious obligations and with morality subject to religious sanction. When the government initiates an effort to place this statement alone in public view, a religious object is unmistakable.

B

Once the Counties were sued, they modified the exhibits and invited additional insight into their purpose in a display that hung for about six months. This new one was the product of forthright and nearly identical Pulaski and McCreary County resolutions listing a series of American historical documents with theistic and Christian references, which were to be posted in order to furnish a setting for displaying the Ten Commandments and any "other Kentucky and American historical document" without raising concern about "any Christian or religious references" in them. As mentioned, the resolutions expressed support for an Alabama judge who posted the Commandments in his courtroom, and cited the fact the Kentucky Legislature once adjourned a session in honor of "Jesus Christ, Prince of Ethics."

In this second display, unlike the first, the Commandments were not hung in isolation, merely leaving the Counties' purpose to emerge from the pervasively religious text of the Commandments themselves. Instead, the second version was required to include the statement of the government's purpose expressly set out in the county resolutions, and underscored it by juxtaposing the Commandments to other documents with highlighted references to God as their sole common element. The display's unstinting focus was on religious passages, showing that the Counties were posting the Commandments precisely because of their sectarian content. That demonstration of the government's objective was enhanced by serial religious references and the accompanying resolution's claim about the embodiment of ethics in Christ. Together, the display and resolution presented an indisputable, and undisputed, showing of an impermissible purpose.

C

1

After the Counties changed lawyers, they mounted a third display, without a new resolution or repeal of the old one. The result was the "Foundations of American Law and Government" exhibit, which placed the Commandments in the company of other documents the Counties thought especially significant in the historical foundation of American government. In trying to persuade the District Court to lift the preliminary injunction, the Counties cited several new purposes for the third version, including a desire "to educate the citizens of the county regarding some of the documents that played a significant role in the foundation of our system of law and government." The Counties' claims did not, however, persuade the court, intimately familiar with the details of this litigation, or the Court of Appeals, neither of which found a legitimizing secular purpose in this third version of the display. . . .

These new statements of purpose were presented only as a litigating position, there being no further authorizing action by the Counties' governing boards. And although repeal of the earlier county authorizations would not have erased them from the record of evidence bearing on current purpose, the extraordinary resolutions for the second display passed just months earlier were not repealed or otherwise repudiated. Indeed, the sectarian spirit of the common resolution found enhanced expression in the third display, which quoted more of the purely religious language of the Commandments than the first two displays had done. . . . No reasonable observer could swallow the claim that the Counties had cast off the objective so unmistakable in the earlier displays.

Nor did the selection of posted material suggest a clear theme that might prevail over evidence of the continuing religious object. In a collection of documents said to be "foundational" to American government, it is at least odd to include a patriotic anthem, but to omit the Fourteenth Amendment, the most significant structural provision adopted since the original Framing. And it is no less baffling to leave out the original Constitution of 1787 while quoting the 1215 Magna Carta even to the point of its declaration that "fish-weirs shall be removed from the Thames." If an observer found these choices and omissions perplexing in isolation, he would be puzzled for a different reason when he read the Declaration of Independence seeking confirmation for the Counties' posted explanation that the "Ten Commandments' . . . influence is clearly seen in the Declaration"; in fact the observer would find that the Commandments are sanctioned as divine imperatives, while the Declaration of Independence holds that the authority of government to enforce the law derives "from the consent of the governed." If the observer had not thrown up his hands, he would probably suspect that the Counties were simply reaching for any way to keep a religious document on the walls of courthouses constitutionally required to embody religious neutrality.

IV

The importance of neutrality as an interpretive guide is no less true now than it was when the Court broached the principle in *Everson v. Board of Ed. of Ewing,* 330 U.S. 1 (1947), and a word needs to be said about the different view taken in today's dissent. We all agree, of course, on the need for some interpretative help.

V

Given the ample support for the District Court's finding of a predominantly religious purpose behind the Counties' third display, we affirm the Sixth Circuit in upholding the preliminary injunction.

JUSTICE O'CONNOR, concurring.

Given the history of this particular display of the Ten Commandments, the Court correctly finds an Establishment Clause violation. The purpose behind the counties' display is relevant because it conveys an unmistakable message of endorsement to the reasonable observer.

JUSTICE SCALIA, with whom the CHIEF JUSTICE and JUSTICE THOMAS join, and with whom JUSTICE KENNEDY joins as to Parts II and III, dissenting.

I would uphold McCreary County and Pulaski County, Kentucky's (hereinafter Counties) displays of the Ten Commandments. I shall discuss first, why the Court's oft repeated assertion that the government cannot favor religious practice is false; second, why today's opinion extends the scope of that falsehood even beyond prior cases; and third, why even on the basis of the Court's false assumptions the judgment here is wrong.

I

A

On September 11, 2001 I was attending in Rome, Italy, an international conference of judges and lawyers, principally from Europe and the United States. That night and the next morning virtually all of the participants watched, in their hotel rooms, the address to the Nation by the President of the United States concerning the murderous attacks upon the Twin Towers and the Pentagon, in which thousands of Americans had been killed. The address ended, as Presidential addresses often do, with the prayer "God bless America." The next afternoon I was approached by one of the judges from a European country, who, after extending his profound condolences for my country's loss, sadly observed "How I wish that the Head of State of my country, at a similar time of national tragedy and distress, could conclude his address 'God bless _____.' It is of course absolutely forbidden."

That is one model of the relationship between church and state—a model spread across Europe by the armies of Napoleon, and reflected in the Constitution of France, which begins "France is [a] . . . secular . . . Republic." Religion is to be strictly excluded from the public forum. This is not, and never was, the model adopted by America.

These actions of our First President and Congress and the Marshall Court were not idiosyncratic; they reflected the beliefs of the period. Those who wrote the Constitution believed that morality was essential to the well-being of society and that encouragement of religion was the best way to foster morality.

With all of this reality (and much more) staring it in the face, how can the Court *possibly* assert that " 'the First Amendment mandates governmental neutrality between . . . religion and nonreligion,' " and that "manifesting a purpose to favor . . . adherence to religion generally," is unconstitutional? Who says so? Surely not the words of the Constitution. Surely not the history and traditions that reflect our society's constant understanding of those words. Surely not even the current sense of our society, recently reflected in an Act of Congress adopted *unanimously* by the Senate and with only 5 nays in the House of Representatives, criticizing a Court of Appeals opinion that had held "under God" in the Pledge of Allegiance unconstitutional.

What distinguishes the rule of law from the dictatorship of a shifting Supreme Court majority is the absolutely indispensable requirement that judicial opinions be grounded in consistently applied principle. That is what prevents judges from ruling now this way, now that—thumbs up or thumbs down—as their personal preferences dictate. Today's opinion forthrightly (or actually, somewhat less than forthrightly) admits that it does not rest upon consistently applied principle. In a revealing footnote, the Court acknowledges that the "Establishment Clause doctrine" it purports to be applying "lacks the comfort of categorical absolutes." What the Court means by this lovely euphemism is that sometimes the Court chooses to decide cases on the principle that government cannot favor religion, and sometimes it does not. The footnote goes on to say that "in special instances we have found good reason" to dispense with the principle, but "no such reasons present themselves here." It does not identify all of those "special instances," much less identify the "good reason" for their existence.

Historical practices thus demonstrate that there is a distance between the acknowledgment of a single Creator and the establishment of a religion.

II

As bad as the *Lemon* test is, it is worse for the fact that, since its inception, its seemingly simple mandates have been manipulated to fit whatever result the Court aimed to achieve. Today's opinion is no different. In two respects it modifies *Lemon* to ratchet up the Court's hostility to religion. First, the Court justifies inquiry into legislative purpose, not as an end itself, but as a means to ascertain the appearance of the government action to an " 'objective observer.' " Because in the Court's view the true danger to be guarded against is that the objective observer would feel like an "outsider" or "not [a] full member of the political community," its inquiry focuses not on the *actual purpose* of government action, but the "purpose apparent from government action." Under this approach, even if a government could show that its actual purpose was not to advance religion, it would presumably violate the Constitution as long as the Court's objective observer would think otherwise.

III

Even accepting the Court's *Lemon*-based premises, the displays at issue here were constitutional.

A

To any person who happened to walk down the hallway of the McCreary or Pulaski County Courthouse during the roughly nine months when the Foundations Displays were exhibited, the displays must have seemed unremarkable—if indeed they were noticed at all. The walls of both courthouses were already lined with historical documents and other assorted portraits; each Foundations Display was exhibited in the same format as these other displays and nothing in the record suggests that either County took steps to give it greater prominence.

In sum: The first displays did not necessarily evidence an intent to further religious practice; nor did the second displays, or the resolutions authorizing them; and there is in any event no basis for attributing whatever intent motivated the first and second displays to the third. Given the presumption of regularity that always accompanies our review of official action, the Court has identified no evidence of a purpose to advance religion in a way that is inconsistent with our cases. The Court may well be correct in identifying the third displays as the fruit of a desire to display the Ten Commandments, but neither our cases nor our history support its assertion that such a desire renders the fruit poisonous.

FOR DISCUSSION

To what degree, if any, does this decision require the state to "sanitize" displays of historic documents so that they no longer reflect any theological statement?

RELATED CASES

***Stone v. Graham*: 449 U.S. 39 (1980).**

Struck down a requirement that the Ten Commandments be posted in Kentucky public school classrooms.

***Lynch v. Donnelly*: 465 U.S. 668 (1984).**

Upheld a religious crèche that was displayed in the context of a variety of other largely secular symbols of the Christmas season.

***County of Allegheny v. ACLU*: 492 U.S. 573 (1989).**

Struck down the display of a religious crèche at a county courthouse while upholding the display of a large menorah next to a Christmas tree.

***Salazar v. Buono*, 559 U.S. 700 (2010).**

The U.S. district court had not adequately considered the context of a congressional law when it issued an order that prevented the transfer of a Latin cross on public land on Sunrise Rock in the Mojave National Preserve in southeastern California, which the Veterans of Foreign Wars had constructed 70 years earlier to commemorate World War I veterans, to a private party in exchange for other land.

ADDRESS OF SENATOR JOHN F. KENNEDY TO THE GREATER HOUSTON MINISTERIAL ASSOCIATION

September 12, 1960, Rice Hotel, Houston, Texas

While the so-called religious issue is necessarily and properly the chief topic here tonight, I want to emphasize from the outset that we have far more critical issues to face in the 1960 election: the spread of Communist influence, until it now festers 90 miles off the coast of Florida—the humiliating treatment of our President and Vice President by those who no longer respect our power—the hungry children I saw in West Virginia, the old people who cannot pay their doctor bills, the families forced to give up their farms—an America with too many slums, with too few schools, and too late to the moon and outer space.

These are the real issues which should decide this campaign. And they are not religious issues—for war and hunger and ignorance and despair know no religious barriers.

But because I am a Catholic, and no Catholic has ever been elected President, the real issues in this campaign have been obscured—perhaps deliberately, in some quarters less responsible than this. So it is apparently necessary for me to state once again—not what kind of church I believe in, for that should be important only to me—but what kind of America I believe in.

I believe in an America where the separation of church and state is absolute—where no Catholic prelate would tell the President (should he be Catholic) how to act, and no Protestant minister would tell his parishioners for whom to vote—where no church or church school is granted any public funds or political preference—and where no man is denied public office merely because his religion differs from the President who might appoint him or the people who might elect him.

I believe in an America that is officially neither Catholic, Protestant nor Jewish—where no public official either requests or accepts instructions on public policy from the Pope, the National Council of Churches or any other ecclesiastical source—where no religious body seeks to impose its will directly or indirectly upon the general populace or the public acts of its officials—and where religious liberty is so indivisible that an act against one church is treated as an act against all.

For while this year it may be a Catholic against whom the finger of suspicion is pointed, in other years it has been, and may someday be again, a Jew—or a Quaker—or a Unitarian—or a Baptist. It was Virginia's harassment of Baptist preachers, for example, that helped lead to Jefferson's statute of religious freedom. Today I may be the victim—but tomorrow it may be you—until the whole fabric of our harmonious society is ripped at a time of great national peril.

Finally, I believe in an America where religious intolerance will someday end—where all men and all churches are treated as equal—where every man has the same right to attend or not attend the church of his choice—where there is no Catholic vote, no anti-Catholic vote, no bloc voting of any kind—and where Catholics, Protestants and Jews, at both the lay and pastoral level, will refrain from those attitudes of disdain and division which have so often marred their works in the past, and promote instead the American ideal of brotherhood.

That is the kind of America in which I believe. And it represents the kind of Presidency in which I believe—a great office that must neither be humbled by making it the instrument of any one religious group nor tarnished by arbitrarily withholding its occupancy from the members of any one religious group. I believe in a President whose religious views are his own private affair, neither imposed by him upon the nation or imposed by the nation upon him as a condition to holding that office.

I would not look with favor upon a President working to subvert the first amendment's guarantees of religious liberty. Nor would our system of checks and balances permit him to do so—and neither do I look with favor upon those who would work to subvert Article VI of the Constitution by requiring a religious test—even by indirection—for it. If they disagree with that safeguard they should be out openly working to repeal it.

I want a Chief Executive whose public acts are responsible to all groups and obligated to none—who can attend any ceremony, service or dinner his office may appropriately require of him—and whose fulfillment of his Presidential oath is not limited or conditioned by any religious oath, ritual or obligation.

This is the kind of America I believe in—and this is the kind I fought for in the South Pacific, and the kind my brother died for in Europe. No one suggested then that we may have a "divided loyalty," that we did "not believe in liberty," or that we belonged to a disloyal group that threatened the "freedoms for which our forefathers died."

And in fact this is the kind of America for which our forefathers died—when they fled here to escape religious test oaths that denied office to members of less favored churches—when they fought for the Constitution, the Bill of Rights, and the Virginia Statute of Religious Freedom—and when they fought at the shrine I visited today, the Alamo. For side by side with Bowie and Crockett died McCafferty and Bailey and Carey—but no one knows whether they were Catholic or not. For there was no religious test at the Alamo.

I ask you tonight to follow in that tradition—to judge me on the basis of my record of 14 years in Congress—on my declared stands against an Ambassador to the Vatican, against unconstitutional aid to parochial schools, and against any boycott of the public schools (which I have attended myself)—instead of judging me on the basis of these pamphlets and publications we all have seen that carefully select quotations out of context from the statements of Catholic church leaders, usually in other countries, frequently in other centuries, and always omitting, of course, the statement of the American Bishops in 1948 which strongly endorsed church-state separation, and which more nearly reflects the views of almost every American Catholic.

I do not consider these other quotations binding upon my public acts—why should you? But let me say, with respect to other countries, that I am wholly opposed to the state being used by any religious group, Catholic or Protestant, to compel, prohibit, or persecute the free exercise of any other religion. And I hope that you and I condemn with equal fervor those nations which deny their Presidency to Protestants and those which deny it to Catholics. And rather than cite the misdeeds of those who differ, I would cite the record of the Catholic Church in such nations as Ireland and France—and the independence of such statesmen as Adenauer and De Gaulle.

But let me stress again that these are my views—for contrary to common newspaper usage, I am not the Catholic candidate for President. I am the Democratic Party's candidate for President who happens also to be a Catholic. I do not speak for my church on public matters—and the church does not speak for me.

Whatever issue may come before me as President—on birth control, divorce, censorship, gambling or any other subject—I will make my decision in accordance with these views, in accordance with what my conscience tells me to be the national interest, and without regard to outside religious pressures or dictates. And no power or threat of punishment could cause me to decide otherwise.

But if the time should ever come—and I do not concede any conflict to be even remotely possible—when my office would require me to either violate my conscience or violate the national interest, then I would resign the office; and I hope any conscientious public servant would do the same.

But I do not intend to apologize for these views to my critics of either Catholic or Protestant faith—nor do I intend to disavow either my views or my church in order to win this election.

If I should lose on the real issues, I shall return to my seat in the Senate, satisfied that I had tried my best and was fairly judged. But if this election is decided on the basis that 40 million Americans lost their chance of being President on the day they were baptized, then it is the whole nation that will be the loser, in the eyes of Catholics and non-Catholics around the world, in the eyes of history, and in the eyes of our own people.

But if, on the other hand, I should win the election, then I shall devote every effort of mind and spirit to fulfilling the oath of the Presidency—practically identical, I might add, to the oath I have taken for 14 years in the Congress. For without reservation, I can "solemnly swear that I will faithfully execute the office of President of the United States, and will to the best of my ability preserve, protect, and defend the Constitution . . . so help me God."

FOR DISCUSSION

In December 2007, former Massachusetts governor Mitt Romney, a member of the Church of Jesus Christ of Latter-day Saints, gave a similar speech after concerns were raised about his Mormon faith. Although, like Kennedy, he stressed that he was running as a party candidate and not as a member of a church, he pursued a more accommodative stance on church and state, emphasizing much more than had Kennedy, the role that religion had played in the foundation of the nation. Do you think this reflects a change in attitudes toward church and state from 1960 to 2007, greater religious commitment on the part of Romney, or something else?

The Free Exercise Clause

Whereas the Establishment Clause prevents official state sponsorship of religion, the Free Exercise Clause limits governmentally imposed restrictions on, or punishments for, religious beliefs. It protects religious worship and forbids the government from distinguishing among denominations.

The Belief-Action Dichotomy

In *Reynolds v. United States* (98 U.S. 145, 1879), the Supreme Court decided that freedom of belief did not always equate to freedom of action. It accordingly upheld a conviction of a bigamist who attempted to justify his actions on the basis of his religious beliefs (Reynolds was a member of the Church of Jesus Christ of Latter-day Saints, which, at the time, supported plural marriages), despite criminal laws to the contrary. The Court decided that the Free Exercise Clause did not give a free pass to those who would violate the laws, especially when the laws hurt others.

If the Free Exercise Clause does not permit bigamy or child sacrifice, however, what, if any, actions, or inactions, can it justify? The Court faced a test of this question in 1940 in reaching its decision in *Minersville School District v. Gobitis* (310 U.S. 586) and again three years later in *West Virginia State Board of Education v. Barnette* (319 U.S. 624). At issue were state-prescribed rules requiring students in public schools to salute the American flag. Jehovah's Witnesses, whose beliefs often brought adherents into conflict with state laws, believe that such salutes constitute a form of idolatry, forbidden by the Ten Commandments; in its first decision, however, the Court found that school boards could require flag salutes as a way of fostering patriotism. This decision unintentionally encouraged widespread acts of violence against Jehovah's Witnesses, who were also pacifists, at a time when the country was gearing up for World War II. The war also brought reports of individuals in Germany marching in lockstep and saluting Adolf Hitler.

By 1943, the Court majority was willing to acknowledge that it had made a mistake, and it reversed course. Scholars still debate whether the decision rested primarily on the Court's interpretation of freedom of speech or whether it rested chiefly on First Amendment rights of freedom of speech, which almost surely also include the right *not* to speak. However it is interpreted, many scholars view Justice Robert Jackson's expansive language in this case to be one of the Court's most eloquent statements of First Amendment freedoms.

The Compelling State Interest Test Applied

The decision in *Sherbert v. Verner* (374 U.S. 398, 1963) centered on the beliefs of another religious minority, namely, the Seventh-day Adventists. Like Orthodox Jews, Adventists believe that they are required to honor the Sabbath by abstaining from work on that day. When Sherbert was fired from a job for refusing to work on Saturdays and the state of North Carolina denied her unemployment compensation, she sued and eventually won her case before the Supreme Court. Unlike *Reynolds*, this case did not involve the violation of a criminal law, and here the Court decided that the government should not penalize the exercise of religious faith without first showing a "compelling state interest," The Court then ruled that such an interest was absent in the present case. The Court majority thought a state imposition on religious faith required more than mere administrative convenience, while dissenters feared that the decision converted a provision designed to shield citizens from negative governmental actions into a provision designed to guarantee positive entitlements.

The decision in *Wisconsin v. Yoder,* 406 U.S. 205 (1972), seems largely cut from the same cloth as *Sherbert.* Members of a religious minority known as the Old Order Amish, who believe that high school education has a corrupting influence on their youth, had decided to substitute apprenticeship programs for formal education of their children beyond the eighth grade. When it heard the state's appeal of the case that had resulted, the Court again decided that the state's interest in such formal education was not compelling. Only Justice Douglas worried that the Court had not, in protecting the rights of the parents, adequately secured the rights of students. Even so, he did not appear to have disagreed with the compelling state interest standard that the Court applied.

The Compelling State Interest Test Reconsidered

Perhaps the *Sherbert* and *Yoder* decisions encouraged complacency; perhaps commentators read them to say more than they intended. In any event, many scholars were shocked by the Court's decision in *Employment Division, Department of Human Resources of Oregon v. Smith* (494 U.S. 872, 1990). Like the appellant in *Sherbert v. Verner*, the appellee in *Smith*, who had been fired from his job for practicing his religion, had then been denied state unemployment benefits. In this case, however, the act of worship did not involve skipping work on Saturday but ingesting peyote, which the state of Oregon had made illegal. Justice Scalia rested his decision opposing *Smith* on this distinction. The fact that Smith had violated a criminal law was enough for Scalia, who thought that the compelling state interest test was too high a standard for the state to meet in such circumstances. Justice O'Connor wanted to retain the compelling state interest test but thought the state's interest in combating drugs was sufficient to meet it. Dissenting justices detected a tectonic shift in the earlier standard, which they had hoped to continue to apply.

Members of Congress were also concerned that the Court had undervalued the Free Exercise Clause. Attempting to use congressional powers as outlined in Section 5 of the Fourteenth Amendment, Congress in the Religious Freedom Restoration Act (1993) directed the Court to apply its earlier compelling state interest test. In *Boerne v. Flores* (521 U.S. 507, 1997), the Court decided that Congress had moved from seeking to *enforce* the Fourteenth Amendment to seeking to *rewrite* it and accordingly voided the application of the law in a case involve church zoning. In *Cutter v. Wilkinson* (544 U.S. 709, 2005), however, the Court did uphold an application of the Religious Land Use and Institutionalized Persons Act of 2000 to individuals confined in government institutions, and so the dialogue on this subject is likely to continue. The boundaries between acceptable governmental accommodation of religious exercise and improper "establishment" of religion will rarely be completely distinct, but whatever tensions there might be between them, the two clauses work together to enhance liberty.

West Virginia State Board of Education v. Barnette

319 U.S. 624, 63 S.Ct. 1178, 87 L.Ed. 1628 (1943)

The West Virginia State Board of Education adopted a resolution requiring a salute and pledge of allegiance to the flag. The penalty for failure to comply was expulsion from school, with the parents subject to a fine. The Jehovah's Witnesses, who have successfully engaged in litigation over a wide variety of church-state issues and who considered the flag salute to be a form of idolatry forbidden by the Ten Commandments, challenged the constitutionality of this regulation. This decision is remarkable because it overturns the ruling in *Minersville School District v. Gobitis* (310 U.S. 586, 1940), which the Court had announced just three years earlier. That decision had led to acts of widespread violence against the Jehovah's Witnesses. *West Virginia v. Barnette* is also noteworthy, and difficult to know where to place within a casebook because, like many other decisions in recent years, it mixes issues of religious exercise with issues of freedom of expression.

Vote: 6–3

Justice Jackson delivered the opinion of the Court.

. . . The freedom asserted by these appellees does not bring them into collision with rights asserted by any other individual. It is such conflicts which most frequently require intervention of the State to determine where the rights of one end and those of another begin. But the refusal of these persons to participate in the ceremony does not interfere with or deny rights of others to do so. Nor is there any question in this case that their behavior is peaceable and orderly. The sole conflict is between authority and rights of the individual. The State asserts power to condition access to public education on making a prescribed sign and profession and at the same time to coerce attendance by punishing both parent and child. The latter stand on a right of self-determination in matters that touch individual opinion and personal attitude.

As the present Chief Justice said in dissent in the *Gobitis* case, the State may "require teaching by instruction and study of all in our history and in the structure and organization of our government, including the guaranties of civil liberty, which tend to inspire patriotism and love of country." Here, however, we are dealing with a compulsion of students to declare a belief. They are not merely made acquainted with the flag salute so that they may be informed as to what it is or even what it means. The issue here is whether this slow and easily neglected route to aroused loyalties constitutionally may be short-cut by substituting a compulsory salute and slogan. . . .

Whether the First Amendment to the Constitution will permit officials to order observance of ritual of this nature does not depend upon whether as a voluntary exercise we would think it to be good, bad or merely innocuous. Any credo of nationalism is likely to include what some disapprove or to omit what others think essential, and to give off different overtones as it takes on different accents or interpretations. If official power exists to coerce acceptance of any patriotic creed, what it shall contain cannot be decided by courts, but must be largely discretionary with the ordaining authority, whose power to prescribe would no doubt include power to amend. Hence validity of the asserted power to force an American citizen publicly to profess any statement of belief or to engage in any ceremony of assent to one, presents questions of power that must be considered independently of any idea we may have as to the utility of the ceremony in question. . . .

The Fourteenth Amendment, as now applied to the States, protects the citizen against the State itself and all of its creatures—Boards of Education not excepted. These have, of course, important, delicate, and highly discretionary functions, but none that they may not perform within the limits of the Bill of Rights. That they are educating the young for citizenship is reason for scrupulous protection of Constitutional freedoms of the individual, if we are not to strangle the free mind at its source and teach youth to discount important principles of our government as mere platitudes.

Such Boards are numerous and their territorial jurisdiction often small. But small and local authority may feel less sense of responsibility to the Constitution, and agencies of publicity may be less vigilant in calling it to account. The action of Congress in making flag observance voluntary and respecting the conscience of the objector in a matter so vital as raising the Army contrasts sharply with these local regulations in matters relatively trivial to the welfare of the nation. There are village tyrants as well as village Hampdens, but none who acts under color of law is beyond reach of the Constitution.

The *Gobitis* opinion reasoned that this is a field "where courts possess no marked and certainly no controlling competence," that it is committed to the legislatures as well as the courts to guard cherished liberties and that it is constitutionally appropriate to "fight out the wise use of legislative authority in the forum of public opinion and before legislative assemblies rather than to transfer such a contest to the judicial arena," since all the "effective means of inducing political changes are left free."

The very purpose of a Bill of Rights was to withdraw certain subjects from the vicissitudes of political controversy, to place them beyond the reach of majorities and officials and to establish them as legal principles to be applied by the courts. One's rights to life, liberty, and property, to free speech, a free press, freedom of worship and assembly, and other fundamental rights may not be submitted to vote; they depend on the outcome of no elections.

In weighing arguments of the parties it is important to distinguish between the due process clause of the Fourteenth Amendment as an instrument for transmitting the principles of the First Amendment and those cases in which it is applied for its own sake. The test of legislation which collides with the Fourteenth Amendment, because it also collides with the principles of the First, is much more definite than the test when only the Fourteenth is involved. Much of the vagueness of the due process clause disappears when the specific prohibitions of the First become its standard. The right of a State to regulate, for example, a public utility may well include, so far as the due process test is concerned, power to impose all of the restrictions which a legislature may have a "rational basis" for adopting. But freedoms of speech and of press, of assembly, and of worship may not be infringed on such slender grounds. They are susceptible of restriction only to prevent grave and immediate danger to interests which the state may lawfully protect. It is important to note that while it is the Fourteenth Amendment which bears directly upon the State it is the more specific limiting principles of the First Amendment that finally govern this case. It seems trite but necessary to say that the First Amendment to our Constitution was designed to avoid those ends by avoiding these beginnings. There is no mysticism in the American concept of the State or of the nature or origin of its authority. We set up government by consent of the governed, and the Bill of Rights denies those in power any legal opportunity to coerce that consent. Authority here is to be controlled by public opinion, not public opinion by authority. If there is any fixed star in our constitutional constellation, it is that no official, high or petty, can prescribe what shall be orthodox in politics, nationalism, religion, or other matters of opinion or force citizens to confess by word or act their faith therein. If there are any circumstances which permit an exception, they do not now occur to us.

We think the action of the local authorities in compelling the flag salute and pledge transcends constitutional limitations on their power and invades the sphere of intellect and spirit which it is the purpose of the First Amendment to our Constitution to reserve from all official control.

The decision of this Court in *Minersville School District v. Gobitis* and the holdings of those few *per curiam* decisions which preceded and foreshadowed it are overruled, and the judgment enjoining enforcement of the West Virginia Regulation is Affirmed.

JUSTICE BLACK and JUSTICE DOUGLAS, concurring.

No well-ordered society can leave to the individuals an absolute right to make final decisions, unassailable by the State, as to everything they will or will not do. The First Amendment does not go so far. Religious faiths, honestly held, do not free individuals from responsibility to conduct themselves obediently to laws which are either imperatively necessary to protect society as a whole from grave and pressingly imminent dangers or which, without any general prohibition, merely regulate time, place or manner of religious activity. Decision as to the constitutionality of particular laws which strike at the substance of religious tenets and practices must be made by this Court. The duty is a solemn one, and in meeting it we cannot say that a failure, because of religious scruples, to assume a particular physical position and to repeat the words of a patriotic formula creates a grave danger to the nation. Such a statutory exaction is a form of test oath, and the test oath has always been abhorrent in the United States.

JUSTICE MURPHY, concurring.

A reluctance to interfere with considered state action, the fact that the end sought is a desirable one, the emotion aroused by the flag as a symbol for which we have fought and are now fighting again—all of these are understandable. But there is before us the right of freedom to believe, freedom to worship one's Maker according to the dictates of one's conscience, a right which the Constitution specifically shelters. Reflection has convinced me that as a judge I have no loftier duty or responsibility than to uphold that spiritual freedom to its farthest reaches. . . .

Official compulsion to affirm what is contrary to one's religious beliefs is the antithesis of freedom of worship which, it is well to recall, was achieved in this country only after what Jefferson characterized as the "severest contest in which I have ever been engaged."

JUSTICE FRANKFURTER, dissenting.

One who belongs to the most vilified and persecuted minority in history is not likely to be insensible to the freedoms guaranteed by our Constitution. Were my purely personal attitude relevant I should wholeheartedly associate myself with the general libertarian views in the Court's opinion, representing as they do the thought and action of a lifetime. But as judges we are neither Jew nor Gentile, neither Catholic nor agnostic. We owe equal attachment to the Constitution and are equally bound by our judicial obligations whether we derive our citizenship from the earliest or the latest immigrants to these shores. As a member of this Court I am not justified in writing my private notions of policy into the Constitution, no matter how deeply I may cherish them or how mischievous I may deem their disregard. The duty of a judge who must decide which of two claims before the Court shall prevail, that of a State to enact and enforce laws within its general competence or that of an individual to refuse obedience because of the demands of his conscience, is not that of the ordinary person. It can never be emphasized too much that one's own opinion about the wisdom or evil of a law should be excluded altogether when one is doing one's duty on the bench. The only opinion of our own even looking in that direction that is material is our opinion whether legislators could in reason have enacted such a law. In the light of all the circumstances, including the history of this question in this Court, it would require more daring than I possess to deny that reasonable legislators could have taken the action which is before us for review. Most unwillingly, therefore, I must differ from my brethren with regard to legislation like this. I cannot bring my mind to believe that the "liberty" secured by the Due Process Clause gives this Court authority to deny to the State of West Virginia the attainment of that which we all recognize as a legitimate legislative end, namely, the promotion of good citizenship, by employment of the means here chosen. . . .

FOR DISCUSSION

If members of another religious group believed they were required to salute the flag each day, and the school had not made provisions for them to do so, do you think the Free Exercise Clause would have required the accommodation of their beliefs?

RELATED CASES

***Reynolds v. United States:* 98 U.S. 145 (1879).**

Religious liberty does not include the performance of immoral or criminal acts even if those acts happen to be sanctioned by religious doctrine. The act in question here was polygamy.

***Davis v. Beason:* 133 U.S. 333 (1890).**

An Idaho statute denying the right to vote or hold office to any person practicing, advocating, or belonging to any organization that practices or advocates bigamy or polygamy was found to be an exercise of legislative power and not open to constitutional or legal objection. It was never intended that the First Amendment prohibit legislation punishing acts inimical to the peace, good order, and morals of society.

***Pierce v. Society of Sisters*: 268 U.S. 510 (1925).**

The liberty of parents to educate their children and the sanctity of property of schools was held to preclude the state from enacting legislation requiring attendance at public schools when nonpublic schools are available.

***Cantwell v. Connecticut*: 310 U.S. 196 (1940).**

The Court applied the Free Exercise Clause to the states via the Due Process Clause of the Fourteenth Amendment and decided that a municipality cannot require Jehovah's Witnesses to get a permit before beginning to solicit money for religious purposes.

***Hamilton v. Regents of the University of California*: 293 U.S. 245 (1934).**

The Court ruled that requiring students at a state university to take a course in military science and tactics is not a deprivation of liberty without due process.

***Jones v. Opelika*: 316 U.S. 584 (1942).**

Nondiscriminatory taxes that impose no special burden on those who sell religious literature are not invalid. In 1943 this decision was reversed by *Murdock* (see below).

***Jamison v. Texas*: 318 U.S. 413 (1943).**

The right to distribute handbills on religious subjects on the public streets cannot be prohibited at all times, at all places, and under all circumstances. Here an ordinance of Dallas was held void.

***Largent v. Texas*: 318 U.S. 418 (1943).**

Requiring a permit for the distribution of religious handbills is prior restraint and void. The handbills in question "seek in a lawful fashion to promote the raising of funds for religious purposes." Such handbills are to be distinguished from commercial handbills. Distribution of the latter can be regulated or prohibited. See also *Jamison v. Texas,* 318 U.S. 413 (1943).

***Murdock v. Pennsylvania*: 319 U.S. 105 (1943).**

Voided an ordinance of the city of Jeannette, Pennsylvania. requiring all solicitors to secure a license from the treasurer of the borough before beginning their activity.

***United States v. Ballard*: 322 U.S. 78 (1944).**

The truth or falsity of religious doctrine is not a proper matter for consideration by a jury.

***Cleveland v. United States*: 329 U.S. 14 (1946).**

The Mann Act applies to transportation of a woman across a state line for the purpose of entering into a plural marriage with her even though the marriage contemplated is motivated by religious doctrine.

***Marsh v. Alabama*: 326 U.S. 501 (1946).**

One may remain on private property contrary to the will of the owner and the law of the state as long as the only objective of the nonowner's presence is the exercise of an asserted right to spread his religious views. The alleged offense took place in Chickasaw, a company-owned town, a suburb of Mobile, which the Court held was no different from any other city. Thus, the "company town" was held to be performing a function that was basically governmental. Therefore it was bound by constitutional guarantees.

***Kunz v. New York*: 340 U.S. 290 (1951).**

When an administrative official is given administrative discretion to issue permits for speeches on religious matters, "the ordinance is clearly invalid as a prior restraint on the exercise of First Amendment rights."

***McGowan v. Maryland*: 366 U.S. 420 (1961).**

Sunday closing laws, or "blue laws," are not laws respecting the establishment of religion within the meaning of the First Amendment because the legislation is not religiously motivated; rather, its aim is to provide a uniform day of rest for all citizens. Since the classifications involved are reasonable, the legislation does not violate the Equal Protection Clause of the Fourteenth Amendment.

***Cox v. Louisiana*: 379 U.S. 536 (1965).**

Local officials cannot be permitted unfettered discretion in regulating the use of streets for peaceful parades and assemblies, although a state has the right to impose nondiscriminatory restrictions.

***Elk Grove Unified School District v. Newdow*: 542 U.S. 1 (2004).**

The Court decided that Newdow did not have standing to challenge to the words "under God" in the pledge of allegiance that was said in public schools even though, under precedent established by *West Virginia v. Barnette*, those who in fact had standing had been exempted from reciting those words.

SHERBERT V. VERNER

374 U.S. 398, 83 S.Ct. 1790, 10 L.Ed.2d 965 (1963)

In this case, the Supreme Court had to decide whether the Free Exercise Clause requires a state to provide unemployment compensation to a Seventh-day Adventist who had lost her job because of her refusal to work on Saturday, her denomination's day of worship and rest. In part, it had to decide whether giving such a benefit to promote her free exercise of religion constituted an improper establishment of religion.

Vote 7–2

JUSTICE BRENNAN delivered the opinion of the Court.

Appellant, a member of the Seventh-day Adventist Church, was discharged by her South Carolina employer because she would not work on Saturday, the Sabbath Day of her faith. When she was unable to obtain other employment because from conscientious scruples she would not take Saturday work, she filed a claim for unemployment compensation benefits under the South Carolina Unemployment Compensation Act. That law provides that, to be eligible for benefits, a claimant must be "able to work and . . . available for work"; and, further, that a claimant is ineligible for benefits "if . . . he has failed, without good cause . . . to accept available suitable work when offered him by the employment office or the employer. . . ." The appellee Employment Security Commission, in administrative proceedings under the statute, found that appellant's restriction upon her availability for Saturday work brought her within the provision disqualifying for benefits insured workers who fail, without good cause, to accept "suitable work when offered . . . by the employment office or the employer. . . ." The Commission's finding was sustained by the Court of Common Pleas for Spartanburg County. That court's judgment was in turn affirmed by the South Carolina Supreme Court, which rejected appellant's contention that, as applied to her, the disqualifying provisions of the South Carolina statute abridged her right to the free exercise of her religion secured under the Free Exercise Clause of the First Amendment through the Fourteenth Amendment. The State Supreme Court held specifically that appellant's ineligibility infringed no constitutional liberties because such a construction of the statute "places no restriction upon the appellant's freedom of religion nor does it in any way prevent her in the exercise of her right and freedom to observe her religious beliefs in accordance with the dictates of her conscience." We noted probable jurisdiction of appellant's appeal. We reverse the judgment of the South Carolina Supreme Court and remand for further proceedings not inconsistent with this opinion.

I

The door of the Free Exercise Clause stands tightly closed against any governmental regulation of religious *beliefs* as such, *Cantwell v. Connecticut,* 310 U.S. 296 (1940). Government may neither compel affirmation of a repugnant belief, *Torcaso v. Watkins,* 367 U.S. 488 (1961); nor penalize or discriminate against individuals or groups because they hold religious views abhorrent to the authorities, *Fowler v. Rhode Island,* 345 U.S. 67 (1953); nor employ the taxing power to inhibit the dissemination of particular religious views, *Murdock v. Pennsylvania,* 319 U.S. 105 (1943); *Follett v. McCormick,* 321 U.S. 573 (1944). On the other hand, the Court has rejected challenges under the Free Exercise Clause to governmental regulation of certain overt acts prompted by religious beliefs or principles, for "even when the action is in accord with one's religious convictions, [it] is not totally free from legislative restrictions." *Braunfeld v. Brown,* 366 U.S. 599 (1961). The conduct or actions so regulated have invariably posed some substantial threat to public safety, peace or order.

Plainly enough, appellant's conscientious objection to Saturday work constitutes no conduct prompted by religious principles of a kind within the reach of state legislation. If, therefore, the decision of the South Carolina Supreme Court is to withstand appellant's constitutional challenge, it must be either because her disqualification as a beneficiary represents no infringement by the State of her constitutional rights of free exercise, or because any incidental burden on the free exercise of appellant's religion may be justified by a "compelling state interest in the regulation of a subject within the State's constitutional power to regulate. . . ."

II

We turn first to the question whether the disqualification for benefits imposes any burden on the free exercise of appellant's religion. We think it is clear that it does. In a sense the consequences of such a disqualification to religious principles and practices may be only an indirect result of welfare legislation within the State's general competence to enact; it is true that no criminal sanctions directly compel appellant to work a six-day week. But this is only the beginning, not the end, of our inquiry. For "if the purpose or effect of a law is to impede the observance of one or all religions or is to discriminate invidiously between religions, that law is constitutionally invalid even though the burden may be characterized as being only indirect." *Braunfeld v. Brown.* Here not only is it apparent that appellant's declared ineligibility for benefits derives solely from the practice of her religion, but the pressure upon her to forego that practice is unmistakable. The ruling forces her to choose between following the precepts of her religion and forfeiting benefits, on the one hand, and abandoning one of the precepts of her religion in order to accept work, on the other hand. Governmental imposition of such a choice puts the same kind of burden upon the free exercise of religion as would a fine imposed against appellant for her Saturday worship.

Nor may the South Carolina court's construction of the statute be saved from constitutional infirmity on the ground that unemployment compensation benefits are not appellant's "right" but merely a "privilege." It is too late in the day to doubt that the liberties of religion and expression may be infringed by the denial of or placing of conditions upon a benefit or privilege. For example, in *Flemming v. Nestor,* 363 U.S. 603 (1960), the

Court recognized with respect to Federal Social Security benefits that "the interest of a covered employee under the Act is of sufficient substance to fall within the protection from arbitrary governmental action afforded by the Due Process Clause." In *Speiser v. Randall*, 357 U.S. 513 (1958), we emphasized that conditions upon public benefits cannot be sustained if they so operate, whatever their purpose, as to inhibit or deter the exercise of First Amendment freedoms. We there struck down a condition which limited the availability of a tax exemption to those members of the exempted class who affirmed their loyalty to the state government granting the exemption. While the State was surely under no obligation to afford such an exemption, we held that the imposition of such a condition upon even a gratuitous benefit inevitably deterred or discouraged the exercise of First Amendment rights of expression and thereby threatened to "produce a result which the State could not command directly. . . .To deny an exemption to claimants who engage in certain forms of speech is in effect to penalize them for such speech." Likewise, to condition the availability of benefits upon this appellant's willingness to violate a cardinal principle of her religious faith effectively penalizes the free exercise of her constitutional liberties.

Significantly South Carolina expressly saves the Sunday worshipper from having to make the kind of choice which we here hold infringes the Sabbatarian's religious liberty. When in times of "national emergency" the textile plants are authorized by the State Commissioner of Labor to operate on Sunday, "no employee shall be required to work on Sunday . . . who is conscientiously opposed to Sunday work; and if any employee should refuse to work on Sunday on account of conscientious . . . objections he or she shall not jeopardize his or her seniority by such refusal or be discriminated against in any other manner." No question of the disqualification of a Sunday worshipper for benefits is likely to arise, since we cannot suppose that an employer will discharge him in violation of this statute. The unconstitutionality of the disqualification of the Sabbatarian is thus compounded by the religious discrimination which South Carolina's general statutory scheme necessarily effects.

III

We must next consider whether some compelling state interest enforced in the eligibility provisions of the South Carolina statute justifies the substantial infringement of appellant's First Amendment right. It is basic that no showing merely of a rational relationship to some colorable state interest would suffice; in this highly sensitive constitutional area, "only the gravest abuses, endangering paramount interests, give occasion for permissible limitation," *Thomas v. Collins,* 323 U.S. 516 (1945). No such abuse or danger has been advanced in the present case. The appellees suggest no more than a possibility that the filing of fraudulent claims by unscrupulous claimants feigning religious objections to Saturday work might not only dilute the unemployment compensation fund but also hinder the scheduling by employers of necessary Saturday work. But that possibility is not apposite here because no such objection appears to have been made before the South Carolina Supreme Court, and we are unwilling to assess the importance of an asserted state interest without the views of the state court. Nor, if the contention had been made below, would the record appear to sustain it; there is no proof whatever to warrant such fears of malingering or deceit as those which the respondents now advance. Even if consideration of such evidence is not foreclosed by the prohibition against judicial inquiry into the truth or falsity of religious beliefs, *United States v. Ballard,* 322 U.S. 78 (1944)—a question as to which we intimate no view since it is not before us—it is highly doubtful whether such evidence would be sufficient to warrant a substantial infringement of religious liberties. For even if the possibility of spurious claims did threaten to dilute the fund and disrupt the scheduling of work, it would plainly be incumbent upon the appellees to demonstrate that no alternative forms of regulation would combat such abuses without infringing First Amendment rights.

In these respects, then, the state interest asserted in the present case is wholly dissimilar to the interests which were found to justify the less direct burden upon religious practices in *Braunfeld v. Brown.* The Court recognized that the Sunday closing law which that decision sustained undoubtedly served "to make the practice of [the Orthodox Jewish merchants'] . . . religious beliefs more expensive." But the statute was nevertheless saved by a countervailing factor which finds no equivalent in the instant case—a strong state interest in providing one uniform day of rest for all workers. That secular objective could be achieved, the Court found, only by declaring Sunday to be that day of rest. Requiring exemptions for Sabbatarians, while theoretically possible, appeared to present an administrative problem of such magnitude, or to afford the exempted class so great a competitive advantage, that such a requirement would have rendered the entire statutory scheme unworkable. In the present case no such justifications underlie the determination of the state court that appellant's religion makes her ineligible to receive benefits.

IV

In holding as we do, plainly we are not fostering the "establishment" of the Seventh-day Adventist religion in South Carolina, for the extension of unemployment benefits to Sabbatarians in common with Sunday worshippers reflects nothing more than the governmental obligation of neutrality in the face of religious differences, and does not represent that involvement of religious with secular institutions which it is the object of the Establishment Clause to forestall. Nor does the recognition of the appellant's right to unemployment benefits under the state statute serve to abridge any other person's religious liberties. Nor do we, by our decision today, declare the existence of a constitutional right to unemployment benefits on the part of all persons whose religious convictions are the cause of their unemployment. This is not a case in which an employee's religious convictions serve to make him a nonproductive member of society. Finally, nothing we say today constrains the States to adopt any particular form or scheme of unemployment compensation. Our holding today is only that South Carolina may not constitutionally apply the eligibility provisions so as to constrain a worker to abandon his religious convictions respecting the day of rest. This holding but reaffirms a principle that we announced a decade and a half ago, namely that no State may "exclude individual Catholics, Lutherans, Mohammedans, Baptists, Jews, Methodists, Non-believers, Presbyterians, or the members of any other faith, *because of their faith, or lack of it*, from receiving the benefits of public welfare legislation." *Everson v. Board of Education,* 330 U.S. 1 (1947).

JUSTICE DOUGLAS, concurring.

This case is resolvable not in terms of what an individual can demand of government, but solely in terms of what government may not do to an individual in violation of his religious scruples. The fact that government cannot exact from me a surrender of one iota of my religious scruples does not, of course, mean that I can demand of government a sum of money, the better to exercise them. For the Free Exercise Clause is written in terms of what the government cannot do to the individual, not in terms of what the individual can exact from the government.

Those considerations, however, are not relevant here. If appellant is otherwise qualified for unemployment benefits, payments will be made to her not as a Seventh-day Adventist, but as an unemployed worker. Conceivably these payments will indirectly benefit her church, but no more so than does the salary of any public employee. Thus, this case does not involve the problems of direct or indirect state assistance to a religious organization—matters relevant to the Establishment Clause, not in issue here.

JUSTICE STEWART, concurring in the result.

Although fully agreeing with the result which the Court reaches in this case, I cannot join the Court's opinion. This case presents a double-barreled dilemma, which in all candor I think the Court's opinion has not succeeded in papering over. The dilemma ought to be resolved.

To require South Carolina to so administer its laws as to pay public money to the appellant under the circumstances of this case is thus clearly to require the State to violate the Establishment Clause as construed by this Court. This poses no problem for me, because I think the Court's mechanistic concept of the Establishment Clause is historically unsound and constitutionally wrong. I think the process of constitutional decision in the area of the relationships between government and religion demands considerably more than the invocation of broad-brushed rhetoric of the kind I have quoted. And I think that the guarantee of religious liberty embodied in the Free Exercise Clause affirmatively requires government to create an atmosphere of hospitality and accommodation to individual belief or disbelief. In short, I think our Constitution commands the positive protection by government of religious freedom—not only for a minority, however small—not only for the majority, however large—but for each of us.

JUSTICE HARLAN, whom JUSTICE WHITE joins, dissenting.

Today's decision is disturbing both in its rejection of existing precedent and in its implications for the future. The significance of the decision can best be understood after an examination of the state law applied in this case.

. . . What the Court is holding is that if the State chooses to condition unemployment compensation on the applicant's availability for work, it is constitutionally compelled to *carve out an exception*—and to provide benefits—for those whose unavailability is due to their religious convictions. Such a holding has particular significance in two respects.

First, despite the Court's protestations to the contrary, the decision necessarily overrules *Braunfeld v. Brown*, 366 U.S. 599 (1961), which held that it did not offend the "Free Exercise" Clause of the Constitution for a State to forbid a Sabbatarian to do business on Sunday. The secular purpose of the statute before us today is even clearer than that involved in *Braunfeld*. And just as in *Braunfeld*—where exceptions to the Sunday closing laws for Sabbatarians would have been inconsistent with the purpose to achieve a uniform day of rest and would have required case-by-case inquiry into religious beliefs—so here, an exception to the rules of eligibility based on religious convictions would necessitate judicial examination of those convictions and would be at odds with the limited purpose of the statute to smooth out the economy during periods of industrial instability. Finally, the indirect financial burden of the present law is far less than that involved in *Braunfeld*. Forcing a store owner to close his business on Sunday may well have the effect of depriving him of a satisfactory livelihood if his religious convictions require him to close on Saturday as well. Here we are dealing only with temporary benefits, amounting to a fraction of regular weekly wages and running for not more than 22 weeks. Clearly, any differences between this case and *Braunfeld* cut against the present appellant.

Second, the implications of the present decision are far more troublesome than its apparently narrow dimensions would indicate at first glance. The meaning of today's holding, as already noted, is that the State must furnish unemployment benefits to one who is unavailable for work if the unavailability stems from the exercise of religious convictions. The State, in other words, must *single out* for financial assistance those whose behavior is religiously motivated, even though it denies such assistance to others whose identical behavior (in this case, inability to work on Saturdays) is not religiously motivated.

It has been suggested that such singling out of religious conduct for special treatment may violate the constitutional limitations on state action. My own view, however, is that at least under the circumstances of this case it would be a permissible accommodation of religion for the State, if it *chose* to do so, to create an exception to its eligibility requirements for persons like the appellant. The constitutional obligation of "neutrality," is not so narrow a channel that the slightest deviation from an absolutely straight course leads to condemnation. There are too many instances in which no such course can be charted, too many areas in which the pervasive activities of the State justify some special provision for religion to prevent it from being submerged by an all-embracing secularism. The State violates its obligation of neutrality when, for example, it mandates a daily religious exercise in its public schools, with all the attendant pressures on the school children that such an exercise entails. But there is, I believe, enough flexibility in the Constitution to permit a legislative judgment accommodating an unemployment compensation law to the exercise of religious beliefs such as appellant's.

For very much the same reasons, however, I cannot subscribe to the conclusion that the State is constitutionally *compelled* to carve out an exception to its general rule of eligibility in the present case. Those situations in which the Constitution may require special treatment on account of religion are, in my view, few and far between, and this view is amply supported by the course of constitutional litigation in this area. . . .

FOR DISCUSSION

To what extent, if any, do you think this decision was influenced by the fact that South Carolina provided for exemptions for Sunday, as opposed to Saturday, work? Do you think the Court's recognition of the rights of Sabbatarians in any way tends toward the "establishment" of such religion? Is this decision consistent with blue laws that require all businesses (including those by Orthodox Jews and others who would normally close on Saturdays) to close on Sundays?

RELATED CASES

***Thomas v. Review Board of Indiana Employment Security Division:* 450 U.S. 707 (1981).**

A Jehovah's Witness who was transferred to a plant that produced tanks was entitled to unemployment compensation after quitting his new job because of religious convictions.

***Hobbie v. Unemployment Commission of Florida:* 480 U.S. 136 (1987).**

An individual who converted to the Seventh-day Adventist faith was entitled to unemployment compensation when she subsequently quit her job, which required her to work on Saturdays.

WISCONSIN V. YODER

406 U.S. 205, 92 S.Ct. 1526, 32 L.Ed.2d 15 (1972)

Religion often provides its members with the courage to differ, but what should be done when religious practices might adversely affect youth? In *Pierce v. Society of Sisters* (268 U.S. 510, 1925), the Supreme Court had decided that parents had the right to send their children to parochial schools. In Yoder the Court confronts the issue of whether members of the Old Order Amish should be permitted to withdraw their students from school after the eighth grade but prior to the state-mandated attendance age of sixteen.

Vote: 6–1

CHIEF JUSTICE BURGER delivered the opinion of the Court.

Respondents Jonas Yoder and Wallace Miller are members of the Old Order Amish religion, and respondent Adin Yutzy is a member of the Conservative Amish Mennonite Church. They and their families are residents of Green County, Wisconsin. Wisconsin's compulsory school-attendance law required them to cause their children to attend public or private school until reaching age 16 but the respondents declined to send their children, ages 14 and 15, to public school after they completed the eighth grade. The children were not enrolled in any private school, or within any recognized exception to the compulsory-attendance law, and they are conceded to be subject to the Wisconsin statute.

On complaint of the school district administrator for the public schools, respondents were charged, tried, and convicted of violating the compulsory-attendance law in Green County Court and were fined the sum of $5 each. Respondents defended on the ground that the application of the compulsory-attendance law violated their rights under the First and Fourteenth Amendments. The trial testimony showed that respondents believed, in accordance with the tenets of Old Order Amish communities generally, that their children's attendance at high school, public or private, was contrary to the Amish religion and way of life. They believed that by sending their children to high school, they would not only expose themselves to the danger of the censure of the church community, but, as found by the county court, also endanger their own salvation and that of their children. The State stipulated that respondents' religious beliefs were sincere.

A related feature of Old Order Amish communities is their devotion to a life in harmony with nature and the soil, as exemplified by the simple life of the early Christian era that continued in America during much of our early national life. Amish beliefs require members of the community to make their living by farming or closely related activities. Broadly speaking, the Old Order Amish religion pervades and determines the entire mode of life of its adherents. Their conduct is regulated in great detail by the *Ordnung*, or rules, of the church community. Adult baptism, which occurs in late adolescence, is the time at which Amish young people voluntarily undertake heavy obligations, not unlike the Bar Mitzvah of the Jews, to abide by the rules of the church community.

Amish objection to formal education beyond the eighth grade is firmly grounded in these central religious concepts. They object to the high school, and higher education generally, because the values they teach are in marked variance with Amish values and the Amish way of life; they view secondary school education as an impermissible exposure of their children to a "worldly" influence in conflict with their beliefs. The high school tends to emphasize intellectual and scientific accomplishments, self-distinction, competitiveness, worldly success, and social life with other students. Amish society emphasizes informal learning-through-doing; a life of "goodness," rather than a life of intellect; wisdom, rather than technical knowledge; community welfare, rather than competition; and separation from, rather than integration with, contemporary worldly society.

Formal high school education beyond the eighth grade is contrary to Amish beliefs, not only because it places Amish children in an environment hostile to Amish beliefs with increasing emphasis on competition in class work and sports and with pressure to conform to the styles, manners, and ways of the peer group, but also because it takes them away from their community, physically and emotionally, during the crucial and formative adolescent period of life. During this period, the children must acquire Amish attitudes favoring manual work and self-reliance and the specific skills needed to perform the adult role of an Amish farmer or housewife. They must learn to enjoy physical labor. Once a child has learned basic reading, writing, and elementary mathematics, these traits, skills, and attitudes admittedly fall within the category of those best learned through example and "doing" rather than in a classroom. And, at this time in life, the Amish child must also grow in his faith and his relationship to the Amish community if he is to be prepared to accept the heavy obligations imposed by adult baptism. In short, high school attendance with teachers who are not of the Amish faith—and may even be hostile to it—interposes a serious barrier to the integration of the Amish child into the Amish religious community. Dr. John Hostetler, one of the experts on Amish society, testified that the modern high school is not equipped, in curriculum or social environment, to impart the values promoted by Amish society.

The Amish do not object to elementary education through the first eight grades as a general proposition because they agree that their children must have basic skills in the "three R's" in order to read the Bible, to be good farmers and citizens, and to be able to deal with non-Amish people when necessary in the course of daily affairs. They view such a basic education as acceptable because it does not significantly expose their children to worldly values or interfere with their development in the Amish community during the crucial adolescent period. While Amish accept compulsory elementary education generally, wherever possible they have established their own elementary schools in many respects like the small local schools of the past. In the Amish belief higher learning tends to develop values they reject as influences that alienate man from God.

On the basis of such considerations, Dr. Hostetler testified that compulsory high school attendance could not only result in great psychological harm to Amish children, because of the conflicts it would produce, but would also, in his opinion, ultimately result in the destruction of the Old Order Amish church community as it exists in the United States today. The testimony of Dr. Donald A. Erickson, an expert witness on education, also showed that the Amish succeed in preparing their high school age children to be productive members of the Amish community. He described their system of learning through doing the skills directly relevant to their adult roles in the Amish community as "ideal" and perhaps superior to ordinary high school education. The evidence also showed that the Amish have an excellent record as law-abiding and generally self-sufficient members of society.

Although the trial court in its careful findings determined that the Wisconsin compulsory school-attendance law "does interfere with the freedom of the Defendants to act in accordance with their sincere religious belief" it also concluded that the requirement of high school attendance until age 16 was a "reasonable and constitutional" exercise of governmental power, and therefore denied the motion to dismiss the charges. The Wisconsin Circuit Court affirmed the convictions. The Wisconsin Supreme Court, however, sustained respondents' claim under the Free Exercise Clause of the First Amendment and reversed the convictions. A majority of the court was of the opinion that the State had failed to make an adequate showing that its interest in "establishing and maintaining an educational system overrides the defendants' right to the free exercise of their religion."

I

There is no doubt as to the power of a State, having a high responsibility for education of its citizens, to impose reasonable regulations for the control and duration of basic education. Providing public schools ranks at the very apex of the function of a State. Yet even this paramount responsibility was, in *Pierce v. Society of Sisters,* 268 U.S. 510 (1925), made to yield to the right of parents to provide an equivalent education in a privately operated system. There the Court held that Oregon's statute compelling attendance in a public school from age eight to age 16 unreasonably interfered with the interest of parents in directing the rearing of their offspring, including their education in church-operated schools. As that case suggests, the values of parental direction of the religious upbringing and education of their children in their early and formative years have a high place in our society. A State's interest in universal education, however highly we rank it, is not totally free from a balancing process when it impinges on fundamental rights and interests, such as those specifically protected by the Free Exercise Clause of the First Amendment, and the traditional interest of parents with respect to the religious upbringing of their children so long as they, in the words of *Pierce,* "prepare [them] for additional obligations."

It follows that in order for Wisconsin to compel school attendance beyond the eighth grade against a claim that such attendance interferes with the practice of a legitimate religious belief, it must appear either that the State does not deny the free exercise of religious belief by its requirement, or that there is a state interest of sufficient magnitude to override the interest claiming protection under the Free Exercise Clause. Long before there was general acknowledgment of the need for universal formal education, the Religion Clauses had specifically and firmly fixed the right to free exercise of religious beliefs, and buttressing this fundamental right was an equally firm, even if less explicit, prohibition against the establishment of any religion by government. The values underlying these two provisions relating to religion have been zealously protected, sometimes even at the expense of other interests of admittedly high social importance. The invalidation of financial aid to parochial schools by government grants for a salary subsidy for teachers is but one example of the extent to which courts have gone in this regard, notwithstanding that such aid programs were legislatively determined to be in the public interest and the service of sound educational policy by States and by Congress.

The essence of all that has been said and written on the subject is that only those interests of the highest order and those not otherwise served can overbalance legitimate claims to the free exercise of religion. We can accept it as settled, therefore, that, however strong the State's interest in universal compulsory education, it is by no means absolute to the exclusion or subordination of all other interests.

II

We come then to the quality of the claims of the respondents concerning the alleged encroachment of Wisconsin's compulsory school-attendance statute on their rights and the rights of their children to the free exercise of the religious beliefs they and their forebears have adhered to for almost three centuries. In evaluating those claims we must be careful to determine whether the Amish religious faith and their mode of life are, as they claim, inseparable and interdependent. A way of life, however virtuous and admirable, may not be interposed as a barrier to reasonable state regulation of education if it is based on purely secular considerations; to have the protection of the Religion Clauses, the claims must be rooted in religious belief. Although a determination of what is a "religious" belief or practice entitled to constitutional protection may present a most delicate question, the very concept of ordered liberty precludes allowing every person to make his own standards on matters of conduct in which society as a whole has important interests. Thus, if the Amish asserted their claims because of their subjective evaluation and rejection of the contemporary secular values accepted by the majority, much as Thoreau rejected the social values of his time and isolated himself at Walden Pond, their claims would not rest on a religious basis. Thoreau's choice was philosophical and personal rather than religious, and such belief does not rise to the demands of the Religion Clauses.

Giving no weight to such secular considerations, however, we see that the record in this case abundantly supports the claim that the traditional way of life of the Amish is not merely a matter of personal preference, but one of deep religious conviction, shared by an organized group, and intimately related to daily living. . . .

The record shows that the respondents' religious beliefs and attitude toward life, family, and home have remained constant—perhaps some would say static—in a period of unparalleled progress in human knowledge generally and great changes in education. The respondents freely concede, and indeed assert as an article of faith, that their religious beliefs and what we would today call "life style" have not altered in fundamentals for centuries. Their way of life in a church-oriented community, separated from the outside world and "worldly" influences, their attachment to nature and the soil, is a way inherently simple and uncomplicated, albeit difficult to preserve against the pressure to conform. Their rejection of telephones, automobiles, radios, and television, their mode of dress, of speech, their habits of manual work do indeed set them apart from much of contemporary society; these customs are both symbolic and practical.

As the society around the Amish has become more populous, urban, industrialized, and complex, particularly in this century, government regulation of human affairs has correspondingly become more detailed and pervasive. The Amish mode of life has thus come into conflict increasingly with requirements of contemporary society exerting a hydraulic insistence on conformity to majoritarian standards. So long as compulsory education laws were confined to eight grades of elementary basic education imparted in a nearby rural schoolhouse, with a large proportion of students of the Amish faith, the Old Order Amish had little basis to fear that school attendance would expose their children to the worldly influence they reject. But modern compulsory secondary education in rural areas is now largely carried on in a consolidated school, often remote from the student's home and alien to his daily home life. As the record so strongly shows, the values and programs of the modern secondary school are in sharp conflict with the fundamental mode of life mandated by the Amish religion; modern laws requiring compulsory secondary education have accordingly engendered great concern and conflict. The conclusion is inescapable that secondary schooling, by exposing Amish children to worldly influences in terms of attitudes, goals, and values contrary to beliefs, and by substantially interfering with the religious development of the Amish child and his integration into the way of life of the Amish faith community at the crucial adolescent stage of development, contravenes the basic religious tenets and practice of the Amish faith, both as to the parent and the child.

The impact of the compulsory-attendance law on respondents' practice of the Amish religion is not only severe, but inescapable, for the Wisconsin law affirmatively compels them, under threat of criminal sanction, to perform acts undeniably at odds with fundamental tenets of their religious beliefs. Nor is the impact of the compulsory-attendance law confined to grave interference with important Amish religious tenets from a subjective point of view. It carries with it precisely the kind of objective danger to the free exercise of religion that the First Amendment was designed to prevent. As the record shows, compulsory school attendance to age 16 for Amish children carries with it a very real threat of undermining the Amish community and religious practice as they exist today; they must either abandon belief and be assimilated into society at large, or be forced to migrate to some other and more tolerant region.

III

Neither the findings of the trial court nor the Amish claims as to the nature of their faith are challenged in this Court by the State of Wisconsin. Its position is that the State's interest in universal compulsory formal secondary education to age 16 is so great that it is paramount to the undisputed claims of respondents that their mode of preparing their youth for Amish life, after the traditional elementary education, is an essential part of their religious belief and practice. Nor does the State undertake to meet the claim that the Amish mode of life and education is inseparable from and a part of the basic tenets of their religion—indeed, as much a part of their religious belief and practices as baptism, the confessional, or a sabbath may be for others.

Wisconsin concedes that under the Religion Clauses religious beliefs are absolutely free from the State's control, but it argues that "actions," even though religiously grounded, are outside the protection of the First Amendment. But our decisions have rejected the idea that religiously grounded conduct is always outside the protection of the Free Exercise Clause. It is true that activities of individuals, even when religiously based, are often subject to regulation by the States in the exercise of their undoubted power to promote the health, safety, and general welfare, or the Federal Government in the exercise of its delegated powers. But to agree that religiously grounded conduct must often be subject to the broad police power of the State is not to deny that there are areas of conduct protected by the Free Exercise Clause of the First Amendment and thus beyond the power of the State to control, even under regulations of general applicability. This case, therefore, does not become easier because respondents were convicted for their "actions" in refusing to send their children to the public high school; in this context belief and action cannot be neatly confined in logic-tight compartments.

Nor can this case be disposed of on the grounds that Wisconsin's requirement for school attendance to age 16 applies uniformly to all citizens of the State and does not, on its face, discriminate against religions or a particular religion, or that it is motivated by legitimate secular concerns. A regulation neutral on its face may, in its application, nonetheless offend the constitutional requirement for governmental neutrality if it unduly burdens the free exercise of religion. The Court must not ignore the danger that an exception from a general obligation of citizenship on religious grounds may run afoul of the Establishment Clause, but that danger cannot be allowed to prevent any exception no matter how vital it may be to the protection of values promoted by the right of free exercise.

We turn, then, to the State's broader contention that its interest in its system of compulsory education is so compelling that even the established religious practices of the Amish must give way. Where fundamental claims of religious freedom are at stake, however, we cannot accept such a sweeping claim; despite its admitted validity in the generality of cases, we must searchingly examine the interests that the State seeks to promote by its requirement for compulsory education to age 16, and the impediment to those objectives that would flow from recognizing the claimed Amish exemption.

The State advances two primary arguments in support of its system of compulsory education. It notes, as Thomas Jefferson pointed out early in our history, that some degree of education is necessary to prepare citizens to participate effectively and intelligently in our open political system if we are to preserve freedom and independence. Further, education prepares individuals to be self-reliant and self-sufficient participants in society. We accept these propositions.

However, the evidence adduced by the Amish in this case is persuasively to the effect that an additional one or two years of formal high school for Amish children in place of their long-established program of informal vocational education would do little to serve those interests. . . .

The State, however, supports its interest in providing an additional one or two years of compulsory high school education to Amish children because of the possibility that some such children will choose to leave the Amish community, and that if this occurs they will be ill-equipped for life. The State argues that if Amish children leave their church they should not be in the position of making their way in the world without the education available in the one or two additional years the State requires. However, on this record, that argument is highly speculative. There is no specific evidence of the loss of Amish adherents by attrition, nor is there any showing that upon leaving the Amish community Amish children, with their practical agricultural training and habits of industry and self-reliance, would become burdens on society because of educational short-comings. Indeed, this argument of the State appears to rest primarily on the State's mistaken assumption, already noted, that the Amish do not provide "any education for their children beyond the eighth grade, but allow them to grow in ignorance." To the contrary, not only do the Amish accept the necessity for formal schooling through the eighth grade level, but continue to provide what has been characterized by the undisputed testimony of expert educators as an "ideal" vocational education for their children in the adolescent years.

In these terms, Wisconsin's interest in compelling the school attendance of Amish children to age 16 emerges as somewhat less substantial than requiring such attendance for children generally. For, while agricultural employment is not totally outside the legitimate concerns of the child labor laws, employment of children under parental guidance and on the family farm from age 14 to age 16 is an ancient tradition that lies at the periphery of the objectives of such laws. There is no intimation that the Amish employment of their children on family farms is in any way deleterious to their health or that Amish parents exploit children at tender years. Any such inference would be contrary to the record before us. Moreover, employment of Amish children on the family farm does not present the undesirable economic aspects of eliminating jobs that might otherwise be held by adults.

IV

Finally, the State, on authority of *Prince v. Massachusetts*, 321 U.S. 158 (1944), argues that a decision exempting Amish children from the State's requirement fails to recognize the substantive right of the Amish child to a secondary education, and fails to give due regard to the power of the State as *parens patriae* to extend the benefit of secondary education to children regardless of the wishes of their parents. . . .

This case, of course, is not one in which any harm to the physical or mental health of the child or to the public safety, peace, order, or welfare has been demonstrated or may be properly inferred. The record is to the contrary, and any reliance on that theory would find no support in the evidence.

Contrary to the suggestion of the dissenting opinion of Mr. Justice Douglas, our holding today in no degree depends on the assertion of the religious interest of the child as contrasted with that of the parents. It is the parents who are subject to prosecution here for failing to cause their children to attend school, and it is their right of free exercise, not that of their children, that must determine Wisconsin's power to impose criminal penalties on the parent.

JUSTICE DOUGLAS, dissenting in part.

I agree with the Court that the religious scruples of the Amish are opposed to the education of their children beyond the grade schools, yet I disagree with the Court's conclusion that the matter is within the dispensation of parents alone. The Court's analysis assumes that the only interests at stake in the case are those of the Amish parents on the one hand, and those of the State on the other. The difficulty with this approach is that, despite the Court's claim, the parents are seeking to vindicate not only their own free exercise claims, but also those of their high-school-age children.

It is argued that the right of the Amish children to religious freedom is not presented by the facts of the case, as the issue before the Court involves only the Amish parents' religious freedom to defy a state criminal statute imposing upon them an affirmative duty to cause their children to attend high school.

First, respondents' motion to dismiss in the trial court expressly asserts, not only the religious liberty of the adults, but also that of the children, as a defense to the prosecutions. It is, of course, beyond question that the parents have standing as defendants in a criminal prosecution to assert the religious interests of their children as a defense. Although the lower courts and a majority of this Court assume an identity of interest between parent and child, it is clear that they have treated the religious interest of the child as a factor in the analysis.

Second, it is essential to reach the question to decide the case, not only because the question was squarely raised in the motion to dismiss, but also because no analysis of religious-liberty claims can take place in a vacuum. If the parents in this case are allowed a religious exemption, the inevitable effect is to impose the parents' notions of religious duty upon their children. Where the child is mature enough to express potentially conflicting desires, it would be an invasion of the child's rights to permit such an imposition without canvassing his views. As in *Prince v. Massachusetts*, 321 U.S. 158 (1944), it is an imposition resulting from this very litigation. As the child has no other effective forum, it is in this litigation that his rights should be considered. And, if an Amish child desires to attend high school, and is mature enough to have that desire respected, the State may well be able to override the parents' religiously motivated objections.

Religion is an individual experience. It is not necessary, nor even appropriate, for every Amish child to express his views on the subject in a prosecution of a single adult. Crucial, however, are the views of the child whose parent is the subject of the suit. Frieda Yoder has in fact testified that her own religious views are opposed to high-school education. I therefore join the judgment of the Court as to respondent Jonas Yoder. But Frieda Yoder's views may not be those of Vernon Yutzy or Barbara Miller. I must dissent, therefore, as to respondents Adin Yutzy and Wallace Miller as their motion to dismiss also raised the question of their children's religious liberty.

FOR DISCUSSION

Do you agree with Justice Douglas that the Court should have investigated whether the wishes of parents and children might have diverged in this case? If the Court had conducted such an investigation and had found that the wishes of the students and parents differed, to whose wishes should it have deferred? Why?

EMPLOYMENT DIVISION, DEPARTMENT OF HUMAN RESOURCES OF OREGON V. SMITH

494 U.S. 872, 110 S.Ct. 1595, 108 L.Ed.2d 876 (1990)

The Free Exercise Clause suggests that governments should not seek to criminalize religious practices because of their perceived truth or untruth. But what application should governments give to criminal laws that fall with greater severity on one group of believers than on another? In this case, the Court wrestles with a law, criminalizing the use of peyote that fell with particular force on the Native American Church, which employed the mildly hallucinogenic drug as part of its worship. The case has ignited a major, and still controversial, reassessment of such legislation that continues to this day.

Vote 6–3

JUSTICE SCALIA delivered the opinion of the Court.

This case requires us to decide whether the Free Exercise Clause of the First Amendment permits the State of Oregon to include religiously inspired peyote use within the reach of its general criminal prohibition on use of that drug, and thus permits the State to deny unemployment benefits to persons dismissed from their jobs because of such religiously inspired use.

I

Oregon law prohibits the knowing or intentional possession of a "controlled substance" unless the substance has been prescribed by a medical practitioner. The law defines "controlled substance" as a drug classified in Schedules I through V of the Federal Controlled Substances Act, as modified by the State Board of Pharmacy. Persons who violate this provision by possessing a controlled substance listed on Schedule I are "guilty of a Class B felony." As compiled by the State Board of Pharmacy under its statutory authority, Schedule I contains the drug peyote, a hallucinogen derived from the plant *Lophophora williamsii Lemaire.*

Respondents Alfred Smith and Galen Black (hereinafter respondents) were fired from their jobs with a private drug rehabilitation organization because they ingested peyote for sacramental purposes at a ceremony of the Native American Church, of which both are members. When respondents applied to petitioner Employment Division (hereinafter petitioner) for unemployment compensation, they were determined to be ineligible for benefits because they had been discharged for work-related "misconduct." The Oregon Court of Appeals reversed that determination, holding that the denial of benefits violated respondents' free exercise rights under the First Amendment.

On appeal to the Oregon Supreme Court, petitioner argued that the denial of benefits was permissible because respondents' consumption of peyote was a crime under Oregon law. The Oregon Supreme Court reasoned, however, that the criminality of respondents' peyote use was irrelevant to resolution of their constitutional claim—since the purpose of the "misconduct" provision under which respondents had been disqualified was not to enforce the State's criminal laws but to preserve the financial integrity of the compensation fund, and since that purpose was inadequate to justify the burden that disqualification imposed on respondents' religious practice. Citing our decisions in *Sherbert v. Verner,* 374 U.S. 398 (1963), and *Thomas v. Review Bd. of Indiana Employment Security Div.,* 450 U.S. 707 (1981), the court concluded that respondents were entitled to payment of unemployment benefits. We granted certiorari.

Before this Court in 1987, petitioner continued to maintain that the illegality of respondents' peyote consumption was relevant to their constitutional claim. We agreed, concluding that "if a State has prohibited through its criminal laws certain kinds of religiously motivated conduct without violating the First Amendment, it certainly follows that it may impose the lesser burden of denying unemployment compensation benefits to persons who engage in that conduct." We noted, however, that the Oregon Supreme Court had not decided whether respondents' sacramental use of peyote was in fact proscribed by Oregon's controlled substance law, and that this issue was a matter of dispute between the parties. Being "uncertain about the legality of the religious use of peyote in Oregon," we determined that it would not be "appropriate for us to decide whether the practice is protected by the Federal Constitution." Accordingly, we vacated the judgment of the Oregon Supreme Court and remanded for further proceedings.

On remand, the Oregon Supreme Court held that respondents' religiously inspired use of peyote fell within the prohibition of the Oregon statute, which "makes no exception for the sacramental use" of the drug. It then considered whether that prohibition was valid under the Free Exercise Clause, and concluded that it was not. The court therefore reaffirmed its previous ruling that the State could not deny unemployment benefits to respondents for having engaged in that practice.

We again granted certiorari.

II

Respondents' claim for relief rests on our decisions in *Sherbert v. Verner, Thomas v. Review Bd. of Indiana Employment Security Div.,* and *Hobbie v. Unemployment Appeals Comm'n of Florida*, 480 U.S. 136 (1987), in which we held that a State could not condition the availability of unemployment insurance on an individual's willingness to forgo conduct required by his religion. As we observed in *Smith I*, 485 U.S. 660 (1988), however, the conduct at issue in those cases was not prohibited by law. We held that distinction to be critical, for "if Oregon does prohibit the religious use of peyote, and if that prohibition is consistent with the Federal Constitution, there is no federal right to engage in that conduct in Oregon," and "the State is free to withhold unemployment compensation from respondents for engaging in work-related misconduct, despite its religious motivation." Now that the Oregon Supreme Court has confirmed that Oregon does prohibit the religious use of peyote, we proceed to consider whether that prohibition is permissible under the Free Exercise Clause.

A

The Free Exercise Clause of the First Amendment, which has been made applicable to the States by incorporation into the Fourteenth Amendment, see *Cantwell v. Connecticut,* 310 U.S. 296 (1940), provides that "Congress shall make no law respecting an establishment of religion, or *prohibiting the free exercise thereof. . . .*" The free exercise of religion means, first and foremost, the right to believe and profess whatever religious doctrine one desires. Thus, the First Amendment obviously excludes all "governmental regulation of religious *beliefs* as such." *Sherbert v. Verner,* 374 U.S. 398 (1963). The government may not compel affirmation of religious belief, see *Torcaso v. Watkins,* 367 U.S. 488 (1961), punish the expression of religious doctrines it believes to be false, *United States v. Ballard,* 322 U.S. 78 (1944), impose special disabilities on the basis of religious views or religious status, see *McDaniel v. Paty*, 435 U.S. 618 (1978); *Fowler v. Rhode Island,* 345 U.S. 67 (1953), or lend its power to one or the other side in controversies over religious authority or dogma.

But the "exercise of religion" often involves not only belief and profession but the performance of (or abstention from) physical acts: assembling with others for a worship service, participating in sacramental use of bread and wine, proselytizing, abstaining from certain foods or certain modes of transportation. It would be true, we think (though no case of ours has involved the point), that a State would be "prohibiting the free exercise [of religion]" if it sought to ban such acts or abstentions only when they are engaged in for religious reasons, or only because of the religious belief that they display. It would doubtless be unconstitutional, for example, to ban the casting of "statues that are to be used for worship purposes," or to prohibit bowing down before a golden calf.

Respondents in the present case, however, seek to carry the meaning of "prohibiting the free exercise [of religion]" one large step further. They contend that their religious motivation for using peyote places them beyond the reach of a criminal law that is not specifically directed at their religious practice, and that is concededly constitutional as applied to those who use the drug for other reasons. They assert, in other words, that "prohibiting the free exercise [of religion]" includes requiring any individual to observe a generally applicable law that requires (or forbids) the performance of an act that his religious belief forbids (or requires). As a textual matter, we do not think the words must be given that meaning. It is no more necessary to regard the collection of a general tax, for example, as "prohibiting the free exercise [of religion]" by those citizens who believe support of organized government to be sinful, than it is to regard the same tax as "abridging the freedom . . . of the press" of those publishing companies that must pay the tax as a condition of staying in business. It is a permissible reading of the text, in the one case as in the other, to say that if prohibiting the exercise of religion (or burdening the activity of printing) is not the object of the tax but merely the incidental effect of a generally applicable and otherwise valid provision, the First Amendment has not been offended.

Our decisions reveal that the latter reading is the correct one. We have never held that an individual's religious beliefs excuse him from compliance with an otherwise valid law prohibiting conduct that the State is free to regulate. On the contrary, the record of more than a century of our free exercise jurisprudence contradicts that proposition. As described succinctly by Justice Frankfurter in *Minersville School Dist. Bd. of Ed. v. Gobitis,* 310 U. S. 586 (1940): "Conscientious scruples have not, in the course of the long struggle for religious toleration, relieved the individual from obedience to a general law not aimed at the promotion or restriction of religious beliefs. The mere possession of religious convictions which contradict the relevant concerns of a political society does not relieve the citizen from the discharge of political responsibilities." We first had occasion to assert that principle in *Reynolds v. United States,* 98 U.S. 145 (1879), where we rejected the claim that criminal laws against polygamy could not be constitutionally applied to those whose religion commanded the practice. "Laws," we said, "are made for the government of actions, and while they cannot interfere with mere religious belief and opinions, they may with practices. . . . Can a man excuse his practices to the contrary because of his religious belief? To permit this would be to make the professed doctrines of religious belief superior to the law of the land, and in effect to permit every citizen to become a law unto himself."

Subsequent decisions have consistently held that the right of free exercise does not relieve an individual of the obligation to comply with a "valid and neutral law of general applicability on the ground that the law proscribes (or prescribes) conduct that his religion prescribes (or proscribes)." In *Prince v. Massachusetts,* 321 U.S. 158 (1944), we held that a mother could be prosecuted under the child labor laws for using her children to dispense literature in the streets, her religious motivation notwithstanding. We found no constitutional infirmity in "excluding [these children] from doing there what no other children may do." In *Braunfeld v. Brown,* 366 U.S. 599 (1961), we upheld Sunday-closing laws against the claim that they burdened the religious practices of persons whose religions compelled them to refrain from work on other days. In *Gillette v. United States,* 401 U.S. 437 (1971), we sustained the military Selective Service System against the claim that it violated free exercise by conscripting persons who opposed a particular war on religious grounds.

Our most recent decision involving a neutral, generally applicable regulatory law that compelled activity forbidden by an individual's religion was *United States v. Lee,* 455 U.S. 252 (1982). There, an Amish employer, on behalf of himself and his employees, sought exemption from collection and payment of Social Security taxes on the ground that the Amish faith prohibited participation in governmental support programs. We rejected the claim that an exemption was constitutionally required. There would be no way, we observed, to distinguish the Amish believer's objection to Social Security taxes from the religious objections that others might have to the collection or use of other taxes. "If, for example, a religious adherent believes war is a sin, and if a certain percentage of the federal budget can be identified as devoted to war-related activities, such individuals would have a similarly valid claim to be exempt from paying that percentage of the income tax. The tax system could not function if denominations were allowed to challenge the tax system because tax payments were spent in a manner that violates their religious belief.

The only decisions in which we have held that the First Amendment bars application of a neutral, generally applicable law to religiously motivated action have involved not the Free Exercise Clause alone, but the Free Exercise Clause in conjunction with other constitutional protections, such as freedom of speech and of the press, see *Cantwell v. Connecticut* (invalidating a licensing system for religious and charitable solicitations under which the administrator had discretion to deny a license to any cause he deemed nonreligious); *Murdock v. Pennsylvania,* 319 U. S. 105 (1943) (invalidating a flat tax on solicitation as applied to the dissemination of religious ideas); *Follett v. McCormick*, 321 U.S. 573 (1944) (same), or the right of parents, acknowledged in *Pierce v. Society of Sisters* (1925), to direct the education of their children, see *Wisconsin* v. *Yoder,* 406 U.S. 205 (1972) (invalidating compulsory school-attendance laws as applied to Amish parents who refused on religious grounds to send their children to school). Some of our cases prohibiting compelled expression, decided exclusively upon free speech grounds, have also involved freedom of religion, cf. *Wooley v. Maynard,* 430 U.S. 705 (1977) (invalidating compelled display of a license plate slogan that offended individual religious beliefs); *West Virginia Bd. of Education* v. *Barnette,* 319 U.S. 624 (1943) (invalidating compulsory flag salute statute challenged by religious objectors). And it is easy to envision a case in which a challenge on freedom of association grounds would likewise be reinforced by Free Exercise Clause concerns.

The present case does not present such a hybrid situation, but a free exercise claim unconnected with any communicative activity or parental right. Respondents urge us to hold, quite simply, that when otherwise prohibitable conduct is accompanied by religious convictions, not only the convictions but the conduct itself must be free from governmental regulation. We have never held that, and decline to do so now. There being no contention that Oregon's drug law represents an attempt to regulate religious beliefs, the communication of religious beliefs, or the raising of one's children in those beliefs, the rule to which we have adhered ever since *Reynolds* plainly controls. "Our cases do not at their farthest reach support the proposition that a stance of conscientious opposition relieves an objector from any colliding duty fixed by a democratic government." *Gillette v. United States,* 401 U.S. 437 (1971).

B

Respondents argue that even though exemption from generally applicable criminal laws need not automatically be extended to religiously motivated actors, at least the claim for a religious exemption must be evaluated under the balancing test set forth in *Sherbert v. Verner* (1963). Under the *Sherbert* test, governmental actions that substantially burden a religious practice must be justified by a compelling governmental interest. Applying that test we have, on three occasions, invalidated state unemployment compensation rules that conditioned the availability of benefits upon an applicant's willingness to work under conditions forbidden by his religion. See *Sherbert v. Verner; Thomas v. Review Bd. of Indiana Employment Security Div.* (1981); *Hobbie v. Unemployment Appeals Comm'n of Florida* (1987). We have never invalidated any governmental action on the basis of the *Sherbert* test except the denial of unemployment compensation. Although we have sometimes purported to apply the *Sherbert* test in contexts other than that, we have always found the test satisfied. In recent years we have abstained from applying the *Sherbert* test (outside the unemployment compensation field) at all. In *Bowen v. Roy*, 476 U.S. 693 (1986), we declined to apply *Sherbert* analysis to a federal statutory scheme that required benefit applicants and recipients to provide their Social Security numbers. The plaintiffs in that case asserted that it would violate their religious beliefs to obtain and provide a Social Security number for their daughter. We held the statute's application to the plaintiffs valid regardless of whether it was necessary to effectuate a compelling interest. In *Lyng v. Northwest Indian Cemetery Protective Assn.*, 485 U. S. 439 (1988), we declined to apply *Sherbert* analysis to the Government's logging and road construction activities on lands used for religious purposes by several Native American Tribes, even though it was undisputed that the activities "could have devastating effects on traditional Indian religious practices." In *Goldman v. Weinberger,* 475 U.S. 503 (1986), we rejected application of the *Sherbert* test to military dress regulations that forbade the wearing of yarmulkes. In *O'Lone v. Estate of*

Shabazz, 482 U.S. 342 (1987), we sustained, without mentioning the *Sherbert* test, a prison's refusal to excuse inmates from work requirements to attend worship services.

Even if we were inclined to breathe into *Sherbert* some life beyond the unemployment compensation field, we would not apply it to require exemptions from a generally applicable criminal law. The *Sherbert* test, it must be recalled, was developed in a context that lent itself to individualized governmental assessment of the reasons for the relevant conduct. As a plurality of the Court noted in *Roy*, a distinctive feature of unemployment compensation programs is that their eligibility criteria invite consideration of the particular circumstances behind an applicant's unemployment: "The statutory conditions [in *Sherbert* and *Thomas*] provided that a person was not eligible for unemployment compensation benefits if, 'without good cause,' he had quit work or refused available work. The 'good cause' standard created a mechanism for individualized exemptions." As the plurality pointed out in *Roy*, our decisions in the unemployment cases stand for the proposition that where the State has in place a system of individual exemptions, it may not refuse to extend that system to cases of "religious hardship" without compelling reason.

Whether or not the decisions are that limited, they at least have nothing to do with an across-the-board criminal prohibition on a particular form of conduct. Although, as noted earlier, we have sometimes used the *Sherbert* test to analyze free exercise challenges to such laws, we have never applied the test to invalidate one. We conclude today that the sounder approach, and the approach in accord with the vast majority of our precedents, is to hold the test inapplicable to such challenges. The government's ability to enforce generally applicable prohibitions of socially harmful conduct, like its ability to carry out other aspects of public policy, "cannot depend on measuring the effects of a governmental action on a religious objector's spiritual development." To make an individual's obligation to obey such a law contingent upon the law's coincidence with his religious beliefs, except where the State's interest is "compelling"—permitting him, by virtue of his beliefs, "to become a law unto himself," *Reynolds v. United States*, 345 U.S. 1 (1953)—contradicts both constitutional tradition and common sense.

The "compelling government interest" requirement seems benign, because it is familiar from other fields. But using it as the standard that must be met before the government may accord different treatment on the basis of race, see, *e. g., Palmore v. Sidoti,* 466 U.S. 429 (1984), or before the government may regulate the content of speech, is not remotely comparable to using it for the purpose asserted here. What it produces in those other fields—equality of treatment and an unrestricted flow of contending speech—are constitutional norms; what it would produce here—a private right to ignore generally applicable laws—is a constitutional anomaly.

Nor is it possible to limit the impact of respondents' proposal by requiring a "compelling state interest" only when the conduct prohibited is "central" to the individual's religion. It is no more appropriate for judges to determine the "centrality" of religious beliefs before applying a "compelling interest" test in the free exercise field, than it would be for them to determine the "importance" of ideas before applying the "compelling interest" test in the free speech field.

If the "compelling interest" test is to be applied at all, then, it must be applied across the board, to all actions thought to be religiously commanded. Moreover, if "compelling interest" really means what it says (and watering it down here would subvert its rigor in the other fields where it is applied), many laws will not meet the test. Any society adopting such a system would be courting anarchy, but that danger increases in direct proportion to the society's diversity of religious beliefs, and its determination to coerce or suppress none of them. Precisely because "we are a cosmopolitan nation made up of people of almost every conceivable religious preference," *Braunfeld v. Brown*, and precisely because we value and protect that religious divergence, we cannot afford the luxury of deeming *presumptively invalid*, as applied to the religious objector, every regulation of conduct that does not protect an interest of the highest order. The rule respondents favor would open the prospect of constitutionally required religious exemptions from civic obligations of almost every conceivable kind.

Values that are protected against government interference through enshrinement in the Bill of Rights are not thereby banished from the political process. Just as a society that believes in the negative protection accorded to the press by the First Amendment is likely to enact laws that affirmatively foster the dissemination of the printed word, so also a society that believes in the negative protection accorded to religious belief can be expected to be solicitous of that value in its legislation as well. It is therefore not surprising that a number of States have made an exception to their drug laws for sacramental peyote use. But to say that a nondiscriminatory religious-practice exemption is permitted, or even that it is desirable, is not to say that it is constitutionally required, and that the appropriate occasions for its creation can be discerned by the courts. It may fairly be said that leaving accommodation to the political process will place at a relative disadvantage those religious practices that are not widely engaged in; but that unavoidable consequence of democratic government must be preferred to a system in which each conscience is a law unto itself or in which judges weigh the social importance of all laws against the centrality of all religious beliefs.

JUSTICE O'CONNOR, concurring.

Although I agree with the result the Court reaches in this case, I cannot join its opinion. In my view, today's holding dramatically departs from well-settled First Amendment jurisprudence, appears unnecessary to resolve the question presented, and is incompatible with our Nation's fundamental commitment to individual religious liberty.

II

The Court today extracts from our long history of free exercise precedents the single categorical rule that "if prohibiting the exercise of religion . . . is . . . merely the incidental effect of a generally applicable and otherwise valid provision, the First Amendment has not been offended." Indeed, the Court holds that where the law is a generally applicable criminal prohibition, our usual free exercise jurisprudence does not even apply. To reach this sweeping result, however, the Court must not only give a strained reading of the First Amendment but must also disregard our consistent application of free exercise doctrine to cases involving generally applicable regulations that burden religious conduct.

A

The Free Exercise Clause of the First Amendment commands that "Congress shall make no law . . . prohibiting the free exercise [of religion]." In *Cantwell v. Connecticut,* 310 U.S. 296 (1940), we held that this prohibition applies to the States by incorporation into the Fourteenth Amendment and that it categorically forbids government regulation of religious beliefs. As the Court recognizes, however, the "free *exercise*" of religion often, if not invariably, requires the performance of (or abstention from) certain acts. Because the First Amendment does not distinguish between religious belief and religious conduct, conduct motivated by sincere religious belief, like the belief itself, must be at least presumptively protected by the Free Exercise Clause.

The Court today, however, interprets the Clause to permit the government to prohibit, without justification, conduct mandated by an individual's religious beliefs, so long as that prohibition is generally applicable. But a law that prohibits certain conduct—conduct that happens to be an act of worship for someone—manifestly does prohibit that person's free exercise of his religion. A person who is barred from engaging in religiously motivated conduct is barred from freely exercising his religion. Moreover, that person is barred from freely exercising his religion regardless of whether the law prohibits the conduct only when engaged in for religious reasons, only by members of that religion, or by all persons. It is difficult to deny that a law that prohibits religiously motivated conduct, even if the law is generally applicable, does not at least implicate First Amendment concerns.

The Court responds that generally applicable laws are "one large step" removed from laws aimed at specific religious practices. The First Amendment, however, does not distinguish between laws that are generally applicable and laws that target particular religious practices. Indeed, few States would be so naive as to enact a law directly prohibiting or burdening a religious practice as such. Our free exercise cases have all concerned generally applicable laws that had the effect of significantly burdening a religious practice. If the First Amendment is to have any vitality, it ought not be construed to cover only the extreme and hypothetical situation in which a State directly targets a religious practice. As we have noted in a slightly different context, " '[s]uch a test has no basis in precedent and relegates a serious First Amendment value to the barest level of minimum scrutiny that the Equal Protection Clause already provides.' "

To say that a person's right to free exercise has been burdened, of course, does not mean that he has an absolute right to engage in the conduct. Under our established First Amendment jurisprudence, we have recognized that the freedom to act, unlike the freedom to believe, cannot be absolute. Instead, we have respected both the First Amendment's express textual mandate and the governmental interest in regulation of conduct by requiring the government to justify any substantial burden on religiously motivated conduct by a compelling state interest and by means narrowly tailored to achieve that interest. The compelling interest test effectuates the First Amendment's command that religious liberty is an independent liberty, that it occupies a preferred position, and that the Court will not permit encroachments upon this liberty, whether direct or indirect, unless required by clear and compelling governmental interests "of the highest order." "Only an especially important governmental interest pursued by narrowly tailored means can justify exacting a sacrifice of First Amendment freedoms as the price for an equal share of the rights, benefits, and privileges enjoyed by other citizens." *Bowen v. Roy*, 476 U.S. 693, 728 (1986).

The Court attempts to support its narrow reading of the Clause by claiming that "[w]e have never held that an individual's religious beliefs excuse him from compliance with an otherwise valid law prohibiting conduct that the State is free to regulate." But as the Court later notes, as it must, in cases such as *Cantwell* and *Yoder* we have in fact interpreted the Free Exercise Clause to forbid application of a generally applicable prohibition to religiously motivated conduct.

The Court endeavors to escape from our decisions in *Cantwell* and *Yoder* by labeling them "hybrid" decisions, but there is no denying that both cases expressly relied on the Free Exercise Clause, and that we have consistently regarded those cases as part of the mainstream of our free exercise jurisprudence. Moreover, in each of the other cases cited by the Court to support its categorical rule, we rejected the particular constitutional claims before us only after carefully weighing the competing interests. See *Prince v. Massachusetts,* 321 U. S. 158 (1944) (state interest in regulating children's activities justifies denial of religious exemption from child labor laws); *Braunfeld v. Brown* (1961) (state interest in uniform day of rest justifies denial of religious exemption from Sunday closing law); *Gillette* (state interest in military affairs justifies denial of religious exemption from conscription laws); *Lee* (state interest in comprehensive Social Security system justifies denial of religious exemption from mandatory participation requirement). That we rejected the free exercise claims in those cases hardly calls into question the applicability of First Amendment doctrine in the first place. Indeed, it is surely unusual to judge the vitality of a constitutional doctrine by looking to the win-loss record of the plaintiffs who happen to come before us.

B

Respondents, of course, do not contend that their conduct is automatically immune from all governmental regulation simply because it is motivated by their sincere religious beliefs. The Court's rejection of that argument might therefore be regarded as merely harmless dictum. Rather, respondents invoke our traditional compelling interest test to argue that the Free Exercise Clause requires the State to grant them a limited exemption from its general criminal prohibition against the possession of peyote. The Court today, however, denies them even the opportunity to make that argument, concluding that "the sounder approach, and the approach in accord with the vast majority of our precedents, is to hold the [compelling interest] test inapplicable to" challenges to general criminal prohibitions.

In my view, however, the essence of a free exercise claim is relief from a burden imposed by government on religious practices or beliefs, whether the burden is imposed directly through laws that prohibit or compel specific religious practices, or indirectly through laws that, in effect, make abandonment of one's own religion or conformity to the religious beliefs of others the price of an equal place in the civil community.

A State that makes criminal an individual's religiously motivated conduct burdens that individual's free exercise of religion in the severest manner possible, for it "results in the choice to the individual of either abandoning his religious principle or facing criminal prosecution." I would have thought it beyond argument that such laws implicate free exercise concerns.

Indeed, we have never distinguished between cases in which a State conditions receipt of a benefit on conduct prohibited by religious beliefs and cases in which a State affirmatively prohibits such conduct. The *Sherbert* compelling interest test applies in both kinds of cases.

I would reaffirm that principle today: A neutral criminal law prohibiting conduct that a State may legitimately regulate is, if anything, *more* burdensome than a neutral civil statute placing legitimate conditions on the award of a state benefit.

C

Thus, the critical question in this case is whether exempting respondents from the State's general criminal prohibition "will unduly interfere with fulfillment of the governmental interest." Although the question is close, I would conclude that uniform application of Oregon's criminal prohibition is "essential to accomplish," its overriding interest in preventing the physical harm caused by the use of a Schedule I controlled substance. Oregon's criminal prohibition represents that State's judgment that the possession and use of controlled substances, even by only one person, is inherently harmful and dangerous. Because the health effects caused by the use of controlled substances exist regardless of the motivation of the user, the use of such substances, even for religious purposes, violates the very purpose of the laws that prohibit them. Moreover, in view of the societal interest in preventing trafficking in controlled substances, uniform application of the criminal prohibition at issue is essential to the effectiveness of Oregon's stated interest in preventing any possession of peyote.

For these reasons, I believe that granting a selective exemption in this case would seriously impair Oregon's compelling interest in prohibiting possession of peyote by its citizens. Under such circumstances, the Free Exercise Clause does not require the State to accommodate respondents' religiously motivated conduct.

JUSTICE BLACKMUN, with whom JUSTICES BRENNAN and MARSHALL join, dissenting.

This Court over the years painstakingly has developed a consistent and exacting standard to test the constitutionality of a state statute that burdens the free exercise of religion. Such a statute may stand only if the law in general, and the State's refusal to allow a religious exemption in particular, are justified by a compelling interest that cannot be served by less restrictive means.

Until today, I thought this was a settled and inviolate principle of this Court's First Amendment jurisprudence. The majority, however, perfunctorily dismisses it as a "constitutional anomaly." As carefully detailed in Justice O'Connor's concurring opinion, the majority is able to arrive at this view only by mischaracterizing this Court's precedents.

This distorted view of our precedents leads the majority to conclude that strict scrutiny of a state law burdening the free exercise of religion is a "luxury" that a well-ordered society cannot afford, and that the repression of minority religions is an "unavoidable consequence of democratic government." I do not believe the Founders thought their dearly bought freedom from religious persecution a "luxury," but an essential element of liberty—and they could not have thought religious intolerance "unavoidable," for they drafted the Religion Clauses precisely in order to avoid that intolerance.

For these reasons, I agree with Justice O'Connor's analysis of the applicable free exercise doctrine, and I join parts I and II of her opinion. As she points out, "the critical question in this case is whether exempting respondents from the State's general criminal prohibition 'will unduly interfere with fulfillment of the governmental interest.' " I do disagree, however, with her specific answer to that question.

I

In weighing the clear interest of respondents Smith and Black (hereinafter respondents) in the free exercise of their religion against Oregon's asserted interest in enforcing its drug laws, it is important to articulate in precise terms the state interest involved. It is not the State's broad interest in fighting the critical "war on drugs" that must be weighed against respondents' claim, but the State's narrow interest in refusing to make an exception for the religious, ceremonial use of peyote.

The State's interest in enforcing its prohibition, in order to be sufficiently compelling to outweigh a free exercise claim, cannot be merely abstract or symbolic. The State cannot plausibly assert that unbending application of a criminal prohibition is essential to fulfill any compelling interest, if it does not, in fact, attempt to enforce that prohibition. In this case, the State actually has not evinced any concrete interest in enforcing its drug laws against religious users of peyote. Oregon has never sought to prosecute respondents, and does not claim that it has made significant enforcement efforts against other religious users of peyote. The State's asserted interest thus amounts only to the symbolic preservation of an unenforced prohibition. But a government interest in "symbolism, even symbolism for so worthy a cause as the abolition of unlawful drugs," cannot suffice to abrogate the constitutional rights of individuals.

Similarly, this Court's prior decisions have not allowed a government to rely on mere speculation about potential harms, but have demanded evidentiary support for a refusal to allow a religious exception.

The State proclaims an interest in protecting the health and safety of its citizens from the dangers of unlawful drugs. It offers, however, no evidence that the religious use of peyote has ever harmed anyone. The factual findings of other courts cast doubt on the State's assumption that religious use of peyote is harmful.

The fact that peyote is classified as a Schedule I controlled substance does not, by itself, show that any and all uses of peyote, in any circumstance, are inherently harmful and dangerous. The Federal Government, which created the classifications of unlawful drugs from which Oregon's drug laws are derived, apparently does not find peyote so dangerous as to preclude an exemption for religious use. Moreover, other Schedule I drugs have lawful uses.

The carefully circumscribed ritual context in which respondents used peyote is far removed from the irresponsible and unrestricted recreational use of unlawful drugs. The Native American Church's internal restrictions on, and supervision of, its members' use of peyote substantially obviate the State's health and safety concerns.

Moreover, just as in *Yoder*, the values and interests of those seeking a religious exemption in this case are congruent, to a great degree, with those the State seeks to promote through its drug laws. Not only does the church's doctrine forbid nonreligious use of peyote; it also generally advocates self-reliance, familial responsibility, and abstinence from alcohol.

Finally, the State argues that granting an exception for religious peyote use would erode its interest in the uniform, fair, and certain enforcement of its drug laws. The State fears that, if it grants an exemption for religious peyote use, a flood of other claims to religious exemptions will follow. It would then be placed in a dilemma, it says, between allowing a patchwork of exemptions that would hinder its law enforcement efforts, and risking a violation of the Establishment Clause by arbitrarily limiting its religious exemptions. This argument, however, could be made in almost any free exercise case.

The State's apprehension of a flood of other religious claims is purely speculative. Almost half the States, and the Federal Government, have maintained an exemption for religious peyote use for many years, and apparently have not found themselves overwhelmed by claims to other religious exemptions. Allowing an exemption for religious peyote use would not necessarily oblige the State to grant a similar exemption to other religious groups. The unusual circumstances that make the religious use of peyote compatible with the State's interests in health and safety and in preventing drug trafficking would not apply to other religious claims.

II

Finally, although I agree with Justice O'Connor that courts should refrain from delving into questions whether, as a matter of religious doctrine, a particular practice is "central" to the religion, I do not think this means that the courts must turn a blind eye to the severe impact of a State's restrictions on the adherents of a minority religion.

The American Indian Religious Freedom Act, in itself, may not create rights enforceable against government action restricting religious freedom, but this Court must scrupulously apply its free exercise analysis to the religious claims of Native Americans, however unorthodox they may be. Otherwise, both the First Amendment and the stated policy of Congress will offer to Native Americans merely an unfulfilled and hollow promise.

FOR DISCUSSION

How does Scalia attempt to distinguish this case from the precedents of *Sherbert v. Verner* and *Wisconsin v. Yoder*? Do you think he succeeds? What arguments are there for applying, or not applying, the "compelling state interest" test in cases where a criminal law falls with disproportionate impact on one religious group rather than another?

It is unlikely that Oregon would have adopted a law outlawing all alcohol and making the use of wine in communion illegal. Had it done so, do you think the Court would have ruled in a similar fashion?

RELATED CASES

***Lyng v. Northwest Indians Cemetery Protective Association:* 485 U.S. 439 (1988).**

Ruled that the Free Exercise Clause does not prevent the government from harvesting timber in a site in a national forest that Native Americans considered to be sacred.

***Church of the Lukumi Babalu Aye v. City of Hialeah:* 508 U.S. 520 (1993).**

Struck down a city ordinance prohibiting the ritual sacrifice of animals that appeared to target members of the Santeria religion.

***Boerne v. Flores:* 521 U.S. 507 (1997).**

In a 6–3 vote, the Court, led by Justice Kennedy struck down a provision of the Religious Freedom Restoration Act of 1995 designed to require that the government show a "compelling state interest" when applying a law of general applicability that falls with particular force on groups of religious believers. Thus rejecting a church's attempt to exempt itself from a historic landmark ordinance, the Court ruled that Congress had exceeded its power under Section 5 of the Fourteenth Amendment (the Enforcement Clause) by seeking to redefine, rather than enforce the Amendment.

CUTTER V. WILKINSON

544 U.S. 709, 125 S.Ct. 2113, 161 L.Ed.2d 1020 (2005)

After the Court's decision in *Employment Division v. Smith* (494 U.S. 872, 1990), Congress adopted the Religious Freedom Restoration Act (RFRA), which attempted to require the Court to reimpose the compelling state interest test in Free Exercise cases. Congress justified the law under Section 5 of the Fourteenth Amendment, which invests the national legislature with power to "enforce" the amendment. In Boerne v. Flores (521 U.S. 507, 1997), the Court overturned this application of RFRA on the grounds that Congress had attempted to reinterpret the Fourteenth Amendment and reverse judgments on constitutionality, as opposed to enforcing the amendment. Congress then adopted the Religious Land Use and Institutionalized Persons Act of 2000 (RLUIPA), which attempted to reapply the compelling state interest test to individuals confined in governmental institutions. In Cutter the Supreme Court upholds the more limited law against charges that RLUIPA improperly advances religion contrary to the Establishment Clause.

Vote: 9–0

JUSTICE GINSBURG delivered the opinion of the Court.

Section 3 of the Religious Land Use and Institutionalized Persons Act of 2000 (RLUIPA), provides in part: "No government shall impose a substantial burden on the religious exercise of a person residing in or confined to an institution," unless the burden furthers "a compelling governmental interest" " and does so by "the least restrictive means." Plaintiffs below, petitioners here, are current and former inmates of institutions operated by the Ohio Department of Rehabilitation and Correction and assert that they are adherents of "nonmainstream" religions: the Satanist, Wicca, and Asatru religions, and the Church of Jesus Christ Christian. They complain that Ohio prison officials (respondents here), in violation of RLUIPA, have failed to accommodate their religious exercise in a variety of different ways, including retaliating and discriminating against them for exercising their nontraditional faiths, denying them access to religious literature, denying them the same opportunities for group worship that are granted to adherents of mainstream religions, forbidding them to adhere to the dress and appearance mandates of their religions, withholding religious ceremonial items that are substantially identical to those that the adherents of mainstream religions are permitted, and failing to provide a chaplain trained in their faith.

In response to petitioners' complaints, respondent prison officials have mounted a facial challenge to the institutionalized-persons provision of RLUIPA; respondents contend, *inter alia*, that the Act improperly advances religion in violation of the First Amendment's Establishment Clause. The District Court denied respondents' motion to dismiss petitioners' complaints, but the Court of Appeals reversed that determination. The appeals court held, as the prison officials urged, that the portion of RLUIPA applicable to institutionalized persons, violates the Establishment Clause. We reverse the Court of Appeals' judgment.

"This Court has long recognized that the government may . . . accommodate religious practices . . . without violating the Establishment Clause." *Hobbie* v. *Unemployment Appeals Comm'n of Fla.,* 480 U.S. 136 (1987). Just last Term, in *Locke* v. *Davey,* 540 U.S. 712 (2004), the Court reaffirmed that "there is room for play in the joints between" the Free Exercise and Establishment Clauses, allowing the government to accommodate religion beyond free exercise requirements, without offense to the Establishment Clause. "At some point, accommodation may devolve into 'an unlawful fostering of religion.' " *Corporation of Presiding Bishop of Church of Jesus Christ of Latter-day Saints* v. *Amos,* 483 U.S. 327 (1987) (quoting *Hobbie*). But § 3 of RLUIPA, we hold, does not, on its face, exceed the limits of permissible government accommodation of religious practices.

I A

RLUIPA is the latest of long-running congressional efforts to accord religious exercise heightened protection from government-imposed burdens, consistent with this Court's precedents. Ten years before RLUIPA's enactment, the Court held, in *Employment Div., Dept. of Human Resources of Ore. v. Smith*, 484 U.S. 872 (1990), that the First Amendment's Free Exercise Clause does not inhibit enforcement of otherwise valid laws of general application that incidentally burden religious conduct. In particular, we ruled that the Free Exercise Clause did not bar Oregon from enforcing its blanket ban on peyote possession with no allowance for sacramental use of the drug. Accordingly, the State could deny unemployment benefits to persons dismissed from their jobs because of their religiously inspired peyote use. The Court recognized, however, that the political branches could shield religious exercise through legislative accommodation, for example, by making an exception to proscriptive drug laws for sacramental peyote use.

Responding to *Smith*, Congress enacted the Religious Freedom Restoration Act of 1993 (RFRA), [which] "prohibits 'government' from 'substantially burdening' a person's exercise of religion even if the burden results from a rule of general applicability unless the government can demonstrate the burden '(1) is in furtherance of a compelling governmental interest; and (2) is the least restrictive means of furthering that compelling governmental interest.' " "Universal" in its coverage, RFRA "applied to all Federal and State law," but notably lacked a Commerce Clause underpinning or a Spending Clause limitation to recipients of federal funds. In *City of Boerne*, this Court invalidated RFRA as applied to States and their subdivisions, holding that the Act exceeded Congress' remedial powers under the Fourteenth Amendment.

Congress again responded, this time by enacting RLUIPA. Less sweeping than RFRA, and invoking federal authority under the Spending and Commerce Clauses, RLUIPA targets two areas: Section 2 of the Act concerns land-use regulation, § 3 relates to religious exercise by institutionalized persons, § 2000cc–1. Section 3, at issue here, provides that "no [state or local] government shall impose a substantial burden on the religious exercise of a person residing in or confined to an institution," unless the government shows that the burden furthers "a compelling governmental interest" and does so by "the least restrictive means." The Act defines "religious exercise" to include "any exercise of religion, whether or not compelled by, or central to, a system of religious belief." Section 3 applies when "the substantial burden [on religious exercise] is imposed in a program or activity that receives Federal financial assistance," or "the substantial burden affects, or removal of that substantial burden would affect, commerce with foreign nations, among the several States, or with Indian tribes." "A person may assert a violation of [RLUIPA] as a claim or defense in a judicial proceeding and obtain appropriate relief against a government."

Before enacting § 3, Congress documented, in hearings spanning three years, that "frivolous or arbitrary" barriers impeded institutionalized persons' religious exercise. To secure redress for inmates who encountered undue barriers to their religious observances, Congress carried over from RFRA the "compelling governmental interest"/"least restrictive means" standard. Lawmakers anticipated, however, that courts entertaining complaints under § 3 would accord "due deference to the experience and expertise of prison and jail administrators."

II A

The Religion Clauses of the First Amendment provide: "Congress shall make no law respecting an establishment of religion, or prohibiting the free exercise thereof." The first of the two Clauses, commonly called the Establishment Clause, commands a separation of church and state. The second, the Free Exercise Clause, requires government respect for, and noninterference with, the religious beliefs and practices of our Nation's people. While the two Clauses express complementary values, they often exert conflicting pressures.

Our decisions recognize that "there is room for play in the joints" between the Clauses, some space for legislative action neither compelled by the Free Exercise Clause nor prohibited by the Establishment Clause. In accord with the majority of Courts of Appeals that have ruled on the question, we hold that § 3 of RLUIPA fits within the corridor between the Religion Clauses: On its face, the Act qualifies as a permissible legislative accommodation of religion that is not barred by the Establishment Clause.

Foremost, we find RLUIPA's institutionalized-persons provision compatible with the Establishment Clause because it alleviates exceptional government-created burdens on private religious exercise.

Furthermore, the Act on its face does not founder on shoals our prior decisions have identified: Properly applying RLUIPA, courts must take adequate account of the burdens a requested accommodation may impose on nonbeneficiaries; and they must be satisfied that the Act's prescriptions are and will be administered neutrally among different faiths.

"The 'exercise of religion' often involves not only belief and profession but the performance of . . . physical acts [such as] assembling with others for a worship service [or] participating in sacramental use of bread and wine. . . ." *Smith.* Section 3 covers state-run institutions—mental hospitals, prisons, and the like—in which the government exerts a degree of control unparalleled in civilian society and severely disabling to private religious exercise. RLUIPA thus protects institutionalized persons who are unable freely to attend to their religious needs and are therefore dependent on the government's permission and accommodation for exercise of their religion.

We note in this regard the Federal Government's accommodation of religious practice by members of the military. . . .

We do not read RLUIPA to elevate accommodation of religious observances over an institution's need to maintain order and safety. Our decisions indicate that an accommodation must be measured so that it does not override other significant interests. In *Estate of Thornton v. Caldor,* 472 U.S. 703 (1985), the Court struck down a Connecticut law that "armed Sabbath observers with an absolute and unqualified right not to work on whatever day they designated as their Sabbath." We held the law invalid under the Establishment Clause because it "unyieldingly weighted" the interests of Sabbatarians "over all other interests."

We have no cause to believe that RLUIPA would not be applied in an appropriately balanced way, with particular sensitivity to security concerns. While the Act adopts a "compelling governmental interest" standard, "context matters" in the application of that standard. Lawmakers supporting RLUIPA were mindful of the urgency of discipline, order, safety, and security in penal institutions. They anticipated that courts would apply the Act's standard with "due deference to the experience and expertise of prison and jail administrators in establishing necessary regulations and procedures to maintain good order, security and discipline, consistent with consideration of costs and limited resources."

Finally, RLUIPA does not differentiate among bona fide faiths. In *Kiryas Joel Village School v. Grumet,* 512 U.S. 687 (1994), we invalidated a state law that carved out a separate school district to serve exclusively a community of highly religious Jews, the Satmar Hasidim. We held that the law violated the Establishment Clause, in part because it "singled out a particular religious sect for special treatment." RLUIPA presents no such defect. It confers no privileged status on any particular religious sect, and singles out no bona fide faith for disadvantageous treatment.

B

The Sixth Circuit misread our precedents to require invalidation of RLUIPA as "impermissibly advancing religion by giving greater protection to religious rights than to other constitutionally protected rights." Our decision in *Corporation of Presiding Bishop of Church of Jesus Christ of Latter-day Saints v. Amos,* 483 U. S. 327 (1987) counsels otherwise. There, we upheld against an Establishment Clause challenge a provision exempting "religious organizations from Title VII's prohibition against discrimination in employment on the basis of religion." The District Court in *Amos*, reasoning in part that the exemption improperly "singled out religious entities for a benefit," had "declared the statute unconstitutional as applied to secular activity." Religious accommodations, we held, need not "come packaged with benefits to secular entities."

Were the Court of Appeals' view the correct reading of our decisions, all manner of religious accommodations would fall. Congressional permission for members of the military to wear religious apparel while in uniform would fail, as would accommodations Ohio itself makes. Ohio could not, as it now does, accommodate "traditionally recognized" religions: The State provides inmates with chaplains "but not with publicists or political consultants," and allows "prisoners to assemble for worship, but not for political rallies."

In upholding RLUIPA's institutionalized-persons provision, we emphasize that respondents "have raised a facial challenge to [the Act's] constitutionality, and have not contended that under the facts of any of [petitioners'] specific cases . . . [that] applying RLUIPA would produce unconstitutional results." The District Court, noting the underdeveloped state of the record, concluded: A finding "that it is *factually impossible* to provide the kind of accommodations that RLUIPA will require without significantly compromising prison security or the levels of service provided to other inmates" cannot be made at this juncture.

Should inmate requests for religious accommodations become excessive, impose unjustified burdens on other institutionalized persons, or jeopardize the effective functioning of an institution, the facility would be free to resist the imposition. In that event, adjudication in as-applied challenges would be in order.

JUSTICE THOMAS, concurring.

I join the opinion of the Court. I agree with the Court that the Religious Land Use and Institutionalized Persons Act of 2000 (RLUIPA) is constitutional under our modern Establishment Clause case law. I write to explain why a proper historical understanding of the Clause as a federalism provision leads to the same conclusion.

I

The Establishment Clause provides that "Congress shall make no law respecting an establishment of religion." As I have explained, an important function of the Clause was to "make clear that Congress could not interfere with state establishments." The Clause, then, "is best understood as a federalism provision" that "protects state establishments from federal interference." Ohio contends that this federalism understanding of the Clause prevents federal oversight of state choices within the " 'play in the joints' " between the Free Exercise and Establishment Clauses. In other words, Ohio asserts that the Clause protects the States from federal interference with otherwise constitutionally permissible choices regarding religious policy. In Ohio's view, RLUIPA intrudes on such state policy choices and hence violates the Clause.

Ohio's vision of the range of protected state authority overreads the Clause. Ohio and its *amici* contend that, even though "States can no longer establish preferred churches" because the Clause has been incorporated against the States through the Fourteenth Amendment, "Congress is as unable as ever to contravene constitutionally permissible *State choices regarding religious policy*." That is not what the Clause says. The Clause prohibits Congress from enacting legislation "respecting an *establishment* of religion;" it does not prohibit Congress from enacting legislation "respecting religion" or "taking cognizance of religion."

II

On its face—the relevant inquiry, as this is a facial challenge—RLUIPA is not a law "respecting an establishment of religion." RLUIPA provides, as relevant: "No government shall impose a substantial burden on the religious exercise of a person residing in or confined to an institution, . . . even if the burden results from a rule of general applicability, unless the government demonstrates that imposition of the burden on that person," first, "furthers a compelling governmental interest," and second, "is the least restrictive means of furthering that compelling governmental interest." This provision does not prohibit or interfere with state establishments, since no State has established (or constitutionally could establish, given an incorporated Clause) a religion. Nor does the provision require a State to establish a religion: It does not force a State to coerce religious observance or payment of taxes supporting clergy, or require a State to prefer one religious sect over another. It is a law respecting religion, but not one respecting an establishment of religion.

In addition, RLUIPA's text applies to all laws passed by state and local governments, including "rules of general applicability," whether or not they concern an establishment of religion. State and local governments obviously have many laws that have nothing to do with religion, let alone establishments thereof. Numerous applications of RLUIPA therefore do not contravene the Establishment Clause, and a facial challenge based on the Clause must fail.

It also bears noting that Congress, pursuant to its Spending Clause authority, conditioned the States' receipt of federal funds on their compliance with RLUIPA. As noted above, RLUIPA may well exceed the spending power. Nonetheless, while Congress' condition stands, the States subject themselves to that condition by voluntarily accepting federal funds. The States' voluntary acceptance of Congress' condition undercuts Ohio's argument that Congress is encroaching on its turf.

FOR DISCUSSION

What do the last two cases and the legislative responses to them say about the respective roles of the legislative and judicial branches in making and interpreting laws?

RELATED CASE

***Gonzales v. O Centro Espirita Beneficente Uniao do Vegetal:* 546 U.S. 418 (2006).**

The Religious Freedom Restoration Act protected the rights of a Christian Spiritist group from Brazil to import a hallucinogenic sacramental tea against attempts by the U.S. Customs Agency to confiscate it.

EQUAL EMPLOYMENT OPPORTUNITY COMMISSION V. ABERCROMBIE & FITCH STORES

575 U.S. ___, 135 S.Ct. 2028, 192 L.Ed.2d 35 (2015)

Many of the protections within the Bill of Rights are fleshed out in legislation that Congress adopts. Few laws have been more important than the Civil Rights Act of 1964, which is best known for outlawing racial discrimination in places of public accommodation. At issue in this case is a provision of the law that prohibits prospective employers from refusing to hire individuals simply to avoid accommodating their religious faith if the employer can do so without undue hardship. In this case, The Equal Employment Opportunity Commission (EEOC) filed a case on behalf of Samantha Elauf, a practicing Muslim who showed up for her interview with Abercrombie & Fitch (a clothing store) in a headscarf. Although deemed otherwise employable, Abercrombie & Fitch thought that a headscarf would be inconsistent with its dress code for employees and decided not to hire her without her actually asking for an accommodation. The District Court had awarded Elauf $20,000 in damages, but the Tenth Circuit had reversed.

Vote: 8 ½ to ½

J. ALITO filing a concurring opinion and J. THOMAS concurring in part and dissenting in part.

JUSTICE SCALIA delivered the opinion of the Court.

Title VII of the Civil Rights Act of 1964 prohibits a prospective employer from refusing to hire an applicant in order to avoid accommodating a religious practice that it could accommodate without undue hardship. The question presented is whether this prohibition applies only where an applicant has informed the employer of his need for an accommodation. . . .

II

Title VII of the Civil Rights Act of 1964 78 Stat. 253, as amended, prohibits two categories of employment practices. It is unlawful for an employer:

> "(1) to fail or refuse to hire or to discharge any individual, or otherwise to discriminate against any individual with respect to his compensation, terms, conditions, or privileges of employment, because of such individual's race, color, religion, sex, or national origin; or
>
> (2) to limit, segregate, or classify his employees or applicants for employment in any way which would deprive or tend to deprive any individual of employment opportunities or otherwise adversely affect his status as an employee, because of such individual's race, color, religion, sex, or national origin." 42 U. S. C. § 2000e–2(a).

These two proscriptions, often referred to as the "disparate treatment" (or "intentional discrimination") provision and the "disparate impact" provision, are the only causes of action under Title VII. The word "religion" is defined to "includ[e] all aspects of religious observance and practice, as well as belief, unless an employer demonstrates that he is unable to reasonably accommodate to" a "religious observance or practice without undue hardship on the conduct of the employer's business." § 2000e(j).

Abercrombie's primary argument is that an applicant cannot show disparate treatment without first showing that an employer has "actual knowledge" of the applicant's need for an accommodation. We disagree. Instead, an applicant need only show that his need for an accommodation was a motivating factor in the employer's decision.

The disparate-treatment provision forbids employers to:

> (1) "fail . . . to hire" an applicant (2) "because of" (3) "such individual's . . . religion" (which includes his religious practice). Here, of course, Abercrombie (1) failed to hire Elauf. The parties concede that (if Elauf sincerely believes that her religion so requires) Elauf's wearing of a head-scarf is (3) a "religious practice." All that remains is whether she was not hired (2) "because of" her religious practice.

The term "because of" appears frequently in antidiscrimination laws. It typically imports, at a minimum, the traditional standard of but-for causation. *University of Tex. Southwestern Medical Center* v. *Nassar*, 570 U. S. ___ (2013). Title VII relaxes this standard, however, to prohibit even making a protected characteristic a "motivating factor" in an employment decision. 42 U. S. C. § 2000e– 2(m). "Because of" in § 2000e–2(a)(1) links the forbidden consideration to each of the verbs preceding it; an individual's actual religious practice may not be a motivating factor in failing to hire, in refusing to hire, and so on.

It is significant that § 2000e–2(a)(1) does not impose a knowledge requirement. As Abercrombie acknowledges, some antidiscrimination statutes do. For example, the Americans with Disabilities Act of 1990 defines discrimination to include an employer's failure to make "reasonable accommodations to the *known* physical or mental limitations" of an applicant. § 12112(b)(5)(A) (emphasis added). Title VII contains no such limitation.

Instead, the intentional discrimination provision prohibits certain *motives*, regardless of the state of the actor's knowledge. Motive and knowledge are separate concepts. An employer who has actual knowledge of the need for an accommodation does not violate Title VII by refusing to hire an applicant if avoiding that accommodation is not his *motive*. Conversely, an employer who acts with the motive of avoiding accommodation may violate Title VII even if he has no more than an unsubstantiated suspicion that accommodation would be needed.

Thus, the rule for disparate-treatment claims based on a failure to accommodate a religious practice is straightforward: An employer may not make an applicant's religious practice, confirmed or otherwise, a factor in employment decisions. For example, suppose that an employer thinks (though he does not know for certain) that a job applicant may be an orthodox Jew who will observe the Sabbath, and thus be unable to work on Saturdays. If the applicant actually requires an accommodation of that religious practice, and the employer's desire to avoid the prospective accommodation is a motivating factor in his decision, the employer violates Title VII.

Abercrombie urges this Court to adopt the Tenth Circuit's rule "allocat[ing] the burden of raising a religious conflict." Brief for Respondent 46. This would require the employer to have actual knowledge of a conflict between an applicant's religious practice and a work rule. The problem with this approach is the one that inheres in most incorrect interpretations of statutes: It asks us to add words to the law to produce what is thought to be a desirable result. That is Congress's province. We construe Title VII's silence as exactly that: silence. Its disparate-treatment provision prohibits actions taken with the *motive* of avoiding the need for accommodating a religious practice. A request for accommodation, or the employer's certainty that the practice exists, may make it easier to infer motive, but is not a necessary condition of liability.

Abercrombie argues in the alternative that a claim based on a failure to accommodate an applicant's religious practice must be raised as a disparate-impact claim, not a disparate-treatment claim. We think not. That might have been true if Congress had limited the meaning of "religion" in Title VII to religious *belief*—so that discriminating against a particular religious *practice* would not be disparate treatment though it might have disparate impact. In fact, however, Congress defined "religion," for Title VII's purposes, as "includ[ing] all aspects of religious observance and practice, as well as belief." 42 U. S. C.§ 2000e(j). Thus, religious practice is one of the protected characteristics that cannot be accorded disparate treatment and must be accommodated.

Nor does the statute limit disparate-treatment claims to only those employer policies that treat religious practices less favorably than similar secular practices. Abercrombie's argument that a neutral policy cannot constitute "intentional discrimination" may make sense in other contexts. But Title VII does not demand mere neutrality with regard to religious practices—that they be treated no worse than other practices. Rather, it gives them favored treatment, affirmatively obligating employers not "to fail or refuse to hire or discharge any individual . . . because of such individual's" "religious observance and practice." An employer is surely entitled to have, for example, a no- headwear policy as an ordinary matter. But when an applicant requires an accommodation as an "aspec[t] of religious . . . practice," it is no response that the subsequent "fail[ure] . . . to hire" was due to an otherwise-neutral policy. Title VII requires otherwise-neutral policies to give way to the need for an accommodation.

* * *

The Tenth Circuit misinterpreted Title VII's requirements in granting summary judgment. We reverse its judgment and remand the case for further consideration consistent with this opinion.

It is so ordered.

JUSTICE THOMAS, concurring in part and dissenting in part.

I agree with the Court that there are two—and only two—causes of action under Title VII of the Civil Rights Act of 1964 as understood by our precedents: a disparate-treatment (or intentional-discrimination) claim and a disparate-impact claim. *Ante,* at 3. Our agreement ends there. Unlike the majority, I adhere to what I had thought before today was an undisputed proposition: Mere application of a neutral policy cannot constitute "intentional discrimination." Because the Equal Employment Opportunity Commission (EEOC) can prevail here only if Abercrombie engaged in intentional discrimination, and because Abercrombie's application of its neutral Look Policy does not meet that description, I would affirm the judgment of the Tenth Circuit.

GLOSSARY

Accommodationists: Those who believe that government may accommodate religious exercises as long as it does not favor one religion over another.

Endorsement Test: A test devised by Justice Sandra Day O'Connor, which allows general accommodation of religion as long as such accommodation does not send the message that it is endorsing a religion or making adherents to any religious view feel as though the government is seeking to give benefits on the basis of religious beliefs.

Establishment Clause: Provision in the First Amendment prohibiting Congress from making any law "respecting an establishment of religion." This clause is usually linked to the concept of separation of church and state.

Free Exercise Clause: Language in the First Amendment providing for the exercise of religion without interference from government.

***Lemon* Test:** A three-part test, formulated in *Lemon v. Kurtzman* (403 U.S. 602, 1971), designed to ascertain whether laws violate the Establishment Clause. The test seeks to establish whether laws have a secular legislative purpose, whether their primary effect advances or inhibits religion, and whether they promote excessive entanglement between church and state.

Neutrality: An approach to the Establishment Clause that may either stress the need for the government to treat religions similarly or seek to treat religious adherents no better or worse than individuals who adhere to no religion.

Strict Separationists: Individuals who interpret the Constitution to provide for a high wall of separation between church and state.

Test Oaths: Affirmations of religious beliefs made as a condition to taking public office. Forbidden by a provision of Article VI of the Constitution.

SELECTED BIBLIOGRAPHY

Abraham, Henry J., and Barbara A. Perry. 2003. *Freedom and the Court: Civil Rights and Liberties in the United States*, 8th ed. Lawrence: University Press of Kansas.

Adams, Arlin M., and Charles J. Emmerich. 1990. *A Nation Dedicated to Religious Liberty: The Constitutional Heritage of the Religious Clauses.* Philadelphia: University of Pennsylvania Press.

Davis, Derek. 1991. *Original Intent: Chief Justice Rehnquist and the Course of American Church/State Relations*. Buffalo, NY: Prometheus Books.

Davis, Derek. 2005. *Religion and the Continental Congress, 1774–1789: Contributions to Original Intent.* New York: Oxford University Press.

Dunn, Charles, ed. 2008. *The Future of Religion in American Politics.* Lexington: University Press of Kentucky.

Guliuzza, Frank III. 2000. *Over the Wall: Protecting Religious Expression in the Public Square.* Albany: State University of New York Press.

Ivers, Gregg. 1993. *Redefining the First Freedom: The Supreme Court and the Consolidation of State Power.* New Brunswick, NJ: Transaction Publishers.

Levy, Leonard W. 1986. *The Establishment Clause and the First Amendment.* New York: Macmillan.

Miller, Nicholas P. 2012. *The Religious Roots of the First Amendment: Dissenting Protestants and the Separation of Church and State.* New York: Oxford University Press.

Monsma, Stephen V. 1993. *Positive Neutrality: Letting Religious Freedom Ring.* Westport, CT: Greenwood Press.

Noll, Mark A., ed. 1990. *Religion and American Politics: From the Colonial Period to the 1980s.* New York: Oxford University Press.

Reichley, A. James. 1985. *Religion in American Public Life.* Washington, DC: The Brookings Institution.

Sehat, David. 2015. *The Myth of American Religious Freedom*, updated edition. New York: Oxford University Press.

Sorauf, Frank J. 1976. *The Wall of Separation: The Constitutional Politics of Church and State.* Princeton, NJ: Princeton University Press.

Vile, John R., David Hudson, and David Schultz. 2008. *The Encyclopedia of the First Amendment.* Washington, DC: Congressional Quarterly.

CHAPTER III

Freedom of Speech

Timeline: Freedom of Speech

1787 The U.S. Constitution is written.

1791 States ratify the first ten amendments to the Constitution, beginning with Amendment I, which guarantees freedom of speech.

1798 The Sedition Act makes it a crime to criticize the government or the president of the United States.

1800 The Virginia Report challenges the constitutionality of the Sedition Act.

1801 The Democratic Republican Party wins the national election. Jefferson pardons individuals convicted under the Sedition Act.

1833 The Supreme Court decides in *Barron v. Baltimore* that the provisions in the Bill of Rights limit the national government only.

1859 British philosopher John Stuart Mill publishes *On Liberty*, an influential defense of freedom of speech.

1873 The Comstock Act makes it illegal to send obscene materials through the mail.

1902 The Free Speech League is founded in New York to commit itself to protecting all forms of expression. The League, the first such organization in the United States, was formed, largely in reaction to laws designed to target anarchism.

1917 The United States enters World War I. Congress enacts Espionage Act.

1919 Justice Oliver Wendell Holmes Jr. formulates the "clear and present danger test" in *Schenck v. United States*, which upholds the conviction of an American socialist who mailed antiwar literature to potential draftees.

1925 *Gitlow v. New York* upholds a conviction based on a publication that the Court believed had a "bad tendency" to bring about evils that Congress was empowered to prevent.

1938 In his *Carolene Products* Footnote 4, Justice Harlan Fiske Stone justifies a "double standard" that warrants greater scrutiny by the Court to First Amendment claims.

1940 The Smith Act makes it illegal to advocate the violent overthrow of the U.S. government.

1942 *Chaplinsky v. New Hampshire* allows for the prosecution of "fighting words."

1949 *Kovacs v. Cooper* permits the regulation of sound trucks as a reasonable "time, place, and manner" restriction. *Terminiello v. Chicago* overturns a "disorderly conduct" conviction of a priest who delivered a fiery speech.

1951 In *Dennis v. United States*, the Supreme Court upholds the application to leading Communists of the Smith Act, ruling that the law had weighed the "gravity of the evil" of such speech against the unlikelihood that it would succeed. In *Feiner v. New York* the Court allows for prosecution of speech that it thought threatened to create a "breach of the peace."

1952 *Beauharnais v. Illinois* recognizes the possibility of "group libel."

1968 *United States v. O'Brien* upholds a law punishing individuals who burn draft cards but indicating that government has to justify restraints on such symbolic speech.

1969 *Brandenburg v. Ohio* permits provocative speech by a Klan leader, ruling that it had not created the likelihood of "imminent lawless action." *Tinker v. Des Moines Independent School District* extends some protections to speech in public high schools.

1971 *Cohen v. California* decides that First Amendment protection of freedom of speech allows an individual to wear a jacket with a vulgar word in public.

1978 A circuit court decision in *Collin v. Smith* recognizes the rights of Nazis to march in uniform despite the provocative nature of such displays.

1986 *Bethel School District No. 403 v. Fraser* indicates that high school students can be punished for speech that is considered to be lewd or inappropriate for the audience.

1987 *Rankin v. McPherson* distinguishes between careless and hurtful words and "true threats" that the government may punish.

1988 *Hazelwood v. Kuhlmeier* allows a high school principal to censor a school newspaper.

1991 In *Rust v. Sullivan* the Court indicates that the government may legally restrict information that individuals working for it may disperse.

1989 *Ward v. Rock Against Racism* further articulates occasions when restrictions are reasonable in terms of time, place, and manner. *Texas v. Johnson* overturns the conviction of a protester who burned a U.S. flag.

1992 *R.A.V. v. City of St. Paul* strikes down a hate speech ordinance that seems to disfavor one kind of speech more than others.

1993 *Wisconsin v. Mitchell* allows courts to include consideration of whether crimes were motivated by "hate" in deciding on appropriate penalties.

1998 *National Endowment for the Arts v. Finley* upholds a restriction that Congress imposes on funding for the arts.

2000 *Wisconsin v. Southworth* rejects pleas from students who think that they should be able to limit the dispersal of activity fees to causes with which they agree.

2003 *Virginia v. Black* allows states to punish individuals who burned crosses but only when that action was used to for purposes of intimidation.

2007 *Morse v. Frederick* allows a school principal to discipline a student who sent a message that could be interpreted as favoring drug use.

2009 *Pleasant Grove City, Utah v. Summum* uses the doctrine of "government speech" to allow a city to refuse accepting a monument with the Seven Aphorisms of Summum.

2011 In *Brown v. Entertainment Merchants Ass'n,* the Supreme Court strikes down a state law seeking to ban and regulate the sale and distribution of violent video games.

2011 The Supreme Court *in Snyder v. Phelps* relies on free speech guarantees to overturn a jury verdict against individuals for infliction of emotional distress who had protested with anti-gay messages at the funeral of a member of the military. *Brown v. Entertainment Merchants Association* overturns a state law banning the sale of violent video games to minors.

2014 In *McCullen v. Coakley* the Supreme Court invalidates a 35-foot buffer zone between patients seeking abortions at clinics and individuals who wish to counsel these women in terms of not seeking to terminate their pregnancies.

2015 *Elonis v. United States* established that under the First Amendment, an individual must show more than negligence to collect damages for the posting of a violent rap lyric when the lyrics contain a disclaimer indicating that the threats are fictitious.

Walker v. Texas Division, Sons of Confederate Veterans, allows Texas to reject the display of a confederate flag on its license plates.

First Amendment:

Congress shall make no law . . . abridging the freedom of speech.

INTRODUCTION

Like the clauses in the First Amendment prohibiting an establishment of religion and protecting religious exercise, the phrase protecting freedom of speech is among the provisions that Americans most cherish. Freedom of speech is closely allied to the accompanying right of freedom of the press, which is treated in the next chapter. The rights of freedom of speech and press are important not only for individual personal development but also for the proper working of **republican**, or representative, government.

The rights to expressive freedoms protected in the First Amendment are broad. The entire amendment (excluding the religion clauses) protects the rights to freedom of speech, press, peaceful assembly, and to petition the government. All these freedoms are essential to the protection of free expression. Consequently, over the last two hundred plus years, the Supreme Court, as well as the lower federal and state courts, have a rich accumulation of literally tens of thousands of cases seeking to address two basic questions: What types of communication are covered by the First Amendment, and, among the types covered, what is the extent of the constitutional protections to which they are entitled? Both questions are the subject of an enormous amount of legal scholarship and often form the core of one or more classes on the First Amendment in law school.

No one book, let alone a single chapter, can provide an exhaustive account of what the First Amendment expressive freedoms mean and how the amendment protects them. In this volume, the topic has been divided into two chapters. This chapter looks at the core cases surrounding what is "speech" and the protections assigned to it under the First Amendment by the Supreme Court. The next chapter treats the other expressive rights, press and association, as well as special categories of speech, including obscenity, pornography, and commercial speech. The division of the First Amendment expressive freedoms into two chapters is meant to illuminate first what the Court has said core "free speech" is for individuals, but in some cases other entities, such as corporations, are also entitled to speak on some matters. However, the First Amendment is complex, rich with special categories of speech depending on its content or the identity of the person uttering it.

Theories of Free Speech

Even before the First Amendment was adopted, Article I, Section 6, contained a provision, called the **Speech and Debate Clause**, exempting members of Congress from being questioned in court about statements they made in that body. The right to choose representatives, which is so essential to republican government, would be difficult to exercise responsibly if candidates or voters could not freely express their views.

Like the free exercise of religion of the First Amendment, freedom of speech follows logically from the democratic proposition that no individual has the right to tell others what they must believe. Some democratic theorists further associate freedom of speech with the "**marketplace of ideas**." According to this theory, good ideas, like good products, are more likely to win popular favor than ideas that cannot be backed by sound arguments. Just as Americans increasingly resort to presidential debates to sort out political candidates, many seem confident that the cure for improvident, or unwise, speech is more speech rather than increased governmental restrictions.

The English utilitarian philosopher John Stuart Mill (1806–1873) was among those who argued that free speech not only enhances individual personal development but also promotes the general good. In his book *On Liberty* (first published in 1869), Mill maintained that that without challenge, individuals would come to hold their opinions as prejudices rather than really thinking through and understanding their own views.

Freedom of speech may come close to an absolute right; Justices Hugo Black and William O. Douglas, both appointed to the Court by Franklin D. Roosevelt, certainly thought so. They often argued that this right occupied a "**preferred position**" among constitutional guarantees. Such a position shifted the presumption to the side of the claimed right, rather than to the side of laws designed to limit it. Others continue to emphasize that however important First Amendment rights may be, they must be "balanced" against the very need for government. Such arguments are especially prominent in discussions of perceived threats to national order.

Speech That Criticizes the Government or Seems to Threaten Public Order: An Early Controversy

Largely because of the First Amendment, speech has been relatively unconstrained by federal law throughout American history, but there have been some exceptions. One of the earliest and most notable occurred in the administration of John Adams, during which the United States was engaged in an unofficial war with France, and bitter controversies over whether America should be supporting England or France spilled over into U.S. domestic policy.

Faced with this situation, Congress, dominated by members of the Federalist Party (largely founded by Alexander Hamilton), adopted the **Alien and Sedition Acts**. The former hindered the naturalization of aliens (immigrants who were not yet citizens), many of whom favored Democratic-Republicans, the other major political party that Thomas Jefferson and James Madison had founded. The latter directly impinged on First Amendment rights of free speech and press by making it a crime to criticize the president or government of the United States. This controversial law is the first reading in this chapter.

The Sedition Act was set to expire at the end of Adams's first term, and, partly as a consequence, the Supreme Court never reviewed its constitutionality. However, it clearly lost in the court of public opinion. To be sure, not everyone agreed with the Virginia and Kentucky Resolutions, which James Madison and Thomas Jefferson anonymously authored to oppose the law, but the primary disagreement focused on a single controversial idea that the Resolutions expressed: that states might "interpose" themselves against such laws in the hopes that other states would rally with them. Although other states did not rush to join Virginia and Kentucky Resolutions (discussed in Volume I of this textbook), an electoral majority did vote the Federalists out of office, bringing Jefferson's Democratic-Republican Party to power. Jefferson, in turn, pardoned those who had been convicted under the law.

Prior to the ratification of the Fourteenth Amendment in 1868, states regulated speech issues relative to blasphemy, obscenity, libel, and the like. Lincoln authorized some arrests of inflammatory editors and speakers during his wartime presidency, but federal laws on the subject were largely limited to acts, like the Comstock Act of 1876, that attempted to limit sending obscene materials through the mails.

SEDITION ACT

July 14, 1798

SECTION 1. Be it enacted by the Senate and House of Representatives of the United States of America, in Congress assembled, That if any persons shall unlawfully combine or conspire together, with intent to oppose any measure or measures of the government of the United States, which are or shall be directed by proper authority, or to impede the operation of any law of the United States, or to intimidate or prevent any person holding a place or office in or under the government of the United States, from undertaking, performing or executing his trust or duty, and if any person or persons, with intent as aforesaid, shall counsel, advise or attempt to procure any insurrection, riot, unlawful assembly, or combination, whether such conspiracy, threatening, counsel, advice, or attempt shall have the proposed effect or not, he or they shall be deemed guilty of a high misdemeanor, and on conviction, before any court of the United States having jurisdiction thereof, shall be punished by a fine not exceeding five thousand dollars, and by imprisonment during a term not less than six months nor exceeding five years; and further, at the discretion of the court may be ho]den to find sureties for his good behaviour in such sum, and for such time, as the said court may direct.

SEC. 2. And be it farther enacted, That if any person shall write, print, utter or publish, or shall cause or procure to be written, printed, uttered or published, or shall knowingly and willingly assist or aid in writing, printing, uttering or publishing any false, scandalous and malicious writing or writings against the government of the United States, or either house of the Congress of the United States, or the President of the United States, with intent to defame the said government, or either house of the said Congress, or the said President, or to bring them, or either of them, into contempt or disrepute; or to excite against them, or either or any of them, the hatred of the good people of the United States, or to stir up sedition within the United States, or to excite any unlawful combinations therein, for opposing or resisting any law of the United States, or any act of the President of the United States, done in pursuance of any such law, or of the powers in him vested by the constitution of the United States, or to resist, oppose, or defeat any such law or act, or to aid, encourage or abet any hostile designs of any foreign nation against United States, their people or government, then such person, being thereof convicted before any court of the United States having jurisdiction thereof, shall be punished by a fine not exceeding two thousand dollars, and by imprisonment not exceeding two years.

SEC. 3. And be it further enacted and declared, That if any person shall be prosecuted under this act, for the writing or publishing any libel aforesaid, it shall be lawful for the defendant, upon the trial of the cause, to give in evidence in his defence, the truth of the matter contained in the publication charged as a libel. And the jury who shall try the cause, shall have a right to determine the law and the fact, under the direction of the court, as in other cases.

SEC. 4. And be it further enacted, That this act shall continue and be in force until the third day of March, one thousand eight hundred and one, and no longer: Provided, that the expiration of the act shall not prevent or defeat a prosecution and punishment of any offence against the law, during the time it shall be in force.

FOR DISCUSSION

Advocates of the Sedition Act thought that it represented a major advance over legislation in England in that it specifically permitted individuals to use the truthfulness of what they had said to defend themselves in jury trials. Assuming that this language was an improvement, why might Democratic-Republicans have thought it was inadequate?

Responses to the Alien and Sedition Acts

Democratic-Republicans believed the Sedition Act violated the First Amendment. The states of Virginia and Kentucky adopted resolutions attempting to rally other state legislatures against the law. Anonymously authored by James Madison and Thomas Jefferson (then serving as vice president), these acts are chiefly known today for their view of federalism; they seem to elevate state review of legislation deemed to be unconstitutional over judicial review at a time when Federalists, who supported the laws, dominated the judiciary and never found occasion to invalidate such laws. The Virginia and Kentucky Resolutions remain an affirmation of a broad reading of the First Amendment long after they have largely ceased to be regarded as a viable approach to the relations between the states and the national government.

VIRGINIA RESOLUTION

RESOLVED, That the General Assembly of Virginia, doth unequivocably express a firm resolution to maintain and defend the Constitution of the United States and the Constitution of this State, against every aggression either foreign or domestic, and that they will support the government of the United States in all measures warranted by the former.

That the General Assembly doth particularly protest against the palpable and alarming infractions of the Constitution in the two late cases of the "Alien and Sedition Acts" passed at the last session of Congress; the first of which exercises a power no where delegated to the federal government, and which by uniting legislative and judicial powers to those of executive, subverts the general principles of free government; as well as the particular organization, and positive provisions of the federal constitution; and the other of which acts, exercises in like manner, a power not delegated by the constitution, but on the contrary, expressly and positively forbidden by one of the amendments thererto; a power, which more than any other, ought to produce universal alarm, because it is levelled against that right of freely examining public characters and measures, and of free communication among the people thereon, which has ever been justly deemed, the only effectual guardian of every other right.

That this state having by its Convention, which ratified the federal Constitution, expressly declared, that among other essential rights, "the Liberty of Conscience and of the Press cannot be cancelled, abridged, restrained, or modified by any authority of the United States," and from its extreme anxiety to guard these rights from every possible attack of sophistry or ambition, having with other states, recommended an amendment for that purpose, which amendment was, in due time, annexed to the Constitution; it would mark a reproachable inconsistency, and criminal degeneracy, if an indifference were now shewn, to the most palpable violation of one of the Rights, thus declared and secured; and to the establishment of a precedent which may be fatal to the other.

That the good people of this commonwealth, having ever felt, and continuing to feel, the most sincere affection for their brethren of the other states; the truest anxiety for establishing and perpetuating the union of all; and the most scrupulous fidelity to that constitution, which is the pledge of mutual friendship, and the instrument of mutual happiness; the General Assembly doth solemnly appeal to the like dispositions of the other states, in confidence that they will concur with this commonwealth in declaring, as it does hereby declare, that the acts aforesaid, are unconstitutional; and that the necessary and proper measures will be taken by each, for co-operating with this state, in maintaining the Authorities, Rights, and Liberties, referred to the States respectively, or to the people. . . .

Agreed to by the Senate, December 24, 1798.

FOR DISCUSSION

The Virginia and Kentucky Resolutions are more known for their defense of states' rights than for their articulation of First Amendment freedoms, but perhaps the latter is ultimately more important. Can you think of other occasions in which one or more states were more sympathetic to First Amendment rights than was Congress?

World War I and Beyond

The next set of federal laws that restricted political speech were the Espionage Act of 1917 and the Sedition Act of 1918. Congress adopted both during World War I when the national government mounted a vigorous campaign to enforce loyalty. After the passage of these acts, Attorney General A. Mitchell Palmer launched the so-called Palmer raids in which governmental personnel confiscated inflammatory materials from radical organizations.

The first case to emerge from these laws was *Schenck v. United States* (249 U.S. 47, 1919). Charles Schenck and Elizabeth Baer had been convicted for mailing literature to potential draftees comparing conscription to a form of involuntary servitude that was contrary to the Thirteenth Amendment. Justice Oliver Wendell Holmes Jr. decided that although in ordinary times and places the First Amendment would protect such speech. in the case at hand, the actions needed to be judged in the framework of wartime exigencies. Although he set a relatively high bar for suppressing speech, Holmes used the illustration of falsely shouting fire in a theater to indicate that this freedom was not absolute. He thus upheld the convictions on the basis that the speech in question posed a "**clear and present danger**" against which Congress had a right to legislate.

Later that year, Holmes dissented in *Abrams v. United States* (250 U.S. 616, 1919), where the Court majority purported to use his test to uphold another in a series of convictions of Russian immigrants who had distributed pamphlets opposing U.S. intervention in their homeland. Holmes did not believe such pamphleteering posed a similarly clear or present danger, and argued for a "free trade in ideas."

Holmes continued in dissent in *Gitlow v. New York* (268 U.S. 652, 1925), when the Court used New York's Criminal Anarchy Statute to uphold the conviction of Benjamin Gitlow and other socialists for publishing pamphlets advocating a proletariat revolution. The majority, concerned that "a single revolutionary spark may kindle a fire" that resulted in a "destructive conflagration," focused on the "bad tendency" of the literature in question to foment revolution. This standard was probably closer to the one that many states had been applying to free speech issues prior to *Schenck*. Ironically, while the Court upheld Gitlow's conviction, it was this case, highlighted in Chapter 1 of this volume on incorporation, in which the Court first explicitly announced that it would use the Fourteenth Amendment to declare unconstitutional state laws it saw as infringing on freedom of speech.

In 1940 Congress adopted the Smith Act, which made it a crime to advocate the violent overthrow of the national government. As World War II gave way to a world-wide cold war in which the United States and the Soviet Union were the major protagonists, representing, respectively, the free world and state-supported communism, the Communist Party of the USA continued to ally with Soviet policies, and the government launched an attack on its leaders through the Smith Act.

In *Dennis v. United States* (341 U.S. 494, 1951), the Court tried again to fashion a test that would properly weigh such actions in the Cold War context. Drawing from an appellate court decision that Judge Learned Hand had fashioned, the majority chose the "gravity of the evil" test, which allowed consideration of the weight of such evil (in this case, violent overthrow of the government) against its improbability in upholding the conviction of Communist Party leaders. *Yates v. United States* (354 U.S. 298, 1957) and other cases largely limited the application of *Dennis* to party founders, but Justices Hugo Black and William O. Douglas were among those who thought previous decisions had already compromised First Amendment protections.

Brandenburg v. Ohio (395 U.S. 444, 1969) ultimately provided the occasion for the Court to go beyond even the clear and present danger test to decide that it would overturn the conviction of a Ku Klux Klansman whose incoherent ramblings to an isolated crowd did not, in the Court's judgment, present the "threat of imminent lawless action." Justices Black and Douglas openly crowed over what they considered to be the demise of the clear and present danger test. Others hoped that the era of prosecuting people simply for provocative speech was at an end.

This section ends with *Brown v. Entertainment Merchants Ass'n*, 564 U.S. 786 (2011) and *McCullen v. Coakley*, 573 U.S. ___; 134 S.Ct. 2518 (2014). The first case involved a state law seeking to ban or regulate the sale and distribution of violent video games. The Court viewed this effort as **content-based** regulation of speech, finding that violent video games were protected by the First Amendment. The second case addressed the constitutionality of content and viewpoint neutral law that imposed a 35-foot buffer zone between women seeking abortions at clinics and individuals who wished to counsel them against that choice. Both cases address different forms and types of regulation of speech that pit contrasting rights or rights and policy against one another. In *McCullen* decision should be read alongside the abortion and reproductive rights cases found in Chapter IX.

In general, when the Court examines challenges raising First Amendment free speech claims, it uses strict scrutiny. The Court is especially skeptical of either content-based regulations, efforts to limit speech based on what is said, or **viewpoint regulations** that seek to limit a specific message or target a specific person or speaker.

SCHENCK V. UNITED STATES

249 U.S. 47, 39 S.Ct. 247, 63 L.Ed. 470 (1919)

The Espionage Act of 1917 forbade any circulation of false statements made with intent to hinder the military effort; included in this classification were attempts to cause disloyalty in the armed forces or to obstruct recruiting. Schenck, general secretary of the Socialist Party, sent out about fifteen thousand leaflets to persons who had been drafted, urging them to oppose the Conscription Act. Arrested, he challenged the validity of the Espionage Act under the First Amendment guarantees of freedom of speech and press.

Vote: 9–0

JUSTICE HOLMES delivered the opinion of the Court.

. . . We admit that in many places and in ordinary times the defendants in saying all that was said in the circular would have been within their constitutional rights. But the character of every act depends upon the circumstances in which it is done. The most stringent protection of free speech would not protect a man in falsely shouting fire in a theatre and causing a panic. It does not even protect a man from an injunction against uttering words that may have all the effect of force. . . .

The question in every case is whether the words are used in such circumstances and are of such a nature as to create a clear and present danger that they will bring about the substantive evils that Congress has a right to prevent. It is a question of proximity and degree. When a nation is at war many things that might be said in time of peace are such a hindrance to its effort that their utterance will not be endured so long as men fight and that no court could regard them as protected by any constitutional right. It seems to be admitted that if an actual obstruction of the recruiting service were proved, liability for words that produced that effect might be enforced. The statute of 1917 in § 4 punishes conspiracies to obstruct as well as actual obstruction. If the act (speaking, or circulating a paper), its tendency, and the intent with which it is done are the same, we perceive no ground for saying that success alone warrants making the act a crime. . . . Judgments affirmed.

FOR DISCUSSION

Do you find that Justice Holmes's analogy of falsely shouting fire in a theater is sufficient to establish that freedom of speech is not absolute? Do you think Schenck's actions in this case were equivalent to such an example? Did the actions constitute a clear and present danger to the war effort? To the nation as a whole? Explain.

GITLOW V. NEW YORK

268 U.S. 652, 45 S.Ct. 625, 69 L.Ed. 1138 (1925)

This case, parts of which were also printed in the first chapter dealing with incorporation of the Bill of Rights into the Fourteenth Amendment, advanced the **"bad tendency" test**, which seemed less deferential to speech than the "clear and present danger" test articulated by Holmes in *Schenck*. Gitlow and three other socialists had been indicted and convicted under New York's Criminal Anarchy Law, which called for the punishment of individuals who advocated "the duty, necessity or propriety of overthrowing or overturning organized by force or violence." Gitlow had arranged for the printing and distribution of socialist pamphlets.

Vote: 7–2

JUSTICE SANFORD delivered the opinion of the Court.

The indictment was in two counts. The first charged that the defendant had advocated, advised and taught the duty, necessity and propriety of overthrowing and overturning organized government by force, violence and unlawful means, by certain writings therein set forth entitled "The Left Wing Manifesto"; the second that he had printed, published and knowingly circulated and distributed a certain paper called "The Revolutionary Age," containing the writings set forth in the first count advocating, advising and teaching the doctrine that organized government should be overthrown by force, violence and unlawful means.

There was no evidence of any effect resulting from the publication and circulation of the Manifesto.

Extracts from the Manifesto are set forth in the margin. Coupled with a review of the rise of Socialism, it condemned the dominant "moderate Socialism" for its recognition of the necessity of the democratic parliamentary state; repudiated its policy of introducing Socialism by legislative measures; and advocated, in plain and unequivocal language, the necessity of accomplishing the "Communist Revolution" by a militant and "revolutionary Socialism", based on "the class struggle" and mobilizing the "power of the proletariat in action," through mass industrial revolts developing into mass political strikes and "revolutionary mass action", for the purpose of conquering and destroying the parliamentary state and establishing in its place, through a "revolutionary dictatorship of the proletariat", the system of Communist Socialism. . . .

The precise question presented, and the only question which we can consider under this writ of error, then is, whether the statute, as construed and applied in this case by the state courts, deprived the defendant of his liberty of expression in violation of the due process clause of the Fourteenth Amendment.

The statute does not penalize the utterance or publication of abstract "doctrine" or academic discussion having no quality of incitement to any concrete action. It is not aimed against mere historical or philosophical essays. It does not restrain the advocacy of changes in the form of government by constitutional and lawful means. What it prohibits is language advocating, advising or teaching the overthrow of organized government by unlawful means. These words imply urging to action. . . .

The Manifesto, plainly, is neither the statement of abstract doctrine nor, as suggested by counsel, mere prediction that industrial disturbances and revolutionary mass strikes will result spontaneously in an inevitable process of evolution in the economic system. It advocates and urges in fervent language mass action which shall progressively foment industrial disturbances and through political mass strikes and revolutionary mass action overthrow and destroy organized parliamentary government. It concludes with a call to action in these words: "The proletariat revolution and the Communist reconstruction of society—*the struggle for these*—is now indispensable. . . . The Communist International calls the proletariat of the world to the final struggle!" This is not the expression of philosophical abstraction, the mere prediction of future events; it is the language of direct incitement.

The means advocated for bringing about the destruction of organized parliamentary government, namely, mass industrial revolts usurping the functions of municipal government, political mass strikes directed against the parliamentary state, and revolutionary mass action for its final destruction, necessarily imply the use of force and violence, and in their essential nature are inherently unlawful in a constitutional government of law and order. That the jury were warranted in finding that the Manifesto advocated not merely the abstract doctrine of overthrowing organized government by force, violence and unlawful means, but action to that end, is clear.

For present purposes we may and do assume that freedom of speech and of the press—which are protected by the First Amendment from abridgment by Congress—are among the fundamental personal rights and "liberties" protected by the due process clause of the Fourteenth Amendment from impairment by the States.

It is a fundamental principle, long established, that the freedom of speech and of the press which is secured by the Constitution, does not confer an absolute right to speak or publish, without responsibility, whatever one may choose, or an unrestricted and unbridled license that gives immunity for every possible use of language and prevents the punishment of those who abuse this freedom.

That a State in the exercise of its police power may punish those who abuse this freedom by utterances inimical to the public welfare, tending to corrupt public morals, incite to crime, or disturb the public peace, is not open to question. . . . .

And, for yet more imperative reasons, a State may punish utterances endangering the foundations of organized government and threatening its overthrow by unlawful means. These imperil its own existence as a constitutional State. Freedom of speech and press. . . does not protect disturbances to the public peace or the attempt to subvert the government. It does not protect publications or teachings which tend to subvert or imperil the government or to impede or hinder it in the performance of its governmental duties.

By enacting the present statute the State has determined, through its legislative body, that utterances advocating the overthrow of organized government by force, violence and unlawful means, are so inimical to the general welfare and involve such danger of substantive evil that they may be penalized in the exercise of its police power. That determination must be given great weight. Every presumption is to be indulged in favor of the validity of the statute. *Mugler v. Kansas,* 123 U.S. 623 [(1887)]. And the case is to be considered "in the light of the principle that the State is primarily the judge of regulations required in the interest of public safety and welfare;" and that its police "statutes may only be declared unconstitutional where they are arbitrary or unreasonable attempts to exercise authority vested in the State in the public interest." *Great Northern Ry. v. Clara City,* 246 U.S. 434 (1918). That utterances inciting to the overthrow of organized government by unlawful means, present a sufficient danger of substantive evil to bring their punishment within the range of legislative discretion, is clear. Such utterances, by their very nature, involve danger to the public peace and to the security of the State. They threaten breaches of the peace and ultimate revolution. And the immediate danger is none the less real and substantial, because the effect of a given utterance cannot be accurately foreseen. The State cannot reasonably be required to measure the danger from every such utterance in the nice balance of a jeweler's scale. A single revolutionary spark may kindle a fire that, smouldering for a time, may burst into a sweeping and destructive conflagration. It cannot be said that the State is acting arbitrarily or unreasonably when in the exercise of its judgment as to the measures necessary to protect the public peace and safety, it seeks to extinguish the spark without waiting until it has enkindled the flame or blazed into the conflagration. It cannot reasonably be required to defer the adoption of measures for its own peace and safety until the revolutionary utterances lead to actual disturbances of the public peace or imminent and immediate danger of its own destruction; but it may, in the exercise of its judgment, suppress the threatened danger in its incipiency. . . .

We cannot hold that the present statute is an arbitrary or unreasonable exercise of the police power of the State unwarrantably infringing the freedom of speech or press; and we must and do sustain its constitutionality.

This being so it may be applied to every utterance—not too trivial to be beneath the notice of the law—which is of such a character and used with such intent and purpose as to bring it within the prohibition of the statute. . . .

It is clear that the question in such cases is entirely different from that involved in those cases where the statute merely prohibits certain acts involving the danger of substantive evil, without any reference to language itself, and it is sought to apply its provisions to language used by the defendant for the purpose of bringing about the prohibited results. There, if it be contended that the statute cannot be applied to the language used by the defendant because of its protection by the freedom of speech or press, it must necessarily be found, as an original question, without any previous determination by the legislative body, whether the specific language used involved such likelihood of bringing about the substantive evil as to deprive it of the constitutional protection. In such cases it has been held that the general provisions of the statute may be constitutionally applied to the specific utterance of the defendant if its natural tendency and probable effect was to bring about the substantive evil which the legislative body might prevent. And the general statement in the *Schenck* [*v. United States*, 249 U.S. 47 (1919)] *Case* that the "question in every case is whether the words are used in such circumstances and are of such a nature as to create a clear and present danger that they will bring about the substantive evils,"—upon which great reliance is placed in the defendant's argument—was manifestly intended, as shown by the context, to apply only in cases of this class, and has no application to those like the present, where the legislative body itself has previously determined the danger of substantive evil arising from utterances of a specified character.

JUSTICE HOLMES, dissenting.

Mr. Justice Brandeis and I are of opinion that this judgment should be reversed. The general principle of free speech, it seems to me, must be taken to be included in the Fourteenth Amendment, in view of the scope that has been given to the word 'liberty' as there used, although perhaps it may be accepted with a somewhat larger latitude of interpretation than is allowed to Congress by the sweeping language that governs or ought to govern the laws of the United States. If I am right, then I think that the criterion sanctioned by the full Court in

Schenck v. United States [249 U.S. 47 (1919)] applies. "The question in every case is whether the words used are used in such circumstances and are of such a nature as to create a clear and present danger that they will bring about the substantive evils that [the State] has a right to prevent." It is true that in my opinion this criterion was departed from in *Abrams v. United States* [250 U.S. 616 (1919)], but the convictions that I expressed in that case are too deep for it to be possible for me as yet to believe that it and *Schaefer v. United States* [251 U.S. 466 (1920)] have settled the law. If what I think the correct test is applied, it is manifest that there was no present danger of an attempt to overthrow the government by force on the part of the admittedly small minority who shared the defendant's views. It is said that this manifesto was more than a theory, that it was an incitement. Every idea is an incitement. It offers itself for belief and if believed it is acted on unless some other belief outweighs it or some failure of energy stifles the movement at its birth. The only difference between the expression of an opinion and an incitement in the narrower sense is the speaker's enthusiasm for the result. Eloquence may set fire to reason. But whatever may be thought of the redundant discourse before us it had no chance of starting a present conflagration. If in the long run the beliefs expressed in proletarian dictatorship are destined to be accepted by the dominant forces of the community, the only meaning of free speech is that they should be given their chance and have their way.

If the publication of this document had been laid as an attempt to induce an uprising against government at once and not at some indefinite time in the future it would have presented a different question. The object would have been one with which the law might deal, subject to the doubt whether there was any danger that the publication could produce any result, or in other words, whether it was not futile and too remote from possible consequences. But the indictment alleges the publication and nothing more.

FOR DISCUSSION

Is the majority decision in this case an explication, or a repudiation, of the clear and present danger test? Do you think the Court would have ruled unanimously if the publication in question had set a specific date for a proletariat revolution? What if the date had been fifty years in the future?

RELATED CASES

***Frohwerk v. United States:* 249 U.S. 204 (1919).**

The insertion in a German-language newspaper of articles bringing into question the purposes of U.S. participation in World War I, as well as the legal and practical justification of the draft, is not protected by the Constitution. Here there was "clear and present danger" to the war effort.

***Debs v. United States:* 249 U.S. 211 (1919).**

The delivery of a speech with such words and in such circumstances that the probable effect will be to prevent recruiting—and with that intent—is punishable under the Espionage Act of 1917 as amended in 1918.

***Abrams v. United States:* 250 U.S. 616 (1919).**

The publication of pamphlets opposing the sending of troops to Russia and urging a strike in the munitions industry is not protected by the Constitution. Holmes's dissent, advocating the clear and present danger test over the bad tendency test, is famous.

***Schaefer v. United States:* 251 U.S. 466 (1920).**

Persons editing a newspaper who systematically took news dispatches from other papers and published them with omissions, additions and changes, with intent to promote the success of Germany and obstruct U.S. enlistment and recruiting efforts, could be prosecuted under the Espionage Act.

***Pierce v. United States:* 252 U.S. 239 (1920).**

When a publication may "have a tendency to cause insubordination, disloyalty, and refusal of duty in the military and naval forces of the United States," those responsible for distributing the publication may be held liable.

***Hartzel v. United States:* 322 U.S. 680 (1944).**

The government must prove, beyond reasonable doubt, that a certain publication was distributed with the specific intent of interfering with the war effort, and there must be a clear and present danger that these subversive activities will succeed.

***Bond v. Floyd:* 385 U.S. 116 (1966).**

A majority of state legislators cannot test the sincerity with which another duly elected legislator can swear to uphold the Constitution. A state cannot apply to a legislator a First Amendment standard stricter than that applicable to a private citizen.

DENNIS V. UNITED STATES

341 U.S. 494, 71 S.Ct. 857, 95 L.Ed. 1137 (1951)

Congress passed the Alien Registration Act—the Smith Act—in 1940. It forbade the advocacy of force to overthrow the government or membership in an organization that advocates such forceful overthrow. Eleven Communist leaders were indicted for knowingly conspiring to organize the Communist Party of the United States as a group teaching and advocating the violent overthrow of the government of the United States; the defendants were also indicted as individuals for having taught and advocated such overthrow. The trial was held in District Judge Harold Medina's court in New York City. The Smith Act was challenged as being contrary to free speech. In its decision, the Supreme Court relied heavily on a reformulation of the clear and present danger test by Learned Hand, a distinguished circuit court judge. This reformulation is generally known as the "**gravity of the evil**" test.

Vote: 6–2

CHIEF JUSTICE VINSON delivered the opinion of the Court.

. . . The obvious purpose of the statute is to protect existing Government, not from change by peaceable; lawful and constitutional means, but from change by violence, revolution and terrorism. That it is within the *power* of the Congress to protect the Government of the United States from armed rebellion is a proposition which requires little discussion. Whatever theoretical merit there may be to the argument that there is a "right" to rebellion against dictatorial governments is without force where the existing structure of the government provides for peaceful and orderly change. We reject any principle of governmental helplessness in the face of preparation for revolution, which principle, carried to its logical conclusion, must lead to anarchy. No one could conceive that it is not within the power of Congress to prohibit acts intended to overthrow the Government by force and violence. The question with which we are concerned here is not whether Congress has such *power,* but whether the *means* which it has employed conflict with the First and Fifth Amendments to the Constitution.

One of the bases for the contention that the means which Congress has employed are invalid takes the form of an attack on the fact of the statute on the grounds that by its terms it prohibits academic discussion of the merits of Marxism-Leninism, that it stifles ideas and is contrary to all concepts of a free speech and a free press. Although we do not agree that the language itself has that significance, we must bear in mind that it is the duty of the federal courts to interpret federal legislation in a manner not inconsistent with the demands of the Constitution. . . . This is a federal statute which we must interpret as well as judge. . . .

The very language of the Smith Act negates the interpretation which petitioners would have us impose on that Act. It is directed at advocacy, not discussion. Thus, the trial judge properly charged the jury that they could not convict if they found that petitioners did "no more than pursue peaceful studies and discussions or teaching and advocacy in the realm of ideas." He further charged that it was not unlawful "to conduct in an American college and university a course explaining the philosophical theories set forth in the books which have been placed in evidence." Such a charge is in strict accord with the statutory language, and illustrates the meaning to be placed on those words. Congress did not intend to eradicate the free discussion of political theories, to destroy the traditional rights of Americans to discuss and evaluate ideas without fear of governmental sanction. Rather Congress was concerned with the very kind of activity in which the evidence showed these petitioners engaged. . . .

We pointed out in *Communications Assn. v. Douds*, 339 U.S. 382 (1950) that the basis of the First Amendment is the hypothesis that speech can rebut speech, propaganda will answer propaganda, free debate of ideas will result in the wisest governmental policies. It is for this reason that this Court has recognized the inherent value of free discourse. An analysis of the leading cases in this Court which have involved direct limitations on speech, however, will demonstrate that both the majority of the Court and the dissenters in particular cases have recognized that this is not an unlimited, unqualified right, but that the societal value of speech must, on occasion, be subordinated to other values and considerations. . . .

. . . Speech is not an absolute, above and beyond control by the legislature when its judgment, subject to review here, is that certain kinds of speech are so undesirable as to warrant criminal sanction. Nothing is more certain in modern society than the principle that there are no absolutes, that a name, a phrase, a standard has meaning only when associated with the considerations which gave birth to the nomenclature. To those who would paralyze our Government in the face of impending threat by encasing it in a semantic straitjacket we must reply that all concepts are relative.

In this case we are squarely presented with the application of the "clear and present danger" test, and must decide what that phrase imports. We first note that many of the cases in which this Court has reversed convictions by use of this or similar tests have been based on the fact that the interest which the State was attempting to protect was itself too insubstantial to warrant restriction of speech. . . . Overthrow of the Government by force and violence is certainly a substantial enough interest for the Government to limit speech. Indeed, this is the ultimate value of any society, for if a society cannot protect its very structure from armed internal attack, it must follow that no subordinate value can be protected. If, then, this interest may be protected, the literal problem which is presented is what has been meant by the use of the phrase "clear and present danger" of the utterances bringing about the evil within the power of Congress to punish.

Obviously, the words cannot mean that before the Government may act, it must wait until the *putsch* is about to be executed, the plans have been laid and the signal is awaited. If Government is aware that a group aiming at its overthrow is attempting to indoctrinate its members and to commit them to a course whereby they will strike when the leaders feel the circumstances permit, action by the Government is required. The argument that there is no need for Government to concern itself, for Government is strong, it possesses ample powers to put down a rebellion, it may defeat the revolution with ease needs no answer. For that is not the question. Certainly an attempt to overthrow the Government by force, even though doomed from the outset because of inadequate numbers or power of the revolutionists, is a sufficient evil for Congress to prevent. The damage which such attempts create both physically and politically to a nation makes it impossible to measure the validity in terms of the probability of success, or the immediacy of a successful attempt. In the instant case the trial judge charged the jury that they could not convict unless they found that petitioners intended to overthrow the Government "as speedily as circumstances would permit." This does not mean, and could not properly mean, that they would not strike until there was certainty of success. What was meant was that the revolutionists would strike when they thought the time was ripe. We must therefore reject the contention that success or probability of success is the criterion.

The situation with which Justices Holmes and Brandeis were concerned in *Gitlow* v. *New York*, 268 U.S. 652 (1925), was a comparatively isolated event bearing little relation in their minds to any substantial threat to the safety of the community. . . . They were not confronted with any situation comparable to the instant one—the development of an apparatus designed and dedicated to the overthrow of the Government, in the context of world crisis after crisis.

Chief Judge Learned Hand, writing for the majority below, interpreted the phrase as follows: "In each case [courts] must ask whether the gravity of the 'evil,' discounted by its improbability, justifies such invasion of free speech as is necessary to avoid the danger." We adopt this statement of the rule. As articulated by Chief Judge Hand, it is as succinct and inclusive as any other we might devise at this time. It takes into consideration those factors which we deem relevant, and relates their significances. More we cannot expect from words.

Likewise, we are in accord with the court below, which affirmed the trial court's finding that the requisite danger existed. The mere fact that from the period 1945 to 1948 petitioner's activities did not result in an attempt to overthrow the Government by force and violence is of course no answer to the fact that there was a group that was ready to make the attempt. The formation by petitioners of such a highly organized conspiracy, with rigidly disciplined members subject to call when the leaders, these petitioners, felt that the time had come for action, coupled with the inflammable nature of world conditions, similar uprisings in other countries, and the touch-and-go nature of our relations with countries with whom petitioners were in the very least ideologically attuned, convince us that their convictions were justified on this score. And this analysis disposes of the contention that a conspiracy to advocate, as distinguished from the advocacy itself, cannot be constitutionally restrained, because it comprises only the preparation. It is the existence of the conspiracy which creates the danger. . . . If the ingredients of the reaction are present, we cannot bind the Government to wait until the catalyst is added. . . .

When facts are found that establish the violation of a statute the protection against conviction afforded by the First Amendment is a matter of law. The doctrine that there must be a clear and present danger of a substantive evil that Congress has a right to prevent is a judicial rule to be applied as a matter of law by the courts. The guilt is established by proof of facts. Whether the First Amendment protects the activity which constitutes the violation of the statute must depend upon a judicial determination of the scope of the First Amendment applied to the circumstances of the case. . . .

JUSTICE FRANKFURTER concurred.

. . . Free speech cases are not an exception to the principle that we are not legislators, that direct policy-making is not our province. How best to reconcile competing interests is the business of legislatures, and the balance they strike is a judgment not to be displaced by ours, but to be respected unless outside the pale of fair judgment. . . .

It is not for us to decide how we would adjust the clash of interests which this case presents were the primary responsibility for reconciling it ours. Congress has determined that the danger created by advocacy of overthrow justifies the ensuing restriction on freedom of speech. The determination was made after due deliberation, and the seriousness of the congressional purpose is attested by the volume of legislation passed to effectuate the same ends. . . .

JUSTICE JACKSON concurred.

. . . The "clear and present danger" test was an innovation by Mr. Justice Holmes in the *Schenck* [v. *United States*, 249 U.S. 47 (1919),] case, reiterated and refined by him and Mr. Brandeis in later cases, all arising before the era of World War II revealed the subtlety and efficacy of modernized revolutionary techniques used by totalitarian parties. In those cases, they were faced with convictions under so-called criminal syndicalism statutes aimed at anarchists but which, loosely construed, had been applied to punish socialism, pacifism, and left-wing ideologies, the charges often resting on far-fetched inferences which, if true, would establish only technical or trivial violations. They proposed "clear and present danger" as a test for the sufficiency of evidence in particular cases. . . .

I think reason is lacking for applying that test to this case. . . .

The authors of the clear and present danger test never applied it to a case like this, nor would I. If applied as it is proposed here, it means that the Communist plotting is protected during its period of incubation; its preliminary stages of organization and preparation are immune from the law; the Government can move only after imminent action is manifest, when it would, of course, be too late. . . .

JUSTICE BLACK dissented.

. . . At the outset I want to emphasize what the crime involved in this case is, and what it is not. These petitioners were not charged with an attempt to overthrow the Government. They were not even charged with overt acts of any kind designed to overthrow the Government. They were not even charged with saying anything or writing anything designed to overthrow the Government. The charge was that they agreed to assemble and to talk and publish certain ideas at a later date. The indictment is that they conspired to organize the Communist Party and to use speech or newspapers and other publications in the future to teach and advocate the forcible overthrow of the Government. No matter how it is worded, this is a virulent form of prior censorship of speech and press, which I believe the First Amendment forbids. I would hold § 3 of the Smith Act authorizing this prior restraint unconstitutional on its face and as applied. . . .

Public opinion being what it now is, few will protest the conviction of these Communist petitioners. There is hope, however, that in calmer times, when present pressures, passions and fears subside, this or some later Court will restore the First Amendment liberties to the high preferred place where they belong in a free society.

JUSTICE DOUGLAS dissented.

. . . The Act, as construed, requires the element of intent—that those who teach the creed believe in it. The crime then depends not on what is taught but on who the teacher is. That is to make freedom of speech turn not on *what is said,* but on the intent with which it is said. Once we start down that road we enter territory dangerous to the liberties of every citizen. . . .

FOR DISCUSSION

Some justices found it significant that the Communist Party USA did not operate by the same rules as the two major political parties. To what degree do you think the Court could reasonably take into consideration the "conspiratorial" nature of the party?

RELATED CASES

***Yates v. United States*: 354 U.S. 298 (1957).**

The Court overturned the conviction of regional leaders of the Communist Party USA, observing that the statute of limitations had expired for members who had helped organize the Communist Party and ruling that the government had not adequately distinguished between theoretical discussions of revolution and actual attempts to carry it into effect.

***Lightfoot v. United States:* 355 U.S. 2 (1957).**

In this case, the Supreme Court, on the authority of *Jencks v. United States,* 353 U.S. 657 (1956), reversed *per curiam* a judgment of the Seventh Circuit Court of Appeals, affirming defendant's conviction for violation of the Smith Act. The Seventh Circuit had held constitutional the "membership clause" of the Smith Act, which subjected a member of a group advocating the overthrow of the government by force or violence to a criminal penalty, provided he knew of the group's purposes.

***Communist Party v. Subversive Activities Control Board:* 367 U.S. 1 (1961).**

Registration provisions of the Subversive Activities Control Act of 1950 held valid.

***Scales v. United States:* 367 U.S. 203 (1961).**

Active membership in an organization engaged in illegal advocacy by one having guilty knowledge and intent is a violation of the Smith Act. In this matter the Smith Act does not violate the Due Process guarantee of the Constitution.

BRANDENBURG V. OHIO

395 U.S. 444, 89 S.Ct. 1827, 23 L.Ed. 2d 430 (1969)

As the decision in *Dennis v. United States*, 341 U.S. 494 (1951), showed, the reformulated clear and present danger test generally emphasized the degree of dangerousness of perceived threats rather than their likelihood. In *Brandenburg*, the Court sought to correct this imbalance by focusing on both the likelihood and the imminence of the threatened danger.

Vote: 8–0

***PER CURIAM* opinion.**

The appellant, a leader of a Ku Klux Klan group, was convicted under the Ohio Criminal Syndicalism statute for "advocat[ing] . . . the duty, necessity, or propriety of crime, sabotage, violence, or unlawful methods of terrorism as a means of accomplishing industrial or political reform" and for "voluntarily assembl[ing] with any society, group, or assemblage of persons formed to teach or advocate the doctrines of criminal syndicalism." He was fined $1,000 and sentenced to one to 10 years' imprisonment. The appellant challenged the constitutionality of the criminal syndicalism statute under the First and Fourteenth Amendments to the United States Constitution, but the intermediate appellate court of Ohio affirmed his conviction without opinion. The Supreme Court of Ohio dismissed his appeal. . . . We reverse.

The record shows that a man, identified at trial as the appellant, telephoned an announcer-reporter on the staff of a Cincinnati television station and invited him to come to a Ku Klux Klan "rally" to be held at a farm in Hamilton County. With the cooperation of the organizers, the reporter and a cameraman attended the meeting and filmed the events. Portions of the films were later broadcast on the local station and on a national network.

One film showed 12 hooded figures, some of whom carried firearms. They were gathered around a large wooden cross, which they burned. No one was present other than the participants and the newsmen who made the film. Most of the words uttered during the scene were incomprehensible when the film was projected, but scattered phrases could be understood that were derogatory of Negroes and, in one instance, of Jews. Another scene on the same film showed the appellant, in Klan regalia, making a speech. The speech, in full, was as follows: "This is an organizers' meeting. We have had quite a few members here today which are—we have hundreds, hundreds of members throughout the State of Ohio. I can quote from a newspaper clipping from the Columbus, Ohio Dispatch, five weeks ago Sunday morning. The Klan has more members in the State of Ohio than does any other organization. We're not a revengent organization, but if our President, our Congress, our Supreme Court, continues to suppress the white, Caucasian race, it's possible that there might have to be some revengeance taken.

"We are marching on Congress July the Fourth, four hundred thousand strong. From there we are dividing into two groups, one group to march on St. Augustine, Florida, the other group to march into Mississippi. Thank you."

The second film showed six hooded figures one of whom, later identified as the appellant, repeated a speech very similar to that recorded on the first film. The reference to the possibility of "revengeance" was omitted, and one sentence was added: "Personally, I believe the nigger should be returned to Africa, the Jew returned to Israel." Though some of the figures in the films carried weapons, the speaker did not.

The Ohio Criminal Syndicalism Statute was enacted in 1919. From 1917 to 1920, identical or quite similar laws were adopted by 20 States and two territories. In 1927, this Court sustained the constitutionality of California's Criminal Syndicalism Act, the text of which is quite similar to that of the laws of Ohio. *Whitney v. California,* 274 U.S. 357 (1927). The Court upheld the statute on the ground that, without more, "advocating" violent means to effect political and economic change involves such danger to the security of the State that the State may outlaw it. But *Whitney* has been thoroughly discredited by later decisions. These later decisions have fashioned the principle that the constitutional guarantees of free speech and free press do not permit a State to forbid or proscribe advocacy of the use of force or of law violation except where such advocacy is directed to inciting or producing imminent lawless action and is likely to incite or produce such action. [The Court cites a number of post-*Whitney* precedents.] . . .

Measured by this test, Ohio's Criminal Syndicalism Act cannot be sustained. The Act punishes persons who "advocate or teach the duty, necessity, or propriety" of violence "as a means of accomplishing industrial or political reform"; or who publish or circulate or display any book or paper containing such advocacy; or who "justify" the commission of violent acts "with intent to exemplify, spread or advocate the propriety of the doctrines of criminal syndicalism"; or who "voluntarily assemble" with a group formed "to teach or advocate the doctrines of criminal syndicalism." Neither the indictment nor the trial judge's instructions to the jury in any way refined the statute's bald definition of the crime in terms of mere advocacy not distinguished from incitement to imminent lawless action.

Accordingly, we are here confronted with a statute which, by its own words and as applied, purports to punish mere advocacy and to forbid, on pain of criminal punishment, assembly with others merely to advocate the described type of action. Such a statute falls within the condemnation of the First and Fourteenth Amendments. The contrary teaching of *Whitney v. California*, cannot be supported, and that decision is therefore overruled.

JUSTICE BLACK, concurring.

I agree with the views expressed by Mr. Justice Douglas in his concurring opinion in this case that the "clear and present danger" doctrine should have no place in the interpretation of the First Amendment. I join the Court's opinion, which, as I understand it, simply cites *Dennis v. United States*, 341 U.S. 494 (1951), but does not indicate any agreement on the Court's part with the "clear and present danger" doctrine on which *Dennis* purported to rely.

JUSTICE DOUGLAS, concurring.

While I join the opinion of the Court, I desire to enter a *caveat.* [Douglas begins with a discussion of *Schenck v. United States*, 249 U.S. 47 (1919), and other precedents that articulated the clear and present danger test.]

My own view is quite different. I see no place in the regime of the First Amendment for any "clear and present danger" test, whether strict and tight as some would make it, or free-wheeling as the Court in *Dennis v. United States*, 341 U.S. 494 (1951), rephrased it.

When one reads the opinions closely and sees when and how the "clear and present danger" test has been applied, great misgivings are aroused. First, the threats were often loud but always puny and made serious only by judges so wedded to the *status quo* that critical analysis made them nervous. Second, the test was so twisted and perverted in *Dennis* as to make the trial of those teachers of Marxism an all-out political trial which was part and parcel of the cold war that has eroded substantial parts of the First Amendment.

Action is often a method of expression and within the protection of the First Amendment.

Suppose one tears up his own copy of the Constitution in eloquent protest to a decision of this Court. May he be indicted?

Suppose one rips his own Bible to shreds to celebrate his departure from one "faith" and his embrace of atheism. May he be indicted?

[Douglas examines *United States v. O'Brien*, 391 U.S. 367 (1968) and other precedents.] The line between what is permissible and not subject to control and what may be made impermissible and subject to regulation is the line between ideas and overt acts.

The example usually given by those who would punish speech is the case of one who falsely shouts fire in a crowded theatre.

This is, however, a classic case where speech is brigaded with action. See *Speiser* v. *Randall,* 357 U.S. 513 (1958). They are indeed inseparable and a prosecution can be launched for the overt acts actually caused. Apart from rare instances of that kind, speech is, I think, immune from prosecution. Certainly there is no constitutional line between advocacy of abstract ideas as in *Yates v. United States*, 354 U.S. 298 (1957), and advocacy of political action as in *Scales v. United States*, 367 U.S. 203 (1961). The quality of advocacy turns on the depth of the conviction; and government has no power to invade that sanctuary of belief and conscience.

FOR DISCUSSION

Under what set of conditions do you think the Court might have upheld Brandenburg's conviction in this case?

BROWN V. ENTERTAINMENT MERCHANTS ASS'N

564 U.S. 786, 131 S.Ct. 2729, 180 L.Ed.2d 708 (2011)

The state of California passed a law imposing restrictions and labeling requirements on the sale or rental of "violent video games" to minors. Manufacturers and distributors of these games sued, claiming a violation of their First and Fourteenth Amendment rights. The federal district court permanently enjoining enforcement of the law, the Court of Appeals affirmed, and Supreme Court granted certiorari and affirmed.

Vote: 7–2

JUSTICE SCALIA delivered the opinion of the Court, in which JUSTICES KENNEDY, GINSBURG, SOTOMAYER, and KAGAN joined.

I

California Assembly Bill 1179 (2005), Cal. Civ.Code Ann. §§ 1746–1746.5 (West 2009) (Act), prohibits the sale or rental of "violent video games" to minors, and requires their packaging to be labeled "18." The Act covers games "in which the range of options available to a player includes killing, maiming, dismembering, or sexually assaulting an image of a human being, if those acts are depicted" in a manner that "[a] reasonable person, considering the game as a whole, would find appeals to a deviant or morbid interest of minors," that is "patently offensive to prevailing standards in the community as to what is suitable for minors," and that "causes the game, as a whole, to lack serious literary, artistic, political, or scientific value for minors." § 1746(d)(1)(A). Violation of the Act is punishable by a civil fine of up to $1,000. § 1746.3.

II

California correctly acknowledges that video games qualify for First Amendment protection. The Free Speech Clause exists principally to protect discourse on public matters, but we have long recognized that it is difficult to distinguish politics from entertainment, and dangerous to try. "Everyone is familiar with instances of propaganda through fiction. What is one man's amusement, teaches another's doctrine." *Winters v. New York,* 333 U.S. 507, 510 (1948). Like the protected books, plays, and movies that preceded them, video games communicate ideas—and even social messages—through many familiar literary devices (such as characters, dialogue, plot, and music) and through features distinctive to the medium (such as the player's interaction with the virtual world). That suffices to confer First Amendment protection. Under our Constitution, "esthetic and moral judgments about art and literature . . . are for the individual to make, not for the Government to decree, even with the mandate or approval of a majority." And whatever the challenges of applying the Constitution to ever-advancing technology, "the basic principles of freedom of speech and the press, like the First Amendment's command, do not vary" when a new and different medium for communication appears.

The most basic of those principles is this: "[A]s a general matter, . . . government has no power to restrict expression because of its message, its ideas, its subject matter, or its content." There are of course exceptions. " 'From 1791 to the present,' . . . the First Amendment has 'permitted restrictions upon the content of speech in a few limited areas,' and has never 'include[d] a freedom to disregard these traditional limitations.' " These limited areas—such as obscenity, incitement, and fighting words, represent "well-defined and narrowly limited classes of speech, the prevention and punishment of which have never been thought to raise any Constitutional problem."

Last Term, in [*United States v.] Stevens,* [559 U.S. 460 (2010)], we held that new categories of unprotected speech may not be added to the list by a legislature that concludes certain speech is too harmful to be tolerated. *Stevens* concerned a federal statute purporting to criminalize the creation, sale, or possession of certain depictions of animal cruelty. The statute covered depictions "in which a living animal is intentionally maimed, mutilated, tortured, wounded, or killed" if that harm to the animal was illegal where the "the creation, sale, or possession t[ook] place." A saving clause largely borrowed from our obscenity jurisprudence, see *Miller v. California,* 413 U.S. 15, 24 (1973), exempted depictions with "serious religious, political, scientific, educational, journalistic, historical, or artistic value." We held that statute to be an impermissible content-based restriction on speech.

There was no American tradition of forbidding the *depiction of* animal cruelty—though States have long had laws against *committing* it.

The Government argued in *Stevens* that lack of a historical warrant did not matter; that it could create new categories of unprotected speech by applying a "simple balancing test" that weighs the value of a particular category of speech against its social costs and then punishes that category of speech if it fails the test. We emphatically rejected that "startling and dangerous" proposition. "Maybe there are some categories of speech that have been historically unprotected, but have not yet been specifically identified or discussed as such in our case law." But without persuasive evidence that a novel restriction on content is part of a long (if heretofore unrecognized) tradition of proscription, a legislature may not revise the "judgment [of] the American people," embodied in the First Amendment, "that the benefits of its restrictions on the Government outweigh the costs."

That holding controls this case. As in *Stevens,* California has tried to make violent-speech regulation look like obscenity regulation by appending a saving clause required for the latter. That does not suffice. Our cases have been clear that the obscenity exception to the First Amendment does not cover whatever a legislature finds shocking, but only depictions of "sexual conduct," *Miller,* at 24. See also *Cohen v. California,* 403 U.S. 15, 20, (1971).

Stevens was not the first time we have encountered and rejected a State's attempt to shoehorn speech about violence into obscenity. In *Winters,* we considered a New York criminal statute "forbid[ding] the massing of stories of bloodshed and lust in such a way as to incite to crime against the person," The New York Court of Appeals upheld the provision as a law against obscenity. "[T]here can be no more precise test of written indecency or obscenity," it said, "than the continuing and changeable experience of the community as to what types of books are likely to bring about the corruption of public morals or other analogous injury to the public order." That is of course the same expansive view of governmental power to abridge the freedom of speech based on interest-balancing that we rejected in *Stevens.* Our opinion in *Winters,* which concluded that the New York statute failed a heightened vagueness standard applicable to restrictions upon speech entitled to First Amendment protection, made clear that violence is not part of the obscenity that the Constitution permits to be regulated. The speech reached by the statute contained "no indecency or obscenity in any sense heretofore known to the law."

Because speech about violence is not obscene, it is of no consequence that California's statute mimics the New York statute regulating obscenity-for-minors that we upheld in *Ginsberg v. New York,* 390 U.S. 629 (1968). That case approved a prohibition on the sale to minors of *sexual* material that would be obscene from the perspective of a child. We held that the legislature could "adjus[t] the definition of obscenity 'to social realities by permitting the appeal of this type of material to be assessed in terms of the sexual interests . . .' of . . . minors." And because "obscenity is not protected expression," the New York statute could be sustained so long as the legislature's judgment that the proscribed materials were harmful to children "was not irrational."

The California Act is something else entirely. It does not adjust the boundaries of an existing category of unprotected speech to ensure that a definition designed for adults is not uncritically applied to children. California does not argue that it is empowered to prohibit selling offensively violent works *to adults*—and it is wise not to, since that is but a hair's breadth from the argument rejected in *Stevens.* Instead, it wishes to create a wholly new category of content-based regulation that is permissible only for speech directed at children.

That is unprecedented and mistaken. "[M]inors are entitled to a significant measure of First Amendment protection, and only in relatively narrow and well-defined circumstances may government bar public dissemination of protected materials to them." No doubt a State possesses legitimate power to protect children from harm, but that does not include a free-floating power to restrict the ideas to which children may be exposed. "Speech that is neither obscene as to youths nor subject to some other legitimate proscription cannot be suppressed solely to protect the young from ideas or images that a legislative body thinks unsuitable for them."

California's argument would fare better if there were a longstanding tradition in this country of specially restricting children's access to depictions of violence, but there is none. Certainly the *books* we give children to read—or read to them when they are younger—contain no shortage of gore. *Grimm's Fairy Tales*, for example, are grim indeed. As her just deserts for trying to poison Snow White, the wicked queen is made to dance in red hot slippers "till she fell dead on the floor, a sad example of envy and jealousy." Cinderella's evil stepsisters have their eyes pecked out by doves. And Hansel and Gretel (children!) kill their captor by baking her in an oven.

High-school reading lists are full of similar fare. Homer's Odysseus blinds Polyphemus the Cyclops by grinding out his eye with a heated stake. ("Even so did we seize the fiery-pointed brand and whirled it round in his eye, and the blood flowed about the heated bar. And the breath of the flame singed his eyelids and brows all about, as the ball of the eye burnt away, and the roots thereof crackled in the flame"). In the *Inferno*, Dante and Virgil watch corrupt politicians struggle to stay submerged beneath a lake of boiling pitch, lest they be skewered by devils above the surface. And Golding's *Lord of the Flies* recounts how a schoolboy called Piggy is savagely murdered *by other children* while marooned on an island.

This is not to say that minors' consumption of violent entertainment has never encountered resistance. In the 1800's, dime novels depicting crime and "penny dreadfuls" (named for their price and content) were blamed in some quarters for juvenile delinquency. When motion pictures came along, they became the villains instead. "The days when the police looked upon dime novels as the most dangerous of textbooks in the school for crime are drawing to a close . . . . They say that the moving picture machine . . . tends even more than did the dime novel to turn the thoughts of the easily influenced to paths which sometimes lead to prison." Moving Pictures as Helps to Crime, N.Y. Times, Feb. 21, 1909, quoted in Brief for Cato Institute, at 8. For a time, our Court did permit broad censorship of movies because of their capacity to be "used for evil." Radio dramas were next, and then came comic books. Many in the late 1940's and early 1950's blamed comic books for fostering a "preoccupation with violence and horror" among the young, leading to a rising juvenile crime rate. But efforts to convince Congress to restrict comic books failed. And, of course, after comic books came television and music lyrics.

California claims that video games present special problems because they are "interactive," in that the player participates in the violent action on screen and determines its outcome. The latter feature is nothing new: Since at least the publication of *The Adventures of You: Sugarcane Island* in 1969, young readers of choose-your-own-adventure stories have been able to make decisions that determine the plot by following instructions about which page to turn to. As for the argument that video games enable participation in the violent action, that seems to us more a matter of degree than of kind. As Judge Posner has observed, all literature is interactive. "[T]he better it is, the more interactive. Literature when it is successful draws the reader into the story, makes him identify with the characters, invites him to judge them and quarrel with them, to experience their joys and sufferings as the reader's own." *American Amusement Machine Assn. v. Kendrick,* 244 F.3d 572, 577 (C.A.7 2001) (striking down a similar restriction on violent video games).

III

Because the Act imposes a restriction on the content of protected speech, it is invalid unless California can demonstrate that it passes strict scrutiny—that is, unless it is justified by a compelling government interest and is narrowly drawn to serve that interest. The State must specifically identify an "actual problem" in need of solving, and the curtailment of free speech must be actually necessary to the solution. That is a demanding standard. "It is rare that a regulation restricting speech because of its content will ever be permissible."

California cannot meet that standard. At the outset, it acknowledges that it cannot show a direct causal link between violent video games and harm to minors. Rather, relying upon our decision in *Turner Broadcasting System, Inc. v. FCC,* 512 U.S. 622 (1994), the State claims that it need not produce such proof because the legislature can make a predictive judgment that such a link exists, based on competing psychological studies. But reliance on

Turner Broadcasting is misplaced. That decision applied *intermediate scrutiny* to a content-neutral regulation. California's burden is much higher, and because it bears the risk of uncertainty, ambiguous proof will not suffice.

The State's evidence is not compelling. California relies primarily on the research of Dr. Craig Anderson and a few other research psychologists whose studies purport to show a connection between exposure to violent video games and harmful effects on children. These studies have been rejected by every court to consider them, and with good reason: They do not prove that violent video games *cause* minors to *act* aggressively (which would at least be a beginning). Instead, "[n]early all of the research is based on correlation, not evidence of causation, and most of the studies suffer from significant, admitted flaws in methodology." They show at best some correlation between exposure to violent entertainment and minuscule real-world effects, such as children's feeling more aggressive or making louder noises in the few minutes after playing a violent game than after playing a nonviolent game.

Even taking for granted Dr. Anderson's conclusions that violent video games produce some effect on children's feelings of aggression, those effects are both small and indistinguishable from effects produced by other media. In his testimony in a similar lawsuit, Dr. Anderson admitted that the "effect sizes" of children's exposure to violent video games are "about the same" as that produced by their exposure to violence on television. And he admits that the *same* effects have been found when children watch cartoons starring Bugs Bunny or the Road Runner, or when they play video games like Sonic the Hedgehog that are rated "E" (appropriate for all ages), or even when they "vie[w] a picture of a gun."

Of course, California has (wisely) declined to restrict Saturday morning cartoons, the sale of games rated for young children, or the distribution of pictures of guns. The consequence is that its regulation is wildly underinclusive when judged against its asserted justification, which in our view is alone enough to defeat it. Underinclusiveness raises serious doubts about whether the government is in fact pursuing the interest it invokes, rather than disfavoring a particular speaker or viewpoint.

The Act is also seriously underinclusive in another respect—and a respect that renders irrelevant the contentions of the concurrence and the dissents that video games are qualitatively different from other portrayals of violence. The California Legislature is perfectly willing to leave this dangerous, mind-altering material in the hands of children so long as one parent (or even an aunt or uncle) says it's OK. And there are not even any requirements as to how this parental or avuncular relationship is to be verified; apparently the child's or putative parent's, aunt's, or uncle's say-so suffices. That is not how one addresses a serious social problem.

California claims that the Act is justified in aid of parental authority: By requiring that the purchase of violent video games can be made only by adults, the Act ensures that parents can decide what games are appropriate. At the outset, we note our doubts that punishing third parties for conveying protected speech to children *just in case* their parents disapprove of that speech is a proper governmental means of aiding parental authority. Accepting that position would largely vitiate the rule that "only in relatively narrow and well-defined circumstances may government bar public dissemination of protected materials to [minors]."

But leaving that aside, California cannot show that the Act's restrictions meet a substantial need of parents who wish to restrict their children's access to violent video games but cannot do so. The video-game industry has in place a voluntary rating system designed to inform consumers about the content of games. The system, implemented by the Entertainment Software Rating Board (ESRB), assigns age-specific ratings to each video game submitted: EC (Early Childhood); E (Everyone); E10+ (Everyone 10 and older); T (Teens); M (17 and older); and AO (Adults Only—18 and older). The Video Software Dealers Association encourages retailers to prominently display information about the ESRB system in their stores; to refrain from renting or selling adults-only games to minors; and to rent or sell "M" rated games to minors only with parental consent. In 2009, the Federal Trade Commission (FTC) found that, as a result of this system, "the video game industry outpaces the movie and music industries" in "(1) restricting target-marketing of mature-rated products to children; (2) clearly and prominently disclosing rating information; and (3) restricting children's access to mature-rated products at retail." This system does much to ensure that minors cannot purchase seriously violent games on their own, and that parents who care about the matter can readily evaluate the games their children bring home. Filling the remaining modest gap in concerned-parents' control can hardly be a compelling state interest.

And finally, the Act's purported aid to parental authority is vastly overinclusive. Not all of the children who are forbidden to purchase violent video games on their own have parents who *care* whether they purchase violent video games. While some of the legislation's effect may indeed be in support of what some parents of the restricted children actually want, its entire effect is only in support of what the State thinks parents *ought* to want. This is not the narrow tailoring to "assisting parents" that restriction of First Amendment rights requires.

* * *

California's effort to regulate violent video games is the latest episode in a long series of failed attempts to censor violent entertainment for minors. While we have pointed out above that some of the evidence brought forward to support the harmfulness of video games is unpersuasive, we do not mean to demean or disparage the concerns that underlie the attempt to regulate them—concerns that may and doubtless do prompt a good deal of parental oversight. We have no business passing judgment on the view of the California Legislature that violent video games (or, for that matter, any other forms of speech) corrupt the young or harm their moral development. Our task is only to say whether or not such works constitute a "well-defined and narrowly limited clas[s] of speech, the prevention and punishment of which have never been thought to raise any Constitutional problem," *Chaplinsky* [*v. New Hampshire*], 315 U.S.[568], at 571–572 (the answer plainly is no); and if not, whether the regulation of such works is justified by that high degree of necessity we have described as a compelling state interest (it is not). Even where the protection of children is the object, the constitutional limits on governmental action apply.

We affirm the judgment below.

FOR DISCUSSION

If California could produce evidence showing that some video games do encourage its players to become more violent, would that be enough to support limits or bans on their sale and distribution?

RELATED CASES

***United States v. Alvarez:* 567 U.S. 709 (2012).**

Supreme Court strikes down as content-based regulation Stolen Valor Act which made makes it a crime to falsely claim receipt of military decorations or medals and provides an enhanced penalty if the Congressional Medal of Honor is involved.

***Reed v. Town of Gilbert, Arizona:* 576 U.S. ___ (2015).**

A town's sign ordinance, restricting size, duration, and location of temporary directional signs is a content-based restriction on free speech.

***City of Ladue v. Gilleo:* 512 U.S. 43 (1994).**

A city sign ordinance that prohibited individuals from placing political signs in their yards (Gilleo was protesting war in the Persian Gulf) constituted viewpoint discrimination against such messages when the City allowed for signs for other purposes.

McCullen v. Coakley

573 U.S. ___, 134 S.Ct. 2518, 189 L.Ed. 2d. 502 (2014)

Individuals brought action on free speech grounds against the Massachusetts Attorney General, challenging the constitutionality of a Massachusetts statute that made it a crime to knowingly stand on a public way or sidewalk within 35 feet of an entrance or driveway to any place, other than a hospital, where abortions were performed. The district court denied both the facial and applied challenges; the Court of Appeals affirmed the decision.

Vote: 9–0

Chief Justice Roberts wrote the opinion for the Court.

A Massachusetts statute makes it a crime to knowingly stand on a "public way or sidewalk" within 35 feet of an entrance or driveway to any place, other than a hospital, where abortions are performed. Petitioners are individuals who approach and talk to women outside such facilities, attempting to dissuade them from having abortions. The statute prevents petitioners from doing so near the facilities' entrances. The question presented is whether the statute violates the First Amendment.

I

A

In 2000, the Massachusetts Legislature enacted the Massachusetts Reproductive Health Care Facilities Act. The law was designed to address clashes between abortion opponents and advocates of abortion rights that were occurring outside clinics where abortions were performed. The Act established a defined area with an 18-foot radius around the entrances and driveways of such facilities. Anyone could enter that area, but once within it, no one (other than certain exempt individuals) could knowingly approach within six feet of another person—unless that person consented—"for the purpose of passing a leaflet or handbill to, displaying a sign to, or engaging in oral protest, education, or counseling with such other person." A separate provision subjected to criminal punishment anyone who "knowingly obstructs, detains, hinders, impedes or blocks another person's entry to or exit from a reproductive health care facility."

The statute was modeled on a similar Colorado law that this Court had upheld in *Hill v. Colorado,* 530 U.S. 703 (2000). Relying on *Hill,* the United States Court of Appeals for the First Circuit sustained the Massachusetts statute against a First Amendment challenge.

By 2007, some Massachusetts legislators and law enforcement officials had come to regard the 2000 statute as inadequate. At legislative hearings, multiple witnesses recounted apparent violations of the law. Massachusetts Attorney General Martha Coakley, for example, testified that protestors violated the statute "on a routine basis." To illustrate this claim, she played a video depicting protestors approaching patients and clinic staff within the buffer zones, ostensibly without the latter individuals' consent. Clinic employees and volunteers also testified that protestors congregated near the doors and in the driveways of the clinics, with the result that prospective patients occasionally retreated from the clinics rather than try to make their way to the clinic entrances or parking lots.

Captain William B. Evans of the Boston Police Department, however, testified that his officers had made "no more than five or so arrests" at the Planned Parenthood clinic in Boston and that what few prosecutions had been brought were unsuccessful. Witnesses attributed the dearth of enforcement to the difficulty of policing the six-foot no-approach zones. Captain Evans testified that the 18-foot zones were so crowded with protestors that they resembled "a goalie's crease," making it hard to determine whether a protestor had deliberately approached a patient or, if so, whether the patient had consented. For similar reasons, Attorney General Coakley concluded that the six-foot no-approach zones were "unenforceable." What the police needed, she said, was a fixed buffer zone around clinics that protestors could not enter. Captain Evans agreed, explaining that such a zone would "make our job so much easier."

To address these concerns, the Massachusetts Legislature amended the statute in 2007, replacing the six-foot no-approach zones (within the 18-foot area) with a 35-foot fixed buffer zone from which individuals are categorically excluded. The statute now provides:

> "No person shall knowingly enter or remain on a public way or sidewalk adjacent to a reproductive health care facility within a radius of 35 feet of any portion of an entrance, exit or driveway of a reproductive health care facility or within the area within a rectangle created by extending the outside boundaries of any entrance, exit or driveway of a reproductive health care facility in straight lines to the point where such lines intersect the sideline of the street in front of such entrance, exit or driveway."

The 35-foot buffer zone applies only "during a facility's business hours," and the area must be "clearly marked and posted." In practice, facilities typically mark the zones with painted arcs and posted signs on adjacent sidewalks and streets. A first violation of the statute is punishable by a fine of up to $500, up to three months in prison, or both, while a subsequent offense is punishable by a fine of between $500 and $5,000, up to two and a half years in prison, or both.

B

Some of the individuals who stand outside Massachusetts abortion clinics are fairly described as protestors, who express their moral or religious opposition to abortion through signs and chants or, in some cases, more aggressive methods such as face-to-face confrontation. Petitioners take a different tack. They attempt to engage women approaching the clinics in what they call "sidewalk counseling," which involves offering information about alternatives to abortion and help pursuing those options. Petitioner Eleanor McCullen, for instance, will typically initiate a conversation this way: "Good morning, may I give you my literature? Is there anything I can do for you? I'm available if you have any questions." If the woman seems receptive, McCullen will provide additional information. McCullen and the other petitioners consider it essential to maintain a caring demeanor, a calm tone of voice, and direct eye contact during these exchanges. Such interactions, petitioners believe, are a much more effective means of dissuading women from having abortions than confrontational methods such as shouting or brandishing signs, which in petitioners' view tend only to antagonize their intended audience. In unrefuted testimony, petitioners say they have collectively persuaded hundreds of women to forgo abortions.

The buffer zones have displaced petitioners from their previous positions outside the clinics. McCullen offers counseling outside a Planned Parenthood clinic in Boston, as do petitioners Jean Zarrella and Eric Cadin. Petitioner Gregory Smith prays the rosary there. The clinic occupies its own building on a street corner. Its main door is recessed into an open foyer, approximately 12 feet back from the public sidewalk. Before the Act was amended to create the buffer zones, petitioners stood near the entryway to the foyer. Now a buffer zone—marked by a painted arc and a sign—surrounds the entrance. This zone extends 23 feet down the sidewalk in one direction, 26 feet in the other, and outward just one foot short of the curb. The clinic's entrance adds another seven feet to the width of the zone. The upshot is that petitioners are effectively excluded from a 56-foot-wide expanse of the public sidewalk in front of the clinic.

Petitioners at all three clinics claim that the buffer zones have considerably hampered their counseling efforts. Although they have managed to conduct some counseling and to distribute some literature outside the buffer zones—particularly at the Boston clinic—they say they have had many fewer conversations and distributed many fewer leaflets since the zones went into effect.

II

By its very terms, the Massachusetts Act regulates access to "public way[s]" and "sidewalk[s]." Such areas occupy a "special position in terms of First Amendment protection" because of their historic role as sites for discussion and debate. These places—which we have labeled "traditional public fora"—" 'have immemorially been held in trust for the use of the public and, time out of mind, have been used for purposes of assembly, communicating thoughts between citizens, and discussing public questions.' "

It is no accident that public streets and sidewalks have developed as venues for the exchange of ideas. Even today, they remain one of the few places where a speaker can be confident that he is not simply preaching to the choir. With respect to other means of communication, an individual confronted with an uncomfortable message can always turn the page, change the channel, or leave the Web site. Not so on public streets and sidewalks. There, a listener often encounters speech he might otherwise tune out. In light of the First Amendment's purpose "to preserve an uninhibited marketplace of ideas in which truth will ultimately prevail," this aspect of traditional public fora is a virtue, not a vice.

In short, traditional public fora are areas that have historically been open to the public for speech activities. Thus, even though the Act says nothing about speech on its face, there is no doubt—and respondents do not dispute—that it restricts access to traditional public fora and is therefore subject to First Amendment scrutiny.

Consistent with the traditionally open character of public streets and sidewalks, we have held that the government's ability to restrict speech in such locations is "very limited." In particular, the guiding First Amendment principle that the "government has no power to restrict expression because of its message, its ideas, its subject matter, or its content" applies with full force in a traditional public forum. As a general rule, in such a forum the government may not "selectively . . . shield the public from some kinds of speech on the ground that they are more offensive than others."

We have, however, afforded the government somewhat wider leeway to regulate features of speech unrelated to its content. "[E]ven in a public forum the government may impose reasonable restrictions on the time, place, or manner of protected speech, provided the restrictions 'are justified without reference to the content of the regulated speech, that they are narrowly tailored to serve a significant governmental interest, and that they leave open ample alternative channels for communication of the information.' "

While the parties agree that this test supplies the proper framework for assessing the constitutionality of the Massachusetts Act, they disagree about whether the Act satisfies the test's three requirements.

III

Petitioners contend that the Act is not content neutral for two independent reasons: First, they argue that it discriminates against abortion-related speech because it establishes buffer zones only at clinics that perform abortions. Second, petitioners contend that the Act, by exempting clinic employees and agents, favors one viewpoint about abortion over the other. If either of these arguments is correct, then the Act must satisfy strict scrutiny—that is, it must be the least restrictive means of achieving a compelling state interest. Respondents do not argue that the Act can survive this exacting standard.

A

The Act applies only at a "reproductive health care facility," defined as "a place, other than within or upon the grounds of a hospital, where abortions are offered or performed." Given this definition, petitioners argue, "virtually all speech affected by the Act is speech concerning abortion," thus rendering the Act content based.

We disagree. To begin, the Act does not draw content-based distinctions on its face. The Act would be content based if it required "enforcement authorities" to "examine the content of the message that is conveyed to determine whether" a violation has occurred. But it does not. Whether petitioners violate the Act "depends" not "on what they say," but simply on where they say it. Indeed, petitioners can violate the Act merely by standing in a buffer zone, without displaying a sign or uttering a word.

It is true, of course, that by limiting the buffer zones to abortion clinics, the Act has the "inevitable effect" of restricting abortion-related speech more than speech on other subjects. But a facially neutral law does not become content based simply because it may disproportionately affect speech on certain topics. On the contrary, "[a] regulation that serves purposes unrelated to the content of expression is deemed neutral, even if it has an incidental effect on some speakers or messages but not others." The question in such a case is whether the law is " 'justified without reference to the content of the regulated speech.' "

The Massachusetts Act is. Its stated purpose is to "increase forthwith public safety at reproductive health care facilities." Respondents have articulated similar purposes before this Court—namely, "public safety, patient access to healthcare, and the unobstructed use of public sidewalks and roadways."

We have previously deemed the foregoing concerns to be content neutral. Obstructed access and congested sidewalks are problems no matter what caused them. A group of individuals can obstruct clinic access and clog sidewalks just as much when they loiter as when they protest abortion or counsel patients.

B

Petitioners also argue that the Act is content based because it exempts four classes of individuals, one of which comprises "employees or agents of [a reproductive healthcare] facility acting within the scope of their employment." This exemption, petitioners say, favors one side in the abortion debate and thus constitutes viewpoint discrimination—an "egregious form of content discrimination." In particular, petitioners argue that the exemption allows clinic employees and agents—including the volunteers who "escort" patients arriving at the Boston clinic—to speak inside the buffer zones.

There is nothing inherently suspect about providing some kind of exemption to allow individuals who work at the clinics to enter or remain within the buffer zones. In particular, the exemption cannot be regarded as simply a carve-out for the clinic escorts; it also covers employees such as the maintenance worker shoveling a snowy sidewalk or the security guard patrolling a clinic entrance.

We thus conclude that the Act is neither content nor viewpoint based and therefore need not be analyzed under strict scrutiny.

IV

Even though the Act is content neutral, it still must be "narrowly tailored to serve a significant governmental interest." The tailoring requirement does not simply guard against an impermissible desire to censor. The government may attempt to suppress speech not only because it disagrees with the message being expressed, but also for mere convenience. Where certain speech is associated with particular problems, silencing the speech is sometimes the path of least resistance. But by demanding a close fit between ends and means, the tailoring requirement prevents the government from too readily "sacrific[ing] speech for efficiency."

For a content-neutral time, place, or manner regulation to be narrowly tailored, it must not "burden substantially more speech than is necessary to further the government's legitimate interests." Such a regulation, unlike a content-based restriction of speech, "need not be the least restrictive or least intrusive means of" serving the government's interests. But the government still "may not regulate expression in such a manner that a substantial portion of the burden on speech does not serve to advance its goals."

A

As noted, respondents claim that the Act promotes "public safety, patient access to healthcare, and the unobstructed use of public sidewalks and roadways." Petitioners do not dispute the significance of these interests. We have, moreover, previously recognized the legitimacy of the government's interests in "ensuring public safety and order, promoting the free flow of traffic on streets and sidewalks, protecting property rights, and protecting a woman's freedom to seek pregnancy-related services." The buffer zones clearly serve these interests.

At the same time, the buffer zones impose serious burdens on petitioners' speech. At each of the three Planned Parenthood clinics where petitioners attempt to counsel patients, the zones carve out a significant portion of the adjacent public sidewalks, pushing petitioners well back from the clinics' entrances and driveways. The zones thereby compromise petitioners' ability to initiate the close, personal conversations that they view as essential to "sidewalk counseling."

For example, in uncontradicted testimony, McCullen explained that she often cannot distinguish patients from passersby outside the Boston clinic in time to initiate a conversation before they enter the buffer zone. And even when she does manage to begin a discussion outside the zone, she must stop abruptly at its painted border, which she believes causes her to appear "untrustworthy" or "suspicious." Given these limitations, McCullen is often reduced to raising her voice at patients from outside the zone—a mode of communication sharply at odds with the compassionate message she wishes to convey. Clark gave similar testimony about her experience at the Worcester clinic.

These burdens on petitioners' speech have clearly taken their toll. Although McCullen claims that she has persuaded about 80 women not to terminate their pregnancies since the 2007 amendment, she also says that she reaches "far fewer people" than she did before the amendment, Zarrella reports an even more precipitous decline in her success rate: She estimated having about 100 successful interactions over the years before the 2007 amendment, but not a single one since. And as for the Worcester clinic, Clark testified that "only one woman out of 100 will make the effort to walk across [the street] to speak with [her]."

The buffer zones have also made it substantially more difficult for petitioners to distribute literature to arriving patients. As explained, because petitioners in Boston cannot readily identify patients before they enter the zone, they often cannot approach them in time to place literature near their hands—the most effective means of getting the patients to accept it. In Worcester and Springfield, the zones have pushed petitioners so far back from the clinics' driveways that they can no longer even attempt to offer literature as drivers turn into the parking lots. In short, the Act operates to deprive petitioners of their two primary methods of communicating with patients.

In the context of petition campaigns, we have observed that "one-on-one communication" is "the most effective, fundamental, and perhaps economical avenue of political discourse." When the government makes it more difficult to engage in these modes of communication, it imposes an especially significant First Amendment burden.

B

1

The buffer zones burden substantially more speech than necessary to achieve the Commonwealth's asserted interests. At the outset, we note that the Act is truly exceptional: Respondents and their *amici* identify no other State with a law that creates fixed buffer zones around abortion clinics. That of course does not mean that the law is invalid. It does, however, raise concern that the Commonwealth has too readily forgone options that could serve its interests just as well, without substantially burdening the kind of speech in which petitioners wish to engage.

That is the case here. The Commonwealth's interests include ensuring public safety outside abortion clinics, preventing harassment and intimidation of patients and clinic staff, and combating deliberate obstruction of clinic entrances. The Act itself contains a separate provision, subsection (e)—unchallenged by petitioners—that prohibits much of this conduct. That provision subjects to criminal punishment "[a]ny person who knowingly obstructs, detains, hinders, impedes or blocks another person's entry to or exit from a reproductive health care facility." If Massachusetts determines that broader prohibitions along the same lines are necessary, it could enact legislation similar to the federal Freedom of Access to Clinic Entrances Act of 1994 (FACE Act), which subjects to both criminal and civil penalties anyone who "by force or threat of force or by physical obstruction, intentionally injures, intimidates or interferes with or attempts to injure, intimidate or interfere with any person because that person is or has been, or in order to intimidate such person or any other person or any class of persons from, obtaining or providing reproductive health services." Some dozen other States have done so.

The point is not that Massachusetts must enact all or even any of the proposed measures discussed above. The point is instead that the Commonwealth has available to it a variety of approaches that appear capable of serving its interests, without excluding individuals from areas historically open for speech and debate.

2

Respondents have but one reply: "We have tried other approaches, but they do not work." Respondents emphasize the history in Massachusetts of obstruction at abortion clinics, and the Commonwealth's allegedly failed attempts to combat such obstruction with injunctions and individual prosecutions. They also point to the Commonwealth's experience under the 2000 version of the Act, during which the police found it difficult to enforce the six-foot no-approach zones given the "frenetic" activity in front of clinic entrances. According to respondents, this history shows that Massachusetts has tried less restrictive alternatives to the buffer zones, to no avail.

We cannot accept that contention. Although respondents claim that Massachusetts "tried other laws already on the books," they identify not a single prosecution brought under those laws within at least the last 17 years. And while they also claim that the Commonwealth "tried injunctions," the last injunctions they cite date to the 1990s. In short, the Commonwealth has not shown that it seriously undertook to address the problem with less intrusive tools readily available to it. Nor has it shown that it considered different methods that other jurisdictions have found effective.

Petitioners wish to converse with their fellow citizens about an important subject on the public streets and sidewalks—sites that have hosted discussions about the issues of the day throughout history. Respondents assert undeniably significant interests in maintaining public safety on those same streets and sidewalks, as well as in preserving access to adjacent healthcare facilities. But here the Commonwealth has pursued those interests by the extreme step of closing a substantial portion of a traditional public forum to all speakers. It has done so without seriously addressing the problem through alternatives that leave the forum open for its time-honored purposes. The Commonwealth may not do that consistent with the First Amendment.

The judgment of the Court of Appeals for the First Circuit is reversed, and the case is remanded for further proceedings consistent with this opinion.

It is so ordered.

FOR DISCUSSION

Why do sidewalks enjoy a special status in First Amendment law? Why did the Court decide that simply allowing protesting and picketing from outside the buffer zone was inadequate First Amendment protection? In what way does the Court find a neutral protest zone to be a prohibited content-based form of regulation?

Time, Place, and Manner Restrictions

The speech cases discussed above all dealt with the *content* of speech. The Court has posed increasingly high barriers to restricting speech on this basis. To do otherwise is to invest the government with the power of censorship. The issue changes, however, when the government focuses not on the content of the speech but on its context. Scholars thus distinguish between regulations of speech that are **content based** and those that are **content neutral**.

While the government thus subjects content-based regulations to the strictest scrutiny, it applies less scrutiny to general laws designed to secure order that impose indirect impositions on speech. Speech would be hindered rather than furthered if all individuals were permitted to speak simultaneously at the same time and place. Students might initially be amused if fellow classmates tried to talk at the same time as their professors, but in time they would probably expect either that the professor silence the students during scheduled lecture times or that the university refund their tuition for the class.

This chapter includes two milestone cases that illustrate the Court's approach to time, place, and manner restrictions. In *Kovacs v. Cooper* (336 U.S. 77, 1949), the Court upheld a law that restricted "loud and raucous" noises from sound trucks. In *Ward v. Rock Against Racism* (491 U.S. 781, 1989), the Court further upheld a set of regulations in New York's Central Park that were designed to control the volume of rock concerts. Note that the state was not claiming to regulate the content of the speech in either case.

Careless Words Versus True Threats

"True threats" constitute an exception to freedom of speech. Indeed, under criminal law, a person can actually be convicted of assault for uttering words that have the effect of force. As demonstrated by the ruling in *Brandenberg v. Ohio* (395 U.S. 444, 1969), in the preceding section, however, most people are unlikely to feel threatened by generalized threats, and when such words are phrased more in the manner of preferences than threats, they have even less force.

Rankin v. McPherson (483 U.S. 378, 1987) provides a good example. Hearing of the attempted assassination of President Ronald Reagan, a clerical employee in a constable's office, Ardith McPherson, indicated that she hoped the next attempt might succeed. As inappropriate as her words were, the Court ultimately concluded that they constituted legitimate expression of opinion about an issue of public concern. The decision underlined the fact that individuals do not lose their rights to express their opinions even when employed by the government, although the Court would likely have found differently had McPherson uttered her words on the department's behalf!

KOVACS V. COOPER

336 U.S. 77, 69 S.Ct. 448, 93 L.Ed. 513 (1949)

An ordinance of Trenton, New Jersey, prohibited the playing, use, or operation for advertising or any other purpose on the public streets of sound trucks or any instrument that emitted "loud and raucous noises." This ban was challenged as violating freedom of speech.

Vote: 5–4

JUSTICE REED delivered the opinion of the Court,

. . . City streets are recognized as a normal place for the exchange of ideas by speech or paper. But this does not mean the freedom is beyond all control. We think it is a permissible exercise of legislative discretion to bar sound trucks with broadcasts of public interest, amplified to a loud and raucous volume, from the public ways of municipalities. On the business streets of cities like Trenton, with its more than 125,000 people, such distractions would be dangerous to traffic at all hours useful for the dissemination of information, and in the residential thoroughfares the quiet and tranquility so desirable for city dwellers would likewise be at the mercy of advocates of particular religious, social or political persuasions. We cannot believe that rights of free speech compel a municipality to allow such mechanical voice amplification on any of its streets.

The right of free speech is guaranteed every citizen that he may reach the minds of willing listeners and to do so there must be opportunity to win their attention. This is the phase of freedom of speech that is involved here. We do not think the Trenton ordinance abridges that freedom. It is an extravagant extension of due process to say that because of it a city cannot forbid talking on the streets through a loud speaker in a loud and raucous tone. Surely such an ordinance does not violate our people's "concept of ordered liberty" so as to require federal intervention to protect a citizen from the action of his own local government. . . . Opportunity to gain the public's ears by objectionably amplified sound on the streets is no more assured by the right of free speech than is the unlimited opportunity to address gatherings on the streets. The preferred position of freedom of speech in a society that cherishes liberty for all does not require legislators to be insensible to claims by citizens to comfort and convenience. To enforce freedom of speech in disregard of the rights of others would be harsh and arbitrary in itself. That more people may be more easily and cheaply reached by sound trucks, perhaps borrowed without cost from some zealous supporter, is not enough to call forth constitutional protection for what those charged with public welfare reasonably think is a nuisance when easy means of publicity are open. Section 4 of the ordinance bars sound trucks from broadcasting in a loud and raucous manner on the streets. There is no restriction upon the communication of ideas or discussion of issues by the human voice, by newspapers, by pamphlets, by dodgers. We think that the need for reasonable protection in the homes or business houses from the distracting noises of vehicles equipped with such sound amplifying devices justifies the ordinance.

Affirmed.

JUSTICE FRANKFURTER concurred.

. . . Only a disregard of vital differences between natural speech, even of the loudest spellbinder, and the noise of sound trucks would give sound trucks the constitutional rights accorded to the unaided human voice. Nor is it for this Court to devise the terms on which sound trucks should be allowed to operate, if at all. These are matters for the legislative judgment controlled by public opinion. So long as a legislature does not prescribe what ideas may be noisily expressed and what may not be, nor discriminate among those who would make inroads upon the public peace, it is not for us to supervise the limits the legislature may impose in safeguarding the steadily narrowing opportunities for serenity and reflection. Without such opportunities freedom of thought becomes a mocking phrase, and without freedom of thought there can be no free society.

JUSTICE JACKSON concurred.

I join the judgment sustaining the Trenton ordinance because I believe that operation of mechanical sound-amplifying devices conflicts with quiet enjoyment of home and park and with safe and legitimate use of street and market place, and that it is constitutionally subject to regulation or prohibition by the state or municipal authority. No violation of the Due Process Clause of the Fourteenth Amendment by reason of infringement of free speech arises unless such regulation or prohibition undertakes to censor the contents of the broadcasting. Freedom of speech for Kovacs does not, in my view, include freedom to use sound amplifiers to drown out the natural speech of others.

JUSTICE BLACK dissented, joined by JUSTICE DOUGLAS and JUSTICE RUTLEDGE.

. . . In *Saia v. New York,* 334 U.S. 558 (1948), we . . . placed use of loud speakers in public streets and parks on the same constitutional level as freedom to speak on streets without such devices, freedom to speak over radio, and freedom to distribute literature.

In this case the Court denies speech amplifiers the constitutional shelter recognized by our decisions and holding in the *Saia* case. This is true because the Trenton, New Jersey ordinance here sustained goes beyond a mere prior censorship of all loud speakers with authority in the censor to prohibit some of them. This Trenton ordinance wholly bars the use of all loud speakers mounted upon any vehicle in any of the city's public streets.

In my view this repudiation of the prior *Saia* opinion makes a dangerous and unjustifiable breach in the constitutional barriers designed to insure freedom of expression. Ideas and beliefs are today chiefly disseminated to the masses of people through the press, radio, moving pictures, and public address systems. To some extent at least there is competition of ideas between and within these groups.

The basic premise for the First Amendment is that all present instruments of communication, as well as others that inventive genius may bring into being, shall be free from governmental censorship or prohibition. Laws which hamper the free use of some instruments of communication thereby favor competing channels. Thus, unless constitutionally prohibited, laws like this Trenton ordinance can give an overpowering influence to views of owners of legally favored instruments of communication. . . . And it is an obvious fact that public speaking today without sound amplifiers is a wholly inadequate way to reach the people on a large scale. . . . A city ordinance that reasonably restricts the volume of sound, or the hours during which an amplifier may be used does not, in my mind, infringe the constitutionally protected area of free speech. It is because this ordinance does none of these things, but is instead an absolute prohibition of all uses of an amplifier on any of the streets of Trenton at any time that I must dissent. . . . .

FOR DISCUSSION

Would laws limiting the use of sound trucks advantage richer groups over poorer ones? Would it make a difference to the constitutionality of this law if Jehovah's Witnesses constituted the only religious organization to use this means of communication?

NOTE

Justice Black refers in his decision to *Saia v. New York* (334 U.S. 558, 1948). In that case, the Court had ruled that a city could not vest the power in the chief of police to forbid the use of a sound truck on a street, but it prescribed no standards for the exercise of the officer's discretion. *Kovacs* essentially distinguished *Saia* by interpreting the decision in the former case as having invalidated the law, not for prohibiting sound trucks per se, but for improperly vesting the discretion to do so in the hands of a public official.

WARD V. ROCK AGAINST RACISM

491 U.S. 781, 109 S.Ct. 2746, 105 L.Ed. 2d 661 (1989)

This case arose in New York City, which attempted to regulate the volume of music coming from the Naumberg Acoustic Bandshell in the southeast portion of Central Park so as not to disturb people in the Sheep Meadow, an area designed for quiet recreation, and residents of Central Park West. The city required that performers use sound-amplification equipment and a sound technician that it provided. The sponsors of a rock concert had won a challenge to these regulations in a circuit court.

Vote: 6–3

JUSTICE KENNEDY delivered the opinion of the Court.

I

Rock Against Racism, respondent in this case, is an unincorporated association which, in its own words, is "dedicated to the espousal and promotion of antiracist views." Each year from 1979 through 1986, RAR has sponsored a program of speeches and rock music at the bandshell. RAR has furnished the sound equipment and sound technician used by the various performing groups at these annual events.

Over the years, the city received numerous complaints about excessive sound amplification at respondent's concerts from park users and residents of areas adjacent to the park. On some occasions RAR was less than cooperative when city officials asked that the volume be reduced; at one concert, police felt compelled to cut off the power to the sound system, an action that caused the audience to become unruly and hostile. . . . Before the 1984 concert, city officials met with RAR representatives to discuss the problem of excessive noise. It was decided that the city would monitor sound levels at the edge of the concert ground, and would revoke respondent's event permit if specific volume limits were exceeded. Sound levels at the concert did exceed acceptable levels for sustained periods of time, despite repeated warnings and requests that the volume be lowered. Two citations for excessive volume were issued to respondent during the concert. When the power was eventually shut off, the audience became abusive and disruptive.

The following year, when respondent sought permission to hold its upcoming concert at the bandshell, the city declined to grant an event permit, citing its problems with noise and crowd control at RAR's previous concerts. The city suggested some other city-owned facilities as alternative sites for the concert. RAR declined the invitation and filed suit in United States District Court against the city, its mayor, and various police and parks department officials, seeking an injunction directing issuance of an event permit. After respondent agreed to abide by all applicable regulations, the parties reached agreement and a permit was issued.

The city then undertook to develop comprehensive New York City Parks Department Use Guidelines for the Naumberg Bandshell. A principal problem to be addressed by the guidelines was controlling the volume of amplified sound at bandshell events. A major concern was that at some bandshell performances the event sponsors had been unable to "provide the amplification levels required and 'crowds unhappy with the sound became disappointed or unruly.' " The city found that this problem had several causes, including inadequate sound equipment, sound technicians who were either unskilled at mixing sound outdoors or unfamiliar with the acoustics of the bandshell and its surroundings, and the like. Because some performers compensated for poor sound mix by raising volume, these factors tended to exacerbate the problem of excess noise.

The city considered various solutions to the sound-amplification problem. . . . The Use Guidelines were promulgated on March 21, 1986. After learning that it would be expected to comply with the guidelines at its upcoming annual concert in May 1986, respondent returned to the District Court and filed a motion for an injunction against the enforcement of certain aspects of the guidelines. The District Court preliminarily enjoined enforcement of the sound-amplification rule on May 1, 1986. Under the protection of the injunction, and alone among users of the bandshell in the 1986 season, RAR was permitted to use its own sound equipment and technician, just as it had done in prior years. RAR's 1986 concert again generated complaints about excessive noise from park users and nearby residents.

After the concert, respondent amended its complaint to seek damages and a declaratory judgment striking down the guidelines as facially invalid. After hearing five days of testimony about various aspects of the guidelines, the District Court issued its decision upholding the sound-amplification guideline. The court found that the city had been "motivated by a desire to obtain top-flight sound equipment and experienced operators" in selecting an independent contractor to provide the equipment and technician for bandshell events, and that the performers who did use the city's sound system in the 1986 season, in performances "which ran the full cultural gamut from grand opera to salsa to reggae," were uniformly pleased with the quality of the sound provided.

[Kennedy further analyzes the district court opinion.]

The Court of Appeals reversed. After recognizing that "[c]ontent neutral time, place and manner regulations are permissible so long as they are narrowly tailored to serve a substantial government interest and do not unreasonably limit alternative avenues of expression," the court added the proviso that "the method and extent of such regulation must be reasonable, that is, it must be the least intrusive upon the freedom of expression as is reasonably necessary to achieve a legitimate purpose of the regulation." Applying this test, the court determined that the city's guideline was valid only to the extent necessary to achieve the city's legitimate interest in controlling excessive volume, but found there were various alternative means of controlling volume without also intruding on respondent's ability to control the sound mix. For example, the city could have directed respondent's sound technician to keep the volume below specified levels. Alternatively, a volume-limiting device could have been installed; and as a "last resort," the court suggested, "the plug can be pulled on the sound to enforce the volume limit." In view of the potential availability of these seemingly less restrictive alternatives, the Court of Appeals concluded that the sound-amplification guideline was invalid because the city had failed to prove that its regulation "was the least intrusive means of regulating the volume."

II

Music is one of the oldest forms of human expression. From Plato's discourse in the Republic to the totalitarian state in our own times, rulers have known its capacity to appeal to the intellect and to the emotions, and have censored musical compositions to serve the needs of the state. . . . The Constitution prohibits any like attempts in our own legal order. Music, as a form of expression and communication, is protected under the First Amendment. . . .

Here the bandshell was open, apparently, to all performers; and we decide the case as one in which the bandshell is a public forum for performances in which the government's right to regulate expression is subject to the protections of the First Amendment. . . . Our cases make clear, however, that even in a public forum the government may impose reasonable restrictions on the time, place, or manner of protected speech, provided the restrictions "are justified without reference to the content of the regulated speech, that they are narrowly tailored to serve a significant governmental interest, and that they leave open ample alternative channels for communication of the information." *Clark* v. *Community for Creative Non-Violence*, 468 U.S. 288 (1984). . . . We consider these requirements in turn.

A

The principal inquiry in determining content neutrality, in speech cases generally and in time, place, or manner cases in particular, is whether the government has adopted a regulation of speech because of disagreement with the message it conveys. The government's purpose is the controlling consideration. A regulation that serves purposes unrelated to the content of expression is deemed neutral, even if it has an incidental effect on some speakers or messages but not others. . . .

The principal justification for the sound-amplification guideline is the city's desire to control noise levels at bandshell events, in order to retain the character of the Sheep Meadow and its more sedate activities, and to avoid undue intrusion into residential areas and other areas of the park. This justification for the guideline "ha[s] nothing to do with content," *Boos v. Barry*, 485 U.S. 312 (1988), and it satisfies the requirement that time, place, or manner regulations be content neutral.

The only other justification offered below was the city's interest in "ensur[ing] the quality of sound at Bandshell events." Respondent urges that this justification is not content neutral because it is based upon the quality, and thus the content, of the speech being regulated. In respondent's view, the city is seeking to assert artistic control over performers at the bandshell by enforcing a bureaucratically determined, value-laden conception of good sound. That all performers who have used the city's sound equipment have been completely satisfied is of no moment, respondent argues, because "[t]he First Amendment does not permit and cannot tolerate state control of artistic expression merely because the State claims that [its] efforts will lead to 'top-quality' results."

While respondent's arguments that the government may not interfere with artistic judgment may have much force in other contexts, they are inapplicable to the facts of this case. The city has disclaimed in express terms any interest in imposing its own view of appropriate sound mix on performers. . . .

B

The city's regulation is also "narrowly tailored to serve a significant governmental interest." *Community for Creative Non-Violence*. . . .

We think it also apparent that the city's interest in ensuring the sufficiency of sound amplification at bandshell events is a substantial one. The record indicates that inadequate sound amplification has had an adverse affect on the ability of some audiences to hear and enjoy performances at the bandshell. The city enjoys a substantial interest in ensuring the ability of its citizens to enjoy whatever benefits the city parks have to offer, from amplified music to silent meditation.

The Court of Appeals recognized the city's substantial interest in limiting the sound emanating from the bandshell. The court concluded, however, that the city's sound-amplification guideline was not narrowly tailored to further this interest, because "it has not [been] shown . . . that the requirement of the use of the city's sound system and technician was the *least intrusive means* of regulating the volume." In the court's judgment, there were several alternative methods of achieving the desired end that would have been less restrictive of respondent's First Amendment rights.

The Court of Appeals erred in sifting through all the available or imagined alternative means of regulating sound volume in order to determine whether the city's solution was "the least intrusive means" of achieving the desired end. This "less-restrictive-alternative analysis . . . has never been a part of the inquiry into the validity of a time, place, and manner regulation." Instead, our cases quite clearly hold that restrictions on the time, place, or manner of protected speech are not invalid "simply because there is some imaginable alternative that might be less burdensome on speech." *United States* v. *Albertini,* 472 U.S. 675 (1985).

Lest any confusion on the point remain, we reaffirm today that a regulation of the time, place, or manner of protected speech must be narrowly tailored to serve the government's legitimate, content-neutral interests but that it need not be the least restrictive or least intrusive means of doing so. Rather, the requirement of narrow tailoring is satisfied "so long as the . . . regulation promotes a substantial government interest that would be achieved less effectively absent the regulation." *United States* v. *Albertini.*

It is undeniable that the city's substantial interest in limiting sound volume is served in a direct and effective way by the requirement that the city's sound technician control the mixing board during performances. Absent this requirement, the city's interest would have been served less well, as is evidenced by the complaints about excessive volume generated by respondent's past concerts. The alternative regulatory methods hypothesized by the Court of Appeals reflect nothing more than a disagreement with the city over how much control of volume is appropriate or how that level of control is to be achieved. See *Clark v. Community for Creative Non-Violence,*468 U.S. 288 (1984). The Court of Appeals erred in failing to defer to the city's reasonable determination that its interest in controlling volume would be best served by requiring bandshell performers to utilize the city's sound technician.

C

The final requirement, that the guideline leave open ample alternative channels of communication, is easily met. Indeed, in this respect the guideline is far less restrictive than regulations we have upheld in other cases, for it does not attempt to ban any particular manner or type of expression at a given place or time. Rather, the guideline continues to permit expressive activity in the bandshell, and has no effect on the quantity or content of that expression beyond regulating the extent of amplification. That the city's limitations on volume may reduce to some degree the potential audience for respondent's speech is of no consequence, for there has been no showing that the remaining avenues of communication are inadequate.

III

The city's sound-amplification guideline is narrowly tailored to serve the substantial and content-neutral governmental interests of avoiding excessive sound volume and providing sufficient amplification within the bandshell concert ground, and the guideline leaves open ample channels of communication. Accordingly, it is valid under the First Amendment as a reasonable regulation of the place and manner of expression. The judgment of the Court of Appeals is *Reversed.*

JUSTICE MARSHALL, with whom JUSTICES BRENNAN and STEVENS JOIN, dissented.

No one can doubt that government has a substantial interest in regulating the barrage of excessive sound that can plague urban life. Unfortunately, the majority plays to our shared impatience with loud noise to obscure the damage that it does to our First Amendment rights. Until today, a key safeguard of free speech has been government's obligation to adopt the least intrusive restriction necessary to achieve its goals. By abandoning the requirement that time, place, and manner regulations must be narrowly tailored, the majority replaces constitutional scrutiny with mandatory deference. The majority's willingness to give government officials a free hand in achieving their policy ends extends so far as to permit, in this case, government control of speech in advance of its dissemination. Because New York City's Use Guidelines (Guidelines) are not narrowly tailored to serve its interest in regulating loud noise, and because they constitute an impermissible prior restraint, I dissent.

I

The majority sets forth the appropriate standard for assessing the constitutionality of the Guidelines. A time, place, and manner regulation of expression must be content neutral, serve a significant government interest, be narrowly tailored to serve that interest, and leave open ample alternative channels of communication. . . .

My complaint is with the majority's serious distortion of the narrow tailoring requirement. Our cases have not, as the majority asserts, "clearly" rejected a less-restrictive-alternative test. On the contrary, just last Term, we held that a statute is narrowly tailored only "if it targets and eliminates no more than the exact source of the 'evil' it seeks to remedy." While there is language in a few opinions which, taken out of context, supports the majority's position, in practice, the Court has interpreted the narrow tailoring requirement to mandate an examination of alternative methods of serving the asserted governmental interest and a determination whether the greater efficacy of the challenged regulation outweighs the increased burden it places on protected speech. . . .

The Court's past concern for the extent to which a regulation burdens speech more than would a satisfactory alternative is noticeably absent from today's decision. The majority requires only that government show that its interest cannot be served as effectively without the challenged restriction. It will be enough, therefore, that the challenged regulation advances the government's interest only in the slightest, for any differential burden on speech that results does not enter the calculus. Despite its protestations to the contrary, the majority thus has abandoned the requirement that restrictions on speech be narrowly tailored in any ordinary use of the phrase. Indeed, after today's decision, a city could claim that bans on handbill distribution or on door-to-door solicitation are the most effective means of avoiding littering and fraud, or that a ban on loudspeakers and radios in a public park is the most effective means of avoiding loud noise. Logically extended, the majority's analysis would permit such far-reaching restrictions on speech.

II

[Marshall addresses the prior restraint issue.]

III

Today's decision has significance far beyond the world of rock music. Government no longer need balance the effectiveness of regulation with the burdens on free speech. After today, government need only assert that it is most effective to control speech in advance of its expression. Because such a result eviscerates the First Amendment, I dissent.

FOR DISCUSSION

Does your campus have regulations that are similar to those that the Court affirmed in this case? Does it treat speech in open areas and speech in classrooms the same? Do public universities differ in how they must treat speech in comparison to private ones?

RELATED CASE

F.C.C. v. Pacifica Foundation: 438 U.S. 726 (1968).

Justice Stevens ruled that the Federal Communications Commission could regulate vulgar speech on the radio. The station in question had broadcast comedian George Carlin's monologue entitled "Seven Dirty Words" at 2 P.M. The Court largely focused on the pervasiveness of this medium and its accessibility to children.

RANKIN V. MCPHERSON

483 U.S. 378, 107 S.Ct. 2891, 97 L.Ed. 315 (1987)

Freedom of speech does not allow individuals to threaten physical harm to others (a form of assault); but the line between such "true threats" and mere "letting off steam" is sometimes elusive. In McPherson, a clerical employee of a county constable's office contested her discharge when, after hearing of an attempt on the life of President Reagan, she said, "If they go for him again, I hope they get him"

Vote: 5–4

JUSTICE MARSHALL delivered the opinion of the Court.

I

On January 12, 1981, respondent Ardith McPherson was appointed a deputy in the office of the Constable of Harris County, Texas. The Constable is an elected official who functions as a law enforcement officer. At the time of her appointment, McPherson, a black woman, was 19 years old and had attended college for a year, studying secretarial science. Her appointment was conditional for a 90-day probationary period.

Although McPherson's title was "deputy constable," this was the case only because all employees of the Constable's office, regardless of job function, were deputy constables. She was not a commissioned peace officer, did not wear a uniform, and was not authorized to make arrests or permitted to carry a gun. McPherson's duties were purely clerical.

On March 30, 1981, McPherson and some fellow employees heard on an office radio that there had been an attempt to assassinate the President of the United States. Upon hearing that report, McPherson engaged a co-worker, Lawrence Jackson, who was apparently her boyfriend, in a brief conversation, which according to McPherson's uncontroverted testimony went as follows:

Q: What did you say?

A: I said I felt that that would happen sooner or later.

Q: Okay. And what did Lawrence say?

A: Lawrence said, yeah, agreeing with me.

Q: Okay. Now, when you—after Lawrence spoke, then what was your next comment?

A: Well, we were talking—it's a wonder why they did that. I felt like it would be a black person that did that, because I feel like most of my kind is on welfare and CETA, and they use medicaid, and at the time, I was thinking that's what it was.

. . . But then after I said that, and then Lawrence said, yeah, he's cutting back medicaid and food stamps. And I said, yeah, welfare and CETA. I said, shoot, if they go for him again, I hope they get him.

McPherson's last remark was overheard by another Deputy Constable, who, unbeknownst to McPherson, was in the room at the time. The remark was reported to Constable Rankin, who summoned McPherson. McPherson readily admitted that she had made the statement, but testified that she told Rankin, upon being asked if she made the statement, "Yes, but I didn't mean anything by it." After their discussion, Rankin fired McPherson.

[Marshall reviews lower court rulings that ultimately decided that McPherson's firing had been unconstitutional.]

II

It is clearly established that a State may not discharge an employee on a basis that infringes that employee's constitutionally protected interest in freedom of speech. *Perry v. Sindermann*, 408 U.S. 593 (1972). Even though McPherson was merely a probationary employee, and even if she could have been discharged for any reason or for no reason at all, she may nonetheless be entitled to reinstatement if she was discharged for exercising her constitutional right to freedom of expression. . . .

The determination whether a public employer has properly discharged an employee for engaging in speech requires "a balance between the interests of the [employee], as a citizen, in commenting upon matters of public concern and the interest of the State, as an employer, in promoting the efficiency of the public services it performs through its employees." *Pickering v. Board of Education,* 391 U.S. 563 (1968); *Connick v. Myers,* 461 U.S. 138 (1983). This balancing is necessary in order to accommodate the dual role of the public employer as a provider of public services and as a government entity operating under the constraints of the First Amendment. On the one hand, public employers are employers, concerned with the efficient function of their operations; review of every personnel decision made by a public employer could, in the long run, hamper the performance of public functions. On the other hand, "the threat of dismissal from public employment is . . . a potent means of inhibiting speech." *Pickering.* Vigilance is necessary to ensure that public employers do not use authority over employees to silence discourse, not because it hampers public functions but simply because superiors disagree with the content of employees' speech.

A

The threshold question in applying this balancing test is whether McPherson's speech may be "fairly characterized as constituting speech on a matter of public concern." *Connick.* "Whether an employee's speech addresses a matter of public concern must be determined by the content, form, and context of a given statement, as revealed by the whole record." . . .

Considering the statement in context, as *Connick* requires, discloses that it plainly dealt with a matter of public concern. The statement was made in the course of a conversation addressing the policies of the President's administration. It came on the heels of a news bulletin regarding what is certainly a matter of heightened public attention: an attempt on the life of the President. While a statement that amounted to a threat to kill the President would not be protected by the First Amendment, the District Court concluded, and we agree, that McPherson's statement did not amount to a threat punishable under 18 U.S.C. 871(a) or 18 U.S.C. 2385, or, indeed, that could properly be criminalized at all.

B

Because McPherson's statement addressed a matter of public concern, *Pickering* next requires that we balance McPherson's interest in making her statement against "the interest of the State, as an employer, in promoting the efficiency of the public services it performs through its employees." The State bears a burden of justifying the discharge on legitimate grounds.

In performing the balancing, the statement will not be considered in a vacuum; the manner, time, and place of the employee's expression are relevant, as is the context in which the dispute arose. We have previously recognized as pertinent considerations whether the statement impairs discipline by superiors or harmony among co-workers, has a detrimental impact on close working relationships for which personal loyalty and confidence are necessary, or impedes the performance of the speaker's duties or interferes with the regular operation of the enterprise.

These considerations, and indeed the very nature of the balancing test, make apparent that the state interest element of the test focuses on the effective functioning of the public employer's enterprise. Interference with work, personnel relationships, or the speaker's job performance can detract from the public employer's function; avoiding such interference can be a strong state interest. From this perspective, however, petitioners fail to demonstrate a state interest that outweighs McPherson's First Amendment rights. While McPherson's statement was made at the workplace, there is no evidence that it interfered with the efficient functioning of the office. The Constable was evidently not afraid that McPherson had disturbed or interrupted other employees—he did not inquire to whom respondent had made the remark and testified that he "was not concerned who she had made it to." In fact, Constable Rankin testified that the possibility of interference with the functions of the Constable's office had not been a consideration in his discharge of respondent and that he did not even inquire whether the remark had disrupted the work of the office.

Nor was there any danger that McPherson had discredited the office by making her statement in public. McPherson's speech took place in an area to which there was ordinarily no public access; her remark was evidently made in a private conversation with another employee. . . .

. . . [I]t is undisputed that he fired McPherson based on the content of her speech. Evidently because McPherson had made the statement, and because the Constable believed that she "meant it," he decided that she was not a suitable employee to have in a law enforcement agency. But in weighing the State's interest in discharging an employee based on any claim that the content of a statement made by the employee somehow undermines the mission of the public employer, some attention must be paid to the responsibilities of the employee within the agency. The burden of caution employees bear with respect to the words they speak will vary with the extent of authority and public accountability the employee's role entails. Where, as here, an employee serves no confidential, policymaking, or public contact role, the danger to the agency's successful functioning from that employee's private speech is minimal. . . .

This is such a case. McPherson's employment-related interaction with the Constable was apparently negligible. Her duties were purely clerical and were limited solely to the civil process function of the Constable's office. There is no indication that she would ever be in a position to further—or indeed to have any involvement with—the minimal law enforcement activity engaged in by the Constable's office. Given the function of the agency, McPherson's position in the office, and the nature of her statement, we are not persuaded that Rankin's interest in discharging her outweighed her rights under the First Amendment.

Because we agree with the Court of Appeals that McPherson's discharge was improper, the judgment of the Court of Appeals is Affirmed.

JUSTICE SCALIA, with whom CHIEF JUSTICE REHNQUIST, and JUSTICES WHITE and O'CONNOR join, dissenting.

I agree with the proposition, felicitously put by Constable Rankin's counsel, that no law enforcement agency is required by the First Amendment to permit one of its employees to "ride with the cops and cheer for the robbers." . . . The Court, applying the two-prong analysis of *Connick v. Myers*, 461 U.S. 138 (1983), holds that McPherson's statement was protected by the First Amendment because (1) it "addressed a matter of public concern," and (2) McPherson's interest in making the statement outweighs Rankin's interest in suppressing it. In so doing, the Court significantly and irrationally expands the definition of "public concern"; it also carves out a new and very large class of employees—i. e., those in "nonpolicymaking" positions - who, if today's decision is to be believed, can never be disciplined for statements that fall within the Court's expanded definition. Because I believe the Court's conclusions rest upon a distortion of both the record and the Court's prior decisions, I dissent.

I

To appreciate fully why the majority errs in reaching its first conclusion, it is necessary to recall the origins and purposes of Connick's "public concern" requirement. The Court long ago rejected Justice Holmes' approach to the free speech rights of public employees, that "[a policeman] may have a constitutional right to talk politics, but he has no constitutional right to be a policeman," *McAuliffe v. Mayor of New Bedford*, 155 Mass. 216 (1892). We have, however, recognized that the government's power as an employer to make hiring and firing decisions on the basis of what its employees and prospective employees say has a much greater scope than its power to regulate expression by the general public.

Specifically, we have held that the First Amendment's protection against adverse personnel decisions extends only to speech on matters of "public concern," which we have variously described as those matters dealing in some way with "the essence of self-government," . . ., matters as to which "free and open debate is vital to informed decisionmaking by the electorate," . . ., and matters as to which " 'debate . . . [must] be uninhibited, robust, and wide-open,' " . . .

McPherson fails this threshold requirement. The statement for which she was fired—and the only statement reported to the Constable—was, "If they go for him again, I hope they get him." It is important to bear in mind the District Judge's finding that this was not hyperbole. . . .

Given the meaning of the remark, there is no basis for the Court's suggestion that McPherson's criticisms of the President's policies that immediately preceded the remark can illuminate it in such fashion as to render it constitutionally protected. Those criticisms merely reveal the speaker's motive for expressing the desire that the next attempt on the President's life succeed, in the same way that a political assassin's remarks to his victim before pulling the trigger might reveal a motive for that crime. The majority's magical transformation of the motive for McPherson's statement into its content is as misguided as viewing a political assassination preceded by a harangue as nothing more than a strong denunciation of the victim's political views.

That McPherson's statement does not constitute speech on a matter of "public concern" is demonstrated by comparing it with statements that have been found to fit that description in prior decisions involving public employees. . . . .

McPherson's statement is indeed so different from those that it is only one step removed from statements that we have previously held entitled to no First Amendment protection even in the nonemployment context—including assassination threats against the President (which are illegal under 18 U.S.C. 871). . . . A statement lying so near the category of completely unprotected speech cannot fairly be viewed as lying within the "heart" of the First Amendment's protection; it lies within that category of speech that can neither be characterized as speech on matters of public concern nor properly subject to criminal penalties. Once McPherson stopped explicitly criticizing the President's policies and expressed a desire that he be assassinated, she crossed the line.

The Court reaches the opposite conclusion only by distorting the concept of "public concern." It does not explain how a statement expressing approval of a serious and violent crime—assassination of the President—can possibly fall within that category.

II

Even if I agreed that McPherson's statement was speech on a matter of "public concern," I would still find it unprotected. It is important to be clear on what the issue is in this part of the case. It is not, as the Court suggests, whether "Rankin's interest in discharging [McPherson] outweighed her rights under the First Amendment." Rather, it is whether his interest in preventing the expression of such statements in his agency outweighed her First Amendment interest in making the statement. We are not deliberating, in other words, (or at least should not be) about whether the sanction of dismissal was, as the concurrence puts it, "an . . . intemperat[e] employment decision." It may well have been—and personally I think it was. But we are not sitting as a panel to develop sound principles of proportionality for adverse actions in the state civil service. We are asked to determine whether, given the interests of this law enforcement office, McPherson had a right to say what she did—so that she could not only not be fired for it, but could not be formally reprimanded for it, or even prevented from repeating it endlessly into the future. It boggles the mind to think that she has such a right.

FOR DISCUSSION

The most notable statement in this opinion is probably Justice Scalia's comment that one should not be able to "ride with the cops and cheer for the robbers." Why do you think the Court majority ultimately finds this analogy unconvincing? Would it diminish your faith in the criminal justice system if you thought your local constable was employing an individual who would make a remark like that at issue in this case? In recent years, there has been news coverage of public officials who have posted racist or sexist comments on public Facebook pages that identifies their employers. Are these different scenarios? What facts would be relevant in determining whether or not *McPherson* should apply?

RELATED CASE

***Garcetti v. Ceballos:* 547 U.S. 410 (2006).**

A 5–4 Court ruled that a public employee who made comments that he was denied a promotion because of his prior criticism of a warrant did not have his First Amendment rights violated because these comments were made in his capacity as a public employee and not as a private citizen.

The Government as Speaker

Rankin v. McPherson (483 U.S. 378, 1987) demonstrates that it is not always easy to separate the rights of speakers from those of the institution for which they work. An old proverb says "One who pays the piper calls the tune"; but to what degree does government increase its power over speech as it increases the number of programs that it funds?

Three successive cases in this chapter illustrate the issues that sometimes arise in this area. *Rust v. Sullivan* (500 U.S. 173, 1991) combines controversies over speech with those over abortion. The close 5–4 vote over whether individuals employed under Title X of the Public Health Services Act could be forbidden from providing information about abortion services is but one indication of the conflicting values that are in play.

National Endowment for the Arts v. Finley (524 U.S. 569, 1998) further applies this principle to funding for the arts. Again, the majority upholds a regulation against charges that it is designed to be a form of censorship, but the policy was relatively tame and did not impose any categorical requirements.

Finally, in *Board of Regents of University of Wisconsin v. Southworth* (529 U.S. 217, 2000), the Court addresses limits on student activity fees. In *Rosenberger v. Rectors and Visitors of the University of Virginia* (515 U.S. 819, 1995), the Court had decided that a university could not withhold student activity fees from religious groups. In *Southworth* it decided that students cannot selectively exempt themselves from contributing funds to organizations that support political opinions with which they might disagree. Since, however, the Court put considerable emphasis on the fact that university campuses are designed to provide a forum for a wide variety of opinions, the decision might be relatively difficult to generalize.

RUST V. SULLIVAN

500 U.S. 173, 111 S.Ct. 1759, 114 L.Ed. 2d 233 (1991)

As described later in this volume (Chapter IX), the Supreme Court recognized in *Roe v. Wade* (410 U.S. 113, 1973) that the liberty protected by the Fourteenth Amendment was sufficient to allow a woman to choose whether to have an abortion, especially in the months prior to viability. Later, in *Maher v. Roe* (432 U.S. 464, 1977), the justices decided that the Court's recognition of a right to abortions did not necessarily require the government to fund the procedures. *Rust* raises the further issue of whether government can restrict individuals who work for the government from giving abortion counseling. This particular case involves a "**facial challenge**" to the regulations as a whole. Consideration of their application to a particular case—for example, a situation in which lack of advice about abortions might directly threaten a woman's life—is called an "as applied challenge."

Vote: 5–4

CHIEF JUSTICE REHNQUIST delivered the opinion of the Court.

These cases concern a facial challenge to Department of Health and Human Services (HHS) regulations which limit the ability of Title X fund recipients to engage in abortion-related activities. The United States Court of Appeals for the Second Circuit upheld the regulations, finding them to be a permissible construction of the statute as well as consistent with the First and Fifth Amendments to the Constitution. We granted certiorari to resolve a split among the Courts of Appeals. We affirm.

I

A

In 1970, Congress enacted Title X of the Public Health Service Act (Act), 84 Stat. 1506, as amended, which provides federal funding for family-planning services. The Act authorizes the Secretary to "make grants to and enter into contracts with public or nonprofit private entities to assist in the establishment and operation of voluntary family planning projects which shall offer a broad range of acceptable and effective family planning methods and services." Grants and contracts under Title X must "be made in accordance with such regulations as the Secretary may promulgate." § 300a–4(a). Section 1008 of the Act, however, provides that "none of the funds appropriated under this subchapter shall be used in programs where abortion is a method of family planning." That restriction was intended to ensure that Title X funds would "be used only to support preventive family planning services, population research, infertility services, and other related medical, informational, and educational activities."

In 1988, the Secretary promulgated new regulations designed to provide " 'clear and operational guidance' to grantees about how to preserve the distinction between Title X programs and abortion as a method of family planning." . . ..

The regulations attach three principal conditions on the grant of federal funds for Title X projects. First, the regulations specify that a "Title X project may not provide counseling concerning the use of abortion as a method of family planning or provide referral for abortion as a method of family planning." Because Title X is limited to preconceptional services, the program does not furnish services related to childbirth. . . .

Second, the regulations broadly prohibit a Title X project from engaging in activities that "encourage, promote or advocate abortion as a method of family planning." Forbidden activities include lobbying for legislation that would increase the availability of abortion as a method of family planning, developing or disseminating materials advocating abortion as a method of family planning, providing speakers to promote abortion as a method of family planning, using legal action to make abortion available in any way as a method of family planning, and paying dues to any group that advocates abortion as a method of family planning as a substantial part of its activities.

Third, the regulations require that Title X projects be organized so that they are "physically and financially separate" from prohibited abortion activities. . . .

B

Petitioners are Title X grantees and doctors who supervise Title X funds suing on behalf of themselves and their patients. Respondent is the Secretary of HHS. . . .

[Rehnquist reviews the lower court decisions.]

II

We begin by pointing out the posture of the cases before us. Petitioners are challenging the *facial* validity of the regulations. Thus, we are concerned only with the question whether, on their face, the regulations are both authorized by the Act and can be construed in such a manner that they can be applied to a set of individuals without infringing upon constitutionally protected rights. Petitioners face a heavy burden in seeking to have the regulations invalidated as facially unconstitutional. "A facial challenge to a legislative Act is, of course, the most difficult challenge to mount successfully, since the challenger must establish that no set of circumstances exists under which the Act would be valid. The fact that [the regulations] might operate unconstitutionally under some conceivable set of circumstances is insufficient to render [them] wholly invalid." *United States* v. *Salerno,* 481 U.S. 739 (1987). [Rehnquist concludes in Section A that the Secretary's construction of the statute is permissible and in Section B that the "program integrity" provisions of the statute are constitutional.]

III

Petitioners contend that the regulations violate the First Amendment by impermissibly discriminating based on viewpoint because they prohibit "all discussion about abortion as a lawful option—including counseling, referral, and the provision of neutral and accurate information about ending a pregnancy—while compelling the clinic or counselor to provide information that promotes continuing a pregnancy to term." They assert that the regulations violate the "free speech rights of private health care organizations that receive Title X funds, of their staff, and of their patients" by impermissibly imposing "viewpoint-discriminatory conditions on government subsidies" and thus "penalize speech funded with non-Title X monies." Because "Title X continues to fund speech ancillary to pregnancy testing in a manner that is not evenhanded with respect to views and information about abortion, it invidiously discriminates on the basis of viewpoint." Relying on *Regan v. Taxation with Representation of Wash.*, 461 U.S. 540 (1983), and *Arkansas Writers' Project, Inc. v. Ragland*, 481 U.S. 221 (1987), petitioners also assert that while the Government may place certain conditions on the receipt of federal subsidies, it may not "discriminate invidiously in its subsidies in such a way as to 'aim at the suppression of dangerous ideas.' "

There is no question but that the statutory prohibition contained in § 1008 is constitutional. In *Maher v. Roe*, 432 U.S. 464 (1977), we upheld a state welfare regulation under which Medicaid recipients received payments for services related to childbirth, but not for nontherapeutic abortions. The Court rejected the claim that this unequal subsidization worked a violation of the Constitution. We held that the government may "make a value judgment favoring childbirth over abortion, and . . . implement that judgment by the allocation of public funds." Here the Government is exercising the authority it possesses under *Maher* and *Harris v. McRae*, 448 U.S. 297 (1980), to subsidize family planning services which will lead to conception and childbirth, and declining to "promote or encourage abortion." The Government can, without violating the Constitution, selectively fund a program to encourage certain activities it believes to be in the public interest, without at the same time funding an alternative program which seeks to deal with the problem in another way. In so doing, the Government has not discriminated on the basis of viewpoint; it has merely chosen to fund one activity to the exclusion of the other. . . .

To hold that the Government unconstitutionally discriminates on the basis of viewpoint when it chooses to fund a program dedicated to advance certain permissible goals, because the program in advancing those goals necessarily discourages alternative goals, would render numerous Government programs constitutionally suspect. When Congress established a National Endowment for Democracy to encourage other countries to adopt democratic principles, it was not constitutionally required to fund a program to encourage competing lines of political philosophy such as communism and fascism. Petitioners' assertions ultimately boil down to the position that if the Government chooses to subsidize one protected right, it must subsidize analogous counterpart rights. But the Court has soundly rejected that proposition. Within far broader limits than petitioners are willing to concede, when the Government appropriates public funds to establish a program it is entitled to define the limits of that program.

Petitioners rely heavily on their claim that the regulations would not, in the circumstance of a medical emergency, permit a Title X project to refer a woman whose pregnancy places her life in imminent peril to a provider of abortions or abortion-related services. These cases, of course, involve only a facial challenge to the regulations, and we do not have before us any application by the Secretary to a specific fact situation. On their face, we do not read the regulations to bar abortion referral or counseling in such circumstances. . . .

Petitioners also contend that the restrictions on the subsidization of abortion-related speech contained in the regulations are impermissible because they condition the receipt of a benefit, in these cases Title X funding, on the relinquishment of a constitutional right, the right to engage in abortion advocacy and counseling. Relying on *Perry v. Sindermann*, 408 U.S. 593, 597 (1972), and *FCC v. League of Women Voters of Cal.*, 468 U.S. 364 (1984), petitioners argue that "even though the government may deny [a] . . . benefit for any number of reasons, there are some reasons upon which the government may not rely. It may not deny a benefit to a person on a basis that infringes his constitutionally protected interests—especially, his interest in freedom of speech."

Petitioners' reliance on these cases is unavailing, however, because here the Government is not denying a benefit to anyone, but is instead simply insisting that public funds be spent for the purposes for which they were authorized. . . .

In contrast, our "unconstitutional conditions" cases involve situations in which the Government has placed a condition on the *recipient* of the subsidy rather than on a particular program or service, thus effectively prohibiting the recipient from engaging in the protected conduct outside the scope of the federally funded program. . . .

By requiring that the Title X grantee engage in abortion-related activity separately from activity receiving federal funding, Congress has, consistent with our teachings in *League of Women Voters* and *Regan*, not denied it the right to engage in abortion-related activities. Congress has merely refused to fund such activities out of the public fisc, and the Secretary has simply required a certain degree of separation from the Title X project in order to ensure the integrity of the federally funded program.

The same principles apply to petitioners' claim that the regulations abridge the free speech rights of the grantee's staff. Individuals who are voluntarily employed for a Title X project must perform their duties in accordance with the regulation's restrictions on abortion counseling and referral. The employees remain free, however, to pursue abortion-related activities when they are not acting under the auspices of the Title X project.

This is not to suggest that funding by the Government, even when coupled with the freedom of the fund recipients to speak outside the scope of the Government-funded project, is invariably sufficient to justify Government control over the content of expression. For example, this Court has recognized that the existence of a Government "subsidy," in the form of Government-owned property, does not justify the restriction of speech in areas that have "been traditionally open to the public for expressive activity," *United States v. Kokinda*, 497 U.S. 720 (1990); *Hague v. CIO*, 307 U.S. 496, 515 (1939), or have been "expressly dedicated to speech activity." Similarly, we have recognized that the university is a traditional sphere of free expression so fundamental to the functioning of our society that the Government's ability to control speech within that sphere by means of conditions attached to the expenditure of Government funds is restricted by the vagueness and overbreadth doctrines of the First Amendment, *Keyishian v. Board of Regents, State Univ. of N.Y.* [385 U.S. 589] (1967).

JUSTICE BLACKMUN, with whom JUSTICE MARSHALL joins, with whom JUSTICE STEVENS joins as to Parts II and III, and with whom JUSTICE O'CONNOR joins as to Part I, dissenting.

Casting aside established principles of statutory construction and administrative jurisprudence, the majority in these cases today unnecessarily passes upon important questions of constitutional law. In so doing, the Court, for the first time, upholds viewpoint-based suppression of speech solely because it is imposed on those dependent upon the Government for economic support. Under essentially the same rationale, the majority upholds direct regulation of dialogue between a pregnant woman and her physician when that regulation has both the purpose and the effect of manipulating her decision as to the continuance of her pregnancy. I conclude that the Secretary's regulation of referral, advocacy, and counseling activities exceeds his statutory authority, and, also, that the regulations violate the First and Fifth Amendments of our Constitution. Accordingly, I dissent and would reverse the divided-vote judgment of the Court of Appeals.

I

[Blackmun addresses the construction of federal statutes.]

II

I also strongly disagree with the majority's disposition of petitioners' constitutional claims, and because I feel that a response thereto is indicated, I move on to that issue.

A

Until today, the Court never has upheld viewpoint-based suppression of speech simply because that suppression was a condition upon the acceptance of public funds. Whatever may be the Government's power to condition the receipt of its largess upon the relinquishment of constitutional rights, it surely does not extend to a condition that suppresses the recipient's cherished freedom of speech based solely upon the content or viewpoint of that speech. [Blackmun cites a number of cases.]

It cannot seriously be disputed that the counseling and referral provisions at issue in the present cases constitute content-based regulation of speech. . . .

The regulations are also clearly viewpoint based. While suppressing speech favorable to abortion with one hand, the Secretary compels antiabortion speech with the other. . . .

The Government's articulated interest in distorting the doctor-patient dialogue—ensuring that federal funds are not spent for a purpose outside the scope of the program—falls far short of that necessary to justify the suppression of truthful information and professional medical opinion regarding constitutionally protected conduct. Moreover, the offending regulation is not narrowly tailored to serve this interest. For example, the governmental interest at stake could be served by imposing rigorous bookkeeping standards to ensure financial separation or adopting content-neutral rules for the balanced dissemination of family-planning and health information. By failing to balance or even to consider the free speech interests claimed by Title X physicians against the Government's asserted interest in suppressing the speech, the Court falters in its duty to implement the protection that the First Amendment clearly provides for this important message.

C

Finally, it is of no small significance that the speech the Secretary would suppress is truthful information regarding constitutionally protected conduct of vital importance to the listener. One can imagine no legitimate governmental interest that might be served by suppressing such information. Concededly, the abortion debate is among the most divisive and contentious issues that our Nation has faced in recent years. "But freedom to differ is not limited to things that do not matter much. That would be a mere shadow of freedom. The test of its substance is the right to differ as to things that touch the heart of the existing order." *West Virginia Bd. of Ed. v. Barnette*, 319 U.S. 624 (1943).

JUSTICE STEVENS, dissenting.

In my opinion, the Court has not paid sufficient attention to the language of the controlling statute or to the consistent interpretation accorded the statute by the responsible cabinet officers during four different Presidencies and 18 years. . . .

FOR DISCUSSION

To what degree, if any, do you think the opinions of individual justices on the speech issue in this case were also influenced by their opinions as to the constitutionality of antiabortion legislation? Based on this decision, do you think the government should be able to instruct a doctor who thinks abortion is morally wrong to tell patients about this procedural option?

NATIONAL ENDOWMENT FOR THE ARTS V. FINLEY

524 U.S. 569, 118 S.Ct. 2168, 141 L.Ed. 2d 500 (1998)

Like *Rust v. Sullivan* (500 U.S. 173, 1991), this case deals in part with conditions that government can impose as a condition of funding. The case was prompted by a law that Congress adopted in the wake of criticisms that art projects it had supported offended public sensibilities. As in *Rust*, this case involves a facial challenge, which is more difficult to establish than would an "as-applied" challenge to a specific denial of funding.

Vote: 8–1

JUSTICE O'CONNOR delivered the opinion of the Court.

The National Foundation on the Arts and Humanities Act, as amended in 1990, requires the Chairperson of the National Endowment for the Arts (NEA) to ensure that "artistic excellence and artistic merit are the criteria by which [grant] applications are judged, taking into consideration general standards of decency and respect for the diverse beliefs and values of the American public." In this case, we review the Court of Appeals' determination that § 954(d)(1), on its face, impermissibly discriminates on the basis of viewpoint and is void for vagueness under the First and Fifth Amendments. We conclude that § 954(d)(1) is facially valid, as it neither inherently interferes with First Amendment rights nor violates constitutional vagueness principles.

I

A

With the establishment of the NEA in 1965, Congress embarked on a "broadly conceived national policy of support for the . . . arts in the United States," pledging federal funds to "help create and sustain not only a climate encouraging freedom of thought, imagination, and inquiry but also the material conditions facilitating the release of . . . creative talent." The enabling statute vests the NEA with substantial discretion to award grants; it identifies only the broadest funding priorities, including "artistic and cultural significance, giving emphasis to American creativity and cultural diversity," "professional excellence," and the encouragement of "public knowledge, education, understanding, and appreciation of the arts."

[O'Connor reviews both how the NEA chooses projects and the types of projects that it has funded.]

Throughout the NEA's history, only a handful of the agency's roughly 100,000 awards have generated formal complaints about misapplied funds or abuse of the public's trust. Two provocative works, however, prompted public controversy in 1989 and led to congressional revaluation of the NEA's funding priorities and efforts to increase oversight of its grant-making procedures. The Institute of Contemporary Art at the University of Pennsylvania had used $30,000 of a visual arts grant it received from the NEA to fund a 1989 retrospective of photographer Robert Mapplethorpe's work. The exhibit, entitled *The Perfect Moment*, included homoerotic photographs that several Members of Congress condemned as pornographic. Members also denounced artist Andres Serrano's work *Piss Christ*, a photograph of a crucifix immersed in urine. Serrano had been awarded a $15,000 grant from the Southeast Center for Contemporary Art, an organization that received NEA support.

[O'Connor reviews congressional reactions to these exhibits, including the provision at issue in this case.]

II

A

Respondents raise a facial constitutional challenge to § 954(d)(1), and consequently they confront "a heavy burden" in advancing their claim. Facial invalidation "is, manifestly, strong medicine" that "has been employed by the Court sparingly and only as a last resort." *Broadrick v. Oklahoma,* 413 U.S. 601 (1973). To prevail, respondents must demonstrate a substantial risk that application of the provision will lead to the suppression of speech.

Respondents argue that the provision is a paradigmatic example of viewpoint discrimination because it rejects any artistic speech that either fails to respect mainstream values or offends standards of decency. The premise of respondents' claim is that § 954(d)(1) constrains the agency's ability to fund certain categories of artistic expression. The NEA, however, reads the provision as merely hortatory, and contends that it stops well short of an absolute restriction. Section 954(d)(1) adds "considerations" to the grant-making process; it does not preclude awards to projects that might be deemed "indecent" or "disrespectful," nor place conditions on grants, or even specify that those factors must be given any particular weight in reviewing an application. Indeed, the agency asserts that it has adequately implemented § 954(d)(1) merely by ensuring the representation of various backgrounds and points of view on the advisory panels that analyze grant applications. . . .

Furthermore, like the plain language of § 954(d), the political context surrounding the adoption of the "decency and respect" clause is inconsistent with respondents' assertion that the provision compels the NEA to deny funding on the basis of viewpoint discriminatory criteria. The legislation was a bipartisan proposal introduced as a counterweight to amendments aimed at eliminating the NEA's funding or substantially constraining its grant-making authority. . . .

That § 954(d)(1) admonishes the NEA merely to take "decency and respect" into consideration, and that the legislation was aimed at reforming procedures rather than precluding speech, undercut respondents' argument that the provision inevitably will be utilized as a tool for invidious viewpoint discrimination. In cases where we have struck down legislation as facially unconstitutional, the dangers were both more evident and more substantial. . . .

In contrast, the "decency and respect" criteria do not silence speakers by expressly "threatening censorship of ideas." Thus, we do not perceive a realistic danger that § 954(d)(1) will compromise First Amendment values.

As respondents' own arguments demonstrate, the considerations that the provision introduces, by their nature, do not engender the kind of directed viewpoint discrimination that would prompt this Court to invalidate a statute on its face. Respondents assert, for example, that "one would be hard-pressed to find two people in the United States who could agree on what the 'diverse beliefs and values of the American public' are, much less on whether a particular work of art 'respects' them"; and they claim that " 'decency' is likely to mean something very different to a septuagenarian in Tuscaloosa and a teenager in Las Vegas." The NEA likewise views the considerations enumerated in § 954(d)(1) as susceptible to multiple interpretations. . . . Accordingly, the provision does not introduce considerations that, in practice, would effectively preclude or punish the expression of particular views. Indeed, one could hardly anticipate how "decency" or "respect" would bear on grant applications in categories such as funding for symphony orchestras.

Respondents' claim that the provision is facially unconstitutional may be reduced to the argument that the criteria in § 954(d)(1) are sufficiently subjective that the agency could utilize them to engage in viewpoint discrimination. Given the varied interpretations of the criteria and the vague exhortation to "take them into consideration," it seems unlikely that this provision will introduce any greater element of selectivity than the determination of "artistic excellence" itself. . . .

The NEA's enabling statute contemplates a number of indisputably constitutional applications for both the "decency" prong of § 954(d)(1) and its reference to "respect for the diverse beliefs and values of the American public." Educational programs are central to the NEA's mission. . . . And it is well established that "decency" is a permissible factor where "educational suitability" motivates its consideration. . . .

Permissible applications of the mandate to consider "respect for the diverse beliefs and values of the American public" are also apparent. In setting forth the purposes of the NEA, Congress explained that "it is vital to democracy to honor and preserve its multicultural artistic heritage." The agency expressly takes diversity into account, giving special consideration to "projects and productions . . . that reach, or reflect the culture of, a minority, inner city, rural, or tribal community," as well as projects that generally emphasize "cultural diversity." Respondents do not contend that the criteria in § 954(d)(1) are impermissibly applied when they may be justified, as the statute contemplates, with respect to a project's intended audience.

We recognize, of course, that reference to these permissible applications would not alone be sufficient to sustain the statute against respondents' First Amendment challenge. But neither are we persuaded that, in other applications, the language of § 954(d)(1) itself will give rise to the suppression of protected expression. Any content-based considerations that may be taken into account in the grant-making process are a consequence of the nature of arts funding. . . .

[O'Connor distinguishes this decision from the decision in *Rosenberger v. Rector and Visitors of Univ. of Va.* (515 U.S. 819, 1995) relative to the distribution of funds collected from student activity fees.]

Respondents do not allege discrimination in any particular funding decision. (In fact, after filing suit to challenge § 954(d)(1), two of the individual respondents received NEA grants. Thus, we have no occasion here to address an as-applied challenge in a situation where the denial of a grant may be shown to be the product of invidious viewpoint discrimination. If the NEA were to leverage its power to award subsidies on the basis of subjective criteria into a penalty on disfavored viewpoints, then we would confront a different case. . . .

B

Finally, although the First Amendment certainly has application in the subsidy context, we note that the Government may allocate competitive funding according to criteria that would be impermissible were direct regulation of speech or a criminal penalty at stake. So long as legislation does not infringe on other constitutionally protected rights, Congress has wide latitude to set spending priorities. . . . .

III

The lower courts also erred in invalidating § 954(d)(1) as unconstitutionally vague. Under the First and Fifth Amendments, speakers are protected from arbitrary and discriminatory enforcement of vague standards. See *NAACP v. Button,* 371 U.S. 415 (1963). The terms of the provision are undeniably opaque, and if they appeared in a criminal statute or regulatory scheme, they could raise substantial vagueness concerns. It is unlikely, however, that speakers will be compelled to steer too far clear of any "forbidden area" in the context of grants of this nature. . . . We recognize, as a practical matter, that artists may conform their speech to what they believe to be the decision-making criteria in order to acquire funding. But when the Government is acting as patron rather than as sovereign, the consequences of imprecision are not constitutionally severe.

In the context of selective subsidies, it is not always feasible for Congress to legislate with clarity. Indeed, if this statute is unconstitutionally vague, then so too are all government programs awarding scholarships and grants on the basis of subjective criteria such as "excellence." . . .

Section 954(d)(1) merely adds some imprecise considerations to an already subjective selection process. It does not, on its face, impermissibly infringe on First or Fifth Amendment rights. Accordingly, the judgment of the Court of Appeals is reversed and the case is remanded for further proceedings consistent with this opinion.

It is so ordered.

JUSTICE SCALIA, with whom JUSTICE THOMAS joins, concurring in the judgment.

"The operation was a success, but the patient died." What such a procedure is to medicine, the Court's opinion in this case is to law. It sustains the constitutionality of 20 U.S.C. § 954(d)(1) by gutting it. The most avid congressional opponents of the provision could not have asked for more. I write separately because, unlike the Court, I think that § 954(d)(1) must be evaluated as written, rather than as distorted by the agency it was meant to control. By its terms, it establishes content- and viewpoint-based criteria upon which grant applications are to be evaluated. And that is perfectly constitutional.

JUSTICE SOUTER, dissenting.

The question here is whether the italicized segment of this statute is unconstitutional on its face: "artistic excellence and artistic merit are the criteria by which applications [for grants from the National Endowment for the Arts] are judged, *taking into consideration general standards of decency and respect for the diverse beliefs and values of the American public.*" It is.

The decency and respect proviso mandates viewpoint-based decisions in the disbursement of government subsidies, and the Government has wholly failed to explain why the statute should be afforded an exemption from the fundamental rule of the First Amendment that viewpoint discrimination in the exercise of public authority over expressive activity is unconstitutional. The Court's conclusions that the proviso is not viewpoint based, that it is not a regulation, and that the NEA may permissibly engage in viewpoint-based discrimination, are all patently mistaken. Nor may the question raised be answered in the Government's favor on the assumption that some constitutional applications of the statute are enough to satisfy the demand of facial constitutionality, leaving claims of the proviso's obvious invalidity to be dealt with later in response to challenges of specific applications of the discriminatory standards. This assumption is irreconcilable with our long standing and sensible doctrine of facial overbreadth, applicable to claims brought under the First Amendment's speech clause. I respectfully dissent.

I

"If there is a bedrock principle underlying the First Amendment, it is that the government may not prohibit the expression of an idea simply because society finds the idea itself offensive or disagreeable." . . .

It goes without saying that artistic expression lies within this First Amendment protection. . . . The constitutional protection of artistic works turns not on the political significance that may be attributable to such productions, though they may indeed comment on the political, but simply on their expressive character, which falls within a spectrum of protected "speech" extending outward from the core of overtly political declarations. Put differently, art is entitled to full protection because our "cultural life," just like our native politics, "rests upon [the] ideal" of governmental viewpoint neutrality.

When called upon to vindicate this ideal, we characteristically begin by asking "whether the government has adopted a regulation of speech because of disagreement with the message it conveys. The government's purpose is the controlling consideration." *Ward v. Rock Against Racism,* 491 U.S. 781 (1989). The answer in this case is damning. One need do nothing more than read the text of the statute to conclude that Congress's purpose in imposing the decency and respect criteria was to prevent the funding of art that conveys an offensive message; the decency and respect provision on its face is quintessentially viewpoint based, and quotations from the *Congressional Record* merely confirm the obvious legislative purpose. In the words of a cosponsor of the bill that enacted the proviso, "works which deeply offend the sensibilities of significant portions of the public ought not to be supported with public funds." [Souter provides additional supporting quotations.]

II

In the face of such clear legislative purpose, so plainly expressed, the Court has its work cut out for it in seeking a constitutional reading of the statute.

A

The Court says, first, that because the phrase "general standards of decency and respect for the diverse beliefs and values of the American public" is imprecise and capable of multiple interpretations, "the considerations that the provision introduces, by their nature, do not engender the kind of directed viewpoint discrimination that would prompt this Court to invalidate a statute on its face." Unquestioned case law, however, is clearly to the contrary.

B

Another alternative for avoiding unconstitutionality that the Court appears to regard with some favor is the Government's argument that the NEA may comply with § 954(d) merely by populating the advisory panels that analyze grant applications with members of diverse backgrounds. Would that it were so easy; this asserted implementation of the law fails even to "reflect a plausible construction of the plain language of the statute." *Rust v. Sullivan* [500 U.S. 173] (1991).

C

A third try at avoiding constitutional problems is the Court's disclaimer of any constitutional issue here because "section 954(d)(1) adds 'considerations' to the grant-making process; it does not preclude awards to projects that might be deemed 'indecent' or 'disrespectful,' nor place conditions on grants, or even specify that those factors must be given any particular weight in reviewing an application." Since "§ 954(d)(1) admonishes the NEA merely to take 'decency and respect' into consideration," not to make funding decisions specifically on those grounds, the Court sees no constitutional difficulty.

That is not a fair reading. . . .

III

A second basic strand in the Court's treatment of today's question . . . in effect assumes that whether or not the statute mandates viewpoint discrimination, there is no constitutional issue here because government art subsidies fall within a zone of activity free from First Amendment restraints. The Government calls attention to the roles of government-as-speaker and government-as-buyer, in which the government is of course entitled to engage in viewpoint discrimination: if the Food and Drug Administration launches an advertising campaign on the subject of smoking, it may condemn the habit without also having to show a cowboy taking a puff on the opposite page; and if the Secretary of Defense wishes to buy a portrait to decorate the Pentagon, he is free to prefer George Washington over George the Third.

The Government freely admits, however, that it neither speaks through the expression subsidized by the NEA, nor buys anything for itself with its NEA grants. . . .

IV

[This section critiques the majority's general approach to facial challenges.]

V

The Court does not strike down the proviso, however. Instead, it preserves the irony of a statutory mandate to deny recognition to virtually any expression capable of causing offense in any quarter as the most recent manifestation of a scheme enacted to "create and sustain . . . a climate encouraging freedom of thought, imagination, and inquiry."

FOR DISCUSSION

Justice Scalia quips, "The operation was a success, but the patient died." What does he mean by this? Is he correct? Does the case end up chiefly showing the scope or the limits of governmental restrictions on the spending of funds?

BOARD OF REGENTS OF UNIVERSITY OF WISCONSIN V. SOUTHWORTH

529 U.S. 217, 120 S.Ct. 1346, 146 L.Ed. 2d 193 (2000)

In *Rosenberg v. Board of Visitors and Rectors of the University of Virginia* (515 U.S. 810, 1995), the Supreme Court decided that a public university could not deny student activity fees to an organization on the basis of its religious character. This case deals with a related issue: whether universities can continue to collect student monies for organizations advocating causes with which students might individually disagree.

Vote: 9–0

JUSTICE KENNEDY delivered the opinion of the Court.

For the second time in recent years we consider constitutional questions arising from a program designed to facilitate extracurricular student speech at a public university. Respondents are a group of students at the University of Wisconsin. They brought a First Amendment challenge to a mandatory student activity fee imposed by petitioner Board of Regents of the University of Wisconsin and used in part by the University to support student organizations engaging in political or ideological speech. Respondents object to the speech and expression of some of the student organizations. Relying upon our precedents which protect members of unions and bar associations from being required to pay fees used for speech the members find objectionable, both the District Court and the Court of Appeals invalidated the University's student fee program. The University contends that its mandatory student activity fee and the speech which it supports are appropriate to further its educational mission.

We reverse. The First Amendment permits a public university to charge its students an activity fee used to fund a program to facilitate extracurricular student speech if the program is viewpoint neutral. We do not sustain, however, the student referendum mechanism of the University's program, which appears to permit the exaction of fees in violation of the viewpoint neutrality principle. As to that aspect of the program, we remand for further proceedings.

I

[Kennedy proceeds to describe the University of Wisconsin system.]

The responsibility for governing the University of Wisconsin System is vested by law with the board of regents. The same law empowers the students to share in aspects of the University's governance. One of those functions is to administer the student activities fee program. By statute the "students in consultation with the chancellor and subject to the final confirmation of the board [of regents] shall have the responsibility for the disposition of those student fees which constitute substantial support for campus student activities." The students do so, in large measure, through their student government, called the Associated Students of Madison (ASM), and various ASM subcommittees. The program the University maintains to support the extracurricular activities undertaken by many of its student organizations is the subject of the present controversy.

It seems that since its founding the University has required full-time students enrolled at its Madison campus to pay a nonrefundable activity fee. For the 1995–1996 academic year, when this suit was commenced, the activity fee amounted to $331.50 per year. The fee is segregated from the University's tuition charge. Once collected, the activity fees are deposited by the University into the accounts of the State of Wisconsin. The fees are drawn upon by the University to support various campus services and extracurricular student activities. In the University's view, the activity fees "enhance the educational experience" of its students by "promoting extracurricular activities," "stimulating advocacy and debate on diverse points of view," enabling "participation in political activity," "promoting student participation in campus administrative activity," and providing "opportunities to develop social skills," all consistent with the University's mission.

The board of regents classifies the segregated fee into allocable and nonallocable portions. The nonallocable portion approximates 80% of the total fee and covers expenses such as student health services, intramural sports, debt service, and the upkeep and operations of the student union facilities. Respondents did not challenge the purposes to which the University commits the nonallocable portion of the segregated fee.

The allocable portion of the fee supports extracurricular endeavors pursued by the University's registered student organizations or RSO's. To qualify for RSO status students must organize as a not-for-profit group, limit membership primarily to students, and agree to undertake activities related to student life on campus. During the 1995–1996 school year, 623 groups had RSO status on the Madison campus. To name but a few, RSO's included the Future Financial Gurus of America; the International Socialist Organization; the College Democrats; the College Republicans; and the American Civil Liberties Union Campus Chapter. As one would expect, the expressive activities undertaken by RSO's are diverse in range and content, from displaying posters and circulating newsletters throughout the campus, to hosting campus debates and guest speakers, and to what can best be described as political lobbying.

RSO's may obtain a portion of the allocable fees in one of three ways. Most do so by seeking funding from the Student Government Activity Fund (SGAF), administered by the ASM. SGAF moneys may be issued to support an RSO's operations and events, as well as travel expenses "central to the purpose of the organization." As an alternative, an RSO can apply for funding from the General Student Services Fund (GSSF), administered through the ASM's finance committee. During the 1995–1996 academic year, 15 RSO's received GSSF funding. . . .

The GSSF, as well as the SGAF, consists of moneys originating in the allocable portion of the mandatory fee. The parties have stipulated that, with respect to SGAF and GSSF funding, "the process for reviewing and approving allocations for funding is administered in a viewpoint-neutral fashion," and that the University does not use the fee program for "advocating a particular point of view."

A student referendum provides a third means for an RSO to obtain funding. While the record is sparse on this feature of the University's program, the parties inform us that the student body can vote either to approve or to disapprove an assessment for a particular RSO. One referendum resulted in an allocation of $45,000 to WISPIRG during the 1995–1996 academic year. At oral argument, counsel for the University acknowledged that a referendum could also operate to defund an RSO or to veto a funding decision of the ASM. In October 1996, for example, the student body voted to terminate funding to a national student organization to which the University belonged. . . .

II

It is inevitable that government will adopt and pursue programs and policies within its constitutional powers but which nevertheless are contrary to the profound beliefs and sincere convictions of some of its citizens. The government, as a general rule, may support valid programs and policies by taxes or other exactions binding on protesting parties. . . . The case we decide here, however, does not raise the issue of the government's right, or, to be more specific, the state-controlled University's right, to use its own funds to advance a particular message. The University's whole justification for fostering the challenged expression is that it springs from the initiative of the students, who alone give it purpose and content in the course of their extracurricular endeavors.

The University having disclaimed that the speech is its own, we do not reach the question whether traditional political controls to ensure responsible government action would be sufficient to overcome First Amendment objections and to allow the challenged program under the principle that the government can speak for itself. If the challenged speech here were financed by tuition dollars and the University and its officials were responsible for its content, the case might be evaluated on the premise that the government itself is the speaker. That is not the case before us.

The University of Wisconsin exacts the fee at issue for the sole purpose of facilitating the free and open exchange of ideas by, and among, its students. We conclude the objecting students may insist upon certain safeguards with respect to the expressive activities which they are required to support. . . . The standard of viewpoint neutrality found in the public forum cases provides the standard we find controlling. We decide that the viewpoint neutrality requirement of the University program is in general sufficient to protect the rights of the objecting students. The student referendum aspect of the program for funding speech and expressive activities, however, appears to be inconsistent with the viewpoint neutrality requirement.

We must begin by recognizing that the complaining students are being required to pay fees which are subsidies for speech they find objectionable, even offensive. The *Abood* and *Keller* cases, then, provide the beginning point for our analysis. *Abood v. Detroit Bd. of Ed.,* 431 U.S. 209 (1977); *Keller v. State Bar of Cal.,* 496 U.S. 1 (1990). While those precedents identify the interests of the protesting students, the means of implementing First Amendment protections adopted in those decisions are neither applicable nor workable in the context of extracurricular student speech at a university.

In *Abood,* some nonunion public school teachers challenged an agreement requiring them, as a condition of their employment, to pay a service fee equal in amount to union dues. The objecting teachers alleged that the union's use of their fees to engage in political speech violated their freedom of association guaranteed by the First and Fourteenth Amendments. The Court agreed and held that any objecting teacher could "prevent the Union's spending a part of their required service fees to contribute to political candidates and to express political views unrelated to its duties as exclusive bargaining representative." The principles outlined in *Abood* provided the foundation for our later decision in *Keller.* There we held that lawyers admitted to practice in California could be required to join a state bar association and to fund activities "germane" to the association's mission of "regulating the legal profession and improving the quality of legal services." The lawyers could not, however, be required to fund the bar association's own political expression.

The proposition that students who attend the University cannot be required to pay subsidies for the speech of other students without some First Amendment protection follows from the *Abood* and *Keller* cases. Students enroll in public universities to seek fulfillment of their personal aspirations and of their own potential. If the University conditions the opportunity to receive a college education, an opportunity comparable in importance to joining a labor union or bar association, on an agreement to support objectionable, extracurricular expression by other students, the rights acknowledged in *Abood* and *Keller* become implicated. It infringes on the speech and beliefs of the individual to be required, by this mandatory student activity fee program, to pay subsidies for the objectionable speech of others without any recognition of the State's corresponding duty to him or her. Yet recognition must be given as well to the important and substantial purposes of the University, which seeks to facilitate a wide range of speech.

In *Abood* and *Keller* the constitutional rule took the form of limiting the required subsidy to speech germane to the purposes of the union or bar association. The standard of germane speech as applied to student speech at a university is unworkable, however, and gives insufficient protection both to the objecting students and to the University program itself. . . .

The speech the University seeks to encourage in the program before us is distinguished not by discernable limits but by its vast, unexplored bounds. To insist upon asking what speech is germane would be contrary to the very goal the University seeks to pursue. It is not for the Court to say what is or is not germane to the ideas to be pursued in an institution of higher learning.

Just as the vast extent of permitted expression makes the test of germane speech inappropriate for intervention, so too does it underscore the high potential for intrusion on the First Amendment rights of the objecting students. It is all but inevitable that the fees will result in subsidies to speech which some students find objectionable and offensive to their personal beliefs. If the standard of germane speech is inapplicable, then, it might be argued the remedy is to allow each student to list those causes which he or she will or will not support. If a university decided that its students' First Amendment interests were better protected by some type of optional or refund system it would be free to do so. We decline to impose a system of that sort as a constitutional requirement, however. The restriction could be so disruptive and expensive that the program to support extracurricular speech would be ineffective. The First Amendment does not require the University to put the program at risk.

The University may determine that its mission is well served if students have the means to engage in dynamic discussions of philosophical, religious, scientific, social, and political subjects in their extracurricular campus life outside the lecture hall. If the University reaches this conclusion, it is entitled to impose a mandatory fee to sustain an open dialogue to these ends.

The University must provide some protection to its students' First Amendment interests, however. The proper measure, and the principal standard of protection for objecting students, we conclude, is the requirement of viewpoint neutrality in the allocation of funding support. Viewpoint neutrality was the obligation to which we gave substance in *Rosenberger v. Rector and Visitors of Univ. of Va.*, 515 U.S. 819 (1995). . . .

The parties have stipulated that the program the University has developed to stimulate extracurricular student expression respects the principle of viewpoint neutrality. If the stipulation is to continue to control the case, the University's program in its basic structure must be found consistent with the First Amendment.

Our decision ought not to be taken to imply that in other instances the University, its agents or employees, or—of particular importance—its faculty, are subject to the First Amendment analysis which controls in this case. Where the University speaks, either in its own name through its regents or officers, or in myriad other ways through its diverse faculties, the analysis likely would be altogether different. . . .

III

It remains to discuss the referendum aspect of the University's program. While the record is not well developed on the point, it appears that by majority vote of the student body a given RSO may be funded or defunded. It is unclear to us what protection, if any, there is for viewpoint neutrality in this part of the process. To the extent the referendum substitutes majority determinations for viewpoint neutrality it would undermine the constitutional protection the program requires. The whole theory of viewpoint neutrality is that minority views are treated with the same respect as are majority views. Access to a public forum, for instance, does not depend upon majoritarian consent. That principle is controlling here. A remand is necessary and appropriate to resolve this point; and the case in all events must be reexamined in light of the principles we have discussed.

JUSTICE SOUTER, with whom JUSTICES STEVENS and BREYER join, concurring in the judgment.

The majority today validates the University's student activity fee after recognizing a new category of First Amendment interests and a new standard of viewpoint neutrality protection. I agree that the University's scheme is permissible, but do not believe that the Court should take the occasion to impose a cast-iron viewpoint neutrality requirement to uphold it. Instead, I would hold that the First Amendment interest claimed by the student respondents here is simply insufficient to merit protection by anything more than the viewpoint neutrality already accorded by the University, and I would go no further.

FOR DISCUSSION

Cases have established that nonunion members can be assessed for work that unions do on their behalf but not for materials that such unions produce advocating political messages. Would it be appropriate to apply such a principle in this case? What would be its advantages or disadvantages?

RELATED CASE

***Pleasant Grove City, Utah v. Summum:* 555 U.S. 460 (2009).**

The Court unanimously decided that a city did not have to accept a permanent monument in a public park donated by a religious group called Summum, even though the city had previously accepted a monument with the Ten Commandments. The city sought to exclude the monument, which displayed the Seven Aphorisms of Summum, on the basis that the object was neither directly related to the city's history nor donated by a group with long-standing community ties. Justice Alito's majority decision said that a permanent monument became "government speech" in a way that allowing individuals to speak or pass out flyers does not and that the monument was not therefore subject to strict scrutiny. In a concurring opinion, Justices Scalia and Thomas specifically indicated that they did not think the case raised legitimate First Amendment Establishment Clause issues.

***Abood v. Detroit Board of Education:* 431 U.S. 209 (1977).**

A unanimous Supreme Court ruled that a public sector union may collect fees from employees who were not members of the union to help defray the costs of collective bargaining even if these employees objected to the political activities and speech of the union. The Court said that these employee's First Amendment rights were not violated so long as their dues were not used for ideological or political purposes.

***Knox v. SEIU No. 10–112:* 567 U.S. 310 (2012).**

Court ruled that labor union had to give notice to members that some of their union dues would be used for political purposes so that they could exercise their First Amendment right to opt out.

***Harris v. Quinn:* 573 U.S. ___ (2014).**

Court ruled that the State of Illinois could not force non-union personal health care workers to pay dues and fees to a labor union because they were not government employees, but instead hired by individual patients.

***Walker v. Texas Division, Sons of Confederate Veterans:* 576 U.S. ___ (2015).**

The Texas Division of the Son of Confederate Veterans sought to require the State of Texas to issue a specialty license plate for their group that would depict the Confederate flag. When the State refused, the Son of Confederates sued, claiming their First Amendment free speech rights had been violated. In a 5–4 decision, the Court ruled that license plates were government speech, and therefore Texas did not violate the Sons' speech in refusing to create a license plate with the Confederate flag on it.

***Reed v. Town of Gilbert:* 576 U.S. ___ (2015).**

The Court invalidated a town ordinance that prohibited the display of certain outdoor signs without a permit but exempted certain ideological, political, and temporary direction signs. The Court ruled that the regulation, which the town had applied to signs announcing the time and location of religious services, resulted in impermissible content discrimination that required strict scrutiny.

Student Speech

Among the most fascinating time, place, and manner restrictions on speech are those that involve students. This chapter includes four cases that restrict the freedom of speech or press rights of high school students. The lead case, *Tinker v. Des Moines Independent School District* (393 U.S. 503, 1969), is also important to the discussion under "Speech Plus," because it involves symbolic speech—junior high school students wearing black armbands in protest of the Vietnam War. Justice Abe Fortas's majority opinion in this case remains one of the clearest judicial affirmations of the First Amendment rights of students (and teachers) in classroom settings. Note, however, that the Court majority indicates that the "speech" in question was acceptable precisely because it did not, in the Court's judgment, cause substantial disruption. The "silent" nature of the "speech" also made the activity less likely to interfere with the rights of others.

Bethel School District No. 403 v. Fraser (478 U.S. 675, 1986) indicates that speech within a school setting will still be judged according to the appropriateness of the school's educational mission and the maturity level of the students involved. The Court upholds the right of a principal to punish a student for lewd (but not obscene) words that he delivers to a school assembly that includes junior high school students. Similarly, in *Hazelwood School District v. Kuhlmeier* (484 U.S. 260, 1988), which should be considered in light of other cases in this book related to freedom of the press, the Court allows a high school principal to censor a student newspaper in a way that would never be acceptable outside a school setting. In *Morse v. Frederick* (551 U.S. 393, 2007), the Court further allows a principal to punish a student for an ambiguous message ("BONG HiTS 4 Jesus") that might simply be nonsensical or might be interpreted to favor drug use.

Scholars continue to debate whether the last three cases represent a retreat from *Tinker.* Although they have yet to do so, in time, courts will tease out the degree to which these decisions apply to college students.

Tinker v. Des Moines Independent Community School District

393 U.S. 503, 89 S.Ct. 722, 21 L.Ed. 2d 731 (1969)

This landmark case dealt with the constitutionality of a policy that principals in Des Moines schools adopted to discourage public school students from wearing black armbands to school in protest over the Vietnam War. Three students who wore armbands were suspended in accordance with the policy, and they appealed; lower federal courts upheld the principals' actions.

Vote: 7–2

Justice Fortas delivered the opinion of the Court.

I

The District Court recognized that the wearing of an armband for the purpose of expressing certain views is the type of symbolic act that is within the Free Speech Clause of the First Amendment. . . . As we shall discuss, the wearing of armbands in the circumstances of this case was entirely divorced from actually or potentially disruptive conduct by those participating in it. It was closely akin to "pure speech" which, we have repeatedly held, is entitled to comprehensive protection under the First Amendment. . . .

First Amendment rights, applied in light of the special characteristics of the school environment, are available to teachers and students. It can hardly be argued that either students or teachers shed their constitutional rights to freedom of speech or expression at the schoolhouse gate. This has been the unmistakable holding of this Court for almost 50 years. . . .

On the other hand, the Court has repeatedly emphasized the need for affirming the comprehensive authority of the States and of school officials, consistent with fundamental constitutional safeguards, to prescribe and control conduct in the schools. See *Epperson v. Arkansas,* 393 U.S. 97 (1968); *Meyer v. Nebraska,* 262 U.S. 390 (1923). Our problem lies in the area where students in the exercise of First Amendment rights collide with the rules of the school authorities.

II

The problem posed by the present case does not relate to regulation of the length of skirts or the type of clothing, to hair style, or deportment. . . . It does not concern aggressive, disruptive action or even group demonstrations. Our problem involves direct, primary First Amendment rights akin to "pure speech."

The school officials banned and sought to punish petitioners for a silent, passive expression of opinion, unaccompanied by any disorder or disturbance on the part of petitioners. There is here no evidence whatever of petitioners' interference, actual or nascent, with the schools' work or of collision with the rights of other students to be secure and to be let alone. Accordingly, this case does not concern speech or action that intrudes upon the work of the schools or the rights of other students.

Only a few of the 18,000 students in the school system wore the black armbands. Only five students were suspended for wearing them. There is no indication that the work of the schools or any class was disrupted. Outside the classrooms, a few students made hostile remarks to the children wearing armbands, but there were no threats or acts of violence on school premises.

The District Court concluded that the action of the school authorities was reasonable because it was based upon their fear of a disturbance from the wearing of the armbands. But, in our system, undifferentiated fear or apprehension of disturbance is not enough to overcome the right to freedom of expression. Any departure from absolute regimentation may cause trouble. Any variation from the majority's opinion may inspire fear. Any word spoken, in class, in the lunchroom, or on the campus, that deviates from the views of another person may start an argument or cause a disturbance. But our Constitution says we must take this risk, *Terminiello v. Chicago*, 337 U.S. 1 (1949); and our history says that it is this sort of hazardous freedom—this kind of openness—that is the basis of our national strength and of the independence and vigor of Americans who grow up and live in this relatively permissive, often disputatious, society.

In order for the State in the person of school officials to justify prohibition of a particular expression of opinion, it must be able to show that its action was caused by something more than a mere desire to avoid the discomfort and unpleasantness that always accompany an unpopular viewpoint. Certainly where there is no finding and no showing that engaging in the forbidden conduct would "materially and substantially interfere with the requirements of appropriate discipline in the operation of the school," the prohibition cannot be sustained.

In the present case, the District Court made no such finding, and our independent examination of the record fails to yield evidence that the school authorities had reason to anticipate that the wearing of the armbands would substantially interfere with the work of the school or impinge upon the rights of other students. . . .

On the contrary, the action of the school authorities appears to have been based upon an urgent wish to avoid the controversy which might result from the expression, even by the silent symbol of armbands, of opposition to this Nation's part in the conflagration in Vietnam. . . .

It is also relevant that the school authorities did not purport to prohibit the wearing of all symbols of political or controversial significance. The record shows that students in some of the schools wore buttons relating to national political campaigns, and some even wore the Iron Cross, traditionally a symbol of Nazism. The order prohibiting the wearing of armbands did not extend to these. Instead, a particular symbol—black armbands worn to exhibit opposition to this Nation's involvement in Vietnam—was singled out for prohibition. Clearly, the prohibition of expression of one particular opinion, at least without evidence that it is necessary to avoid material and substantial interference with schoolwork or discipline, is not constitutionally permissible.

In our system, state-operated schools may not be enclaves of totalitarianism. School officials do not possess absolute authority over their students. Students in school as well as out of school are "persons" under our Constitution. They are possessed of fundamental rights which the State must respect, just as they themselves must respect their obligations to the State. In our system, students may not be regarded as closed-circuit recipients of only that which the State chooses to communicate. They may not be confined to the expression of those sentiments that are officially approved. In the absence of a specific showing of constitutionally valid reasons to regulate their speech, students are entitled to freedom of expression of their views. . . .

In *Meyer v. Nebraska,* Mr. Justice McReynolds expressed this Nation's repudiation of the principle that a State might so conduct its schools as to "foster a homogeneous people." He said: "In order to submerge the individual and develop ideal citizens, Sparta assembled the males at seven into barracks and intrusted their subsequent education and training to official guardians. Although such measures have been deliberately approved by men of great genius, their ideas touching the relation between individual and State were wholly different from those upon which our institutions rest; and it hardly will be affirmed that any legislature could impose such restrictions upon the people of a State without doing violence to both letter and spirit of the Constitution."

This principle has been repeated by this Court on numerous occasions during the intervening years. . . .

The principle of these cases is not confined to the supervised and ordained discussion which takes place in the classroom. The principal use to which the schools are dedicated is to accommodate students during prescribed hours for the purpose of certain types of activities. Among those activities is personal intercommunication among the students. This is not only an inevitable part of the process of attending school;

it is also an important part of the educational process. A student's rights, therefore, do not embrace merely the classroom hours. . . .

Under our Constitution, free speech is not a right that is given only to be so circumscribed that it exists in principle but not in fact. Freedom of expression would not truly exist if the right could be exercised only in an area that a benevolent government has provided as a safe haven for crackpots. The Constitution says that Congress (and the States) may not abridge the right to free speech. This provision means what it says. We properly read it to permit reasonable regulation of speech-connected activities in carefully restricted circumstances. But we do not confine the permissible exercise of First Amendment rights to a telephone booth or the four corners of a pamphlet, or to supervised and ordained discussion in a school classroom.

If a regulation were adopted by school officials forbidding discussion of the Vietnam conflict, or the expression by any student of opposition to it anywhere on school property except as part of a prescribed classroom exercise, it would be obvious that the regulation would violate the constitutional rights of students, at least if it could not be justified by a showing that the students' activities would materially and substantially disrupt the work and discipline of the school.

JUSTICE STEWART, concurring.

Although I agree with much of what is said in the Court's opinion, and with its judgment in this case, I cannot share the Court's uncritical assumption that, school discipline aside, the First Amendment rights of children are co-extensive with those of adults.

JUSTICE BLACK, dissenting.

The Court's holding in this case ushers in what I deem to be an entirely new era in which the power to control pupils by the elected "officials of state supported public schools . . ." in the United States is in ultimate effect transferred to the Supreme Court. . . .

While I have always believed that under the First and Fourteenth Amendments neither the State nor the Federal Government has any authority to regulate or censor the content of speech, I have never believed that any person has a right to give speeches or engage in demonstrations where he pleases and when he pleases.

While the record does not show that any of these armband students shouted, used profane language, or were violent in any manner, detailed testimony by some of them shows their armbands caused comments, warnings by other students, the poking of fun at them, and a warning by an older football player that other, nonprotesting students had better let them alone. There is also evidence that a teacher of mathematics had his lesson period practically "wrecked" chiefly by disputes with Mary Beth Tinker, who wore her armband for her "demonstration." Even a casual reading of the record shows that this armband did divert students' minds from their regular lessons, and that talk, comments, etc., made John Tinker "self-conscious" in attending school with his armband. . . .

[Black ties the Court decision to pre–New Deal cases in which courts substituted their ideas of reasonableness for those of legislators.]

I deny, therefore, that it has been the "unmistakable holding of this Court for almost 50 years" that "students" and "teachers" take with them into the "schoolhouse gate" constitutional rights to "freedom of speech or expression." . . .

In my view, teachers in state-controlled public schools are hired to teach there. Although Mr. Justice McReynolds may have intimated to the contrary in *Meyer* v. *Nebraska,* certainly a teacher is not paid to go into school and teach subjects the State does not hire him to teach as a part of its selected curriculum. Nor are public school students sent to the schools at public expense to broadcast political or any other views to educate and inform the public. The original idea of schools, which I do not believe is yet abandoned as worthless or out of date, was that children had not yet reached the point of experience and wisdom which enabled them to teach all of their elders. It may be that the Nation has outworn the old-fashioned slogan that "children are to be seen not heard," but one may, I hope, be permitted to harbor the thought that taxpayers send children to school on the premise that at their age they need to learn, not teach.

One does not need to be a prophet or the son of a prophet to know that after the Court's holding today some students in Iowa schools and indeed in all schools will be ready, able, and willing to defy their teachers on practically all orders. This is the more unfortunate for the schools since groups of students all over the land are already running loose, conducting break-ins, sit-ins, lie-ins, and smash-ins. Many of these student groups, as is all too familiar to all who read the newspapers and watch the television news programs, have already engaged in rioting, property seizures, and destruction. They have picketed schools to force students not to cross their picket lines and have too often violently attacked earnest but frightened students who wanted an education that the pickets did not want them to get. Students engaged in such activities are apparently confident that they know far more about how to operate public school systems than do their parents, teachers, and elected school officials. It is no answer to say that the particular students here have not yet reached such high points in their demands to attend classes in order to exercise their political pressures. Turned loose with lawsuits for damages and injunctions against their teachers as they are here, it is nothing but wishful thinking to imagine that young, immature students will not soon believe it is their right to control the schools rather than the right of the States that collect the taxes to hire the teachers for the benefit of the pupils. This case, therefore, wholly without constitutional reasons in my judgment, subjects all the public schools in the country to the whims and caprices of their loudest-mouthed, but maybe not their brightest, students. I, for one, am not fully persuaded that school pupils are wise enough, even with this Court's expert help from Washington, to run the 23,390 public school systems in our 50 States. I wish, therefore, wholly to disclaim any purpose on my part to hold that the Federal Constitution compels the teachers, parents, and elected school officials to surrender control of the American public school system to public school students. I dissent.

FOR DISCUSSION

Justice Hugo Black was typically one of the Court's staunchest supporters of freedom of speech, and yet in this case he found himself dissenting. What were his concerns? Were they justified? Do you think his dissent was based chiefly on the speech/conduct distinction or on the fact that the case involved students? Which position do you think is stronger? Why?

BETHEL SCHOOL DISTRICT NO. 403 V. FRASER

478 U.S. 675, 106 S.Ct. 3159, 92 L.Ed. 2d 549 (1986)

Although the speech in Tinker was symbolic, it was clearly politically oriented. By contrast, this case involves the action of a school district that punished a student for giving a lewd speech to a school assembly.

Vote: 7–2

CHIEF JUSTICE BURGER delivered the majority opinion.

We granted certiorari to decide whether the First Amendment prevents a school district from disciplining a high school student for giving a lewd speech at a school assembly.

I

A

On April 26, 1983, respondent Matthew N. Fraser, a student at Bethel High School in Pierce County, Washington, delivered a speech nominating a fellow student for student elective office. Approximately 600 high school students, many of whom were 14-year-olds, attended the assembly. Students were required to attend the assembly or to report to the study hall. The assembly was part of a school-sponsored educational program in self-government. Students who elected not to attend the assembly were required to report to study hall. During the entire speech, Fraser referred to his candidate in terms of an elaborate, graphic, and explicit sexual metaphor.

Two of Fraser's teachers, with whom he discussed the contents of his speech in advance, informed him that the speech was "inappropriate and that he probably should not deliver it," and that his delivery of the speech might have "severe consequences."

During Fraser's delivery of the speech, a school counselor observed the reaction of students to the speech. Some students hooted and yelled; some by gestures graphically simulated the sexual activities pointedly alluded to in respondent's speech. Other students appeared to be bewildered and embarrassed by the speech. One teacher reported that on the day following the speech, she found it necessary to forgo a portion of the scheduled class lesson in order to discuss the speech with the class.

B

Bethel High School disciplinary rule prohibiting the use of obscene language in the school provides: "Conduct which materially and substantially interferes with the educational process is prohibited, including the use of obscene, profane language or gestures."

The morning after the assembly, the Assistant Principal called Fraser into her office and notified him that the school considered his speech to have been a violation of this rule. Fraser was presented with copies of five letters submitted by teachers, describing his conduct at the assembly; he was given a chance to explain his conduct, and he admitted to having given the speech described and that he deliberately used sexual innuendo in the speech. Fraser was then informed that he would be suspended for three days, and that his name would be removed from the list of candidates for graduation speaker at the school's commencement exercises.

B

[Burger reviews U.S. District Court and Ninth Circuit Court decisions favoring Fraser and awarding him damages.]

II

This Court acknowledged in *Tinker v. Des Moines Independent Community School Dist.,* 393 U.S. 503 (1969), that students do not "shed their constitutional rights to freedom of speech or expression at the schoolhouse gate." . . . . .

The marked distinction between the political "message" of the armbands in *Tinker* and the sexual content of respondent's speech in this case seems to have been given little weight by the Court of Appeals.

III

The role and purpose of the American public school system were well described by two historians, who stated: "[Public] education must prepare pupils for citizenship in the Republic. . . It must inculcate the habits and manners of civility as values in themselves conducive to happiness and as indispensable to the practice of self-government in the community and the nation." In *Ambach v. Norwick*, 441 U.S. 68 (1979), we echoed the essence of this statement of the objectives of public education as the "[inculcation of] fundamental values necessary to the maintenance of a democratic political system."

These fundamental values of "habits and manners of civility" essential to a democratic society must, of course, include tolerance of divergent political and religious views, even when the views expressed may be unpopular. But these "fundamental values" must also take into account consideration of the sensibilities of others, and, in the case of a school, the sensibilities of fellow students. The undoubted freedom to advocate unpopular and controversial views in schools and classrooms must be balanced against the society's countervailing interest in teaching students the boundaries of socially appropriate behavior. Even the most heated political discourse in a democratic society requires consideration for the personal sensibilities of the other participants and audiences.

In our Nation's legislative halls, where some of the most vigorous political debates in our society are carried on, there are rules prohibiting the use of expressions offensive to other participants in the debate. . . . Can it be that what is proscribed in the halls of Congress is beyond the reach of school officials to regulate?

The First Amendment guarantees wide freedom in matters of adult public discourse. A sharply divided Court upheld the right to express an antidraft viewpoint in a public place, albeit in terms highly offensive to most citizens. See *Cohen v. California*, 403 U.S. 15 (1971). It does not follow, however, that simply because the use of an offensive form of expression may not be prohibited to adults making what the speaker considers a political point, the same latitude must be permitted to children in a public school. . . .

Surely it is a highly appropriate function of public school education to prohibit the use of vulgar and offensive terms in public discourse. Indeed, the "fundamental values necessary to the maintenance of a democratic political system" disfavor the use of terms of debate highly offensive or highly threatening to others. Nothing in the Constitution prohibits the states from insisting that certain modes of expression are inappropriate and subject to sanctions. . . .

The process of educating our youth for citizenship in public schools is not confined to books, the curriculum, and the civics class; schools must teach by example the shared values of a civilized social order. Consciously or otherwise, teachers—and indeed the older students—demonstrate the appropriate form of civil discourse and political expression by their conduct and deportment in and out of class. Inescapably, like parents, they are role models. The schools, as instruments of the state, may determine that the essential lessons of civil, mature conduct cannot be conveyed in a school that tolerates lewd, indecent, or offensive speech and conduct such as that indulged in by this confused boy.

The pervasive sexual innuendo in Fraser's speech was plainly offensive to both teachers and students—indeed to any mature person. By glorifying male sexuality, and in its verbal content, the speech was acutely insulting to teenage girl students. The speech could well be seriously damaging to its less mature audience, many of whom were only 14 years old and on the threshold of awareness of human sexuality. Some students were reported as bewildered by the speech and the reaction of mimicry it provoked.

This Court's First Amendment jurisprudence has acknowledged limitations on the otherwise absolute interest of the speaker in reaching an unlimited audience where the speech is sexually explicit and the audience may include children. . . .

We have also recognized an interest in protecting minors from exposure to vulgar and offensive spoken language. In *FCC* v. *Pacifica Foundation*, 438 U.S. 726 (1978), we dealt with the power of the Federal Communications Commission to regulate a radio broadcast described as "indecent but not obscene." . . .

We hold that petitioner School District acted entirely within its permissible authority in imposing sanctions upon Fraser in response to his offensively lewd and indecent speech. Unlike the sanctions imposed on the students wearing armbands in *Tinker*, the penalties imposed in this case were unrelated to any political viewpoint. The First Amendment does not prevent the school officials from determining that to permit a vulgar and lewd speech such as respondent's would undermine the school's basic educational mission. A high school assembly or classroom is no place for a sexually explicit monologue directed towards an unsuspecting audience of teenage students. Accordingly, it was perfectly appropriate for the school to disassociate itself to make the point to the pupils that vulgar speech and lewd conduct is wholly inconsistent with the "fundamental values" of public school education. Justice Black, dissenting in *Tinker*, made a point that is especially relevant in this case: "I wish therefore, . . . to disclaim any purpose . . . to hold that the Federal Constitution compels the teachers, parents, and elected school officials to surrender control of the American public school system to public school students."

IV

[Burger further rejects the argument that the student's due process rights were violated.]

JUSTICE STEVENS, dissenting.

"Frankly, my dear, I don't give a damn."

When I was a high school student, the use of those words in a public forum shocked the Nation. Today Clark Gable's four-letter expletive is less offensive than it was then. Nevertheless, I assume that high school administrators may prohibit the use of that word in classroom discussion and even in extracurricular activities that are sponsored by the school and held on school premises. For I believe a school faculty must regulate the content as well as the style of student speech in carrying out its educational mission. It does seem to me, however, that if a student is to be punished for using offensive speech, he is entitled to fair notice of the scope of the prohibition and the consequences of its violation. The interest in free speech protected by the First Amendment and the interest in fair procedure protected by the Due Process Clause of the Fourteenth Amendment combine to require this conclusion.

This respondent was an outstanding young man with a fine academic record. The fact that he was chosen by the student body to speak at the school's commencement exercises demonstrates that he was respected by his peers. This fact is relevant for two reasons. It confirms the conclusion that the discipline imposed on him—a 3-day suspension and ineligibility to speak at the school's graduation exercises—was sufficiently serious to justify invocation of the School District's grievance procedures. See *Goss* v. *Lopez*, 419 U.S. 565 (1975). More importantly, it indicates that he was probably in a better position to determine whether an audience composed of 600 of his contemporaries would be offended by the use of a four-letter word—or a sexual metaphor—than is a group of judges who are at least two generations and 3,000 miles away from the scene of the crime.

The fact that the speech may not have been offensive to his audience—or that he honestly believed that it would be inoffensive—does not mean that he had a constitutional right to deliver it. For the school—not the student—must prescribe the rules of conduct in an educational institution. But it does mean that he should not be disciplined for speaking frankly in a school assembly if he had no reason to anticipate punitive consequences. [Stevens examined three theories under which the student might have been thought to know that he would be punished and rejected all of them.]

FOR DISCUSSION

Do you think the Court would have ruled the same if the speech at issue had been delivered by a faculty member? To what degree do you think the First Amendment rights of students and faculty members are linked? Which group do you think ultimately has more freedom? Why?

HAZELWOOD SCHOOL DISTRICT V. KUHLMEIER

484 U.S. 260, 108 S.Ct. 562, 98 L.Ed. 2d 592 (1988)

Citing privacy concerns, a high school principal refused to permit a school-funded student newspaper to publish articles about pregnant students at the school or the effects of divorce on students. The students appealed the administrative decision to a district court, which ruled against them. The Eighth District Court of Appeals ruled for the students and reversed. The school district appealed to the Supreme Court which reversed.

Vote: 5–3

JUSTICE WHITE delivered the majority opinion of the Court.

I

[White observes that the student newspaper at issue was written and edited by a school journalism class and funded by the board of education.]

The practice at Hazelwood East during the spring 1983 semester was for the journalism teacher [Emerson] to submit page proofs of each *Spectrum* issue to Principal Reynolds for his review prior to publication. On May 10, Emerson delivered the proofs of the May 13 edition to Reynolds, who objected to two of the articles scheduled to appear in that edition. One of the stories described three Hazelwood East students' experiences with pregnancy; the other discussed the impact of divorce on students at the school.

Reynolds was concerned that, although the pregnancy story used false names "to keep the identity of these girls a secret," the pregnant students still might be identifiable from the text. He also believed that the article's references to sexual activity and birth control were inappropriate for some of the younger students at the school. In addition, Reynolds was concerned that a student identified by name in the divorce story had complained that her father "wasn't spending enough time with my mom, my sister and I" prior to the divorce, "was always out of town on business or out late playing cards with the guys," and "always argued about everything" with her mother. Reynolds believed that the student's parents should have been given an opportunity to respond to these remarks or to consent to their publication. He was unaware that Emerson had deleted the student's name from the final version of the article.

Reynolds believed that there was no time to make the necessary changes in the stories before the scheduled press run and that the newspaper would not appear before the end of the school year if printing were delayed to any significant extent. He concluded that his only options under the circumstances were to publish a four-page newspaper instead of the planned six-page newspaper, eliminating the two pages on which the offending stories appeared, or to publish no newspaper at all. Accordingly, he directed Emerson to withhold from publication the two pages containing the stories on pregnancy and divorce. He informed his superiors of the decision, and they concurred.

[White reviews the District Court's reasoning supporting the school officials and the Court of Appeals decision that sided with the students.]

II

Students in the public schools do not "shed their constitutional rights to freedom of speech or expression at the schoolhouse gate." *Tinker.* They cannot be punished merely for expressing their personal views on the school premises—whether "in the cafeteria, or on the playing field, or on the campus during the authorized hours"—unless school authorities have reason to believe that such expression will "substantially interfere with the work of the school or impinge upon the rights of other students."

We have nonetheless recognized that the First Amendment rights of students in the public schools "are not automatically coextensive with the rights of adults in other settings," *Bethel School District No. 403 v. Fraser* (1986), and must be "applied in light of the special characteristics of the school environment." *Tinker.* A school need not tolerate student speech that is inconsistent with its "basic educational mission," *Fraser, supra*, at 685, even though the government could not censor similar speech outside the school.

A

We deal first with the question whether *Spectrum* may appropriately be characterized as a forum for public expression. The public schools do not possess all of the attributes of streets, parks, and other traditional public forums that "time out of mind, have been used for purposes of assembly, communicating thoughts between citizens, and discussing public questions." *Hague v. CIO*, 307 U.S. 496 (1939). . . .

School officials did not deviate in practice from their policy that production of *Spectrum* was to be part of the educational curriculum and a "regular classroom activit[y]." The District Court found that Robert Stergos, the journalism teacher during most of the 1982–1983 school year, "both had the authority to exercise and in fact exercised a great deal of control over *Spectrum*." . . . These factual findings are amply supported by the record, and were not rejected as clearly erroneous by the Court of Appeals.

The evidence relied upon by the Court of Appeals in finding *Spectrum* to be a public forum, is equivocal at best.

B

The question whether the First Amendment requires a school to tolerate particular student speech—the question that we addressed in *Tinker*—is different from the question whether the First Amendment requires a school affirmatively to promote particular student speech. The former question addresses educators' ability to silence a student's personal expression that happens to occur on the school premises. The latter question concerns educators' authority over school-sponsored publications, theatrical productions, and other expressive activities that students, parents, and members of the public might reasonably perceive to bear the imprimatur of the school. These activities may fairly be characterized as part of the school curriculum, whether or not they occur in a traditional classroom setting, so long as they are supervised by faculty members and designed to impart particular knowledge or skills to student participants and audiences.

Educators are entitled to exercise greater control over this second form of student expression to assure that participants learn whatever lessons the activity is designed to teach, that readers or listeners are not exposed to material that may be inappropriate for their level of maturity, and that the views of the individual speaker are not erroneously attributed to the school. Hence, a school may in its capacity as publisher of a school newspaper or producer of a school play "disassociate itself," *Fraser*, not only from speech that would "substantially interfere with [its] work . . . or impinge upon the rights of other students," *Tinker*, but also from speech that is, for example, ungrammatical, poorly written, inadequately researched, biased or prejudiced, vulgar or profane, or unsuitable for immature audiences. A school must be able to set high standards for the student speech that is disseminated under its auspices—standards that may be higher than those demanded by some newspaper publishers or theatrical producers in the "real" world—and may refuse to disseminate student speech that does not meet those standards. In addition, a school must be able to take into account the emotional maturity of the intended audience in determining whether to disseminate student speech on potentially sensitive topics, which might range from the existence of Santa Claus in an elementary school setting to the particulars of teenage sexual activity in a high school setting. A school must also retain the authority to refuse to sponsor student speech that might reasonably be perceived to advocate drug or alcohol use, irresponsible sex, or conduct otherwise inconsistent with "the shared values of a civilized social order," *Fraser*, or to associate the school with any position other than neutrality on matters of political controversy. Otherwise, the schools would be unduly constrained from fulfilling their role as "a principal instrument in awakening the child to cultural values, in preparing him for later professional training, and in helping him to adjust normally to his environment." *Brown v. Board of Education*, 347 U.S. 483 (1954).

Accordingly, we conclude that the standard articulated in *Tinker* for determining when a school may punish student expression need not also be the standard for determining when a school may refuse to lend its name and resources to the dissemination of student expression. Instead, we hold that educators do not offend the First Amendment by exercising editorial control over the style and content of student speech in school-sponsored expressive activities so long as their actions are reasonably related to legitimate pedagogical concerns.

This standard is consistent with our oft-expressed view that the education of the Nation's youth is primarily the responsibility of parents, teachers, and state and local school officials, and not of federal judges. It is only when the decision to censor a school-sponsored publication, theatrical production, or other vehicle of student expression has no valid educational purpose that the First Amendment is so "directly and sharply implicate[d]," as to require judicial intervention to protect students' constitutional rights.

III

We also conclude that Principal Reynolds acted reasonably in requiring the deletion from the May 13 issue of *Spectrum* of the pregnancy article, the divorce article, and the remaining articles that were to appear on the same pages of the newspaper.

In sum, we cannot reject as unreasonable Principal Reynolds' conclusion that neither the pregnancy article nor the divorce article was suitable for publication in *Spectrum*. Reynolds could reasonably have concluded that the students who had written and edited these articles had not sufficiently mastered those portions of the Journalism II curriculum that pertained to the treatment of controversial issues and personal attacks, the need to protect the privacy of individuals whose most intimate concerns are to be revealed in the newspaper, and "the legal, moral, and ethical restrictions imposed upon journalists within [a] school community" that includes adolescent subjects and readers. Finally, we conclude that the principal's decision to delete two pages of *Spectrum*, rather than to delete only the offending articles or to require that they be modified, was reasonable under the circumstances as he understood them. Accordingly, no violation of First Amendment rights occurred.

The judgment of the Court of Appeals for the Eighth Circuit is therefore *Reversed.*

JUSTICE BRENNAN, with whom JUSTICES MARSHALL and BLACKMUN join, dissenting.

In my view the principal broke more than just a promise. He violated the First Amendment's prohibitions against censorship of any student expression that neither disrupts classwork nor invades the rights of others, and against any censorship that is not narrowly tailored to serve its purpose.

I

Public education serves vital national interests in preparing the Nation's youth for life in our increasingly complex society and for the duties of citizenship in our democratic Republic. . . .

In *Tinker v. Des Moines Independent Community School District,* 393 U.S. 503 (1969), this Court struck the balance. We held that official censorship of student expression—there the suspension of several students until they removed their armbands protesting the Vietnam war—is unconstitutional unless the speech "materially disrupts classwork or involves substantial disorder or invasion of the rights of others . . . ." School officials may not suppress "silent, passive expression of opinion, unaccompanied by any disorder or disturbance on the part of" the speaker. The "mere desire to avoid the discomfort and unpleasantness that always accompany an unpopular viewpoint," *id.*, at 509, or an unsavory subject, *Fraser*, does not justify official suppression of student speech in the high school.

This Court applied the *Tinker* test just a Term ago in *Fraser,* upholding an official decision to discipline a student for delivering a lewd speech in support of a student-government candidate. The Court today casts no doubt on *Tinker*'s vitality. Instead it erects a taxonomy of school censorship, concluding that *Tinker* applies to one category and not another. On the one hand is censorship "to silence a student's personal expression that happens to occur on the school premises." On the other hand is censorship of expression that arises in the context of "school-sponsored . . . expressive activities that students, parents, and members of the public might reasonably perceive to bear the imprimatur of the school."

The Court does not, for it cannot, purport to discern from our precedents the distinction it creates. One could, I suppose, readily characterize the students' symbolic speech in *Tinker* as "personal expression that happens to [have] occur[red] on school premises," although *Tinker* did not even hint that the personal nature of the speech was of any (much less dispositive) relevance. But that same description could not by any stretch of the imagination fit Fraser's speech. He did not just "happen" to deliver his lewd speech to an ad hoc gathering on the playground. As the second paragraph of *Fraser* evinces, if ever a forum for student expression was "school-sponsored," Fraser's was: "Fraser . . . delivered a speech nominating a fellow student for student elective office. Approximately 600 high school students . . . attended the assembly. Students were required to attend the assembly or to report to the study hall. The assembly was part of a *school-sponsored* educational program in self-government."

II

Even if we were writing on a clean slate, I would reject the Court's rationale for abandoning *Tinker* in this case. The Court offers no more than an obscure tangle of three excuses to afford educators "greater control" over school-sponsored speech than the *Tinker* test would permit: the public educator's prerogative to control curriculum; the pedagogical interest in shielding the high school audience from objectionable viewpoints and sensitive topics; and the school's need to dissociate itself from student expression. None of the excuses, once disentangled, supports the distinction that the Court draws. *Tinker* fully addresses the first concern; the second is illegitimate; and the third is readily achievable through less oppressive means. [In the remainder of this section, Brennan examines each of these three rationales.]

III

Since the censorship served no legitimate pedagogical purpose, it cannot by any stretch of the imagination have been designed to prevent "materia[l] disrup[tion of] classwork," *Tinker.* Nor did the censorship fall within the category that *Tinker* described as necessary to prevent student expression from "inva[ding] the rights of others." If that term is to have any content, it must be limited to rights that are protected by law. "Any yardstick less exacting than [that] could result in school officials curtailing speech at the slightest fear of disturbance," a prospect that would be completely at odds with this Court's pronouncement that the "undifferentiated fear or apprehension of disturbance is not enough [even in the public school context] to overcome the right to freedom of expression." *Tinker.* And, as the Court of Appeals correctly reasoned, whatever journalistic impropriety these articles may have contained, they could not conceivably be tortious, much less criminal.

Finally, even if the majority were correct that the principal could constitutionally have censored the objectionable material, I would emphatically object to the brutal manner in which he did so. Where "[t]he separation of legitimate from illegitimate speech calls for more sensitive tools" *Speiser v. Randall*, 357 U.S. 513 (1958), the principal used a paper shredder. He objected to some material in two articles, but excised six entire articles. He did not so much as inquire into obvious alternatives, such as precise deletions or additions (one of which had already been made), rearranging the layout, or delaying publication. Such unthinking contempt for individual rights is intolerable from any state official. It is particularly insidious from one to whom the public entrusts the task of inculcating in its youth an appreciation for the cherished democratic liberties that our Constitution guarantees.

IV

The Court opens its analysis in this case by purporting to reaffirm *Tinker*'s time-tested proposition that public school students "do not 'shed their constitutional rights to freedom of speech or expression at the schoolhouse gate.' " That is an ironic introduction to an opinion that denudes high school students of much of the First Amendment protection that *Tinker* itself prescribed. Instead of "teach[ing] children to respect the diversity of ideas that is fundamental to the American system," *Board of Education v. Pico*, 457 U.S. 853 (1982), and "that our Constitution is a living reality, not parchment preserved under glass," *Shanley v. Northeast Independent School Dist., Bexar Cty., Tex.*, 462 F. 2d 960 (1972), the Court today "teach[es] youth to discount important principles of our government as mere platitudes." *West Virginia Board of Education v. Barnette*, 319 U.S. 624 (1943). The young men and women of Hazelwood East expected a civics lesson, but not the one the Court teaches them today.

I dissent.

FOR DISCUSSION

If you review the decisions in the chapter on freedom of the press, you will see that this case represents a classic case of "prior restraint." Generally, there is a very strong presumption against such censorship. Do you think the principal had adequate reasons to act in this case? Do you think he could have opened himself or the school to a civil suit had he ruled otherwise?

RELATED CASE

***United States of America v. Progressive, Inc.*, 467 F. Supp. 990 (W.D. Wis.1979).**

The US government sought and secured a temporary restraining order to prevent *Progressive Magazine* from publishing an article describing how to make a hydrogen bomb. The government eventually dropped the case, and the Seventh Circuit Court of Appeals dismissed it because other sources had published similar information.

MORSE V. FREDERICK

127 S.Ct. 2618, 168 L.Ed. 2d 290 (2007)

In this opinion, the Court had to decide whether Morse, a high school principal in Juneau, Alaska, could suspend a student (Frederick) for holding up a banner in front of the school at a school-approved Olympic Torch Relay that said "BONG HiTS 4 Jesus," an expression that could be interpreted either as favoring drug use or as completely nonsensical. The Court in effect needed to determine whether the student's expression in this case came closer to that in *Tinker v. Des Moines* (393 U.S. 503, 1969) or to that in *Bethel v. Fraser* (478 U.S. 675, 1986) and *Hazelwood School District v. Kuhlmeier* (484 U.S. 260, 1988). The District Court had upheld the principal's action, but the Ninth U.S. Circuit Court had reversed.

Vote: 5.5–3.5

CHIEF JUSTICE ROBERTS delivered the opinion of the Court.

Our cases make clear that students do not "shed their constitutional rights to freedom of speech or expression at the schoolhouse gate." *Tinker v. Des Moines Independent Community School Dist.*, 393 U.S. 503 (1969). At the same time, we have held that "the constitutional rights of students in public school are not automatically coextensive with the rights of adults in other settings," *Bethel School District No. 403 v. Fraser*, 478 U.S. 675 (1986), and that the rights of students "must be 'applied in light of the special characteristics of the school environment.'" *Hazelwood School Distr. v. Kuhlmeier*, 484 U.S. 260 (1988). Consistent with these principles, we hold that schools may take steps to safeguard those entrusted to their care from speech that can reasonably be regarded as encouraging illegal drug use. We conclude that the school officials in this case did not violate the First Amendment by confiscating the pro-drug banner and suspending the student responsible for it.

I

We granted certiorari on two questions: whether Frederick had a First Amendment right to wield his banner, and, if so, whether that right was so clearly established that the principal may be held liable for damages. We resolve the first question against Frederick, and therefore have no occasion to reach the second.

II

At the outset, we reject Frederick's argument that this is not a school speech case—as has every other authority to address the question. The event occurred during normal school hours. It was sanctioned by Principal Morse "as an approved social event or class trip," and the school district's rules expressly provide that pupils in "approved social events and class trips are subject to district rules for student conduct." Teachers and administrators were interspersed among the students and charged with supervising them. The high school band and cheerleaders performed. Frederick, standing among other [Juneau-Douglas High School] students across the street from the school [JDHS], directed his banner toward the school, making it plainly visible to most students. Under these circumstances, we agree with the superintendent that Frederick cannot "stand in the midst of his fellow students, during school hours, at a school-sanctioned activity and claim he is not at school." . . .

III

The message on Frederick's banner is cryptic. It is no doubt offensive to some, perhaps amusing to others. To still others, it probably means nothing at all. Frederick himself claimed "that the words were just nonsense meant to attract television cameras." But Principal Morse thought the banner would be interpreted by those viewing it as promoting illegal drug use, and that interpretation is plainly a reasonable one.

As Morse later explained in a declaration, when she saw the sign, she thought that "the reference to a 'bong hit' would be widely understood by high school students and others as referring to smoking marijuana." She further believed that "display of the banner would be construed by students, District personnel, parents and others witnessing the display of the banner, as advocating or promoting illegal drug use"—in violation of school policy. . . .

We agree with Morse. At least two interpretations of the words on the banner demonstrate that the sign advocated the use of illegal drugs. First, the phrase could be interpreted as an imperative: "[Take] bong hits . . ."—a message equivalent, as Morse explained in her declaration, to "smoke marijuana" or "use an illegal drug." Alternatively, the phrase could be viewed as celebrating drug use—"bong hits [are a good thing]," or "[we take] bong hits"—and we discern no meaningful distinction between celebrating illegal drug use in the midst of fellow students and outright advocacy or promotion.

The pro-drug interpretation of the banner gains further plausibility given the paucity of alternative meanings the banner might bear. The best Frederick can come up with is that the banner is "meaningless and funny." The dissent similarly refers to the sign's message as "curious," "ambiguous," "nonsense," "ridiculous," "obscure," "silly," "quixotic," and "stupid." Gibberish is surely a possible interpretation of the words on the banner, but it is not the only one, and dismissing the banner as meaningless ignores its undeniable reference to illegal drugs.

The dissent mentions Frederick's "credible and uncontradicted explanation for the message—he just wanted to get on television." But that is a description of Frederick's *motive* for displaying the banner; it is not an interpretation of what the banner says. The *way* Frederick was going to fulfill his ambition of appearing on television was by unfurling a pro-drug banner at a school event, in the presence of teachers and fellow students.

Elsewhere in its opinion, the dissent emphasizes the importance of political speech and the need to foster "national debate about a serious issue," as if to suggest that the banner is political speech. But not even Frederick argues that the banner conveys any sort of political or religious message. Contrary to the dissent's suggestion, this is plainly not a case about political debate over the criminalization of drug use or possession.

IV

The question thus becomes whether a principal may, consistent with the First Amendment, restrict student speech at a school event, when that speech is reasonably viewed as promoting illegal drug use. We hold that she may.

In *Tinker*, this Court made clear that "First Amendment rights, applied in light of the special characteristics of the school environment, are available to teachers and students." *Tinker* involved a group of high school students who decided to wear black armbands to protest the Vietnam War. School officials learned of the plan and then adopted a policy prohibiting students from wearing armbands. When several students nonetheless wore armbands to school, they were suspended. The students sued, claiming that their First Amendment rights had been violated, and this Court agreed.

Tinker held that student expression may not be suppressed unless school officials reasonably conclude that it will "materially and substantially disrupt the work and discipline of the school." The essential facts of *Tinker* are quite stark, implicating concerns at the heart of the First Amendment. The students sought to engage in political speech, using the armbands to express their "disapproval of the Vietnam hostilities and their advocacy of a truce, to make their views known, and, by their example, to influence others to adopt them." Political speech, of course, is "at the core of what the First Amendment is designed to protect." *Virginia v. Black*, 538 U.S. 343 (2003). The only interest the Court discerned underlying the school's actions was the "mere desire to avoid the discomfort and unpleasantness that always accompany an unpopular viewpoint," or "an urgent wish to avoid the controversy which might result from the expression." That interest was not enough to justify banning "a silent, passive expression of opinion, unaccompanied by any disorder or disturbance."

This Court's next student speech case was *Fraser*. Matthew Fraser was suspended for delivering a speech before a high school assembly in which he employed what this Court called "an elaborate, graphic, and explicit sexual metaphor." Analyzing the case under *Tinker*, the District Court and Court of Appeals found no disruption, and therefore no basis for disciplining Fraser. This Court reversed, holding that the "School District acted entirely within its permissible authority in imposing sanctions upon Fraser in response to his offensively lewd and indecent speech."

. . . [I]t is enough to distill from *Fraser* two basic principles. First, *Fraser*'s holding demonstrates that "the constitutional rights of students in public school are not automatically coextensive with the rights of adults in other settings." Had Fraser delivered the same speech in a public forum outside the school context, it would have been protected. In school, however, Fraser's First Amendment rights were circumscribed "in light of the special characteristics of the school environment." Second, *Fraser* established that the mode of analysis set forth in *Tinker* is not absolute. Whatever approach *Fraser* employed, it certainly did not conduct the "substantial disruption" analysis prescribed by *Tinker.*

Our most recent student speech case, *Kuhlmeier*, concerned "expressive activities that students, parents, and members of the public might reasonably perceive to bear the imprimatur of the school." Staff members of a high school newspaper sued their school when it chose not to publish two of their articles. The Court of Appeals analyzed the case under *Tinker*, ruling in favor of the students because it found no evidence of material disruption to classwork or school discipline. This Court reversed, holding that "educators do not offend the First Amendment by exercising editorial control over the style and content of student speech in school-sponsored expressive activities so long as their actions are reasonably related to legitimate pedagogical concerns."

Kuhlmeier does not control this case because no one would reasonably believe that Frederick's banner bore the school's imprimatur. The case is nevertheless instructive because it confirms both principles cited above. *Kuhlmeier* acknowledged that schools may regulate some speech "even though the government could not censor similar speech outside the school." And, like *Fraser*, it confirms that the rule of *Tinker* is not the only basis for restricting student speech.

Drawing on the principles applied in our student speech cases, we have held in the Fourth Amendment context that "while children assuredly do not 'shed their constitutional rights . . . at the schoolhouse gate,' . . . the nature of those rights is what is appropriate for children in school." *Veronia Sch. Dist. 47J v. Acton*, 515 U.S. 646 (1995). In particular, "the school setting requires some easing of the restrictions to which searches by public authorities are ordinarily subject."

The problem remains serious today. About half of American 12th graders have used an illicit drug, as have more than a third of 10th graders and about one-fifth of 8th graders. Nearly one in four 12th graders has used an illicit drug in the past month. Some 25% of high schoolers say that they have been offered, sold, or given an illegal drug on school property within the past year.

Congress has declared that part of a school's job is educating students about the dangers of illegal drug use. It has provided billions of dollars to support state and local drug-prevention programs, and required that schools receiving federal funds under the Safe and Drug-Free Schools and Communities Act of 1994 certify that their drug prevention programs "convey a clear and consistent message that . . . the illegal use of drugs [is] wrong and harmful."

The "special characteristics of the school environment," and the governmental interest in stopping student drug abuse—reflected in the policies of Congress and myriad school boards, including JDHS—allow schools to restrict student expression that they reasonably regard as promoting illegal drug use. *Tinker* warned that schools may not prohibit student speech because of "undifferentiated fear or apprehension of disturbance" or "a mere desire to avoid the discomfort and unpleasantness that always accompany an unpopular viewpoint." The danger here is far more serious and palpable. The particular concern to prevent student drug abuse at issue here, embodied in established school policy, extends well beyond an abstract desire to avoid controversy.

Petitioners urge us to adopt the broader rule that Frederick's speech is proscribable because it is plainly "offensive" as that term is used in *Fraser.* We think this stretches *Fraser* too far; that case should not be read to encompass any speech that could fit under some definition of "offensive." After all, much political and religious speech might be perceived as offensive to some. The concern here is not that Frederick's speech was offensive, but that it was reasonably viewed as promoting illegal drug use.

Although accusing this decision of doing "serious violence to the First Amendment" by authorizing "viewpoint discrimination," the dissent concludes that "it might well be appropriate to tolerate some targeted viewpoint discrimination in this unique setting." Nor do we understand the dissent to take the position that schools are required to tolerate student advocacy of illegal drug use at school events, even if that advocacy falls short of inviting "imminent" lawless action. And even the dissent recognizes that the issues here are close enough that the principal should not be held liable in damages, but should instead enjoy qualified immunity for her actions. Stripped of rhetorical flourishes, then, the debate between the dissent and this opinion is less about constitutional first principles than about whether Frederick's banner constitutes promotion of illegal drug use. We have explained our view that it does. The dissent's contrary view on that relatively narrow question hardly justifies sounding the First Amendment bugle.

JUSTICE THOMAS, concurring.

The Court today decides that a public school may prohibit speech advocating illegal drug use. I agree and therefore join its opinion in full. I write separately to state my view that the standard set forth in *Tinker v. Des Moines Independent School District,* 393 U.S. 503 (1969), is without basis in the Constitution.

I

The First Amendment states that "Congress shall make no law . . . abridging the freedom of speech." As this Court has previously observed, the First Amendment was not originally understood to permit all sorts of speech; instead, "there are certain well-defined and narrowly limited classes of speech, the prevention and punishment of which have never been thought to raise any Constitutional problem." In my view, the history of public education suggests that the First Amendment, as originally understood, does not protect student speech in public schools. Although colonial schools were exclusively private, public education proliferated in the early 1800's. By the time the States ratified the Fourteenth Amendment, public schools had become relatively common. If students in public schools were originally understood as having free-speech rights, one would have expected 19th-century public schools to have respected those rights and courts to have enforced them. They did not.

II

Tinker effected a sea change in students' speech rights, extending them well beyond traditional bounds. . . .

Justice Black dissented, criticizing the Court for "subjecting all the public schools in the country to the whims and caprices of their loudest-mouthed, but maybe not their brightest, students." He emphasized the instructive purpose of schools: "Taxpayers send children to school on the premise that at their age they need to learn, not teach." In his view, the Court's decision "surrendered control of the American public school system to public school students."

Of course, *Tinker's* reasoning conflicted with the traditional understanding of the judiciary's role in relation to public schooling, a role limited by *in loco parentis.* Perhaps for that reason, the Court has since scaled back *Tinker*'s standard, or rather set the standard aside on an ad hoc basis. . . . .

III

In light of the history of American public education, it cannot seriously be suggested that the First Amendment "freedom of speech" encompasses a student's right to speak in public schools. Early public schools gave total control to teachers, who expected obedience and respect from students. And courts routinely deferred to schools' authority to make rules and to discipline students for violating those rules. Several points are clear: (1) under *in loco parentis*, speech rules and other school rules were treated identically; (2) the *in loco parentis* doctrine imposed almost no limits on the types of rules that a school could set while students were in school; and (3) schools and teachers had tremendous discretion in imposing punishments for violations of those rules.

And because *Tinker* utterly ignored the history of public education, courts (including this one) routinely find it necessary to create ad hoc exceptions to its central premise. This doctrine of exceptions creates confusion without fixing the underlying problem by returning to first principles. Just as I cannot accept *Tinker*'s standard,

I cannot subscribe to *Kuhlmeier*'s alternative. Local school boards, not the courts, should determine what pedagogical interests are "legitimate" and what rules "reasonably relate" to those interests.

Justice Black may not have been "a prophet or the son of a prophet," but his dissent in *Tinker* has proved prophetic. In the name of the First Amendment, *Tinker* has undermined the traditional authority of teachers to maintain order in public schools. "Once a society that generally respected the authority of teachers, deferred to their judgment, and trusted them to act in the best interest of school children, we now accept defiance, disrespect, and disorder as daily occurrences in many of our public schools." Dupre, Should Students Have Constitutional Rights? Keeping Order in the Public Schools, 65 *Geo. Wash. L. Rev.* 49, 50 (1996). We need look no further than this case for an example: Frederick asserts a constitutional right to utter at a school event what is either "gibberish," or an open call to use illegal drugs. To elevate such impertinence to the status of constitutional protection would be farcical and would indeed be to "surrender control of the American public school system to public school students."

I join the Court's opinion because it erodes *Tinker*'s hold in the realm of student speech, even though it does so by adding to the patchwork of exceptions to the *Tinker* standard. I think the better approach is to dispense with *Tinker* altogether, and given the opportunity, I would do so.

JUSTICE ALITO, with whom JUSTICE KENNEDY joins, concurring.

I join the opinion of the Court on the understanding that (a) it goes no further than to hold that a public school may restrict speech that a reasonable observer would interpret as advocating illegal drug use and (b) it provides no support for any restriction of speech that can plausibly be interpreted as commenting on any political or social issue, including speech on issues such as "the wisdom of the war on drugs or of legalizing marijuana for medicinal use."

JUSTICE BREYER, concurring in the judgment in part and dissenting in part.

This Court need not and should not decide this difficult First Amendment issue on the merits. Rather, I believe that it should simply hold that qualified immunity bars the student's claim for monetary damages and say no more.

JUSTICE STEVENS, with whom JUSTICE SOUTHER and JUSTICE GINSBURG join, dissenting.

A significant fact barely mentioned by the Court sheds a revelatory light on the motives of both the students and the principal of Juneau-Douglas High School (JDHS). On January 24, 2002, the Olympic Torch Relay gave those Alaska residents a rare chance to appear on national television. As Joseph Frederick repeatedly explained, he did not address the curious message—"BONG HiTS 4 JESUS"—to his fellow students. He just wanted to get the camera crews' attention. Moreover, concern about a nationwide evaluation of the conduct of the JDHS student body would have justified the principal's decision to remove an attention-grabbing 14-foot banner, even if it had merely proclaimed "Glaciers Melt!"

I agree with the Court that the principal should not be held liable for pulling down Frederick's banner. I would hold, however, that the school's interest in protecting its students from exposure to speech "reasonably regarded as promoting illegal drug use," . . ., cannot justify disciplining Frederick for his attempt to make an ambiguous statement to a television audience simply because it contained an oblique reference to drugs. The First Amendment demands more, indeed, much more.

In my judgment, the First Amendment protects student speech if the message itself neither violates a permissible rule nor expressly advocates conduct that is illegal and harmful to students. This nonsense banner does neither, and the Court does serious violence to the First Amendment in upholding—indeed, lauding—a school's decision to punish Frederick for expressing a view with which it disagreed.

III

Although this case began with a silly, nonsensical banner, it ends with the Court inventing out of whole cloth a special First Amendment rule permitting the censorship of any student speech that mentions drugs, at least so long as someone could perceive that speech to contain a latent pro-drug message. Our First Amendment jurisprudence has identified some categories of expression that are less deserving of protection than others—fighting words, obscenity, and commercial speech, to name a few. Rather than reviewing our opinions discussing such categories, I mention two personal recollections that have no doubt influenced my conclusion that it would be profoundly unwise to create special rules for speech about drug and alcohol use.

Even in high school, a rule that permits only one point of view to be expressed is less likely to produce correct answers than the open discussion of countervailing views. In the national debate about a serious issue, it is the expression of the minority's viewpoint that most demands the protection of the First Amendment. Whatever the better policy may be, a full and frank discussion of the costs and benefits of the attempt to prohibit the use of marijuana is far wiser than suppression of speech because it is unpopular.

I respectfully dissent.

FOR DISCUSSION

Do you think the Court would have decided this case differently if, instead of making a possible allusion to drugs, the sign simply appeared to be blasphemous? The Court has long since given up regulating blasphemy in movies. Might it ever be appropriate to have regulations concerning blasphemy in public schools? On what basis does Justice Thomas question whether First Amendment freedoms apply to a school setting? What is the primary method of constitutional interpretation that he uses to arrive at this conclusion?

Fighting Words, Hate Speech, and Hostile Audiences

Hate or offensive speech, like obscenity and libel, has occupied an ambiguous and not always constitutionally clear role under the First Amendment. On the one hand, offensive words can be viewed simply as means to offend or incite others, and therefore not worthy of constitutional protection. On the other hand, the fact that the words arouse in others feelings, perhaps of anger or rage, may well be proof that offensive words have speech content deserving of First Amendment protection, especially if used in a way designed to get listeners' attention or when communicated in the context of a political rally.

Still, what should the Court do if, instead of simply getting listeners' attention, a speaker incites people to riot, protest, or engage in other types of reaction that could threaten the speaker or public safety? As none other than Justice Oliver Wendell Holmes Jr. noted in formulating the "clear and present danger" test, some ideas may in fact be the spark that incites a flame of rioting or lawlessness that could be dangerous.

Chaplinsky v. State of New Hampshire (315 U.S. 568, 1942) remains the Supreme Court's classic articulation of the doctrine of "fighting words." Focusing on face-to-face exchanges that are more likely to lead to a fight than to reasoned discussion, the Court identifies such "fighting words" as an exception to free speech. (The speech at issue here consisted of derogatory words that a Jehovah's Witness directed to a police officer). The fact that subsequent cases have affirmed the exception without identifying other examples indicates that the exception was intended to be relatively narrow.

Notably, in *Terminiello v. Chicago* (337 U.S. 1, 1949), the Court majority did not think a speech that a Catholic priest delivered in a crowded auditorium constituted such fighting words, even though it was provocative enough to lead to hurled rocks and broken windows. The Court was undoubtedly wary of allowing crowd reactions to determine the constitutionality of the speaker's words. By contrast, in *Feiner v. New York* (340 U.S. 315, 1951), the Court upheld a "breach of the peace" conviction of a college student who directed a similarly provocative speech to a group gathered on a street corner.

The decision in *Beauharnais v. Illinois* (343 U.S. 250, 1952) complicates the picture still further. Although it remains a fairly solitary precedent, it suggests that governments may be able to prosecute individuals for "group libel." Few racist tirades would escape censure under such a standard.

Although it is a circuit court decision, *Collin v. Smith* (578 F.2d 1197, 1978) appears to be correct in its application of subsequent Supreme Court decisions to a highly emotional issue. In allowing Nazis to parade in uniform in a neighborhood whose residents included survivors of the Nazi holocaust, the Court rejected claims that the uniforms are either a form of "fighting words," largely because individuals could avert their eyes. The Court made it clear that the First Amendment applies to speech that citizens hate.

Three additional cases round out this discussion. In *R. A. V. v. City of St. Paul* (505 U.S. 377, 1992), the Court employs the strong presumption against content regulation to strike down a law that attempts to punish derogatory speech directed to some groups but not to others. In *Wisconsin v. Mitchell* (508 U.S. 476, 1993), by contrast, it allows consideration of motive to influence appropriate punishments. Finally, in *Snyder v. Phelps*, 562 U.S. 443 (2011), the issue was anti-gay demonstrating by church members at funerals of members of the military who had died while serving their country. *Snyder,* like *R.A.V.,* stands for a strong presumption that all forms of speech, even that which is unpopular and offensive, is protected against being banned.

CHAPLINSKY V. STATE OF NEW HAMPSHIRE

315 U.S. 568, 62 S.Ct. 766, 86 L.Ed. 1031 (1942)

The appellant, Chaplinsky, a Jehovah's Witness, had been convicted under a New Hampshire ordinance for violating a law providing that "No person shall address any offensive, derisive or annoying word to any other person who is lawfully in any street or other public place, nor call him by any offensive or derisive name, nor make any noise or exclamation in his presence and hearing with intent to deride, offend or annoy him, or to prevent him from pursuing his lawful business or occupation." The Court had to decide whether Chaplinsky's speech was protected by the First Amendment.

Vote: 9–0

JUSTICE MURPHY delivered the opinion of the Court.

The complaint charged that appellant 'with force and arms, in a certain public place in said city of Rochester, to wit, on the public sidewalk on the easterly side of Wakefield Street, near unto the entrance of the City Hall, did unlawfully repeat, the words following, addressed to the complainant, that is to say, 'You are a God damned racketeer' and 'a damned Fascist and the whole government of Rochester are Fascists or agents of Fascists' the same being offensive, derisive and annoying words and names'.

Upon appeal there was a trial de novo of appellant before a jury in the Superior Court. He was found guilty and the judgment of conviction was affirmed by the Supreme Court of the State.

By motions and exceptions, appellant raised the questions that the statute was invalid under the Fourteenth Amendment of the Constitution of the United States in that it placed an unreasonable restraint on freedom of speech, freedom of the press, and freedom of worship, and because it was vague and indefinite. These contentions were overruled and the case comes here on appeal.

There is no substantial dispute over the facts. Chaplinsky was distributing the literature of his sect on the streets of Rochester on a busy Saturday afternoon. Members of the local citizenry complained to the City Marshal, Bowering, that Chaplinsky was denouncing all religion as a 'racket'. Bowering told them that Chaplinsky was lawfully engaged, and then warned Chaplinsky that the crowd was getting restless. Sometime later a disturbance occurred and the traffic officer on duty at the busy intersection started with Chaplinsky for the police station, but did not inform him that he was under arrest or that he was going to be arrested. On the way they encountered Marshal Bowering who had been advised that a riot was under way and was therefore hurrying to the scene. Bowering repeated his earlier warning to Chaplinsky who then addressed to Bowering the words set forth in the complaint.

Chaplinsky's version of the affair was slightly different. He testified that when he met Bowering, he asked him to arrest the ones responsible for the disturbance. In reply Bowering cursed him and told him to come along. Appellant admitted that he said the words charged in the complaint with the exception of the name of the Deity.

Over appellant's objection the trial court excluded as immaterial testimony relating to appellant's mission 'to preach the true facts of the Bible', his treatment at the hands of the crowd, and the alleged neglect of duty on the part of the police. This action was approved by the court below which held that neither provocation nor the truth of the utterance would constitute a defense to the charge.

It is now clear that "Freedom of speech and freedom of the press, which are protected by the First Amendment from infringement by Congress, are among the fundamental personal rights and liberties which are protected by the Fourteenth Amendment from invasion by state."

Appellant here pitches his argument on the due process clause of the Fourteenth Amendment. Appellant assails the statute as a violation of all three freedoms, speech, press and worship, but only an attack on the basis of free speech is warranted. The spoken, not the written, word is involved. And we cannot conceive that cursing a public officer is the exercise of religion in any sense of the term. But even if the activities of the appellant which preceded the incident could be viewed as religious in character, and therefore entitled to the protection of the Fourteenth Amendment, they would not cloak him with immunity from the legal consequences for concomitant acts committed in violation of a valid criminal statute. We turn, therefore, to an examination of the statute itself.

Allowing the broadest scope to the language and purpose of the Fourteenth Amendment, it is well understood that the right of free speech is not absolute at all times and under all circumstances. There are certain well-defined and narrowly limited classes of speech, the prevention and punishment of which has never been thought to raise any Constitutional problem. These include the lewd and obscene, the profane, the libelous, and the insulting or "fighting" words—those which by their very utterance inflict injury or tend to incite an immediate breach of the peace. It has been well observed that such utterances are no essential part of any exposition of ideas, and are of such slight social value as a step to truth that any benefit that may be derived from them is clearly outweighed by the social interest in order and morality. "Resort to epithets or personal abuse is not in any proper sense communication of information or opinion safeguarded by the Constitution, and its punishment as a criminal act would raise no question under that instrument." *Cantwell v. Connecticut*, 310 U.S. 296, 309–310.

On the authority of its earlier decisions, the state court declared that the statute's purpose was to preserve the public peace, no words being "forbidden except such as have a direct tendency to cause acts of violence by the person to whom, individually, the remark is addressed." It was further said: "The word 'offensive' is not to be defined in terms of what a particular addressee thinks. . . . The test is what men of common intelligence would understand would be words likely to cause an average addressee to fight. . . . The English language has a number of words and expressions which by general consent are 'fighting words' when said without a disarming smile. . . . Such words, as ordinary men know, are likely to cause a fight. So are threatening, profane or obscene revilings. Derisive and annoying words can be taken as coming within the purview of the statute as heretofore interpreted only when they have this characteristic of plainly tending to excite the addressee to a breach of the peace. . . . The statute, as construed, does no more than prohibit the face-to-face words plainly likely to cause a breach of the peace by the addressee, words whose speaking constitute a breach of the peace by the speaker—including 'classical fighting words', words in current use less 'classical' but equally likely to cause violence, and other disorderly words, including profanity, obscenity and threats."

Nor can we say that the application of the statute to the facts disclosed by the record substantially or unreasonably impinges upon the privilege of free speech. Argument is unnecessary to demonstrate that the appellations "damn racketeer" and "damn Fascist" are epithets likely to provoke the average person to retaliation, and thereby cause a breach of the peace.

Affirmed.

FOR DISCUSSION

Considering the words that demonstrators hurled at police officers in the 1960s and 1970s, do you think the words used in *Chaplinsky, decades earlier,* would still be considered to be fighting words?

TERMINIELLO V. CITY OF CHICAGO

337 U.S. 169, S.Ct. 894, 93 L.Ed. 1131 (1949)

In this case the Court had to decide whether a priest's provocative words to an audience were the kinds of "fighting words" that it had identified in *Chaplinsky v. State of New Hampshire* (315 U.S. 568, 1942).

Vote: 5–4

JUSTICE DOUGLAS delivered the opinion of the Court.

Petitioner after jury trial was found guilty of disorderly conduct in violation of a city ordinance of Chicago and fined. The case grew out of an address he delivered in an auditorium in Chicago under the auspices of the Christian Veterans of America. The meeting commanded considerable public attention. The auditorium was filled to capacity with over eight hundred persons present. Others were turned away. Outside of the auditorium a crowd of about one thousand persons gathered to protest against the meeting. A cordon of policemen was assigned to the meeting to maintain order; but they were not able to prevent several disturbances. The crowd outside was angry and turbulent.

Petitioner in his speech condemned the conduct of the crowd outside and vigorously, if not viciously, criticized various political and racial groups whose activities he denounced as inimical to the nation's welfare.

The trial court charged that 'breach of the peace' consists of any "misbehavior which violates the public peace and decorum"; and that the "misbehavior may constitute a breach of the peace if it stirs the public to anger, invites dispute, brings about a condition of unrest, or creates a disturbance, or if it molests the inhabitants in the enjoyment of peace and quiet by arousing alarm." Petitioner did not take exception to that instruction. But he maintained at all times that the ordinance as applied to his conduct violated his right of free speech under the Federal Constitution. The judgment of conviction was affirmed by the Illinois Appellate Court, and by the

Illinois Supreme Court. The case is here on a petition for certiorari which we granted because of the importance of the question presented.

The argument here has been focused on the issue of whether the content of petitioner's speech was composed of derisive, fighting words, which carried it outside the scope of the constitutional guarantees. We do not reach that question, for there is a preliminary question that is dispositive of the case.

The vitality of civil and political institutions in our society depends on free discussion. As Chief Justice Hughes wrote in *De Jonge v. Oregon*, 299 U.S. 353 (1937), it is only through free debate and free exchange of ideas that government remains responsive to the will of the people and peaceful change is effected. The right to speak freely and to promote diversity of ideas and programs is therefore one of the chief distinctions that sets us apart from totalitarian regimes.

Accordingly a function of free speech under our system of government is to invite dispute. It may indeed best serve its high purpose when it induces a condition of unrest, creates dissatisfaction with conditions as they are, or even stirs people to anger. Speech is often provocative and challenging. It may strike at prejudices and preconceptions and have profound unsettling effects as it presses for acceptance of an idea. That is why freedom of speech, though not absolute, *Chaplinsky v. New Hampshire*, is nevertheless protected against censorship or punishment, unless shown likely to produce a clear and present danger of a serious substantive evil that rises far above public inconvenience, annoyance, or unrest. There is no room under our Constitution for a more restrictive view. For the alternative would lead to standardization of ideas either by legislatures, courts, or dominant political or community groups.

The ordinance as construed by the trial court seriously invaded this province. It permitted conviction of petitioner if his speech stirred people to anger, invited public dispute, or brought about a condition of unrest. A conviction resting on any of those grounds may not stand.

The statute as construed in the charge to the jury was passed on by the Illinois courts and sustained by them over the objection that as so read it violated the Fourteenth Amendment. The fact that the parties did not dispute its construction makes the adjudication no less ripe for our review, as the *Stromberg v. California*, 283 U.S. 359 (1931), decision indicates. We can only take the statute as the state courts read it. From our point of view it is immaterial whether the state law question as to its meaning was controverted or accepted. The pinch of the statute is in its application. It is that question which the petitioner has brought here. To say therefore that the question on this phase of the case is whether the trial judge gave a wrong charge is wholly to misconceive the issue.

But it is said that throughout the appellate proceedings the Illinois courts assumed that the only conduct punishable and punished under the ordinance was conduct constituting "fighting words." That emphasizes, however, the importance of the rule of the *Stromberg* case. Petitioner was not convicted under a statute so narrowly construed. For all anyone knows he was convicted under the parts of the ordinance (as construed) which, for example, make it an offense merely to invite dispute or to bring about a condition of unrest. We cannot avoid that issue by saying that all Illinois did was to measure petitioner's conduct, not the ordinance, against the Constitution. Petitioner raised both points—that his speech was protected by the constitution; that the inclusion of his speech within the ordinance was a violation of the Constitution. We would, therefore, strain at technicalities to conclude that the constitutionality of the ordinance as construed and applied to petitioner was not before the Illinois courts. The record makes clear that petitioner at all times challenged the constitutionality of the ordinance as construed and applied to him.

Reversed.

FOR DISCUSSION

To what degree, if any, should audience reaction determine the legitimacy of a speaker's words? To what degree, if any, did the clear and present danger test call for such considerations?

FEINER V. NEW YORK

340 U.S. 315, 71 S.Ct. 303: 95 L.Ed. 295 (1951)

The petitioner, Irving Feiner, a university student, addressed an open-air meeting in an African American neighborhood in Syracuse, New York. His speech appeared to police officers to be arousing the crowd, and they asked him repeatedly to stop speaking. Ultimately arrested for disorderly conduct, Feiner challenged the arrest as having violated his right of free speech under the Fourteenth Amendment.

Vote: 6–3

CHIEF JUSTICE VINSON delivered the opinion of the Court.

The language of *Cantwell v. Connecticut,* 310 U.S. 296 (1940), is appropriate here. "The offense known as breach of the peace embraces a great variety of conduct destroying or menacing public order and tranquility. It includes not only violent acts but acts and words likely to produce violence in others. No one would have the hardihood to suggest that the principle of freedom of speech sanctions incitement to riot or that religious liberty connotes the privilege to exhort others to physical attack upon those belonging to another sect. When clear and present danger of riot, disorder, interference with traffic upon the public streets, or other immediate threat to public safety, peace, or order, appears, the power of the State to prevent or punish is obvious." The findings of the New York courts as to the condition of the crowd and the refusal of petitioner to obey the police requests, supported as they are by the record of this case, are persuasive that the conviction of petitioner for violation of public peace, order and authority does not exceed the bounds of proper state action. This Court respects, as it must, the interest of the community in maintaining peace and order on its streets. . . . We cannot say that the preservation of that interest here encroaches on the constitutional rights of this petitioner.

We are well aware that the ordinary murmurings and objections of a hostile audience cannot be allowed to silence a speaker, and are also mindful of the possible danger of giving overzealous police officials complete discretion to break up otherwise lawful public meetings. "A state may not unduly suppress free communication of views, religious or other, under the guise of conserving desirable conditions." [*Cantwell v. Connecticut.*]

But we are not faced here with such a situation. It is one thing to say that the police cannot be used as an instrument for the suppression of unpopular views, and another to say that, when as here the speaker passes the bounds of argument or persuasion and undertakes incitement to riot, they are powerless to prevent a breach of the peace. Nor in this case can we condemn the considered judgment of three New York courts approving the means which the police, faced with a crisis, used in the exercise of their power and duty to preserve peace and order. The findings of the state courts as to the existing situation and the imminence of greater disorder coupled with petitioner's deliberate defiance of the police officers convince us that we should not reverse this conviction in the name of free speech.

Affirmed.

JUSTICE BLACK dissented.

. . . Moreover, assuming that the "facts" did indicate a critical situation, I reject the implication of the Court's opinion that the police had no obligation to protect petitioner's constitutional right to talk. The police of course have power to prevent breaches of the peace. But if, in the name of preserving order, they ever can interfere with a lawful public speaker, they first must make all reasonable efforts to protect him. Here the policemen did not even pretend to try to protect petitioner. According to the officers' testimony, the crowd was restless but there is no showing of any attempt to quiet it; pedestrians were forced to walk into the street, but there was no effort to clear a path on the sidewalk; one person threatened to assault petitioner but the officers did nothing to discourage this when even a word might have sufficed. Their duty was to protect petitioner's right to talk, even to the extent of arresting the man who threatened to interfere. Instead, they shirked that duty and acted only to suppress the right to speak. . . .

JUSTICE DOUGLAS dissented, with the concurrence of JUSTICE MINTON.

. . . A speaker may not, of course, incite a riot any more than he may incite a breach of the peace by the use of "fighting words." See *Chaplinsky v. New Hampshire.* But this record shows no such extremes. It shows an unsympathetic audience and the threat of one man to haul the speaker from the stage. It is against that kind of threat the speakers need police protection. If they do not receive it and instead the police throw their weight on the side of those who would break up the meetings, the police become the new censors of speech. Police censorship has all the vices of censorship from city halls which we have repeatedly struck down. . . .

FOR DISCUSSION

Do you think it is possible to reconcile the decisions in *Feiner* and *Terminiello*? If so, how can you account for the differing outcomes in cases that seem in many respects to be the same?

BEAUHARNAIS V. ILLINOIS

343 U.S. 250, 72 S.Ct. 725, 98 L.Ed. 919 (1952)

Hate speech may be directed to groups as well as to individuals. This case involves just such a circumstance. Students should keep this case in mind when considering cases related to libel in the next chapter, on freedom of the press.

Vote: 5–4

JUSTICE FRANKFURTER delivered the opinion of the Court.

The petitioner was convicted upon information in the Municipal Court of Chicago of violating § 224a of Division 1 of the Illinois Criminal Code. He was fined $200. The section provides:

> It shall be unlawful for any person, firm or corporation to manufacture, sell, or offer for sale, advertise or publish, present or exhibit in any public place in this state any lithograph, moving picture, play, drama or sketch, which publication or exhibition portrays depravity, criminality, unchastity, or lack of virtue of a class of citizens, of any race, color, creed or religion which said publication or exhibition exposes the citizens of any race, color, creed or religion to contempt, derision, or obloquy or which is productive of breach of the peace or riots.

Beauharnais challenged the statute as violating the liberty of speech and of the press guaranteed as against the States by the Due Process Clause of the Fourteenth Amendment, and as too vague, under the restrictions implicit in the same Clause, to support conviction for crime. The Illinois courts rejected these contentions and sustained defendant's conviction. We granted certiorari in view of the serious questions raised concerning the limitations imposed by the Fourteenth Amendment on the power of a State to punish utterances promoting friction among racial and religious groups.

The information, cast generally in the terms of the statute, charged that Beauharnais "did unlawfully . . . exhibit in public places lithographs, which publications portray depravity, criminality, unchastity or lack of virtue of citizens of Negro race and color and which exposes (sic) citizens of Illinois of the Negro race and color to contempt, derision, or obloquy . . . ." The lithograph complained of was a leaflet setting forth a petition calling on the Mayor and City Council of Chicago "to halt the further encroachment, harassment and invasion of white people, their property, neighborhoods and persons, by the Negro. . . ." Below was a call for "One million self respecting white people in Chicago to unite. . ." with the statement added that "If persuasion and the need to prevent the white race from becoming mongrelized by the negro will not unite us, then the aggressions . . . rapes, robberies, knives, guns and marijuana of the negro, surely will." This, with more language, similar if not so violent, concluded with an attached application for membership in the White Circle League of America, Inc.

The testimony at the trial was substantially undisputed. From it the jury could find that Beauharnais was president of the White Circle League; that, at a meeting on January 6, 1950, he passed out bundles of the lithographs in question, together with other literature, to volunteers for distribution on downtown Chicago street corners the following day; that he carefully organized that distribution, giving detailed instructions for it; and that the leaflets were in fact distributed on January 7 in accordance with his plan and instructions. The court, together with other charges on burden of proof and the like, told the jury "if you find . . . that the defendant, Joseph Beauharnais, did . . . manufacture, sell, or offer for sale, advertise or publish, present or exhibit in any public place the lithograph . . . then you are to find the defendant guilty. . . ." He refused to charge the jury, as requested by the defendant, that in order to convict they must find "that the article complained of was likely to produce a clear and present danger of a serious substantive evil that rises for above public inconvenience, annoyance or unrest." Upon this evidence and these instructions, the jury brought in the conviction here for review.

Libel of an individual was a common-law crime, and thus criminal in the colonies. Indeed, at common law, truth or good motives was no defense. In the first decades after the adoption of the Constitution, this was changed by judicial decision, statute or constitution in most States, but nowhere was there any suggestion that the crime of libel be abolished. Today, every American jurisdiction—the forty-eight States, the District of Columbia, Alaska, Hawaii and Puerto Rico—punishes libels directed at individuals. "There are certain well-defined and narrowly limited classes of speech, the prevention and punishment of which has never been thought to raise any Constitutional problem. These include the lewd and obscene, the profane, the libelous, and the insulting or 'fighting' words—those which by their very utterance inflict injury or tend to incite an immediate breach of the peace. It has been well observed that such utterances are no essential part of any exposition of ideas, and are of such slight social value as a step to truth that any benefit that may be derived from them is clearly outweighed by the social interest in order and morality." "Resort to epithets or personal abuse is not in any proper sense communication of information or opinion safeguarded by the Constitution, and its punishment as a criminal act would raise no question under that instrument." Such were the views of a unanimous Court in *Chaplinsky v. State of New Hampshire,*315 U.S. 568 (1942).

No one will gainsay that it is libelous falsely to charge another with being a rapist, robber, carrier of knives and guns, and user of marijuana. The precise question before us, then, is whether the protection of 'liberty' in the Due Process Clause of the Fourteenth Amendment prevents a State from punishing such libels—as criminal libel has been defined, limited and constitutionally recognized time out of mind—directed at designated collectivities and flagrantly disseminated. There is even authority, however dubious, that such utterances were also crimes at common law. It is certainly clear that some American jurisdictions have sanctioned their punishment under ordinary criminal libel statutes. We cannot say, however, that the question is concluded by history and practice. But if an utterance directed at an individual may be the object of criminal sanctions, we cannot deny to a State power to punish the same utterance directed at a defined group, unless we can say that this a willful and purposeless restriction unrelated to the peace and well-being of the State.

Long ago this Court recognized that the economic rights of an individual may depend for the effectiveness of their enforcement on rights in the group, even though not formally corporate, to which he belongs. Such group-protection on behalf of the individual may, for all we know, be a need not confined to the part that a trade union plays in effectuating rights abstractly recognized as belonging to its members. It is not within our competence to confirm or deny claims of social scientists as to the dependence of the individual on the position of his racial or religious group in the community. It would, however, be arrant dogmatism, quite outside the scope of our authority in passing on the powers of a State, for us to deny that the Illinois Legislature may warrantably believe that a man's job and his educational opportunities and the dignity accorded him may depend as much on the reputation of the racial and religious group to which he willy-nilly belongs, as on his own merits. This being so, we are precluded from saying that speech concededly punishable when immediately directed at individuals cannot be outlawed if directed at groups with whose position and esteem in society the affiliated individual may be inextricably involved.

Affirmed.

JUSTICE BLACK, with whom JUSTICE DOUGLAS concurs, dissenting.

This case is here because Illinois inflicted criminal punishment on Beauharnais for causing the distribution of leaflets in the city of Chicago. The conviction rests on the leaflet's contents, not on the time, manner or place of distribution. Beauharnais is head of an organization that opposes amalgamation and favors segregation of white and colored people. After discussion, an assembly of his group decided to petition the mayor and council of Chicago to pass laws for segregation. Volunteer members of the group agreed to stand on street corners, solicit signers to petitions addressed to the city authorities, and distribute leaflets giving information about the group, its beliefs and its plans. In carrying out this program a solicitor handed out a leaflet which was the basis of this prosecution. Since the Court opinion quotes only parts of the leaflet, I am including all of it as an appendix to this dissent.

I

That Beauharnais and his group were making a genuine effort to petition their elected representatives is not disputed. Even as far back as 1689, the Bill of Rights exacted of William & Mary said: "It is the Right of the Subjects to petition the King, and all Commitments and Prosecutions for such petitioning are illegal." And 178 years ago the Declaration of Rights of the Continental Congress proclaimed to the monarch of that day that his American subjects had "a right peaceably to assemble, consider of their grievances, and petition the King; and that all prosecutions, prohibitory proclamations, and commitments for the same, are illegal." After independence was won, Americans stated as the first unequivocal command of their Bill of Rights: "Congress shall make no law . . . abridging the freedom of speech, or of the press; or the right of the people peaceably to assemble, and to petition the Government for a redress of grievances." Without distortion, this First Amendment could not possibly be read so as to hold that Congress has power to punish Beauharnais and others for petitioning Congress as they have here sought to petition the Chicago authorities. And we have held in a number of prior cases that the Fourteenth Amendment makes the specific prohibitions of the First Amendment equally applicable to the states.

In view of these prior holdings, how does the Court justify its holding today that states can punish people for exercising the vital freedoms intended to be safeguarded from suppression by the First Amendment? The prior holdings are not referred to; the Court simply acts on the bland assumption that the First Amendment is wholly irrelevant. It is not even accorded the respect of a passing mention.

Today's case degrades First Amendment freedoms to the "rational basis" level. It is now a certainty that the new "due process" coverall offers far less protection to liberty than would adherence to our former cases compelling states to abide by the unequivocal First Amendment command that its defined freedoms shall not be abridged.

FOR DISCUSSION

The *Beauharnais* ruling says that hate speech directed at a specific racial, ethnic, or religious group lacks constitutional protection. The case technically has never been overturned, but how viable a precedent is it in light of *Brandenburg v. Ohio*?

COLLIN V. SMITH

578 F.2d 1197 (7th Cir. 1978)

This circuit court decision deals in part with the issue of hate speech and in part with the issue of symbolic speech.

PELL, CIRCUIT JUDGE.

Plaintiff-appellee, the National Socialist Party of America (NSPA), is a political group described by its leader, plaintiff-appellee Frank Collin, as a Nazi party. Among NSPA's more controversial and generally unacceptable beliefs are that black persons are biologically inferior to white persons, and should be expatriated to Africa as soon as possible; that American Jews have "inordinate . . . political and financial power" in the world and are "in the forefront of the international Communist revolution." NSPA members affect a uniform reminiscent of those worn by members of the German Nazi Party during the Third Reich, and display a swastika thereon and on a red, white, and black flag they frequently carry.

In Collin's words:

> We wear brown shirts with a dark brown tie, a swastika pin on the tie, a leather shoulder strap, a black belt with buckle, dark brown trousers, black engineer boots, and either a steel helmet or a cloth cap, depending on the situation, plus a swastika arm band on the left arm and an American flag patch on the right arm.

The Village of Skokie, Illinois, a defendant-appellant, is a suburb north of Chicago. It has a large Jewish population, including as many as several thousand survivors of the Nazi holocaust in Europe before and during World War II. Other defendants-appellants are Village officials.

When Collin and NSPA announced plans to march in front of the Village Hall in Skokie on May 1, 1977, Village officials responded by obtaining in state court a preliminary injunction against the demonstration. After state courts refused to stay the injunction pending appeal, the United States Supreme Court ordered a stay. The injunction was subsequently reversed. On May 2, 1977, the Village enacted three ordinances to prohibit demonstrations such as the one Collin and NSPA had threatened. This lawsuit seeks declaratory and injunctive relief against enforcement of the ordinances.

Village Ordinance No. 77–5–N–994 (hereinafter designated, for convenience of reference, as 994) is a comprehensive permit system for all parades or public assemblies of more than 50 persons. It requires permit applicants to obtain $300,000 in public liability insurance and $50,000 in property damage insurance. One of the prerequisites for a permit is a finding by the appropriate official(s) that the assembly will not portray criminality, depravity or lack of virtue in, or incite violence, hatred, abuse or hostility toward a person or group of persons by reason of reference to religious, racial, ethnic, national or regional affiliation. Another is a finding that the permit activity will not be conducted "for an unlawful purpose." None of this ordinance applies to activities of the Village itself or of a governmental agency, and any provision of the ordinance may be waived by unanimous consent of the Board of Trustees of the Village. To parade or assemble without a permit is a crime, punishable by fines from $5 to $500.

Collin and NSPA applied for a permit to march on July 4, 1977, which was denied on the ground the application disclosed an intention to violate 996. The Village apparently applies 994 § 27–56(i) so that an intention to violate 995 or 996 establishes an "unlawful purpose" for the march or assembly. The permit application stated that the march would last about a half hour, and would involve 30 to 50 demonstrators wearing uniforms including swastikas and carrying a party banner with a swastika and placards with statements thereon such as "White Free Speech," "Free Speech for the White Man," and "Free Speech for White America." A single file sidewalk march that would not disrupt traffic was proposed, without speeches or the distribution of handbills or literature. Counsel for the Village advises us that the Village does not maintain that Collin and NSPA will behave other than as described in the permit application(s).

The district court, after considering memoranda, exhibits, depositions, and live testimony, issued a comprehensive and thorough opinion granting relief to Collin and NSPA. The insurance requirements of 994 were invalidated as insuperable obstacles to free speech in Skokie, and §§ 27–56(c) & (i) (the latter when used to deny permits on the basis of anticipated violations of 995 or 996) were adjudged impermissible prior restraints. Ordinance 995 was determined to be fatally vague and overbroad, and 996 was invalidated as overbroad and patently unjustified.

On its appeal, the Village concedes the invalidity of the insurance requirements as applied to these plaintiffs and of the uniform prohibition of 996.

I

The conflict underlying this litigation has commanded substantial public attention, and engendered considerable and understandable emotion. We would hopefully surprise no one by confessing personal views that NSPA's beliefs and goals are repugnant to the core values held generally by residents of this country, and, indeed, to much of what we cherish in civilization. As judges sworn to defend the Constitution, however, we cannot decide this or any case on that basis. Ideological tyranny, no matter how worthy its motivation, is forbidden as much to appointed judges as to elected legislators.

But our task here is to decide whether the First Amendment protects the activity in which appellees wish to engage, not to render moral judgment on their views or tactics. No authorities need be cited to establish the proposition, which the Village does not dispute, that First Amendment rights are truly precious and fundamental to our national life. Nor is this truth without relevance to the saddening historical images this case inevitably arouses. It is, after all, in part the fact that our constitutional system protects minorities unpopular at a particular time or place from governmental harassment and intimidation, that distinguishes life in this country from life under the Third Reich.

Before undertaking specific analysis of the clash between the Village ordinances and appellees' desires to demonstrate in Skokie, it will be helpful to establish some general principles of pertinence to the decision required of us. Putting to one side for the moment the question of whether the content of appellees' views and symbols makes a constitutional difference here, we find we are unable to deny that the activities in which the appellees wish to engage are within the ambit of the First Amendment.

Legislating against the content of First Amendment activity, however, launches the government on a slippery and precarious path.

But analysis of content restrictions must begin with a healthy respect for the truth that they are the most direct threat to the vitality of First Amendment rights.

II

We first consider ordinance 995, prohibiting the dissemination of materials which would promote hatred towards persons on the basis of their heritage. The Village would apparently apply this provision to NSPA's display of swastikas, their uniforms, and, perhaps, to the content of their placards.

The ordinance cannot be sustained on the basis of some of the more obvious exceptions to the rule against content control. While some would no doubt be willing to label appellees' views and symbols obscene, the constitutional rule that obscenity is unprotected applies only to material with erotic content. Furthermore, although the Village introduced evidence in the district court tending to prove that some individuals, at least, might have difficulty restraining their reactions to the Nazi demonstration, the Village tells us that it does not rely on a fear of responsive violence to justify the ordinance, and does not even suggest that there will be any physical violence if the march is held.

Four basic arguments are advanced by the Village to justify the content restrictions of 995. First, it is said that the content criminalized by 995 is "totally lacking in social content," and that it consists of "false statements of fact" in which there is "no constitutional value." We disagree that, if applied to the proposed demonstration, the ordinance can be said to be limited to "statements of fact," false or otherwise. No handbills are to be distributed; no speeches are planned. To the degree that the symbols in question can be said to assert anything specific, it must be the Nazi ideology, which cannot be treated as a mere false "fact."

We may agree with the district court that

> if any philosophy should be regarded as completely unacceptable to civilized society, that of plaintiffs, who, while disavowing on the witness stand any advocacy of genocide, have nevertheless deliberately identified themselves with a regime whose record of brutality and barbarism is unmatched in modern history, would be a good place to start. But there can be no legitimate start down such a road.

Under the First Amendment there is no such thing as a false idea. However pernicious an opinion may seem, we depend for its correction not on the conscience of judges and juries but on the competition of other ideas.

In the words of Justice Jackson, "every person must be his own watchman for truth, because the forefathers did not trust any government to separate the true from the false for us." The asserted falseness of Nazi dogma, and, indeed, its general repudiation, simply do not justify its suppression.

The Village's second argument, and the one on which principal reliance is placed, centers on *Beauharnais v. Illinois,* 343 U.S. 250 (1952). There a conviction was upheld under a statute prohibiting, in language substantially (and perhaps not unintentionally) similar to that used in the ordinance here, the dissemination of materials promoting racial or religious hatred. The closely-divided Court stated that the criminal punishment of libel of an Individual raised no constitutional problems, relying on *Chaplinsky v. New Hampshire,* 315 U.S. 568 (1942).

In our opinion *Beauharnais* does not support ordinance 995, for two independent reasons. First, the rationale of that decision turns quite plainly on the strong tendency of the prohibited utterances to cause violence and disorder. The Illinois Supreme Court had so limited the statute's application, as the United States Supreme Court noted. The latter Court also pointed out that the tendency to induce breach of the peace was the traditional justification for the criminal libel laws which had always been thought to be immune from the First Amendment. After stating the issue (whether Illinois could extend criminal libel to groups) the Court turned to Illinois' history of racial strife "and its frequent obligato of extreme racial and religious propaganda," and concluded that the Illinois legislature could reasonably connect the strife and the propaganda and criminalize the latter to prevent the former.

It may be questioned, after cases such as *Cohen v. California,* 403 U.S. 15 (1971); *Gooding v. Wilson*, 405 U.S. 518 (1972); *and Brandenburg v. Ohio*, 395 U.S. 444 (1969), whether the tendency to induce violence approach sanctioned implicitly in *Beauharnais* would pass constitutional muster today. Assuming that it would, however, it does not support ordinance 995, because the Village, as we have indicated, does not assert appellees' possible violence, an audience's possible responsive violence, or possible violence against third parties by those incited by appellees, as justifications for 995. Ordinance 995 would apparently be applied in the absence of any such threat. The rationale of *Beauharnais*, then, simply does not apply here.

The Village's third argument is that it has a policy of fair housing, which the dissemination of racially defamatory material could undercut. We reject this argument without extended discussion. That the effective exercise of First Amendment rights may undercut a given government's policy on some issue is, indeed, one of the purposes of those rights. No distinction is constitutionally admissible that turns on the intrinsic justice of the particular policy in issue.

The Village's fourth argument is that the Nazi march, involving as it does the display of uniforms and swastikas, will create a substantive evil that it has a right to prohibit: the infliction of psychic trauma on resident holocaust survivors and other Jewish residents. The Village points out that Illinois recognizes the "new tort" of intentional infliction of severe emotional distress. Assuming that specific individuals could proceed in tort under this theory to recover damages provably occasioned by the proposed march, and that a First Amendment defense would not bar the action, it is nonetheless quite a different matter to criminalize protected First Amendment conduct in anticipation of such results.

FOR DISCUSSION

Given the last paragraph of Judge Pell's decision, do you think it is possible that the Supreme Court would accept a civil action by a bystander who claimed that seeing the Nazis in uniform constituted an intentional infliction of emotional distress? Would it matter if the individual had been the victim of Nazi atrocities in World War II? This decision states that under the First Amendment "there is no such thing as a false idea." What does that statement mean? In your judgment, is the statement correct?

RELATED CASE

Frisby v. Schultz: **487 U.S. 474 (1988).**

Writing for the Court, Justice O'Connor held that an ordinance that banned residential picketing directed at a particular household did not violate the First Amendment because it was meant to shield a captive audience from offensive speech. Unlike the ruling in *Smith,* where the Court observed that the parade was short in duration, that it was not directed at any particular household, and that residents had the option of staying in their homes (or ignoring the demonstration), the plaintiff, a doctor who performed abortions, was subject to a constant barrage of protesters outside his door, making it impossible for him to escape their message. The Court ruled that Schultz, unlike the residents of Skokie, was a captive audience who had no choice but to listen to the speech of the protesters. The protection of a captive audience receives different constitutional treatment from the protection of the hostile audiences in *Feiner* and *Terminiello.*

R.A.V. v. City of St. Paul

505 U.S. 377, 112 S.Ct. 2538, 120 L.Ed. 2d 305 (1992)

Like flag burning, the issue raised in *Texas v. Johnson* (491 U.S. 397, 1989), cross burning is a highly controversial act, often associated with intimidation. In this case, the Court struggled with a city ordinance that regulated this behavior as part of a municipal bias-motivated crime ordinance. In addressing the issue, the Court had to decide in part whether the law was overly broad or whether it constituted improper regulation of the content of speech.

Vote: 9–0

JUSTICE SCALIA delivered the opinion of the Court.

In the predawn hours of June 21, 1990, petitioner and several other teenagers allegedly assembled a crudely made cross by taping together broken chair legs. They then allegedly burned the cross inside the fenced yard of a black family that lived across the street from the house where petitioner was staying. Although this conduct could have been punished under any of a number of laws, one of the two provisions under which respondent city of St. Paul chose to charge petitioner (then a juvenile) was the St. Paul Bias-Motivated Crime Ordinance, St. Paul, Minn., Legis. Code § 292.02 (1990), which provides:

> Whoever places on public or private property a symbol, object, appellation, characterization or graffiti, including, but not limited to, a burning cross or Nazi swastika, which one knows or has reasonable grounds to know arouses anger, alarm or resentment in others on the basis of race, color, creed, religion or gender commits disorderly conduct and shall be guilty of a misdemeanor.

Petitioner moved to dismiss this count on the ground that the St. Paul ordinance was substantially overbroad and impermissibly content based and therefore facially invalid under the First Amendment. The trial court granted this motion, but the Minnesota Supreme Court reversed. That court rejected petitioner's overbreadth claim because, as construed in prior Minnesota cases, the modifying phrase "arouses anger, alarm or resentment in others" limited the reach of the ordinance to conduct that amounts to "fighting words," *i.e.,* "conduct that itself inflicts injury or tends to incite immediate violence . . .," and therefore the ordinance reached only expression "that the first amendment does not protect." The court also concluded that the ordinance was not impermissibly content based because, in its view, "the ordinance is a narrowly tailored means toward accomplishing the compelling governmental interest in protecting the community against bias-motivated threats to public safety and order." We granted certiorari.

I

In construing the St. Paul ordinance, we are bound by the construction given to it by the Minnesota court. Accordingly, we accept the Minnesota Supreme Court's authoritative statement that the ordinance reaches only those expressions that constitute "fighting words" within the meaning of *Chaplinsky v. State of New Hampshire,* 315 U.S. 568 (1942). Petitioner and his *amici* urge us to modify the scope of the *Chaplinsky* formulation, thereby invalidating the ordinance as "substantially overbroad." We find it unnecessary to consider this issue. Assuming, *arguendo,* that all of the expression reached by the ordinance is proscribable under the "fighting words" doctrine, we nonetheless conclude that the ordinance is facially unconstitutional in that it prohibits otherwise permitted speech solely on the basis of the subjects the speech addresses.

The First Amendment generally prevents government from proscribing speech. From 1791 to the present, however, our society, like other free but civilized societies, has permitted restrictions upon the content of speech in a few limited areas, which are "of such slight social value as a step to truth that any benefit that may be derived from them is clearly outweighed by the social interest in order and morality." We have recognized that "the freedom of speech" referred to by the First Amendment does not include a freedom to disregard these traditional limitations. Our decisions since the 1960's have narrowed the scope of the traditional categorical exceptions for defamation,

We have sometimes said that these categories of expression are "not within the area of constitutionally protected speech," or that the "protection of the First Amendment does not extend" to them. Such statements must be taken in context, however, and are no more literally true than is the occasionally repeated shorthand characterizing obscenity "as not being speech at all." What they mean is that these areas of speech can, consistently with the First Amendment, be regulated *because of their constitutionally proscribable content* (obscenity, defamation, etc.)—not that they are categories of speech entirely invisible to the Constitution, so that they may be made the vehicles for content discrimination unrelated to their distinctively proscribable content. Thus, the government may proscribe libel; but it may not make the further content discrimination of proscribing *only* libel critical of the government.

Our cases surely do not establish the proposition that the First Amendment imposes no obstacle whatsoever to regulation of particular instances of such proscribable expression, so that the government "may regulate [them] freely." That would mean that a city council could enact an ordinance prohibiting only those legally obscene works that contain criticism of the city government or, indeed, that do not include endorsement of the city government. Such a simplistic, all-or-nothing-at-all approach to First Amendment protection is at odds with common sense and with our jurisprudence as well. It is not true that "fighting words" have at most a "*de minimis*" expressive content, or that their content is *in all respects* "worthless and undeserving of constitutional protection," sometimes they are quite expressive indeed. We have not said that they constitute "*no* part of the expression of ideas," but only that they constitute "no *essential* part of any exposition of ideas."

The proposition that a particular instance of speech can be proscribable on the basis of one feature (*e.g.,* obscenity) but not on the basis of another (*e.g.,* opposition to the city government) is commonplace and has found application in many contexts. We have long held, for example, that nonverbal expressive activity can be banned because of the action it entails, but not because of the ideas it expresses—so that burning a flag in violation of an ordinance against outdoor fires could be punishable, whereas burning a flag in violation of an ordinance against dishonoring the flag is not. And just as the power to proscribe particular speech on the basis of a noncontent element (*e.g.,* noise) does not entail the power to proscribe the same speech on the basis of a content element; so also, the power to proscribe it on the basis of *one* content element (*e.g.,* obscenity) does not entail the power to proscribe it on the basis of *other* content elements.

In other words, the exclusion of "fighting words" from the scope of the First Amendment simply means that, for purposes of that Amendment, the unprotected features of the words are, despite their verbal character, essentially a "nonspeech" element of communication. Fighting words are thus analogous to a noisy sound truck: Each is, as Justice Frankfurter recognized, a "mode of speech"; both can be used to convey an idea; but neither has, in and of itself, a claim upon the First Amendment. As with the sound truck, however, so also with fighting words: The government may not regulate use based on hostility—or favoritism—towards the underlying message expressed.

II

Applying these principles to the St. Paul ordinance, we conclude that, even as narrowly construed by the Minnesota Supreme Court, the ordinance is facially unconstitutional. Although the phrase in the ordinance, "arouses anger, alarm or resentment in others," has been limited by the Minnesota Supreme Court's construction to reach only those symbols or displays that amount to "fighting words," the remaining, unmodified terms make clear that the ordinance applies only to "fighting words" that insult, or provoke violence, "on the basis of race, color, creed, religion or gender." Displays containing abusive invective, no matter how vicious or severe, are permissible unless they are addressed to one of the specified disfavored topics. Those who wish to use "fighting words" in connection with other ideas—to express hostility, for example, on the basis of political affiliation, union membership, or homosexuality—are not covered. The First Amendment does not permit St. Paul to impose special prohibitions on those speakers who express views on disfavored subjects.

In its practical operation, moreover, the ordinance goes even beyond mere content discrimination, to actual viewpoint discrimination. Displays containing some words—odious racial epithets, for example—would be prohibited to proponents of all views. But "fighting words" that do not themselves invoke race, color, creed, religion, or gender—aspersions upon a person's mother, for example—would seemingly be usable *ad libitum* in the placards of those arguing *in favor* of racial, color, etc., tolerance and equality, but could not be used by those speakers' opponents. One could hold up a sign saying, for example, that all "anti-Catholic bigots" are misbegotten; but not that all "papists" are, for that would insult and provoke violence "on the basis of religion." St. Paul has no such authority to license one side of a debate to fight freestyle, while requiring the other to follow Marquis of Queensberry rules.

What we have here, it must be emphasized, is not a prohibition of fighting words that are directed at certain persons or groups (which would be *facially* valid if it met the requirements of the Equal Protection Clause); but rather, a prohibition of fighting words that contain (as the Minnesota Supreme Court repeatedly emphasized) messages of "bias-motivated" hatred and in particular, as applied to this case, messages "based on virulent notions of racial supremacy." One must wholeheartedly agree with the Minnesota Supreme Court that "[i]t is the responsibility, even the obligation, of diverse communities to confront such notions in whatever form they appear," but the manner of that confrontation cannot consist of selective limitations upon speech. St. Paul's brief asserts that a general "fighting words" law would not meet the city's needs because only a content-specific measure can communicate to minority groups that the "group hatred" aspect of such speech "is not condoned by the majority." The point of the First Amendment is that majority preferences must be expressed in some fashion other than silencing speech on the basis of its content.

Let there be no mistake about our belief that burning a cross in someone's front yard is reprehensible. But St. Paul has sufficient means at its disposal to prevent such behavior without adding the First Amendment to the fire.

The judgment of the Minnesota Supreme Court is reversed, and the case is remanded for proceedings not inconsistent with this opinion.

It is so ordered.

JUSTICE WHITE, with whom JUSTICES BLACKMUN and O'CONNOR join, and with whom JUSTICE STEVENS joins except as to Part I–A, concurring in the judgment.

I agree with the majority that the judgment of the Minnesota Supreme Court should be reversed. However, our agreement ends there.

This case could easily be decided within the contours of established First Amendment law by holding, as petitioner argues, that the St. Paul ordinance is fatally overbroad because it criminalizes not only unprotected expression but expression protected by the First Amendment. Instead, "find[ing] it unnecessary" to consider the questions upon which we granted review, the Court holds the ordinance facially unconstitutional on a ground that was never presented to the Minnesota Supreme Court, a ground that has not been briefed by the parties before this Court, a ground that requires serious departures from the teaching of prior cases.

FOR DISCUSSION

Can you think of other laws that the City of St. Paul might have used to restrict cross-burning? Why do you suppose they decided not to use these laws?

WISCONSIN V. MITCHELL

508 U.S. 476, 113 S.Ct. 2194, 124 L.Ed. 2d 436 (1993)

Here the Court had to decide whether it could enhance a criminal sentence because the crime was racially motivated.

Vote: 9–0

CHIEF JUSTICE REHNQUIST delivered the opinion of the Court.

Respondent Todd Mitchell's sentence for aggravated battery was enhanced because he intentionally selected his victim on account of the victim's race. The question presented in this case is whether this penalty enhancement is prohibited by the First and Fourteenth Amendments. We hold that it is not.

On the evening of October 7, 1989, a group of young black men and boys, including Mitchell, gathered at an apartment complex in Kenosha, Wisconsin. Several members of the group discussed a scene from the motion picture "Mississippi Burning," in which a white man beat a young black boy who was praying. The group moved outside and Mitchell asked them: " 'Do you all feel hyped up to move on some white people?' " Shortly thereafter, a young white boy approached the group on the opposite side of the street where they were standing. As the boy walked by, Mitchell said: " 'You all want to fuck somebody up? There goes a white boy; go get him.' " Mitchell counted to three and pointed in the boy's direction. The group ran toward the boy, beat him severely, and stole his tennis shoes. The boy was rendered unconscious and remained in a coma for four days.

After a jury trial in the Circuit Court for Kenosha County, Mitchell was convicted of aggravated battery. That offense ordinarily carries a maximum sentence of two years' imprisonment. But because the jury found that Mitchell had intentionally selected his victim because of the boy's race, the maximum sentence for Mitchell's offense was increased to seven years under § 939.645. That provision enhances the maximum penalty for an offense whenever the defendant "[i]ntentionally selects the person against whom the crime . . . is committed . . . because of the race, religion, color, disability, sexual orientation, national origin or ancestry of that person. . . ." The Circuit Court sentenced Mitchell to four years' imprisonment for the aggravated battery.

Mitchell unsuccessfully sought postconviction relief in the Circuit Court. Then he appealed his conviction and sentence, challenging the constitutionality of Wisconsin's penalty-enhancement provision on First Amendment grounds. The Wisconsin Court of Appeals rejected Mitchell's challenge, but the Wisconsin Supreme Court reversed. The Supreme Court held that the statute "violates the First Amendment directly by punishing what the legislature has deemed to be offensive thought."

The Supreme Court also held that the penalty-enhancement statute was unconstitutionally overbroad. It reasoned that, in order to prove that a defendant intentionally selected his victim because of the victim's protected status, the State would often have to introduce evidence of the defendant's prior speech, such as racial epithets he may have uttered before the commission of the offense. This evidentiary use of protected speech, the court thought, would have a "chilling effect" on those who feared the possibility of prosecution for offenses subject to penalty enhancement. Finally, the court distinguished antidiscrimination laws, which have long been held constitutional, on the ground that the Wisconsin statute punishes the "subjective mental process" of selecting a victim because of his protected status, whereas antidiscrimination laws prohibit "objective acts of discrimination."

We granted certiorari because of the importance of the question presented and the existence of a conflict of authority among state high courts on the constitutionality of statutes similar to Wisconsin's penalty-enhancement provision. We reverse.

Mitchell argues that we are bound by the Wisconsin Supreme Court's conclusion that the statute punishes bigoted thought and not conduct. But here the Wisconsin Supreme Court did not, strictly speaking, construe the Wisconsin statute in the sense of defining the meaning of a particular statutory word or phrase. Rather, it merely characterized the "practical effect" of the statute for First Amendment purposes. This assessment does not bind us. Once any ambiguities as to the meaning of the statute are resolved, we may form our own judgment as to its operative effect.

The State argues that the statute does not punish bigoted thought, as the Supreme Court of Wisconsin said, but instead punishes only conduct. While this argument is literally correct, it does not dispose of Mitchell's First Amendment challenge. To be sure, our cases reject the "view that an apparently limitless variety of conduct can be labeled 'speech' whenever the person engaging in the conduct intends thereby to express an idea." Thus, a physical assault is not by any stretch of the imagination expressive conduct protected by the First Amendment.

But the fact remains that under the Wisconsin statute the same criminal conduct may be more heavily punished if the victim is selected because of his race or other protected status than if no such motive obtained. Thus, although the statute punishes criminal conduct, it enhances the maximum penalty for conduct motivated by a discriminatory point of view more severely than the same conduct engaged in for some other reason or for no reason at all. Because the only reason for the enhancement is the defendant's discriminatory motive for selecting his victim, Mitchell argues (and the Wisconsin Supreme Court held) that the statute violates the First Amendment by punishing offenders' bigoted beliefs.

Traditionally, sentencing judges have considered a wide variety of factors in addition to evidence bearing on guilt in determining what sentence to impose on a convicted defendant. The defendant's motive for committing the offense is one important factor. Thus, in many States the commission of a murder, or other capital offense, for pecuniary gain is a separate aggravating circumstance under the capital sentencing statute.

But it is equally true that a defendant's abstract beliefs, however obnoxious to most people, may not be taken into consideration by a sentencing judge. In *Dawson v. Delaware* [503 U.S. 159 (1992)], the State introduced evidence at a capital sentencing hearing that the defendant was a member of a white supremacist prison gang. Because "the evidence proved nothing more than [the defendant's] abstract beliefs," we held that its admission violated the defendant's First Amendment rights. In so holding, however, we emphasized that "the Constitution does not erect a *per se* barrier to the admission of evidence concerning one's beliefs and associations at sentencing simply because those beliefs and associations are protected by the First Amendment." Thus, in *Barclay v. Florida*, 463 U.S. 939 (1983), we allowed the sentencing judge to take into account the defendant's racial animus towards his victim. The evidence in that case showed that the defendant's membership in the Black Liberation Army and desire to provoke a "race war" were related to the murder of a white man for which he was convicted. Because "the elements of racial hatred in [the] murder" were relevant to several aggravating factors, we held that the trial judge permissibly took this evidence into account in sentencing the defendant to death.

Mitchell argues that the Wisconsin penalty-enhancement statute is invalid because it punishes the defendant's discriminatory motive, or reason, for acting. But motive plays the same role under the Wisconsin statute as it does under federal and state antidiscrimination laws, which we have previously upheld against constitutional challenge.

Nothing in our decision last Term in *R.A.V. v. City of St. Paul*, 505 U.S. 377 (1992), compels a different result here. That case involved a First Amendment challenge to a municipal ordinance prohibiting the use of " 'fighting words' that insult, or provoke violence, 'on the basis of race, color, creed, religion or gender.' " Because the ordinance only proscribed a class of "fighting words" deemed particularly offensive by the city—*i.e.,* those "that contain . . . messages of 'bias-motivated' hatred, we held that it violated the rule against content-based discrimination But whereas the ordinance struck down in *R.A.V.* was explicitly directed at expression (*i.e.,* "speech" or "messages"), the statute in this case is aimed at conduct unprotected by the First Amendment.

Moreover, the Wisconsin statute singles out for enhancement bias-inspired conduct because this conduct is thought to inflict greater individual and societal harm. For example, according to the State and its *amici,* bias-motivated crimes are more likely to provoke retaliatory crimes, inflict distinct emotional harms on their victims, and incite community unrest The State's desire to redress these perceived harms provides an adequate explanation for its penalty-enhancement provision over and above mere disagreement with offenders' beliefs or biases. As Blackstone said long ago, "it is but reasonable that among crimes of different natures those should be most severely punished, which are the most destructive of the public safety and happiness."

Finally, there remains to be considered Mitchell's argument that the Wisconsin statute is unconstitutionally overbroad because of its "chilling effect" on free speech. Mitchell argues (and the Wisconsin Supreme Court agreed) that the statute is "overbroad" because evidence of the defendant's prior speech or associations may be used to prove that the defendant intentionally selected his victim on account of the victim's protected status. Consequently, the argument goes, the statute impermissibly chills free expression with respect to such matters by those concerned about the possibility of enhanced sentences if they should in the future commit a criminal offense covered by the statute. We find no merit in this contention.

The sort of chill envisioned here is far more attenuated and unlikely than that contemplated in traditional "overbreadth" cases. We must conjure up a vision of a Wisconsin citizen suppressing his unpopular bigoted opinions for fear that if he later commits an offense covered by the statute, these opinions will be offered at trial to establish that he selected his victim on account of the victim's protected status, thus qualifying him for penalty enhancement. To stay within the realm of rationality, we must surely put to one side minor misdemeanor offenses covered by the statute, such as negligent operation of a motor vehicle; for it is difficult, if not impossible, to conceive of a situation where such offenses would be racially motivated. We are left, then, with the prospect of a citizen suppressing his bigoted beliefs for fear that evidence of such beliefs will be introduced against him at trial if he commits a more serious offense against person or property. This is simply too speculative a hypothesis to support Mitchell's overbreadth claim.

For the foregoing reasons, we hold that Mitchell's First Amendment rights were not violated by the application of the Wisconsin penalty-enhancement provision in sentencing him. The judgment of the Supreme Court of Wisconsin is therefore reversed, and the case is remanded for further proceedings not inconsistent with this opinion.

It is so ordered.

FOR DISCUSSION

How did the Court attempt to distinguish this case from *R.A.V.*? To what degree does the motivation for a crime enhance or diminish the culpability of its perpetrator? Do you see a different motive here than in the *R.A.V.* case?

SNYDER V. PHELPS

562 U.S. 443, 131 S.Ct. 1207, 179 L.Ed.2d 172 (2011)

Albert Snyder, the father of a deceased military service member, brought action against the Westboro Baptist Church, arising from the latter's anti-homosexual demonstration near his son's funeral. Among other allegations, Snyder claimed that the protest was an intentional infliction of emotional distress. The jury issued a verdict for the father, the United States District Court for the District of Maryland remitted aggregate punitive damages award, and the defendants appealed. The United States Court of Appeals for the Fourth Circuit, reversed.

Vote: 8–1

CHIEF JUSTICE ROBERTS delivered the opinion of the Court.

A jury held members of the Westboro Baptist Church liable for millions of dollars in damages for picketing near a soldier's funeral service. The picket signs reflected the church's view that the United States is overly tolerant of sin and that God kills American soldiers as punishment. The question presented is whether the First Amendment shields the church members from tort liability for their speech in this case.

I

A

Fred Phelps founded the Westboro Baptist Church in Topeka, Kansas, in 1955. The church's congregation believes that God hates and punishes the United States for its tolerance of homosexuality, particularly in America's military. The church frequently communicates its views by picketing, often at military funerals. In the more than 20 years that the members of Westboro Baptist have publicized their message, they have picketed nearly 600 funerals.

Marine Lance Corporal Matthew Snyder was killed in Iraq in the line of duty. Lance Corporal Snyder's father selected the Catholic church in the Snyders' hometown of Westminster, Maryland, as the site for his son's funeral. Local newspapers provided notice of the time and location of the service.

Phelps became aware of Matthew Snyder's funeral and decided to travel to Maryland with six other Westboro Baptist parishioners (two of his daughters and four of his grandchildren) to picket. On the day of the memorial service, the Westboro congregation members picketed on public land adjacent to public streets near the Maryland State House, the United States Naval Academy, and Matthew Snyder's funeral. The Westboro picketers carried signs that were largely the same at all three locations. They stated, for instance: "God Hates the USA/Thank God for 9/11," "America is Doomed," "Don't Pray for the USA," "Thank God for IEDs," "Thank God for Dead Soldiers," "Pope in Hell," "Priests Rape Boys," "God Hates Fags," "You're Going to Hell," and "God Hates You."

The church had notified the authorities in advance of its intent to picket at the time of the funeral, and the picketers complied with police instructions in staging their demonstration. The picketing took place within a 10-

by-25-foot plot of public land adjacent to a public street, behind a temporary fence. That plot was approximately 1,000 feet from the church where the funeral was held. Several buildings separated the picket site from the church. The Westboro picketers displayed their signs for about 30 minutes before the funeral began and sang hymns and recited Bible verses. None of the picketers entered church property or went to the cemetery. They did not yell or use profanity, and there was no violence associated with the picketing.

The funeral procession passed within 200 to 300 feet of the picket site. Although Snyder testified that he could see the tops of the picket signs as he drove to the funeral, he did not see what was written on the signs until later that night, while watching a news broadcast covering the event.

B

Snyder filed suit against Phelps, Phelps's daughters, and the Westboro Baptist Church (collectively Westboro or the church) in the United States District Court for the District of Maryland under that court's diversity jurisdiction. Snyder alleged five state tort law claims: defamation, publicity given to private life, intentional infliction of emotional distress, intrusion upon seclusion, and civil conspiracy. Westboro moved for summary judgment contending, in part, that the church's speech was insulated from liability by the First Amendment.

The District Court awarded Westboro summary judgment on Snyder's claims for defamation and publicity given to private life, concluding that Snyder could not prove the necessary elements of those torts. A trial was held on the remaining claims. At trial, Snyder described the severity of his emotional injuries. He testified that he is unable to separate the thought of his dead son from his thoughts of Westboro's picketing, and that he often becomes tearful, angry, and physically ill when he thinks about it. Expert witnesses testified that Snyder's emotional anguish had resulted in severe depression and had exacerbated pre-existing health conditions.

A jury found for Snyder on the intentional infliction of emotional distress, intrusion upon seclusion, and civil conspiracy claims, and held Westboro liable for $2.9 million in compensatory damages and $8 million in punitive damages. Westboro filed several post-trial motions, including a motion contending that the jury verdict was grossly excessive and a motion seeking judgment as a matter of law on all claims on First Amendment grounds. The District Court remitted the punitive damages award to $2.1 million, but left the jury verdict otherwise intact.

In the Court of Appeals, Westboro's primary argument was that the church was entitled to judgment as a matter of law because the First Amendment fully protected Westboro's speech. The Court of Appeals agreed. The court reviewed the picket signs and concluded that Westboro's statements were entitled to First Amendment protection because those statements were on matters of public concern, were not provably false, and were expressed solely through hyperbolic rhetoric.

We granted certiorari.

II

To succeed on a claim for intentional infliction of emotional distress in Maryland, a plaintiff must demonstrate that the defendant intentionally or recklessly engaged in extreme and outrageous conduct that caused the plaintiff to suffer severe emotional distress. The Free Speech Clause of the First Amendment—"Congress shall make no law . . . abridging the freedom of speech"—can serve as a defense in state tort suits, including suits for intentional infliction of emotional distress.

Whether the First Amendment prohibits holding Westboro liable for its speech in this case turns largely on whether that speech is of public or private concern, as determined by all the circumstances of the case. "[S]peech on 'matters of public concern' . . . is 'at the heart of the First Amendment's protection.' " *Dun & Bradstreet, Inc. v. Greenmoss Builders, Inc.*, 472 U.S. 749, 758–759 (1985). The First Amendment reflects "a profound national commitment to the principle that debate on public issues should be uninhibited, robust, and wide-open." *New York Times Co. v. Sullivan,* 376 U.S. 254, 270 (1964). That is because "speech concerning public affairs is more than self-expression; it is the essence of self-government." *Garrison v. Louisiana,* 379 U.S. 64, 74–75 (1964). Accordingly, "speech on public issues occupies the highest rung of the hierarchy of First Amendment values, and is entitled to special protection." *Connick v. Myers,* 461 U.S. 138, 145 (1983).

" '[N]ot all speech is of equal First Amendment importance,' " however, and where matters of purely private significance are at issue, First Amendment protections are often less rigorous. That is because restricting speech on purely private matters does not implicate the same constitutional concerns as limiting speech on matters of public interest: "[T]here is no threat to the free and robust debate of public issues; there is no potential interference with a meaningful dialogue of ideas"; and the "threat of liability" does not pose the risk of "a reaction of self-censorship" on matters of public import. *Dun & Bradstreet.*

We noted a short time ago, in considering whether public employee speech addressed a matter of public concern, that "the boundaries of the public concern test are not well defined." *San Diego v. Roe,* 543 U.S. 77, 83 (2004) (*per curiam*). Although that remains true today, we have articulated some guiding principles, principles that accord broad protection to speech to ensure that courts themselves do not become inadvertent censors.

Speech deals with matters of public concern when it can "be fairly considered as relating to any matter of political, social, or other concern to the community," or when it "is a subject of legitimate news interest; that is, a subject of general interest and of value and concern to the public." The arguably "inappropriate or controversial character of a statement is irrelevant to the question whether it deals with a matter of public concern." *Rankin v. McPherson,* 483 U.S. 378, 387 (1987).

The "content" of Westboro's signs plainly relates to broad issues of interest to society at large, rather than matters of "purely private concern." The placards read "God Hates the USA/Thank God for 9/11," "America is Doomed," "Don't Pray for the USA," "Thank God for IEDs," "Fag Troops," "Semper Fi Fags," "God Hates Fags," "Maryland Taliban," "Fags Doom Nations," "Not Blessed Just Cursed," "Thank God for Dead Soldiers," "Pope in Hell," "Priests Rape Boys," "You're Going to Hell," and "God Hates You." While these messages may fall short of refined social or political commentary, the issues they highlight—the political and moral conduct of the United States and its citizens, the fate of our Nation, homosexuality in the military, and scandals involving the Catholic clergy—are matters of public import. The signs certainly convey Westboro's position on those issues, in a manner designed, unlike the private speech in *Dun & Bradstreet,* to reach as broad a public audience as possible. And even if a few of the signs—such as "You're Going to Hell" and "God Hates You"—were viewed as containing messages related to Matthew Snyder or the Snyders specifically, that would not change the fact that the overall thrust and dominant theme of Westboro's demonstration spoke to broader public issues.

Apart from the content of Westboro's signs, Snyder contends that the "context" of the speech—its connection with his son's funeral—makes the speech a matter of private rather than public concern. The fact that Westboro spoke in connection with a funeral, however, cannot by itself transform the nature of Westboro's speech. Westboro's signs, displayed on public land next to a public street, reflect the fact that the church finds much to condemn in modern society. Its speech is "fairly characterized as constituting speech on a matter of public concern," and the funeral setting does not alter that conclusion.

Snyder argues that the church members in fact mounted a personal attack on Snyder and his family, and then attempted to "immunize their conduct by claiming that they were actually protesting the United States' tolerance of homosexuality or the supposed evils of the Catholic Church." We are not concerned in this case that Westboro's speech on public matters was in any way contrived to insulate speech on a private matter from liability. Westboro had been actively engaged in speaking on the subjects addressed in its picketing long before it became aware of Matthew Snyder, and there can be no serious claim that Westboro's picketing did not represent its "honestly believed" views on public issues. There was no pre-existing relationship or conflict between Westboro and Snyder that might suggest Westboro's speech on public matters was intended to mask an attack on Snyder over a private matter.

Snyder goes on to argue that Westboro's speech should be afforded less than full First Amendment protection "not only because of the words" but also because the church members exploited the funeral "as a platform to bring their message to a broader audience." There is no doubt that Westboro chose to stage its picketing at the Naval Academy, the Maryland State House, and Matthew Snyder's funeral to increase publicity for its views and because of the relation between those sites and its views—in the case of the military funeral, because Westboro believes that God is killing American soldiers as punishment for the Nation's sinful policies.

Westboro's choice to convey its views in conjunction with Matthew Snyder's funeral made the expression of those views particularly hurtful to many, especially to Matthew's father. The record makes clear that the applicable legal term—"emotional distress"—fails to capture fully the anguish Westboro's choice added to Mr. Snyder's already incalculable grief. But Westboro conducted its picketing peacefully on matters of public concern at a public place adjacent to a public street. Such space occupies a "special position in terms of First Amendment protection." *United States v. Grace,* 461 U.S. 171, 180 (1983). "[W]e have repeatedly referred to public streets as the archetype of a traditional public forum," noting that " '[t]ime out of mind' public streets and sidewalks have been used for public assembly and debate."

We have identified a few limited situations where the location of targeted picketing can be regulated under provisions that the Court has determined to be content neutral. In *Frisby* [*v. Schultz,* 487 U.S. 474 (1988)], for example, we upheld a ban on such picketing "before or about" a particular residence. In *Madsen v. Women's Health Center, Inc.,* 512 U.S. 753 (1994), we approved an injunction requiring a buffer zone between protesters and an abortion clinic entrance. The facts here are obviously quite different, both with respect to the activity being regulated and the means of restricting those activities.

Simply put, the church members had the right to be where they were. Westboro alerted local authorities to its funeral protest and fully complied with police guidance on where the picketing could be staged. The picketing was conducted under police supervision some 1,000 feet from the church, out of the sight of those at the church. The protest was not unruly; there was no shouting, profanity, or violence.

The record confirms that any distress occasioned by Westboro's picketing turned on the content and viewpoint of the message conveyed, rather than any interference with the funeral itself. A group of parishioners standing at the very spot where Westboro stood, holding signs that said "God Bless America" and "God Loves You," would not have been subjected to liability. It was what Westboro said that exposed it to tort damages.

Given that Westboro's speech was at a public place on a matter of public concern, that speech is entitled to "special protection" under the First Amendment. Such speech cannot be restricted simply because it is upsetting or arouses contempt. "If there is a bedrock principle underlying the First Amendment, it is that the government may not prohibit the expression of an idea simply because society finds the idea itself offensive or disagreeable.". Indeed, "the point of all speech protection . . . is to shield just those choices of content that in someone's eyes are misguided, or even hurtful."

The jury here was instructed that it could hold Westboro liable for intentional infliction of emotional distress based on a finding that Westboro's picketing was "outrageous." "Outrageousness," however, is a highly malleable standard with "an inherent subjectiveness about it which would allow a jury to impose liability on the basis of the jurors' tastes or views, or perhaps on the basis of their dislike of a particular expression." In a case such as this, a jury is "unlikely to be neutral with respect to the content of [the] speech," posing "a real danger of becoming an instrument for the suppression of . . . 'vehement, caustic, and sometimes unpleasan[t]' " expression. Such a risk is unacceptable; "in public debate [we] must tolerate insulting, and even outrageous, speech in order to provide adequate 'breathing space' to the freedoms protected by the First Amendment."

What Westboro said, in the whole context of how and where it chose to say it, is entitled to "special protection" under the First Amendment, and that protection cannot be overcome by a jury finding that the picketing was outrageous.

For all these reasons, the jury verdict imposing tort liability on Westboro for intentional infliction of emotional distress must be set aside.

IV

Our holding today is narrow. We are required in First Amendment cases to carefully review the record, and the reach of our opinion here is limited by the particular facts before us. As we have noted, "the sensitivity and significance of the interests presented in clashes between First Amendment and [state law] rights counsel relying on limited principles that sweep no more broadly than the appropriate context of the instant case."

Westboro believes that America is morally flawed; many Americans might feel the same about Westboro. Westboro's funeral picketing is certainly hurtful and its contribution to public discourse may be negligible. But Westboro addressed matters of public import on public property, in a peaceful manner, in full compliance with the guidance of local officials. The speech was indeed planned to coincide with Matthew Snyder's funeral, but did not itself disrupt that funeral, and Westboro's choice to conduct its picketing at that time and place did not alter the nature of its speech.

Speech is powerful. It can stir people to action, move them to tears of both joy and sorrow, and—as it did here—inflict great pain. On the facts before us, we cannot react to that pain by punishing the speaker. As a Nation we have chosen a different course—to protect even hurtful speech on public issues to ensure that we do not stifle public debate. That choice requires that we shield Westboro from tort liability for its picketing in this case.

The judgment of the United States Court of Appeals for the Fourth Circuit is affirmed.

It is so ordered.

JUSTICE ALITO, dissenting.

Our profound national commitment to free and open debate is not a license for the vicious verbal assault that occurred in this case.

Petitioner Albert Snyder is not a public figure. He is simply a parent whose son, Marine Lance Corporal Matthew Snyder, was killed in Iraq. Mr. Snyder wanted what is surely the right of any parent who experiences such an incalculable loss: to bury his son in peace. But respondents, members of the Westboro Baptist Church, deprived him of that elementary right. They first issued a press release and thus turned Matthew's funeral into a tumultuous media event. They then appeared at the church, approached as closely as they could without trespassing, and launched a malevolent verbal attack on Matthew and his family at a time of acute emotional vulnerability. As a result, Albert Snyder suffered severe and lasting emotional injury. The Court now holds that the First Amendment protected respondents' right to brutalize Mr. Snyder. I cannot agree.

FOR DISCUSSION

If the protestors had been on private property, would the results of the case have been different?

Speech Plus

The First Amendment protects words both in oral (speech) and written (press) form. As the rulings in *Tinker v. Des Moines Ind. Comm. School Dist.* (393 U.S. 503, 1969) and *Collin v. Smith* (578 F.2d 1197, 1978) demonstrate, the Court also recognizes that one may "speak" through actions—wearing armbands, participating in parades or pickets, waving placards, etc. The last four cases in this chapter all deal, in one manner or another, with speech combined with action.

United States v. O'Brien (391 U.S. 367, 1968) bears some resemblance to cases involving place, time, and manner restrictions. Although protesters could certainly demonstrate their opposition to the Vietnam War, this did not mean that every form of protest was acceptable. In deciding whether individuals had the right to burn their draft cards, the Court attempted to formulate a principle that it could apply in other such cases.

Like O'Brien, Cohen opposed the Vietnam War and the draft that supported it. However inappropriate a jacket with the words "Fuck the Draft" might be in polite company, the words conveyed a clear political message, the speech that most scholars consider to be at the very core of the First Amendment. In *Cohen v. California* (403 U.S. 15, 1971), the Court decided that the words were not obscene because they were not erotic; moreover, they were not "fighting words," because observers could avert their eyes.

It might be difficult to avert one's eyes from an individual who is burning the nation's most sacred symbol. In any event, in 1984 the police arrested Gregory Lee Johnson when he burned an American flag outside the Reunion Arena in Dallas, where the Republican National Convention was being held. In *Texas v. Johnson* (491 U.S. 397, 1989), the Court ruled that that the law at issue was an impermissible content regulation of speech. Several presidents and members of most sessions of Congress have attempted, unsuccessfully, to overturn the decision by constitutional amendment.

Virginia v. Black (538 U.S. 343, 2003), shows how issues of symbolic speech sometimes overlap issues of hate speech. In America, the Ku Klux Klan has long employed the burning cross as a symbol of hate and intimidation. Yet, in upholding a conviction in *Black*, the Court was careful to specify that the state could not outlaw burning a cross per se, but only instances in which such conduct was specifically tied to intimidation.

The First Amendment has helped assure that freedom of speech remains the rule and suppression of speech the exception, but the Court's conviction that even this right is not absolute has often obliged it to draw the line between regulations of speech that are acceptable and those that are not. The Court will continue to draw from the past as it interprets the Constitution for the future.

UNITED STATES V. O'BRIEN

391 U.S. 367, 88 S.Ct. 1673, 20 L.Ed. 2d 672 (1968)

This case, like that of *Tinker v. Des Moines Ind. Comm. School Dist.* (393 U.S. 503, 1969), grew out of protests against the war in Vietnam. Also as in Tinker, this case involved the use of symbolic speech: here, O'Brien's burning of a Selective Service, or draft, card, on the steps of the South Boston Courthouse. The case set forth a three-part standard that courts continue to use in cases entailing allegations that a regulation of conduct is really designed to target protected speech.

Vote: 7–1

CHIEF JUSTICE WARREN delivered the opinion of the Court.

The indictment upon which he [O'Brien] was tried charged that he "willfully and knowingly did mutilate, destroy, and change by burning . . . [his] Registration Certificate in violation of Title 50, App., United States

Code, Section 462 (b)." Section 462 (b) is part of the Universal Military Training and Service Act of 1948. Section 462 (b) (3), one of six numbered subdivisions of 462 (b), was amended by Congress in 1965, so that at the time O'Brien burned his certificate an offense was committed by any person, "who forges, alters, knowingly destroys, knowingly mutilates, or in any manner changes any such certificate. . . ." [Warren next reviews the District Court decision upholding the law, and the First Circuit Court of Appeals decision ruling that it was unconstitutional.]

I

[In this section, Warren reviews the information on the card, its role in the Selective Service System, and legislative actions designed to protect such cards.]

II

O'Brien first argues that the 1965 Amendment is unconstitutional as applied to him because his act of burning his registration certificate was protected "symbolic speech" within the First Amendment. His argument is that the freedom of expression which the First Amendment guarantees includes all modes of "communication of ideas by conduct," and that his conduct is within this definition because he did it in "demonstration against the war and against the draft."

We cannot accept the view that an apparently limitless variety of conduct can be labeled "speech" whenever the person engaging in the conduct intends thereby to express an idea. However, even on the assumption that the alleged communicative element in O'Brien's conduct is sufficient to bring into play the First Amendment, it does not necessarily follow that the destruction of a registration certificate is constitutionally protected activity. This Court has held that when "speech" and "nonspeech" elements are combined in the same course of conduct, a sufficiently important governmental interest in regulating the nonspeech element can justify incidental limitations on First Amendment freedoms. To characterize the quality of the governmental interest which must appear, the Court has employed a variety of descriptive terms: compelling; substantial; subordinating; paramount; cogent; strong. Whatever imprecision inheres in these terms, we think it clear that a government regulation is sufficiently justified if it is within the constitutional power of the Government; if it furthers an important or substantial governmental interest; if the governmental interest is unrelated to the suppression of free expression; and if the incidental restriction on alleged First Amendment freedoms is no greater than is essential to the furtherance of that interest. We find that the 1965 Amendment to 12 (b) (3) of the Universal Military Training and Service Act meets all of these requirements, and consequently that O'Brien can be constitutionally convicted for violating it.

The constitutional power of Congress to raise and support armies and to make all laws necessary and proper to that end is broad and sweeping. . . . The power of Congress to classify and conscript manpower for military service is "beyond question." *Lichter v. United States,* 334 U.S. 742 (1948). Pursuant to this power, Congress may establish a system of registration for individuals liable for training and service, and may require such individuals within reason to cooperate in the registration system. The issuance of certificates indicating the registration and eligibility classification of individuals is a legitimate and substantial administrative aid in the functioning of this system. And legislation to insure the continuing availability of issued certificates serves a legitimate and substantial purpose in the system's administration.

[Warren proceeds to characterize the draft card as an essential element of the Selective Service System.]

1. The registration certificate serves as proof that the individual described thereon has registered for the draft. The classification certificate shows the eligibility classification of a named but undescribed individual. Voluntarily displaying the two certificates is an easy and painless way for a young man to dispel a question as to whether he might be delinquent in his Selective Service obligations. . . .

2. The information supplied on the certificates facilitates communication between registrants and local boards, simplifying the system and benefiting all concerned. . . .

3. Both certificates carry continual reminders that the registrant must notify his local board of any change of address, and other specified changes in his status. The smooth functioning of the system requires that local boards be continually aware of the status and whereabouts of registrants, and the destruction of certificates deprives the system of a potentially useful notice device.

4. The regulatory scheme involving Selective Service certificates includes clearly valid prohibitions against the alteration, forgery, or similar deceptive misuse of certificates. The destruction or mutilation of certificates obviously increases the difficulty of detecting and tracing abuses such as these. Further, a mutilated certificate might itself be used for deceptive purposes.

The many functions performed by Selective Service certificates establish beyond doubt that Congress has a legitimate and substantial interest in preventing their wanton and unrestrained destruction and assuring their continuing availability by punishing people who knowingly and willfully destroy or mutilate them. And we are unpersuaded that the pre-existence of the nonpossession regulations in any way negates this interest.

In the absence of a question as to multiple punishment, it has never been suggested that there is anything improper in Congress' providing alternative statutory avenues of prosecution to assure the effective protection of one and the same interest. . . .

We think it apparent that the continuing availability to each registrant of his Selective Service certificates substantially furthers the smooth and proper functioning of the system that Congress has established to raise armies. We think it also apparent that the Nation has a vital interest in having a system for raising armies that functions with maximum efficiency and is capable of easily and quickly responding to continually changing circumstances. For these reasons, the Government has a substantial interest in assuring the continuing availability of issued Selective Service certificates.

It is equally clear that the 1965 Amendment specifically protects this substantial governmental interest. We perceive no alternative means that would more precisely and narrowly assure the continuing availability of issued Selective Service certificates than a law which prohibits their willful mutilation or destruction. The 1965 Amendment prohibits such conduct and does nothing more. In other words, both the governmental interest and the operation of the 1965 Amendment are limited to the noncommunicative aspect of O'Brien's conduct. The governmental interest and the scope of the 1965 Amendment are limited to preventing harm to the smooth and efficient functioning of the Selective Service System. When O'Brien deliberately rendered unavailable his registration certificate, he willfully frustrated this governmental interest. For this noncommunicative impact of his conduct, and for nothing else, he was convicted.

The case at bar is therefore unlike one where the alleged governmental interest in regulating conduct arises in some measure because the communication allegedly integral to the conduct is itself thought to be harmful. In *Stromberg v. California*, 283 U.S. 359 (1931), for example, this Court struck down a statutory phrase which punished people who expressed their "opposition to organized government" by displaying "any flag, badge, banner, or device." Since the statute there was aimed at suppressing communication it could not be sustained as a regulation of noncommunicative conduct.

In conclusion, we find that because of the Government's substantial interest in assuring the continuing availability of issued Selective Service certificates, because amended 462 (b) is an appropriately narrow means of protecting this interest and condemns only the independent noncommunicative impact of conduct within its reach, and because the noncommunicative impact of O'Brien's act of burning his registration certificate frustrated the Government's interest, a sufficient governmental interest has been shown to justify O'Brien's conviction.

JUSTICE DOUGLAS, dissenting.

[Douglas wanted the Court to consider whether Congress had the right to conscript troops absent a congressional declaration of war.]

FOR DISCUSSION

The Court puts considerable emphasis on the fact that the draft card is government property and that it is essential to the continued viability of the draft. Would the state be able to prosecute someone for burning a copy of his draft card? Would it make any difference if the audience thought the item being burned were the original?

COHEN V. CALIFORNIA

403 U.S. 15, 91 S.Ct. 1780, 29 L.Ed. 2d 284 (1971)

This case deals with the public display of a four-letter word generally regarded as vulgar. In *Chaplinsky v. New Hampshire* (315 U.S. 568, 1942), the Court had created a class of speech (highly derogatory words said face to face) identified as "**fighting words**" that it did not think was protected by the First Amendment. In this case, the Court distinguished the word in question both from such words in the category of obscenity, which will be examined in the next chapter, and from arguments that the speech was thrust upon unwilling recipients.

Vote: 5–4

JUSTICE HARLAN delivered the opinion of the Court.

This case may seem at first blush too inconsequential to find its way into our books, but the issue it presents is of no small constitutional significance.

Appellant Paul Robert Cohen was convicted in the Los Angeles Municipal Court of violating that part of California Penal Code § 415 which prohibits "maliciously and willfully disturb[ing] the peace or quiet of any neighborhood or person . . . by . . . offensive conduct. . . ." He was given 30 days' imprisonment. The facts upon which his conviction rests are detailed in the opinion of the Court of Appeal of California, Second Appellate District, as follows: "On April 26, 1968, the defendant was observed in the Los Angeles County Courthouse in the corridor outside of division 20 of the municipal court wearing a jacket bearing the words 'Fuck the Draft' which were plainly visible. There were women and children present in the corridor. The defendant was arrested. The defendant testified that he wore the jacket knowing that the words were on the jacket as a means of informing the public of the depth of his feelings against the Vietnam War and the draft. The defendant did not engage in, nor threaten to engage in, nor did anyone as the result of his conduct in fact commit or threaten to commit any act of violence. The defendant did not make any loud or unusual noise, nor was there any evidence that he uttered any sound prior to his arrest."

In affirming the conviction the Court of Appeal held that "offensive conduct" means "behavior which has a tendency to provoke *others* to acts of violence or to in turn disturb the peace," and that the State had proved this element because, on the facts of this case, "it was certainly reasonably foreseeable that such conduct might cause others to rise up to commit a violent act against the person of the defendant or attempt to forceably remove his jacket." The California Supreme Court declined review by a divided vote. We brought the case here, postponing the consideration of the question of our jurisdiction over this appeal to a hearing of the case on the merits. We now reverse. [The Court further dismisses another jurisdictional issue.]

In order to lay hands on the precise issue which this case involves, it is useful first to canvass various matters which this record does *not* present.

The conviction quite clearly rests upon the asserted offensiveness of the *words* Cohen used to convey his message to the public. The only "conduct" which the State sought to punish is the fact of communication. Thus, we deal here with a conviction resting solely upon "speech," not upon any separately identifiable conduct which allegedly was intended by Cohen to be perceived by others as expressive of particular views but which, on its face, does not necessarily convey any message and hence arguably could be regulated without effectively repressing Cohen's ability to express himself. Further, the State certainly lacks power to punish Cohen for the underlying content of the message the inscription conveyed. At least so long as there is no showing of an intent to incite disobedience to or disruption of the draft, Cohen could not, consistently with the First and Fourteenth Amendments, be punished for asserting the evident position on the inutility or immorality of the draft his jacket reflected. *Yates* v. *United States*, 354 U.S. 298 (1957).

Appellant's conviction, then, rests squarely upon his exercise of the "freedom of speech" protected from arbitrary governmental interference by the Constitution and can be justified, if at all, only as a valid regulation of the manner in which he exercised that freedom, not as a permissible prohibition on the substantive message it conveys. This does not end the inquiry, of course, for the First and Fourteenth Amendments have never been thought to give absolute protection to every individual to speak whenever or wherever he pleases, or to use any form of address in any circumstances that he chooses. In this vein, too, however, we think it important to note that several issues typically associated with such problems are not presented here.

In the first place, Cohen was tried under a statute applicable throughout the entire State. Any attempt to support this conviction on the ground that the statute seeks to preserve an appropriately decorous atmosphere in the courthouse where Cohen was arrested must fail in the absence of any language in the statute that would have put appellant on notice that certain kinds of otherwise permissible speech or conduct would nevertheless, under California law, not be tolerated in certain places. No fair reading of the phrase "offensive conduct" can be said sufficiently to inform the ordinary person that distinctions between certain locations are thereby created.

In the second place, as it comes to us, this case cannot be said to fall within those relatively few categories of instances where prior decisions have established the power of government to deal more comprehensively with certain forms of individual expression simply upon a showing that such a form was employed. This is not, for example, an obscenity case. Whatever else may be necessary to give rise to the States' broader power to prohibit obscene expression, such expression must be, in some significant way, erotic. *Roth* v. *United States*, 354 U.S. 476 (1957). It cannot plausibly be maintained that this vulgar allusion to the Selective Service System would conjure up such psychic stimulation in anyone likely to be confronted with Cohen's crudely defaced jacket.

This Court has also held that the States are free to ban the simple use, without a demonstration of additional justifying circumstances, of so-called "fighting words," those personally abusive epithets which, when addressed to the ordinary citizen, are, as a matter of common knowledge, inherently likely to provoke violent reaction. *Chaplinsky* v. *New Hampshire*, 315 U.S. 568 (1942). While the four-letter word displayed by Cohen in relation to the draft is not uncommonly employed in a personally provocative fashion, in this instance it was clearly not "directed to the person of the hearer." *Cantwell* v. *Connecticut*, 310 U.S. 296 (1940). No individual actually or likely to be present could reasonably have regarded the words on appellant's jacket as a direct personal insult. Nor do we have here an instance of the exercise of the State's police power to prevent a speaker from intentionally provoking a given group to hostile reaction. There is, as noted above, no showing that anyone who saw Cohen was in fact violently aroused or that appellant intended such a result.

Finally, in arguments before this Court much has been made of the claim that Cohen's distasteful mode of expression was thrust upon unwilling or unsuspecting viewers, and that the State might therefore legitimately act as it did in order to protect the sensitive from otherwise unavoidable exposure to appellant's crude form of protest. Of course, the mere presumed presence of unwitting listeners or viewers does not serve automatically to justify curtailing all speech capable of giving offense. While this Court has recognized that government may properly act in many situations to prohibit intrusion into the privacy of the home of unwelcome views and ideas which cannot be totally banned from the public dialogue, we have at the same time consistently stressed that "we are often 'captives' outside the sanctuary of the home and subject to objectionable speech." . . ..

In this regard, persons confronted with Cohen's jacket were in a quite different posture than, say, those subjected to the raucous emissions of sound trucks blaring outside their residences. Those in the Los Angeles courthouse could effectively avoid further bombardment of their sensibilities simply by averting their eyes. And, while it may be that one has a more substantial claim to a recognizable privacy interest when walking through a courthouse corridor than, for example, strolling through Central Park, surely it is nothing like the interest in being free from unwanted expression in the confines of one's own home. . . .

II

Against this background, the issue flushed by this case stands out in bold relief. It is whether California can excise, as "offensive conduct," one particular scurrilous epithet from the public discourse, either upon the theory of the court below that its use is inherently likely to cause violent reaction or upon a more general assertion that the States, acting as guardians of public morality, may properly remove this offensive word from the public vocabulary. The rationale of the California court is plainly untenable. At most it reflects an "undifferentiated fear or apprehension of disturbance [which] is not enough to overcome the right to freedom of expression." *Tinker* v. *Des Moines Indep. Community School Dist.*, 393 U.S. 503, 508 (1969). We have been shown no evidence that substantial numbers of citizens are standing ready to strike out physically at whoever may assault their sensibilities with execrations like that uttered by Cohen. . . .

Admittedly, it is not so obvious that the First and Fourteenth Amendments must be taken to disable the States from punishing public utterance of this unseemly expletive in order to maintain what they regard as a suitable level of discourse within the body politic. We think, however, that examination and reflection will reveal the shortcomings of a contrary viewpoint.

At the outset, we cannot overemphasize that, in our judgment, most situations where the State has a justifiable interest in regulating speech will fall within one or more of the various established exceptions, discussed above but not applicable here, to the usual rule that governmental bodies may not prescribe the form or content of individual expression. Equally important to our conclusion is the constitutional backdrop against which our decision must be made. The constitutional right of free expression is powerful medicine in a society as diverse and populous as ours. It is designed and intended to remove governmental restraints from the arena of public discussion, putting the decision as to what views shall be voiced largely into the hands of each of us, in the hope that use of such freedom will ultimately produce a more capable citizenry and more perfect polity and in the belief that no other approach would comport with the premise of individual dignity and choice upon which our political system rests. See *Whitney v. California*, 274 U.S. 357 (1927).

To many, the immediate consequence of this freedom may often appear to be only verbal tumult, discord, and even offensive utterance. These are, however, within established limits, in truth necessary side effects of the broader enduring values which the process of open debate permits us to achieve. That the air may at times seem filled with verbal cacophony is, in this sense, not a sign of weakness but of strength. . . .

Against this perception of the constitutional policies involved, we discern certain more particularized considerations that peculiarly call for reversal of this conviction. First, the principle contended for by the State seems inherently boundless. How is one to distinguish this from any other offensive word? Surely the State has no right to cleanse public debate to the point where it is grammatically palatable to the most squeamish among us. Yet no readily ascertainable general principle exists for stopping short of that result were we to affirm the judgment below. For, while the particular four-letter word being litigated here is perhaps more distasteful than most others of its genre, it is nevertheless often true that one man's vulgarity is another's lyric. Indeed, we think it is largely because governmental officials cannot make principled distinctions in this area that the Constitution leaves matters of taste and style so largely to the individual.

Additionally, we cannot overlook the fact, because it is well illustrated by the episode involved here, that much linguistic expression serves a dual communicative function: it conveys not only ideas capable of relatively precise, detached explication, but otherwise inexpressible emotions as well. In fact, words are often chosen as much for their emotive as their cognitive force. We cannot sanction the view that the Constitution, while solicitous of the cognitive content of individual speech, has little or no regard for that emotive function which, practically speaking, may often be the more important element of the overall message sought to be communicated. Indeed, as Mr. Justice Frankfurter has said, "one of the prerogatives of American citizenship is the right to criticize public men and measures—and that means not only informed and responsible criticism but the freedom to speak foolishly and without moderation." *Baumgartner v. United States,* 322 U.S. 665 (1944).

Finally, and in the same vein, we cannot indulge the facile assumption that one can forbid particular words without also running a substantial risk of suppressing ideas in the process. Indeed, governments might soon seize upon the censorship of particular words as a convenient guise for banning the expression of unpopular views. We have been able, as noted above, to discern little social benefit that might result from running the risk of opening the door to such grave results.

It is, in sum, our judgment that, absent a more particularized and compelling reason for its actions, the State may not, consistently with the First and Fourteenth Amendments, make the simple public display here involved of this single four-letter expletive a criminal offense. Because that is the only arguably sustainable rationale for the conviction here at issue, the judgment below must be *Reversed.*

JUSTICE BLACKMUN, with whom CHIEF JUSTICE BURGER and JUSTICE BLACK join.

I dissent, and I do so for two reasons:

1. Cohen's absurd and immature antic, in my view, was mainly conduct and little speech. . . . Further, the case appears to me to be well within the sphere of *Chaplinsky* v. *New Hampshire,* 315 U.S. 568 (1942), where Mr. Justice Murphy, a known champion of First Amendment freedoms, wrote for a unanimous bench. As a consequence, this Court's agonizing over First Amendment values seems misplaced and unnecessary.

2. I am not at all certain that the California Court of Appeal's construction of § 415 is now the authoritative California construction. . . . [Blackmun does not believe the law was intended to apply to nonviolent acts that did not create a clear and present danger of violence.]

FOR DISCUSSION

Scholars continue to debate the importance of this decision. Was it a milestone, or was the matter so silly that the Court should have declined to hear the case? If the Court had upheld this conviction, do you think it would ultimately have had to distinguish which words were forbidden and which were not? Would there have been any principled way to do that? If so, what would it have been?

TEXAS V. JOHNSON

491 U.S. 397, 109 S.Ct. 2533, 105 L.Ed.2d 342 (1989)

Few issues are more emotional than those connected to the American flag. In this case, the Court had to decide whether Gregory Johnson was guilty of desecrating a venerated object when he burned an American flag outside the Republican National Convention in 1984. Johnson had accompanied his actions with criticisms of the United States. A Texas Court of Criminal Appeals had overturned Johnson's conviction in a lower Texas court.

Vote: 5–4

JUSTICE BRENNAN delivered the opinion of the Court.

After publicly burning an American flag as a means of political protest, Gregory Lee Johnson was convicted of desecrating a flag in violation of Texas law. This case presents the question whether his conviction is consistent with the First Amendment. We hold that it is not.

I

[Brennan reviews Johnson's actions and those of the lower courts.]

II

Johnson was convicted of flag desecration for burning the flag rather than for uttering insulting words. This fact somewhat complicates our consideration of his conviction under the First Amendment. We must first determine whether Johnson's burning of the flag constituted expressive conduct, permitting him to invoke the First Amendment in challenging his conviction. See, *Spence v. Washington*, 418 U.S. 405 (1974). If his conduct was expressive, we next decide whether the State's regulation is related to the suppression of free expression. If the State's regulation is not related to expression, then the less stringent standard we announced in *United States v. O'Brien,* 391 U.S. 367 (1968), for regulations of noncommunicative conduct controls. If it is, then we are outside of *O'Brien*'s test, and we must ask whether this interest justifies Johnson's conviction under a more demanding standard. A third possibility is that the State's asserted interest is simply not implicated on these facts, and in that event the interest drops out of the picture.

The First Amendment literally forbids the abridgment only of "speech," but we have long recognized that its protection does not end at the spoken or written word. . . .

[Brennan illustrates with a wide variety of cases concentrating specifically on those relative to flag desecration.]

We have not automatically concluded, however, that any action taken with respect to our flag is expressive. Instead, in characterizing such action for First Amendment purposes, we have considered the context in which it occurred. In *Spence v. Washington*, 418 U.S. 405 (1974), for example, we emphasized that Spence's taping of a peace sign to his flag was "roughly simultaneous with and concededly triggered by the Cambodian incursion and the Kent State tragedy." The State of Washington had conceded, in fact, that Spence's conduct was a form of communication, and we stated that "the State's concession is inevitable on this record."

The State of Texas conceded for purposes of its oral argument in this case that Johnson's conduct was expressive conduct and this concession seems to us as prudent as was Washington's in *Spence*. Johnson burned an American flag as part—indeed, as the culmination—of a political demonstration that coincided with the convening of the Republican Party and its renomination of Ronald Reagan for President. . . . .

III

The government generally has a freer hand in restricting expressive conduct than it has in restricting the written or spoken word. It may not, however, proscribe particular conduct *because* it has expressive elements. "[W]hat might be termed the more generalized guarantee of freedom of expression makes the communicative nature of conduct an inadequate *basis* for singling out that conduct for proscription. A law *directed at* the communicative nature of conduct must, like a law directed at speech itself, be justified by the substantial showing of need that the First Amendment requires." It is, in short, not simply the verbal or nonverbal nature of the expression, but the governmental interest at stake, that helps to determine whether a restriction on that expression is valid.

Thus, although we have recognized [in *O'Brien*] that where " 'speech' and 'nonspeech' elements are combined in the same course of conduct, a sufficiently important governmental interest in regulating the nonspeech element can justify incidental limitations on First Amendment freedoms," we have limited the applicability of *O'Brien*'s relatively lenient standard to those cases in which "the governmental interest is unrelated to the suppression of free expression." In stating, moreover, that *O'Brien*'s test "in the last analysis is little, if any, different from the standard applied to time, place, or manner restrictions," *Clark v. Community for Creative Non-Violence*, 468 U.S. 288 (1984), we have highlighted the requirement that the governmental interest in question be unconnected to expression in order to come under *O'Brien*'s less demanding rule.

In order to decide whether *O'Brien*'s test applies here, therefore, we must decide whether Texas has asserted an interest in support of Johnson's conviction that is unrelated to the suppression of expression. If we find that an interest asserted by the State is simply not implicated on the facts before us, we need not ask whether *O'Brien*'s test applies. The State offers two separate interests to justify this conviction: preventing breaches of the peace and preserving the flag as a symbol of nationhood and national unity. We hold that the first interest is not implicated on this record and that the second is related to the suppression of expression.

A

Texas claims that its interest in preventing breaches of the peace justifies Johnson's conviction for flag desecration. However, no disturbance of the peace actually occurred or threatened to occur because of Johnson's burning of the flag. . . .

The State's position, therefore, amounts to a claim that an audience that takes serious offense at particular expression is necessarily likely to disturb the peace and that the expression may be prohibited on this basis. Our precedents do not countenance such a presumption. On the contrary, they recognize that a principal "function of free speech under our system of government is to invite dispute. . . ."

Nor does Johnson's expressive conduct fall within that small class of "fighting words" that are "likely to provoke the average person to retaliation, and thereby cause a breach of the peace." *Chaplinsky v. New Hampshire*, 315 U.S. 568 (1942). No reasonable onlooker would have regarded Johnson's generalized expression of dissatisfaction with the policies of the Federal Government as a direct personal insult or an invitation to exchange fisticuffs.

We thus conclude that the State's interest in maintaining order is not implicated on these facts. The State need not worry that our holding will disable it from preserving the peace. We do not suggest that the First Amendment forbids a State to prevent "imminent lawless action." And, in fact, Texas already has a statute specifically prohibiting breaches of the peace, which tends to confirm that Texas need not punish this flag desecration in order to keep the peace. See *Boos v. Barry* [485 U.S. 312 (1988)].

B

The State also asserts an interest in preserving the flag as a symbol of nationhood and national unity. In *Spence*, we acknowledged that the government's interest in preserving the flag's special symbolic value "is directly related to expression in the context of activity" such as affixing a peace symbol to a flag. We are equally persuaded that this interest is related to expression in the case of Johnson's burning of the flag. The State, apparently, is concerned that such conduct will lead people to believe either that the flag does not stand for nationhood and national unity, but instead reflects other, less positive concepts, or that the concepts reflected in the flag do not in fact exist, that is, that we do not enjoy unity as a Nation. These concerns blossom only when a person's treatment of the flag communicates some message, and thus are related "to the suppression of free expression" within the meaning of *O'Brien*. We are thus outside of *O'Brien*'s test altogether.

IV

It remains to consider whether the State's interest in preserving the flag as a symbol of nationhood and national unity justifies Johnson's conviction.

As in *Spence*, "[w]e are confronted with a case of prosecution for the expression of an idea through activity," and "[a]ccordingly, we must examine with particular care the interests advanced by [petitioner] to support its prosecution." Johnson was not, we add, prosecuted for the expression of just any idea; he was prosecuted for his expression of dissatisfaction with the policies of this country, expression situated at the core of our First Amendment values.

Moreover, Johnson was prosecuted because he knew that his politically charged expression would cause "serious offense." If he had burned the flag as a means of disposing of it because it was dirty or torn, he would not have been convicted of flag desecration under this Texas law: federal law designates burning as the preferred means of disposing of a flag "when it is in such condition that it is no longer a fitting emblem for display," and Texas has no quarrel with this means of disposal. The Texas law is thus not aimed at protecting the physical integrity of the flag in all circumstances, but is designed instead to protect it only against impairments that would cause serious offense to others. . . .

Whether Johnson's treatment of the flag violated Texas law thus depended on the likely communicative impact of his expressive conduct. Our decision in *Boos v. Barry,* tells us that this restriction on Johnson's expression is content based. In *Boos*, we considered the constitutionality of a law prohibiting "the display of any sign within 500 feet of a foreign embassy if that sign tends to bring that foreign government into 'public odium' or 'public disrepute.' " Rejecting the argument that the law was content neutral because it was justified by "our international law obligation to shield diplomats from speech that offends their dignity," we held that "[t]he emotive impact of speech on its audience is not a 'secondary effect' " unrelated to the content of the expression itself. According to the principles announced in *Boos*, Johnson's political expression was restricted because of the content of the message he conveyed. We must therefore subject the State's asserted interest in preserving the special symbolic character of the flag to "the most exacting scrutiny." *Boos* v. *Barry*.

Texas argues that its interest in preserving the flag as a symbol of nationhood and national unity survives this close analysis. Quoting extensively from the writings of this Court chronicling the flag's historic and symbolic role in our society, the State emphasizes the " 'special place' " reserved for the flag in our Nation. The State's argument is not that it has an interest simply in maintaining the flag as a symbol of *something*, no matter what it symbolizes; indeed, if that were the State's position, it would be difficult to see how that interest is endangered by highly symbolic conduct such as Johnson's. Rather, the State's claim is that it has an interest in preserving the flag as a symbol of *nationhood* and *national unity*, a symbol with a determinate range of meanings. According to Texas, if one physically treats the flag in a way that would tend to cast doubt on either the idea that nationhood and national unity are the flag's referents or that national unity actually exists, the message conveyed thereby is a harmful one and therefore may be prohibited.

If there is a bedrock principle underlying the First Amendment, it is that the government may not prohibit the expression of an idea simply because society finds the idea itself offensive or disagreeable. [Brennan cites a variety of precedents.]

Texas' focus on the precise nature of Johnson's expression, moreover, misses the point of our prior decisions: their enduring lesson, that the government may not prohibit expression simply because it disagrees with its message, is not dependent on the particular mode in which one chooses to express an idea. If we were to hold that a State may forbid flag burning wherever it is likely to endanger the flag's symbolic role, but allow it wherever burning a flag promotes that role—as where, for example, a person ceremoniously burns a dirty flag—we would be saying that when it comes to impairing the flag's physical integrity, the flag itself may be used as a symbol—as a substitute for the written or spoken word or a "short cut from mind to mind"—only in one direction. We would be permitting a State to "prescribe what shall be orthodox" by saying that one may burn the flag to convey one's attitude toward it and its referents only if one does not endanger the flag's representation of nationhood and national unity.

There is, moreover, no indication—either in the text of the Constitution or in our cases interpreting it—that a separate juridical category exists for the American flag alone. Indeed, we would not be surprised to learn that the persons who framed our Constitution and wrote the Amendment that we now construe were not known for their reverence for the Union Jack. The First Amendment does not guarantee that other concepts virtually sacred to our Nation as a whole—such as the principle that discrimination on the basis of race is odious and destructive—will go unquestioned in the market-place of ideas. See *Brandenburg v. Ohio*, 395 U.S. 444 (1969). We decline, therefore, to create for the flag an exception to the joust of principles protected by the First Amendment.

It is not the State's ends, but its means, to which we object. It cannot be gainsaid that there is a special place reserved for the flag in this Nation, and thus we do not doubt that the government has a legitimate interest in making efforts to "preserv[e] the national flag as an unalloyed symbol of our country." *Spence.* We reject the suggestion, urged at oral argument by counsel for Johnson, that the government lacks "any state interest whatsoever" in regulating the manner in which the flag may be displayed. Congress has, for example, enacted precatory regulations describing the proper treatment of the flag, and we cast no doubt on the legitimacy of its interest in making such recommendations. To say that the government has an interest in encouraging proper treatment of the flag, however, is not to say that it may criminally punish a person for burning a flag as a means of political protest. "National unity as an end which officials may foster by persuasion and example is not in question. The problem is whether under our Constitution compulsion as here employed is a permissible means for its achievement." [*West Virginia Board of Education v. Barnette,* 319 U.S. 624 (1943).]

We are fortified in today's conclusion by our conviction that forbidding criminal punishment for conduct such as Johnson's will not endanger the special role played by our flag or the feelings it inspires. To paraphrase Justice Holmes, we submit that nobody can suppose that this one gesture of an unknown man will change our Nation's attitude towards its flag. See *Abrams* v. *United States,* 250 U.S. 616 (1919). Indeed, Texas' argument that the burning of an American flag " 'is an act having a high likelihood to cause a breach of the peace,' " and its statute's implicit assumption that physical mistreatment of the flag will lead to "serious offense," tend to confirm that the flag's special role is not in danger; if it were, no one would riot or take offense because a flag had been burned.

We are tempted to say, in fact, that the flag's deservedly cherished place in our community will be strengthened, not weakened, by our holding today. Our decision is a reaffirmation of the principles of freedom and inclusiveness that the flag best reflects, and of the conviction that our toleration of criticism such as Johnson's is a sign and source of our strength. . . .

The way to preserve the flag's special role is not to punish those who feel differently about these matters. It is to persuade them that they are wrong. . . .

V

Johnson was convicted for engaging in expressive conduct. The State's interest in preventing breaches of the peace does not support his conviction because Johnson's conduct did not threaten to disturb the peace. Nor does the State's interest in preserving the flag as a symbol of nationhood and national unity justify his criminal conviction for engaging in political expression. The judgment of the Texas Court of Criminal Appeals is therefore *Affirmed.*

JUSTICE KENNEDY, concurring.

The hard fact is that sometimes we must make decisions we do not like. We make them because they are right, right in the sense that the law and the Constitution, as we see them, compel the result. And so great is our commitment to the process that, except in the rare case, we do not pause to express distaste for the result, perhaps for fear of undermining a valued principle that dictates the decision. This is one of those rare cases.

CHIEF JUSTICE REHNQUIST, with whom JUSTICES WHITE and O'CONNOR join, dissenting.

In holding this Texas statute unconstitutional, the Court ignores Justice Holmes' familiar aphorism that "a page of history is worth a volume of logic." *New York Trust Co. v. Eisner*, 256 U.S. 345 (1921). For more than 200 years, the American flag has occupied a unique position as the symbol of our Nation, a uniqueness that justifies a governmental prohibition against flag burning in the way respondent Johnson did here.

[Rehnquist proceeds to examine references to the U.S. flag throughout American history.]

The American flag, then, throughout more than 200 years of our history, has come to be the visible symbol embodying our Nation. It does not represent the views of any particular political party, and it does not represent any particular political philosophy. The flag is not simply another "idea" or "point of view" competing for recognition in the marketplace of ideas. Millions and millions of Americans regard it with an almost mystical reverence regardless of what sort of social, political, or philosophical beliefs they may have. I cannot agree that the First Amendment invalidates the Act of Congress, and the laws of 48 of the 50 States, which make criminal the public burning of the flag.

Here it may equally well be said that the public burning of the American flag by Johnson was no essential part of any exposition of ideas, and at the same time it had a tendency to incite a breach of the peace. Johnson was free to make any verbal denunciation of the flag that he wished; indeed, he was free to burn the flag in private. He could publicly burn other symbols of the Government or effigies of political leaders. He did lead a march through the streets of Dallas, and conducted a rally in front of the Dallas City Hall. He engaged in a "die-in" to protest nuclear weapons. He shouted out various slogans during the march, including: "Reagan, Mondale which will it be? Either one means World War III"; "Ronald Reagan, killer of the hour, Perfect example of U.S. power"; and "red, white and blue, we spit on you, you stand for plunder, you will go under." For none of these acts was he arrested or prosecuted; it was only when he proceeded to burn publicly an American flag stolen from its rightful owner that he violated the Texas statute.

The result of the Texas statute is obviously to deny one in Johnson's frame of mind one of many means of "symbolic speech." Far from being a case of "one picture being worth a thousand words," flag burning is the equivalent of an inarticulate grunt or roar that, it seems fair to say, is most likely to be indulged in not to express any particular idea, but to antagonize others. . . .

The Court concludes its opinion with a regrettably patronizing civics lecture, presumably addressed to the Members of both Houses of Congress, the members of the 48 state legislatures that enacted prohibitions against flag burning, and the troops fighting under that flag in Vietnam who objected to its being burned: "The way to preserve the flag's special role is not to punish those who feel differently about these matters. It is to persuade them that they are wrong." The Court's role as the final expositor of the Constitution is well established, but its role as a Platonic guardian admonishing those responsible to public opinion as if they were truant schoolchildren has no similar place in our system of government. The cry of "no taxation without representation" animated those who revolted against the English Crown to found our Nation—the idea that those who submitted to government should have some say as to what kind of laws would be passed. Surely one of the high purposes of a democratic society is to legislate against conduct that is regarded as evil and profoundly offensive to the majority of people—whether it be murder, embezzlement, pollution, or flag burning.

Our Constitution wisely places limits on powers of legislative majorities to act, but the declaration of such limits by this Court "is, at all times, a question of much delicacy, which ought seldom, if ever, to be decided in the affirmative, in a doubtful case." *Fletcher v. Peck*, 6 Cranch 87 (1810). Uncritical extension of constitutional protection to the burning of the flag risks the frustration of the very purpose for which organized governments are instituted. The Court decides that the American flag is just another symbol, about which not only must opinions pro and con be tolerated, but for which the most minimal public respect may not be enjoined. The government may conscript men into the Armed Forces where they must fight and perhaps die for the flag, but the government may not prohibit the public burning of the banner under which they fight. I would uphold the Texas statute as applied in this case.

JUSTICE STEVENS, dissenting.

As the Court analyzes this case, it presents the question whether the State of Texas, or indeed the Federal Government, has the power to prohibit the public desecration of the American flag. The question is unique. In my judgment rules that apply to a host of other symbols, such as state flags, armbands, or various privately promoted emblems of political or commercial identity, are not necessarily controlling. Even if flag burning could be considered just another species of symbolic speech under the logical application of the rules that the Court has developed in its interpretation of the First Amendment in other contexts, this case has an intangible dimension that makes those rules inapplicable.

A country's flag is a symbol of more than "nationhood and national unity." It also signifies the ideas that characterize the society that has chosen that emblem as well as the special history that has animated the growth and power of those ideas. . . .

So it is with the American flag. It is more than a proud symbol of the courage, the determination, and the gifts of nature that transformed 13 fledgling Colonies into a world power. It is a symbol of freedom, of equal opportunity, of religious tolerance, and of good will for other peoples who share our aspirations. The symbol carries its message to dissidents both at home and abroad who may have no interest at all in our national unity or survival.

The value of the flag as a symbol cannot be measured. Even so, I have no doubt that the interest in preserving that value for the future is both significant and legitimate. Conceivably that value will be enhanced by the Court's conclusion that our national commitment to free expression is so strong that even the United States as ultimate guarantor of that freedom is without power to prohibit the desecration of its unique symbol. But I am unpersuaded. The creation of a federal right to post bulletin boards and graffiti on the Washington Monument might enlarge the market for free expression, but at a cost I would not pay. Similarly, in my considered judgment, sanctioning the public desecration of the flag will tarnish its value—both for those who cherish the ideas for which it waves and for those who desire to don the robes of martyrdom by burning it. That tarnish is not justified by the trivial burden on free expression occasioned by requiring that an available, alternative mode of expression—including uttering words critical of the flag, see *Street v. New York*, 394 U.S. 576 (1969)—be employed.

The Court is therefore quite wrong in blandly asserting that respondent "was prosecuted for his expression of dissatisfaction with the policies of this country, expression situated at the core of our First Amendment values." Respondent was prosecuted because of the method he chose to express his dissatisfaction with those policies. Had he chosen to spray-paint—or perhaps convey with a motion picture projector—his message of dissatisfaction on the facade of the Lincoln Memorial, there would be no question about the power of the Government to prohibit his means of expression. The prohibition would be supported by the legitimate interest in preserving the quality of an important national asset. Though the asset at stake in this case is intangible, given its unique value, the same interest supports a prohibition on the desecration of the American flag.

The ideas of liberty and equality have been an irresistible force in motivating leaders like Patrick Henry, Susan B. Anthony, and Abraham Lincoln, schoolteachers like Nathan Hale and Booker T. Washington, the Philippine Scouts who fought at Bataan, and the soldiers who scaled the bluff at Omaha Beach. If those ideas are worth fighting for—and our history demonstrates that they are—it cannot be true that the flag that uniquely symbolizes their power is not itself worthy of protection from unnecessary desecration.

I respectfully dissent.

[Congress responded to this decision by adopting the Flag Protection Act of 1989, providing for the criminal conviction of individuals who committed flag desecration. The Supreme Court invalidated this law in *United States v. Eichman*, 496 U.S. 310 (1990).]

FOR DISCUSSION

One can approach this case by asking whether it is a proper interpretation of the First Amendment or by asking whether, if it is, the Constitution should be changed. What do you think? What would be the pros and cons of such an amendment? Should the Court be more reluctant to adopt amendments modifying interpretations of provisions of the Bill of Rights than of other constitutional provisions? Why or why not?

VIRGINIA V. BLACK

538 U.S. 343, 123 S.Ct. 1536, 155 L.Ed. 2d 535 (2003)

Few actions can be more intimidating than burning a cross—an event often associated with violence by the Ku Klux Klan against African Americans, Jews, and immigrants. In this case the Court was to decide on the constitutionality of a Virginia law that made burning a cross for the purpose of intimidation illegal and considered cross burning prima facie evidence of an intent to intimidate.

Vote: 6–3; 5–4

JUSTICE O'CONNOR delivered the opinion of the Court

In this case we consider whether the Commonwealth of Virginia's statute banning cross burning with "an intent to intimidate a person or group of persons" violates the First Amendment. We conclude that while a State, consistent with the First Amendment, may ban cross burning carried out with the intent to intimidate, the provision in the Virginia statute treating any cross burning as prima facie evidence of intent to intimidate renders the statute unconstitutional in its current form.

I

Respondents Barry Black, Richard Elliott, and Jonathan O'Mara were convicted separately of violating Virginia's cross-burning statute, § 18.2–423. [O'Connor observes that Black was convicted of a cross burning that occurred at a Klan rally on private property with the owner's consent in a relatively secluded place. At trial, the Court instructed the jury that "the burning of a cross by itself is sufficient evidence from which you may infer the required intent [to intimidate]." Elliott and O'Mara, who were not Klan members, had been convicted of attempting to burn a cross of the yard of a next-door neighbor in Virginia Beach, Virginia, with whom they had previously quarreled about using the backyard for a firing range. In a split decision, the Virginia Supreme Court had held that the statute was facially unconstitutional.]

II

Cross burning originated in the 14th century as a means for Scottish tribes to signal each other. See M. Newton & J. Newton, *The Ku Klux Klan: An Encyclopedia* 145 (1991). Sir Walter Scott used cross burnings for dramatic effect in *The Lady of the Lake*, where the burning cross signified both a summons and a call to arms. Cross burning in this country, however, long ago became unmoored from its Scottish ancestry. Burning a cross in the United States is inextricably intertwined with the history of the Ku Klux Klan.

The first Ku Klux Klan began in Pulaski, Tennessee, in the spring of 1866. Although the Ku Klux Klan started as a social club, it soon changed into something far different. The Klan fought Reconstruction and the corresponding drive to allow freed blacks to participate in the political process. Soon the Klan imposed "a veritable reign of terror" throughout the South. The Klan employed tactics such as whipping, threatening to burn people at the stake, and murder. The Klan's victims included blacks, southern whites who disagreed with the Klan, and "carpetbagger" northern whites.

The activities of the Ku Klux Klan prompted legislative action at the national level. . . .

The genesis of the second Klan began in 1905, with the publication of Thomas Dixon's *The Clansmen: An Historical Romance of the Ku Klux Klan*. . . .

From the inception of the second Klan, cross burnings have been used to communicate both threats of violence and messages of shared ideology. . . .

Often, the Klan used cross burnings as a tool of intimidation and a threat of impending violence. [O'Connor cites further examples.]

Throughout the history of the Klan, cross burnings have also remained potent symbols of shared group identity and ideology. The burning cross became a symbol of the Klan itself and a central feature of Klan gatherings. According to the Klan constitution (called the kloran), the "fiery cross" was the "emblem of that sincere, unselfish devotedness of all klansmen to the sacred purpose and principles we have espoused." The Ku Klux Klan Hearings before the House Committee on Rules, 67th Cong. And the Klan has often published its newsletters and magazines under the name *The Fiery Cross*.

At Klan gatherings across the country, cross burning became the climax of the rally or the initiation.

To this day, regardless of whether the message is a political one or whether the message is also meant to intimidate, the burning of a cross is a "symbol of hate." *Capitol Square Review and Advisory Bd. v. Pinette,* 515 U.S. 753 (1995). And while cross burning sometimes carries no intimidating message, at other times the intimidating message is the *only* message conveyed. For example, when a cross burning is directed at a particular person not affiliated with the Klan, the burning cross often serves as a message of intimidation, designed to inspire in the victim a fear of bodily harm. Moreover, the history of violence associated with the Klan shows that the possibility of injury or death is not just hypothetical. The person who burns a cross directed at a particular person often is making a serious threat, meant to coerce the victim to comply with the Klan's wishes unless the victim is willing to risk the wrath of the Klan. . . . .

In sum, while a burning cross does not inevitably convey a message of intimidation, often the cross burner intends that the recipients of the message fear for their lives. And when a cross burning is used to intimidate, few if any messages are more powerful.

III

A

[O'Connor cites the purpose of the First Amendment in protecting "free trade in ideas" and its application to "symbolic or expressive conduct as well as to actual speech."]

"True threats" encompass those statements where the speaker means to communicate a serious expression of an intent to commit an act of unlawful violence to a particular individual or group of individuals. The speaker need not actually intend to carry out the threat. Rather, a prohibition on true threats "protects individuals from the fear of violence" and "from the disruption that fear engenders," in addition to protecting people "from the possibility that the threatened violence will occur." Intimidation in the constitutionally proscribable sense of the word is a type of true threat, where a speaker directs a threat to a person or group of persons with the intent of placing the victim in fear of bodily harm or death. Respondents do not contest that some cross burnings fit within this meaning of intimidating speech, and rightly so. As noted in Part II, the history of cross burning in this country shows that cross burning is often intimidating, intended to create a pervasive fear in victims that they are a target of violence.

B

The Supreme Court of Virginia ruled that in light of *R. A. V. v. City of St. Paul*, 505 U.S. 377 (1992), even if it is constitutional to ban cross burning in a content-neutral manner, the Virginia cross-burning statute is unconstitutional because it discriminates on the basis of content and viewpoint. It is true, as the Supreme Court of Virginia held, that the burning of a cross is symbolic expression. . . .

The fact that cross burning is symbolic expression, however, does not resolve the constitutional question. The Supreme Court of Virginia relied upon *R. A. V.* v. *City of St. Paul*, to conclude that once a statute discriminates on the basis of this type of content, the law is unconstitutional. We disagree.

In *R. A. V.*, we held that a local ordinance that banned certain symbolic conduct, including cross burning, when done with the knowledge that such conduct would " 'arouse anger, alarm or resentment in others on the basis of race, color, creed, religion or gender' " was unconstitutional. We held that the ordinance did not pass constitutional muster because it discriminated on the basis of content by targeting only those individuals who "provoke violence" on a basis specified in the law. The ordinance did not cover "those who wish to use 'fighting words' in connection with other ideas—to express hostility, for example, on the basis of political affiliation, union membership, or homosexuality." This content-based discrimination was unconstitutional because it allowed the city "to impose special prohibitions on those speakers who express views on disfavored subjects."

We did not hold in *R. A. V.* that the First Amendment prohibits *all* forms of content-based discrimination within a proscribable area of speech. Rather, we specifically stated that some types of content discrimination did not violate the First Amendment:

"When the basis for the content discrimination consists entirely of the very reason the entire class of speech at issue is proscribable, no significant danger of idea or viewpoint discrimination exists. Such a reason, having been adjudged neutral enough to support exclusion of the entire class of speech from First Amendment protection, is also neutral enough to form the basis of distinction within the class."

Similarly, Virginia's statute does not run afoul of the First Amendment insofar as it bans cross burning with intent to intimidate. Unlike the statute at issue in *R. A. V.*, the Virginia statute does not single out for opprobrium only that speech directed toward "one of the specified disfavored topics." It does not matter whether an individual burns a cross with intent to intimidate because of the victim's race, gender, or religion, or because of the victim's "political affiliation, union membership, or homosexuality." Moreover, as a factual matter it is not true that cross burners direct their intimidating conduct solely to racial or religious minorities.

IV

The Supreme Court of Virginia ruled in the alternative that Virginia's cross-burning statute was unconstitutionally overbroad due to its provision stating that "any such burning of a cross shall be prima facie evidence of an intent to intimidate a person or group of persons."

. . . The provision permits the Commonwealth to arrest, prosecute, and convict a person based solely on the fact of cross burning itself.

It is apparent that the provision as so interpreted " 'would create an unacceptable risk of the suppression of ideas.' " The act of burning a cross may mean that a person is engaging in constitutionally proscribable intimidation. But that same act may mean only that the person is engaged in core political speech. The prima facie evidence provision in this statute blurs the line between these two meanings of a burning cross. As interpreted by the jury instruction, the provision chills constitutionally protected political speech because of the possibility that a State will prosecute—and potentially convict—somebody engaging only in lawful political speech at the core of what the First Amendment is designed to protect.

As the history of cross burning indicates, a burning cross is not always intended to intimidate. Rather, sometimes the cross burning is a statement of ideology, a symbol of group solidarity. . . . The prima facie provision makes no effort to distinguish among these different types of cross burnings. It does not distinguish between a cross burning done with the purpose of creating anger or resentment and a cross burning done with the purpose of threatening or intimidating a victim. It does not distinguish between a cross burning at a public rally or a cross burning on a neighbor's lawn. It does not treat the cross burning directed at an individual differently from the cross burning directed at a group of like-minded believers. It allows a jury to treat a cross burning on the property of another with the owner's acquiescence in the same manner as a cross burning on the property of another without the owner's permission. . . .

It may be true that a cross burning, even at a political rally, arouses a sense of anger or hatred among the vast majority of citizens who see a burning cross. But this sense of anger or hatred is not sufficient to ban all cross burnings. . . .

For these reasons, the prima facie evidence provision, as interpreted through the jury instruction and as applied in Barry Black's case, is unconstitutional on its face.

V

With respect to Barry Black, we agree with the Supreme Court of Virginia that his conviction cannot stand, and we affirm the judgment of the Supreme Court of Virginia. With respect to Elliott and O'Mara, we vacate the judgment of the Supreme Court of Virginia, and remand the case for further proceedings.

It is so ordered.

JUSTICE THOMAS, dissenting.

In every culture, certain things acquire meaning well beyond what outsiders can comprehend. That goes for both the sacred, see *Texas* v. *Johnson*, 491 U.S. 397 (1989), and the profane. I believe that cross burning is the paradigmatic example of the latter.

I

Although I agree with the majority's conclusion that it is constitutionally permissible to "ban . . . cross burning carried out with intent to intimidate," I believe that the majority errs in imputing an expressive component to the activity in question. In my view, whatever expressive value cross burning has, the legislature simply wrote it out by banning only intimidating conduct undertaken by a particular means. A conclusion that the statute prohibiting cross burning with intent to intimidate sweeps beyond a prohibition on certain conduct into the zone of expression overlooks not only the words of the statute but also reality.

A

"In holding [the ban on cross burning with intent to intimidate] unconstitutional, the Court ignores Justice Holmes' familiar aphorism [in New York Trust Co. v. Eisner, 256 U.S. 345 (1921)] that 'a page of history is worth a volume of logic.' " . . .

"The world's oldest, most persistent terrorist organization is not European or even Middle Eastern in origin. Fifty years before the Irish Republican Army was organized, a century before Al Fatah declared its holy war on Israel, the Ku Klux Klan was actively harassing, torturing and murdering in the United States. Today . . . its members remain fanatically committed to a course of violent opposition to social progress and racial equality in the United States." M. Newton & J. Newton, *The Ku Klux Klan: An Encyclopedia* vii (1991).

To me, the majority's brief history of the Ku Klux Klan only reinforces this common understanding of the Klan as a terrorist organization, which, in its endeavor to intimidate, or even eliminate those its dislikes, uses the most brutal of methods.

Such methods typically include cross burning—"a tool for the intimidation and harassment of racial minorities, Catholics, Jews, Communists, and any other groups hated by the Klan." *Capitol Square Review and Advisory Bd. v. Pinette*, 515 U.S. 753 (1995). For those not easily frightened, cross burning has been followed by more extreme measures, such as beatings and murder. Juan Williams, *Eyes on the Prize: America's Civil Rights Years 1954–1965*, (1965). As the Solicitor General points out, the association between acts of intimidating cross burning and violence is well documented in recent American history. Indeed, the connection between cross burning and violence is well ingrained, and lower courts have so recognized.

In our culture, cross burning has almost invariably meant lawlessness and understandably instills in its victims well-grounded fear of physical violence.

B

[Thomas illustrates the role that cross burning has played in intimidating minorities in Virginia.]

Accordingly, this statute prohibits only conduct, not expression. And, just as one cannot burn down someone's house to make a political point and then seek refuge in the First Amendment, those who hate cannot terrorize and intimidate to make their point. In light of my conclusion that the statute here addresses only conduct, there is no need to analyze it under any of our First Amendment tests.

II

Even assuming that the statute implicates the First Amendment, in my view, the fact that the statute permits a jury to draw an inference of intent to intimidate from the cross burning itself presents no constitutional problems. Therein lies my primary disagreement with the plurality.

A

"The threshold inquiry is ascertaining the constitutional analysis applicable to [a jury instruction involving a presumption] is to determine the nature of the presumption it describes." *Francis v. Franklin*, 471 U.S. 307 (1985). We have categorized the presumptions as either permissive inferences or mandatory presumptions.

To the extent we do have a construction of this statute by the Virginia Supreme Court, we know that both the majority and the dissent agreed that the presumption was "a statutorily supplied *inference*." Under Virginia law, the term "inference" has a well-defined meaning and is distinct from the term "presumption."

A presumption is a rule of law that compels the fact finder to draw a certain conclusion or a certain inference from a given set of facts. The primary significance of a presumption is that it operates to shift to the opposing party the burden of producing evidence tending to rebut the presumption. No presumption, however, can operate to shift the ultimate burden of persuasion from the party upon whom it was originally cast.

Because the prima facie clause here is an inference, not an irrebuttable presumption, there is all the more basis under our Due Process precedents to sustain this statute.

B

The plurality, however, is troubled by the presumption because this is a First Amendment case. The plurality laments the fate of an innocent cross-burner who burns a cross, but does so without an intent to intimidate. The plurality fears the chill on expression because, according to the plurality, the inference permits "the Commonwealth to arrest, prosecute and convict a person based solely on the fact of cross burning itself." First, it is, at the very least, unclear that the inference comes into play during arrest and initiation of a prosecution, that is, prior to the instructions stage of an actual trial. Second, as I explained above, the inference is rebuttable and, as the jury instructions given in this case demonstrate, Virginia law still requires the jury to find the existence of each element, including intent to intimidate, beyond a reasonable doubt.

Moreover, even in the First Amendment context, the Court has upheld such regulations where conduct that initially appears culpable, ultimately results in dismissed charges.

III

Because I would uphold the validity of this statute, I respectfully dissent.

FOR DISCUSSION

To what degree do you think this decision is compatible with the Court's decision in *Brandenburg v. Ohio*? With *R.A.V.*? What would be the advantages and disadvantages of a constitutional amendment that classified all cross burnings as hate speech?

GLOSSARY

Alien and Sedition Acts:. Acts passed by Federalists in 1798 that made it more difficult for immigrants to become citizens and also punished individuals who criticized the government or president of the United States.

Bad Tendency Test: A test, generally less deferential to speech than the clear and present danger test, whereby the Court allowed Congress to legislate against speech that has an inclination toward inciting or causing illegal activities.

Clear and Present Danger Test: First articulated by Justice Oliver Wendell Holmes in *Schenck v. United States,* 249 U.S. 47 (1919): Congress had the right to legislate against actions that led to a clear and present danger that Congress, in turn, had the right to prevent.

Content-Based [Regulation]: Courts subject regulations based on the content of speech to the strictest scrutiny. In a related vein, the Supreme Court also looks with disfavor on viewpoint discrimination, which limits speech based on the ideology of the speaker.

Content-Neutral [Speech Regulation]: Regulation based not on the content of the speech but on the time, place, or manner of its dissemination.

Facial Challenge: A lawsuit that claims that a law is invalid on its face. Such challenges are generally more difficult to prove than "as-applied" challenges, which focus more specifically on the way that a law is being applied or enforced.

Fighting Words: Highly insulting face-to-face speech that the Court has decided is exempt from First Amendment protections because such words are more likely to evoke emotional than rational responses.

Gravity of the Evil Test: The test used by the Supreme Court in *Dennis v. United States*, in which it considered the perceived gravity of the unwanted result that speech might elicit in determining whether its suppression was justified.

Marketplace of Ideas: Analogy often used in discussions of freedom of speech and expression; it suggests that the best and truest ideas will be most likely to get assent by the greatest number of people.

Preferred Position: The place of freedom of speech in contemporary law: namely, that it is paramount and generally trumps any rights with which it comes into conflict.

Republican Government: A term used in the Constitution, and by America's Founding Fathers, to refer to representative government.

Speech and Debate Clause: A provision in Article I, Section 6, predating the First Amendment and exempting members of Congress from prosecution for things that they said before Congress.

Time, Place, and Manner Restrictions: Because courts are generally deferential to the people's right to freedom of speech, regulations that are related to the time, place, and manner of speech, rather than to its content, are subject to limitation.

Viewpoint Restrictions: Regulation or restriction of speech based on its particular message which is disfavored by the government.

SELECTED BIBLIOGRAPHY

Abraham, Henry J., and Barbara A. Perry. 2003. *Freedom and the Court: Civil Rights and Liberties in the United States.* 8th ed. Lawrence: University Press of Kansas.

Chaffee, Zechariah, Jr. 1964. *Free Speech in the United States.* Cambridge, MA: Harvard University Press.

Curtis, Michael Kent. 2000. *Free Speech: The People's Darling Privilege.* Durham, NC: Duke University Press.

Dupre, Anne P. 2009. *Speaking Up: The Unintended Costs of Free Speech in Public Schools.* Cambridge, MA: Harvard University Press.

Ellis, Richard J. 2005. *To the Flag: The Unlikely History of the Pledge of Allegiance* Lawrence: University Press of Kansas.

Finan, Christopher M. 2007. *From the Palmer Raids to the Patriot Act: A History of the Fight for Free Speech in America.* Boston: Beacon Press.

Kalven, Harry, Jr. 1988. *A Worthy Tradition: Freedom of Speech in America.* New York: Harper & Row.

Poe, Lucan A., Jr. 1991. *The Fourth Estate and the Constitution: Freedom of the Press in America.* Berkeley: University of California Press.

Rabban, David M. 1997. *Free Speech in Its Forgotten Years.* New York: Cambridge University Press.

Shiffrin, Steven H. 2016. *What's Wrong with the First Amendment.* New York: Cambridge University Press.

Smolla, A. 1992. *Free Speech in an Open Society.* New York: Alfred A. Knopf.

Tedford, Thomas, and Dale A. Herbeck. 2005. *Freedom of Speech in the United States.* 5th ed. State College, PA: Strata Publishing.

Tushnet, Mark V. and Alan K. Chen. 2017. *Free Speech Beyond Words: The Surprising Reach of the First Amendment.* New York: New York University Press.

Van Alstyne, William W. 1984. *Interpretations of the First Amendment.* Durham, NC: Duke University Press.

Vile, John R., David L. Hudson Jr., and David Schultz. 2009. *Encyclopedia of the First Amendment.* Washington, DC: CQ Press.

Weaver, Russell L., and Donald E. Lively. 2003. *Understanding the First Amendment.* New York: Matthew Bender.

CHAPTER IV

Free Press, Assembly, Petition, and Other Types of Speech

Timeline: Free Press Assembly, and Petition

1735 New York newspaper publisher Peter Zenger is acquitted of charges of seditious libel against the British governor of New York.

1917 The United States enters World War I.

1931 In *Near v. Minnesota* the Supreme Court rules that the First Amendment Freedom of Press Clause was incorporated to apply to the states by way of the Fourteenth Amendment.

1936 The Supreme Court rules in *Grosjean v. American Press Co.* that a tax on newspapers violated the First Amendment's Freedom of the Press Clause.

1940 The Smith Act makes it illegal to advocate the violent overthrow of the U.S. government.

1941 The United States enters World War II.

1941 The Supreme Court rules in *Bridges v. California and Times-Mirror Co. v. Superior Court of California* that a decision by a newspaper to print a telegram by labor officials critical of a court decision was protected by the First Amendment.

1945 The United States drops two atomic bombs on Japan, ending World War II.

1946 Winston Churchill gives his famous Iron Curtain speech at Westminster College in Fulton, Missouri.

1947 The fairness doctrine is adopted.

1949 USSR explodes its first nuclear bomb.

1949 The cold war between the United States and the Soviet Union begins.

1950 The Supreme Court rules in *American Communications Association v. Douds* that part of the 1947 Taft-Hartley Act does not violate the First Amendment; the provision in question barred any investigation by the National Labor Relations Board unless all officers of a labor organization involved in a dispute have signed an affidavit certifying that they are not Communists.

1950 The Korean War begins.

1950 Senator Joseph McCarthy of Wisconsin gives a speech asserting that the State Department is employing individuals known to be members of the Communist Party.

1951 The Supreme Court upholds the constitutionality of the Smith Act in *Dennis v. United States.*

1952 The Supreme Court rules in *Burstyn v. Wilson* that films and motion pictures are protected by the First Amendment.

1952 The Supreme Court rules in *Adler v. Board of Education* that a New York State law barring employment in the public schools any person who is a member of an organization advocating the unlawful overthrow of the government of the United States does not violate the First Amendment.

1953 Julius and Ethel Rosenberg are executed as spies.

1953 Truce is declared in the Korean War.

1957 The Supreme Court rules in *Roth v. United States* that obscenity is not protected by the First Amendment.

1957 The Supreme Court overturns the conviction of several members of the American Communist Party under the Smith Act in *Yates v. United States.*

1958 The Supreme Court rules in *National Association for the Advancement of Colored People v. State of Alabama* that a state law requiring a nonprofit organization to divulge its membership list violates the First Amendment.

1959 The Supreme Court rules in *Kingsley International Pictures Corporation v. Regents* that a New York State law applied to ban the film *Lady Chatterley's Lover* violates the First Amendment.

1963 In *Edwards v. South Carolina* the Supreme Court rules that a march to the courthouse is protected under the assembly and petition clauses of the First Amendment.

1964 The Supreme Court rules in *New York Times Co. v. Sullivan* that an individual suing a newspaper for libel cannot prevail unless it can be shown that the paper demonstrated a reckless disregard for the truth.

1964 Congress adopts of the Gulf of Tonkin Resolution.

1967 The Supreme Court rules in *Keyishian v. Board of Regents of the University of the State of New York* that a state law requiring teachers to sign loyalty oaths violates the First Amendment.

1968 North Vietnamese launch the Tet Offensive.

1968 Secretary of Defense Robert McNamara commissions the study of U.S. involvement in Vietnam. The study is referred to as the Pentagon Papers.

1969 The Supreme Court rules in *Stanley v. Georgia* that the First Amendment protects the right of individuals to possess obscene materials for private viewing.

1969 The Supreme Court upholds the constitutionality of the fairness doctrine in *Red Lion Broadcasting, Co. v. F.C.C.*

1969 Police in New York City raid the Stonewall Inn, a gay bar, and beat up several patrons.

1971 The *Washington Post* and the *New York Times* begin the publication of the Pentagon Papers.

1971 The Supreme Court rules in *New York Times Co. v. United States* that the First Amendment protects the right of a newspaper to publish the Pentagon Papers.

1972 The Supreme Court rules in *Branzburg v. Hayes* that the First Amendment does not shield a newspaper reporter from having to disclose a source for a story.

1973 The Supreme Court develops in *Miller v. California* a constitutional test to determine obscenity.

1976 The Supreme Court rules in *Virginia State Board of Pharmacy v. Virginia Citizens Consumer Council, Inc.* that commercial speech is entitled to some First Amendment protection.

1978 The Supreme Court rules in *Federal Communications Commission v. Pacifica Foundation* that George Carlin's "Seven Dirty Words" may be restricted from broadcast on the radio during certain hours when children would likely be listening.

1979 A U.S. district court judge issues an injunction in *United States v. The Progressive, Inc.* preventing a the magazine from publishing an article describing how to make a nuclear bomb. The Seventh Circuit Court voided this order after being made aware that such information was already available in public sources.

1979 The Supreme Court rules in *Gannett Co. v. DePasquale* that a judge can close a criminal trial and prevent the press from covering it to protect the defendant's Sixth Amendment rights.

1980 The Supreme Court rules in *Richmond Newspapers, Inc. v. Virginia* that the First Amendment protects the right of the media to cover criminal trials.

1980 The Supreme Court develops in *Central Hudson Gas & Elec. Corp. v. Public Service Commission of New York* a test for determining when commercial speech may be regulated without violating the First Amendment.

1984 The Supreme Court rules in *Roberts v. United States Jaycees* that a group's right to freedom of association was not violated by a law that required it to admit women as members.

1985 The Seventh Circuit Court of Appeals rules in *American Booksellers Association, Inc. v. Hudnut* that a city law making it a crime to show pornography that depicts women as victims of violence or in positions subordinate to males violates the First Amendment.

1986 The Supreme Court rules in *City of Renton v. Playtime Theatres, Inc.* that a law aimed at addressing the "secondary effects" of adult entertainment establishments does not violate the First Amendment.

1986 The Supreme Court upholds in *Posadas de Puerto Rico Associates v. Tourism Co. of Puerto Rico* a law preventing casino and gambling advertising directed toward residents of Puerto Rico even though the same advertising was permitted to be directed toward tourists.

1988 The Supreme Court rules in *Hazelwood School Dist. v. Kuhlmeier* that a principal of a public high school did not violate the First Amendment when he prevented a student newspaper from publishing an article about pregnant students.

1991 The Supreme Court rules in *Barnes v. Glen Theatre, Inc.* that nonobscene nude dancing is entitled to only a marginal amount of First Amendment protection.

1992 The Canadian Supreme Court rules in *Regina v. Butler* that a law making it illegal to depict women and others in exploitive or violent sexual situations does not violate the Canadian Bill of Rights.

1992 Mosaic, the first Web browser, is developed.

1995 The Supreme Court rules in *Hurley v. Irish-American Gay, Lesbian & Bisexual Group of Boston, Inc.* that the organizers of the Boston St. Patrick's Day parade may refuse to allow gays and lesbians to march in the parade.

1996 The Supreme Court rules in *44 Liquormart, Inc. v. Rhode Island* that a state law banning the advertising of prices for alcohol products violated the First Amendment.

1999 The Court of Appeals for the District Columbia rules in *Hutchins v. District of Columbia* ruled that a youth curfew law did not violate the First Amendment.

2000 In *Boy Scouts of America v. James Dale,* the Supreme Court rules that the Boys Scouts may expel a leader in the organization because of his sexual orientation.

2004 The Supreme Court rules in *Ashcroft v. American Civil Liberties Union* that the Child Online Protection Act that sought to regulate sexual content on the Internet was a violation of the First Amendment.

2010 The Supreme Court rules in *Citizens United v. Federal Election Commission* that laws limiting the ability of corporations to expend money to influence elections violate their First Amendment rights. The same rule also applies to labor unions.

2011 In *Brown v. Entertainment Merchants Ass'n,* the Supreme Court strikes down a state law seeking to ban and regulate the sale and distribution of violent video games.

2016 In *Bollea v Gawker*, a Florida jury awards Hulk Hogan (Bollea) $115 million in damages because Gawker Media invaded his privacy by publishing a sex tape featuring him.

First Amendment:

Congress shall make no law . . . abridging the freedom of . . . the press; or the right of the people peaceably to assemble, and to petition the government for a redress of grievances.

INTRODUCTION

As pointed out in Chapter III, the First Amendment is expansive, covering a wide range of freedoms. But despite its breadth, there are limits to its reach. Two conclusions are clear: First, when the First Amendment was drafted, its Framers could not have envisioned all the forms of communication and association that now exist. Second, the Framers did not view all existing forms of communication as coming under its protection.

The world of 1791 when the Bill of Rights was formally adopted by the states was one of face-to-face contact and the distribution of ideas through speeches, newspapers, or pamphlets. The Framers definitely did not have in mind today's forms of communications such as radio and television, major media corporations, and now the Internet, with innovative Web sites and streaming data like YouTube, Twitter, and other tools of the social media. Nor did they have any concept of cyberspace venues such as chat rooms and Facebook as ways of social interaction. In addition, it is debatable whether the Framers would have considered either sexually explicit materials or commercial speech such as the advertisements to be forms of protected speech. Over time, works by writers such as Walt Whitman, Mark Twain, Henry Miller, and Kurt Vonnegut have been targeted by censors, demonstrating that what might count as literature for some is objectionable to others. Moreover, in drafting the First Amendment the Framers' focus was on individual political speech; it was impossible for them to even consider that the advertising familiar today on television and over the Internet might be a form of speech deserving of any legal protection.

The challenge in applying the First Amendment in the twenty-first century lies in deciding what ideas can be protected and in what format. This chapter follows up on the discussion in Chapter III, which examined cases involving what free speech means primarily to individuals. It looked at what "speech" is and the protections it deserves. This chapter begins by examining **obscenity** and pornography, and commercial speech, seeking to determine if, when, and how these entities are to receive constitutional protection. It then turns to freedom of the press, examining what forms of communication now constitute the media and the scope of the regulations on newspapers, broadcasters, and other information outlets that the government may impose. Finally, the chapter looks at the forgotten part of the First Amendment, freedom of assembly and petition, and the conditions under which interpersonal relations may be directed or regulated by the government.

In examining of these different types of communications, one should ask: Are they protected by the First Amendment? If so, do they deserve the same level of protection received by individuals engaged in political discussion? If not, how much legal protection, if any, do they deserve? Finally, are there some events or circumstances that would permit some limits on these various forms of expression? For example, should war, national security, or the nature of the speaker (journalist, television show, spy, or child) be an important factor in deciding the level of constitutional protection afforded? Should it matter if the content is sexually explicit, discusses classified national security material, or mentions the price of beer? All these issues or variables have been the subject of many of the cases examined in this chapter.

Obscenity, Pornography, and Censorship

The First Amendment states that "Congress shall make no law . . . abridging the freedom of speech, or of religion." As simple as this declaration is, it should be clear by now that determining what constitutes "speech" for the purposes of constitutional protection is not so easy. While some literalists and absolutists such as Justice Hugo Black have contended that all forms of utterances and statements made orally or in writing qualify as speech and therefore deserve constitutional protection, few would accept this assertion without reservation. For example, written or oral statements to extort money from others may well be a form of communication; generally, however, one cannot use the First Amendment as a defense against criminal blackmail charges.

Historically, two classes of communication have been viewed as outside the tent of First Amendment protected speech. The first is libelous speech, the other is obscenity. Regulation of obscenity, and the closely related concept of pornographic material, has deep historical roots that trace back to England. In England, the Lord Campbell Act of 1857 sought to regulate the discussion of certain sexual matters, while in the United States the Comstock Act of 1873 made it illegal to use the mails to ship obscene or indecent materials. Margaret Sanger, who distributed information promoting and discussing birth control, was arrested for these activities because they were said to be violations of the Comstock Act.

Generally, obscenity and pornography laws have been directed at sexually explicit materials. Some contend that the United States inherited the generally conservative, prudish, or later Victorian attitudes of England toward sex and sexuality. Others root the desire for censorship in America's Puritan origins and the historical authority of state governments to use their police powers to protect the health, safety, welfare, and *morals* of the people. Still others contend that obscene and pornographic materials corrupt individuals, leading to sex crimes or other deviant behavior. While there is little or mixed social science evidence supporting this last claim, some nevertheless justify censorship of sexually explicit material on assertions that it either hurts users or victimizes others. Finally, some seek to keep such materials from minors, or to limit adult access to such materials to prevent them from falling into the hands of minors. In 1986, the report of the Attorney General's Commission on Pornography drew on many of these themes when it advocated more limits on pornography. This document, nearly two thousand pages long, is often called the Meese Report because it was produced under Attorney General Ed Meese.

Over time many books—both sexually explicit works and those that are not—have been the target of censors. *The Tropic of Cancer,* by Henry Miller, now recognized as a classic of literature, was once declared obscene by state courts and banned from distribution. *Lady Chatterley's Lover,* by D. H. Lawrence, also was a frequent object of scorn. But in addition to books, regulators are now seeking to limit access to pornographic materials by scrutinizing plays and performances, movies, records, and now material on the Web. At one time in the United States, motion pictures or movies were not rated for content. However, local governments had boards that issued such ratings of movies. When these boards were effectively shut down by court rulings, the Motion Picture Association of America began the use of voluntary ratings. Lenny Bruce, a famous comedian in the 1950s and 1960s, was arrested repeatedly in places such as New York and Chicago because of the sexually explicit content of his routine. Even album covers and lyrics have borne the criticism of some who see in them sexually explicit or violent messages that should be restricted in their distribution, or at least kept from minors.

If obscene materials are not protected by the First Amendment, it becomes necessary to ask what "obscene" means. Supreme Court Justice Potter Stewart is often mocked for a line in one of his opinions in which he said that he could not define obscenity, but "I know it when I see it." However, not all agree on what constitutes obscenity, necessitating a definition or test. One of the first such tests dates to 1868 in a British case, *Regina v. Hicklin* (LR 3 QB 360, i). Here Chief Justice Lord Alexander Cockburn declared: "The test of obscenity is whether the tendency of the matter charged as obscenity is to deprave and corrupt those whose minds are open to such immoral influences and into whose hands a publication of this sort may fall." The *Hicklin* test, as it came to be known, was used to separate the obscene from the mere pornographic. In the United States, the *Hicklin* test would be used to separate sexually explicit materials not protected from the First Amendment from those receiving such protection. Yet even material that was deemed not to be obscene nevertheless offended some people, who would then seek to censor it.

The United States abandoned the *Hicklin* test or rule in the United States in *Roth v. United States* (354 U.S. 476, 1957). *Roth* is significant for two reasons. It is the first case in which the Court formally and clearly states that obscene materials are outside the protection of the First Amendment, although the dissents by Justices Douglas and Black suggest that at least some would not have reached this conclusion. *Roth* also sought to improve upon the *Hicklin* test, offering a definition of obscenity: "[W]hether to the average person, applying contemporary community standards, the dominant theme of the material taken as a whole appeals to the prurient interest." This test would eventually prove unworkable, forcing the Court to revise it several times before settling on a new definition in *Miller v. California* (413 U.S. 15, 1973).

In *Miller v. California,* the Court constructs a three-part test to determine if material is obscene. The ***Miller* test** asks "(a) whether 'the average person, applying contemporary community standards' would find that the work, taken as a whole, appeals to the prurient interest; (b) whether the work depicts or describes, in a patently offensive way, sexual conduct specifically defined by the applicable state law; and (c) whether the work, taken as a whole, lacks serious literary, artistic, political, or scientific value." Does the *Miller* test clarify any of the problems inherent in the *Roth* test? To Douglas it did not. But despite some of its problems, and some refinement over the years, it remains the basic test for obscenity, using local community standards for determining obscenity. Does not such a test effectively create different standards for different communities? How should such a test be applied now, in the age of the Internet, when material is broadcast from one location and potentially received in numerous places across the United States? What now constitutes a local community?

Along with seeking to define what is obscene, another issue turns to the way an idea is expressed. While books have been subject to censorship and the chapter on free speech discussed briefly some of the issue surrounding book bans, turning written material into video raises a different set of issues. The Framers had no idea or conception that modes of communication such as television or movies could ever exist, leaving open the question of whether such technologies should be given First Amendment Protection. That issue was put to rest in *Burstyn v. Wilson* (343 U.S. 495, 1952). In this case the Court had to address the issue of whether films or motion pictures received First Amendment protection. Here the Court made "official" the dictum of *United States v. Paramount Pictures, Inc.* (334 U.S. 131, 1948), which had declared movies to be a part of the "press" of the country as encompassed by the First Amendment. Movies were simply recognized as a significant means of communication. Prior censorship was condemned here also, and there was as well language about the "vice of vagueness" regarding the lack of adequate standards. Public interest in the matter—the protection of religious sensibilities—was held not sufficient to justify the sort of restriction involved in *Burstyn*.

The significance of this ruling was played out in *Kingsley International Pictures Corporation v. Regents* (360 U.S. 684, 1959). Here New York State sought to prevent the distribution and viewing of the movie *Lady Chatterley's Lover* because the film advocated or appeared to endorse adultery. The Court struck down the ban on First Amendment grounds, finding that that this constituted censorship. The basic point in *Kingsley* is that there may be no official prior restraint on the expression and advocacy of opinions or ideas, no matter how unconventional they may be. Because there was no need to determine the matter in reaching the decision, the Court did not pass on whether a state may provide for the licensing of movies. By way of summation, from the Court's decisions it appears that states may ban motion pictures only if the movies are obscene as defined by the *Miller* test.

Obscenity put on public view is one thing, but what about obscenity in private? Sexually explicit materials raise a series of legal issues depending on where they are displayed or consumed. One question specifically: Do individuals have a First Amendment right to possess and view obscene materials privately, such as in homes? In *Stanley v. Georgia* (394 U.S. 557, 1969), the Supreme Court said "yes." This decision appeared to offer significant First Amendment to materials in private that otherwise would not be given such protection if viewed publicly. The public display of sexual materials poses problems that private consumption does not. Specifically, many assert that adult entertainment establishments create **secondary effects** problems. They may be engulfed or surrounded by persons engaged in illegal behavior, such as prostitution. They may expose children to obscenity. Thus, many communities sought to use their zoning laws to restrict the location of adult businesses to certain areas of town, often away from schools, for example. In *City of Renton v. Playtime Theatres, Inc.* (475 U.S. 41, 1986), the Court upheld zoning laws or regulations of these types, ruling that the secondary effects were constitutional time, manner, and place restrictions. Another issue related to regulating secondary effects addresses what type of sexually explicit material can be displayed. In *Barnes v. Glen Theatre, Inc.* (501 U.S. 560, 1991), the Court upheld an Indiana law banning totally nude dancing. The Court ruled that non-obscene nude dancing deserved only marginal First Amendment protection and it could therefore be regulated. *Barnes* appears to create a new constitutional category for sexually explicit materials. Instead of the "on-off switch" that either grants or withholds constitutional protection, *Barnes* recognizes that some form of sexually explicit or nude dancing is protected by the First Amendment, but only marginally. This marginal protection gives communities potentially more leeway to regulate businesses featuring this type of live entertainment.

Do sexually explicit materials cause harm? The assumption of *Renton* and the secondary effects doctrine suggests that they do, at least indirectly. But one assumption of advocates of those seeking to regulate forms of expression that are both obscene and pornographic is that these materials corrupt their consumers or users. In the 1980s, feminist scholars Catharine A. MacKinnon and Andrea Dworkin, further developed the argument that some graphic pornography incites violence against women. While the two women's efforts in Minneapolis failed, they succeeded in securing passage of a law in Indianapolis, Indiana, that declared some pornography a form of violence against women that could be banned. The Seventh Circuit disagreed in *American Booksellers Association, Inc., v. Hudnut* (771 F.2d 323, 7th Cir. 1985). The Court ruled that *Miller* was controlling and that the Indianapolis ordinance was simply an effort to bypass the First Amendment. Compare this case to one from the Canadian Supreme Court, *Regina v. Butler* (1 S.C.R. 452, 1992), for contrasting approaches to defining free expression and addressing pornography, *Butler* and *Hudnut* reach different conclusions regarding the respective constitutional protection for violent but non-obscene sexually oriented materials. In the United States, the *Miller* test seems to be dispositive in determining whether sexually oriented materials receive First Amendment protection. In *Hudnut*, the court finds that efforts to regulate materials that have been deemed non-obscene by way of declaring them illegal if violent are unconstitutional. Canadian law has less of this "light switch" or all-or-nothing approach, seeming to create a new category of violent pornography that is not protected. For some feminists, all pornography involves violence or depicts women in subordinate positions, while for others the pornographic display of women is not inherently discriminatory or exploitive. In many ways, the handling of violent pornography as discussed in these cases raises many of the same issues seen in the discussion of hate speech in the preceding chapter. Ideas and displays that many find noxious still receive First Amendment protection.

Like television in the mid-twentieth century, the Internet and the World Wide Web have more recently made it possible to bring many new forms of entertainment into homes, but this time using individual computer terminals. It did not take long for people to exploit the Web for sexual purposes, using it as a way to distribute pornographic materials or to solicit sex. Many in Congress worried that minors would become victims of the new Internet sex industry, and they passed legislation to protect them. The Communications Decency Act (CDA) of 1996, intended to regulate the distribution of pornographic materials, was declared unconstitutional in *Reno v. ACLU* (521 U.S. 844, 1997). Congress responded with the Child Online Protection Act. In *Ashcroft v. American Civil Liberties Union* (542 U.S. 656, 2004), the Court again ruled, as it had in *Reno*, that efforts to regulate non-obscene but sexually explicit material on the Web violated the First Amendment. Again, the *Miller* test seemed to control what can be regulated. Moreover, the Court also seems to suggest that there are less restrictive ways to regulate the Internet to make it more difficult for children to access some materials. These might include filters, or perhaps even better, parental supervision over what children access or view.

While not about obscenity per se, concern about the effects of violent video games on children has led to calls to regulate or ban their sale and distribution. In *Brown v. Entertainment Merchants Ass'n* (564 U.S. 786, 2011) the Supreme Court invalidated a California law that sought to do exactly that. In its justification for the law the State sought to draw parallels between obscenity and violent video games, both in terms of trying to argue that were not protected by the First Amendment and by trying to address their secondary effects. The Court rejected both lines of arguments.

In the end, the First Amendment has proved to pose a thorny problem for those seeking to regulate the distribution, publication, and display of sexually explicit materials. While obscenity is not protected, ascertaining what is obscene has been found to be quite difficult to determine. The problem is only enhanced more as new forms of communication make such materials more accessible, and as tastes change, affecting what standards are used to determine what is considered obscene.

BURSTYN V. WILSON

343 U.S. 495, 72 S.Ct. 777, 96 L.Ed. 1098 (1952)

A statute of the state of New York permitted the state board of regents to ban motion picture films because they were "sacrilegious." The highly controversial Italian film The Miracle had been so judged by the board, and this decision, under power granted by the statute, was challenged in the courts as being in conflict with the First and Fourteenth Amendments.

Vote: No dissent

JUSTICE CLARK delivered the opinion of the Court.

. . . It cannot be doubted that motion pictures are a significant medium for the communication of ideas. They may affect public attitudes and behavior in a variety of ways, ranging from direct espousal of a political or social doctrine to the subtle shaping of thought which characterizes all artistic expression. The importance of motion pictures as an organ of public opinion is not lessened by the fact that they are designed to entertain as well as to inform. . . .

It is urged that motion pictures do not fall within the First Amendment's aegis because their production, distribution, and exhibition is a large-scale business conducted for private profit. We cannot agree. That books, newspapers, and magazines are published and sold for profit does not prevent them from being a form of expression whose liberty is safeguarded by the First Amendment. We fail to see why operation for profit should have any different effect in the case of motion pictures.

It is further urged that motion pictures possess a greater capacity for evil, particularly among the youth of a community, than other modes of expression. Even if one were to accept this hypothesis, it does not follow that motion pictures should be disqualified from First Amendment protection. If there be capacity for evil it may be relevant in determining the permissible scope of community control, but it does not authorize substantially unbridled censorship such as we have here.

For the foregoing reasons, we conclude that expression by means of motion pictures is included within the free speech and free press guaranty of the First and Fourteenth Amendments. To the extent that language in the opinion in *Mutual Film Corp. v. Industrial Commission of Ohio*, 236 U.S. 230 (1915), is out of harmony with the views here set forth, we no longer adhere to it.

To hold that liberty of expression by means of motion pictures is guaranteed by the First and Fourteenth Amendments, however, is not the end of our problem. It does not follow that the Constitution requires absolute freedom to exhibit every motion picture of every kind at all times and all places. That much is evident from the series of decisions of this Court with respect to other media of communication of ideas. Nor does it follow that motion pictures are necessarily subject to the precise rules governing any other particular method of expression. Each method tends to present its own peculiar problems. But the basic principles of freedom of speech and the press, like the First Amendment's command, do not vary. Those principles, as they have frequently been enunciated by this Court, make freedom of expression the rule. There is no justification in this case for making an exception to that rule. . . .

New York's highest court says there is "nothing mysterious" about the statutory provision applied in this case: "It is simply this: that no religion, as that word is understood by the ordinary, reasonable person, shall be treated with contempt, mockery, scorn and ridicule. . . ." This is far from the kind of narrow exception to freedom of expression which a state may carve out to satisfy the adverse demands of other interests of society. In seeking to apply the broad and all-inclusive definition of "sacrilegious" given by the New York courts, the censor is set adrift upon a boundless sea amid a myriad of conflicting currents of religious views, with no charts but those provided by the most vocal and powerful orthodoxies. New York cannot vest such unlimited restraining control over motion pictures in a censor. . . . Under such a standard the most careful and tolerant censor would find it virtually impossible to avoid favoring one religion over another, and he would be subject to an inevitable tendency to ban the expression of unpopular sentiments sacred to a religious minority. Application of the "sacrilegious" test, in these or other respects, might raise substantial questions under the First Amendment's guaranty of separate church and state with freedom of worship for all. However, from the standpoint of freedom of speech and the press, it is enough to point out that the state has no legitimate interest in protecting any or all religions from views distasteful to them which is sufficient to justify prior restraints upon the expression of those views. It is not the business of government in our nation to suppress real or imagined attacks upon a particular religious doctrine, whether they appear in publications, speeches, or motion pictures.

Since the term "sacrilegious" is the sole standard under attack here, it is not necessary for us to decide, for example, whether a state may censor motion pictures under a clearly-drawn statute designed and applied to prevent the showing of obscene films. That is a very different question from the one now before us. We hold only that under the First and Fourteenth Amendments a state may not ban a film on the basis of a censor's conclusion that it is a "sacrilegious."

Reversed.

JUSTICE FRANKFURTER, whom JUSTICES JACKSON and BURTON joined, concurring.

. . . In *Cantwell v. Connecticut,* 310 U.S. 296, 310 (1940), Mr. Justice Roberts, speaking for the whole Court, said: "In the realm of religious faith, and in that of political belief, sharp differences arise. In both fields the tenets of one man may seem the rankest error to his neighbor." Conduct and beliefs dear to one may seem the rankest "sacrilege" to another. A few examples suffice to show the difficulties facing a conscientious censor or motion picture producer or distributor in determining what the New York statute condemns as sacrilegious. A motion picture portraying Christ as divine—for example, a movie showing medieval Church art—would offend the religious opinions of the members of several Protestant denominations who do not believe in the Trinity, as well as those of a non-Christian faith. Conversely, one showing Christ as merely an ethical teacher could not but offend millions of Christians of many denominations. Which is "sacrilegious"? The doctrine of transubstantiation, and the veneration of relics or particular stone and wood embodiments of saints or divinity, both sacred to Catholics, are offensive to a great many Protestants, and therefore for them sacrilegious in the view of the New York court. Is a picture treating either subject, whether sympathetically, unsympathetically, or neutrally, "sacrilegious"? It is not a sufficient answer to say that "sacrilegious" is definite, because all subjects that in any way might be interpreted as offending the religious beliefs of anyone of the 300 sects of the United States are banned in New York. To allow such vague, undefinable powers of censorship to be exercised is bound to have stultifying consequences on the creative process of literature and art—for the films are derived largely from literature. History does not encourage reliance on the wisdom and moderation of the censor as a safeguard in the exercise of such drastic power over the mind of men. We not only do not know but cannot know what is condemnable by "sacrilegious." And if we cannot tell, how are those to be governed by the statute to tell?

It is this impossibility of knowing how far the form of words by which the New York Court of Appeals explained "sacrilegious" carries the proscription of religious subjects that makes the term unconstitutionally vague. . . .

. . . Prohibition through words that fail to convey what is permitted and what is prohibited for want of appropriate objective standards, offends Due Process in two ways. First, it does not sufficiently apprise those bent on obedience of law of what may reasonably be foreseen to be found illicit by the law-enforcing authority, whether court or jury or administrative agency. Secondly, where licensing is rested, in the first instance, in an administrative agency, the available judicial review is in effect rendered inoperative. On the basis of such a portmanteau word as "sacrilegious," the judiciary has no standards with which to judge the validity of administrative action which necessarily involves, at least in large measure, subjective determinations. Thus, the administrative first step becomes the last step. . . .

FOR DISCUSSION

Are motion picture or movie ratings codes (G, PG, R, NC–17) unconstitutional? Does it matter that these ratings are done voluntarily by the motion picture or music industry? What if the government issued these ratings?

RELATED CASE

***Mutual Film Corp. v. Industrial Commission of Ohio*: 236 U.S. 230 (1915).**

The moving picture censorship act of Ohio of 1913 is not unconstitutional: it does not deprive the owners of moving pictures of their property without due process of law; it is not a burden on interstate commerce; and it does not abridge freedom and liberty of speech and opinion. Motion pictures do not come under the constitutional guarantee of freedom of the press. This case antedated the Court's vital concern with civil rights and liberties problems.

ROTH V. UNITED STATES

354 U.S. 476, 77 S.Ct. 1304, 1 L.Ed.2d 1498 (1957)

A bookseller of adult products advertised his books, photos, and other materials by means of circulars distributed on the street. He was convicted on several charges of selling obscene materials, and he appealed. His case—Roth—was heard along with another case.

Vote: 6–3

JUSTICE BRENNAN delivered the opinion of the Court.

The constitutionality of a criminal obscenity statute is the question [here]. In *Roth v. United States*, 354 U.S. 476 (1957), the primary constitutional question is whether the federal obscenity statute violates the provision of the First Amendment that "Congress shall make no law abridging the freedom of speech, or of the press." In *Alberts v. California*, 354 U.S. 476 (1957), the primary constitutional question is whether the obscenity provisions of the California Penal Code invade the freedoms of speech and press as they may be incorporated in the liberty protected from state action by the Due Process Clause of the Fourteenth Amendment.

Roth conducted a business in New York in the publication and sale of books, photographs and magazines. He used circulars and advertising matter to solicit sales. He was convicted by a jury in the District Court for the Southern District of New York upon 4 counts of a 26-count indictment charging him with mailing obscene circulars and advertising, and an obscene book, in violation of the federal obscenity statute. His conviction was affirmed by the Court of Appeals for the Second Circuit. We granted certiorari.

Alberts conducted a mail-order business from Los Angeles. He was convicted by the Judge of the Municipal Court of the Beverly Hills Judicial District (having waived a jury trial) under a misdemeanor complaint which charged him with lewdly keeping for sale obscene and indecent books, and with writing, composing and publishing an obscene advertisement of them, in violation of the California Penal Code. The conviction was affirmed by the Appellate Department of the Superior Court of the State of California in and for the County of Los Angeles. We noted probable jurisdiction.

The dispositive question is whether obscenity is utterance within the area of protected speech and press. Although this is the first time the question has been squarely presented to this Court, either under the First Amendment or under the Fourteenth Amendment, expressions found in numerous opinions indicate that this Court has always assumed that obscenity is not protected by the freedoms of speech and press.

The guaranties of freedom of expression in effect in 10 of the 14 States which by 1792 had ratified the Constitution, gave no absolute protection for every utterance. Thirteen of the 14 States provided for the prosecution of libel, and all of those States made either blasphemy or profanity, or both, statutory crimes. As early as 1712, Massachusetts made it criminal to publish 'any filthy, obscene, or profane song, pamphlet, libel or mock sermon' in imitation or mimicking of religious services. Thus, profanity and obscenity were related offenses.

In light of this history, it is apparent that the unconditional phrasing of the First Amendment was not intended to protect every utterance. This phrasing did not prevent this Court from concluding that libelous utterances are not within the area of constitutionally protected speech. At the time of the adoption of the First Amendment, obscenity law was not as fully developed as libel law, but there is sufficiently contemporaneous evidence to show that obscenity, too, was outside the protection intended for speech and press.

The protection given speech and press was fashioned to assure unfettered interchange of ideas for the bringing about of political and social changes desired by the people.

All ideas having even the slightest redeeming social importance—unorthodox ideas, controversial ideas, even ideas hateful to the prevailing climate of opinion—have the full protection of the guaranties, unless excludable because they encroach upon the limited area of more important interests. But implicit in the history of the First Amendment is the rejection of obscenity as utterly without redeeming social importance. This rejection for that reason is mirrored in the universal judgment that obscenity should be restrained, reflected in the international agreement of over 50 nations, in the obscenity laws of all of the 48 States, and in the 20 obscenity laws enacted by the Congress from 1842 to 1956.

We hold that obscenity is not within the area of constitutionally protected speech or press.

The judgments are affirmed.

CHIEF JUSTICE WARREN, concurring in the result.

I agree with the result reached by the Court in these cases, but, because we are operating in a field of expression and because broad language used here may eventually be applied to the arts and sciences and freedom of communication generally, I would limit our decision to the facts before us and to the validity of the statutes in question as applied.

That there is a social problem presented by obscenity is attested by the expression of the legislatures of the forty-eight States as well as the Congress. To recognize the existence of a problem, however, does not require that we sustain any and all measures adopted to meet that problem. The history of the application of laws designed to suppress the obscene demonstrates convincingly that the power of government can be invoked under them against great art or literature, scientific treatises, or works exciting social controversy. Mistakes of the past prove that there is a strong countervailing interest to be considered in the freedoms guaranteed by the First and Fourteenth Amendments.

The line dividing the salacious or pornographic from literature or science is not straight and unwavering. Present laws depend largely upon the effect that the materials may have upon those who receive them. It is manifest that the same object may have a different impact, varying according to the part of the community it reached. But there is more to these cases. It is not the book that is on trial; it is a person.

JUSTICE DOUGLAS, with whom JUSTICE BLACK concurs, dissenting.

When we sustain these convictions, we make the legality of a publication turn on the purity of thought which a book or tract instills in the mind of the reader. I do not think we can approve that standard and be faithful to the command of the First Amendment, which by its terms is a restraint on Congress and which by the Fourteenth is a restraint on the States.

The test of obscenity the Court endorses today gives the censor free range over a vast domain. To allow the State to step in and punish mere speech or publication that the judge or the jury thinks has an undesirable impact on thoughts but that is not shown to be a part of unlawful action is drastically to curtail the First Amendment. As recently stated by two of our outstanding authorities on obscenity, "The danger of influencing a change in the current moral standards of the community, or of shocking or offending readers, or of stimulating sex thoughts or desires apart from objective conduct, can never justify the losses to society that result from interference with literary freedom." Lockhart & McClure, Literature, The Law of Obscenity, and the Constitution, 38 *Minn. L. Rev.* 295, 387.

I would give the broad sweep of the First Amendment full support. I have the same confidence in the ability of our people to reject noxious literature as I have in their capacity to sort out the true from the false in theology, economics, politics, or any other field.

FOR DISCUSSION

Would the dissenting justices provide constitutional protection to obscene materials? Why or why not? Does the First Amendment protect all forms of expression?

KINGSLEY INTERNATIONAL PICTURES CORPORATION V. REGENTS

360 U.S. 684, 79 S.Ct 1362, 3 L.Ed.2d. 1512 (1959)

The Kingsley Corporation was the distributor for a motion picture entitled Lady Chatterley's Lover, and, in accordance with the provisions of the New York Education Law, requested a license to exhibit the movie. This was refused on the grounds that the film presented adultery "as being right and desirable for certain people under certain circumstances." This denial was upheld by the New York Court of Appeals against the contention that the proceeding violated the First Amendment guarantees of free speech and press as applied to the states by means of the Fourteenth Amendment.

Vote: 9–0

JUSTICE STEWART delivered the opinion of the Court.

. . . What New York has done . . . is to prevent the exhibition of a motion picture because that picture advocates an idea—that adultery under certain circumstances may be proper behavior. Yet the First Amendment's basic guarantee is of freedom to advocate ideas. The State, quite simply, has thus struck at the very heart of constitutionally protected liberty.

It is contended that the State's action was justified because the motion picture attractively portrays a relationship which is contrary to the moral standards, the religious precepts, and the legal code of its citizenry. This argument misconceives what it is that the Constitution protects. Its guarantee is not confined to the expression of ideas that are conventional or shared by a majority. It protects advocacy of the opinion that adultery may sometimes be proper, no less than advocacy of socialism or the single tax. And in the realm of ideas it protects expression which is eloquent no less than that which is unconvincing.

Advocacy of conduct proscribed by law is not, as Mr. Justice Brandeis long ago pointed out, "a justification for denying free speech where the advocacy falls short of incitement and there is nothing to indicate that the advocacy would be immediately acted on." *Whitney v. California,* 274 U.S. 357, at 376 (concurring opinion) (1927). "Among free men, the deterrents ordinarily to be applied to prevent crime are education and punishment for violations of the law, not abridgment of the rights of free speech. . . ."

The inflexible command which the New York Court of Appeals has attributed to the State Legislature thus cuts so close to the core of constitutional freedom as to make it quite needless in this case to examine the periphery. Specifically, there is not occasion to consider the appellant's contention that the State is entirely without power to require films of any kind to be licensed prior to their exhibition. Nor need we here determine whether despite problems peculiar to motion pictures, the controls which a State may impose upon this medium of expression are precisely coextensive with those allowable for newspapers, books, or individual speech. It is enough for the present case to reaffirm that motion pictures are within the First and Fourteenth Amendments' basic protection. . . .

Reversed.

FOR DISCUSSION

Would a film with a theme or message such as *Lady Chatterley's Lover* be considered offensive today? What if a film advocated sex with minors? Would the Roberts Court rule any differently? Why or why not?

RELATED CASES

In a series of *per curiam* decisions following the *Burstyn* case, which included *United Artists Corp. v. Board of Censors* (339 U.S. 952, 1950), *Holmby Productions, Inc. v. Vaugh,*(350 U.S. 870, 1955), and *Gelling v. Texas* (343 U.S. 960, 1952), and citing *Gelling,* the Court held invalid attempts by various states and cities to censor movies.

***Adams Newark Theater Co. v. Newark:* 354 U.S. 931 (1957).**

The Supreme Court in a *per curiam* opinion affirmed a judgment of the Supreme Court of New Jersey declaring that ordinances specifically placing certain types of conduct within the general terms of previous ordinances condemning lewdness, obscenity, or indecency are not unconstitutional violations of the right of free speech. It was held that some of the behaviors prohibited are so violently contrary to good morals and decency as to be condemnable even though some behavior that would otherwise be classified as lewd, indecent, or obscene is not subject to censorship because of free speech.

***Times Film Corp. v. City of Chicago:* 365 U.S. 43 (1961).**

Chicago's municipal code provision that all motion pictures be submitted for examination before a license for their public exhibition could be granted was challenged. The Court upheld the ordinance and noted that there is no complete and absolute freedom to exhibit, at least once, any and every kind of motion picture. Freedom from prior restraint is not an absolute privilege under the First Amendment.

***Freedman v. Maryland:* 380 U.S. 51 (1965).**

A noncriminal process that requires the prior submission of a movie film to a censor avoids constitutional infirmity only if it takes place under procedural safeguards designed to obviate the dangers of a censorship system. Among other things, such safeguards must include assurance of a prompt final judicial determination of obscenity.

***Jacobellis v. State of Ohio:* 378 U.S. 184 (1964).**

Obscenity in movies is not subject to constitutional protection, and the Court must make an independent constitutional judgment on the facts of an obscenity case as to whether the material involved is constitutionally protected.

***Ginsberg v. New York:* 390 U.S. 629 (1968).**

Obscenity is not within the area of protected speech and press. New York's regulation in defining obscenity on the basis of appeal to minors under seventeen is valid.

MILLER V. CALIFORNIA

413 U.S. 15, 93 S.Ct. 2607, 37 L.Ed.2d 419 (1973)

Miller, as the owner of a store, used mass mailings to advertise products, including those he described as adult oriented. He was convicted under a state obscenity statute and appealed.

Vote: 5–4

CHIEF JUSTICE BURGER delivered the opinion of the Court.

This is one of a group of 'obscenity-pornography' cases being reviewed by the Court in a re-examination of standards enunciated in earlier cases involving what Mr. Justice Harlan called 'the intractable obscenity problem.'

Appellant conducted a mass mailing campaign to advertise the sale of illustrated books, euphemistically called 'adult' material. After a jury trial, he was convicted of violating California Penal Code s 311.2(a), a misdemeanor, by knowingly distributing obscene matter, and the Appellate Department, Superior Court of California, County of Orange, summarily affirmed the judgment without opinion. Appellant's conviction was specifically based on his conduct in causing five unsolicited advertising brochures to be sent through the mail in an envelope addressed to a restaurant in Newport Beach, California. The envelope was opened by the manager of the restaurant and his mother. They had not requested the brochures; they complained to the police.

The brochures advertise four books entitled "Intercourse," "Man-Woman," "Sex Orgies Illustrated," and "An Illustrated History of Pornography," and a film entitled "Marital Intercourse." While the brochures contain some descriptive printed material, primarily they consist of pictures and drawings very explicitly depicting men and women in groups of two or more engaging in a variety of sexual activities, with genitals often prominently displayed.

I

This case involves the application of a State's criminal obscenity statute to a situation in which sexually explicit materials have been thrust by aggressive sales action upon unwilling recipients who had in no way indicated any desire to receive such materials. This Court has recognized that the States have a legitimate interest in prohibiting dissemination or exhibition of obscene material when the mode of dissemination carries with it a significant danger of offending the sensibilities of unwilling recipients or of exposure to juveniles. It is in this context that we are called on to define the standards which must be used to identify obscene material that a State may regulate without infringing on the First Amendment as applicable to the States through the Fourteenth Amendment.

The dissent of Mr. Justice Brennan reviews the background of the obscenity problem, but since the Court now undertakes to formulate standards more concrete than those in the past, it is useful for us to focus on two of the landmark cases in the somewhat tortured history of the Court's obscenity decisions. In *Roth v. United States,* 354 U.S. 476 (1957), the Court sustained a conviction under a federal statute punishing the mailing of "obscene, lewd, lascivious or filthy . . ." materials. The key to that holding was the Court's rejection of the claim that obscene materials were protected by the First Amendment. Five Justices joined in the opinion stating:

> "All ideas having even the slightest redeeming social importance—unorthodox ideas, controversial ideas, even ideas hateful to the prevailing climate of opinion—have the full protection of the (First Amendment) guaranties, unless excludable because they encroach upon the limited area of more important interests. But implicit in the history of the First Amendment is the rejection of obscenity as utterly without redeeming social importance. This is the same judgment expressed by this Court in *Chaplinsky v. New Hampshire,* 315 U.S. 568, 571–572:
>
> ". . . There are certain well-defined and narrowly limited classes of speech, the prevention and punishment of which have never been thought to raise any Constitutional problem. These include the lewd and obscene . . . . It has been well observed that such utterances are no essential part of any exposition of ideas, and are of such slight social value as a step to truth that any benefit that may be derived from them is clearly outweighed by the social interest in order and morality. . . ."

We hold that obscenity is not within the area of constitutionally protected speech or press.

Nine years later, in *Memoirs v. Massachusetts,* 383 U.S. 413 (1966), the Court veered sharply away from the *Roth* concept and, with only three Justices in the plurality opinion, articulated a new test of obscenity. The plurality held that under the *Roth* definition

> as elaborated in subsequent cases, three elements must coalesce: it must be established that (a) the dominant theme of the material taken as a whole appeals to a prurient interest in sex; (b) the material is patently offensive because if affronts contemporary community standards relating to the description or representation of sexual matters; and (c) the material is utterly without redeeming social value.

The sharpness of the break with *Roth*, represented by the third element of the *Memoirs* test and emphasized by Mr. Justice White's dissent, was further underscored when the *Memoirs* plurality went on to state:

> The Supreme Judicial Court erred in holding that a book need not be "unqualifiedly worthless before it can be deemed obscene." A book cannot be proscribed unless it is found to be utterly without redeeming social value.

While *Roth* presumed 'obscenity' to be 'utterly without redeeming social importance,' *Memoirs* required that to prove obscenity it must be affirmatively established that the material is 'utterly without redeeming social value.' Thus, even as they repeated the words of *Roth*, the *Memoirs* plurality produced a drastically altered test that called on the prosecution to prove a negative, i.e., that the material was 'utterly without redeeming social value'—a burden virtually impossible to discharge under our criminal standards of proof. Such considerations caused Mr. Justice Harlan to wonder if the 'utterly without redeeming social value' test had any meaning at all.

Apart from the initial formulation in the *Roth* case, no majority of the Court has at any given time been able to agree on a standard to determine what constitutes obscene, pornographic material subject to regulation under the States' police power. We have seen 'a variety of views among the members of the Court unmatched in any other course of constitutional adjudication.' This is not remarkable, for in the area of freedom of speech and press the courts must always remain sensitive to any infringement on genuinely serious literary, artistic, political, or scientific expression. This is an area in which there are few eternal verities.

II

This much has been categorically settled by the Court, that obscene material is unprotected by the First Amendment. 'The First and Fourteenth Amendments have never been treated as absolutes. We acknowledge, however, the inherent dangers of undertaking to regulate any form of expression. State statutes designed to regulate obscene materials must be carefully limited. As a result, we now confine the permissible scope of such regulation to works which depict or describe sexual conduct. That conduct must be specifically defined by the applicable state law, as written or authoritatively construed. A state offense must also be limited to works which, taken as a whole, appeal to the prurient interest in sex, which portray sexual conduct in a patently offensive way, and which, taken as a whole, do not have serious literary, artistic, political, or scientific value.

The basic guidelines for the trier of fact must be: (a) whether "the average person, applying contemporary community standards" would find that the work, taken as a whole, appeals to the prurient interest; (b) whether the work depicts or describes, in a patently offensive way, sexual conduct specifically defined by the applicable state law; and (c) whether the work, taken as a whole, lacks serious literary, artistic, political, or scientific value. We do not adopt as a constitutional standard the "utterly without redeeming social value" test of *Memoirs v. Massachusetts*; that concept has never commanded the adherence of more than three Justices at one time. If a state law that regulates obscene material is thus limited, as written or construed, the First Amendment values applicable to the States through the Fourteenth Amendment are adequately protected by the ultimate power of appellate courts to conduct an independent review of constitutional claims when necessary.

We emphasize that it is not our function to propose regulatory schemes for the States. That must await their concrete legislative efforts. It is possible, however, to give a few plain examples of what a state statute could define for regulation under part (b) of the standard announced in this opinion:

(a) Patently offensive representations or descriptions of ultimate sexual acts, normal or perverted, actual or simulated.

(b) Patently offensive representation or descriptions of masturbation, excretory functions, and lewd exhibition of the genitals.

Sex and nudity may not be exploited without limit by films or pictures exhibited or sold in places of public accommodation any more than live sex and nudity can be exhibited or sold without limit in such public places. At a minimum, prurient, patently offensive depiction or description of sexual conduct must have serious literary, artistic, political, or scientific value to merit First Amendment protection. For example, medical books for the education of physicians and related personnel necessarily use graphic illustrations and descriptions of human anatomy. In resolving the inevitably sensitive questions of fact and law, we must continue to rely on the jury system, accompanied by the safeguards that judges, rules of evidence, presumption of innocence, and other protective features provide, as we do with rape, murder, and a host of other offenses against society and its individual members.

JUSTICE DOUGLAS, dissenting.

I

Today we leave open the way for California to send a man to prison for distributing brochures that advertise books and a movie under freshly written standards defining obscenity which until today's decision were never the part of any law.

II

[Douglas objects to the lack of precision in the Court's definition of obscenity.]

III

The idea that the First Amendment permits government to ban publications that are "offensive" to some people puts an ominous gloss on freedom of the press. That test would make it possible to ban any paper or any journal or magazine in some benighted place. The First Amendment was designed "to invite dispute," to induce "a condition of unrest," to "create dissatisfaction with conditions as they are," and even to stir "people' to anger." *Termininiello v. Chicago*, 337 U.S. 1, 4 [(1949)]. The idea that the First Amendment permits punishment for ideas that are "offensive" to the particular judge or jury sitting in judgment is astounding. No greater leveler of speech or literature has ever been designed. To give the power to the censor, as we do today, is to make a sharp and radical break with the traditions of a free society. The First Amendment was not fashioned as a vehicle for dispensing tranquilizers to the people. Its prime function was to keep debate open to "offensive" as well as to "staid" people. The tendency throughout history has been to subdue the individual and to exalt the power of government. The use of the standard "offensive" gives authority to government that cuts the very vitals out of the First Amendment. As is intimated by the Court's opinion, the materials before us may be garbage. But so is much of what is said in political campaigns, in the daily press, on TV, or over the radio. By reason of the First Amendment—and solely because of it—speakers and publishers have not been threatened or subdued because their thoughts and ideas may be "offensive" to some.

If there are to be restraints on what is obscene, then a constitutional amendment should be the way of achieving the end. There are societies where religion and mathematics are the only free segments. It would be a dark day for America if that were our destiny. But the people can make it such if they choose to write obscenity into the Constitution and define it.

We deal with highly emotional, not rational, questions. To many the Song of Solomon is obscene. I do not think we, the judges, were ever given the constitutional power to make definitions of obscenity. If it is to be defined, let the people debate and decide by a constitutional amendment what they want to ban as obscene and what standards they want the legislatures and the courts to apply. Perhaps the people will decide that the path towards a mature, integrated society requires that all ideas competing for acceptance must have no censor. Perhaps they will decide otherwise. Whatever the choice, the courts will have some guidelines. Now we have none except our own predilections.

FOR DISCUSSION

Does the *Miller* test provide a clear rule for determining what is obscene? Does the decision provide a clear guide for someone thinking of producing sexually explicit materials?

RELATED CASE

***Pope v. Illinois:* 481 U.S. 497 (1987).**

The majority modified the *Miller* test to require that determinations of whether materials lack "serious value" must be undertaken from a national level as judged by a reasonable person.

STANLEY V. GEORGIA

394 U.S. 557, 89 S.Ct. 1243, 22 L.Ed.2d 542 (1969)

While executing a warrant to search a home for evidence of illegal gambling activities, the police discovered films and concluded that they were obscene. The homeowner was convicted of violating a state obscenity law, and he appealed.

Vote: 9–0

JUSTICE MARSHALL delivered the opinion of the Court.

An investigation of appellant's alleged bookmaking activities led to the issuance of a search warrant for appellant's home. Under authority of this warrant, federal and state agents secured entrance. They found very little evidence of bookmaking activity, but while looking through a desk drawer in an upstairs bedroom, one of the federal agents, accompanied by a state officer, found three reels of eight-millimeter film. Using a projector and screen found in an upstairs living room, they viewed the films. The state officer concluded that they were obscene and seized them. Since a further examination of the bedroom indicated that appellant occupied it, he was charged with possession of obscene matter and placed under arrest. He was later indicted for 'knowingly hav(ing) possession of obscene matter' in violation of Georgia law. Appellant was tried before a jury and convicted. The Supreme Court of Georgia affirmed.

Appellant raises several challenges to the validity of his conviction. We find it necessary to consider only one. Appellant argues here, and argued below, that the Georgia obscenity statute, insofar as it punishes mere private possession of obscene matter, violates the First Amendment, as made applicable to the States by the Fourteenth Amendment. For reasons set forth below, we agree that the mere private possession of obscene matter cannot constitutionally be made a crime.

It is now well established that the Constitution protects the right to receive information and ideas. "This freedom (of speech and press) . . . necessarily protects the right to receive. . ." *Martin v. City of Struthers*, 319 U.S. 141, 143 (1943). This right to receive information and ideas, regardless of their social worth is fundamental to our free society. Moreover, in the context of this case—a prosecution for mere possession of printed or filmed matter in the privacy of a person's own home—that right takes on an added dimension. For also fundamental is the right to be free, except in very limited circumstances, from unwanted governmental intrusions into one's privacy.

These are the rights that appellant is asserting in the case before us. He is asserting the right to read or observe what he pleases—the right to satisfy his intellectual and emotional needs in the privacy of his own home. He is asserting the right to be free from state inquiry into the contents of his library. Georgia contends that appellant does not have these rights, that there are certain types of materials that the individual may not read or even possess. Georgia justifies this assertion by arguing that the films in the present case are obscene. But we think that mere categorization of these films as 'obscene' is insufficient justification for such a drastic invasion of personal liberties guaranteed by the First and Fourteenth Amendments. Whatever may be the justifications for other statutes regulating obscenity, we do not think they reach into the privacy of one's own home. If the First Amendment means anything, it means that a State has no business telling a man, sitting alone in his own house, what books he may read or what films he may watch. Our whole constitutional heritage rebels at the thought of giving government the power to control men's minds.

And yet, in the face of these traditional notions of individual liberty, Georgia asserts the right to protect the individual's mind from the effects of obscenity. We are not certain that this argument amounts to anything more than the assertion that the State has the right to control the moral content of a person's thoughts. To some, this may be a noble purpose, but it is wholly inconsistent with the philosophy of the First Amendment. As the Court said in *Kingsley International Pictures Corp. v. Regents*, 360 U.S. 684 (1959), "(t)his argument misconceives what it is that the Constitution protects. Its guarantee is not confined to the expression of ideas that are conventional or shared by a majority. And in the realm of ideas it protects expression which is eloquent no less than that which is unconvincing." Nor is it relevant that obscene materials in general, or the particular films before the Court, are arguably devoid of any ideological content. The line between the transmission of ideas and mere entertainment is much too elusive for this Court to draw, if indeed such a line can be drawn at all. Whatever the power of the state to control public dissemination of ideas inimical to the public morality, it cannot constitutionally premise legislation on the desirability of controlling a person's private thoughts.

Given the present state of knowledge, the State may no more prohibit mere possession of obscene matter on the ground that it may lead to antisocial conduct than it may prohibit possession of chemistry books on the ground that they may lead to the manufacture of homemade spirits.

We hold that the First and Fourteenth Amendments prohibit making mere private possession of obscene material a crime. *Roth* and the cases following that decision are not impaired by today's holding. As we have said, the States retain broad power to regulate obscenity; that power simply does not extend to mere possession by the individual in the privacy of his own home. Accordingly, the judgment of the court below is reversed and the case is remanded for proceedings not inconsistent with this opinion.

FOR DISCUSSION

Why should obscene materials be given more protection in private homes than in venues open to the public? Is it that the materials are being protected here, or is there a different First Amendment issue involved?

Communities unable to ban non-obscene but still sexually oriented establishments such as those featuring adult movies, stripping, or other adult entertainment sought ways to regulate the businesses, often through zoning. The courts invalidated many of these laws, finding that complete zoning bans violated the First Amendment. Yet a different tactic in regulation was, instead of attempting to control the materials these establishments contained, such as books or videos, to seek to confine or address some of the problems that often crop up in neighborhoods in which adult establishments are present.

RELATED CASE

***Osborne v. Ohio:* 495 U.S. 103 (1990).**

Although the Court found that the state had proved all the elements of the offense in this case, it ruled that states could enforce laws against the private possession of child pornography.

CITY OF RENTON V. PLAYTIME THEATRES, INC.

475 U.S. 41, 106 S.Ct. 925, 89 L.Ed.2d 29 (1986)

The City of Renton, Washington, enacted a zoning ordinance that prevented adult theaters from locating within a thousand feet of churches, schools, and residential areas. The owner of an adult theater challenged the ordinance as a violation of his First Amendment rights.

Vote: 7–2

JUSTICE REHNQUIST delivered the opinion of the Court.

This case involves a constitutional challenge to a zoning ordinance, enacted by appellant city of Renton, Washington, that prohibits adult motion picture theaters from locating within 1,000 feet of any residential zone, single- or multiple-family dwelling, church, park, or school. Appellees, Playtime Theatres, Inc., and Sea-First Properties, Inc., filed an action in the United States District Court for the Western District of Washington seeking a declaratory judgment that the Renton ordinance violated the First and Fourteenth Amendments and a permanent injunction against its enforcement. The District Court ruled in favor of Renton and denied the permanent injunction, but the Court of Appeals for the Ninth Circuit reversed and remanded for reconsideration. We noted probable jurisdiction, and now reverse the judgment of the Ninth Circuit.

In our view, the resolution of this case is largely dictated by our decision in *Young v. American Mini Theatres, Inc.*, 427 U. S. 50 (1976). There, although five Members of the Court did not agree on a single rationale for the decision, we held that the city of Detroit's zoning ordinance, which prohibited locating an adult theater within 1,000 feet of any two other "regulated uses" or within 500 feet of any residential zone, did not violate the First and Fourteenth Amendments. The Renton ordinance, like the one in *American Mini Theatres,* does not ban adult theaters altogether, but merely provides that such theaters may not be located within 1,000 feet of any residential zone, single- or multiple-family dwelling, church, park, or school. The ordinance is therefore properly analyzed as a form of time, place, and manner regulation.

Describing the ordinance as a time, place, and manner regulation is, of course, only the first step in our inquiry. This Court has long held that regulations enacted for the purpose of restraining speech on the basis of its content presumptively violate the First Amendment. On the other hand, so-called "content-neutral" time, place, and manner regulations are acceptable so long as they are designed to serve a substantial governmental interest and do not unreasonably limit alternative avenues of communication.

At first glance, the Renton ordinance, like the ordinance in *Young v. American Mini Theatres,* 427 U.S. 50 (1976), does not appear to fit neatly into either the "content-based" or the "content-neutral" category. To be sure, the ordinance treats theaters that specialize in adult films differently from other kinds of theaters. Nevertheless, as the District Court concluded, the Renton ordinance is aimed not at the *content* of the films shown at "adult motion picture theatres," but rather at the *secondary effects* of such theaters on the surrounding community. The District Court found that the City Council's "*predominate* concerns" were with the secondary effects of adult theaters, and not with the content of adult films themselves.

It was with this understanding in mind that, in *American Mini Theatres,* a majority of this Court decided that, at least with respect to businesses that purvey sexually explicit materials, zoning ordinances designed to combat the undesirable secondary effects of such businesses are to be reviewed under the standards applicable to "content-neutral" time, place, and manner regulations. Justice Stevens, writing for the plurality, concluded that the city of Detroit was entitled to draw a distinction between adult theaters and other kinds of theaters "without violating the government's paramount obligation of neutrality in its regulation of protected communication," noting that "[i]t is th[e] secondary effect which these zoning ordinances attempt to avoid, not the dissemination of 'offensive' speech,"

> [The] dissent misconceives the issue in this case by insisting that it involves an impermissible time, place, and manner restriction based on the content of expression. It involves nothing of the kind. We have here merely a decision by the city to treat certain movie theaters differently because they have markedly different effects upon their surroundings. . . . Moreover, even if this were a case involving a special governmental response to the content of one type of movie, it is possible that the result would be supported by a line of cases recognizing that the government can tailor its reaction to different types of speech according to the degree to which its special and overriding interests are implicated.

In sum, we find that the Renton ordinance represents a valid governmental response to the "admittedly serious problems" created by adult theaters. Renton has not used "the power to zone as a pretext for suppressing expression," but rather has sought to make some areas available for adult theaters and their patrons, while at the same time preserving the quality of life in the community at large by preventing those theaters from locating in other areas. This, after all, is the essence of zoning. Here, as in *American Mini Theatres,* the city has enacted a zoning ordinance that meets these goals while also satisfying the dictates of the First Amendment. The judgment of the Court of Appeals is therefore

Reversed.

JUSTICE BRENNAN, with whom JUSTICE MARSHALL joins, dissenting.

Renton's zoning ordinance selectively imposes limitations on the location of a movie theater based exclusively on the content of the films shown there. The constitutionality of the ordinance is therefore not correctly analyzed under standards applied to content-neutral time, place, and manner restrictions. But even assuming that the ordinance may fairly be characterized as content neutral, it is plainly unconstitutional under the standards established by the decisions of this Court. Although the Court's analysis is limited to cases involving "businesses that purvey sexually explicit materials," and thus does not affect our holdings in cases involving state regulation of other kinds of speech, I dissent.

I

"[A] constitutionally permissible time, place, or manner restriction may not be based upon either the content or subject matter of speech." *Consolidated Edison Co. v. Public Service Comm'n of N.Y.*, 447 U.S. 530, 536 (1980). The Court asserts that the ordinance is "aimed not at the *content* of the films shown at 'adult motion picture theatres,' but rather at the *secondary effects* of such theaters on the surrounding community," and thus is simply a time, place, and manner regulation. This analysis is misguided.

The fact that adult movie theaters may cause harmful "secondary" land-use effects may arguably give Renton a compelling reason to regulate such establishments; it does not mean, however, that such regulations are content neutral. Because the ordinance imposes special restrictions on certain kinds of speech on the basis of *content,* I cannot simply accept, as the Court does, Renton's claim that the ordinance was not designed to suppress the content of adult movies. "[W]hen regulation is based on the content of speech, governmental action must be scrutinized more carefully to ensure that communication has not been prohibited 'merely because public officials disapprove the speaker's views.' " "[B]efore deferring to [Renton's] judgment, [we] must be convinced that the city is seriously and comprehensively addressing" secondary-land use effects associated with adult movie theaters. In this case, both the language of the ordinance and its dubious legislative history belie the Court's conclusion that "the city's pursuit of its zoning interests here was unrelated to the suppression of free expression."

FOR DISCUSSION

Identify other secondary effects that might be subject to regulation. How expansive is the *Renton* ruling in terms of what it permits?

BARNES V. GLEN THEATRE, INC.

501 U.S. 560, 111 S.Ct. 2456, 115 L.Ed.2d 504 (1991)

An owner of two adult establishments challenged a state law prohibiting totally nude dancing.

Vote: 5–4

CHIEF JUSTICE REHNQUIST delivered the opinion of the Court.

Respondents are two establishments in South Bend, Indiana, that wish to provide totally nude dancing as entertainment, and individual dancers who are employed at these establishments. They claim that the First Amendment's guarantee of freedom of expression prevents the State of Indiana from enforcing its public indecency law to prevent this form of dancing. We reject their claim.

The facts appear from the pleadings and findings of the District Court and are uncontested here. The Kitty Kat Lounge, Inc. (Kitty Kat), is located in the city of South Bend. It sells alcoholic beverages and presents "go-go dancing." Its proprietor desires to present "totally nude dancing," but an applicable Indiana statute regulating public nudity requires that the dancers wear "pasties" and "G-strings" when they dance. The dancers are not paid an hourly wage, but work on commission. They receive a 100 percent commission on the first $60 in drink sales during their performances. Darlene Miller, one of the respondents in the action, had worked at the Kitty Kat for about two years at the time this action was brought. Miller wishes to dance nude because she believes she would make more money doing so.

Respondent Glen Theatre, Inc., is an Indiana corporation with a place of business in South Bend. Its primary business is supplying so-called adult entertainment through written and printed materials, movie showings, and live entertainment at an enclosed "bookstore." The live entertainment at the "bookstore" consists of nude and seminude performances and showings of the female body through glass panels. Customers sit in a booth and insert coins into a timing mechanism that permits them to observe the live nude and seminude dancers for a period of time. One of Glen Theatre's dancers, Gayle Ann Marie Sutro, has danced, modeled, and acted professionally for more than 15 years, and in addition to her performances at the Glen Theatre, can be seen in a pornographic movie at a nearby theater.

Respondents sued in the United States District Court for the Northern District of Indiana to enjoin the enforcement of the Indiana public indecency statute, asserting that its prohibition against complete nudity in public places violated the First Amendment. The District Court originally granted respondents' prayer for an injunction, finding that the statute was facially overbroad. The Court of Appeals for the Seventh Circuit reversed, deciding that previous litigation with respect to the statute in the Supreme Court of Indiana and this Court precluded the possibility of such a challenge, and remanded to the District Court in order for the plaintiffs to pursue their claim that the statute violated the First Amendment as applied to their dancing. On remand, the District Court concluded that "the type of dancing these plaintiffs wish to perform is not expressive activity protected by the Constitution of the United States," and rendered judgment in favor of the defendants. The case was again appealed to the Seventh Circuit, and a panel of that court reversed the District Court, holding that the nude dancing involved here was expressive conduct protected by the First Amendment. The Court of Appeals then heard the case en banc, and the court rendered a series of comprehensive and thoughtful opinions. The majority concluded that nonobscene nude dancing performed for entertainment is expression protected by the First Amendment, and that the public indecency statute was an improper infringement of that expressive activity because its purpose was to prevent the message of eroticism and sexuality conveyed by the dancers. We granted certiorari, and now hold that the Indiana statutory requirement that the dancers in the establishments involved in this case must wear pasties and G-strings does not violate the First Amendment.

The "time, place, or manner" test was developed for evaluating restrictions on expression taking place on public property which had been dedicated as a "public forum," although we have on at least one occasion applied it to conduct occurring on private property. In *Clark v. Community for Nonviolence*, 468 U.S. 288 (1984), we observed that this test has been interpreted to embody much the same standards as those set forth in *United States v. O'Brien,* 391 U.S. 367 (1968), and we turn, therefore, to the rule enunciated in *O'Brien.*

O'Brien burned his draft card on the steps of the South Boston Courthouse in the presence of a sizable crowd, and was convicted of violating a statute that prohibited the knowing destruction or mutilation of such a card. He claimed that his conviction was contrary to the First Amendment because his act was "symbolic speech"—expressive conduct. The Court rejected his contention that symbolic speech is entitled to full First Amendment protection, saying:

> [E]ven on the assumption that the alleged communicative element in O'Brien's conduct is sufficient to bring into play the First Amendment, it does not necessarily follow that the destruction of a registration certificate is constitutionally protected activity. This Court has held that when 'speech' and 'nonspeech' elements are combined in the same course of conduct, a sufficiently important governmental interest in regulating the nonspeech element can justify incidental limitations on First Amendment freedoms. To characterize the quality of the governmental interest which must appear, the Court has employed a variety of descriptive terms: compelling; substantial; subordinating; paramount; cogent; strong. Whatever imprecision inheres in these terms, we think it clear that a government regulation is sufficiently justified if it is within the constitutional power of the Government; if it furthers an important or substantial governmental interest; if the governmental

interest is unrelated to the suppression of free expression; and if the incidental restriction on alleged First Amendment freedoms is no greater than is essential to the furtherance of that interest.

Applying the four-part *O'Brien* test enunciated above, we find that Indiana's public indecency statute is justified despite its incidental limitations on some expressive activity. The public indecency statute is clearly within the constitutional power of the State and furthers substantial governmental interests. It is impossible to discern, other than from the text of the statute, exactly what governmental interest the Indiana legislators had in mind when they enacted this statute, for Indiana does not record legislative history, and the State's highest court has not shed additional light on the statute's purpose. Nonetheless, the statute's purpose of protecting societal order and morality is clear from its text and history. Public indecency statutes of this sort are of ancient origin and presently exist in at least 47 States. Public indecency, including nudity, was a criminal offense at common law, and this Court recognized the common-law roots of the offense of "gross and open indecency" in *Winters v. New York,* 333 U.S. 507 (1948). Public nudity was considered an act *malum in se.* Public indecency statutes such as the one before us reflect moral disapproval of people appearing in the nude among strangers in public places. . . .

[P]ublic indecency statutes were designed to protect morals and public order. The traditional police power of the States is defined as the authority to provide for the public health, safety, and morals, and we have upheld such a basis for legislation.

Thus, the public indecency statute furthers a substantial government interest in protecting order and morality.

This interest is unrelated to the suppression of free expression. Some may view restricting nudity on moral grounds as necessarily related to expression. We disagree. It can be argued, of course, that almost limitless types of conduct—including appearing in the nude in public—are "expressive," and in one sense of the word this is true. People who go about in the nude in public may be expressing something about themselves by so doing.

The judgment of the Court of Appeals accordingly is

Reversed.

JUSTICE SCALIA, concurring in the judgment.

I agree that the judgment of the Court of Appeals must be reversed. In my view, however, the challenged regulation must be upheld, not because it survives some lower level of First Amendment scrutiny, but because, as a general law regulating conduct and not specifically directed at expression, it is not subject to First Amendment scrutiny at all.

JUSTICE WHITE, with whom JUSTICES MARSHALL, BLACKMUN, and STEVENS join, dissenting.

The first question presented to us in this case is whether nonobscene nude dancing performed as entertainment is expressive conduct protected by the First Amendment. The Court of Appeals held that it is, observing that our prior decisions permit no other conclusion. Not surprisingly, then, the plurality now concedes that "nude dancing of the kind sought to be performed here is expressive conduct within the outer perimeters of the First Amendment. . . ." This is no more than recognizing, as the Seventh Circuit observed, that dancing is an ancient art form and "inherently embodies the expression and communication of ideas and emotions."

The Indiana law, as applied to nude dancing, targets the expressive activity itself; in Indiana nudity in a dancing performance is a crime because of the message such dancing communicates. In *Employment Div., Dept. of Human Resources of Oregon v. Smith,* 485 U.S. 660 (1988), the use of drugs was not criminal because the use was part of or occurred within the course of an otherwise protected religious ceremony, but because a general law made it so and was supported by the same interests in the religious context as in others.

Accordingly, I would affirm the judgment of the Court of Appeals, and dissent from this Court's judgment.

FOR DISCUSSION

Under *Barnes*, could a city totally ban all forms of nude dancing? Could it require dancers to be fully clothed? Are laws that require women to cover their breasts in public such at a beach, constitutional? Are nude protests against political causes protected speech?

AMERICAN BOOKSELLERS ASSOCIATION, INC. V. HUDNUT

771 F.2d 323 (7th Cir. 1985)

The City of Indianapolis enacted a law making it a crime to show pornography that depicts women as victims of violence or in positions subordinate to males. The law also gave women standing to sue in court owners or distributors of such materials. Bookstore owners challenged the law as a violation of their First Amendment rights.

CIRCUIT JUDGE EASTERBROOK delivered the opinion of the court.

Indianapolis enacted an ordinance defining "pornography" as a practice that discriminates against women. "Pornography" is to be redressed through the administrative and judicial methods used for other discrimination. The City's definition of "pornography" is considerably different from "obscenity," which the Supreme Court has held is not protected by the First Amendment.

> "Pornography" under the ordinance is "the graphic sexually explicit subordination of women, whether in pictures or in words, that also includes one or more of the following:
>
> (1) Women are presented as sexual objects who enjoy pain or humiliation; or
>
> (2) Women are presented as sexual objects who experience sexual pleasure in being raped; or
>
> (3) Women are presented as sexual objects tied up or cut up or mutilated or bruised or physically hurt, or as dismembered or truncated or fragmented or severed into body parts; or
>
> (4) Women are presented as being penetrated by objects or animals; or
>
> (5) Women are presented in scenarios of degradation, injury, abasement, torture, shown as filthy or inferior, bleeding, bruised, or hurt in a context that makes these conditions sexual; or
>
> (6) Women are presented as sexual objects for domination, conquest, violation, exploitation, possession, or use, or through postures or positions of servility or submission or display."

The statute provides that the "use of men, children, or transsexuals in the place of women in paragraphs (1) through (6) above shall also constitute pornography under this section." The ordinance as passed in April 1984 defined "sexually explicit" to mean actual or simulated intercourse or the uncovered exhibition of the genitals, buttocks or anus. An amendment in June 1984 deleted this provision, leaving the term undefined.

The Indianapolis ordinance does not refer to the prurient interest, to offensiveness, or to the standards of the community. It demands attention to particular depictions, not to the work judged as a whole. It is irrelevant under the ordinance whether the work has literary, artistic, political, or scientific value. The City and many amici point to these omissions as virtues. They maintain that pornography influences attitudes, and the statute is a way to alter the socialization of men and women rather than to vindicate community standards of offensiveness.

And as one of the principal drafters of the ordinance has asserted, "if a woman is subjected, why should it matter that the work has other value?" Catharine A. MacKinnon, Pornography, Civil Rights, and Speech, 20 *Harv.Civ.Rts.—Civ.Lib.L.Rev.* 1, 21 (1985).

We do not try to balance the arguments for and against an ordinance such as this. The ordinance discriminates on the ground of the content of the speech. Speech treating women in the approved way—in sexual encounters "premised on equality"—is lawful no matter how sexually explicit. Speech treating women in the disapproved way—as submissive in matters sexual or as enjoying humiliation—is unlawful no matter how significant the literary, artistic, or political qualities of the work taken as a whole. The state may not ordain preferred viewpoints in this way. The Constitution forbids the state to declare one perspective right and silence opponents.

The ordinance contains four prohibitions. People may not "traffic" in pornography, "coerce" others into performing in pornographic works, or "force" pornography on anyone. Anyone injured by someone who has seen or read pornography has a right of action against the maker or seller.

Trafficking is defined in § 16–3(g)(4) as the "production, sale, exhibition, or distribution of pornography." The offense excludes exhibition in a public or educational library, but a "special display" in a library may be sex discrimination. Section 16–3(g)(4)(C) provides that the trafficking paragraph "shall not be construed to make isolated passages or isolated parts actionable."

"Coercion into pornographic performance" is defined in § 16–3(g)(5) as "[c]oercing, intimidating or fraudulently inducing any person . . . into performing for pornography. . . ." The ordinance specifies that proof of any of the following "shall not constitute a defense: I. That the person is a woman; . . . VI. That the person has previously posed for sexually explicit pictures . . . with anyone. . .; . . . VIII. That the person actually consented to a use of the performance that is changed into pornography; . . . IX. That the person knew that the purpose of the acts or events in question was to make pornography; . . . XI. That the person signed a contract, or made statements affirming a willingness to cooperate in the production of pornography; XII. That no physical force, threats, or weapons were used in the making of the pornography; or XIII. That the person was paid or otherwise compensated."

"Forcing pornography on a person," according to § 16–3(g)(5), is the "forcing of pornography on any woman, man, child, or transsexual in any place of employment, in education, in a home, or in any public place." The statute does not define forcing, but one of its authors states that the definition reaches pornography shown to medical students as part of their education or given to language students for translation.

Section 16–3(g)(7) defines as a prohibited practice the "assault, physical attack, or injury of any woman, man, child, or transsexual in a way that is directly caused by specific pornography."

For purposes of all four offenses, it is generally "not . . . a defense that the respondent did not know or intend that the materials were pornography. . . ." But the ordinance provides that damages are unavailable in trafficking cases unless the complainant proves "that the respondent knew or had reason to know that the materials were pornography." It is a complete defense to a trafficking case that all of the materials in question were pornography only by virtue of category (6) of the definition of pornography. In cases of assault caused by pornography, those who seek damages from "a seller, exhibitor or distributor" must show that the defendant knew or had reason to know of the material's status as pornography. By implication, those who seek damages from an author need not show this.

III

"If there is any fixed star in our constitutional constellation, it is that no official, high or petty, can prescribe what shall be orthodox in politics, nationalism, religion, or other matters of opinion or force citizens to confess by word or act their faith therein." *West Virginia State Board of Education v. Barnette,* 319 U.S. 624 (1943). Under the First Amendment the government must leave to the people the evaluation of ideas. Bald or subtle, an idea is as powerful as the audience allows it to be. A belief may be pernicious—the beliefs of Nazis led to the death of millions, those of the Klan to the repression of millions. A pernicious belief may prevail. Totalitarian governments today rule much of the planet, practicing suppression of billions and spreading dogma that may enslave others. One of the things that separates our society from theirs is our absolute right to propagate opinions that the government finds wrong or even hateful.

The ideas of the Klan may be propagated. Communists may speak freely and run for office. The Nazi Party may march through a city with a large Jewish population. People may criticize the President by misrepresenting his positions, and they have a right to post their misrepresentations on public property. People may teach religions that others despise. People may seek to repeal laws guaranteeing equal opportunity in employment or to revoke the constitutional amendments granting the vote to blacks and women. They may do this because "above all else, the First Amendment means that government has no power to restrict expression because of its message [or] its ideas. . . ."

Under the ordinance graphic sexually explicit speech is "pornography" or not depending on the perspective the author adopts. Speech that "subordinates" women and also, for example, presents women as enjoying pain, humiliation, or rape, or even simply presents women in "positions of servility or submission or display" is forbidden, no matter how great the literary or political value of the work taken as a whole. Speech that portrays women in positions of equality is lawful, no matter how graphic the sexual content. This is thought control. It establishes an "approved" view of women, of how they may react to sexual encounters, of how the sexes may relate to each other. Those who espouse the approved view may use sexual images; those who do not, may not.

Indianapolis justifies the ordinance on the ground that pornography affects thoughts. Men who see women depicted as subordinate are more likely to treat them so. Pornography is an aspect of dominance. It does not persuade people so much as change them. It works by socializing, by establishing the expected and the permissible. In this view pornography is not an idea; pornography is the injury.

There is much to this perspective. Beliefs are also facts. People often act in accordance with the images and patterns they find around them. People raised in a religion tend to accept the tenets of that religion, often without independent examination. People taught from birth that black people are fit only for slavery rarely rebelled against that creed; beliefs coupled with the self-interest of the masters established a social structure that inflicted great harm while enduring for centuries. Words and images act at the level of the subconscious before they persuade at the level of the conscious. Even the truth has little chance unless a statement fits within the framework of beliefs that may never have been subjected to rational study.

Yet this simply demonstrates the power of pornography as speech. All of these unhappy effects depend on mental intermediation. Pornography affects how people see the world, their fellows, and social relations. If pornography is what pornography does, so is other speech. Hitler's orations affected how some Germans saw Jews. Communism is a world view, not simply a *Manifesto* by Marx and Engels or a set of speeches. Efforts to suppress communist speech in the United States were based on the belief that the public acceptability of such ideas would increase the likelihood of totalitarian government. Religions affect socialization in the most pervasive way.

Racial bigotry, anti-semitism, violence on television, reporters' biases—these and many more influence the culture and shape our socialization. None is directly answerable by more speech, unless that speech too finds its place in the popular culture. Yet all is protected as speech, however insidious. Any other answer leaves the government in control of all of the institutions of culture, the great censor and director of which thoughts are good for us.

Sexual responses often are unthinking responses, and the association of sexual arousal with the subordination of women therefore may have a substantial effect. But almost all cultural stimuli provoke unconscious responses. Religious ceremonies condition their participants. Teachers convey messages by selecting what not to cover; the implicit message about what is off limits or unthinkable may be more powerful than the messages for which they present rational argument. Television scripts contain unarticulated assumptions. People may be conditioned in subtle ways. If the fact that speech plays a role in a process of conditioning were enough to permit governmental regulation, that would be the end of freedom of speech.

It is possible to interpret the claim that the pornography is the harm in a different way. Indianapolis emphasizes the injury that models in pornographic films and pictures may suffer. The record contains materials depicting sexual torture, penetration of women by red-hot irons and the like. These concerns have nothing to do with written materials subject to the statute, and physical injury can occur with or without the "subordination" of women.

IV

The definition of "pornography" is unconstitutional. No construction or excision of particular terms could save it. The offense of trafficking in pornography necessarily falls with the definition. We express no view on the district court's conclusions that the ordinance is vague and that it establishes a prior restraint. Neither is necessary to our judgment. We also express no view on the argument presented by several amici that the ordinance is itself a form of discrimination on account of sex.

No amount of struggle with particular words and phrases in this ordinance can leave anything in effect. The district court came to the same conclusion. Its judgment is therefore

AFFIRMED.

FOR DISCUSSION

Suppose it were shown beyond dispute that a real link existed between the pornography at issue in this case and violence against women. Would that showing justify the law? Is this case about obscenity and violence or about advocacy?

REGINA V. BUTLER

1992 Carswell Man 100 (Supreme Court of Canada)

Canada enacted a law similar to the one found unconstitutional in Indianapolis (see *Hudnut* case, above) that made it illegal to depict women and others in exploitive or violent sexual situations. A bookstore owner challenged the law as a violation of the Canadian Charter of Rights and Freedoms (the Canadian version of the American Bill of Rights).

1. Facts and Proceedings

The Court summaries the applicable laws and jurisdiction in the case.

2 In August 1987, the appellant, Donald Victor Butler, opened the Avenue Video Boutique located in Winnipeg, Manitoba. The shop sells and rents "hard-core" videotapes and magazines as well as sexual paraphernalia. Outside the store is a sign which reads:

Avenue Video Boutique; a private members only adult video/visual club.

Notice: if sex oriented material offends you, please do not enter.

No admittance to persons under 18 years.

3 On August 21, 1987 the city of Winnipeg police entered the appellant's store with a search warrant and seized all the inventory. The appellant was charged with 173 counts in the first indictment: three counts of selling obscene material contrary to § 159(2)(*a*) of the *Criminal Code*, R.S.C. 1970, ¶ C–34 (now § 163(2)(*a*)), 41 counts of possessing obscene material for the purpose of distribution contrary to § 159(1)(*a*) (now § 163(1)(*a*)) of the *Criminal Code*, 128 counts of possessing obscene material for the purpose of sale contrary to s. 159(2)(*a*) of the *Criminal Code* and one count of exposing obscene material to public view contrary to § 159(2)(*a*) of the *Criminal Code.*

4 On October 19, 1987, the appellant reopened the store at the same location. As a result of a police operation a search warrant was executed on October 29, 1987, resulting in the arrest of an employee, Norma McCord. The appellant was arrested at a later date.

5 A joint indictment was laid against the appellant doing business as Avenue Video Boutique and Norma McCord. The joint indictment contains 77 counts under § 159 (now § 163) of the *Criminal Code*: two counts of selling obscene material contrary to § 159(2)(*a*), 73 counts of possessing obscene material for the purpose of distribution contrary to § 159(1)(*a*), one count of possessing obscene material for the purpose of sale contrary to § 159(2)(*a*) and one count of exposing obscene material to public view contrary to § 159(2)(*a*).

6 The trial judge convicted the appellant on eight counts relating to eight films. Convictions were entered against the co-accused McCord with respect to two counts relating to two of the films. Fines of $1,000 per offence were imposed on the appellant. Acquittals were entered on the remaining charges.

7 The Crown appealed the 242 acquittals with respect to the appellant and the appellant cross-appealed the convictions. The majority of the Manitoba Court of Appeal allowed the appeal of the Crown and entered convictions for the appellant with respect to all of the counts, Twaddle and Helper JJ.A. dissenting.

2. Relevant Legislation

Criminal Code, R.S.C. 1985, ¶ C–46

28. 163.(1) Everyone commits an offence who,

(*a*) makes, prints, publishes, distributes, circulates, or has in his possession for the purpose of publication, distribution or circulation any obscene written matter, picture, model, phonograph record or other thing whatever; or

(*b*) makes, prints, publishes, distributes, sells or has in his possession for the purpose of publication, distribution or circulation a crime comic.

(8) For the purposes of this Act, any publication a dominant characteristic of which is the undue exploitation of sex, or of sex and any one or more of the following subjects, namely, crime, horror, cruelty and violence, shall be deemed to be obscene.

3. Issues

29 The following constitutional questions are raised by this appeal:

30 1. Does § 163 of the *Criminal Code* of Canada, R.S.C. 1985, ¶ C–46, violate § 2(*b*) of the *Canadian Charter of Rights and Freedoms*?

31 2. If § 163 of the *Criminal Code* of Canada, R.S.C. 1985, c. C–46, violates § 2(*b*) of the *Canadian Charter of Rights and Freedoms*, can § 163 of the *Criminal Code* of Canada be demonstrably justified under § 1 of the *Canadian Charter of Rights and Freedoms* as a reasonable limit prescribed by law?

Analysis

B. Judicial Interpretation of § 163(8)

(a) Section 163(8) to be Exclusive Test

42 Any doubt that § 163(8) was intended to provide an exhaustive test of obscenity was settled in R. *v. Dechow*, (1978) 1 S.C.R. 951. Laskin C.J.C. stated (at p. 962) [S.C.R.]:

> I am not only satisfied to regard § 159(8) [now s. 163(8)] as prescribing an exhaustive test of obscenity in respect of a publication which has sex as a theme or characteristic but I am also of the opinion that this Court should apply that test in respect of other provisions of the *Code*, such as §§ 163 and 164, in cases in which the allegation of obscenity revolves around sex considerations. Since the view that I take, in line with that expressed by Judson J. in the *Brodie* case, is that the *Hicklin* rule has been displaced by § 159(8) in respect of publications, I would not bring it back under any other sections of the *Code*, such as §§ 159, 163 and 164, to provide a back-up where a sexual theme or sexual factors are the basis upon which obscenity charges are laid and the charges fail because the test prescribed by s. 159(8) has not been met.

(b) Tests of "Undue Exploitation of Sex"

44 In order for the work or material to qualify as "obscene," the exploitation of sex must not only be its dominant characteristic, but such exploitation must be "undue." In determining when the exploitation of sex will be considered "undue," the courts have attempted to formulate workable tests. The most important of these is the "community standard of tolerance" test.

53 In *Towne Cinema*, Dickson C.J.C. considered the "degradation" or "dehumanization" test to be the principal indicator of "undueness" without specifying what role the community tolerance test plays in respect of this issue. He did observe, however, that the community might tolerate some forms of exploitation that caused harm that were nevertheless undue. The relevant passages appear at p. 505:

> Sex related publications which portray persons in a degrading manner as objects of violence, cruelty or other forms of dehumanizing treatment, may be "undue" for the purpose of § 159(8). No one should be subject to the degradation and humiliation inherent in publications which link sex with violence, cruelty, and other forms of dehumanizing treatment. It is not likely that at a given moment in a society's history, such publications will be tolerated. . . .

C. Does § 163 Violate § 2(b) of the Charter?

77 In assessing whether § 163(8) prescribes an intelligible standard, consideration must be given to the manner in which the provision has been judicially interpreted.

78 Standards which escape precise technical definition, such as "undue," are an inevitable part of the law. The *Criminal Code* contains other such standards. Without commenting on their constitutional validity, I note that the terms "indecent," "immoral" or "scurrilous," found in §§ 167, 168, 173 and 175, are nowhere defined in the *Code*. It is within the role of the judiciary to attempt to interpret these terms. If such interpretation yields an intelligible standard, the threshold test for the application of § 1 is met. In my opinion, the interpretation of § 163(8) in prior judgments which I have reviewed, as supplemented by these reasons, provides an intelligible standard.

(b) Objective

79 The respondent argues that there are several pressing and substantial objectives which justify overriding the freedoms to distribute obscene materials. Essentially, these objectives are the avoidance of harm resulting from antisocial attitudinal changes that exposure to obscene material causes and the public interest in

maintaining a "decent society." On the other hand, the appellant argues that the objective of § 163 is to have the state act as "moral custodian" in sexual matters and to impose subjective standards of morality.

84 In my view, however, the overriding objective of § 163 is not moral disapprobation but the avoidance of harm to society. In *Towne Cinema*, Dickson C.J.C. stated, "It is harm to society from undue exploitation that is aimed at by the section, not simply lapses in propriety or good taste."

85 The harm was described in the following way in the Report on Pornography by the Standing Committee on Justice and Legal Affairs ("MacGuigan Report") (1978)(at p. 18:4):

> The clear and unquestionable danger of this type of material is that it reinforces some unhealthy tendencies in Canadian society. The effect of this type of material is to reinforce male-female stereotypes to the detriment of both sexes. It attempts to make degradation, humiliation, victimization, and violence in human relationships appear normal and acceptable. A society which holds that egalitarianism, non-violence, consensualism, and mutuality are basic to any human interaction, whether sexual or other, is clearly justified in controlling and prohibiting any medium of depiction, description or advocacy which violates these principles.

5. Conclusion

128 I conclude that while § 163(8) infringes § 2(*b*) of the *Charter*, freedom of expression, it constitutes a reasonable limit and is saved by virtue of the provisions of § 1. The trial judge convicted the appellant only with respect to materials which contained scenes involving violence or cruelty intermingled with sexual activity or depicted lack of consent to sexual contact or otherwise could be said to dehumanize men or women in a sexual context. The majority of the Court of Appeal, on the other hand, convicted the appellant on all charges.

FOR DISCUSSION

How does one explain the difference between this decision and the one in *Hudnut*? Is it sufficient to say that the United States cares more about free expression and Canada more about women?

ASHCROFT V. AMERICAN CIVIL LIBERTIES UNION

542 U.S. 656, 124 S.Ct. 2783, 159 L.Ed.2d 690 (2004)

Congress enacted the Child Online Protection Act (COPA) in an effort to protect children from adult sexual materials and sexual predators. COPA was enacted after the Supreme Court had declared a previous congressional effort to regulate sexual content on the Internet to be a violation of the First Amendment, hence unconstitutional. COPA was challenged because it, too, was believed to be unconstitutional, for similar reasons.

Vote: 5–4

JUSTICE KENNEDY delivered the opinion of the Court.

This case presents a challenge to a statute enacted by Congress to protect minors from exposure to sexually explicit materials on the Internet, the Child Online Protection Act (COPA). We must decide whether the Court of Appeals was correct to affirm a ruling by the District Court that enforcement of COPA should be enjoined because the statute likely violates the First Amendment.

In enacting COPA, Congress gave consideration to our earlier decisions on this subject, in particular the decision in *Reno v. American Civil Liberties Union,* 521 U.S. 844 (1997). For that reason, "the Judiciary must proceed with caution and . . . with care before invalidating the Act." The imperative of according respect to the Congress, however, does not permit us to depart from well-established First Amendment principles. Instead, we must hold the Government to its constitutional burden of proof.

Content-based prohibitions, enforced by severe criminal penalties, have the constant potential to be a repressive force in the lives and thoughts of a free people. To guard against that threat the Constitution demands that content-based restrictions on speech be presumed invalid, and that the Government bear the burden of showing their constitutionality. This is true even when Congress twice has attempted to find a constitutional means to restrict, and punish, the speech in question.

I

A

COPA is the second attempt by Congress to make the Internet safe for minors by criminalizing certain Internet speech. The first attempt was the Communications Decency Act of 1996. The Court held the CDA unconstitutional because it was not narrowly tailored to serve a compelling governmental interest and because less restrictive alternatives were available.

In response to the Court's decision in *Reno,* Congress passed COPA. COPA imposes criminal penalties of a $50,000 fine and six months in prison for the knowing posting, for "commercial purposes," of World Wide Web content that is "harmful to minors." Material that is "harmful to minors" is defined as:

any communication, picture, image, graphic image file, article, recording, writing, or other matter of any kind that is obscene or that—

> (A) the average person, applying contemporary community standards, would find, taking the material as a whole and with respect to minors, is designed to appeal to, or is designed to pander to, the prurient interest;
>
> (B) depicts, describes, or represents, in a manner patently offensive with respect to minors, an actual or simulated sexual act or sexual contact, an actual or simulated normal or perverted sexual act, or a lewd exhibition of the genitals or post-pubescent female breast; and
>
> (C) taken as a whole, lacks serious literary, artistic, political, or scientific value for minors.

"Minors" are defined as "any person under 17 years of age." § 231(e)(7). A person acts for "commercial purposes only if such person is engaged in the business of making such communications." "Engaged in the business," in turn,

> means that the person who makes a communication, or offers to make a communication, by means of the World Wide Web, that includes any material that is harmful to minors, devotes time, attention, or labor to such activities, as a regular course of such person's trade or business, with the objective of earning a profit as a result of such activities (although it is not necessary that the person make a profit or that the making or offering to make such communications be the person's sole or principal business or source of income).

While the statute labels all speech that falls within these definitions as criminal speech, it also provides an affirmative defense to those who employ specified means to prevent minors from gaining access to the prohibited materials on their Web site. A person may escape conviction under the statute by demonstrating that he has restricted access by minors to material that is harmful to minors—

(A) by requiring use of a credit card, debit account, adult access code, or adult personal identification number;

(B) by accepting a digital certificate that verifies age, or

(C) by any other reasonable measures that are feasible under available technology.

II

A

The District Court, in deciding to grant the preliminary injunction, concentrated primarily on the argument that there are plausible, less restrictive alternatives to COPA. A statute that "effectively suppresses a large amount of speech that adults have a constitutional right to receive and to address to one another . . . is unacceptable if less restrictive alternatives would be at least as effective in achieving the legitimate purpose that the statute was enacted to serve." When plaintiffs challenge a content-based speech restriction, the burden is on the Government to prove that the proposed alternatives will not be as effective as the challenged statute.

In considering this question, a court assumes that certain protected speech may be regulated, and then asks what is the least restrictive alternative that can be used to achieve that goal. The purpose of the test is not to consider whether the challenged restriction has some effect in achieving Congress' goal, regardless of the restriction it imposes. The purpose of the test is to ensure that speech is restricted no further than necessary to achieve the goal, for it is important to ensure that legitimate speech is not chilled or punished. For that reason, the test does not begin with the status quo of existing regulations, then ask whether the challenged restriction has some additional ability to achieve Congress' legitimate interest. Any restriction on speech could be justified under that analysis. Instead, the court should ask whether the challenged regulation is the least restrictive means among available, effective alternatives.

In deciding whether to grant a preliminary injunction stage, a district court must consider whether the plaintiffs have demonstrated that they are likely to prevail on the merits. The court also considers whether the plaintiff has shown irreparable injury, but the parties in this case do not contest the correctness of the District Court's conclusion that a likelihood of irreparable injury had been established. As the Government bears the burden of proof on the ultimate question of COPA's constitutionality, respondents must be deemed likely to prevail unless the Government has shown that respondents' proposed less restrictive alternatives are less effective than COPA. Applying that analysis, the District Court concluded that respondents were likely to prevail. That conclusion was not an abuse of discretion, because on this record there are a number of plausible, less restrictive alternatives to the statute.

The primary alternative considered by the District Court was blocking and filtering software. Blocking and filtering software is an alternative that is less restrictive than COPA, and, in addition, likely more effective as a means of restricting children's access to materials harmful to them. The District Court, in granting the preliminary injunction, did so primarily because the plaintiffs had proposed that filters are a less restrictive alternative to COPA and the Government had not shown it would be likely to disprove the plaintiffs' contention at trial.

Filters are less restrictive than COPA. They impose selective restrictions on speech at the receiving end, not universal restrictions at the source. Under a filtering regime, adults without children may gain access to speech they have a right to see without having to identify themselves or provide their credit card information. Even adults with children may obtain access to the same speech on the same terms simply by turning off the filter on their home computers. Above all, promoting the use of filters does not condemn as criminal any category of speech, and so the potential chilling effect is eliminated, or at least much diminished. All of these things are true, moreover, regardless of how broadly or narrowly the definitions in COPA are construed.

Filters also may well be more effective than COPA. First, a filter can prevent minors from seeing all pornography, not just pornography posted to the Web from America. The District Court noted in its fact findings that one witness estimated that 40% of harmful-to-minors content comes from overseas. COPA does not prevent minors from having access to those foreign harmful materials. That alone makes it possible that filtering software might be more effective in serving Congress' goals. Effectiveness is likely to diminish even further if COPA is upheld, because the providers of the materials that would be covered by the statute simply can move their operations overseas. It is not an answer to say that COPA reaches some amount of materials that are harmful to minors; the question is whether it would reach more of them than less restrictive alternatives. In addition, the District Court found that verification systems may be subject to evasion and circumvention, for example by minors who have their own credit cards. Finally, filters also may be more effective because they can be applied to all forms of Internet communication, including e-mail, not just communications available via the World Wide Web.

The Government's burden is not merely to show that a proposed less restrictive alternative has some flaws; its burden is to show that it is less effective. It is not enough for the Government to show that COPA has some effect. Nor do respondents bear a burden to introduce, or offer to introduce, evidence that their proposed alternatives are more effective. The Government has the burden to show they are less so. The Government having failed to carry its burden, it was not an abuse of discretion for the District Court to grant the preliminary injunction.

On this record, the Government has not shown that the less restrictive alternatives proposed by respondents should be disregarded. Those alternatives, indeed, may be more effective than the provisions of COPA. The District Court did not abuse its discretion when it entered the preliminary injunction. The judgment of the Court of Appeals is affirmed, and the case is remanded for proceedings consistent with this opinion.

It is so ordered.

JUSTICE STEVENS, with whom JUSTICE GINSBURG joins, concurring.

When it first reviewed the constitutionality of the Child Online Protection Act (COPA), the Court of Appeals held that the statute's use of "contemporary community standards" to identify materials that are "harmful to minors" was a serious, and likely fatal, defect. I have already explained at some length why I agree with that holding. I continue to believe that the Government may not penalize speakers for making available to the general World Wide Web audience that which the least tolerant communities in America deem unfit for their children's consumption, and consider that principle a sufficient basis for deciding this case.

But COPA's use of community standards is not the statute's only constitutional defect. Today's decision points to another: that, as far as the record reveals, encouraging deployment of user-based controls, such as filtering software, would serve Congress' interest in protecting minors from sexually explicit Internet materials as well or better than attempting to regulate the vast content of the World Wide Web at its source, and at a far less significant cost to First Amendment values.

JUSTICE BREYER, with whom CHIEF JUSTICE REHNQUIST and JUSTICE O'CONNOR join, dissenting.

The Child Online Protection Act (Act) seeks to protect children from exposure to commercial pornography placed on the Internet. It does so by requiring commercial providers to place pornographic material behind Internet "screens" readily accessible to adults who produce age verification. The Court recognizes that we should " 'proceed . . . with care before invalidating the Act,' " while pointing out that the "imperative of according respect to the Congress . . . does not permit us to depart from well-established First Amendment principles." I agree with these generalities. Like the Court, I would subject the Act to "the most exacting scrutiny," requiring the Government to show that any restriction of nonobscene expression is "narrowly drawn" to further a "compelling interest" and that the restriction amounts to the "least restrictive means" available to further that interest.

Nonetheless, my examination of (1) the burdens the Act imposes on protected expression, (2) the Act's ability to further a compelling interest, and (3) the proposed "less restrictive alternatives" convinces me that the Court is wrong. I cannot accept its conclusion that Congress could have accomplished its statutory objective—protecting children from commercial pornography on the Internet—in other, less restrictive ways.

III

I turn, then, to the actual "less restrictive alternatives" that the Court proposes. The Court proposes two real alternatives, *i.e.,* two potentially less restrictive ways in which Congress might alter the status quo in order to achieve its "compelling" objective.

First, the Government might "act to encourage" the use of blocking and filtering software. The problem is that any argument that rests upon this alternative proves too much. If one imagines enough government resources devoted to the problem and perhaps additional scientific advances, then, of course, the use of software might become as effective and less restrictive. Obviously, the Government could give all parents, schools, and Internet cafes free computers with filtering programs already installed, hire federal employees to train parents and teachers on their use, and devote millions of dollars to the development of better software. The result might be an alternative that is extremely effective.

But the Constitution does not, because it cannot, require the Government to disprove the existence of magic solutions, *i.e.,* solutions that, put in general terms, will solve any problem less restrictively but with equal effectiveness. Otherwise, "the undoubted ability of lawyers and judges," who are not constrained by the budgetary worries and other practical parameters within which Congress must operate, "to imagine *some* kind of slightly less drastic or restrictive an approach would make it impossible to write laws that deal with the harm that called the statute into being." As Justice Blackmun recognized, a "judge would be unimaginative indeed if he could not come up with something a little less 'drastic' or a little less 'restrictive' in almost any situation, and thereby enable himself to vote to strike legislation down." Illinois Bd. of Elections v. Socialist Workers Party, 440 U.S. 173, 188–189, 59 L. Ed. 2d 230, 99 S. Ct. 983 (1979) (concurring opinion). Perhaps that is why no party has argued seriously that additional expenditure of government funds to encourage the use of screening is a "less restrictive alternative."

FOR DISCUSSION

What are some other ways in place to protect children from online pornography and sexual predators? Is there anything Congress can do, or is the matter up to parents?

RELATED CASES

***Ashcroft v. Free Speech Coalition:* 535 U.S. 234 (2002).**

The Court struck down portions of the Child Pornography Prevention Act of 1996 (CPPA). Specifically, the Court ruled that the portion of CPPA that banned depictions of minors engaged in sexual activity, including computer-simulated depictions, was overbroad. The Court noted that by the definitions of CPPA, many works of literature, such as *Romeo and Juliet,* would be banned.

Federal Communications Commission v. Fox Television Stations: **567 U.S. 229 (2012).**

Ruled that the FCC rules on fleeting expletives and fleeting nudity had not provided proper notice to stations, which was essential to due process. J. Kennedy's majority opinion specifically noted that he was not reconsidering the opinion in *FCC v. Pacifica* (1978)

Fox v. Federal Communications Commission: **556 U.S. 502 (2009).**

Upheld by a 5–4 vote the contention that an FCC had not acted in an arbitrary fashion in regulating the airing of four-letter words called "fleeting expletives" from the news or live shows. The Court did not specifically decide whether the speech itself was constitutional or not.

Federal Communications Commission v. Pacifica Foundation: **438 U.S. 726 (1978).**

Upheld the authority of the FCC to ban the radio broadcasting of George Carlin's "Seven Dirty Words" comedy routine.

Brown v. Entertainment Merchants Ass'n

564 U.S. 786, 131 S.Ct. 2729, 180 L.Ed.2d 708 (2011)

Located in Chapter III, page 185.

FOR DISCUSSION

What is the expressive content or speech in violent video games? Is it clear what "violent" means? *America's Army* is the official video game of the US Military, used for both training and recruitment purposes, and it is available to play or download on the Internet. How might have its use and distribution by the Military been affected by the California law and how does it use by the military affect the First Amendment arguments here, especially when it comes to the argument about regulating violence?

Commercial Speech

Anyone who watches television, listens to the radio, surfs the Web, or reads a newspaper or magazine is bombarded with commercials and advertisements for products and services. These may be for legitimate products from reputable dealers, or they may constitute no more than spam or junk advertising from dubious hustlers. How these ads are viewed varies from consumer to consumer. But whatever the merit of advertising, is it certain that this speech deserved First Amendment protection?

At the time when the Supreme Court first began protecting freedom of speech, it did not extend First Amendment protection to commercial speech, which includes communications by corporations or speech that involves business transactions such as solicitations or advertising. Generally, it was assumed that the core of the Free Speech Clause protected political communications by individuals; eventually, other forms of speech such as self-expression or symbolic speech were recognized either as constitutionally equal or as receiving some form of lesser protection. Other forms of communication, such as those defined as obscene and commercial speech, fell outside the ambit of the First Amendment.

In *Valentine v. Chrestensen* (316 U.S. 52, 1942) the issue was whether the public distribution of handbills advertising a boat was protected speech. Justice Roberts quickly dismissed the case, contending that the First

Amendment did not protect commercial speech. In *Pittsburgh Press v. Pittsburgh Commission on Human Relations* (413 U.S. 376, 1973), the Court upheld an ordinance making it illegal to run help-wanted ads in sex columns. Again, the Court ruled that commercial speech stood outside the pale of constitutional protection. Moreover, even in the area of political speech, the 1907 Tillman Act barred corporations from expending money to influence federal elections, thereby restricting the political activity of these entities, although in the *Citizens United v. Federal Election Commission*, 558 U.S. 310, 2010), the Supreme Court expanded the political free speech rights of corporations (and labor unions) to spend money to influence elections. (The *Citizens United* case is discussed in more detail in Chapter IX and in volume one of this textbook where the political rights of corporations are examined). Yet while it was deemed unworthy of First Amendment protection, commercial speech was defined narrowly. In 1964 the case of *New York Times v. Sullivan* (376 U.S. 254), a major decision regarding press freedom and libel discussed elsewhere in this volume, the Supreme Court rejected arguments that the alleged libelous language stood outside the First Amendment because it appeared in a paid advertisement in the newspaper. In this case, Justice Brennan, writing for the Court, defined *Valentine* narrowly and distinguished it from the ad in the *New York Times* case, indicating that in *New York Times* civil rights groups had purchased the speech to communicate their opinions. In *Valentine*, the handbills merely proposed a commercial transaction. Thus, at least until the early 1970s, the constitutional consensus seemed to be that commercial speech fell outside the First Amendment.

Yet the crack in the commercial speech wall occurred in *Bigelow v. Virginia* (421 U.S. 809, 1975). Here a newspaper sought to run an advertisement in Virginia, where state law barred the advertising of abortion services, for a legal abortion service in New York. In part, the advertisement stated:

UNWANTED PREGNANCY
LET US HELP YOU
Abortions are now legal in New York.
There are no residency requirements.
FOR IMMEDIATE PLACEMENT IN ACCREDITED
HOSPITALS AND CLINICS AT LOW COST
Contact
WOMEN'S PAVILION
515 Madison Avenue
New York, N.Y. 10022

The Supreme Court overturned the Virginia law, ruling that the ad contained not only a commercial solicitation for services: "The advertisement published in appellant's newspaper did more than simply propose a commercial transaction. It contained factual material of clear 'public interest.' Portions of its message, most prominently the lines, 'Abortions are now legal in New York. There are no residency requirements,' involve the exercise of the freedom of communicating information and disseminating opinion." Stating that "speech is not stripped of First Amendment protection merely because it appears in that form" (i.e., the form of an advertisement), the Court found that the abortion ad and some forms of commercial speech were entitled to First Amendment protection.

The move to protect more traditional commercial solicitations or ads with the First Amendment began a year later in *Virginia State Board of Pharmacy v. Virginia Citizens Consumer Council, Inc.* (425 U.S. 748, 1976). Virginia had adopted a law preventing the advertising of prescription drug prices, supported by the rationale that such a ban was necessary to protect consumers. The Court saw the issue differently, focusing on the on the First Amendment right of the consumer to receive information through advertising and thus invalidating the law.

After the *Virginia Board of Pharmacy* ruling, commercial speech was deemed to come within the scope of the First Amendment. Striking down of the ban on drug price advertising also had a cascade effect into other areas of commercial speech. For example, the Court used the reasoning in the *Virginia Board of Pharmacy* decision to invalidate long-standing rules by states and bar associations barring lawyers from advertising.

However, while *Virginia Board of Pharmacy* ruled that commercial speech deserved some First Amendment protection, the Court did not articulate how much. Did it enjoy a status equal to that of other forms of communication, such as political speech? Were there circumstances under which it could be restricted? These questions were unresolved until *Central Hudson Gas & Elec. Corp. v. Public Service Commission of New York* (447 U.S. 557, 1980). *Central Hudson* is important because it created an important test (the ***Central Hudson* test**) outlining the scope of government regulation of commercial speech. For the Court:

> In commercial speech cases, then, a four-part analysis has developed. At the outset, we must determine whether the expression is protected by the First Amendment. For commercial speech to come within that provision, it at least must concern lawful activity and not be misleading. Next, we ask whether the asserted governmental interest is substantial. If both inquiries yield positive answers, we must determine whether the regulation directly advances the governmental interest asserted, and whether it is not more extensive than is necessary to serve that interest.

Central Hudson's four-part test for regulation of commercial speech remains the basic criterion in determining whether advertising materials or communications by businesses are entitled to constitutional protection. But just because the test seemed to offer constitutional protection to commercial speech did not mean that all forms of this type of communication would be protected. In some cases, commercial speech protections gave way to police power authority to protect the welfare of the people.

The next two cases demonstrate the contrasting ways in which the *Central Hudson* test has been used either to protect the public or give them information they may want or need as consumers.

The first case, *Posadas de Puerto Rico Associates v. Tourism Co. of P. R.* (478 U.S. 328, 1986), upholds the constitutionality of a ban in Puerto Rico on gaming and casino ads to residents while at the same time permitting such promotions to be directed toward tourists. The Court, using the four-part test, finds that the government's interest in protecting the health, safety, welfare, and morals of Puerto Rico's residents is substantial and that it outweighs the First Amendment rights of the casinos. Here, Justice Rehnquist found that protecting residents against the prostitution, organized crime, and what might be called the secondary effects of gaming justified the limits on advertising. While gambling was not illegal, nonetheless the Court found that the ban on advertising was a legitimate effort to protect residents. Conversely, in *44 Liquormart, Inc. v. Rhode Island* (517 U.S. 484, 1996), the Court declared a state ban on liquor price advertising unconstitutional. The decision in this case seems to be almost a simple repeat of the decision in *Virginia Board of Pharmacy.*

In reading *Posadas* and *44Liquormart,* ask why the Puerto Rican ban was upheld but the ban in Rhode Island was not. Both cases were decided using the *Central Hudson* test. Is there a clear rationale that distinguishes the two types of advertising? Many critics of the former decision think not.

One consequence of the increase in protection for commercial speech was a 1996 federal law permitting drug and pharmaceutical companies to advertise prescription drugs directly to consumers. Such advertising is a highly profitable venture, generating billions in revenue for drug manufacturers. While some assert that these ads produce better informed consumers who can make better judgments about their health, others respond that freedom to reach out to consumers directly has changed the practice of medicine, undermining the traditional doctor-patient relationship as individuals go to their physicians insisting that the cure to their ailments rests in a prescription for a specific brand-name drug. Given the decisions in the commercial speech cases, can it be said that all regulations on advertising, as long as not deceptive, are beyond the scope of regulation? What is the level of constitutional protection commercial speech effectively has as a result of these decisions? Does it look as though the longer-term trend is to elevate commercial speech to the same status as political speech? These are some of the questions to ponder as one looks at these cases.

VIRGINIA STATE BOARD OF PHARMACY V. VIRGINIA CITIZENS CONSUMER COUNCIL, INC.

425 U.S. 748, 96 S.Ct. 1817, 48 L.Ed.2d 346 (1976)

The State of Virginia made it illegal for pharmacists to advertise prescription prices. A consumer group challenged the law, seeking to obtain prescription prices to help buyers make price comparisons.

Vote: 8–1

JUSTICE BLACKMUN delivered the opinion of the Court.

The plaintiff-appellees in this case attack, as violative of the First and Fourteenth Amendments, that portion of s 54–524.35 of Va.Code Ann. (1974), which provides that a pharmacist licensed in Virginia is guilty of unprofessional conduct if he "(3) publishes, advertises or promotes, directly or indirectly, in any manner whatsoever, any amount, price, fee, premium, discount, rebate or credit terms . . . for any drugs which may be dispensed only by prescription." The three-judge District Court declared the quoted portion of the statute "void and of no effect" and enjoined the defendant-appellants, the Virginia State Board of Pharmacy and the individual members of that Board, from enforcing it.

I

[This section describes the status of pharmacists under Virginia law.]

II

This is not the first challenge to the constitutionality of § 54–524.35 and what is now its third-numbered phrase. Shortly after the phrase was added to the statute in 1968, a suit seeking to enjoin its operation was instituted by a drug retailing company and one of its pharmacists. Although the First Amendment was invoked, the challenge appears to have been based primarily on the Due Process and Equal Protection Clauses of the Fourteenth Amendment. In any event, the prohibition on drug price advertising was upheld. The three-judge court did find that the dispensation of prescription drugs "affects the public health, safety and welfare." No appeal was taken.

The present, and second, attack on the statute is one made not by one directly subject to its prohibition, that is, a pharmacist, but by prescription drug consumers who claim that they would greatly benefit if the prohibition were lifted and advertising freely allowed. The plaintiffs are an individual Virginia resident who suffers from diseases that require her to take prescription drugs on a daily basis, and two nonprofit organizations. Their claim that the First Amendment entitles the user of prescription drugs to receive information that pharmacists wish to communicate to them through advertising and other promotional means, concerning the prices of such drugs.

Certainly that information may be of value. Drug prices in Virginia, for both prescription and nonprescription items, strikingly vary from outlet to outlet even within the same locality. It is stipulated, for example, that in Richmond "the cost of 40 Achromycin tablets ranges from $2.59 to $6.00, a difference of 140% (Sic)," and that in the Newport News-Hampton area the cost of tetracycline ranges from $1.20 to $9.00, a difference of 650%.

III

The question first arises whether, even assuming that First Amendment protection attaches to the flow of drug price information, it is a protection enjoyed by the appellees as recipients of the information, and not solely, if at all, by the advertisers themselves who seek to disseminate that information.

Freedom of speech presupposes a willing speaker. But where a speaker exists, as is the case here, the protection afforded is to the communication, to its source and to its recipients both. This is clear from the decided cases. In *Lamont v. Postmaster General,* 381 U.S. 301 (1965), the Court upheld the First Amendment rights of citizens to receive political publications sent from abroad. More recently, in *Kleindienst v. Mandel,* 408 U.S. 753 (1972), we acknowledged that this Court has referred to a First Amendment right to "receive information and ideas," and that freedom of speech " 'necessarily protects the right to receive.' " And in *Procunier v. Martinez,* 416 U.S. 396 (1974), where censorship of prison inmates' mail was under examination, we thought it unnecessary to assess the First Amendment rights of the inmates themselves, for it was reasoned that such censorship equally infringed the rights of noninmates to whom the correspondence was addressed. There are numerous other expressions to the same effect in the Court's decisions. If there is a right to advertise, there is a reciprocal right to receive the advertising, and it may be asserted by these appellees.

IV

The appellants contend that the advertisement of prescription drug prices is outside the protection of the First Amendment because it is "commercial speech." There can be no question that in past decisions the Court has given some indication that commercial speech is unprotected. In *Valentine v. Chrestensen,* 316 U.S. 52 (1942), the Court upheld a New York statute that prohibited the distribution of any "handbill, circular . . . or other advertising matter whatsoever in or upon any street." The Court concluded that, although the First Amendment would forbid the banning of all communication by handbill in the public thoroughfares, it imposed "no such restraint on government as respects purely commercial advertising." Further support for a "commercial speech" exception to the First Amendment may perhaps be found in *Breard v. Alexandria,* 341 U.S. 622 (1951), where the Court upheld a conviction for violation of an ordinance prohibiting door-to-door solicitation of magazine subscriptions. The Court reasoned: "The selling . . . brings into the transaction a commercial feature," and it distinguished *Martin v. Struthers,* 319 U.S. 141 (1943), where it had reversed a conviction for door-to-door distribution of leaflets publicizing a religious meeting, as a case involving "no element of the commercial." Moreover, the Court several times has stressed that communications to which First Amendment protection was given were not "purely commercial."

Since the decision in *Breard,* however, the Court has never denied protection on the ground that the speech in issue was "commercial speech." That simplistic approach, which by then had come under criticism or was regarded as of doubtful validity by Members of the Court, was avoided in *Pittsburgh Press Co. v. Human Relations Comm'n,* 413 U.S. 376 (1973). There the Court upheld an ordinance prohibiting newspapers from listing employment advertisements in columns according to whether male or female employees were sought to be hired. The Court, to be sure, characterized the advertisements as "classic examples of commercial speech," and a newspaper's printing of the advertisements as of the same character. The Court, however, upheld the ordinance on the ground that the restriction it imposed was permissible because the discriminatory hirings proposed by the advertisements, and by their newspaper layout, were themselves illegal.

Last Term, in *Bigelow v. Virginia,* 421 U.S. 809 (1975), the notion of unprotected "commercial speech" all but passed from the scene. We reversed a conviction for violation of a Virginia statute that made the circulation of any publication to encourage or promote the processing of an abortion in Virginia a misdemeanor. The defendant had published in his newspaper the availability of abortions in New York. The advertisement in question, in addition to announcing that abortions were legal in New York, offered the services of a referral agency in that State. We rejected the contention that the publication was unprotected because it was commercial.

Chrestensen's continued validity was questioned and its holding was described as "distinctly a limited one" that merely upheld "a reasonable regulation of the manner in which commercial advertising could be distributed." We concluded that "the Virginia courts erred in their assumptions that advertising, as such, was entitled to no First Amendment protection," and we observed that the "relationship of speech to the marketplace of products or of services does not make it valueless in the marketplace of ideas."

Here, in contrast, the question whether there is a First Amendment exception for "commercial speech" is squarely before us. Our pharmacist does not wish to editorialize on any subject, cultural, philosophical, or political. He does not wish to report any particularly newsworthy fact, or to make generalized observations even about commercial matters. The "idea" he wishes to communicate is simply this: "I will sell you the X prescription drug at the Y price." Our question, then, is whether this communication is wholly outside the protection of the First Amendment.

V

We begin with several propositions that already are settled or beyond serious dispute. It is clear, for example, that speech does not lose its First Amendment protection because money is spent to project it, as in a paid advertisement of one form or another.

Speech likewise is protected even though it is carried in a form that is "sold" for profit, and even though it may involve a solicitation to purchase or otherwise pay or contribute money.

If there is a kind of commercial speech that lacks all First Amendment protection, therefore, it must be distinguished by its content. Yet the speech whose content deprives it of protection cannot simply be speech on a commercial subject. No one would contend that our pharmacist may be prevented from being heard on the subject of whether, in general, pharmaceutical prices should be regulated, or their advertisement forbidden. Nor can it be dispositive that a commercial advertisement is noneditorial, and merely reports a fact. Purely factual matter of public interest may claim protection.

Our question is whether speech which does "no more than propose a commercial transaction, is so removed from any "exposition of ideas, and from " 'truth, science, morality, and arts in general, in its diffusion of liberal sentiments on the administration of Government,' " that it lacks all protection. Our answer is that it is not.

Focusing first on the individual parties to the transaction that is proposed in the commercial advertisement, we may assume that the advertiser's interest is a purely economic one. That hardly disqualifies him from protection under the First Amendment.

As to the particular consumer's interest in the free flow of commercial information, that interest may be as keen, if not keener by far, than his interest in the day's most urgent political debate. Appellees' case in this respect is a convincing one. Those whom the suppression of prescription drug price information hits the hardest are the poor, the sick, and particularly the aged. A disproportionate amount of their income tends to be spent on prescription drugs; yet they are the least able to learn, by shopping from pharmacist to pharmacist, where their scarce dollars are best spent. When drug prices vary as strikingly as they do, information as to who is charging what becomes more than a convenience. It could mean the alleviation of physical pain or the enjoyment of basic necessities.

Generalizing, society also may have a strong interest in the free flow of commercial information. Even an individual advertisement, though entirely "commercial," may be of general public interest. The facts of decided cases furnish illustrations: advertisements stating that referral services for legal abortions are available, *Bigelow v. Virginia*; that a manufacturer of artificial furs promotes his product as an alternative to the extinction by his competitors of fur-bearing mammals. Obviously, not all commercial messages contain the same or even a very great public interest element. There are few to which such an element, however, could not be added. Our pharmacist, for example, could cast himself as a commentator on store-to-store disparities in drug prices, giving his own and those of a competitor as proof. We see little point in requiring him to do so, and little difference if he does not.

Moreover, there is another consideration that suggests that no line between publicly "interesting" or "important" commercial advertising and the opposite kind could ever be drawn. Advertising, however tasteless and excessive it sometimes may seem, is nonetheless dissemination of information as to who is producing and selling what product, for what reason, and at what price. So long as we preserve a predominantly free enterprise economy, the allocation of our resources in large measure will be made through numerous private economic decisions. It is a matter of public interest that those decisions, in the aggregate, be intelligent and well informed. To this end, the free flow of commercial information is indispensable. And if it is indispensable to the proper allocation of resources in a free enterprise system, it is also indispensable to the formation of intelligent opinions as to how that system ought to be regulated or altered. Therefore, even if the First Amendment were thought to be primarily an instrument to enlighten public decision making in a democracy, we could not say that the free flow of information does not serve that goal.

Arrayed against these substantial individual and societal interests are a number of justifications for the advertising ban. These have to do principally with maintaining a high degree of professionalism on the part of licensed pharmacists. Indisputably, the State has a strong interest in maintaining that professionalism. It is exercised in a number of ways for the consumer's benefit. There is the clinical skill involved in the compounding of drugs, although, as has been noted, these now make up only a small percentage of the prescriptions filled. Yet, even with respect to manufacturer-prepared compounds, there is room for the pharmacist to serve his customer well or badly. Drugs kept too long on the shelf may lose their efficacy or become adulterated. They can be packaged for the user in such a way that the same results occur. The expertise of the pharmacist may supplement that of the prescribing physician, if the latter has not specified the amount to be dispensed or the directions that are to appear on the label. The pharmacist, a specialist in the potencies and dangers of drugs, may even be consulted by the physician as to what to prescribe. He may know of a particular antagonism between the prescribed drug and another that the customer is or might be taking, or with an allergy the customer may suffer. The pharmacist himself may have supplied the other drug or treated the allergy. Some pharmacists, concededly not a large number, "monitor" the health problems and drug consumptions of customers who come to them repeatedly. A pharmacist who has a continuous relationship with his customer is in the best position, of course, to exert professional skill for the customer's protection.

Price advertising, it is argued, will place in jeopardy the pharmacist's expertise and, with it, the customer's health. It is claimed that the aggressive price competition that will result from unlimited advertising will make it impossible for the pharmacist to supply professional services in the compounding, handling, and dispensing of prescription drugs. Such services are time consuming and expensive; if competitors who economize by eliminating them are permitted to advertise their resulting lower prices, the more painstaking and conscientious pharmacist will be forced either to follow suit or to go out of business. It is also claimed that prices might not necessarily fall as a result of advertising. If one pharmacist advertises, others must, and the resulting expense will inflate the cost of drugs. It is further claimed that advertising will lead people to shop for their prescription drugs among the various pharmacists who offer the lowest prices, and the loss of stable pharmacist-customer relationships will make individual attention and certainly the practice of monitoring impossible. Finally, it is argued that damage will be done to the professional image of the pharmacist. This image, that of a skilled and specialized craftsman, attracts talent to the profession and reinforces the better habits of those who are in it. Price advertising, it is said, will reduce the pharmacist's status to that of a mere retailer

The challenge now made, however, is based on the First Amendment. This casts the Board's justifications in a different light, for on close inspection it is seen that the State's protectiveness of its citizens rests in large measure on the advantages of their being kept in ignorance. The advertising ban does not directly affect professional standards one way or the other. It affects them only through the reactions it is assumed people will have to the free flow of drug price information. There is no claim that the advertising ban in any way prevents the cutting of corners by the pharmacist who is so inclined. That pharmacist is likely to cut corners in any event. The only effect the advertising ban has on him is to insulate him from price competition and to open the way for him to make a substantial, and perhaps even excessive, profit in addition to providing an inferior service. The more painstaking pharmacist is also protected but, again, it is a protection based in large part on public ignorance.

VI

In concluding that commercial speech, like other varieties, is protected, we of course do not hold that it can never be regulated in any way. Some forms of commercial speech regulation are surely permissible. We mention a few only to make clear that they are not before us and therefore are not foreclosed by this case.

There is no claim, for example, that the prohibition on prescription drug price advertising is a mere time, place, and manner restriction. We have often approved restrictions of that kind provided that they are justified without reference to the content of the regulated speech, that they serve a significant governmental interest, and that in so doing they leave open ample alternative channels for communication of the information. Whatever may be the proper bounds of time, place, and manner restrictions on commercial speech, they are plainly exceeded by this Virginia statute, which singles out speech of a particular content and seeks to prevent its dissemination completely.

Nor is there any claim that prescription drug price advertisements are forbidden because they are false or misleading in any way. Untruthful speech, commercial or otherwise, has never been protected for its own sake. Obviously, much commercial speech is not provably false, or even wholly false, but only deceptive or misleading. We foresee no obstacle to a State's dealing effectively with this problem. The First Amendment, as we construe it today, does not prohibit the State from insuring that the stream of commercial information flow cleanly as well as freely.

FOR DISCUSSION

What interests does the state offer in seeking to prohibit price advertising? Whose First Amendment interests are raised in this case, and why do those interests defeat the state interests?

RELATED CASE

***Bates v. State Bar of Arizona*: 433 U.S. 350 (1977).**

In a 6–3 opinion, the Court ruled that a ban on ads quoting the prices for legal services was unconstitutional. The Court found that the information conveyed in the advertising copy under consideration communicated important information to the public.

Central Hudson Gas & Elec. Corp. v. Public Service Commission of New York

447 U.S. 557, 100 S.Ct. 2343, 65 L.Ed.2d 341 (1980)

The New York State Public Utilities Commission issued an order that banned utility companies from advertising and promoting the use of electricity. The commission supported the order by arguing that there was insufficient power in the state to sustain demand. Central Hudson contested the ban, claiming that it violated the utility's First Amendment rights.

Vote: 8–1

Justice Powell delivered the opinion of the Court.

This case presents the question whether a regulation of the Public Service Commission of the State of New York violates the First and Fourteenth Amendments because it completely bans promotional advertising by an electrical utility.

I

In December 1973, the Commission, appellee here, ordered electric utilities in New York State to cease all advertising that "promot[es] the use of electricity." The order was based on the Commission's finding that "the interconnected utility system in New York State does not have sufficient fuel stocks or sources of supply to continue furnishing all customer demands for the 1973–1974 winter."

Three years later, when the fuel shortage had eased, the Commission requested comments from the public on its proposal to continue the ban on promotional advertising. Central Hudson Gas & Electric Corp., the appellant in this case, opposed the ban on First Amendment grounds. After reviewing the public comments, the Commission extended the prohibition in a Policy Statement issued on February 25, 1977.

The Policy Statement divided advertising expenses "into two broad categories: promotional—advertising intended to stimulate the purchase of utility services—and institutional and informational, a broad category inclusive of all advertising not clearly intended to promote sales." The Commission declared all promotional advertising contrary to the national policy of conserving energy. It acknowledged that the ban is not a perfect vehicle for conserving energy. For example, the Commission's order prohibits promotional advertising to develop consumption during periods when demand for electricity is low. By limiting growth in "off-peak" consumption, the ban limits the "beneficial side effects" of such growth in terms of more efficient use of existing power-plants. And since oil dealers are not under the Commission's jurisdiction and thus remain free to advertise, it was recognized that the ban can achieve only "piecemeal conservationism." Still, the Commission adopted the restriction because it was deemed likely to "result in some dampening of unnecessary growth" in energy consumption.

The Commission's order explicitly permitted "informational" advertising designed to encourage "shifts of consumption" from peak demand times to periods of low electricity demand. (emphasis in original). Informational advertising would not seek to increase aggregate consumption, but would invite a leveling of demand throughout any given 24-hour period. The agency offered to review "specific proposals by the companies for specifically described [advertising] programs that meet these criteria."

When it rejected requests for rehearing on the Policy Statement, the Commission supplemented its rationale for the advertising ban. The agency observed that additional electricity probably would be more expensive to produce than existing output. Because electricity rates in New York were not then based on marginal cost, the Commission feared that additional power would be priced below the actual cost of generation.

This additional electricity would be subsidized by all consumers through generally higher rates. The state agency also thought that promotional advertising would give "misleading signals" to the public by appearing to encourage energy consumption at a time when conservation is needed.

Appellant challenged the order in state court, arguing that the Commission had restrained commercial speech in violation of the First and Fourteenth Amendments

II

The Commission's order restricts only commercial speech, that is, expression related solely to the economic interests of the speaker and its audience. The First Amendment, as applied to the States through the Fourteenth Amendment, protects commercial speech from unwarranted governmental regulation. Commercial expression not only serves the economic interest of the speaker, but also assists consumers and furthers the societal interest in the fullest possible dissemination of information. In applying the First Amendment to this area, we have rejected the "highly paternalistic" view that government has complete power to suppress or regulate commercial speech. "[P]eople will perceive their own best interests if only they are well enough informed, and . . . the best means to that end is to open the channels of communication rather than to close them. . . ." Even when advertising communicates only an incomplete version of the relevant facts, the First Amendment presumes that some accurate information is better than no information at all. Nevertheless, our decisions have recognized "the 'commonsense' distinction between speech proposing a commercial transaction, which occurs in an area traditionally subject to government regulation, and other varieties of speech." The Constitution therefore accords a lesser protection to commercial speech than to other constitutionally guaranteed expression. The protection available for particular commercial expression turns on the nature both of the expression and of the governmental interests served by its regulation.

The First Amendment's concern for commercial speech is based on the informational function of advertising. Consequently, there can be no constitutional objection to the suppression of commercial messages that do not accurately inform the public about lawful activity. The government may ban forms of communication more likely to deceive the public than to inform it, or commercial speech related to illegal activity.

If the communication is neither misleading nor related to unlawful activity, the government's power is more circumscribed. The State must assert a substantial interest to be achieved by restrictions on commercial speech. Moreover, the regulatory technique must be in proportion to that interest. The limitation on expression must be designed carefully to achieve the State's goal. Compliance with this requirement may be measured by two criteria. First, the restriction must directly advance the state interest involved; the regulation may not be sustained if it provides only ineffective or remote support for the government's purpose. Second, if the governmental interest could be served as well by a more limited restriction on commercial speech, the excessive restrictions cannot survive.

In commercial speech cases, then, a four-part analysis has developed. At the outset, we must determine whether the expression is protected by the First Amendment. For commercial speech to come within that provision, it at least must concern lawful activity and not be misleading. Next, we ask whether the asserted governmental interest is substantial. If both inquiries yield positive answers, we must determine whether the regulation directly advances the governmental interest asserted, and whether it is not more extensive than is necessary to serve that interest.

III

We now apply this four-step analysis for commercial speech to the Commission's arguments in support of its ban on promotional advertising.

A

[The Court observes that the speech at issue is neither inaccurate nor related to unlawful activity.]

B

The Commission offers two state interests as justifications for the ban on promotional advertising. The first concerns energy conservation. Any increase in demand for electricity—during peak or off-peak periods—means greater consumption of energy. The Commission argues, and the New York court agreed, that the State's interest in conserving energy is sufficient to support suppression of advertising designed to increase consumption of electricity. In view of our country's dependence on energy resources beyond our control, no one can doubt the importance of energy conservation. Plainly, therefore, the state interest asserted is substantial.

The Commission also argues that promotional advertising will aggravate inequities caused by the failure to base the utilities' rates on marginal cost. The utilities argued to the Commission that if they could promote the use of electricity in periods of low demand, they would improve their utilization of generating capacity. The Commission responded that promotion of off-peak consumption also would increase consumption during peak periods. If peak demand were to rise, the absence of marginal cost rates would mean that the rates charged for the additional power would not reflect the true costs of expanding production. Instead, the extra costs would be borne by all consumers through higher overall rates. Without promotional advertising, the Commission stated, this inequitable turn of events would be less likely to occur. The choice among rate structures involves difficult and important questions of economic supply and distributional fairness. The State's concern that rates be fair and efficient represents a clear and substantial governmental interest.

We come finally to the critical inquiry in this case: whether the Commission's complete suppression of speech ordinarily protected by the First Amendment is no more extensive than necessary to further the State's interest in energy conservation. The Commission's order reaches all promotional advertising, regardless of the impact of the touted service on overall energy use. But the energy conservation rationale, as important as it is, cannot justify suppressing information about electric devices or services that would cause no net increase in total energy use. In addition, no showing has been made that a more limited restriction on the content of promotional advertising would not serve adequately the State's interests.

Appellant insists that but for the ban, it would advertise products and services that use energy efficiently. These include the "heat pump," which both parties acknowledge to be a major improvement in electric heating, and the use of electric heat as a "backup" to solar and other heat sources. Although the Commission has questioned the efficiency of electric heating before this Court, neither the Commission's Policy Statement nor its order denying rehearing made findings on this issue. In the absence of authoritative findings to the contrary, we must credit as within the realm of possibility the claim that electric heat can be an efficient alternative in some circumstances.

The Commission's order prevents appellant from promoting electric services that would reduce energy use by diverting demand from less efficient sources, or that would consume roughly the same amount of energy as do alternative sources. In neither situation would the utility's advertising endanger conservation or mislead the public. To the extent that the Commission's order suppresses speech that in no way impairs the State's interest in energy conservation, the Commission's order violates the First and Fourteenth Amendments and must be invalidated.

The Commission also has not demonstrated that its interest in conservation cannot be protected adequately by more limited regulation of appellant's commercial expression. To further its policy of conservation, the Commission could attempt to restrict the format and content of Central Hudson's advertising. It might, for example, require that the advertisements include information about the relative efficiency and expense of the offered service, both under current conditions and for the foreseeable future. In the absence of a showing that more limited speech regulation would be ineffective, we cannot approve the complete suppression of Central Hudson's advertising.

IV

Our decision today in no way disparages the national interest in energy conservation. We accept without reservation the argument that conservation, as well as the development of alternative energy sources, is an imperative national goal. Administrative bodies empowered to regulate electric utilities have the authority—and indeed the duty—to take appropriate action to further this goal. When, however, such action involves the suppression of speech, the First and Fourteenth Amendments require that the restriction be no more extensive than is necessary to serve the state interest. In this case, the record before us fails to show that the total ban on promotional advertising meets this requirement.

Reversed.

JUSTICE REHNQUIST, dissenting.

The Court today invalidates an order issued by the New York Public Service Commission designed to promote a policy that has been declared to be of critical national concern. The order was issued by the Commission in 1973 in response to the Mideastern oil embargo crisis. It prohibits electric corporations "from promoting the use of electricity through the use of advertising, subsidy payments . . ., or employee incentives." Although the immediate crisis created by the oil embargo has subsided, the ban on promotional advertising remains in effect. The regulation was re-examined by the New York Public Service Commission in 1977. Its constitutionality was subsequently upheld by the New York Court of Appeals, which concluded that the paramount national interest in energy conservation justified its retention.

The Court's analysis in my view is wrong in several respects. Initially, I disagree with the Court's conclusion that the speech of a state-created monopoly, which is the subject of a comprehensive regulatory scheme, is entitled to protection under the First Amendment. I also think that the Court errs here in failing to recognize that the state law is most accurately viewed as an economic regulation and that the speech involved (if it falls within the scope of the First Amendment at all) occupies a significantly more subordinate position in the hierarchy of First Amendment values than the Court gives it today. Finally, the Court in reaching its decision improperly substitutes its own judgment for that of the State in deciding how a proper ban on promotional advertising should be drafted. With regard to this latter point, the Court adopts as its final part of a four-part test a "no more extensive than necessary" analysis that will unduly impair a state legislature's ability to adopt legislation reasonably designed to promote interests that have always been rightly thought to be of great importance to the State.

FOR DISCUSSION

Does the test proposed in this case provide clear rules for when commercial speech may be regulated? What action could the government take to ban advertising that was clearly deceptive or false? In a given case, who decides what is "deceptive" or "false"?

RELATED CASES

***First National Bank of Boston v. Bellotti:* 435 U.S. 765 (1978).**

The First Amendment protects the right of a nonprofit corporation to expend money for the purposes of expressing its opinions on elections issues as long as the funds are not spent to support or oppose an individual candidate.

Corporate speech is protected under the First Amendment for the general purposes of expressing opinions on matters of political concern.

***Citizens United v. Federal Election Commission:* 558 U.S. 310 (2010).**

A 5–4 majority of the Court led by Justice Kennedy struck down the portion of the Bipartisan Campaign Reform Act of 2002 (BCRA) that prohibited corporations and unions from making independent expenditures that name candidates for office for campaigns 30 days prior to a primary election while upholding disclaimer and disclosure requirements.

POSADAS DE PUERTO RICO ASSOCIATES V. TOURISM CO. OF P. R.

478 U.S. 328, 106 S.Ct. 2968, 92 L.Ed.2d 266 (1986)

While Puerto Rico permits gambling and the operation of casinos in some areas of the island and directs advertisements of such activity toward tourists, it banned the advertisement of these activities to its residents. A casino and hotel operator challenged the ban on advertising to residents, and the lower courts upheld it against First Amendment claims.

Vote: 5–4

JUSTICE REHNQUIST delivered the opinion of the Court.

In this case we address the facial constitutionality of a Puerto Rico statute and regulations restricting advertising of casino gambling aimed at the residents of Puerto Rico. Appellant Posadas de Puerto Rico Associates, doing business in Puerto Rico as Condado Holiday Inn Hotel and Sands Casino, filed suit against appellee Tourism Company of Puerto Rico in the Superior Court of Puerto Rico, San Juan Section. Appellant sought a declaratory judgment that the statute and regulations, both facially and as applied by the Tourism Company, impermissibly suppressed commercial speech in violation of the First Amendment and the equal protection and due process guarantees of the United States Constitution. The Superior Court held that the advertising restrictions had been unconstitutionally applied to appellant's past conduct. But the court adopted a narrowing construction of the statute and regulations and held that, based on such a construction, both were facially constitutional. The Supreme Court of Puerto Rico dismissed an appeal on the ground that it "d[id] not present a substantial constitutional question." We postponed consideration of the question of jurisdiction until the hearing on the merits. We now hold that we have jurisdiction to hear the appeal, and we affirm the decision of the Supreme Court of Puerto Rico with respect to the facial constitutionality of the advertising restrictions.

In 1948, the Puerto Rico Legislature legalized certain forms of casino gambling. The Games of Chance Act of 1948, Act No. 221 of May 15, 1948 (Act), authorized the playing of roulette, dice, and card games in licensed "gambling rooms." Bingo and slot machines were later added to the list of authorized games of chance under the Act. See Act of June 7, 1948, No. 21, § 1 (bingo); Act of July 30, 1974, No. 2, pt. 2, § 2 (slot machines). The legislature's intent was set forth in the Act's Statement of Motives:

> The purpose of this Act is to contribute to the development of tourism by means of the authorization of certain games of chance which are customary in the recreation places of the great tourist centers of the world, and by the establishment of regulations for and the strict surveillance of said games by the government, in order to ensure for tourists the best possible safeguards, while at the same time opening for the Treasurer of Puerto Rico an additional source of income.

The Act also provided that "[n]o gambling room shall be permitted to advertise or otherwise offer their facilities to the public of Puerto Rico."

In 1975, appellant Posadas de Puerto Rico Associates, a partnership organized under the laws of Texas, obtained a franchise to operate a gambling casino and began doing business under the name Condado Holiday Inn Hotel and Sands Casino. In 1978, appellant was twice fined by the Tourism Company for violating the advertising restrictions in the Act and implementing regulations. Appellant protested the fines in a series of letters to the Tourism Company.

Because this case involves the restriction of pure commercial speech which does "no more than propose a commercial transaction," *Virginia Pharmacy Board v. Virginia Citizens Consumer Council, Inc.,* 425 U.S. 748 (1976), our First Amendment analysis is guided by the general principles identified in *Central Hudson Gas & Electric Corp. v. Public Service Comm'n of New York,* 447 U.S. 557 (1980). Under *Central Hudson,* commercial speech receives a limited form of First Amendment protection so long as it concerns a lawful activity and is not misleading or fraudulent. Once it is determined that the First Amendment applies to the particular kind of commercial speech at issue, then the speech may be restricted only if the government's interest in doing so is substantial, the restrictions directly advance the government's asserted interest, and the restrictions are no more extensive than necessary to serve that interest.

The particular kind of commercial speech at issue here, namely, advertising of casino gambling aimed at the residents of Puerto Rico, concerns a lawful activity and is not misleading or fraudulent, at least in the abstract. We must therefore proceed to the three remaining steps of the *Central Hudson* analysis in order to determine whether Puerto Rico's advertising restrictions run afoul of the First Amendment. The first of these three steps involves an assessment of the strength of the government's interest in restricting the speech. The interest at stake in this case, as determined by the Superior Court, is the reduction of demand for casino gambling by the residents of Puerto Rico. Appellant acknowledged the existence of this interest in its February 24, 1982, letter to the Tourism Company. The Tourism Company's brief before this Court explains the legislature's belief that "[e]xcessive casino gambling among local residents . . . would produce serious harmful effects on the health, safety and welfare of the Puerto Rican citizens, such as the disruption of moral and cultural patterns, the increase in local crime, the fostering of prostitution, the development of corruption, and the infiltration of organized crime." These are some of the very same concerns, of course, that have motivated the vast majority of the 50 States to prohibit casino gambling. We have no difficulty in concluding that the Puerto Rico Legislature's interest in the health, safety, and welfare of its citizens constitutes a "substantial" governmental interest.

The last two steps of the *Central Hudson* analysis basically involve a consideration of the "fit" between the legislature's ends and the means chosen to accomplish those ends. Step three asks the question whether the challenged restrictions on commercial speech "directly advance" the government's asserted interest. In the instant case, the answer to this question is clearly "yes." The Puerto Rico Legislature obviously believed, when it enacted the advertising restrictions at issue here, that advertising of casino gambling aimed at the residents of Puerto Rico would serve to increase the demand for the product advertised. We think the legislature's belief is a reasonable one, and the fact that appellant has chosen to litigate this case all the way to this Court indicates that appellant shares the legislature's view.

We also think it clear beyond peradventure that the challenged statute and regulations satisfy the fourth and last step of the *Central Hudson* analysis, namely, whether the restrictions on commercial speech are no more extensive than necessary to serve the government's interest. The narrowing constructions of the advertising restrictions announced by the Superior Court ensure that the restrictions will not affect advertising of casino gambling aimed at tourists, but will apply only to such advertising when aimed at the residents of Puerto Rico. Appellant contends, however, that the First Amendment requires the Puerto Rico Legislature to reduce demand for casino gambling among the residents of Puerto Rico not by suppressing commercial speech that might *encourage* such gambling, but by promulgating additional speech designed to *discourage* it. We reject this contention. We think it is up to the legislature to decide whether or not such a "counterspeech" policy would be as effective in reducing the demand for casino gambling as a restriction on advertising. The legislature could conclude, as it apparently did here, that residents of Puerto Rico are already aware of the risks of casino gambling, yet would nevertheless be induced by widespread advertising to engage in such potentially harmful conduct.

In short, we conclude that the statute and regulations at issue in this case, as construed by the Superior Court, pass muster under each prong of the *Central Hudson* test. We therefore hold that the Supreme Court of Puerto Rico properly rejected appellant's First Amendment claim.

It is so ordered.

JUSTICE BRENNAN, with whom JUSTICES MARSHALL and BLACKMUN join, dissenting.

The Puerto Rico Games of Chance Act of 1948, Act No. 221 of May 15, 1948, legalizes certain forms of casino gambling in Puerto Rico. Section 8 of the Act nevertheless prohibits gambling casinos from "advertis[ing] or otherwise offer[ing] their facilities to the public of Puerto Rico." § 8, codified, as amended, at P.R. Laws Ann., Tit. 15, § 77 (1972). Because neither the language of § 8 nor the applicable regulations define what constitutes "advertis[ing] or otherwise offer[ing gambling] facilities to the public of Puerto Rico," appellee Tourism Company was found to have applied the Act in an arbitrary and confusing manner. To ameliorate this problem, the Puerto Rico Superior Court, to avoid a declaration of the unconstitutionality of § 8, construed it to ban only advertisements or offerings directed to the residents of Puerto Rico, and listed examples of the kinds of advertisements that the court considered permissible under the Act. I doubt that this interpretation will assure that arbitrary and unreasonable applications of § 8 will no longer occur. However, even assuming that appellee will now enforce § 8 in a nonarbitrary manner, I do not believe that Puerto Rico constitutionally may suppress truthful commercial speech in order to discourage its residents from engaging in lawful activity.

I

It is well settled that the First Amendment protects commercial speech from unwarranted governmental regulation. Our decisions have recognized, however, "the 'common-sense' distinction between speech proposing a commercial transaction, which occurs in an area traditionally subject to government regulation, and other varieties of speech." We have therefore held that the Constitution "accords less protection to commercial speech than to other constitutionally safeguarded forms of expression." *Bolger v. Youngs Drug Products Corp.*, 463 U.S. 60, 64–65 (1983). Thus, while the First Amendment ordinarily prohibits regulation of speech based on the content of the communicated message, the government may regulate the content of commercial speech in order to prevent the dissemination of information that is false, deceptive, or misleading, or that proposes an illegal transaction. We have, however, consistently invalidated restrictions designed to deprive consumers of accurate information about products and services legally offered for sale.

I see no reason why commercial speech should be afforded less protection than other types of speech where, as here, the government seeks to suppress commercial speech in order to deprive consumers of accurate information concerning lawful activity. Commercial speech is considered to be different from other kinds of protected expression because advertisers are particularly well suited to evaluate "the accuracy of their messages and the lawfulness of the underlying activity,"

"Even though 'commercial' speech is involved, [this kind of restriction] strikes at the heart of the First Amendment. This is because it is a covert attempt by the State to manipulate the choices of its citizens, not by persuasion or direct regulation, but by depriving the public of the information needed to make a free choice. . . . [T]he State's policy choices are insulated from the visibility and scrutiny that direct regulation would entail and the conduct of citizens is molded by the information that government chooses to give them."

I respectfully dissent.

FOR DISCUSSION

Why is it permitted to advertise to tourists but not residents? How can such a distinction be justified?

---

44 LIQUORMART, INC. V. RHODE ISLAND

517 U.S. 484, 116 S.Ct. 1495, 134 L.Ed.2d 711 (1996)

A multistate liquor store ran an advertisement in a Rhode Island newspaper listing the prices of its snack foods and sodas. The ad depicted liquor bottles with the word "WOW" next to the illustration. The Rhode Island Liquor Control Board determined that this ad violated the state ban on price advertising for alcohol products, and it fined the owner of the store. The owner challenged the fine and ban on alcohol price advertising as a First Amendment violation.

Vote: 9–0

JUSTICE STEVENS delivered the opinion of the Court with respect to Parts I, II, VII, and VIII; JUSTICES KENNEDY, SOUTER, and GINSBURG joined Parts III and V; JUSTICES KENNEDY, THOMAS, and GINSBURG joined Part VI; and, JUSTICES KENNEDY and GINSBURG joined Part IV.

Last Term we held that a federal law abridging a brewer's right to provide the public with accurate information about the alcoholic content of malt beverages is unconstitutional. *Rubin v. Coors Brewing Co.,* 514 U.S. 476 (1995). We now hold that Rhode Island's statutory prohibition against advertisements that provide the public with accurate information about retail prices of alcoholic beverages is also invalid. Our holding rests on the conclusion that such an advertising ban is an abridgment of speech protected by the First Amendment and that it is not shielded from constitutional scrutiny by the Twenty-first Amendment.

I

In 1956, the Rhode Island Legislature enacted two separate prohibitions against advertising the retail price of alcoholic beverages. The first applies to vendors licensed in Rhode Island as well as to out-of-state manufacturers, wholesalers, and shippers. It prohibits them from "advertising in any manner whatsoever" the price of any alcoholic beverage offered for sale in the State; the only exception is for price tags or signs displayed with the merchandise within licensed premises and not visible from the street. The second statute applies to the Rhode Island news media. It contains a categorical prohibition against the publication or broadcast of any advertisements—even those referring to sales in other States—that "make reference to the price of any alcoholic beverages."

In two cases decided in 1985, the Rhode Island Supreme Court reviewed the constitutionality of these two statutes. In *S & S Liquor Mart, Inc. v. Pastore*, 497 A.2d 729 (R.I. 1985), a liquor retailer located in Westerly, Rhode Island, a town that borders the State of Connecticut, having been advised that his license would be revoked if he advertised his prices in a Connecticut paper, sought to enjoin enforcement of the first statute. Over the dissent of one justice, the court upheld the statute. It concluded that the statute served the substantial state interest in " 'the promotion of temperance.' " Because the plaintiff failed to prove that the statute did not serve that interest, the court held that he had not carried his burden of establishing a violation of the First Amendment. In response to the dissent's argument that the court had placed the burden on the wrong party, the majority reasoned that the Twenty-first Amendment gave the statute " 'an added presumption [of] validity.' " Although that presumption had not been overcome in that case, the State Supreme Court assumed that in a future case the record might "support the proposition that these advertising restrictions do not further temperance objectives."

III

Advertising has been a part of our culture throughout our history. Even in colonial days, the public relied on "commercial speech" for vital information about the market. Early newspapers displayed advertisements for goods and services on their front pages, and town criers called out prices in public squares. Indeed, commercial messages played such a central role in public life prior to the founding that Benjamin Franklin authored his early defense of a free press in support of his decision to print, of all things, an advertisement for voyages to Barbados.

In accord with the role that commercial messages have long played, the law has developed to ensure that advertising provides consumers with accurate information about the availability of goods and services. In the early years, the common law, and later, statutes, served the consumers' interest in the receipt of accurate information in the commercial market by prohibiting fraudulent and misleading advertising. It was not until the 1970's, however, that this Court held that the First Amendment protected the dissemination of truthful and nonmisleading commercial messages about lawful products and services.

In *Bigelow v. Virginia,* 421 U.S. 809 (1975), we held that it was error to assume that commercial speech was entitled to no First Amendment protection or that it was without value in the marketplace of ideas. The following Term in *Virginia Bd. of Pharmacy v. Virginia Citizens Consumer Council, Inc.,* 425 U.S. 748 (1976), we expanded on our holding in *Bigelow* and held that the State's blanket ban on advertising the price of prescription drugs violated the First Amendment.

Virginia Bd. of Pharmacy reflected the conclusion that the same interest that supports regulation of potentially misleading advertising, namely, the public's interest in receiving accurate commercial information, also supports an interpretation of the First Amendment that provides constitutional protection for the dissemination of accurate and nonmisleading commercial messages. We explained:

> Advertising, however tasteless and excessive it sometimes may seem, is nonetheless dissemination of information as to who is producing and selling what product, for what reason, and at what price. So long as we preserve a predominantly free enterprise economy, the allocation of our resources in large measure will be made through numerous private economic decisions. It is a matter of public interest that those decisions, in the aggregate, be intelligent and well informed. To this end, the free flow of commercial information is indispensable.

In *Central Hudson Gas & Elec. Corp. v. Public Serv. Comm'n of N.Y.,* 447 U.S. 557 (1980), we took stock of our developing commercial speech jurisprudence. In that case, we considered a regulation "completely" banning all promotional advertising by electric utilities. Our decision acknowledged the special features of commercial speech but identified the serious First Amendment concerns that attend blanket advertising prohibitions that do not protect consumers from commercial harms.

Five Members of the Court recognized that the state interest in the conservation of energy was substantial, and that there was "an immediate connection between advertising and demand for electricity." Nevertheless, they concluded that the regulation was invalid because respondent commission had failed to make a showing that a more limited speech regulation would not have adequately served the State's interest.

In reaching its conclusion, the majority explained that although the special nature of commercial speech may require less than strict review of its regulation, special concerns arise from "regulations that entirely suppress commercial speech in order to pursue a nonspeech-related policy." In those circumstances, "a ban on speech could screen from public view the underlying governmental policy." As a result, the Court concluded that "special care" should attend the review of such blanket bans, and it pointedly remarked that "in recent years this

Court has not approved a blanket ban on commercial speech unless the expression itself was flawed in some way, either because it was deceptive or related to unlawful activity."

IV

As our review of the case law reveals, Rhode Island errs in concluding that *all* commercial speech regulations are subject to a similar form of constitutional review simply because they target a similar category of expression. The mere fact that messages propose commercial transactions does not in and of itself dictate the constitutional analysis that should apply to decisions to suppress them.

When a State regulates commercial messages to protect consumers from misleading, deceptive, or aggressive sales practices, or requires the disclosure of beneficial consumer information, the purpose of its regulation is consistent with the reasons for according constitutional protection to commercial speech and therefore justifies less than strict review. However, when a State entirely prohibits the dissemination of truthful, nonmisleading commercial messages for reasons unrelated to the preservation of a fair bargaining process, there is far less reason to depart from the rigorous review that the First Amendment generally demands.

The special dangers that attend complete bans on truthful, nonmisleading commercial speech cannot be explained away by appeals to the "commonsense distinctions" that exist between commercial and noncommercial speech. Regulations that suppress the truth are no less troubling because they target objectively verifiable information, nor are they less effective because they aim at durable messages. As a result, neither the "greater objectivity" nor the "greater hardiness" of truthful, nonmisleading commercial speech justifies reviewing its complete suppression with added deference.

Precisely because bans against truthful, nonmisleading commercial speech rarely seek to protect consumers from either deception or overreaching, they usually rest solely on the offensive assumption that the public will respond "irrationally" to the truth. The First Amendment directs us to be especially skeptical of regulations that seek to keep people in the dark for what the government perceives to be their own good.

V

In this case, there is no question that Rhode Island's price advertising ban constitutes a blanket prohibition against truthful, nonmisleading speech about a lawful product. There is also no question that the ban serves an end unrelated to consumer protection. Accordingly, we must review the price advertising ban with "special care," mindful that speech prohibitions of this type rarely survive constitutional review.

The State argues that the price advertising prohibition should nevertheless be upheld because it directly advances the State's substantial interest in promoting temperance, and because it is no more extensive than necessary. Although there is some confusion as to what Rhode Island means by temperance, we assume that the State asserts an interest in reducing alcohol consumption.

Although the record suggests that the price advertising ban may have some impact on the purchasing patterns of temperate drinkers of modest means, the State has presented no evidence to suggest that its speech prohibition will *significantly* reduce marketwide consumption. Indeed, the District Court's considered and uncontradicted finding on this point is directly to the contrary. Moreover, the evidence suggests that the abusive drinker will probably not be deterred by a marginal price increase, and that the true alcoholic may simply reduce his purchases of other necessities.

The State also cannot satisfy the requirement that its restriction on speech be no more extensive than necessary. It is perfectly obvious that alternative forms of regulation that would not involve any restriction on speech would be more likely to achieve the State's goal of promoting temperance. As the State's own expert conceded, higher prices can be maintained either by direct regulation or by increased taxation. Per capita purchases could be limited as is the case with prescription drugs. Even educational campaigns focused on the problems of excessive, or even moderate, drinking might prove to be more effective.

FOR DISCUSSION

After this decision, is it clear how much First Amendment protection commercial speech receives, or deserves? Should commercial speech receive the same protection as political speech, or should it be treated the same as nude dancing in *Barnes*?

Freedom of the Press

At least from 1735, the year of the New York City trial of journalist Peter Zenger, freedom of the press has been an important right in the American constitutional tradition. The defendant had been accused of publishing seditious libel of New York governor William Crosby in the *New York Weekly Journal.* Zenger's attorney, Andrew Hamilton, asserted that truth was his client's defense and that the law itself was deficient. The jury returned a verdict of "not guilty," which was taken as a statement that a free press had a right to criticize the government even if its officials did not like what they were reading.

During the Revolutionary War and in the early years of the American republic, freedom of the press was often tested. Much of the ideological battle took place in pamphlets, with small presses churning out the pros and cons of independence and criticizing the British rule. During the debates surrounding the adoption of the Constitution, James Madison, Alexander Hamilton, and John Jay published their arguments in favor of the document in New York newspapers. These arguments, now known as *The Federalist Papers*, may have been the 1787 equivalent of the modern political ads seen on television or on YouTube today. The Anti-Federalists similarly used the presses to develop and publicize their positions. Unfortunately, on the darker side, freedom of the press was challenged by the Alien and Sedition Acts of 1798, which led to the jailing of some men who had published remarks critical of President John Adams.

The First Amendment states that no law shall be passed that abridges freedom of the press. As with the other clauses of the First Amendment, the language seems absolute, but it is not always so clear what the law covers. Does it allow for criticism of government officials, even if the allegations are not correct? Does it allow for the publication of top-secret information, such as the design for nuclear weapons? Can reporters refuse to disclose their sources? Are newspapers, television, social media, or the Web covered by the First Amendment? Can the government regulate media content, require that some material be published, or restrict the publication of content of other types? All these are questions that dominate the development of constitutional law with respect to freedom of the press. The cases included in this section chart the efforts to apply this constitutional provision in a changing world that has seen the extension of "publishing" beyond small printers such as Benjamin Franklin to massive multinational media empires that cover numerous forms of communication reaching diverse audiences.

The starting point for freedom of the press claims is *Near v. Minnesota* (283 U.S. 697, 1931). The *Near* case, beyond its legal doctrines, is also wonderful for its fact pattern, which involves muckraking and accusations of graft and corruption. In *Near* the Court applied to freedom of the press the "*Gitlow* doctrine," discussed in the preceding chapter, and for the first time held a statute void on that basis. The Court especially condemned prior restraint of publication. Here the attempt had been made to stop future publication on the basis of past activities.

Bridges v. California (314 U.S. 252, 1941) and Times-Mirror Co. v. Superior Court of California (314 U.S. 252, 1941) also involved criticism. Here, a newspaper sought to reprint a telegram from union officials criticizing a judge. In its ruling, the Court overturned a contempt of court citation against the paper and the union officials. As in free speech cases, the Court found no evidence that the publication constituted a "clear and present danger" that government had a right to prevent.

If seeking to prevent publication implicates freedom of the press concerns, so do efforts to retaliate against the media after a story has been published or an issue brought to the attention of the public. The case of *Grosjean v. American Press Co* (297 U.S. 233, 1936), involved a tax on newspapers that had published articles critical of the Louisiana governor. While the tax appeared to be neutral, it was not, and the Court ruled that it violated the amendment. The *Grosjean* opinion includes a good account of attempts that have been made over the years to restrict the free press by taxation. Here the taxing power rather than the police power was at issue; but the Court looked beyond the face of the statute to discover the true purpose of the legislation. Special taxes are not void unless they are discriminatory.

New York Times v. Sullivan (376 U.S. 254, 1964) is a landmark decision in the realm of freedom of the press. The case grew out of the civil rights revolution in the 1960s, when the northern media increasingly covered and criticized local southern officials who fought integration. Here the *New York Times* is sued for libel because it printed an advertisement criticizing an Alabama sheriff that contained some factual errors. A lower court awarded damages in excess of several hundreds of thousands of dollars—a hefty sum at that time. The libel resided in the factual errors. The Supreme Court had to decide whether those errors rose to the level of libel. The Court stated no, and in the process created a rule that protected press freedom: for public officials to prevail in a libel suit against a newspaper, they must show reckless disregard for the truth, or malice. The idea here is that for the sake of promoting an open and accountable government, newspapers should generally be permitted to criticize the government and its officials, even if some factual errors are published. Thus, *Sullivan* narrows the grounds for finding that the media have engaged in libel, liberating them to publish and criticize public figures, even if they do not always get the facts one hundred percent correct. The "absence of malice" standard articulated in the case was justified as an effort to promote wide-open and robust criticism, a function that is consistent with the core goals of the First Amendment Free Press Clause.

The 1960s produced several events that implicated freedom of the press. These included the civil rights revolution, the Vietnam War, and protests against the war itself and against and the U.S. government. The national media covered many of these events, and the *New York Times* published a steady stream of articles. One topic that came to dominate the government's public relations efforts and the nation's headlines was how the United States came to be involved in Vietnam and why its forces were fighting in the war. In 1967 Secretary of Defense Robert McNamara commissioned a study to investigate these questions. The report was to be classified as top secret. However, Daniel Ellsberg leaked the report, now known as the Pentagon Papers, to the press. Both the *Washington Post* and the *New York Times* obtained copies and sought to publish excerpts of the report in 1971. President Richard Nixon wanted an injunction to prevent publication. After lower courts had rejected his request, the Supreme Court in *New York Times Company v. United States* (403 U.S. 713, 1971), heard the case and also denied the injunction. The *New York Times* case, otherwise known as the Pentagon Papers case, produced a clear result in favor of the media; yet the opinion of the six-person majority yielded no consistent or agreed-upon reasoning. The dissenters, including Chief Justice Warren Burger, expressed concern that the published materials had been stolen. Yet the fractured majority opinions left open the possibility that despite the ruling in *Near*, some type of prior restraint for national security reasons might be sustainable.

While an injunction to restrain publication was rejected in the Pentagon Papers case, a judge did enjoin *Progressive Magazine* from publishing an article describing how to make a hydrogen bomb. This lower court decision, in *United States of America v. The Progressive, Inc.* (467 F.Supp. 990, D. Wisc. 1979), is the only case in American history of a federal court restraining the publication of an article. A court of appeals dismissed the case after the government abandoned the appeal, and *Progressive* did eventually publish the article.

When reporters cover the news they often need to interview individuals as sources of information. Oftentimes the identity of the source can be revealed, but some persons supplying information request to remain anonymous. They do so for many reasons: to protect themselves from reprisals such as loss of a job, for example, or to protect others. In other cases, reporters interview individuals who have broken the law or know something about illegal activity. Journalists do not want to divulge the identity of these sources. What if they are subpoenaed by a court? Reporters and the media claim a **reporter's privilege**—protection against official requests to identify their sources on the basis of the First Amendment's Freedom of the Press Clause. But does the First Amendment protect reporters from having to reveal sources? This was the issue raised in *Branzburg v. Hayes* (408 U.S. 665, 1972), and in a narrow 5–4 opinion the Court ruled that there was no reporter's privilege, rejecting assertions that the Constitution shields reporters from revealing sources. After this case several states adopted shield laws to protect reporters from having to reveal their sources. Similar efforts at the federal level have failed. In 2005 *New York Times* reporter Judith Miller was ordered jailed by a federal judge for her refusal to disclose a source in a case investigating the leaking of the name of CIA agent Valerie Plame.

A different issue associated with freedom of the press entails the differences between print media, such as newspapers, and television and radio, which broadcast over the airwaves. Newspapers are privately owned, and in theory there is no limit to the number of papers that could exist. However, there is a finite number of broadcast frequencies; and if there were no regulation of broadcasting, different radio and television stations might drown one another out. In creating the regulatory environment for radio, and later television, the 1934 Telecommunications Act declared the broadcast frequencies or airwaves to be owned by the public. Individuals who wished to broadcast had to obtain a license from the Federal Communications Commission (FCC). Because of the limited number of broadcast licenses, the FCC in 1947 began to enforce the f**airness doctrine**, the requirement that television stations give airtime to opposing viewpoints on matters of public importance. The argument in favor of the doctrine rested partly in the monopoly position that broadcasters appeared to have; in addition, since the airwaves were owned by the public, the government could place some conditions or limits upon ownership if one wanted a license. However, broadcasters claimed the doctrine violated their First Amendment rights. In *Red Lion Broadcasting Co. v. F.C.C.* (395 U.S. 367, 1969), the Supreme Court unanimously disagreed with the broadcasters. In reading the opinion, note how the Court looked not at the rights of the broadcasters but of the public. After pitting the First Amendment rights of both interested parties, it weighed in on the side of the consumer and the public.

The FCC repealed the fairness doctrine in 1987, contending that it was unconstitutional and that with the rise of new forms of media, such as cable television, the doctrine no longer made sense. Some argue that the rule makes even less sense today in a world with the Web, where network television is breaking down and cable television, radio, and online information sources are increasing in importance. Conversely, some in 2008 and 2009 began to argue that despite all these information sources there was still a lack of diversity in viewpoints. When President Barack Obama took office in 2009 there was some rumor and talk that he might reinstitute the fairness doctrine. The fear of this development came mostly from Rush Limbaugh and conservative talk radio. Congress early in 2009 voted to prevent the FCC from reinstituting the rule, dispelling, for now, worries about the return of the earlier policy.

Both the public ownership of the airwaves and concern to protect children from objectionable language are central to the decision in *Federal Communications Commission v. Pacifica Foundation* (438 U.S. 726, 1978). The FCC had composed a list of seven words that it considered obscene, which could not be broadcast on radio or television. Comedian George Carlin created a comic skit, referred to as "Seven Dirty Words," to mock this instance of government censorship. A radio station broadcast the comedy routine, and a parent complained to the FCC that he had heard it with his minor child present. The FCC placed a letter in the station's file (to be considered when its license was renewed), and the latter appealed. The Court upheld this sanction, rejecting the First Amendment arguments here.

Since Pacifica and *Red Lion,* even though the FCC has created space for cable television and non-prime time network television and radio to broadcast more adult-oriented themes and language, standards on prime time are strictly enforced. The FCC fined CBS for the display of Janet Jackson's bare breast during the 2004 Super Bowl half-time show, and Howard Stern faced numerous fines for having used indecent language on his morning New York City radio show. The "seven dirty words" still cannot be legally broadcast on mainstream television.

A recurrent theme in criminal law is the **free press/fair trial** conflict. It pits a free press against a fair trial when concern arises that intense media exposure, including pretrial publicity, will make it impossible for a defendant to receive a fair trial. In *Sheppard v. Maxwell* (384 U.S. 333, 1986), the Court overturned the conviction of Dr. Sam Sheppard, who had been accused of murdering his wife. The case, which became the basis of the 1960s television series (and later movie) *The Fugitive*, was dominated by intense media coverage that included megaphones set up in the courtroom to broadcast the proceedings to listeners outside. The Court ruled that the pretrial and trial coverage rendered a fair trial impossible.

In some cases, it might be to the advantage of defendants to close a trial to the media. Routinely, legal proceedings involving minors are closed. However, what about cases of adults who wish to close a hearing? This was the issue in *Gannett Co., Inc. v. Depasquale* (443 U.S. 368, 1979). The defendant moved to close the hearing and the prosecutor did not object, but the press did. The Supreme Court upheld the closing of the court proceeding. *Gannett* was a Sixth Amendment decision that generated an avalanche of criticism, forcing Chief Justice Burger to state publicly that the decision did not reflect judicial support for the routine closing of trials. Less than a year later, the Court revisited the issue, this time deciding on First Amendment grounds.

Richmond Newspapers, Inc. v. Virginia (448 U.S. 555, 1980) used the First Amendment effectively to overrule the Sixth Amendment decision in *Gannett.* The press has an independent right to view criminal trials regardless of the objections of the plaintiffs, save for a narrow band of exceptions to preserve a fair trial from adverse pretrial or trial publicity.

In *Tinker v. Des Moines School District* (393 U.S. 503, 1969), the Court stated that the Constitution and the First Amendment do not stop at the schoolhouse gate. But how far do those rights extend? In *Bethel School District No. 403 v. Fraser* (478 U.S. 675, 1986), the Court stated that the rights of students are not coextensive with those of adults and that the needs of the educational environment might necessitate the drawing of some limits on the former. Do these limits permit schools to censor or restrict school newspapers? In *Hazelwood School Dist. v. Kuhlmeier* (484 U.S. 260, 1988), the Supreme Court gave school principals more authority to censor student newspapers sponsored by the school. *Kuhlmeier,* which was decided in the context of a public school setting, held that the school district as publisher may restrict student presses in order to promote its educational mission and to protect others from objectionable material. Other factors also critical to the case were the school's funding of the newspaper and the association of the publication with a class project. In the case of private schools, the First Amendment does not apply, and school administrators may be freer to regulate student papers. At the college level, public university administrators have less leeway to censor, especially if the student-run papers are funded by student fees.

Overall, the freedom of the press cases raise a host of important issues that place many compelling values into conflict. They test the limits about what can be printed or broadcast, and to whom, and they force consideration of whether the differences in the medium (print or broadcast) make a difference. Web-based modes of communication such as YouTube and blogs, and now Twitter, only make these issues even more complex. They do so in many ways. First, with the rise of blogs and other forms of internet communications, it is becoming more and more difficult to determine what is a legitimate press or not. Is a blog a press protected by the First Amendment? If so, are blog writers journalists? Moreover, with the press becoming ever more controlled by for-profit corporations, what and where is the line to be drawn between commercial speech, which traditionally received lesser First Amendment protection, and journalism. Third, the *New York Times v. Sullivan* standards are being challenged in cases such as *Terry Bollea v. Gawker Media*, 2016 WL 4073660 (Fla. Cir. Ct.). Bollea, better known as the professional wrestler Hulk Hogan, was awarded in 2016 $115 million by a Florida jury when they ruled that Gawker Media, an on-line publication, had invaded Hogan's privacy by publishing a sex tape featuring him. The case raised interesting issues about who or what it means to be a public figure and what constituted harm and invasion of privacy. Some saw in the verdict an effort by the jury to hold the press more responsible for their actions, perhaps signaling a retreat or rethinking of the broad protections *New York Times v. Sullivan* established.

Finally, as the 2016 US presidential election revealed, there appears to be many "fake news" sites flourishing on the web emerging from both foreign and domestic sources. How should these sites be treated—as legitimate journalistic venues or publications, or something else?

BRIDGES V. CALIFORNIA, AND TIMES-MIRROR CO. V. SUPERIOR COURT OF CALIFORNIA

314 U.S. 252, 62 S.Ct. 190, 86 L.Ed 1098 (1941)

At the time that a motion for a new trial was pending in a case involving a dispute between an AFL union and a CIO union of which Harry Bridges was an officer, Bridges sent a telegramto the secretary of labor, which he released to the press. This telegram termed the judge's decision "outrageous" and threatened that an attempt to enforce the decision would tie up the Port of Los Angeles and would involve the entire Pacific Coast. The action against the newspaper was based on the publication of three editorials. Two members of a labor union in Los Angeles had been found guilty of assaulting nonunion truck drivers, and the date for sentence had been set by the court. The editorial said the judge would make a serious mistake if he granted probation.

Both Bridges and the Times-Mirror company, which owned a number of newspapers including the LA Times and the Denver Post, were cited for contempt and convicted, and these convictions were challenged as violating freedom of speech and press.

Vote: 5–4

JUSTICE BLACK delivered the opinion of the Court.

. . . What finally emerges from the "clear and present danger" cases is a working principle that the substantive evil must be extremely serious and the degree of imminence extremely high before utterances can be punished. Those cases do not purport to mark the furthermost constitutional boundaries of protected expression, nor do we here. They do no more than recognize a minimum compulsion of the Bill of Rights. For the First Amendment does not speak equivocally. It prohibits any law "abridging the freedom of speech or of the press." It must be taken as a command of the broadest scope that explicit language, read in the context of a liberty-loving society, will allow. . . .

. . . We must therefore turn to the particular utterances here in question and the circumstances of their publication to determine to what extent the substantive evil of unfair administration of justice was a likely consequence, and whether the degree of likelihood was sufficient to justify summary punishment. . . .

This editorial, given the most intimidating construction it will bear, did no more than threaten future adverse criticism which was reasonably to be expected anyway in the event of a lenient disposition of the pending case. To regard it, therefore, as in itself of substantial influence upon the course of justice would be to impute to judges a lack of firmness, wisdom, or honor, which we cannot accept as a major premise.

Let us assume that the telegram could be construed as an announcement of Bridges' intention to call a strike, something which, it is admitted, neither the general law of California nor the court's degree prohibited. With an eye on the realities of the situation, we cannot assume that Judge Schmidt was unaware of the possibility of a strike as a consequence of his decision. If he was not intimidated by the facts themselves, we do not believe that the most explicit statement of them could have sidetracked the course of justice. Again, we find exaggeration in the conclusion that the utterance even "tended" to interfere with justice. If there was electricity in the atmosphere, it was generated by the facts; the charge added by the Bridges telegram can be dismissed as negligible. . . .

JUSTICE FRANKFURTER dissented, joined by CHIEF JUSTICE STONE and JUSTICES ROBERTS and BYRNES.

. . . Our duty is not ended with the recitation of phrases that are the short-hand of a complicated historic process. . . . The fact that the communication to the Secretary of Labor may have been privileged does not constitutionally protect whatever extraneous use may have been made of the communication. It is said that the possibility of a strike, in case of an adverse ruling, must in any event have suggested itself to the private thoughts of a sophisticated judge. Therefore the publication of the Bridges telegram, we are told, merely gave that possibility public expression. To afford constitutional shelter for a definite attempt at coercing a court into a favorable decision because of the contingencies of frustration to which all judicial action is subject, is to hold, in effect, that the Constitution subordinates the judicial settlement of conflicts to the unfettered indulgence of violent speech. The mere fact that after an unfavorable decision men may, upon full consideration of their responsibilities as well as their rights, engage in a strike or a lockout, is a poor reason for denying a state the power to protect its courts from being bludgeoned by serious threats while a decision is hanging in the judicial balance. A vague, undetermined possibility that a decision of a court may lead to a serious manifestation of protest is one thing. The impact of a definite threat of action to prevent a decision is a wholly different matter. To deny such realities is to stultify law. Rights must be judged in their context and not *in vacuo*.

FOR DISCUSSION

Are there ever any circumstances when a judge should be permitted to prevent the publication or broadcasting of a story? What if the story would cause publicity that would damage a court proceeding? Was the latter possibility the true issue in this case?

RELATED CASES

***Toledo Newspaper Co. v. United States:* 247 U.S. 402 (1918).**

A newspaper's publication of comment on a case pending in a federal court and on the conduct of the judge in the case was held to have a reasonable tendency to obstruct the administration of justice.

***Craig v. Hecht:* 263 U.S. 255 (1923).**

Review of a conviction for contempt handed down by a U.S. District Court can be made only by a federal circuit court of appeals. It is improper for a convicted party to seek review of his conviction by a proceeding in habeas corpus in the district court.

***Nye v. United States:* 313 U.S. 33 (1941).**

Overruled the *Toledo* decision by holding invalid a citation for contempt for actions that took place more than one hundred miles from the court, specifically influencing a plaintiff to withdraw a suit.

***Pennekamp v. Florida:* 328 U.S. 331 (1946).**

The publication of editorials concerning the attitude of a judge toward persons charged with crime has too remote an effect on juries to be a clear and present danger to justice. See also *Maryland v. Baltimore Radio Show* (1950).

***Craig v. Harney:* 331 U.S. 367 (1947).**

An inaccurate news story about a trial and an editorial written in intemperate language do not constitute a real danger to the administration of justice. See also the concurrence by Justices Frankfurter and Jackson in *Shepherd v. Florida* (1951).

***Fisher v. Pace:* 336 U.S. 132 (1949).**

Citation for contempt of a lawyer who refused to stop talking on orders from the judge is not a denial of free speech in the courtroom.

***Maryland v. Baltimore Radio Show:* 338 U.S. 912 (1950).**

A broadcasting company had been convicted of contempt for permitting the broadcast of prejudicial matter concerning a pending murder trial. A lower court had reversed the conviction, and the Supreme Court then refused certiorari. Justice Frankfurter's opinion is notable for its explanation of why the Court denies petitions for certiorari.

***Shepherd v. Florida:* 341 U.S. 50 (1951).**

In a *per curiam* opinion, the Court here reversed a Florida conviction for rape of an African American defendant. The Court cited *Cassell v. Texas* (339 U.S. 282, 1950) as its authority. In the concurring opinion by Justice Jackson, it was stated that the Fourteenth Amendment right to a fair trial has not been observed if a defendant is tried in an atmosphere of violent prejudice against him.

***Sacher v. United States:* 343 U.S. 1 (1952).**

A federal judge may summarily dispose of a contempt charge if he certifies "that he saw or heard the conduct constituting the contempt and that it was committed in the actual presence of the court." The case involved the lawyers for the eleven Communist Party leaders tried before Judge Harold Medina in 1951 under the Smith Act.

NEAR V. MINNESOTA

283 U.S. 697, 51 S.Ct. 623, 75 L.Ed. 1357 (1931)

A statute of the state of Minnesota provided for the abatement, as a public nuisance, of a "malicious, scandalous and defamatory newspaper, magazine or other periodical." The Saturday Press, published by the defendants in Minneapolis, was charged by the county attorney of Hennepin County with being such a publication, and the attorney brought suit to enjoin publication. The periodical had accused certain public officials of gross negligence and misconduct in office.

Vote: 5–4

CHIEF JUSTICE HUGHES delivered the opinion of the Court.

. . . This statute, for the suppression as a public nuisance of a newspaper or periodical, is unusual, if not unique, and raises questions of grave importance transcending the local interests involved in the particular action. It is no longer open to doubt that the liberty of the press, and of speech, is within the liberty safeguarded by the due process clause of the Fourteenth Amendment from invasion by state action. . . . In maintaining this guaranty, the authority of the State to enact laws to promote the health, safety, morals and general welfare of its people is necessarily admitted. The limits of this sovereign power must always be determined with appropriate regard to the particular subject of its exercise. . . . Liberty of speech and of the press is also not an absolute right, and the state may punish its abuse. . . . Liberty, in each of its phases, has its history and connotation and, in the present instance, the inquiry is as to the historic conception of the liberty of the press and whether the statute under review violates the essential attributes of that liberty. . . .

If we cut through mere details of procedure, the operation and effect of the statute in substance is that public authorities may bring the owner or publisher of a newspaper or periodical before a judge upon a charge of conducting a business of publishing scandalous and defamatory matter—in particular that the matter consists of charges against public officers of official dereliction—and unless the owner or publisher is able and disposed to bring competent evidence to satisfy the judge that the charges are true and are published with good motives and for justifiable ends, his newspaper or periodical is suppressed and further publication is made punishable as a contempt. This is of the essence of censorship.

The question is whether a statute authorizing such proceedings in restraint of publication is consistent with the conception of the liberty of the press as historically conceived and guaranteed. . . .

The exceptional nature of its limitations places in a strong light the general conception that liberty of the press, historically considered and taken up by the Federal Constitution, has meant, principally although not exclusively, immunity from previous restraints or censorship. The conception of the liberty of the press in this country had broadened with the exigencies of the colonial period and with the efforts to secure freedom from oppressive administration. That liberty was especially cherished for the immunity it afforded from previous restraint of the publication of censure of public officers and charges of official misconduct. . . .

The importance of this immunity has not lessened. While reckless assaults upon public men, and efforts to bring obloquy upon those who are endeavoring faithfully to discharge official duties, exert a baleful influence and deserve the severest condemnation in public opinion, it cannot be said that this abuse is greater, and it is believed to be less, than that which characterized the period in which our institutions took shape. Meanwhile, the administration of government has become more complex, the opportunities for malfeasance and corruption have multiplied, crime has grown to most serious proportions, and the danger of its protection by unfaithful officials and of the impairment of the fundamental security of life and property by criminal alliances and official neglect, emphasizes the primary need of a vigilant and courageous press, especially in great cities. The fact that the liberty of the press may be abused by miscreant purveyors of scandal does not make any the less necessary the immunity of the press from previous restraint in dealing with official misconduct. Subsequent punishment for such abuses as may exist is the appropriate remedy, consistent with constitutional privilege. . . .

Equally unavailing is the insistence that the statute is designed to prevent the circulation of scandal which tends to disturb the public peace and to provoke assaults and the commission of crime. Charges of reprehensible conduct, and in particular of official malfeasance, unquestionably create a public scandal, but the theory of the constitutional guaranty is that even a more serious public evil would be caused by authority to prevent publication. . . . There is nothing new in the fact that charges of reprehensible conduct may create resentment and the disposition to resort to violent means of redress, but this well-understood tendency did not alter the determination to protect the press against censorship and restraint upon publication. . . . The danger of violent reactions becomes greater with effective organization of defiant groups resenting exposure, and if this consideration warranted legislative interference with the initial freedom of publication, the constitutional protection would be reduced to a mere form of words.

For these reasons we hold the statute, so far as it authorized the proceedings in this action under clause (b) of section one, to be an infringement of the liberty of the press guaranteed by the Fourteenth Amendment. We should add that this decision rests upon the operation and effect of the statute, without regard to the question of the truth of the charges contained in the particular periodical. The fact that the public officers named in this case, and those associated with the charges of official dereliction, may be deemed to be impeccable, cannot affect the conclusion that the statute imposes an unconstitutional restraint upon publication. Judgment reversed.

JUSTICE BUTLER dissented, joined by JUSTICES VAN DEVANTER, MCREYNOLDS and SUTHERLAND.

Defendant concedes that the editions of the newspapers complained of are "defamatory *per se.*" And he says: "It has been asserted that the constitution was never intended to be a shield for malice, scandal, and defamation when untrue, or published with bad motives, or for unjustifiable ends. . . . The contrary is true; every person *does* have a constitutional right to publish malicious, scandalous, and defamatory matter though untrue, and with bad motives, and for unjustifiable ends, *in the first instance,* though he is subject to responsibility therefore *afterwards.*" The record, when the substance of the article is regarded, require that concession here. And this Court is required to pass on the validity of the state law on that basis. . . .

The Minnesota statute does not operate as a *previous* restraint on publication within the proper meaning of that phrase. It does not authorize administrative control in advance such as was formerly exercised by the licensers and censors, but prescribes a remedy to be enforced by a suit in equity. In this case there was previous publication made in the course of the business of regularly producing malicious, scandalous, and defamatory periodicals. The business and publications unquestionably constitute an abuse of the right of free press. The statute denounces the things done as a nuisance on the ground, as stated by the state supreme court, that they threaten morals, peace, and good order. There is no question of the power of the State to denounce such transgressions. The restraint authorized is only in respect of continuing to do what has been duly adjudged to constitute a nuisance. . . . There is nothing in the statute purporting to prohibit publications that have not been adjudged to constitute a nuisance. It is fanciful to suggest similarity between the granting of enforcement of the decree authorized by this statute to prevent *further* publication of malicious, scandalous, and defamatory articles and the *previous restraint* upon the press by licensers as referred to by Blackstone and described in the history of the times to which he alludes. . . .

The judgment should be affirmed.

FOR DISCUSSION

If, in fact, what the newspaper wanted to print was libelous or false, should the First Amendment protect its publication?

RELATED CASES

United States v. Paramount Picture: **334 U.S. 131 (1948).**

Held that "moving pictures, like newspapers and radio, are included in the press whose freedom is guaranteed by the First Amendment."

Kingsley Books v. Brown: **354 U.S. 436 (1957).**

A state (here New York) may provide for restraint of circulation of material already published if a judicial hearing determines that the material is obscene.

GROSJEAN V. AMERICAN PRESS CO.

297 U.S. 233, 56 S.Ct. 444, 80 L.Ed. 660 (1936)

A group of newspapers in Louisiana brought this suit to prevent the enforcement of a statute that levied a 2 percent gross receipts tax on newspapers having a circulation of 80,000 copies per week; in practice, the tax was applicable to only thirteen newspapers. All but one of these had openly opposed Senator Huey P. Long, under whose influence the law had been passed. The statute was challenged as abridging the freedom of the press contrary to the Due Process Clause and the equal protection guarantees of the Fourteenth Amendment.

Vote: 9–0

JUSTICE SUTHERLAND delivered the opinion of the Court.

. . . Judge Cooley has laid down the test to be applied—"The evils to be prevented were not the censorship of the press merely, but any action of the government by means of which it might prevent such free and general discussion of public matters as seems absolutely essential to prepare the people for an intelligent exercise of their rights as citizens" 2 Cooley's *Constitutional Limitations* (8th Ed.) p. 886.

It is not intended by anything we have said to suggest that the owners of newspapers are immune from any of the ordinary forms of taxation for support of the government. But this is not an ordinary form of tax, but one single in kind, with a long history of hostile misuse against the freedom of the press.

The predominant purpose of the grant of immunity here invoked was to preserve an untrammeled press as a vital source of public information. The newspapers, magazines and other journals of the country, it is safe to say, have shed and continue to shed, more light on the public and business affairs of the nation than any other instrumentality of publicity; and since informed public opinion is the most potent of all restraints upon misgovernment, the suppression or abridgement of the publicity afforded by a free press cannot be regarded otherwise than with grave concern. The tax here involved is bad not because it takes money from the pockets of the appellees. If that were all, a wholly different question would be presented. It is bad because, in the light of its history and of its present setting, it is seen to be a deliberate and calculated device in the guise of a tax to limit the circulation of information to which the public is entitled in virtue of the constitutional guarantees. A free press stands as one of the great interpreters between the government and the people. To allow it to be fettered is to fetter ourselves.

In view of the persistent search for new subjects of taxation, it is not without significance that, with the single exception of the Louisiana statute, so far as we can discover, no state during the one hundred fifty years of our national existence has undertaken to impose a tax like that now in question.

The form in which the tax is imposed is in itself suspicious. It is not measured or limited by the volume of advertisements. It is measured alone by the extent of the circulation of the publication in which the advertisements are carried, with the plain purpose of penalizing the publishers and curtailing the circulation of a selected group of newspapers.

Having reached the conclusion that the act imposing the tax in question is unconstitutional under the due process of law clause because it abridges the freedom of the press, we deem it unnecessary to consider the further ground assigned that it also constitutes a denial of the equal protection of the laws.

Decree affirmed.

FOR DISCUSSION

What if the tax in this case had not been directed toward newspapers that were being critical of the governor? Is a truly "neutral" tax on newspapers unconstitutional? What about a tax on television, radio, or Internet broadcasts of news?

RELATED CASES

***Associated Press v. NLRB:* 301 U.S. 103 (1937).**

The Associated Press was held to be engaged in interstate commerce. Its operations involved the constant use of the means of interstate and foreign communication: "Interstate communication of a business nature, whatever the means of such communication, is interstate commerce regulable by Congress under the Constitution." Further such regulation is not violative of freedom of the press.

***United States v. Associated Press:* 326 U.S. 1 (1945).**

The Court held the AP in violation of the Sherman Antitrust Act in that the organization's bylaws were in restraint of trade. Freedom of the press does not include the right to combine to restrain trade in news.

***Oklahoma Press Publishing Co. v. Walling:* 327 U.S. 186 (1946).**

Congress may subject newspapers to the wage and hour provisions of the Fair Labor Standards Act. There is no denial of freedom of the press; there is no restraint upon expression; and publishers of newspapers have been placed on the same plane with other businesses.

***Minneapolis Star and Tribune v. Minnesota:* 460 U.S. 575 (1983).**

A state tax on newsprint and ink was held to violate the First Amendment.

NEW YORK TIMES CO. V. SULLIVAN

376 U.S. 254, 84 S.Ct. 710, 11 L.Ed.2d 686 (1964)

A county commissioner sued for libel the company that publishes the *New York Times*, claiming that an ad run in the paper contained factual inaccuracies and suggestions regarding the plaintiff's involvement in terrorizing and threatening civil rights demonstrators. A jury found for the commissioner, and the company that published the paper appealed.

Vote: 9–0

JUSTICE BRENNAN delivered the opinion of the Court.

We are required in this case to determine for the first time the extent to which the constitutional protections for speech and press limit a State's power to award damages in a libel action brought by a public official against critics of his official conduct.

Respondent L. B. Sullivan is one of the three elected Commissioners of the City of Montgomery, Alabama. He testified that he was "Commissioner of Public Affairs and the duties are supervision of the Police Department, Fire Department, Department of Cemetery and Department of Scales." He brought this civil libel action against the four individual petitioners, who are Negroes and Alabama clergymen, and against petitioner the New York Times Company, a New York corporation which publishes the *New York Times*, a daily newspaper.

A jury in the Circuit Court of Montgomery County awarded him damages of $500,000, the full amount claimed, against all the petitioners, and the Supreme Court of Alabama affirmed.

Respondent's complaint alleged that he had been libeled by statements in a full-page advertisement that was carried in the New York Times on March 29, 1960. Entitled "Heed Their Rising Voices," the advertisement began by stating that "As the whole world knows by now, thousands of Southern Negro students are engaged in widespread non-violent demonstrations in positive affirmation of the right to live in human dignity as guaranteed by the U.S. Constitution and the Bill of Rights." It went on to charge that "in their efforts to uphold these guarantees, they are being met by an unprecedented wave of terror by those who would deny and negate that document which the whole world looks upon as setting the pattern for modern freedom. . . ." Succeeding paragraphs purported to illustrate the "wave of terror" by describing certain alleged events. The text concluded with an appeal for funds for three purposes: support of the student movement, "the struggle for the right-to-vote," and the legal defense of Dr. Martin Luther King, Jr., leader of the movement, against a perjury indictment then pending in Montgomery.

The text appeared over the names of 64 persons, many widely known for their activities in public affairs, religion, trade unions, and the performing arts. Below these names, and under a line reading "We in the south who are struggling daily for dignity and freedom warmly endorse this appeal," appeared the names of the four individual petitioners and of 16 other persons, all but two of whom were identified as clergymen in various Southern cities. The advertisement was signed at the bottom of the page by the "Committee to Defend Martin Luther King and the Struggle for Freedom in the South," and the officers of the Committee were listed.

Of the 10 paragraphs of text in the advertisement, the third and a portion of the sixth were the basis of respondent's claim of libel. They read as follows:

> Third paragraph:
>
> In Montgomery, Alabama, after students sang "My Country, 'Tis of Thee" on the State Capitol steps, their leaders were expelled from school, and truckloads of police armed with shotguns and tear-gas ringed the Alabama State College Campus. When the entire student body protested to state authorities by refusing to re-register, their dining hall was padlocked in an attempt to starve them into submission.
>
> Sixth paragraph:
>
> Again and again the Southern violators have answered Dr. King's peaceful protests with intimidation and violence. They have bombed his home almost killing his wife and child. They have assaulted his person. They have arrested him seven times—for "speeding," "loitering" and similar "offenses." And now they have charged him with "perjury"—a felony under which they could imprison him for ten years. . . .

Although neither of these statements mentions respondent by name, he contended that the word "police" in the third paragraph referred to him as the Montgomery Commissioner who supervised the Police Department, so that he was being accused of "ringing" the campus with police. He further claimed that the paragraph would be read as imputing to the police, and hence to him, the padlocking of the dining hall in order to starve the students into submission. As to the sixth paragraph, he contended that since arrests are ordinarily made by the police, the statement "They have arrested [Dr. King] seven times" would be read as referring to him; he further contended that the "They" who did the arresting would be equated with the "They" who committed the other described acts and with the "Southern violators." Thus, he argued, the paragraph would be read as accusing the Montgomery police, and hence him, of answering Dr. King's protests with "intimidation and violence," bombing his home, assaulting his person, and charging him with perjury. Respondent and six other Montgomery residents testified that they read some or all of the statements as referring to him in his capacity as Commissioner.

It is uncontroverted that some of the statements contained in the paragraphs were not accurate descriptions of events which occurred in Montgomery. Although Negro students staged a demonstration on the State Capitol steps, they sang the National Anthem and not "My Country, 'Tis of Thee." Although nine students were expelled by the State Board of Education, this was not for leading the demonstration at the Capitol, but for demanding service at a lunch counter in the Montgomery County Courthouse on another day. Not the entire student body, but most of it, had protested the expulsion, not by refusing to register, but by boycotting classes on a single day; virtually all the students did register for the ensuing semester. The campus dining hall was not padlocked on any occasion, and the only students who may have been barred from eating there were the few who had neither signed a preregistration application nor requested temporary meal tickets. Although the police were deployed near the campus in large numbers on three occasions, they did not at any time "ring" the campus, and they were not called to the campus in connection with the demonstration on the State Capitol steps, as the third paragraph implied. Dr. King had not been arrested seven times, but only four; and although he claimed to have been assaulted some years earlier in connection with his arrest for loitering outside a courtroom, one of the officers who made the arrest denied that there was such an assault.

Under Alabama law as applied in this case, a publication is "libelous per se" if the words "tend to injure a person . . . in his reputation" or to "bring [him] into public contempt"; the trial court stated that the standard was met if the words are such as to "injure him in his public office, or impute misconduct to him in his office, or want of official integrity, or want of fidelity to a public trust . . . ." The jury must find that the words were published "of and concerning" the plaintiff, but where the plaintiff is a public official his place in the governmental hierarchy is sufficient evidence to support a finding that his reputation has been affected by statements that reflect upon the agency of which he is in charge. Once "libel per se" has been established, the defendant has no defense as to stated facts unless he can persuade the jury that they were true in all their particulars.

The question before us is whether this rule of liability, as applied to an action brought by a public official against critics of his official conduct, abridges the freedom of speech and of the press that is guaranteed by the First and Fourteenth Amendments.

The general proposition that freedom of expression upon public questions is secured by the First Amendment has long been settled by our decisions. The constitutional safeguard, we have said, "was fashioned to assure unfettered interchange of ideas for the bringing about of political and social changes desired by the people."

"The maintenance of the opportunity for free political discussion to the end that government may be responsive to the will of the people and that changes may be obtained by lawful means, an opportunity essential to the security of the Republic, is a fundamental principle of our constitutional system." *Stromberg v. California*, 283 U.S. 359 (1931), "[I]t is a prized American privilege to speak one's mind, although not always with perfect good taste, on all public institutions," *Bridges v. California*, 314 U.S. 252, 270 (1941), and this opportunity is to be afforded for "vigorous advocacy" no less than "abstract discussion." The First Amendment, said Judge Learned Hand, "presupposes that right conclusions are more likely to be gathered out of a multitude of tongues, than through any kind of authoritative selection. To many this is, and always will be, folly; but we have staked upon it our all." *United States v. Associated Press*, 326 U.S. 1 (1945). Mr. Justice Brandeis, in his concurring opinion in *Whitney v. California*, 274 U.S. 357 (1927), gave the principle its classic formulation:

> Those who won our independence believed . . . that public discussion is a political duty; and that this should be a fundamental principle of the American government. They recognized the risks to which all human institutions are subject. But they knew that order cannot be secured merely through fear

of punishment for its infraction; that it is hazardous to discourage thought, hope and imagination; that fear breeds repression; that repression breeds hate; that hate menaces stable government; that the path of safety lies in the opportunity to discuss freely supposed grievances and proposed remedies; and that the fitting remedy for evil counsels is good ones. Believing in the power of reason as applied through public discussion, they eschewed silence coerced by law— the argument of force in its worst form. Recognizing the occasional tyrannies of governing majorities, they amended the Constitution so that free speech and assembly should be guaranteed.

A rule compelling the critic of official conduct to guarantee the truth of all his factual assertions—and to do so on pain of libel judgments virtually unlimited in amount—leads to a comparable "self-censorship." Allowance of the defense of truth, with the burden of proving it on the defendant, does not mean that only false speech will be deterred.

Even courts accepting this defense as an adequate safeguard have recognized the difficulties of adducing legal proofs that the alleged libel was true in all its factual particulars.

Under such a rule, would-be critics of official conduct may be deterred from voicing their criticism, even though it is believed to be true and even though it is in fact true, because of doubt whether it can be proved in court or fear of the expense of having to do so. They tend to make only statements which "steer far wider of the unlawful zone." The rule thus dampens the vigor and limits the variety of public debate. It is inconsistent with the First and Fourteenth Amendments.

The constitutional guarantees require, we think, a federal rule that prohibits a public official from recovering damages for a defamatory falsehood relating to his official conduct unless he proves that the statement was made with "actual malice"—that is, with knowledge that it was false or with reckless disregard of whether it was false or not. An oft-cited statement of a like rule, which has been adopted by a number of state courts, is found in the Kansas case of *Coleman v. MacLennan,* 78 Kan. 711, 98 P. 281, 285 (1908).

FOR DISCUSSION

What obligation do publishers have to prevent factual errors in advertisements in their publications? Does this case permit the press to make any errors? What standard should apply if one is not dealing with elected or public officials? For example, should the legal standard in this case be the same for celebrities or private individuals?

RELATED CASES

***Associated Press v. Walker:* 388 U.S. 180 (1967).**

Public figures such as army generals are treated the same as public officials when it comes to assessing claims of libel against the media.

***Monitor Patriot Co. v. Roy:* 401 U.S. 265 (1971).**

Candidates for public office are treated the same as public officials in cases of libel.

***Gertz v. Robert Welch, Inc.:* 418 U.S. 323 (1974).**

The *New York Times v. Sullivan* standards for assessing liability in libel do not apply to private individuals, in this case a lawyer. The latter enjoy more protection than public officials or figures.

***Hustler Magazine v. Falwell:* 485 U.S. 46 (1988).**

Writing for the Court, Chief Justice Rehnquist ruled that public figures and officials who were the subject of a mass media parody could not recover for the tort of intentional infliction of emotional distress unless the *New York Times* standard had been met.

NEW YORK TIMES COMPANY V. UNITED STATES

403 U.S. 713, 91 S.Ct. 2140, 29 L.Ed.2d 822 (1971)

The Attorney General and the U.S. government sought to prevent the New York Times from publishing classified materials describing U.S. involvement in the Vietnam War. The D.C. Circuit Court affirmed a District Court decision not to enjoin publication, but the Second Circuit remanded the case to the district court to reconsider its decision refusing to do so to enjoin publication, and the government appealed to the Supreme Court.

Vote: 6–3

PER CURIAM.

We granted certiorari in these cases in which the United States seeks to enjoin the *New York Times* and the *Washington Post* from publishing the contents of a classified study entitled "History of U.S. Decision-Making Process on Viet Nam Policy."

"Any system of prior restraints of expression comes to this Court bearing a heavy presumption against its constitutional validity.' " The Government "thus carries a heavy burden of showing justification for the imposition of such a restraint." The District Court for the Southern District of New York in the *New York Times* case, and the District Court for the District of Columbia and the Court of Appeals for the District of Columbia Circuit, in the *Washington Post* case held that the Government had not met that burden. We agree.

The judgment of the Court of Appeals for the District of Columbia Circuit is therefore affirmed. The order of the Court of Appeals for the Second Circuit is reversed, and the case is remanded with directions to enter a judgment affirming the judgment of the District Court for the Southern District of New York. The stays entered June 25, 1971, by the Court are vacated. The judgments shall issue forthwith.

JUSTICE BLACK, with whom JUSTICE DOUGLAS joins, concurring.

I adhere to the view that the Government's case against the *Washington Post* should have been dismissed and that the injunction against the *New York Times* should have been vacated without oral argument when the cases were first presented to this Court. I believe that every moment's continuance of the injunctions against these newspapers amounts to a flagrant, indefensible, and continuing violation of the First Amendment. Furthermore, after oral argument, I agree completely that we must affirm the judgment of the Court of Appeals for the District of Columbia Circuit and reverse the judgment of the Court of Appeals for the Second Circuit for the reasons stated by my Brothers Douglas and Brennan. In my view it is unfortunate that some of my Brethren are apparently willing to hold that the publication of news may sometimes be enjoined. Such a holding would make a shambles of the First Amendment.

Our Government was launched in 1789 with the adoption of the Constitution. The Bill of Rights, including the First Amendment, followed in 1791. Now, for the first time in the 182 years since the founding of the Republic, the federal courts are asked to hold that the First Amendment does not mean what it says, but rather means that the Government can halt the publication of current news of vital importance to the people of this country.

In seeking injunctions against these newspapers and in its presentation to the Court, the Executive Branch seems to have forgotten the essential purpose and history of the First Amendment. When the Constitution was adopted, many people strongly opposed it because the document contained no Bill of Rights to safeguard certain basic freedoms. They especially feared that the new powers granted to a central government might be interpreted to permit the government to curtail freedom of religion, press, assembly, and speech. In response to an overwhelming public clamor, James Madison offered a series of amendments to satisfy citizens that these great liberties would remain safe and beyond the power of government to abridge. Madison proposed what later became the First Amendment in three parts, . . . one of which proclaimed: "The people shall not be deprived or abridged of their right to speak, to write, or to publish their sentiments; and the freedom of the press, as one of the great bulwarks of liberty, shall be inviolable." The amendments were offered to curtail and restrict the general powers granted to the Executive, Legislative, and Judicial Branches two years before in the original Constitution. The Bill of Rights changed the original Constitution into a new charter under which no branch of government could abridge the people's freedoms of press, speech, religion, and assembly. Yet the Solicitor General argues and some members of the Court appear to agree that the general powers of the Government adopted in the original Constitution should be interpreted to limit and restrict the specific and emphatic guarantees of the Bill of Rights adopted later. I can imagine no greater perversion of history. Madison and the other Framers of the First Amendment, able men that they were, wrote in language they earnestly believed could never be misunderstood: "Congress shall make no law abridging the freedom of the press." Both the history and language of the First Amendment support the view that the press must be left free to publish news, whatever the source, without censorship, injunctions, or prior restraints.

In the First Amendment the Founding Fathers gave the free press the protection it must have to fulfill its essential role in our democracy. The press was to serve the governed, not the governors. The Government's power to censor the press was abolished so that the press would remain forever free to censure the Government. The press was protected so that it could bare the secrets of government and inform the people. Only a free and unrestrained press can effectively expose deception in government. And paramount among the responsibilities of a free press is the duty to prevent any part of the government from deceiving the people and sending them off to distant lands to die of foreign fevers and foreign shot and shell. In my view, far from deserving condemnation for their courageous reporting, the *New York Times*, the *Washington Post*, and other newspapers should be commended for serving the purpose that the Founding Fathers saw so clearly. In revealing the workings of government that led to the Vietnam war, the newspapers nobly did precisely that which the Founders hoped and trusted they would do.

In other words, we are asked to hold that despite the First Amendment's emphatic command, the Executive Branch, the Congress, and the Judiciary can make laws enjoining publication of current news and abridging freedom of the press in the name of "national security." The Government does not even attempt to rely on any act of Congress. Instead it makes the bold and dangerously far-reaching contention that the courts should take it upon themselves to "make" a law abridging freedom of the press in the name of equity, presidential power and national security, even when the representatives of the people in Congress have adhered to the command of the First Amendment and refused to make such a law. To find that the President has "inherent power" to halt the publication of news by resort to the courts would wipe out the First Amendment and destroy the fundamental liberty and security of the very people the Government hopes to make "secure." No one can read the history of the adoption of the First Amendment without being convinced beyond any doubt that it was injunctions like those sought here that Madison and his collaborators intended to outlaw in this Nation for all time.

JUSTICE DOUGLAS, with whom JUSTICE BLACK joins, concurring.

The dominant purpose of the First Amendment was to prohibit the widespread practice of governmental suppression of embarrassing information. It is common knowledge that the First Amendment was adopted against the widespread use of the common law of seditious libel to punish the dissemination of material that is embarrassing to the powers-that-be. The present cases will, I think, go down in history as the most dramatic illustration of that principle. A debate of large proportions goes on in the Nation over our posture in Vietnam. That debate antedated the disclosure of the contents of the present documents. The latter are highly relevant to the debate in progress.

Secrecy in government is fundamentally anti-democratic, perpetuating bureaucratic errors. Open debate and discussion of public issues are vital to our national health. On public questions there should be 'uninhibited, robust, and wide-open' debate.

I would affirm the judgment of the Court of Appeals in the *Post* case, vacate the stay of the Court of Appeals in the *Times* case and direct that it affirm the District Court.

The stays in these cases that have been in effect for more than a week constitute a flouting of the principles of the First Amendment as interpreted in *Near v. Minnesota ex rel. Olson,* 283 U.S. 697 (1931).

JUSTICE BRENNAN, concurring.

I

I write separately in these cases only to emphasize what should be apparent: that our judgments in the present cases may not be taken to indicate the propriety, in the future, of issuing temporary stays and restraining orders to block the publication of material sought to be suppressed by the Government. So far as I can determine, never before has the United States sought to enjoin a newspaper from publishing information in its possession. The relative novelty of the questions presented, the necessary haste with which decisions were reached, the magnitude of the interests asserted, and the fact that all the parties have concentrated their arguments upon the question whether permanent restraints were proper may have justified at least some of the restraints heretofore imposed in these cases. Certainly it is difficult to fault the several courts below for seeking to assure that the issues here involved were preserved for ultimate review by this Court. But even if it be assumed that some of the interim restraints were proper in the two cases before us, that assumption has no bearing upon the propriety of similar judicial action in the future. To begin with, there has now been ample time for reflection and judgment; whatever values there may be in the preservation of novel questions for appellate review may not support any restraints in the future. More important, the First Amendment stands as an absolute bar to the imposition of judicial restraints in circumstances of the kind presented by these cases.

JUSTICE WHITE, with whom JUSTICE STEWART joins, concurring.

I concur in today's judgments, but only because of the concededly extraordinary protection against prior restraints enjoyed by the press under our constitutional system. I do not say that in no circumstances would the First Amendment permit an injunction against publishing information about government plans or operations. Nor, after examining the materials the Government characterizes as the most sensitive and destructive, can I deny that revelation of these documents will do substantial damage to public interests. Indeed, I am confident that their disclosure will have that result. But I nevertheless agree that the United States has not satisfied the very heavy burden that it must meet to warrant an injunction against publication in these cases, at least in the absence of express and appropriately limited congressional authorization for prior restraints in circumstances such as these.

FOR DISCUSSION

Why in this case did it not matter to the majority that the Pentagon Papers were stolen? Should it be illegal to publish state secrets, as it is in some countries, such as Great Britain? Even if not illegal, should the press publish the date and time of a military troop deployment or attack if it has that information?

UNITED STATES V. THE PROGRESSIVE, INC.

467 F.Supp. 990 (D. Wisc. 1979)

The United States sought to enjoin the Progressive magazine from publishing an article allegedly describing how to make a nuclear bomb; the article was based on information gathered from declassified sources.

WARREN, DISTRICT JUDGE.

MEMORANDUM AND ORDER

On March 9, 1979, this Court, at the request of the government, but after hearing from both parties, issued a temporary restraining order enjoining defendants, their employees, and agents from publishing or otherwise communicating or disclosing in any manner any restricted data contained in the article: "The H-Bomb Secret: How We Got It, Why We're Telling It."

In keeping with the Court's order that the temporary restraining order should be in effect for the shortest time possible, a preliminary injunction hearing was scheduled for one week later, on March 16, 1979. At the request of the parties and with the Court's acquiescence, the preliminary injunction hearing was rescheduled for 10:00 A.M. today in order that both sides might have additional time to file affidavits and arguments. The Court continued the temporary restraining order until 5:00 P.M. today.

In order to grant a preliminary injunction, the Court must find that plaintiff has a reasonable likelihood of success on the merits, and that the plaintiff will suffer irreparable harm if the injunction does not issue. In addition, the Court must consider the interest of the public and the balance of the potential harm to plaintiff and defendants.

Under the facts here alleged, the question before this Court involves a clash between allegedly vital security interests of the United States and the competing constitutional doctrine against prior restraint in publication.

In its argument and briefs, plaintiff relies on national security, as enunciated by Congress in The Atomic Energy Act of 1954, as the basis for classification of certain documents. Plaintiff contends that, in certain areas, national preservation and self-interest permit the retention and classification of government secrets. The government argues that its national security interest also permits it to impress classification and censorship upon information originating in the public domain, if when drawn together, synthesized and collated, such information acquires the character of presenting immediate, direct and irreparable harm to the interests of the United States.

Defendants argue that freedom of expression as embodied in the First Amendment is so central to the heart of liberty that prior restraint in any form becomes anathema. They contend that this is particularly true when a nation is not at war and where the prior restraint is based on surmise or conjecture. While acknowledging that freedom of the press is not absolute, they maintain that the publication of the projected article does not rise to the level of immediate, direct and irreparable harm which could justify incursion into First Amendment freedoms.

Hence, although embodying deep and fundamental principles of democratic philosophy, the issue also requires a factual determination by a federal court sitting in equity. At the level of a temporary restraining order, or a preliminary injunction, such matters are customarily dealt with through affidavits.

Thus far the affidavits filed are numerous and complex. They come from individuals of learning and renown. They deal with how the information at issue was assembled, what it means, and how injurious the affiant believes it to be.

The Court notes the *amici curiae* briefs filed by the American Civil Liberties Union, the Wisconsin Civil Liberties Union, the Federation of American Scientists and the Fund for Open Information and Accountability, Inc., and expresses thanks for them. The Court gave consideration to the suggestion that a panel of experts be appointed to serve as witnesses for the Court to assist it in determining whether the dangers of publication are as great as the government asserts or as inconsequential as *The Progressive* states. However, the Court concluded that such a procedure really would merely proliferate the opinions of experts arrayed on both sides of the issue.

Both parties have already marshalled impressive opinions covering all aspects of the case. The Court has read all this material and has now heard extensive argument. It is time for decision.

From the founding days of this nation, the rights to freedom of speech and of the press have held an honored place in our constitutional scheme. The establishment and nurturing of these rights is one of the true achievements of our form of government.

Because of the importance of these rights, any prior restraint on publication comes into court under a heavy presumption against its constitutional validity.

However, First Amendment rights are not absolute. They are not boundless.

In *Near v. Minnesota*, 283 U.S. 697 (1931), the Supreme Court specifically recognized an extremely narrow area, involving national security, in which interference with First Amendment rights might be tolerated and a prior restraint on publication might be appropriate. The Court stated:

> When a nation is at war many things that might be said in time of peace are such a hindrance to its effort that their utterance will not be endured so long as men fight and that no Court could regard them as protected by any constitutional right." No one would question but that a government might prevent actual obstruction to its recruiting service or the publication of the sailing dates of transports or the number and location of troops.

Thus, it is clear that few things, save grave national security concerns, are sufficient to override First Amendment interests. A court is well admonished to approach any requested prior restraint with a great deal of skepticism.

Juxtaposed against the right to freedom of expression is the government's contention that the national security of this country could be jeopardized by publication of the article.

The Court is convinced that the government has a right to classify certain sensitive documents to protect its national security. The problem is with the scope of the classification system.

Defendants contend that the projected article merely contains data already in the public domain and readily available to any diligent seeker. They say other nations already have the same information or the opportunity to obtain it. How then, they argue, can they be in violation of 42 U.S.C. §§ 2274(b) and 2280 which purport to authorize injunctive relief against one who would disclose restricted data "with reason to believe such data will be utilized to injure the United States or to secure an advantage to any foreign nation . . ."?

Although the government states that some of the information is in the public domain, it contends that much of the data is not, and that the Morland article contains a core of information that has never before been published.

Furthermore, the government's position is that whether or not specific information is "in the public domain" or has been "declassified" at some point is not determinative. The government states that a court must look at the nature and context of prior disclosures and analyze what the practical impact of the prior disclosures are as contrasted to that of the present revelation.

The government feels that the mere fact that the author, Howard Morland, could prepare an article explaining the technical processes of thermonuclear weapons does not mean that those processes are available to everyone. They lay heavy emphasis on the argument that the danger lies in the exposition of certain concepts never heretofore disclosed in conjunction with one another.

In an impressive affidavit, Dr. Hans A. Bethe, whose affidavit was introduced by the government and whose article, The Hydrogen Bomb: II, was a source document for Theodore Postol's affidavit filed by the defendants, states that sizeable portions of the Morland text should be classified as restricted data because the processes outlined in the manuscript describe the essential design and operation of thermonuclear weapons. He later concludes "that the design and operational concepts described in the manuscript are not expressed or revealed in the public literature nor do I believe they are known to scientists not associated with the government weapons programs."

The Court has grappled with this difficult problem and has read and studied the affidavits and other documents on file. After all this, the Court finds concepts within the article that it does not find in the public realm concepts that are vital to the operation of the hydrogen bomb.

Does the article provide a "do-it-yourself" guide for the hydrogen bomb? Probably not. A number of affidavits make quite clear that a sine qua non to thermonuclear capability is a large, sophisticated industrial capability coupled with a coterie of imaginative, resourceful scientists and technicians. One does not build a hydrogen bomb in the basement. However, the article could possibly provide sufficient information to allow a medium size nation to move faster in developing a hydrogen weapon. It could provide a ticket to by-pass blind alleys.

What is involved here is information dealing with the most destructive weapon in the history of mankind, information of sufficient destructive potential to nullify the right to free speech and to endanger the right to life itself.

Stripped to its essence then, the question before the Court is a basic confrontation between the First Amendment right to freedom of the press and national security.

Our Founding Fathers believed, as we do, that one is born with certain inalienable rights which, as the Declaration of Independence intones, include the right to life, liberty and the pursuit of happiness. The Constitution, including the Bill of Rights, was enacted to make those rights operable in everyday life.

The Court believes that each of us is born seized of a panoply of basic rights, that we institute governments to secure these rights and that there is a hierarchy of values attached to these rights which is helpful in deciding the clash now before us.

Certain of these rights have an aspect of imperativeness or centrality that make them transcend other rights. Somehow it does not seem that the right to life and the right to not have soldiers quartered in your home can be of equal import in the grand scheme of things. While it may be true in the long-run, as Patrick Henry instructs us, that one would prefer death to life without liberty, nonetheless, in the short-run, one cannot enjoy freedom of speech, freedom to worship or freedom of the press unless one first enjoys the freedom to live.

Faced with a stark choice between upholding the right to continued life and the right to freedom of the press, most jurists would have no difficulty in opting for the chance to continue to breathe and function as they work to achieve perfect freedom of expression. Is the choice here so stark? Only time can give us a definitive answer. But considering another aspect of this panoply of rights we all have is helpful in answering the question now before us. This aspect is the disparity of the risk involved. The destruction of various human rights can come about in differing ways and at varying speeds. Freedom of the press can be obliterated overnight by some dictator's imposition of censorship or by the slow nibbling away at a free press through successive bits of repressive legislation enacted by a nation's lawmakers. Yet, even in the most drastic of such situations, it is always possible for a dictator to be overthrown, for a bad law to be repealed or for a judge's error to be subsequently rectified. Only when human life is at stake are such corrections impossible. The case at bar is so difficult precisely because the consequences of error involve human life itself and on such an awesome scale. The Secretary of State states that publication will increase thermonuclear proliferation and that this would "irreparably impair the national security of the United States." The Secretary of Defense says that dissemination of the Morland paper will mean a substantial increase in the risk of thermonuclear proliferation and lead to use or threats that would "adversely affect the national security of the United States." Howard Morland asserts that "if the information in my article were not in the public domain, it should be put there . . . so that ordinary citizens may have informed opinions about nuclear weapons." The Court is faced with the difficult task of weighing and resolving these divergent views. A mistake in ruling against The Progressive will seriously infringe cherished First Amendment rights. If a preliminary injunction is issued, it will constitute the first instance of prior restraint against a publication in this fashion in the history of this country, to this Court's knowledge. Such notoriety is not to be sought. It will curtail defendants' First Amendment rights in a drastic and substantial fashion. It will infringe upon our right to know and to be informed as well. A mistake in ruling against the United States could pave the way for thermonuclear annihilation for us all. In that event, our right to life is extinguished and the right to publish becomes moot. In the *Near* case, the Supreme Court recognized that publication of troop movements in time of war would threaten national security and could therefore be restrained. Times have changed significantly since 1931 when *Near* was decided. Now war by foot soldiers has been replaced in large part by war by machines and bombs. No longer need there be any advance warning or any preparation time before a nuclear war could be commenced. In light of these factors, this Court concludes that publication of the technical information on the hydrogen bomb contained in the article is analogous to publication of troop movements or locations in time of war and falls within the extremely narrow exception to the rule against prior restraint.

FINDINGS OF FACT

19. After careful review of the Morland article and other documents filed in this case, the Court finds that publication or other disclosure of the Secret Restricted Data contained in the Morland article would irreparably harm the national security of the United States.

20. The United States and its citizens will suffer irreparable harm and the public interest will be disserved if a preliminary injunction is not issued. On balance, the defendants will not be substantially harmed by the issuance of such a preliminary injunction.

21. Publication of the Restricted Data in the Morland article will result in direct, immediate and irreparable damage to the United States by accelerating the capacity of certain non-thermonuclear nations to manufacture thermonuclear weapons.

CONCLUSIONS OF LAW

This Court has jurisdiction over the subject matter of this action pursuant to 42 U.S.C. § 2280 and 28 U.S.C. § 1345. Publication or other disclosure or communication of the Restricted Data contained in the Morland article would likely constitute a violation of the Atomic Energy Act, 42 U.S.C. § 2274(b). The pertinent provisions of the Atomic Energy Act, 42 U.S.C. § 2274(b) and § 2280, apply to the defendants and are not constitutionally vague or over broad. Because defendants intend imminently to publish the Restricted Data contained in the Morland article, unless restrained by order of the court, plaintiff, United States of America, is entitled to a preliminary injunction, prohibiting publication or disclosure of the article pursuant to 42 U.S.C. § 2280. In view of the showing of harm made by the United States, a preliminary injunction would be warranted even in the absence of statutory authorization because of the existence of the likelihood of direct, immediate and irreparable injury to our nation and its people The facts and circumstances as presented here fall within the extremely narrow recognized area, involving national security, in which a prior restraint on publication is appropriate. Issuance of a preliminary injunction does not, under the circumstances presented to the Court, violate defendants' First Amendment rights. Plaintiff has proven all necessary prerequisites for issuance of a preliminary injunction restraining defendants from publishing or disclosing any Restricted Data contained in the Morland article until a final determination in this action has been made by the Court.

FOR DISCUSSION

Should publication of information about nuclear or other weapons be enjoined in order to prevent terrorists from obtaining it? Is some military or technological information so inherently dangerous that it should not be allowed to be published for general audiences?

BRANZBURG V. HAYES

408 U.S. 665, 92 S.Ct. 2646, 33 L.Ed.2d 626 (1972)

A Kentucky newspaper ran a story describing how individuals made illegal drugs for sale. The writer of the story was subpoenaed and asked to reveal the identities of these individuals. He refused, claiming a reporter's privilege under state law and the First Amendment. State courts rejected these claims and the reporter appealed to the Supreme Court. The Court reviewed this case in conjunction with *In re Pappas* and *United States v. Caldwell*, cases involving investigations of the Black Panthers.

Vote: 5–4

Opinion of the Court by JUSTICE WHITE, announced by the CHIEF JUSTICE.

The issue in these cases is whether requiring newsmen to appear and testify before state or federal grand juries abridges the freedom of speech and press guaranteed by the First Amendment. We hold that it does not.

I

The writ of certiorari in *Branzburg v. Hayes,* 408 U.S. 665 (1972), and *Branzburg v. Meigs*, 503 S.W.2d 748 (1971), brings before us two judgments of the Kentucky Court of Appeals, both involving petitioner Branzburg, a staff reporter for the *Courier-Journal*, a daily newspaper published in Louisville, Kentucky.

On November 15, 1969, the *Courier-Journal* carried a story under petitioner's by-line describing in detail his observations of two young residents of Jefferson County synthesizing hashish from marihuana, an activity which, they asserted, earned them about $5,000 in three weeks. The article included a photograph of a pair of hands working above a laboratory table on which was a substance identified by the caption as hashish. The article stated that petitioner had promised not to reveal the identity of the two hashish makers. Petitioner was shortly subpoenaed by the Jefferson County grand jury; he appeared, but refused to identify the individuals he had seen possessing marihuana or the persons he had seen making hashish from marihuana. A state trial court judge ordered petitioner to answer these questions and rejected his contention that the Kentucky reporters' privilege statute, the First Amendment of the United States Constitution, or §§ 1, 2 and 8 of the Kentucky Constitution authorized his refusal to answer. Petitioner then sought prohibition and mandamus in the Kentucky Court of Appeals on the same grounds, but the Court of Appeals denied the petition. It held that petitioner had abandoned his First Amendment argument in a supplemental memorandum he had filed and tacitly rejected his argument based on the Kentucky Constitution. It also construed Ky.Rev.Stat. § 421.100 as affording a newsman the privilege of refusing to divulge the identity of an informant who supplied him with information, but held that the statute did not permit a reporter to refuse to testify about events he had observed personally, including the identities of those persons he had observed.

The second case involving petitioner Branzburg arose out of his later story published on January 10, 1971, which described in detail the use of drugs in Frankfort, Kentucky. The article reported that in order to provide a comprehensive survey of the "drug scene" in Frankfort, petitioner had "spent two weeks interviewing several dozen drug users in the capital city" and had seen some of them smoking marihuana. A number of conversations with and observations of several unnamed drug users were recounted. Subpoenaed to appear before a Franklin County grand jury "to testify in the matter of violation of statutes concerning use and sale of drugs," petitioner Branzburg moved to quash the summons; the motion was denied, although an order was issued protecting Branzburg from revealing "confidential associations, sources or information" but requiring that he "answer any questions which concern or pertain to any criminal act, the commission of which was actually observed by (him)." Prior to the time he was slated to appear before the grand jury, petitioner sought mandamus and prohibition from the Kentucky Court of Appeals, arguing that if he were forced to go before the grand jury or to answer questions regarding the identity of informants or disclose information given to him in confidence, his effectiveness as a reporter would be greatly damaged. The Court of Appeals once again denied the requested writs, reaffirming its construction of Ky.Rev.Stat. § 421.100, and rejecting petitioner's claim of a First Amendment privilege.

II

Petitioners Branzburg and Pappas and respondent Caldwell press First Amendment claims that may be simply put: that to gather news it is often necessary to agree either not to identify the source of information published or to publish only part of the facts revealed, or both; that if the reporter is nevertheless forced to reveal these confidences to a grand jury, the source so identified and other confidential sources of other reporters will be measurably deterred from furnishing publishable information, all to the detriment of the free flow of information protected by the First Amendment. Although the newsmen in these cases do not claim an absolute privilege against official interrogation in all circumstances, they assert that the reporter should not be forced either to appear or to testify before a grand jury or at trial until and unless sufficient grounds are shown for believing that the reporter possesses information relevant to a crime the grand jury is investigating, that the information the reporter has is unavailable from other sources, and that the need for the information is sufficiently compelling to override the claimed invasion of First Amendment interests occasioned by the disclosure. Principally relied upon are prior cases emphasizing the importance of the First Amendment guarantees to individual development and to our system of representative government, decisions requiring that official action with adverse impact on First Amendment rights be justified by a public interest that is "compelling" or "paramount," and those precedents establishing the principle that justifiable governmental goals may not be achieved by unduly broad means having an unnecessary impact on protected rights of speech, press, or association. The heart of the claim is that the burden on news gathering resulting from compelling reporters to disclose confidential information outweighs any public interest in obtaining the information.

We do not question the significance of free speech, press, or assembly to the country's welfare. Nor is it suggested that news gathering does not quality for First Amendment protection; without some protection for seeking out the news, freedom of the press could be eviscerated. But these cases involve no intrusions upon speech or assembly, no prior restraint or restriction on what the press may publish, and no express or implied command that the press publish what it prefers to withhold. No exaction or tax for the privilege of publishing, and no penalty, civil or criminal, related to the content of published material is at issue here. The use of confidential sources by the press is not forbidden or restricted; reporters remain free to seek news from any source by means within the law. No attempt is made to require the press to publish its sources of information or indiscriminately to disclose them on request.

The sole issue before us is the obligation of reporters to respond to grand jury subpoenas as other citizens do and to answer questions relevant to an investigation into the commission of crime. Citizens generally are not constitutionally immune from grand jury subpoenas; and neither the First Amendment nor any other constitutional provision protects the average citizen from disclosing to a grand jury information that he has received in confidence. The claim is, however, that reporters are exempt from these obligations because if forced to respond to subpoenas and identify their sources or disclose other confidences, their informants will refuse or be reluctant to furnish newsworthy information in the future. This asserted burden on news gathering is said to make compelled testimony from newsmen constitutionally suspect and to require a privileged position for them.

It is clear that the First Amendment does not invalidate every incidental burdening of the press that may result from the enforcement of civil or criminal statutes of general applicability. Under prior cases, otherwise valid laws serving substantial public interests may be enforced against the press as against others, despite the possible burden that may be imposed. The Court has emphasized that "(t)he publisher of a newspaper has no special immunity from the application of general laws. He has no special privilege to invade the rights and liberties of others." It was there held that the Associated Press, a news-gathering and disseminating organization, was not exempt from the requirements of the National Labor Relations Act. The holding was reaffirmed in *Oklahoma Press Publishing Co. v. Walling,* 327 U. S. 186 (1946), where the Court rejected the claim that applying the Fair Labor Standards Act to a newspaper publishing business would abridge the freedom of press guaranteed by the First Amendment. *Associated Press v. United States*, 326 U. S. 1 (1945), similarly overruled assertions that the First Amendment precluded application of the Sherman Act to a news-gathering and disseminating organization.

The prevailing view is that the press is not free to publish with impunity everything and anything it desires to publish. Although it may deter or regulate what is said or published, the press may not circulate knowing or reckless falsehoods damaging to private reputation without subjecting itself to liability for damages, including punitive damages, or even criminal prosecution.

It has generally been held that the First Amendment does not guarantee the press a constitutional right of special access to information not available to the public generally.

It is thus not surprising that the great weight of authority is that newsmen are not exempt from the normal duty of appearing before a grand jury and answering questions relevant to a criminal investigation. At common law, courts consistently refused to recognize the existence of any privilege authorizing a newsman to refuse to reveal confidential information to a grand jury In 1958, a news gatherer asserted for the first time that the First Amendment exempted confidential information from public disclosure pursuant to a subpoena issued in a civil suit, but the claim was denied, and this argument has been almost uniformly rejected since then although there are occasional dicta that, in circumstances not presented here, a newsman might be excused

A number of States have provided newsmen a statutory privilege of varying breadth, but the majority have not done so, and none has been provided by federal statute. Until now the only testimonial privilege for unofficial witnesses that is rooted in the Federal Constitution is the Fifth Amendment privilege against compelled self-incrimination. We are asked to create another by interpreting the First Amendment to grant newsmen a testimonial privilege that other citizens do not enjoy. This we decline to do. Fair and effective law enforcement aimed at providing security for the person and property of the individual is a fundamental function of government, and the grand jury plays an important, constitutionally mandated role in this process. On the records now before us, we perceive no basis for holding that the public interest in law enforcement and in ensuring effective grand jury proceedings is insufficient to override the consequential, but uncertain, burden on news gathering that is said to result from insisting that reporters, like other citizens, respond to relevant questions put to them in the course of a valid grand jury investigation or criminal trial.

Thus, we cannot seriously entertain the notion that the First Amendment protects a newsman's agreement to conceal the criminal conduct of his source, or evidence thereof, on the theory that it is better to write about crime than to do something about it. Insofar as any reporter in these cases undertook not to reveal or testify about the crime he witnessed, his claim of privilege under the First Amendment presents no substantial question. The crimes of news sources are no less reprehensible and threatening to the public interest when witnessed by a reporter than when they are not.

The argument that the flow of news will be diminished by compelling reporters to aid the grand jury in a criminal investigation is not irrational, nor are the records before us silent on the matter. But we remain unclear how often and to what extent informers are actually deterred from furnishing information when newsmen are forced to testify before a grand jury. The available data indicate that some newsmen rely a great deal on confidential sources and that some informants are particularly sensitive to the threat of exposure and may be silenced if it is held by this Court that, ordinarily, newsmen must testify pursuant to subpoenas, but the evidence fails to demonstrate that there would be a significant construction of the flow of news to the public if this Court reaffirms the prior common-law and constitutional rule regarding the testimonial obligations of newsmen. Estimates of the inhibiting effect of such subpoenas on the willingness of informants to make disclosures to newsmen are widely divergent and to a great extent speculative. It would be difficult to canvass the views of the informants themselves; surveys of reporters on this topic are chiefly opinions of predicted informant behavior and must be viewed in the light of the professional self-interest of the interviewees. Reliance by the press on confidential informants does not mean that all such sources will in fact dry up because of the later possible appearance of the newsman before a grand jury. The reporter may never be called and if he objects to testifying, the prosecution may not insist. Also, the relationship of many informants to the press is a symbiotic one which is unlikely to be greatly inhibited by the threat of subpoena: quite often, such informants are members of a minority political or cultural group that relies heavily on the media to propagate its views, publicize its aims, and magnify its exposure to the public. Moreover, grand juries characteristically conduct secret proceedings, and law enforcement officers are themselves experienced in dealing with informers, and have their own methods for protecting them without interference with the effective administration of Justice. There is little before us indicating that informants whose interest in avoiding exposure is that it may threaten job security, personal safety, or peace of mind, would in fact be in a worse position, or would think they would be, if they risked placing their trust in public officials as well as reporters. We doubt if the informer who prefers anonymity but is sincerely interested in furnishing evidence of crime will always or very often be deterred by the prospect of dealing with those public authorities characteristically charged with the duty to protect the public interest as well as his.

JUSTICE POWELL, concurring.

I add this brief statement to emphasize what seems to me to be the limited nature of the Court's holding. The Court does not hold that newsmen, subpoenaed to testify before a grand jury, are without constitutional rights with respect to the gathering of news or in safeguarding their sources. Certainly, we do not hold, as suggested in Mr. Justice Stewart's dissenting opinion, that state and federal authorities are free to "annex" the news media as "an investigative arm of government." The solicitude repeatedly shown by this Court for First Amendment freedoms should be sufficient assurance against any such effort, even if one seriously believed that the media—properly free and untrammeled in the fullest sense of these terms—were not able to protect themselves.

JUSTICE STEWART, with whom JUSTICES BRENNAN and MARSHALL join, dissenting.

The Court's crabbed view of the First Amendment reflects a disturbing insensitivity to the critical role of an independent press in our society. The question whether a reporter has a constitutional right to a confidential relationship with his source is of first impression here, but the principles that should guide our decision are as basic as any to be found in the Constitution. While Mr. Justice Powell's enigmatic concurring opinion gives some hope of a more flexible view in the future, the Court in these cases holds that a newsman has no First Amendment right to protect his sources when called before a grand jury. The Court thus invites state and federal authorities to undermine the historic independence of the press by attempting to annex the journalistic profession as an investigative arm of government. Not only will this decision impair performance of the press' constitutionally protected functions, but it will, I am convinced, in the long run, harm rather than help the administration of Justice.

I respectfully dissent.

I

The reporter's constitutional right to a confidential relationship with his source stems from the broad societal interest in a full and free flow of information to the public. It is this basic concern that underlies the Constitution's protection of a free press, because the guarantee is "not for the benefit of the press so much as for the benefit of all of us."

A

In keeping with this tradition, we have held that the right to publish is central to the First Amendment and basic to the existence of constitutional democracy.

A corollary of the right to publish must be the right to gather news. The full flow of information to the public protected by the free-press guarantee would be severely curtailed if no protection whatever were afforded to the process by which news is assembled and disseminated. We have, therefore, recognized that there is a right to publish without prior governmental approval, and a right to receive printed matter.

No less important to the news dissemination process is the gathering of information. News must not be unnecessarily cut off at its source, for without freedom to acquire information the right to publish would be impermissibly compromised. Accordingly, a right to gather news, of some dimensions, must exist

B

The right to gather news implies, in turn, a right to a confidential relationship between a reporter and his source. This proposition follows as a matter of simple logic once three factual predicates are recognized: (1) newsmen require informants to gather news; (2) confidentiality—the promise or understanding that names or certain aspects of communications will be kept off the record—is essential to the creation and maintenance of a news-gathering relationship with informants; and (3) an unbridled subpoena power—the absence of a constitutional right protecting, in any way, a confidential relationship from compulsory process—will either deter sources from divulging information or deter reporters from gathering and publishing information.

FOR DISCUSSION

Does the threat of a reporter's having to disclose sources hurt the ability to gather news and information? If reporters are granted a privilege against revealing sources, does that give them more First Amendment rights than nonjournalists? Should reporters have these "extra" rights? Who qualifies as a reporter? Should a person who creates a blog be considered a journalist?

RED LION BROADCASTING CO. V. F.C.C.

395 U.S. 367, 89 S.Ct. 1794, 23 L.Ed. 2d 371 (1969)

A radio station aired a talk show in which the author of a book was attacked verbally by an individual. The author requested a right to respond under the FCC fairness doctrine, and the FCC ordered the station to offer him airtime to respond. The station appealed the FCC order.

Vote: 9–0

JUSTICE WHITE delivered the opinion of the Court.

The Federal Communications Commission has for many years imposed on radio and television broadcasters the requirement that discussion of public issues be presented on broadcast stations, and that each side of those issues must be given fair coverage. This is known as the fairness doctrine, which originated very early in the history of broadcasting and has maintained its present outlines for some time. It is an obligation whose content has been defined in a long series of FCC rulings in particular cases, and which is distinct from the statutory requirement of s 315 of the Communications Act[1] that equal time be allotted all qualified candidates for public office. Two aspects of the fairness doctrine, relating to personal attacks in the context of controversial public issues and to political editorializing, were codified more precisely in the form of FCC regulations in 1967. The two cases before us now, which were decided separately below, challenge the constitutional and statutory bases of the doctrine and component rules. Red Lion involves the application of the fairness doctrine to a particular broadcast, and RTNDA arises as an action to review the FCC's 1967 promulgation of the personal attack and political editorializing regulations, which were laid down after the Red Lion litigation had begun.

1. Communications Act of 1934, Tit. III, 48 Stat. 1081, as amended, 47 U.S.C. s 301 et seq. Section 315 now reads:

315. Candidates for public office; facilities; rules.

(a) If any licensee shall permit any person who is a legally qualified candidate for any public office to use a broadcasting station, he shall afford equal opportunities to all other such candidates for that office in the use of such broadcasting station: Provided, That such licensee shall have no power of censorship over the material broadcast under the provisions of this section. No obligation is imposed upon any licensee to allow the use of its station by any such candidate. Appearance by a legally qualified candidate on any—

(1) bona fide newscast,

(2) bona fide news interview,

(3) bona fide news documentary (if the appearance of the candidate is incidental to the presentation of the subject or subjects covered by the news documentary), or

(4) on-the-spot coverage of bona fide news events (including but not limited to political conventions and activities incidental thereto),

shall not be deemed to be use of a broadcasting station within the meaning of this subsection. Nothing in the foregoing sentence shall be construed as relieving broadcasters, in connection with the presentation of newscasts, news interviews, news documentaries, and on-the-spot coverage of news events, from the obligation imposed upon them under this chapter to operate in the public interest and to afford reasonable opportunity for the discussion of conflicting views on issues of public importance.

(b) The charges made for the use of any broadcasting station for any of the purposes set forth in this section shall not exceed the charges made for comparable use of such station for other purposes.

(c) The Commission shall prescribe appropriate rules and regulations to carry out the provisions of this section.

I

A

The Red Lion Broadcasting Company is licensed to operate a Pennsylvania radio station, WGCB. On November 27, 1964, WGCB carried a 15-minute broadcast by the Reverend Billy James Hargis as part of a "Christian Crusade" series. A book by Fred J. Cook entitled *Goldwater—Extremist on the Right* was discussed by Hargis, who said that Cook had been fired by a newspaper for making false charges against city officials; that Cook had then worked for a Communist-affiliated publication; that he had defended Alger Hiss and attacked J. Edgar Hoover and the Central Intelligence Agency; and that he had now written a "book to smear and destroy Barry Goldwater." When Cook heard of the broadcast he concluded that he had been personally attacked and demanded free reply time, which the station refused. After an exchange of letters among Cook, Red Lion, and the FCC, the FCC declared that the Hargis broadcast constituted a personal attack on Cook; that Red Lion had failed to meet its obligation under the fairness doctrine as expressed in Times-Mirror Broadcasting Co., to send a tape, transcript, or summary of the broadcast to Cook and offer him reply time; and that the station must provide reply time whether or not Cook would pay for it. On review in the Court of Appeals for the District of Columbia Circuit. the FCC's position was upheld as constitutional and otherwise proper.

III

The broadcasters challenge the fairness doctrine and its specific manifestations in the personal attack and political editorial rules on conventional First Amendment grounds, alleging that the rules abridge their freedom of speech and press. Their contention is that the First Amendment protects their desire to use their allotted frequencies continuously to broadcast whatever they choose, and to exclude whomever they choose from ever using that frequency. No man may be prevented from saying or publishing what he thinks, or from refusing in his speech or other utterances to give equal weight to the views of his opponents This right, they say, applies equally to broadcasters.

A

Although broadcasting is clearly a medium affected by a First Amendment interest, differences in the characteristics of new media justify differences in the First Amendment standards applied to them. For example, the ability of new technology to produce sounds more raucous than those of the human voice justifies restrictions on the sound level, and on the hours and places of use, of sound trucks so long as the restrictions are reasonable and applied without discrimination.

Just as the Government may limit the use of sound-amplifying equipment potentially so noisy that it drowns out civilized private speech, so may the Government limit the use of broadcast equipment. The right of free speech of a broadcaster, the user of a sound truck, or any other individual does not embrace a right to snuff out the free speech of others.

When two people converse face to face, both should not speak at once if either is to be clearly understood. But the range of the human voice is so limited that there could be meaningful communications if half the people in the United States were talking and the other half listening. Just as clearly, half the people might publish and the other half read. But the reach of radio signals is incomparably greater than the range of the human voice and the problem of interference is a massive reality. The lack of know-how and equipment may keep many from the air, but only a tiny fraction of those with resources and intelligence can hope to communicate by radio at the same time if intelligible communication is to be had, even if the entire radio spectrum is utilized in the present state of commercially acceptable technology.

Where there are substantially more individuals who want to broadcast than there are frequencies to allocate, it is idle to posit an unabridgeable First Amendment right to broadcast comparable to the right of every individual to speak, write, or publish. If 100 persons want broadcast licenses but there are only 10 frequencies to allocate, all of them may have the same right to a license; but if there is to be any effective communication by radio, only a few can be licensed and the rest must be barred from the airwaves. It would be strange if the First Amendment, aimed at protecting and furthering communications, prevented the Government from making radio communication possible by requiring licenses to broadcast and by limiting the number of licenses so as not to overcrowd the spectrum.

This has been the consistent view of the Court. Congress unquestionably has the power to grant and deny licenses and to eliminate existing stations. No one has a First Amendment right to a license or to monopolize a radio frequency; to deny a station license because the public interest requires it is not a denial of free speech.

By the same token, as far as the First Amendment is concerned those who are licensed stand no better than those to whom licenses are refused. A license permits broadcasting, but the licensee has no constitutional right to be the one who holds the license or to monopolize a radio frequency to the exclusion of his fellow citizens. There is nothing in the First Amendment which prevents the Government from requiring a licensee to share his frequency with others and to conduct himself as a proxy or fiduciary with obligations to present those views and voices which are representative of his community and which would otherwise, by necessity, be barred from the airwaves.

B

Rather than confer frequency monopolies on a relatively small number of licensees, in a Nation of 200,000,000, the Government could surely have decreed that each frequency should be shared among all or some of those who wish to use it, each being assigned a portion of the broadcast day or the broadcast week. The ruling and regulations at issue here do not go quite so far. They assert that under specified circumstances, a licensee must offer to make available a reasonable amount of broadcast time to those who have a view different from that which has already been expressed on his station. The expression of a political endorsement, or of a personal attack while dealing with a controversial public issue, simply triggers this time sharing. As we have said, the First Amendment confers no right on licensees to prevent others from broadcasting on their frequencies and no right to an unconditional monopoly of a scarce resource which the Government has denied others the right to use.

In terms of constitutional principle, and as enforced sharing of a scarce resource, the personal attack and political editorial rules are indistinguishable from the equal-time provision of § 315, a specific enactment of Congress requiring stations to set aside reply time under specified circumstances and to which the fairness doctrine and these constituent regulations are important complements. That provision, which has been part of the law since 1927, Radio Act of 1927, § 18, 44 Stat. 1170, has been held valid by this Court as an obligation of the licensee relieving him of any power in any way to prevent or censor the broadcast, and thus insulating him from liability for defamation. The constitutionality of the statute under the First Amendment was unquestioned.

Nor can we say that it is inconsistent with the First Amendment goal of producing an informed public capable of conducting its own affairs to require a broadcaster to permit answers to personal attacks occurring in the course of discussing controversial issues, or to require that the political opponents of those endorsed by the station be given a chance to communicate with the public. Otherwise, station owners and a few networks would have unfettered power to make time available only to the highest bidders, to communicate only their own views on public issues, people and candidates, and to permit on the air only those with whom they agreed. There is no sanctuary in the First Amendment for unlimited private censorship operating in a medium not open to all. Freedom of the press from governmental interference under the First Amendment does not sanction repression of that freedom by private

D

We need not and do not now ratify every past and future decision by the FCC with regard to programming. There is no question here of the Commission's refusal to permit the broadcaster to carry a particular program or to publish his own views; of a discriminatory refusal to require the licensee to broadcast certain views which have been denied access to the airwaves; of government censorship of a particular program contrary to § 326; or of the official government view dominating public broadcasting. Such questions would raise more serious First Amendment issues. But we do hold that the Congress and the Commission do not violate the First Amendment when they require a radio or television station to give reply time to answer personal attacks and political editorials.

E

It is argued that even if at one time the lack of available frequencies for all who wished to use them justified the Government's choice of those who would best serve the public interest by acting as proxy for those who would present differing views, or by giving the latter access directly to broadcast facilities, this condition no longer prevails so that continuing control is not justified. To this there are several answers.

Scarcity is not entirely a thing of the past. Advances in technology, such as microwave transmission, have led to more efficient utilization of the frequency spectrum, but uses for that spectrum have also grown apace. Portions of the spectrum must be reserved for vital uses unconnected with human communication, such as radio-navigational aids used by aircraft and vessels. Conflicts have even emerged between such vital functions as defense preparedness and experimentation in methods of averting midair collisions through radio warning devices. Land mobile services such as police, ambulance, fire department, public utility, and other communications systems have been occupying an increasingly crowded portion of the frequency spectrum and there are, apart from licensed amateur radio operators' equipment, 5,000,000 transmitters operated on the citizens' band which is also increasingly congested. Among the various uses for radio frequency space, including marine, aviation, amateur, military, and common carrier users, there are easily enough claimants to permit use of the whole with an even smaller allocation to broadcast radio and television uses than now exists.

The rapidity with which technological advances succeed one another to create more efficient use of spectrum space on the one hand, and to create new uses for that space by ever growing numbers of people on the other, makes it unwise to speculate on the future allocation of that space. It is enough to say that the resource is one of considerable and growing importance whose scarcity impelled its regulation by an agency authorized by Congress. Nothing in this record, or in our own researches, convinces us that the resource is no longer one for which there are more immediate and potential uses than can be accommodated, and for which wise planning is essential. This does not mean, of course, that every possible wavelength must be occupied at every hour by some vital use in order to sustain the congressional judgment. The substantial capital investment required for many uses, in addition to the potentiality for confusion and interference inherent in any scheme for continuous kaleidoscopic reallocation of all available space, may make this unfeasible. The allocation need not be made at such a breakneck pace that the objectives of the allocation are themselves.

Even where there are gaps in spectrum utilization, the fact remains that existing broadcasters have often attained their present position because of their initial government selection in competition with others before new technological advances opened new opportunities for further uses. Long experience in broadcasting, confirmed habits of listeners and viewers, network affiliation, and other advantages in program procurement give existing broadcasters a substantial advantage over new entrants, even where new entry is technologically possible. These advantages are the fruit of a preferred position conferred by the Government. Some present possibility for new entry by competing stations is not enough, in itself, to render unconstitutional the Government's effort to assure that a broadcaster's programming ranges widely enough to serve the public interest.

In view of the scarcity of broadcast frequencies, the Government's role in allocating those frequencies, and the legitimate claims of those unable without governmental assistance to gain access to those frequencies for expression of their views, we hold the regulations and ruling at issue here are both authorized by statute and constitutional. The judgment of the Court of Appeals in Red Lion is affirmed and that in RTNDA reversed and the causes remanded for proceedings consistent with this opinion.

It is so ordered.

FOR DISCUSSION

Whose First Amendment rights does the Court side with in this case? For example, is the need for the fairness doctrine now rendered moot, given the rise, since this decision was handed down in 1972, of the Internet and other new communication services, such as podcasting and Twitter?

FEDERAL COMMUNICATIONS COMMISSION V. PACIFICA FOUNDATION

438 U.S. 726, 98 S.Ct. 3026, 57 L.Ed.2d 1073 (1978)

A radio station broadcast a comedy routine by George Carlin making fun of the seven words that the FCC had proscribed from being used on the air. A parent complained to the FCC that he had heard the routine with his minor child present. The FCC put this complaint in the station's file, and the latter appealed.

Vote: 5–4

JUSTICE STEVENS delivered the opinion of the Court (Parts I, II, III, and IV–C) and an opinion in which CHIEF JUSTICE BURGER and JUSTICE REHNQUIST joined (Parts IV–A and IV–B).

This case requires that we decide whether the Federal Communications Commission has any power to regulate a radio broadcast that is indecent but not obscene.

A satiric humorist named George Carlin recorded a 12-minute monologue entitled "Filthy Words" before a live audience in a California theater. He began by referring to his thoughts about "the words you couldn't say on the public, ah, airwaves, um, the ones you definitely wouldn't say, ever." He proceeded to list those words and repeat them over and over again in a variety of colloquialisms. The transcript of the recording, which is appended to this opinion, indicates frequent laughter from the audience.

At about 2 o'clock in the afternoon on Tuesday, October 30, 1973, a New York radio station, owned by respondent Pacifica Foundation, broadcast the "Filthy Words" monologue. A few weeks later a man, who stated that he had heard the broadcast while driving with his young son, wrote a letter complaining to the Commission.

He stated that, although he could perhaps understand the "record's being sold for private use, I certainly cannot understand the broadcast of same over the air that, supposedly, you control."

The complaint was forwarded to the station for comment. In its response, Pacifica explained that the monologue had been played during a program about contemporary society's attitude toward language and that, immediately before its broadcast, listeners had been advised that it included "sensitive language which might be regarded as offensive to some." Pacifica characterized George Carlin as "a significant social satirist" who "like Twain and Sahl before him, examines the language of ordinary people. . . . Carlin is not mouthing obscenities, he is merely using words to satirize as harmless and essentially silly our attitudes towards those words." Pacifica stated that it was not aware of any other complaints about the broadcast.

On February 21, 1975, the Commission issued a declaratory order granting the complaint and holding that Pacifica "could have been the subject of administrative sanctions." The Commission did not impose formal sanctions, but it did state that the order would be "associated with the station's license file, and in the event that subsequent complaints are received, the Commission will then decide whether it should utilize any of the available sanctions it has been granted by Congress.

In its memorandum opinion the commission stated that it intended to "clarify the standards which will be utilized in considering" the growing number of complaints about indecent speech on the airwaves. Advancing several reasons for treating broadcast speech differently from other forms of expression, the Commission found a power to regulate indecent broadcasting in two statutes: 18 U.S.C. § 1464 (1976 ed.), which forbids the use of "any obscene, indecent, or profane language by means of radio communications," and 47 U.S.C. § 303(g), which requires the Commission to "encourage the larger and more effective use of radio in the public interest."

The Commission characterized the language used in the Carlin monologue as "patently offensive," though not necessarily obscene, and expressed the opinion that it should be regulated by principles analogous to those found in the law of nuisance where the "law generally speaks to *channeling* behavior more than actually prohibiting it. . . . [T]he concept of 'indecent' is intimately connected with the exposure of children to language that describes, in terms patently offensive as measured by contemporary community standards for the broadcast medium, sexual or excretory activities and organs at times of the day when there is a reasonable risk that children may be in the audience."

Applying these considerations to the language used in the monologue as broadcast by respondent, the Commission concluded that certain words depicted sexual and excretory activities in a patently offensive manner, noted that they "were broadcast at a time when children were undoubtedly in the audience (i.e., in the early afternoon)," and that the prerecorded language, with these offensive words "repeated over and over," was "deliberately broadcast." In summary, the Commission stated: "We therefore hold that the language as broadcast was indecent and prohibited by 18 U.S.C. [§] 1464."

IV

Pacifica makes two constitutional attacks on the Commission's order. First, it argues that the Commission's construction of the statutory language broadly encompasses so much constitutionally protected speech that reversal is required even if Pacifica's broadcast of the "Filthy Words" monologue is not itself protected by the First Amendment. Second, Pacifica argues that inasmuch as the recording is not obscene, the Constitution forbids any abridgment of the right to broadcast it on the radio.

A

The first argument fails because our review is limited to the question whether the Commission has the authority to proscribe this particular broadcast. As the Commission itself emphasized, its order was "issued in a specific factual context." That approach is appropriate for courts as well as the Commission when regulation of indecency is at stake, for indecency is largely a function of context—it cannot be adequately judged in the abstract.

It is true that the Commission's order may lead some broadcasters to censor themselves. At most, however, the Commission's definition of indecency will deter only the broadcasting of patently offensive references to excretory and sexual organs and activities. While some of these references may be protected, they surely lie at the periphery of First Amendment concern. The danger dismissed so summarily in *Red Lion Broadcasting, Co. v. FCC*, 395 U.S. 367 (1969), in contrast, was that broadcasters would respond to the vagueness of the regulations by refusing to present programs dealing with important social and political controversies. Invalidating any rule on the basis of its hypothetical application to situations not before the Court is "strong medicine" to be applied "sparingly and only as a last resort." We decline to administer that medicine to preserve the vigor of patently offensive sexual and excretory speech.

B

When the issue is narrowed to the facts of this case, the question is whether the First Amendment denies government any power to restrict the public broadcast of indecent language in any circumstances. For if the government has any such power, this was an appropriate occasion for its exercise.

The words of the Carlin monologue are unquestionably "speech" within the meaning of the First Amendment. It is equally clear that the Commission's objections to the broadcast were based in part on its content. The order must therefore fall if, as Pacifica argues, the First Amendment prohibits all governmental regulation that depends on the content of speech. Our past cases demonstrate, however, that no such absolute rule is mandated by the Constitution.

The classic exposition of the proposition that both the content and the context of speech are critical elements of First Amendment analysis is Mr. Justice Holmes' statement for the Court in *Schenck v. United States,* 249 U.S. 47 (1919):

> We admit that in many places and in ordinary times the defendants in saying all that was said in the circular would have been within their constitutional rights. But the character of every act depends upon the circumstances in which it is done. . . . The most stringent protection of free speech would not protect a man in falsely shouting fire in a theatre and causing a panic. It does not even protect a man from an injunction against uttering words that may have all the effect of force. . . . The question in every case is whether the words used are used in such circumstances and are of such a nature as to create a clear and present danger that they will bring about the substantive evils that Congress has a right to prevent.

Other distinctions based on content have been approved in the years since *Schenck.* The government may forbid speech calculated to provoke a fight. It may pay heed to the " 'commonsense differences' between commercial speech and other varieties." It may treat libels against private citizens more severely than libels against public officials. Obscenity may be wholly prohibited. And only two Terms ago we refused to hold that a "statutory classification is unconstitutional because it is based on the content of communication protected by the First Amendment."

The question in this case is whether a broadcast of patently offensive words dealing with sex and excretion may be regulated because of its content. Obscene materials have been denied the protection of the First Amendment because their content is so offensive to contemporary moral standards. But the fact that society may find speech offensive is not a sufficient reason for suppressing it. Indeed, if it is the speaker's opinion that gives offense, that consequence is a reason for according it constitutional protection. For it is a central tenet of the First Amendment that the government must remain neutral in the marketplace of ideas. If there were any reason to believe that the Commission's characterization of the Carlin monologue as offensive could be traced to its political content—or even to the fact that it satirized contemporary attitudes about four-letter words—First Amendment protection might be required. But that is simply not this case. These words offend for the same reasons that obscenity offends. Their place in the hierarchy of First Amendment values was aptly sketched by Mr. Justice Murphy when he said: "Such utterances are no essential part of any exposition of ideas, and are of such slight social value as a step to truth that any benefit that may be derived from them is clearly outweighed by the social interest in order and morality."

Although these words ordinarily lack literary, political, or scientific value, they are not entirely outside the protection of the First Amendment. Some uses of even the most offensive words are unquestionably protected. Nonetheless, the constitutional protection accorded to a communication containing such patently offensive sexual and excretory language need not be the same in every context. It is a characteristic of speech such as this that both its capacity to offend and its "social value," to use Mr. Justice Murphy's term, vary with the circumstances. Words that are commonplace in one setting are shocking in another. To paraphrase Mr. Justice Harlan, one occasion's lyric is another's vulgarity.

In this case it is undisputed that the content of Pacifica's broadcast was "vulgar," "offensive," and "shocking."

C

We have long recognized that each medium of expression presents special First Amendment problems. And of all forms of communication, it is broadcasting that has received the most limited First Amendment protection. Thus, although other speakers cannot be licensed except under laws that carefully define and narrow official discretion, a broadcaster may be deprived of his license and his forum if the Commission decides that such an action would serve "the public interest, convenience, and necessity." Similarly, although the First Amendment protects newspaper publishers from being required to print the replies of those whom they criticize, it affords no such protection to broadcasters; on the contrary, they must give free time to the victims of their criticism.

The reasons for these distinctions are complex, but two have relevance to the present case. First, the broadcast media have established a uniquely pervasive presence in the lives of all Americans. Patently offensive, indecent material presented over the airwaves confronts the citizen, not only in public, but also in the privacy of the home, where the individual's right to be left alone plainly outweighs the First Amendment rights of an intruder. Because the broadcast audience is constantly tuning in and out, prior warnings cannot completely protect the listener or viewer from unexpected program content. To say that one may avoid further offense by turning off the radio when he hears indecent language is like saying that the remedy for an assault is to run away after the first blow. One may hang up on an indecent phone call, but that option does not give the caller a constitutional immunity or avoid a harm that has already taken place.

Second, broadcasting is uniquely accessible to children, even those too young to read. Although Carlin's written message might have been incomprehensible to a first grader, Pacifica's broadcast could have enlarged a child's vocabulary in an instant. Other forms of offensive expression may be withheld from the young without restricting the expression at its source. Bookstores and motion picture theaters, for example, may be prohibited from making indecent material available to children. We held in *Ginsberg v. New York,* 390 U.S. 629 (1968), that the government's interest in the "well-being of its youth" and in supporting "parents' claim to authority in their own household" justified the regulation of otherwise protected expression. The ease with which children may obtain access to broadcast material, coupled with the concerns recognized in *Ginsberg,* amply justify special treatment of indecent broadcasting.

The judgment of the Court of Appeals is reversed.

It is so ordered.

FOR DISCUSSION

Was Carlin's "Seven Dirty Words" obscene? What is the basis for preventing that comedy routine and those words from being broadcast on the radio? Should the FCC be allowed to screen certain words in order to prevent children or those who object to them from hearing them? Are there alternatives to banning their utterance or broadcast?

GANNETT CO., INC. V. DEPASQUALE

443 U.S. 368, 99 S.Ct. 2898, 61 L.Ed.2d 608 (1979)

Defense attorneys in a murder trial sought to close a court hearing owing to pretrial publicity. With no objection from the prosecutor, the judge granted the motion. Subsequently a reporter contested the order to close the hearing.

Vote: 5–4

JUSTICE STEWART delivered the opinion of the Court.

The question presented in this case is whether members of the public have an independent constitutional right to insist upon access to a pretrial judicial proceeding, even though the accused, the prosecutor, and the trial judge all have agreed to the closure of that proceeding in order to assure a fair trial.

I

The motions to suppress came on before Judge DePasquale on November 4. At this hearing, defense attorneys argued that the unabated buildup of adverse publicity had jeopardized the ability of the defendants to receive a fair trial. They thus requested that the public and the press be excluded from the hearing. The District Attorney did not oppose the motion. Although Carol Ritter, a reporter employed by the petitioner, was present in the courtroom, no objection was made at the time of the closure motion. The trial judge granted the motion. The next day, however, Ritter wrote a letter to the trial judge asserting a "right to cover this hearing," and requesting that "we . . . be given access to the transcript." The judge responded later the same day. He stated that the suppression hearing had concluded and that any decision on immediate release of the transcript had been reserved. The petitioner then moved the court to set aside its exclusionary order. The trial judge scheduled a hearing on this motion for November 16 after allowing the parties to file briefs. At this proceeding, the trial judge stated that, in his view, the press had a constitutional right of access although he deemed it "unfortunate" that no representative of the petitioner had objected at the time of the closure motion. Despite his acceptance of the existence of this right, however, the judge emphasized that it had to be balanced against the constitutional right of the defendants to a fair trial. After finding on the record that an open suppression hearing would pose a "reasonable probability of prejudice to these defendants," the judge ruled that the interest of the press and the public was outweighed in this case by the defendants' right to a fair trial. The judge thus refused to vacate his exclusion order or grant the petitioner immediate access to a transcript of the pretrial hearing. The following day, an original proceeding in the nature of prohibition and mandamus, challenging the closure orders on First, Sixth, and Fourteenth Amendment grounds, was commenced by the petitioner in the Supreme Court of the State of New York, Appellate Division, Fourth Department. On December 17, 1976, that court held that the exclusionary orders transgressed the public's vital interest in open judicial proceedings and further constituted an unlawful prior restraint in violation of the First and Fourteenth Amendments. It accordingly vacated the trial court's orders. On appeal, the New York Court of Appeals held that the case was technically moot but, because of the critical importance of the issues involved, retained jurisdiction and reached the merits. The court noted that under state law, "[c]riminal trials are presumptively open to the public, including the press," but held that this presumption was overcome in this case because of the danger posed to the defendants' ability to receive a fair trial. Thus, the Court of Appeals upheld the exclusion of the press and the public from the pretrial proceeding.

IV

A

The Sixth Amendment, applicable to the States through the Fourteenth, surrounds a criminal trial with guarantees such as the rights to notice, confrontation, and compulsory process that have as their overriding purpose the protection of the accused from prosecutorial and judicial abuses. Among the guarantees that the Amendment provides to a person charged with the commission of a criminal offense, and to him alone, is the "right to a speedy and public trial, by an impartial jury." The Constitution nowhere mentions any right of access to a criminal trial on the part of the public; its guarantee, like the others enumerated, is personal to the accused. Our cases have uniformly recognized the public trial guarantee as one created for the benefit of the defendant. In *In re Oliver*, 333 U.S. 257 (1948), this Court held that the secrecy of a criminal contempt trial violated the accused's right to a public trial under the Fourteenth Amendment. The right to a public trial, the Court stated, "has always been recognized as a safeguard against any attempt to employ our courts as instruments of persecution. The knowledge that every criminal trial is subject to contemporaneous review in the forum of public opinion is an effective restraint on possible abuse of judicial power." In an explanatory footnote, the Court stated that the public trial guarantee

. . . "is for the protection of all persons accused of crime—the innocently accused, that they may not become the victim of an unjust prosecution, as well as the guilty, that they may be awarded a fair trial—that one rule [as to public trials] must be observed and applied to all." Frequently quoted is the statement in [1] Cooley, *Constitutional Limitations* (8th ed. 1927) at 647: "The requirement of a public trial is for the benefit of the accused; that the public may see he is fairly dealt with and not unjustly condemned, and that the presence of interested spectators may keep his triers keenly alive to a sense of their responsibility and to the importance of their functions . . . ."

Similarly, in *Estes v. Texas,* 381 U.S. 532 (1965), the Court held that a defendant was deprived of his right to due process of law under the Fourteenth Amendment by the televising and broadcasting of his trial. In rejecting the claim that the media representatives had a constitutional right to televise the trial, the Court stated that "[t]he purpose of the requirement of a public trial was to guarantee that the accused would be fairly dealt with and not unjustly condemned." . . .

Thus, both the *Oliver* and *Estes* cases recognized that the constitutional guarantee of a public trial is for the benefit of the defendant. There is not the slightest suggestion in either case that there is any correlative right in members of the public to insist upon a public trial.

B

While the Sixth Amendment guarantees to a defendant in a criminal case the right to a public trial, it does not guarantee the right to compel a private trial. "The ability to waive a constitutional right does not ordinarily carry with it the right to insist upon the opposite of that right." But the issue here is not whether the defendant can compel a private trial. Rather, the issue is whether members of the public have an enforceable right to a public trial that can be asserted independently of the parties in the litigation. There can be no blinking the fact that there is a strong societal interest in public trials. Openness in court proceedings may improve the quality of testimony, induce unknown witnesses to come forward with relevant testimony, cause all trial participants to perform their duties more conscientiously, and generally give the public an opportunity to observe the judicial system. But there is a strong societal interest in other constitutional guarantees extended to the accused as well.

The public, for example, has a definite and concrete interest in seeing that Justice is swiftly and fairly administered. Similarly, the public has an interest in having a criminal case heard by a jury, an interest distinct from the defendant's interest in being tried by a jury of his peers. Recognition of an independent public interest in the enforcement of Sixth Amendment guarantees is a far cry, however, from the creation of a constitutional right on the part of the public. In an adversary system of criminal Justice, the public interest in the administration of Justice is protected by the participants in the litigation. Thus, because of the great public interest in jury trials as the preferred mode of fact-finding in criminal cases, a defendant cannot waive a jury trial without the consent of the prosecutor and judge. But if the defendant waives his right to a jury trial, and the prosecutor and the judge consent, it could hardly be seriously argued that a member of the public could demand a jury trial because of the societal interest in that mode of fact-finding.

VI

The petitioner also argues that members of the press and the public have a right of access to the pretrial hearing by reason of the First and Fourteenth Amendments. In *Pell v. Procunier,* 417 U.S. 817 (1974), and *Houchins v. KQED, Inc.*, 438 U.S. 1 (1978), this Court upheld prison regulations that denied to members of the press access to prisons superior to that afforded to the public generally. Some Members of the Court, however, took the position in those cases that the First and Fourteenth Amendments do guarantee to the public in general, or the press in particular, a right of access that precludes their complete exclusion in the absence of a significant governmental interest. Several factors lead to the conclusion that the actions of the trial judge here were consistent with any right of access the petitioner may have had under the First and Fourteenth Amendments. First, none of the spectators present in the courtroom, including the reporter employed by the petitioner, objected when the defendants made the closure motion. Despite this failure to make a contemporaneous objection, counsel for the petitioner was given an opportunity to be heard at a proceeding where he was allowed to voice the petitioner's objections to closure of the pretrial hearing. At this proceeding, which took place after the filing of briefs, the trial court balanced the "constitutional rights of the press and the public" against the "defendants' right to a fair trial." The trial judge concluded after making this appraisal that the press and the public could be excluded from the suppression hearing and could be denied immediate access to a transcript, because an open proceeding would pose a "reasonable probability of prejudice to these defendants." Thus, the trial court found that the representatives of the press did have a right of access of constitutional dimension, but held, under the circumstances of this case, that this right was outweighed by the defendants' right to a fair trial. Furthermore, any denial of access in this case was not absolute but only temporary. Once the danger of prejudice had dissipated, a transcript of the suppression hearing was made available. The press and the public then had a full opportunity to scrutinize the suppression hearing. Unlike the case of an absolute ban on access, therefore, the press here had the opportunity to inform the public of the details of the pretrial hearing accurately and completely. Under these circumstances, any First and Fourteenth Amendment right of the petitioner to attend a criminal trial was not violated.

VII

For all of the reasons discussed in this opinion, we hold that the Constitution provides no such right. Accordingly, the judgment of the New York Court of Appeals is affirmed. *It is so ordered.*

CHIEF JUSTICE BURGER, concurring.

I join the opinion of the Court, but I write separately to emphasize my view of the nature of the proceeding involved in today's decision. By definition, a hearing on a motion before trial to suppress evidence is not a *trial*; it is a *pre* trial hearing. The Sixth Amendment tells us that "[i]n all criminal prosecutions, the *accused* SHALL ENJOY THE RIGHT TO A . . . PUBLIC TRIAL." (Emphasis Supplied.) It is the practice of Western societies, and has been part of the common-law tradition for centuries, that trials generally be public. This is an important prophylaxis of the system of Justice that constitutes the adhesive element of our society. The public has an interest in observing the performance not only of the litigants and the witnesses, but also of the advocates and the presiding judge. Similarly, if the accused testifies, there is a proper public interest in that testimony. But interest alone does not create a constitutional right.

JUSTICE REHNQUIST, concurring.

While I concur in the opinion of the Court, I write separately to emphasize what should be apparent from the Court's Sixth Amendment holding and to address the First Amendment issue that the Court appears to reserve. The Court today holds, without qualification, that "members of the public have no constitutional right under the Sixth and Fourteenth Amendments to attend criminal trials." In this case, the trial judge closed the suppression hearing because he concluded that an open hearing might have posed a danger to the defendants' ability to receive a fair trial. But the Court's recitation of this fact and its discussion of the need to preserve the defendant's right to a fair trial, should not be interpreted to mean that under the Sixth Amendment a trial court can close a pretrial hearing or trial only when there is a danger that prejudicial publicity will harm the defendant. To the contrary, since the Court holds that the public does not have *any* Sixth Amendment right of access to such proceedings, it necessarily follows that if the parties agree on a closed proceeding, the trial court is not required by the Sixth Amendment to advance any reason whatsoever for declining to open a pretrial hearing or trial to the public. "There is no question that the Sixth Amendment permits and even presumes open trials as a norm." But, as the Court today holds, the Sixth Amendment does not require a criminal trial or hearing to be opened to the public if the participants to the litigation agree for any reason, no matter how jurisprudentially appealing or unappealing, that it should be closed.

FOR DISCUSSION

Why was this decision so controversial? Did the Court say that all court proceedings could be closed to prevent media or press coverage? Under what circumstances may legal proceedings be closed?

RICHMOND NEWSPAPERS, INC. V. VIRGINIA

448 U.S. 555, 100 S.Ct. 2814, 65 L.Ed.2d 973 (1980)

In a murder trial, the defense attorney asked the judge to close the proceedings to the public. The prosecutor did not object, and the judge ordered the trial closed. No one else objected to the closure at the time. Subsequently a Virginia newspaper contested the closing as a First Amendment violation.

Vote: 8–1

CHIEF JUSTICE BURGER announced the judgment of the Court and delivered an opinion, in which JUSTICES WHITE and STEVENS joined.

The narrow question presented in this case is whether the right of the public and press to attend criminal trials is guaranteed under the United States Constitution.

I

In March 1976, one Stevenson was indicted for the murder of a hotel manager who had been found stabbed to death on December 2, 1975. Tried promptly in July 1976, Stevenson was convicted of second-degree murder in the Circuit Court of Hanover County, Va. The Virginia Supreme Court reversed the conviction in October

1977, holding that a bloodstained shirt purportedly belonging to Stevenson had been improperly admitted into evidence.

Stevenson was retried in the same court. This second trial ended in a mistrial on May 30, 1978, when a juror asked to be excused after trial had begun and no alternate was available. A third trial, which began in the same court on June 6, 1978, also ended in a mistrial. It appears that the mistrial may have been declared because a prospective juror had read about Stevenson's previous trials in a newspaper and had told other prospective jurors about the case before the retrial began.

Stevenson was tried in the same court for a fourth time beginning on September 11, 1978. Present in the courtroom when the case was called were appellants Wheeler and McCarthy, reporters for appellant Richmond Newspapers, Inc. Before the trial began, counsel for the defendant moved that it be closed to the public. The trial judge, who had presided over two of the three previous trials, asked if the prosecution had any objection to clearing the courtroom. The prosecutor stated he had no objection and would leave it to the discretion of the court. Presumably referring to Va. Code § 19.2–266 (Supp.1980), the trial judge then announced: "[T]he statute gives me that power specifically and the defendant has made the motion." He then ordered "that the Courtroom be kept clear of all parties except the witnesses when they testify." The record does not show that any objections to the closure order were made by anyone present at the time, including appellants Wheeler and McCarthy.

II

We begin consideration of this case by noting that the precise issue presented here has not previously been before this Court for decision. In *Gannett Co. v. DePasquale*, 443 U.S. 368 (1979), the Court was not required to decide whether a right of access to *trials*, as distinguished from hearings on *pre* trial motions, was constitutionally guaranteed. The Court held that the Sixth Amendment's guarantee to the accused of a public trial gave neither the public nor the press an enforceable right of access to a *pre* trial suppression hearing. One concurring opinion specifically emphasized that "a hearing on a motion before trial to suppress evidence is not a *trial*. . . ." Moreover, the Court did not decide whether the First and Fourteenth Amendments guarantee a right of the public to attend trials.

In prior cases the Court has treated questions involving conflicts between publicity and a defendant's right to a fair trial; as we observed in *Nebraska Press Assn. v. Stuart,* 427 U.S. 539 (1976), "[t]he problems presented by this [conflict] are almost as old as the Republic. But here for the first time the Court is asked to decide whether a criminal trial itself may be closed to the public upon the unopposed request of a defendant, without any demonstration that closure is required to protect the defendant's superior right to a fair trial, or that some other overriding consideration requires closure.

A

The origins of the proceeding which has become the modern criminal trial in Anglo-American Justice can be traced back beyond reliable historical records. We need not here review all details of its development, but a summary of that history is instructive. What is significant for present purposes is that throughout its evolution, the trial has been open to all who care to observe.

In the days before the Norman Conquest, cases in England were generally brought before moots, such as the local court of the hundred or the county court, which were attended by the freemen of the community. Somewhat like modern jury duty, attendance at these early meetings was compulsory on the part of the freemen, who were called upon to render judgment

From these early times, although great changes in courts and procedures took place, one thing remained constant: the public character of the trial at which guilt or innocence was decided. Sir Thomas Smith, writing in 1565 about "the definitive proceedings in causes criminall," explained that, while the indictment was put in writing as in civil law countries: We have found nothing to suggest that the presumptive openness of the trial, which English courts were later to call "one of the essential qualities of a court of Justice, was not also an attribute of the judicial systems of colonial America. In Virginia, for example, such records as there are of early criminal trials indicate that they were open, and nothing to the contrary has been cited. Indeed, when in the mid-1600's the Virginia Assembly felt that the respect due the courts was "by the clamorous unmannerlynes of the people lost, and order, gravity and decoram which should manifest the authority of a court in the court it selfe neglected," the response was not to restrict the openness of the trials to the public, but instead to prescribe rules for the conduct of those attending them.

B

As we have shown, and as was shown in both the Court's opinion and the dissent in *Gannett*, the historical evidence demonstrates conclusively that at the time when our organic laws were adopted, criminal trials both here and in England had long been presumptively open. This is no quirk of history; rather, it has long been recognized as an indispensible attribute of an Anglo-American trial. Both Hale in the 17th century and Blackstone in the 18th saw the importance of openness to the proper functioning of a trial; it gave assurance that the proceedings were conducted fairly to all concerned, and it discouraged perjury, the misconduct of participants, and decisions based on secret bias or partiality. . . .

Looking back, we see that when the ancient "town meeting" form of trial became too cumbersome, 12 members of the community were delegated to act as its surrogates, but the community did not surrender its right to observe the conduct of trials. The people retained a "right of visitation" which enabled them to satisfy themselves that Justice was in fact being done.

People in an open society do not demand infallibility from their institutions, but it is difficult for them to accept what they are prohibited from observing. When a criminal trial is conducted in the open, there is at least an opportunity both for understanding the system in general and its workings in a particular case.

C

From this unbroken, uncontradicted history, supported by reasons as valid today as in centuries past, we are bound to conclude that a presumption of openness inheres in the very nature of a criminal trial under our system of Justice. This conclusion is hardly novel; without a direct holding on the issue, the Court has voiced its recognition of it in a variety of contexts over the years. Despite the history of criminal trials being presumptively open since long before the Constitution, the State presses its contention that neither the Constitution nor the Bill of Rights contains any provision which by its terms guarantees to the public the right to attend criminal trials. Standing alone, this is correct, but there remains the question whether, absent an explicit provision, the Constitution affords protection against exclusion of the public from criminal trials.

III

A

The First Amendment, in conjunction with the Fourteenth, prohibits governments from "abridging the freedom of speech, or of the press; or the right of the people peaceably to assemble, and to petition the Government for a redress of grievances." These expressly guaranteed freedoms share a common core purpose of assuring freedom of communication on matters relating to the functioning of government. Plainly it would be difficult to single out any aspect of government of higher concern and importance to the people than the manner in which criminal trials are conducted; as we have shown, recognition of this pervades the centuries-old history of open trials and the opinions of this Court. The Bill of Rights was enacted against the backdrop of the long history of trials being presumptively open. Public access to trials was then regarded as an important aspect of the process itself; the conduct of trials "before as many of the people as chuse to attend" was regarded as one of "the inestimable advantages of a free English constitution of government." In guaranteeing freedoms such as those of speech and press, the First Amendment can be read as protecting the right of everyone to attend trials so as to give meaning to those explicit guarantees. "[T]he First Amendment goes beyond protection of the press and the self-expression of individuals to prohibit government from limiting the stock of information from which members of the public may draw." Free speech carries with it some freedom to listen. "In a variety of contexts this Court has referred to a First Amendment right to 'receive information and ideas.' " What this means in the context of trials is that the First Amendment guarantees of speech and press, standing alone, prohibit government from summarily closing courtroom doors which had long been open to the public at the time that Amendment was adopted.

D

Having concluded there was a guaranteed right of the public under the First and Fourteenth Amendments to attend the trial of Stevenson's case, we return to the closure order challenged by appellants. The Court in *Gannett* made clear that although the Sixth Amendment guarantees the accused a right to a public trial, it does not give a right to a private trial. Despite the fact that this was the fourth trial of the accused, the trial judge made no findings to support closure; no inquiry was made as to whether alternative solutions would have met the need to ensure fairness; there was no recognition of any right under the Constitution for the public or press to attend the trial. In contrast to the pretrial proceeding dealt with in *Gannett*, there exist in the context of the trial itself various tested alternatives to satisfy the constitutional demands of fairness. There was no suggestion that any problems with witnesses could not have been dealt with by their exclusion from the courtroom or their sequestration during the trial. Nor is there anything to indicate that sequestration of the jurors would not have guarded against their being subjected to any improper information. All of the alternatives admittedly present difficulties for trial courts, but none of the factors relied on here was beyond the realm of the manageable. Absent an overriding interest articulated in findings, the trial of a criminal case must be open to the public. Accordingly, the judgment under review is *Reversed.*

JUSTICE POWELL took no part in the consideration or decision of this case.

JUSTICE WHITE, concurring.

This case would have been unnecessary had *Gannett Co. v. DePasquale*, 427 U.S. 539 (1976), construed the Sixth Amendment to forbid excluding the public from criminal proceedings except in narrowly defined circumstances. But the Court there rejected the submission of four of us to this effect, thus requiring that the First Amendment issue involved here be addressed. On this issue, I concur in the opinion of The Chief Justice.

JUSTICE STEVENS, concurring.

This is a watershed case. Until today the Court has accorded virtually absolute protection to the dissemination of information or ideas, but never before has it squarely held that the acquisition of newsworthy matter is entitled to any constitutional protection whatsoever.

JUSTICE BRENNAN, with whom JUSTICE MARSHALL joins, concurring in the judgment.

Gannett Co. v. DePasquale held that the Sixth Amendment right to a public trial was personal to the accused, conferring no right of access to pretrial proceedings that is separately enforceable by the public or the press. The instant case raises the question whether the First Amendment, of its own force and as applied to the States through the Fourteenth Amendment, secures the public an independent right of access to trial proceedings. Because I believe that the First Amendment—of itself and as applied to the States through the Fourteenth Amendment—secures such a public right of access, I agree with those of my Brethren who hold that, without more, agreement of the trial judge and the parties cannot constitutionally close a trial to the public.

FOR DISCUSSION

Did this decision overturn *Gannett Co., Inc. v. DePasquale?* What was the legal basis of the decision in this case? Does this decision foreclose the possibility of ever closing a court proceeding? Does the decision mean that the press has a First Amendment right to bring cameras into a courtroom and broadcast the proceedings?

RELATED CASE

***Nebraska Press Association v. Stuart:* 427 U.S. 539 (1976).**

Writing for the Court, Chief Justice Burger struck down an order by a judge preventing the media from reporting on events occurring in the court before the jury was impaneled. Burger contended that there was a heavy burden against prior restraints on the press covering trials and events occurring in the courtroom.

HAZELWOOD SCHOOL DIST. V. KUHLMEIER

484 U.S. 260, 108 S.Ct. 562, 98 L.Ed.2d 592 (1988)

See Chapter III, page 232.

FOR DISCUSSION

Do student newspapers have any First Amendment rights? Does it matter if the students are in a public or a private school? College or K–12?

Freedom of Assembly and Petition

Freedom of assembly (association) and petition are perhaps the forgotten rights. The importance of individuals being able to associate for religious, political, and other purposes is nonetheless a highly valued and important right, as is a right to submit a list of grievances one has against the government. In fact, the Declaration of Independence could be viewed as the first and perhaps best expression of the right to petition the government. In this case, it was, as the second half of the Declaration reads, a bill of particulars the American colonies had against the English King George III. Moreover, in 1841, in his famous book *Democracy in America*, Alexis de Toqueville described uniquely how Americans had a tendency to join voluntary associations to promote a variety of civic purposes. Yet the right to freedom of association is not explicitly mentioned in the Constitution or the Bill of Rights. Instead, it has been found to exist, or is constructed, out of the other rights named in the First Amendment, such as speech, religion, and assembly. Freedom of association and petition are tightly connected and also often are wrapped together with freedom of speech and press.

As the Court would eventually describe it, freedom of association entails two rights. The first is a right to freely associate with individuals with whom we choose. Individuals have a right to select their friends, political associates, and to join others who will accept them into worship, if they so choose. Conversely, individuals also have a right not to associate with others. The second right is to associate without undue government intrusion or surveillance of one's whereabouts. The government should neither be watching nor should keeping tabs on whom individuals associate with, and it also not intrude into these relationships by asking people about their associates or friends.

The issues of freedom of association first surfaced in the early years of the American republic, with the 1798 Alien and Sedition Acts. Not only did these acts criminalize criticism of government officials, specifically the president of the United States, but they also appeared to determine one's guilt based upon association with others. While the Alien and Sedition Acts never faced the scrutiny of the Supreme Court, they were the first federal laws to implicate freedom of association rights.

Criticism of the government, as well as protests and demonstrations, often bring with them the greatest challenges to associational claims. Early in twentieth century, protests around World War I led to the passage of the Espionage Act of 1917 and the Sedition Act of 1918 as anti-German hysteria translated into crackdowns against war protesters. The Russian Revolution in 1917 further inflamed fears; and in the United States, raids were conducted at the behest of Attorney General A. Mitchell Palmer with the goal of deporting aliens viewed as disloyal. From these events, fears of Communists, and their possible infiltration into the labor movements, government, and eventually the civil rights movements of the 1950s and 1960s, led subsequent attorneys general and FBI directors such as J. Edgar Hoover to order the surveillance of individuals such as Martin Luther King Jr.

After World War II, fears of Communists intensified, and President Truman ordered the use of loyalty oaths for federal employees. Similar oaths become popular at all levels of government. In 1947 Truman also ordered the creation of the Attorney General's List of Subversive Organizations. This list was maintained until the early 1970s. Passage of the Internal Security Act of 1950 mandated that Communist organizations register with the Attorney General. Wisconsin Senator Joseph McCarthy's hearings during the 1950s, and the House Un-American Activities Committee (HUAC) beginning in the 1940s, also subpoenaed many individuals, suspected Communists or not, to testify about their political associations and memberships. Some of these hearings looked to Communist involvement in Hollywood and the motion picture industry, leading to the blacklisting of actors, screenwriters, and directors. In many of these McCarthy or HUAC hearings, individuals invoked the Fifth Amendment right against self-incrimination, but such assertions were often ridiculed and tended to be seen by some as de facto admissions of guilt.

Dennis v. United States (341 U.S. 494, 1951) is one of the first cases to examine freedom of association in the context of the Cold War. In this case at issue was a law passed by Congress in 1940, the Alien Registration Act, otherwise known as the Smith Act, which forbade the advocacy of force to overthrow the government, as well as membership in an organization advocating forceful overthrow. Eleven members of the Communist Party were convicted of violation of the Smith Act. The Supreme Court upheld these convictions, ruling that the Act was directed at advocacy, not discussion of ideas, and that the government should not sit by quietly while some plot violent means to overthrow the government. While many view the *Dennis* case as one about free speech, can one separate speech from association, especially if the speech or discussion take place when one gathers with others who share similar views? Conversations or discussions may in fact require one to associate with others, and here some critics argue that *Dennis* targeted those who opted to join the Communist Party. *Dennis* can take its place alongside *Marbury v. Madison* (5 U.S. 137, 1803) and *Dred Scott v. Sandford* (60 U.S. 393, 1857) as cases that need never have happened. The Court here could very well have interpreted the Smith Act as not applying to the actions of the defendants in this case. However, was it a combination of the Cold War atmosphere, fear, and prejudice that led to the result? Note also the statement of Judge Learned Hand, which the Court adopted, means simply that for a grave evil, there need be slight probability of the occurrence to justify restrictions on speech; but for a slight evil, there must be great probability of its happening before limits on speech can be justified.

Yates v. United States (354 U.S. 298, 1957) supposedly "clarified" *Dennis,* the Court going to great lengths to emphasize that *Dennis* had not been overruled. In *Yates,* Frankfurter and Burton changed their votes from their stand in the *Dennis* case. The other members of the majority in *Dennis* had either died or retired from the Court. The lone dissenter in *Yates,* Justice Clark, did not participate in *Dennis.* Obviously the conditions set down in *Yates* make very difficult the securing of convictions under the Smith Act. The opinion made several points. Any charge of "organizing" a subversive group must be considered in connection with the statute of limitations. The trial judge's charge to the jury must distinguish between advocacy of abstract doctrine (not illegal) and advocacy directed at promoting unlawful action (illegal). The Court also set forth some rules of evidence that must be abided by in the prosecution of persons under the statute. Some measure of the difficulties posed by the decision is indicated by the fact that six months after *Yates* indictments against the remaining nine defendants were dismissed by the Department of Justice. Overall, was *Yates* decided as it was because it simply served to clarify *Dennis,* or did the change in Court personnel and the circumstances of the Cold War explain the holding?

American Communications Ass'n v. Douds (339 U.S. 382, 1950) is the first of several cases challenging loyalty oaths. Here at issue was Section 9(h) of the Taft-Hartley Act of 1947, which barred any investigation by the National Labor Relations Board unless all officers of a labor organization involved in a dispute signed an affidavit certifying that they were not Communists. The Court upheld the registration requirement by circumventing the First Amendment. In *Douds,* the Court avoided the real constitutional difficulty involved by holding that the oath requirement was a regulation of commerce rather than a regulation of freedom of speech. The "Non-Communist Oath" requirement of Taft-Hartley was repealed by the Landrum-Griffin Act of 1959—the Labor-Management Reporting and Disclosure Act—but the provision that union officers cannot be members of the Communist Party was held to be a **bill of attainder**, hence void, in *United States v. Brown* (381 U.S. 437, 1965).

Adler v. Board of Education (342 U.S. 485, 1952) is another case addressing loyalty oaths or requirements. The New York State's Feinberg Law specifically makes ineligible for employment in the public schools of the state any person who is a member of an organization advocating the unlawful overthrow of the government of the United States. Again the Court upheld the law. The statute in question in *Adler,* in spite of its implied assertion of "guilt by association," had no retroactive effect; it allowed teachers to use the defense that their membership was innocent, and organizations were to be labeled as subversive only after notice and hearing. These points must have influenced the Court in the sense that individuals have some opportunity to prove their innocence or correct any misunderstandings before they faced discipline or dismissal. This case is yet another iteration of the maxim that public employment is not a personal right.

But *Keyishian v. Board of Regents of the University of the State of New York* (385 U.S. 589, 1967) stands in contrast to *Douds* and *Adler.* Here several public university faculty members challenged the New York State loyalty oath. This time the Court found the oath unconstitutional under the First Amendment. The law was attacked as overbroad and vague, infringing on some protected activities. Critical to this opinion perhaps is the setting: a university, not primary school (K–12). Moreover, *Keyishian* focuses on the right of a professor or teacher to discuss and espouse ideas in the classroom as part of a learning exercise. The opinion is considered famous for suggesting that the First Amendment protects the **academic freedom** of professors to discuss controversial ideas in their teaching and research without fear of discipline. Ward Churchill offered this defense in 2009 in contesting his firing from the University of Colorado. He alleged that the school fired him because he referred to some of the victims of the 9/11 bombings in New York City as "little Eichmanns" [Adolf Eichmann was a high-ranking Nazi who helped organize the holocaust]. His comments created a firestorm of controversy. The school claimed he was fired for academic dishonesty; he asserted that it was for the provocative statements. A jury agreed with Churchill but awarded him damages of only one dollar.

In addition to the anticommunist hysteria of the Cold War, civil rights protesters drew increasing scrutiny, especially in the South during the 1950s and 1960s. One especially active group, the National Association for the Advancement of Colored People (NAACP), was targeted by officials in states such as Alabama because of its advocacy for African Americans. In an effort to break up the NAACP, the state of Alabama sought disclosure of the organization's membership list. Such disclosure clearly would have chilled recruitment and membership retention efforts, as fear of reprisal and intimidation would have prevented many from joining the organization or continuing to be associated with it. In *National Association for the Advancement of Colored People v. State of Alabama* (357 U.S. 449, 1958), the Supreme Court ruled that the membership lists of organizations such as NAACP were protected by the First Amendment. The decision may be the first clear articulation of the statement that the First Amendment embodies a right to a freedom of association. According to the Court:

> Effective advocacy of both public and private points of view, particularly controversial ones, is undeniably enhanced by group association, as this Court has more than once recognized by remarking upon the close nexus between the freedoms of speech and assembly. It is beyond debate that freedom to engage in association for the advancement of beliefs and ideas is an inseparable aspect of the 'liberty' assured by the Due Process Clause of the Fourteenth Amendment, which embraces freedom of speech.

How broadly should this dictum and the case be read? Does the freedom of association protect organizations from compelled disclosure of donor lists, for example? Does it extend to individuals who make political donations? Could the government create a registry or list of individuals whom considers to be terrorists or security risks, simply based on their membership in some group or association?

While for the most part the right to freedom of association protects civil rights demonstrators and political protesters, others issues persist. One source of contention involves gender and gay rights. Is exclusion of women or gays, lesbians, bisexuals, and transsexuals (GLBT) from membership in organizations a form of discrimination and therefore illegal, or is it a right to freedom of association and therefore protected by the First Amendment? The next three cases look at the intersection of the right to associate, not to associate, and to discriminate. First, in *Roberts v. United States Jaycees* (468 U.S. 609, 1984) the Supreme Court ruled that the First Amendment did not prevent the enforcement of a Minnesota civil rights law that made it illegal for public accommodations to discriminate against women. In this case, the argument was that the Jaycees were a "public accommodation" under a Minnesota civil rights law and therefore the exclusion of women from the organization was illegal. The Jaycees, at least the national chapter of the organization, contended that the organization had a First Amendment right to exclude women. In part the Jaycees contended that accepting women would hurt the organization. The Supreme Court rejected that argument, finding, in part, that women were already joining the Minnesota chapter of the Jaycees and the organization was not damaged.

However, contrast the decision in *Roberts* with the next two cases. First in *Boy Scouts of America v. Dale* (530 U.S. 640, 2000), an individual challenged his removal from the Boys Scouts because he was gay. The Scouts had a policy that forbids gays from being affiliated with the organization. James Dale challenged his exclusion under a New Jersey civil rights law that was almost identical to the Minnesota act that figured in the *Roberts* case. The state courts ruled that the Scouts were a public accommodation under New Jersey law and therefore could not exclude Dale. The Supreme Court disagreed. Whereas in *Roberts* gender was seen to be irrelevant to the mission of the organization, the Court in *Dale* ruled that sexual orientation—specifically, being heterosexual—was central to the mission of the Boy Scouts. In reaching this conclusion the Court referred, among other sources, to the Boy Scout oath. Some critics of the decision, who contend that there was no difference in the legal issues between *Roberts* and *Dale*, say further that homophobia is the only explanation for the different holdings. Others argue that there was a difference in terms of mission between the two organizations, which had a bearing on how the First Amendment applies. As you read the two cases, what do you think?

The other case to examine is *Hurley v. Irish-American Gay, Lesbian and Bisexual Group of Boston* (515 U.S. 557, 1995). Annually the City of Boston issues a parade permit to an organization of Irish-Americans to hold the St. Patrick's Day parade. A group representing gay, lesbian, and bisexual Irish-Americans, which had been refused permission to march in the parade, sought to compel the group sponsoring the event to allow their participation. Lower courts ordered their inclusion in the parade and the Supreme Court reversed. In a unanimous opinion the Court ruled against the Irish-American Gay, Lesbian and Bisexual Group of Boston. The Court stated: "But whatever the reason, it boils down to the choice of a speaker not to propound a particular point of view, and that choice is presumed to lie beyond the government's power to control." In effect, the organizers of the parade have a right to control their parade and include or exclude those whom they want. The right to associate also includes the right not to associate. Would such an argument have been persuasive during the civil rights era in reference to whites not wanting to associate with blacks? Critics of *Hurley* think not.

Among various techniques tried in efforts to address youth crime and victimization, curfew laws are often adopted because they offer ways to restrict the times and places when individuals under the age of eighteen may be in public, and their reasons for gathering. These laws raise numerous constitutional issues, including associational claims. Is freedom of association something enjoyed by minors? Yes, but according to the Court in *Hutchins v. District of Columbia* (188 F.3d 531, 338, C.A.D.C., 1999), that right is qualified. The majority argued that those under eighteen do not have an unqualified right to be on the streets alone without adult supervision, whereas the dissent saw age as immaterial to the right to freedom of association. While some courts have ruled that youth curfew laws are unconstitutional, decisions such as *Hutchins* and *Kuhlmeier* suggest that the courts are not prepared to extend First Amendment rights fully to minors.

When it comes to the petition right, it is curious to note the paucity or cases that are decided on that issue. One of the few, *United Mine Workers of America, Dist. 12 v. Illinois State Bar Ass'n,* 389 U.S. 217 (1967), dealt with the question of whether a labor union could employ a licensed attorney on a salary basis to represent any of its members who wished his services to prosecute workmen's compensation claims before the Illinois Industrial Commission. The Supreme Court ruled in favor of the union, contending that spending money for this purpose was a legitimate form of petitioning the government. In *Edwards v. South Carolina*, 372 U.S. 229 (1963), the Court ruled that a march to the state courthouse to protest racial discrimination was protected under the speech, assembly, and petition parts of the First Amendment, although it is not so clear how much of the holding rests on the latter two provisions. But it does appear that in some cases assembling for political purposes is also a form of petition.

Overall, these freedom-of-assembly-and-petition decisions raise important questions about the rights of individuals to join organizations, the right of organizations to control their membership, and the authority of the government to regulate the behavior of both.

DENNIS V. UNITED STATES

341 U.S. 494, 71 S.Ct. 857, 95 L.Ed.2d 1356 (1951)

See Chapter III, page 179.

FOR DISCUSSION

How likely was it that the discussion among a handful of Communist Party members was going to lead to a violent revolution? Where does the Court draw the lines here between discussion, advocacy, and action? What should the First Amendment protect?

YATES V. UNITED STATES

354 U.S. 298, 77 S.Ct. 1064, 1 L.Ed. 517 (1957)

This case—which might be called "the second *Dennis* case"—involved the convictions of fourteen Communists for violation of the Smith Act. They were convicted of having conspired to advocate and to teach forceful overthrow of the government of the United States and of having conspired to organize the Communist Party of the United States. These were the same basic charges of *Dennis v. United States* (341 U.S. 494, 1951); but the persons involved here were lesser or "second-string" members of the Communist Party.

Vote: 6–1

JUSTICE HARLAN delivered the opinion of the Court.

. . . Petitioners claim that "organize" means to "establish," "found," or "bring into existence," and that in this sense the Communist Party was organized by 1945 at the latest. On this basis petitioners contend that this part of the indictment, returned in 1951, was barred by the three-year statute of limitations. . . .

We conclude, therefore, that since the Communist Party came into being in 1945, and the indictment was not returned until 1951, the three-year statute of limitations had run out on the "organizing" charge, and required the withdrawal of that part of the indictment from the jury's consideration. . . .

In failing to distinguish between advocacy of forcible overthrow as an abstract doctrine and advocacy of action to that end, the District Court appears to have been led astray by the holding in *Dennis* that advocacy of violent action to be taken at some future time was enough. It seems to have considered that, since "inciting" speech is usually thought of as calculated to induce immediate action, and since *Dennis v. United States*, 341 U.S. 494 (1951), held advocacy of action for future overthrow sufficient, this meant that advocacy, irrespective of its tendency to generate action, is punishable, provided only that it is uttered with a specific intent to accomplish overthrow. In other words, the District Court apparently thought that *Dennis* obliterated the traditional dividing line between advocacy of abstract doctrine and advocacy of action.

This misconceives the situation confronting the Court in *Dennis* and what was held there. Although the jury's verdict, interpreted in light of the trial court's instructions, did not justify the conclusion that the defendants' advocacy was directed at, or created any danger of, immediate overthrow, it did establish that the advocacy was aimed at building up a seditious group and maintaining it in readiness for action at a propitious time. . . . The essence of the *Dennis* holding was that indoctrination of a group in preparation for future violent action, as well as exhortation to immediate action, by advocacy found to be directed to "action for the accomplishment" of forcible overthrow, to violence "as a rule or principle of action," and employing "language of incitement," is not constitutionally protected when the group is of sufficient size and cohesiveness, is sufficiently oriented towards action, and other circumstances are such as reasonably to justify apprehension that action will occur. This is quite a different thing from the view of the District Court here that mere doctrinal justification of forcible overthrow, if engaged in with the intent to accomplish overthrow, is punishable per se under the Smith Act. That sort of advocacy, even though uttered with the hope that it may ultimately lead to violent revolution, is too remote from concrete action to be regarded as the kind of indoctrination preparatory to action which was condemned in *Dennis*. As one of the concurring opinions in *Dennis* put it: Throughout our decisions there has recurred a distinction between the statement of an idea which may prompt its hearers to take unlawful action, and advocacy that such action be taken. There is nothing in *Dennis* which makes that historic distinction obsolete. . . .

In light of the foregoing we are unable to regard the District Court's charge upon this aspect of the case as adequate. The jury was never told that the Smith Act does not denounce advocacy in the sense of preaching abstractly the forcible overthrow of the Government. We think that the trial court's statement that the proscribed advocacy must include the "urging," "necessity," and "duty" of forcible overthrow, and not merely its "desirability" and "propriety," may not be regarded as a sufficient substitute for charging that the Smith Act reaches only advocacy of action for the overthrow of government by force and violence. The essential distinction is that those to whom the advocacy is addressed must be urged to *do* something, now or in the future, rather than merely to *believe* in something. At best the expressions used by the trial court were equivocal, since in the absence of any instructions differentiating advocacy of abstract doctrine from advocacy of action, they were as consistent with the former as they were with the latter. . . .

[Of the fourteen persons involved in this proceeding, the Court ordered the acquittal of five because there was no evidence to connect them with the conspiracy except the fact of party membership. New trials were ordered for the remaining nine: the Court held that because they had been active individually in a way other than party membership, the possibility existed that a jury might convict them]

JUSTICES BRENNAN and WHITTAKER took no part in the consideration or decision of this case.

JUSTICE BLACK, with whom JUSTICE DOUGLAS joined, concurred in part and dissented in part.

I would reverse every one of these convictions and direct that all the defendants be acquitted. In my judgment the statutory provisions on which these prosecutions are based abridge freedom of speech, press and assembly in violation of the First Amendment to the United States Constitution. . . .

. . . I cannot agree that "justice" requires this Court to send these cases back to put these defendants in jeopardy again in violation of the spirit if not the letter of the Fifth Amendment's provision against double jeopardy. . . .

In essence, petitioners were tried upon the charge that they believe in and want to foist upon this country a different and to us a despicable form of authoritarian government in which voices criticizing the existing order are summarily silenced. I fear that the present type of prosecutions are more in line with the philosophy of authoritarian government than with that expressed by our First Amendment. . . .

JUSTICE CLARK dissented.

. . . The conspiracy charged here is the same as in *Dennis*, except that here it is geared to California conditions, and brought, for the period 1948 to 1951, under the general conspiracy statute, 18 U.S.C. § 371, rather than the old conspiracy section of the Smith Act. The indictment charges petitioners with a conspiracy to violate two sections of the Smith Act, as recodified in 18 U.S.C. § 2385 by knowingly and willfully (1) teaching and advocating the violent overthrow of the government of the United States, and (2) organizing in California through the creation of groups, cells, schools, assemblies of persons, and the like, the communist Party, a society which teaches or advocates the violent overthrow of the Government.

The conspiracy includes the same group of defendants as in the *Dennis* case though petitioners here occupied a lower echelon in the party hierarchy. They, nevertheless, served in the same army and engaged in the same mission. . . .

FOR DISCUSSION

Does this case overturn *Dennis*? Constitutionally, what is different in this case? Politically?

RELATED CASES

***Lightfoot v. United States:* 355 U.S. 2 (1957).**

In this case the Supreme Court on the authority of *Jencks* reversed *per curiam* a judgment of the Seventh Circuit Court of Appeals, affirming defendant's conviction for violation of the Smith Act. The Seventh Circuit had held constitutional the "membership clause" of the Smith Act, which subjected a member of a group advocating the overthrow of the government by force or violence to a criminal penalty, provided he knew of the group's purposes.

***Nowak v. United States:* 356 U.S. 660 (1958).**

Naturalization can be voided only by a showing of illegal acquisition that is clear, unequivocal, and convincing. See also *Schneiderman v. United States* (320 U.S. 118, 1943) and *Maisenberg v. United States* (356 U.S. 670, 1958).

***Communist Party v. Subversive Activities Control Board:* 367 U.S. 1 (1961).**

Registration provisions of the Subversive Activities Control Act of 1950 were held valid.

AMERICAN COMMUNICATIONS ASS'N V. DOUDS

339 U.S. 382, 70 S.Ct. 674, 94 L.Ed. 925 (1950)

The non-Communist affidavit provision of the Labor Management Relations Act of 1947—the Taft-Hartley Act—was brought into question here. This provision—Section 9(h)—barred any investigation by the National Labor Relations Board unless all officers of the labor organization involved in a dispute signed an affidavit certifying that they were not Communists and did not advocate the overthrow of the U.S. government by force or by illegal means.

Vote: 5–1 (Three Justices abstained)

CHIEF JUSTICE VINSON delivered the opinion of the Court.

. . . The unions contend that the necessary effect of § 9(h) is to make it impossible for persons who cannot sign the oath to be officers of labor unions. They urge that such a statute violates fundamental rights guaranteed by the First Amendment: the right of union officers to hold what political views they choose and to associate with what political groups they will, and the right of unions to choose their officers without interference from government. The Board has argued, on the other hand, that § 9 (h) presents no First Amendment problem because its sole sanction is the withdrawal from noncomplying unions of the "privilege" of using its facilities. . . .

Neither contention states the problem with complete accuracy. . . . The practicalities of the situation place the proscriptions of § 9(h) somewhere between those two extremes. The difficult question that emerges is whether, consistently with the First Amendment, Congress, by statute, may exert these pressures upon labor unions to deny positions of leadership to certain persons who are identified by particular beliefs and political affiliations.

There can be no doubt that Congress may, under its constitutional power to regulate commerce among the several States, attempt to prevent political strikes and other kinds of direct action designed to burden and interrupt the free flow of commerce. We think it is clear, in addition, that the remedy provided by § 9 (h) bears reasonable relation to the evil which the statute was designed to reach. Congress could rationally find that the Communist Party is not like other political parties in its utilization of positions of union leadership as means by which to bring about strikes and other obstructions of commerce for purposes of political advantage, and that many persons who believe in overthrow of the Government by force and violence are also likely to resort to such tactics when, as officers, they formulate union policy.

The fact that the statute identifies persons by their political affiliations and beliefs, which are circumstances ordinarily irrelevant to permissible subjects of government action, does not lead to the conclusion that such circumstances are never relevant. . . . If accidents of birth and ancestry under some circumstances justify an inference concerning future conduct, it can hardly be doubted that voluntary affiliations and beliefs justify a similar inference when drawn by the legislature on the basis of its investigations.

. . . Government's interest here is not in preventing the dissemination of Communist doctrine or the holding of particular beliefs because it is feared that unlawful action will result there from if free speech is practiced. Its interest is in protecting the free flow of commerce from what Congress considers to be substantial evils of conduct that are not the products of speech at all. Section 9 (h), in other words, does not interfere with speech because Congress fears the consequences of speech; it regulates harmful conduct which Congress has determined is carried on by persons who may be identified by their political affiliations and beliefs. The Board does not contend that political strikes, the substantive evil at which § 9 (h) is aimed, are the present or impending products of advocacy of the doctrines of Communism or the expression of belief in overthrow of the Government by force. On the contrary, it points out that such strikes are called by persons who, so Congress has found, have the will and power to do so *without* advocacy or persuasion that seeks acceptance in the competition of the market. Speech may be fought with speech. Falsehoods and fallacies must be exposed, not suppressed, unless there is not sufficient time to avert the evil consequences of noxious doctrine by argument and education. That is the command of the First Amendment. But force may and must be met with force. Section 9 (h) is designed to protect the public not against what Communists and others identified therein advocate or believe, but against what Congress has concluded they have done and are likely to do again. . . .

On the other hand, legitimate attempts to protect the public, not from the remote possible effects of noxious ideologies, but from present excesses of direct, active conduct, are not presumptively bad because they interfere with and, in some of its manifestations, restrain the exercise of First Amendment rights.

. . . In essence, the problem is one of weighing the probable effects of the statute upon the free exercise of the right of speech and assembly against the congressional determination that political strikes are evils of conduct which cause substantial harm to interstate commerce and that Communists and others identified by § 9 (h) pose continuing threats to that public interest when in positions of union leadership. . . .

. . . Those who, so Congress has found, would subvert the public interest cannot escape all regulation because, at the same time, they carry on legitimate political activities. . . . To encourage unions to displace them from positions of great power over the national economy, while at the same time leaving free the outlets by which they may pursue legitimate political activities of persuasion and advocacy, does not seem to us to contravene the purposes of the First Amendment. That Amendment requires that one be permitted to believe what he will. It requires that one be permitted to advocate what he will unless there is a clear and present danger that a substantial public evil will result there from. It does not require that he be permitted to be the keeper of the arsenal. . . .

Section 9 (h) is designed to protect the public not against what Communists and others identified therein advocate or believe but against what Congress has concluded they have done and are likely to do again.

[The Court found no merit in the contention that this was a bill of attainder or *ex post facto* legislation or unconstitutionally vague.]

We conclude that § 9 (h) of the Labor Management Relations Act, as herein construed, is compatible with the Federal Constitution and may stand. The judgments of the courts below are therefore Affirmed.

JUSTICES DOUGLAS, CLARK, and MINTON took no part in the consideration or decision of these cases.

JUSTICE JACKSON, concurred in part and dissented in part.

If the statute before us required labor union officers to forswear membership in the Republican Party, the Democratic Party or the Socialist Party, I suppose all agree that it would be unconstitutional. But why, if it is valid as to the Communist Party?

The answer, for me, is in the decisive differences between the Communist Party and every other party of any importance in the long experience of the United States with party government. In order that today's decision may not be useful as a precedent for suppression of any political opposition compatible with our free institutions, I limit concurrence to grounds and distinctions explicitly set forth herein, without which I should regard this Act as unconstitutional. . . .

1. *The goal of the Communist Party is to seize powers of government by and for a minority rather than to acquire power through the vote of a free electorate.* It seeks not merely a change of administration, or of Congress, or reform legislation within the constitutional framework. Its program is not merely to socialize property more rapidly and extensively than the other parties are doing. While the difference between other parties in these matters is largely as to pace, the Communist Party's difference is one of direction. . . .

2. *The Communist Party alone among American parties past or present is dominated and controlled by a foreign government.* It is a satrap party which, to the threat of civil disorder, adds the threat of betrayal into alien hands. . . .

3. *Violent and undemocratic means are the calculated and indispensable methods to attain the Communist Party's goal.* It would be incredible naïveté to expect the American branch of this movement to forego the only methods by which a Communist Party has anywhere come into power. In not one of the countries it now dominates was the Communist Party chosen by a free or contestable election; in not one can it be evicted by any election. The international police state has crept over Eastern Europe by deception, coercion, *coup d'état,* terrorism and assassination. Not only has it overpowered its critics and opponents; it has usually liquidated them. The American Communist Party has copied the organizational structure and its leaders have been schooled in the same technique and by the same tutors. . . .

4. *The Communist Party has sought to gain this leverage and hold on the American population by acquiring control of the labor movement.* All political parties have wooed labor and its leaders. But what other parties seek is principally the vote of labor. The Communist Party, on the other hand, is not primarily interested in labor's vote, for it does not expect to win by votes. It strives for control of labor's coercive power—the strike, the sit-down, the slow-down, sabotage, or other means of producing industrial paralysis. Congress has legalized the strike as labor's weapon for improving its own lot. But where Communists have labor control, the strike can be and sometimes is perverted to a party weapon. In 1940 and 1941, undisclosed Communists used their labor offices to sabotage this Nation's effort to rebuild its own defenses. Disguised as leaders of free American labor, they were in truth secret partisans of Stalin, who, in partnership with Hitler, was overrunning Europe, sending honest labor leaders to concentration camps, and reducing labor to slavery in every land either of them was able to occupy. No other important political party in our history has attempted to use the strike to nullify a foreign or a domestic policy adopted by those chosen under our representative system. . . .

5. *Every member of the Communist Party is an agent to execute the Communist program.* What constitutes a party? Major political parties in the United States have never been closely knit or secret organizations. Anyone who usually votes the party ticket is reckoned a member, although he has not applied for or been admitted to membership, pays no dues, has taken no pledge, and is free to vote, speak and act as he wills. Followers are held together by rather casual acceptance of general principles, the influence of leaders, and sometimes by the cohesive power of patronage. Membership in the party carries with it little assurance that the member

understands or believes in its principles and none at all that he will take orders from its leaders. One may quarrel with the party and bolt its candidates and return again as much a member as those who were regular. And it is often a source of grief to those who have labored long in the vineyard that late arrivals are taken into the party councils from other parties without scrutiny. Of course, when party organization is of this character, there is little ground for inference that all members are committed to party plans or that they are agents for their execution.

Membership in the Communist Party is totally different. The Party is a secret conclave. Members are admitted only upon acceptance as reliable and after indoctrination in its policies, to which the member is fully committed. They are provided with cards or credentials, usually issued under false names so that the identification can only be made by officers of the Party who hold the code. Moreover, each pledges unconditional obedience to party authority. Adherents are known by secret or code names. They constitute "cells" in the factory, the office, the political society, or the labor union. For any deviation from the party line they are purged and excluded. . . .

Congress has, however, required an additional disclaimer, which in my view does encounter serious constitutional objections. A union officer must also swear that "he does not believe in . . . the overthrow of the United States Government by force or by any illegal or unconstitutional methods." . . .

The men who led the struggle forcibly to overthrow lawfully constituted British authority found moral support by asserting a natural law under which their revolution was justified, and they broadly proclaimed these beliefs in the document basic to our freedom. Such sentiments have also been given ardent and rather extravagant expression by Americans of undoubted patriotism. Most of these utterances were directed against a tyranny which left no way to change by suffrage. It seems to me a perversion of their meaning to quote them, as the Communists often do, to sanction violent attacks upon a representative government which does afford such means. But while I think Congress may make it a crime to take one overt step to use or to incite violence or force against our Government, I do not see how in the light of our history, a mere belief that one has a natural right under some circumstances to do so can subject an American citizen to prejudice any more than possession of any other erroneous belief. Can we say that men of our time must not even think about the propositions on which our own Revolution was justified? . . .

JUSTICE FRANKFURTER concurred except as to Part VII involving chiefly the vagueness of the legislation.

JUSTICE BLACK dissented.

. . . Under such circumstances, restrictions imposed on proscribed groups are seldom static, even though the rate of expansion may not move in geometric progression from discrimination to arm-band to ghetto and worse. Thus I cannot regard the Court's holding as one which merely bars Communists from holding union office and nothing more. For its reasoning would apply just as forcibly to statutes barring Communists and their suspected sympathizers from election to political office, mere membership in unions, and in fact from getting or holding any jobs whereby they could earn a living. . . .

FOR DISCUSSION

Should the government even be asking individuals about their political views or about their memberships in groups or organizations? Why did the Court not find a First Amendment violation here?

RELATED CASES

***United States v. Robel:* 389 U.S. 258 (1967).**

Under the Subversive Activities Control Act, no member of the Communist-Action organization could be employed in any defense facility. The Court held that the First Amendment forbids use of guilt by association alone as a basis for such a ban without regard to the quality and degree of membership in an organization.

***Schneider v. Smith:* 390 U.S. 17 (1968).**

Although Congress can enact legislation to safeguard American shipping from subversive activity, the action in this case—of the Coast Guard, which refused to process Schneider's merchant mariner's document—was not justified. The refusal was based on ideas or beliefs rather than actions.

ADLER V. BOARD OF EDUCATION

342 U.S. 485, 72 S.Ct. 380, 96 L.Ed. 517 (1952)

New York State's Feinberg Law specifically makes ineligible for employment in the public schools of the state any person who is a member of an organization advocating the unlawful overthrow of the government of the United States. Under the law, the Board of Regents is to compile a list, after conducting a hearing to ascertain which organizations belong on this list. Any person who is disqualified for employment under the terms of this law is entitled to a full hearing with the privilege of representation by counsel and the right of judicial review.

Vote: 6–3

JUSTICE MINTON delivered the opinion of the Court.

. . . A teacher works in a sensitive area in a schoolroom. There he shapes the attitude of young minds towards the society in which they live. In this, the state has a vital concern. It must preserve the integrity of the schools. That the school authorities have the right and the duty to screen the officials, teachers, and employees as to their fitness to maintain the integrity of the schools as a part of ordered society, cannot be doubted. One's associates, past and present, as well as one's conduct, may properly be considered in determining fitness and loyalty. From time immemorial, one's reputation has been determined in part by the company he keeps. In the employment of officials and teachers of the school system, the state may very properly inquire into the company they keep, and we know of no rule, constitutional or otherwise, that prevents the state, when determining the fitness and loyalty of such persons, from considering the organizations and persons with whom they associate.

If, under the procedure set up in the New York law, a person is found to be unfit and is disqualified from employment in the public school system because of membership in a listed organization, he is not thereby denied the right of free speech and assembly. His freedom of choice between membership in the organization and employment in the school system might be limited, but not his freedom of speech or assembly, except in the remote sense that limitation is inherent in every choice. Certainly such limitation is not one the state may not make in the exercise of its police power to protect the schools from pollution and thereby to defend its own existence. . . .

Membership in a listed organization found to be within the statute and known by the member to be within the statute is a legislative finding that the member by his membership supports the thing the organization stands for, namely, the overthrow of government by unlawful means. We cannot say that such a finding is contrary to fact or that "generality of experience" points to a different conclusion. Disqualification follows therefore as a reasonable presumption from such membership and support. Nor is there here a problem of procedural due process. The presumption is not conclusive but arises only in a hearing where the person against whom it may arise has full opportunity to rebut it. . . .

Where, as here, the relation between the fact found and the presumption is clear and direct and is not conclusive, the requirements of due process are satisfied. . . .

We find no constitutional infirmity in § 12 (a) of the Civil Service Law of New York or in the Feinberg Law which implemented it, and the judgment is affirmed.

JUSTICE FRANKFURTER dissented, holding that the Court should have declined jurisdiction.

JUSTICE BLACK dissented.

. . . This policy of freedom is in my judgment embodied in the First Amendment and made applicable to the states by the Fourteenth. Because of this policy public officials cannot be constitutionally vested with powers to select the ideas people can think about, censor the public views they can express, or choose the persons or groups people can associate with. Public officials with such power are not public servants; they are public masters.

I dissent from the Court's judgment sustaining this law which effectively penalizes school teachers for their thoughts and their associates.

JUSTICE DOUGLAS dissented, with the concurrence of JUSTICE BLACK.

. . . The present law proceeds on a principle repugnant to our society—guilt by association. A teacher is disqualified because of her membership in an organization found to be "subversive." . . . The mere fact of membership in the organization raises a *prima facie* case of her own guilt. She may, it is said, show her innocence. But innocence in this case turns on knowledge; and when the witch hunt is on, one who must rely on ignorance leans on a feeble reed.

The very threat of such a procedure is certain to raise havoc with academic freedom. Youthful indiscretions, mistaken causes, misguided enthusiasms—all long forgotten—become the ghosts of a harrowing present. Any organization committed to a liberal cause, any group organized to revolt against an hysterical trend, any committee launched to sponsor an unpopular program becomes suspect. These are the organizations into which Communists often infiltrate. Their presence infects the whole, even though the project was not conceived in sin. A teacher caught in that mesh is almost certain to stand condemned. Fearing condemnation, she will tend to shrink from any association that stirs controversy. In that manner freedom of expression will be stifled. . . .

FOR DISCUSSION

What is called "at-will employment" is the general rule for employment in the United States. By that rule, employees can be hired or fired at the will of the employer. How much is the at-will doctrine behind this decision? How much of the decision is premised upon the fact that no one has a right to a job? How much of this is about the involvement of minors (i.e., students in the public schools)?

RELATED CASES

***Cramp v. Board of Public Instruction of Orange County:* 368 U.S. 278 (1961).**

A state cannot, consistently with the Due Process Clause of the Fourteenth Amendment, force an employee to either take a loyalty oath that is vague and uncertain at the risk of subsequent prosecution for perjury or face immediate dismissal from public service.

***Baggett v. Bullitt:* 377 U.S. 360 (1964).**

The Court declared a Washington State loyalty oath statute void because of vagueness. The requirement was held not open to one or a few interpretations but to an indefinite number. This decision overruled Gerende v. Board of Supervisors of Elections (341 U.S. 56, 1951).

KEYISHIAN V. BOARD OF REGENTS OF THE UNIVERSITY OF THE STATE OF NEW YORK

385 U.S. 589, 87 S.Ct. 675, 17 L.Ed. 192 (1967)

Appellants, faculty members of the State University of New York and a non-faculty employee, brought this action for declaratory and injunctive relief, claiming that New York's teacher loyalty laws and regulations were unconstitutional. Their continued employment had been terminated or was threatened when each appellant faculty member refused to comply with a requirement of the university trustees that he certify that he was not a Communist and that, if he had ever been one, he had so advised the university president; the nonfaculty employee refused to state under oath whether he had advocated or been a member of a group that advocated forceful overthrow of the government. Under § 3021 of New York's Education Law, "treasonable or seditious" utterances or acts are grounds for dismissal from the public school system: Section 3022 (the Feinberg Law) of the Education Law requires the State Board of Regents to issue regulations for the disqualification or removal on loyalty grounds of faculty or other personnel in the state educational system, to make a list of "subversive" organizations, and to provide that membership therein constitutes prima facie evidence of disqualification for employment. The Board listed the national and state Communist parties as "subversive organizations" under the law. Shortly before the trial of this case, however, the university trustees' certificate requirement was rescinded and it was announced that no person would be ineligible for employment "solely" because he refused to sign the certificate.

Vote: 5–4

JUSTICE BRENNAN delivered the opinion of the Court.

. . . We emphasize once again that ". . . precision of regulation must be the touchstone in an area so closely touching our most precious freedoms," *NAACP v. Button,* 371 U.S. 415, 438 (1963); ". . . for standards of permissible statutory vagueness are strict in the area of free expression. . . . Because First Amendment freedoms need breathing space to survive, government may regulate in the area only with narrow specificity." *Id.,* at 432–433. New York's complicated and intricate scheme plainly violates that standard. When one must guess what conduct or utterance may lose him his position, one necessarily will "steer far wider of the unlawful zone. . . ." *Speiser v. Randall,* 357 U.S. 513, 526 (1958).

. . . Vagueness of wording is aggravated by prolixity and profusion of statutes, regulations, and administrative machinery, and by manifold cross-references to interrelated enactments and rules.

We therefore hold that § 3021 of the Education Law and subdivisions 1 (a), 1 (b) and 3 of § 105 of the Civil Service Law as implemented by the machinery created pursuant to § 3022 of the Education Law are unconstitutional.

. . . Subdivision 2 of the Feinberg Law was, however, before the Court in *Adler* and its constitutionality was sustained. But constitutional doctrine which has emerged since that decision has rejected its major premise. That premise was that public employment, including academic employment, may be conditioned upon the surrender of constitutional rights which could not be abridged by direct government action. Teachers, the Court said in *Adler* v. *Board of Educ. of City of New York*, 342 U.S. 485 (1952), "may work for the school system upon the reasonable terms laid down by the proper authorities of New York. If they do not choose to work on such terms, they are at liberty to retain their beliefs and associations and go elsewhere." 342 U.S., at 492.

. . . We proceed then to the question of the validity of the provisions of subdivision 1 (c) of § 105 and subdivision 2 of § 3022, barring employment to members of listed organizations. Here again constitutional doctrine has developed since *Adler*. Mere knowing membership without a specific intent to further the unlawful aims of an organization is not a constitutionally adequate basis for exclusion from such positions as those held by appellants.

. . . Measured against this standard, both Civil Service Law § 105, subd. 1 (c), and Education Law § 3022, subd. 2, sweep overbroadly into association which may not be proscribed. . . . Where statutes have an overbroad sweep, just as where they are vague, "the hazard of loss or substantial impairment of those precious rights may be critical," *Dombrowski v. Pfister,* 380 U.S. 479 (1965) at 486, since those covered by the statute are bound to limit their behavior to that which is unquestionably safe. . . .

We therefore hold that Civil Service Law § 105, subd. 1 (c), and Education Law § 3022, subd. 2, are invalid insofar as they proscribe mere knowing membership without any showing of specific intent to further the unlawful aims of the Communist Party of the United States or of the State of New York.

The judgment of the District Court is reversed and the case is remanded for further proceedings consistent with this opinion.

Reversed and remanded.

JUSTICE CLARK dissented.

. . . It is clear that the Feinberg Law, in which this Court found "no constitutional infirmity" in 1952, has been given its death blow today. Just as the majority here finds that there "can be no doubt of the legitimacy of New York's interest in protecting its education system from subversion" there can also be no doubt that "the be-all and end-all" of New York's effort is here. And, regardless of its correctness, neither New York nor the several States that have followed the teaching of *Adler v. Board of Education,* 342 U.S. 485 (1952), for some 15 years, can ever put the pieces together again. No court has ever reached out so far to destroy so much with so little. . . .

In view of this long list of decisions covering over 15 years of this Court's history, in which no opinion of this Court even questioned the validity of the *Adler* line of cases, it is strange to me that the Court now finds that the "constitutional doctrine which has emerged since. . . has rejected [*Adler*'s] major premise." With due respect, as I read them, our cases have done no such thing. . . .

The majority says that the Feinberg Law is bad because it has an "overbroad sweep." I regret to say—and I do so with deference—that the majority has by its broadside swept away one of our most precious rights, namely, the right of self-preservation. Our public educational system is the genius of our democracy. The minds of our youth are developed there and the character of that development will determine the future of our land. Indeed, our very existence depends upon it. The issue here is a very narrow one. It is not freedom of speech, freedom of thought, freedom of press, freedom of assembly, or of association, even in the Communist Party. It is simply this: May the State provide that one who, after a hearing with full judicial review, is found to have willfully and deliberately advocated, advised, or taught that our Government should be overthrown by force or violence or other unlawful means; or to have willfully and deliberately printed, published, etc., any book or paper that so advocated *and to have personally* advocated such doctrine himself; or to have willfully and deliberately become a member of an organization that advocates such doctrine, is *prima facie* disqualified from teaching in its university? My answer, in keeping with all of our cases up until today, is "Yes"!

I dissent.

FOR DISCUSSION

Is the difference between the holding in this case and that in *Adler* due to the respective settings: in one case a university, and in the other primary school (grades K–12)?

RELATED CASE

***Pickering v. Board of Education of Township High School District:* 391 U.S. 563 (1968).**

Absent proof of false statements knowingly or recklessly made by a teacher (here a letter to a local newspaper), the exercise of one's right to speak on issues of public importance may not furnish the basis for dismissal from public employment.

NATIONAL ASSOCIATION FOR THE ADVANCEMENT OF COLORED PEOPLE V. STATE OF ALABAMA

357 U.S. 449, 78 S.Ct. 1163, 2 L.Ed.2d 1488 (1958)

In accordance with one of its laws, the state of Alabama sought the membership list of the Alabama NAACP as a condition of permitting the civil rights organization to do business in the state. The NAACP objected, claiming that its list of members was protected by the First Amendment. The state courts ruled against the organization, which ultimately appealed to the Supreme Court.

Vote: 9–0

JUSTICE HARLAN delivered the opinion of the Court.

We review from the standpoint of its validity under the Federal Constitution a judgment of civil contempt entered against petitioner, the National Association for the Advancement of Colored People, in the courts of Alabama. The question presented is whether Alabama, consistently with the Due Process Clause of the Fourteenth Amendment, can compel petitioner to reveal to the State's Attorney General the names and addresses of all its Alabama members and agents, without regard to their positions or functions in the Association. The judgment of contempt was based upon petitioner's refusal to comply fully with a court order requiring in part the production of membership lists. Petitioner's claim is that the order, in the circumstances shown by this record, violated rights assured to petitioner and its members under the Constitution.

Alabama has a statute similar to those of many other States which requires a foreign corporation, except as exempted, to qualify before doing business by filing its corporate charter with the Secretary of State and designating a place of business and an agent to receive service of process. The statute imposes a fine on a corporation transacting intrastate business before qualifying and provides for criminal prosecution of officers of such a corporation. The National Association for the Advancement of Colored People is a nonprofit membership corporation organized under the laws of New York. Its purposes, fostered on a nationwide basis, are those indicated by its name, and it operates through chartered affiliates which are independent unincorporated associations, with membership therein equivalent to membership in petitioner. The first Alabama affiliates were chartered in 1918. Since that time the aims of the Association have been advanced through activities of its affiliates, and in 1951 the Association itself opened a regional office in Alabama, at which it employed two supervisory persons and one clerical worker. The Association has never complied with the qualification statute, from which it considered itself exempt.

In 1956 the Attorney General of Alabama brought an equity suit in the State Circuit Court, Montgomery County, to enjoin the Association from conducting further activities within, and to oust it from, the State. Among other things the bill in equity alleged that the Association had opened a regional office and had organized various affiliates in Alabama; had recruited members and solicited contributions within the State; had given financial support and furnished legal assistance to Negro students seeking admission to the state university; and had supported a Negro boycott of the bus lines in Montgomery to compel the seating of passengers without regard to race. The bill recited that the Association, by continuing to do business in Alabama without complying with the qualification statute, was 'causing irreparable injury to the property and civil rights of the residents and citizens of the State of Alabama for which criminal prosecution and civil actions at law afford no adequate relief.' On the day the complaint was filed, the Circuit Court issued ex parte an order restraining the Association, *pendente lite* [while the litigation is pending], from engaging in further activities within the State and forbidding it to take any steps to qualify itself to do business therein.

Petitioner demurred to the allegations of the bill and moved to dissolve the restraining order. It contended that its activities did not subject it to the qualification requirements of the statute and that in any event what the State sought to accomplish by its suit would violate rights to freedom of speech and assembly guaranteed under the Fourteenth Amendment to the Constitution of the United States. Before the date set for a hearing on this motion, the State moved for the production of a large number of the Association's records and papers, including bank statements, leases, deeds, and records containing the names and addresses of all Alabama "members" and "agents" of the Association. It alleged that all such documents were necessary for adequate preparation for the hearing, in view of petitioner's denial of the conduct of intrastate business within the meaning of the qualification statute. Over petitioner's objections, the court ordered the production of a substantial part of the requested records, including the membership lists, and postponed the hearing on the restraining order to a date later than the time ordered for production.

III

We thus reach petitioner's claim that the production order in the state litigation trespasses upon fundamental freedoms protected by the Due Process Clause of the Fourteenth Amendment. Petitioner argues that in view of the facts and circumstances shown in the record, the effect of compelled disclosure of the membership lists will be to abridge the rights of its rank-and-file members to engage in lawful association in support of their common beliefs. It contends that governmental action which, although not directly suppressing association, nevertheless carries this consequence, can be justified only upon some overriding valid interest of the State.

Effective advocacy of both public and private points of view, particularly controversial ones, is undeniably enhanced by group association, as this Court has more than once recognized by remarking upon the close nexus between the freedoms of speech and assembly. It is beyond debate that freedom to engage in association for the advancement of beliefs and ideas is an inseparable aspect of the 'liberty' assured by the Due Process Clause of the Fourteenth Amendment, which embraces freedom of speech. Of course, it is immaterial whether the beliefs sought to be advanced by association pertain to political, economic, religious or cultural matters, and state action which may have the effect of curtailing the freedom to associate is subject to the closest scrutiny.

The fact that Alabama, so far as is relevant to the validity of the contempt judgment presently under review, has taken no direct action to restrict the right of petitioner's members to associate freely, does not end inquiry into the effect of the production order. In the domain of these indispensable liberties, whether of speech, press, or association, the decisions of this Court recognize that abridgement of such rights, even though unintended, may inevitably follow from varied forms of governmental action. Thus in *American Communications Association v. Douds,* 339 U.S. 382 (1950), the Court stressed that the legislation there challenged, which on its face sought to regulate labor unions and to secure stability in interstate commerce, would have the practical effect 'of discouraging' the exercise of constitutionally protected political rights, and it upheld that statute only after concluding that the reasons advanced for its enactment were constitutionally sufficient to justify its possible deterrent effect upon such freedoms. Similar recognition of possible unconstitutional intimidation of the free exercise of the right to advocate underlay this Court's narrow construction of the authority of a congressional committee investigating lobbying and of an Act regulating lobbying, although in neither case was there an effort to suppress speech. The governmental action challenged may appear to be totally unrelated to protected liberties. Statutes imposing taxes upon rather than prohibiting particular activity have been struck down when perceived to have the consequence of unduly curtailing the liberty of freedom of press assured under the Fourteenth Amendment.

It is hardly a novel perception that compelled disclosure of affiliation with groups engaged in advocacy may constitute as effective a restraint on freedom of association as the forms of governmental action in the cases above were thought likely to produce upon the particular constitutional rights there involved. This Court has recognized the vital relationship between freedom to associate and privacy in one's associations. When referring to the varied forms of governmental action which might interfere with freedom of assembly, it said in *American Communications Ass'n v. Douds*: "A requirement that adherents of particular religious faiths or political parties wear identifying arm-bands, for example, is obviously of this nature." Compelled disclosure of membership in an organization engaged in advocacy of particular beliefs is of the same order. Inviolability of privacy in group association may in many circumstances be indispensable to preservation of freedom of association, particularly where a group espouses dissident beliefs.

We think that the production order, in the respects here drawn in question, must be regarded as entailing the likelihood of a substantial restraint upon the exercise by petitioner's members of their right to freedom of association. Petitioner has made an uncontroverted showing that on past occasions revelation of the identity of its rank-and-file members has exposed these members to economic reprisal, loss of employment, threat of physical coercion, and other manifestations of public hostility. Under these circumstances, we think it apparent that compelled disclosure of petitioner's Alabama membership is likely to affect adversely the ability of petitioner and its members to pursue their collective effort to foster beliefs which they admittedly have the right to advocate, in that it may induce members to withdraw from the Association and dissuade others from joining it because of fear of exposure of their beliefs shown through their associations and of the consequences of this exposure. For the reasons stated, the judgment of the Supreme Court of Alabama must be reversed and the case remanded for proceedings not inconsistent with this opinion.

Reversed.

FOR DISCUSSION

How broadly does the Court construct the right to freedom of association in this case? Does this right prevent the government from ever asking groups or individuals to make disclosures? Is there a right to remain anonymous?

ROBERTS V. UNITED STATES JAYCEES

468 U.S. 609, 104 S.Ct. 3244, 82 L.Ed.2d 462 (1984)

Minnesota chapters of Jaycees, in violation of the national policy of the organization, admitted women into their membership. The national Jaycees objected and ordered the state chapters to exclude women. The state chapters refused to comply and filed a complaint contending that the exclusion of women violated a state public accommodations law banning discrimination against women. The Minnesota Department of Human Rights and the state supreme court ruled against the United States Jaycees, and the organization appealed.

Vote: 9–0

JUSTICE BRENNAN delivered the opinion of the Court.

This case requires us to address a conflict between a State's efforts to eliminate gender-based discrimination against its citizens and the constitutional freedom of association asserted by members of a private organization. In the decision under review, the Court of Appeals for the Eighth Circuit concluded that, by requiring the United States Jaycees to admit women as full voting members, the Minnesota Human Rights Act violates the First and Fourteenth Amendment rights of the organization's members. We noted probable jurisdiction, and now reverse.

I

A

The United States Jaycees (Jaycees), founded in 1920 as the Junior Chamber of Commerce, is a nonprofit membership corporation, incorporated in Missouri with national headquarters in Tulsa, Okla. The objective of the Jaycees, as set out in its bylaws, is to pursue

> such educational and charitable purposes as will promote and foster the growth and development of young men's civic organizations in the United States, designed to inculcate in the individual membership of such organization a spirit of genuine Americanism and civic interest, and as a supplementary education institution to provide them with opportunity for personal development and achievement and an avenue for intelligent participation by young men in the affairs of their community, state and nation, and to develop true friendship and understanding among young men of all nations.

The organization's bylaws establish seven classes of membership, including individual or regular members, associate individual members, and local chapters. Regular membership is limited to young men between the ages of 18 and 35, while associate membership is available to individuals or groups ineligible for regular membership, principally women and older men. An associate member, whose dues are somewhat lower than those charged regular members, may not vote, hold local or national office, or participate in certain leadership training and awards programs. The bylaws define a local chapter as "[a]ny young men's organization of good repute existing in any community within the United States, organized for purposes similar to and consistent with those" of the national organization. The ultimate policymaking authority of the Jaycees rests with an annual national convention, consisting of delegates from each local chapter, with a national president and board of directors. At the time of trial in August 1981, the Jaycees had approximately 295,000 members in 7,400 local chapters affiliated with 51 state organizations. There were at that time about 11,915 associate members. The national organization's executive vice president estimated at trial that women associate members make up about two percent of the Jaycees' total membership.

New members are recruited to the Jaycees through the local chapters, although the state and national organizations are also actively involved in recruitment through a variety of promotional activities. A new regular member pays an initial fee followed by annual dues; in exchange, he is entitled to participate in all of the activities of the local, state, and national organizations. The national headquarters employs a staff to develop "program kits" for use by local chapters that are designed to enhance individual development, community development, and members' management skills. These materials include courses in public speaking and personal finances as well as community programs related to charity, sports, and public health. The national office also makes available to members a range of personal products, including travel accessories, casual wear, pins, awards, and other gifts. The programs, products, and other activities of the organization are all regularly featured in publications made available to the membership, including a magazine entitled "Future."

B

In 1974 and 1975, respectively, the Minneapolis and St. Paul chapters of the Jaycees began admitting women as regular members. Currently, the memberships and boards of directors of both chapters include a substantial proportion of women. As a result, the two chapters have been in violation of the national organization's bylaws for about 10 years. The national organization has imposed a number of sanctions on the Minneapolis and St. Paul chapters for violating the bylaws, including denying their members eligibility for state or national office or awards programs, and refusing to count their membership in computing votes at national conventions.

In December 1978, the president of the national organization advised both chapters that a motion to revoke their charters would be considered at a forthcoming meeting of the national board of directors in Tulsa. Shortly after receiving this notification, members of both chapters filed charges of discrimination with the Minnesota Department of Human Rights. The complaints alleged that the exclusion of women from full membership required by the national organization's bylaws violated the Minnesota Human Rights Act (Act).

After an investigation, the Commissioner of the Minnesota Department of Human Rights found probable cause to believe that the sanctions imposed on the local chapters by the national organization violated the statute and ordered that an evidentiary hearing be held before a state hearing examiner. Before that hearing took place, however, the national organization brought suit against various state officials, appellants here, in the United States District Court for the District of Minnesota, seeking declaratory and injunctive relief to prevent enforcement of the Act. The complaint alleged that, by requiring the organization to accept women as regular members, application of the Act would violate the male members' constitutional rights of free speech and association. With the agreement of the parties, the District Court dismissed the suit without prejudice, stating that it could be renewed in the event the state administrative proceeding resulted in a ruling adverse to the Jaycees.

The proceeding before the Minnesota Human Rights Department hearing examiner then went forward and, upon its completion, the examiner filed findings of fact and conclusions of law. The examiner concluded that the Jaycees organization is a "place of public accommodation" within the Act and that it had engaged in an unfair discriminatory practice by excluding women from regular membership. He ordered the national organization to cease and desist from discriminating against any member or applicant for membership on the basis of sex and from imposing sanctions on any Minnesota affiliate for admitting women. The Jaycees then filed a renewed complaint in the District Court, which in turn certified to the Minnesota Supreme Court the question whether the Jaycees organization is a "place of public accommodation" within the meaning of the State's Human Rights Act.

With the record of the administrative hearing before it, the Minnesota Supreme Court answered that question in the affirmative.

II

Our decisions have referred to constitutionally protected "freedom of association" in two distinct senses. In one line of decisions, the Court has concluded that choices to enter into and maintain certain intimate human relationships must be secured against undue intrusion by the State because of the role of such relationships in safeguarding the individual freedom that is central to our constitutional scheme. In this respect, freedom of association receives protection as a fundamental element of personal liberty. In another set of decisions, the Court has recognized a right to associate for the purpose of engaging in those activities protected by the First Amendment—speech, assembly, petition for the redress of grievances, and the exercise of religion. The Constitution guarantees freedom of association of this kind as an indispensable means of preserving other individual liberties.

The intrinsic and instrumental features of constitutionally protected association may, of course, coincide. In particular, when the State interferes with individuals' selection of those with whom they wish to join in a common endeavor, freedom of association in both of its forms may be implicated. The Jaycees contend that this is such a case. Still, the nature and degree of constitutional protection afforded freedom of association may vary depending on the extent to which one or the other aspect of the constitutionally protected liberty is at stake in a given case. We therefore find it useful to consider separately the effect of applying the Minnesota statute to the Jaycees on what could be called its members' freedom of intimate association and their freedom of expressive association.

A

The Court has long recognized that, because the Bill of Rights is designed to secure individual liberty, it must afford the formation and preservation of certain kinds of highly personal relationships a substantial measure of sanctuary from unjustified interference by the State. Without precisely identifying every consideration that may underlie this type of constitutional protection, we have noted that certain kinds of personal bonds have played a critical role in the culture and traditions of the Nation by cultivating and transmitting shared ideals and beliefs; they thereby foster diversity and act as critical buffers between the individual and the power of the State. Moreover, the constitutional shelter afforded such relationships reflects the realization that individuals draw much of their emotional enrichment from close ties with others. Protecting these relationships from unwarranted state interference therefore safeguards the ability independently to define one's identity that is central to any concept of liberty.

The personal affiliations that exemplify these considerations, and that therefore suggest some relevant limitations on the relationships that might be entitled to this sort of constitutional protection, are those that attend the creation and sustenance of a family—marriage; childbirth; the raising and education of children; and cohabitation with one's relatives. Family relationships, by their nature, involve deep attachments and commitments to the necessarily few other individuals with whom one shares not only a special community of thoughts, experiences, and beliefs but also distinctively personal aspects of one's life. Among other things, therefore, they are distinguished by such attributes as relative smallness, a high degree of selectivity in decisions to begin and maintain the affiliation, and seclusion from others in critical aspects of the relationship. As a general matter, only relationships with these sorts of qualities are likely to reflect the considerations that have led to an understanding of freedom of association as an intrinsic element of personal liberty. Conversely, an association lacking these qualities—such as a large business enterprise—seems remote from the concerns giving rise to this constitutional protection. Accordingly, the Constitution undoubtedly imposes constraints on the State's power to control the selection of one's spouse that would not apply to regulations affecting the choice of one's fellow employees.

Between these poles, of course, lies a broad range of human relationships that may make greater or lesser claims to constitutional protection from particular incursions by the State. Determining the limits of state authority over an individual's freedom to enter into a particular association therefore unavoidably entails a careful assessment of where that relationship's objective characteristics locate it on a spectrum from the most intimate to the most attenuated of personal attachments.

B

An individual's freedom to speak, to worship, and to petition the government for the redress of grievances could not be vigorously protected from interference by the State unless a correlative freedom to engage in group effort toward those ends were not also guaranteed. According protection to collective effort on behalf of shared goals is especially important in preserving political and cultural diversity and in shielding dissident expression from suppression by the majority. Consequently, we have long understood as implicit in the right to engage in activities protected by the First Amendment a corresponding right to associate with others in pursuit of a wide variety of political, social, economic, educational, religious, and cultural ends. In view of the various protected activities in which the Jaycees engages, that right is plainly implicated in this case.

Government actions that may unconstitutionally infringe upon this freedom can take a number of forms. Among other things, government may seek to impose penalties or withhold benefits from individuals because of their membership in a disfavored group; it may attempt to require disclosure of the fact of membership in a group seeking anonymity, and it may try to interfere with the internal organization or affairs of the group. By requiring the Jaycees to admit women as full voting members, the Minnesota Act works an infringement of the last type. There can be no clearer example of an intrusion into the internal structure or affairs of an association than a regulation that forces the group to accept members it does not desire.

The right to associate for expressive purposes is not, however, absolute. Infringements on that right may be justified by regulations adopted to serve compelling state interests, unrelated to the suppression of ideas, that cannot be achieved through means significantly less restrictive of associational freedoms. We are persuaded that Minnesota's compelling interest in eradicating discrimination against its female citizens justifies the impact that application of the statute to the Jaycees may have on the male members' associational freedoms.

On its face, the Minnesota Act does not aim at the suppression of speech, does not distinguish between prohibited and permitted activity on the basis of viewpoint, and does not license enforcement authorities to administer the statute on the basis of such constitutionally impermissible criteria. Nor does the Jaycees contend that the Act has been applied in this case for the purpose of hampering the organization's ability to express its views. Instead, as the Minnesota Supreme Court explained, the Act reflects the State's strong historical commitment to eliminating discrimination and assuring its citizens equal access to publicly available goods and services. That goal, which is unrelated to the suppression of expression, plainly serves compelling state interests of the highest order.

By prohibiting gender discrimination in places of public accommodation, the Minnesota Act protects the State's citizenry from a number of serious social and personal harms.

In applying the Act to the Jaycees, the State has advanced those interests through the least restrictive means of achieving its ends. Indeed, the Jaycees has failed to demonstrate that the Act imposes any serious burdens on the male members' freedom of expressive association.

In any event, even if enforcement of the Act causes some incidental abridgment of the Jaycees' protected speech, that effect is no greater than is necessary to accomplish the State's legitimate purposes. As we have explained, acts of invidious discrimination in the distribution of publicly available goods, services, and other advantages cause unique evils that government has a compelling interest to prevent—wholly apart from the point of view such conduct may transmit. Accordingly, like violence or other types of potentially expressive activities that produce special harms distinct from their communicative impact, such practices are entitled to no constitutional protection.

FOR DISCUSSION

What does it mean to be a "public accommodation"? Why did the Court not see gender as core to the mission of the Jaycees?

BOY SCOUTS OF AMERICA V. JAMES DALE

530 U.S. 640, 120 S.Ct. 2446, 147 L.Ed.2d 554 (2000)

A New Jersey chapter of the Boy Scouts of America revoked the membership of a former Eagle Scout when they learned that he had publicly announced that he was gay. The Scouts believed being gay was inconsistent with the values of their organization. The New Jersey Supreme Court ruled the revocation of the membership illegal under a state public accommodations law. The Boy Scouts appealed.

Vote: 5–4

CHIEF JUSTICE REHNQUIST delivered the opinion of the Court.

Petitioners are the Boy Scouts of America and the Monmouth Council, a division of the Boy Scouts of America (collectively, Boy Scouts). The Boy Scouts is a private, not-for-profit organization engaged in instilling its system of values in young people. The Boy Scouts asserts that homosexual conduct is inconsistent with the values it seeks to instill. Respondent is James Dale, a former Eagle Scout whose adult membership in the Boy Scouts was revoked when the Boy Scouts learned that he is an avowed homosexual and gay rights activist. The New Jersey Supreme Court held that New Jersey's public accommodations law requires that the Boy Scouts readmit Dale. This case presents the question whether applying New Jersey's public accommodations law in this way violates the Boy Scouts' First Amendment right of expressive association. We hold that it does.

I

James Dale entered Scouting in 1978 at the age of eight by joining Monmouth Council's Cub Scout Pack 142. Dale became a Boy Scout in 1981 and remained a Scout until he turned 18. By all accounts, Dale was an exemplary Scout. In 1988, he achieved the rank of Eagle Scout, one of Scouting's highest honors.

Dale applied for adult membership in the Boy Scouts in 1989. The Boy Scouts approved his application for the position of assistant scoutmaster of Troop 73. Around the same time, Dale left home to attend Rutgers University. After arriving at Rutgers, Dale first acknowledged to himself and others that he is gay. He quickly became involved with, and eventually became the copresident of, the Rutgers University Lesbian/Gay Alliance. In 1990, Dale attended a seminar addressing the psychological and health needs of lesbian and gay teenagers. A newspaper covering the event interviewed Dale about his advocacy of homosexual teenagers' need for gay role models. In early July 1990, the newspaper published the interview and Dale's photograph over a caption identifying him as the copresident of the Lesbian/Gay Alliance.

Later that month, Dale received a letter from Monmouth Council Executive James Kay revoking his adult membership. Dale wrote to Kay requesting the reason for Monmouth Council's decision. Kay responded by letter that the Boy Scouts "specifically forbid membership to homosexuals."

II

In *Roberts v. United States Jaycees,* 468 U.S. 609 (1984), we observed that "implicit in the right to engage in activities protected by the First Amendment" is "a corresponding right to associate with others in pursuit of a wide variety of political, social, economic, educational, religious, and cultural ends." This right is crucial in preventing the majority from imposing its views on groups that would rather express other, perhaps unpopular, ideas. [See *ibid.* (stating that protection of the right to expressive association is "especially important in preserving political and cultural diversity and in shielding dissident expression from suppression by the majority"). Can this be deleted? MDD] Government actions that may unconstitutionally burden this freedom may take many forms, one of which is "intrusion into the internal structure or affairs of an association" like a "regulation that forces the group to accept members it does not desire." Forcing a group to accept certain members may impair the ability of the group to express those views, and only those views, that it intends to express. Thus, "[f]reedom of association . . . plainly presupposes a freedom not to associate."

The forced inclusion of an unwanted person in a group infringes the group's freedom of expressive association if the presence of that person affects in a significant way the group's ability to advocate public or private viewpoints. But the freedom of expressive association, like many freedoms, is not absolute. We have held that the freedom could be overridden "by regulations adopted to serve compelling state interests, unrelated to the suppression of ideas, that cannot be achieved through means significantly less restrictive of associational freedoms."

To determine whether a group is protected by the First Amendment's expressive associational right, we must determine whether the group engages in "expressive association." The First Amendment's protection of expressive association is not reserved for advocacy groups. But to come within its ambit, a group must engage in some form of expression, whether it be public or private.

Because this is a First Amendment case where the ultimate conclusions of law are virtually inseparable from findings of fact, we are obligated to independently review the factual record to ensure that the state court's judgment does not unlawfully intrude on free expression. The record reveals the following. The Boy Scouts is a private, nonprofit organization. According to its mission statement:

It is the mission of the Boy Scouts of America to serve others by helping to instill values in young people and, in other ways, to prepare them to make ethical choices over their lifetime in achieving their full potential.

The values we strive to instill are based on those found in the Scout Oath and Law:

Scout Oath

On my honor I will do my best

To do my duty to God and my country

and to obey the Scout Law;

To help other people at all times;

To keep myself physically strong,

mentally awake, and morally straight.

Scout Law

A Scout is:

Trustworthy Obedient

Loyal Cheerful

Helpful Thrifty

Friendly Brave

Courteous Clean

Kind Reverent.

Thus, the general mission of the Boy Scouts is clear: "[T]o instill values in young people." The Boy Scouts seeks to instill these values by having its adult leaders spend time with the youth members, instructing and engaging them in activities like camping, archery, and fishing. During the time spent with the youth members, the scoutmasters and assistant scoutmasters inculcate them with the Boy Scouts' values—both expressly and by example. It seems indisputable that an association that seeks to transmit such a system of values engages in expressive activity.

Given that the Boy Scouts engages in expressive activity, we must determine whether the forced inclusion of Dale as an assistant scoutmaster would significantly affect the Boy Scouts' ability to advocate public or private viewpoints. This inquiry necessarily requires us first to explore, to a limited extent, the nature of the Boy Scouts' view of homosexuality.

The values the Boy Scouts seeks to instill are "based on" those listed in the Scout Oath and Law. App. 184. The Boy Scouts explains that the Scout Oath and Law provide "a positive moral code for living; they are a list of 'do's' rather than 'don'ts.' " The Boy Scouts asserts that homosexual conduct is inconsistent with the values embodied in the Scout Oath and Law, particularly with the values represented by the terms "morally straight" and "clean."

Obviously, the Scout Oath and Law do not expressly mention sexuality or sexual orientation. And the terms "morally straight" and "clean" are by no means self-defining. Different people would attribute to those terms very different meanings. For example, some people may believe that engaging in homosexual conduct is not at odds with being "morally straight" and "clean." And others may believe that engaging in homosexual conduct is contrary to being "morally straight" and "clean." The Boy Scouts says it falls within the latter category.

The Boy Scouts asserts that it "teach[es] that homosexual conduct is not morally straight," and that it does "not want to promote homosexual conduct as a legitimate form of behavior." We accept the Boy Scouts' assertion. We need not inquire further to determine the nature of the Boy Scouts' expression with respect to homosexuality. But because the record before us contains written evidence of the Boy Scouts' viewpoint, we look to it as instructive, if only on the question of the sincerity of the professed beliefs.

The New Jersey Supreme Court determined that the Boy Scouts' ability to disseminate its message was not significantly affected by the forced inclusion of Dale as an assistant scoutmaster because of the following findings:

> "oy Scout members do not associate for the purpose of disseminating the belief that homosexuality is immoral; Boy Scouts discourages its leaders from disseminating *any* views on sexual issues; and Boy Scouts includes sponsors and members who subscribe to different views in respect of homosexuality.

We disagree with the New Jersey Supreme Court's conclusion drawn from these findings.

First, associations do not have to associate for the "purpose" of disseminating a certain message in order to be entitled to the protections of the First Amendment. An association must merely engage in expressive activity that could be impaired in order to be entitled to protection. For example, the purpose of the St. Patrick's

Day parade in *Hurley* [*v. Irish-American Gay, Lesbian & Bisexual Group of Boston, Inc.,* 515 U.S. 557, 1995] was not to espouse any views about sexual orientation, but we held that the parade organizers had a right to exclude certain participants nonetheless.

Second, even if the Boy Scouts discourages Scout leaders from disseminating views on sexual issues—a fact that the Boy Scouts disputes with contrary evidence—the First Amendment protects the Boy Scouts' method of expression. If the Boy Scouts wishes Scout leaders to avoid questions of sexuality and teach only by example, this fact does not negate the sincerity of its belief discussed above.

Third, the First Amendment simply does not require that every member of a group agree on every issue in order for the group's policy to be "expressive association." The Boy Scouts takes an official position with respect to homosexual conduct, and that is sufficient for First Amendment purposes. In this same vein, Dale makes much of the claim that the Boy Scouts does not revoke the membership of heterosexual Scout leaders that openly disagree with the Boy Scouts' policy on sexual orientation. But if this is true, it is irrelevant. The presence of an avowed homosexual and gay rights activist in an assistant scoutmaster's uniform sends a distinctly different message from the presence of a heterosexual assistant scoutmaster who is on record as disagreeing with Boy Scouts policy. The Boy Scouts has a First Amendment right to choose to send one message but not the other. The fact that the organization does not trumpet its views from the housetops, or that it tolerates dissent within its ranks, does not mean that its views receive no First Amendment protection.

Having determined that the Boy Scouts is an expressive association and that the forced inclusion of Dale would significantly affect its expression, we inquire whether the application of New Jersey's public accommodations law to require that the Boy Scouts accept Dale as an assistant scoutmaster runs afoul of the Scouts' freedom of expressive association. We conclude that it does.

The judgment of the New Jersey Supreme Court is reversed, and the case is remanded for further proceedings not inconsistent with this opinion.

FOR DISCUSSION

How does this case differ from *Roberts*? How is the Scout's oath used in this case? Are you persuaded by the majority about the differences between the two cases in terms of how they justify their holdings to apply or rejection application of civil rights laws to the two organizations?

HURLEY V. IRISH-AMERICAN GAY, LESBIAN AND BISEXUAL GROUP OF BOSTON, INC.

515 U.S. 557, 115 S.Ct. 2338, 132 L.Ed.2d 487 (1995)

Annually the City of Boston issues a parade permit to an organization of Irish-Americans to hold the St. Patrick's Day parade. A group representing gay, lesbian, and bisexual Irish-Americans sought to compel the group sponsoring the parade to let them march in it after the latter refused. The state courts ordered the Irish-American Gay, Lesbian and Bisexual Group of Boston to be allowed to march in the St. Patrick's Day parade, and its organizers appealed.

Vote: 9–0

JUSTICE SOUTER delivered the opinion of the Court.

The issue in this case is whether Massachusetts may require private citizens who organize a parade to include among the marchers a group imparting a message the organizers do not wish to convey. We hold that such a mandate violates the First Amendment.

I

March 17 is set aside for two celebrations in South Boston. As early as 1737, some people in Boston observed the feast of the apostle to Ireland, and since 1776 the day has marked the evacuation of royal troops and Loyalists from the city, prompted by the guns captured at Ticonderoga and set up on Dorchester Heights under General Washington's command. Washington himself reportedly drew on the earlier tradition in choosing "St. Patrick" as the response to "Boston," the password used in the colonial lines on evacuation day. Although the General Court of Massachusetts did not officially designate March 17 as Evacuation Day until 1938, the City Council of Boston had previously sponsored public celebrations of Evacuation Day, including notable commemorations on the centennial in 1876, and on the 125th anniversary in 1901, with its parade, salute, concert, and fireworks display.

Through 1992, the city allowed the Council to use the city's official seal, and provided printing services as well as direct funding.

In 1992, a number of gay, lesbian, and bisexual descendants of the Irish immigrants joined together with other supporters to form the respondent organization, GLIB, to march in the parade as a way to express pride in their Irish heritage as openly gay, lesbian, and bisexual individuals, to demonstrate that there are such men and women among those so descended, and to express their solidarity with like individuals who sought to march in New York's St. Patrick's Day Parade. Although the Council denied GLIB's application to take part in the 1992 parade, GLIB obtained a state-court order to include its contingent, which marched "uneventfully" among that year's 10,000 participants and 750,000 spectators.

In 1993, after the Council had again refused to admit GLIB to the upcoming parade, the organization and some of its members filed this suit against the Council, the individual petitioner John J. "Wacko" Hurley, and the city of Boston, alleging violations of the State and Federal Constitutions and of the state public accommodations law, which prohibits "any distinction, discrimination or restriction on account of . . . sexual orientation . . . relative to the admission of any person to, or treatment in any place of public accommodation, resort or amusement."

II

Given the scope of the issues as originally joined in this case, it is worth noting some that have fallen aside in the course of the litigation, before reaching us. Although the Council presents us with a First Amendment claim, respondents do not. Neither do they press a claim that the Council's action has denied them equal protection of the laws in violation of the Fourteenth Amendment. While the guarantees of free speech and equal protection guard only against encroachment by the government and "erec[t] no shield against merely private conduct, respondents originally argued that the Council's conduct was not purely private, but had the character of state action. The trial court's review of the city's involvement led it to find otherwise, however, and although the Supreme Judicial Court did not squarely address the issue, it appears to have affirmed the trial court's decision on that point as well as the others. In any event, respondents have not brought that question up either in a cross-petition for certiorari or in their briefs filed in this Court. When asked at oral argument whether they challenged the conclusion by the Massachusetts' courts that no state action is involved in the parade, respondents' counsel answered that they "do not press that issue here." In this Court, then, their claim for inclusion in the parade rests solely on the Massachusetts public accommodations law.

There is no corresponding concession from the other side, however, and certainly not to the state courts' characterization of the parade as lacking the element of expression for purposes of the First Amendment.

III

A

If there were no reason for a group of people to march from here to there except to reach a destination, they could make the trip without expressing any message beyond the fact of the march itself. Some people might call such a procession a parade, but it would not be much of one. Real "[p]arades are public dramas of social relations, and in them performers define who can be a social actor and what subjects and ideas are available for communication and consideration." Hence, we use the word "parade" to indicate marchers who are making some sort of collective point, not just to each other but to bystanders along the way. Indeed, a parade's dependence on watchers is so extreme that nowadays, as with Bishop Berkeley's celebrated tree, "if a parade or demonstration receives no media coverage, it may as well not have happened." Parades are thus a form of expression, not just motion, and the inherent expressiveness of marching to make a point explains our cases involving protest marches. In *Gregory v. City of Chicago,* 394 U.S. 111 (1969), for example, petitioners had taken part in a procession to express their grievances to the city government, and we held that such a "march, if peaceful and orderly, falls well within the sphere of conduct protected by the First Amendment." Similarly, in *Edwards v. South Carolina,* 372 U.S. 229 (1963), where petitioners had joined in a march of protest and pride, carrying placards and singing The Star Spangled Banner, we held that the activities "reflect an exercise of these basic constitutional rights in their most pristine and classic form.

The protected expression that inheres in a parade is not limited to its banners and songs, however, for the Constitution looks beyond written or spoken words as mediums of expression. Noting that "[s]ymbolism is a primitive but effective way of communicating ideas," our cases have recognized that the First Amendment shields such acts as saluting a flag (and refusing to do so), wearing an armband to protest a war, displaying a red flag, and even "[m]arching, walking or parading" in uniforms displaying the swastika.

C

"Since *all* speech inherently involves choices of what to say and what to leave unsaid," one important manifestation of the principle of free speech is that one who chooses to speak may also decide "what not to say," Although the State may at times "prescribe what shall be orthodox in commercial advertising" by requiring the dissemination of "purely factual and uncontroversial information," outside that context it may not compel affirmance of a belief with which the speaker disagrees. Indeed this general rule, that the speaker has the right to tailor the speech, applies not only to expressions of value, opinion, or endorsement, but equally to statements of fact the speaker would rather avoid subject, perhaps, to the permissive law of defamation, Nor is the rule's benefit restricted to the press, being enjoyed by business corporations generally and by ordinary people engaged in unsophisticated expression as well as by professional publishers. Its point is simply the point of all speech protection, which is to shield just those choices of content that in someone's eyes are misguided, or even hurtful.

Petitioners' claim to the benefit of this principle of autonomy to control one's own speech is as sound as the South Boston parade is expressive. Rather like a composer, the Council selects the expressive units of the parade from potential participants, and though the score may not produce a particularized message, each contingent's expression in the Council's eyes comports with what merits celebration on that day. Even if this view gives the Council credit for a more considered judgment than it actively made, the Council clearly decided to exclude a message it did not like from the communication it chose to make, and that is enough to invoke its right as a private speaker to shape its expression by speaking on one subject while remaining silent on another.

The message it disfavored is not difficult to identify. Although GLIB's point (like the Council's) is not wholly articulate, a contingent marching behind the organization's banner would at least bear witness to the fact that some Irish are gay, lesbian, or bisexual, and the presence of the organized marchers would suggest their view that people of their sexual orientations have as much claim to unqualified social acceptance as heterosexuals and indeed as members of parade units organized around other identifying characteristics. The parade's organizers may not believe these facts about Irish sexuality to be so, or they may object to unqualified social acceptance of gays and lesbians or have some other reason for wishing to keep GLIB's message out of the parade. But whatever the reason, it boils down to the choice of a speaker not to propound a particular point of view, and that choice is presumed to lie beyond the government's power to control.

IV

Our holding today rests not on any particular view about the Council's message but on the Nation's commitment to protect freedom of speech. Disapproval of a private speaker's statement does not legitimize use of the Commonwealth's power to compel the speaker to alter the message by including one more acceptable to others. Accordingly, the judgment of the Supreme Judicial Court is reversed, and the case is remanded for proceedings not inconsistent with this opinion.

It is so ordered.

FOR DISCUSSION

Should groups have a right to decide who gets to join or maintain membership in their respective organizations? Do you think the decision in *Hurley* would have been different if the parade organizers wanted to exclude women or people of color? What if Dale had been a minor scout rather than an adult leader? Could private individuals decide they do not want to associate with gays, lesbians, transsexuals, or same-sex married couples?

HUTCHINS V. DISTRICT OF COLUMBIA

188 F.3d 531, 338 (C.A.D.C., 1999) *En banc*

The District of Columbia enacted a youth curfew ordinance banning individuals under the age of eighteen from being out in public during certain hours. The ordinance allowed several exceptions (called "defenses") to the ban. Parents, minors, and business owners challenged the curfew in court as a violation of the First Amendment.

Vote: 6–5

JUDGE SILBERMAN delivered the majority opinion.

The District of Columbia appeals the district court's grant of summary judgment to plaintiffs/appellees, a group of minors, parents, and a private business, enjoining enforcement of the District's Juvenile Curfew, and holding that it violates the fundamental rights of minors and their parents and is unconstitutionally vague. A divided panel of our circuit affirmed the district court, and rehearing *en banc* was granted. A plurality believes that the curfew implicates no fundamental rights of minors or their parents. Even assuming the curfew does implicate such rights, we hold that it survives heightened scrutiny. And, it does not violate the First or Fourth Amendment rights of minors.

I

The District of Columbia Council, determining that juvenile crime and victimization in the District was a serious problem—and growing worse—unanimously adopted the Juvenile Curfew Act of 1995, which bars juveniles 16 and under from being in a public place unaccompanied by a parent or without equivalent adult supervision from 11:00 P.M. on Sunday through Thursday to 6:00 A.M. on the following day and from midnight to 6:00 A.M. on Saturday and Sunday, subject to certain enumerated defenses. The curfew contains eight "defenses": it is not violated if the minor is (1) accompanied by the minor's parent or guardian or any other person 21 years or older authorized by a parent to be a caretaker for the minor; (2) on an errand at the direction of the minor's parent, guardian, or caretaker, without any detour or stop; (3) in a vehicle involved in interstate travel; (4) engaged in certain employment activity, or going to or from employment, without any detour or stop; (5) involved in an emergency; (6) on the sidewalk that abuts the minor's or the next-door neighbor's residence, if the neighbor has not complained to the police; (7) in attendance at an official school, religious, or other recreational activity sponsored by the District of Columbia, a civic organization, or another similar entity that takes responsibility for the minor, or going to or from, without any detour or stop, such an activity supervised by adults; or (8) exercising First Amendment rights, including free exercise of religion, freedom of speech, and the right of assembly. If, after questioning an apparent offender to determine his age and reason for being in a public place, a police officer reasonably believes that an offense has occurred under the curfew law and that no defense exists, the minor will be detained by the police and then released into the custody of the minor's parent, guardian, or an adult acting *in loco parentis*. If no one claims responsibility for the minor, the minor may be taken either to his residence or placed into the custody of the Family Services Administration until 6:00 A.M. the following morning. Minors found in violation of the curfew may be ordered to perform up to 25 hours of community service for each violation, while parents violating the curfew may be fined up to $500 or required to perform community service, and may be required to attend parenting classes.

II

A

Appellees contend (and the district court determined) that the curfew infringes on a *substantive* fundamental right—the right to free movement—and as a substantive right it cannot be taken away merely through "due process." Of course a right to free movement is a synonym for the right to liberty; when one is put in jail it is obvious that one's right to free movement has been curtailed, but that is constitutionally permissible if the person whose liberty has been curtailed is afforded due process. But any government impingement on a *substantive* fundamental right to free movement would be measured under a strict scrutiny standard and would be justified only if the infringement is narrowly tailored to serve a compelling state interest.

We think that juveniles do not have a fundamental right to be on the streets at night without adult supervision. The Supreme Court has already rejected the idea that juveniles have a right to "come and go at will" because "juveniles, unlike adults, are always in some form of custody," and we see no reason why the asserted right here would fare any better. That the rights of juveniles are not necessarily coextensive with those of adults is undisputed, and "unemancipated minors lack some of the most fundamental rights of self-determination—including even the right of liberty in its narrow sense, *i.e.*, the right to come and go at will." While appellees claim that this reasoning obscures the difference between parental custody and governmental custody, appellees necessarily concede that juveniles are always in *some* form of custody. Not only is it anomalous to say that juveniles have a right to be unsupervised when they are always in some form of custody, but the recognition of such a right would fly in the face of the state's well-established powers of *parens patriae* in preserving and promoting the welfare of children. The state's authority over children's activities is unquestionably broader than that over like actions of adults. See *Prince v. Massachusetts,* 321 U.S. 158 (1944), (observing that the state's power to prohibit street preaching by "children not accompanied by an older person hardly seems open to question").

And it would be inconsistent to find a fundamental right here, when the Court has concluded that the state may intrude upon the "freedom" of juveniles in a variety of similar circumstances without implicating fundamental rights, and can do so in far more intrusive ways than is contemplated here.

Neither does the asserted right here have deep roots in our "history and tradition." As the District noted, juvenile curfews were not uncommon early in our history, nor are they uncommon now. That juvenile curfews are common is, of course, not conclusive in determining whether they comport with due process, but the historical prevalence of such laws is "plainly worth considering" in determining whether the practice " 'offends some principle of justice so deeply rooted in the traditions and conscience of our people as to be ranked as fundamental.' " In sum, neither history nor precedent supports the existence of a fundamental right for juveniles to be in a public place without adult supervision during curfew hours, and we decline to recognize one here.

TATEL, CIRCUIT JUDGE, dissenting.

I agree with Judge Rogers that the District of Columbia juvenile curfew implicates a fundamental right to free movement and that the right should be defined without regard to the age of the right-holder. I join Judge Rogers's conclusion that this curfew fails to survive even intermediate scrutiny. Modeled nearly verbatim on a Dallas juvenile curfew "without apparent determination that circumstances here warranted exactly the same solution," and made permanent by the D.C. Council without any assessment of its effectiveness simply to avoid mooting this litigation when the initial temporary measure expired, the D.C. curfew applies at specific times to juveniles of specific ages despite virtually no record evidence that the particular restrictions will deter crime by and against the city's youth.

FOR DISCUSSION

Should age be a factor determining the extent of First Amendment rights for individuals? What if, in this case, parents had permitted their children to be outside during curfew hours? Would there have been a different First Amendment issue here?

RELATED CASE

Other state and federal courts have litigated youth curfew laws, and some of these acts have been upheld. In *Hodgkins ex rel. Hodgkins v. Peterson* (355 F.3d 1048, 7th Cir., 2004), the Seventh Circuit Court of Appeals invalidated an Indiana youth curfew law, holding that it violated the First Amendment expressive rights of the minors, as well as those of parents.

UNITED MINE WORKERS OF AMERICA, DIST. 12 V. ILLINOIS STATE BAR ASS'N

389 U.S. 217, 88 S.Ct. 353, 19 L.Ed.2d 426 (1967)

Labor union hired an attorney on a salaried basis to assist its members with workers compensation issues. Illinois State Bar Association and others to enjoin union from engaging in practices alleged to constitute unauthorized practice of law. The Circuit Court ruled in favor of the bar association and the Illinois Supreme Court affirmed. On certiorari to the US Supreme Court they vacated the judgment and remanded.

Vote: 8–1

JUSTICE BLACK wrote for the Court.

The Illinois State Bar Association and others filed this complaint to enjoin the United Mine Workers of America, District 12, from engaging in certain practices alleged to constitute the unauthorized practice of law. The essence of the complaint was that the Union had employed a licensed attorney on a salary basis to represent any of its members who wished his services to prosecute workmen's compensation claims before the Illinois Industrial Commission. The trial court found from facts that were not in dispute that employment of an attorney by the association for this purpose did constitute unauthorized practice and permanently enjoined the Union from '(e)mploying attorneys on salary or retainer basis to represent its members with respect to Workmen's Compensation claims and any and all other claims which they may have under the statutes and laws of Illinois.' The Illinois Supreme Court rejected the Mine Workers' contention that this decree abridged their freedom of speech, petition, and assembly under the First and Fourteenth Amendments and affirmed.

The Illinois Supreme Court rejected petitioner's contention that its members had a right, protected by the First and Fourteenth Amendments, to join together and assist one another in the assertion of their legal rights by collectively hiring an attorney to handle their claims. That court held that our decision in *Railroad Trainmen v. Virginia Bar*, [149 S.E.2d 265 (1966)], protected plans under which workers were advised to consult specific attorneys, but did not extend to protect plans involving an explicit hiring of such attorneys by the union. The Illinois court recognized that in *NAACP v. Button*, [371 U.S. 415 (1963)], we also held protected a plan under which the attorneys recommended to members were actually paid by the association, but the Illinois court viewed the *Button* case as concerned chiefly with litigation that can be characterized as a form of political expression. We do not think our decisions in *Trainmen* and *Button* can be so narrowly limited. We hold that the freedom of speech, assembly, and petition guaranteed by the First and Fourteenth Amendments gives petitioner the right to hire attorneys on a salary basis to assist its members in the assertion of their legal rights.

We start with the premise that the rights to assemble peaceably and to petition for a redress or grievances are among the most precious of the liberties safeguarded by the Bill of Rights. These rights, moreover, are intimately connected both in origin and in purpose, with the other First Amendment rights of free speech and free press. The First Amendment would, however, be a hollow promise if it left government free to destroy or erode its guarantees by indirect restraints so long as no law is passed that prohibits free speech, press, petition, or assembly as such. We have therefore repeatedly held that laws which actually affect the exercise of these vital rights cannot be sustained merely because they were enacted for the purpose of dealing with some evil within the State's legislative competence, or even because the laws do in fact provide a helpful means of dealing with such an evil.

The decree at issue here thus substantially impairs the associational rights of the Mine Workers and is not needed to protect the State's interest in high standards of legal ethics. In the many years the program has been in operation, there has come to light, so far as we are aware, not one single instance of abuse, of harm to clients, of any actual disadvantage to the public or to the profession, resulting from the mere fact of the financial connection between the Union and the attorney who represents its members. Since the operative portion of the decree prohibits any financial connection between the attorney and the Union, the decree cannot stand; and to the extent any other part of the decree forbids this arrangement it too must fall.

The judgment and decree are vacated and the case is remanded for proceedings not inconsistent with this opinion. It is so ordered.

Judgment and decree vacated and case remanded.

FOR DISCUSSION

Does the case stand for the proposition that the right to petition the government involves challenging government actions in court?

EDWARDS V. SOUTH CAROLINA

372 U.S. 229, 83 S.Ct. 680, 9 L.Ed.2d 697 (1963)

African-American individuals wishing to protest racial discrimination marched to the state fairgrounds where they were arrested and convicted for breach of peace. The South Carolina Supreme Court affirmed the convictions, and on certiorari the US Supreme Court reversed.

Vote: 8–1

JUSTICE STEWART wrote for the Court.

The petitioners, 187 in number, were convicted in a magistrate's court in Columbia, South Carolina, of the common law crime of breach of the peace. Their convictions were ultimately affirmed by the South Carolina Supreme Court. We granted certiorari, to consider the claim that these convictions cannot be squared with the Fourteenth Amendment of the United States Constitution.

There was no substantial conflict in the trial evidence. Late in the morning of March 2, 1961, the petitioners, high school and college students of the Negro race, met at the Zion Baptist Church in Columbia. From there, at about noon, they walked in separate groups of about 15 to the South Carolina State House grounds, an area of two city blocks open to the general public. Their purpose was 'to submit a protest to the citizens of South Carolina, along with the Legislative Bodies of South Carolina, our feelings and our dissatisfaction with the present condition of discriminatory actions against Negroes, in general, and to let them know that we were dissatisfied and that we would like for the laws which prohibited Negro privileges in this State to be removed.'

Already on the State House grounds when the petitioners arrived were 30 or more law enforcement officers, who had advance knowledge that the petitioners were coming.[2] Each group of petitioners entered the grounds through a driveway and parking area known in the record as the 'horseshoe.' As they entered, they were told by the law enforcement officials that 'they had a right, as a citizen, to go through the State House grounds, as any other citizen has, as long as they were peaceful.' During the next half hour or 45 minutes, the petitioners, in the same small groups, walked single file or two abreast in an orderly way through the grounds, each group carrying placards bearing such messages as 'I am proud to be a Negro' and 'Down with segregation.'

During this time a crowd of some 200 to 300 onlookers had collected in the horseshoe area and on the adjacent sidewalks. There was no evidence to suggest that these onlookers were anything but curious, and no evidence at all of any threatening remarks, hostile gestures, or offensive language on the part of any member of the crowd. The City Manager testified that he recognized some of the onlookers, whom he did not identify, as 'possible trouble makers,' but his subsequent testimony made clear that nobody among the crowd actually caused or threatened any trouble.[4] There was no obstruction of pedestrian or vehicular traffic within the State House grounds.[5] No vehicle was prevented from entering or leaving the horseshoe area. Although vehicular traffic at a nearby street intersection was slowed down somewhat, an officer was dispatched to keep traffic moving. There were a number of bystanders on the public sidewalks adjacent to the State House grounds, but they all moved on when asked to do so, and there was no impediment of pedestrian traffic. Police protection at the scene was at all times sufficient to meet any foreseeable possibility of disorder.

In the situation and under the circumstances thus described, the police authorities advised the petitioners that they would be arrested if they did not disperse within 15 minutes. Instead of dispersing, the petitioners engaged in what the City Manager described as 'boisterous,' 'loud,' and 'flamboyant' conduct, which, as his later testimony made clear, consisted of listening to a 'religious harangue' by one of their leaders, and loudly singing 'The Star Spangled Banner' and other patriotic and religious songs, while stamping their feet and clapping their hands. After 15 minutes had passed, the police arrested the petitioners and marched them off to jail.

Upon this evidence the state trial court convicted the petitioners of breach of the peace, and imposed sentences ranging from a $10 fine or five days in jail, to a $100 fine or 30 days in jail. In affirming the judgments, the Supreme Court of South Carolina said that under the law of that State the offense of breach of the peace 'is not susceptible of exact definition,' but that the 'general definition of the offense' is as follows:

'In general terms, a breach of the peace is a violation of public order, a disturbance of the public tranquility, by any act or conduct inciting to violence, it includes any violation of any law enacted to preserve peace and good order. It may consist of an act of violence or an act likely to produce violence. It is not necessary that the peace be actually broken to lay the foundation for a prosecution for this offense. If what is done is unjustifiable and unlawful, tending with sufficient directness to break the peace, no more is required. Nor is actual personal violence an essential element in the offense.

'By 'peace,' as used in the law in this connection, is meant the tranquility enjoyed by citizens of a municipality or community where good order reigns among its members, which is the natural right of all persons in political society.'

The petitioners contend that there was a complete absence of any evidence of the commission of this offense, and that they were thus denied one of the most basic elements of due process of law. Whatever the merits of this contention, we need not pass upon it in the present case. The state courts have held that the petitioners' conduct constituted breach of the peace under state law, and we may accept their decision as binding upon us to that extent. But it nevertheless remains our duty in a case such as this to make an independent examination of the whole record. And it is clear to us that in arresting, convicting, and punishing the petitioners under the circumstances disclosed by this record, South Carolina infringed the petitioners' constitutionally protected rights of free speech, free assembly, and freedom to petition for redress of their grievances.

It has long been established that these First Amendment freedoms are protected by the Fourteenth Amendment from invasion by the States. The circumstances in this case reflect an exercise of these basic constitutional rights in their most pristine and classic form. The petitioners felt aggrieved by laws of South Carolina which allegedly 'prohibited Negro privileges in this State.' They peaceably assembled at the site of the State Government and there peaceably expressed their grievances 'to the citizens of South Carolina, along with the Legislative Bodies of South Carolina.' Not until they were told by police officials that they must disperse on pain of arrest did they do more. Even then, they but sang patriotic and religious songs after one of their leaders had delivered a 'religious harangue.' There was no violence or threat of violence on their part, or on the part of any member of the crowd watching them. Police protection was 'ample.'

The Fourteenth Amendment does not permit a State to make criminal the peaceful expression of unpopular views. '(A) function of free speech under our system of government is to invite dispute. It may indeed best serve its high purpose when it induces a condition of unrest, creates dissatisfaction with conditions as they are, or even stirs people to anger. Speech is often provocative and challenging. It may strike at prejudices and preconceptions and have profound unsettling effects as it presses for acceptance of an idea. That is why freedom of speech is protected against censorship or punishment, unless shown likely to produce a clear and present danger of a serious substantive evil that rises far above public inconvenience, annoyance, or unrest.

There is no room under our Constitution for a more restrictive view. For the alternative would lead to standardization of ideas either by legislatures, courts, or dominant political or community groups.' As in the *Terminiello* [v. *City of Chicago*, 337 U.S. 1 (1949)] case, the courts of South Carolina have defined a criminal offense so as to permit conviction of the petitioners if their speech 'stirred people to anger, invited public dispute, or brought about a condition of unrest. A conviction resting on any of those grounds may not stand.'

For these reasons we conclude that these criminal convictions cannot stand.

Reversed.

FOR DISCUSSION

Did the Court actually decide this case on the basis of freedom of petition? How are petition and assembly related? Under what circumstances is simply a march a form of petition?

GLOSSARY

Academic Freedom: The right of instructors to teach or espouse ideas in the classroom or in their writings. Academic freedom is recognized as a First Amendment right. in *Keyishian v. Board of Regents of the University of the State of New York.*

Bill of Attainder: Legislation naming or labeling a specific person as guilty of a crime and punishing them without a trial. Bills of attainder are prohibited under Article I, sections 9 and 10 of the Constitution.

***Central Hudson Gas & Electric* Test:** In *Central Hudson Gas & Elec. Corp. v. Public Service Commission of New York* (447 U.S. 557, 1980), the Court devised a four-part test to determine whether commercial speech may be regulated. First, the expression must be protected by the First Amendment. For commercial speech to come within that provision, it must at least concern lawful activity and not be misleading. Second, the Court will ask if the asserted governmental interest to regulate the speech is substantial. If the expression is both protected and meets the "lawful but not misleading" condition, the Court will then ask if the regulation directly advances the governmental interest asserted. Finally, there must be assurance that the regulation is not more extensive than is necessary to serve the stated interest. If all four conditions are met, the commercial speech may be regulated.

Commercial Speech: Traditionally a form of speech that included advertising that was not protected under the First Amendment. However, beginning with *Virginia State Board of Pharmacy v. Virginia Citizens Consumer Council* (425 U.S. 748, 1976), the Court has provided constitutional protection for this form of speech, as long as it is truthful. Commercial speech does not receive the same level of protection accorded individual political speech. In *Central Hudson Gas & Elec. Corp. v. Public Service Commission of New York* the Court devised a test to determine when commercial speech may be regulated.

Fairness Doctrine: A principle adopted by the Federal Communications Commission as a result of congressional legislation requiring television and radio stations to give each side fair coverage in the discussing of public issues. Although upheld as constitutional in *Red Lion Broadcasting Co. v. F.C.C,* (395 U.S. 367, 1969), the fairness doctrine was repudiated by the FCC in 1987.

Free Press/Fair Trial: A constitutional tension between the First Amendment right of the press and the public to observe open trials versus the Sixth Amendment right of criminal defendants to have a fair and impartial trial, a right that could be impaired by adverse publicity before and during trial.

***Miller* test:** This is the test to determine what sexually explicit materials are obscene. The test asks "(a) whether 'the average person, applying contemporary community standards' would find that the work, taken as a whole, appeals to the prurient interest; (b) whether the work depicts or describes, in a patently offensive way, sexual conduct specifically defined by the applicable state law; and (c) whether the work, taken as a whole, lacks serious literary, artistic, political, or scientific value." See **obscenity.**

Non-obscene Nude Dancing: A form of expression that receives minimal First Amendment protection according to the Court in *Barnes v. Glen Theatre, Inc.* (501 U.S. 560, 1991).

Obscenity: The quality of sexually explicit materials that is not protected by the First Amendment. The *Miller* test, from *Miller v. California* (413 U.S. 15, 1973), is used to determine what is obscene.

Pornography: Sexually explicit materials that receive some First Amendment free speech protection.

Prior Restraint: The prevention of the media from publishing a story or idea for national security or other reasons. The government carries a very high burden to enjoin a publication; only one federal district court decision in American history—*United States of America, v. The Progressive, Inc.*—has allowed for prior restraint, and its ruling was overturned on appeal.

Public Officials: Elected or appointed government officers who, according to the Court in *New York Times v. Sullivan* (376 U.S. 254, 1964), need to show actual malice or reckless disregard for the truth in order to win a libel suit against the media or others who criticize them. The actual malice test was devised to protect the media from libel suits even if some of the statements alleged as facts are not completely accurate. The rationale for this standard is to protect freedom of press, as guaranteed by the First Amendment.

Reckless Disregard for the Truth: The standard of proof the Court defined in *New York Times v. Sullivan* (376 U.S. 254, 1964), which must be met to establish libel of public officials by the media. Subsequently in *Associated Press v. Walker* (389 U.S. 28, 1967), the Court applied the same standard of proof to those attempting to show libel against public figures.

Reporter's Privilege: The right of a news reporter to refuse to divulge the source of a story when subpoenaed by a court. In *Branzburg v. Hayes* (408 U.S. 665, 1972), the Court rejected arguments that the First Amendment protects this privilege.

Secondary Effects: These include the prevalence of drugs, prostitution, and other forms of crime often found in association with the operation of adult entertainment establishments. In *City of Renton v. Playtime Theatres, Inc.* (475 U.S. 41, 1986), the Court stated that state and local governments can address concerns about the secondary effects of adult entertainment by means of regulations such as zoning laws without violating the First Amendment.

Youth Curfew Laws: Laws that prohibit minors from being out in public during certain times unless accompanied by the parents or for specified reasons. Courts are split on the constitutionality of these laws.

SELECTED BIBLIOGRAPHY

Alexander, Larry. 2005. *Is There a Right of Freedom of Expression?* New York: Cambridge University Press.

Bobbitt, Philip. 1991. *Constitutional Interpretation.* Cambridge, MA: Blackwell.

Bollinger, Lee C. 1986. *The Tolerant Society.* New York: Clarendon Press.

Bosmajian, Haig. 1999. *The Freedom Not to Speak.* New York: NYU Press.

Chaffee, Zechariah, Jr. 1964. *Free Speech in the United States* Cambridge, MA: Harvard University Press.

Graber, Mark A. 1991. *Transforming Free Speech: The Ambiguous Legacy of Civil Libertarianism.* Berkeley: University of California Press.

Greenwalt, Kent. 1989. *Speech, Crime, and the Uses of Language.* New York: Oxford University Press.

Kalven, Harry, Jr. 1988. *A Worthy Tradition: Freedom of Speech in America.* New York: Harper & Row.

Levy, Leonard W. 1985. *Emergence of a Free Press.* New York: Oxford University Press.

Levy, Leonard W. 1989. *Original Intent and the Framers' Constitution.* New York: Macmillan.

Poe, Lucas A., Jr. 1991. *The Fourth Estate and the Constitution: Freedom of the Press in America.* Berkeley: University of California Press.

Russell, Margaret M. 2010. *Freedom of Assembly and Petition: The First Amendment, Its Constitutional History and the Contemporary Debate.* New York: Prometheus Books.

Shiffrin, Steven H. 1990. *The First Amendment, Democracy, and Romance.* Cambridge, MA: Harvard University Press.

Smith, Jeffrey Alan. 1999. *War and Press Freedom: The Problem of Prerogative Power.* Chicago: Chicago University Press.

Tedford, Thomas. 1985. *Freedom of Speech in the United States.* New York: Random House.

Tribe, Laurence H., and Michael C. Dorf. 1991. *On Reading the Constitution.* Cambridge, MA: Harvard University Press.

Van Alstyne, William W. 1984. *Interpretations of the First Amendment.* Durham, NC: Duke University Press.

CHAPTER V

The Second Amendment: The Right to Bear Arms

Timeline: The Second Amendment: The Right to Bear Arms

1689	English Bill of Rights allowed Protestants to own guns for their protection
c1700	The long rifle (often called the Kentucky or Pennsylvania rifle) became a staple of the American frontier.
1775	Battles of Lexington and Concord were precipitated by British attempts to confiscate rebel military supplies.
1787	Constitutional Convention meeting in Philadelphia drafts U.S. Constitution, which recognizes rights of states to maintain their own militia.
1789	Constitution goes into effect. Congress proposes 12 amendments that will become the Bill of Rights.
1791	The Second Amendment was ratified as the second of 10 amendments now known as the Bill of Rights.
1860	The Henry Rifle repeating rifle went into production.
1861	The U.S. Civil War began
1862	The Gatling gun, a precursor to machine guns, was patented.
1865	U.S. Civil War ends with a Union victory.
	John Wilkes Booth assassinated President Abraham Lincoln with a handgun.
	Southern states begin adopting Black Codes, which sought to limit African-American gun ownership.
1866	Ku Klux Klan (KKK) founded in Pulaski, Tennessee and quickly became associated with physical intimidation of African-Americans.
	First Winchester repeating rifle.
1868	The Fourteenth Amendment extends certain rights of citizens to all persons born or naturalized within the United States.
1870–71	Congress adopts Enforcement Acts, designed to protect the rights of newly-freed African-Americans.
1871	National Rifle Association was founded.

1875 In *United States v. Cruikshank* the Supreme Court determined that the Fourteenth Amendment does not incorporate the Second Amendment to the states or protect citizens from civil rights violations from private citizens.

1886 The Supreme Court in *Presser v. Illinois* does not prohibit states from regulating private militias.

1920 St. Valentine's Day Massacre, which involved death of seven gang members in Chicago drew attention to problems of gun violence, much of which was connected to national alcoholic prohibition.

1934 National Firearms Act required the registration of certain weapons such as fully automatic weapons and sawed-off shotguns.

1939 In *United States v. Miller* the Supreme Court recognized the right of states to regulate the private ownership of firearms.

1963 President John F. Kennedy assassinated with a rifle in Dallas, Texas.

1968 New York Senator Robert F. Kennedy and civil rights leader Martin Luther King, Jr. assassinated in separate incidents.

1968 Congress adopts a gun control act prohibiting gun ownership by certain individuals deemed to be threats to public safety.

1980 Mark David Chapman kills John Lennon of the Beatles with a .38-calibar pistol.

1981 John Hinkley, Jr. unsuccessfully attempts to assassinate President Ronald Reagan but wounds him and Press Secretary, James Brady.

1993 Brady Handgun Violence Prevention Act establishes a National Instant Criminal Background Check System that applies to most purchasers of handguns.

1994 Violent Gun Control and Law Enforcement Act banned most semiautomatic assault weapons.

1997 *Printz v. United States* invalidates interim provision of the Brady law, which required state officials to conduct criminal background checks of gun purchasers. In a concurring opinion, Justice Thomas argues that gun ownership is an individual right.

2008 The Supreme Court in *District of Columbia v. Heller* found the Second Amendment confers an individual right to own a firearm for self-defense and other lawful purposes.

2009 *United States v. Hayes* upheld provision of Gun Control Act of 1968 restricting gun ownership by individuals convicted of domestic violence.

2010 In *McDonald v. City of Chicago, Illinois,* the Supreme Court applied the Second Amendment to the states via the Fourteenth Amendment

2012 The massacre of 20 first-graders and 6 teachers in Newtown, Connecticut, like previous firearm attacks, leads both to renewed calls for stricter gun control laws and to calls for giving citizens greater freedom to protect themselves.

2016 Omar Mateen, a 29-year-old security guard, killed 49 people and wounded 53 others in the gay nightclub The Pulse, in Orlando, Florida using a semiautomatic rifle and a handgun.

Second Amendment:

A well regulated militia, being necessary to the security of a free state, the right of the people to keep and bear arms, shall not be infringed.

The Supreme Court's first decision interpreting the Bill of Rights was in 1833 in *Barron v. Baltimore*, 32 U.S. 243. In the over 175 years since that case was decided, the Supreme Court has pronounced hundreds if not thousands of decisions expounding on both incorporation and the meaning of the Bill of Rights. Surprisingly, though, the Court has had little to say about the Second Amendment to the Constitution. Five decisions are regularly cited regarding the interpretation of the meaning of the Second Amendment. In the earliest decisions, rendered in the aftermath of the Civil War and the ratification of the Fourteenth Amendment, the Court ensured that state militias could support the government by maintaining public order. This interpretation meant that the "right to bear arms" was seen as a collective, not individual right, regulated by Congress and the states.

As noted in Chapter VIII, soon after the passage of the Fourteenth Amendment—with its requirement that due process and equal protection rights, and the privileges and immunities of citizenship, be protected by the states for their own citizens—the Court quickly defined these restrictions on the states very narrowly. The rapid consequence was that the Fourteenth Amendment did not protect citizens in the states from other private groups who wished to deny them their constitutional rights—such as voting, owning private property, or even protecting their lives against violence. This meant that the newly freed people in the South, for whom the Fourteenth Amendment was designed in part to protect, could only rely on the Fourteenth Amendment to protect them against direct state action, not against the states' refusal to prosecute white supremacist mobs like the Ku Klux Klan who began a reign of violence in the South. The first case which provided the Supreme Court's interpretation of the Second Amendment, *United States v. Cruikshank* (92 U.S. 542, 1875), rose in that legal context.

A private militia of former Confederate soldiers and members of the Ku Klux Klan attacked a group of black citizens, who had occupied a courthouse to protect Republican office holders, resulting in the Colfax Massacre of many African-Americans. The federal government prosecuted a small number of the almost 100 accused perpetrators under the Fourteenth Amendment claim that these white individuals had denied basic constitutional rights (the right to vote, bear arms, assemble, etc.) to the black citizens they had attacked and/or executed. The Supreme Court found these charges to be vague, and all of the charges were eventually dismissed. The majority opinion noted, "[t]his is one of the amendments that has no other effect than to restrict the powers of the national government." The Court did not find the Second Amendment applicable to the states or to limiting the actions of other individuals. This decision was reinforced by the only two other decisions rendered by the Court on the Second Amendment in the 20th Century.

The 1886 case of *Presser v. Illinois* (116 U.S. 252), while arising under different circumstances, reinforced the *Cruikshank* interpretation of the Second Amendment. Brought by a private white militia in Illinois, which had been constrained by state law from publicly drilling with their weapons, the Court found the Amendment to be "a limitation only on the power of Congress and the national government, and not of the states." Similarly, *United States v. Miller* (307 U.S. 174, 1939), which upheld the constitutionality of the National Firearms Act of 1934, requiring the registering of certain weapons, reinforced the notion that the Second Amendment was a barrier against Congress passing laws that would preclude the state from maintaining an armed militia of its citizens. Because the Second Amendment was seen as a collective right, not an individual right, these decisions made it clear the Court understood the Second Amendment as allowing states to regulate firearm possession and ownership, not inherent to "the preservation or efficiency of a well-regulated militia." The standard of judicial decision making noted in *Miller* was the lowest test of "some reasonable relationship" between the regulation and the constitutional guarantee. While this was the status of the constitutional interpretation, the scope of the Second Amendment was not a closed debate post-1939.

Continuing controversies included the following: Does the text of the amendment protect an individual right to keep and bear arms, or is that a collective right maintained within the context of a militia? Until *District of Columbia v. Heller* (554 U.S. 570) in 2008, the Court had not explicitly addressed this question. The debate between Justices Scalia and Stevens highlights the contrasting ways the Court uses test, history, and precedent in seeking to understand how the language of the Bill of Rights applies in a society centuries removed from that of the Framers.

In *Heller* the Court stated only that the Second Amendment protects an individual right. The decision, as Justice Scalia indicates, does not specify what that right is actually protecting, and he went out of his way to assert that the ruling would not invalidate many traditional restrictions on gun ownership. Moreover, the ruling affects the District of Columbia and the federal government only. The *Heller* decision did not incorporate the Second Amendment to apply to the states, leaving them, presumably, free to restrict gun ownership as before. As a result of *Heller,* many questions remained about the meaning of the Second Amendment. Among them, should the logic of *Carolene Products* footnote number 4 apply? This footnote notes that legislation which is directed against particular minority groups which have been victims of prejudice should be "subjected to more exacting judicial scrutiny."

Heller resolved the debate regarding whether the Second Amendment protects an individual or a collective right, with the majority ruling in the former. Who do you think offered a more persuasive reading of the Second Amendment? Who made the more compelling uses of textual or historical evidence for his reading of the amendment, Justice Scalia or Justice Stevens?

While *Heller* did resolve the individual-collective right issue, it did not answer three other legal questions. First, the Court did not address the scope of the privileges protected by the Second Amendment. Since the First Amendment is not absolute, there is no reason to think the Second will be found to be either, thereby suggesting that the Court will continue to allow some limits on guns. Second, the Court did not describe the level of analysis or degree of scrutiny it would apply in gun cases under the Second Amendment. If the right to bear arms is a fundamental right, will it receive strict scrutiny analysis? Finally, because this was a case arising out of the District of Columbia and not a state the Court did not address the incorporation issue. Is the Second Amendment a right that is incorporated to apply to states via the Fourteenth Amendment? The Court did not address these questions until 2010 in *McDonald v. Chicago* (561 U.S. 742).

In this case the Supreme Court used the Fourteenth Amendment to apply the Second Amendment to the States, requiring them to respect this new individual constitutional right in their regulations of citizen access to firearms. This ruling did not strike down all forms of gun control passed by the states, just as *Heller* did not invalidate all forms of federal gun regulations. It is clear from the majority opinion by Justice Alito that the Second Amendment, like the First, is not an absolute right and can be limited by the state and federal government. However, the decision also opened up challenges to many of the current state laws regulating the ownership and carrying of firearms.

By 2016, all states allowed individuals to carry a concealed weapon; only the District of Columbia prohibited it. Many states adopted "Stand Your Ground" laws that recognize an individual's right to respond to an imminent threat, without a responsibility to retreat, as long as that individual has a right to be there. Other states passed "Duty to Retreat" laws, which prohibits people from resorting to deadly force in self-defense if they are able to avoid harm by running away or other means. There is also great variance in laws regarding the carrying of concealed weapons on college campuses across the country.

Since *McDonald*, a large number of cases have been litigated on these and other grounds, but because there is still no clear standard for constitutional analysis for these cases, there have been mixed results in the lower federal courts. Some state regulations have been upheld as constitutional, while others have been struck down. Among the notable decisions have been that a State may ban firearms on college campuses, *DiGiacinto v. Rector and Visitors of George Mason University*, 281 Va. 127 (2011); juveniles have no right to carry a handgun, *U.S. v. Rene E.*, 583 F.3d 8 (1st Cir. 2009); the Constitution does not protect the right to possess machine guns, *Hamblen v. U.S.*, 591 F. 3d 471 (6th Cir. 2009); states may ban felons from possessing firearms, *U.S. v. Williams*, 616 F. 3d 685 (7th Cir. 2010); and, states may ban persons convicted of domestic violence from possessing firearms, *U.S. v. Skoien*, 614 F. 3d 638 (7th Cir. 2010). These decisions speak to the dicta penned by Scalia in *Heller* that many long-standing gun laws may be constitutional and that the Second Amendment, as seems to be the case with other amendments, is not absolute.

A spate of recent gun massacres, some involving ties to international terrorism, have heighted calls both for stricter gun regulations and for giving citizens more effective measures of protecting themselves. These pressures, and mixed results in the lower federal courts, will likely lead to additional Supreme Court decisions to help clarify the constitutional standard used in applying the Second Amendment to the regulation of weapons.

UNITED STATES V. CRUIKSHANK

92 U.S. 542, 2 Otto 542, 23 L.Ed. 588 (1875)

This case arose after a local white militia in Louisiana murdered an unknown number of Black men (memorialized at 105, reported between 65 and 169). Concerned that local Democrats would try to take control of the parish government, which was evenly divided between black and white officials, an all-black militia took control of the courthouse. Quickly, a white mob of 150 consisting of former Confederate soldiers, members of the Ku Klux Klan, and other violent white supremacist groups surrounded the Courthouse and after a battle, the occupants surrendered and many were murdered. The Colfax Massacre has been remembered by historians as the "bloodiest single instance of racial carnage in the Reconstruction era." Despite the indictment of 97 members of the white mob, only nine men including William J. Cruikshank were charged with violating the Enforcement Acts of 1870 and 1871 (the Ku Klux Klan Acts) to violate the civil rights of black citizens. The counts included denying other citizens lawful assembly, bearing arms, due process of law, equal protection of laws, and the right to vote.

Vote: 5–4

CHIEF JUSTICE WAITE delivered the opinion of the court.

This case comes here with a certificate by the judges of the Circuit Court for the District of Louisiana that they were divided in opinion upon a question which occurred at the hearing. It presents for our consideration an indictment containing sixteen counts, divided into two series of eight counts each, based upon sect. 6 of the Enforcement Act of May 31, 1870. That section is as follows:

> "That if two or more persons shall band or conspire together, or go in disguise upon the public highway, or upon the premises of another, with intent to violate any provision of this act, or to injure, oppress, threaten, or intimidate any citizen, with intent to prevent or hinder his free exercise and enjoyment of any right or privilege granted or secured to him by the Constitution or laws of the United States, or because of his having exercised the same, such persons shall be held guilty of felony, and, on conviction thereof, shall be fined or imprisoned, or both, at the discretion of the court—the fine not to exceed $5,000, and the imprisonment not to exceed ten years—and shall, moreover, be

> thereafter ineligible to, and disabled from holding, any office or place of honor, profit, or trust created by the Constitution or laws of the United States."

The question certified arose upon a motion in arrest of judgment after a verdict of guilty generally upon the whole sixteen counts, and is stated to be whether "the said sixteen counts of said indictment are severally good and sufficient in law, and contain charges of criminal matter indictable under the laws of the United States."

The general charge in the first eight counts is that of "banding," and in the second eight that of "conspiring" together to injure, oppress, threaten, and intimidate Levi Nelson and Alexander Tillman, citizens of the United States, of African descent and persons of color, with the intent thereby to hinder and prevent them in their free exercise and enjoyment of rights and privileges "granted and secured" to them "in common with all other good citizens of the United States by the Constitution and laws of the United States."

We have in our political system a government of the United States and a government of each of the several States. Each one of these governments is distinct from the others, and each has citizens of its own who owe it allegiance and whose rights, within its jurisdiction, it must protect. The same person may be at the same time a citizen of the United States and a citizen of a State, but his rights of citizenship under one of these governments will be different from those he has under the other.

Citizens are the members of the political community to which they belong. They are the people who compose the community, and who, in their associated capacity, have established or submitted themselves to the dominion of a government for the promotion of their general welfare and the protection of their individual as well as their collective rights. In the formation of a government, the people may confer upon it such powers as they choose. The government, when so formed, may, and when called upon should, exercise all the powers it has for the protection of the rights of its citizens and the people within its jurisdiction, but it can exercise no other. The duty of a government to afford protection is limited always by the power it possesses for that purpose.

Experience made the fact known to the people of the United States that they required a national government for national purposes. The separate governments of the separate States, bound together by the articles of confederation alone, were not sufficient for the promotion of the general welfare of the people in respect to foreign nations, or for their complete protection as citizens of the confederated States. For this reason, the people of the United States, "in order to form a more perfect union, establish justice, insure domestic tranquillity, provide for the common defence, promote the general welfare, and secure the blessings of liberty" to themselves and their posterity, ordained and established the government of the United States, and defined its powers by a Constitution, which they adopted as its fundamental law, and made its rule of action.

The government thus established and defined is to some extent a government of the States in their political capacity. It is also, for certain purposes, a government of the people. Its powers are limited in number, but not in degree. Within the scope of its powers, as enumerated and defined, it is supreme, and above the States; but beyond, it has no existence. It was erected for special purposes, and endowed with all the powers necessary for its own preservation and the accomplishment of the ends its people had in view. It can neither grant nor secure to its citizens any right or privilege not expressly or by implication placed under its jurisdiction.

The people of the United States resident within any State are subject to two governments—one State and the other National—but there need be no conflict between the two. The powers which one possesses the other does not. They are established for different purposes, and have separate jurisdictions. Together, they make one whole, and furnish the people of the United States with a complete government, ample for the protection of all their rights at home and abroad. True, it may sometimes happen that a person is amenable to both jurisdictions for one and the same act. Thus, if a marshal of the United States is unlawfully resisted while executing the process of the courts within a State, and the resistance is accompanied by an assault on the officer, the sovereignty of the United States is violated by the resistance, and that of the State by the breach of peace in the assault. So, too, if one passes counterfeited coin of the United States within a State, it may be an offence against the United States and the State: the United States because it discredits the coin, and the State because of the fraud upon him to whom it is passed. This does not, however, necessarily imply that the two governments possess powers in common, or bring them into conflict with each other. It is the natural consequence of a citizenship which owes allegiance to two sovereignties and claims protection from both. The citizen cannot complain, because he has voluntarily submitted himself to such a form of government. He owes allegiance to the two departments, so to speak, and, within their respective spheres, must pay the penalties which each exacts for disobedience to its laws. In return, he can demand protection from each within its own jurisdiction.

The Government of the United States is one of delegated powers alone. Its authority is defined and limited by the Constitution. All powers not granted to it by that instrument are reserved to the States or the people. No rights can be acquired under the Constitution or laws of the United States, except such as the Government of the United States has the authority to grant or secure. All that cannot be so granted or secured are left under the protection of the States.

We now proceed to an examination of the indictment, to ascertain whether the several rights, which it is alleged the defendants intended to interfere with, are such as had been in law and in fact granted or secured by the Constitution or laws of the United States.

The first and ninth counts state the intent of the defendants to have been to hinder and prevent the citizens named in the free exercise and enjoyment of their "lawful right and privilege to peaceably assemble together with each other and with other citizens of the United States for a peaceful and lawful purpose." . . . .

The second and tenth counts are equally defective. The right there specified is that of "bearing arms for a lawful purpose." This is not a right granted by the Constitution. Neither is it in any manner dependent upon that instrument for its existence. The second amendment declares that it shall not be infringed, but this, as has been seen, means no more than that it shall not be infringed by Congress. This is one of the amendments that has no other effect than to restrict the powers of the national government, leaving the people to look for their protection against any violation by their fellow citizens of the rights it recognizes, to what is called, in *The City of New York v. Miln,* 11 Pet. 139, the "powers which relate to merely municipal legislation, or what was, perhaps, more properly called internal police," "not surrendered or restrained" by the Constitution of the United States.

Another objection is made to these counts that they are too vague and uncertain. This will be considered hereafter, in connection with the same objection to other counts.

Inasmuch, therefore, as it does not appear in these counts that the intent of the defendants was to prevent these parties from exercising their right to vote on account of their race, &c., it does not appear that it was their intent to interfere with any right granted or secured by the Constitution or laws of the United States. We may suspect that race was the cause of the hostility, but it is not so averred. This is material to a description of the substance of the offence, and cannot be supplied by implication. Everything essential must be charged positively, and not inferentially. The defect here is not in form, but in substance.

We are therefore of the opinion that the first, second, third, fourth, sixth, seventh, ninth, tenth, eleventh, twelfth, fourteenth, and fifteenth counts do not contain charges of a criminal nature made indictable under the laws of the United States, and that consequently they are not good and sufficient in law. They do not show that it was the intent of the defendants, by their conspiracy, to hinder or prevent the enjoyment of any right granted or secured by the Constitution.

According to the view we take of these counts, the question is not whether it is enough, in general, to describe a statutory offence in the language of the statute, but whether the offence has here been described at all. The statute provides for the punishment of those who conspire "to injure, oppress, threaten, or intimidate any citizen, with intent to prevent or hinder his free exercise and enjoyment of any right or privilege granted or secured to him by the Constitution or laws of the United States."

These counts in the indictment charge, in substance that the intent in this case was to hinder and prevent these citizens in the free exercise and enjoyment of "every, each, all, and singular" the rights granted them by the Constitution, &c. There is no specification of any particular right. The language is broad enough to cover all.

But it is needless to pursue the argument further. The conclusion is irresistible that these counts are too vague and general. They lack the certainty and precision required by the established rules of criminal pleading. It follows that they are not good and sufficient in law. They are so defective that no judgment of conviction should be pronounced upon them.

The order of the Circuit Court arresting the judgment upon the verdict is, therefore, affirmed; and the cause remanded, with instructions to discharge the defendants.

JUSTICE CLIFFORD, dissented.

FOR DISCUSSION

While this case has been cited to justify the limited scope of the Second Amendment and the allowance of state gun control laws, it was decided prior to the incorporation of the Bill of Rights to the states under the Fourteenth Amendment. Should the Fourteenth Amendment protect against citizens violating the constitutional rights of other citizens? Do the extreme facts of this case influence your interpretation? What other remedies might there be when the state is unwilling or unable to protect its own citizens from private forms of violence?

PRESSER V. ILLINOIS

116 U.S. 252, 6 S.Ct. 580, 29 L.Ed. 615 (1886)

The facts of the case are found in the final paragraphs of the decision.

Vote: 9–0

JUSTICE WILLIAM B. WOODS delivered the majority opinion.

The doctrine that statutes constitutional in part only will be upheld as to what is constitutional if it can he separated from the unconstitutional provisions reasserted.

A state statute providing that all able-bodied male citizens of the state between eighteen and forty-five, except those exempted, shall be subject to military duty, and shall be enrolled and designated as the state militia, and prohibiting all bodies of men other than the regularly organized volunteer militia of the state and the troops of the United States from associating together as military organizations or drilling or parading with arms in any city of the state without license from the governor as to these provisions is constitutional, and does not infringe the laws of the United States, and it is sustained as to them, although the act contains other provisions, separable from the foregoing, which it was contended infringed upon the powers vested in the United States by the Constitution or upon laws enacted by Congress in pursuance thereof.

The provision in the Second Amendment to the Constitution, that "The right of the people to keep and bear arms shall not be infringed" is a limitation only on the power of Congress and the national government, and not of the states. But in view of the fact that all citizens capable of bearing arms constitute the reserved military force of the national government as well as in view of its general powers, the states cannot prohibit the people from keeping and bearing arms so as to deprive the United States of their rightful resource for maintaining the public security.

The provision in the Fourteenth Amendment to the Constitution that "No state shall make or enforce any law which shall abridge the privileges or immunities of citizens of the United States" does not prevent a state from passing such laws to regulate the privileges and immunities of its own citizens as do not abridge their privileges and immunities as citizens of the United States.

Unless restrained by their own constitutions, state legislatures may enact statutes to control and regulate all organizations, drilling, and parading of military bodies and associations except those which are authorized by the militia laws of the United States.

Herman Presser, the plaintiff in error, was indicted on September 24, 1879, in the Criminal Court of Cook County, Illinois, far a violation of the following sections of Art. XI of the Military Code of that state, Act of May 28, 1879, Laws of 1879, 192.

> "§ 5. It shall not be lawful for any body of men whatever other than the regular organized volunteer militia of this state and the troops of the United States to associate themselves together as a military company or organization, or to drill or parade with arms in any city or town of this state without the license of the Governor thereof, which license may at any time be revoked, *and provided further* that students in educational institutions where military science is a part of the course of instruction may, with the consent of the Governor, drill and parade with arms in public under the superintendence of their instructors, and may take part in any regimental or brigade encampment under command of their military instructor, and while so encamped shall be governed by the provisions of this act. They shall be entitled only to transportation and subsistence, and shall report and be subject to the commandant of such encampment, *provided* that nothing herein contained shall be construed so as to prevent benevolent or social organizations from wearing swords."

> "§ 6. Whoever offends against the provisions of the preceding section or belongs to or parades with any such unauthorized body of men with arms shall be punished by a fine not exceeding the sum of ten dollars ($10), or by imprisonment in the common jail for a term not exceeding six months, or both."

The indictment charged in substance that Presser, on September 24, 1879, in the County of Cook, in the State of Illinois "did unlawfully belong to and did parade and drill in the City of Chicago with an unauthorized body of men with arms who had associated themselves together as a military company and organization without having a license from the governor, and not being a part of or belonging to 'the regular organized volunteer militia' of the State of Illinois or the troops of the United States."

A motion to quash the indictment was overruled. Presser then pleaded not guilty, and, both parties having waived a jury, the case was tried by the court, which found Presser guilty and sentenced him to pay a fine of $10.

The **bill of exceptions** taken upon the trial set out all the evidence, from which it appeared that Presser was thirty-one years old, a citizen of the United States and of the State of Illinois, and a voter; that he belonged to a society called the "Lehr und Wehr Verein," a corporation organized April 16, 1875, in due form, under chapter 32, Revised Statutes of Illinois, called the "General Incorporation Laws of Illinois," "for the purpose," as expressed by its certificate of association, "of improving the mental and bodily condition of its members so as to qualify them for the duties of citizens of a republic. Its members shall therefore obtain, in the meetings of the association, a knowledge of our laws and political economy, and shall also be instructed in military and gymnastic exercises;" that Presser, in December, 1879, marched at the head of said company, about four hundred in number, in the streets of the City of Chicago, he riding on horseback and in command; that the company was armed with rifles, and Presser with a cavalry sword; that the company had no license from the Governor of Illinois to drill or parade as a part of the militia of the state, and was not a part of the regular organized militia of the state, nor a part of troops of the United States, and had no organization under the militia law of the United States. The evidence showed no other facts. Exceptions were reserved to the ruling of the court upon the motion to quash the indictment, to the finding of guilty, and to the judgment thereon. The case was taken to the Supreme Court of Illinois, where the judgment was affirmed. Thereupon Presser brought the present writ of error for a review of the judgment of affirmance.

FOR DISCUSSION

Prior to the decision to incorporate the Second Amendment to the states, the cases of *Presser* and *Cruikshank* were cited by advocates of state control laws and those who interpreted the Second Amendment as protecting an individual right to bear arms. How could *Presser* be interpreted as supporting both perspectives?

RELATED CASE

***Quilici v. Village of Morton Grove:* 695 F. 2d 261, 7th Cir. (1982).**

The circuit court noted that both parties litigating a handgun regulation argued *Presser* was the primary precedent. They stated they could not read *Presser* in any way but as allowing for state (and local government) regulation of firearms.

UNITED STATES V. MILLER

307 U.S. 174, 59 S.Ct. 816, 83 L. Ed 1206 (1939)

Jack Miller and Frank Layton were charged with violating the National Firearms Act of 1934 by carrying from Claremore, Oklahoma to Siloam Springs, Arkansas a double barrel 12-gauge Stevens shotgun with a barrel less than the 18 inches required by statute. They were accused of not having registered the firearm as required by federal code and having no evidence of ownership of the weapon. The federal district court found one section of the law to violate the Second Amendment, and the case was appealed directly to the Supreme Court.

Vote: 8–0

JUSTICE MCREYNOLDS delivered the opinion of the Court.

In the absence of any evidence tending to show that possession or use of a "shotgun having a barrel of less than eighteen inches in length" at this time has some reasonable relationship to the preservation or efficiency of a well regulated militia, we cannot say that the Second Amendment guarantees the right to keep and bear such an instrument. Certainly it is not within judicial notice that this weapon is any part of the ordinary military equipment, or that its use could contribute to the common defense.

The Constitution, as originally adopted, granted to the Congress power—

> To provide for calling forth the Militia to execute the Laws of the Union, suppress Insurrections and repel Invasions; To provide for organizing, arming, and disciplining, the Militia, and for governing such Part of them as may be employed in the Service of the United States, reserving to the States

respectively, the Appointment of the Officers, and the Authority of training the Militia according to the discipline prescribed by Congress.

With obvious purpose to assure the continuation and render possible the effectiveness of such forces, the declaration and guarantee of the Second Amendment were made. It must be interpreted and applied with that end in view.

The Militia which the States were expected to maintain and train is set in contrast with Troops which they were forbidden to keep without the consent of Congress. The sentiment of the time strongly disfavored standing armies; the common view was that adequate defense of country and laws could be secured through the Militia—civilians primarily, soldiers on occasion.

The signification attributed to the term Militia appears from the debates in the Convention, the history and legislation of Colonies and States, and the writings of approved commentators. These show plainly enough that the Militia comprised all males physically capable of acting in concert for the common defense. "A body of citizens enrolled for military discipline." And further, that ordinarily, when called for service these men were expected to appear bearing arms supplied by themselves and of the kind in common use at the time.

In a militia, the character of the labourer, artificer, or tradesman, predominates over that of the soldier: in a standing army, that of the soldier predominates over every other character, and in this distinction seems to consist the essential difference between those two different species of military force.

"The American Colonies In The 17th Century," Osgood, Vol. 1, ch. XIII, affirms in reference to the early system of defense in New England—

> In all the colonies, as in England, the militia system was based on the principle of the assize of arms. This implied the general obligation of all adult male inhabitants to possess arms, and, with certain exceptions, to cooperate in the work of defence.

The possession of arms also implied the possession of ammunition, and the authorities paid quite as much attention to the latter as to the former.

A year later [1632] it was ordered that any single man who had not furnished himself with arms might be put out to service, and this became a permanent part of the legislation of the colony [Massachusetts].

Also, Clauses intended to insure the possession of arms and ammunition by all who were subject to military service appear in all the important enactments concerning military affairs. Fines were the penalty for delinquency, whether of towns or individuals. According to the usage of the times, the infantry of Massachusetts consisted of pikemen and musketeers. The law, as enacted in 1649 and thereafter, provided that each of the former should be armed with a pike, corselet, head-piece, sword, and knapsack. The musketeer should carry a "good fixed musket," not under bastard musket bore, not less than three feet, nine inches, nor more than four feet three inches in length, a priming wire, scourer, and mould, a sword, rest, bandoleers, one pound of powder, twenty bullets, and two fathoms of match. The law also required that two-thirds of each company should be musketeers.

The General Court of Massachusetts, January Session 1784, provided for the organization and government of the Militia. It directed that the Train Band should "contain all able bodied men, from sixteen to forty years of age, and the Alarm List, all other men under sixty years of age, . . ."

Also, [t]hat every noncommissioned officer and private soldier of the said militia not under the controul of parents, masters or guardians, and being of sufficient ability therefor in the judgment of the Selectmen of the town in which he shall dwell, shall equip himself, and be constantly provided with a good fire arm, etc.

By an Act passed April 4, 1786, the New York Legislature directed:

> That every able-bodied Male Person, being a Citizen of this State, or of any of the United States, and residing in this State, (except such Persons as are hereinafter excepted) and who are of the Age of Sixteen, and under the Age of Forty-five Years, shall, by the Captain or commanding Officer of the Beat in which such Citizens shall reside, within four Months after the passing of this Act, be enrolled in the Company of such Beat. . . . That every Citizen so enrolled and notified shall, within three Months thereafter, provide himself, at his own Expense, with a good Musket or Firelock, a sufficient Bayonet and Belt, a Pouch with a Box therein to contain not less than Twenty-four Cartridges suited to the Bore of his Musket or Firelock, each Cartridge containing a proper Quantity of Powder and Ball, two spare Flints, a Blanket and Knapsack; . . .

The General Assembly of Virginia, October, 1785, (12 Hening's Statutes) declared,

> The defense and safety of the commonwealth depend upon having its citizens properly armed and taught the knowledge of military duty.

It further provided for organization and control of the Militia, and directed that "All free male persons between the ages of eighteen and fifty years," with certain exceptions, "shall be inrolled or formed into companies." "There shall be a private muster of every company once in two months."

Also that

> Every officer and soldier shall appear at his respective muster-field on the day appointed, by eleven o'clock in the forenoon, armed, equipped, and accoutred, as follows: . . . every non-commissioned officer and private with a good, clean musket carrying an ounce ball, and three feet eight inches long in the barrel, with a good bayonet and iron ramrod well fitted thereto, a cartridge box properly made, to contain and secure twenty cartridges fitted to his musket, a good knapsack and canteen, and moreover, each non-commissioned officer and private shall have at every muster one pound of good powder, and four pounds of lead, including twenty blind cartridges, and each serjeant shall have a pair of moulds fit to cast balls for their respective companies, to be purchased by the commanding officer out of the monies arising on delinquencies. *Provided,* That the militia of the counties westward of the Blue Ridge, and the counties below adjoining thereto, shall not be obliged to be armed with muskets, but may have good rifles with proper accoutrements, in lieu thereof. And every of the said officers, non-commissioned officers, and privates, shall constantly keep the aforesaid arms, accoutrements, and ammunition ready to be produced whenever called for by his commanding officer. If any private shall make it appear to the satisfaction of the court hereafter to be appointed for trying delinquencies under this act that he is so poor that he cannot purchase the arms herein required, such court shall cause them to be purchased out of the money arising from delinquents.

Most if not all of the States have adopted provisions touching the right to keep and bear arms. Differences in the language employed in these have naturally led to somewhat variant conclusions concerning the scope of the right guaranteed. But none of them seems to afford any material support for the challenged ruling of the court below.

We are unable to accept the conclusion of the court below, and the challenged judgment must be reversed. The cause will be remanded for further proceedings.

JUSTICE DOUGLAS took no part in the consideration or decision of this cause.

FOR DISCUSSION

Because the Supreme Court provided such limited guidance to the interpretation of the Second Amendment, this case remained the solitary Supreme Court precedent from the ratification of the Fourteenth Amendment in 1868 until the decision in *District of Columbia v. Heller* in 2008. What doctrine do you derive from this brief majority decision? Does it provide clear guidance to the states as to how they may exercise their police powers? Does the National Firearms Act limit these police powers?

RELATED CASES

United States v. Oakes: **564 F.2d 384 (10th Cir. 1977).**

The Second Amendment does not recognize an individual right to bear arms; participation in a citizen's militia unrecognized by state government is not protected by the Second Amendment.

Hickman v. Block: **81 F.3d 981 (9th Cir. 1996).**

A city's refusal to grant a concealed carry permit to a private citizen does not constitute a denial of Second Amendment rights.

United States v. Emerson: **270 F.3d 203 (5th Cir. 2001).**

The Second Amendment protects the individual's right to bear arms from federal involvement; it is not, however, an absolute right.

DISTRICT OF COLUMBIA V. HELLER

554 U.S. 570, 171 L.Ed. 2d 637, 128 S.Ct. 2783 (2008)

A District of Columbia law regulating handgun possession made it illegal to carry an unregistered firearm and banned the registration of handguns. The law also proscribed the carrying of an unlicensed handgun, but authorized the police chief to issue 1-year licenses. Residents with licensed firearms were required to keep them unloaded and dissembled or bound by a trigger lock or similar device. Heller, a special policeman in the District, applied to register a handgun he wished to keep at home. Permission was refused, and Heller filed suit on Second Amendment grounds, to enjoin the city from enforcing the bar on handgun registration. He also challenged both the licensing requirement that prohibits keeping an unlicensed firearm in the home, and the trigger-lock requirement.

Vote: 5–4

JUSTICE SCALIA delivered the opinion of the Court.

We consider whether a District of Columbia prohibition on the possession of usable handguns in the home violates the Second Amendment to the Constitution.

I

The District of Columbia generally prohibits the possession of handguns. It is a crime to carry an unregistered firearm, and the registration of handguns is prohibited. Wholly apart from that prohibition, no person may carry a handgun without a license, but the chief of police may issue licenses for 1-year periods. District of Columbia law also requires residents to keep their lawfully owned firearms, such as registered long guns, "unloaded and dissembled or bound by a trigger lock or similar device" unless they are located in a place of business or are being used for lawful recreational activities.

Respondent Dick Heller is a D.C. special police officer authorized to carry a handgun while on duty at the Federal Judicial Center. He applied for a registration certificate for a handgun that he wished to keep at home, but the District refused. He thereafter filed a lawsuit in the Federal District Court for the District of Columbia seeking, on Second Amendment grounds, to enjoin the city from enforcing the bar on the registration of handguns, the licensing requirement insofar as it prohibits the carrying of a firearm in the home without a license, and the trigger-lock requirement insofar as it prohibits the use of "functional firearms within the home." The District Court dismissed respondent's complaint. The Court of Appeals for the District of Columbia Circuit, construing his complaint as seeking the right to render a firearm operable and carry it about his home in that condition only when necessary for self-defense, reversed. It held that the Second Amendment protects an individual right to possess firearms and that the city's total ban on handguns, as well as its requirement that firearms in the home be kept nonfunctional even when necessary for self-defense, violated that right. The Court of Appeals directed the District Court to enter summary judgment for respondent.

We granted certiorari.

II

We turn first to the meaning of the Second Amendment.

A

The Second Amendment provides: "A well regulated Militia, being necessary to the security of a free State, the right of the people to keep and bear Arms, shall not be infringed." In interpreting this text, we are guided by the principle that "[t]he Constitution was written to be understood by the voters; its words and phrases were used in their normal and ordinary as distinguished from technical meaning." Normal meaning may of course include an idiomatic meaning, but it excludes secret or technical meanings that would not have been known to ordinary citizens in the founding generation.

The two sides in this case have set out very different interpretations of the Amendment. Petitioners and today's dissenting Justices believe that it protects only the right to possess and carry a firearm in connection with militia service. Respondent argues that it protects an individual right to possess a firearm unconnected with service in a militia, and to use that arm for traditionally lawful purposes, such as self-defense within the home.

The Second Amendment is naturally divided into two parts: its prefatory clause and its operative clause. The former does not limit the latter grammatically, but rather announces a purpose. The Amendment could be rephrased, "Because a well regulated Militia is necessary to the security of a free State, the right of the people to keep and bear Arms shall not be infringed." Although this structure of the Second Amendment is unique in our Constitution, other legal documents of the founding era, particularly individual-rights provisions of state constitutions, commonly included a prefatory statement of purpose.

Logic demands that there be a link between the stated purpose and the command. The Second Amendment would be nonsensical if it read, "A well regulated Militia, being necessary to the security of a free State, the right of the people to petition for redress of grievances shall not be infringed." That requirement of logical connection may cause a prefatory clause to resolve an ambiguity in the operative clause ("The separation of church and state being an important objective, the teachings of canons shall have no place in our jurisprudence." The preface makes clear that the operative clause refers not to canons of interpretation but to clergymen.) But apart from that clarifying function, a prefatory clause does not limit or expand the scope of the operative clause. "It is nothing unusual in acts . . . for the enacting part to go beyond the preamble; the remedy often extends beyond the particular act or mischief which first suggested the necessity of the law." Therefore, while we will begin our textual analysis with the operative clause, we will return to the prefatory clause to ensure that our reading of the operative clause is consistent with the announced purpose.

1. Operative Clause

a. **"Right of the People."** The first salient feature of the operative clause is that it codifies a "right of the people." The unamended Constitution and the Bill of Rights use the phrase "right of the people" two other times, in the First Amendment's Assembly-and-Petition Clause and in the Fourth Amendment's Search-and-Seizure Clause. The Ninth Amendment uses very similar terminology ("The enumeration in the Constitution, of certain rights, shall not be construed to deny or disparage others retained by the people"). All three of these instances unambiguously refer to individual rights, not "collective" rights, or rights that may be exercised only through participation in some corporate body.

Three provisions of the Constitution refer to "the people" in a context other than "rights"—the famous preamble ("We the people"), § 2 of Article I (providing that "the people" will choose members of the House), and the Tenth Amendment (providing that those powers not given the Federal Government remain with "the States" or "the people"). Those provisions arguably refer to "the people" acting collectively—but they deal with the exercise or reservation of powers, not rights. Nowhere else in the Constitution does a "right" attributed to "the people" refer to anything other than an individual right.[6]

What is more, in all six other provisions of the Constitution that mention "the people," the term unambiguously refers to all members of the political community, not an unspecified subset.

This contrasts markedly with the phrase "the militia" in the prefatory clause. As we will describe below, the "militia" in colonial America consisted of a subset of "the people"—those who were male, able bodied, and within a certain age range. Reading the Second Amendment as protecting only the right to "keep and bear Arms" in an organized militia therefore fits poorly with the operative clause's description of the holder of that right as "the people."

We start therefore with a strong presumption that the Second Amendment right is exercised individually and belongs to all Americans.

b. **"Keep and bear Arms."** We move now from the holder of the right—"the people"—to the substance of the right: "to keep and bear Arms."

Before addressing the verbs "keep" and "bear," we interpret their object: "Arms." The 18th-century meaning is no different from the meaning today.

The term was applied, then as now, to weapons that were not specifically designed for military use and were not employed in a military capacity. Some have made the argument, bordering on the frivolous, that only those arms in existence in the 18th century are protected by the Second Amendment. We do not interpret constitutional rights that way. Just as the First Amendment protects modern forms of communications, *e.g., Reno v. American Civil Liberties Union,* 521 U.S. 844, 849 (1997), and the Fourth Amendment applies to modern forms

---

6 If we look to other founding-era documents, we find that some state constitutions used the term "the people" to refer to the people collectively, in contrast to "citizen," which was used to invoke individual rights. See Heyman, Natural Rights and the Second Amendment, in *The Second Amendment in Law and History* 179, 193–195 (C. Bogus ed.2000) (hereinafter Bogus). But that usage was not remotely uniform. See, *e.g.,* N.C. Declaration of Rights § XIV (1776), in 5 *The Federal and State Constitutions, Colonial Charters, and Other Organic Laws* 2787, 2788 (F. Thorpe ed.1909) (hereinafter Thorpe) (jury trial); Md. Declaration of Rights § XVIII (1776), in 3 *id.,* at 1686, 1688 (vicinage requirement); Vt. Declaration of Rights ch. 1, § XI (1777), in 6 *id.,* at 3737, 3741 (searches and seizures); Pa. Declaration of Rights § XII (1776), in 5 *id.,* at 3081, 3083 (free speech). And, most importantly, it was clearly not the terminology used in the Federal Constitution, given the First, Fourth, and Ninth Amendments.

of search, *e.g., Kyllo v. United States,* 533 U.S. 27, 35–36 (2001), the Second Amendment extends, prima facie, to all instruments that constitute bearable arms, even those that were not in existence at the time of the founding.

The phrase "keep arms" was not prevalent in the written documents of the founding period that we have found, but there are a few examples, all of which favor viewing the right to "keep Arms" as an individual right unconnected with militia service. William Blackstone, for example, wrote that Catholics convicted of not attending service in the Church of England suffered certain penalties, one of which was that they were not permitted to "keep arms in their houses." Petitioners point to militia laws of the founding period that required militia members to "keep" arms in connection with militia service, and they conclude from this that the phrase "keep Arms" has a militia-related connotation. This is rather like saying that, since there are many statutes that authorize aggrieved employees to "file complaints" with federal agencies, the phrase "file complaints" has an employment-related connotation. "Keep arms" was simply a common way of referring to possessing arms, for militiamen *and everyone else.*

From our review of founding-era sources, we conclude that this natural meaning was also the meaning that "bear arms" had in the 18th century. In numerous instances, "bear arms" was unambiguously used to refer to the carrying of weapons outside of an organized militia. The most prominent examples are those most relevant to the Second Amendment: Nine state constitutional provisions written in the 18th century or the first two decades of the 19th, which enshrined a right of citizens to "bear arms in defense of themselves and the state" or "bear arms in defense of himself and the state." It is clear from those formulations that "bear arms" did not refer only to carrying a weapon in an organized military unit.

The phrase "bear Arms" also had at the time of the founding an idiomatic meaning that was significantly different from its natural meaning: "to serve as a soldier, do military service, fight" or "to wage war." But it *unequivocally* bore that idiomatic meaning only when followed by the preposition "against," which was in turn followed by the target of the hostilities. Every example given by petitioners' *amici* for the idiomatic meaning of "bear arms" from the founding period either includes the preposition "against" or is not clearly idiomatic.

In any event, the meaning of "bear arms" that petitioners and Justice Stevens propose is *not even* the (sometimes) idiomatic meaning. Rather, they manufacture a hybrid definition, whereby "bear arms" connotes the actual carrying of arms (and therefore is not really an idiom) but only in the service of an organized militia. No dictionary has ever adopted that definition, and we have been apprised of no source that indicates that it carried that meaning at the time of the founding. But it is easy to see why petitioners and the dissent are driven to the hybrid definition. Giving "bear Arms" its idiomatic meaning would cause the protected right to consist of the right to be a soldier or to wage war—an absurdity that no commentator has ever endorsed. Worse still, the phrase "keep and bear Arms" would be incoherent. The word "Arms" would have two different meanings at once: "weapons" (as the object of "keep") and (as the object of "bear") one-half of an idiom. It would be rather like saying "He filled and kicked the bucket" to mean "He filled the bucket and died." Grotesque.

Finally, Justice Stevens suggests that "keep and bear Arms" was some sort of term of art, presumably akin to "hue and cry" or "cease and desist." (This suggestion usefully evades the problem that there is no evidence whatsoever to support a military reading of "keep arms.") Justice Stevens believes that the unitary meaning of "keep and bear Arms" is established by the Second Amendment's calling it a "right" (singular) rather than "rights" (plural). There is nothing to this. State constitutions of the founding period routinely grouped multiple (related) guarantees under a singular "right," and the First Amendment protects the "right [singular] of the people peaceably to assemble, and to petition the Government for a redress of grievances." And even if "keep and bear Arms" were a unitary phrase, we find no evidence that it bore a military meaning. Although the phrase was not at all common (which would be unusual for a term of art), we have found instances of its use with a clearly nonmilitary connotation.

Meaning of the Operative Clause. Putting all of these textual elements together, we find that they guarantee the individual right to possess and carry weapons in case of confrontation. This meaning is strongly confirmed by the historical background of the Second Amendment. We look to this because it has always been widely understood that the Second Amendment, like the First and Fourth Amendments, codified a *pre-existing* right. The very text of the Second Amendment implicitly recognizes the pre-existence of the right and declares only that it "shall not be infringed."

There seems to us no doubt, on the basis of both text and history, that the Second Amendment conferred an individual right to keep and bear arms. Of course the right was not unlimited, just as the First Amendment's right of free speech was not. Thus, we do not read the Second Amendment to protect the right of citizens to carry arms for *any sort* of confrontation, just as we do not read the First Amendment to protect the right of citizens to speak for *any purpose.* Before turning to limitations upon the individual right, however, we must determine whether the prefatory clause of the Second Amendment comports with our interpretation of the operative clause.

2. Prefatory Clause

The prefatory clause reads: "A well regulated Militia, being necessary to the security of a free State. . . ."

a. "Well-Regulated Militia." In *United States v. Miller,* 307 U.S. 174, 179 (1939), we explained that "the Militia comprised all males physically capable of acting in concert for the common defense." That definition comports with founding-era sources.

Petitioners take a seemingly narrower view of the militia, stating that "[m]ilitias are the state- and congressionally-regulated military forces described in the Militia Clauses (art. I, § 8, cls. 15–16)." Although we agree with petitioners' interpretive assumption that "militia" means the same thing in Article I and the Second Amendment, we believe that petitioners identify the wrong thing, namely, the organized militia. Unlike armies and navies, which Congress is given the power to create ("to raise . . . Armies"; "to provide . . . a Navy," Art. I, § 8, cls. 12–13), the militia is assumed by Article I already to be *in existence.* Congress is given the power to "provide for calling forth the militia," § 8, cl. 15; and the power not to create, but to "organiz[e]" it—and not to organize "a" militia, which is what one would expect if the militia were to be a federal creation, but to organize "the" militia, connoting a body already in existence, *ibid.,* cl. 16. This is fully consistent with the ordinary definition of the militia as all able-bodied men. From that pool, Congress has plenary power to organize the units that will make up an effective fighting force. That is what Congress did in the first militia Act, which specified that "each and every free able-bodied white male citizen of the respective states, resident therein, who is or shall be of the age of eighteen years, and under the age of forty-five years (except as is herein after excepted) shall severally and respectively be enrolled in the militia." Act of May 8, 1792, 1 Stat. 271. To be sure, Congress need not conscript every able-bodied man into the militia, because nothing in Article I suggests that in exercising its power to organize, discipline, and arm the militia, Congress must focus upon the entire body. Although the militia consists of all able-bodied men, the federally organized militia may consist of a subset of them.

Finally, the adjective "well-regulated" implies nothing more than the imposition of proper discipline and training.

b. "Security of a Free State." The phrase "security of a free state" meant "security of a free polity," not security of each of the several States as the dissent below argued. It is true that the term "State" elsewhere in the Constitution refers to individual States, but the phrase "security of a free state" and close variations seem to have been terms of art in 18th-century political discourse, meaning a " 'free country' " or free polity. Moreover, the other instances of "state" in the Constitution are typically accompanied by modifiers making clear that the reference is to the several States—"each state," "several states," "any state," "that state," "particular states," "one state," "no state." And the presence of the term "foreign state" in Article I and Article III shows that the word "state" did not have a single meaning in the Constitution.

3. Relationship between Prefatory Clause and Operative Clause

We reach the question, then: Does the preface fit with an operative clause that creates an individual right to keep and bear arms? It fits perfectly, once one knows the history that the founding generation knew and that we have described above. That history showed that the way tyrants had eliminated a militia consisting of all the able-bodied men was not by banning the militia but simply by taking away the people's arms, enabling a select militia or standing army to suppress political opponents. This is what had occurred in England that prompted codification of the right to have arms in the English Bill of Rights.

It is therefore entirely sensible that the Second Amendment's prefatory clause announces the purpose for which the right was codified: to prevent elimination of the militia. The prefatory clause does not suggest that preserving the militia was the only reason Americans valued the ancient right; most undoubtedly thought it even more important for self-defense and hunting. But the threat that the new Federal Government would destroy the citizens' militia by taking away their arms was the reason that right—unlike some other English rights—was codified in a written Constitution. We affirm the judgment of the Court of Appeals.

JUSTICE STEVENS, with whom JUSTICES SOUTER, GINSBURG, and BREYER join, dissenting.

The question presented by this case is not whether the Second Amendment protects a "collective right" or an "individual right." Surely it protects a right that can be enforced by individuals. But a conclusion that the Second Amendment protects an individual right does not tell us anything about the scope of that right.

Guns are used to hunt, for self-defense, to commit crimes, for sporting activities, and to perform military duties. The Second Amendment plainly does not protect the right to use a gun to rob a bank; it is equally clear that it *does* encompass the right to use weapons for certain military purposes. Whether it also protects the right to possess and use guns for nonmilitary purposes like hunting and personal self-defense is the question presented by this case. The text of the Amendment, its history, and our decision in *United States v. Miller,* 307 U.S. 174 (1939), provide a clear answer to that question.

The Second Amendment was adopted to protect the right of the people of each of the several States to maintain a well-regulated militia. It was a response to concerns raised during the ratification of the Constitution that the power of Congress to disarm the state militias and create a national standing army posed an intolerable threat to the sovereignty of the several States. Neither the text of the Amendment nor the arguments advanced by its proponents evidenced the slightest interest in limiting any legislature's authority to regulate private civilian uses of firearms. Specifically, there is no indication that the Framers of the Amendment intended to enshrine the common-law right of self-defense in the Constitution.

In 1934, Congress enacted the National Firearms Act, the first major federal firearms law. Upholding a conviction under that Act, this Court held that, "[i]n the absence of any evidence tending to show that possession or use of a 'shotgun having a barrel of less than eighteen inches in length' at this time has some reasonable relationship to the preservation or efficiency of a well regulated militia, we cannot say that the Second Amendment guarantees the right to keep and bear such an instrument." The view of the Amendment we took in *Miller*—that it protects the right to keep and bear arms for certain military purposes, but that it does not curtail the Legislature's power to regulate the nonmilitary use and ownership of weapons—is both the most natural reading of the Amendment's text and the interpretation most faithful to the history of its adoption.

Even if the textual and historical arguments on both sides of the issue were evenly balanced, respect for the well-settled views of all of our predecessors on this Court, and for the rule of law itself, would prevent most jurists from endorsing such a dramatic upheaval in the law. As Justice Cardozo observed years ago, the "labor of judges would be increased almost to the breaking point if every past decision could be reopened in every case, and one could not lay one's own course of bricks on the secure foundation of the courses laid by others who had gone before him."

In this dissent I shall first explain why our decision in *Miller* was faithful to the text of the Second Amendment and the purposes revealed in its drafting history. I shall then comment on the postratification history of the Amendment, which makes abundantly clear that the Amendment should not be interpreted as limiting the authority of Congress to regulate the use or possession of firearms for purely civilian purposes.

I

The text of the Second Amendment is brief. It provides: "A well regulated Militia, being necessary to the security of a free State, the right of the people to keep and bear Arms, shall not be infringed."

Three portions of that text merit special focus: the introductory language defining the Amendment's purpose, the class of persons encompassed within its reach, and the unitary nature of the right that it protects.

"A well regulated Militia, being necessary to the security of a free State"

The preamble to the Second Amendment makes three important points. It identifies the preservation of the militia as the Amendment's purpose; it explains that the militia is necessary to the security of a free State; and it recognizes that the militia must be "well regulated." In all three respects it is comparable to provisions in several State Declarations of Rights that were adopted roughly contemporaneously with the Declaration of Independence. Those state provisions highlight the importance members of the founding generation attached to the maintenance of state militias; they also underscore the profound fear shared by many in that era of the dangers posed by standing armies. While the need for state militias has not been a matter of significant public interest for almost two centuries, that fact should not obscure the contemporary concerns that animated the Framers.

The parallels between the Second Amendment and these state declarations, and the Second Amendment's omission of any statement of purpose related to the right to use firearms for hunting or personal self-defense, is especially striking in light of the fact that the Declarations of Rights of Pennsylvania and Vermont *did* expressly protect such civilian uses at the time. The contrast between those two declarations and the Second Amendment reinforces the clear statement of purpose announced in the Amendment's preamble. It confirms that the Framers' single-minded focus in crafting the constitutional guarantee "to keep and bear arms" was on military uses of firearms, which they viewed in the context of service in state militias.

The preamble thus both sets forth the object of the Amendment and informs the meaning of the remainder of its text.

The Court today tries to denigrate the importance of this clause of the Amendment by beginning its analysis with the Amendment's operative provision and returning to the preamble merely "to ensure that our reading of the operative clause is consistent with the announced purpose." That is not how this Court ordinarily reads such texts, and it is not how the preamble would have been viewed at the time the Amendment was adopted. While the Court makes the novel suggestion that it need only find some "logical connection" between the preamble and the operative provision, it does acknowledge that a prefatory clause may resolve an ambiguity in the text. Without identifying any language in the text that even mentions civilian uses of firearms, the Court proceeds to "find" its preferred reading in what is at best an ambiguous text, and then concludes that its reading is not foreclosed by the preamble. Perhaps the Court's approach to the text is acceptable advocacy, but it is surely an unusual approach for judges to follow.

"The right of the people"

The centerpiece of the Court's textual argument is its insistence that the words "the people" as used in the Second Amendment must have the same meaning, and protect the same class of individuals, as when they are used in the First and Fourth Amendments. According to the Court, in all three provisions—as well as the Constitution's preamble, section 2 of Article I, and the Tenth Amendment—"the term unambiguously refers to all members of the political community, not an unspecified subset." But the Court *itself* reads the Second Amendment to protect a "subset" significantly narrower than the class of persons protected by the First and Fourth Amendments; when it finally drills down on the substantive meaning of the Second Amendment, the Court limits the protected class to "law-abiding, responsible citizens." But the class of persons protected by the First and Fourth Amendments is *not* so limited; for even felons (and presumably irresponsible citizens as well) may invoke the protections of those constitutional provisions. The Court offers no way to harmonize its conflicting pronouncements.

The Court also overlooks the significance of the way the Framers used the phrase "the people" in these constitutional provisions. In the First Amendment, no words define the class of individuals entitled to speak, to publish, or to worship; in that Amendment it is only the right peaceably to assemble, and to petition the Government for a redress of grievances, that is described as a right of "the people." These rights contemplate collective action. While the right peaceably to assemble protects the individual rights of those persons participating in the assembly, its concern is with action engaged in by members of a group, rather than any single individual. Likewise, although the act of petitioning the Government is a right that can be exercised by individuals, it is primarily collective in nature. For if they are to be effective, petitions must involve groups of individuals acting in concert.

Similarly, the words "the people" in the Second Amendment refer back to the object announced in the Amendment's preamble. They remind us that it is the collective action of individuals having a duty to serve in the militia that the text directly protects and, perhaps more importantly, that the ultimate purpose of the Amendment was to protect the States' share of the divided sovereignty created by the Constitution.

As used in the Fourth Amendment, "the people" describes the class of persons protected from unreasonable searches and seizures by Government officials. It is true that the Fourth Amendment describes a right that need not be exercised in any collective sense. But that observation does not settle the meaning of the phrase "the people" when used in the Second Amendment. For, as we have seen, the phrase means something quite different in the Petition and Assembly Clauses of the First Amendment. Although the abstract definition of the phrase "the people" could carry the same meaning in the Second Amendment as in the Fourth Amendment, the preamble of the Second Amendment suggests that the uses of the phrase in the First and Second Amendments are the same in referring to a collective activity. By way of contrast, the Fourth Amendment describes a right *against* governmental interference rather than an affirmative right *to* engage in protected conduct, and so refers to a right to protect a purely individual interest. As used in the Second Amendment, the words "the people" do not enlarge the right to keep and bear arms to encompass use or ownership of weapons outside the context of service in a well-regulated militia.

"To keep and bear Arms"

Although the Court's discussion of these words treats them as two "phrases"—as if they read "to keep" and "to bear"—they describe a unitary right: to possess arms if needed for military purposes and to use them in conjunction with military activities.

As a threshold matter, it is worth pausing to note an oddity in the Court's interpretation of "to keep and bear arms." Unlike the Court of Appeals, the Court does not read that phrase to create a right to possess arms for "lawful, private purposes." Instead, the Court limits the Amendment's protection to the right "to possess and carry weapons in case of confrontation." No party or *amicus* urged this interpretation; the Court appears to have fashioned it out of whole cloth. But although this novel limitation lacks support in the text of the Amendment, the Amendment's text *does* justify a different limitation: the "right to keep and bear arms" protects only a right to possess and use firearms in connection with service in a state-organized militia.

The term "bear arms" is a familiar idiom; when used unadorned by any additional words, its meaning is "to serve as a soldier, do military service, fight." Had the Framers wished to expand the meaning of the phrase "bear arms" to encompass civilian possession and use, they could have done so by the addition of phrases such as "for the defense of themselves," as was done in the Pennsylvania and Vermont Declarations of Rights. The *unmodified* use of "bear arms," by contrast, refers most naturally to a military purpose, as evidenced by its use in literally dozens of contemporary texts. The absence of any reference to civilian uses of weapons tailors the text of the Amendment to the purpose identified in its preamble. But when discussing these words, the Court simply ignores the preamble.

The Court argues that a "qualifying phrase that contradicts the word or phrase it modifies is unknown this side of the looking glass." But this fundamentally fails to grasp the point. The stand-alone phrase "bear arms" most naturally conveys a military meaning *unless* the addition of a qualifying phrase signals that a different meaning is intended. When, as in this case, there is no such qualifier, the most natural meaning is the military one; and, in the absence of any qualifier, it is all the more appropriate to look to the preamble to confirm the natural meaning of the text. The Court's objection is particularly puzzling in light of its own contention that the addition of the modifier "against" changes the meaning of "bear arms."

The Amendment's use of the term "keep" in no way contradicts the military meaning conveyed by the phrase "bear arms" and the Amendment's preamble. To the contrary, a number of state militia laws in effect at the time of the Second Amendment's drafting used the term "keep" to describe the requirement that militia members store their arms at their homes, ready to be used for service when necessary. "[K]eep and bear arms" thus perfectly describes the responsibilities of a framing-era militia member.

This reading is confirmed by the fact that the clause protects only one right, rather than two. It does not describe a right "to keep arms" and a separate right "to bear arms." Rather, the single right that it does describe is both a duty and a right to have arms available and ready for military service, and to use them for military purposes when necessary. Different language surely would have been used to protect nonmilitary use and possession of weapons from regulation if such an intent had played any role in the drafting of the Amendment.

When each word in the text is given full effect, the Amendment is most naturally read to secure to the people a right to use and possess arms in conjunction with service in a well-regulated militia. So far as appears, no more than that was contemplated by its drafters or is encompassed within its terms. Even if the meaning of the text were genuinely susceptible to more than one interpretation, the burden would remain on those advocating a departure from the purpose identified in the preamble and from settled law to come forward with persuasive new arguments or evidence. The textual analysis offered by respondent and embraced by the Court falls far short of sustaining that heavy burden. And the Court's emphatic reliance on the claim "that the Second Amendment . . . codified a *pre-existing* right," is of course beside the point because the right to keep and bear arms for service in a state militia was also a pre-existing right.

Indeed, not a word in the constitutional text even arguably supports the Court's overwrought and novel description of the Second Amendment as "elevat[ing] above all other interests" "the right of law-abiding, responsible citizens to use arms in defense of hearth and home."

II

Madison, charged with the task of assembling the proposals for amendments sent by the ratifying States, was the principal draftsman of the Second Amendment. He had before him, or at the very least would have been aware of, all of these proposed formulations. In addition, Madison had been a member, some years earlier, of the committee tasked with drafting the Virginia Declaration of Rights. That committee considered a proposal by Thomas Jefferson that would have included within the Virginia Declaration the following language: "No freeman shall ever be debarred the use of arms [within his own lands or tenements]." 1 *Papers of Thomas Jefferson* 363 (J. Boyd ed. 1950). But the committee rejected that language, adopting instead the provision drafted by George Mason.

With all of these sources upon which to draw, it is strikingly significant that Madison's first draft omitted any mention of nonmilitary use or possession of weapons. Rather, his original draft repeated the essence of the two proposed amendments sent by Virginia, combining the substance of the two provisions succinctly into one, which read: "The right of the people to keep and bear arms shall not be infringed; a well armed, and well regulated militia being the best security of a free country; but no person religiously scrupulous of bearing arms, shall be compelled to render military service in person."

Madison's decision to model the Second Amendment on the distinctly military Virginia proposal is therefore revealing, since it is clear that he considered and rejected formulations that would have unambiguously protected civilian uses of firearms. When Madison prepared his first draft, and when that draft was debated and modified, it is reasonable to assume that all participants in the drafting process were fully aware of the other formulations that would have protected civilian use and possession of weapons and that their choice to craft the Amendment as they did represented a rejection of those alternative formulations.

Madison's initial inclusion of an exemption for conscientious objectors sheds revelatory light on the purpose of the Amendment. It confirms an intent to describe a duty as well as a right, and it unequivocally identifies the military character of both. The objections voiced to the conscientious-objector clause only confirm the central meaning of the text. Although records of the debate in the Senate, which is where the conscientious-objector clause was removed, do not survive, the arguments raised in the House illuminate the perceived problems with the clause: Specifically, there was concern that Congress "can declare who are those religiously scrupulous, and prevent them from bearing arms." The ultimate removal of the clause, therefore, only serves to confirm the purpose of the Amendment-to protect against congressional disarmament, by whatever means, of the States' militias.

The history of the adoption of the Amendment thus describes an overriding concern about the potential threat to state sovereignty that a federal standing army would pose, and a desire to protect the States' militias as the means by which to guard against that danger. But state militias could not effectively check the prospect of a federal standing army so long as Congress retained the power to disarm them, and so a guarantee against such disarmament was needed. As we explained in *Miller*: "With obvious purpose to assure the continuation and render possible the effectiveness of such forces the declaration and guarantee of the Second Amendment were made. It must be interpreted and applied with that end in view." The evidence plainly refutes the claim that the Amendment was motivated by the Framers' fears that Congress might act to regulate any civilian uses of weapons. And even if the historical record were genuinely ambiguous, the burden would remain on the parties advocating a change in the law to introduce facts or arguments " 'newly ascertained' "; the Court is unable to identify any such facts or arguments.

FOR DISCUSSION

In light of the Court's precedents excluding the interpretation of the Second Amendment as an individual right, do you find the Court's justification compelling? Why or why not? How do the judicial philosophies of the individual justices impact their interpretations in this case?

RELATED CASES

***United States v. Brunson:* 2008 U.S. App LEXIS 19456 (4th Cir. 2008).**

A challenge against a federal law barring felon ownership of guns was "presumed valid."

***Maloney v. Cuomo:* 554 F.3d 56 (2d Cir. 2009).**

Relied on *Cruikshank* and *Presser*, finding the Second Amendment does not prohibit state or local regulations of guns.

***Printz v. United States:* 521 U.S. 898 (1997)**

In striking down an interim provision of the Brady Bill that required state officials to conduct criminal background checks of gun buyers, Justice Thomas filed a concurring opinion in which he argued that the Second Amendment protected an individual right to bear arms.

OTIS MCDONALD V. CITY OF CHICAGO, ILLINOIS

561 U.S. 742, 130 S.Ct. 3020, 177 L.Ed. 2d 894 (2010)

Otis McDonald, Adam Orlov, Colleen Lawson, and David Lawson were residents of Chicago who were unable to possess handguns in their homes because of the city ordinances that limited handgun possession to the few private citizens who could qualify for a registration certificate. The petitioners claimed that post-*Heller*, the Chicago ordinances violated the Second and Fourteenth Amendments. The District Court rejected this argument, noting that *District of Columbia v. Heller* did not determine the incorporation of the Second Amendment to the states, and the appellate court affirmed noted that *U.S. v. Cruikshank*, 92 U.S. 542 (1876); *Presser v. Illinois*, 116 U.S. 252 (1886), and M*iller v. Texas*, 153 U.S. 535 (1894) were the relevant precedents.

Vote: 5–4

JUSTICE ALITO announced the judgment of the Court and delivered the opinion of the Court with respect to Parts I, II–A, II–B, II–D, III–A, and III–B, in which CHIEF JUSTICE ROBERTS, JUSTICE SCALIA, JUSTICE KENNEDY, and JUSTICE THOMAS join, and an opinion with respect to Parts II–C, IV, and V, in which CHIEF JUSTICE ROBERTS, JUSTICE SCALIA, and JUSTICE KENNEDY join.

Two years ago, in *District of Columbia v. Heller*, 554 U. S. [570] (2008), we held that the Second Amendment protects the right to keep and bear arms for the purpose of self-defense, and we struck down a District of Columbia law that banned the possession of handguns in the home. The city of Chicago (City) and the village of Oak Park, a Chicago suburb, have laws that are similar to the District of Columbia's, but Chicago and Oak Park argue that their laws are constitutional because the Second Amendment has no application to the States. We have previously held that most of the provisions of the Bill of Rights apply with full force to both the Federal Government and the States. Applying the standard that is well established in our case law, we hold that the Second Amendment right is fully applicable to the States.

I

[Provided a statement of facts]

II

A

Petitioners argue that the Chicago and Oak Park laws violate the right to keep and bear arms for two reasons. Petitioners' primary submission is that this right is among the "privileges or immunities of citizens of the United States" and that the narrow interpretation of the Privileges or Immunities Clause adopted in the *Slaughter-House Cases*, [16 Wall. 36 (1873)], should now be rejected. As a secondary argument, petitioners contend that the Fourteenth Amendment's Due Process Clause "incorporates" the Second Amendment right.

Chicago and Oak Park (municipal respondents) maintain that a right set out in the Bill of Rights applies to the States only if that right is an indispensable attribute of any "civilized" legal system. If it is possible to imagine a civilized country that does not recognize the right, the municipal respondents tell us, then that right is not protected by due process. And since there are civilized countries that ban or strictly regulate the private possession of handguns, the municipal respondents maintain that due process does not preclude such measures. In light of the parties' far-reaching arguments, we begin by recounting this Court's analysis over the years of the relationship between the provisions of the Bill of Rights and the States.

B

The Bill of Rights, including the Second Amendment, originally applied only to the Federal Government. In *Barron v. Baltimore*, 7 Pet. 243 (1833), the Court, in an opinion by Chief Justice Marshall, explained that this question was "of great importance" but "not of much difficulty." In less than four pages, the Court firmly rejected the proposition that the first eight Amendments operate as limitations on the States, holding that they apply only to the Federal Government.

The constitutional Amendments adopted in the aftermath of the Civil War fundamentally altered our country's federal system. The provision at issue in this case, § 1 of the Fourteenth Amendment, provides, among other things, that a State may not abridge "the privileges or immunities of citizens of the United States" or deprive "any person of life, liberty, or property, without due process of law."

Four years after the adoption of the Fourteenth Amendment, this Court was asked to interpret the Amendment's reference to "the privileges or immunities of citizens of the United States." The *Slaughter-House Cases* involved challenges to a Louisiana law permitting the creation of a state-sanctioned monopoly on the butchering of animals within the city of New Orleans. Justice Samuel Miller's opinion for the Court concluded that the Privileges or Immunities Clause protects only those rights "which owe their existence to the Federal government, its National character, its Constitution, or its laws." The Court held that other fundamental rights—rights that predated the creation of the Federal Government and that "the State governments were created to establish and secure"—were not protected by the Clause.

In drawing a sharp distinction between the rights of federal and state citizenship, the Court relied on two principal arguments. First, the Court emphasized that the Fourteenth Amendment's Privileges or Immunities Clause spoke of "the privileges or immunities of citizens of the United States," and the Court contrasted this phrasing with the wording in the first sentence of the Fourteenth Amendment and in the Privileges and Immunities Clause of Article IV, both of which refer to state citizenship. Second, the Court stated that a contrary reading would "radically chang[e] the whole theory of the relations of the State and Federal governments to each other and of both these governments to the people," and the Court refused to conclude that such a change had been made "in the absence of language which expresses such a purpose too clearly to admit of doubt." Finding the phrase "privileges or immunities of citizens of the United States" lacking by this high standard, the Court reasoned that the phrase must mean something more limited.

Under the Court's narrow reading, the Privileges or Immunities Clause protects such things as the right

> "to come to the seat of government to assert any claim [a citizen] may have upon that government, to transact any business he may have with it, to seek its protection, to share its offices, to engage in administering its functions . . . [and to] become a citizen of any State of the Union by a bonâ fide residence therein, with the same rights as other citizens of that State." [*Slaughter-House Cases*] at 79–80.

Finding no constitutional protection against state intrusion of the kind envisioned by the Louisiana statute, the Court upheld the statute.

Today, many legal scholars dispute the correctness of the narrow *Slaughter-House* interpretation.

Three years after the decision in the Slaughter-House Cases, the Court decided *Cruikshank*, the first of the three 19th-century cases on which the Seventh Circuit relied. In that case, the Court reviewed convictions stemming from the infamous Colfax Massacre in Louisiana on Easter Sunday 1873. Dozens of blacks, many unarmed, were slaughtered by a rival band of armed white men. Cruikshank himself allegedly marched unarmed African-American prisoners through the streets and then had them summarily executed. Ninety-seven men were indicted for participating in the massacre, but only nine went to trial. Six of the nine were acquitted of all charges; the remaining three were acquitted of murder but convicted under the Enforcement Act of 1870, for banding and conspiring together to deprive their victims of various constitutional rights, including the right to bear arms.

The Court reversed all of the convictions, including those relating to the deprivation of the victims' right to bear arms. The Court wrote that the right of bearing arms for a lawful purpose "is not a right granted by the Constitution" and is not "in any manner dependent upon that instrument for its existence." "The second amendment," the Court continued, "declares that it shall not be infringed; but this . . . means no more than that it shall not be infringed by Congress." "Our later decisions in *Presser v. Illinois*, 116 U. S. 252, 265 (1886), and *Miller v. Texas*, 153 U. S. 535, 538 (1894), reaffirmed that the Second Amendment applies only to the Federal Government." *Heller*, 554 U. S., at [620], n. 23.

C

As previously noted, the Seventh Circuit concluded that *Cruikshank*, *Presser*, and *Miller* doomed petitioners' claims at the Court of Appeals level. Petitioners argue, however, that we should overrule those decisions and hold that the right to keep and bear arms is one of the "privileges or immunities of citizens of the United States." In petitioners' view, the Privileges or Immunities Clause protects all of the rights set out in the Bill of Rights, as well as some others, but petitioners are unable to identify the Clause's full scope. Nor is there any consensus on that question among the scholars who agree that the Slaughter-House Cases' interpretation is flawed.

We see no need to reconsider that interpretation here. For many decades, the question of the rights protected by the Fourteenth Amendment against state infringement has been analyzed under the Due Process Clause of that Amendment and not under the Privileges or Immunities Clause. We therefore decline to disturb the *Slaughter-House* holding.

At the same time, however, this Court's decisions in *Cruikshank*, *Presser*, and *Miller* do not preclude us from considering whether the Due Process Clause of the Fourteenth Amendment makes the Second Amendment right binding on the States. None of those cases "engage[d] in the sort of Fourteenth Amendment inquiry required by our later cases." As explained more fully below, *Cruikshank*, *Presser*, and *Miller* all preceded the era in which the Court began the process of "selective incorporation" under the Due Process Clause, and we have never previously addressed the question whether the right to keep and bear arms applies to the States under that theory.

Indeed, *Cruikshank* has not prevented us from holding that other rights that were at issue in that case are binding on the States through the Due Process Clause. In *Cruikshank*, the Court held that the general "right of the people peaceably to assemble for lawful purposes," which is protected by the First Amendment, applied only against the Federal Government and not against the States. Nonetheless, over 60 years later the Court held that the right of peaceful assembly was a "fundamental righ[t] . . . safeguarded by the due process clause of the Fourteenth Amendment." *De Jonge v. Oregon*, 299 U. S. 353, 364 (1937). We follow the same path here and thus consider whether the right to keep and bear arms applies to the States under the Due Process Clause.

D

1

In the late 19th century, the Court began to consider whether the Due Process Clause prohibits the States from infringing rights set out in the Bill of Rights. See *Hurtado v. California*, 110 U. S. 516 (1884) (due process does not require grand jury indictment); *Chicago, B. & Q. R. Co. v. Chicago*, 166 U. S. 226 (1897) (due process prohibits States from taking of private property for public use without just compensation). Five features of the approach taken during the ensuing era should be noted.

First, the Court viewed the due process question as entirely separate from the question whether a right was a privilege or immunity of national citizenship. See *Twining v. New Jersey*, 211 U. S. 78, 99 (1908).

Second, the Court explained that the only rights protected against state infringement by the Due Process Clause were those rights "of such a nature that they are included in the conception of due process of law." See also, e.g., *Betts v. Brady*, 316 U. S. 455 (1942); *Palko v. Connecticut*, 302 U. S. 319 (1937); *Powell v. Alabama*, 287 U. S. 45 (1932). While it was "possible that some of the personal rights safeguarded by the first eight Amendments against National action [might] also be safeguarded against state action," the Court stated, this was "not because those rights are enumerated in the first eight Amendments." *Twining* at 99.

Third, in some cases decided during this era the Court "can be seen as having asked, when inquiring into whether some particular procedural safeguard was required of a State, if a civilized system could be imagined that would not accord the particular protection." *Duncan v. Louisiana*, 391 U. S. 145, 149, n. 14 (1968).

Fourth, the Court during this era was not hesitant to hold that a right set out in the Bill of Rights failed to meet the test for inclusion within the protection of the Due Process Clause. The Court found that some such rights qualified. See, e.g., *Gitlow v. New York*, 268 U. S. 652, 666 (1925) (freedom of speech and press); *Near v. Minnesota*, 283 U. S. 697 (1931) (same); Powell, supra (assistance of counsel in capital cases); *De Jonge* (freedom of assembly); *Cantwell v. Connecticut*, 310 U. S. 296 (1940) (free exercise of religion). But others did not. See, e.g., *Hurtado*, supra (grand jury indictment requirement); *Twining* (privilege against self-incrimination).

Finally, even when a right set out in the Bill of Rights was held to fall within the conception of due process, the protection or remedies afforded against state infringement sometimes differed from the protection or remedies provided against abridgment by the Federal Government.

2

An alternative theory regarding the relationship between the Bill of Rights and § 1 of the Fourteenth Amendment was championed by Justice Black. This theory held that § 1 of the Fourteenth Amendment totally incorporated all of the provisions of the Bill of Rights. As Justice Black noted, the chief congressional proponents of the Fourteenth Amendment espoused the view that the Amendment made the Bill of Rights applicable to the States and, in so doing, overruled this Court's decision in *Barron*. Nonetheless, the Court never has embraced Justice Black's "total incorporation" theory.

3

While Justice Black's theory was never adopted, the Court eventually moved in that direction by initiating what has been called a process of "selective incorporation," i.e., the Court began to hold that the Due Process Clause fully incorporates particular rights contained in the first eight Amendments.

The decisions during this time abandoned three of the previously noted characteristics of the earlier period. [T]he Court inquired whether a particular Bill of Rights guarantee is fundamental to our scheme of ordered liberty and system of justice.

The Court also shed any reluctance to hold that rights guaranteed by the Bill of Rights met the requirements for protection under the Due Process Clause. The Court eventually incorporated almost all of the provisions of the Bill of Rights. Only a handful of the Bill of Rights protections remain unincorporated.

Finally, the Court abandoned "the notion that the Fourteenth Amendment applies to the States only a watered-down, subjective version of the individual guarantees of the Bill of Rights," stating that it would be "incongruous" to apply different standards "depending on whether the claim was asserted in a state or federal court." Instead, the Court decisively held that incorporated Bill of Rights protections "are all to be enforced against the States under the Fourteenth Amendment according to the same standards that protect those personal rights against federal encroachment."

Employing this approach, the Court overruled earlier decisions in which it had held that particular Bill of Rights guarantees or remedies did not apply to the States.

III

With this framework in mind, we now turn directly to the question whether the Second Amendment right to keep and bear arms is incorporated in the concept of due process. In answering that question, as just explained, we must decide whether the right to keep and bear arms is fundamental to our scheme of ordered liberty, or as we have said in a related context, whether this right is "deeply rooted in this Nation's history and tradition," *Washington v. Glucksberg*, 521 U. S. 702, 721 (1997).

A

Our decision in *Heller* points unmistakably to the answer. Self-defense is a basic right, recognized by many legal systems from ancient times to the present day, and in *Heller*, we held that individual self-defense is "the central component" of the Second Amendment right. Explaining that "the need for defense of self, family, and property is most acute" in the home, we found that this right applies to handguns because they are "the most preferred firearm in the nation to 'keep' and use for protection of one's home and family." Thus, we concluded, citizens must be permitted "to use [handguns] for the core lawful purpose of self-defense."

Heller makes it clear that this right is "deeply rooted in this Nation's history and tradition." *Heller* explored the right's origins, noting that the 1689 English Bill of Rights explicitly protected a right to keep arms for self-defense, and that by 1765, Blackstone was able to assert that the right to keep and bear arms was "one of the fundamental rights of Englishmen."

Blackstone's assessment was shared by the American colonists. As we noted in *Heller*, King George III's attempt to disarm the colonists in the 1760's and 1770's "provoked polemical reactions by Americans invoking their rights as Englishmen to keep arms."

This understanding persisted in the years immediately following the ratification of the Bill of Rights. In addition to the four States that had adopted Second Amendment analogues before ratification, nine more States adopted state constitutional provisions protecting an individual right to keep and bear arms between 1789 and 1820. Founding-era legal commentators confirmed the importance of the right to early Americans. St. George Tucker, for example, described the right to keep and bear arms as "the true palladium of liberty" and explained that prohibitions on the right would place liberty "on the brink of destruction."

B

1

By the 1850's, the perceived threat that had prompted the inclusion of the Second Amendment in the Bill of Rights—the fear that the National Government would disarm the universal militia—had largely faded as a popular concern, but the right to keep and bear arms was highly valued for purposes of self-defense. Abolitionist authors wrote in support of the right. And when attempts were made to disarm "Free-Soilers" in "Bloody Kansas," Senator Charles Sumner, who later played a leading role in the adoption of the Fourteenth Amendment, proclaimed that "[n]ever was [the rifle] more needed in just self-defense than now in Kansas." Indeed, the 1856 Republican Party Platform protested that in Kansas the constitutional rights of the people had been "fraudulently and violently taken from them" and the "right of the people to keep and bear arms" had been "infringed."

After the Civil War, many of the over 180,000 African Americans who served in the Union Army returned to the States of the old Confederacy, where systematic efforts were made to disarm them and other blacks. The laws of some States formally prohibited African Americans from possessing firearms. For example, a Mississippi law provided that "no freedman, free negro or mulatto, not in the military service of the United States government, and not licensed so to do by the board of police of his or her county, shall keep or carry fire-arms of any kind, or any ammunition, dirk or bowie knife."

Throughout the South, armed parties, often consisting of ex-Confederate soldiers serving in the state militias, forcibly took firearms from newly freed slaves. In the first session of the 39th Congress, Senator Wilson told his colleagues: "In Mississippi rebel State forces, men who were in the rebel armies, are traversing the State, visiting the freedmen, disarming them, perpetrating murders and outrages upon them; and the same things are done in other sections of the country." The Report of the Joint Committee on Reconstruction—which was widely reprinted in the press and distributed by Members of the 39th Congress to their constituents shortly after Congress approved the Fourteenth Amendment—contained numerous examples of such abuses. In one town, the "marshal [took] all arms from returned colored soldiers, and [was] very prompt in shooting the blacks whenever an opportunity occur[red]." As Senator Wilson put it during the debate on a failed proposal to disband Southern militias: "There is one unbroken chain of testimony from all people that are loyal to this country, that the greatest outrages are perpetrated by armed men who go up and down the country searching houses, disarming people, committing outrages of every kind and description."

Union Army commanders took steps to secure the right of all citizens to keep and bear arms, but the 39th Congress concluded that legislative action was necessary. Its efforts to safeguard the right to keep and bear arms demonstrate that the right was still recognized to be fundamental.

The most explicit evidence of Congress' aim appears in § 14 of the Freedmen's Bureau Act of 1866, which provided that "the right . . . to have full and equal benefit of all laws and proceedings concerning personal liberty, personal security, and the acquisition, enjoyment, and disposition of estate, real and personal, including the constitutional right to bear arms, shall be secured to and enjoyed by all the citizens . . . without respect to race or color, or previous condition of slavery." Section 14 thus explicitly guaranteed that "all the citizens," black and white, would have "the constitutional right to bear arms."

The Civil Rights Act of 1866, which was considered at the same time as the Freedmen's Bureau Act, similarly sought to protect the right of all citizens to keep and bear arms. Section 1 of the Civil Rights Act guaranteed the "full and equal benefit of all laws and proceedings for the security of person and property, as is enjoyed by white citizens." This language was virtually identical to language in § 14 of the Freedmen's Bureau Act. And as noted, the latter provision went on to explain that one of the "laws and proceedings concerning personal liberty, personal security, and the acquisition, enjoyment, and disposition of estate, real and personal" was "the constitutional right to bear arms." Representative Bingham believed that the Civil Rights Act protected the same rights as enumerated in the Freedmen's Bureau bill, which of course explicitly mentioned the right to keep and bear arms. The unavoidable conclusion is that the Civil Rights Act, like the Freedmen's Bureau Act, aimed to protect "the constitutional right to bear arms" and not simply to prohibit discrimination.

Congress, however, ultimately deemed these legislative remedies insufficient. Southern resistance, Presidential vetoes, and this Court's pre-Civil-War precedent persuaded Congress that a constitutional amendment was necessary to provide full protection for the rights of blacks. Today, it is generally accepted that the Fourteenth Amendment was understood to provide a constitutional basis for protecting the rights set out in the Civil Rights Act of 1866.

In debating the Fourteenth Amendment, the 39th Congress referred to the right to keep and bear arms as a fundamental right deserving of protection. Senator Samuel Pomeroy described three "indispensable" "safeguards of liberty under our form of Government." One of these, he said, was the right to keep and bear arms:

"Every man . . . should have the right to bear arms for the defense of himself and family and his homestead. And if the cabin door of the freedman is broken open and the intruder enters for purposes as vile as were known to slavery, then should a well-loaded musket be in the hand of the occupant to send the polluted wretch to another world, where his wretchedness will forever remain complete."

Even those who thought the Fourteenth Amendment unnecessary believed that blacks, as citizens, "have equal right to protection, and to keep and bear arms for self-defense."

Evidence from the period immediately following the ratification of the Fourteenth Amendment only confirms that the right to keep and bear arms was considered fundamental. In an 1868 speech addressing the disarmament of freedmen, Representative Stevens emphasized the necessity of the right: "Disarm a community and you rob them of the means of defending life. Take away their weapons of defense and you take away the inalienable right of defending liberty." "The fourteenth amendment, now so happily adopted, settles the whole question." And in debating the Civil Rights Act of 1871, Congress routinely referred to the right to keep and bear arms and decried the continued disarmament of blacks in the South. Finally, legal commentators from the period emphasized the fundamental nature of the right.

The right to keep and bear arms was also widely protected by state constitutions at the time when the Fourteenth Amendment was ratified. In 1868, 22 of the 37 States in the Union had state constitutional provisions explicitly protecting the right to keep and bear arms. Quite a few of these state constitutional guarantees, moreover, explicitly protected the right to keep and bear arms as an individual right to self-defense. What is more, state constitutions adopted during the Reconstruction era by former Confederate States included a right to keep and bear arms. A clear majority of the States in 1868, therefore, recognized the right to keep and bear arms as being among the foundational rights necessary to our system of Government.

In sum, it is clear that the Framers and ratifiers of the Fourteenth Amendment counted the right to keep and bear arms among those fundamental rights necessary to our system of ordered liberty.

2

Despite all this evidence, municipal respondents contend that Congress, in the years immediately following the Civil War, merely sought to outlaw "discriminatory measures taken against freedmen, which it addressed by adopting a non-discrimination principle" and that even an outright ban on the possession of firearms was regarded as acceptable, "so long as it was not done in a discriminatory manner." They argue that Members of Congress overwhelmingly viewed § 1 of the Fourteenth Amendment "as an antidiscrimination rule," and they cite statements to the effect that the section would outlaw discriminatory measures. This argument is implausible.

First, while § 1 of the Fourteenth Amendment contains "an antidiscrimination rule," namely, the Equal Protection Clause, municipal respondents can hardly mean that § 1 does no more than prohibit discrimination. If that were so, then the First Amendment, as applied to the States, would not prohibit nondiscriminatory abridgments of the rights to freedom of speech or freedom of religion; the Fourth Amendment, as applied to the States, would not prohibit all unreasonable searches and seizures but only discriminatory searches and seizures—and so on. We assume that this is not municipal respondents' view, so what they must mean is that the Second Amendment should be singled out for special—and specially unfavorable—treatment. We reject that suggestion.

Second, municipal respondents' argument ignores the clear terms of the Freedmen's Bureau Act of 1866, which acknowledged the existence of the right to bear arms. If that law had used language such as "the equal benefit of laws concerning the bearing of arms," it would be possible to interpret it as simply a prohibition of racial discrimination. But § 14 speaks of and protects "the constitutional right to bear arms," an unmistakable reference to the right protected by the Second Amendment. And it protects the "full and equal benefit" of this right in the States. It would have been nonsensical for Congress to guarantee the full and equal benefit of a constitutional right that does not exist.

Third, if the 39th Congress had outlawed only those laws that discriminate on the basis of race or previous condition of servitude, African Americans in the South would likely have remained vulnerable to attack by many of their worst abusers: the state militia and state peace officers. In the years immediately following the Civil War, a law banning the possession of guns by all private citizens would have been nondiscriminatory only in the formal sense. Any such law—like the Chicago and Oak Park ordinances challenged here—presumably would have permitted the possession of guns by those acting under the authority of the State and would thus have left firearms in the hands of the militia and local peace officers. And as the Report of the Joint Committee on Reconstruction revealed, those groups were widely involved in harassing blacks in the South.

Fourth, municipal respondents' purely antidiscrimination theory of the Fourteenth Amendment disregards the plight of whites in the South who opposed the Black Codes. If the 39th Congress and the ratifying public had simply prohibited racial discrimination with respect to the bearing of arms, opponents of the Black Codes would have been left without the means of self-defense—as had abolitionists in Kansas in the 1850's.

Fifth, the 39th Congress' response to proposals to disband and disarm the Southern militias is instructive. Despite recognizing and deploring the abuses of these militias, the 39th Congress balked at a proposal to disarm them. Disarmament, it was argued, would violate the members' right to bear arms, and it was ultimately decided to disband the militias but not to disarm their members. It cannot be doubted that the right to bear arms was regarded as a substantive guarantee, not a prohibition that could be ignored so long as the States legislated in an evenhanded manner.

IV

Municipal respondents' remaining arguments are at war with our central holding in Heller: that the Second Amendment protects a personal right to keep and bear arms for lawful purposes, most notably for self-defense within the home. Municipal respondents, in effect, ask us to treat the right recognized in *Heller* as a second-class right, subject to an entirely different body of rules than the other Bill of Rights guarantees that we have held to be incorporated into the Due Process Clause.

Municipal respondents' main argument is nothing less than a plea to disregard 50 years of incorporation precedent and return (presumably for this case only) to a bygone era. Municipal respondents submit that the Due Process Clause protects only those rights "recognized by all temperate and civilized governments, from a deep and universal sense of [their] justice." According to municipal respondents, if it is possible to imagine any civilized legal system that does not recognize a particular right, then the Due Process Clause does not make that right binding on the States. Therefore, the municipal respondents continue, because such countries as England, Canada, Australia, Japan, Denmark, Finland, Luxembourg, and New Zealand either ban or severely limit handgun ownership, it must follow that no right to possess such weapons is protected by the Fourteenth Amendment.

This line of argument is, of course, inconsistent with the long-established standard we apply in incorporation cases. And the present-day implications of municipal respondents' argument are stunning. For example, many of the rights that our Bill of Rights provides for persons accused of criminal offenses are virtually unique to this country. If our understanding of the right to a jury trial, the right against self-incrimination, and the right to counsel were necessary attributes of any civilized country, it would follow that the United States is the only civilized Nation in the world.

Municipal respondents attempt to salvage their position by suggesting that their argument applies only to substantive as opposed to procedural rights. But even in this trimmed form, municipal respondents' argument flies in the face of more than a half-century of precedent. For example, in *Everson v. Board of Ed. of Ewing*, 330 U. S. 1, 8 (1947), the Court held that the Fourteenth Amendment incorporates the Establishment Clause of the First Amendment. Yet several of the countries that municipal respondents recognize as civilized have established state churches. If we were to adopt municipal respondents' theory, all of this Court's Establishment Clause precedents involving actions taken by state and local governments would go by the boards.

Municipal respondents maintain that the Second Amendment differs from all of the other provisions of the Bill of Rights because it concerns the right to possess a deadly implement and thus has implications for public safety. And they note that there is intense disagreement on the question whether the private possession of guns in the home increases or decreases gun deaths and injuries.

The right to keep and bear arms, however, is not the only constitutional right that has controversial public safety implications. All of the constitutional provisions that impose restrictions on law enforcement and on the prosecution of crimes fall into the same category. Municipal respondents cite no case in which we have refrained from holding that a provision of the Bill of Rights is binding on the States on the ground that the right at issue has disputed public safety implications.

We likewise reject municipal respondents' argument that we should depart from our established incorporation methodology on the ground that making the Second Amendment binding on the States and their subdivisions is inconsistent with principles of federalism and will stifle experimentation. Municipal respondents point out—quite correctly—that conditions and problems differ from locality to locality and that citizens in different jurisdictions have divergent views on the issue of gun control. Municipal respondents therefore urge us to allow state and local governments to enact any gun control law that they deem to be reasonable, including a complete ban on the possession of handguns in the home for self-defense.

There is nothing new in the argument that, in order to respect federalism and allow useful state experimentation, a federal constitutional right should not be fully binding on the States. This argument was made repeatedly and eloquently by Members of this Court who rejected the concept of incorporation and urged retention of the two-track approach to incorporation. Throughout the era of "selective incorporation," Justice Harlan in particular, invoking the values of federalism and state experimentation, fought a determined rearguard action to preserve the two-track approach.

Time and again, however, those pleas failed. Unless we turn back the clock or adopt a special incorporation test applicable only to the Second Amendment, municipal respondents' argument must be rejected. Under our precedents, if a Bill of Rights guarantee is fundamental from an American perspective, then, unless stare decisis counsels otherwise, that guarantee is fully binding on the States and thus limits (but by no means eliminates) their ability to devise solutions to social problems that suit local needs and values. As noted by the 38 States that have appeared in this case as amici supporting petitioners, "[s]tate and local experimentation with reasonable firearms regulations will continue under the Second Amendment."

Municipal respondents and their amici complain that incorporation of the Second Amendment right will lead to extensive and costly litigation, but this argument applies with even greater force to constitutional rights and remedies that have already been held to be binding on the States.

Municipal respondents assert that, although most state constitutions protect firearms rights, state courts have held that these rights are subject to "interest-balancing" and have sustained a variety of restrictions. In *Heller*, however, we expressly rejected the argument that the scope of the Second Amendment right should be determined by judicial interest balancing, and this Court decades ago abandoned "the notion that the Fourteenth Amendment applies to the States only a watered-down, subjective version of the individual guarantees of the Bill of Rights."

As evidence that the Fourteenth Amendment has not historically been understood to restrict the authority of the States to regulate firearms, municipal respondents and supporting amici cite a variety of state and local firearms laws that courts have upheld. But what is most striking about their research is the paucity of precedent sustaining bans comparable to those at issue here and in *Heller*. Municipal respondents cite precisely one case (from the late 20th century) in which such a ban was sustained. It is important to keep in mind that Heller, while striking down a law that prohibited the possession of handguns in the home, recognized that the right to keep and bear arms is not "a right to keep and carry any weapon whatsoever in any manner whatsoever and for whatever purpose." We made it clear in *Heller* that our holding did not cast doubt on such longstanding regulatory measures as "prohibitions on the possession of firearms by felons and the mentally ill," "laws forbidding the carrying of firearms in sensitive places such as schools and government buildings, or laws imposing conditions and qualifications on the commercial sale of arms." We repeat those assurances here. Despite municipal respondents' doomsday proclamations, incorporation does not imperil every law regulating firearms.

Municipal respondents argue, finally, that the right to keep and bear arms is unique among the rights set out in the first eight Amendments "because the reason for codifying the Second Amendment (to protect the militia) differs from the purpose (primarily, to use firearms to engage in self-defense) that is claimed to make the right implicit in the concept of ordered liberty." Municipal respondents suggest that the Second Amendment right differs from the rights heretofore incorporated because the latter were "valued for [their] own sake." But we have never previously suggested that incorporation of a right turns on whether it has intrinsic as opposed to instrumental value, and quite a few of the rights previously held to be incorporated—for example the right to counsel and the right to confront and subpoena witnesses—are clearly instrumental by any measure. Moreover, this contention repackages one of the chief arguments that we rejected in *Heller*, *i.e.,* that the scope of the Second Amendment right is defined by the immediate threat that led to the inclusion of that right in the Bill of Rights. In *Heller*, we recognized that the codification of this right was prompted by fear that the Federal Government would disarm and thus disable the militias, but we rejected the suggestion that the right was valued only as a means of preserving the militias. On the contrary, we stressed that the right was also valued because the possession of firearms was thought to be essential for self-defense. As we put it, self-defense was "the central component of the right itself."

V

A

We turn, finally, to the two dissenting opinions. Justice Stevens' eloquent opinion covers ground already addressed, and therefore little need be added in response. Justice Stevens would "ground the prohibitions against state action squarely on due process, without intermediate reliance on any of the first eight Amendments." The question presented in this case, in his view, "is whether the particular right asserted by petitioners applies to the States because of the Fourteenth Amendment itself, standing on its own bottom." He would hold that "[t]he rights protected against state infringement by the Fourteenth Amendment's Due Process Clause need not be identical in shape or scope to the rights protected against Federal Government infringement by the various provisions of the Bill of Rights."

As we have explained, the Court, for the past half-century, has moved away from the two-track approach. If we were now to accept Justice Stevens' theory across the board, decades of decisions would be undermined. We assume that this is not what is proposed. What is urged instead, it appears, is that this theory be revived solely for the individual right that *Heller* recognized, over vigorous dissents.

The relationship between the Bill of Rights' guarantees and the States must be governed by a single, neutral principle. It is far too late to exhume what Justice Brennan, writing for the Court 46 years ago, derided as "the notion that the Fourteenth Amendment applies to the States only a watered-down, subjective version of the individual guarantees of the Bill of Rights."

B

Justice Breyer's dissent makes several points to which we briefly respond. To begin, while there is certainly room for disagreement about Heller's analysis of the history of the right to keep and bear arms, nothing written since Heller persuades us to reopen the question there decided. Few other questions of original meaning have been as thoroughly explored.

Justice Breyer's conclusion that the Fourteenth Amendment does not incorporate the right to keep and bear arms appears to rest primarily on four factors: First, "there is no popular consensus" that the right is fundamental; second, the right does not protect minorities or persons neglected by those holding political power; third, incorporation of the Second Amendment right would "amount to a significant incursion on a traditional and important area of state concern, altering the constitutional relationship between the States and the Federal Government" and preventing local variation; and fourth, determining the scope of the Second Amendment right in cases involving state and local laws will force judges to answer difficult empirical questions regarding matters that are outside their area of expertise. Even if we believed that these factors were relevant to the incorporation inquiry, none of these factors undermines the case for incorporation of the right to keep and bear arms for self-defense.

First, we have never held that a provision of the Bill of Rights applies to the States only if there is a "popular consensus" that the right is fundamental, and we see no basis for such a rule. But in this case, as it turns out, there is evidence of such a consensus. An amicus brief submitted by 58 Members of the Senate and 251 Members of the House of Representatives urges us to hold that the right to keep and bear arms is fundamental. Another brief submitted by 38 States takes the same position.

Second, petitioners and many others who live in high-crime areas dispute the proposition that the Second Amendment right does not protect minorities and those lacking political clout. The plight of Chicagoans living in high-crime areas was recently highlighted when two Illinois legislators representing Chicago districts called on the Governor to deploy the Illinois National Guard to patrol the City's streets. The legislators noted that the number of Chicago homicide victims during the current year equaled the number of American soldiers killed during that same period in Afghanistan and Iraq and that 80% of the Chicago victims were black. Amici supporting incorporation of the right to keep and bear arms contend that the right is especially important for women and members of other groups that may be especially vulnerable to violent crime. If, as petitioners believe, their safety and the safety of other law-abiding members of the community would be enhanced by the possession of handguns in the home for self-defense, then the Second Amendment right protects the rights of minorities and other residents of high-crime areas whose needs are not being met by elected public officials.

Third, Justice Breyer is correct that incorporation of the Second Amendment right will to some extent limit the legislative freedom of the States, but this is always true when a Bill of Rights provision is incorporated. Incorporation always restricts experimentation and local variations, but that has not stopped the Court from incorporating virtually every other provision of the Bill of Rights. "[T]he enshrinement of constitutional rights necessarily takes certain policy choices off the table." *Heller*, 554 U. S., at ___. This conclusion is no more remarkable with respect to the Second Amendment than it is with respect to all the other limitations on state power found in the Constitution.

Finally, Justice Breyer is incorrect that incorporation will require judges to assess the costs and benefits of firearms restrictions and thus to make difficult empirical judgments in an area in which they lack expertise. As we have noted, while his opinion in *Heller* recommended an interest-balancing test, the Court specifically rejected that suggestion. "The very enumeration of the right takes out of the hands of government—even the Third Branch of Government—the power to decide on a case-by-case basis whether the right is really worth insisting upon." *Heller* at [683].

* * *

In *Heller*, we held that the Second Amendment protects the right to possess a handgun in the home for the purpose of self-defense. Unless considerations of stare decisis counsel otherwise, a provision of the Bill of Rights that protects a right that is fundamental from an American perspective applies equally to the Federal Government and the States. We therefore hold that the Due Process Clause of the Fourteenth Amendment incorporates the Second Amendment right recognized in *Heller*. The judgment of the Court of Appeals is reversed, and the case is remanded for further proceedings.

It is so ordered.

JUSTICE SCALIA, concurring.

I join the Court's opinion. Despite my misgivings about Substantive Due Process as an original matter, I have acquiesced in the Court's incorporation of certain guarantees in the Bill of Rights "because it is both long established and narrowly limited." *Albright v. Oliver*, 510 U. S. 266, 275 (1994). This case does not require me to reconsider that view, since straightforward application of settled doctrine suffices to decide it.

I write separately only to respond to some aspects of Justice Stevens' dissent. Not that aspect which disagrees with the majority's application of our precedents to this case, which is fully covered by the Court's opinion. But much of what Justice Stevens writes is a broad condemnation of the theory of interpretation which underlies the Court's opinion, a theory that makes the traditions of our people paramount. He proposes a different theory, which he claims is more "cautiou[s]" and respectful of proper limits on the judicial role. It is that claim I wish to address.

I

A

After stressing the substantive dimension of what he has renamed the "liberty clause," Justice Stevens proceeds to urge readoption of the theory of incorporation articulated in *Palko v. Connecticut*, 302 U. S. 319, 325 (1937). But in fact he does not favor application of that theory at all. For whether *Palko* requires only that "a fair and enlightened system of justice would be impossible without" the right sought to be incorporated, or requires in addition that the right be rooted in the "traditions and conscience of our people," many of the rights Justice Stevens thinks are incorporated could not pass muster under either test: abortion, homosexual sodomy, the right to have excluded from criminal trials evidence obtained in violation of the Fourth Amendment, and the right to teach one's children foreign languages, among others.

That Justice Stevens is not applying any version of *Palko* is clear from comparing, on the one hand, the rights he believes are covered, with, on the other hand, his conclusion that the right to keep and bear arms is not covered. Rights that pass his test include not just those "relating to marriage, procreation, contraception, family relationships, and child rearing and education," but also rights against "[g]overnment action that shocks the conscience, pointlessly infringes settled expectations, trespasses into sensitive private realms or life choices without adequate justification, [or] perpetrates gross injustice." Not all such rights are in, however, since only "some fundamental aspects of personhood, dignity, and the like" are protected. Exactly what is covered is not clear. But whatever else is in, he knows that the right to keep and bear arms is out, despite its being as "deeply rooted in this Nation's history and tradition," as a right can be, see *District of Columbia v. Heller*, 554 U. S. [570] (2008). I can find no other explanation for such certitude except that Justice Stevens, despite his forswearing of "personal and private notions," deeply believes it should be out.

The subjective nature of Justice Stevens' standard is also apparent from his claim that it is the courts' prerogative—indeed their duty—to update the Due Process Clause so that it encompasses new freedoms the Framers were too narrow-minded to imagine. Courts, he proclaims, must "do justice to [the Clause's] urgent call and its open texture" by exercising the "interpretive discretion the latter embodies." (Why the people are not up to the task of deciding what new rights to protect, even though it is they who are authorized to make changes, see U. S. Const., Art. V, is never explained.) And it would be "judicial abdication" for a judge to "tur[n] his back" on his task of determining what the Fourteenth Amendment covers by "outsourc[ing]" the job to "historical sentiment,"—that is, by being guided by what the American people throughout our history have thought. It is only we judges, exercising our "own reasoned judgment," who can be entrusted with deciding the Due Process Clause's scope—which rights serve the Amendment's "central values,"—which basically means picking the rights we want to protect and discarding those we do not.

II

If Justice Stevens' account of the constraints of his approach did not demonstrate that they do not exist, his application of that approach to the case before us leaves no doubt. He offers several reasons for concluding that the Second Amendment right to keep and bear arms is not fundamental enough to be applied against the States. None is persuasive, but more pertinent to my purpose, each is either intrinsically indeterminate, would preclude incorporation of rights we have already held incorporated, or both. His approach therefore does nothing to stop a judge from arriving at any conclusion he sets out to reach.

III

Justice Stevens' response to this concurrence makes the usual rejoinder of "living Constitution" advocates to the criticism that it empowers judges to eliminate or expand what the people have prescribed: The traditional, historically focused method, he says, reposes discretion in judges as well. Historical analysis can be difficult; it sometimes requires resolving threshold questions, and making nuanced judgments about which evidence to consult and how to interpret it.

I will stipulate to that. But the question to be decided is not whether the historically focused method is a perfect means of restraining aristocratic judicial Constitution-writing; but whether it is the best means available in an imperfect world. Or indeed, even more narrowly than that: whether it is demonstrably much better than what Justice Stevens proposes. I think it beyond all serious dispute that it is much less subjective, and intrudes much less upon the democratic process. It is less subjective because it depends upon a body of evidence susceptible of reasoned analysis rather than a variety of vague ethico-political First Principles whose combined conclusion can be found to point in any direction the judges favor. In the most controversial matters brought before this Court—for example, the constitutionality of prohibiting abortion, assisted suicide, or homosexual sodomy, or the constitutionality of the death penalty—any historical methodology, under any plausible standard of proof, would lead to the same conclusion. Moreover, the methodological differences that divide historians, and the varying interpretive assumptions they bring to their work are nothing compared to the differences among the American people (though perhaps not among graduates of prestigious law schools) with regard to the moral judgments Justice Stevens would have courts pronounce. And whether or not special expertise is needed to answer historical questions, judges most certainly have no "comparative . . . advantage," in resolving moral disputes. What is more, his approach would not eliminate, but multiply, the hard questions courts must confront, since he would not replace history with moral philosophy, but would have courts consider both.

And the Court's approach intrudes less upon the democratic process because the rights it acknowledges are those established by a constitutional history formed by democratic decisions; and the rights it fails to acknowledge are left to be democratically adopted or rejected by the people, with the assurance that their decision is not subject to judicial revision. Justice Stevens' approach, on the other hand, deprives the people of that power, since whatever the Constitution and laws may say, the list of protected rights will be whatever courts wish it to be. After all, he notes, the people have been wrong before and courts may conclude they are wrong in the future. Justice Stevens abhors a system in which "majorities or powerful interest groups always get their way," but replaces it with a system in which unelected and life-tenured judges always get their way. That such usurpation is effected unabashedly—with "the judge's cards . . . laid on the table"—makes it even worse. In a vibrant democracy, usurpation should have to be accomplished in the dark. It is Justice Stevens' approach, not the Court's, that puts democracy in peril.

JUSTICE THOMAS, concurring in part and concurring in the judgment.

I agree with the Court that the Fourteenth Amendment makes the right to keep and bear arms set forth in the Second Amendment "fully applicable to the States." I write separately because I believe there is a more straightforward path to this conclusion, one that is more faithful to the Fourteenth Amendment's text and history.

Applying what is now a well-settled test, the plurality opinion concludes that the right to keep and bear arms applies to the States through the Fourteenth Amendment's Due Process Clause because it is "fundamental" to the American "scheme of ordered liberty," and "deeply rooted in this Nation's history and tradition." I agree with that description of the right. But I cannot agree that it is enforceable against the States through a clause that speaks only to "process." Instead, the right to keep and bear arms is a privilege of American citizenship that applies to the States through the Fourteenth Amendment's Privileges or Immunities Clause.

I

In *District of Columbia v. Heller*, 554 U. S. [570] (2008), this Court held that the Second Amendment protects an individual right to keep and bear arms for the purpose of self-defense, striking down a District of Columbia ordinance that banned the possession of handguns in the home. The question in this case is whether the Constitution protects that right against abridgment by the States.

As the Court explains, if this case were litigated before the Fourteenth Amendment's adoption in 1868, the answer to that question would be simple. In *Barron v. Baltimore*, 7 Pet. 243 (1833), this Court held that the Bill of Rights applied only to the Federal Government.

Nearly three decades after *Barron*, the Nation was splintered by a civil war fought principally over the question of slavery. As was evident to many throughout our Nation's early history, slavery, and the measures designed to protect it, were irreconcilable with the principles of equality, government by consent, and inalienable rights proclaimed by the Declaration of Independence and embedded in our constitutional structure.

After the war, a series of constitutional amendments were adopted to repair the Nation from the damage slavery had caused. The provision at issue here, § 1 of the Fourteenth Amendment, significantly altered our system of government. The first sentence of that section provides that "[a]ll persons born or naturalized in the United States and subject to the jurisdiction thereof, are citizens of the United States and of the State wherein they reside." This unambiguously overruled this Court's contrary holding in *Dred Scott v. Sandford*, 19 How. 393 (1857), that the Constitution did not recognize black Americans as citizens of the United States or their own State.

The meaning of § 1's next sentence has divided this Court for many years. That sentence begins with the command that "[n]o State shall make or enforce any law which shall abridge the privileges or immunities of citizens of the United States." On its face, this appears to grant the persons just made United States citizens a certain collection of rights—i.e., privileges or immunities—attributable to that status.

This Court's precedents accept that point, but define the relevant collection of rights quite narrowly. In the *Slaughter-House Cases*, 16 Wall. 36 (1873), decided just five years after the Fourteenth Amendment's adoption, the Court interpreted this text, now known as the Privileges or Immunities Clause, for the first time. In a closely divided decision, the Court drew a sharp distinction between the privileges and immunities of state citizenship and those of federal citizenship, and held that the Privileges or Immunities Clause protected only the latter category of rights from state abridgment. The Court defined that category to include only those rights "which owe their existence to the Federal government, its National character, its Constitution, or its laws." This arguably left open the possibility that certain individual rights enumerated in the Constitution could be considered privileges or immunities of federal citizenship. But the Court soon rejected that proposition, interpreting the Privileges or Immunities Clause even more narrowly in its later cases.

Chief among those cases is *United States v. Cruikshank*, 92 U. S. 542 (1876). There, the Court held that members of a white militia who had brutally murdered as many as 165 black Louisianians congregating outside a courthouse had not deprived the victims of their privileges as American citizens to peaceably assemble or to keep and bear arms. According to the Court, the right to peaceably assemble codified in the First Amendment was not a privilege of United States citizenship because "[t]he right . . . existed long before the adoption of the Constitution." Similarly, the Court held that the right to keep and bear arms was not a privilege of United States citizenship because it was not "in any manner dependent upon that instrument for its existence." In other words, the reason the Framers codified the right to bear arms in the Second Amendment—its nature as an inalienable right that pre-existed the Constitution's adoption—was the very reason citizens could not enforce it against States through the Fourteenth.

That circular reasoning effectively has been the Court's last word on the Privileges or Immunities Clause. In the intervening years, the Court has held that the Clause prevents state abridgment of only a handful of rights, such as the right to travel, that are not readily described as essential to liberty.

As a consequence of this Court's marginalization of the Clause, litigants seeking federal protection of fundamental rights turned to the remainder of § 1 in search of an alternative fount of such rights. They found one in a most curious place—that section's command that every State guarantee "due process" to any person before depriving him of "life, liberty, or property." . . . .

While this Court has at times concluded that a right gains "fundamental" status only if it is essential to the American "scheme of ordered liberty" or "deeply rooted in this Nation's history and tradition," the Court has just as often held that a right warrants Due Process Clause protection if it satisfies a far less measurable range of criteria. Using the latter approach, the Court has determined that the Due Process Clause applies rights against the States that are not mentioned in the Constitution at all, even without seriously arguing that the Clause was originally understood to protect such rights.

All of this is a legal fiction. The notion that a constitutional provision that guarantees only "process" before a person is deprived of life, liberty, or property could define the substance of those rights strains credulity for even the most casual user of words. Moreover, this fiction is a particularly dangerous one. The one theme that links the Court's substantive due process precedents together is their lack of a guiding principle to distinguish "fundamental" rights that warrant protection from nonfundamental rights that do not. Today's decision illustrates the point. Replaying a debate that has endured from the inception of the Court's substantive due process jurisprudence, the dissents laud the "flexibility" in this Court's substantive due process doctrine, while the plurality makes yet another effort to impose principled restraints on its exercise. But neither side argues that the meaning they attribute to the Due Process Clause was consistent with public understanding at the time of its ratification.

I cannot accept a theory of constitutional interpretation that rests on such tenuous footing. This Court's substantive due process framework fails to account for both the text of the Fourteenth Amendment and the history that led to its adoption, filling that gap with a jurisprudence devoid of a guiding principle. I believe the original meaning of the Fourteenth Amendment offers a superior alternative, and that a return to that meaning would allow this Court to enforce the rights the Fourteenth Amendment is designed to protect with greater clarity and predictability than the substantive due process framework has so far managed.

I acknowledge the volume of precedents that have been built upon the substantive due process framework, and I further acknowledge the importance of stare decisis to the stability of our Nation's legal system. But stare decisis is only an "adjunct" of our duty as judges to decide by our best lights what the Constitution means. Moreover, as judges, we interpret the Constitution one case or controversy at a time. The question presented in this case is not whether our entire Fourteenth Amendment jurisprudence must be preserved or revised, but only whether, and to what extent, a particular clause in the Constitution protects the particular right at issue here. With the inquiry appropriately narrowed, I believe this case presents an opportunity to reexamine, and begin the process of restoring, the meaning of the Fourteenth Amendment agreed upon by those who ratified it.

II

The Privileges or Immunities Clause of the Fourteenth Amendment declares that "[n]o State . . . shall abridge the privileges or immunities of citizens of the United States." In interpreting this language, it is important to recall that constitutional provisions are "written to be understood by the voters." *Heller*, 554 U. S., at ___. Thus, the objective of this inquiry is to discern what "ordinary citizens" at the time of ratification would have understood the Privileges or Immunities Clause to mean.

A

* * *

The text examined so far demonstrates three points about the meaning of the Privileges or Immunities Clause in § 1. First, "privileges" and "immunities" were synonyms for "rights." Second, both the States and the Federal Government had long recognized the inalienable rights of their citizens. Third, Article IV, § 2 of the Constitution protected traveling citizens against state discrimination with respect to the fundamental rights of state citizenship.

Two questions still remain, both provoked by the textual similarity between § 1's Privileges or Immunities Clause and Article IV, § 2. The first involves the nature of the rights at stake: Are the privileges or immunities of "citizens of the United States" recognized by § 1 the same as the privileges and immunities of "citizens in the several States" to which Article IV, § 2 refers? The second involves the restriction imposed on the States: Does § 1, like Article IV, § 2, prohibit only discrimination with respect to certain rights if the State chooses to recognize them, or does it require States to recognize those rights? I address each question in turn.

B

* * *

This evidence plainly shows that the ratifying public understood the Privileges or Immunities Clause to protect constitutionally enumerated rights, including the right to keep and bear arms. As the Court demonstrates, there can be no doubt that § 1 was understood to enforce the Second Amendment against the States. In my view, this is because the right to keep and bear arms was understood to be a privilege of American citizenship guaranteed by the Privileges or Immunities Clause.

C

The next question is whether the Privileges or Immunities Clause merely prohibits States from discriminating among citizens if they recognize the Second Amendment's right to keep and bear arms, or whether the Clause requires States to recognize the right. The municipal respondents, Chicago and Oak Park, argue for the former interpretation. They contend that the Second Amendment, as applied to the States through the Fourteenth, authorizes a State to impose an outright ban on handgun possession such as the ones at issue here so long as a State applies it to all citizens equally. The Court explains why this antidiscrimination-only reading of § 1 as a whole is "implausible." I agree, but because I think it is the Privileges or Immunities Clause that applies this right to the States, I must explain why this Clause in particular protects against more than just state discrimination, and in fact establishes a minimum baseline of rights for all American citizens. . . .

This history confirms what the text of the Privileges or Immunities Clause most naturally suggests: Consistent with its command that "[n]o State shall . . . abridge" the rights of United States citizens, the Clause establishes a minimum baseline of federal rights, and the constitutional right to keep and bear arms plainly was among them.

III

My conclusion is contrary to this Court's precedents, which hold that the Second Amendment right to keep and bear arms is not a privilege of United States citizenship. I must, therefore, consider whether stare decisis requires retention of those precedents. As mentioned at the outset, my inquiry is limited to the right at issue here. Thus, I do not endeavor to decide in this case whether, or to what extent, the Privileges or Immunities Clause applies any other rights enumerated in the Constitution against the States. Nor do I suggest that the stare decisis considerations surrounding the application of the right to keep and bear arms against the States would be the same as those surrounding another right protected by the Privileges or Immunities Clause. I consider stare decisis only as it applies to the question presented here.

A

This inquiry begins with the *Slaughter-House Cases.* The Court held that the Privileges or Immunities Clause protected only rights of federal citizenship—those "which owe their existence to the Federal government, its National character, its Constitution, or its laws"—and did not protect any of the rights of state citizenship. In other words, the Court defined the two sets of rights as mutually exclusive.

After separating these two sets of rights, the Court defined the rights of state citizenship as "embrac[ing] nearly every civil right for the establishment and protection of which organized government is instituted"—that is, all those rights listed in *Corfield.*

I reject that understanding. There was no reason to interpret the Privileges or Immunities Clause as putting the Court to the extreme choice of interpreting the "privileges and immunities" of federal citizenship to mean either all those rights listed in *Corfield,* or almost no rights at all. If the Privileges or Immunities Clause were understood to protect every conceivable civil right from state abridgment, the Fifteenth Amendment would have been redundant.

The better view, in light of the States and Federal Government's shared history of recognizing certain inalienable rights in their citizens, is that the privileges and immunities of state and federal citizenship overlap.

B

Three years after *Slaughter-House,* the Court in *Cruikshank* squarely held that the right to keep and bear arms was not a privilege of American citizenship, thereby overturning the convictions of militia members responsible for the brutal Colfax Massacre. *Cruikshank* is not a precedent entitled to any respect. The flaws in its interpretation of the Privileges or Immunities Clause are made evident by the preceding evidence of its original meaning, and I would reject the holding on that basis alone. But, the consequences of *Cruikshank* warrant mention as well.

Cruikshank's holding that blacks could look only to state governments for protection of their right to keep and bear arms enabled private forces, often with the assistance of local governments, to subjugate the newly freed slaves and their descendants through a wave of private violence designed to drive blacks from the voting booth and force them into peonage, an effective return to slavery. Without federal enforcement of the inalienable right to keep and bear arms, these militias and mobs were tragically successful in waging a campaign of terror against the very people the Fourteenth Amendment had just made citizens.

Take, for example, the Hamburg Massacre of 1876. There, a white citizen militia sought out and murdered a troop of black militiamen for no other reason than that they had dared to conduct a celebratory Fourth of July parade through their mostly black town. The white militia commander, "Pitchfork" Ben Tillman, later described this massacre with pride. None of the perpetrators of the Hamburg murders was ever brought to justice.

Organized terrorism like that perpetuated by Tillman and his cohorts proliferated in the absence of federal enforcement of constitutional rights. Militias such as the Ku Klux Klan, the Knights of the White Camellia, the White Brotherhood, the Pale Faces, and the '76 Association spread terror among blacks and white Republicans by breaking up Republican meetings, threatening political leaders, and whipping black militiamen.

Although Congress enacted legislation to suppress these activities, Klan tactics remained a constant presence in the lives of Southern blacks for decades. Between 1882 and 1968, there were at least 3,446 reported lynchings of blacks in the South. They were tortured and killed for a wide array of alleged crimes, without even the slightest hint of due process.

The use of firearms for self-defense was often the only way black citizens could protect themselves from mob violence.

In my view, the record makes plain that the Framers of the Privileges or Immunities Clause and the ratifying-era public understood—just as the Framers of the Second Amendment did—that the right to keep and bear arms was essential to the preservation of liberty. The record makes equally plain that they deemed this right necessary to include in the minimum baseline of federal rights that the Privileges or Immunities Clause established in the wake of the War over slavery. There is nothing about *Cruikshank's* contrary holding that warrants its retention.

* * *

I agree with the Court that the Second Amendment is fully applicable to the States. I do so because the right to keep and bear arms is guaranteed by the Fourteenth Amendment as a privilege of American citizenship.

JUSTICE STEVENS, dissenting.

In *District of Columbia v. Heller*, 554 U. S. ____ (2008), the Court answered the question whether a federal enclave's "prohibition on the possession of usable handguns in the home violates the Second Amendment to the Constitution." The question we should be answering in this case is whether the Constitution "guarantees individuals a fundamental right," enforceable against the States, "to possess a functional, personal firearm, including a handgun, within the home." That is a different—and more difficult—inquiry than asking if the Fourteenth Amendment "incorporates" the Second Amendment. The so-called incorporation question was squarely and, in my view, correctly resolved in the late 19th century.

Before the District Court, petitioners focused their pleadings on the special considerations raised by domestic possession, which they identified as the core of their asserted right. In support of their claim that the city of Chicago's handgun ban violates the Constitution, they now rely primarily on the Privileges or Immunities Clause of the Fourteenth Amendment. They rely secondarily on the Due Process Clause of that Amendment.

Neither submission requires the Court to express an opinion on whether the Fourteenth Amendment places any limit on the power of States to regulate possession, use, or carriage of firearms outside the home.

I agree with the plurality's refusal to accept petitioners' primary submission. Their briefs marshal an impressive amount of historical evidence for their argument that the Court interpreted the Privileges or Immunities Clause too narrowly in the *Slaughter-House Cases*, 16 Wall. 36 (1873). But the original meaning of the Clause is not as clear as they suggest—and not nearly as clear as it would need to be to dislodge 137 years of precedent. The burden is severe for those who seek radical change in such an established body of constitutional doctrine. Moreover, the suggestion that invigorating the Privileges or Immunities Clause will reduce judicial discretion, strikes me as implausible, if not exactly backwards. "For the very reason that it has so long remained a clean slate, a revitalized Privileges or Immunities Clause holds special hazards for judges who are mindful that their proper task is not to write their personal views of appropriate public policy into the Constitution."

I further agree with the plurality that there are weighty arguments supporting petitioners' second submission, insofar as it concerns the possession of firearms for lawful self-defense in the home. But these arguments are less compelling than the plurality suggests; they are much less compelling when applied outside the home; and their validity does not depend on the Court's holding in *Heller*. For that holding sheds no light on the meaning of the Due Process Clause of the Fourteenth Amendment. Our decisions construing that Clause to render various procedural guarantees in the Bill of Rights enforceable against the States likewise tell us little about the meaning of the word "liberty" in the Clause or about the scope of its protection of nonprocedural rights.

This is a substantive due process case.

I

Section 1 of the Fourteenth Amendment decrees that no State shall "deprive any person of life, liberty, or property, without due process of law." The Court has filled thousands of pages expounding that spare text. As I read the vast corpus of substantive due process opinions, they confirm several important principles that ought to guide our resolution of this case. The principal opinion's lengthy summary of our "incorporation" doctrine, and its implicit (and untenable) effort to wall off that doctrine from the rest of our substantive due process jurisprudence, invite a fresh survey of this old terrain.

Substantive Content

The first, and most basic, principle established by our cases is that the rights protected by the Due Process Clause are not merely procedural in nature. At first glance, this proposition might seem surprising, given that the Clause refers to "process." But substance and procedure are often deeply entwined. Upon closer inspection, the text can be read to "impos[e] nothing less than an obligation to give substantive content to the words 'liberty' and 'due process of law,' " *Washington v. Glucksberg*, 521 U. S. 702, 764 (1997), lest superficially fair procedures be permitted to "destroy the enjoyment" of life, liberty, and property, and the Clause's prepositional modifier be permitted to swallow its primary command. Procedural guarantees are hollow unless linked to substantive interests; and no amount of process can legitimize some deprivations.

Liberty

The second principle woven through our cases is that substantive due process is fundamentally a matter of personal liberty. For it is the liberty clause of the Fourteenth Amendment that grounds our most important holdings in this field. It is the liberty clause that enacts the Constitution's "promise" that a measure of dignity and self-rule will be afforded to all persons. It is the liberty clause that reflects and renews "the origins of the American heritage of freedom [and] the abiding interest in individual liberty that makes certain state intrusions on the citizen's right to decide how he will live his own life intolerable." Our substantive due process cases have episodically invoked values such as privacy and equality as well, values that in certain contexts may intersect with or complement a subject's liberty interests in profound ways. But as I have observed on numerous occasions, "most of the significant [20th-century] cases raising Bill of Rights issues have, in the final analysis, actually interpreted the word 'liberty' in the Fourteenth Amendment."

Federal/ State Divergence

The third precept to emerge from our case law flows from the second: The rights protected against state infringement by the Fourteenth Amendment's Due Process Clause need not be identical in shape or scope to the rights protected against Federal Government infringement by the various provisions of the Bill of Rights. As drafted, the Bill of Rights directly constrained only the Federal Government. Although the enactment of the Fourteenth Amendment profoundly altered our legal order, it "did not unstitch the basic federalist pattern woven into our constitutional fabric." Nor, for that matter, did it expressly alter the Bill of Rights. The Constitution still envisions a system of divided sovereignty, still "establishes a federal republic where local differences are to be cherished as elements of liberty" in the vast run of cases, still allocates a general "police power . . . to the States and the States alone." Elementary considerations of constitutional text and structure suggest there may be legitimate reasons to hold state governments to different standards than the Federal Government in certain areas.

II

So far, I have explained that substantive due process analysis generally requires us to consider the term "liberty" in the Fourteenth Amendment, and that this inquiry may be informed by but does not depend upon the content of the Bill of Rights. How should a court go about the analysis, then? Our precedents have established, not an exact methodology, but rather a framework for decisionmaking. In this respect, too, the Court's narrative fails to capture the continuity and flexibility in our doctrine.

More fundamentally, a rigid historical methodology is unfaithful to the Constitution's command. For if it were really the case that the Fourteenth Amendment's guarantee of liberty embraces only those rights "so rooted in our history, tradition, and practice as to require special protection," then the guarantee would serve little function, save to ratify those rights that state actors have already been according the most extensive protection. That approach is unfaithful to the expansive principle Americans laid down when they ratified the Fourteenth Amendment and to the level of generality they chose when they crafted its language; it promises an objectivity it cannot deliver and masks the value judgments that pervade any analysis of what customs, defined in what manner, are sufficiently "rooted"; it countenances the most revolting injustices in the name of continuity, for we must never forget that not only slavery but also the subjugation of women and other rank forms of discrimination are part of our history; and it effaces this Court's distinctive role in saying what the law is, leaving the development and safekeeping of liberty to majoritarian political processes. It is judicial abdication in the guise of judicial modesty.

No, the liberty safeguarded by the Fourteenth Amendment is not merely preservative in nature but rather is a "dynamic concept." Its dynamism provides a central means through which the Framers enabled the Constitution to "endure for ages to come," *McCulloch v. Maryland*, 4 Wheat. 316, 415 (1819). . . . The judge who would outsource the interpretation of "liberty" to historical sentiment has turned his back on a task the Constitution assigned to him and drained the document of its intended vitality.

III

At this point a difficult question arises. In considering such a majestic term as "liberty" and applying it to present circumstances, how are we to do justice to its urgent call and its open texture—and to the grant of interpretive discretion the latter embodies—without injecting excessive subjectivity or unduly restricting the States' "broad latitude in experimenting with possible solutions to problems of vital local concern," *Whalen v.*

Roe, 429 U. S. 589, 597 (1977)? One part of the answer, already discussed, is that we must ground the analysis in historical experience and reasoned judgment, and never on "merely personal and private notions." *Rochin v. California*, 342 U. S. 165, 170 (1952). Our precedents place a number of additional constraints on the decisional process. Although "guideposts for responsible decisionmaking in this unchartered area are scarce and open-ended," *Collins v. Harker Heights*, 503 U. S. 115, 125 (1992), significant guideposts do exist.[23]

The most basic is that we have eschewed attempts to provide any all-purpose, top-down, totalizing theory of "liberty." That project is bound to end in failure or worse. The Framers did not express a clear understanding of the term to guide us, and the now-repudiated Lochner v. New York, 198 U.S. 45 (1905)] line of cases attests to the dangers of judicial overconfidence in using substantive due process to advance a broad theory of the right or the good. In its most durable precedents, the Court "has not attempted to define with exactness the liberty . . . guaranteed" by the Fourteenth Amendment. By its very nature, the meaning of liberty cannot be "reduced to any formula; its content cannot be determined by reference to any code."

Yet while "the 'liberty' specially protected by the Fourteenth Amendment" is "perhaps not capable of being fully clarified," it is capable of being refined and delimited. We have insisted that only certain types of especially significant personal interests may qualify for especially heightened protection. Ever since "the deviant economic due process cases [were] repudiated," our doctrine has steered away from "laws that touch economic problems, business affairs, or social conditions," and has instead centered on "matters relating to marriage, procreation, contraception, family relationships, and child rearing and education," *Paul v. Davis*, 424 U. S. 693, 713 (1976). These categories are not exclusive. Government action that shocks the conscience, pointlessly infringes settled expectations, trespasses into sensitive private realms or life choices without adequate justification, perpetrates gross injustice, or simply lacks a rational basis will always be vulnerable to judicial invalidation. Nor does the fact that an asserted right falls within one of these categories end the inquiry. More fundamental rights may receive more robust judicial protection, but the strength of the individual's liberty interests and the State's regulatory interests must always be assessed and compared. No right is absolute.

Rather than seek a categorical understanding of the liberty clause, our precedents have thus elucidated a conceptual core. The clause safeguards, most basically, "the ability independently to define one's identity," *Roberts v. United States Jaycees*, 468 U. S. 609, 619 (1984), "the individual's right to make certain unusually important decisions that will affect his own, or his family's, destiny," and the right to be respected as a human being. Self-determination, bodily integrity, freedom of conscience, intimate relationships, political equality, dignity and respect—these are the central values we have found implicit in the concept of ordered liberty.

Another key constraint on substantive due process analysis is respect for the democratic process. If a particular liberty interest is already being given careful consideration in, and subjected to ongoing calibration by, the States, judicial enforcement may not be appropriate. When the Court declined to establish a general right to physician-assisted suicide, for example, it did so in part because "the States [were] currently engaged in serious, thoughtful examinations of physician-assisted suicide and other similar issues," rendering judicial intervention both less necessary and potentially more disruptive. Conversely, we have long appreciated that more "searching" judicial review may be justified when the rights of "discrete and insular minorities"—groups that may face systematic barriers in the political system—are at stake. *United States v. Carolene Products Co.*, 304 U. S. 144, 153, n. 4 (1938). Courts have a "comparative . . . advantage" over the elected branches on a limited, but significant, range of legal matters.

Recognizing a new liberty right is a momentous step. It takes that right, to a considerable extent, "outside the arena of public debate and legislative action." Sometimes that momentous step must be taken; some fundamental aspects of personhood, dignity, and the like do not vary from State to State, and demand a baseline level of protection. But sensitivity to the interaction between the intrinsic aspects of liberty and the practical realities of contemporary society provides an important tool for guiding judicial discretion.

This sensitivity is an aspect of a deeper principle: the need to approach our work with humility and caution. Because the relevant constitutional language is so "spacious," I have emphasized that "[t]he doctrine of judicial self-restraint requires us to exercise the utmost care whenever we are asked to break new ground in this field." Many of my colleagues and predecessors have stressed the same point, some with great eloquence. Historical study may discipline as well as enrich the analysis. But the inescapable reality is that no serious theory of Section 1 of the Fourteenth Amendment yields clear answers in every case, and "[n]o formula could serve as a substitute, in this area, for judgment and restraint."

Several rules of the judicial process help enforce such restraint. In the substantive due process field as in others, the Court has applied both the doctrine of stare decisis—adhering to precedents, respecting reliance interests, prizing stability and order in the law—and the common-law method—taking cases and controversies as they present themselves, proceeding slowly and incrementally, building on what came before. This restrained methodology was evident even in the heyday of "incorporation" during the 1960's. Although it would have been much easier for the Court simply to declare certain Amendments in the Bill of Rights applicable to the States in toto, the Court took care to parse each Amendment into its component guarantees, evaluating them one by one. This piecemeal approach allowed the Court to scrutinize more closely the right at issue in any given dispute, reducing both the risk and the cost of error.

Relatedly, rather than evaluate liberty claims on an abstract plane, the Court has "required in substantive-due-process cases a 'careful description' of the asserted fundamental liberty interest." And just as we have required such careful description from the litigants, we have required of ourselves that we "focus on the allegations in the complaint to determine how petitioner describes the constitutional right at stake." This does not mean that we must define the asserted right at the most specific level, thereby sapping it of a universal valence and a moral force it might otherwise have. It means, simply, that we must pay close attention to the precise liberty interest the litigants have asked us to vindicate.

Our holdings should be similarly tailored. Even if the most expansive formulation of a claim does not qualify for substantive due process recognition, particular components of the claim might. Even if a State's interest in regulating a certain matter must be permitted, in the general course, to trump the individual's countervailing liberty interest, there may still be situations in which the latter "is entitled to constitutional protection."

As this discussion reflects, to acknowledge that the task of construing the liberty clause requires judgment is not to say that it is a license for unbridled judicial lawmaking. To the contrary, only an honest reckoning with our discretion allows for honest argumentation and meaningful accountability.

IV

[Discusses the Self-Defense Claim of Plaintiff]

VI

The preceding sections have already addressed many of the points made by Justice Scalia in his concurrence. But in light of that opinion's fixation on this one, it is appropriate to say a few words about Justice Scalia's broader claim: that his preferred method of substantive due process analysis, a method "that makes the traditions of our people paramount," is both more restrained and more facilitative of democracy than the method I have outlined. Colorful as it is, Justice Scalia's critique does not have nearly as much force as does his rhetoric. His theory of substantive due process, moreover, comes with its own profound difficulties.

Although Justice Scalia aspires to an "objective," "neutral" method of substantive due process analysis, his actual method is nothing of the sort. Under the "historically focused" approach he advocates, numerous threshold questions arise before one ever gets to the history. At what level of generality should one frame the liberty interest in question? What does it mean for a right to be "deeply rooted in this Nation's history and tradition"? By what standard will that proposition be tested? Which types of sources will count, and how will those sources be weighed and aggregated? There is no objective, neutral answer to these questions. There is not even a theory—at least, Justice Scalia provides none—of how to go about answering them.

Nor is there any escaping *Palko*, it seems. To qualify for substantive due process protection, Justice Scalia has stated, an asserted liberty right must be not only deeply rooted in American tradition, "but it must also be implicit in the concept of ordered liberty." Applying the latter, *Palko*-derived half of that test requires precisely the sort of reasoned judgment—the same multifaceted evaluation of the right's contours and consequences—that Justice Scalia mocks in his concurrence today.

So does applying the first half. It is hardly a novel insight that history is not an objective science, and that its use can therefore "point in any direction the judges favor." Yet 21 years after the point was brought to his attention by Justice Brennan, Justice Scalia remains "oblivious to the fact that [the concept of 'tradition'] can be as malleable and elusive as 'liberty' itself." Even when historical analysis is focused on a discrete proposition, such as the original public meaning of the Second Amendment, the evidence often points in different directions. The historian must choose which pieces to credit and which to discount, and then must try to assemble them into a coherent whole. In *Heller*, Justice Scalia preferred to rely on sources created much earlier and later in time than the Second Amendment itself; I focused more closely on sources contemporaneous with the Amendment's drafting and ratification. No mechanical yardstick can measure which of us was correct, either with respect to the materials we chose to privilege or the insights we gleaned from them.

The malleability and elusiveness of history increase exponentially when we move from a pure question of original meaning, as in *Heller*, to Justice Scalia's theory of substantive due process. At least with the former sort of question, the judge can focus on a single legal provision; the temporal scope of the inquiry is (or should be) relatively bounded; and there is substantial agreement on what sorts of authorities merit consideration. With Justice Scalia's approach to substantive due process, these guideposts all fall away. The judge must canvas the entire landscape of American law as it has evolved through time, and perhaps older laws as well, pursuant to a standard (deeply rootedness) that has never been defined. In conducting this rudderless, panoramic tour of American legal history, the judge has more than ample opportunity to "look over the heads of the crowd and pick out [his] friends," *Roper v. Simmons*, 543 U. S. 551, 617 (2005) (Scalia, J., dissenting).

My point is not to criticize judges' use of history in general or to suggest that it always generates indeterminate answers; I have already emphasized that historical study can discipline as well as enrich substantive due process analysis. My point is simply that Justice Scalia's defense of his method, which holds out objectivity and restraint as its cardinal—and, it seems, only—virtues, is unsatisfying on its own terms. For a limitless number of subjective judgments may be smuggled into his historical analysis. Worse, they may be buried in the analysis. At least with my approach, the judge's cards are laid on the table for all to see, and to critique. The judge must exercise judgment, to be sure. When answering a constitutional question to which the text provides no clear answer, there is always some amount of discretion; our constitutional system has always depended on judges' filling in the document's vast open spaces. But there is also transparency.

Justice Scalia's approach is even less restrained in another sense: It would effect a major break from our case law outside of the "incorporation" area. Justice Scalia does not seem troubled by the fact that his method is largely inconsistent with the Court's canonical substantive due process decisions. To the contrary, he seems to embrace this dissonance. My method seeks to synthesize dozens of cases on which the American people have relied for decades. Justice Scalia's method seeks to vaporize them. So I am left to wonder, which of us is more faithful to this Nation's constitutional history? And which of us is more faithful to the values and commitments of the American people, as they stand today? In 1967, when the Court held in Loving [v. Virginia], 388 U. S. 1, that adults have a liberty-based as well as equality-based right to wed persons of another race, interracial marriage was hardly "deeply rooted" in American tradition. Racial segregation and subordination were deeply rooted. The Court's substantive due process holding was nonetheless correct—and we should be wary of any interpretive theory that implies, emphatically, that it was not.

Which leads me to the final set of points I wish to make: Justice Scalia's method invites not only bad history, but also bad constitutional law. As I have already explained, in evaluating a claimed liberty interest (or any constitutional claim for that matter), it makes perfect sense to give history significant weight: Justice Scalia's position is closer to my own than he apparently feels comfortable acknowledging. But it makes little sense to give history dispositive weight in every case. And it makes especially little sense to answer questions like whether the right to bear arms is "fundamental" by focusing only on the past, given that both the practical significance and the public understandings of such a right often change as society changes. What if the evidence had shown that, whereas at one time firearm possession contributed substantially to personal liberty and safety, nowadays it contributes nothing, or even tends to undermine them? Would it still have been reasonable to constitutionalize the right?

The concern runs still deeper. Not only can historical views be less than completely clear or informative, but they can also be wrong. Some notions that many Americans deeply believed to be true, at one time, turned out not to be true. Some practices that many Americans believed to be consistent with the Constitution's guarantees of liberty and equality, at one time, turned out to be inconsistent with them. The fact that we have a written Constitution does not consign this Nation to a static legal existence. Although we should always "pa[y] a decent regard to the opinions of former times," it "is not the glory of the people of America" to have "suffered a blind veneration for antiquity." *The Federalist* No. 14. It is not the role of federal judges to be amateur historians. And it is not fidelity to the Constitution to ignore its use of deliberately capacious language, in an effort to transform foundational legal commitments into narrow rules of decision.

As for "the democratic process," a method that looks exclusively to history can easily do more harm than good. Just consider this case. The net result of Justice Scalia's supposedly objective analysis is to vest federal judges—ultimately a majority of the judges on this Court—with unprecedented lawmaking powers in an area in which they have no special qualifications, and in which the give-and-take of the political process has functioned effectively for decades. Why this "intrudes much less upon the democratic process," ante, at 14, than an approach that would defer to the democratic process on the regulation of firearms is, to say the least, not self-evident. I cannot even tell what, under Justice Scalia's view, constitutes an "intrusion."

It is worth pondering, furthermore, the vision of democracy that underlies Justice Scalia's critique. Because very few of us would welcome a system in which majorities or powerful interest groups always get their way. Under our constitutional scheme, I would have thought that a judicial approach to liberty claims such as the one I have outlined—an approach that investigates both the intrinsic nature of the claimed interest and the practical significance of its judicial enforcement, that is transparent in its reasoning and sincere in its effort to incorporate constraints, that is guided by history but not beholden to it, and that is willing to protect some rights even if they have not already received uniform protection from the elected branches—has the capacity to improve, rather than "[im]peril," our democracy. It all depends on judges' exercising careful, reasoned judgment. As it always has, and as it always will.

JUSTICE BREYER, with whom JUSTICE GINSBURG and JUSTICE SOTOMAYOR join, dissenting.

In my view, Justice Stevens has demonstrated that the Fourteenth Amendment's guarantee of "substantive due process" does not include a general right to keep and bear firearms for purposes of private self-defense. As he argues, the Framers did not write the Second Amendment with this objective in view. Unlike other forms of substantive liberty, the carrying of arms for that purpose often puts others' lives at risk. And the use of arms for private self-defense does not warrant federal constitutional protection from state regulation.

The Court, however, does not expressly rest its opinion upon "substantive due process" concerns. Rather, it directs its attention to this Court's "incorporation" precedents and asks whether the Second Amendment right to private self-defense is "fundamental" so that it applies to the States through the Fourteenth Amendment.

I shall therefore separately consider the question of "incorporation." I can find nothing in the Second Amendment's text, history, or underlying rationale that could warrant characterizing it as "fundamental" insofar as it seeks to protect the keeping and bearing of arms for private self-defense purposes. Nor can I find any justification for interpreting the Constitution as transferring ultimate regulatory authority over the private uses of firearms from democratically elected legislatures to courts or from the States to the Federal Government. I therefore conclude that the Fourteenth Amendment does not "incorporate" the Second Amendment's right "to keep and bear Arms." And I consequently dissent. . . .

In sum, the police power, the superiority of legislative decisionmaking, the need for local decisionmaking, the comparative desirability of democratic decisionmaking, the lack of a manageable judicial standard, and the life-threatening harm that may flow from striking down regulations all argue against incorporation. Where the incorporation of other rights has been at issue, some of these problems have arisen. But in this instance all these problems are present, all at the same time, and all are likely to be present in most, perhaps nearly all, of the cases in which the constitutionality of a gun regulation is at issue. At the same time, the important factors that favor incorporation in other instances—e.g., the protection of broader constitutional objectives—are not present here. The upshot is that all factors militate against incorporation—with the possible exception of historical factors.

III

In sum, the Framers did not write the Second Amendment in order to protect a private right of armed self-defense. There has been, and is, no consensus that the right is, or was, "fundamental." No broader constitutional interest or principle supports legal treatment of that right as fundamental. To the contrary, broader constitutional concerns of an institutional nature argue strongly against that treatment.

Moreover, nothing in 18th-, 19th-, 20th-, or 21st-century history shows a consensus that the right to private armed self-defense, as described in *Heller*, is "deeply rooted in this Nation's history or tradition" or is otherwise "fundamental." Indeed, incorporating the right recognized in Heller may change the law in many of the 50 States. Read in the majority's favor, the historical evidence is at most ambiguous. And, in the absence of any other support for its conclusion, ambiguous history cannot show that the Fourteenth Amendment incorporates a private right of self-defense against the States.

With respect, I dissent.

FOR DISCUSSION

The concurring and dissenting opinions articulate a clear disagreement between Justices Scalia and Stevens over the interpretation of the proper role and sources of judicial decisionmaking. How do they characterize their own positions? What are the points of contention? In what way does this philosophy impact their determination around the Second Amendment?

RELATED CASES

***United States v. Skoien:* 587 F.3d 803 (7th Cir. 2010).**

Upheld a federal law precluding gun ownership by those convicted of specific domestic violence claims.

***Wrenn v. District of Columbia:* 2015 U.S. Dist. LEXIS 71383 (2015).**

Struck down the District of Columbia's concealed carry requirement, which had necessitated applicants to demonstrate a good reason to carry as too vague and thus in violation of the Second Amendment.

***Peruta v. County of San Diego:* 824 F.3d 919 (9th Cir. 2016).**

In a challenge to California's severely limited concealed carry law, the court found the Second Amendment does not provide the right to carry a concealed weapon to members of the public.

GLOSSARY

Bill of Exceptions: A written statement from a trial judge to the appellate court detailing litigant objections to court decisions during the trial and the rationale for protest.

Incorporation: The theory that with the adoption of the Due Process Clause of the Fourteenth Amendment, some or all of the provisions of the Bill of Rights also limit the actions of state and local governments.

Selective Incorporation: The theory that the Due Process Clause of the Fourteenth Amendment applies only to certain parts or sections of the Bill of Rights to state and local governments. Using this theory, the Supreme Court has incorporated all but the Third and parts of the Seventh Amendment.

SELECTED BIBLIOGRAPHY

Cornell, Saul. 2006. *A Well-Regulated Militia: The Founding Fathers and the Origins of Gun Control in America.* New York: NY: Oxford University Press.

Cornell, Saul A. and Nelson Kozuskanich, editors. 2013. *The Second Amendment on Trial: Critical Essays on* District of Columbia v. Heller. Amherst, MA: University of Massachusetts Press.

Goldman, Robert M. 2001. *Reconstruction and Black Suffrage: Losing the Vote in* Reese *and* Cruikshank. Lawrence, KS: Kansas University Press.

Halbrook, Stephen P. 2008. *The Founders' Second Amendment.* Chicago: The Independent Institute.

Lane, Charles. 2008. *The Day Freedom Died: The Colfax Massacre, The Supreme Court, and the Betrayal of Reconstruction.* New York: Henry Holt.

Malcolm, Joyce Lee. 1994. *To Keep and Bear Arms: The Origins of an Anglo-American Right.* Cambridge, MA: Harvard University Press.

Spitzer, Robert J. 2015. *Guns Across America: Reconciling Gun Rules and Rights.* New York: Oxford University Press.

Uviller, H. Richard and William G. Merkel. 2002. *The Militia and the Right to Bear Arms, or How the Second Amendment Fell Silent.* Durham, NC: Duke University Press.

Waldman, Michael. 2014. *The Second Amendment: A Biography.* New York: Simon & Schuster.

CHAPTER VI

The Eighth Amendment and Cruel and Unusual Punishment

Timeline: The Eighth Amendment and Cruel and Unusual Punishment

1689 The English Bill of Rights provides that "excessive bail ought not to be required, nor excessive fines imposed, nor cruel and unusual punishments inflicted."

1787 The Northwest Ordinance prohibits cruel and unusual punishments.

1791 States adopt the Bill of Rights.

1833 *Barron v. Baltimore* finds that the provisions in the Bill of Rights apply only to the national government.

1868 States ratify the Fourteenth Amendment.

1910 *Weems v. United States* voids a Philippine law on the basis that sentencing an individual who had falsified a document to fifteen years of hard labor, in accordance with the law, constituted cruel and unusual punishment.

1947 *State of Louisiana ex rel. Francis v. Resweber* yields the ruling that a state does not inflict "cruel and unusual punishment" when it executes an individual by electrocution after the failure of a prior attempt to carry out the sentence.

1958 In *Trop v. Dulles* the Supreme Court says that the Eighth Amendment "must draw its meaning from the evolving standards of decency that mark the progress of a maturing society."

1962 In *Robinson v. California* the Supreme Court uses the Eighth and Fourteenth Amendments to strike down a state law making it a crime to be a drug addict.

1972 The Supreme Court in *Furman v. Georgia* declares the death penalty unconstitutional as it was then administered.

1976 *Gregg v. Georgia* accepts a death penalty statute that provides for bifurcated trials and considerations of mitigating and aggravating circumstances.

1976 *Woodson v. North Carolina* outlaws mandatory death penalty statutes.

1977 Gary Gilmore (Utah) becomes the first person to be executed under new rules under *Gregg v. Georgia.* He had dropped appeals and asked that his sentence be carried out.

1977 *Coker v. Georgia* decides that absent a resulting death, the rape of an adult woman cannot be punished by the death penalty.

1980 *Rummel v. Estelle* upholds a "three strikes and you're out" law.

1987 *McCleskey v. Kemp* rejects a quantitative attempt to demonstrate that the death penalty is arbitrarily administered on the basis of race and thereby unconstitutional.

1989 *Penry v. Lynaugh* decides that the Eighth Amendment does not prohibit capital punishment of the mentally retarded.

1989 *Stanford v. Kentucky* upholds imposition of the death penalty on individuals who were fifteen to seventeen years old when the crime was committed.

1991 *Harmelin v. Michigan* upholds a sentence for narcotics possession against claims that the punishment is disproportionate.

1993 *Herrera v. Collins* rejects a claim of "actual innocence."

2002 *Atkins v. Virginia* rejects infliction of the death penalty on individuals who are mentally retarded.

2002 *Ring v. Arizona* rules that juries (not judges) must decide on aggravating factors and that their findings must be certain beyond a reasonable doubt.

2005 *Roper v. Simmons* (2005) rejects infliction of the death penalty on individuals who have been sentenced for crime committed prior to their eighteenth birthday.

2007 New Jersey becomes the first state to repeal the death penalty since the Supreme Court began questioning its constitutionality.

2008 The Supreme Court decides in *Kennedy v. Louisiana* that the death penalty is not appropriate punishment for the rape of a child that does not result in death.

2008 The Court decides in *Baze v. Rees* that the "cocktail" of drugs used for lethal injections does not constitute "cruel and unusual punishment."

2011 In *Brown v. Plata*, the Supreme Court upheld an order by a 3-judge court mandating that California reduce its prison population after finding that overcrowding has so stretched medical treatments as to constitute cruel and unusual punishment.

2014 A 5–4 decision in *Hall v. Florida* decides that a state had violated the Eighth Amendment when it had relied solely on an IQ test to determine whether a defendant was mentally retarded under guidelines established in *Atkins v. Virginia.*

2016 Supreme Court overturns a death penalty decision in Georgia in the case of *Foster v. Chapman* after new evidence reveals that the prosecution attempted to exclude blacks from the jury.

Eighth Amendment:

Excessive bail shall not be required, nor excessive fines imposed, nor cruel and unusual punishments inflicted.

INTRODUCTION: CONSTITUTIONAL FOUNDATIONS

The provision in the Eighth Amendment is the most recognized limitation on criminal punishments, but it has constitutional antecedents. Article I, Section 3, limits the punishments for governmental officials who are convicted by the U.S. Senate for impeachable offenses to removal from office and possible exclusion from future offices (although they may subsequently be tried and sentenced for other crimes through the regular judicial system).

Similarly, Article I, Sections 9 and 10—the former limiting Congress and the latter limiting the states—both prohibit **bills of attainder** and **ex post facto laws.** The term *bill of attainder* refers to a punishment imposed by a legislature on specific individuals without benefit of a trial (a practice of the English Parliament with which Americans were familiar). As the chapter on property rights in the companion volume to this book explains, according to Supreme Court decisions on the subject, the ex post facto laws do not refer to any retroactive law but only to such criminal laws, either making a previously legal act illegal and punishing individuals for its violation or punishing individuals more severely than the law permitted at the time of the offense.

Recognizing the enormity of treason, the last provision of Article III, Section 3, also provides that "no Attainder of Treason shall work Corruption of Blood, or Forfeiture except during the Life of the Person attainted." By prohibiting **corruption of blood**, this provision prevents Congress from visiting punishments for crimes of fathers and mothers on their children, thus emphasizing the principle of personal, rather than collective, responsibility. The Due Process Clause of the Fifth Amendment, later also included in the Fourteenth Amendment, provides for due process relative to punishments that affect one's "life, liberty, or property."

The Death Penalty and Proportionality

The Eighth Amendment was adopted as part of the national Bill of Rights, ratified in 1791. The Fifth and Sixth Amendments, which precede the Eighth, deal chiefly with the rights of individuals who are accused of, or on trial for, crimes. (The Seventh Amendment deals with civil, rather than criminal, matters.) Similarly, the first provision of the Eighth Amendment applies to criminal matters by prohibiting "excessive" bail or "excessive" fines. **Bail** is a refundable monetary payment that persons accused of a crime make to guarantee that they will show up for trial. Although the Eighth Amendment prohibits "excessive bail," it does not guarantee that every individual will be entitled to it—governments would not want to release a dangerous psychopath even if such an individual offered to post bail of a million dollars! Similarly, the government might fine a criminally negligent shipping company millions of dollars for an oil spill without such a fine being considered excessive.

The most litigated provision of the Eighth Amendment prohibits "**cruel and unusual punishments**." Perhaps in part because there was relatively little discussion of this provision in the Congress that proposed it, commentators and judges still debate whether the determination of cruelty and unusualness is primarily one for legislators or for judges to make. Even those who think legislators have primary responsibility could probably think of horrendous (albeit not altogether likely) examples that would be so excessive as to call for judicial intervention.

The discussion of cruel and unusual punishments is linked to the debate between advocates of interpreting the Constitution through **original intent** and proponents of a more flexible, **"living" Constitution**. The former typically seek to solve legal controversies by reference to prohibitions or punishments in force when the Eighth Amendment was adopted, whereas the latter emphasize the idea that the meaning of the amendment might expand over time. Proponents of the expansionist viewpoint argue that the term "cruel and unusual" was intentionally designed to change with contemporary conceptions. In a frequently cited observation made in a ruling that the government could not strip a wartime deserter of citizenship, Chief Justice Earl Warren observed that the Eighth Amendment "must draw its meaning from the evolving standards of decency that mark the progress of a maturing society" (*Trop v. Dulles,* 356 U.S. 86, 1958).

As the majority of cases selected for inclusion in this chapter will demonstrate, most of the debate over cruel and unusual punishments has focused on **capital punishment** (the death penalty). Since this sentence clearly is both more severe and more final than others, fair and just governments are rightly concerned that they not impose it on innocent persons.

In a phrase that the Fourteenth Amendment later repeated, the Fifth Amendment of the Constitution contains a clause that prohibits deprivation of "life, liberty, or property, without due process of law." Like other Europeans, the English, from whom many American laws derived, executed individuals for a wide variety of crimes. The reference to "life" in the Fifth and Fourteenth Amendments indicates that Americans had relatively few reservations in 1791 or in 1868 about imposition of the death penalty per se. The means of carrying out the penalty did somewhat change over time, with electrocution often replacing hanging or death by firing squad, and in recent years, lethal injection has largely replaced earlier methods. In one of the Court's most notorious decisions, *Louisiana ex rel. Francis v. Resweber* (329 U.S. 459, 1947), the justices ruled that an initial failure of an electric chair did not preclude a state from trying a second time. It was not until *Robinson v. California* (370 U.S. 660, 1962), however, that the Supreme Court decided that the "cruel and unusual" provision of the Eighth Amendment applied to the states under the Fourteenth Amendment. In *Robinson,* the Court invalidated a California law that made it a crime to be addicted to illegal drugs.

Most of the judicial debate over capital punishment has occurred since 1972 when, for the first time in history, the Supreme Court decided that the death penalty, as then administered, was unconstitutional (*Furman v. Georgia,* 408 U.S. 238, 1972). The varied opinions in this case give insights into continuing controversies in this area and provide students with a chance to hone their analytical skills and compare and contrast arguments.

In the *Furman* ruling, Justice William O. Douglas led off by expressing concerns over the way that race might affect imposition of the death penalty. Justice William J. Brennan believed that capital punishment was inconsistent with governmental recognition of human dignity; Brennan, Justice Thurgood Marshall, and, later, Justice Harry Blackmun, would conclude that the penalty was thus, per se, unconstitutional. Although he spoke only for himself, Justice Potter Stewart's opinion may ultimately have carried the day; he found the imposition of the death penalty as then administered to be wanton and unpredictable (he likened it to lightning). Justice Byron White had similar reservations about the imposition of the penalty and questioned whether it was an effective deterrent. Justice Marshall concluded that the penalty was unconstitutional in part by questioning whether it achieved its stated objectives; he did not think the public supported the penalty. By contrast, Chief Justice Warren Burger and Justice Blackmun, along with Justices Lewis Powell and William Rehnquist, all thought the Court had unwisely become involved in an issue that the Constitution had chiefly reserved to legislative judgment.

Legislatures certainly did not take the decision in *Furman* to be the end of the matter. As Congress joined a large majority of states in reenacting death penalty legislation, the Court was faced again, in *Gregg v. Georgia* (428 U.S. 153, 1976), with new statutes that sought to make imposition of the penalty less capricious. The Court ultimately accepted legislation that required juries to consider **aggravating, extenuating, and mitigating** factors; another requirement was the **bifurcated** proceeding, which separated the trial phase of the prosecution from the penalty phase. Two justices, however, were unconvinced that the death penalty could ever be appropriate.

Simultaneous with the decision in *Gregg,* the Court ruled in *Woodson v. North Carolina* (428 U.S. 280, 1976) and *Roberts v. Louisiana* (428 U.S. 325, 1976) that mandatory death sentences were unconstitutional. In so doing, the Court continued to emphasize the importance of individualized sentencing. Ironically, individualized penalties would arguably lead to even greater diversity in sentences.

Prior to *Furman,* juries, especially in the South, often imposed the death penalty on men who had committed rape. In *Coker v. Georgia* (433 U.S. 584, 1977), the Court decided that, despite the heinousness of this crime, it did not by itself merit such a penalty, at least not when the victim was an adult woman. It was not until

2008 that the Court in *Kennedy v. Louisiana* (554 U.S. 407) finally extended this same prohibition to the rape of minors, albeit not without generating considerable controversy.

In *Furman v. Georgia*, Justice Douglas raised concerns about whether the race of the perpetrators was influencing sentencing. This issue reemerged in *McCleskey v. Kemp* (481 U.S. 279, 1987), when the Court was confronted with a scholarly statistical study that also considered the race of the victims. Although the Court ultimately rejected this challenge to the state law, questions of racial justice continue to bedevil the issue and arguably undermine support for the penalty.

Gregg v. Georgia indicated that all capital cases should be subject to mandatory review to ensure consistency and fairness. Because the United States has a federal system, however, such reviews can take place at either the state or the national level. Although the Warren Court was known as relatively generous in granting habeas corpus review, in *Stone v. Powell* (428 U.S. 466, 1976), the Burger Court narrowed the range oases it would hear in matters related to the Fourth Amendment. In *Herrera v. Collins* (506 U.S. 390, 1993), the Rehnquist Court extended this thinking to death penalty cases that had already received full state review, deciding that a state's review of "actual innocence" claims was sufficient without an additional federal review.

As states have turned increasingly away from electrocution to lethal injections, there have been some well-publicized cases where states, sometimes finding it difficult to find supplies of lethal drugs, have varied the drug cocktail that they administer to induce death and where the process of dying has been prolonged as a result. To date, the Supreme Court has largely deferred to state choices on the subject. Thus, in *Glossip v. Gross*, 576 U.S. ___ (2015), applying earlier principles that the Court had set forth in *Baze v. Rees*, 553 U.S. 35 (2008), the Court refused to issue an injunction against an Oklahoma law permitting the use of a cocktail including the sedative midazolam, which had been implicated in an earlier procedure in which the recipient awoke and lingered for about 40 minutes before dying. The case was especially notable for Justice Stephen Breyer's dissent, joined by three other justices, in which he questioned whether the death penalty was any longer constitutional.

Special Circumstances

The death penalty is generally tied to culpability. The rationales of **deterrence** and **retribution** are both predicated to a large degree on the idea that those who are being punished had control of their actions. But what of those who may not fit this model because of diminished capacity? This question has been raised in at least two circumstances.

After first ruling, in *Penry v. Lynaugh* (492 U.S. 302, 1989), that punishments of individuals who were mentally challenged did not violate the cruel and unusual punishment provision, the Court reconsidered and reversed this decision in *Atkins v. Virginia* (536 U.S. 304, 2002). The Court weighed not only the possibility that individuals who were mentally handicapped might be less successful in aiding in their own defense but also reviewed trends in state lawmaking in that area. The dissenters questioned whether the Court has ascertained or manufactured the consensus that it purported to find. More generally, the dissents point to some of the difficulties of applying the "living Constitution" approach to this issue.

This critique did not prevent the Court from making a similar turnabout in *Roper v. Simmons* (543 U.S. 551, 2005), which overturned *Stanford v. Kentucky* (492 U.S. 361, 1989). An earlier decision (*Thompson v. Oklahoma,* 487 U.S. 815, 1988) had already excluded those below the age of sixteen from the death penalty; in *Roper* the court ruled that juveniles from sixteen to eighteen were less culpable than adults, and therefore to sentence them to death was a violation of the Eighth Amendment. *Roper* was a particularly difficult case because Simmons had committed his crime at least in part because he thought his age might help him avoid the consequences. *Roper* also raises the issue of the degree, if any, to which American judges and justices should consider practices in other nations in deciding on the appropriateness of penalties.

FURMAN V. GEORGIA

408 U.S. 238, 92 S.Ct. 2726, 33 L.Ed.2d 346 (1972)

This extremely lengthy Supreme Court case, with multiple opinions, was the first to examine whether the death penalty per se could constitute cruel and unusual punishment. All three defendants were black, and two had been sentenced to death for rape of adult women, a penalty that is contrary to current law. The Court's brief **per curiam** opinion, representing the views of five justices, ultimately put the death penalty, as then administered, on hold. While for three justices, no constitutional infirmity was associated with the death penalty, others thought that the penalty itself, not merely its application, violated the Eighth and Fourteenth Amendments. Although it is not first, Justice Stewart's concurring opinion is often cited as best, encapsulating the thinking of the majority of justices who decided this case.

Vote: 5–4

JUSTICE DOUGLAS, concurring.

It has been assumed in our decisions that punishment by death is not cruel, unless the manner of execution can be said to be inhuman and barbarous. *In re Kemmler*, 136 U.S. 436, 447 (1889). It is also said in our opinions that the proscription of cruel and unusual punishments "is not fastened to the obsolete but may acquire meaning as public opinion becomes enlightened by a humane justice." *Weems v. United States*, 217 U.S. 349 (1910). A like statement was made in *Trop v. Dulles*, 356 U.S. 86 (1958), that the Eighth Amendment "must draw its meaning from the evolving standards of decency that mark the progress of a maturing society."

The generality of a law inflicting capital punishment is one thing. What may be said of the validity of a law on the books and what may be done with the law in its application do, or may, lead to quite different conclusions.

It would seem to be incontestable that the death penalty inflicted on one defendant is "unusual" if it discriminates against him by reason of his race, religion, wealth, social position, or class, or if it is imposed under a procedure that gives room for the play of such prejudices.

There is evidence that the provision of the English Bill of Rights of 1689, from which the language of the Eighth Amendment was taken, was concerned primarily with selective or irregular application of harsh penalties and that its aim was to forbid arbitrary and discriminatory penalties of a severe nature. . . .

The English Bill of Rights, enacted December 16, 1689, stated that "excessive bail ought not to be required, nor excessive fines imposed, nor cruel and unusual punishments inflicted." These were the words chosen for our Eighth Amendment. A like provision had been in Virginia's Constitution of 1776 and in the constitutions of seven other States. The Northwest Ordinance, enacted under the Articles of Confederation, included a prohibition of cruel and unusual punishments. But the debates of the First Congress on the Bill of Rights throw little light on its intended meaning. All that appears is the following:

> Mr. SMITH, of South Carolina, objected to the words "nor cruel and unusual punishments"; the import of them being too indefinite.
>
> Mr. LIVERMORE: The clause seems to express a great deal of humanity, on which account I have no objection to it; but as it seems to have no meaning in it, I do not think it necessary. What is meant by the terms excessive bail? Who are to be the judges? What is understood by excessive fines? It lies with the court to determine. No cruel and unusual punishment is to be inflicted; it is sometimes necessary to hang a man, villains often deserve whipping, and perhaps having their ears cut off; but are we in future to be prevented from inflicting these punishments because they are cruel? If a more lenient mode of correcting vice and deterring others from the commission of it could be invented, it

would be very prudent in the Legislature to adopt it; but until we have some security that this will be done, we ought not to be restrained from making necessary laws by any declaration of this kind.

The words "cruel and unusual" certainly include penalties that are barbaric. But the words, at least when read in light of the English proscription against selective and irregular use of penalties, suggest that it is "cruel and unusual" to apply the death penalty—or any other penalty—selectively to minorities whose numbers are few, who are outcasts of society, and who are unpopular, but whom society is willing to see suffer though it would not countenance general application of the same penalty across the board. . . .

We cannot say from facts disclosed in these records that these defendants were sentenced to death because they were black. Yet our task is not restricted to an effort to divine what motives impelled these death penalties. Rather, we deal with a system of law and of justice that leaves to the uncontrolled discretion of judges or juries the determination whether defendants committing these crimes should die or be imprisoned. Under these laws no standards govern the selection of the penalty. People live or die, dependent on the whim of one man or of 12.

[Most of the remainder of Douglas's opinion focuses on what he considers to be the equal protection difficulty in jury application of the death penalty.]

JUSTICE BRENNAN, concurring.

I

We have very little evidence of the Framers' intent in including the Cruel and Unusual Punishments Clause among those restraints upon the new Government enumerated in the Bill of Rights. . . .

Several conclusions thus emerge from the history of the adoption of the Clause. We know that the Framers' concern was directed specifically at the exercise of legislative power. They included in the Bill of Rights a prohibition upon "cruel and unusual punishments" precisely because the legislature would otherwise have had the unfettered power to prescribe punishments for crimes. Yet we cannot now know exactly what the Framers thought "cruel and unusual punishments" were. Certainly they intended to ban torturous punishments, but the available evidence does not support the further conclusion that *only* torturous punishments were to be outlawed. . . .

Judicial enforcement of the Clause, then, cannot be evaded by invoking the obvious truth that legislatures have the power to prescribe punishments for crimes. That is precisely the reason the Clause appears in the Bill of Rights. The difficulty arises, rather, in formulating the "legal principles to be applied by the courts" when a legislatively prescribed punishment is challenged as "cruel and unusual." In formulating those constitutional principles, we must avoid the insertion of "judicial conception[s] of . . . wisdom or propriety," *Weems v. United States*, yet we must not, in the guise of "judicial restraint," abdicate our fundamental responsibility to enforce the Bill of Rights. Were we to do so, the "constitution would indeed be as easy of application as it would be deficient in efficacy and power. Its general principles would have little value and be converted by precedent into impotent and lifeless formulas. Rights declared in words might be lost in reality." The Cruel and Unusual Punishments Clause would become, in short, "little more than good advice." *Trop v. Dulles.*

II

Ours would indeed be a simple task were we required merely to measure a challenged punishment against those that history has long condemned. That narrow and unwarranted view of the Clause, however, was left behind with the 19th century. Our task today is more complex. We know "that the words of the [Clause] are not precise, and that their scope is not static." We know, therefore, that the Clause "must draw its meaning from the evolving standards of decency that mark the progress of a maturing society." That knowledge, of course, is but the beginning of the inquiry. At bottom, then, the Cruel and Unusual Punishments Clause prohibits the infliction of uncivilized and inhuman punishments. The State, even as it punishes, must treat its members with respect for their intrinsic worth as human beings. A punishment is "cruel and unusual," therefore, if it does not comport with human dignity.

This formulation, of course, does not of itself yield principles for assessing the constitutional validity of particular punishments. Nevertheless, even though "this Court has had little occasion to give precise content to the [Clause]," there are principles recognized in our cases and inherent in the Clause sufficient to permit a judicial determination whether a challenged punishment comports with human dignity.

The primary principle is that a punishment must not be so severe as to be degrading to the dignity of human beings. Pain, certainly, may be a factor in the judgment. The infliction of an extremely severe punishment will often entail physical suffering. See *Weems v. United States*. Yet the Framers also knew "that there could be exercises of cruelty by laws other than those which inflicted bodily pain or mutilation." Even though "there may be involved no physical mistreatment, no primitive torture," *Trop v. Dulles,* severe mental pain may be inherent in the infliction of a particular punishment. See *Weems v. United States*. That, indeed, was one of the conclusions underlying the holding of the plurality in *Trop v. Dulles* that the punishment of expatriation violates the Clause. And the physical and mental suffering inherent in the punishment of *cadena temporal*, was an obvious basis for the Court's decision in *Weems v. United States* that the punishment was "cruel and unusual."

More than the presence of pain, however, is comprehended in the judgment that the extreme severity of a punishment makes it degrading to the dignity of human beings. The barbaric punishments condemned by history, "punishments which inflict torture, such as the rack, the thumbscrew, the iron boot, the stretching of limbs and the like," are, of course, "attended with acute pain and suffering." *O'Neil v. Vermont*, 144 U.S. 323 (1892). When we consider why they have been condemned, however, we realize that the pain involved is not the only reason. The true significance of these punishments is that they treat members of the human race as nonhumans, as objects to be toyed with and discarded. They are thus inconsistent with the fundamental premise of the Clause that even the vilest criminal remains a human being possessed of common human dignity.

The infliction of an extremely severe punishment, then, like the one before the Court in *Weems v. United States*, from which "no circumstance of degradation [was] omitted," may reflect the attitude that the person punished is not entitled to recognition as a fellow human being. . . .

In determining whether a punishment comports with human dignity, we are aided also by a second principle inherent in the Clause—that the State must not arbitrarily inflict a severe punishment. This principle derives from the notion that the State does not respect human dignity when, without reason, it inflicts upon some people a severe punishment that it does not inflict upon others. . . .

As *Wilkerson v. Utah,* 99 U.S. 130 (1878), suggests, when a severe punishment is inflicted "in the great majority of cases" in which it is legally available, there is little likelihood that the State is inflicting it arbitrarily. If, however, the infliction of a severe punishment is "something different from that which is generally done" in such cases, *Trop v. Dulles*, there is a substantial likelihood that the State, contrary to the requirements of regularity and fairness embodied in the Clause, is inflicting the punishment arbitrarily. This principle is especially important today. There is scant danger, given the political processes "in an enlightened democracy such as ours," that extremely severe punishments will be widely applied. The more significant function of the Clause, therefore, is to protect against the danger of their arbitrary infliction.

A third principle inherent in the Clause is that a severe punishment must not be unacceptable to contemporary society. Rejection by society, of course, is a strong indication that a severe punishment does not comport with human dignity. . . .

The final principle inherent in the Clause is that a severe punishment must not be excessive. A punishment is excessive under this principle if it is unnecessary: The infliction of a severe punishment by the State cannot comport with human dignity when it is nothing more than the pointless infliction of suffering. If there is a significantly less severe punishment adequate to achieve the purposes for which the punishment is inflicted, *Robinson v. California*, 70 U.S. 660 (1962); *Trop v. Dulles*, the punishment inflicted is unnecessary and therefore excessive.

Since the Bill of Rights was adopted, this Court has adjudged only three punishments to be within the prohibition of the Clause. See *Weems v. United States* (1910) (12 years in chains at hard and painful labor); *Trop v. Dulles* (1958) (expatriation); *Robinson v. California*, (1962) (imprisonment for narcotics addiction). . . .

III

The punishment challenged in these cases is death. Death, of course, is a "traditional" punishment, *Trop v. Dulles,* one that "has been employed throughout our history," and its constitutional background is accordingly an appropriate subject of inquiry.

There is, first, a textual consideration raised by the Bill of Rights itself. The Fifth Amendment declares that if a particular crime is punishable by death, a person charged with that crime is entitled to certain procedural protections. We can thus infer that the Framers recognized the existence of what was then a common punishment. We cannot, however, make the further inference that they intended to exempt this particular punishment from the express prohibition of the Cruel and Unusual Punishments Clause. Nor is there any indication in the debates on the Clause that a special exception was to be made for death. If anything, the indication is to the contrary, for Livermore specifically mentioned death as a candidate for future proscription under the Clause. Finally, it does not advance analysis to insist that the Framers did not believe that adoption of the Bill of Rights would immediately prevent the infliction of the punishment of death; neither did they believe that it would immediately prevent the infliction of other corporal punishments that, although common at the time, are now acknowledged to be impermissible.

There is also the consideration that this Court has decided three cases involving constitutional challenges to particular methods of inflicting this punishment. In *Wilkerson v. Utah*, 99 U.S. 130 (1879), and *In re Kemmler*, 136 U.S. 436 (1890), the Court, expressing in both cases the since-rejected "historical" view of the Clause, approved death by shooting and death by electrocution. In *Wilkerson*, the Court concluded that shooting was a common method of execution; in *Kemmler*, the Court held that the Clause did not apply to the States. In *Louisiana ex rel. Francis v. Resweber,* 329 U.S. 459 (1947), the Court approved a second attempt at electrocution after the first had failed. . . . These three decisions thus reveal that the Court, while ruling upon various methods of inflicting death, has assumed in the past that death was a constitutionally permissible punishment. Past assumptions, however, are not sufficient to limit the scope of our examination of this punishment today. The constitutionality of death itself under the Cruel and Unusual Punishments Clause is before this Court for the first time; we cannot avoid the question by recalling past cases that never directly considered it.

The question, then, is whether the deliberate infliction of death is today consistent with the command of the Clause that the State may not inflict punishments that do not comport with human dignity. I will analyze the punishment of death in terms of the principles set out above and the cumulative test to which they lead: It is a denial of human dignity for the State arbitrarily to subject a person to an unusually severe punishment that society has indicated it does not regard as acceptable, and that cannot be shown to serve any penal purpose more effectively than a significantly less drastic punishment. Under these principles and this test, death is today a "cruel and unusual" punishment.

Death is a unique punishment in the United States. In a society that so strongly affirms the sanctity of life, not surprisingly the common view is that death is the ultimate sanction. This natural human feeling appears all about us. There has been no national debate about punishment, in general or by imprisonment, comparable to the debate about the punishment of death. No other punishment has been so continuously restricted, nor has any State yet abolished prisons, as some have abolished this punishment. And those States that still inflict death reserve it for the most heinous crimes. Juries, of course, have always treated death cases differently, as have governors exercising their commutation powers. . . .

The only explanation for the uniqueness of death is its extreme severity. Death is today an unusually severe punishment, unusual in its pain, in its finality, and in its enormity. No other existing punishment is comparable to death in terms of physical and mental suffering. Although our information is not conclusive, it appears that there is no method available that guarantees an immediate and painless death. Since the discontinuance of flogging as a constitutionally permissible punishment, *Jackson* v. *Bishop*, 404 F.2d 571 (8th Cir. 1968), death remains as the only punishment that may involve the conscious infliction of physical pain. In addition, we know that mental pain is an inseparable part of our practice of punishing criminals by death, for the prospect of pending execution exacts a frightful toll during the inevitable long wait between the imposition of sentence and the actual infliction of death. . . .

The unusual severity of death is manifested most clearly in its finality and enormity. Death, in these respects, is in a class by itself. . . .

Death is truly an awesome punishment. The calculated killing of a human being by the State involves, by its very nature, a denial of the executed person's humanity. The contrast with the plight of a person punished by imprisonment is evident. An individual in prison does not lose "the right to have rights." . . .

In comparison to all other punishments today, then, the deliberate extinguishment of human life by the State is uniquely degrading to human dignity. I would not hesitate to hold, on that ground alone, that death is today a "cruel and unusual" punishment, were it not that death is a punishment of longstanding usage and acceptance in this country. I therefore turn to the second principle—that the State may not arbitrarily inflict an unusually severe punishment.

The outstanding characteristic of our present practice of punishing criminals by death is the infrequency with which we resort to it. The evidence is conclusive that death is not the ordinary punishment for any crime.

There has been a steady decline in the infliction of this punishment in every decade since the 1930's, the earliest period for which accurate statistics are available. . . ..

Although it is difficult to imagine what further facts would be necessary in order to prove that death is, as my Brother Stewart puts it, "wantonly and . . . freakishly" inflicted, I need not conclude that arbitrary infliction is patently obvious. I am not considering this punishment by the isolated light of one principle. The probability of arbitrariness is sufficiently substantial that it can be relied upon, in combination with the other principles, in reaching a judgment on the constitutionality of this punishment.

When there is a strong probability that an unusually severe and degrading punishment is being inflicted arbitrarily, we may well expect that society will disapprove of its infliction. I turn, therefore, to the third principle. An examination of the history and present operation of the American practice of punishing criminals by death reveals that this punishment has been almost totally rejected by contemporary society.

The progressive decline in, and the current rarity of, the infliction of death demonstrate that our society seriously questions the appropriateness of this punishment today. . . .

The final principle to be considered is that an unusually severe and degrading punishment may not be excessive in view of the purposes for which it is inflicted. . . .

The States' primary claim is that death is a necessary punishment because it prevents the commission of capital crimes more effectively than any less severe punishment. The first part of this claim is that the infliction of death is necessary to stop the individuals executed from committing further crimes. The sufficient answer to this is that if a criminal convicted of a capital crime poses a danger to society, effective administration of the

State's pardon and parole laws can delay or deny his release from prison, and techniques of isolation can eliminate or minimize the danger while he remains confined.

The more significant argument is that the threat of death prevents the commission of capital crimes because it deters potential criminals who would not be deterred by the threat of imprisonment. The argument is not based upon evidence that the threat of death is a superior deterrent. Indeed, as my Brother Marshall establishes, the available evidence uniformly indicates, although it does not conclusively prove, that the threat of death has no greater deterrent effect than the threat of imprisonment. The States argue, however, that they are entitled to rely upon common human experience, and that experience, they say, supports the conclusion that death must be a more effective deterrent than any less severe punishment. Because people fear death the most, the argument runs, the threat of death must be the greatest deterrent.

It is important to focus upon the precise import of this argument. It is not denied that many, and probably most, capital crimes cannot be deterred by the threat of punishment. Thus the argument can apply only to those who think rationally about the commission of capital crimes. Particularly is that true when the potential criminal, under this argument, must not only consider the risk of punishment, but also distinguish between two possible punishments. The concern, then, is with a particular type of potential criminal, the rational person who will commit a capital crime knowing that the punishment is long-term imprisonment, which may well be for the rest of his life, but will not commit the crime knowing that the punishment is death. On the face of it, the assumption that such persons exist is implausible.

In any event, this argument cannot be appraised in the abstract. . . . We are concerned with the practice of punishing criminals by death as it exists in the United States today. Proponents of this argument necessarily admit that its validity depends upon the existence of a system in which the punishment of death is invariably and swiftly imposed. Our system, of course, satisfies neither condition. . . .

There is, however, another aspect to the argument that the punishment of death is necessary for the protection of society. The infliction of death, the States urge, serves to manifest the community's outrage at the commission of the crime. It is, they say, a concrete public expression of moral indignation that inculcates respect for the law and helps assure a more peaceful community. . . .

The question, however, is not whether death serves these supposed purposes of punishment, but whether death serves them more effectively than imprisonment. There is no evidence whatever that utilization of imprisonment rather than death encourages private blood feuds and other disorders. . . .

There is, then, no substantial reason to believe that the punishment of death, as currently administered, is necessary for the protection of society. The only other purpose suggested, one that is independent of protection for society, is retribution. Shortly stated, retribution in this context means that criminals are put to death because they deserve it.

Although it is difficult to believe that any State today wishes to proclaim adherence to "naked vengeance," *Trop v. Dulles*, the States claim, in reliance upon its statutory authorization, that death is the only fit punishment for capital crimes and that this retributive purpose justifies its infliction. . . .

In sum, the punishment of death is inconsistent with all four principles: Death is an unusually severe and degrading punishment; there is a strong probability that it is inflicted arbitrarily; its rejection by contemporary society is virtually total; and there is no reason to believe that it serves any penal purpose more effectively than the less severe punishment of imprisonment. The function of these principles is to enable a court to determine whether a punishment comports with human dignity. Death, quite simply, does not.

JUSTICE STEWART, concurring.

The penalty of death differs from all other forms of criminal punishment, not in degree but in kind. It is unique in its total irrevocability. It is unique in its rejection of **rehabilitation** of the convict as a basic purpose of criminal justice. And it is unique, finally, in its absolute renunciation of all that is embodied in our concept of humanity.

For these and other reasons, at least two of my Brothers have concluded that the infliction of the death penalty is constitutionally impermissible in all circumstances under the Eighth and Fourteenth Amendments. Their case is a strong one. But I find it unnecessary to reach the ultimate question they would decide.

If we were reviewing death sentences imposed under these or similar laws [requiring mandatory penalties for all persons convicted of certain crimes], we would be faced with the need to decide whether capital punishment is unconstitutional for all crimes and under all circumstances. We would need to decide whether a legislature—state or federal—could constitutionally determine that certain criminal conduct is so atrocious that society's interest in deterrence and retribution wholly outweighs any considerations of reform or rehabilitation of the perpetrator, and that, despite the inconclusive empirical evidence, only the automatic penalty of death will provide maximum deterrence.

On that score I would say only that I cannot agree that retribution is a constitutionally impermissible ingredient in the imposition of punishment. The instinct for retribution is part of the nature of man, and channeling that instinct in the administration of criminal justice serves an important purpose in promoting the stability of a society governed by law. When people begin to believe that organized society is unwilling or unable to impose upon criminal offenders the punishment they "deserve," then there are sown the seeds of anarchy—of self-help, vigilante justice, and lynch law.

Instead, the death sentences now before us are the product of a legal system that brings them, I believe, within the very core of the Eighth Amendment's guarantee against cruel and unusual punishments, a guarantee applicable against the States through the Fourteenth Amendment. *Robinson v. California,* 370 U.S. 660 (1962). In the first place, it is clear that these sentences are "cruel" in the sense that they excessively go beyond, not in degree but in kind, the punishments that the state legislatures have determined to be necessary. *Weems v. United States,* 217 U.S. 349 (1910). In the second place, it is equally clear that these sentences are "unusual" in the sense that the penalty of death is infrequently imposed for murder, and that its imposition for rape is extraordinarily rare. But I do not rest my conclusion upon these two propositions alone.

These death sentences are cruel and unusual in the same way that being struck by lightning is cruel and unusual. For, of all the people convicted of rapes and murders in 1967 and 1968, many just as reprehensible as these, the petitioners are among a capriciously selected random handful upon whom the sentence of death has in fact been imposed. My concurring Brothers have demonstrated that, if any basis can be discerned for the selection of these few to be sentenced to die, it is the constitutionally impermissible basis of race. See *McLaughlin v. Florida*, 379 U.S. 184 (1964). But racial discrimination has not been proved, and I put it to one side. I simply conclude that the Eighth and Fourteenth Amendments cannot tolerate the infliction of a sentence of death under legal systems that permit this unique penalty to be so wantonly and so freakishly imposed.

For these reasons I concur in the judgments of the Court.

JUSTICE WHITE, concurring.

The facial constitutionality of statutes requiring the imposition of the death penalty for first-degree murder, for more narrowly defined categories of murder, or for rape would present quite different issues under the Eighth Amendment than are posed by the cases before us. In joining the Court's judgments, therefore, I do not at all intimate that the death penalty is unconstitutional *per se* or that there is no system of capital punishment that would comport with the Eighth Amendment. That question, ably argued by several of my Brethren, is not presented by these cases and need not be decided.

The narrower question to which I address myself concerns the constitutionality of capital punishment statutes under which (1) the legislature authorizes the imposition of the death penalty for murder or rape; (2) the legislature does not itself mandate the penalty in any particular class or kind of case (that is, legislative will is not frustrated if the penalty is never imposed), but delegates to judges or juries the decisions as to those cases, if any, in which the penalty will be utilized; and (3) judges and juries have ordered the death penalty with such infrequency that the odds are now very much against imposition and execution of the penalty with respect to any convicted murderer or rapist. It is in this context that we must consider whether the execution of these petitioners would violate the Eighth Amendment.

I begin with what I consider a near truism: that the death penalty could so seldom be imposed that it would cease to be a credible deterrent or measurably to contribute to any other end of punishment in the criminal justice system. It is perhaps true that no matter how infrequently those convicted of rape or murder are executed, the penalty so imposed is not disproportionate to the crime and those executed may deserve exactly what they received. It would also be clear that executed defendants are finally and completely **incapacitated** from again committing rape or murder or any other crime. But when imposition of the penalty reaches a certain degree of infrequency, it would be very doubtful that any existing general need for retribution would be measurably satisfied. Nor could it be said with confidence that society's need for specific deterrence justifies death for so few when for so many in like circumstances life imprisonment or shorter prison terms are judged sufficient, or that community values are measurably reinforced by authorizing a penalty so rarely invoked.

Most important, a major goal of the criminal law—to deter others by punishing the convicted criminal—would not be substantially served where the penalty is so seldom invoked that it ceases to be the credible threat essential to influence the conduct of others. For present purposes I accept the morality and utility of punishing one person to influence another. I accept also the effectiveness of punishment generally and need not reject the death penalty as a more effective deterrent than a lesser punishment. But common sense and experience tell us that seldom-enforced laws become ineffective measures for controlling human conduct and that the death penalty, unless imposed with sufficient frequency, will make little contribution to deterring those crimes for which it may be exacted.

The imposition and execution of the death penalty are obviously cruel in the dictionary sense. But the penalty has not been considered cruel and unusual punishment in the constitutional sense because it was thought justified by the social ends it was deemed to serve. At the moment that it ceases realistically to further these purposes, however, the emerging question is whether its imposition in such circumstances would violate the Eighth Amendment. It is my view that it would, for its imposition would then be the pointless and needless extinction of life with only marginal contributions to any discernible social or public purposes. A penalty with such negligible returns to the State would be patently excessive and cruel and unusual punishment violative of the Eighth Amendment.

It is also my judgment that this point has been reached with respect to capital punishment as it is presently administered under the statutes involved in these cases. . . .

JUSTICE MARSHALL, concurring.

The criminal acts with which we are confronted are ugly, vicious, reprehensible acts. Their sheer brutality cannot and should not be minimized. But, we are not called upon to condone the penalized conduct; we are asked only to examine the penalty imposed on each of the petitioners and to determine whether or not it violates the Eighth Amendment. . . .

The elasticity of the constitutional provision under consideration presents dangers of too little or too much self-restraint. Hence, we must proceed with caution to answer the question presented. By first examining the historical derivation of the Eighth Amendment and the construction given it in the past by this Court, and then exploring the history and attributes of capital punishment in this country, we can answer the question presented with objectivity and a proper measure of self-restraint.

Perhaps the most important principle in analyzing "cruel and unusual" punishment questions is one that is reiterated again and again in the prior opinions of the Court: *i. e.*, the cruel and unusual language "must draw its meaning from the evolving standards of decency that mark the progress of a maturing society." Thus, a penalty that was permissible at one time in our Nation's history is not necessarily permissible today.

Faced with an open question, we must establish our standards for decision. The decisions discussed in the previous section imply that a punishment may be deemed cruel and unusual for any one of four distinct reasons.

First, there are certain punishments that inherently involve so much physical pain and suffering that civilized people cannot tolerate them—*e.g.*, use of the rack, the thumbscrew, or other modes of torture. . . . . .

Second, there are punishments that are unusual, signifying that they were previously unknown as penalties for a given offense. If these punishments are intended to serve a humane purpose, they may be constitutionally permissible. Prior decisions leave open the question of just how much the word "unusual" adds to the word "cruel." I have previously indicated that use of the word "unusual" in the English Bill of Rights of 1689 was inadvertent, and there is nothing in the history of the Eighth Amendment to give flesh to its intended meaning. . . .

Third, a penalty may be cruel and unusual because it is excessive and serves no valid legislative purpose. *Weems v. United States*, 217 U.S. 349 (1910). The decisions previously discussed are replete with assertions that one of the primary functions of the cruel and unusual punishments clause is to prevent excessive or unnecessary penalties, ...

Fourth, where a punishment is not excessive and serves a valid legislative purpose, it still may be invalid if popular sentiment abhors it. . . .

It is immediately obvious, then, that since capital punishment is not a recent phenomenon, if it violates the Constitution, it does so because it is excessive or unnecessary, or because it is abhorrent to currently existing moral values.

We must proceed to the history of capital punishment in the United States.

IV

Capital punishment has been used to penalize various forms of conduct by members of society since the beginnings of civilization. Its precise origins are difficult to perceive, but there is some evidence that its roots lie in violent retaliation by members of a tribe or group, or by the tribe or group itself, against persons committing hostile acts toward group members. Thus, infliction of death as a penalty for objectionable conduct appears to have its beginnings in private vengeance.

As individuals gradually ceded their personal prerogatives to a sovereign power, the sovereign accepted the authority to punish wrongdoing as part of its "divine right" to rule. Individual vengeance gave way to the vengeance of the state, and capital punishment became a public function. Capital punishment worked its way into the laws of various countries, and was inflicted in a variety of macabre and horrific ways. . . .

V

In order to assess whether or not death is an excessive or unnecessary penalty, it is necessary to consider the reasons why a legislature might select it as punishment for one or more offenses, and examine whether less severe penalties would satisfy the legitimate legislative wants as well as capital punishment. If they would, then the death penalty is unnecessary cruelty, and, therefore, unconstitutional.

There are six purposes conceivably served by capital punishment: retribution, deterrence, prevention of repetitive criminal acts, encouragement of guilty pleas and confessions, eugenics, and economy. These are considered *seriatim* below.

A

The concept of retribution is one of the most misunderstood in all of our criminal jurisprudence. The principal source of confusion derives from the fact that, in dealing with the concept, most people confuse the question "why do men in fact punish?" with the question "what justifies men in punishing?" Men may punish for any number of reasons, but the one reason that punishment is morally good or morally justifiable is that someone has broken the law. Thus, it can correctly be said that breaking the law is the *sine qua non* of punishment, or, in other words, that we only tolerate punishment as it is imposed on one who deviates from the norm established by the criminal law.

The fact that the State may seek retribution against those who have broken its laws does not mean that retribution may then become the State's sole end in punishing. Our jurisprudence has always accepted deterrence in general, deterrence of individual recidivism, isolation of dangerous persons, and rehabilitation as proper goals of punishment. Retaliation, vengeance, and retribution have been roundly condemned as intolerable aspirations for a government in a free society. The history of the Eighth Amendment supports only the conclusion that retribution for its own sake is improper.

B

The most hotly contested issue regarding capital punishment is whether it is better than life imprisonment as a deterrent to crime. While the contrary position has been argued, it is my firm opinion that the death penalty is a more severe sanction than life imprisonment. . . .

It must be kept in mind, then, that the question to be considered is not simply whether capital punishment is a deterrent, but whether it is a better deterrent than life imprisonment.

[After extensive review, Marshall concludes that it is not.]

C

Much of what must be said about the death penalty as a device to prevent recidivism is obvious—if a murderer is executed, he cannot possibly commit another offense. The fact is, however, that murderers are extremely unlikely to commit other crimes either in prison or upon their release. . . .

D

The three final purposes which may underlie utilization of a capital sanction—encouraging guilty pleas and confessions, eugenics, and reducing state expenditures—may be dealt with quickly. If the death penalty is used to encourage guilty pleas and thus to deter suspects from exercising their rights under the Sixth Amendment to jury trials, it is unconstitutional. Its elimination would do little to impair the State's bargaining position in criminal cases, since life imprisonment remains a severe sanction which can be used as leverage for bargaining for pleas or confessions in exchange either for charges of lesser offenses or recommendations of leniency.

Moreover, to the extent that capital punishment is used to encourage confessions and guilty pleas, it is not being used for punishment purposes. A State that justifies capital punishment on its utility as part of the conviction process could not profess to rely on capital punishment as a deterrent. Such a State's system would be structured with twin goals only: obtaining guilty pleas and confessions and imposing *imprisonment* as the maximum sanction. Since life imprisonment is sufficient for bargaining purposes, the death penalty is excessive if used for the same purposes.

In light of the previous discussion on deterrence, any suggestions concerning the eugenic benefits of capital punishment are obviously meritless. . . .

As for the argument that it is cheaper to execute a capital offender than to imprison him for life, even assuming that such an argument, if true, would support a capital sanction, it is simply incorrect. A disproportionate amount of money spent on prisons is attributable to death row. . . .

E

There is but one conclusion that can be drawn from all of this—*i. e.*, the death penalty is an excessive and unnecessary punishment that violates the Eighth Amendment.

In addition, even if capital punishment is not excessive, it nonetheless violates the Eighth Amendment because it is morally unacceptable to the people of the United States at this time in their history. . . .

In other words, the question with which we must deal is not whether a substantial proportion of American citizens would today, if polled, opine that capital punishment is barbarously cruel, but whether they would find it to be so in the light of all information presently available.

Assuming knowledge of all the facts presently available regarding capital punishment, the average citizen would, in my opinion, find it shocking to his conscience and sense of justice. For this reason alone capital punishment cannot stand.

CHIEF JUSTICE BURGER, with whom JUSTICES BLACKMUN, POWELL, and REHNQUIST join, dissenting.

Justice Stewart and Justice White have concluded that petitioners' death sentences must be set aside because prevailing sentencing practices do not comply with the Eighth Amendment. For the reasons set forth in Part V of this opinion, I believe this approach fundamentally misconceives the nature of the Eighth Amendment guarantee and flies directly in the face of controlling authority of extremely recent vintage.

I

If we were possessed of legislative power, I would either join with Mr. Justice Brennan and Mr. Justice Marshall or, at the very least, restrict the use of capital punishment to a small category of the most heinous crimes. Our constitutional inquiry, however, must be divorced from personal feelings as to the morality and efficacy of the death penalty, and be confined to the meaning and applicability of the uncertain language of the Eighth Amendment. . . . Yet it is essential to our role as a court that we not seize upon the enigmatic character of the guarantee as an invitation to enact our personal predilections into law.

II

Counsel for petitioners properly concede that capital punishment was not impermissibly cruel at the time of the adoption of the Eighth Amendment. Not only do the records of the debates indicate that the Founding Fathers were limited in their concern to the prevention of torture, but it is also clear from the language of the Constitution itself that there was no thought whatever of the elimination of capital punishment. The opening sentence of the Fifth Amendment is a guarantee that the death penalty not be imposed "unless on a presentment or indictment of a Grand Jury." The Double Jeopardy Clause of the Fifth Amendment is a prohibition against being "twice put in jeopardy of life" for the same offense. Similarly, the Due Process Clause commands "due process of law" before an accused can be "deprived of life, liberty, or property." Thus, the explicit language of the Constitution affirmatively acknowledges the legal power to impose capital punishment; it does not expressly or by implication acknowledge the legal power to impose any of the various punishments that have been banned as cruel since 1791. Since the Eighth Amendment was adopted on the same day in 1791 as the Fifth Amendment, it hardly needs more to establish that the death penalty was not "cruel" in the constitutional sense at that time.

In the 181 years since the enactment of the Eighth Amendment, not a single decision of this Court has cast the slightest shadow of a doubt on the constitutionality of capital punishment. . . .

Before recognizing such an instant evolution in the law, it seems fair to ask what factors have changed that capital punishment should now be "cruel" in the constitutional sense as it has not been in the past. It is apparent that there has been no change of constitutional significance in the nature of the punishment itself. Twentieth century modes of execution surely involve no greater physical suffering than the means employed at the time of the Eighth Amendment's adoption. . . .

The Court's quiescence in this area can be attributed to the fact that in a democratic society legislatures, not courts, are constituted to respond to the will and consequently the moral values of the people. . . .

III

There are no obvious indications that capital punishment offends the conscience of society to such a degree that our traditional deference to the legislative judgment must be abandoned. It is not a punishment such as burning at the stake that everyone would ineffably find to be repugnant to all civilized standards. Nor is it a punishment so roundly condemned that only a few aberrant legislatures have retained it on the statute books. Capital punishment is authorized by statute in 40 States, the District of Columbia, and in the federal courts for the commission of certain crimes. On four occasions in the last 11 years Congress has added to the list of federal crimes punishable by death. In looking for reliable indicia of contemporary attitude, none more trustworthy has been advanced.

[Burger also states that public opinion polls have not shown overwhelming condemnation of the penalty.]

Counsel for petitioners rely on a different body of empirical evidence. They argue, in effect, that the number of cases in which the death penalty is imposed, as compared with the number of cases in which it is statutorily available, reflects a general revulsion toward the penalty that would lead to its repeal if only it were more generally and widely enforced. It cannot be gainsaid that by the choice of juries—and sometimes judges—the death penalty is imposed in far fewer than half the cases in which it is available. To go further and characterize the rate of imposition as "freakishly rare," as petitioners insist, is unwarranted hyperbole. And regardless of its characterization, the rate of imposition does not impel the conclusion that capital punishment is now regarded as intolerably cruel or uncivilized.

The selectivity of juries in imposing the punishment of death is properly viewed as a refinement on, rather than a repudiation of, the statutory authorization for that penalty. Legislatures prescribe the categories of crimes for which the death penalty should be available, and, acting as "the conscience of the community," juries are entrusted to determine in individual cases that the ultimate punishment is warranted. . . .

The rate of imposition of death sentences falls far short of providing the requisite unambiguous evidence that the legislatures of 40 States and the Congress have turned their backs on current or evolving standards of decency in continuing to make the death penalty available. . . .

IV

Capital punishment has also been attacked as violative of the Eighth Amendment on the ground that it is not needed to achieve legitimate penal aims and is thus "unnecessarily cruel." As a pure policy matter, this approach has much to recommend it, but it seeks to give a dimension to the Eighth Amendment that it was never intended to have and promotes a line of inquiry that this Court has never before pursued.

The Eighth Amendment, as I have noted, was included in the Bill of Rights to guard against the use of torturous and inhuman punishments, not those of limited efficacy. . . .

The less esoteric but no less controversial question is whether the death penalty acts as a superior deterrent. Those favoring abolition find no evidence that it does. Those favoring retention start from the intuitive notion that capital punishment should act as the most effective deterrent and note that there is no convincing evidence that it does not. Escape from this empirical stalemate is sought by placing the burden of proof on the States and concluding that they have failed to demonstrate that capital punishment is a more effective deterrent than life imprisonment. Numerous justifications have been advanced for shifting the burden, and they are not without their rhetorical appeal. However, these arguments are not descended from established constitutional principles, but are born of the urge to bypass an unresolved factual question. . . .

V

Today the Court has not ruled that capital punishment is *per se* violative of the Eighth Amendment; nor has it ruled that the punishment is barred for any particular class or classes of crimes. The substantially similar concurring opinions of Mr. Justice Stewart and Mr. Justice White, which are necessary to support the judgment setting aside petitioners' sentences, stop short of reaching the ultimate question. The actual scope of the Court's ruling, which I take to be embodied in these concurring opinions, is not entirely clear. This much, however, seems apparent: if the legislatures are to continue to authorize capital punishment for some crimes, juries and judges can no longer be permitted to make the sentencing determination in the same manner they have in the past. This approach—not urged in oral arguments or briefs—misconceives the nature of the constitutional command against "cruel and unusual punishments," disregards controlling case law, and demands a rigidity in capital cases which, if possible of achievement, cannot be regarded as a welcome change. Indeed the contrary seems to be the case.

As I have earlier stated, the Eighth Amendment forbids the imposition of punishments that are so cruel and inhumane as to violate society's standards of civilized conduct. The Amendment does not prohibit all punishments the States are unable to prove necessary to deter or control crime. The Amendment is not concerned with the process by which a State determines that a particular punishment is to be imposed in a particular case. And the Amendment most assuredly does not speak to the power of legislatures to confer sentencing discretion on juries, rather than to fix all sentences by statute.

The critical factor in the concurring opinions of both Mr. Justice Stewart and Mr. Justice White is the infrequency with which the penalty is imposed. This factor is taken not as evidence of society's abhorrence of capital punishment—the inference that petitioners would have the Court draw—but as the earmark of a deteriorated system of sentencing. It is concluded that petitioners' sentences must be set aside, not because the punishment is impermissibly cruel, but because juries and judges have failed to exercise their sentencing discretion in acceptable fashion.

To be sure, there is a recitation cast in Eighth Amendment terms: petitioners' sentences are "cruel" because they exceed that which the legislatures have deemed necessary for all cases; petitioners' sentences are "unusual" because they exceed that which is imposed in most cases. This application of the words of the Eighth Amendment suggests that capital punishment can be made to satisfy Eighth Amendment values if its rate of imposition is somehow multiplied; it seemingly follows that the flexible sentencing system created by the legislatures, and carried out by juries and judges, has yielded more mercy than the Eighth Amendment can stand. The implications of this approach are mildly ironical. . . .

This novel formulation of Eighth Amendment principles—albeit necessary to satisfy the terms of our limited grant of certiorari—does not lie at the heart of these concurring opinions. The decisive grievance of the opinions—not translated into Eighth Amendment terms—is that the present system of discretionary sentencing in capital cases has failed to produce evenhanded justice; the problem is not that too few have been sentenced to die, but that the selection process has followed no rational pattern. This claim of arbitrariness is not only lacking in empirical support, but also it manifestly fails to establish that the death penalty is a "cruel and unusual" punishment. The Eighth Amendment was included in the Bill of Rights to assure that certain types of punishments would never be imposed, not to channelize the sentencing process. The approach of these concurring opinions has no antecedent in the Eighth Amendment cases. It is essentially and exclusively a procedural due process argument.

While I would not undertake to make a definitive statement as to the parameters of the Court's ruling, it is clear that if state legislatures and the Congress wish to maintain the availability of capital punishment, significant statutory changes will have to be made. . . .

It seems remarkable to me that with our basic trust in lay jurors as the keystone in our system of criminal justice, it should now be suggested that we take the most sensitive and important of all decisions away from them. I could more easily be persuaded that mandatory sentences of death, without the intervening and ameliorating impact of lay jurors, are so arbitrary and doctrinaire that they violate the Constitution. The very infrequency of death penalties imposed by jurors attests their cautious and discriminating reservation of that penalty for the most extreme cases. I had thought that nothing was clearer in history, as we noted in *McGautha v. California,* 402 U.S. 183 (1971), one year ago, than the American abhorrence of "the common-law rule imposing a mandatory death sentence on all convicted murderers." . . ..

VI

. . . While I cannot endorse the process of decisionmaking that has yielded today's result and the restraints that that result imposes on legislative action, I am not altogether displeased that legislative bodies have been given the opportunity, and indeed unavoidable responsibility, to make a thorough re-evaluation of the entire subject of capital punishment. If today's opinions demonstrate nothing else, they starkly show that this is an area where legislatures can act far more effectively than courts.

JUSTICE BLACKMUN, dissenting.

Cases such as these provide for me an excruciating agony of the spirit. I yield to no one in the depth of my distaste, antipathy, and, indeed, abhorrence, for the death penalty, with all its aspects of physical distress and fear and of moral judgment exercised by finite minds. That distaste is buttressed by a belief that capital punishment serves no useful purpose that can be demonstrated. For me, it violates childhood's training and life's experiences, and is not compatible with the philosophical convictions I have been able to develop. It is antagonistic to any sense of "reverence for life." Were I a legislator, I would vote against the death penalty for the policy reasons argued by counsel for the respective petitioners and expressed and adopted in the several opinions filed by the Justices who vote to reverse these judgments.

[Blackmun goes on to say that he does not think precedents allow him, as a justice, to invalidate capital punishment.]

JUSTICE POWELL, with whom CHIEF JUSTICE BURGER, and JUSTICES BLACKMUN and REHNQUIST join, dissenting.

I

The Constitution itself poses the first obstacle to petitioners' argument that capital punishment is *per se* unconstitutional. The relevant provisions are the Fifth, Eighth, and Fourteenth Amendments. . . .

II

Petitioners assert that the constitutional issue is an open one uncontrolled by prior decisions of this Court. They view the several cases decided under the Eighth Amendment as assuming the constitutionality of the death penalty without focusing squarely upon the issue. I do not believe that the case law can be so easily cast aside. . . .

III

Petitioners seek to avoid the authority of the foregoing cases, and the weight of express recognition in the Constitution itself, by reasoning which will not withstand analysis. The thesis of petitioners' case derives from several opinions in which members of this Court have recognized the dynamic nature of the prohibition against cruel and unusual punishments. . . .

The prior opinions of this Court point with great clarity to reasons why those of us who sit on this Court at a particular time should act with restraint before assuming, contrary to a century of precedent, that we now know the answer for all time to come. First, where as here, the language of the applicable provision provides great leeway and where the underlying social policies are felt to be of vital importance, the temptation to read personal preference into the Constitution is understandably great. . . .

The second consideration dictating judicial self-restraint arises from a proper recognition of the respective roles of the legislative and judicial branches. The designation of punishments for crimes is a matter peculiarly within the sphere of the state and federal legislative bodies. . . .

IV

Although determining the range of available punishments for a particular crime is a legislative function, the very presence of the Cruel and Unusual Punishments Clause within the Bill of Rights requires, in the context of a specific case, that courts decide whether particular acts of the Congress offend that Amendment. The Due Process Clause of the Fourteenth Amendment imposes on the judiciary a similar obligation to scrutinize state legislation. But the proper exercise of that constitutional obligation in the cases before us today must be founded on a full recognition of the several considerations set forth above—the affirmative references to capital punishment in the Constitution, the prevailing precedents of this Court, the limitations on the exercise of our power imposed by tested principles of judicial self-restraint, and the duty to avoid encroachment on the powers conferred upon state and federal legislatures. . . .

Petitioners' contentions are premised, as indicated above, on the long-accepted view that concepts embodied in the Eighth and Fourteenth Amendments evolve. They present, with skill and persistence, a list of "objective indicators" which are said to demonstrate that prevailing standards of human decency have progressed to the final point of requiring the Court to hold, for all cases and for all time, that capital punishment is unconstitutional.

Briefly summarized, these proffered indicia of contemporary standards of decency include the following: (i) a worldwide trend toward the disuse of the death penalty; (ii) the reflection in the scholarly literature of a progressive rejection of capital punishment founded essentially on moral opposition to such treatment; (iii) the decreasing numbers of executions over the last 40 years and especially over the last decade; (iv) the small number of death sentences rendered in relation to the number of cases in which they might have been imposed; and (v) the indication of public abhorrence of the penalty reflected in the circumstance that executions are no longer public affairs. The foregoing is an incomplete summary but it touches the major bases of petitioners' presentation. Although they are not appropriate for consideration as objective evidence, petitioners strongly urge two additional propositions. They contend, first, that the penalty survives public condemnation only through the infrequency, arbitrariness, and discriminatory nature of its application, and, second, that there no longer exists any legitimate justification for the utilization of the ultimate penalty. These contentions, which have proved persuasive to several of the Justices constituting the majority, deserve separate consideration and will be considered in the ensuing sections. Before turning to those arguments, I first address the argument based on "objective" factors.

Any attempt to discern contemporary standards of decency through the review of objective factors must take into account several overriding considerations which petitioners choose to discount or ignore. In a democracy the first indicator of the public's attitude must always be found in the legislative judgments of the people's chosen representatives. . . .

This recent history of activity with respect to legislation concerning the death penalty abundantly refutes the abolitionist position.

The second and even more direct source of information reflecting the public's attitude toward capital punishment is the jury. . . .

One must conclude, contrary to petitioners' submission, that the indicators most likely to reflect the public's view—legislative bodies, state referenda and the juries which have the actual responsibility—do not support the contention that evolving standards of decency require total abolition of capital punishment. . . .

V

Petitioners seek to salvage their thesis by arguing that the infrequency and discriminatory nature of the actual resort to the ultimate penalty tend to diffuse public opposition. We are told that the penalty is imposed exclusively on uninfluential minorities—"the poor and powerless, personally ugly and socially unacceptable." It is urged that this pattern of application assures that large segments of the public will be either uninformed or unconcerned and will have no reason to measure the punishment against prevailing moral standards.

Implicitly, this argument concedes the unsoundness of petitioners' contention, examined above under Part IV, that objective evidence shows a present and widespread community rejection of the death penalty. It is now said, in effect, not that capital punishment presently offends our citizenry, but that the public *would* be offended *if* the penalty were enforced in a nondiscriminatory manner against a significant percentage of those charged with capital crimes, and *if* the public were thereby made aware of the moral issues surrounding capital punishment. Rather than merely registering the objective indicators on a judicial balance, we are asked ultimately to rest a far-reaching constitutional determination on a prediction regarding the subjective judgments of the mass of our people under hypothetical assumptions that may or may not be realistic.

Apart from the impermissibility of basing a constitutional judgment of this magnitude on such speculative assumptions, the argument suffers from other defects. If, as petitioners urge, we are to engage in speculation, it is not at all certain that the public would experience deep-felt revulsion if the States were to execute as many sentenced capital offenders this year as they executed in the mid-1930's. It seems more likely that public reaction, rather than being characterized by undifferentiated rejection, would depend upon the facts and circumstances surrounding each particular case.

Members of this Court know, from the petitions and appeals that come before us regularly, that brutish and revolting murders continue to occur with disquieting frequency. Indeed, murders are so commonplace in our society that only the most sensational receive significant and sustained publicity. It could hardly be suggested that in any of these highly publicized murder cases—the several senseless assassinations or the too numerous shocking multiple murders that have stained this country's recent history—the public has exhibited any signs of "revulsion" at the thought of executing the convicted murderers. The public outcry, as we all know, has been quite to the contrary. . .

As Mr. Justice Marshall's opinion today demonstrates, the argument does have a more troubling aspect. It is his contention that if the average citizen were aware of the disproportionate burden of capital punishment borne by the "poor, the ignorant, and the underprivileged," he would find the penalty "shocking to his conscience and sense of justice" and would not stand for its further use. This argument, like the apathy rationale, calls for further speculation on the part of the Court. . . .

Finally, yet another theory for abolishing the death penalty—reflected in varying degrees in each of the concurring opinions today—is predicated on the discriminatory impact argument. . . . Whatever may be the facts with respect to jury sentencing, this argument calls for a reconsideration of the "standards" aspects of the Court's decision in *McGautha v. California*, 402 U.S. 183 (1971). Although that is the unmistakable thrust of these opinions today, I see no reason to reassess the standards question considered so carefully in Mr. Justice Harlan's opinion for the Court last Term. Having so recently reaffirmed our historic dedication to entrusting the sentencing function to the jury's "untrammeled discretion," it is difficult to see how the Court can now hold the entire process constitutionally defective under the Eighth Amendment. . . .

VI

Petitioner in *Branch v. Texas,* 408 U.S. 238 (1972), and to a lesser extent the petitioners in the other cases before us today, urge that capital punishment is cruel and unusual because it no longer serves any rational legislative interests. Before turning to consider whether any of the traditional aims of punishment justify the death penalty, I should make clear the context in which I approach this aspect of the cases.

First, I find no support—in the language of the Constitution, in its history, or in the cases arising under it—for the view that this Court may invalidate a category of penalties because we deem less severe penalties adequate to serve the ends of penology. . . .

Secondly, if we were free to question the justifications for the use of capital punishment, a heavy burden would rest on those who attack the legislatures' judgments to prove the lack of rational justifications. . . .

I come now to consider, subject to the reservations above expressed, the two justifications most often cited for the retention of capital punishment. The concept of retribution—though popular for centuries—is now criticized as unworthy of a civilized people. Yet this Court has acknowledged the existence of a retributive element in criminal sanctions and has never heretofore found it impermissible. . . .

While retribution alone may seem an unworthy justification in a moral sense, its utility in a system of criminal justice requiring public support has long been recognized.

Deterrence is a more appealing justification, although opinions again differ widely. . . .

As I noted at the outset of this section, legislative judgments as to the efficacy of particular punishments are presumptively rational and may not be struck down under the Eighth Amendment because this Court may think that some alternative sanction would be more appropriate. Even if such judgments were within the judicial prerogative, petitioners have failed to show that there exist no justifications for the legislative enactments challenged in these cases. . . .

JUSTICE REHNQUIST, with whom CHIEF JUSTICE BURGER, and JUSTICES BLACKMUN and POWELL join, dissenting.

Rigorous attention to the limits of this Court's authority is likewise enjoined because of the natural desire that beguiles judges along with other human beings into imposing their own views of goodness, truth, and justice upon others. Judges differ only in that they have the power, if not the authority, to enforce their desires. This is doubtless why nearly two centuries of judicial precedent from this Court counsel the sparing use of that power. The most expansive reading of the leading constitutional cases does not remotely suggest that this Court has been granted a roving commission, either by the Founding Fathers or by the framers of the Fourteenth Amendment, to strike down laws that are based upon notions of policy or morality suddenly found unacceptable by a majority of this Court. . . .

FOR DISCUSSION

This set of opinions is rife with contradictions; an adequate brief would attempt to take each of them into account. Justice Douglas is especially concerned about the influence of race. Can you think of a way that his concerns might be mitigated?

Justice Brennan is especially concerned about "human dignity." Is this chiefly a constitutional, or an extraconstitutional, standard? How, if at all, do you think proponents of the death penalty might respond?

Justice Stewart is especially troubled by the capriciousness of the death penalty as he thought it was then being administered. How, if at all, do you think this capriciousness might be mitigated? What about a mandatory death penalty for certain specified crimes? Would such a penalty be consistent with individualized sentencing?

Justice Marshall focuses on the specific functions of punishment in general and of the death penalty in particular. What functions does he identify? What is his attitude toward retribution? Do you think this is ever appropriate in death sentencing? Is it possible to distinguish vengeance from retribution? If so, how?

What is Justice Blackmun's dilemma in this case? Keep this dilemma in mind as you read future decisions that he authored on the same subject. How often do you think justices uphold the constitutionality of legislation the wisdom or justice or which they dispute? Do you think the dissenters in this case find it easier to uphold the death penalty because they believe it is a legitimate exercise of governmental power?

Justice Stewart questions the deterrent effect of capital punishment. Do you think that scientific evidence can conclusively establish whether the death penalty does or does not deter crime?

Do you think the dissenters are ultimately most influenced by their view of the death penalty or by their conception of the judicial function? How do they respond to the argument that the Eighth Amendment was intended to enforce contemporary standards rather than those of the founding period?

As you read the next case, consider whether you think the Court's imposition in this area ultimately proved to be beneficial.

GREGG V. GEORGIA

428 U.S. 153, 96 S.Ct. 2909, 49 L.Ed.2d 859 (1976)

After *Furman v. Georgia* (408 U.S. 238, 1972), numerous states attempted to adopt new death penalty legislation that they hoped would comport with the standards established by the majority in that case. The legislation at issue separated the trial phase from the penalty phase of the trial and had the jury consider aggravating, extenuating, and mitigating factors; all such verdicts were subject to appellate review. Gregg had been convicted of armed robbery and murder.

Vote: 7–2

Judgment of the Court, and opinion of JUSTICES STEWART, POWELL, and STEVENS, announced by JUSTICE STEWART.

The issue in this case is whether the imposition of the sentence of death for the crime of murder under the law of Georgia violates the Eighth and Fourteenth Amendments.

I

[Stewart reviews facts of the case.]

Finally, the judge instructed the jury that it "would not be authorized to consider [imposing] the penalty of death" unless it first found beyond a reasonable doubt one of these aggravating circumstances:

"One—That the offense of murder was committed while the offender was engaged in the commission of two other capital felonies, to-wit the armed robbery of [Simmons and Moore].

"Two—That the offender committed the offense of murder for the purpose of receiving money and the automobile described in the indictment.

"Three—The offense of murder was outrageously and wantonly vile, horrible and inhuman, in that they *[sic]* involved the depravity of [the] mind of the defendant."

Finding the first and second of these circumstances, the jury returned verdicts of death on each count.

II

Before considering the issues presented it is necessary to understand the Georgia statutory scheme for the imposition of the death penalty. The Georgia statute, as amended after our decision in *Furman v. Georgia,* 408 U.S. 238 (1972), retains the death penalty for six categories of crime: murder, kidnapping for ransom or where the victim is harmed, armed robbery, rape, treason, and aircraft hijacking. The capital defendant's guilt or innocence is determined in the traditional manner, either by a trial judge or a jury, in the first stage of a bifurcated trial.

If trial is by jury, the trial judge is required to charge lesser included offenses when they are supported by any view of the evidence. After a verdict, finding, or plea of guilty to a capital crime, a presentence hearing is conducted before whoever made the determination of guilt. The sentencing procedures are essentially the same in both bench and jury trials. . . .

In the assessment of the appropriate sentence to be imposed the judge is also required to consider or to include in his instructions to the jury "any mitigating circumstances or aggravating circumstances otherwise authorized by law and any of [ten] statutory aggravating circumstances which may be supported by the evidence. . . ."

In addition to the conventional appellate process available in all criminal cases, provision is made for special expedited direct review by the Supreme Court of Georgia of the appropriateness of imposing the sentence of death in the particular case. . . .

The court is directed to consider "the punishment as well as any errors enumerated by way of appeal," and to determine:

(1) Whether the sentence of death was imposed under the influence of passion, prejudice, or any other arbitrary factor, and

(2) Whether, in cases other than treason or aircraft hijacking, the evidence supports the jury's or judge's finding of a statutory aggravating circumstance as enumerated in section 27.2534.1 (b), and

(3) Whether the sentence of death is excessive or disproportionate to the penalty imposed in similar cases, considering both the crime and the defendant.

If the court affirms a death sentence, it is required to include in its decision reference to similar cases that it has taken into consideration. . . .

III

The Court on a number of occasions has both assumed and asserted the constitutionality of capital punishment. . . But until *Furman v. Georgia* the Court never confronted squarely the fundamental claim that the punishment of death always, regardless of the enormity of the offense or the procedure followed in imposing the sentence, is cruel and unusual punishment in violation of the Constitution. Although this issue was presented and addressed in *Furman,* it was not resolved by the Court. . . . We now hold that the punishment of death does not invariably violate the Constitution.

A

[Stewart reviews history of "cruel and unusual" punishments.]

Of course, the requirements of the Eighth Amendment must be applied with an awareness of the limited role to be played by the courts. . . .

But, while we have an obligation to insure that constitutional bounds are not overreached, we may not act as judges as we might as legislators. . . .

Therefore, in assessing a punishment selected by a democratically elected legislature against the constitutional measure, we presume its validity. We may not require the legislature to select the least severe penalty possible so long as the penalty selected is not cruelly inhumane or disproportionate to the crime involved. And a heavy burden rests on those who would attack the judgment of the representatives of the people.

C

The imposition of the death penalty for the crime of murder has a long history of acceptance both in the United States and in England. . . .

It is apparent from the text of the Constitution itself that the existence of capital punishment was accepted by the Framers. At the time the Eighth Amendment was ratified, capital punishment was a common sanction in every State. . . .

The petitioners in the capital cases before the Court today renew the "standards of decency" argument, but developments during the four years since *Furman* have undercut substantially the assumptions upon which their argument rested. Despite the continuing debate, dating back to the 19th century, over the morality and utility of capital punishment, it is now evident that a large proportion of American society continues to regard it as an appropriate and necessary criminal sanction.

The most marked indication of society's endorsement of the death penalty for murder is the legislative response to *Furman.* The legislatures of at least 35 States have enacted new statutes that provide for the death penalty for at least some crimes that result in the death of another person. And the Congress of the United States, in 1974, enacted a statute providing the death penalty for aircraft piracy that results in death. These recently adopted statutes have attempted to address the concerns expressed by the Court in *Furman* primarily (i) by specifying the factors to be weighed and the procedures to be followed in deciding when to impose a capital sentence, or (ii) by making the death penalty mandatory for specified crimes. But all of the post-*Furman* statutes make clear that capital punishment itself has not been rejected by the elected representatives of the people.

In the only statewide referendum occurring since *Furman* and brought to our attention, the people of California adopted a constitutional amendment that authorized capital punishment. . . .

. . . the actions of juries in many States since *Furman* are fully compatible with the legislative judgments, reflected in the new statutes, as to the continued utility and necessity of capital punishment in appropriate cases. At the close of 1974 at least 254 persons had been sentenced to death since *Furman,* and by the end of March 1976, more than 460 persons were subject to death sentences.

As we have seen, however, the Eighth Amendment demands more than that a challenged punishment be acceptable to contemporary society. The Court also must ask whether it comports with the basic concept of human dignity at the core of the Amendment. . . .

The death penalty is said to serve two principal social purposes: retribution and deterrence of capital crimes by prospective offenders.

In part, capital punishment is an expression of society's moral outrage at particularly offensive conduct. This function may be unappealing to many, but it is essential in an ordered society that asks its citizens to rely on legal processes rather than self-help to vindicate their wrongs. . . .

Statistical attempts to evaluate the worth of the death penalty as a deterrent to crimes by potential offenders have occasioned a great deal of debate. . . .

Although some of the studies suggest that the death penalty may not function as a significantly greater deterrent than lesser penalties, there is no convincing empirical evidence either supporting or refuting this view. We may nevertheless assume safely that there are murderers, such as those who act in passion, for whom the threat of death has little or no deterrent effect. But for many others, the death penalty undoubtedly is a significant deterrent. There are carefully contemplated murders, such as murder for hire, where the possible penalty of death may well enter into the cold calculus that precedes the decision to act. And there are some categories of murder, such as murder by a life prisoner, where other sanctions may not be adequate.

The value of capital punishment as a deterrent of crime is a complex factual issue the resolution of which properly rests with the legislatures, which can evaluate the results of statistical studies in terms of their own local conditions and with a flexibility of approach that is not available to the courts.

Finally, we must consider whether the punishment of death is disproportionate in relation to the crime for which it is imposed. There is no question that death as a punishment is unique in its severity and irrevocability. When a defendant's life is at stake, the Court has been particularly sensitive to insure that every safeguard is observed. But we are concerned here only with the imposition of capital punishment for the crime of murder, and when a life has been taken deliberately by the offender, we cannot say that the punishment is invariably disproportionate to the crime. It is an extreme sanction, suitable to the most extreme of crimes.

We hold that the death penalty is not a form of punishment that may never be imposed, regardless of the circumstances of the offense, regardless of the character of the offender, and regardless of the procedure followed in reaching the decision to impose it.

IV

We now consider whether Georgia may impose the death penalty on the petitioner in this case.

A

While *Furman* did not hold that the infliction of the death penalty *per se* violates the Constitution's ban on cruel and unusual punishments, it did recognize that the penalty of death is different in kind from any other punishment imposed under our system of criminal justice. Because of the uniqueness of the death penalty, *Furman* held that it could not be imposed under sentencing procedures that created a substantial risk that it would be inflicted in an arbitrary and capricious manner. . . .

Furman mandates that where discretion is afforded a sentencing body on a matter so grave as the determination of whether a human life should be taken or spared, that discretion must be suitably directed and limited so as to minimize the risk of wholly arbitrary and capricious action.

These procedures require the jury to consider the circumstances of the crime and the criminal before it recommends sentence. No longer can a Georgia jury do as Furman's jury did: reach a finding of the defendant's guilt and then, without guidance or direction, decide whether he should live or die. Instead, the jury's attention is directed to the specific circumstances of the crime: Was it committed in the course of another capital felony? Was it committed for money? Was it committed upon a peace officer or judicial officer? Was it committed in a particularly heinous way or in a manner that endangered the lives of many persons? In addition, the jury's attention is focused on the characteristics of the person who committed the crime: Does he have a record of prior convictions for capital offenses? Are there any special facts about this defendant that mitigate against imposing capital punishment (*e.g.,* his youth, the extent of his cooperation with the police, his emotional state at the time of the crime). As a result, while some jury discretion still exists, "the discretion to be exercised is controlled by clear and objective standards so as to produce non-discriminatory application."

As an important additional safeguard against arbitrariness and caprice, the Georgia statutory scheme provides for automatic appeal of all death sentences to the State's Supreme Court. . . .

V

The basic concern of *Furman* centered on those defendants who were being condemned to death capriciously and arbitrarily. Under the procedures before the Court in that case, sentencing authorities were not directed to give attention to the nature or circumstances of the crime committed or to the character or record of the defendant. Left unguided, juries imposed the death sentence in a way that could only be called freakish. The new Georgia sentencing procedures, by contrast, focus the jury's attention on the particularized nature of the crime and the particularized characteristics of the individual defendant. While the jury is permitted to consider any aggravating or mitigating circumstances, it must find and identify at least one statutory aggravating factor before it may impose a penalty of death. In this way the jury's discretion is channeled. No longer can a jury wantonly and freakishly impose the death sentence; it is always circumscribed by the legislative guidelines. In addition, the review function of the Supreme Court of Georgia affords additional assurance that the concerns that prompted our decision in *Furman* are not present to any significant degree in the Georgia procedure applied here.

JUSTICE WHITE, with whom CHIEF JUSTICE BURGER and JUSTICE REHNQUIST join, concurring in the judgment.

III

The threshold question in this case is whether the death penalty may be carried out for murder under the Georgia legislative scheme consistent with the decision in *Furman v. Georgia,* 408 U.S. 238 (1972). In *Furman,* this Court held that as a result of giving the sentencer unguided discretion to impose or not to impose the death penalty for murder, the penalty was being imposed discriminatorily, wantonly and freakishly, and so infrequently that any given death sentence was cruel and unusual. Petitioner argues that, as in *Furman,* the jury is still the sentencer; that the statutory criteria to be considered by the jury on the issue of sentence under Georgia's new statutory scheme are vague and do not purport to be all-inclusive; and that, in any event, there are *no* circumstances under which the jury is required to impose the death penalty. Consequently, the petitioner argues that the death penalty will inexorably be imposed in as discriminatory, standardless, and rare a manner as it was imposed under the scheme declared invalid in *Furman.*

The argument is considerably overstated. The Georgia Legislature has made an effort to identify those aggravating factors which it considers necessary and relevant to the question whether a defendant convicted of capital murder should be sentenced to death. The jury which imposes sentence is instructed on all statutory aggravating factors which are supported by the evidence, and is told that it may not impose the death penalty unless it unanimously finds at least one of those factors to have been established beyond a reasonable doubt. The Georgia Legislature has plainly made an effort to guide the jury in the exercise of its discretion, while at the same time permitting the jury to dispense mercy on the basis of factors too intangible to write into a statute, and I cannot accept the naked assertion that the effort is bound to fail. . . .

JUSTICE BRENNAN, dissenting.

The Cruel and Unusual Punishments Clause "must draw its meaning from the evolving standards of decency that mark the progress of a maturing society." . . .

In *Furman v. Georgia,* 408 U.S. 238 (1972), I read "evolving standards of decency" as requiring focus upon the essence of the death penalty itself and not primarily or solely upon the procedures under which the determination to inflict the penalty upon a particular person was made. . . .

The fatal constitutional infirmity in the punishment of death is that it treats "members of the human race as nonhumans, as objects to be toyed with and discarded. [It is] thus inconsistent with the fundamental premise of the Clause that even the vilest criminal remains a human being possessed of common human dignity." As such it is a penalty that "subjects the individual to a fate forbidden by the principle of civilized treatment guaranteed by the [Clause]." I therefore would hold, on that ground alone, that death is today a cruel and unusual punishment prohibited by the Clause. "Justice of this kind is obviously no less shocking than the crime itself, and the new 'official' murder, far from offering redress for the offense committed against society, adds instead a second defilement to the first." [Quoted from Camus's *Reflections on the Guillotine.*]

JUSTICE MARSHALL, dissenting.

In *Furman v. Georgia*, 408 U.S. 238 (1972), I concluded that the death penalty is constitutionally invalid for two reasons. First, the death penalty is excessive. And second, the American people, fully informed as to the purposes of the death penalty and its liabilities, would in my view reject it as morally unacceptable.

Since the decision in *Furman,* the legislatures of 35 States have enacted new statutes authorizing the imposition of the death sentence for certain crimes, and Congress has enacted a law providing the death penalty for air piracy resulting in death. I would be less than candid if I did not acknowledge that these developments have a significant bearing on a realistic assessment of the moral acceptability of the death penalty to the American people. But if the constitutionality of the death penalty turns, as I have urged, on the opinion of an *informed* citizenry, then even the enactment of new death statutes cannot be viewed as conclusive. In *Furman,* I observed that the American people are largely unaware of the information critical to a judgment on the morality of the death penalty, and concluded that if they were better informed they would consider it shocking, unjust, and unacceptable. A recent study, conducted after the enactment of the post-*Furman* statutes, has confirmed that the American people know little about the death penalty, and that the opinions of an informed public would differ significantly from those of a public unaware of the consequences and effects of the death penalty.

Even assuming, however, that the post-*Furman* enactment of statutes authorizing the death penalty renders the prediction of the views of an informed citizenry an uncertain basis for a constitutional decision, the enactment of those statutes has no bearing whatsoever on the conclusion that the death penalty is unconstitutional because it is excessive. An excessive penalty is invalid under the Cruel and Unusual Punishments Clause "even though popular sentiment may favor" it. . . .

FOR DISCUSSION

How, if at all, did the adoption of state and federal legislation since the decision in *Furman v. Georgia* affect the Court's evaluation as to the acceptability of the penalty in the court of public opinion? According to the majority opinion in the case, does the death penalty deter crime? Who should ultimately decide this question? The adoption of subsequent legislation seemed to call into question Justice Marshall's view that the American opinion rejected the death penalty. How did he attempt to deal with this development?

COKER v. GEORGIA

433 U.S. 584, 97 S.Ct. 2861, 53 L.Ed.2d 982 (1977)

This case involves the question of whether a state can impose the death penalty for the rape of an adult woman when the victim did not die.

Vote: 7–2

JUSTICE WHITE delivered the opinion of the Court.

III

That question, with respect to rape of an adult woman, is now before us. We have concluded that a sentence of death is grossly disproportionate and excessive punishment for the crime of rape and is therefore forbidden by the Eighth Amendment as cruel and unusual punishment.

As advised by recent cases, we seek guidance in history and from the objective evidence of the country's present judgment concerning the acceptability of death as a penalty for rape of an adult woman. At no time in the last 50 years have a majority of the States authorized death as a punishment for rape. In 1925, 18 States, the District of Columbia, and the Federal Government authorized capital punishment for the rape of an adult female. By 1971 just prior to the decision in *Furman* v. *Georgia,* 408 U.S. 238 (1972), that number had declined, but not substantially, to 16 States plus the Federal Government. . . .

But if the "most marked indication of society's endorsement of the death penalty for murder is the legislative response to *Furman,*" *Gregg v. Georgia,* 428 U.S. 153 (1976), it should also be a telling datum that the public judgment with respect to rape, as reflected in the statutes providing the punishment for that crime, has been dramatically different. In reviving death penalty laws to satisfy *Furman*'s mandate, none of the States that had not previously authorized death for rape chose to include rape among capital felonies. Of the 16 States in which rape had been a capital offense, only three provided the death penalty for rape of an adult woman in their revised statutes—Georgia, North Carolina, and Louisiana. In the latter two States, the death penalty was mandatory for those found guilty, and those laws were invalidated by *Woodson* and *Roberts*. . . .

Georgia argues that 11 of the 16 States that authorized death for rape in 1972 attempted to comply with *Furman* by enacting arguably mandatory death penalty legislation and that it is very likely that, aside from Louisiana and North Carolina, these States simply chose to eliminate rape as a capital offense rather than to *require* death for *each* and *every* instance of rape. The argument is not without force; but 4 of the 16 States did not take the mandatory course and also did *not* continue rape of an adult woman as a capital offense. Further, as we have indicated, the legislatures of 6 of the 11 arguably mandatory States have revised their death penalty laws since *Woodson v. North Carolina,* 428 U.S. 280 (1976), and *Roberts v. Louisiana,* 428 U.S. 325 (1976), without enacting a new death penalty for rape. And this is to say nothing of 19 other States that enacted nonmandatory, post-*Furman* statutes and chose not to sentence rapists to death.

B

It was also observed in *Gregg* that "[t]he jury . . . is a significant and reliable objective index of contemporary values because it is so directly involved," and that it is thus important to look to the sentencing decisions that juries have made in the course of assessing whether capital punishment is an appropriate penalty for the crime being tried. Of course, the jury's judgment is meaningful only where the jury has an appropriate measure of choice as to whether the death penalty is to be imposed. As far as execution for rape is concerned, this is now true only in Georgia and in Florida; and in the latter State, capital punishment is authorized only for the rape of children.

According to the factual submissions in this Court, out of all rape convictions in Georgia since 1973—and that total number has not been tendered—63 cases had been reviewed by the Georgia Supreme Court as of the time of oral argument; and of these, 6 involved a death sentence, 1 of which was set aside, leaving 5 convicted rapists now under sentence of death in the State of Georgia. Georgia juries have thus sentenced rapists to death six times since 1973. This obviously is not a negligible number; and the State argues that as a practical matter juries simply reserve the extreme sanction for extreme cases of rape and that recent experience surely does not prove that jurors consider the death penalty to be a disproportionate punishment for every conceivable instance of rape, no matter how aggravated. Nevertheless, it is true that in the vast majority of cases, at least 9 out of 10, juries have not imposed the death sentence.

IV

Rape is without doubt deserving of serious punishment; but in terms of moral depravity and of the injury to the person and to the public, it does not compare with murder, which does involve the unjustified taking of human life. . . .

Although it may be accompanied by another crime, rape by definition does not include the death of or even the serious injury to another person. The murderer kills; the rapist, if no more than that, does not. Life is over for the victim of the murderer; for the rape victim, life may not be nearly so happy as it was, but it is not over and normally is not beyond repair. We have the abiding conviction that the death penalty, which "is unique in its severity and irrevocability," *Gregg* v. *Georgia,* is an excessive penalty for the rapist who, as such, does not take human life.

JUSTICE BRENNAN, concurring in the judgment.

Adhering to my view that the death penalty is in all circumstances cruel and unusual punishment prohibited by the Eighth and Fourteenth Amendments, *Gregg* v. *Georgia,* 428 U.S. 153 (1976), I concur in the judgment of the Court setting aside the death sentence imposed under the Georgia rape statute.

CHIEF JUSTICE BURGER, with whom JUSTICE REHNQUIST joins, dissenting.

In a case such as this, confusion often arises as to the Court's proper role in reaching a decision. Our task is not to give effect to our individual views on capital punishment; rather, we must determine what the Constitution permits a State to do under its reserved powers. In striking down the death penalty imposed upon the petitioner in this case, the Court has overstepped the bounds of proper constitutional adjudication by substituting its policy judgment for that of the state legislature. I accept that the Eighth Amendment's concept of disproportionality bars the death penalty for minor crimes. But rape is not a minor crime; hence the Cruel and Unusual Punishments Clause does not give the Members of this Court license to engraft their conceptions of proper public policy onto the considered legislative judgments of the States. Since I cannot agree that Georgia lacked the constitutional power to impose the penalty of death for rape, I dissent from the Court's judgment.

The analysis of the plurality opinion is divided into two parts: (a) an "objective" determination that most American jurisdictions do not presently make rape a capital offense, and (b) a subjective judgment that death is an excessive punishment for rape because the crime does not, in and of itself, cause the death of the victim. I take issue with each of these points.

More to the point, however, it is myopic to base sweeping constitutional principles upon the narrow experience of the past five years. . . . .

In any case, when considered in light of the experience since the turn of this century, where more than one-third of American jurisdictions have consistently provided the death penalty for rape, the plurality's focus on the experience of the immediate past must be viewed as truly disingenuous. Having in mind the swift changes in positions of some Members of this Court in the short span of five years, can it rationally be considered a relevant indicator of what our society deems "cruel and unusual" to look solely to what legislatures have *refrained* from doing under conditions of great uncertainty arising from our less than lucid holdings on the Eighth Amendment? Far more representative of societal mores of the 20th century is the accepted practice in a substantial number of jurisdictions preceding the *Furman* decision. . . .

However, even were one to give the most charitable acceptance to the plurality's statistical analysis, it still does not, to my mind, support its conclusion. The most that can be claimed is that for the past year Georgia has been the only State whose adult rape death penalty statute has not otherwise been invalidated; two other state legislatures had enacted rape death penalty statutes in the last five years, but these were invalidated for reasons unrelated to rape under the Court's decisions last Term. Even if these figures could be read as indicating that no other States view the death penalty as an appropriate punishment for the rape of an adult woman, it would not necessarily follow that Georgia's imposition of such sanction violates the Eighth Amendment.

The Court has repeatedly pointed to the reserve strength of our federal system which allows state legislatures, within broad limits, to experiment with laws, both criminal and civil, in the effort to achieve socially desirable results. . . .

The question of whether the death penalty is an appropriate punishment for rape is surely an open one. . . .

In order for Georgia's legislative program to develop it must be given time to take effect so that data may be evaluated for comparison with the experience of States which have not enacted death penalty statutes. . . .

(b)

The subjective judgment that the death penalty is simply disproportionate to the crime of rape is even more disturbing than the "objective" analysis discussed *supra.* The plurality's conclusion on this point is based upon the bare fact that murder necessarily results in the physical death of the victim, while rape does not. However, no Member of the Court explains why this distinction has relevance, much less constitutional significance. It is, after all, not irrational—nor constitutionally impermissible—for a legislature to make the penalty more severe than the criminal act it punishes in the hope it would deter wrongdoing. . . .

Whatever our individual views as to the wisdom of capital punishment, I cannot agree that it is constitutionally impermissible for a state legislature to make the "solemn judgment" to impose such penalty for the crime of rape. Accordingly, I would leave to the States the task of legislating in this area of the law.

FOR DISCUSSION

In *Kennedy v. Louisiana* (2008) the Court extended the rationale of *Coker* to exclude child rapists, in this case a stepfather, from the death penalty as well. One of the issues raised was whether a rape could have such a traumatic effect on a child that the crime could be said to be equivalent to murder. What do you think?

McCleskey v. Kemp

481 U.S. 279, 107 S.Ct. 1756, 95 L.Ed.2d 262 (1987)

Here an African American defendant attempts to use a statistical study to prove that capital punishment was being administered in a racially discriminatory fashion. This case is thus appropriate for consideration not only with respect to the Eighth Amendment but also in the following chapter, which deals with equal protection. Students might find it productive to compare the decision in *McCleskey* with that in *Batson v. Kentucky* (476 U.S. 79, 1986), involving considerations of race in jury selection.

Vote: 5–4

Justice Powell delivered the opinion of the Court.

This case presents the question whether a complex statistical study that indicates a risk that racial considerations enter into capital sentencing determinations proves that petitioner McCleskey's capital sentence is unconstitutional under the Eighth or Fourteenth Amendment.

I

[Powell reviews the facts of the case involving the murder of a white police officer by a black man during the commission of an armed robbery of a furniture store.]

McCleskey . . . raised 18 claims, one of which was that the Georgia capital sentencing process is administered in a racially discriminatory manner in violation of the Eighth and Fourteenth Amendments to the United States Constitution. In support of his claim, McCleskey proffered a statistical study performed by Professors David C. Baldus, Charles Pulaski, and George Woodworth (the Baldus study) that purports to show a disparity in the imposition of the death sentence in Georgia based on the race of the murder victim and, to a lesser extent, the race of the defendant. The Baldus study is actually two sophisticated statistical studies that examine over 2,000 murder cases that occurred in Georgia during the 1970's. The raw numbers collected by Professor Baldus indicate that defendants charged with killing white persons received the death penalty in 11% of the cases, but defendants charged with killing blacks received the death penalty in only 1% of the cases. The raw numbers also indicate a reverse racial disparity according to the race of the defendant: 4% of the black defendants received the death penalty, as opposed to 7% of the white defendants.

Baldus also divided the cases according to the combination of the race of the defendant and the race of the victim. He found that the death penalty was assessed in 22% of the cases involving black defendants and white victims; 8% of the cases involving white defendants and white victims; 1% of the cases involving black defendants and black victims; and 3% of the cases involving white defendants and black victims. Similarly, Baldus found that prosecutors sought the death penalty in 70% of the cases involving black defendants and white victims; 32% of the cases involving white defendants and white victims; 15% of the cases involving black defendants and black victims; and 19% of the cases involving white defendants and black victims.

Baldus subjected his data to an extensive analysis, taking account of 230 variables that could have explained the disparities on nonracial grounds. One of his models concludes that, even after taking account of 39 nonracial variables, defendants charged with killing white victims were 4.3 times as likely to receive a death sentence as defendants charged with killing blacks. According to this model, black defendants were 1.1 times as likely to receive a death sentence as other defendants. Thus, the Baldus study indicates that black defendants, such as McCleskey, who kill white victims have the greatest likelihood of receiving the death penalty.

[Powell reviews the district and circuit courts' rejection of this plea.]

II

McCleskey's first claim is that the Georgia capital punishment statute violates the Equal Protection Clause of the Fourteenth Amendment. He argues that race has infected the administration of Georgia's statute in two ways: persons who murder whites are more likely to be sentenced to death than persons who murder blacks, and black murderers are more likely to be sentenced to death than white murderers. As a black defendant who killed a white victim, McCleskey claims that the Baldus study demonstrates that he was discriminated against because of his race and because of the race of his victim. In its broadest form, McCleskey's claim of discrimination extends to every actor in the Georgia capital sentencing process, from the prosecutor who sought the death penalty and the jury that imposed the sentence, to the State itself that enacted the capital punishment statute and allows it to remain in effect despite its allegedly discriminatory application. We agree with the Court of Appeals, and every other court that has considered such a challenge, that this claim must fail.

A

Our analysis begins with the basic principle that a defendant who alleges an equal protection violation has the burden of proving "the existence of purposeful discrimination." *Whitus v. Georgia,* 385 U.S. 545 (1967). A corollary to this principle is that a criminal defendant must prove that the purposeful discrimination "had a discriminatory effect" on him. *Wayte v. United States,* 470 U.S. 598 (1985). Thus, to prevail under the Equal Protection Clause, McCleskey must prove that the decisionmakers in *his* case acted with discriminatory purpose. He offers no evidence specific to his own case that would support an inference that racial considerations played a part in his sentence. Instead, he relies solely on the Baldus study. . . .

The Court has accepted statistics as proof of intent to discriminate in certain limited contexts. First, this Court has accepted statistical disparities as proof of an equal protection violation in the selection of the jury venire in a particular district. Although statistical proof normally must present a "stark" pattern to be accepted as the sole proof of discriminatory intent under the Constitution, "because of the nature of the jury-selection task, . . . we have permitted a finding of constitutional violation even when the statistical pattern does not approach [such] extremes." *Arlington Heights v. Metropolitan Housing Dev. Corp.*, 429 U.S. 252 (1977). Second, this Court has accepted statistics in the form of multiple-regression analysis to prove statutory violations under Title VII of the Civil Rights Act of 1964.

But the nature of the capital sentencing decision, and the relationship of the statistics to that decision, are fundamentally different from the corresponding elements in the venire-selection or Title VII cases. Most importantly, each particular decision to impose the death penalty is made by a petit jury selected from a properly constituted venire. Each jury is unique in its composition, and the Constitution requires that its decision rest on consideration of innumerable factors that vary according to the characteristics of the individual defendant and the facts of the particular capital offense. Thus, the application of an inference drawn from the general statistics to a specific decision in a trial and sentencing simply is not comparable to the application of an inference drawn from general statistics to a specific venire-selection or Title VII case. In those cases, the statistics relate to fewer entities, and fewer variables are relevant to the challenged decisions.

Another important difference between the cases in which we have accepted statistics as proof of discriminatory intent and this case is that, in the venire-selection and Title VII contexts, the decisionmaker has an opportunity to explain the statistical disparity. Here, the State has no practical opportunity to rebut the Baldus study. . . .

Finally, McCleskey's statistical proffer must be viewed in the context of his challenge. McCleskey challenges decisions at the heart of the State's criminal justice system. "One of society's most basic tasks is that of protecting the lives of its citizens and one of the most basic ways in which it achieves the task is through criminal laws against murder." *Gregg* v. *Georgia*, 428 U.S. 153, 226 (1976) (White, J., concurring). Implementation of these laws necessarily requires discretionary judgments. Because discretion is essential to the criminal justice process, we would demand exceptionally clear proof before we would infer that the discretion has been abused. The unique nature of the decisions at issue in this case also counsels against adopting such an inference from the disparities indicated by the Baldus study. Accordingly, we hold that the Baldus study is clearly insufficient to support an inference that any of the decisionmakers in McCleskey's case acted with discriminatory purpose.

B

McCleskey also suggests that the Baldus study proves that the State as a whole has acted with a discriminatory purpose. He appears to argue that the State has violated the Equal Protection Clause by adopting the capital punishment statute and allowing it to remain in force despite its allegedly discriminatory application. But " 'discriminatory purpose' . . . implies more than intent as volition or intent as awareness of consequences. It implies that the decisionmaker, in this case a state legislature, selected or reaffirmed a particular course of action at least in part 'because of,' not merely 'in spite of,' its adverse effects upon an identifiable group." For this claim to prevail, McCleskey would have to prove that the Georgia Legislature enacted or maintained the death penalty statute *because of* an anticipated racially discriminatory effect. In *Gregg v. Georgia,* 428 U.S. 153 (1976), this Court found that the Georgia capital sentencing system could operate in a fair and neutral manner. There was no evidence then, and there is none now, that the Georgia Legislature enacted the capital punishment statute to further a racially discriminatory purpose.

Nor has McCleskey demonstrated that the legislature maintains the capital punishment statute because of the racially disproportionate impact suggested by the Baldus study. . . .

III

A–C

[Powell reviews precedents.]

D

In sum, our decisions since *Furman* have identified a constitutionally permissible range of discretion in imposing the death penalty. First, there is a required threshold below which the death penalty cannot be imposed. In this context, the State must establish rational criteria that narrow the decisionmaker's judgment as to whether the circumstances of a particular defendant's case meet the threshold. Moreover, a societal consensus that the death penalty is disproportionate to a particular offense prevents a State from imposing the death penalty for that offense. Second, States cannot limit the sentencer's consideration of any relevant circumstance that could cause it to decline to impose the penalty. In this respect, the State cannot channel the sentencer's discretion, but must allow it to consider any relevant information offered by the defendant.

IV

A

In light of our precedents under the Eighth Amendment, McCleskey cannot argue successfully that his sentence is "disproportionate to the crime in the traditional sense." He does not deny that he committed a murder in the course of a planned robbery, a crime for which this Court has determined that the death penalty constitutionally may be imposed. His disproportionality claim "is of a different sort." McCleskey argues that the sentence in his case is disproportionate to the sentences in other murder cases.

On the one hand, he cannot base a constitutional claim on an argument that his case differs from other cases in which defendants *did* receive the death penalty. On automatic appeal, the Georgia Supreme Court found that McCleskey's death sentence was not disproportionate to other death sentences imposed in the State. . . .

On the other hand, absent a showing that the Georgia capital punishment system operates in an arbitrary and capricious manner, McCleskey cannot prove a constitutional violation by demonstrating that other defendants who may be similarly situated did *not* receive the death penalty. In *Gregg*, the Court confronted the argument that "the opportunities for discretionary action that are inherent in the processing of any murder case under Georgia law," specifically the opportunities for discretionary leniency, rendered the capital sentences imposed arbitrary and capricious. We rejected this contention. . .

Because McCleskey's sentence was imposed under Georgia sentencing procedures that focus discretion "on the particularized nature of the crime and the particularized characteristics of the individual defendant," we lawfully may presume that McCleskey's death sentence was not "wantonly and freakishly" imposed, and thus that the sentence is not disproportionate within any recognized meaning under the Eighth Amendment.

B

Although our decision in *Gregg* as to the facial validity of the Georgia capital punishment statute appears to foreclose McCleskey's disproportionality argument, he further contends that the Georgia capital punishment system is arbitrary and capricious in *application*, and therefore his sentence is excessive, because racial considerations may influence capital sentencing decisions in Georgia. We now address this claim.

To evaluate McCleskey's challenge, we must examine exactly what the Baldus study may show. Even Professor Baldus does not contend that his statistics *prove* that race enters into any capital sentencing decisions or that race was a factor in McCleskey's particular case. Statistics at most may show only a likelihood that a particular factor entered into some decisions. There is, of course, some risk of racial prejudice influencing a jury's decision in a criminal case. There are similar risks that other kinds of prejudice will influence other criminal trials. The question "is at what point that risk becomes constitutionally unacceptable," *Turner v. Murray*, 476 U.S. 28 (1986). McCleskey asks us to accept the likelihood allegedly shown by the Baldus study as the constitutional measure of an unacceptable risk of racial prejudice influencing capital sentencing decisions. This we decline to do.

Because of the risk that the factor of race may enter the criminal justice process, we have engaged in "unceasing efforts" to eradicate racial prejudice from our criminal justice system. *Batson v. Kentucky,* 476 U.S. 79 (1986). Our efforts have been guided by our recognition that "the inestimable privilege of trial by jury . . . is a vital principle, underlying the whole administration of criminal justice," *Ex parte Milligan,* 71 U.S. 2 (1866). . . .

McCleskey's argument that the Constitution condemns the discretion allowed decisionmakers in the Georgia capital sentencing system is antithetical to the fundamental role of discretion in our criminal justice system. Discretion in the criminal justice system offers substantial benefits to the criminal defendant. Not only can a jury decline to impose the death sentence, it can decline to convict or choose to convict of a lesser offense. . . .

C

At most, the Baldus study indicates a discrepancy that appears to correlate with race. Apparent disparities in sentencing are an inevitable part of our criminal justice system. The discrepancy indicated by the Baldus study is "a far cry from the major systemic defects identified in *Furman v. Georgia,* 408 U.S. 238 (1972)," *Pulley* v. *Harris,* 465 U.S. 37 (1984). . . .

Two additional concerns inform our decision in this case. First, McCleskey's claim, taken to its logical conclusion, throws into serious question the principles that underlie our entire criminal justice system. The Eighth Amendment is not limited in application to capital punishment, but applies to all penalties. Thus, if we accepted McCleskey's claim that racial bias has impermissibly tainted the capital sentencing decision, we could soon be faced with similar claims as to other types of penalty. Moreover, the claim that his sentence rests on the irrelevant factor of race easily could be extended to apply to claims based on unexplained discrepancies that correlate to membership in other minority groups, and even to gender. Similarly, since McCleskey's claim relates to the race of his victim, other claims could apply with equally logical force to statistical disparities that correlate with the race or sex of other actors in the criminal justice system, such as defense attorneys or judges.

Also, there is no logical reason that such a claim need be limited to racial or sexual bias. If arbitrary and capricious punishment is the touchstone under the Eighth Amendment, such a claim could—at least in theory—be based upon any arbitrary variable, such as the defendant's facial characteristics, or the physical attractiveness of the defendant or the victim, that some statistical study indicates may be influential in jury decisionmaking. As these examples illustrate, there is no limiting principle to the type of challenge brought by McCleskey. The Constitution does not require that a State eliminate any demonstrable disparity that correlates with a potentially irrelevant factor in order to operate a criminal justice system that includes capital punishment. As we have stated specifically in the context of capital punishment, the Constitution does not "plac[e] totally unrealistic conditions on its use." *Gregg v. Georgia.*

Second, McCleskey's arguments are best presented to the legislative bodies. It is not the responsibility—or indeed even the right—of this Court to determine the appropriate punishment for particular crimes. It is the legislatures, the elected representatives of the people, that are "constituted to respond to the will and consequently the moral values of the people." *Furman v. Georgia.* . . .

Accordingly, we affirm the judgment of the Court of Appeals for the Eleventh Circuit.

It is so ordered.

JUSTICE BRENNAN, with whom JUSTICE MARSHALL joins, and with whom JUSTICES BLACKMUN and STEVENS join in all but Part I, dissenting.

I

Adhering to my view that the death penalty is in all circumstances cruel and unusual punishment forbidden by the Eighth and Fourteenth Amendments, I would vacate the decision below insofar as it left undisturbed the death sentence imposed in this case. . . .

Even if I did not hold this position, however, I would reverse the Court of Appeals, for petitioner McCleskey has clearly demonstrated that his death sentence was imposed in violation of the Eighth and Fourteenth Amendments. . . .

II

At some point in this case, Warren McCleskey doubtless asked his lawyer whether a jury was likely to sentence him to die. A candid reply to this question would have been disturbing. First, counsel would have to tell McCleskey that few of the details of the crime or of McCleskey's past criminal conduct were more important than the fact that his victim was white. Furthermore, counsel would feel bound to tell McCleskey that defendants charged with killing white victims in Georgia are 4.3 times as likely to be sentenced to death as defendants charged with killing blacks. In addition, frankness would compel the disclosure that it was more likely than not that the race of McCleskey's victim would determine whether he received a death sentence: 6 of every 11 defendants convicted of killing a white person would not have received the death penalty if their victims had been black, while, among defendants with aggravating and mitigating factors comparable to McCleskey's, 20 of every 34 would not have been sentenced to die if their victims had been black. Finally, the assessment would not be complete without the information that cases involving black defendants and white victims are more likely to result in a death sentence than cases featuring any other racial combination of defendant and victim. . . .

III

A

It is important to emphasize at the outset that the Court's observation that McCleskey cannot prove the influence of race on any particular sentencing decision is irrelevant in evaluating his Eighth Amendment claim. Since *Furman v. Georgia*, 408 U.S. 238 (1972), the Court has been concerned with the *risk* of the imposition of an arbitrary sentence, rather than the proven fact of one. *Furman* held that the death penalty "may not be imposed under sentencing procedures that create a substantial risk that the punishment will be inflicted in an arbitrary and capricious manner." *Godfrey v. Georgia,* 446 U.S. 420 (1980). . . .

Defendants challenging their death sentences thus never have had to prove that impermissible considerations have actually infected sentencing decisions. We have required instead that they establish that the system under which they were sentenced posed a significant risk of such an occurrence. McCleskey's claim does differ, however, in one respect from these earlier cases: it is the first to base a challenge not on speculation about how a system *might* operate, but on empirical documentation of how it *does* operate.

B

The Baldus study indicates that, after taking into account some 230 nonracial factors that might legitimately influence a sentencer, the jury *more likely than not* would have spared McCleskey's life had his victim been black. The study distinguishes between those cases in which (1) the jury exercises virtually no discretion because the strength or weakness of aggravating factors usually suggests that only one outcome is appropriate; and (2) cases reflecting an "intermediate" level of aggravation, in which the jury has considerable discretion in choosing a sentence. McCleskey's case falls into the intermediate range. In such cases, death is imposed in 34% of white-victim crimes and 14% of black-victim crimes, a difference of 139% in the rate of imposition of the death penalty. In other words, just under 59%—almost 6 in 10—defendants comparable to McCleskey would not have received the death penalty if their victims had been black.

McCleskey's statistics have particular force because most of them are the product of sophisticated multiple-regression analysis. Such analysis is designed precisely to identify patterns in the aggregate, even though we may not be able to reconstitute with certainty any individual decision that goes to make up that pattern. Multiple-regression analysis is particularly well suited to identify the influence of impermissible considerations in sentencing, since it is able to control for permissible factors that may explain an apparent arbitrary pattern. . . .

The statistical evidence in this case thus relentlessly documents the risk that McCleskey's sentence was influenced by racial considerations. This evidence shows that there is a better than even chance in Georgia that race will influence the decision to impose the death penalty: a majority of defendants in white-victim crimes would not have been sentenced to die if their victims had been black. . . .

C

Evaluation of McCleskey's evidence cannot rest solely on the numbers themselves. We must also ask whether the conclusion suggested by those numbers is consonant with our understanding of history and human experience. Georgia's legacy of a race-conscious criminal justice system, as well as this Court's own recognition of the persistent danger that racial attitudes may affect criminal proceedings, indicates that McCleskey's claim is not a fanciful product of mere statistical artifice.

IV

The Court cites four reasons for shrinking from the implications of McCleskey's evidence: the desirability of discretion for actors in the criminal justice system, the existence of statutory safeguards against abuse of that discretion, the potential consequences for broader challenges to criminal sentencing, and an understanding of the contours of the judicial role. While these concerns underscore the need for sober deliberation, they do not justify rejecting evidence as convincing as McCleskey has presented.

The Court maintains that petitioner's claim "is antithetical to the fundamental role of discretion in our criminal justice system." It states that "where the discretion that is fundamental to our criminal process is involved, we decline to assume that what is unexplained is invidious."

Reliance on race in imposing capital punishment, however, is antithetical to the very rationale for granting sentencing discretion. Discretion is a means, not an end. . . .

Considering the race of a defendant or victim in deciding if the death penalty should be imposed is completely at odds with this concern that an individual be evaluated as a unique human being. . . .

The Court also declines to find McCleskey's evidence sufficient in view of "the safeguards designed to minimize racial bias in the [capital sentencing] process." *Gregg v. Georgia* 428 U.S. 153 (1976) upheld the Georgia capital sentencing statute against a facial challenge which Justice White described in his concurring opinion as based on "simply an assertion of lack of faith" that the system could operate in a fair manner. Justice White observed that the claim that prosecutors might act in an arbitrary fashion was "unsupported by any facts," and that prosecutors must be assumed to exercise their charging duties properly "absent facts to the contrary." It is clear that *Gregg* bestowed no permanent approval on the Georgia system. It simply held that the State's statutory safeguards were assumed sufficient to channel discretion without evidence otherwise.

It has now been over 13 years since Georgia adopted the provisions upheld in *Gregg*. Professor Baldus and his colleagues have compiled data on almost 2,500 homicides committed during the period 1973–1979. They have taken into account the influence of 230 nonracial variables, using a multitude of data from the State itself, and have produced striking evidence that the odds of being sentenced to death are significantly greater than average if a defendant is black or his or her victim is white. The challenge to the Georgia system is not speculative or theoretical; it is empirical. . . . .

The Court next states that its unwillingness to regard petitioner's evidence as sufficient is based in part on the fear that recognition of McCleskey's claim would open the door to widespread challenges to all aspects of criminal sentencing. Taken on its face, such a statement seems to suggest a fear of too much justice. Yet surely the majority would acknowledge that if striking evidence indicated that other minority groups, or women, or even persons with blond hair, were disproportionately sentenced to death, such a state of affairs would be repugnant to deeply rooted conceptions of fairness. . . .

It hardly needs reiteration that this Court has consistently acknowledged the uniqueness of the punishment of death. . . .

The Court's projection of apocalyptic consequences for criminal sentencing is thus greatly exaggerated. . . .

Finally, the Court justifies its rejection of McCleskey's claim by cautioning against usurpation of the legislatures' role in devising and monitoring criminal punishment. The Court is, of course, correct to emphasize the gravity of constitutional intervention and the importance that it be sparingly employed. The fact that "capital punishment is now the law in more than two thirds of our States," however, does not diminish the fact that capital punishment is the most awesome act that a State can perform. The judiciary's role in this society counts for little if the use of governmental power to extinguish life does not elicit close scrutiny. . . .

FOR DISCUSSION

Southern states execute far more individuals than do states in other regions of the nation. Do you think it is fair that an individual who commits a crime in one state, or one area of the nation, has a greater chance of being executed than persons who commit comparable crimes in another? Most, but surely not all, individuals who are executed are men. Should that effect the constitutionality of the procedure?

HERRERA V. COLLINS

506 U.S. 390, 113 S.Ct. 853, 122 L.Ed.2d 203 (1993)

Although we have included this case here, it could just as easily fit in chapters dealing with due process rights; indeed, a dissenter suggests that the case actually involves "substantive" due process. On the surface the issue seems absurd. The Court appears to be rejecting a death penalty appeal on the basis of a defendant's "actual innocence." Are there other, deeper issues?

Vote: 6–3

CHIEF JUSTICE REHNQUIST delivered the opinion of the Court.

Petitioner Leonel Torres Herrera was convicted of capital murder and sentenced to death in January 1982. He unsuccessfully challenged the conviction on direct appeal and state collateral proceedings in the Texas state courts, and in a federal habeas petition. In February 1992—10 years after his conviction—he urged in a second federal habeas petition that he was "actually innocent" of the murder for which he was sentenced to death, and that the Eighth Amendment's prohibition against cruel and unusual punishment and the Fourteenth Amendment's guarantee of due process of law therefore forbid his execution. He supported this claim with affidavits tending to show that his now-dead brother, rather than he, had been the perpetrator of the crime. Petitioner urges us to hold that this showing of innocence entitles him to relief in this federal habeas proceeding. We hold that it does not.

Shortly before 11 P.M. on an evening in late September 1981, the body of Texas Department of Public Safety Officer David Rucker was found by a passer-by on a stretch of highway about six miles east of Los Fresnos, Texas, a few miles north of Brownsville in the Rio Grande Valley. Rucker's body was lying beside his patrol car. He had been shot in the head.

At about the same time, Los Fresnos Police Officer Enrique Carrisalez observed a speeding vehicle traveling west towards Los Fresnos, away from the place where Rucker's body had been found, along the same road. Carrisalez, who was accompanied in his patrol car by Enrique Hernandez, turned on his flashing red lights and pursued the speeding vehicle. After the car had stopped briefly at a red light, it signaled that it would pull over and did so. The patrol car pulled up behind it. Carrisalez took a flashlight and walked toward the car of the speeder. The driver opened his door and exchanged a few words with Carrisalez before firing at least one shot at Carrisalez' chest. The officer died nine days later.

Petitioner Herrera was arrested a few days after the shootings and charged with the capital murder of both Carrisalez and Rucker. He was tried and found guilty of the capital murder of Carrisalez in January 1982, and sentenced to death. In July 1982, petitioner pleaded guilty to the murder of Rucker.

At petitioner's trial for the murder of Carrisalez, Hernandez, who had witnessed Carrisalez' slaying from the officer's patrol car, identified petitioner as the person who had wielded the gun. A declaration by Officer Carrisalez to the same effect, made while he was in the hospital, was also admitted. Through a license plate check, it was shown that the speeding car involved in Carrisalez' murder was registered to petitioner's "live-in" girlfriend. Petitioner was known to drive this car, and he had a set of keys to the car in his pants pocket when he was arrested. Hernandez identified the car as the vehicle from which the murderer had emerged to fire the fatal shot. He also testified that there had been only one person in the car that night.

The evidence showed that Herrera's Social Security card had been found alongside Rucker's patrol car on the night he was killed. Splatters of blood on the car identified as the vehicle involved in the shootings, and on petitioner's blue jeans and wallet were identified as type A blood—the same type which Rucker had. (Herrera has type O blood.) Similar evidence with respect to strands of hair found in the car indicated that the hair was Rucker's and not Herrera's. A handwritten letter was also found on the person of petitioner when he was arrested, which strongly implied that he had killed Rucker.

Petitioner appealed his conviction and sentence, arguing, among other things, that Hernandez' and Carrisalez' identifications were unreliable and improperly admitted. The Texas Court of Criminal Appeals affirmed, and we denied certiorari. Petitioner's application for state habeas relief was denied. . . .

Petitioner next returned to state court and filed a second habeas petition, raising, among other things, a claim of "actual innocence" based on newly discovered evidence. In support of this claim petitioner presented the affidavits of Hector Villarreal, an attorney who had represented petitioner's brother, Raul Herrera, Sr., and of Juan Franco Palacious, one of Raul, Senior's former cellmates. Both individuals claimed that Raul, Senior, who died in 1984, had told them that he—and not petitioner—had killed Officers Rucker and Carrisalez. The State District Court denied this application, finding that "no evidence at trial remotely suggest[ed] that anyone other than [petitioner] committed the offense." The Texas Court of Criminal Appeals affirmed, and we denied certiorari.

In February 1992, petitioner lodged the instant habeas petition—his second—in federal court, alleging, among other things, that he is innocent of the murders of Rucker and Carrisalez, and that his execution would thus violate the Eighth and Fourteenth Amendments. In addition to proffering the above affidavits, petitioner presented the affidavits of Raul Herrera, Jr., Raul, Senior's son, and Jose Ybarra, Jr., a schoolmate of the Herrera brothers. Raul, Junior, averred that he had witnessed his father shoot Officers Rucker and Carrisalez and petitioner was not present. Raul, Junior, was nine years old at the time of the killings. Ybarra alleged that Raul, Senior, told him one summer night in 1983 that he had shot the two police officers. Petitioner alleged that law enforcement officials were aware of this evidence, and had withheld it in violation of *Brady v. Maryland*, 373 U.S. 83 (1963).

[Rehnquist reviews lower court decisions.]

Petitioner asserts that the Eighth and Fourteenth Amendments to the United States Constitution prohibit the execution of a person who is innocent of the crime for which he was convicted. This proposition has an elemental appeal, as would the similar proposition that the Constitution prohibits the imprisonment of one who is innocent of the crime for which he was convicted. After all, the central purpose of any system of criminal justice is to convict the guilty and free the innocent. But the evidence upon which petitioner's claim of innocence rests was not produced at his trial, but rather eight years later. In any system of criminal justice, "innocence" or "guilt" must be determined in some sort of a judicial proceeding. Petitioner's showing of innocence, and indeed his constitutional claim for relief based upon that showing, must be evaluated in the light of the previous proceedings in this case, which have stretched over a span of 10 years.

A person when first charged with a crime is entitled to a presumption of innocence, and may insist that his guilt be established beyond a reasonable doubt. Other constitutional provisions also have the effect of ensuring against the risk of convicting an innocent person. . . . In capital cases, we have required additional protections because of the nature of the penalty at stake. See, *e. g., Beck v. Alabama*, 447 U.S. 625 (1980) (jury must be given option of convicting the defendant of a lesser offense). All of these constitutional safeguards, of course, make it more difficult for the State to rebut and finally overturn the presumption of innocence which attaches to every criminal defendant. But we have also observed that "due process does not require that every conceivable step be taken, at whatever cost, to eliminate the possibility of convicting an innocent person." *Patterson v. New York*,

432 U.S. 197 (1977). To conclude otherwise would all but paralyze our system for enforcement of the criminal law.

Once a defendant has been afforded a fair trial and convicted of the offense for which he was charged, the presumption of innocence disappears. . . .

Claims of actual innocence based on newly discovered evidence have never been held to state a ground for federal habeas relief absent an independent constitutional violation occurring in the underlying state criminal proceeding. . . .

This rule is grounded in the principle that federal habeas courts sit to ensure that individuals are not imprisoned in violation of the Constitution—not to correct errors of fact. . . .

The dissent fails to articulate the relief that would be available if petitioner were to meets its "probable innocence" standard. Would it be commutation of petitioner's death sentence, new trial, or unconditional release from imprisonment? The typical relief granted in federal habeas corpus is a conditional order of release unless the State elects to retry the successful habeas petitioner, or in a capital case a similar conditional order vacating the death sentence. Were petitioner to satisfy the dissent's "probable innocence" standard, therefore, the District Court would presumably be required to grant a conditional order of relief, which would in effect require the State to retry petitioner 10 years after his first trial, not because of any constitutional violation which had occurred at the first trial, but simply because of a belief that in light of petitioner's new-found evidence a jury might find him not guilty at a second trial.

Yet there is no guarantee that the guilt or innocence determination would be any more exact. To the contrary, the passage of time only diminishes the reliability of criminal adjudications. . . .

Petitioner asserts that this case is different because he has been sentenced to death. But we have "refused to hold that the fact that a death sentence has been imposed requires a different standard of review on federal habeas corpus." *Murray v. Giarratano*, 492 U.S. 1 (1989). . . .

The Constitution itself, of course, makes no mention of new trials. New trials in criminal cases were not granted in England until the end of the 17th century. And even then, they were available only in misdemeanor cases, though the writ of error *coram nobis* was available for some errors of fact in felony cases. . . .

The early federal cases adhere to the common-law rule that a new trial may be granted only during the term of court in which the final judgment was entered. . . .

The practice in the States today, while of limited relevance to our historical inquiry, is divergent. Texas is one of 17 States that requires a new trial motion based on newly discovered evidence to be made within 60 days of judgment. One State adheres to the common-law rule and requires that such a motion be filed during the term in which judgment was rendered. Eighteen jurisdictions have time limits ranging between one and three years, with 10 States and the District of Columbia following the 2-year federal time limit. Only 15 States allow a new trial motion based on newly discovered evidence to be filed more than three years after conviction. Of these States, four have waivable time limits of less than 120 days, two have waivable time limits of more than 120 days, and nine States have no time limits.

In light of the historical availability of new trials, our own amendments to Rule 33 [setting a 2-year time limit for filing new trial motions based on newly discovered evidence], and the contemporary practice in the States, we cannot say that Texas' refusal to entertain petitioner's newly discovered evidence eight years after his conviction transgresses a principle of fundamental fairness "rooted in the traditions and conscience of our people." *Patterson v. New York*, 432 U.S. 197 (1977). This is not to say, however, that petitioner is left without a forum to raise his actual innocence claim. For under Texas law, petitioner may file a request for executive clemency. . . .

[Rehnquist further reviews this mechanism.]

We may assume, for the sake of argument in deciding this case, that in a capital case a truly persuasive demonstration of "actual innocence" made after trial would render the execution of a defendant unconstitutional, and warrant federal habeas relief if there were no state avenue open to process such a claim. But because of the very disruptive effect that entertaining claims of actual innocence would have on the need for finality in capital cases, and the enormous burden that having to retry cases based on often stale evidence would place on the States, the threshold showing for such an assumed right would necessarily be extraordinarily high. The showing made by petitioner in this case falls far short of any such threshold.

Petitioner's newly discovered evidence consists of affidavits. In the new trial context, motions based solely upon affidavits are disfavored because the affiants' statements are obtained without the benefit of cross-examination and an opportunity to make credibility determinations. . . .

The affidavits filed in this habeas proceeding were given over eight years after petitioner's trial. No satisfactory explanation has been given as to why the affiants waited until the 11th hour—and, indeed, until after the alleged perpetrator of the murders himself was dead—to make their statements. Equally troubling, no explanation has been offered as to why petitioner, by hypothesis an innocent man, pleaded guilty to the murder of Rucker.

Moreover, the affidavits themselves contain inconsistencies, and therefore fail to provide a convincing account of what took place on the night Officers Rucker and Carrisalez were killed. . . .

Finally, the affidavits must be considered in light of the proof of petitioner's guilt at trial—proof which included two eyewitness identifications, numerous pieces of circumstantial evidence, and a handwritten letter in which petitioner apologized for killing the officers and offered to turn himself in under certain conditions. That proof, even when considered alongside petitioner's belated affidavits, points strongly to petitioner's guilt.

This is not to say that petitioner's affidavits are without probative value. Had this sort of testimony been offered at trial, it could have been weighed by the jury, along with the evidence offered by the State and petitioner, in deliberating upon its verdict. Since the statements in the affidavits contradict the evidence received at trial, the jury would have had to decide important issues of credibility. But coming 10 years after petitioner's trial, this showing of innocence falls far short of that which would have to be made in order to trigger the sort of constitutional claim which we have assumed, *arguendo*, to exist.

The judgment of the Court of Appeals is *Affirmed.*

JUSTICE SCALIA, with whom JUSTICE THOMAS joins, concurring.

. . . There is no basis in text, tradition, or even in contemporary practice (if that were enough) for finding in the Constitution a right to demand judicial consideration of newly discovered evidence of innocence brought forward after conviction. In saying that such a right exists, the dissenters apply nothing but their personal opinions to invalidate the rules of more than two-thirds of the States, and a Federal Rule of Criminal Procedure for which this Court itself is responsible. If the system that has been in place for 200 years (and remains widely approved) "shock[s]" the dissenters' consciences, perhaps they should doubt the calibration of their consciences, or, better still, the usefulness of "conscience shocking" as a legal test.

JUSTICE BLACKMUN, with whom JUSTICES STEVENS and SOUTER join with respect to Parts I–IV, dissenting.

Nothing could be more contrary to contemporary standards of decency, see *Ford v. Wainwright*, 477 U.S. 399 (1986), or more shocking to the conscience, see *Rochin v. California*, 342 U.S. 165 (1952), than to execute a person who is actually innocent.

I therefore must disagree with the long and general discussion that precedes the Court's disposition of this case. That discussion, of course, is dictum because the Court assumes, "for the sake of argument in deciding this case, that in a capital case a truly persuasive demonstration of 'actual innocence' made after trial would render the execution of a defendant unconstitutional." Without articulating the standard it is applying, however, the Court then decides that this petitioner has not made a sufficiently persuasive case. Because I believe that in the first instance the District Court should decide whether petitioner is entitled to a hearing and whether he is entitled to relief on the merits of his claim, I would reverse the order of the Court of Appeals and remand this case for further proceedings in the District Court.

I

The Court's enumeration, of the constitutional rights of criminal defendants surely is entirely beside the point. These protections sometimes fail. . . .

A

I believe it contrary to any standard of decency to execute someone who is actually innocent. Because the Eighth Amendment applies to questions of guilt or innocence, and to persons upon whom a valid sentence of death has been imposed, I also believe that petitioner may raise an Eighth Amendment challenge to his punishment on the ground that he is actually innocent.

B

Execution of the innocent is equally offensive to the Due Process Clause of the Fourteenth Amendment. The majority's discussion misinterprets petitioner's Fourteenth Amendment claim as raising a procedural, rather than a substantive, due process challenge. . . .

II

The majority's discussion of petitioner's constitutional claims is even more perverse when viewed in the light of this Court's recent habeas jurisprudence. Beginning with a trio of decisions in 1986, this Court shifted the focus of federal habeas review of successive, abusive, or defaulted claims away from the preservation of constitutional rights to a fact-based inquiry into the habeas petitioner's guilt or innocence. . . .

A

Whatever procedures a State might adopt to hear actual-innocence claims, one thing is certain: The possibility of executive clemency is *not* sufficient to satisfy the requirements of the Eighth and Fourteenth Amendments. The majority correctly points out: " 'A pardon is an act of grace.' " The vindication of rights guaranteed by the Constitution has never been made to turn on the unreviewable discretion of an executive official or administrative tribunal. . . .

B

Texas provides no judicial procedure for hearing petitioner's claim of actual innocence and his habeas petition was properly filed in district court under § 2254. The district court is entitled to dismiss the petition summarily only if "it plainly appears from the face of the petition and any exhibits annexed to it that the petitioner is not entitled to relief." If, as is the case here, the petition raises factual questions and the State has failed to provide a full and fair hearing, the district court is required to hold an evidentiary hearing.

C

. . . I would hold that, to obtain relief on a claim of actual innocence, the petitioner must show that he probably is innocent. This standard is supported by several considerations. First, new evidence of innocence may be discovered long after the defendant's conviction. Given the passage of time, it may be difficult for the

State to retry a defendant who obtains relief from his conviction or sentence on an actual-innocence claim. The actual-innocence proceeding thus may constitute the final word on whether the defendant may be punished. In light of this fact, an otherwise constitutionally valid conviction or sentence should not be set aside lightly. Second, conviction after a constitutionally adequate trial strips the defendant of the presumption of innocence. . . . . The actual-innocence inquiry is therefore distinguishable from review for sufficiency of the evidence, where the question is not whether the defendant is innocent but whether the government has met its constitutional burden of proving the defendant's guilt beyond a reasonable doubt. When a defendant seeks to challenge the determination of guilt after he has been validly convicted and sentenced, it is fair to place on him the burden of proving his innocence, not just raising doubt about his guilt.

IV

In this case, the District Court determined that petitioner's newly discovered evidence warranted further consideration. Because the District Court doubted its own authority to consider the new evidence, it thought that petitioner's claim of actual innocence should be brought in state court, but it clearly did not think that petitioner's evidence was so insubstantial that it could be dismissed without any hearing at all. I would reverse the order of the Court of Appeals and remand the case to the District Court to consider whether petitioner has shown, in light of all the evidence, that he is probably actually innocent.

FOR DISCUSSION

Based on the evidence presented in this case, do you think the defendant was actually innocent? Do you think the Court majority did? The dissenters? If proof emerged that the state had recently executed an innocent individual, would that affect the constitutionality of the death penalty? What if proof emerged that several innocent persons had been executed?

ATKINS V. VIRGINIA

536 U.S. 304, 122 S.Ct. 2242, 153 L.Ed.2d 335 (2002)

This decision reconsiders an earlier ruling in *Penry v. Lynaugh* (492 U.S. 302, 1989), in which the Supreme Court had held that the Eighth Amendment does not prohibit capital punishment of cognitively impaired persons.

Vote: 6–3

JUSTICE STEVENS delivered the opinion of the Court.

Those mentally retarded persons who meet the law's requirements for criminal responsibility should be tried and punished when they commit crimes. Because of their disabilities in areas of reasoning, judgment, and control of their impulses, however, they do not act with the level of moral culpability that characterizes the most serious adult criminal conduct. Moreover, their impairments can jeopardize the reliability and fairness of capital proceedings against mentally retarded defendants. Presumably for these reasons, in the 13 years since we decided *Penry v. Lynaugh*, 492 U.S. 302 (1989), the American public, legislators, scholars, and judges have deliberated over the question whether the death penalty should ever be imposed on a mentally retarded criminal. The consensus reflected in those deliberations informs our answer to the question presented by this case: whether such executions are "cruel and unusual punishments" prohibited by the Eighth Amendment to the Federal Constitution.

I

Petitioner, Daryl Renard Atkins, was convicted of abduction, armed robbery, and capital murder, and sentenced to death. At approximately midnight on August 16, 1996, Atkins and William Jones, armed with a semiautomatic handgun, abducted Eric Nesbitt, robbed him of the money on his person, drove him to an automated teller machine in his pickup truck where cameras recorded their withdrawal of additional cash, then took him to an isolated location where he was shot eight times and killed.

Jones and Atkins both testified in the guilt phase of Atkins' trial. Each confirmed most of the details in the other's account of the incident, with the important exception that each stated that the other had actually shot and killed Nesbitt. Jones' testimony, which was both more coherent and credible than Atkins', was obviously credited by the jury and was sufficient to establish Atkins' guilt. At the penalty phase of the trial, the State introduced victim impact evidence and proved two aggravating circumstances: future dangerousness and "vileness of the offense." To prove future dangerousness, the State relied on Atkins' prior felony convictions as well as the testimony of four victims of earlier robberies and assaults. To prove the second aggravator, the prosecution relied upon the trial record, including pictures of the deceased's body and the autopsy report.

In the penalty phase, the defense relied on one witness, Dr. Evan Nelson, a forensic psychologist who had evaluated Atkins before trial and concluded that he was "mildly mentally retarded." His conclusion was based on interviews with people who knew Atkins, a review of school and court records, and the administration of a standard intelligence test which indicated that Atkins had a full scale IQ of 59.

The jury sentenced Atkins to death. . . .

II

The Eighth Amendment succinctly prohibits "excessive" sanctions. It provides: "Excessive bail shall not be required, nor excessive fines imposed, nor cruel and unusual punishments inflicted." In *Weems v. United States,* 217 U.S. 349 (1910), we held that a punishment of 12 years jailed in irons at hard and painful labor for the crime of falsifying records was excessive. We explained "that it is a precept of justice that punishment for crime should be graduated and proportioned to the offense." We have repeatedly applied this proportionality precept in later cases interpreting the Eighth Amendment. [Stevens cites cases.]

Guided by our approach in these cases, we shall first review the judgment of legislatures that have addressed the suitability of imposing the death penalty on the mentally retarded and then consider reasons for agreeing or disagreeing with their judgment.

III

The parties have not called our attention to any state legislative consideration of the suitability of imposing the death penalty on mentally retarded offenders prior to 1986. In that year, the public reaction to the execution of a mentally retarded murderer in Georgia apparently led to the enactment of the first state statute prohibiting such executions. In 1988, when Congress enacted legislation reinstating the federal death penalty, it expressly provided that a "sentence of death shall not be carried out upon a person who is mentally retarded." In 1989, Maryland enacted a similar prohibition. It was in that year that we decided *Penry*, and concluded that those two state enactments, "even when added to the 14 States that have rejected capital punishment completely, do not provide sufficient evidence at present of a national consensus."

Much has changed since then. Responding to the national attention received by the Bowden execution [of a man with an I.Q. of 65 in 1986 by the state of Georgia] and our decision in *Penry*, state legislatures across the country began to address the issue. In 1990 Kentucky and Tennessee enacted statutes similar to those in Georgia and Maryland, as did New Mexico in 1991, and Arkansas, Colorado, Washington, Indiana, and Kansas in 1993 and 1994. In 1995, when New York reinstated its death penalty, it emulated the Federal Government by expressly exempting the mentally retarded. Nebraska followed suit in 1998. There appear to have been no similar enactments during the next two years, but in 2000 and 2001 six more States—South Dakota, Arizona, Connecticut, Florida, Missouri, and North Carolina—joined the procession. The Texas Legislature unanimously adopted a similar bill, and bills have passed at least one house in other States, including Virginia and Nevada.

It is not so much the number of these States that is significant, but the consistency of the direction of change. Given the well-known fact that anticrime legislation is far more popular than legislation providing protections for persons guilty of violent crime, the large number of States prohibiting the execution of mentally retarded persons (and the complete absence of States passing legislation reinstating the power to conduct such executions) provides powerful evidence that today our society views mentally retarded offenders as categorically less culpable than the average criminal. The evidence carries even greater force when it is noted that the legislatures that have addressed the issue have voted overwhelmingly in favor of the prohibition. Moreover, even in those States that allow the execution of mentally retarded offenders, the practice is uncommon. . . .

IV

This consensus unquestionably reflects widespread judgment about the relative culpability of mentally retarded offenders, and the relationship between mental retardation and the penological purposes served by the death penalty. Additionally, it suggests that some characteristics of mental retardation undermine the strength of the procedural protections that our capital jurisprudence steadfastly guards.

As discussed above, clinical definitions of mental retardation require not only subaverage intellectual functioning, but also significant limitations in adaptive skills such as communication, self-care, and self-direction that became manifest before age 18. Mentally retarded persons frequently know the difference between right and wrong and are competent to stand trial. Because of their impairments, however, by definition they have diminished capacities to understand and process information, to communicate, to abstract from mistakes and learn from experience, to engage in logical reasoning, to control impulses, and to understand the reactions of others. There is no evidence that they are more likely to engage in criminal conduct than others, but there is abundant evidence that they often act on impulse rather than pursuant to a premeditated plan, and that in group settings they are followers rather than leaders. Their deficiencies do not warrant an exemption from criminal sanctions, but they do diminish their personal culpability. In light of these deficiencies, our death penalty jurisprudence provides two reasons consistent with the legislative consensus that the mentally retarded should be categorically excluded from execution. First, there is a serious question as to whether either justification that we have recognized as a basis for the death penalty applies to mentally retarded offenders. . . .

With respect to retribution—the interest in seeing that the offender gets his "just deserts"—the severity of the appropriate punishment necessarily depends on the culpability of the offender. . . .

With respect to deterrence—the interest in preventing capital crimes by prospective offenders—"it seems likely that 'capital punishment can serve as a deterrent only when murder is the result of premeditation and deliberation,' " *Enmund v. Florida*, 458 U.S. 782 (1982). Exempting the mentally retarded from that punishment will not affect the "cold calculus that precedes the decision" of other potential murderers. Indeed, that sort of calculus is at the opposite end of the spectrum from behavior of mentally retarded offenders. . . .

The reduced capacity of mentally retarded offenders provides a second justification for a categorical rule making such offenders ineligible for the death penalty. The risk "that the death penalty will be imposed in spite of factors which may call for a less severe penalty," *Lockett v. Ohio*, 438 U.S. 586 (1978), is enhanced, not only by the possibility of false confessions, but also by the lesser ability of mentally retarded defendants to make a persuasive showing of mitigation in the face of prosecutorial evidence of one or more aggravating factors. Mentally retarded defendants may be less able to give meaningful assistance to their counsel and are typically poor witnesses, and their demeanor may create an unwarranted impression of lack of remorse for their crimes.

CHIEF JUSTICE REHNQUIST, with whom JUSTICES SCALIA and THOMAS join, dissenting.

The question presented by this case is whether a national consensus deprives Virginia of the constitutional power to impose the death penalty on capital murder defendants like petitioner, *i.e.*, those defendants who indisputably are competent to stand trial, aware of the punishment they are about to suffer and why, and whose mental retardation has been found an insufficiently compelling reason to lessen their individual responsibility for the crime. The Court pronounces the punishment cruel and unusual primarily because 18 States recently have passed laws limiting the death eligibility of certain defendants based on mental retardation alone, despite the fact that the laws of 19 other States besides Virginia continue to leave the question of proper punishment to the individuated consideration of sentencing judges or juries familiar with the particular offender and his or her crime.

I agree with Justice Scalia, that the Court's assessment of the current legislative judgment regarding the execution of defendants like petitioner more resembles a *post hoc* rationalization for the majority's subjectively preferred result rather than any objective effort to ascertain the content of an evolving standard of decency. I write separately, however, to call attention to the defects in the Court's decision to place weight on foreign laws, the views of professional and religious organizations, and opinion polls in reaching its conclusion. The Court's suggestion that these sources are relevant to the constitutional question finds little support in our precedents and, in my view, is antithetical to considerations of federalism, which instruct that any "permanent prohibition upon all units of democratic government must [be apparent] in the operative acts (laws and the application of laws) that the people have approved." . . .

In my view, these two sources—the work product of legislatures and sentencing jury determinations—ought to be the sole indicators by which courts ascertain the contemporary American conceptions of decency for purposes of the Eighth Amendment. They are the only objective indicia of contemporary values firmly supported by our precedents. More importantly, however, they can be reconciled with the undeniable precepts that the democratic branches of government and individual sentencing juries are, by design, better suited than courts to evaluating and giving effect to the complex societal and moral considerations that inform the selection of publicly acceptable criminal punishments.

JUSTICE SCALIA, with whom the CHIEF JUSTICE REHNQUIST and JUSTICE THOMAS join, dissenting.

Today's decision is the pinnacle of our Eighth Amendment death-is-different jurisprudence. Not only does it, like all of that jurisprudence, find no support in the text or history of the Eighth Amendment; it does not even have support in current social attitudes regarding the conditions that render an otherwise just death penalty inappropriate. Seldom has an opinion of this Court rested so obviously upon nothing but the personal views of its members.

II

As the foregoing history demonstrates, petitioner's mental retardation was a *central issue* at sentencing. The jury concluded, however, that his alleged retardation was not a compelling reason to exempt him from the death penalty in light of the brutality of his crime and his long demonstrated propensity for violence. "In upsetting this particularized judgment on the basis of a constitutional absolute," the Court concludes that no one who is even slightly mentally retarded can have sufficient "moral responsibility" to be subjected to capital punishment for any crime. As a sociological and moral conclusion that is implausible; and it is doubly implausible as an interpretation of the United States Constitution." *Thompson v. Oklahoma,* 487 U.S. 815 (1988).

The Court makes no pretense that execution of the mildly mentally retarded would have been considered "cruel and unusual" in 1791. Only the *severely* or *profoundly* mentally retarded, commonly known as "idiots," enjoyed any special status under the law at that time. They, like lunatics, suffered a "deficiency in will" rendering them unable to tell right from wrong. . . .

The Court is left to argue, therefore, that execution of the mildly retarded is inconsistent with the "evolving standards of decency that mark the progress of a maturing society." *Trop v. Dulles,* 356 U.S. 86 (1958). Before today, our opinions consistently emphasized that Eighth Amendment judgments regarding the existence of social "standards" "should be informed by objective factors to the maximum possible extent" and "should not be, or appear to be, merely the subjective views of individual Justices." . . . "First" among these objective factors are the "statutes passed by society's elected representatives," *Stanford v. Kentucky*, 492 U.S. 361 (1989); because it "will rarely if ever be the case that the Members of this Court will have a better sense of the evolution in views of the American people than do their elected representatives," *Thompson v. Oklahoma,* 487 U.S. 815 (1988).

The Court pays lip service to these precedents as it miraculously extracts a "national consensus" forbidding execution of the mentally retarded, from the fact that 18 States—less than *half* (47%) of the 38 States that permit capital punishment (for whom the issue exists)—have very recently enacted legislation barring execution of the mentally retarded. Even that 47% figure is a distorted one. If one is to say, as the Court does today, that *all* executions of the mentally retarded are so morally repugnant as to violate our national "standards of decency," surely the "consensus" it points to must be one that has set its righteous face against *all* such executions. Not 18 States, but only seven—18% of death penalty jurisdictions—have legislation of that scope. . . .

But let us accept, for the sake of argument, the Court's faulty count. That bare number of States alone—*18*—should be enough to convince any reasonable person that no "national consensus" exists. How is it possible that agreement among 47% of the death penalty jurisdictions amounts to "consensus"? . . .

Moreover, a major factor that the Court entirely disregards is that the legislation of all 18 States it relies on is still in its infancy. The oldest of the statutes is only 14 years old; five were enacted last year; over half were enacted within the past eight years. Few, if any, of the States have had sufficient experience with these laws to know whether they are sensible in the long term. . . .

The Court attempts to bolster its embarrassingly feeble evidence of "consensus" with the following: "It is not so much the number of these States that is significant, but the *consistency* of the direction of change." But in what *other* direction *could we possibly* see change? Given that 14 years ago *all* the death penalty statutes included the mentally retarded, *any* change (except precipitate undoing of what had just been done) was *bound to be* in the one direction the Court finds significant enough to overcome the lack of real consensus. That is to say, to be accurate the Court's "*consistency*-of-the-direction-of-change" point should be recast into the following unimpressive observation: "No State has yet undone its exemption of the mentally retarded, one for as long as 14 whole years." . . .

Even less compelling (if possible) is the Court's argument, that evidence of "national consensus" is to be found in the infrequency with which retarded persons are executed in States that do not bar their execution. To begin with, what the Court takes as true is in fact quite doubtful. . . . *If,* however, execution of the mentally retarded *is* "uncommon"; and if it is not a sufficient explanation of this that the retarded comprise a tiny fraction of society (1% to 3%); then surely the explanation is that mental retardation is a constitutionally mandated mitigating factor at sentencing. For that reason, even if there were uniform national sentiment in *favor* of executing the retarded in appropriate cases, one would still expect execution of the mentally retarded to be "uncommon." . . .

But the Prize for the Court's Most Feeble Effort to fabricate "national consensus" must go to its appeal (deservedly relegated to a footnote) to the views of assorted professional and religious organizations, members of the so-called "world community," and respondents to opinion polls. . . .

III

Beyond the empty talk of a "national consensus," the Court gives us a brief glimpse of what really underlies today's decision: pretension to a power confined *neither* by the moral sentiments originally enshrined in the

Eighth Amendment (its original meaning) *nor even* by the current moral sentiments of the American people. " 'The Constitution,' " the Court says, "contemplates that in the end *our own judgment* will be brought to bear on the question of the acceptability of the death penalty under the Eighth Amendment.' " (The unexpressed reason for this unexpressed "contemplation" of the Constitution is presumably that really good lawyers have moral sentiments superior to those of the common herd, whether in 1791 or today.) The arrogance of this assumption of power takes one's breath away. And it explains, of course, why the Court can be so cavalier about the evidence of consensus. It is just a game, after all. "In the end," it is the *feelings* and *intuition* of a majority of the Justices that count—"the perceptions of decency, or of penology, or of mercy, entertained . . . by a majority of the small and unrepresentative segment of our society that sits on this Court."

The genuinely operative portion of the opinion, then, is the Court's statement of the reasons why it agrees with the contrived consensus it has found, that the "diminished capacities" of the mentally retarded render the death penalty excessive. The Court's analysis rests on two fundamental assumptions: (1) that the Eighth Amendment prohibits excessive punishments, and (2) that sentencing juries or judges are unable to account properly for the "diminished capacities" of the retarded. The first assumption is wrong, as I explained at length in *Harmelin* v. *Michigan,* 501 U.S. 957 (1991). The Eighth Amendment is addressed to always-and-everywhere "cruel" punishments, such as the rack and the thumbscrew. But where the punishment is in itself permissible, "the Eighth Amendment is not a ratchet, whereby a temporary consensus on leniency for a particular crime fixes a permanent constitutional maximum, disabling the States from giving effect to altered beliefs and responding to changed social conditions." The second assumption—inability of judges or juries to take proper account of mental retardation—is not only unsubstantiated, but contradicts the immemorial belief, here and in England, that they play an *indispensable* role in such matters. . . .

Proceeding from these faulty assumptions, the Court gives two reasons why the death penalty is an excessive punishment for all mentally retarded offenders. First, the "diminished capacities" of the mentally retarded raise a "serious question" whether their execution contributes to the "social purposes" of the death penalty, viz., retribution and deterrence. . . . Retribution is not advanced, the argument goes, because the mentally retarded are *no more culpable* than the average murderer, whom we have already held lacks sufficient culpability to warrant the death penalty. Who says so? Is there an established correlation between mental acuity and the ability to conform one's conduct to the law in such a rudimentary matter as murder? Are the mentally retarded really more disposed (and hence more likely) to commit willfully cruel and serious crime than others? In my experience, the opposite is true: being childlike generally suggests innocence rather than brutality.

As for the other social purpose of the death penalty that the Court discusses, deterrence: That is not advanced, the Court tells us, because the mentally retarded are "less likely" than their non-retarded counterparts to "process the information of the possibility of execution as a penalty and . . . control their conduct based upon that information." Of course this leads to the same conclusion discussed earlier—that the mentally retarded (because they are less deterred) are more likely to kill—which neither I nor the society at large believes. In any event, even the Court does not say that *all* mentally retarded individuals cannot "process the information of the possibility of execution as a penalty and . . . control their conduct based upon that information"; it merely asserts that they are "less likely" to be able to do so. . . .

The Court throws one last factor into its grab bag of reasons why execution of the retarded is "excessive" in all cases: Mentally retarded offenders "face a special risk of wrongful execution" because they are less able "to make a persuasive showing of mitigation," "to give meaningful assistance to their counsel," and to be effective witnesses. "Special risk" is pretty flabby language (even flabbier than "less likely")—and I suppose a similar "special risk" could be said to exist for just plain stupid people, inarticulate people, even ugly people. If this unsupported claim has any substance to it (which I doubt) it might support a due process claim in all criminal prosecutions of the mentally retarded; but it is hard to see how it has anything to do with an *Eighth Amendment* claim that execution of the mentally retarded is cruel and unusual. We have never before held it to be cruel and unusual punishment to impose a sentence in violation of some *other* constitutional imperative.

FOR DISCUSSION

To what degree is the majority influenced by concerns that individuals who are mentally retarded might find it difficult to help with their own defense? What security, if any, does the Court provide to prevent individuals from claiming to be mentally handicapped when they are not? Why do you think the Court has continued to allow states to choose whether to have capital punishment while refusing to allow them to decide whether to execute individuals who are mentally handicapped?

RELATED CASES

***Payne v. Tennessee:* 501 U.S. 808 (1991).**

Overruled previous decisions in *Booth v. Maryland* (482 U.S. 496, 1987) and *South Carolina v. Gathers* (490 U.S. 804, 1989) and allowed the use of victim-impact statements at the penalty phase of a capital trial.

***Ring v. Arizona:* 536 U.S. 584 (1992).**

Decided that a jury, rather than a judge, had to engage in fact-finding to determine whether aggravating factors, which might lead to the death penalty, were involved.

***Hall v. Florida:* 572 U.S. ___ (2014).**

Decided that a Florida court erred when it relied exclusively on an IQ test to determine that the defendant was not mentally challenged and was therefore eligible for the death penalty.

ROPER V. SIMMONS

543 U.S. 551, 125 S.Ct. 1183, 161 L.Ed.2d (2005)

Decisions in one case often influence those in related cases. Here the Court reassesses its ruling in *Stanford v. Kentucky* (492 U.S. 361, 1989), where it had upheld the death sentence of a juvenile offender older than fifteen but younger than eighteen on the basis of its decision in Atkins relative to inflicting such punishments on the cognitively impaired.

Vote: 5–4

JUSTICE KENNEDY delivered the opinion of the Court.

This case requires us to address, for the second time in a decade and a half, whether it is permissible under the Eighth and Fourteenth Amendments of the Constitution of the United States to execute a juvenile offender who was older than 15 but younger than 18 when he committed a capital crime. In *Stanford v. Kentucky*, 492 U.S. 361 (1989), a divided Court rejected the proposition that the Constitution bars capital punishment for juvenile offenders in this age group. We reconsider the question.

I

[Kennedy describes Simmons' offense, committed when he was 17 years old, which consisting of planning and executing a crime of committing murder and then tying up the victim and throwing her off a bridge and drowning her. Kennedy notes that "Simmons assured his friends they could 'get away with it' because they were minors." Kennedy also notes that Simmons had told friends "he had killed a woman 'because the bitch seen my face.' " In imposing a sentence, the jury had considered age as a possible mitigating factor. The Missouri Supreme Court had subsequently overturned the decision in light of the reasoning in *Atkins v. Virginia,* 536 U.S. 304 (2002).]

II

The prohibition against "cruel and unusual punishments," like other expansive language in the Constitution, must be interpreted according to its text, by considering history, tradition, and precedent, and with due regard for its purpose and function in the constitutional design. To implement this framework we have established the propriety and affirmed the necessity of referring to "the evolving standards of decency that mark the progress of a maturing society" to determine which punishments are so disproportionate as to be cruel and unusual.

In *Thompson* v. *Oklahoma*, 487 U.S. 815 (1988), a plurality of the Court determined that our standards of decency do not permit the execution of any offender under the age of 16 at the time of the crime. The plurality opinion explained that no death penalty State that had given express consideration to a minimum age for the death penalty had set the age lower than 16. The plurality also observed that "[t]he conclusion that it would offend civilized standards of decency to execute a person who was less than 16 years old at the time of his or her offense is consistent with the views that have been expressed by respected professional organizations, by other nations that share our Anglo-American heritage, and by the leading members of the Western European community." The opinion further noted that juries imposed the death penalty on offenders under 16 with exceeding rarity; the last execution of an offender for a crime committed under the age of 16 had been carried out in 1948, 40 years prior.

The next year, in *Stanford v. Kentucky*, 492 U.S. 361 (1989), the Court, over a dissenting opinion joined by four Justices, referred to contemporary standards of decency in this country and concluded the Eighth and Fourteenth Amendments did not proscribe the execution of juvenile offenders over 15 but under 18. The Court noted that 22 of the 37 death penalty States permitted the death penalty for 16-year-old offenders, and, among these 37 States, 25 permitted it for 17-year-old offenders. These numbers, in the Court's view, indicated there was no national consensus "sufficient to label a particular punishment cruel and unusual." . . .

The same day the Court decided *Stanford*, it held that the Eighth Amendment did not mandate a categorical exemption from the death penalty for the mentally retarded. *Penry v. Lynaugh*, 492 U.S. 302 (1989). . . .

Three Terms ago the subject was reconsidered in *Atkins*. We held that standards of decency have evolved since *Penry* and now demonstrate that the execution of the mentally retarded is cruel and unusual punishment. . . .

III

A

The evidence of national consensus against the death penalty for juveniles is similar, and in some respects parallel, to the evidence *Atkins* held sufficient to demonstrate a national consensus against the death penalty for the mentally retarded. When *Atkins* was decided, 30 States prohibited the death penalty for the mentally retarded. This number comprised 12 that had abandoned the death penalty altogether, and 18 that maintained it but excluded the mentally retarded from its reach. By a similar calculation in this case, 30 States prohibit the juvenile death penalty, comprising 12 that have rejected the death penalty altogether and 18 that maintain it but, by express provision or judicial interpretation, exclude juveniles from its reach. Since *Penry*, only five States had executed offenders known to have an IQ under 70. In the present case, too, even in the 20 States without a formal prohibition on executing juveniles, the practice is infrequent. Since *Stanford*, six States have executed prisoners for crimes committed as juveniles. In the past 10 years, only three have done so: Oklahoma, Texas, and Virginia. . . .

There is, to be sure, at least one difference between the evidence of consensus in *Atkins* and in this case. Impressive in *Atkins* was the rate of abolition of the death penalty for the mentally retarded. Sixteen States that permitted the execution of the mentally retarded at the time of *Penry* had prohibited the practice by the time we heard *Atkins*. By contrast, the rate of change in reducing the incidence of the juvenile death penalty, or in taking specific steps to abolish it, has been slower. Five States that allowed the juvenile death penalty at the time of *Stanford* have abandoned it in the intervening 15 years—four through legislative enactments and one through judicial decision.

Though less dramatic than the change from *Penry* to *Atkins*, we still consider the change from *Stanford* to this case to be significant. As noted in *Atkins*, with respect to the States that had abandoned the death penalty for the mentally retarded since *Penry*, "[i]t is not so much the number of these States that is significant, but the consistency of the direction of change." In particular we found it significant that, in the wake of *Penry*, no State that had already prohibited the execution of the mentally retarded had passed legislation to reinstate the penalty. The number of States that have abandoned capital punishment for juvenile offenders since *Stanford* is smaller than the number of States that abandoned capital punishment for the mentally retarded after *Penry;* yet we think the same consistency of direction of change has been demonstrated. . . .

The slower pace of abolition of the juvenile death penalty over the past 15 years, moreover, may have a simple explanation. When we heard *Penry*, only two death penalty States had already prohibited the execution of the mentally retarded. When we heard *Stanford*, by contrast, 12 death penalty States had already prohibited the execution of any juvenile under 18, and 15 had prohibited the execution of any juvenile under 17. If anything, this shows that the impropriety of executing juveniles between 16 and 18 years of age gained wide recognition earlier than the impropriety of executing the mentally retarded. . . .

B

A majority of States have rejected the imposition of the death penalty on juvenile offenders under 18, and we now hold this is required by the Eighth Amendment.

Three general differences between juveniles under 18 and adults demonstrate that juvenile offenders cannot with reliability be classified among the worst offenders. First, as any parent knows and as the scientific and sociological studies respondent and his *amici* cite tend to confirm, "[a] lack of maturity and an underdeveloped sense of responsibility are found in youth more often than in adults and are more understandable among the young. These qualities often result in impetuous and ill-considered actions and decisions." *Johnson v. Texas* 509 U.S. 350, at 367 (1993). . . .

The second area of difference is that juveniles are more vulnerable or susceptible to negative influences and outside pressures, including peer pressure. . . .

The third broad difference is that the character of a juvenile is not as well formed as that of an adult. The personality traits of juveniles are more transitory, less fixed.

These differences render suspect any conclusion that a juvenile falls among the worst offenders. The susceptibility of juveniles to immature and irresponsible behavior means "their irresponsible conduct is not as morally reprehensible as that of an adult." *Thompson*. Their own vulnerability and comparative lack of control over their immediate surroundings mean juveniles have a greater claim than adults to be forgiven for failing to escape negative influences in their whole environment. See *Stanford*. . . .

In *Thompson*, a plurality of the Court recognized the import of these characteristics with respect to juveniles under 16, and relied on them to hold that the Eighth Amendment prohibited the imposition of the death penalty on juveniles below that age. We conclude the same reasoning applies to all juvenile offenders under 18.

Once the diminished culpability of juveniles is recognized, it is evident that the penological justifications for the death penalty apply to them with lesser force than to adults. We have held there are two distinct social purposes served by the death penalty: " 'retribution and deterrence of capital crimes by prospective offenders.' " *Atkins*. As for retribution, we remarked in *Atkins* that "[i]f the culpability of the average murderer is insufficient to justify the most extreme sanction available to the State, the lesser culpability of the mentally retarded offender surely does not merit that form of retribution." The same conclusions follow from the lesser culpability of the juvenile offender. . . .

As for deterrence, it is unclear whether the death penalty has a significant or even measurable deterrent effect on juveniles, as counsel for the petitioner acknowledged at oral argument. . . .

It is difficult even for expert psychologists to differentiate between the juvenile offender whose crime reflects unfortunate yet transient immaturity, and the rare juvenile offender whose crime reflects irreparable corruption. . . .

Drawing the line at 18 years of age is subject, of course, to the objections always raised against categorical rules. The qualities that distinguish juveniles from adults do not disappear when an individual turns 18. By the same token, some under 18 have already attained a level of maturity some adults will never reach. For the reasons we have discussed, however, a line must be drawn. . . .

These considerations mean *Stanford* v. *Kentucky* should be deemed no longer controlling on this issue. To the extent *Stanford* was based on review of the objective indicia of consensus that obtained in 1989, it suffices to note that those indicia have changed. . . .

IV

Our determination that the death penalty is disproportionate punishment for offenders under 18 finds confirmation in the stark reality that the United States is the only country in the world that continues to give official sanction to the juvenile death penalty. This reality does not become controlling, for the task of interpreting the Eighth Amendment remains our responsibility. Yet at least from the time of the Court's decision in *Trop*, the Court has referred to the laws of other countries and to international authorities as instructive for its interpretation of the Eighth Amendment's prohibition of "cruel and unusual punishments." . . .

Respondent and his *amici* have submitted, and petitioner does not contest, that only seven countries other than the United States have executed juvenile offenders since 1990: Iran, Pakistan, Saudi Arabia, Yemen, Nigeria, the Democratic Republic of Congo, and China. Since then each of these countries has either abolished capital punishment for juveniles or made public disavowal of the practice. In sum, it is fair to say that the United States now stands alone in a world that has turned its face against the juvenile death penalty.

JUSTICE STEVENS, with whom JUSTICE GINSBURG joins, concurring.

Perhaps even more important than our specific holding today is our reaffirmation of the basic principle that informs the Court's interpretation of the Eighth Amendment. If the meaning of that Amendment had been frozen when it was originally drafted, it would impose no impediment to the execution of 7-year-old children today. See *Stanford v. Kentucky,* 492 U.S. 361 (1989). The evolving standards of decency that have driven our construction of this critically important part of the Bill of Rights foreclose any such reading of the Amendment. In the best tradition of the common law, the pace of that evolution is a matter for continuing debate; but that our understanding of the Constitution does change from time to time has been settled since John Marshall breathed life into its text. If great lawyers of his day—Alexander Hamilton, for example—were sitting with us today, I would expect them to join Justice Kennedy's opinion for the Court. In all events, I do so without hesitation.

JUSTICE O'CONNOR, dissenting.

The Court's decision today establishes a categorical rule forbidding the execution of any offender for any crime committed before his 18th birthday, no matter how deliberate, wanton, or cruel the offense. Neither the objective evidence of contemporary societal values, nor the Court's moral proportionality analysis, nor the two in tandem suffice to justify this ruling.

Although the Court finds support for its decision in the fact that a majority of the States now disallow capital punishment of 17-year-old offenders, it refrains from asserting that its holding is compelled by a genuine national consensus. Indeed, the evidence before us fails to demonstrate conclusively that any such consensus has emerged in the brief period since we upheld the constitutionality of this practice in *Stanford v. Kentucky*, 492 U.S. 361 (1989).

Instead, the rule decreed by the Court rests, ultimately, on its independent moral judgment that death is a disproportionately severe punishment for any 17-year-old offender. I do not subscribe to this judgment. Adolescents *as a class* are undoubtedly less mature, and therefore less culpable for their misconduct, than adults. But the Court has adduced no evidence impeaching the seemingly reasonable conclusion reached by many state legislatures: that at least *some* 17-year-old murderers are sufficiently mature to deserve the death penalty in an appropriate case. Nor has it been shown that capital sentencing juries are incapable of accurately assessing a youthful defendant's maturity or of giving due weight to the mitigating characteristics associated with youth.

On this record—and especially in light of the fact that so little has changed since our recent decision in *Stanford*—I would not substitute our judgment about the moral propriety of capital punishment for 17-year-old murderers for the judgments of the Nation's legislatures. Rather, I would demand a clearer showing that our society truly has set its face against this practice before reading the Eighth Amendment categorically to forbid it.

JUSTICE SCALIA, with whom CHIEF JUSTICE REHNQUIST and JUSTICE THOMAS join, dissenting.

[Scalia quotes Alexander Hamilton's argument in *Federalist* No. 78 that the Court would be bound down by precedents.] What a mockery today's opinion makes of Hamilton's expectation, announcing the Court's conclusion that the meaning of our Constitution has changed over the past 15 years—not, mind you, that this Court's decision 15 years ago was *wrong*, but that the Constitution *has changed*. The Court reaches this implausible result by purporting to advert, not to the original meaning of the Eighth Amendment, but to "the evolving standards of decency," of our national society. It then finds, on the flimsiest of grounds, that a national consensus which could not be perceived in our people's laws barely 15 years ago now solidly exists. Worse still, the Court says in so many words that what our people's laws say about the issue does not, in the last analysis, matter: "[I]n the end our own judgment will be brought to bear on the question of the acceptability of the death penalty under the Eighth Amendment." The Court thus proclaims itself sole arbiter of our Nation's moral standards—and in the course of discharging that awesome responsibility purports to take guidance from the views of foreign courts and legislatures. Because I do not believe that the meaning of our Eighth Amendment, any more than the meaning of other provisions of our Constitution, should be determined by the subjective views of five Members of this Court and like-minded foreigners, I dissent.

FOR DISCUSSION

Should it make any difference that Simmons appears to have participated in this crime in part because he thought his age would likely exempt him from the death penalty? Dissenting justices are concerned about the majority's use of trends in other nations. In your view, is it appropriate for the Court to consider the jurisprudence of countries other than the United States in deciding whether the death penalty violates contemporary standards?

Issues Not Involving the Death Penalty

Rummel v. Estelle (445 U.S. 263, 1980) raises yet another issue tied to the Eighth Amendment but not to the death penalty, namely, the constitutionality of anti-recidivism statutes known as "**three strikes and you're out**" laws. Such laws result in dramatically enhanced sentences for repeat offenders. In deciding this issue, the Court confronted the more general issue of proportionality. Justice Rehnquist ultimately decided that precedents applying the principle of proportionality to the death penalty should stop there and not be widened further. Even while focusing on an issue not involving capital punishment, the Court made it clear that it continued to view such punishments as substantially different from others.

In *Harmelin v. Michigan* (501 U.S. 957, 1991), the Court majority again declined to equate the "cruel and unusual punishment" provision with that of "proportionality," in this case upholding a life sentence for illegal drug possession. It is by no means clear that this will be the last word on the subject.

In *Brown v. Plata*, 563 U.S. 493, (2011), the Supreme Court ruled that prison overcrowding in California was so acute as to constitute cruel and unusual punishment and to justify a decision by a 3-judge federal court mandating that the overcrowding be reduced. Critics questioned whether the Court was stepping into decision-making that was properly vested in the state legislature.

RUMMEL V. ESTELLE

445 U.S. 263, 100 S.Ct. 1133, 63 L.Ed.2d 382 (1980)

States looking to combat crime have paid particular attention to repeat offenders, or **recidivists**. Many states have adopted "three strikes and you're out" legislation, like that at issue in this case, where the Supreme Court was to decide whether the application of a law that can impose a harsh prison sentence after a relatively minor third offense constitutes "cruel and unusual punishment." Note the dispute between the majority and the dissenters as to whether the Court should apply similar or different standards in capital and noncapital cases.

Vote: 5–4

JUSTICE REHNQUIST delivered the opinion of the Court.

Petitioner William James Rummel is presently serving a life sentence imposed by the State of Texas in 1973 under its "recidivist statute," formerly Art. 63 of its Penal Code, which provided that "[whoever] shall have been three times convicted of a felony less than capital shall on such third conviction be imprisoned for life in the penitentiary." On January 19, 1976, Rummel sought a writ of habeas corpus in the United States District Court for the Western District of Texas, arguing that life imprisonment was "grossly disproportionate" to the three felonies that formed the predicate for his sentence and that therefore the sentence violated the ban on cruel and unusual punishments of the Eighth and Fourteenth Amendments. The District Court and the United States Court of Appeals for the Fifth Circuit rejected Rummel's claim, finding no unconstitutional disproportionality. We granted certiorari and now affirm.

I

In 1964 the State of Texas charged Rummel with fraudulent use of a credit card to obtain $80 worth of goods or services. Because the amount in question was greater than $50, the charged offense was a felony punishable by a minimum of 2 years and a maximum of 10 years in the Texas Department of Corrections. Rummel eventually pleaded guilty to the charge and was sentenced to three years' confinement in a state penitentiary.

In 1969 the State of Texas charged Rummel with passing a forged check in the amount of $28.36, a crime punishable by imprisonment in a penitentiary for not less than two nor more than five years. Rummel pleaded guilty to this offense and was sentenced to four years' imprisonment.

In 1973 Rummel was charged with obtaining $120.75 by false pretenses. Because the amount obtained was greater than $50, the charged offense was designated "felony theft," which, by itself, was punishable by confinement in a penitentiary for not less than 2 nor more than 10 years. The prosecution chose, however, to proceed against Rummel under Texas' recidivist statute, and cited in the indictment his 1964 and 1969 convictions as requiring imposition of a life sentence if Rummel were convicted of the charged offense. A jury convicted Rummel of felony theft and also found as true the allegation that he had been convicted of two prior felonies. As a result, on April 26, 1973, the trial court imposed upon Rummel the life sentence mandated by Art. 63.

[Rehnquist summarizes actions of other courts in the case.]

II

Initially, we believe it important to set forth two propositions that Rummel does not contest. First, Rummel does not challenge the constitutionality of Texas' recidivist statute as a general proposition. In *Spencer v. Texas,* 385 U.S. 554 (1967), this Court upheld the very statute employed here, noting in the course of its opinion that similar statutes had been sustained against contentions that they violated "constitutional strictures dealing with double jeopardy, *ex post facto* laws, cruel and unusual punishment, due process, equal protection, and privileges and immunities." Here, Rummel attacks only the result of applying this concededly valid statute to the facts of his case.

Second, Rummel does not challenge Texas' authority to punish each of his offenses as felonies, that is, by imprisoning him in a state penitentiary. . . .

This Court has on occasion stated that the Eighth Amendment prohibits imposition of a sentence that is grossly disproportionate to the severity of the crime. In recent years this proposition has appeared most frequently in opinions dealing with the death penalty. . . .

This theme, the unique nature of the death penalty for purposes of Eighth Amendment analysis, has been repeated time and time again in our opinions. . . .

Outside the context of capital punishment, successful challenges to the proportionality of particular sentences have been exceedingly rare. . . .

. . . Thus the interest of the State of Texas here is not simply that of making criminal the unlawful acquisition of another person's property; it is in addition the interest, expressed in all recidivist statutes, in dealing in a harsher manner with those who by repeated criminal acts have shown that they are simply incapable of conforming to the norms of society as established by its criminal law. By conceding the validity of recidivist statutes generally, Rummel himself concedes that the State of Texas, or any other State, has a valid interest in so dealing with that class of persons.

Undaunted by earlier cases . . . Rummel attempts to ground his proportionality attack on an alleged "nationwide" trend away from mandatory life sentences and toward "lighter, discretionary sentences." According to Rummel, "[no] jurisdiction in the United States or the Free World punishes habitual offenders as harshly as Texas." In support of this proposition, Rummel offers detailed charts and tables documenting the history of recidivist statutes in the United States since 1776.

[Rehnquist examines the operation of the Texas law and does not find that it differs significantly from others.]

Rummel's charts and tables do appear to indicate that he might have received more lenient treatment in almost any State other than Texas, West Virginia, or Washington. The distinctions, however, are subtle rather than gross. A number of States impose a mandatory life sentence upon conviction of four felonies rather than three. Other States require one or more of the felonies to be "violent" to support a life sentence. Still other States leave the imposition of a life sentence after three felonies within the discretion of a judge or jury. It is one thing for a court to compare those States that impose capital punishment for a specific offense with those States that do not. It is quite another thing for a court to attempt to evaluate the position of any particular recidivist scheme within Rummel's complex matrix.

Nor do Rummel's extensive charts even begin to reflect the complexity of the comparison he asks this Court to make. . . .

Perhaps, as asserted in *Weems v. United States*, 217 U. S. 349 (1910), "time works changes" upon the Eighth Amendment, bringing into existence "new conditions and purposes." We all, of course, would like to think that we are "moving down the road toward human decency." *Furman v. Georgia,* 408 U.S. 238 (1972). Within the confines of this judicial proceeding, however, we have no way of knowing in which direction that road lies. Penologists themselves have been unable to agree whether sentences should be light or heavy, discretionary or determinate. This uncertainty reinforces our conviction that any "nationwide trend" toward lighter, discretionary sentences must find its source and its sustaining force in the legislatures, not in the federal courts.

III

The most casual review of the various criminal justice systems now in force in the 50 States of the Union shows that the line dividing felony theft from petty larceny, a line usually based on the value of the property taken, varies markedly from one State to another. We believe that Texas is entitled to make its own judgment as to where such lines lie, subject only to those strictures of the Eighth Amendment that can be informed by objective factors. See *Coker v. Georgia,* 433 U.S. 584 (1977). Moreover, given Rummel's record, Texas was not required to treat him in the same manner as it might treat him were this his first "petty property offense." Having twice imprisoned him for felonies, Texas was entitled to place upon Rummel the onus of one who is simply unable to bring his conduct within the social norms prescribed by the criminal law of the State.

The purpose of a recidivist statute such as that involved here is not to simplify the task of prosecutors, judges, or juries. Its primary goals are to deter repeat offenders and, at some point in the life of one who repeatedly commits criminal offenses serious enough to be punished as felonies, to segregate that person from the rest of society for an extended period of time. This segregation and its duration are based not merely on that person's most recent offense but also on the propensities he has demonstrated over a period of time during which he has been convicted of and sentenced for other crimes. Like the line dividing felony theft from petty larceny, the point at which a recidivist will be deemed to have demonstrated the necessary propensities and the amount of time that the recidivist will be isolated from society are matters largely within the discretion of the punishing jurisdiction.

We therefore hold that the mandatory life sentence imposed upon this petitioner does not constitute cruel and unusual punishment under the Eighth and Fourteenth Amendments. The judgment of the Court of Appeals is *Affirmed.*

JUSTICE STEWART, concurring.

I am moved to repeat the substance of what I had to say on another occasion about the recidivist legislation of Texas:

If the Constitution gave me a roving commission to impose upon the criminal courts of Texas my own notions of enlightened policy, I would not join the Court's opinion. For it is clear to me that the recidivist procedures adopted in recent years by many other States . . . are far superior to those utilized [here]. But the question for decision is not whether we applaud or even whether we personally approve the procedures followed in [this case]. The question is whether those procedures fall below the minimum level the [Constitution] will tolerate. Upon that question I am constrained to join the opinion and judgment of the Court. *Spencer v. Texas,* 385 U.S. 554 (1967).

JUSTICE POWELL, with whom JUSTICES BRENNAN, MARSHALL, and STEVENS join, dissenting.

I

This Court today affirms the Fifth Circuit's decision. I dissent because I believe that (i) the penalty for a noncapital offense may be unconstitutionally disproportionate, (ii) the possibility of parole should not be considered in assessing the nature of the punishment, (iii) a mandatory life sentence is grossly disproportionate as applied to petitioner, and (iv) the conclusion that this petitioner has suffered a violation of his Eighth Amendment rights is compatible with principles of judicial restraint and federalism.

II

B

The scope of the Cruel and Unusual Punishments Clause extends not only to barbarous methods of punishment, but also to punishments that are grossly disproportionate. Disproportionality analysis measures the relationship between the nature and number of offenses committed and the severity of the punishment inflicted upon the offender. The inquiry focuses on whether a person deserves such punishment, not simply on whether punishment would serve a utilitarian goal. A statute that levied a mandatory life sentence for overtime parking might well deter vehicular lawlessness, but it would offend our felt sense of justice. The Court concedes today that the principle of disproportionality plays a role in the review of sentences imposing the death penalty, but suggests that the principle may be less applicable when a noncapital sentence is challenged. Such a limitation finds no support in the history of Eighth Amendment jurisprudence.

The principle of disproportionality is rooted deeply in English constitutional law. The Magna Carta of 1215 insured that "[a] free man shall not be [fined] for a trivial offence, except in accordance with the degree of the offence; and for a serious offence he shall be [fined] according to its gravity." By 1400, the English common law had embraced the principle, not always followed in practice, that punishment should not be excessive either in severity or length. One commentator's survey of English law demonstrates that the "cruel and unusual punishments" clause of the English Bill of Rights of 1689 "was first, an objection to the imposition of punishments which were unauthorized by statute and outside the jurisdiction of the sentencing court, and second, a reiteration of the English policy against disproportionate penalties."

In *Weems v. United States,* 217 U.S. 349 (1910), a public official convicted for falsifying a public record claimed that he suffered cruel and unusual punishment when he was sentenced to serve 15 years' imprisonment in hard labor with chains. The sentence also subjected Weems to loss of civil rights and perpetual surveillance after his release. This Court agreed that the punishment was cruel and unusual. The Court was attentive to the methods of the punishment, but its conclusion did not rest solely upon the nature of punishment. The Court relied explicitly upon the relationship between the crime committed and the punishment imposed. . . .

In sum, a few basic principles emerge from the history of the Eighth Amendment. Both barbarous forms of punishment and grossly excessive punishments are cruel and unusual. A sentence may be excessive if it serves no acceptable social purpose, or is grossly disproportionate to the seriousness of the crime. The principle of disproportionality has been acknowledged to apply to both capital and noncapital sentences.

III

Under Texas law, petitioner has been sentenced to a mandatory life sentence. Even so, the Court of Appeals rejected the petitioner's Eighth Amendment claim primarily because it concluded that the petitioner probably would not serve a life sentence. In view of good-time credits available under the Texas system, the court concluded that Rummel might serve no more than 10 years. Thus, the Court of Appeals equated petitioner's sentence to 10 years of imprisonment without the possibility of parole.

It is true that imposition in Texas of a mandatory life sentence does not necessarily mean that petitioner will spend the rest of his life behind prison walls. If petitioner attains sufficient good-time credits, he may be eligible for parole within 10 or 12 years after he begins serving his life sentence. But petitioner will have no right to early release; he will merely be eligible for parole. And parole is simply an act of executive grace.

A holding that the possibility of parole discounts a prisoner's sentence for the purposes of the Eighth Amendment would be cruelly ironic. The combined effect of our holdings under the Due Process Clause of the Fourteenth Amendment and the Eighth Amendment would allow a State to defend an Eighth Amendment claim by contending that parole is probable even though the prisoner cannot enforce that expectation. Such an approach is inconsistent with the Eighth Amendment. The Court has never before failed to examine a prisoner's Eighth Amendment claim because of the speculation that he might be pardoned before the sentence was carried out.

IV

The Eighth Amendment commands this Court to enforce the constitutional limitation of the Cruel and Unusual Punishments Clause. In discharging this responsibility, we should minimize the risk of constitutionalizing the personal predilictions of federal judges by relying upon certain objective factors. Among these are (i) the nature of the offense, see *Coker v. Georgia,* 433 U.S. 584 (1977); (ii) the sentence imposed for commission of the same crime in other jurisdictions; *Weems* v. *United States*; cf. *Trop* v. *Dulles*, 356 U.S. 86 (1958); and (iii) the sentence imposed upon other criminals in the same jurisdiction, *Weems.*

B

Apparently, only 12 States have ever enacted habitual offender statutes imposing a mandatory life sentence for the commission of two or three nonviolent felonies and only 3, Texas, Washington, and West Virginia, have retained such a statute.

More than three-quarters of American jurisdictions have never adopted a habitual offender statute that would commit the petitioner to mandatory life imprisonment. The jurisdictions that currently employ habitual offender statutes either (i) require the commission of more than three offenses, (ii) require the commission of at least one violent crime, (iii) limit a mandatory penalty to less than life, or (iv) grant discretion to the sentencing authority. In none of the jurisdictions could the petitioner have received a mandatory life sentence merely upon the showing that he committed three nonviolent property-related offenses.

The federal habitual offender statute also differs materially from the Texas statute. Title 18 U.S.C. § 3575 provides increased sentences for "dangerous special offenders" who have been convicted of a felony. . . .

C

Finally, it is necessary to examine the punishment that Texas provides for other criminals. First and second offenders who commit more serious crimes than the petitioner may receive markedly less severe sentences. . . .

D

Examination of the objective factors traditionally employed by the Court to assess the proportionality of a sentence demonstrates that petitioner suffers a cruel and unusual punishment. . . .

V

The Court today agrees with the State's arguments that a decision in petitioner's favor would violate principles of federalism and, because of difficulty in formulating standards to guide the decision of the federal courts, would lead to excessive interference with state sentencing decisions. Neither contention is convincing.

. . . But even as the Constitution recognizes a sphere of state activity free from federal interference, it explicitly compels the States to follow certain constitutional commands. When we apply the Cruel and Unusual Punishments Clause against the States, we merely enforce an obligation that the Constitution has created. . . .

Because the State believes that the federal courts can formulate no practicable standard to identify grossly disproportionate sentences, it fears that the courts would intervene into state criminal justice systems at will. Such a "floodgates" argument can be easy to make and difficult to rebut. But in this case we can identify and apply objective criteria that reflect constitutional standards of punishment and minimize the risk of judicial subjectivity. Moreover, we can rely upon the experience of the United States Court of Appeals for the Fourth Circuit in applying criteria similar to those that I believe should govern this case.

VI

I recognize that the difference between the petitioner's grossly disproportionate sentence and other prisoners' constitutionally valid sentences is not separated by the clear distinction that separates capital from noncapital punishment. "But the fact that a line has to be drawn somewhere does not justify its being drawn anywhere." *Pearce v. Commissioner*, 315 U.S. 543 (1942). The Court has, in my view, chosen the easiest line rather than the best.

FOR DISCUSSION

What are the strengths and weaknesses of "three strikes and you're out" legislation? To what degree do you think the justices in this case attempted to separate their own view of the wisdom of such legislation from its constitutionality?

HARMELIN V. MICHIGAN

501 U.S. 957, 111 S.Ct. 2680, 115 L.Ed.2d 836 (1991)

In this case the Court has to decide whether sentencing an individual to life in prison without possibility of parole for possession of 672 grams of cocaine constitutes cruel and unusual punishment.

Vote: 5–4

JUSTICE SCALIA delivered the majority opinion.

Petitioner claims that his sentence is unconstitutionally "cruel and unusual" for two reasons: first, because it is "significantly disproportionate" to the crime he committed; second, because the sentencing judge was statutorily required to impose it, without taking into account the particularized circumstances of the crime and of the criminal.

I

A

The Eighth Amendment, which applies against the States by virtue of the Fourteenth Amendment, see *Robinson v. California,* 370 U.S. 660 (1962), provides: "Excessive bail shall not be required, nor excessive fines imposed, nor cruel and unusual punishments inflicted." In *Rummel v. Estelle*, 445 U.S. 263 (1980), we held that it did not constitute "cruel and unusual punishment" to impose a life sentence, under a recidivist statute, upon a defendant who had been convicted, successively, of fraudulent use of a credit card to obtain $80 worth of goods or services, passing a forged check in the amount of $28.36, and obtaining $120.75 by false pretenses. . . .

Two years later, in *Hutto v. Davis*, 454 U.S. 370 (1982), we similarly rejected an Eighth Amendment challenge to a prison term of 40 years and fine of $20,000 for possession and distribution of approximately nine ounces of marijuana. . . .

A year and a half after *Davis* we uttered what has been our last word on this subject to date. *Solem v. Helm*, 463 U.S. 277 (1983), set aside under the Eighth Amendment, because it was disproportionate, a sentence of life imprisonment without possibility of parole, imposed under a South Dakota recidivist statute for successive offenses that included three convictions of third-degree burglary, one of obtaining money by false pretenses, one of grand larceny, one of third-offense driving while intoxicated, and one of writing a "no account" check with intent to defraud. . . .

It should be apparent from the above discussion that our 5-to-4 decision eight years ago in *Solem* was scarcely the expression of clear and well accepted constitutional law. . . .

B

Solem based its conclusion principally upon the proposition that a right to be free from disproportionate punishments was embodied within the "cruell and unusuall Punishments" provision of the English Declaration of Rights of 1689, and was incorporated, with that language, in the Eighth Amendment. . . .

[Scalia extensively examines the history of this provision.]

In all these contemporaneous discussions, as in the prologue of the Declaration, a punishment is not considered objectionable because it is disproportionate, but because it is "out of [the Judges'] Power," "contrary to Law and ancient practice," without "Precedents" or "express Law to warrant," "unusual," "illegal," or imposed by "Pretence to a discretionary Power." Moreover, the phrase "cruell and unusuall" is treated as interchangeable with "cruel and illegal." In other words, the "illegall and cruell Punishments" of the Declaration's prologue are the same thing as the "cruell and unusuall Punishments" of its body. . . .

In sum, we think it most unlikely that the English Cruell and Unusuall Punishments Clause was meant to forbid "disproportionate" punishments. There is even less likelihood that proportionality of punishment was one of the traditional "rights and privileges of Englishmen" apart from the Declaration of Rights, which happened to be included in the Eighth Amendment. . . .

C

Unless one accepts the notion of a blind incorporation, however, the ultimate question is not what "cruell and unusuall punishments" meant in the Declaration of Rights, but what its meaning was to the Americans who adopted the Eighth Amendment. . . .

Wrenched out of its common-law context, and applied to the actions of a legislature, the word "unusual" could hardly mean "contrary to law." But it continued to mean (as it continues to mean today) "such as [does not] occur in ordinary practice," *Webster's American Dictionary* (1828), "such as is [not] in common use," *Webster's Second International Dictionary* 2807 (1954). . . .

The language bears the construction, however—and here we come to the point crucial to resolution of the present case—that "cruelty and unusualness" are to be determined not solely with reference to the punishment at issue ("Is life imprisonment a cruel and unusual punishment?") but with reference to the crime for which it is imposed as well ("Is life imprisonment cruel and unusual punishment for possession of unlawful drugs?"). The latter interpretation would make the provision a form of proportionality guarantee. The arguments against it, however, seem to us conclusive.

First of all, to use the phrase "cruel and unusual punishment" to describe a requirement of proportionality would have been an exceedingly vague and oblique way of saying what Americans were well accustomed to saying more directly. The notion of "proportionality" was not a novelty (though then as now there was little agreement over what it entailed). . . .

Secondly, it would seem quite peculiar to refer to cruelty and unusualness *for the offense in question*, in a provision having application only to a new government that had never before defined offenses, and that would be defining new and peculiarly national ones. Finally, and most conclusively, as we proceed to discuss, the fact that what was "cruel and unusual" under the Eighth Amendment was to be determined without reference to the particular offense is confirmed by all available evidence of contemporary understanding.

The early commentary on the Clause contains no reference to disproportionate or excessive sentences, and again indicates that it was designed to outlaw particular *modes* of punishment. . . .

Many other Americans apparently agreed that the Clause only outlawed certain *modes* of punishment: During the 19th century several States ratified constitutions that prohibited "cruel and unusual," "cruel or unusual," or simply "cruel" punishments *and* required *all* punishments to be proportioned to the offense. . . .

Throughout the 19th century, state courts interpreting state constitutional provisions with identical or more expansive wording (*i. e.*, "cruel *or* unusual") concluded that these provisions did not proscribe disproportionality but only certain modes of punishment. . . .

II

We think it enough that those who framed and approved the Federal Constitution chose, for whatever reason, not to include within it the guarantee against disproportionate sentences that some State Constitutions contained. It is worth noting, however, that there was good reason for that choice—a reason that reinforces the necessity of overruling *Solem*. While there are relatively clear historical guidelines and accepted practices that enable judges to determine which *modes* of punishment are "cruel and unusual," *proportionality* does not lend itself to such analysis. . . .

This becomes clear, we think, from a consideration of the three factors that *Solem* found relevant to the proportionality determination: (1) the inherent gravity of the offense, (2) the sentences imposed for similarly grave offenses in the same jurisdiction, and (3) sentences imposed for the same crime in other jurisdictions. As to the first factor: Of course some offenses, involving violent harm to human beings, will always and everywhere be regarded as serious, but that is only half the equation. The issue is *what else* should be regarded to be *as serious* as these offenses, or even to be *more serious* than some of them. On that point, judging by the statutes that Americans have enacted, there is enormous variation—even within a given age, not to mention across the many generations ruled by the Bill of Rights.

The second factor suggested in *Solem* fails for the same reason. One cannot compare the sentences imposed by the jurisdiction for "similarly grave" offenses if there is no objective standard of gravity. Judges will be comparing what *they* consider comparable. . . .

As for the third factor mentioned by *Solem*—the character of the sentences imposed by other States for the same crime—it must be acknowledged that that can be applied with clarity and ease. The only difficulty is that it has no conceivable relevance to the Eighth Amendment.

III

Our 20th-century jurisprudence has not remained entirely in accord with the proposition that there is no proportionality requirement in the Eighth Amendment, but neither has it departed to the extent that *Solem* suggests. . . .

The first holding of this Court unqualifiedly applying a requirement of proportionality to criminal penalties was issued 185 years after the Eighth Amendment was adopted. In *Coker v. Georgia,* the Court held that, because of the disproportionality, it was a violation of the Cruel and Unusual Punishments Clause to impose capital punishment for rape of an adult woman. Five years later, in *Enmund v. Florida*, 458 U.S. 782 (1982), we held that it violates the Eighth Amendment, because of disproportionality, to impose the death penalty upon a participant in a felony that results in murder, without any inquiry into the participant's intent to kill. *Rummel v. Estelle*, 445 U.S. 263 (1980), treated this line of authority as an aspect of our death penalty jurisprudence, rather than a generalizable aspect of Eighth Amendment law. We think that is an accurate explanation, and we reassert it. Proportionality review is one of several respects in which we have held that "death is different," and have imposed protections that the Constitution nowhere else provides. . . .

IV

Petitioner claims that his sentence violates the Eighth Amendment for a reason in addition to its alleged disproportionality. He argues that it is "cruel and unusual" to impose a mandatory sentence of such severity, without any consideration of so-called mitigating factors such as, in his case, the fact that he had no prior felony convictions. . . .

As our earlier discussion should make clear, this claim has no support in the text and history of the Eighth Amendment. Severe, mandatory penalties may be cruel, but they are not unusual in the constitutional sense, having been employed in various forms throughout our Nation's history. . . .

Petitioner's "required mitigation" claim, like his proportionality claim, does find support in our death penalty jurisprudence. We have held that a capital sentence is cruel and unusual under the Eighth Amendment if it is imposed without an individualized determination that that punishment is "appropriate"—whether or not the sentence is "grossly disproportionate." Petitioner asks us to extend this so-called "individualized capital sentencing doctrine," *Sumner v. Shuman*, 483 U.S. 66 (1987), to an "individualized mandatory life in prison without parole sentencing doctrine." We refuse to do so.

Our cases creating and clarifying the "individualized capital sentencing doctrine" have repeatedly suggested that there is no comparable requirement outside the capital context, because of the qualitative difference between death and all other penalties. . . .

JUSTICE KENNEDY, with whom JUSTICES O'CONNOR and SOUTER join, concurring in part and concurring in the judgment.

. . . [S]*tare decisis* counsels our adherence to the narrow proportionality principle that has existed in our Eighth Amendment jurisprudence for 80 years. Although our proportionality decisions have not been clear or consistent in all respects, they can be reconciled, and they require us to uphold petitioner's sentence.

I

A

Our decisions recognize that the Cruel and Unusual Punishments Clause encompasses a narrow proportionality principle. . . .

B

Though our decisions recognize a proportionality principle, its precise contours are unclear. This is so in part because we have applied the rule in few cases and even then to sentences of different types. . . .

. . . . Despite these tensions, close analysis of our decisions yields some common principles that give content to the uses and limits of proportionality review.

The first of these principles is that the fixing of prison terms for specific crimes involves a substantive penological judgment that, as a general matter, is "properly within the province of legislatures, not courts." *Rummel v. Estelle*, 445 U.S. 263 (1980). . . .

The second principle is that the Eighth Amendment does not mandate adoption of any one penological theory. . . .

Third, marked divergences both in underlying theories of sentencing and in the length of prescribed prison terms are the inevitable, often beneficial, result of the federal structure. . . .

The fourth principle at work in our cases is that proportionality review by federal courts should be informed by " 'objective factors to the maximum possible extent.' " *Rummel*. . . .

All of these principles—the primacy of the legislature, the variety of legitimate penological schemes, the nature of our federal system, and the requirement that proportionality review be guided by objective factors—inform the final one: The Eighth Amendment does not require strict proportionality between crime and sentence. Rather, it forbids only extreme sentences that are "grossly disproportionate" to the crime. . . .

II

[Kennedy applies these principles to the length and mandatory nature of the penalty in the present case.]

III

. . . The dangers flowing from drug offenses and the circumstances of the crime committed here demonstrate that the Michigan penalty scheme does not surpass constitutional bounds. Michigan may use its criminal law to address the issue of drug possession in wholesale amounts in the manner that it has in this sentencing scheme. . . .

JUSTICE WHITE, with whom JUSTICE BLACKMUN and STEVENS join, dissenting.

The language of the Amendment does not refer to proportionality in so many words, but it does forbid "excessive" fines, a restraint that suggests that a determination of excessiveness should be based at least in part on whether the fine imposed is disproportionate to the crime committed. Nor would it be unreasonable to conclude that it would be both cruel and unusual to punish overtime parking by life imprisonment, see *Rummel v. Estelle,* 445 U.S. 263 (1980), or, more generally, to impose any punishment that is grossly disproportionate to the offense for which the defendant has been convicted. . . .

[White proceeds to summarize Scalia's arguments as well as prior cases that applied the proportionality principle.]

If Justice Scalia really means what he says—"the Eighth Amendment contains no proportionality guarantee," it is difficult to see how any of the above holdings and declarations about the proportionality requirement of the Amendment could survive. Later in his opinion, however, Justice Scalia backtracks and appears to accept that the Amendment does indeed insist on proportional punishments in a particular class of cases, those that involve sentences of death. His fallback position is that outside the capital cases, proportionality review is not required by the Amendment. . . .

. . .[T]he Court's jurisprudence concerning the scope of the prohibition against cruel and unusual punishments has long understood the limitations of a purely historical analysis. . . .

The Court therefore has recognized that a punishment may violate the Eighth Amendment if it is contrary to the "evolving standards of decency that mark the progress of a maturing society." *Trop v. Dulles,* 356 U.S. 86 (1958). . . .

Two dangers lurk in Justice Scalia's analysis. First, he provides no mechanism for addressing a situation such as that proposed in *Rummel,* in which a legislature makes overtime parking a felony punishable by life imprisonment. He concedes that "one can imagine extreme examples"—perhaps such as the one described in *Rummel*—"that no rational person, in no time or place, could accept," but attempts to offer reassurance by claiming that "for the same reason these examples are easy to decide, they are certain never to occur." This is cold comfort indeed, for absent a proportionality guarantee, there would be no basis for deciding such cases should they arise.

Second, as I have indicated, Justice Scalia's position that the Eighth Amendment addresses only modes or methods of punishment is quite inconsistent with our capital punishment cases, which do not outlaw death as a mode or method of punishment, but instead put limits on its application. If the concept of proportionality is downgraded in the Eighth Amendment calculus, much of this Court's capital penalty jurisprudence will rest on quicksand.

While Justice Scalia seeks to deliver a swift death sentence to *Solem v. Helm,* 463 U.S. 277 (1983), Justice Kennedy prefers to eviscerate it, leaving only an empty shell. The analysis Justice Kennedy proffers is contradicted by the language of *Solem* itself and by our other cases interpreting the Eighth Amendment.

[White proceeds to examine Kennedy's concurrence.]

The first *Solem* factor requires a reviewing court to assess the gravity of the offense and the harshness of the penalty. The mandatory sentence of life imprisonment without possibility of parole "is the most severe punishment that the State could have imposed on any criminal for any crime," for Michigan has no death penalty.

Although these factors are "by no means exhaustive," in evaluating the gravity of the offense, it is appropriate to consider "the harm caused or threatened to the victim or society," based on such things as the degree of violence involved in the crime and "the absolute magnitude of the crime," and "the culpability of the offender," including the degree of requisite intent and the offender's motive in committing the crime.

Drugs are without doubt a serious societal problem. To justify such a harsh mandatory penalty as that imposed here, however, the offense should be one which will *always* warrant that punishment. Mere possession of drugs—even in such a large quantity—is not so serious an offense that it will always warrant, much less mandate, life imprisonment without possibility of parole. Unlike crimes directed against the persons and property of others, possession of drugs affects the criminal who uses the drugs most directly. The ripple effect on society caused by possession of drugs, through related crimes, lost productivity, health problems, and the like, is often not the direct consequence of possession, but of the resulting addiction, something which this Court held in *Robinson v. California*, 370 U.S. 660 (1962), cannot be made a crime.

To be constitutionally proportionate, punishment must be tailored to a defendant's personal responsibility and moral guilt. See *Enmund v. Florida*, 458 U.S. 782 (1982). Justice Kennedy attempts to justify the harsh mandatory sentence imposed on petitioner by focusing on the subsidiary effects of drug use, and thereby ignores this aspect of our Eighth Amendment jurisprudence. . . .

The "absolute magnitude" of petitioner's crime is not exceptionally serious. Because possession is necessarily a lesser included offense of possession with intent to distribute, it is odd to punish the former as severely as the latter. Nor is the requisite intent for the crime sufficient to render it particularly grave. To convict someone under the possession statute, it is only necessary to prove that the defendant knowingly possessed a mixture containing narcotics which weighs at least 650 grams. There is no *mens rea* requirement of intent to distribute the drugs, as there is in the parallel statute. . . .

The second prong of the *Solem* analysis is an examination of "the sentences imposed on other criminals in the same jurisdiction." As noted above, there is no death penalty in Michigan; consequently, life without parole, the punishment mandated here, is the harshest penalty available. It is reserved for three crimes: first-degree murder; manufacture, distribution, or possession with intent to manufacture or distribute 650 grams or more of narcotics; and possession of 650 grams or more of narcotics. Crimes directed against the persons and property of others—such as second-degree murder; rape; and armed robbery—do not carry such a harsh mandatory sentence, although they do provide for the possibility of a life sentence in the exercise of judicial discretion. It is clear that petitioner "has been treated in the same manner as, or more severely than, criminals who have committed far more serious crimes."

The third factor set forth in *Solem* examines "the sentences imposed for commission of the same crime in other jurisdictions." No other jurisdiction imposes a punishment nearly as severe as Michigan's for possession of the amount of drugs at issue here. Of the remaining 49 States, only Alabama provides for a mandatory sentence of life imprisonment without possibility of parole for a first-time drug offender, and then only when a defendant possesses *10 kilograms* or more of cocaine. . . .

JUSTICE MARSHALL, dissenting.

I agree with Justice White's dissenting opinion, except insofar as it asserts that the Eighth Amendment's Cruel and Unusual Punishments Clause does not proscribe the death penalty. I adhere to my view that capital punishment is in all instances unconstitutional. . . .

JUSTICE STEVENS, with whom JUSTICE BLACKMUN joins, dissenting.

. . . Nevertheless, a mandatory sentence of life imprisonment without the possibility of parole does share one important characteristic of a death sentence: The offender will never regain his freedom. Because such a sentence does not even purport to serve a rehabilitative function, the sentence must rest on a rational determination that the punished "criminal conduct is so atrocious that society's interest in deterrence and retribution wholly outweighs any considerations of reform or rehabilitation of the perpetrator." Serious as this defendant's crime was, I believe it is irrational to conclude that every similar offender is wholly incorrigible.

FOR DISCUSSION

Is the Court justified in distinguishing the proportionality of death penalty legislation from the proportionality of other penalties? Do the opinions of the lead justices in this case seem specifically tailored to the issue, or do you think they are reflections of the writers' larger judicial philosophies? Considering what you know of federalism, what are the advantages and disadvantages of allowing states to have leeway in this area? If you had been the Michigan governor, do you think you would have issued a pardon to Harmelin? Explain. What do you think would be comparative advantages and disadvantages of allowing such matters to be settled through executive discretion rather than through judicial discretion?

RELATED CASES

***Ewing v. California:* 538 U.S. 11 (2003).**

Upheld a California "three strikes and you're out" law that permitted a judge to decide whether some crimes, designated as "wobblers," would be considered to be misdemeanors or felonies.

***Lockyer v. Andrade:* 538 U.S. 63 (2003).**

Rejected a federal habeas corpus appeal of the "three strikes and you're out" law on the basis that the law was not contrary to clearly established law.

***Gall v. United States:* 552 U.S. 38 (2007).**

The Court ruled that appellate courts should give deference to trial court judges who have decided to depart from Federal Sentencing Guidelines for drug offenses. Here a judge had ordered probation, rather than jail time, for Brian Gall, who had conquered a drug habit and withdrawn from an Ecstasy drug ring that, when Gall was a student at the University of Iowa, had distributed 2,500 grams of the controlled substance.

***Kimbrough v. United States:* 552 U.S. 85 (2007).**

The Court again decided that appellate courts should defer to a district judge—in this case, one who had departed from Federal Sentencing Guidelines relative to drug offenses. The judge had modified recommendations that were resulting in sentences 100 times greater for individuals who owned crack than for those dealing in powdered cocaine. Critics had argued that this law was resulting in disproportionate penalties for those, often disadvantaged African Americans, whose convictions entailed the latter. Neither *Gall* nor *Kimbrough* was specifically based on the Eighth Amendment.

***Greenlaw v. United States:* 544 U.S. 237 (2008).**

The Supreme Court ruled that absent a governmental appeal or cross appeal, a federal appeals court lacked authority to substitute a fifty-two-year sentence for the thirty-seven-year sentence that had been imposed by a U.S. district court.

GLOSSARY

Aggravating, Extenuating, and Mitigating Factors: The Supreme Court has ruled that juries must take these into account when arriving at sentencing verdicts in death penalty cases.

Bail: A refundable payment that defendants are required to post in order to assure that they will return to court for trial. The Eighth Amendment prohibits bail from being "excessive." "excessive

Bifurcated: Divided into two parts. The Supreme Court has ruled that the guilt and sentencing phases of capital punishment cases are to be so separated.

Bills of Attainder: Legislative punishments without benefit of a trial, forbidden by Article I, Sections 8 and 9, of the Constitution.

Capital Punishment: Imposition of the death penalty.

Corruption of Blood: The principle, once used in England, that prohibited individuals attainted of (i.e., "corrupted by") some crimes from inheriting or passing on property. Article III outlaws corruption of blood as a punishment for treason.

Cruel and Unusual Punishments: Prohibited by the Eighth Amendment.

Deterrence: The stated goal of using punishment, especially capital punishment, as a way of discouraging others from committing crimes.

Ex Post Facto Law: Makes a previously legal action a crime and punishes a person for it; such legislation is banned under Article I, Section 9, which is now understood to outlaw the imposition of a penalty more severe than the law had assessed when a given crime was committed.

Incapacitated: Punishments designed to keep criminals "off the streets," so they do not pose threats to others, are said to render the offenders incapacitated.

***Per Curiam* Opinion:** An unsigned opinion, generally quite short, announcing the Court's opinion on behalf of a group of justices.

Proportionality: Essentially, the concept that the punishment should fit the crime. Justices debate the degree to which the cruel and unusual punishment provision in the Eighth Amendment includes a requirement for proportionality.

Recidivists: Repeat criminal offenders.

Rehabilitation: The attempt to bring about positive behaviors, sometimes through punishments.

Retribution: The goal of the use of punishment to recompense for an offender's crimes. Opponents of retribution think it is too closely tied to earlier ideas of personal vengeance.

"Three Strikes and You're Out" Laws: Laws that impose more several penalties on recidivists than on persons convicted of a first or second offense.

SELECTED BIBLIOGRAPHY

Banner, Stuart. 2002. *The Death Penalty: An American History*. Cambridge, MA: Harvard University Press.

Bedau, Hugo, ed. 1997. *The Death Penalty in America: Current Controversies*. New York: Oxford University Press.

Berns, Walter. 1979. *For Capital Punishment: Crime and the Morality of the Death Penalty*. New York: Basic Books.

Bessler, John D. 2013. *Cruel and Unusual: The American Death Penalty and the Founders' Eighth Amendment*. Lebanon, NH: Northeastern.

Hood, Roger. 1996. *The Death Penalty: A World-wide Perspective*, 2nd ed. Oxford: Clarendon Press.

Megivern, James J. 1997. *The Death Penalty: An Historical and Theological Survey*. New York: Paulist Press.

Melsner, Michael. 1974. *Cruel and Unusual: The Supreme Court and Capital Punishment*. New York: William Morrow.

Steiker, Carol S. and Jordan M. Steiker. 2016. *Courting Death: The Supreme Court and Capital Punishment*. Belknap Press: Cambridge, MA.

Vandiver, Margaret. 2006. *Lethal Punishment: Lynchings and Legal Executions in the South*. New Brunswick, NJ: Rutgers University Press.

Zimring, Franklin E. 2003. *The Contradictions of American Capital Punishment*. New York: Oxford University Press.

CHAPTER VII

Criminal Due Process

Timeline: Criminal Due Process

1789 Congress proposes the Bill of Rights.

1791 The states ratify the Bill of Rights.

1886 In *Boyd v. United States* the Supreme Court links interpretation of the Fourth and Fifth Amendments.

1908 *Twining v. New Jersey* determines that the Fourteenth Amendment does not require states to provide the Fifth Amendment guarantee against self-incrimination in criminal trials.

1914 In its ruling in *Weeks v. United States* the Supreme Court forbids the federal government from using evidence obtained in violation of the Fourth Amendment against the criminally accused.

1949 *Wolf v. Colorado*, however, allows states to determine whether they will or will not use illegally obtained evidence in criminal prosecutions.

1953 Newly inaugurated president Dwight D. Eisenhower nominates Earl Warren as chief justice of the United States.

1960 The Supreme Court in *Elkins v. United States* closes the "silver platter" loophole that had allowed federal officials to give to state officials, for use in criminal prosecutions, evidence obtained in violation of the Fourth Amendment. John F. Kennedy is elected president.

1961 *Mapp v. Ohio,* overturning *Wolf v. Colorado*, prohibits states from using illegal evidence in criminal prosecutions. Exclusionary rule applies to the states, as well as to the federal government.

1963 President Kennedy is assassinated; Vice President Lyndon B. Johnson becomes president. Court's ruling in *Gideon v. Wainwright* requires that states provide counsel for indigent defendants in criminal trials.

1964 *Escobedo v. Illinois* determines that a confession obtained while a suspect was denied access to his attorney cannot be used against him or her.

1966 *Miranda v. Arizona* rules that suspects questioned while in police custody must be clearly informed of their constitutional rights.

1966 *Schmerber v. California* narrows the protection provided by the self-incrimination guarantees of the Due Process Clause.

1967 In *Katz v. United States* the Court rules that the expectation of privacy might determine the need for the warrant, as opposed to the location of the search, thereby restricting the use of warrantless wiretapping.

1967 In *Warden v. Hayden* the Court rules that in a warrantless search, there is no constitutional distinction between the discovery of items of evidence and contraband items.

1967 Widespread urban uprisings occur across America.

1968 The Supreme Court finds in *Terry v. Ohio* that a brief investigatory stop and a warrantless external pat-down based on an articulable suspicion does not violate the Fourth Amendment rights of the person so treated.

1968 President Johnson signs into law the Omnibus Crime Control and Safe Streets Act of 1968, a major piece of legislation that sought to address the rise of crime and rioting occurring across the country.

1968 The Kerner Commission, established by President Johnson and officially known as the National Advisory Commission on Civil Disorders, issues its report on the causes of the 1967 race uprisings in the United States.

1969 Richard M. Nixon is inaugurated as president; he soon appoints Warren Burger as the chief justice of the United States.

1969 In *Chimel v. California* the Court rules that arresting officers may perform a warrantless search in the immediate area of the accused.

1971 President Nixon declares the war on drugs when he proclaims that "America's public enemy number one in the United States is drug abuse."

1972 Watergate scandal begins.

1974 Nixon is impeached and resigns as president; Vice President Gerald Ford becomes president.

1977 According to *Pennsylvania v. Mimms,* if a traffic stop turns into a criminal stop, officers may ask the driver to step outside the car.

1980 In *United States v. Mendenhall* the Court finds that when a suspect is free to leave an officer's presence, any consent to search provided has not been coerced.

1980 Ronald Reagan is elected president.

1983 *Illinois v. Gates* creates the totality-of-circumstances test for determining probable cause.

1984 In *United States v. Leon* the Court recognizes a good faith exception for police enforcement of a search warrant. *New York v. Quarles* discovers a public safety exception to the *Miranda* requirement.

1986 Associate Justice William Rehnquist is appointed chief justice by President Reagan.

1987 First Lady Nancy Reagan launches the "Just so no" to drugs campaign.

1988 George H. W. Bush is elected president.

1990 In *New York v. Harris* the Court rules that a Mirandized police station confession obtained after an illegal arrest does not violate the detainee's constitutional rights.

1991 In *Florida v. Bostick* the Court determines that a search is consensual when a suspect feels free to walk away, but instead stays and allows a search.

1992 Bill Clinton is elected president.

1993 Congress passes the Handgun Violence Prevention Act (also known as the Brady Bill), which requires a five-day waiting period before the purchase of a handgun.

1994 Violent Crime Control and Law Enforcement Act, signed by President Clinton, increases funding for crime prevention and the hiring of new officers.

1995 Oklahoma City Federal Building bombing; there are 168 deaths.

1996 In *Whren v. United States* the Court rules that officers can search a vehicle stopped for a traffic violation even if the stop was pretextual for a criminal investigation. The Antiterrorism and Effective Penalty Act, passed in response to the Oklahoma City bombing, alters habeas corpus requirements, provides mandatory victim restitution and protections, and makes provisions for the prosecution of persons accused of terrorism.

1999 Columbine School shooting in Littleton, Colorado.

2001 In *Kyllo v. U.S.* the Court determines that a search can be invalid even if the petitioner's property is not physically invaded.

2001 The ruling in *Atwater v. City of Lago Vista* allows a warrantless arrest for minor offenses, even if punishable only by a fine.

2001 In the wake of the September 11 attacks on the United States, Congress passes the U.S. Patriot Act.

2006 In *Georgia v. Randolph* the Court rules that a spouse may not permit a search of a residence over the objections of his or her husband or wife.

2009 The Supreme Court in *Safford United School District v. Redding* found a public middle school student's Fourth Amendment rights were violated when she was stripped to her underwear to find ibuprofen.

2012 In *United States v. Jones* the Court found that the warrantless installation of a GPS tracking device on a vehicle violates the Fourth Amendment's protection against unlawful searches.

2014 The Supreme Court in *Heien v. North Carolina* determined that a legitimate mistake by a police officer in making a traffic stop can provide reasonable suspicion for a search.

INTRODUCTION

Congress proposed and the states ratified the Fourth, Fifth, and Sixth Amendments to the Constitution as part of the Bill of Rights. These amendments, which initially applied only to the national government but now also apply to the states (see Chapter I), protect the rights of individuals accused of, or on trial for, a crime. Since anyone can be so accused, these rights protect everyone. Governments seek to protect their citizens in part by preventing and punishing crime. As important as this is, it is also important to see that the innocent are not caught in the same net as the guilty. The Supreme Court must often adjudicate cases that involve potential conflicts between personal security and individual rights. The Supreme Court builds new decisions on past precedents often linking rulings on these amendments to other rulings dealing with the right to privacy

These criminal due process clauses contain not only **procedural protections** from abuses by the government—the right to due process, certain types of guarantees at trial, recognitions on the limitations on the power of the government to punish those convicted, and limits to governmental searches—but also have been interpreted by the Supreme Court to provide **substantive protections**. Substantive protections, unlike procedural protections, are not clearly articulated within the amendments; rather, they are rights that the Court believes are necessary to protect and ensure fair treatment to individuals. Consider the prohibition against police brutality discussed later in this chapter as a key substantive right that requires federal enforcement.

The Fourth Amendment

The Fourth Amendment of the Constitution consists of two clauses. The first prohibits unreasonable searches and seizures, and the second provides procedures for search warrants. Jurists and scholars continue to argue about the relationship between the two clauses. Historians know that the Framers were particularly concerned about general warrants, and writs of assistance. These orders, which were issued by British and colonial authorities, did not identify specific persons or places to be searched or items to be seized. The Supreme Court generally requires such a specific warrant, with the accompanying requirements of probable cause, before it will accept the results of a government search. During Chief Justice Earl Warren's tenure (1953–1969), the Court significantly expanded the protections of the Fourth Amendment; but, subsequent courts have recognized an increased number of exceptions as constitutionally reasonable.

The Fifth Amendment

The Fifth Amendment contains numerous guarantees for individuals accused of crime. These include the requirement of indictment by grand juries, the prohibition of procedures that would result in double jeopardy, the prohibition against self-incrimination, and the Takings Clause (prohibiting the taking of property for public use without just compensation), which was discussed extensively in the first volume of this work. One of the Fifth Amendment's most important guarantee for persons accused of crimes prohibits the federal government from depriving individuals of life, liberty, or property without due process of law; the Fourteenth Amendment provides the same guarantee to the citizens of the states. While, as with the Fourth Amendment, the meaning of the guarantee of due process has evolved over time, jurists and scholars generally interpret it to require fundamental fairness. The section of the chapter devoted to the Fourth Amendment will demonstrate not only that our understanding of what constitutes "fairness" changes, but so does the role the Court plays in defining the notion of fairness. Central to the Fifth Amendment are such issues as protection against self-incrimination and the necessity of informing persons accused of a crime, once in custody, of their constitutional rights.

Sixth Amendment

The notion of criminal due process also includes the provisions of the Sixth Amendment, which determine the limits of governmental power during the trial of an individual accused of a crime. Initially limited to the federal government and selectively applied to the states over time, the Sixth Amendment guarantees the following procedural rights: to be notified of the charges against the accused, to have a speedy and public trial, to confront all witnesses, to have access to an attorney, and to be tried before a local impartial jury. This section of the chapter will particularly focus on access to representation for the poor and the impact of racial and gender discrimination on our understanding of what constitutes a jury of peers.

FOURTH AMENDMENT: SEARCH AND SEIZURE

***U.S. Constitution*, Fourth Amendment:**

The right of the people to be secure in their persons, houses, papers, and effects, against unreasonable searches and seizures, shall not be violated, and no Warrants shall issue, but upon probable cause, supported by Oath or affirmation, and particularly describing the place to be searched, and the persons or things to be seized.

The Framers designed the Fourth Amendment of the Constitution, like the First Amendment, to protect the people from abuses by the federal government. Relying on the observations of the protections provided to citizens by the English **Magna Carta** and on the history of the abuses of the British government against its own citizens and against the colonists, the Founders framed the Fourth Amendment to prohibit unlimited blanket searches of property and seizure of evidence. It was not until the case of *Boyd v. United States* (116 U.S. 616, 1886) that the meaning and implications of the amendment began to be explicitly framed. In that case, the Court held that the compulsory production of papers for a customs investigation actually implicated both the Fourth Amendment's search and seizure provision and the Self-Incrimination Clause of the Fifth Amendment. One of the most litigated areas in constitutional law comprises the determination of when a **warrant** is necessary for a search to be legitimate and when evidence deriving from an illegal search can be admitted in criminal proceedings, for it is here that key provisions of the Fourth Amendment are ambiguous.

For the Supreme Court, the key question has been how to protect the individual from potential abuses by the state while simultaneously protecting the larger citizenry from those who would endanger the community. Over the last 125 years, the Court has explicated the meaning of the warrant requirement and the appropriate exceptions that need to be allowed—may police engage in a warrantless search when there is immediate danger to themselves or the public? the possibility of danger? the potential disposal of evidence?

The Exclusionary Rule

An equally important question has centered on the enforceability of the Fourth Amendment. Specifically, when the police illegally obtain evidence demonstrating guilt, may the government use it in prosecuting the citizen who has been accused? Through the judicially developed doctrine of the **exclusionary rule**, the Court created tests for determining when problematic evidence may be used in court and when it must excluded. As new technology emerges and law enforcement moves from a physical search of a contained physical space to the digital search of sound, heat, and words—the Court's application of the Fourth Amendment continues to evolve.

In 1914 the Supreme Court, in *Weeks v. United States* (232 U.S. 383), prohibited the federal government from using in its criminal prosecutions evidence obtained through violation of the Fourth Amendment. However, in *Wolf v. Colorado* (338 U.S. 25, 1949), the Supreme Court applied provisions of the Fourth Amendment to the states via the Due Process Clause of the Fourteenth Amendment without applying the corresponding exclusionary rule to enforce it. Although the federal government could not use similar material in its criminal prosecutions until 1960, following the decision in *Elkins v. United States* (364 U.S. 206), it could hand over to the states evidence that could not be used in federal prosecutions for use in state judicial actions. This so-called **silver platter doctrine** provided federal law enforcement officers a means of avoiding the constraints of the *Weeks* ruling. The Supreme Court closed this loophole in the *Elkins* decision.

One year later, in the case of *Mapp v. Ohio* (367 U.S. 643, 1961), the Supreme Court extended the *Weeks* rule of exclusion of evidence secured by unreasonable search and seizure to state courts. This decision came only after years of inconclusiveness illustrated in *Wolf v. Colorado*. *Mapp* also represents a further extension of the "*Gitlow* doctrine"—referencing the 1925 decision of *Gitlow v. New York* (268 U.S. 652)—but, this time applying the Fourth Amendment to the states through the "liberty" and "due process" provisions of the Fourteenth Amendment via selective incorporation. (For more information on this topic see the discussion in Chapter I of the concepts of incorporation and interpretation of the Bill of Rights.) While the facts of *Mapp* focused on the constitutionality of the Ohio obscenity law under which the appellant Dollree Mapp was convicted, many of the *amicus curiae* ("friend of the court") briefs filed with the Supreme Court focused on the exclusionary rule question that the Court ended up addressing. The Supreme Court also decided that while the questions brought on appeal focused on the state of Ohio's obscenity statutes, a majority believed that this case was the ideal vehicle to overturn *Wolf v. Colorado*.

Evidentiary Requirements and Exceptions

After the decisions of *Mapp* and *Elkins* made it clear that the Supreme Court would be enforcing the exclusionary clause and closing the previous exceptions, the need increased for law enforcement officers to have a clearer understanding of the elements of a legitimate search and seizure. A series of cases followed that raised these questions. In *Warden v. Hayden* (387 U.S. 294, 1967), a warrantless—yet legitimate—search of a home for an armed robber whose victims had followed him revealed weapons, ammunition, and clothing that the robber had been described as wearing. The Court had to determine whether the Fourth Amendment provided a different constitutional standard for objects significant only in evidentiary value than for contraband items that can always be legitimately seized—"instrumentalities and means by which a crime is committed, the fruits of crime such as stolen property, weapons by which escape of the person arrested might be affected, and property the possession of which is a crime." The Court, in this case, found nothing in the Fourth Amendment to distinguish between the two. In his majority opinion, Justice Brennan, argues that the primary goal of the Fourth Amendment is to protect privacy and not property, and there is no difference in the violation of privacy whether police seize evidence of crime, fruits of crime, instrumentalities of criminal action, or contraband.

As in the constitutional arena of speech, press, privacy, and expression, the Fourth Amendment provides a lesser protection for minors than it does for adults. The Court has ruled consistently since the case of *Tinker v. Des Moines Independent Community School District* (393 U.S. 503, 1969) that the requirements of the school environment can place a limit on the freedom of students but that minors, especially those attending public schools, still have clearly protected constitutional rights. The concerns for the learning environment and legitimate school interests must be balanced with the liberty rights of students. In *New Jersey v. T.L.O.* (468 U.S. 1214, 1984), the Court considered a case of a student who was stopped on suspicion of smoking, which was against school policies. The student denied the charge, but during questioning by a principal and a cursory search of her purse, cigarettes and rolling papers were discovered. A more thorough search revealed marijuana, a pipe, and items believed to comprise evidence of drug dealing; at this juncture the student's mother was called and the student was turned over to the police. In determining the constitutionality of the search, the Supreme Court reduced the standard used for a constitutional search on school property from one of "probable cause" to the less strict Fourth Amendment requirement of "reasonableness."

In 2009 the Supreme Court had the opportunity to revisit the *T.L.O.* precedent in *Safford v. Redding* (557 U.S. 364, 2009), when a thirteen-year-old girl suspected of possessing prescription-strength ibuprofen and over-the-counter naproxen pills was questioned, asked to strip down to her underwear and then demonstrate that she had secreted nothing in her underwear. The Court characterized this as a "strip search" and was then obliged to determine if the *T.L.O.* precedent still stood and if so, whether the "reasonableness" standard had been met. In the years since President Nixon declared a War on Drugs, many rights of minors—such as the right to privacy and the right to expression—have been lessened. Consider for instance, the allowance of suspicionless drug tests of public school athletes (*Vernonia School District 47J v. Acton*, 515 U.S. 646, 1995) and its extension to all public school students engaging in extracurricular activities (*Board of Education v. Earls,* 536 U.S. 822, 2002), or the justification of the suspension of a student who, excused from school to view the Olympic Torch run, held up a banner saying "Bong Hits 4 Jesus" (*Morse v. Frederick,* 551 U.S. 393, 2007). Many Court watchers remain alert as to whether the War on Drugs will continue to narrow the rights of minors.

Electronic Surveillance

In 1967, the year of the *Warden v. Hayden ruling,* the Court heard a case in which a man had been convicted based in part on a conversation that the Federal Bureau of Investigation (FBI) had recorded (*Katz v. United States,* 389 U.S. 347). Katz had used the telephone in a public booth to make calls that entailed his transmission of wagering information. The Court determined that although the eavesdropping and recording devices had been attached outside the booth, the evidence obtained thereby could not be used because the FBI had failed to get a warrant for the recording of conversations. In *Olmstead v. United States* (277 U.S. 438, 1928), Chief Justice William Howard Taft, who did not think that conversations could be seized under the "persons, papers, or effects" language of the Fourth Amendment, had allowed for warrantless wiretaps that did not require a physical trespass or the use of force. By contrast, in *Olmstead* the Court decided to give the words of the Fourth Amendment a broader meaning that focused less on the protection of specific places than on individual privacy. What an individual seeks to keep private, even in a publicly accessible space, may be constitutionally protected. Moreover, what a person consciously makes public—even in a private space—is not protected by the Fourth Amendment. Even though agents had not physically penetrated the booth, the Court found that Katz had an expectation of privacy and therefore the FBI needed a warrant to listen to or tape these conversations. The passage of the 2001 Patriot Act and its subsequent amendments, as well as other executive and legislative actions expanding the scope of law enforcement authority over citizens while investigating "terrorism," has extended the relevance of *Katz*. Its influence can still be seen in litigation surrounding the use of technology in law enforcement, such as in the governmental reliance on mass data collection and in the use of GPS trackers.

Technology continues to challenge the boundaries of the meanings of "search" and "seizure" under the Fourth Amendment. As law enforcement officers move beyond physical searches to virtual electronic searches, the courts are forced to redefine the nature of place, physicality, and privacy. This dilemma is exemplified in *Kyllo v. United States* (533 U.S. 27, 2001). Here the police had used thermal imaging to discover the use of heat lamps, which are typically relied upon to facilitate the indoor growth of plants like marijuana. When the intensity of heat emanating from Kyllo's home indicated the possible growth of marijuana, officers had used this evidence, along with other tips and utility bills, to get a warrant to physically search the house. The Court confronted the question of whether such a warrantless scan of a private home from outside the property constitutes a search of premises that would violate the resident's Fourth Amendment rights. The Court could imagine the other ways in which police officers could search private homes—listening, watching, photographing, or recording—all without physically invading the property. Is this technology, rapidly becoming available to everyone in the public domain, being used to create a search or merely to observe what is already in public view?

This question was initially addressed in 2012. The expansion of Global Positioning System (GPS) technology, which allows individuals to be tracked, frequently without their knowledge, has also had Fourth Amendment implications. In the case of the *United States v. Jones*, 565 U.S. 400 (2012), Antoine Jones was arrested for drug possession after he was followed by police for a month. Without a warrant, the District of Columbia police had attached a GPS device to Jones' jeep and followed his movements 24 hours a day for a month. The Supreme Court found that there was a reasonable expectation of privacy when an individual drove on public roads and that private property rights had been violated as well. This limit on technology means that police need a warrant supported by probable cause prior to obtaining this type of evidence.

Stop and Frisk

The case of *Terry v. Ohio* (392 U.S. 1, 1968) raised another question regarding the scope of authority for law enforcement officers. In this case, an officer in plain clothes observed two individuals engaging in repetitive and suspicious behavior, leading him to believe that they were planning an imminent robbery. The officer stopped the suspects, and after identifying himself and briefly questioning them, patted down their clothing, an activity that revealed two revolvers and bullets. This case resulted in Chief Justice Warren's majority defining the scope of a legitimate "*Terry* frisk." In trying to balance the right of innocent citizens not to be challenged by an abusive state against the legitimate crime control concerns of law enforcement officers, the Court created a new test for Fourth Amendment legitimacy. While the Court still recognized such a routine of stopping and frisking as a seizure and search, it ruled that an officer who has an articulable suspicion, which is supported by a discussion with suspects that heightens the officer's concern for personal and public safety, may conduct a limited search of the outer clothing of the subject in a search for weapons that could threaten the officer. Concerns have been raised that implicit bias and racial profiling by police officers result in a disproportionate number of Black and Latino males being subjected to such searches.

Searches Incident to Arrest

The Court continued to be concerned about the legitimacy of searches in the absence of a search warrant. While it may not be feasible to expect the state to provide a search warrant in every circumstance, the Court needed to construct standards so strict that officers could predict when evidence secured in a given manner would be deemed illegally obtained and thereby excluded from court proceedings under the Fourth Amendment. In *Chimel v. California* (395 U.S. 752, 1969), the Court confronted a case in which officers, in the course of administering an arrest warrant, searched the suspect's entire home over his objections and without a search warrant. The officers then used objects they had recovered in the search to obtain a conviction against Chimel in state court. The Supreme Court was asked to decide how much variance state actors have in searching a space pursuant to a lawful arrest in the absence of a search warrant. What type of search is allowable "incident to the arrest"? The *Chimel* decision reemphasizes the norm of "advanced judicial approval of searches and seizures through the warrant procedure," recognizing the need to ensure officers' safety. To balance these two key principles, the Court found that in a legitimate "search incident to arrest" officers can search the person arrested to remove potential weapons or evidence. In addition, the area immediately under the individual's control prior to the arrest could be searched to prevent weapons or evidence from being concealed or destroyed. This ruling, however, clearly noted that an entire search of a room, let alone an entire house, would require a search warrant and its concomitant accountability.

The Vehicular Exception to the Warrant Requirement

Like other forms of new technology, the automobile added a new complication to search and seizure law. Like a house, a car represents assumed privacy and property ownership; yet a car is more public than a house, and the vehicle's mobility means that time spent seeking a warrant could result in the disappearance of the item of interest. In *Carroll v. United States* (267 U.S. 132, 1925), the Court carved out an automobile exception to the warrant requirement based on reasonable suspicion of criminal activity.

The case of *Pennsylvania v. Mimms* (434 U.S. 106, 1977), labored on the foregoing distinction. Police stopped Harry Mimms for driving with expired plates. When the two officers asked Mimms to step out of the car and surrender his registration and license, they observed a bulge in his jacket. A subsequent search revealed a revolver and ammunition; it was also discovered that Mimms's passenger was similarly armed. The Pennsylvania Supreme Court argued that while the stop was legitimate and the search based on the "bulge" was clear, Mimms could not legitimately be ordered out of the car, and therefore all actions following were excluded from consideration as constitutionally invalid. The Supreme Court of the United States did not share Pennsylvania's concern for the seizure of Mimms. As dissents by Justices Marshall, Stevens, and Brennan reveal, the decision arguably represents a shift from the Warren Court's concern for privacy and the Burger Court's greater emphasis on the officers' safety and its liberalization of the *Terry* test.

The Court has returned to the question of the constitutional rights inherent in a vehicle many times since *Pennsylvania v. Mimms* (1977). In the unanimously decided case of *Whren v. United States* (517 U.S. 806, 1996), the Court evaluated whether an officer may constitutionally detain a motorist if the officer has probable cause to believe the motorist has committed a traffic violation that is not punishable under criminal law. Within the context of the War on Drugs, the Court was considering the validity of the "pretextual stop," that is, a traffic stop of a vehicle the police have reason, but not probable cause, to believe is involved in criminal activity. Although the officer cannot detain the car on a "fishing expedition," police would often ask a driver to pull over for questioning about a civil violation hoping that during the course of the routine traffic stop, probable cause for criminal scrutiny could be obtained. The petitioners, in this case, thought the selective enforcement of traffic laws to engage in criminal investigation violated the Fourth Amendment's limitations on seizures. While the Court agreed that such traffic stops are seizures under the Fourth Amendment, determining whether a stop is pretextual was not a decision-making process in which the Court wanted to engage, preferring to trust the judgment of the officer.

Consent Searches

The automobile exception to the warrant requirement emerged out of attempts to prosecute individuals for alcohol possession, distribution, or consumption during national Prohibition (i.e., the years during which the Eighteenth Amendment was in effect). Similarly, the modern declaration of the War on Drugs and the growth of the policing power of such regulatory agencies as the Drug Enforcement Authority (DEA) has led to new questions and conflicts under the Fourth Amendment. More significantly, the governmental emphasis on the interdiction of drugs and the increased criminalization of personal drug use generated increased pressure to privilege the power of the state over the rights of the individual, in the name of societal good. The consequences of the conflict were revealed in the 1980 case of *United States v. Mendenhall* (446 U.S. 544). After disembarking from a cross-country flight, two DEA officers observed Sylvia Mendenhall acting consistently with a profile of the behavior of drug couriers. After having approached, questioned, and identified Mendenhall, and having examined her ticket, the officials were suspicious enough to escort her to an office where she consented to a preliminary search, leading to a full body search, which revealed drugs. This case forced the Court to address the question of what constitutes consent to a search and what are the necessary elements of a seizure. In this case, the Court uses a "reasonable person" test to gauge whether Mendenhall was free to leave the officers' custody: barring physical restraint, the suspect is free to leave; and if she was not seized, her consent to be searched must not be found to be coerced.

The Supreme Court returned to the attributes of consent to a warrantless search in 2006, when a case challenged the assertion that a wife could legitimately consent to a search of jointly shared property for drugs that her husband allegedly held. Again, this case demonstrates the impact of the War on Drugs on the interpretation of the Fourth Amendment. *Georgia v. Randolph* (547 U.S. 103, 2006) required the Supreme Court to decide what it means when the two occupants of a dwelling conflict over whether they are providing a consensual search. The justices did not find that the search was consensual because one of the occupants was present and denied consent to the search. Justice Souter, in writing the majority opinion, noted "in the balancing of competing individual and governmental interests entailed by the bar to unreasonable searches . . . the cooperative occupant's invitation adds nothing to the government's side to counter the force of an objecting individual's claim to security against the government's intrusion into his dwelling place." The police, however, had been called to this residence because of the wife's claim of domestic violence. The dissenters (Chief Justice Roberts and Justices Scalia and Thomas) claim that this decision will protect abusers and violent roommates, leaving their victims unshielded by the law. In many ways the facts of this case represent the tension articulated in the Fourth Amendment—the privacy rights of the accused and the security of the citizens and the state.

In general the Supreme Court has stated that warrants are presumptively required when search a private home or apartment, *Kyllo v. United States*, 533 U.S. 27 (2001). Moreover, warrants are also generally required to do searches and the Exclusionary Rule generally excludes illegally obtained evidence from being used in Court to convict someone of a crime. Yet, as noted above, the Court has also enunciated numerous exceptions to the Fourth Amendment's warrant requirement. The following table summarizes these exceptions.

Exceptions to the Fourth Amendment Warrant Requirements

Automobile searches	*Carroll v. United States,* 267 U.S. 132 (1925)
Risk of evidence being destroyed	*U.S. v. MacDonald*, 335 U.S.451 (1948)
Administrative inventory searches	*Camera v. Municipal Court*, 387 U.S. 523 (1967)
Hot pursuit	*Warden v. Hayden,* 387 U.S. 294 (1967)
Stop and frisk	*Terry v. Ohio,* 392 U.S. 1, 19 (1968)
Search incident to arrest	*Chimel v. California*, 395 U.S. 752 (1969)
Consent	*Schneckloth v Bustamonte*, 412 U.S. 218 (1972)
Border searches	*Almeida-Sanchez v. U.S.*, 413 U.S. 266 (1973)
Exigent circumstances	*United States v. Watson*, 423 U.S. 411 (1976)
Good Faith	*United States v. Leon,* 468 U.S. 897 (1984)
Public safety	*New York v. Quarles*, 467 U.S. 649 (1984)
Inevitable discovery	*Nix v. Williams,* 467 U.S. 431 (1984)
Plain view of police	*Arizona v. Hicks 480* U.S. 321 (1987)
Reasonable mistake for traffic stop	*Heien v. North Carolina*, 574 U.S. ___ (2014)

Ascertaining Probable Cause

As the political pressure on law enforcement officers to stop the drug trade increased, so did the pressure on judges and magistrates to be "tough on crime" and to provide assistance in the policing and prosecution of drug offenders. It was almost inevitable that a case would come before the Supreme Court in which claims for the validity of a search were based on the credibility of the probable cause supporting the warrant. In *Illinois v. Gates* (462 U.S. 213, 1983), the justices decided such a case. Based on an anonymous letter accusing a local couple of trafficking and selling drugs, police in Bloomingdale, Illinois, began an investigation of Sue and Lance Gates's travel itinerary. After verifying some of the details of the accusatory note, a judge found probable cause and awarded a search warrant of the Gates's automobile and home. Subsequent evidence discovered pursuant to the search resulted in a conviction, which in turn generated an appeal. In this decision, the Court retreats from a series of specific tests outlined in prior cases to define legitimate probable cause and crafted a broader "totality-of-circumstances" test. In so doing, the Burger Court continued tilting the balance of the Fourth Amendment in favor of state powers to enforce laws.

Exceptions to the Exclusionary Rule

Accompanying the War on Drugs, the constraints of the **exclusionary rule** came under enhanced scrutiny, not only by the courts but also by the political system. Designed by the Court in cases like *Weeks v. United States* and *Mapp v. Ohio*, the exclusionary rule states that illegally obtained evidence cannot be used in a criminal trial. Judges reason that if the tree (the search) is poisonous, then the fruit of the poisonous tree (the evidence obtained by the illegal search) is also poisonous, hence illegal.

What happens when police officers have acted in good faith with what they assumed was a valid warrant to obtain evidence necessary for prosecution, but later the warrant is found to be invalid for lack of probable cause? In *United States v. Leon* (468 U.S. 897, 1984), the Supreme Court considered another case involving "a confidential informant of unproven reliability," suspected drug dealers, and a problematic search warrant. After arguing that the primary purpose of the exclusionary rule is to minimize unconstitutional police conduct, the justices decided to make a good faith exception for the police. If the fault is with the magistrate, the Court asks, why punish the constable and, with that officer, society?

This case was decided with the companion case of *Massachusetts v. Sheppard* (468 U.S. 981, 1984), which also legitimized "good faith" exception to the exclusionary rule. The Supreme Court used the good faith exception to continue the identification of exceptions to the application of the exclusionary rule, tilting the balance even further toward the state's crime control functions over the individual's right of privacy. Such exceptions included the inevitable discovery of evidence (*Nix v. Williams*, 467 U. S. 431, 1984), the creation of anticipatory search warrants when there is probable cause that a criminal action is imminent (*U.S. v. Grubbs*, 547 U.S. 90, 2006), and the expansion of the good faith exception to police reliance on erroneous records of outstanding arrest warrants (*Arizona v. Evans*, 514 U.S. 1, 1995).

The expansion of the police powers continued into the Rehnquist Court (1986–2005). While the Court held the line on the need for warrants and the significance of the Fourth Amendment law, it continued to weaken the exclusionary rule. In *New York v. Harris* (495 U.S. 14, 1990), the police went to Harris's home, without an arrest warrant, to take him into custody for the murder of Thelma Stanton. Harris opened the door and let the officers enter, whereupon they read Harris his ***Miranda* rights**, which explains the constitutional rights of a person accused in our legal system. Harris acknowledged his understanding of these rights, the police questioned him, and he confessed to the murder. After these events, Harris was taken to the police station, where he was Mirandized again, and he then provided a written confession. The lower court excluded his first confession because the absence of probable cause made his arrest illegal, and the Supreme Court agreed. The Court, however, found no constitutional grounds to exclude the police station confession subsequent to the illegal arrest. Over the next fifteen years, the Court continued to expand the state's ability to arrest individuals with a warrant by weakening the traditional "knock and announce" rule (see, e.g., *Wilson v. Arkansas*, 520 U.S. 385, 1997; *U.S. v. Ramirez*, 523 U.S. 65, 1998; *Hudson v. Michigan*, 547 U. S. 586, 2006).

The need to clarify the concept of uncoerced consent continued to haunt the Court throughout the Rehnquist Court years. In another drug trafficking case, *Florida v. Bostick* (501 U.S. 429, 1991), police searched the luggage of a passenger on an interstate bus and discovered a significant amount of cocaine. the bus was stopped far from the final destination and two armed officers, with no articulable suspicion, asked for Bostick's ticket and identification, noted that they were narcotics agents, and asked to search Bostick's luggage. In this case, which might also apply to other forms of public transportation in which individuals are far from home and in enclosed spaces with limited exits, like planes and trains, the Court ruled that Bostick had granted permission.

By 2002, in *U.S. v. Drayton* (536 U.S. 194), the Court no longer required bus passengers to be informed of their right to refuse consent. Both the majority and dissenting opinions clearly indicate the impact of the War on Drugs on individual expectations of privacy and Fourth Amendment interpretation alike. As expectations of privacy lessen, does the power of the state expand in search and seizure litigation? While the Court appeared to accept the relationship between these two concepts in *Minnesota v. Dickerson* (508 U.S. 366, 1993), allowing police to seize contraband they discovered through "plain feel," the Court challenged this notion in 2000. In *Bond v. U.S.* (529 U.S. 334, 2000), the Court recognized an expectation of privacy in luggage transported on a passenger bus, thus limiting the ability of officers to engage in exploratory search, but a post-9/11 Court might render a different decision.

While the interpretation of the Fourth Amendment has evolved over time, initially enforced by the Warren Court, political and technological pressures have affected the nature of the questions facing the Supreme Court. The value of the importance of balancing the individual rights to be secure in one's home and to be protected from an unwarranted intrusion of the state into individual privacy against the government's clear interest in crime control and society's security remains. The exclusionary rule is still the primary means of enforcing the constitutional provisions of the Fourth Amendment. On the one hand, with the changing governmental priorities of the War on Drugs and the War on Terror, the exceptions by which law enforcement officers have through which to escape the limitations of constitutional constraints have expanded. Technology has also resulted in additional governmental flexibility. On the other hand, the Supreme Court under the leadership of Chief Justice John Roberts (2005–) has expanded the circumstances in which a warrant is needed before a search or seizure.

Racial Profiling

One criticism directed against law enforcement officers and agencies is that people of color are more often targeted for stops, searches, seizures, and arrests than are Caucasians. The use of race in law enforcement raises difficult questions, among the most important are is race ever a legitimate factor to consider in policing? For some, race—in terms of identifying a suspect—may be important in help solve a crime, especially if victims identify suspects based in part on their race. But what if race is used more generically, whether intentionally or unintentionally, in law enforcement? What if one can show that police are more likely to stop people, such as drivers, of a specific race? Or what if race is used as a factor in police use of force, or in making predictions regarding who is likely to commit a crime? These are questions that raise equal protection issues, and well as those regarding police civil liability for discrimination. Chapter XI on State Action examines some of the constitutional issues regarding allegations of police use of excessive force. But here, the question is about what some label as **racial profiling.**

The issue of racial profiling first came to attention in the 1970s and 1980s as law enforcement agencies mobilized to interdict illegal drug distribution. The Drug Enforcement Agency (DEA) crafted a drug courier profile that included racial characteristics of suspected individuals who might be carrying drugs on their persons or in their vehicles. Using Supreme Court precedents such as *Terry v. Ohio* and *United States v. Whren,* law enforcement officials were encouraged to use stop and frisk and routine traffic violations as opportunities to stop and search individuals and vehicles for drugs. These are called **pretextual stops.** But evidence soon surfaced that the DEA program Operation Pipeline in Florida was targeting people of color. Then in New Jersey evidence surfaced of state troopers targeting people of color, and in other states such as Maryland studies emerged that police were more likely to stop, detain for long periods, and search people of color, especially African-Americans, than Caucasians. Some called this "driving while black." Similar pressures were placed on individuals of obvious Hispanic or Latino descent and this was dubbed "driving while brown."

Numerous studies have been undertaken since the 1990s documenting racial disparities in law enforcement. Critics contend this is unlawful discrimination. In response, others argue that race can be a legitimate factor to consider in policing and the fact that in many cases stops and searches turn up evidence of crimes, such as illegal possession of drugs or weapons, demonstrates that such profiling may simply be good policing and that the law should allow police to act on their instincts derived from their experiences in law enforcement. In response, critics argue that allowing police to act on these hunches simply reinforces racial biases.

The issue of racial profiling took on a new meaning after the terrorist attacks on September 11, 2001, where there were demands to subject Muslims or those of Arab or Middle Eastern descent to special examination. Those calls were again renewed by Donald Trump during the 2016 presidential race where he called for either a ban on Muslims entering the United States or the creation of a special registry for those who are Muslim. These issues raise Equal Protection issues beyond the scope of this chapter. Yet here the book presents *Brown v. City of Oneonta, New York*, 221 F.3d 329 (2nd. Cir. 1999). In this case a Court of Appeals rejected claims that stopping and questioning all African-American males at a college as part of a criminal assault investigation was an unconstitutional use of race.

WOLF V. COLORADO

338 U.S. 25, 69 S.Ct. 1359, 93 L.Ed. 1782 (1949)

Weeks v. United States (232 U.S. 383, 1914) prohibited the federal government from using in prosecutions evidence obtained through searches and seizures that were illegal according to the Fourth Amendment. This judicial prohibition is known as the exclusionary rule. *Wolf v. Colorado* is the combination of several cases in which the Supreme Court of Colorado upheld state convictions based on evidence admitted at trial that had been obtained unconstitutionally according to federal law. While the Supreme Court determined in *Weeks* that the Fifth Amendment requires the federal government to secure the search and seizure requirements of the Fourth Amendment, it was necessary here to decide whether the Fourteenth Amendment made the same requirement on the state governments.

Vote: 6–3

JUSTICE FRANKFURTER delivered the opinion of the Court.

[This case is presented in Chapter I: Incorporation and the Interpretation of the Bill of Rights.]

FOR DISCUSSION

Why might the Court decide to extend the requirements of the Fourteenth Amendment to the states? Is a uniform policy among the states necessary to fulfill the guarantees of the Fourth Amendment? Why or why not?

RELATED CASES

***Rochin v. California:* 342 U.S. 165 (1952).**

The conduct of officers in securing evidence from an accused person may in and of itself deny due process even though the evidence had been admitted to the court record under the *Wolf v. Colorado* rule.

***Irvine v. California:* 347 U.S. 128 (1954).**

Evidence secured by officers by "trespass and probably a burglary" may be entered in a prosecution in a state court for a state offense.

***Breithaupt v. Abram:* 352 U.S. 432 (1957).**

The taking of a blood sample by a technician while the accused was unconscious following an accident and the use of the results of a subsequent blood test later in a prosecution for involuntary manslaughter did not deprive the accused of due process of law.

***Elkins v. United States:* 364 U.S. 206 (1960).**

Ended the "silver platter" doctrine, which allowed federal officials to give illegally obtained evidence to states for prosecution.

***Missouri v. McNeely:* 569 U.S. 141 (2013).**

When investigating drunk driving, the time limitations of blood alcohol tests are not enough of an emergency to take blood without a warrant.

MAPP V. OHIO

367 U.S. 643, 81 S.Ct. 1684, 6 L.Ed.2d 1081 (1961)

On May 23, 1957, three Cleveland police officers went to Dollree Mapp's home because they had information that a person involved in a recent bombing was hiding there. The police knocked and demanded entry; Mapp, after a phone call to her attorney, refused to admit the officers. Returning three hours later with police reinforcements, the officers forcibly entered Mapp's home. Her lawyer arrived and was denied access to the house. When Mapp asked to see the warrant, a paper was held up; she grabbed it and placed it down her shirt. The police then recovered the page, which was blank, and handcuffed Mapp. The search, which extended to Mapp's daughter's room and the home's basement and attic, included photo albums and personal papers. From a trunk in the basement, the police recovered items that were deemed obscene under Ohio law and for which Mapp was brought to trial. At the trial, no search warrant was presented, nor was the absence of such a document explained. The state convicted Mapp for possession of obscene material, and although the Ohio Supreme Court questioned the methods used by the police, the state court upheld the conviction because the police had not taken evidence from Mapp's person "by the use of brutal or offensive physical force against the defendant."

Vote: 6–3

JUSTICE CLARK delivered the opinion of the Court.

This case is presented in Chapter I: Incorporation and the Interpretation of the Bill of Rights.

FOR DISCUSSION

Under what circumstances should the Supreme Court overturn precedents? Do those circumstances reveal themselves in this case? How?

RELATED CASES

***Stanford v. Texas:* 379 U.S. 476 (1965).**

Under a warrant for the search of a home for books, pamphlets, and other written instruments concerning the Communist Party of Texas, two thousand items were seized. The Court held that the writ in question was the very type of warrant the Fourth Amendment was designed to forbid; instead, the ruling stated, the Fourth Amendment requires precision in describing the place to be searched, and the person or things to be seized.

***Linkletter v. Walker:* 381 U.S. 618 (1965).**

The Court held that to make the rule of *Mapp v. Ohio* retroactive would tax the administration of justice to the utmost. The Constitution neither prohibits nor requires that retroactive effect be given to a new rule.

***Lewis v. United States:* 385 U.S. 206 (1966).**

When a home is converted into a commercial center to which outsiders are invited for purposes of transacting unlawful business, that business is entitled to no greater sanctity than it would enjoy if it were carried on in a store or other public place.

WARDEN, MARYLAND PENITENTIARY V. HAYDEN

387 U.S. 294, 87 S.Ct. 1642, 18 L.Ed.2d 782 (1967)

On the morning of March 17, 1962, an armed robber held up the Baltimore Diamond Cab Company for $363. Two cab drivers followed a suspect to a residential address and then called the police with a description of the alleged robber and his location. When the police arrived, the homeowner, Mrs. Hayden, did not object to a search of her home for the suspect. Mr. Hayden, who matched the taxi drivers' description, was found in a bedroom "feigning sleep." After a search in which no other man was found, Hayden was arrested. Subsequent searching revealed a shotgun and a pistol in a toilet tank, ammunition for the guns in the bedroom, clothing and a cap—meeting the description of that worn by the person described by the drivers—in the washing machine. A Maryland court convicted Hayden of armed robbery based on this evidence. A district court of appeals reversed, upholding the validity of the search based on *Harris v. U.S.* (331 U.S. 145. 1947), but finding that the seized clothing could not be used because, unlike the guns and ammunition, it had evidentiary value only and therefore could not be lawfully seized without a warrant.

Vote: 6–3

JUSTICE BRENNAN delivered the opinion of the Court.

We review in this case the validity of the proposition that there is under the Fourth Amendment a "distinction between merely evidentiary materials, on the one hand, which may not be seized either under the authority of a search warrant or during the course of a search incident to arrest, and on the other hand, those objects which may validly be seized including the instrumentalities and means by which a crime is committed, the fruits of crime such as stolen property, weapons by which escape of the person arrested might be effected, and property the possession of which is a crime" [*Harris v. United States*, 331 U.S. 145, 154 (1947)].

II

We agree with the Court of Appeals that neither the entry without warrant to search for the robber, nor the search for him without warrant was invalid. Under the circumstances of this case, "the exigencies of the situation made that course imperative." *McDonald v. United States*, 335 U.S. 451, 456 (1948).

We do not rely upon *Harris v. United States*, in sustaining the validity of the search. The principal issue in *Harris* was whether the search there could properly be regarded as incident to the lawful arrest, since Harris was in custody before the search was made and the evidence seized. Here, the seizures occurred prior to or immediately contemporaneous with Hayden's arrest, as part of an effort to find a suspected felon, armed, within the house into which he had run only minutes before the police arrived. The permissible scope of search must, therefore, at the least, be as broad as may reasonably be necessary to prevent the dangers that the suspect at large in the house may resist or escape.

It is argued that, while the weapons, ammunition, and cap may have been seized in the course of a search for weapons, the officer who seized the clothing was searching neither for the suspect nor for weapons when he looked into the washing machine in which he found the clothing. But even if we assume, although we do not decide, that the exigent circumstances in this case made lawful a search without warrant only for the suspect or his weapons, it cannot be said on this record that the officer who found the clothes in the washing machine was not searching for weapons. He testified that he was searching for the man or the money, but his failure to state explicitly that he was searching for weapons, in the absence of a specific question to that effect, can hardly be accorded controlling weight. He knew that the robber was armed and he did not know that some weapons had been found at the time he opened the machine. In these circumstances the inference that he was in fact also looking for weapons is fully justified.

III

We come, then, to the question whether, even though the search was lawful, the Court of Appeals was correct in holding that the seizure and introduction of the items of clothing violated the Fourth Amendment because they are "mere evidence." The distinction made by some of our cases between seizure of items of evidential value only and seizure of instrumentalities, fruits, or contraband has been criticized by courts and commentators. The Court of Appeals, however, felt "obligated to adhere to it." We today reject the distinction as based on premises no longer accepted as rules governing the application of the Fourth Amendment.

Nothing in the language of the Fourth Amendment supports the distinction between "mere evidence" and instrumentalities, fruits of crime, or contraband. Privacy is disturbed no more by a search directed to a purely evidentiary object than it is by a search directed to an instrumentality, fruit, or contraband. A magistrate can intervene in both situations, and the requirements of probable cause and specificity can be preserved intact. Moreover, nothing in the nature of property seized as evidence renders it more private than property seized, for example, as an instrumentality; quite the opposite may be true. Indeed, the distinction is wholly irrational, since, depending on the circumstances, the same "papers and effects" may be "mere evidence" in one case and "instrumentality" in another.

In *Gouled v. United States,* 255 U.S. 298, 309 (1921), the Court said that search warrants "may not be used as a means of gaining access to a man's house or office and papers solely for the purpose of making search to secure evidence to be used against him in a criminal or penal proceeding. . . ."

The items of clothing involved in this case are not "testimonial" or "communicative" in nature, and their introduction therefore did not compel respondent to become a witness against himself in violation of the Fifth Amendment. *Schmerber v. California*, 384 U.S. 757 [(1966)]. This case thus does not require that we consider whether there are items of evidential value whose very nature precludes them from being the object of a reasonable search and seizure.

The premise that property interests control the right of the Government to search and seize has been discredited. Searches and seizures may be "unreasonable" within the Fourth Amendment even though the Government asserts a superior property interest at common law. We have recognized that the principal object of the Fourth Amendment is the protection of privacy rather than property, and have increasingly discarded fictional and procedural barriers rested on property concepts. This shift in emphasis from property to privacy has come about through a subtle interplay of substantive and procedural reform. The remedial structure finally escaped the bounds of common law property limitations in *Silverthorne Lumber Co. v. United States*, 251 U.S. 385 (1920), and *Gouled v. United States* when it became established that suppression might be sought during a criminal trial, and under circumstances which would not sustain an action in trespass or replevin. Recognition that the role of the Fourth Amendment was to protect against invasions of privacy demanded a remedy to condemn the seizure in *Silverthorne*, although no possible common law claim existed for the return of the copies made by the Government of the papers it had seized. The remedy of suppression, necessarily involving only the limited, functional consequence of excluding the evidence from trial, satisfied that demand.

The development of search and seizure law since *Silverthorne* and *Gouled* is replete with examples of the transformation in substantive law brought about through the interaction of the felt need to protect privacy from unreasonable invasions and the flexibility in rulemaking made possible by the remedy of exclusion.

The premise in *Gouled* that government may not seize evidence simply for the purpose of proving crime has likewise been discredited. The requirement that the Government assert in addition some property interest in material it seizes has long been a fiction, obscuring the reality that government has an interest in solving crime. The requirements of the Fourth Amendment can secure the same protection of privacy whether the search is for "mere evidence" or for fruits, instrumentalities or contraband. There must, of course, be a nexus—automatically provided in the case of fruits, instrumentalities or contraband—between the item to be seized and criminal behavior. Thus in the case of "mere evidence," probable cause must be examined in terms of cause to believe that the evidence sought will aid in a particular apprehension or conviction. In so doing, consideration of police purposes will be required. But no such problem is presented in this case. The clothes found in the washing machine matched the description of those worn by the robber and the police therefore could reasonably believe that the items would aid in the identification of the culprit.

The survival of the *Gouled* distinction is attributable more to chance than considered judgment. Legislation has helped perpetuate it. Thus, Congress has never authorized the issuance of search warrants for the seizure of mere evidence of crime.

The Fourth Amendment allows intrusions upon privacy under these circumstances, and there is no viable reason to distinguish intrusions to secure "mere evidence" from intrusions to secure fruits, instrumentalities, or contraband.

The judgment of the Court of Appeals is Reversed.

JUSTICE BLACK concurs in the result.

JUSTICE FORTAS, with whom CHIEF JUSTICE WARREN joins, concurring.

While I agree that the Fourth Amendment should not be held to require exclusion from evidence of the clothing as well as the weapons and ammunition found by the officers during the search, I cannot join in the majority's broad—and in my judgment, totally unnecessary—repudiation of the so-called "mere evidence" rule.

Our Constitution envisions that searches will ordinarily follow procurement by police of a valid search warrant. Such warrants are to issue only on probable cause, and must describe with particularity the persons or things to be seized. There are exceptions to this rule. Searches may be made incident to a lawful arrest, and—as today's decision indicates—in the course of "hot pursuit." But searches under each of these exceptions have, until today, been confined to those essential to fulfill the purpose of the exception: that is, we have refused to permit use of articles the seizure of which could not be strictly tied to and justified by the exigencies which excused the warrantless search. The use in evidence of weapons seized in a "hot pursuit" search or search incident to arrest satisfies this criterion because of the need to protect the arresting officers from weapons to which the suspect might resort. The search for and seizure of fruits are, of course, justifiable on independent grounds: The fruits are an object of the pursuit or arrest of the suspect, and should be restored to their true owner.

Similarly, we have forbidden the use of articles seized in such a search unless obtained from the person of the suspect or from the immediate vicinity. Since a warrantless search is justified only as incident to an arrest or "hot pursuit," this Court and others have held that its scope does not include permission to search the entire building in which the arrest occurs, or to rummage through locked drawers and closets, or to search at another time or place.

In the present case, the articles of clothing admitted into evidence are not within any of the traditional categories which describe what materials may be seized, either with or without a warrant. The restrictiveness of these categories has been subjected to telling criticism, and although I believe that we should approach expansion of these categories with the diffidence which their imposing provenance commands, I agree that the use of identifying clothing worn in the commission of a crime and seized during "hot pursuit" is within the spirit and intendment of the "hot pursuit" exception to the search-warrant requirement. That is because the clothing is pertinent to identification of the person hotly pursued as being, in fact, the person whose pursuit was justified by connection with the crime. I would frankly place the ruling on that basis. I would not drive an enormous and dangerous hole in the Fourth Amendment to accommodate a specific and, I think, reasonable exception.

JUSTICE DOUGLAS, dissenting.

We start with the Fourth Amendment. . . .

This constitutional guarantee, now as applicable to the States (*Mapp v. Ohio*, 367 U.S. 643, 1961) as to the Federal Government, has been thought, until today, to have two faces of privacy:

> (1) One creates a zone of privacy that may not be invaded by the police through raids, by the legislators through laws, or by magistrates through the issuance of warrants.
>
> (2) A second creates a zone of privacy that may be invaded either by the police in hot pursuit or by a search incident to arrest or by a warrant issued by a magistrate on a showing of probable cause.

The first has been recognized from early days in Anglo-American law.

Our question is whether the Government, though armed with a proper search warrant or though making a search incident to an arrest, may seize, and use at the trial, testimonial evidence, whether it would otherwise be barred by the Fifth Amendment or would be free from such strictures. The teaching of *Boyd* v. *United States*, 116 U.S. 616 (1886) is that such evidence, though seized pursuant to a lawful search, is inadmissible.

That doctrine had its full flowering in *Gouled v. United States*, 255 U.S. 298 (1921), where an opinion was written by Mr. Justice Clarke for a unanimous Court that included both Mr. Justice Holmes and Mr. Justice Brandeis. The prosecution was for defrauding the Government under procurement contracts. Documents were taken from defendant's business office under a search warrant and used at the trial as evidence against him. Stolen or forged papers could be so seized, the Court said; so could lottery tickets; so could contraband; so could property in which the public had an interest, for reasons tracing back to warrants allowing the seizure of stolen property. But the papers or documents fell in none of those categories and the Court therefore held that even though they had been taken under a warrant, they were inadmissible at the trial as not even a warrant, though otherwise proper and regular, could be used "for the purpose of making search to secure evidence" of a crime. The use of those documents against the accused might, of course, violate the Fifth Amendment. But whatever may be the intrinsic nature of the evidence, the owner is then "the unwilling source of the evidence," there being no difference so far as the Fifth Amendment is concerned "whether he be obliged to supply evidence against himself or whether such evidence be obtained by an illegal search of his premises and seizure of his private papers."

The right of privacy protected by the Fourth Amendment relates in part of course to the precincts of the home or the office. But it does not make them sanctuaries where the law can never reach. There are such places in the world. A policeman in "hot pursuit" or an officer with a search warrant can enter any house, any room, any building, any office. The privacy of those places is of course protected against invasion except in limited situations. The full privacy protected by the Fourth Amendment is, however, reached when we come to books, pamphlets, papers, letters, documents, and other personal effects. Unless they are contraband or instruments of the crime, they may not be reached by any warrant nor may they be lawfully seized by the police who are in "hot pursuit." By reason of the Fourth Amendment the police may not rummage around among these personal effects, no matter how formally perfect their authority may appear to be. They may not seize them. If they do, those articles may not be used in evidence. Any invasion whatsoever of those personal effects is "unreasonable" within the meaning of the Fourth Amendment.

The constitutional philosophy is, I think, clear. The personal effects and possessions of the individual (all contraband and the like excepted) are sacrosanct from prying eyes, from the long arm of the law, from any rummaging by police. Privacy involves the choice of the individual to disclose or to reveal what he believes, what he thinks, what he possesses. Those who wrote the Bill of Rights believed that every individual needs both to communicate with others and to keep his affairs to himself. That dual aspect of privacy means that the individual should have the freedom to select for himself the time and circumstances when he will share his secrets with others and decide the extent of that sharing. This is his prerogative not the States'.

It was in that tradition that we held in *Griswold v. Connecticut*, 381 U.S. 479 (1965), that lawmakers could not, as respects husband and wife at least, make the use of contraceptives a crime.

This right of privacy, sustained in *Griswold*, is kin to the right of privacy created by the Fourth Amendment. That there is a zone that no police can enter—whether in "hot pursuit" or armed with a meticulously proper warrant—has been emphasized by *Boyd v. United States*, 116 U.S. 616 (1866) and by *Gouled v. United States*, 255 U.S. 298 (1921). They have been consistently and continuously approved. I would adhere to them and leave with the individual the choice of opening his private effects (apart from contraband and the like) to the police or keeping their contents a secret and their integrity inviolate. The existence of that choice is the very essence of the right of privacy. Without it the Fourth Amendment and the Fifth are ready instruments for the police state that the Framers sought to avoid.

FOR DISCUSSION

How is the right to privacy enmeshed with the Fourth Amendment? What is significant in the Fourth Amendment for protecting privacy and not property? What is the primary source of conflict between Justice Brennan in his majority opinion and Justice Douglas in his dissent?

RELATED CASES

Wong Sun v. United States: 371 U.S. 471 (1963).

This decision extends the exclusionary rule to verbal evidence discovered during a warrantless search. The Court finds that confessions made without probable cause and subsequent to an arrest were a fruit of the poisonous tree and therefore inadmissible.

Silverman v. United States: 365 U.S. 505 (1961).

The Court found that a warrantless tapping of a house with a "spike mike" that penetrated a heating duct violated the Due Process Clause because it actually physically intruded into the home. Personal conversations are worthy of constitutional protection.

***Florida v. Jardines:* 569 U.S. 1 (2013).**

The use of a trained dog to sniff for drugs at the door of a private residence is a search, requiring both probable cause and a warrant.

SAFFORD UNIFIED SCHOOL DISTRICT #1 v. REDDING

557 U.S. 364, 129 S.Ct. 2633, 174 L.Ed.2d 354 (2009)

The facts are provided in the majority opinion, which follows.

Vote: 8–1

JUSTICE SOUTER delivered the opinion of the Court, in which CHIEF JUSTICE ROBERTS and JUSTICES SCALIA, KENNEDY, BREYER, ALITO, STEVENS, and GINSBURG joined.

I

The events immediately prior to the search in question began in 13-year-old Savana Redding's math class at Safford Middle School one October day in 2003. The assistant principal of the school, Kerry Wilson, came into the room and asked Savana to go to his office. There, he showed her a day planner, unzipped and open flat on his desk, in which there were several knives, lighters, a permanent marker, and a cigarette. Wilson asked Savana whether the planner was hers; she said it was, but that a few days before she had lent it to her friend, Marissa Glines. Savana stated that none of the items in the planner belonged to her.

Wilson then showed Savana four white prescription-strength ibuprofen 400-mg pills, and one over-the-counter blue naproxen 200-mg pill, all used for pain and inflammation but banned under school rules without advance permission. He asked Savana if she knew anything about the pills. Savana answered that she did not. Wilson then told Savana that he had received a report that she was giving these pills to fellow students; Savana denied it and agreed to let Wilson search her belongings. Helen Romero, an administrative assistant, came into the office, and together with Wilson they searched Savana's backpack, finding nothing.

At that point, Wilson instructed Romero to take Savana to the school nurse's office to search her clothes for pills. Romero and the nurse, Peggy Schwallier, asked Savana to remove her jacket, socks, and shoes, leaving her in stretch pants and a T-shirt (both without pockets), which she was then asked to remove. Finally, Savana was told to pull her bra out and to the side and shake it, and to pull out the elastic on her underpants, thus exposing her breasts and pelvic area to some degree. No pills were found.

Savana's mother filed suit against Safford Unified School District # 1, Wilson, Romero, and Schwallier for conducting a strip search in violation of Savana's Fourth Amendment rights. The District Court for the District of Arizona granted [a motion for summary judgment] on the ground that there was no Fourth Amendment violation, and a panel of the Ninth Circuit affirmed.

A closely divided Circuit sitting en banc, however, reversed. Following the two-step protocol for evaluating claims of qualified immunity, the Ninth Circuit held that the strip search was unjustified under the Fourth Amendment test for searches of children by school officials set out in *New Jersey v. T.L.O.*, 469 U.S. 325 (1985).

II

The Fourth Amendment "right of the people to be secure in their persons . . . against unreasonable searches and seizures" generally requires a law enforcement officer to have probable cause for conducting a search. "Probable cause exists where 'the facts and circumstances within [an officer's] knowledge and of which [he] had reasonably trustworthy information [are] sufficient in themselves to warrant a man of reasonable caution in the belief that' an offense has been or is being committed," *Brinegar v. United States*, 338 U.S. 160, 175–176 (1949), and that evidence bearing on that offense will be found in the place to be searched.

In *New Jersey v. T.L.O.* we recognized that the school setting "requires some modification of the level of suspicion of illicit activity needed to justify a search" and held that for searches by school officials "a careful balancing of governmental and private interests suggests that the public interest is best served by a Fourth Amendment standard of reasonableness that stops short of probable cause." We have thus applied a standard of reasonable suspicion to determine the legality of a school administrator's search of a student and have held that a school search "will be permissible in its scope when the measures adopted are reasonably related to the objectives of the search and not excessively intrusive in light of the age and sex of the student and the nature of the infraction."

Perhaps the best that can be said generally about the required knowledge component of probable cause for a law enforcement officer's evidence search is that it raise a "fair probability," *Illinois v. Gates*, 462 U.S. 213 at 238 (1983), or a "substantial chance," of discovering evidence of criminal activity. The lesser standard for school searches could as readily be described as a moderate chance of finding evidence of wrongdoing.

III

A

In this case, the school's policies strictly prohibit the nonmedical use, possession, or sale of any drug on school grounds, including " '[a]ny prescription or over-the-counter drug, except those for which permission to use in school has been granted pursuant to Board policy.' " . . .[W]hile she denied knowledge of the contraband, Savana admitted that the day planner was hers and that she had lent it to Marissa. Wilson had other reports of their friendship from staff members, who had identified Savana and Marissa as part of an unusually rowdy group at the school's opening dance in August, during which alcohol and cigarettes were found in the girls' bathroom. Wilson had reason to connect the girls with this contraband, for Wilson knew that [another student] had told the principal that before [a recent school] dance, he had been at a party at Savana's house where alcohol was served. Marissa's statement that the pills came from Savana was thus sufficiently plausible to warrant suspicion that Savana was involved in pill distribution.

This suspicion of Wilson's was enough to justify a search of Savana's backpack and outer clothing. If a student is reasonably suspected of giving out contraband pills, she is reasonably suspected of carrying them on her person and in the carryall that has become an item of student uniform in most places today. If Wilson's reasonable suspicion of pill distribution were not understood to support searches of outer clothes and backpack, it would not justify any search worth making. And the look into Savana's bag, in her presence and in the relative privacy of Wilson's office, was not excessively intrusive, any more than Romero's subsequent search of her outer clothing.

B

Here it is that the parties part company, with Savana's claim that extending the search at Wilson's behest to the point of making her pull out her underwear was constitutionally unreasonable. The exact label for this final step in the intrusion is not important, though strip search is a fair way to speak of it. Romero and Schwallier directed Savana to remove her clothes down to her underwear, and then "pull out" her bra and the elastic band on her underpants. Although Romero and Schwallier stated that they did not see anything when Savana followed their instructions, we would not define strip search and its Fourth Amendment consequences in a way that would guarantee litigation about who was looking and how much was seen. The very fact of Savana's pulling her underwear away from her body in the presence of the two officials who were able to see her necessarily exposed her breasts and pelvic area to some degree, and both subjective and reasonable societal expectations of personal privacy support the treatment of such a search as categorically distinct, requiring distinct elements of justification on the part of school authorities for going beyond a search of outer clothing and belongings.

Savana's subjective expectation of privacy against such a search is inherent in her account of it as embarrassing, frightening, and humiliating. Changing for gym is getting ready for play; exposing for a search is responding to an accusation reserved for suspected wrongdoers and fairly understood as so degrading that a number of communities have decided that strip searches in schools are never reasonable and have banned them no matter what the facts may be.

The indignity of the search does not, of course, outlaw it, but it does implicate the rule of reasonableness as stated in *T.L.O.*, that "the search as actually conducted [be] reasonably related in scope to the circumstances which justified the interference in the first place." 469 U.S., at 341. The scope will be permissible, that is, when it is "not excessively intrusive in light of the age and sex of the student and the nature of the infraction."

Here, the content of the suspicion failed to match the degree of intrusion. Wilson knew beforehand that the pills were prescription-strength ibuprofen and over-the-counter naproxen, common pain relievers equivalent to two Advil, or one Aleve. He must have been aware of the nature and limited threat of the specific drugs he was searching for, and while just about anything can be taken in quantities that will do real harm, Wilson had no reason to suspect that large amounts of the drugs were being passed around, or that individual students were receiving great numbers of pills.

Nor could Wilson have suspected that Savana was hiding common painkillers in her underwear. Petitioners suggest, as a truth universally acknowledged, that "students . . . hid[e] contraband in or under their clothing." But when the categorically extreme intrusiveness of a search down to the body of an adolescent requires some justification in suspected facts, general background possibilities fall short; a reasonable search that extensive calls for suspicion that it will pay off. But nondangerous school contraband does not raise the specter of stashes in intimate places, and there is no evidence in the record of any general practice among Safford Middle School students of hiding that sort of thing in underwear. . . .

In sum, what was missing from the suspected facts that pointed to Savana was any indication of danger to the students from the power of the drugs or their quantity, and any reason to suppose that Savana was carrying pills in her underwear. We think that the combination of these deficiencies was fatal to finding the search reasonable.

In so holding, we mean to cast no ill reflection on the assistant principal, for the record raises no doubt that his motive throughout was to eliminate drugs from his school and protect students from what Jordan Romero had gone through. Parents are known to overreact to protect their children from danger, and a school official with responsibility for safety may tend to do the same. The difference is that the Fourth Amendment places limits on the official, even with the high degree of deference that courts must pay to the educator's professional judgment.

We do mean, though, to make it clear that the *T.L.O.* concern to limit a school search to reasonable scope requires the support of reasonable suspicion of danger or of resort to underwear for hiding evidence of wrongdoing before a search can reasonably make the quantum leap from outer clothes and backpacks to exposure of intimate parts. The meaning of such a search, and the degradation its subject may reasonably feel, place a search that intrusive in a category of its own demanding its own specific suspicions.

JUSTICE THOMAS, dissenting.

I

"Although the underlying command of the Fourth Amendment is always that searches and seizures be reasonable, what is reasonable depends on the context within which a search takes place." Thus, although public school students retain Fourth Amendment rights under this Court's precedent, those rights "are different . . . than elsewhere; the 'reasonableness' inquiry cannot disregard the schools' custodial and tutelary responsibility for children," *Vernonia School Dist. 47J v. Acton*, 515 U.S. 646, 656 (1995); see also *T.L.O.*, 469 U.S., at 339 (identifying "the substantial interest of teachers and administrators in maintaining discipline in the classroom and on school grounds"). For nearly 25 years this Court has understood that "[m]aintaining order in the classroom has never been easy, but in more recent years, school disorder has often taken particularly ugly forms: drug use and violent crime in the schools have become major social problems."

For this reason, school officials retain broad authority to protect students and preserve "order and a proper educational environment" under the Fourth Amendment. This authority requires that school officials be able to engage in the "close supervision of schoolchildren, as well as . . . enforc[e] rules against conduct that would be perfectly permissible if undertaken by an adult." Seeking to reconcile the Fourth Amendment with this unique public school setting, the Court in *T.L.O.* held that a school search is "reasonable" if it is " 'justified at its inception' " and " 'reasonably related in scope to the circumstances which justified the interference in the first place.' " The search under review easily meets this standard.

A

A "search of a student by a teacher or other school official will be 'justified at its inception' when there are reasonable grounds for suspecting that the search will turn up evidence that the student has violated or is violating either the law or the rules of the school." *T.L.O.*, at 341–342. As the majority rightly concedes, this search was justified at its inception because there were reasonable grounds to suspect that Redding possessed medication that violated school rules. A finding of reasonable suspicion "does not deal with hard certainties, but with probabilities." *United States v. Cortez*, 449 U.S. 411, 418 (1981). To satisfy this standard, more than a mere "hunch" of wrongdoing is required, but "considerably" less suspicion is needed than would be required to "satisf[y] a preponderance of the evidence standard." *United States v. Arvizu*, 534 U.S. 266, 274 (2002).

Furthermore, in evaluating whether there is a reasonable "particularized and objective" basis for conducting a search based on suspected wrongdoing, government officials must consider the "totality of the circumstances." School officials have a specialized understanding of the school environment, the habits of the students, and the concerns of the community, which enables them to " 'formulat[e] certain common-sense conclusions about human behavior.' " *United States v. Sokolow*, 490 U.S. 1, 8 (1989). And like police officers, school officials are "entitled to make an assessment of the situation in light of [this] specialized training and familiarity with the customs of the [school]."

Here, petitioners had reasonable grounds to suspect that Redding was in possession of prescription and nonprescription drugs in violation of the school's prohibition of the "non-medical use, possession, or sale of a drug" on school property or at school events. As an initial matter, school officials were aware that a few years earlier, a student had become "seriously ill" and "spent several days in intensive care" after ingesting prescription medication obtained from a classmate. Fourth Amendment searches do not occur in a vacuum; rather, context must inform the judicial inquiry. In this instance, the suspicion of drug possession arose at a middle school that had "a history of problems with students using and distributing prohibited and illegal substances on campus." . . .

Thus, as the majority acknowledges, the totality of relevant circumstances justified a search of Redding for pills.

B

The remaining question is whether the search was reasonable in scope. Under *T.L.O.*, "a search will be permissible in its scope when the measures adopted are reasonably related to the objectives of the search and not excessively intrusive in light of the age and sex of the student and the nature of the infraction." 469 U.S., at 342. According to the majority, to be reasonable, this school search required a showing of "danger to the students from the power of the drugs or their quantity" or a "reason to suppose that [Redding] was carrying pills in her underwear." Each of these additional requirements is an unjustifiable departure from bedrock Fourth Amendment law in the school setting, where this Court has heretofore read the Fourth Amendment to grant considerable leeway to school officials. Because the school officials searched in a location where the pills could have been hidden, the search was reasonable in scope under *T.L.O.*

1

The Court has generally held that the reasonableness of a search's scope depends only on whether it is limited to the area that is capable of concealing the object of the search. See, e.g., *Wyoming v. Houghton*, 526 U.S. 295, 307 (1999) (Police officers "may inspect passengers' belongings found in the car that are capable of concealing the object of the search"); *Florida v. Jimeno*, 500 U.S. 248, 251 (1991) ("The scope of a search is generally defined by its expressed object"); *United States v. Johns*, 469 U.S. 478, 487 (1985) (search reasonable because "there is no plausible argument that the object of the search could not have been concealed in the packages"); *United States v. Ross*, 456 U.S. 798, 820 (1982) ("A lawful search . . . generally extends to the entire area in which the object of the search may be found").

In keeping with this longstanding rule, the "nature of the infraction" referenced in *T.L.O.* delineates the proper scope of a search of students in a way that is identical to that permitted for searches outside the school—i.e., the search must be limited to the areas where the object of that infraction could be concealed. A search of a student therefore is permissible in scope under *T.L.O.* so long as it is objectively reasonable to believe that the area searched could conceal the contraband.

The analysis of whether the scope of the search here was permissible under that standard is straightforward. Indeed, the majority does not dispute that "general background possibilities" establish that students conceal "contraband in their underwear." It acknowledges that school officials had reasonable suspicion to look in Redding's backpack and outer clothing because if "Wilson's reasonable suspicion of pill distribution were not understood to support searches of outer clothes and backpack, it would not justify any search worth making." The majority nevertheless concludes that proceeding any further with the search was unreasonable. But there is no support for this conclusion. The reasonable suspicion that Redding possessed the pills for distribution purposes did not dissipate because the search of her backpack turned up nothing. It was eminently reasonable to conclude that the backpack was empty because Redding was secreting the pills in a place she thought no one would look.

Redding would not have been the first person to conceal pills in her undergarments. Nor will she be the last after today's decision, which announces the safest place to secrete contraband in school.

2

The majority's decision in this regard also departs from another basic principle of the Fourth Amendment: that law enforcement officials can enforce with the same vigor all rules and regulations irrespective of the perceived importance of any of those rules.

The majority has placed school officials in this "impossible spot" by questioning whether possession of Ibuprofen and Naproxen causes a severe enough threat to warrant investigation. Had the suspected infraction involved a street drug, the majority implies that it would have approved the scope of the search. In effect, then, the majority has replaced a school rule that draws no distinction among drugs with a new one that does. As a result, a full search of a student's person for prohibited drugs will be permitted only if the Court agrees that the drug in question was sufficiently dangerous. Such a test is unworkable and unsound. School officials cannot be expected to halt searches based on the possibility that a court might later find that the particular infraction at issue is not severe enough to warrant an intrusive investigation.

Judges are not qualified to second-guess the best manner for maintaining quiet and order in the school environment. It is a mistake for judges to assume the responsibility for deciding which school rules are important enough to allow for invasive searches and which rules are not.

3

Even if this Court were authorized to second-guess the importance of school rules, the Court's assessment of the importance of this district's policy is flawed. It is a crime to possess or use prescription-strength Ibuprofen without a prescription. By prohibiting unauthorized prescription drugs on school grounds—and conducting a search to ensure students abide by that prohibition—the school rule here was consistent with a routine provision of the state criminal code. It hardly seems unreasonable for school officials to enforce a rule that, in effect, proscribes conduct that amounts to a crime.

II

By declaring the search unreasonable in this case, the majority has " 'surrender[ed] control of the American public school system to public school students' " by invalidating school policies that treat all drugs equally and by second-guessing swift disciplinary decisions made by school officials. The Court's interference in these matters of great concern to teachers, parents, and students illustrates why the most constitutionally sound approach to the question of applying the Fourth Amendment in local public schools would in fact be the complete restoration of the common-law doctrine of *in loco parentis.*

So empowered, schoolteachers and administrators had almost complete discretion to establish and enforce the rules they believed were necessary to maintain control over their classrooms. The perils of judicial policymaking inherent in applying Fourth Amendment protections to public schools counsel in favor of a return to the understanding that existed in this Nation's first public schools, which gave teachers discretion to craft the rules needed to carry out the disciplinary responsibilities delegated to them by parents.

If the common-law view that parents delegate to teachers their authority to discipline and maintain order were to be applied in this case, the search of Redding would stand. There can be no doubt that a parent would have had the authority to conduct the search at issue in this case.

In light of this relationship, the Court has indicated that a parent can authorize a third-party search of a child by consenting to such a search, even if the child denies his consent. Certainly, a search by the parent himself is no different, regardless of whether or not a child would prefer to be left alone.

In the end, the task of implementing and amending public school policies is beyond this Court's function. Parents, teachers, school administrators, local politicians, and state officials are all better suited than judges to determine the appropriate limits on searches conducted by school officials. Preservation of order, discipline, and safety in public schools is simply not the domain of the Constitution. And, common sense is not a judicial monopoly or a Constitutional imperative.

III

"[T]he nationwide drug epidemic makes the war against drugs a pressing concern in every school." *Bd. of Educ. v. Earls*, 536 U.S. 822, 834 (2002). And yet the Court has limited the authority of school officials to conduct searches for the drugs that the officials believe pose a serious safety risk to their students. By doing so, the majority has confirmed that a return to the doctrine of *in loco parentis* is required to keep the judiciary from essentially seizing control of public schools. Only then will teachers again be able to " 'govern the[ir] pupils, quicken the slothful, spur the indolent, restrain the impetuous, and control the stubborn' " by making " 'rules, giv[ing] commands, and punish[ing] disobedience' " without interference from judges. By deciding that it is better equipped to decide what behavior should be permitted in schools, the Court has undercut student safety and undermined the authority of school administrators and local officials. Even more troubling, it has done so in a case in which the underlying response by school administrators was reasonable and justified. I cannot join this regrettable decision. I, therefore, respectfully dissent from the Court's determination that this search violated the Fourth Amendment.

FOR DISCUSSION

Does this case strengthen or weaken the precedent of *New Jersey v. T.L.O.*? How? What might be the consequences of the Court returning to Justice Thomas' recommendation of *in loco parentis*?

RELATED CASE

***New Jersey v. T.L.O.*: 469 U.S. 325 (1985).**

For students who are being searched by school officials for contraband, the Fourth Amendment does not require a standard of probable cause; instead, officials must meet the less-strict standard of "reasonableness."

KATZ V. UNITED STATES

389 U.S. 347, 88 S.Ct. 507, 19 L.Ed. 2d 576 (1967)

Petitioner Katz was convicted under an indictment charging him with transmitting wagering information by telephone across state lines in violation of federal statute. Evidence of Katz's portion of the conversations was introduced at the trial. The conversations were overheard and taped by FBI agents who had attached an electronic listening and recording device—without a warrant—to the outside of the telephone booth from which the calls were made. There was no physical entrance by the officers or the listening device into the actual phone booth.

Vote: 7–1

JUSTICE STEWART delivered the opinion of the Court.

Because of the misleading way the issues have been formulated, the parties have attached great significance to the characterization of the telephone booth from which the petitioner placed his calls. The petitioner has strenuously argued that the booth was a "constitutionally protected area." The Government has maintained with equal vigor that it was not. But this effort to decide whether or not a given "area," viewed in the abstract, is "constitutionally protected" deflects attention from the problem presented by this case. For the Fourth Amendment protects people, not places. What a person knowingly exposes to the public, even in his own home or office, is not a subject of Fourth Amendment protection. But what he seeks to preserve as private, even in an area accessible to the public, may be constitutionally protected.

The Government stresses the fact that the telephone booth from which the petitioner made his calls was constructed partly of glass, so that he was as visible after he entered it as he would have been if he had remained outside. But what he sought to exclude when he entered the booth was not the intruding eye—it was the uninvited ear. He did not shed his right to do so simply because he made his calls from a place where he might be seen. No less than an individual in a business office, in a friend's apartment, or in a taxicab, a person in a telephone booth may rely upon the protection of the Fourth Amendment. One who occupies it, shuts the door behind him, and pays the toll that permits him to place a call is surely entitled to assume that the words he utters into the mouthpiece will not be broadcast to the world. To read the Constitution more narrowly is to ignore the vital role that the public telephone has come to play in private communication.

The Government contends, however, that the activities of its agents in this case should not be tested by Fourth Amendment requirements, for the surveillance technique they employed involved no physical penetration of the telephone booth from which the petitioner placed his calls. It is true that the absence of such penetration was at one time thought to foreclose further Fourth Amendment inquiry, *Olmstead v. United States*, 277 U.S. 438 (1928); *Goldman v. United States*, 316 U.S. 129 (1942), for that Amendment was thought to limit only searches and seizures of tangible property. But "the premise that property interests control the right of the Government to search and seize has been discredited." *Warden v. Hayden*, 387 U.S. 294, 304 (1967). Once this much is acknowledged, and once it is recognized that the Fourth Amendment protects people—and not simply "areas"—against unreasonable searches and seizures, it becomes clear that the reach of that Amendment cannot turn upon the presence or absence of a physical intrusion into any given enclosure.

We conclude that the underpinnings of *Olmstead* and *Goldman* have been so eroded by our subsequent decisions that the "trespass" doctrine there enunciated can no longer be regarded as controlling. The Government's activities in electronically listening to and recording the petitioner's words violated the privacy upon which he justifiably relied while using the telephone booth and thus constituted a "search and seizure" within the meaning of the Fourth Amendment. The fact that the electronic device employed to achieve that end did not happen to penetrate the wall of the booth can have no constitutional significance.

The question remaining for decision, then, is whether the search and seizure conducted in this case complied with constitutional standards.

. . . [I]t is clear that this surveillance was so narrowly circumscribed that a duly authorized magistrate, properly notified of the need for such investigation, specifically informed of the basis on which it was to proceed, and clearly apprised of the precise intrusion it would entail, could constitutionally have authorized, with appropriate safeguards, the very limited search and seizure that the Government asserts in fact took place.

The Government urges that, because its agents relied upon the decisions in *Olmstead* and *Goldman*, and because they did no more here than they might properly have done with prior judicial sanction, we should retroactively validate their conduct. That we cannot do. It is apparent that the agents in this case acted with restraint. Yet the inescapable fact is that this restraint was imposed by the agents themselves, not by a judicial officer. They were not required, before commencing the search, to present their estimate of probable cause for detached scrutiny by a neutral magistrate. They were not compelled, during the conduct of the search itself, to observe precise limits established in advance by a specific court order. Nor were they directed, after the search had been completed, to notify the authorizing magistrate in detail of all that had been seized. In the absence of such safeguards, this Court has never sustained a search upon the sole ground that officers reasonably expected to find evidence of a particular crime and voluntarily confined their activities to the least intrusive means consistent with that end. "Over and again this Court has emphasized that the mandate of the [Fourth] Amendment requires adherence to judicial processes," *United States v. Jeffers*, 342 U.S. 48 (1951) and that searches conducted outside the judicial process, without prior approval by judge or magistrate, are per se unreasonable under the Fourth Amendment—subject only to a few specifically established and well-delineated exceptions.

It is difficult to imagine how any of those exceptions could ever apply to the sort of search and seizure involved in this case. The Government does not question these basic principles. Rather, it urges the creation of a new exception to cover this case. It argues that surveillance of a telephone booth should be exempted from the usual requirement of advance authorization by a magistrate upon a showing of probable cause. We cannot agree.

Wherever a man may be, he is entitled to know that he will remain free from unreasonable searches and seizures. The government agents here ignored "the procedure of antecedent justification . . . that is central to the Fourth Amendment," a procedure that we hold to be a constitutional precondition of the kind of electronic surveillance involved in this case. Because the surveillance here failed to meet that condition, and because it led to the petitioner's conviction, the judgment must be reversed.

JUSTICE MARSHALL took no part in the consideration or decision of this case.

JUSTICE DOUGLAS, with whom JUSTICE BRENNAN joins, concurring.

While I join the opinion of the Court, I feel compelled to reply to the separate concurring opinion of my Brother White, which I view as a wholly unwarranted green light for the Executive Branch to resort to electronic eavesdropping without a warrant in cases which the Executive Branch itself labels "national security" matters.

Neither the President nor the Attorney General is a magistrate. In matters where they believe national security may be involved they are not detached, disinterested, and neutral as a court or magistrate must be. Under the separation of powers created by the Constitution, the Executive Branch is not supposed to be neutral and disinterested. Rather it should vigorously investigate and prevent breaches of national security and prosecute those who violate the pertinent federal laws. The President and Attorney General are properly interested parties, cast in the role of adversary, in national security cases. They may even be the intended victims of subversive action. Since spies and saboteurs are as entitled to the protection of the Fourth Amendment as suspected gamblers like petitioner, I cannot agree that where spies and saboteurs are involved adequate protection of Fourth Amendment rights is assured when the President and Attorney General assume both the position of adversary-and-prosecutor and disinterested, neutral magistrate.

JUSTICE HARLAN, concurring.

I join the opinion of the Court, which I read to hold only (a) that an enclosed telephone booth is an area where, like a home, *Weeks v. United States*, 232 U.S. 383 (1914), and unlike a field, *Hester v. United States*, 265 U.S. 57 (1924), a person has a constitutionally protected reasonable expectation of privacy; (b) that electronic as well as physical intrusion into a place that is in this sense private may constitute a violation of the Fourth Amendment; and (c) that the invasion of a constitutionally protected area by federal authorities is, as the Court has long held, presumptively unreasonable in the absence of a search warrant.

The critical fact in this case is that "one who occupies it, [a telephone booth] shuts the door behind him, and pays the toll that permits him to place a call is surely entitled to assume" that his conversation is not being intercepted. The point is not that the booth is "accessible to the public" at other times, but that it is a temporarily private place whose momentary occupants' expectations of freedom from intrusion are recognized as reasonable.

Finally, I do not read the Court's opinion to declare that no interception of a conversation one-half of which occurs in a public telephone booth can be reasonable in the absence of a warrant. As elsewhere under the Fourth Amendment, warrants are the general rule, to which the legitimate needs of law enforcement may demand specific exceptions. It will be time enough to consider any such exceptions when an appropriate occasion presents itself, and I agree with the Court that this is not one.

JUSTICE WHITE, concurring.

I agree that the official surveillance of petitioner's telephone conversations in a public booth must be subjected to the test of reasonableness under the Fourth Amendment and that on the record now before us the particular surveillance undertaken was unreasonable absent a warrant properly authorizing it. This application of the Fourth Amendment need not interfere with legitimate needs of law enforcement.

In joining the Court's opinion, I note the Court's acknowledgment that there are circumstances in which it is reasonable to search without a warrant. In this connection, in footnote 23 the Court points out that today's decision does not reach national security cases. Wiretapping to protect the security of the Nation has been authorized by successive Presidents. The present Administration would apparently save national security cases from restrictions against wiretapping. We should not require the warrant procedure and the magistrate's judgment if the President of the United States or his chief legal officer, the Attorney General, has considered the requirements of national security and authorized electronic surveillance as reasonable.

JUSTICE BLACK, dissenting.

If I could agree with the Court that eavesdropping carried on by electronic means (equivalent to wiretapping) constitutes a "search" or "seizure," I would be happy to join the Court's opinion.

My basic objection is twofold: (1) I do not believe that the words of the Amendment will bear the meaning given them by today's decision, and (2) I do not believe that it is the proper role of this Court to rewrite the Amendment in order "to bring it into harmony with the times" and thus reach a result that many people believe to be desirable.

Goldman v. United States, 316 U.S. 129 (1942), is an even clearer example of this Court's traditional refusal to consider eavesdropping as being covered by the Fourth Amendment. There federal agents used a detectaphone, which was placed on the wall of an adjoining room, to listen to the conversation of a defendant carried on in his private office and intended to be confined within the four walls of the room. This Court, referring to *Olmstead v. United States*, 277 U.S. 438 (1928), found no Fourth Amendment violation.

It should be noted that the Court in *Olmstead* based its decision squarely on the fact that wiretapping or eavesdropping does not violate the Fourth Amendment.

. . . I think that although the Court attempts to convey the impression that for some reason today *Olmstead* and *Goldman* are no longer good law, it must face up to the fact that these cases have never been overruled or even "eroded." I must align myself with all those judges who up to this year have never been able to impute such a meaning to the words of the Amendment.

Since I see no way in which the words of the Fourth Amendment can be construed to apply to eavesdropping, that closes the matter for me. In interpreting the Bill of Rights, I willingly go as far as a liberal construction of the language takes me, but I simply cannot in good conscience give a meaning to words which they have never before been thought to have and which they certainly do not have in common ordinary usage. I will not distort the words of the Amendment in order to "keep the Constitution up to date" or "to bring it into harmony with the times." It was never meant that this Court have such power, which in effect would make us a continuously functioning constitutional convention.

With this decision the Court has completed, I hope, its rewriting of the Fourth Amendment, which started only recently when the Court began referring incessantly to the Fourth Amendment not so much as a law against unreasonable searches and seizures as one to protect an individual's privacy.

The Fourth Amendment protects privacy only to the extent that it prohibits unreasonable searches and seizures of "persons, houses, papers, and effects." No general right is created by the Amendment so as to give this Court the unlimited power to hold unconstitutional everything which affects privacy. Certainly the Framers, well acquainted as they were with the excesses of governmental power, did not intend to grant this Court such omnipotent lawmaking authority as that. The history of governments proves that it is dangerous to freedom to repose such powers in courts.

For these reasons I respectfully dissent.

FOR DISCUSSION

How might the expectation of privacy be evaluated in a more digital world than the one in which phone booths were common? What happens to this standard in a world in which the expectation of privacy has diminished?

RELATED CASES

***Berger v. State of New York:* 388 U.S. 41 (1967).**

The Court struck down an eavesdropping statute and acknowledged that eavesdropping was a violation of privacy that may be done only by the state, by agents equipped with a warrant showing probable cause and other specific limitations.

***Riley v. California:* 573 U.S. ___ (2014).**

The digital data in a phone cannot be searched without a warrant when seized during an arrest, but during an emergency there may be an exception.

DANNY LEE KYLLO V. UNITED STATES

533 U.S. 27, 121 S.Ct. 2038, 150 L.Ed. 2d 94 (2001)

U.S. Department of Interior officers suspected Danny Kyllo of growing marijuana in his Oregon home. Using a thermal imager to ascertain that the amount of heat necessary for this endeavor emanated from Kyllo's home, agents found support for their suspicions. Scanning from their car, parked in the public streets, the agents had determined that parts of Kyllo's home were substantially warmer than others, and hotter than the homes of his neighbors. Based on informer tips, utility bills, and the thermal imaging results consistent with the use of high-intensity lamps for growing plants indoors, a warrant authorizing a search for marijuana plants was granted. Kyllo was convicted on the evidence thus obtained. He challenged the validity of the search, but it was upheld in the district and appellate court.

Vote: 5–4

JUSTICE SCALIA delivered the opinion of the Court.

This case presents the question whether the use of a thermal-imaging device aimed at a private home from a public street to detect relative amounts of heat within the home constitutes a "search" within the meaning of the Fourth Amendment.

II

With few exceptions, the question whether a warrantless search of a home is reasonable and hence constitutional must be answered no.

On the other hand, the antecedent question of whether or not a Fourth Amendment "search" has occurred is not so simple under our precedent. The permissibility of ordinary visual surveillance of a home used to be clear because, well into the 20th century, our Fourth Amendment jurisprudence was tied to common-law trespass. Visual surveillance was unquestionably lawful because " 'the eye cannot by the laws of England be guilty of a trespass.' "

Boyd v. United States, 116 U.S. 616, 628 (1886). We have since decoupled violation of a person's Fourth Amendment rights from trespassory violation of his property, but the lawfulness of warrantless visual surveillance of a home has still been preserved. As we observed in *California v. Ciraolo*, 476 U.S. 207, 213 (1986), "the Fourth Amendment protection of the home has never been extended to require law enforcement officers to shield their eyes when passing by a home on public thoroughfares."

One might think that the new validating rationale would be that examining the portion of a house that is in plain public view, while it is a "search" despite the absence of trespass, is not an "unreasonable" one under the Fourth Amendment. But in fact we have held that visual observation is no "search" at all—perhaps in order to preserve somewhat more intact our doctrine that warrantless searches are presumptively unconstitutional. In assessing when a search is not a search, we have applied somewhat in reverse the principle first enunciated in

Katz v. United States, 389 U.S. 347 (1967). *Katz* involved eavesdropping by means of an electronic listening device placed on the outside of a telephone booth—a location not within the catalog ("persons, houses, papers, and effects") that the Fourth Amendment protects against unreasonable searches. We held that the Fourth Amendment nonetheless protected *Katz* from the warrantless eavesdropping because he "justifiably relied" upon the privacy of the telephone booth. We have subsequently applied this principle to hold that a Fourth Amendment search does not occur—even when the explicitly protected location of a house is concerned—unless "the individual manifested a subjective expectation of privacy in the object of the challenged search," and "society [is] willing to recognize that expectation as reasonable." *Ciraolo*, at 211. We have applied this test in holding that it is not a search for the police to use a pen register at the phone company to determine what numbers were dialed in a private home, *Smith v. Maryland*, 442 U.S. 735 (1979), and we have applied the test on two different occasions in holding that aerial surveillance of private homes and surrounding areas does not constitute a search, *Ciraolo*, supra; *Florida v. Riley*, 488 U.S. 445 (1989).

The present case involves officers on a public street engaged in more than naked-eye surveillance of a home. We have previously reserved judgment as to how much technological enhancement of ordinary perception from such a vantage point, if any, is too much.

III

It would be foolish to contend that the degree of privacy secured to citizens by the Fourth Amendment has been entirely unaffected by the advance of technology. For example, as the cases discussed above make clear, the technology enabling human flight has exposed to public view (and hence, we have said, to official observation) uncovered portions of the house and its curtilage that once were private. The question we confront today is what limits there are upon this power of technology to shrink the realm of guaranteed privacy.

The *Katz* test—whether the individual has an expectation of privacy that society is prepared to recognize as reasonable—has often been criticized as circular, and hence subjective and unpredictable. While it may be difficult to refine *Katz* when the search of areas such as telephone booths, automobiles, or even the curtilage and uncovered portions of residences are at issue, in the case of the search of the interior of homes—the prototypical and hence most commonly litigated area of protected privacy—there is a ready criterion, with roots deep in the common law, of the minimal expectation of privacy that exists, and that is acknowledged to be reasonable. To withdraw protection of this minimum expectation would be to permit police technology to erode the privacy guaranteed by the Fourth Amendment. We think that obtaining by sense-enhancing technology any information regarding the interior of the home that could not otherwise have been obtained without physical "intrusion into a constitutionally protected area," *Silverman v. United States*, 365 U.S. 505, 512 (1961), constitutes a search—at least where (as here) the technology in question is not in general public use. This assures preservation of that degree of privacy against government that existed when the Fourth Amendment was adopted. On the basis of this criterion, the information obtained by the thermal imager in this case was the product of a search.

We have said that the Fourth Amendment draws "a firm line at the entrance to the house," *Payton v. New York*, 445 U.S. 573, 590 (1980). That line, we think, must be not only firm but also bright—which requires clear specification of those methods of surveillance that require a warrant. While it is certainly possible to conclude from the videotape of the thermal imaging that occurred in this case that no "significant" compromise of the homeowner's privacy has occurred, we must take the long view, from the original meaning of the Fourth Amendment forward.

> The Fourth Amendment is to be construed in the light of what was deemed an unreasonable search and seizure when it was adopted, and in a manner which will conserve public interests as well as the interests and rights of individual citizens. *Carroll v. United States*, 267 U.S. 132, 149 (1925).

Where, as here, the Government uses a device that is not in general public use, to explore details of the home that would previously have been unknowable without physical intrusion, the surveillance is a "search" and is presumptively unreasonable without a warrant.

Since we hold the Thermovision imaging to have been an unlawful search, it will remain for the District Court to determine whether, without the evidence it provided, the search warrant issued in this case was supported by probable cause—and if not, whether there is any other basis for supporting admission of the evidence that the search pursuant to the warrant produced.

JUSTICE STEVENS, with whom CHIEF JUSTICE REHNQUIST and JUSTICES O'CONNOR and KENNEDY join, dissenting.

There is, in my judgment, a distinction of constitutional magnitude between "through-the-wall surveillance" that gives the observer or listener direct access to information in a private area, on the one hand, and the thought processes used to draw inferences from information in the public domain, on the other hand. The Court has crafted a rule that purports to deal with direct observations of the inside of the home, but the case before us merely involves indirect deductions from "off-the-wall" surveillance, that is, observations of the exterior of the home. Those observations were made with a fairly primitive thermal imager that gathered data exposed on the outside of petitioner's home but did not invade any constitutionally protected interest in privacy. Moreover, I believe that the supposedly "bright-line" rule the Court has created in response to its concerns about future technological developments is unnecessary, unwise, and inconsistent with the Fourth Amendment.

I

There is no need for the Court to craft a new rule to decide this case, as it is controlled by established principles from our Fourth Amendment jurisprudence. One of those core principles, of course, is that "searches and seizures inside a home without a warrant are presumptively unreasonable." *Payton v. New York*, 445 U.S. 573, 586 (1980). But it is equally well settled that searches and seizures of property in plain view are presumptively reasonable. That is the principle implicated here.

While the Court "takes the long view" and decides this case based largely on the potential of yet-to-be-developed technology that might allow "through-the-wall surveillance," this case involves nothing more than off-the-wall surveillance by law enforcement officers to gather information exposed to the general public from the outside of petitioner's home. All that the infrared camera did in this case was passively measure heat emitted from the exterior surfaces of petitioner's home; all that those measurements showed were relative differences in emission levels, vaguely indicating that some areas of the roof and outside walls were warmer than others. As still images from the infrared scans show, no details regarding the interior of petitioner's home were revealed.

Unlike an x-ray scan, or other possible "through-the-wall" techniques, the detection of infrared radiation emanating from the home did not accomplish "an unauthorized physical penetration into the premises," *Silverman v. United States*, 365 U.S. 505, 509 (1961), nor did it "obtain information that it could not have obtained by observation from outside the curtilage of the house," *United States v. Karo*, 468 U.S. 705, 715 (1984).

Indeed, the ordinary use of the senses might enable a neighbor or passerby to notice the heat emanating from a building, particularly if it is vented, as was the case here. Additionally, any member of the public might notice that one part of a house is warmer than another part or a nearby building if, for example, rainwater evaporates or snow melts at different rates across its surfaces. Such use of the senses would not convert into an unreasonable search if, instead, an adjoining neighbor allowed an officer onto her property to verify her perceptions with a sensitive thermometer. Nor, in my view, does such observation become an unreasonable search if made from a distance with the aid of a device that merely discloses that the exterior of one house, or one area of the house, is much warmer than another. Nothing more occurred in this case.

To be sure, the homeowner has a reasonable expectation of privacy concerning what takes place within the home, and the Fourth Amendment's protection against physical invasions of the home should apply to their functional equivalent. But the equipment in this case did not penetrate the walls of petitioner's home, and while it did pick up "details of the home" that were exposed to the public, it did not obtain "any information regarding the interior of the home."

Notwithstanding the implications of today's decision, there is a strong public interest in avoiding constitutional litigation over the monitoring of emissions from homes, and over the inferences drawn from such monitoring.

II

Instead of trying to answer the question whether the use of the thermal imager in this case was even arguably unreasonable, the Court has fashioned a rule that is intended to provide essential guidance for the day when "more sophisticated systems" gain the "ability to 'see' through walls and other opaque barriers." The newly minted rule encompasses "obtaining [1] by sense-enhancing technology [2] any information regarding the interior of the home [3] that could not otherwise have been obtained without physical intrusion into a constitutionally protected area . . . [4] at least where (as here) the technology in question is not in general public use." In my judgment, the Court's new rule is at once too broad and too narrow, and is not justified by the Court's explanation for its adoption. As I have suggested, I would not erect a constitutional impediment to the use of sense-enhancing technology unless it provides its user with the functional equivalent of actual presence in the area being searched.

Despite the Court's attempt to draw a line that is "not only firm but also bright," the contours of its new rule are uncertain because its protection apparently dissipates as soon as the relevant technology is "in general public use." Yet how much use is general public use is not even hinted at by the Court's opinion, which makes the somewhat doubtful assumption that the thermal imager used in this case does not satisfy that criterion.

III

Although the Court is properly and commendably concerned about the threats to privacy that may flow from advances in the technology available to the law enforcement profession, it has unfortunately failed to heed the tried and true counsel of judicial restraint. Instead of concentrating on the rather mundane issue that is actually presented by the case before it, the Court has endeavored to craft an all-encompassing rule for the future. It would be far wiser to give legislators an unimpeded opportunity to grapple with these emerging issues rather than to shackle them with prematurely devised constitutional constraints. I respectfully dissent.

FOR DISCUSSION

Would the decision be different if the technology used were widely available to the general public? Why or why not? What does your answer predict for the future of the Fourth Amendment?

RELATED CASES

***California v. Ciraolo:* 476 U.S. 207 (1986).**

The Court found that police observation by aerial surveillance of a backyard screened by a high fence did not constitute a warrantless search.

***California v. Greenwood:* 486 U.S. 35 (1988).**

Residential garbage, placed at the curb for collection, does not benefit from the presumption of privacy and therefore is unprotected by the Fourth Amendment.

UNITED STATES V. JONES

565 U.S. 400, 132 S.Ct. 945, 181 L.Ed. 2d 911 (2012)

Antoine Jones was placed under surveillance by a joint task force of the FBI and the District of Columbia Metropolitan Police Department because of suspected drug trafficking. FBI agents in Maryland installed a global-positioning system (GPS) tracking device on Jones' jeep when it was parked in a public parking lot. The car was monitored for 28 days. Based on the resulting 2000 pages of data. Jones was convicted and given a life sentence for drug trafficking. With a motion to suppress the evidence because a warrant in Maryland was not obtained, the Appellate Court reversed the conviction noting the use of evidence obtained without a warrant violated the Fourth Amendment.

Vote: 9–0.

JUSTICE SCALIA delivered the opinion of the Court.

II

A

The Fourth Amendment provides in relevant part that "[t]he right of the people to be secure in their persons, houses, papers, and effects, against unreasonable searches and seizures, shall not be violated." It is beyond dispute that a vehicle is an "effect" as that term is used in the Amendment. We hold that the Government's installation of a GPS device on a target's vehicle, and its use of that device to monitor the vehicle's movements, constitutes a "search."

It is important to be clear about what occurred in this case: The Government physically occupied private property for the purpose of obtaining information. We have no doubt that such a physical intrusion would have been considered a "search" within the meaning of the Fourth Amendment when it was adopted.

The text of the Fourth Amendment reflects its close connection to property, since otherwise it would have referred simply to "the right of the people to be secure against unreasonable searches and seizures"; the phrase "in their persons, houses, papers, and effects" would have been superfluous.

Consistent with this understanding, our Fourth Amendment jurisprudence was tied to common-law trespass, at least until the latter half of the 20th century. *Kyllo* v. *United States*, 533 U. S. 27, 31 (2001). Thus, in *Olmstead* v. *United States*, 277 U. S. 438, 464 (1928), we held that wiretaps attached to telephone wires on the public streets did not constitute a Fourth Amendment search because "[t]here was no entry of the houses or offices of the defendants."

Our later cases, of course, have deviated from that exclusively property-based approach. In *Katz* v. *United States*, 389 U. S. 347, 351 (1967), we said that "the Fourth Amendment protects people, not places," and found a violation in attachment of an eavesdropping device to a public telephone booth. Our later cases have applied the analysis of Justice Harlan's concurrence in that case, which said that a violation occurs when government officers violate a person's "reasonable expectation of privacy." The Government contends that the Harlan standard shows that no search occurred here, since Jones had no "reasonable expectation of privacy" in the area of the Jeep accessed by Government agents (its underbody) and in the locations of the Jeep on the public roads, which were visible to all. But we need not address the Government's contentions, because Jones's Fourth Amendment rights do not rise or fall with the *Katz* formulation. At bottom, we must "assur[e] preservation of that degree of privacy against government that existed when the Fourth Amendment was adopted." *Kyllo* at 34. As explained, for most of our history the Fourth Amendment was understood to embody a particular concern for government trespass upon the areas ("persons, houses, papers, and effects") it enumerates. *Katz* did not repudiate that understanding. Less than two years later the Court upheld defendants' contention that the Government could not introduce against them conversations between *other* people obtained by warrantless placement of electronic surveillance devices in their homes. The opinion rejected the dissent's contention that there was no Fourth Amendment violation "unless the conversational privacy of the homeowner himself is invaded." *Alderman* v. *United States*, 394 U. S. 165, 176 (1969). "[W]e [do not] believe that *Katz*, by holding that the Fourth Amendment protects persons and their private conversations, was intended to withdraw any of the protection which the Amendment extends to the home . . . ." *Id.*, at 180.

More recently, in *Soldal* v. *Cook County*, 506 U. S. 56, 62 (1992), the Court unanimously rejected the argument that although a "seizure" had occurred "in a 'technical' sense" when a trailer home was forcibly removed, no Fourth Amendment violation occurred because law enforcement had not "invade[d] the [individuals'] privacy." *Katz*, the Court explained, established that "property rights are not the sole measure of Fourth Amendment violations," but did not "snuf[f] out the previously recognized protection for property." 506 U. S., at 64. As Justice Brennan explained in his concurrence in *United States v. Knotts*, 460 U.S. 276, 286 (1983), *Katz* did not erode the principle "that, when the Government *does* engage in physical intrusion of a constitutionally protected area in order to obtain information, that intrusion may constitute a violation of the Fourth Amendment."

The Government contends that several of our post-*Katz* cases foreclose the conclusion that what occurred here constituted a search. It relies principally on two cases in which we rejected Fourth Amendment challenges to "beepers," electronic tracking devices that represent another form of electronic monitoring. The first case, *Knotts*, upheld against Fourth Amendment challenge the use of a "beeper" that had been placed in a container of chloroform, allowing law enforcement to monitor the location of the container. We said that there had been no infringement of Knotts' reasonable expectation of privacy since the information obtained—the location of the automobile carrying the container on public roads, and the location of the off-loaded container in open fields near Knotts' cabin—had been voluntarily conveyed to the public. But as we have discussed, the *Katz* reasonable-expectation-of-privacy test has been *added to*, not *substituted for*, the common-law trespassory test. The holding in *Knotts* addressed only the former, since the latter was not at issue. The beeper had been placed in the container before it came into Knotts' possession, with the consent of the then-owner. *Knotts* did not challenge that installation, and we specifically declined to consider its effect on the Fourth Amendment analysis.

The second "beeper" case, *United States* v. *Karo*, 468 U. S. 705 (1984), does not suggest a different conclusion. There we addressed the question left open by *Knotts*, whether the installation of a beeper in a container amounted to a search or seizure. As in *Knotts*, at the time the beeper was installed the container belonged to a third party, and it did not come into possession of the defendant until later. Thus, the specific question we considered was whether the installation "*with the consent of the original owner* constitute[d] a search or seizure . . . when the container is delivered to a buyer having no knowledge of the presence of the beeper." *Id.*, at 707. We held not. The Government, we said, came into physical contact with the container only before it belonged to the defendant Karo; and the transfer of the container with the unmonitored beeper inside did not convey any information and thus did not invade Karo's privacy. That conclusion is perfectly consistent with the one we reach here. Karo accepted the container as it came to him, beeper and all, and was therefore not entitled to object to the beeper's presence, even though it was used to monitor the container's location. Jones, who possessed the Jeep at the time the Government trespassorily inserted the information-gathering device, is on much different footing.

By attaching the device to the Jeep, officers encroached on a protected area.

B

The concurrence begins by accusing us of applying "18th-century tort law." That is a distortion. What we apply is an 18th-century guarantee against un-reasonable searches, which we believe must provide *at a minimum* the degree of protection it afforded when it was adopted. The concurrence does not share that belief. It would apply *exclusively Katz*'s reasonable-expectation-of-privacy test, even when that eliminates rights that previously existed.

The concurrence faults our approach for "present[ing] particularly vexing problems" in cases that do not involve physical contact, such as those that involve the transmission of electronic signals. We entirely fail to understand that point. For unlike the concurrence, which would make *Katz* the *exclusive* test, we do not make trespass the exclusive test. Situations involving merely the transmission of electronic signals without trespass would *remain* subject to *Katz* analysis.

In fact, it is the concurrence's insistence on the exclusivity of the *Katz* test that needlessly leads us into "particularly vexing problems" in the present case. This Court has to date not deviated from the understanding that mere visual observation does not constitute a search. We accordingly held in *Knotts* that "[a] person traveling in an automobile on public thoroughfares has no reasonable expectation of privacy in his movements from one place to another." 460 U. S., at 281. Thus, even assuming that the concurrence is correct to say that "[t]raditional surveillance" of Jones for a 4-week period "would have required a large team of agents, multiple vehicles, and perhaps aerial assistance," our cases suggest that such visual observation is constitutionally permissible. It may be that achieving the same result through electronic means, without an accompanying trespass, is an unconstitutional invasion of privacy, but the present case does not require us to answer that question.

And answering it affirmatively leads us needlessly into additional thorny problems. The concurrence posits that "relatively short-term monitoring of a person's movements on public streets" is okay, but that "the use of longer term GPS monitoring in investigations *of most offenses*" is no good. That introduces yet another novelty into our jurisprudence. There is no precedent for the proposition that whether a search has occurred depends on the nature of the crime being investigated. And even accepting that novelty, it remains unexplained why a 4-week investigation is "surely" too long and why a drug-trafficking conspiracy involving substantial amounts of cash and narcotics is not an "extra-ordinary offens[e]" which may permit longer observation. What of a 2-day monitoring of a suspected purveyor of stolen electronics? Or of a 6-month monitoring of a suspected terrorist? We may have to grapple with these "vexing problems" in some future case where a classic trespassory search is not involved and resort must be had to *Katz* analysis; but there is no reason for rushing forward to resolve them here.

* * *

The judgment of the Court of Appeals for the D. C. Circuit is affirmed.

It is so ordered.

JUSTICE SOTOMAYOR, concurring.

I join the Court's opinion because I agree that a search within the meaning of the Fourth Amendment occurs, at a minimum, "[w]here, as here, the Government obtains information by physically intruding on a constitutionally protected area." The Government usurped Jones' property for the purpose of conducting surveillance on him, thereby invading privacy interests long afforded, and undoubtedly entitled to, Fourth Amendment protection.

Of course, the Fourth Amendment is not concerned only with trespassory intrusions on property. Rather, even in the absence of a trespass, "a Fourth Amendment search occurs when the government violates a subjective expectation of privacy that society recognizes as reasonable." *Kyllo* v. *United States*, 533 U. S. 27–33 (2001). In *Katz* v. *United States*, 389 U. S. 347, 361 (1967), this Court enlarged its then-prevailing focus on property rights by announcing that the reach of the Fourth Amendment does not "turn upon the presence or absence of a physical intrusion." As the majority's opinion makes clear, however, *Katz*'s reasonable-expectation-of-privacy test augmented, but did not displace or diminish, the common-law trespassory test that preceded it. Thus, "when the Government *does* engage in physical intrusion of a constitutionally protected area in order to obtain information, that intrusion may constitute a violation of the Fourth Amendment." *United States* v. *Knotts*, 460 U. S. 276, 286 (1983). Justice Alito's approach, which discounts altogether the constitutional relevance of the Government's physical intrusion on Jones' Jeep, erodes that longstanding protection for privacy expectations inherent in items of property that people possess or control. By contrast, the trespassory test applied in the majority's opinion reflects an irreducible constitutional minimum: When the Government physically invades personal property to gather information, a search occurs. The reaffirmation of that principle suffices to decide this case.

Nonetheless, as Justice Alito notes, physical intrusion is now unnecessary to many forms of surveillance. With increasing regularity, the Government will be capable of duplicating the monitoring undertaken in this case by enlisting factory- or owner-installed vehicle tracking devices or GPS-enabled smartphones. In cases of electronic or other novel modes of surveillance that do not depend upon a physical invasion on property, the majority opinion's trespassory test may provide little guidance. As Justice Alito incisively observes, the same technological advances that have made possible nontrespassory surveillance techniques will also affect the *Katz* test by shaping the evolution of societal privacy expectations. Under that rubric, I agree with Justice Alito that, at the very least, "longer term GPS monitoring in investigations of most offenses impinges on expectations of privacy."

In cases involving even short-term monitoring, some unique attributes of GPS surveillance relevant to the *Katz* analysis will require particular attention. GPS monitoring generates a precise, comprehensive record of a person's public movements that reflects a wealth of detail about her familial, political, professional, religious, and sexual associations. The Government can store such records and efficiently mine them for information years into the future. And because GPS monitoring is cheap in comparison to conventional surveillance techniques and, by design, proceeds surreptitiously, it evades the ordinary checks that constrain abusive law enforcement practices: "limited police resources and community hostility."

Awareness that the Government may be watching chills associational and expressive freedoms. And the Government's unrestrained power to assemble data that reveal private aspects of identity is susceptible to abuse. The net result is that GPS monitoring—by making available at a relatively low cost such a substantial quantum of intimate information about any person whom the Government, in its unfettered discretion, chooses to track—may "alter the relationship between citizen and government in a way that is inimical to democratic society."

I would take these attributes of GPS monitoring into account when considering the existence of a reasonable societal expectation of privacy in the sum of one's public movements. I would ask whether people reasonably expect that their movements will be recorded and aggregated in a manner that enables the Government to ascertain, more or less at will, their political and religious beliefs, sexual habits, and so on. I do not regard as dispositive the fact that the Government might obtain the fruits of GPS monitoring through lawful conventional surveillance techniques. I would also consider the appropriateness of entrusting to the Executive, in the absence of any oversight from a coordinate branch, a tool so amenable to misuse, especially in light of the Fourth Amendment's goal to curb arbitrary exercises of police power to and prevent "a too permeating police surveillance."

More fundamentally, it may be necessary to reconsider the premise that an individual has no reasonable expectation of privacy in information voluntarily disclosed to third parties. This approach is ill suited to the digital age, in which people reveal a great deal of information about themselves to third parties in the course of carrying out mundane tasks. People disclose the phone numbers that they dial or text to their cellular providers; the URLs that they visit and the e-mail addresses with which they correspond to their Internet service providers; and the books, groceries, and medications they purchase to online retailers. Perhaps, as Justice Alito notes, some people may find the "tradeoff" of privacy for convenience "worthwhile," or come to accept this "diminution of privacy" as "inevitable," and perhaps not. I for one doubt that people would accept without complaint the warrantless disclosure to the Government of a list of every Web site they had visited in the last week, or month, or year. But whatever the societal expectations, they can attain constitutionally protected status only if our Fourth Amendment jurisprudence ceases to treat secrecy as a prerequisite for privacy. I would not assume that all information voluntarily disclosed to some member of the public for a limited purpose is, for that reason alone, disentitled to Fourth Amendment protection.

Resolution of these difficult questions in this case is unnecessary, however, because the Government's physical intrusion on Jones' Jeep supplies a narrower basis for decision. I therefore join the majority's opinion.

JUSTICE ALITO, with whom JUSTICES GINSBURG, BREYER, and KAGAN join, concurring in the judgment.

This case requires us to apply the Fourth Amendment's prohibition of unreasonable searches and seizures to a 21st-century surveillance technique, the use of a Global Positioning System (GPS) device to monitor a vehicle's movements for an extended period of time. Ironically, the Court has chosen to decide this case based on 18th-century tort law. By attaching a small GPS device to the underside of the vehicle that respondent drove, the law enforcement officers in this case engaged in conduct that might have provided grounds in 1791 for a suit for trespass to chattels. And for this reason, the Court concludes, the installation and use of the GPS device constituted a search.

This holding, in my judgment, is unwise. It strains the language of the Fourth Amendment; it has little if any support in current Fourth Amendment case law; and it is highly artificial.

I would analyze the question presented in this case by asking whether respondent's reasonable expectations of privacy were violated by the long-term monitoring of the movements of the vehicle he drove.

I

A

The Fourth Amendment prohibits "unreasonable searches and seizures," and the Court makes very little effort to explain how the attachment or use of the GPS device fits within these terms. The Court does not contend that there was a seizure. A seizure of property occurs when there is "some meaningful interference with an individual's possessory interests in that property," *United States* v. *Jacobsen,* 466 U. S. 109, 113 (1984), and here there was none. Indeed, the success of the surveillance technique that the officers employed was dependent on the fact that the GPS did not interfere in any way with the operation of the vehicle, for if any such interference had been detected, the device might have been discovered.

The Court does claim that the installation and use of the GPS constituted a search, but this conclusion is dependent on the questionable proposition that these two procedures cannot be separated for purposes of Fourth Amendment analysis. If these two procedures are analyzed separately, it is not at all clear from the Court's opinion why either should be regarded as a search. It is clear that the attachment of the GPS device was not itself a search; if the device had not functioned or if the officers had not used it, no information would have been obtained. And the Court does not contend that the use of the device constituted a search either. On the contrary, the Court accepts the holding in *United States* v. *Knotts,* 460 U. S. 276 (1983), that the use of a surreptitiously planted electronic device to monitor a vehicle's movements on public roads did not amount to a search.

The Court argues—and I agree—that "we must 'assur[e] preservation of that degree of privacy against government that existed when the Fourth Amendment was adopted.' " But it is almost impossible to think of late-18th-century situations that are analogous to what took place in this case. (Is it possible to imagine a case in which a constable secreted himself somewhere in a coach and remained there for a period of time in order to monitor the movements of the coach's owner?) The Court's theory seems to be that the concept of a search, as originally understood, comprehended any technical trespass that led to the gathering of evidence, but we know that this is incorrect. At common law, any unauthorized intrusion on private property was actionable, but a trespass on open fields, as opposed to the "curtilage" of a home, does not fall within the scope of the Fourth Amendment because private property outside the curtilage is not part of a "hous[e]" within the meaning of the Fourth Amendment.

B

The Court's reasoning in this case is very similar to that in the Court's early decisions involving wiretapping and electronic eavesdropping, namely, that a technical trespass followed by the gathering of evidence constitutes a search. In the early electronic surveillance cases, the Court concluded that a Fourth Amendment search occurred when private conversations were monitored as a result of an "unauthorized physical penetration into the premises occupied" by the defendant. In *Silverman* v. *United States,* 365 U. S. 505, 509 (1961), police officers listened to conversations in an attached home by inserting a "spike mike" through the wall that this house shared with the vacant house next door. This procedure was held to be a search because the mike made contact with a heating duct on the other side of the wall and thus "usurp[ed] . . . an integral part of the premises."

By contrast, in cases in which there was no trespass, it was held that there was no search. Thus, in *Olmstead* v. *United States,* 277 U. S. 438 (1928), the Court found that the Fourth Amendment did not apply because "[t]he taps from house lines were made in the streets near the houses." Similarly, the Court concluded that no search occurred in *Goldman* v. *United States,* 316 U. S. 129, 135 (1942), where a "detectaphone" was placed on the outer wall of defendant's office for the purpose of overhearing conversations held within the room.

This trespass-based rule was repeatedly criticized. In *Olmstead,* Justice Brandeis wrote that it was "immaterial where the physical connection with the telephone wires was made." Although a private conversation transmitted by wire did not fall within the literal words of the Fourth Amendment, he argued, the Amendment should be understood as prohibiting "every unjustifiable intrusion by the government upon the privacy of the individual."

Katz v. *United States,* 389 U. S. 347 (1967), finally did away with the old approach, holding that a trespass was not required for a Fourth Amendment violation. *Katz* involved the use of a listening device that was attached to the outside of a public telephone booth and that allowed police officers to eavesdrop on one end of the target's phone conversation. This procedure did not physically intrude on the area occupied by the target, but the *Katz* Court, "repudiate[ed]" the old doctrine and held that "[t]he fact that the electronic device employed . . . did not happen to penetrate the wall of the booth can have no constitutional significance." What mattered, the Court now held, was whether the conduct at issue "violated the privacy upon which [the defendant] justifiably relied while using the telephone booth."

Under this approach, as the Court later put it when addressing the relevance of a technical trespass, "an actual trespass is neither necessary *nor sufficient* to establish a constitutional violation," *United States* v. *Karo,* 468 U. S. 705, 713 (1984).

II

The majority suggests that two post-*Katz* decisions—*Soldal v. Cook County*, 506 U. S. 56 (1992), and *Alderman v. United States*, 394 U. S. 165 (1969)—show that a technical trespass is sufficient to establish the existence of a search, but they provide little support. In *Soldal*, the Court held that towing away a trailer home without the owner's consent constituted a seizure even if this did not invade the occupants' personal privacy. But in the present case, the Court does not find that there was a seizure, and it is clear that none occurred. In *Alderman,* the Court held that the Fourth Amendment rights of homeowners were implicated by the use of a surreptitiously planted listening device to monitor third-party conversations that occurred within their home. *Alderman* is best understood to mean that the homeowners had a legitimate expectation of privacy in all conversations that took place under their roof. In sum, the majority is hard pressed to find support in post-*Katz* cases for its trespass-based theory.

III

Disharmony with a substantial body of existing case law is only one of the problems with the Court's approach in this case.

I will briefly note four others. First, the Court's reasoning largely disregards what is really important (the *use* of a GPS for the purpose of long-term tracking) and instead attaches great significance to something that most would view as relatively minor (attaching to the bottom of a car a small, light object that does not interfere in any way with the car's operation). Attaching such an object is generally regarded as so trivial that it does not provide a basis for recovery under modern tort law. But under the Court's reasoning, this conduct may violate the Fourth Amendment. By contrast, if long-term monitoring can be accomplished without committing a technical trespass—suppose, for example, that the Federal Government required or persuaded auto manufacturers to include a GPS tracking device in every car—the Court's theory would provide no protection.

Second, the Court's approach leads to incongruous results. If the police attach a GPS device to a car and use the device to follow the car for even a brief time, under the Court's theory, the Fourth Amendment applies. But if the police follow the same car for a much longer period using unmarked cars and aerial assistance, this tracking is not subject to any Fourth Amendment constraints. In the present case, the Fourth Amendment applies, the Court concludes, because the officers installed the GPS device after respondent's wife, to whom the car was registered, turned it over to respondent for his exclusive use. But if the GPS had been attached prior to that time, the Court's theory would lead to a different result. So if the GPS device had been installed before respondent's wife gave him the keys, respondent would have no claim for trespass—and, presumably, no Fourth Amendment claim either.

Third, under the Court's theory, the coverage of the Fourth Amendment may vary from State to State. If the events at issue here had occurred in a community property State or a State that has adopted the Uniform Marital Property Act, respondent would likely be an owner of the vehicle, and it would not matter whether the GPS was installed before or after his wife turned over the keys. In non-community-property States, on the other hand, the registration of the vehicle in the name of respondent's wife would generally be regarded as presumptive evidence that she was the sole owner.

Fourth, the Court's reliance on the law of trespass will present particularly vexing problems in cases involving surveillance that is carried out by making electronic, as opposed to physical, contact with the item to be tracked. For example, suppose that the officers in the present case had followed respondent by surreptitiously activating a stolen vehicle detection system that came with the car when it was purchased. Would the sending of a radio signal to activate this system constitute a trespass to chattels? Trespass to chattels has traditionally required a physical touching of the property. In recent years, courts have wrestled with the application of this old tort in cases involving unwanted electronic contact with computer systems, and some have held that even the transmission of electrons that occurs when a communication is sent from one computer to another is enough. But may such decisions be followed in applying the Court's trespass theory? Assuming that what matters under the Court's theory is the law of trespass as it existed at the time of the adoption of the Fourth Amendment, do these recent decisions represent a change in the law or simply the application of the old tort to new situations?

IV

A

The *Katz* expectation-of-privacy test avoids the problems and complications noted above, but it is not without its own difficulties. It involves a degree of circularity, and judges are apt to confuse their own expectations of privacy with those of the hypothetical reasonable person to which the *Katz* test looks. In addition, the *Katz* test rests on the assumption that this hypothetical reasonable person has a well-developed and stable set of privacy expectations. But technology can change those expectations. Dramatic technological change may lead to periods in which popular expectations are in flux and may ultimately produce significant changes in popular attitudes. New technology may provide increased convenience or security at the expense of privacy, and many people may find the tradeoff worthwhile. And even if the public does not welcome the diminution of privacy that new technology entails, they may eventually reconcile themselves to this development as inevitable.

On the other hand, concern about new intrusions on privacy may spur the enactment of legislation to protect against these intrusions. This is what ultimately happened with respect to wiretapping. After *Katz*, Congress did not leave it to the courts to develop a body of Fourth Amendment case law governing that complex subject. Instead, Congress promptly enacted a comprehensive statute and since that time, the regulation of wiretapping has been governed primarily by statute and not by case law. In an ironic sense, although *Katz* overruled *Olmstead*, Chief Justice Taft's suggestion in the latter case that the regulation of wiretapping was a matter better left for Congress has been borne out.

B

Recent years have seen the emergence of many new devices that permit the monitoring of a person's movements. In some locales, closed-circuit television video monitoring is becoming ubiquitous. On toll roads, automatic toll collection systems create a precise record of the movements of motorists who choose to make use of that convenience. Many motorists purchase cars that are equipped with devices that permit a central station to ascertain the car's location at any time so that roadside assistance may be provided if needed and the car may be found if it is stolen.

Perhaps most significant, cell phones and other wireless devices now permit wireless carriers to track and record the location of users—and as of June 2011, it has been reported, there were more than 322 million wireless devices in use in the United States. For older phones, the accuracy of the location information depends on the density of the tower network, but new "smart phones," which are equipped with a GPS device, permit more precise tracking. For example, when a user activates the GPS on such a phone, a provider is able to monitor the phone's location and speed of movement and can then report back real-time traffic conditions after combining ("crowdsourcing") the speed of all such phones on any particular road. Similarly, phone-location-tracking services are offered as "social" tools, allowing consumers to find (or to avoid) others who enroll in these services. The availability and use of these and other new devices will continue to shape the average person's expectations about the privacy of his or her daily movements.

V

In the pre-computer age, the greatest protections of privacy were neither constitutional nor statutory, but practical. Traditional surveillance for any extended period of time was difficult and costly and therefore rarely undertaken. The surveillance at issue in this case—constant monitoring of the location of a vehicle for four weeks—would have required a large team of agents, multiple vehicles, and perhaps aerial assistance. Only an investigation of unusual importance could have justified such an expenditure of law enforcement resources. Devices like the one used in the present case, however, make long-term monitoring relatively easy and cheap. In circumstances involving dramatic technological change, the best solution to privacy concerns may be legislative. A legislative body is well situated to gauge changing public attitudes, to draw detailed lines, and to balance privacy and public safety in a comprehensive way.

To date, however, Congress and most States have not enacted statutes regulating the use of GPS tracking technology for law enforcement purposes. The best that we can do in this case is to apply existing Fourth Amendment doctrine and to ask whether the use of GPS tracking in a particular case involved a degree of intrusion that a reasonable person would not have anticipated.

Under this approach, relatively short-term monitoring of a person's movements on public streets accords with expectations of privacy that our society has recognized as reasonable. But the use of longer term GPS monitoring in investigations of most offenses impinges on expectations of privacy. For such offenses, society's expectation has been that law enforcement agents and others would not—and indeed, in the main, simply could not—secretly monitor and catalogue every single movement of an individual's car for a very long period. In this case, for four weeks, law enforcement agents tracked every movement that respondent made in the vehicle he was driving. We need not identify with precision the point at which the tracking of this vehicle became a search, for the line was surely crossed before the 4-week mark. Other cases may present more difficult questions. But where uncertainty exists with respect to whether a certain period of GPS surveillance is long enough to constitute a Fourth Amendment search, the police may always seek a warrant. We also need not consider whether prolonged GPS monitoring in the context of investigations involving extraordinary offenses would similarly intrude on a constitutionally protected sphere of privacy. In such cases, long-term tracking might have been mounted using previously available techniques.

* * *

For these reasons, I conclude that the lengthy monitoring that occurred in this case constituted a search under the Fourth Amendment. I therefore agree with the majority that the decision of the Court of Appeals must be affirmed.

FOR DISCUSSION

How might continuing changes in technology impact the Fourth Amendment? Does this case provide some guidelines which could be applicable as technology which can help police evolves?

RELATED CASE

***Grady v. North Carolina:* 575 U.S. ___ (2015).**

GPS placed on a convicted felon to monitor his movements constitutes an unlawful search and seizure in the Fourth Amendment.

TERRY V. OHIO

392 U.S. 1, 88 S.Ct. 1868, 20 L.Ed.2d 889 (1968)

Terry and his codefendant, Richard Chilton, were prosecuted and convicted based on two revolvers and bullets obtained in a challenged search by a police detective in Cleveland. Officer Martin McFadden was patrolling in plain clothes when Chilton and Terry behaved in a way that attracted his attention. The men's actions led him to suspect that the subjects were casing a store prior to an attempt at a daytime robbery. Soon after making this observation, McFadden identified himself as a police officer, and in response to the actions of Terry and Chilton, patted down their clothing. The trial court denied a motion to suppress the evidence, ruling that this frisk was essential to the performance of the officer's investigatory duties. The suspects were found guilty, and the Ohio Court of Appeals affirmed.

Vote: 8–1

CHIEF JUSTICE WARREN delivered the opinion of the Court.

I

We have recently held that "the Fourth Amendment protects people, not places," *Katz v. United States*, 389 U.S. 347, 351 (1967), and wherever an individual may harbor a reasonable "expectation of privacy," he is entitled to be free from unreasonable governmental intrusion. Of course, the specific content and incidents of this right must be shaped by the context in which it is asserted. For "what the Constitution forbids is not all searches and seizures, but unreasonable searches and seizures." *Elkins v. United States*, 364 U.S. 206, 222 (1960). Unquestionably petitioner was entitled to the protection of the Fourth Amendment as he walked down the street in Cleveland. The question is whether in all the circumstances of this on-the-street encounter, his right to personal security was violated by an unreasonable search and seizure.

We would be less than candid if we did not acknowledge that this question thrusts to the fore difficult and troublesome issues regarding a sensitive area of police activity—issues which have never before been squarely presented to this Court. Reflective of the tensions involved are the practical and constitutional arguments pressed with great vigor on both sides of the public debate over the power of the police to "stop and frisk"—as it is sometimes euphemistically termed—suspicious persons.

On the one hand, it is frequently argued that in dealing with the rapidly unfolding and often dangerous situations on city streets the police are in need of an escalating set of flexible responses, graduated in relation to the amount of information they possess. For this purpose it is urged that distinctions should be made between a "stop" and an "arrest" (or a "seizure" of a person), and between a "frisk" and a "search."

On the other side the argument is made that the authority of the police must be strictly circumscribed by the law of arrest and search as it has developed to date in the traditional jurisprudence of the Fourth Amendment. It is contended with some force that there is not—and cannot be—a variety of police activity which does not depend solely upon the voluntary cooperation of the citizen and yet which stops short of an arrest based upon probable cause to make such an arrest.

In this context we approach the issues in this case mindful of the limitations of the judicial function in controlling the myriad daily situations in which policemen and citizens confront each other on the street. The State has characterized the issue here as "the right of a police officer . . . to make an on-the-street stop, interrogate and pat down for weapons (known in street vernacular as 'stop and frisk')." But this is only partly accurate. For the issue is not the abstract propriety of the police conduct, but the admissibility against petitioner of the evidence uncovered by the search and seizure. Ever since its inception, the rule excluding evidence seized in violation of the Fourth Amendment has been recognized as a principal mode of discouraging lawless police conduct. See *Weeks v. United States*, 232 U.S. 383, 391–393 (1914). Thus its major thrust is a deterrent one, and experience has taught that it is the only effective deterrent to police misconduct in the criminal context, and that without it the constitutional guarantee against unreasonable searches and seizures would be a mere "form of words." *Mapp v. Ohio*, 367 U.S. 643, 655 (1961). The rule also serves another vital function—"the imperative of judicial integrity." *Elkins v. United States*, 364 U.S. 206, 222 (1960).

The exclusionary rule has its limitations, however, as a tool of judicial control. It cannot properly be invoked to exclude the products of legitimate police investigative techniques on the ground that much conduct which is closely similar involves unwarranted intrusions upon constitutional protections. Moreover, in some contexts the rule is ineffective as a deterrent.

Proper adjudication of cases in which the exclusionary rule is invoked demands a constant awareness of these limitations. The wholesale harassment by certain elements of the police community, of which minority groups, particularly Negroes, frequently complain, will not be stopped by the exclusion of any evidence from any criminal trial. Yet a rigid and unthinking application of the exclusionary rule, in futile protest against practices which it can never be used effectively to control, may exact a high toll in human injury and frustration of efforts to prevent crime.

II

Our first task is to establish at what point in this encounter the Fourth Amendment becomes relevant. That is, we must decide whether and when Officer McFadden "seized" Terry and whether and when he conducted a "search." There is some suggestion in the use of such terms as "stop" and "frisk" that such police conduct is outside the purview of the Fourth Amendment because neither action rises to the level of a "search" or "seizure" within the meaning of the Constitution. We emphatically reject this notion. It is quite plain that the Fourth Amendment governs "seizures" of the person which do not eventuate in a trip to the station house and prosecution for crime—"arrests" in traditional terminology. It must be recognized that whenever a police officer accosts an individual and restrains his freedom to walk away, he has "seized" that person. And it is nothing less than sheer torture of the English language to suggest that a careful exploration of the outer surfaces of a person's clothing all over his or her body in an attempt to find weapons is not a "search." Moreover, it is simply fantastic to urge that such a procedure performed in public by a policeman while the citizen stands helpless, perhaps facing a wall with his hands raised, is a "petty indignity." It is a serious intrusion upon the sanctity of the person, which may inflict great indignity and arouse strong resentment, and it is not to be undertaken lightly.

We therefore reject the notions that the Fourth Amendment does not come into play at all as a limitation upon police conduct if the officers stop short of something called a "technical arrest" or a "full-blown search."

In this case there can be no question, then, that Officer McFadden "seized" petitioner and subjected him to a "search" when he took hold of him and patted down the outer surfaces of his clothing. We must decide whether at that point it was reasonable for Officer McFadden to have interfered with petitioner's personal security as he did. And in determining whether the seizure and search were "unreasonable" our inquiry is a dual one—whether the officer's action was justified at its inception, and whether it was reasonably related in scope to the circumstances which justified the interference in the first place.

III

If this case involved police conduct subject to the Warrant Clause of the Fourth Amendment, we would have to ascertain whether "probable cause" existed to justify the search and seizure which took place. However, that is not the case. . . . [W]e deal here with an entire rubric of police conduct—necessarily swift action predicated upon the on-the-spot observations of the officer on the beat—which historically has not been, and as a practical matter could not be, subjected to the warrant procedure. Instead, the conduct involved in this case must be tested by the Fourth Amendment's general proscription against unreasonable searches and seizures.

In order to assess the reasonableness of Officer McFadden's conduct as a general proposition, it is necessary "first to focus upon the governmental interest which allegedly justifies official intrusion upon the constitutionally protected interests of the private citizen," for there is "no ready test for determining reasonableness other than by balancing the need to search [or seize] against the invasion which the search [or seizure] entails." *Camara v. Municipal Court*, 387 U.S. 523, 534–535 (1967). And in justifying the particular intrusion the police officer must be able to point to specific and articulable facts which, taken together with rational inferences from those facts, reasonably warrant that intrusion. Anything less would invite intrusions upon constitutionally guaranteed rights based on nothing more substantial than inarticulate hunches, a result this Court has consistently refused to sanction.

Applying these principles to this case, we consider first the nature and extent of the governmental interests involved. One general interest is of course that of effective crime prevention and detection; it is this interest which underlies the recognition that a police officer may in appropriate circumstances and in an appropriate manner approach a person for purposes of investigating possibly criminal behavior even though there is no probable cause to make an arrest. It was this legitimate investigative function Officer McFadden was discharging when he decided to approach petitioner and his companions. He had observed Terry, Chilton, and Katz [a third man who had joined Terry and Chilton] go through a series of acts, each of them perhaps innocent in itself, but which taken together warranted further investigation. It would have been poor police work indeed for an officer of 30 years' experience in the detection of thievery from stores in this same neighborhood to have failed to investigate this behavior further.

The crux of this case, however, is not the propriety of Officer McFadden's taking steps to investigate petitioner's suspicious behavior, but rather, whether there was justification for McFadden's invasion of Terry's personal security by searching him for weapons in the course of that investigation. We are now concerned with more than the governmental interest in investigating crime; in addition, there is the more immediate interest of the police officer in taking steps to assure himself that the person with whom he is dealing is not armed with a weapon that could unexpectedly and fatally be used against him. American criminals have a long tradition of armed violence, and every year in this country many law enforcement officers are killed in the line of duty, and thousands more are wounded.

In view of these facts, we cannot blind ourselves to the need for law enforcement officers to protect themselves and other prospective victims of violence in situations where they may lack probable cause for an arrest.

We must still consider, however, the nature and quality of the intrusion on individual rights which must be accepted if police officers are to be conceded the right to search for weapons in situations where probable cause to arrest for crime is lacking. Even a limited search of the outer clothing for weapons constitutes a severe, though brief, intrusion upon cherished personal security, and it must surely be an annoying, frightening, and perhaps humiliating experience.

Our evaluation of the proper balance that has to be struck in this type of case leads us to conclude that there must be a narrowly drawn authority to permit a reasonable search for weapons for the protection of the police officer, where he has reason to believe that he is dealing with an armed and dangerous individual, regardless of whether he has probable cause to arrest the individual for a crime. The officer need not be absolutely certain that the individual is armed; the issue is whether a reasonably prudent man in the circumstances would be warranted in the belief that his safety or that of others was in danger. And in determining whether the officer acted reasonably in such circumstances, due weight must be given, not to his inchoate and unparticularized suspicion or "hunch," but to the specific reasonable inferences which he is entitled to draw from the facts in light of his experience.

IV

We must now examine the conduct of Officer McFadden in this case to determine whether his search and seizure of petitioner were reasonable, both at their inception and as conducted. We think on the facts and circumstances Officer McFadden detailed before the trial judge a reasonably prudent man would have been warranted in believing petitioner was armed and thus presented a threat to the officer's safety while he was investigating his suspicious behavior. The actions of Terry and Chilton were consistent with McFadden's hypothesis that these men were contemplating a daylight robbery—which, it is reasonable to assume, would be likely to involve the use of weapons—and nothing in their conduct from the time he first noticed them until the time he confronted them and identified himself as a police officer gave him sufficient reason to negate that hypothesis.

V

We conclude that the revolver seized from Terry was properly admitted in evidence against him. At the time he seized petitioner and searched him for weapons, Officer McFadden had reasonable grounds to believe that petitioner was armed and dangerous, and it was necessary for the protection of himself and others to take swift measures to discover the true facts and neutralize the threat of harm if it materialized. The policeman carefully restricted his search to what was appropriate to the discovery of the particular items which he sought. We merely hold today that where a police officer observes unusual conduct which leads him reasonably to conclude in light of his experience that criminal activity may be afoot and that the persons with whom he is dealing may be armed and presently dangerous, where in the course of investigating this behavior he identifies himself as a policeman and makes reasonable inquiries, and where nothing in the initial stages of the encounter serves to dispel his reasonable fear for his own or others' safety, he is entitled for the protection of himself and others in the area to conduct a carefully limited search of the outer clothing of such persons in an attempt to discover weapons which might be used to assault him. Such a search is a reasonable search under the Fourth Amendment, and any weapons seized may properly be introduced in evidence against the person from whom they were taken.

Affirmed.

JUSTICE BLACK concurs in the judgment.

JUSTICE HARLAN, concurring.

While I unreservedly agree with the Court's ultimate holding in this case, I am constrained to fill in a few gaps, as I see them, in its opinion. I do this because what is said by this Court today will serve as initial guidelines for law enforcement authorities and courts throughout the land as this important new field of law develops.

The state courts held, . . ., that when an officer is lawfully confronting a possibly hostile person in the line of duty he has a right, springing only from the necessity of the situation and not from any broader right to disarm, to frisk for his own protection. This holding, with which I agree and with which I think the Court agrees, offers the only satisfactory basis I can think of for affirming this conviction. The holding has, however, two logical corollaries that I do not think the Court has fully expressed.

In the first place, if the frisk is justified in order to protect the officer during an encounter with a citizen, the officer must first have constitutional grounds to insist on an encounter, to make a forcible stop. Any person, including a policeman, is at liberty to avoid a person he considers dangerous. If and when a policeman has a right instead to disarm such a person for his own protection, he must first have a right not to avoid him but to be in his presence. I would make it perfectly clear that the right to frisk in this case depends upon the reasonableness of a forcible stop to investigate a suspected crime.

Where such a stop is reasonable, however, the right to frisk must be immediate and automatic if the reason for the stop is, as here, an articulable suspicion of a crime of violence.

I would affirm this conviction for what I believe to be the same reasons the Court relies on. I would, however, make explicit what I think is implicit in affirmance on the present facts. Officer McFadden's right to interrupt Terry's freedom of movement and invade his privacy arose only because circumstances warranted forcing an encounter with Terry in an effort to prevent or investigate a crime. Once that forced encounter was justified, however, the officer's right to take suitable measures for his own safety followed automatically.

JUSTICE WHITE, concurring.

There is nothing in the Constitution which prevents a policeman from addressing questions to anyone on the streets. Absent special circumstances, the person approached may not be detained or frisked but may refuse to cooperate and go on his way. However, given the proper circumstances, such as those in this case, it seems to me the person may be briefly detained against his will while pertinent questions are directed to him. Of course, the person stopped is not obliged to answer, answers may not be compelled, and refusal to answer furnishes no basis for an arrest, although it may alert the officer to the need for continued observation. In my view, it is temporary detention, warranted by the circumstances, which chiefly justifies the protective frisk for weapons.

JUSTICE DOUGLAS, dissenting.

I agree that petitioner was "seized" within the meaning of the Fourth Amendment. I also agree that frisking petitioner and his companions for guns was a "search." But it is a mystery how that "search" and that "seizure" can be constitutional by Fourth Amendment standards, unless there was "probable cause" to believe that (1) a crime had been committed or (2) a crime was in the process of being committed or (3) a crime was about to be committed.

The opinion of the Court disclaims the existence of "probable cause." If loitering were in issue and that was the offense charged, there would be "probable cause" shown. But the crime here is carrying concealed weapons; and there is no basis for concluding that the officer had "probable cause" for believing that that crime was being committed. Had a warrant been sought, a magistrate would, therefore, have been unauthorized to issue one, for he can act only if there is a showing of "probable cause." We hold today that the police have greater authority to make a "seizure" and conduct a "search" than a judge has to authorize such action. We have said precisely the opposite over and over again.

To give the police greater power than a magistrate is to take a long step down the totalitarian path. Perhaps such a step is desirable to cope with modern forms of lawlessness. But if it is taken, it should be the deliberate choice of the people through a constitutional amendment. Until the Fourth Amendment, which is closely allied with the Fifth, is rewritten, the person and the effects of the individual are beyond the reach of all government agencies until there are reasonable grounds to believe (probable cause) that a criminal venture has been launched or is about to be launched.

There have been powerful hydraulic pressures throughout our history that bear heavily on the Court to water down constitutional guarantees and give the police the upper hand. That hydraulic pressure has probably never been greater than it is today.

Yet if the individual is no longer to be sovereign, if the police can pick him up whenever they do not like the cut of his jib, if they can "seize" and "search" him in their discretion, we enter a new regime. The decision to enter it should be made only after a full debate by the people of this country.

FOR DISCUSSION

Why is Justice Douglas concerned about the construction of the *Terry* frisk exception? Does this *Terry* frisk fulfill Chief Justice Warren's desire to maintain a balance between the privacy concern of individual citizens and the crime control interests of the state? When New York based its crime control modeled on *Terry* searches, the city found that Latino and African American men were disproportionately stopped. How can *Terry* and the potential for racial profiling be reconciled?

RELATED CASES

***Sibron v. New York:* 392 U.S. 1 (1968).**

Applying the *Terry* standard, the Supreme Court found that a police officer who placed his hand in a suspect's pockets for the sole purpose of locating narcotics—not for his own protection—had executed an illegal search under the Fourth Amendment.

***United States v. Sokolow:* 490 U.S. 1 (1989).**

The Court declared that the constitutional standard for a legitimate *Terry* search is the totality of circumstances resulting in reasonable suspicion, not probable cause.

***Illinois v. Wardlow:* 528 U.S. 119 (2000).**

Only reasonable suspicion is required for a forcible stop and frisk.

***Floyd v. City of New York:* 959 F. Supp2d 540 (2013).**

A federal district found a New York City Police "stop and frisk" policy, which targeted young men of color, was "indiscrete racial profiling" and violated the Fourth Amendment.

***Heien v. North Carolina:* 574 U.S. ___ (2015).**

In a vehicle, reasonable suspicion to stop and search may rest on a reasonable mistake.

CHIMEL V. CALIFORNIA

395 U.S. 752, 89 S.Ct. 2034, 23 L.Ed. 2d 685 (1969)

Pursuant to administering an arrest warrant against petitioner Chimel for the burglary of a coin shop, three officers knocked on the door of his home, identified themselves to the petitioner's wife, and asked to enter. Upon Chimel's arrival from work, they administered the arrest warrant and asked to "look around." Despite his objections and the lack of search warrant, the police advised Chimel that pursuant to a lawful arrest they could search his premises. Over approximately an hour, the officers searched the entire home and seized several items that were used against Chimel in his trial. Despite his objections, he was convicted, and this conviction was confirmed by both the California Court of Appeals and California Supreme Court.

Vote: 6–2

JUSTICE STEWART delivered the opinion of the Court.

Without deciding the question, we proceed on the hypothesis that the California courts were correct in holding that the arrest of the petitioner was valid under the Constitution. This brings us directly to the question whether the warrantless search of the petitioner's entire house can be constitutionally justified as incident to that arrest. The decisions of this Court bearing upon that question have been far from consistent, as even the most cursory review makes evident.

Approval of a warrantless search incident to a lawful arrest seems first to have been articulated by the Court in 1914 as dictum in *Weeks v. United States*, 232 U.S. 383, at 392, in which the Court stated:

> What then is the present case? Before answering that inquiry specifically, it may be well by a process of exclusion to state what it is not. It is not an assertion of the right on the part of the Government, always recognized under English and American law, to search the person of the accused when legally arrested to discover and seize the fruits or evidences of crime.

That statement made no reference to any right to search the place where an arrest occurs, but was limited to a right to search the "person."

Without explanation, however, the principle emerged in expanded form a few months later in *Agnello v. United States*, 269 U.S. 20 at 30 (1925)—although still by way of dictum:

> The right without a search warrant contemporaneously to search persons lawfully arrested while committing crime and to search the place where the arrest is made in order to find and seize things connected with the crime as its fruits or as the means by which it was committed, as well as weapons and other things to effect an escape from custody, is not to be doubted.

And in *Marron v. United States*, 275 U.S. 192 (1927), two years later, the dictum of *Agnello* appeared to be the foundation of the Court's decision. In that case federal agents had secured a search warrant authorizing the seizure of liquor and certain articles used in its manufacture. In searching a closet for the items listed in the warrant they came across an incriminating ledger, concededly not covered by the warrant, which they also seized. The Court upheld the seizure of the ledger by holding that since the agents had made a lawful arrest, "they had a right without a warrant contemporaneously to search the place in order to find and seize the things used to carry on the criminal enterprise."

That the *Marron* opinion did not mean all that it seemed to say became evident, however, a few years later in *Go-Bart Importing Co. v. United States*, 282 U.S. 344 (1931), and *United States v. Lefkowitz*, 285 U.S. 452 (1932). In *Go-Bart*, agents had searched the office of persons whom they had lawfully arrested, and had taken several papers from a desk, a safe, and other parts of the office. The Court noted that no crime had been committed in the agents' presence, and that although the agent in charge "had an abundance of information and time to swear out a valid [search] warrant, he failed to do so." In holding the search and seizure unlawful, the Court stated:

> Plainly the case before us is essentially different from *Marron v. United States*. . . As an incident to the arrest [the federal agents] seized a ledger in a closet where the liquor or some of it was kept and some bills beside the cash register. These things were visible and accessible and in the offender's immediate custody. There was no threat of force or general search or rummaging of the place. 282 U.S., at 358.

This limited characterization of *Marron* was reiterated in *Lefkowitz*, a case in which the Court held unlawful a search of desk drawers and a cabinet despite the fact that the search had accompanied a lawful arrest.

The limiting views expressed in *Go-Bart* and *Lefkowitz* were thrown to the winds, however, in *Harris v. United States*, 331 U.S. 145, decided in 1947. In that case, officers had obtained a warrant for Harris' arrest on the basis of his alleged involvement with the cashing and interstate transportation of a forged check. He was arrested in the living room of his four-room apartment, and in an attempt to recover two canceled checks thought to have been used in effecting the forgery, the officers undertook a thorough search of the entire apartment. Inside a desk drawer they found a sealed envelope marked "George Harris, personal papers." The envelope, which was then torn open, was found to contain altered Selective Service documents, and those documents were used to secure Harris' conviction for violating the Selective Training and Service Act of 1940. The Court rejected Harris' Fourth Amendment claim, sustaining the search as "incident to arrest."

Only a year after *Harris*, however, the pendulum swung again. In *Trupiano v. United States*, 334 U.S. 699, [(1948)] agents raided the site of an illicit distillery, saw one of several conspirators operating the still, and arrested him, contemporaneously "seiz[ing] the illicit distillery." The Court held that the arrest and others made subsequently had been valid, but that the unexplained failure of the agents to procure a search warrant—in spite of the fact that they had had more than enough time before the raid to do so—rendered the search unlawful.

In 1950, two years after *Trupiano*, came *United States v. Rabinowitz*, 339 U.S. 56, the decision upon which California primarily relies in the case now before us. In *Rabinowitz*, federal authorities had been informed that the defendant was dealing in stamps bearing forged overprints. On the basis of that information they secured a warrant for his arrest, which they executed at his one-room business office. At the time of the arrest, the officers "searched the desk, safe, and file cabinets in the office for about an hour and a half," and seized 573 stamps with forged overprints. The stamps were admitted into evidence at the defendant's trial, and this Court affirmed his conviction, rejecting the contention that the warrantless search had been unlawful. The Court held that the search in its entirety fell within the principle giving law enforcement authorities "the right 'to search the place where the arrest is made in order to find and seize things connected with the crime. . . .' " *Harris* was regarded as "ample authority" for that conclusion. The opinion rejected the rule of *Trupiano* that "in seizing goods and articles, law enforcement agents must secure and use search warrants wherever reasonably practicable." The test, said the Court, "is not whether it is reasonable to procure a search warrant, but whether the search was reasonable."

Rabinowitz has come to stand for the proposition, *inter alia*, that a warrantless search "incident to a lawful arrest" may generally extend to the area that is considered to be in the "possession" or under the "control" of the person arrested. And it was on the basis of that proposition that the California courts upheld the search of the petitioner's entire house in this case. That doctrine, however, at least in the broad sense in which it was applied by the California courts in this case, can withstand neither historical nor rational analysis.

Even limited to its own facts, the *Rabinowitz* decision was, as we have seen, hardly founded on an unimpeachable line of authority. As Mr. Justice Frankfurter commented in dissent in that case, the "hint" contained in *Weeks* was, without persuasive justification, "loosely turned into dictum and finally elevated to a decision." And the approach taken in cases such as *Go-Bart*, *Lefkowitz*, and *Trupiano* was essentially disregarded by the *Rabinowitz* Court.

Nor is the rationale by which the State seeks here to sustain the search of the petitioner's house supported by a reasoned view of the background and purpose of the Fourth Amendment. Mr. Justice Frankfurter wisely pointed out in his *Rabinowitz* dissent that the Amendment's proscription of "unreasonable searches and seizures" must be read in light of "the history that gave rise to the words"—a history of "abuses so deeply felt by the Colonies as to be one of the potent causes of the Revolution. . . ." 339 U.S., at 69. The Amendment was in large part a reaction to the general warrants and warrantless searches that had so alienated the colonists and had helped speed the movement for independence. In the scheme of the Amendment, therefore, the requirement that "no Warrants shall issue, but upon probable cause," plays a crucial part. As the Court put it in *McDonald v. United States*, 335 U.S. 451:

We are not dealing with formalities. The presence of a search warrant serves a high function. Absent some grave emergency, the Fourth Amendment has interposed a magistrate between the citizen and the police. This was done not to shield criminals nor to make the home a safe haven for illegal activities. It was done so that an objective mind might weigh the need to invade that privacy in order to enforce the law. The right of privacy was deemed too precious to entrust to the discretion of those whose job is the detection of crime and the arrest of criminals. . . . And so the Constitution requires a magistrate to pass on the desires of the police before they violate the privacy of the home. We cannot be true to that constitutional requirement and excuse the absence of a search warrant without a showing by those who seek exemption from the constitutional mandate that the exigencies of the situation made that course imperative.

Only last Term in *Terry v. Ohio*, 392 U.S. 1 [(1968)], we emphasized that "the police must, whenever practicable, obtain advance judicial approval of searches and seizures through the warrant procedure," and that "the scope of [a] search must be 'strictly tied to and justified by' the circumstances which rendered its initiation permissible."

A similar analysis underlies the "search incident to arrest" principle, and marks its proper extent. When an arrest is made, it is reasonable for the arresting officer to search the person arrested in order to remove any weapons that the latter might seek to use in order to resist arrest or effect his escape. Otherwise, the officer's safety might well be endangered, and the arrest itself frustrated. In addition, it is entirely reasonable for the arresting officer to search for and seize any evidence on the arrestee's person in order to prevent its concealment or destruction. And the area into which an arrestee might reach in order to grab a weapon or evidentiary items must, of course, be governed by a like rule. A gun on a table or in a drawer in front of one who is arrested can be as dangerous to the arresting officer as one concealed in the clothing of the person arrested. There is ample justification, therefore, for a search of the arrestee's person and the area "within his immediate control"—construing that phrase to mean the area from within which he might gain possession of a weapon or destructible evidence.

There is no comparable justification, however, for routinely searching any room other than that in which an arrest occurs—or, for that matter, for searching through all the desk drawers or other closed or concealed areas in that room itself. Such searches, in the absence of well-recognized exceptions, may be made only under the authority of a search warrant.

Rabinowitz and *Harris* have been the subject of critical commentary for many years, and have been relied upon less and less in our own decisions. It is time, for the reasons we have stated, to hold that on their own facts, and insofar as the principles they stand for are inconsistent with those that we have endorsed today, they are no longer to be followed.

Application of sound Fourth Amendment principles to the facts of this case produces a clear result. The search here went far beyond the petitioner's person and the area from within which he might have obtained either a weapon or something that could have been used as evidence against him. There was no constitutional justification, in the absence of a search warrant, for extending the search beyond that area. The scope of the search was, therefore, "unreasonable" under the Fourth and Fourteenth Amendments, and the petitioner's conviction cannot stand.

Reversed.

JUSTICE HARLAN, concurring.

The only thing that has given me pause in voting to overrule *Harris* and *Rabinowitz* is that as a result of *Mapp v. Ohio*, 367 U.S. 643 (1961), and *Ker v. California*, 374 U.S. 23 (1963), every change in Fourth Amendment law must now be obeyed by state officials facing widely different problems of local law enforcement. We simply do not know the extent to which cities and towns across the Nation are prepared to administer the greatly expanded warrant system which will be required by today's decision; nor can we say with assurance that in each and every local situation, the warrant requirement plays an essential role in the protection of those fundamental liberties protected against state infringement by the Fourteenth Amendment.

Thus, one is now faced with the dilemma . . . of choosing between vindicating sound Fourth Amendment principles at the possible expense of state concerns, long recognized to be consonant with the Fourteenth Amendment before *Mapp* and *Ker* came on the books, or diluting the Federal Bill of Rights in the interest of leaving the States at least some elbow room in their methods of criminal law enforcement.

This federal-state factor has not been an easy one for me to resolve, but in the last analysis I cannot in good conscience vote to perpetuate bad Fourth Amendment law.

JUSTICE WHITE, with whom JUSTICE BLACK joins, dissenting.

Few areas of the law have been as subject to shifting constitutional standards over the last 50 years as that of the search "incident to an arrest." There has been a remarkable instability in this whole area, which has seen at least four major shifts in emphasis. Today's opinion makes an untimely fifth. In my view, the Court should not now abandon the old rule.

II

The rule which has prevailed, but for very brief or doubtful periods of aberration, is that a search incident to an arrest may extend to those areas under the control of the defendant and where items subject to constitutional seizure may be found. The justification for this rule must, under the language of the Fourth Amendment, lie in the reasonableness of the rule.

In terms, then, the Court must decide whether a given search is reasonable. The Amendment does not proscribe "warrantless searches" but instead it proscribes "unreasonable searches" and this Court has never held nor does the majority today assert that warrantless searches are necessarily unreasonable.

Applying this reasonableness test to the area of searches incident to arrests, one thing is clear at the outset. Search of an arrested man and of the items within his immediate reach must in almost every case be reasonable.

This is not to say that a search can be reasonable without regard to the probable cause to believe that seizable items are on the premises. But when there are exigent circumstances, and probable cause, then the search may be made without a warrant, reasonably. An arrest itself may often create an emergency situation making it impracticable to obtain a warrant before embarking on a related search. Again assuming that there is probable cause to search premises at the spot where a suspect is arrested, it seems to me unreasonable to require the police to leave the scene in order to obtain a search warrant when they are already legally there to make a valid arrest, and when there must almost always be a strong possibility that confederates of the arrested man will in the meanwhile remove the items for which the police have probable cause to search. This must so often be the case that it seems to me as unreasonable to require a warrant for a search of the premises as to require a warrant for search of the person and his very immediate surroundings.

IV

If circumstances so often require the warrantless arrest that the law generally permits it, the typical situation will find the arresting officers lawfully on the premises without arrest or search warrant. Like the majority, I would permit the police to search the person of a suspect and the area under his immediate control either to assure the safety of the officers or to prevent the destruction of evidence. And like the majority, I see nothing in the arrest alone furnishing probable cause for a search of any broader scope. However, whereas here the existence of probable cause is independently established and would justify a warrant for a broader search for evidence, I would follow past cases and permit such a search to be carried out without a warrant, since the fact of arrest supplies an exigent circumstance justifying police action before the evidence can be removed, and also alerts the suspect to the fact of the search so that he can immediately seek judicial determination of probable cause in an adversary proceeding, and appropriate redress.

FOR DISCUSSION

How does the decision in *Chimel v. California* balance the competing interests before the Court? Does the ruling overly constrain the state, as claimed by the dissenters? Is there a case to be made that it defers too much to the state? If so, how would you make this argument?

RELATED CASE

***Arizona v. Hicks:* 480 U.S. 321 (1987).**

Police must have probable cause before seizing an item during an unrelated warrantless, yet legitimate, search and seizure.

PENNSYLVANIA V. MIMMS

434 U.S. 106, 98 S.Ct. 330, 54 L.Ed.2d 331 (1977)

While patrolling, two Philadelphia police officers stopped Harry Mimms for driving a car with an expired license plate. The officer who asked Mimms to step out of the car and show his license and registration observed what could have been a weapon under Mimms's sports coat. The officer frisked Mimms and found a revolver and ammunition. The passenger in the car was similarly armed. This evidence was used to secure a conviction of Mimms for carrying a concealed deadly weapon and unlawfully carrying an unlicensed firearm. Mimms appealed, and the Pennsylvania Supreme Court reversed the conviction, holding that the weapon should have been suppressed as evidence because its seizure violated Mimms's rights under the Fourth and Fifth Amendments. The state supreme court found that the stop had been valid and ruled that the search would have been valid once the bulge was observed. The court argued, however, that ordering Mimms out of the car was an impermissible "seizure" and the subsequent search was invalid. The Commonwealth of Pennsylvania asked the Supreme Court of the United States to review this decision.

Vote: 6–3

PER CURIAM.

In this case, unlike *Terry v. Ohio,* 392 U.S. 1 (1968), there is no question about the propriety of the initial restrictions on respondent's freedom of movement. Respondent was driving an automobile with expired license tags in violation of the Pennsylvania Motor Vehicle Code. Deferring for a moment the legality of the "frisk" once the bulge had been observed, we need presently deal only with the narrow question of whether the order to get out of the car, issued after the driver was lawfully detained, was reasonable and thus permissible under the Fourth Amendment.

Placing the question in this narrowed frame, we look first to that side of the balance which bears the officer's interest in taking the action that he did. The State freely concedes the officer had no reason to suspect foul play from the particular driver at the time of the stop, there having been nothing unusual or suspicious about his behavior. It was apparently his practice to order all drivers out of their vehicles as a matter of course whenever they had been stopped for a traffic violation. The State argues that this practice was adopted as a precautionary measure to afford a degree of protection to the officer and that it may be justified on that ground. Establishing a face-to-face confrontation diminishes the possibility, otherwise substantial, that the driver can make unobserved movements; this, in turn, reduces the likelihood that the officer will be the victim of an assault.

We think it too plain for argument that the State's proffered justification—the safety of the officer—is both legitimate and weighty. And we have specifically recognized the inordinate risk confronting an officer as he approaches a person seated in an automobile.

Against this important interest we are asked to weigh the intrusion into the driver's personal liberty occasioned not by the initial stop of the vehicle, which was admittedly justified, but by the order to get out of the car. We think this additional intrusion can only be described as de minimis. The driver is being asked to expose to view very little more of his person than is already exposed. The police have already lawfully decided that the driver shall be briefly detained; the only question is whether he shall spend that period sitting in the driver's seat of his car or standing alongside it.

There remains the second question of the propriety of the search once the bulge in the jacket was observed. We have as little doubt on this point as on the first; the answer is controlled by *Terry v. Ohio.* In that case we thought the officer justified in conducting a limited search for weapons once he had reasonably concluded that the person whom he had legitimately stopped might be armed and presently dangerous. Under the standard enunciated in that case . . . there is little question the officer was justified. The bulge in the jacket permitted the officer to conclude that Mimms was armed and thus posed a serious and present danger to the safety of the officer. In these circumstances, any man of "reasonable caution" would likely have conducted the "pat-down."

JUSTICE MARSHALL, dissenting.

I join my Brother Stevens' dissenting opinion, but I write separately to emphasize the extent to which the Court today departs from the teachings of *Terry v. Ohio*, 392 U.S. 1 (1968).

The "stop and frisk" in *Terry* was . . . justified by the probability, not only that a crime was about to be committed, but also that the crime "would be likely to involve the use of weapons." The Court confined its holding to situations in which the officer believes that "the persons with whom he is dealing may be armed and presently dangerous" and "fear[s] for his own or others' safety."

In the instant case, the officer did not have even the slightest hint, prior to ordering respondent out of the car, that respondent might have a gun. Yet the Court holds that, once the officer had made this routine stop, he was justified in imposing the additional intrusion of ordering respondent out of the car, regardless of whether there was any individualized reason to fear respondent.

Such a result cannot be explained by *Terry*, which limited the nature of the intrusion by reference to the reason for the stop. In *Terry* there was an obvious connection, emphasized by the Court, between the officer's suspicion that an armed robbery was being planned and his frisk for weapons. In the instant case "the circumstance . . . which justified the interference in the first place" was an expired license plate. There is simply no relation at all between that circumstance and the order to step out of the car.

The institutional aspects of the Court's decision trouble me as much as does the Court's substantive result. The Court extends *Terry's* expressly narrow holding, solely on the basis of certiorari papers, and in the process summarily reverses the considered judgment of Pennsylvania's highest court. Such a disposition cannot engender respect for the work of this Court.

JUSTICE STEVENS, with whom JUSTICES BRENNAN and MARSHALL join, dissenting.

Almost ten years ago in *Terry v. Ohio*, 392 U.S. 1 (1968), the Court held that "probable cause" was not required to justify every seizure of the person by a police officer. That case was decided after six months of deliberation following full argument and unusually elaborate briefing. The approval in *Terry* of a lesser standard for certain limited situations represented a major development in Fourth Amendment jurisprudence.

Today, without argument, the Court adopts still another—and even lesser—standard of justification for a major category of police seizures. More importantly, it appears to abandon "the central teaching of this Court's Fourth Amendment jurisprudence"—which has ordinarily required individualized inquiry into the particular facts justifying every police intrusion—in favor of a general rule covering countless situations. But what is most disturbing is the fact that this important innovation is announced almost casually, in the course of explaining the summary reversal of a decision the Court should not even bother to review.

Since Mimms has already served his sentence, the importance of reinstating his conviction is minimal at best. Even if the Pennsylvania Supreme Court has afforded him greater protection than is required by the Federal Constitution, the conviction may be invalid under state law.

Moreover, the Pennsylvania Supreme Court may still construe its own constitution to prohibit what it described as the "indiscriminate procedure" of ordering all traffic offenders out of their vehicles. In all events, whatever error the state court has committed affects only the Commonwealth of Pennsylvania. Its decision creates no conflict requiring resolution by this Court on a national level. In most cases, these considerations would cause us to deny certiorari.

No doubt it is a legitimate concern about the safety of police officers throughout the Nation that prompts the Court to give this case such expeditious treatment. I share that concern and am acutely aware that almost every decision of this Court holding that an individual's Fourth Amendment rights have been invaded makes law enforcement somewhat more difficult and hazardous. That, however, is not a sufficient reason for this Court to reach out to decide every new Fourth Amendment issue as promptly as possible. In this area of constitutional adjudication, as in all others, it is of paramount importance that the Court have the benefit of differing judicial evaluations of an issue before it is finally resolved on a nationwide basis.

This case illustrates two ways in which haste can introduce a new element of confusion into an already complex set of rules. First, the Court has based its legal ruling on a factual assumption about police safety that is dubious at best; second, the Court has created an entirely new legal standard of justification for intrusions on the liberty of the citizen.

Obviously, it is not my purpose to express an opinion on the safest procedure to be followed in making traffic arrests or to imply that the arresting officer faces no significant hazard, even in the apparently routine situation. I do submit, however, that no matter how hard we try we cannot totally eliminate the danger associated with law enforcement, and that, before adopting a nationwide rule, we should give further consideration to the infinite variety of situations in which today's holding may be applied.

Until today the law applicable to seizures of a person has required individualized inquiry into the reason for each intrusion, or some comparable guarantee against arbitrary harassment. A factual demonstration of probable cause is required to justify an arrest; an articulable reason to suspect criminal activity and possible violence is needed to justify a stop and frisk. But to eliminate any requirement that an officer be able to explain the reasons for his actions signals an abandonment of effective judicial supervision of this kind of seizure and leaves police discretion utterly without limits. Some citizens will be subjected to this minor indignity while others—perhaps those with more expensive cars, or different bumper stickers, or different-colored skin—may escape it entirely.

If this new rule is truly predicated on a safety rationale—rather than a desire to permit pretextual searches—it should also justify a frisk for weapons, or at least an order directing the driver to lean on the hood of the car with legs and arms spread out. For unless such precautionary measures are also taken, the added safety—if any—in having the driver out of the car is of no value when a truly dangerous offender happens to be caught.

I respectfully dissent from the grant of certiorari and from the decision on the merits without full argument and briefing.

FOR DISCUSSION

How can the Court recognize the legitimate concern for officer safety without allowing it to supersede any and all privacy claims with respect to state action under the Fourth Amendment? Was the dissent correct in stating that the decision in *Mimms* was a revision of *Terry*? Why or why not?

RELATED CASES

***Maryland v. Wilson:* 519 U.S. 408 (1997).**

Extended *Pennsylvania v. Mimms* to allow police officers to require both passengers and the driver to exit a car the officers have lawfully stopped for a routine traffic violation. While the Court recognized the personal liberty of the passengers, it also recognized the legitimacy of governmental concern for officer safety.

***Alabama v. White:* 496 U.S. 325 (1990).**

The police are allowed to stop and question individuals in their cars based on an anonymous tip if that tip has been corroborated and if the officers have established reasonable suspicion of criminal activity.

***Atwater v. Lago Vista:* 532 U.S. 318 (2001).**

The Court allowed police to arrest and detain drivers who have been stopped for routine traffic violations, even if the violations are misdemeanors punished only by a fine.

***Thornton v. United States:* 541 U.S. 615 (2004).**

Police may search the passenger compartment of a car after the driver has vacated the vehicle and a superficial search has revealed drugs in his pocket under the "search incident to arrest" exception to the Fourth Amendment.

WHREN V. UNITED STATES

517 U.S. 806, 116 S.Ct. 1769, 135 L.Ed.2d 89 (1996)

The facts of the case are explained in the Court's opinion.

Vote: 9–0

JUSTICE SCALIA delivered the opinion of the Court.

In this case we decide whether the temporary detention of a motorist who the police have probable cause to believe has committed a civil traffic violation is inconsistent with the Fourth Amendment's prohibition against unreasonable seizures unless a reasonable officer would have been motivated to stop the car by a desire to enforce the traffic laws.

I

On the evening of June 10, 1993, plainclothes vice-squad officers of the District of Columbia Metropolitan Police Department were patrolling a "high drug area" of the city in an unmarked car. Their suspicions were aroused when they passed a dark Pathfinder truck with temporary license plates and youthful occupants waiting at a stop sign, the driver looking down into the lap of the passenger at his right. The truck remained stopped at the intersection for what seemed an unusually long time—more than 20 seconds. When the police car executed a U-turn in order to head back toward the truck, the Pathfinder turned suddenly to its right, without signaling, and sped off at an "unreasonable" speed. The policemen followed, and in a short while overtook the Pathfinder when it stopped behind other traffic at a red light. They pulled up alongside, and Officer Ephraim Soto stepped out and approached the driver's door, identifying himself as a police officer and directing the driver, petitioner Brown, to put the vehicle in park. When Soto drew up to the driver's window, he immediately observed two large plastic bags of what appeared to be crack cocaine in petitioner Whren's hands. Petitioners were arrested, and quantities of several types of illegal drugs were retrieved from the vehicle.

Petitioners were charged in a four-count indictment with violating various federal drug laws. . . . At a pretrial suppression hearing, they challenged the legality of the stop and the resulting seizure of the drugs. They argued that the stop had not been justified by probable cause to believe, or even reasonable suspicion, that petitioners were engaged in illegal drug-dealing activity; and that Officer Soto's asserted ground for approaching the vehicle—to give the driver a warning concerning traffic violations—was pretextual. The District Court denied the suppression motion, concluding that "the facts of the stop were not controverted". . . .

Petitioners were convicted of the counts at issue here. The Court of Appeals affirmed the convictions. . . .

II

The Fourth Amendment guarantees "the right of the people to be secure in their persons, houses, papers, and effects, against unreasonable searches and seizures." Temporary detention of individuals during the stop of an automobile by the police, even if only for a brief period and for a limited purpose, constitutes a "seizure" of "persons" within the meaning of this provision. An automobile stop is thus subject to the constitutional imperative that it not be "unreasonable" under the circumstances. As a general matter, the decision to stop an automobile is reasonable where the police have probable cause to believe that a traffic violation has occurred.

Petitioners accept that Officer Soto had probable cause to believe that various provisions of the District of Columbia traffic code had been violated. They argue, however, that "in the unique context of civil traffic regulations" probable cause is not enough. Since, they contend, the use of automobiles is so heavily and minutely regulated that total compliance with traffic and safety rules is nearly impossible, a police officer will almost invariably be able to catch any given motorist in a technical violation. This creates the temptation to use traffic stops as a means of investigating other law violations, as to which no probable cause or even articulable suspicion exists. Petitioners, who are both black, further contend that police officers might decide which motorists to stop based on decidedly impermissible factors, such as the race of the car's occupants. To avoid this danger, they say, the Fourth Amendment test for traffic stops should be, not the normal one . . . of whether probable cause existed to justify the stop; but rather, whether a police officer, acting reasonably, would have made the stop for the reason given.

A

Not only have we never held, outside the context of inventory search or administrative inspection . . . that an officer's motive invalidates objectively justifiable behavior under the Fourth Amendment; but we have repeatedly held and asserted the contrary. In *United States v. Villamonte-Marquez*, 462 U.S. 579 (1983), we held that an otherwise valid warrantless boarding of a vessel by customs officials was not rendered invalid "because the customs officers were accompanied by a Louisiana state policeman, and were following an informant's tip that a vessel in the ship channel was thought to be carrying marihuana." We flatly dismissed the idea that an ulterior motive might serve to strip the agents of their legal justification. In *United States v. Robinson*, 414 U.S. 218 (1973), we held that a traffic-violation arrest (of the sort here) would not be rendered invalid by the fact that it was "a mere pretext for a narcotics search"; and that a lawful post-arrest search of the person would not be rendered invalid by the fact that it was not motivated by the officer-safety concern that justifies such searches.

We think these cases foreclose any argument that the constitutional reasonableness of traffic stops depends on the actual motivations of the individual officers involved. We of course agree with petitioners that the Constitution prohibits selective enforcement of the law based on considerations such as race. But the constitutional basis for objecting to intentionally discriminatory application of laws is the Equal Protection Clause, not the Fourth Amendment. Subjective intentions play no role in ordinary, probable-cause Fourth Amendment analysis.

B

Recognizing that we have been unwilling to entertain Fourth Amendment challenges based on the actual motivations of individual officers, petitioners disavow any intention to make the individual officer's subjective good faith the touchstone of "reasonableness." They insist that the standard they have put forward—whether the officer's conduct deviated materially from usual police practices, so that a reasonable officer in the same circumstances would not have made the stop for the reasons given—is an "objective" one.

But although framed in empirical terms, this approach is plainly and indisputably driven by subjective considerations. Its whole purpose is to prevent the police from doing under the guise of enforcing the traffic code what they would like to do for different reasons.

. . .[I]t seems to us somewhat easier to figure out the intent of an individual officer than to plumb the collective consciousness of law enforcement in order to determine whether a "reasonable officer" would have been moved to act upon the traffic violation. While police manuals and standard procedures may sometimes provide objective assistance, ordinarily one would be reduced to speculating about the hypothetical reaction of a hypothetical constable—an exercise that might be called virtual subjectivity.

Moreover, police enforcement practices, even if they could be practicably assessed by a judge, vary from place to place and from time to time. We cannot accept that the search and seizure protections of the Fourth Amendment are so variable and can be made to turn upon such trivialities.

III

In what would appear to be an elaboration on the "reasonable officer" test, petitioners argue that the balancing inherent in any Fourth Amendment inquiry requires us to weigh the governmental and individual interests implicated in a traffic stop such as we have here. That balancing, petitioners claim, does not support investigation of minor traffic infractions by plainclothes police in unmarked vehicles; such investigation only minimally advances the government's interest in traffic safety, and may indeed retard it by producing motorist confusion and alarm—a view said to be supported by the Metropolitan Police Department's own regulations generally prohibiting this practice.

It is of course true that in principle every Fourth Amendment case, since it turns upon a "reasonableness" determination, involves a balancing of all relevant factors. With rare exceptions not applicable here, however, the result of that balancing is not in doubt where the search or seizure is based upon probable cause. That is why petitioners must rely upon cases like *Delaware v. Prouse,* 440 U.S. 648 (1979), to provide examples of actual "balancing" analysis. There, the police action in question was a random traffic stop for the purpose of checking a motorist's license and vehicle registration, a practice that—like the practices at issue in the inventory search and administrative inspection cases upon which petitioners rely in making their "pretext" claim—involves police intrusion without the probable cause that is its traditional justification. Our opinion in *Prouse* expressly distinguished the case from a stop based on precisely what is at issue here: "probable cause to believe that a driver is violating any one of the multitude of applicable traffic and equipment regulations." It noted approvingly that "the foremost method of enforcing traffic and vehicle safety regulations . . . is acting upon observed violations," which afford the " 'quantum of individualized suspicion' " necessary to ensure that police discretion is sufficiently constrained (quoting *United States v. Martinez-Fuerte,* 428 U.S. at 560). What is true of *Prouse* is also true of other cases that engaged in detailed "balancing" to decide the constitutionality of automobile stops, such as *Martinez-Fuerte,* which upheld checkpoint stops, and *United States v. Brignoni-Ponce,* 422 U.S. 873 (1975), which disallowed so-called "roving patrol" stops: The detailed "balancing" analysis was necessary because they involved seizures without probable cause.

Petitioners urge as an extraordinary factor in this case that the "multitude of applicable traffic and equipment regulations" is so large and so difficult to obey perfectly that virtually everyone is guilty of violation, permitting the police to single out almost whomever they wish for a stop. But we are aware of no principle that would allow us to decide at what point a code of law becomes so expansive and so commonly violated that infraction itself can no longer be the ordinary measure of the lawfulness of enforcement. And even if we could identify such exorbitant codes, we do not know by what standard (or what right) we would decide, as petitioners would have us do, which particular provisions are sufficiently important to merit enforcement.

For the run-of-the-mill case, which this surely is, we think there is no realistic alternative to the traditional common-law rule that probable cause justifies a search and seizure.

FOR DISCUSSION

In what way might the Equal Protection Clause be applicable to pretextual stops, as suggested by the Court's opinion? Should the motivations or intentions of officer matter in constitutional enforcement of the Fourth Amendment? Why or why not?

RELATED CASES

***New York v. Belton:* 453 U.S. 454 (1981).**

The Supreme Court extended the *Chimel* rule regarding searching incident to arrest to the search of the passenger compartment of an automobile upon the arrest of any occupant of that car.

***Illinois v. Caballes:* 543 U.S. 405 (2005).**

The Supreme Court found that the use of a drug-detection dog to sniff a vehicle during a legitimate traffic stop is not a search under the Fourth Amendment.

***Arizona v. Gant:* 556 U.S. 332 (2009).**

The Court narrowed *New York v. Belton*, ruling that vehicles could be searched only when the person arrested is close enough to the car that the police might be concerned that the suspect could seize a weapon or tamper with evidence or when the police reasonably believe that the car has evidence relevant to the crime precipitating the arrest.

UNITED STATES V. MENDENHALL

446 U.S. 544, 100 S.Ct. 1870, 64 L.Ed.2d 497 (1980)

Sylvia Mendenhall flew from Los Angeles to Detroit in the early morning. When she disembarked, two Drug Enforcement Administration (DEA) agents who were at the airport to detect narcotics trafficking observed her and perceived that her conduct was characteristic of individuals who engage as narcotics carriers. They subsequently approached Mendelhall, identified themselves as federal agents, and asked for her identification and ticket; her responses and behavior raised their suspicions and they asked her to accompany them to their airport office, where she consented to a search of her person and purse. Findings from this search caused the agents to ask a female officer to conduct a full search, which uncovered drugs. Upon this evidence, Mendenhall was convicted for possession with intent to sell. The district court dismissed her challenge of these search and seizure activities, and the court of appeals reversed, finding the search of Mendenhall to be unlawful.

Vote: 5–4

JUSTICE STEWART announced the judgment of the Court and delivered an opinion, in which JUSTICE REHNQUIST joined. [CHIEF JUSTICE BURGER, JUSTICE BLACKMUN, and JUSTICE POWELL also join all but Part II-A of this opinion.]

II

The Fourth Amendment provides that "the right of the people to be secure in their persons, houses, papers, and effects, against unreasonable searches and seizures, shall not be violated. . . ." There is no question in this case that the respondent possessed this constitutional right of personal security as she walked through the Detroit Airport, for "the Fourth Amendment protects people, not places," *Katz v. United States*, 389 U.S. 347, 351 (1967). Here the Government concedes that its agents had neither a warrant nor probable cause to believe that the respondent was carrying narcotics when the agents conducted a search of the respondent's person. It is the Government's position, however, that the search was conducted pursuant to the respondent's consent, and thus was excepted from the requirements of both a warrant and probable cause. Evidently, the Court of Appeals concluded that the respondent's apparent consent to the search was in fact not voluntarily given and was in any event the product of earlier official conduct violative of the Fourth Amendment. We must first consider, therefore, whether such conduct occurred, either on the concourse or in the DEA office at the airport.

A

. . . [I]f the respondent was "seized" when the DEA agents approached her on the concourse and asked questions of her, the agents' conduct in doing so was constitutional only if they reasonably suspected the respondent of wrongdoing. But "[obviously], not all personal intercourse between policemen and citizens involves 'seizures' of persons. Only when the officer, by means of physical force or show of authority, has in some way restrained the liberty of a citizen may we conclude that a 'seizure' has occurred." *Terry v. Ohio*, 392 U.S. 1 (1968).

We adhere to the view that a person is "seized" only when, by means of physical force or a show of authority, his freedom of movement is restrained. Only when such restraint is imposed is there any foundation whatever for invoking constitutional safeguards. As long as the person to whom questions are put remains free to disregard the questions and walk away, there has been no intrusion upon that person's liberty or privacy as would under the Constitution require some particularized and objective justification.

Moreover, characterizing every street encounter between a citizen and the police as a "seizure," while not enhancing any interest secured by the Fourth Amendment, would impose wholly unrealistic restrictions upon a wide variety of legitimate law enforcement practices. The Court has on other occasions referred to the acknowledged need for police questioning as a tool in the effective enforcement of the criminal laws.

We conclude that a person has been "seized" within the meaning of the Fourth Amendment only if, in view of all of the circumstances surrounding the incident, a reasonable person would have believed that he was not free to leave. Examples of circumstances that might indicate a seizure, even where the person did not attempt to leave, would be the threatening presence of several officers, the display of a weapon by an officer, some physical touching of the person of the citizen, or the use of language or tone of voice indicating that compliance with the officer's request might be compelled. In the absence of some such evidence, otherwise inoffensive contact between a member of the public and the police cannot, as a matter of law, amount to a seizure of that person.

On the facts of this case, no "seizure" of the respondent occurred. In short, nothing in the record suggests that the respondent had any objective reason to believe that she was not free to end the conversation in the concourse and proceed on her way, and for that reason we conclude that the agents' initial approach to her was not a seizure.

Our conclusion that no seizure occurred is not affected by the fact that the respondent was not expressly told by the agents that she was free to decline to cooperate with their inquiry, for the voluntariness of her responses does not depend upon her having been so informed.

B

Although we have concluded that the initial encounter between the DEA agents and the respondent on the concourse at the Detroit Airport did not constitute an unlawful seizure, it is still arguable that the respondent's Fourth Amendment protections were violated when she went from the concourse to the DEA office. Such a violation might in turn infect the subsequent search of the respondent's person.

The District Court specifically found that the respondent accompanied the agents to the office " 'voluntarily in a spirit of apparent cooperation.' " Notwithstanding this determination by the trial court, the Court of Appeals evidently concluded that the agents' request that the respondent accompany them converted the situation into an arrest requiring probable cause in order to be found lawful. But because the trial court's finding was sustained by the record, the Court of Appeals was mistaken in substituting for that finding its view of the evidence.

The question whether the respondent's consent to accompany the agents was in fact voluntary or was the product of duress or coercion, express or implied, is to be determined by the totality of all the circumstances, and is a matter which the Government has the burden of proving. The Government's evidence showed that the respondent was not told that she had to go to the office, but was simply asked if she would accompany the officers.

On the other hand, it is argued that the incident would reasonably have appeared coercive to the respondent, who was 22 years old and had not been graduated from high school. It is additionally suggested that the respondent, a female and a Negro, may have felt unusually threatened by the officers, who were white males.

While these factors were not irrelevant, neither were they decisive, and the totality of the evidence in this case was plainly adequate to support the District Court's finding that the respondent voluntarily consented to accompany the officers to the DEA office.

C

Because the search of the respondent's person was not preceded by an impermissible seizure of her person, it cannot be contended that her apparent consent to the subsequent search was infected by an unlawful detention. There remains to be considered whether the respondent's consent to the search was for any other reason invalid. The District Court explicitly credited the officers' testimony and found that the "consent was freely and voluntarily given". . . . There was more than enough evidence in this case to sustain that view. First, we note that the respondent, who was 22 years old and had an 11th-grade education, was plainly capable of a knowing consent. Second, it is especially significant that the respondent was twice expressly told that she was free to decline to consent to the search, and only thereafter explicitly consented to it. And, perhaps more important for present purposes, the fact that the officers themselves informed the respondent that she was free to withhold her consent substantially lessened the probability that their conduct could reasonably have appeared to her to be coercive.

Counsel for the respondent has also argued that because she was within the DEA office when she consented to the search, her consent may have resulted from the inherently coercive nature of those surroundings. But in view of the District Court's finding that the respondent's presence in the office was voluntary, the fact that she was there is little or no evidence that she was in any way coerced. And in response to the argument that the respondent would not voluntarily have consented to a search that was likely to disclose the narcotics that she carried, we repeat that the question is not whether the respondent acted in her ultimate self-interest, but whether she acted voluntarily.

III

We conclude that the District Court's determination that the respondent consented to the search of her person "freely and voluntarily" was sustained by the evidence and that the Court of Appeals was, therefore, in error in setting it aside. Accordingly, the judgment of the Court of Appeals is reversed, and the case is remanded to that court for further proceedings.

JUSTICE POWELL, with whom CHIEF JUSTICE BURGER and JUSTICE BLACKMUN join, concurring in part and concurring in the judgment.

I join Parts I, II-B, II-C, and III of the Court's opinion. Because neither of the courts below considered the question, I do not reach the Government's contention that the agents did not "seize" the respondent within the meaning of the Fourth Amendment. In my view, we may assume for present purposes that the stop did constitute a seizure. I would hold—as did the District Court—that the federal agents had reasonable suspicion that the respondent was engaging in criminal activity, and, therefore, that they did not violate the Fourth Amendment by stopping the respondent for routine questioning.

II

Terry v. Ohio, 392 U.S. 1 (1968), establishes that a reasonable investigative stop does not offend the Fourth Amendment. The reasonableness of a stop turns on the facts and circumstances of each case. In particular, the Court has emphasized (i) the public interest served by the seizure, (ii) the nature and scope of the intrusion, and (iii) the objective facts upon which the law enforcement officer relied in light of his knowledge and expertise.

A

The public has a compelling interest in detecting those who would traffic in deadly drugs for personal profit. Few problems affecting the health and welfare of our population, particularly our young, cause greater concern than the escalating use of controlled substances. Much of the drug traffic is highly organized and conducted by sophisticated criminal syndicates. The profits are enormous. And many drugs, including heroin, may be easily concealed. As a result, the obstacles to detection of illegal conduct may be unmatched in any other area of law enforcement.

B

Our cases demonstrate that "the scope of [a] particular intrusion, in light of all the exigencies of the case, [is] a central element in the analysis of reasonableness." *Terry v. Ohio*, supra, at 18, n. 15. The intrusion in this case was quite modest. . . . Unlike the petitioner in *Terry*,. the respondent was not physically restrained. The agents did not display weapons. The questioning was brief. In these circumstances, the respondent could not reasonably have felt frightened or isolated from assistance.

C

In reviewing the factors that led the agents to stop and question the respondent, it is important to recall that a trained law enforcement agent may be "able to perceive and articulate meaning in given conduct which would be wholly innocent to the untrained observer." *Brown v. Texas*, 443 U.S. 47 (1979) at 52, n. 2. Among the circumstances that can give rise to reasonable suspicion are the agent's knowledge of the methods used in recent criminal activity and the characteristics of persons engaged in such illegal practices. Law enforcement officers may rely on the "characteristics of the area," and the behavior of a suspect who appears to be evading police contact.

III

The District Court, which had an opportunity to hear Agent Anderson's testimony and judge his credibility, concluded that the decision to stop the respondent was reasonable. I agree. The public interest in preventing drug traffic is great, and the intrusion upon the respondent's privacy was minimal. The specially trained agents acted pursuant to a well-planned, and effective, federal law enforcement program. They observed respondent engaging in conduct that they reasonably associated with criminal activity. Furthermore, the events occurred in an airport known to be frequented by drug couriers. In light of all of the circumstances, I would hold that the agents possessed reasonable and articulable suspicion of criminal activity when they stopped the respondent in a public place and asked her for identification.

JUSTICE WHITE, with whom JUSTICES BRENNAN, MARSHALL, and STEVENS join, dissenting.

The Court today concludes that agents of the Drug Enforcement Administration (DEA) acted lawfully in stopping a traveler changing planes in an airport terminal and escorting her to a DEA office for a strip-search of her person. This result is particularly curious because a majority of the Members of the Court refuse to reject the conclusion that Ms. Mendenhall was "seized," while a separate majority decline to hold that there were reasonable grounds to justify a seizure. Justice Stewart concludes that the DEA agents acted lawfully, regardless of whether there were any reasonable grounds for suspecting Ms. Mendenhall of criminal activity, because he finds that Ms. Mendenhall was not "seized" by the DEA agents, even though throughout the proceedings below the Government never questioned the fact that a seizure had occurred necessitating a showing of antecedent reasonable suspicion. Justice Powell's opinion concludes that even though Ms. Mendenhall may have been "seized," the seizure was lawful because her behavior while changing planes in the airport provided reasonable suspicion that she was engaging in criminal activity. The Court then concludes, based on the absence of evidence that Ms. Mendenhall resisted her detention, that she voluntarily consented to being taken to the DEA office, even though she in fact had no choice in the matter. This conclusion is inconsistent with our recognition that consent cannot be presumed from a showing of acquiescence to authority, and it cannot be reconciled with our decision last Term in *Dunaway v. New York*, 442 U.S. 200 (1979).

I

Mr. Justice Stewart believes that a "seizure" within the meaning of the Fourth Amendment occurs when an individual's freedom of movement is restrained by means of physical force or a show of authority. Although it is undisputed that Ms. Mendenhall was not free to leave after the DEA agents stopped her and inspected her identification, Mr. Justice Stewart concludes that she was not "seized" because he finds that, under the totality of the circumstances, a reasonable person would have believed that she was free to leave. While basing this finding on an alleged absence from the record of objective evidence indicating that Ms. Mendenhall was not free to ignore the officer's inquiries and continue on her way, Mr. Justice Stewart's opinion brushes off the fact that this asserted evidentiary deficiency may be largely attributable to the fact that the "seizure" question was never raised below. Even if one believes the Government should be permitted to raise the "seizure" question in this Court, the proper course would be to direct a remand to the District Court for an evidentiary hearing on the question, rather than to decide it in the first instance in this Court.

II

Assuming, as we should, that Ms. Mendenhall was "seized" within the meaning of the Fourth Amendment when she was stopped by the DEA agents, the legality of that stop turns on whether there were reasonable grounds for suspecting her of criminal activity at the time of the stop.

At the time they stopped Ms. Mendenhall, the DEA agents' suspicion that she was engaged in criminal activity was based solely on their brief observations of her conduct at the airport. The officers had no advance information that Ms. Mendenhall, or anyone on her flight, would be carrying drugs. What the agents observed Ms. Mendenhall do in the airport was not "unusual conduct" which would lead an experienced officer reasonably to conclude that criminal activity was afoot, but rather the kind of behavior that could reasonably be expected of anyone changing planes in an airport terminal.

None of the aspects of Ms. Mendenhall's conduct, either alone or in combination, were sufficient to provide reasonable suspicion that she was engaged in criminal activity. The fact that Ms. Mendenhall was the last person to alight from a flight originating in Los Angeles was plainly insufficient to provide a basis for stopping her. Nor was the fact that her flight originated from a "major source city," for the mere proximity of a person to areas with a high incidence of drug activity or to persons known to be drug addicts, does not provide the necessary reasonable suspicion for an investigatory stop. Under the circumstances of this case, the DEA agents' observations that Ms. Mendenhall claimed no luggage and changed airlines were also insufficient to provide reasonable suspicion.

III

Whatever doubt there may be concerning whether Ms. Mendenhall's Fourth Amendment interests were implicated during the initial stages of her confrontation with the DEA agents, she undoubtedly was "seized" within the meaning of the Fourth Amendment when the agents escorted her from the public area of the terminal to the DEA office for questioning and a strip-search of her person. In *Dunaway v. New York*, 442 U.S. 200 (1979), we held that a person who accompanied police officers to a police station for purposes of interrogation undoubtedly "was 'seized' in the Fourth Amendment sense," even though "he was not told he was under arrest." We found it significant that the suspect was taken to a police station, "was never informed that he was 'free to go,' " and "would have been physically restrained if he had refused to accompany the officers or had tried to escape their custody." Like the "seizure" in *Dunaway*, the nature of the intrusion to which Ms. Mendenhall was subjected when she was escorted by DEA agents to their office and detained there for questioning and a strip-search was so great that it "was in important respects indistinguishable from a traditional arrest." Although Ms. Mendenhall was not told that she was under arrest, she in fact was not free to refuse to go to the DEA office and was not told that she was. Furthermore, once inside the office, Ms. Mendenhall would not have been permitted to leave without submitting to a strip-search.

Because the intrusion to which Ms. Mendenhall was subjected when she was escorted to the DEA office is of the same character as that involved in *Dunaway*, probable cause, which concededly was absent, was required to support the intrusion.

The Court recognizes that the Government has the burden of proving that Ms. Mendenhall consented to accompany the officers, but it nevertheless holds that the "totality of evidence was plainly adequate" to support a finding of consent. On the record before us, the Court's conclusion can only be based on the notion that consent can be assumed from the absence of proof that a suspect resisted police authority.

Because Ms. Mendenhall was being illegally detained at the time of the search of her person, her suppression motion should have been granted in the absence of evidence to dissipate the taint.

FOR DISCUSSION

What should be required to demonstrate that an individual fully consents to a search? What constitutes a legal seizure under the Fourth Amendment? According to the Supreme Court in *Mendenhall*?

RELATED CASES

***Brown v. Texas:* 443 U.S. 47 (1979).**

Unless there is a reasonable suspicion of potential criminal activity, police may not detain people on the street for identity checks.

***Ybarra v. Illinois:* 444 U.S. 85 (1979).**

A warrant that authorized a search of a bar and its bartender for drugs did not justify *Terry* searches of the establishment's customers.

***Hiibel v. Sixth Judicial District Court of Nevada:* 524 U.S. 177 (2004).**

The Court found that someone who is stopped subject to a lawful *Terry* search (with reasonable suspicion) can be required to provide his or her name to the detaining officer.

GEORGIA V. RANDOLPH

547 U.S. 103, 126 S.Ct. 1515, 164 L.Ed.2d 208 (2006)

While responding to a domestic abuse call at a married couple's house in Georgia, the police officer was told by the wife, in the presence of the husband, that there was evidence in the house of the man's illegal drug use. The information was given voluntarily. The husband unequivocally refused the officer's request for permission for a warrantless search of the house. However, the wife then consented to a search and led the officer to the evidence. The police seized this material and, after obtaining a search warrant, seized further evidence of drug use. The husband was indicted under state law for cocaine possession. He moved to suppress the evidence in question on the asserted basis that it had been obtained as a result of an illegal search. However, the state trial court, ruling that the wife had common authority to consent to the search, denied the motion.

Vote: 5–3

JUSTICE SOUTER delivered the opinion of the Court.

The Fourth Amendment recognizes a valid warrantless entry and search of premises when police obtain the voluntary consent of an occupant who shares, or is reasonably believed to share, authority over the area in common with a co-occupant who later objects to the use of evidence so obtained. *Illinois v. Rodriguez*, 497 U.S. 177 (1990); *United States v. Matlock*, 415 U.S. 164 (1974). The question here is whether such an evidentiary seizure is likewise lawful with the permission of one occupant when the other, who later seeks to suppress the evidence, is present at the scene and expressly refuses to consent. We hold that, in the circumstances here at issue, a physically present co-occupant's stated refusal to permit entry prevails, rendering the warrantless search unreasonable and invalid as to him.

II

To the Fourth Amendment rule ordinarily prohibiting the warrantless entry of a person's house as unreasonable per se, *Payton v. New York*, 445 U.S. 573 (1980); *Coolidge v. New Hampshire*, 403 U.S. 443 (1971), one "jealously and carefully drawn" exception, *Jones v. United States*, 357 U.S. 493 (1958), recognizes the validity of searches with the voluntary consent of an individual possessing authority. That person might be the householder against whom evidence is sought, *Schneckloth v. Bustamonte*, 412 U.S. 218 (1973), or a fellow occupant who shares common authority over property, when the suspect is absent, and the exception for consent extends even to entries and searches with the permission of a co-occupant whom the police reasonably, but erroneously, believe to possess shared authority as an occupant. None of our co-occupant consent-to-search cases, however, has presented the further fact of a second occupant physically present and refusing permission to search, and later moving to suppress evidence so obtained. The significance of such a refusal turns on the underpinnings of the co-occupant consent rule, as recognized since *Matlock*.

D

Since the co-tenant wishing to open the door to a third party has no recognized authority in law or social practice to prevail over a present and objecting co-tenant, his disputed invitation, without more, gives a police officer no better claim to reasonableness in entering than the officer would have in the absence of any consent at all. Accordingly, in the balancing of competing individual and governmental interests entailed by the bar to unreasonable searches, the cooperative occupant's invitation adds nothing to the government's side to counter the force of an objecting individual's claim to security against the government's intrusion into his dwelling place. Since we hold to the "centuries-old principle of respect for the privacy of the home," *Wilson v. Layne*, 526 U.S. 603, 610 (1999), "it is beyond dispute that the home is entitled to special protection as the center of the private lives of our people," *Minnesota v. Carter*, 525 U.S. 83, 99 (1998). We have, after all, lived our whole national history with an understanding of "the ancient adage that a man's home is his castle [to the point that t]he poorest man may in his cottage bid defiance to all the forces of the Crown," *Miller v. United States*, 357 U.S. 301, 307 (1958).

Disputed permission is thus no match for this central value of the Fourth Amendment, and the State's other countervailing claims do not add up to outweigh it. Yes, we recognize the consenting tenant's interest as a citizen in bringing criminal activity to light, and we understand a co-tenant's legitimate self-interest in siding with the police to deflect suspicion raised by sharing quarters with a criminal.

But society can often have the benefit of these interests without relying on a theory of consent that ignores an inhabitant's refusal to allow a warrantless search. The co-tenant acting on his own initiative may be able to deliver evidence to the police, and can tell the police what he knows, for use before a magistrate in getting a warrant.

Nor should this established policy of Fourth Amendment law be undermined by the principal dissent's claim that it shields spousal abusers and other violent co-tenants who will refuse to allow the police to enter a dwelling when their victims ask the police for help. It is not that the dissent exaggerates violence in the home; we recognize that domestic abuse is a serious problem in the United States.

But this case has no bearing on the capacity of the police to protect domestic victims. The dissent's argument rests on the failure to distinguish two different issues: when the police may enter without committing a trespass, and when the police may enter to search for evidence. No question has been raised, or reasonably could be, about the authority of the police to enter a dwelling to protect a resident from domestic violence; so long as they have good reason to believe such a threat exists, it would be silly to suggest that the police would commit a tort by entering, say, to give a complaining tenant the opportunity to collect belongings and get out safely, or to determine whether violence (or threat of violence) has just occurred or is about to (or soon will) occur, however much a spouse or other co-tenant objected. (And since the police would then be lawfully in the premises, there is no question that they could seize any evidence in plain view or take further action supported by any consequent probable cause. Thus, the question whether the police might lawfully enter over objection in order to provide any protection that might be reasonable is easily answered yes. The undoubted right of the police to enter in order to protect a victim, however, has nothing to do with the question in this case, whether a search with the consent of one co-tenant is good against another, standing at the door and expressly refusing consent.

This is the line we draw, and we think the formalism is justified. So long as there is no evidence that the police have removed the potentially objecting tenant from the entrance for the sake of avoiding a possible objection, there is practical value in the simple clarity of complementary rules, one recognizing the co-tenant's permission when there is no fellow occupant on hand, the other according dispositive weight to the fellow occupant's contrary indication when he expresses it. For the very reason that *Rodriguez* held it would be unjustifiably impractical to require the police to take affirmative steps to confirm the actual authority of a consenting individual whose authority was apparent, we think it would needlessly limit the capacity of the police to respond to ostensibly legitimate opportunities in the field if we were to hold that reasonableness required the police to take affirmative steps to find a potentially objecting co-tenant before acting on the permission they had already received. There is no ready reason to believe that efforts to invite a refusal would make a difference in many cases, whereas every co-tenant consent case would turn into a test about the adequacy of the police's efforts to consult with a potential objector. Better to accept the formalism of distinguishing *Matlock* from this case than to impose a requirement, time-consuming in the field and in the courtroom, with no apparent systemic justification. The pragmatic decision to accept the simplicity of this line is, moreover, supported by the substantial number of instances in which suspects who are asked for permission to search actually consent, albeit imprudently, a fact that undercuts any argument that the police should try to locate a suspected inhabitant because his denial of consent would be a foregone conclusion.

JUSTICE ALITO took no part in the consideration or decision of this case.

JUSTICE STEVENS, concurring.

This case illustrates why even the most dedicated adherent to an approach to constitutional interpretation that places primary reliance on the search for original understanding would recognize the relevance of changes in our society.

At least since 1604 it has been settled that in the absence of exigent circumstances, a government agent has no right to enter a "house" or "castle" unless authorized to do so by a valid warrant. The issue in this case relates to the content of the advice that the officer should provide when met at the door by a man and a woman who are apparently joint tenants or joint owners of the property.

In the 18th century, when the Fourth Amendment was adopted, the advice would have been quite different from what is appropriate today. Given the then-prevailing dramatic differences between the property rights of the husband and the far lesser rights of the wife, only the consent of the husband would matter. Whether "the master of the house" consented or objected, his decision would control. Thus if "original understanding" were to govern the outcome of this case, the search was clearly invalid because the husband did not consent. History, however, is not dispositive because it is now clear, as a matter of constitutional law, that the male and the female are equal partners. *Reed v. Reed*, 404 U.S. 71 (1971).

In today's world the only advice that an officer could properly give should make it clear that each of the partners has a constitutional right that he or she may independently assert or waive. Assuming that both spouses are competent, neither one is a master possessing the power to override the other's constitutional right to deny entry to their castle.

With these observations, I join the Court's opinion.

JUSTICE BREYER, concurring.

If Fourth Amendment law forced us to choose between two bright-line rules, (1) a rule that always found one tenant's consent sufficient to justify a search without a warrant and (2) a rule that never did, I believe we should choose the first. That is because, as The Chief Justice's dissent points out, a rule permitting such searches can serve important law enforcement needs (for example, in domestic abuse cases) and the consenting party's joint tenancy diminishes the objecting party's reasonable expectation of privacy.

If a possible abuse victim invites a responding officer to enter a home or consents to the officer's entry request, that invitation (or consent) itself could reflect the victim's fear about being left alone with an abuser. It could also indicate the availability of evidence, in the form of an immediate willingness to speak, that might not otherwise exist. In that context, an invitation (or consent) would provide a special reason for immediate, rather than later, police entry. And, entry following invitation or consent by one party ordinarily would be reasonable even in the face of direct objection by the other. That being so, contrary to The Chief Justice's suggestion, today's decision will not adversely affect ordinary law enforcement practices.

Given the case-specific nature of the Court's holding, and with these understandings, I join the Court's holding and its opinion.

CHIEF JUSTICE ROBERTS, with whom JUSTICE SCALIA joins, dissenting.

The Court creates constitutional law by surmising what is typical when a social guest encounters an entirely atypical situation. The rule the majority fashions does not implement the high office of the Fourth Amendment to protect privacy, but instead provides protection on a random and happenstance basis, protecting, for example, a co-occupant who happens to be at the front door when the other occupant consents to a search, but not one napping or watching television in the next room. And the cost of affording such random protection is great, as demonstrated by the recurring cases in which abused spouses seek to authorize police entry into a home they share with a nonconsenting abuser.

The correct approach to the question presented is clearly mapped out in our precedents: The Fourth Amendment protects privacy. If an individual shares information, papers, or places with another, he assumes the risk that the other person will in turn share access to that information or those papers or places with the government. And just as an individual who has shared illegal plans or incriminating documents with another cannot interpose an objection when that other person turns the information over to the government, just because the individual happens to be present at the time, so too someone who shares a place with another cannot interpose an objection when that person decides to grant access to the police, simply because the objecting individual happens to be present.

A warrantless search is reasonable if police obtain the voluntary consent of a person authorized to give it. Co-occupants have "assumed the risk that one of their number might permit [a] common area to be searched." *United States v. Matlock*, 415 U.S. 164, 171, n. 7 (1974). Just as Mrs. Randolph could walk upstairs, come down, and turn her husband's cocaine straw over to the police, she can consent to police entry and search of what is, after all, her home, too.

The law acknowledges that although we might not expect our friends and family to admit the government into common areas, sharing space entails risk. A person assumes the risk that his co-occupants—just as they might report his illegal activity or deliver his contraband to the government—might consent to a search of areas over which they have access and control.

JUSTICE SCALIA, dissenting.

I join the dissent of The Chief Justice, but add these few words in response to Justice Stevens' concurrence.

It is not as clear to me as it is to Justice Stevens that, at the time the Fourth Amendment was adopted, a police officer could enter a married woman's home over her objection, and could not enter with only her consent. Nor is it clear to me that the answers to these questions depended solely on who owned the house. It is entirely clear, however, that if the matter did depend solely on property rights, a latter-day alteration of property rights would also produce a latter-day alteration of the Fourth Amendment outcome—without altering the Fourth Amendment itself.

Finally, I must express grave doubt that today's decision deserves Justice Stevens' celebration as part of the forward march of women's equality. Given the usual patterns of domestic violence, how often can police be expected to encounter the situation in which a man urges them to enter the home while a woman simultaneously demands that they stay out? The most common practical effect of today's decision, insofar as the contest between the sexes is concerned, is to give men the power to stop women from allowing police into their homes—which is, curiously enough, precisely the power that Justice Stevens disapprovingly presumes men had in 1791.

JUSTICE THOMAS, dissenting.

The Court has long recognized that "[i]t is an act of responsible citizenship for individuals to give whatever information they may have to aid in law enforcement." *Miranda v. Arizona*, 384 U.S. 436, 477–478 (1966). Consistent with this principle, the Court held in *Coolidge v. New Hampshire*, 403 U.S. 443 (1971), that no Fourth Amendment search occurs where, as here, the spouse of an accused voluntarily leads the police to potential evidence of wrongdoing by the accused. Because *Coolidge* squarely controls this case, the Court need not address whether police could permissibly have conducted a general search of the Randolph home, based on Mrs. Randolph's consent. I respectfully dissent.

FOR DISCUSSION

When does a co-resident have the right to provide permission for a search? Is the majority or the dissent correct in the interpretations advanced of the Fourth Amendment? Why? How significant is the fact that the officers were called to the house on a charge of domestic abuse?

RELATED CASES

***United States v. Matlock:* 415 U.S. 164 (1974).**

The police can search a shared bedroom without violating the Fourth Amendment when one of the occupants provides consent.

***Illinois v. Rodriguez:* 497 U.S. 177 (1990).**

If the police were provided access to a home by a person they mistakenly believed was authorized to provide consent, evidence obtained from that warrantless search may be used at trial.

ILLINOIS V. GATES

462 U.S. 213, 103 S.Ct. 2317, 76 L.Ed.2d 527 (1983)

Subsequent to receiving an anonymous letter claiming that a couple named Sue and Lance Gates were selling and trafficking drugs, police in Bloomingdale, Illinois, engaged in preliminary investigation of the Gateses. The anonymous note indicated that the couple's connections were in Florida and that their travel involved combinations of drives and flights. The note specifically mentioned dates, and the Bloomingdale police detective, Mader, was able to verify through surveillance many of details provided. Presented with the anonymous communication and the verifying evidence, a judge found probable cause and issued a search warrant for the residence and automobile of Sue and Lance Gates. The drug and weapons evidence found was suppressed by the Illinois circuit court on the basis of the argument that the judge did not have probable cause to issue the warrant. The Illinois Appellate Court and the Supreme Court of Illinois affirmed this decision.

Vote: 6–3

JUSTICE REHNQUIST delivered the opinion of the Court.

II

The Illinois Supreme Court concluded—and we are inclined to agree—that, standing alone, the anonymous letter sent to the Bloomingdale Police Department would not provide the basis for a magistrate's determination that there was probable cause to believe contraband would be found in the Gateses' car and home. The letter provides virtually nothing from which one might conclude that its author is either honest or his information reliable; likewise, the letter gives absolutely no indication of the basis for the writer's predictions regarding the Gateses' criminal activities. Something more was required, then, before a magistrate could conclude that there was probable cause to believe that contraband would be found in the Gateses' home and car.

The Illinois Supreme Court also properly recognized that Detective Mader's affidavit might be capable of supplementing the anonymous letter with information sufficient to permit a determination of probable cause. In holding that the affidavit in fact did not contain sufficient additional information to sustain a determination of probable cause, the Illinois court applied a "two-pronged test," derived from our decision in *Spinelli v. United States*, 393 U.S. 410 (1969). The Illinois Supreme Court, like some others, apparently understood *Spinelli* as requiring that the anonymous letter satisfy each of two independent requirements before it could be relied on. According to this view, the letter, as supplemented by Mader's affidavit, first had to adequately reveal the "basis of knowledge" of the letterwriter—the particular means by which he came by the information given in his report. Second, it had to provide facts sufficiently establishing either the "veracity" of the affiant's informant, or, alternatively, the "reliability" of the informant's report in this particular case.

The Illinois court, alluding to an elaborate set of legal rules that have developed among various lower courts to enforce the "two-pronged test," found that the test had not been satisfied.

We agree with the Illinois Supreme Court that an informant's "veracity," "reliability," and "basis of knowledge" are all highly relevant in determining the value of his report. We do not agree, however, that these elements should be understood as entirely separate and independent requirements to be rigidly exacted in every case, which the opinion of the Supreme Court of Illinois would imply. Rather, as detailed below, they should be understood simply as closely intertwined issues that may usefully illuminate the commonsense, practical question whether there is "probable cause" to believe that contraband or evidence is located in a particular place.

III

This totality-of-the-circumstances approach is far more consistent with our prior treatment of probable cause than is any rigid demand that specific "tests" be satisfied by every informant's tip.

We also have recognized that affidavits "are normally drafted by nonlawyers in the midst and haste of a criminal investigation. Technical requirements of elaborate specificity once exacted under common law pleadings have no proper place in this area." *United States v. Ventresca*, 380 U.S. 102, 108 (1965). Likewise, search and arrest warrants long have been issued by persons who are neither lawyers nor judges, and who certainly do not remain abreast of each judicial refinement of the nature of "probable cause." The rigorous inquiry into the *Spinelli* prongs and the complex superstructure of evidentiary and analytical rules that some have seen implicit in our *Spinelli* decision, cannot be reconciled with the fact that many warrants are—quite properly—issued on the basis of nontechnical, common-sense judgments of laymen applying a standard less demanding than those used in more formal legal proceedings.

Similarly, we have repeatedly said that after-the-fact scrutiny by courts of the sufficiency of an affidavit should not take the form of *de novo* review. A magistrate's "determination of probable cause should be paid great deference by reviewing courts." *Spinelli* at 419.

The strictures that inevitably accompany the "two-pronged test" cannot avoid seriously impeding the task of law enforcement. If, as the Illinois Supreme Court apparently thought, that test must be rigorously applied in every case, anonymous tips would be of greatly diminished value in police work. Ordinary citizens, like ordinary witnesses, generally do not provide extensive recitations of the basis of their everyday observations. Likewise, as the Illinois Supreme Court observed in this case, the veracity of persons supplying anonymous tips is by hypothesis largely unknown, and unknowable. As a result, anonymous tips seldom could survive a rigorous application of either of the *Spinelli* prongs. Yet, such tips, particularly when supplemented by independent police investigation, frequently contribute to the solution of otherwise "perfect crimes." While a conscientious assessment of the basis for crediting such tips is required by the Fourth Amendment, a standard that leaves virtually no place for anonymous citizen informants is not.

For all these reasons, we conclude that it is wiser to abandon the "two-pronged test" established by our decisions in *Aguilar v. Texas*, 378 U.S. 108 (1964), and *Spinelli*. In its place we reaffirm the totality-of-the-circumstances analysis that traditionally has informed probable-cause determinations. The task of the issuing magistrate is simply to make a practical, common-sense decision whether, given all the circumstances set forth in the affidavit before him, including the "veracity" and "basis of knowledge" of persons supplying hearsay information, there is a fair probability that contraband or evidence of a crime will be found in a particular place. And the duty of a reviewing court is simply to ensure that the magistrate had a "substantial basis for . . . [concluding]" that probable cause existed. *Jones v. United States*, 362 U.S. 257 at 271 (1960). We are convinced that this flexible, easily applied standard will better achieve the accommodation of public and private interests that the Fourth Amendment requires than does the approach that has developed from *Aguilar* and *Spinelli*.

IV

Our decisions applying the totality-of-the-circumstances analysis outlined above have consistently recognized the value of corroboration of details of an informant's tip by independent police work. In *Jones v. United States* we held that an affidavit relying on hearsay "is not to be deemed insufficient on that score, so long as a substantial basis for crediting the hearsay is presented." Likewise, we recognized the probative value of corroborative efforts of police officials in *Aguilar*—the source of the "two-pronged test"—by observing that if the police had made some effort to corroborate the informant's report at issue, "an entirely different case" would have been presented.

Our decision in *Draper v. United States*, 358 U.S. 307 (1959), however, is the classic case on the value of corroborative efforts of police officials. There, an informant named Hereford reported that Draper would arrive in Denver on a train from Chicago on one of two days, and that he would be carrying a quantity of heroin. The informant also supplied a fairly detailed physical description of Draper, and predicted that he would be wearing a light colored raincoat, brown slacks, and black shoes, and would be walking "real fast." Hereford gave no indication of the basis for his information.

On one of the stated dates police officers observed a man matching this description exit a train arriving from Chicago; his attire and luggage matched Hereford's report and he was walking rapidly. We explained in *Draper* that, by this point in his investigation, the arresting officer "had personally verified every facet of the information given him by Hereford except whether petitioner had accomplished his mission and had the three ounces of heroin on his person or in his bag. And surely, with every other bit of Hereford's information being thus personally verified, [the officer] had 'reasonable grounds' to believe that the remaining unverified bit of Hereford's information—that Draper would have the heroin with him—was likewise true"...

The showing of probable cause in the present case was fully as compelling as that in *Draper*. Even standing alone, the facts obtained through the independent investigation of Mader and the DEA at least suggested that the Gateses were involved in drug trafficking

In addition, the judge could rely on the anonymous letter, which had been corroborated in major part by Mader's efforts—just as had occurred in *Draper*. The Supreme Court of Illinois reasoned that Draper involved an informant who had given reliable information on previous occasions, while the honesty and reliability of the anonymous informant in this case were unknown to the Bloomingdale police. While this distinction might be an apt one at the time the Police Department received the anonymous letter, it became far less significant after Mader's independent investigative work occurred.

Finally, the anonymous letter contained a range of details relating not just to easily obtained facts and conditions existing at the time of the tip, but to future actions of third parties ordinarily not easily predicted. The letter writer's accurate information as to the travel plans of each of the Gateses was of a character likely obtained only from the Gateses themselves, or from someone familiar with their not entirely ordinary travel plans. Of course, the Gateses' travel plans might have been learned from a talkative neighbor or travel agent; under the "two-pronged test" developed from *Spinelli*, the character of the details in the anonymous letter might well not permit a sufficiently clear inference regarding the letterwriter's "basis of knowledge." But, as discussed previously, probable cause does not demand the certainty we associate with formal trials. It is enough that there was a fair probability that the writer of the anonymous letter had obtained his entire story either from the Gateses or someone they trusted. And corroboration of major portions of the letter's predictions provides just this probability. It is apparent, therefore, that the judge issuing the warrant had a "substantial basis for . . . [concluding]" that probable cause to search the Gateses' home and car existed. The judgment of the Supreme Court of Illinois therefore must be Reversed.

JUSTICE WHITE, concurring in the judgment.

III

Abandoning the "two-pronged test" of *Aguilar v. Texas*, 378 U.S. 108 (1964), and *Spinelli v. United States*, 393 U.S. 410 (1969), the Court upholds the validity of the warrant under a new "totality of the circumstances" approach. Although I agree that the warrant should be upheld, I reach this conclusion in accordance with the *Aguilar-Spinelli* framework.

A

In the present case, it is undisputed that the anonymous tip, by itself, did not furnish probable cause. The question is whether those portions of the affidavit describing the results of the police investigation of the respondents, when considered in light of the tip, "would permit the suspicions engendered by the informant's report to ripen into a judgment that a crime was probably being committed." *Spinelli* at 418.

The critical issue is not whether the activities observed by the police are innocent or suspicious. Instead, the proper focus should be on whether the actions of the suspects, whatever their nature, give rise to an inference that the informant is credible and that he obtained his information in a reliable manner.

But *Aguilar* and *Spinelli*, like our other cases, do not require that certain guilt be established before a warrant may properly be issued. "[Only] the probability, and not a prima facie showing, of criminal activity is the standard of probable cause." *Spinelli* at 419 (citing *Beck v. Ohio*, 379 U.S. 89, 96 (1964)). I therefore conclude that the judgment of the Illinois Supreme Court invalidating the warrant must be reversed.

B

The Court agrees that the warrant was valid, but, in the process of reaching this conclusion, it overrules the *Aguilar-Spinelli* tests and replaces them with a "totality of the circumstances" standard. As shown above, it is not at all necessary to overrule *Aguilar-Spinelli* in order to reverse the judgment below. Therefore, because I am inclined to believe that, when applied properly, the *Aguilar-Spinelli* rules play an appropriate role in probable-cause determinations, and because the Court's holding may foretell an evisceration of the probable-cause standard, I do not join the Court's holding.

The Court reasons that the "veracity" and "basis of knowledge" tests are not independent, and that a deficiency as to one can be compensated for by a strong showing as to the other. Thus, a finding of probable cause may be based on a tip from an informant "known for the unusual reliability of his predictions" or from "an unquestionably honest citizen," even if the report fails thoroughly to set forth the basis upon which the information was obtained. If this is so, then it must follow a fortiori that "the affidavit of an officer, known by the magistrate to be honest and experienced, stating that [contraband] is located in a certain building" must be acceptable. It would be "quixotic" if a similar statement from an honest informant, but not one from an honest officer, could furnish probable cause. But we have repeatedly held that the unsupported assertion or belief of an officer does not satisfy the probable-cause requirement. Thus, this portion of today's holding can be read as implicitly rejecting the teachings of these prior holdings.

Thus, as I read the majority opinion, it appears that the question whether the probable-cause standard is to be diluted is left to the common-sense judgments of issuing magistrates. I am reluctant to approve any standard that does not expressly require, as a prerequisite to issuance of a warrant, some showing of facts from which an inference may be drawn that the informant is credible and that his information was obtained in a reliable way. The Court is correctly concerned with the fact that some lower courts have been applying *Aguilar-Spinelli* in an unduly rigid manner. I believe, however, that with clarification of the rule of corroborating information, the lower courts are fully able to properly interpret *Aguilar-Spinelli* and avoid such unduly rigid applications. I may be wrong; it ultimately may prove to be the case that the only profitable instruction we can provide to magistrates is to rely on common sense. But the question whether a particular anonymous tip provides the basis for issuance of a warrant will often be a difficult one, and I would at least attempt to provide more precise guidance by clarifying *Aguilar-Spinelli* and the relationship of those cases with *Draper v. United States*, 358 U.S. 307 (1959), before totally abdicating our responsibility in this area. Hence, I do not join the Court's opinion rejecting the *Aguilar-Spinelli* rules.

JUSTICE BRENNAN, with whom JUSTICE MARSHALL joins, dissenting.

Although I join Justice Stevens' dissenting opinion and agree with him that the warrant is invalid even under the Court's newly announced "totality of the circumstances" test, I write separately to dissent from the Court's unjustified and ill-advised rejection of the two-prong test for evaluating the validity of a warrant based on hearsay announced in *Aguilar v. Texas*, 378 U.S. 108 (1964), and refined in *Spinelli v. United States*, 393 U.S. 410 (1969).

I

Until today the Court has never squarely addressed the application of the *Aguilar* and *Spinelli* standards to tips from anonymous informants. Both *Aguilar* and *Spinelli* dealt with tips from informants known at least to the police. And surely there is even more reason to subject anonymous informants' tips to the tests established by *Aguilar* and *Spinelli*. By definition nothing is known about an anonymous informant's identity, honesty, or reliability. One commentator has suggested that anonymous informants should be treated as presumptively unreliable. In any event, there certainly is no basis for treating anonymous informants as presumptively reliable. Nor is there any basis for assuming that the information provided by an anonymous informant has been obtained in a reliable way. If we are unwilling to accept conclusory allegations from the police, who are presumptively reliable, or from informants who are known, at least to the police, there cannot possibly be any rational basis for accepting conclusory allegations from anonymous informants.

To suggest that anonymous informants' tips are subject to the tests established by *Aguilar* and *Spinelli* is not to suggest that they can never provide a basis for a finding of probable cause. It is conceivable that police corroboration of the details of the tip might establish the reliability of the informant under *Aguilar's* veracity prong, as refined in *Spinelli*, and that the details in the tip might be sufficient to qualify under the "self-verifying detail" test established by *Spinelli* as a means of satisfying *Aguilar's* basis of knowledge prong. The *Aguilar* and *Spinelli* tests must be applied to anonymous informants' tips, however, if we are to continue to insure that findings of probable cause, and attendant intrusions, are based on information provided by an honest or credible person who has acquired the information in a reliable way.

In light of the important purposes served by *Aguilar* and *Spinelli*, I would not reject the standards they establish. If anything, I simply would make more clear that *Spinelli*, properly understood, does not depart in any fundamental way from the test established by *Aguilar*.

II

In rejecting the *Aguilar-Spinelli* standards, the Court suggests that a "totality-of-the circumstances approach is far more consistent with our prior treatment of probable cause than is any rigid demand that specific 'tests' be satisfied by every informant's tip."

At the heart of the Court's decision to abandon *Aguilar* and *Spinelli* appears to be its belief that "the direction taken by decisions following *Spinelli* poorly serves '[the] most basic function of any government': 'to provide for the security of the individual and of his property.' " This conclusion rests on the judgment that *Aguilar* and *Spinelli* "seriously [impede] the task of law enforcement" and render anonymous tips valueless in police work. Surely, the Court overstates its case. But of particular concern to all Americans must be that the Court gives virtually no consideration to the value of insuring that findings of probable cause are based on information that a magistrate can reasonably say has been obtained in a reliable way by an honest or credible person. I share Justice White's fear that the Court's rejection of *Aguilar* and *Spinelli* and its adoption of a new totality-of-the-circumstances test "may foretell an evisceration of the probable-cause standard. . . ."

III

The Court's complete failure to provide any persuasive reason for rejecting *Aguilar* and *Spinelli* doubtlessly reflects impatience with what it perceives to be "overly technical" rules governing searches and seizures under the Fourth Amendment. Words such as "practical," "nontechnical," and "common sense," as used in the Court's opinion, are but code words for an overly permissive attitude towards police practices in derogation of the rights secured by the Fourth Amendment. Everyone shares the Court's concern over the horrors of drug trafficking, but under our Constitution only measures consistent with the Fourth Amendment may be employed by government to cure this evil. We must be ever mindful of Justice Stewart's admonition in *Coolidge v. New Hampshire*, 403 U.S. 443 (1971): "In times of unrest, whether caused by crime or racial conflict or fear of internal subversion, this basic law and the values that it represents may appear unrealistic or 'extravagant' to some. But the values were those of the authors of our fundamental constitutional concepts." In the same vein, *Glasser v. United States*, 315 U.S. 60 at 86 (1942), warned that "[steps] innocently taken may, one by one, lead to the irretrievable impairment of substantial liberties."

JUSTICE STEVENS, with whom JUSTICE BRENNAN joins, dissenting.

The fact that Lance and Sue Gates made a 22-hour nonstop drive from West Palm Beach, Florida, to Bloomingdale, Illinois, only a few hours after Lance had flown to Florida provided persuasive evidence that they were engaged in illicit activity. That fact, however, was not known to the judge when he issued the warrant to search their home.

What the judge did know at that time was that the anonymous informant had not been completely accurate in his or her predictions. The informant had indicated that " 'Sue . . . drives their car to Florida where she leaves it to be loaded up with drugs. . . . Sue [flies] back after she drops the car off in Florida.' " Yet Detective Mader's affidavit reported that she " 'left the West Palm Beach area driving the Mercury northbound.' "

The discrepancy between the informant's predictions and the facts known to Detective Mader is significant for three reasons. First, it cast doubt on the informant's hypothesis that the Gates already had " 'over [$100,000] worth of drugs in their basement[.]' " The informant had predicted an itinerary that always kept one spouse in Bloomingdale, suggesting that the Gates did not want to leave their home unguarded because something valuable was hidden within. That inference obviously could not be drawn when it was known that the pair was actually together over a thousand miles from home.

Second, the discrepancy made the Gates' conduct seem substantially less unusual than the informant had predicted it would be. It would have been odd if, as predicted, Sue had driven down to Florida on Wednesday, left the car, and flown right back to Illinois. But the mere facts that Sue was in West Palm Beach with the car, that she was joined by her husband at the Holiday Inn on Friday, and that the couple drove north together the next morning are neither unusual nor probative of criminal activity.

Third, the fact that the anonymous letter contained a material mistake undermines the reasonableness of relying on it as a basis for making a forcible entry into a private home.

FOR DISCUSSION

What is the key source of conflict between the majority and dissent in determining the validity of a claim of probable cause? Does this decision enhance or constrain the discretion of the magistrate or judge in awarding a search warrant? What are the potential consequences of this decision for Fourth Amendment jurisprudence?

RELATED CASES

***Massachusetts v. Upton:* 466 U.S. 727 (1984).**

Judges may determine if a warrant is justified by the "totality of circumstances" presented by the police to provide the necessary probable cause.

***Groh v. Ramirez:* 520 U.S. 551 (2004).**

Judges can issue valid search warrants only when they identify the items to be seized, not just the location to be searched.

UNITED STATES V. LEON

468 U.S. 897, 104 S.Ct. 3405, 82 L.Ed.2d 677 (1984)

The facts of this case are articulated in the opinion.

Vote: 6–3

JUSTICE WHITE delivered the opinion of the Court.

This case presents the question whether the Fourth Amendment exclusionary rule should be modified so as not to bar the use in the prosecution's case in chief of evidence obtained by officers acting in reasonable reliance on a search warrant issued by a detached and neutral magistrate but ultimately found to be unsupported by probable cause. To resolve this question, we must consider once again the tension between the sometimes competing goals of, on the one hand, deterring official misconduct and removing inducements to unreasonable invasions of privacy and, on the other, establishing procedures under which criminal defendants are "acquitted or convicted on the basis of all the evidence which exposes the truth." *Alderman v. United States*, 394 U.S. 165, 175 (1969).

I

In August 1981, a confidential informant of unproven reliability informed an officer of the Burbank Police Department that two persons known to him as "Armando" and "Patsy" were selling large quantities of cocaine and methaqualone from their residence at 620 Price Drive in Burbank, Cal. The informant also indicated that he had witnessed a sale of methaqualone by "Patsy" at the residence approximately five months earlier and had observed at that time a shoebox containing a large amount of cash that belonged to "Patsy." He further declared that "Armando" and "Patsy" generally kept only small quantities of drugs at their residence and stored the remainder at another location in Burbank.

On the basis of this information, the Burbank police initiated an extensive investigation focusing first on the Price Drive residence and later on two other residences as well. Cars parked at the Price Drive residence were determined to belong to respondents Armando Sanchez, who had previously been arrested for possession of marihuana, and Patsy Stewart, who had no criminal record. During the course of the investigation, officers observed an automobile belonging to respondent Ricardo Del Castillo, who had previously been arrested for possession of 50 pounds of marihuana, arrive at the Price Drive residence. The driver of that car entered the house, exited shortly thereafter carrying a small paper sack, and drove away. A check of Del Castillo's probation records led the officers to respondent Alberto Leon, whose telephone number Del Castillo had listed as his employer's. Leon had been arrested in 1980 on drug charges, and a companion had informed the police at that time that Leon was heavily involved in the importation of drugs into this country. Before the current investigation began, the Burbank officers had learned that an informant had told a Glendale police officer that Leon stored a large quantity of methaqualone at his residence in Glendale. During the course of this investigation, the Burbank officers learned that Leon was living at 716 South Sunset Canyon in Burbank.

Subsequently, the officers observed several persons, at least one of whom had prior drug involvement, arriving at the Price Drive residence and leaving with small packages; observed a variety of other material activity at the two residences as well as at a condominium at 7902 Via Magdalena; and witnessed a variety of relevant activity involving respondents' automobiles. The officers also observed respondents Sanchez and Stewart board separate flights for Miami. The pair later returned to Los Angeles together, consented to a search of their luggage that revealed only a small amount of marihuana, and left the airport. Based on these and other observations summarized in the affidavit, Officer Cyril Rombach of the Burbank Police Department, an experienced and well-trained narcotics investigator, prepared an application for a warrant to search 620 Price Drive, 716 South Sunset Canyon, 7902 Via Magdalena, and automobiles registered to each of the respondents for an extensive list of items believed to be related to respondents' drug-trafficking activities. Officer Rombach's extensive application was reviewed by several Deputy District Attorneys.

A facially valid search warrant was issued in September 1981 by a State Superior Court Judge. The ensuing searches produced large quantities of drugs at the Via Magdalena and Sunset Canyon addresses and a small quantity at the Price Drive residence. Other evidence was discovered at each of the residences and in Stewart's and Del Castillo's automobiles. Respondents were indicted by a grand jury in the District Court for the Central District of California and charged with conspiracy to possess and distribute cocaine and a variety of substantive counts.

The respondents then filed motions to suppress the evidence seized pursuant to the warrant. The District Court held an evidentiary hearing and, while recognizing that the case was a close one, granted the motions to suppress in part. It concluded that the affidavit was insufficient to establish probable cause, but did not suppress all of the evidence as to all of the respondents because none of the respondents had standing to challenge all of the searches. In to a request from the Government, the court made clear that Officer Rombach had acted in good faith, but it rejected the Government's suggestion that the Fourth Amendment exclusionary rule should not apply where evidence is seized in reasonable, good-faith reliance on a search warrant.

The District Court denied the Government's motion for reconsideration, and a divided panel of the Court of Appeals for the Ninth Circuit affirmed. The Court of Appeals first concluded that Officer Rombach's affidavit could not establish probable cause to search the Price Drive residence. The affidavit, moreover, failed to establish the informant's credibility. Accordingly, the Court of Appeals concluded that the information provided by the informant was inadequate under both prongs of the two-part test established in *Aguilar v. Texas*, 378 U.S. 108 (1964), and *Spinelli v. United States*, 393 U.S. 410 (1969). The Court of Appeals refused the Government's invitation to recognize a good-faith exception to the Fourth Amendment exclusionary rule.

We granted certiorari to consider the propriety of such a modification. Although it undoubtedly is within our power to consider the question whether probable cause existed under the "totality of the circumstances" test announced last Term in *Illinois v. Gates*, 462 U.S. 213 (1983), that question has not been briefed or argued; and it is also within our authority, which we choose to exercise, to take the case as it comes to us, accepting the Court of Appeals' conclusion that probable cause was lacking under the prevailing legal standards.

We have concluded that, in the Fourth Amendment context, the exclusionary rule can be modified somewhat without jeopardizing its ability to perform its intended functions. Accordingly, we reverse the judgment of the Court of Appeals.

II

Language in opinions of this Court and of individual Justices has sometimes implied that the exclusionary rule is a necessary corollary of the Fourth Amendment, *Mapp v. Ohio*, 367 U.S. 643 (1961); *Olmstead v. United States*, 277 U.S. 438 (1928), or that the rule is required by the conjunction of the Fourth and Fifth Amendments. These implications need not detain us long. The Fifth Amendment theory has not withstood critical analysis or the test of time, and the Fourth Amendment "has never been interpreted to proscribe the introduction of illegally seized evidence in all proceedings or against all persons." *Stone v. Powell*, 428 U.S. 465, 486 (1976).

A

The substantial social costs exacted by the exclusionary rule for the vindication of Fourth Amendment rights have long been a source of concern. An objectionable collateral consequence of this interference with the criminal justice system's truth-finding function is that some guilty defendants may go free or receive reduced sentences as a result of favorable plea bargains. Particularly when law enforcement officers have acted in objective good faith or their transgressions have been minor, the magnitude of the benefit conferred on such guilty defendants offends basic concepts of the criminal justice system.

B

As yet, we have not recognized any form of good-faith exception to the Fourth Amendment exclusionary rule. But the balancing approach that has evolved during the years of experience with the rule provides strong support for the modification currently urged upon us. As we discuss below, our evaluation of the costs and benefits of suppressing reliable physical evidence seized by officers reasonably relying on a warrant issued by a detached and neutral magistrate leads to the conclusion that such evidence should be admissible in the prosecution's case in chief.

III

A

Because a search warrant "provides the detached scrutiny of a neutral magistrate, which is a more reliable safeguard against improper searches than the hurried judgment of a law enforcement officer 'engaged in the often competitive enterprise of ferreting out crime,'" *United States v. Chadwick*, 433 U.S. 1, 9 (1977), we have expressed a strong preference for warrants and declared that "in a doubtful or marginal case a search under a warrant may be sustainable where without one it would fall." *United States v. Ventresca*, 380 U.S. 102, 106 (1965). Reasonable minds frequently may differ on the question whether a particular affidavit establishes probable cause, and we have thus concluded that the preference for warrants is most appropriately effectuated by according "great deference" to a magistrate's determination.

Deference to the magistrate, however, is not boundless. It is clear, first, that the deference accorded to a magistrate's finding of probable cause does not preclude inquiry into the knowing or reckless falsity of the affidavit on which that determination was based. Second, the courts must also insist that the magistrate purport to "perform his 'neutral and detached' function and not serve merely as a rubber stamp for the police." *Aguilar v. Texas* at 111.

Third, reviewing courts will not defer to a warrant based on an affidavit that does not "provide the magistrate with a substantial basis for determining the existence of probable cause." *Illinois v. Gates*, 462 U.S., at 239.

Only in the first of these three situations, however, has the Court set forth a rationale for suppressing evidence obtained pursuant to a search warrant; in the other areas, it has simply excluded such evidence without considering whether Fourth Amendment interests will be advanced. To the extent that proponents of exclusion rely on its behavioral effects on judges and magistrates in these areas, their reliance is misplaced. First, the exclusionary rule is designed to deter police misconduct rather than to punish the errors of judges and magistrates. Second, there exists no evidence suggesting that judges and magistrates are inclined to ignore or subvert the Fourth Amendment or that lawlessness among these actors requires application of the extreme sanction of exclusion.

Third, and most important, we discern no basis, and are offered none, for believing that exclusion of evidence seized pursuant to a warrant will have a significant deterrent effect on the issuing judge or magistrate. And, to the extent that the rule is thought to operate as a "systemic" deterrent on a wider audience, it clearly can have no such effect on individuals empowered to issue search warrants. Judges and magistrates are not adjuncts to the law enforcement team; as neutral judicial officers, they have no stake in the outcome of particular criminal prosecutions. The threat of exclusion thus cannot be expected significantly to deter them.

B

If exclusion of evidence obtained pursuant to a subsequently invalidated warrant is to have any deterrent effect, therefore, it must alter the behavior of individual law enforcement officers or the policies of their departments.

C

We conclude that the marginal or nonexistent benefits produced by suppressing evidence obtained in objectively reasonable reliance on a subsequently invalidated search warrant cannot justify the substantial costs of exclusion. We do not suggest, however, that exclusion is always inappropriate in cases where an officer has obtained a warrant and abided by its terms. Nevertheless, the officer's reliance on the magistrate's probable-cause determination and on the technical sufficiency of the warrant he issues must be objectively reasonable, and it is clear that in some circumstances the officer will have no reasonable grounds for believing that the warrant was properly issued.

Suppression therefore remains an appropriate remedy if the magistrate or judge in issuing a warrant was misled by information in an affidavit that the affiant knew was false or would have known was false except for his reckless disregard of the truth. *Franks v. Delaware*, 438 U.S. 154 (1978). Finally, depending on the circumstances of the particular case, a warrant may be so facially deficient—i.e., in failing to particularize the place to be searched or the things to be seized—that the executing officers cannot reasonably presume it to be valid.

In so limiting the suppression remedy, we leave untouched the probable-cause standard and the various requirements for a valid warrant.

JUSTICE BLACKMUN, concurring.

The Court today holds that evidence obtained in violation of the Fourth Amendment by officers acting in objectively reasonable reliance on a search warrant issued by a neutral and detached magistrate need not be excluded, as a matter of federal law, from the case in chief of federal and state criminal prosecutions. In so doing, the Court writes another chapter in the volume of Fourth Amendment law opened by *Weeks v. United States*, 232 U.S. 383 (1914). I join the Court's opinion in this case and the one in *Massachusetts v. Sheppard*, 468 U.S. 981 (1984), because I believe that the rule announced today advances the legitimate interests of the criminal justice system without sacrificing the individual rights protected by the Fourth Amendment. I write separately, however, to underscore what I regard as the unavoidably provisional nature of today's decisions.

As the Court's opinion in this case makes clear, the Court has narrowed the scope of the exclusionary rule because of an empirical judgment that the rule has little appreciable effect in cases where officers act in objectively reasonable reliance on search warrants.

What must be stressed, however, is that any empirical judgment about the effect of the exclusionary rule in a particular class of cases necessarily is a provisional one. By their very nature, the assumptions on which we proceed today cannot be cast in stone. To the contrary, they now will be tested in the real world of state and federal law enforcement, and this Court will attend to the results. If it should emerge from experience that, contrary to our expectations, the good-faith exception to the exclusionary rule results in a material change in police compliance with the Fourth Amendment, we shall have to reconsider what we have undertaken here. The logic of a decision that rests on untested predictions about police conduct demands no less.

If a single principle may be drawn from this Court's exclusionary rule decisions, from *Weeks* through *Mapp v. Ohio*, 367 U.S. 643 (1961), to the decisions handed down today, it is that the scope of the exclusionary rule is subject to change in light of changing judicial understanding about the effects of the rule outside the confines of the courtroom. It is incumbent on the Nation's law enforcement officers, who must continue to observe the Fourth Amendment in the wake of today's decisions, to recognize the double-edged nature of that principle.

JUSTICE BRENNAN, with whom JUSTICE MARSHALL joins, dissenting.

Ten years ago in *United States v. Calandra*, 414 U.S. 338 (1974), I expressed the fear that the Court's decision "may signal that a majority of my colleagues have positioned themselves to reopen the door [to evidence secured by official lawlessness] still further and abandon altogether the exclusionary rule in search-and-seizure cases." Since then, in case after case, I have witnessed the Court's gradual but determined strangulation of the rule. It now appears that the Court's victory over the Fourth Amendment is complete. That today's decisions represent the piece de resistance of the Court's past efforts cannot be doubted, for today the Court sanctions the use in the prosecution's case in chief of illegally obtained evidence against the individual whose rights have been violated—a result that had previously been thought to be foreclosed.

The Court seeks to justify this result on the ground that the "costs" of adhering to the exclusionary rule in cases like those before us exceed the "benefits." But the language of deterrence and of cost/benefit analysis, if used indiscriminately, can have a narcotic effect. It creates an illusion of technical precision and ineluctability. It suggests that not only constitutional principle but also empirical data support the majority's result. When the Court's analysis is examined carefully, however, it is clear that we have not been treated to an honest assessment of the merits of the exclusionary rule, but have instead been drawn into a curious world where the "costs" of excluding illegally obtained evidence loom to exaggerated heights and where the "benefits" of such exclusion are made to disappear with a mere wave of the hand.

The majority ignores the fundamental constitutional importance of what is at stake here. While the machinery of law enforcement and indeed the nature of crime itself have changed dramatically since the Fourth Amendment became part of the Nation's fundamental law in 1791, what the Framers understood then remains true today—that the task of combating crime and convicting the guilty will in every era seem of such critical and pressing concern that we may be lured by the temptations of expediency into forsaking our commitment to protecting individual liberty and privacy. It was for that very reason that the Framers of the Bill of Rights insisted that law enforcement efforts be permanently and unambiguously restricted in order to preserve personal freedoms. In the constitutional scheme they ordained, the sometimes unpopular task of ensuring that the government's enforcement efforts remain within the strict boundaries fixed by the Fourth Amendment was entrusted to the courts. As James Madison predicted in his address to the First Congress on June 8, 1789:

> If [these rights] are incorporated into the Constitution, independent tribunals of justice will consider themselves in a peculiar manner the guardians of those rights; they will be an impenetrable bulwark

against every assumption of power in the Legislative or Executive; they will be naturally led to resist every encroachment upon rights expressly stipulated for in the Constitution by the declaration of rights. 1 Annals of Cong. 439. If those independent tribunals lose their resolve, however, as the Court has done today, and give way to the seductive call of expediency, the vital guarantees of the Fourth Amendment are reduced to nothing more than a "form of words." *Silverthorne Lumber Co. v. United States*, 251 U.S. 385, 392 (1920).

A proper understanding of the broad purposes sought to be served by the Fourth Amendment demonstrates that the principles embodied in the exclusionary rule rest upon a far firmer constitutional foundation than the shifting sands of the Court's deterrence rationale. But even if I were to accept the Court's chosen method of analyzing the question posed by these cases, I would still conclude that the Court's decision cannot be justified.

IV

When the public, as it quite properly has done in the past as well as in the present, demands that those in government increase their efforts to combat crime, it is all too easy for those government officials to seek expedient solutions. In contrast to such costly and difficult measures as building more prisons, improving law enforcement methods, or hiring more prosecutors and judges to relieve the overburdened court systems in the country's metropolitan areas, the relaxation of Fourth Amendment standards seems a tempting, costless means of meeting the public's demand for better law enforcement. In the long run, however, we as a society pay a heavy price for such expediency, because as Justice Jackson observed, the rights guaranteed in the Fourth Amendment "are not mere second-class rights but belong in the catalog of indispensable freedoms." *Brinegar v. United States*, 338 U.S. 160, 180 (1949) (dissenting opinion). Once lost, such rights are difficult to recover. There is hope, however, that in time this or some later Court will restore these precious freedoms to their rightful place as a primary protection for our citizens against overreaching officialdom. I dissent.

Justice Stevens, concurred in the judgment in *Massachusetts v. Sheppard* [a companion case also involving a "good faith" exception to the exclusionary rule] and dissented in *United States v. Leon.*

FOR DISCUSSION

The majority of the Court notes, "the exclusionary rule is designed to deter police misconduct rather than to punish the errors of judges and magistrates," What are the other purposes of the exclusionary rule? How, if at all, might the decision here affect these other functions?

RELATED CASES

***Nix v. Williams:* 467 U.S. 431 (1984).**

Court upheld a new exception to the exclusionary rule, namely, acknowledging situations in which police would have inevitably discovered the evidence, in this case a body discovered as the result of an improper confession but at the time that a search of the area was in progress that would have led to the body at a time of cold weather when the body would be essentially in the same condition.

***Arizona v. Evans:* 514 U.S. 1 (1995).**

Court expanded the good faith exception of the exclusionary rule to include police reliance on computer records that erroneously listed certain arrest warrants as outstanding.

***United States v. Grubbs:* 547 U.S. 90 (2006).**

The Court noted that the Fourth Amendment allowance for "anticipatory" search warrants is founded on probable cause that a criminal act is imminent.

NEW YORK V. HARRIS

495 U.S. 14, 110 S.Ct. 1640, 109 L.Ed.2d 13 (1990)

See facts provided in the majority opinion, which follows.

Vote: 5–4

JUSTICE WHITE delivered the opinion of the Court.

On January 11, 1984, New York City police found the body of Ms. Thelma Staton murdered in her apartment. Various facts gave the officers probable cause to believe that the respondent in this case, Bernard Harris, had killed Ms. Staton. As a result, on January 16, 1984, three police officers went to Harris' apartment to take him into custody. They did not first obtain an arrest warrant.

When the police arrived, they knocked on the door, displaying their guns and badges. Harris let them enter. Once inside, the officers read Harris his rights under *Miranda v. Arizona*, 384 U.S. 436 (1966). Harris acknowledged that he understood the warnings, and agreed to answer the officers' questions. At that point, he reportedly admitted that he had killed Ms. Staton.

Harris was arrested, taken to the station house, and again informed of his *Miranda* rights. He then signed a written inculpatory statement. The police subsequently read Harris the *Miranda* warnings a third time and videotaped an incriminating interview between Harris and a district attorney, even though Harris had indicated that he wanted to end the interrogation.

The trial court suppressed Harris' first and third statements; the State does not challenge those rulings. The sole issue in this case is whether Harris' second statement—the written statement made at the station house—should have been suppressed because the police, by entering Harris' home without a warrant and without his consent, violated *Payton v. New York*, 445 U.S. 573 (1980), which held that the Fourth Amendment prohibits the police from effecting a warrantless and nonconsensual entry into a suspect's home in order to make a routine felony arrest. The New York trial court concluded that the statement was admissible. Following a bench trial, Harris was convicted of second-degree murder. The Appellate Division affirmed.

A divided New York Court of Appeals reversed. We granted certiorari to resolve the admissibility of the station house statement.

For present purposes, we accept the finding below that Harris did not consent to the police officers' entry into his home and the conclusion that the police had probable cause to arrest him. It is also evident, in light of *Payton*, that arresting Harris in his home without an arrest warrant violated the Fourth Amendment. . . . [We decline to apply the exclusionary rule in this context because the rule in *Payton* was designed to protect the physical integrity of the home; it was not intended to grant criminal suspects, like Harris, protection for statements made outside their premises where the police have probable cause to arrest the suspect for committing a crime.]

Payton itself emphasized that our holding in that case stemmed from the "overriding respect for the sanctity of the home that has been embedded in our traditions since the origins of the Republic." 445 U.S. at 601. Although it had long been settled that a warrantless arrest in a public place was permissible as long as the arresting officer had probable cause, *Payton* nevertheless drew a line at the entrance to the home. The arrest warrant was required to "interpose the magistrate's determination of probable cause" to arrest before the officers could enter a house to effect an arrest.

Nothing in the reasoning of that case suggests that an arrest in a home without a warrant but with probable cause somehow renders unlawful continued custody of the suspect once he is removed from the house. Because the officers had probable cause to arrest Harris for a crime, Harris was not unlawfully in custody when he was removed to the station house, given *Miranda* warnings, and allowed to talk. For Fourth Amendment purposes, the legal issue is the same as it would be had the police arrested Harris on his doorstep, illegally entered his home to search for evidence, and later interrogated Harris at the station house. Similarly, if the police had made a warrantless entry into Harris' home, not found him there, but arrested him on the street when he returned, a later statement made by him after proper warnings would no doubt be admissible.

This case is therefore different from *Brown v. Illinois*, 422 U.S. 590 (1975), *Dunaway v. New York*, 442 U.S. 200 (1979), and *Taylor v. Alabama*, 457 U.S. 687 (1982). In each of those cases, evidence obtained from a criminal defendant following arrest was suppressed because the police lacked probable cause. The three cases stand for the familiar proposition that the indirect fruits of an illegal search or arrest should be suppressed when they bear a sufficiently close relationship to the underlying illegality.

Harris' statement taken at the police station was not the product of being in unlawful custody. Neither was it the fruit of having been arrested in the home rather than someplace else.

We do not hold, as the dissent suggests, that a statement taken by the police while a suspect is in custody is always admissible as long as the suspect is in legal custody. Statements taken during legal custody would of course be inadmissible, for example, if they were the product of coercion, if *Miranda* warnings were not given, or if there was a violation of the rule of *Edwards v. Arizona*, 451 U.S. 477 (1981). We do hold that the station house statement in this case was admissible because Harris was in legal custody, as the dissent concedes, and because the statement, while the product of an arrest and being in custody, was not the fruit of the fact that the arrest was made in the house rather than someplace else.

To put the matter another way, suppressing the statement taken outside the house would not serve the purpose of the rule that made Harris' in-house arrest illegal. The warrant requirement for an arrest in the home is imposed to protect the home, and anything incriminating the police gathered from arresting Harris in his home, rather than elsewhere, has been excluded, as it should have been; the purpose of the rule has thereby been vindicated. We are not required by the Constitution to go further and suppress statements later made by Harris in order to deter police from violating *Payton*. "As cases considering the use of unlawfully obtained evidence in criminal trials themselves make clear, it does not follow from the emphasis on the exclusionary rule's deterrent value that 'anything which deters illegal searches is thereby commanded by the Fourth Amendment.' " *United States v. Leon*, 468 U.S. 897, 910 (1984). Even though we decline to suppress statements made outside the home following a *Payton* violation, the principal incentive to obey *Payton* still obtains: the police know that a warrantless entry will lead to the suppression of any evidence found, or statements taken, inside the home.

We hold that, where the police have probable cause to arrest a suspect, the exclusionary rule does not bar the State's use of a statement made by the defendant outside of his home, even though the statement is taken after an arrest made in the home in violation of *Payton*. The judgment of the court below is accordingly Reversed.

JUSTICE MARSHALL, with whom JUSTICES BRENNAN, BLACKMUN, and STEVENS join, dissenting.

Police officers entered Bernard Harris' home and arrested him there. They did not have an arrest warrant, he did not consent to their entry, and exigent circumstances did not exist. An arrest in such circumstances violates the Fourth Amendment. About an hour after his arrest, Harris made an incriminating statement, which the government subsequently used at his trial. The majority concedes that the fruits of that illegal entry must be suppressed. The sole question before us is whether Harris' statement falls within that category.

The majority answers this question by adopting a broad and unprecedented principle, holding that "where the police have probable cause to arrest a suspect, the exclusionary rule does not bar the State's use of a statement made by the defendant outside of his home, even though the statement is taken after an arrest made in the home in violation of Payton." The majority's conclusion is wrong. Its reasoning amounts to nothing more than an analytical sleight of hand, resting on errors in logic, misreadings of our cases, and an apparent blindness to the incentives the Court's ruling creates for knowing and intentional constitutional violations by the police. I dissent.

I

In recent years, this Court has repeatedly stated that the principal purpose of the Fourth Amendment's exclusionary rule is to eliminate incentives for police officers to violate that Amendment. A police officer who violates the Constitution usually does so to obtain evidence that he could not secure lawfully. The best way to deter him is to provide that any evidence so obtained will not be admitted at trial.

Because deterrence is a principal purpose of the exclusionary rule, our attenuation analysis must be driven by an understanding of how extensive exclusion must be to deter violations of the Fourth Amendment. We have long held that where police have obtained a statement after violating the Fourth Amendment, the interest in deterrence does not disappear simply because the statement was voluntary, as required by the Fifth Amendment. Police officers are well aware that simply because a statement is "voluntary" does not mean that it was entirely unaffected by the Fourth Amendment violation.

Accordingly, we have identified several factors as relevant to the issue of attenuation: the length of time between the arrest and the statement, the presence of intervening circumstances, and the "purpose and flagrancy" of the violation.

We have identified the last factor as "particularly" important. When a police officer intentionally violates what he knows to be a constitutional command, exclusion is essential to conform police behavior to the law. Such a "flagrant" violation is in marked contrast to a violation that is the product of a good-faith misunderstanding of the relevant constitutional requirements.

An application of the *Brown v. Illinois*, 422 U.S. 590 (1975), factors to this case compels the conclusion that Harris' statement at the station house must be suppressed. About an hour elapsed between the illegal arrest and Harris' confession, without any intervening factor other than the warnings required by *Miranda v. Arizona*, 384 U.S. 436 (1966). Indeed, in *Brown*, we held that a statement made almost two hours after an illegal arrest, and after *Miranda* warnings had been given, was not sufficiently removed from the violation so as to dissipate the taint.

As to the flagrancy of the violation, petitioner does not dispute that the officers were aware that the Fourth Amendment prohibited them from arresting Harris in his home without a warrant.

II

Had the Court analyzed this case as our precedents dictate that it should, I could end my discussion here—the dispute would reduce to an application of the *Brown* factors to the constitutional wrong and the inculpatory statement that followed. But the majority chooses no such unremarkable battleground. Instead, the Court redrafts our cases in the service of conclusions they straightforwardly and explicitly reject. Specifically, the Court finds suppression unwarranted on the authority of its newly fashioned per se rule. In the majority's view, when police officers make a warrantless home arrest in violation of *Payton*, their physical exit from the suspect's home necessarily breaks the causal chain between the illegality and any subsequent statement by the suspect, such that the statement is admissible regardless of the *Brown* factors.

B

The majority's reading of our cases similarly lacks foundation. In the majority's view, our attenuation cases are not concerned with the lingering taint of an illegal arrest; rather, they focus solely on whether a subsequently obtained statement is made during an illegal detention of the suspect. In the Court's view, if (and only if) the detention is illegal at the moment the statement is made will it be suppressed. Unlike an arrest without probable cause, a *Payton* violation alone does not make the subsequent detention of the suspect illegal. Thus, the Court argues, no statement made after a Payton violation has ended is suppressible by reason of the Fourth Amendment violation as long as the police have probable cause.

The majority's theory lacks any support in our cases. In each case presenting issues similar to those here, we have asked the same question: whether the invasion of privacy occasioned by the illegal arrest taints a statement made after the violation has ended—stated another way, whether the arrest caused the statement. Never before today has this Court asked whether the illegality itself was continuing at the time the evidence was secured.

Indeed, such an approach would render irrelevant the first and second of the *Brown* factors, which focus, respectively, on the passage of time and the existence of intervening factors between the illegality and the subsequently obtained statement.

C

Perhaps the most alarming aspect of the Court's ruling is its practical consequences for the deterrence of *Payton* violations. Imagine a police officer who has probable cause to arrest a suspect but lacks a warrant. The officer knows if he were to break into the home to make the arrest without first securing a warrant, he would violate the Fourth Amendment and any evidence he finds in the house would be suppressed. Of course, if he does not enter the house, he will not be able to use any evidence inside the house either, for the simple reason that he will never see it. The officer also knows, though, that waiting for the suspect to leave his house before arresting him could entail a lot of waiting, and the time he would spend getting a warrant would be better spent arresting criminals. The officer could leave the scene to obtain a warrant, thus avoiding some of the delay, but that would entail giving the suspect an opportunity to flee.

More important, the officer knows that if he breaks into the house without a warrant and drags the suspect outside, the suspect, shaken by the enormous invasion of privacy he has just undergone, may say something incriminating. Before today's decision, the government would only be able to use that evidence if the Court found that the taint of the arrest had been attenuated; after the decision, the evidence will be admissible regardless of whether it was the product of the unconstitutional arrest. Thus, the officer envisions the following best-case scenario if he chooses to violate the Constitution: He avoids a major expenditure of time and effort, ensures that the suspect will not escape, and procures the most damaging evidence of all, a confession. His worst-case scenario is that he will avoid a major expenditure of effort, ensure that the suspect will not escape, and will see evidence in the house (which would have remained unknown absent the constitutional violation) that cannot be used in the prosecution's case in chief. The Court thus creates powerful incentives for police officers to violate the Fourth Amendment. In the context of our constitutional rights and the sanctity of our homes, we cannot afford to presume that officers will be entirely impervious to those incentives. I dissent.

FOR DISCUSSION

The dissent in this case claims that the decision creates powerful incentives for police officers to violate the Fourth Amendment. Do you agree? How would the majority refute this argument?

RELATED CASES

***Wilson v. Arkansas:* 514 U.S. 927 (1995).**

The Supreme Court recognized that an officer's enforcement of an arrest warrant in a home might be constitutionally implemented even if the officer had not knocked on the door. The Court declined to create guidelines.

***Richards v. Wisconsin:* 520 U.S. 385 (1997).**

The Court identified the need to create "case-specific" guidelines that identify circumstances in which police can deviate from the "knock and announce" rule (e.g., safety of officers).

***United States v. Ramirez:* 523 U.S. 65 (1998).**

Noting that the Fourth Amendment does not require a higher standard than reasonable suspicion that knocking and announcing could be dangerous, could impede investigation or the crime, or could be futile, the Court reinforced its related verdict of 1997 *(Richards v. Wisconsin).*

***Hudson v. Michigan:* 547 U. S. 586 (2006).**

When an otherwise valid search violates the "knock and announce" rule of serving a warrant, the exclusionary rule is not triggered and evidence does not need to be suppressed.

FLORIDA V. BOSTICK

501 U.S. 429, 111 S.Ct. 2382, 115 L.Ed. 2d 389 (1991)

Terrance Bostick was on a bus traveling from Miami to Atlanta. During a stop in Fort Lauderdale, Florida, two armed officers with badges boarded the bus, picked out Bostick with no claim of articulable suspicion, and asked to inspect his ticket and identification. Bostic complied; both documents were returned to him, and the police then identified themselves as narcotics agents and asked to search his luggage. Contraband discovered in Bostick's luggage was later used to convict him. Bostick challenged allegations that he had consented to the search and sought to suppress the evidence that had resulted. The Florida District Court of Appeal affirmed, but certified the question to the Florida Supreme Court. The Florida Supreme Court overturned the decision.

Vote: 6–3

JUSTICE O'CONNOR delivered the opinion of the Court.

We have held that the Fourth Amendment permits police officers to approach individuals at random in airport lobbies and other public places to ask them questions and to request consent to search their luggage, so long as a reasonable person would understand that he or she could refuse to cooperate. This case requires us to determine whether the same rule applies to police encounters that take place on a bus.

I

Drug interdiction efforts have led to the use of police surveillance at airports, train stations, and bus depots. Law enforcement officers stationed at such locations routinely approach individuals, either randomly or because they suspect in some vague way that the individuals may be engaged in criminal activity, and ask them potentially incriminating questions. Broward County has adopted such a program. County Sheriff's Department officers routinely board buses at scheduled stops and ask passengers for permission to search their luggage.

In this case, two officers discovered cocaine when they searched a suitcase belonging to Terrance Bostick.

Two facts are particularly worth noting. First, the police specifically advised Bostick that he had the right to refuse consent. Bostick appears to have disputed the point, but, as the Florida Supreme Court noted explicitly, the trial court resolved this evidentiary conflict in the State's favor. Second, at no time did the officers threaten Bostick with a gun. The Florida Supreme Court indicated that one officer carried a zipper pouch containing a pistol—the equivalent of carrying a gun in a holster—but the court did not suggest that the gun was ever removed from its pouch, pointed at Bostick, or otherwise used in a threatening manner. The dissent's characterization of the officers as "gun-wielding inquisitor[s]," is colorful, but lacks any basis in fact.

II

The sole issue presented for our review is whether a police encounter on a bus of the type described above necessarily constitutes a "seizure" within the meaning of the Fourth Amendment. The State concedes, and we accept for purposes of this decision, that the officers lacked the reasonable suspicion required to justify a seizure and that, if a seizure took place, the drugs found in Bostick's suitcase must be suppressed as tainted fruit.

Our cases make it clear that a seizure does not occur simply because a police officer approaches an individual and asks a few questions. So long as a reasonable person would feel free "to disregard the police and go about his business," *California v. Hodari D.*, 499 U.S. 621, 628 (1991), the encounter is consensual and no reasonable suspicion is required. The encounter will not trigger Fourth Amendment scrutiny unless it loses its consensual nature. The Court made precisely this point in *Terry v. Ohio*, 392 U.S. 1, 19, n. 16 (1968): "Obviously, not all personal intercourse between policemen and citizens involves 'seizures' of persons. Only when the officer, by means of physical force or show of authority, has in some way restrained the liberty of a citizen may we conclude that a 'seizure' has occurred."

Since *Terry*, we have held repeatedly that mere police questioning does not constitute a seizure.

There is no doubt that if this same encounter had taken place before Bostick boarded the bus or in the lobby of the bus terminal, it would not rise to the level of a seizure. We have stated that even when officers have no basis for suspecting a particular individual, they may generally ask questions of that individual, see *INS v. Delgado*, 466 U.S. 210, 216 (1984); ask to examine the individual's identification, see *United States v. Mendenhall*, 446 U.S. 544, 557–558 (1980); and request consent to search his or her luggage, see *Florida v. Royer*, 460 U.S. 491, at 501 (1983)—as long as the police do not convey a message that compliance with their requests is required.

Bostick insists that this case is different because it took place in the cramped confines of a bus. A police encounter is much more intimidating in this setting, he argues, because police tower over a seated passenger and there is little room to move around. Bostick claims to find support in language from *Michigan v. Chesternut*, 486 U.S. 567, 573 (1988), and other cases, indicating that a seizure occurs when a reasonable person would believe that he or she is not "free to leave." Bostick maintains that a reasonable bus passenger would not have felt free to leave under the circumstances of this case because there is nowhere to go on a bus. Also, the bus was about to depart. Had Bostick disembarked, he would have risked being stranded and losing whatever baggage he had locked away in the luggage compartment.

The Florida Supreme Court found this argument persuasive, so much so that it adopted a per se rule prohibiting the police from randomly boarding buses as a means of drug interdiction. The state court erred, however, in focusing on whether Bostick was "free to leave" rather than on the principle that those words were intended to capture.

Here, for example, the mere fact that Bostick did not feel free to leave the bus does not mean that the police seized him. Bostick was a passenger on a bus that was scheduled to depart. He would not have felt free to leave the bus even if the police had not been present.

In this respect, the Court's decision in *INS v. Delgado* is dispositive. At issue there was the INS' practice of visiting factories at random and questioning employees to determine whether any were illegal aliens. Several INS agents would stand near the building's exits, while other agents walked through the factory questioning workers. The Court acknowledged that the workers may not have been free to leave their worksite, but explained that this was not the result of police activity: "Ordinarily, when people are at work their freedom to move about has been meaningfully restricted, not by the actions of law enforcement officials, but by the workers' voluntary obligations to their employers." We concluded that there was no seizure because, even though the workers were not free to leave the building without being questioned, the agents' conduct should have given employees "no reason to believe that they would be detained if they gave truthful answers to the questions put to them or if they simply refused to answer."

The present case is analytically indistinguishable from *Delgado*. Like the workers in that case, Bostick's freedom of movement was restricted by a factor independent of police conduct—i.e., by his being a passenger on a bus. Accordingly, the "free to leave" analysis on which Bostick relies is inapplicable. In such a situation, the appropriate inquiry is whether a reasonable person would feel free to decline the officers' requests or otherwise terminate the encounter. This formulation follows logically from prior cases and breaks no new ground.

This Court, as the dissent correctly observes, is not empowered to suspend constitutional guarantees so that the Government may more effectively wage a "war on drugs." If that war is to be fought, those who fight it must respect the rights of individuals, whether or not those individuals are suspected of having committed a crime. By the same token, this Court is not empowered to forbid law enforcement practices simply because it considers them distasteful. The Fourth Amendment proscribes unreasonable searches and seizures; it does not proscribe voluntary cooperation. The cramped confines of a bus are one relevant factor that should be considered in evaluating whether a passenger's consent is voluntary. We cannot agree, however, with the Florida Supreme Court that this single factor will be dispositive in every case.

We adhere to the rule that, in order to determine whether a particular encounter constitutes a seizure, a court must consider all the circumstances surrounding the encounter to determine whether the police conduct would have communicated to a reasonable person that the person was not free to decline the officers' requests or otherwise terminate the encounter. That rule applies to encounters that take place on a city street or in an airport lobby, and it applies equally to encounters on a bus.

The judgment of the Florida Supreme Court is reversed, and the case is remanded for further proceedings not inconsistent with this opinion.

JUSTICE MARSHALL, with whom JUSTICES BLACKMUN and STEVENS join, dissenting.

Our Nation, we are told, is engaged in a "war on drugs." No one disputes that it is the job of law-enforcement officials to devise effective weapons for fighting this war. But the effectiveness of a law-enforcement technique is not proof of its constitutionality. The general warrant, for example, was certainly an effective means of law enforcement. Yet it was one of the primary aims of the Fourth Amendment to protect citizens from the tyranny of being singled out for search and seizure without particularized suspicion notwithstanding the effectiveness of this method. In my view, the law-enforcement technique with which we are confronted in this case—the suspicionless police sweep of buses in intrastate or interstate travel—bears all of the indicia of coercion and unjustified intrusion associated with the general warrant. Because I believe that the bus sweep at issue in this case violates the core values of the Fourth Amendment, I dissent.

I

The question for this Court . . . is whether the suspicionless, dragnet-style sweep of buses in intrastate and interstate travel is consistent with the Fourth Amendment. The majority suggests that this latest tactic in the drug war is perfectly compatible with the Constitution. I disagree.

II

I have no objection to the manner in which the majority frames the test for determining whether a suspicionless bus sweep amounts to a Fourth Amendment "seizure." I agree that the appropriate question is whether a passenger who is approached during such a sweep "would feel free to decline the officers' requests or otherwise terminate the encounter." What I cannot understand is how the majority can possibly suggest an affirmative answer to this question.

. . . [T]he issue is . . . whether such a passenger—without being apprised of his rights—would have felt free to terminate the antecedent encounter with the police.

Unlike the majority, I have no doubt that the answer to this question is no. Apart from trying to accommodate the officers, respondent had only two options. First, he could have remained seated while obstinately refusing to respond to the officers' questioning. But in light of the intimidating show of authority that the officers made upon boarding the bus, respondent reasonably could have believed that such behavior would only arouse the officers' suspicions and intensify their interrogation.

Second, respondent could have tried to escape the officers' presence by leaving the bus altogether. But because doing so would have required respondent to squeeze past the gunwielding inquisitor who was blocking the aisle of the bus, this hardly seems like a course that respondent reasonably would have viewed as available to him.

Even if respondent had perceived that the officers would let him leave the bus, moreover, he could not reasonably have been expected to resort to this means of evading their intrusive questioning. The vulnerability that an intrastate or interstate traveler experiences when confronted by the police outside of his "own familiar territory" surely aggravates the coercive quality of such an encounter.

The case on which the majority primarily relies, *INS v. Delgado*, 466 U.S. 210 (1984), is distinguishable in every relevant respect. In *Delgado*, this Court held that workers approached by law-enforcement officials inside of a factory were not "seized" for purposes of the Fourth Amendment. The Court was careful to point out, however, that the presence of the agents did not furnish the workers with a reasonable basis for believing that they were not free to leave the factory, as at least some of them did. Unlike passengers confronted by law-enforcement officials on a bus stopped temporarily at an intermediate point in its journey, workers approached by law-enforcement officials at their workplace need not abandon personal belongings and venture into unfamiliar environs in order to avoid unwanted questioning. Moreover, the workers who did not leave the building in *Delgado* remained free to move about the entire factory, a considerably less confining environment than a bus. Finally, contrary to the officer who confronted respondent, the law-enforcement officials in Delgado did not conduct their interviews with guns in hand.

Rather than requiring the police to justify the coercive tactics employed here, the majority blames respondent for his own sensation of constraint. The majority concedes that respondent "did not feel free to leave the bus" as a means of breaking off the interrogation by the Broward County officers. But this experience of confinement, the majority explains, "was the natural result of his decision to take the bus." Thus, in the majority's view, because respondent's "freedom of movement was restricted by a factor independent of police conduct—i.e., by his being a passenger on a bus,"—respondent was not seized for purposes of the Fourth Amendment.

This reasoning borders on sophism and trivializes the values that underlie the Fourth Amendment. Obviously, a person's "voluntary decision" to place himself in a room with only one exit does not authorize the police to force an encounter upon him by placing themselves in front of the exit. It is no more acceptable for the police to force an encounter on a person by exploiting his "voluntary decision" to expose himself to perfectly legitimate personal or social constraints. By consciously deciding to single out persons who have undertaken interstate or intrastate travel, officers who conduct suspicionless, dragnet-style sweeps put passengers to the choice of cooperating or of exiting their buses and possibly being stranded in unfamiliar locations. It is exactly because this "choice" is no "choice" at all that police engage this technique.

In my view, the Fourth Amendment clearly condemns the suspicionless, dragnet-style sweep of intrastate or interstate buses. Withdrawing this particular weapon from the government's drug-war arsenal would hardly leave the police without any means of combating the use of buses as instrumentalities of the drug trade. The police would remain free, for example, to approach passengers whom they have a reasonable, articulable basis to suspect of criminal wrongdoing. Alternatively, they could continue to confront passengers without suspicion so long as they took simple steps, like advising the passengers confronted of their right to decline to be questioned, to dispel the aura of coercion and intimidation that pervades such encounters. There is no reason to expect that such requirements would render the Nation's buses law-enforcement-free zones.

III

The majority attempts to gloss over the violence that today's decision does to the Fourth Amendment with empty admonitions. "If the [war on drugs] is to be fought," the majority intones, "those who fight it must respect the rights of individuals, whether or not those individuals are suspected of having committed a crime." The majority's actions, however, speak louder than its words. I dissent.

FOR DISCUSSION

In what way has the War on Drugs influenced our interpretation of the Fourth Amendment and our understanding of how to balance individual interests and societal concerns? Is Justice O'Connor realistic in noting that Terrance Bostick could have simply refrained from consenting? What are the necessary components of consent?

RELATED CASES

Minnesota v. Dickerson: **508 U.S. 366 (1993).**

Within the bounds of a *Terry* search, found contraband in the "plain feel of an officer" may be seized and used as evidence.

Bond v. United States: **529 U.S. 334 (2000).**

A citizen has an expectation of privacy in luggage brought on a Greyhound bus in an opaque bag that is kept above the passenger's seat. An agent's physical manipulation of the bag in an exploratory search is a violation of the Fourth Amendment.

United States v. Drayton: **536 U.S. 194 (2002).**

The Fourth Amendment does not require officers to advise bus passengers of their right to refuse to consent to a search.

Arizona v. United States

567 U.S. 387, 132 S.Ct. 2492, 183 L.Ed. 2d 351, 2012 U.S. LEXIS 4872 (2012)

Facts of the case are contained in the majority opinion.

Vote: 5–3

Justice Kagan took no part in the consideration or decision of the case.

Justice Kennedy delivered the opinion of the Court.

To address pressing issues related to the large number of aliens within its borders who do not have a lawful right to be in this country, the State of Arizona in 2010 enacted a statute called the Support Our Law Enforcement and Safe Neighborhoods Act. The law is often referred to as S. B. 1070, the version introduced in the state senate. Its stated purpose is to "discourage and deter the unlawful entry and presence of aliens and economic activity by persons unlawfully present in the United States." The law's provisions establish an official state policy of "attrition through enforcement." The question before the Court is whether federal law preempts and renders invalid four separate provisions of the state law.

I

The United States filed this suit against Arizona, seeking to enjoin S. B. 1070 as preempted. [Two provisions of the law explore state authority to address immigration issues within the state.] Two other provisions give specific arrest authority and investigative duties with respect to certain aliens to state and local law enforcement officers. Section 6 authorizes officers to arrest without a warrant a person "the officer has probable cause to believe . . . has committed any public offense that makes the person removable from the United States." § 13–3883(A)(5). Section 2(B) provides that officers who conduct a stop, detention, or arrest must in some circumstances make efforts to verify the person's immigration status with the Federal Government.

The United States District Court for the District of Arizona issued a preliminary injunction preventing the four provisions at issue from taking effect. The Court of Appeals for the Ninth Circuit affirmed. This Court granted certiorari to resolve important questions concerning the interaction of state and federal power with respect to the law of immigration and alien status.

II

A

The Government of the United States has broad, undoubted power over the subject of immigration and the status of aliens. This authority rests, in part, on the National Government's constitutional power to "establish an uniform Rule of Naturalization," U. S. Const., Art. I, § 8, cl. 4, and its inherent power as sovereign to control and conduct relations with foreign nations.

The federal power to determine immigration policy is well settled. Immigration policy can affect trade, investment, tourism, and diplomatic relations for the entire Nation, as well as the perceptions and expectations of aliens in this country who seek the full protection of its laws. Perceived mistreatment of aliens in the United States may lead to harmful reciprocal treatment of American citizens abroad.

It is fundamental that foreign countries concerned about the status, safety, and security of their nationals in the United States must be able to confer and communicate on this subject with one national sovereign, not the 50 separate States. This Court has reaffirmed that "[o]ne of the most important and delicate of all international relationships . . . has to do with the protection of the just rights of a country's own nationals when those nationals are in another country." *Hines v. Davidowitz*, 312 U.S. 52, 64 (1941).

Federal governance of immigration and alien status is extensive and complex. Congress has specified categories of aliens who may not be admitted to the United States. Unlawful entry and unlawful reentry into the country are federal offenses. Once here, aliens are required to register with the Federal Government and to carry proof of status on their person. Failure to do so is a federal misdemeanor. Federal law also authorizes States to deny noncitizens a range of public benefits; and it imposes sanctions on employers who hire unauthorized workers.

Congress has specified which aliens may be removed from the United States and the procedures for doing so. Aliens may be removed if they were inadmissible at the time of entry, have been convicted of certain crimes, or meet other criteria set by federal law. Removal is a civil, not criminal, matter. A principal feature of the removal system is the broad discretion exercised by immigration officials. Federal officials, as an initial matter, must decide whether it makes sense to pursue removal at all. If removal proceedings commence, aliens may seek asylum and other discretionary relief allowing them to remain in the country or at least to leave without formal removal.

Discretion in the enforcement of immigration law embraces immediate human concerns. Unauthorized workers trying to support their families, for example, likely pose less danger than alien smugglers or aliens who commit a serious crime. The equities of an individual case may turn on many factors, including whether the alien has children born in the United States, long ties to the community, or a record of distinguished military service. Some discretionary decisions involve policy choices that bear on this Nation's international relations. Returning an alien to his own country may be deemed inappropriate even where he has committed a removable offense or fails to meet the criteria for admission. The foreign state may be mired in civil war, complicit in political persecution, or enduring conditions that create a real risk that the alien or his family will be harmed upon return. The dynamic nature of relations with other countries requires the Executive Branch to ensure that enforcement policies are consistent with this Nation's foreign policy with respect to these and other realities.

Agencies in the Department of Homeland Security play a major role in enforcing the country's immigration laws. United States Customs and Border Protection (CBP) is responsible for determining the admissibility of aliens and securing the country's borders. In 2010, CBP's Border Patrol apprehended almost half a million people. Immigration and Customs Enforcement (ICE), a second agency, "conducts criminal investigations involving the enforcement of immigration-related statutes." ICE also operates the Law Enforcement Support Center. LESC, as the Center is known, provides immigration status information to federal, state, and local officials around the clock. ICE officers are responsible "for the identification, apprehension, and removal of illegal aliens from the United States." Hundreds of thousands of aliens are removed by the Federal Government every year . . . . there were 387,242 removals, and 476,405 returns without a removal order, in 2010.

B

The pervasiveness of federal regulation does not diminish the importance of immigration policy to the States. Arizona bears many of the consequences of unlawful immigration. Hundreds of thousands of deportable aliens are apprehended in Arizona each year. Unauthorized aliens who remain in the State comprise, by one estimate, almost six percent of the population. And in the State's most populous county, these aliens are reported to be responsible for a disproportionate share of serious crime.

Statistics alone do not capture the full extent of Arizona's concerns. Accounts in the record suggest there is an "epidemic of crime, safety risks, serious property damage, and environmental problems" associated with the influx of illegal migration across private land near the Mexican border. Phoenix is a major city of the United States, yet signs along an interstate highway 30 miles to the south warn the public to stay away. One reads, "DANGER—PUBLIC WARNING—TRAVEL NOT RECOMMENDED / Active Drug and Human Smuggling Area / Visitors May Encounter Armed Criminals and Smuggling Vehicles Traveling at High Rates of Speed." The problems posed to the State by illegal immigration must not be underestimated.

These concerns are the background for the formal legal analysis that follows. The issue is whether, under preemption principles, federal law permits Arizona to implement the state-law provisions in dispute.

III

Federalism, central to the constitutional design, adopts the principle that both the National and State Governments have elements of sovereignty the other is bound to respect. From the existence of two sovereigns follows the possibility that laws can be in conflict or at cross-purposes. The Supremacy Clause provides a clear rule that federal law "shall be the supreme Law of the Land; and the Judges in every State shall be bound thereby, any Thing in the Constitution or Laws of any State to the Contrary notwithstanding." Art. VI, cl. 2. Under this principle, Congress has the power to preempt state law. There is no doubt that Congress may withdraw specified powers from the States by enacting a statute containing an express preemption provision.

State law must also give way to federal law in at least two other circumstances. First, the States are precluded from regulating conduct in a field that Congress, acting within its proper authority, has determined must be regulated by its exclusive governance. The intent to displace state law altogether can be inferred from a framework of regulation "so pervasive . . . that Congress left no room for the States to supplement it" or where there is a "federal interest . . . so dominant that the federal system will be assumed to preclude enforcement of state laws on the same subject." *Rice v. Santa Fe Elevator Corp.*, 331 U.S. 218, 230 (1947).

Second, state laws are preempted when they conflict with federal law. This includes cases where "compliance with both federal and state regulations is a physical impossibility," *Florida Lime & Avocado Growers, Inc. v. Paul*, 373 U.S. 132, 142–143 (1963), and those instances where the challenged state law "stands as an obstacle to the accomplishment and execution of the full purposes and objectives of Congress." In preemption analysis, courts should assume that "the historic police powers of the States" are not superseded "unless that was the clear and manifest purpose of Congress." *Rice* at 230.

The . . . challenged provisions of the state law each must be examined under these preemption principles.

IV

C

Section 6

Section 6 of S. B. 1070 provides that a state officer, "without a warrant, may arrest a person if the officer has probable cause to believe . . . [the person] has committed any public offense that makes [him] removable from the United States." The United States argues that arrests authorized by this statute would be an obstacle to the removal system Congress created.

As a general rule, it is not a crime for a removable alien to remain present in the United States. If the police stop someone based on nothing more than possible removability, the usual predicate for an arrest is absent. When an alien is suspected of being removable, a federal official issues an administrative document called a Notice to Appear. The form does not authorize an arrest. Instead, it gives the alien information about the proceedings, including the time and date of the removal hearing. If an alien fails to appear, an in absentia order may direct removal.

The federal statutory structure instructs when it is appropriate to arrest an alien during the removal process. For example, the Attorney General can exercise discretion to issue a warrant for an alien's arrest and detention "pending a decision on whether the alien is to be removed from the United States." And if an alien is ordered removed after a hearing, the Attorney General will issue a warrant. In both instances, the warrants are executed by federal officers who have received training in the enforcement of immigration law.

Section 6 attempts to provide state officers even greater authority to arrest aliens on the basis of possible removability than Congress has given to trained federal immigration officers. Under state law, officers who believe an alien is removable by reason of some "public offense" would have the power to conduct an arrest on that basis regardless of whether a federal warrant has issued or the alien is likely to escape. This state authority could be exercised without any input from the Federal Government about whether an arrest is warranted in a particular case. This would allow the State to achieve its own immigration policy. The result could be unnecessary harassment of some aliens (for instance, a veteran, college student, or someone assisting with a criminal investigation) whom federal officials determine should not be removed.

This is not the system Congress created. Federal law specifies limited circumstances in which state officers may perform the functions of an immigration officer. A principal example is when the Attorney General has granted that authority to specific officers in a formal agreement with a state or local government. There are significant complexities involved in enforcing federal immigration law, including the determination whether a person is removable. As a result, the agreements reached with the Attorney General must contain written certification that officers have received adequate training to carry out the duties of an immigration officer.

By authorizing state officers to decide whether an alien should be detained for being removable, § 6 violates the principle that the removal process is entrusted to the discretion of the Federal Government. Decisions of this nature touch on foreign relations and must be made with one voice.

In defense of § 6, Arizona notes a federal statute permitting state officers to "cooperate with the Attorney General in the identification, apprehension, detention, or removal of aliens not lawfully present in the United States." There may be some ambiguity as to what constitutes cooperation under the federal law; but no coherent understanding of the term would incorporate the unilateral decision of state officers to arrest an alien for being removable absent any request, approval, or other instruction from the Federal Government. The Department of Homeland Security gives examples of what would constitute cooperation under federal law. These include situations where States participate in a joint task force with federal officers, provide operational support in executing a warrant, or allow federal immigration officials to gain access to detainees held in state facilities. State officials can also assist the Federal Government by responding to requests for information about when an alien will be released from their custody. But the unilateral state action to detain authorized by § 6 goes far beyond these measures, defeating any need for real cooperation.

Congress has put in place a system in which state officers may not make warrantless arrests of aliens based on possible removability except in specific, limited circumstances. By nonetheless authorizing state and local officers to engage in these enforcement activities as a general matter, § 6 creates an obstacle to the full purposes and objectives of Congress. Section 6 is preempted by federal law.

D

Section 2(B)

Section 2(B) of S. B. 1070 requires state officers to make a "reasonable attempt . . . to determine the immigration status" of any person they stop, detain, or arrest on some other legitimate basis if "reasonable suspicion exists that the person is an alien and is unlawfully present in the United States." The law also provides that "[a]ny person who is arrested shall have the person's immigration status determined before the person is released." The accepted way to perform these status checks is to contact ICE, which maintains a database of immigration records.

Three limits are built into the state provision. First, a detainee is presumed not to be an alien unlawfully present in the United States if he or she provides a valid Arizona driver's license or similar identification. Second, officers "may not consider race, color or national origin . . . except to the extent permitted by the United States [and] Arizona Constitution[s]." Third, the provisions must be "implemented in a manner consistent with federal law regulating immigration, protecting the civil rights of all persons and respecting the privileges and immunities of United States citizens

The United States and its amici contend that, even with these limits, the State's verification requirements pose an obstacle to the framework Congress put in place. The first concern is the mandatory nature of the status checks. The second is the possibility of prolonged detention while the checks are being performed.

1

Consultation between federal and state officials is an important feature of the immigration system. Congress has made clear that no formal agreement or special training needs to be in place for state officers to "communicate with the [Federal Government] regarding the immigration status of any individual, including reporting knowledge that a particular alien is not lawfully present in the United States." And Congress has obligated ICE to respond to any request made by state officials for verification of a person's citizenship or immigration status. ICE's Law Enforcement Support Center operates "24 hours a day, seven days a week, 365 days a year" and provides, among other things, "immigration status, identity information and real-time assistance to local, state and federal law enforcement agencies. LESC responded to more than one million requests for information in 2009 alone.

The United States argues that making status verification mandatory interferes with the federal immigration scheme. It is true that § 2(B) does not allow state officers to consider federal enforcement priorities in deciding whether to contact ICE about someone they have detained. In other words, the officers must make an inquiry even in cases where it seems unlikely that the Attorney General would have the alien removed. This might be the case, for example, when an alien is an elderly veteran with significant and longstanding ties to the community.

Congress has done nothing to suggest it is inappropriate to communicate with ICE in these situations, however. Indeed, it has encouraged the sharing of information about possible immigration violations. A federal statute regulating the public benefits provided to qualified aliens in fact instructs that "no State or local government entity may be prohibited, or in any way restricted, from sending to or receiving from [ICE] information regarding the immigration status, lawful or unlawful, of an alien in the United States." The federal scheme thus leaves room for a policy requiring state officials to contact ICE as a routine matter.

2

Some who support the challenge to § 2(B) argue that, in practice, state officers will be required to delay the release of some detainees for no reason other than to verify their immigration status. Detaining individuals solely to verify their immigration status would raise constitutional concerns. And it would disrupt the federal framework to put state officers in the position of holding aliens in custody for possible unlawful presence without federal direction and supervision The program put in place by Congress does not allow state or local officers to adopt this enforcement mechanism.

But § 2(B) could be read to avoid these concerns. To take one example, a person might be stopped for jaywalking in Tucson and be unable to produce identification. The first sentence of § 2(B) instructs officers to make a "reasonable" attempt to verify his immigration status with ICE if there is reasonable suspicion that his presence in the United States is unlawful. The state courts may conclude that, unless the person continues to be suspected of some crime for which he may be detained by state officers, it would not be reasonable to prolong the stop for the immigration inquiry.

To take another example, a person might be held pending release on a charge of driving under the influence of alcohol. As this goes beyond a mere stop, the arrestee (unlike the jaywalker) would appear to be subject to the categorical requirement in the second sentence of § 2(B) that "[a]ny person who is arrested shall have the person's immigration status determined before [he] is released." State courts may read this as an instruction to initiate a status check every time someone is arrested, or in some subset of those cases, rather than as a command to hold the person until the check is complete no matter the circumstances. Even if the law is read as an instruction to complete a check while the person is in custody, moreover, it is not clear at this stage and on this record that the verification process would result in prolonged detention.

However the law is interpreted, if § 2(B) only requires state officers to conduct a status check during the course of an authorized, lawful detention or after a detainee has been released, the provision likely would survive preemption—at least absent some showing that it has other consequences that are adverse to federal law and its objectives. There is no need in this case to address whether reasonable suspicion of illegal entry or another immigration crime would be a legitimate basis for prolonging a detention, or whether this too would be preempted by federal law.

The nature and timing of this case counsel caution in evaluating the validity of § 2(B). The Federal Government has brought suit against a sovereign State to challenge the provision even before the law has gone into effect. There is a basic uncertainty about what the law means and how it will be enforced. At this stage, without the benefit of a definitive interpretation from the state courts, it would be inappropriate to assume § 2(B) will be construed in a way that creates a conflict with federal law. As a result, the United States cannot prevail in its current challenge. This opinion does not foreclose other preemption and constitutional challenges to the law as interpreted and applied after it goes into effect.

V

Immigration policy shapes the destiny of the Nation. On May 24, 2012, at one of this Nation's most distinguished museums of history, a dozen immigrants stood before the tattered flag that inspired Francis Scott Key to write the National Anthem. There they took the oath to become American citizens. These naturalization ceremonies bring together men and women of different origins who now share a common destiny. They swear a common oath to renounce fidelity to foreign princes, to defend the Constitution, and to bear arms on behalf of the country when required by law. The history of the United States is in part made of the stories, talents, and lasting contributions of those who crossed oceans and deserts to come here.

The National Government has significant power to regulate immigration. With power comes responsibility, and the sound exercise of national power over immigration depends on the Nation's meeting its responsibility to base its laws on a political will informed by searching, thoughtful, rational civic discourse. Arizona may have understandable frustrations with the problems caused by illegal immigration while that process continues, but the State may not pursue policies that undermine federal law.

* * *

The United States has established that §§ 3, 5(C), and 6 of S. B. 1070 are preempted. It was improper, however, to enjoin § 2(B) before the state courts had an opportunity to construe it and without some showing that enforcement of the provision in fact conflicts with federal immigration law and its objectives.

The judgment of the Court of Appeals for the Ninth Circuit is affirmed in part and reversed in part. The case is remanded for further proceedings consistent with this opinion.

It is so ordered.

JUSTICE SCALIA, concurring in part and dissenting in part.

The United States is an indivisible "Union of sovereign States." Today's opinion, approving virtually all of the Ninth Circuit's injunction against enforcement of the four challenged provisions of Arizona's law, deprives States of what most would consider the defining characteristic of sovereignty: the power to exclude from the sovereign's territory people who have no right to be there. Neither the Constitution itself nor even any law passed by Congress supports this result. I dissent.

. . . .

As is often the case, discussion of the dry legalities that are the proper object of our attention suppresses the very human realities that gave rise to the suit. Arizona bears the brunt of the country's illegal immigration problem. Its citizens feel themselves under siege by large numbers of illegal immigrants who invade their property, strain their social services, and even place their lives in jeopardy. Federal officials have been unable to remedy the problem, and indeed have recently shown that they are unwilling to do so. Thousands of Arizona's estimated 400,000 illegal immigrants—including not just children but men and women under 30—are now assured immunity from enforcement, and will be able to compete openly with Arizona citizens for employment.

Arizona has moved to protect its sovereignty—not in contradiction of federal law, but in complete compliance with it. The laws under challenge here do not extend or revise federal immigration restrictions, but merely enforce those restrictions more effectively. If securing its territory in this fashion is not within the power of Arizona, we should cease referring to it as a sovereign State. I dissent.

JUSTICE THOMAS, concurring in part and dissenting in part.

I agree with Justice Scalia that federal immigration law does not pre-empt any of the challenged provisions of S. B. 1070. I reach that conclusion, however, for the simple reason that there is no conflict between the "ordinary meanin[g]" of the relevant federal laws and that of the four provisions of Arizona law at issue here.

Section 2(B) of S. B. 1070 provides that, when Arizona law enforcement officers reasonably suspect that a person they have lawfully stopped, detained, or arrested is unlawfully present, "a reasonable attempt shall be made, when practicable, to determine the immigration status of the person" pursuant to the verification procedure established by Congress in 8 U. S. C. § 1373(c). Nothing in the text of that or any other federal statute prohibits Arizona from directing its officers to make immigration-related inquiries in these situations. To the contrary, federal law expressly states that "no State or local government entity may be prohibited, or in any way restricted, from sending to or receiving from" federal officials "information regarding the immigration status" of an alien. And, federal law imposes an affirmative obligation on federal officials to respond to a State's immigration-related inquiries.

Section 6 of S. B. 1070 authorizes Arizona law enforcement officers to make warrantless arrests when there is probable cause to believe that an arrestee has committed a public offense that renders him removable under federal immigration law. States, as sovereigns, have inherent authority to conduct arrests for violations of federal law, unless and until Congress removes that authority. Here, no federal statute purports to withdraw that authority. As Justice Scalia notes, federal law does limit the authority of federal officials to arrest removable aliens, but those statutes do not apply to state officers. And, federal law expressly recognizes that state officers may "cooperate with the Attorney General" in the "apprehension" and "detention" of "aliens not lawfully present in the United States." Nothing in that statute indicates that such cooperation requires a prior "request, approval, or other instruction from the Federal Government."

Despite the lack of any conflict between the ordinary meaning of the Arizona law and that of the federal laws at issue here, the Court holds that various provisions of the Arizona law are pre-empted because they "stan[d] as an obstacle to the accomplishment and execution of the full purposes and objectives of Congress." I have explained that the "purposes and objectives" theory of implied pre-emption is inconsistent with the Constitution because it invites courts to engage in freewheeling speculation about congressional purpose that roams well beyond statutory text. Under the Supremacy Clause, pre-emptive effect is to be given to congressionally enacted laws, not to judicially divined legislative purposes. Thus, even assuming the existence of some tension between Arizona's law and the supposed "purposes and objectives" of Congress, I would not hold that any of the provisions of the Arizona law at issue here are pre-empted on that basis.

JUSTICE ALITO, concurring in part and dissenting in part.

While I agree with the Court on § 2(B) . . ., I part ways on . . . § 6. Like § 2(B), § 6 adds virtually nothing to the authority that Arizona law enforcement officers already exercise. And whatever little authority they have gained is consistent with federal law.

FOR DISCUSSION

The majority of the Court notes that while § 2(B) is not unconstitutional as written, they could be applied and enforced in such a way as to raise constitutional questions? In what ways would such a constitutional challenge be made? Does the intent of Arizona in passing the law raise constitutional questions or do you believe the way the law is enforced determines constitutional status? Are there any constitutional rights people should possess regardless of their immigration status?

RELATED CASE

***Melendres v. Arpaio:* 989 F.Supp. 2d 822 (D.C. Arizona) 2012: 784 F. 3d 1254 (9th Cir.) 2012.**

A class-action lawsuit finding that Maricopa County (Arizona) sheriff Joe Arpaio unlawfully relied on racial profiling and illegal detention to target Latinos. Federal court found county in contempt for violating court injunctions.

BROWN V. CITY OF ONEONTA, NEW YORK

221 F.3d 329 (2d Cir. 1999)

A 77 year old women is assaulted in her home and as part of her description of the assailant she depicts him as a young, African-American male. The assault occurred in a city of 10,000, populated by mostly Caucasians, except for a small population of African-Americans residing at the state university. Police asked the university for a list of African-American males enrolled there and they proceeded to stop and question them. Many of these individuals sue, contending a violation of their constitutional rights. Lower courts largely reject these claims, the cases are appealed and the Court of Appeals affirms.

Vote: 3–0

Before: OAKES and WALKER, CIRCUIT JUDGES, and GOLDBERG, JUDGE.

JOHN M. WALKER, CIRCUIT JUDGE: Plaintiffs-appellants, black residents of Oneonta, New York, appeal from the September 9, 1998 judgment of the United States District Court for the Northern District of New York (Thomas J. McAvoy, *Chief Judge*). Plaintiffs' claims arise from their interactions with police authorities during an investigation conducted by the New York State and Oneonta Police Departments based on a victim's description of a suspect that consisted primarily of the suspect's race. Plaintiffs asserted claims under 42 U.S.C. § 1983 alleging violations of the Equal Protection Clause and the Fourth Amendment, claims under 42 U.S.C. §§ 1981, 1985(3) and 1986, and other related federal and state causes of action. The district court granted summary judgment for defendants on some of plaintiffs' claims and dismissed others on the pleadings, and the parties stipulated to the discontinuance and dismissal of the remaining claims.

This case bears on the question of the extent to which law enforcement officials may utilize race in their investigation of a crime. We hold that under the circumstances of this case, where law enforcement officials possessed a description of a criminal suspect, even though that description consisted primarily of the suspect's race and gender, absent other evidence of discriminatory racial animus, they could act on the basis of that description without violating the Equal Protection Clause. Accordingly, we affirm the dismissal of plaintiffs' § 1983 claims under the Fourteenth Amendment as well as their claims under 42 U.S.C. §§ 1981, 1985(3) and 1986.

Police action is still subject to the constraints of the Fourth Amendment, however, and a description of race and gender alone will rarely provide reasonable suspicion justifying a police search or seizure. In this case, certain individual plaintiffs were subjected to seizures by defendant law enforcement officials, and those individuals may proceed with their claims under the Fourth Amendment.

BACKGROUND

I. *Factual Background*

Oneonta, a small town in upstate New York about sixty miles west of Albany, has about 10,000 full-time residents. In addition, some 7,500 students attend and reside at the State University of New York College at Oneonta ("SUCO"). The people in Oneonta are for the most part white. Fewer than three hundred blacks live in the town, and just two percent of the students at SUCO are black.

On September 4, 1992, shortly before 2:00 a.m., someone broke into a house just outside Oneonta and attacked a seventy-seven-year-old woman. The woman told the police who responded to the scene that she could not identify her assailant's face, but that he was wielding a knife; that he was a black man, based on her view of his hand and forearm; and that he was young, because of the speed with which he crossed her room. She also told the police that, as they struggled, the suspect had cut himself on the hand with the knife. A police canine unit tracked the assailant's scent from the scene of the crime toward the SUCO campus, but lost the trail after several hundred yards.

The police immediately contacted SUCO and requested a list of its black male students. An official at SUCO supplied the list, and the police attempted to locate and question every black male student at SUCO. This endeavor produced no suspects. Then, over the next several days, the police conducted a "sweep" of Oneonta, stopping and questioning non-white persons on the streets and inspecting their hands for cuts. More than two hundred persons were questioned during that period, but no suspect was apprehended. Those persons whose names appeared on the SUCO list and those who were approached and questioned by the police, believing that they had been unlawfully singled out because of their race, decided to seek redress.

II. *Procedural History*

In early 1993, the SUCO students whose names appeared on the list and other persons questioned during the sweep of Oneonta filed this action in the district court against the City of Oneonta, the State of New York, SUCO, certain SUCO officials, and various police departments and police officers. Plaintiffs sought certification of two plaintiff classes consisting of the 78 students on the list as Class I, and those persons, whether students or not, stopped and questioned by the police as Class II.

In their amended complaint, plaintiffs asserted, under 42 U.S.C. § 1983, that defendants violated their rights under the Fourth Amendment and the Equal Protection Clause of the United States Constitution by questioning the black SUCO students and by conducting the sweep of Oneonta. Plaintiffs also alleged related claims under 42 U.S.C. §§ 1981, 1985(3) & 1986, and under Title VI, 42 U.S.C. § 2000d, and asserted various state law claims. Plaintiffs whose names appeared on the list also asserted claims under §§ 1983, 1985(3) and 1986 alleging that certain defendants had violated their rights under the Family Educational Rights and Privacy Act of 1974 ("FERPA"), 20 U.S.C. § 1232g, by releasing the list to the police.

DISCUSSION

On appeal, plaintiffs raise several contentions of error: first, that the district court improperly dismissed their § 1983 claims under the Equal Protection Clause using an incorrect pleading standard; second, that the district court made the same error in dismissing their § 1981 claims; third, that the district court erroneously dismissed or granted summary judgment against plaintiffs on their § 1983 claims under the Fourth Amendment; and finally, that the district court improperly dismissed their "derivative" claims under §§ 1985(3) and 1986. We affirm the dismissal of plaintiffs' equal protection and § 1981 claims, but we reverse in part the district court's rulings on plaintiffs' claims under the Fourth Amendment. We will discuss the particulars of each of plaintiffs' claims in turn.

I. *Equal Protection Claims*

The Fourteenth Amendment to the United States Constitution declares that "[n]o State shall . . . deny to any person within its jurisdiction the equal protection of the laws." U.S. Const. amend. XIV, § 1. The Equal Protection Clause "is essentially a direction that all persons similarly situated should be treated alike." To state a race-based claim under the Equal Protection Clause, a plaintiff must allege that a government actor intentionally discriminated against him on the basis of his race.

There are several ways for a plaintiff to plead intentional discrimination that violates the Equal Protection Clause. A plaintiff could point to a law or policy that "expressly classifies persons on the basis of race." (citing *Adarand Constructors, Inc. v. Pena,* 515 U.S. 200, 213, 227–29 (1995)). Or, a plaintiff could identify a facially neutral law or policy that has been applied in an intentionally discriminatory manner. *See Yick Wo v. Hopkins,* 118 U.S. 356, 373–74 (1886). A plaintiff could also allege that a facially neutral statute or policy has an adverse effect and that it was motivated by discriminatory animus. *See Village of Arlington Heights v. Metropolitan Hous. Dev. Corp.,* 429 U.S. 252, 264–65 (1977); *Johnson v. Wing,* 178 F.3d 611, 615 (2d Cir.1999).

Plaintiffs seek to plead an equal protection violation by the first method enumerated above. They contend that defendants utilized an express racial classification by stopping and questioning plaintiffs solely on the basis of their race. Plaintiffs assert that the district court erred in requiring them to plead the existence of a similarly situated group of non-minority individuals that were treated differently in the investigation of a crime.

When pleading a violation of the Equal Protection Clause, it is sometimes necessary to allege the existence of a similarly situated group that was treated differently. For example, if a plaintiff seeks to prove selective prosecution on the basis of his race, he "must show that similarly situated individuals of a different race were not prosecuted."

Plaintiffs are correct, however, that it is not necessary to plead the existence of a similarly situated non-minority group when challenging a law or policy that contains an express, racial classification. These classifications are subject to strict judicial scrutiny, and strict scrutiny analysis in effect addresses the question of whether people of different races are similarly situated with regard to the law or policy at issue. This does not avail plaintiffs in this case, however, because they have not identified any law or policy that contains an express racial classification.

Plaintiffs do not allege that upon hearing that a violent crime had been committed, the police used an established profile of violent criminals to determine that the suspect must have been black. Nor do they allege that the defendant law enforcement agencies have a regular policy based upon racial stereotypes that all black Oneonta residents be questioned whenever a violent crime is reported. In short, plaintiffs' factual premise is not supported by the pleadings: they were not questioned solely on the basis of their race. They were questioned on the altogether legitimate basis of a physical description given by the victim of a crime. Defendants' policy was race-neutral on its face; their policy was to investigate crimes by interviewing the victim, getting a description of the assailant, and seeking out persons who matched that description. This description contained not only race, but also gender and age, as well as the possibility of a cut on the hand. In acting on the description provided by the victim of the assault—a description that included race as one of several elements—defendants did not engage in a suspect racial classification that would draw strict scrutiny. The description, which originated not with the state but with the victim, was a legitimate classification within which potential suspects might be found.

Plaintiffs cite to cases holding that initiating an investigation of a person based solely upon that person's race violates the Equal Protection Clause. In *United States v. Avery,* 137 F.3d 343 (6th Cir.1997), the defendant claimed that he was stopped by law enforcement solely on the basis of his race. While the court affirmed his conviction, citing other factors utilized by the police in choosing to follow the defendant, the court stated that "[i]f law enforcement . . . takes steps to initiate an investigation of a citizen based solely upon that citizen's race, without more, then a violation of the Equal Protection Clause has occurred." Here, the police were not routinely patrolling an airport for possible drug smuggling, as in *Avery*. Instead, it is alleged that they were searching for a particular perpetrator of a violent assault, relying in their search on the victim's description of the perpetrator as a young black man with a cut on his hand. As the police therefore are not alleged to have investigated "based solely upon . . . race, without more," plaintiffs have failed to state an actionable claim under the Equal Protection Clause.

Police practices that mirror defendants' behavior in this case—attempting to question every person fitting a general description—may well have a disparate impact on small minority groups in towns such as Oneonta. If there are few black residents who fit the general description, for example, it would be more useful for the police to use race to find a black suspect than a white one. It may also be practicable for law enforcement to attempt to contact every black person who was a young male, but quite impossible to contact every such white person. If a community were primarily black with very few white residents and the search were for a young white male, the impact would be reversed. The Equal Protection Clause, however, has long been interpreted to extend to governmental action that has a disparate impact on a minority group only when that action was undertaken with discriminatory intent. Without additional evidence of discriminatory animus, the disparate impact of an investigation such as the one in this case is insufficient to sustain an equal protection claim.

In this case, plaintiffs do not sufficiently allege discriminatory intent. They do allege that at least one woman, Sheryl Champen, was stopped by law enforcement officials during their sweep of Oneonta. This allegation is significant because it may indicate that defendants considered race more strongly than other parts of the victim's description. However, this single incident, to the extent that it was related to the investigation, is not sufficient in our view to support an equal protection claim under the circumstances of this case.

We are not blind to the sense of frustration that was doubtlessly felt by those questioned by the police during this investigation. The actions of the police were understandably upsetting to the innocent plaintiffs who were stopped to see if they fit the victim's description of the suspect. The plaintiffs have argued that there is little difference between what occurred here and unlawful profiling based on a racial stereotype. While we disagree as a matter of law and believe that the conduct of the police in the circumstances presented here did not constitute a violation of the equal protection rights of the plaintiffs, we do not establish any rule that would govern circumstances giving rise to liability that are not present in this case. Any such rule will have to wait for the appropriate case. Nor do we hold that under no circumstances may the police, when acting on a description of a suspect, violate the equal protection rights of non-suspects, whether or not the police only stop persons conforming to the description of the suspect given by the victim.

We are also not unmindful of the impact of this police action on community relations. Law enforcement officials should always be cognizant of the impressions they leave on a community, lest distrust of law enforcement undermine its effectiveness. Yet our role is not to evaluate whether the police action in question was the appropriate response under the circumstances, but to determine whether what was done violated the

Equal Protection Clause. We hold that it did not, and therefore affirm the district court's dismissal of plaintiffs' § 1983 claims alleging equal protection violations.

II. *Section 1981 Claims*

To establish a claim under 42 U.S.C. § 1981, plaintiffs must allege facts supporting the following elements: (1) plaintiffs are members of a racial minority; (2) defendants' intent to discriminate on the basis of race; and (3) discrimination concerning one of the statute's enumerated activities. Those enumerated activities include the rights "to make and enforce contracts, to sue, be parties, give evidence, and to the full and equal benefit of all laws and proceedings for the security of persons and property." 42 U.S.C. § 1981(a).

Plaintiffs' claims under 42 U.S.C. § 1981 suffer from the same shortcomings as their equal protection claims. Section 1981, like the Equal Protection Clause, only prohibits intentional racial discrimination. Accordingly, plaintiffs must meet the same pleading standard for their § 1981 claims as for their § 1983 claims under the Equal Protection Clause, and these claims were insufficiently pleaded for the reasons stated above. We therefore affirm the dismissal of plaintiffs' § 1981 claims.

III. *Fourth Amendment Claims*

Plaintiffs' § 1983 claims also allege a violation of their Fourth Amendment rights during defendants' sweep of Oneonta. The district court dismissed many of these claims and granted summary judgment for defendants on other claims because, in its view, plaintiffs had not been subject to "seizures" under the Fourth Amendment. For the reasons that follow, we vacate the summary judgment against plaintiffs Jamel Champen, Jean Cantave, Ricky Brown, and Sheryl Champen, and affirm the district court's dismissal or grant of summary judgment with regard to the remaining claims.

In *Terry v. Ohio,* 392 U.S. 1 (1968), the Supreme Court established that the Fourth Amendment does not prohibit the police from stopping a person for questioning when the police have a reasonable suspicion that a person may be armed and dangerous, even when that suspicion does not amount to the probable cause necessary to make an arrest. Defendants would have difficulty demonstrating reasonable suspicion in this case, and indeed, they do not attempt to do so. Defendants instead argue that the district court correctly determined that no reasonable suspicion was necessary, because no seizure—not even a *Terry* stop—occurred in this case.

To prevail on a § 1983 claim under the Fourth Amendment based on an allegedly unlawful *Terry* stop, a plaintiff first must prove that he was seized. "[A] seizure does not occur simply because a police officer approaches an individual and asks a few questions." However, a seizure does occur when, "by means of physical force or show of authority," a police officer detains a person such that "a reasonable person would have believed that he was not free to leave," Pertinent factors identifying a police seizure can include

> the threatening presence of several officers; the display of a weapon; physical touching of the person by the officer; language or tone indicating that compliance with the officer was compulsory; prolonged retention of a person's personal effects, such as airplane tickets or identification; and a request by the officer to accompany him to the police station or a police room.

Whether a seizure occurred is a question of law to be reviewed *de novo,* while the factual findings underlying that determination are reviewed for clear error.

Jamel Champen, in his affidavit, alleges that a police officer pointed a spotlight at him and said "What, are you stupid? Come here. I want to talk to you." He was then told to show his hands. While it is arguably a close case, we conclude that a reasonable person in Champen's circumstances would have considered the police officer's request to be compulsory. Accordingly, we hold that Champen was seized and vacate the summary judgment for defendants on his Fourth Amendment claim.

Jean Cantave avers that he was driving in Oneonta when he was pulled over by a police car with a siren and flashing lights. Cantave was ordered out of the car and instructed to place his hands on top of the car. The Supreme Court has stated that the "[t]emporary detention of individuals during the stop of an automobile by the police, even if only for a brief period and for a limited purpose, constitutes a 'seizure' of 'persons' " under the Fourth Amendment. Under *Whren,* we have no doubt that Cantave was seized, and accordingly we vacate the summary judgment for defendants on Cantave's claim.

Ricky Brown's affidavit states that three police officers stopped him on the street. The police officers questioned him about whether he was a student and where he had been. They asked for his identification card, passed it around, and returned it to Brown. At one point, the officers "formed a circle around" Brown. When Brown asked if he had permission to leave, they told him that he was free to go. When Brown started to leave, however, one officer told him to come back and asked to see his hands. We conclude that a reasonable person in Brown's position—directed to return by one of the police officers who, just moments before, had encircled him—would not have felt free to leave. We therefore vacate the district court's grant of summary judgment on Brown's claim.

Sheryl Champen alleges that a police officer approached her at a bus station and told her that if she wanted to board the bus for which she was waiting, she would have to produce some identification. This contact is plainly a seizure under the caselaw because the police officer made it clear that he was detaining her. Accordingly, we vacate the summary judgment for defendants on Sheryl Champen's claim.

Raishawn Morris alleges that he encountered two police officers in his dorm lobby, and that they asked him to show them his hands. This does not rise to the level of a seizure, and we affirm the summary judgment for defendants on Morris's claim.

Finally, we also affirm the district court's dismissal of the remaining Fourth Amendment claims. The other plaintiffs did not submit any affidavits describing the details of their contacts with defendants, and the complaint fails to allege facts stating a claim that they were seized by defendants.

IV. *Claims Under §§ 1985(3) & 1986*

Plaintiffs also asserted causes of action under 42 U.S.C. §§ 1985(3) and 1986. The elements of a claim under § 1985(3) are: "(1) a conspiracy; (2) for the purpose of depriving, either directly or indirectly, any person or class of persons of equal protection of the laws, . . .; (3) an act in furtherance of the conspiracy; (4) whereby a person is . . . deprived of any right of a citizen of the United States." The conspiracy must be motivated by racial animus. Because a claim under § 1985(3) requires proof of discriminatory racial animus, we affirm the district court's dismissal of plaintiffs' § 1985(3) claims for the same reasons that we dismissed plaintiffs' equal protection and § 1981 claims, discussed in detail above. And because "a § 1986 claim must be predicated on a valid § 1985 claim," plaintiffs' § 1986 claim was properly dismissed as well.

CONCLUSION

We affirm the dismissal of plaintiffs' § 1983 claims under the Equal Protection Clause. We also affirm the dismissal of plaintiffs' claims under §§ 1981, 1985(3) and 1986. With regard to the plaintiffs' § 1983 claims under the Fourth Amendment, we affirm the district court's dismissal of these claims except those of plaintiffs Jamel Champen, Jean Cantave, Ricky Brown and Sheryl Champen. We vacate the district court's grant of summary judgment on those claims, and remand the case to the district court for further proceedings. Jamel Champen, Jean Cantave, Ricky Brown, and Sheryl Champen may continue to litigate their § 1983 claims of Fourth Amendment violations against all law enforcement defendants except Redmond and Olsen, against whom their claims were previously dismissed.

Affirmed in part, vacated in part, and remanded. Each party shall bear its own costs.

FOR DISCUSSION

Why did the Court say this use of race was permissible? Do you agree? Do you think it was racial profiling?

FIFTH AMENDMENT: SELF-INCRIMINATION

Fifth Amendment:

No person shall be held to answer for a capital, or otherwise infamous crime, unless on a presentment or indictment of a Grand Jury, except in cases arising in the land or naval forces, or in the Militia, when in actual service in time of War or public danger; nor shall any person be subject for the same offence to be twice put in jeopardy of life or limb; nor shall be compelled in any criminal case to be a witness against himself, nor be deprived of life, liberty, or property, without due process of law; nor shall private property be taken for public use, without just compensation. *U.S. Constitution*, Fifth Amendment

The Fifth Amendment to the Constitution provides that the federal government shall not deprive a person of life, liberty, or property without the protection of due process of law. The Fourteenth Amendment is now interpreted as levying this same restriction on the states. In *Twining v. New Jersey* (211 U.S. 78, 1908), the Supreme Court found that certain protections in the Bill of Rights "are of such a nature that they are included in the conception of due process of law." Because the Fourteenth Amendment contains a guarantee that states must protect the due process rights of its citizens, some criminal protections have been incorporated by it. "Due process," however, is a nebulous term that is subject to repeated redefinition. While its specific meaning has evolved over time and through court decisions, due process can be said to embody the concept of fundamental fairness. This conception includes both **substantive due process**—*what* is done by the government and its actors to individuals—as well as **procedural due process**—*how* something is done under governmental authority. As the following cases demonstrate, the notion of what is fair evolves over time, as does the role the Court perceives due process to play in articulating what constitutes substantive due process. For example, is it necessary that citizens clearly understand the rights that are granted them under the Constitution? How do we balance the interest of the government in protecting the larger society with the privacy rights of the individual?

Informing Individuals of Their Rights

Probably the best-known case in constitutional law is that of *Miranda v. Arizona* (384 U.S. 436, 1966). Memorialized in the minds of most Americans because of countless television police dramas, *Miranda's* consequence is that the accused must articulate an understanding of his or her rights guaranteed under the Fourth, Fifth, and Sixth Amendments of the Constitution. There must not merely be a generic waiver of an individual's rights; rather, a "knowing and intelligent waiver [is] required to relinquish constitutional rights."

Miranda followed a controversial decision in *Escobedo v. Illinois* (378 U.S. 478, 1964), with a similar fact pattern, in which a young man was questioned in police custody until he confessed. During four hours of interrogation, Escobedo was standing and handcuffed, denied access to his attorney despite his request to see counsel; moreover, the attorney was barred from seeing the detainee. The confession was used to gain a conviction; but the Supreme Court later held that under the circumstances Escobedo's statements were illegally obtained and should not have been admissible. Chief Justice Warren, in *Miranda's* majority opinion, claimed that the decisions in both *Miranda* and *Escobedo* are "not an innovation in our jurisprudence, but . . . an application of principles long recognized and applied in our settings. . . ."

Exceptions to Miranda

While *Miranda* continues to be valid constitutional law, numerous exceptions to the rule have been carved out over time. Similar to Fourth Amendment protections, exceptions recognizing the concerns of officer safety, emergency or exigent circumstances, and public safety have been recognized by the Supreme Court. Public commentary surrounding these cases during the Rehnquist Court years frequently noted an expectation for the "end of the *Miranda* era," but in all these cases the *Miranda* precedent was affirmed and recognized as inherent to the Constitution's due process protections (see *Dickerson v. United States*, 530 U.S. 428, 2000). In 1984, in *New York v. Quarles* (467 U.S. 649, 1984), an individual who had been described by witnesses as armed was arrested while wearing an empty holster near a grocery store. Officers questioned Benjamin Quarles about the location of the weapon after the arrest but before Quarles had received his *Miranda* warning. The weapon was found where Quarles had indicated. The City of New York brought suit when both the trial court and the New York appellate court excluded the confession and weapon as valid evidence. The Supreme Court, after a discussion of the purpose of *Miranda*, noted that there was a public safety exclusion to its ruling. In 2004, in *United States v. Patane* (542 U.S. 630), the Court expanded this constitutional exemption to apply to all physical evidence obtained through an uncoerced, yet un-Mirandized statement. In addition, the Supreme Court has also ruled in various cases that un-Mirandized statements of those accused of crimes can be used to impeach them if they take the witness stand. These statements may also be used in grand jury proceedings and in sentencing.

Links Between the Fifth and Sixth Amendments

The case of *Miranda,* along with the Sixth Amendment cases of *Escobedo v. Illinois* and *Gideon v. Wainwright* (372 U.S. 335, 1963), represented a new high standard set by the Supreme Court in interpreting and applying the requirement of counsel in criminal cases. The Court has long recognized the importance of the guarantee of counsel; but these and similar cases shoved the point at which the right to counsel is triggered back almost to the moment of arrest. The matter of coerced confessions and the impact of such civil liberties abuses on the Fifth and Sixth Amendment guarantees have been almost merged with the right to counsel (see, e.g., *Massiah v. United States,* 377 U.S. 201, 1964). The decisions in these cases generated much bitter criticism of the Court, and while the justices have revisited these issues occasionally, finding numerous exceptions to the guidelines, the ultimate standard of *Miranda* has been sustained.

The Shock the Conscience Test

The complexity of determining the meaning of **substantive due process** in the arena of criminal procedure is especially evident in the "shock the conscience" cases. *Rochin v. California* (342 U.S. 165, 1952) introduced this concept in an attempt to explain the scope of the Fifth Amendment due process protections. For the judicial majority in *Rochin* and subsequent cases, the Due Process Clause is violated when officers of the government engage in crime control behavior that "shocks the conscience" of the average person. The Court used this test to determine in subsequent nonconsensual search and warrantless cases whether such actions as pumping a suspect's stomach for evidence or taking a blood sample were so extreme that they shocked the conscience. If so, they could be interpreted as violating the Constitution. Despite the Court's endorsement of this test (and its occasional reappearance over time), many of the justices have been uncomfortable with the subjective nature of the test and the way in which the individual conscience of the evaluating judge would serve as a gauge of the degree to which police action infringed upon the Due Process Clause.

While in the case of *Breithaupt v. Abram* (352 U.S. 432, 1956) the Court found that withdrawing blood from an unconscious driver suspected of drunk driving did not "shock the conscience," the Court returned to the question in *Schmerber v. California* (384 U.S. 757, 1966). The fact pattern was similar: a driver was conscious and refused a blood alcohol test; a sample was drawn, despite the subject's objection. The Court did not use the shock the conscience test, but instead narrowed the coverage of the self-incrimination protection of the Due Process Clause. Specifically, in a 5–4 majority, Justice Brennan found that only testimony or "enforced communication" was protected by the right against self-incrimination.

MIRANDA V. ARIZONA

384 U.S. 436, 86 S.Ct. 1602, 16 L.Ed. 2d 694 (1966)

The Court simultaneously decided four cases; in the principal case, Ernesto Miranda was questioned in an isolated interrogation room while in police custody. None of the defendants in the combined cases was given a full and effective warning of his rights at the outset of the interrogation process. In all four cases, the questioning elicited oral admissions. In three of the cases, the defendants also signed statements, which were admitted at their trials. All the defendants were convicted, and all the convictions, except one from a California court, were affirmed on appeal.

Vote: 5–4

CHIEF JUSTICE WARREN delivered the opinion of the Court.

The cases before us raise questions which go to the roots of our concepts of American criminal jurisprudence: the restraints society must observe consistent with the Federal Constitution in prosecuting individuals for crime. More specifically, we deal with the admissibility of statements obtained from an individual who is subjected to custodial police interrogation and the necessity for procedures which assure that the individual is accorded his privilege under the Fifth Amendment to the Constitution not to be compelled to incriminate himself.

We dealt with certain phases of this problem recently in *Escobedo v. Illinois,* 378 U.S. 478 (1964). There, as in the four cases before us, law enforcement officials took the defendant into custody and interrogated him in a police station for the purpose of obtaining a confession. The police did not effectively advise him of his right to remain silent or of his right to consult with his attorney. Rather, they confronted him with an alleged accomplice who accused him of having perpetrated a murder. When the defendant denied the accusation and said "I didn't shoot Manuel, you did it," they handcuffed him and took him to an interrogation room. There, while handcuffed and standing, he was questioned for four hours until he confessed. During this interrogation, the police denied his request to speak to his attorney, and they prevented his retained attorney, who had come to the police station, from consulting with him. At his trial, the State, over his objection, introduced the confession against him. We held that the statements thus made were constitutionally inadmissible. . . .

We start here, as we did in *Escobedo,* with the premise that our holding is not an innovation in our jurisprudence, but is an application of principles long recognized and applied in other settings. . . .

Our holding will be spelled out with some specificity in the pages which follow but briefly stated it is this: the prosecution may not use statements, whether exculpatory or inculpatory, stemming from custodial interrogation of the defendant unless it demonstrates the use of procedural safeguards effective to secure the privilege against self-incrimination. By custodial interrogation, we mean questioning initiated by law enforcement officers after a person has been taken into custody or otherwise deprived of his freedom of action in any significant way. As for the procedural safeguards to be employed, unless other fully effective means are devised to inform accused persons of their right of silence and to assure a continuous opportunity to exercise it, the following measures are required. Prior to any questioning, the person must be warned that he has a right to remain silent, that any statement he does make may be used as evidence against him, and that he has a right to the presence of an attorney, either retained or appointed. The defendant may waive effectuation of these rights, provided the waiver is made voluntarily, knowingly and intelligently. If, however, he indicates in any manner and at any stage of the process that he wishes to consult with an attorney before speaking there can be no questioning. Likewise, if the individual is alone and indicates in any manner that he does not wish to be interrogated, the police may not question him. The mere fact that he may have answered some questions or volunteered some statements on his own does not deprive him of the right to refrain from answering any further inquiries until he has consulted with an attorney and thereafter consents to be questioned.

I

The constitutional issue we decide in each of these cases is the admissibility of statements obtained from a defendant questioned while in custody and deprived of his freedom of action. In each, the defendant was questioned by police officers, detectives, or a prosecuting attorney in a room in which he was cut off from the outside world. In none of these cases was the defendant given a full and effective warning of his rights at the outset of the interrogation process. In all the cases, the questioning elicited oral admissions, and in three of them, signed statements as well which were admitted at their trials. They all thus share salient features—incommunicado interrogation of individuals in a police-dominated atmosphere, resulting in self-incriminating statements without full warnings of constitutional rights. . . .

In the cases before us today, given this background, we concern ourselves primarily with this interrogation atmosphere and the evils it can bring. In No.759, *Miranda v. Arizona,* the police arrested the defendant and took him to a special interrogation room where they secured a confession. In No.760, *Vignera v. New York,* the defendant made oral admissions to the police after interrogation in the afternoon, and then signed an inculpatory statement upon being questioned by an assistant district attorney later the same evening. In No.761, *Westover v. United States,* the defendant was handed over to the Federal Bureau of Investigation by local authorities after they had detained and interrogated him for a lengthy period, both at night and the following morning. After some two hours of questioning, the federal officers had obtained signed statements from the defendant. Lastly, in No. 584, *California v. Stewart,* the local police held the defendant five days in the station and interrogated him of nine separate occasions before they secured his inculpatory statement. . . .

From the foregoing, we can readily perceive an intimate connection between the privilege against self-incrimination and police custodial questioning. It is fitting to turn to history and precedent underlying the Self-Incrimination Clause to determine its applicability in this situation.

II

We sometimes forget how long it has taken to establish the privilege against self-incrimination, the sources from which it came and the fervor with which it was defended. Its roots go back into ancient times. . . .

At the outset, if a person in custody is to be subjected to interrogation, he must first be informed in clear and unequivocal terms that he has the right to remain silent. For those unaware of the privilege, the warning is needed simply to make them aware of it—the threshold requirement for an intelligent decision as to its exercise. More important, such a warning is an absolute prerequisite in overcoming the inherent pressures of the interrogation atmosphere. It is not just the subnormal or woefully ignorant who succumb to an interrogator's imprecations, whether implied or expressly stated, that the interrogation will continue until a confession is obtained or that silence in the face of accusation is itself damning and will bode ill when presented to a jury. Further, the warning will show the individual that his interrogators are prepared to recognize his privilege should he choose to exercise it. . . .

The warning of the right to remain silent must be accompanied by the explanation that anything said can and will be used against the individual in court. This warning is needed in order to make him aware not only of the privilege, but also of the consequences of forgoing it. It is only through an awareness of these consequences that there can be any assurance of real understanding and intelligent exercise of the privilege. Moreover, this warning may serve to make the individual more acutely aware that he is faced with a phase of the adversary system—that he is not in the presence of persons acting solely in his interest.

The circumstances surrounding in-custody interrogation can operate very quickly to overbear the will of one merely made aware of his privilege by his interrogators. Therefore, the right to have counsel present at the interrogation is indispensable to the protection of the Fifth Amendment privilege under the system we delineate today. . . .

The presence of counsel at the interrogation may serve several significant subsidiary functions as well. If the accused decides to talk to his interrogators, the assistance of counsel can mitigate the dangers of untrustworthiness. With a lawyer present the likelihood that the police will practice coercion is reduced, and if coercion is nevertheless exercised the lawyer can testify to it in court. The presence of a lawyer can also help to guarantee that the accused gives a fully accurate statement to the police and that the statement is rightly reported by the prosecution at trial. . . .

An individual need not make a pre-interrogation request for a lawyer. While such request affirmatively secures his right to have one, his failure to ask for a lawyer does not constitute a waiver. . . .

Accordingly we hold that an individual held for interrogation must be clearly informed that he has the right to consult with a lawyer and to have the lawyer with him during interrogation under the system for protecting the privilege we delineate today. As with the warnings of the right to remain silent and that anything stated can be used in evidence against him, this warning is an absolute prerequisite to interrogation. . . .

If an individual indicates that he wishes the assistance of counsel before any interrogation occurs, the authorities cannot rationally ignore or deny his request on the basis that the individual does not have or cannot afford a retained attorney. The financial ability of the individual has no relationship to the scope of the rights involved here. The privilege against self-incrimination secured by the Constitution applies to all individuals. The need for counsel in order to protect the privilege exists for the indigent as well as the affluent. . . .

In order fully to apprise a person interrogated of the extent of his rights under this system then, it is necessary to warn him not only that he has the right to consult with an attorney, but also that if he is indigent a lawyer will be appointed to represent him. Without this additional warning, the admonition of the right to consult with counsel would often be understood as meaning only that he can consult with a lawyer if he has one or has the funds to obtain one. . . .

If the interrogation continues without the presence of an attorney and a statement is taken, a heavy burden rests on the government to demonstrate that the defendant knowingly and intelligently waived his privilege against self-incrimination and his right to retained or appointed counsel.

Moreover, where in-custody interrogation is involved, there is no room for the contention that the privilege is waived if the individual answers some questions or gives some information on his own prior to invoking his right to remain silent when interrogated. . . .

The principles announced today deal with the protection which must be given to the privilege against self-incrimination when the individual is first subjected to police interrogation while in custody at the station or otherwise deprived of his freedom of action in any way. It is at this point that our adversary system of criminal proceedings commences, distinguishing itself at the outset from the inquisitorial system recognized in some countries. Under the system of warnings we delineate today or under any other system which may be devised and found effective, the safeguards to be erected about the privilege must come into play at this point. . . .

To summarize, we hold that when an individual is taken into custody or otherwise deprived of his freedom by the authorities and is subjected to questioning, the privilege against self-incrimination is jeopardized. Procedural safeguards must be employed to protect the privilege, and unless other fully effective means are adopted to notify the person of his right of silence and to assure that the exercise of the right will be scrupulously honored, the following measures are required. He must be warned prior to any questioning that he has the right to remain silent, that anything he says can be used against him in a court of law, that he has the right to the presence of an attorney, and that if he cannot afford an attorney one will be appointed for him prior to any questioning if he so desires. Opportunity to exercise these rights must be afforded to him throughout the interrogation. After such warnings have been given, and such opportunity afforded him, the individual may knowingly and intelligently waive these rights and agree to answer questions or make a statement. But unless and until such warnings and waiver are demonstrated by the prosecution at trial, no evidence obtained as a result of interrogation can be used against him. . . .

We reverse. From the testimony of the officers and by the admission of respondent, it is clear that Miranda was not in any way apprised of his right to consult with an attorney and to have one present during the interrogation, nor was his right not to be compelled to incriminate himself effectively protected in any other manner. Without these warnings the statements were inadmissible. The mere fact that he signed a statement which contained a typed-in clause stating that he had "full knowledge" of his "legal rights" does not approach the knowing and intelligent waiver required to relinquish constitutional rights. . . .

JUSTICE CLARK dissented.

Rather than employing the arbitrary Fifth Amendment rule which the Court lays down I would follow the more pliable dictates of Due Process Clauses of the Fifth and Fourteenth Amendments which we are accustomed to administering and which we know from our cases are effective instruments in protecting persons in police custody. In this way we would not be acting in the dark nor in one full sweep changing the traditional rules of custodial interrogation which this Court has for so long recognized as a justifiable and proper tool in balancing individual rights against the rights of society. It will be soon enough to go further when we are able to appraise with somewhat better accuracy the effect of such a holding. . . .

JUSTICE HARLAN dissenting, joined by JUSTICE STEWART and JUSTICE WHITE.

To incorporate this notion into the Constitution requires a strained reading of history and precedent and a disregard of the very pragmatic concerns that alone may on occasion justify such strains. I believe that reasoned examination will show that the Due Process Clauses provided an adequate tool for coping with confessions and that, even if the Fifth Amendment privilege against self-incrimination be invoked, its precedents taken as a whole do not sustain the present rules. Viewed as a choice base on pure policy, these new rules prove to be a highly debatable if not one-sided appraisal of the competing interests, imposed over widespread objection, at the very time when judicial restraint is most called for by the circumstances.

JUSTICE WHITE dissenting, joined by JUSTICE HARLAN and JUSTICE STEWART.

The proposition that the privilege against self-incrimination forbids in-custody interrogation without the warnings specified in the majority opinion and without a clear waiver of counsel has no significant support in the history of the privilege or in the language of the Fifth Amendment. As for the English authorities and the common-law history, the privilege, firmly established in the second half of the seventeenth century, was never applied except to prohibit compelled judicial interrogations. . . .

Our own constitutional provision provides that no person "shall be compelled in any criminal case to be a witness against himself." These words, when "[c]onsidered in the light to be shed by grammar and the dictionary . . . appear to signify simply that nobody shall be compelled to give oral testimony against himself in a criminal proceeding under way in which he is defendant." Corwin, The Supreme Court's Construction of the Self-Incrimination Clause, 29 *Mich. L. Rev.* 1, 2. . . .

But if the Court is here and now to announce new and fundamental policy to govern certain aspects of our affairs, it is wholly legitimate to examine the mode of this or any other constitutional decision in this Court and to inquire into the advisability of its end product in terms of the long-range interest of the country. . . .

FOR DISCUSSION

How is the actual ruling in *Miranda* generally understood in popular American culture? How does this misinterpret the decision? What might be the consequences of such a misrepresentation of *Miranda* by a large portion of the general population?

RELATED CASES

***Jackson v. Denno:* 378 U.S. 368 (1964).**

A defendant in a criminal case is deprived of due process of law if his conviction is founded, in whole or in part, upon an involuntary confession, without regard for the truth or falsity of the confession and even though there is ample evidence aside from the confession to support the conviction.

***Berghuis v. Thompkins:* 560 U.S. 370 (2010).**

The accused must explicitly and unambiguously invoke *Miranda* rights to remain silent and to be provided counsel.

***JDB v. North Carolina:* 564 U.S. 261 (2011).**

The age of the child being questioned must be considered when determining if a minor is in police custody and must be Mirandized.

NEW YORK V. QUARLES

467 U.S. 649, 104 S.Ct. 2626, 81 L.Ed.2d 550 (1984)

After a witness described Benjamin Quarles, indicated that he was armed, and said that he had entered a local supermarket, Quarles was apprehended and charged with criminal possession of a weapon. The suspect was subdued, after which he was discovered wearing an empty holster. Prior to receiving a *Miranda* warning, a police officer named Kraft asked where the gun was, and Quarles indicated the location at which the gun was subsequently found. The gun and Quarles's statement were excluded in trial court. The decision was affirmed by the New York Court of Appeals.

Vote: 5–4

JUSTICE REHNQUIST delivered the opinion of the Court.

[T]he only issue before us is whether Officer Kraft was justified in failing to make available to respondent the procedural safeguards associated with the privilege against compulsory self-incrimination since *Miranda.*

We hold that on these facts there is a "public safety" exception to the requirement that *Miranda* warnings be given before a suspect's answers may be admitted into evidence, and that the availability of that exception does not depend upon the motivation of the individual officers involved. In a kaleidoscopic situation such as the one confronting these officers, where spontaneity rather than adherence to a police manual is necessarily the order of the day, the application of the exception which we recognize today should not be made to depend on post hoc findings at a suppression hearing concerning the subjective motivation of the arresting officer. Undoubtedly most police officers, if placed in Officer Kraft's position, would act out of a host of different, instinctive, and largely unverifiable motives—their own safety, the safety of others, and perhaps as well the desire to obtain incriminating evidence from the suspect.

Whatever the motivation of individual officers in such a situation, we do not believe that the doctrinal underpinnings of *Miranda* [*v. Arizona*, 384 U.S. 436, 1966)] require that it be applied in all its rigor to a situation in which police officers ask questions reasonably prompted by a concern for the public safety. The *Miranda* decision was based in large part on this Court's view that the warnings which it required police to give to suspects in custody would reduce the likelihood that the suspects would fall victim to constitutionally impermissible practices of police interrogation in the presumptively coercive environment of the station house.

The police in this case, in the very act of apprehending a suspect, were confronted with the immediate necessity of ascertaining the whereabouts of a gun which they had every reason to believe the suspect had just removed from his empty holster and discarded in the supermarket. So long as the gun was concealed somewhere in the supermarket, with its actual whereabouts unknown, it obviously posed more than one danger to the public safety: an accomplice might make use of it, a customer or employee might later come upon it.

We conclude that the need for answers to questions in a situation posing a threat to the public safety outweighs the need for the prophylactic rule protecting the Fifth Amendment's privilege against self-incrimination. We decline to place officers such as Officer Kraft in the untenable position of having to consider, often in a matter of seconds, whether it best serves society for them to ask the necessary questions without the *Miranda* warnings and render whatever probative evidence they uncover inadmissible, or for them to give the warnings in order to preserve the admissibility of evidence they might uncover but possibly damage or destroy their ability to obtain that evidence and neutralize the volatile situation confronting them.

JUSTICE O'CONNOR, concurring in the judgment in part and dissenting in part.

In my view, a "public safety" exception unnecessarily blurs the edges of the clear line heretofore established and makes *Miranda's* requirements more difficult to understand. In some cases, police will benefit because a reviewing court will find that an exigency excused their failure to administer the required warnings. But in other cases, police will suffer because, though they thought an exigency excused their noncompliance, a reviewing court will view the "objective" circumstances differently and require exclusion of admissions hereby obtained. The end result will be a finespun new doctrine on public safety exigencies incident to custodial interrogation, complete with the hair-splitting distinctions that currently plague our Fourth Amendment jurisprudence.

Miranda has never been read to prohibit the police from asking questions to secure the public safety. Rather, the critical question *Miranda* addresses is who shall bear the cost of securing the public safety when such questions are asked and answered: the defendant or the State. *Miranda*, for better or worse, found the resolution of that question implicit in the prohibition against compulsory self-incrimination and placed the burden on the

State. When police ask custodial questions without administering the required warnings, *Miranda* quite clearly requires that the answers received be presumed compelled and that they be excluded from evidence at trial.

In my view, since there is nothing about an exigency that makes custodial interrogation any less compelling, a principled application of *Miranda* requires that respondent's statement be suppressed.

JUSTICE MARSHALL, with whom JUSTICES BRENNAN and STEVENS join, dissenting.

The majority's entire analysis rests on the factual assumption that the public was at risk during Quarles' interrogation. This assumption is completely in conflict with the facts as found by New York's highest court. Before the interrogation began, Quarles had been "reduced to a condition of physical powerlessness." Contrary to the majority's speculations, Quarles was not believed to have, nor did he in fact have, an accomplice to come to his rescue. When the questioning began, the arresting officers were sufficiently confident of their safety to put away their guns. As Officer Kraft acknowledged at the suppression hearing, "the situation was under control." Based on Officer Kraft's own testimony, the New York Court of Appeals found: "Nothing suggests that any of the officers was by that time concerned for his own physical safety." The Court of Appeals also determined that there was no evidence that the interrogation was prompted by the arresting officers' concern for the public's safety.

The majority attempts to slip away from these unambiguous findings of New York's highest court by proposing that danger be measured by objective facts rather than the subjective intentions of arresting officers.

II

The majority's treatment of the legal issues presented in this case is no less troubling than its abuse of the facts. Before today's opinion, the Court had twice concluded that, under *Miranda v. Arizona*, 384 U.S. 436 (1966), police officers conducting custodial interrogations must advise suspects of their rights before any questions concerning the whereabouts of incriminating weapons can be asked. *Rhode Island v. Innis*, 446 U.S. 291, 298–302 (1980) (dicta); *Orozco v. Texas*, 394 U.S. 324 (1969) (holding). Now the majority departs from these cases and rules that police may withhold *Miranda* warnings whenever custodial interrogations concern matters of public safety.

III

Though unfortunate, the difficulty of administering the "public-safety" exception is not the most profound flaw in the majority's decision. The majority has lost sight of the fact that *Miranda v. Arizona* and our earlier custodial-interrogation cases all implemented a constitutional privilege against self-incrimination. The rules established in these cases were designed to protect criminal defendants against prosecutions based on coerced self-incriminating statements. The majority today turns its back on these constitutional considerations, and invites the government to prosecute through the use of what necessarily are coerced statements.

FOR DISCUSSION

What similarities do you perceive among the exceptions given by the Court to the Fourth Amendment search and seizure guarantees? What differences? Do these exceptions recognize the legitimate concerns of the state in protecting society, erode the meaning of these constitutional guarantees, or have an entirely different effect?

RELATED CASES

***Rhode Island v. Innis:* 446 U.S. 291 (1980).**

The guarantees provided by *Miranda v. Arizona* do not apply until the police actually begin explicit questioning; they do not apply during casual conversation en route to the police station.

***Arizona v. Fulminante:* 499 U.S. 279 (1991).**

A coerced confession can be used at trial if other evidence used at trial, which was obtained independently of the confession, was sufficient for a guilty verdict. The coerced confession cannot be used against the defendant.

***Dickerson v. United States:* 530 U.S. 428 (2000).**

The Court holds that *Miranda* determines the admissibility of statements made during both state and federal custodial interrogations.

***Salinas v. Texas:* 570 U.S. ___ (2013).**

The Fifth Amendment protection against self-incrimination does not protect a defendant's decision to remain mute during question prior to arrest.

SCHMERBER V. CALIFORNIA

384 U.S. 757, 86 S.Ct. 1826, 16 L.Ed.2d 908 (1966)

Schmerber was convicted of driving under the influence; the conviction was based on a blood sample drawn at a hospital after a car accident. The procedure took place at the request of a police officer and over the objections of the petitioner. The petitioner challenged the use of the blood alcohol evidence as an illegal search and seizure in violation of the Fourth and Fourteenth Amendments, a violation of the right against self-incrimination protected by the Fifth Amendment, and a violation of the Due Process Clause of the Fourteenth Amendment.

Vote: 5–4

JUSTICE BRENNAN delivered the opinion of the Court.

I

THE DUE PROCESS CLAUSE CLAIM.

Breithaupt v. Abram 352 U.S. 432 (1956) was also a case in which police officers caused blood to be withdrawn from the driver of an automobile involved in an accident, and in which there was ample justification for the officer's conclusion that the driver was under the influence of alcohol. There, as here, the extraction was made by a physician in a simple, medically acceptable manner in a hospital environment. There, however, the driver was unconscious at the time the blood was withdrawn and hence had no opportunity to object to the procedure. We affirmed the conviction there resulting from the use of the test in evidence, holding that under such circumstances the withdrawal did not offend "that 'sense of justice' of which we spoke in *Rochin v. California*, 342 U.S. 165 1952)." 352 U.S., at 435. *Breithaupt* thus requires the rejection of petitioner's due process argument, and nothing in the circumstances of this case or in supervening events persuades us that this aspect of *Breithaupt* should be overruled.

II

THE PRIVILEGE AGAINST SELF-INCRIMINATION CLAIM.

Breithaupt summarily rejected an argument that the withdrawal of blood and the admission of the analysis report involved in that state case violated the Fifth Amendment privilege of any person not to "be compelled in any criminal case to be a witness against himself." But that case, holding that the protections of the Fourteenth Amendment do not embrace this Fifth Amendment privilege, has been succeeded by *Malloy v. Hogan*, 378 U.S. 1, 8 (1964). We there held that "the Fourteenth Amendment secures against state invasion the same privilege that the Fifth Amendment guarantees against federal infringement." We therefore must now decide whether the withdrawal of the blood and admission in evidence of the analysis involved in this case violated petitioner's privilege.

It could not be denied that in requiring petitioner to submit to the withdrawal and chemical analysis of his blood the State compelled him to submit to an attempt to discover evidence that might be used to prosecute him for a criminal offense. He submitted only after the police officer rejected his objection and directed the physician to proceed. The officer's direction to the physician to administer the test over petitioner's objection constituted compulsion for the purposes of the privilege. The critical question, then, is whether petitioner was thus compelled "to be a witness against himself."

Not even a shadow of testimonial compulsion upon or enforced communication by the accused was involved either in the extraction or in the chemical analysis. Petitioner's testimonial capacities were in no way implicated; indeed, his participation, except as a donor, was irrelevant to the results of the test, which depend on chemical analysis and on that alone. Since the blood test evidence, although an incriminating product of compulsion, was neither petitioner's testimony nor evidence relating to some communicative act or writing by the petitioner, it was not inadmissible on privilege grounds.

IV

THE SEARCH AND SEIZURE CLAIM.

In *Breithaupt*, as here, it was also contended that the chemical analysis should be excluded from evidence as the product of an unlawful search and seizure in violation of the Fourth and Fourteenth Amendments. The Court did not decide whether the extraction of blood in that case was unlawful, but rejected the claim on the basis of *Wolf v. Colorado*, 338 U.S. 25 (1949). That case had held that the Constitution did not require, in state prosecutions for state crimes, the exclusion of evidence obtained in violation of the Fourth Amendment's provisions. We have since overruled *Wolf* in that respect, holding in *Mapp v. Ohio*, 367 U.S. 643 (1961), that the exclusionary rule adopted for federal prosecutions in *Weeks v. United States*, 232 U.S. 383 (1914), must also be applied in criminal prosecutions in state courts. The question is squarely presented therefore, whether the chemical analysis introduced in evidence in this case should have been excluded as the product of an unconstitutional search and seizure.

In this case, as will often be true when charges of driving under the influence of alcohol are pressed, these questions arise in the context of an arrest made by an officer without a warrant. Here, there was plainly probable cause for the officer to arrest petitioner and charge him with driving an automobile while under the influence of intoxicating liquor. The police officer who arrived at the scene shortly after the accident smelled liquor on petitioner's breath, and testified that petitioner's eyes were "bloodshot, watery, sort of a glassy appearance."

Although the facts which established probable cause to arrest in this case also suggested the required relevance and likely success of a test of petitioner's blood for alcohol, the question remains whether the arresting officer was permitted to draw these inferences himself, or was required instead to procure a warrant before proceeding with the test.

The officer in the present case, however, might reasonably have believed that he was confronted with an emergency, in which the delay necessary to obtain a warrant, under the circumstances, threatened "the destruction of evidence," *Preston v. United States*, 376 U.S. 364, 367 (1964). We are told that the percentage of alcohol in the blood begins to diminish shortly after drinking stops, as the body functions to eliminate it from the system. Particularly in a case such as this, where time had to be taken to bring the accused to a hospital and to investigate the scene of the accident, there was no time to seek out a magistrate and secure a warrant.

Similarly, we are satisfied that the test chosen to measure petitioner's blood-alcohol level was a reasonable one.

Finally, the record shows that the test was performed in a reasonable manner.

We thus conclude that the present record shows no violation of petitioner's right under the Fourth and Fourteenth Amendments to be free of unreasonable searches and seizures. It bears repeating, however, that we reach this judgment only on the facts of the present record. The integrity of an individual's person is a cherished value of our society. That we today hold that the Constitution does not forbid the States minor intrusions into an individual's body under stringently limited conditions in no way indicates that it permits more substantial intrusions, or intrusions under other conditions.

JUSTICE HARLAN, whom JUSTICE STEWART joins, concurring.

While agreeing with the Court that the taking of this blood test involved no testimonial compulsion, I would go further and hold that apart from this consideration the case in no way implicates the Fifth Amendment.

CHIEF JUSTICE WARREN, dissenting.

I believe it is sufficient for me to reiterate my dissenting opinion in *Breithaupt v. Abram*, 352 U.S. 432, 440, as the basis on which to reverse this conviction.

JUSTICE BLACK with whom JUSTICE DOUGLAS joins, dissenting.

I would reverse petitioner's conviction. . . . I disagree with the Court's holding that California did not violate petitioner's constitutional right against self-incrimination when it compelled him, against his will, to allow a doctor to puncture his blood vessels in order to extract a sample of blood and analyze it for alcoholic content, and then used that analysis as evidence to convict petitioner of a crime.

JUSTICE DOUGLAS, dissenting.

I adhere to the views of The Chief Justice in his dissent in *Breithaupt v. Abram*, 352 U.S. 432, 440, and to the views I stated in my dissent in that case.

We are dealing with the right of privacy which, since the *Breithaupt* case, we have held to be within the penumbra of some specific guarantees of the Bill of Rights. *Griswold v. Connecticut*, 381 U.S. 479 (1965). Thus, the Fifth Amendment marks "a zone of privacy" which the Government may not force a person to surrender. Likewise the Fourth Amendment recognizes that right when it guarantees the right of the people to be secure "in their persons." No clearer invasion of this right of privacy can be imagined than forcible bloodletting of the kind involved here.

JUSTICE FORTAS, dissenting.

I would reverse. In my view, petitioner's privilege against self-incrimination applies. I would add that, under the Due Process Clause, the State, in its role as prosecutor, has no right to extract blood from an accused or anyone else, over his protest. As prosecutor, the State has no right to commit any kind of violence upon the person, or to utilize the results of such a tort, and the extraction of blood, over protest, is an act of violence.

FOR DISCUSSION

Some types of technologies today require the passive consent of the individual to whom they are applied. Which of these might be used to provide evidence against an accused person? Would use of these technologies violate the Due Process Clause according to *Schmerber* and the following cases? Why or why not?

RELATED CASES

***United States v. Dionisio:* 410 U.S. 1 (1973).**

The Court finds that providing as evidence to a grand jury samples of the defendant's voice obtained without that person's consent does not violate self-incrimination protections.

***Cupp v. Murphy:* 412 U.S. 291 (1973).**

The Supreme Court decides that the use of a fingernail scraping obtained without a warrant from a suspect voluntarily cooperating with police does not violate the individual's constitutional rights.

***Estelle v. Williams:* 425 U.S. 501 (1976).**

According to the Supreme Court, compelling a defendant to wear prison attire during a criminal trial violates the Fifth Amendment's protection against self-incrimination.

SIXTH AMENDMENT: FAIR TRIAL PROVISIONS

U.S. Constitution, Sixth Amendment:

In all criminal prosecutions, the accused shall enjoy the right to a speedy and public trial, by an impartial jury of the State and district wherein the crime shall have been committed, which district shall have been previously ascertained by law, and to be informed of the nature and cause of the accusation; to be confronted with the witnesses against him; to have compulsory process for obtaining witnesses in his favor, and to have the Assistance of Counsel for his defense.

After someone has been accused of a crime by the state, the Constitution ensures specific guarantees to protect the that person during trial. Because all the resources of the state are mobilized against the individual during the trial, the Constitution—specifically the Fourth, Fifth, and Sixth Amendment—attempts to balance this power by limiting the extent of the state's authority. More specifically, the concept of criminal due process also encompasses the provisions of the Sixth Amendment. This amendment provides basic rights to those who are accused of criminal offenses by the government and are placed on trial. While these procedural rights to a speedy and public trial, with an impartial local jury, notification of charges, confronting of witnesses, and access to counsel were initially seen as rights guaranteed from encroachment by the federal government, under selective incorporation they were expanded to protect from state encroachment as well (see: confrontation of witnesses, *Pointer v. Texas*, 380 U.S. 400, 1965; impartial jury, *Parker v. Gladden*, 385 U.S. 363, 1966; speedy trial, *Klopfer v. North Carolina*, 386 U.S. 213, 1967; and presentation of witnesses to establish a defense, *Washington v. Texas*, 388 U.S. 14, 1967).

These particular provisions were designed to prevent the government from taking individuals in secrecy, concealing their arrest and trial, and convicting the persons without allowing a defense against criminal charges or prosecutorial witnesses. These protections hold the government accountable: they force prosecutors, while making a convincing case to the community, to assume the burden of demonstrating the guilt of the accused. While these protections make it harder for the state to garner a conviction, it becomes correspondingly less likely that an innocent person will be convicted. An **adversarial due process system**, as in the United States, in which "truth" is determined by advocates for both the state and the accused making persuasive arguments before judges and juries, requires a degree of equality between the parties. Hence, as the following cases demonstrate, the provision of an attorney for the accused is particularly necessary for fairness.

The Right to Counsel

In the 1963 case of *Gideon v. Wainwright* (372 U.S. 335), an indigent man who had not had the benefit of counsel was convicted of breaking and entry. This crime is a noncapital felony in Florida, and the state allowed for the appointment of a public defender in capital cases only. Previously, in *Betts v. Brady* (316 U.S. 455, 1942), the Supreme Court had ruled that the Due Process Clause did not require that the government provide counsel in all felony cases because the right to an attorney is not a fundamental right, necessary for a fair trial. In *Gideon*, the Court reconsidered this analysis of the fundamental requirements of the Due Process Clause. This landmark decision not only requires that all indigent individuals accused of a felony crime and facing a felony sentence be provided a state attorney to meet the procedural requirements of due process, but also overturned *Betts v. Brady*.

The right to an attorney was extended a year later in *Escobedo v. Illinois* (378 U.S. 478). In this case, a young man was denied access to his attorney while being held for questioning by the police. A statement elicited from Danny Escobedo at that time was used to convict him of murder in a subsequent trial. In this case, the Court noted that the police and Escobedo disagreed on what Escobedo was promised during the questioning; but it was clear that Escobedo's ignorance of the law was a factor in his willingness to provide a statement to the police. The Court applied *Gideon* and found that when the police question a suspect—in custody—for the purpose of eliciting incriminating statements, access to counsel may not be denied without violating the Due Process Clause.

A Jury of One's Peers

The Supreme Court has been repeatedly considered the characteristics required of the members of a jury of peers. Does a jury have to mirror the race, gender, and economic status of an accused individual in order to fulfill the fair trial requirements of the Sixth Amendment? In the 1990 case of *Holland v. Illinois* (493 U.S. 474), the Supreme Court ruled that all the Sixth Amendment requires is a fair jury, not a representative jury. At times, however, one or more persons have been explicitly excluded from the jury pool because of race or gender. Recognition of these circumstances has led to an evolution in the Court's understanding of the Sixth Amendment's requirements. In *Batson v. Kentucky* (476 U.S. 79, 1986), a judge had allowed the prosecutor during **voir dire** to eliminate all black members of a potential jury; as a result, a black male was tried before an all-white jury. According to *Swain v. Alabama* (380 U.S. 202, 1965), such circumstances required a criminal defendant to demonstrate that the use of **preemptive challenges** resulted in an equal protection violation. The Court reaffirmed the potential for such juries violating the Equal Protection Clause in *Batson*, noting that once the accused has demonstrated the appearance of discrimination, the burden shifts to the state to make a neutral explanation for the removal of black jurors. Over time, the Supreme Court has expanded this decision to all cases in which the defendant and the excluded jurors are of different races (*Powers v. Ohio*, 499 U.S. 400, 1991), to civil cases tried before a jury (*Edmonson v. Leesville Concrete*, 500 U.S. 614, 1991), and to gender discrimination cases (*J.E.B. v. Alabama ex. rel. T.B.*, 511 U.S. 127, 1994).

As the Supreme Court has clarified the requirements of the Sixth Amendment in a manner that the lower courts can interpret and apply, new circumstances have developed. The protections of citizens during the trial process can be particularly hard for the Court as it attempts to secure individual rights while balancing the state's interest in crime control. As the Court has struggled with this balance, two larger questions have emerged from the language of the Sixth Amendment—what does the right of representation mean for those who cannot afford an attorney, and what impact does racial and gender discrimination have on the ability of the government to provide a jury of peers?

GIDEON V. WAINWRIGHT

372 U.S. 335, 83 S.Ct. 792, 9 L.Ed.2d 799 (1963)

Clarence Earl Gideon was charged in a Florida state court with having broken into and entered a poolroom with intent to commit a misdemeanor. This is a noncapital felony under Florida law. The defendant appeared in court without funds and without counsel and asked the court to appoint counsel for him. This was denied because Florida law permitted appointment of counsel for indigent defendants only in capital cases. Gideon conducted his own defense, was convicted and sentenced to prison. Subsequently he applied for a writ of habeas corpus on the ground that the trial court's refusal to appoint counsel denied him rights under the Constitution. The state supreme court denied all relief.

Vote: 9–0

JUSTICE BLACK delivered the opinion of the Court.

This ruling is presented in Chapter I in the section on the Bill of Rights and the Fourteenth Amendment.

FOR DISCUSSION

Why does our system require access to an attorney in seeking to provide fundamental fairness and criminal due process? Is this requirement unique to systems of adversarial due process?

RELATED CASES

***Betts v. Brady:* 316 U.S. 455 (1942).**

Due process does not obligate a state to furnish counsel in every case. Most states do not consider appointment of counsel a fundamental right, essential to a fair trial. This is a matter of legislative policy.

***Lane v. Brown:* 372 U.S. 477 (1963).**

When a public defender cuts off the appeal of an indigent in a criminal case because of the belief that an appeal will be unsuccessful, there is a denial of due process.

***Draper v. Washington:* 372 U.S. 487 (1963).**

A trial judge's determination that an indigent's appeal in a criminal case is frivolous inadequately substitutes for the full appellate review available to nonindigents when the effect of that finding is to prevent an appellate examination based upon a sufficiently complete record of the trial proceedings themselves.

ESCOBEDO v. ILLINOIS

378 U.S. 478, 84 S.Ct. 1758, 12 L.Ed.2d 977 (1964)

Twenty-two-year-old Danny Escobedo was arrested in Chicago with his sister and taken to police headquarters for interrogation in connection with the fatal shooting, about eleven days earlier, of his brother-in-law. The young man, who was of Mexican extraction, had been arrested shortly after the shooting but had made no statement and was not released until after his lawyer obtained a writ of habeas corpus from a state court. While in custody, petitioner made several requests to see his lawyer, who, though present in the building, was refused access to his client. Petitioner was not advised by the police of his right to remain silent and, after persistent questioning by the police, made a damaging statement to an assistant state's attorney; that statement was admitted at the trial. Convicted of murder, Escobedo appealed to the state supreme court, which affirmed the conviction.

Vote: 5–4

JUSTICE GOLDBERG delivered the opinion of the Court.

The critical question in this case is whether, under the circumstances, the refusal by the police to honor petitioner's request to consult with his lawyer during the course of an interrogation constitutes a denial of "the Assistance of Counsel" in violation of the Sixth Amendment to the Constitution as "made obligatory upon the States by the Fourteenth Amendment," *Gideon v. Wainwright,* 372 U.S. 335, 342 (1963), and thereby renders inadmissible in a state criminal trial any incriminating statement elicited by the police during the interrogation. . . .

Notwithstanding repeated requests by each, petitioner and his retained lawyer were afforded no opportunity to consult during the course of the entire interrogation. At one point, as previously noted, petitioner and his attorney came into each other's view for a few moments but the attorney was quickly ushered away. Petitioner testified "that he heard a detective telling the attorney the latter would not be allowed to talk to [him] 'until they were done' " and that he heard the attorney being refused permission to remain in the adjoining room. A police officer testified that he had told the lawyer that he could not see petitioner until "we were through interrogating" him.

There is testimony by the police that during the interrogation, petitioner, a 22-year-old of Mexican extraction with no record of previous experience with the police, "was handcuffed" in a standing position and that he "was nervous, he had circles under his eyes and he was upset" and was "agitated" because "he had not slept well in over a week."

It is undisputed that during the course of the interrogation Officer Montejano, who "grew up" in petitioner's neighborhood, who knew his family, and who uses "Spanish language in [his] police work," conferred alone with petitioner "for about a quarter of an hour. . . ." Petitioner testified that the officer said to him "in Spanish that my sister and I could go home if I pinned it on Benedict DiGerlando," that "he would see to it that we would go home and be held only as witnesses, if anything, if we had made a statement against DiGerlando . . ., that we would be able to go home that night." Petitioner testified that he made the statement in issue because of this assurance. Officer Montejano denied offering any such assurance. . . . Petitioner, a layman, was undoubtedly unaware that under Illinois law an admission of "mere" complicity in the murder plot was legally as damaging as an admission of firing of the fatal shots. The "guiding hand of counsel" was essential to advise petitioner of his rights in this delicate situation. This was the "stage when legal aid and advice" were most critical to petitioner. . . .

We hold, therefore, that where, as here, the investigation is no longer a general inquiry into an unsolved crime but has begun to focus on a particular suspect, the suspect has been taken into police custody, the police carry out a process of interrogations that lends itself to eliciting incriminating statements, the suspect has requested and been denied an opportunity to consult with his lawyer, and the police have not effectively warned him of his absolute constitutional right to remain silent, the accused has been denied "the Assistance of Counsel" in violation of the Sixth Amendment to the Constitution as "made obligatory upon the States by the Fourteenth Amendment," *Gideon v. Wainwright,* 372 U.S., at 342, and that no statement elicited by the police during the interrogation may be used against him at a criminal trial. . . .

Nothing we have said today affects the powers of the police to investigate "an unsolved crime," *Spano v. New York,* 360 U.S. 315, 327, by gathering information from witnesses and by other "proper investigative efforts." *Haynes v. Washington,* 373 U.S. 503, 519. We hold only that when the process shifts from investigatory to accusatory—when its focus is on the accused and its purpose is to elicit a confession—our adversary system begins to operate, and, under the circumstances here, the accused must be permitted to consult with his lawyer.

The judgment of the Illinois Supreme Court is reversed and the case remanded for proceedings not inconsistent with this opinion.

Reversed and remanded.

JUSTICE STEWART dissented.

. . . The confession which the Court today holds inadmissible was a voluntary one. It was given during the course of a perfectly legitimate police investigation of an unsolved murder. The Court says that what happened during this investigation "affected" the trial. I had always supposed that the whole purpose of a police investigation of a murder was to "affect" the trial of the murderer, and that it would be only an incompetent, unsuccessful, or corrupt investigation which would not do so. The Court further says that the Illinois police officers did not advise the petitioner of his "constitutional rights" before he confessed to the murder. This Court has never held that the Constitution requires the police to give any "advice" under circumstances such as these.

Supported by no stronger authority than its own rhetoric, the Court today converts a routine police investigation of an unsolved murder into a distorted analogue of a judicial trial. It imports into this investigation constitutional concepts historically applicable only after the onset of formal prosecutorial proceedings. By doing so, I think the Court perverts those precious constitutional guarantees, and frustrates the vital interests of society in preserving the legitimate and proper function of honest and purposeful police investigation. . . .

JUSTICE WHITE dissented, joined by JUSTICES CLARK and STEWART

By abandoning the voluntary-involuntary test for admissibility of confessions, the Court seems driven by the notion that it is uncivilized law enforcement to use an accused's own admissions against him at his trial. It attempts to find a home for this new and nebulous rule of due process by attaching it to the right to counsel guaranteed in the federal system by the Sixth Amendment and binding upon the States by virtue of the due process guarantee of the Fourteenth Amendment. *Gideon v. Wainwright,* 372 U.S. 335 (1963). The right to counsel now not only entitles the accused to counsel's advice and aid in preparing for trial but stands as an impenetrable barrier to any interrogation once the accused has become a suspect. From that very moment apparently his right to counsel attaches, a rule wholly unworkable and impossible to administer unless police cars are equipped with public defenders and undercover agents and police informants have defense counsel at their side. I would not abandon the Court's prior cases defining with some care and analysis the circumstances requiring the presence or aid of counsel and substitute the amorphous and wholly unworkable principle that counsel is constitutionally required whenever he would or could be helpful. . . .

> Under this new approach one might just as well argue that a potential defendant is constitutionally entitled to a lawyer before, not after, he commits a crime, since it is then that crucial incriminating evidence is put within the reach of the Government by the would-be accused. Until now there simply has been no right guaranteed by the Federal Constitution to be free from the use at trial of a voluntary admission made prior to indictment. . . .

Today's decision cannot be squared with other provisions of the Constitution which, in my view, define the system of criminal justice this Court is empowered to administer. . . .

FOR DISCUSSION

Why do you think the Court so carefully distinguished between questioning in the course of investigation and questioning to make a case against a particular subject? Should this be relevant for due process, why or why not?

RELATED CASES

***Massiah v. United States:* 377 U.S. 201 (1964).**

After his indictment and in the absence of his counsel, an accused person was denied the basic protections of the Sixth Amendment when federal agents had deliberately elicited from him (here by means of a hidden radio transmitter) incriminating evidence.

***Estes v. Texas:* 381 U.S. 532 (1965).**

The impact of televised trial proceedings on the jurors, witnesses, the trial judge, and the defendant can potentially strip the accused of a fair trial. The Court recognized this judgment had necessarily been based on the case at hand and could be malleable in the future.

***Sheppard v. Maxwell:* 384 U.S. 333 (1966).**

Dr. Samuel H. Sheppard did not receive a fair trial consistent with the Due Process Clause of the Fourteenth Amendment because of the trial judge's failure to protect the defendant from the massive, pervasive, and prejudicial publicity that attended his prosecution.

***Chandler v. Florida:* 49 U.S. 560 (1981).**

The Court found that *Estes v. Texas* (1965) did not mean that all radio, television, and photographic coverage of a criminal trial with public exposure violates constitutional protections. States are allowed to experiment with technology in the courtroom, especially when, as in Florida, there are clear guidelines designed to protect defendants' Sixth and Fourteenth Amendment rights.

BATSON V. KENTUCKY

476 U.S. 79, 106 S.Ct. 1712, 90 L.Ed.2d 69 (1986)

During the trial of an African American man, the judge allowed the prosecutor to use his discretionary preemptory challenges during **voir dire** to discharge all the potential jury members who were black and thus empanel an all-white jury. This challenged the segment of *Swain v. Alabama* (380 U.S. 202, 1965) regarding the "evidentiary burden placed on a criminal defendant who claims that he has been denied equal protection through the State's use of peremptory challenges to exclude members of his race from the . . . jury."

Vote: 7–2

JUSTICE POWELL delivered the opinion of the Court.

II

In *Swain v. Alabama*, 380 U.S. 202, [203–204] (1965), this Court recognized that a "State's purposeful or deliberate denial to Negroes on account of race of participation as jurors in the administration of justice violates the Equal Protection Clause." This principle has been "consistently and repeatedly" reaffirmed in numerous decisions of this Court both preceding and following *Swain*. We reaffirm the principle today.

A

More than a century ago, the Court decided that the State denies a black defendant equal protection of the laws when it puts him on trial before a jury from which members of his race have been purposefully excluded. *Strauder v. West Virginia*, 100 U.S. 303 (1880). That decision laid the foundation for the Court's unceasing efforts to eradicate racial discrimination in the procedures used to select the venire from which individual jurors are drawn.

In holding that racial discrimination in jury selection offends the Equal Protection Clause, the Court in *Strauder* recognized, however, that a defendant has no right to a "petit jury composed in whole or in part of persons of his own race."

Racial discrimination in selection of jurors harms not only the accused whose life or liberty they are summoned to try. Competence to serve as a juror ultimately depends on an assessment of individual qualifications and ability impartially to consider evidence presented at a trial. A person's race simply "is unrelated to his fitness as a juror." As long ago as *Strauder*, therefore, the Court recognized that by denying a person participation in jury service on account of his race, the State unconstitutionally discriminated against the excluded juror.

B

In *Strauder*, the Court invalidated a state statute that provided that only white men could serve as jurors. We can be confident that no State now has such a law. The Constitution requires, however, that we look beyond the face of the statute defining juror qualifications and also consider challenged selection practices to afford "protection against action of the State through its administrative officers in effecting the prohibited discrimination." *Norris v. Alabama*, 294 U.S. 587, at 589 (1935). Thus, the Court has found a denial of equal protection where the procedures implementing a neutral statute operated to exclude persons from the venire on racial grounds, and has made clear that the Constitution prohibits all forms of purposeful racial discrimination in selection of jurors. While decisions of this Court have been concerned largely with discrimination during selection of the venire, the principles announced there also forbid discrimination on account of race in selection of the petit jury. Since the Fourteenth Amendment protects an accused throughout the proceedings bringing him to justice, *Hill v. Texas*, 316 U.S. 400, 406 (1942), the State may not draw up its jury lists pursuant to neutral procedures but then resort to discrimination at "other stages in the selection process," *Avery v. Georgia*, 345 U.S. 559, 562 (1953).

Accordingly, the component of the jury selection process at issue here, the State's privilege to strike individual jurors through peremptory challenges, is subject to the commands of the Equal Protection Clause. Although a prosecutor ordinarily is entitled to exercise permitted peremptory challenges "for any reason at all, as long as that reason is related to his view concerning the outcome" of the case to be tried, *United States v. Robinson*, 421 F.Supp. 467, 473 (Conn. 1976). *United States v. Newman*, 549 F.2d 240 (CA2 1977), the Equal Protection Clause forbids the prosecutor to challenge potential jurors solely on account of their race or on the assumption that black jurors as a group will be unable impartially to consider the State's case against a black defendant.

III

The principles announced in *Strauder* never have been questioned in any subsequent decision of this Court. Rather, the Court has been called upon repeatedly to review the application of those principles to particular facts. A recurring question in these cases, as in any case alleging a violation of the Equal Protection Clause, was whether the defendant had met his burden of proving purposeful discrimination on the part of the State. *Whitus v. Georgia*, 385 U.S. 545, 550 (1967); *Hernandez v. Texas*, [347 U.S. 475 (1954)], at 478–481; *Akins v. Texas*, 325 U.S., at 403–404; *Martin v. Texas*, 200 U.S. 316 (1906). That question also was at the heart of the portion of Swain v. Alabama we reexamine today.

B

Since the decision in *Swain*, we have explained that our cases concerning selection of the venire reflect the general equal protection principle that the "invidious quality" of governmental action claimed to be racially discriminatory "must ultimately be traced to a racially discriminatory purpose." *Washington v. Davis*, 426 U.S. 229, 240 (1976). As in any equal protection case, the "burden is, of course," on the defendant who alleges discriminatory selection of the venire "to prove the existence of purposeful discrimination." *Whitus v. Georgia*, 385 U.S., at 550. In deciding if the defendant has carried his burden of persuasion, a court must undertake "a sensitive inquiry into such circumstantial and direct evidence of intent as may be available." *Arlington Heights v. Metropolitan Housing Development Corp.*, 429 U.S. 252, 266 (1977). Circumstantial evidence of invidious intent may include proof of disproportionate impact. We have observed that under some circumstances proof of discriminatory impact "may for all practical purposes demonstrate unconstitutionality because in various circumstances the discrimination is very difficult to explain on nonracial grounds." For example, "total or seriously disproportionate exclusion of Negroes from jury venires," "is itself such an 'unequal application of the law . . . as to show intentional discrimination,' " id., at 241.

Moreover, since *Swain*, we have recognized that a black defendant alleging that members of his race have been impermissibly excluded from the venire may make out a prima facie case of purposeful discrimination by showing that the totality of the relevant facts gives rise to an inference of discriminatory purpose. Once the defendant makes the requisite showing, the burden shifts to the State to explain adequately the racial exclusion. The State cannot meet this burden on mere general assertions that its officials did not discriminate or that they properly performed their official duties. Rather, the State must demonstrate that "permissible racially neutral selection criteria and procedures have produced the monochromatic result." *Alexander v. Louisiana* at 632.

The showing necessary to establish a prima facie case of purposeful discrimination in selection of the venire may be discerned in this Court's decisions. The defendant initially must show that he is a member of a racial group capable of being singled out for differential treatment. In combination with that evidence, a defendant may then make a prima facie case by proving that in the particular jurisdiction members of his race have not been summoned for jury service over an extended period of time. Proof of systematic exclusion from the venire raises an inference of purposeful discrimination because the "result bespeaks discrimination." *Hernandez v. Texas*, 347 U.S., at 482.

Once the defendant makes a prima facie showing, the burden shifts to the State to come forward with a neutral explanation for challenging black jurors. Though this requirement imposes a limitation in some cases on the full peremptory character of the historic challenge, we emphasize that the prosecutor's explanation need not rise to the level [of] justifying exercise of a challenge for cause. But the prosecutor may not rebut the defendant's prima facie case of discrimination by stating merely that he challenged jurors of the defendant's race on the assumption—or his intuitive judgment—that they would be partial to the defendant because of their shared race. Just as the Equal Protection Clause forbids the States to exclude black persons from the venire on the assumption that blacks as a group are unqualified to serve as jurors, so it forbids the States to strike black veniremen on the assumption that they will be biased in a particular case simply because the defendant is black. The core guarantee of equal protection, ensuring citizens that their State will not discriminate on account of race, would be meaningless were we to approve the exclusion of jurors on the basis of such assumptions, which arise solely from the jurors' race. Nor may the prosecutor rebut the defendant's case merely by denying that he had a discriminatory motive or "[affirming] [his] good faith in making individual selections." *Alexander v. Louisiana*, 405 U.S., at 632. If these general assertions were accepted as rebutting a defendant's prima facie case, the Equal Protection Clause "would be but a vain and illusory requirement." *Norris v. Alabama* at 598. The prosecutor therefore must articulate a neutral explanation related to the particular case to be tried. The trial court then will have the duty to determine if the defendant has established purposeful discrimination.

JUSTICE MARSHALL, concurring.

I join Justice Powell's eloquent opinion for the Court, which takes a historic step toward eliminating the shameful practice of racial discrimination in the selection of juries. The Court's opinion cogently explains the pernicious nature of the racially discriminatory use of peremptory challenges, and the repugnancy of such discrimination to the Equal Protection Clause. The Court's opinion also ably demonstrates the inadequacy of any burden of proof for racially discriminatory use of peremptories that requires that "justice . . . sit supinely by" and be flouted in case after case before a remedy is available. I nonetheless write separately to express my views. The decision today will not end the racial discrimination that peremptories inject into the jury-selection process. That goal can be accomplished only by eliminating peremptory challenges entirely.

II

I wholeheartedly concur in the Court's conclusion that use of the peremptory challenge to remove blacks from juries, on the basis of their race, violates the Equal Protection Clause. I would go further, however, in fashioning a remedy adequate to eliminate that discrimination. Merely allowing defendants the opportunity to challenge the racially discriminatory use of peremptory challenges in individual cases will not end the illegitimate use of the peremptory challenge.

III

The inherent potential of peremptory challenges to distort the jury process by permitting the exclusion of jurors on racial grounds should ideally lead the Court to ban them entirely from the criminal justice system.

Our criminal justice system "requires not only freedom from any bias against the accused, but also from any prejudice against his prosecution. Between him and the state the scales are to be evenly held." *Hayes v. Missouri*, 120 U.S. 68, 70 (1887). We can maintain that balance, not by permitting both prosecutor and defendant to engage in racial discrimination in jury selection, but by banning the use of peremptory challenges by prosecutors and by allowing the States to eliminate the defendant's peremptories as well.

JUSTICE REHNQUIST, with whom CHIEF JUSTICE BURGER joins, dissenting.

The Court states, in the opening line of its opinion, that this case involves only a reexamination of that portion of *Swain v. Alabama*, 380 U.S. 202 (1965), concerning "the evidentiary burden placed on a criminal defendant who claims that he has been denied equal protection through the State's use of peremptory challenges to exclude members of his race from the petit jury." But in reality the majority opinion deals with much more than "evidentiary [burdens]." With little discussion and less analysis, the Court also overrules one of the fundamental substantive holdings of *Swain*, namely, that the State may use its peremptory challenges to remove from the jury, on a case-specific basis, prospective jurors of the same race as the defendant. Because I find the

Court's rejection of this holding both ill-considered and unjustifiable under established principles of equal protection, I dissent.

I cannot subscribe to the Court's unprecedented use of the Equal Protection Clause to restrict the historic scope of the peremptory challenge, which has been described as "a necessary part of trial by jury." *Swain*, 380 U.S., at 219. In my view, there is simply nothing "unequal" about the State's using its peremptory challenges to strike blacks from the jury in cases involving black defendants, so long as such challenges are also used to exclude whites in cases involving white defendants, Hispanics in cases involving Hispanic defendants, Asians in cases involving Asian defendants, and so on. This case-specific use of peremptory challenges by the State does not single out blacks, or members of any other race for that matter, for discriminatory treatment. Such use of peremptories is at best based upon seat-of-the-pants instincts, which are undoubtedly crudely stereotypical and may in many cases be hopelessly mistaken. But as long as they are applied across-the-board to jurors of all races and nationalities, I do not see—and the Court most certainly has not explained—how their use violates the Equal Protection Clause.

Nor does such use of peremptory challenges by the State infringe upon any other constitutional interests. The Court does not suggest that exclusion of blacks from the jury through the State's use of peremptory challenges results in a violation of either the fair-cross-section or impartiality component of the Sixth Amendment. And because the case-specific use of peremptory challenges by the State does not deny blacks the right to serve as jurors in cases involving nonblack defendants, it harms neither the excluded jurors nor the remainder of the community.

The use of group affiliations, such as age, race, or occupation, as a "proxy" for potential juror partiality, based on the assumption or belief that members of one group are more likely to favor defendants who belong to the same group, has long been accepted as a legitimate basis for the State's exercise of peremptory challenges. Indeed, given the need for reasonable limitations on the time devoted to voir dire, the use of such "proxies" by both the State and the defendant may be extremely useful in eliminating from the jury persons who might be biased in one way or another. The Court today holds that the State may not use its peremptory challenges to strike black prospective jurors on this basis without violating the Constitution. But I do not believe there is anything in the Equal Protection Clause, or any other constitutional provision, that justifies such a departure from the substantive holding contained in Part II of *Swain*. Petitioner in the instant case failed to make a sufficient showing to overcome the presumption announced in *Swain* that the State's use of peremptory challenges was related to the context of the case. I would therefore affirm the judgment of the court below.

FOR DISCUSSION

When might a jury composed of members of a single race or gender be constitutionally valid under the Sixth Amendment. According to *Batson*, how could this case be made?

RELATED CASES

***Patton v. Mississippi:* 332 U.S. 463 (1947).**

Supreme Court overturned a death penalty conviction, asserting that the exclusion of citizens from jury duty on the basis of race led to unconstitutional indictments and verdicts. In this case no blacks had served on a jury in the county in 30 years even though a third of the population was black.

***Holland v. Illinois:* 493 U.S. 474 (1990).**

The Supreme Court holds that the Sixth Amendment guarantees only a fair jury; it does not guarantee a representative jury.

***Powers v. Ohio:* 499 U.S. 400 (1991).**

The *Batson* precedent is applied to cases in which the defendant and the excluded jurors are of different races.

***Edmonson v. Leesville Concrete Company, Inc.:* 500 U.S. 614 (1991).**

The *Batson* precedent is applied to civil cases.

***Hernandez v. New York:* 500 U.S. 352 (1991).**

Unlawful race-based discrimination does not exist when a prosecuting attorney offers a race-neutral basis for his preemptory strikes of Latino jurors. In this case, the attorney was concerned about whether the jurors would be able to listen to and follow an interpreter.

***J.E.B. v. Alabama ex. rel. T.B.:* 511 U.S. 127 (1994).**

The Equal Protection Clause prohibits gender discrimination in jury selection, and the exclusion of potential jurors solely on the basis of gender is unconstitutional.

GLOSSARY

Adversarial Due Process: A system in which lawyers bear the burden of making persuasive cases regarding the interpretation of the facts and the disposition of the law. Frequently, in this system, judges serve as referees and juries make determinations.

Exclusionary Rule: A judicially designed interpretation of the Fourth Amendment as forbidding unconstitutionally obtained evidence from being used in a trial against an individual accused of a crime.

Magna Carta: English legal document, dated 1215, which constrains the monarch, forcing him or her to abide by particular legal procedures when prosecuting British subjects.

***Miranda* Rights:** Guarantees recognized by the Supreme Court in the 1966 case of *Miranda v. Arizona* with a view to ensuring that individuals in the custody of the state, having been accused of a crime, are notified of their constitutional rights prior to questioning.

Precedental Consistency: The ideal that law decided by judges should be based on previously determined cases (precedents) to ensure that legal reasoning remains predictable and constant.

Preemptive Challenge: An attorney-initiated request made during *voir dire* to have a potential jurist removed from the jury panel without explanation or justification.

Pretextual Stops: The use of minor traffic offenses such as broken taillights as the basis of stopping someone suspected of committing or having committed a more serious crime such as drug or weapons possession.

Procedural Due Process: The guarantees by the government as to what processes will be provided before rights to life, liberty, and property may be limited. Laws and the Constitution explicitly provide these limitations on governmental action.

Procedural Protections: Specific guarantees provided in the Constitution and designed to protect citizens from governmental intrusions; the protections include the right to an attorney, the right to a speedy trial, and the definition of certain searches and seizures as unlawful.

Racial Profiling: The intentional or unintentional use of race in law enforcement to stop or search individuals suspected of violating the law.

Substantive Due Process: The guarantee of fundamental fairness that the courts have found reflected in the Due Process Clause of the Constitution. Instead of protecting citizens from how the government exercises its authority, substantive due process covers what the government and its actors do to citizens.

Substantive Protections: The judiciary's interpretation of the Constitution to ensure that the government provides fundamental fairness to its citizens.

Tort: A civil wrong or harm committed by one individual against another. Tort claims are part of a state's common law. Individuals who believe that they have been subject to illegal law enforcement activity may bring tort actions against police officers.

***Voir Dire*:** The process in which attorneys representing both the state and the defendant query the people in the jury pool about their demographic characteristics and biases in order to create an impartial jury.

SELECTED BIBLIOGRAPHY

Bloom, Robert M. 2003. *Searches, Seizures, and Warrants: A Reference Guide to the United States.* Westport, CT: Praeger Publishers.

Clancey, Thomas K. 2008. *The Fourth Amendment: Its History and Interpretation.* Durham: Carolina Academic Press.

Cuddihy, William J. 2009. *The Fourth Amendment: Origins and Original Meaning 1602–1791.* New York: Oxford University Press.

Dash, Samuel. 2004. *The Intruders: Unreasonable Searches and Seizures from King John to John Ashcroft.* Rutgers, NJ: Rutgers University Press.

Diffie, Whitfield, and Susan Landau. 1998. *Privacy on the Line: The Politics of Wiretapping and Encryption.* Cambridge, MA: MIT Press.

Gizzi, Michael C. and R. Craig Curtis. 2016. *The Fourth Amendment in Flux: The Roberts Court, Crime Control, and Digital Privacy.* Lawrence, KS: University of Kansas Press.

Hubbart, Phillip A. 2005. *Making Sense of Search and Seizure Law: A Fourth Amendment Handbook.* Durham, NC: Carolina Academic Press.

Kappeler, Victor. 2007. *Critical Issues in Police Civil Liability,* 4th ed. Long Grove, IL: Waveland Press.

Lewis, Anthony. 1964. *Gideon's Trumpet.* New York: Random House.

Long, Carolyn N. 2006. Mapp v. Ohio: *Guarding Against Unreasonable Searches and Seizures.* Lawrence: University Press of Kansas.

McInnis, Thomas N. 2001. *The Christian Burial Case: An Introduction to Criminal and Judicial Procedure.* Westport, CT: Praeger Publishers.

Norris, Clive, Jade Moran, and Gary Armstrong (eds.). 1998. *Surveillance, Closed Circuit Television and Social Control.* Brookfield, VT: Ashgate Publishing.

Shapiro, Barbara J. 1991. *Beyond Reasonable Doubt and Probable Cause: Historical Perspectives on the Anglo-American Law of Evidence.* Berkeley: University of California Press.

CHAPTER VIII

Equal Protection of the Laws

Timeline: Equal Protection of the Laws

1776	Declaration of Independence is signed, announcing a formal split with England and asserting "that all men are created equal."
1848	Seneca Falls Declaration is written to challenge the traditional understanding of women's rights under the Constitution.
1861	The American Civil War begins.
1863	The Emancipation Proclamation, freeing enslaved peoples in the states of the Confederacy, is signed by President Lincoln.
1865	The Thirteenth Amendment is ratified, abolishing slavery in the United States.
	Southern reconstruction begins with the registration of black voters in the South.
1868	The Fourteenth Amendment, granting rights to newly freed slaves, also provides enforcement powers to Congress.
1870	The Fifteenth Amendment, designed to protect voting rights of males regardless of previous condition of servitude or race, is ratified.
1873	*Bradwell v. Illinois* determines that the Equal Protection Clause of the Fourteenth Amendment does not prohibit sex-based classifications by the states.
1877	Federal troops are withdrawn from the South, marking the end of Reconstruction.
1896	The Supreme Court in *Plessy v. Ferguson* interprets the Fourteenth Amendment as allowing state segregation laws that provide for "separate but equal" accommodations.
1908	Race riots in Springfield, Illinois, result in the deaths of black people and destruction of their property.
1909	In the wake of the violence in Illinois, the interracial National Association for the Advancement of Colored People (NAACP) is founded.
1913	Woman suffrage march in Washington, D.C., during the inauguration of President Woodrow Wilson; the new president imprisons women who were protesting outside the White House.
1920	The Nineteenth Amendment, ensuring women's right to vote, is ratified.
1948	In *Shelley v. Kraemer* the Court rules that while racially restrictive housing covenants are constitutionally allowable, their enforcement by a state court violates the Fourteenth Amendment.

1950 The Court in *Sweatt v Painter* and *McLaurin v. Oklahoma State Regents* determined that facilities and education must be close to equal to sustain segregated graduate education under the Equal Protection Clause.

1954 *Brown v. Board of Education I* overturns *Plessy v. Ferguson's* interpretation of the Equal Protection Clause; in *Hernandez v. Texas* the Court rules that the Fourteenth Amendment grants equal protection to Mexican Americans and people of all races.

1954 *Bolling v. Sharpe* announces that the federal government is required to provide equal protection of the laws through the Due Process Clause of the Fifth Amendment.

1955 In *Brown v. Board of Education II* the Court delegates to district courts the implementation of the 1954 *Brown* decision in segregated public schools.

1955 Immediately after the arrest of Rosa Parks, the Montgomery Improvement Association calls for a city-wide bus boycott to secure better treatment of blacks on the segregated public buses; the action lasts for 385 days.

1961 In *Hoyt v. Florida*, the Court rules that a fair jury system does not have to require women to be part of jury pools.

1964 Student Nonviolent Coordinating Committee declare Freedom Summer in Mississippi, registering voters and hosting freedom schools; the Mississippi Freedom Democratic Party challenges the state's segregated Democratic Party at the Democratic National Convention in Atlantic City.

1964 The Civil Rights Act is ratified, prohibiting discrimination based on race, gender, and religion in the workplace, in education, in housing, and in other areas of American life.

1964 In *Heart of Atlanta Motel v. United States* the Court finds the new Civil Rights Act constitutional under the commerce powers of Congress.

1965 Bloody Sunday in Selma, Alabama: peaceful protesters are shown on national television being brutally abused by police.

1965 Voting Rights Act is ratified, providing for federal enforcement of voting rights and the prohibition of discriminatory voting practices.

1967 President Lyndon B. Johnson appoints the first African American justice of the Supreme Court: Thurgood Marshall.

1968 Martin Luther King, Jr. is assassinated in Memphis, Tennessee, where he had been supporting the Memphis Sanitation Workers' strike.

1971 In *Swann v. Charlotte-Mecklenburg* the Supreme Court allows for busing, construction changes, and pupil assignment programs to ensure desegregation of public schools.

1971 In *Reed v. Reed* the Supreme Court finds for the first time that the Equal Protection Clause incorporates gender in its coverage.

1973 According to the ruling in *Frontiero v. Richardson,* an Air Force policy that treats dependents' benefits differently, depending on the gender of the personnel covered, violates the Equal Protection Clause.

1973 In *San Antonio Independent School v. Rodriguez* the Court states that the Fourteenth Amendment does not imply a constitutional right to an equal education.

1976 In *Craig v. Boren* the Supreme Court determines that underage drinking laws that distinguish between the genders must be substantially related to an important governmental function.

1976 The Court in *Washington v. Davis* rules that to challenge race-neutral governmental actions that have a discriminatory impact, the plaintiff must demonstrate intent to discriminate.

1978 In *Regents of the University of California v. Bakke* the Court rejects strict quotas but says that educational institutions may use race in addition to other factors in making admissions decisions.

1979 In *Ambach v. Norwick* the Supreme Court holds that the hiring of noncitizens could constitutionally be prohibited from some state jobs.

1981 Sandra Day O'Connor becomes the first woman appointed to the Supreme Court, named by President Ronald Reagan.

1981 Ruling in *Michael M. v. Superior Court of Sonoma County,* the Court finds a compelling governmental interest in treating males and females differently in cases of statutory rape.

1981 The case of *Rostker v. Goldberg* results in the finding that the male-only selective service regulations were constitutional under the Equal Protection Clause.

1982 The Court's ruling in *Plyler v. Doe* ensures access to public education for the children of undocumented aliens.

1982 In *Mississippi University for Women v. Hogan* the Court bans the practice of denying males admission to a state-funded nursing program.

1983 The Supreme Court determines in *City of Richmond v. J. A. Croson* that race-conscious remedies created by governmental bodies must be designed to remedy past harm.

1985 *City of Cleburne v. Cleburne Living Center* places state laws discriminating against the mentally disabled under the lowest standard of equal protection scrutiny, but still decides that the law is unconstitutional.

1989 In *Edgewood Independent School District v. Kirby* the Texas Supreme Court finds that funding education based on property taxes violates the state constitution.

1990 In *Metro Broadcasting v. Federal Communications Commission,* the Court uses a legal standard less stringent than that in *Kirby* to determine whether race may be used in remedial policies.

1991 Upon the retirement of Justice Thurgood Marshall, President George Herbert Walker Bush nominates as his replacement Clarence Thomas, who becomes the second African American to be named to the Supreme Court.

1992 *United States v. Fordice* requires states with dual systems of higher education, even those no longer mandated by state law, ensure that such systems are dismantled.

1993 President Bill Clinton names Ruth Bader Ginsburg to the Supreme Court; she is the second female justice.

1995 The Court requires a heightened standard to evaluate the validity of race-conscious policies in *Adarand Constructors v. Pena.*

1996 In *Romer v. Evans* the Court finds that a state constitutional amendment prohibiting communities from forbidding discrimination on the basis of sexual preference violates the Equal Protection Clause.

1996 The males-only admissions policy at a public educational institution, Virginia Military Institute, is held to be unconstitutional in *United States v. Virginia.*

2003	In the twin cases of *Grutter v. Bollinger* and *Gratz v. Bollinger* the Court finds that the state did have a compelling interest in fostering diversity in higher education but finds further that all forms of race-conscious admissions programs are not constitutional.
2007	The Court rules in *Parents Involved in Community Schools v. Seattle School District No. 1* that the states' compelling interest in diversity does not apply to primary and secondary education pupil assignment programs.
2009	The first African American president of the United States, Barack Obama, is inaugurated. He appoints Sonia Sotomayor to the Court, the third woman, and the first Latino to serve in such a position.
2010	President Obama appoints Elena Kagan to the Supreme Court as the fourth female Associate Justice.
2013	The Supreme Court finds in *United States v. Windsor* that § 3 of the federal Defense of Marriage Act is unconstitutional.
2015	In *Obergefell v. Hodges* the Supreme Court found the Due Process and Equal Protection Clauses guarantee same-sex couples a right to marry.
2016	The Supreme Court in *Fisher v. University of Texas* decided that admission officials can consider race as one factor among others in constructing a more diverse college student body.

Fourteenth Amendment, Section 1:

All persons born or naturalized in the United States, and subject to the jurisdiction thereof, are citizens of the United States and of the state wherein they reside. No state shall make or enforce any law which shall abridge the privileges or immunities of citizens of the United States; nor shall any state deprive any person of life, liberty, or property, without due process of law; nor deny to any person within its jurisdiction the equal protection of the laws.

INTRODUCTION

The delegates to the Constitutional Convention of 1787 chose to ensure and strengthen a national government rather than address the matter of slavery, a source of division among the various state delegations. Despite this choice, the issue resulted in three important compromises prior to ratification. The Three-fifths Clause of Article I, Section 2, provided that both representation in the U.S. House of Representatives—otherwise apportioned according to population—and direct taxes would be determined by counting those enslaved (for whom a euphemism was used) as three-fifths of a person, thus advantaging the slave states in their representation in Congress. Section 9 of Article I prohibited Congress from limiting the importation of slaves until 1808. Article IV, Section 2, generally called the Fugitive Slave Clause, further required states to return individuals who fled their "Service or Labour in one State" to "the Party to whom such Service or Labour may be due." The Constitution did not provide a definition of national citizenship. As a consequence, the Court was able to state in *Dred Scott v. Sandford* (19 How. 393, 1857) that blacks were not, and could not become, U.S. citizens, even if individual states granted them citizenship.

Citizenship, according to the majority opinion of Chief Justice Roger B. Taney, was defined by the founding documents of the nation, especially the Declaration of Independence and the Constitution, as well as in the records of the debates at the Constitutional Convention. These writings excluded African Americans from citizenship, according to Taney, based on their race, not on the institution of slavery.

> The legislation of the States therefore shows, in a manner not to be mistaken, the inferior and subject condition of that race at the time the Constitution was adopted, and long afterwards, . . . and it is hardly consistent with the respect due to these States, to suppose that they regarded at that time, as fellow-citizens and members of the sovereignty, a class of beings whom they had thus stigmatized; . . . and upon whom they had impressed such deep and enduring marks of inferiority and degradation; or, that when they met in convention to form the Constitution, they looked upon them as portion of their constituents, or designed to include them in the provisions so carefully inserted for the security and protection of the liberties and rights of their citizens. It cannot be supposed that they intended to secure to them rights, and privileges, and rank, in the new political body throughout the Union, which every one of them denied within the limits of its own dominion. More especially, it cannot be believed that the large slaveholding States regarded them as included in the citizens, or would have consented to a Constitution which might compel them to receive them in that character from another State.

One result of *Dred Scott* was to securely place citizenship on a racial foundation, not one based on condition of servitude. One of the post-Civil War amendments, the Fourteenth Amendment, was ratified in 1868; its opening sentence was designed to overturn *Dred Scott's* racial definition of citizenship, but interpretations of other segments of this amendment evolved in many directions. For example, in *Yick Wo v. Hopkins*, 118 U.S. 356 (1886), the Supreme Court ruled that the Fourteenth Amendment applied to all, regardless of race, color, or nationality. In *Hernandez v. Texas*, 347 U.S. 475 (1954), the Supreme Court determined that the Fourteenth Amendment's Equal Protection Clause applies to Mexican Americans and, by extension, to citizens of all races.

The Fourteenth Amendment has also been understood as requiring states to guarantee their citizens the due process of law, the privileges and immunities of citizenship, and the equal protection of the laws. Over time, through the process of selective incorporation, the Supreme Court has determined that the states must also provide the majority of the Bill of Rights guarantees to its citizens. The "Enforcement Clause" (Section 5 of the Fourteenth Amendment) grants that "The Congress shall have the power to enforce, by appropriate legislation, the provisions of this article." While the written meaning of the Fourteenth Amendment may seem quite clear, this has not been the case in the century and half since ratification. The extent of the federal government's powers to enforce state compliance has been continuously challenged (see volume I, Chapter V, "Federalism"); the determination of the scope of the Bill of Rights incorporated under the Fourteenth Amendment has regularly engaged the Court (see Chapter I, this volume); and the appropriateness and constitutionality of state action relative to racial protections have been evaluated (see Chapter XI, "State Action"). Continuously, the Court has struggled to identify which groups are included under the Equal Protection Clause and how stringently their rights must be observed. From Justice Miller's observation in the *Slaughterhouse Cases* (16 Wall. 36, 1873) that "[w]e doubt very much whether any action of a state not directed by way of discrimination against the Negroes as a class, or on account of their race, will ever be held to come within the purview of this provision," through the years when corporations were the chief beneficiaries of this guarantee against unreasonable classification and discrimination, to the late twentieth century when racial and gender disparity challenges dominated under this provision, and in the present, when persons in previously ignored categories are asserting group identity, the Court has wound a weary way.

The inscription on the frieze of the Supreme Court building, "Equal Justice Under Law," encapsulates the equal protection provision of the Fourteenth Amendment. By requiring that "no state shall deny to any person within its jurisdiction the equal protection of the law," the Equal Protection Clause of the Fourteenth Amendment forces courts to determine when state laws, distinguishing among classes of people, violate the rights of individuals. Contemporary interpretations of this constitutional amendment perceive it as meaning that all are equal in the eyes of the law and that characteristics such as race, gender, wealth, or age can rarely enter into statutory determinations.

Yet laws cannot treat people identically; consequently, certain types of classification remain valid under the Equal Protection Clause. For example, states often designate lower speed limits for drivers of tractor-trailer trucks than for drivers of cars because trucks are heavier and require longer stopping distances. Although the law is not supposed to treat persons who are in approximately the same circumstances differently from one another, it may utilize classifications of persons based on property, location, or occupations to achieve governmental objectives. Thus women, under certain circumstances, may be treated differently in the law from men in order to make the genders more equal. Reasonable distinctions under law can be made constitutionally. One of the struggles of the Court has been the determination of tests and standards to allow lower courts and states to determine when these classifications are constitutional.

This chapter is divided into four segments, covering the following areas: race and equal protection, gender and equal protection, affirmative action, and other classifications. The primary issue surrounding the issue of race in equal protection law has been determining the nature and meaning of equality. In light of the origins of the Fourteenth Amendment, it is not surprising that a large number, perhaps most, of the related constitutional decisions have focused on the status of African Americans. It has been state laws that have primarily regulated such contested areas as criminal court procedures, property rights and protections, transportation, education, and the just administration of the laws. In all these areas the courts would be forced to carve through the legal remnants of slavery and the perpetuation of racial bigotry to determine when the Fourteenth Amendment applied. Increasing the difficulty of the task were early Court precedents limiting the scope of the Fourteenth Amendment. Passed to prohibit states from discriminating against their own citizens, the Supreme Court quickly determined that the new constitutional provision did not require states to protect black citizens from the animus and discrimination of private white citizens. Not until the case of *Heart of Atlanta Motel v. United States* (379 U.S. 241, 1964) would the Court interpret other constitutional provisions (e.g., the Commerce Clause, Article I, § 8, ¶ 3) as empowering the federal government to protect citizens from private racial discrimination.

In the arena of gender and equal protection law, the primary concern of the Supreme Court has been identifying the appropriate **judicial standard** to use in evaluating the constitutionality of a challenged law. Because the Constitution has never explicitly distinguished between men and women (except in section 2 of the Fourteenth Amendment), the historical challenge would be one of correcting assumptions and stereotypes regarding inclusion. State laws, on the other hand, were built on the common law understanding of women as the property of their male relations and thus clearly distinguished between men and women. The argument that such classifications are rooted in biology and the need to protect the socially, economically, and physically more vulnerable females was difficult to challenge constitutionally. In addition, racial and economic prejudices, as well as political conflicts, would make it difficult for women to assert full political rights.

Once women were understood to be included under the Equal Protection Clause, in the 1971 case of *Reed v. Reed* (404 U.S. 71), the Supreme Court spent the next several decades wading through state legislation that had been challenged because it made distinctions between men and women. In determining which of these laws were constitutionally appropriate, the Court found itself continuously questioning the constitutional tests regarding legitimate statutory distinctions between men and women. Were women more comparable to African Americans, for whom statutory distinctions from dominant whites could rarely be legitimate, or more like the drivers of cars and tractor-trailer trucks, with respect to whom the interests of society were so different that separate legal provisions were necessary to regulate the two populations?

This quandary of the Court points to an ongoing issue related to equal protection and race and gender. What obligations does the state government have to ensure equality for its citizens? Is the constitutional requirement for the law to treat everyone the same (formal equality), or must the law recognize historical, social, and economic barriers to equality and compensate parties claiming to have been damaged (substantive equality)? Affirmative action is an attempt to prove substantive equality. Recognizing a history of discrimination both statutorily and personally against white women and against people of color of both genders, affirmative action is the deliberate inclusion of members of these groups, by employers and institutions, through hiring, promotions, and admissions processes. Private institutions and companies can voluntarily assume affirmative action policies; such programs become constitutionally controversial only when state and federal governments require similar compliance. This is because when some people are explicitly included, some who have historically benefited from exclusionary policies now must compete for inclusion. In addition, the very equal protection claims on which affirmative action is based can be perceived as no longer protecting white males. For the Supreme Court, the pivotal question to be answered is whether there is a constitutional distinction between the racial and gender statutory classifications designed to include citizens in society (**benevolent legislation**) and those crafted to exclude (**invidious legislation**).

The final section of the chapter examines how groups identified by factors other than race and gender are defined and protected by the Equal Protection Clause. As society recognizes the unique attributes of various self-identified groups, and acknowledges a national history of animus and discrimination toward people the dominant culture has framed as "other," the Supreme Court has had to determine where in the Equal Protection Clause equality is found. For instance, when is it appropriate to distinguish children, the mentally ill, the indigent, the aged, and the mentally or physically handicapped under state and federal law? While distinctions based on race and fundamental constitutional rights (e.g., freedom of religious exercise) are given the highest scrutiny under the Constitution, and gender is given only an intermediate level of protection, there was little guidance regarding the constitutional protection guaranteed other groups. In the latter half of the twentieth century, the Supreme Court proved to be very reluctant to provide a high level of protection to these groups of individuals, even when they met the established constitutional tests. Instead, the Court insisted on guaranteeing the ability of state and federal legislatures to provide the protections perceived to be necessary for these classes of citizens.

Race

Belatedly, the prediction of Justice Miller in the *Slaughterhouse Cases* has been realized, and the interpretation of the equal protection provision in relation to racial matters has become a primary concern of the Court. The scope of these cases has been broad—ranging from court procedure, through property rights, to transportation and education, and the just administration of the laws. One complication in the interpretation of equal protection has been that the early definitions of equality were framed against a long history of slavery based on race. In a judicial system based on **precedent,** legal protections and definitions evolve slowly; accordingly, the pace of evolution in equal protection jurisprudence has often been glacial. The fundamental contradiction of the claims of the Declaration of Independence and the Constitution with the racist treatment of African Americans and other peoples of color, despite Chief Justice Taney's interpretation in *Dred Scott v. Sandford* (19 How. 393, 1857), has throughout our history produced unresolved conflicts for the Supreme Court and the citizens of the nation.

The claims of the Declaration of Independence for the equality of men based on their natural, God-ordained rights of liberty ring hollow when examined in the context of the race-based **chattel slavery** society to which it was addressed. Frederick Douglass, in his famous 1852 speech "The Meaning of July Fourth for the Negro," picks up on these inherent contradictions as revealed in the lives of both free and enslaved blacks.

> Whether we turn to the declarations of the past, or to the professions of the present, the conduct of the nation seems equally hideous and revolting. America is false to the past, false to the present, and solemnly binds herself to be false to the future. Standing with God and the crushed and bleeding slave on this occasion, I will, in the name of humanity which is outraged, in the name of liberty which

> is fettered, in the name of the constitution and the Bible which are disregarded and trampled upon, dare to call in question and to denounce, with all the emphasis I can command, everything that serves to perpetuate slavery—the great sin and shame of America!

This speech clearly articulates the political, economic, and legal realities of blacks in America—they were not citizens. This status, carefully justified in Chief Justice Taney's opinion in *Dred Scott*, was not because of the economic system of slavery; it was because of a race-based structure that permeated all aspects of American life, affecting both free and enslaved blacks.

After the Civil War and the 1868 ratification of the Fourteenth Amendment, the Radical Republicans in Congress passed a number of federal statutes designed to ameliorate the impact of the newly endorsed Black Codes, state statutes designed to regulate the lives of black citizens. South Carolina and Mississippi, in 1865, passed two of the earliest codes. The states justified these laws as protecting the rights of the new African-American citizens to marry, own property, and negotiate contracts. In practice, however, these codes were very like the pre–Civil War slave codes: they controlled black mobility and labor, as well as race relations.

In response to the Black Codes, the formation of the Ku Klux Klan in 1865, and growing violence against the newly freed people, Congress passed a series of federal statutes collectively designated the Enforcement Acts. The Ku Klux Klan Act of 1871, which was designed to stop private violence against blacks, criminalized conspiracies to deny citizens their civil rights. Twelve years later, in *United States v. Harris* (106 U.S. 626, 1883), the Supreme Court determined that the focus of the Fourteenth Amendment was state activity against American citizens, not the violation of the rights of former slaves by private citizens acting either collectively or individually. Because the amendment's Enforcement Clause was the only authority the federal government had to infringe upon state regulations toward its own citizens, the Ku Klux Klan Act was gutted by the decision. According to *Harris*, states had to protect citizens from other citizens, and most states were not willing to protect their black citizens from violence and infringement of their rights by whites.

The Civil Rights Act of 1875 can be seen as a forerunner of the Civil Rights Act of 1964. The nineteenth-century act prohibited discrimination against individuals because of their race in public accommodations, such as railroad cars, hotels, restaurants, and theaters. In the *Civil Rights Cases* (109 U.S. 3, 1883), the Supreme Court, as in *Harris*, found the 1875 act to be unconstitutional because the Fourteenth Amendment is directed at state action, not at private behavior that violates civil rights. According to the decision, if a state refuses to protect its citizens, there is nothing the federal government can do about it and no remedy available from the Constitution. It would be eighty-one years before the courts or Congress would redress this decision by allowing federal prohibition of private acts of discrimination protected by state law. Subsequently, one of the only surviving elements of these laws include a segment of the Civil Rights Act of 1870—42 U.S.C. § 1983—which allows the federal government to criminally pursue individuals such as county sheriffs or state police officers who, while acting under "color of law," violate citizens' civil rights.

By 1896, many states had adopted Jim Crow laws, which specifically mandated racial segregation. These laws led to segregation in transportation, schools, restaurants, and graveyards. It affected drinking fountains, rest rooms, and even the Bible on which witnesses in courts were asked to swear. In *Plessy v. Ferguson* (163 U.S. 537, 1896) the Supreme Court had to decide if a Louisiana state law requiring African Americans to be seated in a separate railway car from whites violated the Equal Protection Clause of the Fourteenth Amendment. A group of black citizens calling themselves the Citizens' Committee to Test the Constitutionality of the Separate Car Law was organized to generate this action against the Louisville and Nashville Railroad Company as a test case. In a 7–1 decision, the Court found that such state segregation laws were constitutional under the Equal Protection Clause of the Fourteenth Amendment.

The Court would not use the Equal Protection Clause to prevent racially targeted legislation until the mid-twentieth century. In the World War II case of *Korematsu v. United States* (323 U.S. 214, 1944), the Supreme Court upheld Presidential Executive Order 9066, which authorized the military to exclude citizens of Japanese background from regions that were deemed to be essential for the national defense because they were potential targets for espionage by Japan. The majority found this exercise of presidential power to be constitutional on the ground of military necessity and denied that its effects unconstitutionally targeted a particular racial group; the dissent by Justice Murphy is now seen as prescient in its recognition of the racism underlying the decision. The U.S. government has now admitted that its wartime policy was flawed and has made reparations to the Japanese Americans who lost property because of it. The *Korematsu* decision is much more thoroughly discussed in Chapter I, where the case is excerpted.

By the early twentieth century, the form of state-mandated segregation known as Jim Crow, and approved in *Plessy v. Ferguson,* was ensconced across the South, and segregation was also a common practice throughout much of the North. In the intervening years, the "separate but equal" principle was applied to a variety of cases in the areas of education, public spaces, housing, and public accommodations. By 1905, however, boycotts of public transportation by black residents had been documented in every state of the former Confederacy and in virtually every major southern metropolis. Although unsuccessful in stopping state-sanctioned segregation, these acts of collective action were the precursors of the Montgomery bus boycott in 1955, from which Rosa Parks and Martin Luther King Jr. rose to public visibility. It would take the decision in *Brown v. Board of Education* (347 U.S. 483) in 1954 to overturn *Plessy's* interpretation of the Equal Protection Clause. Later, statutory acts provided change in the laws for public accommodation and transportation.

In the mid-twentieth century the Supreme Court, under relentless pressure from the Legal Defense Fund (LDF) of the National Association for the Advancement of Colored People (NAACP), began addressing state-mandated school segregation. The LDF had developed a legal strategy of challenging primary school systems and institutions of higher education on the basis of proof that the education provided to blacks was not equivalent to that received by whites. LDF strategists had assumed that to truly equalize the two systems would bankrupt state governments.

In a series of cases, beginning with *Missouri ex rel. Gaines v. Canada* (305 U.S. 337, 1938), the Supreme Court became increasingly insistent that the "separate but equal" formula required greater equality between segregated institutions, if not less separateness, than previously assumed. For instance, in the two 1950 cases of *Sweatt v. Painter* (339 U.S. 629) and *McLaurin v. Oklahoma State Regents* (339 U.S. 637), the Supreme Court considered whether the Equal Protection Clause limited the ability of a state to distinguish between graduate and professional students of different races in its public universities. Howard Sweatt had been rejected from the University of Texas Law School on racial grounds and, under state court order, Texas created a new law school for him; Sweatt argued that a nascent law school that was understaffed and underfunded could not compete with the education provided by the established legal program at the prestigious University of Texas. The Supreme Court held that the facilities were not equal, and the state was ordered to provide "equal protection" by admitting Sweatt to the University of Texas. Despite this and similar advances in equal protection jurisprudence, mandated segregation in and of itself was still not considered to be violative of equal protection.

Segregation's legitimacy under the Equal Protection Clause would not be demolished until 1954 in *Brown v. Board of Education* (347 U.S. 483), one of the most momentous Supreme Court decisions of the twentieth century. This case made it clear that *Plessy v. Ferguson's* interpretation of the Equal Protection Clause of the Fourteenth Amendment—which allowed mandated segregation as long as parallel facilities were provided for both races—was no longer acceptable. Several elements distinguish the judicial opinion and its justification, including the absence of precedents and the use of sociological evidence. Two points in connection with *Brown* (and as borne out in subsequent cases) need emphasis: (1) that the Court did not mandate integration but simply outlawed segregation on a racial basis, and (2) that the segregation thus outlawed had been based *solely* on race.

The Court emphasized the second point repeatedly in the course of the opinion in *Brown*. In later cases the Court held that integration must be positively sought.

The 1954 *Brown* decision, and the ruling known as *Brown II* (349 U.S. 294, 1955), which soon followed, evolved from five challenges stemming from the poor quality of segregated public schools in school districts in Kansas, South Carolina, Virginia, Delaware, and the District of Columbia. While the four states' cases could be decided under the Fourteenth Amendment's Equal Protection Clause, the District of Columbia—which is not a state—was not protected by that clause but by the Due Process Clause of the Fifth Amendment

The Court's decision in *Bolling v. Sharpe* (347 U.S. 497, 1954), following that in *Hurd v. Hodge* (334 U.S. 24, 1948), has been regarded as nationalizing the Equal Protection Clause of the Fourteenth Amendment in that the Due Process Clause of the Fifth Amendment is now broadly interpreted to include the basic concepts involved in "equal protection." As *Bolling v. Sharpe* demonstrates, in certain instances the Due Process Clause can be used as an effective substitute for the Equal Protection Clause. After the *Brown* and *Bolling* decisions in 1954, the Court held a hearing in 1955 and handed down a "mandate decision" to implement its original judgment. Specifically, in *Brown II*, the Court decided that lower federal courts would be responsible for ensuring full compliance with the *Brown I* ruling. They were given the authority to consider

> problems related to administration, arising from physical condition of the school plant, the school transportation system, personnel, revision of school districts and attendance areas into compact units to achieve a system of determining admission to the public schools on a nonracial basis, and revision of local laws and regulations which may be necessary in solving the foregoing problems.

This authority of the federal judges and the intransigence of the state policymakers resulted in a long parade of school desegregation and integration cases. Initially, these Supreme Court cases involved desegregation: the demolishing of state laws and policies that prevented students from attending schools of their choice. Later, there were challenges to various court- and schoolboard-designed programs to ensure that students attended racially mixed (integrated) schools. The line between desegregation and integration is inherently blurred.

Busing school children had a long history, especially in rural districts. It developed a new connotation after the 1971 case of *Swann v. Charlotte-Mecklenburg Board of Education* (402 U.S. 1), which confronted the scope of authority of the federal judges and the responsibility of school districts in implementing *Brown I.* A large administrative entity, the Charlotte-Mecklenburg school district in North Carolina only had 29 percent African American students, but two-thirds of them attended schools that were more than 99 percent African American. Under the supervision of a federal court-appointed expert, the district created a new plan that included new school construction decisions and student assignment programs, including the use of busing. A unanimous Court determined that the techniques proposed in the plan could be legitimate means of integrating school systems. The South was not the only region that experienced such legal supervision. In the first northern school decision case, *Keyes v. School District No. 1, Denver, Colorado* (413 U.S. 189, 1973), the Court determined that evidence of deliberate discrimination through policies and practice, even if not lawfully compelled, can demonstrate a finding of *de jure* discrimination in a school system.

Keyes was soon followed by the many more school busing conflicts of the 1970s and the development of a newer phenomenon of "white flight," in which wealthier white residents simply moved from districts that had mandated desegregation to suburban districts under no such compulsion. The battle for desegregation through busing barely outlasted the decade. The dual decisions of *Milliken v. Bradley (Milliken I)* (418 U.S. 717, 1974) and *Milliken v. Bradley (Milliken II)* (433 U.S. 267, 1977) resulted in limiting metropolitan busing for the purpose of compensating for white flight. In the first ruling, which permitted only school segregation remedies that were narrowly tailored to fit a given violation and designed to correct the unconstitutional condition, Chief Justice Burger, writing for the majority, stated:

> Before the boundaries of separate and autonomous school districts may be set aside by consolidating the separate units for remedial purposes or by imposing a cross-district remedy, it must first be shown that there has been a constitutional violation within one district that produces a significant segregative effect in another district. Specifically, it must be shown that racially discriminatory acts of the state or local school districts, or of a single school district have been a substantial cause of inter-district segregation. Thus, an inter-district remedy might be in order where the racially discriminatory acts of one or more school districts caused racial segregation in an adjacent district, or where district lines have been deliberately drawn on the basis of race. In such circumstances, an inter-district remedy would be appropriate to eliminate the inter-district segregation directly caused by the constitutional violation. Conversely, without an inter-district violation and inter-district effect, there is no constitutional wrong calling for an inter-district remedy (418 U.S. 744–745).

These decisions clearly limited the power of federal judges to construct plans individually crafted to eliminate the remnants of de facto and de jure segregation "root and branch." As Justice Marshall noted in his dissent in *Milliken I*,

> After 20 years of small, often difficult steps toward that great end, the Court today takes a giant step backwards. Notwithstanding a record showing widespread and pervasive racial segregation in the educational system provided by the State of Michigan for children in Detroit, this Court holds that the District Court was powerless to require the State to remedy its constitutional violation in any meaningful fashion. Ironically purporting to base its result on the principle that the scope of the remedy in a desegregation case should be determined by the nature and the extent of the constitutional violation, the Court's answer is to provide no remedy at all for the violation proved in this case, thereby guaranteeing that Negro children in Detroit will receive the same separate and inherently unequal education in the future as they have been unconstitutionally afforded in the past (418 U.S. 782).

Columbus Board of Education v. Penick (443 U.S. 449, 1979) was the last Supreme Court decision that fully empowered a federal district judge, Robert Duncan, to dismantle a district's de jure segregation. By the late 1990s, many schools were still segregated, but cases challenging as inadequate school district efforts to diversify fell under the category of affirmative action case law because such policies were no longer in direct response to state actions that created segregation, but to social and economic forces enforcing segregated housing patterns.

Much of the law preventing employment discrimination falls under Title VII of the Civil Rights Act of 1964; however, the Equal Protection Clause was frequently averred in cases challenging discrimination in the governmental employment. In the case of *Washington v. Davis* (426 U.S. 229, 1976), two African American police officers challenged the District of Columbia Metropolitan Police Department's promotion policy as racially discriminatory. As part of the promotion decision process, the department had used a written personnel test; officers' scores on this test had resulted in the exclusion of a disproportionate number of African Americans from eligibility for promotion. The test, developed by the federal Civil Service Commission, evaluated verbal skills, vocabulary, and reading comprehension. These plaintiffs were able to make an equal protection claim under the Due Process Clause of the Fifth Amendment as a result of *Bolling v. Sharpe*, over twenty years earlier. *Washington v. Davis* established a new requirement—the submission of evidence of discriminatory intent or purpose—for those who would successfully challenge the race neutrality of governmental actions. The impact of this controversial decision is seen in later housing, school desegregation, and voting rights cases. After 1972, when Title VII of the Civil Rights Act of 1964 was amended to apply to governmental employees, employment discrimination cases no longer needed to be brought under the higher standard of the Equal Protection Clause.

In the early 1990s one consequence of centuries of state-mandated discrimination and segregation came before the Court in *United States v. Fordice/Ayers v. Fordice* (505 U.S. 717, 1992). The state of Mississippi maintained a de jure system of segregation in higher education, with five predominantly white public colleges and three historically black public institutions. A group of black citizens initiated a lawsuit in 1975 charging that Mississippi had created and maintained a dual system of higher education. The federal government intervened, finding that the state had not dismantled the dual system, even after the legal obligation to maintain it had been rescinded. This case called into question the role and function of public historically black colleges and universities (HBCU) in a post-segregation society. The Court found that Mississippi had not met its affirmative duty to destroy the dual system, and therefore *Fordice* was remanded to the lower courts for remedial determination. For Mississippi, the problem of supporting twice as many public schools as the population required continued to be a budgetary challenge; but the elimination of the schools established to comprise the sole educational opportunity for black Mississippians was not a political, or practical, option. How can a dual system be completely eliminated, root and branch, in an era of limited resources?

The implications of race and the Equal Protection Clause continue to be important in such arenas as housing discrimination, voting rights and challenges, and in affirmative action claims. Many of these relationships are discussed in other chapters of this volume.

THE DECLARATION OF INDEPENDENCE

1776

This document was approved by the Second Continental Congress on July 4, 1776 to explain why the thirteen North American colonies were revolting against England. The chief author was Thomas Jefferson, a Virginia slaveholder, who would later help found the Democratic-Republican Party and become the nation's third president. In modifying the document, the Continental Congress tempered his original indictment, which blamed American slavery on the English king.

We hold these truths to be self-evident, that all men are created equal, that they are endowed by their Creator with certain unalienable Rights, that among these are Life, Liberty and the pursuit of Happiness. That to secure these rights, Governments are instituted among Men, deriving their just powers from the consent of the governed. That whenever any Form of Government becomes destructive of these ends, it is the Right of the People to alter or to abolish it, and to institute new Government, laying its foundation on such principles and organizing its powers in such form, as to them shall seem most likely to effect their Safety and Happiness. . . .

FREDERICK DOUGLASS, "THE MEANING OF JULY FOURTH FOR THE NEGRO"

Rochester, New York, speech delivered on July 5, 1852

After his escape from slavery as a young man, Frederick Douglass became a noted essayist and orator, as well as the publisher of the *North Star*, an abolitionist newspaper. All his endeavors were directed toward the abolition of slavery in the United States; many of his arguments were directed against the inherent contradictions between the promise of the American Constitution and Declaration of Independence and the realities of life in the United States for both free and enslaved African Americans. One of his best-known speeches, "The Meaning of July Fourth for the Negro," was delivered in Rochester, New York, on July 5, 1852. Douglass later revised the speech and published it as a pamphlet. In 1852 he had been invited to speak about what the Fourth of July means for America's black population, and while the first part of his speech praises what the founding fathers did for this country, his remarks soon moved into a condemnation of the attitude of American society toward slavery.

Fellow-citizens, pardon me, allow me to ask, why am I called upon to speak here today? What have I, or those I represent, to do with your national independence? Are the great principles of political freedom and of natural justice, embodied in that Declaration of Independence, extended to us? and am I, therefore, called upon to bring our humble offering to the national altar, and to confess the benefits and express devout gratitude for the blessings resulting from your independence to us?

But such is not the state of the case. I say it with a sad sense of the disparity between us. I am not included within the pale of glorious anniversary! Your high independence only reveals the immeasurable distance between us. The blessings in which you, this day, rejoice, are not enjoyed in common. The rich inheritance of justice, liberty, prosperity and independence, bequeathed by your fathers, is shared by you, not by me. The sunlight that brought light and healing to you, has brought stripes and death to me. This Fourth July is yours, not mine. You may rejoice, I must mourn. To drag a man in fetters into the grand illuminated temple of liberty, and call upon him to join you in joyous anthems, were inhuman mockery and sacrilegious irony. Do you mean, citizens, to mock me, by asking me to speak today? If so, there is a parallel to your conduct. And let me warn you that it is dangerous to copy the example of a nation whose crimes, towering up to heaven, were thrown down by the breath of the Almighty, burying that nation in irrevocable ruin! I can today take up the plaintive lament of a peeled and woe-smitten people!

Fellow-citizens, above your national, tumultuous joy, I hear the mournful wail of millions! whose chains, heavy and grievous yesterday, are, today, rendered more intolerable by the jubilee shouts that reach them. If I do forget, if I do not faithfully remember those bleeding children of sorrow this day, "may my right hand forget her cunning, and may my tongue cleave to the roof of my mouth!" To forget them, to pass lightly over their wrongs, and to chime in with the popular theme, would be treason most scandalous and shocking, and would make me a reproach before God and the world. My subject, then, fellow-citizens, is American slavery. I shall see this day and its popular characteristics from the slave's point of view. Standing there identified with the American bondman, making his wrongs mine, I do not hesitate to declare, with all my soul, that the character and conduct of this nation never looked blacker to me than on this 4th of July! Whether we turn to the declarations of the past, or to the professions of the present, the conduct of the nation seems equally hideous and revolting. America is false to the past, false to the present, and solemnly binds herself to be false to the future. Standing with God and the crushed and bleeding slave on this occasion, I will, in the name of humanity which is outraged, in the name of liberty which is fettered, in the name of the constitution and the Bible which are disregarded and trampled upon, dare to call in question and to denounce, with all the emphasis I can command, everything that serves to perpetuate slavery—the great sin and shame of America!

Must I undertake to prove that the slave is a man? That point is conceded already. Nobody doubts it. The slaveholders themselves acknowledge it in the enactment of laws for their government. They acknowledge it when they punish disobedience on the part of the slave. There are seventy-two crimes in the State of Virginia which, if committed by a black man (no matter how ignorant he be), subject him to the punishment of death; while only two of the same crimes will subject a white man to the like punishment. What is this but the acknowledgment that the slave is a moral, intellectual, and responsible being? The manhood of the slave is conceded. It is admitted in the fact that Southern statute books are covered with enactments forbidding, under severe fines and penalties, the teaching of the slave to read or to write. When you can point to any such laws in reference to the beasts of the field, then I may consent to argue the manhood of the slave.

For the present, it is enough to affirm the equal manhood of the Negro race. Is it not astonishing that, while we are ploughing, planting, and reaping, using all kinds of mechanical tools, erecting houses, constructing bridges, building ships, working in metals of brass, iron, copper, silver and gold; that, while we are reading, writing and ciphering, acting as clerks, merchants and secretaries, having among us lawyers, doctors, ministers, poets, authors, editors, orators and teachers; that, while we are engaged in all manner of enterprises common to other men, digging gold in California, capturing the whale in the Pacific, feeding sheep and cattle on the hill-side, living, moving, acting, thinking, planning, living in families as husbands, wives and children, and, above all, confessing and worshipping the Christian's God, and looking hopefully for life and immortality beyond the grave, we are called upon to prove that we are men!

What, to the American slave, is your 4th of July? I answer; a day that reveals to him, more than all other days in the year, the gross injustice and cruelty to which he is the constant victim. To him, your celebration is a sham; your boasted liberty, an unholy license; your national greatness, swelling vanity; your sounds of rejoicing are empty and heartless; your denunciation of tyrants, brass fronted impudence; your shouts of liberty and equality, hollow mockery; your prayers and hymns, your sermons and thanksgivings, with all your religious parade and solemnity, are, to Him, mere bombast, fraud, deception, impiety, and hypocrisy—a thin veil to cover up crimes which would disgrace a nation of savages. There is not a nation on the earth guilty of practices more shocking and bloody than are the people of the United States, at this very hour.

Allow me to say, in conclusion, notwithstanding the dark picture I have this day presented, of the state of the nation, I do not despair of this country. There are forces in operation which must inevitably work the downfall of slavery. "The arm of the Lord is not shortened," and the doom of slavery is certain. I, therefore, leave off where I began, with hope. While drawing encouragement from "the Declaration of Independence," the great principles it contains, and the genius of American Institutions, my spirit is also cheered by the obvious tendencies of the age. Nations do not now stand in the same relation to each other that they did ages ago. No nation can now shut itself up from the surrounding world and trot round in the same old path of its fathers without interference. The time was when such could be done. Long established customs of hurtful character could formerly fence themselves in, and do their evil work with social impunity. Knowledge was then confined and enjoyed by the privileged few, and the multitude walked on in mental darkness. But a change has now come over the affairs of mankind.

PLESSY V. FERGUSON

163 U.S. 537, 3 S.Ct. 18, 41 L.Ed. 256 (1896)

In 1890, the state of Louisiana passed a law that required separate railway carriages for white and black passengers. Homer Plessy, who although of mixed race and could pass as white was identified under the law as an African American, sat in the "Whites Only" car and refused to comply with the conductor's order to move to the "Colored" car. After his forced removal and arrest, Plessy was in a position to challenge the Louisiana law as a violation of the Thirteenth Amendment's abolition of slavery and a violation of his rights under the Fourteenth Amendment. The lower court upheld the constitutionality of the Louisiana law.

Vote: 7–1

JUSTICE BROWN delivered the opinion of the Court.

That [the Louisiana law] does not conflict with the Thirteenth Amendment, which abolished slavery and involuntary servitude, except as a punishment for crime, is too clear for argument. Slavery implies involuntary servitude—a state of bondage; the ownership of mankind as a chattel, or at least the control of the labor and services of one man for the benefit of another, and the absence of a legal right to the disposal of his own person, property and services. . . . [T]his amendment was regarded by the statesmen of that day as insufficient to protect the colored race from certain laws which had been enacted in the Southern States, imposing upon the colored race onerous disabilities and burdens, and curtailing their rights in the pursuit of life, liberty and property to such an extent that their freedom was of little value; and that the Fourteenth Amendment was devised to meet this exigency.

A statute which implies merely a legal distinction between the white and colored races—a distinction which is founded in the color of the two races, and which must always exist so long as white men are distinguished from the other race by color—has no tendency to destroy the legal equality of the two races, or reestablish a state of involuntary servitude.

The object of the [Fourteenth A]mendment was undoubtedly to enforce the absolute equality of the two races before the law, but in the nature of things it could not have been intended to abolish distinctions based upon color, or to enforce social, as distinguished from political equality, or a commingling of the two races upon terms unsatisfactory to either. Laws permitting, and even requiring, their separation in places where they are liable to be brought into contact do not necessarily imply the inferiority of either race to the other, and have been generally, if not universally, recognized as within the competency of the state legislatures in the exercise of their police power.

In the *Civil Rights Cases*, 109 U.S. 3 (1883), it was held that an act of Congress, entitling all persons within the jurisdiction of the United States to the full and equal enjoyment of the accommodations, advantages, facilities and privileges of inns, public conveyances, on land or water, theatres and other places of public amusement, and made applicable to citizens of every race and color, regardless of any previous condition of servitude, was unconstitutional and void, upon the ground that the Fourteenth Amendment was prohibitory upon the States only, and the legislation authorized to be adopted by Congress for enforcing it was not direct legislation on matters respecting which the States were prohibited from making or enforcing certain laws, or doing certain acts, but was corrective legislation, such as might be necessary or proper for counteracting and redressing the effect of such laws or acts.

So far, then, as a conflict with the Fourteenth Amendment is concerned, the case reduces itself to the question whether the statute of Louisiana is a reasonable regulation, and with respect to this there must necessarily be a large discretion on the part of the legislature. In determining the question of reasonableness it is at liberty to act with reference to the established usages, customs and traditions of the people, and with a view to the promotion of their comfort, and the preservation of the public peace and good order. Gauged by this standard, we cannot say that a law which authorizes or even requires the separation of the two races in public conveyances is unreasonable, or more obnoxious to the Fourteenth Amendment than the acts of Congress requiring separate schools for colored children in the District of Columbia, the constitutionality of which does not seem to have been questioned, or the corresponding acts of state legislatures.

We consider the underlying fallacy of the plaintiff's argument to consist in the assumption that the enforced separation of the two races stamps the colored race with a badge of inferiority. If this be so, it is not by reason of anything found in the act, but solely because the colored race chooses to put that construction upon it. . . . Legislation is powerless to eradicate racial instincts or to abolish distinctions based upon physical differences, and the attempt to do so can only result in accentuating the difficulties of the present situation. If the civil and political rights of both races be equal one cannot be inferior to the other civilly or politically. If one race be inferior to the other socially, the Constitution of the United States cannot put them upon the same plane.

The judgment of the court below is, therefore, Affirmed.

JUSTICE HARLAN, dissenting.

[W]e have before us a state enactment that compels, under penalties, the separation of the two races in railroad passenger coaches, and makes it a crime for a citizen of either race to enter a coach that has been assigned to citizens of the other race.

Thus the State regulates the use of a public highway by citizens of the United States solely upon the basis of race.

However apparent the injustice of such legislation may be, we have only to consider whether it is consistent with the Constitution of the United States.

In respect of civil rights, common to all citizens, the Constitution of the United States does not, I think, permit any public authority to know the race of those entitled to be protected in the enjoyment of such rights. Every true man has pride of race, and under appropriate circumstances when the rights of others, his equals before the law, are not to be affected, it is his privilege to express such pride and to take such action based upon it as to him seems proper. But I deny that any legislative body or judicial tribunal may have regard to the race of citizens when the civil rights of those citizens are involved. Indeed, such legislation, as that here in question, is inconsistent not only with that equality of rights which pertains to citizenship, National and State, but with the personal liberty enjoyed by everyone within the United States.

The Thirteenth Amendment does not permit the withholding or the deprivation of any right necessarily inhering in freedom. It not only struck down the institution of slavery as previously existing in the United States, but it prevents the imposition of any burdens or disabilities that constitute badges of slavery or servitude. It decreed universal civil freedom in this country. . . . But that amendment having been found inadequate to the protection of the rights of those who had been in slavery, it was followed by the Fourteenth Amendment, which added greatly to the dignity and glory of American citizenship, and to the security of personal liberty. . . . These two amendments, if enforced according to their true intent and meaning, will protect all the civil rights that pertain to freedom and citizenship. Finally, and to the end that no citizen should be denied, on account of his race, the privilege of participating in the political control of his country, it was declared by the Fifteenth Amendment that "the right of citizens of the United States to vote shall not be denied or abridged by the United States or by any State on account of race, color or previous condition of servitude."

It was said in argument that the statute of Louisiana does not discriminate against either race, but prescribes a rule applicable alike to white and colored citizens. But this argument does not meet the difficulty. Every one knows that the statute in question had its origin in the purpose, not so much to exclude white persons from railroad cars occupied by blacks, as to exclude colored people from coaches occupied by or assigned to white persons. The fundamental objection . . . to the statute is that it interferes with the personal freedom of citizens. If a white man and a black man choose to occupy the same public conveyance on a public highway, it is their right to do so, and no government, proceeding alone on grounds of race, can prevent it without infringing the personal liberty of each.

The white race deems itself to be the dominant race in this country. And so it is, in prestige, in achievements, in education, in wealth and in power. So, I doubt not, it will continue to be for all time, if it remains true to its great heritage and holds fast to the principles of constitutional liberty. But in view of the Constitution, in the eye of the law, there is in this country no superior, dominant, ruling class of citizens. There is no caste here. Our Constitution is color-blind, and neither knows nor tolerates classes among citizens. In respect of civil rights, all citizens are equal before the law. The humblest is the peer of the most powerful. The law regards man as man, and takes no account of his surroundings or of his color when his civil rights as guaranteed by the supreme law of the land are involved. It is, therefore, to be regretted that this high tribunal, the final expositor of the fundamental law of the land, has reached the conclusion that it is competent for a State to regulate the enjoyment by citizens of their civil rights solely upon the basis of race.

In my opinion, the judgment this day rendered will, in time, prove to be quite as pernicious as the decision made by this tribunal in the *Dred Scott,* 19 How. 393 (1856), case.

The arbitrary separation of citizens, on the basis of race, while they are on a public highway, is a badge of servitude wholly inconsistent with the civil freedom and the equality before the law established by the Constitution. It cannot be justified upon any legal grounds.

FOR DISCUSSION

What does the exclusion of black "nurses attending children of the other race" written into the Louisiana Separate Cars Act clarify regarding the function of the law? Outside of *Plessy*, can the mandated separation of races ever be constitutional under the Equal Protection Clause? Why or why not?

RELATED CASES

***Hall v. DeCuir:* 95 U.S. 485 (1878).**

A Louisiana statute passed during the Reconstruction period prohibited segregation on public carriers. The Court held that the state had improperly invaded a field reserved for Congress, since the matter required uniformity of practice to avoid burdening interstate commerce.

***Chiles v. Chesapeake and Ohio Railway Company:* 218 U.S. 71 (1910).**

Upheld a Kentucky law mandating segregation on interstate trains in Kentucky.

***McCabe v. Atchison, Topeka and Santa Fe Railway Co.:* 235 U.S. 151 (1914).**

An Oklahoma statute that permitted railroads to provide Pullman and dining cars for the exclusive use of whites while not providing them on demand for African Americans was not affording to all customers the "substantial equality" required by the Interstate Commerce Act.

***Mitchell v. United States:* 313 U.S. 80 (1941).**

Denial of Pullman accommodations to African Americans is unjust discrimination under the Interstate Commerce Act, as well as contrary to the substantial equality demanded by the Fourteenth Amendment.

***Morgan v. Virginia:* 328 U.S. 373 (1946).**

A state statute requiring segregation on all buses, both interstate and intrastate, was held invalid. Seating arrangements on interstate buses must be governed by a uniform rule to avoid imposing a burden on interstate commerce.

***Gayle v. Browder:* 352 U.S. 903 (1956).**

An ordinance of the City of Montgomery and an Alabama statute that required segregation on intrastate buses was held to be contrary to the Equal Protection and Due Process clauses of the Fourteenth Amendment. The Montgomery bus boycott was initiated to challenge this form of racial discrimination; respondents Browder and four other African American women had registered complaints against the city bus system.

SWEATT V. PAINTER

39 U.S. 629, 70 S.Ct. 848, 94 L.Ed. 1114 (1950)

Herbert Sweatt, an African American applied for admission to the University of Texas Law School and was rejected on the basis of his race. At the time, Texas had no law school open to blacks. The Texas state courts had earlier required the creation of a law school that blacks could attend, but the contemplated institution would not have offered the facilities or the staff available at the state law school. Sweatt continued his appeals on the grounds that the separate law school violated his equal protection rights; the Texas courts did not agree.

Vote: 9–0

CHIEF JUSTICE VINSON delivered the opinion of the Court.

This case and *McLaurin v. Oklahoma State Regents*, 339 U.S. 637 (1950), present different aspects of this general question: To what extent does the Equal Protection Clause of the Fourteenth Amendment limit the power of a state to distinguish between students of different races in professional and graduate education in a state university?

The University of Texas Law School, from which petitioner was excluded, was staffed by a faculty of sixteen full-time and three part-time professors, some of whom are nationally recognized authorities in their field. Its student body numbered 850. The library contained over 65,000 volumes. Among the other facilities available to the students were a law review, moot court facilities, scholarship funds, and Order of the Coif affiliation. The school's alumni occupy the most distinguished positions in the private practice of the law and in the public life of the State. It may properly be considered one of the nation's ranking law schools.

The law school for Negroes which was to have opened in February, 1947, would have had no independent faculty or library. The teaching was to be carried on by four members of the University of Texas Law School faculty, who were to maintain their offices at the University of Texas while teaching at both institutions. Few of the 10,000 volumes ordered for the library had arrived; nor was there any full-time librarian. The school lacked accreditation.

Since the trial of this case, respondents report the opening of a law school at the Texas State University for Negroes. It is apparently on the road to full accreditation. It has a faculty of five full-time professors; a student body of 23; a library of some 16,500 volumes serviced by a full-time staff; a practice court and legal aid association; and one alumnus who has become a member of the Texas Bar.

Whether the University of Texas Law School is compared with the original or the new law school for Negroes, we cannot find substantial equality in the educational opportunities offered white and Negro law students by the State. In terms of number of the faculty, variety of courses and opportunity for specialization, size of the student body, scope of the library, availability of law review and similar activities, the University of Texas Law School is superior. What is more important, the University of Texas Law School possesses to a far greater degree those qualities which are incapable of objective measurement but which make for greatness in a law school.

Such qualities, to name but a few, include reputation of the faculty, experience of the administration, position and influence of the alumni, standing in the community, traditions and prestige. It is difficult to believe that one who had a free choice between these law schools would consider the question close.

The law school to which Texas is willing to admit petitioner excludes from its student body members of the racial groups which number 85% of the population of the State and include most of the lawyers, witnesses, jurors, judges and other officials with whom petitioner will inevitably be dealing when he becomes a member of the Texas Bar. With such a substantial and significant segment of society excluded, we cannot conclude that the education offered petitioner is substantially equal to that which he would receive if admitted to the University of Texas Law School.

It may be argued that excluding petitioner from that school is no different from excluding white students from the new law school. This contention overlooks realities. It is unlikely that a member of a group so decisively in the majority, attending a school with rich traditions and prestige which only a history of consistently maintained excellence could command, would claim that the opportunities afforded him for legal education were unequal to those held open to petitioner. That such a claim, if made, would be dishonored by the State, is no answer. "Equal protection of the laws is not achieved through indiscriminate imposition of inequalities." *Shelley v. Kraemer*, 334 U.S. 1, 22 (1948).

This Court has stated Unanimously that "The State must provide [legal education] for [petitioner] in conformity with the equal protection clause of the Fourteenth Amendment and provide it as soon as it does for applicants of any other group." *Sipuel v. Board of Regents*, 332 U.S. 631, 633 (1948). In *Missouri ex rel. Gaines v. Canada*, 305 U.S. 337, 351 (1938), the Court, speaking through Chief Justice Hughes, declared that "petitioner's right was a personal one. It was as an individual that he was entitled to the equal protection of the laws, and the State was bound to furnish him within its borders facilities for legal education substantially equal to those which the State there afforded for persons of the white race, whether or not other negroes sought the same opportunity." These are the only cases in this Court which present the issue of the constitutional validity of race distinctions in state-supported graduate and professional education.

In accordance with these cases, petitioner may claim his full constitutional right: legal education equivalent to that offered by the State to students of other races. Such education is not available to him in a separate law school as offered by the State.

We hold that the Equal Protection Clause of the Fourteenth Amendment requires that petitioner be admitted to the University of Texas Law School.

Reversed.

FOR DISCUSSION

How does the definition of equal protection change between *Plessy v. Ferguson* and *Sweatt v. Painter*? How might this evolution of equal protection jurisprudence be explained?

RELATED CASES

***Cumming v. Richmond County Board of Education:* 175 U.S. 528 (1899).**

A Georgia school board's discontinuance of a black high school while leaving undisturbed the high school for whites was held valid on the basis of lack of county finances. The Court held that closing the white school would not help the African Americans. Further, private schools were available for African Americans at no additional cost to them. Finally, the Court said, since education is primarily a state matter, there should be intervention only when constitutional rights are clearly violated.

***Berea College v. Kentucky:* 211 U.S. 45 (1908).**

Because of its power to control corporations, a state may forbid a private school from integrating its student body.

***Gong Lum v. Rice:* 275 U.S. 78 (1927).**

The Court held that it was not denial of equal protection to require a Chinese student to attend a black school instead of a white school.

***Missouri ex rel. Gaines v. Canada:* 305 U.S. 337 (1938).**

A state cannot exclude African Americans from its law school by offering to pay their tuition at law schools in neighboring states. The Court held that a state can guarantee equal protection only where its laws operate, within its own jurisdiction. The contention of Gaines, an African American, against S. W. Canada, registrar of the University of Missouri, was upheld.

***Sipuel v. Board of Regents of the University of Oklahoma:* 332 U.S. 631 (1948).**

An African American woman was held to be denied equal protection when her application for admission to the law school of the University of Oklahoma was rejected.

***McLaurin v. Oklahoma State Regents:* 339 U.S. 637 (1950).**

Segregated practices in a graduate school requiring McLaurin's separation from other students in classrooms, library, and cafeteria have the effect of denying equal protection. They "impair and inhibit [McLaurin's] ability to study, to engage in discussions and exchange views with other students, and, in general, to learn his profession."

BROWN V. BOARD OF EDUCATION

347 U.S. 483, 74 S.Ct. 686, 98 L.Ed. 873 (1954)

Plaintiffs from Kansas, South Carolina, Virginia, and Delaware challenged their segregated public schools as a violation of the Fourteenth Amendments guarantee of equal protection of the laws. In each of these states, the district court applied *Plessy v. Ferguson's* "separate but equal" doctrine and found the segregated schools constitutional. In Delaware, the state supreme court affirmed the "separate but equal" doctrine but ordered plaintiffs admitted to white schools because the white and black schools were not equal.

Vote: 9–0

CHIEF JUSTICE WARREN delivered the opinion of the Court.

These cases come to us from the States of Kansas, South Carolina, Virginia, and Delaware. They are premised on different facts and different local conditions, but a common legal question justifies their consideration together in this consolidated opinion.

The plaintiffs contend that segregated public schools are not "equal" and cannot be made "equal," and that hence they are deprived of the equal protection of the laws. Because of the obvious importance of the question presented, the Court took jurisdiction. Argument was heard in the 1952 Term, and reargument was heard this Term on certain questions propounded by the Court.

Reargument was largely devoted to the circumstances surrounding the adoption of the Fourteenth Amendment in 1868. This discussion and our own investigation convince us that, although these sources cast some light, it is not enough to resolve the problem with which we are faced. At best, they are inconclusive. The most avid proponents of the post–[Civil] War Amendments undoubtedly intended them to remove all legal distinctions among "all persons born or naturalized in the United States." Their opponents, just as certainly, were antagonistic to both the letter and the spirit of the Amendments and wished them to have the most limited effect.

An additional reason for the inconclusive nature of the Amendment's history, with respect to segregated schools, is the status of public education at that time. In the South, the movement toward free common schools, supported by general taxation, had not yet taken hold. Education of white children was largely in the hands of private groups. Education of Negroes was almost nonexistent, and practically all of the race were illiterate. In fact, any education of Negroes was forbidden by law in some states. As a consequence, it is not surprising that there should be so little in the history of the Fourteenth Amendment relating to its intended effect on public education.

In the first cases in this Court construing the Fourteenth Amendment, decided shortly after its adoption, the Court interpreted it as proscribing all state-imposed discriminations against the Negro race. The doctrine of "separate but equal" did not make its appearance in this Court until 1896 in the case of *Plessy v. Ferguson,* 163 U.S. 537 (1896), involving not education but transportation. American courts have since labored with the doctrine for over half a century. In this Court, there have been six cases involving the "separate but equal" doctrine in the field of public education. In *Cumming v. County Board of Education*, 175 U.S. 528 (1899), and *Gong Lum v. Rice*, 275 U.S. 78 (1927), the validity of the doctrine itself was not challenged. In more recent cases, all on the graduate school level, inequality was found in that specific benefits enjoyed by white students were denied to Negro students of the same educational qualifications. *Missouri ex rel. Gaines v. Canada*, 305 U.S. 337 (1938); *Sipuel v. Oklahoma*, 332 U.S. 631 (1948); *Sweatt v. Painter*, 339 U.S. 629 (1950); *McLaurin v. Oklahoma State Regents*, 339 U.S. 637 (1950). In none of these cases was it necessary to re-examine the doctrine to grant relief to the Negro plaintiff. And in *Sweatt v. Painter*, the Court expressly reserved decision on the question whether *Plessy v. Ferguson* should be held inapplicable to public education.

In the instant cases, that question is directly presented. Here, unlike *Sweatt v. Painter*, there are findings below that the Negro and white schools involved have been equalized, or are being equalized, with respect to buildings, curricula, qualifications and salaries of teachers, and other "tangible" factors. Our decision, therefore, cannot turn on merely a comparison of these tangible factors in the Negro and white schools involved in each of the cases. We must look instead to the effect of segregation itself on public education.

Today, education is perhaps the most important function of state and local governments. Compulsory school attendance laws and the great expenditures for education both demonstrate our recognition of the importance of education to our democratic society. It is required in the performance of our most basic public responsibilities, even service in the armed forces. It is the very foundation of good citizenship. In these days, it is doubtful that any child may reasonably be expected to succeed in life if he is denied the opportunity of an education. Such an opportunity, where the state has undertaken to provide it, is a right which must be made available to all on equal terms.

We come then to the question presented: Does segregation of children in public schools solely on the basis of race, even though the physical facilities and other "tangible" factors may be equal, deprive the children of the minority group of equal educational opportunities? We believe that it does.

In *Sweatt v. Painter*, in finding that a segregated law school for Negroes could not provide them equal educational opportunities, this Court relied in large part on "those qualities which are incapable of objective measurement but which make for greatness in a law school." In *McLaurin v. Oklahoma State Regents*, the Court, in requiring that a Negro admitted to a white graduate school be treated like all other students, again resorted to intangible considerations: ". . . his ability to study, to engage in discussions and exchange views with other students, and, in general, to learn his profession" 339 U.S. 637, 641. Such considerations apply with added force to children in grade and high schools. To separate them from others of similar age and qualifications solely because of their race generates a feeling of inferiority as to their status in the community that may affect their hearts and minds in a way unlikely ever to be undone.

Whatever may have been the extent of psychological knowledge at the time of *Plessy v. Ferguson*, this finding is amply supported by modern authority. Any language in *Plessy v. Ferguson* contrary to this finding is rejected.

We conclude that in the field of public education the doctrine of "separate but equal" has no place. Separate educational facilities are inherently unequal. Therefore, we hold that the plaintiffs and others similarly situated for whom the actions have been brought are, by reason of the segregation complained of, deprived of the equal protection of the laws guaranteed by the Fourteenth Amendment. This disposition makes unnecessary any discussion whether such segregation also violates the Due Process Clause of the Fourteenth Amendment.

Because these are class actions, because of the wide applicability of this decision, and because of the great variety of local conditions, the formulation of decrees in these cases presents problems of considerable complexity. On reargument, the consideration of appropriate relief was necessarily subordinated to the primary question—the constitutionality of segregation in public education. We have now announced that such segregation is a denial of the equal protection of the laws. In order that we may have the full assistance of the parties in formulating decrees, the cases will be restored to the docket, and the parties are requested to present further argument . . . this Term.

It is so ordered.

FOR DISCUSSION

How does the Court explain its reasoning in overturning a sixty-year-old precedent? What resources does the Court use to justify its decision in this case? What do you think of the Court's use of psychological data? Was this use similar, or dissimilar, to what it had done in *Plessy v. Ferguson*?

RELATED CASES

***Florida ex rel. Hawkins v. Board of Control:* 350 U.S. 413 (1956).**

Even though Florida had a "substantially equal" law school for African Americans, Hawkins was entitled to "prompt admission" to the white law school.

***Cooper v. Aaron:* 358 U.S. 1 (1958).**

Forbids state and local officials from postponing public school desegregation. The Court ruled that the Supremacy Clause (of Article VI) made *Brown v. Board of Education* the controlling precedent for all states.

***Shuttlesworth v. Birmingham Board of Education:* 358 U.S. 101 (1958).**

The Court upheld placement of pupils in schools "upon a basis of individual merit without regard to their race or color."

BOLLING V. SHARPE

347 U.S. 497, 74 S.Ct. 693, 98 L.Ed. 884 (1954)

This case, the fifth action in the *Brown v. Board of Education* litigation, originated in the District of Columbia. Because Washington, D.C., is not a state, it is not covered under the Equal Protection Clause of the Fourteenth Amendment. The Court had to decide the degree to which the Due Process Clause of the Fifth Amendment might apply.

Vote: 9–0

CHIEF JUSTICE WARREN delivered the opinion of the Court.

This case challenges the validity of segregation in the public schools of the District of Columbia. The petitioners, minors of the Negro race, allege that such segregation deprives them of due process of law under the Fifth Amendment. They were refused admission to a public school attended by white children solely because of their race.

We have this day held that the Equal Protection Clause of the Fourteenth Amendment prohibits the states from maintaining racially segregated public schools. The legal problem in the District of Columbia is somewhat different, however. The Fifth Amendment, which is applicable in the District of Columbia, does not contain an equal protection clause as does the Fourteenth Amendment which applies only to the states. But the concepts of equal protection and due process, both stemming from our American ideal of fairness, are not mutually exclusive. The "equal protection of the laws" is a more explicit safeguard of prohibited unfairness than "due process of law," and, therefore, we do not imply that the two are always interchangeable phrases. But, as this Court has recognized, discrimination may be so unjustifiable as to be violative of due process.

Classifications based solely upon race must be scrutinized with particular care, since they are contrary to our traditions and hence constitutionally suspect. As long ago as 1896, this Court declared the principle "that the Constitution of the United States, in its present form, forbids, so far as civil and political rights are concerned, discrimination by the General Government, or by the States, against any citizen because of his race." And in *Buchanan v. Warley*, 245 U.S. 60 (1917), the Court held that a statute which limited the right of a property owner to convey his property to a person of another race was, as an unreasonable discrimination, a denial of due process of law.

Although the Court has not assumed to define "liberty" with any great precision, that term is not confined to mere freedom from bodily restraint. Liberty under law extends to the full range of conduct which the individual is free to pursue, and it cannot be restricted except for a proper governmental objective. Segregation in public education is not reasonably related to any proper governmental objective, and thus it imposes on Negro children of the District of Columbia a burden that constitutes an arbitrary deprivation of their liberty in violation of the Due Process Clause.

In view of our decision that the Constitution prohibits the states from maintaining racially segregated public schools, it would be unthinkable that the same Constitution would impose a lesser duty on the Federal Government. We hold that racial segregation in the public schools of the District of Columbia is a denial of the due process of law guaranteed by the Fifth Amendment to the Constitution.

For the reasons set out in *Brown v. Board of Education*, this case will be restored to the docket for reargument. . . .

FOR DISCUSSION

What implications might arise from a refusal to recognize an implicit right to equal protection in the Fifth Amendment? Is this an appropriate role for the Supreme Court? Why or why not?

BROWN V. BOARD OF EDUCATION II

349 U.S. 294, 75 S.Ct. 753, 99 L.Ed. 1083 (1955)

After the ruling in *Brown I* that the application to public education of the separate but equal doctrine from Plessy violated the Equal Protection Clause of the Fourteenth Amendment, the Supreme Court was left with the question of a suitable remedy. All the previous parties, plus the attorneys general of all the states that permitted or required racial discrimination in public education, were invited to submit briefs on the question and/or to participate in oral arguments.

Vote: 9–0

CHIEF JUSTICE WARREN delivered the opinion of the Court.

Full implementation of these constitutional principles may require solution of varied local school problems. School authorities have the primary responsibility for elucidating, assessing, and solving these problems; courts will have to consider whether the action of school authorities constitutes good faith implementation of the governing constitutional principles. Because of their proximity to local conditions and the possible need for further hearings, the courts which originally heard these cases can best perform this judicial appraisal. Accordingly, we believe it appropriate to remand the cases to those courts.

In fashioning and effectuating the decrees, the courts will be guided by equitable principles. Traditionally, equity has been characterized by a practical flexibility in shaping its remedies and by a facility for adjusting and reconciling public and private needs. These cases call for the exercise of these traditional attributes of equity power. At stake is the personal interest of the plaintiffs in admission to public schools as soon as practicable on a nondiscriminatory basis. To effectuate this interest may call for elimination of a variety of obstacles in making the transition to school systems operated in accordance with the constitutional principles set forth in our May 17, 1954, decision. Courts of equity may properly take into account the public interest in the elimination of such obstacles in a systematic and effective manner. But it should go without saying that the vitality of these constitutional principles cannot be allowed to yield simply because of disagreement with them.

While giving weight to these public and private considerations, the courts will require that the defendants make a prompt and reasonable start toward full compliance with our May 17, 1954, ruling. Once such a start has been made, the courts may find that additional time is necessary to carry out the ruling in an effective manner. The burden rests upon the defendants to establish that such time is necessary in the public interest and is consistent with good faith compliance at the earliest practicable date. To that end, the courts may consider problems related to administration, arising from the physical condition of the school plant, the school transportation system, personnel, revision of school districts and attendance areas into compact units to achieve a system of determining admission to the public schools on a nonracial basis, and revision of local laws and regulations which may be necessary in solving the foregoing problems. They will also consider the adequacy of any plans the defendants may propose to meet these problems and to effectuate a transition to a racially nondiscriminatory school system. During this period of transition, the courts will retain jurisdiction of these cases.

The judgments below, except that in the Delaware case, are accordingly reversed and the cases are remanded to the District Courts to take such proceedings and enter such orders and decrees consistent with this opinion as are necessary and proper to admit to public schools on a racially nondiscriminatory basis with all deliberate speed the parties to these cases. The judgment in the Delaware case—ordering the immediate admission of the plaintiffs to schools previously attended only by white children—is affirmed on the basis of the principles stated in our May 17, 1954, opinion, but the case is remanded to the Supreme Court of Delaware for such further proceedings as that Court may deem necessary in light of this opinion.

It is so ordered.

FOR DISCUSSION

Would a different basis for decision making in *Brown I* affect the implementation of *Brown II*? What was the outcome of the Supreme Court's reliance on lower federal courts for implementation? What was the justices' rationale for such a reliance?

RELATED CASES

***Griffin v. County School Board of Prince Edward County:* 377 U.S. 218 (1964).**

For the county board to close public schools while at the same time tuition grants and tax concessions are being made to assist white children in private segregated schools is a denial of equal protection under the Fourteenth Amendment. The Court noted that a lower federal court could order the county board to levy taxes to operate a public school system in the county.

***Green v. County School Board of New Kent County, Virginia:* 391 U.S. 430 (1968).**

School boards must formulate positive plans that promise realistically to bring about promptly a unitary, nonracial, nondiscriminatory school system. In the same vein, on the same day the Court also decided Raney v. Board of Education of Gould School District (Arkansas) (391 U.S. 443) and Monroe v. Board of Commissioners of the City of Jackson (Tennessee) (391 U.S. 450).

***United States v. Montgomery County Board of Education:* 395 U.S. 225 (1969).**

A U.S. district court order to the local school board setting a ratio of white to black teachers in each school in the district was held valid as a means of implementing a desegregated system.

***Alexander v. Holmes County Board of Education:* 391 U.S. 19 (1969).**

All dual school systems must be eliminated immediately and re-formed into unitary school systems.

SWANN V. CHARLOTTE-MECKLENBURG BOARD OF EDUCATION

402 U.S. 1, 91 S.Ct. 1267, 28 L.Ed.2d 554 (1971)

This case addressed the scope of authority of the federal judges and the responsibility of school districts in implementing *Brown I.* The Charlotte-Mecklenburg school district in North Carolina was a large district in which 71 percent of students were Caucasian and 29 percent were African American, but two-thirds of black pupils attended schools that were more than 99 percent African American. After a thorough investigation, the district court appointed an outside expert to provide an alternative desegregation plan to the one suggested by the board of education. The Court adopted a combination of the plans; the state court of appeals rejected some elements. The Supreme Court had to decide on the legitimacy of school construction decisions and student assignment programs, including the use of busing.

Vote: 9–0

CHIEF JUSTICE BURGER delivered the opinion of the Court.

This case and those argued with it arose in States having a long history of maintaining two sets of schools in a single school system deliberately operated to carry out a governmental policy to separate pupils in schools solely on the basis of race. That was what *Brown v. Board of Education* was all about. These cases present us with the problem of defining in more precise terms than heretofore the scope of the duty of school authorities and district courts in implementing *Brown I* and the mandate to eliminate dual systems and establish unitary systems at once. Meanwhile district courts and courts of appeals have struggled in hundreds of cases with a multitude and variety of problems under this Court's general directive. Understandably, in an area of evolving remedies, those courts had to improvise and experiment without detailed or specific guidelines. This Court, in *Brown I,* appropriately dealt with the large constitutional principles; other federal courts had to grapple with the flinty, intractable realities of day-to-day implementation of those constitutional commands. Their efforts, of necessity, embraced a process of "trial and error," and our effort to formulate guidelines must take into account their experience.

I

[This section summarizes the plans proposed for Charlotte/Mecklenburg County and the actions in the lower courts.]

II

Over the 16 years since *Brown II*, many difficulties were encountered in implementation of the basic constitutional requirement that the State not discriminate between public school children on the basis of their race. Nothing in our national experience prior to 1955 prepared anyone for dealing with changes and adjustments of the magnitude and complexity encountered since then. Deliberate resistance of some to the Court's mandates has impeded the good-faith efforts of others to bring school systems into compliance. The details and nature of these dilatory tactics have been noted frequently by this Court and other courts.

By the time the Court considered *Green v. County School Board*, 391 U.S. 430, in 1968, very little progress had been made in many areas where dual school systems had historically been maintained by operation of state laws. In *Green*, the Court was confronted with a record of a freedom-of-choice program that the District Court had found to operate in fact to preserve a dual system more than a decade after *Brown II*.

Alexander v. Holmes County Board of Education, 396 U.S. 19 (1969), restated the basic obligation asserted in *Griffin v. School Board*, 377 U.S. 218, 234 (1964), and *Green*, that the remedy must be implemented forthwith.

The problems encountered by the district courts and courts of appeals make plain that we should now try to amplify guidelines, however incomplete and imperfect, for the assistance of school authorities and courts. The failure of local authorities to meet their constitutional obligations aggravated the massive problem of converting from the state-enforced discrimination of racially separate school systems. This process has been rendered more difficult by changes since 1954 in the structure and patterns of communities, the growth of student population, movement of families, and other changes, some of which had marked impact on school planning, sometimes neutralizing or negating remedial action before it was fully implemented. Rural areas accustomed for half a century to the consolidated school systems implemented by bus transportation could make adjustments more readily than metropolitan areas with dense and shifting population, numerous schools, congested and complex traffic patterns.

III

If school authorities fail in their affirmative obligations under these holdings, judicial authority may be invoked. Once a right and a violation have been shown, the scope of a district court's equitable powers to remedy past wrongs is broad, for breadth and flexibility are inherent in equitable remedies.

This allocation of responsibility once made, the Court attempted from time to time to provide some guidelines for the exercise of the district judge's discretion and for the reviewing function of the courts of appeals. However, a school desegregation case does not differ fundamentally from other cases involving the framing of equitable remedies to repair the denial of a constitutional right. The task is to correct, by a balancing of the individual and collective interests, the condition that offends the Constitution.

In seeking to define even in broad and general terms how far this remedial power extends it is important to remember that judicial powers may be exercised only on the basis of a constitutional violation. Remedial judicial authority does not put judges automatically in the shoes of school authorities whose powers are plenary. Judicial authority enters only when local authority defaults.

School authorities are traditionally charged with broad power to formulate and implement educational policy and might well conclude, for example, that in order to prepare students to live in a pluralistic society each school should have a prescribed ratio of Negro to white students reflecting the proportion for the district as a whole. To do this as an educational policy is within the broad discretionary powers of school authorities; absent a finding of a constitutional violation, however, that would not be within the authority of a federal court. As with any equity case, the nature of the violation determines the scope of the remedy. In default by the school authorities of their obligation to proffer acceptable remedies, a district court has broad power to fashion a remedy that will assure a unitary school system.

The school authorities argue that the equity powers of federal district courts have been limited by Title IV of the Civil Rights Act of 1964, 42 U.S.C. § 2000c. The language and the history of Title IV show that it was enacted not to limit but to define the role of the Federal Government in the implementation of the *Brown I* decision. It authorizes the Commissioner of Education to provide technical assistance to local boards in the preparation of desegregation plans, to arrange "training institutes" for school personnel involved in desegregation efforts, and to make grants directly to schools to ease the transition to unitary systems.

In short, there is nothing in the Act that provides us material assistance in answering the question of remedy for state-imposed segregation in violation of *Brown I.* The basis of our decision must be the prohibition of the Fourteenth Amendment that no State shall "deny to any person within its jurisdiction the equal protection of the laws."

IV

We turn now to the problem of defining with more particularity the responsibilities of school authorities in desegregating a state-enforced dual school system in light of the Equal Protection Clause.

The construction of new schools and the closing of old ones are two of the most important functions of local school authorities and also two of the most complex. They must decide questions of location and capacity in light of population growth, finances, land values, site availability, through an almost endless list of factors to be considered. The result of this will be a decision which, when combined with one technique or another of student assignment, will determine the racial composition of the student body in each school in the system.

In the past, choices in this respect have been used as a potent weapon for creating or maintaining a state-segregated school system. In addition to the classic pattern of building schools specifically intended for Negro or white students, school authorities have sometimes, since *Brown*, closed schools which appeared likely to become racially mixed through changes in neighborhood residential patterns.

In ascertaining the existence of legally imposed school segregation, the existence of a pattern of school construction and abandonment is thus a factor of great weight. In devising remedies where legally imposed segregation has been established, it is the responsibility of local authorities and district courts to see to it that future school construction and abandonment are not used and do not serve to perpetuate or re-establish the dual system. When necessary, district courts should retain jurisdiction to assure that these responsibilities are carried out.

V

The central issue in this case is that of student assignment, and there are essentially four problem areas:

(1) to what extent racial balance or racial quotas may be used as an implement in a remedial order to correct a previously segregated system;

(2) whether every all-Negro and all-white school must be eliminated as an indispensable part of a remedial process of desegregation;

(3) what the limits are, if any, on the rearrangement of school districts and attendance zones, as a remedial measure; and

(4) what the limits are, if any, on the use of transportation facilities to correct state-enforced racial school segregation.

1. Racial Balances or Racial Quotas

Our objective in dealing with the issues presented by these cases is to see that school authorities exclude no pupil of a racial minority from any school, directly or indirectly, on account of race; it does not and cannot embrace all the problems of racial prejudice, even when those problems contribute to disproportionate racial concentrations in some schools.

In this case it is urged that the District Court has imposed a racial balance requirement of 71%–29% on individual schools.

As the voluminous record in this case shows, the predicate for the District Court's use of the 71%–29% ratio was twofold: first, its express finding, approved by the Court of Appeals and not challenged here, that a dual school system had been maintained by the school authorities at least until 1969; second, its finding, also approved by the Court of Appeals, that the school board had totally defaulted in its acknowledged duty to come forward with an acceptable plan of its own, notwithstanding the patient efforts of the District Judge who, on at least three occasions, urged the board to submit plans. It was because of this total failure of the school board that the District Court was obliged to turn to other qualified sources, and Dr. Finger [the court-appointed expert] designated to assist the District Court to do what the board should have done.

We see therefore that the use made of mathematical ratios was no more than a starting point in the process of shaping a remedy, rather than an inflexible requirement. From that starting point the District Court proceeded to frame a decree that was within its discretionary powers, as an equitable remedy for the particular circumstances. Awareness of the racial composition of the whole school system is likely to be a useful starting point in shaping a remedy to correct past constitutional violations. In sum, the very limited use made of mathematical ratios was within the equitable remedial discretion of the District Court.

2. One-Race Schools

The record in this case reveals the familiar phenomenon that in metropolitan areas minority groups are often found concentrated in one part of the city. In some circumstances certain schools may remain all or largely of one race until new schools can be provided or neighborhood patterns change. Schools all or predominately of one race in a district of mixed population will require close scrutiny to determine that school assignments are not part of state-enforced segregation.

In light of the above, it should be clear that the existence of some small number of one-race, or virtually one-race, schools within a district is not in and of itself the mark of a system that still practices segregation by law. The district judge or school authorities should make every effort to achieve the greatest possible degree of actual desegregation and will thus necessarily be concerned with the elimination of one-race schools. The court should scrutinize such schools, and the burden upon the school authorities will be to satisfy the court that their racial composition is not the result of present or past discriminatory action on their part.

Provision for optional transfer of those in the majority racial group of a particular school to other schools where they will be in the minority is an indispensable remedy for those students willing to transfer to other schools in order to lessen the impact on them of the state-imposed stigma of segregation.

3. Remedial Altering of Attendance Zones

The maps submitted in these cases graphically demonstrate that one of the principal tools employed by school planners and by courts to break up the dual school system has been a frank—and sometimes drastic—gerrymandering of school districts and attendance zones. An additional step was pairing, "clustering," or "grouping" of schools with attendance assignments made deliberately to accomplish the transfer of Negro students out of formerly segregated Negro schools and transfer of white students to formerly all-Negro schools. More often than not, these zones are neither compact nor contiguous; indeed they may be on opposite ends of the city. As an interim corrective measure, this cannot be said to be beyond the broad remedial powers of a court.

Absent a constitutional violation there would be no basis for judicially ordering assignment of students on a racial basis. All things being equal, with no history of discrimination, it might well be desirable to assign pupils to schools nearest their homes. But all things are not equal in a system that has been deliberately constructed and maintained to enforce racial segregation. The remedy for such segregation may be administratively awkward, inconvenient, and even bizarre in some situations and may impose burdens on some; but all awkwardness and inconvenience cannot be avoided in the interim period when remedial adjustments are being made to eliminate the dual school systems.

No fixed or even substantially fixed guidelines can be established as to how far a court can go, but it must be recognized that there are limits. The objective is to dismantle the dual school system.

We hold that the pairing and grouping of noncontiguous school zones is a permissible tool and such action is to be considered in light of the objectives sought.

4. Transportation of Students

Bus transportation has been an integral part of the public education system for years, and was perhaps the single most important factor in the transition from the one-room schoolhouse to the consolidated school. Eighteen million of the Nation's public school children, approximately 39%, were transported to their schools by bus in 1969–1970 in all parts of the country.

The District Court's conclusion that assignment of children to the school nearest their home serving their grade would not produce an effective dismantling of the dual system is supported by the record.

Thus the remedial techniques used in the District Court's order were within that court's power to provide equitable relief; implementation of the decree is well within the capacity of the school authority.

In these circumstances, we find no basis for holding that the local school authorities may not be required to employ bus transportation as one tool of school desegregation. Desegregation plans cannot be limited to the walk-in school.

An objection to transportation of students may have validity when the time or distance of travel is so great as to either risk the health of the children or significantly impinge on the educational process.

VI

At some point, these school authorities and others like them should have achieved full compliance with this Court's decision in *Brown I*. The systems would then be "unitary" in the sense required by our decisions in *Green* and *Alexander*.

It does not follow that the communities served by such systems will remain demographically stable, for in a growing, mobile society, few will do so. Neither school authorities nor district courts are constitutionally required to make year-by-year adjustments of the racial composition of student bodies once the affirmative duty to desegregate has been accomplished and racial discrimination through official action is eliminated from the system. This does not mean that federal courts are without power to deal with future problems; but in the absence of a showing that either the school authorities or some other agency of the State has deliberately attempted to fix or alter demographic patterns to affect the racial composition of the schools, further intervention by a district court should not be necessary.

FOR DISCUSSION

How does this case demonstrate how the core civic values of liberty and equality are frequently in conflict in constitutional interpretation? How would a citizen who privileges liberty over equality respond to this case? How would one who privileges equality over liberty?

RELATED CASES

***Davis v. Board of School Commissions of Mobile County*: 402 U.S. 33 (1971).**

The Supreme Court allows all desegregation techniques, including the redrawing of attendance zones, to be considered in order to maximize school system desegregation.

***Keyes v. School District No. 1, Denver, CO:* 413 U.S. 189 (1973).**

In this first northern school desegregation case, the Court found that evidence of deliberate discrimination, even if not lawfully compelled, can demonstrate a finding of *de jure* discrimination in a school system.

***Milliken v. Bradley (Milliken I):* 418 U.S. 717 (1974).**

A metropolitan (Detroit) remedy that covers multiple districts cannot be imposed if there is no evidence that the outlying district contributed to the segregation of the city. White flight cannot be compensated for by metropolitan busing.

***Milliken v. Bradley (Milliken II):* 433 U.S. 267 (1977).**

The Court ruled that school segregation remedies that are narrowly tailored to fit the violation and correct the unconstitutional condition are permissible.

***Washington v. Seattle School District, No. 1:* 458 U.S. 457 (1982).**

The Court found that Washington State's Initiative 350, which prohibited busing for school desegregation, was in violation of the Equal Protection Clause.

***Board of Education of Oklahoma City Public Schools v. Dowell:* 498 U.S. 237 (1991).**

School districts that were previously segregated and under a desegregation decree must be removed from the decree when they have moved to eliminate the "vestiges of past discrimination," regardless of whether the district is desegregated.

***Freeman v. Pitts:* 503 U.S. 467 (1992).**

District court judges may release a school district from their supervision in stages before there is full compliance to each of the court desegregation decrees.

WASHINGTON V. DAVIS

426 U.S. 229, 96 S.Ct. 2040, 48 L.Ed.2d 597 (1976)

Two African American police officers challenged the promotion plans of the District of Columbia Metropolitan Police Department as racially discriminatory. To make promotion decisions, the department considered, among other factors, the results of a written personnel test (Test 21) that had the effect of excluding from eligibility for promotion a disproportionate number of African American officers. The instrument, developed by the federal Civil Service Commission, tested verbal skills, vocabulary, reading, and comprehension. Plaintiffs charged a violation of their due process rights under the Fifth Amendment. The test was upheld by the district court and invalidated by the court of appeals.

Vote: 7–2

JUSTICE WHITE delivered the opinion of the Court.

I

[This section summarized the facts of the case and the lower court actions.]

II

The central purpose of the Equal Protection Clause of the Fourteenth Amendment is the prevention of official conduct discriminating on the basis of race. It is also true that the Due Process Clause of the Fifth Amendment contains an equal protection component prohibiting the United States from invidiously discriminating between individuals or groups. *Bolling v. Sharpe*, 347 U.S. 497 (1954). But our cases have not embraced the proposition that a law or other official act, without regard to whether it reflects a racially discriminatory purpose, is unconstitutional solely because it has a racially disproportionate impact.

Almost 100 years ago, *Strauder v. West Virginia*, 100 U.S. 303 (1880), established that the exclusion of Negroes from grand and petit juries in criminal proceedings violated the Equal Protection Clause, but the fact that a particular jury or a series of juries does not statistically reflect the racial composition of the community does not in itself make out an invidious discrimination forbidden by the Clause. "A purpose to discriminate must be present which may be proven by systematic exclusion of eligible jurymen of the proscribed race or by unequal application of the law to such an extent as to show intentional discrimination." *Akins v. Texas*, 325 U.S. 398, 403–404 (1945).

The school desegregation cases have also adhered to the basic equal protection principle that the invidious quality of a law claimed to be racially discriminatory must ultimately be traced to a racially discriminatory purpose. That there are both predominantly black and predominantly white schools in a community is not alone violative of the Equal Protection Clause.

This is not to say that the necessary discriminatory racial purpose must be express or appear on the face of the statute, or that a law's disproportionate impact is irrelevant in cases involving Constitution-based claims of racial discrimination. A statute, otherwise neutral on its face, must not be applied so as invidiously to discriminate on the basis of race. *Yick Wo v. Hopkins*, 118 U.S. 356 (1886).

Necessarily, an invidious discriminatory purpose may often be inferred from the totality of the relevant facts, including the fact, if it is true, that the law bears more heavily on one race than another. It is also not infrequently true that the discriminatory impact . . . may for all practical purposes demonstrate unconstitutionality because in various circumstances the discrimination is very difficult to explain on nonracial grounds. Nevertheless, we have not held that a law, neutral on its face and serving ends otherwise within the power of government to pursue, is invalid under the Equal Protection Clause simply because it may affect a greater proportion of one race than of another. Disproportionate impact is not irrelevant, but it is not the sole touchstone of an invidious racial discrimination forbidden by the Constitution. Standing alone, it does not trigger the rule, *McLaughlin v. Florida*, 379 U.S. 184 (1964), that racial classifications are to be subjected to the strictest scrutiny and are justifiable only by the weightiest of considerations.

As an initial matter, we have difficulty understanding how a law establishing a racially neutral qualification for employment is nevertheless racially discriminatory and denies "any person . . . equal protection of the laws" simply because a greater proportion of Negroes fail to qualify than members of other racial or ethnic groups. Had respondents, along with all others who had failed Test 21, whether white or black, brought an action claiming that the test denied each of them equal protection of the laws as compared with those who had passed with high enough scores to qualify them as police recruits, it is most unlikely that their challenge would have been sustained.

Nor on the facts of the case before us would the disproportionate impact of Test 21 warrant the conclusion that it is a purposeful device to discriminate against Negroes and hence an infringement of the constitutional rights of respondents as well as other black applicants. As we have said, the test is neutral on its face and rationally may be said to serve a purpose the Government is constitutionally empowered to pursue.

Under Title VII, Congress provided that when hiring and promotion practices disqualifying substantially disproportionate numbers of blacks are challenged, discriminatory purpose need not be proved, and that it is an insufficient response to demonstrate some rational basis for the challenged practices. It is necessary, in addition, that they be "validated" in terms of job performance in any one of several ways, perhaps by ascertaining the minimum skill, ability, or potential necessary for the position at issue and determining whether the qualifying tests are appropriate for the selection of qualified applicants for the job in question. However this process proceeds, it involves a more probing judicial review of, and less deference to, the seemingly reasonable acts of administrators and executives than is appropriate under the Constitution where special racial impact, without discriminatory purpose, is claimed. We are not disposed to adopt this more rigorous standard for the purposes of applying the Fifth and the Fourteenth Amendments in cases such as this.

A rule that a statute designed to serve neutral ends is nevertheless invalid, absent compelling justification, if in practice it benefits or burdens one race more than another would be far reaching and would raise serious questions about, and perhaps invalidate, a whole range of tax, welfare, public service, regulatory, and licensing statutes that may be more burdensome to the poor and to the average black than to the more affluent white.

Given that rule, such consequences would perhaps be likely to follow. However, in our view, extension of the rule beyond those areas where it is already applicable by reason of statute, such as in the field of public employment, should await legislative prescription.

JUSTICE STEVENS, concurring.

There are two reasons why I am convinced that the challenge to Test 21 is insufficient. First, the test serves the neutral and legitimate purpose of requiring all applicants to meet a uniform minimum standard of literacy. Reading ability is manifestly relevant to the police function, there is no evidence that the required passing grade was set at an arbitrarily high level, and there is sufficient disparity among high schools and high school graduates to justify the use of a separate uniform test. Second, the same test is used throughout the federal service. The applicants for employment in the District of Columbia Police Department represent such a small fraction of the total number of persons who have taken the test that their experience is of minimal probative value in assessing the neutrality of the test itself. That evidence, without more, is not sufficient to overcome the presumption that a test which is this widely used by the Federal Government is in fact neutral in its effect as well as its "purpose" as that term is used in constitutional adjudication.

JUSTICE BRENNAN, with whom JUSTICE MARSHALL joins, dissenting.

III

Albemarle Paper Company v. Moody, 422 U.S. 405 (1975) read *Griggs v. Duke Power Company*, 401 U.S. 421 (1971) to require that a discriminatory test be validated through proof "by professionally acceptable methods" that it is " 'predictive of or significantly correlated with important elements of work behavior which comprise or are relevant to the job or jobs for which candidates are being evaluated.' " 422 U.S., at 431 . . . Further, we rejected the employer's attempt to validate a written test by proving that it was related to supervisors' job performance ratings, because there was no demonstration that the ratings accurately reflected job performance. We were unable "to determine whether the criteria actually considered were sufficiently related to the [employer's] legitimate interest in job-specific ability to justify a testing system with a racially discriminatory impact." 422 U.S., at 433. To me, therefore, these cases read Title VII as requiring proof of a significant relationship to job performance to establish the validity of a discriminatory test. Petitioners do not maintain that there is a demonstrated correlation between Test 21 scores and job performance. Moreover, their validity study was unable to discern a significant positive relationship between training averages and job performance. Thus, there is no proof of a correlation—either direct or indirect—between Test 21 and performance of the job of being a police officer.

[I]t should be observed that every federal court, except the District Court in this case, presented with proof identical to that offered to validate Test 21 has reached a conclusion directly opposite to that of the Court today. Sound policy considerations support the view that, at a minimum, petitioners should have been required to prove that the police training examinations either measure job-related skills or predict job performance. Where employers try to validate written qualification tests by proving a correlation with written examinations in a training course, there is a substantial danger that people who have good verbal skills will achieve high scores on both tests due to verbal ability, rather than "job-specific ability." As a result, employers could validate any entrance examination that measures only verbal ability by giving another written test that measures verbal ability at the end of a training course. Any contention that the resulting correlation between examination scores would be evidence that the initial test is "job related" is plainly erroneous. It seems to me, however, that the Court's holding in this case can be read as endorsing this dubious proposition. Today's result will prove particularly unfortunate if it is extended to govern Title VII cases.

FOR DISCUSSION

How might this decision be applicable to cases in housing discrimination, school desegregation, or in issues related to voting rights? How could the intent to discriminate be demonstrated? What should be more relevant: intent or discriminatory outcomes? Why?

RELATED CASES

***Arlington Heights v. Metropolitan Housing Development Corporation:* 429 U.S. 252 (1977).**

To challenge the denial of a rezoning request, an entity wishing to build federally subsidized, integrated, low-income housing must demonstrate racially discriminatory intent.

***Personnel Administrator of Massachusetts v. Feeney:* 442 U.S. 256 (1979).**

The Court upheld a neutral Massachusetts law granting preferences to veterans in hiring, despite its disproportionate impact on women because of their lack of opportunities for military service, stating that the law did not violate women's equal protection rights. The Court relied on *Washington v. Davis*, which required evidence of intentional discrimination to demonstrate equal protection violations.

UNITED STATES V. FORDICE; AYERS V. FORDICE

505 U.S. 717, 112 S.Ct. 2727, 120 L.Ed.2d 575 (1992)

The state of Mississippi maintained a de jure system of segregation in higher education consisting of five predominantly white public institutions and three historically black public institutions. A group of black citizens initiated a lawsuit in 1975 charging that Mississippi "had maintained the racially segregative effects of its prior dual system of postsecondary education in violation of the Fifth, Ninth, Thirteenth, and Fourteenth Amendments, 42 U. S. C. §§ 1981 and 1983, and Title VI of the Civil Rights Act of 1964, 42 U. S. C. § 2000d" Shortly thereafter, the United States filed its complaint in intervention, charging that state officials had failed to satisfy their obligation under the Equal Protection Clause of the Fourteenth Amendment and Title VI to dismantle Mississippi's dual system of higher education. After fifteen years of negotiation and litigation, the district court found that Mississippi had demonstrated that it was disestablishing the former segregated system of higher education. The court of appeals concurred.

Vote: 8–1

JUSTICE WHITE delivered the opinion of the Court.

III

The District Court, the Court of Appeals, and respondents recognize and acknowledge that the State of Mississippi had the constitutional duty to dismantle the dual school system that its laws once mandated. Nor is there any dispute that this obligation applies to its higher education system. If the State has not discharged this duty, it remains in violation of the Fourteenth Amendment. *Brown v. Board of Education,* 347 U.S. 483 (1954), and its progeny clearly mandate this observation. Thus, the primary issue in these cases is whether the State has met its affirmative duty to dismantle its prior dual university system.

Our decisions establish that a State does not discharge its constitutional obligations until it eradicates policies and practices traceable to its prior de jure dual system that continue to foster segregation. Thus we have consistently asked whether existing racial identifiability is attributable to the State; and examined a wide range of factors to determine whether the State has perpetuated its formerly de jure segregation in any facet of its institutional system.

We do not agree with the Court of Appeals or the District Court, however, that the adoption and implementation of race-neutral policies alone suffice to demonstrate that the State has completely abandoned its prior dual system. That college attendance is by choice and not by assignment does not mean that a race-neutral admissions policy cures the constitutional violation of a dual system. In a system based on choice, student attendance is determined not simply by admissions policies, but also by many other factors. Although some of these factors clearly cannot be attributed to state policies, many can be. If policies traceable to the de jure system are still in force and have discriminatory effects, those policies too must be reformed to the extent practicable and consistent with sound educational practices.

IV

Had the Court of Appeals applied the correct legal standard, it would have been apparent from the undisturbed factual findings of the District Court that there are several surviving aspects of Mississippi's prior dual system which are constitutionally suspect; for even though such policies may be race neutral on their face, they substantially restrict a person's choice of which institution to enter, and they contribute to the racial identifiability of the eight public universities. Mississippi must justify these policies or eliminate them.

[W]e address four policies of the present system: admissions standards, program duplication, institutional mission assignments, and continued operation of all eight public universities. . . .

Because the former de jure segregated system of public universities in Mississippi impeded the free choice of prospective students, the State in dismantling that system must take the necessary steps to ensure that this choice now is truly free. The full range of policies and practices must be examined with this duty in mind. That an institution is predominantly white or black does not in itself make out a constitutional violation. But surely the State may not leave in place policies rooted in its prior officially segregated system that serve to maintain the racial identifiability of its universities if those policies can practicably be eliminated without eroding sound educational policies.

Because the District Court and the Court of Appeals failed to consider the State's duties in their proper light, the cases must be remanded. To the extent that the State has not met its affirmative obligation to dismantle its prior dual system, it shall be adjudged in violation of the Constitution and Title VI and remedial proceedings shall be conducted.

JUSTICE O'CONNOR, concurring.

I write separately to emphasize that it is Mississippi's burden to prove that it has undone its prior segregation, and that the circumstances in which a State may maintain a policy or practice traceable to de jure segregation that has segregative effects are narrow. In my view, it also follows from the State's obligation to prove that it has "taken all steps" to eliminate policies and practices traceable to de jure segregation that if the State shows that maintenance of certain remnants of its prior system is essential to accomplish its legitimate goals, then it still must prove that it has counteracted and minimized the segregative impact of such policies to the extent possible. Only by eliminating a remnant that unnecessarily continues to foster segregation or by negating insofar as possible its segregative impact can the State satisfy its constitutional obligation to dismantle the discriminatory system that should, by now, be only a distant memory.

JUSTICE THOMAS, concurring.

I agree with the Court that a State does not satisfy its obligation to dismantle a dual system of higher education merely by adopting race-neutral policies for the future administration of that system. I agree that this statement defines the appropriate standard to apply in the higher education context. I write separately to emphasize that this standard is far different from the one adopted to govern the grade-school context in *Green v. School Bd. of New Kent County*, 391 U.S. 430 (1968), and its progeny. In particular, because it does not compel the elimination of all observed racial imbalance, it portends neither the destruction of historically black colleges nor the severing of those institutions from their distinctive histories and traditions.

In particular, we do not foreclose the possibility that there exists "sound educational justification" for maintaining historically black colleges as such. Despite the shameful history of state-enforced segregation, these institutions have survived and flourished. Indeed, they have expanded as opportunities for blacks to enter historically white institutions have expanded.

I think it undisputable that these institutions have succeeded in part because of their distinctive histories and traditions; for many, historically black colleges have become "a symbol of the highest attainments of black culture." J. Preer, *Lawyers v. Educators: Black Colleges and Desegregation in Public Higher Education* 2 (1982). Obviously, a State cannot maintain such traditions by closing particular institutions, historically white or historically black, to particular racial groups. Nonetheless, it hardly follows that a State cannot operate a diverse assortment of institutions—including historically black institutions—open to all on a race-neutral basis, but with established traditions and programs that might disproportionately appeal to one race or another. Although I agree that a State is not constitutionally required to maintain its historically black institutions as such, I do not understand our opinion to hold that a State is forbidden to do so. It would be ironic, to say the least, if the institutions that sustained blacks during segregation were themselves destroyed in an effort to combat its vestiges.

JUSTICE SCALIA, concurring in the judgment in part and dissenting in part.

With some of what the Court says today, I agree. I agree, of course, that the Constitution compels Mississippi to remove all discriminatory barriers to its state-funded universities. *Brown v. Board of Education*, 347 U.S. 483 (1954) (*Brown* I). I agree that the Constitution does not compel Mississippi to remedy funding disparities between its historically black institutions (HBI's) and historically white institutions (HWI's). And I agree that Mississippi's American College Testing Program (ACT) requirements need further review. I reject, however, the effectively unsustainable burden the Court imposes on Mississippi, and all States that formerly operated segregated universities, to demonstrate compliance with *Brown I*. That requirement, which resembles what we prescribed for primary and secondary schools in *Green v. School Bd. of New Kent County*, 391 U.S. 430 (1968), has no proper application in the context of higher education, provides no genuine guidance to States and lower courts, and is as likely to subvert as to promote the interests of those citizens on whose behalf the present suit was brought.

* * *

The Court was asked to decide today whether, in the provision of university education, a State satisfies its duty under *Brown I* by removing discriminatory barriers to admissions. That question required us to choose between the standards established in *Green* and *Bazemore v. Friday, 478 U.S. 385 (1986)*], both of which involved (as, for the most part, this does) free-choice plans that failed to end de facto segregation. Once the confusion engendered by the Court's something-for-all, guidance-to-none opinion has been dissipated, it will become apparent that, essentially, the Court has adopted *Green.*

I would not predict, however, that today's opinion will succeed in producing the same result as *Green*—viz., compelling the States to compel racial "balance" in their schools—because of several practical imperfections: because the Court deprives district judges of the most efficient (and perhaps the only effective) *Green* remedy, mandatory student assignment; because some contradictory elements of the opinion (its suggestion, for example, that Mississippi's mission designations foster, rather than deter, segregation) will prevent clarity of application; and because the virtually standardless discretion conferred upon district judges will permit them to do pretty much what they please. What I do predict is a number of years of litigation-driven confusion and destabilization in the university systems of all the formerly de jure States, that will benefit neither blacks nor whites, neither predominantly black institutions nor predominantly white ones. Nothing good will come of this judicially ordained turmoil, except the public recognition that any court that would knowingly impose it must hate segregation. We must find some other way of making that point.

FOR DISCUSSION

How can a dual system be completely eliminated in an era of limited resources without destroying the institutions established when laws enforcing segregation were in effect? In a post-segregation era, what should be the role of HBCUs, tribal colleges, and institutions serving Hispanic populations?

RELATED CASES

***Florida ex. rel. Hawkins v. Board of Control:* 350 U.S. 413 (1956).**

In this case the Supreme Court applied the ruling in *Brown v. Board of Education* to higher education.

***Adams v. Richardson:* 351 F. 2d 636 [D.C. Cir.] (1972).**

This litigation challenged all nineteen border and southern states as still operating segregated and discriminatory systems of higher education. In 1999 the federal court ruled that Adams and the other plaintiffs lacked the appropriate standing to pursue litigation.

***Regents of the University of California v. Bakke:* 438 U.S. 265 (1978).**

Overturned the admissions policy at the University of California at Davis Medical School, which used a form of racial quota system. The Court argued that race-conscious admissions programs were constitutional as long as race was not the only factor used.

***Grutter v. Bollinger:* 539 U.S. 306 (2003).**

Upheld the affirmative action admissions policy of the University of Michigan Law School. The Court found that the narrowly tailored use of race in admissions was allowable when the intent was to pursue a compelling interest in maintaining the educational benefits resulting from a diverse student body.

Gender

From its origination, the Constitution has provided limited protections for women. With the exception of voting rights guaranteed by the Nineteenth Amendment (1920), it has been the Court's interpretation of the Constitution that has evolved, rather than the explicit language of the text, to allow the expansion of basic citizenship protections to women. Although the original document made general references to "persons" and "citizens" without specifying gender, the political rights of women of color and white women alike remained severely restricted. In 1848 two feminists, Elizabeth Cady Stanton and Lucretia Mott, presented the "Seneca Falls Declaration of Sentiments and Resolutions" to a group of three hundred people gathered to discuss the situation of white women as similar to and distinct from the concerns of the enslaved men and women of African descent. The *Declaration of Sentiments* used much of the language of the *Declaration of Independence.* Instead of the colonists declaring their independence from England, however, women declared their independence from men: "The history of mankind is a history of repeated injuries and usurpations on the part of man toward woman, having in direct object the establishment of an absolute tyranny over her." While this document has no policy significance, it does illustrate the philosophical arguments regarding suffrage and equality debated twenty years prior to the Civil War. It was not until the ratification of the Fourteenth Amendment in 1868 that the Court began formal consideration of the constitutionally protected rights of women. The Fourteenth Amendment requires states to provide equal protection of the laws for its citizens and to protect the privileges and immunities of citizenship. Those who hoped that the progress of women and African Americans would be parallel, however, were disappointed by the wording of Section 2, which imposes penalties only on states that limited *male* citizens' right to vote.

Fourteenth Amendment § 2:

Representatives shall be apportioned among the several States according to their respective numbers, counting the whole number of persons in each State, excluding Indians not taxed. But when the right to vote at any election for the choice of electors for President and Vice President of the United States, Representatives in Congress, the Executive and Judicial officers of a State, or the members of the Legislature thereof, is denied to any of the male inhabitants of such State, being twenty-one years of age, and citizens of the United States, or in any way abridged, except for participation in rebellion, or other crime, the basis of representation therein shall be reduced in the proportion which the number of such male citizens shall bear to the whole number of male citizens twenty-one years of age in such State.

Two cases decided by the Supreme Court immediately after the passage of the Fourteenth Amendment made it clear that the Constitution still did not equally protect the rights of women. *Bradwell v. Illinois* (83 U.S. 130, 1873) found that equal protection did not prohibit sex-based classifications by states. States have the authority to determine the scope of rights, in this case the right to practice law, which women automatically receive because they are U.S. citizens. As the concurring opinion by Justice Joseph Bradley in *Bradwell* demonstrates, constitutional interpretation of the day perceived women as existing primarily in the role of mothers and wives. He stated "the civil law, as well as nature herself, has always recognized a wide difference in the respective spheres and destinies of man and woman. . . . The paramount destiny and mission of woman are to fulfill the noble and benign office of wife and mother." *Bradwell v. Illinois* was announced the day after the Supreme Court delivered its seminal decision in the *Slaughterhouse Cases* (83 U.S. 36, 1873), where the Court decided that the Fourteenth Amendment's Privileges and Immunities Clause protects only the rights of national citizenship. The Court also noted that the Equal Protection Clause was designed primarily to secure the constitutional concerns of African Americans. While the Court did not absolutely exclude women from its coverage, it would be many decades before coverage would extend to women. The Supreme Court in *Bradwell* did not address the question of whether the Illinois law violated the Equal Protection Clause of the Fourteenth Amendment, even though Bradwell's attorney had raised the issue in his brief.

In the second case that made it clear that citizenship did not guarantee the right to vote, *Minor v. Happersett* (88 U.S. 162, 1875), the Court argued that the Fourteenth Amendment protects only rights that people previously possessed; it does not create new ones. The Court believed that states could extend additional citizenship rights to women independently, but that the federal constitution did not automatically do so.

By the early twentieth century, as women entered the workforce in greater numbers, state legislatures began regulating the number of hours that women could work, determining what occupations were appropriate for women, and delineating other terms of female employment. The justification for such protective legislation was found in *Muller v. Oregon* (208 U.S. 412, 1908), a decision that was influenced by the first "Brandeis brief" (so-named to honor Justice Louis Brandeis, who as an attorney in this case introduced the consideration of contemporary social science data in reaching a verdict). In *Muller* the Court found that "healthy mothers are essential to vigorous offspring, the physical well-being of women becomes an object of public interest and care in order to preserve the strength and vigor of the race." This point of view began to dominate the Court's thinking, and the justices upheld legislation designed to protect women from discrimination in the civic sphere into the 1980s. For instance, the Court in *Goesaert v. Cleary* (335 U.S. 464, 1948) decided that a woman could be prevented from working in a bar unless her father or husband owned the establishment. The 1961 case of *Hoyt v. Florida* (368 U.S. 57) determined that women have the right to serve on juries; because the woman is "the center of home and family life," however, she does not, unlike men, have the duty to serve. *Hoyt* was overturned in 1975 in the case of *Taylor v. Louisiana* (419 U.S. 522, 1975), where the Court found that a fair jury system must draw from all segments of society and not exclude half of the population through an exception devised to keep women out.

A similar piece of protective legislation in California was upheld in *Michael M. v. Superior Court of Sonoma County* (1981), although in this case males were found liable for statutory rape charges even when similarly situated women were not. Here the Court declared a compelling governmental interest in maintaining the statutory distinction between men and women because of the biological differences between the genders: that is, young women can become pregnant. In the same year, *Rostker v. Goldberg* (453 U.S. 57, 1981) clarified that women's exemption from the selective service registration and the draft is not a form of unconstitutional discrimination, "but rather realistically reflects the fact that the sexes [in part because congressional law prohibited women from serving in combat] are not similarly situated." Because this case involves an equal protection challenge to a federal statute, it falls under the Due Process Clause of the Fifth Amendment. Unlike the Due Process Clause of the Fourteenth Amendment, which applies to the states, the federal promise of due process does not contain an explicit equal protection guarantee. In *Bolling v. Sharpe,* and the District of Columbia's case in *Washington v. Davis,* the Supreme Court found an inherent guarantee of equal protection in the Due Process Clause of the Fifth Amendment. While the Supreme Court in subsequent decisions changed its rulings regarding working hours, barroom employment, and jury service, and California changed its mind regarding the gender distinctions in statutory rape laws, *Rostker* is still the law of the land although legislative challenges may be forthcoming, especially as the armed services open more combat positions to women.

Evolving Judicial Standards

Over the years, the Supreme Court has developed three different standards to help determine the constitutionality of state laws under the Equal Protection Clause. The lowest, the **"minimal rationality"** standard, applies to most forms of classification—for example, the treatment of minors compared to adults. To meet this standard of ordinary scrutiny, the state must simply demonstrate that there is a rational foundation for the discriminatory law. If the state can show that there is a rational relationship between the distinction of groups under the contested law and a legitimate objective of the state, the law is not deemed to be in violation of the Fourteenth Amendment. If the state is unable to demonstrate such a relationship, then the Court will strike the law down as a violation of the Equal Protection Clause.

The highest standard, called **"strict scrutiny,"** applies to laws that violate fundamental freedoms (such as religion, speech, and press) or pertain to "suspect" classifications, such as racial distinctions. This standard requires the state to demonstrate to the judiciary that the challenged classification is necessary to achieve a permissible state objective. While gender fits many of the attributes inherent to suspect classification—it is an **immutable characteristic,** and there is a history of **"invidious" discrimination** or emotionally based antagonism toward women—the Supreme Court has not held that it meets the criteria required of a **suspect classification**.

In cases such as *Hoyt v. Florida* (1961), the Court argued that laws that distinguished between men and women had to have only a rational foundation to justify this discrimination. Because women are mothers, unlike men, they were not traditionally expected to spend time away from their families on juries. But in 1971 the Supreme Court, for the first time ever, found a law that treated men and women differently to be unconstitutional. In *Reed v. Reed* (404 U.S. 71), the justices asked whether an equal protection violation was present in the Idaho Probate Code, which required that in determining between equally entitled applicants to administer an estate, the male must be privileged over the female. By its ruling, the Court created a new standard: to be found constitutional, any law discriminating on the basis of gender must meet an important governmental function and be substantially related to that purpose.

Despite the use of a new standard, it would not be until the 1976 case of *Craig v. Boren* (429 U.S. 190) that the Supreme Court recognized that it had been using this new standard of "semi-strict" classification, or **intermediate scrutiny**, since *Reed v. Reed.* In this challenge to an Oklahoma statute that regulated the sale of alcoholic beverages, the Court found that allowing women over the age of eighteen to purchase 3.2 percent beer while forbidding men under the age of twenty-one to buy it was not constitutional under the Equal Protection Clause. The Court noted "*Reed v. Reed* has . . . provided the underpinning for decisions that have invalidated statutes employing gender as an inaccurate proxy for other, more germane bases of classification." Justice Rehnquist, who dissented, preferred what he considered to be a more appropriate reliance on the traditional rational basis test for gender challenges under equal protection.

The reliance on intermediate scrutiny for gender challenges on the basis of equal protection has been consistent, even when men challenge laws that treat them less advantageously than women, as happened in *Mississippi University for Women v. Hogan* (458 U.S. 718, 1982). In this case, Joe Hogan applied to the School of Nursing at the Mississippi University for Women and was denied admission on the basis of his gender. The Court found that under these circumstances, Mississippi was unable to demonstrate that its stated justification of compensating for discriminatory barriers confronting women was the actual purpose in creating a discriminatory classification. At the time, 98 percent of all registered nurses were women. Constitutionally, the university needed to allow males to enroll for credit in the School of Nursing; here again, the Equal Protection Clause was used to protect a man from gender discrimination.

In the 1973 case of *Frontiero v. Richardson* (411 U.S. 677), the Supreme Court implied that if the proposed Equal Rights Amendment (ERA) to the Constitution were ratified, gender might become a suspect classification, similar to racial classifications.

> Section 1. Equality of rights under the law shall not be denied or abridged by the United States or by any state on account of sex.
>
> Section 2. The Congress shall have the power to enforce, by appropriate legislation, the provisions of this article.
>
> Section 3. This amendment shall take effect two years after the date of ratification.

Proposed Equal Rights Amendment

Sharron Frontiero was a lieutenant in the U.S. Air Force who wanted dependent benefits for her spouse, the same benefits her male colleagues automatically received for their wives. Frontiero was denied the benefits because she could not demonstrate that her husband received over half of his support from her income. The Court found that this Air Force policy clearly violated the values of equal protection. While eight justices agreed with this verdict, only Justices Douglas, White, and Marshall joined Justice Brennan in basing the decision on strict scrutiny. The other four justices filed a variety of concurring opinions in which they agreed with the outcome of the decision, but not the constitutional reasoning. Justice Rehnquist dissented from the decision. Because *Frontiero* is a plurality decision, rather than a majority decision, the Court in later cases does not consider as precedent the argument made by Brennan—namely, that sex is a suspect classification that should, like race, fall under suspect scrutiny. Despite the optimism of the plurality, the ERA was very controversial. Many people were afraid that if it passed, women would lose the legal protections they possessed—the exemption from being drafted, the right to have special protections as mothers, and the financial guarantees provided by federal programs. Consequently, the amendment has consistently failed to get the necessary votes for ratification and to amend the Constitution.

While the lower court in *Michael M. v. Superior Court of Sonoma County* relied on suspect classification in its decision, the Supreme Court has not consistently applied strict scrutiny to all its gender discrimination cases.

Instead, the Court has occasionally rethought the intermediate standard of scrutiny. In the 1996 case of *United States v. Virginia* (518 U. S. 515), the Supreme Court examined the male-only admissions policy of Virginia Military Institute (VMI), which is a public, state-supported college. In her majority opinion, Justice Ruth Bader Ginsburg argued that the state must show "exceedingly persuasive justification" for differential treatment, in this case the exclusion of women from VMI. This is a higher requirement for the state than originally articulated in *Craig v. Boren* and a stronger constitutional protection against gender discrimination. While the Court has used this phrasing occasionally over the last thirty years (*Personnel Administrator of Massachusetts v. Feeney*, 442 U.S. 256, 1979; *Miller v. Albright*, 523 U.S. 420, 1998), the new standard has not been cited consistently in discrimination cases and does not appear to be new equal protection standard for gender. Only eight justices, divided seven to one, decided the VMI case; Justice Thomas had **recused** himself because his son was at that time enrolled in the military academy.

The difference in legal standards used by the Supreme Court in evaluating gender challenges to the Equal Protection Clause, as opposed to racial challenges, is significant. The consequences for women of color in challenging statutes and policies that might intertwine race and gender barriers is also significant. This is an issue that has not been completely resolved, as society's understanding of gender as both a biological reality and a socially constructed one is still evolving and transforming. Because the importance of social stereotypes in constituting gender and the way in which these perceptions change over time, it is possible that this area of law may not be settled for many years. As more women become engaged in the process of writing law, interpreting law, and enforcing law, the nation's understanding of the law itself may also be transformed. Regardless of this potential for change, the Constitution does not explicitly guarantee equality based on gender. The guarantee of equal rights for women has been provided by federal statutes, state laws and constitutions, and federal and state court decisions, but not by the explicit language of the Constitution.

SENECA FALLS DECLARATION OF SENTIMENTS AND RESOLUTIONS

(1848)

Written by Elizabeth Cady Stanton and Lucretia Mott in response to the exclusion of women from participation in the 1840 World's Anti-Slavery Convention in London, the Declaration was presented in Seneca Falls, New York, in 1848. In the audience were three hundred people who had gathered to consider the situation of women as unique from, but connected to, the claims of African slaves. Similar to Frederick Douglass's speech, "The Meaning of July Fourth for the Negro," the Seneca Falls Declaration asserts that the promises of the Declaration of Independence have failed with respect to the attempts by women to secure equal rights. This writing, like that of Douglass, roots the demands of the disenfranchised in the very heart of the American political tradition.

When, in the course of human events, it becomes necessary for one portion of the family of man to assume among the people of the earth a position different from that which they have hitherto occupied, but one to which the laws of nature and of nature's God entitle them, a decent respect to the opinions of mankind requires that they should declare the causes that impel them to such a course.

We hold these truths to be self-evident: that all men and women are created equal; that they are endowed by their Creator with certain inalienable rights; that among these are life, liberty, and the pursuit of happiness; that to secure these rights governments are instituted, deriving their just powers from the consent of the governed. Whenever any form of government becomes destructive of these ends, it is the right of those who suffer from it to refuse allegiance to it, and to insist upon the institution of a new government, laying its foundation on such principles, and organizing its powers in such form, as to them shall seem most likely to effect their safety and happiness. Prudence, indeed, will dictate that governments long established should not be changed for light and transient causes; and accordingly all experience hath shown that mankind are more disposed to suffer, while evils are sufferable, than to right themselves by abolishing the forms to which they were accustomed. But when a long train of abuses and usurpations, pursuing invariably the same object, evinces a design to reduce them under absolute despotism, it is their duty to throw off such government, and to provide new guards for their future security. Such has been the patient sufferance of the women under this government, and such is now the necessity which constrains them to demand the equal station to which they are entitled.

The history of mankind is a history of repeated injuries and usurpations on the part of man toward woman, having in direct object the establishment of an absolute tyranny over her. To prove this, let facts be submitted to a candid world.

He has never permitted her to exercise her inalienable right to the elective franchise.

He has compelled her to submit to laws, in the formation of which she had no voice.

He has withheld from her rights which are given to the most ignorant and degraded men—both natives and foreigners.

Having deprived her of this first right of a citizen, the elective franchise, thereby leaving her without representation in the halls of legislation, he has oppressed her on all sides.

He has made her, if married, in the eye of the law, civilly dead.

He has taken from her all right in property, even to the wages she earns.

He has made her, morally, an irresponsible being, as she can commit many crimes with impunity, provided they be done in the presence of her husband. In the covenant of marriage, she is compelled to promise obedience to her husband, he becoming to all intents and purposes, her master—the law giving him power to deprive her of her liberty, and to administer chastisement.

He has so framed the laws of divorce, as to what shall be the proper causes, and in case of separation, to whom the guardianship of the children shall be given, as to be wholly regardless of the happiness of women—the law, in all cases, going upon a false supposition of the supremacy of man, and giving all power into his hands.

After depriving her of all rights as a married woman, if single, and the owner of property, he has taxed her to support a government which recognizes her only when her property can be made profitable to it.

He has monopolized nearly all the profitable employments, and from those she is permitted to follow, she receives but a scanty remuneration. He closes against her all the avenues to wealth and distinction which he considers most honorable to himself. As a teacher of theology, medicine, or law, she is not known.

He has denied her the facilities for obtaining a thorough education, all colleges being closed against her.

He allows her in Church, as well as State, but a subordinate position, claiming Apostolic authority for her exclusion from the ministry, and, with some exceptions, from any public participation in the affairs of the Church.

He has created a false public sentiment by giving to the world a different code of morals for men and women, by which moral delinquencies which exclude women from society, are not only tolerated, but deemed of little account in man.

He has usurped the prerogative of Jehovah himself, claiming it as his right to assign for her a sphere of action, when that belongs to her conscience and to her God.

He has endeavored, in every way that he could, to destroy her confidence in her own powers, to lessen her self-respect, and to make her willing to lead a dependent and abject life.

Now, in view of this entire disfranchisement of one-half the people of this country, their social and religious degradation—in view of the unjust laws above mentioned, and because women do feel themselves aggrieved, oppressed, and fraudulently deprived of their most sacred rights, we insist that they have immediate admission to all the rights and privileges which belong to them as citizens of the United States.

In entering upon the great work before us, we anticipate no small amount of misconception, misrepresentation, and ridicule; but we shall use every instrumentality within our power to affect our object. We shall employ agents, circulate tracts, petition the State and National legislatures, and endeavor to enlist the pulpit and the press in our behalf. We hope this Convention will be followed by a series of Conventions embracing every part of the country.

BRADWELL V. ILLINOIS

83 U.S. (16 Wall.) 130 (1873)

Myra Bradwell had studied for the Illinois bar examination under the guidance of her husband, an attorney. She passed the exam, but the state of Illinois refused to allow her to practice law on the grounds of her gender. Iowa had already admitted the first woman to the state bar, in 1869. Bradwell is the first Supreme Court case to challenge sex-based classification under the Fourteenth Amendment.

Vote: 8–1

JUSTICE MILLER delivered the opinion of the Court.

As regards the provision of the Constitution that citizens of each State shall be entitled to all the privileges and immunities of citizens in the several States, the plaintiff in her affidavit has stated very clearly a case to which it is inapplicable.

The protection designed by that clause, as has been repeatedly held, has no application to a citizen of the State whose laws are complained of. If the plaintiff was a citizen of the State of Illinois, that provision of the Constitution gave her no protection against its courts or its legislation.

The [F]ourteenth [A]mendment declares that citizens of the United States are citizens of the State within which they reside; therefore the plaintiff was, at the time of making her application, a citizen of the United States and a citizen of the State of Illinois.

We do not here mean to say that there may not be a temporary residence in one State, with intent to return to another, which will not create citizenship in the former. But the plaintiff states nothing to take her case out of the definition of citizenship of a State as defined by the first section of the [F]ourteenth [A]mendment.

In regard to that amendment counsel for the plaintiff in this court truly says that there are certain privileges and immunities which belong to a citizen of the United States as such; otherwise it would be nonsense for the fourteenth amendment to prohibit a State from abridging them, and he proceeds to argue that admission to the bar of a State of a person who possesses the requisite learning and character is one of those which a State may not deny. In this latter proposition we are not able to concur with counsel. We agree with him that there are privileges and immunities belonging to citizens of the United States, in that relation and character, and that it is these and these alone which a State is forbidden to abridge. But the right to admission to practice in the courts of a State is not one of them. This right in no sense depends on citizenship of the United States. It has not, as far as we know, ever been made in any State, or in any case, to depend on citizenship at all. Certainly many prominent and distinguished lawyers have been admitted to practice, both in the State and Federal courts, who were not citizens of the United States or of any State. But, on whatever basis this right may be placed, so far as it can have any relation to citizenship at all, it would seem that, as to the courts of a State, it would relate to citizenship of the State, and as to Federal courts, it would relate to citizenship of the United States.

The opinion just delivered in the *Slaughterhouse Cases,* 83 U.S. 36 (1873), renders elaborate argument in the present case unnecessary; for, unless we are wholly and radically mistaken in the principles on which those cases are decided, the right to control and regulate the granting of license to practice law in the courts of a State is one of those powers which are not transferred for its protection to the Federal government, and its exercise is in no manner governed or controlled by citizenship of the United States in the party seeking such license.

JUSTICE BRADLEY, joined by JUSTICES SWAYNE and FIELD, concurring.

The claim that, under the fourteenth amendment of the Constitution, which declares that no State shall make or enforce any law which shall abridge the privileges and immunities of citizens of the United States, the statute law of Illinois, or the common law prevailing in that State, can no longer be set up as a barrier against the right of females to pursue any lawful employment for a livelihood (the practice of law included), assumes that it is one of the privileges and immunities of women as citizens to engage in any and every profession, occupation, or employment in civil life. It certainly cannot be affirmed, as an historical fact, that this has ever been established as one of the fundamental privileges and immunities of the sex. On the contrary, the civil law, as well as nature herself, has always recognized a wide difference in the respective spheres and destinies of man and woman. Man is, or should be, woman's protector and defender. The natural and proper timidity and delicacy which belongs to the female sex evidently unfits it for many of the occupations of civil life. The constitution of the family organization, which is founded in the divine ordinance, as well as in the nature of things, indicates the domestic sphere as that which properly belongs to the domain and functions of womanhood. The harmony, not to say identity, of interest and views which belong, or should belong, to the family institution is repugnant to the idea of a woman adopting a distinct and independent career from that of her husband. So firmly fixed was this sentiment in the founders of the common law that it became a maxim of that system of jurisprudence that a woman had no legal existence separate from her husband, who was regarded as her head and representative in the social state; and, notwithstanding some recent modifications of this civil status, many of the special rules of law flowing from and dependent upon this cardinal principle still exist in full force in most States. One of these is, that a married woman is incapable, without her husband's consent, of making contracts which shall be binding on her or him. This very incapacity was one circumstance which the Supreme Court of Illinois deemed important in rendering a married woman incompetent fully to perform the duties and trusts that belong to the office of an attorney and counsellor.

It is true that many women are unmarried and not affected by any of the duties, complications, and incapacities arising out of the married state, but these are exceptions to the general rule. The paramount destiny and mission of woman are to fulfill the noble and benign offices of wife and mother. This is the law of the Creator. And the rules of civil society must be adapted to the general constitution of things, and cannot be based upon exceptional cases.

The humane movements of modern society, which have for their object the multiplication of avenues for woman's advancement, and of occupations adapted to her condition and sex, have my heartiest concurrence. But I am not prepared to say that it is one of her fundamental rights and privileges to be admitted into every office and position, including those which require highly special qualifications and demanding special responsibilities.

FOR DISCUSSION

How did the cultural assumptions of the Court impact the way the justices interpreted the Equal Protection Clause's coverage of women? What are the rights inherent to citizenship?

RELATED CASES

***United States v. Susan B. Anthony:* 24 F. Cas. 829 (N.D.N.Y.) 1873.**

In this case, the voting rights activist Susan B. Anthony was arrested and charged with having voted, which was against the law in New York. The judge refused to allow Anthony to testify on her own behalf. She lost in federal court and was fined, but would not pay the amount specified. The judge then refused to imprison her, and because of this, she was unable to appeal to the Supreme Court.

***Minor v. Happersett:* 88 U.S. (21 Wall.) 162 (1875).**

Similar to *Anthony*, this case produced a ruling that the Fourteenth Amendment's guarantee of the privileges and immunities of citizenship does not include the right of women to vote. This is one of the last cases to attempt to use the Privileges and Immunities Clause to obtain citizenship equality. Future cases would focus on the Equal Protection Clause.

HOYT V. FLORIDA

368 U.S. 57, 82 S.Ct. 159, 7 L.Ed. 2d 118 (1961)

The appellant, Hoyt, was convicted in a Florida court for the murder of her husband. Her appeal claimed that because her case had been tried before an all-male jury, her rights under the Fourteenth Amendment had been violated. Florida Statute 1959, § 40.01 (1) required all juries to be composed of male and female citizens. The law provided that no female could be taken for jury service unless she had registered with the clerk of the circuit court her desire to be placed on the jury list. The Florida Supreme Court confirmed Hoyt's conviction.

Vote: 9–0

JUSTICE HARLAN delivered the opinion of the Court.

At the core of appellant's argument is the claim that the nature of the crime of which she was convicted peculiarly demanded the inclusion of persons of her own sex on the jury. She was charged with killing her husband by assaulting him with a baseball bat. As described by the Florida Supreme Court, the affair occurred in the context of a marital upheaval involving, among other things, the suspected infidelity of appellant's husband, and culminating in the husband's final rejection of his wife's efforts at reconciliation. It is claimed, in substance, that women jurors would have been more understanding or compassionate than men in assessing the quality of appellant's act and her defense of "temporary insanity." No claim is made that the jury as constituted was otherwise afflicted by any elements of supposed unfairness.

Of course, these premises misconceive the scope of the right to an impartially selected jury assured by the Fourteenth Amendment. That right does not entitle one accused of crime to a jury tailored to the circumstances of the particular case, whether relating to the sex or other condition of the defendant, or to the nature of the charges to be tried. It requires only that the jury be indiscriminately drawn from among those eligible in the community for jury service, untrammelled by any arbitrary and systematic exclusions. The result of this appeal must therefore depend on whether such an exclusion of women from jury service has been shown.

I

We address ourselves first to appellant's challenge to the statute on its face.

We of course recognize that the Fourteenth Amendment reaches not only arbitrary class exclusions from jury service based on race or color, but also all other exclusions which "single out" any class of persons "for different treatment not based on some reasonable classification." *Hernandez v. Texas*, 347 U.S. 475, 478 (1954). We need not, however, accept appellant's invitation to canvass in this case the continuing validity of this Court's dictum in *Strauder v. West Virginia*, 100 U.S. 303, 310 (1880), to the effect that a State may constitutionally "confine" jury duty "to males."

Manifestly, Florida's § 40.01 (1) does not purport to exclude women from state jury service. It accords women an absolute exemption from jury service unless they expressly waive that privilege. This is not to say, however, that what in form may be only an exemption of a particular class of persons can in no circumstances be regarded as an exclusion of that class.

In the selection of jurors Florida has differentiated between men and women in two respects. It has given women an absolute exemption from jury duty based solely on their sex, no similar exemption obtaining as to men. And it has provided for its effectuation in a manner less onerous than that governing exemptions exercisable by men: women are not to be put on the jury list unless they have voluntarily registered for such service; men, on the other hand, even if entitled to an exemption, are to be included on the list unless they have filed a written claim of exemption as provided by law.

In neither respect can we conclude that Florida's statute is not "based on some reasonable classification," and that it is thus infected with unconstitutionality. Despite the enlightened emancipation of women from the restrictions and protections of bygone years, and their entry into many parts of community life formerly considered to be reserved to men, woman is still regarded as the center of home and family life. We cannot say that it is constitutionally impermissible for a State, acting in pursuit of the general welfare, to conclude that a woman should be relieved from the civic duty of jury service unless she herself determines that such service is consistent with her own special responsibilities.

Florida is not alone in so concluding. Women are now eligible for jury service in all but three States of the Union. Of the forty-seven States where women are eligible, seventeen besides Florida, as well as the District of Columbia, have accorded women an absolute exemption based solely on their sex, exercisable in one form or another. [W]e cannot regard it as irrational for a state legislature to consider preferable a broad exemption, whether born of the State's historic public policy or of a determination that it would not be administratively feasible to decide in each individual instance whether the family responsibilities of a prospective female juror were serious enough to warrant an exemption.

Appellant argues that whatever may have been the design of this Florida enactment, the statute in practical operation results in an exclusion of women from jury service, because women, like men, can be expected to be available for jury service only under compulsion. In this connection she points out that by 1957, when this trial took place, only some 220 women out of approximately 46,000 registered female voters in Hillsborough County—constituting about 40 per cent of the total voting population of that county—had volunteered for jury duty since the limitation of jury service to males, was removed by § 40.01 (1) in 1949.

This argument, however, is surely beside the point. Given the reasonableness of the classification involved in § 40.01 (1), the relative paucity of women jurors does not carry the constitutional consequence appellant would have it bear.

II

Appellant's attack on the statute as applied in this case fares no better.

This case in no way resembles those involving race or color in which the circumstances shown were found by this Court to compel a conclusion of purposeful discriminatory exclusions from jury service. E.g., *Hernandez v. Texas*; *Norris v. Alabama*, 294 U.S. 587 (1935); *Smith v. Texas*, 311 U.S. 128 (1940); *Hill v. Texas*, 316 U.S. 400 (1942); *Eubanks v. Louisiana*, 356 U.S. 584 (1958). There is present here neither the unfortunate atmosphere of ethnic or racial prejudices which underlay the situations depicted in those cases, nor the long course of discriminatory administrative practice which the statistical showing in each of them evinced.

In the circumstances here depicted, it indeed "taxes our credulity," to attribute to these administrative officials a deliberate design to exclude the very class whose eligibility for jury service the state legislature, after many years of contrary policy, had declared only a few years before. It is sufficiently evident from the record that the presence on the jury list of no more than ten or twelve women in the earlier years, and the failure to add in 1957 more women to those already on the list, are attributable not to any discriminatory motive, but to a purpose to put on the list only those women who might be expected to be qualified for service if actually called. Nor is there the slightest suggestion that the list was the product of any plan to place on it only women of a particular economic or other community or organizational group.

Finally, the disproportion of women to men on the list independently carries no constitutional significance. In the administration of the jury laws proportional class representation is not a constitutionally required factor.

Finding no substantial evidence whatever in this record that Florida has arbitrarily undertaken to exclude women from jury service, a showing which it was incumbent on appellant to make, we must sustain the judgment of the Supreme Court of Florida.

Affirmed.

THE CHIEF JUSTICE, JUSTICE BLACK and JUSTICE DOUGLAS, concurring.

We cannot say from this record that Florida is not making a good faith effort to have women perform jury duty without discrimination on the ground of sex. Hence we concur in the result, for the reasons set forth in Part II of the Court's opinion.

FOR DISCUSSION

Is there a way to protect vulnerable groups from civic responsibilities without relying on social stereotypes? How? What might be the implications for citizenship?

RELATED CASES

***Quong Wing v. Kirkendall*: 223 U.S. 62 (1912).**

A male Chinese American who operated a hand laundry challenged a Montana law that gave tax benefits to small laundries owned by women but no similar benefits to men. The Court upheld the law under the Equal Protection Clause.

***Breedlove v. Shuttles:* 302 U.S. 277 (1937).**

The Court rejected the equal protection claims of a man challenging gender-based discrimination in tax laws. All sighted males between twenty-one and sixty years of age had to pay the tax regardless of voting status; women had to pay the tax only if they registered to vote.

***Goesaert v. Cleary, Liquor Control Commission of Michigan:* 335 U.S. 464 (1948).**

The Court upheld a Michigan law that prevented women from working behind a bar unless the establishment was owned by their husband or their father. The Court saw no violation of the Equal Protection Clause, reporting that the state may have made the provision because bartending by women might "give rise to moral and social problems against which it may devise preventative measures."

Taylor v. Louisiana: **419 U.S. 522 (1975).**

The Court overturns the decision of *Hoyt v. Florida* and rules that a fair jury system must draw from a cross section of the entire society and not exclude over half the population.

J.E.B. v. Alabama ex. rel. T.B.: **511 U.S. 127 (1994).**

The Equal Protection Clause prohibits excluding potential members from a jury on the basis of gender, just as selection cannot be based on race.

REED V. REED

404 U.S. 71, 92 S.Ct. 251, 30 L.Ed.2d 225 (1971)

Richard Reed died without a will and while estranged from his parents. Sally Reed, the appellant, filed a petition to be named the administrator of the estate of Richard Reed, who was her adopted son. The decedent's father, appellee Cecil Reed, filed a competing petition to be named the same. The probate court decided that §§ 15–312 and 15–314 of the Idaho Probate Code were controlling and that the law required that males be preferred to females when equally entitled people sought to administer an estate. Sally Reed appealed, and the district court found that the Idaho law violated the Equal Protection Clause of the Fourteenth Amendment. Cecil Reed's appeal to the Idaho Supreme Court resulted in the reversal of the district court's ruling and a rejection of the equal protection claim.

Vote: 9–1

CHIEF JUSTICE BURGER delivered the opinion of the Court.

Having examined the record and considered the briefs and oral arguments of the parties, we have concluded that the arbitrary preference established in favor of males by § 15–314 of the Idaho Code cannot stand in the face of the Fourteenth Amendment's command that no State deny the equal protection of the laws to any person within its jurisdiction.

Idaho does not, of course, deny letters of administration to women altogether. Indeed, under § 15–312, a woman whose spouse dies intestate has a preference over a son, father, brother, or any other male relative of the decedent. Moreover, we can judicially notice that in this country, presumably due to the greater longevity of women, a large proportion of estates, both intestate and under wills of decedents, are administered by surviving widows.

Section 15–314 is restricted in its operation to those situations where competing applications for letters of administration have been filed by both male and female members of the same entitlement class established by § 15–312. In such situations, § 15–314 provides that different treatment be accorded to the applicants on the basis of their sex; it thus establishes a classification subject to scrutiny under the Equal Protection Clause.

In applying that clause, this Court has consistently recognized that the Fourteenth Amendment does not deny to States the power to treat different classes of persons in different ways. *Barbier v. Connolly*, 113 U.S. 27 (1885); *Lindsley v. Natural Carbonic Gas Co.*, 220 U.S. 61 (1911); *Railway Express Agency v. New York*, 336 U.S. 106 (1949); *McDonald v. Board of Election Commissioners*, 394 U.S. 802 (1969). The Equal Protection Clause of that amendment does, however, deny to States the power to legislate that different treatment be accorded to persons placed by a statute into different classes on the basis of criteria wholly unrelated to the objective of that statute. A classification "must be reasonable, not arbitrary, and must rest upon some ground of difference having a fair and substantial relation to the object of the legislation, so that all persons similarly circumstanced shall be treated alike." *Royster Guano Co. v. Virginia*, 253 U.S. 412, 415 (1920). The question presented by this case, then, is whether a difference in the sex of competing applicants for letters of administration bears a rational relationship to a state objective that is sought to be advanced by the operation of §§ 15–312 and 15–314.

Clearly the objective of reducing the workload on probate courts by eliminating one class of contests is not without some legitimacy. The crucial question, however, is whether § 15–314 advances that objective in a manner consistent with the command of the Equal Protection Clause. We hold that it does not. To give a mandatory preference to members of either sex over members of the other, merely to accomplish the elimination of hearings on the merits, is to make the very kind of arbitrary legislative choice forbidden by the Equal Protection Clause of the Fourteenth Amendment; and whatever may be said as to the positive values of avoiding intrafamily controversy, the choice in this context may not lawfully be mandated solely on the basis of sex.

The judgment of the Idaho Supreme Court is reversed and the case remanded for further proceedings not inconsistent with this opinion.

Reversed and remanded.

FOR DISCUSSION

What types of state statutes, classified on the basis of gender, might be constitutional under this constitutional standard? Why is this decision a significant precedent?

FURTHER CASES

***Kahn v. Shevin:* 416 U.S. 351 (1974).**

The Court upheld against an equal protection challenge a Florida law that provided widows, but not widowers, a $500 annual exemption on their property tax. The Court cited the *Reed* precedent, but cited "reasonableness" as the standard.

***Orr v. Orr:* 440 U.S. 268 (1979).**

Court upheld an equal protection challenge of an Alabama statute that allowed for men to pay alimony to former wives but did not allow for the possibility of greater-earning women being obliged to pay alimony to their former husbands.

FRONTIERO V. RICHARDSON

411 U.S. 677, 93 S.Ct. 1764, 36 L.Ed.2d 583 (1973)

Sharron Frontiero was a U.S. Air Force lieutenant who sought the typical dependent benefits because she was married: increased quarters allowance, housing, and medical benefits for her spouse. Wives of male military members were automatically awarded such benefits. Frontiero was denied her application because she did not document that her husband relied on her for over half of his support. Frontiero challenged this policy as unlawful sex discrimination in violation of the Due Process Clause of the Fifth Amendment. The federal district court for the Middle District of Alabama rejected this claim and upheld the constitutionality of the federal statutes that mandated the nature of spousal benefits.

Vote: 8–1

JUSTICE BRENNAN announced the plurality decision.

I

In an effort to attract career personnel through reenlistment, Congress established a scheme for the provision of fringe benefits to members of the uniformed services on a competitive basis with business and industry. Thus, under 37 U.S.C. § 403, a member of the uniformed services with dependents is entitled to an increased "basic allowance for quarters" and, under 10 U.S.C. § 1076, a member's dependents are provided comprehensive medical and dental care.

Although the legislative history of these statutes sheds virtually no light on the purposes underlying the differential treatment accorded male and female members, a majority of the three-judge District Court surmised that Congress might reasonably have concluded that, since the husband in our society is generally the "breadwinner" in the family—and the wife typically the "dependent" partner—"it would be more economical to require married female members claiming husbands to prove actual dependency than to extend the presumption of dependency to such members." Indeed, given the fact that approximately 99% of all members of the uniformed services are male, the District Court speculated that such differential treatment might conceivably lead to a "considerable saving of administrative expense and manpower."

II

At the outset, appellants contend that classifications based upon sex, like classifications based upon race, alienage, and national origin, are inherently suspect and must therefore be subjected to close judicial scrutiny. We agree and, indeed, find at least implicit support for such an approach in our unanimous decision only last Term in *Reed v. Reed*, 404 U.S. 71 (1971).

The Court . . . held that, even though the State's interest in achieving administrative efficiency "is not without some legitimacy," "to give a mandatory preference to members of either sex over members of the other, merely to accomplish the elimination of hearings on the merits, is to make the very kind of arbitrary legislative choice forbidden by the [Constitution]. . . ." This departure from "traditional" rational-basis analysis with respect to sex-based classifications is clearly justified.

There can be no doubt that our Nation has had a long and unfortunate history of sex discrimination. Traditionally, such discrimination was rationalized by an attitude of "romantic paternalism" which, in practical effect, put women, not on a pedestal, but in a cage. Indeed, this paternalistic attitude became so firmly rooted in our national consciousness that, 100 years ago, a distinguished Member of this Court was able to proclaim:

> . . .The paramount destiny and mission of woman are to fulfil the noble and benign offices of wife and mother. This is the law of the Creator. *Bradwell v. State* (16 Wall. 130, 141, 1873) (Bradley, J., concurring).

As a result of notions such as these, our statute books gradually became laden with gross, stereotyped distinctions between the sexes and, indeed, throughout much of the 19th century the position of women in our society was, in many respects, comparable to that of blacks under the pre–Civil War slave codes. Neither slaves nor women could hold office, serve on juries, or bring suit in their own names, and married women traditionally were denied the legal capacity to hold or convey property or to serve as legal guardians of their own children.

It is true, of course, that the position of women in America has improved markedly in recent decades. Nevertheless, it can hardly be doubted that, in part because of the high visibility of the sex characteristic, women still face pervasive, although at times more subtle, discrimination in our educational institutions, in the job market and, perhaps most conspicuously, in the political arena.

Moreover, since sex, like race and national origin, is an immutable characteristic determined solely by the accident of birth, the imposition of special disabilities upon the members of a particular sex because of their sex would seem to violate "the basic concept of our system that legal burdens should bear some relationship to individual responsibility. . . ." *Weber v. Aetna Casualty & Surety Co.*, 406 U.S. 164, 175 (1972). And what differentiates sex from such nonsuspect statuses as intelligence or physical disability, and aligns it with the recognized suspect criteria, is that the sex characteristic frequently bears no relation to ability to perform or contribute to society. As a result, statutory distinctions between the sexes often have the effect of invidiously relegating the entire class of females to inferior legal status without regard to the actual capabilities of its individual members.

We might also note that, over the past decade, Congress has itself manifested an increasing sensitivity to sex-based classifications. In Tit[le] VII of the Civil Rights Act of 1964, for example, Congress expressly declared that no employer, labor union, or other organization subject to the provisions of the Act shall discriminate against any individual on the basis of "race, color, religion, sex, or national origin." Thus, Congress itself has concluded that classifications based upon sex are inherently invidious, and this conclusion of a coequal branch of Government is not without significance to the question presently under consideration.

With these considerations in mind, we can only conclude that classifications based upon sex, like classifications based upon race, alienage, or national origin, are inherently suspect, and must therefore be subjected to strict judicial scrutiny. Applying the analysis mandated by that stricter standard of review, it is clear that the statutory scheme now before us is constitutionally invalid.

III

The sole basis of the classification established in the challenged statutes is the sex of the individuals involved.

Moreover, the Government concedes that the differential treatment accorded men and women under these statutes serves no purpose other than mere "administrative convenience." In essence, the Government maintains that, as an empirical matter, wives in our society frequently are dependent upon their husbands, while husbands rarely are dependent upon their wives. Thus, the Government argues that Congress might reasonably have concluded that it would be both cheaper and easier simply conclusively to presume that wives of male members are financially dependent upon their husbands, while burdening female members with the task of establishing dependency in fact.

The Government offers no concrete evidence, however, tending to support its view that such differential treatment in fact saves the Government any money. In order to satisfy the demands of strict judicial scrutiny, the Government must demonstrate, for example, that it is actually cheaper to grant increased benefits with respect to all male members, than it is to determine which male members are in fact entitled to such benefits and to grant increased benefits only to those members whose wives actually meet the dependency requirement. Here, however, there is substantial evidence that, if put to the test, many of the wives of male members would fail to qualify for benefits.

In any case, our prior decisions make clear that, although efficacious administration of governmental programs is not without some importance, "the Constitution recognizes higher values than speed and efficiency." *Stanley v. Illinois*, 405 U.S. 645, 656 (1972). And when we enter the realm of "strict judicial scrutiny," there can be no doubt that "administrative convenience" is not a shibboleth, the mere recitation of which dictates constitutionality. We therefore conclude that, by according differential treatment to male and female members of the uniformed services for the sole purpose of achieving administrative convenience, the challenged statutes violate the Due Process Clause of the Fifth Amendment insofar as they require a female member to prove the dependency of her husband.

Reversed.

JUSTICE POWELL, with whom THE CHIEF JUSTICE and JUSTICE BLACKMUN join, concurring in the judgment.

I agree that the challenged statutes constitute an unconstitutional discrimination against servicewomen in violation of the Due Process Clause of the Fifth Amendment, but I cannot join the opinion of Mr. Justice Brennan, which would hold that all classifications based upon sex, "like classifications based upon race, alienage, and national origin," are "inherently suspect and must therefore be subjected to close judicial scrutiny." It is unnecessary for the Court in this case to characterize sex as a suspect classification, with all of the far-reaching implications of such a holding. *Reed v. Reed*, 404 U.S. 71 (1971), which abundantly supports our decision today, did not add sex to the narrowly limited group of classifications which are inherently suspect. In my view, we can and should decide this case on the authority of *Reed* and reserve for the future any expansion of its rationale.

There is another, and I find compelling, reason for deferring a general categorizing of sex classifications as invoking the strictest test of judicial scrutiny. The Equal Rights Amendment, which if adopted will resolve the substance of this precise question, has been approved by the Congress and submitted for ratification by the States. If this Amendment is duly adopted, it will represent the will of the people accomplished in the manner prescribed by the Constitution. By acting prematurely and unnecessarily, as I view it, the Court has assumed a decisional responsibility at the very time when state legislatures, functioning within the traditional democratic process, are debating the proposed Amendment. It seems to me that this reaching out to pre-empt by judicial action a major political decision which is currently in process of resolution does not reflect appropriate respect for duly prescribed legislative processes.

There are times when this Court, under our system, cannot avoid a constitutional decision on issues which normally should be resolved by the elected representatives of the people. But democratic institutions are weakened, and confidence in the restraint of the Court is impaired, when we appear unnecessarily to decide sensitive issues of broad social and political importance at the very time they are under consideration within the prescribed constitutional processes.

FOR DISCUSSION

What is the key conflict between the justices' opinions that resulted in this case being a plurality and not a majority opinion? Why is the constitutional standard used by the Court to determine an equal protection violation so significant?

RELATED CASES

***Schlesinger v. Ballard:* 419 U.S. 498 (1975).**

The Court upheld a system used by the U.S. Navy that allowed women four more years of duty to achieve promotion before they are forced out of the service by discharge. Citing *Reed* and *Frontiero*, the Court argued that the system was not based on administrative convenience or outmoded stereotypes, but reflected the occupational differences in treatment for men and women in the Navy.

***Weinberger v. Wiesenfeld:* 420 U.S. 636 (1975).**

The Court found unconstitutional a social security system that awarded death benefits to widows, but not to widowers. The justices ruled that this violated the equal protection rights of the deceased female wage earner.

Craig v. Boren

429 U.S. 190, 97 S.Ct. 451, 50 L.Ed.2d 397 (1976)

The state of Oklahoma prohibited the sale of 3.2 percent beer to males under the age of twenty-one and to females under the age of eighteen. Craig, a man between the ages of eighteen and twenty-one, and Whitener, a woman who was a vendor of 3.2 percent beer, challenged the gender-based age differential on the grounds that it demonstrated invidious discrimination against men between the ages of eighteen and twenty in violation of the Equal Protection Clause of the Fourteenth Amendment. The federal district court upheld the constitutionality of the law.

Vote: 7–2

Justice Brennan delivered the opinion of the Court.

II

A

Analysis may appropriately begin with the reminder that *Reed* [*v. Reed,* 404 U.S. 71 (1971)] emphasized that statutory classifications that distinguish between males and females are "subject to scrutiny under the Equal Protection Clause." To withstand constitutional challenge, previous cases establish that classifications by gender must serve important governmental objectives and must be substantially related to achievement of those objectives. Thus, in *Reed*, the objectives of "reducing the workload on probate courts," and "avoiding intrafamily controversy," were deemed of insufficient importance to sustain use of an overt gender criterion in the appointment of administrators of intestate decedents' estates. Decisions following *Reed* similarly have rejected administrative ease and convenience as sufficiently important objectives to justify gender-based classifications. See, *Stanley v. Illinois*, 405 U.S. 645, 656 (1972); *Frontiero v. Richardson*, 411 U.S. 677, 690 (1973); *Schlesinger v. Ballard*, 419 U.S. 498, 506–507 (1975).

Reed v. Reed has also provided the underpinning for decisions that have invalidated statutes employing gender as an inaccurate proxy for other, more germane bases of classification. Similarly, increasingly outdated misconceptions concerning the role of females in the home rather than in the "marketplace and world of ideas" were rejected as loose-fitting characterizations incapable of supporting state statutory schemes that were premised upon their accuracy. In light of the weak congruence between gender and the characteristic or trait that gender purported to represent, it was necessary that the legislatures choose either to realign their substantive laws in a gender-neutral fashion, or to adopt procedures for identifying those instances where the sex-centered generalization actually comported with fact.

We turn then to the question whether, under *Reed*, the difference between males and females with respect to the purchase of 3.2% beer warrants the differential in age drawn by the Oklahoma statute. We conclude that it does not.

B

[Cites the district court reliance on the important governmental objective in *Reed v. Reed*.]

C

Clearly, the protection of public health and safety represents an important function of state and local governments. However, appellees' statistics in our view cannot support the conclusion that the gender-based distinction closely serves to achieve that objective and therefore the distinction cannot under *Reed* withstand equal protection challenge.

The appellees introduced a variety of statistical surveys. First, an analysis of arrest statistics for 1973 demonstrated that 18–20-year-old male arrests for "driving under the influence" and "drunkenness" substantially exceeded female arrests for that same age period. Similarly, youths aged 17–21 were found to be overrepresented among those killed or injured in traffic accidents, with males again numerically exceeding females in this regard. Third, a random roadside survey in Oklahoma City revealed that young males were more inclined to drive and drink beer than were their female counterparts. Fourth, Federal Bureau of Investigation nationwide statistics exhibited a notable increase in arrests for "driving under the influence." Finally, statistical evidence gathered in other jurisdictions, particularly Minnesota and Michigan, was offered to corroborate Oklahoma's experience by indicating the pervasiveness of youthful participation in motor vehicle accidents following the imbibing of alcohol. Conceding that "the case is not free from doubt," the District Court nonetheless concluded that this statistical showing substantiated "a rational basis for the legislative judgment underlying the challenged classification."

Even were this statistical evidence accepted as accurate, it nevertheless offers only a weak answer to the equal protection question presented here. Viewed in terms of the correlation between sex and the actual activity that Oklahoma seeks to regulate—driving while under the influence of alcohol—the statistics broadly establish that.18% of females and 2% of males in that age group were arrested for that offense. While such a disparity is not trivial in a statistical sense, it hardly can form the basis for employment of a gender line as a classifying device.

Moreover, the statistics exhibit a variety of other shortcomings that seriously impugn their value to equal protection analysis. Setting aside the obvious methodological problems, the surveys do not adequately justify the salient features of Oklahoma's gender-based traffic-safety law. None purports to measure the use and dangerousness of 3.2% beer as opposed to alcohol generally, a detail that is of particular importance since, in light of its low alcohol level, Oklahoma apparently considers the 3.2% beverage to be "nonintoxicating."

It is unrealistic to expect either members of the judiciary or state officials to be well versed in the rigors of experimental or statistical technique. But this merely illustrates that proving broad sociological propositions by statistics is a dubious business, and one that inevitably is in tension with the normative philosophy that underlies the Equal Protection Clause. Suffice to say that the showing offered by the appellees does not satisfy us that sex represents a legitimate, accurate proxy for the regulation of drinking and driving. In fact, when it is further recognized that Oklahoma's statute prohibits only the selling of 3.2% beer to young males and not their drinking the beverage once acquired (even after purchase by their 18–20-year-old female companions), the relationship between gender and traffic safety becomes far too tenuous to satisfy Reed's requirement that the gender-based difference be substantially related to achievement of the statutory objective.

We hold, therefore, that under *Reed*, Oklahoma's 3.2% beer statute invidiously discriminates against males 18–20 years of age.

JUSTICE REHNQUIST, dissenting.

The Court's disposition of this case is objectionable on two grounds. First is its conclusion that men challenging a gender-based statute which treats them less favorably than women may invoke a more stringent standard of judicial review than pertains to most other types of classifications. Second is the Court's enunciation of this standard, without citation to any source, as being that "classifications by gender must serve important governmental objectives and must be substantially related to achievement of those objectives." The only redeeming feature of the Court's opinion, to my mind, is that it apparently signals a retreat by those who joined the plurality opinion in *Frontiero v. Richardson*, 411 U.S. 677 (1973), from their view that sex is a "suspect" classification for purposes of equal protection analysis.

I think the Oklahoma statute challenged here need pass only the "rational basis" equal protection analysis expounded in cases such as *McGowan v. Maryland*, 366 U.S. 420 (1961), and *Williamson v. Lee Optical Co.*, 348 U.S. 483 (1955), and I believe that it is constitutional under that analysis.

I

In *Frontiero v. Richardson*, the opinion for the plurality sets forth the reasons of four Justices for concluding that sex should be regarded as a suspect classification for purposes of equal protection analysis. These reasons center on our Nation's "long and unfortunate history of sex discrimination," 411 U.S., at 684, which has been reflected in a whole range of restrictions on the legal rights of women, not the least of which have concerned the ownership of property and participation in the electoral process. Noting that the pervasive and persistent nature of the discrimination experienced by women is in part the result of their ready identifiability, the plurality rested its invocation of strict scrutiny largely upon the fact that "statutory distinctions between the sexes often have the effect of invidiously relegating the entire class of females to inferior legal status without regard to the actual capabilities of its individual members."

Subsequent to *Frontiero*, the Court has declined to hold that sex is a suspect class, *Stanton v. Stanton*, and no such holding is imported by the Court's resolution of this case. However, The Court's application here of an elevated or "intermediate" level scrutiny, like that invoked in cases dealing with discrimination against females, raises the question of why the statute here should be treated any differently from countless legislative classifications unrelated to sex which have been upheld under a minimum rationality standard.

Most obviously unavailable to support any kind of special scrutiny in this case, is a history or pattern of past discrimination, such as was relied on by the plurality in *Frontiero* to support its invocation of strict scrutiny. There is no suggestion in the Court's opinion that males in this age group are in any way peculiarly disadvantaged, subject to systematic discriminatory treatment, or otherwise in need of special solicitude from the courts.

The Court does not discuss the nature of the right involved, and there is no reason to believe that it sees the purchase of 3.2% beer as implicating any important interest, let alone one that is "fundamental" in the constitutional sense of invoking strict scrutiny. Indeed, the Court's accurate observation that the statute affects the selling but not the drinking of 3.2% beer, further emphasizes the limited effect that it has on even those persons in the age group involved. There is, in sum, nothing about the statutory classification involved here to suggest that it affects an interest, or works against a group, which can claim under the Equal Protection Clause that it is entitled to special judicial protection.

The Court's conclusion that a law which treats males less favorably than females "must serve important governmental objectives and must be substantially related to achievement of those objectives" apparently comes out of thin air. The Equal Protection Clause contains no such language, and none of our previous cases adopt that standard. I would think we have had enough difficulty with the two standards of review which our cases have recognized—the norm of "rational basis," and the "compelling state interest" required where a "suspect classification" is involved—so as to counsel weightily against the insertion of still another "standard" between those two. How is this Court to divine what objectives are important? How is it to determine whether a particular law is "substantially" related to the achievement of such objective, rather than related in some other way to its achievement? Both of the phrases used are so diaphanous and elastic as to invite subjective judicial preferences or prejudices relating to particular types of legislation, masquerading as judgments whether such legislation is directed at "important" objectives or, whether the relationship to those objectives is "substantial" enough.

FOR DISCUSSION

Why does Justice Rehnquist in his dissent believe that a rational basis test would be most appropriate in this case? What is the primary distinction between decisions in *Frontiero v. Richardson* and the *Reed v. Reed* and the facts of this case?

RELATED CASES

***Stanton v. Stanton:* 421 U.S. 7 (1975).**

The Court held that *Reed v. Reed* required the invalidation of a Utah differential age-of-majority statute, in which girls became adults at age eighteen and boys at twenty-one. The Supreme Court disregarded the state's claimed purpose: preparing boys for their expected performance in the economic and political worlds.

***Califano v. Goldfarb:* 430 U.S. 199 (1977).**

A social security regulation that allowed widows to receive surviving spouse benefits if the husband's benefits were greater than the widow's own social security benefits, but required widowers to demonstrate their dependency on their wife's benefits, was found to violate the Equal Protection Clause.

***Califano v. Webster:* 420 U.S. 313 (1977).**

The Supreme Court upheld another social security law that provided for all women who retired prior to 1975 benefits in addition to those paid to men retiring at the same time. The Court found that this benefit was designed to compensate for "economic disabilities" faced by women and thereby allowable under the Equal Protection Clause.

ROSTKER V. GOLDBERG

453 U.S. 57, 101 S.Ct. 2646, 69 L.Ed.2d 478 (1981)

In 1980, shortly after the Soviet invasion of Afghanistan, the Military Selective Service Act (MSSA) was reactivated to require registration of all male citizens between the ages of eighteen and twenty-six in case of a need for a national military draft. Despite President Carter's recommendation that the MSSA be amended to allow for the registration and possible conscription of women, after a long debate Congress declined to expand the scope of the act. A lawsuit initiated by several young men in 1971 was heard before the federal district court of the Eastern District of Pennsylvania. The court struck down the act, ruling that it violated the Due Process Clause of the Fifth Amendment.

Vote: 6–3

JUSTICE REHNQUIST delivered the opinion of the Court.

II

The case arises in the context of Congress' authority over national defense and military affairs, and perhaps in no other area has the Court accorded Congress greater deference. In rejecting the registration of women, Congress explicitly relied upon its constitutional powers under Art. I, § 8, cls. 12–14.

This Court has consistently recognized Congress' "broad constitutional power" to raise and regulate armies and navies, *Schlesinger v. Ballard*, 419 U.S. 498, 510 (1975).

In *Schlesinger v. Ballard*, the Court considered a due process challenge, brought by males, to the Navy policy of according females a longer period than males in which to attain promotions necessary to continued service. The Court distinguished previous gender-based discriminations held unlawful in *Reed v. Reed*, 404 U.S. 71 (1971), and *Frontiero v. Richardson*, 411 U.S. 677 (1973). In those cases, the classifications were based on "overbroad generalizations." In the case before it, however, the Court noted:

> [The] different treatment of men and women naval officers . . . reflects, not archaic and overbroad generalizations, but, instead, the demonstrable fact that male and female line officers in the Navy are not similarly situated with respect to opportunities for professional service. Appellee has not challenged the current restrictions on women officers' participation in combat and in most sea duty. Id., at 508.

In light of the combat restrictions, women did not have the same opportunities for promotion as men, and therefore it was not unconstitutional for Congress to distinguish between them.

None of this is to say that Congress is free to disregard the Constitution when it acts in the area of military affairs. In that area, as any other, Congress remains subject to the limitations of the Due Process Clause; *Hamilton v. Kentucky Distilleries & Warehouse Co.*, 251 U.S. 146, 156 (1919), but the tests and limitations to be applied may differ because of the military context. We of course do not abdicate our ultimate responsibility to decide the constitutional question, but simply recognize that the Constitution itself requires such deference to congressional choice.

No one could deny that under the test of *Craig v. Boren*, 429 US. 190 (1976), the Government's interest in raising and supporting armies is an "important governmental interest." Congress and its Committees carefully considered and debated two alternative means of furthering that interest: the first was to register only males for potential conscription, and the other was to register both sexes. Congress chose the former alternative. When that decision is challenged on equal protection grounds, the question a court must decide is not which alternative it would have chosen, had it been the primary decisionmaker, but whether that chosen by Congress denies equal protection of the laws.

Schlesinger v. Ballard did not purport to apply a different equal protection test because of the military context, but did stress the deference due congressional choices among alternatives in exercising the congressional authority to raise and support armies and make rules for their governance. In light of the floor debate and the Report of the Senate Armed Services Committee hereinafter discussed, it is apparent that Congress was fully aware not merely of the many facts and figures presented to it by witnesses who testified before its Committees, but of the current thinking as to the place of women in the Armed Services. In such a case, we cannot ignore Congress' broad authority conferred by the Constitution to raise and support armies when we are urged to declare unconstitutional its studied choice of one alternative in preference to another for furthering that goal.

III

This case is quite different from several of the gender-based discrimination cases we have considered in that, despite appellees' assertions, Congress did not act "unthinkingly" or "reflexively and not for any considered reason." The question of registering women for the draft not only received considerable national attention and was the subject of wide-ranging public debate, but also was extensively considered by Congress in hearings, floor debate, and in committee. Hearings held by both Houses of Congress in response to the President's request for authorization to register women adduced extensive testimony and evidence concerning the issue.

The foregoing clearly establishes that the decision to exempt women from registration was not the " 'accidental by-product of a traditional way of thinking about females.' " *Califano v. Webster*, 430 U.S. 313, 320 (1977). The issue was considered at great length, and Congress clearly expressed its purpose and intent.

Congress determined that any future draft, which would be facilitated by the registration scheme, would be characterized by a need for combat troops. The Senate Report explained, in a specific finding later adopted by both Houses, that "[if] mobilization were to be ordered in a wartime scenario, the primary manpower need would be for combat replacements." The purpose of registration, therefore, was to prepare for a draft of combat troops.

Women as a group, however, unlike men as a group, are not eligible for combat. The restrictions on the participation of women in combat in the Navy and Air Force are statutory. Under 10 U S.C. § 6015, "women may not be assigned to duty on vessels or in aircraft that are engaged in combat missions," and under 10 U.S.C. § 8549 female members of the Air Force "may not be assigned to duty in aircraft engaged in combat missions." The Army and Marine Corps preclude the use of women in combat as a matter of established policy. Congress specifically recognized and endorsed the exclusion of women from combat in exempting women from registration.

The existence of the combat restrictions clearly indicates the basis for Congress' decision to exempt women from registration. The purpose of registration was to prepare for a draft of combat troops. Since women are excluded from combat, Congress concluded that they would not be needed in the event of a draft, and therefore decided not to register them.

Congress' decision to authorize the registration of only men, therefore, does not violate the Due Process Clause. The exemption of women from registration is not only sufficiently but also closely related to Congress' purpose in authorizing registration. The fact that Congress and the Executive have decided that women should not serve in combat fully justifies Congress in not authorizing their registration, since the purpose of registration is to develop a pool of potential combat troops. As was the case in *Schlesinger v. Ballard*, "the gender classification is not individious, but rather realistically reflects the fact that the sexes are not similarly situated" in this case. The Constitution requires that Congress treat similarly situated persons similarly, not that it engage in gestures of superficial equality.

In holding the MSSA constitutionally invalid the District Court relied heavily on the President's decision to seek authority to register women and the testimony of members of the Executive Branch and the military in support of that decision. As stated by the administration's witnesses before Congress, however, the President's "decision to ask for authority to register women is based on equity."

Although the military experts who testified in favor of registering women uniformly opposed the actual drafting of women, there was testimony that in the event of a draft of 650,000 the military could absorb some 80,000 female inductees. The 80,000 would be used to fill noncombat positions, freeing men to go to the front. In relying on this testimony in striking down the MSSA, the District Court palpably exceeded its authority when it ignored Congress' considered response to this line of reasoning.

. . . Congress simply did not consider it worth the added burdens of including women in draft and registration plans.

Congress also concluded that whatever the need for women for noncombat roles during mobilization, whether 80,000 or less, it could be met by volunteers.

Most significantly, Congress determined that staffing noncombat positions with women during a mobilization would be positively detrimental to the important goal of military flexibility.

In sum, Congress carefully evaluated the testimony that 80,000 women conscripts could be usefully employed in the event of a draft and rejected it in the permissible exercise of its constitutional responsibility. The District Court was quite wrong in undertaking an independent evaluation of this evidence, rather than adopting an appropriately deferential examination of Congress' evaluation of that evidence.

In light of the foregoing, we conclude that Congress acted well within its constitutional authority when it authorized the registration of men, and not women, under the Military Selective Service Act. The decision of the District Court holding otherwise is accordingly Reversed.

JUSTICE MARSHALL, with whom JUSTICE BRENNAN joins, dissenting.

The Court today places its imprimatur on one of the most potent remaining public expressions of "ancient canards about the proper role of women," *Phillips v. Martin Marietta Corp.*, 400 U.S. 542, 545 (1971) (Marshall, J., concurring). It upholds a statute that requires males but not females to register for the draft, and which thereby categorically excludes women from a fundamental civic obligation. Because I believe the Court's decision is inconsistent with the Constitution's guarantee of equal protection of the laws, I dissent.

I

A

It bears emphasis . . . that the only question presented by this case is whether the exclusion of women from registration under the Military Selective Service Act contravenes the equal protection component of the Due Process Clause of the Fifth Amendment. Although the purpose of registration is to assist preparations for drafting civilians into the military, we are not asked to rule on the constitutionality of a statute governing conscription.

B

By now it should be clear that statutes like the MSSA, which discriminate on the basis of gender, must be examined under the "heightened" scrutiny mandated by *Craig v. Boren*, 429 U.S. 190 (1976). Under this test, a gender-based classification cannot withstand constitutional challenge unless the classification is substantially related to the achievement of an important governmental objective. This test applies whether the classification discriminates against males or females. The party defending the challenged classification carries the burden of demonstrating both the importance of the governmental objective it serves and the substantial relationship between the discriminatory means and the asserted end. Consequently before we can sustain the MSSA, the Government must demonstrate that the gender-based classification it employs bears "a close and substantial relationship to [the achievement of] important governmental objectives," *Personnel Administrator of Massachusetts v. Feeney*, 442 U.S. 256, 273 (1979).

C

The MSSA states that "an adequate armed strength must be achieved and maintained to insure the security of this Nation." I agree with the majority, that "[no] one could deny that . . . the Government's interest in raising and supporting armies is an 'important governmental interest.' " Consequently, the first part of the *Craig v. Boren* test is satisfied. But the question remains whether the discriminatory means employed itself substantially serves the statutory end.

When, as here, a federal law that classifies on the basis of gender is challenged as violating this constitutional guarantee, it is ultimately for this Court, not Congress, to decide whether there exists the constitutionally required "close and substantial relationship" between the discriminatory means employed and the asserted governmental objective. In my judgment, there simply is no basis for concluding in this case that excluding women from registration is substantially related to the achievement of a concededly important governmental interest in maintaining an effective defense.

FOR DISCUSSION

Is this case based on societal stereotypes or legitimate governmental interests? Is it outmoded protectionist legislation, rational policy making, or something else? How do you believe this case might be decided if it were heard today?

RELATED CASES

***Geduldig v. Aiello:* 417 U.S. 484 (1974).**

The Court determined that a state policy that excluded pregnancy benefits in the disability policy was not unconstitutional. The Court used the lowest level of scrutiny and found that the law was not based on gender differences.

***Personnel Administrator of Massachusetts v. Feeney:* 442 U.S. 256 (1979).**

Court upheld decision that a neutral Massachusetts law granting preferences to veterans in hiring did not violate the equal protection rights of women despite the law's disproportionate impact on them because of their lack of opportunities for military service. The Court relied on the 1976 case of *Washington v. Davis* (426 U.S. 229, 1979), which required evidence of intentional discrimination to demonstrate equal protection violations.

MICHAEL M. V. SUPERIOR COURT OF SONOMA COUNTY

450 U.S. 464, 101 S.Ct. 1200, 67 L.Ed.2d 437 (1981)

The petitioner, Michael M., a seventeen-year-old-male, was charged with the statutory rape of a female under the age of eighteen. California's statutory rape law (§ 261.5 of the penal code) made males criminally liable for having sex with a female only if she were under eighteen years of age. The petitioner challenged the law as violating the Equal Protection Clause of the Fourteenth Amendment. The California district and appellate courts denied the petitioner's claim, but the Supreme Court of California held that § 261.5 "discriminates on the basis of sex because only females may be victims and only males may violate the section." The Court relied on strict scrutiny in assessing the equal protection claim but nevertheless found that the state had met its burden of demonstrating a compelling governmental interest; the constitutionality of the statute was upheld.

Vote: 5–4

JUSTICE REHNQUIST announced the judgment of the Court and delivered an opinion, in which THE CHIEF JUSTICE, JUSTICE STEWART, and JUSTICE POWELL joined.

As is evident from our opinions, the Court has had some difficulty in agreeing upon the proper approach and analysis in cases involving challenges to gender-based classifications. Unlike the California Supreme Court, we have not held that gender-based classifications are "inherently suspect" and thus we do not apply so-called "strict scrutiny" to those classifications. See *Stanton v. Stanton*, 421 U.S. 7 (1975). Our cases have held, however, that the traditional minimum rationality test takes on a somewhat "sharper focus" when gender-based classifications are challenged. In *Reed v. Reed*, 404 U.S. 71 (1971), for example, the Court stated that a gender-based classification will be upheld if it bears a "fair and substantial relationship" to legitimate state ends, while in *Craig v. Boren*, 429 U.S. 190 at 197 (1976), the Court restated the test to require the classification to bear a "substantial relationship" to "important governmental objectives."

Underlying these decisions is the principle that a legislature may not "make overbroad generalizations based on sex which are entirely unrelated to any differences between men and women or which demean the ability or social status of the affected class." *Parham v. Hughes*, 441 U.S. 347, 354 (1979). But because the Equal Protection Clause does not "demand that a statute necessarily apply equally to all persons" or require " 'things which are different in fact . . . to be treated in law as though they were the same,' " *Rinaldi v. Yeager*, 384 U.S. 305, 309 (1966), quoting *Tigner v. Texas*, 310 U.S. 141, 147 (1940), this Court has consistently upheld statutes where the gender classification is not invidious, but rather realistically reflects the fact that the sexes are not similarly situated in certain circumstances. As the Court has stated, a legislature may "provide for the special problems of women." *Weinberger v. Wiesenfeld*, 420 U.S. 636, 653 (1975).

Applying those principles to this case, the fact that the California Legislature criminalized the act of illicit sexual intercourse with a minor female is a sure indication of its intent or purpose to discourage that conduct. Precisely why the legislature desired that result is of course somewhat less clear. Some legislators may have been concerned about preventing teenage pregnancies, others about protecting young females from physical injury or from the loss of "chastity," and still others about promoting various religious and moral attitudes towards premarital sex.

The justification for the statute offered by the State, and accepted by the Supreme Court of California, is that the legislature sought to prevent illegitimate teenage pregnancies. That finding, of course, is entitled to great deference.

We are satisfied not only that the prevention of illegitimate pregnancy is at least one of the "purposes" of the statute, but also that the State has a strong interest in preventing such pregnancy.

We need not be medical doctors to discern that young men and young women are not similarly situated with respect to the problems and the risks of sexual intercourse. Only women may become pregnant, and they suffer disproportionately the profound physical, emotional, and psychological consequences of sexual activity.

The question thus boils down to whether a State may attack the problem of sexual intercourse and teenage pregnancy directly by prohibiting a male from having sexual intercourse with a minor female. We hold that such a statute is sufficiently related to the State's objectives to pass constitutional muster.

Because virtually all of the significant harmful and inescapably identifiable consequences of teenage pregnancy fall on the young female, a legislature acts well within its authority when it elects to punish only the participant who, by nature, suffers few of the consequences of his conduct. It is hardly unreasonable for a legislature acting to protect minor females to exclude them from punishment. Moreover, the risk of pregnancy itself constitutes a substantial deterrence to young females. No similar natural sanctions deter males. A criminal sanction imposed solely on males thus serves to roughly "equalize" the deterrents on the sexes.

It is argued that this statute is not necessary to deter teenage pregnancy because a gender-neutral statute, where both male and female would be subject to prosecution, would serve that goal equally well. The relevant inquiry, however, is not whether the statute is drawn as precisely as it might have been, but whether the line chosen by the California Legislature is within constitutional limitations.

State persuasively contends that a gender-neutral statute would frustrate its interest in effective enforcement. Its view is that a female is surely less likely to report violations of the statute if she herself would be subject to criminal prosecution. In an area already fraught with prosecutorial difficulties, we decline to hold that the Equal Protection Clause requires a legislature to enact a statute so broad that it may well be incapable of enforcement.

In upholding the California statute we also recognize that this is not a case where a statute is being challenged on the grounds that it "invidiously discriminates" against females. To the contrary, the statute places a burden on males which is not shared by females. But we find nothing to suggest that men, because of past discrimination or peculiar disadvantages, are in need of the special solicitude of the courts. As we have held, the statute instead reasonably reflects the fact that the consequences of sexual intercourse and pregnancy fall more heavily on the female than on the male.

Accordingly the judgment of the California Supreme Court is Affirmed.

JUSTICE STEWART, concurring.

B

The Constitution is violated when government, state or federal, invidiously classifies similarly situated people on the basis of the immutable characteristics with which they were born. Thus, detrimental racial classifications by government always violate the Constitution, for the simple reason that, so far as the Constitution is concerned, people of different races are always similarly situated. See *Fullilove v. Klutznick*, 448 U.S. 448, 522 (1980) (dissenting opinion); *McLaughlin v. Florida*, 379 U.S. 184, 198 (1964) (concurring opinion); *Brown v. Board of Ed.*, 347 U.S. 483 (1954); *Plessy v. Ferguson*, 163 U.S. 537, 552 (1896) (dissenting opinion). By contrast, while detrimental gender classifications by government often violate the Constitution, they do not always do so, for the reason that there are differences between males and females that the Constitution necessarily recognizes. In this case we deal with the most basic of these differences: females can become pregnant as the result of sexual intercourse; males cannot.

As was recognized in *Parham v. Hughes*, 441 U.S. 347, 354 (1979), "a State is not free to make overbroad generalizations based on sex which are entirely unrelated to any differences between men and women or which demean the ability or social status of the affected class." Gender-based classifications may not be based upon administrative convenience, or upon archaic assumptions about the proper roles of the sexes. *Craig v. Boren*, 429 U.S. 190 (1976); *Frontiero v. Richardson*, 411 U.S. 677 (1973); *Reed v. Reed*, 404 U.S. 71 (1971). But we have recognized that in certain narrow circumstances men and women are not similarly situated; in these circumstances a gender classification based on clear differences between the sexes is not invidious, and a legislative classification realistically based upon those differences is not unconstitutional. "[Gender]-based classifications are not invariably invalid. When men and women are not in fact similarly situated in the area covered by the legislation in question, the Equal Protection Clause is not violated." *Caban v. Mohammed*, 441 U.S. 380, 398 (1979) (dissenting opinion).

Applying these principles to the classification enacted by the California Legislature, it is readily apparent that § 261.5 does not violate the Equal Protection Clause. Young women and men are not similarly situated with respect to the problems and risks associated with intercourse and pregnancy, and the statute is realistically related to the legitimate state purpose of reducing those problems and risks.

E

In short, the Equal Protection Clause does not mean that the physiological differences between men and women must be disregarded. While those differences must never be permitted to become a pretext for invidious discrimination, no such discrimination is presented by this case. The Constitution surely does not require a State to pretend that demonstrable differences between men and women do not really exist.

JUSTICE BRENNAN, with whom JUSTICES WHITE and MARSHALL join, dissenting.

I

It is disturbing to find the Court so splintered on a case that presents such a straightforward issue: Whether the admittedly gender-based classification in Cal. Penal Code Ann. § 261.5 bears a sufficient relationship to the State's asserted goal of preventing teenage pregnancies to survive the "mid-level" constitutional scrutiny mandated by *Craig v. Boren*, 429 U.S. 190 (1976). Applying the analytical framework provided by our precedents,

I am convinced that there is only one proper resolution of this issue: the classification must be declared unconstitutional. I fear that the plurality opinion and Justices Stewart and Blackmun reach the opposite result by placing too much emphasis on the desirability of achieving the State's asserted statutory goal—prevention of teenage pregnancy—and not enough emphasis on the fundamental question of whether the sex-based discrimination in the California statute is substantially related to the achievement of that goal.

III

Until very recently, no California court or commentator had suggested that the purpose of California's statutory rape law was to protect young women from the risk of pregnancy. Indeed, the historical development of § 261.5 demonstrates that the law was initially enacted on the premise that young women, in contrast to young men, were to be deemed legally incapable of consenting to an act of sexual intercourse. Because their chastity was considered particularly precious, those young women were felt to be uniquely in need of the State's protection. In contrast, young men were assumed to be capable of making such decisions for themselves; the law therefore did not offer them any special protection.

It is perhaps because the gender classification in California's statutory rape law was initially designed to further these outmoded sexual stereotypes, rather than to reduce the incidence of teenage pregnancies, that the State has been unable to demonstrate a substantial relationship between the classification and its newly asserted goal. But whatever the reason, the State has not shown that Cal. Penal Code § 261.5 is any more effective than a gender-neutral law would be in deterring minor females from engaging in sexual intercourse. It has therefore not met its burden of proving that the statutory classification is substantially related to the achievement of its asserted goal.

FOR DISCUSSION

Do you agree with Justice Brennan's dissent that the California law furthers outdated stereotypes or the majority's claim that it represents a legitimate state interest in reducing teenage pregnancies? Why or why not?

MISSISSIPPI UNIVERSITY FOR WOMEN V. HOGAN

458 U.S. 718, 102 S.Ct. 3331, 73 L.Ed. 2d 1090 (1982)

Joe Hogan, the respondent, applied for admission to the state of Mississippi's only public single-sex institution of higher education, the Mississippi University for Women (MUW). More particularly, he was interested in enrolling in the School of Nursing. He was denied admission solely on the grounds of his gender. He challenged the MUW School of Nursing's single-sex admissions policy as violating the Equal Protection Clause of the Fourteenth Amendment. The federal district court ruled summarily for the state of Mississippi, but the court of appeals reversed this decision.

Vote: 5–4

JUSTICE O'CONNOR delivered the opinion of the Court.

II

We begin our analysis aided by several firmly established principles. Because the challenged policy expressly discriminates among applicants on the basis of gender, it is subject to scrutiny under the Equal Protection Clause of the Fourteenth Amendment. *Reed v. Reed*, 404 U.S. 71, 75 (1971). That this statutory policy discriminates against males rather than against females does not exempt it from scrutiny or reduce the standard of review. Our decisions also establish that the party seeking to uphold a statute that classifies individuals on the basis of their gender must carry the burden of showing an "exceedingly persuasive justification" for the classification. The burden is met only by showing at least that the classification serves "important governmental objectives and that the discriminatory means employed" are "substantially related to the achievement of those objectives." *Wengler v. Druggists Mutual Ins. Co.*, 446 U.S. 142, 150 (1980).

Although the test for determining the validity of a gender-based classification is straightforward, it must be applied free of fixed notions concerning the roles and abilities of males and females. Care must be taken in ascertaining whether the statutory objective itself reflects archaic and stereotypic notions. Thus, if the statutory objective is to exclude or "protect" members of one gender because they are presumed to suffer from an inherent handicap or to be innately inferior, the objective itself is illegitimate. See *Frontiero v. Richardson*, 411 U.S. 677, 684–685 (1973) (plurality opinion).

If the State's objective is legitimate and important, we next determine whether the requisite direct, substantial relationship between objective and means is present. The purpose of requiring that close relationship is to assure that the validity of a classification is determined through reasoned analysis rather than through the mechanical application of traditional, often inaccurate, assumptions about the proper roles of men and women. The need for the requirement is amply revealed by reference to the broad range of statutes already invalidated by this Court, statutes that relied upon the simplistic, outdated assumption that gender could be used as a "proxy for other, more germane bases of classification," *Craig v. Boren*, 429 U.S. 190, 198 (1976), to establish a link between objective and classification.

III

A

The State's primary justification for maintaining the single-sex admissions policy of MUW's School of Nursing is that it compensates for discrimination against women and, therefore, constitutes educational affirmative action. As applied to the School of Nursing, we find the State's argument unpersuasive.

In limited circumstances, a gender-based classification favoring one sex can be justified if it intentionally and directly assists members of the sex that is disproportionately burdened.

It is readily apparent that a State can evoke a compensatory purpose to justify an otherwise discriminatory classification only if members of the gender benefited by the classification actually suffer a disadvantage related to the classification.

A similar pattern of discrimination against women influenced our decision in *Schlesinger v. Ballard*. There, we considered a federal statute that granted female Naval officers a 13-year tenure of commissioned service before mandatory discharge, but accorded male officers only a 9-year tenure. We recognized that, because women were barred from combat duty, they had had fewer opportunities for promotion than had their male counterparts. By allowing women an additional four years to reach a particular rank before subjecting them to mandatory discharge, the statute directly compensated for other statutory barriers to advancement.

In sharp contrast, Mississippi has made no showing that women lacked opportunities to obtain training in the field of nursing or to attain positions of leadership in that field when the MUW School of Nursing opened its door or that women currently are deprived of such opportunities. When MUW's School of Nursing began operation, nearly 98 percent of all employed registered nurses were female.

Rather than compensate for discriminatory barriers faced by women, MUW's policy of excluding males from admission to the School of Nursing tends to perpetuate the stereotyped view of nursing as an exclusively woman's job. Thus, we conclude that, although the State recited a "benign, compensatory purpose," it failed to establish that the alleged objective is the actual purpose underlying the discriminatory classification.

The policy is invalid also because it fails the second part of the equal protection test, for the State has made no showing that the gender-based classification is substantially and directly related to its proposed compensatory objective. To the contrary, MUW's policy of permitting men to attend classes as auditors fatally undermines its claim that women, at least those in the School of Nursing, are adversely affected by the presence of men.

MUW permits men who audit to participate fully in classes. The uncontroverted record reveals that admitting men to nursing classes does not affect teaching style, that the presence of men in the classroom would not affect the performance of the female nursing students, and that men in coeducational nursing schools do not dominate the classroom. In sum, the record in this case is flatly inconsistent with the claim that excluding men from the School of Nursing is necessary to reach any of MUW's educational goals.

Thus, considering both the asserted interest and the relationship between the interest and the methods used by the State, we conclude that the State has fallen far short of establishing the "exceedingly persuasive justification" needed to sustain the gender-based classification. Accordingly, we hold that MUW's policy of denying males the right to enroll for credit in its School of Nursing violates the Equal Protection Clause of the Fourteenth Amendment.

JUSTICE BLACKMUN, dissenting.

While the Court purports to write narrowly, declaring that it does not decide the same issue with respect to "separate but equal" undergraduate institutions for females and males, or with respect to units of MUW other than its School of Nursing, there is inevitable spillover from the Court's ruling today. That ruling, it seems to me, places in constitutional jeopardy any state-supported educational institution that confines its student body in any area to members of one sex, even though the State elsewhere provides an equivalent program to the complaining applicant. The Court's reasoning does not stop with the School of Nursing of the Mississippi University for Women.

JUSTICE POWELL, with whom JUSTICE REHNQUIST joins, dissenting.

II

The issue in this case is whether a State transgresses the Constitution when—within the context of a public system that offers a diverse range of campuses, curricula, and educational alternatives—it seeks to accommodate the legitimate personal preferences of those desiring the advantages of an all-women's college. In my view, the Court errs seriously by assuming—without argument or discussion—that the equal protection standard generally applicable to sex discrimination is appropriate here. That standard was designed to free women from "archaic and overbroad generalizations. . . ." *Schlesinger v. Ballard*, 419 U.S. 498, 508 (1975). In no previous case have we applied it to invalidate state efforts to expand women's choices. Nor are there prior sex discrimination decisions by this Court in which a male plaintiff, as in this case, had the choice of an equal benefit.

The cases cited by the Court therefore do not control the issue now before us. In most of them women were given no opportunity for the same benefit as men. Cases involving male plaintiffs are equally inapplicable.

By applying heightened equal protection analysis to this case, the Court frustrates the liberating spirit of the Equal Protection Clause. It prohibits the States from providing women with an opportunity to choose the type of university they prefer. And yet it is these women whom the Court regards as the victims of an illegal, stereotyped perception of the role of women in our society. The Court reasons this way in a case in which no woman has complained, and the only complainant is a man who advances no claims on behalf of anyone else. His claim, it should be recalled, is not that he is being denied a substantive educational opportunity, or even the right to attend an all-male or a coeducational college. It is only that the colleges open to him are located at inconvenient distances.

III

The Court views this case as presenting a serious equal protection claim of sex discrimination. I do not, and I would sustain Mississippi's right to continue MUW on a rational-basis analysis.

FOR DISCUSSION

According to the majority, when might a public single-sex institution be allowed as constitutional under the Equal Protection Clause? Is the dissent's analysis of the majority opinion correct—that is, is a new standard being professed?

RELATED CASES

***Kirstein v. Rector and Visitors of the University of Virginia:* 309 F.Supp 184 (E.D. Va.) (1970).**

The University of Virginia denied women admission to the Charlottesville campus, the most prestigious branch of the state university system. While the district court refused to abolish single-sex education in the state (the Virginia Military Institute was also a male-only university at the time), the court encouraged the University of Virginia's governing board to adopt a three-year plan to admit men and women on an equal basis; this settled the case.

***Williams v. McNair:* 316 F.Supp. 134 (D.S.C.) (1970).**

The district court upheld an equal protection challenge to South Carolina's system of higher education. The state had two public single-sex institutions, the Citadel for men and Winthrop College for women. A male sought admission to Winthrop, and the court found no constitutional violation in restricting admissions only to women.

***Vorchheimer v. School District of Philadelphia:* 532 F.2d 880 (3rd Circ.) (1976).**

A court of appeals upheld the constitutionality of Philadelphia's two single-sex public high schools—Central High (males) and Girls High. The court justified the decision by observing that both sexes were affected equally and cited evidence that students of both sexes could benefit from single-sex education at the high school level.

UNITED STATES V. VIRGINIA

518 U.S. 515, 116 S.Ct. 2264, 135 L.Ed.2d 735 (1996)

The Virginia Military Institute (VMI) was the only single-sex school funded by the Commonwealth of Virginia. Its stated mission is to train "citizen-soldiers," and it uses the "adversative method" of instruction. In 1990, after receiving a complaint from a female high school student, the United States sued Virginia and the military school, claiming that VMI's male-only admissions policy violated the Equal Protection Clause of the Fourteenth Amendment. The federal district court ruled in favor of VMI and, using Mississippi University for Women v. Hogan as precedent, dismissed the equal protection claim. The court of appeals disagreed and found no legitimate state policy to justify on constitutional grounds the continuation of VMI's single-sex status. In response, the Commonwealth of Virginia proposed a parallel program for women—the Virginia Women's Institute for Leadership (VWIL)—to be housed at Mary Baldwin College, which was then all-female. Although sharing a common mission—the training of "citizen-soldiers"—VMI and the proposed VWIL varied greatly in terms of degree offerings, financial resources, and pedagogical approaches. Unlike VMI, Mary Baldwin

College offered degrees in the liberal arts and sciences only, not in the sciences or engineering. Mary Baldwin did not have the faculty or the financial resources of VMI. Most significantly, VWIL did not use the adversative method of pedagogy but a "cooperative method which reinforces self-esteem." The district court upheld the two institutions as meeting the requirements of the equal protection clause and the Fourth Circuit Court of Appeals affirmed.

Vote: 7–1

JUSTICE GINSBURG delivered the opinion of the Court.

II

A

VMI today enrolls about 1,300 men as cadets. Its academic offerings in the liberal arts, sciences, and engineering are also available at other public colleges and universities in Virginia. But VMI's mission is special. It is the mission of the school to produce educated and honorable men, prepared for the varied work of civil life, imbued with love of learning, confident in the functions and attitudes of leadership, possessing a high sense of public service, advocates of the American democracy and free enterprise system, and ready as citizen-soldiers to defend their country in time of national peril. Mission Study Committee of the VMI Board of Visitors, Report, May 16, 1986.

In contrast to the federal service academies, institutions maintained "to prepare cadets for career service in the armed forces," VMI's program "is directed at preparation for both military and civilian life"; "only about 15% of VMI cadets enter career military service." 766 F. Supp., at 1432.

VMI produces its "citizen-soldiers" through "an adversative, or doubting, model of education" which features "physical rigor, mental stress, absolute equality of treatment, absence of privacy, minute regulation of behavior, and indoctrination in desirable values." As one Commandant of Cadets described it, the adversative method " 'dissects the young student,' " and makes him aware of his " 'limits and capabilities,' " so that he knows " 'how far he can go with his anger, . . . how much he can take under stress, . . . exactly what he can do when he is physically exhausted.' "

VMI cadets live in spartan barracks where surveillance is constant and privacy nonexistent; they wear uniforms, eat together in the mess hall, and regularly participate in drills. Entering students are incessantly exposed to the rat line, "an extreme form of the adversative model," comparable in intensity to Marine Corps boot camp. Tormenting and punishing, the rat line bonds new cadets to their fellow sufferers and, when they have completed the 7-month experience, to their former tormentors.

VMI attracts some applicants because of its reputation as an extraordinarily challenging military school, and "because its alumni are exceptionally close to the school." "Women have no opportunity anywhere to gain the benefits of [the system of education at VMI]."

III

The cross-petitions in this case present two ultimate issues. First, does Virginia's exclusion of women from the educational opportunities provided by VMI—extraordinary opportunities for military training and civilian leadership development—deny to women "capable of all of the individual activities required of VMI cadets," the equal protection of the laws guaranteed by the Fourteenth Amendment? Second, if VMI's "unique" situation—as Virginia's sole single-sex public institution of higher education—offends the Constitution's equal protection principle, what is the remedial requirement?

IV

We note, once again, the core instruction of this Court's pathmarking decisions in J. *E. B. v. Alabama ex rel. T. B.,* 511 U.S. 127, 136–137 (1994), and *Mississippi Univ. for Women*, 458 U.S. at 724: Parties who seek to defend gender-based government action must demonstrate an "exceedingly persuasive justification" for that action.

Without equating gender classifications, for all purposes, to classifications based on race or national origin, the Court, in post-*Reed* [v. *Reed*, 404 U.S. 71 (1971)] decisions, has carefully inspected official action that closes a door or denies opportunity to women (or to men). To summarize the Court's current directions for cases of official classification based on gender: Focusing on the differential treatment or denial of opportunity for which relief is sought, the reviewing court must determine whether the proffered justification is "exceedingly persuasive." The burden of justification is demanding and it rests entirely on the State. The State must show "at least that the [challenged] classification serves 'important governmental objectives and that the discriminatory means employed' are 'substantially related to the achievement of those objectives.' " The justification must be genuine, not hypothesized or invented post hoc in response to litigation. And it must not rely on overbroad generalizations about the different talents, capacities, or preferences of males and females.

The heightened review standard our precedent establishes does not make sex a proscribed classification. Supposed "inherent differences" are no longer accepted as a ground for race or national origin classifications. Physical differences between men and women, however, are enduring: "The two sexes are not fungible; a community made up exclusively of one [sex] is different from a community composed of both." *Ballard v. United States*, 329 U.S. 187, 193 (1946).

Measuring the record in this case against the review standard just described, we conclude that Virginia has shown no "exceedingly persuasive justification" for excluding all women from the citizen-soldier training afforded by VMI. We therefore affirm the Fourth Circuit's initial judgment, which held that Virginia had violated the Fourteenth Amendment's Equal Protection Clause. Because the remedy proffered by Virginia—the Mary Baldwin VWIL program—does not cure the constitutional violation, i.e., it does not provide equal opportunity, we reverse the Fourth Circuit's final judgment in this case.

V

Virginia challenges that "liability" ruling and asserts two justifications in defense of VMI's exclusion of women. First, the Commonwealth contends, "single-sex education provides important educational benefits," and the option of single-sex education contributes to "diversity in educational approaches." Second, the Commonwealth argues, "the unique VMI method of character development and leadership training," the school's adversative approach, would have to be modified were VMI to admit women. We consider these two justifications in turn.

A

[W]e find no persuasive evidence in this record that VMI's male-only admission policy "is in furtherance of a state policy of 'diversity.' " No such policy, the Fourth Circuit observed, can be discerned from the movement of all other public colleges and universities in Virginia away from single-sex education. A purpose genuinely to advance an array of educational options, as the Court of Appeals recognized, is not served by VMI's historic and constant plan—a plan to "afford a unique educational benefit only to males." However "liberally" this plan serves the Commonwealth's sons, it makes no provision whatever for her daughters. That is not equal protection.

B

Virginia next argues that VMI's adversative method of training provides educational benefits that cannot be made available, unmodified, to women. Alterations to accommodate women would necessarily be "radical," so "drastic," Virginia asserts, as to transform, indeed "destroy," VMI's program. Neither sex would be favored by the transformation, Virginia maintains: Men would be deprived of the unique opportunity currently available to them; women would not gain that opportunity because their participation would "eliminate the very aspects of [the] program that distinguish [VMI] from . . . other institutions of higher education in Virginia."

The notion that admission of women would downgrade VMI's stature, destroy the adversative system and, with it, even the school, is a judgment hardly proved, a prediction hardly different from other "self-fulfilling prophec[ies]," see *Mississippi Univ. for Women*, 458 U.S. at 730, once routinely used to deny rights or opportunities. When women first sought admission to the bar and access to legal education, concerns of the same order were expressed.

Women's successful entry into the federal military academies, and their participation in the Nation's military forces, indicate that Virginia's fears for the future of VMI may not be solidly grounded. The Commonwealth's justification for excluding all women from "citizen-soldier" training for which some are qualified, in any event, cannot rank as "exceedingly persuasive," as we have explained and applied that standard.

VI

In the second phase of the litigation, Virginia presented its remedial plan—maintain VMI as a male-only college and create VWIL as a separate program for women. Inspecting the VMI and VWIL educational programs to determine whether they "afforded to both genders benefits comparable in substance, [if] not in form and detail," the Court of Appeals concluded that Virginia had arranged for men and women opportunities "sufficiently comparable" to survive equal protection evaluation. The United States challenges this "remedial" ruling as pervasively misguided.

A

Virginia chose not to eliminate, but to leave untouched, VMI's exclusionary policy. For women only, however, Virginia proposed a separate program, different in kind from VMI and unequal in tangible and intangible facilities. Having violated the Constitution's equal protection requirement, Virginia was obliged to show that its remedial proposal "directly addressed and related to" the violation, i.e., the equal protection denied to women ready, willing, and able to benefit from educational opportunities of the kind VMI offers. Virginia described VWIL as a "parallel program," and asserted that VWIL shares VMI's mission of producing "citizen-soldiers" and VMI's goals of providing "education, military training, mental and physical discipline, character . . . and leadership development." If the VWIL program could not "eliminate the discriminatory effects of the past," could it at least "bar like discrimination in the future"? A comparison of the programs said to be "parallel" informs our answer. In exposing the character of, and differences in, the VMI and VWIL programs, we recapitulate facts earlier presented.

VWIL affords women no opportunity to experience the rigorous military training for which VMI is famed. Instead, the VWIL program "deemphasize[s]" military education, and uses a "cooperative method" of education "which reinforces self-esteem."

VWIL students receive their "leadership training" in seminars, externships, and speaker series, episodes and encounters lacking the "physical rigor, mental stress, . . . minute regulation of behavior, and indoctrination in desirable values" made hallmarks of VMI's citizen-soldier training. Kept away from the pressures, hazards, and psychological bonding characteristic of VMI's adversative training, VWIL students will not know the "feeling of tremendous accomplishment" commonly experienced by VMI's successful cadets.

Virginia maintains that these methodological differences are "justified pedagogically," based on "important differences between men and women in learning and developmental needs," "psychological and sociological differences" Virginia describes as "real" and "not stereotypes."

As earlier stated, generalizations about "the way women are," estimates of what is appropriate for most women, no longer justify denying opportunity to women whose talent and capacity place them outside the average description. Notably, Virginia never asserted that VMI's method of education suits most men.

B

In myriad respects other than military training, VWIL does not qualify as VMI's equal. VWIL's student body, faculty, course offerings, and facilities hardly match VMI's. Nor can the VWIL graduate anticipate the benefits associated with VMI's 157-year history, the school's prestige, and its influential alumni network.

Virginia, in sum, while maintaining VMI for men only, has failed to provide any "comparable single-gender women's institution." Instead, the Commonwealth has created a VWIL program fairly appraised as a "pale shadow" of VMI in terms of the range of curricular choices and faculty stature, funding, prestige, alumni support and influence.

C

The Fourth Circuit plainly erred in exposing Virginia's VWIL plan to a deferential analysis, for "all gender-based classifications today" warrant "heightened scrutiny." Valuable as VWIL may prove for students who seek the program offered, Virginia's remedy affords no cure at all for the opportunities and advantages withheld from women who want a VMI education and can make the grade. In sum, Virginia's remedy does not match the constitutional violation; the Commonwealth has shown no "exceedingly persuasive justification" for withholding from women qualified for the experience premier training of the kind VMI affords.

CHIEF JUSTICE REHNQUIST, concurring in the judgment.

II

The Court defines the constitutional violation in these cases as "the categorical exclusion of women from an extraordinary educational opportunity afforded to men." By defining the violation in this way, and by emphasizing that a remedy for a constitutional violation must place the victims of discrimination in " 'the position they would have occupied in the absence of [discrimination],' " the Court necessarily implies that the only adequate remedy would be the admission of women to the all-male institution. As the foregoing discussion suggests, I would not define the violation in this way; it is not the "exclusion of women" that violates the Equal Protection Clause, but the maintenance of an all-men school without providing any—much less a comparable—institution for women.

Accordingly, the remedy should not necessarily require either the admission of women to VMI or the creation of a VMI clone for women. An adequate remedy in my opinion might be a demonstration by Virginia that its interest in educating men in a single-sex environment is matched by its interest in educating women in a single-sex institution. To demonstrate such, the Commonwealth does not need to create two institutions with the same number of faculty Ph.D.'s, similar SAT scores, or comparable athletic fields. Nor would it necessarily require that the women's institution offer the same curriculum as the men's; one could be strong in computer science, the other could be strong in liberal arts. It would be a sufficient remedy, I think, if the two institutions offered the same quality of education and were of the same overall caliber.

If a State decides to create single-sex programs, the State would, I expect, consider the public's interest and demand in designing curricula. And rightfully so. But the State should avoid assuming demand based on stereotypes; it must not assume a priori, without evidence, that there would be no interest in a women's school of civil engineering, or in a men's school of nursing.

In the end, the women's institution Virginia proposes, VWIL, fails as a remedy, because it is distinctly inferior to the existing men's institution and will continue to be for the foreseeable future. VWIL simply is not, in any sense, the institution that VMI is. In particular, VWIL is a program appended to a private college, not a self-standing institution; and VWIL is substantially underfunded as compared to VMI. I therefore ultimately agree with the Court that Virginia has not provided an adequate remedy.

JUSTICE SCALIA, dissenting.

I

I shall devote most of my analysis to evaluating the Court's opinion on the basis of our current equal protection jurisprudence, which regards this Court as free to evaluate everything under the sun by applying one of three tests: "rational basis" scrutiny, intermediate scrutiny, or strict scrutiny. These tests are no more scientific than their names suggest, and a further element of randomness is added by the fact that it is largely up to us which test will be applied in each case. Strict scrutiny, we have said, is reserved for state "classifications based on race or national origin and classifications affecting fundamental rights," *Clark v. Jeter*, 486 U.S. 456, 46 (1988). It is my position that the term "fundamental rights" should be limited to "interest[s] traditionally protected by our society," *Michael H. v. Gerald D.*, 491 U.S. 110, 122 (1989); but the Court has not accepted that view, so that strict scrutiny will be applied to the deprivation of whatever sort of right we consider "fundamental." We have no established criterion for "intermediate scrutiny" either, but essentially apply it when it seems like a good idea to load the dice. So far it has been applied to content-neutral restrictions that place an incidental burden on speech, to disabilities attendant to illegitimacy, and to discrimination on the basis of sex.

I have no problem with a system of abstract tests such as rational basis, intermediate, and strict scrutiny (though I think we can do better than applying strict scrutiny and intermediate scrutiny whenever we feel like it). Such formulas are essential to evaluating whether the new restrictions that a changing society constantly imposes upon private conduct comport with that "equal protection" our society has always accorded in the past. But in my view the function of this Court is to preserve our society's values regarding (among other things) equal protection, not to revise them; to prevent backsliding from the degree of restriction the Constitution imposed upon democratic government, not to prescribe, on our own authority, progressively higher degrees. For that reason it is my view that, whatever abstract tests we may choose to devise, they cannot supersede—and indeed ought to be crafted so as to reflect—those constant and unbroken national traditions that embody the people's understanding of ambiguous constitutional texts. More specifically, it is my view that "when a practice not expressly prohibited by the text of the Bill of Rights bears the endorsement of a long tradition of open, widespread, and unchallenged use that dates back to the beginning of the Republic, we have no proper basis for striking it down." *Rutan v. Republican Party of Ill.*, 497 U.S. 62 (1990) (Scalia, J., dissenting). The same applies, *mutatis mutandis* [the necessary changes having been made], to a practice asserted to be in violation of the post-Civil War Fourteenth Amendment.

The all-male constitution of VMI comes squarely within such a governing tradition. Founded by the Commonwealth of Virginia in 1839 and continuously maintained by it since, VMI has always admitted only men. And in that regard it has not been unusual. In other words, the tradition of having government-funded military schools for men is as well rooted in the traditions of this country as the tradition of sending only men into military combat. The people may decide to change the one tradition, like the other, through democratic processes; but the assertion that either tradition has been unconstitutional through the centuries is not law, but politics-smuggled-into-law.

And the same applies, more broadly, to single-sex education in general, which, as I shall discuss, is threatened by today's decision with the cutoff of all state and federal support. Government-run nonmilitary educational institutions for the two sexes have until very recently also been part of our national tradition. These traditions may of course be changed by the democratic decisions of the people, as they largely have been.

Today, however, change is forced upon Virginia, and reversion to single-sex education is prohibited nationwide, not by democratic processes but by order of this Court. Even while bemoaning the sorry, bygone days of "fixed notions" concerning women's education, the Court favors current notions so fixedly that it is willing to write them into the Constitution of the United States by application of custom-built "tests." This is not the interpretation of a Constitution, but the creation of one.

II

To reject the Court's disposition today, however, it is not necessary to accept my view that the Court's made-up tests cannot displace longstanding national traditions as the primary determinant of what the Constitution means. It is only necessary to apply honestly the test the Court has been applying to sex-based classifications for the past two decades. It is well settled, as Justice O'Connor stated some time ago for a unanimous Court, that we evaluate a statutory classification based on sex under a standard that lies "between the extremes of rational basis review and strict scrutiny." *Clark v. Jeter*, 486 U.S. at 461. We have denominated this standard "intermediate scrutiny" and under it have inquired whether the statutory classification is "substantially related to an important governmental objective."

Although the Court in two places recites the test as stated in *Hogan*, which asks whether the State has demonstrated "that the classification serves important governmental objectives and that the discriminatory means employed are substantially related to the achievement of those objectives," the Court never answers the question presented in anything resembling that form. When it engages in analysis, the Court instead prefers the phrase "exceedingly persuasive justification" from *Hogan*. The Court's nine invocations of that phrase, and even its fanciful description of that imponderable as "the core instruction" of the Court's decisions in *J. E. B. v. Alabama ex rel. T. B.,* 511 U.S. 127 (1994), and *Hogan* would be unobjectionable if the Court acknowledged that whether a "justification" is "exceedingly persuasive" must be assessed by asking "[whether] the classification serves important governmental objectives and [whether] the discriminatory means employed are substantially related to the achievement of those objectives." Instead, however, the Court proceeds to interpret "exceedingly persuasive justification" in a fashion that contradicts the reasoning of *Hogan* and our other precedents.

That is essential to the Court's result, which can only be achieved by establishing that intermediate scrutiny is not survived if there are some women interested in attending VMI, capable of undertaking its activities, and able to meet its physical demands.

Only the amorphous "exceedingly persuasive justification" phrase, and not the standard elaboration of intermediate scrutiny, can be made to yield this conclusion that VMI's single-sex composition is unconstitutional because there exist several women (or, one would have to conclude under the Court's reasoning, a single woman) willing and able to undertake VMI's program. Intermediate scrutiny has never required a least-restrictive-means analysis, but only a "substantial relation" between the classification and the state interests that it serves.

Not content to execute a de facto abandonment of the intermediate scrutiny that has been our standard for sex-based classifications for some two decades, the Court purports to reserve the question whether, even in principle, a higher standard (i.e., strict scrutiny) should apply. "The Court has," it says, "thus far reserved most stringent judicial scrutiny for classifications based on race or national origin . . .," and it describes our earlier cases as having done no more than decline to "equate gender classifications, for all purposes, to classifications based on race or national origin". The wonderful thing about these statements is that they are not actually false—just as it would not be actually false to say that "our cases have thus far reserved the 'beyond a reasonable doubt' standard of proof for criminal cases," or that "we have not equated tort actions, for all purposes, to criminal prosecutions." But the statements are misleading, insofar as they suggest that we have not already categorically held strict scrutiny to be inapplicable to sex-based classifications. And the statements are irresponsible, insofar as they are calculated to destabilize current law. Our task is to clarify the law—not to muddy the waters, and not to exact overcompliance by intimidation. The States and the Federal Government are entitled to know before they act the standard to which they will be held, rather than be compelled to guess about the outcome of Supreme Court peek-a-boo.

The Court's intimations are particularly out of place because it is perfectly clear that, if the question of the applicable standard of review for sex-based classifications were to be regarded as an appropriate subject for reconsideration, the stronger argument would be not for elevating the standard to strict scrutiny, but for reducing it to rational-basis review. The latter certainly has a firmer foundation in our past jurisprudence: Whereas no majority of the Court has ever applied strict scrutiny in a case involving sex-based classifications, we routinely applied rational-basis review until the 1970's. And of course normal, rational-basis review of sex-based classifications would be much more in accord with the genesis of heightened standards of judicial review, the famous footnote in *United States v. Carolene Products Co.*, 304 U.S. 144 (1938), which said (intimatingly) that we did not have to inquire in the case at hand whether prejudice against discrete and insular minorities may be a special condition, which tends seriously to curtail the operation of those political processes ordinarily to be relied upon to protect minorities, and which may call for a correspondingly more searching judicial inquiry. Id., at 152–153, n. 4.

It is hard to consider women a "discrete and insular minority" unable to employ the "political processes ordinarily to be relied upon," when they constitute a majority of the electorate. And the suggestion that they are incapable of exerting that political power smacks of the same paternalism that the Court so roundly condemns. Moreover, a long list of legislation proves the proposition false. See, e.g., Equal Pay Act of 1963, 29 U.S.C. § 206(d); Title VII of the Civil Rights Act of 1964, 42 U.S.C. § 2000e–2; Title IX of the Education Amendments of 1972, 20 U.S.C. § 1681; Women's Business Ownership Act of 1988, Pub. L. 100–533, 102 Stat. 2689; Violence Against Women Act of 1994, Pub. L. 103–322, Title IV, 108 Stat. 1902.

FOR DISCUSSION

Does the "exceedingly persuasive justification" test significantly vary from the intermediate scrutiny used in *Mississippi University of Women v. Hogan*? What constitutional standard should courts use in evaluating gender challenges to the Equal Protection Clause? Why?

RELATED CASES

***Miller v. Albright:* 523 U.S. 420 (1998).**

The Court found that a federal immigration law could convey citizenship to children born to unmarried mothers while denying citizenship to children born to unmarried fathers. The justices could not agree on the constitutional grounds on which they upheld this law.

***Nguyen and Boulais v. INS:* 533 U.S. 53 (2001).**

Court upheld the federal law denying citizenship to children born to unmarried fathers unless the father had demonstrated paternity before the child turned eighteen. The Court determined that rather than relying on stereotypes of parenting, the law merely represented the biological differences in the circumstances of birth for the mother and the father. The majority used the language of the *VMI* and *Hogan* precedents and found that the law passed the intermediate scrutiny test.

Affirmative Action

For many years, the laws, federal and state constitutions, policies, and attitudes of the nation discriminated against people of color and women of all races, prohibiting them from competing in the workplace, earning money to support their families, or attending colleges, universities, and professional schools. After the mid-twentieth century, when the laws allowing for segregation and many forms of discrimination were eliminated, large gaps in salary, education, wealth, and advancement continued. There had been programs since before the New Deal and World War II that had benefited certain groups in recognition of their sacrifices for the nation or their particular need (e.g., the GI bill for veterans, agricultural subsidies for farmers). These forms of governmental assistance aided some groups to the detriment of others and were frequently administered in a fashion that continued patterns of racial and gender discrimination. The conflict over the use of similar policies with the goal of redressing governmental and private discrimination arose over the consistency of those policies with the Equal Protection Clause of the Fourteenth and Fifth Amendments. Private institutions and companies can voluntarily assume affirmative action policies; they become constitutionally controversial only when state and federal governments require similar compliance.

Advocates of affirmative action argued that the state and federal courts have upheld acts of private and governmental discrimination as legally acceptable. These advocates noted the continuous use of racial covenants in housing contracts, discrimination in the armed forces, regulations that discriminate against women in the workplace, and a long line of cases maintaining both a Jim Crow segregated society and segregation in education. The proponents of affirmative action demonstrated that discriminatory laws and policies existed in the North as well as the South, negatively affecting both women and citizens of color. For these litigants, the years of being handicapped and hindered in the marketplace required that the government and private sector take affirmative steps to allow those previously disadvantaged to compete, changing the current policies and structure to eliminate any vestiges of discrimination. Race and gender must be considered, they argued, to remove these vestiges and ensure fair treatment in the workplace and in schools. To ignore race and gender would be naïve and merely a continuation of discriminatory patterns.

Critics of affirmative action generally acknowledged the clear history of gender and racial discrimination and the role of the courts and governments in maintaining that history. For these critics, previous actions had not succeeded because they had taken citizens' characteristics of race and gender into account inappropriately. With the reinterpretation of the Fourteenth Amendment in *Brown v. Board of Education* (347 U.S. 483, 1954), disallowing separate but equal legislation, and the *Heart of Atlanta Motel* (379 U.S. 241, 1964) decision, which upheld the constitutionality of the Civil Rights Act of 1964, these litigants viewed the consideration of race and gender by the government as automatically suspect. If these protected statuses were taken into account by legislation, then the Court must ensure that the government had a compelling interest in implementing this policy, and that the law was narrowly tailored to that interest. For these critics, a color-blind Constitution required strict scrutiny for any form of race-conscious legislation and intermediate scrutiny for any form of gender-conscious legislation, regardless of the intent of the law.

As the struggle over affirmative action evolved, the question that faced the Court was whether, if the Constitution prohibited discrimination based on race or gender, it could allow remedial programs that take race and gender into account. If strict scrutiny were accepted as the appropriate standard for evaluating racial discrimination, did it matter if that discrimination was **benevolent** or **invidious** in intent?

One of the earliest cases in which this conflict was addressed was a challenge to an affirmative action program at the University of California at Davis Medical School in 1978. *Regents of the University of California v. Bakke* (438 U.S. 265) arose when Allan Bakke, a white male, applied to the program and was turned down twice; in both years some applicants who were admitted to the school through a special admissions program had grade point averages, standardized test scores, and admissions committee rankings significantly lower than Bakke's. As part of the medical school's admissions process, the committee considered applicants who were a member of a "minority group" or "economically and/or educationally disadvantaged." Sixteen slots were set aside in each class for students to be specially admitted; Bakke claimed that this program excluded him from admission on the basis of his race in violation of the Equal Protection Clause of the Fourteenth Amendment. In a complex decision, the Court decided that while race could be explicitly considered in the admissions process, it could not be a quota and it needed to be considered among such other factors as socio-economic class, region, and experience. In this decision, four justices argued for the constitutionality of the program and four argued against it. Justice Powell, who agreed with elements of both blocs of justices, cast the deciding vote. Because he was the only person who agreed with his decision, the result was not a majority decision, but a weaker plurality. Regardless of the decision's form, this precedent set the guidelines for the Court as it would address future cases of affirmative action that existed primarily in the workplace.

For almost a decade, the Court upheld a wide variety of state and local affirmative action programs targeted toward employment. Typically, as in *Local 28 Sheet Metal Workers' Union v. EEOC* (478 U.S. 421, 1986), the Court found that lower courts could allow race-conscious measures in the workplace as a means of remedying demonstrated acts of past discrimination. Throughout this period, remedial legislation—like affirmative action—as long as it could demonstrate its connection to a past injustice, was generally held to a lower equal protection standard than legislation designed to exclude people from participating. The Court would emphasize the significance of the aspect of "remedy" in *City of Richmond v. J. A. Croson Company* (488 U.S. 469, 1989). In 1983 the Richmond City Council adopted the Minority Business Utilization Plan, which required contractors for the city to subcontract at least 30 percent of the work to minority business enterprises (MBEs). The city adopted the definition of "minority" from federal statutes that had passed Supreme Court muster in *Fullilove v. Klutznick* (448 U.S. 448, 1980) and covered U.S. citizens who are black, Spanish-speaking, Asian, Indian, Eskimo, or Aleut. According to the language of the city's plan, the program was remedial in nature and designed to increase the participation of minority business enterprises in public projects. This case is significant because in a 6–3 decision, the Court emphasized that any color-conscious policies must be crafted to remedy a particular past harm. According to Justice O'Connor's majority opinion,

> Classifications based on race carry a danger of stigmatic harm. Unless they are strictly reserved for remedial settings, they may in fact promote notions of racial inferiority and lead to politics of racial hostility. . . . [T]he standard of review under the Equal Protection Clause is not dependent on the race of those burdened or benefited by a particular classification.

Because there was no history of city discrimination against "Oriental, Indian, Eskimo, or Aleut" residents of Richmond, Virginia, the Court found that the statute was neither narrowly defined nor remedial in nature. For the justices who contributed dissenting opinions, the irony of the assertion that the capital of the former Confederacy did not have a history of discrimination deserving of remediation was overwhelming.

By 1990, when the Court heard the case of *Metro Broadcasting, Inc. v. Federal Communications Commission* (497 U.S. 547), a prominent concern was identifying a legal standard appropriate for use in evaluating equal protection challenges of affirmative action policies. *Metro Broadcasting* combined two challenges to the federal agency's policy of awarding preferences to minority owners during comparative licensing proceedings. While the Court found the federal government's consideration of race in this decision acceptable, *Metro Broadcasting* is more significant because of the Court's 5–4 acceptance of intermediate scrutiny in the evaluation of race-conscious policies intended to achieve remediation. This meant that if a government could demonstrate that a program was substantially related to an important governmental objective, it had met the requirements of equal protection.

The *Metro Broadcasting* decision would not stand for long. Five years later, in the case of *Adarand Constructors v. Pena* (515 U.S. 200, 1995), the Court would rule that strict scrutiny should be used to evaluate all government programs that consider race, regardless of whether the policy had come from a federal, local, or state agency. In *Adarand*, the petitioner claimed that the federal government's practice of providing general contractors financial incentives to hire subcontractors controlled by "socially and economically disadvantaged individuals," and more specifically, the government's use of race to identify subcontractors that met this requirement, was a violation of the equal protection component of the Fifth Amendment's Due Process Clause. The Court in *Adarand* set the precedent that for a race-conscious governmental program to be constitutional, the government must demonstrate that the policy both serves a compelling state interest and is necessary to meet that interest. Consequently, most governmental set-aside programs were placed under review, and governmental bodies were much less likely to pursue race-conscious remedies even for purposes of addressing past or current discrimination.

A clear example of this hesitancy is found in *Hopwood v. Texas* (78 F.3d 932, 5th Cir., 1996). In March 1996, a three-judge panel ruled that the University of Texas School of Law could not use race as a factor in admissions for any of the following reasons: to diversify the student body; to change a perceived hostile environment; to challenge the school's poor reputation in the local community; or to eliminate any effects of past discrimination by agents other than themselves. *Hopwood*, while applicable only to the Fifth Circuit, was seen as a significant challenge to race-based affirmative action programs in higher education. Similar determinations, however, were made in other states: voter referendums in California, Washington, and Michigan, as well as gubernatorial intervention in Florida, made affirmative action programs in higher education admissions illegal. By contrast, federal courts in the Sixth and Ninth circuits ruled that the universities of Tennessee, Michigan, and Washington were able to weigh race as a factor in admitting students. Clearly, there was great variance within the nation and among the circuit courts regarding the legitimacy of affirmative action in higher education admissions. The Supreme Court finally decided to resolve this conflict in *Grutter v. Bollinger* (539 U.S. 306) and *Gratz v. Bollinger* (539 U.S. 244), which were decided in 2003.

In *Grutter* the Court examined the admissions process of the law school at the University of Michigan. As part of the admissions process, the law school winnowed over 3,500 applications to an entering class of approximately 350 students annually. The school's policy was to prioritize not only academically competitive students with legal promise, but also individuals who represented a mix of backgrounds and experiences; in addition, it explicitly stated that while results on the Law School Admissions Test and undergraduate grade point averages mattered, neither was a guarantee of either admission or disqualification. The law school application of Barbara Grutter, the petitioner, a white Michigan resident with a high grade point average and test score, was rejected. In the *Grutter* decision, the Court upheld as constitutional the practice of considering race in admissions decisions when the goal was to achieve the educational benefits of a diverse student body. Justice O'Connor authored the majority opinion, in which she expressed the belief that in twenty-five years the Court would no longer need to consider race in selecting students. O'Connor made clear that the University of Michigan Law School could consider race as a factor in selecting students because of the multiple educational benefits that flow from a diverse student body. Justice Ginsburg authored a concurring opinion in which she backed major portions of O'Connor's decision, but questioned the section that stressed that universities would be barred from weighing race as a factor in selecting students in twenty-five years. Justices Thomas and Scalia dissented, but both agreed with O'Connor's view that in twenty-five years, universities should discontinue using race in making admissions decisions. In fact, they interpreted O'Connor's language as stipulating a deadline after which universities could no longer utilize race in the admission process.

Although the Michigan law school's admission process was ruled constitutional in *Grutter*, in the other case, *Gratz v. Bollinger*, the justices explored the admissions process of the University of Michigan's undergraduate program and came to a contrary conclusion. Although the Court did maintain that diversity can be a compelling state interest, it ruled that the use of affirmative action in Michigan's undergraduate admissions program was not sufficiently narrowly tailored to avoid violating the Equal Protection Clause.

In 2007 the Supreme Court decided to merge that traditional debate over school integration into the larger debate related to affirmative action and reexamine what approaches are constitutional in trying to balance the racial composition of schools to prevent re-segregation. In the case of *Parents Involved in Community Schools v.*

Seattle School District No. 1 et al. (551 U.S. 701, 2007), the Court examined two school districts in which voluntarily adopted student assignment plans relied on race to determine which public schools children could attend. In each instance, the school district relied on race in assigning individual students to particular schools, so that the racial balance in each school would fall within a range that had been determined on the basis of the racial composition of the school district as a whole. Parents of students who were denied assignment to particular schools under these plans solely because of their race brought suit, contending that allocating children to different public schools on the basis of race violated the Fourteenth Amendment guarantee of equal protection. In both cases, the Court was presented with the same fundamental question—may a public school that had not operated de jure segregated schools, or has been found to be unitary in the federal courts, choose to classify students by race and use that classification in making school assignments? The Court did not find the precedents of *Gratz* and *Grutter*, with their allowance of racial diversity as a compelling governmental interest, to be applicable with respect to primary and secondary education. Therefore, applying strict scrutiny, the Court did not find that the two school districts had demonstrated a compelling governmental interest that justified their race-conscious policies. Consequently, both pupil assignment programs fell as violating the Equal Protection Clause.

In 2016, the Supreme Court revisited the *Grutter* decision in its second consideration of the *Hopwood* case in *Fisher v. University of Texas (Fisher II)* (579 U.S. ___). When the Court first heard the case in 2013 (*Fisher v. University of Texas* (*Fisher I*), 570 U.S. ___), it noted that the lower court did not apply strict scrutiny in its evaluation of the university's policy under the Equal Protection Clause. In *Fisher II* the Court determined that the University of Texas' consideration of race as a single factor among many to select the remaining students in the class—after all students who graduated in the top ten percent of their high school class are admitted—is narrowly tailored to the goal of a diverse college class. Consequently, this affirmative action program does not violate the Equal Protection Clause.

Affirmative action has been a highly contested arena for the Supreme Court and continues as such. Over the last thirty years, the Court has wrestled with the task of arriving at a proper standard for use in evaluating race-conscious remedies, just as the nation has grappled with questions of the constitutional legitimacy and necessity of race-conscious measures to overcome the legacy of racism and discrimination. The large number of plurality opinions on affirmative action, the many justices who split their decisions between concurring and dissenting opinions, the often strident tone of the debate, and the sheer length of these cases point to the complexity and contentiousness of discussions of the constitutionality of race-conscious policies. This issue promises to continue to be emotionally contested well into the foreseeable future.

REGENTS OF THE UNIVERSITY OF CALIFORNIA V. BAKKE

438 U.S. 265, 98 S.Ct. 2733, 57 L.Ed.2d 750 (1978)

Allan Bakke, a white male, applied to the University of California at Davis Medical School program in 1973 and 1974. He was turned down twice and learned that in both years, applicants whose grade point averages (GPA), Medical College Admissions Test (MCAT) scores, and overall admissions committee rankings were significantly lower than his had been admitted into the school through a special admissions program. The special admissions committee considered applicants who were "economically and/or educationally disadvantaged" or belonged to a "minority group." After reviewing these applicants separately, the special admissions committee recommended the best of the candidates for admission until the number of slots reserved in the new class had been met. Bakke claimed that this special admissions program had excluded him from admission on the basis of his race, in violation of the Equal Protection Clause of the Fourteenth Amendment. The Superior Court of California found the program in violation of the federal constitution and enjoined the university from considering race in admissions decisions. The Supreme Court of California upheld this decision.

Vote: ***Per curiam***

JUSTICE POWELL announced the judgment of the Court.

III

A

Petitioner does not deny that decisions based on race or ethnic origin by faculties and administrations of state universities are reviewable under the Fourteenth Amendment. For his part, respondent does not argue that all racial or ethnic classifications are per se invalid. The parties do disagree as to the level of judicial scrutiny to be applied to the special admissions program. Petitioner argues that the court below erred in applying strict scrutiny, as this inexact term has been applied in our cases. That level of review, petitioner asserts, should be reserved for classifications that disadvantage "discrete and insular minorities." Respondent, on the other hand, contends that the California court correctly rejected the notion that the degree of judicial scrutiny accorded a particular racial or ethnic classification hinges upon membership in a discrete and insular minority and duly recognized that the "rights established [by the Fourteenth Amendment] are personal rights." *Shelley v. Kraemer*, 334 U.S. 1, 22 (1948).

En route to this crucial battle over the scope of judicial review, the parties fight a sharp preliminary action over the proper characterization of the special admissions program. Petitioner prefers to view it as establishing a "goal" of minority representation in the Medical School. Respondent, echoing the courts below, labels it a racial quota.

This semantic distinction is beside the point: The special admissions program is undeniably a classification based on race and ethnic background. To the extent that there existed a pool of at least minimally qualified minority applicants to fill the 16 special admissions seats, white applicants could compete only for 84 seats in the entering class, rather than the 100 open to minority applicants. Whether this limitation is described as a quota or a goal, it is a line drawn on the basis of race and ethnic status.

The guarantees of the Fourteenth Amendment extend to all persons. Its language is explicit: "No State shall . . . deny to any person within its jurisdiction the equal protection of the laws." It is settled beyond question that the "rights created by the first section of the Fourteenth Amendment are, by its terms, guaranteed to the individual. The rights established are personal rights," *Shelley v. Kraemer,* at 22. The guarantee of equal protection cannot mean one thing when applied to one individual and something else when applied to a person of another color. If both are not accorded the same protection, then it is not equal.

Nevertheless, petitioner argues that the court below erred in applying strict scrutiny to the special admissions program because white males, such as respondent, are not a "discrete and insular minority" requiring extraordinary protection from the majoritarian political process. *Carolene Products Co.*, 304 U.S. 144 (1938), at 152–153, n. 4. This rationale, however, has never been invoked in our decisions as a prerequisite to subjecting racial or ethnic distinctions to strict scrutiny. Nor has this Court held that discreteness and insularity constitute necessary preconditions to a holding that a particular classification is invidious. These characteristics may be relevant in deciding whether or not to add new types of classifications to the list of "suspect" categories or whether a particular classification survives close examination. Racial and ethnic classifications, however, are subject to stringent examination without regard to these additional characteristics. We declared as much in the first cases explicitly to recognize racial distinctions as suspect:

> Distinctions between citizens solely because of their ancestry are by their very nature odious to a free people whose institutions are founded upon the doctrine of equality. *Hirabayashi v. United States*, 320 U.S. 81 (1943), at 100.
>
> [All] legal restrictions which curtail the civil rights of a single racial group are immediately suspect. That is not to say that all such restrictions are unconstitutional. It is to say that courts must subject them to the most rigid scrutiny. *Korematsu v. United States*, 323 U.S. 214 (1944), at 216.

The Court has never questioned the validity of those pronouncements. Racial and ethnic distinctions of any sort are inherently suspect and thus call for the most exacting judicial examination.

IV

We have held that in "order to justify the use of a suspect classification, a State must show that its purpose or interest is both constitutionally permissible and substantial, and that its use of the classification is 'necessary . . . to the accomplishment' of its purpose or the safeguarding of its interest." *In re Griffiths*, 413 U.S. 717, 721–722 (1973). The special admissions program purports to serve the purposes of: (i) "reducing the historic deficit of traditionally disfavored minorities in medical schools and in the medical profession"; (ii) countering the effects of societal discrimination; (iii) increasing the number of physicians who will practice in communities currently underserved; and (iv) obtaining the educational benefits that flow from an ethnically diverse student body. It is necessary to decide which, if any, of these purposes is substantial enough to support the use of a suspect classification.

A

If petitioner's purpose is to assure within its student body some specified percentage of a particular group merely because of its race or ethnic origin, such a preferential purpose must be rejected not as insubstantial but as facially invalid. Preferring members of any one group for no reason other than race or ethnic origin is discrimination for its own sake. This the Constitution forbids.

B

The State certainly has a legitimate and substantial interest in ameliorating, or eliminating where feasible, the disabling effects of identified discrimination.

. . . [T]he purpose of helping certain groups whom the faculty of the Davis Medical School perceived as victims of "societal discrimination" does not justify a classification that imposes disadvantages upon persons like respondent, who bear no responsibility for whatever harm the beneficiaries of the special admissions program are thought to have suffered. To hold otherwise would be to convert a remedy heretofore reserved for violations of legal rights into a privilege that all institutions throughout the Nation could grant at their pleasure to whatever groups are perceived as victims of societal discrimination. That is a step we have never approved.

C

Petitioner simply has not carried its burden of demonstrating that it must prefer members of particular ethnic groups over all other individuals in order to promote better health-care delivery to deprived citizens. Indeed, petitioner has not shown that its preferential classification is likely to have any significant effect on the problem.

D

The fourth goal asserted by petitioner is the attainment of a diverse student body. This clearly is a constitutionally permissible goal for an institution of higher education. Academic freedom, though not a specifically enumerated constitutional right, long has been viewed as a special concern of the First Amendment.

The freedom of a university to make its own judgments as to education includes the selection of its student body.

Thus, in arguing that its universities must be accorded the right to select those students who will contribute the most to the "robust exchange of ideas," petitioner invokes a countervailing constitutional interest, that of the First Amendment. In this light, petitioner must be viewed as seeking to achieve a goal that is of paramount importance in the fulfillment of its mission.

Ethnic diversity, however, is only one element in a range of factors a university properly may consider in attaining the goal of a heterogeneous student body. Although a university must have wide discretion in making the sensitive judgments as to who should be admitted, constitutional limitations protecting individual rights may not be disregarded. Respondent urges—and the courts below have held—that petitioner's dual admissions program is a racial classification that impermissibly infringes his rights under the Fourteenth Amendment. As the interest of diversity is compelling in the context of a university's admissions program, the question remains whether the program's racial classification is necessary to promote this interest.

V

A

It may be assumed that the reservation of a specified number of seats in each class for individuals from the preferred ethnic groups would contribute to the attainment of considerable ethnic diversity in the student body. But petitioner's argument that this is the only effective means of serving the interest of diversity is seriously flawed. In a most fundamental sense the argument misconceives the nature of the state interest that would justify consideration of race or ethnic background. It is not an interest in simple ethnic diversity, in which a specified percentage of the student body is in effect guaranteed to be members of selected ethnic groups, with the remaining percentage an undifferentiated aggregation of students. The diversity that furthers a compelling state interest encompasses a far broader array of qualifications and characteristics of which racial or ethnic origin is but a single though important element. Petitioner's special admissions program, focused solely on ethnic diversity, would hinder rather than further attainment of genuine diversity.

The experience of other university admissions programs, which take race into account in achieving the educational diversity valued by the First Amendment, demonstrates that the assignment of a fixed number of places to a minority group is not a necessary means toward that end. An illuminating example is found in the Harvard College program[.]

In such an admissions program, race or ethnic background may be deemed a "plus" in a particular applicant's file, yet it does not insulate the individual from comparison with all other candidates for the available seats. The file of a particular black applicant may be examined for his potential contribution to diversity without the factor of race being decisive when compared, for example, with that of an applicant identified as an Italian-American if the latter is thought to exhibit qualities more likely to promote beneficial educational pluralism. Such qualities could include exceptional personal talents, unique work or service experience, leadership potential, maturity, demonstrated compassion, a history of overcoming disadvantage, ability to communicate with the poor, or other qualifications deemed important. In short, an admissions program operated in this way is flexible enough to consider all pertinent elements of diversity in light of the particular qualifications of each applicant, and to place them on the same footing for consideration, although not necessarily according them the same weight. Indeed, the weight attributed to a particular quality may vary from year to year depending upon the "mix" both of the student body and the applicants for the incoming class.

This kind of program treats each applicant as an individual in the admissions process. The applicant who loses out on the last available seat to another candidate receiving a "plus" on the basis of ethnic background will not have been foreclosed from all consideration for that seat simply because he was not the right color or had the wrong surname. It would mean only that his combined qualifications, which may have included similar nonobjective factors, did not outweigh those of the other applicant. His qualifications would have been weighed fairly and competitively, and he would have no basis to complain of unequal treatment under the Fourteenth Amendment.

B

In summary, it is evident that the Davis special admissions program involves the use of an explicit racial classification never before countenanced by this Court. It tells applicants who are not Negro, Asian, or Chicano that they are totally excluded from a specific percentage of the seats in an entering class. No matter how strong their qualifications, quantitative and extracurricular, including their own potential for contribution to educational diversity, they are never afforded the chance to compete with applicants from the preferred groups for the special admissions seats. At the same time, the preferred applicants have the opportunity to compete for every seat in the class.

The fatal flaw in petitioner's preferential program is its disregard of individual rights as guaranteed by the Fourteenth Amendment. *Shelley v. Kraemer*, 334 U.S., at 22. Such rights are not absolute. But when a State's distribution of benefits or imposition of burdens hinges on ancestry or the color of a person's skin, that individual is entitled to a demonstration that the challenged classification is necessary to promote a substantial state interest. Petitioner has failed to carry this burden. For this reason, that portion of the California court's judgment holding petitioner's special admissions program invalid under the Fourteenth Amendment must be affirmed.

C

In enjoining petitioner from ever considering the race of any applicant, however, the courts below failed to recognize that the State has a substantial interest that legitimately may be served by a properly devised admissions program involving the competitive consideration of race and ethnic origin. For this reason, so much of the California court's judgment as enjoins petitioner from any consideration of the race of any applicant must be reversed.

JUSTICES BRENNAN, WHITE, MARSHALL, and BLACKMUN, concurring in the judgment in part and dissenting in part.

The Court today, in reversing in part the judgment of the Supreme Court of California, affirms the constitutional power of Federal and State Governments to act affirmatively to achieve equal opportunity for all. The difficulty of the issue presented—whether government may use race-conscious programs to redress the continuing effects of past discrimination—and the mature consideration which each of our Brethren has brought to it have resulted in many opinions, no single one speaking for the Court. But this should not and must not mask the central meaning of today's opinions: Government may take race into account when it acts not to demean or insult any racial group, but to remedy disadvantages cast on minorities by past racial prejudice, at least when appropriate findings have been made by judicial, legislative, or administrative bodies with competence to act in this area.

I

Our Nation was founded on the principle that "all Men are created equal." Yet candor requires acknowledgment that the Framers of our Constitution, to forge the 13 Colonies into one Nation, openly compromised this principle of equality with its antithesis: slavery. The consequences of this compromise are well known and have aptly been called our "American Dilemma."

Against this background, claims that law must be "colorblind" or that the datum of race is no longer relevant to public policy must be seen as aspiration rather than as description of reality. This is not to denigrate aspiration; for reality rebukes us that race has too often been used by those who would stigmatize and oppress minorities. Yet we cannot . . . let color blindness become myopia which masks the reality that many "created equal" have been treated within our lifetimes as inferior both by the law and by their fellow citizens.

III

A

The assertion of human equality is closely associated with the proposition that differences in color or creed, birth or status, are neither significant nor relevant to the way in which persons should be treated. Nonetheless, the position that such factors must be "constitutionally an irrelevance," *Edwards v. California*, 314 U.S. 160, 185 (1941) (Jackson, J., concurring), summed up by the shorthand phrase "[our] Constitution is color-blind," *Plessy v. Ferguson*, 163 U.S. 537, 559 (1896) (Harlan, J., dissenting), has never been adopted by this Court as the proper meaning of the Equal Protection Clause. Indeed, we have expressly rejected this proposition on a number of occasions.

Our cases have always implied that an "overriding statutory purpose," *McLaughlin v. Florida*, 379 U.S. 184, 192 (1964), could be found that would justify racial classifications. See, e.g., *Loving v. Virginia*, 388 U.S. 1, 11 (1967); *Korematsu v. United States*, 323 U.S. 214, 216 (1944); *Hirabayashi v. United States*, 320 U.S. 81, 100–101 (1943).

We conclude, therefore, that racial classifications are not per se invalid under the Fourteenth Amendment. Accordingly, we turn to the problem of articulating what our role should be in reviewing state action that expressly classifies by race.

B

Unquestionably we have held that a government practice or statute which restricts "fundamental rights" or which contains "suspect classifications" is to be subjected to "strict scrutiny" and can be justified only if it furthers a compelling government purpose and, even then, only if no less restrictive alternative is available. But no fundamental right is involved here. Nor do whites as a class have any of the "traditional indicia of suspectness: the class is not saddled with such disabilities, or subjected to such a history of purposeful unequal treatment, or relegated to such a position of political powerlessness as to command extraordinary protection from the majoritarian political process." See *United States v. Carolene Products Co.*, 304 U.S. 144, 152 n. 4 (1938).

Moreover, if the University's representations are credited, this is not a case where racial classifications are "irrelevant and therefore prohibited." *Hirabayashi*, at 100.

On the other hand, the fact that this case does not fit neatly into our prior analytic framework for race cases does not mean that it should be analyzed by applying the very loose rational-basis standard of review that is the very least that is always applied in equal protection cases.

In sum, because of the significant risk that racial classifications established for ostensibly benign purposes can be misused, causing effects not unlike those created by invidious classifications, it is inappropriate to inquire only whether there is any conceivable basis that might sustain such a classification. Instead, to justify such a classification an important and articulated purpose for its use must be shown. In addition, any statute must be stricken that stigmatizes any group or that singles out those least well represented in the political process to bear the brunt of a benign program. Thus, our review under the Fourteenth Amendment should be strict—not " 'strict' in theory and fatal in fact," because it is stigma that causes fatality—but strict and searching nonetheless.

IV

Davis' articulated purpose of remedying the effects of past societal discrimination is, under our cases, sufficiently important to justify the use of race-conscious admissions programs where there is a sound basis for concluding that minority underrepresentation is substantial and chronic, and that the handicap of past discrimination is impeding access of minorities to the Medical School.

A

At least since *Green v. County School Board*, 391 U.S. 430 (1968), it has been clear that a public body which has itself been adjudged to have engaged in racial discrimination cannot bring itself into compliance with the Equal Protection Clause simply by ending its unlawful acts and adopting a neutral stance. Moreover, we stated that school boards, even in the absence of a judicial finding of past discrimination, could voluntarily adopt plans which assigned students with the end of creating racial pluralism by establishing fixed ratios of black and white students in each school. *Swann v. Charlotte-Mecklenburg*, 402 U.S. 1 (1971). In each instance, the creation of unitary school systems, in which the effects of past discrimination had been "eliminated root and branch," *Green* at 438, was recognized as a compelling social goal justifying the overt use of race.

B

Properly construed, therefore, our prior cases unequivocally show that a state government may adopt race-conscious programs if the purpose of such programs is to remove the disparate racial impact its actions might otherwise have and if there is reason to believe that the disparate impact is itself the product of past discrimination, whether its own or that of society at large. There is no question that Davis' program is valid under this test.

C

The second prong of our test—whether the Davis program stigmatizes any discrete group or individual and whether race is reasonably used in light of the program's objectives—is clearly satisfied by the Davis program.

It is not even claimed that Davis' program in any way operates to stigmatize or single out any discrete and insular, or even any identifiable, nonminority group. Nor will harm comparable to that imposed upon racial minorities by exclusion or separation on grounds of race be the likely result of the program. True, whites are excluded from participation in the special admissions program, but this fact only operates to reduce the number of whites to be admitted in the regular admissions program in order to permit admission of a reasonable percentage—less than their proportion of the California population—of otherwise underrepresented qualified minority applicants.

D

We disagree with the lower courts' conclusion that the Davis program's use of race was unreasonable in light of its objectives. First, as petitioner argues, there are no practical means by which it could achieve its ends in the foreseeable future without the use of race-conscious measures. With respect to any factor (such as poverty or family educational background) that may be used as a substitute for race as an indicator of past discrimination, whites greatly outnumber racial minorities simply because whites make up a far larger percentage of the total population and therefore far outnumber minorities in absolute terms at every socioeconomic level.

Second, the Davis admissions program does not simply equate minority status with disadvantage. Rather, Davis considers on an individual basis each applicant's personal history to determine whether he or she has likely been disadvantaged by racial discrimination. The record makes clear that only minority applicants likely to have been isolated from the mainstream of American life are considered in the special program; other minority applicants are eligible only through the regular admissions program.

E

Finally, Davis' special admissions program cannot be said to violate the Constitution simply because it has set aside a predetermined number of places for qualified minority applicants rather than using minority status as a positive factor to be considered in evaluating the applications of disadvantaged minority applicants. For purposes of constitutional adjudication, there is no difference between the two approaches.

The "Harvard" program, as those employing it readily concede, openly and successfully employs a racial criterion for the purpose of ensuring that some of the scarce places in institutions of higher education are allocated to disadvantaged minority students. That the Harvard approach does not also make public the extent of the preference and the precise workings of the system while the Davis program employs a specific, openly stated number, does not condemn the latter plan for purposes of Fourteenth Amendment adjudication. It may be that the Harvard plan is more acceptable to the public than is the Davis "quota." But there is no basis for preferring a particular preference program simply because in achieving the same goals that the Davis Medical School is pursuing, it proceeds in a manner that is not immediately apparent to the public.

JUSTICE WHITE wrote a concurring opinion.

JUSTICE MARSHALL wrote an opinion concurring with the Court.

I agree with the judgment of the Court only insofar as it permits a university to consider the race of an applicant in making admissions decisions. I do not agree that petitioner's admissions program violates the Constitution. For it must be remembered that, during most of the past 200 years, the Constitution as interpreted by this Court did not prohibit the most ingenious and pervasive forms of discrimination against the Negro. Now, when a State acts to remedy the effects of that legacy of discrimination, I cannot believe that this same Constitution stands as a barrier.

IV

While I applaud the judgment of the Court that a university may consider race in its admissions process, it is more than a little ironic that, after several hundred years of class-based discrimination against Negroes, the Court is unwilling to hold that a class-based remedy for that discrimination is permissible. In declining to so hold, today's judgment ignores the fact that for several hundred years Negroes have been discriminated against, not as individuals, but rather solely because of the color of their skins. It is unnecessary in 20th-century America to have individual Negroes demonstrate that they have been victims of racial discrimination; the racism of our society has been so pervasive that none, regardless of wealth or position, has managed to escape its impact. The experience of Negroes in America has been different in kind, not just in degree, from that of other ethnic groups. It is not merely the history of slavery alone but also that a whole people were marked as inferior by the law. And that mark has endured. The dream of America as the great melting pot has not been realized for the Negro; because of his skin color he never even made it into the pot.

These differences in the experience of the Negro make it difficult for me to accept that Negroes cannot be afforded greater protection under the Fourteenth Amendment where it is necessary to remedy the effects of past discrimination. In the *Civil Rights Cases*, 109 U.S. 3 (1883), the Court wrote that the Negro emerging from slavery must cease "to be the special favorite of the laws." We cannot in light of the history of the last century yield to that view. Had the Court in that decision and others been willing to "do for human liberty and the fundamental rights of American citizenship, what it did . . . for the protection of slavery and the rights of the masters of fugitive slaves," we would not need now to permit the recognition of any "special wards."

Most importantly, had the Court been willing in 1896, in *Plessy v. Ferguson,* 163 U.S. 537 (1896), to hold that the Equal Protection Clause forbids differences in treatment based on race, we would not be faced with this dilemma in 1978. We must remember, however, that the principle that the "Constitution is colorblind" appeared only in the opinion of the lone dissenter. The majority of the Court rejected the principle of color blindness, and for the next 60 years, from *Plessy* to *Brown v. Board of Education*, ours was a Nation where, by law, an individual could be given "special" treatment based on the color of his skin.

It is because of a legacy of unequal treatment that we now must permit the institutions of this society to give consideration to race in making decisions about who will hold the positions of influence, affluence, and prestige in America. For far too long, the doors to those positions have been shut to Negroes. If we are ever to become a fully integrated society, one in which the color of a person's skin will not determine the opportunities available to him or her, we must be willing to take steps to open those doors. I do not believe that anyone can truly look into America's past and still find that a remedy for the effects of that past is impermissible.

It has been said that this case involves only the individual, *Bakke*, and this University. I doubt, however, that there is a computer capable of determining the number of persons and institutions that may be affected by the decision in this case. For example, we are told by the Attorney General of the United States that at least 27 federal agencies have adopted regulations requiring recipients of federal funds to take " 'affirmative action to overcome the effects of conditions which resulted in limiting participation . . . by persons of a particular race, color, or national origin.' " I cannot even guess the number of state and local governments that have set up affirmative-action programs, which may be affected by today's decision.

I fear that we have come full circle. After the Civil War our Government started several "affirmative action" programs. This Court in the *Civil Rights Cases* and *Plessy v. Ferguson* destroyed the movement toward complete equality. For almost a century no action was taken, and this nonaction was with the tacit approval of the courts. Then we had *Brown v. Board of Education* [347 U.S. 483 (1954)] and the Civil Rights Acts of Congress, followed by numerous affirmative-action programs. Now, we have this Court again stepping in, this time to stop affirmative-action programs of the type used by the University of California.

JUSTICE BLACKMUN wrote a separate opinion concurring with the Court.

JUSTICE STEVENS, with whom CHIEF JUSTICE BURGER, JUSTICES STEWART and REHNQUIST join, concurring in the judgment in part and dissenting in part.

It is always important at the outset to focus precisely on the controversy before the Court. It is particularly important to do so in this case because correct identification of the issues will determine whether it is necessary or appropriate to express any opinion about the legal status of any admissions program other than petitioner's.

I

This is not a class action. The controversy is between two specific litigants. Allan Bakke challenged petitioner's special admissions program, claiming that it denied him a place in medical school because of his race in violation of the Federal and California Constitutions and of Title VI of the Civil Rights Act of 1964, 42 U.S.C. § 2000d et seq. The California Supreme Court upheld his challenge and ordered him admitted. If the state court was correct in its view that the University's special program was illegal, and that Bakke was therefore unlawfully excluded from the Medical School because of his race, we should affirm its judgment, regardless of our views about the legality of admissions programs that are not now before the Court.

The judgment as originally entered by the trial court contained four separate paragraphs, two of which are of critical importance. Paragraph 3 declared that the University's special admissions program violated the Fourteenth Amendment, the State Constitution, and Title VI. The trial court did not order the University to admit Bakke because it concluded that Bakke had not shown that he would have been admitted if there had been no special program. Instead, in paragraph 2 of its judgment it ordered the University to consider Bakke's application for admission without regard to his race or the race of any other applicant. The order did not include any broad prohibition against any use of race in the admissions process; its terms were clearly limited to the

University's consideration of Bakke's application. Because the University has since been ordered to admit Bakke, paragraph 2 of the trial court's order no longer has any significance.

The California Supreme Court, in a holding that is not challenged, ruled that the trial court incorrectly placed the burden on Bakke of showing that he would have been admitted in the absence of discrimination. The University then conceded "that it [could] not meet the burden of proving that the special admissions program did not result in Mr. Bakke's failure to be admitted." Accordingly, the California Supreme Court directed the trial court to enter judgment ordering Bakke's admission. Since that order superseded paragraph 2 of the trial court's judgment, there is no outstanding injunction forbidding any consideration of racial criteria in processing applications.

It is therefore perfectly clear that the question whether race can ever be used as a factor in an admissions decision is not an issue in this case, and that discussion of that issue is inappropriate.

II

Both petitioner and respondent have asked us to determine the legality of the University's special admissions program by reference to the Constitution. Our settled practice, however, is to avoid the decision of a constitutional issue if a case can be fairly decided on a statutory ground. "If there is one doctrine more deeply rooted than any other in the process of constitutional adjudication, it is that we ought not to pass on questions of constitutionality . . . unless such adjudication is unavoidable." *Spector Motor Co. v. McLaughlin*, 323 U.S. 101, 105 [(1944)]. The more important the issue, the more force there is to this doctrine. In this case, we are presented with a constitutional question of undoubted and unusual importance. Since, however, a dispositive statutory claim was raised at the very inception of this case, and squarely decided in the portion of the trial court judgment affirmed by the California Supreme Court, it is our plain duty to confront it. Only if petitioner should prevail on the statutory issue would it be necessary to decide whether the University's admissions program violated the Equal Protection Clause of the Fourteenth Amendment.

III

The University's special admissions program violated Title VI of the Civil Rights Act of 1964 by excluding Bakke from the Medical School because of his race. It is therefore our duty to affirm the judgment ordering Bakke admitted to the University.

FOR DISCUSSION

What is the consequence of *Bakke* being reported as a plurality decision, as opposed to a majority decision? How would you characterize the key point of contention among the concurring members of the Court? Among the dissenters? Do you agree with Justice Powell that there is a difference between the use of race in the California Davis admission's plan and the use of race at Harvard?

RELATED CASES

***Fullilove v. Klutznick:* 448 U.S. 448 (1980).**

Congressional legislation setting aside at least 10 percent of local public works programs to contract or subcontract with minority-owned businesses was a legitimate exercise of congressional authority under the Spending Clause in Article I. Because it was a remedial act, the Court did not need to review it in terms of whether it was or was not colorblind.

Wygant v. Jackson Board of Education: **476 U.S. 267 (1986).**

A collective bargaining agreement resulted in more recently hired black teachers being retained during layoffs while whites with more seniority were laid off. The Supreme Court found this to be an unconstitutional violation of the Equal Protection Clause. The Court specifically noted that the racial classification needed to be justified with a compelling state interest, and the means chosen by the state needed to be narrowly tailored to their goal.

United States v. Paradise: **480 U.S. 149 (1987).**

The Supreme Court upheld the constitutionality of a remedial promotion plan that allowed one black officer to be promoted to certain ranks for every white officer (contingent on their being enough black officers in the pool). The Alabama Department of Public Safety was responding to a series of civil lawsuits it had lost in the early 1970s.

Local 28 Sheet Metal Workers' Union v. EEOC: **478 U.S. 421 (1986).**

Title VII of the Civil Rights Act of 1964 does not prevent courts from allowing race-conscious (affirmative action) measures to remedy demonstrated acts of past discrimination. This ruling allows federal courts to move beyond injunctions to stop discriminatory behavior.

CITY OF RICHMOND V. J. A. CROSON COMPANY

488 U.S. 469, 109 S.Ct. 706, 102 L.Ed.2d 854 (1989)

In 1983 the Richmond City Council adopted a program, the Minority Business Utilization Plan, that required contractors for the city to subcontract at least 30 percent of the city's work to minority business enterprises (MBEs). For the purpose of the plan, the city adopted the definition of "minority" from federal language and so classified U.S. citizens who are black, Spanish-speaking, oriental, Indian, Eskimo, or Aleut. According to the language of the plan, it was remedial and designed to increase the participation of MBEs in public projects. The managers of J. A. Croson Company challenged the law after they were denied a city contract because they had been unable to find a MBE to handle a sufficient percentage of the work at a competitive cost. The federal district court upheld the city's plan and Fourth Circuit affirmed. The case was then appealed to the Supreme Court, which vacated the decision of the appellate court and remanded it in light of the ruling in *Wygant v. Jackson Board of Education* (476 U.S. 267, 1986), which required a showing of compelling governmental interest to institute such a plan. The court of appeals then found that the Richmond set-aside program violated the Equal Protection Clause of the Fourteenth Amendment.

Vote: 6–3

JUSTICE O'CONNOR announced the judgment of the Court and delivered the opinion of the Court with respect to Parts I, III-B, and IV, an opinion with respect to Part II, in which CHIEF JUSTICE REHNQUIST and JUSTICE WHITE join, and an opinion with respect to Parts III-A and V, in which CHIEF JUSTICE REHNQUIST, and JUSTICES WHITE and KENNEDY join.

In this case, we confront once again the tension between the Fourteenth Amendment's guarantee of equal treatment to all citizens, and the use of race-based measures to ameliorate the effects of past discrimination on the opportunities enjoyed by members of minority groups in our society. In *Fullilove v. Klutznick*, 448 U.S. 448 (1980), we held that a congressional program requiring that 10% of certain federal construction grants be awarded to minority contractors did not violate the equal protection principles embodied in the Due Process Clause of the Fifth Amendment. Relying largely on our decision in *Fullilove*, some lower federal courts have applied a similar standard of review in assessing the constitutionality of state and local minority set-aside provisions under the Equal Protection Clause of the Fourteenth Amendment. Since our decision two Terms ago in *Wygant v. Jackson Board of Education*, 476 U.S. 267 (1986), the lower federal courts have attempted to apply its standards in evaluating the constitutionality of state and local programs which allocate a portion of public contracting opportunities exclusively to minority-owned businesses. We noted probable jurisdiction in this case to consider the applicability of our decision in *Wygant* to a minority set-aside program adopted by the city of Richmond, Virginia.

II

The parties and their supporting amici fight an initial battle over the scope of the city's power to adopt legislation designed to address the effects of past discrimination. Relying on our decision in *Wygant*, appellee argues that the city must limit any race-based remedial efforts to eradicating the effects of its own prior discrimination. This is essentially the position taken by the Court of Appeals below. Appellant argues that our decision in *Fullilove* is controlling, and that as a result the city of Richmond enjoys sweeping legislative power to define and attack the effects of prior discrimination in its local construction industry. We find that neither of these two rather stark alternatives can withstand analysis.

In *Fullilove*, we upheld the minority set-aside contained in § 103(f)(2) of the Public Works Employment Act of 1977, Pub. L. 95–28, 91 Stat. 116, 42 U S.C. § 6701 et seq. (Act) against a challenge based on the equal protection component of the Due Process Clause.

The principal opinion in *Fullilove*, written by Chief Justice Burger, did not employ "strict scrutiny" or any other traditional standard of equal protection review. The Chief Justice noted at the outset that although racial classifications call for close examination, the Court was at the same time "bound to approach [its] task with appropriate deference to the Congress, a co-equal branch charged by the Constitution with the power to 'provide for the. . . general Welfare of the United States' and 'to enforce by appropriate legislation,' the equal protection guarantees of the Fourteenth Amendment." The principal opinion asked two questions: first, were the objectives of the legislation within the power of Congress? Second, was the limited use of racial and ethnic criteria a permissible means for Congress to carry out its objectives within the constraints of the Due Process Clause?

On the issue of congressional power, the Chief Justice found that Congress' commerce power was sufficiently broad to allow it to reach the practices of prime contractors on federally funded local construction projects. Congress could mandate state and local government compliance with the set-aside program under its § 5 power to enforce the Fourteenth Amendment.

The Chief Justice next turned to the constraints on Congress' power to employ race-conscious remedial relief. His opinion stressed two factors in upholding the MBE set-aside. First was the unique remedial powers of Congress under § 5 of the Fourteenth Amendment[.]

Because of these unique powers, the Chief Justice concluded that "Congress not only may induce voluntary action to assure compliance with existing federal statutory or constitutional antidiscrimination provisions, but also, where Congress has authority to declare certain conduct unlawful, it may, as here, authorize and induce state action to avoid such conduct."

In reviewing the legislative history behind the Act, the principal opinion focused on the evidence before Congress that a nationwide history of past discrimination had reduced minority participation in federal construction grants. The Chief Justice also noted that Congress drew on its experience under § 8(a) of the Small Business Act of 1953, which had extended aid to minority businesses. The Chief Justice concluded that "Congress had abundant historical basis from which it could conclude that traditional procurement practices, when applied to minority businesses, could perpetuate the effects of prior discrimination."

The second factor emphasized by the principal opinion in *Fullilove* was the flexible nature of the 10% set-aside. Two "congressional assumptions" underlay the MBE program: first, that the effects of past discrimination had impaired the competitive position of minority businesses, and second, that "adjustment for the effects of past discrimination" would assure that at least 10% of the funds from the federal grant program would flow to minority businesses. The Chief Justice noted that both of these "assumptions" could be "rebutted" by a grantee seeking a waiver of the 10% requirement. The Chief Justice indicated that without this fine tuning to remedial purpose, the statute would not have "pass[ed] muster."

Appellant and its supporting amici rely heavily on *Fullilove* for the proposition that a city council, like Congress, need not make specific findings of discrimination to engage in race-conscious relief.

What appellant ignores is that Congress, unlike any State or political subdivision, has a specific constitutional mandate to enforce the dictates of the Fourteenth Amendment. The power to "enforce" may at times also include the power to define situations which Congress determines threaten principles of equality and to adopt prophylactic rules to deal with those situations.

That Congress may identify and redress the effects of society-wide discrimination does not mean that, a fortiori, the States and their political subdivisions are free to decide that such remedies are appropriate. Section 1 of the Fourteenth Amendment is an explicit constraint on state power, and the States must undertake any remedial efforts in accordance with that provision. To hold otherwise would be to cede control over the content of the Equal Protection Clause to the 50 state legislatures and their myriad political subdivisions.

It would seem equally clear, however, that a state or local subdivision (if delegated the authority from the State) has the authority to eradicate the effects of private discrimination within its own legislative jurisdiction. This authority must, of course, be exercised within the constraints of § 1 of the Fourteenth Amendment. Our decision in *Wygant* is not to the contrary. *Wygant* addressed the constitutionality of the use of racial quotas by local school authorities pursuant to an agreement reached with the local teachers' union. It was in the context of addressing the school board's power to adopt a race-based layoff program affecting its own work force that the Wygant plurality indicated that the Equal Protection Clause required "some showing of prior discrimination by the governmental unit involved." *Wygant*, 476 U.S., at 274. As a matter of state law, the city of Richmond has legislative authority over its procurement policies, and can use its spending powers to remedy private discrimination, if it identifies that discrimination with the particularity required by the Fourteenth Amendment. To this extent, on the question of the city's competence, the Court of Appeals erred in following *Wygant* by rote in a case involving a state entity which has state-law authority to address discriminatory practices within local commerce under its jurisdiction.

Thus, if the city could show that it had essentially become a "passive participant" in a system of racial exclusion practiced by elements of the local construction industry, we think it clear that the city could take affirmative steps to dismantle such a system. It is beyond dispute that any public entity, state or federal, has a compelling interest in assuring that public dollars, drawn from the tax contributions of all citizens, do not serve to finance the evil of private prejudice.

III

A

The Equal Protection Clause of the Fourteenth Amendment provides that "[n]o State shall . . . deny to any person within its jurisdiction the equal protection of the laws." The Richmond Plan denies certain citizens the opportunity to compete for a fixed percentage of public contracts based solely upon their race. To whatever racial group these citizens belong, their "personal rights" to be treated with equal dignity and respect are implicated by a rigid rule erecting race as the sole criterion in an aspect of public decisionmaking.

Absent searching judicial inquiry into the justification for such race-based measures, there is simply no way of determining what classifications are "benign" or "remedial" and what classifications are in fact motivated by illegitimate notions of racial inferiority or simple racial politics. Indeed, the purpose of strict scrutiny is to "smoke out" illegitimate uses of race by assuring that the legislative body is pursuing a goal important enough to warrant use of a highly suspect tool. The test also ensures that the means chosen "fit" this compelling goal so closely that there is little or no possibility that the motive for the classification was illegitimate racial prejudice or stereotype.

Classifications based on race carry a danger of stigmatic harm. Unless they are strictly reserved for remedial settings, they may in fact promote notions of racial inferiority and lead to a politics of racial hostility. We thus reaffirm the view expressed by the plurality in *Wygant* that the standard of review under the Equal Protection Clause is not dependent on the race of those burdened or benefited by a particular classification.

Under the standard proposed by Justice Marshall's dissent, "race-conscious classifications designed to further remedial goals," are forthwith subject to a relaxed standard of review. The dissent's watered-down version of equal protection review effectively assures that race will always be relevant in American life, and that the "ultimate goal" of "eliminat[ing] entirely from governmental decisionmaking such irrelevant factors as a human being's race," *Wygant*, at 320 (Stevens, J., dissenting), will never be achieved.

Justice Powell's opinion in *Regents of the University of California v. Bakke*, 438 U.S. 265 (1978), applied heightened scrutiny under the Equal Protection Clause to the racial classification at issue. His opinion decisively rejected the first justification for the racially segregated admissions plan. The desire to have more black medical students or doctors, standing alone, was not merely insufficiently compelling to justify a racial classification, it was "discrimination for its own sake," forbidden by the Constitution. Nor could the second concern, the history of discrimination in society at large, justify a racial quota in medical school admissions. Justice Powell contrasted the "focused" goal of remedying "wrongs worked by specific instances of racial discrimination" with "the remedying of the effects of 'societal discrimination,' an amorphous concept of injury that may be ageless in its reach into the past." He indicated that for the governmental interest in remedying past discrimination to be triggered "judicial, legislative, or administrative findings of constitutional or statutory violations" must be made. Only then does the government have a compelling interest in favoring one race over another.

B

While there is no doubt that the sorry history of both private and public discrimination in this country has contributed to a lack of opportunities for black entrepreneurs, this observation, standing alone, cannot justify a rigid racial quota in the awarding of public contracts in Richmond, Virginia. Like the claim that discrimination in primary and secondary schooling justifies a rigid racial preference in medical school admissions, an amorphous claim that there has been past discrimination in a particular industry cannot justify the use of an unyielding racial quota.

It is sheer speculation how many minority firms there would be in Richmond absent past societal discrimination, just as it was sheer speculation how many minority medical students would have been admitted to the medical school at Davis absent past discrimination in educational opportunities. Defining these sorts of injuries as "identified discrimination" would give local governments license to create a patchwork of racial preferences based on statistical generalizations about any particular field of endeavor.

In sum, none of the evidence presented by the city points to any identified discrimination in the Richmond construction industry. We, therefore, hold that the city has failed to demonstrate a compelling interest in apportioning public contracting opportunities on the basis of race. To accept Richmond's claim that past societal discrimination alone can serve as the basis for rigid racial preferences would be to open the door to competing claims for "remedial relief" for every disadvantaged group. The dream of a Nation of equal citizens in a society where race is irrelevant to personal opportunity and achievement would be lost in a mosaic of shifting preferences based on inherently unmeasurable claims of past wrongs.

The foregoing analysis applies only to the inclusion of blacks within the Richmond set-aside program. There is absolutely no evidence of past discrimination against Spanish speaking, Oriental, Indian, Eskimo, or Aleut persons in any aspect of the Richmond construction industry. The random inclusion of racial groups that, as a practical matter, may never have suffered from discrimination in the construction industry in Richmond suggests that perhaps the city's purpose was not in fact to remedy past discrimination.

If a 30% set-aside was "narrowly tailored" to compensate black contractors for past discrimination, one may legitimately ask why they are forced to share this "remedial relief" with an Aleut citizen who moves to Richmond tomorrow? The gross overinclusiveness of Richmond's racial preference strongly impugns the city's claim of remedial motivation.

IV

[I]t is almost impossible to assess whether the Richmond Plan is narrowly tailored to remedy prior discrimination since it is not linked to identified discrimination in any way. We limit ourselves to two observations in this regard.

First, there does not appear to have been any consideration of the use of race-neutral means to increase minority business participation in city contracting. There is no evidence in this record that the Richmond City Council has considered any alternatives to a race-based quota.

Second, the 30% quota cannot be said to be narrowly tailored to any goal, except perhaps outright racial balancing. It rests upon the "completely unrealistic" assumption that minorities will choose a particular trade in lockstep proportion to their representation in the local population.

Since the city must already consider bids and waivers on a case-by-case basis, it is difficult to see the need for a rigid numerical quota.

Given the existence of an individualized procedure, the city's only interest in maintaining a quota system rather than investigating the need for remedial action in particular cases would seem to be simple administrative convenience. But the interest in avoiding the bureaucratic effort necessary to tailor remedial relief to those who truly have suffered the effects of prior discrimination cannot justify a rigid line drawn on the basis of a suspect classification. Under Richmond's scheme, a successful black, Hispanic, or Oriental entrepreneur from anywhere in the country enjoys an absolute preference over other citizens based solely on their race. We think it obvious that such a program is not narrowly tailored to remedy the effects of prior discrimination.

V

Because the city of Richmond has failed to identify the need for remedial action in the awarding of its public construction contracts, its treatment of its citizens on a racial basis violates the dictates of the Equal Protection Clause. Accordingly, the judgment of the Court of Appeals for the Fourth Circuit is Affirmed.

JUSTICE STEVENS, concurring in part and concurring in the judgment.

A central purpose of the Fourteenth Amendment is to further the national goal of equal opportunity for all our citizens. In order to achieve that goal we must learn from our past mistakes, but I believe the Constitution requires us to evaluate our policy decisions—including those that govern the relationships among different racial and ethnic groups—primarily by studying their probable impact on the future. I therefore do not agree with the premise that seems to underlie today's decision, as well as the decision in *Wygant v. Jackson Board of Education*, 476 U.S. 267 (1986), that a governmental decision that rests on a racial classification is never permissible except as a remedy for a past wrong.

First, the city makes no claim that the public interest in the efficient performance of its construction contracts will be served by granting a preference to minority-business enterprises. This case is therefore completely unlike *Wygant*. . . . As I pointed out in my dissent in that case, even if we completely disregard our history of racial injustice, race is not always irrelevant to sound governmental decisionmaking.

Second, this litigation involves an attempt by a legislative body, rather than a court, to fashion a remedy for a past wrong. Thus, in cases involving the review of judicial remedies imposed against persons who have been proved guilty of violations of law, I would allow the courts in racial discrimination cases the same broad discretion that chancellors enjoy in other areas of the law.

Third, instead of engaging in a debate over the proper standard of review to apply in affirmative-action litigation, I believe it is more constructive to try to identify the characteristics of the advantaged and disadvantaged classes that may justify their disparate treatment. In this case that approach convinces me that, instead of carefully identifying the characteristics of the two classes of contractors that are respectively favored and disfavored by its ordinance, the Richmond City Council has merely engaged in the type of stereotypical analysis that is a hallmark of violations of the Equal Protection Clause. Whether we look at the class of persons benefited by the ordinance or at the disadvantaged class, the same conclusion emerges.

The ordinance is equally vulnerable because of its failure to identify the characteristics of the disadvantaged class of white contractors that justify the disparate treatment. Thus, the composition of the disadvantaged class of white contractors presumably includes some who have been guilty of unlawful discrimination, some who practiced discrimination before it was forbidden by law, and some who have never discriminated against anyone on the basis of race. Imposing a common burden on such a disparate class merely because each member of the class is of the same race stems from reliance on a stereotype rather than fact or reason.

Accordingly, I concur in Parts I, III-B, and IV of the Court's opinion, and in the judgment.

JUSTICE KENNEDY, concurring in part and concurring in the judgment.

I join all but Part II of Justice O'Connor's opinion and give this further explanation.

Part II examines our case law upholding congressional power to grant preferences based on overt and explicit classification by race. With the acknowledgment that the summary in Part II is both precise and fair, I must decline to join it. The process by which a law that is an equal protection violation when enacted by a State becomes transformed to an equal protection guarantee when enacted by Congress poses a difficult proposition for me; but as it is not before us, any reconsideration of that issue must await some further case. For purposes of the ordinance challenged here, it suffices to say that the State has the power to eradicate racial discrimination and its effects in both the public and private sectors, and the absolute duty to do so where those wrongs were caused intentionally by the State itself. The Fourteenth Amendment ought not to be interpreted to reduce a State's authority in this regard, unless, of course, there is a conflict with federal law or a state remedy is itself a violation of equal protection. The latter is the case presented here.

Nevertheless, given that a rule of automatic invalidity for racial preferences in almost every case would be a significant break with our precedents that require a case-by-case test, I am not convinced we need adopt it at this point. On the assumption that it will vindicate the principle of race neutrality found in the Equal Protection Clause, I accept the less absolute rule contained in Justice O'Connor's opinion, a rule based on the proposition that any racial preference must face the most rigorous scrutiny by the courts.

The ordinance before us falls far short of the standard we adopt. We are left with an ordinance and a legislative record open to the fair charge that it is not a remedy but is itself a preference which will cause the same corrosive animosities that the Constitution forbids in the whole sphere of government and that our national policy condemns in the rest of society as well. This ordinance is invalid under the Fourteenth Amendment.

JUSTICE SCALIA, concurring in the judgment.

I agree with much of the Court's opinion, and, in particular, with Justice O'Connor's conclusion that strict scrutiny must be applied to all governmental classification by race, whether or not its asserted purpose is "remedial" or "benign." I do not agree, however, with Justice O'Connor's dictum suggesting that, despite the Fourteenth Amendment, state and local governments may in some circumstances discriminate on the basis of race in order (in a broad sense) "to ameliorate the effects of past discrimination." The benign purpose of compensating for social disadvantages, whether they have been acquired by reason of prior discrimination or otherwise, can no more be pursued by the illegitimate means of racial discrimination than can other assertedly benign purposes we have repeatedly rejected. The difficulty of overcoming the effects of past discrimination is as nothing compared with the difficulty of eradicating from our society the source of those effects, which is the tendency—fatal to a Nation such as ours—to classify and judge men and women on the basis of their country of origin or the color of their skin. A solution to the first problem that aggravates the second is no solution at all.

In my view there is only one circumstance in which the States may act by race to "undo the effects of past discrimination": where that is necessary to eliminate their own maintenance of a system of unlawful racial classification. If, for example, a state agency has a discriminatory pay scale compensating black employees in all positions at 20% less than their nonblack counterparts, it may assuredly promulgate an order raising the salaries of "all black employees" to eliminate the differential. This distinction explains our school desegregation cases, in which we have made plain that States and localities sometimes have an obligation to adopt race conscious remedies.

It is plainly true that in our society blacks have suffered discrimination immeasurably greater than any directed at other racial groups. But those who believe that racial preferences can help to "even the score" display, and reinforce, a manner of thinking by race that was the source of the injustice and that will, if it endures within our society, be the source of more injustice still.

Since I believe that the appellee here had a constitutional right to have its bid succeed or fail under a decisionmaking process uninfected with racial bias, I concur in the judgment of the Court.

JUSTICE MARSHALL, with whom JUSTICES BRENNAN and BLACKMUN join, dissenting.

It is a welcome symbol of racial progress when the former capital of the Confederacy acts forthrightly to confront the effects of racial discrimination in its midst. In my view, nothing in the Constitution can be construed to prevent Richmond, Virginia, from allocating a portion of its contracting dollars for businesses owned or controlled by members of minority groups. Indeed, Richmond's set-aside program is indistinguishable in all meaningful respects from—and in fact was patterned upon—the federal set-aside plan which this Court upheld in *Fullilove v. Klutznick*, 448 U.S. 448 (1980).

A majority of this Court holds today, however, that the Equal Protection Clause of the Fourteenth Amendment blocks Richmond's initiative. The essence of the majority's position is that Richmond has failed to catalog adequate findings to prove that past discrimination has impeded minorities from joining or participating fully in Richmond's construction contracting industry. I find deep irony in second-guessing Richmond's judgment on this point. As much as any municipality in the United States, Richmond knows what racial discrimination is; a century of decisions by this and other federal courts has richly documented the city's disgraceful history of public and private racial discrimination. In any event, the Richmond City Council has supported its determination that minorities have been wrongly excluded from local construction contracting. Its proof includes statistics showing that minority-owned businesses have received virtually no city contracting dollars and rarely if ever belonged to area trade associations; testimony by municipal officials that discrimination has been widespread in the local construction industry; and the same exhaustive and widely publicized federal studies relied on in *Fullilove*, studies which showed that pervasive discrimination in the Nation's tight-knit construction industry had operated to exclude minorities from public contracting. These are precisely the types of statistical and testimonial evidence which, until today, this Court had credited in cases approving of race conscious measures designed to remedy past discrimination.

More fundamentally, today's decision marks a deliberate and giant step backward in this Court's affirmative-action jurisprudence. Cynical of one municipality's attempt to redress the effects of past racial discrimination in a particular industry, the majority launches a grapeshot attack on race-conscious remedies in general. The majority's unnecessary pronouncements will inevitably discourage or prevent governmental entities, particularly States and localities, from acting to rectify the scourge of past discrimination. This is the harsh reality of the majority's decision, but it is not the Constitution's command.

III

A

Today, for the first time, a majority of this Court has adopted strict scrutiny as its standard of Equal Protection Clause review of race-conscious remedial measures. This is an unwelcome development. A profound difference separates governmental actions that themselves are racist, and governmental actions that seek to remedy the effects of prior racism or to prevent neutral governmental activity from perpetuating the effects of such racism.

Racial classifications "drawn on the presumption that one race is inferior to another or because they put the weight of government behind racial hatred and separatism" warrant the strictest judicial scrutiny because of the very irrelevance of these rationales. By contrast, racial classifications drawn for the purpose of remedying the effects of discrimination that itself was race based have a highly pertinent basis: the tragic and indelible fact that discrimination against blacks and other racial minorities in this Nation has pervaded our Nation's history and continues to scar our society. As I stated in *Fullilove*: "Because the consideration of race is relevant to remedying the continuing effects of past racial discrimination, and because governmental programs employing racial classifications for remedial purposes can be crafted to avoid stigmatization, . . . such programs should not be subjected to conventional 'strict scrutiny' — scrutiny that is strict in theory, but fatal in fact." *Fullilove*, at 518–519.

In concluding that remedial classifications warrant no different standard of review under the Constitution than the most brutal and repugnant forms of state-sponsored racism, a majority of this Court signals that it regards racial discrimination as largely a phenomenon of the past, and that government bodies need no longer preoccupy themselves with rectifying racial injustice. I, however, do not believe this Nation is anywhere close to eradicating racial discrimination or its vestiges. In constitutionalizing its wishful thinking, the majority today does a grave disservice not only to those victims of past and present racial discrimination in this Nation whom government has sought to assist, but also to this Court's long tradition of approaching issues of race with the utmost sensitivity.

C

Today's decision, finally, is particularly noteworthy for the daunting standard it imposes upon States and localities contemplating the use of race-conscious measures to eradicate the present effects of prior discrimination and prevent its perpetuation. The majority restricts the use of such measures to situations in which a State or locality can put forth "a prima facie case of a constitutional or statutory violation." In so doing, the majority calls into question the validity of the business set-asides which dozens of municipalities across this Nation have adopted on the authority of *Fullilove*.

Nothing in the Constitution or in the prior decisions of this Court supports limiting state authority to confront the effects of past discrimination to those situations in which a prima facie case of a constitutional or statutory violation can be made out. By its very terms, the majority's standard effectively cedes control of a large component of the content of that constitutional provision to Congress and to state legislatures. If an antecedent Virginia or Richmond law had defined as unlawful the award to nonminorities of an overwhelming share of a city's contracting dollars, for example, Richmond's subsequent set-aside initiative would then satisfy the majority's standard. But without such a law, the initiative might not withstand constitutional scrutiny. The meaning of "equal protection of the laws" thus turns on the happenstance of whether a state or local body has previously defined illegal discrimination. Indeed, given that racially discriminatory cities may be the ones least likely to have tough antidiscrimination laws on their books, the majority's constitutional incorporation of state and local statutes has the perverse effect of inhibiting those States or localities with the worst records of official racism from taking remedial action.

IV

The majority today sounds a full-scale retreat from the Court's longstanding solicitude to race-conscious remedial efforts "directed toward deliverance of the century-old promise of equality of economic opportunity." *Fullilove*, 448 U.S., at 463. The new and restrictive tests it applies scuttle one city's effort to surmount its discriminatory past, and imperil those of dozens more localities. I, however, profoundly disagree with the cramped vision of the Equal Protection Clause which the majority offers today and with its application of that vision to Richmond, Virginia's, laudable set-aside plan. The battle against pernicious racial discrimination or its effects is nowhere near won. I must dissent.

JUSTICE BLACKMUN, with whom JUSTICE BRENNAN joins, dissenting.

I join Justice Marshall's perceptive and incisive opinion revealing great sensitivity toward those who have suffered the pains of economic discrimination in the construction trades for so long.

I never thought that I would live to see the day when the city of Richmond, Virginia, the cradle of the Old Confederacy, sought on its own, within a narrow confine, to lessen the stark impact of persistent discrimination. But Richmond, to its great credit, acted. Yet this Court, the supposed bastion of equality, strikes down Richmond's efforts as though discrimination had never existed or was not demonstrated in this particular litigation. Justice Marshall convincingly discloses the fallacy and the shallowness of that approach. History is irrefutable, even though one might sympathize with those who—though possibly innocent in themselves—benefit from the wrongs of past decades.

So the Court today regresses. I am confident, however, that, given time, it one day again will do its best to fulfill the great promises of the Constitution's Preamble and of the guarantees embodied in the Bill of Rights—a fulfillment that would make this Nation very special.

FOR DISCUSSION

According to the majority, how tightly should a remedy be constrained to address a history of past discrimination by a local government? According to the dissenters? How much discretion should a local government have to make its own policies related to affirmative action?

RELATED CASES

***Teamsters v. United States*: 431 U.S. 324 (1977).**

The Court ruled that because a company had participated in practices of segregation and discrimination after the passage of the Civil Rights Act of 1964, a federal court could order the company to award retroactive seniority under specific circumstances without violating Title VII of the Civil Rights Act.

***United Steelworks of America v. Weber*: 443 U.S. 193 (1979).**

The Supreme Court upheld an affirmative action-guided training program designed to increase the representation of blacks in a company's pool of skilled craft workers. The private sector can take independent steps to eliminate evidence and patterns of racial segregation.

***Bazemore v. Friday*: 478 U.S. 385 (1986).**

A government program that was segregated and racially discriminatory prior to the passage of the Civil Rights Act of 1964 and maintains the same pay scales and policies has continued to discriminate and is liable for the resulting discrepancies.

METRO BROADCASTING, INC. V. FEDERAL COMMUNICATIONS COMMISSION

497 U.S. 547, 110 S.Ct. 2997, 111 L.Ed.2d 445 (1990)

This case combines two similar appeals. Petitioner Metro Broadcasting is challenging the Federal Communications Commission's (FCC) policy of awarding preferences to minority owners during comparative licensing proceedings. The FCC review board denied Metro's proposal to construct and operate a new UHF television station in Orlando, Florida, in favor of Rainbow Broadcasting, with 90 percent Hispanic ownership. After substantial delay, the Court of Appeals for the District of Columbia upheld the FCC board's decision. The second appeal emerges from an attempt to make a minority distress sale by Faith Center, Inc., which held a television station license in Hartford, Connecticut. Several attempts to sell the license failed, and Faith Center, still obliged to sell to a minority-controlled enterprise, then offered the station to Astroline Communication Company Limited Partnership. Shurberg Broadcasting of Hartford, Inc., which had been denied permission to build a television station in Hartford pending minority sale by Faith Center, challenged the FCC distress sale policy as a violation of Shurberg's equal protection rights. The Court of Appeals for the District of Columbia invalidated the FCC's minority distress sale policy.

Vote: 5–4

JUSTICE BRENNAN delivered the opinion of the Court.

The issue in these cases, consolidated for decision today, is whether certain minority preference policies of the Federal Communications Commission violate the equal protection component of the Fifth Amendment. The policies in question are (1) a program awarding an enhancement for minority ownership in comparative proceedings for new licenses, and (2) the minority "distress sale" program, which permits a limited category of existing radio and television broadcast stations to be transferred only to minority-controlled firms. We hold that these policies do not violate equal protection principles.

I

A

The policies before us today can best be understood by reference to the history of federal efforts to promote minority participation in the broadcasting industry. In the Communications Act of 1934, 48 Stat. 1064, as amended, Congress assigned to the Federal Communications Commission (FCC or Commission) exclusive authority to grant licenses, based on "public convenience, interest, or necessity," to persons wishing to construct and operate radio and television broadcast stations in the United States. Although for the past two decades minorities have constituted at least one-fifth of the United States population, during this time relatively few members of minority groups have held broadcast licenses. In 1971, minorities owned only 10 of the approximately 7,500 radio stations in the country and none of the more than 1,000 television stations; in 1978, minorities owned less than 1 percent of the Nation's radio and television stations; and in 1986, they owned just 2.1 percent of the more than 11,000 radio and television stations in the United States. Moreover, these statistics fail to reflect the fact that, as late entrants who often have been able to obtain only the less valuable stations, many minority broadcasters serve geographically limited markets with relatively small audiences.

The Commission has therefore worked to encourage minority participation in the broadcast industry. The FCC began by formulating rules to prohibit licensees from discriminating against minorities in employment. The FCC explained that "broadcasting is an important mass media form which, because it makes use of the airwaves belonging to the public, must obtain a Federal license under a public interest standard and must operate in the public interest in order to obtain periodic renewals of that license." Regulations dealing with employment practices were justified as necessary to enable the FCC to satisfy its obligation under the Communications Act of 1934 to promote diversity of programming.

Describing its actions as only "first steps," the FCC outlined two elements of a minority ownership policy.

First, the Commission pledged to consider minority ownership as one factor in comparative proceedings for new licenses.

Second, the FCC outlined a plan to increase minority opportunities to receive reassigned and transferred licenses through the so-called "distress sale" policy. These two Commission minority ownership policies are at issue today.

II

It is of overriding significance in these cases that the FCC's minority ownership programs have been specifically approved—indeed, mandated—by Congress.

We hold that the FCC minority ownership policies pass muster under the test we announce today. First, we find that they serve the important governmental objective of broadcast diversity. Second, we conclude that they are substantially related to the achievement of that objective.

A

Congress found that "the effects of past inequities stemming from racial and ethnic discrimination have resulted in a severe underrepresentation of minorities in the media of mass communications." H. R. Conf. Rep. No. 97–765, p. 43 (1982). Congress and the Commission do not justify the minority ownership policies strictly as remedies for victims of this discrimination, however. Rather, Congress and the FCC have selected the minority ownership policies primarily to promote programming diversity, and they urge that such diversity is an important governmental objective that can serve as a constitutional basis for the preference policies. We agree.

Against this background, we conclude that the interest in enhancing broadcast diversity is, at the very least, an important governmental objective and is therefore a sufficient basis for the Commission's minority ownership policies. Just as a "diverse student body" contributing to a " 'robust exchange of ideas' " is a "constitutionally-permissible goal" on which a race-conscious university admissions program may be predicated, *Regents of University of California v. Bakke*, 438 U.S. 265, 311–313 (1978), the diversity of views and information on the airwaves serves important First Amendment values.

B

We also find that the minority ownership policies are substantially related to the achievement of the Government's interest. One component of this inquiry concerns the relationship between expanded minority ownership and greater broadcast diversity; both the FCC and Congress have determined that such a relationship exists. Although we do not " 'defer' to the judgment of the Congress and the Commission on a constitutional question," and would not "hesitate to invoke the Constitution should we determine that the Commission has not fulfilled its task with appropriate sensitivity" to equal protection principles, *Columbia Broadcasting System, Inc. v. Democratic National Committee*, 412 U.S. 94, at 103 (1973), we must pay close attention to the expertise of the Commission and the factfinding of Congress when analyzing the nexus between minority ownership and programming diversity. With respect to this "complex" empirical question, we are required to give "great weight to the decisions of Congress and the experience of the Commission."

III

The Commission's minority ownership policies bear the imprimatur of longstanding congressional support and direction and are substantially related to the achievement of the important governmental objective of broadcast diversity. The judgment [with respect to Metro Broadcasting, Inc.] is affirmed, the judgment [with respect to Faith Center, Inc.] is reversed, and the cases are remanded for proceedings consistent with this opinion.

JUSTICE STEVENS, concurring.

Today the Court squarely rejects the proposition that a governmental decision that rests on a racial classification is never permissible except as a remedy for a past wrong. I endorse this focus on the future benefit, rather than the remedial justification, of such decisions.

I remain convinced, of course, that racial or ethnic characteristics provide a relevant basis for disparate treatment only in extremely rare situations and that it is therefore "especially important that the reasons for any such classification be clearly identified and unquestionably legitimate." *Fullilove v. Klutznick*, 448 U.S. 448, 534–535 (1980) (dissenting opinion). The Court's opinion explains how both elements of that standard are satisfied. Specifically, the reason for the classification—the recognized interest in broadcast diversity—is clearly identified and does not imply any judgment concerning the abilities of owners of different races or the merits of different kinds of programming. Neither the favored nor the disfavored class is stigmatized in any way. In addition, the Court demonstrates that these cases fall within the extremely narrow category of governmental decisions for which racial or ethnic heritage may provide a rational basis for differential treatment. The public interest in broadcast diversity—like the interest in an integrated police force, diversity in the composition of a public school faculty, or diversity in the student body of a professional school—is in my view unquestionably legitimate.

JUSTICE O'CONNOR, with whom CHIEF JUSTICE REHNQUIST, and JUSTICES SCALIA and KENNEDY join, dissenting.

At the heart of the Constitution's guarantee of equal protection lies the simple command that the Government must treat citizens "as individuals, not 'as simply components of a racial, religious, sexual or national class.' " *Arizona Governing Comm. for Tax Deferred Annuity and Deferred Compensation Plans v. Norris*, 463 U.S. 1073, 1083 (1983). Social scientists may debate how peoples' thoughts and behavior reflect their background, but the Constitution provides that the Government may not allocate benefits and burdens among individuals based on the assumption that race or ethnicity determines how they act or think. To uphold the challenged programs, the Court departs from these fundamental principles and from our traditional requirement that racial classifications are permissible only if necessary and narrowly tailored to achieve a compelling interest. This departure marks a renewed toleration of racial classifications and a repudiation of our recent affirmation that the Constitution's equal protection guarantees extend equally to all citizens. The Court's application of a lessened equal protection standard to congressional actions finds no support in our cases or in the Constitution. I respectfully dissent.

I

As we recognized last Term, the Constitution requires that the Court apply a strict standard of scrutiny to evaluate racial classifications such as those contained in the challenged FCC distress sale and comparative licensing policies. "Strict scrutiny" requires that, to be upheld, racial classifications must be determined to be necessary and narrowly tailored to achieve a compelling state interest. The Court abandons this traditional safeguard against discrimination for a lower standard of review, and in practice applies a standard like that applicable to routine legislation. Yet the Government's different treatment of citizens according to race is no routine concern. This Court's precedents in no way justify the Court's marked departure from our traditional treatment of race classifications and its conclusion that different equal protection principles apply to these federal actions.

IV

Our traditional equal protection doctrine requires, in addition to a compelling state interest, that the Government's chosen means be necessary to accomplish, and narrowly tailored to further, the asserted interest. The chosen means, resting as they do on stereotyping and so indirectly furthering the asserted end, could not plausibly be deemed narrowly tailored. The Court instead finds the racial classifications to be "substantially related" to achieving the Government's interest, a far less rigorous fit requirement. The FCC's policies fail even this requirement.

D

In sum, the FCC has not met its burden even under the Court's test that approves of racial classifications that are substantially related to an important governmental objective. Of course, the programs even more clearly fail the strict scrutiny that should be applied. The Court has determined, in essence, that Congress and all federal agencies are exempted, to some ill-defined but significant degree, from the Constitution's equal protection requirements. This break with our precedents greatly undermines equal protection guarantees and permits distinctions among citizens based on race and ethnicity which the Constitution clearly forbids. I respectfully dissent.

JUSTICE KENNEDY, with whom JUSTICE SCALIA joins, dissenting.

Almost 100 years ago in *Plessy v. Ferguson*, 163 U.S. 537 (1896), this Court upheld a government-sponsored race-conscious measure, a Louisiana law that required "equal but separate accommodations" for "white" and "colored" railroad passengers. The *Plessy* Court concluded that the "race-conscious measures" it reviewed were reasonable because they served the governmental interest of increasing the riding pleasure of railroad passengers. The fundamental errors in *Plessy*, its standard of review and its validation of rank racial insult by the State, distorted the law for six decades before the Court announced its apparent demise in *Brown v. Board of Education*, 347 U.S. 483 (1954). *Plessy's* standard of review and its explication have disturbing parallels to today's majority opinion that should warn us something is amiss here.

I cannot agree with the Court that the Constitution permits the Government to discriminate among its citizens on the basis of race in order to serve interests so trivial as "broadcast diversity." In abandoning strict scrutiny to endorse this interest the Court turns back the clock on the level of scrutiny applicable to federal race-conscious measures.

The Court insists that the programs under review are "benign." A fundamental error of the *Plessy* Court was its similar confidence in its ability to identify "benign" discrimination: "We consider the underlying fallacy of the plaintiff's argument to consist in the assumption that the enforced separation of the two races stamps the colored race with a badge of inferiority. If this be so, it is not by reason of anything found in the act, but solely because the colored race chooses to put that construction upon it." Although the majority is "confident" that it can determine when racial discrimination is benign, it offers no explanation as to how it will do so.

The history of governmental reliance on race demonstrates that racial policies defended as benign often are not seen that way by the individuals affected by them. Although the majority disclaims it, the FCC policy seems based on the demeaning notion that members of the defined racial groups ascribe to certain "minority views" that must be different from those of other citizens. Special preferences also can foster the view that members of the favored groups are inherently less able to compete on their own. And, rightly or wrongly, special preference programs often are perceived as targets for exploitation by opportunists who seek to take advantage of monetary rewards without advancing the stated policy of minority inclusion.

Perhaps the Court can succeed in its assumed role of case-by-case arbiter of when it is desirable and benign for the Government to disfavor some citizens and favor others based on the color of their skin. Perhaps the tolerance and decency to which our people aspire will let the disfavored rise above hostility and the favored escape condescension. But history suggests much peril in this enterprise, and so the Constitution forbids us to undertake it. I regret that after a century of judicial opinions we interpret the Constitution to do no more than move us from "separate but equal" to "unequal but benign."

FOR DISCUSSION

What are the implications of not adopting a strict scrutiny standard when evaluating governmental race-conscious measures? What has changed since the *Croson* decision?

RELATED CASES

***Red Lion Broadcasting, Co. v. FCC:* 395 U.S. 367 (1969).**

The Supreme Court upheld the Federal Communication Commission's fairness doctrine, which required broadcasters to present public issues in a balanced fashion and limited both personal attacks in debate and editorializing on political issues. The Court found the policy did not violate the First Amendment's guarantee of freedom of speech.

***Columbia Broadcasting System, Inc. v. Democratic National Committee:* 412 U.S. 94 (1973).**

Broadcasting networks do not have to sell broadcast time to political groups for presentation of controversial perspectives.

ADARAND CONSTRUCTORS V. PENA

515 U.S. 200, 115 S.Ct. 2097, 132 L.Ed. 2d 158 (1995)

According to the federal government, all federally funded contracts will reward the key contractor if they subcontract with small businesses that are minority controlled. The law defined this classification as including

Black Americans, Hispanic Americans, Native Americans, Asian Pacific Americans, and other racial minorities. Adarand Constructors submitted the lowest bid as a subcontractor, but was not certified as a minority business; another subcontractor, Gonzales Construction Company, was so certified and was awarded the work. The key contractor would have accepted Adarand Construction's bid, except that he would receive an additional payment for hiring Gonzales Construction.

Vote: 5–4

JUSTICE O'CONNOR announced the judgment of the Court and delivered an opinion with respect to Parts I, II, III–A, III–B, III–D, and IV, which is for the Court except insofar as it might be inconsistent with the views expressed in JUSTICE SCALIA'S concurrence, and an opinion with respect to Part III–C in which JUSTICE KENNEDY joins.

Petitioner Adarand Constructors, Inc., claims that the Federal Government's practice of giving general contractors on Government projects a financial incentive to hire subcontractors controlled by "socially and economically disadvantaged individuals," and in particular, the Government's use of race-based presumptions in identifying such individuals, violates the equal protection component of the Fifth Amendment's Due Process Clause. The Court of Appeals rejected Adarand's claim. We conclude, however, that courts should analyze cases of this kind under a different standard of review than the one the Court of Appeals applied. We therefore vacate the Court of Appeals' judgment and remand the case for further proceedings.

III

Adarand's claim arises under the Fifth Amendment to the Constitution, which provides that "No person shall . . . be deprived of life, liberty, or property, without due process of law." Although this Court has always understood that Clause to provide some measure of protection against arbitrary treatment by the Federal Government, it is not as explicit a guarantee of equal treatment as the Fourteenth Amendment, which provides that "No State shall . . . deny to any person within its jurisdiction the equal protection of the laws." Our cases have accorded varying degrees of significance to the difference in the language of those two Clauses. We think it necessary to revisit the issue here.

A

In *Bolling v. Sharpe*, 347 U.S. 497 (1954), the Court for the first time explicitly questioned the existence of any difference between the obligations of the Federal Government and the States to avoid racial classifications. *Bolling* did note that "the 'equal protection of the laws' is a more explicit safeguard of prohibited unfairness than 'due process of law.' " But *Bolling* then concluded that, "in view of [the] decision that the Constitution prohibits the states from maintaining racially segregated public schools, it would be unthinkable that the same Constitution would impose a lesser duty on the Federal Government."

Later cases in contexts other than school desegregation did not distinguish between the duties of the States and the Federal Government to avoid racial classifications.

The various opinions in *Frontiero v. Richardson*, 411 U.S. 677 (1973), which concerned sex discrimination by the Federal Government, took their equal protection standard of review from *Reed v. Reed*, 404 U.S. 71 (1971), a case that invalidated sex discrimination by a State, without mentioning any possibility of a difference between the standards applicable to state and federal action. Thus, in 1975, the Court stated explicitly that "this Court's approach to Fifth Amendment equal protection claims has always been precisely the same as to equal protection claims under the Fourteenth Amendment." *Weinberger v. Wiesenfeld*, 420 U.S. 636, 638, n. 2 (1975).

B

Most of the cases discussed above involved classifications burdening groups that have suffered discrimination in our society. In 1978, the Court confronted the question whether race-based governmental action designed to benefit such groups should also be subject to "the most rigid scrutiny." *Regents of Univ. of Cal. v. Bakke*, 438 U.S. 265 [(1978)], involved an equal protection challenge to a state-run medical school's practice of reserving a number of spaces in its entering class for minority students. *Bakke* did not produce an opinion for the Court, but Justice Powell's opinion announcing the Court's judgment rejected the argument. In a passage joined by Justice White, Justice Powell wrote that "the guarantee of equal protection cannot mean one thing when applied to one individual and something else when applied to a person of another color." He concluded that "racial and ethnic distinctions of any sort are inherently suspect and thus call for the most exacting judicial examination." On the other hand, four Justices in *Bakke* would have applied a less stringent standard of review to racial classifications "designed to further remedial purposes." And four Justices thought the case should be decided on statutory grounds.

Two years after *Bakke*, the Court faced another challenge to remedial race-based action, this time involving action undertaken by the Federal Government. In *Fullilove v. Klutznick*, 448 U.S. 448 (1980), the Court upheld Congress' inclusion of a 10% set-aside for minority-owned businesses in the Public Works Employment Act of 1977. Chief Justice Burger, in an opinion joined by Justices White and Powell, observed that "[a]ny preference based on racial or ethnic criteria must necessarily receive a most searching examination to make sure that it does not conflict with constitutional guarantees." 448 U.S. at 491. As in *Bakke*, there was no opinion for the Court. That opinion, however, "did not adopt, either expressly or implicitly, the formulas of analysis articulated in such cases as [*Bakke*]." It employed instead a two-part test which asked, first, "whether the objectives of the legislation are within the power of Congress," and second, "whether the limited use of racial and ethnic criteria, in the context presented, is a constitutionally permissible means for achieving the congressional objectives." It then upheld the program under that test, adding at the end of the opinion that the program also "would survive judicial review under either 'test' articulated in the several *Bakke* opinions." Justice Marshall (joined by Justices Brennan and Blackmun) concurred in the judgment, reiterating the view of four Justices in *Bakke* that any race-based governmental action designed to "remedy the present effects of past racial discrimination" should be upheld if it was "substantially related" to the achievement of an "important governmental objective"—i.e., such action should be subjected only to what we now call "intermediate scrutiny."

In *Wygant v. Jackson Bd. of Ed.*, 476 U.S. 267 (1986), the Court considered a Fourteenth Amendment challenge to another form of remedial racial classification. The issue in *Wygant* was whether a school board could adopt race-based preferences in determining which teachers to lay off. Justice Powell's plurality opinion observed that "the level of scrutiny does not change merely because the challenged classification operates against a group that historically has not been subject to governmental discrimination," and stated the two-part inquiry as "whether the layoff provision is supported by a compelling state purpose and whether the means chosen to accomplish that purpose are narrowly tailored." In other words, "racial classifications of any sort must be subjected to 'strict scrutiny.' " Four Justices dissented, three of whom again argued for intermediate scrutiny of remedial race-based government action.

The Court's failure to produce a majority opinion in *Bakke*, *Fullilove*, and *Wygant* left unresolved the proper analysis for remedial race-based governmental action. Lower courts found this lack of guidance unsettling.

The Court resolved the issue, at least in part, in 1989. *Richmond v. J. A. Croson Co.,* 488 U.S. 469 (1989), concerned a city's determination that 30% of its contracting work should go to minority-owned businesses. A majority of the Court in Croson held that "the standard of review under the Equal Protection Clause is not dependent on the race of those burdened or benefited by a particular classification," and that the single standard of review for racial classifications should be "strict scrutiny."

With *Croson*, the Court finally agreed that the Fourteenth Amendment requires strict scrutiny of all race-based action by state and local governments. But *Croson* of course had no occasion to declare what standard of review the Fifth Amendment requires for such action taken by the Federal Government. *Croson* observed simply that the Court's "treatment of an exercise of congressional power in *Fullilove* cannot be dispositive here," because *Croson's* facts did not implicate Congress' broad power under § 5 of the Fourteenth Amendment.

A year later, however, the Court took a surprising turn. *Metro Broadcasting, Inc. v. FCC*, 497 U.S. 547 (1990), involved a Fifth Amendment challenge to two race-based policies of the Federal Communications Commission (FCC). In *Metro Broadcasting*, the Court repudiated the long-held notion that "it would be unthinkable that the same Constitution would impose a lesser duty on the Federal Government" than it does on a State to afford equal protection of the laws, *Bolling* at 500. It did so by holding that "benign" federal racial classifications need only satisfy intermediate scrutiny, even though *Croson* had recently concluded that such classifications enacted by a State must satisfy strict scrutiny. "Benign" federal racial classifications, the Court said,"—even if those measures are not 'remedial' in the sense of being designed to compensate victims of past governmental or societal discrimination—are constitutionally permissible to the extent that they serve important governmental objectives within the power of Congress and are substantially related to achievement of those objectives." *Metro Broadcasting*, 497 U.S. at 564–565. The Court did not explain how to tell whether a racial classification should be deemed "benign," other than to express "confidence that an 'examination of the legislative scheme and its history' will separate benign measures from other types of racial classifications."

By adopting intermediate scrutiny as the standard of review for congressionally mandated "benign" racial classifications, *Metro Broadcasting* departed from prior cases in two significant respects. First, it turned its back on *Croson's* explanation of why strict scrutiny of all governmental racial classifications is essential[.]

Second, *Metro Broadcasting* squarely rejected one of the three propositions established by the Court's earlier equal protection cases, namely, congruence between the standards applicable to federal and state racial classifications, and in so doing also undermined the other two—skepticism of all racial classifications and consistency of treatment irrespective of the race of the burdened or benefited group.

The three propositions undermined by *Metro Broadcasting* all derive from the basic principle that the Fifth and Fourteenth Amendments to the Constitution protect persons, not groups. These ideas have long been central to this Court's understanding of equal protection, and holding "benign" state and federal racial classifications to different standards does not square with them. Accordingly, we hold today that all racial classifications, imposed by whatever federal, state, or local governmental actor, must be analyzed by a reviewing court under strict scrutiny. In other words, such classifications are constitutional only if they are narrowly tailored measures that further compelling governmental interests. To the extent that *Metro Broadcasting* is inconsistent with that holding, it is overruled.

C

"Although adherence to precedent is not rigidly required in constitutional cases, any departure from the doctrine of stare decisis demands special justification." *Arizona v. Rumsey*, 467 U.S. 203, 212 (1984). In deciding whether this case presents such justification, we recall Justice Frankfurter's admonition that "stare decisis is a principle of policy and not a mechanical formula of adherence to the latest decision, however recent and questionable, when such adherence involves collision with a prior doctrine more embracing in its scope, intrinsically sounder, and verified by experience." *Helvering v. Hallock,* 309 U.S. 106 (1940). Remaining true to an "intrinsically sounder" doctrine established in prior cases better serves the values of stare decisis than would following a more recently decided case inconsistent with the decisions that came before it; the latter course would simply compound the recent error and would likely make the unjustified break from previously established doctrine complete. In such a situation, "special justification" exists to depart from the recently decided case.

As we have explained, *Metro Broadcasting* undermined important principles of this Court's equal protection jurisprudence, established in a line of cases stretching back over 50 years. Those principles together stood for an "embracing" and "intrinsically sound" understanding of equal protection "verified by experience," namely, that the Constitution imposes upon federal, state, and local governmental actors the same obligation to respect the personal right to equal protection of the laws. We cannot adhere to our most recent decision without colliding with an accepted and established doctrine. We also note that *Metro Broadcasting's* application of different standards of review to federal and state racial classifications has been consistently criticized by commentators.

By refusing to follow *Metro Broadcasting*, then, we do not depart from the fabric of the law; we restore it. We also note that reliance on a case that has recently departed from precedent is likely to be minimal, particularly where, as here, the rule set forth in that case is unlikely to affect primary conduct in any event.

Justice Stevens takes us to task for what he perceives to be an erroneous application of the doctrine of stare decisis. But as we have described, we think that well-settled legal principles pointed toward a conclusion different from that reached in *Metro Broadcasting*, and we therefore disagree with Justice Stevens that "the law at the time of that decision was entirely open to the result the Court reached." We also disagree with Justice Stevens that Justice Stewart's dissenting opinion in *Fullilove* supports his "novelty" argument. There is nothing new about the notion that Congress, like the States, may treat people differently because of their race only for compelling reasons.

Metro Broadcasting's untenable distinction between state and federal racial classifications lacks support in our precedent, and undermines the fundamental principle of equal protection as a personal right. In this case, as between that principle and "its later misapplications," the principle must prevail.

D

Federal racial classifications, like those of a State, must serve a compelling governmental interest, and must be narrowly tailored to further that interest. Of course, it follows that to the extent (if any) that *Fullilove* held federal racial classifications to be subject to a less rigorous standard, it is no longer controlling.

We think that requiring strict scrutiny is the best way to ensure that courts will consistently give racial classifications that kind of detailed examination, both as to ends and as to means.

Finally, we wish to dispel the notion that strict scrutiny is "strict in theory, but fatal in fact." The unhappy persistence of both the practice and the lingering effects of racial discrimination against minority groups in this country is an unfortunate reality, and government is not disqualified from acting in response to it. When race-based action is necessary to further a compelling interest, such action is within constitutional constraints if it satisfies the "narrow tailoring" test this Court has set out in previous cases.

JUSTICE SCALIA, concurring in part and concurring in the judgment.

I join the opinion of the Court . . . and except insofar as it may be inconsistent with the following: In my view, government can never have a "compelling interest" in discriminating on the basis of race in order to "make up" for past racial discrimination in the opposite direction. Individuals who have been wronged by unlawful racial discrimination should be made whole; but under our Constitution there can be no such thing as either a creditor or a debtor race. That concept is alien to the Constitution's focus upon the individual, and its rejection of dispositions based on race, or based on blood. To pursue the concept of racial entitlement—even for the most admirable and benign of purposes—is to reinforce and preserve for future mischief the way of thinking that produced race slavery, race privilege and race hatred. In the eyes of government, we are just one race here. It is American.

It is unlikely, if not impossible, that the challenged program would survive under this understanding of strict scrutiny, but I am content to leave that to be decided on remand.

JUSTICE THOMAS, concurring in part and concurring in the judgment.

I agree with the majority's conclusion that strict scrutiny applies to all government classifications based on race. I write separately, however, to express my disagreement with the premise underlying Justice Stevens' and Justice Ginsburg's dissents: that there is a racial paternalism exception to the principle of equal protection. I believe that there is a "moral [and] constitutional equivalence," between laws designed to subjugate a race and those that distribute benefits on the basis of race in order to foster some current notion of equality. Government cannot make us equal; it can only recognize, respect, and protect us as equal before the law.

That these programs may have been motivated, in part, by good intentions cannot provide refuge from the principle that under our Constitution, the government may not make distinctions on the basis of race. As far as the Constitution is concerned, it is irrelevant whether a government's racial classifications are drawn by those who wish to oppress a race or by those who have a sincere desire to help those thought to be disadvantaged. There can be no doubt that the paternalism that appears to lie at the heart of this program is at war with the principle of inherent equality that underlies and infuses our Constitution.

These programs not only raise grave constitutional questions, they also undermine the moral basis of the equal protection principle. Purchased at the price of immeasurable human suffering, the equal protection principle reflects our Nation's understanding that such classifications ultimately have a destructive impact on the individual and our society. But there can be no doubt that racial paternalism and its unintended consequences can be as poisonous and pernicious as any other form of discrimination. So-called "benign" discrimination teaches many that because of chronic and apparently immutable handicaps, minorities cannot compete with them without their patronizing indulgence. Inevitably, such programs engender attitudes of superiority or, alternatively, provoke resentment among those who believe that they have been wronged by the government's use of race. These programs stamp minorities with a badge of inferiority and may cause them to develop dependencies or to adopt an attitude that they are "entitled" to preferences.

In my mind, government-sponsored racial discrimination based on benign prejudice is just as noxious as discrimination inspired by malicious prejudice. In each instance, it is racial discrimination, plain and simple.

JUSTICE STEVENS, with whom Justice Ginsburg joins, dissenting.

Instead of deciding this case in accordance with controlling precedent, the Court today delivers a disconcerting lecture about the evils of governmental racial classifications.

IV

This is the third time in the Court's entire history that it has considered the constitutionality of a federal affirmative-action program. On each of the two prior occasions, the first in 1980, *Fullilove v. Klutznick*, 448 U.S. 448, and the second in 1990, *Metro Broadcasting, Inc. v. FCC*, 497 U.S. 547, the Court upheld the program. Today the Court explicitly overrules *Metro Broadcasting* (at least in part), and undermines *Fullilove* by recasting the standard on which it rested and by calling even its holding into question. By way of explanation, Justice O'Connor advises the federal agencies and private parties that have made countless decisions in reliance on those cases that "we do not depart from the fabric of the law; we restore it."

In the Court's view, our decision in *Metro Broadcasting* was inconsistent with the rule announced in *Richmond v. J. A. Croson Co.*, 488 U.S. 469 (1989). But two decisive distinctions separate those two cases. First, *Metro Broadcasting* involved a federal program, whereas *Croson* involved a city ordinance. *Metro Broadcasting* thus drew primary support from *Fullilove*, which predated *Croson* and which *Croson* distinguished on the grounds of the federal-state dichotomy that the majority today discredits. Although Members of today's majority trumpeted the importance of that distinction in *Croson*, they now reject it in the name of "congruence." It is therefore quite wrong for the Court to suggest today that overruling *Metro Broadcasting* merely restores the status quo ante, for the law at the time of that decision was entirely open to the result the Court reached. Today's decision is an unjustified departure from settled law.

Second, *Metro Broadcasting's* holding rested on more than its application of "intermediate scrutiny." Indeed, I have always believed that, labels notwithstanding, the Federal Communications Commission (FCC) program we upheld in that case would have satisfied any of our various standards in affirmative-action cases—including the one the majority fashions today. What truly distinguishes *Metro Broadcasting* from our other affirmative-action precedents is the distinctive goal of the federal program in that case. Instead of merely seeking to remedy past discrimination, the FCC program was intended to achieve future benefits in the form of broadcast diversity.

Thus, prior to *Metro Broadcasting*, the interest in diversity had been mentioned in a few opinions, but it is perfectly clear that the Court had not yet decided whether that interest had sufficient magnitude to justify a racial classification. *Metro Broadcasting*, of course, answered that question in the affirmative. The majority today overrules *Metro Broadcasting* only insofar as it is "inconsistent with [the] holding" that strict scrutiny applies to "benign" racial classifications promulgated by the Federal Government. The proposition that fostering diversity may provide a sufficient interest to justify such a program is not inconsistent with the Court's holding today—indeed, the question is not remotely presented in this case—and I do not take the Court's opinion to diminish that aspect of our decision in *Metro Broadcasting*.

The Court's suggestion that it may be necessary in the future to overrule *Fullilove* in order to restore the fabric of the law, is even more disingenuous than its treatment of *Metro Broadcasting*. For the Court endorses the "strict scrutiny" standard that Justice Powell applied in *Bakke*, and acknowledges that he applied that standard in *Fullilove* as well. Moreover, Chief Justice Burger also expressly concluded that the program we considered in *Fullilove* was valid under any of the tests articulated in *Bakke*, which of course included Justice Powell's. The Court thus adopts a standard applied in *Fullilove* at the same time it questions that case's continued vitality and accuses it of departing from prior law. As was true of *Metro Broadcasting*, the Court in *Fullilove* decided an important, novel, and difficult question. Providing a different answer to a similar question today cannot fairly be characterized as merely "restoring" previously settled law.

JUSTICE SOUTER, joined by JUSTICES GINSBURG and BREYER, wrote a separate dissenting opinion.

JUSTICE GINSBURG, with whom JUSTICE BREYER joins, dissenting.

. . . [I]n view of the attention the political branches are currently giving the matter of affirmative action, I see no compelling cause for the intervention the Court has made in this case. I further agree with Justice Stevens that, in this area, large deference is owed by the Judiciary to "Congress' institutional competence and constitutional authority to overcome historic racial subjugation." I write separately to underscore not the differences the several opinions in this case display, but the considerable field of agreement—the common understandings and concerns—revealed in opinions that together speak for a majority of the Court.

I

The statutes and regulations at issue, as the Court indicates, were adopted by the political branches in response to an "unfortunate reality": "the unhappy persistence of both the practice and the lingering effects of racial discrimination against minority groups in this country." The United States suffers from those lingering effects because, for most of our Nation's history, the idea that "we are just one race," was not embraced. For generations, our lawmakers and judges were unprepared to say that there is in this land no superior race, no race inferior to any other.

The divisions in this difficult case should not obscure the Court's recognition of the persistence of racial inequality and a majority's acknowledgment of Congress' authority to act affirmatively, not only to end discrimination, but also to counteract discrimination's lingering effects. Those effects, reflective of a system of racial caste only recently ended, are evident in our workplaces, markets, and neighborhoods. Job applicants with identical resumes, qualifications, and interview styles still experience different receptions, depending on their race. White and African-American consumers still encounter different deals. People of color looking for housing still face discriminatory treatment by landlords, real estate agents, and mortgage lenders. Minority entrepreneurs sometimes fail to gain contracts though they are the low bidders, and they are sometimes refused work even after winning contracts. Bias both conscious and unconscious, reflecting traditional and unexamined habits of thought, keeps up barriers that must come down if equal opportunity and nondiscrimination are ever genuinely to become this country's law and practice.

Given this history and its practical consequences, Congress surely can conclude that a carefully designed affirmative action program may help to realize, finally, the "equal protection of the laws" the Fourteenth Amendment has promised since 1868.

II

The lead opinion uses one term, "strict scrutiny," to describe the standard of judicial review for all governmental classifications by race. But that opinion's elaboration strongly suggests that the strict standard announced is indeed "fatal" for classifications burdening groups that have suffered discrimination in our society. That seems to me, and, I believe, to the Court, the enduring lesson one should draw from *Korematsu v. United States*, 323 U.S. 214 (1944); for in that case, scrutiny the Court described as "most rigid," nonetheless yielded a pass for an odious, gravely injurious racial classification. A *Korematsu*-type classification, as I read the opinions in this case, will never again survive scrutiny: Such a classification, history and precedent instruct, properly ranks as prohibited.

For a classification made to hasten the day when "we are just one race," however, the lead opinion has dispelled the notion that "strict scrutiny" is " 'fatal in fact.' " Properly, a majority of the Court calls for review that is searching, in order to ferret out classifications in reality malign, but masquerading as benign. The Court's once lax review of sex-based classifications demonstrates the need for such suspicion. Today's decision thus usefully reiterates that the purpose of strict scrutiny "is precisely to distinguish legitimate from illegitimate uses of race in governmental decisionmaking," "to 'differentiate between' permissible and impermissible governmental use of race," to distinguish " 'between a "No Trespassing" sign and a welcome mat.' "

Close review also is in order for this further reason. As Justice Souter points out, and as this very case shows, some members of the historically favored race can be hurt by catchup mechanisms designed to cope with the lingering effects of entrenched racial subjugation. Court review can ensure that preferences are not so large as to trammel unduly upon the opportunities of others or interfere too harshly with legitimate expectations of persons in once-preferred groups.

While I would not disturb the programs challenged in this case, and would leave their improvement to the political branches, I see today's decision as one that allows our precedent to evolve, still to be informed by and responsive to changing conditions.

FOR DISCUSSION

What has changed since *Metro Broadcasting* to lead the Court to render this decision? Why might people say that strict scrutiny is "strict in theory, fatal in fact"? Should affirmative action laws and other forms of race-conscious legislation be treated differently under the Equal Protection Clause? Why or why not?

RELATED CASES

***Piscataway Board of Education v. Taxman:* 91 F.3d 1547 (1998).**

This case is most significant because the Supreme Court never heard it. *Taxman* was an affirmative action case generated when a school board needed to eliminate a teacher's position and the most recently hired teachers had been hired on the same day; one teacher, who was black, was retained, and the other teacher, who was white, sued, citing affirmative action concerns. The Supreme Court accepted the case, but civil rights groups concerned about the potential for a contrary ruling by the Court, provided the money to settle the litigation prior to oral arguments.

***Ricci v. DeStefano:* 557 U.S. 557 (2009).**

Results of a city's test for firefighters hoping to be promoted to management positions had excluded most African American and Hispanic candidates. The Supreme Court narrowly ruled that the test could not be discarded on the grounds of disparate impact. Rather, to avoid violating Title VII of the Civil Rights Act of 1964 by throwing out a test, the city must have strong evidence that the use of the test would subject the city to disparate impact liability in the federal courts.

GRUTTER V. BOLLINGER

539 U.S. 306, 123 S.Ct. 2325, 156 L.Ed.2d 304 (2003)

As part of the admissions process, the University of Michigan Law School winnows over 3,500 applications to an entering class of approximately 350 students every year. The law school wants students with legal promise who not only are academically competitive but also represent a mix of backgrounds and experiences. The school's written policy makes it clear that while results of the Law School Admission Test (LSAT) and undergraduate grade point average (GPA) matter, they are not a guarantee of either admission or disqualification. While recognizing various forms of diversity, the school formally reaffirms a commitment to the inclusion of students who have been historically discriminated against and who "without this commitment might not be represented in our student body in meaningful numbers." The petitioner Barbara Grutter, a white Michigan resident with a 3.8 GPA and 161 LSAT score, was ultimately rejected by the University of Michigan for admission to law school. She alleged that the university had discriminated against her on the basis of race and in violation of the Fourteenth Amendment. After a bench trial, the district court found that the law school's use of race in admissions decisions was unlawful. The Sixth Circuit Court of Appeals reversed the decision of the district court.

Vote: 5–4

JUSTICE O'CONNOR delivered the opinion of the Court.

We granted certiorari, to resolve the disagreement among the Courts of Appeals on a question of national importance: Whether diversity is a compelling interest that can justify the narrowly tailored use of race in selecting applicants for admission to public universities.

II

A

We last addressed the use of race in public higher education over 25 years ago. In the landmark [*Regents of the University of California v.*] *Bakke* case, we reviewed a racial set-aside program that reserved 16 out of 100 seats in a medical school class for members of certain minority groups. 438 U.S. 265 (1978). The decision produced six separate opinions, none of which commanded a majority of the Court. Four Justices would have upheld the program against all attack on the ground that the government can use race to "remedy disadvantages cast on minorities by past racial prejudice." Four other Justices avoided the constitutional question altogether and struck down the program on statutory grounds. Justice Powell provided a fifth vote not only for invalidating the set-aside program, but also for reversing the state court's injunction against any use of race whatsoever. The only holding for the Court in *Bakke* was that a "State has a substantial interest that legitimately may be served by a properly devised admissions program involving the competitive consideration of race and ethnic origin." Thus, we reversed that part of the lower court's judgment that enjoined the university "from any consideration of the race of any applicant."

Since this Court's splintered decision in *Bakke*, Justice Powell's opinion announcing the judgment of the Court has served as the touchstone for constitutional analysis of race-conscious admissions policies. Public and private universities across the Nation have modeled their own admissions programs on Justice Powell's views on permissible race-conscious policies.

First, Justice Powell rejected an interest in " 'reducing the historic deficit of traditionally disfavored minorities in medical schools and in the medical profession' " as an unlawful interest in racial balancing. Second, Justice Powell rejected an interest in remedying societal discrimination because such measures would risk placing unnecessary burdens on innocent third parties "who bear no responsibility for whatever harm the beneficiaries of the special admissions program are thought to have suffered." Third, Justice Powell rejected an interest in "increasing the number of physicians who will practice in communities currently underserved," concluding that even if such an interest could be compelling in some circumstances the program under review was not "geared to promote that goal."

Justice Powell approved the university's use of race to further only one interest: "the attainment of a diverse student body." With the important proviso that "constitutional limitations protecting individual rights may not be disregarded," Justice Powell grounded his analysis in the academic freedom that "long has been viewed as a special concern of the First Amendment."

Justice Powell was, however, careful to emphasize that in his view race "is only one element in a range of factors a university properly may consider in attaining the goal of a heterogeneous student body."

In the wake of our fractured decision in *Bakke*, courts have struggled to discern whether Justice Powell's diversity rationale, set forth in part of the opinion joined by no other Justice, is nonetheless binding precedent. . . .

B

We have held that all racial classifications imposed by government "must be analyzed by a reviewing court under strict scrutiny." This means that such classifications are constitutional only if they are narrowly tailored to further compelling governmental interests. "Absent searching judicial inquiry into the justification for such race-based measures," we have no way to determine what "classifications are 'benign' or 'remedial' and what classifications are in fact motivated by illegitimate notions of racial inferiority or simple racial politics." *Richmond v. J. A. Croson Co.*, 488 U.S. 469 (1989) (plurality opinion). We apply strict scrutiny to all racial classifications to " 'smoke out' illegitimate uses of race by assuring that [government] is pursuing a goal important enough to warrant use of a highly suspect tool."

Strict scrutiny is not "strict in theory, but fatal in fact." *Adarand Constructors, Inc. v. Pena*, 515 U.S. 200, at 237 (1995). Although all governmental uses of race are subject to strict scrutiny, not all are invalidated by it. When race-based action is necessary to further a compelling governmental interest, such action does not violate the constitutional guarantee of equal protection so long as the narrow-tailoring requirement is also satisfied.

Not every decision influenced by race is equally objectionable and strict scrutiny is designed to provide a framework for carefully examining the importance and the sincerity of the reasons advanced by the governmental decisionmaker for the use of race in that particular context.

III

A

With these principles in mind, we turn to the question whether the Law School's use of race is justified by a compelling state interest. Before this Court, as they have throughout this litigation, respondents assert only one justification for their use of race in the admissions process: obtaining "the educational benefits that flow from a diverse student body." In other words, the Law School asks us to recognize, in the context of higher education, a compelling state interest in student body diversity.

We first wish to dispel the notion that the Law School's argument has been foreclosed, either expressly or implicitly, by our affirmative-action cases decided since *Bakke*. It is true that some language in those opinions might be read to suggest that remedying past discrimination is the only permissible justification for race-based governmental action. But we have never held that the only governmental use of race that can survive strict scrutiny is remedying past discrimination. Nor, since *Bakke*, have we directly addressed the use of race in the context of public higher education. Today, we hold that the Law School has a compelling interest in attaining a diverse student body.

As part of its goal of "assembling a class that is both exceptionally academically qualified and broadly diverse," the Law School seeks to "enroll a 'critical mass' of minority students." The Law School's interest is not simply "to assure within its student body some specified percentage of a particular group merely because of its race or ethnic origin." *Bakke*, 438 U.S., at 307. That would amount to outright racial balancing, which is patently unconstitutional. Rather, the Law School's concept of critical mass is defined by reference to the educational benefits that diversity is designed to produce.

The Law School does not premise its need for critical mass on "any belief that minority students always (or even consistently) express some characteristic minority viewpoint on any issue." To the contrary, diminishing the force of such stereotypes is both a crucial part of the Law School's mission, and one that it cannot accomplish with only token numbers of minority students. Just as growing up in a particular region or having particular professional experiences is likely to affect an individual's views, so too is one's own, unique experience of being a racial minority in a society, like our own, in which race unfortunately still matters. The Law School has determined, based on its experience and expertise, that a "critical mass" of underrepresented minorities is necessary to further its compelling interest in securing the educational benefits of a diverse student body.

B

Even in the limited circumstance when drawing racial distinctions is permissible to further a compelling state interest, government is still "constrained in how it may pursue that end: [T]he means chosen to accomplish the [government's] asserted purpose must be specifically and narrowly framed to accomplish that purpose." *Shaw v. Hunt*, 517 U.S. 899, 908 (1996). The purpose of the narrow tailoring requirement is to ensure that "the means chosen 'fit' . . . the compelling goal so closely that there is little or no possibility that the motive for the classification was illegitimate racial prejudice or stereotype." *Richmond v. J. A. Croson Co.*, 488 U.S., at 493.

Since *Bakke*, we have had no occasion to define the contours of the narrow-tailoring inquiry with respect to race-conscious university admissions programs. That must be calibrated to fit the distinct issues raised by the use of race to achieve student body diversity in public higher education.

To be narrowly tailored, a race-conscious admissions program cannot use a quota system—it cannot "insulate each category of applicants with certain desired qualifications from competition with all other applicants." *Bakke* at 315. Instead, a university may consider race or ethnicity only as a " 'plus' in a particular applicant's file," without "insulating the individual from comparison with all other candidates for the available seats." In other words, an admissions program must be "flexible enough to consider all pertinent elements of diversity in light of the particular qualifications of each applicant, and to place them on the same footing for consideration, although not necessarily according them the same weight."

We find that the Law School's admissions program bears the hallmarks of a narrowly tailored plan. As Justice Powell made clear in *Bakke*, truly individualized consideration demands that race be used in a flexible, nonmechanical way. It follows from this mandate that universities cannot establish quotas for members of certain racial groups or put members of those groups on separate admissions tracks. Nor can universities insulate applicants who belong to certain racial or ethnic groups from the competition for admission. Universities can, however, consider race or ethnicity more flexibly as a "plus" factor in the context of individualized consideration of each and every applicant.

We are satisfied that the Law School's admissions program, like the Harvard plan described by Justice Powell, does not operate as a quota. Properly understood, a "quota" is a program in which a certain fixed number or proportion of opportunities are "reserved exclusively for certain minority groups." *Richmond v. J. A. Croson Co.* at 496.

The Law School's goal of attaining a critical mass of underrepresented minority students does not transform its program into a quota.

The Chief Justice believes that the Law School's policy conceals an attempt to achieve racial balancing, and cites admissions data to contend that the Law School discriminates among different groups within the critical mass. But, as the Chief Justice concedes, the number of underrepresented minority students who ultimately enroll in the Law School differs substantially from their representation in the applicant pool and varies considerably for each group from year to year.

That a race-conscious admissions program does not operate as a quota does not, by itself, satisfy the requirement of individualized consideration. When using race as a "plus" factor in university admissions, a university's admissions program must remain flexible enough to ensure that each applicant is evaluated as an individual and not in a way that makes an applicant's race or ethnicity the defining feature of his or her application. The importance of this individualized consideration in the context of a race-conscious admissions program is paramount.

Here, the Law School engages in a highly individualized, holistic review of each applicant's file, giving serious consideration to all the ways an applicant might contribute to a diverse educational environment.

What is more, the Law School actually gives substantial weight to diversity factors besides race. The Law School frequently accepts nonminority applicants with grades and test scores lower than underrepresented minority applicants (and other nonminority applicants) who are rejected. This shows that the Law School seriously weighs many other diversity factors besides race that can make a real and dispositive difference for nonminority applicants as well.

Petitioner and the United States argue that the Law School's plan is not narrowly tailored because race-neutral means exist to obtain the educational benefits of student body diversity that the Law School seeks. We disagree. Narrow tailoring does not require exhaustion of every conceivable race-neutral alternative. Nor does it require a university to choose between maintaining a reputation for excellence or fulfilling a commitment to provide educational opportunities to members of all racial groups.

To be narrowly tailored, a race-conscious admissions program must not "unduly burden individuals who are not members of the favored racial and ethnic groups." *Metro Broadcasting, Inc. v. FCC*, 497 U.S. 547, 630 (1990).

We are satisfied that the Law School's admissions program does not. Because the Law School considers "all pertinent elements of diversity," it can (and does) select nonminority applicants who have greater potential to enhance student body diversity over underrepresented minority applicants.

In the context of higher education, the durational requirement can be met by sunset provisions in race-conscious admissions policies and periodic reviews to determine whether racial preferences are still necessary to achieve student body diversity. Universities in California, Florida, and Washington State, where racial preferences in admissions are prohibited by state law, are currently engaged in experimenting with a wide variety of alternative approaches. Universities in other States can and should draw on the most promising aspects of these race-neutral alternatives as they develop.

The requirement that all race-conscious admissions programs have a termination point "assures all citizens that the deviation from the norm of equal treatment of all racial and ethnic groups is a temporary matter, a measure taken in the service of the goal of equality itself." *Richmond v. J. A. Croson Co.*, 488 U.S., at 510.

We take the Law School at its word that it would "like nothing better than to find a race-neutral admissions formula" and will terminate its race-conscious admissions program as soon as practicable. It has been 25 years since Justice Powell first approved the use of race to further an interest in student body diversity in the context of public higher education. Since that time, the number of minority applicants with high grades and test scores has indeed increased. We expect that 25 years from now, the use of racial preferences will no longer be necessary to further the interest approved today.

IV

In summary, the Equal Protection Clause does not prohibit the Law School's narrowly tailored use of race in admissions decisions to further a compelling interest in obtaining the educational benefits that flow from a diverse student body. The judgment of the Court of Appeals for the Sixth Circuit, accordingly, is affirmed.

JUSTICE GINSBURG, with whom JUSTICE BREYER joins, concurring.

The Court's observation that race-conscious programs "must have a logical end point," accords with the international understanding of the office of affirmative action. The International Convention on the Elimination of All Forms of Racial Discrimination, ratified by the United States in 1994, endorses "special and concrete measures to ensure the adequate development and protection of certain racial groups or individuals belonging to them, for the purpose of guaranteeing them the full and equal enjoyment of human rights and fundamental freedoms." But such measures, the Convention instructs, "shall in no case entail as a consequence the maintenance of unequal or separate rights for different racial groups after the objectives for which they were taken have been achieved."

The Court further observes that "it has been 25 years since Justice Powell [in *Regents of Univ. of Cal. v. Bakke*, 438 U.S. 265 (1978)] first approved the use of race to further an interest in student body diversity in the context of public higher education." For at least part of that time, however, the law could not fairly be described as "settled," and in some regions of the Nation, overtly race-conscious admissions policies have been proscribed. Moreover, it was only 25 years before *Bakke* that this Court declared public school segregation unconstitutional, a declaration that, after prolonged resistance, yielded an end to a law-enforced racial caste system, itself the legacy of centuries of slavery.

It is well documented that conscious and unconscious race bias, even rank discrimination based on race, remain alive in our land, impeding realization of our highest values and ideals. As to public education, data for the years 2000–2001 show that 71.6% of African-American children and 76.3% of Hispanic children attended a school in which minorities made up a majority of the student body. And schools in predominantly minority communities lag far behind others measured by the educational resources available to them.

However strong the public's desire for improved education systems may be, it remains the current reality that many minority students encounter markedly inadequate and unequal educational opportunities. Despite these inequalities, some minority students are able to meet the high threshold requirements set for admission to the country's finest undergraduate and graduate educational institutions. As lower school education in minority communities improves, an increase in the number of such students may be anticipated. From today's vantage point, one may hope, but not firmly forecast, that over the next generation's span, progress toward nondiscrimination and genuinely equal opportunity will make it safe to sunset affirmative action.

CHIEF JUSTICE REHNQUIST, with whom JUSTICES SCALIA, KENNEDY, and THOMAS join, dissenting.

I agree with the Court that, "in the limited circumstance when drawing racial distinctions is permissible," the government must ensure that its means are narrowly tailored to achieve a compelling state interest. I do not believe, however, that the University of Michigan Law School's (Law School) means are narrowly tailored to the interest it asserts. The Law School claims it must take the steps it does to achieve a " 'critical mass' " of underrepresented minority students. But its actual program bears no relation to this asserted goal. Stripped of its "critical mass" veil, the Law School's program is revealed as a naked effort to achieve racial balancing.

Before the Court's decision today, we consistently applied the same strict scrutiny analysis regardless of the government's purported reason for using race and regardless of the setting in which race was being used. We rejected calls to use more lenient review in the face of claims that race was being used in "good faith" because " 'more than good motives should be required when government seeks to allocate its resources by way of an explicit racial classification system.' " *Adarand* [*Constructors, Inc. v. Pena*, 515 U.S. 200] at 226 (1995). We likewise rejected calls to apply more lenient review based on the particular setting in which race is being used. Indeed, even in the specific context of higher education, we emphasized that "constitutional limitations protecting individual rights may not be disregarded." *Bakke* at 314.

Although the Court recites the language of our strict scrutiny analysis, its application of that review is unprecedented in its deference.

Respondents' asserted justification for the Law School's use of race in the admissions process is "obtaining 'the educational benefits that flow from a diverse student body.' "

In practice, the Law School's program bears little or no relation to its asserted goal of achieving "critical mass." Respondents explain that the Law School seeks to accumulate a "critical mass" of each underrepresented minority group. But the record demonstrates that the Law School's admissions practices with respect to these groups differ dramatically and cannot be defended under any consistent use of the term "critical mass."

From 1995 through 2000, the Law School admitted between 1,130 and 1,310 students. Of those, between 13 and 19 were Native American, between 91 and 108 were African-Americans, and between 47 and 56 were Hispanic. If the Law School is admitting between 91 and 108 African-Americans in order to achieve "critical mass," thereby preventing African-American students from feeling "isolated or like spokespersons for their race," one would think that a number of the same order of magnitude would be necessary to accomplish the same purpose for Hispanics and Native Americans. Similarly, even if all of the Native American applicants admitted in a given year matriculate, which the record demonstrates is not at all the case, * how can this possibly constitute a "critical mass" of Native Americans in a class of over 350 students? In order for this pattern of admission to be consistent with the Law School's explanation of "critical mass," one would have to believe that the objectives of "critical mass" offered by respondents are achieved with only half the number of Hispanics and one-sixth the number of Native Americans as compared to African-Americans. But respondents offer no race-specific reasons for such disparities. Instead, they simply emphasize the importance of achieving "critical mass," without any explanation of why that concept is applied differently among the three underrepresented minority groups.

I do not believe that the Constitution gives the Law School such free rein in the use of race. The Law School has offered no explanation for its actual admissions practices and, unexplained, we are bound to conclude that the Law School has managed its admissions program, not to achieve a "critical mass," but to extend offers of admission to members of selected minority groups in proportion to their statistical representation in the applicant pool. But this is precisely the type of racial balancing that the Court itself calls "patently unconstitutional."

Finally, I believe that the Law School's program fails strict scrutiny because it is devoid of any reasonably precise time limit on the Law School's use of race in admissions. Our previous cases have required some limit on the duration of programs such as this because discrimination on the basis of race is invidious.

The Court suggests a possible 25-year limitation on the Law School's current program. Respondents, on the other hand, remain more ambiguous, explaining that "the Law School of course recognizes that race-conscious programs must have reasonable durational limits, and the Sixth Circuit properly found such a limit in the Law School's resolve to cease considering race when genuine race-neutral alternatives become available." These discussions of a time limit are the vaguest of assurances. In truth, they permit the Law School's use of racial preferences on a seemingly permanent basis. Thus, an important component of strict scrutiny—that a program be limited in time—is casually subverted.

The Court, in an unprecedented display of deference under our strict scrutiny analysis, upholds the Law School's program despite its obvious flaws. We have said that when it comes to the use of race, the connection between the ends and the means used to attain them must be precise. But here the flaw is deeper than that; it is not merely a question of "fit" between ends and means. Here the means actually used are forbidden by the Equal Protection Clause of the Constitution.

JUSTICE KENNEDY, dissenting.

The separate opinion by Justice Powell in *Regents of Univ. of Cal. v. Bakke*, 438 U.S. 265 (1978), is based on the principle that a university admissions program may take account of race as one, nonpredominant factor in a system designed to consider each applicant as an individual, provided the program can meet the test of strict scrutiny by the judiciary. This is a unitary formulation. If strict scrutiny is abandoned or manipulated to distort its real and accepted meaning, the Court lacks authority to approve the use of race even in this modest, limited way. The opinion by Justice Powell, in my view, states the correct rule for resolving this case. The Court, however, does not apply strict scrutiny. By trying to say otherwise, it undermines both the test and its own controlling precedents.

Justice Powell's approval of the use of race in university admissions reflected a tradition, grounded in the First Amendment, of acknowledging a university's conception of its educational mission. Our precedents provide a basis for the Court's acceptance of a university's considered judgment that racial diversity among students can further its educational task, when supported by empirical evidence.

It is unfortunate, however, that the Court takes the first part of Justice Powell's rule but abandons the second. Having approved the use of race as a factor in the admissions process, the majority proceeds to nullify the essential safeguard Justice Powell insisted upon as the precondition of the approval. The safeguard was rigorous judicial review, with strict scrutiny as the controlling standard. This Court has reaffirmed, subsequent to *Bakke*, the absolute necessity of strict scrutiny when the state uses race as an operative category. In the context of university admissions the objective of racial diversity can be accepted based on empirical data known to us, but deference is not to be given with respect to the methods by which it is pursued. Preferment by race, when resorted to by the State, can be the most divisive of all policies, containing within it the potential to destroy confidence in the Constitution and in the idea of equality. The majority today refuses to be faithful to the settled principle of strict review designed to reflect these concerns.

The Court, in a review that is nothing short of perfunctory, accepts the University of Michigan Law School's assurances that its admissions process meets with constitutional requirements. The majority fails to confront the reality of how the Law School's admissions policy is implemented. The dissenting opinion by The Chief Justice, which I join in full, demonstrates beyond question why the concept of critical mass is a delusion used by the Law School to mask its attempt to make race an automatic factor in most instances and to achieve numerical goals indistinguishable from quotas.

It is regrettable the Court's important holding allowing racial minorities to have their special circumstances considered in order to improve their educational opportunities is accompanied by a suspension of the strict scrutiny which was the predicate of allowing race to be considered in the first place. If the Court abdicates its constitutional duty to give strict scrutiny to the use of race in university admissions, it negates my authority to approve the use of race in pursuit of student diversity. The Constitution cannot confer the right to classify on the basis of race even in this special context absent searching judicial review. For these reasons, though I reiterate my approval of giving appropriate consideration to race in this one context, I must dissent in the present case.

JUSTICE SCALIA, with whom JUSTICE THOMAS joins, concurring in part and dissenting in part.

I join the opinion of The Chief Justice. As he demonstrates, the University of Michigan Law School's mystical "critical mass" justification for its discrimination by race challenges even the most gullible mind. The admissions statistics show it to be a sham to cover a scheme of racially proportionate admissions.

I also join Parts I through VII of Justice Thomas's opinion. I find particularly unanswerable his central point: that the allegedly "compelling state interest" at issue here is not the incremental "educational benefit" that emanates from the fabled "critical mass" of minority students, but rather Michigan's interest in maintaining a "prestige" law school whose normal admissions standards disproportionately exclude blacks and other minorities. If that is a compelling state interest, everything is.

I add the following: The "educational benefit" that the University of Michigan seeks to achieve by racial discrimination consists, according to the Court, of " 'cross-racial understanding,' " and " 'better prepar[ation of] students for an increasingly diverse workforce and society,' " all of which is necessary not only for work, but also for good "citizenship." This is not, of course, an "educational benefit" on which students will be graded on their Law School transcript (Works and Plays Well with Others: B+) or tested by the bar examiners (Q: Describe in 500 words or less your cross-racial understanding). For it is a lesson of life rather than law—essentially the same lesson taught to (or rather learned by, for it cannot be "taught" in the usual sense) people three feet shorter and twenty years younger than the full-grown adults at the University of Michigan Law School, in institutions ranging from Boy Scout troops to public-school kindergartens. If properly considered an "educational benefit" at all, it is surely not one that is either uniquely relevant to law school or uniquely "teachable" in a formal educational setting. And therefore: If it is appropriate for the University of Michigan Law School to use racial discrimination for the purpose of putting together a "critical mass" that will convey generic lessons in socialization and good citizenship, surely it is no less appropriate—indeed, particularly appropriate—for the civil service system of the State of Michigan to do so. There, also, those exposed to "critical masses" of certain races will presumably become better Americans, better Michiganders, better civil servants. And surely private employers cannot be criticized—indeed, should be praised—if they also "teach" good citizenship to their adult employees through a patriotic, all-American system of racial discrimination in hiring. The nonminority individuals who are deprived of a legal education, a civil service job, or any job at all by reason of their skin color will surely understand.

Unlike a clear constitutional holding that racial preferences in state educational institutions are impermissible, or even a clear anticonstitutional holding that racial preferences in state educational institutions are OK, today's *Grutter-Gratz* split double header seems perversely designed to prolong the controversy and the litigation. I do not look forward to any of these cases. The Constitution proscribes government discrimination on the basis of race, and state-provided education is no exception.

JUSTICE THOMAS, with whom JUSTICE SCALIA joins as to Parts I–VII, concurring in part and dissenting in part.

Frederick Douglass, speaking to a group of abolitionists almost 140 years ago, delivered a message lost on today's majority:

> In regard to the colored people, there is always more that is benevolent, I perceive, than just, manifested towards us. What I ask for the negro is not benevolence, not pity, not sympathy, but simply justice. The American people have always been anxious to know what they shall do with us. . . . I have had but one answer from the beginning. Do nothing with us! Your doing with us has already played the mischief with us. Do nothing with us! If the apples will not remain on the tree of their own strength, if they are worm-eaten at the core, if they are early ripe and disposed to fall, let them fall! . . . And if the negro cannot stand on his own legs, let him fall also. All I ask is, give him a chance to stand on his own legs! Let him alone! . . . Your interference is doing him positive injury. What the Black Man Wants: An Address Delivered in Boston, Massachusetts, on 26 January 1865, reprinted in 4 *The Frederick Douglass Papers* 59, 68 (J. Blassingame & J. McKivigan eds. 1991).

Like Douglass, I believe blacks can achieve in every avenue of American life without the meddling of university administrators. Because I wish to see all students succeed whatever their color, I share, in some respect, the sympathies of those who sponsor the type of discrimination advanced by the University of Michigan Law School (Law School). The Constitution does not, however, tolerate institutional devotion to the status quo in admissions policies when such devotion ripens into racial discrimination. Nor does the Constitution countenance the unprecedented deference the Court gives to the Law School, an approach inconsistent with the very concept of "strict scrutiny."

No one would argue that a university could set up a lower general admission standard and then impose heightened requirements only on black applicants. Similarly, a university may not maintain a high admission standard and grant exemptions to favored races. The Law School, of its own choosing, and for its own purposes, maintains an exclusionary admissions system that it knows produces racially disproportionate results. Racial discrimination is not a permissible solution to the self-inflicted wounds of this elitist admissions policy.

The majority upholds the Law School's racial discrimination not by interpreting the people's Constitution, but by responding to a faddish slogan of the cognoscenti. Nevertheless, I concur in part in the Court's opinion. First, I agree with the Court insofar as its decision, which approves of only one racial classification, confirms that further use of race in admissions remains unlawful. Second, I agree with the Court's holding that racial discrimination in higher education admissions will be illegal in 25 years. I respectfully dissent from the remainder of the Court's opinion and the judgment, however, because I believe that the Law School's current use of race violates the Equal Protection Clause and that the Constitution means the same thing today as it will in 300 months.

V

Putting aside the absence of any legal support for the majority's reflexive deference, there is much to be said for the view that the use of tests and other measures to "predict" academic performance is a poor substitute for a system that gives every applicant a chance to prove he can succeed in the study of law. The rallying cry that in the absence of racial discrimination in admissions there would be a true meritocracy ignores the fact that the entire process is poisoned by numerous exceptions to "merit." The Equal Protection Clause does not, however, prohibit the use of unseemly legacy preferences or many other kinds of arbitrary admissions procedures. What the Equal Protection Clause does prohibit are classifications made on the basis of race. So while legacy preferences can stand under the Constitution, racial discrimination cannot. I will not twist the Constitution to invalidate legacy preferences or otherwise impose my vision of higher education admissions on the Nation. The majority should similarly stay its impulse to validate faddish racial discrimination the Constitution clearly forbids.

VII

As the foregoing makes clear, I believe the Court's opinion to be, in most respects, erroneous. I do, however, find two points on which I agree.

A

First, I note that the issue of unconstitutional racial discrimination among the groups the Law School prefers is not presented in this case, because petitioner has never argued that the Law School engages in such a practice, and the Law School maintains that it does not. I join the Court's opinion insofar as it confirms that this type of racial discrimination remains unlawful. Like the Court, I express no opinion as to whether the Law School's current admissions program runs afoul of this prohibition.

B

The Court also holds that racial discrimination in admissions should be given another 25 years before it is deemed no longer narrowly tailored to the Law School's fabricated compelling state interest. While I agree that in 25 years the practices of the Law School will be illegal, they are, for the reasons I have given, illegal now. The majority does not and cannot rest its time limitation on any evidence that the gap in credentials between black and white students is shrinking or will be gone in that timeframe. No one can seriously contend, and the Court does not, that the racial gap in academic credentials will disappear in 25 years. Nor is the Court's holding that racial discrimination will be unconstitutional in 25 years made contingent on the gap closing in that time.

For the immediate future, however, the majority has placed its imprimatur on a practice that can only weaken the principle of equality embodied in the Declaration of Independence and the Equal Protection Clause. It has been nearly 140 years since Frederick Douglass asked the intellectual ancestors of the Law School to "[d]o nothing with us!" and the Nation adopted the Fourteenth Amendment. Now we must wait another 25 years to see this principle of equality vindicated. I therefore respectfully dissent from the remainder of the Court's opinion and the judgment.

FOR DISCUSSION

Is this decision consistent with or challenging to the *Adarand,* case? Does it contain clear guidelines for the lower federal courts to follow? Justice O'Connor states in the majority opinion, "We expect that 25 years from now, the use of racial preferences will no longer be necessary to further the interest approved today." How do you interpret this? Do you agree with Justices Thomas and Scalia or Justice Ginsburg? Why?

RELATED CASES

***Hopwood v. Texas:* 78 F.3d 932 (CA5 1996) (*Hopwood I*).**

Diversity in higher education is not a compelling state interest; therefore affirmative action programs in higher education admissions cannot be justified by such an objective and are in violation of the Equal Protection Clause of the Fourteenth Amendment.

***Smith v. University of Wash. Law School:* 233 F.3d 1188 (CA9 2000).**

Diversity in higher education is a compelling state interest; therefore an affirmative action program in higher education admissions justified by such an objective does not automatically violate the Equal Protection Clause of the Fourteenth Amendment.

***Gratz* v. *Bollinger:* 539 U.S. 244, 270 (2003).**

Although the Court agrees that diversity can be a compelling state interest, the justices found that the use of affirmative action in the University of Michigan's undergraduate admissions program was not sufficiently narrowly tailored to avoid violating the Equal Protection Clause.

***Fisher v. University of Texas:* 579 U.S. ___ (2016).**

The University of Texas policy of using race as one factor among many to ensure a racially diverse college campus was sufficiently narrowly tailored and did not violate the Equal Protection Clause.

PARENTS INVOLVED IN COMMUNITY SCHOOLS V. SEATTLE SCHOOL DISTRICT NO. 1 ET AL.

551 U.S. 701, 127 S.Ct. 2738, 75 U.S.L.W. 4577 (2007)

See the case for a discussion of the facts.

Vote: 5–4

CHIEF JUSTICE ROBERTS announced the judgment of the Court, and delivered the opinion of the Court with respect to Parts I, II, III-A, and III-C, and an opinion with respect to Parts III-B and IV, in which JUSTICES SCALIA, THOMAS, and ALITO join.

The school districts in these cases voluntarily adopted student assignment plans that rely upon race to determine which public schools certain children may attend. The Seattle school district classifies children as white or nonwhite; the Jefferson County school district as black or "other." In Seattle, this racial classification is used to allocate slots in oversubscribed high schools. In Jefferson County, it is used to make certain elementary school assignments and to rule on transfer requests. In each case, the school district relies upon an individual student's race in assigning that student to a particular school, so that the racial balance at the school falls within a predetermined range based on the racial composition of the school district as a whole. Parents of students denied assignment to particular schools under these plans solely because of their race brought suit, contending that allocating children to different public schools on the basis of race violated the Fourteenth Amendment guarantee of equal protection. The Courts of Appeals below upheld the plans. We granted certiorari, and now reverse.

I

Both cases present the same underlying legal question—whether a public school that had not operated legally segregated schools or has been found to be unitary may choose to classify students by race and rely upon that classification in making school assignments. Although we examine the plans under the same legal framework, the specifics of the two plans, and the circumstances surrounding their adoption, are in some respects quite different.

III

A

It is well established that when the government distributes burdens or benefits on the basis of individual racial classifications, that action is reviewed under strict scrutiny. As the Court recently reaffirmed, " 'racial classifications are simply too pernicious to permit any but the most exact connection between justification and classification.' " *Gratz* v. *Bollinger*, 539 U.S. 244, 270 (2003). In order to satisfy this searching standard of review, the school districts must demonstrate that the use of individual racial classifications in the assignment plans here under review is "narrowly tailored" to achieve a "compelling" government interest.

Without attempting in these cases to set forth all the interests a school district might assert, it suffices to note that our prior cases, in evaluating the use of racial classifications in the school context, have recognized two interests that qualify as compelling. The first is the compelling interest of remedying the effects of past intentional discrimination. Yet the Seattle public schools have not shown that they were ever segregated by law, and were not subject to court-ordered desegregation decrees. The Jefferson County public schools were previously segregated by law and were subject to a desegregation decree entered in 1975. In 2000, the District Court that entered that decree dissolved it, finding that Jefferson County had "eliminated the vestiges associated with the former policy of segregation and its pernicious effects," and thus had achieved "unitary" status. Jefferson County accordingly does not rely upon an interest in remedying the effects of past intentional discrimination in defending its present use of race in assigning students.

Nor could it. Once Jefferson County achieved unitary status, it had remedied the constitutional wrong that allowed race-based assignments. Any continued use of race must be justified on some other basis.

The second government interest we have recognized as compelling for purposes of strict scrutiny is the interest in diversity in higher education upheld in *Grutter v. Bollinger*, 539 U.S. 306 (2003). The specific interest found compelling in *Grutter* was student body diversity "in the context of higher education."

The entire gist of the analysis in *Grutter* was that the admissions program at issue there focused on each applicant as an individual, and not simply as a member of a particular racial group. The point of the narrow tailoring analysis in which the *Grutter* Court engaged was to ensure that the use of racial classifications was indeed part of a broader assessment of diversity, and not simply an effort to achieve racial balance, which the Court explained would be "patently unconstitutional."

In the present cases, by contrast, race is not considered as part of a broader effort to achieve "exposure to widely diverse people, cultures, ideas, and viewpoints;" race, for some students, is determinative standing alone. The districts argue that other factors, such as student preferences, affect assignment decisions under their plans, but under each plan when race comes into play, it is decisive by itself. It is not simply one factor weighed with others in reaching a decision, as in *Grutter*; it is *the* factor. Like the University of Michigan undergraduate plan struck down in *Gratz v. Bollinger*, the plans here "do not provide for a meaningful individualized review of applicants" but instead rely on racial classifications in a "nonindividualized, mechanical" way, at 276, 280.

Even when it comes to race, the plans here employ only a limited notion of diversity, viewing race exclusively in white/nonwhite terms in Seattle and black/"other" terms in Jefferson County. It is hard to understand how a plan that could allow these results can be viewed as being concerned with achieving enrollment that is " 'broadly diverse,' " *Grutter* at 329.

In upholding the admissions plan in *Grutter*, though, this Court relied upon considerations unique to institutions of higher education, noting that in light of "the expansive freedoms of speech and thought associated with the university environment, universities occupy a special niche in our constitutional tradition." 539 U.S., at 329. The Court in *Grutter* expressly articulated key limitations on its holding—defining a specific type of broad-based diversity and noting the unique context of higher education—but these limitations were largely disregarded by the lower courts in extending *Grutter* to uphold race-based assignments in elementary and secondary schools. The present cases are not governed by *Grutter*.

B

Perhaps recognizing that reliance on *Grutter* cannot sustain their plans, both school districts assert additional interests, distinct from the interest upheld in *Grutter*, to justify their race-based assignments. Each school district argues that educational and broader socialization benefits flow from a racially diverse learning environment, and each contends that because the diversity they seek is racial diversity—not the broader diversity at issue in *Grutter*—it makes sense to promote that interest directly by relying on race alone.

. . . [I]t is clear that the racial classifications employed by the districts are not narrowly tailored to the goal of achieving the educational and social benefits asserted to flow from racial diversity. In design and operation, the plans are directed only to racial balance, pure and simple, an objective this Court has repeatedly condemned as illegitimate.

In fact, in each case the extreme measure of relying on race in assignments is unnecessary to achieve the stated goals, even as defined by the districts. When the actual racial breakdown is considered, enrolling students without regard to their race yields a substantially diverse student body under any definition of diversity.

In *Grutter*, the number of minority students the school sought to admit was an undefined "meaningful number" necessary to achieve a genuinely diverse student body. Although the matter was the subject of disagreement on the Court, the majority concluded that the law school did not count back from its applicant pool to arrive at the "meaningful number" it regarded as necessary to diversify its student body. Here the racial balance the districts seek is a defined range set solely by reference to the demographics of the respective school districts.

This working backward to achieve a particular type of racial balance, rather than working forward from some demonstration of the level of diversity that provides the purported benefits, is a fatal flaw under our existing precedent. *Grutter* itself reiterated that "outright racial balancing" is "patently unconstitutional." 539 U.S., at 330.

Accepting racial balancing as a compelling state interest would justify the imposition of racial proportionality throughout American society, contrary to our repeated recognition that "[a]t the heart of the Constitution's guarantee of equal protection lies the simple command that the Government must treat citizens as individuals, not as simply components of a racial, religious, sexual or national class." *Miller* v. *Johnson*, 515 U.S. 900, 911 (1995). Allowing racial balancing as a compelling end in itself would "effectively assur[e] that race will always be relevant in American life, and that the 'ultimate goal' of 'eliminating entirely from governmental decisionmaking such irrelevant factors as a human being's race' will never be achieved." *Croson,* at 495. An interest "linked to nothing other than proportional representation of various races . . . would support indefinite use of racial classifications, employed first to obtain the appropriate mixture of racial views and then to ensure that the [program] continues to reflect that mixture." *Metro Broadcasting*, at 614.

The principle that racial balancing is not permitted is one of substance, not semantics. Racial balancing is not transformed from "patently unconstitutional" to a compelling state interest simply by relabeling it "racial diversity." While the school districts use various verbal formulations to describe the interest they seek to promote-racial diversity, avoidance of racial isolation, racial integration—they offer no definition of the interest that suggests it differs from racial balance.

However closely related race-based assignments may be to achieving racial balance, that itself cannot be the goal, whether labeled "racial diversity" or anything else. To the extent the objective is sufficient diversity so that students see fellow students as individuals rather than solely as members of a racial group, using means that treat students solely as members of a racial group is fundamentally at cross-purposes with that end.

C

The districts assert, as they must, that the way in which they have employed individual racial classifications is necessary to achieve their stated ends. The minimal effect these classifications have on student assignments, however, suggests that other means would be effective. Seattle's racial tiebreaker results, in the end, only in shifting a small number of students between schools.

Similarly, Jefferson County's use of racial classifications has only a minimal effect on the assignment of students.

While we do not suggest that *greater* use of race would be preferable, the minimal impact of the districts' racial classifications on school enrollment casts doubt on the necessity of using racial classifications. In *Grutter*, the consideration of race was viewed as indispensable in more than tripling minority representation at the law school—from 4 to 14.5 percent. Here the most Jefferson County itself claims is that "because the guidelines provide a firm definition of the Board's goal of racially integrated schools, they 'provide administrators with the authority to facilitate, negotiate and collaborate with principals and staff to maintain schools within the 15–50% range.' " Classifying and assigning schoolchildren according to a binary conception of race is an extreme approach in light of our precedents and our Nation's history of using race in public schools, and requires more than such an amorphous end to justify it.

The districts have also failed to show that they considered methods other than explicit racial classifications to achieve their stated goals. Narrow tailoring requires "serious, good faith consideration of workable race-neutral alternatives," *Grutter* at 339, and yet in Seattle several alternative assignment plans—many of which would not have used express racial classifications—were rejected with little or no consideration. Jefferson County has failed to present any evidence that it considered alternatives, even though the district already claims that its goals are achieved primarily through means other than the racial classifications.

IV

If the need for the racial classifications embraced by the school districts is unclear, even on the districts' own terms, the costs are undeniable. Government action dividing us by race is inherently suspect because such classifications promote "notions of racial inferiority and lead to a politics of racial hostility," [*City of Richmond v. J.A.*] *Croson* [*Co.,* 488 U.S. 469,] at 493 (1989), "reinforce the belief, held by too many for too much of our history, that individuals should be judged by the color of their skin," *Shaw* v. *Reno*, 509 U.S. 630, 657 (1993), and "endorse race-based reasoning and the conception of a Nation divided into racial blocs, thus contributing to an escalation of racial hostility and conflict." *Metro Broadcasting*, 497 U.S., at 603.

All this is true enough in the contexts in which these statements were made—government contracting, voting districts, allocation of broadcast licenses, and electing state officers—but when it comes to using race to assign children to schools, history will be heard. In *Brown* v. *Board of Education*, 347 U.S. 483 (1954) (*Brown I*), we held that segregation deprived black children of equal educational opportunities regardless of whether school facilities and other tangible factors were equal, because government classification and separation on grounds of race themselves denoted inferiority. It was not the inequality of the facilities but the fact of legally separating children on the basis of race on which the Court relied to find a constitutional violation in 1954.

Before *Brown*, schoolchildren were told where they could and could not go to school based on the color of their skin. The school districts in these cases have not carried the heavy burden of demonstrating that we should allow this once again—even for very different reasons. For schools that never segregated on the basis of race, such as Seattle, or that have removed the vestiges of past segregation, such as Jefferson County, the way "to achieve a system of determining admission to the public schools on a nonracial basis," *Brown II* [349 U.S., at 300–301 (1955)], is to stop assigning students on a racial basis. The way to stop discrimination on the basis of race is to stop discriminating on the basis of race.

The judgments of the Courts of Appeals for the Sixth and Ninth Circuits are reversed, and the cases are remanded for further proceedings.

JUSTICE THOMAS, concurring.

Today, the Court holds that state entities may not experiment with race-based means to achieve ends they deem socially desirable. I wholly concur in The Chief Justice's opinion. I write separately to address several of the contentions in Justice Breyer's dissent. Contrary to the dissent's arguments, resegregation is not occurring in Seattle or Louisville; these school boards have no present interest in remedying past segregation; and these race-based student-assignment programs do not serve any compelling state interest. Accordingly, the plans are unconstitutional. Disfavoring a color-blind interpretation of the Constitution, the dissent would give school boards a free hand to make decisions on the basis of race—an approach reminiscent of that advocated by the segregationists in *Brown* v. *Board of Education,* 347 U.S. 483 (1954). This approach is just as wrong today as it was a half-century ago. The Constitution and our cases require us to be much more demanding before permitting local school boards to make decisions based on race.

JUSTICE KENNEDY, concurring in part and concurring in the judgment.

The Nation's schools strive to teach that our strength comes from people of different races, creeds, and cultures uniting in commitment to the freedom of all. In these cases two school districts in different parts of the country seek to teach that principle by having classrooms that reflect the racial makeup of the surrounding community. That the school districts consider these plans to be necessary should remind us our highest aspirations are yet unfulfilled. But the solutions mandated by these school districts must themselves be lawful. To make race matter now so that it might not matter later may entrench the very prejudices we seek to overcome. In my view the state-mandated racial classifications at issue, official labels proclaiming the race of all persons in a broad class of citizens—elementary school students in one case, high school students in another—are unconstitutional as the cases now come to us.

I agree with The Chief Justice that we have jurisdiction to decide the cases before us and join Parts I and II of the Court's opinion. I also join Parts III-A and III-C. . . . My views do not allow me to join the balance of the opinion by The Chief Justice, which seems to me to be inconsistent in both its approach and its implications with the history, meaning, and reach of the Equal Protection Clause. Justice Breyer's dissenting opinion, on the other hand, rests on what in my respectful submission is a misuse and mistaken interpretation of our precedents. This leads it to advance propositions that, in my view, are both erroneous and in fundamental conflict with basic equal protection principles. As a consequence, this separate opinion is necessary to set forth my conclusions in the two cases before the Court.

I

The opinion of the Court and Justice Breyer's dissenting opinion describe in detail the history of integration efforts in Louisville and Seattle. These plans classify individuals by race and allocate benefits and burdens on that basis; and as a result, they are to be subjected to strict scrutiny. The dissent finds that the school districts have identified a compelling interest in increasing diversity, including for the purpose of avoiding racial isolation. The plurality, by contrast, does not acknowledge that the school districts have identified a compelling interest here. For this reason, among others, I do not join Parts III-B and IV. Diversity, depending on its meaning and definition, is a compelling educational goal a school district may pursue.

II

Our Nation from the inception has sought to preserve and expand the promise of liberty and equality on which it was founded. Today we enjoy a society that is remarkable in its openness and opportunity. Yet our tradition is to go beyond present achievements, however significant, and to recognize and confront the flaws and injustices that remain. This is especially true when we seek assurance that opportunity is not denied on account of race. The enduring hope is that race should not matter; the reality is that too often it does.

This is by way of preface to my respectful submission that parts of the opinion by The Chief Justice imply an all-too-unyielding insistence that race cannot be a factor in instances when, in my view, it may be taken into account. The plurality opinion is too dismissive of the legitimate interest government has in ensuring all people have equal opportunity regardless of their race. The plurality's postulate that "[t]he way to stop discrimination on the basis of race is to stop discriminating on the basis of race" is not sufficient to decide these cases. Fifty years of experience since *Brown v. Board of Education*, 347 U.S. 483 (1954), should teach us that the problem before us defies so easy a solution. School districts can seek to reach Brown's objective of equal educational opportunity. The plurality opinion is at least open to the interpretation that the Constitution requires school districts to ignore the problem of de facto resegregation in schooling. I cannot endorse that conclusion. To the extent the plurality opinion suggests the Constitution mandates that state and local school authorities must accept the status quo of racial isolation in schools, it is, in my view, profoundly mistaken.

In the cases before us it is noteworthy that the number of students whose assignment depends on express racial classifications is limited. I join Part III-C of the Court's opinion because I agree that in the context of these plans, the small number of assignments affected suggests that the schools could have achieved their stated ends through different means. These include the facially race-neutral means set forth above or, if necessary, a more nuanced, individual evaluation of school needs and student characteristics that might include race as a component. The latter approach would be informed by *Grutter v. Bollinger*, 539 U.S. 306 (2003), though of course the criteria relevant to student placement would differ based on the age of the students, the needs of the parents, and the role of the schools.

III

The dissent rests on the assumptions that these sweeping race-based classifications of persons are permitted by existing precedents; that its confident endorsement of race categories for each child in a large segment of the community presents no danger to individual freedom in other, prospective realms of governmental regulation; and that the racial classifications used here cause no hurt or anger of the type the Constitution prevents. Each of these premises is, in my respectful view, incorrect.

* * *

This Nation has a moral and ethical obligation to fulfill its historic commitment to creating an integrated society that ensures equal opportunity for all of its children. A compelling interest exists in avoiding racial isolation, an interest that a school district, in its discretion and expertise, may choose to pursue. Likewise, a district may consider it a compelling interest to achieve a diverse student population. Race may be one component of that diversity, but other demographic factors, plus special talents and needs, should also be considered. What the government is not permitted to do, absent a showing of necessity not made here, is to classify every student on the basis of race and to assign each of them to schools based on that classification. Crude measures of this sort threaten to reduce children to racial chits valued and traded according to one school's supply and another's demand.

That statement, to be sure, invites this response: A sense of stigma may already become the fate of those separated out by circumstances beyond their immediate control. But to this the replication must be: Even so, measures other than differential treatment based on racial typing of individuals first must be exhausted.

The decision today should not prevent school districts from continuing the important work of bringing together students of different racial, ethnic, and economic backgrounds. Due to a variety of factors—some influenced by government, some not—neighborhoods in our communities do not reflect the diversity of our Nation as a whole. Those entrusted with directing our public schools can bring to bear the creativity of experts, parents, administrators, and other concerned citizens to find a way to achieve the compelling interests they face without resorting to widespread governmental allocation of benefits and burdens on the basis of racial classifications.

With this explanation I concur in the judgment of the Court.

JUSTICE STEVENS, dissenting.

While I join Justice Breyer's eloquent and unanswerable dissent in its entirety, it is appropriate to add these words.

There is a cruel irony in The Chief Justice's reliance on our decision in *Brown v. Board of Education*, 349 U.S. 294 (1955). The first sentence in the concluding paragraph of his opinion states: "Before *Brown*, schoolchildren were told where they could and could not go to school based on the color of their skin." This sentence reminds me of Anatole France's observation: "[T]he majestic equality of the la[w], forbid[s] rich and poor alike to sleep under bridges, to beg in the streets, and to steal their bread." The Chief Justice fails to note that it was only black schoolchildren who were so ordered; indeed, the history books do not tell stories of white children struggling to attend black schools. In this and other ways, The Chief Justice rewrites the history of one of this Court's most important decisions.

The Chief Justice rejects the conclusion that the racial classifications at issue here should be viewed differently than others, because they do not impose burdens on one race alone and do not stigmatize or exclude. The only justification for refusing to acknowledge the obvious importance of that difference is the citation of a few recent opinions—none of which even approached unanimity—grandly proclaiming that all racial classifications must be analyzed under "strict scrutiny."

If we look at cases decided during the interim between *Brown* and *Adarand [Constructors v. Pena,* 515 U.S. 200 (1995)], we can see how a rigid adherence to tiers of scrutiny obscures *Brown's* clear message. Perhaps the best example is provided by our approval of the decision of the Supreme Judicial Court of Massachusetts in 1967 upholding a state statute mandating racial integration in that State's school system. See *School Comm. of Boston v. Board of Education*, 352 Mass. 693, 227 N. E. 2d 729. Rejecting arguments comparable to those that the plurality accepts today, that court noted: "It would be the height of irony if the racial imbalance act, enacted as it was with the laudable purpose of achieving equal educational opportunities, should, by prescribing school pupil allocations based on race, founder on unsuspected shoals in the Fourteenth Amendment."

Invoking our mandatory appellate jurisdiction, the Boston plaintiffs prosecuted an appeal in this Court. Our ruling on the merits simply stated that the appeal was "dismissed for want of a substantial federal question." *School Comm. of Boston v. Board of Education*, 389 U.S. 572 (1968). That decision not only expressed our appraisal of the merits of the appeal, but it constitutes a precedent that the Court overrules today. The subsequent statements by the unanimous Court in *Swann v. Charlotte-Mecklenburg Bd. of Ed.*, 402 U.S. 1, 16 (1971), by then-Justice Rehnquist in chambers in *Bustop, Inc. v. Los Angeles Bd. of Ed.*, 439 U.S. 1380, 1383 (1978), and by the host of state court decisions cited by Justice Breyer, were fully consistent with that disposition. Unlike today's decision, they were also entirely loyal to *Brown*.

The Court has changed significantly since it decided *School Comm. of Boston* in 1968. It was then more faithful to *Brown* and more respectful of our precedent than it is today. It is my firm conviction that no Member of the Court that I joined in 1975 would have agreed with today's decision.

JUSTICE BREYER, with whom JUSTICE STEVENS, JUSTICE SOUTER, and JUSTICE GINSBURG join, dissenting.

These cases consider the longstanding efforts of two local school boards to integrate their public schools. The school board plans before us resemble many others adopted in the last 50 years by primary and secondary schools throughout the Nation. All of those plans represent local efforts to bring about the kind of racially integrated education that *Brown v. Board of Education*, 347 U.S. 483 (1954), long ago promised—efforts that this Court has repeatedly required, permitted, and encouraged local authorities to undertake. This Court has recognized that the public interests at stake in such cases are "compelling." We have approved of "narrowly tailored" plans that are no less race-conscious than the plans before us. And we have understood that the Constitution permits local communities to adopt desegregation plans even where it does not require them to do so.

The plurality pays inadequate attention to this law, to past opinions' rationales, their language, and the contexts in which they arise. As a result, it reverses course and reaches the wrong conclusion. In doing so, it distorts precedent, it misapplies the relevant constitutional principles, it announces legal rules that will obstruct efforts by state and local governments to deal effectively with the growing resegregation of public schools, it threatens to substitute for present calm a disruptive round of race-related litigation, and it undermines *Brown's* promise of integrated primary and secondary education that local communities have sought to make a reality. This cannot be justified in the name of the Equal Protection Clause.

VI

The plans before us satisfy the requirements of the Equal Protection Clause. And it is the plurality's opinion, not this dissent that "fails to ground the result it would reach in law."

Four basic considerations have led me to this view. First, the histories of Louisville and Seattle reveal complex circumstances and a long tradition of conscientious efforts by local school boards to resist racial segregation in public schools. Segregation at the time of *Brown* gave way to expansive remedies that included busing, which in turn gave rise to fears of white flight and resegregation. For decades now, these school boards have considered and adopted and revised assignment plans that sought to rely less upon race, to emphasize greater student choice, and to improve the conditions of all schools for all students, no matter the color of their skin, no matter where they happen to reside. The plans under review—which are less burdensome, more egalitarian, and more effective than prior plans—continue in that tradition. And their history reveals school district goals whose remedial, educational, and democratic elements are inextricably intertwined each with the others.

Second, since this Court's decision in *Brown*, the law has consistently and unequivocally approved of both voluntary and compulsory race-conscious measures to combat segregated schools. The Equal Protection Clause, ratified following the Civil War, has always distinguished in practice between state action that excludes and thereby subordinates racial minorities and state action that seeks to bring together people of all races. From *Swann v. Charlotte-Mecklenburg Bd. of Ed.*, 402 U.S. 1 (1971) to *Grutter v. Bollinger*, 539 U.S. 306 (2003), this Court's decisions have emphasized this distinction, recognizing that the fate of race relations in this country depends upon unity among our children, "for unless our children begin to learn together, there is little hope that our people will ever learn to live together." *Milliken v. Bradley*, 418 U.S. 717 (1974), at 783 (Marshall, J., dissenting).

Third, the plans before us, subjected to rigorous judicial review, are supported by compelling state interests and are narrowly tailored to accomplish those goals. Just as diversity in higher education was deemed compelling in *Grutter*, diversity in public primary and secondary schools—where there is even more to gain—must be, a fortiori, a compelling state interest. Even apart from *Grutter*, five Members of this Court agree that "avoiding racial isolation" and "achiev[ing] a diverse student population" remain today compelling interests. These interests combine remedial, educational, and democratic objectives. For the reasons discussed above, however, I disagree with Justice Kennedy that Seattle and Louisville have not done enough to demonstrate that their present plans are necessary to continue upon the path set by *Brown*. These plans are more "narrowly tailored" than the race-conscious law school admissions criteria at issue in *Grutter*. Hence, their lawfulness follows a fortiori from this Court's prior decisions.

Fourth, the plurality's approach risks serious harm to the law and for the Nation. Its view of the law rests either upon a denial of the distinction between exclusionary and inclusive use of race-conscious criteria in the context of the Equal Protection Clause, or upon such a rigid application of its "test" that the distinction loses practical significance. Consequently, the Court's decision today slows down and sets back the work of local school boards to bring about racially diverse schools.

Indeed, the consequences of the approach the Court takes today are serious. Yesterday, the plans under review were lawful. Today, they are not. Yesterday, the citizens of this Nation could look for guidance to this Court's unanimous pronouncements concerning desegregation. Today, they cannot. Yesterday, school boards had available to them a full range of means to combat segregated schools. Today, they do not.

The Court's decision undermines other basic institutional principles as well. What has happened to stare decisis? The history of the plans before us, their educational importance, their highly limited use of race—all these and more—make clear that the compelling interest here is stronger than in *Grutter*. The plans here are more narrowly tailored than the law school admissions program there at issue. Hence, applying *Grutter's* strict test, their lawfulness follows a fortiori. To hold to the contrary is to transform that test from "strict" to "fatal in fact"—the very opposite of what *Grutter* said. And what has happened to *Swann*? . . . . To *School Committee of Boston v. Board of Education*, 352 Mass. 693, 1968? After decades of vibrant life, they would all, under the plurality's logic, be written out of the law.

And what of respect for democratic local decisionmaking by States and school boards? For several decades this Court has rested its public school decisions upon *Swann's* basic view that the Constitution grants local school districts a significant degree of leeway where the inclusive use of race-conscious criteria is at issue. Now localities will have to cope with the difficult problems they face (including resegregation) deprived of one means they may find necessary.

And what of law's concern to diminish and peacefully settle conflict among the Nation's people? Instead of accommodating different good-faith visions of our country and our Constitution, today's holding upsets settled expectations, creates legal uncertainty, and threatens to produce considerable further litigation, aggravating race-related conflict.

And what of the long history and moral vision that the Fourteenth Amendment itself embodies? The plurality cites in support those who argued in Brown against segregation, and Justice Thomas likens the approach that I have taken to that of segregation's defenders. But segregation policies did not simply tell schoolchildren "where they could and could not go to school based on the color of their skin;" they perpetuated a caste system rooted in the institutions of slavery and 80 years of legalized subordination. The lesson of history, is not that efforts to continue racial segregation are constitutionally indistinguishable from efforts to achieve racial integration. Indeed, it is a cruel distortion of history to compare Topeka, Kansas, in the 1950's to Louisville and Seattle in the modern day—to equate the plight of Linda Brown (who was ordered to attend a Jim Crow school) to the circumstances of Joshua McDonald (whose request to transfer to a school closer to home was initially declined). This is not to deny that there is a cost in applying "a state-mandated racial label." But that cost does not approach, in degree or in kind, the terrible harms of slavery, the resulting caste system, and 80 years of legal racial segregation.

Finally, what of the hope and promise of *Brown*? For much of this Nation's history, the races remained divided. It was not long ago that people of different races drank from separate fountains, rode on separate buses, and studied in separate schools. In this Court's finest hour, *Brown v. Board of Education* challenged this history and helped to change it. For *Brown* held out a promise. It was a promise embodied in three Amendments designed to make citizens of slaves. It was the promise of true racial equality—not as a matter of fine words on paper, but as a matter of everyday life in the Nation's cities and schools. It was about the nature of a democracy that must work for all Americans. It sought one law, one Nation, one people, not simply as a matter of legal principle but in terms of how we actually live.

Not everyone welcomed this Court's decision in *Brown*. Three years after that decision was handed down, the Governor of Arkansas ordered state militia to block the doors of a white schoolhouse so that black children could not enter. The President of the United States dispatched the 101st Airborne Division to Little Rock, Arkansas, and federal troops were needed to enforce a desegregation decree. See *Cooper v. Aaron*, 358 U.S. 1 (1958). Today, almost 50 years later, attitudes toward race in this Nation have changed dramatically. Many parents, white and black alike, want their children to attend schools with children of different races. Indeed, the very school districts that once spurned integration now strive for it. The long history of their efforts reveals the complexities and difficulties they have faced. And in light of those challenges, they have asked us not to take from their hands the instruments they have used to rid their schools of racial segregation, instruments that they believe are needed to overcome the problems of cities divided by race and poverty. The plurality would decline their modest request.

The plurality is wrong to do so. The last half-century has witnessed great strides toward racial equality, but we have not yet realized the promise of *Brown*. To invalidate the plans under review is to threaten the promise of *Brown*. The plurality's position, I fear, would break that promise. This is a decision that the Court and the Nation will come to regret.

I must dissent.

FOR DISCUSSION

Should diversity in the classroom be a fundamental concern for local school boards? Is it a compelling justification for governmental intervention? Consider the competing discussions of *Brown v. Board of Education* by Justice Stevens and Chief Justice Roberts. Which best captures your understanding of *Brown*? Why?

Additional Classifications

The protected categories of race and gender have been developed within the Court's constitutional interpretation since the mid-to-late-twentieth century, although the implications of the provisions of the Equal Protection Clause have yet to be fully developed. Other groups, which have been less obviously distinguished by the law, have been more slowly integrated into equal protection jurisprudence as judges have wrestled with how children, immigrants, the aged, the mentally ill, the indigent, the physically or mentally disabled, and gays, bisexuals, lesbians, or transgendered people are to be treated constitutionally. Fundamental rights (those rights explicitly protected in the Constitution like free exercise of religion) and race have been given the highest level of protections under the Equal Protection Clause. Typically, the courts have determined that only groups that are immutable or unchanging in their essential characteristic (like racial groups) and have faced a history of invidious discrimination based on such characteristics are classified as a "suspect" class, worthy of the strictest of scrutiny. Yet, as this chapter has demonstrated, gender has been placed most typically under intermediate scrutiny. The Supreme Court has proven to be very reluctant to place other groups under the higher levels of scrutiny, even when persons coming under those classifications are proven to possess an immutable characteristic and a history of invidious discrimination against them. Instead, the Supreme Court has been reluctant to interfere with the ability of the state and federal legislatures to provide the protections they perceive to be necessary for these more vulnerable classes of citizens.

Alienage

Although the Fourteenth Amendment limits citizenship to "All persons born or naturalized in the United States and subject to the jurisdiction thereof" (the latter provision is generally applied to children born in the US to foreign diplomats) its due process and equal protections clauses apply to "any person" within state jurisdiction. The Court has accordingly provided some protection for noncitizen aliens, particularly with respect to employment and education.

Congress is responsible for naturalization, the process of converting non-native-born individuals into citizens, but state policies often also affect individuals who have not yet become citizens. In early America, congressional laws limited naturalization to free white immigrants who resided in the United States for a certain period of time. Later in the nineteenth century, the U.S. sought to restrict immigration from China and Japan, while states adopted laws limiting the rights of such individuals to purchase property. As late as 1922 [*Ozawa v. United States*, 260 U.S. 178] and 1923 [*United States v. Thind*, 262 US. 204] the Supreme Court interpreted federal laws to deny naturalization to an individual from Japan and another from India. In *Yick Wo v. Hopkins*, 118 U.S. 356 (1886), the Court did strike down San Francisco ordinance that allowed city officials unfairly to discriminate against Chinese laundries, and in *United States v. Wong Kim Ark*, 169 U.S. 649 (1898), it ruled that the Fourteenth Amendment provided that individuals who were born in the United States of Chinese parents were U.S. citizens.

For many years, individuals with "alien" status in the United States faced a backdrop of state legislation prohibiting their employment in a variety of civil service jobs, including teaching. New York law, for instance, did not allow individuals to be certified as a public school teacher unless they were either a U.S. citizen or had demonstrated the intent to apply for citizenship. Certification is necessary in New York to teach in a public elementary or secondary school. The 1979 case of *Ambach v. Norwick* (441 U.S. 68) was brought by two long-term residents, married to U.S. citizens but still retaining citizenship in their homeland. In this case, the Supreme Court found that precedent had consistently noted that "some state functions are so bound up with the operation of the State as a governmental entity as to permit the exclusion from those functions of all persons who have not become part of the process of self-government." In fact, the Court had previously found that New York could exclude aliens from the police force with such a justification (*Foley v. Connelie*, 435 U.S. 291, 1978). Teaching is a similar governmental function in that the inculcation of citizenship is a key part of the profession; therefore, a citizenship requirement to teach in the public schools bears a rational relationship to a legitimate state interest. Using the lowest standard—the rational relations test—of the Equal Protection Clause, the Court found the New York law constitutional.

In the case of *Cabell v. Chavez-Salido* (454 U.S. 432, 1982), the Court expanded the ruling in *Ambach* to uphold a California statute that prohibited aliens from working as probation officers for the state. The dissenters in *Ambach* also dissented in *Cabell.* In 1984 the Supreme Court considered the constitutionality of a Texas law that mandated U.S. citizenship for notaries public. The Court decided in *Bernal v. Fainter* (467 U.S. 216, 1984) that state laws that discriminate against aliens must survive strict scrutiny under the Equal Protection Clause unless the discrimination demonstrably meets an important public function; at this junction the classification for notaries falls under regular scrutiny.

While the Supreme Court has been clear that undocumented aliens do not possess protected status under the Constitution, their children, according to *Plyler v. Doe* (457 U.S. 202, 1982), are given protection, particularly in the arena of public education. This case emerged from the 1975 revision of a Texas state statute in order to prohibit the state from funding of the education of children not legally admitted to the United States; under the revision, local school boards were also authorized to deny these children enrollment in the public schools. Parents of schoolchildren of Mexican origin who had been excluded from the Tyler Independent school district initiated this class action lawsuit. In its ruling the Court clearly stated, "The Equal Protection Clause was intended to work nothing less than the abolition of all caste-based and invidious class-based legislation. . . . [I]llegal aliens who are plaintiffs in these cases may claim the benefit of the Fourteenth Amendment's guarantee of equal protection. . . ." While the Court found that undocumented aliens could not claim suspect classification, and the justices explicitly stated that education is not a fundamental constitutional right, they also said that without a substantial state interest to deny these children access to public education, the state of Texas was in violation of the Equal Protection Clause.

The equal protection standard the Court uses in cases related to immigration and alienage vary. At times the Court has applied the strict scrutiny standard—for example, in *Sugarman v. Dougall* (413 U.S. 634, 1973) and *Nyquist v. Mauclet* (432 U.S. 1, 1977). The Court has also applied a lower level of scrutiny in cases limiting alien entry into the political community (e.g., *Foley v. Connelie*, 435 U.S. 291, 1978; *Ambach v. Norwick*, 441 U.S. 68, 1979; and *Cabell v. Chavez-Salido*, 454 U.S. 432, 1982), although state legislation in these cases frequently has not sustained the scrutiny.

Although the Fourteenth Amendment recognizes both those who are born in the United States and those who are naturalized as citizens, it is less clear about individuals who are born abroad to citizen parents (they qualify under the law of *jus sanguinis*, or the law of blood, rather than under that of *jus soli*, the law of the soil). An early case excluded Native Americans who had been born on reservations from citizenship (See *Elk v. Wilkins*, 112 U.S. 94 (1884)), although the Indian Citizenship Act of 1924 later remedied this.

In *Perez v. Brownell*, 356 U.S. 44 (1958), the U.S. ruled that an individual who had been born in the United States lost his citizenship by departing from the U.S. during World War II and voting in a Mexican election. In *Trop v. Dulles*, 356 U.S. 86 (1958), however, it decided that the U.S. could not strip citizenship from a native-born individual who deserted from the army; the Court concluded that this was cruel and unusual punishment. In 1971, the Court ruled in *Rogers v. Bellei*, 401 U.S. 815 that congressional laws required individuals who were born abroad to American citizens to reside in the United States for specified periods in order to claim this citizenship. In *Nguyen v. Immigration and Naturalization Service*, 533 U.S. 53 (2001), the Court decided that the status of mothers being easier to ascertain than that of fathers, Congress could establish stricter rules for individuals claiming citizenship through a father than through a mother. More recently, in *Torres v. Lynch*, 578 U.S. ___ (2016), the Court held that a lawful resident who came to the U.S. as a youth could be expelled from the U.S. for committing an aggravated felony.

Social scientists dispute whether undocumented immigrants chiefly take jobs from US citizens or whether they primarily take jobs that native US citizens would not, and the degree to which immigrants give back in taxes in comparison to their use of social services, like welfare, medical benefits, and education. Recent years have witnessed rising concern over the number of individuals who have come to the U.S. from Mexico and Central American countries without following proper immigration procedures, but Congress has to date been unable to craft a solution. At a time when some legislators have recommended extending citizenship to individuals who arrived in the United States as children, have been in the country for a number of years, have obeyed the laws, and who have joined the military or enrolled in college (the proposed Dream Act), President Donald Trump rose to national prominence by referring to many Mexican immigrants as "rapists and murderers" and by promising to deport illegal aliens and build a big wall to keep new ones out. His critique was launched at a time when several European countries were being swamped by a flood of refugees fleeing war and persecution in Libya, Syria, Afghanistan and neighboring nations and were facing increasing terrorist incidents often tied to their homelands.

Cognitively and Physically Impaired Persons

The legal status of cognitively and physically impaired persons has been statutorily protected since the passage of the Americans with Disabilities Act of 1990; the constitutional status of these groups under the Equal Protection Clause has been less clear. The Court has been unwilling to extend higher protective status to disabled individuals out of fear that the measure would constrain the state and federal governments from passing the forms of protective legislation they deem necessary. The case of *City of Cleburne, Texas v. Cleburne Living Center, Inc.* (473 U.S. 432, 1985) demonstrates that actions of the state designed to limit the involvement of disabled citizens will fail regular scrutiny if it is not tied to a clear governmental purpose. The Cleburne Living Center had attempted to establish a group home for the cognitively impaired in a residential community. Although the proposed home passed all city regulations, the Cleburne City Council required special hearing for such residential facilities like this group home; after a public hearing, the residential housing permit was denied. The Supreme Court found the denial of the permit to "rest on an irrational prejudice against the mentally retarded"; therefore, the city's decision did not pass the lowest level of equal protection scrutiny. The Court is clear in *City of Cleburne* that it will not extend to the mentally disabled an intermediate suspect classification with its concomitant higher standard of judicial review. In this case, the Court was unwilling to grant "quasi-suspect status" to the mentally disabled or to rely on intermediate or strict scrutiny to evaluate legislative action for its discriminatory impact on this group. The Supreme Court instead determined that basic scrutiny or the "rational relation" test would guard against invidious discrimination.

Sexual Orientation and Same-Sex Marriage

The evolution of sexual orientation as a protected status has been more intense than the corresponding progress of many citizenship groups; yet the Supreme Court has been very unwilling to use the Equal Protection Clause to address sexual orientation, preferring to rely on the Due Process Clause when possible. This stance may be partially due to a historic preference of the Court to perceive sexuality as a behavior, protected under the right of privacy, as opposed to an identity secured under the Equal Protection Clause. Many of the cases with which this chapter concludes are also discussed in volume one in the chapter on federalism.

As the 1986 case of *Bowers v. Hardwick* (478 U.S. 186) demonstrates, state laws formerly exhibited uniformity in their definitions of acceptable behavior. A Georgia law, passed in 1816, prohibited all sexual acts that were considered to be sodomy (oral and anal sex) regardless of the genders of the persons participating in the sexual activity; as written, the law applied to both heterosexual and homosexual couples. The private location of the activity or its consensual nature was irrelevant to the enforcement of the law. Although the Georgia statute applied to all couples, regardless of sexual orientation, the majority opinion in this case focused on whether there was a fundamental constitutional right for a gay person to engage in sexual acts characterized as "sodomy." The Court did note the evolution of social values regarding homosexual behavior: in 1961 all fifty states had criminalized sodomy; by 1986 only twenty-five states had such laws. Justice White, writing for the Court, emphasized that state legislatures needed to address this criminalization:

> Against this background, to claim that a right to engage in such conduct is "deeply rooted in this Nation's history and tradition" or "implicit in the concept of ordered liberty" is, at best, facetious. Nor are we inclined to take a more expansive view of our authority to discover new fundamental rights imbedded in the Due Process Clause. The Court is most vulnerable and comes nearest to illegitimacy when it deals with judge-made constitutional law having little or no cognizable roots in

> the language or design of the Constitution. There should be, therefore, great resistance to expand the substantive reach of those Clauses, particularly if it requires redefining the category of rights deemed to be fundamental. Otherwise, the Judiciary necessarily takes to itself further authority to govern the country without express constitutional authority. The claimed right pressed on us today falls far short of overcoming this resistance.

Because the Court found there was no fundamental right "to commit homosexual sodomy," the Georgia rule was allowed to stand. The dissenters in this case challenged the Court's characterization, noting that the case was about the larger right to privacy in light of the broad sweep of the law and its potential for selective enforcement.

In 1998 the state of Georgia reevaluated its own statute. In *Powell v. The State* (270 Ga. 327) the law was challenged as a violation of the right to privacy—not as a federally protected right, but as a value that had been guaranteed through the Georgia constitution and in Georgia case law. The Georgia Supreme Court noted that their decision to find the state sodomy statute unconstitutional was based not on its own "personal notions of morality," but on the observation that the law infringes on the constitutional standards of both Georgia and the United States. "While many believe that acts of sodomy, even those involving consenting adults, are morally reprehensible, this repugnance alone does not create a compelling justification for state regulation of the activity." For the dissenting opinion, the mere fact that the law had been perceived as constitutional for ninety years called into question the new discovery that this statute was now unconstitutional. Where should these types of changes occur—through the judiciary or through the legislature? At the federal level or within the states themselves?

A clear exception to the reliance on the Due Process Clause and state privacy protections was recorded in the 1996 Colorado case of *Romer v. Evans* (517 U.S. 620). This case developed in the wake of a 1992 state constitutional referendum labeled "Amendment 2," which arose from a series of municipal ordinances that had banned discrimination on the basis of sexual orientation in housing, employment, education, public accommodations, and health and welfare services. The amendment repealed all such ordinances and prohibited any state or local governmental action—whether executive, legislative, or judicial—designed to protect gays, lesbians, or bisexuals. The plaintiffs claimed that the enforcement of Amendment 2 exposed them to a substantial risk of discrimination.

While the state of Colorado claimed that the new amendment simply meant that all citizens would be treated the same, with none receiving special protections, the Supreme Court interpreted the amendment as separating out individuals on the basis of their sexual orientation: "The amendment withdraws from homosexuals, but no others, specific legal protection from the injuries caused by discrimination, and it forbids reinstatement of these laws and policies." Consequently, the Court found the referendum unconstitutional in that it appeared to have no state purpose besides animosity to a particular classification of people. The amendment failed even the most rudimentary scrutiny and was declared to have no rational relation to a legitimate governmental purpose. Despite recent rulings striking down discriminatory legislation against homosexuals, the Court has not applied a higher standard of protection to legislation regarding sexual orientation than that by which other forms of social legislation are evaluated.

After more than two decades, the Supreme Court returned to consider the issue initially addressed in *Bowers v. Hardwick* in the case of *Lawrence v. Texas* (539 U.S. 558, 2003). Unlike the Georgia statute, the Texas law prohibited sodomy only with an individual of the same sex; that is, it specifically targeted homosexual sexual behavior. Unlike *Bowers*, the Texas law was not challenged under the right to privacy; rather, a violation of the Equal Protection Clause of the constitutions of both the federal government and the state of was asserted. Because the Texas statute allowed the same behavior to be legally engaged in by heterosexual couples, it fell under the scope of equal protection case law, which requires that similarly situated groups be treated similarly under the law unless there is a valid reason by the state to differentiate.

The Court, under the Equal Protection Clause of the Fourteenth Amendment, has created a series of standards to evaluate the constitutionality of challenged statutes depending on who is targeted by the legislation. For instance, legislation that distinguishes on the basis of race is given the highest degree of scrutiny by the Court; legislation based on gender is given an intermediate degree of scrutiny; and legislation distinguishing between drivers of commercial trucks and drivers of passenger cars is given the lowest level of scrutiny. The Court has determined that such features as a history of invidious discrimination (targeted, focused discrimination based on hatred of the group) and the immutability of a group's characteristics help determine the degree of protection provided by the Constitution.

In *Romer*, the Court had considered a Colorado constitutional amendment that had prohibited municipalities from passing ordinances that banned discrimination based on sexual preference. In this case, the Court placed sexual orientation under the weakest standard of protection under the Equal Protection Clause and still found the amendment unconstitutional because it had no rational relationship to a legitimate governmental function. Thus the Court overturned *Bowers v. Hardwick* as incorrectly decided and on that ground ruled that the Texas statute was similarly unconstitutional. However, the Court did not determine if the Texas statute was unconstitutional on the basis of an equal protection violation. This left the law interestingly situated—clear that the right of privacy provides some protections against laws targeting sexual orientation, but not clear what type of protection the Equal Protection Clause provides for homosexuals, bisexuals, transgendered persons, or those with a non-binary sexual identity. This law will continue to evolve and develop, often with the states pushing for protections more expansive than those provided by the federal government.

One example of this phenomenon of state expansion of rights is seen in the law surrounding same-sex marriage and demonstrated by the Massachusetts Supreme Court decision of *Goodridge v. Department of Public Health* (440 Mass. 309, 2003). In this case, several same-sex couples sued the Massachusetts Department of Public Health for having denied them marriage licenses on the ground that the state did not then recognize same-sex marriages as legal. The majority opinion agreed that the Massachusetts law clearly defined marriage as being between a man and a woman only. The justices did not, however, believe that the state's rationale for this definition met the rational basis test (lowest level of scrutiny) for either the Due Process or the Equal Protection Clause. Consequently, the Court decided that the Massachusetts constitutional provisions of both individual liberty and equality required that "the protections, benefits, and obligations of civil marriage" be extended to same-sex couples. A few states have also passed laws legitimizing same-sex marriages or civil unions; several other states have provided spousal benefits to gay couples, in the absence of legal unions. In response to these changes in state law, more than half the states have modified their constitutions by means of what are called "Defense of Marriage" amendments, which limit the legal definition of marriage to unions between a man and a woman. In recent years, there has been a movement to adopt a federal constitutional amendment of the same nature. Since, however, the regulating and recording of marriages is traditionally reserved to the states, it is difficult to predict the grounds on which the federal government would assume the power to establish the parameters of the definition of marriage.

In 1996 the federal government did indeed make such an attempt. The Federal Defense of Marriage Act was initially passed in response to *Baehr v. Miike* (852 P.2d 44, 1993), a decision by the Hawaiian Supreme Court that found a Hawaiian statute limiting the definition of marriage to opposite-sex couples to be a violation of the Hawaiian Constitution's Equal Protection Clause. Although the state amended its constitution in 1998 to grant the state legislature the power to limit marriage to opposite-sex couples, which it did, Congress had already passed the Defense of Marriage Act. The federal law was designed to prevent the Equal Protection Clause and the Due Process Clause of the Fourteenth Amendment from being interpreted as forcing the federal government to expand the definition of marriage to same-sex couples (Section 1). It was also intended to ensure that any interpretation of the Full Faith and Credit Clause (Article IV, Section 1) of the Constitution could not be used to compel a state that does not allow same-sex marriage to recognize such marriages legitimized by another state (Section 2).

Subsequently, most state courts that extended the protection of marriage to same-sex couples relied upon their own state constitutions, not the federal Constitution. Over the next twenty years, the issue maintained its prominence as states wrestled with their own definitions of marriage in referendums, statehouses, and courthouses.

The 2013 case of *United States v. Windsor* (570 U.S. ___) raised the question of how the federal government could assume the power to define the parameters of the definition of marriage, which states had traditionally exercised. This decision allowed the Supreme Court to examine the constitutionality of the federal definition of marriage as limited to a male and female under the DOMA. While the Court found that the DOMA allowed states to define marriage as they desire, the federal definition controlled over 1,000 federal statutes and innumerable regulations. The President of the United States and the Justice department decided not to defend the constitutionality of this key part of the statute, and the Supreme Court found in the liberty interest of the Fifth Amendment protections of equal protection of the laws for those in legally sanctioned same-sex marriages. The Court framed this as a federalism case, noting "[t]he federal statute is invalid, for no legitimate purpose overcomes the purpose and effect to disparage and to injure those whom the State, by its marriage laws, sought to protect in personhood and dignity."

The dissenting opinions challenge this characterization of the DOMA; Chief Justice Roberts, in particular, notes that this very federalism argument should protect the diversity of state opinions on the matter of same-sex marriage, but he noted his fear that it would not. This concern arose in part around the debate in California that reached the Supreme Court at the same time. After the California Supreme Court found that the denial of same-sex couples the right to marry violated the California Constitution, the citizens passed Proposition 8, which amended the state constitution to preclude same-sex marriage. Between the time of the Supreme Court decision and Proposition 8, the state recorded many marriages and then suspended them until appeals could be heard in the federal courts. The federal courts eventually determined that Proposition 8 was not valid and same-sex marriages were constitutionally required in the state.

Similar complexities arose in the Sixth Circuit of the federal court of appeals, where state DOMA legislation prevented same-sex marriages, and several federal district court judges found such barriers to violate the Fourteenth Amendment. Claims from Michigan, Kentucky, Ohio, and Tennessee were consolidated and brought before the Supreme Court in *Obergefell v. Hodges* (576 U.S. ___, 2015). In his majority decision, Justice Kennedy emphasized that "[a]fter years of litigation, legislation, referenda, and the discussions that attended these public acts, the States are now divided on the issue of same-sex marriage."

In fact, despite the appellate court's concern that the issue should remain in the state legislatures for the time being, the majority argued that "[l]eaving the current state of affairs in place would maintain and promote instability and uncertainty." This point drew one of the strongest critiques from the dissenting opinions written by the multiple author combinations of Chief Justice Roberts and Justices Scalia, Thomas, and Alito. These opinions repeatedly argued that the federal courts' intervention "usurped" the "constitutional right" of states and citizens to define the institution of marriage. Justice Kennedy and the majority, on the other hand, emphasized that both liberty and equality interests were inherent in the question of same-sex marriage and that understandings of both concepts—as well as the institution of marriage—had evolved over time.

While the constitutional and federal definition of marriage has been resolved, questions involving sexuality and rights continue. Concerns regarding enforcement of these protections, the obligation of state and local employees to obey laws they believe challenge their religious understanding, and the First Amendment rights of religious institutions to define marriage for themselves continue. Questions of the rights afforded to transgendered populations and issues of sexual identity are currently being addressed under statutory law (e.g., Title VII of the Civil Rights Act of 1964 and in Title IX), but, like many contentious issues, will be constitutionally challenged at some future point.

Transgendered People and Gender Identity

While the laws protecting people who identify as lesbian, gay, or bisexual have had a longer history, only in the last several years have transgendered people and those challenging a binary sexual identity received significant federal legal attention. Within the United States, between .3 and .5 percent of the population identify as transgendered, translating into approximately 700,000 to 1 million individuals; however, violence against this population has been disproportionately high. In 2014, the FBI provided the first data on violence based on the victim's sexual identity; their findings reveal that while hate crimes had decreased over most categories, it had increased based on the sexual identity of the victim. Title VII of the Civil Rights Act of 1964 and Title IX of the Education Act of 1972 both ban discrimination based on "sex" and was interpreted by the Obama Administration as incorporating gender identity. As a consequence, federal agencies and some federal district and appellate courts have found discrimination against the transgendered to be an illegal form of sex discrimination in the workplace and in public schools. The Equal Employment Opportunity Commission (EEOC) issued its first ruling protecting transgendered individuals in 2012. In 2014, the EEOC provided public guidance to protect students who had experienced sexual violence based on their gender identity, and the Justice Department endorsed the EEOC's interpretation of Title IX.

Although transgendered activists have advocated for legal protections in employment, housing, and public accommodations (stores, hotels, transportation), a major focus has been in obtaining access to public restrooms that match their self-identified gender. This has proven to be politically controversial. After the city of Houston, Texas passed laws guaranteeing access to public restrooms, and college campuses provided gender-neutral bathrooms, voters in Houston overturned the ordinance with the articulated fear of men using women's restrooms for predatory purposes. Tennessee legislators considered laws that criminalize the use of restrooms designed for a gender not assigned at birth. The state of North Carolina passed a highly publicized law that requires transgendered persons from using the bathroom for the sex identified on their birth certificates. A number of other states attempted unsuccessfully to pass similar laws in 2015 and 2016.

In Spring 2016, the Obama Administration released a letter from the Education and Justice Departments to provide guidance to public schools to prevent discrimination against transgendered students by peer harassment or unlawful school policies, particularly related to bathroom policies. In response, nine states (Alabama, Georgia, Louisiana, Oklahoma, Tennessee, Texas, Utah, West Virginia, Wisconsin), a governor (Maine), and a state education department (Arizona) filed a federal lawsuit in Texas arguing that the Obama Administration was trying to revise Title IX through executive authority. In August, the federal district judge enjoined the Obama administration from enforcing the guidelines as they contradicted the current legislative text. In Illinois, in Fall 2016, a federal district judge ruled the other direction siding with the Department of Education's position. By February 2017, the new Trump Administration withdrew their support from these guidelines and from the federal litigation raising questions as to their position regarding the protection of transgendered students and gender identity under Title IX.

While these cases and others have been litigated in the lower federal courts, the Supreme Court has not engaged this issue directly until its 2016 term when it decided to rule on this question of the expansion of the federal regulations to transgendered public school students. *Gloucester County School Board v. GG* is a fourth circuit case in which a transgendered boy was originally allowed to use the boys' restroom in his Virginia public school until the school board created a policy requiring students to use the bathroom that corresponds to their biological gender or use a private bathroom. A divided appellate court found the board policy discriminatory and a trial judge ordered school officials to allow the litigant Gavin Grimm to use the bathroom. The Supreme Court had accepted this case for oral arguments in early 2017, but after the Trump Administration rescinded the federal guidelines the Court remanded the case back to the Fourth Circuit for consideration.

Poverty/Right to an Equal Education

The Court has not been willing to extend to the category "poverty" a blanket guarantee of heightened scrutiny. In fact, in many cases, particularly outside the issues of criminal procedures, the class of poverty has remained at a regular level of scrutiny. As for the right to an equal education from the state, the Court has made it very clear that it neither finds a constitutional guarantee regarding equality of education in the Fourteenth Amendment or a fundamental right to a public education specified in the U.S. Constitution. In Texas, funding of public education through the use of property taxes had resulted in a bifurcated system of education based on wealth, and consequently, race. In *San Antonio Independent School District v. Rodriguez* (411 U.S. 1, 1973), the plaintiffs compared the San Antonio area's least affluent district (Edgewood Independent School District: 90 percent Mexican American and 6 percent African American) to its most affluent district (Alamo Heights Independent School District: 18 percent Mexican American, less than 1 percent African American, the remaining students Anglo). The Edgewood district, based on assessed fees from property taxes, state dollars, and federal funds, spent $356 per pupil during the 1967–1968 school year, while the Alamo Heights district spent $594. The plaintiffs argued that this discrepancy resulted in a violation of the Equal Protection Clause. In its decision, the Supreme Court refused to apply a heightened level of scrutiny because the justices did not believe that the correlation between education and wealth could be used to support the assertion that the Equal Protection Clause mandated equal advantages or absolute equality.

One consequence of the *Rodriguez* case was the subsequent finding in the Texas courts that the state's school financing system was in violation of the state constitution (*Edgewood Independent School District v. Kirby,* 33 Tex. Sup. J. 12, 1989). Rather than ruling against the state funding system on equal protection grounds, however, the Texas justice cited Article VII, Section 1, of the Texas constitution, which requires an "efficient system of public free schools." The state court found that the enormous disparities in educational resources based on the relative wealth of the various districts conflicts with the state's mission "to educate its populace efficiently and provide for a general diffusion of knowledge statewide." Although the Supreme Court of the United States had ruled that the Texas statutory scheme was constitutional under the Equal Protection Clause of the Fourteenth Amendment, other states have challenged similar funding schemes under the various provisions of their respective constitutions. The *Edgewood Independent School District* decision is merely one of many similar cases.

Since its decision in *Rodriguez*, the Supreme Court has not revisited the finding that the Constitution implies no fundamental right to education. The Supreme Court has found a fundamental right to vote, the right to marry or divorce the person of the opposite sex of one's choice, the right to procedural fairness in the criminal process, and the right to run as a candidate for public office. On the other hand, the Court has made it clear that there is no fundamental right to education or to receive welfare payments (*Shapiro v. Thompson*, 394 U.S. 618, 1969).

Outside race and gender, the Court has been very unwilling to place vulnerable groups under any form of heightened review. Documented aliens and children born illegitimately have received greater protections; but the poor, the physically and mentally disabled, the mentally ill, and those whom the law has distinguished for their sexual orientation or gender identity have not. The Court has articulated different reasons for not providing stricter review of legislation disfavoring these groups, but it is clear that these cases will continue to confront the Court as discriminatory legislation is passed by the state and federal legislatures.

AMBACH V. NORWICK

441 U.S. 68, 99 S.Ct. 1589, 60 L.Ed.2d 49 (1979)

According to New York law, the state cannot certify as a public school teacher a person who is neither a U.S. citizen nor in the process of becoming one, as demonstrated by an announced intention to apply for citizenship. Without certification, a person may not teach in a public elementary or secondary school in the state. The appellees, Norwick and Dachinger, are respectively, British and Finnish citizens, long-term residents who married U.S. citizens but retained their home citizenship despite eligibility for U.S. citizenship. A three-judge district court held that the applicable statute, New York Education Law 3001(3), discriminated against aliens in violation of the Equal Protection Clause.

Vote: 5–4

JUSTICE POWELL delivered the opinion of the Court.

II

A

The decisions of this Court regarding the permissibility of statutory classifications involving aliens have not formed an unwavering line over the years. State regulation of the employment of aliens long has been subject to constitutional constraints. In *Yick Wo v. Hopkins*, 118 U.S. 356 (1886), the Court struck down an ordinance which was applied to prevent aliens from running laundries, and in *Truax v. Raich*, 239 U.S. 33 (1915), a law requiring at least 80% of the employees of certain businesses to be citizens was held to be an unconstitutional infringement of an alien's "right to work for a living in the common occupations of the community. . . ." At the same time, however, the Court also has recognized a greater degree of latitude for the States when aliens were sought to be excluded from public employment. Hence, as part of a larger authority to forbid aliens from owning land, *Frick v. Webb*, 263 U.S. 326 (1923); *Webb v. O'Brien*, 263 U.S. 313 (1923); *Porterfield v. Webb*, 263 U.S. 225 (1923); *Terrace v. Thompson*, 263 U.S. 197 (1923); *Blythe v. Hinckley*, 180 U.S. 333 (1901); *Hauenstein v. Lynham*, 100 U.S. 483 (1880); harvesting wildlife, *Patsone v. Pennsylvania*, 232 U.S. 138 (1914); *McCready v. Virginia*, 94 U.S. 391 (1877); or maintaining an inherently dangerous enterprise, *Ohio ex rel. Clarke v. Deckebach*, 274 U.S. 392 (1927), States permissibly could exclude aliens from working on public construction projects, *Crane v. New York*, 239 U.S. 195 (1915), and, it appears, from engaging in any form of public employment at all.

Over time, the Court's decisions gradually have restricted the activities from which States are free to exclude aliens. The first sign that the Court would question the constitutionality of discrimination against aliens even in areas affected with a "public interest" appeared in *Oyama v. California*, 332 U.S. 633 (1948). The Court there held that statutory presumptions designed to discourage evasion of California's ban on alien landholding discriminated against the citizen children of aliens. This process of withdrawal from the former doctrine culminated in *Graham v. Richardson*, which for the first time treated classifications based on alienage as "inherently suspect and subject to close judicial scrutiny." 403 U.S., at 372. Applying *Graham*, this Court has held invalid statutes that prevented aliens from entering a State's classified civil service, *Sugarman v. Dougall*, 413 U.S. 634 (1973), practicing law, *In re Griffiths*, 413 U.S. 717 (1973), working as an engineer, *Examining Board v. Flores de Otero*, 426 U.S. 572 (1976), and receiving state educational benefits, *Nyquist v. Mauclet*, 432 U.S. 1 (1977).

Although our more recent decisions have departed substantially from the public-interest doctrine of *Truax's* day, they have not abandoned the general principle that some state functions are so bound up with the operation of the State as a governmental entity as to permit the exclusion from those functions of all persons who have not become part of the process of self-government.

Applying the rational-basis standard, we held last Term that New York could exclude aliens from the ranks of its police force. *Foley v. Connelie*, 435 U.S. 291 (1978). Because the police function fulfilled "a most fundamental obligation of government to its constituency" and by necessity cloaked policemen with substantial discretionary powers, we viewed the police force as being one of those appropriately defined classes of positions for which a citizenship requirement could be imposed. Accordingly, the State was required to justify its classification only "by a showing of some rational relationship between the interest sought to be protected and the limiting classification."

The distinction between citizens and aliens, though ordinarily irrelevant to private activity, is fundamental to the definition and government of a State. The Constitution itself refers to the distinction no less than 11 times, indicating that the status of citizenship was meant to have significance in the structure of our government. It is because of this special significance of citizenship that governmental entities, when exercising the functions of government, have wider latitude in limiting the participation of noncitizens.

B

In determining whether, for purposes of equal protection analysis, teaching in public schools constitutes a governmental function, we look to the role of public education and to the degree of responsibility and discretion teachers possess in fulfilling that role.

The importance of public schools in the preparation of individuals for participation as citizens, and in the preservation of the values on which our society rests, long has been recognized by our decisions[.]

Within the public school system, teachers play a critical part in developing students' attitude toward government and understanding of the role of citizens in our society. Alone among employees of the system, teachers are in direct, day-to-day contact with students both in the classrooms and in the other varied activities of a modern school. In shaping the students' experience to achieve educational goals, teachers by necessity have wide discretion over the way the course material is communicated to students. They are responsible for presenting and explaining the subject matter in a way that is both comprehensible and inspiring. No amount of standardization of teaching materials or lesson plans can eliminate the personal qualities a teacher brings to bear in achieving these goals. Further, a teacher serves as a role model for his students, exerting a subtle but important influence over their perceptions and values. Thus, through both the presentation of course materials and the example he sets, a teacher has an opportunity to influence the attitudes of students toward government, the political process, and a citizen's social responsibilities. This influence is crucial to the continued good health of a democracy.

Furthermore, it is clear that all public school teachers, and not just those responsible for teaching the courses most directly related to government, history, and civic duties, should help fulfill the broader function of the public school system. More importantly, a State properly may regard all teachers as having an obligation to promote civic virtues and understanding in their classes, regardless of the subject taught. In light of the foregoing considerations, we think it clear that public school teachers come well within the "governmental function" principle recognized in *Sugarman* and *Foley*. Accordingly, the Constitution requires only that a citizenship requirement applicable to teaching in the public schools bear a rational relationship to a legitimate state interest.

III

As the legitimacy of the State's interest in furthering the educational goals outlined above is undoubted, it remains only to consider whether 3001 (3) bears a rational relationship to this interest. The restriction is carefully framed to serve its purpose, as it bars from teaching only those aliens who have demonstrated their unwillingness to obtain United States citizenship. Appellees, and aliens similarly situated, in effect have chosen to classify themselves. They prefer to retain citizenship in a foreign country with the obligations it entails of primary duty and loyalty. They have rejected the open invitation extended to qualify for eligibility to teach by applying for citizenship in this country. The people of New York, acting through their elected representatives, have made a judgment that citizenship should be a qualification for teaching the young of the State in the public schools, and 3001 (3) furthers that judgment. Reversed.

JUSTICE BLACKMUN, with whom JUSTICES BRENNAN, MARSHALL, and STEVENS join, dissenting.

Once again the Court is asked to rule upon the constitutionality of one of New York's many statutes that impose a requirement of citizenship upon a person before that person may earn his living in a specified occupation. These New York statutes, for the most part, have their origin in the frantic and overreactive days of the First World War when attitudes of parochialism and fear of the foreigner were the order of the day.

As the Court acknowledges, its decisions regarding the permissibility of statutory classifications concerning aliens "have not formed an unwavering line over the years." Thus, just last Term, in *Foley v. Connelie*, 435 U.S. 291 (1978), the Court upheld against equal protection challenge the New York statute limiting appointment of members of the state police force to citizens of the United States. The touchstone, the Court indicated, was that citizenship may be a relevant qualification for fulfilling " 'important nonelective executive, legislative, and judicial positions' held by 'officers who participate directly in the formulation, execution, or review of broad public policy.' " Id., at 296, quoting *Sugarman v. Dougall*, 413 U.S. 634, 647 (1973). For such positions, a State need show only some rational relationship between the interest sought to be protected and the limiting classification. The propriety of making citizenship a qualification for a narrowly defined class of positions was also recognized, in passing, in *Sugarman v. Dougall*, and in *Nyquist v. Mauclet*, 432 U.S. 1, 11 (1977).

On the other hand, the Court frequently has invalidated a state provision that denies a resident alien the right to engage in specified occupational activity: *Yick Wo v. Hopkins*, 118 U.S. 356 (1886) (ordinance applied so as to prevent Chinese subjects from engaging in the laundry business); *Truax v. Raich*, 239 U.S. 33 (1915) (statute requiring an employer's work force to be composed of not less than 80% "qualified electors or native-born citizens"); *Takahashi v. Fish & Game Comm'n*, 334 U.S. 410 (1948) (limitation of commercial fishing licenses to persons not "ineligible to citizenship"); *Sugarman v. Dougall* (New York statute relating to permanent positions in the "competitive class" of the state civil service); *In re Griffiths*, 413 U.S. 717 (1973) (the practice of law); *Nelson v. Miranda*, 413 U.S. 902 (1973), (social service worker and teacher); *Examining Board v. Flores de Otero*, 426 U.S. 572 (1976) (the practice of civil engineering).

Indeed, the Court has held more than once that state classifications based on alienage are "inherently suspect and subject to close judicial scrutiny." *Graham v. Richardson*, 403 U.S. 365, 372 (1971). And "[a]lienage classifications by a State that do not withstand this stringent examination cannot stand."

There is thus a line, most recently recognized in *Foley v. Connelie*, between those employments that a State in its wisdom constitutionally may restrict to United States citizens, on the one hand, and those employments, on the other, that the State may not deny to resident aliens. For me, the present case falls on the *Sugarman-Griffiths-Flores de Otero-Mauclet* side of that line, rather than on the narrowly isolated Foley side.

But the Court, to the disadvantage of appellees, crosses the line from *Griffiths* to *Foley* by saying, that the "distinction between citizens and aliens, though ordinarily irrelevant to private activity, is fundamental to the definition and government of a State." It then concludes that public school teaching "constitutes a governmental function," and that public school teachers may be regarded as performing a task that goes "to the heart of representative government." The Court speaks of the importance of public schools in the preparation of individuals for participation as citizens, and in the preservation of the values on which our society rests. After then observing that teachers play a critical part in all this, the Court holds that New York's citizenship requirement is constitutional because it bears a rational relationship to the State's interest in furthering these educational goals.

I perceive a number of difficulties along the easy road the Court takes to this conclusion:

First, the New York statutory structure itself refutes the argument. Section 3001 (3), the very statute at issue here, provides for exceptions with respect to alien teachers "employed pursuant to regulations adopted by the commissioner of education permitting such employment."

Second, the New York statute is all-inclusive in its disqualifying provisions: "No person shall be employed or authorized to teach in the public schools of the state who is . . . [n]ot a citizen." It sweeps indiscriminately. It is "neither narrowly confined nor precise in its application," nor limited to the accomplishment of substantial state interests. *Sugarman v. Dougall*, 413 U.S., at 643.

Third, the New York classification is irrational. The route to "diverse and conflicting elements" and their being "brought together on a broad but common ground," which the Court so emphasizes, is hardly to be achieved by disregarding some of the diverse elements that are available, competent, and contributory to the richness of our society and of the education it could provide.

Fourth, it is logically impossible to differentiate between this case concerning teachers and *In re Griffiths* concerning attorneys. One may speak proudly of the role model of the teacher, of his ability to mold young minds, of his inculcating force as to national ideals, and of his profound influence in the impartation of our society's values. Are the attributes of an attorney any the less?

If an attorney has a constitutional right to take a bar examination and practice law, despite his being a resident alien, it is impossible for me to see why a resident alien, otherwise completely competent and qualified, as these appellees concededly are, is constitutionally disqualified from teaching in the public schools of the great State of New York. I respectfully dissent.

FOR DISCUSSION

What criteria might the Court consider in determining when a position meets an important public function? How might a state craft legislation to ensure that its classification on the basis of citizenship will withstand constitutional scrutiny?

RELATED CASES

***Sugarman v. Dougall:* 413 U.S. 634 (1973).**

The Court found that the Equal Protection Clause prohibits the state of New York from denying to aliens jobs with the state.

***Hampton v. Mow Sun Wong:* 426 U.S. 88 (1976).**

The substantive right of equal justice guaranteed by the Fifth Amendment's Due Process Clause prevents the federal government from excluding noncitizens (or natives of Samoa) from employment in civil service.

PLYLER V. DOE

457 U.S. 202, 102 S.Ct. 2382, 72 L.Ed.2d 786 (1982)

In 1975 the Texas legislature revised state law § 21.031 to prohibit the state funding of education for children who had not been legally admitted to the United States; local school boards were also authorized to deny enrollment in public schools to these children. The Court here combined two challenges to the new statute. *Plyler v. Doe* was a class action brought by parents of children of Mexican origin who had been excluded from the Tyler Independent School District. The federal court located in the Eastern District of Texas held that illegal aliens were entitled to the protection of the Equal Protection Clause of the Fourteenth Amendment and that the Texas law was in violation. The court of appeals upheld the district court on this determination. *In re Alien Children Education Litigation* was a consolidation of a number of challenges from the other sections of Texas against the same state legislation. The federal court for the Southern District of Texas also found § 21.031 in violation of the Equal Protection Clause of the Fourteenth Amendment. The appellate court affirmed.

Vote: 5–4

JUSTICE BRENNAN delivered the opinion of the Court.

II

The Fourteenth Amendment provides that "[no] State shall . . . deprive any person of life, liberty, or property, without due process of law; nor deny to any person within its jurisdiction the equal protection of the laws." Appellants argue at the outset that undocumented aliens, because of their immigration status, are not "persons within the jurisdiction" of the State of Texas, and that they therefore have no right to the equal protection of Texas law. We reject this argument. Whatever his status under the immigration laws, an alien is surely a "person" in any ordinary sense of that term. Aliens, even aliens whose presence in this country is unlawful, have long been recognized as "persons" guaranteed due process of law by the Fifth and Fourteenth Amendments. *Shaughnessy v. Mezei*, 345 U.S. 206, 212 (1953); *Wong Wing v. United States*, 163 U.S. 228, 238 (1896); *Yick Wo v. Hopkins*, 118 U.S. 356, 369 (1886). Indeed, we have clearly held that the Fifth Amendment protects aliens whose presence in this country is unlawful from invidious discrimination by the Federal Government. *Mathews v. Diaz*, 426 U.S. 67, 77 (1976).

Appellants seek to distinguish our prior cases, emphasizing that the Equal Protection Clause directs a State to afford its protection to persons within its jurisdiction while the Due Process Clauses of the Fifth and Fourteenth Amendments contain no such assertedly limiting phrase. In appellants' view, persons who have entered the United States illegally are not "within the jurisdiction" of a State even if they are present within a State's boundaries and subject to its laws. Neither our cases nor the logic of the Fourteenth Amendment supports that constricting construction of the phrase "within its jurisdiction."

There is simply no support for appellants' suggestion that "due process" is somehow of greater stature than "equal protection" and therefore available to a larger class of persons. To the contrary, each aspect of the Fourteenth Amendment reflects an elementary limitation on state power. To permit a State to employ the phrase "within its jurisdiction" in order to identify subclasses of persons whom it would define as beyond its jurisdiction, thereby relieving itself of the obligation to assure that its laws are designed and applied equally to those persons, would undermine the principal purpose for which the Equal Protection Clause was incorporated in the Fourteenth Amendment. The Equal Protection Clause was intended to work nothing less than the abolition of all caste-based and invidious class-based legislation. That objective is fundamentally at odds with the power the State asserts here to classify persons subject to its laws as nonetheless excepted from its protection.

Our conclusion that the illegal aliens who are plaintiffs in these cases may claim the benefit of the Fourteenth Amendment's guarantee of equal protection only begins the inquiry. The more difficult question is whether the Equal Protection Clause has been violated by the refusal of the State of Texas to reimburse local school boards for the education of children who cannot demonstrate that their presence within the United States is lawful, or by the imposition by those school boards of the burden of tuition on those children. It is to this question that we now turn.

III

B

Undocumented aliens cannot be treated as a suspect class because their presence in this country in violation of federal law is not a "constitutional irrelevancy." Nor is education a fundamental right; a State need not justify by compelling necessity every variation in the manner in which education is provided to its population. But more is involved in these cases than the abstract question whether § 21.031 discriminates against a suspect class, or whether education is a fundamental right. Section 21.031 imposes a lifetime hardship on a discrete class of children not accountable for their disabling status. The stigma of illiteracy will mark them for the rest of their lives. By denying these children a basic education, we deny them the ability to live within the structure of our civic institutions, and foreclose any realistic possibility that they will contribute in even the smallest way to the progress of our Nation. In determining the rationality of § 21.031, we may appropriately take into account its costs to the Nation and to the innocent children who are its victims. In light of these countervailing costs, the discrimination contained in § 21.031 can hardly be considered rational unless it furthers some substantial goal of the State.

IV

It is the State's principal argument, and apparently the view of the dissenting Justices, that the undocumented status of these children [or not] establishes a sufficient rational basis for denying them benefits that a State might choose to afford other residents. Indeed, in the State's view, Congress' apparent disapproval of the presence of these children within the United States, and the evasion of the federal regulatory program that is the mark of undocumented status, provides authority for its decision to impose upon them special disabilities. Faced with an equal protection challenge respecting the treatment of aliens, we agree that the courts must be attentive to congressional policy; the exercise of congressional power might well affect the State's prerogatives to afford differential treatment to a particular class of aliens. But we are unable to find in the congressional immigration scheme any statement of policy that might weigh significantly in arriving at an equal protection balance concerning the State's authority to deprive these children of an education.

As we recognized in *De Canas v. Bica*, 424 U.S. 351 (1976), the States do have some authority to act with respect to illegal aliens, at least where such action mirrors federal objectives and furthers a legitimate state goal. In contrast, there is no indication that the disability imposed by § 21.031 corresponds to any identifiable congressional policy. The State does not claim that the conservation of state educational resources was ever a congressional concern in restricting immigration. More importantly, the classification reflected in § 21.031 does not operate harmoniously within the federal program.

V

Appellants argue that the classification at issue furthers an interest in the "preservation of the state's limited resources for the education of its lawful residents." Of course, a concern for the preservation of resources standing alone can hardly justify the classification used in allocating those resources. *Graham v. Richardson*, 403 U.S. 365, 374–375 (1971). The State must do more than justify its classification with a concise expression of an intention to discriminate. Apart from the asserted state prerogative to act against undocumented children solely on the basis of their undocumented status—an asserted prerogative that carries only minimal force in the circumstances of these cases—we discern three colorable state interests that might support § 21.031.

First, appellants appear to suggest that the State may seek to protect itself from an influx of illegal immigrants. While a State might have an interest in mitigating the potentially harsh economic effects of sudden shifts in population, § 21.031 hardly offers an effective method of dealing with an urgent demographic or economic problem. There is no evidence in the record suggesting that illegal entrants impose any significant burden on the State's economy.

Second, while it is apparent that a State may "not . . . reduce expenditures for education by barring [some arbitrarily chosen class of] children from its schools," *Shapiro v. Thompson*, 394 U.S. 618, 633 (1969), appellants suggest that undocumented children are appropriately singled out for exclusion because of the special burdens they impose on the State's ability to provide high-quality public education. But the record in no way supports the claim that exclusion of undocumented children is likely to improve the overall quality of education in the State.

Finally, appellants suggest that undocumented children are appropriately singled out because their unlawful presence within the United States renders them less likely than other children to remain within the boundaries of the State, and to put their education to productive social or political use within the State. Even assuming that such an interest is legitimate, it is an interest that is most difficult to quantify. In any event, the record is clear that many of the undocumented children disabled by this classification will remain in this country indefinitely, and that some will become lawful residents or citizens of the United States. It is difficult to understand precisely what the State hopes to achieve by promoting the creation and perpetuation of a subclass of illiterates within our boundaries, surely adding to the problems and costs of unemployment, welfare, and crime.

VI

If the State is to deny a discrete group of innocent children the free public education that it offers to other children residing within its borders, that denial must be justified by a showing that it furthers some substantial state interest. No such showing was made here. Accordingly, the judgment of the Court of Appeals in each of these cases is Affirmed.

JUSTICE MARSHALL, concurring.

While I join the Court opinion, I do so without in any way retreating from my opinion in *San Antonio Independent School District v. Rodriguez*, 411 U.S. 1, 70–133 (1973) (dissenting). I continue to believe that an individual's interest in education is fundamental, and that this view is amply supported "by the unique status accorded public education by our society, and by the close relationship between education and some of our most basic constitutional values." Furthermore, I believe that the facts of these cases demonstrate the wisdom of rejecting a rigidified approach to equal protection analysis, and of employing an approach that allows for varying levels of scrutiny depending upon "the constitutional and societal importance of the interest adversely affected and the recognized invidiousness of the basis upon which the particular classification is drawn." It continues to be my view that a class-based denial of public education is utterly incompatible with the Equal Protection Clause of the Fourteenth Amendment.

JUSTICE BLACKMUN, concurring.

I join the opinion and judgment of the Court.

I write separately, however, because in my view the nature of the interest at stake is crucial to the proper resolution of these cases.

In my view, when the State provides an education to some and denies it to others, it immediately and inevitably creates class distinctions of a type fundamentally inconsistent with those purposes, mentioned above, of the Equal Protection Clause. Children denied an education are placed at a permanent and insurmountable competitive disadvantage, for an uneducated child is denied even the opportunity to achieve. And when those children are members of an identifiable group, that group—through the State's action—will have been converted into a discrete underclass.

But classifications involving the complete denial of education are in a sense unique, for they strike at the heart of equal protection values by involving the State in the creation of permanent class distinctions. In a sense, then, denial of an education is the analogue of denial of the right to vote: the former relegates the individual to second-class social status; the latter places him at a permanent political disadvantage.

This conclusion is fully consistent with *San Antonio Independent School District v. Rodriguez*, 911 U.S. 1 (1973). The Court there reserved judgment on the constitutionality of a state system that "occasioned an absolute denial of educational opportunities to any of its children," noting that "no charge fairly could be made that the system [at issue in *Rodriguez*] fails to provide each child with an opportunity to acquire . . . basic minimal skills." . . . *Rodriguez* held, and the Court now reaffirms, that "a State need not justify by compelling necessity every variation in the manner in which education is provided to its population." Similarly, it is undeniable that education is not a "fundamental right" in the sense that it is constitutionally guaranteed. Here, however, the State has undertaken to provide an education to most of the children residing within its borders. And, in contrast to the situation in *Rodriguez*, it does not take an advanced degree to predict the effects of a complete denial of education upon those children targeted by the State's classification. In such circumstances, the voting decisions suggest that the State must offer something more than a rational basis for its classification.

Because I believe that the Court's carefully worded analysis recognizes the importance of the equal protection and preemption interests I consider crucial, I join its opinion as well as its judgment.

JUSTICE POWELL, concurring.

I join the opinion of the Court, and write separately to emphasize the unique character of the cases before us.

The classification at issue deprives a group of children of the opportunity for education afforded all other children simply because they have been assigned a legal status due to a violation of law by their parents. These children thus have been singled out for a lifelong penalty and stigma. A legislative classification that threatens the creation of an underclass of future citizens and residents cannot be reconciled with one of the fundamental purposes of the Fourteenth Amendment. In these unique circumstances, the Court properly may require that the State's interests be substantial and that the means bear a "fair and substantial relation" to these interests.

In my view, the State's denial of education to these children bears no substantial relation to any substantial state interest. Both of the District Courts found that an uncertain but significant percentage of illegal alien children will remain in Texas as residents and many eventually will become citizens. One need not go so far to conclude that the exclusion of appellees' class of children from state-provided education is a type of punitive discrimination based on status that is impermissible under the Equal Protection Clause.

In reaching this conclusion, I am not unmindful of what must be the exasperation of responsible citizens and government authorities in Texas and other States similarly situated. Their responsibility, if any, for the influx of aliens is slight compared to that imposed by the Constitution on the Federal Government. So long as the ease of entry remains inviting, and the power to deport is exercised infrequently by the Federal Government, the additional expense of admitting these children to public schools might fairly be shared by the Federal and State Governments. But it hardly can be argued rationally that anyone benefits from the creation within our borders of a subclass of illiterate persons many of whom will remain in the State, adding to the problems and costs of both State and National Governments attendant upon unemployment, welfare, and crime.

CHIEF JUSTICE BURGER, with whom JUSTICES WHITE, REHNQUIST, and O'CONNOR join, dissenting.

Were it our business to set the Nation's social policy, I would agree without hesitation that it is senseless for an enlightened society to deprive any children—including illegal aliens—of an elementary education. I fully agree that it would be folly—and wrong—to tolerate creation of a segment of society made up of illiterate persons, many having a limited or no command of our language. However, the Constitution does not constitute us as "Platonic Guardians" nor does it vest in this Court the authority to strike down laws because they do not meet our standards of desirable social policy, "wisdom," or "common sense." We trespass on the assigned function of the political branches under our structure of limited and separated powers when we assume a policymaking role as the Court does today.

The Court makes no attempt to disguise that it is acting to make up for Congress' lack of "effective leadership" in dealing with the serious national problems caused by the influx of uncountable millions of illegal aliens across our borders. The failure of enforcement of the immigration laws over more than a decade and the inherent difficulty and expense of sealing our vast borders have combined to create a grave socioeconomic dilemma. It is a dilemma that has not yet even been fully assessed, let alone addressed. However, it is not the function of the Judiciary to provide "effective leadership" simply because the political branches of government fail to do so.

The Court's holding today manifests the justly criticized judicial tendency to attempt speedy and wholesale formulation of "remedies" for the failures—or simply the laggard pace—of the political processes of our system of government. The Court employs, and in my view abuses, the Fourteenth Amendment in an effort to become an omnipotent and omniscient problem solver. That the motives for doing so are noble and compassionate does not alter the fact that the Court distorts our constitutional function to make amends for the defaults of others.

B

Once it is conceded—as the Court does—that illegal aliens are not a suspect class, and that education is not a fundamental right, our inquiry should focus on and be limited to whether the legislative classification at issue bears a rational relationship to a legitimate state purpose. *Vance v. Bradley*, 440 U.S. 93, 97 (1979); *Dandridge v. Williams*, 397 U.S. 471, 485–487 (1970).

The State contends primarily that § 21.031 serves to prevent undue depletion of its limited revenues available for education, and to preserve the fiscal integrity of the State's school-financing system against an ever-increasing flood of illegal aliens—aliens over whose entry or continued presence it has no control. Of course such fiscal concerns alone could not justify discrimination against a suspect class or an arbitrary and irrational denial of benefits to a particular group of persons. Yet I assume no Member of this Court would argue that prudent conservation of finite state revenues is per se an illegitimate goal. The significant question here is whether the requirement of tuition from illegal aliens who attend the public schools—as well as from residents of other states, for example—is a rational and reasonable means of furthering the State's legitimate fiscal ends.

Without laboring what will undoubtedly seem obvious to many, it simply is not "irrational" for a state to conclude that it does not have the same responsibility to provide benefits for persons whose very presence in the state and this country is illegal as it does to provide for persons lawfully present. By definition, illegal aliens have no right whatever to be here, and the state may reasonably, and constitutionally, elect not to provide them with governmental services at the expense of those who are lawfully in the state. In *De Canas v. Bica*, 424 U.S. 351, 357 (1976), we held that a State may protect its "fiscal interests and lawfully resident labor force from the deleterious effects on its economy resulting from the employment of illegal aliens." The Court has failed to offer even a plausible explanation why illegality of residence in this country is not a factor that may legitimately bear upon the bona fides of state residence and entitlement to the benefits of lawful residence.

II

The Constitution does not provide a cure for every social ill, nor does it vest judges with a mandate to try to remedy every social problem. Moreover, when this Court rushes in to remedy what it perceives to be the failings of the political processes, it deprives those processes of an opportunity to function. When the political institutions are not forced to exercise constitutionally allocated powers and responsibilities, those powers, like muscles not used, tend to atrophy. Today's cases, I regret to say, present yet another example of unwarranted judicial action which in the long run tends to contribute to the weakening of our political processes.

The solution to this seemingly intractable problem is to defer to the political processes, unpalatable as that may be to some.

FOR DISCUSSION

Why does it matter to the Court that these are children of undocumented aliens? What substantial state interest could Texas claim to justify the exclusionary legislation? Would a finding of substantial state interest satisfy the Equal Protection Clause?

RELATED CASES

Graham v. Richardson: **403 U.S. 465 (1971).**

The Supreme Court determined that alien status falls under suspect classification with respect to the Equal Protection Clause; here, Arizona's limitations of welfare benefits based on citizenship was found to violate the clause.

Nyquist v. Mauclet: **432 U.S. 1 (1977).**

Court found unconstitutional a New York law that limited state scholarships and financial aid to citizens and denied access to such assistance to resident aliens.

Toll v. Moreno: **458 U.S. 1 (1982).**

The Supreme Court found that a Maryland law that denied in-state tuition rates at state institutions to nonimmigrant aliens who held federal visas and were state residents violated federal policy. Consequently, the Court found the state law invalid under the Supremacy Clause.

CITY OF CLEBURNE, TEXAS V. CLEBURNE LIVING CENTER, INC.

473 U.S. 432, 105 S.Ct. 3249, 87 L.Ed. 2d 313 (1985)

Cleburne Living Center, Inc. (CLC) sought to lease a building to serve as a group home for thirteen mentally handicapped men and women. The residents would be under live-in supervision by CLC staff. The organization was in compliance with all state and federal laws. The City of Cleburne required a special-use permit for the facility because of its contemplated use, although no special permit was necessary for residential facilities of other types. An application was submitted and a public hearing was held, after which the city council denied the special-use permit. The CLC went to federal court, alleging that the zoning ordinance requiring such a permit was unconstitutional because it discriminated against the mentally handicapped in violation of the Equal Protection Clause of the Fourteenth Amendment. The district court upheld the Cleburne ordinance as constitutional.

Vote: 6–3

JUSTICE WHITE delivered the opinion of the Court.

The Court of Appeals for the Fifth Circuit held that mental retardation is a "quasi-suspect" classification and that the ordinance violated the Equal Protection Clause because it did not substantially further an important governmental purpose. We hold that a lesser standard of scrutiny is appropriate, but conclude that under that standard the ordinance is invalid as applied in this case.

II

The Equal Protection Clause of the Fourteenth Amendment commands that no State shall "deny to any person within its jurisdiction the equal protection of the laws," which is essentially a direction that all persons similarly situated should be treated alike. *Plyler v. Doe*, 457 U.S. 202, 216 (1982). Section 5 of the Amendment empowers Congress to enforce this mandate, but absent controlling congressional direction, the courts have themselves devised standards for determining the validity of state legislation or other official action that is challenged as denying equal protection. The general rule is that legislation is presumed to be valid and will be sustained if the classification drawn by the statute is rationally related to a legitimate state interest. *Schweiker v. Wilson*, 450 U.S. 221, 230 (1981); *United States Railroad Retirement Board v. Fritz*, 449 U.S. 166, 174–175 (1980); *Vance v. Bradley*, 440 U.S. 93, 97 (1979); *New Orleans v. Dukes*, 427 U.S. 297, 303 (1976).

The general rule gives way, however, when a statute classifies by race, alienage, or national origin. These factors are so seldom relevant to the achievement of any legitimate state interest that laws grounded in such considerations are deemed to reflect prejudice and antipathy—a view that those in the burdened class are not as worthy or deserving as others. For these reasons and because such discrimination is unlikely to be soon rectified by legislative means, these laws are subjected to strict scrutiny and will be sustained only if they are suitably tailored to serve a compelling state interest. *McLaughlin v. Florida*, 379 U.S. 184, 192 (1964); *Graham v. Richardson*, 403 U.S. 365 (1971). Similar oversight by the courts is due when state laws impinge on personal rights protected by the Constitution.

Legislative classifications based on gender also call for a heightened standard of review. That factor generally provides no sensible ground for differential treatment. "[What] differentiates sex from such nonsuspect statuses as intelligence or physical disability . . . is that the sex characteristic frequently bears no relation to ability to perform or contribute to society." *Frontiero v. Richardson*, 411 U.S. 677, 686 (1973) (plurality opinion). Rather than resting on meaningful considerations, statutes distributing benefits and burdens between the sexes in different ways very likely reflect outmoded notions of the relative capabilities of men and women. A gender classification fails unless it is substantially related to a sufficiently important governmental interest. *Mississippi University for Women v. Hogan*, 458 U.S. 718 (1982); *Craig v. Boren*, 429 U.S. 190 (1976). Those restrictions "will survive equal protection scrutiny to the extent they are substantially related to a legitimate state interest." *Mills v. Habluetzel*, 456 U.S. 91, 99 (1982).

The lesson of [*Massachusetts Board of Retirement v.*] *Murgia* [427 U.S. 307 (1976)] is that where individuals in the group affected by a law have distinguishing characteristics relevant to interests the State has the authority to implement, the courts have been very reluctant, as they should be in our federal system and with our respect for the separation of powers, to closely scrutinize legislative choices as to whether, how, and to what extent those interests should be pursued. In such cases, the Equal Protection Clause requires only a rational means to serve a legitimate end.

III

Against this background, we conclude for several reasons that the Court of Appeals erred in holding mental retardation a quasi-suspect classification calling for a more exacting standard of judicial review than is normally accorded economic and social legislation. First, it is undeniable, and it is not argued otherwise here, that those who are mentally retarded have a reduced ability to cope with and function in the everyday world. How this large and diversified group is to be treated under the law is a difficult and often a technical matter, very much a task for legislators guided by qualified professionals and not by the perhaps ill-informed opinions of the judiciary. Heightened scrutiny inevitably involves substantive judgments about legislative decisions, and we doubt that the predicate for such judicial oversight is present where the classification deals with mental retardation.

Second, the distinctive legislative response, both national and state, to the plight of those who are mentally retarded demonstrates not only that they have unique problems, but also that the lawmakers have been addressing their difficulties in a manner that belies a continuing antipathy or prejudice and a corresponding need for more intrusive oversight by the judiciary.

Such legislation thus singling out the retarded for special treatment reflects the real and undeniable differences between the retarded and others. That a civilized and decent society expects and approves such legislation indicates that governmental consideration of those differences in the vast majority of situations is not only legitimate but also desirable. It may be, as CLC contends, that legislation designed to benefit, rather than disadvantage, the retarded would generally withstand examination under a test of heightened scrutiny. The relevant inquiry, however, is whether heightened scrutiny is constitutionally mandated in the first instance.

Third, the legislative response, which could hardly have occurred and survived without public support, negates any claim that the mentally retarded are politically powerless in the sense that they have no ability to attract the attention of the lawmakers. Any minority can be said to be powerless to assert direct control over the legislature, but if that were a criterion for higher level scrutiny by the courts, much economic and social legislation would now be suspect.

Fourth, if the large and amorphous class of the mentally retarded were deemed quasi-suspect for the reasons given by the Court of Appeals, it would be difficult to find a principled way to distinguish a variety of other groups who have perhaps immutable disabilities setting them off from others, who cannot themselves mandate the desired legislative responses, and who can claim some degree of prejudice from at least part of the public at large.

Our refusal to recognize the retarded as a quasi-suspect class does not leave them entirely unprotected from invidious discrimination. To withstand equal protection review, legislation that distinguishes between the mentally retarded and others must be rationally related to a legitimate governmental purpose. This standard, we believe, affords government the latitude necessary both to pursue policies designed to assist the retarded in realizing their full potential, and to freely and efficiently engage in activities that burden the retarded in what is essentially an incidental manner. The State may not rely on a classification whose relationship to an asserted goal is so attenuated as to render the distinction arbitrary or irrational.

IV

The constitutional issue is clearly posed. The city does not require a special use permit . . . for apartment houses, multiple dwellings, boarding and lodging houses, fraternity or sorority houses, dormitories, apartment hotels, hospitals, sanitariums, nursing homes for convalescents or the aged (other than for the insane or feebleminded or alcoholics or drug addicts), private clubs or fraternal orders, and other specified uses. It does, however, insist on a special permit for the Featherston home, and it does so, as the District Court found, because it would be a facility for the mentally retarded. May the city require the permit for this facility when other care and multiple-dwelling facilities are freely permitted?

The District Court found that the City Council's insistence on the permit rested on several factors. First, the Council was concerned with the negative attitude of the majority of property owners located within 200 feet of the [CLC] facility, as well as with the fears of elderly residents of the neighborhood. But mere negative attitudes, or fear, unsubstantiated by factors which are properly cognizable in a zoning proceeding, are not permissible bases for treating a home for the mentally retarded differently from apartment houses, multiple dwellings, and the like.

Second, the Council had two objections to the location of the facility. It was concerned that the facility was across the street from a junior high school, and it feared that the students might harass the occupants of the [CLC] home. But the school itself is attended by about 30 mentally retarded students, and denying a permit based on such vague, undifferentiated fears is again permitting some portion of the community to validate what would otherwise be an equal protection violation. The other objection to the home's location was that it was located on "a five hundred year flood plain." This concern with the possibility of a flood, however, can hardly be based on a distinction between the [CLC] home and, for example, nursing homes, homes for convalescents or the aged, or sanitariums or hospitals, any of which could be located on the [CLC] site without obtaining a special use permit. The same may be said of another concern of the Council—doubts about the legal responsibility for actions which the mentally retarded might take.

Fourth, the Council was concerned with the size of the home and the number of people that would occupy it. The District Court found, and the Court of Appeals repeated, that "[if] the potential residents of the [CLC] home were not mentally retarded, but the home was the same in all other respects, its use would be permitted under the city's zoning ordinance."

The short of it is that requiring the permit in this case appears to us to rest on an irrational prejudice against the mentally retarded, including those who would occupy the [CLC] facility and who would live under the closely supervised and highly regulated conditions expressly provided for by state and federal law.

The judgment of the Court of Appeals is affirmed insofar as it invalidates the zoning ordinance as applied to the [CLC] home. The judgment is otherwise vacated, and the case is remanded.

JUSTICE STEVENS, with whom CHIEF JUSTICE BURGER joins, concurring.

The Court of Appeals disposed of this case as if a critical question to be decided were which of three clearly defined standards of equal protection review should be applied to a legislative classification discriminating against the mentally retarded. In fact, our cases have not delineated three—or even one or two—such well-defined standards. Rather, our cases reflect a continuum of judgmental responses to differing classifications which have been explained in opinions by terms ranging from "strict scrutiny" at one extreme to "rational basis" at the other. I have never been persuaded that these so-called "standards" adequately explain the decisional process. Cases involving classifications based on alienage, illegal residency, illegitimacy, gender, age, or—as in this case—mental retardation, do not fit well into sharply defined classifications.

In every equal protection case, we have to ask certain basic questions. What class is harmed by the legislation, and has it been subjected to a "tradition of disfavor" by our laws? What is the public purpose that is being served by the law? What is the characteristic of the disadvantaged class that justifies the disparate treatment? In most cases the answer to these questions will tell us whether the statute has a "rational basis." The answers will result in the virtually automatic invalidation of racial classifications and in the validation of most economic classifications, but they will provide differing results in cases involving classifications based on alienage, gender, or illegitimacy. But that is not because we apply an "intermediate standard of review" in these cases; rather it is because the characteristics of these groups are sometimes relevant and sometimes irrelevant to a valid public purpose, or, more specifically, to the purpose that the challenged laws purportedly intended to serve.

Every law that places the mentally retarded in a special class is not presumptively irrational.

Although the city argued in the Court of Appeals that legitimate interests of the neighbors justified the restriction, the court unambiguously rejected that argument. In this Court, the city has argued that the discrimination was really motivated by a desire to protect the mentally retarded from the hazards presented by the neighborhood. Zoning ordinances are not usually justified on any such basis, and in this case, for the reasons explained by the Court, I find that justification wholly unconvincing. I cannot believe that a rational member of this disadvantaged class could ever approve of the discriminatory application of the city's ordinance in this case.

JUSTICE MARSHALL, with whom JUSTICES BRENNAN and BLACKMUN join, concurring in the judgment in part and dissenting in part.

The Court holds that all retarded individuals cannot be grouped together as the "feebleminded" and deemed presumptively unfit to live in a community. Underlying this holding is the principle that mental retardation per se cannot be a proxy for depriving retarded people of their rights and interests without regard to variations in individual ability. With this holding and principle I agree. The Equal Protection Clause requires attention to the capacities and needs of retarded people as individuals.

I cannot agree, however, with the way in which the Court reaches its result or with the narrow, as-applied remedy it provides for the city of Cleburne's equal protection violation. The Court holds the ordinance invalid on rational-basis grounds and disclaims that anything special, in the form of heightened scrutiny, is taking place. Yet Cleburne's ordinance surely would be valid under the traditional rational-basis test applicable to economic and commercial regulation. In my view, it is important to articulate, as the Court does not, the facts and principles that justify subjecting this zoning ordinance to the searching review—the heightened scrutiny—that actually leads to its invalidation. Moreover, in invalidating Cleburne's exclusion of the "feebleminded" only as applied to respondents, rather than on its face, the Court radically departs from our equal protection precedents. Because I dissent from this novel and truncated remedy, and because I cannot accept the Court's disclaimer that no "more exacting standard" than ordinary rational-basis review is being applied, I write separately.

I

I share the Court's criticisms of the overly broad lines that Cleburne's zoning ordinance has drawn. But if the ordinance is to be invalidated for its imprecise classifications, it must be pursuant to more powerful scrutiny than the minimal rational-basis test used to review classifications affecting only economic and commercial matters. The same imprecision in a similar ordinance that required opticians but not optometrists to be licensed to practice, or that excluded new but not old businesses from parts of a community, would hardly be fatal to the statutory scheme.

The refusal to acknowledge that something more than minimum rationality review is at work here is, in my view, unfortunate in at least two respects. The suggestion that the traditional rational-basis test allows this sort of searching inquiry creates precedent for this Court and lower courts to subject economic and commercial classifications to similar and searching "ordinary" rational-basis review—a small and regrettable step back toward the days of *Lochner v. New York*, 198 U.S. 45 (1905). Moreover, by failing to articulate the factors that justify today's "second order" rational-basis review, the Court provides no principled foundation for determining when more searching inquiry is to be invoked. Lower courts are thus left in the dark on this important question, and this Court remains unaccountable for its decisions employing, or refusing to employ, particularly searching scrutiny. Candor requires me to acknowledge the particular factors that justify invalidating Cleburne's zoning ordinance under the careful scrutiny it today receives.

V

The Court's opinion approaches the task of principled equal protection adjudication in what I view as precisely the wrong way. The formal label under which an equal protection claim is reviewed is less important than careful identification of the interest at stake and the extent to which society recognizes the classification as an invidious one. Yet in focusing obsessively on the appropriate label to give its standard of review, the Court fails to identify the interests at stake or to articulate the principle that classifications based on mental retardation must be carefully examined to assure they do not rest on impermissible assumptions or false stereotypes regarding individual ability and need. No guidance is thereby given as to when the Court's freewheeling, and potentially dangerous, "rational-basis standard" is to be employed, nor is attention directed to the invidiousness of grouping all retarded individuals together. Moreover, the Court's narrow, as-applied remedy fails to deal adequately with the overbroad presumption that lies at the heart of this case. Rather than leaving future retarded individuals to run the gauntlet of this overbroad presumption, I would affirm the judgment of the Court of Appeals in its entirety and would strike down on its face the provision at issue. I therefore concur in the judgment in part and dissent in part.

FOR DISCUSSION

Under what criteria does the Court find that mentally handicapped persons should receive the least stringent standard of equal protection review? In what way are these arguments similar to or different from those in Court decisions regarding the protection of race or gender?

RELATED CASE

***Heller v. Doe*: 509 U.S. 312 (1993).**

The Court refused to expand the application of heightened scrutiny under the Equal Protection Clause to mentally ill persons.

BOWERS V. HARDWICK

478 U.S. 186, 106 S.Ct. 2841, 92 L.Ed. 2d 140 (1986)

A police officer had found Michael Hardwick in the bedroom of his home, committing an act of sodomy. Hardwick was then charged with violating the Georgia law that prohibited sexual acts so classified. The district attorney declined to bring the charges to the grand jury. In response, Hardwick challenged the Georgia law in federal court as unconstitutional in that it criminalized consensual sodomy. He claimed that the Georgia law, as currently administered, placed him in "imminent danger of arrest." The district court granted a motion to dismiss for failure to submit a claim and the Supreme Court summarily affirmed. The Court of Appeals for the Eleventh Circuit reversed, finding that the Georgia statute violated Hardwick's fundamental rights. The court ruled that Hardwick's sexual activities were private and intimate activities that the Ninth Amendment and the Due Process Clause of the Fourteenth Amendment prohibited the state from regulating. The case was remanded for trial. The Supreme Court accepted the attorney general's petition to determine whether the sodomy statute violated Hardwick's fundamental rights. In that case, for the Georgia statute to withstand constitutional challenge, the state would have to demonstrate that the law was supported by a compelling state interest and was narrowly tailored.

Vote: 5–4

JUSTICE WHITE delivered the opinion of the Court.

This case does not require a judgment on whether laws against sodomy between consenting adults in general, or between homosexuals in particular, are wise or desirable. It raises no question about the right or propriety of state legislative decisions to repeal their laws that criminalize homosexual sodomy, or of state-court decisions invalidating those laws on state constitutional grounds. The issue presented is whether the Federal Constitution confers a fundamental right upon homosexuals to engage in sodomy and hence invalidates the laws of the many States that still make such conduct illegal and have done so for a very long time. The case also calls for some judgment about the limits of the Court's role in carrying out its constitutional mandate.

We first register our disagreement with the Court of Appeals and with respondent that the Court's prior cases have construed the Constitution to confer a right of privacy that extends to homosexual sodomy and for all intents and purposes have decided this case. The reach of this line of cases was sketched in *Carey v. Population Services International*, 431 U.S. 678, 685 (1977). *Pierce v. Society of Sisters*, 268 U.S. 510 (1925), and *Meyer v. Nebraska*, 262 U.S. 390 (1923), were described as dealing with child rearing and education; *Prince v. Massachusetts*, 321 U.S. 158 (1944), with family relationships; *Skinner v. Oklahoma ex rel. Williamson*, 316 U.S. 535 (1942), with procreation; *Loving v. Virginia*, 388 U.S. 1 (1967), with marriage; *Griswold v. Connecticut*, 381 U.S. 479 (1965), and *Eisenstadt v. Baird*, 405 U.S. 438 (1972), with contraception; and *Roe v. Wade*, 410 U.S. 113 (1973), with abortion. The latter three cases were interpreted as construing the Due Process Clause of the Fourteenth Amendment to confer a fundamental individual right to decide whether or not to beget or bear a child.

Accepting the decisions in these cases and the above description of them, we think it evident that none of the rights announced in those cases bears any resemblance to the claimed constitutional right of homosexuals to engage in acts of sodomy that is asserted in this case. No connection between family, marriage, or procreation on the one hand and homosexual activity on the other has been demonstrated, either by the Court of Appeals or by respondent. Precedent aside, however, respondent would have us announce, as the Court of Appeals did, a fundamental right to engage in homosexual sodomy. This we are quite unwilling to do. It is true that despite the language of the Due Process Clauses of the Fifth and Fourteenth Amendments, which appears to focus only on the processes by which life, liberty, or property is taken, the cases are legion in which those Clauses have been interpreted to have substantive content, subsuming rights that to a great extent are immune from federal or state regulation or proscription. Among such cases are those recognizing rights that have little or no textual support in the constitutional language. *Meyer*, *Prince*, and *Pierce* fall in this category, as do the privacy cases from *Griswold* to *Carey*.

Striving to assure itself and the public that announcing rights not readily identifiable in the Constitution's text involves much more than the imposition of the Justices' own choice of values on the States and the Federal Government, the Court has sought to identify the nature of the rights qualifying for heightened judicial protection. In *Palko v. Connecticut*, 302 U.S. 319, 325, 326 (1937), it was said that this category includes those fundamental liberties that are "implicit in the concept of ordered liberty," such that "neither liberty nor justice would exist if [they] were sacrificed." A different description of fundamental liberties appeared in *Moore v. East Cleveland*, 431 U.S. 494, 503 (1977), where they are characterized as those liberties that are "deeply rooted in this Nation's history and tradition."

It is obvious to us that neither of these formulations would extend a fundamental right to homosexuals to engage in acts of consensual sodomy. Proscriptions against that conduct have ancient roots. Sodomy was a criminal offense at common law and was forbidden by the laws of the original 13 States when they ratified the Bill of Rights. In 1868, when the Fourteenth Amendment was ratified, all but 5 of the 37 States in the Union had criminal sodomy laws. In fact, until 1961, all 50 States outlawed sodomy, and today, 24 States and the District of Columbia continue to provide criminal penalties for sodomy performed in private and between consenting adults. Against this background, to claim that a right to engage in such conduct is "deeply rooted in this Nation's history and tradition" or "implicit in the concept of ordered liberty" is, at best, facetious.

Nor are we inclined to take a more expansive view of our authority to discover new fundamental rights imbedded in the Due Process Clause. The Court is most vulnerable and comes nearest to illegitimacy when it deals with judge-made constitutional law having little or no cognizable roots in the language or design of the Constitution. There should be, therefore, great resistance to expand the substantive reach of those Clauses, particularly if it requires redefining the category of rights deemed to be fundamental. Otherwise, the Judiciary necessarily takes to itself further authority to govern the country without express constitutional authority. The claimed right pressed on us today falls far short of overcoming this resistance.

Respondent, however, asserts that the result should be different where the homosexual conduct occurs in the privacy of the home. He relies on *Stanley v. Georgia*, 394 U.S. 557, 565 (1969), where the Court held that the First Amendment prevents conviction for possessing and reading obscene material in the privacy of one's home: "If the First Amendment means anything, it means that a State has no business telling a man, sitting alone in his house, what books he may read or what films he may watch."

Stanley did protect conduct that would not have been protected outside the home, and it partially prevented the enforcement of state obscenity laws; but the decision was firmly grounded in the First Amendment. The right pressed upon us here has no similar support in the text of the Constitution, and it does not qualify for recognition under the prevailing principles for construing the Fourteenth Amendment. Its limits are also difficult to discern.

Even if the conduct at issue here is not a fundamental right, respondent asserts that there must be a rational basis for the law and that there is none in this case other than the presumed belief of a majority of the electorate in Georgia that homosexual sodomy is immoral and unacceptable. This is said to be an inadequate rationale to support the law. The law, however, is constantly based on notions of morality, and if all laws representing essentially moral choices are to be invalidated under the Due Process Clause, the courts will be very busy indeed. Even respondent makes no such claim, but insists that majority sentiments about the morality of homosexuality should be declared inadequate. We do not agree, and are unpersuaded that the sodomy laws of some 25 States should be invalidated on this basis.

CHIEF JUSTICE BURGER, concurring.

I join the Court's opinion, but I write separately to underscore my view that in constitutional terms there is no such thing as a fundamental right to commit homosexual sodomy.

As the Court notes, the proscriptions against sodomy have very "ancient roots." Decisions of individuals relating to homosexual conduct have been subject to state intervention throughout the history of Western civilization. Condemnation of those practices is firmly rooted in Judeo-Christian moral and ethical standards. In 1816 the Georgia Legislature passed the statute at issue here, and that statute has been continuously in force in one form or another since that time. To hold that the act of homosexual sodomy is somehow protected as a fundamental right would be to cast aside millennia of moral teaching.

This is essentially not a question of personal "preferences" but rather of the legislative authority of the State. I find nothing in the Constitution depriving a State of the power to enact the statute challenged here.

JUSTICE POWELL, concurring.

I join the opinion of the Court. I agree with the Court that there is no fundamental right—i.e., no substantive right under the Due Process Clause—such as that claimed by respondent Hardwick, and found to exist by the Court of Appeals. This is not to suggest, however, that respondent may not be protected by the Eighth Amendment of the Constitution. The Georgia statute at issue in this case, authorizes a court to imprison a person for up to 20 years for a single private, consensual act of sodomy. In my view, a prison sentence for such conduct—certainly a sentence of long duration—would create a serious Eighth Amendment issue.

In this case, however, respondent has not been tried, much less convicted and sentenced. Moreover, respondent has not raised the Eighth Amendment issue below. For these reasons this constitutional argument is not before us.

JUSTICE BLACKMUN, with whom JUSTICES BRENNAN, MARSHALL, and STEVENS join, dissenting.

This case is no more about "a fundamental right to engage in homosexual sodomy," as the Court purports to declare, than *Stanley v. Georgia*, 394 U.S. 557 (1969), was about a fundamental right to watch obscene movies, or *Katz v. United States*, 389 U.S. 347 (1967), was about a fundamental right to place interstate bets from a telephone booth. Rather, this case is about "the most comprehensive of rights and the right most valued by civilized men," namely, "the right to be let alone." *Olmstead v. United States*, 277 U.S. 438, 478 (1928) (Brandeis, J., dissenting).

I believe we must analyze respondent Hardwick's claim in the light of the values that underlie the constitutional right to privacy. If that right means anything, it means that, before Georgia can prosecute its citizens for making choices about the most intimate aspects of their lives, it must do more than assert that the choice they have made is an " 'abominable crime not fit to be named among Christians.' " *Herring v. State*, 119 Ga. 709, 721 (1904).

I

First, the Court's almost obsessive focus on homosexual activity is particularly hard to justify in light of the broad language Georgia has used. Unlike the Court, the Georgia Legislature has not proceeded on the assumption that homosexuals are so different from other citizens that their lives may be controlled in a way that would not be tolerated if it limited the choices of those other citizens. Rather, Georgia has provided that "[a] person commits the offense of sodomy when he performs or submits to any sexual act involving the sex organs of one person and the mouth or anus of another." The sex or status of the persons who engage in the act is irrelevant as a matter of state law. In fact, to the extent I can discern a legislative purpose for Georgia's 1968 enactment of § 16–6–2, that purpose seems to have been to broaden the coverage of the law to reach heterosexual as well as homosexual activity. I therefore see no basis for the Court's decision to treat this case as an "as applied" challenge to § 16–6–2, or for Georgia's attempt, both in its brief and at oral argument, to defend § 16–6–2 solely on the grounds that it prohibits homosexual activity. Michael Hardwick's standing may rest in significant part on Georgia's apparent willingness to enforce against homosexuals a law it seems not to have any desire to enforce against heterosexuals. But his claim that § 16–6–2 involves an unconstitutional intrusion into his privacy and his right of intimate association does not depend in any way on his sexual orientation.

Second, I disagree with the Court's refusal to consider whether § 16–6–2 runs afoul of the Eighth or Ninth Amendments or the Equal Protection Clause of the Fourteenth Amendment. Respondent's complaint expressly invoked the Ninth Amendment, and he relied heavily before this Court on *Griswold v. Connecticut*, 381 U.S. 479, 484 (1965), which identifies that Amendment as one of the specific constitutional provisions giving "life and substance" to our understanding of privacy. More importantly, the procedural posture of the case requires that we affirm the Court of Appeals' judgment if there is any ground on which respondent may be entitled to relief.

III

First, petitioner asserts that the acts made criminal by the statute may have serious adverse consequences for "the general public health and welfare," such as spreading communicable diseases or fostering other criminal activity. Inasmuch as this case was dismissed by the District Court on the pleadings, it is not surprising that the record before us is barren of any evidence to support petitioner's claim.

The core of petitioner's defense of § 16–6–2, however, is that respondent and others who engage in the conduct prohibited by § 16–6–2 interfere with Georgia's exercise of the " 'right of the Nation and of the States to maintain a decent society,' " *Paris Adult Theatre I v. Slaton*, 413 U.S. 49, at 59–60 (1973). Essentially, petitioner argues, and the Court agrees, that the fact that the acts described in § 16–6–2 "for hundreds of years, if not thousands, have been uniformly condemned as immoral" is a sufficient reason to permit a State to ban them today.

I cannot agree that either the length of time a majority has held its convictions or the passions with which it defends them can withdraw legislation from this Court's scrutiny. It is precisely because the issue raised by this case touches the heart of what makes individuals what they are that we should be especially sensitive to the rights of those whose choices upset the majority.

The assertion that "traditional Judeo-Christian values proscribe" the conduct involved cannot provide an adequate justification for § 16–6–2. That certain, but by no means all, religious groups condemn the behavior at issue gives the State no license to impose their judgments on the entire citizenry. The legitimacy of secular legislation depends instead on whether the State can advance some justification for its law beyond its conformity to religious doctrine.

Certainly, some private behavior can affect the fabric of society as a whole. Petitioner and the Court fail to see the difference between laws that protect public sensibilities and those that enforce private morality. Statutes banning public sexual activity are entirely consistent with protecting the individual's liberty interest in decisions concerning sexual relations: the same recognition that those decisions are intensely private which justifies protecting them from governmental interference can justify protecting individuals from unwilling exposure to the sexual activities of others. But the mere fact that intimate behavior may be punished when it takes place in public cannot dictate how States can regulate intimate behavior that occurs in intimate places.

This case involves no real interference with the rights of others, for the mere knowledge that other individuals do not adhere to one's value system cannot be a legally cognizable interest, let alone an interest that can justify invading the houses, hearts, and minds of citizens who choose to live their lives differently.

IV

It took but three years for the Court to see the error in its analysis in *Minersville School District v. Gobitis*, 310 U.S. 586 (1940), and to recognize that the threat to national cohesion posed by a refusal to salute the flag was vastly outweighed by the threat to those same values posed by compelling such a salute. I can only hope that here, too, the Court soon will reconsider its analysis and conclude that depriving individuals of the right to choose for themselves how to conduct their intimate relationships poses a far greater threat to the values most deeply rooted in our Nation's history than tolerance of nonconformity could ever do. Because I think the Court today betrays those values, I dissent.

JUSTICE STEVENS, with whom JUSTICES BRENNAN and MARSHALL join, dissenting.

Like the statute that is challenged in this case, the rationale of the Court's opinion applies equally to the prohibited conduct regardless of whether the parties who engage in it are married or unmarried, or are of the same or different sexes. Sodomy was condemned as an odious and sinful type of behavior during the formative period of the common law. That condemnation was equally damning for heterosexual and homosexual sodomy. Moreover, it provided no special exemption for married couples. The license to cohabit and to produce legitimate offspring simply did not include any permission to engage in sexual conduct that was considered a "crime against nature."

The history of the Georgia statute before us clearly reveals this traditional prohibition of heterosexual, as well as homosexual, sodomy. Indeed, at one point in the 20th century, Georgia's law was construed to permit certain sexual conduct between homosexual women even though such conduct was prohibited between heterosexuals. The history of the statutes cited by the majority as proof for the proposition that sodomy is not constitutionally protected, and similarly reveals a prohibition on heterosexual, as well as homosexual, sodomy.

Because the Georgia statute expresses the traditional view that sodomy is an immoral kind of conduct regardless of the identity of the persons who engage in it, I believe that a proper analysis of its constitutionality requires consideration of two questions: First, may a State totally prohibit the described conduct by means of a neutral law applying without exception to all persons subject to its jurisdiction? If not, may the State save the statute by announcing that it will only enforce the law against homosexuals? The two questions merit separate discussion.

I

Our prior cases make two propositions abundantly clear. First, the fact that the governing majority in a State has traditionally viewed a particular practice as immoral is not a sufficient reason for upholding a law prohibiting the practice; neither history nor tradition could save a law prohibiting miscegenation from constitutional attack. Second, individual decisions by married persons, concerning the intimacies of their physical relationship, even when not intended to produce offspring, are a form of "liberty" protected by the Due Process Clause of the Fourteenth Amendment.

II

If the Georgia statute cannot be enforced as it is written—if the conduct it seeks to prohibit is a protected form of liberty for the vast majority of Georgia's citizens—the State must assume the burden of justifying a selective application of its law. Either the persons to whom Georgia seeks to apply its statute do not have the same interest in "liberty" that others have, or there must be a reason why the State may be permitted to apply a generally applicable law to certain persons that it does not apply to others.

The first possibility is plainly unacceptable. Although the meaning of the principle that "all men are created equal" is not always clear, it surely must mean that every free citizen has the same interest in "liberty" that the members of the majority share. From the standpoint of the individual, the homosexual and the heterosexual have the same interest in deciding how he will live his own life, and, more narrowly, how he will conduct himself in his personal and voluntary associations with his companions. State intrusion into the private conduct of either is equally burdensome.

The second possibility is similarly unacceptable. A policy of selective application must be supported by a neutral and legitimate interest—something more substantial than a habitual dislike for, or ignorance about, the disfavored group. Neither the State nor the Court has identified any such interest in this case. The Court has posited as a justification for the Georgia statute "the presumed belief of a majority of the electorate in Georgia that homosexual sodomy is immoral and unacceptable." But the Georgia electorate has expressed no such belief—instead, its representatives enacted a law that presumably reflects the belief that all sodomy is immoral and unacceptable. Unless the Court is prepared to conclude that such a law is constitutional, it may not rely on the work product of the Georgia Legislature to support its holding. For the Georgia statute does not single out homosexuals as a separate class meriting special disfavored treatment.

III

The Court orders the dismissal of respondent's complaint even though the State's statute prohibits all sodomy; even though that prohibition is concededly unconstitutional with respect to heterosexuals; and even though the State's post hoc explanations for selective application are belied by the State's own actions. At the very least, I think it clear at this early stage of the litigation that respondent has alleged a constitutional claim sufficient to withstand a motion to dismiss.

I respectfully dissent.

FOR DISCUSSION

When should a federal court be willing to enforce new constitutional substantive rights that result in the finding that state laws are unconstitutional? Consider the impact of such cases as *Brown v. Board of Education* (1954), *Mapp v. Ohio* (1961), and *Reed v. Reed* (1971).

RELATED CASE

***Powell v. The State:* 270 Ga. 327 (1998).**

The Georgia anti-sodomy law was challenged as a violation of the right to privacy—not as a federally protected right, but as a value that had been guaranteed through the Georgia constitution and in Georgia case law.

ROMER V. EVANS

517 U.S. 620, 116 S.Ct. 1620, 134 L.Ed.2d 855 (1996)

In 1992 the voters of Colorado amended their constitution through a statewide referendum referenced as "Amendment 2." This vote resulted from a series of municipal ordinances that had recently banned discrimination on the basis of sexual orientation in housing, employment, education, public accommodations, and health and welfare services. Amendment 2 repealed all these ordinances and prohibited any state or local governmental action, whether executive, legislative, or judicial in origination, designed to protect homosexuals, lesbians, or bisexuals. The plaintiffs claimed that the enforcement of Amendment 2 exposed them to a substantial risk of discrimination. The trial court granted a preliminary injunction, and the Supreme Court of Colorado held that Amendment 2 was subject to strict scrutiny under the Fourteenth Amendment. The trial court, applying the ruling, enjoined enforcement of Amendment 2, and the state supreme court affirmed the ruling.

Vote: 6–3

JUSTICE KENNEDY delivered the opinion of the Court.

One century ago, the first Justice Harlan admonished this Court that the Constitution "neither knows nor tolerates classes among citizens." *Plessy v. Ferguson*, 163 U.S. 537, 559 (1896) (dissenting opinion). Unheeded then, those words now are understood to state a commitment to the law's neutrality where the rights of persons are at stake. The Equal Protection Clause enforces this principle and today requires us to hold invalid a provision of Colorado's Constitution.

II

The State's principal argument in defense of Amendment 2 is that it puts gays and lesbians in the same position as all other persons. So, the State says, the measure does no more than deny homosexuals special rights. This reading of the amendment's language is implausible.

Sweeping and comprehensive is the change in legal status effected by this law. Homosexuals, by state decree, are put in a solitary class with respect to transactions and relations in both the private and governmental spheres. The amendment withdraws from homosexuals, but no others, specific legal protection from the injuries caused by discrimination, and it forbids reinstatement of these laws and policies.

The change Amendment 2 works in the legal status of gays and lesbians in the private sphere is far reaching, both on its own terms and when considered in light of the structure and operation of modern antidiscrimination laws. That structure is well illustrated by contemporary statutes and ordinances prohibiting discrimination by providers of public accommodations. "At common law, innkeepers, smiths, and others who 'made profession of a public employment,' were prohibited from refusing, without good reason, to serve a customer." *Hurley v. Irish-American Gay, Lesbian and Bisexual Group of Boston, Inc.*, 515 U.S. 557, 571 (1995). The duty was a general one and did not specify protection for particular groups. The common-law rules, however, proved insufficient in many instances, and it was settled early that the Fourteenth Amendment did not give Congress a general power to prohibit discrimination in public accommodations, *Civil Rights Cases*, 109 U.S. 3, 25 (1883). In consequence, most states have chosen to counter discrimination by enacting detailed statutory schemes.

Colorado's state and municipal laws typify this emerging tradition of statutory protection and follow a consistent pattern.

. . . Colorado's state and local governments have not limited antidiscrimination laws to groups that have so far been given the protection of heightened equal protection scrutiny under our cases. Rather, they set forth an extensive catalog of traits which cannot be the basis for discrimination, including age, military status, marital status, pregnancy, parenthood, custody of a minor child, political affiliation, physical or mental disability of an individual or of his or her associates—and, in recent times, sexual orientation.

Amendment 2 bars homosexuals from securing protection against the injuries that these public-accommodations laws address. That in itself is a severe consequence, but there is more. Amendment 2, in addition, nullifies specific legal protections for this targeted class in all transactions in housing, sale of real estate, insurance, health and welfare services, private education, and employment. Not confined to the private sphere, Amendment 2 also operates to repeal and forbid all laws or policies providing specific protection for gays or lesbians from discrimination by every level of Colorado government.

Amendment 2's reach may not be limited to specific laws passed for the benefit of gays and lesbians. It is a fair, if not necessary, inference from the broad language of the amendment that it deprives gays and lesbians even of the protection of general laws and policies that prohibit arbitrary discrimination in governmental and private settings. At some point in the systematic administration of these laws, an official must determine whether homosexuality is an arbitrary and, thus, forbidden basis for decision. Yet a decision to that effect would itself amount to a policy prohibiting discrimination on the basis of homosexuality, and so would appear to be no more valid under Amendment 2 than the specific prohibitions against discrimination the state court held invalid.

If this consequence follows from Amendment 2, as its broad language suggests, it would compound the constitutional difficulties the law creates. The state court did not decide whether the amendment has this effect, however, and neither need we.

III

The Fourteenth Amendment's promise that no person shall be denied the equal protection of the laws must coexist with the practical necessity that most legislation classifies for one purpose or another, with resulting disadvantage to various groups or persons. We have attempted to reconcile the principle with the reality by stating that, if a law neither burdens a fundamental right nor targets a suspect class, we will uphold the legislative classification so long as it bears a rational relation to some legitimate end.

Amendment 2 fails, indeed defies, even this conventional inquiry. First, the amendment has the peculiar property of imposing a broad and undifferentiated disability on a single named group, an exceptional and, as we shall explain, invalid form of legislation. Second, its sheer breadth is so discontinuous with the reasons offered for it that the amendment seems inexplicable by anything but animus toward the class it affects; it lacks a rational relationship to legitimate state interests.

Taking the first point, even in the ordinary equal protection case calling for the most deferential of standards, we insist on knowing the relation between the classification adopted and the object to be attained. In the ordinary case, a law will be sustained if it can be said to advance a legitimate government interest, even if the law seems unwise or works to the disadvantage of a particular group, or if the rationale for it seems tenuous. By requiring that the classification bear a rational relationship to an independent and legitimate legislative end, we ensure that classifications are not drawn for the purpose of disadvantaging the group burdened by the law.

Amendment 2 confounds this normal process of judicial review. It is at once too narrow and too broad. It identifies persons by a single trait and then denies them protection across the board. The resulting disqualification of a class of persons from the right to seek specific protection from the law is unprecedented in our jurisprudence. The absence of precedent for Amendment 2 is itself instructive; "discriminations of an unusual character especially suggest careful consideration to determine whether they are obnoxious to the constitutional provision." *Louisville Gas & Elec. Co. v. Coleman*, 277 U.S. 32, 37–38 (1928).

A second and related point is that laws of the kind now before us raise the inevitable inference that the disadvantage imposed is born of animosity toward the class of persons affected. Even laws enacted for broad and ambitious purposes often can be explained by reference to legitimate public policies which justify the incidental disadvantages they impose on certain persons. Amendment 2, however, in making a general announcement that gays and lesbians shall not have any particular protections from the law, inflicts on them immediate, continuing, and real injuries that outrun and belie any legitimate justifications that may be claimed for it. We conclude that, in addition to the far-reaching deficiencies of Amendment 2 that we have noted, the principles it offends, in another sense, are conventional and venerable; a law must bear a rational relationship to a legitimate governmental purpose, *Kadrmas v. Dickinson Public Schools*, 487 U.S. 450 (1988), and Amendment 2 does not.

The primary rationale the State offers for Amendment 2 is respect for other citizens' freedom of association, and in particular the liberties of landlords or employers who have personal or religious objections to homosexuality. Colorado also cites its interest in conserving resources to fight discrimination against other groups. The breadth of the Amendment is so far removed from these particular justifications that we find it impossible to credit them. We cannot say that Amendment 2 is directed to any identifiable legitimate purpose or discrete objective. It is a status-based enactment divorced from any factual context from which we could discern a relationship to legitimate state interests; it is a classification of persons undertaken for its own sake, something the Equal Protection Clause does not permit. "Class legislation . . . [is] obnoxious to the prohibitions of the Fourteenth Amendment. . . ." *Civil Rights Cases*, 109 U.S. at 24.

We must conclude that Amendment 2 classifies homosexuals not to further a proper legislative end but to make them unequal to everyone else. This Colorado cannot do. A State cannot so deem a class of persons a stranger to its laws. Amendment 2 violates the Equal Protection Clause, and the judgment of the Supreme Court of Colorado is affirmed.

JUSTICE SCALIA, with whom CHIEF JUSTICE REHNQUIST and JUSTICE THOMAS join, dissenting.

The Court has mistaken a Kulturkampf for a fit of spite. The constitutional amendment before us here is not the manifestation of a " 'bare . . . desire to harm' " homosexuals, but is rather a modest attempt by seemingly tolerant Coloradans to preserve traditional sexual mores against the efforts of a politically powerful minority to revise those mores through use of the laws. That objective, and the means chosen to achieve it, are not only unimpeachable under any constitutional doctrine hitherto pronounced (hence the opinion's heavy reliance upon principles of righteousness rather than judicial holdings); they have been specifically approved by the Congress of the United States and by this Court.

In holding that homosexuality cannot be singled out for disfavorable treatment, the Court contradicts a decision, unchallenged here, pronounced only 10 years ago, see *Bowers v. Hardwick*, 478 U.S. 186 (1986), and places the prestige of this institution behind the proposition that opposition to homosexuality is as reprehensible as racial or religious bias. Whether it is or not is precisely the cultural debate that gave rise to the Colorado constitutional amendment (and to the preferential laws against which the amendment was directed). Since the Constitution of the United States says nothing about this subject, it is left to be resolved by normal democratic means, including the democratic adoption of provisions in state constitutions. This Court has no business imposing upon all Americans the resolution favored by the elite class from which the Members of this institution are selected, pronouncing that "animosity" toward homosexuality is evil. I vigorously dissent.

I

The only denial of equal treatment [the Court's opinion] contends homosexuals have suffered is this: They may not obtain preferential treatment without amending the state constitution.

The central thesis of the Court's reasoning is that any group is denied equal protection when, to obtain advantage (or, presumably, to avoid disadvantage), it must have recourse to a more general and hence more difficult level of political decisionmaking than others. The world has never heard of such a principle, which is why the Court's opinion is so long on emotive utterance and so short on relevant legal citation. And it seems to me most unlikely that any multilevel democracy can function under such a principle. For whenever a disadvantage is imposed, or conferral of a benefit is prohibited, at one of the higher levels of democratic decisionmaking (i.e., by the state legislature rather than local government, or by the people at large in the state constitution rather than the legislature), the affected group has (under this theory) been denied equal protection. To take the simplest of examples, consider a state law prohibiting the award of municipal contracts to relatives of mayors or city councilmen. Once such a law is passed, the group composed of such relatives must, in order to get the benefit of city contracts, persuade the state legislature—unlike all other citizens, who need only persuade the municipality. It is ridiculous to consider this a denial of equal protection, which is why the Court's theory is unheard of.

The Court might reply that the example I have given is not a denial of equal protection only because the same "rational basis" (avoidance of corruption) which renders constitutional the substantive discrimination against relatives (i.e., the fact that they alone cannot obtain city contracts) also automatically suffices to sustain what might be called the electoral-procedural discrimination against them (i.e., the fact that they must go to the state level to get this changed). This is of course a perfectly reasonable response, and would explain why "electoral-procedural discrimination" has not hitherto been heard of: A law that is valid in its substance is automatically valid in its level of enactment. But the Court cannot afford to make this argument, for as I shall discuss next, there is no doubt of a rational basis for the substance of the prohibition at issue here.

II

I turn next to whether there was a legitimate rational basis for the substance of the constitutional amendment—for the prohibition of special protection for homosexuals. It is unsurprising that the Court avoids discussion of this question, since the answer is so obviously yes. The case most relevant to the issue before us today is not even mentioned in the Court's opinion: In *Bowers v. Hardwick*, 478 U.S. 186 (1986), we held that the Constitution does not prohibit what virtually all States had done from the founding of the Republic until very recent years—making homosexual conduct a crime. That holding is unassailable, except by those who think that the Constitution changes to suit current fashions.

Moreover, even if the provision regarding homosexual "orientation" were invalid, respondents' challenge to Amendment 2—which is a facial challenge—must fail. "A facial challenge to a legislative Act is, of course, the most difficult challenge to mount successfully, since the challenger must establish that no set of circumstances exists under which the Act would be valid." *United States v. Salerno*, 481 U.S. 739, 745 (1987). It would not be enough for respondents to establish (if they could) that Amendment 2 is unconstitutional as applied to those of homosexual "orientation"; since, under *Bowers*, Amendment 2 is unquestionably constitutional as applied to those who engage in homosexual conduct, the facial challenge cannot succeed. Some individuals of homosexual "orientation" who do not engage in homosexual acts might successfully bring an as-applied challenge to Amendment 2, but so far as the record indicates, none of the respondents is such a person.

III

The foregoing suffices to establish what the Court's failure to cite any case remotely in point would lead one to suspect: No principle set forth in the Constitution, nor even any imagined by this Court in the past 200 years, prohibits what Colorado has done here. But the case for Colorado is much stronger than that. What it has done is not only unprohibited, but eminently reasonable, with close, congressionally approved precedent in earlier constitutional practice.

First, as to its eminent reasonableness. The Court's opinion contains grim, disapproving hints that Coloradans have been guilty of "animus" or "animosity" toward homosexuality, as though that has been established as un-American. Of course it is our moral heritage that one should not hate any human being or class of human beings. But I had thought that one could consider certain conduct reprehensible—murder, for example, or polygamy, or cruelty to animals—and could exhibit even "animus" toward such conduct. The Colorado amendment does not, to speak entirely precisely, prohibit giving favored status to people who are homosexuals; they can be favored for many reasons—for example, because they are senior citizens or members of racial minorities. But it prohibits giving them favored status because of their homosexual conduct—that is, it prohibits favored status for homosexuality.

The Court's portrayal of Coloradans as a society fallen victim to pointless, hate-filled "gay-bashing" is so false as to be comical. Colorado not only is one of the 25 States that have repealed their antisodomy laws, but was among the first to do so. But the society that eliminates criminal punishment for homosexual acts does not necessarily abandon the view that homosexuality is morally wrong and socially harmful; often, abolition simply reflects the view that enforcement of such criminal laws involves unseemly intrusion into the intimate lives of citizens.

That is where Amendment 2 came in. It sought to counter both the geographic concentration and the disproportionate political power of homosexuals by (1) resolving the controversy at the statewide level, and (2) making the election a single-issue contest for both sides. It put directly, to all the citizens of the State, the question: Should homosexuality be given special protection? They answered no. The Court today asserts that this most democratic of procedures is unconstitutional. Lacking any cases to establish that facially absurd proposition, it simply asserts that it must be unconstitutional, because it has never happened before.

Today's opinion has no foundation in American constitutional law, and barely pretends to. The people of Colorado have adopted an entirely reasonable provision which does not even disfavor homosexuals in any substantive sense, but merely denies them preferential treatment. Amendment 2 is designed to prevent piecemeal deterioration of the sexual morality favored by a majority of Coloradans, and is not only an appropriate means to that legitimate end, but a means that Americans have employed before. Striking it down is an act, not of judicial judgment, but of political will. I dissent.

FOR DISCUSSION

What would be the constitutional arguments for placing sexual preference legislation under due process or equal protection guarantees? What would be the legal consequences of each of these choices?

RELATED CASE

***Boy Scouts of America v. Dale:* 530 U.S. 640 (2000).**

After the state of New Jersey amended its discrimination laws to protect sexual orientation, the Boy Scouts revoked a local leader's adult membership because of his homosexuality. The Court upheld the right of the Boy Scouts of America to control its membership as a private organization.

See also the discussion of sexual preference cases in volume one in the chapter on federalism, and in this volume in the discussion of freedom of association (Chapter IV).

LAWRENCE V. TEXAS

539 U.S. 558, 123 S.Ct. 2472, 156 L.Ed.2d 508 (2003)

Upon entering an apartment to investigate a weapons disturbance complaint, two Harris County police officers observed John Geddes Lawrence and Tyrone Garner engaged in a sexual act. The men were arrested on the charge of "deviate sexual intercourse," or sodomy with an individual of the same sex. The petitioner challenged the Texas statute as a violation of both the Equal Protection Clause of the Fourteenth Amendment and a similar provision in the Texas constitution. The criminal court rejected these claims and fined the petitioners $200 each, plus court costs. The Texas Court of Appeals (14th District) rejected the challenge and affirmed the criminal court.

Vote: 6–3

JUSTICE KENNEDY delivered the opinion of the Court.

I

We granted certiorari to consider three questions:

1. Whether Petitioners' criminal convictions under the Texas "Homosexual Conduct" law—which criminalizes sexual intimacy by same-sex couples, but not identical behavior by different-sex couples—violate the Fourteenth Amendment guarantee of equal protection of laws?

2. Whether Petitioners' criminal convictions for adult consensual sexual intimacy in the home violate their vital interests in liberty and privacy protected by the Due Process Clause of the Fourteenth Amendment?

3. Whether *Bowers v. Hardwick*, 478 U.S. 186 (1986), should be overruled?

II

We conclude the case should be resolved by determining whether the petitioners were free as adults to engage in the private conduct in the exercise of their liberty under the Due Process Clause of the Fourteenth Amendment to the Constitution. For this inquiry we deem it necessary to reconsider the Court's holding in *Bowers*.

The facts in *Bowers* had some similarities to the instant case. A police officer, whose right to enter seems not to have been in question, observed Hardwick, in his own bedroom, engaging in intimate sexual conduct with another adult male. The conduct was in violation of a Georgia statute making it a criminal offense to engage in sodomy. One difference between the two cases is that the Georgia statute prohibited the conduct whether or not the participants were of the same sex, while the Texas statute, as we have seen, applies only to participants of the same sex. Hardwick was not prosecuted, but he brought an action in federal court to declare the state statute invalid. He alleged he was a practicing homosexual and that the criminal prohibition violated rights guaranteed to him by the Constitution. The Court, in an opinion by Justice White, sustained the Georgia law. Chief Justice Burger and Justice Powell joined the opinion of the Court and filed separate, concurring opinions. Four Justices dissented.

The Court began its substantive discussion in *Bowers* as follows: "The issue presented is whether the Federal Constitution confers a fundamental right upon homosexuals to engage in sodomy and hence invalidates the laws of the many States that still make such conduct illegal and have done so for a very long time." Id., at 190. That statement, we now conclude, discloses the Court's own failure to appreciate the extent of the liberty at stake. To say that the issue in *Bowers* was simply the right to engage in certain sexual conduct demeans the claim the individual put forward, just as it would demean a married couple were it to be said marriage is simply about the right to have sexual intercourse. The laws involved in *Bowers* and here are, to be sure, statutes that purport to do no more than prohibit a particular sexual act. Their penalties and purposes, though, have more far-reaching consequences, touching upon the most private human conduct, sexual behavior, and in the most private of places, the home. The statutes do seek to control a personal relationship that, whether or not entitled to formal recognition in the law, is within the liberty of persons to choose without being punished as criminals.

Having misapprehended the claim of liberty there presented to it, and thus stating the claim to be whether there is a fundamental right to engage in consensual sodomy, the *Bowers* Court said: "Proscriptions against that conduct have ancient roots." Id., at 192. In academic writings, and in many of the scholarly amicus briefs filed to assist the Court in this case, there are fundamental criticisms of the historical premises relied upon by the majority and concurring opinions in *Bowers*. We need not enter this debate in the attempt to reach a definitive historical judgment, but the following considerations counsel against adopting the definitive conclusions upon which *Bowers* placed such reliance.

At the outset it should be noted that there is no longstanding history in this country of laws directed at homosexual conduct as a distinct matter.

Laws prohibiting sodomy do not seem to have been enforced against consenting adults acting in private. Instead of targeting relations between consenting adults in private, 19th-century sodomy prosecutions typically involved relations between men and minor girls or minor boys, relations between adults involving force, relations between adults implicating disparity in status, or relations between men and animals.

It was not until the 1970's that any State singled out same-sex relations for criminal prosecution, and only nine States have done so. Post-*Bowers* even some of these States did not adhere to the policy of suppressing homosexual conduct. Over the course of the last decades, States with same-sex prohibitions have moved toward abolishing them.

Of even more importance, almost five years before *Bowers* was decided the European Court of Human Rights considered a case with parallels to *Bowers* and to today's case. An adult male resident in Northern Ireland alleged he was a practicing homosexual who desired to engage in consensual homosexual conduct. The laws of Northern Ireland forbade him that right. He alleged that he had been questioned, his home had been searched, and he feared criminal prosecution. The court held that the laws proscribing the conduct were invalid under the European Convention on Human Rights. *Dudgeon v. United Kingdom*, 45 Eur. Ct. H. R. (1981) P 52. Authoritative in all countries that are members of the Council of Europe (21 nations then, 45 nations now), the decision is at odds with the premise in *Bowers* that the claim put forward was insubstantial in our Western civilization.

In our own constitutional system the deficiencies in *Bowers* became even more apparent in the years following its announcement. The 25 States with laws prohibiting the relevant conduct referenced in the Bowers decision are reduced now to 13, of which 4 enforce their laws only against homosexual conduct. In those States where sodomy is still proscribed, whether for same-sex or heterosexual conduct, there is a pattern of nonenforcement with respect to consenting adults acting in private.

Two principal cases decided after *Bowers* cast its holding into even more doubt. In *Planned Parenthood of Southeastern Pa. v. Casey*, 505 U.S. 833 (1992), the Court reaffirmed the substantive force of the liberty protected by the Due Process Clause. The *Casey* decision again confirmed that our laws and tradition afford constitutional protection to personal decisions relating to marriage, procreation, contraception, family relationships, child rearing, and education.

The second post-*Bowers* case of principal relevance is *Romer v. Evans*, 517 U.S. 620 (1996). There the Court struck down class-based legislation directed at homosexuals as a violation of the Equal Protection Clause. We concluded that the provision was "born of animosity toward the class of persons affected" and further that it had no rational relation to a legitimate governmental purpose.

Equality of treatment and the due process right to demand respect for conduct protected by the substantive guarantee of liberty are linked in important respects, and a decision on the latter point advances both interests. If protected conduct is made criminal and the law which does so remains unexamined for its substantive validity, its stigma might remain even if it were not enforceable as drawn for equal protection reasons. When homosexual conduct is made criminal by the law of the State, that declaration in and of itself is an invitation to subject homosexual persons to discrimination both in the public and in the private spheres. The central holding of *Bowers* has been brought in question by this case, and it should be addressed. Its continuance as precedent demeans the lives of homosexual persons.

The foundations of *Bowers* have sustained serious erosion from our recent decisions in *Casey* and *Romer.*

To the extent *Bowers* relied on values we share with a wider civilization, it should be noted that the reasoning and holding in *Bowers* have been rejected elsewhere. The European Court of Human Rights has followed not *Bowers* but its own decision in *Dudgeon v. United Kingdom.*

Other nations, too, have taken action consistent with an affirmation of the protected right of homosexual adults to engage in intimate, consensual conduct.

The doctrine of *stare decisis* is essential to the respect accorded to the judgments of the Court and to the stability of the law. It is not, however, an inexorable command. The holding in *Bowers*, however, has not induced detrimental reliance comparable to some instances where recognized individual rights are involved. Indeed, there has been no individual or societal reliance on *Bowers* of the sort that could counsel against overturning its holding once there are compelling reasons to do so. *Bowers* itself causes uncertainty, for the precedents before and after its issuance contradict its central holding.

Bowers was not correct when it was decided, and it is not correct today. It ought not to remain binding precedent. *Bowers v. Hardwick* should be and now is overruled.

Had those who drew and ratified the Due Process Clauses of the Fifth Amendment or the Fourteenth Amendment known the components of liberty in its manifold possibilities, they might have been more specific. They did not presume to have this insight. They knew times can blind us to certain truths and later generations can see that laws once thought necessary and proper in fact serve only to oppress. As the Constitution endures, persons in every generation can invoke its principles in their own search for greater freedom.

The judgment of the Court of Appeals for the Texas Fourteenth District is reversed, and the case is remanded for further proceedings not inconsistent with this opinion.

JUSTICE O'CONNOR, concurring in the judgment.

The Court today overrules *Bowers v. Hardwick*, 478 U.S. 186 (1986). I joined *Bowers*, and do not join the Court in overruling it. Nevertheless, I agree with the Court that Texas' statute banning same-sex sodomy is unconstitutional. Rather than relying on the substantive component of the Fourteenth Amendment's Due Process Clause, as the Court does, I base my conclusion on the Fourteenth Amendment's Equal Protection Clause.

The Equal Protection Clause of the Fourteenth Amendment "is essentially a direction that all persons similarly situated should be treated alike." *Cleburne v. Cleburne Living Center, Inc.*, 473 U.S. 432, 439 (1985); see also *Plyler v. Doe*, 457 U.S. 202, 216 (1982). Under our rational basis standard of review, "legislation is presumed to be valid and will be sustained if the classification drawn by the statute is rationally related to a legitimate state interest." *Cleburne v. Cleburne Living Center*, at 440.

We have consistently held, however, that some objectives, such as "a bare . . . desire to harm a politically unpopular group," are not legitimate state interests. When a law exhibits such a desire to harm a politically unpopular group, we have applied a more searching form of rational basis review to strike down such laws under the Equal Protection Clause.

We have been most likely to apply rational basis review to hold a law unconstitutional under the Equal Protection Clause where, as here, the challenged legislation inhibits personal relationships.

The statute at issue here makes sodomy a crime only if a person "engages in deviate sexual intercourse with another individual of the same sex." Sodomy between opposite-sex partners, however, is not a crime in Texas. That is, Texas treats the same conduct differently based solely on the participants. Those harmed by this law are people who have a same-sex sexual orientation and thus are more likely to engage in behavior prohibited by § 21.06.

The Texas statute makes homosexuals unequal in the eyes of the law by making particular conduct—and only that conduct—subject to criminal sanction. It appears that prosecutions under Texas' sodomy law are rare. This case shows, however, that prosecutions under § 21.06 do occur. And while the penalty imposed on petitioners in this case was relatively minor, the consequences of conviction are not. As the Court notes, petitioners' convictions, if upheld, would disqualify them from or restrict their ability to engage in a variety of professions, including medicine, athletic training, and interior design. Indeed, were petitioners to move to one of four States, their convictions would require them to register as sex offenders to local law enforcement.

Texas attempts to justify its law, and the effects of the law, by arguing that the statute satisfies rational basis review because it furthers the legitimate governmental interest of the promotion of morality. In *Bowers*, we held that a state law criminalizing sodomy as applied to homosexual couples did not violate substantive due process. We rejected the argument that no rational basis existed to justify the law, pointing to the government's interest in promoting morality. The only question in front of the Court in Bowers was whether the substantive component of the Due Process Clause protected a right to engage in homosexual sodomy. *Bowers* did not hold that moral disapproval of a group is a rational basis under the Equal Protection Clause to criminalize homosexual sodomy when heterosexual sodomy is not punished.

Texas argues, however, that the sodomy law does not discriminate against homosexual persons. Instead, the State maintains that the law discriminates only against homosexual conduct. While it is true that the law applies only to conduct, the conduct targeted by this law is conduct that is closely correlated with being homosexual.

A State can of course assign certain consequences to a violation of its criminal law. But the State cannot single out one identifiable class of citizens for punishment that does not apply to everyone else, with moral disapproval as the only asserted state interest for the law.

That this law as applied to private, consensual conduct is unconstitutional under the Equal Protection Clause does not mean that other laws distinguishing between heterosexuals and homosexuals would similarly fail under rational basis review. Texas cannot assert any legitimate state interest here, such as national security or preserving the traditional institution of marriage.

Unlike the moral disapproval of same-sex relations—the asserted state interest in this case—other reasons exist to promote the institution of marriage beyond mere moral disapproval of an excluded group.

A law branding one class of persons as criminal solely based on the State's moral disapproval of that class and the conduct associated with that class runs contrary to the values of the Constitution and the Equal Protection Clause, under any standard of review. I therefore concur in the Court's judgment that Texas' sodomy law banning "deviate sexual intercourse" between consenting adults of the same sex, but not between consenting adults of different sexes, is unconstitutional.

JUSTICE SCALIA, with whom THE CHIEF JUSTICE and JUSTICE THOMAS join, dissenting.

"Liberty finds no refuge in a jurisprudence of doubt." *Planned Parenthood of Southeastern Pa. v. Casey*, 505 U.S. 833, 844 (1992). That was the Court's sententious response, barely more than a decade ago, to those seeking to overrule *Roe v. Wade*, 410 U.S. 113 (1973). The Court's response today, to those who have engaged in a 17-year crusade to overrule *Bowers v. Hardwick*, 478 U.S. 186 (1986), is very different. The need for stability and certainty presents no barrier.

I

I begin with the Court's surprising readiness to reconsider a decision rendered a mere 17 years ago in *Bowers v. Hardwick*. I do not myself believe in rigid adherence to stare decisis in constitutional cases; but I do believe that we should be consistent rather than manipulative in invoking the doctrine.

Today, however, the widespread opposition to *Bowers*, a decision resolving an issue as "intensely divisive" as the issue in *Roe*, is offered as a reason in favor of overruling it. Gone, too, is any "enquiry" (of the sort conducted in *Casey*) into whether the decision sought to be overruled has "proven 'unworkable,' " *Casey*, at 855.

Today's approach to *stare decisis* invites us to overrule an erroneously decided precedent (including an "intensely divisive" decision) if: (1) its foundations have been "eroded" by subsequent decisions; (2) it has been subject to "substantial and continuing" criticism; and (3) it has not induced "individual or societal reliance" that counsels against overturning. The problem is that *Roe* itself—which today's majority surely has no disposition to overrule—satisfies these conditions to at least the same degree as *Bowers*.

II

Having decided that it need not adhere to *stare decisis*, the Court still must establish that *Bowers* was wrongly decided and that the Texas statute, as applied to petitioners, is unconstitutional.

Texas Penal Code Ann. § 21.06(a) (2003) undoubtedly imposes constraints on liberty. So do laws prohibiting prostitution, recreational use of heroin, and, for that matter, working more than 60 hours per week in a bakery. But there is no right to "liberty" under the Due Process Clause, though today's opinion repeatedly makes that claim. The Fourteenth Amendment expressly allows States to deprive their citizens of "liberty," so long as "due process of law" is provided: "No state shall . . . deprive any person of life, liberty, or property, without due process of law."

IV

I turn now to the ground on which the Court squarely rests its holding: the contention that there is no rational basis for the law here under attack. This proposition is so out of accord with our jurisprudence—indeed, with the jurisprudence of any society we know—that it requires little discussion.

The Texas statute undeniably seeks to further the belief of its citizens that certain forms of sexual behavior are "immoral and unacceptable," *Bowers*, at 196—the same interest furthered by criminal laws against fornication, bigamy, adultery, adult incest, bestiality, and obscenity. *Bowers* held that this was a legitimate state interest. The Court today reaches the opposite conclusion. This effectively decrees the end of all morals legislation. If, as the Court asserts, the promotion of majoritarian sexual morality is not even a legitimate state interest, none of the above-mentioned laws can survive rational-basis review.

V

Finally, I turn to petitioners' equal-protection challenge, which no Member of the Court save Justice O'Connor embraces: On its face § 21.06(a) applies equally to all persons. Men and women, heterosexuals and homosexuals, are all subject to its prohibition of deviate sexual intercourse with someone of the same sex. To be sure, § 21.06 does distinguish between the sexes insofar as concerns the partner with whom the sexual acts are performed: men can violate the law only with other men, and women only with other women. But this cannot itself be a denial of equal protection, since it is precisely the same distinction regarding partner that is drawn in state laws prohibiting marriage with someone of the same sex while permitting marriage with someone of the opposite sex.

Today's opinion is the product of a Court, which is the product of a law-profession culture, that has largely signed on to the so-called homosexual agenda, by which I mean the agenda promoted by some homosexual activists directed at eliminating the moral opprobrium that has traditionally attached to homosexual conduct. I noted in an earlier opinion the fact that the American Association of Law Schools (to which any reputable law school must seek to belong) excludes from membership any school that refuses to ban from its job-interview facilities a law firm (no matter how small) that does not wish to hire as a prospective partner a person who openly engages in homosexual conduct.

One of the most revealing statements in today's opinion is the Court's grim warning that the criminalization of homosexual conduct is "an invitation to subject homosexual persons to discrimination both in the public and in the private spheres." It is clear from this that the Court has taken sides in the culture war, departing from its role of assuring, as neutral observer, that the democratic rules of engagement are observed. Many Americans do not want persons who openly engage in homosexual conduct as partners in their business, as scoutmasters for their children, as teachers in their children's schools, or as boarders in their home. They view this as protecting themselves and their families from a lifestyle that they believe to be immoral and destructive. The Court views it as "discrimination" which it is the function of our judgments to deter. So imbued is the Court with the law profession's anti-anti-homosexual culture, that it is seemingly unaware that the attitudes of that culture are not obviously "mainstream"; that in most States what the Court calls "discrimination" against those who engage in homosexual acts is perfectly legal; that proposals to ban such "discrimination" under Title VII have repeatedly been rejected by Congress; that in some cases such "discrimination" is mandated by federal statute; and that in some cases such "discrimination" is a constitutional right.

Let me be clear that I have nothing against homosexuals, or any other group, promoting their agenda through normal democratic means. Social perceptions of sexual and other morality change over time, and every group has the right to persuade its fellow citizens that its view of such matters is the best. That homosexuals have achieved some success in that enterprise is attested to by the fact that Texas is one of the few remaining

States that criminalize private, consensual homosexual acts. But persuading one's fellow citizens is one thing, and imposing one's views in absence of democratic majority will is something else.

The matters appropriate for this Court's resolution are only three: Texas's prohibition of sodomy neither infringes a "fundamental right" (which the Court does not dispute), nor is unsupported by a rational relation to what the Constitution considers a legitimate state interest, nor denies the equal protection of the laws. I dissent.

JUSTICE THOMAS, dissenting.

I join Justice Scalia's dissenting opinion. I write separately to note that the law before the Court today "is . . . uncommonly silly." *Griswold v. Connecticut*, 381 U.S. 479, 527 (1965) (Stewart, J., dissenting). If I were a member of the Texas Legislature, I would vote to repeal it. Punishing someone for expressing his sexual preference through noncommercial consensual conduct with another adult does not appear to be a worthy way to expend valuable law enforcement resources.

Notwithstanding this, I recognize that as a member of this Court I am not empowered to help petitioners and others similarly situated. My duty, rather, is to "decide cases 'agreeably to the Constitution and laws of the United States.' " And, just like Justice Stewart, I "can find [neither in the Bill of Rights nor any other part of the Constitution a] general right of privacy," or as the Court terms it today, the "liberty of the person both in its spatial and more transcendent dimensions."

FOR DISCUSSION

What is the significance of the Court's decision to place protection against same-sex discrimination within the Due Process Clause as opposed to the Equal Protection Clause? How do you respond to Justice Thomas's claim that while it is an "uncommonly silly" law, it needs to be addressed by the Texas legislature and not the federal Supreme Court?

RELATED CASE

***Rumsfeld v. Forum for Academic and Institutional Rights:* 547 U.S. 47 (2006).**

Law schools that refuse access to military recruiters because of conflict between the military's "don't ask, don't tell" policy and the law schools' antidiscrimination policy regarding sexual orientation are still subject to the penalties of a federal law known as the Solomon Amendment, which denies federal funding to institutions that do not allow military recruiters access to students.

UNITED STATES V. WINDSOR

570 U.S. ___, 133 S.Ct. 2675, 186 L.Ed.2d 808 (2013)

Edith Windsor and Thea Spyer were legally married in Ontario, Canada in 2007, subsequently returning to their home in New York City. After Spyer's death in 2009, her estate was left to Windsor, but the Defense of Marriage Act, which explicitly excluded a same-sex partner from being considered a "spouse," prohibited her from claiming the spousal exemption to the estate tax. This statutory prohibition left Windsor with over a $360,000 tax bill. She paid the tax and filed a lawsuit challenging the constitutionality of this provision. Both a federal district court and the court of appeals found this portion of the statute to be unconstitutional, ordering the United States to pay Windsor a refund.

Vote: 5–4

JUSTICE KENNEDY delivered the majority opinion.

I

In 1996, as some States were beginning to consider the concept of same-sex marriage, see, *e.g.*, *Baehr* v. *Lewin*, 74 Haw. 530, 852 P. 2d 44 (1993), and before any State had acted to permit it, Congress enacted the Defense of Marriage Act (DOMA), 110 Stat. 2419. DOMA contains two operative sections: Section 2, which has not been challenged here, allows States to refuse to recognize same-sex marriages performed under the laws of other States. Section 3 is at issue here. It amends the Dictionary Act in Title 1, § 7, of the United States Code to provide a federal definition of "marriage" and "spouse."

The definitional provision does not by its terms forbid States from enacting laws permitting same-sex marriages or civil unions or providing state benefits to residents in that status. The enactment's comprehensive definition of marriage for purposes of all federal statutes and other regulations or directives covered by its terms, however, does control over 1,000 federal laws in which marital or spousal status is addressed as a matter of federal law.

While the tax refund suit was pending, the Attorney General of the United States notified the Speaker of the House of Representatives that the Department of Justice would no longer defend the constitutionality of DOMA's § 3. Noting that "the Department has previously defended DOMA against . . . challenges involving legally married same-sex couples," the Attorney General informed Congress that "the President has concluded that given a number of factors, including a documented history of discrimination, classifications based on sexual orientation should be subject to a heightened standard of scrutiny."

Although "the President . . . instructed the Department not to defend the statute in *Windsor*," he also decided "that Section 3 will continue to be enforced by the Executive Branch" and that the United States had an "interest in providing Congress a full and fair opportunity to participate in the litigation of those cases." The stated rationale for this dual-track procedure (determination of unconstitutionality coupled with ongoing enforcement) was to "recogniz[e] the judiciary as the final arbiter of the constitutional claims raised."

In response to the notice from the Attorney General, the Bipartisan Legal Advisory Group (BLAG) of the House of Representatives voted to intervene in the litigation to defend the constitutionality of § 3 of DOMA. The Department of Justice did not oppose limited intervention by BLAG.

In granting certiorari on the question of the constitutionality of § 3 of DOMA, the Court requested argument on two additional questions: whether the United States' agreement with Windsor's legal position precludes further review and whether BLAG has standing to appeal the case.

III

When at first Windsor and Spyer longed to marry, neither New York nor any other State granted them that right. After waiting some years, in 2007 they traveled to Ontario to be married there. It seems fair to conclude that, until recent years, many citizens had not even considered the possibility that two persons of the same sex might aspire to occupy the same status and dignity as that of a man and woman in lawful marriage. For marriage between a man and a woman no doubt had been thought of by most people as essential to the very definition of that term and to its role and function throughout the history of civilization. That belief, for many who long have held it, became even more urgent, more cherished when challenged. For others, however, came the beginnings of a new perspective, a new insight. Accordingly some States concluded that same-sex marriage ought to be given recognition and validity in the law for those same-sex couples who wish to define themselves by their commitment to each other. The limitation of lawful marriage to heterosexual couples, which for centuries had been deemed both necessary and fundamental, came to be seen in New York and certain other States as an unjust exclusion.

Slowly at first and then in rapid course, the laws of New York came to acknowledge the urgency of this issue for same-sex couples who wanted to affirm their commitment to one another before their children, their family, their friends, and their community. And so New York recognized same-sex marriages performed elsewhere; and then it later amended its own marriage laws to permit same-sex marriage. New York, in common with, as of this writing, 11 other States and the District of Columbia, decided that same-sex couples should have the right to marry and so live with pride in themselves and their union and in a status of equality with all other married persons. After a statewide deliberative process that enabled its citizens to discuss and weigh arguments for and against same-sex marriage, New York acted to enlarge the definition of marriage to correct what its citizens and elected representatives perceived to be an injustice that they had not earlier known or understood.

Against this background of lawful same-sex marriage in some States, the design, purpose, and effect of DOMA should be considered as the beginning point in deciding whether it is valid under the Constitution. By history and tradition the definition and regulation of marriage . . . has been treated as being within the authority and realm of the separate States. Yet it is further established that Congress, in enacting discrete statutes, can make determinations that bear on marital rights and privileges.

[P]recedents involving congressional statutes which affect marriages and family status . . . illustrate this point. In addressing the interaction of state domestic relations and federal immigration law Congress determined that marriages "entered into for the purpose of procuring an alien's admission [to the United States] as an immigrant" will not qualify the noncitizen for that status, even if the noncitizen's marriage is valid and proper for state-law purposes. And in establishing income-based criteria for Social Security benefits, Congress decided that although state law would determine in general who qualifies as an applicant's spouse, common-law marriages also should be recognized, regardless of any particular State's view on these relationships.

Though these discrete examples establish the constitutionality of limited federal laws that regulate the meaning of marriage in order to further federal policy, DOMA has a far greater reach; for it enacts a directive applicable to over 1,000 federal statutes and the whole realm of federal regulations. And its operation is directed to a class of persons that the laws of New York, and of 11 other States, have sought to protect. See *Goodridge* v. *Department of Public Health*, 440 Mass. 309, 798 N. E. 2d 941 (2003).

In order to assess the validity of that intervention it is necessary to discuss the extent of the state power and authority over marriage as a matter of history and tradition. State laws defining and regulating marriage, of course, must respect the constitutional rights of persons; but, subject to those guarantees, "regulation of domestic relations" is "an area that has long been regarded as a virtually exclusive province of the States." *Sosna v. Iowa*, 419 U.S. 393, 403 (1975).

The recognition of civil marriages is central to state domestic relations law applicable to its residents and citizens. The definition of marriage is the foundation of the State's broader authority to regulate the subject of domestic relations with respect to the "[p]rotection of offspring, property interests, and the enforcement of marital responsibilities." *Williams v. North Carolina*, 317 U.S. 287, 298 (1942). "[T]he states, at the time of the adoption of the Constitution, possessed full power over the subject of marriage and divorce... [and] the Constitution delegated no authority to the Government of the United States on the subject of marriage and divorce." *Haddock v. Haddock*, 201 U.S. 562, 575 (1906).

Consistent with this allocation of authority, the Federal Government, through our history, has deferred to state-law policy decisions with respect to domestic relations. In order to respect this principle, the federal courts, as a general rule, do not adjudicate issues of marital status even when there might otherwise be a basis for federal jurisdiction.

The significance of state responsibilities for the definition and regulation of marriage dates to the Nation's beginning; for "when the Constitution was adopted the common understanding was that the domestic relations of husband and wife and parent and child were matters reserved to the States." *Ohio ex rel. Popovici v. Angler*, 280 U.S. 379–384 (1930). Marriage laws vary in some respects from State to State. For example, the required minimum age is 16 in Vermont, but only 13 in New Hampshire. Likewise the permissible degree of consanguinity can vary (most States permit first cousins to marry, but a handful—such as Iowa and Washington—prohibit the practice). But these rules are in every event consistent within each State.

Against this background DOMA rejects the long-established precept that the incidents, benefits, and obligations of marriage are uniform for all married couples within each State, though they may vary, subject to constitutional guarantees, from one State to the next. Despite these considerations, it is unnecessary to decide whether this federal intrusion on state power is a violation of the Constitution because it disrupts the federal balance. The State's power in defining the marital relation is of central relevance in this case quite apart from principles of federalism. Here the State's decision to give this class of persons the right to marry conferred upon them a dignity and status of immense import. When the State used its historic and essential authority to define the marital relation in this way, its role and its power in making the decision enhanced the recognition, dignity, and protection of the class in their own community. DOMA, because of its reach and extent, departs from this history and tradition of reliance on state law to define marriage.

The Federal Government uses this state-defined class for the opposite purpose—to impose restrictions and disabilities. That result requires this Court now to address whether the resulting injury and indignity is a deprivation of an essential part of the liberty protected by the Fifth Amendment. What the State of New York treats as alike the federal law deems unlike by a law designed to injure the same class the State seeks to protect. In acting first to recognize and then to allow same-sex marriages, New York was responding "to the initiative of those who [sought] a voice in shaping the destiny of their own times." These actions were without doubt a proper exercise of its sovereign authority within our federal system, all in the way that the Framers of the Constitution intended. The dynamics of state government in the federal system are to allow the formation of consensus respecting the way the members of a discrete community treat each other in their daily contact and constant interaction with each other.

The States' interest in defining and regulating the marital relation, subject to constitutional guarantees, stems from the understanding that marriage is more than a routine classification for purposes of certain statutory benefits. Private, consensual sexual intimacy between two adult persons of the same sex may not be punished by the State, and it can form "but one element in a personal bond that is more enduring." *Lawrence* v. *Texas*, 539 U. S. 558, 567 (2003). By its recognition of the validity of same-sex marriages performed in other jurisdictions and then by authorizing same-sex unions and same-sex marriages, New York sought to give further protection and dignity to that bond. *Bond v. U.S.*, 564 U.S. [211] (2011). For same-sex couples who wished to be married, the State acted to give their lawful conduct a lawful status. This status is a far-reaching legal acknowledgment of the intimate relationship between two people, a relationship deemed by the State worthy of dignity in the community equal with all other marriages. It reflects both the community's considered perspective on the historical roots of the institution of marriage and its evolving understanding of the meaning of equality.

IV

DOMA seeks to injure the very class New York seeks to protect. By doing so it violates basic due process and equal protection principles applicable to the Federal Government. The Constitution's guarantee of equality "must at the very least mean that a bare congressional desire to harm a politically unpopular group cannot" justify disparate treatment of that group. In determining whether a law is motived by an improper animus or purpose, " '[d]iscriminations of an unusual character' " especially require careful consideration. DOMA cannot survive under these principles. The responsibility of the States for the regulation of domestic relations is an important indicator of the substantial societal impact the State's classifications have in the daily lives and customs of its people. DOMA's unusual deviation from the usual tradition of recognizing and accepting state definitions of marriage here operates to deprive same-sex couples of the benefits and responsibilities that come with the federal recognition of their marriages. This is strong evidence of a law having the purpose and effect of disapproval of that class. The avowed purpose and practical effect of the law here in question are to impose a disadvantage, a separate status, and so a stigma upon all who enter into same-sex marriages made lawful by the unquestioned authority of the States.

The history of DOMA's enactment and its own text demonstrate that interference with the equal dignity of same-sex marriages, a dignity conferred by the States in the exercise of their sovereign power, was more than an incidental effect of the federal statute. It was its essence. The House Report announced its conclusion that "it is both appropriate and necessary for Congress to do what it can to defend the institution of traditional heterosexual marriage. . . . H. R. 3396 is appropriately entitled the 'Defense of Marriage Act.' The effort to redefine 'marriage' to extend to homosexual couples is a truly radical proposal that would fundamentally alter the institution of marriage." The House concluded that DOMA expresses "both moral disapproval of homosexuality, and a moral conviction that heterosexuality better comports with traditional (especially Judeo-Christian) morality." The stated purpose of the law was to promote an "interest in protecting the traditional moral teachings reflected in heterosexual-only marriage laws." Were there any doubt of this far-reaching purpose, the title of the Act confirms it: The Defense of Marriage.

DOMA's operation in practice confirms this purpose. When New York adopted a law to permit same-sex marriage, it sought to eliminate inequality; but DOMA frustrates that objective through a system-wide enactment with no identified connection to any particular area of federal law. DOMA writes inequality into the entire United States Code. The particular case at hand concerns the estate tax, but DOMA is more than a simple determination of what should or should not be allowed as an estate tax refund. Among the over 1,000 statutes and numerous federal regulations that DOMA controls are laws pertaining to Social Security, housing, taxes, criminal sanctions, copyright, and veterans' benefits.

DOMA's principal effect is to identify a subset of state-sanctioned marriages and make them unequal. The principal purpose is to impose inequality, not for other reasons like governmental efficiency. Responsibilities, as well as rights, enhance the dignity and integrity of the person. And DOMA contrives to deprive some couples married under the laws of their State, but not other couples, of both rights and responsibilities. By creating two contradictory marriage regimes within the same State, DOMA forces same-sex couples to live as married for the purpose of state law but unmarried for the purpose of federal law, thus diminishing the stability and predictability of basic personal relations the State has found it proper to acknowledge and protect. By this dynamic DOMA undermines both the public and private significance of state- sanctioned same-sex marriages; for it tells those couples, and all the world, that their otherwise valid marriages are unworthy of federal recognition. This places same-sex couples in an unstable position of being in a second-tier marriage. The differentiation demeans the couple, whose moral and sexual choices the Constitution protects, see *Lawrence*, 539 U. S. 558, and whose relationship the State has sought to dignify. And it humiliates tens of thousands of children now being raised by same-sex couples. The law in question makes it even more difficult for the children to understand the integrity and closeness of their own family and its concord with other families in their community and in their daily lives.

* * *

The power the Constitution grants it also restrains. And though Congress has great authority to design laws to fit its own conception of sound national policy, it cannot deny the liberty protected by the Due Process Clause of the Fifth Amendment.

What has been explained to this point should more than suffice to establish that the principal purpose and the necessary effect of this law are to demean those persons who are in a lawful same-sex marriage. This requires the Court to hold, as it now does, that DOMA is unconstitutional as a deprivation of the liberty of the person protected by the Fifth Amendment of the Constitution.

The liberty protected by the Fifth Amendment's Due Process Clause contains within it the prohibition against denying to any person the equal protection of the laws. While the Fifth Amendment itself withdraws from Government the power to degrade or demean in the way this law does, the equal protection guarantee of the Fourteenth Amendment makes that Fifth Amendment right all the more specific and all the better understood and preserved.

The class to which DOMA directs its restrictions and restraints are those persons who are joined in same-sex marriages made lawful by the State. DOMA singles out a class of persons deemed by a State entitled to recognition and protection to enhance their own liberty. It imposes a disability on the class by refusing to acknowledge a status the State finds to be dignified and proper. DOMA instructs all federal officials, and indeed all persons with whom same-sex couples interact, including their own children, that their marriage is less worthy than the marriages of others. The federal statute is invalid, for no legitimate purpose overcomes the purpose and effect to disparage and to injure those whom the State, by its marriage laws, sought to protect in personhood and dignity. By seeking to displace this protection and treating those persons as living in marriages less respected than others, the federal statute is in violation of the Fifth Amendment. This opinion and its holding are confined to those lawful marriages.

The judgment of the Court of Appeals for the Second Circuit is affirmed.

It is so ordered.

CHIEF JUSTICE ROBERTS, dissenting.

On the merits of the constitutional dispute the Court decides to decide, I . . . agree with Justice Scalia that Congress acted constitutionally in passing the Defense of Marriage Act (DOMA). Interests in uniformity and stability amply justified Congress's decision to retain the definition of marriage that, at that point, had been adopted by every State in our Nation, and every nation in the world.

The majority sees a more sinister motive, pointing out that the Federal Government has generally (though not uniformly) deferred to state definitions of marriage in the past. That is true, of course, but none of those prior state-by-state variations had involved differences over something—as the majority puts it—"thought of by most people as essential to the very definition of [marriage] and to its role and function throughout the history of civilization." That the Federal Government treated this fundamental question differently than it treated variations over consanguinity or minimum age is hardly surprising—and hardly enough to support a conclusion that the "principal purpose," of the 342 Representatives and 85 Senators who voted for it, and the President who signed it, was a bare desire to harm. Nor do the snippets of legislative history and the banal title of the Act to which the majority points suffice to make such a showing. At least without some more convincing evidence that the Act's principal purpose was to codify malice, and that it furthered *no* legitimate government interests, I would not tar the political branches with the brush of bigotry.

But while I disagree with the result to which the majority's analysis leads it in this case, I think it more important to point out that its analysis leads no further. The Court does not have before it, and the logic of its opinion does not decide, the distinct question whether the States, in the exercise of their "historic and essential authority to define the marital relation," may continue to utilize the traditional definition of marriage.

The majority goes out of its way to make this explicit in the penultimate sentence of its opinion. It states that "[t]his opinion and its holding are confined to those lawful marriages,"—referring to same-sex marriages that a State has already recognized as a result of the local "community's considered perspective on the historical roots of the institution of marriage and its evolving understanding of the meaning of equality." Justice Scalia believes this is a " 'bald, unreasoned disclaime[r].' " In my view, though, the disclaimer is a logical and necessary consequence of the argument the majority has chosen to adopt. The dominant theme of the majority opinion is that the Federal Government's intrusion into an area "central to state domestic relations law applicable to its residents and citizens" is sufficiently "unusual" to set off alarm bells. I think the majority goes off course, as I have said, but it is undeniable that its judgment is based on federalism.

The majority extensively chronicles DOMA's departure from the normal allocation of responsibility between State and Federal Governments, emphasizing that DOMA "rejects the long-established precept that the incidents, benefits, and obligations of marriage are uniform for all married couples within each State." But there is no such departure when one State adopts or keeps a definition of marriage that differs from that of its neighbor, for it is entirely expected that state definitions would "vary, subject to constitutional guarantees, from one State to the next." Thus, while "[t]he State's power in defining the marital relation is of central relevance" to the majority's decision to strike down DOMA here, that power will come into play on the other side of the board in future cases about the constitutionality of state marriage definitions. So too will the concerns for state diversity and sovereignty that weigh against DOMA's constitutionality in this case.

We may in the future have to resolve challenges to state marriage definitions affecting same-sex couples. That issue, however, is not before us in this case. . . . I write only to highlight the limits of the majority's holding and reasoning today, lest its opinion be taken to resolve not only a question that I believe is not properly before us—DOMA's constitutionality—but also a question that all agree, and the Court explicitly acknowledges, is not at issue.

JUSTICE SCALIA, with whom JUSTICE THOMAS joins, and with whom THE CHIEF JUSTICE joins as to Part I, dissenting.

This case is about power in several respects. It is about the power of our people to govern themselves, and the power of this Court to pronounce the law. Today's opinion aggrandizes the latter, with the predictable consequence of diminishing the former. We have no power to decide this case. And even if we did, we have no power under the Constitution to invalidate this democratically adopted legislation. The Court's errors on both points spring forth from the same diseased root: an exalted conception of the role of this institution in America.

I A

The Court is eager—*hungry*—to tell everyone its view of the legal question at the heart of this case. Standing in the way is an obstacle, a technicality of little interest to anyone but the people of We the People, who created it as a barrier against judges' intrusion into their lives. They gave judges, in Article III, only the "judicial Power," a power to decide not abstract questions but real, concrete "Cases" and "Controversies." Yet the plaintiff and the Government agree entirely on what should happen in this lawsuit. They agree that the court below got it right; and they agreed in the court below that the court below that one got it right as well. What, then, are we *doing* here?

The answer lies at the heart of the jurisdictional portion of today's opinion, where a single sentence lays bare the majority's vision of our role. The Court says that we have the power to decide this case because if we did not, then our "primary role in determining the constitutionality of a law" (at least one that "has inflicted real injury on a plaintiff") would "become only secondary to the President's." But wait, the reader wonders—Windsor won below, and so *cured* her injury, and the President was glad to see it. True, says the majority, but judicial review must march on regardless, lest we "undermine the clear dictate of the separation-of-powers principle that when an Act of Congress is alleged to conflict with the Constitution, it is emphatically the province and duty of the judicial department to say what the law is."

That is jaw-dropping. It is an assertion of judicial supremacy over the people's Representatives in Congress and the Executive. It envisions a Supreme Court standing (or rather enthroned) at the apex of government, empowered to decide all constitutional questions, always and everywhere "primary" in its role.

Our authority begins and ends with the need to adjudge the rights of an injured party who stands before us seeking redress.

That is completely absent here. Windsor's injury was cured by the judgment in her favor. And while, in ordinary circumstances, the United States is injured by a directive to pay a tax refund, this suit is far from ordinary. Whatever injury the United States has suffered will surely not be redressed by the action that it, as a litigant, asks us to take. The final sentence of the Solicitor General's brief on the merits reads: "For the foregoing reasons, the judgment of the court of appeals *should be affirmed*." That will not cure the Government's injury, but carve it into stone. One could spend many fruitless afternoons ransacking our library for any other petitioner's brief seeking an affirmance of the judgment against it. What the petitioner United States asks us to do in the case before us is exactly what the respondent Windsor asks us to do: not to provide relief from the judgment below but to say that that judgment was correct. And the same was true in the Court of Appeals: Neither party sought to undo the judgment for Windsor, and so that court should have dismissed the appeal (just as we should dismiss) for lack of jurisdiction. Since both parties agreed with the judgment of the District Court for the Southern District of New York, the suit should have ended there. The further proceedings have been a contrivance, having no object in mind except to elevate a District Court judgment that has no precedential effect in other courts, to one that has precedential effect throughout the Second Circuit, and then (in this Court) precedential effect throughout the United States.

II

For the reasons above, I think that this Court has, and the Court of Appeals had, no power to decide this suit. We should vacate the decision below and remand to the Court of Appeals for the Second Circuit, with instructions to dismiss the appeal. Given that the majority has volunteered its view of the merits, however, I proceed to discuss that as well.

A

There are many remarkable things about the majority's merits holding. The first is how rootless and shifting its justifications are. For example, the opinion starts with seven full pages about the traditional power of States to define domestic relations—initially fooling many readers, I am sure, into thinking that this is a federalism opinion. But we are eventually told that "it is unnecessary to decide whether this federal intrusion on state power is a violation of the Constitution," and that "[t]he State's power in defining the marital relation is of central relevance in this case quite apart from principles of federalism" because "the State's decision to give this class of persons the right to marry conferred upon them a dignity and status of immense import." But no one questions the power of the States to define marriage (with the concomitant conferral of dignity and status), so what is the point of devoting seven pages to describing how long and well established that power is? Even after the opinion has formally disclaimed reliance upon principles of federalism, mentions of "the usual tradition of recognizing and accepting state definitions of marriage" continue. What to make of this? The opinion never explains. My guess is that the majority, while reluctant to suggest that defining the meaning of "marriage" in federal statutes is unsupported by any of the Federal Government's enumerated powers, nonetheless needs some rhetorical basis to support its pretense that today's prohibition of laws excluding same-sex marriage is confined to the Federal Government (leaving the second, state-law shoe to be dropped later, maybe next Term). But I am only guessing.

Equally perplexing are the opinion's references to "the Constitution's guarantee of equality." Near the end of the opinion, we are told that although the "equal protection guarantee of the Fourteenth Amendment makes

[the] Fifth Amendment [due process] right all the more specific and all the better understood and preserved"—what can *that* mean?—"the Fifth Amendment itself withdraws from Government the power to degrade or demean in the way this law does." The only possible interpretation of this statement is that the Equal Protection Clause, even the Equal Protection Clause as incorporated in the Due Process Clause, is not the basis for today's holding. But the portion of the majority opinion that explains why DOMA is unconstitutional (Part IV) begins by citing . . . equal-protection cases. And those three cases are the *only* authorities that the Court cites in Part IV about the Constitution's meaning, except for its citation of *Lawrence* v. *Texas*, 539 U. S. 558 (2003) (not an equal-protection case) to support its passing assertion that the Constitution protects the "moral and sexual choices" of same-sex couples.

Moreover, if this is meant to be an equal-protection opinion, it is a confusing one. The opinion does not resolve and indeed does not even mention what had been the central question in this litigation: whether, under the Equal Protection Clause, laws restricting marriage to a man and a woman are reviewed for more than mere rationality. That is the issue that divided the parties and the court below. In accord with my previously expressed skepticism about the Court's "tiers of scrutiny" approach, I would review this classification only for its rationality. As nearly as I can tell, the Court agrees with that; its opinion does not apply strict scrutiny, and its central propositions are taken from rational-basis cases like *Moreno*. But the Court certainly does not *apply* anything that resembles that deferential framework.

The majority opinion need not get into the strict-vs-rational-basis scrutiny question, and need not justify its holding under either, because it says that DOMA is unconstitutional as "a deprivation of the liberty of the person protected by the Fifth Amendment of the Constitution," that it violates "basic due process" principles, and that it inflicts an "injury and indignity" of a kind that denies "an essential part of the liberty protected by the Fifth Amendment." The majority never utters the dread words "substantive due process," perhaps sensing the disrepute into which that doctrine has fallen, but that is what those statements mean. Yet the opinion does not argue that same-sex marriage is "deeply rooted in this Nation's history and tradition," a claim that would of course be quite absurd. So would the further suggestion (also necessary, under our substantive-due-process precedents) that a world in which DOMA exists is one bereft of " 'ordered liberty.' "

Some might conclude that this loaf could have used a while longer in the oven. But that would be wrong; it is already overcooked. The most expert care in preparation cannot redeem a bad recipe. The sum of all the Court's nonspecific hand-waving is that this law is invalid (maybe on equal-protection grounds, maybe on substantive-due-process grounds, and perhaps with some amorphous federalism component playing a role) because it is motivated by a " 'bare . . . desire to harm' " couples in same-sex marriages. It is this proposition with which I will therefore engage.

B

As I have observed before, the Constitution does not forbid the government to enforce traditional moral and sexual norms. I will not swell the U. S. Reports with restatements of that point. It is enough to say that the Constitution neither requires nor forbids our society to approve of same-sex marriage, much as it neither requires nor forbids us to approve of no-fault divorce, polygamy, or the consumption of alcohol.

However, even setting aside traditional moral disapproval of same-sex marriage (or indeed same-sex sex), there are many perfectly valid—indeed, downright boring—justifying rationales for this legislation. Their existence ought to be the end of this case. For they give the lie to the Court's conclusion that only those with hateful hearts could have voted "aye" on this Act. And more importantly, they serve to make the contents of the legislators' hearts quite irrelevant: "It is a familiar principle of constitutional law that this Court will not strike down an otherwise constitutional statute on the basis of an alleged illicit legislative motive." *United States* v. *O'Brien*, 391 U. S. 367, 383 (1968). Or at least it *was* a familiar principle. By holding to the contrary, the majority has declared open season on any law that (in the opinion of the law's opponents and any panel of like-minded federal judges) can be characterized as mean-spirited.

The majority concludes that the only motive for this Act was the "bare . . . desire to harm a politically unpopular group." Bear in mind that the object of this condemnation is not the legislature of some once-Confederate Southern state (familiar objects of the Court's scorn, but our respected coordinate branches, the Congress and Presidency of the United States. Laying such a charge against them should require the most extraordinary evidence, and I would have thought that every attempt would be made to indulge a more anodyne explanation for the statute. The majority does the opposite—affirmatively concealing from the reader the arguments that exist in justification. It makes only a passing mention of the "arguments put forward" by the Act's defenders, and does not even trouble to paraphrase or describe them. I imagine that this is because it is harder to maintain the illusion of the Act's supporters as unhinged members of a wild-eyed lynch mob when one first describes their views as *they* see them.

* * *

By formally declaring anyone opposed to same-sex marriage an enemy of human decency, the majority arms well every challenger to a state law restricting marriage to its traditional definition. Henceforth those challengers will lead with this Court's declaration that there is "no legitimate purpose" served by such a law, and will claim that the traditional definition has "the purpose and effect to disparage and to injure" the "personhood and dignity" of same-sex couples. The majority's limiting assurance will be meaningless in the face of language like that, as the majority well knows. That is why the language is there. The result will be a judicial distortion of our society's debate over marriage—a debate that can seem in need of our clumsy "help" only to a member of this institution.

As to that debate: Few public controversies touch an institution so central to the lives of so many, and few inspire such attendant passion by good people on all sides. Few public controversies will ever demonstrate so vividly the beauty of what our Framers gave us, a gift the Court pawns today to buy its stolen moment in the spotlight: a system of government that permits us to rule *ourselves*. Since DOMA's passage, citizens on all sides of the question have seen victories and they have seen defeats. There have been plebiscites, legislation, persuasion, and loud voices—in other words, democracy. Victories in one place are offset by victories in other places for others. Even in a *single State*, the question has come out differently on different occasions.

In the majority's telling, this story is black-and-white: Hate your neighbor or come along with us. The truth is more complicated. It is hard to admit that one's political opponents are not monsters, especially in a struggle like this one, and the challenge in the end proves more than today's Court can handle. Too bad. A reminder that disagreement over something so fundamental as marriage can still be politically legitimate would have been a fit task for what in earlier times was called the judicial temperament. We might have covered ourselves with honor today, by promising all sides of this debate that it was theirs to settle and that we would respect their resolution. We might have let the People decide.

But that the majority will not do. Some will rejoice in today's decision, and some will despair at it; that is the nature of a controversy that matters so much to so many. But the Court has cheated both sides, robbing the winners of an honest victory, and the losers of the peace that comes from a fair defeat. We owed both of them better. I dissent.

JUSTICE ALITO, with whom JUSTICE THOMAS joins as to Parts II and III, dissenting.

Our Nation is engaged in a heated debate about same-sex marriage. That debate is, at bottom, about the nature of the institution of marriage. Respondent Edith Windsor, supported by the United States, asks this Court to intervene in that debate, and although she couches her argument in different terms, what she seeks is a holding that enshrines in the Constitution a particular understanding of marriage under which the sex of the partners makes no difference. The Constitution, however, does not dictate that choice. It leaves the choice to the people, acting through their elected representatives at both the federal and state levels. I would therefore hold that Congress did not violate Windsor's constitutional rights by enacting § 3 of the Defense of Marriage Act (DOMA), which defines the meaning of marriage under federal statutes that either confer upon married persons certain federal benefits or impose upon them certain federal obligations.

II

Windsor and the United States argue that § 3 of DOMA violates the equal protection principles that the Court has found in the Fifth Amendment's Due Process Clause. The Court rests its holding on related arguments.

Same-sex marriage presents a highly emotional and important question of public policy—but not a difficult question of constitutional law. The Constitution does not guarantee the right to enter into a same-sex marriage. Indeed, no provision of the Constitution speaks to the issue.

The Court has sometimes found the Due Process Clauses to have a substantive component that guarantees liberties beyond the absence of physical restraint. And the Court's holding that "DOMA is unconstitutional as a deprivation of the liberty of the person protected by the Fifth Amendment of the Constitution," suggests that substantive due process may partially underlie the Court's decision today. But it is well established that any "substantive" component to the Due Process Clause protects only "those fundamental rights and liberties which are, objectively, 'deeply rooted in this Nation's history and tradition,' " as well as " 'implicit in the concept of ordered liberty,' such that 'neither liberty nor justice would exist if they were sacrificed.' "

It is beyond dispute that the right to same-sex marriage is not deeply rooted in this Nation's history and tradition. In this country, no State permitted same-sex marriage until the Massachusetts Supreme Judicial Court held in 2003 that limiting marriage to opposite-sex couples violated the State Constitution. Nor is the right to same-sex marriage deeply rooted in the traditions of other nations. No country allowed same-sex couples to marry until the Netherlands did so in 2000.

What Windsor and the United States seek, therefore, is not the protection of a deeply rooted right but the recognition of a very new right, and they seek this innovation not from a legislative body elected by the people, but from unelected judges. Faced with such a request, judges have cause for both caution and humility.

The family is an ancient and universal human institution. Family structure reflects the characteristics of a civilization, and changes in family structure and in the popular understanding of marriage and the family can have profound effects. Past changes in the understanding of marriage—for example, the gradual ascendance of the idea that romantic love is a prerequisite to marriage—have had far-reaching consequences. But the process by which such consequences come about is complex, involving the interaction of numerous factors, and tends to occur over an extended period of time.

We can expect something similar to take place if same-sex marriage becomes widely accepted. The long-term consequences of this change are not now known and are unlikely to be ascertainable for some time to come. There are those who think that allowing same-sex marriage will seriously undermine the institution of marriage. Others think that recognition of same-sex marriage will fortify a now-shaky institution.

At present, no one—including social scientists, philosophers, and historians—can predict with any certainty what the long-term ramifications of widespread acceptance of same-sex marriage will be. And judges are certainly not equipped to make such an assessment. The Members of this Court have the authority and the responsibility to interpret and apply the Constitution. Thus, if the Constitution contained a provision guaranteeing the right to marry a person of the same sex, it would be our duty to enforce that right. But the Constitution simply does not speak to the issue of same-sex marriage. In our system of government, ultimate sovereignty rests with the people, and the people have the right to control their own destiny. Any change on a question so fundamental should be made by the people through their elected officials.

III

Perhaps because they cannot show that same-sex marriage is a fundamental right under our Constitution, Windsor and the United States couch their arguments in equal protection terms. They argue that § 3 of DOMA discriminates on the basis of sexual orientation, that classifications based on sexual orientation should trigger a form of "heightened" scrutiny, and that § 3 cannot survive such scrutiny. They further maintain that the governmental interests that § 3 purports to serve are not sufficiently important and that it has not been adequately shown that § 3 serves those interests very well. The Court's holding, too, seems to rest on "the equal protection guarantee of the Fourteenth Amendment"—although the Court is careful not to adopt most of Windsor's and the United States' argument.

In my view, the approach that Windsor and the United States advocate is misguided. Our equal protection framework, upon which Windsor and the United States rely, is a judicial construct that provides a useful mechanism for analyzing a certain universe of equal protection cases. But that framework is ill suited for use in evaluating the constitutionality of laws based on the traditional understanding of marriage, which fundamentally turn on what marriage is.

JUSTICE ALITO, dissenting.

III.

Underlying our equal protection jurisprudence is the central notion that "[a] classification 'must be reasonable, not arbitrary, and must rest upon some ground of difference having a fair and substantial relation to the object of the legislation, so that all persons similarly circumstanced shall be treated alike.' " *Reed v. Reed*, 404 U.S. 71, 76 (1971). The modern tiers of scrutiny—on which Windsor and the United States rely so heavily—are a heuristic to help judges determine when classifications have that "fair and substantial relation to the object of the legislation," *Reed*, at 76.

In asking the Court to determine that § 3 of DOMA is subject to and violates heightened scrutiny, Windsor and the United States thus ask us to rule that the presence of two members of the opposite sex is as rationally related to marriage as white skin is to voting or a Y-chromosome is to the ability to administer an estate. That is a striking request and one that unelected judges should pause before granting. Acceptance of the argument would cast all those who cling to traditional beliefs about the nature of marriage in the role of bigots or superstitious fools.

By asking the Court to strike down DOMA as not satisfying some form of heightened scrutiny, Windsor and the United States are really seeking to have the Court resolve a debate between two competing views of marriage.

The first and older view, which I will call the "traditional" or "conjugal" view, sees marriage as an intrinsically opposite-sex institution. [The Bipartisan Legal Advisory Group of the House of Representatives (BLAG)] notes that virtually every culture, including many not influenced by the Abrahamic religions, has limited marriage to people of the opposite sex. And BLAG attempts to explain this phenomenon by arguing that the institution of marriage was created for the purpose of channeling heterosexual intercourse into a structure that supports child rearing.

Others explain the basis for the institution in more philosophical terms. They argue that marriage is essentially the solemnizing of a comprehensive, exclusive, permanent union that is intrinsically ordered to producing new life, even if it does not always do so. While modern cultural changes have weakened the link between marriage and procreation in the popular mind, there is no doubt that, throughout human history and across many cultures, marriage has been viewed as an exclusively opposite-sex institution and as one inextricably linked to procreation and biological kinship.

The other, newer view is what I will call the "consent-based" vision of marriage, a vision that primarily defines marriage as the solemnization of mutual commitment—marked by strong emotional attachment and sexual attraction—between two persons. At least as it applies to heterosexual couples, this view of marriage now plays a very prominent role in the popular understanding of the institution. Indeed, our popular culture is infused with this understanding of marriage. Proponents of same-sex marriage argue that because gender differentiation is not relevant to this vision, the exclusion of same-sex couples from the institution of marriage is rank discrimination. The Constitution does not codify either of these views of marriage (although I suspect it would have been hard at the time of the adoption of the Constitution or the Fifth Amendment to find Americans who did not take the traditional view for granted). The silence of the Constitution on this question should be enough to end the matter as far as the judiciary is concerned. Yet, Windsor and the United States implicitly ask us to endorse the consent-based view of marriage and to reject the traditional view, thereby arrogating to ourselves the power to decide a question that philosophers, historians, social scientists, and theologians are better qualified to explore. Because our constitutional order assigns the resolution of questions of this nature to the people, I would not presume to enshrine either vision of marriage in our constitutional jurisprudence.

Legislatures, however, have little choice but to decide between the two views. We have long made clear that neither the political branches of the Federal Government nor state governments are required to be neutral between competing visions of the good, provided that the vision of the good that they adopt is not countermanded by the Constitution. Accordingly, both Congress and the States are entitled to enact laws recognizing either of the two understandings of marriage. And given the size of government and the degree to which it now regulates daily life, it seems unlikely that either Congress or the States could maintain complete neutrality even if they tried assiduously to do so.

Rather than fully embracing the arguments made by Windsor and the United States, the Court strikes down § 3 of [The Defense of Marriage Act (DOMA)] as a classification not properly supported by its objectives. The Court reaches this conclusion in part because it believes that § 3 encroaches upon the States' sovereign prerogative to define marriage. Indeed, the Court's ultimate conclusion is that DOMA falls afoul of the Fifth Amendment because it "singles out a class of persons deemed *by a State* entitled to recognition and protection to enhance their own liberty" and "imposes a disability on the class by refusing to acknowledge a status *the State finds* to be dignified and proper."

To the extent that the Court takes the position that the question of same-sex marriage should be resolved primarily at the state level, I wholeheartedly agree. I hope that the Court will ultimately permit the people of each State to decide this question for themselves. Unless the Court is willing to allow this to occur, the whiffs of federalism in the today's opinion of the Court will soon be scattered to the wind.

In any event, § 3 of DOMA, in my view, does not encroach on the prerogatives of the States, assuming of course that the many federal statutes affected by DOMA have not already done so. Section 3 does not prevent any State from recognizing same-sex marriage or from extending to same-sex couples any right, privilege, benefit, or obligation stemming from state law. All that § 3 does is to define a class of persons to whom federal law extends certain special benefits and upon whom federal law imposes certain special burdens. In these provisions, Congress used marital status as a way of defining this class—in part, I assume, because it viewed marriage as a valuable institution to be fostered and in part because it viewed married couples as comprising a unique type of economic unit that merits special regulatory treatment. Assuming that Congress has the power under the Constitution to enact the laws affected by § 3, Congress has the power to define the category of persons to whom those laws apply.

FOR DISCUSSION

The opinions articulate different understandings of the role of the court in addressing conflicts between states, federal legislatures, and the executive. What are these interpretations? Did § 3 of DOMA impinge on the authority of the state to regulate marriage? Why or why not?

RELATED CASE

***Hollingsworth v. Perry:* 570 U.S. ___ (2013).**

The US Supreme Court determined advocates for California's Proposition 8, which overturned a State Supreme Court decision allowing for same sex marriage, did not have standing to appeal a district court decision countermanding the referendum as violating the Equal Protection Clause of the Constitution.

OBERGEFELL V. HODGES, DIRECTOR, OHIO DEPARTMENT OF HEALTH

576 U. S. ___, 135 S.Ct. 2071, 191 L.Ed. 2d 953 (2015)

Fourteen same-sex couples and two men whose partners were deceased challenged state laws in Michigan, Kentucky, Ohio, and Tennessee that prohibited same-sex marriages. They brought a Fourteenth Amendment claim against their state officials responsible for enforcing these state laws. The petitioners argued that states violated the federal constitution when states denied them the right to marry or refused to recognize their marriage when lawfully performed in another state. Each of the federal district courts ruled in favor of the petitioners. Upon the four states' appeal, the Sixth Circuit consolidated these cases and reversed the lower courts in *DeBoer v. Synder*, 772 F.3d 388 (2014).

Vote: 5–4

JUSTICE KENNEDY delivered the opinion of the Court.

The Constitution promises liberty to all within its reach, a liberty that includes certain specific rights that allow persons, within a lawful realm, to define and express their identity. The petitioners in these cases seek to find that liberty by marrying someone of the same sex and having their marriages deemed lawful on the same terms and conditions as marriages between persons of the opposite sex.

I

These cases come from Michigan, Kentucky, Ohio, and Tennessee, States that define marriage as a union between one man and one woman.

This Court granted review, limited to two questions. The first, presented by the cases from Michigan and Kentucky, is whether the Fourteenth Amendment requires a State to license a marriage between two people of the same sex. The second, presented by the cases from Ohio, Tennessee, and, again, Kentucky, is whether the Fourteenth Amendment requires a State to recognize a same-sex marriage licensed and performed in a State which does grant that right.

II

Before addressing the principles and precedents that govern these cases, it is appropriate to note the history of the subject now before the Court.

A

From their beginning to their most recent page, the annals of human history reveal the transcendent importance of marriage. The lifelong union of a man and a woman always has promised nobility and dignity to all persons, without regard to their station in life. Marriage is sacred to those who live by their religions and offers unique fulfillment to those who find meaning in the secular realm. Its dynamic allows two people to find a life that could not be found alone, for a marriage becomes greater than just the two persons. Rising from the most basic human needs, marriage is essential to our most profound hopes and aspirations.

The centrality of marriage to the human condition makes it unsurprising that the institution has existed for millennia and across civilizations

That history is the beginning of these cases. The respondents say it should be the end as well. To them, it would demean a timeless institution if the concept and lawful status of marriage were extended to two persons of the same sex. Marriage, in their view, is by its nature a gender-differentiated union of man and woman. This view long has been held—and continues to be held—in good faith by reasonable and sincere people here and throughout the world.

The petitioners acknowledge this history but contend that these cases cannot end there. Were their intent to demean the revered idea and reality of marriage, the petitioners' claims would be of a different order. But that is neither their purpose nor their submission. To the contrary, it is the enduring importance of marriage that underlies the petitioners' contentions. This, they say, is their whole point. Far from seeking to devalue marriage, the petitioners seek it for themselves because of their respect—and need—for its privileges and responsibilities. And their immutable nature dictates that same-sex marriage is their only real path to this profound commitment.

Recounting the circumstances of three of these cases illustrates the urgency of the petitioners' cause from their perspective. Petitioner James Obergefell, a plaintiff in the Ohio case, met John Arthur over two decades ago. They fell in love and started a life together, establishing a lasting, committed relation. In 2011, however, Arthur was diagnosed with amyotrophic lateral sclerosis, or ALS. This debilitating disease is progressive, with no known cure. Two years ago, Obergefell and Arthur decided to commit to one another, resolving to marry before Arthur died. To fulfill their mutual promise, they traveled from Ohio to Maryland, where same-sex marriage was legal. It was difficult for Arthur to move, and so the couple was wed inside a medical transport plane as it remained on the tarmac in Baltimore. Three months later, Arthur died. Ohio law does not permit Obergefell to be listed as the surviving spouse on Arthur's death certificate. By statute, they must remain strangers even in death, a state-imposed separation Obergefell deems "hurtful for the rest of time." He brought suit to be shown as the surviving spouse on Arthur's death certificate.

April DeBoer and Jayne Rowse are co-plaintiffs in the case from Michigan. They celebrated a commitment ceremony to honor their permanent relation in 2007. They both work as nurses, DeBoer in a neonatal unit and Rowse in an emergency unit. In 2009, DeBoer and Rowse fostered and then adopted a baby boy. Later that same year, they welcomed another son into their family. The new baby, born prematurely and abandoned by his biological mother, required around-the-clock care. The next year, a baby girl with special needs joined their family. Michigan, however, permits only opposite-sex married couples or single individuals to adopt, so each child can have only one woman as his or her legal parent. If an emergency were to arise, schools and hospitals may treat the three children as if they had only one parent. And, were tragedy to befall either DeBoer or Rowse, the other would have no legal rights over the children she had not been permitted to adopt. This couple seeks relief from the continuing uncertainty their unmarried status creates in their lives.

Army Reserve Sergeant First Class Ijpe DeKoe and his partner Thomas Kostura, co-plaintiffs in the Tennessee case, fell in love. In 2011, DeKoe received orders to deploy to Afghanistan. Before leaving, he and Kostura married in New York. A week later, DeKoe began his deployment, which lasted for almost a year.

When he returned, the two settled in Tennessee, where DeKoe works full-time for the Army Reserve. Their lawful marriage is stripped from them whenever they reside in Tennessee, returning and disappearing as they travel across state lines. DeKoe, who served this Nation to preserve the freedom the Constitution protects, must endure a substantial burden.

B

The ancient origins of marriage confirm its centrality, but it has not stood in isolation from developments in law and society. The history of marriage is one of both continuity and change. That institution—even as confined to opposite-sex relations—has evolved over time.

Under the centuries-old doctrine of coverture, a married man and woman were treated by the State as a single, male-dominated legal entity. As women gained legal, political, and property rights, and as society began to understand that women have their own equal dignity, the law of coverture was abandoned. These and other developments in the institution of marriage over the past centuries were not mere superficial changes. Rather, they worked deep transformations in its structure, affecting aspects of marriage long viewed by many as essential.

This dynamic can be seen in the Nation's experiences with the rights of gays and lesbians. Until the mid-20th century, same-sex intimacy long had been condemned as immoral by the state itself in most Western nations, a belief often embodied in the criminal law. For this reason, among others, many persons did not deem homosexuals to have dignity in their own distinct identity. A truthful declaration by same-sex couples of what was in their hearts had to remain unspoken. Even when a greater awareness of the humanity and integrity of homosexual persons came in the period after World War II, the argument that gays and lesbians had a just claim to dignity was in conflict with both law and widespread social conventions. Same-sex intimacy remained a crime in many States. Gays and lesbians were prohibited from most government employment, barred from military service, excluded under immigration laws, targeted by police, and burdened in their rights to associate.

In the late 20th century, following substantial cultural and political developments, same-sex couples began to lead more open and public lives and to establish families. This development was followed by a quite extensive discussion of the issue in both governmental and private sectors and by a shift in public attitudes toward greater tolerance. As a result, questions about the rights of gays and lesbians soon reached the courts, where the issue could be discussed in the formal discourse of the law.

This Court first gave detailed consideration to the legal status of homosexuals in *Bowers* v. *Hardwick*, 478 U. S. 186 (1986). There it upheld the constitutionality of a Georgia law deemed to criminalize certain homosexual acts. Ten years later, in *Romer* v. *Evans*, 517 U. S. 620 (1996), the Court invalidated an amendment to Colorado's Constitution that sought to foreclose any branch or political subdivision of the State from protecting persons against discrimination based on sexual orientation. Then, in 2003, the Court overruled *Bowers*, holding that laws making same-sex intimacy a crime "demea[n] the lives of homosexual persons." *Lawrence* v. *Texas*, 539 U. S. 558, 575.

Against this background, the legal question of same-sex marriage arose. In 1993, the Hawaii Supreme Court held Hawaii's law restricting marriage to opposite-sex couples constituted a classification on the basis of sex and was therefore subject to strict scrutiny under the Hawaii Constitution. *Baehr* v. *Lewin*, 74 Haw. 530, 852 P. 2d 44. Although this decision did not mandate that same-sex marriage be allowed, some States were concerned by its implications and reaffirmed in their laws that marriage is defined as a union between opposite-sex partners. So too in 1996, Congress passed the Defense of Marriage Act (DOMA), 110 Stat. 2419, defining marriage for all federal-law purposes as "only a legal union between one man and one woman as husband and wife."

The new and widespread discussion of the subject led other States to a different conclusion. In 2003, the Supreme Judicial Court of Massachusetts held the State's Constitution guaranteed same-sex couples the right to marry. See *Goodridge* v. *Department of Public Health*, 440 Mass. 309, 798 N. E. 2d 941 (2003). After that ruling, some additional States granted marriage rights to same-sex couples, either through judicial or legislative processes. Two Terms ago, in *United States* v. *Windsor*, 570 U. S. ___ (2013), this Court invalidated DOMA to the extent it barred the Federal Government from treating same-sex marriages as valid even when they were lawful in the State where they were licensed. DOMA, the Court held, impermissibly disparaged those same-sex couples "who wanted to affirm their commitment to one another before their children, their family, their friends, and their community."

Numerous cases about same-sex marriage have reached the United States Courts of Appeals in recent years. In accordance with the judicial duty to base their decisions on principled reasons and neutral discussions, without scornful or disparaging commentary, courts have written a substantial body of law considering all sides of these issues. That case law helps to explain and formulate the underlying principles this Court now must consider. With the exception of the opinion here under review and one other, the Courts of Appeals have held that excluding same-sex couples from marriage violates the Constitution. There also have been many thoughtful District Court decisions addressing same-sex marriage—and most of them, too, have concluded same-sex couples must be allowed to marry. In addition the highest courts of many States have contributed to this ongoing dialogue in decisions interpreting their own State Constitutions.

After years of litigation, legislation, referenda, and the discussions that attended these public acts, the States are now divided on the issue of same-sex marriage.

III

Under the Due Process Clause of the Fourteenth Amendment, no State shall "deprive any person of life, liberty, or property, without due process of law." The fundamental liberties protected by this Clause include most of the rights enumerated in the Bill of Rights. In addition these liberties extend to certain personal choices central to individual dignity and autonomy, including intimate choices that define personal identity and beliefs.

The nature of injustice is that we may not always see it in our own times. The generations that wrote and ratified the Bill of Rights and the Fourteenth Amendment did not presume to know the extent of freedom in all of its dimensions, and so they entrusted to future generations a charter protecting the right of all persons to enjoy liberty as we learn its meaning. When new insight reveals discord between the Constitution's central protections and a received legal stricture, a claim to liberty must be addressed. Applying these established tenets, the Court has long held the right to marry is protected by the Constitution. In *Loving* v. *Virginia*, 388 U. S. 1, 12 (1967), which invalidated bans on interracial unions, a unanimous Court held marriage is "one of the vital personal rights essential to the orderly pursuit of happiness by free men." The Court reaffirmed that holding in *Zablocki* v. *Redhail*, 434 U. S. 374, 384 (1978), which held the right to marry was burdened by a law prohibiting fathers who were behind on child support from marrying. The Court again applied this principle in *Turner* v. *Safley*, 482 U. S. 78, 95 (1987), which held the right to marry was abridged by regulations limiting the privilege of prison inmates to marry. Over time and in other contexts, the Court has reiterated that the right to marry is fundamental under the Due Process Clause.

It cannot be denied that this Court's cases describing the right to marry presumed a relationship involving opposite-sex partners. The Court, like many institutions, has made assumptions defined by the world and time of which it is a part.

This analysis compels the conclusion that same-sex couples may exercise the right to marry. The four principles and traditions to be discussed demonstrate that the reasons marriage is fundamental under the Constitution apply with equal force to same-sex couples.

A first premise of the Court's relevant precedents is that the right to personal choice regarding marriage is inherent in the concept of individual autonomy. This abiding connection between marriage and liberty is why *Loving* invalidated interracial marriage bans under the Due Process Clause. Like choices concerning contraception, family relationships, procreation, and childrearing, all of which are protected by the Constitution, decisions concerning marriage are among the most intimate that an individual can make.

The nature of marriage is that, through its enduring bond, two persons together can find other freedoms, such as expression, intimacy, and spirituality. This is true for all persons, whatever their sexual orientation. There is dignity in the bond between two men or two women who seek to marry and in their autonomy to make such profound choices.

A second principle in this Court's jurisprudence is that the right to marry is fundamental because it supports a two-person union unlike any other in its importance to the committed individuals. This point was central to *Griswold* v. *Connecticut* [381 U.S. 479 (1965)], which held the Constitution protects the right of married couples to use contraception. Suggesting that marriage is a right "older than the Bill of Rights," *Griswold* described marriage this way:

> "Marriage is a coming together for better or for worse, hopefully enduring, and intimate to the degree of being sacred. It is an association that promotes a way of life, not causes; a harmony in living, not political faiths; a bilateral loyalty, not commercial or social projects. Yet it is an association for as noble a purpose as any involved in our prior decisions." [381 U.S., at 486.]

Marriage responds to the universal fear that a lonely person might call out only to find no one there. It offers the hope of companionship and understanding and assurance that while both still live there will be someone to care for the other.

As this Court held in *Lawrence [v. Texas,* 539 U.S. 558 (2003)], same-sex couples have the same right as opposite-sex couples to enjoy intimate association. *Lawrence* invalidated laws that made same-sex intimacy a criminal act. And it acknowledged that "[w]hen sexuality finds overt expression in intimate conduct with another person, the conduct can be but one element in a personal bond that is more enduring." 539 U. S., at 567. But while *Lawrence* confirmed a dimension of freedom that allows individuals to engage in intimate association without criminal liability, it does not follow that freedom stops there. Outlaw to outcast may be a step forward, but it does not achieve the full promise of liberty.

A third basis for protecting the right to marry is that it safeguards children and families and thus draws meaning from related rights of childrearing, procreation, and education. Under the laws of the several States, some of marriage's protections for children and families are material. But marriage also confers more profound benefits.

As all parties agree, many same-sex couples provide loving and nurturing homes to their children, whether biological or adopted. And hundreds of thousands of children are presently being raised by such couples. Most States have allowed gays and lesbians to adopt, either as individuals or as couples, and many adopted and foster children have same-sex parents. This provides powerful confirmation from the law itself that gays and lesbians can create loving, supportive families.

Excluding same-sex couples from marriage thus conflicts with a central premise of the right to marry. Without the recognition, stability, and predictability marriage offers, their children suffer the stigma of knowing their families are somehow lesser. They also suffer the significant material costs of being raised by unmarried parents, relegated through no fault of their own to a more difficult and uncertain family life. The marriage laws at issue here thus harm and humiliate the children of same-sex couples.

That is not to say the right to marry is less meaningful for those who do not or cannot have children. An ability, desire, or promise to procreate is not and has not been a prerequisite for a valid marriage in any State. In light of precedent protecting the right of a married couple not to procreate, it cannot be said the Court or the States have conditioned the right to marry on the capacity or commitment to procreate.

Fourth and finally, this Court's cases and the Nation's traditions make clear that marriage is a keystone of our social order. This idea has been reiterated even as the institution has evolved in substantial ways over time, superseding rules related to parental consent, gender, and race once thought by many to be essential. Marriage remains a building block of our national community. For that reason, just as a couple vows to support each other, so does society pledge to support the couple, offering symbolic recognition and material benefits to protect and nourish the union. Indeed, while the States are in general free to vary the benefits they confer on all married couples, they have throughout our history made marriage the basis for an expanding list of governmental rights, benefits, and responsibilities. These aspects of marital status include: taxation; inheritance and property rights; rules of intestate succession; spousal privilege in the law of evidence; hospital access; medical decision-making authority; adoption rights; the rights and benefits of survivors; birth and death certificates; professional ethics rules; campaign finance restrictions; workers' compensation benefits; health insurance; and child custody, support, and visitation rules. Valid marriage under state law is also a significant status for over a thousand provisions of federal law. The States have contributed to the fundamental character of the marriage right by placing that institution at the center of so many facets of the legal and social order.

There is no difference between same- and opposite-sex couples with respect to this principle. Yet by virtue of their exclusion from that institution, same-sex couples are denied the constellation of benefits that the States have linked to marriage. This harm results in more than just material burdens. Same-sex couples are consigned to an instability many opposite-sex couples would deem intolerable in their own lives. As the State itself makes marriage all the more precious by the significance it attaches to it, exclusion from that status has the effect of teaching that gays and lesbians are unequal in important respects. It demeans gays and lesbians for the State to lock them out of a central institution of the Nation's society. Same-sex couples, too, may aspire to the transcendent purposes of marriage and seek fulfillment in its highest meaning.

The limitation of marriage to opposite-sex couples may long have seemed natural and just, but its inconsistency with the central meaning of the fundamental right to marry is now manifest. With that knowledge must come the recognition that laws excluding same-sex couples from the marriage right impose stigma and injury of the kind prohibited by our basic charter.

Objecting that this does not reflect an appropriate framing of the issue, the respondents refer to *Washington* v. *Glucksberg*, 521 U. S. 702, 721 (1997), which called for a " 'careful description' " of fundamental rights. They assert the petitioners do not seek to exercise the right to marry but rather a new and nonexistent "right to same-sex marriage." *Glucksberg* did insist that liberty under the Due Process Clause must be defined in a most circumscribed manner, with central reference to specific historical practices. Yet while that approach may have been appropriate for the asserted right there involved (physician-assisted suicide), it is inconsistent with the approach this Court has used in discussing other fundamental rights, including marriage and intimacy. *Loving* did not ask about a "right to inter-racial marriage"; *Turner* did not ask about a "right of inmates to marry"; and *Zablocki* did not ask about a "right of fathers with unpaid child support duties to marry." Rather, each case inquired about the right to marry in its comprehensive sense, asking if there was a sufficient justification for excluding the relevant class from the right.

That principle applies here. If rights were defined by who exercised them in the past, then received practices could serve as their own continued justification and new groups could not invoke rights once denied. This Court has rejected that approach, both with respect to the right to marry and the rights of gays and lesbians. Under the Constitution, same-sex couples seek in marriage the same legal treatment as opposite-sex couples, and it would disparage their choices and diminish their personhood to deny them this right.

The right of same-sex couples to marry that is part of the liberty promised by the Fourteenth Amendment is derived, too, from that Amendment's guarantee of the equal protection of the laws. The Due Process Clause and the Equal Protection Clause are connected in a profound way, though they set forth independent principles.

Rights implicit in liberty and rights secured by equal protection may rest on different precepts and are not always co-extensive, yet in some instances each may be instructive as to the meaning and reach of the other. In any particular case one Clause may be thought to capture the essence of the right in a more accurate and comprehensive way, even as the two Clauses may converge in the identification and definition of the right. This interrelation of the two principles furthers our understanding of what freedom is and must become.

Each concept—liberty and equal protection—leads to a stronger understanding of the other. Indeed, in interpreting the Equal Protection Clause, the Court has recognized that new insights and societal understandings can reveal unjustified inequality within our most fundamental institutions that once passed unnoticed and unchallenged.

Other cases confirm this relation between liberty and equality. In *Lawrence* the Court acknowledged the interlocking nature of these constitutional safeguards in the context of the legal treatment of gays and lesbians. Although *Lawrence* elaborated its holding under the Due Process Clause, it acknowledged, and sought to remedy, the continuing inequality that resulted from laws making intimacy in the lives of gays and lesbians a crime against the State. *Lawrence* therefore drew upon principles of liberty and equality to define and protect the rights of gays and lesbians, holding the State "cannot demean their existence or control their destiny by making their private sexual conduct a crime." *Id.*, at 578.

This dynamic also applies to same-sex marriage. It is now clear that the challenged laws burden the liberty of same-sex couples, and it must be further acknowledged that they abridge central precepts of equality. Here the marriage laws enforced by the respondents are in essence unequal: same-sex couples are denied all the benefits afforded to opposite-sex couples and are barred from exercising a fundamental right. Especially against a long history of disapproval of their relationships, this denial to same-sex couples of the right to marry works a grave and continuing harm. The imposition of this disability on gays and lesbians serves to disrespect and subordinate them. And the Equal Protection Clause, like the Due Process Clause, prohibits this unjustified infringement of the fundamental right to marry.

These considerations lead to the conclusion that the right to marry is a fundamental right inherent in the liberty of the person, and under the Due Process and Equal Protection Clauses of the Fourteenth Amendment couples of the same-sex may not be deprived of that right and that liberty. The Court now holds that same-sex couples may exercise the fundamental right to marry. No longer may this liberty be denied to them. . . .[T]he State laws challenged by Petitioners in these cases are now held invalid to the extent they exclude same-sex couples from civil marriage on the same terms and conditions as opposite-sex couples.

IV

There may be an initial inclination in these cases to proceed with caution—to await further legislation, litigation, and debate. The respondents warn there has been insufficient democratic discourse before deciding an issue so basic as the definition of marriage. In its ruling on the cases now before this Court, the majority opinion for the Court of Appeals made a cogent argument that it would be appropriate for the respondents' States to await further public discussion and political measures before licensing same-sex marriages.

Yet there has been far more deliberation than this argument acknowledges. There have been referenda, legislative debates, and grassroots campaigns, as well as countless studies, papers, books, and other popular and scholarly writings. There has been extensive litigation in state and federal courts. Judicial opinions addressing the issue have been informed by the contentions of parties and counsel, which, in turn, reflect the more general, societal discussion of same-sex marriage and its meaning that has occurred over the past decades. As more than 100 *amici* make clear in their filings, many of the central institutions in American life—state and local governments, the military, large and small businesses, labor unions, religious organizations, law enforcement, civic groups, professional organizations, and universities—have devoted substantial attention to the question.

This has led to an enhanced understanding of the issue—an understanding reflected in the arguments now presented for resolution as a matter of constitutional law.

Of course, the Constitution contemplates that democracy is the appropriate process for change, so long as that process does not abridge fundamental rights.

The dynamic of our constitutional system is that individuals need not await legislative action before asserting a fundamental right. The Nation's courts are open to injured individuals who come to them to vindicate their own direct, personal stake in our basic charter. An individual can invoke a right to constitutional protection when he or she is harmed, even if the broader public disagrees and even if the legislature refuses to act. The issue before the Court here is the legal question whether the Constitution protects the right of same-sex couples to marry.

This is not the first time the Court has been asked to adopt a cautious approach to recognizing and protecting fundamental rights. In *Bowers* [*v. Hardwick,* 478 U.S. 186 (1986)], a bare majority upheld a law criminalizing same-sex intimacy. That approach might have been viewed as a cautious endorsement of the democratic process, which had only just begun to consider the rights of gays and lesbians. Yet, in effect, *Bowers* upheld state action that denied gays and lesbians a fundamental right and caused them pain and humiliation. As evidenced by the dissents in that case, the facts and principles necessary to a correct holding were known to the *Bowers* Court. That is why *Lawrence* held *Bowers* was "not correct when it was decided." 539 U. S., at 578. Although *Bowers* was eventually repudiated in *Lawrence*, men and women were harmed in the interim, and the substantial effects of these injuries no doubt lingered long after *Bowers* was overruled. Dignitary wounds cannot always be healed with the stroke of a pen.

A ruling against same-sex couples would have the same effect—and, like *Bowers*, would be unjustified under the Fourteenth Amendment. The petitioners' stories make clear the urgency of the issue they present to the Court. James Obergefell now asks whether Ohio can erase his marriage to John Arthur for all time. April DeBoer and Jayne Rowse now ask whether Michigan may continue to deny them the certainty and stability all mothers desire to protect their children, and for them and their children the childhood years will pass all too soon. Ijpe DeKoe and Thomas Kostura now ask whether Tennessee can deny to one who has served this Nation the basic dignity of recognizing his New York marriage. Properly presented with the petitioners' cases, the Court has a duty to address these claims and answer these questions.

Indeed, faced with a disagreement among the Courts of Appeals—a disagreement that caused impermissible geographic variation in the meaning of federal law—the Court granted review to determine whether same-sex couples may exercise the right to marry. Were the Court to uphold the challenged laws as constitutional, it would teach the Nation that these laws are in accord with our society's most basic compact. Were the Court to stay its hand to allow slower, case-by-case determination of the required availability of specific public benefits to same-sex couples, it still would deny gays and lesbians many rights and responsibilities intertwined with marriage.

The respondents also argue allowing same-sex couples to wed will harm marriage as an institution by leading to fewer opposite-sex marriages. This may occur, the respondents contend, because licensing same-sex marriage severs the connection between natural procreation and marriage. That argument, however, rests on a counterintuitive view of opposite-sex couple's decisionmaking processes regarding marriage and parenthood. Decisions about whether to marry and raise children are based on many personal, romantic, and practical considerations; and it is unrealistic to conclude that an opposite-sex couple would choose not to marry simply because same-sex couples may do so. The respondents have not shown a foundation for the conclusion that allowing same-sex marriage will cause the harmful outcomes they describe. Indeed, with respect to this asserted basis for excluding same-sex couples from the right to marry, it is appropriate to observe these cases involve only the rights of two consenting adults whose marriages would pose no risk of harm to themselves or third parties.

Finally, it must be emphasized that religions, and those who adhere to religious doctrines, may continue to advocate with utmost, sincere conviction that, by divine precepts, same-sex marriage should not be condoned. The First Amendment ensures that religious organizations and persons are given proper protection as they seek to teach the principles that are so fulfilling and so central to their lives and faiths, and to their own deep aspirations to continue the family structure they have long revered. The same is true of those who oppose same-sex marriage for other reasons. In turn, those who believe allowing same-sex marriage is proper or indeed essential, whether as a matter of religious conviction or secular belief, may engage those who disagree with their view in an open and searching debate. The Constitution, however, does not permit the State to bar same-sex couples from marriage on the same terms as accorded to couples of the opposite sex.

V

These cases also present the question whether the Constitution requires States to recognize same-sex marriages validly performed out of State. As made clear by the case of Obergefell and Arthur, and by that of DeKoe and Kostura, the recognition bans inflict substantial and continuing harm on same-sex couples.

Leaving the current state of affairs in place would maintain and promote instability and uncertainty. For some couples, even an ordinary drive into a neighboring State to visit family or friends risks causing severe hardship in the event of a spouse's hospitalization while across state lines. In light of the fact that many States already allow same-sex marriage—and hundreds of thousands of these marriages already have occurred—the disruption caused by the recognition bans is significant and ever-growing.

As counsel for the respondents acknowledged at argument, if States are required by the Constitution to issue marriage licenses to same-sex couples, the justifications for refusing to recognize those marriages performed elsewhere are undermined. The Court, in this decision, holds same-sex couples may exercise the fundamental right to marry in all States. It follows that the Court also must hold—and it now does hold—that there is no lawful basis for a State to refuse to recognize a lawful same-sex marriage performed in another State on the ground of its same-sex character.

* * *

No union is more profound than marriage, for it embodies the highest ideals of love, fidelity, devotion, sacrifice, and family. In forming a marital union, two people become something greater than once they were. As some of the petitioners in these cases demonstrate, marriage embodies a love that may endure even past death. It would misunderstand these men and women to say they disrespect the idea of marriage. Their plea is that they do respect it, respect it so deeply that they seek to find its fulfillment for themselves. Their hope is not to be condemned to live in loneliness, excluded from one of civilization's oldest institutions. They ask for equal dignity in the eyes of the law. The Constitution grants them that right.

The judgment of the Court of Appeals for the Sixth Circuit is reversed.

It is so ordered.

CHIEF JUSTICE ROBERTS, with whom JUSTICES SCALIA and THOMAS join, dissenting.

Petitioners make strong arguments rooted in social policy and considerations of fairness. They contend that same-sex couples should be allowed to affirm their love and commitment through marriage, just like opposite-sex couples. That position has undeniable appeal; over the past six years, voters and legislators in eleven States and the District of Columbia have revised their laws to allow marriage between two people of the same sex.

But this Court is not a legislature. Whether same-sex marriage is a good idea should be of no concern to us. Under the Constitution, judges have power to say what the law is, not what it should be.

Although the policy arguments for extending marriage to same-sex couples may be compelling, the legal arguments for requiring such an extension are not. The fundamental right to marry does not include a right to make a State change its definition of marriage. And a State's decision to maintain the meaning of marriage that has persisted in every culture throughout human history can hardly be called irrational. In short, our Constitution does not enact any one theory of marriage. The people of a State are free to expand marriage to include same-sex couples, or to retain the historic definition.

Today, however, the Court takes the extraordinary step of ordering every State to license and recognize same-sex marriage. Many people will rejoice at this decision, and I begrudge none their celebration. But for those who believe in a government of laws, not of men, the majority's approach is deeply disheartening. Supporters of same-sex marriage have achieved considerable success persuading their fellow citizens—through the democratic process—to adopt their view. That ends today. Five lawyers have closed the debate and enacted their own vision of marriage as a matter of constitutional law. Stealing this issue from the people will for many cast a cloud over same-sex marriage, making a dramatic social change that much more difficult to accept.

The majority's decision is an act of will, not legal judgment. The right it announces has no basis in the Constitution or this Court's precedent. The majority expressly disclaims judicial "caution" and omits even a pretense of humility, openly relying on its desire to remake society according to its own "new insight" into the "nature of injustice." As a result, the Court invalidates the marriage laws of more than half the States and orders the transformation of a social institution that has formed the basis of human society for millennia, for the Kalahari Bushmen and the Han Chinese, the Carthaginians and the Aztecs. Just who do we think we are?

It can be tempting for judges to confuse our own preferences with the requirements of the law. But as this Court has been reminded throughout our history, the Constitution "is made for people of fundamentally differing views." *Lochner* v. *New York*, 198 U. S. 45, 76 (1905) (Holmes, J., dissenting). Accordingly, "courts are not concerned with the wisdom or policy of legislation." *Id.*, at 69 (Harlan, J., dissenting). The majority today neglects that restrained conception of the judicial role. It seizes for itself a question the Constitution leaves to the people, at a time when the people are engaged in a vibrant debate on that question. And it answers that question based not on neutral principles of constitutional law, but on its own "understanding of what freedom is and must become." I have no choice but to dissent.

Understand well what this dissent is about: It is not about whether, in my judgment, the institution of marriage should be changed to include same-sex couples. It is instead about whether, in our democratic republic, that decision should rest with the people acting through their elected representatives, or with five lawyers who happen to hold commissions authorizing them to resolve legal disputes according to law. The Constitution leaves no doubt about the answer.

IV

The Court's accumulation of power does not occur in a vacuum. It comes at the expense of the people. And they know it. Here and abroad, people are in the midst of a serious and thoughtful public debate on the issue of same-sex marriage. They see voters carefully considering same-sex marriage, casting ballots in favor or opposed, and sometimes changing their minds. They see political leaders similarly reexamining their positions, and either reversing course or explaining adherence to old convictions confirmed anew. They see governments and businesses modifying policies and practices with respect to same-sex couples, and participating actively in the civic discourse. They see countries overseas democratically accepting profound social change, or declining to do so. This deliberative process is making people take seriously questions that they may not have even regarded as questions before. When decisions are reached through democratic means, some people will inevitably be disappointed with the results. But those whose views do not prevail at least know that they have had their say, and accordingly are—in the tradition of our political culture—reconciled to the result of a fair and honest debate. In addition, they can gear up to raise the issue later, hoping to persuade enough on the winning side to think again.

But today the Court puts a stop to all that. By deciding this question under the Constitution, the Court removes it from the realm of democratic decision. There will be consequences to shutting down the political process on an issue of such profound public significance. Closing debate tends to close minds. People denied a voice are less likely to accept the ruling of a court on an issue that does not seem to be the sort of thing courts usually decide. Indeed, however heartened the proponents of same-sex marriage might be on this day, it is worth acknowledging what they have lost, and lost forever: the opportunity to win the true acceptance that comes from persuading their fellow citizens of the justice of their cause. And they lose this just when the winds of change were freshening at their backs.

Federal courts are blunt instruments when it comes to creating rights. They have constitutional power only to resolve concrete cases or controversies; they do not have the flexibility of legislatures to address concerns of parties not before the court or to anticipate problems that may arise from the exercise of a new right. Today's decision, for example, creates serious questions about religious liberty. Many good and decent people oppose same-sex marriage as a tenet of faith, and their freedom to exercise religion is—unlike the right imagined by the majority—actually spelled out in the Constitution.

Respect for sincere religious conviction has led voters and legislators in every State that has adopted same-sex marriage democratically to include accommodations for religious practice. The majority's decision imposing same-sex marriage cannot, of course, create any such accommodations. The majority graciously suggests that religious believers may continue to "advocate" and "teach" their views of marriage. The First Amendment guarantees, however, the freedom to "*exercise*" religion. Ominously, that is not a word the majority uses.

Hard questions arise when people of faith exercise religion in ways that may be seen to conflict with the new right to same-sex marriage—when, for example, a religious college provides married student housing only to opposite-sex married couples, or a religious adoption agency declines to place children with same-sex married couples. Indeed, the Solicitor General candidly acknowledged that the tax exemptions of some religious institutions would be in question if they opposed same-sex marriage. There is little doubt that these and similar questions will soon be before this Court. Unfortunately, people of faith can take no comfort in the treatment they receive from the majority today.

Perhaps the most discouraging aspect of today's decision is the extent to which the majority feels compelled to sully those on the other side of the debate. The majority offers a cursory assurance that it does not intend to disparage people who, as a matter of conscience, cannot accept same-sex marriage. That disclaimer is hard to square with the very next sentence, in which the majority explains that "the necessary consequence" of laws codifying the traditional definition of marriage is to "demea[n] or stigmatiz[e]" same-sex couples. The majority reiterates such characterizations over and over. By the majority's account, Americans who did nothing more than follow the understanding of marriage that has existed for our entire history—in particular, the tens of millions of people who voted to reaffirm their States' enduring definition of marriage—have acted to "lock . . . out," "disparage," "disrespect and subordinate," and inflict "[d]ignitary wounds" upon their gay and lesbian neighbors. These apparent assaults on the character of fairminded people will have an effect, in society and in court. Moreover, they are entirely gratuitous. It is one thing for the majority to conclude that the Constitution protects a right to same-sex marriage; it is something else to portray everyone who does not share the majority's "better informed understanding" as bigoted.

In the face of all this, a much different view of the Court's role is possible. That view is more modest and restrained. It is more skeptical that the legal abilities of judges also reflect insight into moral and philosophical issues. It is more sensitive to the fact that judges are unelected and unaccountable, and that the legitimacy of their power depends on confining it to the exercise of legal judgment. It is more attuned to the lessons of history, and what it has meant for the country and Court when Justices have exceeded their proper bounds. And it is less pretentious than to suppose that while people around the world have viewed an institution in a particular way for thousands of years, the present generation and the present Court are the ones chosen to burst the bonds of that history and tradition.

* * *

If you are among the many Americans—of whatever sexual orientation—who favor expanding same-sex marriage, by all means celebrate today's decision. Celebrate the achievement of a desired goal. Celebrate the opportunity for a new expression of commitment to a partner. Celebrate the availability of new benefits. But do not celebrate the Constitution. It had nothing to do with it. I respectfully dissent.

JUSTICE SCALIA, with whom JUSTICE THOMAS joins, dissenting.

I join The Chief Justice's opinion in full. I write separately to call attention to this Court's threat to American democracy.

The substance of today's decree is not of immense personal importance to me. The law can recognize as marriage whatever sexual attachments and living arrangements it wishes, and can accord them favorable civil consequences, from tax treatment to rights of inheritance. Those civil consequences—and the public approval that conferring the name of marriage evidences—can perhaps have adverse social effects, but no more adverse than the effects of many other controversial laws. So it is not of special importance to me what the law says about marriage. It is of overwhelming importance, however, who it is that rules me. Today's decree says that my Ruler, and the Ruler of 320 million Americans coast-to-coast, is a majority of the nine lawyers on the Supreme Court. The opinion in these cases is the furthest extension in fact—and the furthest extension one can even imagine—of the Court's claimed power to create "liberties" that the Constitution and its Amendments neglect to mention. This practice of constitutional revision by an unelected committee of nine, always accompanied (as it is today) by extravagant praise of liberty, robs the People of the most important liberty they asserted in the Declaration of Independence and won in the Revolution of 1776: the freedom to govern themselves.

I

Until the courts put a stop to it, public debate over same-sex marriage displayed American democracy at its best. Individuals on both sides of the issue passionately, but respectfully, attempted to persuade their fellow citizens to accept their views. Americans considered the arguments and put the question to a vote. The electorates of 11 States, either directly or through their representatives, chose to expand the traditional definition of marriage. Many more decided not to. Win or lose, advocates for both sides continued pressing their cases, secure in the knowledge that an electoral loss can be negated by a later electoral win. That is exactly how our system of government is supposed to work.

But the Court ends this debate, in an opinion lacking even a thin veneer of law. Buried beneath the mummeries and straining-to-be-memorable passages of the opinion is a candid and startling assertion: No matter *what* it was the People ratified, the Fourteenth Amendment protects those rights that the Judiciary, in its "reasoned judgment," thinks the Fourteenth Amendment ought to protect. That is so because "[t]he generations that wrote and ratified the Bill of Rights and the Fourteenth Amendment did not presume to know the extent of freedom in all of its dimensions . . . ." One would think that sentence would continue: ". . . and therefore they provided for a means by which the People could amend the Constitution," or perhaps ". . . and therefore they left the creation of additional liberties, such as the freedom to marry someone of the same sex, to the People, through the never-ending process of legislation." But no. What logically follows, in the majority's judge-empowering estimation, is: "and so they entrusted to future generations a charter protecting the right of all persons to enjoy liberty as we learn its meaning." The "we," needless to say, is the nine of us. "History and tradition guide and discipline [our] inquiry but do not set its outer boundaries." Thus, rather than focusing on *the People's* understanding of "liberty"—at the time of ratification or even today—the majority focuses on four "principles and traditions" that, *in the majority's view*, prohibit States from defining marriage as an institution consisting of one man and one woman.

This is a naked judicial claim to legislative—indeed, *super*-legislative—power; a claim fundamentally at odds with our system of government. Except as limited by a constitutional prohibition agreed to by the People, the States are free to adopt whatever laws they like, even those that offend the esteemed Justices' "reasoned judgment." A system of government that makes the People subordinate to a committee of nine unelected lawyers does not deserve to be called a democracy.

II

But what really astounds is the hubris reflected in today's judicial Putsch. The five Justices who compose today's majority are entirely comfortable concluding that every State violated the Constitution for all of the 135 years between the Fourteenth Amendment's ratification and Massachusetts' permitting of same-sex marriages in 2003. *Goodridge* v. *Department of Public Health*, 440 Mass. 309, 798 N. E.2d 941 (2003). They have discovered in the Fourteenth Amendment a "fundamental right" overlooked by every person alive at the time of ratification, and almost everyone else in the time since. They see what lesser legal minds—minds like Thomas Cooley, John Marshall Harlan, Oliver Wendell Holmes, Jr., Learned Hand, Louis Brandeis, William Howard Taft, Benjamin Cardozo, Hugo Black, Felix Frankfurter, Robert Jackson, and Henry Friendly—could not. They are certain that the People ratified the Fourteenth Amendment to bestow on them the power to remove questions from the democratic process when that is called for by their "reasoned judgment."

The opinion is couched in a style that is as pretentious as its content is egotistic. It is one thing for separate concurring or dissenting opinions to contain extravagances, even silly extravagances, of thought and expression; it is something else for the official opinion of the Court to do so. Of course the opinion's showy profundities are often profoundly incoherent. "The nature of marriage is that, through its enduring bond, two persons together can find other freedoms, such as expression, intimacy, and spirituality." (Really? Who ever thought that intimacy and spirituality [whatever that means] were freedoms? And if intimacy is, one would think Freedom of Intimacy is abridged rather than expanded by marriage. Ask the nearest hippie. Expression, sure enough, *is* a freedom, but anyone in a long-lasting marriage will attest that that happy state constricts, rather than expands, what one can prudently say.) Rights, we are told, can "rise . . . from a better informed understanding of how constitutional imperatives define a liberty that remains urgent in our own era." (Huh? How can a better informed understanding of how constitutional imperatives [whatever that means] define [whatever that means] an urgent liberty [never mind], give birth to a right?) And we are told that, "[i]n any particular case," either the Equal Protection or Due Process Clause "may be thought to capture the essence of [a] right in a more accurate and comprehensive way," than the other, "even as the two Clauses may converge in the identification and definition of the right." (What say? What possible "essence" does substantive due process "capture" in an "accurate and comprehensive way"? It stands for nothing whatever, except those freedoms and entitlements that this Court *really* likes. And the Equal Protection Clause, as employed today, identifies nothing except a difference in treatment that this Court *really* dislikes. Hardly a distillation of essence. If the opinion is correct that the two clauses "converge in the identification and definition of [a] right," that is only because the majority's likes and dislikes are predictably compatible.) I could go on. The world does not expect logic and precision in poetry or inspirational pop-philosophy; it demands them in the law. The stuff contained in today's opinion has to diminish this Court's reputation for clear thinking and sober analysis.

* * *

Hubris is sometimes defined as o'erweening pride; and pride, we know, goeth before a fall. The Judiciary is the "least dangerous" of the federal branches because it has "neither Force nor Will, but merely judgment; and must ultimately depend upon the aid of the executive arm" and the States, "even for the efficacy of its judgments." *The Federalist* No. 78, pp. 522, 523 (J. Cooke ed. 1961) (A. Hamilton). With each decision of ours that takes from the People a question properly left to them—with each decision that is unabashedly based not on law, but on the "reasoned judgment" of a bare majority of this Court—we move one step closer to being reminded of our impotence.

JUSTICE THOMAS, with whom JUSTICE SCALIA joins, dissenting.

The Court's decision today is at odds not only with the Constitution, but with the principles upon which our Nation was built. Since well before 1787, liberty has been understood as freedom from government action, not entitlement to government benefits. The Framers created our Constitution to preserve that understanding of liberty. Yet the majority invokes our Constitution in the name of a "liberty" that the Framers would not have recognized, to the detriment of the liberty they sought to protect. Along the way, it rejects the idea—captured in our Declaration of Independence—that human dignity is innate and suggests instead that it comes from the Government. This distortion of our Constitution not only ignores the text, it inverts the relationship between the individual and the state in our Republic. I cannot agree with it.

II B

Whether we define "liberty" as locomotion or freedom from governmental action more broadly, petitioners have in no way been deprived of it.

Petitioners cannot claim, under the most plausible definition of "liberty," that they have been imprisoned or physically restrained by the States for participating in same-sex relationships. To the contrary, they have been able to cohabitate and raise their children in peace. They have been able to hold civil marriage ceremonies in States that recognize same-sex marriages and private religious ceremonies in all States. They have been able to travel freely around the country, making their homes where they please. Far from being incarcerated or physically restrained, petitioners have been left alone to order their lives as they see fit.

Nor, under the broader definition, can they claim that the States have restricted their ability to go about their daily lives as they would be able to absent governmental restrictions. Petitioners do not ask this Court to order the States to stop restricting their ability to enter same-sex relationships, to engage in intimate behavior, to make vows to their partners in public ceremonies, to engage in religious wedding ceremonies, to hold themselves out as married, or to raise children. The States have imposed no such restrictions. Nor have the States prevented petitioners from approximating a number of incidents of marriage through private legal means, such as wills, trusts, and powers of attorney.

Instead, the States have refused to grant them governmental entitlements. Petitioners claim that as a matter of "liberty," they are entitled to access privileges and benefits that exist solely *because of* the government. They want, for example, to receive the State's *imprimatur* on their marriages—on state issued marriage licenses, death certificates, or other official forms. And they want to receive various monetary benefits, including reduced inheritance taxes upon the death of a spouse, compensation if a spouse dies as a result of a work-related injury, or loss of consortium damages in tort suits. But receiving governmental recognition and benefits has nothing to do with any understanding of "liberty" that the Framers would have recognized.

JUSTICE ALITO, with whom JUSTICES SCALIA and THOMAS join, dissenting.

Until the federal courts intervened, the American people were engaged in a debate about whether their States should recognize same-sex marriage. The question in these cases, however, is not what States *should* do about same-sex marriage but whether the Constitution answers that question for them. It does not. The Constitution leaves that question to be decided by the people of each State.

III

Today's decision usurps the constitutional right of the people to decide whether to keep or alter the traditional understanding of marriage. The decision will also have other important consequences.

It will be used to vilify Americans who are unwilling to assent to the new orthodoxy. In the course of its opinion, the majority compares traditional marriage laws to laws that denied equal treatment for African-Americans and women. The implications of this analogy will be exploited by those who are determined to stamp out every vestige of dissent.

Perhaps recognizing how its reasoning may be used, the majority attempts, toward the end of its opinion, to reassure those who oppose same-sex marriage that their rights of conscience will be protected. We will soon see whether this proves to be true. I assume that those who cling to old beliefs will be able to whisper their thoughts in the recesses of their homes, but if they repeat those views in public, they will risk being labeled as bigots and treated as such by governments, employers, and schools.

The system of federalism established by our Constitution provides a way for people with different beliefs to live together in a single nation. If the issue of same-sex marriage had been left to the people of the States, it is likely that some States would recognize same-sex marriage and others would not. It is also possible that some States would tie recognition to protection for conscience rights. The majority today makes that impossible. By imposing its own views on the entire country, the majority facilitates the marginalization of the many Americans who have traditional ideas. Recalling the harsh treatment of gays and lesbians in the past, some may think that turn-about is fair play. But if that sentiment prevails, the Nation will experience bitter and lasting wounds.

Today's decision will also have a fundamental effect on this Court and its ability to uphold the rule of law. If a bare majority of Justices can invent a new right and impose that right on the rest of the country, the only real limit on what future majorities will be able to do is their own sense of what those with political power and cultural influence are willing to tolerate. Even enthusiastic supporters of same-sex marriage should worry about the scope of the power that today's majority claims.

Today's decision shows that decades of attempts to restrain this Court's abuse of its authority have failed. A lesson that some will take from today's decision is that preaching about the proper method of interpreting the Constitution or the virtues of judicial self-restraint and humility cannot compete with the temptation to achieve what is viewed as a noble end by any practicable means. I do not doubt that my colleagues in the majority sincerely see in the Constitution a vision of liberty that happens to coincide with their own. But this sincerity is cause for concern, not comfort. What it evidences is the deep and perhaps irremediable corruption of our legal culture's conception of constitutional interpretation.

Most Americans—understandably—will cheer or lament today's decision because of their views on the issue of same-sex marriage. But all Americans, whatever their thinking on that issue, should worry about what the majority's claim of power portends.

FOR DISCUSSION

It may be surprising to some readers to see that the majority opinion focuses on the expanding understanding of the Fourteenth Amendment to encompass same-sex marriage and the dissenting opinions focuses on the appropriate role of the Court in interpreting the Constitution. How do you attempt to reconcile these two positions? Is it possible? As Justice Scalia suggests in *Windsor v. U.S.* (2013), was this decision inevitable after *Windsor*?

SAN ANTONIO INDEPENDENT SCHOOL DISTRICT V. RODRIGUEZ

411 U.S. 1, 93 S.Ct. 1278, 36 L.Ed.2d 16 (1973)

Mexican American parents in San Antonio, Texas, filed a class action lawsuit challenging the state's system of financing public education. The suit was brought on behalf of Texas schoolchildren who were either racial minorities or residing in districts with low property taxes because their parents were poor. The complaint argued that the practice of financing school systems based on property taxes and a state contribution was a violation of the Fourteenth Amendment. To demonstrate the inequities, the plaintiffs compared two districts in the San Antonio area: the least affluent (Edgewood Independent School District, 90 percent Mexican American and 6 percent African American) and the most affluent (Alamo Heights Independent School District, 18 percent Mexican American, less than 1 percent African American, the remaining students being Anglo). The Edgewood district, based on assessed fees from property taxes, state dollars, and federal funds spent $356 per pupil during the 1967–1968 school year, while the Alamo Heights district spent $594. The district court had found the Texas school financing system unconstitutional under the Equal Protection Clause of the Fourteenth Amendment.

Vote: 5–4

JUSTICE POWELL delivered the opinion of the Court.

I

We must decide, first, whether the Texas system of financing public education operates to the disadvantage of some suspect class or impinges upon a fundamental right explicitly or implicitly protected by the Constitution, thereby requiring strict judicial scrutiny. If so, the judgment of the District Court should be affirmed. If not, the Texas scheme must still be examined to determine whether it rationally furthers some legitimate, articulated state purpose and therefore does not constitute an invidious discrimination in violation of the Equal Protection Clause of the Fourteenth Amendment.

II

We are unable to agree that this case, which in significant aspects is sui generis [of its own kind, or unique], may be so neatly fitted into the conventional mosaic of constitutional analysis under the Equal Protection Clause. Indeed, for the several reasons that follow, we find neither the suspect-classification nor the fundamental-interest analysis persuasive.

A

Examination of the District Court's opinion and of appellees' complaint, briefs, and contentions at oral argument suggests, however, at least three ways in which the discrimination claimed here might be described. The Texas system of school financing might be regarded as discriminating (1) against "poor" persons whose incomes fall below some identifiable level of poverty or who might be characterized as functionally "indigent," or (2) against those who are relatively poorer than others, or (3) against all those who, irrespective of their personal incomes, happen to reside in relatively poorer school districts. Our task must be to ascertain whether, in fact, the Texas system has been shown to discriminate on any of these possible bases and, if so, whether the resulting classification may be regarded as suspect.

The precedents of this Court provide the proper starting point. The individuals, or groups of individuals, who constituted the class discriminated against in our prior cases shared two distinguishing characteristics:

because of their impecunity they were completely unable to pay for some desired benefit, and as a consequence, they sustained an absolute deprivation of a meaningful opportunity to enjoy that benefit.

In *Griffin v. Illinois*, 351 U.S. 12 (1956), and its progeny, the Court invalidated state laws that prevented an indigent criminal defendant from acquiring a transcript, or an adequate substitute for a transcript, for use at several stages of the trial and appeal process.

Likewise, in *Douglas v. California*, 372 U.S. 353 (1963), a decision establishing an indigent defendant's right to court-appointed counsel on direct appeal, the Court dealt only with defendants who could not pay for counsel from their own resources and who had no other way of gaining representation.

Williams v. Illinois, 399 U.S. 235 (1970), and *Tate v. Short*, 401 U.S. 395 (1971), struck down criminal penalties that subjected indigents to incarceration simply because of their inability to pay a fine.

Finally, in *Bullock v. Carter*, 405 U.S. 134 (1972), the Court invalidated the Texas filing-fee requirement for primary elections.

Only appellees' first possible basis for describing the class disadvantaged by the Texas school-financing system—discrimination against a class of definably "poor" persons—might arguably meet the criteria established in these prior cases. Even a cursory examination, however, demonstrates that neither of the two distinguishing characteristics of wealth classifications can be found here. First, in support of their charge that the system discriminates against the "poor," appellees have made no effort to demonstrate that it operates to the peculiar disadvantage of any class fairly definable as indigent, or as composed of persons whose incomes are beneath any designated poverty level.

Second, neither appellees nor the District Court addressed the fact that, unlike each of the foregoing cases, lack of personal resources has not occasioned an absolute deprivation of the desired benefit.

For these two reasons—the absence of any evidence that the financing system discriminates against any definable category of "poor" people or that it results in the absolute deprivation of education—the disadvantaged class is not susceptible of identification in traditional terms.

. . . [I]t is clear that appellees' suit asks this Court to extend its most exacting scrutiny to review a system that allegedly discriminates against a large, diverse, and amorphous class, unified only by the common factor of residence in districts that happen to have less taxable wealth than other districts. The system of alleged discrimination and the class it defines have none of the traditional indicia of suspectness: the class is not saddled with such disabilities, or subjected to such a history of purposeful unequal treatment, or relegated to such a position of political powerlessness as to command extraordinary protection from the majoritarian political process.

We thus conclude that the Texas system does not operate to the peculiar disadvantage of any suspect class. But in recognition of the fact that this Court has never heretofore held that wealth discrimination alone provides an adequate basis for invoking strict scrutiny, appellees have not relied solely on this contention. They also assert that the State's system impermissibly interferes with the exercise of a "fundamental" right and that accordingly the prior decisions of this Court require the application of the strict standard of judicial review. *Graham v. Richardson*, 403 U.S. 365, 375–376 (1971); *Kramer v. Union School District*, 395 U.S. 621 (1969); *Shapiro v. Thompson*, 394 U.S. 618 (1969). It is this question—whether education is a fundamental right, in the sense that it is among the rights and liberties protected by the Constitution—which has so consumed the attention of courts and commentators in recent years.

B

Nothing this Court holds today in any way detracts from our historic dedication to public education. We are in complete agreement with the conclusion of the three-judge panel below that "the grave significance of education both to the individual and to our society" cannot be doubted. But the importance of a service performed by the State does not determine whether it must be regarded as fundamental for purposes of examination under the Equal Protection Clause.

It is not the province of this Court to create substantive constitutional rights in the name of guaranteeing equal protection of the laws. Thus, the key to discovering whether education is "fundamental" is not to be found in comparisons of the relative societal significance of education as opposed to subsistence or housing. Nor is it to be found by weighing whether education is as important as the right to travel. Rather, the answer lies in assessing whether there is a right to education explicitly or implicitly guaranteed by the Constitution.

Education, of course, is not among the rights afforded explicit protection under our Federal Constitution. Nor do we find any basis for saying it is implicitly so protected. As we have said, the undisputed importance of education will not alone cause this Court to depart from the usual standard for reviewing a State's social and economic legislation. It is appellees' contention, however, that education is distinguishable from other services and benefits provided by the State because it bears a peculiarly close relationship to other rights and liberties accorded protection under the Constitution. Specifically, they insist that education is itself a fundamental personal right because it is essential to the effective exercise of First Amendment freedoms and to intelligent utilization of the right to vote. In asserting a nexus between speech and education, appellees urge that the right to speak is meaningless unless the speaker is capable of articulating his thoughts intelligently and persuasively. The "marketplace of ideas" is an empty forum for those lacking basic communicative tools. Likewise, they argue that the corollary right to receive information becomes little more than a hollow privilege when the recipient has not been taught to read, assimilate, and utilize available knowledge.

A similar line of reasoning is pursued with respect to the right to vote.

We need not dispute any of these propositions. The Court has long afforded zealous protection against unjustifiable governmental interference with the individual's rights to speak and to vote. Yet we have never presumed to possess either the ability or the authority to guarantee to the citizenry the most effective speech or the most informed electoral choice. That these may be desirable goals of a system of freedom of expression and of a representative form of government is not to be doubted. These are indeed goals to be pursued by a people whose thoughts and beliefs are freed from governmental interference. But they are not values to be implemented by judicial intrusion into otherwise legitimate state activities.

Even if it were conceded that some identifiable quantum of education is a constitutionally protected prerequisite to the meaningful exercise of either right, we have no indication that the present levels of educational expenditure in Texas provide an education that falls short. Whatever merit appellees' argument might have if a State's financing system occasioned an absolute denial of educational opportunities to any of its children, that argument provides no basis for finding an interference with fundamental rights where only relative differences in spending levels are involved and where—as is true in the present case—no charge fairly could be made that the system fails to provide each child with an opportunity to acquire the basic minimal skills necessary for the enjoyment of the rights of speech and of full participation in the political process.

In one further respect we find this a particularly inappropriate case in which to subject state action to strict judicial scrutiny. The present case, in another basic sense, is significantly different from any of the cases in which the Court has applied strict scrutiny to state or federal legislation touching upon constitutionally protected rights. Each of our prior cases involved legislation which "deprived," "infringed," or "interfered" with the free exercise of some such fundamental personal right or liberty. A critical distinction between those cases and the one now before us lies in what Texas is endeavoring to do with respect to education.

III

In sum, to the extent that the Texas system of school financing results in unequal expenditures between children who happen to reside in different districts, we cannot say that such disparities are the product of a system that is so irrational as to be invidiously discriminatory. Texas has acknowledged its shortcomings and has persistently endeavored—not without some success—to ameliorate the differences in levels of expenditures without sacrificing the benefits of local participation. The Texas plan is not the result of hurried, ill-conceived legislation. It certainly is not the product of purposeful discrimination against any group or class. On the contrary, it is rooted in decades of experience in Texas and elsewhere, and in major part is the product of responsible studies by qualified people. One also must remember that the system here challenged is not peculiar to Texas or to any other State. In its essential characteristics, the Texas plan for financing public education reflects what many educators for a half century have thought was an enlightened approach to a problem for which there is no perfect solution. The constitutional standard under the Equal Protection Clause is whether the challenged state action rationally furthers a legitimate state purpose or interest. *McGinnis v. Royster*, 410 U.S. 263, 270 (1973). We hold that the Texas plan abundantly satisfies this standard.

JUSTICE STEWART, concurring

The method of financing public schools in Texas, as in almost every other State, has resulted in a system of public education that can fairly be described as chaotic and unjust. It does not follow, however, and I cannot find, that this system violates the Constitution of the United States. I join the opinion and judgment of the Court because I am convinced that any other course would mark an extraordinary departure from principled adjudication under the Equal Protection Clause of the Fourteenth Amendment. The uncharted directions of such a departure are suggested, I think, by the imaginative dissenting opinion my Brother Marshall has filed today.

Unlike other provisions of the Constitution, the Equal Protection Clause confers no substantive rights and creates no substantive liberties. The function of the Equal Protection Clause, rather, is simply to measure the validity of classifications created by state laws.

JUSTICE BRENNAN, dissenting.

Although I agree with my Brother White that the Texas statutory scheme is devoid of any rational basis, and for that reason is violative of the Equal Protection Clause, I also record my disagreement with the Court's rather distressing assertion that a right may be deemed "fundamental" for the purposes of equal protection analysis only if it is "explicitly or implicitly guaranteed by the Constitution." As my Brother Marshall convincingly demonstrates, our prior cases stand for the proposition that "fundamentality" is, in large measure, a function of the right's importance in terms of the effectuation of those rights which are in fact constitutionally guaranteed.

Here, there can be no doubt that education is inextricably linked to the right to participate in the electoral process and to the rights of free speech and association guaranteed by the First Amendment. This being so, any classification affecting education must be subjected to strict judicial scrutiny, and since even the State concedes that the statutory scheme now before us cannot pass constitutional muster under this stricter standard of review, I can only conclude that the Texas school-financing scheme is constitutionally invalid.

JUSTICE WHITE, with whom JUSTICES DOUGLAS and BRENNAN join, dissenting.

I cannot disagree with the proposition that local control and local decisionmaking play an important part in our democratic system of government.

The difficulty with the Texas system, however, is that it provides a meaningful option to Alamo Heights and like school districts but almost none to Edgewood and those other districts with a low per-pupil real estate tax base.

The Equal Protection Clause permits discriminations between classes but requires that the classification bear some rational relationship to a permissible object sought to be attained by the statute.

Neither Texas nor the majority heeds this rule. If the State aims at maximizing local initiative and local choice, by permitting school districts to resort to the real property tax if they choose to do so, it utterly fails in achieving its purpose in districts with property tax bases so low that there is little if any opportunity for interested parents, rich or poor, to augment school district revenues. Requiring the State to establish only that unequal treatment is in furtherance of a permissible goal, without also requiring the State to show that the means chosen to effectuate that goal are rationally related to its achievement, makes equal protection analysis no more than an empty gesture. In my view, the parents and children in Edgewood, and in like districts, suffer from an invidious discrimination violative of the Equal Protection Clause.

This does not, of course, mean that local control may not be a legitimate goal of a school financing system. Nor does it mean that the State must guarantee each district an equal per-pupil revenue from the state school-financing system. Nor does it mean, as the majority appears to believe, that, by affirming the decision below, this Court would be "imposing on the States inflexible constitutional restraints that could circumscribe or handicap the continued research and experimentation so vital to finding even partial solutions to educational problems and to keeping abreast of ever-changing conditions." On the contrary, it would merely mean that the State must fashion a financing scheme which provides a rational basis for the maximization of local control, if local control is to remain a goal of the system, and not a scheme with "different treatment be[ing] accorded to persons placed by a statute into different classes on the basis of criteria wholly unrelated to the objective of that statute." *Reed v. Reed*, 404 U.S. 71, 75–76 (1971).

Perhaps the majority believes that the major disparity in revenues provided and permitted by the Texas system is inconsequential. I cannot agree, however, that the difference of the magnitude appearing in this case can sensibly be ignored, particularly since the State itself considers it so important to provide opportunities to exceed the minimum state educational expenditures.

JUSTICE MARSHALL, with whom JUSTICE DOUGLAS concurs, dissenting.

The Court today decides, in effect, that a State may constitutionally vary the quality of education which it offers its children in accordance with the amount of taxable wealth located in the school districts within which they reside. The majority's decision represents an abrupt departure from the mainstream of recent state and federal court decisions concerning the unconstitutionality of state educational financing schemes dependent upon taxable local wealth. More unfortunately, though, the majority's holding can only be seen as a retreat from our historic commitment to equality of educational opportunity and as unsupportable acquiescence in a system which deprives children in their earliest years of the chance to reach their full potential as citizens. The Court does this despite the absence of any substantial justification for a scheme which arbitrarily channels educational resources in accordance with the fortuity of the amount of taxable wealth within each district.

In my judgment, the right of every American to an equal start in life, so far as the provision of a state service as important as education is concerned, is far too vital to permit state discrimination on grounds as tenuous as those presented by this record. Nor can I accept the notion that it is sufficient to remit these appellees to the vagaries of the political process which, contrary to the majority's suggestion, has proved singularly unsuited to the task of providing a remedy for this discrimination. I, for one, am unsatisfied with the hope of an ultimate "political" solution sometime in the indefinite future while, in the meantime, countless children unjustifiably receive inferior educations that "may affect their hearts and minds in a way unlikely ever to be undone." *Brown v. Board of Education*, 347 U.S. 483, 494 (1954). I must therefore respectfully dissent.

I

The Court acknowledges that "substantial interdistrict disparities in school expenditures" exist in Texas, and that these disparities are "largely attributable to differences in the amounts of money collected through local property taxation." But instead of closely examining the seriousness of these disparities and the invidiousness of the Texas financing scheme, the Court undertakes an elaborate exploration of the efforts Texas has purportedly made to close the gaps between its districts in terms of levels of district wealth and resulting educational funding. Yet, however praiseworthy Texas' equalizing efforts, the issue in this case is not whether Texas is doing its best to ameliorate the worst features of a discriminatory scheme but, rather, whether the scheme itself is in fact unconstitutionally discriminatory in the face of the Fourteenth Amendment's guarantee of equal protection of the laws. When the Texas financing scheme is taken as a whole, I do not think it can be doubted that it produces a discriminatory impact on substantial numbers of the schoolage children of the State of Texas.

B

The appellants do not deny the disparities in educational funding caused by variations in taxable district property wealth. They do contend, however, that whatever the differences in per-pupil spending among Texas districts, there are no discriminatory consequences for the children of the disadvantaged districts. But appellants reject the suggestion that the quality of education in any particular district is determined by money. . . . In their view, there is simply no denial of equal educational opportunity to any Texas schoolchildren as a result of the widely varying per-pupil spending power provided districts under the current financing scheme.

In my view . . . it is inequality—not some notion of gross inadequacy—of educational opportunity that raises a question of denial of equal protection of the laws. I find any other approach to the issue unintelligible and without directing principle. Here appellees have made a substantial showing of wide variations in educational funding and the resulting educational opportunity afforded to the school children of Texas. This discrimination is, in large measure, attributable to significant disparities in the taxable wealth of local Texas school districts. This is a sufficient showing to raise a substantial question of discriminatory state action in violation of the Equal Protection Clause.

C

But this Court has consistently recognized that where there is in fact discrimination against individual interests, the constitutional guarantee of equal protection of the laws is not inapplicable simply because the discrimination is based upon some group characteristic such as geographic location. Texas has chosen to provide free public education for all its citizens, and it has embodied that decision in its constitution. Yet, having established public education for its citizens, the State, as a direct consequence of the variations in local property wealth endemic to Texas' financing scheme, has provided some Texas schoolchildren with substantially less resources for their education than others. Thus, while on its face the Texas scheme may merely discriminate between local districts, the impact of that discrimination falls directly upon the children whose educational opportunity is dependent upon where they happen to live.

II

A

I . . . cannot accept the majority's labored efforts to demonstrate that fundamental interests, which call for strict scrutiny of the challenged classification, encompass only established rights which we are somehow bound to recognize from the text of the Constitution itself. To be sure, some interests which the Court has deemed to be fundamental for purposes of equal protection analysis are themselves constitutionally protected rights. Thus, discrimination against the guaranteed right of freedom of speech has called for strict judicial scrutiny.

I would like to know where the Constitution guarantees the right to procreate, *Skinner v. Oklahoma*, 316 U.S. 535, 541 (1942), or the right to vote in state elections, e.g., *Reynolds v. Sims*, 377 U.S. 533 (1964), or the right to an appeal from a criminal conviction, e.g., *Griffin v. Illinois*, 351 U.S. 12 (1956). These are instances in which, due to the importance of the interests at stake, the Court has displayed a strong concern with the existence of discriminatory state treatment. But the Court has never said or indicated that these are interests which independently enjoy full-blown constitutional protection.

In summary, it seems to me inescapably clear that this Court has consistently adjusted the care with which it will review state discrimination in light of the constitutional significance of the interests affected and the invidiousness of the particular classification. In the context of economic interests, we find that discriminatory state action is almost always sustained, for such interests are generally far removed from constitutional guarantees. But the situation differs markedly when discrimination against important individual interests with constitutional implications and against particularly disadvantaged or powerless classes is involved. The majority suggests, however, that a variable standard of review would give this Court the appearance of a "superlegislature." I cannot agree. Such an approach seems to me a part of the guarantees of our Constitution and of the historic experiences with oppression of and discrimination against discrete, powerless minorities which underlie that document. In truth, the Court itself will be open to the criticism raised by the majority so long as it continues on its present course of effectively selecting in private which cases will be afforded special consideration without acknowledging the true basis of its action. Such obfuscated action may be appropriate to a political body such as a legislature, but it is not appropriate to this Court. Open debate of the bases for the Court's action is essential to the rationality and consistency of our decisionmaking process. Only in this way can we avoid the label of legislature and ensure the integrity of the judicial process.

Nevertheless, the majority today attempts to force this case into the same category for purposes of equal protection analysis as decisions involving discrimination affecting commercial interests. By so doing, the majority singles this case out for analytic treatment at odds with what seems to me to be the clear trend of recent decisions in this Court, and thereby ignores the constitutional importance of the interest at stake and the invidiousness of the particular classification, factors that call for far more than the lenient scrutiny of the Texas financing scheme which the majority pursues. Yet if the discrimination inherent in the Texas scheme is scrutinized with the care demanded by the interest and classification present in this case, the unconstitutionality of that scheme is unmistakable.

FOR DISCUSSION

Why might the Supreme Court be unwilling to declare education to be a fundamental right, subject to the provisions of equal protection? What could be the societal consequences of such a decision?

EDGEWOOD INDEPENDENT SCHOOL DISTRICT V. KIRBY

777 S.W.2d 391, 1989 Tex. LEXIS 129, 33 Tex. Sup. J. 12 (1989)

The facts of the case are given in the opinion, which follows.

Vote: 2–1

JUSTICE OSCAR H. MAUZY, delivered the opinion of the Texas Supreme Court.

At issue is the constitutionality of the Texas system for financing the education of public school children. Edgewood Independent School District, sixty-seven other school districts, and numerous individual school children and parents filed suit seeking a declaration that the Texas school financing system violates the Texas Constitution. The trial court rendered judgment to that effect and declared that the system violates the Texas Constitution, article I, section 3, article I, section 19, and article VII, section 1. By a 2–1 vote, the court of appeals reversed that judgment and declared the system constitutional. We reverse the judgment of the court of appeals and, with modification, affirm that of the trial court.

The basic facts of this cause are not in dispute. The only question is whether those facts describe a public school financing system that meets the requirements of the Constitution. As summarized and excerpted, the facts are as follows.

There are approximately three million public school children in Texas. The legislature finances the education of these children through a combination of revenues supplied by the state itself and revenues supplied by local school districts which are governmental subdivisions of the state. Of total education costs, the state provides about forty-two percent, school districts provide about fifty percent, and the remainder comes from various other sources including federal funds. School districts derive revenues from local ad valorem property taxes, and the state raises funds from a variety of sources including the sales tax and various severance and excise taxes.

There are glaring disparities in the abilities of the various school districts to raise revenues from property taxes because taxable property wealth varies greatly from district to district. The wealthiest district has over $14,000,000 of property wealth per student, while the poorest has approximately $20,000; this disparity reflects a 700 to 1 ratio. The 300,000 students in the lowest-wealth schools have less than 3% of the state's property wealth to support their education while the 300,000 students in the highest-wealth schools have over 25% of the state's property wealth; thus the 300,000 students in the wealthiest districts have more than eight times the property value to support their education as the 300,000 students in the poorest districts.

The state has tried for many years to lessen the disparities through various efforts to supplement the poorer districts.

Because of the disparities in district property wealth, spending per student varies widely, ranging from $2,112 to $19,333. Under the existing system, an average of $2,000 more per year is spent on each of the 150,000 students in the wealthiest districts than is spent on the 150,000 students in the poorest districts.

The lower expenditures in the property-poor districts are not the result of lack of tax effort.

Property-poor districts are trapped in a cycle of poverty from which there is no opportunity to free themselves. Because of their inadequate tax base, they must tax at significantly higher rates in order to meet minimum requirements for accreditation; yet their educational programs are typically inferior. The location of new industry and development is strongly influenced by tax rates and the quality of local schools. Thus, the property-poor districts with their high tax rates and inferior schools are unable to attract new industry or development and so have little opportunity to improve their tax base.

The amount of money spent on a student's education has a real and meaningful impact on the educational opportunity offered that student. High-wealth districts are able to provide for their students broader educational experiences including more extensive curricula, more up-to-date technological equipment, better libraries and library personnel, teacher aides, counseling services, lower student-teacher ratios, better facilities, parental involvement programs, and drop-out prevention programs. They are also better able to attract and retain experienced teachers and administrators.

Based on these facts, the trial court concluded that the school financing system violates the Texas Constitution's equal rights guarantee of article I, section 3, the due course of law guarantee of article I, section 19, and the "efficiency" mandate of article VII, section 1. The court of appeals reversed. We reverse the judgment of the court of appeals and, with modification, affirm the judgment of the trial court.

Article VII, section 1 of the Texas Constitution provides:

A general diffusion of knowledge being essential to the preservation of the liberties and rights of the people, it shall be the duty of the Legislature of the State to establish and make suitable provision for the support and maintenance of an efficient system of public free schools.

The State argues that, as used in article VII, section 1, the word "efficient" was intended to suggest a simple and inexpensive system. Under the Reconstruction Constitution of 1869, the people had been subjected to a militaristic school system with the state exercising absolute authority over the training of children. Thus, the State contends that delegates to the 1875 Constitutional Convention deliberately inserted into this provision the word "efficient" in order to prevent the establishment of another Reconstruction-style, highly centralized school system.

If our state's population had grown at the same rate in each district and if the taxable wealth in each district had also grown at the same rate, efficiency could probably have been maintained within the structure of the present system. That did not happen. Wealth, in its many forms, has not appeared with geographic symmetry. The economic development of the state has not been uniform. Some cities have grown dramatically, while their sister communities have remained static or have shrunk. Formulas that once fit have been knocked askew. Although local conditions vary, the constitutionally imposed state responsibility for an efficient education system is the same for all citizens regardless of where they live.

We conclude that, in mandating "efficiency," the constitutional framers and ratifiers did not intend a system with such vast disparities as now exist. Instead, they stated clearly that the purpose of an efficient system was to provide for a "general diffusion of knowledge." The present system, by contrast, provides not for a diffusion that is general, but for one that is limited and unbalanced. The resultant inequalities are thus directly contrary to the constitutional vision of efficiency.

By statutory directives, the legislature has attempted through the years to reduce disparities and improve the system. There have been good faith efforts on the part of many public officials, and some progress has been made. However, as the undisputed facts of this case make painfully clear, the reality is that the constitutional mandate has not been met.

The legislature's recent efforts have focused primarily on increasing the state's contributions. More money allocated under the present system would reduce some of the existing disparities between districts but would at best only postpone the reform that is necessary to make the system efficient. A band-aid will not suffice; the system itself must be changed.

We hold that the state's school financing system is neither financially efficient nor efficient in the sense of providing for a "general diffusion of knowledge" statewide, and therefore that it violates article VII, section 1 of the Texas Constitution. Efficiency does not require a per capita distribution, but it also does not allow concentrations of resources in property-rich school districts that are taxing low when property-poor districts that are taxing high cannot generate sufficient revenues to meet even minimum standards. There must be a direct and close correlation between a district's tax effort and the educational resources available to it; in other words, districts must have substantially equal access to similar revenues per pupil at similar levels of tax effort. Children who live in poor districts and children who live in rich districts must be afforded a substantially equal opportunity to have access to educational funds. Certainly, this much is required if the state is to educate its populace efficiently and provide for a general diffusion of knowledge statewide.

Some have argued that reform in school finance will eliminate local control, but this argument has no merit. An efficient system does not preclude the ability of communities to exercise local control over the education of their children. It requires only that the funds available for education be distributed equitably and evenly. An efficient system will actually allow for more local control, not less. It will provide property-poor districts with economic alternatives that are not now available to them. Only if alternatives are indeed available can a community exercise the control of making choices.

Our decision today is not without precedent. Courts in nine other states with similar school financing systems have ruled those systems to be unconstitutional for varying reasons. *DuPree v. Alma School Dist. No. 30*, 279 Ark. 340, 651 S.W.2d 90 (1983); *Serrano v. Priest*, 5 Cal.3d 584, 96 Cal.Rptr. 601, 487 P.2d 1241 (1971); *Horton v. Meskill*, 172 Conn. 615, 376 A.2d 359 (Conn. 1977); *Rose v. Council for Better Educ.*, No. 88–SC–804–TG, 790 S.W.2d 186 (Ky. June 8, 1989); *Helena Elementary School Dist. No. 1 v. State*, 236 Mont. 44, 769 P.2d 684 (Mont. 1989); *Robinson v. Cahill*, 62 N.J. 473, 303 A.2d 273, cert. denied, 414 U.S. 976 (1973); *Seattle School Dist. No. 1 v. State*, 90 Wash.2d 476, 585 P.2d 71 (1978); *Pauley v. Kelly*, 162 W.Va. 672, 255 S.E.2d 859 (1979); *Washakie County School Dist. No. 1 v. Herschler*, 606 P.2d 310 (Wyo.), cert. denied, 449 U.S. 824 (1980).

Although we have ruled the school financing system to be unconstitutional, we do not now instruct the legislature as to the specifics of the legislation it should enact; nor do we order it to raise taxes. The legislature has primary responsibility to decide how best to achieve an efficient system. We decide only the nature of the constitutional mandate and whether that mandate has been met. Because we hold that the mandate of efficiency has not been met, we reverse the judgment of the court of appeals. The legislature is duty-bound to provide for an efficient system of education, and only if the legislature fulfills that duty can we launch this great state into a strong economic future with educational opportunity for all.

GLOSSARY

Benevolent Discrimination: Statutory distinctions made between groups of individuals to enable a previously excluded group to more fully participate in society or to be better able to economically compete.

Chattel Slavery: A system in which human beings are owned; not only with respect to their labor but also in their physical bodies, similar to livestock.

Malevolent Discrimination: A form of discrimination enabled by statutory distinctions that prevent some people from fully participating in society or fully competing economically.

Minimal Rationality: The lowest standard of scrutiny under the Equal Protection Clause. To meet this standard, the state must demonstrate that a rational reason exists for the law challenged as discriminatory. If the government can demonstrate a rational relationship between the distinction of groups under the challenged law, as well as a legitimate state objective, the law is not in violation of the Fourteenth Amendment. If the state cannot demonstrate a rational relation, then the law is in violation of the Equal Protection Clause.

Intermediate Scrutiny: A standard under the Equal Protection Clause that requires that a law discriminating against a protected class meet an important governmental function and be substantially related to that purpose. Also known as "semi-strict" scrutiny.

Invidious Discrimination: The result of a law reflecting an emotionally based antagonism toward the distinguished group.

Recused: Describing the voluntary removal of a judge or justice from participation in the decision of a case; judges frequently recuse themselves to avoid the appearance of a conflict of interest.

Strict Scrutiny: The highest standard used in determining whether discriminatory legislation has violated the Equal Protection Clause. This standard requires the government to demonstrate that the statute's challenged classification is necessary in order to achieve a permissible state objective and that the law is narrowly tailored to the achievement of that objective. Strict scrutiny is used in the evaluation of laws that impinge upon fundamental freedoms (such as religion, speech, and press) or that pertain to "suspect" classifications, such as racial distinctions.

Suspect Classification: Legislation that falls into this category is given the highest scrutiny under the Equal Protection Clause. It distinguishes laws affecting a group whose members are immutable or unchanging in their essential characteristics (such as race) and have faced a history of invidious discrimination based on this characteristic.

SELECTED BIBLIOGRAPHY

Anderson, Terry H. 2004. *The Pursuit of Fairness: A History of Affirmative Action.* Oxford and New York: Oxford University Press.

Baer, Judith. 1983. *Equality under the Constitution: Reclaiming the Fourteenth Amendment.* Ithaca, NY: Cornell University Press.

Baer, Judith A. 1999. *Our Lives before the Law: Constructing a Feminist Jurisprudence.* Princeton, NJ: Princeton University Press.

Baer, Judith A., and Leslie Goldstein. 2006. *The Constitutional and Legal Rights of Women: Cases in Law and Social Change.* Sweet Springs, MO: Roxbury Press.

Bedi, Sonu. 2013. *Beyond Race, Sex, and Sexual Orientation: Legal Equality Without Identity.* New York: Cambridge University Press.

Berry, Mary Francis. 1994. *Black Americans, White Law: A History of Constitutional Racism in America.* New York: Penguin Books.

Caplan, Lincoln. 1997. *Up against the Law: Affirmative Action and the Supreme Court.* New York: Twentieth Century Fund Press.

Davis, Abraham L., and Barbara Luck Graham. 1995. *The Supreme Court, Race, and Civil Rights.* Thousand Oaks, CA: Sage.

DuBois, Ellen Carol. 1998. *Woman Suffrage & Women's Rights.* New York: New York University Press.

Dyer, Justin Buckley. 2013. *Slavery, Abortion, and the Politics of Constitutional Meaning.* New York, NY: Cambridge University Press.

Edelman, Lauren B. 2016. *Working Law: Courts, Corporations, and Symbolic Civil Rights.* Chicago, IL: University of Chicago Press.

Failer, Judith Lynn. 2002. *Who Qualifies for Rights? Homelessness, Mental Illness and Civil Commitment.* Ithaca, NY: Cornell University Press.

Fehrenbacher, Dan. 1978. *The* Dred Scott *Case: Its Significance in American Law and Politics.* New York: Oxford University Press.

Glenn, Evelyn Nakano. 2002. *Unequal Freedom: How Race and Gender Shaped American Citizenship and Labor.* Cambridge, MA: Harvard University Press.

Graham, Hugh Davis. 1992. *Civil Rights and the Presidency: Race and Gender in American Politics.* New York: Oxford University Press.

Higginbotham, A. Leon. 1978. *In the Matter of Color.* New York: Oxford University Press.

Higginbotham, A. Leon. 1996. *Shades of Freedom: Racial Politics and the Presumptions of the American Legal Process.* New York: Oxford University Press.

Hill, Herbert, and J. Jones., eds. 1993. *Race in America: The Struggle for Equality.* Madison: University of Wisconsin Press.

Karst, Kenneth. 1989. *Belonging to America: Equal Citizenship and the Constitution.* New Haven, CT: Yale University Press.

Katznelson, Ira. 2005. *When Affirmative Action Was White: An Untold History of Racial Inequality in Twentieth Century America.* New York: W. W. Norton.

Kerber, Linda K. 1998. *No Constitutional Right to Be Ladies: Women and the Obligation of Citizenship.* New York: Hill and Wang.

Kessler-Harris, Alice. 2001. *In Pursuit of Equality: Women, Men, and the Quest for Economic Citizenship in 20th Century America.* New York: Oxford University Press.

Klarman, Michael J. 2004. *From Jim Crow to Civil Rights: The Supreme Court and the Struggle for Racial Equality.* New York: Oxford University Press.

Kluger, Richard. 2004. *Simple Justice: The History of* Brown v. Board of Education *and Black American's Struggle for Equality, rev. ed.* New York: Alfred A. Knopf.

Lawrence, Susan. 1990. *The Poor in Court.* Princeton, NJ: Princeton University Press.

Lively, Donald. 1992. *The Constitution and Race.* Westport, CT: Praeger Publishing.

Lofgren, Charles A. 1987. *The* Plessy *Case: A Legal-Historical Interpretation.* New York: Oxford University Press.

Mezey, Susan Gluck. 1992. *In Pursuit of Equality: Women, Public Policy, and the Federal Courts.* New York: St. Martin's Press.

Mezey, Susan Gluck. 2003. *Elusive Equality: Women's Rights, Public Policy, and the Law.* Boulder, CO: Lynne Rienner Publishing.

Nieman, Donald G. 1991. *Promises to Keep: African-Americans and the Constitutional Order, 1776 to the Present.* New York: Oxford University Press.

Olivas, Michael A. 2012. *No Undocumented Child Left Behind: Plyler v. Doe and the Education of Undocumented Schoolchildren.* New York: New York University Press.

Perry, Barbara A. 2007. *The Michigan Affirmative Action Cases.* Lawrence: University Press of Kansas.

Pinello, Daniel R. 2003. *Gay Rights and American Law.* New York: Cambridge University Press.

Sracic, Paul A. 2006. San Antonio v. Rodriguez *and the Pursuit of Equal Education: The Debate over Discrimination and School Funding.* Lawrence: University Press of Kansas.

Strum, Philippa. 2002. *Women in the Barracks: The VMI Case and Equal Rights.* Lawrence: University Press of Kansas.

Tushnet, Mark V. 1987. *The NAACP's Legal Strategy against Segregated Education, 1925–1950.* Chapel Hill: University of North Carolina Press.

Vile, John R., ed. 2016. *American Immigration and Citizenship: A Documentary History.* Lanham, MD: Rowman & Littlefield.

Zeitlow, Rebecca E. 2006. *Enforcing Equality: Congress, the Constitution, and the Protection of Individual Rights.* New York: New York University Press.

CHAPTER IX

Privacy and Reproductive Rights

Timeline: Privacy and Reproductive Rights

1873 The Comstock Act makes it a criminal offense to send contraception or birth control information through the U.S. mail and to sell such devices through interstate commerce.

1890 *Harvard Law Review* publishes "The Right to Privacy," an essay by Samuel Warren and Louis D. Brandeis arguing that common law protections of privacy (i.e., "the right to be left alone") can be applied to contemporary jurisprudence.

1891 In *Union Pacific Railroad Company v. Botsford* the Supreme Court recognizes a right of personal privacy under the Constitution.

1923 In *Meyer v. Nebraska* the Supreme Court rules that parents have the liberty to raise and educate their children as they deem appropriate.

1925 The Supreme Court determines in *Pierce v. Society of Sisters* that parents have the right to meet their educational responsibilities to their minor children through private education.

1928 In his dissent in *Olmstead v. United States*, Justice Brandeis defines the right to privacy as the "right to be left alone."

1965 *Griswold v. Connecticut* is the Court's first formal recognition that a right to privacy is inherent in the Constitution. Therefore, married couples have the right to choose to be informed about and use contraception.

1971 The Supreme Court finds that the right of privacy does not guarantee a right to abortion in *United States v. Vuitch*.

1972 *Eisenstadt v. Baird* declares that unmarried couples also have the right to privacy with respect to contraception.

1973 The Supreme Court finds in *Roe v. Wade* that women's right of privacy, which includes a right to have an abortion, can be of greater constitutional importance than the states' interest in protecting health and welfare of individual mothers.

1976 In *Planned Parenthood of Central Maryland v. Danforth* the Supreme Court expands the right to an abortion to minors who have been determined by courts to be "mature."

1976 In *Bellotti v. Baird (Bellotti I)*, the Court finds unconstitutional a Massachusetts statute requiring all minors seeking abortions to have parental consent for the procedure.

1977 *Carey v. Population Services International* declares unconstitutional a Pennsylvania law prohibiting the sale or distribution of contraception to minors under the age of sixteen, as well as the advertising of birth control.

1979 In *Bellotti v. Baird II* the Court revisits *Bellotti I* and allows a requirement for parental consent for a minor's abortion where procedural access for a mature minor to judicially bypass the requirement is statutorily available.

1980 *Harris v. McRae* upholds the constitutionality of a federal law, the Hyde Amendment, which restricts federal funding of abortions.

1981 In *H.L. v. Matheson* the Supreme Court upholds a Utah law requiring parental notification of unemancipated minors seeking abortions.

1982 Pennsylvania passes the Abortion Control Act of 1982.

1983 In *Akron v. Akron Center for Reproductive Health Inc.,* the Supreme Court overturns a local ordinance regulating abortion because it does not reflect a legitimate governmental interest.

1986 The Supreme Court, in *Thornburgh v. American College of Obstetricians and Gynecologists,* finds a Pennsylvania statute unconstitutional because it elevates policy interests of the state over the privacy interests of the woman.

1989 In *Webster v. Reproductive Health Services* the Court rules that although *Roe* remains law, states may constitutionally require a number of restrictions on the right to abortion.

1990 In *Cruzan v. Director, Missouri Department of Health,* the Court identifies a right of competent individuals to remove themselves from life support.

1990 In *Hodgson v. Minnesota* the Supreme Court rejects a Minnesota law requiring dual parental notification before a minor can have an abortion but approves the practice of making available judicial bypass opportunities. Simultaneously, the Court decides *Ohio v. Akron Center for Reproductive Health,* approving a state requirement for single parental notification by a minor seeking an abortion, when the statute provides for an exception through a judicial bypass procedure.

1992 *Planned Parenthood of Southeastern Pennsylvania v. Casey* upholds both *Roe* and the state of Pennsylvania's limitations on access to abortion, ruling that the latter were not an undue burden on women seeking the procedure.

1994 Oregon passes its Death with Dignity Act.

1995 In *Vernonia School District v. Acton* the Court determines that the random suspicionless drug testing of athletes in public high schools is allowable because the government's legitimate concern to protect minors from illegal drug use justifies a minimal intrusion on student privacy.

1997 In *Washington v. Glucksberg* the Supreme Court finds no right in the Due Process Clause to physician-assisted suicide. Similarly, in *Vacco v. Quill* the Court finds no such right in the Equal Protection Clause of the Fourteenth Amendment.

2000 The Supreme Court in *Stenberg v. Carhart* overturns a Nebraska statute banning "partial-birth abortions," ruling that the language of the law was too broad.

2002 In *Board of Education of Independent School District No. 92 of Pottawatomie City v. Earls* the Supreme Court extends the *Vernonia* decision to all students participating in extracurricular activities, justifying the ruling on the grounds that such students have a diminished expectation of privacy and that drug tests are only minimally intrusive.

2003 Congress passes the Partial-Birth Abortion Ban Act.

2006 The Supreme Court determines in *Oregon v. Gonzales* that the Controlled Substances Act of 1970 does not allow the U.S. attorney general to prosecute physicians in Oregon who participate in state-protected acts of physician-assisted suicide.

2007 In *Gonzales v. Carhart* the Supreme Court upholds the constitutionality of the federal Partial-Birth Abortion Ban Act.

2014 In *Burwell v. Hobby Lobby* the Supreme Court allowed public corporations with religious missions to receive the free exercise of religion exemption in the Affordable Care Act regarding the provision of birth control to its employees.

2016 The Supreme Court in *Zubick v. Hobby Lobby* returned to the lower federal courts the question of the constitutionality of a federal accommodation for religious employers allowing them to not pay for or notify employees that birth control was provided by insurance companies under the Affordable Care Act.

2016 In *Whole Woman's Health v. Hellerstedt* the Court found a Texas law that closed abortion clinics through regulation to construe a substantial burden on the right to privacy.

INTRODUCTION

Unlike the rights long understood to be guaranteed by Equal Protection Clause or the Due Process Clause, a right to privacy is not explicitly mentioned in the text of the Constitution or in the Bill of Rights. Instead, in over a century of law, the judiciary has discovered among the values and liberties protected by the Constitution a right to individual privacy. Formally unrecognized by Congress, this right has instead been identified by the courts, which have articulated its scope and applied its protections. Considering the degree of debate and contention over the scope and meaning of the Due Process and Equal Protection clauses that appear in the text of the Constitution, it is not surprising that the right to privacy has generated similar controversy. For most twenty-first-century Americans, however, the right to privacy is so inherent in the definition of individual liberty that its guarantee is assumed to be embedded in the Constitution itself, as opposed to being rooted in our cultural traditions. As expressed initially in academic writing and later in the language of the Supreme Court, this "right to be left alone" is perceived as applying to an individual's home, body, and property. It is known that government may not interfere with this right to privacy without a valid justification as to the necessity for superseding the liberty of an individual.

The more recent controversy over the right to privacy is less closely related to the significance and existence of the concept than to issues of the individual's right to control his or her own body. In particular, the debate has spanned the right to use contraception, the right to have legal access to abortion, and the right to die on one's own terms. This chapter will examine how the understanding of the right to privacy has evolved over the last century and the conflict between the state's defense of its articulated interests—health and safety of the mother, protection of the rights of the fetus, and the need for assurance that the vulnerable ill are not pushed to end their lives prematurely—and the right of the individual to be left alone. It is within the realm of these conflicts that the right of privacy is being currently defined.

The Right to Privacy

The question of the relationship between the individual's right to privacy and the Constitution is intriguing and continuously controversial. Unlike the names of many **fundamental rights**—the right to vote, the right to procedural due process, the right to free speech and press—the term "privacy" is not textually found in the

Constitution. In fact, while the value of personal privacy is reflected in many places in the Constitution—for example, the freedom to speak, worship, and assemble, the protection of one's home from quartering troops, and the protection against self-incrimination—and while personal privacy is honored in both common law and the American political tradition, there is no language directly guaranteeing one's privacy in the face of intrusion by the state.

But what does privacy mean for the individual in relation to governmental intrusion? As with every liberty secured by the Constitution, the right to privacy cannot be absolute; otherwise the government would not be able to pursue its obligations to promote the general welfare. It is ironic, however, that the earliest manifestations of a legal notion of privacy are based on civil litigation claiming that privacy violations were committed by one individual against another. One such example is found in an 1880 state supreme court decision involving a woman who gave birth attended by a physician and his friend, whom the woman and her husband had erroneously understood to also be a doctor. In *John H. DeMay and Alfred B. Scattergood v. Alvira Roberts* (46 Mich. Reports 160, 165–166, 1880), the Michigan Supreme Court explicitly noted that "the plaintiff had a legal right to the privacy of her apartment at such a time, and the law secures to her this right by requiring others to observe it, and to abstain from its violation." While this decision had no precedental value for federal or state courts outside Michigan, it marked the beginning of a formal, legal recognition of the right to privacy.

Ten years later, two Boston lawyers, Samuel Warren and future Supreme Court justice Louis D. Brandeis, published "The Right to Privacy" in the *Harvard Law Review*. Warren and Brandeis were attempting to construct an argument that would allow their clients to seek damages from newspapers that had printed unflattering or personal information, even if that information did not meet the standards of libel or slander. The article's impact was more significant in the **jurisprudence** of privacy than in the two attorneys' civil litigation practice. As Warren and Brandeis noted, "the protection afforded to the thoughts, sentiments, and emotions . . . is merely an instance of the enforcement of the more general right of the individual to be let alone."

The concept of a "right to privacy" continued to develop in the context of an increasing number of state and federal acts of **protectionistic legislation** designed to safeguard citizens from the consequences of their own decisions. In 1873, for instance, Congress passed the Act for the Suppression of Trade in, and Circulation of, Obscene Literature and Articles of Immoral Use. Known popularly as the Comstock Act, this law criminalized both the sending of birth control information or contraceptive devices through the U.S. mail and the selling of contraceptives through interstate commerce. In 1919 Nebraska passed a law requiring that all school curricula be taught in English and forbade the teaching of foreign languages to students before the ninth grade. In the case of *Meyer v. Nebraska* (262 U.S. 390, 1923), the Court found that the value of liberty encompasses not only physical liberty and the ability to make contracts but the freedom to "engage in any of the common occupations of life, to acquire useful knowledge . . . establish a home and bring up children . . . and generally to enjoy those privileges long recognized at common law as essential to the orderly pursuit of happiness by free men." Similarly, Oregon passed the Compulsory Education Act of 1922, which required all children between the ages of eight and sixteen to attend public schools. In *Pierce v. Society of Sisters* (268 U.S. 510, 1925), the Supreme Court found that the act

> unreasonably interferes with the liberty of parents and guardians to direct the upbringing and education of children under their control. As often heretofore pointed out, rights guaranteed by the Constitution may not be abridged by legislation which has no reasonable relation to some purpose within the competency of the State. . . . The child is not the mere creature of the State; those who nurture him and direct his destiny have the right, coupled with the high duty, to recognize and prepare him for additional obligations.

Within three years, the relationship between the Fourth Amendment's protection against unreasonable search and seizure and an individual's right to personal privacy was clarified in *Olmstead v. United States* (277 U.S.

438, 1928). This case emerged when Olmstead and others were convicted of a conspiracy to violate the National Prohibition Act through possessing, transporting, or selling of intoxicating liquors. The conspiracy was largely discovered by four federal Prohibition officers, who intercepted private telephone messages by the conspirators through wiretaps that were installed and monitored without physically trespassing in the defendants' private property. The Supreme Court found that the use of such evidence of the content of private telephone conversations did not violate the Fourth Amendment's ban on unreasonable search and seizure or the Fifth Amendments' prohibition against self-incrimination. In terms of privacy jurisprudence, however, the case is more notable for its dissenting opinions. Justice Brandeis's assertion that the right to privacy is essentially the "right to be left alone" is one of the most influential definitions of privacy. This phrase, which is recited repeatedly in later analyses, echoes Brandeis and Warren's argument regarding the right to privacy in their 1890 *Harvard Law Review* article.

Not until the seminal case of *Griswold v. Connecticut* (381 U.S. 479, 1965), however, would the Supreme Court formally recognize a right of privacy within the Constitution. The right to privacy is one that claims many ancient roots, but it is also one that the Court identifies from the **penumbras** or shadows **of the Constitution** and then articulates as a foundational right essential for democracy and citizenship. In justifying this decision in *Griswold*, the Court provides a litany of ways in which the Court had identified and recognized zones of privacy throughout the twentieth century. This recitation of cases will become familiar to readers as the right to privacy develops in later case law; the zones of privacy that Court focuses on are the home (search and seizure provisions, implicit assumptions of protection from the state); the person (right to privacy in thought and intimate choices); and the family (the raising and bearing of children). Although these zones overlap, the Court identifies specific amendments to the Constitution that protect these interests: the First, Third, Fourth, Fifth, Ninth, and Fourteenth Amendments.

The conflict among scholars and justices over the legitimacy of such a claim of constitutionally protected privacy is often based on concern over the consequences for our continuing jurisprudence. The issue for some is the inherently problematic nature of an electorally unaccountable body, whose members can be removed only by impeachment, making substantive decisions about the Constitution. For these individuals, these are questions best resolved by legislative bodies; see, for example, Justice Scalia's dissents in the abortion cases. Others wonder about the potential consequences of isolating more areas of an individual's life (such as sexual preferences and reproductive choices) from the scrutiny and regulation of the state. Still others focus on the necessity of protecting individuals' privacy that is developing as technology changes, our understanding of citizenship expands, and the role of the private and personal in the expression of our public selves evolves. These issues of privacy move beyond the typical exploration of reproductive rights to questions of personal privacy in an era of great national security concerns and to issues of the individual's right to die when technology can sustain life beyond personal preferences. Our understanding of the Constitution has changed as we have confronted these issues; the conflict between the individual and state, and the tension between personal liberty and community interest has remained.

SAMUEL WARREN AND LOUIS D. BRANDEIS, "THE RIGHT TO PRIVACY"

Written by two Boston lawyers, this 1890 *Harvard Law Review* (4: 193) article addressed the need for protection against harmful, but not defamatory, reporting in newspapers. Moving outside the legal categories of slander and libel, which were against the law at the time, the authors were contriving a legal argument to be used on behalf of individuals seeking damages as a result of unflattering and private information published by newspapers.

That the individual shall have full protection in person and in property is a principle as old as the common law; but it has been found necessary from time to time to define anew the exact nature and extent of such protection. Political, social, and economic changes entail the recognition of new rights, and the common law, in its eternal youth, grows to meet the demands of society. Thus, in very early times, the law gave a remedy only for physical interference with life and property, for trespasses *vi et armis*. Then the "right to life" served only to protect the subject from battery in its various forms; liberty meant freedom from actual restraint; and the right to property secured to the individual his lands and his cattle. Later, there came a recognition of man's spiritual nature, of his feelings and his intellect. Gradually the scope of these legal rights broadened; and now the right to life has come to mean the right to enjoy life—the right to be let alone, the right to liberty secures the exercise of extensive civil privileges; and the term "property" has grown to comprise every form of possession—intangible, as well as tangible.

This development of the law was inevitable. The intense intellectual and emotional life, and the heightening of sensations which came with the advance of civilization, made it clear to man that only a part of the pain, pleasure, and profit of life lay in physical things. Thoughts, emotions, and sensations demanded legal recognition, and the beautiful capacity for growth which characterizes the common law enabled the judges to afford the requisite protection, without the interposition of the legislature.

It is our purpose to consider whether the existing law affords a principle which can properly be invoked to protect the privacy of the individual; and, if it does, what the nature and extent of such protection is.

The common law secures to each individual the right of determining, ordinarily, to what extent his thoughts, sentiments, and emotions shall be communicated to others. Under our system of government, he can never be compelled to express them (except when upon the witness stand); and even if he has chosen to give them expression, he generally retains the power to fix the limits of the publicity which shall be given them. The existence of this right does not depend upon the particular method of expression adopted. It is immaterial whether it be by word or by signs, in painting, by sculpture, or in music. Neither does the existence of the right depend upon the nature or value of the thought or emotion, nor upon the excellence of the means of expression. The same protection is accorded to a casual letter or an entry in a diary and to the most valuable poem or essay, to a botch or daub and to a masterpiece. In every such case the individual is entitled to decide whether that which is his shall be given to the public.

These considerations lead to the conclusion that the protection afforded to thoughts, sentiments, and emotions, expressed through the medium of writing or of the arts, so far as it consists in preventing publication, is merely an instance of the enforcement of the more general right of the individual to be let alone. It is like the right not to be assaulted or beaten, the right not to be imprisoned, the right not to be maliciously prosecuted, the right not to be defamed. In each of these rights, as indeed in all other rights recognized by the law, there inheres the quality of being owned or possessed—and (as that is the distinguishing attribute of property) there may be some propriety in speaking of those rights as property. But, obviously, they bear little resemblance to what is ordinarily comprehended under that term. The principle which protects personal writings and all other personal productions, not against theft and physical appropriation, but against publication in any form, is in reality not the principle of private property, but that of an inviolate personality.

If we are correct in this conclusion, the existing law affords a principle which may be invoked to protect the privacy of the individual from invasion either by the too enterprising press, the photographer, or the possessor of any other modern device for recording or reproducing scenes or sounds. For the protection afforded is not confined by the authorities to those cases where any particular medium or form of expression has been adopted, nor to products of the intellect.

We must therefore conclude that the rights, so protected, whatever their exact nature, are not rights arising from contract or from special trust, but are rights as against the world; and, as above stated, the principle which has been applied to protect these rights is in reality not the principle of private property, unless that word be used in an extended and unusual sense. The principle which protects personal writings and any other productions of the intellect or of the emotions, is the right to privacy, and the law has no new principle to formulate when it extends this protection to the personal appearance, sayings, acts, and to personal relations, domestic or otherwise.

It remains to consider what are the limitations of this right to privacy, and what remedies may be granted for the enforcement of the right. To determine in advance of experience the exact line at which the dignity and convenience of the individual must yield to the demands of the public welfare or of private justice would be a difficult task; but the more general rules are furnished by the legal analogies already developed in the law of slander and libel, and in the law of literary and artistic property.

First. The right to privacy does not prohibit any publication of matter which is of public or general interest.

Second. The right to privacy does not prohibit the communication of any matter, though in its nature private, when the publication is made under circumstances which would render it a privileged communication according to the law of slander and libel.

Third. The law would probably not grant any redress for the invasion of privacy by oral publication in the absence of special damage.

Fourth. The right to privacy ceases upon the publication of the facts by the individual, or with his consent.

Fifth. The truth of the matter published does not afford a defense.

Sixth. The absence of "malice" in the publisher does not afford a defense.

The remedies for an invasion of the right of privacy are also suggested by those administered in the law of defamation, and in the law of literary and artistic property, namely:

1. An action of tort for damages in all cases. Even in the absence of special damages, substantial compensation could be allowed for injury to feelings as in the action of slander and libel.

2. An injunction, in perhaps a very limited class of cases.

It would doubtless be desirable that the privacy of the individual should receive the added protection of the criminal law, but for this, legislation would be required. Perhaps it would be deemed proper to bring the criminal liability for such publication within narrower limits; but that the community has an interest in preventing such invasions of privacy, sufficiently strong to justify the introduction of such a remedy, cannot be doubted. Still, the protection of society must come mainly through a recognition of the rights of the individual. Each man is responsible for his own acts and omissions only. If he condones what he reprobates, with a weapon at hand equal to his defense, he is responsible for the results. If he resists, public opinion will rally to his support. Has he then such a weapon? It is believed that the common law provides him with one, forged in the slow fire of the centuries, and today fitly tempered to his hand. The common law has always recognized a man's house as his castle, impregnable, often even to its own officers engaged in the execution of its commands. Shall the courts thus close the front entrance to constituted authority, and open wide the back door to idle or prurient curiosity?

FOR DISCUSSION

What might be the consequence of Warren and Brandeis's argument that the right of privacy is "in reality not the principle of private property, but that of an inviolate personality"?

PIERCE V. SOCIETY OF SISTERS

268 U.S. 510, 45 S.Ct. 571, 69 L.Ed. 1070 (1925)

The Society of Sisters, an educational organization based in Oregon, challenged the Compulsory Education Act of 1922. The law required children between the ages of eight and sixteen to attend public schools, beginning no later than September 1, 1926. The Society of Sisters claimed that the law would cause pupils to withdraw from its school, diminishing the group's income and decreasing the value of its property. The Society of Sisters believed that the Compulsory Education Act conflicted with the right of parents to choose their children's educational and religious training. A second appellee, Hill Military Academy, made a similar claim under the Fourteenth Amendment. Lower courts granted preliminary orders restraining the state of Oregon from threatening or attempting to enforce the act. The state appealed to the Supreme Court.

Vote: 9–0

JUSTICE MCREYNOLDS delivered the opinion of the Court.

No question is raised concerning the power of the State reasonably to regulate all schools, to inspect, supervise and examine them, their teachers and pupils; to require that all children of proper age attend some school, that teachers shall be of good moral character and patriotic disposition, that certain studies plainly essential to good citizenship must be taught, and that nothing be taught which is manifestly inimical to the public welfare.

The inevitable practical result of enforcing the Act under consideration would be destruction of appellees' primary schools, and perhaps all other private primary schools for normal children within the State of Oregon. These parties are engaged in a kind of undertaking not inherently harmful, but long regarded as useful and meritorious. Certainly there is nothing in the present records to indicate that they have failed to discharge their obligations to patrons, students or the State. And there are no peculiar circumstances or present emergencies which demand extraordinary measures relative to primary education.

Under the doctrine of *Meyer v. Nebraska*, 262 U.S. 390 [1923], we think it entirely plain that the Act of 1922 unreasonably interferes with the liberty of parents and guardians to direct the upbringing and education of children under their control. As often heretofore pointed out, rights guaranteed by the Constitution may not be abridged by legislation which has no reasonable relation to some purpose within the competency of the State. The fundamental theory of liberty upon which all governments in this Union repose excludes any general power of the State to standardize its children by forcing them to accept instruction from public teachers only. The child is not the mere creature of the State; those who nurture him and direct his destiny have the right, coupled with the high duty, to recognize and prepare him for additional obligations.

Appellees are corporations and therefore, it is said, they cannot claim for themselves the liberty which the Fourteenth Amendment guarantees. Accepted in the proper sense, this is true. But they have business and property for which they claim protection. These are threatened with destruction through the unwarranted compulsion which appellants are exercising over present and prospective patrons of their schools. And this court has gone very far to protect against loss threatened by such action.

The courts of the State have not construed the Act, and we must determine its meaning for ourselves. Evidently it was expected to have general application and cannot be construed as though merely intended to amend the charters of certain private corporations, as in *Berea College v. Kentucky*, 211 U.S. 45 [1908]. No argument in favor of such view has been advanced.

Generally it is entirely true, as urged by counsel, that no person in any business has such an interest in possible customers as to enable him to restrain exercise of proper power of the State upon the ground that he will be deprived of patronage. But the injunctions here sought are not against the exercise of any proper power. Plaintiffs asked protection against arbitrary, unreasonable and unlawful interference with their patrons and the consequent destruction of their business and property. Their interest is clear and immediate, within the rule approved in *Truax v. Raich,* 239 U.S. 33 (1915), *Truax v. Corrigan,* 257 U.S. 312 (1921), and *Terrace v. Thompson,* 263 U.S. 197 (1923), and many other cases where injunctions have issued to protect business enterprises against interference with the freedom of patrons or customers.

FOR DISCUSSION

How does the case of *Pierce v. Society of Sisters* advance the analysis of a constitutionally protected right of privacy? Is this reasoning consistent with the Warren/Brandeis argument, or does it challenge it?

FURTHER CASES

***Buck v. Bell*: 274 U.S. 200 (1927).**

The Court upheld a Virginia law that allowed the compulsory sterilization of women who had been committed to mental hospitals. The law did require a hearing before the procedure was initiated; the challenge was based on the substantive issue, not the procedural.

***Skinner v. Oklahoma ex rel. Williamson*: 316 U.S. 535 (1942).**

The Supreme Court overturned the Oklahoma Criminal Sterilization Act, which had allowed the state to sterilize "habitual criminals." The Court found that the act violated the Equal Protection Clause of the Fourteenth Amendment.

***Loving v. Virginia*: 388 U.S. 1 (1967).**

The Court determined that Virginia's anti-miscegenation law, which criminalized interracial marriages, violated the Equal Protection Clause of the Fourteenth Amendment. In the unanimous decision, the Court argued that race-based distinctions are subject to strict scrutiny.

OLMSTEAD V. UNITED STATES

277 U.S. 438, 48 S.Ct. 564, 72 L.Ed. 944 (1928)

Olmstead and others were convicted of a conspiracy to violate the National Prohibition Act through the possession, transportation, or sale of intoxicating liquors. Olmstead was the leading conspirator and the general manager of the business. The conspiracy was largely discovered by the work of four federal Prohibition officers, who intercepted private telephone messages of the conspirators. The wiretaps were installed and monitored without physically trespassing in the petitioners' private property. The Ninth Circuit Court of Appeals did not find any violation of the Fourth and Fifth Amendments. The Supreme Court agreed to hear arguments on the single question of whether the use as evidence of private telephone conversations between Olmstead and the others, intercepted by means of wiretapping, violated the petitioners' rights under the Fourth and Fifth Amendments.

Vote: 9–0

CHIEF JUSTICE TAFT delivered the opinion of the Court.

The Fourth Amendment provides—"The right of the people to be secure in their persons, houses, papers, and effects against unreasonable searches and seizures shall not be violated; and no warrants shall issue but upon probable cause, supported by oath or affirmation and particularly describing the place to be searched and the persons or things to be seized." And the Fifth: "No person . . . shall be compelled, in any criminal case, to be a witness against himself."

It will be helpful to consider the chief cases in this Court which bear upon the construction of these Amendments.

Boyd v. United States, 116 U.S. 616 (1886), was an information filed by the District Attorney in the federal court in a cause of seizure and forfeiture against thirty-five cases of plate glass, which charged that the owner and importer, with intent to defraud the revenue, made an entry of the imported merchandise by means of a fraudulent or false invoice. It became important to show the quantity and value of glass contained in twenty-nine cases previously imported. The fifth section of the Act of June 22, 1874, provided that in cases not criminal under the revenue laws, the United States Attorney, whenever he thought an invoice, belonging to the defendant, would tend to prove any allegation made by the United States, might by a written motion describing the invoice and setting forth the allegation which he expected to prove, secure a notice from the court to the defendant to produce the invoice, and if the defendant refused to produce it, the allegations stated in the motion should be taken as confessed, but if produced, the United States Attorney should be permitted, under the direction of the court, to make an examination of the invoice, and might offer the same in evidence.

The court held the Act of 1874 repugnant to the Fourth and Fifth Amendments.

The statute provided an official demand for the production of a paper or document by the defendant for official search and use as evidence on penalty that by refusal he should be conclusively held to admit the incriminating character of the document as charged. It was certainly no straining of the language to construe the search and seizure under the Fourth Amendment to include such official procedure.

The next case, and perhaps the most important, is *Weeks v. United States*, 232 U.S. 383 (1914),—a conviction for using the mails to transmit coupons or tickets in a lottery enterprise. The defendant was arrested by a police officer without a warrant. After his arrest other police officers and the United States marshal went to his house, got the key from a neighbor, entered the defendant's room and searched it, and took possession of various papers and articles. Neither the marshal nor the police officers had a search warrant. The defendant filed a petition in court asking the return of all his property. The court ordered the return of everything not pertinent to the charge, but denied return of relevant evidence. This court held that such taking of papers by an official of the United States, acting under color of his office, was in violation of the constitutional rights of the defendant, and upon making seasonable application he was entitled to have them restored, and that by permitting their use upon the trial, the trial court erred.

There is no room in the present case for applying the Fifth Amendment unless the Fourth Amendment was first violated. There was no evidence of compulsion to induce the defendants to talk over their many telephones. They were continually and voluntarily transacting business without knowledge of the interception. Our consideration must be confined to the Fourth Amendment.

The striking outcome of the *Weeks* case and those which followed it was the sweeping declaration that the Fourth Amendment, although not referring to or limiting the use of evidence in courts, really forbade its introduction if obtained by government officers through a violation of the Amendment. Theretofore many had supposed that under the ordinary common law rules, if the tendered evidence was pertinent, the method of obtaining it was unimportant. But in the *Weeks* case, and those which followed, this Court decided with great emphasis, and established as the law for the federal courts, that the protection of the Fourth Amendment would be much impaired unless it was held that not only was the official violator of the rights under the Amendment subject to action at the suit of the injured defendant, but also that the evidence thereby obtained could not be received.

The well known historical purpose of the Fourth Amendment, directed against general warrants and writs of assistance, was to prevent the use of governmental force to search a man's house, his person, his papers and his effects; and to prevent their seizure against his will. This phase of the misuse of governmental power of compulsion is the emphasis of the opinion of the Court in the *Boyd* case. This appears too in the *Weeks* case. . . .

Gouled v. United States, 255 U.S. 298 (1921), carried the inhibition against unreasonable searches and seizures to the extreme limit. Its authority is not to be enlarged by implication and must be confined to the precise state of facts disclosed by the record. A representative of the Intelligence Department of the Army, having by stealth obtained admission to the defendant's office, seized and carried away certain private papers valuable for evidential purposes. This was held an unreasonable search and seizure within the Fourth Amendment. A stealthy entrance in such circumstances became the equivalent to an entry by force. There was actual entrance into the private quarters of defendant and the taking away of something tangible. Here we have testimony only of voluntary conversations secretly overheard.

The Amendment itself shows that the search is to be of material things—the person, the house, his papers or his effects. The description of the warrant necessary to make the proceeding lawful, is that it must specify the place to be searched and the person or things to be seized.

The United States takes no such care of telegraph or telephone messages as of mailed sealed letters. The Amendment does not forbid what was done here. There was no searching. There was no seizure. The evidence was secured by the use of the sense of hearing and that only. There was no entry of the houses of offices of the defendants.

By the invention of the telephone, fifty years ago, and its application for the purpose of extending communications, one can talk with another at a far distant place. The language of the Amendment can not be extended and expanded to include telephone wires reaching to the whole world from the defendant's house of office. The intervening wires are not part of his house of office any more than are the highways along which they are stretched.

Justice Bradley in the *Boyd* case, and Justice Clarke in the *Gouled* case, said that the Fifth Amendment and the Fourth Amendment were to be liberally construed to effect the purpose of the framers of the Constitution in the interest of liberty. But that can not justify enlargement of the language employed beyond the possible practical meaning of houses, persons, papers, and effects, or so to apply the words search and seizure as to forbid hearing or sight.

Congress may of course protect the secrecy of telephone messages by making them, when intercepted, inadmissible in evidence in federal criminal trials, by direct legislation, and thus depart from the common law of evidence. But the courts may not adopt such a policy by attributing an enlarged and unusual meaning to the Fourth Amendment. The reasonable view is that one who installs in his house a telephone instrument with connecting wires intends to project his voice to those quite outside, and that the wires beyond his house and messages while passing over them are not within the protection of the Fourth Amendment. Here those who intercepted the projected voices were not in the house of either party to the conversation.

Neither the cases we have cited nor any of the many federal decisions brought to our attention hold the Fourth Amendment to have been violated as against a defendant unless there has been an official search and seizure of his person, or such a seizure of his papers or his tangible material effects, or an actual physical invasion of his house "or curtilage" for the purpose of making a seizure.

We think, therefore, that the wire tapping here disclosed did not amount to a search or seizure within the meaning of the Fourth Amendment.

The judgments of the Circuit Court of Appeals are affirmed.

JUSTICE HOLMES, dissenting.

While I do not deny it, I am not prepared to say that the penumbra of the Fourth and Fifth Amendments covers the defendant, although I fully agree that Courts are apt to err by sticking too closely to the words of a law where those words import a policy that goes beyond them. But I think, as Mr. Justice Brandeis says, that apart from the Constitution the Government ought not to use evidence obtained and only obtainable by a criminal act. There is no body of precedents by which we are bound, and which confines us to logical deduction from established rules. Therefore we must consider the two objects of desire, both of which we cannot have, and make up our minds which to choose. It is desirable that criminals should be detected, and to that end that all available evidence should be used. It also is desirable that the Government should not itself foster and pay for other crimes, when they are the means by which the evidence is to be obtained. We have to choose, and for my part I think it a less evil that some criminals should escape than that the Government should play an ignoble part.

JUSTICE BRANDEIS, dissenting.

The defendants were convicted of conspiring to violate the National Prohibition Act. Before any of the persons now charged had been arrested or indicted, the telephones by means of which they habitually communicated with one another and with others had been tapped by federal officers. To this end, a lineman of long experience in wire-tapping was employed, on behalf of the Government and at its expense. He tapped eight telephones, some in the homes of the persons charged, some in their offices. Acting on behalf of the Government and in their official capacity, at least six other prohibition agents listened over the tapped wires and reported the messages taken. Their operations extended over a period of nearly five months. The typewritten record of the notes of conversations overheard occupies 775 typewritten pages. By objections seasonably made and persistently renewed, the defendants objected to the admission of the evidence obtained by wire-tapping, on the ground that the Government's wire-tapping constituted an unreasonable search and seizure, in violation of the Fourth Amendment; and that the use as evidence of the conversations overheard compelled the defendants to be witnesses against themselves, in violation of the Fifth Amendment.

When the Fourth and Fifth Amendments were adopted, "the form that evil had theretofore taken," had been necessarily simple. Force and violence were then the only means known to man by which a Government could directly effect self-incrimination. It could compel the individual to testify—a compulsion effected, if need be, by torture. It could secure possession of his papers and other articles incident to his private life—a seizure effected, if need be, by breaking and entry. Protection against such invasion of "the sanctities of a man's home and the privacies of life" was provided in the Fourth and Fifth Amendments by specific language. But "time works changes, brings into existence new conditions and purposes." *Weems v. United States,* 217 U.S. 349, 1910. Subtler and more far-reaching means of invading privacy have become available to the Government. Discovery and invention have made it possible for the Government, by means far more effective than stretching upon the rack, to obtain disclosure in court of what is whispered in the closet.

Moreover, "in the application of a constitution, our contemplation cannot be only of what has been but of what may be." The progress of science in furnishing the Government with means of espionage is not likely to stop with wire-tapping. Ways may some day be developed by which the Government, without removing papers from secret drawers, can reproduce them in court, and by which it will be enabled to expose to a jury the most intimate occurrences of the home. Advances in the psychic and related sciences may bring means of exploring unexpressed beliefs, thoughts and emotions. Can it be that the Constitution affords no protection against such invasions of individual security?

A sufficient answer is found in *Boyd v. United States*, 116 U.S. 616, 627–630 [(1886)], a case that will be remembered as long as civil liberty lives in the United States.

Time and again, this Court in giving effect to the principle underlying the Fourth Amendment, has refused to place an unduly literal construction upon it. This was notably illustrated in the *Boyd* case itself. Taking language in its ordinary meaning, there is no "search" or "seizure" when a defendant is required to produce a document in the orderly process of a court's procedure. "The right of the people to be secure in their persons, houses, papers, and effects, against unreasonable searches and seizures," would not be violated, under any ordinary construction of language, by compelling obedience to a subpoena. But this Court holds the evidence inadmissible simply because the information leading to the issue of the subpoena has been unlawfully secured.

Decisions of this Court applying the principle of the *Boyd* case have settled these things. Unjustified search and seizure violates the Fourth Amendment, whatever the character of the paper; whether the paper when taken by the federal officers was in the home, in an office or elsewhere; whether the taking was effected by force, by fraud, or in the orderly process of a court's procedure. From these decisions, it follows necessarily that the Amendment is violated by the officer's reading the paper without a physical seizure, without his even touching it; and that use, in any criminal proceeding, of the contents of the paper so examined—as where they are testified to by a federal officer who thus saw the document or where, through knowledge so obtained, a copy has been procured elsewhere—any such use constitutes a violation of the Fifth Amendment.

The protection guaranteed by the Amendments is much broader in scope. The makers of our Constitution undertook to secure conditions favorable to the pursuit of happiness. They recognized the significance of man's spiritual nature, of his feelings and of his intellect. They knew that only a part of the pain, pleasure and satisfactions of life are to be found in material things. They sought to protect Americans in their beliefs, their thoughts, their emotions and their sensations. They conferred, as against the Government, the right to be let alone—the most comprehensive of rights and the right most valued by civilized men. To protect that right, every unjustifiable intrusion by the Government upon the privacy of the individual, whatever the means employed, must be deemed a violation of the Fourth Amendment. And the use, as evidence in a criminal proceeding, of facts ascertained by such intrusion must be deemed a violation of the Fifth.

Applying to the Fourth and Fifth Amendments the established rule of construction, the defendants' objections to the evidence obtained by wire-tapping must, in my opinion, be sustained. It is, of course, immaterial where the physical connection with the telephone wires leading into the defendants' premises was made. And it is also immaterial that the intrusion was in aid of law enforcement. Experience should teach us to be most on our guard to protect liberty when the Government's purposes are beneficent. Men born to freedom are naturally alert to repel invasion of their liberty by evil-minded rulers. The greatest dangers to liberty lurk in insidious encroachment by men of zeal, well-meaning but without understanding.

JUSTICE BUTLER, dissenting.

The single question for consideration is this: May the Government, consistently with that clause, have its officers whenever they see fit, tap wires, listen to, take down and report, the private messages and conversations transmitted by telephones?

The United States maintains that "The 'wire tapping' operations of the federal prohibition agents were not a 'search and seizure' in violation of the security of the 'persons, houses, papers and effects' of the petitioners in the constitutional sense or within the intendment of the Fourth Amendment." The Court, adhering to and reiterating the principles laid down and applied in prior decisions construing the search and seizure clause, in substance adopts the contention of the Government.

The question at issue depends upon a just appreciation of the facts. Telephones are used generally for transmission of messages concerning official, social, business and personal affairs including communications that are private and privileged—those between physician and patient, lawyer and client, parent and child, husband and wife. The contracts between telephone companies and users contemplate the private use of the facilities employed in the service. The communications belong to the parties between whom they pass. During their transmission the exclusive use of the wire belongs to the persons served by it. Wire tapping involves interference with the wire while being used. Tapping the wires and listening in by the officers literally constituted a search for evidence. As the communications passed, they were heard and taken down.

In *Boyd v. United States*, 116 U.S. 616 (1886), there was no "search or seizure" within the literal or ordinary meaning of the words, nor was Boyd—if these constitutional provisions were read strictly according to the letter—compelled in a "criminal case" to be a "witness" against himself. The statute, there held unconstitutional because repugnant to the search and seizure clause, merely authorized judgment for sums claimed by the Government on account of revenue if the defendant failed to produce his books, invoices and papers. The principle of that case has been followed, developed and applied in this and many other courts. And it is in harmony with the rule of liberal construction that always has been applied to provisions of the Constitution safeguarding personal rights, as well as to those granting governmental powers.

This Court has always construed the Constitution in the light of the principles upon which it was founded. The direct operation or literal meaning of the words used do not measure the purpose or scope of its provisions. Under the principles established and applied by this Court, the Fourth Amendment safeguards against all evils that are like and equivalent to those embraced within the ordinary meaning of its words. That construction is consonant with sound reason and in full accord with the course of decisions since *McCulloch v. Maryland*. That is the principle directly applied in the *Boyd* case.

When the facts in these cases are truly estimated, a fair application of that principle decides the constitutional question in favor of the petitioners. With great deference, I think they should be given a new trial.

JUSTICE STONE also wrote a dissenting opinion.

FOR DISCUSSION

How do the dissenting opinions articulate a relationship between the right of privacy and the protections granted by the Fourth and Fifth Amendments?

RELATED CASES

***Vernonia School District v. Acton:* 515 U.S. 646 (1995).**

The Court found that suspicionless drug testing of high school athletes attending public schools does not violate search and seizure protections of the Fourth Amendment. The government's concern to protect minors from illegal drug use justifies minimal intrusion of the athletes' privacy.

***Board of Education of Independent School District No. 92 of Pottawatomie City v. Earls:* 536 U.S. 822 (2002).**

In a 5–4 decision, the Supreme Court upheld the constitutionality of the student activities drug testing policy of this Oklahoma school system, which required all students participating in extracurricular activities to consent to suspicionless testing for drugs. The Court found that students participating in the activities had a diminished expectation of privacy and that the tests in question were minimally intrusive.

***United States v. Jones:* 565 U.S. 400 (2012).**

The Supreme Court found that the warrantless installation of GPS tracking unit on Jones' car violated his privacy and the Fourth Amendment.

GRISWOLD V. CONNECTICUT

381 U.S. 479, 85 S.Ct. 1678, 14 L.Ed.2d 510 (1965)

Griswold, executive director of the Planned Parenthood League of Connecticut, and Buxton, a licensed physician and professor at Yale Medical School, were arrested for giving married couples information, instruction, and medical advice regarding contraceptives, in violation of a Connecticut law (§ 53–32). The statute made the use of birth control punishable by a fine of at least fifty dollars and/or imprisonment from sixty days to one year. Section 54–196 allows for the prosecution of anyone who assists or counsels the use of contraceptives as if he or she were the primary offender (i.e., the user). Griswold and Buxton were found guilty and fined $100 each under § 54–196. The appellate division of the circuit court affirmed, as did the Connecticut Supreme Court of Errors.

Vote: 7–2

JUSTICE DOUGLAS delivered the opinion of the Court.

[This case is found in Chapter I, Creating the Modern Federal Judiciary: Incorporation and Interpretation of the Bill of Rights.]

FOR DISCUSSION

Do you find the majority's opinion regarding the existence of a right of privacy that can be inferred from the other constitutional guarantees compelling? Why or why not?

RELATED CASES

***John H. DeMay and Alfred B. Scattergood v. Alvira Roberts:* 46 Mich. Reports 160 (1880).**

This early state Supreme Court decision found that the "plaintiff had a legal right to the privacy of her apartment at such a time, and the law secures to her this right by requiring others to observe it, and to abstain from its violation" (165–166).

***Eisenstadt v. Baird:* 405 U.S. 438 (1972).**

In a 6–1 decision, the Court decided that a Massachusetts law that denied single people access to birth control was unconstitutional. The Court did not rely on its Griswold ruling; instead, it found that the state's distinction between married and single people's legal access to contraceptives lacked the rational reason required to satisfy the guarantees of the Fourteenth Amendment's Equal Protection Clause.

***Carey v. Population Services International:* 431 U.S. 678 (1977).**

The Court held unconstitutional a Pennsylvania law that prohibited the distribution or sale of birth control devices to minors under the age of sixteen, declared illegal the distribution of contraceptives by anyone but a licensed pharmacist, and prohibited the advertising of contraceptives.

***Burwell v. Hobby Lobby:* 573 U.S. ___ (2014).**

The Court allowed public corporations with religious missions to receive a free exercise of religion exemption to the Affordable Care Act regarding the provision of birth control to its employees. See Chapter X on Personhood for a full discussion of this case.

***Zubik v. Burwell:* 578 U.S. ___ (2016).**

The Supreme Court returned to the lower courts the question of the constitutionality of a federal accommodation for religious employers allowing them neither to pay for nor to notify employees that birth control was provided by insurance companies under the Affordable Care Act.

The Right to Abortion

The right to privacy, with its roots in the access to contraception, was quickly expanded to protect people from other ways in which the state interfered with issues of reproduction—more specifically, the issue of abortion. In *Roe v. Wade* (410 U.S. 113, 1973), the Court found that the right to privacy in reproductive choices superseded the numerous state regulations and statutes that had provided blanket prohibitions of abortion. The Court determined that there is a liberty interest possessed by the woman and a state interest in protecting the health and well-being of the mother. Thus, the Court in *Roe* held that an adult woman has a fundamental constitutional right to terminate her pregnancy under certain delineated circumstances. In this seminal case, the Court used a complex structure predicated on the trimesters of pregnancy to balance the interests of the woman and of the state; this system was challenged in later cases as medical technology pushed **fetal viability** to occur increasingly earlier in the pregnancy. In addition, in later cases it became clear that the Court's interest in safeguarding the right of a woman to determine the use of her own body was balanced not only by the responsibility of the state to protect the health of the mother, but the concerns of the parents of a pregnant minor. In time, the judiciary also faced political disagreements over the states' legislative ability to determine the beginning of life through statutory regulation, to articulate constitutional rights of the fetus, and to limit abortion through the regulation of medical facilities and procedures. While *Roe* has withstood such statutory challenges, its strength has diminished, and the ruling is now supported by a more tentative majority coalition.

In *Planned Parenthood of Central Missouri v. Danforth* (428 U.S. 52, 1976), the Court extended this fundamental right (i.e., to abortion) to minors who were deemed mature; the justices noted that "constitutional rights do not mature and come magically into being only when one attains the state-defined age of majority." Three years later, in *Bellotti v. Baird* (443 U.S. 622, 1979: *Bellotti II*), the Court determined that a state could require parental consent prior to a minor's termination of her pregnancy. To ensure to the mature minor a means of exercising her fundamental right to abort, however, the Court ruled that minors must have the option of judicially bypassing the requirement for parental consent. In 1989, the Supreme Court had the opportunity to rethink the question of the fundamental nature of the right to access to abortion; the case of *Webster v. Reproductive Health* (492 U.S. 490) tested the Missouri statute that regulated abortions in that state. According to the statute, life began at conception, and from that moment, "unborn children" had an interest in life and health that the state should protect to the same degree that it protected the interests of all other people. This proposition was challenged, along with two other aspects of the law: (1) after twenty weeks of pregnancy, a doctor who contemplated performing an abortion must first decide that the fetus was not viable and (2) the use of any public resources for any abortion not necessary to save the mother's life was prohibited.

Webster was the first significant challenge to *Roe v. Wade,* and it prompted a record-setting number of **amicus curiae**, or friend of the court, briefs. While the Court did not agree with the state's determination that conception marked the point delineating where the state has an interest in protecting life over the mother's privacy interests, the Court held the state's interest in protecting potential human life as legitimate. The challenged elements of the Missouri law were sustained. However, to the disappointment of opponents of abortion, the Court found the case distinctive enough from *Roe* to prevent the overturning of the 1973 decision, even though *Roe*'s trimester system of regulation was narrowed.

On June 25, 1990, the Supreme Court issued two decisions about the powers of the states to regulate the availability of abortions for minors. Both *Hodgson v. Minnesota* (497 U.S. 417 1990) and *Ohio v. Akron Center for Reproductive Health* (497 U.S. 502, 1990) examined the constitutionality of state laws requiring doctors to ensure that parents are alerted to daughters' intent to abort. A divided majority in *Hodgson* determined that a Minnesota statute requiring a minor to notify both parents before having an abortion was unconstitutional; however, the provision of a judicial process by which exceptions could be granted under specific circumstances (judicial bypass) was upheld as constitutional. The prohibition of the dual parental notification requirement in Hodgson reflected the Court's acknowledgment that pregnant girls might be estranged from or abandoned by one parent, or that the minor's father could have sired the fetus. In *Akron* the Court upheld a state requirement that the minor must either notify one parent or obtain a judicial bypass prior to aborting. The *Hodgson* decision ruled that certain minors must have a way to avoid parental involvement: these exceptions include a minor who was mature enough to make the decision without parental consultation, a minor who might be psychologically or physically endangered if her parents were notified, and a minor whose best interests definitely would be served by the abortion. The Ohio statute required the notification of only one parent, but both states provided a version of the *Bellotti II* judicial bypass procedure. The issue in both cases was whether the respective state notification statute was constitutional under such previous cases as *Bellotti I* and *Danforth.*

While *Roe v. Wade* remained the law of the land, the battle over the constitutionality of abortion protections typically was waged in the state legislatures, as states attempted to find ways of limited access to abortion without banning the procedure. For instance, the Pennsylvania Abortion Control Act of 1982 required a woman seeking an abortion to provide informed consent; wait twenty-four hours; if a minor, obtain consent from one parent or go through the steps needed to secure a judicial bypass option; and, if married, verify that she had notified her husband. In addition, facilities that provide abortion services were given specific reporting requirements. In the 1992 case of *Planned Parenthood of Southeastern Pennsylvania v. Casey* (505 U.S. 833), the Supreme Court again reconsidered the constitutionality of *Roe* and again reaffirmed its essential ruling. The Court upheld most of the provisions passed by Pennsylvania but excluded the requirement of spousal notification. Most of the provisions were held to be legitimate reflections of the interests of the state (e.g., protecting the health of the mother, safety of the procedure, interest of minors), which did not place an undue burden on the woman's right to have an abortion.

Federal courts have not been the only ones wrestling with the constitutionality of state legislation; state courts have assumed similar responsibilities. For instance, the Minnesota legislature passed several statutes limiting the use of public funds for abortion-related medical services to cases of medical necessity, rape, or incest, but allowing the same funds to be used for childbirth-related medical services. This distinction within the statutes was challenged as violating both a woman's right to privacy and the right to equal protection of the laws because it had the effect of favoring favored one reproductive choice over another. The case of *Women of the State of Minnesota v. Gomez* (542 N.W.2d 17, 1995) is especially interesting because these claims are brought under the Minnesota constitution, as opposed to the federal document.

After *Casey*, the Supreme Court generally avoided cases focused on abortion. While *Roe v. Wade* was still the law, the Court allowed states to provide many limitations to this protected liberty, as long as states demonstrate that they are protecting their own constitutionally defined interests. In 2000 the issue of abortion again faced the Supreme Court in the case of *Stenberg v. Carhart* (530 U.S. 914) the famed "partial birth abortion" case. Some commentators speculate that the Court was willing to hear this case because there had been disagreement among the federal circuit courts as to the constitutionality of such provisions and discussions of a federal "partial birth abortion" ban. *Carhart* was a challenge to a Nebraska statute banning the use of the "dilation and extraction" method of abortion in all cases except when necessary to save the life of the mother. This issue was particularly contentious because abortion rights advocates feared the vague language of the statute could be used to ban virtually all abortions and because antiabortion advocates found the nature of the medical procedure to be particularly offensive to fetal rights. The Supreme Court determined that the law was unconstitutional because it provided no exceptions to the ban beyond protecting the life of the mother—for instance, it did not include considerations of the health of the mother—and because the law was so broad that it could be construed to outlaw most forms of abortion.

In 2003 the federal government passed a Partial-Birth Abortion Ban Act, which defined a partial-birth abortion as any procedure in which the fetal death occurs when "the entire fetal head . . . or . . . any part of the fetal trunk past the navel is outside the body of the mother." Several physicians challenged its constitutionality, arguing that this description of partial-birth abortion could apply to the more typical "dilation and evacuation" abortion procedure. They argued that the act would ban most late-term abortions and that it violated the *Planned Parenthood v. Casey* "undue burden" standard. The Supreme Court in *Gonzales v. Carhart* (550 U.S. 124, 2007) upheld the constitutionality of the congressional act under the *Casey* and *Roe* decisions. However, the Court found that the federal legislation differed from the Nebraska statute sustained in *Stenberg v. Casey* and did not reverse this precedent.

Since the decision in *Casey* upholding the right to abortion but allowing the states to regulate the procedure as long as such limitations are not an "undue burden" on a woman seeking an abortion, many states have increased their regulation of the procedure. By 2016, forty-three states prohibited abortions after a specific point in the pregnancy, generally fetal viability, however the state determined it. Other states have regulated the sites at which abortions can be performed, often resulting in a state only having one location available to provide this service. Other regulations include restrictions on the use of public funds affecting indigent women's access to abortion, mandatory trans-vaginal ultrasounds prior to an abortions, a requirement that a second doctor attend the procedure, mandated counseling, and required waiting periods; additional state laws allow institutions to refuse to provide abortions for religious or other grounds, to restrict private insurance coverage of abortion, and to require parental involvement. The Court had not considered any of these regulations to be "undue burdens" on the right to abortion until its 2016 decision in *Whole Woman's Health v. Hellerstedt*, 579 U.S. ___

(2016). In this case, the Supreme Court found a Texas law that mandated regulations for abortion clinics (such as meeting all legal requirements established for ambulatory surgical centers) to be a substantial burden on a woman seeking an abortion. The Court ruled that judges, in evaluating such state laws, should determine the extent to which the regulations serve the articulated state interest (e.g., protecting the health and welfare of the mother) versus the imposed burden (e.g., access to abortion).

ROE V. WADE

410 U.S. 113, 93 S.Ct. 705, 35 L.Ed.2d 147 (1973)

This case combines three complaints regarding state prohibitions on abortion. Jane Roe, a pseudonym for an unmarried pregnant woman (Norma McCorvey), who had tried unsuccessfully to obtain an abortion, challenged a Texas law that allowed the procedure only when the mother's life was in danger. James Hubert Hallford, a licensed physician in Texas, had been arrested for violations of the Texas abortion statutes and had two prosecutions pending against him. Both litigants claimed that the Texas statutes were vague and uncertain, violated the Fourteenth Amendment, and violated doctor and patient rights to privacy as guaranteed by the First, Fourth, Fifth, Ninth, and Fourteenth Amendments. John and Mary Doe (also pseudonomyous names) claimed that Mary Doe had been advised to avoid pregnancy, although the condition would not risk her life. John and Mary Doe sued the state because Mary Doe would want a safe, medical abortion if she became pregnant. The cases were combined, and a three-judge district court held that the statutes were overbroad and thereby void, but dismissed claims for injunctive relief. The state district attorney and the plaintiffs cross-appealed. Both the district court and the U.S. Supreme Court found that the Does did not have standing to bring this litigation.

Vote: 7–2

JUSTICE BLACKMUN delivered the opinion of the Court.

This Texas federal appeal and its Georgia companion, *Doe v. Bolton,* 410 U.S. 179 (1973), present constitutional challenges to state criminal abortion legislation. The Texas statutes under attack here are typical of those that have been in effect in many States for approximately a century. The Georgia statutes, in contrast, have a modern cast and are a legislative product that, to an extent at least, obviously reflects the influences of recent attitudinal change, of advancing medical knowledge and techniques, and of new thinking about an old issue.

We forthwith acknowledge our awareness of the sensitive and emotional nature of the abortion controversy, of the vigorous opposing views, even among physicians, and of the deep and seemingly absolute convictions that the subject inspires. One's philosophy, one's experiences, one's exposure to the raw edges of human existence, one's religious training, one's attitudes toward life and family and their values, and the moral standards one establishes and seeks to observe, are all likely to influence and to color one's thinking and conclusions about abortion.

In addition, population growth, pollution, poverty, and racial overtones tend to complicate and not to simplify the problem.

Our task, of course, is to resolve the issue by constitutional measurement, free of emotion and of predilection. We seek earnestly to do this, and, because we do, we have inquired into, and in this opinion place some emphasis upon, medical and medical-legal history and what that history reveals about man's attitudes toward the abortion procedure over the centuries. We bear in mind, too, Mr. Justice Holmes' admonition in his now-vindicated dissent in *Lochner v. New York*, 198 U.S. 45, 76 (1905):

[The Constitution] is made for people of fundamentally differing views, and the accident of our finding certain opinions natural and familiar or novel and even shocking ought not to conclude our judgment upon the question whether statutes embodying them conflict with the Constitution of the United States.

V

The principal thrust of appellant's attack on the Texas statutes is that they improperly invade a right, said to be possessed by the pregnant woman, to choose to terminate her pregnancy. Appellant would discover this right in the concept of personal "liberty" embodied in the Fourteenth Amendment's Due Process Clause; or in personal, marital, familial, and sexual privacy said to be protected by the Bill of Rights or its penumbras, see *Griswold v. Connecticut*, 381 U.S. 479 (1965); *Eisenstadt v. Baird*, 405 U.S. 438 (1972); id., at 460; or among those rights reserved to the people by the Ninth Amendment, *Griswold v. Connecticut*, 381 U.S., at 486.

VIII

The Constitution does not explicitly mention any right of privacy. In a line of decisions, however, going back perhaps as far as *Union Pacific R. Co. v. Botsford*, 141 U.S. 250, 251 (1891), the Court has recognized that a right of personal privacy, or a guarantee of certain areas or zones of privacy, does exist under the Constitution. In varying contexts, the Court or individual Justices have, indeed, found at least the roots of that right in the First Amendment, *Stanley v. Georgia*, 394 U.S. 557, 564 (1969); in the Fourth and Fifth Amendments, *Terry v. Ohio*, 392 U.S. 1, 8–9 (1968), *Katz v. United States*, 389 U.S. 347, 350 (1967), *Boyd v. United States*, 116 U.S. 616 (1886), see *Olmstead v. United States*, 277 U.S. 438, 478 (1928) (Brandeis, J., dissenting); in the penumbras of the Bill of Rights, *Griswold v. Connecticut*, 381 U.S., at 484–485; in the Ninth Amendment, id., at 486; or in the concept of liberty guaranteed by the first section of the Fourteenth Amendment, see *Meyer v. Nebraska*, 262 U.S. 390, 399 (1923). These decisions make it clear that only personal rights that can be deemed "fundamental" or "implicit in the concept of ordered liberty," *Palko v. Connecticut*, 302 U.S. 319, 325 (1937), are included in this guarantee of personal privacy. They also make it clear that the right has some extension to activities relating to marriage, *Loving v. Virginia*, 388 U.S. 1, 12 (1967); procreation, *Skinner v. Oklahoma*, 316 U.S. 535, 541–542 (1942); contraception, *Eisenstadt v. Baird*, 405 U.S., at 453–454; id., at 460, 463–465; family relationships, *Prince v. Massachusetts*, 321 U.S. 158, 166 (1944); and child rearing and education, *Pierce v. Society of Sisters*, 268 U.S. 510, 535 (1925), *Meyer v. Nebraska*.

This right of privacy, whether it be founded in the Fourteenth Amendment's concept of personal liberty and restrictions upon state action, as we feel it is, or, as the District Court determined, in the Ninth Amendment's reservation of rights to the people, is broad enough to encompass a woman's decision whether or not to terminate her pregnancy. The detriment that the State would impose upon the pregnant woman by denying this choice altogether is apparent. Specific and direct harm medically diagnosable even in early pregnancy may be involved. Maternity, or additional offspring, may force upon the woman a distressful life and future. Psychological harm may be imminent. Mental and physical health may be taxed by child care. There is also the distress, for all concerned, associated with the unwanted child, and there is the problem of bringing a child into a family already unable, psychologically and otherwise, to care for it. In other cases, as in this one, the additional difficulties and continuing stigma of unwed motherhood may be involved. All these are factors the woman and her responsible physician necessarily will consider in consultation.

On the basis of elements such as these, appellant and some amici argue that the woman's right is absolute and that she is entitled to terminate her pregnancy at whatever time, in whatever way, and for whatever reason she alone chooses. With this we do not agree. Appellant's arguments that Texas either has no valid interest at all in regulating the abortion decision, or no interest strong enough to support any limitation upon the woman's sole determination, are unpersuasive. The Court's decisions recognizing a right of privacy also acknowledge that some state regulation in areas protected by that right is appropriate. As noted above, a State may properly assert important interests in safeguarding health, in maintaining medical standards, and in protecting potential life. At some point in pregnancy, these respective interests become sufficiently compelling to sustain regulation of the factors that govern the abortion decision. The privacy right involved, therefore, cannot be said to be absolute. In fact, it is not clear to us that the claim asserted by some amici that one has an unlimited right to do with one's body as one pleases bears a close relationship to the right of privacy previously articulated in the Court's decisions. The Court has refused to recognize an unlimited right of this kind in the past. *Jacobson v. Massachusetts*, 197 U.S. 11 (1905) (vaccination); *Buck v. Bell*, 274 U.S. 200 (1927) (sterilization).

We, therefore, conclude that the right of personal privacy includes the abortion decision, but that this right is not unqualified and must be considered against important state interests in regulation.

We note that those federal and state courts that have recently considered abortion law challenges have reached the same conclusion. A majority, in addition to the District Court in the present case, have held state laws unconstitutional, at least in part, because of vagueness or because of overbreadth and abridgment of rights.

Others have sustained state statutes.

Although the results are divided, most of these courts have agreed that the right of privacy, however based, is broad enough to cover the abortion decision; that the right, nonetheless, is not absolute and is subject to some limitations; and that at some point the state interests as to protection of health, medical standards, and prenatal life, become dominant. We agree with this approach.

Where certain "fundamental rights" are involved, the Court has held that regulation limiting these rights may be justified only by a "compelling state interest," *Kramer v. Union Free School District*, 395 U.S. 621, 627 (1969); *Shapiro v. Thompson*, 394 U.S. 618, 634 (1969), *Sherbert v. Verner*, 374 U.S. 398, 406 (1963), and that legislative enactments must be narrowly drawn to express only the legitimate state interests at stake. *Griswold v. Connecticut*, 381 U.S., at 485.

In the recent abortion cases, courts have recognized these principles. Those striking down state laws have generally scrutinized the State's interests in protecting health and potential life, and have concluded that neither interest justified broad limitations on the reasons for which a physician and his pregnant patient might decide that she should have an abortion in the early stages of pregnancy. Courts sustaining state laws have held that the State's determinations to protect health or prenatal life are dominant and constitutionally justifiable.

IX

A

The appellee and certain amici argue that the fetus is a "person" within the language and meaning of the Fourteenth Amendment. In support of this, they outline at length and in detail the well-known facts of fetal development. If this suggestion of personhood is established, the appellant's case, of course, collapses, for the fetus' right to life would then be guaranteed specifically by the Amendment. The appellant conceded as much on reargument. On the other hand, the appellee conceded on reargument that no case could be cited that holds that a fetus is a person within the meaning of the Fourteenth Amendment.

The Constitution does not define "person" in so many words. Section 1 of the Fourteenth Amendment contains three references to "person." But in nearly all these instances, the use of the word is such that it has application only postnatally. None indicates, with any assurance, that it has any possible pre-natal application.

All this, together with our observation . . . that throughout the major portion of the 19th century prevailing legal abortion practices were far freer than they are today, persuades us that the word "person," as used in the Fourteenth Amendment, does not include the unborn.

B

The pregnant woman cannot be isolated in her privacy. She carries an embryo and, later, a fetus, if one accepts the medical definitions of the developing young in the human uterus. The situation therefore is inherently different from marital intimacy, or bedroom possession of obscene material, or marriage, or procreation, or education, with which *Eisenstadt* and *Griswold*, *Stanley*, *Loving*, *Skinner*, and *Pierce* and *Meyer* were respectively concerned. As we have intimated above, it is reasonable and appropriate for a State to decide that at some point in time another interest, that of health of the mother or that of potential human life, becomes significantly involved. The woman's privacy is no longer sole and any right of privacy she possesses must be measured accordingly.

Texas urges that, apart from the Fourteenth Amendment, life begins at conception and is present throughout pregnancy, and that, therefore, the State has a compelling interest in protecting that life from and after conception. We need not resolve the difficult question of when life begins. When those trained in the respective disciplines of medicine, philosophy, and theology are unable to arrive at any consensus, the judiciary, at this point in the development of man's knowledge, is not in a position to speculate as to the answer.

It should be sufficient to note briefly the wide divergence of thinking on this most sensitive and difficult question.

X

In view of all this, we do not agree that, by adopting one theory of life, Texas may override the rights of the pregnant woman that are at stake. We repeat, however, that the State does have an important and legitimate interest in preserving and protecting the health of the pregnant woman, whether she be a resident of the State or a nonresident who seeks medical consultation and treatment there, and that it has still another important and legitimate interest in protecting the potentiality of human life. These interests are separate and distinct. Each grows in substantiality as the woman approaches term and, at a point during pregnancy, each becomes "compelling."

With respect to the State's important and legitimate interest in the health of the mother, the "compelling" point, in the light of present medical knowledge, is at approximately the end of the first trimester. This is so because of the now-established medical fact, that until the end of the first trimester mortality in abortion may be less than mortality in normal childbirth. It follows that, from and after this point, a State may regulate the abortion procedure to the extent that the regulation reasonably relates to the preservation and protection of maternal health. Examples of permissible state regulation in this area are requirements as to the qualifications of the person who is to perform the abortion; as to the licensure of that person; as to the facility in which the procedure is to be performed, that is, whether it must be a hospital or may be a clinic or some other place of less-than-hospital status; as to the licensing of the facility; and the like.

This means, on the other hand, that, for the period of pregnancy prior to this "compelling" point, the attending physician, in consultation with his patient, is free to determine, without regulation by the State, that, in his medical judgment, the patient's pregnancy should be terminated. If that decision is reached, the judgment may be effectuated by an abortion free of interference by the State.

With respect to the State's important and legitimate interest in potential life, the "compelling" point is at viability. This is so because the fetus then presumably has the capability of meaningful life outside the mother's womb. State regulation protective of fetal life after viability thus has both logical and biological justifications. If the State is interested in protecting fetal life after viability, it may go so far as to proscribe abortion during that period, except when it is necessary to preserve the life or health of the mother.

Measured against these standards, Art. 1196 of the Texas Penal Code, in restricting legal abortions to those "procured or attempted by medical advice for the purpose of saving the life of the mother," sweeps too broadly. The statute makes no distinction between abortions performed early in pregnancy and those performed later, and it limits to a single reason, "saving" the mother's life, the legal justification for the procedure. The statute, therefore, cannot survive the constitutional attack made upon it here.

This conclusion makes it unnecessary for us to consider the additional challenge to the Texas statute asserted on grounds of vagueness.

JUSTICE STEWART, concurring.

In 1963, this Court, in *Ferguson v. Skrupa*, 372 U.S. 726, purported to sound the death knell for the doctrine of substantive due process, a doctrine under which many state laws had in the past been held to violate the Fourteenth Amendment.

Barely two years later, in *Griswold v. Connecticut*, 381 U.S. 479 (1965), the Court held a Connecticut birth control law unconstitutional. In view of what had been so recently said in *Skrupa*, the Court's opinion in Griswold understandably did its best to avoid reliance on the Due Process Clause of the Fourteenth Amendment as the ground for decision. Yet, the Connecticut law did not violate any provision of the Bill of Rights, nor any other specific provision of the Constitution. So it was clear to me then, and it is equally clear to me now, that the Griswold decision can be rationally understood only as a holding that the Connecticut statute substantively invaded the "liberty" that is protected by the Due Process Clause of the Fourteenth Amendment. As so understood, *Griswold* stands as one in a long line of pre-*Skrupa* cases decided under the doctrine of substantive due process, and I now accept it as such.

Several decisions of this Court make clear that freedom of personal choice in matters of marriage and family life is one of the liberties protected by the Due Process Clause of the Fourteenth Amendment. *Loving v. Virginia*, 388 U.S. 1, 12 (1967); *Griswold v. Connecticut*; *Pierce v. Society of Sisters,* 268 U.S. 510 (1925); *Meyer v. Nebraska,* 262 U.S. 390 (1923). As recently as last Term, in *Eisenstadt v. Baird*, 405 U.S. 438, 453, we recognized "the right of the individual, married or single, to be free from unwarranted governmental intrusion into matters so fundamentally affecting a person as the decision whether to bear or beget a child." That right necessarily includes the right of a woman to decide whether or not to terminate her pregnancy.

Clearly, therefore, the Court today is correct in holding that the right asserted by Jane Roe is embraced within the personal liberty protected by the Due Process Clause of the Fourteenth Amendment.

It is evident that the Texas abortion statute infringes that right directly. Indeed, it is difficult to imagine a more complete abridgment of a constitutional freedom than that worked by the inflexible criminal statute now in force in Texas. The question then becomes whether the state interests advanced to justify this abridgment can survive the "particularly careful scrutiny" that the Fourteenth Amendment here requires.

The asserted state interests are protection of the health and safety of the pregnant woman, and protection of the potential future human life within her. These are legitimate objectives, amply sufficient to permit a State to regulate abortions as it does other surgical procedures, and perhaps sufficient to permit a State to regulate abortions more stringently or even to prohibit them in the late stages of pregnancy. But such legislation is not before us, and I think the Court today has thoroughly demonstrated that these state interests cannot constitutionally support the broad abridgment of personal liberty worked by the existing Texas law. Accordingly, I join the Court's opinion holding that that law is invalid under the Due Process Clause of the Fourteenth Amendment.

JUSTICE REHNQUIST, dissenting.

The Court's opinion brings to the decision of this troubling question both extensive historical fact and a wealth of legal scholarship. While the opinion thus commands my respect, I find myself nonetheless in fundamental disagreement with those parts of it that invalidate the Texas statute in question, and therefore dissent.

II

I have difficulty in concluding, as the Court does, that the right of "privacy" is involved in this case. Texas, by the statute here challenged, bars the performance of a medical abortion by a licensed physician on a plaintiff such as Roe. A transaction resulting in an operation such as this is not "private" in the ordinary usage of that word. Nor is the "privacy" that the Court finds here even a distant relative of the freedom from searches and seizures protected by the Fourth Amendment to the Constitution, which the Court has referred to as embodying a right to privacy. *Katz v. United States*, 389 U.S. 347 (1967).

If the Court means by the term "privacy" no more than that the claim of a person to be free from unwanted state regulation of consensual transactions may be a form of "liberty" protected by the Fourteenth Amendment, there is no doubt that similar claims have been upheld in our earlier decisions on the basis of that liberty. But the Court's sweeping invalidation of any restrictions on abortion during the first trimester is impossible to justify under that standard, and the conscious weighing of competing factors that the Court's opinion apparently substitutes for the established test is far more appropriate to a legislative judgment than to a judicial one.

The Court eschews the history of the Fourteenth Amendment in its reliance on the "compelling state interest" test. But the Court adds a new wrinkle to this test by transposing it from the legal considerations associated with the Equal Protection Clause of the Fourteenth Amendment to this case arising under the Due Process Clause of the Fourteenth Amendment. Unless I misapprehend the consequences of this transplanting of the "compelling state interest test," the Court's opinion will accomplish the seemingly impossible feat of leaving this area of the law more confused than it found it.

As in *Lochner v. New York*, 198 U.S. 45 (1905), and similar cases applying substantive due process standards to economic and social welfare legislation, the adoption of the compelling state interest standard will inevitably require this Court to examine the legislative policies and pass on the wisdom of these policies in the very process of deciding whether a particular state interest put forward may or may not be "compelling." The decision here to break pregnancy into three distinct terms and to outline the permissible restrictions the State may impose in each one, for example, partakes more of judicial legislation than it does of a determination of the intent of the drafters of the Fourteenth Amendment.

The fact that a majority of the States reflecting, after all, the majority sentiment in those States, have had restrictions on abortions for at least a century is a strong indication, it seems to me, that the asserted right to an abortion is not "so rooted in the traditions and conscience of our people as to be ranked as fundamental," *Snyder v. Massachusetts*, 291 U.S. 97, 105 (1934). Even today, when society's views on abortion are changing, the very existence of the debate is evidence that the "right" to an abortion is not so universally accepted as the appellant would have us believe.

To reach its result, the Court necessarily has had to find within the scope of the Fourteenth Amendment a right that was apparently completely unknown to the drafters of the Amendment. As early as 1821, the first state law dealing directly with abortion was enacted by the Connecticut Legislature. By the time of the adoption of the Fourteenth Amendment in 1868, there were at least 36 laws enacted by state or territorial legislatures limiting abortion. While many States have amended or updated their laws, 21 of the laws on the books in 1868 remain in effect today. Indeed, the Texas statute struck down today was, as the majority notes, first enacted in 1857 and "has remained substantially unchanged to the present time."

There apparently was no question concerning the validity of this provision or of any of the other state statutes when the Fourteenth Amendment was adopted. The only conclusion possible from this history is that the drafters did not intend to have the Fourteenth Amendment withdraw from the States the power to legislate with respect to this matter.

FOR DISCUSSION

How does the majority root the right to abortion within the right of privacy? Why does Justice Rehnquist, in his dissent, find this problematic? Is there a stronger textual source of this right in the Constitution?

RELATED CASES

***United States v. Vuitch:* 402 U.S. 62 (1971).**

The Court refused to interpret the right to privacy as providing for a right to abortion.

***Doe v. Bolton:* 410 U.S. 179 (1973).**

The companion case to *Roe v. Wade:* the Court held that states were not allowed to criminalize abortion or extensively legislate against the procedure—for example, by limiting abortion providers to licensed hospitals, requiring preapproval by hospital committees, or requiring physician conferral.

***Akron v. Akron Center for Reproductive Health, Inc.:* 462 U.S. 416 (1983).**

The Court applied the reasoning in *Roe v. Wade* to invalidate provisions of an Akron, Ohio, municipal ordinance regulating abortion. The Court found that many of the provisions were designed to prevent women from selecting an abortion as opposed to protecting the medical interests of the State.

WEBSTER V. REPRODUCTIVE HEALTH SERVICES

492 U.S. 490, 109 S.Ct. 3040, 106 L.Ed. 2d 410 (1989)

See the majority opinion for the statement of facts.

Vote: 5–4

CHIEF JUSTICE REHNQUIST announced the judgment of the Court and delivered the opinion of the Court with respect to Parts I, II–A, II–B, and II–C, and an opinion with respect to Parts II–D and III, in which JUSTICES WHITE and KENNEDY join.

This appeal concerns the constitutionality of a Missouri statute regulating the performance of abortions. The United States Court of Appeals for the Eighth Circuit struck down several provisions of the statute on the ground that they violated this Court's decision in *Roe v. Wade*, 410 U.S. 113 (1973), and cases following it. We noted probable jurisdiction, 488 U.S. 1003 (1989), and now reverse.

I

In June 1986, the Governor of Missouri signed into law Missouri Senate Committee Substitute for House Bill No. 1596 (hereinafter Act or statute), which amended existing state law concerning unborn children and abortions. The Act consisted of 20 provisions, 5 of which are now before the Court. The first provision, or preamble, contains "findings" by the state legislature that "[t]he life of each human being begins at conception," and that "unborn children have protectable interests in life, health, and well-being." The Act further requires that all Missouri laws be interpreted to provide unborn children with the same rights enjoyed by other persons, subject to the Federal Constitution and this Court's precedents. Among its other provisions, the Act requires that, prior to performing an abortion on any woman whom a physician has reason to believe is 20 or more weeks pregnant, the physician ascertain whether the fetus is viable by performing "such medical examinations and tests as are necessary to make a finding of the gestational age, weight, and lung maturity of the unborn child." The Act also prohibits the use of public employees and facilities to perform or assist abortions not necessary to save the mother's life, and it prohibits the use of public funds, employees, or facilities for the purpose of "encouraging or counseling" a woman to have an abortion not necessary to save her life.

In July 1986, five health professionals employed by the State and two nonprofit corporations brought this class action in the United States District Court for the Western District of Missouri to challenge the constitutionality of the Missouri statute. Plaintiffs, appellees in this Court, sought declaratory and injunctive relief on the ground that certain statutory provisions violated the First, Fourth, Ninth, and Fourteenth Amendments to the Federal Constitution. They asserted violations of various rights, including the "privacy rights of pregnant women seeking abortions"; the "woman's right to an abortion"; the "righ[t] to privacy in the physician-patient relationship"; the physician's "righ[t] to practice medicine"; the pregnant woman's "right to life due to inherent risks involved in childbirth"; and the woman's right to "receive . . . adequate medical advice and treatment" concerning abortions.

II

Decision of this case requires us to address four sections of the Missouri Act: (a) the preamble; (b) the prohibition on the use of public facilities or employees to perform abortions; (c) the prohibition on public funding of abortion counseling; and (d) the requirement that physicians conduct viability tests prior to performing abortions. We address these seriatim.

A

The Act's preamble, as noted, sets forth "findings" by the Missouri Legislature that "[t]he life of each human being begins at conception," and that "[u]nborn children have protectable interests in life, health, and well-being." The Act then mandates that state laws be interpreted to provide unborn children with "all the rights, privileges, and immunities available to other persons, citizens, and residents of this state," subject to the Constitution and this Court's precedents. In invalidating the preamble, the Court of Appeals relied on this Court's dictum that " 'a State may not adopt one theory of when life begins to justify its regulation of abortions.' "

In our view, the Court of Appeals misconceived the meaning of the *Akron* [*v. Akron Center for Reproductive Health, Inc.*: 462 U.S. 416 (1983)] dictum, which was only that a State could not "justify" an abortion regulation otherwise invalid under *Roe v. Wade* on the ground that it embodied the State's view about when life begins.

We think the extent to which the preamble's language might be used to interpret other state statutes or regulations is something that only the courts of Missouri can definitively decide.

It will be time enough for federal courts to address the meaning of the preamble should it be applied to restrict the activities of appellees in some concrete way.

B

Section 188.210 provides that "[i]t shall be unlawful for any public employee within the scope of his employment to perform or assist an abortion, not necessary to save the life of the mother," while § 188.215 makes it "unlawful for any public facility to be used for the purpose of performing or assisting an abortion not necessary to save the life of the mother."

Nothing in the Constitution requires States to enter or remain in the business of performing abortions. Nor, as appellees suggest, do private physicians and their patients have some kind of constitutional right of access to public facilities for the performance of abortions. Indeed, if the State does recoup all of its costs in performing abortions, and no state subsidy, direct or indirect, is available, it is difficult to see how any procreational choice is burdened by the State's ban on the use of its facilities or employees for performing abortions.

Maher v. Roe, 432 U.S. 464 (1977), *Poelker v. Doe,* 432 U.S. 519 (1977), and *Harris v. McRae,* 448 U.S. 297 (1980), all support the view that the State need not commit any resources to facilitating abortions, even if it can turn a profit by doing so. Thus we uphold the Act's restrictions on the use of public employees and facilities for the performance or assistance of nontherapeutic abortions.

C

The Missouri Act contains three provisions relating to "encouraging or counseling a woman to have an abortion not necessary to save her life." Section 188.205 states that no public funds can be used for this purpose; § 188.210 states that public employees cannot, within the scope of their employment, engage in such speech; and § 188.215 forbids such speech in public facilities. The Court of Appeals . . . held that all three of these provisions were unconstitutionally vague. . . .

Missouri has chosen only to appeal the Court of Appeals' invalidation of the public funding provision, § 188.205. A threshold question is whether this provision reaches primary conduct, or whether it is simply an instruction to the State's fiscal officers not to allocate funds for abortion counseling. We accept, for purposes of decision, the State's claim that § 188.205 "is not directed at the conduct of any physician or health care provider, private or public," but "is directed solely at those persons responsible for expending public funds."

Appellees contend that they are not "adversely" affected under the State's interpretation of § 188.205, and therefore that there is no longer a case or controversy before us on this question. A majority of the Court agrees with appellees that the controversy over § 188.205 is now moot, because appellees' argument amounts to a decision to no longer seek a declaratory judgment that § 188.205 is unconstitutional and accompanying declarative relief.

D

Section 188.029 of the Missouri Act provides:

Before a physician performs an abortion on a woman he has reason to believe is carrying an unborn child of twenty or more weeks gestational age, the physician shall first determine if the unborn child is viable by using and exercising that degree of care, skill, and proficiency commonly exercised by the ordinarily skillful, careful, and prudent physician engaged in similar practice under the same or similar conditions. In making this determination of viability, the physician shall perform or cause to be performed such medical examinations and tests as are necessary to make a finding of the gestational age, weight, and lung maturity of the unborn child and shall enter such findings and determination of viability in the medical record of the mother.

As with the preamble, the parties disagree over the meaning of this statutory provision.

If we construe this provision to require a physician to perform those tests needed to make the three specified findings in all circumstances, including when the physician's reasonable professional judgment indicates that the tests would be irrelevant to determining viability or even dangerous to the mother and the fetus, the second sentence of § 188.029 would conflict with the first sentence's requirement that a physician apply his reasonable professional skill and judgment.

The viability-testing provision of the Missouri Act is concerned with promoting the State's interest in potential human life rather than in maternal health. Section 188.029 creates what is essentially a presumption of viability at 20 weeks, which the physician must rebut with tests indicating that the fetus is not viable prior to performing an abortion.

In *Roe v. Wade*, the Court recognized that the State has "important and legitimate" interests in protecting maternal health and in the potentiality of human life. 410 U.S., at 162. During the second trimester, the State "may, if it chooses, regulate the abortion procedure in ways that are reasonably related to maternal health." After viability, when the State's interest in potential human life was held to become compelling, the State "may, if it chooses, regulate, and even proscribe, abortion except where it is necessary, in appropriate medical judgment, for the preservation of the life or health of the mother."

In *Colautti v. Franklin*, 439 U.S. 379 (1979), upon which appellees rely, the Court held that a Pennsylvania statute regulating the standard of care to be used by a physician performing an abortion of a possibly viable fetus was void for vagueness. But in the course of reaching that conclusion, the Court reaffirmed its earlier statement in *Planned Parenthood of Central Mo. v. Danforth*, 428 U.S. 52, 64 (1976), that " 'the determination of whether a particular fetus is viable is, and must be, a matter for the judgment of the responsible attending physician.' " 439 U.S., at 396.

We think that the doubt cast upon the Missouri statute by these cases is not so much a flaw in the statute as it is a reflection of the fact that the rigid trimester analysis of the course of a pregnancy enunciated in *Roe* has resulted in subsequent cases like *Colautti* and *Akron* making constitutional law in this area a virtual Procrustean bed. Statutes specifying elements of informed consent to be provided abortion patients, for example, were invalidated if they were thought to "structur[e] . . . the dialogue between the woman and her physician." *Thornburgh v. American College of Obstetricians and Gynecologists*, 476 U.S. 747, 763 (1986).

Stare decisis is a cornerstone of our legal system, but it has less power in constitutional cases, where, save for constitutional amendments, this Court is the only body able to make needed changes.

In the first place, the rigid *Roe* framework is hardly consistent with the notion of a Constitution cast in general terms, as ours is, and usually speaking in general principles, as ours does. The key elements of the *Roe* framework—trimesters and viability—are not found in the text of the Constitution or in any place else one would expect to find a constitutional principle.

In the second place, we do not see why the State's interest in protecting potential human life should come into existence only at the point of viability, and that there should therefore be a rigid line allowing state regulation after viability but prohibiting it before viability.

The tests that § 188.029 requires the physician to perform are designed to determine viability. The State here has chosen viability as the point at which its interest in potential human life must be safeguarded. But we are satisfied that the requirement of these tests permissibly furthers the State's interest in protecting potential human life, and we therefore believe § 188.029 to be constitutional.

III

Both appellants and the United States as amicus curiae have urged that we overrule our decision in *Roe v. Wade*. The facts of the present case, however, differ from those at issue in *Roe*. Here, Missouri has determined that viability is the point at which its interest in potential human life must be safeguarded. In *Roe*, on the other hand, the Texas statute criminalized the performance of all abortions, except when the mother's life was at stake. This case therefore affords us no occasion to revisit the holding of *Roe*, which was that the Texas statute unconstitutionally infringed the right to an abortion derived from the Due Process Clause, and we leave it undisturbed. To the extent indicated in our opinion, we would modify and narrow *Roe* and succeeding cases.

Because none of the challenged provisions of the Missouri Act properly before us conflict with the Constitution, the judgment of the Court of Appeals is Reversed.

JUSTICE O'CONNOR, concurring in part and concurring in the judgment.

I concur in Parts I, II-A, II-B, and II-C of the Court's opinion.

I

Nothing in the record before us or the opinions below indicates that subsections 1(1) and 1(2) of the preamble to Missouri's abortion regulation statute will affect a woman's decision to have an abortion.

II

In its interpretation of Missouri's "determination of viability" provision, Mo. Rev. Stat. § 188.029 (1986), the plurality has proceeded in a manner unnecessary to deciding the question at hand.

Unlike the plurality, I do not understand these viability testing requirements to conflict with any of the Court's past decisions concerning state regulation of abortion. Therefore, there is no necessity to accept the State's invitation to reexamine the constitutional validity of *Roe v. Wade*, 410 U.S. 113 (1973). Where there is no need to decide a constitutional question, it is a venerable principle of this Court's adjudicatory processes not to do so, for "[t]he Court will not 'anticipate a question of constitutional law in advance of the necessity of deciding it.' " *Ashwander v. TVA*, 297 U.S. 288, 346 (1936). Neither will it generally "formulate a rule of constitutional law broader than is required by the precise facts to which it is to be applied." 297 U.S., at 347. The Court today has accepted the State's every interpretation of its abortion statute and has upheld, under our existing precedents, every provision of that statute which is properly before us. Precisely for this reason reconsideration of Roe falls not into any "good-cause exception" to this "fundamental rule of judicial restraint. . . ." *Three Affiliated Tribes of Fort Berthold Reservation v. Wold Engineering, P. C.,* 467 U.S. 138, 157 (1984). When the constitutional invalidity of a State's abortion statute actually turns on the constitutional validity of *Roe v. Wade*, there will be time enough to reexamine *Roe*. And to do so carefully.

It is clear to me that requiring the performance of examinations and tests useful to determining whether a fetus is viable, when viability is possible, and when it would not be medically imprudent to do so, does not impose an undue burden on a woman's abortion decision. On this ground alone I would reject the suggestion that § 188.029 as interpreted is unconstitutional. More to the point, however, just as I see no conflict between § 188.029 and *Colautti* or any decision of this Court concerning a State's ability to give effect to its interest in potential life, I see no conflict between § 188.029 and the Court's opinion in *Akron*. The second-trimester hospitalization requirement struck down in *Akron* imposed, in the majority's view, "a heavy, and unnecessary, burden," 462 U.S., at 438, more than doubling the cost of "women's access to a relatively inexpensive, otherwise accessible, and safe abortion procedure." By contrast, the cost of examinations and tests that could usefully and prudently be performed when a woman is 20–24 weeks pregnant to determine whether the fetus is viable would only marginally, if at all, increase the cost of an abortion.

Moreover, the examinations and tests required by § 188.029 are to be performed when viability is possible. This feature of § 188.029 distinguishes it from the second-trimester hospitalization requirement struck down by the *Akron* majority. As the Court recognized in *Thornburgh*, the State's compelling interest in potential life postviability renders its interest in determining the critical point of viability equally compelling. Under the Court's precedents, the same cannot be said for the *Akron* second-trimester hospitalization requirement. As I understand the Court's opinion in *Akron*, therefore, the plurality's suggestion today that *Akron* casts doubt on the validity of § 188.029, even as the Court has interpreted it, is without foundation and cannot provide a basis for reevaluating *Roe*. Accordingly, because the Court of Appeals misinterpreted § 188.029, and because, properly interpreted, § 188.029 is not inconsistent with any of this Court's prior precedents, I would reverse the decision of the Court of Appeals.

JUSTICE SCALIA, concurring in part and concurring in the judgment.

I join Parts I, II–A, II–B, and II–C of the opinion of the Court. As to Part II–D, I share Justice Blackmun's view that it effectively would overrule *Roe v. Wade*, 410 U.S. 113 (1973). I think that should be done, but would do it more explicitly. Since today we contrive to avoid doing it, and indeed to avoid almost any decision of national import, I need not set forth my reasons, some of which have been well recited in dissents of my colleagues in other cases.

The outcome of today's case will doubtless be heralded as a triumph of judicial statesmanship. It is not that, unless it is statesmanlike needlessly to prolong this Court's self-awarded sovereignty over a field where it has little proper business since the answers to most of the cruel questions posed are political and not juridical—a sovereignty which therefore quite properly, but to the great damage of the Court, makes it the object of the sort of organized public pressure that political institutions in a democracy ought to receive.

The real question . . . is whether there are valid reasons to go beyond the most stingy possible holding today. It seems to me there are not only valid but compelling ones. Ordinarily, speaking no more broadly than is absolutely required avoids throwing settled law into confusion; doing so today preserves a chaos that is evident to anyone who can read and count. Alone sufficient to justify a broad holding is the fact that our retaining control, through *Roe*, of what I believe to be, and many of our citizens recognize to be, a political issue, continuously distorts the public perception of the role of this Court. We can now look forward to at least another Term with carts full of mail from the public, and streets full of demonstrators, urging us—their unelected and life tenured judges who have been awarded those extraordinary, undemocratic characteristics precisely in order that we might follow the law despite the popular will—to follow the popular will. Indeed, I expect we can look forward to even more of that than before, given our indecisive decision today. And if these reasons for taking the unexceptional course of reaching a broader holding are not enough, then consider the nature of the constitutional question we avoid: In most cases, we do no harm by not speaking more broadly than the decision requires. Anyone affected by the conduct that the avoided holding would have prohibited will be able to challenge it himself and have his day in court to make the argument. Not so with respect to the harm that many States believed, pre-*Roe*, and many may continue to believe, is caused by largely unrestricted abortion. That will continue to occur if the States have the constitutional power to prohibit it, and would do so, but we skillfully avoid telling them so. Perhaps those abortions cannot constitutionally be proscribed. That is surely an arguable question, the question that reconsideration of *Roe v. Wade* entails. But what is not at all arguable, it seems to me, is that we should decide now and not insist that we be run into a corner before we grudgingly yield up our judgment. The only sound reason for the latter course is to prevent a change in the law—but to think that desirable begs the question to be decided.

It was an arguable question today whether § 188.029 of the Missouri law contravened this Court's understanding of *Roe v. Wade*, and I would have examined *Roe* rather than examining the contravention. Given the Court's newly contracted abstemiousness, what will it take, one must wonder, to permit us to reach that fundamental question? The result of our vote today is that we will not reconsider that prior opinion, even if most of the Justices think it is wrong, unless we have before us a statute that in fact contradicts it—and even then (under our newly discovered "no-broader-than-necessary" requirement) only minor problematical aspects of *Roe* will be reconsidered, unless one expects state legislatures to adopt provisions whose compliance with *Roe* cannot even be argued with a straight face. It thus appears that the mansion of constitutionalized abortion law, constructed overnight in *Roe v. Wade*, must be disassembled doorjamb by doorjamb, and never entirely brought down, no matter how wrong it may be.

Of the four courses we might have chosen today—to reaffirm *Roe*, to overrule it explicitly, to overrule it sub silentio, or to avoid the question—the last is the least responsible. On the question of the constitutionality of § 188.029, I concur in the judgment of the Court and strongly dissent from the manner in which it has been reached.

JUSTICE BLACKMUN, with whom JUSTICES BRENNAN and MARSHALL join, concurring in part and dissenting in part.

Today, *Roe v. Wade*, 410 U.S. 113 (1973), and the fundamental constitutional right of women to decide whether to terminate a pregnancy, survive but are not secure. Although the Court extricates itself from this case without making a single, even incremental, change in the law of abortion, the plurality and Justice Scalia would overrule *Roe* (the first silently, the other explicitly) and would return to the States virtually unfettered authority to control the quintessentially intimate, personal, and life-directing decision whether to carry a fetus to term. Although today, no less than yesterday, the Constitution and the decisions of this Court prohibit a State from enacting laws that inhibit women from the meaningful exercise of that right, a plurality of this Court implicitly invites every state legislature to enact more and more restrictive abortion regulations in order to provoke more and more test cases, in the hope that sometime down the line the Court will return the law of procreative freedom to the severe limitations that generally prevailed in this country before January 22, 1973. Never in my memory has a plurality announced a judgment of this Court that so foments disregard for the law and for our standing decisions.

Nor in my memory has a plurality gone about its business in such a deceptive fashion. At every level of its review, from its effort to read the real meaning out of the Missouri statute, to its intended evisceration of precedents and its deafening silence about the constitutional protections that it would jettison, the plurality obscures the portent of its analysis. With feigned restraint, the plurality announces that its analysis leaves Roe "undisturbed," albeit "modif[ied] and narrow[ed]." But this disclaimer is totally meaningless. The plurality opinion is filled with winks, and nods, and knowing glances to those who would do away with Roe explicitly, but turns a stone face to anyone in search of what the plurality conceives as the scope of a woman's right under the Due Process Clause to terminate a pregnancy free from the coercive and brooding influence of the State. The simple truth is that *Roe* would not survive the plurality's analysis, and that the plurality provides no substitute for *Roe's* protective umbrella.

I fear for the future. I fear for the liberty and equality of the millions of women who have lived and come of age in the 16 years since *Roe* was decided. I fear for the integrity of, and public esteem for, this Court.

I dissent.

I

D

Thus, "not with a bang, but a whimper," the plurality discards a landmark case of the last generation, and casts into darkness the hopes and visions of every woman in this country who had come to believe that the Constitution guaranteed her the right to exercise some control over her unique ability to bear children. The plurality does so either oblivious or insensitive to the fact that millions of women, and their families, have ordered their lives around the right to reproductive choice, and that this right has become vital to the full participation of women in the economic and political walks of American life. The plurality would clear the way once again for government to force upon women the physical labor and specific and direct medical and psychological harms that may accompany carrying a fetus to term.

II

For today, at least, the law of abortion stands undisturbed. For today, the women of this Nation still retain the liberty to control their destinies. But the signs are evident and very ominous, and a chill wind blows.

JUSTICE STEVENS, concurring in part and dissenting in part.

II

To the extent that the Missouri statute interferes with contraceptive choices, I have no doubt that it is unconstitutional under the Court's holdings in *Griswold v. Connecticut*, 381 U.S. 479 (1965); *Eisenstadt v. Baird*, 405 U.S. 438 (1972); and *Carey v. Population Services International*, 431 U.S. 678 (1977).

One might argue that the *Griswold* holding applies to devices "preventing conception," 381 U.S., at 480—that is, fertilization—but not to those preventing implantation, and therefore, that *Griswold* does not protect a woman's choice to use an IUD or take a morning-after pill. There is unquestionably a theological basis for such an argument, just as there was unquestionably a theological basis for the Connecticut statute that the Court invalidated in *Griswold*. Our jurisprudence, however, has consistently required a secular basis for valid legislation. Because I am not aware of any secular basis for differentiating between contraceptive procedures that are effective immediately before and those that are effective immediately after fertilization, I believe it inescapably follows that the preamble to the Missouri statute is invalid under *Griswold* and its progeny.

Indeed, I am persuaded that the absence of any secular purpose for the legislative declarations that life begins at conception and that conception occurs at fertilization makes the relevant portion of the preamble invalid under the Establishment Clause of the First Amendment to the Federal Constitution.

As a secular matter, there is an obvious difference between the state interest in protecting the freshly fertilized egg and the state interest in protecting a 9-month-gestated, fully sentient fetus on the eve of birth. There can be no interest in protecting the newly fertilized egg from physical pain or mental anguish, because the capacity for such suffering does not yet exist; respecting a developed fetus, however, that interest is valid.

Bolstering my conclusion that the preamble violates the First Amendment is the fact that the intensely divisive character of much of the national debate over the abortion issue reflects the deeply held religious convictions of many participants in the debate. The Missouri Legislature may not inject its endorsement of a particular religious tradition into this debate, for "[t]he Establishment Clause does not allow public bodies to foment such disagreement."

In my opinion the preamble to the Missouri statute is unconstitutional for two reasons. To the extent that it has substantive impact on the freedom to use contraceptive procedures, it is inconsistent with the central holding in *Griswold*. To the extent that it merely makes "legislative findings without operative effect," as the State argues, it violates the Establishment Clause of the First Amendment. Contrary to the theological "finding" of the Missouri Legislature, a woman's constitutionally protected liberty encompasses the right to act on her own belief that—to paraphrase St. Thomas Aquinas—until a seed has acquired the powers of sensation and movement, the life of a human being has not yet begun.

FOR DISCUSSION

How do you explain the highly fragmented nature of this decision? How could the Court uphold all the contested elements of the Missouri statute and still not overturn *Roe v. Wade*?

RELATED CASES

H.L. v. Matheson: **450 U.S. 398 (1981).**

The Court examined a Utah statute that forced physicians to notify parents when a minor daughter sought an abortion if the young woman was not financially emancipated or had not presented evidence of her emotional or physical independence from her parents. The Court found this to be an acceptable balance of the State's interest in the health and welfare of the minor against the minor's right to privacy.

***Thornburgh v. American College of Obstetricians and Gynecologists:* 476 U.S. 747, 763 (1986).**

In this Pennsylvania case, the Court evaluated the constitutionality of a statute that required (1) that the woman be informed of medical and legal options available for child support, (2) that the physician inform the woman of potential risks of abortion; (3) that doctors report to the state all abortions performed; (4) that in cases of late-term abortions, care be taken to save the life of the fetus; and (5) that the presence of two physicians be guaranteed during all abortions. The Court found these that provisions elevated the interest of the state in preventing abortions over the liberty and privacy interests of the woman and were therefore unconstitutional.

HODGSON V. MINNESOTA

497 U.S. 417, 110 S.Ct. 2926, 111 L.Ed.2d 344 (1990)

See facts as discussed in the majority opinion.

Vote: 5–4

JUSTICE STEVENS announced the judgment of the Court and delivered the opinion of the Court with respect to Parts I, II, IV, and VII, an opinion with respect to Part III in which JUSTICE BRENNAN joins, an opinion with respect to Parts V and VI in which JUSTICE O'CONNOR joins, and a dissenting opinion with respect to Part VIII.

A Minnesota statute, Minn. Stat. §§ 144.343(2)–(7) (1988), provides, with certain exceptions, that no abortion shall be performed on a woman under 18 years of age until at least 48 hours after both of her parents have been notified. In subdivisions 2–4 of the statute the notice is mandatory unless (1) the attending physician certifies that an immediate abortion is necessary to prevent the woman's death and there is insufficient time to provide the required notice; (2) both of her parents have consented in writing; or (3) the woman declares that she is a victim of parental abuse or neglect, in which event notice of her declaration must be given to the proper authorities. The United States Court of Appeals for the Eighth Circuit, sitting en banc, unanimously held these provisions unconstitutional. In No. 88–1309, we granted the State's petition to review that holding. Subdivision 6 of the same statute provides that if a court enjoins the enforcement of subdivision 2, the same notice requirement shall be effective unless the pregnant woman obtains a court order permitting the abortion to proceed. By a vote of 7 to 3, the Court of Appeals upheld the constitutionality of subdivision 6. In No. 88–1125, we granted the plaintiffs' petition to review that holding.

For reasons that follow, we now conclude that the requirement of notice to both of the pregnant minor's parents is not reasonably related to legitimate state interests and that subdivision 2 is unconstitutional. A different majority of the Court, for reasons stated in separate opinions, concludes that subdivision 6 is constitutional. Accordingly, the judgment of the Court of Appeals in its entirety is affirmed.

III

In cases involving abortion, as in cases involving the right to travel or the right to marry, the identification of the constitutionally protected interest is merely the beginning of the analysis. State regulation of travel and of marriage is obviously permissible even though a State may not categorically exclude nonresidents from its borders, *Shapiro v. Thompson*, 394 U.S. 618, 631 (1969), or deny prisoners the right to marry, *Turner v. Safley*, 482 U.S. 78, 94–99 (1987). But the regulation of constitutionally protected decisions, such as where a person shall reside or whom he or she shall marry, must be predicated on legitimate state concerns other than disagreement with the choice the individual has made. In the abortion area, a State may have no obligation to spend its own money, or use its own facilities, to subsidize nontherapeutic abortions for minors or adults. A State's value judgment favoring childbirth over abortion may provide adequate support for decisions involving such allocation of public funds, but not for simply substituting a state decision for an individual decision that a woman has a right to make for herself. Otherwise, the interest in liberty protected by the Due Process Clause would be a nullity.

In these cases the State of Minnesota does not rest its defense of this statute on any such value judgment. Indeed, it affirmatively disavows that state interest as a basis for upholding this law. Moreover, it is clear that the state judges who have interpreted the statute in over 3,000 decisions implementing its bypass procedures have found no legislative intent to disfavor the decision to terminate a pregnancy. On the contrary, in all but a handful of cases they have approved such decisions. Because the Minnesota statute unquestionably places obstacles in the pregnant minor's path to an abortion, the State has the burden of establishing its constitutionality. Under any analysis, the Minnesota statute cannot be sustained if the obstacles it imposes are not reasonably related to legitimate state interests.

IV

The Court has considered the constitutionality of statutes providing for parental consent or parental notification in six abortion cases decided during the last 14 years. Although the Massachusetts statute reviewed in *Bellotti v. Baird*, 428 U.S. 132 (1976) (*Bellotti I*), and *Bellotti* [*v. Baird*, 443 U.S. 622 (1979) (*Bellotti II*)] required the consent of both parents, and the Utah statute reviewed in *H. L. v. Matheson*, 450 U.S. 398 (1981), required notice to "the parents," none of the opinions in any of those cases focused on the possible significance of making the consent or the notice requirement applicable to both parents instead of just one.

V

Three separate but related interests—the interest in the welfare of the pregnant minor, the interest of the parents, and the interest of the family unit—are relevant to our consideration of the constitutionality of the 48-hour waiting period and the two-parent notification requirement.

The State has a strong and legitimate interest in the welfare of its young citizens, whose immaturity, inexperience, and lack of judgment may sometimes impair their ability to exercise their rights wisely. That interest, which justifies state-imposed requirements that a minor obtain his or her parent's consent before undergoing an operation, marrying, or entering military service extends also to the minor's decision to terminate her pregnancy. Although the Court has held that parents may not exercise "an absolute, and possibly arbitrary, veto" over that decision, *Planned Parenthood of Central Missouri v. Danforth*, 428 U.S. 52 at 74 (1976), it has never challenged a State's reasonable judgment that the decision should be made after notification to and consultation with a parent.

Parents have an interest in controlling the education and upbringing of their children but that interest is "a counterpart of the responsibilities they have assumed." *Lehr v. Robertson*, 463 U.S. 248, 257 (1983). But the demonstration of commitment to the child through the assumption of personal, financial, or custodial responsibility may give the natural parent a stake in the relationship with the child rising to the level of a liberty interest.

While the State has a legitimate interest in the creation and dissolution of the marriage contract, the family has a privacy interest in the upbringing and education of children and the intimacies of the marital relationship which is protected by the Constitution against undue state interference.

A natural parent who has demonstrated sufficient commitment to his or her children is thereafter entitled to raise the children free from undue state interference.

VI

We think it is clear that a requirement that a minor wait 48 hours after notifying a single parent of her intention to get an abortion would reasonably further the legitimate state interest in ensuring that the minor's decision is knowing and intelligent. To the extent that subdivision 2 of the Minnesota statute requires notification of only one parent, it does just that. The brief waiting period provides the parent the opportunity to consult with his or her spouse and a family physician, and it permits the parent to inquire into the competency of the doctor performing the abortion, discuss the religious or moral implications of the abortion decision, and provide the daughter needed guidance and counsel in evaluating the impact of the decision on her future.

The 48-hour delay imposes only a minimal burden on the right of the minor to decide whether or not to terminate her pregnancy.

VII

It is equally clear that the requirement that both parents be notified, whether or not both wish to be notified or have assumed responsibility for the upbringing of the child, does not reasonably further any legitimate state interest. The usual justification for a parental consent or notification provision is that it supports the authority of a parent who is presumed to act in the minor's best interest and thereby assures that the minor's decision to terminate her pregnancy is knowing, intelligent, and deliberate. In the ideal family setting, of course, notice to either parent would normally constitute notice to both. A statute requiring two-parent notification would not further any state interest in those instances. In many families, however, the parent notified by the child would not notify the other parent. In those cases the State has no legitimate interest in questioning one parent's judgment that notice to the other parent would not assist the minor or in presuming that the parent who has assumed parental duties is incompetent to make decisions regarding the health and welfare of the child.

Not only does two-parent notification fail to serve any state interest with respect to functioning families, it disserves the state interest in protecting and assisting the minor with respect to dysfunctional families. The record reveals that in the thousands of dysfunctional families affected by this statute, the two-parent notice requirement proved positively harmful to the minor and her family.

The State does not rely primarily on the best interests of the minor in defending this statute. Rather, it argues that, in the ideal family, the minor should make her decision only after consultation with both parents who should naturally be concerned with the child's welfare and that the State has an interest in protecting the independent right of the parents "to determine and strive for what they believe to be best for their children." Neither of these reasons can justify the two-parent notification requirement.

Nor can any state interest in protecting a parent's interest in shaping a child's values and lifestyle overcome the liberty interests of a minor acting with the consent of a single parent or court.

Unsurprisingly, the Minnesota two-parent notification requirement is an oddity among state and federal consent provisions governing the health, welfare, and education of children. In virtually every State, the consent of one parent is enough to obtain a driver's license or operator's permit. The same may be said with respect to the decision to submit to any medical or surgical procedure other than an abortion. Indeed, the only other Minnesota statute that the State has identified which requires two-parent consent is that authorizing the minor to change his name. These statutes provide testimony to the unreasonableness of the Minnesota two-parent notification requirement and to the ease with which the State can adopt less burdensome means to protect the minor's welfare. We therefore hold that this requirement violates the Constitution.

JUSTICE O'CONNOR, concurring in part and concurring in the judgment in part.

I

I join all but Parts III and VIII of Justice Stevens' opinion. While I agree with some of the central points made in Part III, I cannot join the broader discussion. I agree that the Court has characterized "[a] woman's decision to conceive or to bear a child [as] a component of her liberty that is protected by the Due Process Clause of the Fourteenth Amendment to the Constitution." 497 U.S. at 434. This Court extended that liberty interest to minors in *Bellotti v. Baird*, 443 U.S. 622 (1979) (*Bellotti II*), and *Planned Parenthood of Central Mo. v. Danforth*, 428 U.S. 52, 74 (1976), albeit with some important limitations: "Parental notice and consent are qualifications that typically may be imposed by the State on a minor's right to make important decisions. As immature minors often lack the ability to make fully informed choices that take account of both immediate and long-range consequences, a State reasonably may determine that parental consultation often is desirable and in the best interest of the minor." *Bellotti II*, 443 U.S. at 640–641.

It has been my understanding in this area that "if the particular regulation does not 'unduly burden' the fundamental right, . . . then our evaluation of that regulation is limited to our determination that the regulation rationally relates to a legitimate state purpose." *Akron v. Akron Center for Reproductive Health, Inc.*, 462 U.S. 416, 453 (1983). It is with that understanding that I agree with Justice Stevens' statement that the "statute cannot be sustained if the obstacles it imposes are not reasonably related to legitimate state interests."

Minnesota's two-parent notice requirement is all the more unreasonable when one considers that only half of the minors in the State of Minnesota reside with both biological parents. A third live with only one parent. Given its broad sweep and its failure to serve the purposes asserted by the State in too many cases, I join the Court's striking of subdivision 2.

II

In a series of cases, this Court has explicitly approved judicial bypass as a means of tailoring a parental consent provision so as to avoid unduly burdening the minor's limited right to obtain an abortion.

Subdivision 6 passes constitutional muster because the interference with the internal operation of the family required by subdivision 2 simply does not exist where the minor can avoid notifying one or both parents by use of the bypass procedure.

JUSTICE STEVENS delivered a dissenting opinion in Part VIII.

VIII

The Court holds that the constitutional objection to the two-parent notice requirement is removed by the judicial bypass option provided in subdivision 6 of the Minnesota statute. I respectfully dissent from that holding.

A judicial bypass that is designed to handle exceptions from a reasonable general rule, and thereby preserve the constitutionality of that rule, is quite different from a requirement that a minor—or a minor and one of her parents—must apply to a court for permission to avoid the application of a rule that is not reasonably related to legitimate state goals. A requirement that a minor acting with the consent of both parents apply to a court for permission to effectuate her decision clearly would constitute an unjustified official interference with the privacy of the minor and her family. The requirement that the bypass procedure must be invoked when the minor and one parent agree that the other parent should not be notified represents an equally unjustified governmental intrusion into the family's decisional process. When the parents are living together and have joint custody over the child, the State has no legitimate interest in the communication between father and mother about the child. "Where the parents are divorced, the minor and/or custodial parent, and not a court, is in the best position to determine whether notifying the non-custodial parent would be in the child's best interests." As the Court of

Appeals panel originally concluded, the "minor and custodial parent, . . . by virtue of their major interest and superior position, should alone have the opportunity to decide to whom, if anyone, notice of the minor's abortion decision should be given." I agree with that conclusion.

The judgment of the Court of Appeals in its entirety is affirmed. It is so ordered.

JUSTICE MARSHALL, with whom JUSTICES BRENNAN and BLACKMUN join, concurring in part, concurring in the judgment in part, and dissenting in part.

I concur in Parts I, II, IV, and VII of Justice Stevens' opinion for the Court in No. 88–1309. Although I do not believe that the Constitution permits a State to require a minor to notify or consult with a parent before obtaining an abortion, I am in substantial agreement with the remainder of the reasoning in Part V of Justice Stevens' opinion. For the reasons stated by the Court, Minnesota's two-parent notification requirement is not even reasonably related to a legitimate state interest. Therefore, that requirement surely would not pass the strict scrutiny applicable to restrictions on a woman's fundamental right to have an abortion.

I dissent from the judgment of the Court . . . that the judicial bypass option renders the parental notification and 48-hour delay requirements constitutional. The bypass procedure cannot save those requirements because the bypass itself is unconstitutional both on its face and as applied. At the very least, this scheme substantially burdens a woman's right to privacy without advancing a compelling state interest. More significantly, in some instances it usurps a young woman's control over her own body by giving either a parent or a court the power effectively to veto her decision to have an abortion.

IV

A majority of the Court today strikes down an unreasonable and vastly overbroad requirement that a pregnant minor notify both her parents of her decision to obtain an abortion. With that decision I agree. At the same time, though, a different majority holds that a State may require a young woman to notify one or even both parents and then wait 48 hours before having an abortion, as long as the State provides a judicial bypass procedure. From that decision I vehemently dissent. This scheme forces a young woman in an already dire situation to choose between two fundamentally unacceptable alternatives: notifying a possibly dictatorial or even abusive parent and justifying her profoundly personal decision in an intimidating judicial proceeding to a black-robed stranger. For such a woman, this dilemma is more likely to result in trauma and pain than in an informed and voluntary decision.

JUSTICE SCALIA, concurring in the judgment in part and dissenting in part.

As I understand the various opinions today: One Justice holds that two-parent notification is unconstitutional (at least in the present circumstances) without judicial bypass, but constitutional with bypass, four Justices would hold that two-parent notification is constitutional with or without bypass, four Justices would hold that two-parent notification is unconstitutional with or without bypass, though the four apply two different standards, six Justices hold that one-parent notification with bypass is constitutional, though for two different sets of reasons, and three Justices would hold that one-parent notification with bypass is unconstitutional. One will search in vain the document we are supposed to be construing for text that provides the basis for the argument over these distinctions; and will find in our society's tradition regarding abortion no hint that the distinctions are constitutionally relevant, much less any indication how a constitutional argument about them ought to be resolved. The random and unpredictable results of our consequently unchanneled individual views make it increasingly evident, Term after Term, that the tools for this job are not to be found in the lawyer's—and hence not in the judge's—workbox. I continue to dissent from this enterprise of devising an Abortion Code, and from the illusion that we have authority to do so.

JUSTICE KENNEDY, with whom CHIEF JUSTICE REHNQUIST, and JUSTICES WHITE and SCALIA join, concurring in the judgment in part and dissenting in part.

Today, the Court holds that a statute requiring a minor to notify both parents that she plans to have an abortion is not a permissible means of furthering the interest described with such specificity in *Bellotti v. Baird,* 443 U.S. 622 (1979) *Bellotti II.* This conclusion, which no doubt will come as a surprise to most parents, is incompatible with our constitutional tradition and any acceptable notion of judicial review of legislative enactments. I dissent from the portion of the Court's judgment affirming the Court of Appeals' conclusion that the Minnesota two-parent notice statute is unconstitutional.

The Minnesota statute also provides, however, that if the two-parent notice requirement is invalidated, the same notice requirement is effective unless the pregnant minor obtains a court order permitting the abortion to proceed. The Court of Appeals sustained this portion of the statute, in effect a two-parent notice requirement with a judicial bypass. Five Members of the Court, the four who join this opinion and Justice O'Connor, agree with the Court of Appeals' decision on this aspect of the statute. As announced by Justice Stevens, who dissents from this part of the Court's decision, the Court of Appeals' judgment on this portion of the statute is therefore affirmed.

II

The welfare of the child has always been the central concern of laws with regard to minors. The law does not give to children many rights given to adults, and provides, in general, that children can exercise the rights they do have only through and with parental consent. Legislatures historically have acted on the basis of the qualitative differences in maturity between children and adults, and not without reason. Age is a rough but fair approximation of maturity and judgment, and a State has an interest in seeing that a child, when confronted with serious decisions such as whether or not to abort a pregnancy, has the assistance of her parents in making the choice. If anything is settled by our previous cases dealing with parental notification and consent laws, it is this point.

A State pursues a legitimate end under the Constitution when it attempts to foster and preserve the parent-child relationship by giving all parents the opportunity to participate in the care and nurture of their children. We have held that parents have a liberty interest, protected by the Constitution, in having a reasonable opportunity to develop close relations with their children. We have recognized, of course, that there are limits to the constitutional right of parents to have custody of, or to participate in decisions affecting, their children. If a parent has relinquished the opportunity to develop a relationship with the child, and his or her only link to the child is biological, the Constitution does not require a State to allow parental participation. But the fact that the Constitution does not protect the parent-child relationship in all circumstances does not mean that the State cannot attempt to foster parental participation where the Constitution does not demand that it do so. A State may seek to protect and facilitate the parent-child bond on the assumption that parents will act in their child's best interests. Indeed, we have held that a State cannot terminate parental rights based upon a presumption that a class of parents is unfit without affording individual parents an opportunity to rebut the presumption. If a State cannot legislate on the broad assumption that classes of parents are unfit and undeserving of parental rights without affording an opportunity to rebut the assumption, it is at least permissible for a State to legislate on the premise that parents, as a general rule, are interested in their children's welfare and will act in accord with it.

All that Minnesota asserts is an interest in seeing that parents know about a vital decision facing their child. That interest is a valid one without regard to whether the child is living with either one or both parents, or to the attachment between the minor's parents. How the family unit responds to such notice is, for the most part, beyond the State's control.

Minnesota has done no more than act upon the commonsense proposition that, in assisting their daughter in deciding whether to have an abortion, parents can best fulfill their roles if they have the same information about their own child's medical condition and medical choices as the child's doctor does; and that to deny parents this knowledge is to risk, or perpetuate, estrangement or alienation from the child when she is in the greatest need of parental guidance and support. The Court does the State, and our constitutional tradition, sad disservice by impugning the legitimacy of these elemental objectives.

Given the societal interest that underlies parental notice and consent laws, it comes as no surprise that most States have enacted statutes requiring that, in general, a physician must notify or obtain the consent of at least one of her parents or legal guardian before performing an abortion on a minor. Five States, including Minnesota, appear to require, as a general rule, the notification of both parents before a physician may perform an abortion on a minor. Another six States appear to require, with varying exceptions, the consent of both parents.

III

At least two Members of the Court concede, as they must, that a State has a legitimate interest in the welfare of the pregnant minor and that, in furtherance of this interest, the State may require the minor to notify, and consult with, one of her parents. The Court nonetheless holds the Minnesota statute unconstitutional because it requires the minor to notify not one parent, but both parents, a requirement that the Court says bears no reasonable relation to the minor's welfare. The Court also concludes that Minnesota does not have a legitimate interest in facilitating the participation of both parents in the care and upbringing of their children. Given the substantial protection that minors have under Minnesota law generally, and under the statute in question, the judicial bypass provisions of the law are not necessary to its validity. The two-parent notification law enacted by Minnesota is, in my view, valid without the judicial bypass provision of subdivision 6.

B

I acknowledge that in some cases notifying both parents will not produce desirable results despite the fact that no actual instance is in the record before us, as the two-parent notification requirement was enjoined before it went into effect. We need not decide today, however, whether the Constitution permits a State to require that a physician notify both biological parents before performing an abortion on any minor, for the simple reason that Minnesota has not enacted such a law.

The Minnesota statute in fact contains exceptions to ensure that the statutory notice requirement does not apply if it proves a serious threat to the minor's health or safety. First, the statute does not require notice at all costs; to comply with the law, a physician need only use "reasonably diligent effort" to locate and notify both of the minor's parents.

Second, even where both parents can be located, notice is not required if the physician certifies that the abortion is necessary to prevent the woman's death and there is insufficient time to provide the required notice; if the minor's parents have authorized the abortion in writing; or if the minor declares that she is the victim of sexual abuse, neglect, or physical abuse.

IV

Because a majority of the Court holds that the two-parent notice requirement contained in subdivision 2 is unconstitutional, it is necessary for the Court to consider whether the same notice requirement is constitutional if the minor has the option of obtaining a court order permitting the abortion to proceed in lieu of the required notice. Assuming, as I am bound to do for this part of the analysis, that the notice provisions standing alone are invalid, I conclude that the two-parent notice requirement with the judicial bypass alternative is constitutional.

If a two-parent notification law may be constitutional as applied to immature minors whose best interests are served by the law, but not as applied to minors who are mature or whose best interests are not so served, a judicial bypass is an expeditious and efficient means by which to separate the applications of the law which are constitutional from those which are not. If a judicial bypass is mandated by the Constitution at all, it must be because a general consent rule is unreasonable in at least some of its applications, and the bypass is necessary to save the statute. No reason can be given for refusing to apply a similar analysis to the less demanding case of a notice statute. It follows that a similar result should obtain: A law that requires notice to one or both parents is constitutional with a bypass. I thus concur in that portion of the judgment announced, but not agreed with, by Justice Stevens which affirms the Court of Appeals' conclusion that § 144.343(6) is constitutional.

FOR DISCUSSION

How do you understand the legal difference between statutes requiring parental notification and those that mandate parental consent? Do you perceive that judicial bypass requirements solve the constitutional conflict for minors? How else could the law balance the state's interest in protecting minors and the liberty interest of minors?

RELATED CASES

***Planned Parenthood of Central Missouri v. Danforth:* 428 U.S. 52 (1976).**

The Court allowed the state to impose informed consent requirements and reporting requirements only when they are related to maternal health and do not interfere with the patient-physician relationship. The fetal protection statutes were found to be unconstitutional.

***Bellotti v. Baird:* 428 U.S. 132 (1976).**

The Supreme Court found a Massachusetts law that required all minors to obtain parental consent for abortions to be unconstitutional in that it provided no alternatives (e.g., a judicial bypass procedure) for minors.

***Bellotti v. Baird II:* 443 U.S. 622 (1979).**

The Supreme Court addressed a Massachusetts law that required minors to obtain parental consent before receiving an abortion; minors could obtain judicial consent if the parents refused consent. The Court held that the statute was unconstitutional because judges could deny authorization to a mature and emancipated minor and because there was no statutory provision for a judicial bypass in the event that the minor preferred not to seek parental consent.

PLANNED PARENTHOOD OF SOUTHEASTERN PENNSYLVANIA V. CASEY

505 U.S. 833, 112 S.Ct. 2791, 120 L.Ed.2d 674 (1992)

Five abortion clinics and one physician who provided abortion services challenged the constitutionality of five provisions of the Pennsylvania Abortion Control Act of 1982, as amended in 1988 and 1989. The act required that a woman seeking an abortion provide informed consent and wait twenty-four hours; if a minor, she was obliged to obtain consent from one parent or go through the steps necessary to take advantage of a judicial bypass option; and, if married, she had to verify that she had notified her husband. In addition, facilities that provide abortion services were given specific reporting requirements. The district court found all five requirements to be unconstitutional; the Court of Appeals for the Third Circuit affirmed in part and reversed in part—upholding all the regulations except the requirement of spousal notification.

Vote: 5–4

JUSTICES O'CONNOR, KENNEDY, and SOUTER announced the judgment of the Court and delivered the opinion of the Court with respect to Parts I, II, III, V–A, V–C, and VI, an opinion with respect to Part V–E, in which JUSTICE STEVENS joins, and an opinion with respect to Parts IV, V–B, and V–D.

I

Liberty finds no refuge in a jurisprudence of doubt. Yet 19 years after our holding that the Constitution protects a woman's right to terminate her pregnancy in its early stages, *Roe v. Wade*, 410 U.S. 113 (1973), that definition of liberty is still questioned. Joining the respondents as amicus curiae, the United States, as it has done in five other cases in the last decade, again asks us to overrule *Roe.*

After considering the fundamental constitutional questions resolved by *Roe*, principles of institutional integrity, and the rule of stare decisis, we are led to conclude this: the essential holding of *Roe v. Wade* should be retained and once again reaffirmed.

It must be stated at the outset and with clarity that *Roe's* essential holding, the holding we reaffirm, has three parts. First is a recognition of the right of the woman to choose to have an abortion before viability and to obtain it without undue interference from the State. Before viability, the State's interests are not strong enough to support a prohibition of abortion or the imposition of a substantial obstacle to the woman's effective right to elect the procedure. Second is a confirmation of the State's power to restrict abortions after fetal viability, if the law contains exceptions for pregnancies which endanger the woman's life or health. And third is the principle that the State has legitimate interests from the outset of the pregnancy in protecting the health of the woman and the life of the fetus that may become a child. These principles do not contradict one another; and we adhere to each.

II

Constitutional protection of the woman's decision to terminate her pregnancy derives from the Due Process Clause of the Fourteenth Amendment. It declares that no State shall "deprive any person of life, liberty, or property, without due process of law."

The most familiar of the substantive liberties protected by the Fourteenth Amendment are those recognized by the Bill of Rights. We have held that the Due Process Clause of the Fourteenth Amendment incorporates most of the Bill of Rights against the States. It is tempting, as a means of curbing the discretion of federal judges, to suppose that liberty encompasses no more than those rights already guaranteed to the individual against federal interference by the express provisions of the first eight Amendments to the Constitution. But of course this Court has never accepted that view.

It is also tempting, for the same reason, to suppose that the Due Process Clause protects only those practices, defined at the most specific level, that were protected against government interference by other rules of law when the Fourteenth Amendment was ratified. But such a view would be inconsistent with our law. It is a promise of the Constitution that there is a realm of personal liberty which the government may not enter. We have vindicated this principle before. Marriage is mentioned nowhere in the Bill of Rights and interracial marriage was illegal in most States in the 19th century, but the Court was no doubt correct in finding it to be an aspect of liberty protected against state interference by the substantive component of the Due Process Clause in *Loving v. Virginia*, 388 U.S. 1, 12 (1967). Similar examples may be found in *Turner v. Safley*, 482 U.S. 78, 94–99 (1987); in *Carey v. Population Services International*, 431 U.S. 678, 684–686 (1977); in *Griswold v. Connecticut*, 381 U.S. 479, 481–482 (1965); in *Pierce v. Society of Sisters*, 268 U.S. 510, 534–535 (1925); and in *Meyer v. Nebraska*, 262 U.S. 390, 399–403 (1923).

Our law affords constitutional protection to personal decisions relating to marriage, procreation, contraception, family relationships, child rearing, and education. These matters, involving the most intimate and personal choices a person may make in a lifetime, choices central to personal dignity and autonomy, are central to the liberty protected by the Fourteenth Amendment. At the heart of liberty is the right to define one's own concept of existence, of meaning, of the universe, and of the mystery of human life. Beliefs about these matters could not define the attributes of personhood were they formed under compulsion of the State.

These considerations begin our analysis of the woman's interest in terminating her pregnancy but cannot end it, for this reason: though the abortion decision may originate within the zone of conscience and belief, it is more than a philosophic exercise. Abortion is a unique act. It is an act fraught with consequences for others: for the woman who must live with the implications of her decision; for the persons who perform and assist in the procedure; for the spouse, family, and society which must confront the knowledge that these procedures exist, procedures some deem nothing short of an act of violence against innocent human life; and, depending on one's beliefs, for the life or potential life that is aborted. Though abortion is conduct, it does not follow that the State is entitled to proscribe it in all instances. That is because the liberty of the woman is at stake in a sense unique to the human condition and so unique to the law. The mother who carries a child to full term is subject to anxieties, to physical constraints, to pain that only she must bear. That these sacrifices have from the beginning of the human race been endured by woman with a pride that ennobles her in the eyes of others and gives to the infant a bond of love cannot alone be grounds for the State to insist she make the sacrifice. Her suffering is too intimate and personal for the State to insist, without more, upon its own vision of the woman's role, however dominant that vision has been in the course of our history and our culture. The destiny of the woman must be shaped to a large extent on her own conception of her spiritual imperatives and her place in society.

It should be recognized, moreover, that in some critical respects the abortion decision is of the same character as the decision to use contraception, to which *Griswold v. Connecticut*, *Eisenstadt v. Baird*, and *Carey v. Population Services International* afford constitutional protection. We have no doubt as to the correctness of those decisions. They support the reasoning in *Roe* relating to the woman's liberty because they involve personal decisions concerning not only the meaning of procreation but also human responsibility and respect for it. The same concerns are present when the woman confronts the reality that, perhaps despite her attempts to avoid it, she has become pregnant.

It was this dimension of personal liberty that *Roe* sought to protect, and its holding invoked the reasoning and the tradition of the precedents we have discussed, granting protection to substantive liberties of the person. The extent to which the legislatures of the States might act to outweigh the interests of the woman in choosing to terminate her pregnancy was a subject of debate both in *Roe* itself and in decisions following it.

III

A

3

No evolution of legal principle has left *Roe's* doctrinal footings weaker than they were in 1973. No development of constitutional law since the case was decided has implicitly or explicitly left Roe behind as a mere survivor of obsolete constitutional thinking.

4

We have seen how time has overtaken some of *Roe's* factual assumptions: advances in maternal health care allow for abortions safe to the mother later in pregnancy than was true in 1973, and advances in neonatal care have advanced viability to a point somewhat earlier. But these facts go only to the scheme of time limits on the realization of competing interests, and the divergences from the factual premises of 1973 have no bearing on the validity of *Roe*'s central holding, that viability marks the earliest point at which the State's interest in fetal life is constitutionally adequate to justify a legislative ban on nontherapeutic abortions.

The Court's duty in the present cases is clear. In 1973, it confronted the already-divisive issue of governmental power to limit personal choice to undergo abortion, for which it provided a new resolution based on the due process guaranteed by the Fourteenth Amendment. Whether or not a new social consensus is developing on that issue, its divisiveness is no less today than in 1973, and pressure to overrule the decision, like pressure to retain it, has grown only more intense. A decision to overrule *Roe's* essential holding under the existing circumstances would address error, if error there was, at the cost of both profound and unnecessary damage to the Court's legitimacy, and to the Nation's commitment to the rule of law. It is therefore imperative to adhere to the essence of *Roe's* original decision, and we do so today.

IV

From what we have said so far it follows that it is a constitutional liberty of the woman to have some freedom to terminate her pregnancy. We conclude that the basic decision in Roe was based on a constitutional analysis which we cannot now repudiate. The woman's liberty is not so unlimited, however, that from the outset the State cannot show its concern for the life of the unborn, and at a later point in fetal development the State's interest in life has sufficient force so that the right of the woman to terminate the pregnancy can be restricted.

The woman's right to terminate her pregnancy before viability is the most central principle of *Roe v. Wade*. It is a rule of law and a component of liberty we cannot renounce.

On the other side of the equation is the interest of the State in the protection of potential life. . . . [W]e are satisfied that the immediate question is not the soundness of *Roe's* resolution of the issue, but the precedential force that must be accorded to its holding. And we have concluded that the essential holding of Roe should be reaffirmed.

We reject the trimester framework, which we do not consider to be part of the essential holding of *Roe*. Measures aimed at ensuring that a woman's choice contemplates the consequences for the fetus do not necessarily interfere with the right recognized in *Roe*, although those measures have been found to be inconsistent with the rigid trimester framework announced in that case. The trimester framework suffers from these basic flaws: in its formulation it misconceives the nature of the pregnant woman's interest; and in practice it undervalues the State's interest in potential life, as recognized in *Roe*.

The concept of an undue burden has been utilized by the Court as well as individual Members of the Court, including two of us, in ways that could be considered inconsistent. Because we set forth a standard of general application to which we intend to adhere, it is important to clarify what is meant by an undue burden.

A finding of an undue burden is a shorthand for the conclusion that a state regulation has the purpose or effect of placing a substantial obstacle in the path of a woman seeking an abortion of a nonviable fetus. A statute with this purpose is invalid because the means chosen by the State to further the interest in potential life must be calculated to inform the woman's free choice, not hinder it.

Some guiding principles should emerge. What is at stake is the woman's right to make the ultimate decision, not a right to be insulated from all others in doing so. Regulations which do no more than create a structural mechanism by which the State, or the parent or guardian of a minor, may express profound respect for the life of the unborn are permitted, if they are not a substantial obstacle to the woman's exercise of the right to choose. Unless it has that effect on her right of choice, a state measure designed to persuade her to choose childbirth over abortion will be upheld if reasonably related to that goal. Regulations designed to foster the health of a woman seeking an abortion are valid if they do not constitute an undue burden.

We give this summary:

(a) An undue burden exists, and therefore a provision of law is invalid, if its purpose or effect is to place a substantial obstacle in the path of a woman seeking an abortion before the fetus attains viability.

(b) We reject the rigid trimester framework of *Roe v. Wade*. To promote the State's profound interest in potential life, throughout pregnancy the State may take measures to ensure that the woman's choice is informed, and measures designed to advance this interest will not be invalidated as long as their purpose is to persuade the woman to choose childbirth over abortion. These measures must not be an undue burden on the right.

(c) As with any medical procedure, the State may enact regulations to further the health or safety of a woman seeking an abortion. Unnecessary health regulations that have the purpose or effect of presenting a substantial obstacle to a woman seeking an abortion impose an undue burden on the right.

(d) Our adoption of the undue burden analysis does not disturb the central holding of *Roe v. Wade*, and we reaffirm that holding. Regardless of whether exceptions are made for particular circumstances, a State may not prohibit any woman from making the ultimate decision to terminate her pregnancy before viability.

(e) We also reaffirm *Roe's* holding that "subsequent to viability, the State in promoting its interest in the potentiality of human life may, if it chooses, regulate, and even proscribe, abortion except where it is necessary, in appropriate medical judgment, for the preservation of the life or health of the mother." *Roe v. Wade*, 410 U.S. at 164–165.

These principles control our assessment of the Pennsylvania statute, and we now turn to the issue of the validity of its challenged provisions.

V

A

Because it is central to the operation of various other requirements, we begin with the statute's definition of medical emergency. Under the statute, a medical emergency is that condition which, on the basis of the physician's good faith clinical judgment, so complicates the medical condition of a pregnant woman as to necessitate the immediate abortion of her pregnancy to avert her death or for which a delay will create serious risk of substantial and irreversible impairment of a major bodily function. 18 Pa. Cons. Stat. § 3203 (1990)

The District Court found that there were three serious conditions which would not be covered by the statute: pre-eclampsia, inevitable abortion, and premature ruptured membrane. Yet, as the Court of Appeals observed, it is undisputed that under some circumstances each of these conditions could lead to an illness with substantial and irreversible consequences. While the definition could be interpreted in an unconstitutional manner, the Court of Appeals construed the phrase "serious risk" to include those circumstances. We adhere to that course today, and conclude that, as construed by the Court of Appeals, the medical emergency definition imposes no undue burden on a woman's abortion right.

B

We next consider the informed consent requirement. Except in a medical emergency, the statute requires that at least 24 hours before performing an abortion a physician inform the woman of the nature of the procedure, the health risks of the abortion and of childbirth, and the "probable gestational age of the unborn child." The physician or a qualified nonphysician must inform the woman of the availability of printed materials published by the State describing the fetus and providing information about medical assistance for childbirth, information about child support from the father, and a list of agencies which provide adoption and other services as alternatives to abortion. An abortion may not be performed unless the woman certifies in writing that she has been informed of the availability of these printed materials and has been provided them if she chooses to view them.

We do not doubt that, as the District Court held, the waiting period has the effect of "increasing the cost and risk of delay of abortions," but the District Court did not conclude that the increased costs and potential delays amount to substantial obstacles. Rather, applying the trimester framework's strict prohibition of all regulation designed to promote the State's interest in potential life before viability, the District Court concluded that the waiting period does not further the state "interest in maternal health" and "infringes the physician's discretion to exercise sound medical judgment." Yet, as we have stated, under the undue burden standard a State is permitted to enact persuasive measures which favor childbirth over abortion, even if those measures do not further a health interest. And while the waiting period does limit a physician's discretion, that is not, standing alone, a reason to invalidate it. In light of the construction given the statute's definition of medical emergency by the Court of Appeals, and the District Court's findings, we cannot say that the waiting period imposes a real health risk.

We are left with the argument that the various aspects of the informed consent requirement are unconstitutional because they place barriers in the way of abortion on demand. Even the broadest reading of *Roe*, however, has not suggested that there is a constitutional right to abortion on demand. Rather, the right protected by *Roe* is a right to decide to terminate a pregnancy free of undue interference by the State. Because the informed consent requirement facilitates the wise exercise of that right, it cannot be classified as an interference with the right Roe protects. The informed consent requirement is not an undue burden on that right.

C

Section 3209 of Pennsylvania's abortion law provides, except in cases of medical emergency, that no physician shall perform an abortion on a married woman without receiving a signed statement from the woman that she has notified her spouse that she is about to undergo an abortion.

Section 3209 embodies a view of marriage consonant with the common-law status of married women but repugnant to our present understanding of marriage and of the nature of the rights secured by the Constitution. Women do not lose their constitutionally protected liberty when they marry. The Constitution protects all individuals, male or female, married or unmarried, from the abuse of governmental power, even where that power is employed for the supposed benefit of a member of the individual's family. These considerations confirm our conclusion that § 3209 is invalid.

D

We next consider the parental consent provision. Except in a medical emergency, an unemancipated young woman under 18 may not obtain an abortion unless she and one of her parents (or guardian) provides informed consent as defined above.

We have been over most of this ground before. Our cases establish, and we reaffirm today, that a State may require a minor seeking an abortion to obtain the consent of a parent or guardian, provided that there is an adequate judicial bypass procedure. Under these precedents, in our view, the one-parent consent requirement and judicial bypass procedure are constitutional.

E

Under the recordkeeping and reporting requirements of the statute, every facility which performs abortions is required to file a report stating its name and address as well as the name and address of any related entity, such as a controlling or subsidiary organization. In the case of state-funded institutions, the information becomes public.

In *Danforth*, 428 U.S. at 80, we held that recordkeeping and reporting provisions "that are reasonably directed to the preservation of maternal health and that properly respect a patient's confidentiality and privacy are permissible." We think that under this standard, all the provisions at issue here, except that relating to spousal notice, are constitutional. Although they do not relate to the State's interest in informing the woman's choice, they do relate to health.

VI

Our Constitution is a covenant running from the first generation of Americans to us and then to future generations. It is a coherent succession. Each generation must learn anew that the Constitution's written terms embody ideas and aspirations that must survive more ages than one. We accept our responsibility not to retreat from interpreting the full meaning of the covenant in light of all of our precedents. We invoke it once again to define the freedom guaranteed by the Constitution's own promise, the promise of liberty.

JUSTICE STEVENS, concurring in part and dissenting in part.

II

My disagreement with the joint opinion begins with its understanding of the trimester framework established in *Roe*. Contrary to the suggestion of the joint opinion, it is not a "contradiction" to recognize that the State may have a legitimate interest in potential human life and, at the same time, to conclude that that interest does not justify the regulation of abortion before viability. The fact that the State's interest is legitimate does not tell us when, if ever, that interest outweighs the pregnant woman's interest in personal liberty.

First, it is clear that, in order to be legitimate, the State's interest must be secular; consistent with the First Amendment the State may not promote a theological or sectarian interest. Moreover, as discussed above, the state interest in potential human life is not an interest in loco parentis, for the fetus is not a person.

Identifying the State's interests—which the States rarely articulate with any precision—makes clear that the interest in protecting potential life is not grounded in the Constitution.

In counterpoise is the woman's constitutional interest in liberty. One aspect of this liberty is a right to bodily integrity, a right to control one's person.

The woman's constitutional liberty interest also involves her freedom to decide matters of the highest privacy and the most personal nature.

Serious questions arise, however, when a State attempts to "persuade the woman to choose childbirth over abortion." Decisional autonomy must limit the State's power to inject into a woman's most personal deliberations its own views of what is best. The State may promote its preferences by funding childbirth, by creating and maintaining alternatives to abortion, and by espousing the virtues of family; but it must respect the individual's freedom to make such judgments.

In my opinion, the principles established in this long line of cases and the wisdom reflected in Justice Powell's opinion for the Court in *Akron* (and followed by the Court just six years ago in *Thornburgh*) should govern our decision today. Under these principles, Pa. Cons. Stat. §§ 3205(a)(2)(i)–(iii) (1990) of the Pennsylvania statute are unconstitutional. Those sections require a physician or counselor to provide the woman with a range of materials clearly designed to persuade her to choose not to undergo the abortion.

Under this same analysis, §§ 3205(a)(1)(i) and (iii) of the Pennsylvania statute are constitutional. Those sections, which require the physician to inform a woman of the nature and risks of the abortion procedure and the medical risks of carrying to term, are neutral requirements comparable to those imposed in other medical procedures. Those sections indicate no effort by the Commonwealth to influence the woman's choice in any way. If anything, such requirements enhance, rather than skew, the woman's decisionmaking.

III

The 24-hour waiting period required by §§ 3205(a)(1)–(2) of the Pennsylvania statute raises even more serious concerns. Such a requirement arguably furthers the Commonwealth's interests in two ways, neither of which is constitutionally permissible.

First, it may be argued that the 24-hour delay is justified by the mere fact that it is likely to reduce the number of abortions, thus furthering the Commonwealth's interest in potential life.

Second, it can more reasonably be argued that the 24-hour delay furthers the Commonwealth's interest in ensuring that the woman's decision is informed and thoughtful. But there is no evidence that the mandated delay benefits women or that it is necessary to enable the physician to convey any relevant information to the patient. The mandatory delay thus appears to rest on outmoded and unacceptable assumptions about the decisionmaking capacity of women.

Part of the constitutional liberty to choose is the equal dignity to which each of us is entitled. A woman who decides to terminate her pregnancy is entitled to the same respect as a woman who decides to carry the fetus to term. The mandatory waiting period denies women that equal respect.

IV

In my opinion, a correct application of the "undue burden" standard leads to the same conclusion concerning the constitutionality of these requirements. A state-imposed burden on the exercise of a constitutional right is measured both by its effects and by its character: A burden may be "undue" either because the burden is too severe or because it lacks a legitimate, rational justification.

The 24-hour delay requirement fails both parts of this test.

The counseling provisions are similarly infirm.

Accordingly, while I disagree with Parts IV, V-B, and V-D of the joint opinion, I join the remainder of the Court's opinion.

JUSTICE BLACKMUN, concurring in part, concurring in the judgment in part, and dissenting in part.

I join Parts I, II, III, V-A, V-C, and VI of the joint opinion of JUSTICES O'CONNOR, KENNEDY, and SOUTER.

Three years ago, in *Webster v. Reproductive Health Services*, 492 U.S. 490 (1989), four Members of this Court appeared poised to "cast into darkness the hopes and visions of every woman in this country" who had come to believe that the Constitution guaranteed her the right to reproductive choice. All that remained between the promise of *Roe* and the darkness of the plurality was a single, flickering flame. Decisions since *Webster* gave little reason to hope that this flame would cast much light. But now, just when so many expected the darkness to fall, the flame has grown bright.

I do not underestimate the significance of today's joint opinion. Yet I remain steadfast in my belief that the right to reproductive choice is entitled to the full protection afforded by this Court before *Webster*. And I fear for the darkness as four Justices anxiously await the single vote necessary to extinguish the light.

I

Make no mistake, the joint opinion of Justices O'Connor, Kennedy, and Souter is an act of personal courage and constitutional principle. In contrast to previous decisions in which Justices O'Connor and Kennedy postponed reconsideration of *Roe v. Wade*, 410 U.S. 113 (1973), the authors of the joint opinion today join Justice Stevens and me in concluding that "the essential holding of *Roe v. Wade* should be retained and once again reaffirmed." In brief, five Members of this Court today recognize that "the Constitution protects a woman's right to terminate her pregnancy in its early stages." *Roe* at 10.

The Court's reaffirmation of *Roe's* central holding is also based on the force of stare decisis. "No erosion of principle going to liberty or personal autonomy has left Roe's central holding a doctrinal remnant; *Roe* portends no developments at odds with other precedent for the analysis of personal liberty; and no changes of fact have rendered viability more or less appropriate as the point at which the balance of interests tips." *Roe* at 18. Indeed, the Court acknowledges that *Roe's* limitation on state power could not be removed "without serious inequity to those who have relied upon it or significant damage to the stability of the society governed by it." *Roe* at 13. In the 19 years since *Roe* was decided, that case has shaped more than reproductive planning—"an entire generation has come of age free to assume *Roe's* concept of liberty in defining the capacity of women to act in society, and to make reproductive decisions." *Roe* at 18. The Court understands that, having "call[ed] the contending sides . . . to end their national division by accepting a common mandate rooted in the Constitution," *Roe* at 24, a decision to overrule *Roe* "would seriously weaken the Court's capacity to exercise the judicial power and to function as the Supreme Court of a Nation dedicated to the rule of law." *Roe* at 22. What has happened today should serve as a model for future Justices and a warning to all who have tried to turn this Court into yet another political branch.

Lastly, while I believe that the joint opinion errs in failing to invalidate the other regulations, I am pleased that the joint opinion has not ruled out the possibility that these regulations may be shown to impose an unconstitutional burden. The joint opinion makes clear that its specific holdings are based on the insufficiency of the record before it. I am confident that in the future evidence will be produced to show that "in a large fraction of the cases in which [these regulations are] relevant, [they] will operate as a substantial obstacle to a woman's choice to undergo an abortion."

II

Today, no less than yesterday, the Constitution and decisions of this Court require that a State's abortion restrictions be subjected to the strictest judicial scrutiny. Our precedents and the joint opinion's principles require us to subject all non-de-minimis abortion regulations to strict scrutiny. Under this standard, the Pennsylvania statute's provisions requiring content-based counseling, a 24-hour delay, informed parental consent, and reporting of abortion-related information must be invalidated.

B

The Court has held that limitations on the right of privacy are permissible only if they survive "strict" constitutional scrutiny—that is, only if the governmental entity imposing the restriction can demonstrate that the limitation is both necessary and narrowly tailored to serve a compelling governmental interest. *Griswold v. Connecticut,* 381 U.S. 479, 485 (1965). We have applied this principle specifically in the context of abortion regulations. *Roe v. Wade,* 410 U.S. at 155.

In my view, application of this analytical framework is no less warranted than when it was approved by seven Members of this Court in *Roe*. Strict scrutiny of state limitations on reproductive choice still offers the most secure protection of the woman's right to make her own reproductive decisions, free from state coercion. No majority of this Court has ever agreed upon an alternative approach. The factual premises of the trimester framework have not been undermined, and the *Roe* framework is far more administrable, and far less manipulable, than the "undue burden" standard adopted by the joint opinion.

In sum, *Roe's* requirement of strict scrutiny as implemented through a trimester framework should not be disturbed. No other approach has gained a majority, and no other is more protective of the woman's fundamental right. Lastly, no other approach properly accommodates the woman's constitutional right with the State's legitimate interests.

III

At long last, The Chief Justice and those who have joined him admit it. Gone are the contentions that the issue need not be (or has not been) considered. There, on the first page, for all to see, is what was expected: "We believe that *Roe* was wrongly decided, and that it can and should be overruled consistently with our traditional approach to stare decisis in constitutional cases." If there is much reason to applaud the advances made by the joint opinion today, there is far more to fear from The Chief Justice's opinion.

The Chief Justice's criticism of *Roe* follows from his stunted conception of individual liberty. While recognizing that the Due Process Clause protects more than simple physical liberty, he then goes on to construe this Court's personal-liberty cases as establishing only a laundry list of particular rights, rather than a principled account of how these particular rights are grounded in a more general right of privacy.

Even more shocking than The Chief Justice's cramped notion of individual liberty is his complete omission of any discussion of the effects that compelled childbirth and motherhood have on women's lives. The only expression of concern with women's health is purely instrumental—for The Chief Justice, only women's psychological health is a concern, and only to the extent that he assumes that every woman who decides to have an abortion does so without serious consideration of the moral implications of her decision. In short, The Chief Justice's view of the State's compelling interest in maternal health has less to do with health than it does with compelling women to be maternal.

IV

In one sense, the Court's approach is worlds apart from that of The Chief Justice and Justice Scalia. And yet, in another sense, the distance between the two approaches is short—the distance is but a single vote.

I am 83 years old. I cannot remain on this Court forever, and when I do step down, the confirmation process for my successor well may focus on the issue before us today. That, I regret, may be exactly where the choice between the two worlds will be made.

CHIEF JUSTICE REHNQUIST, with whom JUSTICES WHITE, SCALIA, and THOMAS join, concurring in the judgment in part and dissenting in part.

The joint opinion, following its newly minted variation on stare decisis, retains the outer shell of *Roe v. Wade*, 410 U.S. 113 (1973), but beats a wholesale retreat from the substance of that case. We believe that *Roe* was wrongly decided, and that it can and should be overruled consistently with our traditional approach to stare decisis in constitutional cases. We would adopt the approach of the plurality in *Webster v. Reproductive Health Services*, 492 U.S. 490 (1989), and uphold the challenged provisions of the Pennsylvania statute in their entirety.

II

The joint opinion of Justices O'Connor, Kennedy, and Souter cannot bring itself to say that *Roe* was correct as an original matter, but the authors are of the view that "the immediate question is not the soundness of *Roe's* resolution of the issue, but the precedential force that must be accorded to its holding." Instead of claiming that *Roe* was correct as a matter of original constitutional interpretation, the opinion therefore contains an elaborate discussion of stare decisis. *Roe* decided that a woman had a fundamental right to an abortion. The joint opinion rejects that view. *Roe* decided that abortion regulations were to be subjected to "strict scrutiny" and could be justified only in the light of "compelling state interests." The joint opinion rejects that view. *Roe* analyzed abortion regulation under a rigid trimester framework, a framework which has guided this Court's decisionmaking for 19 years. The joint opinion rejects that framework.

In our view, authentic principles of stare decisis do not require that any portion of the reasoning in *Roe* be kept intact. Erroneous decisions in such constitutional cases are uniquely durable, because correction through legislative action, save for constitutional amendment, is impossible. It is therefore our duty to reconsider constitutional interpretations that "depart from a proper understanding" of the Constitution. *Garcia v. San Antonio Metropolitan Transit Authority*, 469 U.S. 528 (1985) at 557. Our constitutional watch does not cease merely because we have spoken before on an issue; when it becomes clear that a prior constitutional interpretation is unsound we are obliged to reexamine the question.

Apparently realizing that conventional stare decisis principles do not support its position, the joint opinion advances a belief that retaining a portion of *Roe* is necessary to protect the "legitimacy" of this Court. Because the Court must take care to render decisions "grounded truly in principle," and not simply as political and social compromises, the joint opinion properly declares it to be this Court's duty to ignore the public criticism and protest that may arise as a result of a decision. Few would quarrel with this statement, although it may be doubted that Members of this Court, holding their tenure as they do during constitutional "good behavior," are at all likely to be intimidated by such public protests.

But the joint opinion goes on to state that when the Court "resolves the sort of intensely divisive controversy reflected in *Roe* and those rare, comparable cases," its decision is exempt from reconsideration under established principles of stare decisis in constitutional cases. This is so, the joint opinion contends, because in those "intensely divisive" cases the Court has "called the contending sides of a national controversy to end their national division by accepting a common mandate rooted in the Constitution," and must therefore take special care not to be perceived as "surrendering to political pressure" and continued opposition. This is a truly novel principle, one which is contrary to both the Court's historical practice and to the Court's traditional willingness to tolerate criticism of its opinions. Under this principle, when the Court has ruled on a divisive issue, it is apparently prevented from overruling that decision for the sole reason that it was incorrect, unless opposition to the original decision has died away.

The end result of the joint opinion's paeans of praise for legitimacy is the enunciation of a brand new standard for evaluating state regulation of a woman's right to abortion—the "undue burden" standard. As indicated above, *Roe v. Wade* adopted a "fundamental right" standard under which state regulations could survive only if they met the requirement of "strict scrutiny." While we disagree with that standard, it at least had a recognized basis in constitutional law at the time *Roe* was decided. The same cannot be said for the "undue burden" standard, which is created largely out of whole cloth by the authors of the joint opinion. It is a standard which even today does not command the support of a majority of this Court. And it will not, we believe, result in the sort of "simple limitation," easily applied, which the joint opinion anticipates. In sum, it is a standard which is not built to last.

The sum of the joint opinion's labors in the name of stare decisis and "legitimacy" is this: *Roe v. Wade* stands as a sort of judicial Potemkin Village, which may be pointed out to passers-by as a monument to the importance of adhering to precedent. But behind the facade, an entirely new method of analysis, without any roots in constitutional law, is imported to decide the constitutionality of state laws regulating abortion. Neither stare decisis nor "legitimacy" are truly served by such an effort.

We have stated above our belief that the Constitution does not subject state abortion regulations to heightened scrutiny. Accordingly, we think that the correct analysis is that set forth by the plurality opinion in

Webster. A woman's interest in having an abortion is a form of liberty protected by the Due Process Clause, but States may regulate abortion procedures in ways rationally related to a legitimate state interest.

JUSTICE SCALIA also filed a dissenting opinion, with which THE CHIEF JUSTICE, and JUSTICES WHITE and THOMAS join, concurring in the judgment in part and dissenting in part.

FOR DISCUSSION

What test emerges from this case regarding an "undue burden" that the Court can use in the future to evaluate state abortion statutes? Will this test be easy or difficult to apply? Easy or difficult for legislatures to follow? Why do Justice Blackmun and Chief Justice Rehnquist have such radically different perceptions of the compromise represented by *Casey*?

RELATED CASES

***Stenberg v. Carhart:* 530 U.S. 914 (2000).**

The Court found unconstitutional a Nebraska law prohibiting "partial-birth abortion," outside the exception for preserving the mother's health. The law was said to violate the Due Process Clause of the Fourteenth Amendment, as interpreted in *Roe* and *Casey*.

***Gonzales v. Carhart:* 550 U.S. 124 (2007).**

The Court found that the federal Partial-Birth Abortion Ban Act of 2003 was not unconstitutionally vague and did not impose an undue burden on the right to an abortion, despite the absence of an exception to protect the health of the mother. The Court did not overrule *Stenberg v. Casey*.

***Whole Woman's Health v. Hellerstedt:* 579 U.S. ___ (2016).**

The Court determined that a Texas law restricting abortion clinics through regulations were a substantial burden on women's access to abortion services, without sufficient evidence of meeting state goals.

WOMEN OF MINNESOTA V. GOMEZ

542 N.W.2d 17, 1995 Minn. LEXIS 1036 (1995)

The Minnesota legislature passed several statutes that limit the use of public funds for abortion-related medical services to cases of medical necessity, rape, or incest, but allow these funds to be used for childbirth-related medical services. The plaintiffs claimed that this distinction violated women's right to privacy and the equal protection of the laws with respect to their choices related to reproduction. The claims were brought under the Minnesota constitution, as opposed to the federal Constitution (in *Harris v. McRae*, 448 U.S. 297 (1980), the U.S. Supreme Court had upheld the constitutionality of the Hyde Amendment, which had limited the use of federal Medicaid funds for abortion).

CHIEF JUSTICE KEITH delivered the opinion of the court.

In light of the emotional and political overtones of the abortion issue in this country, we must emphasize that this case presents a very narrow legal issue. This opinion is not based upon the morality or immorality of abortion, or the ethical considerations involved in a woman's individual decision whether or not to bear a child. In this case, the Minnesota legislature has adopted certain restrictions which impact poor women who, for medical reasons or because of rape or incest, choose to have an abortion. A similar constitutional challenge would certainly arise if the Minnesota legislature funded abortions for qualified women to limit the population of the poor, but refused to provide medical care for poor women who choose childbirth. Thus, the constitutional issues in this case concern the protection of either choice from discriminatory governmental treatment.

Both parties agree that women have a fundamental right to obtain an abortion before fetal viability under the Minnesota and United States Constitutions. However, plaintiffs assert that the statutory scheme at issue in this case infringes upon this fundamental right to privacy, and therefore must be subjected to strict scrutiny by this court. Because we agree with plaintiffs and because the State has not convinced us that the statutes in question are necessary to promote a compelling governmental interest, we hold that the challenged provisions are unconstitutional. Our decision is only based upon this court's determination that a pregnant woman, who is eligible for medical assistance and is considering an abortion for therapeutic reasons, cannot be coerced into choosing childbirth over abortion by a legislated funding policy. In reaching our decision, we have interpreted the Minnesota Constitution to afford broader protection than the United States Constitution of a woman's fundamental right to reach a private decision on whether to obtain an abortion, and thus reject the United States Supreme Court's opinion on this issue in *Harris v. McRae*, 448 U.S. 297 (1980). We conclude that the challenged provisions impermissibly infringe upon a woman's fundamental right of privacy under Article I, Sections 2, 7 and 10 of the Minnesota Constitution. Accordingly, we affirm the district court, and therefore find it unnecessary to address the equal protection arguments raised by the plaintiffs.

II

The first issue to be decided by this court is whether the challenged statutory provisions impermissibly infringe on a woman's right of privacy in violation of Article I, Sections 2, 7 and 10 of the Minnesota Constitution.

The right of privacy was first recognized at the federal level. In *Griswold v. Connecticut*, the U.S. Supreme Court recognized a "zone of privacy created by several fundamental constitutional guarantees" protected by the federal constitution. 381 U.S. 479, 485 (1965). Encompassed by this right of privacy under the constitution is every woman's fundamental right to decide to terminate her pregnancy free from unwarranted government intrusion. *Roe v. Wade*, 410 U.S. 113, 153 (1973). This right protects against unduly burdensome interference with procreative decision-making, and only a compelling interest can justify state regulation impinging upon that right. *Maher v. Roe*, 432 U.S. 464, 473–74 (1977); *Roe v. Wade*, 410 U.S. at 155–56.

In 1987, this court recognized a similar right of privacy guaranteed under and protected by the Minnesota Bill of Rights. *State v. Gray*, 413 N.W.2d 107, 111 (Minn. 1987). This court has never directly addressed, however, whether the right of privacy under the Minnesota Constitution encompasses a woman's decision to terminate her pregnancy.

In evaluating this issue, we first note that the right of privacy protects only fundamental rights, and therefore "a law must impermissibly infringe upon a fundamental right before it will be declared unconstitutional as violative of the right of privacy." *Gray*, 413 N.W.2d at 111. Fundamental rights are those "which have their origin in the express terms of the Constitution or which are necessarily to be implied from those terms."

In the present case, plaintiffs allege that the fundamental right implicated in this case is the right of a pregnant woman to decide whether to terminate her pregnancy. The State has conceded this point and has adopted the view that "the state constitution protects a woman's right to choose to have an abortion." We agree.

In *Jarvis v. Levine*, we held that the "right [of privacy] begins with protecting the integrity of one's own body and includes the right not to have it altered or invaded without consent." 418 N.W.2d 139, 148 (Minn. 1988). We therefore found that the right to be free from intrusive medical treatment is a fundamental right encompassed by the right of privacy under the Minnesota Constitution.

We find this characterization equally persuasive in the context of the present case. The right of procreation without state interference has long been recognized as "one of the basic civil rights of man . . . fundamental to the very existence and survival of the race." *Skinner v. Oklahoma ex rel. Williamson*, 316 U.S. 535, 541 (1942). We can think of few decisions more intimate, personal, and profound than a woman's decision between childbirth and abortion. Indeed, this decision is of such great import that it governs whether the woman will undergo extreme physical and psychological changes and whether she will create lifelong attachments and responsibilities. We therefore conclude that the right of privacy under the Minnesota Constitution encompasses a woman's right to decide to terminate her pregnancy.

III

Having made this determination, we next consider whether the challenged statutes impermissibly infringe on this right of privacy.

As noted previously, the U.S. Supreme Court has evaluated this issue in light of the federal constitution. In the companion cases of *Beal v. Doe*, 432 U.S. 438, 447 (1977), and *Maher v. Roe*, 432 U.S. 464 (1977), the Court held that the government may refuse to pay for nontherapeutic abortions without conflicting with Title XIX and without impinging on the fundamental right of privacy recognized in *Roe v. Wade*. *Beal v. Doe*, at 474; *Maher v. Roe*. The Court noted that even though the state's interest in encouraging childbirth is not compelling until after viability, it is nevertheless "a significant state interest existing throughout the course of the woman's pregnancy." *Beal v. Doe*, 432 U.S. at 446. The state can therefore make "a value judgment favoring childbirth over abortion, and . . . implement that judgment by the allocation of public funds." *Maher*, 432 U.S. at 474.

Two [sic] years later, in *Harris v. McRae*, the Supreme Court reviewed the Hyde Amendment restricting federal funding of abortion to determine whether it violated any substantive rights secured by the Constitution. 448 U.S. 297 (1980).

The Court . . . viewed the woman's indigency and not the statute as creating the infringement on the woman's decision to terminate her pregnancy, and it held that the government may refuse to pay for abortions without impinging on the constitutionally protected freedom of choice recognized in *Roe v. Wade*.

In the case before us, the State and the dissent assert that this court should adopt the *McRae* Court's distinction between government action that creates an obstacle to abortion and government action that simply fails to remove a preexisting barrier, and should find no infringement. Inherent in this argument is the assertion of the State and the dissent that the Minnesota Constitution does not require the state to fund the exercise of every fundamental right. The State relies upon the *McRae* Court's statement that "although the liberty protected by the Due Process Clause affords protection against unwarranted government interference with freedom of choice in the context of certain personal decisions, it does not confer an entitlement to such funds as may be necessary to realize all the advantages of that freedom." 448 U.S. at 317–18. The relevant inquiry . . . is whether, having elected to participate in a medical assistance program, the state may selectively exclude from such benefits otherwise eligible persons solely because they make constitutionally protected health care decisions with which the state disagrees.

Plaintiffs urge us to construe the Minnesota Constitution more broadly than the *McRae* Court construed the U.S. Constitution and to find that the "ban on medical assistance funding for abortion services 'interferes' with a woman's choice to have an abortion by adding state created financial considerations to the woman's decision making process." Other state courts have addressed this issue, and a substantial majority of these courts have departed from *McRae*.

In evaluating the opposing arguments, we find the U.S. Supreme Court's decision in *McRae* unpersuasive. As Justice Brennan noted in his dissent to *McRae*, "[the Court has] heretofore never hesitated to invalidate any scheme granting or withholding financial benefits that incidentally or intentionally burdens one manner of exercising a constitutionally protected choice." 448 U.S. at 334.

Accordingly, to the extent that *McRae* stands for the proposition that a legislative funding ban on abortion does not infringe on a woman's right to choose abortion, we depart from *McRae*. This court has long recognized that we may interpret the Minnesota Constitution to offer greater protection of individual rights than the U.S. Supreme Court has afforded under the federal constitution.

In some cases, we have in fact interpreted the Minnesota Constitution to provide more protection than that accorded under the federal constitution or have applied a more stringent constitutional standard of review. We find that this is one of those limited circumstances in which we will interpret our constitution to provide more protection than that afforded under the federal constitution.

Minnesota possesses a long tradition of affording persons on the periphery of society a greater measure of government protection and support than may be available elsewhere. This tradition is evident in legislative actions on behalf of the poor, the ill, the developmentally disabled and other persons largely without influence in society.

This court too, has acted to establish that tradition during other times when the nation was divided on an important issue. Previously, when this nation was split on the question of slavery, this court relied on the Minnesota Constitution to strike legislation denying citizens of secessionist states access to Minnesota courts. These secessionists were politically unpopular in unionist Minnesota. Nonetheless, this court held that government must protect the rights of each of its citizens, regardless of the fact that the larger community may hold them in low esteem. We believe that this tradition compels us to deviate from the federal course on the question of denying funding to indigent women seeking therapeutic abortions.

It is critical to note that the right of privacy under our constitution protects not simply the right to an abortion, but rather it protects the woman's decision to abort; any legislation infringing on the decision-making process, then, violates this fundamental right. In the present case, the infringement is the state's offer of money to women for health care services necessary to carry the pregnancy to term, and the state's ban on health care funding for women who choose therapeutic abortions. Faced with these two options, financially independent women might not feel particularly compelled to choose either childbirth or abortion based on the monetary incentive alone. Indigent women, on the other hand, are precisely the ones who would be most affected by an offer of monetary assistance, and it is these women who are targeted by the statutory funding ban. We simply cannot say that an indigent woman's decision whether to terminate her pregnancy is not significantly impacted by the state's offer of comprehensive medical services if the woman carries the pregnancy to term. We conclude, therefore, that these statutes constitute an infringement on the fundamental right of privacy.

Because the challenged provisions infringe on the fundamental right of privacy, we must subject them to strict scrutiny.

. . . [T]he State indicates that its interest is the preservation of potential human life and the encouragement and support of childbirth. However, a woman's right of privacy encompasses her decision whether to choose health care services necessary to terminate or to continue a pregnancy without interference from the state, "at least until such time as the state's important interest in protecting the potentiality of human life predominates over the right to privacy, which is usually at viability." *State v. Merrill*, 450 N.W.2d 318, 322 (Minn. 1990) (citing *Roe*, 410 U.S. at 163). Under *Roe v. Wade*, then, the state's interest in potential life does not become compelling prior to viability. Because the challenged provisions apply at all stages of pregnancy, including prior to viability, they do not withstand strict scrutiny, and thus must be invalidated.

We emphasize that our decision is limited to the class of plaintiffs certified by the district court and the narrow statutory provisions at issue in this case. Specifically, we hold that the State cannot refuse to provide abortions to [Medicare]-eligible women when the procedure is necessary for therapeutic reasons. The statutory scheme, as it exists, takes the decision from the hands of such women in a manner that, in light of the protections afforded by our own constitution, we simply cannot condone. Contrary to the dissent's allegations, this court's decision will not permit any woman eligible for medical assistance to obtain an abortion "on demand." Rather, under our interpretation of the Minnesota Constitution's guaranteed right to privacy, the difficult decision whether to obtain a therapeutic abortion will not be made by the government, but will be left to the woman and her doctor.

JUSTICE STRINGER took no part in the consideration or decision of this case.

JUSTICE COYNE, dissenting.

I respectfully dissent. Since the early 1970s, I have observed that "abortion," though often posited as the subject of discussion, is seldom discussed. Perhaps because the subject plumbs deeply held philosophical and moral beliefs, speakers oftentimes are prone to abandon reasoned discourse for exhortation either "for" or "against" abortion. Because I believe that the majority's decision today will not only assure the continued divisiveness of the issue but will, indeed, escalate the acrimony attendant upon it, I shall attempt to address the constitutional issues in a reasoned and principled manner without the inflammatory rhetoric that so often attends the subject.

The right of privacy which the Supreme Court recognized in *Roe v. Wade* was a woman's right to address the question whether or not to terminate her pregnancy unfettered by state law criminalizing abortion and to free her decision from the possible burden of complicity in a crime. The decision in *Roe* goes no further.

Misapprehending the *Roe* analysis and its context, the majority suggests that it is the identical right which is at issue here and compels the decision reached by the majority. It is not, however, the same right. At least, it seems to me, despite the majority's insistence that there is a single right at issue here, that there is a very significant difference between a right to decide to terminate a pregnancy by abortion without fear of criminal complicity and a right to compel the state to pay for the abortion.

Even if it is no more "sinful and tyrannical" to tax those who consider abortion to be immoral than it is to tax those who consider war immoral, at the very least, respect for the consciences of those who believe abortion is immoral should count as a legitimate basis for Congress and state legislatures to decide not to devote coerced tax dollars to that use. If, as I believe, the decision whether or not the government should fund abortion is properly a matter for decision by the legislature, the legislature has exercised its authority in what appears to me to be a rational manner. Even though the members of the court may disagree with some or all of the legislature's political decisions with respect to funding abortions, this court should not arrogate unto itself the legislative function. The repeated references in the majority opinion to health care services and therapeutic abortions suggest an expectation that only abortions necessitated by significant health considerations will be state-funded. . . .

For two reasons, however, I consider any such expectation doomed to failure. First, there is the practical problem posed by the court's inability to set any standard for determining when an abortion is "necessary for therapeutic reasons." If a woman has decided that she does not want the child and that she does not want to carry it to term, it seems to me more than likely that she will find a physician who will agree that the stress of continuing an unwanted pregnancy justifies an abortion.

It is possible, of course, that the legislature could alleviate that problem by adopting some standards, but the legislature can do nothing except propose a constitutional amendment to address the second reason, for the court has created an impediment to any limitation on state-funded abortions. The majority has based its decision on a constitutional right which it has defined as a "right of privacy under the Minnesota Constitution [which] encompasses a woman's right to decide to terminate her pregnancy." The majority then affirms an injunction precluding enforcement of statutes and rules on the ground that the statutory provisions which provide for funding childbirth but deny funding for abortion "coerce" a decision in violation of a woman's constitutional right to decide to terminate her pregnancy. Having determined that state-funding of medical services, including delivery of the child, to pregnant women and of some, but not all, abortions "coerces" a pregnant woman's decision whether to give birth or terminate her pregnancy and infringes her constitutional right to decide to terminate her pregnancy, as a matter of constitutional law the court is in no better position than the legislature to deny state-funding because the court does not approve of the reason for the decision to terminate the pregnancy. That the limitations the court imposes are less restrictive than those set by the legislature does not alter the fact that if financial considerations can be said to "coerce" a decision in violation of a constitutional right to decide, any restriction of state-funding is "coercive" and, therefore, violative of the fundamental right of privacy.

I would reverse the decision of the district court and direct the entry of judgment in favor of the [State].

FOR DISCUSSION

How does the Minnesota constitution apply to abortion cases related to the federal Constitution? What differences do you see between this decision of a state supreme court and rulings of the U.S. Supreme Court? Are the differences significant or stylistic?

RELATED CASES

Beal v. Doe: **432 U.S. 438 (1977).**

The U.S. Supreme Court ruled that the federal government may disallow nontherapeutic abortions without violating Medicaid provisions or limiting the fundamental right of privacy protected by *Roe v. Wade.*

Maher v. Roe: **432 U.S. 464 (1977).**

The state is able to favor childbirth over abortion and to support this legislative priority through the allocation of public funds. Financial need does not constitute a suspect classification under the Equal Protection Clause.

Harris v. McRae: **448 U.S. 297 (1980).**

The Supreme Court reviewed the Hyde Amendment, which prohibits the use of federal funds for abortions, to determine whether the law violated any substantive rights secured by the Constitution. The Court found that it was the impoverished state of the woman, not the limitations of the Hyde Amendment, that had prevented the exercise of constitutionally guaranteed freedom of choice surrounding abortion.

The Right to Assisted Suicide

While the right to privacy is a prime example of the many new areas of law that have emerged or been proposed under the substantive liberty interest and substantive equality interest of the Fourteenth Amendment, one of the most controversial incorporates the issues of physician-assisted suicide and the right to die. Unlike involuntary euthanasia, assisted suicide and the right to die imply knowledgeable consent on the part of the individual seeking death; hence privacy is a key component of the constitutional legitimacy of these concepts. While the individual has the interest in making key decisions related to his or her own life and body, the state has a vested interest in ensuring physician accountability and in guaranteeing that the individual making the decision will not be coerced in any way. Frequently, the individual making the decision to die represents a vulnerable population—the chronically ill, the terminally ill, those in constant pain—ripe for exploitation. Individuals claim that such a choice is covered by the right of privacy and that the decision itself is to be made in consultation with a physician. The tension between these two competing interests of the individual and state has been addressed by the Court in several cases. Here, as with respect to the issues of abortion and search and seizure (see Chapter VII: Criminal Due Process), technological developments have influenced the Supreme Court's interpretation of the Constitution.

In its first case in this jurisprudential arena, *Cruzan v. Director, Missouri Department of Health* (497 U.S. 261, 1990), the Court recognized an individual liberty interest in removing oneself from life support, although that liberty was awarded only to those deemed competent to exercise that right. Later the Court explored the limits of both the Due Process Clause (*Washington v. Glucksberg*, 521 U.S. 702, 1997) and the Equal Protection Clause (*Vacco v. Quill*, 521 U.S. 793, 1997) in relation to allowing terminally ill patients to practice physician-assisted suicide. In so doing, the Court also explored the power of the states to construct their own balance between the liberty and equality interests of the individual and the interest of the state in protecting the lives of its citizens. While the Supreme Court decided that there were no such protected interests under the Fourteenth Amendment, the concurrences in these cases recognize the ways in which the issues may evolve in the future.

Several physicians who treat the terminally ill, along with three terminal ill patients and a nonprofit advocacy group, Compassion in Dying, challenged the state of Washington's statute prohibiting physician-assisted suicide. The plaintiffs claimed that the law violates the liberty interest protected by the Due Process Clause of the Fourteenth Amendment. The plaintiffs argued that this legislation prevented terminally ill, yet legally competent individuals from exercising their personal liberty to choose to die. In *Washington v. Glucksberg* the Court considered what was historically understood to be a liberty interest under the Due Process Clause. Because suicide had not been understood traditionally as a personal liberty, the justices ruled, and since the state had a legitimate interest in protecting the terminally ill and disabled from coercion to end their lives, the Washington statute did not violate the Due Process Clause.

Simultaneously, an equal protection challenge was made against a similar New York law that criminalized the commission or attempt of suicide but allowed patients to refuse medication, even when the treatment was necessary to preserve their lives. Petitioners, both physicians and terminally ill patients, challenged the disparity between these statutes under the Equal Protection Clause of the Fourteenth Amendment, which requires states to provide equal protection of the laws to all residents. Petitioners claimed that New York law, which allows individuals to refuse life-sustaining medical treatment but prohibits physician-assisted suicide, was unconstitutional because it treats two substantially similar classes differently. In *Vacco v. Quill* the Supreme Court rejected this equal protection challenge, holding that the state had a legitimate interest in protecting terminally ill and disabled persons from coercion that might encourage them to end their lives prematurely; the Court also cited an interest in protecting medical ethics. As in *Washington v. Glucksberg*, the Court found a clear state interest in preserving human life. The Court ruled that there is a clear difference between assisted suicide and the refusal of medical treatment, for in the first situation the physician has the "intent to cause harm" by aiding or hastening a patient's death.

In both *Glucksberg* and *Quill*, the Court eliminated the two grounds that citizens could use to challenge state prohibitions against physician-assisted suicide. What happens when a state statute protects this "right to die"? Can the federal government challenge that law? In the case of *Gonzales v. Oregon* (546 U.S. 243, 2006), the Supreme Court ruled that Attorney General John Ashcroft had acted illegitimately in 2001 when he attempted to use the federal Controlled Substances Act of 1970 to prosecute Oregon physicians who prescribed lethal doses of controlled drugs to terminally ill patients. This decision ensured that Oregon's 1994 Death with Dignity Act, which authorized such actions on the part of physicians, would not be nullified at the behest of the attorney general. The Court interpreted the Controlled Substances Act as criminalizing drug dealing by physicians, not as affording the attorney general license to prohibit a medical practice protected by state law.

Oregon's Death with Dignity Act was the first state law to protect physician-assisted suicide. In 1997, a challenge to the act by the state legislature resulted in a referendum on the law, which yielded a desire to keep the law by approximately 60 percent of the vote. Currently, the Supreme Court has clearly noted that the right to assisted suicide can be safely protected through legislative initiatives, regardless of the absence of constitutional protection. Unlike reproduction and abortion issues, this privacy concern remains solidly located in the state legislatures and the voting public, not in the judicial branch. This was demonstrated in November 2008 when the voters in Washington State voted for Initiative 1000, modeled on Oregon's right-to-die law, protecting physician-assisted suicide. Vermont (2013, legislature) and California (2015, legislature) have followed suit in the years since. Massachusetts (2012) and Colorado (2015) voters have rejected similar initiatives.

WASHINGTON V. GLUCKSBERG

521 U.S. 702, 117 S.Ct. 2302, 138 L.Ed.2d 772 (1997)

Several physicians who treat the terminally ill, along with three terminal ill patients and a nonprofit advocacy group, Compassion in Dying, challenged the state of Washington's law that prohibits causing or aiding a suicide. The parties claimed that the law violates the liberty interest protected by the Due Process Clause of the Fourteenth Amendment. The district court agreed and also found that the law violated the Equal Protection Clause; the Court of Appeals of the Ninth Circuit reversed, finding no such protected interest in the Fourteenth Amendment. The Ninth Circuit then reheard en banc and found that the state ban on assisted suicide was unconstitutional "as applied to terminally ill competent adults who wish to hasten their deaths with medication prescribed by their physicians." The ruling was based solely on the Due Process Clause; no decision was reached based on the Equal Protection Clause.

Vote: 9–0

CHIEF JUSTICE REHNQUIST delivered the opinion of the Court.

The question presented in this case is whether Washington's prohibition against "causing" or "aiding" a suicide offends the Fourteenth Amendment to the United States Constitution. We hold that it does not.

I

We begin, as we do in all due-process cases, by examining our Nation's history, legal traditions, and practices. In almost every State—indeed, in almost every western democracy—it is a crime to assist a suicide. The States' assisted-suicide bans are not innovations. Rather, they are longstanding expressions of the States' commitment to the protection and preservation of all human life. Indeed, opposition to and condemnation of suicide—and, therefore, of assisting suicide—are consistent and enduring themes of our philosophical, legal, and cultural heritages.

More specifically, for over 700 years, the Anglo-American common-law tradition has punished or otherwise disapproved of both suicide and assisting suicide.

. . . [A]lthough States moved away from Blackstone's treatment of suicide, courts continued to condemn it as a grave public wrong.

That suicide remained a grievous, though nonfelonious, wrong is confirmed by the fact that colonial and early state legislatures and courts did not retreat from prohibiting assisting suicide.

Though deeply rooted, the States' assisted-suicide bans have in recent years been reexamined and, generally, reaffirmed. Because of advances in medicine and technology, Americans today are increasingly likely to die in institutions, from chronic illnesses. Public concern and democratic action are therefore sharply focused on how best to protect dignity and independence at the end of life, with the result that there have been many significant changes in state laws and in the attitudes these laws reflect. Many States, for example, now permit "living wills," surrogate health-care decisionmaking, and the withdrawal or refusal of life-sustaining medical treatment. At the same time, however, voters and legislators continue for the most part to reaffirm their States' prohibitions on assisting suicide.

The Washington statute at issue in this case, Wash. Rev. Code § 9A.36.060 (1994), was enacted in 1975 as part of a revision of that State's criminal code. Four years later, Washington passed its Natural Death Act, which specifically stated that the "withholding or withdrawal of life-sustaining treatment . . . shall not, for any purpose, constitute a suicide" and that "nothing in this chapter shall be construed to condone, authorize, or approve mercy killing . . . ." In 1991, Washington voters rejected a ballot initiative which, had it passed, would have permitted a form of physician-assisted suicide. Washington then added a provision to the Natural Death Act expressly excluding physician-assisted suicide.

Attitudes toward suicide itself have changed . . ., but our laws have consistently condemned, and continue to prohibit, assisting suicide. Despite changes in medical technology and notwithstanding an increased emphasis on the importance of end-of-life decisionmaking, we have not retreated from this prohibition. Against this backdrop of history, tradition, and practice, we now turn to respondents' constitutional claim.

II

The Due Process Clause guarantees more than fair process, and the "liberty" it protects includes more than the absence of physical restraint. The Clause also provides heightened protection against government interference with certain fundamental rights and liberty interests. In a long line of cases, we have held that, in addition to the specific freedoms protected by the Bill of Rights, the "liberty" specially protected by the Due Process Clause includes the rights to marry, *Loving v. Virginia*, 388 U.S. 1 (1967); to have children, *Skinner v. Oklahoma ex rel. Williamson*, 316 U.S. 535 (1942); to direct the education and upbringing of one's children, *Meyer v. Nebraska*, 262 U.S. 390 (1923); *Pierce v. Society of Sisters*, 268 U.S. 510 (1925); to marital privacy, *Griswold v. Connecticut*, 381 U.S. 479 (1965); to use contraception; *Eisenstadt v. Baird*, 405 U.S. 438 (1972); to bodily integrity, *Rochin v. California*, 342 U.S. 165 (1952), and to abortion, *Planned Parenthood v. Casey*, 497 U.S. 833 (1992). We have also assumed, and strongly suggested, that the Due Process Clause protects the traditional right to refuse unwanted lifesaving medical treatment. *Cruzan v. Director, Missouri Dept. of Health*, 497 U.S. 261 at 278–279 (1990).

By extending constitutional protection to an asserted right or liberty interest, we, to a great extent, place the matter outside the arena of public debate and legislative action. Our established method of substantive-due-process analysis has two primary features: First, we have regularly observed that the Due Process Clause specially protects those fundamental rights and liberties which are, objectively, "deeply rooted in this Nation's history and tradition;" *Snyder v. Massachusetts*, 291 U.S. 97, 105 (1934), and "implicit in the concept of ordered liberty," such that "neither liberty nor justice would exist if they were sacrificed," *Palko v. Connecticut*, 302 U.S. 319, 325, 326 (1937). Second, we have required in substantive-due-process cases a "careful description" of the asserted fundamental liberty interest.

We now inquire whether this asserted right [to die] has any place in our Nation's traditions. Here, as discussed above, we are confronted with a consistent and almost universal tradition that has long rejected the asserted right, and continues explicitly to reject it today, even for terminally ill, mentally competent adults. To hold for respondents, we would have to reverse centuries of legal doctrine and practice, and strike down the considered policy choice of almost every State.

The history of the law's treatment of assisted suicide in this country has been and continues to be one of the rejection of nearly all efforts to permit it. That being the case, our decisions lead us to conclude that the asserted "right" to assistance in committing suicide is not a fundamental liberty interest protected by the Due Process Clause. The Constitution also requires, however, that Washington's assisted-suicide ban be rationally related to legitimate government interests. This requirement is unquestionably met here. As the court below recognized, Washington's assisted-suicide ban implicates a number of state interests. First, Washington has an "unqualified interest in the preservation of human life." *Cruzan*, 497 U.S. at 282. The State's prohibition on assisted suicide, like all homicide laws, both reflects and advances its commitment to this interest. This interest is symbolic and aspirational as well as practical[.]

Relatedly, all admit that suicide is a serious public-health problem, especially among persons in otherwise vulnerable groups. The State has an interest in preventing suicide, and in studying, identifying, and treating its causes.

The State also has an interest in protecting the integrity and ethics of the medical profession. And physician-assisted suicide could, it is argued, undermine the trust that is essential to the doctor-patient relationship by blurring the time-honored line between healing and harming.

Next, the State has an interest in protecting vulnerable groups—including the poor, the elderly, and disabled persons—from abuse, neglect, and mistakes. If physician-assisted suicide were permitted, many might resort to it to spare their families the substantial financial burden of end-of-life health-care costs.

The State's interest here goes beyond protecting the vulnerable from coercion; it extends to protecting disabled and terminally ill people from prejudice, negative and inaccurate stereotypes, and "societal indifference." The State's assisted-suicide ban reflects and reinforces its policy that the lives of terminally ill, disabled, and elderly people must be no less valued than the lives of the young and healthy, and that a seriously disabled person's suicidal impulses should be interpreted and treated the same way as anyone else's.

Finally, the State may fear that permitting assisted suicide will start it down the path to voluntary and perhaps even involuntary euthanasia. Thus, it turns out that what is couched as a limited right to "physician-assisted suicide" is likely, in effect, a much broader license, which could prove extremely difficult to police and contain. Washington's ban on assisting suicide prevents such erosion.

Throughout the Nation, Americans are engaged in an earnest and profound debate about the morality, legality, and practicality of physician-assisted suicide. Our holding permits this debate to continue, as it should in a democratic society. The decision of the en banc Court of Appeals is reversed, and the case is remanded for further proceedings consistent with this opinion. It is so ordered.

JUSTICE O'CONNOR, concurring.

Death will be different for each of us. For many, the last days will be spent in physical pain and perhaps the despair that accompanies physical deterioration and a loss of control of basic bodily and mental functions. Some will seek medication to alleviate that pain and other symptoms.

The Court frames the issue in this case as whether the Due Process Clause of the Constitution protects a "right to commit suicide which itself includes a right to assistance in doing so," and concludes that our Nation's history, legal traditions, and practices do not support the existence of such a right. I join the Court's opinions because I agree that there is no generalized right to "commit suicide." But respondents urge us to address the narrower question whether a mentally competent person who is experiencing great suffering has a constitutionally cognizable interest in controlling the circumstances of his or her imminent death. I see no need to reach that question in the context of the facial challenges to the . . . laws at issue here. The parties and amici agree that in these States a patient who is suffering from a terminal illness and who is experiencing great pain has no legal barriers to obtaining medication, from qualified physicians, to alleviate that suffering, even to the point of causing unconsciousness and hastening death. In this light, even assuming that we would recognize such an interest, I agree that the State's interests in protecting those who are not truly competent or facing imminent death, or those whose decisions to hasten death would not truly be voluntary, are sufficiently weighty to justify a prohibition against physician-assisted suicide.

Every one of us at some point may be affected by our own or a family member's terminal illness. There is no reason to think the democratic process will not strike the proper balance between the interests of terminally ill, mentally competent individuals who would seek to end their suffering and the State's interests in protecting those who might seek to end life mistakenly or under pressure. As the Court recognizes, States are presently undertaking extensive and serious evaluation of physician-assisted suicide and other related issues.

In sum, there is no need to address the question whether suffering patients have a constitutionally cognizable interest in obtaining relief from the suffering that they may experience in the last days of their lives. The difficulty in defining terminal illness and the risk that a dying patient's request for assistance in ending his or her life might not be truly voluntary justifies the prohibitions on assisted suicide we uphold here.

JUSTICE STEVENS, concurring in the judgments.

The Court ends its opinion with the important observation that our holding today is fully consistent with a continuation of the vigorous debate about the "morality, legality, and practicality of physician-assisted suicide" in a democratic society. I write separately to make it clear that there is also room for further debate about the limits that the Constitution places on the power of the States to punish the practice. . . .

There may be little distinction between the intent of a terminally-ill patient who decides to remove her life-support and one who seeks the assistance of a doctor in ending her life; in both situations, the patient is seeking to hasten a certain, impending death. The doctor's intent might also be the same in prescribing lethal medication as it is in terminating life support. A doctor who fails to administer medical treatment to one who is dying from a disease could be doing so with an intent to harm or kill that patient. Conversely, a doctor who prescribes lethal medication does not necessarily intend the patient's death—rather that doctor may seek simply to ease the patient's suffering and to comply with her wishes. The illusory character of any differences in intent or causation is confirmed by the fact that the American Medical Association unequivocally endorses the practice of terminal sedation—the administration of sufficient dosages of pain-killing medication to terminally ill patients to protect them from excruciating pain even when it is clear that the time of death will be advanced. The purpose of terminal sedation is to ease the suffering of the patient and comply with her wishes, and the actual cause of death is the administration of heavy doses of lethal sedatives. This same intent and causation may exist when a doctor complies with a patient's request for lethal medication to hasten her death.

Thus, although the differences the majority notes in causation and intent between terminating life-support and assisting in suicide support the Court's rejection of the respondents' facial challenge, these distinctions may be inapplicable to particular terminally ill patients and their doctors. Our holding today in *Vacco v. Quill* that the Equal Protection Clause is not violated by New York's classification, just like our holding in *Washington v. Glucksberg* that the Washington statute is not invalid on its face, does not foreclose the possibility that some applications of the New York statute may impose an intolerable intrusion on the patient's freedom.

There remains room for vigorous debate about the outcome of particular cases that are not necessarily resolved by the opinions announced today. How such cases may be decided will depend on their specific facts. In my judgment, however, it is clear that the so-called "unqualified interest in the preservation of human life," *Cruzan*, 497 U.S. at 282, is not itself sufficient to outweigh the interest in liberty that may justify the only possible means of preserving a dying patient's dignity and alleviating her intolerable suffering.

JUSTICE SOUTER, concurring in the judgment.

Three terminally ill individuals and four physicians who sometimes treat terminally ill patients brought this challenge to the Washington statute making it a crime "knowingly . . . [to] aid another person to attempt suicide," Wash. Rev. Code § 9A.36.060 (1994), claiming on behalf of both patients and physicians that it would violate substantive due process to enforce the statute against a doctor who acceded to a dying patient's request for a drug to be taken by the patient to commit suicide. The question is whether the statute sets up one of those "arbitrary impositions" or "purposeless restraints" at odds with the Due Process Clause of the Fourteenth Amendment. *Poe v. Ullman*, 367 U.S. 497, 543 (1961). I conclude that the statute's application to the doctors has not been shown to be unconstitutional, but I write separately to give my reasons for analyzing the substantive due process claims as I do, and for rejecting this one.

IV

B

The State has put forward several interests to justify the Washington law as applied to physicians treating terminally ill patients, even those competent to make responsible choices: protecting life generally, discouraging suicide even if knowing and voluntary, and protecting terminally ill patients from involuntary suicide and euthanasia, both voluntary and nonvoluntary.

It is not necessary to discuss the exact strengths of the first two claims of justification in the present circumstances, for the third is dispositive for me. That third justification is different from the first two, for it addresses specific features of respondents' claim, and it opposes that claim not with a moral judgment contrary to respondents', but with a recognized state interest in the protection of nonresponsible individuals and those who do not stand in relation either to death or to their physicians as do the patients whom respondents describe. The State claims interests in protecting patients from mistakenly and involuntarily deciding to end their lives, and in guarding against both voluntary and involuntary euthanasia. Leaving aside any difficulties in coming to a clear concept of imminent death, mistaken decisions may result from inadequate palliative care or a terminal prognosis that turns out to be error; coercion and abuse may stem from the large medical bills that family members cannot bear or unreimbursed hospitals decline to shoulder. Voluntary and involuntary euthanasia may result once doctors are authorized to prescribe lethal medication in the first instance, for they might find it pointless to distinguish between patients who administer their own fatal drugs and those who wish not to, and their compassion for those who suffer may obscure the distinction between those who ask for death and those who may be unable to request it. The argument is that a progression would occur, obscuring the line between the ill and the dying, and between the responsible and the unduly influenced, until ultimately doctors and perhaps others would abuse a limited freedom to aid suicides by yielding to the impulse to end another's suffering under conditions going beyond the narrow limits the respondents propose. The State thus argues, essentially, that respondents' claim is not as narrow as it sounds, simply because no recognition of the interest they assert could be limited to vindicating those interests and affecting no others. The State says that the claim, in practical effect, would entail consequences that the State could, without doubt, legitimately act to prevent.

The State, however, goes further, to argue that dependence on the vigilance of physicians will not be enough. First, the lines proposed here (particularly the requirement of a knowing and voluntary decision by the patient) would be more difficult to draw than the lines that have limited other recently recognized due process rights. Limiting a state from prosecuting use of artificial contraceptives by married couples posed no practical threat to the State's capacity to regulate contraceptives in other ways that were assumed at the time of *Poe* to be legitimate; the trimester measurements of *Roe* and the viability determination of *Casey* were easy to make with a real degree of certainty. But the knowing and responsible mind is harder to assess. Second, this difficulty could become the greater by combining with another fact within the realm of plausibility, that physicians simply would not be assiduous to preserve the line. They have compassion, and those who would be willing to assist in suicide at all might be the most susceptible to the wishes of a patient, whether the patient were technically quite responsible or not. Physicians, and their hospitals, have their own financial incentives, too, in this new age of managed care. Whether acting from compassion or under some other influence, a physician who would provide a drug for a patient to administer might well go the further step of administering the drug himself; so, the barrier between assisted suicide and euthanasia could become porous, and the line between voluntary and involuntary euthanasia as well. The case for the slippery slope is fairly made out here, not because recognizing one due process right would leave a court with no principled basis to avoid recognizing another, but because there is a plausible case that the right claimed would not be readily containable by reference to facts about the mind that are matters of difficult judgment, or by gatekeepers who are subject to temptation, noble or not.

Respondents propose an answer to all this, the answer of state regulation with teeth. Legislation proposed in several States, for example, would authorize physician-assisted suicide but require two qualified physicians to confirm the patient's diagnosis, prognosis, and competence; and would mandate that the patient make repeated requests witnessed by at least two others over a specified time span; and would impose reporting requirements and criminal penalties for various acts of coercion.

I take it that the basic concept of judicial review with its possible displacement of legislative judgment bars any finding that a legislature has acted arbitrarily when the following conditions are met: there is a serious factual controversy over the feasibility of recognizing the claimed right without at the same time making it impossible for the State to engage in an undoubtedly legitimate exercise of power; facts necessary to resolve the controversy are not readily ascertainable through the judicial process; but they are more readily subject to discovery through legislative factfinding and experimentation. It is assumed in this case, and must be, that a State's interest in protecting those unable to make responsible decisions and those who make no decisions at all entitles the State to bar aid to any but a knowing and responsible person intending suicide, and to prohibit euthanasia. How, and how far, a State should act in that interest are judgments for the State, but the legitimacy of its action to deny a physician the option to aid any but the knowing and responsible is beyond question.

Since there is little experience directly bearing on the issue, the most that can be said is that whichever way the Court might rule today, events could overtake its assumptions, as experimentation in some jurisdictions confirmed or discredited the concerns about progression from assisted suicide to euthanasia.

Legislatures, on the other hand, have superior opportunities to obtain the facts necessary for a judgment about the present controversy. Not only do they have more flexible mechanisms for factfinding than the Judiciary, but their mechanisms include the power to experiment, moving forward and pulling back as facts emerge within their own jurisdictions. There is, indeed, good reason to suppose that in the absence of a judgment for respondents here, just such experimentation will be attempted in some of the States.

I do not decide here what the significance might be of legislative foot-dragging in ascertaining the facts going to the State's argument that the right in question could not be confined as claimed. Sometimes a court may be bound to act regardless of the institutional preferability of the political branches as forums for addressing constitutional claims. Now, it is enough to say that our examination of legislative reasonableness should consider the fact that the Legislature of the State of Washington is no more obviously at fault than this Court is in being uncertain about what would happen if respondents prevailed today. We therefore have a clear question about which institution, a legislature or a court, is relatively more competent to deal with an emerging issue as to which facts currently unknown could be dispositive. The answer has to be, for the reasons already stated, that the legislative process is to be preferred. There is a closely related further reason as well.

One must bear in mind that the nature of the right claimed, if recognized as one constitutionally required, would differ in no essential way from other constitutional rights guaranteed by enumeration or derived from some more definite textual source than "due process." An unenumerated right should not therefore be recognized, with the effect of displacing the legislative ordering of things, without the assurance that its recognition would prove as durable as the recognition of those other rights differently derived. To recognize a right of lesser promise would simply create a constitutional regime too uncertain to bring with it the expectation of finality that is one of this Court's central obligations in making constitutional decisions.

Legislatures, however, are not so constrained. The experimentation that should be out of the question in constitutional adjudication displacing legislative judgments is entirely proper, as well as highly desirable, when the legislative power addresses an emerging issue like assisted suicide. The Court should accordingly stay its hand to allow reasonable legislative consideration. While I do not decide for all time that respondents' claim should not be recognized, I acknowledge the legislative institutional competence as the better one to deal with that claim at this time.

JUSTICE GINSBURG, concurring in the judgments.

I concur in the Court's judgments in these cases substantially for the reasons stated by Justice O'Connor in her concurring opinion.

JUSTICE BREYER, concurring in the judgments.

I agree with the Court in *Vacco v. Quill*, that the articulated state interests justify the distinction drawn between physician assisted suicide and withdrawal of life-support. I also agree with the Court that the critical question in both of the cases before us is whether "the 'liberty' specially protected by the Due Process Clause includes a right" of the sort that the respondents assert. *Washington v. Glucksberg*. I do not agree, however, with the Court's formulation of that claimed "liberty" interest. The Court describes it as a "right to commit suicide with another's assistance." But I would not reject the respondents' claim without considering a different formulation, for which our legal tradition may provide greater support. That formulation would use words roughly like a "right to die with dignity." But irrespective of the exact words used, at its core would lie personal control over the manner of death, professional medical assistance, and the avoidance of unnecessary and severe physical suffering—combined.

. . . Justice Harlan's dissenting opinion in *Poe v. Ullman*, 367 U.S. 497 (1961), offers some support for such a claim. In that opinion, Justice Harlan referred to the "liberty" that the Fourteenth Amendment protects as including "a freedom from all substantial arbitrary impositions and purposeless restraints" and also as recognizing that "certain interests require particularly careful scrutiny of the state needs asserted to justify their abridgment." Id., at 543. The "certain interests" to which Justice Harlan referred may well be similar (perhaps identical) to the rights, liberties, or interests that the Court today, as in the past, regards as "fundamental."

I do not believe, however, that this Court need or now should decide whether or a not such a right is "fundamental." That is because, in my view, the avoidance of severe physical pain (connected with death) would have to comprise an essential part of any successful claim and because, as Justice O'Connor points out, the laws before us do not force a dying person to undergo that kind of pain.

Were the legal circumstances different—for example, were state law to prevent the provision of palliative care, including the administration of drugs as needed to avoid pain at the end of life—then the law's impact upon serious and otherwise unavoidable physical pain (accompanying death) would be more directly at issue. And as Justice O'Connor suggests, the Court might have to revisit its conclusions in these cases.

FOR DISCUSSION

How does the Court determine what constitutes the "liberty interest" protected by the Due Process Clause? The lower courts argued that this Washington law was inconsistent with the privacy protections extended in *Roe v. Wade* and the undue burden guarantee of *Planned Parenthood v. Casey*; do you agree or disagree with that argument?

RELATED CASE

***Cruzan v. Director, Missouri Dept. of Health:* 497 U.S. 261 (1990).**

The Supreme Court recognized that individuals could refuse medical treatment under the Due Process Clause; however, individuals who were incompetent could not exercise these rights. The Court declared constitutional attempts by the state of Missouri to preserve, against the wishes of her parents, the life of a woman in a permanent vegetative condition.

VACCO V. QUILL

521 U.S. 793, 117 S.Ct. 2293, 138 L.Ed. 2d 834 (1997)

New York law criminalizes the commission or attempting of suicide but allows patients to refuse life-sustaining medical treatment. The petitioners—physicians and terminally ill patients—challenged the state law under the Equal Protection Clause of the Fourteenth Amendment. They argued that because the law allows for the refusal of life-sustaining medical treatment but prohibits physician-assisted suicide, it treats two substantially similar classes differently to an extent that rises to the level of unconstitutionality. The district court disagreed, noting the state's interest in protecting life and the difference between the two groups. The court of appeals reversed, pointing out that the law did not treat equally all terminally ill persons who "wish to hasten their deaths" and finding no legitimate state interest to justify the distinction.

Vote: 9–0

CHIEF JUSTICE REHNQUIST delivered the opinion of the Court.

The Equal Protection Clause commands that no State shall "deny to any person within its jurisdiction the equal protection of the laws." This provision creates no substantive rights. *San Antonio Independent School Dist. v. Rodriguez*, 411 U.S. 1, 33 (1973) at 59 (Stewart, J., concurring). Instead, it embodies a general rule that States must treat like cases alike but may treat unlike cases accordingly. *Plyler v. Doe*, 457 U.S. 202, 216 (1982). If a legislative classification or distinction "neither burdens a fundamental right nor targets a suspect class, we will uphold [it] so long as it bears a rational relation to some legitimate end." *Romer v. Evans*, 517 U.S. 620 (1996).

New York's statutes outlawing assisting suicide affect and address matters of profound significance to all New Yorkers alike. They neither infringe fundamental rights nor involve suspect classifications. These laws are therefore entitled to a "strong presumption of validity." *Heller v. Doe*, 509 U.S. 312, 319 (1993).

On their faces, neither New York's ban on assisting suicide nor its statutes permitting patients to refuse medical treatment treat anyone differently than anyone else or draw any distinctions between persons. Everyone, regardless of physical condition, is entitled, if competent, to refuse unwanted lifesaving medical treatment; no one is permitted to assist a suicide. Generally speaking, laws that apply evenhandedly to all "unquestionably comply" with the Equal Protection Clause.

The Court of Appeals, however, concluded that some terminally ill people—those who are on life-support systems—are treated differently than those who are not, in that the former may "hasten death" by ending treatment, but the latter may not "hasten death" through physician-assisted suicide. This conclusion depends on the submission that ending or refusing lifesaving medical treatment "is nothing more nor less than assisted suicide." Unlike the Court of Appeals, we think the distinction between assisting suicide and withdrawing life-sustaining treatment, a distinction widely recognized and endorsed in the medical profession and in our legal traditions, is both important and logical; it is certainly rational.

The law has long used actors' intent or purpose to distinguish between two acts that may have the same result. Put differently, the law distinguishes actions taken "because of" a given end from actions taken "in spite of" their unintended but foreseen consequences.

This Court has also recognized, at least implicitly, the distinction between letting a patient die and making that patient die. In *Cruzan v. Director, Mo. Dept. of Health*, 497 U.S. 261, 278 (1990), we concluded that "the principle that a competent person has a constitutionally protected liberty interest in refusing unwanted medical treatment may be inferred from our prior decisions," and we assumed the existence of such a right for purposes of that case. But our assumption of a right to refuse treatment was grounded not, as the Court of Appeals supposed, on the proposition that patients have a general and abstract "right to hasten death," but on well established, traditional rights to bodily integrity and freedom from unwanted touching. In fact, we observed that "the majority of States in this country have laws imposing criminal penalties on one who assists another to commit suicide." *Cruzan* therefore provides no support for the notion that refusing life-sustaining medical treatment is "nothing more nor less than suicide."

For all these reasons, we disagree with respondents' claim that the distinction between refusing lifesaving medical treatment and assisted suicide is "arbitrary" and "irrational." Granted, in some cases, the line between the two may not be clear, but certainty is not required, even were it possible. Logic and contemporary practice support New York's judgment that the two acts are different, and New York may therefore, consistent with the Constitution, treat them differently. By permitting everyone to refuse unwanted medical treatment while prohibiting anyone from assisting a suicide, New York law follows a longstanding and rational distinction.

New York's reasons for recognizing and acting on this distinction—including prohibiting intentional killing and preserving life; preventing suicide; maintaining physicians' role as their patients' healers; protecting vulnerable people from indifference, prejudice, and psychological and financial pressure to end their lives; and avoiding a possible slide towards euthanasia—are discussed in greater detail in our opinion in *Glucksberg*. These valid and important public interests easily satisfy the constitutional requirement that a legislative classification bear a rational relation to some legitimate end.

The judgment of the Court of Appeals is reversed.

JUSTICE O'CONNOR, concurring.

I join the Court's opinions because I agree that there is no generalized right to "commit suicide." But respondents urge us to address the narrower question whether a mentally competent person who is experiencing great suffering has a constitutionally cognizable interest in controlling the circumstances of his or her imminent death. I see no need to reach that question in the context of the facial challenges to the New York and Washington laws at issue here. The parties and *amici* agree that in these States a patient who is suffering from a terminal illness and who is experiencing great pain has no legal barriers to obtaining medication, from qualified physicians, to alleviate that suffering, even to the point of causing unconsciousness and hastening death. In this light, even assuming that we would recognize such an interest, I agree that the State's interests in protecting those who are not truly competent or facing imminent death, or those whose decisions to hasten death would not truly be voluntary, are sufficiently weighty to justify a prohibition against physician-assisted suicide.

In sum, there is no need to address the question whether suffering patients have a constitutionally cognizable interest in obtaining relief from the suffering that they may experience in the last days of their lives. There is no dispute that dying patients in Washington and New York can obtain palliative care, even when doing so would hasten their deaths. The difficulty in defining terminal illness and the risk that a dying patient's request for assistance in ending his or her life might not be truly voluntary justifies the prohibitions on assisted suicide we uphold here.

JUSTICE STEVENS, concurring in the judgments.

In New York, a doctor must respect a competent person's decision to refuse or to discontinue medical treatment even though death will thereby ensue, but the same doctor would be guilty of a felony if she provided her patient assistance in committing suicide. Today we hold that the Equal Protection Clause is not violated by the resulting disparate treatment of two classes of terminally ill people who may have the same interest in hastening death. I agree that the distinction between permitting death to ensue from an underlying fatal disease and causing it to occur by the administration of medication or other means provides a constitutionally sufficient basis for the State's classification. Unlike the Court, however, I am not persuaded that in all cases there will in fact be a significant difference between the intent of the physicians, the patients or the families in the two situations.

There may be little distinction between the intent of a terminally-ill patient who decides to remove her life-support and one who seeks the assistance of a doctor in ending her life; in both situations, the patient is seeking to hasten a certain, impending death. The doctor's intent might also be the same in prescribing lethal medication as it is in terminating life support. A doctor who fails to administer medical treatment to one who is dying from a disease could be doing so with an intent to harm or kill that patient. Conversely, a doctor who prescribes lethal medication does not necessarily intend the patient's death—rather that doctor may seek simply to ease the patient's suffering and to comply with her wishes. The illusory character of any differences in intent or causation is confirmed by the fact that the American Medical Association unequivocally endorses the practice of terminal sedation—the administration of sufficient dosages of pain-killing medication to terminally ill patients to protect them from excruciating pain even when it is clear that the time of death will be advanced. The purpose of terminal sedation is to ease the suffering of the patient and comply with her wishes, and the actual cause of death is the administration of heavy doses of lethal sedatives. This same intent and causation may exist when a doctor complies with a patient's request for lethal medication to hasten her death.

Thus, although the differences the majority notes in causation and intent between terminating life-support and assisting in suicide support the Court's rejection of the respondents' facial challenge, these distinctions may be inapplicable to particular terminally ill patients and their doctors. Our holding today in *Vacco v. Quill* that the Equal Protection Clause is not violated by New York's classification, just like our holding in *Washington v. Glucksberg* that the Washington statute is not invalid on its face, does not foreclose the possibility that some applications of the New York statute may impose an intolerable intrusion on the patient's freedom.

JUSTICE SOUTER, concurring in the judgment.

Even though I do not conclude that assisted suicide is a fundamental right entitled to recognition at this time, I accord the claims raised by the patients and physicians in this case and *Washington v. Glucksberg* a high degree of importance, requiring a commensurate justification. The reasons that lead me to conclude in *Glucksberg* that the prohibition on assisted suicide is not arbitrary under the due process standard also support the distinction between assistance to suicide, which is banned, and practices such as termination of artificial life support and death-hastening pain medication, which are permitted. I accordingly concur in the judgment of the Court.

JUSTICE GINSBURG, concurring in the judgments.

I concur in the Court's judgments in these cases substantially for the reasons stated by Justice O'Connor in her concurring opinion.

JUSTICE BREYER, concurring in the judgments.

[See Justice Breyer's concurrence in *Washington v. Glucksberg.*]

FOR DISCUSSION

Is the legitimate state interest of preserving life in conflict with the *Roe v. Wade* line of precedents guaranteeing a right to abortion? Why or why not?

RELATED CASE

***Oregon v. Gonzales:* 546 U.S. 243 (2006).**

The Supreme Court determined that U.S. Attorney General John Ashcroft had erred in 2001 when he attempted to use the federal Controlled Substances Act of 1970 to prosecute physicians who prescribe lethal doses of controlled drugs to terminally ill patients. This decision ensured that Oregon's 1994 Death with Dignity Act, which authorized such actions on the part of physicians, could not be successfully challenged by the attorney general, a federal officer. The Court interpreted the Controlled Substances Act as criminalizing drug dealing by physicians, not as cause for the attorney general to prohibit a medical practice that was protected by state law.

GLOSSARY

***Amicus Curiae* Briefs:** "Friend of the court" briefs: third-party submissions before the Supreme Court, generally by interest groups, states and municipalities, and other interested stakeholders arguing issues facing the justices.

Fetal Viability: The point during pregnancy in which the fetus can survive outside the mother's womb. The location of this point is increasingly dependent on technology.

Fundamental Rights: The rights of an individual that are guaranteed by the Constitution and recognized as necessary for sustaining a democratic society.

Jurisprudence: Decisions and principles used to make a decision in law; includes the body of precedents and laws related to a particular principle or doctrine.

Penumbras of the Constitution: A *penumbra* is the shadow cast around the perimeter of the sun and moon. As used by the Court, the phrase indicates the implied rights and liberties that are a consequence of the enumerated rights and liberties articulated in the Constitution.

Protectionistic Legislation: Statutes, designed to provide guarantees and security for a vulnerable segment of the population, that might also limit the liberties of the targeted group of individuals. For example, laws designed to prevent minors from working an excessive number of hours a week to protect them from exploitation resulted in limitations on the ability of some minors to make a contract with an employer.

SELECTED BIBLIOGRAPHY

Behuniak, Susan M. And Arthur G. Svenson. 2002. *Physician-Assisted Suicide: The Anatomy of a Constitutional Law Issue.* New York: Rowman & Littlefield Publishers.

Cruz, David B. " 'The Sexual Freedom Cases': Contraception, Abortion, Abstinence, and the Constitution." *Harvard Civil Rights—Civil Liberties Law Review* 35 (Summer 2000): 299.

Garrow, David J. 1994. *Liberty & Sexuality: The Right of Privacy and the Making of Roe v. Wade*. New York: Macmillan.

Gorsuch, Neil M. 2009. *The Future of Assisted suicide and Euthanasia.* Princeton, NJ: Princeton University Press.

Hull, N.E.H. and Peter Charles Hoffer. 2010. Roe v. Wade: *The Abortion Rights Controversy in American History*, 2nd Ed. Lawrence, KS: University Press of Kansas.

Johnson, John W. 2005. *Griswold v. Connecticut: Birth Control and the Constitutional Right of Privacy*. Lawrence, KS: University Press of Kansas.

Kenyon, Andrew T. and Megan Richardson, eds. 2006. *New Dimensions in Privacy Law: International and Comparative Perspectives*. Cambridge, MA: Cambridge University Press.

O'Brien, David M. 1979. *Privacy, Law, and Public Policy*. New York: Praeger.

Rosen, Jeffrey and Benjamin Wittes. 2013. *Constitution 3.0: Freedom and Technological Change*. Washington, D.C.: Brookings Institution Press.

Silverstein, Helena. 2007. *Girls on the Stand: How Courts Fail Pregnant Minors*. New York: New York University Press.

Solove, Daniel J. 2013. *Nothing to Hide: The False Tradeoff Between Privacy and Security*. New Haven, CT: Yale University Press.

Tribe, Laurence H. 1992. *Abortion: The Clash of Absolutes*. New York: W. W. Norton.

Tone, Andrea. 2001. *Devices and Desires: A History of Contraceptives in America*. New York: Hill and Wang.

Urofsky, Melvin L. 2000. *Lethal Judgments: Assisted Suicide and American Law*. Lawrence, KS: University Press of Kansas.

Wilson, Joshua. 2016. *The New States of Abortion Politics*. Redwood City, CA: Stanford University Press.

CHAPTER X

The Constitution and Personhood

Timeline: Constitutional Personhood

1776 In proclaiming the colonies' separation from Great Britain, the Declaration of Independence uses the generic phrase, "all men are created equal."

1787 Original draft of the Constitution uses the word "person" 22 times.

1787 Article I, section 2 of the Constitution, referred to as the three-fifths compromise, considers slaves to count as three-fifths persons for the purposes of representation and taxation.

1819 In *Dartmouth College v. Woodward* the Supreme Court uses the Contract Clause to invalidate a state law changing the corporate charter of Dartmouth College, which is described as an artificial being.

1848 The Seneca Falls Convention issues a Declaration that says that "all men and women are created equal."

1857 In *Dred Scott v. Sanford* the Supreme Court rules that African-Americans were not federal citizens on the basis of their race, however, states could extend citizenship rights.

1868 Fourteenth Amendment ratified, declaring that all persons born or naturalized in the U.S. are citizens and protecting their privileges or immunities as citizens and guaranteeing equal protection and due process of law.

1886 In *County of Santa Clara v. Southern Pac. R. Company,* Chief Justice Waite suggests that the Fourteenth Amendment applies to corporations.

1875 The Supreme Court rules in *Minor v. Happersett* that although women are citizens of the United States, they may be denied the right to vote.

1888 In *Pembina Consolidated Silver Min. & Milling Co. v. Commonwealth of Pennsylvania* the Supreme Court declares that corporations are persons for the purposes of the Fourteenth Amendment.

1920 Nineteenth Amendment prohibits discrimination in voting on the basis of sex.

1924 Indian Citizenship Act finally extends citizenship to Native Americans.

1950 Isaac Aismov publishes *I, Robot.*

1973 The Supreme Court decides in *Roe v. Wade* that an unborn fetus is not a person for the purposes of the Constitution.

1990 The Human Genome Project begins, seeking to create an entire map of human DNA and genes.

1996	IBM computer Deep Blue defeats world chess champion Gary Kasparov in the opening game of a six-game chess match.
1996	Dolly, a sheep, is the first successful cloned mammal.
2010	In *Citizens United v. Federal Election Commission*, the Supreme Court rules that imposing limits on corporate political expenditures is a form of censorship and a violation of the free speech rights of corporations.
2011–2016	During this period, 11 states attempted to place constitutional measures on the ballot to extend personhood rights to fetuses, none were successful.
2014	In *Burwell v. Hobby Lobby Stores, Inc*, the Supreme Court rules that under federal law a closely-held for-profit business is a person, and its religious freedom rights are violated if forced to provide for contraceptives for women in its insurance as required under the Affordable Care Act.

INTRODUCTION

"We the people" are the first three words of the Constitution. Legally it should be simple to decide who is part of that "we," but it is not always clear who or what the "we" entails. On one level the discussion might be about whether non-citizens, such as aliens or undocumented individuals—those who are illegally in the United States—are entitled to constitutional protections. Should individuals born on US soil to individuals who are illegally in the country be entitled to US citizenship, as proscribed in Article I of the Fourteenth Amendment? Recent debates over immigration policy have led some to question this provision. On another level, discussion might focus on whether even those who are citizens are entitled to the same rights. For example, individuals under the age of eighteen born in the US to citizens are citizens, but they do not enjoy all the rights that those age eighteen and over have. They cannot vote but they can in some situations be charged with crimes as adults. Individuals convicted of felonies lose the right to vote temporarily or permanently in almost all the states, but they do not forfeit their Eighth Amendment rights against cruel and unusual punishment. Issues persist: What does it mean to be a citizen?; Who is eligible to be a citizen?; and What rights are attached to citizenship?

But "We the people" seems to beg another more fundamental question—are the people only real persons? By that, is a person, for constitutional purposes, only a biological person, *homo sapiens* to use biological classifications, or is a person something that can be construed more broadly? Constitutionally could a person be a thing, or something beyond what is normally thought to be a person is a biological sense? Could something that one considers to be property or a thing have rights? Normally not. In *Lynch v. Household Finance Corporation*, 405 U.S. 538 (1972), the Court declared in terms of drawing the line between persons and property that:

> Such difficulties indicate that the dichotomy between personal liberties and property rights is a false one. Property does not have rights. People have rights. The right to enjoy property without unlawful deprivation, no less than the right to speak or the right to travel, is in truth a "personal" right, whether the "property" in question be a welfare check, a home, or a savings account. In fact, a fundamental interdependence exists between the personal right to liberty and the personal right in property. Neither could have meaning without the other. That rights in property are basic civil rights has long been recognized.

On the one hand, one would think it would be simple—persons have rights, things do not. But as the history of the Constitution reveals (and as discussed in volume one of this textbook), there is a long tradition of the Supreme Court ascribing various rights to property. In fact, many histories of the Supreme Court's jurisprudence declare that the major turning point in its constitutional interpretation came in 1937 when in its famous *U.S. v. Carolene Products* footnote number four it shifted its emphasis from providing heightened scrutiny and protection to property rights and shifted it to individual civil rights and liberties. In effect, it shifted constitutional protection from property and things to real persons.

Thus, one would think that it is simple—persons have rights, property does not. The reality is that throughout American history the constitutional line between property and personhood has been thin and contentious. Who or what is a person constitutionally? The text of the original Constitution uses "person" 22 times. Many instances refer to eligibility to run for office such as president. But two places, Article I sections 1 and 9, refer to "other persons" when discussing enslaved individuals for the purposes of determining congressional representation, apportioning taxes, and regulating slave trade. They and Indians were to be counted as "three-fifths" of white male persons when it came to representation. Additionally, the Bill of Rights in the Fifth Amendment uses the word "person" twice, and the remaining amendments use that word an additional 18 times. The Twelfth and Twenty-Second Amendments, in the context of presidential selection account for most of the reference to the term. But the Fourteenth Amendment, especially section 1, uses the word "person" multiple times.

> All persons born or naturalized in the United States, and subject to the jurisdiction thereof, are citizens of the United States and of the State wherein they reside. No State shall make or enforce any law which shall abridge the privileges or immunities of citizens of the United States; nor shall any State deprive any person of life, liberty, or property, without due process of law; nor deny to any person within its jurisdiction the equal protection of the laws.

Who is a person and what constitutional rights attach to that designation? Answering this question is not just legally difficult, but it too has perplexed philosophers, scientists, and theologians. The reason why this distinction—between person and property or thing—is important, is because the label carries powerful implications. For St. Augustine of Hippo, only humans or real persons had souls, which meant that only they had eternal life and would enjoy life after death in Heaven. Additionally, St. Augustine and others did not see a fetus as initially having a soul—ensoulment—until several weeks of development in the uterus. Until ensoulment they were not persons, and if a miscarriage resulted before that point, theologically a person had not died.

For philosophers, being a person was also critical in terms of rights. Immanuel Kant contended that only persons have a concept of dignity and autonomy, meaning that for ethical purposes, they must be treated with respect and as "ends in themselves." John Locke's *Two Treatises of Government,* an important philosophical basis of the Declaration of Independence, the Constitution, and a major influence on many of the constitutional framers, describes the protections of life, liberty, and estate as the proper purpose of government. Individuals—presumably real persons—enjoy these inalienable natural rights, including a right to own property or things, entities that do not seem to have any rights. Being a person is important constitutionally, but deciding who a person is, is not so easy, as evidenced by the Genome project and identifying the DNA structure that make us uniquely human that distinguishes us from other primates. In some cases, DNA research suggests that there is less than a one-percent DNA difference between *homo sapiens* and some primates. The point here is that there is no definitive answer regarding what constitutes or defines a person. It is a matter of profound moral, religious, scientific, and political debate. Given the complexity of defining personhood from those perspectives, it should not be a surprise that it is equally as difficult defining who or what counts constitutionally as a person.

This chapter examines the concept of constitutional personhood. Two recent lines of court decisions have forced this debate. The first is over abortion, the second over campaign finance and free speech rights for corporations. In the former case, the issue as first raised in *Roe v. Wade,* 410 U.S. 113 (1973) is whether a fetus is a person and therefore entitled to a right to life, the latter as raised in *Citizens United v. Federal Election Commission,* 558 U.S. 310 (2010) is over whether the government can ban or regulate money spent by corporations for political purposes. But both lines of cases have expanded the discussion much further beyond the topic beyond their original issues to encompass questions about under circumstances the government may regulate abortions (the subject of Chapter IX) and whether corporations are persons who have a right to freedom of religion.

Additionally, for reasons to be discussed below, changes in social attitudes and technological developments are potentially pushing other boundaries, asking whether in some circumstances animals enjoy certain rights as persons, and whether robots should similarly enjoy such rights. Finally, in terms of something that might sound a little like science fiction, should space aliens, if they exist and visit the United States, enjoy constitutional protections. This chapter engages these questions in exploring constitutional personhood.

Who Is a Person? Slaves, Women, Children, and Fetuses

The starting point for understanding constitutional personhood is with real natural persons. There is no debate that real biological persons, especially U.S. citizens, age eighteen or older, living in the country, who are not felons, enjoy the full protections of the Constitution and the Bill of Rights. Exactly what those rights are is the subject of this entire volume. Thus one can argue that these individuals enjoy full constitutional personhood, at least today. But what about others? At one time the full range of constitutional protections did not extend to other persons including immigrants—(at least not to those who were here illegally), Native-Americans, African-Americans (both enslaved and free), women, and children. All of these individuals were either denied full or partial constitutional personhood until very recently. In fact, deciding who was a person for representation and taxation purposes was one of the central debates and dividing lines during the 1787 Constitutional Convention.

One of the first major conflicts in Philadelphia during the Constitutional Convention was over the structure of the new Congress. The Virginia delegation, which represented the most populous states, contended for representation based on population. The New Jersey delegation proposed the small state plan which argued for a Congress that continued to allocate representation equally among the states. The compromise Connecticut plan resulted in a bicameral Congress with a Senate based on equal representation and a House of Representatives premised on a per capita proportional representation.

Once that compromise was effected, the second line of debate was between the slave and free states: How should the enslaved and, with that, Native-Americans or Indians be counted both for representation and taxation purposes? Both sides agreed first that Native-Americans would not be counted—they were not US citizens but were distinct sovereign people or persons dwelling within the United States. Not until the Indian Citizenship Act of 1924 would they be considered citizens and counted for the purposes of representation, taxation, and rights as constitutional persons. But slaves were another matter in 1787. Southern states wanted to count them for the purposes of representation, but they did not want them to count for the purposes of taxation. Although eager to tax them, Northern states saw no reason that slaves who were not entitled to vote, and who were disproportionally located in the South, should count toward representation. The result was the famous three-fifths compromise found in Article I, section 2 of the Constitution.

> Representatives and direct Taxes shall be apportioned among the several States which may be included within this Union, according to their respective Numbers, which shall be determined by adding to the whole Number of free Persons, including those bound to Service for a Term of Years, and excluding Indians not taxed, three fifths of all other Persons.

Slaves in the original Constitution, were considered three-fifths persons. But what rights did these slaves have? The Supreme Court addressed that issue in ***Dred Scott v. Sanford*, 60 U.S. 393 (1857)**. The case involved whether an individual who was a slave and was taken from a slave state in the South to free territory in Minnesota became emancipated as a result. When his owner took Dred Scott to Minnesota, he moved the latter across the line demarcating slave versus free territory, as defined by the 1920 Missouri Compromise. Chief Justice Taney declared that slaves were legally property and that the Framers did not intend African Americans to be considered constitutional persons with rights. Using the Fifth Amendment due process provision to protect the rights of slave owners to their property, Taney ruled that the Missouri Compromise had unconstitutionally sought to deprive slave holders ownership of their property rights. African American were not constitutional persons because of their race. In 1868, after the Civil War, the Fourteenth Amendment overturned *Dred* Scott and extended citizenship to all persons born or naturalized within the United States regardless of their race or previous condition of servitude.

But African Americans were not the only individuals denied full constitutional personhood. Women too occupied a subordinate status under the original Constitution. Abigail Adams admonished her husband John Adams to "remember the ladies" when he and the Framers deliberated at the Second Continental Congress in 1776; however, they largely ignored the rights of women. The 1787 Constitution was largely silent on the rights of women, leaving it up to state law to decide issues of voting, property, and other rights for them. Reflecting the western value of **coverture**, women enjoyed few rights where it was assumed their husband or fathers would oversee them. The movement for women's constitutional rights greatly expanded with the 1848 Seneca Falls convention, which was organized by Lucretia Mott and Elizabeth Cady Stanton.

The Convention issued a declaration, reflecting the original Declaration of Independence, stating that "We hold these truths to be self-evident: that all men and women are created equal; that they are endowed by their Creator with certain inalienable rights; that among these are life, liberty, and the pursuit of happiness."

Some women who were part of the abolitionist movement, also urged support for the Fourteenth and Fifteenth Amendments, hoping their passage would lead to giving women equal rights to men, including the right to vote. Two Supreme Court decisions largely crushed that hope. First in *Bradwell v. Illinois*, 83 U.S. 130 (1872), the Court rejected a Fourteenth Amendment claim by Myra Bradwell who argued that a state law preventing women from practicing law was a violation of the Privileges or Immunities clause. Although the Court acknowledged that women were persons and citizens, it ruled nonetheless that the State of Illinois could deny Bradwell the right to practice law. The decision noted that English law denied this right to women. Moreover, the Court declared: "That God designed the sexes to occupy different spheres of action, and that it belonged to men to make, apply, and execute the laws, was regarded as an almost axiomatic truth" (132).

Two years later in *Minor v. Happersett*, 88 U.S. 162 (1874), the Supreme Court again acknowledged that women were citizens but also ruled that voting was not one of the privileges or immunities attached to such citizenship, and that states could therefore deny it to women. The 19th Amendment, ratified in 1920, overturned *Minor*, and prohibited discrimination against women with regard to the right to vote. Long after acknowledging the right of women to practice law and engage in many other traditionally-male occupations, society continues to debate the degree to which women should be able to engage in military combat.

The rights of children, like women, were largely left out of the original Constitution, leaving it up to state law to define when one became an adult and before that point, what rights they had. Fathers had nearly complete power or control over children who were not originally offered constitutional rights. That began to change in the 1960s in cases such as *Tinker v. Des Moines*, 393 U.S. 503 (1969) (found in Chapter III) where the Court declared that First Amendment free speech rights of students do not stop at the school house door. Beginning in the 1960s the Supreme Court has come to recognize, as it said in *Planned Parenthood of Central Missouri v. Danforth*, 428 U.S. 52. 74 (1976), that: "Constitutional rights do not mature and come into being magically only when one attains the state-defined age of majority. Minors, as well as adults, are protected by the Constitution and possess constitutional rights."

Yet the Court also noted in that opinion that a "State has somewhat broader authority to regulate the activities of children than of adults" (75). Parents have a constitutional right to raise their children according to their discretion, and those rights must be balanced against the rights of their children. There is no debate that children are constitutional persons now, but they still do not enjoy the full range of rights that adults do. Those under the age of eighteen do not have a right to vote, and at least one court has limited the Second Amendment rights of minors, declaring juveniles had no right to carry a handgun, *U.S. v. Rene E.*, 583 F.3d 8 (1st Cir. 2009). Many laws remain confused over the rights or privileges or minors, ranging from issues related to determining at what age they may be held civilly or criminally responsible as adults for their acts or crimes, the types of punishments they be exposed to, their privacy rights, and even on questions on when they may purchase or consume tobacco or alcohol products.

But when do people become persons who have constitutional protections and rights? Do fetuses qualify as constitutional persons who are afforded rights? In *Roe v. Wade*, 410 U.S. 113 (1973) the Supreme Court said no, declaring "that the word 'person,' as used in the Fourteenth Amendment, does not include the unborn" (158) but referred only to postnatal life. *Roe* was a decision adjudicating the constitutionality of a Texas abortion law, finding that laws preventing women from terminating their pregnancies under certain circumstances were unconstitutional. Yet even in *Roe* the Court acknowledged some state interests in protecting or regulating abortions in order to promote maternal or fetal health. Even to this day, as the discussion on reproductive rights in Chapter IX points out, the legal framework regulating abortion is not premised upon the constitutional personhood of the fetus. Yet some states have sought to enact state laws declaring the fetus a person, raising questions about their constitutionality, while others have sought to enact fetal protection laws that would make it illegal for pregnant women to harm them though actions such as smoking, taking drugs, or consuming alcohol, or fetal homicide laws that would criminalize the killing of a fetus if its mother is assaulted or killed.

DRED SCOTT V. SANFORD

60 U.S. 393, 19 How. 393, 15 L.Ed. 691 (1857)

Dred Scott, a slave who was owned by an individual living in Missouri, was taken to Fort Snelling in the territory of Minnesota. Minnesota was located in free territory according to the Missouri Compromise. Dred Scott sued for his freedom, claiming that now that he was in free territory, he was a free individual. The case was initially heard in state court and then moved to a federal district court which ruled against Scott. The Supreme Court took the case.

CHIEF JUSTICE TANEY delivered the opinion of the court.

This case has been twice argued. After the argument at the last term, differences of opinion were found to exist among the members of the court; and as the questions in controversy are of the highest importance, and the court was at that time much pressed by the ordinary business of the term, it was deemed advisable to continue the case, and direct a re-argument on some of the points, in order that we might have an opportunity of giving to the whole subject a more deliberate consideration. It has accordingly been again argued by counsel, and considered by the court; and I now proceed to deliver its opinion.

There are two leading questions presented by the record:

1. Had the Circuit Court of the United States jurisdiction to hear and determine the case between these parties? And

2. If it had jurisdiction, is the judgment it has given erroneous or not?

The plaintiff in error, who was also the plaintiff in the court below, was, with his wife and children, held as slaves by the defendant, in the State of Missouri; and he brought this action in the Circuit Court of the United States for that district, to assert the title of himself and his family to freedom.

The declaration is in the form usually adopted in that State to try questions of this description, and contains the averment necessary to give the court jurisdiction; that he and the defendant are citizens of different States; that is, that he is a citizen of Missouri, and the defendant a citizen of New York.

The defendant pleaded in abatement to the jurisdiction of the court, that the plaintiff was not a citizen of the State of Missouri, as alleged in his declaration, being a negro of African descent, whose ancestors were of pure African blood, and who were brought into this country and sold as slaves.

To this plea the plaintiff demurred, and the defendant joined in demurrer. The court overruled the plea, and gave judgment that the defendant should answer over. And he thereupon put in sundry pleas in bar, upon which issues were joined; and at the trial the verdict and judgment were in his favor. Whereupon the plaintiff brought this writ of error.

Before we speak of the pleas in bar, it will be proper to dispose of the questions which have arisen on the plea in abatement.

That plea denies the right of the plaintiff to sue in a court of the United States, for the reasons therein stated.

If the question raised by it is legally before us, and the court should be of opinion that the facts stated in it disqualify the plaintiff from becoming a citizen, in the sense in which that word is used in the Constitution of the United States, then the judgment of the Circuit Court is erroneous, and must be reversed.

It is suggested, however, that this plea is not before us; and that as the judgment in the court below on this plea was in favor of the plaintiff, he does not seek to reverse it, or bring it before the court for revision by his writ of error; and also that the defendant waived this defence by pleading over, and thereby admitted the jurisdiction of the court.

But, in making this objection, we think the peculiar and limited jurisdiction of courts of the United States has not been adverted to. This peculiar and limited jurisdiction has made it necessary, in these courts, to adopt different rules and principles of pleading, so far as jurisdiction is concerned, from those which regulate courts of common law in England, and in the different States of the Union which have adopted the common-law rules.

In these last-mentioned courts, where their character and rank are analogous to that of a Circuit Court of the United States; in other words, where they are what the law terms courts of general jurisdiction; they are presumed to have jurisdiction, unless the contrary appears. No averment in the pleadings of the plaintiff is necessary, in order to give jurisdiction. If the defendant objects to it, he must plead it specially, and unless the fact on which he relies is found to be true by a jury, or admitted to be true by the plaintiff, the jurisdiction cannot be disputed in an appellate court.

Now, it is not necessary to inquire whether in courts of that description a party who pleads over in bar, when a plea to the jurisdiction has been ruled against him, does or does not waive his plea; nor whether upon a judgment in his favor on the pleas in bar, and a writ of error brought by the plaintiff, the question upon the plea in abatement would be open for revision in the appellate court. Cases that may have been decided in such courts, or rules that may have been laid down by common-law pleaders, can have no influence in the decision in this court. Because, under the Constitution and laws of the United States, the rules which govern the pleadings in its courts, in questions of jurisdiction, stand on different principles and are regulated by different laws.

This difference arises, as we have said, from the peculiar character of the Government of the United States. For although it is sovereign and supreme in its appropriate sphere of action, yet it does not possess all the powers which usually belong to the sovereignty of a nation. Certain specified powers, enumerated in the Constitution, have been conferred upon it; and neither the legislative, executive, nor judicial departments of the Government can lawfully exercise any authority beyond the limits marked out by the Constitution. And in regulating the judicial department, the cases in which the courts of the United States shall have jurisdiction are particularly and specifically enumerated and defined; and they are not authorized to take cognizance of any case which does not come within the description therein specified. Hence, when a plaintiff sues in a court of the United States, it is necessary that he should show, in his pleading, that the suit he brings is within the jurisdiction of the court, and that he is entitled to sue there. And if he omits to do this, and should, by any oversight of the Circuit Court, obtain a judgment in his favor, the judgment would be reversed in the appellate court for want of jurisdiction in the court below. The jurisdiction would not be presumed, as in the case of a common-law English or State court, unless the contrary appeared. But the record, when it comes before the appellate court, must show, affirmatively, that the inferior court had authority, under the Constitution, to hear and determine the case. And if the plaintiff claims a right to sue in a Circuit Court of the United States, under that provision of the Constitution which gives jurisdiction in controversies between citizens of different States, he must distinctly aver in his pleading that they are citizens of different States; and he cannot maintain his suit without showing that fact in the pleadings.

If, however, the fact of citizenship is averred in the declaration, and the defendant does not deny it, and put it in issue by plea in abatement, he cannot offer evidence at the trial to disprove it, and consequently cannot avail himself of the objection in the appellate court, unless the defect should be apparent in some other part of the record. For if there is no plea in abatement, and the want of jurisdiction does not appear in any other part of the transcript brought up by the writ of error, the undisputed averment of citizenship in the declaration must be taken in this court to be true. In this case, the citizenship is averred, but it is denied by the defendant in the manner required by the rules of pleading, and the fact upon which the denial is based is admitted by the demurrer. And, if the plea and demurrer, and judgment of the court below upon it, are before us upon this record, the question to be decided is, whether the facts stated in the plea are sufficient to show that the plaintiff is not entitled to sue as a citizen in a court of the United States.

And this being the case in the present instance, the plea in abatement is necessarily under consideration; and it becomes, therefore, our duty to decide whether the facts stated in the plea are or are not sufficient to show that the plaintiff is not entitled to sue as a citizen in a court of the United States.

This is certainly a very serious question, and one that now for the first time has been brought for decision before this court. But it is brought here by those who have a right to bring it, and it is our duty to meet it and decide it.

The question is simply this: Can a negro, whose ancestors were imported into this country, and sold as slaves, become a member of the political community formed and brought into existence by the Constitution of the United States, and as such become entitled to all the rights, and privileges, and immunities, guarantied by that instrument to the citizen? One of which rights is the privilege of suing in a court of the United States in the cases specified in the Constitution.

It will be observed, that the plea applies to that class of persons only whose ancestors were negroes of the African race, and imported into this country, and sold and held as slaves. The only matter in issue before the court, therefore, is, whether the descendants of such slaves, when they shall be emancipated, or who are born of parents who had become free before their birth, are citizens of a State, in the sense in which the word citizen is used in the Constitution of the United States. And this being the only matter in dispute on the pleadings, the court must be understood as speaking in this opinion of that class only, that is, of those persons who are the descendants of Africans who were imported into this country, and sold as slaves.

The situation of this population was altogether unlike that of the Indian race. The latter, it is true, formed no part of the colonial communities, and never amalgamated with them in social connections or in government. But although they were uncivilized, they were yet a free and independent people, associated together in nations or tribes, and governed by their own laws. Many of these political communities were situated in territories to which the white race claimed the ultimate right of dominion. But that claim was acknowledged to be subject to the right of the Indians to occupy it as long as they thought proper, and neither the English nor colonial Governments claimed or exercised any dominion over the tribe or nation by whom it was occupied, nor claimed the right to the possession of the territory, until the tribe or nation consented to cede it. These Indian Governments were regarded and treated as foreign Governments, as much so as if an ocean had separated the red man from the white; and their freedom has constantly been acknowledged, from the time of the first emigration to the English colonies to the present day, by the different Governments which succeeded each other. Treaties have been negotiated with them, and their alliance sought for in war; and the people who compose these Indian political communities have always been treated as foreigners not living under our Government. It is true that the course of events has brought the Indian tribes within the limits of the United States under subjection to the white race; and it has been found necessary, for their sake as well as our own, to regard them as in a state of pupilage, and to legislate to a certain extent over them and the territory they occupy. But they may, without doubt, like the subjects of any other foreign Government, be naturalized by the authority of Congress, and become citizens of a State, and of the United States; and if an individual should leave his nation or tribe, and take up his abode among the white population, he would be entitled to all the rights and privileges which would belong to an emigrant from any other foreign people.

We proceed to examine the case as presented by the pleadings.

The words 'people of the United States' and 'citizens' are synonymous terms, and mean the same thing. They both describe the political body who, according to our republican institutions, form the sovereignty, and who hold the power and conduct the Government through their representatives. They are what we familiarly call the 'sovereign people,' and every citizen is one of this people, and a constituent member of this sovereignty. The question before us is, whether the class of persons described in the plea in abatement compose a portion of this people, and are constituent members of this sovereignty? We think they are not, and that they are not included, and were not intended to be included, under the word 'citizens' in the Constitution, and can therefore claim none of the rights and privileges which that instrument provides for and secures to citizens of the United States. On the contrary, they were at that time considered as a subordinate and inferior class of beings, who had been subjugated by the dominant race, and, whether emancipated or not, yet remained subject to their authority, and had no rights or privileges but such as those who held the power and the Government might choose to grant them.

It is not the province of the court to decide upon the justice or injustice, the policy or impolicy, of these laws. The decision of that question belonged to the political or law-making power; to those who formed the sovereignty and framed the Constitution. The duty of the court is, to interpret the instrument they have framed, with the best lights we can obtain on the subject, and to administer it as we find it, according to its true intent and meaning when it was adopted.

In discussing this question, we must not confound the rights of citizenship which a State may confer within its own limits, and the rights of citizenship as a member of the Union. It does not by any means follow, because he has all the rights and privileges of a citizen of a State, that he must be a citizen of the United States. He may have all of the rights and privileges of the citizen of a State, and yet not be entitled to the rights and privileges of a citizen in any other State. For, previous to the adoption of the Constitution of the United States, every State had the undoubted right to confer on whomsoever it pleased the character of citizen, and to endow him with all its rights. But this character of course was confined to the boundaries of the State, and gave him no rights or privileges in other States beyond those secured to him by the laws of nations and the comity of States. Nor have the several States surrendered the power of conferring these rights and privileges by adopting the Constitution of the United States. Each State may still confer them upon an alien, or any one it thinks proper, or upon any class or description of persons; yet he would not be a citizen in the sense in which that word is used in the

Constitution of the United States, nor entitled to sue as such in one of its courts, nor to the privileges and immunities of a citizen in the other States. The rights which he would acquire would be restricted to the State which gave them. The Constitution has conferred on Congress the right to establish an uniform rule of naturalization, and this right is evidently exclusive, and has always been held by this court to be so. Consequently, no State, since the adoption of the Constitution, can by naturalizing an alien invest him with the rights and privileges secured to a citizen of a State under the Federal Government, although, so far as the State alone was concerned, he would undoubtedly be entitled to the rights of a citizen, and clothed with all the rights and immunities which the Constitution and laws of the State attached to that character.

It is very clear, therefore, that no State can, by any act or law of its own, passed since the adoption of the Constitution, introduce a new member into the political community created by the Constitution of the United States. It cannot make him a member of this community by making him a member of its own. And for the same reason it cannot introduce any person, or description of persons, who were not intended to be embraced in this new political family, which the Constitution brought into existence, but were intended to be excluded from it.

The question then arises, whether the provisions of the Constitution, in relation to the personal rights and privileges to which the citizen of a State should be entitled, embraced the negro African race, at that time in this country, or who might afterwards be imported, who had then or should afterwards be made free in any State; and to put it in the power of a single State to make him a citizen of the United States, and endue him with the full rights of citizenship in every other State without their consent? Does the Constitution of the United States act upon him whenever he shall be made free under the laws of a State, and raised there to the rank of a citizen, and immediately clothe him with all the privileges of a citizen in every other State, and in its own courts?

The court think the affirmative of these propositions cannot be maintained. And if it cannot, the plaintiff in error could not be a citizen of the State of Missouri, within the meaning of the Constitution of the United States, and, consequently, was not entitled to sue in its courts.

It is true, every person, and every class and description of persons, who were at the time of the adoption of the Constitution recognized as citizens in the several States, became also citizens of this new political body; but none other; it was formed by them, and for them and their posterity, but for no one else. And the personal rights and privileges guaranteed to citizens of this new sovereignty were intended to embrace those only who were then members of the several State communities, or who should afterwards by birthright or otherwise become members, according to the provisions of the Constitution and the principles on which it was founded. It was the union of those who were at that time members of distinct and separate political communities into one political family, whose power, for certain specified purposes, was to extend over the whole territory of the United States. And it gave to each citizen rights and privileges outside of his State which he did not before possess, and placed him in every other State upon a perfect equality with its own citizens as to rights of person and rights of property; it made him a citizen of the United States.

It becomes necessary, therefore, to determine who were citizens of the several States when the Constitution was adopted. And in order to do this, we must recur to the Governments and institutions of the thirteen colonies, when they separated from Great Britain and formed new sovereignties, and took their places in the family of independent nations. We must inquire who, at that time, were recognized as the people or citizens of a State, whose rights and liberties had been outraged by the English Government; and who declared their independence, and assumed the powers of Government to defend their rights by force of arms.

In the opinion of the court, the legislation and histories of the times, and the language used in the Declaration of Independence, show, that neither the class of persons who had been imported as slaves, nor their descendants, whether they had become free or not, were then acknowledged as a part of the people, nor intended to be included in the general words used in that memorable instrument.

It is difficult at this day to realize the state of public opinion in relation to that unfortunate race, which prevailed in the civilized and enlightened portions of the world at the time of the Declaration of Independence, and when the Constitution of the United States was framed and adopted. But the public history of every European nation displays it in a manner too plain to be mistaken.

They had for more than a century before been regarded as beings of an inferior order, and altogether unfit to associate with the white race, either in social or political relations; and so far inferior, that they had no rights which the white man was bound to respect; and that the negro might justly and lawfully be reduced to slavery for his benefit. He was bought and sold, and treated as an ordinary article of merchandise and traffic, whenever a profit could be made by it. This opinion was at that time fixed and universal in the civilized portion of the white race. It was regarded as an axiom in morals as well as in politics, which no one thought of disputing, or supposed to be open to dispute; and men in every grade and position in society daily and habitually acted upon it in their private pursuits, as well as in matters of public concern, without doubting for a moment the correctness of this opinion.

And in no nation was this opinion more firmly fixed or more uniformly acted upon than by the English Government and English people. They not only seized them on the coast of Africa, and sold them or held them in slavery for their own use; but they took them as ordinary articles of merchandise to every country where they could make a profit on them, and were far more extensively engaged in this commerce than any other nation in the world.

The opinion thus entertained and acted upon in England was naturally impressed upon the colonies they founded on this side of the Atlantic. And, accordingly, a negro of the African race was regarded by them as an article of property, and held, and bought and sold as such, in every one of the thirteen colonies which united in the Declaration of Independence, and afterwards formed the Constitution of the United States. The slaves were more or less numerous in the different colonies, as slave labor was found more or less profitable. But no one seems to have doubted the correctness of the prevailing opinion of the time.

The legislation of the different colonies furnishes positive and indisputable proof of this fact.

It would be tedious, in this opinion, to enumerate the various laws they passed upon this subject. It will be sufficient, as a sample of the legislation which then generally prevailed throughout the British colonies, to give the laws of two of them; one being still a large slaveholding State, and the other the first State in which slavery ceased to exist.

The province of Maryland, in 1717, (ch. 13, s. 5,) passed a law declaring 'that if any free negro or mulatto intermarry with any white woman, or if any white man shall intermarry with any negro or mulatto woman, such negro or mulatto shall become a slave during life, excepting mulattoes born of white women, who, for such intermarriage, shall only become servants for seven years, to be disposed of as the justices of the county court, where such marriage so happens, shall think fit; to be applied by them towards the support of a public school within the said county. And any white man or white woman who shall intermarry as aforesaid, with any negro or mulatto, such white man or white woman shall become servants during the term of seven years, and shall be disposed of by the justices as aforesaid, and be applied to the uses aforesaid.'

The other colonial law to which we refer was passed by Massachusetts in 1705, (chap. 6.) It is entitled 'An act for the better preventing of a spurious and mixed issue,' &c.; and it provides, that 'if any negro or mulatto shall presume to smite or strike any person of the English or other Christian nation, such negro or mulatto shall be severely whipped, at the discretion of the justices before whom the offender shall be convicted.'

And 'that none of her Majesty's English or Scottish subjects, nor of any other Christian nation, within this province, shall contract matrimony with any negro or mulatto; nor shall any person, duly authorized to solemnize marriage, presume to join any such in marriage, on pain of forfeiting the sum of fifty pounds; one moiety thereof to her Majesty, for and towards the support of the Government within this province, and the other moiety to him or them that shall inform and sue for the same, in any of her Majesty's courts of record within the province, by bill, plaint, or information.'

We give both of these laws in the words used by the respective legislative bodies, because the language in which they are framed, as well as the provisions contained in them, show, too plainly to be misunderstood, the degraded condition of this unhappy race. They were still in force when the Revolution began, and are a faithful index to the state of feeling towards the class of persons of whom they speak, and of the position they occupied throughout the thirteen colonies, in the eyes and thoughts of the men who framed the Declaration of Independence and established the State Constitutions and Governments. They show that a perpetual and impassable barrier was intended to be erected between the white race and the one which they had reduced to slavery, and governed as subjects with absolute and despotic power, and which they then looked upon as so far below them in the scale of created beings, that intermarriages between white persons and negroes or mulattoes were regarded as unnatural and immoral, and punished as crimes, not only in the parties, but in the person who joined them in marriage. And no distinction in this respect was made between the free negro or mulatto and the slave, but this stigma, of the deepest degradation, was fixed upon the whole race.

We refer to these historical facts for the purpose of showing the fixed opinions concerning that race, upon which the statesmen of that day spoke and acted. It is necessary to do this, in order to determine whether the general terms used in the Constitution of the United States, as to the rights of man and the rights of the people, was intended to include them, or to give to them or their posterity the benefit of any of its provisions.

The language of the Declaration of Independence is equally conclusive:

It begins by declaring that, 'when in the course of human events it becomes necessary for one people to dissolve the political bands which have connected them with another, and to *410 assume among the powers of the earth the separate and equal station to which the laws of nature and nature's God entitle them, a decent respect for the opinions of mankind requires that they should declare the causes which impel them to the separation.'

It then proceeds to say: 'We hold these truths to be self-evident: that all men are created equal; that they are endowed by their Creator with certain unalienable rights; that among them is life, liberty, and the pursuit of happiness; that to secure these rights, Governments are instituted, deriving their just powers from the consent of the governed.'

The general words above quoted would seem to embrace the whole human family, and if they were used in a similar instrument at this day would be so understood. But it is too clear for dispute, that the enslaved African race were not intended to be included, and formed no part of the people who framed and adopted this declaration; for if the language, as understood in that day, would embrace them, the conduct of the distinguished men who framed the Declaration of Independence would have been utterly and flagrantly inconsistent with the principles they asserted; and instead of the sympathy of mankind, to which they so confidently appealed, they would have deserved and received universal rebuke and reprobation.

Yet the men who framed this declaration were great men—high in literary acquirements—high in their sense of honor, and incapable of asserting principles inconsistent with those on which they were acting. They perfectly understood the meaning of the language they used, and how it would be understood by others; and they knew that it would not in any part of the civilized world be supposed to embrace the negro race, which, by common consent, had been excluded from civilized Governments and the family of nations, and doomed to slavery. They spoke and acted according to the then established doctrines and principles, and in the ordinary language of the day, and no one misunderstood them. The unhappy black race were separated from the white by indelible marks, and laws long before established, and were never thought of or spoken of except as property, and when the claims of the owner or the profit of the trader were supposed to need protection.

This state of public opinion had undergone no change when the Constitution was adopted, as is equally evident from its provisions and language.

The brief preamble sets forth by whom it was formed, for what purposes, and for whose benefit and protection. It declares that it is formed by the *people* of the United States; that is to say, by those who were members of the different political communities in the several States; and its great object is declared to be to secure the blessings of liberty to themselves and their posterity. It speaks in general terms of the *people* of the United States, and of *citizens* of the several States, when it is providing for the exercise of the powers granted or the privileges secured to the citizen. It does not define what description of persons are intended to be included under these terms, or who shall be regarded as a citizen and one of the people. It uses them as terms so well understood, that no further description or definition was necessary.

But there are two clauses in the Constitution which point directly and specifically to the negro race as a separate class of persons, and show clearly that they were not regarded as a portion of the people or citizens of the Government then formed.

One of these clauses reserves to each of the thirteen States the right to import slaves until the year 1808, if it thinks proper. And the importation which it thus sanctions was unquestionably of persons of the race of which we are speaking, as the traffic in slaves in the United States had always been confined to them. And by the other provision the States pledge themselves to each other to maintain the right of property of the master, by delivering up to him any slave who may have escaped from his service, and be found within their respective territories. By the first above-mentioned clause, therefore, the right to purchase and hold this property is directly sanctioned and authorized for twenty years by the people who framed the Constitution. And by the second, they pledge themselves to maintain and uphold the right of the master in the manner specified, as long as the Government they then formed should endure. And these two provisions show, conclusively, that neither the description of persons therein referred to, nor their descendants, were embraced in any of the other provisions of the Constitution; for certainly these two clauses were not intended to confer on them or their posterity the blessings of liberty, or any of the personal rights so carefully provided for the citizen.

FOR DISCUSSION

Why did Dred Scott lose his case? Did the Court actually rule on the merits of his claim? Note that this is a case about standing and the Court ruled that he was not entitled to sue for his freedom. Why not? Taney did not in this decision refer to the three-fifths clause. Can you figure out why?

MINOR V. HAPPERSETT

88 U.S. 162, 22 L.Ed. 627, 21 Wall. 162 (1874)

Virginia Minor, a leader in the women's suffragette movement, attempted to register to vote and was denied. She challenged as a violation of the Fourteenth Amendment a Missouri constitutional provision that limited the right to vote to male citizens. The Missouri Supreme Court ruled against her, and the case was appealed to the US Supreme Court.

Vote: Missouri Supreme Court decision upheld by a unanimous Supreme Court.

CHIEF JUSTICE WAITE delivered the opinion for the Court.

The question is presented in this case, whether, since the adoption of the fourteenth amendment, a woman, who is a citizen of the United States and of the State of Missouri, is a voter in that State, notwithstanding the provision of the constitution and laws of the State, which confine the right of suffrage to men alone. We might, perhaps, decide the case upon other grounds, but this question is fairly made. From the opinion we find that it was the only one decided in the court below, and it is the only one which has been argued here. The case was undoubtedly brought to this court for the sole purpose of having that question decided by us, and in view of the evident propriety there is of having it settled, so far as it can be by such a decision, we have concluded to waive all other considerations and proceed at once to its determination.

It is contended that the provisions of the constitution and laws of the State of Missouri which confine the right of suffrage and registration therefor to men, are in violation of the Constitution of the United States, and therefore void. The argument is, that as a woman, born or naturalized in the United States and subject to the jurisdiction thereof, is a citizen of the United States and of the State in which she resides, she has the right of suffrage as one of the privileges and immunities of her citizenship, which the State cannot by its laws or constitution abridge.

There is no doubt that women may be citizens. They are persons, and by the fourteenth amendment 'all persons born or naturalized in the United States and subject to the jurisdiction thereof' are expressly declared to be 'citizens of the United States and of the State wherein they reside.' But, in our opinion, it did not need this amendment to give them that position. Before its adoption the Constitution of the United States did not in terms prescribe who should be citizens of the United States or of the several States, yet there were necessarily such citizens without such provision. There cannot be a nation without a people. The very idea of a political community, such as a nation is, implies an association of persons for the promotion of their general welfare. Each one of the persons associated becomes a member of the nation formed by the association. He owes it allegiance and is entitled to its protection. Allegiance and protection are, in this connection, reciprocal obligations. The one is a compensation for the other; allegiance for protection and protection for allegiance.

For convenience it has been found necessary to give a name to this membership. The object is to designate by a title the person and the relation he bears to the nation. For this purpose the words 'subject,' 'inhabitant,' and 'citizen' have been used, and the choice between them is sometimes made to depend upon the form of the government. Citizen is now more commonly employed, however, and as it has been considered better suited to the description of one living under a republican government, it was adopted by nearly all of the States upon their separation from Great Britain, and was afterwards adopted in the Articles of Confederation and in the Constitution of the United States. When used in this sense it is understood as conveying the idea of membership of a nation, and nothing more.

To determine, then, who were citizens of the United States before the adoption of the amendment it is necessary to ascertain what persons originally associated themselves together to form the nation, and what were afterwards admitted to membership.

Looking at the Constitution itself we find that it was ordained and established by 'the people of the United States,' and then going further back, we find that these were the people of the several States that had before dissolved the political bands which connected them with Great Britain, and assumed a separate and equal station among the powers of the earth, and that had by Articles of Confederation and Perpetual Union, in which they took the name of 'the United States of America,' entered into a firm league of friendship with each other for their common defence, the security of their liberties and their mutual and general welfare, binding themselves to assist each other against all force offered to or attack made upon them, or any of them, on account of religion, sovereignty, trade, or any other pretence whatever.

Whoever, then, was one of the people of either of these States when the Constitution of the United States was adopted, became *ipso facto* a citizen—a member of the nation created by its adoption. He was one of the persons associating together to form the nation, and was, consequently, one of its original citizens. As to this there has never been a doubt. Disputes have arisen as to whether or not certain persons or certain classes of persons were part of the people at the time, but never as to their citizenship if they were.

Additions might always be made to the citizenship of the United States in two ways: first, by birth, and second, by naturalization. This is apparent from the Constitution itself, for it provides that 'no person except a natural-born citizen, or a citizen of the United States at the time of the adoption of the Constitution, shall be eligible to the office of President, and that Congress shall have power 'to establish a uniform rule of naturalization.' Thus new citizens may be born or they may be created by naturalization.

The Constitution does not, in words, say who shall be natural-born citizens. Resort must be had elsewhere to ascertain that. At common-law, with the nomenclature of which the framers of the Constitution were familiar, it was never doubted that all children born in a country of parents who were its citizens became themselves, upon their birth, citizens also. These were natives, or natural-born citizens, as distinguished from aliens or foreigners. Some authorities go further and include as citizens children born within the jurisdiction without reference to the citizenship of their parents. As to this class there have been doubts, but never as to the first. For the purposes of this case it is not necessary to solve these doubts. It is sufficient for everything we have now to consider that all children born of citizen parents within the jurisdiction are themselves citizens. The words 'all children' are certainly as comprehensive, when used in this connection, as 'all persons,' and if females are included in the last they must be in the first. That they are included in the last is not denied. In fact the whole argument of the plaintiffs proceeds upon that idea.

As early as 1804 it was enacted by Congress that when any alien who had declared his intention to become a citizen in the manner provided by law died before he was actually naturalized, his widow and children should be considered as citizens of the United States, and entitled to all rights and privileges as such upon taking the necessary oath; and in 1855 it was further provided that any woman who might lawfully be naturalized under the existing laws, married, or who should be married to a citizen of the United States, should be deemed and taken to be a citizen.

But if more is necessary to show that women have always been considered as citizens the same as men, abundant proof is to be found in the legislative and judicial history of the country. Thus, by the Constitution, the judicial power of the United States is made to extend to controversies between citizens of different States. Under this it has been uniformly held that the citizenship necessary to give the courts of the United States jurisdiction of a cause must be affirmatively shown on the record. Its existence as a fact may be put in issue and tried. If found not to exist the case must be dismissed. Notwithstanding this the records of the courts are full of cases in which the jurisdiction depends upon the citizenship of women, and not one can be found, we think, in which objection was made on that account. Certainly none can be found in which it has been held that women could not sue or be sued in the courts of the United States. Again, at the time of the adoption of the Constitution, in many of the States (and in some probably now) aliens could not inherit or transmit inheritance. There are a multitude of cases to be found in which the question has been presented whether a woman was or was not an alien, and as such capable or incapable of inheritance, but in no one has it been insisted that she was not a citizen because she was a woman. On the contrary, her right to citizenship has been in all cases assumed. The only question has been whether, in the particular case under consideration, she had availed herself of the right.

Other proof of like character might be found, but certainly more cannot be necessary to establish the fact that sex has never been made one of the elements of citizenship in the United States. In this respect men have never had an advantage over women. The same laws precisely apply to both. The fourteenth amendment did not affect the citizenship of women any more than it did of men. In this particular, therefore, the rights of Mrs. Minor do not depend upon the amendment. She has always been a citizen from her birth, and entitled to all the privileges and immunities of citizenship. The amendment prohibited the State, of which she is a citizen, from abridging any of her privileges and immunities as a citizen of the United States; but it did not confer citizenship on her. That she had before its adoption.

If the right of suffrage is one of the necessary privileges of a citizen of the United States, then the constitution and laws of Missouri confining it to men are in violation of the Constitution of the United States, as amended, and consequently void. The direct question is, therefore, presented whether all citizens are necessarily voters.

The Constitution does not define the privileges and immunities of citizens. For that definition we must look elsewhere. In this case we need not determine what they are, but only whether suffrage is necessarily one of them.

It certainly is nowhere made so in express terms. The United States has no voters in the States of its own creation. The elective officers of the United States are all elected directly or indirectly by State voters. The members of the House of Representatives are to be chosen by the people of the States, and the electors in each State must have the qualifications requisite for electors of the most numerous branch of the State legislature. Senators are to be chosen by the legislatures of the States, and necessarily the members of the legislature required to make the choice are elected by the voters of the State. Each State must appoint in such manner, as the legislature thereof may direct, the electors to elect the President and Vice-President. The times, places, and manner of holding elections for Senators and Representatives are to be prescribed in each State by the legislature thereof; but Congress may at any time, by law, make or alter such regulations, except as to the place of choosing Senators. It is not necessary to inquire whether this power of supervision thus given to Congress is sufficient to authorize any interference with the State laws prescribing the qualifications of voters, for no such interference has ever been attempted. The power of the State in this particular is certainly supreme until Congress acts.

The amendment did not add to the privileges and immunities of a citizen. It simply furnished an additional guaranty for the protection of such as he already had. No new voters were necessarily made by it. Indirectly it may have had that effect, because it may have increased the number of citizens entitled to suffrage under the constitution and laws of the States, but it operates for this purpose, if at all, through the States and the State laws, and not directly upon the citizen.

It is clear, therefore, we think, that the Constitution has not added the right of suffrage to the privileges and immunities of citizenship as they existed at the time it was adopted. This makes it proper to inquire whether suffrage was coextensive with the citizenship of the States at the time of its adoption. If it was, then it may with force be argued that suffrage was one of the rights which belonged to citizenship, and in the enjoyment of which every citizen must be protected. But if it was not, the contrary may with propriety be assumed.

When the Federal Constitution was adopted, all the States, with the exception of Rhode Island and Connecticut, had constitutions of their own. These two continued to act under their charters from the Crown. Upon an examination of those constitutions we find that in no State were all citizens permitted to vote. Each State determined for itself who should have that power. Thus, in New Hampshire, 'every male inhabitant of each town and parish with town privileges, and places unincorporated in the State, of twenty-one years of age and upwards, excepting paupers and persons excused from paying taxes at their own request,' were its voters; in Massachusetts 'every male inhabitant of twenty-one years of age and upwards, having a freehold estate within the commonwealth of the annual income of three pounds, or any estate of the value of sixty pounds;' in Rhode Island 'such as are admitted free of the company and society' of the colony; in Connecticut such persons as had 'maturity in years, quiet and peaceable behavior, a civil conversation, and forty shillings freehold or forty pounds personal estate,' if so certified by the selectmen; in New York 'every male inhabitant of full age who shall have personally resided within one of the counties of the State for six months immediately preceding the day of election . . . if during the time aforesaid he shall have been a freeholder, possessing a freehold of the value of twenty pounds within the county, or have rented a tenement therein of the yearly value of forty shillings, and been rated and actually paid taxes to the State;' in New Jersey 'all inhabitants . . . of full age who are worth fifty pounds, proclamation-money, clear estate in the same, and have resided in the county in which they claim a vote for twelve months immediately preceding the election;' in Pennsylvania 'every freeman of the age of twenty-one years, having resided in the State two years next before the election, and within that time paid a State or county tax which shall have been assessed at least six months before the election;' in Delaware and Virginia 'as exercised by law at present;' in Maryland 'all freemen above twenty-one years of age having a freehold of fifty acres of land in the county in which they offer to vote and residing therein, and all freemen having property in the State above the value of thirty pounds current money, and having resided in the county in which they offer to vote one whole year next preceding the election;' in North Carolina, for senators, 'all freemen of the age of twenty-one years who have been inhabitants of any one county within the State twelve months immediately preceding the day of election, and possessed of a freehold within the same county of fifty acres of land for six months next before and at the day of election,' and for members of the house of commons 'all freemen of the age of twenty-one years who have been inhabitants in any one county within the State twelve months immediately preceding the day of any election, and shall have paid public taxes;' in South Carolina 'every free white man of the age of twenty-one years, being a citizen of the State and having resided therein two years previous to the day of election, and who hath a freehold of fifty acres of land, or a town lot of which he hath been legally seized and possessed at least six months before such election, or (not having such freehold or town lot), hath been a resident within the election district in which he offers to give his vote six months before said election, and hath paid a tax the preceding year of three shillings sterling towards the support of the government;' and in Georgia such 'citizens and inhabitants of the State as shall have attained to the age of twenty-one years, and shall have paid tax for the year next preceding the election, and shall have resided six months within the county.'

In this condition of the law in respect to suffrage in the several States it cannot for a moment be doubted that if it had been intended to make all citizens of the United States voters, the framers of the Constitution would not have left it to implication. So important a change in the condition of citizenship as it actually existed, if intended, would have been expressly declared.

But if further proof is necessary to show that no such change was intended, it can easily be found both in and out of the Constitution. By Article 4, section 2, it is provided that 'the citizens of each State shall be entitled to all the privileges and immunities of citizens in the several States.' If suffrage is necessarily a part of citizenship, then the citizens of each State must be entitled to vote in the several States precisely as their citizens are. This is more than asserting that they may change their residence and become citizens of the State and thus be voters. It goes to the extent of insisting that while retaining their original citizenship they may vote in any State. This, we think, has never been claimed. And again, by the very terms of the amendment we have been considering (the fourteenth), 'Representatives shall be apportioned among the several States according to their respective numbers, counting the whole number of persons in each State, excluding Indians not taxed. But when the right to vote at any election for the choice of electors for President and Vice-President of the United States, representatives in Congress, the executive and judicial officers of a State, or the members of the legislature thereof, is denied to any of the male inhabitants of such State, being twenty-one years of age and citizens of the United States, or in any way abridged, except for participation in the rebellion, or other crimes, the basis of representation therein shall be reduced in the proportion which the number of such male citizens shall bear to the whole number of male citizens twenty-one years of age in such State.' Why this, if it was not in the power of the legislature to deny the right of suffrage to some male inhabitants? And if suffrage was necessarily one of the absolute rights of citizenship, why confine the operation of the limitation to male inhabitants? Women and children are, as we have seen, 'persons.' They are counted in the enumeration upon which the apportionment is to be made, but if they were necessarily voters because of their citizenship unless clearly excluded, why inflict the penalty for the exclusion of males alone? Clearly, no such form of words would have been selected to express the idea here indicated if suffrage was the absolute right of all citizens.

And still again, after the adoption of the fourteenth amendment, it was deemed necessary to adopt a fifteenth, as follows: 'The right of citizens of the United States to vote shall not be denied or abridged by the United States, or by any State, on account of race, color, or previous condition of servitude.' The fourteenth amendment had already provided that no State should make or enforce any law which should abridge the privileges or immunities of citizens of the United States. If suffrage was one of these privileges or immunities, why amend the Constitution to prevent its being denied on account of race, &c.? Nothing is more evident than that the greater must include the less, and if all were already protected why go through with the form of amending the Constitution to protect a part?

It is true that the United States guarantees to every State a republican form of government. It is also true that no State can pass a bill of attainder, and that no person can be deprived of life, liberty, or property without due process of law. All these several provisions of the Constitution must be construed in connection with the other parts of the instrument, and in the light of the surrounding circumstances.

The guaranty is of a republican form of government. No particular government is designated as republican, neither is the exact form to be guaranteed, in any manner especially designated. Here, as in other parts of the instrument, we are compelled to resort elsewhere to ascertain what was intended.

The guaranty necessarily implies a duty on the part of the States themselves to provide such a government. All the States had governments when the Constitution was adopted. In all the people participated to some extent, through their representatives elected in the manner specially provided. These governments the Constitution did not change. They were accepted precisely as they were, and it is, therefore, to be presumed that they were such as it was the duty of the States to provide. Thus we have unmistakable evidence of what was republican in form, within the meaning of that term as employed in the Constitution. As has been seen, all the citizens of the States were not invested with the right of suffrage. In all, save perhaps New Jersey, this right was only bestowed upon men and not upon all of them. Under these circumstances it is certainly now too late to contend that a government is not republican, within the meaning of this guaranty in the Constitution, because women are not made voters.

The same may be said of the other provisions just quoted. Women were excluded from suffrage in nearly all the States by the express provision of their constitutions and laws. If that had been equivalent to a bill of attainder, certainly its abrogation would not have been left to implication. Nothing less than express language would have been employed to effect so radical a change. So also of the amendment which declares that no person shall be deprived of life, liberty, or property without due process of law, adopted as it was as early as 1791. If suffrage was intended to be included within its obligations, language better adapted to express that intent would most certainly have been employed. The right of suffrage, when granted, will be protected. He who has it can only be deprived of it by due process of law, but in order to claim protection he must first show that he has the right.

But we have already sufficiently considered the proof found upon the inside of the Constitution. That upon the outside is equally effective.

The Constitution was submitted to the States for adoption in 1787, and was ratified by nine States in 1788, and finally by the thirteen original States in 1790. Vermont was the first new State admitted to the Union, and it came in under a constitution which conferred the right of suffrage only upon men of the full age of twenty-one years, having resided. in the State for the space of one whole year next before the election, and who were of quiet and peaceable behavior. This was in 1791. The next year, 1792, Kentucky followed with a constitution confining the right of suffrage to free male citizens of the age of twenty-one years who had resided in the State two years or in the county in which they offered to vote one year next before the election. Then followed Tennessee, in 1796, with voters of freemen of the age of twenty-one years and upwards, possessing a freehold in the county wherein they may vote, and being inhabitants of the State or freemen being inhabitants of any one county in the State six months immediately preceding the day of election. But we need not particularize further. No new State has ever been admitted to the Union which has conferred the right of suffrage upon women, and this has never been considered a valid objection to her admission. On the contrary, as is claimed in the argument, the right of suffrage was withdrawn from women as early as 1807 in the State of New Jersey, without any attempt to obtain the interference of the United States to prevent it. Since then the governments of the insurgent States have been reorganized under a requirement that before their representatives could be admitted to seats in Congress they must have adopted new constitutions, republican in form. In no one of these constitutions was suffrage conferred upon women, and yet the States have all been restored to their original position as States in the Union.

Besides this, citizenship has not in all cases been made a condition precedent to the enjoyment of the right of suffrage. Thus, in Missouri, persons of foreign birth, who have declared their intention to become citizens of the United States, may under certain circumstances vote. The same provision is to be found in the constitutions of Alabama, Arkansas, Florida, Georgia, Indiana, Kansas, Minnesota, and Texas.

Certainly, if the courts can consider any question settled, this is one. For nearly ninety years the people have acted upon the idea that the Constitution, when it conferred citizenship, did not necessarily confer the right of suffrage. If *178 uniform practice long continued can settle the construction of so important an instrument as the Constitution of the United States confessedly is, most certainly it has been done here. Our province is to decide what the law is, not to declare what it should be.

We have given this case the careful consideration its importance demands. If the law is wrong, it ought to be changed; but the power for that is not with us. The arguments addressed to us bearing upon such a view of the subject may perhaps be sufficient to induce those having the power, to make the alteration, but they ought not to be permitted to influence our judgment in determining the present rights of the parties now litigating before us. No argument as to woman's need of suffrage can be considered. We can only act upon her rights as they exist. It is not for us to look at the hardship of withholding. Our duty is at an end if we find it is within the power of a State to withhold.

Being unanimously of the opinion that the Constitution of the United States does not confer the right of suffrage upon any one, and that the constitutions and laws of the several States which commit that important trust to men alone are not necessarily void, we

AFFIRM THE JUDGMENT.

FOR DISCUSSION

Are women persons according to the Court? Are they citizens? If yes to both questions, why are they not allowed to vote? Should not citizenship include the right to vote?

ROE V. WADE

410 U.S. 113, 93 S.Ct. 705, 35 L.Ed.2d 147 (1973)

Case located in Chapter IX starting on page 889.

FOR DISCUSSION

If life begins at conception as some religions (but certainly not all) believe, when does a human embryo become a person with constitutional rights? How are the rights ascribed to an embryo to be ranked or compared to any constitutional rights a woman would have? In cases of some assisted reproductive technologies, or in vitro fertilization, more fertilized human eggs than are necessary are produced. Do the unused ones have constitutional rights? Or what rights to frozen embryos have? Who might be able to assert such rights on the embryos' behalf?

A North Dakota Constitutional Measure No. 1 (Senate Concurrent Resolution No. 4009, 2013 Session Laws, Ch. 519) would have created and enacted a new section to Article I of the North Dakota Constitution that would state "The inalienable right to life of every human being at any stage of development must be recognized and protected." Voters at the polls rejected the amendment. But what if it had passed—would it have made embryos constitutional persons?

Corporate Personhood

As noted above, demarcating the lines between persons and property is often easier said than done. In most law schools 1Ls (as first year law students are called) property law is often a required class. One of the basic questions in that class is: What is property and who can own what? One learns that there are lots of different types of property. It can be classified as real versus personal or tangible versus intangible, for example. Along with these distinctions, the law describes interests in property as present or future interests, partial interests, or having full control over it, referred to as fee simple absolute in the case of land. Finally, when it comes to explaining rights in property there is a classic claim that property is like a bundle of sticks or rights. Property ownership vests individuals with power to use it, exclude others from it, or invest or sell it.

Property, one learns, is a very complex entity. It is different from mere possession of something. Contrary to the old adage that "possession is nine-tenths of the law," I might possess something illegally and therefore have no rights to it. Moreover, not all forms of possession are constitutionally recognized. Once an interest is constitutionally recognized as property, however, its owner has certain rights, among which is a Fifth and Fourteenth Amendment right to compensation if the government takes it for public use through eminent domain. Exactly what interests count as property and what constitutes a taking was discussed in Chapter VI of the first volume of this textbook.

Similarly, figuring out what is a person is difficult and involves philosophical, political, and theological issues. Must an entity have a human form or a certain DNA or genetic code to be a person? To be a person, as opposed to being an animal or a robot for example, must one be able to think at a higher level, be self-aware or reflect? Is personhood about the capacity to empathize? Does it require possession of a soul? Politically, to be a person, must an individual be capable of willing, assenting, or making deliberative choices such that one becomes a member of a political community perhaps through a social contract? Persons who are part of a political community thus secure certain rights, but their roles may vary depending on whether they are citizens or not, whether they are legally within the country, their age, and whether they have committed crimes or not. As is true of property, being a person includes a bundle of rights.

While figuring out what exactly property is and what rights are attached to it, property per se does not really have rights. As the Court said in *Lynch v. Household Finance Corporation*, 405 U.S. 538 (1972), people have rights in property, and one needs to look at a complex relationship between the two. The assumption is that there is a clean line distinguishing property from persons. But that is not always the case. Not all persons have the same rights, and in some cases entities that are not real human persons have rights. In legal fiction, some entities are considered to be persons entitled to legal and constitutional protection. One of the first entities to be ascribed rights were corporations.

One of the very first cases by the Supreme Court that described a corporation is *Trustees of Dartmouth College v. Woodward,* 4 Wheat. 518 (1819). Chief Justice Marshall described a corporation as an "artificial being" that allows real persons to come together for a variety of purposes. *Dartmouth College* is an important constitutional cases adjudicating the Contract clause of the Constitution and the power of a state to alter a corporate charter. Marshall's decision recognized that there is a connection between individuals and the rights they have to property and a need to provide some limits on the ability of the government to regulate the latter. However, the Court never went so far as saying that a corporation was a constitutionally recognized person.

The first instance where the Supreme Court did exactly that came after the ratification of the Fourteenth Amendment. Section one of that Amendment refers to "person" several times in terms of prohibiting states from denying privileges or immunities, due process, or equal protection of the laws to them. Legislative history of the Fourteenth Amendment indicate that its intent was both to overturn the Supreme Court's *Dred Scott* opinion and to afford legal protections to freed slaves. These were the intended persons. Yet in *County of Santa Clara v. Southern Pac. R. Co.* 118 U.S. 394 (1886), an otherwise obscure case regarding corporations and state taxing authority, Chief Justice Waite said at the start of the hearing: "The court does not wish to hear argument on the question whether the provision in the Fourteenth Amendment to the Constitution, which forbids a State to deny to any person within its jurisdiction the equal protection of the laws, applies to these corporations. We are all of opinion that it does." Thus in one sentence the Court seemed to declare that corporations were actually persons protected by the Fourteenth Amendment. It is not clear in reading in the decision that the Justices actually said that (read the case yourself and reach your own conclusion), but many scholars attribute to the *Santa Clara* opinion the origin of the claim, precedent, or legal fiction that corporations are persons.

However, the Court more clearly made that claim two years later in *Pembina Consolidated Silver Min. & Milling Co. v. Commonwealth of Pennsylvania*, 8 S.Ct. 737 (1888), another case addressing the ability of a state to tax an out-of-state company. In upholding the tax the Court unanimously declared:

> The inhibition of the amendment that no state shall deprive any person within its jurisdiction of the equal protection of the laws, was designed to prevent any person or class of persons from being singled out as a special subject for discriminating and hostile legislation. Under the designation of 'person' there is no doubt that a private corporation is included.

Pembina Consolidated is an overlooked case that unlike *Santa Clara* unambiguously states corporations are constitutional persons. Subsequent to this case, literally thousands of other state and federal courts have entertained the corporate personhood legal fiction. But just as courts have had to decide on what rights different types of persons possess, so too, they must establish the rights of corporate personhood.

Over time the Supreme Court has addressed this question several times, generally ruling that the Bill of Rights protections extend only to natural persons. For example, the Privileges and Immunities Clause of the 14th Amendment is limited to natural persons, *Hague v. CIO*, 307 U.S. 496, 514 (1939). Corporations have no privilege against self-incrimination under the 5th Amendment, *U.S. v. Kordel*, 397 U.S. 1 (1970), *Braswell v. United States*, 487 U.S. 99 (1988); *Bellis v. United States*, 417 U.S. 85 (1974); *U.S. v. White*, 322 U.S. 694 (1944); *Hale v. Henkel*, 201 U.S. 43 (1906); *In re Grand Jury Witnesses*, 92 F.3d 710 (8th Cir. 1996); *United States v. Dean*, 989 F.2d 1205 (D.C. Cir. 1993); *U.S. v. Wujkowski*, 929, F.2d. 981 (4th Cir. 1991). Corporations have a right to privacy that is less than that which courts afford to natural persons, *U.S. v. Morton Salt Co.*, 338 U.S. 632, 652 (1950). On the other hand, while corporations can be convicted of violations of criminal laws, they cannot be imprisoned, only fined or forced to dissolve their corporate charter, *U.S. v. Vitek Supply Co.*, 151 F.3d 580, 585 (7th Cir. 1998), cert denied, 119 S.Ct. 1026 (1999).

The issue of corporate personhood has become controversial in the last few years, due to two Supreme Court decisions. The first was *Citizens United v. Federal Election Commission*, 558 U.S. 310 (2010). In *Citizens United* the Court, by a 5–4 majority, struck down one of the major provisions of Bipartisan Campaign Reform Act, (a law to regulate money in political campaigns which was discussed in volume one of this textbook) that imposed the ban on electioneering communication. The decision was controversial because, in part it seemed to suggest that corporations enjoyed the same First Amendment free speech rights in politics as did real natural persons. The second case was *Burwell v. Hobby Lobby Stores, Inc.,* 573 U.S. ___ (2014). In that case the Court, ruled on the constitutionality and legality of rules and the law under the Affordable Care Act (popularly known as Obamacare) that mandated employers provide for contraceptives for women as part of their health insurance. The Court here held that corporations were persons under the **Federal Dictionary Act** and in some cases could refuse for religious reasons to provide birth control. As many people came to interpret the case, *Hobby Lobby* stood for the proposition that corporations enjoy a right to free exercise of religion.

As a result of both *Citizens United* and *Hobby Lobby*, there have been efforts to amend the Constitution to declare corporations are not persons. While is seems unlikely that this amendment will pass, these two decisions do raise questions regarding whether corporations are constitutional persons and what rights they should have if they are.

Trustees of Dartmouth College v. Woodward

4 Wheat. 518, 4 L.Ed. 629 (1819)

Dartmouth College was chartered by the English Crown in 1769. The state legislature of New Hampshire in 1816 attempted by statute a complete reorganization of the government of the College, including changing the name to Dartmouth University. Woodward, secretary-treasurer of the college, had joined the new university movement and retained the seal, records, and other articles of the college. The trustees of the old college brought an action in the state court against Woodward for the recovery of this property. The state court decided against the college trustees.

Vote: 5–1

Chief Justice Marshall delivered the opinion of the Court.

. . . The points for consideration are, 1. Is this contract protected by the Constitution of the United States? 2. Is it impaired by the acts under which the defendant holds? . . .

A corporation is an artificial being, invisible, intangible, and existing only in contemplation of law. Being the mere creature of law, it possesses only those properties which the charter of its creation confers upon it, either expressly or as incidental to its very existence. These are such as are supposed best calculated to effect the object for which it was created. Among the most important are immortality, and, if the expression may be allowed, individuality; properties, by which a perpetual succession of many persons are considered as the same, and may act as a single individual. They enable a corporation to manage its own affairs, and to hold property without the perplexing intricacies, the hazardous and endless necessity, of perpetual conveyances for the purpose of transmitting it from hand to hand. It is chiefly for the purpose of clothing bodies of men in succession with these qualities and capacities that corporations were invented and are in use. By these means, a perpetual succession of individuals are capable of acting for the promotion of the particular object, like one immortal being. . . .

. . . They [the donors] are represented by the corporation. The corporation is the assignee of their rights, stands in their place, and distributes their bounty, as they would themselves have distributed it had they been immortal. So, with respect to the students who are to derive learning from this source, the corporation is a trustee for them also. Their potential rights, which, taken distributively, are imperceptible, amount collectively to a most important interest. These are, in the aggregate, to be exercised, asserted, and protected by the corporation. . . .

This is plainly a contract to which the donors, the trustees, and the crown (to whose rights and obligations New Hampshire succeeds) were the original parties. It is a contract made on a valuable consideration. It is a contract for the security and disposition of property. It is a contract on the faith of which real and personal estate has been conveyed to the corporation. It is then a contract within the letter of the Constitution, and within its spirit also, unless the fact that the property is invested by the donors in trustees for the promotion of religion and education, for the benefit of persons who are perpetually changing, though the objects remain the same, shall create a particular exception, taking this case out of the prohibition contained in the Constitution.

It is more than possible that the preservation of rights of this description was not particularly in the view of the framers of the Constitution when the clause under consideration was introduced into that instrument. It is probable that interferences of more frequent recurrence, to which the temptation was stronger and of which the mischief was more extensive, constituted the great motive for imposing this restriction on the state legislatures. But although a particular and a rare case may not in itself be of sufficient magnitude to induce a rule, yet it must be governed by the rule, when established, unless some plain and strong reason for excluding it can be given. It is not enough to say that this particular case was not in the mind of the convention when the article was framed, nor of the American people when it was adopted. It is necessary to go farther, and to say that, had this particular case been suggested, the language would have been so varied as to exclude it, or it would have been made a special exception. The case, being within the words of the rule, must be within its operation likewise, unless there be something in the literal construction so obviously absurd, or mischievous, or repugnant to the general spirit of the instrument as to justify those who expound the Constitution in making it an exception. . . .

The opinion of the Court, after mature deliberation, is that this is a contract, the obligation of which cannot be impaired without violating the Constitution of the United States. This opinion appears to us to be equally supported by reason and by the former decisions of this court.

2. We next proceed to the inquiry whether its obligation has been impaired by those acts of the Legislature of New Hampshire to which the special verdict refers. . . .

On the effect of this law two opinions cannot be entertained. Between acting directly and acting through the agency of trustees and overseers no essential difference is perceived. The whole power of governing the college is transferred from trustees appointed according to the will of the founder, expressed in the charter, to the executive of New Hampshire. The management and application of the funds of this eleemosynary institution, which are placed by the donors in the hands of trustees named in the charter, and empowered to perpetuate themselves, are placed by this act under the control of the government of the state. The will of the state is substituted for the will of the donors in every essential operation of the college. This is not an immaterial change. The founders of the college contracted, not merely for the perpetual application of the funds which they gave to the objects for which those funds were given, they contracted also to secure that application by the constitution of the corporation. They contracted for a system which should, as far as human foresight can provide, retain forever the government of the literary institution they had formed, in the hands of persons approved by themselves. This system is totally changed. The charter of 1769 exists no longer. It is reorganized, and reorganized in such a manner as to convert a literary institution, moulded according to the will of its founders and placed under the control of private literary men, into a machine entirely subservient to the will of government. This may be for the advantage of this college in particular, and may be for the advantage of literature in general; but it is not according to the will of the donors, and is subversive of that contract on the faith of which their property was given. . . .

Judgment reversed.

JUSTICE STORY concurred.

. . . When a private eleemosynary corporation is thus created by the charter of the crown, it is subject to no other control on the part of the crown, than what is expressly or implicitly reserved by the charter itself. Unless a power be reserved for this purpose, the crown cannot, in virtue of its prerogative, without the consent of the corporation, alter or amend the charter, or divest the corporation of any of its franchises, or add to them, or add to, or diminish, the number of the trustees, or remove any of the members, or change, or control the administration of the charity, or compel the corporation to receive a new charter. This is the uniform language of the authorities, and forms one of the most stubborn, and well settled doctrines of the common law. . . .

JUSTICE WASHINGTON also concurred with the same holding as JUSTICE STORY.

JUSTICE DUVALL dissented without an opinion.

FOR DISCUSSION

What is the relationship between individuals and corporations for Chief Justice Marshall? What advantages do individuals gain when they organize into corporations that they would not otherwise possess?

COUNTY OF SANTA CLARA V. SOUTHERN PAC. R. CO.

118 U.S. 394, 6 S.Ct. 1132, 30 L.Ed. 118 (1886)

Mr. Chief Justice Waite said: "The court does not wish to hear argument on the question whether the provision in the Fourteenth Amendment to the Constitution, which forbids a State to deny to any person within its jurisdiction the equal protection of the laws, applies to these corporations. We are all of opinion that it does."

MR. JUSTICE HARLAN delivered the opinion of the court.

These several actions were brought-the first one in the Superior Court of Santa Clara County, California, the others in the Superior Court of Fresno County, in the same state-for the recovery of certain county and State taxes, claimed to be due from the Southern Pacific Railroad Company and the Central Pacific Railroad Company under assessments made by the State Board of Equalization upon their respective franchises, road ways, road beds, rails, and rolling-stock. In the action by Santa Clara County the amount claimed is $13,366.53 for the fiscal year of 1882. For that sum, with five per cent. penalty, interest at the rate of two per cent. per month from December 27, 1882, cost of advertising, and ten per cent. for attorney's fees, judgment is asked against the Southern Pacific Railroad Company. In the other action against the same company the amount claimed is $5,029.27 for the fiscal year of 1881, with five per cent. added for non-payment of taxes and costs of collection. In the action against the Central Pacific Railroad Company judgment is asked for $25,950.50 for the fiscal year of 1881, with like penalty and costs of collection. The answer in each case puts in issue all the material allegations of the complaint, and sets up various special defenses, to which reference will be made further on. With its answer the defendant, in each case, filed a petition, with a proper bond, for the removal of the action into the Circuit Court of the United States for the District, as one arising under the Constitution and laws of the United States. The right of removal was recognized by the state court, and the action proceeded in the circuit court. Each case—the parties having filed a written stipulation waiving a jury—was tried by the court. There was a special finding of facts, upon which judgment was entered in each case for the defendant. The general question to be determined is, whether the judgment can be sustained upon all, or either, of the grounds upon which the defendants rely.

The case as made by the pleadings and the special finding of facts is as follows:

By an act of Congress approved July 27, 1866, 14 Stat. 292, the Atlantic and Pacific Railroad Company was created, with power to construct and maintain, by certain designated routes, a continuous railroad and telegraph line from Springfield, Missouri, to the Pacific. For the purpose-which is avowed by Congress-of facilitating the construction of the line, and thereby securing the safe and speedy transportation of mails, troops, munitions of war, and public stores, a right of way over the public domain was given to the company, and a liberal grant of the public lands was made to it. The railroad so to be constructed, and every part of it was declared to be a post route and military road, subject to the use of the United States for postal, military, naval, and all other government service, and to such regulations as Congress might impose for restricting the charges for government transportation. By the 18th section of the act, the Southern Pacific Railroad Company—a corporation previously organized under a general statute of California, passed May 20, 1861, Stat. Cal. 1861, p. 607—was authorized to connect with the Atlantic and Pacific Railroad at such point, near the boundary line of that State, as the former company deemed most suitable for a railroad to San Francisco, with 'uniform gauge and rate of freight or fare with said road;' and in consideration thereof, and "to aid in its construction," the act declared that it should have similar grants of land, "subject to all the conditions and limitations" provided in said act of Congress, "and shall be required to construct its road on like regulations, as to time and manner, with the Atlantic and Pacific Railroad." §§ 1, 2, 3, 11 and 18.

In November, 1866, the Atlantic and Pacific Railroad Company and the Southern Pacific Railroad Company filed in the office of the Secretary of the Interior their respective acceptances of the act.

By an act of the legislature of California, passed April 4, 1870, to aid in giving effect to the act of congress relating to the Southern Pacific Railroad Company, it was declared that:

> "To enable the said company to more fully and completely comply with and perform the requirements, provisions, and conditions of the said act of Congress, and all other acts of Congress now in force, or which may hereafter be enacted, the State of California hereby consents to said act, and the said company, its successors and assigns, are hereby authorized to change the line of its railroad so as to reach the eastern boundary line of the State of California by such route as the company shall determine to be the most practicable, and to file new and amendatory articles of association, and the right, power, and privilege is hereby granted to, conferred upon, and vested in them to construct, maintain, and operate by steam or other power the said railroad and telegraph line mentioned in said acts of Congress, hereby confirming to, and vesting in, the said company, its successors and assigns all the rights, privileges, franchises, power and authority conferred upon, granted to, or vested in said company by the said acts of Congress, and any act of Congress which may be hereafter enacted."

Subsequently, by the act of March 3, 1871, 116 Stat. 573, Congress incorporated the Texas Pacific Railroad Company, with power to construct and maintain a continuous railroad and telegraph line from Marshall, in the State of Texas, to a point at or near El Paso, thence through New Mexico and Arizona to San Diego, pursuing, as near as might be, the thirty-second parallel of latitude. To aid in its construction, Congress gave it, also, the right of way over the public domain, and made to it a liberal grant of public lands. The 19th section provided:

> "That the Texas Pacific Railroad Company shall be, and it is hereby, declared to be a military and post road; and for the purpose of insuring the carrying of the mails, troops, munitions of war, supplies, and stores of the United States, no act of the company nor any law of any State or Territory shall impede, delay, or prevent the said company from performing its obligations to the United States in that regard: *Provided,* That said road shall be subject to the use of the United States for postal, military, and all other governmental services, at fair and reasonable rates of compensation, not to exceed the price paid by private parties for the same kind of service, and the government shall at all times have the preference in the use of the same for the purpose aforesaid."

The twenty-third section of that act has special reference to the Southern Pacific Railroad Company, and is as follows:

> "Sec. 23. That, for the purpose of connecting the Texas Pacific Railroad with the city of San Francisco, the Southern Pacific Railroad Company of California is hereby authorized (subject to the laws of California) to construct a line of railroad from a point at or near Tehacapa Pass, by way of Los Angeles, to the Texas Pacific Railroad, at or near the Colorado River, with the same rights, grants, and privileges, and subject to the same limitations, restrictions, and conditions, as were granted to said Southern Pacific Railroad Company of California by the act of July 27, 1866: *provided, however,* that this section shall in no way affect or impair the rights, present or prospective, of the Atlantic and Pacific Railroad Company, or any other railroad company."

Under the authority of this legislation, Federal and State, the Southern Pacific Railroad Company constructed a line of railroad from San Francisco, connecting with the Texas and Pacific Railroad (formerly the Texas Pacific Railroad) at Sierra Banca, in Texas; and with other railroads it is operated as one continuous line (except for that part of the route occupied by the Central Pacific Railroad) from Marshall, Texas, to San Francisco. It is stated in the record that the Southern Pacific Railroad Company of California, since the commencement of this action, has completed its road to the Colorado River, at or near the Needles, to connect with the Atlantic and Pacific Railroad, and that with the latter road it constitutes a continuous line from Springfield, Missouri, to the Pacific, except as to the connection, for a relatively short distance, over the road of the Central Pacific Railroad Company.

On the 17th of December, 1877, the said Southern Pacific Railroad Company, and other railroad corporations, then existing under the laws of California, were legally consolidated, and a new corporation thereby formed, under the name of the Southern Pacific Railroad Company, the present defendant in error, 59.30 miles of whose road is in Santa Clara County and 17.93 miles in Fresno County.

On the 1st of April, 1875, this company was indebted to divers persons in large sums of money advanced to construct and equip its road. To secure that indebtedness, it executed on that day a mortgage for $32,520,000 on its road, franchises, rolling-stock and appurtenances, and on a large number of tracts of land, in different counties of California, aggregating over eleven million acres. These lands were granted to the company by Congress under the above-mentioned acts, and are used for agricultural, grazing, and other purposes not connected with the business of the railroad. Of those patented, 3,138 acres are in Santa Clara County and 18,789 acres in Fresno County. When these proceedings were instituted no part of its above mortgage debt had been paid, except the accruing interest and $1,632,000 of the principal, leaving outstanding against it $30,898,000.

In the year 1852 California, by legislative enactment, granted a right of way through that State to the United States for the purpose of constructing a railroad from the Atlantic to the Pacific Ocean-declaring that the interests of California, as well as the whole Union, "require the immediate action of the Government of the United States, for the construction of a national thoroughfare, connecting the navigable waters of the Atlantic and Pacific Oceans, for the purpose of the national safety, in the event of war, and to promote the highest commercial interests of the Republic." Stat. Cal. 1852, p. 150. By an act passed July 1, 1862, 19 Stat. 489, § 1, 8,

Congress incorporated the Union Pacific Railroad Company, with power to construct and maintain a continuous railroad and telegraph line to the western boundary of what was then Nevada territory, "there to meet and connect with the line of the Central Pacific Railroad Company of California.". The declared object of extending government aid to these enterprises was to effect the construction of a railroad and telegraph line from the Missouri River to the Pacific, which, for all purposes of communication, travel, and transportation, so far as the public and the General Government are concerned, should be operated 'as one connected, continuous line." Ibid. §§ 6, 9, 10, 12, 17, 18.

In 1864 the State of California passed an act to aid in carrying out the provisions of this act of Congress, the first section of which declared that:

> "To enable said company more fully and completely to comply with and perform the provisions and conditions of said act of Congress, the said company, their successors and assigns, are hereby authorized and empowered, and the right, power, and privilege is hereby granted to, conferred upon, and vested in them, to construct, maintain, and operate the said railroad and telegraph line, not only in the State of California, but also in the said Territories lying east of and between said State and the Missouri River, with such branches and extensions of said railroad and telegraph line, or either of them, as said company may deem necessary or proper, and also the right of way for said railroad and telegraph line over any lands belonging to this State, and on, over, and along any streets, roads, highways, rivers, streams, water, and water courses, but the same to be so constructed as not to obstruct or destroy the passage or navigation of the same, and also the right to condemn and appropriate to the use of said company such private property, rights, privileges, and franchises as may be proper, necessary, or convenient for the purposes of said railroad and telegraph, the compensation therefor to be ascertained and paid under and by special proceedings, as prescribed in the act providing for the incorporation of railroad companies, approved May 20, 1861, and the act supplementary and amendatory thereof, said company to be subject to all the laws of this State concerning railroad and telegraph lines, except that messages and property of the United States, of this State, and of said company shall have priority of transportation and transmission over said line of railroad and telegraph, hereby confirming to and vesting in said company all the rights, privileges, franchises, power, and authority conferred upon, granted to, and vested in said company by said act of Congress, hereby repealing all laws and parts of laws inconsistent or in conflict with the provisions of this act, or the rights and privileges herein granted."

In 1870, the Central Pacific Railroad Company of California and the Western Pacific Railroad Company formed themselves into one corporation under the name of the Central Pacific Railroad Company, the defendant in one of these actions, 61.06 miles of whose road is in Fresno County. The company complied with the several acts of congress, and there is in operation a continuous line of railway from the Missouri River to the Pacific ocean, the Central Pacific Railroad Company owning and operating the portion thereof between Ogden, in the Territory of Utah, and San Francisco.

When the present action was instituted against this company the United States had and now have a lien, created by the acts of Congress of 1862 and 1864, for $30,000,000, with a large amount of interest, upon its road, rolling-stock, fixtures and franchises; and there were also outstanding bonds for a like amount issued by the company prior to January 1, 1875, and secured by a mortgage upon the same property.

Such were the relations which these two companies held to the United States and to the State when the assessments in question were made for purposes of taxation.

It is necessary now to refer to those provisions of the constitution and laws of the State which, it is claimed, sustain these assessments.

The constitution of California, adopted in 1879, exempts from taxation growing crops, property used exclusively for public schools, and such as may belong to the United States, or to that State, or to any of her county or municipal corporations, and declares that the legislature "may provide, except in the case of credits secured by mortgage or trust deed, for a reduction from credits of debts due to *bona fide* residents" of the State. It is provided in the first section of article XIII that, with these exceptions—"all property in the State, not exempt under the laws of the United States, shall be taxed in proportion to its value, to be ascertained as provided by law. The word 'property,' as used in this article and section, is hereby declared to include moneys, credits, bonds, stocks, dues, franchises, and all other matters and things, real, personal, and mixed, capable of private ownership."

The fourth section of the same article provides:

"A mortgage, deed of trust, contract, or other obligation by which a debt is secured, shall, for the purposes of assessment and taxation, be deemed and treated as an interest in the property affected thereby. *Except as to railroad and other quasi public corporations*, in case of debts so secured, the value of the property affected by such mortgage, deed of trust, contract, or obligation, less the value of such security, shall be assessed and taxed to the owner of the property, and the value of such security shall be assessed and taxed to the owner thereof, in the county, city, or district in which the property affected thereby is situate. The taxes so levied shall be a lien upon the property and security, and may be paid by either party to such security; if paid by the owner of the security, the tax so levied upon the property affected thereby shall become a part of the debt so secured; if the owner of the property shall pay the tax so levied on such security, it shall constitute a payment thereon, and to the extent of such payment, a full discharge thereof: *provided,* That if any such security or indebtedness shall be paid by any such debtor or debtors, after assessment and before the tax levy, the amount of such levy may likewise be retained by such debtor or debtors, and shall be computed according to the tax levy of the preceding year."

The ninth section makes provision for the election of a State Board of Equalization, "whose duty it shall be to equalize the valuation of the taxable property of the several counties in the State for the purpose of taxation." The boards of supervisors of the several counties constitute boards of equalization for their respective counties, and they equalize the valuation of the taxable property therein for purposes of taxation-assessments, whether by the state or county boards, to "conform to the true value in money of the property" contained in the assessment roll.

The tenth section declares:

> "All property, *except as hereinafter in this section provided*, shall be assessed in the county, city, city and county, town, township, or district in which it is situated, in the manner prescribed by law. The *franchise, roadway, road-bed, rails, and rolling-stock of all railroads operated in more than one county* in this State shall be assessed by the State Board of Equalization at their actual value, and the same shall be apportioned to the counties, cities and counties, cities, towns, townships, and districts in which such railroads are located, in proportion to the number of miles of railway laid in such counties, cities and counties, cities, towns, townships, and districts."

The assessments in question, it is contended, were made in conformity with these constitutional provisions, and with what is known as § 3664 of the Political Code of California. That section made it the duty of the State Board of Equalization, on or before the first Monday in May in each year, to "assess the franchise, roadway, road-bed, rails, and rolling-stock of railroads operated in more than one county-to which class belonged the defendants. It required every corporation of that class, by certain officers, or by such officer as the State Board should designate, to furnish the board with a sworn statement showing, among other things, in detail, for the year ending March 1, the whole number of miles of railway owned, operated, or leased by it in the State, the value thereof per mile, and all of its property of every kind located in the State; the number and value of its engines, passenger, mail, express, baggage, freight, and other cars, or property used in operating and repairing its railway in the State, and on railways which are parts of lines extending beyond the limits of the state. It is also directed that "the said property shall be assessed at its actual value;" that the "assessment shall be made upon the entire railway within the State, and shall include the right of way, road-bed, track, bridges, culverts, and rolling-stock;" and that "the depots, station grounds, shops, buildings, and gravel beds shall be assessed by the assessors of the county where situated, as other property." It further declares:

"On or before the fifteenth day of May, in each year, said board shall transmit to the county assessor of each county through which any railway, operated in more than one county, may run, a statement showing the length of the main track or tracks of such railway within the county, together with a description of the whole of said tracks within the county including the right of way by metes and bounds, or other description sufficient for identification, and the assessed value per mile of the same, as fixed by a *pro rata* distribution per mile of the assessed value of the whole franchise, roadway, road-bed, rails, and rolling-stock of such railway within this State. Said statement shall be entered on the assessment roll of the county. At the first meeting of the board of supervisors, after such statement is received by the county assessor, they shall make and cause to be entered in the proper record-book an order stating and declaring the length of the main track, and the assessed value of such railway lying in each city, town, township, school-district, or lesser taxing district in their county, through which such railway runs, as fixed by the State Board of Equalization, which shall constitute the taxable value of said property for taxable purposes in such city, town, township, school, road, or other district." Stat. Cal. 1881, Ch. 73, § 1, page 82.

These companies, within due time, filed with the state board the detailed statement required by that section.

At the trials below, no record of assessment against the respective defendants, as made by the State Board, was given in evidence, and there was introduced no written evidence of the assessment except an official communication from the State Board to each of the assessors of Santa Clara and Fresno Counties, called, in the special findings, the assessment roll for the particular county. The roll for Fresno county, in 1881, relating to the Southern Pacific Railroad Company, is as follows: There were similar rolls in reference to the Central Pacific Railroad in the same county, for the same year, and the Southern Pacific in Santa Clara County for 1882. For each of those years the board of supervisors of the respective counties made an apportionment of the taxes among the legal subdivisions of such counties.

It is stated in the findings that the delinquent lists for those years, so far as they related to the taxes in question, were duly made up in form corresponding with the original assessment roll; that in pursuance of § 3738 of the Political Code of California, the board of supervisors of the respective counties duly passed an order, entered on the minutes, dispensing with the duplicate assessment roll for that year; that the controller of the State transmitted a letter to the tax collector of the county, in pursuance of the provisions of § 3899 of that Code, directing him to offer the property for sale but once, and if there were no *bona fide* purchasers to withdraw it from sale that the tax collector, in obedience to the provisions of that section, transmitted to the controller, with his indorsement thereon of the action had in the premises, a certified copy of the entry upon the delinquent list relating to the tax in question in these several actions; that such indorsement shows that the tax collector had offered the property for sale and had withdrawn it because there was no purchaser for the same; and that the controller, in pursuance of the provisions of the same section, transmitted to the tax collector of the county a letter directing him to bring suit.

In each case there were also the following findings:

"The State Board of Equalization, in assessing said value of said property to and against defendant, assessed the full cash value of said railroad, roadway, road-bed, rails, rolling-stock, and franchises, without deducting therefrom the value of the mortgage, or any part thereof, given and existing thereon as aforesaid, to secure the indebtedness of said company to the holders of said bonds, notwithstanding they had full knowledge of the existence of the said mortgage; and in making said assessment the said State Board of Equalization did not consider or treat said mortgage as an interest in said property, but assessed the whole value thereof to the defendant, in the same manner as if there had been no mortgage thereon."

"The State Board of Equalization, in making the supposed assessment of said roadway of defendant, did knowingly and designedly include in the valuation of said roadway the value of fences erected upon the line between said roadway and the land of coterminous proprietors. Said fences were valued at $300 per mile."

The special grounds of defense by each of the defendants were: (1) That its road is a part of a continuous postal and military route, constructed and maintained under the authority of the United States, by means in part obtained from the General Government; that the company having, with the consent of the state, become subject to the requirements, conditions, and provisions of the acts of Congress, it thereby ceased to be merely a State corporation, and became one of the agencies or instrumentalities employed by the General Government to execute its constitutional powers; and that the franchise to operate a postal and military route, for the transportation of troops, munitions of war, public stores, and the mails, being derived from the United States, cannot, without their consent, be subjected to state taxation. (2) That the provisions of the constitution and laws of California, in respect to the assessment for taxation of the property of railway corporations operating railroads in more than one county, are in violation of the Fourteenth Amendment of the Constitution, in so far as they require the assessment of their property at its full money value, without making deduction, as in the case of railroads operated in one county, and of other corporations, and of natural persons, for the value of the mortgages covering the property assessed; thus imposing upon the defendant unequal burdens, and to that extent denying to it the equal protection of the laws. (3) That what is known as § 3664 of the Political Code of California, under the authority of which in part the assessment was made, was not constitutionally enacted by the legislature, and had not the force of law. (4) That no valid assessment appears in fact to have been made by the State Board. (5) That no interest is recoverable in this action until after judgment. (6) That the assessment upon which the action is based is void, because it included property which the State Board of Equalization had no jurisdiction, under any circumstances, to assess, and that, as such illegal part was so blended with the balance that it cannot be separated, the entire assessment must be treated as a nullity.

The record contains elaborate opinions stating the grounds upon which judgments were ordered for the defendants. Mr. Justice Field overruled the first of the special defenses above named, but sustained the second. The circuit judge, in addition, held that section 3664 of the Political Code had not been passed in the mode required by the state constitution, and consequently was no part of the law of California. These opinions are reported as the *Santa Clara Railroad Tax Case*, in 9 Sawyer, 165, 210; S. C. 18 Fed. Rep. 385.

The propositions embodied in the conclusions reached in the Circuit Court were discussed with marked ability by counsel who appeared in this court for the respective parties. Their importance cannot well be overestimated; for they not only involve a construction of the recent amendments to the National Constitution in their application to the Constitution and the legislation of a State, but upon their determination, if it were necessary to consider them, would depend the system of taxation devised by that State for raising revenue, from certain corporations, for the support of her government. These questions belong to a class which this court should not decide, unless their determination is essential to the disposal of the case in which they arise. Whether the present cases require a decision of them depends upon the soundness of another proposition, upon which the court below, in view of its conclusions upon other issues, did not deem it necessary to pass. We allude to the claim of the defendant, in each case, that the entire assessment is a nullity, upon the ground that the State Board of Equalization included therein property which it was without jurisdiction to assess for taxation.

The argument in behalf of the defendant is: That the State Board knowingly and designedly included in its assessment of "the franchise, roadway, road-bed, rails, and rolling-stock" of each company, the value of the fences erected upon the line between its roadway and the land of coterminous proprietors; that the fences did not constitute a part of such roadway, and therefore, could only be assessed, for taxation by the proper officer of the several counties in which they were situated; and that an entire assessment which includes property not assessable by the State Board against the party assessed, is void, and, therefore, insufficient to support an action, at least, when-and such is claimed to be the case here-it does not appear, with reasonable certainty, from the face of the assessment or otherwise, what part of the aggregate valuation represents the property so illegally included therein.

If these positions are tenable, there will be no occasion to consider the grave questions of constitutional law upon which the case was determined below; for, in that event, the judgment can be affirmed upon the ground that the assessment cannot properly be the basis of a judgment against the defendant.

That the State Board purposely included in its assessment and valuation the fences erected on the line between the railroads and the lands of adjacent proprietors, at the rate of $300 per mile, is undoubtedly true: for it is so stated in the special finding of facts, and that finding must be taken here to be indisputable. It is equally true that that tribunal has no general power of assessment, but only jurisdiction to assess "the franchise, roadway, road-bed, rails, and rolling-stock" of railroad corporations operating roads in more than one county, and that all other property of such corporations, subject to taxation, is assessable only "in the county, city, city and county, town, township, or district in which it is situated, in the manner prescribed by law." Such is the declaration of the State constitution. *People* v. *Sacramento County*, 59 Cal. 321, 324; article XIII, § 10. It must also be conceded that "fences" erected on the line between these railroads and the lands of adjoining proprietors, were improperly included by the State Board in its assessments, unless they constituted a part of the "roadway." Some light is thrown upon this question by that clause of § 3664 of the Political Code of California-which, in the view we take of these cases, may be regarded as having been legally enacted-providing that 'the depots, station grounds, shops, buildings, and gravel beds' shall be assessed in the county where situated as other property. From this it seems, that there is much of the property daily used in the business of a railroad operated in more than one county, that is not assessable by the State Board, but only by the proper authorities of the municipality where it is situated. So that, even if it appeared that the fences assessed by the State Board were the property of the railroad companies, and not of the adjoining proprietors, they could not be included in an assessment by that board unless they were part of the roadway itself; for, as shown, the jurisdiction of that board is restricted to the assessment of the "franchise, roadway, road-bed, rails, and rolling-stock." We come back, then, to the vital inquiry, whether the fences could be assessed under the head of roadway? We are of opinion that they cannot be regarded as part of the roadway for purposes of taxation.

The Constitution of California provides that "land and improvements thereon shall be separately assessed," (Article XIII, § 2; and, although that instrument does not define what are improvements upon land, the Political Code of the State expressly declares that the term "improvements" includes "all buildings, structures, fixtures, *fences*, and improvements erected upon or affixed to the land." § 3617. It would seem from these provisions that fences erected upon the roadway, even if owned by the railroad company, must be separately assessed, as "improvements," in the mode required in the case of depots, station grounds, shops, and buildings owned by the company; namely, by local officers in the county where they are situated. The same considerations of public interest or convenience upon which rest existing regulations for the assessments of depots, station grounds, shops, and buildings of a railroad company operated in more than one county would apply equally to the assessment and valuation for taxation of fences erected upon the line of railway of the same company.

In *San Francisco & North Pacific Railroad Co.* v. *State Board of Equalization*, 60 Cal. 12, 34, which was an application, on *certiorari*, to annul certain orders of the State Board assessing the property of a railroad corporation, one of the questions was as to the meaning of the words "road-bed" and "roadway." The court there said: "The road-bed is the foundation on which the superstructure of a railroad rests. Webster. The roadway is the right of way, which has been held to be the property liable to taxation. *Appeal of N. B. & M. R. R. Co.*, 32 Cal. 499. The rails in place constitute the superstructure resting upon the road-bed." This definition was approved in *San Francisco* v. *Central Pacific Railroad Co.*, 63 Cal. 467, 469. In the latter case the question was whether certain steamers owned by the railroad company, upon which were laid railroad tracks, and with which its passenger and freight cars were transported from the eastern shore of the bay of San Francisco to its western shore, where the railway again commenced, were to be assessed by the city and county of San Francisco, or by the State Board of Equalization. The contention of the company was that they constituted a part of its road-bed or roadway and must, therefore, be assessed by the State Board. But the Supreme Court of the State held otherwise. After observing that all the property of the company, other than its franchise, roadway, road-bed, rails, and rolling-stock, was required by the Constitution to be assessed by the local assessors, the court said: "They are certainly not the franchise of the defendant corporation. They may constitute an element to be taken into computation to arrive at the value of the franchise of such corporation, but they are not such franchise. It is equally as clear that they are not rails or rolling-stock. Are they, then, embraced within the words roadway or road-bed, in the ordinary and popular acceptation of such words as applied to railroads? These two words, as applied to common roads, ordinarily mean the same thing, but as applied to railroads their meaning is not the same. The *road-bed* referred to in § 10, in our judgment, is the bed or foundation on which the superstructure of the railroad rests. Such is the definition given by both Worcester and Webster, and we think it correct. The *roadway* has a more extended signification as applied to railroads. In addition to the part denominated road-bed, the roadway includes whatever space of ground the company is allowed by law in which to construct its road-bed and lay its track. Such space is defined in subdivision 4 of the 17th section and the 20th section of the act 'to provide for the incorporation of railroad companies,' etc., approved May 20, 1861. Stat. 1861, p. 607; *S. F. & N. P. R. Co.* v. *State Board*, 60 Cal. 12."

The argument in support of the proposition that these steamers-constituting, as they did, a necessary link in the line of the company's railway, and upon which rails were actually laid for the running of cars-were a part either of the road-bed or roadway of the railroad, is much more cogent than the argument that the fences erected upon the line between a roadway and the lands of adjoining proprietors are a part of the roadway itself. It seems to the court that the fences in question are not, within the meaning of the local law, a part of the roadway for purposes of taxation; but are "improvements" assessable by the local authorities of the proper county, and, therefore were improperly included by the State Board in its valuation of the property of the defendants.

The next inquiry that naturally arises is, whether the different kinds of property assessed by the State Board are distinct and separable upon the face of the assessment, so that the company being thereby informed of the amount of taxes levied upon each, could be held to have been in default in not tendering such sum, if any, as was legally due? Upon the transcript before us, this question must be answered in the negative. No record of assessment, as made by the State Board, was introduced at the trial, and presumably, no such record existed. Nor is there any documentary evidence of such assessment, except the official communication of the State Board to the local assessors, called, in the findings, the assessment roll of the county. That roll shows only the aggregate valuation of the company's franchise, roadway, road-bed, rails, and rolling-stock in the State; the length of the company's main track in the State; its length in the county; the assessed value per mile of the railway as fixed by the *pro rata* distribution per mile of the assessed value of its whole franchise, roadway, road-bed, rails, and rolling-stock in the State; and the apportionment of the property so assessed to the county.

It appears, as already stated, from the evidence, that the fences were included in the valuation of the defendants' property; but under what head, whether of franchise, roadway, or road-bed, does not appear. Nor can it be ascertained, with reasonable certainty, either from the assessment roll or from other evidence, what was the aggregate valuation of the fences, or what part of such valuation was apportioned to the respective counties through which the railroad was operated. If the presumption is, that the State Board included in its valuation only such property as it had jurisdiction under the state constitution to assess, namely, such as could be rightfully classified under the heads of franchise, roadway, road-bed, rails, or rolling-stock, that presumption was overthrown by proof that it did, in fact, include, under some one or more of those heads, the fences in question. It was then incumbent upon the plaintiff, by satisfactory evidence, to separate that which was illegal from that which was legal-assuming for the purposes of this case only, that the assessment was, in all other respects, legal-and thus impose upon the defendant the duty of tendering, or enabling the court to render judgment for, such amount, if any, as was justly due. But no such evidence was introduced. The finding that the fences were valued at $300 per mile is too vague and indefinite as a basis for estimating the aggregate valuation of the fences included in the assessment, or the amount thereof apportioned to the respective counties. Were the fences the property of adjacent proprietors? Were they assessed at that rate for every mile of the railroad within the State? Were they erected on the line of the railroad in every county through which it was operated, or only in some of them? Wherever erected, were they assessed for each side of the railway, or only for one side? These questions, so important in determining the extent to which the assessment included a valuation of the fences erected upon the line between the railroad and coterminous proprietors, find no solution in the record presented to this court.

If it be suggested that, under the circumstances, the court might have assumed that the State Board included the fences in their assessment, at the rate of $300 per mile for every mile of the railroad within the State, counting one or both sides of the roadway, and, having thus eliminated from the assessment the aggregate so found, given judgment for such sum, if any, as, upon that basis, would have been due upon the valuation of the franchise, road-bed, roadway, rails, and rolling-stock of the defendant, the answer is, that the plaintiff did not offer to take such a judgment; and the court could not have rendered one of that character without concluding the plaintiff hereafter, and upon a proper assessment, from claiming against the defendant taxes for the years in question, upon such of its property as constituted its franchise, roadway, road-bed, rails, and rolling-stock. The case as presented to the court below, was, therefore, one in which the plaintiff sought judgment for an entire tax arising upon an assessment of different kinds of property as a unit-such assessment including property not legally assessable by the State Board, and the part of the tax assessed against the latter property not being separable from the other part. Upon such an issue, the law, we think, is for the defendant; an assessment of that kind is invalid, and will not support an action for the recovery of the entire tax so levied. Cooley on Taxation, 295–296, and authorities there cited; *Libby* v. *Burnham*, 15 Mass. 144, 147; *State Randolph, S.C.* v. *City of Plainfield*, 38 N. J. Law (9 Vroom), 93; *Gamble* v. *Witty*, 55 Mississippi 26, 35; *Stone* v. *Bean*, 15 Gray, 42, 45; *Mosher* v. *Robie*, 11 Maine (2 Fairfield), 137 *Johnson* v. *Colburn*, 36 Vt. 695; *Wells* v. *Burbank*, 17 N. H. 393, 412.

It results that the court below might have given judgment in each case for the defendant upon the ground that the assessment, which was the foundation of the action, included property of material value, which the State Board was without jurisdiction to assess, and the tax levied upon which cannot, from the record, be separated from that imposed upon other property embraced in the same assessment. As the judgment can be sustained upon this ground it is not necessary to consider any other questions raised by the pleadings and the facts found by the court.

It follows that there is no occasion to determine under what circumstances the plaintiffs would be entitled to judgment against a delinquent tax-payer for penalties, interest, or attorney's fees; for, if the plaintiffs are not entitled to judgment for the taxes arising out of the assessments in question, no liability for penalties, interest, or attorney's fees, could result from a refusal or failure to pay such taxes.

Judgment affirmed.

FOR DISCUSSION

What if anything does this case have to do with corporate personhood and the Constitution?

PEMBINA CONSOLIDATED SILVER MIN. & MILLING CO. v. COMMONWEALTH OF PENNSYLVANIA

125 U.S. 181, 8 S.Ct. 737, 31 L.Ed. 650 (1888)

Pembina was a company incorporated in Colorado but doing business in Pennsylvania. It challenged a state law imposing a tax on out-of-state or foreign corporations unless it shall first have obtained from the auditor general an annual license so to do. Pembina refused to pay the tax, contending that the state law was in violation of both the commerce (article 1, § 8, cl. 3,) and privileges and immunities clauses (article 4, § 2, cl. 1.) The court of common pleas affirmed the validity of the assessment, and the corporation took the case on writ of error to the supreme court of the common wealth, which affirmed the judgment of the common pleas. The US Supreme Court affirmed.

Vote 8–0

MR. JUSTICE FIELD delivered for a unanimous court.

The only questions passed upon by the supreme court of Pennsylvania, which can be considered by us, are those which arise upon its ruling against the contention of the plaintiff in error that the statute of the commonwealth is in conflict with clauses of the federal constitution. Its ruling upon the conformity of the statute with the constitution of the commonwealth does not come under our jurisdiction. The clauses of the federal constitution, with which it was urged in the state supreme court that the statute conflicts, are the one vesting in congress the power to regulate foreign and interstate commerce, the one declaring that the citizens of each state are entitled to the privileges and immunities of citizens in the several states, and the one embodied in the fourteenth amendment declaring that no state shall deny to any person within its jurisdiction the equal protection of the laws.

1. It is not perceived in what way the statute impinges upon the commercial clause of the federal constitution. It imposes no prohibition upon the transportation into Pennsylvania of the products of the corporation, or upon their sale in the commonwealth. It only exacts a license tax from the corporation when it has an office in the commonwealth for the use of its officers, stockholders, agents, or employes. The tax is not for their office, but for the office of the corporation; and the use to which it is put is presumably for the latter's business and interest. For no other purpose can it be supposed that the office would be hired by the corporation. The exaction of a license fee to enable the corporation to have an office for that purpose within the commonwealth is clearly within the competency of its legislature. It was decided long ago, and the doctrine has been often affirmed since, that a corporation created by one state cannot-with some exceptions, to which we shall presently refer-do business in another state without the latter's consent, express or implied. In *Paul* v. *Virginia*, 8 Wall. 168, this court, speaking of a foreign corporation, (and under that definition the plaintiff in error, being created under the laws of Colorado, is to be regarded,) said: 'The recognition of its existence even by other states, and the enforcement of its contracts made therein, depend purely upon the comity of those states; a comity which is never extended where the existence of the corporation or the exercise of its powers, are prejudicial to their interests, or repugnant to their policy. Having no absolute right of recognition in other states, but depending for such recognition and the enforcement of its contracts upon their consent, it follows as a matter of course that such consent may be granted upon such terms and conditions as those states may think proper to impose. They may exclude the foreign corporation entirely; they may restrict its business to particular localities; or they may exact such security for the performance of its contracts with their citizens as in their judgment will best promote the public interests. The whole matter rests in their discretion.' A qualification

of this doctrine was expressed in *Telegraph Co.* v. *Telegraph Co.*, 96 U.S. 12, so far as it applies to corporations engaged in commerce under the authority or with the permission of congress. The act of July 24, 1866, 'to aid in the construction of telegraph lines, and to secure to the government the use of the same for postal, military, and other purposes,' which was considered in that case, declared that any telegraph company then organized, or which might thereafter be organized, under the laws of any state, should have the right to construct, maintain, and operate lines of telegraph through and over any portion of the public domain of the United States, over and along any of the military or post roads of the United States, which had been or might thereafter be declared such by act of congress, and over, under, or across the navigable streams or waters of the United States,' upon certain conditions specified therein; and this court held that the telegraph, as an agency of commerce and intercommunication, came under the controlling power of congress, as against any hostile state legislation; and that the Western Union Telegraph Company, having accepted the conditions of the act, could not be excluded by another state from prosecuting its business within her jurisdiction. The legislature of Florida had granted to another company, for 20 years, the exclusive right to establish and maintain telegraph lines in certain counties of the state, but this exclusive grant was adjudged to be invalid as against the company acting under the law of congress. And undoubtedly a corporation of one state, employed in the business of the general government, may do such business in other states without obtaining a license from them. Thus, to take an illustration from the opinion of Mr. Justice BRADLEY in a case recently decided by him, 'if congress should employ a corporation of ship-builders to construct a man-of-war, they would have the right to purchase the necessary timber and iron in any state of the Union,' and, we may add, without the permission and against the prohibition of the state. *Stockton* v. *Railroad Co.*, 32 Fed. Rep. 9, 14. These exceptions do not touch the general doctrine declared as to corporations not carrying on foreign or interstate commerce, or not employed by the government. As to these corporations, the doctrine of *Paul* v. *Virginia* applies. The Colorado corporation does not come within any of the exceptions. Therefore, the recognition of its existence in Pennsylvania, even to the limited extent of allowing it to have an office within its limits for the use of its officers, stockholders, agents, and employes, was a matter dependent on the will of the state. It could make the grant of the privilege conditional upon the payment of a license tax, and fix the sum according to the amount of the authorized capital of the corporation. The absolute power of exclusion includes the right to allow a conditional and restricted exercise of its corporate powers within the state.

We do not perceive the pertinency of the position advanced by counsel that the tax in question is void as an attempt by the state to tax a franchise not granted by her, and property or business not within her jurisdiction. The fact is otherwise. No tax upon the franchise of the foreign corporation is levied, nor upon its business or property without the state. A license tax only is exacted as a condition of its keeping an office within the state for the use of its officers, stockholders, agents, and employes,-nothing more and nothing less; and in what way this can be considered as a regulation of interstate commerce is not apparent.

Nor does the clause of the constitution declaring that the 'citizens of each state shall be entitled to all privileges and immunities of citizens in the several states' have any bearing upon the question of the validity of the license tax in question. Corporations are not citizens within the meaning of that clause. This was expressly held in *Paul* v. *Virginia*. In that case it appeared that a statute of Virginia, passed in February, 1866, declared that no insurance company not incorporated under the laws of the state should carry on business within her limits without previously obtaining a license for that purpose, and that no license should be received by the corporation until it had deposited with the treasurer of the state bonds of a designated character and amount, the latter varying according to the extent of the capital employed. No such deposit was required of insurance companies incorporated by the state for carrying on their business within her limits. A subsequent statute of Virginia made it a penal offense for a person to act in the state as an agent of a foreign insurance company without such license. One Samuel Paul, having acted in the state as an agent for a New York insurance company without a license, was indicted and convicted in a circuit court in Virginia, and sentenced to pay a fine of $50. On error to the court of appeals of the state the judgment was affirmed, and to review that judgment the case was brought to this court. Here it was contended, as in the present case, that the statute of Virginia was invalid by reason of its discriminating provisions between her corporations and corporations of other states; that in this particular it was in conflict with the clause of the constitution mentioned, that the citizens of each state shall be entitled to all the privileges and immunities of citizens in the several states. But the court answered that corporations are not citizens within the meaning of the clause; that the term 'citizens,' as used in the clause, applies only to natural persons, members of the body politic owing allegiance to the state, not to artificial persons created by the legislature, and possessing only such attributes as the legislature has prescribed; that the privileges and immunities secured to citizens of each state in the several states by the clause in question are those privileges and immunities which are common to the citizens in the latter states, under their constitution and laws, by virtue of their citizenship; that special privileges enjoyed by citizens in their own states are not secured in other states by that provision; that it was not intended that the laws of one state should thereby have any operation in other states; that they can have such operation only by the permission, express or implied, of those states; that special privileges which are conferred must be enjoyed at home, unless the assent of other states to their enjoyment therein be given; and that a grant of corporate existence was a grant of special privileges to the corporators, enabling them to act for certain specified purposes as a single individual, and exempting them, unless otherwise provided, from individual liability, which could, therefore, be enjoyed in other states only by their assent.

3. The application of the fourteenth amendment of the constitution to the statute imposing the license tax in question is not more apparent than the application of the clause of the constitution to the rights of citizens of one state to the privileges and immunities of citizens in other states. The inhibition of the amendment that no state shall deprive any person within its jurisdiction of the equal protection of the laws, was designed to prevent any person or class of persons from being singled out as a special subject for discriminating and hostile legislation. Under the designation of 'person' there is no doubt that a private corporation is included. Such corporations are merely associations of individuals united for a special purpose, and permitted to do business under a particular name, and have a succession of members without dissolution. As said by Chief Justice MARSHALL: 'The great object of a corporation is to bestow the character and properties of individuality on a collective and changing body of men.' *Bank* v. *Billings*, 4 Pet. 514, 562. The equal protection of the laws which these bodies may claim is only such as is accorded to similar associations within the jurisdiction of the state. The plaintiff in error is not a corporation within the jurisdiction of Pennsylvania. The office it hires is within such jurisdiction, and on condition that it pays the required license tax it can claim the same protection in the use of the office that any other corporation having a similar office may claim. It would then have the equal protection of the law so far as it had anything within the jurisdiction of the state, and the constitutional amendment requires nothing more. The state is not prohibited from discriminating in the privileges it may grant to foreign corporations as a condition of their doing business or hiring offices within its limits, provided always such discrimination does not interfere with any transaction by such corporations of interstate or foreign commerce. It is not every corporation, lawful in the state of its creation, that other states may be willing to admit within their jurisdiction, or consent that it have offices in them; such, for example, as a corporation for lotteries. And even where the business of a foreign corporation is not unlawful in other states, the latter may wish to limit the number of such corporations, or to subject their business to such control as would be in accordance with the policy governing domestic corporations of a similar character. The states may, therefore, require for the admission within their limits of the corporations of other states, or of any number of them, such conditions as they may choose, without acting in conflict with the concluding provision of the first section of the fourteenth amendment. As to the meaning and extent of that section of the amendment. The only limitation upon this power of the state to exclude a foreign corporation from doing business within its limits or hiring offices for that purpose, or to exact conditions for allowing the corporation to do business or hire offices there, arises where the corporation is in the employ of the federal government, or where its business is strictly commerce,

interstate or foreign. The control of such commerce being in the federal government, is not to be restricted by state authority. Judgment affirmed.

FOR DISCUSSION

How does constitutional personhood factor into the reasoning or arguments here?

CITIZENS UNITED V. FEDERAL ELECTION COMMISSION

558 U.S. 310, 130 S.Ct. 876, 175 L.Ed. 2d. 753 (2010)

Citizens United was a non-profit company that cite to promote a documentary/movie entitled Hilary. The movie was critical of Senator Hilary Clinton and her 2008 presidential campaign. To promote the documentary Citizens United wanted to produce and air brief ads indicating it was available on video-on-demand. Because of concern that these ads would be in violation of BCRA, Citizens United challenged applicability of one section of the Act addressing electioneering communications. Citizens United lost in lower court and after an initial hearing before the Supreme Court, parties were asked to brief arguments regarding its constitutionality. This decision occurred after the second hearing. The facts in the case are described in more detail by Justice Kennedy.

Vote 5–4

KENNEDY, J., delivered the opinion of the Court, in which ROBERTS, and SCALIA and ALITO, joined, in which THOMAS joined as to all but Part IV, and in which STEVENS, GINSBURG, BREYER, and SOTOMAYOR, joined as to Part IV.

JUSTICE KENNEDY delivered the opinion of the Court.

Federal law prohibits corporations and unions from using their general treasury funds to make independent expenditures for speech defined as an "electioneering communication" or for speech expressly advocating the election or defeat of a candidate. 2 U.S.C. § 441b. Limits on electioneering communications were upheld in *McConnell v. Federal Election Comm'n,* 540 U.S. 93 (2003). The holding of *McConnell* rested to a large extent on an earlier case, *Austin v. Michigan Chamber of Commerce,* 494 U.S. 652, 110 S.Ct. 1391, 108 L.Ed.2d 652 (1990). *Austin* had held that political speech may be banned based on the speaker's corporate identity.

In this case we are asked to reconsider *Austin* and, in effect, *McConnell.* We agree with that conclusion and hold that *stare decisis* does not compel the continued acceptance of *Austin.* The Government may regulate corporate political speech through disclaimer and disclosure requirements, but it may not suppress that speech altogether. We turn to the case now before us.

I

A

Citizens United is a nonprofit corporation. It brought this action in the United States District Court for the District of Columbia. A three-judge court later convened to hear the cause. The resulting judgment gives rise to this appeal.

Citizens United has an annual budget of about $12 million. Most of its funds are from donations by individuals; but, in addition, it accepts a small portion of its funds from for-profit corporations.

In January 2008, Citizens United released a film entitled *Hillary: The Movie*. We refer to the film as *Hillary*. It is a 90-minute documentary about then-Senator Hillary Clinton, who was a candidate in the Democratic Party's 2008 Presidential primary elections. *Hillary* mentions Senator Clinton by name and depicts interviews with political commentators and other persons, most of them quite critical of Senator Clinton. *Hillary* was released in theaters and on DVD, but Citizens United wanted to increase distribution by making it available through video-on-demand.

To implement the proposal, Citizens United was prepared to pay for the video-on-demand; and to promote the film, it produced two 10-second ads and one 30-second ad for *Hillary*. Each ad includes a short (and, in our view, pejorative) statement about Senator Clinton, followed by the name of the movie and the movie's Website address. Citizens United desired to promote the video-on-demand offering by running advertisements on broadcast and cable television.

B

Before the Bipartisan Campaign Reform Act of 2002 (BCRA), federal law prohibited-and still does prohibit-corporations and unions from using general treasury funds to make direct contributions to candidates or independent expenditures that expressly advocate the election or defeat of a candidate, through any form of media, in connection with certain qualified federal elections.

C

Citizens United wanted to make *Hillary* available through video-on-demand within 30 days of the 2008 primary elections. It feared, however, that both the film and the ads would be covered by § 441b's ban on corporate-funded independent expenditures, thus subjecting the corporation to civil and criminal penalties under § 437g. In December 2007, Citizens United sought declaratory and injunctive relief against the FEC. It argued that (1) § 441b is unconstitutional as applied to *Hillary;* and (2) BCRA's disclaimer and disclosure requirements, BCRA §§ 201 and 311, are unconstitutional as applied to *Hillary* and to the three ads for the movie.

III

The First Amendment provides that "Congress shall make no law . . . abridging the freedom of speech." Laws enacted to control or suppress speech may operate at different points in the speech process. The following are just a few examples of restrictions that have been attempted at different stages of the speech process-all laws found to be invalid: restrictions requiring a permit at the outset, imposing a burden by impounding proceeds on receipts or royalties,; seeking to exact a cost after the speech occurs, and subjecting the speaker to criminal penalties.

The law before us is an outright ban, backed by criminal sanctions. Section 441b makes it a felony for all corporations-including nonprofit advocacy corporations-either to expressly advocate the election or defeat of candidates or to broadcast electioneering communications within 30 days of a primary election and 60 days of a general election. Thus, the following acts would all be felonies under § 441b: The Sierra Club runs an ad, within the crucial phase of 60 days before the general election, that exhorts the public to disapprove of a Congressman who favors logging in national forests; the National Rifle Association publishes a book urging the public to vote for the challenger because the incumbent U.S. Senator supports a handgun ban; and the American Civil Liberties Union creates a Web site telling the public to vote for a Presidential candidate in light of that candidate's defense of free speech. These prohibitions are classic examples of censorship.

Section 441b is a ban on corporate speech notwithstanding the fact that a PAC created by a corporation can still speak. See *McConnell,* 540 U.S., at 330–333, 124 S.Ct. 619 (opinion of KENNEDY, J.). A PAC is a separate association from the corporation. So the PAC exemption from § 441b's expenditure ban, § 441b(b)(2), does not allow corporations to speak. Even if a PAC could somehow allow a corporation to speak-and it does not-the option to form PACs does not alleviate the First Amendment problems with § 441b. PACs are burdensome alternatives; they are expensive to administer and subject to extensive regulations. For example, every PAC must appoint a treasurer, forward donations to the treasurer promptly, keep detailed records of the identities of the persons making donations, preserve receipts for three years, and file an organization statement and report changes to this information within 10 days.

PACs have to comply with these regulations just to speak. This might explain why fewer than 2,000 of the millions of corporations in this country have PACs. See Brief for Seven Former Chairmen of FEC et al. as *Amici Curiae* 11 (citing FEC, Summary of PAC Activity 1990–2006, online at http://www.fec.gov/press/press2007/20071009pac/sumhistory.pdf); IRS, Statistics of Income: 2006, Corporation. Income Tax Returns 2 (2009) (hereinafter Statistics of Income) (5.8 million for-profit corporations filed 2006 tax returns). PACs, furthermore, must exist before they can speak. Given the onerous restrictions, a corporation may not be able to establish a PAC in time to make its views known regarding candidates and issues in a current campaign.

Section 441b's prohibition on corporate independent expenditures is thus a ban on speech. As a "restriction on the amount of money a person or group can spend on political communication during a campaign," that statute "necessarily reduces the quantity of expression by restricting the number of issues discussed, the depth of their exploration, and the size of the audience reached." *Buckley v. Valeo,* 424 U.S. 1, 19.

Speech is an essential mechanism of democracy, for it is the means to hold officials accountable to the people. The right of citizens to inquire, to hear, to speak, and to use information to reach consensus is a precondition to enlightened self-government and a necessary means to protect it.

For these reasons, political speech must prevail against laws that would suppress it, whether by design or inadvertence. Laws that burden political speech are "subject to strict scrutiny."

Quite apart from the purpose or effect of regulating content, moreover, the Government may commit a constitutional wrong when by law it identifies certain preferred speakers. By taking the right to speak from some and giving it to others, the Government deprives the disadvantaged person or class of the right to use speech to strive to establish worth, standing, and respect for the speaker's voice. The Government may not by these means deprive the public of the right and privilege to determine for itself what speech and speakers are worthy of consideration. The First Amendment protects speech and speaker, and the ideas that flow from each.

We find no basis for the proposition that, in the context of political speech, the Government may impose restrictions on certain disfavored speakers. Both history and logic lead us to this conclusion.

A

1

The Court has recognized that First Amendment protection extends to corporations.

This protection has been extended by explicit holdings to the context of political speech. Under the rationale of these precedents, political speech does not lose First Amendment protection "simply because its source is a corporation." The Court has thus rejected the argument that political speech of corporations or other associations should be treated differently under the First Amendment simply because such associations are not "natural persons."

At least since the latter part of the 19th century, the laws of some States and of the United States imposed a ban on corporate direct contributions to candidates. Yet not until 1947 did Congress first prohibit independent expenditures by corporations and labor unions in § 304 of the Labor Management Relations Act 1947. For almost three decades thereafter, the Court did not reach the question whether restrictions on corporate and union expenditures are constitutional.

2

In *Buckley,* the Court addressed various challenges to the Federal Election Campaign Act of 1971 (FECA) as amended in 1974. These amendments created 18 U.S.C. § 608(e) (1970 ed., Supp. V), see 88 Stat. 1265, an independent expenditure ban separate from § 610 that applied to individuals as well as corporations and labor unions.

Before addressing the constitutionality of § 608(e)'s independent expenditure ban, *Buckley* first upheld § 608(b), FECA's limits on direct contributions to candidates. The *Buckley* Court recognized a "sufficiently important" governmental interest in "the prevention of corruption and the appearance of corruption." This followed from the Court's concern that large contributions could be given "to secure a political *quid pro quo.*"

The *Buckley* Court explained that the potential for *quid pro quo* corruption distinguished direct contributions to candidates from independent expenditures. The Court emphasized that "the independent expenditure ceiling . . . fails to serve any substantial governmental interest in stemming the reality or appearance of corruption in the electoral process."

Notwithstanding this precedent, Congress recodified § 610's corporate and union expenditure ban at 2 U.S.C. § 441b four months after *Buckley* was decided. See 90 Stat. 490. Section 441b is the independent expenditure restriction challenged here.

Less than two years after *Buckley, Bellotti,* 435 U.S. 765, 98 S.Ct. 1407, 55 L.Ed.2d 707, reaffirmed the First Amendment principle that the Government cannot restrict political speech based on the speaker's corporate identity. *Bellotti* could not have been clearer when it struck down a state-law prohibition on corporate independent expenditures related to referenda issues.

It is important to note that the reasoning and holding of *Bellotti* did not rest on the existence of a viewpoint-discriminatory statute. It rested on the principle that the Government lacks the power to ban corporations from speaking.

Bellotti did not address the constitutionality of the State's ban on corporate independent expenditures to support candidates. In our view, however, that restriction would have been unconstitutional under *Bellotti*'s central principle: that the First Amendment does not allow political speech restrictions based on a speaker's corporate identity. See *ibid.*

3

Thus the law stood until *Austin. Austin* "uph[eld] a direct restriction on the independent expenditure of funds for political speech for the first time in [this Court's] history." 494 U.S., at 695, 110 S.Ct. 1391 (KENNEDY, J., dissenting). There, the Michigan Chamber of Commerce sought to use general treasury funds to run a newspaper ad supporting a specific candidate. Michigan law, however, prohibited corporate independent expenditures that supported or opposed any candidate for state office. A violation of the law was punishable as a felony. The Court sustained the speech prohibition.

To bypass *Buckley* and *Bellotti,* the *Austin* Court identified a new governmental interest in limiting political speech: an antidistortion interest. *Austin* found a compelling governmental interest in preventing "the corrosive and distorting effects of immense aggregations of wealth that are accumulated with the help of the corporate form and that have little or no correlation to the public's support for the corporation's political ideas."

B

The Court is thus confronted with conflicting lines of precedent: a pre-*Austin* line that forbids restrictions on political speech based on the speaker's corporate identity and a post-*Austin* line that permits them. No case before *Austin* had held that Congress could prohibit independent expenditures for political speech based on the speaker's corporate identity. Before *Austin* Congress had enacted legislation for this purpose, and the Government urged the same proposition before this Court.

1

Austin's antidistortion rationale would produce the dangerous, and unacceptable, consequence that Congress could ban political speech of media corporations.

C

Our precedent is to be respected unless the most convincing of reasons demonstrates that adherence to it puts us on a course that is sure error. "Beyond workability, the relevant factors in deciding whether to adhere to the principle of *stare decisis* include the antiquity of the precedent, the reliance interests at stake, and of course whether the decision was well reasoned." *Montejo v. Louisiana,* 556 U.S. ____, ____, 129 S.Ct. 2079, 2088–2089, 173 L.Ed.2d 955 (2009) (overruling *Michigan v. Jackson,* 475 U.S. 625, 106 S.Ct. 1404, 89 L.Ed.2d 631 (1986)). We have also examined whether "experience has pointed up the precedent's shortcomings." *Pearson v. Callahan,* 555 U.S. ____, ____, 129 S.Ct. 808, 816, 172 L.Ed.2d 565 (2009) (overruling *Saucier v. Katz,* 533 U.S. 194, 121 S.Ct. 2151, 150 L.Ed.2d 272 (2001)).

These considerations counsel in favor of rejecting *Austin,* which itself contravened this Court's earlier precedents in *Buckley* and *Bellotti.*

For the reasons above, it must be concluded that *Austin* was not well reasoned.

Rapid changes in technology-and the creative dynamic inherent in the concept of free expression-counsel against upholding a law that restricts political speech in certain media or by certain speakers. See Part II-C, *supra.* Today, 30-second television ads may be the most effective way to convey a political message. Soon, however, it may be that Internet sources, such as blogs and social networking Web sites, will provide citizens with significant information about political candidates and issues. Yet, § 441b would seem to ban a blog post expressly advocating the election or defeat of a candidate if that blog were created with corporate funds. See 2 U.S.C. § 441b(a); *MCFL, supra,* at 249, 107 S.Ct. 616. The First Amendment does not permit Congress to make these categorical distinctions based on the corporate identity of the speaker and the content of the political speech.

No serious reliance interests are at stake. As the Court stated in *Payne v. Tennessee,* 501 U.S. 808, 828, 111 S.Ct. 2597, 115 L.Ed.2d 720 (1991), reliance interests are important considerations in property and contract cases, where parties may have acted in conformance with existing legal rules in order to conduct transactions. Here, though, parties have been prevented from acting-corporations have been banned from making independent expenditures. Legislatures may have enacted bans on corporate expenditures believing that those bans were constitutional. This is not a compelling interest for *stare decisis.* If it were, legislative acts could prevent us from overruling our own precedents, thereby interfering with our duty "to say what the law is." *Marbury v. Madison,* 1 Cranch 137, 177, 2 L.Ed. 60 (1803).

Due consideration leads to this conclusion: *Austin,* should be and now is overruled. We return to the principle established in *Buckley* and *Bellotti* that the Government may not suppress political speech on the basis of the speaker's corporate identity. No sufficient governmental interest justifies limits on the political speech of nonprofit or for-profit corporations.

D

Austin is overruled, so it provides no basis for allowing the Government to limit corporate independent expenditures.

Given our conclusion we are further required to overrule the part of *McConnell* that upheld BCRA § 203's extension of § 441b's restrictions on corporate independent expenditures.

The judgment of the District Court is reversed with respect to the constitutionality of 2 U.S.C. § 441b's restrictions on corporate independent expenditures. The judgment is affirmed with respect to BCRA's disclaimer and disclosure requirements. The case is remanded for further proceedings consistent with this opinion.

It is so ordered.

CHIEF JUSTICE ROBERTS, with whom JUSTICE ALITO joins, concurring.

The Government urges us in this case to uphold a direct prohibition on political speech. It asks us to embrace a theory of the First Amendment that would allow censorship not only of television and radio broadcasts, but of pamphlets, posters, the Internet, and virtually any other medium that corporations and unions might find useful in expressing their views on matters of public concern. Its theory, if accepted, would empower the Government to prohibit newspapers from running editorials or opinion pieces supporting or opposing candidates for office, so long as the newspapers were owned by corporations-as the major ones are. First Amendment rights could be confined to individuals, subverting the vibrant public discourse that is at the foundation of our democracy.

The Court properly rejects that theory, and I join its opinion in full. The First Amendment protects more than just the individual on a soapbox and the lonely pamphleteer. I write separately to address the important principles of judicial restraint and *stare decisis* implicated in this case.

II

The text and purpose of the First Amendment point in the same direction: Congress may not prohibit political speech, even if the speaker is a corporation or union. What makes this case difficult is the need to confront our prior decision in *Austin.*

A

Fidelity to precedent-the policy of *stare decisis*-is vital to the proper exercise of the judicial function. "*Stare decisis* is the preferred course because it promotes the evenhanded, predictable, and consistent development of legal principles, fosters reliance on judicial decisions, and contributes to the actual and perceived integrity of the judicial process." *Payne v. Tennessee,* 501 U.S. 808, 827, 111 S.Ct. 2597, 115 L.Ed.2d 720 (1991). For these reasons, we have long recognized that departures from precedent are inappropriate in the absence of a "special justification." *Arizona v. Rumsey,* 467 U.S. 203, 212, 104 S.Ct. 2305, 81 L.Ed.2d 164 (1984).

At the same time, *stare decisis* is neither an "inexorable command," *Lawrence v. Texas,* 539 U.S. 558, 577, 123 S.Ct. 2472, 156 L.Ed.2d 508 (2003), nor "a mechanical formula of adherence to the latest decision," *Helvering v. Hallock,* 309 U.S. 106, 119, 60 S.Ct. 444, 84 L.Ed. 604 (1940), especially in constitutional cases, see *United States v. Scott,* 437 U.S. 82, 101, 98 S.Ct. 2187, 57 L.Ed.2d 65 (1978). If it were, segregation would be legal, minimum wage laws would be unconstitutional, and the Government could wiretap ordinary criminal suspects without first obtaining warrants. As the dissent properly notes, none of us has viewed *stare decisis* in such absolute terms.

Stare decisis is instead a "principle of policy." When considering whether to reexamine a prior erroneous holding, we must balance the importance of having constitutional questions *decided* against the importance of having them *decided right.*

In conducting this balancing, we must keep in mind that *stare decisis* is not an end in itself. Its greatest purpose is to serve a constitutional ideal-the rule of law. It follows that in the unusual circumstance when fidelity to any particular precedent does more to damage this constitutional ideal than to advance it, we must be more willing to depart from that precedent.

Thus, for example, if the precedent under consideration itself departed from the Court's jurisprudence, returning to the " 'intrinsically sounder' doctrine established in prior cases" may "better serv[e] the values of *stare decisis* than would following [the] more recently decided case inconsistent with the decisions that came before it." Abrogating the errant precedent, rather than reaffirming or extending it, might better preserve the law's coherence and curtail the precedent's disruptive effects.

Likewise, if adherence to a precedent actually impedes the stable and orderly adjudication of future cases, its *stare decisis* effect is also diminished. This can happen in a number of circumstances, such as when the precedent's validity is so hotly contested that it cannot reliably function as a basis for decision in future cases, when its rationale threatens to upend our settled jurisprudence in related areas of law, and when the precedent's underlying reasoning has become so discredited that the Court cannot keep the precedent alive without jury-rigging new and different justifications to shore up the original mistake.

B

These considerations weigh against retaining our decision in *Austin*. First, as the majority explains, that decision was an "aberration" insofar as it departed from the robust protections we had granted political speech in our earlier cases. *Austin* undermined the careful line that *Buckley* drew to distinguish limits on contributions to candidates from limits on independent expenditures on speech.

Austin's reasoning was-and remains-inconsistent with *Buckley*'s explicit repudiation of any government interest in "equalizing the relative ability of individuals and groups to influence the outcome of elections." 424 U.S., at 48–49.

Austin was also inconsistent with *Bellotti*'s clear rejection of the idea that "speech that otherwise would be within the protection of the First Amendment loses that protection simply because its source is a corporation."

Second, the validity of *Austin*'s rationale-itself adopted over two "spirited dissents," The simple fact that one of our decisions remains controversial is, of course, insufficient to justify overruling it. But it does undermine the precedent's ability to contribute to the stable and orderly development of the law. In such circumstances, it is entirely appropriate for the Court-which in this case is squarely asked to reconsider *Austin*'s validity for the first time-to address the matter with a greater willingness to consider new approaches capable of restoring our doctrine to sounder footing.

Third, the *Austin* decision is uniquely destabilizing because it threatens to subvert our Court's decisions even outside the particular context of corporate express advocacy. The First Amendment theory underlying *Austin*'s holding is extraordinarily broad. *Austin*'s logic would authorize government prohibition of political speech by a category of speakers in the name of equality-a point that most scholars acknowledge (and many celebrate), but that the dissent denies.

JUSTICE STEVENS, with whom JUSTICE GINSBURG, JUSTICE BREYER, and JUSTICE SOTOMAYOR join, concurring in part and dissenting in part.

The real issue in this case concerns how, not if, the appellant may finance its electioneering. Citizens United is a wealthy nonprofit corporation that runs a political action committee (PAC) with millions of dollars in assets. Under the Bipartisan Campaign Reform Act of 2002 (BCRA), it could have used those assets to televise and promote *Hillary: The Movie* wherever and whenever it wanted to. It also could have spent unrestricted sums to broadcast *Hillary* at any time other than the 30 days before the last primary election. Neither Citizens United's nor any other corporation's speech has been "banned." All that the parties dispute is whether Citizens United had a right to use the funds in its general treasury to pay for broadcasts during the 30-day period. The notion that the First Amendment dictates an affirmative answer to that question is, in my judgment, profoundly misguided. Even more misguided is the notion that the Court must rewrite the law relating to campaign expenditures by *for-profit* corporations and unions to decide this case.

The basic premise underlying the Court's ruling is its iteration, and constant reiteration, of the proposition that the First Amendment bars regulatory distinctions based on a speaker's identity, including its "identity" as a corporation. While that glittering generality has rhetorical appeal, it is not a correct statement of the law. Nor does it tell us when a corporation may engage in electioneering that some of its shareholders oppose. It does not even resolve the specific question whether Citizens United may be required to finance some of its messages with the money in its PAC. The conceit that corporations must be treated identically to natural persons in the political sphere is not only inaccurate but also inadequate to justify the Court's disposition of this case.

In the context of election to public office, the distinction between corporate and human speakers is significant. Although they make enormous contributions to our society, corporations are not actually members of it. They cannot vote or run for office. Because they may be managed and controlled by nonresidents, their interests may conflict in fundamental respects with the interests of eligible voters. The financial resources, legal structure, and instrumental orientation of corporations raise legitimate concerns about their role in the electoral process. Our lawmakers have a compelling constitutional basis, if not also a democratic duty, to take measures designed to guard against the potentially deleterious effects of corporate spending in local and national races.

The majority's approach to corporate electioneering marks a dramatic break from our past. Congress has placed special limitations on campaign spending by corporations ever since the passage of the Tillman Act in 1907. We have unanimously concluded that this "reflects a permissible assessment of the dangers posed by those entities to the electoral process," and have accepted the "legislative judgment that the special characteristics of the corporate structure require particularly careful regulation." The Court today rejects a century of history when it treats the distinction between corporate and individual campaign spending as an invidious novelty born of *Austin v. Michigan Chamber of Commerce,* Relying largely on individual dissenting opinions, the majority blazes through our precedents, overruling or disavowing a body of case law.

I

The Court's ruling threatens to undermine the integrity of elected institutions across the Nation. The path it has taken to reach its outcome will, I fear, do damage to this institution. Before turning to the question whether to overrule *Austin* and part of *McConnell,* it is important to explain why the Court should not be deciding that question.

Scope of the Case

The first reason is that the question was not properly brought before us. In declaring § 203 of BCRA facially unconstitutional on the ground that corporations' electoral expenditures may not be regulated any more stringently than those of individuals, the majority decides this case on a basis relinquished below, not included in the questions presented to us by the litigants, and argued here only in response to the Court's invitation. This procedure is unusual and inadvisable for a court.

" 'It is only in exceptional cases coming here from the federal courts that questions not pressed or passed upon below are reviewed. " The appellant in this case did not so much as assert an exceptional circumstance, and one searches the majority opinion in vain for the mention of any. That is unsurprising, for none exists.

Setting the case for reargument was a constructive step, but it did not cure this fundamental problem. Essentially, five Justices were unhappy with the limited nature of the case before us, so they changed the case to give themselves an opportunity to change the law.

Narrower Grounds

It is all the more distressing that our colleagues have manufactured a facial challenge, because the parties have advanced numerous ways to resolve the case that would facilitate electioneering by nonprofit advocacy corporations such as Citizens United, without toppling statutes and precedents.

Consider just three of the narrower grounds of decision that the majority has bypassed. First, the Court could have ruled, on statutory grounds, that a feature-length film distributed through video-on-demand does not qualify as an "electioneering communication" under § 203 of BCRA, 2 U.S.C. § 441b.

Second, the Court could have expanded the *MCFL* exemption to cover § 501(c)(4) nonprofits that accept only a *de minimis* amount of money from for-profit corporations.

Finally, let us not forget Citizens United's as-applied constitutional challenge. Precisely because Citizens United looks so much like the *MCFL* organizations we have exempted from regulation, while a feature-length video-on-demand film looks so unlike the types of electoral advocacy Congress has found deserving of regulation, this challenge is a substantial one. As the appellant's own arguments show, the Court could have easily limited the breadth of its constitutional holding had it declined to adopt the novel notion that speakers and speech acts must always be treated identically-and always spared expenditures restrictions-in the political realm. Yet the Court nonetheless turns its back on the as-applied review process that has been a staple of campaign finance litigation since *Buckley v. Valeo,* 424 U.S. 1.

III

The novelty of the Court's procedural dereliction and its approach to *stare decisis* is matched by the novelty of its ruling on the merits. The ruling rests on several premises. First, the Court claims that *Austin* and *McConnell* have "banned" corporate speech. Second, it claims that the First Amendment precludes regulatory distinctions based on speaker identity, including the speaker's identity as a corporation. Third, it claims that *Austin* and *McConnell* were radical outliers in our First Amendment tradition and our campaign finance jurisprudence. Each of these claims is wrong.

The So-Called "Ban"

Pervading the Court's analysis is the ominous image of a "categorical ba[n]" on corporate speech. Indeed, the majority invokes the specter of a "ban" on nearly every page of its opinion. This characterization is highly misleading, and needs to be corrected.

In fact it already has been. Our cases have repeatedly pointed out that, "[c]ontrary to the [majority's] critical assumptions," the statutes upheld in *Austin* and *McConnell* do "not impose an *absolute* ban on all forms of corporate political spending." For starters, both statutes provide exemptions for PACs, separate segregated funds established by a corporation for political purposes. See 2 U.S.C. § 441b(b)(2)(C); Mich. Comp. Laws Ann. § 169.255 (West 2005). "The ability to form and administer separate segregated funds," we observed in *McConnell,* "has provided corporations and unions with a constitutionally sufficient opportunity to engage in express advocacy. That has been this Court's unanimous view." 540 U.S., at 203, 124 S.Ct. 619.

Under BCRA, any corporation's "stockholders and their families and its executive or administrative personnel and their families" can pool their resources to finance electioneering communications. 2 U.S.C. § 441b(b)(4)(A)(i). A significant and growing number of corporations avail themselves of this option.

The laws upheld in *Austin* and *McConnell* leave open many additional avenues for corporations' political speech. Like numerous statutes, it exempts media companies' news stories, commentaries, and editorials from its electioneering restrictions, in recognition of the unique role played by the institutional press in sustaining public debate.

Identity-Based Distinctions

The second pillar of the Court's opinion is its assertion that "the Government cannot restrict political speech based on the speaker's . . . identity."

The Government routinely places special restrictions on the speech rights of students, prisoners, members of the Armed Forces, foreigners, and its own employees When such restrictions are justified by a legitimate governmental interest, they do not necessarily raise constitutional problems. In contrast to the blanket rule that the majority espouses, our cases recognize that the Government's interests may be more or less compelling with respect to different classes of speakers,

The same logic applies to this case with additional force because it is the identity of corporations, rather than individuals, that the Legislature has taken into account. As we have unanimously observed, legislatures are entitled to decide "that the special characteristics of the corporate structure require particularly careful regulation" in an electoral context. Not only has the distinctive potential of corporations to corrupt the electoral process long been recognized, but within the area of campaign finance, corporate spending is also "furthest from the core of political expression, since corporations' First Amendment speech and association interests are derived largely from those of their members and of the public in receiving information."

If taken seriously, our colleagues' assumption that the identity of a speaker has *no* relevance to the Government's ability to regulate political speech would lead to some remarkable conclusions. Such an assumption would have accorded the propaganda broadcasts to our troops by "Tokyo Rose" during World War II the same protection as speech by Allied commanders. More pertinently, it would appear to afford the same protection to multinational corporations controlled by foreigners as to individual Americans.

In short, the Court dramatically overstates its critique of identity-based distinctions, without ever explaining why corporate identity demands the same treatment as individual identity. Only the most wooden approach to the First Amendment could justify the unprecedented line it seeks to draw.

Our First Amendment Tradition

A third fulcrum of the Court's opinion is the idea that *Austin* and *McConnell* are radical outliers, "aberration[s]," in our First Amendment tradition. The Court has it exactly backwards. It is today's holding that is the radical departure from what had been settled First Amendment law. To see why, it is useful to take a long view.

1. *Original Understandings*

Let us start from the beginning. The Court invokes "ancient First Amendment principles," to defend today's ruling, yet it makes only a perfunctory attempt to ground its analysis in the principles or understandings of those who drafted and ratified the Amendment. Perhaps this is because there is not a scintilla of evidence to support the notion that anyone believed it would preclude regulatory distinctions based on the corporate form. To the extent that the Framers' views are discernible and relevant to the disposition of this case, they would appear to cut strongly against the majority's position.

This is not only because the Framers and their contemporaries conceived of speech more narrowly than we now think of it, but also because they held very different views about the nature of the First Amendment right and the role of corporations in society. Those few corporations that existed at the founding were authorized by grant of a special legislative charter. The individualized charter mode of incorporation reflected the "cloud of disfavor under which corporations labored" in the early years of this Nation.

The Framers thus took it as a given that corporations could be comprehensively regulated in the service of the public welfare. Unlike our colleagues, they had little trouble distinguishing corporations from human beings, and when they constitutionalized the right to free speech in the First Amendment, it was the free speech of individual Americans that they had in mind. While individuals might join together to exercise their speech rights, business corporations, at least, were plainly not seen as facilitating such associational or expressive ends.

As a matter of original expectations, then, it seems absurd to think that the First Amendment prohibits legislatures from taking into account the corporate identity of a sponsor of electoral advocacy. As a matter of original meaning, it likewise seems baseless-unless one evaluates the First Amendment's "principles," at such a high level of generality that the historical understandings of the Amendment cease to be a meaningful constraint on the judicial task. This case sheds a revelatory light on the assumption of some that an impartial judge's application of an originalist methodology is likely to yield more determinate answers, or to play a more decisive role in the decisional process, than his or her views about sound policy.

IV

Having explained why this is not an appropriate case in which to revisit *Austin* and *McConnell* and why these decisions sit perfectly well with "First Amendment principles," I come at last to the interests that are at stake. The majority recognizes that *Austin* and *McConnell* may be defended on anticorruption, antidistortion, and shareholder protection rationales. It badly errs both in explaining the nature of these rationales, which overlap and complement each other, and in applying them to the case at hand.

The Anticorruption Interest

Undergirding the majority's approach to the merits is the claim that the only "sufficiently important governmental interest in preventing corruption or the appearance of corruption" is one that is "limited to *quid pro quo* corruption." *Ante,* at 909–910. This is the same "crabbed view of corruption" that was espoused by Justice KENNEDY in *McConnell* and squarely rejected by the Court in that case. 540 U.S., at 152, 124 S.Ct. 619. While it is true that we have not always spoken about corruption in a clear or consistent voice, the approach taken by the majority cannot be right, in my judgment. It disregards our constitutional history and the fundamental demands of a democratic society.

On numerous occasions we have recognized Congress' legitimate interest in preventing the money that is spent on elections from exerting an " 'undue influence on an officeholder's judgment' " and from creating " 'the appearance of such influence,' " beyond the sphere of *quid pro quo* relationships. Bribery may be the paradigm case. But the difference between selling a vote and selling access is a matter of degree, not kind. And selling access is not qualitatively different from giving special preference to those who spent money on one's behalf. Corruption operates along a spectrum, and the majority's apparent belief that *quid pro quo* arrangements can be neatly demarcated from other improper influences does not accord with the theory or reality of politics. It certainly does not accord with the record Congress developed in passing BCRA, a record that stands as a remarkable testament to the energy and ingenuity with which corporations, unions, lobbyists, and politicians may go about scratching each other's backs-and which amply supported Congress' determination to target a limited set of especially destructive practices.

Our "undue influence" cases have allowed the American people to cast a wider net through legislative experiments designed to ensure, to some minimal extent, "that officeholders will decide issues . . . on the merits or the desires of their constituencies," and not "according to the wishes of those who have made large financial contributions"—or expenditures—"valued by the officeholder." *McConnell,* 540 U.S., at 153.

Quid Pro Quo *Corruption*

There is no need to take my side in the debate over the scope of the anticorruption interest to see that the Court's merits holding is wrong. Even under the majority's "crabbed view of corruption," the Government should not lose this case.

"The importance of the governmental interest in preventing [corruption through the creation of political debts] has never been doubted." Even in the cases that have construed the anticorruption interest most narrowly, we have never suggested that such *quid pro quo* debts must take the form of outright vote buying or bribes, which have long been distinct crimes. Rather, they encompass the myriad ways in which outside parties may induce an officeholder to confer a legislative benefit in direct response to, or anticipation of, some outlay of money the parties have made or will make on behalf of the officeholder. It has likewise never been doubted that "[o]f almost equal concern as the danger of actual *quid pro quo* arrangements is the impact of the appearance of corruption." In theory, our colleagues accept this much. As applied to BCRA § 203, however, they conclude "[t]he anticorruption interest is not sufficient to displace the speech here in question."

The majority appears to think it decisive that the BCRA record does not contain "direct examples of votes being exchanged for . . . expenditures." It would have been quite remarkable if Congress had created a record detailing such behavior by its own Members. Proving that a specific vote was exchanged for a specific expenditure has always been next to impossible: Elected officials have diverse motivations, and no one will acknowledge that he sold a vote. Yet, even if "[i]ngratiation and access . . . are not corruption" themselves, *ibid.,* they are necessary prerequisites to it; they can create both the opportunity for, and the appearance of, *quid pro quo* arrangements. The influx of unlimited corporate money into the electoral realm also creates new opportunities for the mirror image of *quid pro quo* deals: threats, both explicit and implicit. Starting today, corporations with large war chests to deploy on electioneering may find democratically elected bodies becoming much more attuned to their interests. The majority both misreads the facts and draws the wrong conclusions when it suggests that the BCRA record provides "only scant evidence that independent expenditures . . . ingratiate," and that, "in any event," none of it matters.

The insight that even technically independent expenditures can be corrupting in much the same way as direct contributions is bolstered by our decision last year in *Caperton v. A.T. Massey Coal Co.,* 556 U.S. ___, 129 S.Ct. 2252, 173 L.Ed.2d 1208 (2009). In that case, Don Blankenship, the chief executive officer of a corporation with a lawsuit pending before the West Virginia high court, spent large sums on behalf of a particular candidate, Brent Benjamin, running for a seat on that court. "In addition to contributing the $1,000 statutory maximum to Benjamin's campaign committee, Blankenship donated almost $2.5 million to 'And For The Sake Of The Kids,' " a § 527 corporation that ran ads targeting Benjamin's opponent. *Id.,* at ___, 129 S.Ct., at 2257. "This was not all. Blankenship spent, in addition, just over $500,000 on independent expenditures . . . ' "to support . . . Brent Benjamin." ' " *Id.,* at ___, 129 S.Ct., at 2257 (second alteration in original). Applying its common sense, this Court accepted petitioners' argument that Blankenship's "pivotal role in getting Justice Benjamin elected created a constitutionally intolerable probability of actual bias" when Benjamin later declined to recuse himself from the appeal by Blankenship's corporation. *Id.,* at ___, 129 S.Ct., at 2262. "Though n[o] . . . bribe or criminal influence" was involved, we recognized that "Justice Benjamin would nevertheless feel a debt of gratitude to Blankenship for his extraordinary efforts to get him elected." *Ibid.* "The difficulties of inquiring into actual bias," we further noted, "simply underscore the need for objective rules," *id.,* at ___, 129 S.Ct., at 2263—rules which will perforce turn on the appearance of bias rather than its actual existence.

In *Caperton,* then, we accepted the premise that, at least in some circumstances, independent expenditures on candidate elections will raise an intolerable specter of *quid pro quo* corruption.

Austin and Corporate Expenditures

Just as the majority gives short shrift to the general societal interests at stake in campaign finance regulation, it also overlooks the distinctive considerations raised by the regulation of *corporate* expenditures. The majority fails to appreciate that *Austin*'s antidistortion rationale is itself an anticorruption rationale, tied to the special concerns raised by corporations. Understood properly, "antidistortion" is simply a variant on the classic governmental interest in protecting against improper influences on officeholders that debilitate the democratic process.

1. *Antidistortion*

The fact that corporations are different from human beings might seem to need no elaboration, except that the majority opinion almost completely elides it. *Austin* set forth some of the basic differences. Unlike natural persons, corporations have "limited liability" for their owners and managers, "perpetual life," separation of ownership and control, "and favorable treatment of the accumulation and distribution of assets . . . that enhance their ability to attract capital and to deploy their resources in ways that maximize the return on their shareholders' investments." Unlike voters in U.S. elections, corporations may be foreign controlled. Unlike other interest groups, business corporations have been "effectively delegated responsibility for ensuring society's economic welfare"; they inescapably structure the life of every citizen. " '[T]he resources in the treasury of a business corporation,' "

It might also be added that corporations have no consciences, no beliefs, no feelings, no thoughts, no desires. Corporations help structure and facilitate the activities of human beings, to be sure, and their "personhood" often serves as a useful legal fiction. But they are not themselves members of "We the People" by whom and for whom our Constitution was established.

These basic points help explain why corporate electioneering is not only more likely to impair compelling governmental interests, but also why restrictions on that electioneering are less likely to encroach upon First Amendment freedoms.

It is an interesting question "who" is even speaking when a business corporation places an advertisement that endorses or attacks a particular candidate. Presumably it is not the customers or employees, who typically have no say in such matters. It cannot realistically be said to be the shareholders, who tend to be far removed from the day-to-day decisions of the firm and whose political preferences may be opaque to management. Perhaps the officers or directors of the corporation have the best claim to be the ones speaking, except their fiduciary duties generally prohibit them from using corporate funds for personal ends. Some individuals associated with the corporation must make the decision to place the ad, but the idea that these individuals are thereby fostering their self-expression or cultivating their critical faculties is fanciful. It is entirely possible that the corporation's electoral message will *conflict* with their personal convictions. Take away the ability to use general treasury funds for some of those ads, and no one's autonomy, dignity, or political equality has been impinged upon in the least.

2. *Shareholder Protection*

There is yet another way in which laws such as § 203 can serve First Amendment values. Interwoven with *Austin*'s concern to protect the integrity of the electoral process is a concern to protect the rights of shareholders from a kind of coerced speech: electioneering expenditures that do not "reflec [t] [their] support." When corporations use general treasury funds to praise or attack a particular candidate for office, it is the shareholders, as the residual claimants, who are effectively footing the bill. Those shareholders who disagree with the corporation's electoral message may find their financial investments being used to undermine their political convictions.

V

Today's decision is backwards in many senses. It elevates the majority's agenda over the litigants' submissions, facial attacks over as-applied claims, broad constitutional theories over narrow statutory grounds, individual dissenting opinions over precedential holdings, assertion over tradition, absolutism over empiricism, rhetoric over reality. Our colleagues have arrived at the conclusion that *Austin* must be overruled and that § 203 is facially unconstitutional only after mischaracterizing both the reach and rationale of those authorities, and after bypassing or ignoring rules of judicial restraint used to cabin the Court's lawmaking power. Their conclusion that the societal interest in avoiding corruption and the appearance of corruption does not provide an adequate justification for regulating corporate expenditures on candidate elections relies on an incorrect description of that interest, along with a failure to acknowledge the relevance of established facts and the considered judgments of state and federal legislatures over many decades.

In a democratic society, the longstanding consensus on the need to limit corporate campaign spending should outweigh the wooden application of judge-made rules. The majority's rejection of this principle "elevate[s] corporations to a level of deference which has not been seen at least since the days when substantive due process was regularly used to invalidate regulatory legislation thought to unfairly impinge upon established economic interests." *Bellotti,* 435 U.S., at 817, n. 13, 98 S.Ct. 1407 (White, J., dissenting). At bottom, the Court's opinion is thus a rejection of the common sense of the American people, who have recognized a need to prevent corporations from undermining self-government since the founding, and who have fought against the distinctive corrupting potential of corporate electioneering since the days of Theodore Roosevelt. It is a strange time to repudiate that common sense. While American democracy is imperfect, few outside the majority of this Court would have thought its flaws included a dearth of corporate money in politics.

I would affirm the judgment of the District Court.

JUSTICE THOMAS, concurring in part and dissenting in part.

I join all but Part IV of the Court's opinion.

Political speech is entitled to robust protection under the First Amendment. Section 203 of the Bipartisan Campaign Reform Act of 2002 (BCRA) has never been reconcilable with that protection. By striking down § 203, the Court takes an important first step toward restoring full constitutional protection to speech that is "indispensable to the effective and intelligent use of the processes of popular government." *McConnell v. Federal Election Comm'n,* 540 U.S. 93, (2003) (THOMAS, J., concurring in part, concurring in judgment in part, and dissenting in part) (internal quotation marks omitted). I dissent from Part IV of the Court's opinion, however, because the Court's constitutional analysis does not go far enough. The disclosure, disclaimer, and reporting requirements in BCRA §§ 201 and 311 are also unconstitutional.

FOR DISCUSSION

What value and role do the different opinions assign to precedent? What grounds do they offer for when precedent should be upheld versus rejected? At one point Chief Justice Roberts asserts that: "There is a difference between judicial restraint and judicial abdication." Do you find his distinction valid here? Does the majority offer persuasive arguments for overruling its decisions in *Austin* and *McConnell*?

Do you think the Constitution should treat different speakers differently? Specifically, should corporations be treated differently in the electoral process from ordinary persons?

BURWELL V. HOBBY LOBBY STORES, INC.

___ U.S. ___, 134 S.Ct. 2751, 189 L.Ed.2d 675 (2014)

Several plaintiffs, including Hobby Lobby, a closely-held corporation, challenged regulations issued under Patient Protection and Affordable Care Act (ACA), based on allegations that the preventive services coverage mandate for employers violated constitutional and statutory protections of religious freedom by forcing them to provide health insurance coverage for abortion-inducing drugs and devices, as well as related education and counseling. United States District Court denied plaintiffs' motion for preliminary injunction. Plaintiffs appealed. The United States Court of Appeals reversed and remanded. Case was appealed to the Supreme Court which affirmed.

Vote: 5–4

JUSTICE ALITO wrote the majority opinion.

We must decide in these cases whether the Religious Freedom Restoration Act of 1993 (RFRA) permits the United States Department of Health and Human Services (HHS) to demand that three closely held corporations provide health-insurance coverage for methods of contraception that violate the sincerely held religious beliefs of the companies' owners. We hold that the regulations that impose this obligation violate RFRA, which prohibits the Federal Government from taking any action that substantially burdens the exercise of religion unless that action constitutes the least restrictive means of serving a compelling government interest.

In holding that the HHS mandate is unlawful, we reject HHS's argument that the owners of the companies forfeited all RFRA protection when they decided to organize their businesses as corporations rather than sole proprietorships or general partnerships. The plain terms of RFRA make it perfectly clear that Congress did not discriminate in this way against men and women who wish to run their businesses as for-profit corporations in the manner required by their religious beliefs.

Since RFRA applies in these cases, we must decide whether the challenged HHS regulations substantially burden the exercise of religion, and we hold that they do. The owners of the businesses have religious objections to abortion, and according to their religious beliefs the four contraceptive methods at issue are abortifacients. If the owners comply with the HHS mandate, they believe they will be facilitating abortions, and if they do not comply, they will pay a very heavy price—as much as $1.3 million per day, or about $475 million per year, in the case of one of the companies. If these consequences do not amount to a substantial burden, it is hard to see what would.

Under RFRA, a Government action that imposes a substantial burden on religious exercise must serve a compelling government interest, and we assume that the HHS regulations satisfy this requirement. But in order for the HHS mandate to be sustained, it must also constitute the least restrictive means of serving that interest, and the mandate plainly fails that test. There are other ways in which Congress or HHS could equally ensure that every woman has cost-free access to the particular contraceptives at issue here and, indeed, to all FDA-approved contraceptives.

In fact, HHS has already devised and implemented a system that seeks to respect the religious liberty of religious nonprofit corporations while ensuring that the employees of these entities have precisely the same access to all FDA-approved contraceptives as employees of companies whose owners have no religious objections to providing such coverage. The employees of these religious nonprofit corporations still have access to insurance coverage without cost sharing for all FDA-approved contraceptives; and according to HHS, this system imposes no net economic burden on the insurance companies that are required to provide or secure the coverage.

Although HHS has made this system available to religious nonprofits that have religious objections to the contraceptive mandate, HHS has provided no reason why the same system cannot be made available when the owners of for-profit corporations have similar religious objections. We therefore conclude that this system constitutes an alternative that achieves all of the Government's aims while providing greater respect for religious liberty. And under RFRA, that conclusion means that enforcement of the HHS contraceptive mandate against the objecting parties in these cases is unlawful.

I

A

Congress enacted RFRA in 1993 in order to provide very broad protection for religious liberty. RFRA's enactment came three years after this Court's decision in *Employment Div., Dept. of Human Resources of Ore. v. Smith,* 494 U.S. 872, 110 S.Ct. 1595, 108 L.Ed.2d 876 (1990), which largely repudiated the method of analyzing free-exercise claims that had been used in cases like *Sherbert v. Verner,* 374 U.S. 398, 83 S.Ct. 1790, 10 L.Ed.2d 965 (1963), and *Wisconsin v. Yoder,* 406 U.S. 205, 92 S.Ct. 1526, 32 L.Ed.2d 15 (1972). In determining whether challenged government actions violated the Free Exercise Clause of the First Amendment, those decisions used a balancing test that took into account whether the challenged action imposed a substantial burden on the practice of religion, and if it did, whether it was needed to serve a compelling government interest. Applying this test, the Court held in *Sherbert* that an employee who was fired for refusing to work on her Sabbath could not be denied unemployment benefits. And in *Yoder*, the Court held that Amish children could not be required to comply with a state law demanding that they remain in school until the age of 16 even though their religion required them to focus on uniquely Amish values and beliefs during their formative adolescent years.

In *Smith,* however, the Court rejected "the balancing test set forth in *Sherbert.*" *Smith* concerned two members of the Native American Church who were fired for ingesting peyote for sacramental purposes. When they sought unemployment benefits, the State of Oregon rejected their claims on the ground that consumption of peyote was a crime, but the Oregon Supreme Court, applying the *Sherbert* test, held that the denial of benefits violated the Free Exercise Clause.

This Court then reversed, observing that use of the *Sherbert* test whenever a person objected on religious grounds to the enforcement of a generally applicable law "would open the prospect of constitutionally required religious exemptions from civic obligations of almost every conceivable kind." The Court therefore held that, under the First Amendment, "neutral, generally applicable laws may be applied to religious practices even when not supported by a compelling governmental interest."

Congress responded to *Smith* by enacting RFRA. "[L]aws [that are] 'neutral' toward religion," Congress found, "may burden religious exercise as surely as laws intended to interfere with religious exercise." In order to ensure broad protection for religious liberty, RFRA provides that "Government shall not substantially burden a person's exercise of religion even if the burden results from a rule of general applicability." If the Government substantially burdens a person's exercise of religion, under the Act that person is entitled to an exemption from the rule unless the Government "demonstrates that application of the burden to the person—(1) is in furtherance of a compelling governmental interest; and (2) is the least restrictive means of furthering that compelling governmental interest."

B

At issue in these cases are HHS regulations promulgated under the Patient Protection and Affordable Care Act of 2010(ACA). ACA generally requires employers with 50 or more full-time employees to offer "a group health plan or group health insurance coverage" that provides "minimum essential coverage." Any covered employer that does not provide such coverage must pay a substantial price. Specifically, if a covered employer provides group health insurance but its plan fails to comply with ACA's group-health-plan requirements, the employer may be required to pay $100 per day for each affected "individual." And if the employer decides to stop providing health insurance altogether and at least one full-time employee enrolls in a health plan and qualifies for a subsidy on one of the government-run ACA exchanges, the employer must pay $2,000 per year for each of its full-time employees.

Unless an exception applies, ACA requires an employer's group health plan or group-health-insurance coverage to furnish "preventive care and screenings" for women without "any cost sharing requirements."

Congress itself, however, did not specify what types of preventive care must be covered. Instead, Congress authorized the Health Resources and Services Administration (HRSA), a component of HHS, to make that important and sensitive decision. The HRSA in turn consulted the Institute of Medicine, a nonprofit group of volunteer advisers, in determining which preventive services to require.

In August 2011, based on the Institute's recommendations, the HRSA promulgated the Women's Preventive Services Guidelines. The Guidelines provide that nonexempt employers are generally required to provide "coverage, without cost sharing" for "[a]ll Food and Drug Administration [(FDA)] approved contraceptive methods, sterilization procedures, and patient education and counseling." Although many of the required, FDA-approved methods of contraception work by preventing the fertilization of an egg, four of those methods (those specifically at issue in these cases) may have the effect of preventing an already fertilized egg from developing any further by inhibiting its attachment to the uterus.

HHS also authorized the HRSA to establish exemptions from the contraceptive mandate for "religious employers." That category encompasses "churches, their integrated auxiliaries, and conventions or associations of churches," as well as "the exclusively religious activities of any religious order." HRSA exempted these organizations from the requirement to cover contraceptive services.

In addition, HHS has effectively exempted certain religious nonprofit organizations, described under HHS regulations as "eligible organizations," from the contraceptive mandate. An "eligible organization" means a nonprofit organization that "holds itself out as a religious organization" and "opposes providing coverage for some or all of any contraceptive services required to be covered . . . on account of religious objections." To qualify for this accommodation, an employer must certify that it is such an organization. When a group-health-insurance issuer receives notice that one of its clients has invoked this provision, the issuer must then exclude contraceptive coverage from the employer's plan and provide separate payments for contraceptive services for plan participants without imposing any cost-sharing requirements on the eligible organization, its insurance plan, or its employee beneficiaries. Although this procedure requires the issuer to bear the cost of these services, HHS has determined that this obligation will not impose any net expense on issuers because its cost will be less than or equal to the cost savings resulting from the services.

In addition to these exemptions for religious organizations, ACA exempts a great many employers from most of its coverage requirements. Employers providing "grandfathered health plans"—those that existed prior to March 23, 2010, and that have not made specified changes after that date—need not comply with many of the Act's requirements, including the contraceptive mandate. 42 U.S.C. §§ 18011(a), (e). And employers with fewer than 50 employees are not required to provide health insurance at all. 26 U.S.C. § 4980H(c)(2).

All told, the contraceptive mandate "presently does not apply to tens of millions of people."

II

B

David and Barbara Green and their three children are Christians who own and operate two family businesses. Forty-five years ago, David Green started an arts-and-crafts store that has grown into a nationwide chain called Hobby Lobby. There are now 500 Hobby Lobby stores, and the company has more than 13,000 employees. Hobby Lobby is organized as a for-profit corporation under Oklahoma law.

One of David's sons started an affiliated business, Mardel, which operates 35 Christian bookstores and employs close to 400 people. Mardel is also organized as a for-profit corporation under Oklahoma law.

Though these two businesses have expanded over the years, they remain closely held, and David, Barbara, and their children retain exclusive control of both companies. David serves as the CEO of Hobby Lobby, and his three children serve as the president, vice president, and vice CEO.

Hobby Lobby's statement of purpose commits the Greens to "[h]onoring the Lord in all [they] do by operating the company in a manner consistent with Biblical principles." Each family member has signed a pledge to run the businesses in accordance with the family's religious beliefs and to use the family assets to support Christian ministries. In accordance with those commitments, Hobby Lobby and Mardel stores close on Sundays, even though the Greens calculate that they lose millions in sales annually by doing so. The businesses refuse to engage in profitable transactions that facilitate or promote alcohol use; they contribute profits to Christian missionaries and ministries; and they buy hundreds of full-page newspaper ads inviting people to "know Jesus as Lord and Savior."

Hobby Lobby. . . sued HHS and other federal agencies and officials to challenge the contraceptive mandate under RFRA and the Free Exercise Clause. The District Court denied a preliminary injunction, and the plaintiffs appealed, moving for initial en banc consideration. The Tenth Circuit granted that motion and reversed in a divided opinion. Contrary to the conclusion of the Third Circuit, the Tenth Circuit held that the Greens' two for-profit businesses are "persons" within the meaning of RFRA and therefore may bring suit under that law.

The court then held that the corporations had established a likelihood of success on their RFRA claim. The court concluded that the contraceptive mandate substantially burdened the exercise of religion by requiring the companies to choose between "compromis[ing] their religious beliefs" and paying a heavy fee—either "close to $475 million more in taxes every year" if they simply refused to provide coverage for the contraceptives at issue, or "roughly $26 million" annually if they "drop[ped] health-insurance benefits for all employees."

The court next held that HHS had failed to demonstrate a compelling interest in enforcing the mandate against the Greens' businesses and, in the alternative, that HHS had failed to prove that enforcement of the mandate was the "least restrictive means" of furthering the Government's asserted interests. After concluding that the companies had "demonstrated irreparable harm," the court reversed and remanded for the District Court to consider the remaining factors of the preliminary-injunction test.

III

A

RFRA prohibits the "Government [from] substantially burden[ing] *a person's* exercise of religion even if the burden results from a rule of general applicability" unless the Government "demonstrates that application of the burden to *the person*—(1) is in furtherance of a compelling governmental interest; and (2) is the least restrictive means of furthering that compelling governmental interest." The first question that we must address is whether this provision applies to regulations that govern the activities of for-profit corporations like Hobby Lobby.

HHS contends that neither these companies nor their owners can even be heard under RFRA. According to HHS, the companies cannot sue because they seek to make a profit for their owners, and the owners cannot be heard because the regulations, at least as a formal matter, apply only to the companies and not to the owners as individuals. HHS's argument would have dramatic consequences.

Consider this Court's decision in *Braunfeld v. Brown,* 366 U.S. 599, 81 S.Ct. 1144, 6 L.Ed.2d 563 (1961) (plurality opinion). In that case, five Orthodox Jewish merchants who ran small retail businesses in Philadelphia challenged a Pennsylvania Sunday closing law as a violation of the Free Exercise Clause. Because of their faith, these merchants closed their shops on Saturday, and they argued that requiring them to remain shut on Sunday threatened them with financial ruin. The Court entertained their claim (although it ruled against them on the merits), and if a similar claim were raised today under RFRA against a jurisdiction still subject to the Act (for example, the District of Columbia, the merchants would be entitled to be heard. According to HHS, however, if these merchants chose to incorporate their businesses—without in any way changing the size or nature of their businesses—they would forfeit all RFRA (and free-exercise) rights. HHS would put these merchants to a difficult choice: either give up the right to seek judicial protection of their religious liberty or forgo the benefits, available to their competitors, of operating as corporations.

As we have seen, RFRA was designed to provide very broad protection for religious liberty. By enacting RFRA, Congress went far beyond what this Court has held is constitutionally required. Is there any reason to think that the Congress that enacted such sweeping protection put small-business owners to the choice that HHS suggests? An examination of RFRA's text, to which we turn in the next part of this opinion, reveals that Congress did no such thing.

As we will show, Congress provided protection by . . . employing a familiar legal fiction: It included corporations within RFRA's definition of "persons." But it is important to keep in mind that the purpose of this fiction is to provide protection for human beings. A corporation is simply a form of organization used by human beings to achieve desired ends. An established body of law specifies the rights and obligations of the *people* (including shareholders, officers, and employees) who are associated with a corporation in one way or another. When rights, whether constitutional or statutory, are extended to corporations, the purpose is to protect the rights of these people. For example, extending Fourth Amendment protection to corporations protects the privacy interests of employees and others associated with the company. Protecting corporations from government seizure of their property without just compensation protects all those who have a stake in the corporations' financial well-being. And protecting the free-exercise rights of corporations like Hobby Lobby, Conestoga, and Mardel protects the religious liberty of the humans who own and control those companies.

In holding that Conestoga, as a "secular, for-profit corporation," lacks RFRA protection, the Third Circuit wrote as follows:

> "General business corporations do not, *separate and apart from the actions or belief systems of their individual owners or employees,* exercise religion. They do not pray, worship, observe sacraments or take other religiously-motivated actions separate and apart from the intention and direction of their individual actors."

All of this is true—but quite beside the point. Corporations, "separate and apart from" the human beings who own, run, and are employed by them, cannot do anything at all.

B

1

As we noted above, RFRA applies to "a person's" exercise of religion, and RFRA itself does not define the term "person." We therefore look to the Dictionary Act, which we must consult "[i]n determining the meaning of any Act of Congress, unless the context indicates otherwise."

Under the Dictionary Act, "the wor[d] 'person' . . . include[s] corporations, companies, associations, firms, partnerships, societies, and joint stock companies, as well as individuals."; see *FCC v. AT & T Inc.,* 562 U.S. ____, ____, 131 S.Ct. 1177, 1182–1183, 179 L.Ed.2d 132 (2011) ("We have no doubt that 'person,' in a legal setting, often refers to artificial entities. The Dictionary Act makes that clear"). Thus, unless there is something about the RFRA context that "indicates otherwise," the Dictionary Act provides a quick, clear, and affirmative answer to the question whether the companies involved in these cases may be heard.

We see nothing in RFRA that suggests a congressional intent to depart from the Dictionary Act definition, and HHS makes little effort to argue otherwise. We have entertained RFRA and free-exercise claims brought by nonprofit corporations, and HHS concedes that a nonprofit corporation can be a "person" within the meaning of RFRA.

This concession effectively dispatches any argument that the term "person" as used in RFRA does not reach the closely held corporations involved in these cases. No known understanding of the term "person" includes *some* but not all corporations. The term "person" sometimes encompasses artificial persons (as the Dictionary Act instructs), and it sometimes is limited to natural persons. But no conceivable definition of the term includes natural persons and nonprofit corporations, but not for-profit corporations. Cf. *Clark v. Martinez*, 543 U.S. 371, 378, 125 S.Ct. 716, 160 L.Ed.2d 734 (2005).

JUSTICE GINSBURG, with whom JUSTICE SOTOMAYOR joins, and with whom JUSTICE BREYER and JUSTICE KAGAN join as to all but Part III–C–1, dissenting.

In a decision of startling breadth, the Court holds that commercial enterprises, including corporations, along with partnerships and sole proprietorships, can opt out of any law (saving only tax laws) they judge incompatible with their sincerely held religious beliefs. Compelling governmental interests in uniform compliance with the law, and disadvantages that religion-based opt-outs impose on others, hold no sway, the Court decides, at least when there is a "less restrictive alternative." And such an alternative, the Court suggests, there always will be whenever, in lieu of tolling an enterprise claiming a religion-based exemption, the government, *i.e.,* the general public, can pick up the tab.

Reading RFRA, as the Court does, to require extension of religion-based exemptions to for-profit corporations surely is not grounded in the pre-*Smith* precedent Congress sought to preserve. Had Congress intended RFRA to initiate a change so huge, a clarion statement to that effect likely would have been made in the legislation. The text of RFRA makes no such statement and the legislative history does not so much as mention for-profit corporations.

The Court notes that for-profit corporations may support charitable causes and use their funds for religious ends, and therefore questions the distinction between such corporations and religious nonprofit organizations. Again, the Court forgets that religious organizations exist to serve a community of believers. For-profit corporations do not fit that bill. Moreover, history is not on the Court's side. Recognition of the discrete characters of "ecclesiastical and lay" corporations dates back to Blackstone, see 1 W. Blackstone, Commentaries on the Laws of England 458 (1765), and was reiterated by this Court centuries before the enactment of the Internal Revenue Code. See *Terrett v. Taylor,* 9 Cranch 43, 49, 3 L.Ed. 650 (1815) (describing religious corporations); *Trustees of Dartmouth College,* 4 Wheat., at 645 (discussing "eleemosynary" corporations, including those "created for the promotion of religion"). To reiterate, "for-profit corporations are different from religious non-profits in that they use labor to make a profit, rather than to perpetuate [the] religious value[s] [shared by a community of believers]." *Gilardi,* 733 F.3d, at 1242 (Edwards, J., concurring in part and dissenting in part) (emphasis deleted).

Citing *Braunfeld v. Brown,* 366 U.S. 599, 81 S.Ct. 1144, 6 L.Ed.2d 563 (1961), the Court questions why, if "a sole proprietorship that seeks to make a profit may assert a free-exercise claim, [Hobby Lobby and Conestoga] can't . . . do the same?" *Ante,* at 2770 (footnote omitted). See also *ante,* at 2767–2768. But even accepting, *arguendo,* the premise that unincorporated business enterprises may gain religious accommodations under the Free Exercise Clause, the Court's conclusion is unsound. In a sole proprietorship, the business and its owner are one and the same. By incorporating a business, however, an individual separates herself from the entity and escapes personal responsibility for the entity's obligations. One might ask why the separation should hold only when it serves the interest of those who control the corporation. In any event, *Braunfeld* is hardly impressive authority for the entitlement Hobby Lobby and Conestoga seek. The free exercise claim asserted there was promptly rejected on the merits.

The Court's determination that RFRA extends to for-profit corporations is bound to have untoward effects. Although the Court attempts to cabin its language to closely held corporations, its logic extends to corporations of any size, public or private. Little doubt that RFRA claims will proliferate, for the Court's expansive notion of corporate personhood—combined with its other errors in construing RFRA—invites for-profit entities to seek religion-based exemptions from regulations they deem offensive to their faith.

FOR DISCUSSION

How does the Court see the relationship between individuals and corporations as different from what was described in the *Dartmouth College* case? Did the Court actually say here that the Constitution grants corporations rights as persons? If one wanted to overturn this decision, how would one do it?

RELATED CASE

***Mohamad v. Palestinian Authority*: 556 U.S. 449 (2012).**

Corporations are not persons who can be held liable under the Torture Victim Protection Act. The Act only applies to natural persons.

Animals as Persons

Dating back to British common law animals have traditionally been thought of as property. In the famous case of *Pierson v. Post*, 3 Cai. R. 175, 2 Am. Dec. 264 (1805), a New York Supreme Court judge declared that one did not come to possess property rights in a wild animal until one took physical possession of it—merely pursuing it was not enough. For law school students *Pierson* is an important case about how one acquires property rights and about the difference between how the law treats wild versus domestic animals, but the case is also important for simply pointing out that animals are property and can be owned, bought, and sold like any other form of property. The US Supreme Court has said the same in *Sentell v. New Orleans & C.R. Co.*, 166 U.S. 698 (1897). As property, owners could do anything they wanted to them, including kill for food, pleasure, or sport.

Animals were not persons and had no rights or legal protections. Dating back to St. Augustine and Christian theology, animals were treated as inferior to humans, and the latter had authority over them. Animals, as St. Augustine contended, had no soul and when they died would not go to heaven. Philosophers such as Rene Descartes saw animals as automata, soulless robots who lacked self-awareness, the capacity to reason, and who could feel no pain. Immanuel Kant's ethics indicated that only moral agents capable of making willing choices deserved respect and dignity. Humans possessed such capacity, animals did not. Therefore, the latter did not garner the same ethical rights or respect as did humans. The point is that animals were not considered persons in any legal sense.

However, over time attitudes and the law regarding animals have changed. Jeremy Bentham, a late eighteenth and early nineteenth century British utilitarian philosopher, was one of the earliest supporters of animals rights. Contrary to Descartes, he saw in animals the capacity to suffer and feel pain. It was not the capacity to reason but to feel pain that should bestow on animals some rights, at least against inhuman or cruel torture or treatment. More recent research is also challenging claims that animals cannot think, reason, or be self-aware. Many of the primates are seen as highly intelligent and capable of engaging in dialogue with humans. Some animals use tools, and there is evidence that elephants and other animals are self-aware, that fish feel pain, and that octopuses might have a form of consciousness. The point is that the clear line once thought to distinguish humans from animals is not so clear for many individuals any more.

Gradually laws were adopted against animal cruelty. Additionally, building upon common law distinctions between wild and domestic animals, and as more individuals started acquiring animals as pets, the laws regarding animals have changed. For example, one would never think of writing a will and leaving all of one's money to a piece of furniture. Why would anyone leave money to a piece of property? Yet in recent years pet owners, concerned about what would happen to their dog or cat after the former died, wanted to leave money to the latter in the will to ensure their care. Yet if animals are property can they be willed money? No. But many people now consider their pets members of the family, and states have changed laws to allow for bequests to or on behalf of their pets. The growing personal affection and proximity that pets have in the lives of many, alongside an emerging body of scientific research, have altered legal views about animals.

As noted above, animals were traditionally viewed as legal property and not as persons. They had no rights and could be sacrificed for human persons. One case pointing out that principle is *Church of the Lukumi Babalu Aye, Inc. v. City of Hialeah,* 508 U.S. 520 (1993). Here a city ordinance sought to use the pretext of animal cruelty laws as a way to ban the religious sacrifice of animals by the Santeria religion. The case is notable on several grounds. First, it pointed out the traditional and ancient role that animal sacrifice plays in religion. Second, it highlighted how in some cases the government could enact legitimate laws to regulate animal cruelty or their slaughter. But third, the right of individual free exercise in many cases would override the state interest in regulating animal cruelty. One of the most notable aspects of the opinion is the absence of a discussion of the rights of animals or any interests they possess. The case is about the rights of a group to practice their religion versus a majority wishing to regulate a practice they do not support.

Contrast that case to *State v. Nix*, 355 Or. 777 (2014). Here, even though Oregon does not recognize animals as persons, it does acknowledged that they can be considered victims of crimes. The issue in this case was whether the ordinary use of the term "victim" could include animals. The Court said "yes." While this decision was eventually vacated by the Oregon Supreme Court on other grounds, the case potentially represented a major step for animal personhood by saying animals could be victims for the purposes of determining penalties for offenders committing multiple crimes. This perspective has been long-held for fetuses, however, and has not ensured their awarding of constitutional personhood.

Finally, consider the case of *The People of The State of New York ex rel. The Nonhuman Rights Project, Inc., on Behalf of Tommy v. Patrick C. Lavery, Individually and as an Officer of Circle L Trailer Sales, Inc., et al.*, 124 A.D.3d 148 (NY App.2014). Tommy was a chimpanzee being held, according to the petitioners, captive against his will by his owners. They sought habeas corpus relief for his freedom. In denying habeas the Court noted that no court had ever held an animal to be a legal person. The court also reviewed the law on what it means to be a person and then it noted the extensive recent scholarship contending for animal rights. The opinion ends by declaring that while it could not grant personhood to Tommy or other animals, the legislature could do so. At present animals are not simply property but they are not persons. Given what research is telling us about animals, should they be given some personhood status?

CHURCH OF THE LUKUMI BABALU AYE, INC. V. CITY OF HIALEAH

508 U.S. 520, 113 S.Ct. 2217, 124 L.Ed.2d 472 (1993)

Church brought action challenging city ordinances dealing with ritual slaughter of animals. The United States District Court for the Southern District of Florida denied relief, and church appealed. The Court of Appeals for the Eleventh Circuit affirmed. The Supreme Court reversed.

Vote: 9–0

JUSTICE KENNEDY delivered the opinion of the Court, except as to Part II–A–2.

I

A

This case involves practices of the Santeria religion, which originated in the 19th century. When hundreds of thousands of members of the Yoruba people were brought as slaves from western Africa to Cuba, their traditional African religion absorbed significant elements of Roman Catholicism. The resulting syncretion, or fusion, is Santeria, "the way of the saints." The Cuban Yoruba express their devotion to spirits, called *orishas,* through the iconography of Catholic saints, Catholic symbols are often present at Santeria rites, and Santeria devotees attend the Catholic sacraments. The Santeria faith teaches that every individual has a destiny from God, a destiny fulfilled with the aid and energy of the *orishas.* The basis of the Santeria religion is the nurture of a personal relation with the *orishas,* and one of the principal forms of devotion is an animal sacrifice. The sacrifice of animals as part of religious rituals has ancient roots. Animal sacrifice is mentioned throughout the Old Testament, and it played an important role in the practice of Judaism before destruction of the second Temple in Jerusalem. In modern Islam, there is an annual sacrifice commemorating Abraham's sacrifice of a ram in the stead of his son.

According to Santeria teaching, the *orishas* are powerful but not immortal. They depend for survival on the sacrifice. Sacrifices are performed at birth, marriage, and death rites, for the cure of the sick, for the initiation of new members and priests, and during an annual celebration. Animals sacrificed in Santeria rituals include chickens, pigeons, doves, ducks, guinea pigs, goats, sheep, and turtles. The animals are killed by the cutting of the carotid arteries in the neck. The sacrificed animal is cooked and eaten, except after healing and death rituals.

Santeria adherents faced widespread persecution in Cuba, so the religion and its rituals were practiced in secret. The open practice of Santeria and its rites remains infrequent. The religion was brought to this Nation most often by exiles from the Cuban revolution. The District Court estimated that there are at least 50,000 practitioners in South Florida today.

B

Petitioner Church of the Lukumi Babalu Aye, Inc. (Church), is a not-for-profit corporation organized under Florida law in 1973. The Church and its congregants practice the Santeria religion. The president of the Church is petitioner Ernesto Pichardo, who is also the Church's priest and holds the religious title of *Italero,* the second highest in the Santeria faith. In April 1987, the Church leased land in the City of Hialeah, Florida, and announced plans to establish a house of worship as well as a school, cultural center, and museum. Pichardo indicated that the Church's goal was to bring the practice of the Santeria faith, including its ritual of animal sacrifice, into the open. The Church began the process of obtaining utility service and receiving the necessary licensing, inspection, and zoning approvals. Although the Church's efforts at obtaining the necessary licenses and permits were far from smooth, it appears that it received all needed approvals by early August 1987.The prospect of a Santeria church in their midst was distressing to many members of the Hialeah community, and the announcement of the plans to open a Santeria church in Hialeah prompted the city council to hold an emergency public session on June 9, 1987. The resolutions and ordinances passed at that and later meetings are set forth in the Appendix following this opinion.

A summary suffices here, beginning with the enactments passed at the June 9 meeting. First, the city council adopted Resolution 87–66, which noted the "concern" expressed by residents of the city "that certain religions may propose to engage in practices which are inconsistent with public morals, peace or safety," and declared that "[t]he City reiterates its commitment to a prohibition against any and all acts of any and all religious groups which are inconsistent with public morals, peace or safety." Next, the council approved an emergency ordinance, Ordinance 87–40, which incorporated in full, except as to penalty, Florida's animal cruelty laws. Fla.Stat. ch. 828 (1987). Among other things, the incorporated state law subjected to criminal punishment "[w]hoever . . . unnecessarily or cruelly . . . kills any animal." § 828.12.

The city council desired to undertake further legislative action, but Florida law prohibited a municipality from enacting legislation relating to animal cruelty that conflicted with state law. § 828.27(4). To obtain clarification, Hialeah's city attorney requested an opinion from the attorney general of Florida as to whether § 828.12 prohibited "a religious group from sacrificing an animal in a religious ritual or practice" and whether the city could enact ordinances "making religious animal sacrifice unlawful." The attorney general responded in mid-July. He concluded that the "ritual sacrifice of animals for purposes other than food consumption" was not a "necessary" killing and so was prohibited by § 828.12. The attorney general appeared to define "unnecessary" as "done without any useful motive, in a spirit of wanton cruelty or for the mere pleasure of destruction without being in any sense beneficial or useful to the person killing the animal." He advised that religious animal sacrifice was against state law, so that a city ordinance prohibiting it would not be in conflict.

The city council responded at first with a hortatory enactment, Resolution 87–90, that noted its residents' "great concern regarding the possibility of public ritualistic animal sacrifices" and the state-law prohibition. The resolution declared the city policy "to oppose the ritual sacrifices of animals" within Hialeah and announced that any person or organization practicing animal sacrifice "will be prosecuted."

In September 1987, the city council adopted three substantive ordinances addressing the issue of religious animal sacrifice. Ordinance 87–52 defined "sacrifice" as "to unnecessarily kill, torment, torture, or mutilate an animal in a public or private ritual or ceremony not for the primary purpose of food consumption," and prohibited owning or possessing an animal "intending to use such animal for food purposes." It restricted application of this prohibition, however, to any individual or group that "kills, slaughters or sacrifices animals for any type of ritual, regardless of whether or not the flesh or blood of the animal is to be consumed." The ordinance contained an exemption for slaughtering by "licensed establishment[s]" of animals "specifically raised for food purposes." Declaring, moreover, that the city council "has determined that the sacrificing of animals within the city limits is contrary to the public health, safety, welfare and morals of the community," the city council adopted Ordinance 87–71. That ordinance defined sacrifice as had Ordinance 87–52, and then provided that "[i]t shall be unlawful for any person, persons, corporations or associations to sacrifice any animal within the corporate limits of the City of Hialeah, Florida." The final Ordinance, 87–72, defined "slaughter" as "the killing of animals for food" and prohibited slaughter outside of areas zoned for slaughterhouse use. The ordinance provided an exemption, however, for the slaughter or processing for sale of "small numbers of hogs and/or cattle per week in accordance with an exemption provided by state law." All ordinances and resolutions passed the city council by unanimous vote. Violations of each of the four ordinances were punishable by fines not exceeding $500 or imprisonment not exceeding 60 days, or both. II

The Free Exercise Clause of the First Amendment, which has been applied to the States through the Fourteenth Amendment, see *Cantwell v. Connecticut,* 310 U.S. 296, 303, 60 S.Ct. 900, 903, 84 L. Ed. 1213 (1940), provides that "Congress shall make no law respecting an establishment of religion, or *prohibiting the free exercise thereof. . . .*" (Emphasis added). The city does not argue that Santeria is not a "religion" within the meaning of the First Amendment. Nor could it. Although the practice of animal sacrifice may seem abhorrent to some, "religious beliefs need not be acceptable, logical, consistent, or comprehensible to others in order to merit First Amendment protection." Neither the city nor the courts below, moreover, have questioned the sincerity of petitioners' professed desire to conduct animal sacrifices for religious reasons. We must consider petitioners' First Amendment claim. In addressing the constitutional protection for free exercise of religion, our cases establish the general proposition that a law that is neutral and of general applicability need not be justified by a compelling governmental interest even if the law has the incidental effect of burdening a particular religious practice. Neutrality and general applicability are interrelated, and, as becomes apparent in this case, failure to satisfy one requirement is a likely indication that the other has not been satisfied. A law failing to satisfy these requirements must be justified by a compelling governmental interest and must be narrowly tailored to advance that interest. These ordinances fail to satisfy the *Smith* requirements. We begin by discussing neutrality.

A.

In our Establishment Clause cases we have often stated the principle that the First Amendment forbids an official purpose to disapprove of a particular religion or of religion in general. These cases, however, for the most part have addressed governmental efforts to benefit religion or particular religions, and so have dealt with a question different, at least in its formulation and emphasis, from the issue here. Petitioners allege an attempt to disfavor their religion because of the religious ceremonies it commands, and the Free Exercise Clause is dispositive in our analysis. At a minimum, the protections of the Free Exercise Clause pertain if the law at issue discriminates against some or all religious beliefs or regulates or prohibits conduct because it is undertaken for religious reasons. Indeed, it was "historical instances of religious persecution and intolerance that gave concern to those who drafted the Free Exercise Clause."

1

Although a law targeting religious beliefs as such is never permissible, if the object of a law is to infringe upon or restrict practices because of their religious motivation, the law is not neutral, and it is invalid unless it is justified by a compelling interest and is narrowly tailored to advance that interest. There are, of course, many ways of demonstrating that the object or purpose of a law is the suppression of religion or religious conduct. To determine the object of a law, we must begin with its text, for the minimum requirement of neutrality is that a law not discriminate on its face. A law lacks facial neutrality if it refers to a religious practice without a secular meaning discernable from the language or context. Petitioners contend that three of the ordinances fail this test of facial neutrality because they use the words "sacrifice" and "ritual," words with strong religious connotations. We agree that these words are consistent with the claim of facial discrimination, but the argument is not conclusive. The words "sacrifice" and "ritual" have a religious origin, but current use admits also of secular meanings. The ordinances, furthermore, define "sacrifice" in secular terms, without referring to religious practices. We reject the contention advanced by the city, see Brief for Respondent 15, that our inquiry must end with the text of the laws at issue. Facial neutrality is not determinative. The Free Exercise Clause, like the Establishment Clause, extends beyond facial discrimination. The Clause "forbids subtle departures from neutrality," and "covert suppression of particular religious beliefs," Official action that targets religious conduct for distinctive treatment cannot be shielded by mere compliance with the requirement of facial neutrality. The Free Exercise Clause protects against governmental hostility which is masked, as well as overt. "The Court must survey meticulously the circumstances of governmental categories to eliminate, as it were, religious gerrymanders."

The record in this case compels the conclusion that suppression of the central element of the Santeria worship service was the object of the ordinances. First, though use of the words "sacrifice" and "ritual" does not compel a finding of improper targeting of the Santeria religion, the choice of these words is support for our conclusion. There are further respects in which the text of the city council's enactments discloses the improper attempt to target Santeria. Resolution 87–66, adopted June 9, 1987, recited that "residents and citizens of the City of Hialeah have expressed their concern that certain religions may propose to engage in practices which are inconsistent with public morals, peace or safety," and "reiterate[d]" the city's commitment to prohibit "any and all [such] acts of any and all religious groups." No one suggests, and on this record it cannot be maintained, that city officials had in mind a religion other than Santeria.

It becomes evident that these ordinances target Santeria sacrifice when the ordinances' operation is considered. Apart from the text, the effect of a law in its real operation is strong evidence of its object. To be sure, adverse impact will not always lead to a finding of impermissible targeting. For example, a social harm may have been a legitimate concern of government for reasons quite apart from discrimination. The subject at hand does implicate, of course, multiple concerns unrelated to religious animosity, for example, the suffering or mistreatment visited upon the sacrificed animals and health hazards from improper disposal. But the ordinances when considered together disclose an object remote from these legitimate concerns. The design of these laws accomplishes instead a "religious gerrymander," an impermissible attempt to target petitioners and their religious practices.

It is a necessary conclusion that almost the only conduct subject to Ordinances 87–40, 87–52, and 87–71 is the religious exercise of Santeria church members. The texts show that they were drafted in tandem to achieve this result. We begin with Ordinance 87–71. It prohibits the sacrifice of animals, but defines sacrifice as "to unnecessarily kill . . . an animal in a public or private ritual or ceremony not for the primary purpose of food consumption." The definition excludes almost all killings of animals except for religious sacrifice, and the primary purpose requirement narrows the proscribed category even further, in particular by exempting kosher slaughter. We need not discuss whether this differential treatment of two religions is itself an independent constitutional violation. It suffices to recite this feature of the law as support for our conclusion that Santeria alone was the exclusive legislative concern. The net result of the gerrymander is that few if any killings of animals are prohibited other than Santeria sacrifice, which is proscribed because it occurs during a ritual or ceremony and its primary purpose is to make an offering to the *orishas,* not food consumption. Indeed, careful drafting ensured that, although Santeria sacrifice is prohibited, killings that are no more necessary or humane in almost all other circumstances are unpunished.

Operating in similar fashion is Ordinance 87–52, which prohibits the "possess [ion], sacrifice, or slaughter" of an animal with the "inten[t] to use such animal for food purposes." This prohibition, extending to the keeping of an animal as well as the killing itself, applies if the animal is killed in "any type of ritual" and there is an intent to use the animal for food, whether or not it is in fact consumed for food. The ordinance exempts, however, "any licensed [food] establishment" with regard to "any animals which are specifically raised for food purposes," if the activity is permitted by zoning and other laws. This exception, too, seems intended to cover kosher slaughter. Again, the burden of the ordinance, in practical terms, falls on Santeria adherents but almost no others: If the killing is—unlike most Santeria sacrifices—unaccompanied by the intent to use the animal for food, then it is not prohibited by Ordinance 87–52; if the killing is specifically for food but does not occur during the course of "any type of ritual," it again falls outside the prohibition; and if the killing is for food and occurs during the course of a ritual, it is still exempted if it occurs in a properly zoned and licensed establishment and involves animals "specifically raised for food purposes." A pattern of exemptions parallels the pattern of narrow prohibitions. Each contributes to the gerrymander.

Ordinance 87–40 incorporates the Florida animal cruelty statute, Fla.Stat. § 828.12 (1987). Its prohibition is broad on its face, punishing "[w]hoever . . . unnecessarily . . . kills any animal." The city claims that this ordinance is the epitome of a neutral prohibition. The problem, however, is the interpretation given to the ordinance by respondent and the Florida attorney general. Killings for religious reasons are deemed unnecessary, whereas most other killings fall outside the prohibition. The city, on what seems to be a *per se* basis, deems hunting, slaughter of animals for food, eradication of insects and pests, and euthanasia as necessary. There is no indication in the record that respondent has concluded that hunting or fishing for sport is unnecessary. Indeed, one of the few reported Florida cases decided under § 828.12 concludes that the use of live rabbits to train greyhounds is not unnecessary.

We also find significant evidence of the ordinances' improper targeting of Santeria sacrifice in the fact that they proscribe more religious conduct than is necessary to achieve their stated ends. It is not unreasonable to infer, at least when there are no persuasive indications to the contrary, that a law which visits "gratuitous restrictions" on religious conduct, seeks not to effectuate the stated governmental interests, but to suppress the conduct because of its religious motivation.

The legitimate governmental interests in protecting the public health and preventing cruelty to animals could be addressed by restrictions stopping far short of a flat prohibition of all Santeria sacrificial practice. If improper disposal, not the sacrifice itself, is the harm to be prevented, the city could have imposed a general regulation on the disposal of organic garbage. It did not do so. Indeed, counsel for the city conceded at oral argument that, under the ordinances, Santeria sacrifices would be illegal even if they occurred in licensed, inspected, and zoned slaughterhouses. Thus, these broad ordinances prohibit Santeria sacrifice even when it does not threaten the city's interest in the public health. The District Court accepted the argument that narrower regulation would be unenforceable because of the secrecy in the Santeria rituals and the lack of any central religious authority to require compliance with secular disposal regulations. It is difficult to understand, however, how a prohibition of the sacrifices themselves, which occur in private, is enforceable if a ban on improper disposal, which occurs in public, is not. The neutrality of a law is suspect if First Amendment freedoms are curtailed to prevent isolated collateral harms not themselves prohibited by direct regulation.

Under similar analysis, narrower regulation would achieve the city's interest in preventing cruelty to animals. With regard to the city's interest in ensuring the adequate care of animals, regulation of conditions and treatment, regardless of why an animal is kept, is the logical response to the city's concern, not a prohibition on possession for the purpose of sacrifice. The same is true for the city's interest in prohibiting cruel methods of killing. Under federal and Florida law and Ordinance 87–40, which incorporates Florida law in this regard, killing an animal by the "simultaneous and instantaneous severance of the carotid arteries with a sharp instrument"—the method used in kosher slaughter—is approved as humane. The District Court found that, though Santeria sacrifice also results in severance of the carotid arteries, the method used during sacrifice is less reliable and therefore not humane. If the city has a real concern that other methods are less humane, however, the subject of the regulation should be the method of slaughter itself, not a religious classification that is said to bear some general relation to it.

Ordinance 87–72—unlike the three other ordinances—does appear to apply to substantial nonreligious conduct and not to be overbroad. For our purposes here, however, the four substantive ordinances may be treated as a group for neutrality purposes. Ordinance 87–72 was passed the same day as Ordinance 87–71 and was enacted, as were the three others, in direct response to the opening of the Church. It would be implausible to suggest that the three other ordinances, but not Ordinance 87–72, had as their object the suppression of religion. We need not decide whether the Ordinance 87–72 could survive constitutional scrutiny if it existed separately; it must be invalidated because it functions, with the rest of the enactments in question, to suppress Santeria religious worship.

FOR DISCUSSION

Could the city or the government ever regulate animal slaughter? Is there a First Amendment right to the religious sacrifice of animals?

STATE V. NIX

355 Or. 777 (2014)

The undisputed facts are aptly summarized by the Court of Appeals:

"Acting on a tip, police officers entered defendant's farm and found dozens of emaciated animals, mostly horses and goats, and several animal carcasses in various states of decay. Defendant owned those animals. Defendant was indicted on 23 counts of first-degree animal neglect, and 70 counts of second-degree animal neglect. Each separate count identified a different animal and charged conduct by defendant toward that animal. All of the separate counts were alleged to have occurred within the same span of time. A jury convicted defendant of 20 counts of second-degree animal [neglect].

"At defendant's sentencing hearing, the state asked the trial court to impose 20 separate convictions because the jury had found defendant guilty of neglecting 20 different animals. Accordingly, the state argued, the convictions 'do not merge based on [ORS 161.067](1), (2) and (3).' " The trial court disagreed and merged the guilty verdicts into a single conviction, explaining that

" '[ORS 161.067(2)] talks about—although violating only one statutory provision, it involves two or more victims. In this case, I agree with the defendant's position that the animals are not victims, as defined by the statute; by the ORS 161.067(2).

" '* * * I don't think that [ORS 161.067(3)] applies because the animals are not victims under the definition of the statute requiring that to be persons.'

"Defendant was sentenced to 90 days in jail and three years of bench probation; the trial court suspended imposition of the jail sentence, and the state appealed."

The state appealed, assigning error to the trial court's merger of the 20 counts of second-degree animal neglect. The state argued that, under *State v. Glaspey,* 337 Or. 558, 563, 100 P.3d 730 (2004), the term "victim" in the anti-merger statute draws its meaning from the underlying substantive criminal statute that defendant violated. In this case, the state argued, the text, context, and legislative history of the second-degree animal neglect statute make clear that the legislature intended the neglected animals as the victims of the offense.

Defendant argued that the ordinary meaning of the term "victim" does not include non-humans. Animals, he argued, are treated by Oregon law as the property of their owners. In defendant's view, because no statute expressly defines the word to include animals, only persons can be victims under the anti-merger statute.

The Court of Appeals reversed. In brief, the court reasoned that, following this court's instruction in *Glaspey,* the meaning of the term "victim" as it is used in the anti-merger statute is determined by reference to the underlying substantive criminal statute that defendant violated. 251 Or.App. at 457–58, 283 P.3d 442. The court explained that the substantive criminal statute at issue in this case, ORS 167.325, evinces a legislative concern with the well-being of animals. Reviewing the text and history of the statute, the court concluded that, although animals are usually considered the property of persons, ORS 167.325 reflects a broader public interest in "protect [ing] individual animals as sentient beings" by ensuring that such animals receive minimum care and are not abused or neglected. *Id.* at 460–61, 283 P.3d 442.

On review before this court, defendant renews his argument that "the ordinary meaning of the word 'victim' means a 'person,' " not an animal. According to defendant, "[a]nimals are defined as property under Oregon law," and "[t]here is no statute that allows property to be seen as a victim" of a criminal offense. In defendant's view, the victim of an animal neglect case is either the public at large or the owner of the animal.

The state responds that the ordinary meaning of the word "victim" is not as narrow as defendant contends and that, to the contrary, it commonly is used to refer both to animals and to human beings. Moreover, because individual animals directly suffer the harm that is central to the crime of animal neglect, as set out in ORS 167.325, they are the "victims" of that crime. According to the state, the text and history of the statute make clear that the legislature was concerned with the capacity of animals to suffer abuse and neglect. Indeed, the state argues, the legislature expressly structured the animal neglect statutes "such that the degree of the crime corresponds to the extent of the animal's suffering." Thus, in the state's view, the statutes evince a concern to protect more than a general public interest in animal welfare; rather, those statutes reflect the legislature's intention to protect individual animals from suffering.

The issue before us is one of statutory construction, which we resolve by applying the familiar principles set out in *PGE v. Bureau of Labor and Industries,* 317 Or. 606, 610–12, 859 P.2d 1143 (1993), and *State v. Gaines,*

346 Or. 160, 171–73, 206 P.3d 1042 (2009). Our goal is to ascertain the meaning of the statute that the legislature most likely intended. *Halperin v. Pitts,* 352 Or. 482, 486, 287 P.3d 1069 (2012).

We begin with the text of the statute, in context. Oregon's anti-merger statute provides that, when a defendant is found guilty of committing multiple crimes during a single criminal episode, those guilty verdicts "merge" into a single conviction, unless they are subject to one of a series of exceptions. One of those exceptions is ORS 161.067(2), which provides that, "[w]hen the same conduct or criminal episode, though violating only one statutory provision [,] involves two or more victims, there are as many separately punishable offenses as there are victims." At issue in this case is the meaning of the word "victims" as it is used in that statute.

In the absence of evidence to the contrary, we assume that the legislature intended that the wording of an enactment to be given its ordinary meaning. *State v. Murray,* 340 Or. 599, 604, 136 P.3d 10 (2006). The ordinary meaning of the word "victim" reflected in a dictionary of common usage is:

> "1: a living being sacrificed to some deity or in the performance of a religious rite 2: someone put to death, tortured, or mulcted by another: a person subjected to oppression, deprivation, or suffering <a ~ of war> <a ~ of intolerance> <fell a ~ to prohibition era gangsters> 3: someone who suffers death, loss, or injury in an undertaking of his own <became a ~ of his own ambition> 4: someone tricked, duped, or subjected to hardship: someone badly used or taken advantage of <felt himself the ~ of his brother's shrewdness—W.F. Davis> <little boys, as well as adolescent girls, became the willing~s of sailors and marines—R.M. Lovett>
>
> "syn PREY, QUARRY: VICTIM applies to anyone who suffers either as a result of ruthless design or incidentally or accidentally <the victim sacrificed on these occasions is a hen, or several hens—J.G. Frazer> <was the girl born to be a victim; to be always disliked and crushed as if she were too fine for this world—Joseph Conrad> <lest such a policy precipitate a hot war of which western Europe would be the victim—Quincy Wright> * * *."

Webster's Third New Int'l Dictionary 2550 (unabridged ed. 1983).

In that light, it can be seen that defendant's contention that the "plain meaning" of the word "victim" refers only to persons, and not to animals, is predicated on a selective reading of the dictionary definitions. The first sense listed in the definition, for example, refers broadly to "a living being," not solely to human beings. And the synonymy gives as an example of the word "victim" the sacrifice of animals. The ordinary meaning of the word "victim," then, is capable of referring either to human beings, animals, or both.

Illustrative examples of the plain meaning of "victim" to refer to animals are not difficult to locate. Especially in the context of animal cruelty, it is common to refer to animals as "victims." As far back as the mid-nineteenth century, John Stuart Mill referred to the "unfortunate slaves and victims of the most brutal part of mankind; the lower animals." John Stuart Mill, 2 *Principles of Political Economy: With Some of Their Applications to Social Philosophy* 579 (1864). Rachel Carson complained of cruelty to all, "whether its victim is human or animal." Letter from Rachel Carson to Oxford University Press, (undated) (on file with Yale University Library). A headline from an early New York Times article referred to "Animal Victims of Railroad Trains." N.Y. Times, Oct. 11, 1914, at 77. A more recent article from 1982 on a series of hunting photographs from India mentioned pictures of "animal victims." *Images of India,* N.Y. Times, April 25, 1982. A 1992 article from the Chicago Tribune similarly is headlined, "Pair Heading to Bosnia to Aid Animal Victims of War." Chi. Trib., Oct. 6, 1992. Closer to home, an article in the Oregon State Bar Bulletin reported that, "[t]he Oregon Legislature has repeatedly and consistently articulated a strong public policy favoring the aggressive prosecution of animal cruelty cases by enacting statutes requiring police officers to make arrests in cases of animal abuse and to pay for and provide care to victim animals." *Full-Time Prosecutor to Litigate Animal Cruelty Cases Statewide,* Or. State Bar Bulletin, May 2013.

Having established the common, ordinary meaning of the term "victim," the question is whether anything in the statute at issue suggests that the legislature meant something different. Certainly nothing in the wording of ORS 161.067(2) suggests that the word "victim" cannot refer to animals. If anything, the phrasing of the statute—which refers to the violation of another statutory provision—suggests that the meaning of the word "victim" will depend on the underlying substantive statute that the defendant violated.

FOR DISCUSSION

If animals are victims of crimes, can they be held criminally or civily responsible for their actions?

The People of the State of New York ex rel. The Nonhuman Rights Project, Inc., on Behalf of Tommy v. Patrick C. Lavery, Individually and as an Officer of Circle L Trailer Sales, Inc., et al.

124 A.D.3d 148 (NY App.2014)

Animal rights group applied for order to show cause to commence habeas corpus proceeding on behalf of chimpanzee pursuant to article 70. Animal rights group appealed from the decision of the Supreme Court, Fulton County, J. Sise, J., denying the application.

Vote: 3–0

Judge Peters wrote for the Court.

Opinion

The subject of this litigation is a chimpanzee, known as Tommy, that is presently being kept by respondents on their property in the City of Gloversville, Fulton County. On behalf of Tommy, petitioner sought an order to show cause to commence a habeas corpus proceeding pursuant to CPLR article 70 on the ground that Tommy was being unlawfully detained by respondents. In support, petitioner submitted the affidavits of several experts in an effort to establish that, in general, chimpanzees have attributes sufficient to consider them "persons" for the purposes of their interest in personal autonomy and freedom from unlawful detention. Collectively, these submissions maintain that chimpanzees exhibit highly complex cognitive functions—such as autonomy, self-awareness and self-determination, among others—similar to those possessed by human beings. Following an ex parte hearing, Supreme Court found that the term "person" under CPLR article 70 did not include chimpanzees and issued a judgment refusing to sign an order to show cause. Petitioner appeals.

This appeal presents the novel question of whether a chimpanzee is a "person" entitled to the rights and protections afforded by the writ of habeas corpus. Notably, we have not been asked to evaluate the quality of Tommy's current living conditions in an effort to improve his welfare. In fact, petitioner's counsel stated at oral argument that it does not allege that respondents are in violation of any state or federal statutes respecting the domestic possession of wild animals. According to petitioner, while respondents are in compliance with state and federal statutes, the statutes themselves are inappropriate. Yet, rather than challenging any such statutes, petitioner requests that this Court enlarge the common-law definition of "person" in order to afford legal rights to an animal. We decline to do so, and conclude that a chimpanzee is not a "person" entitled to the rights and protections afforded by the writ of habeas corpus.

The common law writ of habeas corpus, as codified by CPLR article 70, provides a summary procedure by which a "person" who has been illegally imprisoned or otherwise restrained in his or her liberty can challenge the legality of the detention (CPLR 7002[a]). The statute does not purport to define the term "person," and for good reason. Thus, we must look to the common law surrounding the historic writ of habeas corpus to ascertain the breadth of the writ's reach.

Not surprisingly, animals have never been considered persons for the purposes of habeas corpus relief, nor have they been explicitly considered as persons or entities capable of asserting rights for the purpose of state or federal law (*see e.g. Lewis v. Burger King,* 344 Fed.Appx. 470, 472 [10th Cir.2009], *cert. denied* 558 U.S. 1125, 130 S.Ct. 1083, 175 L.Ed.2d 907 [2010]; *Cetacean Community v. Bush,* 386 F.3d 1169, 1178 [9th Cir.2004]; *Tilikum ex rel. People for the Ethical Treatment of Animals, Inc. v. Sea World Parks & Entertainment, Inc.,* 842 F.Supp.2d 1259, 1263 [S.D.Cal.2012]; *Citizens to End Animal Suffering & Exploitation, Inc. v. New England Aquarium,* 836 F.Supp. 45, 49–50 [D.Mass 1993]). Petitioner does not cite any precedent-and there appears to be none-in state law, or under English common law, that an animal could be considered a "person" for the purposes of common-law habeas corpus relief. In fact, habeas corpus relief has never been provided to any nonhuman entity (*see e.g. United States v. Mett,* 65 F.3d 1531, 1534 [9th Cir.1995], *cert. denied* 519 U.S. 870, 117 S.Ct. 185, 136 L.Ed.2d 124 [1996]; *Waste Management of Wisconsin, Inc. v. Fokakis,* 614 F.2d 138, 139–140 [7th Cir.1980], *cert. denied* 449 U.S. 1060, 101 S.Ct. 782, 66 L.Ed.2d 603 [1980]; *Sisquoc Ranch Co. v. Roth,* 153 F.2d 437, 441 [9th Cir.1946]; *Graham v. State of New York,* 25 A.D.2d 693, 693, 267 N.Y.S.2d 1009 [1966]).

The lack of precedent for treating animals as persons for habeas corpus purposes does not, however, end the inquiry, as the writ has over time gained increasing use given its "great flexibility and vague scope." While petitioner proffers various justifications for affording chimpanzees, such as Tommy, the liberty rights protected by such writ, the ascription of rights has historically been connected with the imposition of societal obligations and duties. Reciprocity between rights and responsibilities stems from principles of social contract, which inspired the ideals of freedom and democracy at the core of our system of government (*see* Richard L. Cupp Jr., *Children, Chimps, and Rights: Arguments From "Marginal" Cases,* 45 Ariz. St. L.J. 1, 12–14 [2013]; Richard L. Cupp Jr., *Moving Beyond Animal Rights: A Legal/ Contractualist Critique,* 46 San Diego L. Rev. 27, 69–70 [2009]; *see also Matter of Gault,* 387 U.S. 1, 20–21, 87 S.Ct. 1428, 18 L.Ed.2d 527 [1967]; *United States v. Barona,* 56 F.3d 1087, 1093–1094 [9th Cir.1995], *cert. denied* 516 U.S. 1092, 116 S.Ct. 813, 133 L.Ed.2d 759 [1996]). Under this view, society extends rights in exchange for an express or implied agreement from its members to submit to social responsibilities. In other words, "rights [are] connected to moral agency and the ability to accept societal responsibility in exchange for [those] rights" (Richard L. Cupp Jr., *Children, Chimps, and Rights: Arguments From "Marginal" Cases,* 45 Ariz. St. L.J. 1, 13 [2013]; *see* Richard L. Cupp Jr., *Moving Beyond Animal Rights: A Legal/ Contractualist Critique,* 46 San Diego L. Rev. 27, 69 [2009]).

Further, although the dispositive inquiry is whether chimpanzees are entitled to the right to be free from bodily restraint such that they may be deemed "persons" subject to the benefits of habeas corpus, legal personhood has consistently been defined in terms of both rights *and duties*. Black's Law Dictionary defines the term "person" as "[a] human being" or, as relevant here, "[a]n entity (such as a corporation) that is recognized by law as having the *rights and duties* [of] a human being" (emphasis added). It then goes on to provide:

> "So far as legal theory is concerned, a person is any being whom the law regards as capable of rights and duties. . . . Persons are the substances of which rights and duties are the attributes. It is only in this respect that persons possess juridical significance, and this is the exclusive point of view from which personality receives legal recognition" (Black's Law Dictionary [7th ed. 1999], citing John Salmond, Jurisprudence 318 [10th ed. 1947].

Case law has always recognized the correlative rights and duties that attach to legal personhood (*see e.g. Smith v. ConAgra Foods, Inc.,* 2013 Ark. 502, 431 S.W.3d 200, 203–204 [Ark.2013], citing *Calaway v. Practice Mgmt.*

Servs., Inc., 2010 Ark. 432, *4 [2010] [defining a "person" as "a human being or an entity that is recognized by law as having the rights and duties of a human being"]; *Wartelle v. Women's & Children's Hosp.,* 704 So.2d 778, 780 [La.1997] [finding that the classification of a being or entity as a "person" is made "solely for the purpose of facilitating determinations about the attachment of legal rights and duties"]; *Amadio v. Levin,* 509 Pa. 199, 225, 501 A.2d 1085, 1098 [1985, Zappala, J., concurring] [noting that " '[p]ersonhood' as a legal concept arises not from the humanity of the subject but from the ascription of rights and duties to the subject"]). Associations of human beings, such as corporations and municipal entities, may be considered legal persons, because they too bear legal duties in exchange for their legal rights (*see e.g. Pembina Consol. Silver Mining & Milling Co. v. Pennsylvania,* 125 U.S. 181, 189, 8 S.Ct. 737, 31 L.Ed. 650 [1888]; *Western Sur. Co. v. ADCO Credit, Inc.,* 251 P.3d 714, 716 [Nev.2011]; *State v. A.M.R.,* 147 Wash.2d 91, 94, 51 P.3d 790, 791 [2002]; *State v. Zain,* 207 W.Va. 54, 61–65, 528 S.E.2d 748, 755–759 [1999], *cert. denied* 529 U.S. 1042, 120 S.Ct. 1541, 146 L.Ed.2d 354 [2000]).

Needless to say, unlike human beings, chimpanzees cannot bear any legal duties, submit to societal responsibilities or be held legally accountable for their actions. In our view, it is this incapability to bear any legal responsibilities and societal duties that renders it inappropriate to confer upon chimpanzees the legal rights—such as the fundamental right to liberty protected by the writ of habeas corpus—that have been afforded to human beings.

Our rejection of a rights paradigm for animals does not, however, leave them defenseless. The Legislature has extended significant protections to animals, subject to criminal penalties, such as prohibiting the torture or unjustifiable killing of animals (*see* Agriculture and Markets Law § 353), the abandonment of animals in a public place (*see* Agriculture and Markets Law § 355), the transportation of animals in cruel or inhuman manners (*see* Agriculture and Markets Law § 359[1]) or by railroad without periodically allowing them out for rest and sustenance (*see* Agriculture and Markets Law § 359[2]), and the impounding of animals and then failing to provide them sustenance (*see* Agriculture and Markets Law § 356). Notably, and although subject to certain express exceptions, New Yorkers may not possess primates as pets (*see* ECL 11–0103[6][e][1]; 11–0512). Thus, while petitioner has failed to establish that common-law relief in the nature of habeas corpus is appropriate here, it is fully able to importune the Legislature to extend further legal protections to chimpanzees.

FOR DISCUSSION

What would a petitioner have to show to prevail in a habeas corpus petition on behalf of an animal?

Clones, Robots, and Space Aliens as Persons

Thus far this chapter has examined the constitutional personhood status of various entities ranging from biological entities that are human—slaves, women, children, and human fetuses—to entities that are not—corporations and animals. The line between property and personhood is presumptively clear, but the case law indicates the contrary. In some cases, property is treated as a person and receives constitutional recognition, while in other cases entities that we presume to be persons, or at least human, are not treated as such constitutionally, or are given lesser rights. To be a person does not guarantee constitutional protection as such, while being property does not always equate to lacking rights. The law is muddled, and so is constitutional personhood. But now consider how scientific advances may pose even more challenges in the future for the concept of constitutional personhood.

DNA cloning is a rapidly evolving technology. In 1996 Dolly, a ewe, was the first mammal to have been successfully cloned from an adult cell. DNA technology and cloning have evolved dramatically since then. At some point, it may be possible to clone humans from DNA cells. If that were to happen would these clones be persons entitled to constitutional protections? In 2013 in *Association for Molecular Pathology v. Myriad Genetics, Inc.*, 569 U.S. ___, 133 S. Ct. 2107 (2013) the Supreme Court of the United States ruled that human genes cannot be patented in the U.S. because DNA is a "product of nature." Naturally occurring human DNA sequences are not capable of being formed into a property interest. Yet the Court did not address the issue of whether altered DNA in the future could be patented and altered.

If cloning of human persons were to take place without altering their DNA, would the resulting new second individual be considered a person? Think of scenarios where real existing biological or natural persons clone themselves for replacement parts, such as to provide a new compatible heart or kidney. The 1982 science fiction motion picture *Blade Runner* featured a plot line where the Tyrell Corporation created cloned humans, known as replicants, who would be used for dangerous labor and work at non-Earth colonies. Could clones be created simply for these purposes, or others, and be denied constitutional personhood, or would they be entitled to all the rights that non-cloned humans are entitled?

A second emerging legal front for personhood involves robots and computers. The 1968 Stanley Kubrick motion picture *2001: A Space Odyssey* featured a malicious computer named Hal who sought to kill Dave, one of the astronauts. At the time the film was a fantasy, but it depicted a self-aware computer possessing the intentionality to cause harm to a human. Robots and computers have significantly advanced since then. IBM's computer Deep Blue won a chess game against a reigning world champion. Some scientists speculate that at a future point a robotic computer will possess such human traits as intelligence, feelings, and self-awareness. In such cases, it may be difficult to argue that it is not a person. Currently, robots are property, and if they use damage or harm another, the human owner is held liable. But if the robot is like Hal and develops self-awareness and intentionality, could it be held legally responsible for its actions? The scientific fiction writer Isaac Asimov once penned the three rules of robotics.

> A robot may not injure a human being or, through inaction, allow a human being to come to harm.
>
> A robot must obey orders given it by human beings except where such orders would conflict with the First Law.
>
> A robot must protect its own existence as long as such protection does not conflict with the First or Second Law.

What if a self-aware or conscious robot kills a human? Could it claim self-defense or that it acted to protect the life of a human? Could or should a robot be read its Miranda rights at the time of arrest? Is the robot entitled to an attorney and would the prohibition against cruel and unusual punishment apply? All these sound like strange questions, but the world of robotics as depicted in the Kubrik film or Asimov's writings may not be far off. Already the issues of self-driving or driverless cars are pushing questions of legal liability in new directions, and so might advanced robotics.

But one need not even reach a fully robotic creature to ask questions about personhood. The actor Lee Majors starred in a 1970s television show entitled *The Six Million Dollar Man.* He was a person rebuilt with many robotic parts after an accident. Imagine a scenario where some entity is a real six-million-dollar person, consisting of perhaps some human parts, including partial human brain, but one that is also augmented by a robotic computer. How much real human or DNA would have to be in this entity for it to be considered a constitutional person? With human science and technology evolving so rapidly, the legal and ethical the possibilities of cloning new persons or using artificial intelligence to create them is possible. But if we were to do that, we should heed the words of Justice Kagan in *Kimble v. Marvel Enterprises, Inc.*, U.S., 135 S.Ct. 2401, 2415 (2015), quoting S. Lee and S. Ditko, Amazing Fantasy No. 15: "Spider-Man," p. 13 (1962) ("[I]n this world, with great power there must also come—great responsibility").

Finally, now push the issue of personhood into a completely different direction—space aliens. Imagine, as the opening to the *Star* Wars movies describe, a long time ago, in a galaxy far, far away, there existed space aliens of higher intelligence who come and visit the United States. Would they be persons? Philosopher Robert Nozick wrote in his 1974 book *Anarchy, State, and Utopia* that much of our modern conceptions of ethics is based on a series of rules that higher ordered or intelligent species may sacrifice those inferior to them. That is the basis for how and why humans feel entitled to use animals for their purposes. His book back then surveyed the current research and arguments supposedly labeling animals as inferior to humans, finding that many of the arguments about intelligence or self-awareness quite confused. But nonetheless he decides to apply the rules we apply to animals and then applies them to space aliens: "Could beings from another galaxy stand to us as it is usually thought we do to animals, and if so, would they be justified in treating us as means a la utilitarianism?" (45)

Assume that the proverbial person from Mars or from a far distant galaxy travels to Earth and settles in the United States. Would such an entity, especially if highly intelligent, be considered a person and given constitutional protection?

GLOSSARY

1924 Indian Citizenship Act: A 1924 law granting US citizenship to Native-Americans.

Constitutional Personhood: Recognition by the Supreme Court or the law that some person or entity is considered a "person" for the purposes of the Constitution or Bill or Rights.

Coverture: A historical legal doctrine in western law in which a woman's rights, upon marriage, are subordinated to her husband. The typical consequence was that a married woman could not hold property or make a binding contract.

Federal Dictionary Act: Title 1, sections 1–8 of the United States Code which define certain terms for federal law purposes, including the term "person."

SELECTED BIBLIOGRAPHY

Berg, Jessica. 2007. "Of Elephants and Embryos: a Proposed Framework for Legal Personhood," 59 *Hastings L.J.* 369–406.

De Waal, Frans. 2016. *Are We Smart Enough to Know How Smart Animals Are?* New York: W.W. Norton.

Hallevy, Gabriel. 2010. "I, Robot—I, Criminal"—when Science Fiction Becomes Reality: Legal Liability of AI Robots Committing Criminal Offenses," 22 *Syracuse Sci. & Tech. L. Rep.* 1–37.

Hubbard, F. Patrick. 2010. "Do Androids Dream?': Personhood and Intelligent Artifacts," *83 Temp. L. Rev.* 405–474.

Martyn, Susan R. 2001. "Human Cloning: The Role of Law," 32 *University of Toledo Law Review*, pp. 375–386.

Nozick, Robert. 1974. *Anarchy, State, and Utopia,* New York: Basic Books.

Radin, Margaret Jane. 1996. *Reinterpreting Property,* Chicago: University of Chicago Press.

Regan, Tom. 2004. "The Day May Come: Legal Rights for Animals," 10 *Animal L.* 11–24

Rivard, Michael D. 1992. "Toward a General Theory of Constitutional Personhood: a Theory of Constitutional Personhood for Transgenic Humanoid Species," 39 *UCLA L. Rev.* 1425–1510.

Sunstein, Cass R. 2003. "The Rights of Animals," 70 *U. Chi. L. Rev.* 387–401.

Zelony, Adiv. 2005. "Don't Throw the Baby out with the Bathwater: Why a Ban on Human Cloning Might Be a Threat to Human Rights," 27 *Loyola International and Comparative Law Review*, pp. 541–568.

CHAPTER XI

State Action

Timeline: State Action

1787 The U.S. Constitution does not specifically mention slavery, but allows it continuance and counts slaves as three-fifths of a person for purposes of state representation in the House of Representatives.

1854 The Supreme Court rules in *Dred Scott v. Sandford* that while enslaved African Americans are property, no African American can be a citizen of the United States based on race.

1860 Abraham Lincoln is elected president.

1861 Civil War begins with the Confederacy firing on Fort Sumter in South Carolina.

1865 Civil War ends with General Lee surrendering to General Grant in Appomattox Courthouse, Virginia.

1865 John Wilkes Booth assassinates President Lincoln at Ford's Theatre.

1865 The Thirteen Amendment, banning slavery, is ratified.

1866 Reconstruction begins.

1866 Congress passes the Civil Rights Act of 1866.

1868 The Fourteenth Amendment is ratified, overturning the *Dred Scott* decision.

1870 The Fifteenth Amendment, granting males the right to vote regardless of previous condition of servitude or race, is ratified.

1871 Congress adopts the Civil Rights Act of 1871, otherwise known as the Ku Klux Klan Act, to prevent the suppression of the rights of former slaves.

1875 Congress adopts the Civil Rights Act of 1875, banning discrimination based on race in all public accommodations.

1877 Reconstruction ends with the removal of federal troops from the South.

1883 The Supreme Court rules in the *Civil Rights Cases* that the Civil Rights Act of 1875 was unconstitutional because neither the Fourteenth nor Fifteenth Amendment empowered Congress to adopt it.

1896 The Supreme Court rules in *Plessy v. Ferguson* that a state law mandating separate train compartments for whites and blacks is constitutional.

1909 The National Association for the Advancement of Colored People (NAACP) is established.

1945 The Supreme Court rules in *Screws v. United States* that Congress had the authority to punish a local government official under federal law for the violation of the civil rights of an individual.

1946 In *Marsh v. State of Alabama* the Supreme Court rules that a company town may not prevent a member of Jehovah's Witnesses from distributing religious literature within its boundaries.

1948 In *Shelley v. Kraemer* the Supreme Court rules that the Fourteenth Amendment prevents courts from enforcing racially restrictive covenants.

1954 In *Brown v. Board of Education*, the Supreme Court overturns *Plessy* in *Brown v. Board of Education.*

1955 Rosa Parks is arrested because of her refusal to give up her seat in the front of a bus and move to the rear of the vehicle.

1964 Congress adopts the Civil Rights Act of 1964, banning discrimination in employment and public accommodations.

1964 In *Heart of Atlanta Motel v. United States* and *Katzenbach v. McClung* the Supreme Court upholds the constitutionality of the 1964 Civil Rights Act.

1972 In *Moose Lodge No. 107 v. Irvis* the Supreme Court rules that the federal government may not ban discrimination in a private club that has been granted a state liquor license.

1974 In *Jackson v. Metropolitan Edison Company* the Supreme Court rules that state action had not occurred when a private utility company regulated by the state terminated service to a customer for a nonpayment of a bill.

1989 The Supreme Court rules in *DeShaney v. Winnebago County Dept. of Social Services* that the county was not liable for damages even though, despite knowledge of ongoing abuse, the county had refused to remove from the custody of his father a child who was permanently injured as a result of severe beatings by that parent.

2005 The Supreme Court rules in *Town of Castle Rock, Colorado v. Gonzales* that police were not liable for damages arising from the murder of the three daughters of a woman who had obtained a restraining order against the children's father. The police failed to arrest the father for violating the court order, and he later abducted and killed his daughters.

2007 In *Fashion Valley Mall, LLC v. N.L.R.B.* a California court rules that a private shopping mall may not prevent a labor union from leafleting outside the property.

2014 The police shooting and death of Michael Brown in Ferguson, Missouri, sparked protests that evolved into the Black Lives Matter movement and resulted in a Justice Department finding that while the shooting was justify there had been systemic mistreatment of African Americans by the local police force.

INTRODUCTION

The Constitution forms a framework that constitutes and limits the power of the federal government. It, along with the Bill of Rights, as the chapter on incorporation demonstrated, places limits on the ability of the national and state governments to interfere with certain rights. As the language of the First Amendment makes clear when it opens with "Congress shall make no law," the Bill of Rights limits government and not private action. This means that while the government may not restrict freedom of speech or of the press, nothing in the language of the Bill of Rights appears to prevent private parties from imposing such restrictions. Thus, as a rule, private schools, housing developments, and employers, for example, may be able to engage in practices that would be prohibited to the government. If these restrictive actions are purely private, and not subject to civil rights laws, groups such as the Boy Scouts are free to make decisions regarding the composition of their membership, in accordance with the ruling in *Boy Scouts v. Dale* (530 U.S. 640, 2000).

Constitutional provisions thus appear to distinguish between permissible private action and **state action.** State action refers to acts that can be attributed to the government and therefore are subject to the restrictions of the Constitution. Conversely, actions that cannot be attributed to the government are private and generally are not subject to the Bill of Rights. This means that while the government may not be able to discriminate on the basis of religion, both the First Amendment Free Exercise Clause and the 1964 Civil Rights Act permit religious organizations to use religion as a factor in hiring decisions. In effect, private and religious groups have the right to decide on who joins them and what rights the groups have, even if they discriminate.

The United States has a long history of discrimination. Discrimination against African Americans and other racial minorities has included slavery, Jim Crow laws, and Ku Klux Klan violence. In addition, women also faced discrimination with respect to voting, property rights, and their choice of occupations. But while there is a long history of discrimination, there is a long history of attempts to outlaw or undo it, too. Chapter VII, on equal protection of the laws, described many of the statutes and court decisions that form part of the history of abating racism and sexism. But it is important to underscore that government is not the only possible agent of discrimination. Prejudicial treatment can occur at the hands of government, such as by the passage of a law; but private parties can engage in it as well.

When private parties discriminate, two constitutional questions emerge. First, can the federal government constitutionally ban discrimination when the actors are private parties? Second, is the discrimination really private, or does it have de facto government sanction? In the latter case, the action is not really private at all. Understanding or determining that action is public (government) or private is critical because it may well determine if the government has the authority to act and regulate the action. There is no question that discriminatory actions undertaken directly by the federal government are unconstitutional. However, can the federal government ban or regulate discrimination in private clubs, restaurants, political party gatherings, and other similar places, or is some conduct of individuals simply beyond the reach of the law? This is where the concept of state action becomes important.

Today the boundaries between "government" and "nongovernment" have become blurred as a result of regulation and the letting of contracts to private and nonprofit entities to perform public services. As a result, it is increasingly difficult to determine the classification into which a given actor falls. This in turn means that deciding what constitutes state action is often difficult. The cases in this chapter offer some insights into how the judiciary has sought to decide what constitutes state action.

Additionally, this chapter examines how citizens are protected against excessive use of force by the state in the course of efforts by law enforcement to protect the larger community. While this is a substantive protection, not a procedural one, and although it is based on a statutory claim, not a constitutional one, the federal statute requires a constitutional violation on the part of the officer before an action meets the standard of excessive force. Most typically, such constitutional claims incorporate the Fourth, Fifth, Sixth, and Fourteenth Amendments. The use of force will be examined in terms of deadly force, non-deadly force, and high-speed vehicle chases.

Historical Developments

The first attempt to understand the concept of state action and the proper scope of the federal government to address private discrimination came in the wake of the Civil War. The Reconstruction Congress, under the leadership of the Radical Republicans, adopted the Thirteenth, Fourteenth, and Fifteenth Amendments, as well as three civil rights acts, in 1866, 1871, and 1875. All the amendments and acts were aimed at barring both public discrimination and in some cases, private acts under some circumstances. For example, the 1871 Civil Rights Act, otherwise known as the Ku Klux Klan Act, sought to address violence against blacks and the suppression of their civil rights by state and local government officials. One portion of that statute, which is now codified as 42 U.S.C. § 1983 (as discussed in an earlier chapter in the context of police brutality), made it illegal for individuals acting under the color of the law to suppress the constitutional rights of another individual. While the phrase **under the color of the law** was directed at government officials who discriminated, the language was also interpreted as covering private individuals who effectively were state actors. Thus, if a person was deemed to be acting under the color of the law, he or she was considered to be a state actor, and the Fourteenth Amendment empowered Congress to step in to regulate the action because it was therefore defined as state action.

However, in 1875 Congress took an additional step. The Civil Rights Act of 1875 sought to bar discrimination in public accommodations such as restaurants. It did so not because the government claimed that the private actor was acting under the color of the law, but instead for the purpose of preventing private discrimination against African Americans. In the *Civil Rights Cases* (109 U.S. 3, 1883), the Supreme Court ruled that in passing the 1875 act, Congress had exceeded its constitutional authority. Here the Court set the pattern for the view that the Fourteenth Amendment applied only to state action, not to private actions. This decision and some others of the Reconstruction period have sometimes been referred to as the Second Civil War, this one won by white southern lawyers in the Supreme Court.

Earlier, in *United States v. Cruikshank* (92 U.S. 542 1876), the Court had noted that the Fourteenth Amendment "adds nothing to the rights of one citizen as against another. It simply furnishes a federal guaranty against any encroachment by the States upon the fundamental rights which belong to every citizen as a member of society." As a result of the *Civil Rights Cases*, a firm wall seemed to constructed—state action and discrimination could be regulated; private discrimination could not be. The decision unleashed a wave of practices in the South, some purely private, but many not so thinly supported by the state, which endorsed "separate but equal" as a social policy and made possible the Jim Crow laws that enforced discrimination against African Americans. Eventually, with the adoption of the Civil Rights Act of 1964, Congress would return to addressing discrimination in public accommodations. The act was upheld in *Heart of Atlanta Motel v. United States* (379 U.S. 241, 1964), where the Court relied chiefly on congressional authority to promote the free flow of interstate commerce.

The 1964 act was the product of decades of work launched to overturn the *Civil Rights Cases*. The interracial National Association for the Advancement of Colored People (NAACP), established in 1909, was formed with the goals of overturning *Plessy*, abolishing separate but equal, and ending discrimination against African Americans. The organization's strategy was one of gradually chipping away at discriminatory laws. In part the strategy called on NAACP attorneys to use the Ku Klux Klan Act to their advantage, to secure judicial notice of the view that certain ostensibly private acts in fact constituted state action, and to obtain passage of new civil rights laws.

Screws v. United States (325 U.S. 91, 1945) provides one example of a successful effort to address discrimination. In this case the Court used federal criminal law to prosecute a sheriff who had arrested and beaten to death a theft suspect who was African American.

Screws is an example of the application to state officials of the provisions of federal laws. The Court has made the terms "under color of" and "under pretense of" state law mutually interchangeable in its interpretation of the applicable federal criminal statute. However, the constitutional difficulties involved in applying federal criminal legislation to individuals are very obvious. Eventually, in *Monell v. Department of Social Services* (436 U.S. 658, 1978), the Supreme Court ruled that 42 U.S.C. § 1983 imposed liabilities on local government officials for violations of constitutional rights, paving the way for law enforcement personnel at the local level to face liability for claims of excessive use of force and other constitutional violations.

Restrictive covenants were a tool used to place limits on what owners can do with their property. Often these agreements are used in private communities to create uniform building standards. But restrictive covenants were also a popular tool of racial discrimination. For example, a homebuyer in a town or community might promise not to sell the property to an African American. As contracts, these covenants were for many years enforceable in court. In *Shelley v. Kraemer* (334 U.S. 1, 1948), however, the Supreme Court held that restrictive covenants could not be enforced because such enforcement constituted a form of state action that violated the Equal Protection Clause.

Shelley does not invalidate restrictive covenants. Such arrangements may still be made between private individuals. All that is changed is that neither federal nor state courts may be used to enforce of such agreements. The equal protection provision of the Fourteenth Amendment is not applicable to private persons, natural or legal. For the Fourteenth Amendment to be applicable, there must be state action; and the Court in *Shelley* held that any action by a state court to enforce restrictive covenants amounted to state participation. In other words, in a matter in which the state legislature could not act under the Fourteenth Amendment, the state courts could not act. The *Shelley* decision was potentially far-reaching. Could one not argue that any agreement or matter that comes to the courts for adjudication constitutes state action?

Prior to *Shelley,* in *Marsh v. State of Alabama* (326 U.S. 501, 1946), the Court confronted a different issue. Here the justices considered whether a company town, founded and run by a corporation, could prevent a member of the Jehovah's Witnesses from distributing religious literature in the downtown area. Under the existing reading of the Fourteenth Amendment, the prohibition of leafleting should have constituted private action, in which case it would be beyond the reach of the law.

At issue in *Marsh* was the constitutionality of a private town's restriction of rights of individuals that could not be similarly limited by government. Here the Court adopted a position that private towns have as much control over individuals as do real governments. The traditional conception of government also brought with it the notion of the public square, a place where people could gather and exercise their First Amendment rights. However, for many, the virtual public square is now the shopping mall. In *PruneYard Shopping Center v. Robins* 447 (U.S. 74, 1980), the Supreme Court upheld a California Supreme Court ruling granting free speech rights to the public in privately owned shopping malls. The decision, resting upon unique California constitutional provisions, saw private malls as occupying a new position in the state. In *Fashion Valley Mall, LLC v. N.L.R.B.* (172 Cal. Rptr.3d 742, Cal. 2007), the California Supreme Court revisited the *PruneYard* decision, finding shopping malls to be almost like state actors for the purpose of speech rights.

Moose Lodge No. 107 v. Irvis (407 U.S. 163, 1972) is a famous state action case. The majority and the dissenters argue over whether the mere issuance of liquor licenses is enough to constitute state action, even though the number of licenses that can be issued is limited. This and the *Shelley* case similarly raise the question of whether any government regulation or oversight is enough to constitute state action. In *Moose Lodge* Justice Rehnquist relies on the state actor-private action distinction from the *Civil Rights Cases* and finds that the issuance of a liquor license is an insufficient nexus to constitute state action. By contrast, the dissenters found state action by focusing on the state regulation surrounding the sale and consumption of alcohol in the state.

State regulation is also an issue in *Jackson v. Metropolitan Edison Company* (419 U.S. 345, 1974). Here a private utility company, regulated and licensed by the state of Pennsylvania, turned off a customer's power owing to nonpayment of a bill. The customer claimed state action. Again here the Court said no, with disagreement over how extensive the regulation had to be before it rose to the level of state action.

A different aspect of state action addresses the liability of governmental employees who violate individual rights. The *Screws* case raised the issue of whether states can he held for damages under § 1983 suits as a result of actions of their staff. A slightly different question is whether states can be held liable for a failure to act. In both *Deshaney v. Winnebago County Department of Social Services* (489 U.S. 189, 1989) and *Town of Castle Rock, Colorado v. Gonzales* (545 U.S. 748, 2005), the Court ruled that damages resulting from the failure of public officials to act to protect individuals did not constitute a form of state action. Both the *Deshaney* and *Castle Rock* decisions draw on and reinforce a theory in the law that a general duty on the part of the government to protect individuals does not in itself imply liability in the event of failure to act. Instead, the government must have established a specific or particularized duty with an individual. Generally, that duty exists when the government takes a person into custody, for example. These two cases rejected the idea that mere notice to the government of a dangerous situation is sufficient to establish liability.

CIVIL RIGHTS CASES

109 U.S. 3, 3 S.Ct. 18, 27 L.Ed. 835 (1883)

Several African Americans had been refused admission to hotels, theaters, and railroad "ladies' cars" by the owners of these facilities. An act of Congress forbade discrimination. Arrests of the various private owners were challenged on the basis that the Fourteenth Amendment does not prohibit discriminatory activity on the part of private citizens.

Vote: 8–1

JUSTICE BRADLEY delivered the opinion of the Court.

The first section of the Fourteenth Amendment, which is the one relied on, after declaring who shall be citizens of the United States, and of the several states, is prohibitory in its character, and prohibitory upon the States. It declares that: "No State shall make or enforce any law which shall abridge the privileges or immunities of citizens of the United States; nor shall any State deprive any person of life, liberty or property without due process of law; nor deny to any person within its jurisdiction the equal protection of the laws." It is State action of a particular character that is prohibited. Individual invasion of individual rights is not the subject-matter of the Amendment. It has a deeper and broader scope. It nullifies and makes void all State legislation, and State action of every kind, which impairs the privileges and immunities of citizens of the United States, or which injures them in life, liberty or property without due process of law, or which denies to any of them the equal protection of the laws. It not only does this, but, in order that the national will, thus declared, may not be a mere *brutum fulmen* [empty threat], the last section of the Amendment invests Congress with power to enforce it by appropriate legislation. To enforce what? To enforce the prohibition. To adopt appropriate legislation for correcting the effects of such prohibited State laws and State Acts, and thus to render them effectually null, void and innocuous. This is the legislative power conferred upon Congress, and this is the whole of it. It does not invest Congress with power to legislate upon subjects which are within the domain of State legislation; but to provide modes of relief against State legislation, or State action, of the kind referred to. It does not authorize Congress to create a code of municipal law for the regulation of private rights; but to provide modes of redress against the operation of State laws, and the action of State officers, executive or judicial, when these are subversive of the fundamental rights specified in the Amendment. Positive rights and privileges are undoubtedly secured by the Fourteenth Amendment; but they are secured by way of prohibition against State laws and State proceedings affecting those rights and privileges, and by power given to Congress to legislate for the purpose of carrying such prohibition into effect; and such legislation must, necessarily, be predicated upon such supposed State laws or State proceedings, and be directed to the correction of their operation and effect.

And so in the present case, until some State law has been passed, or some State action through its officers or agents has been taken, adverse to the rights of citizens sought to be protected by the Fourteenth Amendment, no legislation of the United States under said Amendment, nor any proceedings under such legislation, can be called into activity; for the prohibitions of the Amendment are against State laws and acts done under State authority. Of course, legislation may and should be provided in advance to meet the exigency when it arises; but it should be adapted to the mischief and wrong which the Amendment was intended to provide against; and that is, State laws, or State action of some kind, adverse to the rights of the citizens secured by the Amendment. Such legislation cannot properly cover the whole domain of rights appertaining to life, liberty and property, defining them and providing for their vindication. That would be to establish a code of municipal law regulative of all private rights between man and man in society. It would be to make Congress take the place of the State Legislatures and to supersede them. It is absurd to affirm that, because of the rights of life, liberty and property, which include all civil rights that men have, are, by the Amendment, sought to be protected against invasion on the part of the State without due process of law, Congress may, therefore, provide due process of law for their vindication in every case; and that, because the denial by a State to any persons, of the equal protection of the laws, is prohibited by the Amendment, therefore Congress may establish laws for their equal protection. In fine, the legislation which Congress is authorized to adopt in this behalf is not general legislation upon the rights of the citizen, but corrective legislation, that is, such as may be necessary and proper for counteracting such laws as the States may adopt or enforce, and which, by the Amendment, they are prohibited from making or enforcing, or such acts and proceedings as the States may commit or take, and which, by the Amendment, they are prohibited from committing or taking.

On the whole we are of opinion, that no countenance of authority for the passage of the law in question can be found in either the Thirteenth or Fourteenth Amendment of the Constitution; and no other ground of authority for its passage being suggested, it must necessarily be declared void, at least so far as its operation in the several States is concerned.

JUSTICE HARLAN dissented.

The opinion in these cases proceeds, it seems to me, upon grounds entirely too narrow and artificial. I cannot resist the conclusion that the substance and spirit of the recent amendments of the Constitution have been sacrificed by a subtle and ingenious verbal criticism. "It is not the words of the law but the internal sense of it that makes the law: the letter of the law is the body; the sense and reason of the law is the soul." Constitutional provisions, adopted in the interest of liberty, and for the purpose of securing, through national legislation, if need be, rights inhering in a state of freedom, and belonging to American citizenship, have been so construed as to defeat the ends the people desired to accomplish, which they attempted to accomplish and which they supposed they had accomplished by changes in their fundamental law.

In every material sense applicable to the practical enforcement of the Fourteenth Amendment, railroad corporations, keepers of inns, and managers of places of public amusement are agents or instrumentalities of the States, because they are charged with duties to the public, and are amenable, in respect of their duties and functions, to governmental regulation. It seems to me that, within the principle settled in *Ex parte Virginia,* 100 U.S. 339 (1879), a denial, by these instrumentalities of the State, to the citizen, because of his race, of that equality of civil rights secured to him by law, is a denial by the State, within the meaning of the Fourteenth Amendment. . . .

FOR DISCUSSION

After this decision, did Congress have any authority to ban discrimination in private establishments such as stores or restaurants? What constitutes state action, as opposed to private action?

SCREWS V. UNITED STATES

325 U.S. 91, 65 S.Ct. 1031, 89 L.Ed. 249 (1945)

A Georgia county sheriff by the name of Screws, with the aid of a policeman and a deputy, arrested an African American male on a warrant charging him with the theft of a tire. Upon arrival at the courthouse, the officers proceeded to beat the suspect, Robert Hall, claiming that he had reached for a gun. Hall was rendered unconscious and died at a hospital within an hour. The officers were charged with violation of the Federal Criminal Code, Section 20, according to which it is a federal offense willfully to deprive a person, under color of law, of his rights, privileges, or immunities guaranteed by the Constitution and laws of the United States. The case involved the question of whether Congress has the power to provide for the punishment of state officials for violation of civil rights described in federal law.

Vote: 5–4

JUSTICE DOUGLAS delivered the opinion of the Court.

We hesitate to say that when Congress sought to enforce the Fourteenth Amendment in this fashion it did a vain thing. We hesitate to conclude that for 80 years this effort of Congress, renewed several times, to protect the important rights of the individual guaranteed by the Fourteenth Amendment has been an idle gesture. Yet if the Act falls by reason of vagueness so far as due process of law is concerned, there would seem to be a similar lack of specificity when the privileges and immunities clause . . . and the equal protection clause . . . of the Fourteenth Amendment are involved. Only if no construction can save the Act from this claim of unconstitutionality are we willing to reach that result. We do not reach it, for we are of the view that if § 20 is confined more narrowly than the lower courts confined it, it can be preserved as one of the sanctions to the great rights which the Fourteenth Amendment was designed to secure.

The difficulty here is that this question of intent was not submitted to the jury with the proper instructions. The court charged that petitioners acted illegally if they applied more force than was necessary to make the arrest effectual or to protect themselves from the prisoner's alleged assault. But in view of our construction of the word "willfully" the jury should have been further instructed that it was not sufficient that petitioners had a generally bad purpose. To convict it was necessary for them to find that petitioners had the purpose to deprive the prisoner of a constitutional right, e.g., the right to be tried by a court rather than by ordeal. And in determining whether that requisite bad purpose was present the jury would be entitled to consider all the attendant circumstances—the malice of petitioners, the weapons used in the assault, its character and duration, the provocation, if any, and the like.

It is said, however, that petitioners did not act "under color of any law" within the meaning of § 20 of the Criminal Code. We disagree. We are of the view that petitioners acted under "color" of law in making the arrest of Robert Hall and in assaulting him. They were officers of the law who made the arrest. By their own admissions they assaulted Hall in order to protect themselves and to keep their prisoner from escaping. It was their duty under Georgia law to make the arrest effective. Hence, their conduct comes within the statute.

It is clear that under "color" of law means under "pretense" of law. Thus acts of officers in the ambit of their personal pursuits are plainly excluded. Acts of officers who undertake to perform their official duties are included whether they hew to the line of their authority or overstep it. . . .

Reversed.

JUSTICE MURPHY dissented.

[I]t is unnecessary to send this case back for a further trial on the assumption that the jury was not charged on the matter of the willfulness of the state officials, an issue that was not raised below or before us. The evidence is more than convincing that the officials willfully, or at least with wanton disregard of the consequences, deprived Robert Hall of his life without due process of law. A new trial could hardly make that fact more evident; the failure to charge the jury on willfulness was at most an inconsequential error. Moreover, the presence or absence of willfulness fails to decide the constitutional issue raised before us. Section 20 is very definite and certain in its reference to the right to life as spelled out in the Fourteenth Amendment quite apart from the state of mind of the state officials. A finding of willfulness can add nothing to the clarity of that reference.

JUSTICES ROBERTS, FRANKFURTER, and JACKSON dissented.

The debates in Congress are barren of any indication that the supporters of the legislation now before us had the remotest notion of authorizing the National Government to prosecute State officers for conduct which their State had made a State offense where the settled custom of the State did not run counter to formulated law.

Were it otherwise it would indeed be surprising. It was natural to give the shelter of the Constitution to those basic human rights for the vindication of which the successful conduct of the Civil War was the end of a long process. And the extension of federal authority so as to guard against evasion by any State of these newly created federal rights was on obvious corollary. But to attribute to Congress the making overnight of a revolutionary change in the balance of the political relations between the National Government and the States without reason, is a very different thing. And to have provided for the National Government to take over the administration of criminal justice from the States to the extent of making every lawless action of the policeman on the beat or in the station house, whether by way of third degree or the illegal ransacking for evidence in a man's house . . ., a federal offense, would have constituted a revolutionary break with the past overnight.

The matter concerns policies inherent in our federal system and the undesirable consequences of federal prosecution for crimes which are obviously and predominantly State crimes no matter how much sophisticated argumentation may give them the appearance of federal crimes. Congress has not expressed a contrary purpose, either by the language of its legislation or by anything appearing in the environment out of which its language came. The practice of government for seventy-five years likewise speaks against it. Nor is there a body of judicial opinion which bids us find in the unbridled excess of a State officer, constituting a crime under his State law, action taken "under color of law" which federal law forbids.

In the absence of clear direction by Congress we should leave to the States the enforcement of their criminal law, and not relieve States of the responsibility for vindicating wrongdoing that is essentially local or weaken the habits of local law enforcement by tempting reliance on federal authority for an occasional unpleasant task of local enforcement. . . .

FOR DISCUSSION

In this case, what constitutes the "color of the law" that creates state action? Should states be immune from prosecution for violation of federal civil rights law? How can one make this argument?

RELATED CASES

***Williams v. United States:* 341 U.S. 97 (1951).**

A private detective, also serving as a deputy police officer, beat four suspects until they confessed. He was convicted for violation of Section 242 of the federal code (U.S.C) for depriving persons, under color of law, of the right to be tried by due process of law in accordance with their Fourteenth Amendment rights. Earlier, however, the Court had held that the detective could not be prosecuted under Section 241 of the code because it protects only rights and privileges of U.S. citizenship. The appendix of this case has a good, concise history of changes in the language of federal criminal statutes.

***Griffin v. Maryland:* 378 U.S. 130 (1964).**

The action of an individual is state action if the individual, as a deputy sheriff possessing state authority, purports to act pursuant to that authority. It is immaterial that the deputy could have taken the same action in a purely private capacity or that his actions were not authorized by state law.

SHELLEY V. KRAEMER

334 U.S. 1, 68 S.Ct. 836, 92 L.Ed. 256 (1948)

This case involved restrictive covenants that limited the sale of property to Caucasians in specified locations. Shelley, an African American woman, had purchased property in St. Louis covered by a restrictive covenant that barred blacks. The Supreme Court of Missouri, at the request of owners of other properties subject to the restrictive covenant, ordered Shelley and her family to vacate the property they had recently acquired. This state court order was challenged as a violation of the Equal Protection Clause of the Fourteenth Amendment. A very similar case out of Detroit, *Sipes v. McGhee*, was merged with the Missouri case, and the verdict was the same.

Vote: 6–0

CHIEF JUSTICE VINSON delivered the opinion of the Court.

It is well, at the outset, to scrutinize the terms of the restrictive agreements involved in these cases. In the Missouri case [*Shelley*], the covenant declares that no part of the affected property shall be "occupied by any person not of the Caucasian race, it being intended hereby to restrict the use of said property . . . against the occupancy as owners or tenants of any portion of said property for resident or other purpose by people of the Negro or Mongolian race." Not only does the restriction seek to proscribe use and occupancy of the affected properties by members of the excluded class, but as construed by the Missouri courts, the agreement requires that title of any person who uses his property in violation of the restriction shall be divested.

It cannot be doubted that among the civil rights intended to be protected from discriminatory state action by the Fourteenth Amendment are the rights to acquire, enjoy, own and dispose of property. Equality in the enjoyment of property rights was regarded by the framers of that Amendment as an essential pre-condition to the realization of other basic civil rights and liberties which the Amendment was intended to guarantee. Thus, Sec. 1978 of the Revised Statutes, derived from Sec. 1 of the Civil Rights Act of 1866 which was enacted by Congress while the Fourteenth Amendment was also under consideration provides: "All citizens of the United States shall have the same right, in every State and Territory, as is enjoyed by white citizens thereof to inherit, purchase, lease, sell, hold, and convey real and personal property." This Court has given specific recognition to the same principle. *Buchanan v. Warley*, 245 U.S. 60 (1917).

Since the decision of this Court in the *Civil Rights Cases,* 109 U.S. 3 (1883), the principle has become firmly embedded in our constitutional law that the action inhibited by the first section of the Fourteenth Amendment is only such action as may fairly be said to be that of the States. That Amendment erects no shield against merely private conduct, however discriminatory or wrongful.

We conclude, therefore, that the restrictive agreements standing alone cannot be regarded as a violation of any rights guaranteed to petitioners by the Fourteenth Amendment. So long as the purposes of those agreements are effectuated by voluntary adherence to their terms, it would appear clear that there has been no action by the State and the provisions of the Amendment have not been violated.

But here there was more. These are cases in which the purposes of the agreements were secured only by judicial enforcement by state courts of the restrictive terms of the agreements. The respondents urged that judicial enforcement of private agreements does not amount to state action; or in any event, the participation of the States is so attenuated in character as not to amount to state action within the meaning of the Fourteenth Amendment. Finally, it is suggested, even if the States in these cases may be deemed to have acted in the constitutional sense, their action did not deprive petitioners of rights guaranteed by the Fourteenth Amendment. We move to a consideration of these matters.

That the action of state courts and of judicial officers in their official capacities is to be regarded as action of the State within the meaning of the Fourteenth Amendment, is a proposition which has long been established by decisions of this Court. . . .

The short of the matter is that from the time of the adoption of the Fourteenth Amendment until the present, it has been the consistent ruling of this Court that the action of the States to which the Amendment has reference, includes action of the state courts and state judicial officials. Although, in construing the terms of the Fourteenth Amendment, differences have from time to time been expressed as to whether particular types of state action may be said to offend the Amendment's prohibitory provisions, it has never been suggested that state court action is immunized from the operation of those provisions simply because the act is that of the judicial branch of the state government.

Against this background of judicial construction, extending over a period of some three-quarters of a century, we are called upon to consider whether enforcement by state courts of the restrictive agreements in these cases may be deemed to be the acts of those States; and, if so, whether that action has denied these petitioners the equal protection of the laws which the Amendment was intended to insure.

We have no doubt that there has been state action in these cases in the full and complete sense of the phrase. The undisputed facts disclose that petitioners were willing purchasers of properties upon which they desired to establish homes. The owners of the properties were willing sellers; and contracts of sale were accordingly consummated. It is clear that but for the active intervention of the state courts, supported by the full panoply of state power, petitioners would have been free to occupy the properties in question without restraint.

These are not cases, as has been suggested, in which the States have merely abstained from action, leaving private individuals free to impose such discriminations as they see fit. Rather, these are cases in which the States have made available to such individuals the full coercive power of government to deny to petitioners, on the grounds of race or color, the enjoyment of property rights in premises which petitioners are willing and financially able to acquire and which the grantors are willing to sell. The difference between judicial enforcement and non-enforcement of the restrictive covenants is the difference to petitioners between being denied rights of property available to other members of the community and being accorded full enjoyment of those rights on an equal footing. . . .

We hold that in granting judicial enforcement of the restrictive agreements in these cases, the States have denied petitioners the equal protection of the laws and that, therefore, the action of the state courts cannot stand.

Reversed.

JUSTICES REED, JACKSON, and RUTLEDGE took no part in the hearing or decision of these cases.

FOR DISCUSSION

The *Shelley* decision is potentially far-encompassing. Could one argue that any agreement or matter that comes to the courts for adjudication constitutes state action?

RELATED CASES

***Corrigan v. Buckley:* 271 U.S. 323 (1926).**

This case involved restrictive covenants as applied to property in the District of Columbia. The suit was by one owner against another owner to prevent her from selling to a black person, thus breaking the covenant. The Court held that the Due Process Clause of the Fifth Amendment did not apply because it "is a limitation only upon the powers of the general government, and is not directed against the action of individuals."

***City of Richmond v. Deans:* 281 U.S. 704 (1930).**

In a *per curiam* opinion the Supreme Court affirmed a Fourth Circuit Court of Appeals decree that held as a violation of the Fourteenth Amendment's Due Process Clause a city zoning ordinance prohibiting a person from using as a residence any building on any street between intersecting streets where a majority of residences on such street are occupied by those with whom the person is forbidden to intermarry.

***Hurd v. Hodge:* 334 U.S. 24 (1948).**

In another District of Columbia restrictive covenant case, the Court held that federal courts could not enforce such covenants because this would deny "rights intended by Congress to be protected by the Civil Rights Act." Also, the Court held that for a federal court to enforce an agreement that the state courts could not enforce would be contrary to federal public policy.

***Dorsey v. Stuyvesant Town Corp.:* 339 U.S. 981 (1950).**

Where a state law aided a private corporation in a housing development (here by condemning the land and granting certain tax exemptions), later discrimination against blacks in the selection of tenants by agents of the private corporation did not amount to state action and thus did not violate the Fourteenth Amendment.

MARSH V. STATE OF ALABAMA

326 U.S. 501, 66 S.Ct. 276, 90 L.Ed. 265 (1946)

A private town owned by a corporation barred the distribution of religious materials in the business district. A member of the Jehovah's Witnesses who had been distributing religious materials without a permit was arrested for trespass. She was convicted in a trial, and the conviction was upheld on appeal.

Vote: 6–3

JUSTICE BLACK delivered the opinion of the Court.

In this case we are asked to decide whether a State, consistently with the First and Fourteenth Amendments, can impose criminal punishment on a person who undertakes to distribute religious literature on the premises of a company-owned town contrary to the wishes of the town's management. The town, a suburb of Mobile, Alabama, known as Chickasaw, is owned by the Gulf Shipbuilding Corporation. Except for that it has all the characteristics of any other American town. The property consists of residential buildings, streets, a system of sewers, a sewage disposal plant and a 'business block' on which business places are situated. A deputy of the Mobile County Sheriff, paid by the company, serves as the town's policeman. Merchants and service establishments have rented the stores and business places on the business block and the United States uses one of the places as a post office from which six carriers deliver mail to the people of Chickasaw and the adjacent area. The town and the surrounding neighborhood, which can not be distinguished from the Gulf property by anyone not familiar with the property lines, are thickly settled, and according to all indications the residents use the business block as their regular shopping center. To do so, they now, as they have for many years, make use of a company-owned paved street and sidewalk located alongside the store fronts in order to enter and leave the stores and the post office. Intersecting company-owned roads at each end of the business block lead into a four-lane public highway which runs parallel to the business block at a distance of thirty feet. There is nothing to stop highway traffic from coming onto the business block and upon arrival a traveler may make free use of the facilities available there. In short the town and its shopping district are accessible to and freely used by the public in general and there is nothing to distinguish them from any other town and shopping center except the fact that the title to the property belongs to a private corporation.

Had the title to Chickasaw belonged not to a private but to a municipal corporation and had appellant been arrested for violating a municipal ordinance rather than a ruling by those appointed by the corporation to manage a company-town it would have been clear that appellant's conviction must be reversed. Under our decision in *Lovell v. Griffin*, 303 U.S. 444 (1938), and others which have followed that case, neither a state nor a municipality can completely bar the distribution of literature containing religious or political ideas on its streets, sidewalks and public places or make the right to distribute dependent on a flat license tax or permit to be issued by an official who could deny it at will. Our question then narrows down to this: Can those people who live in or come to Chickasaw be denied freedom of press and religion simply because a single company has legal title to all the town? For it is the state's contention that the mere fact that all the property interests in the town are held by a single company is enough to give that company power, enforceable by a state statute, to abridge these freedoms.

We do not agree that the corporation's property interests settle the question. The State urges in effect that the corporation's right to control the inhabitants of Chickasaw is coextensive with the right of a homeowner to regulate the conduct of his guests. We can not accept that contention. Ownership does not always mean absolute dominion. The more an owner, for his advantage, opens up his property for use by the public in general, the more do his rights become circumscribed by the statutory and constitutional rights of those who use it. Thus, the owners of privately held bridges, ferries, turnpikes and railroads may not operate them as freely as a farmer does his farm. Since these facilities are built and operated primarily to benefit the public and since their operation is essentially a public function, it is subject to state regulation. And, though the issue is not directly analogous to the one before us we do want to point out by way of illustration that such regulation may not result in an operation of these facilities, even by privately owned companies, which unconstitutionally interferes with and discriminates against interstate commerce. Had the corporation here owned the segment of the four-lane highway which runs parallel to the 'business block' and operated the same under a State franchise, doubtless no one would have seriously contended that the corporation's property interest in the highway gave it power to obstruct through traffic or to discriminate against interstate commerce. And even had there been no express franchise but mere acquiescence by the State in the corporation's use of its property as a segment of the four-lane highway, operation of all the highway, including the segment owned by the corporation, would still have been performance of a public function and discrimination would certainly have been illegal.

We do not think it makes any significant constitutional difference as to the relationship between the rights of the owner and those of the public that here the State, instead of permitting the corporation to operate a highway, permitted it to use its property as a town, operate a 'business block' in the town and a street and sidewalk on that business block. Whether a corporation or a municipality owns or possesses the town the public in either case has an identical interest in the functioning of the community in such manner that the channels of communication remain free. As we have heretofore stated, the town of Chickasaw does not function differently from any other town. The 'business block' serves as the community shopping center and is freely accessible and open to the people in the area and those passing through. The managers appointed by the corporation cannot curtail the liberty of press and religion of these people consistently with the purposes of the Constitutional guarantees, and a state statute, as the one here involved, which enforces such action by criminally punishing those who attempt to distribute religious literature clearly violates the First and Fourteenth Amendments to the Constitution.

Many people in the United States live in company-owned towns. These people, just as residents of municipalities, are free citizens of their State and country. Just as all other citizens they must make decisions which affect the welfare of community and nation. To act as good citizens they must be informed. In order to enable them to be properly informed their information must be uncensored. There is no more reason for depriving these people of the liberties guaranteed by the First and Fourteenth Amendments than there is for curtailing these freedoms with respect to any other citizen.

JUSTICE REED, dissenting.

Former decisions of this Court have interpreted generously the Constitutional rights of people in this Land to exercise freedom of religion, of speech and of the press. It has never been held and is not now by this opinion of the Court that these rights are absolute and unlimited either in respect to the manner or the place of their exercise. What the present decision establishes as a principle is that one may remain on private property against the will of the owner and contrary to the law of the state so long as the only objection to his presence is that he is exercising an asserted right to spread there his religious views. This is the first case to extend by law the privilege of religious exercises beyond public places or to private places without the assent of the owner.

THE CHIEF JUSTICE and JUSTICE BURTON join in this dissent.

FOR DISCUSSION

Should large condominium projects, housing projects, or gated communities be considered quasi-public actors under *Marsh?* What factors under *Marsh* need to be examined to determine whether these residential projects are functioning as essentially public actors?

FASHION VALLEY MALL, LLC v. N.L.R.B.

172 Cal. Rptr. 3d 742 (Cal. 2007)

A labor union sought to leaflet inside a privately owned shopping mall in California. When the mall owner refused to allow union members to undertake this activity, the labor organization filed an unfair labor practice complaint with the National Labor Relations Board. The federal agency sought an opinion from the California Supreme Court to determine whether the state constitution treated malls as public spaces. Circuit Judge Ginsburg wrote the Court's majority opinion.

FACTS

On October 15, 1998, Graphic Communications International Union Local 432–M (Union) filed a charge before the National Labor Relations Board (NLRB) alleging that the owners of the Fashion Valley Mall (Mall) in San Diego had "refused to permit employees of the Union-Tribune Publishing Company to leaflet in front of Robinsons-May" department store in the Mall. The NLRB issued a complaint and noticed a hearing, after which an administrative law judge ruled that the Mall had violated section 8(a)(1) of the National Labor Relations Act (29 U.S.C. § 158(a)(1)) by barring the employees from distributing leaflets.

The administrative law judge found that the Union "represents a unit of the pressroom employees at the *San Diego Union-Tribune* (*Union-Tribune*), a major general circulation newspaper in San Diego." The collective bargaining agreement between the employees and the newspaper had expired in 1992 and the parties had been unable to reach a new agreement. The administrative law judge thus found that a "primary labor dispute" existed between the newspaper and its employees at the time of the disputed labor activities in 1998.

On October 4, 1998, 30 to 40 Union members had distributed leaflets to customers entering and leaving the Robinsons-May store at the Mall. The leaflets stated that Robinsons-May advertises in the Union-Tribune, described several ways that the newspaper allegedly treated its employees unfairly, and urged customers who believed "that employers should treat employees fairly" to call the newspaper's "CEO," listing his name and telephone number. The administrative law judge concluded: "From all indications, the leafleters conducted their activity in a courteous and peaceful manner without a disruption of any kind and without hindrance to customers entering or leaving" the store.

Within 15 or 20 minutes, Mall officials "arrived on the scene to stop the leafleting," notifying the Union members that they were trespassing because they had not obtained a permit from the Mall "to engage in expressive activity," and warning them that they "would be subject to civil litigation and/or arrest if they did not leave." A police officer appeared and, following a brief argument, the Union members moved to public property near the entrance to the Mall and continued distributing leaflets briefly before leaving the area.

The Mall has adopted rules requiring persons who desire to engage in expressive activity at the Mall to apply for a permit five business days in advance. The applicant "must agree to abide by" the Mall's rules, including Rule 5.6, which prohibits "impeding, competing or interfering with the business of one or more of the stores or merchants in the shopping center by: Urging, or encouraging in any manner, customers not to purchase the merchandise or services offered by any one or more of the stores or merchants in the shopping center."

The administrative law judge found that the Union "was attempting to engage in a lawful consumer boycott of Robinsons-May because Robinsons-May advertised in the *Union-Tribune* newspaper" and further found "that it would have been utterly futile for the Union to have followed [the Mall]'s enormously burdensome application-permit process because its rules contained express provisions barring the very kind of lawful conduct the Union sought to undertake at the Mall." The administrative law judge thus ordered the Mall to cease and desist prohibiting access to the Union's "leafleters for the purpose of engaging in peaceful consumer boycott handbilling."

On September 26, 2001, the matter was transferred to the NLRB in Washington, D.C. On October 29, 2004, the NLRB issued an opinion affirming as modified the administrative law judge's decision. Citing our decision in *Robins v. Pruneyard Shopping Center,* 23 Cal.3d 899](1979) the NLRB stated: "California law permits the exercise of speech and petitioning in private shopping centers, subject to reasonable time, place, and manner rules adopted by the property owner. Rule 5.6.2, however, is essentially a content-based restriction and not a time, place, and manner restriction permitted under California law. That is, the rule prohibits speech 'urging or encouraging in any manner' customers to boycott one of the shopping center stores. . . . [I]t appears that the purpose and effect of this rule was to shield [the Mall]'s tenants, such as the Robinsons-May department store, from otherwise lawful consumer boycott handbilling.

The Mall petitioned for review before the United States Court of Appeals for the District of Columbia Circuit, which issued an opinion on June 16, 2006. The court of appeals stated it had to resolve two issues: "(1) State law aside, did [the Mall]'s requirement of a permit for expressive activity, conditioned as it was upon the Union's agreement not to urge a boycott of any Mall tenant, violate § 8(a)(1) of the Act? (2) If so, was [the Mall] acting within its rights under California law?" The court answered the first question in the affirmative, which meant that the case turned on the resolution of the second question. The court addressed this question of California law as follows: "Although [the Mall] is correct that there is not substantial evidence the Union intended to boycott any of the Mall's tenants, nothing in the Act prohibits the Union from carrying out a secondary boycott by means of peaceful handbilling. In subjecting the Union to a permit process that required it to forswear use of this lawful tactic, therefore, [the Mall] interfered with the employees' rights under § 7 of the Act. . . . Enforcement of Rule 5.6.2 therefore violated § 8(a)(1)—unless, that is, the Company had the right under California constitutional law to exclude the employees altogether." The court of appeals observed that "no California court has squarely decided whether a shopping center may lawfully ban from its premises speech urging the public to boycott a tenant," and concluded that "whether [the Mall] violated § 8(a)(1) of the Act depends upon whether it could lawfully maintain and enforce an anti-boycott rule—a question no California court has resolved." Accordingly, the United States Court of Appeals for the District of Columbia Circuit filed in this court a request, which we granted, to decide the following question: "Under California law may Fashion Valley maintain and enforce against the Union its Rule 5.6.2?"

DISCUSSION

Article I, section 2, subdivision (a) of the California Constitution declares: "Every person may freely speak, write and publish his or her sentiments on all subjects, being responsible for the abuse of this right. A law may not restrain or abridge liberty of speech or press." Nearly 30 years ago, in *Robins v. Pruneyard Shopping Center,* we held that this provision of our state Constitution grants broader rights to free expression than does the First Amendment to the United States Constitution by holding that a shopping mall is a public forum in which persons may exercise their right to free speech under the California Constitution. We stated that a shopping center "to which the public is invited can provide an essential and invaluable forum for exercising [free speech] rights." We noted that in many cities the public areas of the shopping mall are replacing the streets and sidewalks of the central business district which, "have immemorially been held in trust for the use of the public and, time out of mind, have been used for purposes of assembly, communicating thoughts between citizens, and discussing public questions." Because of the "growing importance of the shopping center[,] . . . to prohibit expressive activity in the centers would impinge on constitutional rights beyond speech rights," particularly the right to petition for redress of grievances. Accordingly, we held that the California Constitution "protect[s] speech and petitioning, reasonably exercised, in shopping centers even when the centers are privately owned." We added the caveat in *Pruneyard* that "[b]y no means do we imply that those who wish to disseminate ideas have free rein," noting our previous "endorsement of time, place, and manner rules."

The Mall in the present case generally allows expressive activity, as mandated by the California Constitution, but requires persons wishing to engage in free speech in the Mall to obtain a permit. Under Rule 5.6.2, the Mall will not issue a permit to engage in expressive activity unless the applicant promises to refrain from conduct "Urging, or encouraging in any manner, customers not to purchase the merchandise or services offered by any one or more of the stores or merchants in the shopping center." We must determine, therefore, whether a shopping center violates California law by banning from its premises speech urging the public to boycott one or more of the shopping center's businesses.

The idea that private property can constitute a public forum for free speech if it is open to the public in a manner similar to that of public streets and sidewalks long predates our decision in *Pruneyard.* The United States Supreme Court recognized more than half a century ago that the right to free speech guaranteed by the First Amendment to the United States Constitution can apply even on privately owned land. In *Marsh v. Alabama,* 326 U.S. 501 (1946), the high court held that a Jehovah's Witness had the right to distribute religious literature on the sidewalk near the post office of a town owned by the Gulf Shipbuilding Corporation, because the town had "all the characteristics of any other American town. . . . In short, the town and its shopping district are accessible to and freely used by the public in general, and there is nothing to distinguish them from any other town and shopping center except the fact that the title to the property belongs to a private corporation." The high court stated: "The more an owner, for his advantage, opens up his property for use by the public in general, the more do his rights become circumscribed by the statutory and constitutional rights of those who use it."

This court followed the high court's decision in *Marsh* to hold that a shopping center could not prohibit a union's peaceful picketing of one of the shopping center's stores. We recognized that peaceful picketing by a labor union "involves an exercise of the constitutionally protected right of freedom of speech." We rejected the shopping center's argument that its right to "the exclusive possession and enjoyment of private property" outweighed the union's right to picket: "Because of the public character of the shopping center, however, the impairment of plaintiff's interest must be largely theoretical. Plaintiff has fully opened his property to the public." In *In re Hoffman,* 67 Cal.2d 845 (1967), we reiterated that private property that was open to the public in the same manner as public streets or parks could constitute a public forum for free expression, holding that protesters had the right to express their opposition to the war in Vietnam by distributing leaflets in Union Station in Los Angeles, "a spacious area open to the community as a center for rail transportation" that was owned by three railroad companies. This court reasoned that, with regard to distributing leaflets, "a railway station is like a public street or park. Noise and commotion are characteristic of the normal operation of a railway station. The railroads seek neither privacy within nor exclusive possession of their station. They therefore cannot invoke the law of trespass against petitioners to protect those interests. Nor was there any other interest that would justify prohibiting petitioners' activities. Those activities in no way interfered with the use of the station.

The Mall argues that its rule banning speech that advocates a boycott is a "reasonable regulation" designed to assure that free expression activities "do not interfere with normal business operations" within the meaning of our decision in *Pruneyard.* According to the Mall, it "has the right to prohibit speech that interferes with the intended purpose of the Mall," which is to promote "the sale of merchandise and services to the shopping public." We disagree.

It has been the law since 1964, and remains the law, that a privately owned shopping center must permit peaceful picketing of businesses in shopping centers, even though such picketing may harm the shopping center's business interests. Our decision in *Diamond v. Bland* (1970) 3 Cal. 3d 653 (*Diamond I)* recognized that citizens have a strengthened interest, not a diminished interest, in speech that presents a grievance against a particular business in a privately owned shopping center, including speech that advocates a boycott.

FOR DISCUSSION

Have shopping malls become the new public squares? Should they be required to permit some forms of First Amendment-type activity? Why?

RELATED CASES

***Minnesota v. Wichlund:* 589 N.W.2d 793 (Minn. 1999).**

The Minnesota Supreme Court ruled that the Mall of America's decision to ban animal rights activists from protesting the sale of fur did not constitute state action even though extensive public funding had been provided to build the mall.

***New Jersey Coalition Against War in the Middle East v. J.M.B. Reality, Corporation:* 650 A.2d 757 (N.J. 1994).**

A shopping mall could not bar antiwar leafleters because such an act would violate the free speech rights of the protesters. The state court ruled that malls had become functionally the equivalent of downtowns and had invited the public into the space they occupy.

MOOSE LODGE NO. 107 V. IRVIS

407 U.S. 163, 92 S.Ct. 1965, 32 L.Ed.2d 627 (1972)

Leroy Irvis, an African American guest, was refused service at Moose Lodge No. 107, a private club, in the state of Pennsylvania. Irvis sued the lodge under federal antidiscrimination law, claiming that because the club held a liquor license from the state, its refusal of service constituted state action.

Vote: 6–3

JUSTICE REHNQUIST delivered the opinion of the Court.

Appellee Irvis, a Negro (hereafter appellee), was refused service by appellant Moose Lodge, a local branch of the national fraternal organization located in Harrisburg, Pennsylvania. Appellee then brought this action under 42 U.S.C. § 1983 for injunctive relief in the United States District Court for the Middle District of Pennsylvania. He claimed that because the Pennsylvania liquor board had issued appellant Moose Lodge a private club license that authorized the sale of alcoholic beverages on its premises, the refusal of service to him was 'state action' for the purposes of the Equal Protection Clause of the Fourteenth Amendment. He named both Moose Lodge and the Pennsylvania Liquor Authority as defendants, seeking injunctive relief that would have required the defendant liquor board to revoke Moose Lodge's license so long as it continued its discriminatory practices. Appellee sought no damages.

A three-judge district court convened at appellee's request, upheld his contention on the merits, and entered a decree declaring invalid the liquor license issued to Moose Lodge 'as long as it follows a policy of racial discrimination in its membership or operating policies or practices.' Moose Lodge alone appealed from the decree, and we postponed decision as to jurisdiction until the hearing on the merits. Appellant urges, in the alternative, that we either vacate the judgment below because there is not presently a case or controversy between the parties, or that we reverse on the merits.

II

Moose Lodge is a private club in the ordinary meaning of that term. It is a local chapter of a national fraternal organization having well-defined requirements for membership. It conducts all of its activities in a building that is owned by it. It is not publicly funded. Only members and guests are permitted in any lodge of the order; one may become a guest only by invitation of a member or upon invitation of the house committee.

Appellee, while conceding the right of private clubs to choose members upon a discriminatory basis, asserts that the licensing of Moose Lodge to serve liquor by the Pennsylvania Liquor Control Board amounts to such state involvement with the club's activities as to make its discriminatory practices forbidden by the Equal Protection Clause of the Fourteenth Amendment. The relief sought and obtained by appellee in the District Court was an injunction forbidding the licensing by the liquor authority of Moose Lodge until it ceased its discriminatory practices. We conclude that Moose Lodge's refusal to serve food and beverages to a guest by reason of the fact that he was a Negro does not, under the circumstances here presented, violate the Fourteenth Amendment.

In 1883, this Court in *The Civil Rights Cases*, 109 U.S. 3 (1883), set forth the essential dichotomy between discriminatory action by the State, which is prohibited by the Equal Protection Clause, and private conduct, 'however discriminatory or wrongful,' against which that clause 'erects no shield,' That dichotomy has been subsequently reaffirmed in *Shelley v. Kraemer,* 334 U.S. 1 (1948), and in *Burton v. Wilmington Parking Authority,* 365 U. S. 715 (1961).

While the principle is easily stated, the question of whether particular discriminatory conduct is private, on the one hand, or amounts to 'state action,' on the other hand, frequently admits of no easy answer. 'Only by sifting facts and weighing circumstances can the nonobvious involvement of the State in private conduct be attributed its true significance.'

Our cases make clear that the impetus for the forbidden discrimination need not originate with the State if it is state action that enforces privately originated discrimination. The Court held in *Burton v. Wilmington Parking Authority*, that a private restaurant owner who refused service because of a customer's race violated the Fourteenth Amendment, where the restaurant was located in a building owned by a state-created parking authority and leased from the authority. The Court, after a comprehensive review of the relationship between the lessee and the parking authority concluded that the latter had 'so far insinuated itself into a position of interdependence with Eagle (the restaurant owner) that it must be recognized as a joint participant in the challenged activity, which, on that account, cannot be considered to have been so 'purely private' as to fall without the scope of the Fourteenth Amendment.'

The Court has never held, of course, that discrimination by an otherwise private entity would be violative of the Equal Protection Clause if the private entity receives any sort of benefit or service at all from the State, or if it is subject to state regulation in any degree whatever. Since state-furnished services include such necessities of life as electricity, water, and police and fire protection, such a holding would utterly emasculate the distinction between private as distinguished from state conduct set forth in *The Civil Rights Cases*, and adhered to in subsequent decisions. Our holdings indicate that where the impetus for the discrimination is private, the State must have 'significantly involved itself with invidious discriminations,' in order for the discriminatory action to fall within the ambit of the constitutional prohibition.

The Pennsylvania Liquor Control Board plays absolutely no part in establishing or enforcing the membership or guest policies of the club that it licenses to serve liquor. There is no suggestion in this record that Pennsylvania law, either as written or as applied, discriminates against minority groups either in their right to apply for club licenses themselves or in their right to purchase and be served liquor in places of public accommodation. The only effect that the state licensing of Moose Lodge to serve liquor can be said to have on the right of any other Pennsylvanian to buy or be served liquor on premises other than those of Moose Lodge is that for some purposes club licenses are counted in the maximum number of licenses that may be issued in a given municipality. Basically each municipality has a quota of one retail license for each 1,500 inhabitants. Licenses issued to hotels, municipal golf courses, and airport restaurants are not counted in this quota, nor are club licenses until the maximum number of retail licenses is reached. Beyond that point, neither additional retail licenses nor additional club licenses may be issued so long as the number of issued and outstanding retail licenses remains at or above the statutory maximum.

However detailed this type of regulation may be in some particulars, it cannot be said to in any way foster or encourage racial discrimination. Nor can it be said to make the State in any realistic sense a partner or even a joint venturer in the club's enterprise. The limited effect of the prohibition against obtaining additional club licenses when the maximum number of retail licenses allotted to a municipality has been issued, when considered together with the availability of liquor from hotel, restaurant, and retail licensees, falls far short of conferring upon club licensees a monopoly in the dispensing of liquor in any given municipality or in the State as a whole. We therefore hold that, with the exception hereafter noted, the operation of the regulatory scheme enforced by the Pennsylvania Liquor Control Board does not sufficiently implicate the State in the discriminatory guest policies of Moose Lodge to make the latter 'state action' within the ambit of the Equal Protection Clause of the Fourteenth Amendment.

Reversed and remanded.

JUSTICE DOUGLAS, with whom JUSTICE MARSHALL joins, dissenting.

My view of the First Amendment and the related guarantees of the Bill of Rights is that they create a zone of privacy which precludes government from interfering with private clubs or groups. The associational rights which our system honors permit all white, all black, all brown, and all yellow clubs to be formed. They also permit all Catholic, all Jewish, or all agnostic clubs to be established. Government may not tell a man or woman who his or her associates must be. The individual can be as selective as he desires. So the fact that the Moose Lodge allows only Caucasians to join or come as guests is constitutionally irrelevant, as is the decision of the Black Muslims to admit to their services only members of their race.

The problem is different, however, where the public domain is concerned. I have indicated in *Garner v. Louisiana,* 368 U.S. 157 (1961), and *Lombard v. Louisiana,* 373 U.S. 267 (1963), that where restaurants or other facilities serving the public are concerned and licenses are obtained from the State for operating the business, the 'public' may not be defined by the proprietor to include only people of his choice; nor may a state or municipal service be granted only to some.

Pennsylvania has a state store system of alcohol distribution. Resale is permitted by hotels, restaurants, and private clubs which all must obtain licenses from the Liquor Control Board. The scheme of regulation is complete and pervasive; and the state courts have sustained many restrictions on the licensees. Once a license is issued the licensee must comply with many detailed requirements or risk suspension or revocation of the license. Among these requirements is Regulation § 113.09 which says: 'Every club licensee shall adhere to all of the provisions of its Constitution and By-laws.' This regulation means, as applied to Moose Lodge, that it must adhere to the racially discriminatory provision of the Constitution of its Supreme Lodge that '(t)he membership of lodges shall be composed of male persons of the Caucasian or White race above the age of twenty-one years, and not married to someone of any other than the Caucasian or White race, who are of good moral character, physically and mentally normal, who shall profess a belief in a Supreme Being.'

It is argued that this regulation only aims at the prevention of subterfuge and at enforcing Pennsylvania's differentiation between places of public accommodation and bona fide private clubs. It is also argued that the regulation only gives effect to the constitutionally protected rights of privacy and of association. But I cannot so read the regulation. While those other purposes are embraced in it, so is the restrictive membership clause. And we have held that 'a State is responsible for the discriminatory act of a private party when the State, by its law, has compelled the act.' It is irrelevant whether the law is statutory, or an administrative regulation. And it is irrelevant whether the discriminatory act was instigated by the regulation, or was independent of it. *Peterson v. City of Greenville*, 373 U.S. 244 (1963). The result, as I see it, is the same as though Pennsylvania had put into its liquor licenses a provision that the license may not be used to dispense liquor to blacks, browns, yellows—or atheists or agnostics. Regulation § 113.09 is thus an invidious form of state action.

Were this regulation the only infirmity in Pennsylvania's licensing scheme, I would perhaps agree with the majority that the appropriate relief would be a decree enjoining its enforcement. But there is another flaw in the scheme not so easily cured. Liquor licenses in Pennsylvania, unlike driver's licenses, or marriage licenses, are not freely available to those who meet racially neutral qualifications. There is a complex quota system, which the majority accurately describes. What the majority neglects to say is that the quota for Harrisburg, where Moose Lodge No. 107 is located, has been full for many years. No more club licenses may be issued in that city.

This state-enforced scarcity of licenses restricts the ability of blacks to obtain liquor, for liquor is commercially available only at private clubs for a significant portion of each week. Access by blacks to places that serve liquor is further limited by the fact that the state quota is filled. A group desiring to form a nondiscriminatory club which would serve blacks must purchase a license held by an existing club, which can exact a monopoly price for the transfer. The availability of such a license is speculative at best, however, for, as Moose Lodge itself concedes, without a liquor license a fraternal organization would be hard pressed to survive.

Thus, the State of Pennsylvania is putting the weight of its liquor license, concededly a valued and important adjunct to a private club, behind racial discrimination.

I would affirm the judgment below.

JUSTICE BRENNAN, with whom JUSTICE MARSHALL joins, dissenting.

When Moose Lodge obtained its liquor license, the State of Pennsylvania became an active participant in the operation of the Lodge bar. Liquor licensing laws are only incidentally revenue measures; they are primarily pervasive regulatory schemes under which the State dictates and continually supervises virtually every detail of the operation of the licensee's business. Very few, if any, other licensed businesses experience such complete state involvement. Yet the Court holds that such involvement does not constitute 'state action' making the Lodge's refusal to serve a guest liquor solely because of his race a violation of the Fourteenth Amendment. The vital flaw in the Court's reasoning is its complete disregard of the fundamental value underlying the 'state action' concept.

Plainly, the State of Pennsylvania's liquor regulations intertwine the State with the operation of the Lodge bar in a 'significant way (and) lend (the State's) authority to the sordid business of racial discrimination.' The opinion of the late Circuit Judge Freedman, for the three-judge District Court, most persuasively demonstrates the 'state action' present in this case:

We believe the decisive factor is the uniqueness and the all-pervasiveness of the regulation by the Commonwealth of Pennsylvania of the dispensing of liquor under licenses granted by the state. The regulation inherent in the grant of a state liquor license is so different in nature and extent from the ordinary licenses issued by the state that it is different in quality.

I therefore dissent and would affirm the final decree entered by the District Court.

FOR DISCUSSION

Why did the majority not find state action here? What is the point of disagreement between the majority and the minority?

JACKSON V. METROPOLITAN EDISON COMPANY

419 U.S. 345, 95 S.Ct. 449, 42 L.Ed.2d 477 (1974)

A privately owned utility company licensed in Pennsylvania discontinued service to a customer because of nonpayment of a bill. The customer sued for damages, claiming that the termination constituted state action. Both the district court and the court of appeals dismissed the complaint.

Vote: 6–3

JUSTICE REHNQUIST delivered the opinion of the Court.

Respondent Metropolitan Edison Co. is a privately owned and operated Pennsylvania corporation which holds a certificate of public convenience issued by the Pennsylvania Public Utility Commission empowering it to deliver electricity to a service area which includes the city of York, Pa. As a condition of holding its certificate, it is subject to extensive regulation by the Commission. Under a provision of its general tariff filed with the Commission, it has the right to discontinue service to any customer on reasonable notice of nonpayment of bills.

Petitioner Catherine Jackson is a resident of York, who has received electricity in the past from respondent. Until September 1970, petitioner received electric service to her home in York under an account with respondent in her own name. When her account was terminated because of asserted delinquency in payments due for service, a new account with respondent was opened in the name of one James Dodson, another occupant of the residence, and service to the residence was resumed. There is a dispute as to whether payments due under the Dodson account for services provided during this period were ever made. In August 1971, Dodson left the residence. Service continued thereafter but concededly no payments were made. Petitioner states that no bills were received during this period.

On October 6, 1971, employees of Metropolitan came to the residence and inquired as to Dodson's present address. Petitioner stated that it was unknown to her. On the following day, another employee visited the residence and informed petitioner that the meter had been tampered with so as not to register amounts used. She disclaimed knowledge of this and requested that the service account for her home be shifted from Dodson's name to that of the Robert Jackson, later identified as her 12-year-old son. Four days later on October 11, 1971, without further notice to petitioner, Metropolitan employees disconnected her service.

Petitioner then filed suit against Metropolitan in the United States District Court for the Middle District of Pennsylvania under the Civil Rights Act of 1871, 42 U.S.C. § 1983, seeking damages for the termination and an injunction requiring Metropolitan to continue providing power to her residence until she had been afforded notice, a hearing, and an opportunity to pay any amounts found due. She urged that under state law she had an entitlement to reasonably continuous electrical service to her home and that Metropolitan's termination of her service for alleged nonpayment, action allowed by a provision of its general tariff filed with the Commission, constituted 'state action' depriving her of property in violation of the Fourteenth Amendment's guarantee of due process of law.

The District Court granted Metropolitan's motion to dismiss petitioner's complaint on the ground that the termination did not constitute state action and hence was not subject to judicial scrutiny under the Fourteenth Amendment. On appeal, the United States Court of Appeals for the Third Circuit affirmed, also finding an absence of state action. We granted certiorari to review this judgment.

The Due Process Clause of the Fourteenth Amendment provides: '(N)or shall any State deprive any person of life, liberty, or property, without due process of law.' In 1883, this Court in the Civil Rights Cases, affirmed the essential dichotomy set forth in that Amendment between deprivation by the State, subject to scrutiny under its provisions, and private conduct, 'however discriminatory or wrongful,' against which the Fourteenth Amendment offers no shield.

We have reiterated that distinction on more than one occasion since then. While the principle that private action is immune from the restrictions of the Fourteenth Amendment is well established and easily stated, the question whether particular conduct is 'private,' on the one hand, or 'state action,' on the other, frequently admits of no easy answer.

Here the action complained of was taken by a utility company which is privately owned and operated, but which in many particulars of its business is subject to extensive state regulation. The mere fact that a business is subject to state regulation does not by itself convert its action into that of the State for purposes of the Fourteenth Amendment. Nor does the fact that the regulation is extensive and detailed, as in the case of most public utilities, do so. It may well be that acts of a heavily regulated utility with at least something of a governmentally protected monopoly will more readily be found to be 'state' acts than will the acts of an entity lacking these characteristics. But the inquiry must be whether there is a sufficiently close nexus between the State and the challenged action of the regulated entity so that the action of the latter may be fairly treated as that of the State itself. The true nature of the State's involvement may not be immediately obvious, and detailed inquiry may be required in order to determine whether the test is met.

Petitioner advances a series of contentions which, in her view, lead to the conclusion that this case should fall on the Burton side of the line drawn in the *Civil Rights Cases* rather than on the Moose Lodge side of that line. We find none of them persuasive.

Petitioner first argues that 'state action' is present because of the monopoly status allegedly conferred upon Metropolitan by the State of Pennsylvania. As a factual matter, it may well be doubted that the State ever granted or guaranteed Metropolitan a monopoly. But assuming that it had, this fact is not determinative in considering whether Metropolitan's termination of service to petitioner was 'state action' for purposes of the Fourteenth Amendment. In *Public Utility Commission of D. C. v. Pollak*, 343 U.S. 451 (1952), where the Court dealt with the activities of the District of Columbia Transit Co., a congressionally established monopoly, we expressly disclaimed reliance on the monopoly status of the transit authority. Similarly, although certain monopoly aspects were presented in *Moose Lodge No. 107 v. Irvis,* 407 U.S. 163 (1972), we found that the Lodge's action was not subject to the provisions of the Fourteenth Amendment. In each of those cases, there was insufficient relationship between the challenged actions of the entities involved and their monopoly status. There is no indication of any greater connection here.

We also reject the notion that Metropolitan's termination is state action because the State 'has specifically authorized and approved' the termination practice. In the instant case, Metropolitan filed with the Public Utility Commission a general tariff—a provision of which states Metropolitan's right to terminate service for nonpayment. This provision has appeared in Metropolitan's previously filed tariffs for many years and has never been the subject of a hearing or other scrutiny by the Commission. Although the Commission did hold hearings on portions of Metropolitan's general tariff relating to a general rate increase, it never even considered the reinsertion of this provision in the newly filed general tariff. The provision became effective 60 days after filing when not disapproved by the Commission.

Affirmed.

JUSTICE DOUGLAS, dissenting.

I reach the opposite conclusion from that reached by the majority on the state-action issue.

The injury alleged took place when respondent discontinued its service to this householder without notice or opportunity to remedy or contest her alleged default, even though its tariff provided that respondent might 'discontinue its service on reasonable notice.' May a State allow a utility—which in this case has no competitor—to exploit its monopoly in violation of its own tariff? May a utility have complete immunity under federal law when the State allows it regulatory agency to become the prisoner of the utility or, by a listless attitude of no concern, to permit the utility to use its monopoly power in a lawless way?

It is not enough to examine seriatim each of the factors upon which a claimant relies and to dismiss each individually as being insufficient to support a finding of state action. It is the aggregate that is controlling.

It is said that the mere fact of respondent's monopoly status, assuming arguendo that that status is state conferred or state protected, 'is not determinative in considering whether Metropolitan's termination of service to petitioner was 'state action' for purposes of the Fourteenth Amendment.' Even so, a state-protected monopoly status is highly relevant in assessing the aggregate weight of a private entity's ties to the State.

It is said that the fact that respondent's services are 'affected with a public interest' is not determinative. I agree that doctors, lawyers, and grocers are not transformed into state actors simply because they provide arguably essential goods and services and are regulated by the State. In the present case, however, respondent is not just one person among many; it is the only public utility furnishing electric power to the city. When power is denied a householder, the home, under modern conditions, is likely to become unlivable.

Respondent's procedures for termination of service may never have been subjected to the same degree of state scrutiny and approval, whether explicit or implicit, that was present in *Public Utilities Comm'n v. Pollak*. Yet in the present case the State is heavily involved in respondent's termination procedures, getting into the approved tariff a requirement of 'reasonable notice.' Pennsylvania has undertaken to regulate numerous aspects of respondent's operations in some detail.

In the aggregate, these factors depict a monopolist providing essential public services as a licensee of the State and within a framework of extensive state supervision and control. The particular regulations at issue, promulgated by the monopolist, were authorized by state law and were made enforceable by the weight and authority of the State. Moreover, the State retains the power of oversight to review and amend the regulations if the public interest so requires. Respondent's actions are sufficiently intertwined with those of the State, and its termination-of-service provisions are sufficiently buttressed by state law to warrant a holding that respondent's actions in terminating this householder's service were 'state action' for the purpose of giving federal jurisdiction over respondent under 42 U.S.C. § 1983.

FOR DISCUSSION

What argument does the dissent offer to find state action? Is the creation of a state-sanctioned monopoly enough to change from private to state action? If Douglas's arguments are accepted, would any state regulation of a private entity suffice to establish state action?

DESHANEY V. WINNEBAGO COUNTY DEPT. OF SOCIAL SERVICES

489 U.S. 189, 109 S.Ct. 998, 103 L.Ed.2d 249 (1989)

A child who was in the custody of his father was severely beaten by the parent. The child and his guardian sued the Winnebago County Department of Social Services, claiming that the agency's refusal to act to remove the child from his father's home after repeated reports of abuse constituted state action.

Vote: 6–3

CHIEF JUSTICE REHNQUIST delivered the opinion of the Court

Petitioner is a boy who was beaten and permanently injured by his father, with whom he lived. Respondents are social workers and other local officials who received complaints that petitioner was being abused by his father and had reason to believe that this was the case, but nonetheless did not act to remove petitioner from his father's custody. Petitioner sued respondents, claiming that their failure to act deprived him of his liberty in violation of the Due Process Clause of the Fourteenth Amendment to the United States Constitution. We hold that it did not.

I

The facts of this case are undeniably tragic. Petitioner Joshua DeShaney was born in 1979. In 1980, a Wyoming court granted his parents a divorce and awarded custody of Joshua to his father, Randy DeShaney. The father shortly thereafter moved to Neenah, a city located in Winnebago County, Wisconsin, taking the infant Joshua with him. There he entered into a second marriage, which also ended in divorce.

The Winnebago County authorities first learned that Joshua DeShaney might be a victim of child abuse in January 1982, when his father's second wife complained to the police, at the time of their divorce, that he had previously "hit the boy causing marks and [was] a prime case for child abuse." The Winnebago County Department of Social Services (DSS) interviewed the father, but he denied the accusations, and DSS did not pursue them further. In January 1983, Joshua was admitted to a local hospital with multiple bruises and abrasions. The examining physician suspected child abuse and notified DSS, which immediately obtained an order from a Wisconsin juvenile court placing Joshua in the temporary custody of the hospital. Three days later, the county convened an ad hoc "Child Protection Team"—consisting of a pediatrician, a psychologist, a police detective, the county's lawyer, several DSS caseworkers, and various hospital personnel—to consider Joshua's situation. At this meeting, the Team decided that there was insufficient evidence of child abuse to retain Joshua in the custody of the court. The Team did, however, decide to recommend several measures to protect Joshua, including enrolling him in a preschool program, providing his father with certain counseling services, and encouraging his father's girlfriend to move out of the home. Randy DeShaney entered into a voluntary agreement with DSS in which he promised to cooperate with them in accomplishing these goals.

Based on the recommendation of the Child Protection Team, the juvenile court dismissed the child protection case and returned Joshua to the custody of his father. A month later, emergency room personnel called the DSS caseworker handling Joshua's case to report that he had once again been treated for suspicious injuries. The caseworker concluded that there was no basis for action. For the next six months, the caseworker made monthly visits to the DeShaney home, during which she observed a number of suspicious injuries on Joshua's head; she also noticed that he had not been enrolled in school, and that the girlfriend had not moved out. The caseworker dutifully recorded these incidents in her files, along with her continuing suspicions that someone in the DeShaney household was physically abusing Joshua, but she did nothing more. In November 1983, the emergency room notified DSS that Joshua had been treated once again for injuries that they believed to be caused by child abuse. On the caseworker's next two visits to the DeShaney home, she was told that Joshua was too ill to see her. Still DSS took no action.

In March 1984, Randy DeShaney beat 4-year-old Joshua so severely that he fell into a life-threatening coma. Emergency brain surgery revealed a series of hemorrhages caused by traumatic injuries to the head inflicted over a long period of time. Joshua did not die, but he suffered brain damage so severe that he is expected to spend the rest of his life confined to an institution for the profoundly retarded. Randy DeShaney was subsequently tried and convicted of child abuse.

Joshua and his mother brought this action under 42 U.S.C. § 1983 in the United States District Court for the Eastern District of Wisconsin against respondents Winnebago County, DSS, and various individual employees of DSS. The complaint alleged that respondents had deprived Joshua of his liberty without due process of law, in violation of his rights under the Fourteenth Amendment, by failing to intervene to protect him against a risk of violence at his father's hands of which they knew or should have known. The District Court granted summary judgment for respondents.

II

The Due Process Clause of the Fourteenth Amendment provides that "[n]o State shall . . . deprive any person of life, liberty, or property, without due process of law." Petitioners contend that the State deprived Joshua of his liberty interest in "free[dom] from . . . unjustified intrusions on personal security," by failing to provide him with adequate protection against his father's violence. The claim is one invoking the substantive rather than the procedural component of the Due Process Clause; petitioners do not claim that the State denied Joshua protection without according him appropriate procedural safeguards, but that it was categorically obligated to protect him in these circumstances.

But nothing in the language of the Due Process Clause itself requires the State to protect the life, liberty, and property of its citizens against invasion by private actors. The Clause is phrased as a limitation on the State's power to act, not as a guarantee of certain minimal levels of safety and security. It forbids the State itself to deprive individuals of life, liberty, or property without "due process of law," but its language cannot fairly be extended to impose an affirmative obligation on the State to ensure that those interests do not come to harm through other means. Nor does history support such an expansive reading of the constitutional text. Like its counterpart in the Fifth Amendment, the Due Process Clause of the Fourteenth Amendment was intended to prevent government "from abusing [its] power, or employing it as an instrument of oppression." Its purpose was to protect the people from the State, not to ensure that the State protected them from each other. The Framers were content to leave the extent of governmental obligation in the latter area to the democratic political processes.

Consistent with these principles, our cases have recognized that the Due Process Clauses generally confer no affirmative right to governmental aid, even where such aid may be necessary to secure life, liberty, or property interests of which the government itself may not deprive the individual. If the Due Process Clause does not require the State to provide its citizens with particular protective services, it follows that the State cannot be held liable under the Clause for injuries that could have been averted had it chosen to provide them. As a general matter, then, we conclude that a State's failure to protect an individual against private violence simply does not constitute a violation of the Due Process Clause.

Petitioners contend, however, that even if the Due Process Clause imposes no affirmative obligation on the State to provide the general public with adequate protective services, such a duty may arise out of certain "special relationships" created or assumed by the State with respect to particular individuals. Petitioners argue that such a "special relationship" existed here because the State knew that Joshua faced a special danger of abuse at his father's hands, and specifically proclaimed, by word and by deed, its intention to protect him against that danger. Having actually undertaken to protect Joshua from this danger—which petitioners concede the State played no part in creating—the State acquired an affirmative "duty," enforceable through the Due Process Clause, to do so in a reasonably competent fashion. Its failure to discharge that duty, so the argument goes, was an abuse of governmental power that so "shocks the conscience, as to constitute a substantive due process violation.

We reject this argument. It is true that in certain limited circumstances the Constitution imposes upon the State affirmative duties of care and protection with respect to particular individuals. In *Estelle v. Gamble,* 429 U.S. 97 (1976), we recognized that the Eighth Amendment's prohibition against cruel and unusual punishment, made applicable to the States through the Fourteenth Amendment's Due Process Clause, requires the State to provide adequate medical care to incarcerated prisoners. We reasoned that because the prisoner is unable " 'by reason of the deprivation of his liberty [to] care for himself,' " it is only " 'just' " that the State be required to care for him.

In *Youngberg v. Romeo*, 457 U.S. 307 (1982), we extended this analysis beyond the Eighth Amendment setting, holding that the substantive component of the Fourteenth Amendment's Due Process Clause requires the State to provide involuntarily committed mental patients with such services as are necessary to ensure their "reasonable safety" from themselves and others.

But these cases afford petitioners no help. Taken together, they stand only for the proposition that when the State takes a person into its custody and holds him there against his will, the Constitution imposes upon it a corresponding duty to assume some responsibility for his safety and general well-being. The affirmative duty to protect arises not from the State's knowledge of the individual's predicament or from its expressions of intent to help him, but from the limitation which it has imposed on his freedom to act on his own behalf. In the substantive due process analysis, it is the State's affirmative act of restraining the individual's freedom to act on his own behalf—through incarceration, institutionalization, or other similar restraint of personal liberty—which is the "deprivation of liberty" triggering the protections of the Due Process Clause, not its failure to act to protect his liberty interests against harms inflicted by other means.

The *Estelle-Youngberg* analysis simply has no applicability in the present case. Petitioners concede that the harms Joshua suffered occurred not while he was in the State's custody, but while he was in the custody of his natural father, who was in no sense a state actor. While the State may have been aware of the dangers that Joshua faced in the free world, it played no part in their creation, nor did it do anything to render him any more vulnerable to them. That the State once took temporary custody of Joshua does not alter the analysis, for when it returned him to his father's custody, it placed him in no worse position than that in which he would have been had it not acted at all; the State does not become the permanent guarantor of an individual's safety by having once offered him shelter. Under these circumstances, the State had no constitutional duty to protect Joshua.

Affirmed.

JUSTICE BRENNAN, with whom JUSTICES MARSHALL and BLACKMUN join, dissenting.

"The most that can be said of the state functionaries in this case," the Court today concludes, "is that they stood by and did nothing when suspicious circumstances dictated a more active role for them." Because I believe that this description of respondents' conduct tells only part of the story and that, accordingly, the Constitution itself "dictated a more active role" for respondents in the circumstances presented here, I cannot agree that respondents had no constitutional duty to help Joshua DeShaney.

It may well be, as the Court decides, that the Due Process Clause as construed by our prior cases creates no general right to basic governmental services. That, however, is not the question presented here; indeed, that question was not raised in the complaint, urged on appeal, presented in the petition for certiorari, or addressed in the briefs on the merits. No one, in short, has asked the Court to proclaim that, as a general matter, the Constitution safeguards positive as well as negative liberties.

This is more than a quibble over dicta; it is a point about perspective, having substantive ramifications. In a constitutional setting that distinguishes sharply between action and inaction, one's characterization of the misconduct alleged under § 1983 may effectively decide the case. Thus, by leading off with a discussion (and rejection) of the idea that the Constitution imposes on the States an affirmative duty to take basic care of their citizens, the Court foreshadows—perhaps even preordains—its conclusion that no duty existed even on the specific facts before us. This initial discussion establishes the baseline from which the Court assesses the DeShaneys' claim that, when a State has—"by word and by deed,"—announced an intention to protect a certain class of citizens and has before it facts that would trigger that protection under the applicable state law, the Constitution imposes upon the State an affirmative duty of protection.

The Court's baseline is the absence of positive rights in the Constitution and a concomitant suspicion of any claim that seems to depend on such rights. From this perspective, the DeShaneys' claim is first and foremost about inaction (the failure, here, of respondents to take steps to protect Joshua), and only tangentially about action (the establishment of a state program specifically designed to help children like Joshua). And from this perspective, holding these Wisconsin officials liable—where the only difference between this case and one involving a general claim to protective services is Wisconsin's establishment and operation of a program to protect children—would seem to punish an effort that we should seek to promote.

I would begin from the opposite direction. I would focus first on the action that Wisconsin *has* taken with respect to Joshua and children like him, rather than on the actions that the State failed to take. Such a method is not new to this Court.

Wisconsin has established a child-welfare system specifically designed to help children like Joshua. Wisconsin law places upon the local departments of social services such as respondent (DSS or Department) a duty to investigate reported instances of child abuse.[.] While other governmental bodies and private persons are largely responsible for the reporting of possible cases of child abuse. Wisconsin law channels all such reports to the local departments of social services for evaluation and, if necessary, further action. Even when it is the sheriff's office or police department that receives a report of suspected child abuse, that report is referred to local social services departments for action; the only exception to this occurs when the reporter fears for the child's *immediate* safety. In this way, Wisconsin law invites—indeed, directs—citizens and other governmental entities to depend on local departments of social services such as respondent to protect children from abuse.

As the Court today reminds us, "the Due Process Clause of the Fourteenth Amendment was intended to prevent government 'from abusing [its] power, or employing it as an instrument of oppression.' " My disagreement with the Court arises from its failure to see that inaction can be every bit as abusive of power as action, that oppression can result when a State undertakes a vital duty and then ignores it. Today's opinion construes the Due Process Clause to permit a State to displace private sources of protection and then, at the critical moment, to shrug its shoulders and turn away from the harm that it has promised to try to prevent. Because I cannot agree that our Constitution is indifferent to such indifference, I respectfully dissent.

FOR DISCUSSION

What factors does the Court point to in showing that the county had no duty to protect Joshua DeShaney? What would constitute an affirmative duty that would give rise to a specific duty in such a case?

TOWN OF CASTLE ROCK, COLORADO V. GONZALES

545 U.S. 748, 125 S.Ct. 2796, 162 L.Ed.2d 658 (2005)

A court issued an order for protection restricting a father of three girls from having contact with them. The man subsequently abducted and killed his daughters. Police in the Town of Castle Rock were sued as a result of their failure to arrest an individual who had violated a court restraining order.

Vote: 7–2

JUSTICE SCALIA delivered the opinion of the Court.

We decide in this case whether an individual who has obtained a state-law restraining order has a constitutionally protected property interest in having the police enforce the restraining order when they have probable cause to believe it has been violated.

I

The horrible facts of this case are contained in the complaint that respondent Jessica Gonzales filed in Federal District Court. Respondent alleges that petitioner, the town of Castle Rock, Colorado, violated the Due Process Clause of the Fourteenth Amendment to the United States Constitution when its police officers, acting pursuant to official policy or custom, failed to respond properly to her repeated reports that her estranged husband was violating the terms of a restraining order.

The restraining order had been issued by a state trial court several weeks earlier in conjunction with respondent's divorce proceedings. The original form order, issued on May 21, 1999, and served on respondent's husband on June 4, 1999, commanded him not to "molest or disturb the peace of [respondent] or of any child," and to remain at least 100 yards from the family home at all times. The bottom of the pre-printed form noted that the reverse side contained "IMPORTANT NOTICES FOR RESTRAINED PARTIES AND LAW ENFORCEMENT OFFICIALS." The preprinted text on the back of the form included the following "**WARNING**":

> **A KNOWING VIOLATION OF A RESTRAINING ORDER IS A CRIME** .... A VIOLATION WILL ALSO CONSTITUTE CONTEMPT OF COURT. **YOU MAY BE ARRESTED** WITHOUT NOTICE IF A LAW ENFORCEMENT OFFICER HAS PROBABLE CAUSE TO BELIEVE THAT YOU HAVE KNOWINGLY VIOLATED THIS ORDER.

The preprinted text on the back of the form also included a "**NOTICE TO LAW ENFORCEMENT OFFICIALS,**" which read in part:

> YOU SHALL USE EVERY REASONABLE MEANS TO ENFORCE THIS RESTRAINING ORDER. YOU SHALL ARREST, OR, IF AN ARREST WOULD BE IMPRACTICAL UNDER THE CIRCUMSTANCES, SEEK A WARRANT FOR THE ARREST OF THE RESTRAINED PERSON WHEN YOU HAVE INFORMATION AMOUNTING TO PROBABLE CAUSE THAT THE RESTRAINED PERSON HAS VIOLATED OR ATTEMPTED TO VIOLATE ANY PROVISION OF THIS ORDER AND THE RESTRAINED PERSON HAS BEEN PROPERLY SERVED WITH A COPY OF THIS ORDER OR HAS RECEIVED ACTUAL NOTICE OF THE EXISTENCE OF THIS ORDER.

On June 4, 1999, the state trial court modified the terms of the restraining order and made it permanent. The modified order gave respondent's husband the right to spend time with his three daughters (ages 10, 9, and 7) on alternate weekends, for two weeks during the summer, and, " 'upon reasonable notice,' " for a mid-week dinner visit " 'arranged by the parties' "; the modified order also allowed him to visit the home to collect the children for such "parenting time."

According to the complaint, at about 5 or 5:30 P.M. on Tuesday, June 22, 1999, respondent's husband took the three daughters while they were playing outside the family home. No advance arrangements had been made for him to see the daughters that evening. When respondent noticed the children were missing, she suspected her husband had taken them. At about 7:30 P.M., she called the Castle Rock Police Department, which dispatched two officers. The complaint continues: "When [the officers] arrived . . ., she showed them a copy of the TRO [temporary restraining order] and requested that it be enforced and the three children be returned to her immediately. [The officers] stated that there was nothing they could do about the TRO and suggested that [respondent] call the Police Department again if the three children did not return home by 10:00 P.M."

At approximately 8:30 P.M., respondent talked to her husband on his cellular telephone. He told her "he had the three children [at an] amusement park in Denver." She called the police again and asked them to "have someone check for" her husband or his vehicle at the amusement park and "put out an [all-points bulletin]" for her husband, but the officer with whom she spoke "refused to do so," again telling her to "wait until 10:00 P.M. and see if" her husband returned the girls.

At approximately 10:10 P.M., respondent called the police and said her children were still missing, but she was now told to wait until midnight. She called at midnight and told the dispatcher her children were still missing. She went to her husband's apartment and, finding nobody there, called the police at 12:10 A.M.; she was told to wait for an officer to arrive. When none came, she went to the police station at 12:50 A.M. and submitted an incident report. The officer who took the report "made no reasonable effort to enforce the TRO or locate the three children. Instead, he went to dinner."

At approximately 3:20 A.M., respondent's husband arrived at the police station and opened fire with a semiautomatic handgun he had purchased earlier that evening. Police shot back, killing him. Inside the cab of his pickup truck, they found the bodies of all three daughters, whom he had already murdered.

On the basis of the foregoing factual allegations, respondent brought an action under Rev. Stat. § 1979, 42 U.S.C. § 1983, claiming that the town violated the Due Process Clause because its police department had "an official policy or custom of failing to respond properly to complaints of restraining order violations" and "tolerate[d] the non-enforcement of restraining orders by its police officers." The complaint also alleged that the town's actions "were taken either willfully, recklessly or with such gross negligence as to indicate wanton disregard and deliberate indifference to" respondent's civil rights.

Before answering the complaint, the defendants filed a motion to dismiss under Federal Rule of Civil Procedure 12(b)(6). The District Court granted the motion, concluding that, whether construed as making a substantive due process or procedural due process claim, respondent's complaint failed to state a claim upon which relief could be granted.

A panel of the Court of Appeals affirmed the rejection of a substantive due process claim, but found that respondent had alleged a cognizable procedural due process claim. On rehearing en banc, a divided court reached the same disposition, concluding that respondent had a "protected property interest in the enforcement of the terms of her restraining order" and that the town had deprived her of due process because "the police never 'heard' nor seriously entertained her request to enforce and protect her interests in the restraining order."

II

The Fourteenth Amendment to the United States Constitution provides that a State shall not "deprive any person of life, liberty, or property, without due process of law." In 42 U.S.C. § 1983, Congress has created a federal cause of action for "the deprivation of any rights, privileges, or immunities secured by the Constitution and laws." Respondent claims the benefit of this provision on the ground that she had a property interest in police enforcement of the restraining order against her husband; and that the town deprived her of this property without due process by having a policy that tolerated nonenforcement of restraining orders.

The procedural component of the Due Process Clause does not protect everything that might be described as a "benefit": "To have a property interest in a benefit, a person clearly must have more than an abstract need or desire" and "more than a unilateral expectation of it. He must, instead, have a legitimate claim of entitlement to it." Such entitlements are " 'of course, . . . not created by the Constitution. Rather, they are created and their dimensions are defined by existing rules or understandings that stem from an independent source such as state law.' "

A

Our cases recognize that a benefit is not a protected entitlement if government officials may grant or deny it in their discretion. The Court of Appeals in this case determined that Colorado law created an entitlement to enforcement of the restraining order because the "court-issued restraining order . . . specifically dictated that its terms must be enforced" and a "state statute command[ed]" enforcement of the order when certain objective conditions were met (probable cause to believe that the order had been violated and that the object of the order had received notice of its existence). Respondent contends that we are obliged "to give deference to the Tenth Circuit's analysis of Colorado law on" whether she had an entitlement to enforcement of the restraining order.

We will not, of course, defer to the Tenth Circuit on the ultimate issue: whether what Colorado law has given respondent constitutes a property interest for purposes of the Fourteenth Amendment. That determination, despite its state-law underpinnings, is ultimately one of federal constitutional law.

B

The critical language in the restraining order came not from any part of the order itself (which was signed by the state-court trial judge and directed to the restrained party, respondent's husband), but from the preprinted notice to law-enforcement personnel that appeared on the back of the order. That notice effectively restated the statutory provision describing "peace officers' duties" related to the crime of violation of a restraining order. At the time of the conduct at issue in this case, that provision read as follows:

> (a) Whenever a restraining order is issued, the protected person shall be provided with a copy of such order. *A peace officer shall use every reasonable means to enforce a restraining order.*
>
> (b) *A peace officer shall arrest, or, if an arrest would be impractical under the circumstances, seek a warrant for the arrest of a restrained person* when the peace officer has information amounting to probable cause that:
>
> > (I) The restrained person has violated or attempted to violate any provision of a restraining order; and
> >
> > (II) The restrained person has been properly served with a copy of the restraining order or the restrained person has received actual notice of the existence and substance of such order.
>
> (c) In making the probable cause determination described in paragraph (b) of this subsection (3), a peace officer shall assume that the information received from the registry is accurate. *A peace officer shall enforce a valid restraining order whether or not there is a record of the restraining order in the registry.*

The Court of Appeals concluded that this statutory provision—especially taken in conjunction with a statement from its legislative history, and with another statute restricting criminal and civil liability for officers making arrests—established the Colorado Legislature's clear intent "to alter the fact that the police were not enforcing domestic abuse retraining orders," and thus its intent "that the recipient of a domestic abuse restraining order have an entitlement to its enforcement."

We do not believe that these provisions of Colorado law truly made enforcement of restraining orders *mandatory*. A well-established tradition of police discretion has long coexisted with apparently mandatory arrest statutes.

"In each and every state there are long-standing statutes that, by their terms, seem to preclude nonenforcement by the police. . . . However, for a number of reasons, including their legislative history, insufficient resources, and sheer physical impossibility, it has been recognized that such statutes cannot be interpreted literally. . . . [T]hey clearly do not mean that a police officer may not lawfully decline to make an arrest. As to third parties in these states, the full-enforcement statutes simply have no effect, and their significance is further diminished.

Against that backdrop, a true mandate of police action would require some stronger indication from the Colorado Legislature than "shall use every reasonable means to enforce a restraining order" (or even "shall arrest . . . or . . . seek a warrant"). That language is not perceptibly more mandatory than the Colorado statute which has long told municipal chiefs of police that they "shall pursue and arrest any person fleeing from justice in any part of the state" and that they "shall apprehend any person in the act of committing any offense . . . and, forthwith and without any warrant, bring such person before a . . . competent authority for examination and trial." It is hard to imagine that a Colorado peace officer would not have some discretion to determine that—despite probable cause to believe a restraining order has been violated—the circumstances of the violation or the competing duties of that officer or his agency counsel decisively against enforcement in a particular instance. The practical necessity for discretion is particularly apparent in a case such as this one, where the suspected violator is not actually present and his whereabouts are unknown.

C

Even if we were to think otherwise concerning the creation of an entitlement by Colorado, it is by no means clear that an individual entitlement to enforcement of a restraining order could constitute a "property" interest for purposes of the Due Process Clause. Such a right would not, of course, resemble any traditional conception of property. Although that alone does not disqualify it from due process protection, as *Board of Regents of State Colleges v. Roth*, 408 U.S. 564 (1972), and its progeny show, the right to have a restraining order enforced does not "have some ascertainable monetary value," as even our "*Roth*-type property-as-entitlement" cases have implicitly required. . . .

III

We conclude, therefore, that respondent did not, for purposes of the Due Process Clause, have a property interest in police enforcement of the restraining order against her husband.

JUSTICE SOUTER, with whom Justice Breyer joins, concurring.

I agree with the Court that Jessica Gonzales has shown no violation of an interest protected by the Fourteenth Amendment's Due Process Clause, and I join the Court's opinion. The Court emphasizes the traditional public focus of law enforcement as reason to doubt that these particular legal requirements to provide police services, however unconditional their form, presuppose enforceable individual rights to a certain level of police protection. The Court also notes that the terms of the Colorado statute involved here recognize and preserve the traditional discretion afforded law enforcement officers. Gonzales's claim of a property right thus runs up against police discretion in the face of an individual demand to enforce, and discretion to ignore an individual instruction not to enforce (because, say, of a domestic reconciliation); no one would argue that the beneficiary of a Colorado order like the one here would be authorized to control a court's contempt power or order the police to refrain from arresting. These considerations argue against inferring any guarantee of a level of protection or safety that could be understood as the object of a "legitimate claim of entitlement," in the nature of property arising under Colorado law. Consequently, the classic predicate for federal due process protection of interests under state law is missing.

JUSTICE STEVENS, joined by GINSBURG, dissented.

FOR DISCUSSION

Did any duty exist to protect the children? Why did the Court find that the existence of the restraining order was insufficient to establish a duty?

Excessive Use of Force

Police and law enforcement officials generally obey the law and the Constitution. But on occasion they do not. When on August 9, 2014, a white police officer shot Michael Brown, an African-American, in Ferguson, Missouri, the issue of the use of force by law enforcement personnel was thrust into the national limelight again. Michael Brown or Ferguson highlighted two issues that had largely been ignored in the mainstream national media for years. The first was simply if and under what conditions are the police justified in using force, including deadly force, to do their job and, with that, if that abuse that authority, what are the legal remedies available to hold police accountable. The other issue that surfaced was about the racial disparity or alleged racism in the use of force. By that, were people of color, especially African-Americans, more likely to be shot or face use of excessive force compared to Caucasians?

The Michael Brown incident raised complex questions. There were disputes over the basic facts in the case. Was Michael Brown armed or not, or did the police officer belief that he was? Did Brown refuse or disobey police instructions? Did the police officer over-react? While the grand jury refused to indict, that did not end thinks. The issues raised by the Ferguson shooting lead to the creation of a new national movement and slogan—"Black Lives Matters."

Black Lives Matters is both a movement and a political statement. As a movement, it has gained powerful strength from other stories or incidents of police officer shootings of other people of color. Stories such as New York City police using a choke hold in 2014 to subdue Eric Garner that eventually killed him, tapes showing a St. Anthony, Minnesota police officer shooting Philando Castile during a routine traffic stop, and a North Charleston, South Carolina, police officer seen on 2015 tape shooting a fleeing Walter Scott in the back (and the subsequent mistrial in 2016), are just some of the examples that have led to questions about when is the use of force by police excessive. The fact that in all of these incidents the victims were people of color added racial bias and Equal Protection claims to issues about police criminal and civil liability.

When law enforcement officials use force of any kind the law generally treats their actions different from civilian use of force. Private citizens generally cannot use force of any kind except for self-defense purposes. The common law rules on assault and battery make it illegal for anyone to use unwanted threatened or actual force against another. These are torts for which one may be civilly liable. Similarly, many types of uses of force are crimes, ranging from first degree murder to negligent homicide and criminal assault. Essentially all forms or uses of physical assault against another are unjustified unless used for self-defense purposes. However, rules on self-defense are complex, but generally they require proportional responses or fleeing. By that, if someone accidently pushes or shoves you, you cannot shoot them in self-defense. And in some cases before you use deadly force you often times have a duty to retreat. The big exception in in your own house or apartment when such a duty does not always exist.

Yet when it comes to police use of force, federal and state law empowers or permits the use of force under some circumstances and within certain bounds. Police can clearly use force to protect themselves, but they may also use it to protect the public. They may use to subdue a suspect or in the case of prison officials, it may be used as part of an appropriate corrections or punishment process. The government use of force is thus different than that deployed by private citizens, and there is a large body of law that defines the framework for when such use is permissible.

The question is, what remedies should exist to address situations when law enforcement officials use excessive force? The Supreme Court has answered this question, in part, when it comes both to illegal searches and seizures and improper interrogational techniques. The exclusionary rule, which is meant to address violations of the Fourth Amendment, mandates that illegally obtained evidence be excluded from use in attempting to demonstrate the guilt of a defendant on trial. Similarly, the *Miranda* warnings are meant to place limits on police interrogation techniques by excluding confessions that were extracted in violation of procedures that guarantee those accused of a crime an opportunity to remain silent or to obtain advice of legal counsel.

But critics of both the exclusionary rule and the *Miranda* warnings say that these constitutional remedies are deficient. Critics argue either that the two remedies fail to deter illegal police behavior or that they otherwise result in the exclusion of evidence that leads to guilty individuals being set free. Paraphrasing Justice Cardozo, the concern is that because the officer blunders, the guilty go free. While there is little evidence that the exclusionary rule and the *Miranda* warnings hamper police behavior or let the guilty go free, it is fair to ask if there are alternative remedies to address situations in which the rights of individuals have been violated by law enforcement officers.

One alternative offered is to allow individuals who claim that their rights have been violated to bring lawsuits against police departments and individual officers. Traditionally under state law, individuals have been able to file a series of claims of intentional or negligent **torts** against police officers. A tort is simply a civil suit by one individual against another, claiming that some type of wrong has been committed or damages have been incurred. Tort liability traces its origins to the British common law. Under state law, traditionally and even today, individuals who believed they were the victims of improper police force could file actions for assault and battery. They could also bring other traditional tort claims of wrongful death, false imprisonment, and false arrest. All these torts were considered to be intentional torts. They all required a demonstration of purposeful or intentional behavior on the part of the police or law enforcement officials to damage or hurt an individual. Demonstrating that the police intended to cause damage was difficult to prove, however. But another host of torts, based on negligence, was theoretically easier to win because the requirement for a showing of intent by police was less. These types of torts included negligent operation of a vehicle (to address high-speed chases that led to accidents) or negligent supervision (when, for example, a suicide occurred in a prison or jail). But even these negligent torts were difficult to win for several reasons.

One of the first reasons it is difficult to win a tort case is that juries are reluctant to rule against police officers, especially if the plaintiff is someone who has been convicted of a crime. Second, states can invoke sovereign immunity (a concept discussed in volume I) to prevent suits being filed against it in its own courts. Third, police officers and departments can invoke a host of common law defenses against tort claims. For example, in a claim asserting use of excessive force, the police could claim that the plaintiff was also negligent in having committed the crime or in having resisted arrest. Thus, doctrines such as assumption of risk or contributory negligence often barred recovery against police. Traditional state tort remedies did not appear to be sufficient to check police behavior.

However, the Supreme Court changed the law on liability in *Monell v. Department of Social Services* (436 U.S. 658, 1978). In that case the Supreme Court ruled that local governments and officials could be held liable for **42 United States Code section 1983** violations (generally known as or referred to as § 1983 suits.). Section 1983 was originally part of the 1871 Civil Rights Act; it was adopted to address violent actions committed by members of the Ku Klux Klan after the Civil War. It permitted blacks to sue the Klan for violations of their rights. The specific language of § 1983 states:

> Every person who under color of any statute, ordinance, regulation, custom, or usage, of any State or Territory or the District of Columbia, subjects, or causes to be subjected, any citizen of the United States or other person within the jurisdiction thereof to the deprivation of any rights, privileges, or immunities secured by the Constitution and laws, shall be liable to the party injured in an action at law, Suit in equity, or other proper proceeding for redress. . . .

Section 1983 creates a class of what are called **constitutional torts** against state and local government officials who are demonstrated to have violated the Constitution. Prior to *Monell* it was difficult to sue police officers for violations of the Constitution. This decision made it easier. In *Bivens v. Six Unknown Named Agents* (403 U.S. 388, 1971), the Supreme Court held that individuals could directly sue the federal government for violations of their constitutional rights. The scope of § 1983 issue is broad. Entire law school classes and legal practices are singularly devoted to § 1983 issues. However, this section examines one aspect of § 1983: excessive use of force.

Law enforcement officials frequently must use force in their work. This use of force might be deadly, such as using a gun to shoot and perhaps kill a suspect, or it might less than that, including perhaps simply restraining individuals either for their own safety or for the protection of others. Oftentimes the news captures high-profile stories and images of police using force. In the early 1990s the image of several Los Angeles police officers clubbing and kicking Rodney King made national headlines. In 1999 New York City police officers shot forty-one times at Amadou Diallo, killing him. Stories from Cincinnati, Ohio, and other cities across the country also profile instances of police apparently using excessive force in their work. But what constitutes excessive force? Is there any recourse when the police exceed the bounds of their authority?

Traditionally, police were allowed almost unlimited authority to use force. On the occasions of allegations that they had exceeded their mandate, state tort law governed claims regarding police brutality. Individuals who sued police could bring claims of assault, battery, or other charges under state law. However, few of these suits succeeded, and they were often costly to bring. In addition, many states exempted their police from these tort laws. Victims of alleged police brutality thus had no realistic hope of prevailing under state law, and they similarly lacked recourse under the U.S. Constitution. All this changed with *Monell v. Department of Social Services* (436 U.S. 658, 1978), as noted earlier.

Under *Monell*, the Supreme Court ruled that municipalities are responsible for acts of their police involving the use of excessive force that have been shown to be the product of official policy or organized custom and practice. More specifically, under a § 1983 claim, individuals charging a law enforcement official with a constitutional violation of their rights would have to make four showings: (1) that the plaintiffs were among the persons intended to be protected under the statute; (2) that the defendant (the police officer) had been acting under the color of the law; (3) that there was an alleged violation of a constitutional right; and (4) that the alleged violation reached a constitutional level. Generally it is easy to meet the first requirement. Just about everyone is an individual protected under § 1983. Second, to establish that the officer was acting under the color of the law, plaintiffs had to show that the police were following official department policy. One could do this by pointing to explicit or unofficial policies. But in addition, one had to show that the police officer was acting as an officer and not as a private actor. There are literally hundreds if not thousands of cases litigating questions about what constitutes the color of the law; and factors critical to answering this question include whether officers were in uniform, whether they were driving personal or departmental cars, and whether they were using their police-issued weapons or personal arms. Finally, a § 1983 suit demands that the claim allege a constitutional violation so severe that it rises to constitutional status. Generally, claims center on the First, Third, Fifth, Sixth, Eighth, and Fourteenth Amendments.

When it comes to the fourth element of demonstrating that the alleged violation was so severe that it reached constitutional status, use of force claims are divided into two types—**deadly force** and **nondeadly force**. Each type of use of force not only establishes a threshold for the § 1983 claim, but also seeks to define the outer boundary for law enforcement officials who use coercion in performing their duties.

In *Tennessee v. Garner* (471 U.S. 1, 1985), the Supreme Court outlined the elements to be used in analyzing a § 1983 claim for excessive use of deadly force under the Constitution. In *Garner* the Court ruled that excessive use of deadly force claims are analyzed under the Fourth Amendment's Search and Seizure Clause. The test in this case mandates a balancing of interests to determine police liability. One balances the nature of the intrusion on the individual's Fourth Amendment right against the interests the government cites to justify the intrusion. Under this test, the citizen or individual interest is substantial: not to die. To overcome citizen interest, police must show that the officer believes that the suspect poses an immediate threat of serious physical harm to officers or others. What is "immediate"? What is "serious"? *Serious* generally means that the suspect is armed, with a deadly weapon. *Immediacy* looks to several factors, including the following: How proximate to the past crime was force used? Is mere possession of a weapon enough? Is past dangerousness valid as an issue? These are questions that are fact specific and dependent on the circumstances. However, the closer in time the crime or the suspect's use of force, potentially the more justified the officer in using excessive force to seize the person.

In *Graham v. Connor* (490 U.S. 386, 1989), the Supreme Court ruled on claims of excessive use of nondeadly force. In the *Graham* test, uses of nondeadly force are examined under the Fourth Amendment, with the law asking whether the force employed by the police was supported by objective reasonableness. The objective reasonableness standard asks whether, viewed from the perspective of a reasonable officer with 20/20 hindsight, the force complained of would have been used. Factors determining reasonableness include asking these questions: Was the suspect an immediate threat to officers or others? What was the severity of the crime? Was the suspect actively resisting arrest? Was the suspect attempting to escape? Again, these are all facts specific to a particular case, left up to a jury or trial judge to determine. As the *Garner* and *Graham* tests make clear, law enforcement officials generally cannot shoot suspects as they flee and they cannot use any level of force they want unless they can justify that force as being necessary. There are clear limits to how much force can be used.

In addition to examining use of force in arrests by police under the Fourth Amendment, the Eighth Amendment's Cruel and Unusual Punishment Clause can be used as a basis of § 1983 claims of excessive force. This is often the case when individuals are incarcerated. There is no question that some force or coercion and discipline might be necessary to maintain order in a prison or jail setting. But how much force is too much? What if prison officials use excessive force? What types of injuries to prisoners rise to the level of constitutional tort?

The problem of excessive force in prison settings has a long history, but events in 1971 brought new exposure to the nature and extent of prison violence. In that year, at Attica Prison in upstate New York, more than two thousand inmates rioted. Governor Nelson Rockefeller brought in the state police to suppress the disturbance, and twenty-eight prisoners were killed. After the Attica riots, the state made significant payouts to inmates and to family members who had suffered damages as a result of the use of force.

The Supreme Court examined the use of excessive force under the Cruel and Unusual Punishment Clause in *Hudson v. McMillian* (503 U.S. 1, 1992). Here the Court addressed two issues. The first was whether excessive use of force could constitute a violation of the Eighth Amendment's Cruel and Unusual Punishment Clause such that an individual could bring a § 1983 claim to remedy the abuse. Here the Court said yes. The second question looked to the level of injury that must be sustained by the prisoner. In this case, an inmate had been handcuffed, shackled, and repeatedly beaten and kicked by corrections officers. His injuries included "minor bruises and swelling of his face, mouth, and lips. The blows also loosened [his] teeth and cracked his partial dental plate." The Supreme Court concluded that the use of force against the inmate was unnecessary. Instead of looking to the level of force or injury to decide if there was a § 1983 violation, the Court instead ruled as follows: "When prison officials maliciously and sadistically use force to cause harm, contemporary standards of decency are always violated." Thus the Court affirmed that the treatment complained of rose to the level of cruel and unusual punishment. The Court's standard in *Hudson* for the use of force looked not to the level of force but to the motive. Conceivably any use of force could be a violation of the Eighth Amendment if deployed in a sadistic fashion. Note though in this case the dissents of Justices Thomas and Scalia. They did see the Cruel and Unusual Punishment Clause as stipulating a minimum level of violence or injury that needed to be inflicted before the Constitution was violated. For them, the injuries suffered by Hudson were minor but not unconstitutional. Does their dissent commitment them to stipulating how much injury must be sustained to be a violation? What should prisoners do if officials inflict just enough punishment to come below that threshold?

Finally, this chapter turns to the issue of high-speed police pursuits. Practically every police movie or show depicts an almost obligatory chase scene depicting police officers engaging in a high-speed chase of some suspect. It shows car crashes and life-threatening feats of driving. But are those chases legal? Under what circumstances are police allowed or should they be allowed to do those types of pursuits? The law generally requires strict policies under which such chases are permitted, where factors such as time of day, nature of the crime involved, weather, and location must be considered. In some cases, such high-speed chases are permitted but in others not. Law enforcement generally must obey routine traffic laws but in some situations the law permits them to violate these normal laws—use of excessive speed or running red lights—under emergency or other situations. The Fourth and Fourteenth Amendments govern or help define the outer limits when such chases are permitted. *Scott v. Harris,* 550 U.S. 372 (2007), represents one of the Supreme Court's most recent cases examining excessive use force and under what conditions police may be held liable for damages as a result.

Overall, the ability to bring § 1983 claims against police and law enforcement officials has dramatically changed the legal landscape. In the nearly 40 years since *Monell,* more and more law enforcement activity has been subject to scrutiny involving constitutional tort liability. While § 1983 claims are easier to establish and win than traditional state tort actions, they are still not easy to win. Juries still more often than not sympathize with law enforcement officials than with prisoners and those accused or convicted of crimes. However, some § 1983 claims do succeed, resulting at times in awards in the millions of dollars. But more importantly, these suits have led to changes in the law and in the overall improvement of police practice and standards. While it is far from clear that § 1983 suits are viable or reasonable remedies for constitutional violations—especially if someone is wrongly killed—they are an important tool used to address civil rights violations and to protect those who come into contact with the criminal justice system.

TENNESSEE V. GARNER

471 U.S. 1, 105 S.Ct. 1694, 85 L.Ed. 2d 1 (1985)

Two Memphis, Tennessee, police officers were dispatched at night to respond to a call about a burglary in progress. When they arrived they found someone trying to break into a house. One officer went to the rear of the property and saw Edward Garner, fleeing. The two officers chased Garner, who halted at a six-foot-high fence and then started to climb over it. One of the officers shot Garner in the head to prevent him from escaping. Garner, who died soon after, was found to have possession of about ten dollars, and a purse stolen from the house. Garner's father sued, claiming that the use of force had been excessive. The district court ruled against Garner, the court of appeals reversed, and the case was brought to the Supreme Court.

Vote: 6–3

JUSTICE WHITE delivered the opinion of the Court.

This case requires us to determine the constitutionality of the use of deadly force to prevent the escape of an apparently unarmed suspected felon. We conclude that such force may not be used unless it is necessary to prevent the escape and the officer has probable cause to believe that the suspect poses a significant threat of death or serious physical injury to the officer or others.

I

At about 10:45 P.M. on October 3, 1974, Memphis Police Officers Elton Hymon and Leslie Wright were dispatched to answer a "prowler inside call." Upon arriving at the scene they saw a woman standing on her porch and gesturing toward the adjacent house. She told them she had heard glass breaking and that "they" or "someone" was breaking in next door. While Wright radioed the dispatcher to say that they were on the scene, Hymon went behind the house. He heard a door slam and saw someone run across the backyard. The fleeing suspect, who was appellee-respondent's decedent, Edward Garner, stopped at a 6-feet-high chain link fence at the edge of the yard. With the aid of a flashlight, Hymon was able to see Garner's face and hands. He saw no sign of a weapon, and, though not certain, was "reasonably sure" and "figured" that Garner was unarmed. He thought Garner was 17 or 18 years old and about 5'5" or 5'7" tall. While Garner was crouched at the base of the fence, Hymon called out "police, halt" and took a few steps toward him. Garner then began to climb over the fence. Convinced that if Garner made it over the fence he would elude capture, Hymon shot him. The bullet hit Garner in the back of the head. Garner was taken by ambulance to a hospital, where he died on the operating table. Ten dollars and a purse taken from the house were found on his body.

In using deadly force to prevent the escape, Hymon was acting under the authority of a Tennessee statute and pursuant to Police Department policy. The statute provides that "[i]f, after notice of the intention to arrest the defendant, he either flee or forcibly resist, the officer may use all the necessary means to effect the arrest." The Department policy was slightly more restrictive than the statute, but still allowed the use of deadly force in cases of burglary. The incident was reviewed by the Memphis Police Firearm's Review Board and presented to a grand jury. Neither took any action.

II

Whenever an officer restrains the freedom of a person to walk away, he has seized that person. While it is not always clear just when minimal police interference becomes a seizure, there can be no question that apprehension by the use of deadly force is a seizure subject to the reasonableness requirement of the Fourth Amendment.

A

A police officer may arrest a person if he has probable cause to believe that person committed a crime. Petitioners and appellant argue that if this requirement is satisfied the Fourth Amendment has nothing to say about *how* that seizure is made. This submission ignores the many cases in which this Court, by balancing the extent of the intrusion against the need for it, has examined the reasonableness of the manner in which a search or seizure is conducted. To determine the constitutionality of a seizure "[w]e must balance the nature and quality of the intrusion on the individual's Fourth Amendment interests against the importance of the governmental interests alleged to justify the intrusion." We have described "the balancing of competing interests" as "the key principle of the Fourth Amendment." Because one of the factors is the extent of the intrusion, it is plain that reasonableness depends on not only when a seizure is made, but also how it is carried out.

B

The same balancing process [. . .]demonstrates that, notwithstanding probable cause to seize a suspect, an officer may not always do so by killing him. The intrusiveness of a seizure by means of deadly force is unmatched. The suspect's fundamental interest in his own life need not be elaborated upon. The use of deadly force also frustrates the interest of the individual, and of society, in judicial determination of guilt and punishment. Against these interests are ranged governmental interests in effective law enforcement. It is argued that overall violence will be reduced by encouraging the peaceful submission of suspects who know that they may be shot if they flee. Effectiveness in making arrests requires the resort to deadly force, or at least the meaningful threat thereof. "Being able to arrest such individuals is a condition precedent to the state's entire system of law enforcement." Petitioner's Brief.

Without in any way disparaging the importance of these goals, we are not convinced that the use of deadly force is a sufficiently productive means of accomplishing them to justify the killing of nonviolent suspects. The use of deadly force is a self-defeating way of apprehending a suspect and so setting the criminal justice mechanism in motion. If successful, it guarantees that that mechanism will not be set in motion. And while the meaningful threat of deadly force might be thought to lead to the arrest of more live suspects by discouraging escape attempts, the presently available evidence does not support this thesis. The fact is that a majority of police departments in this country have forbidden the use of deadly force against nonviolent suspects. If those charged with the enforcement of the criminal law have abjured the use of deadly force in arresting nondangerous felons, there is a substantial basis for doubting that the use of such force is an essential attribute of the arrest power in all felony cases. Petitioners and appellant have not persuaded us that shooting nondangerous fleeing suspects is so vital as to outweigh the suspect's interest in his own life.

The use of deadly force to prevent the escape of all felony suspects, whatever the circumstances, is constitutionally unreasonable. It is not better that all felony suspects die than that they escape. Where the suspect poses no immediate threat to the officer and no threat to others, the harm resulting from failing to apprehend him does not justify the use of deadly force to do so. It is no doubt unfortunate when a suspect who is in sight escapes, but the fact that the police arrive a little late or are a little slower afoot does not always justify killing the suspect. A police officer may not seize an unarmed, nondangerous suspect by shooting him dead. The Tennessee statute is unconstitutional insofar as it authorizes the use of deadly force against such fleeing suspects.

It is not, however, unconstitutional on its face. Where the officer has probable cause to believe that the suspect poses a threat of serious physical harm, either to the officer or to others, it is not constitutionally unreasonable to prevent escape by using deadly force. Thus, if the suspect threatens the officer with a weapon or there is probable cause to believe that he has committed a crime involving the infliction or threatened infliction of serious physical harm, deadly force may be used if necessary to prevent escape, and if, where feasible, some warning has been given. As applied in such circumstances, the Tennessee statute would pass constitutional muster.

IV

The District Court concluded that Hymon was justified in shooting Garner because state law allows, and the Federal Constitution does not forbid, the use of deadly force to prevent the escape of a fleeing felony suspect if no alternative means of apprehension is available. This conclusion made a determination of Garner's apparent dangerousness unnecessary. The court did find, however, that Garner appeared to be unarmed, though Hymon could not be certain that was the case. Restated in Fourth Amendment terms, this means Hymon had no articulable basis to think Garner was armed.

In reversing, the Court of Appeals accepted the District Court's factual conclusions and held that "the facts, as found, did not justify the use of deadly force." We agree. Officer Hymon could not reasonably have believed that Garner—young, slight, and unarmed—posed any threat. Indeed, Hymon never attempted to justify his actions on any basis other than the need to prevent an escape. The District Court stated in passing that "[t]he facts of this case did not indicate to Officer Hymon that Garner was 'non-dangerous.' " This conclusion is not explained, and seems to be based solely on the fact that Garner had broken into a house at night. However, the fact that Garner was a suspected burglar could not, without regard to the other circumstances, automatically justify the use of deadly force. Hymon did not have probable cause to believe that Garner, whom he correctly believed to be unarmed, posed any physical danger to himself or others.

The dissent argues that the shooting was justified by the fact that Officer Hymon had probable cause to believe that Garner had committed a nighttime burglary. While we agree that burglary is a serious crime, we cannot agree that it is so dangerous as automatically to justify the use of deadly force. The FBI classifies burglary as a "property" rather than a "violent" crime. Although the armed burglar would present a different situation, the fact that an unarmed suspect has broken into a dwelling at night does not automatically mean he is physically dangerous. This case demonstrates as much.

V

We wish to make clear what our holding means in the context of this case. The complaint has been dismissed as to all the individual defendants. The State is a party only by virtue of 28 U.S.C. § 2403(b) and is not subject to liability. The possible liability of the remaining defendants—the Police Department and the city of Memphis—hinges on *Monell v. New York City Dept. of Social Services,* and is left for remand. We hold that the statute is invalid insofar as it purported to give Hymon the authority to act as he did. As for the policy of the Police Department, the absence of any discussion of this issue by the courts below, and the uncertain state of the record, preclude any consideration of its validity.

The judgment of the Court of Appeals is affirmed, and the case is remanded for further proceedings consistent with this opinion. *So ordered.*

JUSTICE O'CONNOR, with whom CHIEF JUSTICE BURGER and JUSTICE REHNQUIST join, dissenting.

The Court today holds that the Fourth Amendment prohibits a police officer from using deadly force as a last resort to apprehend a criminal suspect who refuses to halt when fleeing the scene of a nighttime burglary. This conclusion rests on the majority's balancing of the interests of the suspect and the public interest in effective law enforcement. Notwithstanding the venerable common-law rule authorizing the use of deadly force if necessary to apprehend a fleeing felon, and continued acceptance of this rule by nearly half the States. the majority concludes that Tennessee's statute is unconstitutional inasmuch as it allows the use of such force to apprehend a burglary suspect who is not obviously armed or otherwise dangerous. Although the circumstances of this case are unquestionably tragic and unfortunate, our constitutional holdings must be sensitive both to the history of the Fourth Amendment and to the general implications of the Court's reasoning. By disregarding the serious and dangerous nature of residential burglaries and the longstanding practice of many States, the Court effectively creates a Fourth Amendment right allowing a burglary suspect to flee unimpeded from a police officer who has probable cause to arrest, who has ordered the suspect to halt, and who has no means short of firing his weapon to prevent escape. I do not believe that the Fourth Amendment supports such a right, and I accordingly dissent.

II

For purposes of Fourth Amendment analysis, I agree with the Court that Officer Hymon "seized" Garner by shooting him. Whether that seizure was reasonable and therefore permitted by the Fourth Amendment requires a careful balancing of the important public interest in crime prevention and detection and the nature and quality of the intrusion upon legitimate interests of the individual. In striking this balance here, it is crucial to acknowledge that police use of deadly force to apprehend a fleeing criminal suspect falls within the "rubric of police conduct . . . necessarily [involving] swift action predicated upon the on-the-spot observations of the officer on the beat." The clarity of hindsight cannot provide the standard for judging the reasonableness of police decisions made in uncertain and often dangerous circumstances. Moreover, I am far more reluctant than is the Court to conclude that the Fourth Amendment proscribes a police practice that was accepted at the time of the adoption of the Bill of Rights and has continued to receive the support of many state legislatures. Although the Court has recognized that the requirements of the Fourth Amendment must respond to the reality of social and technological change, fidelity to the notion of *constitutiona*—as opposed to purely judicial—limits on governmental action requires us to impose a heavy burden on those who claim that practices accepted when the Fourth Amendment was adopted are now constitutionally impermissible.

The public interest involved in the use of deadly force as a last resort to apprehend a fleeing burglary suspect relates primarily to the serious nature of the crime. Household burglaries not only represent the illegal entry into a person's home, but also "pos[e] real risk of serious harm to others." According to recent Department of Justice statistics, "[t]hree-fifths of all rapes in the home, three-fifths of all home robberies, and about a third of home aggravated and simple assaults are committed by burglars." During the period 1973–1982, 2.8 million such violent crimes were committed in the course of burglaries. Victims of a forcible intrusion into their home by a nighttime prowler will find little consolation in the majority's confident assertion that "burglaries only rarely involve physical violence." Moreover, even if a particular burglary, when viewed in retrospect, does not involve physical harm to others, the "harsh potentialities for violence" inherent in the forced entry into a home preclude characterization of the crime as "innocuous, inconsequential, minor, or 'nonviolent.' "

Because burglary is a serious and dangerous felony, the public interest in the prevention and detection of the crime is of compelling importance. Where a police officer has probable cause to arrest a suspected burglar, the use of deadly force as a last resort might well be the only means of apprehending the suspect. With respect to a particular burglary, subsequent investigation simply cannot represent a substitute for immediate apprehension of the criminal suspect at the scene. Indeed, the Captain of the Memphis Police Department testified that in his city, if apprehension is not immediate, it is likely that the suspect will not be caught. Although some law enforcement agencies may choose to assume the risk that a criminal will remain at large, the Tennessee statute reflects a legislative determination that the use of deadly force in prescribed circumstances will serve generally to protect the public. Such statutes assist the police in apprehending suspected perpetrators of serious crimes and provide notice that a lawful police order to stop and submit to arrest may not be ignored with impunity.

Moreover, the fact that police conduct pursuant to a state statute is challenged on constitutional grounds does not impose a burden on the State to produce social science statistics or to dispel any possible doubts about the necessity of the conduct. This observation, I believe, has particular force where the challenged practice both predates enactment of the Bill of Rights and continues to be accepted by a substantial number of the States.

IV

The Court's opinion sweeps broadly to adopt an entirely new standard for the constitutionality of the use of deadly force to apprehend fleeing felons. Thus, the Court "lightly brushe[s] aside," a long-standing police practice that predates the Fourth Amendment and continues to receive the approval of nearly half of the state legislatures. I cannot accept the majority's creation of a constitutional right to flight for burglary suspects seeking to avoid capture at the scene of the crime. Whatever the constitutional limits on police use of deadly force in order to apprehend a fleeing felon, I do not believe they are exceeded in a case in which a police officer has probable cause to arrest a suspect at the scene of a residential burglary, orders the suspect to halt, and then fires his weapon as a last resort to prevent the suspect's escape into the night. I respectfully dissent.

FOR DISCUSSION

Should the type of crime being committed factor into the determination of whether deadly force may be used? How can police determine if a suspect is dangerous? What alternatives do police have besides deadly force to capture fleeing suspects?

RELATED CASES

Hicks v. Woodruff: **216 F.3d 1087 (10th Cir. 1999).**

The Court ruled that shooting a suspect if there was doubt as to whether the suspect was raised to a shooting position constituted an excessive use of force.

Boyd v. Baeppler: **215 F.3d 594 (6th Cir. 2000).**

Imminent danger exists when a suspect points a gun at a law enforcement official.

Rhoder v. McDaniel: **945 F.2d 117 (6th Cir. 1991).**

Imminent danger exists when a suspect has just committed an act of violence.

Scott v. Harris: **127 S. Ct. 1769 (2007).**

A police officer did not use excessive force in terminating a high-speed car chase by ramming a suspect's car, even though the act risked death or serious bodily harm.

GRAHAM V. CONNOR

490 U.S. 386, 109 S.Ct. 1865, 104 L.Ed.2d 443 (1989)

Graham was a diabetic who asked a friend to give him a ride to a store so that he could purchase orange juice to counteract an insulin reaction. At the store the checkout line was long and Graham decided to abandon his purchase. Police observed this quick departure and became suspicious. They stopped Graham and his friend in their car and called for backup. While waiting for backup Graham exited the car and passed out. Police handcuffed him and placed him on the hood of his friend's car. When he regained consciousness he requested that the police verify his medical condition. They told him to shut up and threw him into the squad car. He sustained injuries that included a broken foot, cuts on the wrists, bruises to the forehead, a shoulder injury, and ringing in one ear. He filed a § 1983 claim, which was rejected by the district court and by the court of appeals, both of which contended that the use of force was not excessive. Graham appealed to the Supreme Court.

Vote: 9–0

CHIEF JUSTICE REHNQUIST delivered the opinion of the Court, joined by JUSTICES WHITE, STEVENS, O'CONNOR, SCALIA, and KENNEDY.

This case requires us to decide what constitutional standard governs a free citizen's claim that law enforcement officials used excessive force in the course of making an arrest, investigatory stop, or other "seizure" of his person. We hold that such claims are properly analyzed under the Fourth Amendment's "objective reasonableness" standard, rather than under a substantive due process standard.

In the years following *Johnson v. Glick,* 481 F.2d 1028 (2d Cir. 1973), the vast majority of lower federal courts have applied its four-part "substantive due process" test indiscriminately to all excessive force claims lodged against law enforcement and prison officials under § 1983, without considering whether the particular application of force might implicate a more specific constitutional right governed by a different standard. Indeed, many courts have seemed to assume, as did the courts below in this case, that there is a generic "right" to be free from excessive force, grounded not in any particular constitutional provision but rather in "basic principles of § 1983 jurisprudence."

We reject this notion that all excessive force claims brought under § 1983 are governed by a single generic standard. As we have said many times, § 1983 "is not itself a source of substantive rights," but merely provides "a method for vindicating federal rights elsewhere conferred." In addressing an excessive force claim brought under § 1983, analysis begins by identifying the specific constitutional right allegedly infringed by the challenged application of force. In most instances, that will be either the Fourth Amendment's prohibition against unreasonable seizures of the person, or the Eighth Amendment's ban on cruel and unusual punishments, which are the two primary sources of constitutional protection against physically abusive governmental conduct. The validity of the claim must then be judged by reference to the specific constitutional standard which governs that right, rather than to some generalized "excessive force" standard.

Where, as here, the excessive force claim arises in the context of an arrest or investigatory stop of a free citizen, it is most properly characterized as one invoking the protections of the Fourth Amendment, which guarantees citizens the right "to be secure in their persons . . . against unreasonable . . . seizures" of the person. This much is clear from our decision in *Tennessee v. Garner,* 471 U.S. 1 (1985). In *Garner,* we addressed a claim that the use of deadly force to apprehend a fleeing suspect who did not appear to be armed or otherwise dangerous violated the suspect's constitutional rights, notwithstanding the existence of probable cause to arrest. Though the complaint alleged violations of both the Fourth Amendment and the Due Process Clause, we analyzed the constitutionality of the challenged application of force solely by reference to the Fourth Amendment's prohibition against unreasonable seizures of the person, holding that the "reasonableness" of a particular seizure depends not only on *when* it is made, but also on *how* it is carried out. Today we make explicit what was implicit in *Garner's* analysis, and hold that *all* claims that law enforcement officers have used excessive force—deadly or not—in the course of an arrest, investigatory stop, or other "seizure" of a free citizen should be analyzed under the Fourth Amendment and its "reasonableness" standard, rather than under a "substantive due process" approach. Because the Fourth Amendment provides an explicit textual source of constitutional protection against this sort of physically intrusive governmental conduct, that Amendment, not the more generalized notion of "substantive due process," must be the guide for analyzing these claims.[10]

Determining whether the force used to effect a particular seizure is "reasonable" under the Fourth Amendment requires a careful balancing of " 'the nature and quality of the intrusion on the individual's Fourth Amendment interests' " against the countervailing governmental interests at stake. Our Fourth Amendment jurisprudence has long recognized that the right to make an arrest or investigatory stop necessarily carries with it the right to use some degree of physical coercion or threat thereof to effect it. Because "[t]he test of reasonableness under the Fourth Amendment is not capable of precise definition or mechanical application," however, its proper application requires careful attention to the facts and circumstances of each particular case, including the severity of the crime at issue, whether the suspect poses an immediate threat to the safety of the officers or others, and whether he is actively resisting arrest or attempting to evade arrest by flight.

The "reasonableness" of a particular use of force must be judged from the perspective of a reasonable officer on the scene, rather than with the 20/20 vision of hindsight. The Fourth Amendment is not violated by

---

10 A "seizure" triggering the Fourth Amendment's protections occurs only when government actors have, "by means of physical force or show of authority, . . . in some way restrained the liberty of a citizen."

an arrest based on probable cause, even though the wrong person is arrested, nor by the mistaken execution of a valid search warrant on the wrong premises, With respect to a claim of excessive force, the same standard of reasonableness at the moment applies: "Not every push or shove, even if it may later seem unnecessary in the peace of a judge's chambers," violates the Fourth Amendment. The calculus of reasonableness must embody allowance for the fact that police officers are often forced to make split-second judgments—in circumstances that are tense, uncertain, and rapidly evolving—about the amount of force that is necessary in a particular situation.

As in other Fourth Amendment contexts, however, the "reasonableness" inquiry in an excessive force case is an objective one: the question is whether the officers' actions are "objectively reasonable" in light of the facts and circumstances confronting them, without regard to their underlying intent or motivation. An officer's evil intentions will not make a Fourth Amendment violation out of an objectively reasonable use of force; nor will an officer's good intentions make an objectively unreasonable use of force constitutional.

It is so ordered.

JUSTICE BLACKMUN, with whom JUSTICES BRENNAN and MARSHALL join, concurring in part and concurring in the judgment.

I join the Court's opinion insofar as it rules that the Fourth Amendment is the primary tool for analyzing claims of excessive force in the prearrest context, and I concur in the judgment remanding the case to the Court of Appeals for reconsideration of the evidence under a reasonableness standard. In light of respondents' concession, however, that the pleadings in this case properly may be construed as raising a Fourth Amendment claim, I see no reason for the Court to find it necessary further to reach out to decide that prearrest excessive force claims are to be analyzed under the Fourth Amendment *rather than* under a substantive due process standard. I also see no basis for the Court's suggestion, that our decision in *Tennessee v. Garner,* 471 U.S. 1 (1985), implicitly so held. Nowhere in *Garner* is a substantive due process standard for evaluating the use of excessive force in a particular case discussed; there is no suggestion that such a standard was offered as an alternative and rejected.

In this case, petitioner apparently decided that it was in his best interest to disavow the continued applicability of substantive due process analysis as an alternative basis for recovery in prearrest excessive force cases. His choice was certainly wise as a matter of litigation strategy in his own case, but does not (indeed, cannot be expected to) serve other potential plaintiffs equally well. It is for that reason that the Court would have done better to leave that question for another day. I expect that the use of force that is not demonstrably unreasonable under the Fourth Amendment only rarely will raise substantive due process concerns. But until I am faced with a case in which that question is squarely raised, and its merits are subjected to adversary presentation, I do not join in foreclosing the use of substantive due process analysis in prearrest cases.

FOR DISCUSSION

Under the objective reasonableness test, what factors must a court weigh or consider in deciding whether excessive force was used? What if the police do not know some critical facts—for example, as in *Graham*, that the suspect was a diabetic? How should police liability be assessed?

RELATED CASE

Palmquist v. Selvik: **111 F.3d 1332 (7th Cir. 1992).**

Evidence not known at the time to the police officer cannot be considered in determining the objective reasonableness of the use of force.

HUDSON V. MCMILLIAN

503 U.S. 1, 112 S.Ct. 995, 117 L.Ed.2d 156 (1992)

Hudson was an inmate at the Angola Prison in Louisiana. He had been handcuffed, shackled, and repeatedly beaten and kicked by corrections officers. His injuries included minor bruises and swelling of his face, mouth, and lips. The blows also loosened Hudson's teeth and cracked his partial dental plate. He sued the officers in a § 1983 suit. He won $800 in the district court but lost at the court of appeals, which ruled that his injuries were minor. He appealed to the Supreme Court.

Vote: 7–2

JUSTICE O'CONNOR delivered the opinion of the Court, joined by JUSTICES REHNQUIST, WHITE, KENNEDY, and SOUTER.

This case requires us to decide whether the use of excessive physical force against a prisoner may constitute cruel and unusual punishment when the inmate does not suffer serious injury. We answer that question in the affirmative.

I

Hudson sued the three corrections officers in Federal District Court under Rev. Stat. § 1979, 42 U.S.C. § 1983, alleging a violation of the Eighth Amendment's prohibition on cruel and unusual punishments and seeking compensatory damages. The parties consented to disposition of the case before a Magistrate, who found that McMillian and Woods used force when there was no need to do so and that Mezo expressly condoned their actions. The Magistrate awarded Hudson damages of $800.

The Court of Appeals for the Fifth Circuit reversed. 929 F.2d 1014 (1990). It held that inmates alleging use of excessive force in violation of the Eighth Amendment must prove: (1) significant injury; (2) resulting "directly and only from the use of force that was clearly excessive to the need"; (3) the excessiveness of which was objectively unreasonable; and (4) that the action constituted an unnecessary and wanton infliction of pain. The court determined that respondents' use of force was objectively unreasonable because no force was required. Furthermore, "[t]he conduct of McMillian and Woods qualified as clearly excessive and occasioned unnecessary and wanton infliction of pain." However, Hudson could not prevail on his Eighth Amendment claim because his injuries were "minor" and required no medical attention.

We granted certiorari, to determine whether the "significant injury" requirement applied by the Court of Appeals accords with the Constitution's dictate that cruel and unusual punishment shall not be inflicted.

II

In *Whitley v. Albers,* 475 U.S. 312 (1986), the principal question before us was what legal standard should govern the Eighth Amendment claim of an inmate shot by a guard during a prison riot. We based our answer on the settled rule that " 'the unnecessary and wanton infliction of pain . . . constitutes cruel and unusual punishment forbidden by the Eighth Amendment.' "

What is necessary to establish an "unnecessary and wanton infliction of pain," we said, varies according to the nature of the alleged constitutional violation. For example, the appropriate inquiry when an inmate alleges that prison officials failed to attend to serious medical needs is whether the officials exhibited "deliberate indifference." This standard is appropriate because the State's responsibility to provide inmates with medical care ordinarily does not conflict with competing administrative concerns.

By contrast, officials confronted with a prison disturbance must balance the threat unrest poses to inmates, prison workers, administrators, and visitors against the harm inmates may suffer if guards use force. Despite the weight of these competing concerns, corrections officials must make their decisions "in haste, under pressure, and frequently without the luxury of a second chance." We accordingly concluded in *Whitley* that application of the deliberate indifference standard is inappropriate when authorities use force to put down a prison disturbance. Instead, "the question whether the measure taken inflicted unnecessary and wanton pain and suffering ultimately turns on 'whether force was applied in a good faith effort to maintain or restore discipline or maliciously and sadistically for the very purpose of causing harm.' "

Many of the concerns underlying our holding in *Whitley* arise whenever guards use force to keep order. Whether the prison disturbance is a riot or a lesser disruption, corrections officers must balance the need "to maintain or restore discipline" through force against the risk of injury to inmates. Both situations may require prison officials to act quickly and decisively. Likewise, both implicate the principle that " '[p]rison administrators . . . should be accorded wide-ranging deference in the adoption and execution of policies and practices that in their judgment are needed to preserve internal order and discipline and to maintain institutional security.' " In recognition of these similarities, we hold that whenever prison officials stand accused of using excessive physical force in violation of the Cruel and Unusual Punishments Clause, the core judicial inquiry is that set out in *Whitley:* whether force was applied in a good-faith effort to maintain or restore discipline, or maliciously and sadistically to cause harm.

A

Under the *Whitley* approach, the extent of injury suffered by an inmate is one factor that may suggest "whether the use of force could plausibly have been thought necessary" in a particular situation, "or instead evinced such wantonness with respect to the unjustified infliction of harm as is tantamount to a knowing willingness that it occur." In determining whether the use of force was wanton and unnecessary, it may also be proper to evaluate the need for application of force, the relationship between that need and the amount of force used, the threat "reasonably perceived by the responsible officials," and "any efforts made to temper the severity of a forceful response." The absence of serious injury is therefore relevant to the Eighth Amendment inquiry, but does not end it.

Respondents nonetheless assert that a significant injury requirement of the sort imposed by the Fifth Circuit is mandated by what we have termed the "objective component" of Eighth Amendment analysis. *Wilson v. Seiter*, 501 U.S. 294 (1991), extended the deliberate indifference standard applied to Eighth Amendment claims involving medical care to claims about conditions of confinement. In taking this step, we suggested that the subjective aspect of an Eighth Amendment claim (with which the Court was concerned) can be distinguished from the objective facet of the same claim. Thus, courts considering a prisoner's claim must ask both if "the officials act[ed] with a sufficiently culpable state of mind" and if the alleged wrongdoing was objectively "harmful enough" to establish a constitutional violation.

With respect to the objective component of an Eighth Amendment violation, *Wilson* announced no new rule. Instead, that decision suggested a relationship between the requirements applicable to different types of Eighth Amendment claims. What is necessary to show sufficient harm for purposes of the Cruel and Unusual Punishments Clause depends upon the claim at issue, for two reasons. First, "[t]he general requirement that an Eighth Amendment claimant allege and prove the unnecessary and wanton infliction of pain should . . . be applied with due regard for differences in the kind of conduct against which an Eighth Amendment objection is lodged." Second, the Eighth Amendment's prohibition of cruel and unusual punishments " 'draw[s] its meaning from the evolving standards of decency that mark the progress of a maturing society,' " and so admits of few absolute limitations.

The objective component of an Eighth Amendment claim is therefore contextual and responsive to "contemporary standards of decency." For instance, extreme deprivations are required to make out a conditions-of-confinement claim. Because routine discomfort is "part of the penalty that criminal offenders pay for their offenses against society," "only those deprivations denying 'the minimal civilized measure of life's necessities' are sufficiently grave to form the basis of an Eighth Amendment violation." A similar analysis applies to medical needs. Because society does not expect that prisoners will have unqualified access to health care, deliberate indifference to medical needs amounts to an Eighth Amendment violation only if those needs are "serious."

In the excessive force context, society's expectations are different. When prison officials maliciously and sadistically use force to cause harm, contemporary standards of decency always are violated. This is true whether or not significant injury is evident. Otherwise, the Eighth Amendment would permit any physical punishment, no matter how diabolic or inhuman, inflicting less than some arbitrary quantity of injury. Such a result would have been as unacceptable to the drafters of the Eighth Amendment as it is today

That is not to say that every malevolent touch by a prison guard gives rise to a federal cause of action. The Eighth Amendment's prohibition of "cruel and unusual" punishments necessarily excludes from constitutional recognition *de minimis* uses of physical force, provided that the use of force is not of a sort " 'repugnant to the conscience of mankind.' "

In this case, the Fifth Circuit found Hudson's claim untenable because his injuries were "minor. Yet the blows directed at Hudson, which caused bruises, swelling, loosened teeth, and a cracked dental plate, are not *de minimis* for Eighth Amendment purposes. The extent of Hudson's injuries thus provides no basis for dismissal of his § 1983 claim.

The judgment of the Court of Appeals is *Reversed.*

JUSTICE BLACKMUN, concurring in the judgment.

The Court today appropriately puts to rest a seriously misguided view that pain inflicted by an excessive use of force is actionable under the Eighth Amendment only when coupled with "significant injury," *e.g.,* injury that requires medical attention or leaves permanent marks. Indeed, were we to hold to the contrary, we might place various kinds of state-sponsored torture and abuse—of the kind ingeniously designed to cause pain but without a telltale "significant injury"—entirely beyond the pale of the Constitution. In other words, the constitutional prohibition of "cruel and unusual punishments" then might not constrain prison officials from lashing prisoners with leather straps, whipping them with rubber hoses, beating them with naked fists, shocking them with electric currents, asphyxiating them short of death, intentionally exposing them to undue heat or cold, or forcibly injecting them with psychosis-inducing drugs. These techniques, commonly thought to be practiced only outside this Nation's borders, are hardly unknown within this Nation's prisons.

Because I was in the dissent in *Whitley v. Albers,* 475 U.S. 312 (1986), I do not join the Court's extension of *Whitley*'s malicious-and-sadistic standard to all allegations of excessive force, even outside the context of a prison riot. Nevertheless, I otherwise join the Court's solid opinion and judgment that the Eighth Amendment does not require a showing of "significant injury" in the excessive-force context.

JUSTICE THOMAS, with whom JUSTICE SCALIA joins, dissenting.

In my view, a use of force that causes only insignificant harm to a prisoner may be immoral, it may be tortious, it may be criminal, and it may even be remediable under other provisions of the Federal Constitution, but it is not cruel and unusual punishment. In concluding to the contrary, the Court today goes far beyond our precedents.

A

Until recent years, the Cruel and Unusual Punishments Clause was not deemed to apply at all to deprivations that were not inflicted as part of the sentence for a crime. For generations, judges and commentators regarded the Eighth Amendment as applying only to torturous punishments meted out by statutes or sentencing judges, and not generally to any hardship that might befall a prisoner during incarceration. In *Weems v. United States,* 217 U.S. 349 (1910), the Court extensively chronicled the background of the Amendment, discussing its English antecedents, its adoption by Congress, its construction by this Court, and the interpretation of analogous provisions by state courts. Nowhere does *Weems* even hint that the Clause might regulate not just criminal sentences but the treatment of prisoners. Scholarly commentary also viewed the Clause as governing punishments that were part of the sentence. Probably any punishment *declared by statute* for an offence which was punishable in the same way at the common law, could not be regarded as cruel or unusual in the constitutional sense.

Surely prison was not a more congenial place in the early years of the Republic than it is today; nor were our judges and commentators so naive as to be unaware of the often harsh conditions of prison life. Rather, they simply did not conceive of the Eighth Amendment as protecting inmates from harsh treatment. Thus, historically, the lower courts routinely rejected prisoner grievances by explaining that the courts had no role in regulating prison life. "[I]t is well settled that it is not the function of the courts to superintend the treatment and discipline of prisoners in penitentiaries, but only to deliver from imprisonment those who are illegally confined. It was not until 1976—185 years after the Eighth Amendment was adopted—that this Court first applied it to a prisoner's complaint about a deprivation suffered in prison.

B

We made clear in *Estelle v. Gamble*, 429 U.S. 97 (1976), that the Eighth Amendment plays a very limited role in regulating prison administration. The case involved a claim that prison doctors had inadequately attended an inmate's medical needs. We rejected the claim because the inmate failed to allege "acts or omissions sufficiently harmful to evidence *deliberate indifference* to *serious* medical needs. From the outset, thus, we specified that the Eighth Amendment does not apply to every deprivation, or even every unnecessary deprivation, suffered by a prisoner, but *only* that narrow class of deprivations involving "serious" injury inflicted by prison officials acting with a culpable state of mind. We have since described these twin elements as the "objective" and "subjective" components of an Eighth Amendment prison claim.

These subjective and objective components, of course, are implicit in the traditional Eighth Amendment jurisprudence, which focuses on penalties meted out by statutes or sentencing judges. Thus, if a State were to pass a statute ordering that convicted felons be broken at the wheel, we would not separately inquire whether the legislature had acted with "deliberate indifference," since a statute, as an intentional act, necessarily satisfies an even higher state-of-mind threshold. Likewise, the inquiry whether the deprivation is objectively serious would be encompassed within our determination whether it was "cruel and unusual."

When we cut the Eighth Amendment loose from its historical moorings and applied it to a broad range of prison deprivations, we found it appropriate to make explicit the limitations described in *Estelle, Rhodes, Whitley v. Albers*, 475 U.S. 312 (1986), and *Wilson v. Seiter*, 501 U.S. 294 (1991). "If the pain inflicted is not formally meted out *as punishment* by the statute or the sentencing judge, some mental element must be attributed to the inflicting officer before it can qualify." Similarly, because deprivations of all sorts are the very essence of imprisonment, we made explicit the *serious* deprivation requirement to ensure that the Eighth Amendment did not transfer wholesale the regulation of prison life from executive officials to judges.

II

Today's expansion of the Cruel and Unusual Punishments Clause beyond all bounds of history and precedent is, I suspect, yet another manifestation of the pervasive view that the Federal Constitution must address all ills in our society. Abusive behavior by prison guards is deplorable conduct that properly evokes outrage and contempt. But that does not mean that it is invariably unconstitutional. The Eighth Amendment is not, and should not be turned into, a National Code of Prison Regulation. To reject the notion that the infliction of concededly "minor" injuries can be considered either "cruel" or "unusual" punishment (much less cruel *and* unusual punishment) is not to say that it amounts to acceptable conduct. Rather, it is to recognize that primary responsibility for preventing and punishing such conduct rests not with the Federal Constitution but with the laws and regulations of the various States.

Because I conclude that, under our precedents, a prisoner seeking to establish that he has been subjected to cruel and unusual punishment must always show that he has suffered a serious injury, I would affirm the judgment of the Fifth Circuit.

FOR DISCUSSION

Bruises, swelling of jaw, loose teeth, and broken dental plate comprise an injury serious enough to establish a cruel and unusual punishment claim, especially if the physical punishment was inflicted with malice or sadism. Does the dissenters' argument suggest that some roughing up and physical abuse is permitted? How grave must an injury be for the majority and for the dissenters, before it rises to a level of a constitutional violation?

RELATED CASE

***Martin v. Board of County Commissioners:* 909 F.2d 402 (10th Cir. 1992).**

Arresting an individual and removing her from a hospital against the advice of medical doctors could constitute excessive use of force by police, even though the latter did not touch the suspect.

SCOTT V. HARRIS

550 U.S. 372, 127 S.Ct. 1769, 167 L.Ed.2d 686 (2007)

Motorist sued county deputy and others claiming, use of excessive force in violation of his Fourth Amendment rights during high-speed chase. District Court denied deputy's motion for summary judgment, affirmed decision to allow Fourth Amendment claim against deputy to proceed to trial. Supreme Court granted certiorari and reversed.

Vote: 8–1

JUSTICE SCALIA wrote for the Court.

We consider whether a law enforcement official can, consistent with the Fourth Amendment, attempt to stop a fleeing motorist from continuing his public-endangering flight by ramming the motorist's car from behind. Put another way: Can an officer take actions that place a fleeing motorist at risk of serious injury or death in order to stop the motorist's flight from endangering the lives of innocent bystanders?

I

In March 2001, a Georgia county deputy clocked respondent's vehicle traveling at 73 miles per hour on a road with a 55-mile-per-hour speed limit. The deputy activated his blue flashing lights indicating that respondent should pull over. Instead, respondent sped away, initiating a chase down what is in most portions a two-lane road, at speeds exceeding 85 miles per hour. The deputy radioed his dispatch to report that he was pursuing a fleeing vehicle, and broadcast its license plate number. Petitioner, Deputy Timothy Scott, heard the radio communication and joined the pursuit along with other officers. In the midst of the chase, respondent pulled into the parking lot of a shopping center and was nearly boxed in by the various police vehicles. Respondent evaded the trap by making a sharp turn, colliding with Scott's police car, exiting the parking lot, and speeding off once again down a two-lane highway.

Following respondent's shopping center maneuvering, which resulted in slight damage to Scott's police car, Scott took over as the lead pursuit vehicle. Six minutes and nearly 10 miles after the chase had begun, Scott decided to attempt to terminate the episode by employing a "Precision Intervention Technique ('PIT') maneuver, which causes the fleeing vehicle to spin to a stop." Instead, Scott applied his push bumper to the rear of respondent's vehicle. As a result, respondent lost control of his vehicle, which left the roadway, ran down an embankment, overturned, and crashed. Respondent was badly injured and was rendered a quadriplegic.

Respondent filed suit against Deputy Scott and others under Rev. Stat. § 1979, 42 U.S.C. § 1983, alleging, *inter alia,* a violation of his federal constitutional rights, viz. use of excessive force resulting in an unreasonable seizure under the Fourth Amendment. In response, Scott filed a motion for summary judgment based on an assertion of qualified immunity.

II

In resolving questions of qualified immunity, courts are required to resolve a "threshold question: Taken in the light most favorable to the party asserting the injury, do the facts alleged show the officer's conduct violated a constitutional right? If, and only if, the court finds a violation of a constitutional right, "the next, sequential step is to ask whether the right was clearly established . . . in light of the specific context of the case." Although this ordering contradicts "[o]ur policy of avoiding unnecessary adjudication of constitutional issues," we have said that such a departure from practice is "necessary to set forth principles which will become the basis for a [future] holding that a right is clearly established," We therefore turn to the threshold inquiry: whether Deputy Scott's actions violated the Fourth Amendment.

III

A

The first step in assessing the constitutionality of Scott's actions is to determine the relevant facts.

"[T]aking the facts from the non-movant's viewpoint, [respondent] remained in control of his vehicle, slowed for turns and intersections, and typically used his indicators for turns. He did not run any motorists off the road. Nor was he a threat to pedestrians in the shopping center parking lot, which was free from pedestrian and vehicular traffic as the center was closed. Significantly, by the time the parties were back on the highway and Scott rammed [respondent], the motorway had been cleared of motorists and pedestrians allegedly because of police blockades of the nearby intersections." (citations omitted).The videotape tells quite a different story. There we see respondent's vehicle racing down narrow, two-lane roads in the dead of night at speeds that are shockingly fast. We see it swerve around more than a dozen other cars, cross the double-yellow line, and force cars traveling in both directions to their respective shoulders to avoid being hit. We see it run multiple red lights and travel for considerable periods of time in the occasional center left-turn-only lane, chased by numerous police cars forced to engage in the same hazardous maneuvers just to keep up. Far from being the cautious and controlled driver the lower court depicts, what we see on the video more closely resembles a Hollywood-style car chase of the most frightening sort, placing police officers and innocent bystanders alike at great risk of serious injury.

B

Judging the matter on that basis, we think it is quite clear that Deputy Scott did not violate the Fourth Amendment. Scott does not contest that his decision to terminate the car chase by ramming his bumper into respondent's vehicle constituted a "seizure." "[A] Fourth Amendment seizure [occurs] . . . when there is a governmental termination of freedom of movement through means intentionally applied." It is also conceded, by both sides, that a claim of "excessive force in the course of making [a] . . . 'seizure' of [the] person . . . [is] properly analyzed under the Fourth Amendment's 'objective reasonableness' standard." *Graham v. Connor,* 490 U.S. 386, 388 (1989). The question we need to answer is whether Scott's actions were objectively reasonable.

1

We must first decide whether the actions Scott took constituted "deadly force." If so, respondent claims that *Garner* prescribes certain preconditions that must be met before Scott's actions can survive Fourth Amendment scrutiny: (1) The suspect must have posed an immediate threat of serious physical harm to the officer or others; (2) deadly force must have been necessary to prevent escape;[9] and (3) where feasible, the officer must have given the suspect some warning. Since these *Garner* preconditions for using deadly force were not met in this case, Scott's actions were *per se* unreasonable.

Respondent's argument falters at its first step; *Garner* did not establish a magical on/off switch that triggers rigid preconditions whenever an officer's actions constitute "deadly force." *Garner* was simply an application of the Fourth Amendment's "reasonableness" test, to the use of a particular type of force in a particular situation. *Garner* held that it was unreasonable to kill a "young, slight, and unarmed" burglary suspect, by shooting him "in the back of the head" while he was running away on foot, and when the officer "could not reasonably have believed that [the suspect] . . . posed any threat," and "never attempted to justify his actions on any basis other than the need to prevent an escape," Whatever *Garner* said about the factors that *might have* justified shooting the suspect in that case, such "preconditions" have scant applicability to this case, which has vastly different facts. "*Garner* had nothing to do with one car striking another or even with car chases in general . . . . A police car's bumping a fleeing car is, in fact, not much like a policeman's shooting a gun so as to hit a person." Nor is the threat posed by the flight on foot of an unarmed suspect even remotely comparable to the extreme danger to human life posed by respondent in this case. Although respondent's attempt to craft an easy-to-apply legal test in the Fourth Amendment context is admirable, in the end we must still slosh our way through the factbound morass of "reasonableness." Whether or not Scott's actions constituted application of "deadly force," all that matters is whether Scott's actions were reasonable.

2

In determining the reasonableness of the manner in which a seizure is effected, "[w]e must balance the nature and quality of the intrusion on the individual's Fourth Amendment interests against the importance of the governmental interests alleged to justify the intrusion." Scott defends his actions by pointing to the paramount governmental interest in ensuring public safety, and respondent nowhere suggests this was not the purpose motivating Scott's behavior. Thus, in judging whether Scott's actions were reasonable, we must consider the risk of bodily harm that Scott's actions posed to respondent in light of the threat to the public that Scott was trying to eliminate. Although there is no obvious way to quantify the risks on either side, it is clear from the videotape that respondent posed an actual and imminent threat to the lives of any pedestrians who might have been present, to other civilian motorists, and to the officers involved in the chase. It is equally clear that Scott's actions posed a high likelihood of serious injury or death to respondent—though not the near *certainty* of death posed by, say, shooting a fleeing felon in the back of the head, or pulling alongside a fleeing motorist's car and shooting the motorist. So how does a court go about weighing the perhaps lesser probability of injuring or killing numerous bystanders against the perhaps larger probability of injuring or killing a single person? We think it appropriate in this process to take into account not only the number of lives at risk, but also their relative culpability. It was respondent, after all, who intentionally placed himself and the public in danger by unlawfully engaging in the reckless, high-speed flight that ultimately produced the choice between two evils that Scott confronted. Multiple police cars, with blue lights flashing and sirens blaring, had been chasing respondent for nearly 10 miles, but he ignored their warning to stop. By contrast, those who might have been harmed had Scott not taken the action he did were entirely innocent. We have little difficulty in concluding it was reasonable for Scott to take the action that he did.

[W]e are loath to lay down a rule requiring the police to allow fleeing suspects to get away whenever they drive *so recklessly* that they put other people's lives in danger. It is obvious the perverse incentives such a rule would create: Every fleeing motorist would know that escape is within his grasp, if only he accelerates to 90 miles per hour, crosses the double-yellow line a few times, and runs a few red lights. The Constitution assuredly does not impose this *386 invitation to impunity-earned-by-recklessness. Instead, we lay down a more sensible rule: A police officer's attempt to terminate a dangerous high-speed car chase that threatens the lives of innocent bystanders does not violate the Fourth Amendment, even when it places the fleeing motorist at risk of serious injury or death.

* * *

The car chase that respondent initiated in this case posed a substantial and immediate risk of serious physical injury to others; no reasonable jury could conclude otherwise. Scott's attempt to terminate the chase by forcing respondent off the road was reasonable, and Scott is entitled to summary judgment. The Court of Appeals' judgment to the contrary is reversed.

It is so ordered.

JUSTICE STEVENS, dissenting.

Today, the Court asks whether an officer may "take actions that place a fleeing motorist at risk of serious injury or death in order to stop the motorist's flight from endangering the lives of innocent bystanders." Depending on the circumstances, the answer may be an obvious "yes," an obvious "no," or sufficiently doubtful that the question of the reasonableness of the officer's actions should be decided by a jury, after a review of the degree of danger and the alternatives available to the officer. A high-speed chase in a desert in Nevada is, after all, quite different from one that travels through the heart of Las Vegas.

Omitted from the Court's description of the initial speeding violation is the fact that respondent was on a four-lane portion of Highway 34 when the officer clocked his speed at 73 miles per hour and initiated the chase. More significantly—and contrary to the Court's assumption that respondent's vehicle "force[d] cars traveling in both directions to their respective shoulders to avoid being hit,"—a fact unmentioned in the text of the opinion explains why those cars pulled over prior to being passed by respondent. The sirens and flashing lights on the police cars following respondent gave the same warning that a speeding ambulance or fire engine would have provided. The 13 cars that respondent passed on his side of the road before entering the shopping center, and both of the cars that he passed on the right after leaving the center, no doubt had already pulled to the side of the road or were driving along the shoulder because they heard the police sirens or saw the flashing lights before respondent or the police cruisers approached. A jury could certainly conclude that those motorists were exposed to no greater risk than persons who take the same action in response to a speeding ambulance, and that their reactions were fully consistent with the evidence that respondent, though speeding, retained full control of his vehicle.

The police sirens also minimized any risk that may have arisen from running "multiple red lights," In fact, respondent and his pursuers went through only two intersections with stop lights and in both cases all other vehicles in sight were stationary, presumably because they had been warned of the approaching speeders. Incidentally, the videos do show that the lights were red when the police cars passed through them but, because the cameras were farther away when respondent did so and it is difficult to discern the color of the signal at that point, it is not entirely clear that *392 he ran either or both of the red lights. In any event, the risk of harm to the stationary vehicles was minimized by the sirens, and there is no reason to believe that respondent would have disobeyed the signals if he were not being pursued.

My colleagues on the jury saw respondent "swerve around more than a dozen other cars," and "force cars traveling in both directions to their respective shoulders," but they apparently discounted the possibility that those cars were already out of the pursuit's path as a result of hearing the sirens. Even if that were not so, passing a slower vehicle on a two-lane road always involves some degree of swerving and is not especially dangerous if there are no cars coming from the opposite direction. At no point during the chase did respondent pull into the opposite lane other than to pass a car in front of him; he did the latter no more than five times and, on most of those occasions, used his turn signal. On none of these occasions was there a car traveling in the opposite direction. In fact, at one point, when respondent found himself behind a car in his own lane and there were cars traveling in the other direction, he slowed and waited for the cars traveling in the other direction to pass before overtaking the car in front of him while using his turn signal to do so. This is hardly the stuff of Hollywood. To the contrary, the video does not reveal any incidents that could even be remotely characterized as "close calls."

In sum, the factual statements by the Court of Appeals quoted by the Court, were entirely accurate. That court did not describe respondent as a "cautious" driver as my colleagues imply, but it did correctly conclude that there is no evidence that he ever lost control of his vehicle. That court also correctly pointed out that the incident in the shopping center parking lot did not create any risk to pedestrians or other vehicles because the chase occurred just before 11 p.m. on a weekday night and the center was closed. It is apparent from the record (including the videotape) that local police had blocked off intersections to keep respondent from entering residential neighborhoods and possibly endangering other motorists. I would add that the videos also show that no pedestrians, parked cars, sidewalks, or residences were visible at any time during the chase. The only "innocent bystanders" who were placed "at great risk of serious injury," were the drivers who either pulled off the road in response to the sirens or passed respondent in the opposite direction when he was driving on his side of the road.

I recognize, of course, that even though respondent's original speeding violation on a four-lane highway was rather ordinary, his refusal to stop and subsequent flight was a serious offense that merited severe punishment. It was not, however, a capital offense, or even an offense that justified the use of deadly force rather than an abandonment of the chase. The Court's concern about the "imminent threat to the lives of any pedestrians who might have been present," *ante,* at 1778, while surely valid in an appropriate case, should be discounted in a case involving a nighttime chase in an area where no pedestrians were present.

What would have happened if the police had decided to abandon the chase? We now know that they could have apprehended respondent later because they had his license plate number.

I respectfully dissent.

FOR DISCUSSION

What constitutional right of his did Harris allege the police department violate? What did the Court disagree? What factors do you think should be considered when determining whether a high-speed pursuit would be permitted?

RELATED CASES

***Plumhoff v. Rickard:* ___ U.S. ___, 134 S.Ct. 2012 (2014).**

Court ruled that officers' conduct in firing 15 shots into suspect's vehicle during a high-speed pursuit did not amount to excessive force.

GLOSSARY

42 United States Code section 1983: This section of the 1871 Civil Rights Act is used by individuals to sue state and local officials when they believe their constitutional rights have been violated or that a constitutional tort has been committed against them. Federal officials can be sued under the doctrine developed in *Bivens v. Six Unknown Named FBI Agents.*

Color of the Law: An individual acting under the color of the law can be sued under 42 U.S.C. § 1983 for a violation of another's constitutional rights. Finding that someone has acted under the color of the law is often one way of determining whether state action exists.

Company Town: Town wholly owned by a corporation. In *Marsh v. Alabama* (326 U.S. 501, 1946), the Supreme Court ruled that private towns may not ban the distribution of religious handbills in public places.

Constitutional Tort: A violation of an individual's rights severe enough to be defined as a violation of the Constitution or the Bill of Rights.

Deadly Force: The use of force that results in death or serious bodily injury. Constitutional claims of use of excessive deadly force, which are examined under the Fourth Amendment, involve a weighing of the intrusion on the individual's Fourth Amendment right against the government's interests, cited to justify the intrusion.

Non-Deadly Force: Force that does not result in death or serious bodily injury. Constitutional claims of use of excessive non-deadly force are examined under the Fourth Amendment by means of an objective reasonableness test.

Objective Reasonableness Test: A test formulated by the Supreme Court in Graham v. Connor, 440 U.S. 386 (1989) to determine if nondeadly use of force by law enforcement officials is constitutionally permissible.

Private Actions: Actions or acts that are not attributable to the government. If an act is deemed to be private, the constitutional protections of the Bills of Rights do not apply.

Restrictive Covenants: Private agreements among property owners that often precluded the sale of homes and other property to African Americans. In *Shelley v. Kraemer* (334 U.S. 1, 1948), the Supreme Court said that judicial enforcement of such agreements constituted state action.

State Actions: Actions or acts that can be attributed to the government. If state action is found to exist, the constitutional protections of the Bill of Rights apply. If the actor is a state or local government, the entity can be sued for a constitutional violation under 42 U.S.C. § 1983.

SELECTED BIBLIOGRAPHY

Choper, Jesse. "Thoughts on State Action," *Washington University Law Quarterly*, 757 (1979).

Comment, "The Impact of *Shelley v. Kraemer* on the State Action Concept," 44 *California Law Review*, 718 (1956).

Curry, Lynne. 2007. *The DeShaney Case: Child Abuse, Family Rights, and the Dilemma of State Intervention*. Lawrence: University Press of Kansas.

Davey, Joseph, Dillon. 2008. *The Bill of Rights Today: Constitutional Limits on the Powers of the Government*. Lanham, MD: University Press of America.

Fee, John. "The Formal State Action Doctrine and Free Speech Analysis," 83 *North Carolina Law Review*, 569–619 (2005).

Gonda, Jeffrey D. 2014. "Litigating Racial Justice at the Grassroots: The Shelley Family, Black Realtors, and Shelley v. Kraemer (1948)," *Journal of Supreme Court History* 39 (November) 329–354.

Halbrook, Stephen P. 2008. *The Founders' Second Amendment: Origin of the Right to Bear Arms*. Chicago: Ivan R. Dee.

Horowitz, Harold W. "The Misleading Search for "State Action' under the Fourteenth Amendment," 30 *Southern California Law Review*, 208 (1957).

Huscroft, Grant. 2008. *Expounding the Constitution: Essays in Constitutional Theory*. New York: Cambridge University Press.

Kappler, Victor E. 2006. *Critical Issues in Police Civil Liability*. Prospects Heights, IL: Waveland Press.

Moore, Nina M. 2015. *The Political Roots of Racial Tracking in American Criminal Justice*. New York: Cambridge University Press.

Note, "State Action: Theories for Applying Constitutional Restrictions to Private Activity," 74 *Columbia Law Review*, 656 (1974).

Peller, Gary, and Mark Tushnet. "State Action and a New Birth of Freedom," 92 *Georgetown Law Journal*, 779–817 (2004).

Schwarzchild, Maimon. "Value Pluralism and the Constitution in Defense of the State Action Doctrine," *Supreme Court Review*, pp. 129–161 (1988).

Appendix

VIRGINIA DECLARATION OF RIGHTS

1776

A declaration of rights made by the representatives of the good people of Virginia, assembled in full and free convention; which rights do pertain to them and their posterity, as the basis and foundation of government.

SECTION I. That all men are by nature equally free and independent and have certain inherent rights, of which, when they enter into a state of society, they cannot, by any compact, deprive or divest their posterity; namely, the enjoyment of life and liberty, with the means of acquiring and possessing property, and pursuing and obtaining happiness and safety.

SEC. 2. That all power is vested in, and consequently derived from, the people; that magistrates are their trustees and servants and at all times amenable to them.

SEC. 3. That government is, or ought to be, instituted for the common benefit, protection, and security of the people, nation, or community; of all the various modes and forms of government, that is best which is capable of producing the greatest degree of happiness and safety and is most effectually secured against the danger of maladministration; and that, when any government shall be found inadequate or contrary to these purposes, a majority of the community hath an indubitable, inalienable, and indefeasible right to reform, alter, or abolish it, in such manner as shall be judged most conducive to the public weal.

SEC. 4. That no man, or set of men, are entitled to exclusive or separate emoluments or privileges from the community, but in consideration of public services; which, not being descendible, neither ought the offices of magistrate, legislator, or judge to be hereditary.

SEC. 5. That the legislative and executive powers of the state should be separate and distinct from the judiciary; and that the members of the two first may be restrained from oppression, by feeling and participating the burdens of the people, they should, at fixed periods, be reduced to a private station, return into that body from which they were originally taken, and the vacancies be supplied by frequent, certain, and regular elections, in which all, or any part, of the former members, to be again eligible, or ineligible, as the laws shall direct.

SEC. 6. That elections of members to serve as representatives of the people, in assembly, ought to be free; and that all men, having sufficient evidence of permanent common interest with, and attachment to, the community, have the right of suffrage and cannot be taxed or deprived of their property for public uses without their own consent, or that of their representatives so elected, nor bound by any law to which they have not, in like manner, assented for the public good.

SEC. 7. That all power of suspending laws, or the execution of laws, by any authority, without consent of the representatives of the people, is injurious to their rights and ought not to be exercised.

SEC. 8. That in all capital or criminal prosecutions a man hath a right to demand the cause and nature of his accusation, to be confronted with the accusers and witnesses, to call for evidence in his favor, and to a speedy trial by an impartial jury of twelve men of his vicinage, without whose unanimous consent he cannot be found guilty; nor can he be compelled to give evidence against himself; that no man be deprived of his liberty, except by the law of the land or the judgment of his peers.

SEC. 9. That excessive bail ought not to be required, nor excessive fines imposed, nor cruel and unusual punishments inflicted.

SEC. 10. That general warrants, whereby an officer or messenger may be commanded to search suspected places without evidence of a fact committed, or to seize any person or persons not named, or whose offense is not particularly described and supported by evidence, are grievous and oppressive and ought not to be granted.

SEC. 11. That in controversies respecting property, and in suits between man and man, the ancient trial by jury is preferable to any other and ought to be held sacred.

SEC. 12. That the freedom of the press is one of the great bulwarks of liberty and can never be restrained but by despotic governments.

SEC. 13. That a well-regulated militia, or composed of the body of the people, trained to arms, is the proper, natural, and safe defense of a free state; that standing armies, in time of peace, should be avoided as dangerous to liberty; and that in all cases the military should be under strict subordination to, and governed by, the civil power.

SEC. 14. That the people have a right to uniform government; and, therefore, that no government separate from or independent of the government of Virginia ought to be erected or established within the limits thereof.

SEC. 15. That no free government, or the blessings of liberty, can be preserved to any people, but by a firm adherence to justice, moderation, temperance, frugality, and virtue, and by frequent recurrence to fundamental principles.

SEC. 16. That religion, or the duty which we owe to our Creator, and the manner of discharging it, can be directed only by reason and conviction, not by force or violence; and therefore all men are equally entitled to the free exercise of religion, according to the dictates of conscience; and that it is the mutual duty of all to practice Christian forbearance, love, and charity toward each other.

ALEXANDER HAMILTON, THE FEDERALIST NO. 84 CERTAIN GENERAL AND MISCELLANEOUS OBJECTIONS TO THE CONSTITUTION CONSIDERED AND ANSWERED

Summer 1788

To the People of the State of New York:

IN THE course of the foregoing review of the Constitution, I have taken notice of, and endeavored to answer most of the objections which have appeared against it. There, however, remain a few which either did not fall naturally under any particular head or were forgotten in their proper places. These shall now be discussed; but as the subject has been drawn into great length, I shall so far consult brevity as to comprise all my observations on these miscellaneous points in a single paper.

The most considerable of the remaining objections is that the plan of the convention contains no bill of rights. Among other answers given to this, it has been upon different occasions remarked that the constitutions of several of the States are in a similar predicament. I add that New York is of the number. And yet the opposers of the new system, in this State, who profess an unlimited admiration for its constitution, are among the most intemperate partisans of a bill of rights. To justify their zeal in this matter, they allege two things: one is that, though the constitution of New York has no bill of rights prefixed to it, yet it contains, in the body of it, various provisions in favor of particular privileges and rights, which, in substance amount to the same thing; the other is, that the Constitution adopts, in their full extent, the common and statute law of Great Britain, by which many other rights, not expressed in it, are equally secured.

To the first I answer, that the Constitution proposed by the convention contains, as well as the constitution of this State, a number of such provisions.

Independent of those which relate to the structure of the government, we find the following: Article 1, section 3, clause 7—"Judgment in cases of impeachment shall not extend further than to removal from office, and disqualification to hold and enjoy any office of honor, trust, or profit under the United States; but the party convicted shall, nevertheless, be liable and subject to indictment, trial, judgment, and punishment according to law." Section 9, of the same article, clause 2—"The privilege of the writ of habeas corpus shall not be suspended, unless when in cases of rebellion or invasion the public safety may require it." Clause 3—"No bill of attainder or ex-post-facto law shall be passed." Clause 7—"No title of nobility shall be granted by the United States; and no person holding any office of profit or trust under them, shall, without the consent of the Congress, accept of any present, emolument, office, or title of any kind whatever, from any king, prince, or foreign state." Article 3, section 2, clause 3—"The trial of all crimes, except in cases of impeachment, shall be by jury; and such trial shall be held in the State where the said crimes shall have been committed; but when not committed within any State, the trial shall be at such place or places as the Congress may by law have directed." Section 3, of the same article—"Treason against the United States shall consist only in levying war against them, or in adhering to their enemies, giving them aid and comfort. No person shall be convicted of treason, unless on the testimony of two witnesses to the same overt act, or on confession in open court." And clause 3, of the same section—"The Congress shall have power to declare the punishment of treason; but no attainder of treason shall work corruption of blood, or forfeiture, except during the life of the person attainted."

It may well be a question, whether these are not, upon the whole, of equal importance with any which are to be found in the constitution of this State. The establishment of the writ of *habeas corpus*, the prohibition of *ex post facto* laws, and of TITLES OF NOBILITY, *to which we have no corresponding provision in our Constitution*, are perhaps greater securities to liberty and republicanism than any it contains. The creation of crimes after the commission of the fact, or, in other words, the subjecting of men to punishment for things which, when they were done, were breaches of no law, and the practice of arbitrary imprisonments, have been, in all ages, the favorite and most formidable instruments of tyranny. The observations of the judicious Blackstone,[1] in reference to the latter, are well worthy of recital: "To bereave a man of life, [says he] or by violence to confiscate his estate, without accusation or trial, would be so gross and notorious an act of despotism, as must at once convey the alarm of tyranny throughout the whole nation; but confinement of the person, by secretly hurrying him to jail, where his sufferings are unknown or forgotten, is a less public, a less striking, and therefore *a more dangerous engine* of arbitrary government." And as a remedy for this fatal evil he is everywhere peculiarly emphatical in his encomiums on the *habeas corpus* act, which in one place he calls "the BULWARK of the British Constitution."[2]

Nothing need be said to illustrate the importance of the prohibition of titles of nobility. This may truly be denominated the corner-stone of republican government; for so long as they are excluded, there can never be serious danger that the government will be any other than that of the people.

To the second that is, to the pretended establishment of the common and state law by the Constitution, I answer, that they are expressly made subject "to such alterations and provisions as the legislature shall from time to time make concerning the same." They are therefore at any moment liable to repeal by the ordinary legislative power, and of course have no constitutional sanction. The only use of the declaration was to recognize the ancient law and to remove doubts which might have been occasioned by the Revolution. This consequently can be considered as no part of a declaration of rights, which under our constitutions must be intended as limitations of the power of the government itself.

It has been several times truly remarked that bills of rights are, in their origin, stipulations between kings and their subjects, abridgements of prerogative in favor of privilege, reservations of rights not surrendered to the prince. Such was MAGNA CHARTA, obtained by the barons, sword in hand, from King John. Such were the subsequent confirmations of that charter by succeeding princes. Such was the *Petition of Right* assented to by Charles I, in the beginning of his reign. Such, also, was the Declaration of Right presented by the Lords and Commons to the Prince of Orange in 1688, and afterwards thrown into the form of an act of parliament called the Bill of Rights. It is evident, therefore, that, according to their primitive signification, they have no application to constitutions professedly founded upon the power of the people, and executed by their immediate representatives and servants. Here, in strictness, the people surrender nothing; and as they retain every thing they have no need of particular reservations. "WE, THE PEOPLE of the United States, to secure the blessings of liberty to ourselves and our posterity, do *ordain* and *establish* this Constitution for the United States of America." Here is a better recognition of popular rights, than volumes of those aphorisms which make the principal figure in several of our State bills of rights, and which would sound much better in a treatise of ethics than in a constitution of government.

But a minute detail of particular rights is certainly far less applicable to a Constitution like that under consideration, which is merely intended to regulate the general political interests of the nation, than to a constitution which has the regulation of every species of personal and private concerns. If, therefore, the loud clamors against the plan of the convention, on this score, are well founded, no epithets of reprobation will be too strong for the constitution of this State. But the truth is, that both of them contain all which, in relation to their objects, is reasonably to be desired.

I go further, and affirm that bills of rights, in the sense and to the extent in which they are contended for, are not only unnecessary in the proposed Constitution, but would even be dangerous. They would contain various exceptions to powers not granted; and, on this very account, would afford a colorable pretext to claim more than were granted. For why declare that things shall not be done which there is no power to do? Why, for instance, should it be said that the liberty of the press shall not be restrained, when no power is given by which restrictions may be imposed? I will not contend that such a provision would confer a regulating power; but it is evident that it would furnish, to men disposed to usurp, a plausible pretense for claiming that power. They might urge with a semblance of reason, that the Constitution ought not to be charged with the absurdity of providing against the abuse of an authority which was not given, and that the provision against restraining the liberty of the press afforded a clear implication, that a power to prescribe proper regulations concerning it was intended to be vested in the national government. This may serve as a specimen of the numerous handles which would be given to the doctrine of constructive powers, by the indulgence of an injudicious zeal for bills of rights.

On the subject of the liberty of the press, as much as has been said, I cannot forbear adding a remark or two: in the first place, I observe, that there is not a syllable concerning it in the constitution of this State; in the next, I contend, that whatever has been said about it in that of any other State, amounts to nothing. What signifies a declaration, that "the liberty of the press shall be inviolably preserved"? What is the liberty of the press? Who can give it any definition which would not leave the utmost latitude for evasion? I hold it to be impracticable; and from this I infer, that its security, whatever fine declarations may be inserted in any constitution respecting it, must altogether depend on public opinion, and on the general spirit of the people and of the government.[3] And here, after all, as is intimated upon another occasion, must we seek for the only solid basis of all our rights.

There remains but one other view of this matter to conclude the point. The truth is, after all the declamations we have heard, that the Constitution is itself, in every rational sense, and to every useful purpose, A BILL OF RIGHTS. The several bills of rights in Great Britain form its Constitution, and conversely the constitution of each State is its bill of rights. And the proposed Constitution, if adopted, will be the bill of rights of the Union. Is it one object of a bill of rights to declare and specify the political privileges of the citizens in the structure and administration of the government? This is done in the most ample and precise manner in the plan of the convention; comprehending various precautions for the public security, which are not to be found in any of the State constitutions. Is another object of a bill of rights to define certain immunities and modes of proceeding, which are relative to personal and private concerns? This we have seen has also been attended to, in a variety of cases, in the same plan. Adverting therefore to the substantial meaning of a bill of rights, it is absurd to allege that it is not to be found in the work of the convention. It may be said that it does not go far enough, though it will not be easy to make this appear; but it can with no propriety be contended that there is no such thing. It certainly must be immaterial what mode is observed as to the order of declaring the rights of the citizens, if they are to be found in any part of the instrument which establishes the government. And hence it must be apparent, that much of what has been said on this subject rests merely on verbal and nominal distinctions, entirely foreign from the substance of the thing.

Another objection which has been made, and which, from the frequency of its repetition, it is to be presumed is relied on, is of this nature: "It is improper [say the objectors] to confer such large powers, as are proposed, upon the national government, because the seat of that government must of necessity be too remote from many of the States to admit of a proper knowledge on the part of the constituent, of the conduct of the representative body." This argument, if it proves any thing, proves that there ought to be no general government whatever. For the powers which, it seems to be agreed on all hands, ought to be vested in the Union, cannot be safely intrusted to a body which is not under every requisite control. But there are satisfactory reasons to show that the objection is in reality not well founded. There is in most of the arguments which relate to distance a palpable illusion of the imagination. What are the sources of information by which the people in Montgomery County must regulate their judgment of the conduct of their representatives in the State legislature? Of personal observation they can have no benefit. This is confined to the citizens on the spot. They must therefore depend on the information of intelligent men, in whom they confide; and how must these men obtain their information? Evidently from the complexion of public measures, from the public prints, from correspondences with their representatives, and with other persons who reside at the place of their deliberations. This does not apply to Montgomery County only, but to all the counties at any considerable distance from the seat of government.

It is equally evident that the same sources of information would be open to the people in relation to the conduct of their representatives in the general government, and the impediments to a prompt communication which distance may be supposed to create, will be overbalanced by the effects of the vigilance of the State governments. The executive and legislative bodies of each State will be so many sentinels over the persons employed in every department of the national administration; and as it will be in their power to adopt and pursue a regular and effectual system of intelligence, they can never be at a loss to know the behavior of those who represent their constituents in the national councils, and can readily communicate the same knowledge to the people. Their disposition to apprise the community of whatever may prejudice its interests from another quarter, may be relied upon, if it were only from the rivalship of power. And we may conclude with the fullest assurance that the people, through that channel, will be better informed of the conduct of their national representatives, than they can be by any means they now possess of that of their State representatives.

It ought also to be remembered that the citizens who inhabit the country at and near the seat of government will, in all questions that affect the general liberty and prosperity, have the same interest with those who are at a distance, and that they will stand ready to sound the alarm when necessary, and to point out the actors in any pernicious project. The public papers will be expeditious messengers of intelligence to the most remote inhabitants of the Union.

Among the many curious objections which have appeared against the proposed Constitution, the most extraordinary and the least colorable is derived from the want of some provision respecting the debts due *to* the United States. This has been represented as a tacit relinquishment of those debts, and as a wicked contrivance to screen public defaulters. The newspapers have teemed with the most inflammatory railings on this head; yet there is nothing clearer than that the suggestion is entirely void of foundation, the offspring of extreme ignorance or extreme dishonesty. In addition to the remarks I have made upon the subject in another place, I shall only observe that as it is a plain dictate of common-sense, so it is also an established doctrine of political law, that *"States neither lose any of their rights, nor are discharged from any of their obligations, by a change in the form of their civil government."*[4]

The last objection of any consequence, which I at present recollect, turns upon the article of expense. If it were even true, that the adoption of the proposed government would occasion a considerable increase of expense, it would be an objection that ought to have no weight against the plan.

The great bulk of the citizens of America are with reason convinced, that Union is the basis of their political happiness. Men of sense of all parties now, with few exceptions, agree that it cannot be preserved under the present system, nor without radical alterations; that new and extensive powers ought to be granted to the national head, and that these require a different organization of the federal government—a single body being an unsafe depositary of such ample authorities. In conceding all this, the question of expense must be given up; for it is impossible, with any degree of safety, to narrow the foundation upon which the system is to stand. The two branches of the legislature are, in the first instance, to consist of only sixty-five persons, which is the same number of which Congress, under the existing Confederation, may be composed. It is true that this number is intended to be increased; but this is to keep pace with the progress of the population and resources of the country. It is evident that a less number would, even in the first instance, have been unsafe, and that a continuance of the present number would, in a more advanced stage of population, be a very inadequate representation of the people.

Whence is the dreaded augmentation of expense to spring? One source indicated, is the multiplication of offices under the new government. Let us examine this a little.

It is evident that the principal departments of the administration under the present government, are the same which will be required under the new. There are now a Secretary of War, a Secretary of Foreign Affairs, a Secretary for Domestic Affairs, a Board of Treasury, consisting of three persons, a Treasurer, assistants, clerks, etc. These officers are indispensable under any system, and will suffice under the new as well as the old. As to ambassadors and other ministers and agents in foreign countries, the proposed Constitution can make no other difference than to render their characters, where they reside, more respectable, and their services more useful. As to persons to be employed in the collection of the revenues, it is unquestionably true that these will form a very

considerable addition to the number of federal officers; but it will not follow that this will occasion an increase of public expense. It will be in most cases nothing more than an exchange of State for national officers. In the collection of all duties, for instance, the persons employed will be wholly of the latter description. The States individually will stand in no need of any for this purpose. What difference can it make in point of expense to pay officers of the customs appointed by the State or by the United States? There is no good reason to suppose that either the number or the salaries of the latter will be greater than those of the former.

Where then are we to seek for those additional articles of expense which are to swell the account to the enormous size that has been represented to us? The chief item which occurs to me respects the support of the judges of the United States. I do not add the President, because there is now a president of Congress, whose expenses may not be far, if any thing, short of those which will be incurred on account of the President of the United States. The support of the judges will clearly be an extra expense, but to what extent will depend on the particular plan which may be adopted in regard to this matter. But upon no reasonable plan can it amount to a sum which will be an object of material consequence.

Let us now see what there is to counterbalance any extra expense that may attend the establishment of the proposed government. The first thing which presents itself is that a great part of the business which now keeps Congress sitting through the year will be transacted by the President. Even the management of foreign negotiations will naturally devolve upon him, according to general principles concerted with the Senate, and subject to their final concurrence. Hence it is evident that a portion of the year will suffice for the session of both the Senate and the House of Representatives; we may suppose about a fourth for the latter and a third, or perhaps half, for the former. The extra business of treaties and appointments may give this extra occupation to the Senate. From this circumstance we may infer that, until the House of Representatives shall be increased greatly beyond its present number, there will be a considerable saving of expense from the difference between the constant session of the present and the temporary session of the future Congress.

But there is another circumstance of great importance in the view of economy. The business of the United States has hitherto occupied the State legislatures, as well as Congress. The latter has made requisitions which the former have had to provide for. Hence it has happened that the sessions of the State legislatures have been protracted greatly beyond what was necessary for the execution of the mere local business of the States. More than half their time has been frequently employed in matters which related to the United States. Now the members who compose the legislatures of the several States amount to two thousand and upwards, which number has hitherto performed what under the new system will be done in the first instance by sixty-five persons, and probably at no future period by above a fourth or fifth of that number. The Congress under the proposed government will do all the business of the United States themselves, without the intervention of the State legislatures, who thenceforth will have only to attend to the affairs of their particular States, and will not have to sit in any proportion as long as they have heretofore done. This difference in the time of the sessions of the State legislatures will be clear gain, and will alone form an article of saving, which may be regarded as an equivalent for any additional objects of expense that may be occasioned by the adoption of the new system.

The result from these observations is that the sources of additional expense from the establishment of the proposed Constitution are much fewer than may have been imagined; that they are counterbalanced by considerable objects of saving; and that while it is questionable on which side the scale will preponderate, it is certain that a government less expensive would be incompetent to the purposes of the Union.

PUBLIUS

1. *Vide* Blackstone's *Commentaries*, Vol. 1, p. 136.

2. *Idem*, Vol. 4, p. 438.

3. To show that there is a power in the Constitution by which the liberty of the press may be affected, recourse has been had to the power of taxation. It is said that duties may be laid upon the publications so high as to amount to a prohibition. I know not by what logic it could be maintained, that the declarations in the State constitutions, in favor of the freedom of the press, would be a constitutional impediment to the imposition of duties upon publications by the State legislatures. It cannot certainly be pretended that any degree of duties, however low, would be an abridgment of the liberty of the press. We know that newspapers are taxed in Great Britain, and yet it is notorious that the press nowhere enjoys greater liberty than in that country. And if duties

of any kind may be laid without a violation of that liberty, it is evident that the extent must depend on legislative discretion, respecting the liberty of the press, will give it no greater security than it will have without them. The same invasions of it may be effected under the State constitutions which contain those declarations through the means of taxation, as under the proposed Constitution, which has nothing of the kind. It would be quite as significant to declare that government ought to be free, that taxes ought not to be excessive, etc., as that the liberty of the press ought not to be restrained.

4. *Vide* Rutherford's *Institutes*, Vol. 2, Book II, Chapter X, Sections XIV and XV. Vide also Grotius, Book II, Chapter IX, Sections VIII and IX.

JAMES MADISON, LETTER TO THOMAS JEFFERSON ON THE NECESSITY OF A BILL OF RIGHTS

October 17, 1788

Dear Sir

[Madison comments on previous correspondence from Jefferson and on the situation in Congress and expresses concern that John Adams might (as he eventually did) become the first vice-president.]

The little pamphlet herewith inclosed will give you a collective view of the alterations which have been proposed for the new Constitution. Various and numerous as they appear they certainly omit many of the true grounds of opposition. The articles relating to Treaties—to paper money, and to contracts, created more enemies than all the errors in the System positive & negative put together. It is true nevertheless that not a few, particularly in Virginia have contended for the proposed alterations from the most honorable & patriotic motives; and that among the advocates for the Constitution, there are some who wish for further guards to public liberty & individual rights. As far as these may consist of a constitutional declaration of the most essential rights, it is probable they will be added; though there are many who think such addition unnecessary, and not a few who think it misplaced in such a Constitution. There is scarce any point on which the party in opposition is so much divided as to its importance and its propriety. My own opinion has always been in favor of a bill of rights; provided it be so framed as not to imply powers not meant to be included in the enumeration. At the same time I have never thought the omission a material defect, nor been anxious to supply it even by subsequent amendment, for any other reason than that it is anxiously desired by others. I have favored it because I supposed it might be of use, and if properly executed could not be of disservice. I have not viewed it in an important light 1. because I conceive that in a certain degree, though not in the extent argued by Mr. [James] Wilson, the rights in question are reserved by the manner in which the federal powers are granted. 2. because there is great reason to fear that a positive declaration of some of the most essential rights could not be obtained in the requisite latitude. I am sure that the rights of Conscience in particular, if submitted to public definition would be narrowed much more than they are likely ever to be by an assumed power. One of the objections in New England was that the Constitution by prohibiting religious tests, opened a door for Jews, Turks & infidels. 3. because the limited powers of the federal Government and the jealousy of the subordinate Governments, afford a security which has not existed in the case of the State Governments, and exists in no other. 4. because experience proves the inefficacy of a bill of rights on those occasions when its controul is most needed. Repeated violations of these parchment barriers have been committed by overbearing majorities in every State. In Virginia I have seen the bill of rights violated in every instance where it has been opposed to a popular current.

Notwithstanding the explicit provision contained in that instrument for the rights of Conscience it is well known that a religious establishment wd. have taken place in that State, if the legislative majority had found as they expected, a majority of the people in favor of the measure; and I am persuaded that if a majority of the people were now of one sect, the measure would still take place and on narrower ground than was then proposed, notwithstanding the additional obstacle which the law has since created. Wherever the real power in a Government lies, there is the danger of oppression. In our Governments the real power lies in the majority of the Community, and the invasion of private rights is chiefly to be apprehended, not from acts of Government contrary to the sense of its constituents, but from acts in which the Government is the mere instrument of the major number of the constituents. This is a truth of great importance, but not yet sufficiently attended to: and is probably more strongly impressed on my mind by facts, and reflections suggested by them, than on yours which has contemplated abuses of power issuing from a very different quarter. Wherever there is an interest and power to do wrong, wrong will generally be done, and not less readily by a powerful & interested party than by a powerful and interested prince. The difference, so far as it relates to the superiority of republics over monarchies, lies in the less degree of probability that interest may prompt abuses of power in the former than in the latter; and in the security in the former agst. oppression of more than the smaller part of the society, whereas in the former it may be extended in a manner to the whole. The difference so far as it relates to the point in question—the efficacy of a bill of rights in controuling abuses of power—lies in this, that in a monarchy the latent force of the nation is superior to that of the sovereign, and a solemn charter of popular rights, must have a great effect, as a standard for trying the validity of public acts, and a signal for rousing & uniting the superior force of the community; whereas in a popular Government, the political and physical power may be considered as vested in the same hands, that is in a majority of the people, and consequently the tyrannical will of the sovereign is not [to] be controuled by the dread of an appeal to any other force within the community. What use then it may be asked can a bill of rights serve in popular Governments? I answer the two following which though less essential than in other Governments, sufficiently recommend the precaution. 1. The political truths declared in that solemn manner acquire by degrees the character of fundamental maxims of free Government, and as they become incorporated with the national sentiment, counteract the impulses of interest and passion. 2. Altho' it be generally true as above stated that the danger of oppression lies in the interested majorities of the people rather than in usurped acts of the Government, yet there may be occasions on which the evil may spring from the latter source; and on such, a bill of rights will be a good ground for an appeal to the sense of the community. Perhaps too there may be a certain degree of danger, that a succession of artful and ambitious rulers, may by gradual & well-timed advances, finally erect an independent Government on the subversion of liberty. Should this danger exist at all, it is prudent to guard against it, especially when the precaution can do no injury. At the same time I must own that I see no tendency in our governments to danger on that side. It has been remarked that there is a tendency in all Governments to an augmentation of power at the expence of liberty. But the remark as usually understood does not appear to me well founded. Power when it has attained a certain degree of energy and independence goes on generally to further degrees. But when below that degree, the direct tendency is to further degrees of relaxation, until the abuses of liberty beget a sudden transition to an undue degree of power. With this explanation the remark may be true; and in the latter sense only, is it in my opinion applicable to the Governments in America. It is a melancholy reflection that liberty should be equally exposed to danger whether the Government have too much or too little power, and that the line which divides these extremes should be so inaccurately defined by experience.

Supposing a bill of rights to be proper the articles which ought to compose it, admit of much discussion. I am inclined to think that absolute restrictions in cases that are doubtful, or where emergencies may overrule them, ought to be avoided. The restrictions however strongly marked on paper will never be regarded when opposed to the decided sense of the public; and after repeated violations in extraordinary cases, they will lose even their ordinary efficacy. Should a Rebellion or insurrection alarm the people as well as the Government, and a suspension of the Hab. corp. be dictated by the alarm, no written prohibitions on earth would prevent the measure. Should an army in time of peace be gradually established in our neighbourhood by Britn. or Spain, declarations on paper would have as little effect in preventing a standing force for the public safety. The best security agst. these evils is to remove the pretext for them. With regard to monopolies they are justly classed among the greatest nusances in Government. But it is clear that as encouragements to literary works and ingenious discoveries, they are not too valuable to be wholly renounced? Would it not suffice to require in all cases a reserved right to the Public to abolish the privilege at a price to be specified in the grant of it? Is there not also infinitely less danger of this abuse in our Governments, than in most others? Monopolies are sacrifices of the many to the few. Where the power is in the few it is natural for them to sacrifice the many to their own partialities and corruptions. Where the power, as with us, is in the many not in the few, the danger can not be very great that the few will be thus favored. It is much more to be dreaded that the few will be unnecessarily sacrificed to the many.

I inclose a paper containing the late proceedings in Kentucky. I wish the ensuing Convention may take no step injurious to the character of the district, and favorable to the views of those who wish ill to the U. States. One of my late letters communicated some circumstances which will not fail to occur on perusing the objects of the proposed Convention in next month. Perhaps however there may be less connection between the two cases than at first one is ready to conjecture.

I am Dr Sir with the sincerest esteem & Affectn, Yours, Js. Madison Jr

Letters of Delegates to Congress: Volume 25 March 1, 1788—December 31, 1789: 427–431.

http://memory.loc.gov/cgi-bin/query/r?ammem/hlaw:@field-DOCID+@let-dg025311%

THOMAS JEFFERSON, LETTER TO JAMES MADISON

Paris, March 15, 1789

Your thoughts on the subject of the declaration of rights in the letter of October the 17th, I have weighed with great satisfaction. Some of them had not occurred to me before, but were acknowledged just in the moment they were presented to my mind. In the arguments in favor of a declaration of rights, you omit one which has great weight with me; the legal check which it puts into the hands of the judiciary. This is a body, which, if rendered independent, and kept strictly to their own department, merits great confidence would be too much, for a body composed of such men as [George] Wythe, [John] Blair, and [Edmund] Pendleton? On characters like these, the "*civium ardor prava jubentium*" [allusion to a phrase of Horace often translated "not by the rage of the crowd"] would make no impression. I am happy to find that, on the whole, you are a friend to this amendment. The declaration of rights is, like all other human blessings, alloyed with some inconveniences, and not accomplishing fully its object. But the good of this instance vastly overweighs the evil. I cannot refrain from making short answers to the objections which your letter states to have raised. 1. That the rights in question are reserved by the manner in which the federal powers are granted. Answer. A constitutive act may, certainly, be so formed, as to need no declaration of rights. The act itself has the force of a declaration, as far as it goes; and if it goes to all material points, nothing more is wanting. In the draught of a constitution which I had once a thought of proposing in Virginia, and printed afterwards, I endeavored to reach all the great objects of public liberty, and did not mean to add a declaration of rights. Probably the object was imperfectly executed; but the deficiencies would have been supplied by others, in the course of discussion. But in a constitutive act which leaves some precious articles unnoticed, and raises implications against others, a declaration of rights becomes necessary, by way of supplement. This is the case of our new federal Constitution. This instrument forms us into one State, as to certain objects, and gives us a legislative and executive body for these objects. It should, therefore, guard us against their abuses of power, within the field submitted to them. 2. A positive declaration of some essential rights could not be obtained in the requisite latitude. Answer. Half a loaf is better than no bread. If we cannot secure all our rights, let us secure what we can. 3. The limited powers of the federal government, and jealousy of the subordinate governments, afford a security which exists in no other instance. Answer. The first member of this seems resolvable into the first objection before stated. The jealousy of the subordinate governments is a precious reliance. But observe that those governments are only agents. They must have principles furnished them, whereon to found their opposition. The declaration of rights will be the text, whereby they will try all the acts of the federal government. In this view, it is necessary to the federal government also; as by the same text they may try the opposition of the subordinate governments. 4. Experience proves the inefficacy of a bill of rights. True. But though it is not absolutely efficacious under all circumstances, it is of great potency always, and rarely inefficacious. A brace the more will often keep up the building which would have fallen with that brace the less. There is a remarkable difference between the character of the inconveniencies which attend a declaration of rights, and those which attend the want of it. The inconveniences of the declaration are, that it may cramp government in its useful exertions. But the evil of this is short-lived, moderate and reparable. The inconveniencies of the want of a declaration are permanent, afflicting and irreparable. They are in constant progression from bad to worse. The executive, in our governments, is not the sole, it is scarcely the principal object of my jealousy. The tyranny of the legislatures is the most formidable dread at present, and will be for many years. That of the executive will come in its turn; but it will be at a remote period. I know there are some among us, who would now establish a monarchy. But they are inconsiderable in number and weight of character. The rising race are all republicans. We were educated in royalism; no wonder if some of us retain that idolatry still. Our young people are educated in republicanism; an apostacy from that to royalism, is unprecedented and impossible. I am much pleased with the prospect that a declaration of rights will be added; and hope it will be done in that way which will not endanger the whole frame of the government, or any essential part of it.

The Papers of Thomas Jefferson. Edited by Julian P. Boyd et al. Princeton: Princeton University Press, 1950. 14:659–661.

JAMES MADISON PROPOSES THE BILL OF RIGHTS TO THE HOUSE OF REPRESENTATIVES

June 8, 1789

I am sorry to be accessory to the loss of a single moment of time by the house. If I had been indulged in my motion, and we had gone into a committee of the whole, I think we might have rose, and resumed the consideration of other business before this time; that is, so far as it depended on what I proposed to bring forward. As that mode seems not to give satisfaction, I will withdraw the motion, and move you, sir, that a select committee be appointed to consider and report such amendments as are proper for Congress to propose to the legislatures of the several States, conformably to the 5th article of the constitution.

I will state my reasons why I think it proper to propose amendments; and state the amendments themselves, so far as I think they ought to be proposed. If I thought I could fulfill the duty which I owe to myself and my constituents, to let the subject pass over in silence, I most certainly should not trespass upon the indulgence of this house. But I cannot do this; and am therefore compelled to beg a patient hearing to what I have to lay before you. And I do most sincerely believe that if congress will devote but one day to this subjects, so far as to satisfy the public that we do not disregard their wishes, it will have a salutary influence on the public councils, and prepare the way for a favorable reception of our future measures.

It appears to me that this house is bound by every motive of prudence, not to let the first session pass over without proposing to the state legislatures some things to be incorporated into the constitution, as will render it as acceptable to the whole people of the United States, as it has been found acceptable to a majority of them. I wish, among other reasons why something should be done, that those who have been friendly to the adoption of this constitution, may have the opportunity of proving to those who were opposed to it, that they were as sincerely devoted to liberty and a republican government, as those who charged them with wishing the adoption of this constitution in order to lay the foundation of an aristocracy or despotism. It will be a desirable thing to extinguish from the bosom of every member of the community any apprehensions, that there are those among his countrymen who wish to deprive them of the liberty for which they valiantly fought and honorably bled. And if there are amendments desired, of such a nature as will not injure the constitution, and they can be engrafted so as to give satisfaction to the doubting part of our fellow citizens; the friends of the federal government will evince that spirit of deference and concession for which they have hitherto been distinguished.

It cannot be a secret to the gentlemen in this house, that, notwithstanding the ratification of this system of government by eleven of the thirteen United States, in some cases unanimously, in others by large majorities; yet still there is a great number of our constituents who are dissatisfied with it; among whom are many respectable for their talents, their patriotism, and respectable for the jealousy they have for their liberty, which, though mistaken in its object, is laudable in its motive. There is a great body of the people falling under this description, who at present feel much inclined to join their support to the cause of federalism, if they were satisfied in this one point: We ought not to disregard their inclination, but, on principles of amity and moderation, conform to their wishes, and expressly declare the great rights of mankind secured under this constitution. The acquiescence which our fellow citizens show under the government, calls upon us for a like return of moderation. But perhaps there is a stronger motive than this for our going into a consideration of the subject; it is to provide those securities for liberty which are required by a part of the community. I allude in a particular manner to those two states who have not thought fit to throw themselves into the bosom of the confederacy: it is a desirable thing, on our part as well as theirs, that a re-union should take place as soon as possible. I have no doubt, if we proceed to take those steps which would be prudent and requisite at this juncture, that in a short time we should see that disposition prevailing in those states that are not come in, that we have seen prevailing [in] those states which are.

But I will candidly acknowledge, that, over and above all these considerations, I do conceive that the constitution may be amended; that is to say, if all power is subject to abuse, that then it is possible the abuse of the powers of the general government may be guarded against in a more secure manner than is now done, while no one advantage, arising from the exercise of that power, shall be damaged or endangered by it. We have in this way something to gain, and, if we proceed with caution, nothing to lose; and in this case it is necessary to proceed with caution; for while we feel all these inducements to go into a revisal of the constitution, we must feel for the constitution itself, and make that revisal a moderate one. I should be unwilling to see a door opened for a re-consideration of the whole structure of the government, for a re-consideration of the principles and the substance of the powers given; because I doubt, if such a door was opened, if we should be very likely to stop at that point which would be safe to the government itself: But I do wish to see a door opened to consider, so far as to incorporate those provisions for the security of rights, against which I believe no serious objection has been made by any class of our constituents, such as would be likely to meet with the concurrence of two-thirds of both houses, and the approbation of three-fourths of the state legislatures. I will not propose a single alteration which I do not wish to see take place, as intrinsically proper in itself, or proper because it is wished for by a respectable number of my fellow citizens; and therefore I shall not propose a single alteration but is likely to meet the concurrence required by the constitution.

There have been objections of various kinds made against the constitution: Some were levelled against its structure, because the president was without a council; because the senate, which is a legislative body, had judicial powers in trials on impeachments; and because the powers of that body were compounded in other respects, in a manner that did not correspond with a particular theory; because it grants more power than is supposed to be necessary for every good purpose; and controls the ordinary powers of the state governments. I know some respectable characters who opposed this government on these grounds; but I believe that the great mass of the people who opposed it, disliked it because it did not contain effectual provision against encroachments on particular rights, and those safeguards which they have been long accustomed to have interposed between them and the magistrate who exercised the sovereign power: nor ought we to consider them safe, while a great number of our fellow citizens think these securities necessary.

It has been a fortunate thing that the objection to the government has been made on the ground I stated; because it will be practicable on that ground to obviate the objection, so far as to satisfy the public mind that their liberties will be perpetual, and this without endangering any part of the constitution, which is considered as essential to the existence of the government by those who promoted its adoption.

The amendments which have occurred to me, proper to be recommended by congress to the state legislatures are these:

First. That there be prefixed to the constitution a declaration—

That all power is originally vested in, and consequently derived from the people.

That government is instituted, and ought to be exercised for the benefit of the people; which consists in the enjoyment of life and liberty, with the right of acquiring and using property, and generally of pursuing and obtaining happiness and safety.

That the people have an indubitable, unalienable, and indefeasible right to reform or change their government, whenever it be found adverse or inadequate to the purposes of its institution.

Secondly. That in article 2nd. section 2, clause 3, these words be struck out, to wit, "The number of representatives shall not exceed one for every thirty thousand, but each state shall have at least one representative, and until such enumeration shall be made." And that in place thereof be inserted these words, to wit, "After the first actual enumeration, there shall be one representative for every thirty thousand, until the number amount to after which the proportion shall be so regulated by congress, that the number shall never be less than nor more than but each state shall after the first enumeration, have at least two representatives; and prior thereto."

Thirdly. That in article 2nd, section 6, clause 1, there be added to the end of the first sentence, these words, to wit, "But no law varying the compensation last ascertained shall operate before the next ensuing election of representatives."

Fourthly. That in article 2nd, section 9, between clauses 3 and 4, be inserted these clauses, to wit,

The civil rights of none shall be abridged on account of religious belief or worship, nor shall any national religion be established, nor shall the full and equal rights of conscience by in any manner, or on any pretext infringed.

The people shall not be deprived or abridged of their right to speak, to write, or to publish their sentiments; and the freedom of the press, as one of the great bulwarks of liberty, shall be inviolable.

The people shall not be restrained from peaceably assembling and consulting for their common good, nor from applying to the legislature by petitions, or remonstrances for redress of their grievances.

The right of the people to keep and bear arms shall not be infringed; a well armed, and well regulated militia being the best security of a free country: but no person religiously scrupulous of bearing arms, shall be compelled to render military service in person.

No soldier shall in time of peace be quartered in any house without the consent of the owner; nor at any time, but in a manner warranted by law.

No person shall be subject, except in cases of impeachment, to more than one punishment, or one trial for the same office; nor shall be compelled to be a witness against himself; nor be deprived of life, liberty, or property without due process of law; nor be obliged to relinquish his property, where it may be necessary for public use, without a just compensation.

Excessive bail shall not be required, nor excessive fines imposed, nor cruel and unusual punishments inflicted.

The rights of the people to be secured in their persons, their houses, their papers, and their other property from all unreasonable searches and seizures, shall not be violated by warrants issued without probable cause, supported by oath or affirmation, or not particularly describing the places to be searched, or the persons or things to be seized.

In all criminal prosecutions, the accused shall enjoy the right to a speedy and public trial, to be informed of the cause and nature of the accusation, to be confronted with his accusers, and the witnesses against him; to have a compulsory process for obtaining witnesses in his favor; and to have the assistance of counsel for his defense.

The exceptions here or elsewhere in the constitution, made in favor of particular rights, shall not be so construed as to diminish the just importance of other rights retained by the people; or as to enlarge the powers delegated by the constitution; but either as actual limitations of such powers, or as inserted merely for greater caution.

Fifthly. That in article 2nd, section 10, between clauses 1 and 2, be inserted this clause, to wit: No state shall violate the equal rights of conscience, or the freedom of the press, or the trial by jury in criminal cases.

Sixthly. That article 3rd, section 2, be annexed to the end of clause 2nd, these words to wit: but no appeal to such court shall be allowed where the value in controversy shall not amount to___dollars: nor shall any fact triable by jury, according to the course of common law, be otherwise re-examinable than may consist with the principles of common law.

Seventhly. That in article 3rd, section 2, the third clause be struck out, and in its place be inserted the classes following, to wit:

The trial of all crimes (except in cases of impeachments, and cases arising in the land or naval forces, or the militia when on actual service in time of war or public danger) shall be by an impartial jury of freeholders of the vicinage, with the requisite of unanimity for conviction, of the right of challenge, and other accustomed requisites; and in all crimes punishable with loss of life or member, presentment or indictment by a grand jury shall be an essential preliminary, provided that in cases of crimes committed within any county which may be in possession of an enemy, or in which a general insurrection may prevail, the trial may by law be authorized in some other county of the same state, as near as may be to the seat of the offence.

In cases of crimes committed not within any county, the trial may by law be in such county as the laws shall have prescribed. In suits at common law, between man and man, the trial by jury, as one of the best securities to the rights of the people, ought to remain inviolate.

Eighthly. That immediately after article 6th, be inserted, as article 7th, the clauses following, to wit:

The powers delegated by this constitution, are appropriated to the departments to which they are respectively distributed: so that the legislative department shall never exercise the powers vested in the executive or judicial; nor the executive exercise the powers vested in the legislative or judicial; nor the judicial exercise the powers vested in the legislative or executive departments.

The powers not delegated by this constitution, nor prohibited by it to the states, are reserved to the States respectively.

Ninthly. That article 7th, be numbered as article 8th.

The first of these amendments, relates to what may be called a bill of rights; I will own that I never considered this provision so essential to the federal constitution, as to make it improper to ratify it, until such an amendment was added; at the same time, I always conceived, that in a certain form and to a certain extent, such a provision was neither improper nor altogether useless. I am aware, that a great number of the most respectable friends to the government and champions for republican liberty, have thought such a provision, not only unnecessary, but even improper, nay, I believe some have gone so far as to think it even dangerous. Some policy has been made use of perhaps by gentlemen on both sides of the question: I acknowledge the ingenuity of those arguments which were drawn against the constitution, by a comparison with the policy of Great Britain, in establishing a declaration of rights; but there is too great a difference in the case to warrant the comparison: therefore the arguments drawn from that source, were in a great measure inapplicable. In the declaration of rights which that country has established, the truth is, they have gone no farther, than to raise a barrier against the power of the crown; the power of the legislature is left altogether indefinite. Although I know whenever the great rights, the trial by jury, freedom of the press, or liberty of conscience, came in question in that body, the invasion of them is resisted by able advocates, yet their Magna Charta does not contain any one provision for the security of those rights, respecting which, the people of America are most alarmed. The freedom of the press and rights of conscience, those choicest privileges of the people, are unguarded in the British constitution.

But although the case may be widely different, and it may not be thought necessary to provide limits for the legislative power in that country, yet a different opinion prevails in the United States. The people of many states, have thought it necessary to raise barriers against power in all forms and departments of government, and I am inclined to believe, if once bills of rights are established in all the states as well as the federal constitution, we shall find the although some of them are rather unimportant, yet, upon the whole, they will have a salutary tendency.

It may be said, in some instances they do no more than state the perfect equality of mankind; this to be sure is an absolute truth, yet it is not absolutely necessary to be inserted at the head of a constitution.

In some instances they assert those rights which are exercised by the people in forming and establishing a plan of government. In other instances, they specify those rights which are retained when particular powers are given up to be exercised by the legislature. In other instances, they specify positive rights, which may seem to result from the nature of the compact. Trial by jury cannot be considered as a natural right, but a right resulting from the social compact which regulates the action of the community, but is as essential to secure the liberty of the people as any one of the pre-existent rights of nature. In other instances they lay down dogmatic maxims with respect to the construction of the government; declaring, that the legislative, executive, and judicial branches shall be kept separate and distinct: Perhaps the best way of securing this in practice is to provide such checks, as will prevent the encroachment of the one upon the other.

But whatever may be form which the several states have adopted in making declarations in favor of particular rights, the great object in view is to limit and qualify the powers of government, by excepting out of the grant of power those cases in which the government ought not to act, or to act only in a particular mode. They point these exceptions sometimes against the abuse of the executive power, sometimes against the legislative, and, in some cases, against the community itself; or, in other words, against the majority in favor of the minority.

In our government it is, perhaps, less necessary to guard against the abuse in the executive department than any other; because it is not the stronger branch of the system, but the weaker: It therefore must be levelled against the legislative, for it is the most powerful, and most likely to be abused, because it is under the least control; hence, so far as a declaration of rights can tend to prevent the exercise of undue power, it cannot be doubted but such declaration is proper. But I confess that I do conceive, that in a government modified like this of the United States, the great danger lies rather in the abuse of the community than in the legislative body. The prescriptions in favor of liberty, ought to be levelled against that quarter where the greatest danger lies, namely, that which possesses the highest prerogative of power: But this [is] not found in either the executive or legislative departments of government, but in the body of the people, operating by the majority against the minority.

It may be thought all paper barriers against the power of the community are too weak to be worthy of attention. I am sensible they are not so strong as to satisfy gentlemen of every description who have seen and examined thoroughly the texture of such a defence; yet, as they have a tendency to impress some degree of respect for them, to establish the public opinion in their favor, and rouse the attention of the whole community, it may be one mean to control the majority from those acts to which they might be otherwise inclined.

It has been said by way of objection to a bill of rights, by many respectable gentlemen out of doors, and I find opposition on the same principles likely to be made by gentlemen on this floor, that they are unnecessary articles of a republican government, upon the presumption that the people have those rights in their own hands, and that is the proper place for them to rest. It would be a sufficient answer to say that this objection lies against such provisions under the state governments as well as under the general government; and there are, I believe, but few gentlemen who are inclined to push their theory so far as to say that a declaration of rights in those cases is either ineffectual or improper.

It has been said that in the federal government they are unnecessary, because the powers are enumerated, and it follows that all that are not granted by the constitution are retained: that the constitution is a bill of powers, the great residuum being the rights of the people; and therefore a bill of rights cannot be so necessary as if the residuum was thrown into the hands of the government. I admit that these arguments are not entirely without foundation; but they are not conclusive to the extent which has been supposed. It is true the powers of the general government are circumscribed; they are directed to particular objects; but even if government keeps within those limits, it has certain discretionary powers with respect to the means, which may admit of abuse to a certain extent, in the same manner as the powers of the state governments under their constitutions may to an indefinite extent; because in the constitution of the United States there is a clause granting to Congress the power to make all laws which shall be necessary and proper for carrying into execution all the powers vested in the government of the United States, or in any department or officer thereof; this enables them to fulfil every purpose for which the government was established. Now, may not laws be considered necessary and proper by Congress, for it is them who are to judge of the necessity and propriety to accomplish those special purposes which they may have in contemplation, which laws in themselves are neither necessary or proper; as well as improper laws could be enacted by the state legislatures, for fulfilling the more extended objects of those governments. I will state an instance which I think in point, and proves that this might be the case. The general government has a right to pass all laws which shall be necessary to collect its revenue; the means for enforcing the collection are within the direction of the legislature: may not general warrants be considered necessary for this purpose, as well as for some purposes which it was supposed at the framing of their constitutions the state governments had in view? If there was reason for restraining the state governments from exercising this power, there is like reason for restraining the federal government.

It may be said, because it has been said, that a bill of rights is not necessary, because the establishment of this government has not repealed those declarations of rights which are added to the several state constitutions: that those rights of the people, which had been established by the most solemn act, could not be annihilated by a subsequent act of the people, who meant, and declared at the head of the instrument, that they ordained and established a new system, for the express purpose of securing to themselves and posterity the liberties they had gained by an arduous conflict.

I admit the force of this observation, but I do not look upon it to be conclusive. In the first place, it is too uncertain ground to leave this provision upon, if a provision is at all necessary to secure rights so important as many of those I have mentioned are conceived to be, by the public in general, as well as those in particular who opposed the adoption of this constitution. Beside some states have no bills of rights, there are others provided with very defective ones, and there are others whose bills of rights are not only defective, but absolutely improper; instead of securing some in the full extent which republican principles would require, they limit them too much to agree with the common ideas of liberty.

It has been objected also against a bill of rights, that, by enumerating particular exceptions to the grant of power, it would disparage those rights which were not placed in that enumeration, and it might follow by implication, that those rights which were not singled out, were intended to be assigned into the hands of the general government, and were consequently insecure. This is one of the most plausible arguments I have ever heard urged against the admission of a bill of rights into this system; but, I conceive, that may be guarded against. I have attempted it, as gentlemen may see by turning to the last clause of the 4th resolution.

It has been said, that it is necessary to load the constitution with this provision, because it was not found effectual in the constitution of the particular states. It is true, there are a few particular states in which some of the most valuable articles have not, at one time or other, been violated; but does it not follow but they may have, to a certain degree, a salutary effect against the abuse of power. If they are incorporated into the constitution, independent tribunals of justice will consider themselves in a peculiar manner the guardians of those rights; they will be an impenetrable bulwark against every assumption of power in the legislative or executive; they will be naturally led to resist every encroachment upon rights expressly stipulated for in the constitution by the declaration of rights. Beside this security, there is a great probability that such a declaration in the federal system would be enforced; because the state legislatures will jealously and closely watch the operation of this government, and be able to resist with more effect every assumption of power than any other power on earth can do; and the greatest opponents to a federal government admit the state legislatures to be sure guardians of the people's liberty. I conclude from this view of the subject, that it will be proper in itself, and highly politic, for the tranquility of the public mind, and the stability of the government, that we should offer something, in the form I have proposed, to be incorporated in the system of government, as a declaration of the rights of the people.

In the next place I wish to see that part of the constitution revised which declares, that the number of representatives shall not exceed the proportion of one for every thirty thousand persons, and allows one representative to every state which rates below that proportion. If we attend to the discussion of this subject, which has taken place in the state conventions, and even in the opinion of the friends to the constitution, an alteration here is proper. It is the sense of the people of America, that the number of representatives ought to be increased, but particularly that it should not be left in the discretion of the government to diminish them, below that proportion which certainly is in the power of the legislature as the constitution now stands; and they may, as the population of the country increases, increase the house of representatives to a very unwieldy degree. I confess I always thought this part of the constitution defective, though not dangerous; and that it ought to be particularly attended to whenever congress should go into the consideration of amendments.

There are several lesser cases enumerated in my proposition, in which I wish also to see some alteration take place. That article which leaves it in the power of the legislature to ascertain its own emolument is one to which I allude. I do not believe this is a power which, in the ordinary course of government, is likely to be abused, perhaps of all the powers granted, it is least likely to abuse; but there is a seeming impropriety in leaving any set of men without control to put their hand into the public coffers, to take out money to put in their pockets; there is a seeming indecorum in such power, which leads me to propose a change. We have a guide to this alteration in several of the amendments which the different conventions have proposed. I have gone therefore so far as to fix it, that no law, varying the compensation, shall operate until there is a change in the legislature; in which case it cannot be for the particular benefit of those who are concerned in determining the value of the service.

I wish also, in revising the constitution, we may throw into that section, which interdicts the abuse of certain powers in the state legislatures, some other provisions of equal if not greater importance than those already made. The words, "No state shall pass any bill of attainder, ex post facto law, &c." were wise and proper restrictions in the constitution. I think there is more danger of those powers being abused by the state governments than by the government of the United States. The same may be said of other powers which they possess, if not controlled by the general principle, that laws are unconstitutional which infringe the rights of the community. I should therefore wish to extend this interdiction, and add, as I have stated in the 5th resolution, that no state shall violate the equal right of conscience, freedom of the press, or trial by jury in criminal cases; because it is proper that every government should be disarmed of powers which trench upon those particular rights. I know in some of the state constitutions the power of the government is controlled by such a declaration, but others are not. I cannot see any reason against obtaining even a double security on those points; and nothing can give a more sincere proof of the attachment of those who opposed this constitution to these great and important rights, than to see them join in obtaining the security I have now proposed; because it must be admitted, on all hands, that the state governments are as liable to attack these invaluable privileges as the general government is, and therefore ought to be as cautiously guarded against.

I think it will be proper, with respect to the judiciary powers, to satisfy the public mind on those points which I have mentioned. Great inconvenience has been apprehended to suitors from the distance they would be dragged to obtain justice in the supreme court of the United States, upon an appeal on an action for a small debt. To remedy this, declare, that no appeal shall be made unless the matter in controversy amounts to a particular sum: This, with the regulations respecting jury trials in criminal cases, and suits at common law, it is to be hoped will quiet and reconcile the minds of the people to that part of the constitution.

I find, from looking into the amendments proposed by the state conventions, that several are particularly anxious that it should be declared in the constitution, that the powers not therein delegated, should be reserved to the several states. Perhaps words which may define this more precisely, than the whole of the instrument now does, may be considered as superfluous. I admit they may be deemed unnecessary; but there can be no harm in making such a declaration, if gentlemen will allow that the fact is as stated. I am sure I understand it so, and do therefore propose it.

These are the points on which I wish to see a revision of the constitution take place. How far they will accord with the sense of this body, I cannot take upon me absolutely to determine; but I believe every gentleman will readily admit that nothing is in contemplation, so far as I have mentioned, that can endanger the beauty of the government in any one important feature, even in the eyes of its most sanguine admirers. I have proposed nothing that does not appear to me as proper in itself, or eligible as patronized by a respectable number of our fellow citizens; and if we can make the constitution better in the opinion of those who are opposed to it, without weakening its frame, or abridging its usefulness, in the judgment of those who are attached to it, we act the part of wise and liberal men to make such alterations as shall produce that effect.

Having done what I conceived was my duty, in bringing before this house the subject of amendments, and also stated such as wish for and approve, and offered the reasons which occurred to me in their support; I shall content myself for the present with moving, that a committee be appointed to consider of and report such amendments as ought to be proposed by congress to the legislatures of the states, to become, if ratified by three-fourths thereof, part of the constitution of the United States. By agreeing to this motion, the subject may be going on in the committee, while other important business is proceeding to a conclusion in the house. I should advocate greater dispatch in the business of amendments, if I was not convinced of the absolute necessity there is of pursuing the organization of the government; because I think we should obtain the confidence of our fellow citizens, in proportion as we fortify the rights of the people against the encroachments of the government.

Congressional Register, I, 423–437 and *Gazette of the U.S.*, 10 and 13 June 1789.

THURGOOD MARSHALL, REFLECTIONS ON THE BICENTENNIAL OF THE UNITED STATES

San Francisco Patent and Trademark Law Association
Maui, Hawaii, May 6, 1987

1987 marks the 200th anniversary of the United States Constitution. A Commission has been established to coordinate the celebration. The official meetings, essay contests, and festivities have begun.

The planned commemoration will span three years, and I am told 1987 is "dedicated to the memory of the Founders and the document they drafted in Philadelphia." We are to "recall the achievements of our Founders and the knowledge and experience that inspired them, the nature of the government they established, its origins, its character, and its ends, and the rights and privileges of citizenship, as well as its attendant responsibilities."

Like many anniversary celebrations, the plan for 1987 takes particular events and holds them up as the source of all the very best that has followed. Patriotic feelings will surely swell, prompting proud proclamations of the wisdom, foresight, and sense of justice shared by the Framers and reflected in a written document now yellowed with age. This is unfortunate not in the patriotism itself, but the tendency for the celebration to oversimplify, and overlook the many other events that have been instrumental to our achievements as a nation. The focus of this celebration invites a complacent belief that the vision of those who debated and compromised in Philadelphia yielded the "more perfect Union" it is said we now enjoy.

I cannot accept this invitation, for I do not believe that the meaning of the Constitution was forever "fixed" at the Philadelphia Convention. Nor do I find the wisdom, foresight, and sense of justice exhibited by the Framers particularly profound. To the contrary, the government they devised was defective from the start, requiring several amendments, a civil war, and momentous social transformation to attain the system of constitutional government, and its respect for the individual freedoms and human rights, we hold as fundamental today. When contemporary Americans cite "The Constitution," they invoke a concept that is vastly different from what the Framers barely began to construct two centuries ago.

For a sense of the evolving nature of the Constitution we need look no further than the first three words of the document's preamble: "We the People." When the Founding Fathers used this phrase in 1787, they did not have in mind the majority of America's citizens. "We the People" included, in the words of the Framers, "the whole Number of free Persons." On a matter so basic as the right to vote, for example, Negro slaves were excluded, although they were counted for representational purposes at three-fifths each. Women did not gain the right to vote for over a hundred and thirty years.

These omissions were intentional. The record of the Framers' debates on the slave question is especially clear: The Southern States acceded to the demands of the New England States for giving Congress broad power to regulate commerce, in exchange for the right to continue the slave trade. The economic interests of the regions coalesced: New Englanders engaged in the "carrying trade" would profit from transporting slaves from Africa as well as goods produced in America by slave labor. The perpetuation of slavery ensured the primary source of wealth in the Southern States.

Despite this clear understanding of the role slavery would play in the new republic, use of the words "slaves" and "slavery" was carefully avoided in the original document. Political representation in the lower House of Congress was to be based on the population of "free Persons" in each State, plus three-fifths of all "other Persons." Moral principles against slavery, for those who had them, were compromised, with no explanation of the conflicting principles for which the American Revolutionary War had ostensibly been fought: the self-evident truths "that all men are created equal, that they are endowed by their Creator with certain unalienable Rights, that among these are Life, Liberty and the pursuit of Happiness."

It was not the first such compromise. Even these ringing phrases from the Declaration of Independence are filled with irony, for an early draft of what became that Declaration assailed the King of England for suppressing legislative attempts to end the slave trade and for encouraging slave rebellions. The final draft adopted in 1776 did not contain this criticism. And so again at the Constitutional Convention eloquent objections to the institution of slavery went unheeded, and its opponents eventually consented to a document which laid a foundation for the tragic events that were to follow.

Pennsylvania's Go[u]vern[eu]r Morris provides an example. He opposed slavery and the counting of slaves in determining the basis for representation in Congress. At the Convention he objected that

The inhabitant of Georgia [or] South Carolina who goes to the coast of Africa, and in defiance of the most sacred laws of humanity tears away his fellow creatures from their dearest connections and damns them to the most cruel bondages, shall have more votes in a Government instituted for protection of the rights of mankind, than the Citizen of Pennsylvania or New Jersey who views with a laudable horror, so nefarious a Practice.

And yet Go[u]vern[eu]r Morris eventually accepted the three-fifths accommodation. In fact, he wrote the final draft of the Constitution, the very document the bicentennial will commemorate.

As a result of compromise, the right of the southern States to continue importing slaves was extended, officially, at least until 1808. We know that it actually lasted a good deal longer, as the Framers possessed no monopoly on the ability to trade moral principles for self-interest. But they nevertheless set an unfortunate example. Slaves could be imported, if the commercial interests of the North were protected. To make the compromise even more palatable, customs duties would be imposed at up to ten dollars per slave as a means of raising public revenues.

No doubt it will be said, when the unpleasant truth of the history of slavery in America is mentioned during this bicentennial year, that the Constitution was a product of its times, and embodied a compromise which, under other circumstances, would not have been made. But the effects of the Framers' compromise have remained for generations. They arose from the contradiction between guaranteeing liberty and justice to all, and denying both to Negroes.

The original intent of the phrase, "We the People," was far too clear for any ameliorating construction. Writing for the Supreme Court in 1857, Chief Justice Taney penned the following passage in the Dred Scott case, on the issue whether, in the eyes of the Framers, slaves were "constituent members of the sovereignty," and were to be included among "We the People":

We think they are not, and that they are not included, and were not intended to be included. . . . They had for more than a century before been regarded as beings of an inferior order, and altogether unfit to associate with the white race . . .; and so far inferior, that they had no rights which the white man was bound to respect; and that the Negro might justly and lawfully be reduced to slavery for his benefit. . . . [A]ccordingly, a Negro of the African race was regarded . . . as an article of property, and held, and bought and sold as such. . . . [N]o one seems to have doubted the correctness of the prevailing opinion of the time.

And so, nearly seven decades after the Constitutional Convention, the Supreme Court reaffirmed the prevailing opinion of the Framers regarding the rights of Negroes in America. It took a bloody civil war before the 13th Amendment could be adopted to abolish slavery, though not the consequences slavery would have for future Americans.

While the Union survived the civil war, the Constitution did not. In its place arose a new, more promising basis for justice and equality, the 14th Amendment, ensuring protection of the life, liberty, and property of all persons against deprivations without due process, and guaranteeing equal protection of the laws. And yet almost another century would pass before any significant recognition was obtained of the rights of black Americans to share equally even in such basic opportunities as education, housing, and employment, and to have their votes counted, and counted equally. In the meantime, blacks joined America's military to fight its wars and invested untold hours working in its factories and on its farms, contributing to the development of this country's magnificent wealth and waiting to share in its prosperity.

What is striking is the role legal principles have played throughout America's history in determining the condition of Negroes. They were enslaved by law, emancipated by law, disenfranchised and segregated by law; and, finally, they have begun to win equality by law. Along the way, new constitutional principles have emerged to meet the challenges of a changing society. The progress has been dramatic, and it will continue.

The men who gathered in Philadelphia in 1787 could not have envisioned these changes. They could not have imagined, nor would they have accepted, that the document they were drafting would one day be construed by a Supreme Court to which had been appointed a woman and the descendent of an African slave. "We the People" no longer enslave, but the credit does not belong to the Framers. It belongs to those who refused to acquiesce in outdated notions of "liberty," "justice," and "equality," and who strived to better them.

And so we must be careful, when focusing on the events which took place in Philadelphia two centuries ago, that we not overlook the momentous events which followed, and thereby lose our proper sense of perspective. Otherwise, the odds are that for many Americans the bicentennial celebration will be little more than a blind pilgrimage to the shrine of the original document now stored in a vault in the National Archives. If we seek, instead, a sensitive understanding of the Constitution's inherent defects, and its promising evolution through 200 years of history, the celebration of the "Miracle at Philadelphia" will, in my view, be a far more meaningful and humbling experience. We will see that the true miracle was not the birth of the Constitution, but its life, a life nurtured through two turbulent centuries of our own making, and a life embodying much good fortune that was not.

Thus, in this bicentennial year, we may not all participate in the festivities with flag-waving fervor. Some may more quietly commemorate the suffering, struggle, and sacrifice that has triumphed over much of what was wrong with the original document, and observe the anniversary with hopes not realized and promises not fulfilled. I plan to celebrate the bicentennial of the Constitution as a living document, including the Bill of Rights and the other amendments protecting individual freedoms and human rights.

Glossary

1924 Indian Citizenship Act: A 1924 law granting US citizenship to Native-Americans.

42 United States Code section 1983: This section of the 1871 Civil Rights Act is used by individuals to sue state and local officials when they believe their constitutional rights have been violated or that a constitutional tort has been committed against them. Federal officials can be sued under the doctrine developed in *Bivens v. Six Unknown Named FBI Agents.*

Academic Freedom: The right of instructors to teach or espouse ideas in the classroom or in their writings. Academic freedom is recognized as a First Amendment right in *Keyishian v. Board of Regents of the University of the State of New York.*

Accommodationists: Those who believe that government may accommodate religious exercises as long as it does not favor one religion over another.

Adversarial Due Process: A system in which lawyers bear the burden of making persuasive cases regarding the interpretation of the facts and the disposition of the law. Frequently, in this system, judges serve as referees and juries make determinations.

Advisory Opinions: Opinions that advise what a court would do in hypothetical situations; U.S. courts do not issue advisory opinions.

Advice and Consent: Constitutional term for the Senate's role in deciding whether to accept or reject treaties and presidential nominations to the judiciary and other posts.

Aggravating, Extenuating, and Mitigating Factors: The Supreme Court has ruled that juries must take these into account when arriving at sentencing verdicts in death penalty cases.

Alien and Sedition Acts: Acts passed by Federalists in 1798 that made it more difficult for immigrants to become citizens and also punished individuals who criticized the government or president of the United States.

***Amicus Curiae* Briefs:** "Friend of the court" briefs filed by nonparties to a suit who want to have a court consider their views on the matter.

Appellants: Losing parties in legal actions who file appeals.

Appellate Jurisdiction: The jurisdiction of higher courts to review judgments of lower trial courts. Courts generally limit appellate review to questions of law rather than determinations of facts.

Appellees: Winning parties in legal actions against whom appeals are filed.

Articles of Confederation: The government for the thirteen states that preceded the U.S. Constitution. Ratified in 1781, the Articles remained in effect until 1789.

***Ashwander* Rules:** A series of rules guiding the Supreme Court's interpretation that seek to avoid, when possible, decisions based on constitutional grounds. The basis for this rule resides in judicial restraint and presumptions of legislative deference found in the concepts of separation of powers.

Bad Tendency Test. A test, generally less deferential to speech than the clear and present danger test, whereby the Court allowed Congress to legislate against speech that has an inclination toward inciting or causing illegal activities.

Bail: A refundable payment that defendants are required to post in order to assure that they will return to court for trial. The Eighth Amendment prohibits bail from being "excessive."

Benevolent Discrimination: Statutory distinctions made between groups of individuals to enable a previously excluded group to participate more fully in society or to be better able to economically compete.

Bifurcated: Divided into two parts. The Supreme Court has ruled that the guilt and sentencing phases of capital punishment cases are to be so separated.

Bill of Exceptions: A written statement from a trial judge to the appellate court detailing litigant objections to court decisions during the trial and the rationale for protest.

Bills of Attainder: Legislative punishments without benefit of a trial, forbidden by Article I, Sections 8 and 9, of the Constitution.

Capital Punishment: Imposition of the death penalty.

***Carolene Products* Footnote Number 4:** This refers to Justice Stone's footnote number 4 in *United States v. Carolene Products,* where the Court articulates a constitutional approach to legislation that gives less presumption to a law's validity when it affects the Bill of Rights, the rights of discrete and insular minorities, and the operation of the political process.

Cases and Controversies: Language used in Article III that courts have interpreted to avoid giving advisory opinions when no litigants in a case have concrete interests at stake.

***Central Hudson Gas & Electric* Test:** In *Central Hudson Gas & Elec. Corp. v. Public Service Commission of New York* (447 U.S. 557, 1980), the Court devised a four-part test to determine whether commercial speech may be regulated. First, the expression must be protected by the First Amendment. For commercial speech to come within that provision, it must at least concern lawful activity and not be misleading. Second, the Court will ask if the asserted governmental interest to regulate the speech is substantial. If the expression is both protected and meets the "lawful but not misleading" condition, the Court will then ask if the regulation directly advances the governmental interest asserted. Finally, there must be assurance that the regulation is not more extensive than is necessary to serve the stated interest. If all four conditions are met, the commercial speech may be regulated.

Chattel Slavery: A system in which human beings are owned; not only with respect to their labor but also in their physical bodies, similar to livestock. This was outlawed in the United States by the Thirteenth Amendment (1865).

Checks and Balances: A system of government in which various branches and levels of government are designed to prevent abuse of powers by the others.

Chief Justice of the United States: Designated by the Constitution to preside over the U.S. Supreme Court, the chief is generally considered to be *primus inter pares*, or first among equals. By tradition, the chief either writes or assigns opinions when the chief is in the majority. The chief also presides over trials of presidential impeachments.

Civil Cases: Cases that involve disputes between private individuals.

Clear and Present Danger Test: First articulated by Justice Oliver Wendell Holmes in *Schenck v. United States,* 249 U.S. 47 (1919): Congress had the right to legislate against speech that led to a clear and present danger that Congress, in turn, had the right to prevent.

Color of the Law: An individual (generally a state actor) acting under the color of the law (e.g., in their official capacity) can be sued under 42 U.S.C. § 1983 for a violation of another's constitutional rights. Finding that someone has acted under the color of the law is often one way of determining whether state action exists.

Commercial Speech: Traditionally a form of speech that included advertising that was not protected under the First Amendment. However, beginning with *Virginia State Board of Pharmacy v. Virginia Citizens Consumer Council* (425 U.S. 748, 1976), the Court has provided constitutional protection for such speech, as long as it is truthful. Commercial speech does not receive the same level of protection accorded individual political speech. In *Central Hudson Gas & Elec. Corp. v. Public Service Commission of New York* the Court devised a test to determine when commercial speech may be regulated.

Common Law: The system of judge-made, or judge-discovered, law prominent in Great Britain, that has been adapted to the system of most U.S. states. Louisiana uses a civil law system, based on French and Spanish codes.

Company Town: Town wholly owned by a corporation. In *Marsh v. Alabama* (326 U.S. 501, 1946), the Supreme Court ruled that private towns may not ban the distribution of religious handbills in public places.

Concurring Opinion: An opinion in which a judge or justice indicates agreement with a court's decision but adds further explanation, sometimes justifying a decision on alternate grounds.

Constitutional Convention of 1787: A convention of fifty-five delegates from twelve of the thirteen states (all but Rhode Island) that wrote the Constitution. Copies of the document were sent to state conventions for ratification, and it became effective in 1789.

Constitutional Personhood: Recognition by the Supreme Court or the law that some person or entity is considered a "person" for the purposes of the Constitution or Bill or Rights.

Constitutional Tort: A violation of an individual's rights severe enough to be defined as a violation of the Constitution or the Bill of Rights.

Content-Based [Regulation]: Courts subject regulations based on the content of speech to the strictest scrutiny. In a related vein, the Supreme Court also looks with disfavor on viewpoint discrimination, which limits speech based on the ideology of the speaker.

Content-Neutral [Speech Regulation]: Regulation based not on the content of the speech but on the time, place, or manner of its dissemination.

Corruption of Blood: The principle, once used in England, that prohibited individuals attainted of (i.e., "corrupted by") some crimes from inheriting or passing on property. Article III outlaws corruption of blood as a punishment for treason.

Coverture: A historical legal doctrine in western law in which a woman's rights, upon marriage, are subordinated to her husband. The typical consequence was that a married woman could not hold property or make a binding contract.

Cruel and Unusual Punishments: Prohibited by the Eighth Amendment.

Deadly Force: The use of force that results in death or serious bodily injury. Constitutional claims of use of excessive deadly force, which are examined under the Fourth Amendment, involve a weighing of the intrusion on the individual's Fourth Amendment right against the government's interests, cited to justify the intrusion.

Declaration of Independence: Drafted largely by Thomas Jefferson for the Second Continental Congress, the statement of the American colonists' reasons for declaring their independence from Britain. The document is probably most famous for articulating the natural rights doctrine that "all men are created equal" and that they are endowed with the rights of "life, liberty, and the pursuit of happiness."

Declaratory Judgment: A judgment of law (not to be confused with advisory opinions) that stems from an actual case and is binding on the parties.

Defendants: Individuals responding either to civil cases filed against them or to government charges of criminal wrongdoing.

Delegated Powers: To justify exercises of powers, departments of government must be able to trace them directly to enumerations of power within the Constitution. Most congressional powers are listed in Article I, Section 8. Delegated powers may form the basis of implied powers.

Deterrence: The stated goal of using punishment, especially capital punishment, as a way of discouraging others from committing crimes.

Dissenting Opinion: An opinion in which a judge or justice disagrees with the majority opinion and explains the jurist's reasoning in hopes of persuading others that the opinion is wrong.

During Good Behavior: The constitutional provision according to which judges and justices will serve until they die, retire, or are impeached, convicted, and removed from office.

En Banc: A meeting of all members of a court, typically a U.S. circuit court, whose members more typically serve on three-judge panels.

Endorsement Test: A test devised by Justice Sandra Day O'Connor, which allows general accommodation of religion as long as such accommodation does not send the message that it is endorsing a religion or making adherents to any religious view feel as though the government is seeking to give benefits on the basis of religious beliefs.

Establishment Clause: Provision in the First Amendment prohibiting Congress from making any law "respecting an establishment of religion." This clause is usually linked to the concept of separation of church and state.

Exclusionary Rule: A judicially designed interpretation of the Fourth Amendment as forbidding unconstitutionally obtained evidence from being used in a trial against an individual accused of a crime.

Ex Post Facto Law: Makes a previously legal action a crime and punishes a person for it; such legislation is banned under Article I, Section 9, which is now understood to outlaw the imposition of a penalty more severe than the law had assessed when a given crime was committed.

Facial Challenge: A lawsuit that claims that a law is invalid on its face. Such challenges are generally more difficult to prove than "as-applied" challenges, which focus more specifically on the way that a law is being applied or enforced.

Fairness Doctrine: A Federal Communications Commission (FCC) doctrine adopted as a result of congressional legislation requiring television and radio stations to give each side fair coverage when discussing of public issues. The fairness doctrine was upheld as constitutional in *Red Lion Broadcasting Co. v. F.C.C,* (395 U.S. 367, 1969), but subsequently repealed by the FCC in 1987.

Federal Dictionary Act Title 1, sections 1–8 of the United States Code which define certain terms for federal law purposes, including the term "person."

Federal System: Divides government between a national government and states. A federal government requires a national constitution to delineate the boundaries and respective responsibilities of the two governing entities. In federal systems, both the national and state governments can act directly on the states.

Federalists: Individuals who supported ratification of the U.S. Constitution. They designated their opponents as Anti-Federalists. One of the first two political parties in the United States subsequently took this name.

Fetal Viability: The point during pregnancy in which the fetus can survive outside the mother's womb. The location of this point, prior to which the Court has allowed fewer restrictions on abortion, is increasingly dependent on technology.

Fighting Words: Highly insulting face-to-face speech that the Court has decided is exempt from First Amendment protections because such words are more likely to evoke emotional than rational responses.

Free Exercise Clause: Language in the First Amendment providing for the exercise of religion without interference from government.

Free Press/Fair Trial: A constitutional tension between the First Amendment right of the press and the public to observe open trials versus the Sixth Amendment right of criminal defendants to have a fair and impartial trial, a right that could be impaired by adverse publicity before and during trial.

Fundamental Rights: Rights of individuals explicitly described in the Constitution or the Bill of Rights, as well outside of plain text of both, which the Supreme Court has declared to be so important that legislation affecting them must be subject to strict scrutiny. These latter rights include marriage, procreation, voting, interstate travel, and access to justice.

Gravity of the Evil Test. The test used by the Supreme Court in *Dennis v. United States*, in which it considered the perceived gravity of the unwanted result that speech might elicit in determining whether its suppression was justified.

Impeachment: A constitutional mechanism through which the president, judges, and other civil offices may be charged by the House of Representatives for "Treason, Bribery, or other High Crimes and Misdemeanors." Impeachment leads to a trial in the U.S. Senate, where a two-thirds vote is required to convict and remove from office an impeached person.

Incapacitated: Punishments designed to keep criminals "off the streets," so they do not pose threats to others, are said to render the offenders incapacitated, that is, incapable of causing further harm to the public.

Incorporation: The theory that with the adoption of the Due Process Clause of the Fourteenth Amendment (1868), some or all of the provisions of the Bill of Rights also limit the actions of state and local governments.

Intermediate Scrutiny: A standard under the Equal Protection Clause that requires that a law discriminating against a protected class (gender, alienage, or illegitimacy) meet an important governmental function and be substantially related to that purpose. Also known as "semi-strict" scrutiny.

Interpretivism: A name sometimes given to the position that jurists who believe their task to be limited to ascertaining and applying the original understanding of constitutional words. Noninterpretivists are more likely to supplement this understanding from extraconstitutional sources.

Invidious Discrimination: The result of a law reflecting an emotionally based antagonism toward a group, as on the basis of racism or sexism.

Judicial Activism and Judicial Restraint: Contrasting styles of judicial interpretation, the first stressing a broad judicial responsibility and the latter typically more deferential to judgments made by the two elected branches of government.

Judicial Review: A power not directly stated in the U.S. Constitution, but based both on constitutional principles and on long-standing precedents by which courts determine whether laws brought before them in cases are consistent with the Constitution. Courts may exercise such review over both state and federal legislation.

Jurisdiction: The scope of a court's authority. Article III of the Constitution grants both original and appellate jurisdiction to the Supreme Court, with the latter being subject to "such Exceptions . . . as the Congress shall make."

Jurisprudence: Decisions and principles used to make a decision in law; includes the body of precedents and laws related to a particular principle or doctrine.

Justiciability: Before a Court will deliver an opinion, the parties must show that the controversy that brings them before the Court and/or the remedy they seek is one that is appropriate for judges to address.

Law and Equity: Two divisions of English law, both of which the United States Constitution entrusts to review by the Supreme Court.

***Lemon* Test:** A three-part test, formulated in *Lemon v. Kurtzman* (403 U.S. 602, 1971), designed to ascertain whether laws violate the Establishment Clause. The test seeks to establish whether laws have a secular legislative purpose, whether their primary effect advances or inhibits religion, and whether they promote excessive entanglement between church and state.

Magna C[h]arta: A document signed by King John in England with his noblemen in England in 1215 and generally regarded as the origin of the British Parliament, and subsequent representative institutions, and of the idea of written constitutionalism.

Majority Opinion: An opinion that reflects a Supreme Court majority and has the effect of operative law.

Malevolent Discrimination: A form of discrimination enabled by statutory distinctions that prevent some people from fully participating in society or fully competing economically.

Marketplace of Ideas: Analogy often used in discussions of freedom of speech and expression; it suggests that the best and truest ideas will be most likely to get assent by the greatest number of people.

***Miller* test:** This is the test to determine what sexually explicit materials are obscene. The test asks "(a) whether 'the average person, applying contemporary community standards' would find that the work, taken as a whole, appeals to the prurient interest; (b) whether the work depicts or describes, in a patently offensive way, sexual conduct specifically defined by the applicable state law; and (c) whether the work, taken as a whole, lacks serious literary, artistic, political, or scientific value." See **obscenity.**

Minimal Rationality: The lowest standard of scrutiny under the Equal Protection Clause. To meet this standard, the state must demonstrate that a rational reason exists for the law challenged as discriminatory. If the government can demonstrate a rational relationship between the distinction of groups under the challenged law, as well as a legitimate state objective, the law is not in violation of the Fourteenth Amendment. If the state cannot demonstrate a rational relation, then the law is in violation of the Equal Protection Clause.

***Miranda* Rights:** Guarantees recognized by the Supreme Court in the 1966 case of *Miranda v. Arizona* with a view to ensuring that individuals in the custody of the state, having been accused of a crime, are notified of their constitutional rights prior to questioning.

Missouri Plan: An arrangement adopted in some states whereby the governor appoints judges, who are later subject to a popular vote as to whether they should be retained or removed from office.

Moot: Describing cases that have been effectively settled before they can be adjudicated; courts refuse to hear moot cases because they no longer present a live "case or controversy."

Natural Rights: Rights like "life, liberty, and the pursuit of happiness," which are mentioned in the Declaration of Independence and are thought to belong to individuals by reason of their personhood. Just governments incorporate natural rights into civil rights.

Neutrality: An approach to the Establishment Clause that may either stress the need for the government to treat religions similarly or seek to treat religious adherents no better or worse than individuals who adhere to no religion.

New Jersey Plan: A plan offered by small states at the Constitutional Convention of 1787 advocating equal state representation in a unicameral congress. This plan favored presidential appointment of federal judges.

Non-Deadly Force: Force that does not result in death or serious bodily injury. Constitutional claims of use of excessive non-deadly force are examined under the Fourth Amendment by means of an objective reasonableness test.

Nonobscene Nude Dancing: A form of expression that receives minimal First Amendment protection according to the Court in *Barnes v. Glen Theatre, Inc.* (501 U.S. 560, 1991).

Objective Reasonableness Test: A test formulated by the Supreme Court to determine if non-deadly use of force by law enforcement officials is constitutionally permissible.

Obscenity: The designation for sexually explicit materials that are not protected by the First Amendment. The *Miller* test, from *Miller v. California* (413 U.S. 15, 1973), is used to determine what is obscene.

Original Intent: A method of constitutional interpretation that emphasizes the intent of those who wrote, ratified, and/or amended the Constitution.

Original Jurisdiction: The location, in the legal system, of cases that arrive before a court for their first hearing. The U.S. Supreme Court exercises relatively little original jurisdiction because most cases come to it on appeal.

Parliamentary Sovereignty: Under British law, the legislative body, or Parliament, is regarded as supreme. Americans rejected this notion as incompatible with natural rights and with a system of checks and balances.

Penumbras of the Constitution: A *penumbra* is the shadow cast around the perimeter of the sun and moon. As used by the Court, the phrase indicates the implied rights and liberties that are a consequence of the enumerated rights and liberties articulated in the Constitution.

***Per Curiam* Opinion:** An unsigned opinion, generally quite short, announcing the Court's opinion on behalf of a group of justices.

Political Questions: Issues on which courts will refuse to rule on the grounds that they are matters for the two political, or elected, branches to handle.

Pornography: Sexually explicit materials that receive some First Amendment free speech protection.

Precedental Consistency: The ideal that law decided by judges should be based on previously determined cases (precedents) to ensure that legal reasoning remains predictable and constant.

Preemptive Challenge: An attorney-initiated request made during voir dire to have a potential jurist removed from the jury panel without explanation or justification.

Preferred Position: The place of freedom of speech in contemporary law: namely, that it is paramount and generally trumps any rights with which it comes into conflict.

Pretextual Stops: The use of minor traffic offenses such as broken taillights as the basis of stopping someone suspected of committing or having committed a more serious crime such as drug or weapons possession.

***Primus Inter Pares*:** First among equals. Often used to describe the role of the chief justice of the United States.

Prior Restraint: The prevention of the media from publishing a story or idea for national security or other reasons. The government carries a very high burden to enjoin a publication; only one federal district court decision in American history—*United States of America v. The Progressive, Inc.*— has allowed for prior restraint, and its ruling was overturned on appeal.

Private Actions: Actions or acts that are not attributable to the government. If an act is deemed to be private, the constitutional protections of the Bills of Rights do not apply.

Procedural Due Process: The guarantees by the government as to what processes will be provided before rights to life, liberty, and property may be limited. Laws and the Constitution explicitly provide these limitations on governmental action.

Procedural Protections: Specific guarantees provided in the Constitution and designed to protect citizens from governmental intrusions; the protections include the right to an attorney, the right to a speedy trial, and the definition of certain searches and seizures as unlawful.

Proportionality: Essentially, the concept that the punishment should fit the crime. Justices debate the degree to which the cruel and unusual punishment provision in the Eighth Amendment includes a requirement for proportionality.

Prosecution: Representative of the government in criminal cases.

Protectionistic Legislation: Statutes, designed to provide guarantees and security for a vulnerable segment of the population, which might also limit the liberties of the targeted group of individuals. For example, laws designed to prevent minors from working an excessive number of hours a week to protect them from exploitation resulted in limitations on the ability of some minors to make a contract with an employer.

Public Officials: Elected or appointed government officers who, according to the Court in *New York Times v. Sullivan* (376 U.S. 254, 1964), need to show actual malice or reckless disregard for the truth in order to win a libel suit against the media or others who criticize them. The actual malice test was devised to protect the media from libel suits even if some of the statements alleged as facts are not completely accurate. The rationale for this standard is to protect freedom of press, as guaranteed by the First Amendment.

Racial Profiling: The intentional or unintentional use of race in law enforcement to stop or search individuals suspected of violating the law.

Rational Basis Test: The basic test the Court uses to examine most legislation or economic legislation adopted by the government. Under this test, plaintiffs must show that the government lacked a rational basis in adopting the legislation.

Recidivists: Repeat criminal offenders.

Reckless Disregard for the Truth: The standard of proof the Court defined in *New York Times v. Sullivan* (376 U.S. 254, 1964), which must be met to establish libel of public officials by the media. Subsequently in *Associated Press v. Walker* (389 U.S. 28, 1967), the Court applied the same standard of proof to those attempting to show libel against public figures.

Recusal: The stepping aside of a judge who has a personal stake or interest in a case. Judges are expected to recuse themselves when such conditions exist.

Recused: Describing the voluntary removal of a judge or justice from participation in the decision of a case; judges frequently recuse themselves to avoid the appearance of a conflict of interest.

Rehabilitation: The attempt to bring about positive behaviors, sometimes through punishments.

Reporter's Privilege: The right of a news reporter to refuse to divulge the source of a story when subpoenaed by a court. In *Branzburg v. Hayes* (408 U.S. 665, 1972), the Court rejected arguments that the First Amendment protects this privilege.

Republican Government: A term used in the Constitution, and by America's Founding Fathers, to refer to representative government.

Restrictive Covenants: Private agreements among property owners that often precluded the sale of homes and other property to African Americans. In *Shelley v. Kraemer* (334 U.S. 1, 1948), the Supreme Court said that judicial enforcement of such agreements constituted state action.

Retribution: The goal of the use of punishment to recompense for an offender's crimes. Opponents of retribution think it is too closely tied to earlier ideas of personal vengeance.

Rule of Four: The Supreme Court will not accept review of a case unless four of the nine justices agree that they want to hear it. The rule points to the wide discretion that the Court has in setting its own docket.

Scheme of Ordered Liberty: A theory of selective incorporation developed in *Palko v. State of Connecticut* (1937) stating that the Fourteenth Amendment's Due Process Clause protects only certain rights against state encroachment.

Secondary Effects: These include the prevalence of drugs, prostitution, and other forms of crime often found in association with the operation of adult entertainment establishments. In *City of Renton v. Playtime Theatres, Inc.* (475 U.S. 41, 1986), the Court stated that state and local governments can address concerns about the secondary effects of adult entertainment by means of regulations such as zoning laws without violating the First Amendment.

Selective Incorporation: The theory that the Due Process Clause of the Fourteenth Amendment applies only certain parts or sections of the Bill of Rights to state and local governments. Using this theory, the Supreme Court has incorporated all but the Third and parts of the Seventh Amendment.

Semi-Suspect Classification: Any classification based on gender, alienage, or illegitimacy, which is automatically subject to an intermediate level of scrutiny.

Separation of Powers: Characteristic of a system that divides powers among various branches of government in order to prevent abuses by any of them. The U.S. Constitution divides the national government into legislative, executive, and judicial branches.

Speech and Debate Clause: A provision in Article I, Section 6, predating the First Amendment and exempting members of Congress from prosecution for things that they said before Congress.

Social Contract: The idea that just governments are based on the consent of the governed. Social contract theorists, most notably Thomas Hobbes, John Locke, and Jean-Jacques Rousseau, argued that if individuals found themselves in a lawless state of nature, they would form a social contract to escape the unpleasantness of a society without laws.

Standing: Before courts will accept a case, parties must establish that they have a proper interest in the case. This showing is called standing.

***Stare Decisis*:** Let [the precedent] stand. Many court decisions are based on adherence to existing precedents.

State Actions: Actions or acts that can be attributed to the government. If state action is found to exist, the constitutional protections of the Bill of Rights apply. If the actor is a state or local government, the entity can be sued for a constitutional violation under 42 U.S.C. § 1983.

State of Nature: A hypothetical pre-political state in which laws would not be established, settled, known, or impartially enforced.

Statutory Interpretation: The power that courts exercise to determine the meaning of legislation.

Strict Scrutiny: The highest standard used in determining whether discriminatory legislation has violated the Equal Protection Clause. This standard requires that the government must show that it has a compelling interest, and also that the law addressing that interest is both narrowly tailored and the least restrictive means of securing that interest. Strict scrutiny is also used in the evaluation of laws that impinge upon fundamental freedoms (such as religion, speech, and press) or that pertain to "suspect" classifications, such as racial distinctions.

Strict Separationists: Individuals who interpret the Constitution to provide for a high wall of separation between church and state.

Substantive Due Process: The guarantee of fundamental fairness that the courts have found reflected in the Due Process Clause of the Constitution. Instead of protecting citizens from how the government exercises its authority, substantive due process covers what the government and its actors do to citizens.

Substantive Protections: The judiciary's interpretation of the Constitution to ensure that the government provides fundamental fairness to its citizens.

Supremacy Clause: The provision in Article VI that affirms the supremacy of the Constitution over conflicting state laws.

Suspect Classification: Legislation that falls into this category is given the highest scrutiny under the Equal Protection Clause. It distinguishes laws affecting a group whose members are immutable or unchanging in their essential characteristics (such as race or religion) and have faced a history of invidious discrimination based on this characteristic.

Test Oaths: Affirmations of religious beliefs made as a condition to taking public office. Forbidden by a provision of Article VI of the Constitution.

"Three Strikes and You're Out" Laws: Laws that impose more severe penalties on recidivists than on persons convicted of a first or second offense.

Time, Place, and Manner Restrictions: Because courts are generally deferential to the people's right to freedom of speech, neutral regulations that are related to the time, place, and manner of speech, rather than to its content, are permitted.

Tort: A civil wrong or harm committed by one individual against another. Tort claims are part of a state's common law. Individuals who believe that they have been subject to illegal law enforcement activity may bring tort actions against police officers.

Unicameral Legislature: A lawmaking body that has a single house, or chamber.

U.S. Circuit Courts: Courts that sit midway between the ninety-four U.S. District Courts and the U.S. Supreme Court. There are currently eleven numbered circuits, a D.C. circuit, and a specialized circuit.

U.S. District Courts: Federal trial courts, of which there are currently ninety-four.

U.S. Supreme Court: The highest court in the federal system, with power over both lower state courts and federal courts. Housed in Washington, D.C., the Court has eight associate justices and a chief justice.

Virginia Plan: The first plan introduced at the Constitutional Convention of 1787. It favored a bicameral Congress in which states would be represented according to population. It introduced the idea of separation of powers among the legislative, executive, and judicial branches. It called for legislative appointment of judges.

Voir Dire: The process in which attorneys representing both the state and the defendant query the people in the jury pool about their demographic characteristics and biases in order to create an impartial jury.

Writ of Appeal: A petition, which the Supreme Court used to be obligated to accept, under which litigants could request review of their cases by the Court.

Writ of Certification: A writ in which a lower court asks a higher court to clarify a matter of law.

Writ of Certiorari: The most common writ, or petition, by which cases come before the U.S. Supreme Court for appellate review.

Writ of Mandamus: A judicial order directed to an executive official ordering the official to produce or deliver a document.

Youth Curfew Laws: Laws that prohibit minors from being out in public during certain times unless accompanied by the parents or for specified reasons. Courts are split on the constitutionality of these laws.

Index